BREWER'S DICTIONARY OF PHRASE & FABLE

BREWER'S DICTIONARY OF PHRASE & FABLE

A Treasury of Words That Have a Tale to Tell

The Classic Edition

ABRIDGED

E. COBHAM BREWER

This edition is published by Tess Press, an imprint of Black Dog and Leventhal Publishers, Inc., 151 West 19th St., New York, New York, 10011.

Design by Martin Lubin

Jacket design by Filip Zawodnik

ISBN: 1-57912-490-9

jihgfedcba

Printed in Canada

A

A. The form of this letter is modified from the Egyptian hieroglyph which represents the eagle. The Phœnician (Hebrew) symbol was א (*aleph*=an ox), which has been thought, probably erroneously, to represent an ox-head in outline. The Greek A (*alpha*) was the symbol of a bad augury in the sacrifices. *See also* SCARLET LETTER.

A in logic denotes a universal affirmative. A asserts, E denies. Thus, syllogisms in bᴀrbᴀrᴀ (*q.v.*) contain three universal affirmative propositions.

A1 means first-rate—the very best. In Lloyd's Register of British and Foreign Shipping, the character of the ship's hull is designated by *letters*, and that of the anchors, cables, and stores by *figures*. A1 means hull first-rate, and also anchors, cables, and stores; A2, hull first-rate, but fittings second-rate. Vessels of an inferior character are classified under the letters Æ, E, and I.

A.B. *See* ABLE-BODIED.

Aback. This was originally a nautical term used when a gust of wind forced the sails back against the mast and suddenly stayed the ship's progress. From this comes the phrase "I was taken aback," meaning "I was astounded, taken by surprise."

Abacus (ăb' à kŭs). A primitive calculating machine, consisting of a small frame with wires stretched across it in one direction, each wire having threaded on it ten balls which can be

–00—00000000–
–0000—000000–
–0—000000000–
–0000000—000–
–00000-00000–
–000000000—0–

shifted backwards or forwards. It is used to teach children addition and subtraction and was employed by the Greeks and Romans for calculations, as a modification of it was used to a much later date by the Chinese. The word is derived from the Greek, ἄβαξ, a cyphering table (a slab covered with sand). The multiplication table invented by Pythagoras is called *Abacus Pythagoricus*.

In architecture the *abacus* is the topmost member of a capital.

Abaddon (à băd' òn). The angel of the bottomless pit (*Rev.* ix, 11), from Heb. *abad*, he perished.

Milton uses the name for the bottomless pit itself:—

> In all her gates Abaddon rues
> Thy bold attempt.
>
> *Paradise Regained*, iv, 624.

Abatement (O.Fr. *batre*, to beat down). In heraldry, a mark of depreciation annexed to coat armour, whereby the honour of it is abated.

Abaton (ăb' à ton) (Gr. *a*, not; βαίνω, I go). *As inaccessible as Abaton.* A name given to various places of antiquity difficult of access.

Abbassides (ăb' à sīdz). A dynasty of thirty-seven caliphs who reigned over the Mohammedan Empire from 750 to 1258. They were descended from Abbas, uncle of Mohammed. Haroun al-Raschid (born 765, reigned 786-808), of the *Arabian Nights*, was one of their number.

Abbot of Misrule. *See* KING OF MISRULE.

Abbotsford. The name given by Sir Walter Scott to Clarty Hole, on the south bank of the Tweed, after it became his residence in 1812. Sir Walter devised it from the fancy that the *abbots* of Melrose Abbey used to pass over the *ford* of the Tweed near by.

A B C. An abbreviation having a number of meanings that can be decided only by the context. Thus, "So-and-so doesn't know his A B C" means that he is intensely ignorant: "he doesn't understand the A B C of engineering" means that he has not mastered its rudiments. So, an *A B C Book*, or *Absey Book*, is a primer which used to be used as a child's first lesson book and contained merely the alphabet and a few rudimentary lessons often set in catechism form, as is evident from Shakespeare's lines:—

> That is question now;
> And then comes answer like an Absey book.
>
> *King John*, i, 1.

Abd in Arabic=slave or servant, as Abdiel (*q.v.*) and Abd-Allah (*servant of God*), Abd-el-Kader (*servant of the Mighty One*), Abd-ul-Latif (*servant of the Gracious One*), etc.

Abdallah (ăb dăl′ à). The father of Mohammed. He died shortly before his famous son was born, and is said to have been so beautiful that when he married Amina, 200 virgins broke their hearts from disappointed love.—See Washington Irving's *Life of Mahomet*.

Abdals (ăb′ dàlz). The name given by Mohammedans to certain mysterious persons whose identity is known only to God, and through whom the world is able to continue in existence. When one of them dies another is secretly appointed by God to fill the vacant place.

Abecedarian (ă bè si dâr′ i àn). Usually, one who teaches or is learning his A B C; but also the name of a 16th-century sect of Anabaptists who regarded the teaching of the Holy Spirit (as extracted by them from the Bible) as sufficient for every purpose in life, and hence despised all learning of every kind, except so much of the A B C as was necessary to enable them to read. The sect was founded in 1520 by Nicholas Stork, a weaver of Zwickau; hence they are also spoken of as "the *Zwickau prophets*."

Abecedarian Hymns. Hymns the lines or other divisions of which are arranged in alphabetical order. In Hebrew the 119th Psalm is abecedarian. See ACROSTIC POETRY.

Abhorrers. See PETITIONERS.

Abidhamma (ăb id a′ ma). The third pitaka of the three Pali texts (Tripitaka) which together form the sacred canon of the Buddhists. The Abidhamma contains "the analytical exercises in the psychological system on which the doctrine is based," in seven treatises. See TRIPITAKA.

Abif. See HIRAM ABIF.

Abigail (ăb′ i gāl). A lady's maid. Abigail, wife of Nabal and afterwards of David, is a well-known Scripture heroine (1 *Sam*. xxv, 3). Marlowe called the daughter of Barrabas, his *Jew of Malta*, by this name, and it was given by Beaumont and Fletcher to the "waiting gentlewoman" in *The Scornful Lady*. Swift, Fielding, and other novelists of the period employ it in their novels, and it was further popularized by the notoriety of Abigail Hill, better known as Mrs. Masham, Queen Anne's Lady in Waiting and personal friend.

Abingdon Law. See CUPAR JUSTICE.

Able-bodied Seaman, An, or, *an able seaman*, is a skilled seaman, a sailor of the first class. A crew is divided into three classes: (1) skilled seamen, termed A.B. (Able-Bodied); (2) ordinary seamen; and (3) boys, which include "green hands," or inexperienced men, without regard to age or size.

Aboard. A ship is said to fall aboard another when it runs against it.

Aboard main tack is an old sea-term meaning to draw one of the lower corners of the mainsail down to the chess-tree.

Abolitionists. In U.S.A. the term applied to those who advocated and agitated for the abolition of Negro slavery. In Australia the name was given to those who between 1820 and 1867 sought to obtain by law the abolition of the transportation of convicts to Australia.

Abolla (à bol′ à). An ancient military garment worn by the Greeks and Romans, opposed to the *toga* or robe of peace. The abolla being worn by the lower orders, was affected by philosophers in the vanity of humility.

Abonde (a bond′). Dame Abonde is the French equivalent of Santa Claus, a good fairy who brings children presents while they are asleep on New Year's Eve.

Abou Hassan (ă boo hăs′ ăn). A rich merchant (in *The Arabian Nights*), transferred during sleep to the bed and palace of the Caliph Haroun al-Raschid. Next morning he was treated as the caliph, and every effort was made to make him forget his identity (*The Sleeper Awakened*). The same story, localized to Shakespeare's own Warwickshire, forms the Induction to *The Taming of the Shrew*, where a tinker, Christopher Sly, takes the place of Abou Hassan. The incident is said by Burton (*Anatomy of Melancholy*, II, iv) actually to have occurred during the wedding festivities of Philip the Good of Burgundy (about 1440). *The Ballad of the Frolicsome Duke, or the Tinker's Good Fortune* in the *Percy Reliques*, and another version in Calderon's play, *Life's a Dream* (c. 1633), go to show how popular and widely spread was this Oriental fable.

Above-board. Honest and open. According to Johnson, this is a figurative expression "borrowed from gamesters, who, when they put their hands under the table, are changing their cards."

Above par. A commercial term meaning that the article referred to is at more than its nominal value. See PAR.

Above your hook. See HOOK.

Ab ovo. From the very beginning. Stasinus, in his *Cypria*, a poem in 11 books belonging to the Homeric cycle and forming an introduction to the *Iliad*, does not rush (as does the *Iliad* itself) *in medias res*, but begins with the eggs of Leda, from one of which Helen was born. If Leda had not laid this egg, Helen would never have been born, therefore Paris could not have eloped with her, therefore there would have been no Trojan War, etc. The English use of the phrase probably derives from the line in Horace's *De Arte Poetica*:—

Nec gemino bellum Troianum orditur ab ovo

Abracadabra. A cabalistic charm, said to be made up from the initials of the Hebrew words Ab (Father), Ben (Son), and Ruach ACadsch (Holy Spirit), and formerly used as a powerful antidote against ague, flux, toothache, etc. The word was written on parchment, and suspended from the neck by a linen thread, in the following form:—

```
A B R A C A D A B R A
A B R A C A D A B R
A B R A C A D A B
A B R A C A D A
A B R A C A D
A B R A C A
A B R A C
A B R A
A B R
A B
A
```

Abracax. *See* ABRAXAS.

Abraham. Mohammedan mythology adds the following legends to those told us in the Bible concerning the patriarch. His parents were Prince Azar and his wife, Adna. As King Nimrod had been told that one shortly to be born would dethrone him, he proclaimed a "massacre of the innocents," and Adna retired to a cave where Abraham was born. He was nourished by sucking two of her fingers, one of which supplied milk and the other honey. At the age of fifteen months Abraham was equal in size to a lad of fifteen, and was so wise that his father introduced him to the court of King Nimrod.

Other Mohammedan traditions relate that Abraham and his son "Ismail" rebuilt for the fourth time the Kaaba over the sacred stone at Mecca; that Abraham destroyed the idols manufactured and worshipped by his father, Terah; and that the mountain (called in the Bible "Mount Moriah") on which he offered up his son was "Arfaday."

The Ghebers say that the infant Abraham was thrown into the fire by Nimrod's order, but the flame turned into a bed of roses, on which he went to sleep. Hence Moore's allusion in *Lalla Rookh*:—

Sweet and welcome as the bed
For their own infant prophet spread,
When pitying Heaven to roses turned
The death-flames that beneath him burned.
Fire Worshippers.

To sham Abraham. *See* ABRAM-MAN.

Abrahamic covenant. The covenant made by God with Abraham (*Gen*. xii, 2, 3, and xvii), interpreted to mean that the Messiah should spring from his seed. This promise was given to Abraham, because he left his father's house to live in a strange land, as God told him.

Abraham Newland, An. A bank-note. So called from the name of the chief cashier at the Bank of England from 1782 to 1807, without whose signature no Bank of England notes were genuine.

Abraham's bosom. The repose of the happy in death—

The sons of Edward sleep in Abraham's bosom.
Richard III, iv, 3.

The allusion is to *Luke* xvi, 22, and refers to the ancient custom of allowing a dear friend to recline on one's bosom, as did John on the bosom of Jesus.

There is no leaping from Delilah's lap into Abraham's bosom—*i.e.* those who live and die in notorious sin must not expect to go to heaven at death.

Abram-colour. "Abram" here is a corruption of *auburn*. In *Coriolanus*, ii, 3, the word is so printed in the first three Folios—

Our heads are some brown, some black, some Abram, some bald.

But in the fourth Folio (1685) and in later editions *auburn* is given. Kyd's tragedy, *Soliman and Perseda* (1588) has:—

Where is the eldest son of Priam, the Abram-coloured Trojan?

And Middleton, in *Blurt, Master Constable* (1601), mentions:—

A goodly, long, thick Abram-coloured beard.

Abram-man, or Abraham cove. A pretended maniac who, in Tudor and early Stuart times, wandered about the country as a begging impostor; a Tom o' Bedlam (*q.v.*); hence the phrase, *to sham Abraham*, meaning to pretend illness or distress, in order to get off work.

Inmates of Bedlam (*q.v.*) who were not dangerously mad were kept in the "Abraham Ward," and allowed out from time to time in a distinctive dress. They were permitted to supplement their scanty rations by begging. This gave an opportunity to impostors, and large numbers availed themselves of it. Says *The Canting Academy* (Richd- Head, 1674), they

"used to array themselves with party-coloured ribbons, tape in their hats, a fox-tail hanging down, a long stick with streamers," and beg alms; but "for all their seeming madness, they had wit enough to steal as they went along."

There is a good picture of them in *King Lear*, ii, 3; and see also Beaumont and

Fletcher's *Beggar's Bush*, ii, i:—

Come, princes of the ragged regiment
And these, what name or title e'er they bear,
Jarkman or *Patrico, Cranke* or *Clapper-dudgeon,*
Frater or *Abram-man,* I speak to all
That stand in fair election for the title
Of King of Beggars.

Abraxas (à brăks' às). A cabalistic word used by the Gnostics to denote the Supreme Being, the source of 365 emanations, the sum of the numbers represented by the Greek letters of the word totalling 365. It was frequently engraved on gems (hence known as *abraxas stones*), that were used as amulets or talismans. *See* BASILIDIANS. By some authorities the name is given as that of one of the horses of Aurora.

Absent. "Out of mind as soon as out of sight." This is the form in which the proverb is given by Fulke Greville, Lord Brooke (d. 1628) in his *56th Sonnet;* but it appears with its more usual wording—"Out of sight, out of mind," as the title of one of Barnabe Googe's *Eclogs* (1563).

The absent are always wrong. The translation of the French proverb, *Les absents ont toujours tort,* which implies that it is always easy to lay the blame on someone who is not present to stand up for himself.

Absence makes the heart grow fonder. A tag of doubtful truth, that comes from a song, *The Isle of Beauty* by T. Haynes Bayly (1797-1839).

Absent flag. A small blue signal flown by a yacht to indicate that the owner is not aboard.

Absolute. A Captain Absolute, a bold, despotic man, determined to have his own way, so called from the character in Sheridan's *Rivals.*

Absolute weight. The weight of a body in vacuum.

Absolute zero. The temperature at which a theoretically perfect gas, kept at constant volume, would exert no pressure. In practice this is—273.1° C.

Absquatulate (ăb skwot' ū lāt). To run away or abscond. An artificial American word, possibly from Lat. *ab*, and *squat*, a squatting being a tenement taken in some unclaimed part, without purchase or permission. It seems to have been first used in 1833, in *The Kentuckian,* a play by W. B. Bernard.

Abstinence is the voluntary total forbearance from taking alcohol, certain foods, etc.; it differs from *temperance*, for this admits of their being taken habitually in moderation. In ecclesiastical parlance Days of Abstinence are those when the eating of meat is not permitted; Fasting Days are when only one full meal is allowed in the twenty-four hours.

Abstract Numbers are numbers considered without reference to anything else: 1, 2, 3; if we say 1 year, 2 feet, 3 men, etc., the numbers are no longer abstract, but *concrete.*

Things are said to be **taken in the abstract** when they are considered absolutely, that is, without reference to other matters or persons. Thus, in the abstract, one man may be as good as another, but is yet not so socially and politically.

An abstract of title is a legal expression, meaning an epitome of the evidences of ownership.

Abstraction. Alexander Bain, in *The Senses and the Intellect* (1855), defines abstraction as "the generalizing of some property, so as to present it to the mind, apart from the other properties that usually go along with it in nature"; or it is, as Locke put it: "Nothing more than leaving out of a number of resembling ideas what is peculiar to each." This process is apt to result in what we call *an empty abstraction*, a mere ideality, of no practical use, and sooner or later we turn away from such unsatisfying ideas, as did Wordsworth:—

Give us, for our abstractions, solid facts;
For our disputes, plain pictures.

Excursion v, 636.

Gladstone furnished an excellent illustration of the meaning of the term when he said, "Laws are abstractions until they are put into execution."

Absurd meant originally "quite deaf," (Lat. *ab*, intensive, and *surdus*, deaf); but the Lat. compound, *absurdus*, had the meaning, "out of time," "discordant," hence "harsh" or "rough," and hence the figurative (and now common) meaning "irrational," "silly" or "senseless."

Reductio ad absurdum. *See* REDUCTIO.

Abudah (à bū' da). Thackeray's allusion:—

Like Abudah, he is always looking out for the Fury, and knows that the night will come with the inevitable hag with it.

is to a story in Ridley's *Tales of the Genii* of a merchant of Bagdad who is haunted every night by an old hag.

Abundant Number, An. A number the sum of whose aliquot parts is greater than itself. Thus 12 is an abundant number, because its divisors, 1, 2, 3, 4, 6 = 16, which is greater than 12. *Cp.* DEFICIENT NUMBER, PERFECT NUMBER.

Abus (ăb' ús). An old name of the river Humber. *See* Spenser's *Faerie Queene,* II, x, 16:—

He [Locrine] then encountred, a confused rout,
Forbye the River that whylome was hight
The ancient Abus . . .

See Geoffrey of Monmouth's *Chronicles,* Bk. ii, 2.

Abyla. *See* CALPE.

Acadia (à kā′ dià). The early name of Nova Scotia, introduced to Europe by the Florentine explorer, Verazzani, who reported in 1524 that it was known by that name to the inhabitants. In 1621 Sir Wm. Alexander obtained a grant of the land, and its name was changed to Nova Scotia. The old French inhabitants refused to take the oath of allegiance to the British crown and were in a state of constant rebellion, so in 1755 they were forcibly evacuated; Longfellow's *Evangeline* tells of the resulting sufferings.

Acadine (ăk′ à dīn). A Sicilian fountain mentioned by Diodorus Siculus as having magic properties. Writings were thrown into it for the purpose of being tested; if genuine they floated, if spurious they sank to the bottom.

Acanthus (à kăn′ thùs). The conventionalized representation of the leaf of *Acanthus mollis* used as a decoration in the capitals of Corinthian and composite columns. The story is that an acanthus sprang up around a basket of flowers that Callimachus had placed on his daughter's grave, and that this so struck the fancy of the architect that he introduced the design into his buildings.

Accents. *See* TYPOGRAPHICAL SIGNS.

Accessory. Accessory before the fact is one who is aware that another intends to commit an offence, but is himself absent when the offence is perpetrated.

Accessory after the fact is one who screens a felon, aids him in eluding justice, or helps him in any way to profit by his crime. Thus, the receiver of stolen goods, knowing or even suspecting them to be stolen, is an accessory *ex post facto*.

Accident. A logical accident is some property of quality which a substance possesses, the removal or change of which would not necessarily affect the substance itself, as the height of our bodies, the redness of a brick, the whiteness of paper, etc. Theologians explain the doctrine of transubstantiation by maintaining that the *substance* of the bread and wine is changed into that of the body and blood of Christ, but their *accidents* (flavour, appearance, and so on) remain the same as before.

Accidental colours. *See* COLOURS.

Accidentals in music are signs indicating sharps, flats, naturals, and double sharps and flats, other than those sharps and flats prescribed by the key-signature.

Accius Nævius (ăk′ si ùs nē′ vi ùs). A legendary Roman augur in the reign of Tarquin the Elder. When he forbade the king to increase the number of centuries (*i.e.* divisions of the army) instituted by Romulus, without consulting the augurs, Tarquin asked him if, according to the augurs, the thought then in his, Tarquin's, mind was feasible of accomplishment. "Undoubtedly," said Accius, after consultation. "Then cut through this whetstone with the razor in your hand." The priest gave a bold cut, and the block fell in two (Livy, i, 36).

Accolade (ăk ō lād′). The touch of a sword on the shoulder in the ceremony of conferring knighthood; originally an embrace or touch by the hand on the neck (Lat. *ad collum*, on the neck). In music the brace ({) that connects two or more staves in the score is called an accolade.

Accommodation. In commercial use, a loan of money.

Accommodation note or **bill.** A bill of exchange for which value has not been received, used for the purpose of raising money on credit.

Accommodation ladder. A flight of steps hung over the side of a ship at the gangway.

Accord means "heart to heart" (Lat. *ad corda*). If two persons like and dislike the same things, they are heart to heart with each other.

Similarly, "concord" means heart with heart; "discord," heart divided from heart; "record"—*i.e. re-cordāre*—properly means to bring again to the mind or heart, and secondarily to set this down in writing.

Account, To open an. To enter a customer's name on your ledger for the first time. (Lat. *accomputāre*, to calculate.)

To keep open account. Merchants are said to keep open account when they agree to honour each other's bills of exchange.

A current account or "account current," *a/c.* A commercial term, meaning the account of a customer who does not pay for goods received at time of purchase.

On account. A commercial phrase implying "in part payment for."

On the account was an old pirates' phrase for sailing a-pirating.

To cast accounts. To give the results of the debits and credits entered, balancing the two, and carrying over the surplus.

The account on the Stock Exchange means: the credit allowed on dealings for the fortnightly settlement, or the fortnightly settlement itself, which is also called *account-day*, or *settling-day*.

To be sent to one's account. To have final judgment passed on one. The Ghost in Hamlet uses the phrase as a synonym for death:—

Sent to my account
With all my imperfections on my head.
Hamlet, i, 5.

Accusative. Calvin was so called by his college companions. An "accusative age" is an obsolete expression denoting an age that is *searching*, one that eliminates error by *accusing* it.

This hath been a very accusative age.—Sir E. DERING (16th century).

Ace. The unit of cards or dice, from *as*, which was the Latin unit of weight. In World War I the French term *as*, applied to an airman who had brought down ten enemy aeroplanes, was imported in its English equivalent *ace*. This sense of the word has since been extended to include any more than usually expert flier, bridge-player, golfer, etc.

Within an ace. Within a hair's breadth of; he who wins within an ace wins within a single mark. *See* AMBSAS.

To bate an ace is to make an abatement, or to give a competitor some start or other advantage, in order to render the combatants more equal. *See* BOLTON. Taylor, the water poet (1580-1654), speaking of certain women, says—

Though bad they be, they will not bate an ace
To be call'd Prudence, Temp'rance, Faith, and Grace.

Achæan League (à kē' àn). The first Achæan League was a religious confederation of the twelve towns of Achæa, lasting from very early times till it was broken up by Alexander the Great. The second was a powerful political federation of the Achæan and many other Greek cities, formed to resist Macedonian domination in 280 B.C., and dissolved by the Romans in 147 B.C.

Achates (à kā' tēz). A *fidus Achates* is a faithful companion, a bosom friend. Achates in Virgil's *Æneid* is the chosen companion of the hero in adventures of all kinds.

Achemon (à ke' mon). According to Greek fable Achemon and his brother Basalas were two Cercopes forever quarrelling. One day they saw Hercules asleep under a tree and insulted him, but Hercules tied them by their feet to his club and walked off with them, heads downwards, like a brace of hare. Everyone laughed at the sight, and it became a proverb among the Greeks, when two men were seen quarrelling—"Look out for Melampygos!" (*i.e.* Hercules):—

Ne insidas in Melampygum.

Acheron (ăk' er on). A Greek word meaning "the River of Sorrows"; the river of the infernal regions into which Phlegethon and Cocytus flow: also the lower world (Hades) itself.

They pass the bitter waves of Acheron
Where many souls sit wailing woefully.
SPENSER: *Faerie Queene*, I, v, 33.

Acherontian Books. *See* TAGES.

Acherusia (ăk er ooz' i à). A cavern on the borders of Pontus, through which Hercules dragged Cerberus to earth from the infernal regions.

Achillea (ăk il ē' à). A genus of herbaceous plants of the aster family, including the common yarrow (*Achillea millefolium*), so called from Achilles. The tale is, that when the Greeks invaded Troy, Telephus, son-in-law of Priam, attempted to stop their landing; but, Bacchus causing him to stumble, Achilles wounded him with his spear. The young Trojan was told by an oracle that "Achilles (meaning milfoil or yarrow) would cure the wound"; instead of seeking the plant he applied to the Grecian chief, and promised to conduct the host to Troy if he would cure the wound. Achilles consented to do so, scraped some rust from his spear, and from the filings rose the plant milfoil, which being applied to the wound, had the desired effect. It is called by the French the *herbe aux charpentiers*—*i.e.* carpenters' wort, because it was supposed to heal wounds made by carpenters' tools.

Achilles (à kil' ēz). In Greek legend, the son of Peleus and Thetis and grandson of Eacus, king of the Myrmidons (in Thessaly), and hero of the *Iliad* (*q.v.*). He is represented as being brave and relentless; but, at the opening of the poem, in consequence of a quarrel between him and Agamemnon, commander-in-chief of the allied Greeks, he refused to fight. The Trojans prevailed, and Achilles sent Patroclus to oppose them. Patroclus fell; and Achilles, rushing into the battle, killed Hector (*q.v.*). He himself, according to later poems, was slain at the Scaean gate, before Troy was taken, by an arrow in his heel. *See* ACHILLES TENDON.

Death of Achilles. It was Paris who wounded Achilles in the heel with an arrow (a post-Homeric story).

Achilles's horses. Balios and Xanthos (*see* HORSE).

Achilles's mistress in Troy. Hippodamia, surnamed Briseis (*q.v.*).

Achilles's tomb. In Sigœum, over which no bird ever flies.—*Pliny*, x, 29.

Achilles's tutors. First, Phœnix, who taught him the elements; then Chiron the centaur, who taught him the uses and virtues of plants.

Achilles's wife. Deidamia (*q.v.*).

Achilles and the tortoise. The allusion is to the following paradox proposed by Zeno: In a race Achilles, who can run ten times as fast as a tortoise, gives the latter 100 yards start; but it is impossible for him to overtake the tortoise and win the race; for, while he is running the first hundred yards the tortoise runs ten, while Achilles runs that ten the tortoise is running one, while Achilles is running one the tortoise runs one-tenth of a yard, and so on *ad infinitum*.

Achilles's spear. Shakespeare's lines:—

That gold must round engirt these brows of mine
Whose smile and frown, like to Achilles' spear,
Is able with the change to kill and cure.
                                   2 *Henry VI*, v, 1.

is an allusion from the story told above (*s.v.* ACHILLEA) of the healing of Telephus. It is also referred to by Chaucer:—

. . . speche of Thelophus the king,
And of Achilles with his queynte spere,
For he coude with it both hele and dere (*harm*).
                                   Squire's Tale, 238.

Achilles tendon. A strong sinew running along the heel to the calf of the leg, frequently strained by athletes. The tale is that Thetis took her son Achilles by the heel, and dipped him in the river Styx to make him invulnerable. The water washed every part, except the heel in his mother's hand. It was on this vulnerable point the hero was slain; and the sinew of the heel is called, in consequence, *tendo Achillis*. A post-Homeric story.

The heel of Achilles. The vulnerable or weak point in a man's character or of a nation.

Aching Void, An. That desolation of heart which arises from the recollection of some cherished endearment no longer possessed.

What peaceful hours I once enjoy'd,
    How sweet their memory still;
But they have left an aching void
    The world can never fill.
                    COWPER: *Walking with God.*

Achitophel (à kit' ō fel). Ahithophel was David's traitorous counsellor, who deserted to Absalom; but his advice being disregarded, he hanged himself (2 *Sam.* xvii, 23). The Achitophel of Dryden's satire (*see* ABSALOM AND ACHITOPHEL) was the Earl of Shaftesbury.

Achor (ā' kôr). Said by Pliny to be the name of the deity prayed to by the Cyreneans for the averting of insect pests. *See* FLIES, GOD OF.

Acid Test. The application of acid is a certain test of gold. Hence the phrase is used of a test or trial which will conclusively decide the value, worth, or reliability of anything.

Ack emma. *See* PIP EMMA.

Acme (ăk' mi) (Gr. a point). The highest pitch of perfection; the term used by old medical writers for the crisis of a disease. They divided the progress of a disease into four periods: the *arche*, or beginning; the *anabasis*, or increase; the *acme*, or term of its utmost violence; and the *paracme*, or decline.

Aconite (ăk' ò nīt). The herb Monkshood or Wolfsbane. Classic fabulists ascribe its poisonous qualities to the foam which dropped from the mouths of the three-headed Cerberus, when Hercules, at the command of Eurystheus, dragged the monster from the infernal regions. (Gr. ἀκόνιτον; Lat. *aconitum*.)

Lurida terribiles miscent Aconita novercæ.
                    OVID: *Metamorphoses*, i, 147.

Acre. O.E. *œcer*, is akin to the Lat. *ager* and Ger. *acker* (a field). **God's Acre**, a cemetery or churchyard. Longfellow calls this an "ancient Saxon phrase," but as a matter of fact it is a modern borrowing from Germany.

Acre-shot. An obsolete name for a land tax. "Shot" is *scot*. *See* SCOT AND LOT.

Acres, Bob. A coward by character in Sheridan's *The Rivals*, whose courage always "oozed out at his fingers' ends." Hence, a man of this kind is sometimes called "a regular Bob Acres."

Acropolis (à krop' ō lis) (Gr. *akros*, point, height; *polis*, city). An elevated citadel, especially of ancient Athens, where was built in the 15th century B.C. the Parthenon, the Erechtheum, and the Propylæa or monumental gate.

Acrostic (Gr. *akros*, extremity; *stichos*, row, line of verse). A piece of verse in which the initial letters of each line read downwards consecutively form a word; if the final letters read in the same way also form a word it is a *double acrostic*; if the middle letters as well it is a *triple acrostic*. The term was first applied to the excessively obscure prophecies of the Erythræan sibyl; they were written on loose leaves, and the initial letters made a word when the leaves were sorted and laid in order. (*Dionys.* iv, 62.)

Acrostic Poetry among the Hebrews consisted of twenty-two lines or stanzas beginning with the letters of the alphabet in succession (*cp.* ABECEDARIAN HYMNS).

Act of Faith. *See* AUTO DA FE.

Act of God. Loss arising from the action of forces uncontrollable by man, such as a hurricane, lightning, etc., is said to be due to an "act of God," and hence has no legal redress. A Devonshire jury once found—"That deceased died by the act of God, brought about by the flooded condition of the river."

Act of Man. The sacrificing of cargo, spars, or furnishings, by the master of a vessel for the preservation of his ship. All persons with an interest in the ship and cargo stand a fair share of the loss.

Act of Parliament. This is the official name for a measure which has become the law of the land. The word Bill is applied to a measure on its introduction, and for it to become an Act it has to be read three times in each House of Parliament (during which time it is debated) and receive the royal assent. The Acts of each session are arranged in chapters and officially quoted according to the year of the reign in which they are passed. *See* REGNAL YEAR. The Acts of the English Parliament go back to 1235.

Actæon (ăk tē' on). In Greek mythology a huntsman who, having surprised Diana bathing, was changed by her into a stag and torn to pieces by his own hounds. A stag being a horned animal, he became a representative of men whose wives are unfaithful. *See* HORN.

> Like Sir Actæon he, with Ringwood at thy heel.
> SHAKESPEARE: *Merry Wives*, ii, 1.
> The Emperors themselves did wear Actæon's badge.
> BURTON: *Anatomy of Melancholy* (1621).

Action Sermon. A sermon (in the Scots Presbyterian Church) preached before the celebration of Communion.

Actresses. Coryat, in his *Crudities* (1611), says "When I went to a theatre (in Venice) I observed certain things that I never saw before; for I saw women acte. . . . I have heard that it hath sometimes been used in London," but the first public appearance of a woman on the stage in England was on 8 Dec., 1660, when Margaret Hughes, Prince Rupert's mistress, played Desdemona in *Othello* at a new theatre in Clare Market, London. Previous to that female parts had always been taken by boys; Edward Kynaston (d. 1706) seems to have been the last male actor to play a woman on the English stage, in serious drama.

> Whereas, women's parts in plays have hitherto been acted by men in the habits of women . . . we do permit and give leave for the time to come that all women's parts be acted by women.
> *Charles II's licence of 1662.*

Acu tetigisti. *See* REM ACU.

Ad inquirendum (ăd in kwī ren' dum) (Lat.). A judicial writ commanding an inquiry to be made into some complaint.

Ad libitum (ăd lib' i tum) (Lat.). To choice, at pleasure, without restraint.

Ad rem (ăd rem') (Lat.). To the point in hand; to the purpose.

Ad valorem (ăd văl ôr' em) (Lat.). According to the price charged. A commercial term used in imposing customs duties according to the value of the goods imported. Thus, if teas pay duty *ad valorem*, the high-priced tea will pay more duty per pound than the lower-priced tea.

Adam. The Talmudists say that Adam lived in Paradise only twelve hours, and account for the time thus:—

I. God collected the dust and animated it.
II. Adam stood on his feet.
IV. He named the animals.
VI. He slept and Eve was created.
VII. He married the woman.
X. He fell.
XII. He was thrust out of Paradise.

Mohammedan legends add to the Bible story the tradition that—

God sent Gabriel, Michael, and Israfel one after the other to fetch seven handfuls of earth from different depths and of different colours for the creation of Adam (thereby accounting for the varying colours of mankind), but that they returned empty-handed because Earth foresaw that the creature to be made from her would rebel against God and draw down His curse on her, whereupon Azrael was sent. He executed the commission, and for that reason was appointed to separate the souls from the bodies and hence became the Angel of Death. The earth he had taken was carried into Arabia to a place between Mecca and Tayef, where it was kneaded by the angels, fashioned into human form by God, and left to dry for either forty days or forty years. It is also said that while the clay was being endowed with life and a soul, when the breath breathed by God into the nostrils had reached as far as the navel, the only half-living Adam tried to rise up and got an ugly fall for his pains. Mohammedan tradition holds that he was buried on Aboucais, a mountain of Arabia.

In Greek the word *Adam* is made up of the four initial letters of the cardinal quarters:—

> *Arktos*, north;   *Dusis*, west;
> *Anatole*, east;   *Mesembria*, south.

The Hebrew word (without vowels) forms an anagram with the initials: A[dam], D[avid], M[essiah].

According to Moslem writers: After the Fall Adam and Eve were separated, Adam being placed on Mt. Vassem, in the east, Eve at Jeddah, on the Red Sea coast of Arabia. The Serpent was exiled to the coast of Ebleh. After a hundred years had been thus spent, Adam and Eve were reunited at Arafat, in the vicinity of Mecca. Adam died on Friday, April 7, at the age of 930 years. His body was wrapped in cerements by the Archangel Michael; Gabriel performed the last rites. The body was buried in the grotto of Ghar' ul Kenz, near Mecca. When Noah went into the Ark he took Adam's coffin with him, after the Flood restoring it to its original burial place.

The old Adam. The offending Adam, etc.

> Consideration, like an angel, came
> And whipped the offending Adam out of him.
> SHAKESPEARE: *Henry V*, i, 1.

Adam, as the head of unredeemed man, stands for "original sin," or "man without regenerating grace."

The second Adam. The new Adam, etc. Jesus Christ is so called.

> The Tempter set
> Our second Adam, in the wilderness,
> To show him all earth's kingdoms and their glory.
> *Paradise Lost*, xi, 383.

Milton probably derived the idea from *Rom.* vi, 6, or 1 *Cor.* xv, 22 :—

For as in Adam all die, even so in Christ shall all be made alive.

Compare the address of God to the Saviour in *Paradise Lost*, iii:—

> Be thou in Adam's room
> The head of all mankind, though Adam's son.
> As in him perish all men, so in thee,
> As from a second root, shall be restored
> As many as are restored.

In the same way Milton calls Mary our "second Eve" (*Paradise Lost*, v, 387, and x, 183).

When Adam delved:—

> When Adam delved and Eve span,
> Who was then the gentleman.

This, according to the *Historia Anglicana* of Thos. Walsingham (d. 1422), was the text of John Ball's speech at Blackheath to the rebels in Wat Tyler's insurrection (1381). It seems to be an adaptation of some lines by Richard Rolle of Hampole (d. *c.* 1349):—

> When Adam dalfe and Eve spanne
> To spire of thou may spede,
> Where was then the pride of man,
> That now marres his meed?

Cp. Jack's as good as his master, under JACK (*phrases*).

Adam Bell. *See* CLYM OF THE CLOUGH.

Adam Cupid—*i.e.* Archer Cupid, probably alluding to Adam Bell. In all the early editions the line in *Romeo and Juliet* (II, i, 13): "Young Adam Cupid, he that shot so trim," reads "Young *Abraham* Cupid," etc. The emendation was suggested by Steevens.

Adam's ale. Water; because the first man had nothing else to drink. In Scotland sometimes called *Adam's Wine.*

Adam's apple. The protuberance in the forepart of the throat, the anterior extremity of the thyroid cartilage of the larynx; so called from the superstition that a piece of the forbidden fruit stuck in Adam's throat.

Adam's needle. *Gen.* iii, 7, tells us that Adam and Eve "sewed fig leaves together;" needles were (presumably) not then obtainable, but certain plants furnish needle-like spines, and to some of these the name has been given. The chief is the Yucca, a native of Mexico and Central America.

Adam's Peak. A mountain in Ceylon where, according to Mohammedan legend, Adam bewailed his expulsion from Paradise, standing on one foot for 200 years to expiate his crime; then Gabriel took him to Mount Arafat, where he found Eve.

In the granite is a curious impression resembling a human foot, above 5 feet long by 2½ broad; the Hindus, however, assert that it was made by Buddha when he ascended into heaven.

Adam's profession. Gardening or agriculture is sometimes so called—for obvious reasons.

There is no ancient gentlemen but gardeners, ditchers, and grave-makers; they hold up Adam's profession.
> SHAKESPEARE: *Hamlet*, v, 1.

Adamites (ăd' á mīts). The name given to various heretical sects who supposed themselves to attain to primitive innocence by rejecting marriage and clothing. There was such a sect in North Africa in the 2nd century; the *Abelites* (*q.v.*) were similar; the heresy reappeared in Savoy in the 14th century, and spread over Bohemia and Moravia in the 15th and 16th. One Picard, of Bohemia, was the leader in 1400, and styled himself "Adam, son of God." There are references to the sect in James Shirley's comedy *Hyde Park* (II, iv) (1632), and in *The Guardian*, No. 134 (1713).

Adamant (from Gr. *a*, not; *damao*, I tame). A word used for any stone or mineral of excessive hardness (especially the diamond, which is really the same word); also for the magnet or loadstone; and, by poets, for hardness or firmness in the abstract.

> In *Midsummer Night's Dream*, ii, 1
> You draw me, you hard-hearted adamant;
> But yet you draw not iron, for my heart
> Is true as steel.

We have an instance of the use of the word in both senses. *Adamant* as a name for the loadstone, or magnet, seems to have arisen through an erroneous derivation of the word by early mediæval Latin writers from Late Lat., *adamare*, to take a liking for, to have an attraction for. Thus Shakespeare:—

> As true as steel, as plantage to the moon,
> As sun to day, as turtle to her mate,
> As iron to adamant.
> *Troilus and Cressida*, iii, 2.

Addison's disease. A state of anæmia, languor, irritable stomach, etc., associated with disease of the suprarenal glands: so named from Dr. Thos. Addison, of Guy's Hospital (1793-1860), who first described it.

Addisonian termination. The name given by Bishop Hurd to the construction which closes a sentence with a preposition, such as— "which the prophet took a distinct view of."

Named from Joseph Addison, who frequently employed it.

Addle is the Old English *adela*, mire, or liquid filth; hence rotten, putrid, worthless.

Addle egg. An egg which has no germ; also one in which the chick has died. Hence, fig., *addle-headed*, *addle-pate*, empty-headed. As an addle-egg produces no living bird so an addle-pate lacks brains.

Adept means one who has attained (Lat. *adeptus*, participle of *adipisci*). The alchemists applied the term *vere adeptus* to those persons who professed to have "attained to the knowledge of" the elixir of life or of the philosopher's stone.

Alchemists tell us there are always 11 adepts, neither more nor less. Like the sacred chickens of Compostella, of which there are only 2 and always 2 — a cock and a hen.

> In Rosicrucian lore as learn'd
> As he that *vere adeptus* earn'd.
> BUTLER: *Hudibras*, I, i, 546.

Adeste Fideles (à des' ti fi dē' lēz) ("O come, all ye faithful"). A Christmas hymn the familiar tune of which was composed by John Reading (1677-1764), organist at Winchester and author of "Dulce Domum."

Adiaphorists (ăd ī ăf' or ists) (Gr. indifferent.) Followers of Melanchthon; moderate Lutherans, who held that some of the dogmas of Luther are matters of indifference. They accepted the Interim of Augsburg (*q.v.*).

Adieu (Fr. to God). An elliptical form for *I commend you to God* (*cp.* GOOD-BYE).

Admiral, corruption of Arabic A*mir* (lord or commander), with the article *al*, as in *Amir-al-ma* (commander of the water), A*mir-al-Omra* (commander of the forces), A*mir-al-Muminim* (commander of the faithful).

Milton uses the old form for the ship itself: speaking of Satan, he says:—

> His spear—to equal which the tallest pine
> Hewn on Norwegian hills, to be the mast
> Of some great ammiral, were but a wand—
> He walked with.
> *Paradise Lost*, i, 292.

In the Royal Navy there are now four grades of Admiral, viz. *Admiral of the Fleet*, *Admiral*, *Vice-Admiral*, and *Rear-Admiral*. There used to be three classes, named from the colour of their flag—*Admiral of the Red*, *Admiral of the White*, and *Admiral of the Blue*, who, in engagements, held the centre, van, and rear respectively. The distinction was abolished in 1864.

Admiral of the Blue (*see above*), used facetiously for a butcher who dresses in blue, or a tapster, from his blue apron.

> As soon as customers begin to stir
> The Admiral of the Blue cries, "Coming, Sir!"
> *Poor Robin* (1731).

Admiral of the Red (*see above*), facetiously applied to a winebibber whose face and nose are red.

Admittance. This word is not synonymous with *admission*. From permission to enter, and thence the right or power to enter, it extends to the physical act of entrance, as "he gained admittance to the church." You may have *admission* to the director's room, but there is no *admittance* except through his secretary's office. An old meaning of the word indicates the privilege of being admitted into good society:—

> Sir John . . . you are a gentleman of excellent breeding . . . of great admittance.
> *Merry Wives of Windsor*, ii, 2.

Admonitionists, or **Admonitioners.** Certain Protestants who in 1571 sent an *admonition* to the Parliament condemning everything in the Church of England which was not in accordance with the doctrines and practices of Geneva.

Adonai (à dō' nī) (Heb. pi. of *adon*, lord). A name given to the Deity by the Hebrews, and used by them in place of Yahweh (Jehovah), the "ineffable name," wherever this occurs. In the Vulgate, and hence in the Wyclif, Coverdale, and Douai versions, it is given for Jehovah in *Exod*. vi, 3, where the A.V. reads:—

> And I appeared unto Abraham, unto Isaac, and unto Jacob, by the name of God Almighty, but by my name JEHOVAH was I not known to them.

Thus James Howell says of the Jews:—

> . . . they sing many tunes, and *Adonai* they make the ordinary name of God: Jehovah is pronounced at high Festivals.
> *Letters*, Bk. i, sec. vi, 14 (3 June, 1633).

Adonists. Those Jews who maintain that the vowels of the word Adonai (*q.v.*) are not the vowels necessary to make the tetra-grammaton (*q.v.*), JHVH, into the name of the Deity. *See also* JEHOVAH.

Adonia (à dō' ni à). The feast of Adonis, celebrated in Assyria, Alexandria, Egypt, Judæa, Persia, Cyprus, and Greece, for eight days. Lucian gives a long description of these feasts, which were generally held at midsummer and at which the women first lamented the death and afterwards rejoiced at the resurrection of Adonis—a custom referred to in the Bible (*Ezek*. viii, 14), where Adonis appears under his Phœnician name, Tammuz (*q.v.*).

Adonis (à dō' nis). In classical mythology a beautiful youth who was beloved by Venus, and was killed by a boar while hunting. Hence, usually ironically, any beautiful young man, as in Massinger's *Parliament of Love*, II, 2:—

> Of all men
> I ever saw yet, in my settled judgment . . .
> Thou art the ugliest creature; and when trimm'd up
> To the height, as thou imagin'st, in mine eyes,
> A leper with a clap-dish (to give notice
> He is infectious), in respect of thee
> Appears a young Adonis.

And Leigh Hunt was sent to prison for libelling George IV when Regent, by calling him "a corpulent Adonis of fifty" (*Examiner*, 1813).

Adonis Flower, according to Bion, the rose; Pliny (i, 23) says it is the anemone; others, the field poppy; but now generally used for the pheasant's eye, called in French *goute-de-sang*, because in fable it sprang from the blood of the gored hunter.

Adonis garden. A worthless toy; very perishable goods.

> Thy promises are like Adonis' gardens
> That one day bloom'd and fruitful were the next.
>   SHAKESPEARE: 1 *Henry VI*, i, vi.

The allusion is to the baskets or pots of earth used at the Adonia (*q.v.*), in which quick-growing plants were sown, tended for eight days, allowed to wither, and then thrown into the sea or river with images of the dead Adonis.

In Spenser's *Faerie Queene* (Bk. III, ca. vi) the Garden of Adonis is where—

> All the goodly flowres,
> Wherewith dame Nature doth her beautifie
> And decks the girlonds of her paramoures,
> Are fetcht: there is the first seminarie
> Of all things that are borne to live and die,
> According to their kindes.

It is to these gardens that Milton also refers in *Paradise Lost* (ix, 440):—

> Spot more delicious than those gardens feigned
> Or of revived Adonis, or renowned
> Alcinous, host of old Laertes' son.

Adonis River. A stream which flows from Lebanon to the sea near Byblos which runs red at the season of the year when the feast of Adonis was held.

> Thammuz came next behind,
> Whose annual wound in Lebanon allured
> The Syrian damsels to lament his fate
> In amorous ditties all a summer's day,
> While smooth Adonis from his native rock
> Ran purple to the sea, supposed with blood
> Of Thammuz yearly wounded.
>   MILTON: *Paradise Lost* i, 446.

Adoption by baptism. Being godfather or godmother to a child. The child by baptism is your godchild.

Adoption Controversy. Elipand, Archbishop of Toledo, and Felix, Bishop of Urgel (in the 8th century), maintained that Christ in his *human* nature was the son of God by adoption

only (*Rom.* viii, 29), though in his pre-existing state he was the "begotten Son of God" in the ordinary catholic acceptation. Duns Scotus, Durandus, and Calixtus were among the **Adoptionists** who supported this view, which was condemned by the Council of Frankfort in 794.

Adoptive Emperors. In Roman history, the five Emperors—Nerva, Trajan, Hadrian, Antoninus Pius, and Marcus Aurelius—each of whom (except Nerva, who was elected by the Senate) was the adopted son of his predecessor. Their period (96-180) is said to have been the happiest in the whole history of Rome.

Adoration of the Cross. *See* ANDREW, ST.

Adrastus (á drăs′ tus). (i) A mythical Greek king of Argos, leader of the expedition of the "Seven Against Thebes" (*see under* SEVEN). (ii) In Tasso's *Jerusalem Delivered* (Bk. xx), an Indian prince who aided the King of Egypt against the crusaders. He was slain by Rinaldo.

Adriatic. *See* BRIDE OF THE SEA.

Adulterous Bible. *See* BIBLE, SPECIALLY NAMED.

Advancer. In venery this is the name given to the second branch of a buck's horns.

Advent (Lat. *adventus*, the coming to). The four weeks immediately preceding Christmas, commemorating the first and second coming of Christ; the first to redeem, and the second to judge the world. The season begins on St. Andrew's Day (30th Nov.), or the Sunday nearest to it.

Adversary, The. A name frequently given in English literature to the Devil (from 1 *Pet.* v, 8).

Advocate (Lat. *ad*, to; *vocare*, to call). One called to assist pleaders in a court of law.

The Devil's Advocate. A carping or adverse critic. From the *Advocatus diaboli*, the person appointed to contest the claims of a candidate for canonization before a papal court. He advances all he can against the candidate, and is opposed by the *Advocatus dei* (God's Advocate), who says all he can in support of the proposal.

Adytum (Gr. *aduton*, not to be entered; *duo*, to go). The Holy of Holies in the Greek and Roman temples, into which the general public were not admitted; hence, a sanctum.

Ædiles. Those who, in ancient Rome, had charge of the public buildings (*ædes*), such as the temples, theatres, baths, aqueducts, sewers, including roads and streets also.

Ægeus. A fabulous king of Athens who gave the name to the Ægean Sea. His son, Theseus, went to Crete to deliver Athens from the tribute exacted by Minos. Theseus said, if he succeeded he would hoist a white sail on his home-voyage, as a signal of his safety. This he neglected to do; and Ægeus, who watched the ship from a rock, thinking his son had perished, threw himself into the sea.

This incident is repeated in the tale of Tristram and Isolde. *See* TRISTRAM.

Æginetan Sculptures. Sculptures discovered in 1811 at the temple of Pallas Athene, in the little island of Ægina. They consist of two groups of five and ten figures representing exploits of Greek heroes at Troy, and probably date from about 500 B.C., *i.e.* a little before Phidias. They were restored by Thorwaldsen, and were long the most remarkable ornaments of the Glyptothek, at Munich.

Ægir (ē' jir, ē' gir). In Norse mythology the god of the ocean, husband of Ran. They had nine daughters (the billows), who wore white robes and veils.

Ægis (ē' jis) (Gr. goat skin). The shield of Jupiter made by Vulcan and covered with the skin of the goat Amalthæa, who had suckled the infant Zeus. It was sometimes lent to Athena, daughter of Zeus, and when in her possession carried the head of the Gorgon. By the shaking of his ægis Zeus produced storms and thunder; in art it is usually represented as a kind of cloak fringed with serpents; and it is symbolical of divine protection—hence the modern use of the word in such phrases as I *throw my ægis over you,* I give you my protection.

Ægrotat (ē grō' tăt) (Lat. he is ill). In university parlance, a medical certificate of indisposition to exempt the bearer from sitting examinations.

'A E I', a common motto on jewellery, is Greek, and stands for "for ever and for aye."

A. E. I. O. U. The device adopted by Frederick V, Archduke of Austria, on becoming the Emperor Frederick III in 1440. The letters had been used by his predecessor, Albert II, and then stood for—

Albertus Electus Imperator Optimus Vivat.

The meaning that Frederick gave them was—

Archidux Electus Imperator Optime Vivat.

Many other versions are known, including—

Austriæ Est Imperare Orbi Universo.
Alles Erdreich Ist Oesterreich Unterthan.
Austria's Empire Is Overall Universal.

To which wags added after the war of 1866—

Austria's Empire Is Ousted Utterly.

Frederick the Great is said to have translated the motto thus:—

Austria Erit In Orbe Ultima (*Austria will be lowest in the world*).

Æneas (ē nē' ås). The hero of Virgil's epic, son of Anchises, king of Dardanus, and Aphrodite. According to Homer he fought against the Greeks in the Trojan War and after the sack of Troy reigned in the Troad. Later legends tell how he carried his father Anchises on his shoulders from the flames of Troy, and after roaming about for many years, came to Italy, where he founded a colony which the Romans claim as their origin. The epithet applied to him is *pius*, meaning "dutiful."

Æneid. The epic poem of Virgil (in twelve books). So called from *Æneas* and the suffix *-is*, plur. *ides* (belonging to).

The story of Sinon (says Macrobius) and the taking of Troy is borrowed from Pisander.

The loves of Dido and Æneas are taken from those of Medea and Jason, in Apollonius of Rhodes.

The story of the Wooden Horse and burning of Troy is from Arctinus of Miletus.

Æolian Harp (ē ō' li ån). The wind harp. A box on which strings are stretched. Being placed where a draught gets to the strings, they utter musical sounds.

Awake, Æolian lyre, awake,
And give to rapture all thy trembling strings.
GRAY: *Progress of Poesy.*

Æolian Mode, in Music, the ninth of the church modes, also called the Hypodorian, the range being from A to A, the dominant F or E, and the mediant E or C. It is characterized as "grand and pompous though sometimes soothing."

Æolian Rocks. A geological term for those rocks the formation and distribution of which has been due more to the agency of wind than to that of water. Most of the New Red Sandstones, and many of the Old Red, are of Æolian origin.

Æolic Digamma (ē ol' ik dī' găm å). The sixth letter of the early Greek alphabet (F), sounded like our *w*. Thus *oinos* with the digamma was sounded *woinos*; whence the Latin *vinum*, our *wine*. Gamma, or *g*, was shaped thus Γ, hence digamma = double g; it was early disused as a letter, but was retained as the symbol for the numeral 6. True Æolic was the dialect of Lesbos.

Æolus (ē' ō lůs), in Roman mythology, was "god of the winds."

Æon (ē'on) (Gr. *aion*). An age of the universe, an immeasurable length of time; hence the personification of an age, a god, any being that is eternal. Basilides reckons there have been 365 such Æons, or gods; but Valentinius restricts the number to 30.

Æsehylus (ēs' ki lûs) (525-456 B.C.), the father of the Greek tragic drama. Titles of seventy-two of his plays are known, but only seven are now extant. Fable has it that he was killed by a tortoise dropped by an eagle (to break the shell) on his bald head, which the bird mistook for a stone.

Æschylus of France. Prosper Jolyot de Crebillon (1674-1762).

Æsculapius (ēs kū lā' pi us). The Latin form of the Greek Asklepios, god of medicine and of healing. Now used for "a medical practitioner." The usual offering to him was a cock, hence the phrase "to sacrifice a cock to Æsculapius"—to return thanks (or pay the doctor's bill) after recovery from an illness.

When men a dangerous disease did scape,
Of old, they gave a cock to Æsculape.
BEN JONSON: *Epigram.*

Legend has it that he assumed the form of a serpent (*q.v.*) when he appeared at Rome during a pestilence; hence it is that the goddess of Health bears in her hand a serpent.

Æsir (ē' zer). The collective name of the celestial gods of Scandinavia, who lived in Asgard (*q.v.*). (1) Odin, the chief; (2) Thor (his eldest son, god of thunder); (3) Tiu (another son, god of wisdom); (4) Balder (another son, Scandinavian Apollo); (5) Bragi (god of poetry); (6) Vidar (god of silence); (7) Hoder the blind (slayer of Balder); (8) Hermoder (Odin's son and messenger); (9) Hœnir (a minor god); (10) Odnir (husband of Freyja, the Scandinavian Venus); (11) Loki (the god of mischief); (12) Vali (Odin's youngest son).

Æson's Bath (ē' son).

I perceive a man may be twice a child before the days of dotage; and stands in need of *Æson's* Bath before three score.—Sir THOMAS BROWNE: *Religio Medici, Section* 42.

The reference is to Medea rejuvenating Æson, father of Jason, with the juices of a concoction made of sundry articles. After Æson had imbibed these juices, Ovid says:—

Barba comæque,
Canitie posita, nigrum rapuere, colorem.
Metamorphoses, vii, 288.

Æsop's Fables (ē' sop) are traditionally ascribed to Æsop, a deformed Phrygian slave of the 6th century B.C.; but many of them are far older, some having been discovered on Egyptian papyri of 800 or 1,000 years earlier.

Babirus, probably an Italian, compiled a collection of 137 of the fables in choliambic verse about A.D. 230, and this version was for long used in the mediæval schools.

Pilpay (*q.v.*) has been called the Æsop of India.

Ætolian Hero, The (ē tō' li an). Diomede, who was king of Ætolia. *Ovid.*

Afreet, Afrit (ăf' rēt). In Mohammedan mythology the most powerful but one (Marids) of the five classes of Jinn, or devils. They are of gigantic stature, very malicious, and inspire great dread. Solomon, we are told, once tamed an Afreet, and made it submissive to his will.

Africa. *Teneo te, Africa.* When Cæsar landed at Adrumetum, in Africa, he tripped and fell—a bad omen; but, with wonderful presence of mind, he pretended that he had done so intentionally, and kissing the soil, exclaimed, "Thus do I take possession of thee, O Africa." The story is told also of Scipio, and of Cæsar again at his landing in Britain, and of others in similar circumstances.

Africa semper aliquid novi affert. "Africa is always producing some novelty." A Greek proverb quoted (in Latin) by Pliny, in allusion to the ancient belief that Africa abounded in strange monsters.

African Sisters, The. The Hesperides (*q.v.*), who lived in Africa.

Afridi (ă frē' di). A Pathan tribe of the Indo-Afghan frontier against whom the British sent several punitive expeditions in the late 19th century.

After-cast. An obsolete expression for something done too late; literally, a throw of the dice after the game is ended.

Ever he playeth an after-cast
Of all that he shall say or do.
GOWER.

After me the deluge. *See* APRÈS MOI LE DÉLUGE.

Agamemnon (ăg à mem' non). In Greek legend, the King of Mycenæ, son of Atreus, and leader of the Greeks at the siege of Troy.

Goodly Agamemnon . . .
The glorie of the stock of Tantalus,
And famous light of all the Greekish hosts,
Under whose conduct most victorious,
The *Dorick* flames consumed the *Iliack* posts.
SPENSER: *Virgil's Gnat.*

His *brother* was Menelaos.

His *daughters* were Iphigenia, Electra, Iphianassa, and Chrysothemis (*Sophocles*).

He was *grandson* of Pelops.

He was *killed* in a bath by his wife Clytemnestra, after his return from Troy.

His *son* was Orestes, who slew his mother for murdering his father, and was called Agamemnonides.

His *wife* was Clytemnestra, who lived in adultery with Egistheus. At Troy he fell in love with Cassandra, a daughter of King Priam.

Vixere fortes ante Agamemnona, a quotation from Horace (*Od.* IV, ix), paraphrased by Byron in *Don Juan* (I, v):

Brave men were living before Agamemnon
And since, exceeding valorous and sage,
A good deal like him too, though quite the same none;
But then they shone not on the poet's page,
And so have been forgotten.

Aganippe (ăg à nip' i). In Greek legend a fountain of Bœotia at the foot of Mount Helicon, dedicated to the Muses, because it had the virtue of imparting poetic inspiration. From this fountain the Muses are sometimes called Aganippides.

Agape (ăg' à pi). A love-feast (Gr. *agape*, love). The early Christians held a love-feast before or after communion when contributions were made for the poor. In course of time they became a scandal, and were condemned at the Council of Carthage, 397. The name is also given by Spenser to the fairy mother of Priamond, Diamond, Triamond, and Cambina. (*Faerie Queene*, IV, ii, 41 ff.).

Agapetæ (ăg à pē' tē) (Gr. beloved). A group of 3rd-century ascetic women who, under vows of virginity, contracted spiritual marriage with the monks and attended to their wants. Owing to the scandals occasioned the custom was condemned by St. Jerome and suppressed by various Councils.

Agate (ăg' àt). So called, says Pliny (xxxvii, 10), from Achates or Gagates, a river in Sicily, near which it is found in abundance.

These, these are they, if we consider well,
That saphirs and the diamonds doe excell,
The pearle, the emerauld, and the turkesse bleu,
The sanguine corrall, amber's golden hiew,
The christall, jacinth, *achate*, ruby red.
                    TAYLOR: *The Waterspout* (1630).

Agate is supposed to render a person invisible, and to turn the sword of foes against themselves.

A very small person has been called an agate, from the old custom of carving the stone with diminutive figures for use as seals. Shakespeare speaks of Queen Mab as no bigger than an agate-stone on the forefinger of an alderman.

I was never manned with an agate till now.
                    SHAKESPEARE: 2 *Henry IV*, i, 2.

For the same reason the very small type between nonpareil and pearl, known in England as "ruby," was called agate in America.

Agatha, St. (ăg' à thà), was tortured and martyred at Catania, in Sicily, during the Decian persecution of 251. She is sometimes represented in art with a pair of shears or pincers, and holding a salver on which are her breasts, these having been cut off. Her feast day is 5 February.

Agave (a gā' vi), named from Agave, daughter of Cadmus (*q.v.*), or "American aloe," a Mexican plant, naturalized in many parts of Europe, and fabled by English gardeners to bloom only once in a hundred years. It was introduced into Spain in 1561, and is used in Mexico, Switzerland, Italy, and elsewhere for fences. The Mohammedans of Egypt regard it as a charm and religious symbol; and pilgrims to Mecca hang a leaf of it over their door as a sign of their pilgrimage and as a charm against evil spirits.

Agdistes (ăg dis' tēz). The name is that of a Phrygian deity connected with the symbolic worship of the powers of Nature and by some identified with Cybele. He was hermaphrodite, and sprang from the stone Agdus, parts of which were taken by Deucalion and Pyrrha to cast over their shoulders for repeopling the world after the flood.

Age. A word used of a long but more or less indefinite period of history, human and pre-human, distinguished by certain real or mythical characteristics and usually named from these characteristics or from persons connected with them, as the *Golden Age* (*q.v.*), the *Middle Ages*, the *Dark Ages* (*qq.v.*), the *Age of the Antonines* (from Antoninus Pius, 138, to Marcus Aurelius, 180), the *Prehistoric Age*, etc. Thus, Hallam calls the 9th century the *Age of the Bishops*, and the 12th, the *Age of the Popes*.

Varro (*Fragments*, p. 219, Scaliger's edition, 1623) recognizes three ages: From the beginning of mankind to the Deluge, a time wholly unknown. From the Deluge to the First Olympiad, called the mythical period. From the first Olympiad to the present time, called the historic period.

Shakespeare's passage on the seven ages of man (*As You Like It*, ii, 7) is well known; and Titian symbolized the three ages of man thus: An infant in a cradle. A shepherd playing a flute. An old man meditating on two skulls.

According to Lucretius also there are three ages, distinguished by the materials employed in implements (v. 1282), viz.: *The age of stone*, when celts or implements of stone were employed. *The age of bronze*, when implements were made of copper or brass. *The age of iron*, when implements were made of iron, as at present.

The term *Stone Age* as now used includes the *Eolithic*, *Palæolithic*, and *Neolithic Ages* (*qq.v.*).

Hesiod names five ages, viz.: The *Golden* or patriarchal, under the care of Saturn. The *Silver* or voluptuous, under the care of Jupiter. The *Brazen* or warlike, under the care of Neptune. The *Heroic* or renaissant, under the care of Mars. The *Iron* or present, under the care of Pluto.

Age of Animals. An old Celtic rhyme, put into modern English, says:—

Thrice the age of a dog is that of a horse;
Thrice the age of a horse is that of a man;
Thrice the age of a man is that of a deer;
Thrice the age of a deer is that of an eagle.

Age of Consent. This is the age at which a girl's consent is valid; beneath that age to have carnal knowledge of her is a criminal offence. In English and Scottish law the age of consent is 16.

Age of Discretion. In English law a subject is deemed capable of using his discretion at the age of 14.

Canonical Age. Ecclesiastical law enjoins that the obligation of fasting begins at the age of 21; profession of religious vows after the age of 16; a bishop must have completed his 30th year.

Age hoc (a' je hok). "Attend to this." In sacrifice the Roman crier perpetually repeated these words to arouse attention. In the Common Prayer Book the attention of the congregation is frequently aroused by the exhortation, "Let us pray," though nearly the whole service is that of prayer.

Agelasta (ăj e lăs' tà) (Gr. joyless). The stone on which Ceres rested when worn down by fatigue in searching for her daughter, Persephone.

Agenor (ă jen' or). A son of Neptune, and founder of a nation in Phœnicia. His descendants, Cadmus, Perseus, Europa, etc., are known as the **Agenorides**.

Agent. Is man a free agent? This is a question of theology, which has long been mooted. The point is this: If God foreordains all our actions, they must take place as he foreordains them, and man acts as a watch or clock; but if, on the other hand, man is responsible for his actions, he must be free to act as his inclination leads him. Those who hold the former view are called *necessitarians*; those who hold the latter, *libertarians*.

Aglaia (á glī' á). One of the three Graces (*see* GRACES).

Aglaonice (ăg lā ō nī' si), the Thessalian, being able to calculate eclipses, pretended to have the moon under her command, and to be able when she chose to draw it from heaven. Her secret being found out, her vaunting became a laughing-stock, and gave birth to the Greek proverb cast at braggarts, "Yes as the Moon obeys Aglaonice."

Agnes, St., was martyred in the Diocletian persecution (about 303) at the age of 13. She was tied to a stake, but the fire went out, and Aspasius, set to watch the martyrdom, drew his sword, and cut off her head. St. Agnes is the patron of young virgins. She is commemorated on January 21st. Upon St. Agnes's night, says Aubrey in his *Miscellany*, though he should have said St. Agnes' Eve, you take a row of pins, and pull out every one, one after another. Saying a paternoster, stick a pin in your sleeve, and you will dream of him or her you shall marry; and in Keats's *The Eve of St. Agnes*, we are told—

how, upon St. Agnes' Eve,
Young virgins might have visions of delight,
And soft adorings from their loves receive
Upon the honey'd middle of the night,
If ceremonies due they did aright;
As, supperless to bed they must retire.

Agnostic (Gr. *a*, not; *gignoskein*, to know). A term coined by Prof. Huxley in 1869 (with allusion to St. Paul's mention of an altar to "the Unknown God") to indicate the mental attitude of those who withhold their assent from whatever is incapable of proof, such as an unseen world, a First Cause, etc. Agnostics neither dogmatically accept nor reject such matters, but simply say *Agnosco*—I do not know—they are not capable of proof. *Cp.* THEIST.

Agnus Bell. *See* AGNUS DEI.

Agnus-castus. *See* VITEX.

Agnus Dei (ăg'n ùs dē' ī, dā' ē). A cake of wax or dough stamped with the figure of a lamb supporting the banner of the Cross, and distributed by the Pope on the Sunday after Easter. This is a relic of the ancient custom of collecting and distributing to the worshippers the wax of the Paschal candle, which was stamped with the lamb. The part of the Mass and English communion service beginning with the words *Agnus Dei, qui tolles peccata mundi* (O Lamb of God, that takest away the sins of the world), is also known as the *Agnus Dei*. In Catholic services it is introduced by the ringing of the *Agnus bell*.

Agog (à gog'). **He is all agog,** in nervous anxiety, on the *qui vive*. The word is connected with the Old French phrase *en gogues*, meaning "in mirth": the origin of O.F. *gogue* and Norman *goguer*, to be mirthful, is unknown.

Agonistes (ă gon is' tēz). This word in *Samson Agonistes* (the title of Milton's drama) is Greek for "champion," so the title means simply "Samson the Champion." *Cp.* AGONY.

Agonistics (ă gon is' tiks). A fanatical sect of peripatetic ascetics, adherents to the Donatist schismatics of the early 4th century. They gave themselves this name (meaning "Champions," or "Soldiers," of the Cross); the Catholics called them the *Circumcelliones*, from their wandering about among the houses of the peasants (*circum cellas*).

Agony, meaning great pain or anguish, is derived through French from the Greek word *agonia*, from *agon*, which meant first "an assembly," then "an arena for contests," and hence the "contest" itself; so *agonia*, meaning first a struggle for mastery in the games, came to be used for any struggle, and hence for mental struggle or anguish.

Agony column. A column in a newspaper containing advertisements of missing relatives and friends.

Agrarian Law (à grâr' i àn) (Lat. *ager*, land). In Roman history, a law regulating landed property or the division of conquered territory; hence, a law for making land the common property of a nation, and not the particular property of individuals. In a modified form, a redistribution of land, giving to each citizen a portion.

Aguecheek. Sir Andrew Aguecheek, a straight-haired country squire, stupid even to silliness, self-conceited, living to eat, and wholly unacquainted with the world of fashion. The character is in Shakespeare's *Twelfth Night*.

Agur's Wish (ā' gerz) (*Prov.* xxx, 8). "Give me neither poverty nor riches."

Ahasuerus (à hăz ū ēr' ùs). Under this name the Emperor Xerxes (486-465 B.C.) appears in the biblical books of Ezra and Esther. The Ahasuerus of Daniel has not been identified. This is also the name given to the Wandering Jew (*q.v.*).

Ahithophel (a hith' ō fel). A treacherous friend and adviser. Ahithophel was David's counsellor, but joined Absalom in revolt, and advised him "like the oracle of God" (2 *Sam.* xvi, 20-23). *See* ACHITOPHEL.

Ahmed, Prince (a' med), in the *Arabian Nights*, is noted for the tent given him by the fairy Paribanou, which would cover a whole army, but might be carried in one's pocket; and for the apple of Samarcand, which would cure all diseases. The qualities ascribed to the magic tent are the common property of many legends and romances. *See* CARPET; and SKIDHBLADHNIR.

Ahriman (a' ri màn). In the dual system of Zoroaster, the spiritual enemy of mankind, also called *Angra Mainyu,* and *Druj* (deceit). He has existed since the beginning of the world, and is in eternal conflict with Ahura Mazda, or Ormuzd (*q.v.*).

Their evil principle, the demon Ahriman, might be represented as the rival or as the creature of The God of Light.

GIBBON: *Decline and Fall*, ch. 1i.

Ahura Mazda. *See* ORMUZD.

Aide toi et le Ciel t'aidera (ād twa ā lė sē ėl tā dė ra'). A line from La Fontaine (vi, 18), meaning "God will help those who help themselves," taken as the motto of a French political society, established in 1824. The society intended to induce the middle classes to resist the Government; it aided in bringing about the Revolution of 1830, and was dissolved in 1832. Guizot was at one time its president, and *Le Globe* and *Le National* its organs.

Aim, to give. A term in archery, meaning to *give* the archers information how near their arrows fall to the mark *aimed at*; hence, to give anybody inside information.

But, gentle people, give me aim awhile,
For nature puts me to a heavy task.
SHAKESPEARE. *Titus Andronicus*, v, 3.

Air. Held by Anaxagoras to be the primary form of matter, and given by Aristotle as one of the four elements. *See* ELEMENT.

The air of the court, the **air of gentility: a good air** (manner, deportment) means the pervading habit; hence, *to give oneself airs*—to assume in manner, appearance, and tone, a superiority to which one has no claim.

The plural is essential in this case; air, in the singular is generally complimentary, but in the plural conveys censure. In Italian, we find the phrase, *Si da delle arie*.

Air (in music) is that melody which predominates and gives its character to the piece.

Hot air. *See* HOT.

To air one's opinion. To state opinions openly, to give air to one's opinions.

Air-brained. A mis-spelling of hare-brained (*q.v.*).

Air-line. A direct line, taken—as a crow flies—through the air. *Cp.* BEE-LINE.

Aisle. The north and south wings of a church, from the Lat., *ala* (*axilla, ascella*), through the French, *aile*, a wing. The intrusive "s" did not take root till the middle of the 18th century, and is probably due to a confusion with "isle." In some church documents the aisles are called *alleys* (walks); the choir of Lincoln Cathedral used to be called the "Chanters' alley"; and Olden tells us that when he came to be churchwarden, in 1638, he made the Puritans "come up the middle alley on their knees to the raile."

Ajax (ā jăks). (1) *The Greater.* The most famous hero of the Trojan War after Achilles; king of Salamis, a man of giant stature, daring, and self-confident, son of Telamon. When the armour of Hector was awarded to Ulysses instead of to himself, he turned mad from vexation and stabbed himself.—Homer and later poets.

(2) *The Less.* Son of Oileus, King of Locris, in Greece. The night Troy was taken, he offered violence to Cassandra, the prophetic daughter of Priam; in consequence of which his ship was driven on a rock, and he perished at sea.—Homer and later poets.

Akbar (ăk' bar). An Arabic title, meaning "Very Great." Akbar Khan, the "very great Khan," is applied especially to the great Mogul emperor in India who reigned 1556-1605. His tomb at Secundra, a few miles from Agra, is one of the wonders of the East.

Alabama (ă là ba' mà). The name of this state of the U.S.A. is the Indian name of a river in the state, the meaning of which is "here we rest."

Alabaster. A stone of great purity and whiteness, used for ornaments. The name is said by Pliny (*Nat. Hist.*, xxxvi, 8) to be from an Egyptian town, Alabastron; but nothing is known of this town, nor of the ultimate origin of the Greek word.

Aladdin, (à lăd' in) in the *Arabian Nights*, obtains a magic lamp, and has a splendid palace built by the genie of the lamp. He marries the daughter of the sultan of China, loses his lamp, and his palace is transported to Africa.

Aladdin's lamp. The source of wealth and good fortune. After Aladdin came to his wealth and was married, he suffered his lamp to hang up and get rusty.

Alamo (al' ăm o). American cottonwood tree. In 1718 Franciscan monks founded the Mission of San Antonio de Valero at San Antonio, Texas. It was commonly called the Alamo Mission since it stood in a grove of cottonwood trees. By 1793 it was no longer a mission but the buildings were sometimes used as a fort. In 1836 a Texan garrison of 180 was besieged, overpowered and slaughtered by 4000 Mexicans under Santa Anna. In the subsequent campaign in which the Texans, under Sam Houston, defeated the Mexicans and captured Santa Anna, "remember the Alamo" became the Texan war cry. The buildings are now a National Monument.

Al Araf (al ā' răf) (Arab. the partition, from *'arafa*, to divide). A region, according to the Koran, between Paradise and Jahannam (hell), for those who are neither morally good nor bad, such as infants, lunatics, and idiots. Others regard it as a place where those whose good and evil deeds were about equally balanced can await their ultimate admission to heaven, a kind of "limbo" (*q.v.*).

Alasnam (à lăs' năm). In *the Arabian Nights* Alasnam had eight diamond statues, but was required to find a ninth more precious still, to fill the vacant pedestal. The prize was found in the woman who became his wife, at once the most beautiful and the most perfect of her race.

Alasnam's mirror. The "touchstone of virtue," given to Alasnam by one of the Genii. If he looked in this mirror and it remained unsullied so would the maiden he had in mind; if it clouded, she would prove faithless.

Albatross. The largest of web-footed birds, called by sailors the *Cape Sheep*, from its frequenting the Cape of Good Hope. Many fables are told of the albatross; it is said to sleep in the air, because its flight is a gliding without any apparent motion of its long wings, and sailors say that it is fatal to shoot one. *See also* ANCIENT MARINER.

Alberich. The all-powerful king of the dwarfs in Scandinavian mythology. In Wagner's version of the *Nibelungenlied* he appears as a hideous gnome and steals the magic gold (*Das Rheingold*) guarded by the Rhine Maidens. Later he is captured by the gods, and is forced to give up all he has in return for his freedom.

Albin. *See* ALBANY.

Albino (al bē' nō) (Lat. *albus*, white). A term originally applied by the Portuguese to those Negroes who were mottled with white spots; but now to persons who, owing to the congenital absence of colouring pigment, are born with red eyes and white hair and skin. The term is also applied to beasts and plants, and even, occasionally, in a purely figurative way:

thus, Oliver Wendell Holmes, in the *Autocrat of the Breakfast Table* (ch. viii), speaks of Kirke White as one of the "sweet Albino poets," whose "plaintive song" he admires; apparently implying some deficiency of virility, and possibly playing upon the name.

Albion. An ancient and poetical name for Great Britain: probably from the white (Lat. *albus*) cliffs that face Gaul, but possibly from the *Celtic alp, ailp* (*see* ALBANY), a rock, cliff, mountain. "Albion" or "Albany" may have been the Celtic name of all Great Britain, but was subsequently restricted to Scotland, and then to the Highlands of Scotland.

Legend gives various origins for the name. One derivation is from a giant son of Neptune, named Albion, who discovered the country and ruled over it for forty-four years. According to another story the fifty daughters of the king of Syria, the eldest of whom was named Albia, were all married on the same day and all murdered their husbands on the wedding-night. As punishment they were packed into a ship and set adrift, eventually reaching this western isle where they went ashore and duly married natives, "a lawless crew of devils."

In *Polyolbion* Michael Drayton says that Albion came from Rome and was the first Christian martyr in Britain.

Although the phrase **Perfide Albion** is attributed to Napoleon, the sentiment is much older, for Bossuet (1627-1704) wrote, "L'Angleterre, ah! la perfide Angleterre."

Al Borak. *See* BORAK.

Album. A blank book for photographs, stamps, autographs, miscellaneous jottings, scraps, and so on. The Romans applied the word to certain tables overlaid with gypsum, on which were inscribed the annals of the chief priests, the edicts of the prætors, and rules relating to civil matters. In the Middle Ages, "album" was the general name of a register or list; so called from being kept either on a white (*albus*) board with black letters, or on a black board with white letters.

Alcaic Verse (ăl kā' ik) or *Alcaics*. A Greek lyrical metre, so called from *Alcœos*, a lyric poet, who is said to have invented it. Alcaic measure is little more than a curiosity in English poetry; probably the best example is Tennyson's: —

O migh | ty-mouthed | in | ventor of | harmonies,
O skilled | to sing | of | Time or E | ternity,
God-gift | ed or | gan-voice | of Eng | land,
Milton, a | name to re | sound for | ages.

Alcantara, Order of (ăl kăn' tả rả). A military and religious order instituted in 1213 (on the foundation of the earlier order of San Juan del Pereyro, which had been created about 1155 to fight the Moors) by Alfonso IX, King of Castile, to commemorate the taking of Alcantara from the Moors. In 1835 the Order, which had been under the Benedictine rule, ceased to exist as a religious body, but it remained as a civil and military order under the Crown.

Alceste (ăl sest')· The hero of Molière's *Misanthrope.* He is not unlike Shakespeare's character of Timon, and was taken by Wycherley for the model of his Manly (*q.v.*).

Alchemilla (ăl kė mil' ȧ). A genus of plants of the rose family; so called because alchemists collected the dew of its leaves for their operations. Also called "Lady's Mantle," from the Virgin Mary, to whom the plant was dedicated.

Alchemy (ăl' kė mi). The derivation of this word is obscure: the *al* is the Arabic article, *the*, and *kimia* the Arabic form of Greek *chemeia*, which seems to have meant Egyptian art; hence "the art of the Egyptians." Its main objects were the transmutation of baser metals into gold, the universal solvent (alkahest, *q.v.*), the panacea (*q.v.*), and the elixir of life.

Alcmena (ălk mē' nȧ). In Greek mythology, daughter of Electryon, king of Mycenæ, wife of Amphitryon, and mother (by Zeus) of Hercules. The legend is that at the conception of Hercules Zeus, for additional pleasure with Alcmena, made the night the length of three ordinary nights.

Alderman. A senior or elder; now applied to certain magistrates in corporate towns. In the City of London aldermen were first appointed by a charter of Henry III in 1242; there are 25 (or, counting the Lord Mayor, or chief magistrate, 26), and they are elected for life, one for each ward. Of the larger cities of England: Birmingham has 34 aldermen; Liverpool, 39; Manchester, 36; Sheffield, 25; Leeds, 26; and Bristol, 28.

Aldine Editions. Editions of the Greek and Latin classics, published and printed under the superintendence of Aldo Manuzio, his father-in-law Andrea of Asolo, and his son Paolo, from 1490 to 1597; most of them are in small octavo, and all are noted for their accuracy. The father invented the type called *italics*, once called *Aldine*, and first used in printing *Virgil*, 1501.

Ale is the Anglo-Saxon *ealu*, connected with the Scandinavian *ol*, and Lithuanian *alus*. Beer is the Anglo-Saxon *beor* (M.E., *bere*), connected with the German *bier* and Icelandic *bjorr*. A beverage made from barley is mentioned by

Tacitus and even Herodotus. Hops were introduced from Holland and used for brewing about 1524, but their use was prohibited by Act of Parliament in 1528—a prohibition which soon fell into disuse. Ale is made from pale malt, whence its light colour; porter and stout from malt more highly dried. The word *beer* is of general application; and in many parts of England it includes ale, porter, and stout. In some parts *ale* is used for the stronger malt liquors and *beer* for the weaker, while in others the terms are reversed.

> Called ale among men; but by the gods called beer
> *The Alvismal (10th-cent. Scandinavian poem).*

See also CHURCH-ALE.

Ale-wife. The landlady of an alehouse. In America a fish of the herring kind, only rather larger, is known as the *ale-wife*. Some think it is a corruption of a North American Indian name, *aloofe*, and some of the French *alose*, a shad.

Alecto (à lek′ tō). In classical mythology, one of the three Furies (*q.v.*); her head was covered with snakes.

> Then like Alecto, terrible to view,
> Or like Medusa, the Circassian grew.
> HOOLE: *Jerusalem Delivered*, Bk. vi.

Alectryomancy (à lek tri ō măn′ si). Divination by a cock. Draw a circle, and write in succession round it the letters of the alphabet, on each of which lay a grain of corn. Then put a cock in the centre of the circle, and watch what grains he eats. The letters will prognosticate the answer. Libanus and Jamblicus thus discovered who was to succeed the emperor Valens. The cock ate the grains over the letters t, h, e, o, d = Theod[orus].

Alexander and the Robber. The story is that the pirate Diomedes, having been captured and brought before Alexander, was asked how he dared to molest the seas. "How darest *thou* molest the earth ?" was the reply. "Because I am the master only of a single galley I am termed a robber; but you who oppress the world with huge squadrons are called a king." Alexander was so struck by this reasoning that he made Diomedes rich, a prince, and a dispenser of justice. *See* the *Gesta Romanorum*, cxlvi.

You are thinking of Parmenio and I of Alexander—*i.e.* you are thinking of what you ought to receive, and I what I ought to give; you are thinking of those castigated or rewarded, but I of my position, and what reward is consistent with my rank. The allusion is to the tale that Alexander said to Parmenio, "I consider not what Parmenio should receive, but what Alexander should give."

Only two Alexanders. Alexander said, "There are but two Alexanders—the invincible son of Philip, and the inimitable painting of the hero by Apelles."

The continence of Alexander. Having gained the battle of Issus (333 B.C.) the family of Darius III fell into his hand; but he treated the women with the greatest decorum. A eunuch, having escaped, reported this to Darius, and the king could not but admire such nobility in a rival. *See* CONTINENCE.

Alexander. So Paris, son of Priam, was called by the shepherds who brought him up.

Alexander of the North. Charles XII of Sweden (1682-1718), so called from his military achievements. He was conquered at Pultowa (1709), by Peter the Great.

> Repressing here
> The frantic Alexander of the North.
> THOMSON: *Winter.*

Alexander's beard. A smooth chin, no beard at all. An Amazonian chin (*q.v.*).

> I like this trustie glasse of Steele
> Wherein I see a Sampson's grim regarde
> Disgraced yet with Alexander's bearde.
> GASCOIGNE: *The Steele Glas.*

Alexandra Day. To celebrate the fiftieth year of her residence in England, Queen Alexandra (1844-1925) inaugurated a fund for the assistance of hospitals, convalescent homes, etc., to be raised by the sale of artificial wild roses made by the blind and cripples. On a day in June these are sold in the streets, the buyers wearing the roses as a sign of having contributed to the fund.

Alexandrian. Anything from the East was so called by the old chroniclers and romancers, because Alexandria was the depot from which Eastern stores reached Europe.

> Reclined on Alexandrian carpets [*i.e.* Persian].
> ROSE: *Orlando Furiosa*, x, 37.

Alexandrian Library. Founded by Ptolemy Soter, in Alexandria, in Egypt. The tale is that it was burnt and partly consumed in 391; but when the city fell into the hands of the calif Omar, in 642, the Arabs found books sufficient to "heat the baths of the city for six months." It is said that it contained 700,000 volumes, and the reason given by the Mohammedan destroyer for the destruction of the library was that the books were unnecessary in any case, for all knowledge that was necessary to man was contained in the Koran, and that any knowledge contained in the library that was not in the Koran must be pernicious.

Alexandrian School. An academy of learning founded about 310 B.C. by Ptolemy Soter, son of Lagus, and Demetrius of Phaleron, especially famous for its grammarians and mathematicians. Of the former the most noted are Aristarchus (c. 220-145 B.C.), Eratosthenes (c. 275-195 B.C.), and Harpocration (A.D. 2nd century); and of its mathematicians, Claudius Ptolemæus (A.D. 2nd century) and Euclid (c. 300 B.C.), the former an astronomer, and the latter the geometer whose *Elements* were once very generally used in schools and colleges.

Alexandrine. In *prosody*, an iambic or trochaic line of twelve syllables or six feet with, usually, a cæsura (break) at the sixth syllable. So called either from the 12th-century French metrical romance, *Alexander the Great* (commenced by Lambert-li-Cort and continued by Alexandre de Bernay), or from the old Castilian verse chronicle, *Poema de Alexandro Magno*, both of which are written in this metre. The final line of the Spenserian stanza is an Alexandrine.

A needless Alexandrine ends the song,
Which, like a wounded snake,—drags its slow length along.
POPE: *Essay on Criticism*, ii, 356.

Alexandrine Age. From about A.D. 323 to 640, when Alexandria, in Egypt, was the centre of science, philosophy, and literature.

Alexandrine Philosophy. A system of philosophy which flourished at Alexandria in the early centuries of the Christian era, characterized by its attempt to combine Christianity and Greek philosophy. It gave rise to Gnosticism and Neoplatonism.

Alexandrite. A variety of chrysoberyl found in the mica-slate of the Urals. So named from Alexander II of Russia, on whose birthday it was discovered. The stone is green by natural and red by artificial light.

Alexis, St. Patron saint of hermits and beggars. The story goes that he lived on his father's estate as a hermit till death, but was never recognized. It is given at length in the *Gesta Romanorum* (Tale xv). His feast day is July 17th. He is represented in art with a pilgrim's habit and staff. Sometimes he is drawn as if extended on a mat, with a letter in his hand, dying.

Alfadir (al fa' der) (father of all). In Scandinavian mythology, one of the epithets of Odin (*q.v.*).

Alfana. *See* HORSE.

Alfonsin, Alfonsine Fables. *See* ALPHONSIN, etc.

Alfred the Great (848?-900). King of Wessex, father of the British Navy and leader of the opposition to the invading Danish armies. In January 878 he was surprised and defeated at Chippenham; with the remains of his forces he withdrew to Athelney and continued his resistance. A legend having no basis in fact says that he fled from Chippenham to Athelney and took refuge in a peasant's hut, where the housewife, not recognizing him in his rags, put him to watching cakes baking by the fire. He was so absorbed in his meditations that he allowed the cakes to burn and was scolded as an idle and useless wretch. After his final victory he built a monastery at Athelney in celebration of and in thanksgiving for his resistance there. In 1693, the beautiful Saxon ornament, bearing his name and known as *Alfred's Jewel*, was found at Athelney. It is now in the Ashmolean Museum, Oxford.

Algarsife (ăl' gar sīf). In Chaucer's unfinished *Squire's Tale*, son of Cambuscan, and brother of Camballo, who "won Theodora to wife."

This noble king, this Tartre Cambuscan,
Had two sones by Elfeta his wife,
Of which the eldest sone highte Algarsife,
That other was ycleped Camballo.
A doghter had this worthy king also
That youngest was and highte Canace.

Hence the reference in Milton's *Il Penseroso*:—

Call him up that left half told
The story of Cambuscan bold,
Of Camball, and of Algarsife,
And who had Canace to wife.

Algebra is the Arabic *al jebr* (the equalization), "the supplementing and equalizing (process)"; so called because the problems are solved by equations, and the equations are made by supplementary terms. Fancifully identified with the Arabian chemist Gebir. *See also* WHETSTONE OF WITTE.

Alhambra (ăl hăm' brà). The citadel and palace built at Granada by the Moorish kings in the 13th century. The word is the Arabic *al-hamra*, or at full length *kal'-at al hamra* (the red castle).

Ali (a' lē). Cousin and son-in-law of Mohammed, the beauty of whose eyes is with the Persians proverbial; in so much that the highest term they employ to express beauty is *Ayn Hali* (eyes of Ali).

Alias (ā' li às). "You have as many aliases as Robin of Bagshot," said to one who passes under many names. The phrase is from Gay's *Beggar's Opera*: Robin of Bagshot, one of Macheath's gang, was *alias* Gordon, *alias* Bluff Bob, *alias* Carbuncle, *alias* Bob Booty.

Ali Baba (ă' lē ba' ba). The hero of a story in the *Arabian Nights Entertainments*, who sees a band of robbers enter a cavern by means of the magic password "Open Sesame." When they have gone away he enters the cave, loads his ass with treasure and returns home. The Forty Thieves discover that Ali Baba has learned their secret and resolve to kill him, but they are finally outwitted by the slave-girl Morgiana.

Alibi (Lat. elsewhere). A plea of having been at another place at the time that an offence is alleged to have been committed. A clock which strikes an hour, while the hands point to a different time, the real time being neither one nor the other, has been humorously called an *alibi clock*.

Never mind the character, and stick to the alley bi. Nothing like an alley bi, Sammy, nothing.—DICKENS: *Pickwick Papers.*

A modern and incorrect usage of this word makes it mean an excuse, a pretext.

Alice in Wonderland and its companion *Through the Looking-glass* are probably the most famous and widely read of children's books. Their author was C. L. Dodgson, an Oxford mathematician who wrote under the pseudonym of Lewis Carroll. *Alice* appeared in 1865 and *Looking-glass* in 1871, both books being illustrated by Sir John Tenniel. The original of Alice was Alice Liddell, daughter of Dean Liddell, himself famous as part-author of Liddell & Scott's Greek Lexicon.

Alien (ā′ li ėn). This term is legally applied to a person living in a different country from that of his birth, and not having acquired citizenship in the land of his residence. Later usage has given the word a pejorative implication. An *alienist* is a physician or scientist who specializes in the study and treatment of insanity.

Alifanfaron (ăl i făn′ fä ron). Don Quixote attacked a flock of sheep, and declared them to be the army of the giant Alifanfaron. Similarly Ajax, in a fit of madness, fell upon a flock of sheep, which he mistook for Grecian princes.

Al Kadr (ăl kădr) (the divine decree). A particular night in the month Ramadan, when Mohammedans say that angels descend to earth, and Gabriel reveals to man the decrees of God.—*Al Koran,* ch. xcvii.

All and Some. An old English expression meaning "one and all," confused sometimes with "all and *sum,*" meaning the whole total. It appears in the early 14th-century romance, *Cœur de Lion:*—

They that wolde nought Crystene become,
Richard lect sleen hem alle and some.

All Fool's Day (April 1st). *See* APRIL FOOL.

To go on all fours is to crawl about on all four limbs, like a quadruped or an infant. The phrase used to be (more correctly) *all four,* as in *Lev.* xi, 42, "whatsoever goeth upon all four."

All-Hallows Summer. Another name for St. Martin's Summer (*see* SUMMER), because it sets in about All Hallows; also called St. Luke's Summer (St. Luke's Day is Oct. 18th), and the Indian summer (*q.v.*). Shakespeare uses the term—

"Farewell, thou latter spring; farewell, All-hallows Summer!"

1 *Henry IV,* i, 2.

All-Hallows' Day. All Saints' Day (Nov. 1st), "hallows" being the Old English *halig,* a holy (man), hence, a saint. The French call it *Toussaint.* Between 603 and 610 the Pope (Boniface IV) changed the heathen Pantheon into a Christian church and dedicated it to the honour of all the martyrs. The festival of All Saints was first held on May 1st, but in the year 834 it was changed to November 1st.

All-Hallows' Eve. Many old folklore customs are connected with All-Hallows' Eve (October 31st), such as bobbing for apples, cracking nuts (mentioned in the *Vicar of Wakefield*), finding by various "tests" whether one's lover is true, etc. Burns's *Hallowe'en* gives a good picture of Scottish customs; and there is a tradition in Scotland that those born on All-Hallows' Eve have the gift of double sight, and commanding powers over spirits. Thus, Mary Avenel, in Scott's *The Monastery,* is made to See the White Lady, invisible to less gifted visions.

All serene (Sp. *seréna*). In Cuba the word was used as a countersign by sentinels, and is about equivalent to our "All right," or "All's well." In the late 19th century it was a colloquial catch-word.

All Souls College, Oxford. This was founded in 1437 by Henry Chichele, Archbishop of Canterbury, as a chantry where masses should be said for the souls of those killed in the wars of Henry V and Henry VI. It has a Warden and fifty fellows, few of whom are in residence, but is unique in having no undergraduates.

All Souls' Day. November 2nd, so called because Catholics on that day seek by prayer and almsgiving to alleviate the sufferings of souls in purgatory. It was instituted in the monastery of Cluny in 993.

According to tradition, a pilgrim, returning from the Holy Land, was compelled by a storm to land on a rocky island, where he found a hermit, who told him that among the cliffs was an opening into the infernal regions through which huge flames ascended, and where the groans of the tormented were distinctly audible. The pilgrim told Odilo, abbot of Cluny, of this; and the abbot appointed the day following, which was November 2nd, to be set apart for the benefit of those souls in purgatory.

All this for a song! Said to be Burleigh's remark when Queen Elizabeth ordered him to give £100 to Spenser as a royal gratuity.

Allah (ăl' à). The Arabic name of the Supreme Being, from *al*, the, *illah*, god. *Allah il Allah*, the Mohammedan war-cry, and also the first clause of their confession of faith, is a corruption of *la illah illa allah*, meaning "there is no God, but the God." Another Mohammedan war-cry is *Allah akbar*, "God is most mighty."

Alley or Ally. A choice, large playing-marble made of stone or alabaster, from which it takes its name. The alley tor (more correctly taw) beloved of Master Bardell (*Pickwick Papers*, 34) was a special ally that had won many taws or games.

Alley, The. An old name for Change Alley in the City of London, where dealings in the public funds, etc., used to take place.

Why did 'Change Alley waste thy precious hours
Among the fools who gap'd for golden show'rs?
No wonder if we found some poets there,
Who live on fancy and can feed on air;
No wonder they were caught by South-Sea schemes,
Who ne'er enjoy'd a guinea but in dreams.

THOMAS GAY, to Mr. T. SNOW, goldsmith.

Alligator. When the Spaniards first saw this reptile in the New World, they called it *el lagarto* (the lizard). Sir Walter Raleigh called these creatures *lagartos*; in the 1st Quarto of *Romeo and Juliet* (v, 1) the animal is called an *aligarta*, and in Ben Jonson's *Bartholomew Fair* an *alligarta*.

Alligator Pear. The name given to the fruit of the West Indian tree, *Persea gratissima*. It is a corruption either of the Carib *aouacate*, called by the Spanish discoverers *avocado* or *avigato*, or of the Aztec *abuacath*, which was transmitted through the Fr. *avocat* and Sp. *aguacate*.

Alliteration. The rhetorical device of commencing adjacent accented syllables with the same letter or sound, as in Quince's ridicule of it in *Midsummer Night's Dream* (v. 1):—

With *b*lade, with *b*loody *b*lameful *b*lade,
He *b*ravely *b*roached his *b*oiling *b*loody *b*reast.

Alliteration was a *sine qua non* in Anglo-Saxon and early English poetry, and in modern poetry it is frequently used with great effect, as in Coleridge's:—

The fair *b*reeze *b*lew, the white *f*oam *f*lew.
The *f*urrow *f*ollowed *f*ree.
Ancient Mariner.

And Tennyson's:—
The moan of doves in *imm*emorial el*m*s,
And *m*urmuring of innumerable bees.
Princess, vii.

Many fantastic examples of excessive alliteration are extant, and a good example from a parody by Swinburne will be found under the heading AMPHIGOURI. Hugbald composed an alliterative poem on Charles the Bald, every word of which begins with *e*, and Henry Harder a poem of 100 lines, in Latin hexameters, on cats, each word beginning with *c*, called *Canum cum Catis certamen carmine compositum currente calamo C Catulli Caninii*. The first line is—

Cattorum canimus certamina clara canumque.

Tusser, who died 1580, has a rhyming poem of twelve lines, every word of which begins with *t*; and in the 1890s there was published a *Serenade* of twenty-eight lines, "sung in M flat by Major Marmaduke Muttinhead to Mademoiselle Madeline Mendoza Marriott," which contained only one word—in the line, "Meet me *by* moonlight, marry me"—not beginning with M.

The alliterative alphabetic poem beginning—

An Austrian army awfully arrayed,
Boldly by battery besieged Belgrade;
Cossack commanders, canonading come,
Dealing destruction's devastating doom; . . .

is well known. It was published in *The Trifler*, May 7th, 1817, ascribed to Rev. B. Poulter, later revised by Alaric A. Watts, though claimed for others.

Another attempt of the same kind begins thus:—

About an age ago, as all agree,
Beauteous Belinda, brewing best Bohea
Carelessly chattered, controverting clean,
Dublin's derisive, disputatious dean . . .

Allopathy (à lop' à thi) is in opposition to Homœopathy (*q.v.*). It is from the Greek, *allo pathos*, a different disease. In homœopathy the principle is that "like is to cure like"; in allopathy the disease is to be cured by its "antidote."

Alma (ăl' mà) (Ital. soul, spirit, essence), in Prior's poem of this name typifies the mind or guiding principles of man. Alma is queen of "Body Castle," and is beset by a rabble rout of evil desires, foul imaginations, and silly conceits for seven years (*the Seven Ages*). In Spenser's *Faerie Queene* (II, ix-xi) Alma typifies the soul. She is mistress of the House of Temperance, and there entertains Prince Arthur and Sir Guyon.

Alma Mater. A collegian so calls the university of which he is a member. The words are Latin for "fostering mother," and in ancient Rome the title was given to several goddesses, especially Ceres and Cybele.

They are also used for other "fostering mothers," as in—

You might divert yourself, too, with Alma Mater, the Church.

HORACE WALPOLE: *Letters* (1778).

Almanac. A mediæval Latin word for a table of days and months with astronomical data, etc.

The derivation of the word is obscure, though it clearly comes from the Sp. Arabic *al*, the; *manakh*, a sun-dial. This is not, however, a true Arabic word, but is probably of Greek origin.

Some early almanacs are:—

Before invention of printing:

By Solomon Jarchi	..	in and after	1150
" Peter de Dacia	.. ..	about	1307
" Walter de Elvendene	.. ..	..	1327
" John Somers, Oxford	.. ..	..	1380
" Nicholas de Lynna	.. ..	..	1386
" Purbach	.. ..		1150-1461

After invention of printing:

First printed by Gutenberg, at Mainz	..	1457
By Regiomontanus, at Nuremberg	..	1474
" Zainer, at Ulm	.. ..	1478
" Richard Pynson (*Sheapeherd's Kalendar*)		1497
" Stoffler, in Venice	.. ..	1499
Poor Robin's Almanack	.. ..	1652
Francis Moore's Almanack between 1698 and		1713
Almanach de Gotha,	first published	1764
Whitaker's Almanack	first published	1869

Almanzor (ăl măn' zŏr). The word means "the invincible" and was adopted as a title by several Mussulman potentates, notably the second Abbasside Caliph Abu Jafar Abdullah. It was a royal title given to the kings of Fez, Morocco, and Algiers:—

The kingdoms of Almansor, Fez, and Sus, Marocco and Algiers. . . .

Paradise Lost, xi, 403.

The Caliph Almanzor founded the city of Bagdad, which he named after a beggar who had prophesied that he would do so.

One of the characters in Dryden's *Conquest of Granada* (1672) is an Almanzor; the name figures also as one of the lackeys in Molière's *Précieuses Ridicules.*

Almighty Dollar. Washington Irving seems to have been the first to use this expression:—

The almighty dollar, that great object of universal devotion throughout our land. . . .

W. IRVING: *Wolfert's Roost, Creole Village* (1837).

Ben Jonson in his *Epistle to Elizabeth, Countess of Rutland,* speaks of "almighty gold."

Alms (amz) "(O.E. *ælmysse*, ultimately from Lat. *elemosina* from Gr. *eleemosyne*, compassion); gifts to the poor.

Dr. Johnson says the word has no *singular*; the O.E.D. says it has no *plural*. It is a singular word which, like *riches* (from Fr. *richesse*), has in modern usage become plural. In the Bible we have "he asked *an* alms" (*Acts* iii, 3), but Dryden gives us "alms *are* but the vehicles of prayer" (*Hind and the Panther,* iii, 106).

Alms-drink. Leavings; the liquor which a drinker finds too much, and therefore hands to another; also, liquor left over from a feast and sent to the alms-people. *See Antony and Cleopatra,* ii, 7.

Alms-fee. Peter's pence (*q.v.*).

Almshouse. A house for the use of the poor, usually supported by the endowment of some wealthy patron who built the houses. Almshouses are generally a number of small dwellings built together, often in a row, and are devoted to housing and supporting persons who find themselves poor or destitute in old age.

Aloe (Gr. *aloe*). A very bitter plant; hence the line in Juvenal's sixth satire (181), *Plus aloes quam mellis habet,* "He has in him more bitters than sweets," said of a writer with a sarcastic pen. The French say, "*Le côte d'Adam contient plus d'aloes que de miel,*" where *côte d'Adam,* of course, means woman or one's wife.

Aloof. A sea term, *to stand aloof,* meaning originally to bear to windward, or *luff.* The *a* is the same prefix as in *afoot* or *asleep,* and means *on; loof* is the Dutch *loef,* windward. *To hold aloof* thus means literally "to keep to the windward," and as one cannot do that except by keeping the head of the ship *away,* it came to mean "to keep away from" as opposed to "to approach."

Alpha (ăl' fà). "*I am Alpha and Omega, the first and the last*" (*Rev.* i, 8). "Alpha" is the first, and "Omega" (Ω) the last letter of the Greek alphabet. *Cp.* TAU.

Alphabet. This is the only word of more than one syllable compounded solely of the names of letters. The Greek *alpha* (a) *beta* (b); our A B C (book), etc.

Some curiosities of the alphabet are these:—

Ezra vii, 21, contains all the letters of the English alphabet, presuming I and J to be identical.

Even the Italian alphabet is capable of more than seventeen trillion combinations; that is, 17 followed by eighteen other figures, as—

17,000,000,000,000,000,000;

while the English alphabet will combine into more than twenty-nine thousand quatrillion combinations; that is, 29 followed by twenty-seven other figures, as—

29,000,000,000,000,000,000,000,000,000.

Yet we have no means of differentiating our vowel-sounds; take *a,* we have *fate, fat, Thames, war, orange, ware, abide, calm, swan,* etc. So with *e*, we have *era, the, there, prey (a), met, England, sew, herb, clerk,* etc. The other vowels are equally indefinite.

See LETTER.

Alpheus and Arethusa (ăl fē' us, ăr e thū' za). The Greek legend is that a youthful hunter named Alpheus was in love with the nymph Arethusa; she fled from him to the island of Ortygia on the Sicilian coast and he was turned into a river of Arcadia in the Peloponnesus. Alpheus pursued her under the sea, and, rising in Ortygia, he and she became one in the fountain hereafter called Arethusa. The myth seems to be designed for the purpose of accounting for the fact that the course of the Alpheus is for some considerable distance underground.

Alpine Race. This is another name for the large Celtic Race and is applied to the thickset men, with broad faces, hazel eyes, and light chestnut hair who inhabited the northwest extremity of France, Savoy, Switzerland, the Ardennes, Vosges, and the Biscayan coasts. They were a midway race between the Scandinavian Nordics and the dark Mediterranean folk; the zenith of their culture was the so-called La Tene period (500 B.C. to A.D. 1).

Al Rakim (ăl ra' kim). The dog in the legend of the Seven Sleepers of Ephesus.

Alruna-wife, An (ăl roo' nå). The Alrunes were the *lares* or *penates* of the ancient Germans; and an Alruna-wife, the household goddess.

Al-Sirat (Arab, the path). In Mohammedan mythology, the bridge leading to paradise; a bridge over mid-hell, no wider than the edge of a sword, across which all who enter heaven must pass.

Altar (Lat. *altus,* high; a high place). The oblong block or table, made of wood, marble, or other stone, consecrated and used for religious sacrifice. In Christian churches the term is applied to the communion table. According to the rubric laid down in the Book of Common Prayer the celebrant at Holy Communion shall stand at the north side of the table, thus sideways to the communicants who can in this way observe his motions in the act of consecration. This was enacted in order to do away with the alleged mystery of the Mass, but it is not always observed to-day.

Led to the altar. Married. Said of a woman who, as a bride, is led up the aisle to the altar-rail where marriages are solemnized.

Alter ego (ăl' ter eg' ō). (Lat. other I, other self). One's double; one's intimate and thoroughly trusted friend; one who has full powers to act for another. *Cf.* "One's second self" *under* SECOND.

Althea. The divine Althea of Richard Lovelace was Lucy Sacheverell, also called by the poet, "Lucasta."

When Love with unconfinëd wings
    Hovers within my gates,
And my divine Althea brings
    To whisper at the grates.

Lovelace was thrown into prison by the Long Parliament for his petition in favour of the king; hence the grates referred to.

Altis. The sacred precinct of Zeus at Olympia, containing the great temple and oval altar of Zeus, the Pelopium (grave of Pelops), the Heræum, with many other buildings and statues. It was connected by an arched passage with the Stadium, where the Olympian games were held.

Alto relievo. Italian for "high relief." A term used in sculpture for figures in wood, stone, marble, etc., so cut as to project at least one-half from the tablet.

Alvina weeps, or "Hark! Alvina weeps," *i.e.* the wind howls loudly, a Flemish saying. Alvina was the daughter of a king, who was cursed by her parents because she married unsuitably. From that day she roamed about the air invisible to the eye of man, but her moans are audible.

Alzire (ăl' zēr). Al daughter of Montezuma invented by Voltaire and made the central character of one of his greatest plays of the same name (1736). The scene is shifted from Mexico to Peru.

A.M. or **M.A.** When the Latin form is intended the A comes first, as *Artium Magister;* but where the English form is meant the M precedes, as *Master of Arts.*

The abbreviation "A.M." also stands for *ante meridiem* (Lat.), before noon, and *anno mundi,* in the year of the world.

Amadis of Gaul (à ma' dis). The hero of a prose romance of the same title, supposed to have been written by the Portuguese, Vasco de Lobeira (*d.* 1403), with additions by the Spaniard Montalvo, and by many subsequent romancers, who added exploits and adventures of other knights and thus swelled the romance to fourteen books. The romance was referred to as early as 1350 (in Egidis Colonna's *De Regimine Principium*); it was first printed in 1508, became immensely popular, and exerted a wide influence on literature far into the 17th century.

Amadis, called the "Lion Knight," from the device on his shield, and "Beltenebros" (darkly beautiful), from his personal appearance, was a love-child of Perion, King of Gaula (Wales), and Elizena, Princess of Brittany. He was cast away at birth and became known as the Child of the Sun, and after many adventures including wars with the race of Giants, a war for the hand of his lady-love Oriana, daughter of Lisuarte, King of Greece, the Ordeal of the Forbidden Chamber, etc., he and Oriana are married. He is represented as a poet and a musician, a linguist and a gallant, a knight-errant and a king, the very model of chivalry.

Other names by which Amadis was called were the *Lovely Obscure*, the *Knight of the Green Sword*, the *Knight of the Dwarf*, etc.

Amadis of Greece. A Spanish continuation of the seventh book of Amadis of Gaul (*q.v.*), supposed to be by Feliciano de Silva. It tells the story of Lisuarte of Greece, a grandson of Amadis.

Amalthæa (ăm ăl thē' à). In Greek mythology, the nurse of Zeus. In Roman legend Amalthea is the name of the Sibyl who sold the Sibylline Books (*q.v.*) to Tarquin.

Amalthea's horn. The cornucopia or "horn of plenty" (*q.v.*). The infant Zeus was fed with goats' milk by Amalthea, one of the daughters of Melisseus, King of Crete. Zeus, in gratitude, broke off one of the goat's horns, and gave it to Amalthea, promising that the possessor should always have in abundance everything desired. *See* ÆGIS.

> When Amalthea's horn
> O'er hill and dale the rose-crowned Flora pours,
> And scatters corn and wine, and fruits and flowers.
> CAMOENS: *Lusiad*, Bk. ii.

Amaranth (ăm' à rănth) (Gr. *amarantos*, everlasting). The name given by Pliny to some real or imaginary fadeless flower. Clement of Alexandria says—*Amarantus flos, symbolum est immortalitatis*. Among the ancients it was the symbol of immortality, because its flowers retain to the last much of their deep blood-red colour.

The best-known species are "Love lies bleeding" (*Amarantus caudatus*), and "Prince's feather" (*Amarantus hypochondriacus*).

> Immortal amarant, a flower which once
> In Paradise, fast by the Tree of Life,
> Began to bloom, but, soon for man's offence
> To heaven removed where first it grew, there grows
> And flowers aloft, shading the Fount of Life. . . .
> With these, that never fade, the Spirits elect
> Bind their resplendent locks.
> MILTON: *Paradise Lost*, iii, 353.

Spenser mentions "sad Amaranthus" as one of the flowers "to which sad lovers were transformed of yore" (*Faerie Queene*, III, vi, 45), but there is no known legend to this effect.

In 1653 Christina, Queen of Sweden, instituted the order of the *Knights of the Amaranth*, but it ceased to exist at the death of the Queen.

Amaryllis (ăm à rĭl' is). A rustic sweetheart. The name is borrowed from a shepherdess in the pastorals of Theocritus and Virgil.

> To sport with Amaryllis in the shade.
> MILTON: *Lycidas*, 68.

In Spenser's *Colin Clout's Come Home Again*, Amaryllis is intended for Alice Spenser, Countess of Derby.

Amasis, Ring of (à mā' sis). Herodotus tells us (iii, 4) that Polycrates, tyrant of Samos, was so fortunate in everything that Amasis, king of Egypt, fearing such unprecedented luck boded ill, advised him to part with something which he highly prized. Polycrates accordingly threw into the sea a ring of great value. A few days afterwards, a fish was presented to the tyrant, in which the ring was found. Amasis now renounced friendship with Polycrates, as a man doomed by the gods; and not long afterwards, a satrap put the too fortunate despot to death by crucifixion.

Amati (à ma' ti). A family famous for making stringed instruments at Cremona (*q.v.*) in the 16th and 17th centuries. Either Andrea Amati or Gaspar da Salo produced the first violin similar to those in use to-day, the earliest surviving Amati instrument being dated 1564.

Amaurote (ăm ô rō' te) (Gr. the shadowy or unknown place), the chief city of Utopia (*q.v.*) in the political romance of that name by Sir Thomas More. Rabelais, in his *Pantagruel*, introduces Utopia and "the great city of the Amaurots" (Bk. II, ch. xxiii). He had evidently read Sir Thomas More's book.

To add to the verisimilitude of the romance, More says he could not recollect whether Hythlodaye had told him it was 500 or 300 paces long; and he requested his friend Peter Giles, of Antwerp, to put the question to the adventurer. Swift, in *Gulliver's Travels*, uses very similar means of throwing dust in his reader's eyes. He says:—

> I cannot recollect whether the reception room of the Spaniard's Castle in the Air is 200 or 300 feet long. I will get the next aeronaut who journeys to the moon to take the exact dimensions for me, and will memorialise the learned society of Laputa.

Amazement. Not afraid with any amazement (I *Pet.* iii, 6), introduced at the close of the marriage service in the Book of Common Prayer. The meaning is, you will be God's children so long as you do his bidding, and are not drawn aside by any sort of bewilderment or distraction. Shakespeare uses the word in the same sense:—

> Behold, distraction, frenzy and amazement,
> Like witless antics one another meet.
>
> *Troilus and Cressida*, v, 3.

Amazon (ăm′ à zon). A Greek word meaning *without breast*, or rather, "deprived of a pap." According to Herodotus there was a race of female warriors, or Amazons, living in Scythia, and other Greek stories speak of a nation of women in Africa of a very warlike character. There were no men in the nation, and if a boy was born, it was either killed or sent to its father, who lived in some neighbouring state. The girls had their right breasts burnt off, that they might the better draw the bow. The term is now applied to any strong, brawny woman of masculine habits.

> She towered, fit person for a Queen
> To lead those ancient Amazonian files;
> Or ruling Bandit's wife among the Grecian isles.
>
> WORDSWORTH: *Poems of the Imagination*, xviii.

Amazonia (ăm à zō′ ni à). An old name for the regions about the river Amazon in South America, which was so called because the early Spanish explorers (1541), under Orellana, thought they saw female warriors on its banks.

Amber. A yellow, translucent, fossilized vegetable resin, the name of which originally belonged to ambergris (*q.v.*). Beaumont and Fletcher use it as a verb meaning to perfume with ambergris:—

> Be sure
> The wines be lusty, high, and full of spirit,
> And amber'd all.
>
> *Custom of the Country*, III, ii.

Legend has it that amber is a concretion, the tears of birds who were the sisters of Meleager and who never ceased weeping for the death of their brother.—OVID: *Metamorphoses*, viii, 270.

> Around thee shall glisten the loveliest amber
> That ever the sorrowing sea-bird hath wept.
>
> T. MOORE: *Fire Worshippers*.

Insects, small leaves, etc., are often preserved in amber; hence such phrases as "preserved for all time in the imperishable amber of his genius."

> Pretty! in amber, to observe the forms
> Of hairs, or straws, or dirt, or grubs or worms,
> The things, we know, are neither rich nor rare,
> But wonder how the devil they got there.
>
> POPE: *Ep. to Arbuthnot*, 169-72.

Amber, meaning a repository, is an obsolete spelling of *ambry* (*q.v.*).

Ambergris. A waxy, aromatic substance found floating on tropical seas and in the intestines of the cachalot. It is a marbled ashy grey in colour and is used in perfumery. Its original name was simply *amber* (see AMBER) from Fr. *ambre*, which denoted only this substance; when it came to be applied to the fossil resin (Fr. *ambre jaune*, yellow amber), this grey substance became known as *amber gris* (grey amber).

Ambidexter properly means both hands right hands, and so one who can use his left hand as deftly as his right; in slang use, a double-dealer.

Ambrose, St., Bishop of Milan (b. *c.* 340). In 384 he instituted reforms in Church music and introduced from the Eastern Church the Ambrosian Chant, which was used until Pope Gregory the Great introduced Gregorian Chant two centuries later. His feast day is December 7th. His emblems are: (1) a beehive, in allusion to the legend that a swarm of bees settled on his mouth when lying in his cradle; (2) a scourge, by which he expelled the Arians from Italy.

Ambrosia (ăm brō′ zi à) (Gr. *a*, privative, *brotos*, mortal). The food of the gods, so called because it made them immortal. Anything delicious to the taste or fragrant in perfume is so called from the notion that whatever is used by the celestials must be excellent.

> . . . So fortunate
> Whom the Pierian sacred sisters love
> That . . . with the Gods, for former vertues meede.
> On nectar and Ambrosia do feede.
>
> SPENSER: *Ruines of Time*, 393.

Amelia. A model of conjugal affection, in Fielding's novel of that name. It is said that the character is intended for his own wife.

The name is also associated with Amelia Sedley, one of the heroines of *Vanity Fair*.

Amen Corner, at the west end of Paternoster Row, London, was where the monks used to finish the *Pater Noster* as they went in procession to St. Paul's Cathedral on Corpus Christi Day. They began in *Paternoster* Row with the Lord's Prayer in Latin, which was continued to the end of the street; then said *Amen*, at the corner or bottom of the Row; then turning down *Ave Maria* Lane, commenced chanting the "Hail, Mary!" then crossing Ludgate, entered *Creed* Lane chanting the *Credo*.

Paternoster Row, Amen Corner, and much of Ave Maria Lane were completely destroyed in an air raid on December 28th, 1940.

Amen-Ra. The supreme King of the Gods among the ancient Egyptians, usually figured as a great man with two long plumes rising straight above his head, but sometimes with a ram's head, the ram being sacred to him. He was the patron of Thebes; his oracle was at the oasis of Jupiter Ammon, and he was identified by the Greeks with Zeus.

Amende honorable. An anglicized French phrase signifying a full and frank apology.

In mediæval France the term was applied to a degrading punishment inflicted on traitors, parricides, and sacrilegious persons, who were brought into court with a rope round their neck, stripped to the shirt, and made to beg pardon of God, the king, and the court.

A mensa et thoro. *See* A VINCULO.

Amenthes (a men' thēz). The Egyptian Hades; the abode of the spirits of the dead who were not yet fully purified.

America. *See* UNITED STATES OF AMERICA.

Amerindian (ăm ér in' di àn). This is a "portmanteau" word combining *American* and *Indian* and is applied descriptively to the native Red Indian races and Eskimos of the North American continent.

Ames-ace. *See* AMBS-AS.

Amethea. *See* HORSE.

Amethyst (ăm' e thist) (Gr. *a*-, not; *methuein*, to be drunken). A violet-blue variety of crystalline quartz supposed by the ancients to prevent intoxication.

Drinking-cups made of amethyst were a charm against inebriety; and it was the most cherished of all precious stones by Roman matrons, from the superstition that it would preserve inviolate the affection of their husbands.

Amiable or **Amicable Numbers.** Any two numbers either of which is the sum of the aliquots of the other: thus, the aliquots of 220 are 1, 2, 4, 5, 10, 11, 20, 22, 44, 55, 110 the sum of which is 284; and the aliquots o 284 are 1, 2, 4, 71, 142, the sum of which is 220; so 220 and 284 are amicable numbers.

Amicus curiæ (à mī' kùs kū' ri ē) (Lat. a friend to the court). One in court who is not engaged in the trial or action, but who is invited or allowed to assist with advice or information. The term is now used to describe a disinterested adviser.

Amiral or **Ammiral.** An early form of the word "admiral" (*q.v.*).

Amis and Amile. *See* AMYS.

Ammon (ăm' on). The Libyan Jupiter; the Greek form of the name of the Egyptian god, Amun (*q.v.*).

Son of Ammon. Alexander the Great, who, on his expedition to Egypt, was thus saluted by the priests of the Libyan temple.

Ammon's great son one shoulder had too high.
POPE: *Epistle to Dr. Arbuthnot*, 117.

His father, Philip, claimed to be a descendant of Hercules, and therefore of Jupiter.

Ammonites (ăm' òn ītz). Fossil molluscs allied to the nautilus and cuttlefish. So called because they resemble the horn upon the ancient statues of Jupiter Ammon. They were set in brooches or as earrings in the mid-19th century.

Also the people of Ammon: that is, the descendants of Lot by the son of his younger daughter, Ben-ammi (*Gen.* xix, 38), who are frequently mentioned in the Old Testament.

Amok. *See* AMUCK.

Amorous, The. Philip I of France (1060-1108); so called because he divorced his wife Berthe to espouse Bertrade, who was already married to Foulques, count of Anjou.

Amour propre (a' moor propr) (Fr.). One's self-love, vanity, or opinion of what is due to self. To *wound his amour propre*, is to gall his good opinion of himself—to wound his vanity.

Ampersand (ăm' per sănd). The character "&" for *and*. In the old horn books, after giving the twenty-six letters, the character & was added (. . . X, Y, Z, &), and was called "Ampersand," a corruption of "and per-se &" (and by itself, and). The symbol is an adaptation of the written *et* (Lat. *and*), the transformation of which can be traced if we look at the italic ampersand—*&*—where the "e" and the cross of the "t" are clearly recognizable. *See* TIRONIAN.

Amphigouri (ăm fi goor' i). A verse composition which, while sounding well, contains no sense or meaning. A good example is Swinburne's well-known parody of his own style, *Nephelidia*, the opening lines of which are:—

From the depth of the dreamy decline of the dawn through a notable nimbus of nebulous noon-shine,
Pallid and pink as the palm of the flag-flower that flickers with fear of the flies as they float,
Are they looks of our lovers that lustrously lean from a marvel of mystic miraculous moonshine,
These that we feel in the blood of our blushes that thicken and threaten with throbs through the throat?

Here there is everything that goes to the making of poetry—except sense; and that is absolutely (and, of course, purposely) lacking.

Amphion (ăm fi' on). The son of Zeus and Antiope who, according to Greek legend, built Thebes by the music of his lute, which was so melodious that the stones danced into walls and houses of their own accord.

The gift to king Amphion
That walled a city with its melody
Was for belief no dream.
WORDSWORTH: *Poems of the Imagination; On the Power of Sound.*

Amphisbœna (ăm fis bē' nà). A fabulous venomous serpent supposed to have a head at each end and to be able to move in either direction:

Complicated monsters head and tail,
Scorpion, and asp, and amphisbœna dire,
Cerastes horn'd, hydrus and elops drear,
And dipas . . .
Paradise Lost, x, 524.

The name is applied to a genus of S. American lizards.

Amphitrite (ăm fi trī′ ti). In classic mythology, the goddess of the sea; wife of Poseidon, daughter of Nereus and Doris. (Gr. *amphitrio* for *tribo*, rubbing or wearing away [the shore] on all sides.)

> His weary chariot sought the bowers
> Of Amphitrite and her tending nymphs.
> THOMSON: *Summer* (1. 1625).

Amphitryon (ăm fit′ ri on). *Le véritable Amphitryon est l'Amphitryon ou l'on dine* (Molière). That is, the person who *provides the feast* (whether master of the house or not) is the real host. The tale is that Jupiter assumed the likeness of Amphitryon for the purpose of visiting the latter's wife, Alcmena (*q.v.*), and gave a banquet at his house; but Amphitryon came home and claimed the honour of being the master of the house. As far as the servants and the guests were concerned, the dispute was soon decided—"he who gave the feast was to them the host."

Amrita (ăm rē′ tà) (Sanskrit). In Hindu mythology, the elixir of immortality, the soma-juice, corresponding to the ambrosia (*q.v.*) of classical mythology.

> Lo, Krishna! lo, the one that thirsts for thee!
> Give him the drink of amrit from thy lips.
> SIR EDWIN ARNOLD: *Indian Song of Songs*.

Amuck. A Malay adjective, *amog*, meaning to be in a state of frenzy. To run amuck is to indulge in physical violence while in a state of frenzy.

> Satire's my weapon, but I'm too discreet
> To run amuck and tilt at all I meet.
> POPE: *Satires*, i, 69-70.

Amulet. Something worn, generally round the neck, as a charm. The word was formerly connected with the Arabic *himalah*, the name given to the cord that secured the Koran to the person and was sometimes regarded as a charm; but it has nothing to do with this, and is from the Latin *amuletum*, a preservative against sickness, through French *amulette*.

The early Christians used to wear amulets called *Ichthus* (*q.v.*). *See also* NOTARIKON.

Amun (ăm′ ùn). An Egyptian deity, usually represented with a ram's head with large curved horns, and a human body, or as a human figure with two long upright plumes springing from the head and holding a sceptre and the symbol of life. An immense number of temples were dedicated to him and he was, identified by the Greeks with Zeus. His oracle was in the oasis of Jupiter Ammon. *See* AMMON.

Amyclæan Silence (ăm i klē′ àn). Amyclæ was a Laconian town in the south of Sparta, ruled by the mythical Tyndareus. The inhabitants had so often been alarmed by false rumours of the approach of the Spartans, that they made a decree forbidding mention of the subject. When the Spartans actually came no one dare give warning, and the town was taken. Hence the proverb, *more silent than Amyclæ*.

Castor and Pollux were born at Amyclæ, and are hence sometimes referred to as the **Amyclæan Brothers.**

Amys and Amylion (ă′ mis, à mil′ i òn). A French romance of the 13th century telling the story of the friendship between two heroes of the Carlovingian wars. The story culminates in Amylon's sacrifice of his children to save his friend.

Anabaptists. Originally, a Christian sect which arose in Germany about 1521, the members of which did not believe in infant baptism and hence were baptized *over again* (Gr. *ana=* over again) on coming to years of discretion.

Applied in England as a nickname, and more or less opprobriously, to the Baptists, a body of Dissenters holding similar views.

Anacharsis (ăn à kar′ sis). A princely Scythian named Anacharsis left his native country to travel in pursuit of knowledge. He reached Athens about 594 B.C. and became acquainted with Solon.

In 1788 the Abbé Barthélemy published *Le voyage du Jeune Anacharsis*, a description of Greece in the time of Pericles and Philip. He worked thirty years on preparing this book and at one time it was extremely popular and had great influence on the young. Baron Jean Baptists: Clootz (1755-1794), a Prussian brought up in France, assumed the name of Anacharsis after travelling about Greece and other countries in search of knowledge. He was caught up in the Revolution, when he took to himself the title of The Orator of the Human Race. He was guillotined by Robespierre in 1794.

Anaclethra. Another name for the *agelastra* (*q.v.*).

Anachronism (Gr. *ana chronos*, out of time). An event placed at a wrong date.

Shakespeare has several more or less glaring examples. In 1 *Henry IV*, ii, 5, the carrier complains that the turkeys in his pannier are quite starved; whereas turkeys were introduced from America, which was not discovered until a century after Henry's time. Again, in *Julius Cæsar*, ii, 1, the clock strikes and Cassius says, "The clock has stricken three." But striking clocks were not invented until some 1400 years after the days of Cæsar. The great mine of literary anachronisms is to be found in the mediæval romances of chivalry, where Charlemagne, Edward III, Saracens and Romans all appear as living persons.

Anagram (Gr. *ana graphein*, to write over again). A word or phrase formed by transposing and writing over again the letters of some other word or phrase. Among the many famous examples are:—

Dame Eleanor Davies (prophetess in the reign of Charles 1) = *Never so mad a ladie.*
Gustavus = *Augustus.*
Horatio Nelson = *Honor est a Nilo.*
Queen Victoria's Jubilee = *I require love in a subject.*
Quid est Veritas (*John* xviii, 38)? = *Vir est qui adest.*
Marie Touchet (mistress of Charles IX, of France) = *Je charme tout* (made by Henry IV).
Voltaire is an anagram of *Árouet l(e)j(eune).*

These are interchangeable words:—
Alcuinus and Calvinus; Amor and Roma; Eros and Rose; Evil and Live; and many more.

Ananas [Peruvian *nanas*]. The pineapple. Through the final "s" having been mistaken for the sign of the plural, an erroneous singular, *anana*, is sometimes used:—

Witness thou, best Anana! thou the pride
Of vegetable life.
THOMSON: *Summer,* 685.

Anathema (à nắth' i mà). A denunciation or curse. The word is Greek, and means "a thing devoted"—originally, a thing devoted to any purpose, *e.g.* to the gods, but later only a thing devoted to evil, hence, an accursed thing. It has allusion to the custom of hanging in the temple of a patron god something devoted to him. Thus Gordius hung up his yoke and beam; the shipwrecked hung up their wet clothes; retired workmen hung up their tools; cured cripples their crutches, etc.

Anatomy. He was like an anatomy—*i.e.* a mere skeleton, very thin, like one whose flesh had been anatomized or cut off. Shakespeare uses *atomy* as a synonym. Thus in 2 *Henry IV,* v, 4, Quickly says to the Beadle: "Thou anatomy, thou!" and Doll Tearsheet caps the phrase with," Come, you thin thing; come you rascal."

Anchor. In Christian symbolism the anchor is the sign of hope, in allusion to *Heb.* vi, 19, "Hope we have as an anchor of the soul." In art it is an attribute of Clement of Rome and Nicholas of Bari. Pope Clement, in A.D. 80, was bound to an anchor and cast into the sea; Nicholas of Bari is the patron saint of sailors.

Anchorite (ăng' kòr īt). This is from a Greek word meaning "recluse," and it was applied to those who retired to the desert or solitary places for a life of contemplation and religious exercises. The classes of such ascetics are: *monks*, who adopt a secluded form of life but live in community; *hermits*, who withdraw to desert places but live in caves and occupy themselves manually; *anchorites*, who choose the greatest solitudes and deny themselves shelter and all but a minimum of food.

Ancien Régime (Fr.). The old order of things; a phrase used during the French Revolution for the old Bourbon monarchy, or the system of government, with all its evils, which existed prior to that great change.

Ancient. A corruption of *ensign*—a flag and the officer who bore it. Pistol was Falstaff's and Iago Othello's.

'Tis one Iago, ancient to the general.
Othello, ii, 1.
My whole charge consists of ancients, corporals, lieutenants, gentlemen of companies. . . .
I *Henry IV,* iv, 2.

Ancient Mariner. The story in Coleridge's *Rime of the Ancient Mariner* (first published in the *Lyrical Ballads,* 1798) is founded partly on a dream told by the author's friend, Cruickshank, and partly on passages in various books that he had read. Wordsworth told him the story of the privateer George Shelvocke who, while rounding Cape Horn in the *Speedwell,* in 1720, shot a black albatross. For many weeks following the vessel encountered bad weather, being driven hither and thither before making the coast of Chile, and this ill luck was attributed to the shooting of the bird. Thomas James's *Strange and Dangerous Voyage* (1683) is thought to have suggested some of the more eerie episodes, while the *Letter of St. Paulinus to Macarius, in which he relates astounding wonders concerning the shipwreck of an old man* (1618), giving a story of how there is only one survivor of a crew and how the ship was navigated by angels and steered by "the Pilot of the World," may have furnished the basis of part of the *Rime.*

Ancile (ăn' sīl). The Palladium of Rome; the sacred buckler said to have fallen from heaven in the time of Numa. To prevent its being stolen, he caused eleven others to be made precisely like it, and confided them to the twelve Salii, dancing priests of Mars (*see* SALIENS), who bore them in procession through the city every year at the beginning of March.

Andiron (ănd' īr òn). A fire-dog; that is, a contrivance consisting of a short horizontal bar projecting from an upright stand or rod, the whole usually of iron, for the purpose of holding up the ends of logs in a wood fire. Though the contrivance is made of iron the word originally had nothing to do with the metal, but is from the Old French *andier*, after the late Latin *and-edus*, *andena*, or *anderius*. The English form of the word—like the Latin—has, even in modern times, had many variations, such as *end-iron* and *hand-iron*. Andiron are also known as *dogs*, or *fire-dogs*.

Androcles and the Lion (ăn drō′ klēz). An Oriental apologue on the benefits to be expected as a result of gratitude; told in Æsop, and by Aulus Gellius, in the *Gesta Romanorum*, etc., but of unknown antiquity.

Androcles was a runaway slave who took refuge in a cavern. A lion entered, and instead of tearing him to pieces, lifted up his fore paw that Androcles might extract from it a thorn. The slave being subsequently captured was doomed to fight with a lion in the Roman arena. It so happened that the same lion was let out against him, and recognizing his benefactor, showed towards him every demonstration of love and gratitude.

Android. An old name for an automaton figure resembling a human being (Gr. *androseidos*, a man's likeness).

Andromache (ăn drom′ à ki). In Greek legend she was the wife of Hector, subsequently of Neoptolemus, and finally of Helenus, Hector's brother. It is also the title of a play of Euripides.

Andromeda (ăn drom′e dà). Daughter of Cepheus and Cassiopeia. Her mother boasted that the beauty of Andromeda surpassed that of the Nereids; so the Nereids induced Neptune to send a sea-monster to the country, and an oracle declared that Andromeda must be given up to it. She was accordingly chained to a rock, but was delivered by Perseus, who married her and, at the wedding, slew Phineus, to whom she had been previously promised, with all his companions. After death she was placed among the stars.

Angel. In post-canonical and apocalyptic literature angels are grouped in varying orders, and the hierarchy thus constructed was adapted to Church uses by the early Christian Fathers. In his *De Hierarchia Celesti* the pseudo-Dionysius (early 5th century) gives the names of the nine orders; they are taken from the Old Testament, *Eph*, i, 21, and *Col*. i, 16, and are as follows:—

Seraphim and Cherubim, in the first circle
Thrones and Dominions, in the second,
Virtues, Powers, Principalities,
Archangels and Angels in the third.

Botticelli's great picture, *The Assumption of the Virgin*, in the National Gallery, London, well illustrates the mediæval conception of the "triple circles."

The seven holy angels are—Michael, Gabriel, Raphael, Uriel, Chamuel, Jophiel, and Zadkiel. Michael and Gabriel are mentioned in the Bible, Raphael in the Apocrypha, and all in the apocryphal book of *Enoch* (viii, 2).

Milton (*Paradise Lost*, Bk. i, 392) gives a list of the fallen angels.

Mohammedans say that angels were created from pure, bright *gems*; the genii, of *fire*; and man, of *clay*.

Angel. An obsolete English coin, current from the time of Edward IV to that of Charles I, its full name being the Angel-noble, as it was originally a reissue of the noble (*q.v.*), bearing the figure of the archangel Michael slaying the dragon. Its value varied from 6s. 8d. in 1465 (when first coined) to 10s. under Edward VI. It was the coin presented to persons touched for the King's Evil (*q.v.*).

Angel visits. Delightful intercourse of short duration and rare occurrence.

> Visits
> Like those of angels, short and far between.,
> > BLAIR: *Grave*, ii, 586.
> Like angel visits, few and far between.
> > CAMPBELL: *Pleasures of Hope*, ii, 378.

Angel-water. An old Spanish cosmetic, made of roses, trefoil, and lavender. So called because it was originally made chiefly of angelica.

> Angel-water was the worst scent about her.
> > *Sedley: Bellam.*

Angelic Brothers. A sect of Dutch Pietists founded in the 16th century by George Gichtel. Their views on marriage were similar to those held by the Abelites and Adamites (*qq.v.*).

Angelic Doctor. Thomas Aquinas was so called, because of the purity and excellence of his teaching. His exposition of the most recondite problems of theology and philosophy was judged to be the fruit of almost more than human intelligence, and within the present century a Pope has laid it down that from St. Thomas and his *Summa Theologica* all teaching must derive.

Angelic Hymn, The. The hymn beginning with *Glory be to God in the highest*, etc. (*Luke* ii, 14); so called because the former part of it was sung by the angel host that appeared to the shepherds of Bethlehem.

Angelic Salutation, The. The Ave Maria (*q.v.*).

Angelical Stone. The speculum of Dr. Dee. He asserted that it was given him by the angels

Raphael and Gabriel. It passed into the possession of the Earl of Peterborough, thence to Lady Betty Germaine, by whom it was given to the Duke of Argyll, whose son presented it to Horace Walpole. It was sold in 1842, at the dispersal of the curiosities of Strawberry Hill.

Angelica (ăn jel' i kà). This beautiful but fickle young woman was the heroine of Boiardo's *Orlando Innamorato* and Ariosto's *Orlando Furioso*. Orlando's unrequited love for her drove him mad. The name was used also by Congreve for the principal character in *Love for Love* and by Farquhar in *The Constant Couple* and *Sir Harry Wildair*.

Angevin Kings of England (ăn' je vin). The early Plantagenet kings, from Henry II to John. Anjou first became connected with England in 1127, when Matilda, daughter of Henry I, married Geoffrey V, Count of Anjou; their son became Henry II of England (and Count of Anjou), and until 1205 Anjou was united to the English crown. *Cp.* PLANTAGENET.

Angles. *Non Angli, sed angeli* (Not Angles, but angels). Pope Gregory the Great (reigned 590-604) who sent St. Augustine to convert the English, is said to have made this remark. He saw some fair-haired boys from England in the Roman slave market and inquired about them. On being told that they were Angles, he said, "Not Angles, but Angels—had they but the Gospel."

Anglo-Saxon Chronicle. This relates the history of England from the birth of Christ to 1154. It is written in Anglo-Saxon, is in prose, and was probably begun in the time of Alfred the Great. It is valuable for the information it gives regarding the 8th and 9th centuries.

Anima Mundi (ăn' i mà mŭn' dì) (the soul of the world), with the oldest of the ancient philosophers, meant "the source of life"; with Plato, it meant "the animating principle of matter," inferior to pure spirit; with the Stoics, it meant "the whole vital force of the universe."

G. E. Stahl (1660-1734) taught that the phenomena of animal life are due to an immortal *anima*, or vital principle distinct from matter.

Animals in Heaven. According to Mohammedan legend the following ten animals have been allowed to enter paradise:—

(1) Jonah's whale; (2) Solomon's ant; (3) the ram caught by Abraham and sacrificed instead of Isaac; (4) the lapwing of Balkis; (5) the camel of the prophet Saleh; (6) Balaam's ass; (7) the ox of Moses; (8) the dog Kratim of the Seven Sleepers; (9) Al Borak, Mohammed's ass; and (10) Noah's dove.

Animals in art. Some animals are appropriated to certain saints: as the calf or ox to St. Luke; the cock to St. Peter; the eagle to St. John the Divine; the lion to St. Mark and St. Jerome; the raven to St. Benedict, etc.

Animals sacred to special deities. To Apollo, the wolf, the griffon, and the crow; to Bacchus, the dragon and the panther; to Diana, the stag; to Æsculapius, the serpent; to Hercules, the deer; to Isis, the heifer; to Jupiter, the eagle; to Juno, the peacock and the lamb; to the Lares, the dog; to Mars, the horse and the vulture; to Mercury, the cock; to Minerva, the owl; to Neptune, the bull; to Tethys, the halcyon; to Venus, the dove, the swan, and the sparrow; to Vulcan, the lion, etc.

Animals in symbolism. The lamb, the pelican, and the unicorn, are symbols of Christ.

The dragon, serpent, and swine, symbolize Satan and his crew.

The ant symbolizes frugality and prevision; ape, uncleanness, malice, lust, and cunning; ass, stupidity; bantam cock, pluckiness, priggishness; bat, blindness; bear, ill-temper, uncouthness; bee, industry; beetle, blindness; bull, strength, straightforwardness; bull-dog, pertinacity; butterfly, sportiveness, living in pleasure; camel, submission; cat, deceit; calf, lumpishness, cowardice; cicada, poetry; cock, vigilance, overbearing insolence; crow, longevity; crocodile, hypocrisy; cuckoo, cuckoldom; dog, fidelity, dirty habits; dove, innocence, harmlessness; duck, deceit (French, *canard*, a hoax); eagle, majesty, inspiration; elephant, sagacity, ponderosity; fly, feebleness, insignificance; fox, cunning, artifice; frog and toad, inspiration; goat, lasciviousness; goose, conceit, folly; gull, gullibility; grasshopper, old age; hare, timidity; hawk, rapacity, penetration; hen, maternal care; hog, impurity; horse, speed, grace; jackdaw, vain assumption, empty conceit; jay, senseless chatter; kitten, playfulness; lamb, innocence, sacrifice; lark, cheerfulness; leopard, sin; lion, noble courage; lynx, suspicious vigilance; magpie, garrulity; mole, blindness, obtuseness; monkey, tricks; mule, obstinacy; nightingale, forlornness; ostrich, stupidity; ox, patience, strength, and pride; owl, wisdom; parrot, mocking verbosity; peacock, pride; pigeon, cowardice (pigeon-livered); pig, obstinacy, dirtiness, gluttony; puppy, conceit; rabbit, fecundity; raven, ill luck; robin redbreast, confiding trust; serpent, wisdom; sheep, silliness, timidity; sparrow, lasciviousness; spider, wiliness; stag, cuckoldom; swan, grace; tiger, ferocity; tortoise, chastity; turkey-cock, official insolence; turtle-dove, conjugal fidelity; vulture, rapine; wolf, cruelty, ferocity; worm, cringing; etc.

Animals, Cries of. To the cry, call, or voice of many animals a special name is given; to apply these names indiscriminately is always wrong and frequently ludicrous. Thus, we do not speak of the "croak" of a dog or the "bark" of a bee. Apes gibber; asses bray; bees hum; beetles drone; bears growl; bitterns boom; blackbirds and thrushes whistle; bulls bellow; cats mew, purr, swear, and caterwaul; calves bleat; chaffinches chirp or pink; chickens peep; cocks crow; cows moo or low; crows caw; cuckoos cry cuckoo; deer bell; dogs bark, bay, howl, and yelp; doves coo; ducks quack; eagles, vultures, and peacocks scream; falcons chant; flies buzz; foxes bark and yelp; frogs croak; geese cackle and hiss; grasshoppers chirp and pitter; guineafowls cry "Come back"; and guinea-pigs and hares squeak; hawks scream; hens cackle and cluck; horses neigh and whinny; hyenas laugh; jays and magpies chatter; kittens mew; linnets chuckle in their call; lions and tigers roar and growl; mice squeak and squeal; monkeys chatter and gibber; nightingales pipe and warble—we also speak of its "jug-jug"; owls hoot and screech; oxen low and bellow; parrots talk; peewits cry pee-wit; pigeons coo; pigs grunt, squeak, and squeal; ravens croak; rooks caw; screech-owls screech or shriek; sheep and lambs baa or bleat; snakes hiss; sparrows chirp; stags bellow and call; swallows twitter; swans cry and are said to sing just before death (see SWAN); turkey-cocks gobble; wolves howl. Most birds, besides many of those here mentioned, sing, but we speak of the chick-chick of the black-cap, the drumming of the grouse, and the chirr of the whitethroat.

Animosity meant originally animation, spirit, as the fire of a horse, called in Latin *equi animositas*. Its present exclusive use in a bad sense is an instance of the tendency which words originally neutral have to assume a bad meaning.

Animula, vagula, etc. (an im' ū là văg' ū là). The opening of a poem to his soul, ascribed by his biographer, Ælius Spartianus, to the dying Emperor Hadrian:—

Animula, vagula, blandula,
Hospes, comesque corporis;
Quae nunc abibis in loca,
Pallidula, rigida, nudula;
Nec ut soles, dabis jocos!

It was Englished by Byron:—

Ah! gentle, fleeting, wavering sprite,
Friend and associate of this clay!
To what unknown region borne,
Wilt thou now wing thy distant flight?
No more with wonted humour gay,
But pallid, cheerless, and forlorn.

Ann, Mother. Ann Lee (1736-1784), the founder and "spiritual mother" of the American Society of Shakers (*q.v.*).

Annates (ăn' ātz) [Lat. *annus*, a year]. One entire year's income claimed by the Pope on the appointment of a bishop or other ecclesiastic in the Catholic Church, also called the *first fruits*. By the Statute of Recusants (25 Hen. VIII, c. 20, and the Confirming Act), the right to English Annates and Tenths was transferred to the Crown; but, in the reign of Queen Anne, annates were given up to form a fund for the augmentation of poor livings. *See* QUEEN ANNE'S BOUNTY.

Anno Domini (ăn' ō dom' i nī) (Lat.). In the Year of our Lord; *i.e.* in the year since the Nativity: generally abbreviated to "A.D." It was Dionysius Exiguus who fixed the date of the Nativity; he lived in the early 6th century, and his computation is probably late by some three to six years.

The phrase is sometimes used as a slang synonym for old age; thus, "Anno Domini is his trouble," means that he is suffering from senile decay.

Annunciation, The Day of the. March 25th, also called *Lady Day*, on which the angel announced to the Virgin Mary that she would be the mother of the Messiah.

Annus Luctus (ăn' ŭs lŭk' tūs) (Lat. the year of mourning). The period during which a widow is supposed to remain unmarried. If she marries within about nine months from the death of her husband and a child is born, a doubt might arise as to its paternity. Such a marriage is not illegal.

Annus Mirabilis (ăn' us mir ăb' i lis). The year of wonders, 1666, memorable for the great fire of London and the successes of English arms over the Dutch. Dryden wrote a poem with this title, in which he described both these events.

Anodyne Necklace, An. An anodyne is a medicine to relieve pain, and the anodyne necklace was an amulet supposed to be efficacious against various diseases. In Johnson's *Idler*, No. 40, we read:—

The true pathos of advertisements must have sunk deep into the heart of every man that remembers the zeal shown by the seller of the *anodyne necklace*, for the ease and safety of poor toothing infants.

The term soon came to be applied to the hangman's noose, and we have George Primrose saying:—

May I die by an anodyne necklace, but I had rather be an under-turnkey than an usher in a boarding-school.—GOLDSMITH: *Vicar of Wakefield*, ch. xx.

Anon. The O.E. *on ane*, in one (state, mind, course, body, etc.), the present meaning—*soon, in a little while*—being a misuse of the earlier meaning—*straightway, at once*—much as *directly* and *immediately* are misused. *Mark* i, 30, gives an instance of the old meaning—

But Simon's wife's mother lay sick of a fever, and anon they tell him of her.

This is the Authorized Version; the Revised Version gives *straightway*. Wordsworth's—

Fast the churchyard fills;—anon
Look again, and they all are gone.
                    White Doe of Rylstone, i, 31.

exemplifies the later meaning. The word also was used by servants, tapsters, etc., as an interjectory reply meaning "Coming, sir!"

Answer is the O.E. *and-swaru*, verb *and-swarian* or *swerian*, where *and* is the preposition = the Lat. *re* in *re-spond-eo*. To *swear* (*q.v.*) means literally "to affirm something," and to *an-swear* is to "say something" by way of rejoinder.

To answer its purpose. To carry out what was expected or what was intended.

Antarctica (ăn tark' tik à). The name given to the great continent that covers the region of the South Pole. Its area is about 5,000,000 sq. miles. It contains mountains from 8,000 to 15,000 ft. in height, with several volcanoes, of which only one, Mt. Erebus, is now active. There are no land animals, but it is notable for its penguins. There is no international agreement as to territorial rights, which lie largely between Britain, the Commonwealth of Australia and Argentina.

Antediluvian. Before the Deluge. The word is colloquially used in a disparaging way for anything that is very out of date.

Anthology. The Greek anthology is a collection of several thousand short Greek poems by many authors of every period of Greek literature from the Persian war to the decadence of Byzantium. The most complete edition was published in 1794-1814.

St. Anthony's fire. Erysipelas is so called from the tradition that those who sought the intercession of St. Anthony recovered from the pestilential erysipelas called the *sacred fire*, which proved so fatal in 1089.

St. Anthony's pig. A pet pig, the smallest of the litter, also called the "tantony pig" (*q.v.*); in allusion to St. Anthony being the patron saint of swineherds.

The term is also used of a sponger or hanger-on. Stow says that the officers of the market used to slit the ears of pigs unfit for food. One day one of the proctors of St. Anthony's Hospital tied a bell about a pig whose ear was slit, and no one would ever hurt it. The pig would follow like a dog anyone who fed it.

Anthroposophy (ăn thrō pos' ō fi). The word comes from the Greek *anthropos*, a man, and *sophia*, knowledge, and is the name given to a system of esoteric philosophy enunciated by Rudolf Steiner (1861-1925) who defined it as "the knowledge of the spiritual human being . . . and of everything which the spirit man can perceive in the spiritual world."

Antichrist. The many legends connected with Antichrist, or the Man of Sin, expected by some to precede the second coming of Christ, that were so popular in the Middle Ages are chiefly founded on 2 *Thes.* ii. 1-12, and *Rev.* xiii. In ancient times Antichrist was identified with Caligula, Nero, etc., and there is little doubt that in 2 *Thes.* ii, 7, St. Paul was referring to the Roman Empire. Mohammed was also called Antichrist, and the name has been given to many disturbers of the world's peace, even to Napoleon and to William II of Germany (*see* NUMBER OF THE BEAST). The Mohammedans have a legend that Christ will slay the Antichrist at the gate of the church at Lydda, in Palestine.

Antigone (ăn tig' ō ni). The subject of a tragedy by Sophocles; she was the daughter of Œdipus by his mother, Jocasta. In consequence of disobeying an edict of Creon she was imprisoned in a cave, where she slew herself. She was famed for her devotion to her brother, Polynices, hence the Duchess of Angoulême (1778-1851), sister and prison companion of Louis XVII, was sometimes called *the Modern Antigone*.

Antimony (an' ti mon i). A word of unknown, but (as it was introduced through alchemy) probably of Arabian, origin. "Popular etymology" has been busy with this word, and Johnson—copying earlier writers—in his Dictionary derives it from the Greek *antimonachos* (bad for monks), telling the story that a prior once gave some of this mineral to his convent pigs, who thrived upon it, and became very fat. He next tried it on the monks, who died from its effects.

Antisthenes (ăn tis' the nēz). Founder of the Cynic School in Athens, born about 444 B.C., died about 370. He wore a ragged cloak, and carried a wallet and staff like a beggar. Socrates, whose pupil he was, wittily said he could "see rank pride peering through the holes of Antisthenes' rags."

Antoninus (ăn tō nī' nŭs). *The Wall of Antoninus.* A wall of regularly laid sods resting on a stone pavement, built by the Romans about 100 miles north of Hadrian's Wall, from Dumbarton on the Clyde to Carriden on the Forth, under the direction of Lollius Urbicus, governor of the province under Antoninus Pius, about A.D. 140. It was probably some 14 ft. thick at the base and about the same height; it was fortified at frequent intervals, and was fronted by a deep ditch.

Antrustions (ăn trŭs' ti ŏnz) (O.Fr., from O.H.Ger. *trost,* trust, fidelity). The chief followers of the Frankish kings, who were specially trusty to them.

None but the king could have antrustions.
STUBBS: *Constitutional History,* I, ix.

Aonian (ā ō' ni an). Poetical, pertaining to the Muses. The Muses, according to Greek mythology, dwelt in Aonia, that part of Bœotia which contains Mount Helicon and the Muses' Fountain. Milton speaks of "the Aonian mount" (*Paradise Lost,* i, 15), and Thomson calls the fraternity of poets

The Aonian hive
Who praised are, and starve right merrily.
Castle of Indolence, ii, 2.

À outrance. *See* À L'OUTRANCE.

Apache (à păch' i). The name of a tribe of North American Indians, given to—or adopted by—the hooligans and roughs of Paris about the opening of the present century (in this case pronounced à păsh'). The use of the name for this purpose has a curious parallel in the Mohocks (*q.v.*) of the 17th century.

Ape. To copy, to imitate.

Apelles (à pel' ēz). A famous Grecian painter, contemporary with Alexander the Great. He was born at Colophon, on the coast of Asia Minor, and is known as the *Chian painter*—

The Chian painter, when he was required
To portrait Venus in her perfect hue,
To make his work more absolute, desired
Of all the fairest maids to have the view.
SPENSER: *Dedicatory Sonnets,* xvii.

Apemantus (ăp e măn 'tŭs). A churlish philosopher, in *Timon of Athens.*

A-per-se (à pēr sē). An A 1; a person or thing of unusual merit. "A" all alone, with no one who can follow, *nemo proximus aut secundus.*

Chaucer calls Cresseide "the floure and A-per-se of Troi and Greek."

London, thou art of townës A-*per-se.*
DUNBAR (1501).

Apex. The topmost height, summit, or tiptop; originally the pointed olive-wood spike on the top of the cap of a Roman flamen; also the crest or spike of a helmet.

Aphrodite (ăf' rō dī ti) (Gr. *aphros,* foam). The Greek Venus; so called because she sprang from the foam of the sea.

Aphrodite's girdle. The cestus (*q.v.*).

Apocalyptic Number. 666 *See* NUMBER OF THE BEAST.

Apocrypha (à pok' ri fà) (Gr. *apokrupto,* hidden); hence, of unknown authorship: the explanation given in the Preface to the Apocrypha in the 1539 Bible that the books are so called "because they were wont to be read not openly . . . but, as it were, in secret and apart" is not tenable. Those books included in the Septuagint and Vulgate versions of the Old Testament, but which, at the Reformation, were excluded from the Sacred Canon by the Protestants, mainly on the grounds that they were not originally written in Hebrew, and were not looked upon as genuine by the Jews. They are not printed in Protestant Bibles in ordinary circulation, but in the Authorized Version, as printed in 1611, they are given immediately after the Old Testament. The books are as follows:—

1 and 2 Esdras. Baruch, with the Epistle of
Tobit. Jeremiah.
Judith. The Song of the Three Children.
The rest of Esther. The Story of Susanna.
Wisdom. The Idol Bel and the Dragon.
Ecclesiasticus. 1 and 2 Maccabees.

The New Testament also has a large number of apocryphal books more or less attached to it: these consist of later gospels and epistles, apocalypses, etc., as well as such recently discovered fragments as the *Logia* (sayings of Jesus) of the Oxyrhynchus papyrus. The best-known books of the New Testament apocrypha are:—

Protevangelium, or the Book of James.
Gospel of Nicodemus, or the Acts of Pilate.
The Ascent of James.
The Acts of Paul and Thecla.
Letters of Abgarus to Christ.
Epistles of Paul to the Laodiceans, and to the Alexandrines, and the Third Epistle to the Corinthians.
The Teaching of the Apostles (Didaché).
The three Books of the Shepherd of Hermas.

Apollinarians (à pol in âr' i anz). An heretical sect founded in the middle of the 4th century by Apollinaris, a presbyter of Laodicea. They denied that Christ had a human soul, and asserted that the *Logos* supplied its place. The heresy was condemned at the Council of Chalcedon, the fourth General Council, 451.

Apollo (à pol' ō). In Greek and Roman mythology, son of Zeus and Leto (Latona), one of the great gods of Olympus, typifying the sun in its light- and life-giving as well as in its destroying power; often identified with Helios, the sun-god. He was god of music, poetry, and the healing art, the latter of which he bestowed on his son, Æsculapius. He is represented in art as the perfection of youthful manhood.

> The fire-robed god,
> Golden Apollo.
>
> SHAKESPEARE: *Winter's Tale*, iv, 4.

> Apollo with the plectrum strook
> The chords, and from beneath his hands a crash
> Of mighty sounds rushed forth, whose music shook
> The soul with sweetness, and like an adept
> His sweeter voice a just accordance kept,
>
> SHELLEY: *Homer's Hymn to Mercury*, lxxxv.

A perfect Apollo is a model of manly beauty, referring to the Apollo Belvedere (*q.v.*).

Apollo of Portugal. Luis Camoëns (c. 1524-1580), author of the *Lusiad*; the great Portuguese poet, who ended his days in poverty.

Apollo Belvedere. An ancient marble statue, supposed to be a Roman-Greek copy of a bronze votive statue set up at Delphi in commemoration of the repulse of an attack by the Gauls on the shrine of Apollo in 279 B.C. It represents the god holding the remains of a bow, or (according to some conjectures) an ægis, in his left hand, and is called Belvedere from the Belvedere Gallery of the Vatican, where it stands. It was discovered in 1495, amidst the ruins of Antium and was purchased by Pope Julius II.

Apollodoros (a pol' ō dôr' ús). Plato says: "who would not rather be a man of sorrows than Apollodoros, envied by all for his enormous wealth, yet nourishing in his heart the scorpions of a guilty conscience?" (*The Republic*). This Apollodorus was the tyrant of Cassandrea. He obtained the supreme power 379 B.C., exercised it with the utmost cruelty, and was put to death by Antigonos Gonatas.

Apollyon (à pol' yón). The Greek name of Abaddon (*q.v.*), king of hell and angel of the bottomless pit. (*Rev.* ix, 11.) His introduction by Bunyan into the *Pilgrim's Progress* has made his name familiar.

Aposiopesis. *See* QUOS EGO.

Apostate, The. Julian, the Roman emperor (331-363). He was brought up as a Christian, but on his accession to the throne (361) he announced his conversion to paganism and proclaimed the free toleration of all religions.

A posteriori (ā pos tē' ri ôr' i) (Lat. from the latter). An *a posteriori* argument is proving the cause from the effect. Thus, if we see a watch we conclude there was a watchmaker. Robinson Crusoe inferred there was another human being on the desert island, because he saw a human footprint in the wet sand. It is thus the existence and character of God are inferred from His works. *See* A PRIORI.

Apostles. In the preamble of the statutes instituting the Order of St. Michael, founded in 1469 by Louis XI, the archangel is styled "my lord," and is created a knight. The apostles had been already ennobled and knighted. We read of "the Earl Peter," "Count Paul," "the Baron Stephen," and so on. Thus, in the introduction of a sermon upon St. Stephen's Day, we have these lines:—

> Contes vous vueille la patron
> De St. Estieul le baron.

> The Apostles were gentlemen of bloude . . . and Christ . . . might, if He had esteemed of the vayne glorye of this world, have borne coat armour.
>
> *The Blazon of Gentrie.*

The badges or symbols of the fourteen apostles (*i.e.* the twelve original apostles with Matthias and Paul).

Andrew, an *X-shaped cross*, because he was crucified on one.

Bartholomew, *a knife*, because he was flayed with a knife.

James the Great, *a scallop shell, a pilgrim's staff*, or *a gourd bottle*, because he is the patron saint of pilgrims. *See* SCALLOP SHELL.

James the Less, *a fuller's pole*, because he was killed by a blow on the head with a pole, dealt him by Simeon the fuller.

John, *a cup with a winged serpent flying out of it*, in allusion to the tradition about Aristodemos, priest of Diana, who challenged John to drink a cup of poison. John made the sign of a cross on the cup, Satan like a dragon flew from it, and John then drank the cup which was quite innocuous.

Judas Iscariot, *a bag*, because he had the bag and "bare what was put therein" (*John* xii, 6).

Jude, *a club*, because he was martyred with a club.

Matthew, *a hatchet* or *halberd*, because he was slain at Nadabar with a halberd.

Matthias, *a battleaxe*, because he was first stoned, and then beheaded with a battleaxe.

Paul, *a sword*, because his head was cut off with a sword. The convent of La Lisla, in Spain, boasts of possessing the very instrument.

Peter, *a bunch of keys*, because Christ gave him the "keys of the kingdom of heaven." A *cock*, because he went out and wept bitterly when he heard the cock crow (*Matt.* xxvi, 75).

Philip, *a long staff surmounted with a cross*, because he suffered death by being suspended by the neck from a tall pillar.

Simon, *a saw*, because he was sawn to death, according to tradition.

Thomas, *a lance*, because he was pierced through the body, at Meliapour, with a lance.

According to Catholic legend, seven of the Apostles are buried at Rome.

ANDREW lies buried at Amalfi (Naples).

BARTHOLOMEW, at Rome, in the church of Bartholomew, on the Tiber Island.

JAMES THE GREAT was buried at St. Jago de Compostella, in Spain.

JAMES THE LESS, at Rome, in the church of SS. Philip and James.

JOHN, at Ephesus.

JUDE, at Rome.

MATTHEW, at Salerno (Naples).

MATTHIAS, at Rome, under the altar of the Basilica.

PAUL, somewhere in Italy.

PETER, at Rome, in the church of St. Peter.

PHILIP, at Rome.

SIMON or SIMEON, at Rome.

THOMAS, at Ortona (Naples). (? Madras.)

The supposed remains of MARK THE EVANGELIST were buried at Venice, about 800.

LUKE THE EVANGELIST is said to have been buried at Padua.

N.B.—Italy claims thirteen of these apostles or evangelists—Rome seven, Naples three, Mark at Venice, Luke at Padua, and Paul at Rome.

See EVANGELISTS.

Twelve Apostles. The last twelve names on the poll or list of ordinary degrees were so called, when the list was arranged in order of merit, and not alphabetically, as now; they were also called the *Chosen Twelve.* The last of the twelve was designated "St. Paul," from a play on the verse 1 *Cor.* xv, 9. The same term was later applied to the last twelve in the Mathematical Tripos.

Apostles' Creed. A Church creed supposed to be an epitome of doctrine taught by the apostles. It was received into the Latin Church, in its present form, in the 11th century, but a formula somewhat like it existed in the 2nd century. Items were added in the 4th and 5th centuries, and verbal alterations much later.

Apostolic Succession. This is the term in use for the doctrine that the mission given to the apostles by Christ (*John* xx, 23 and *Matt.* xxviii, 19) must extend to their legitimate successors in an unbroken line. This means in practice that only those clergy who have been ordained by bishops who are themselves in the succession can administer the sacraments and perform other sacerdotal functions.

Apparel. One meaning of this word used to be "ornament" or "embellishment," especially the embroidery on ecclesiastical vestments. In the 19th century it was revived, and applied to the ornamental parts of the alb at the lower edge and at the wrists. Pugin says:—

The albe should be made with apparels worked in silk or gold, embroidered with ornaments.—*Glossary of Ecclesiastical Ornament* (1844).

Appeal to the Country, To. To ask the nation to express their opinion on some moot question. In order to obtain such public opinion Parliament must be dissolved and a general election held.

Appiades (ăp' i à dēz). Five divinities whose temple stood near the fountains of Appius, in Rome. Their names are Venus, Pallas, Concord, Peace, and Vesta. They were represented on horseback, like Amazons.

Appian Way (ăp' i àn). The oldest and best known of all the Roman roads, leading from Rome to Brundisium (Brindisi) by way of Capua. This "queen of roads" was begun by Appius Claudius, the decemvir, 313 B.C.

Apple. The well-known story of Newton and the Apple originated with Voltaire, who tells us that Mrs. Conduit, Newton's niece, told him that Newton was at Woolsthorpe (visiting his mother) in 1666, when, seeing an apple fall, he was led into the train of thought which resulted in his establishment of the law of gravitation (1685).

Apple of Discord. A cause of dispute; something to contend about. At the marriage of Thetis and Peleus, where all the gods and goddesses met together, Discord (Eris), who had not been invited, threw on the table a golden apple "for the most beautiful." Juno, Minerva, and Venus put in their separate claims; the point was referred to Paris (*q.v.*), who gave judgment in favour of Venus. This brought upon him the vengeance of Juno and Minerva, to whose spite the fall of Troy is attributed.

The apple appears more than once in Greek story; see ATALANTA'S RACE; HESPERIDES.

There is no mention of an apple in the Bible story of Eve's temptation. We have no further particulars than that it was "the fruit of the tree in the midst of the garden," and the Mohammedans leave the matter equally vague, though their commentators hazard the guess that it may have been an ear of wheat, or the fruit of the vine or the fig. The apple is a comparatively late conjecture.

For the story of William Tell and the apple, see TELL.

Apples of Paradise, according to tradition, had a bite on one side, to commemorate the bite given by Eve.

Apples of perpetual youth. In Scandinavian mythology, the golden apples of perpetual youth, in the keeping of Idhunn, daughter of the dwarf Svald, and wife of Bragi. It is by tasting them that the gods preserve their youth.

Apples of Sodom. Thevenot says—"There are apple-trees on the sides of the Dead Sea which bear lovely fruit, but within are full of ashes." Josephus, Strabo, Tacitus, and others speak of these apples, and are probably referring to the gall-nuts produced by the insect *Cynips insana*. The phrase is used figuratively for anything disappointing.

> You see, my lords, what goodly fruit she seems;
> Yet like those apples travellers report
> To sow where Sodom and Gomorrah stood,
> I will but touch her, and straight you will see
> She'll fall to soot and ashes.
> WEBSTER: *The White Devil.*

Apple of the eye. The pupil, because it was anciently supposed to be a round solid ball like an apple. Figuratively applied to anything extremely dear or extremely sensitive.

> He kept him as the apple of his eye.—*Deut.* xxxii, 10.

Apple-cart. To upset the apple-cart. To ruin carefully laid plans. To have one's expectations blighted, as a farmer's might be when his load of apples was overturned. This phrase is recorded as in use as early as 1796.

Apple-pie order. Prim and precise order. The origin of this phrase is still doubtful. Perhaps the suggestion made above of *nappepli* (Fr. *nappes pliées*, folded linen, neat as folded linen) is near the mark.

Apple-polishing. An attempt to win favour by gifts or flattery. From the practice of American schoolchildren of bringing shiny apples to their teachers.

Apple Tree Gang. The name given to John Reid, and his friends, from Scotland, who were responsible for the introduction of Golf into U.S.A. in 1888, at Yonkers, N.Y. The name was coined in 1892 when Reid and his friends moved to their 3rd "course" at Yonkers—a 34-acre orchard which yielded six holes.

Après moi le déluge. After me the deluge— I care not what happens after I am dead and gone. It is recorded that Madame de Pompadour (1721-64), mistress of Louis XV, said, *Après nous le deluge,* when remonstrated with on account of the extravagances of the Court. It is probable that she had heard the phrase on the lips of her royal lover. Metternich, the Austrian statesman (1773-1859), also used the expression, but his meaning was that when his guiding hand was removed, things would probably go to rack and ruin.

April. The month when trees unfold and the womb of Nature opens with young life. (Lat. *aperire*, to open.)

The old Dutch name was *Gras-maand* (grass-month); the old Saxon, *Easter-monath* (orient or pascal-month). In the French Republican calendar it was called *Germinal* (the time of budding, March 21st to April 19th).

April fool. Called in France *un poisson d'Avril* (*q.v.*), and in Scotland a *gowk* (cuckoo). In Hindustan similar tricks are played at the Huli Festival (March 31st). So that it cannot refer to the uncertainty of the weather, nor yet to a mockery of the trial of our Redeemer, the two most popular explanations. A better solution is this: As March 25th used to be New Year's Day, April 1st was its octave, when its festivities culminated and ended.

It may be a relic of the Roman "Cerealia," held at the beginning of April. The tale is that Proserpina was sporting in the Elysian meadows, and had just filled her lap with daffodils, when Pluto carried her off to the lower world. Her mother, Ceres, heard the echo of her screams, and went in search of "the voice"; but her search was a fool's errand, it was hunting the gowk, or looking for the "echo of a scream."

A priori (ā prī ôr 'i) (Lat. from an antecedent). An *a priori* argument is one in which a fact is deduced from something antecedent, as when we infer certain effects from given causes. All mathematical proofs are of the *a priori* kind, whereas judgments in the law courts are usually *a posteriori* (*q.v.*); we infer the animus from the act.

Aqua Regia (ăk' wa rē' jȧ) (Lat. royal water). A mixture of one part of nitric acid, with from two to four of hydrochloric acid; so called because it dissolves gold, *the king of metals.*

Aqua vitæ (ăk' wȧ vī' tē) (Lat. water of life). Brandy; any spirituous liquor; also, formerly, certain ardent spirits used by the alchemists. Ben Jonson terms a seller of such an "acquavitæ man" (*Alchemist,* i. 1). The "elixir of life" (*q.v.*) was made from these spirits. *See* EAU DE VIE.

Aquarius (ȧ kwâr' i ús) (Lat. the water-bearer). The eleventh of the twelve zodiacal constellations, representing the figure of a man with his left hand raised and with his right pouring from a ewer a stream of water; it is the eleventh division of the ecliptic, which the sun enters on January 21st, though this does not now coincide with the constellation.

Aquila non captat muscas (ăk' wi lȧ non căp' tȧt mŭs' kȧs). A Latin phrase, "An eagle does not hawk at flies," a proverbial saying implying that little things are beneath a great man's contempt.

Aquiline. Raymond's matchless steed. *See* HORSE.

Arabesque. An adjective and noun applied to the Arabian and Moorish style of decoration and architecture. One of its chief features is that no representation of animal forms is admitted. During the Spanish wars in the reign of Louis XIV, arabesque decorations were profusely introduced into France.

Arabia. It was Ptolemy who was the author of the threefold division into **Arabia Petræa,** "Stony Arabia"; **Arabia Felix** (*Yemen*), "Fertile Arabia," *i.e.* the south-west coast; and **Arabia Deserta,** "Desert Arabia."

Arabian Bird, The. The phœnix; hence, figuratively, a marvellous or unique person.

All of her that is out of door most rich!
If she be furnish'd with a mind so rare,
She is alone the Arabian bird.
SHAKESPEARE: *Cymbeline,* i, 6.

Arabian Nights Entertainments, The. A collection of ancient Oriental tales, first collected in its present form about 1450, probably in Cairo. The first European translation was the French one by Antoine Galland (12 vols., 1704-8), which is a free rendering of the oldest known MS. (1548). There are English translations founded on this by R. Heron (4 vols., 1792), W. Beloe (4 vols., 1795), and others. In 1840 E. W. Lane published an entirely new translation (3 vols.) made from the latest Arabic edition (Cairo 1835); John Payne's translation appeared in 4 vols., 1882-4. Sir Richard Burton's literal translation was the first unexpurgated edition, and is enriched by a great number of exhaustive notes on Oriental manners and customs. It was issued by the Kamashastra Society of Benares, in 10 vols., 1885-6, followed by 6 vols. of *Supplemental Nights* in 1886-8. The standard French translation is that by J. C. Mardrus, 16 vols., 1899-1994, which has been severely criticized by Arabic scholars.

Arabic Figures. The figures 1, 2, 3, 4, etc. So called because they were introduced into Europe (Spain) by the Moors or Arabs (about the end of the 10th century), who brought them from India about 250 years earlier. They were not generally adopted in Europe till after the invention of printing. Far more important than the characters, is the decimalism of these figures: 1 figure = units, 2 figures = tens, 3 figures = hundreds, and so on *ad infinitum.* *Cp.* NUMERALS

The figures i, ii, iii, iv, v, vi, vii, viii, ix, x, etc., are called Roman figures.

Arachne's Labours (à răk' ni). In Greek legend Arachne was so skilful a spinner that she challenged Minerva to a trial of skill, and hanged herself because the goddess beat her. Minerva then changed her into a spider. Hence **arachnida,** the scientific name for spiders, scorpions, and mites.

Aratus (à rā' tùs). A Greek statesman and general (271-213 B.C.), famous for his patriotism and devotion to freedom. He liberated his native Sicyon from the usurper Nicocles, and would not allow even a picture of a king to exist. He was poisoned by Philip of Macedon.

Aratus, who awhile relumed the soul
Of fondly-lingering liberty in Greece.
THOMSON: *Winter,* 491, 492.

Arbor Day. A day set apart in Canada and the United States for planting trees. It was first inaugurated about 1885 in Nebraska.

Arcadia (ar kā' di à). A district of the Peloponnesus which, according to Virgil, was the home of pastoral simplicity and happiness. The name was taken by Sidney as the title of his romance (1590), and it was soon generally adopted in English.

Arcadian beasts. An old expression, to be found in Plautus, Pliny, etc. *See Persius,* iii, 9:—

Arcadiæ pecuaria rudere credas

and *Rabelais,* V, vii. So called because the ancient Arcadians were renowned as simpletons. *Juvenal* (vii, 160) has *arcadicus juvenis,* meaning a stupid youth.

Archangel. In Christian legend, the title is usually given to Michael, the chief opponent of Satan and his angels and the champion of the Church of Christ on earth. In the mediæval hierarchy (*see* ANGEL) the Archangels comprise an order of the third division.

According to the Koran, there are four archangels: Gabriel, the angel of revelations, who writes down the divine decrees; Michael, the champion, who fights the battles of faith; Azrael, the angel of death; and Israfel, who is commissioned to sound the trumpet of the resurrection.

Archers. The best archers in British history and story are Robin Hood and his two comrades Little John and Will Scarlet.

The famous archers of Henry II were Tepus his bowman of the Guards, Gilbert of the white hind, Hubert of Suffolk, and Clifton of Hampshire.

Nearly equal to these were Egbert of Kent and William of Southampton. *See also* CLYM OF THE CLOUGH.

Domitian, the Roman emperor, we are told, could shoot four arrows between the spread fingers of a man's hand.

Tell, who shot an apple set on the head of his son, is a replica of the Scandinavian tale of Egil, who, at the command of King Nidung, performed a precisely similar feat.

Robin Hood, we are told, could shoot an arrow a mile or more.

Archimedean Principle (ar ki mē′ di ȧn). The quantity of water displaced by any body immersed therein will equal in bulk the bulk of the body immersed. This scientific fact was noted by the philosopher Archimedes of Syracuse (c. 287-212 B.C.). *See* EUREKA.

Archimedean screw. An endless screw, used for raising water, etc., invented by Archimedes.

Architecture, Orders of. These five are the classic orders: Tuscan, Doric, Ionic, Corinthian, and Composite.

In ancient times the following was the *usual* practice:

CORINTHIAN, for temples of Venus, Flora, Proserpine, and the Water Nymphs.

DORIC, for temples of Minerva, Mars, and Hercules.

IONIC, for temples of Juno, Diana, and Bacchus.

TUSCAN, for grottoes and all rural deities.

Archon. In ancient Greece the archon was a chief magistrate; in the 2nd century a sect of the Gnostics, known as Archontics, applied the word as a subordinate power (analogous, perhaps, to the angels), who, at the bidding of God, made the world.

Arcite (ar sī′ ti, ar′ sīt). A young Theban knight, made captive by Duke Theseus, and imprisoned with Palamon at Athens. Both captives fell in love with Emily, the duke's sister, sister-in-law, or daughter (according to different versions), and after they had gained their liberty Emily was promised by the duke to the victor in a tournament. Arcite won, but, as he was riding to receive the prize, he was thrown from his horse and killed. Emily became the bride of Palamon. The story has been told many times and in many versions, notably by Boccaccio, Chaucer (*Knight's Tale*), Dryden, and Fletcher (*Two Noble Kinsmen*).

Arcos Barbs. War steeds of Arcos, in Andalusia, very famous in Spanish ballads. *See* BARB.

Arctic Region means the region of Arcturos (the Bear stars), from Gr. *arktos*, meaning both the animal and the constellation, and *arktikos*, pertaining to the bear, hence, northern. Arcturus (the bear-ward) is the name now given to the brightest star in Boötes that can be readily found by following the curve of the Great Bear's tail; but in *Job* xxxviii, 32, it means the Great Bear itself.

Areopagus (ăr e op′ ȧ gus) (Gr. the hill of Mars, or Ares). The seat of a famous tribunal in Athens; so called from the tradition that the first cause tried there was that of Mars or Ares, accused by Neptune of the death of his son Halirrhothius.

Then Paul stood in the midst of Mars' Hill.—*Acts* xvii, 22.

Ares (ȧr′ ēz). The god of war in Greek mythology, son of Zeus and Hera. In certain aspects he corresponds with the Roman Mars.

Aretinian Syllables. *Ut, re, mi, fa, sol, la,* used by Guido d'Arezzo in the 11th century for his hexachord, or scale of six notes. They are the first syllables of some words in the opening stanza of a hymn for St. John's Day (*see* DOH). *Si,* the seventh note, was not introduced till the 17th century.

Argan (ar′ gȯn). The principal character in Molière's *Malade Imaginaire,* a hypochondriac uncertain whether to think more of his ailments or of his purse.

Argand Lamp. A lamp with a circular wick, through which a current of air flows, to supply oxygen to the flame, and increase its brilliancy. Invented by Aimé Argand, 1789.

Argentine, Argentina (ar′ jen tīn, ar jen tē′ nȧ). The name of this great S. American republic means The Silver Republic and is akin to that of its principal river, Rio de la Plata, turned into English as the River Plate. Buenos Aires, the capital city, was founded in 1535, and direct Spanish rule lasted until 1816, when a republic was declared. Spanish-American politics do not lend themselves to a concise summary; suffice it to say that Argentina is now one of the richest and most powerful states on the S. American continent.

Argo (Gr. *argos,* swift). The galley of Jason that went in search of the Golden Fleece.

The wondred Argo, which in venturous peece,
First through the Euxine seas bore all the flower of Greece.
                    SPENSER. *Faerie Queene,* II, xii, 44.

The story is told by Apollonius of Rhodes. Hence, a ship sailing on any specially adventurous voyage, and figuratively.

Such an Argo, when freighted with such a fleece, will unquestionably be held in chase by many a pirate.
                    BROOKE: *Fool of Quality.*

Argonauts. The sailors of the ship *Argo,* who sailed from Greece to Colchis in quest of the Golden Fleece. The name is also given to the paper-nautilus, a cephalopod mollusc.

Argot (ar' gō). Slang or flash language. The word is French, and was formerly used only for the canting jargon of thieves, rogues, and vagabonds.

Argus-eyed. Jealously watchful. According to Grecian fable, the fabulous creature, Argus, had 100 eyes, and Juno set him to watch Io, of whom she was jealous. Mercury, however, charmed Argus to sleep and slew him; whereupon Juno changed him into a peacock with the eyes in the tail (*cp.* PEACOCK'S FEATHER). Hence the name *Argus* for a genus of Asiatic pheasant.

> Return to your charge, be Argus-eyed,
> Awake to the affair you have in hand.
> > BEN JONSON: *Staple of News*, III, ii.
> So praysen babes the Peacocks spotted traine,
> And wondren at bright Argus blazing eye.
> > SPENSER: *Shepherd's Calendar*, October.

Ariadne (ă ri ăd' ni). In Greek mythology, daughter of the Cretan king, Minos. She helped Theseus to escape from the labyrinth, and later went with him to Naxos, where he deserted her and she became the wife of Bacchus (*q.v.*).

Arians (âr' i ǎnz). The followers of Arius, a presbyter of the Church of Alexandria, in the 4th century. He maintained (1) that the Father and Son are distinct beings; (2) that the Son, though divine, is not equal to the Father; (3) that the Son had a state of existence previous to His appearance on earth, but not from eternity; and (4) that the Messiah was not real man, but a divine being in a case of flesh. Their tenets varied from time to time and also among their different sections. The heresy was formally anathematized at the Council of Nicæa (325), but the sect was not, and never has been, wholly extinguished.

Ariel (âr'iel). The name of a spirit. Used in cabalistic angelology, and in Heywood's *Hierarchie of the Blessed Angels* (1635) for one of the seven angelic "princes" who rule the waters; by Milton for one of the rebel angels (*Paradise Lost*, vi, 371); by Pope (*Rape of the Lock*) for a sylph, the guardian of Belinda; but especially by Shakespeare, in the *Tempest*, for "an ayrie spirit."

He was enslaved to the witch Sycorax, who overtasked him; and in punishment for not doing what was beyond his power, shut him up in a pine-rift for twelve years. On the death of Sycorax, Ariel became the slave of Caliban, who tortured him most cruelly. Prospero liberated him from the pine-rift, and the grateful fairy served him for sixteen years, when he was set free.

Aries (âr'ēz). The Ram. The sign of the Zodiac in which the sun is from March 21st to April 20th; the first portion of the ecliptic, between 0° and 30° longitude.

> At last from Aries rolls the bounteous sun.
> > THOMSON: *Spring*, 20.

The first point of Aries is the spot in the celestial equator occupied by the sun at the spring equinox. It is in celestial mensuration what the meridian of Greenwich is in terrestrial.

Arimanes (a ri ma' nēz). The same as Ahriman (*q.v.*). In *Manfred* Byron introduces him under this name, seated "on a Globe of Fire, surrounded by the Spirits."

Arion (á rī' on). A Greek poet and musician who flourished about 700 B.C., and who, according to legend, was cast into the sea by mariners, but carried to Tænaros on the back of a dolphin.

Ariosto of the North (ăr i os' tō). So Byron called Sir Walter Scott. (*Childe Harold*, iv, 40.)

Aristides (á ris' ti dēz). An Athenian statesman and general, who died about 468 B.C., and was surnamed "The Just." He was present at the battles of Marathon and Salamis, and was in command at Platæa.

> Then Aristides lifts his honest front,
> Spotless of heart; to whom the unflattering voice
> Of Freedom gave the noblest name of "Just."
> > THOMSON: *Winter*, 459.

"The British Aristides" was Andrew Marvell, the poet and satirist (1621-78). "The French Aristides" was François Paul Jules Grévy, president of the Third Republic from 1879 till he was compelled to resign in 1887 in consequence of a scandal connected with the sale of offices and honours.

Aristocracy (Gr. *aristo-cratia*, rule of the best born). Originally, the government of a state by its best citizens. Carlyle uses the term in this sense in his *Latter-day Pamphlets* (iii, 41): "The attainment of a truer and truer Aristocracy, or Government again by the Best." The word is to-day generally applied to the patrician order, or to a class that is, or claims to be, specially privileged by reason of birth or wealth.

Aristophanes (ăr is tof' á nēz). The greatest of the Greek comic dramatists. He was born about 450 B.C. and died about 380 B.C., and is specially notable as a satirist.

The English or modern Aristophanes. Samuel Foote (1720-77).

The French Aristophanes. Molière (1622-73).

Aristotle (ăr′ is totl). One of the greatest of the Greek philosophers, pupil of Plato, and founder of the Peripatetic School. *See* PERIPATETICS.

Aristotelian philosophy (ăr is tot ē′ li ån). Aristotle maintained that four separate causes are necessary before anything exists: the material cause, the formal, the final, and the moving cause. The first is the antecedents from which the thing comes into existence; the second, that which gives it its individuality; the moving or efficient cause is that which causes matter to assume its individual forms; and the final cause is that for which the thing exists. According to Aristotle, matter is eternal.

Aristotelian Unities. *See* DRAMATIC UNITIES.

Arm, Arms. This word, with the meaning of the limb, has given rise to a good many common phrases, such as: —

Arm in arm. Walking in a friendly way with arms linked.

Arm of the sea. A narrow inlet.

Secular arm. Civil, in contra-distinction to ecclesiastical jurisdiction.

The relapsed are delivered to the secular arm.
PRIESTLEY: *Corruptions of Christianity*.

At arm's length. At a good distance; hence, with avoidance of familiarity.

Infant in arms. One that cannot yet walk and so has to be carried, but **a nation in arms** is one in which all the people are prepared for war.

With open arms. Cordially; as persons receive a dear friend when they open their arms for an embrace.

The word "arm" is almost always plural nowadays when denoting implements or accoutrements for fighting, etc., and also in heraldic usage. Among common phrases are: —

To arms. Make ready for battle.

"To arms!" cried Mortimer,
And couched his quivering lance.
GRAY: *The Bard*.

To lay down arms. To cease from armed hostility; to surrender.

Under arms. Prepared for battle; in battle array.

Up in arms. In open rebellion; figuratively, roused to anger.

King of Arms. *See* HERALDS.

The right to bear arms. The right to use an heraldic device, which can be obtained only by direct grant from the College of Heralds (and the payment of certain fees), or by patrimony, *i.e.* direct descent from one on whom the grant has been conferred. In either case a small annual licence must be paid if the coat of arms is used in any way, such as on one's carriage, silver, or stationery. A person having such right is said to be *armigerous*.

The Royal Arms of England. The three lions passant gardant were introduced by Richard Cœur de Lion after his return from the third Crusade; the lion rampant in the second quarter is from the arms of Scotland, it having first been used in the reign of Alexander II (1214-49); and the harp in the fourth quarter represents Ireland; it was assigned to Ireland in the time of Henry VIII; before that time her device was three crowns. The lion supporter is English, and the unicorn Scottish; they were introduced by James I. The crest, a lion statant gardant, first appears on the Great Seal of Edward III.

The correct emblazoning of the arms of the United Kingdom of Great Britain and Ireland is: —

Quarterly, first and fourth gules, three lions passant gardant in pale, or, for England; second or, a lion rampant with a double tressure flory-counter-flory gules, for Scotland; third azure, a harp or, stringed argent, for Ireland; all surrounded by the Garter. *Crest.* — Upon the royal helmet, the imperial crown proper, thereon a lion statant gardant or, imperial crowned proper. *Supporters.* — A lion rampant gardant, or, crowned as the crest. Sinister, a unicorn argent, armed, crined, and unguled proper, gorged with a coronet composed of crosses patée and fleur de lis, a chain affixed thereto passing between the forelegs, and reflexed over the back, also or. *Motto.* — "Dieu et mon Droit" in the compartment below, the shield, with the Union rose, shamrock, and thistle engrafted on the same stem.

From the time of Edward III (1340) until the Union of Great Britain and Ireland (1800) the reigning sovereigns styled themselves "of Great Britain, France and Ireland, King," (Elizabeth I said that if the Salic Law forbade her to be Queen of France she would e'en be King) and the fleur de lys of France was quartered with the arms of England and Scotland. The empty title was abandoned as from 1 January, 1801, and from that date and for that reason all diplomatic correspondence thenceforward was carried on in English instead of French.

Nor has this been the only change in the Royal Arms. On the accession of George I (1714) the White Horse of Hanover was borne in pretence (*i.e.* superimposed in the centre of the royal coat of arms). On the death of William IV (1837) the Salic Law prohibited the accession of Victoria to the throne of Hanover, and on her uncle the Duke of Cumberland succeeding to that throne, the Hanoverian arms were dropped from the British royal arms.

Armada (ar mä′ dà). Originally Spanish for "army," the word is now used, from the Spanish

Armada, for any fleet of large size or strength. Formerly spelt *armado*.

> At length resolv'd t'assert the wat'ry ball,
> He [Charles II] in himself did whole Armadoes bring;
> Him aged seamen might their master call,
> And choose for general, were he not their king.
> > Dryden: *Annus Mirabilis*, xiv.

The Spanish Armada. The fleet assembled by Philip II of Spain, in 1588, for the conquest of England. It consisted of 129 vessels, carried 8,000 sailors, 19,000 soldiers, 2,000 guns and provisions to feed 40,000 men for six months. After battle and storm no more than 54 vessels got back to Spain, carrying a few sick and exhausted men.

Armageddon (ar mȧ ged' ŏn). The name given in the Apocalypse (*Rev.* xvi, 16) to the site of the last great battle that is to be between the nations before the Day of Judgment; hence, any great battle or scene of slaughter.

The place the author of the Apocalypse had in mind was probably the mountainous district near Megiddo, generally identified with the modern Lejjun, about 54 miles due north of Jerusalem.

Armida (ar mē' da). In Tasso's *Jerusalem Delivered* a beautiful sorceress, with whom Rinaldo fell in love, and wasted his time in voluptuous pleasure. After his escape from her, Armida followed him, but not being able to allure him back, set fire to her palace, rushed into a combat, and was slain.

In 1806, Frederick William of Prussia declared war against Napoleon, and his young queen rode about in military costume to arouse the enthusiasm of the people. When Napoleon was told of it, he said, "She is Armida, in her distraction setting fire to her own palace."

Armistice Day. Hostilities in World War I ended at 11 o'clock on November 11th, 1918, when an armistice was signed. In subsequent years November 11th was kept as Armistice Day, marked by a two-minute silence and cessation of work at 11 a.m., followed in various places by ceremonies. In 1946 the old name was changed to Remembrance Day, to include a memorial of the close of the 1939-45 war and it is kept on the Sunday nearest 11th November.

Armour, Coat, or **a Coat of Arms,** was originally a drapery of silk or other rich stuff worn by a knight over his armour and embroidered in colours with his distinguishing device. This practice was adopted by the Crusaders, who found it necessary to cover their steel armour from the rays of the sun.

Armoury. The place where armour and arms are kept.

> The sword
> Of Michael from the armoury of God
> Was given him.
> > Milton: *Paradise Lost*, vi, 320.

The word may also mean armour collectively, as in *Paradise Lost*, iv, 553:—

> nigh at hand
> Celestial armoury, shields, helms, and spears,
> Hung high, with diamond flaming and with gold.

Arnauts (ar' nauts) (Turk. brave men). Albanian mountaineers.

> Stained with the best of Arnaut's blood.
> > Byron: *The Giaour*.

Arod. In Dryden's *Absalom and Achitophel* is designed for Sir William Waller.

> But in the sacred annals of our plot
> Industrious Arod never be forgot,
> The labours of this midnight magistrate
> May vie with Corah's [Titus Oates] to preserve the state.   Part ii.

Arras (ar' ȧs). Tapestry; the cloth of Arras, in Artois, formerly famed for its manufacture. When rooms were hung with tapestry it was easy for persons to hide behind it; thus Hubert hid the two villains who were to put out Arthur's eyes, Polonius was slain by Hamlet while concealed behind the arras, Falstaff proposed to hide behind it at Windsor, etc.

Arria (ăr' i a). The wife of Cæcina Pætus, who, being accused of conspiring against the Emperor Claudius, was condemned to death by suicide. As he hesitated to carry out the sentence Arria stabbed herself, then presenting the dagger to her husband, said; "Pætus, it gives no pain" (*non dolet*). (A.D. 42). *See* Pliny, vii.

Arrière ban. *See* Ban.

Arrière pensée (Fr. "behind-thought"). A hidden or reserved motive, not apparent on the surface.

Artegal, or **Arthegal, Sir** (ar' te gȧl). The hero of Bk. v of Spenser's *Faerie Queene*, lover of Britomart, to whom he is made known by means of a magic mirror. He is emblematic of Justice, and in many of his deeds, such as the rescue of Irena (Ireland) from Grantorto, is typical of Arthur, Lord Grey of Wilton, who went to Ireland as Lord Lieutenant in 1580 with Spenser as his secretary. *See* Elidure.

Artemis. *See* Diana.

Artesian Wells. So called from *Arteis*, the Old French name for Artois, in France, where they were first bored. They are sunk with a boring or drilling apparatus into water or oil-bearing strata from which the liquid rises by its own pressure to the top of the bore.

Artful Dodger. A young thief in Dickens's *Oliver Twist*, pupil of Fagin. His name was Jack

Dawkins, and he became a most perfect adept in villainy.

Arthegal. *See* ARTEGAL.

Arthur. A shadowy British chieftain of the 6th century, first mentioned by Nennius, a Breton monk of the 10th century. He fought many battles and is said to have been a king of the Silures, a tribe of ancient Britons, to have been mortally wounded in the battle of Camlan (537), in Cornwall, during the revolt of his nephew, Modred (who was also slain), and to have been taken to Glastonbury, where he died.

His wife was Guinevere, who committed adultery with Sir Launcelot of the Lake, one of the Knights of the Round Table.

Arthur was the natural son of Uther and Igerna (wife of Gorolis, duke of Cornwall), and was brought up by Sir Ector.

He was born at Tintagel Castle, in Cornwall.

His chief home and the seat of his court was Caerleon, in Wales; and he was buried at Avalon (*q.v.*).

His sword was called Excalibur; his spear, Rone; and his shield, Pridwin. His dog was named Cavall. *See* ROUND TABLE, KNIGHTS OF THE.

Arthurian Romances. The stories which have King Arthur as their central figure appear as early as the 12th century in the *Historia Regum Britanniœ* of Geoffrey of Monmouth (d. 1154), which drew partly from the work of Nennius (*see* ARTHUR), partly—according to the author—from an ancient British or Breton book (lost, if ever existing) lent him by Walter, Archdeacon of Oxford, and partly from sources which are untraced, but the originals of which are probably embedded in Welsh or Celtic legends, most of them being now non-extant. The original Arthur was a very shadowy warrior; Geoffrey of Monmouth, probably at the instigation of Henry I and for the purpose of providing the new nation with a national hero, made many additions; the story was taken up in France and further expanded; Wace, a French poet (who is the first to mention the Round Table, *q.v.*), turned it into a metrical chronicle of some 14,000 lines (*Brut d'Angle-terre*, *c.* 1155); Celtic and other legends, including those of the Grail (*q.v.*) and Sir Tristram, were superadded, and in about 1205 Layamon, the Worcestershire priest, completed his *Brut* (about 30,000 lines), which included Wace's work and amplifications such as the story of the fairies at Arthur's birth, who, at his death, wafted him to Avalon, as well as Sir Gawain and

Sir Bedivere. In France the legends were worked upon by Robert de Borron (fl. 1215), who first attached the story of the Grail (*q.v.*) to the Arthurian Cycle and brought the legend of Merlin into prominence, and Chrestien de Troyes (*c.* 1140-90), who is responsible for the presence in the Cycle of the tale of Enid and Geraint, the tragic loves of Launcelot and Guinevere, the story of Perceval, and other additions for many of which he was indebted to the Welsh *Mabinogion*. Many other legends in the form of ballads, romances, and Welsh and Breton songs and lays were popular, and in the 15th century the whole *corpus* was collected, edited, and more or less worked into a state of homogeneity by Sir Thomas Malory (d. 1471), his *Le Morte d'Arthur* being printed by Caxton in 1485. For the different heroes, sections, etc., of this great Cycle of Romance, *see* the various names throughout this Dictionary.

Articles of Roup. The conditions of sale at a roup (*q.v.*), as announced by a crier.

Arts. Degrees in Arts. In the mediæval ages the full course consisted of the three subjects which constituted the *Trivium*, and the four subjects which constituted the *Quadrivium*:—

The *Trivium* was grammar, logic, and rhetoric.

The *Quadrivium* was music, arithmetic, geometry, and astronomy.

The *Master of Arts* was the person qualified to teach or be the master of students in arts; as the *Doctor* was the person qualified to teach theology, law or medicine.

Aryans. The parent stock of what is called the Indo-European family of nations. Their original home is quite unknown, authorities differing so widely as between a locality enclosed by the river Oxus and the Hindu-kush mountains, and the shores of the Baltic, or Central Europe. The Aryan family of languages includes Sanskrit, Zend, Latin, Greek, Celtic, Persian and Hindu, with all the European, except Basque, Turkish, Hungarian, and Finnish. Sometimes called the Indo-European, sometimes the Indo-Germanic, and sometimes the Japhetic.

Under the Nazi regime in Germany the word was prostituted by being applied to any race, person or thing that was not Semitic, even the Japanese being classified as Aryans.

Arzina. A river that flows into the North Sea, near Wardhus, where Sir Hugh Willoughby's three ships were ice-bound, and the whole crew perished of starvation.

In these fell regions, in Arzina caught,
And to the stony deep his idle ship
Immediate sealed, he with his hapless crew . . .
Froze into statues.
THOMSON: *Winter*, 930.

Ascalaphus. In Greek mythology, an inhabitant of the underworld who, when Pluto gave Proserpine permission to return to the upper world if she had eaten nothing, said that she had partaken of a pomegranate. In revenge Proserpine turned him into an owl by sprinkling him with the water of Phlegethon.

Ascendant. An astrological term. In casting a horoscope the point of the ecliptic or degree of the zodiac which is just rising at the moment of birth is called the ascendant, and the easternmost star represents the house of life (*see* HOUSE), because it is in the act of ascending. This is a man's strongest star, and when his outlook is bright, we say *his star is in the ascendant*.

The house of the Ascendant, includes five degrees of the zodiac above the point just rising, and twenty-five below it. Usually, the point of birth is referred to.

Ascension Day, or Holy Thursday (*q.v.*). The day set apart by the Christian Churches to commemorate the ascent of our Lord from earth to heaven. It is the fortieth day after Easter. *See* BOUNDS, BEATING THE.

Asclepiads, or **Asclepiadic Metre** (ăs kle pī′ ådz) A term in Greek and Latin prosody denoting a verse (invented by Asclepiades) which consists of a spondee, two (or three) choriambi, and an iambus, usually with a central cæsura, thus:—

$$ - \mid \smile \smile \parallel \smile \smile \mid \smile $$

The first ode of Horace is Asclepiadic. The first and last two lines may be translated in the same metre, thus:—

Dear friend, patron of song, sprung from the race of kings;
Thy name ever a grace and a protection brings. . . .
My name, if to the lyre haply you chance to wed,
Pride would high as the stars lift my exalted head.

Ascot Races. A very fashionable meeting, run early in June on Ascot Heath (6 miles from Windsor). These races were instituted early in the 18th century.

Ascræn Poet, or **Sage** (ăs krē′ ån). Hesiod, the Greek didactic poet, born at Ascra in Bœotia. Virgil (*Eclogues*, vii, 70) calls him the "Old Ascræon."

Ash Wednesday. The first Wednesday in Lent, so called from an ancient Roman Catholic custom of sprinkling on the heads of penitents who had confessed that day the ashes of the palms that were consecrated on the previous Palm Sunday which themselves had been consecrated at the altar. The custom, it is said, was introduced by Gregory the Great.

Ashes. Ashes to ashes, dust to dust. A phrase from the English Burial Service, used sometimes to signify total finality. It is founded on various scriptural texts, such as "Dust thou art, and unto dust thou shalt return" (*Gen*. iii, 19), and "I will bring thee to ashes upon the earth in the sight of all them that behold thee" (*Ezek*. xxviii, 18).

Ashes to ashes and dust to dust,
If God won't have him the Devil must.

According to Sir Walter Scott (*see* his edition of Swift's *Journal to Stella*. March 25th, 1710-11), this was the form of burial service given by the sexton to the body of Guiscard, the French refugee who, in 1711, attempted the life of Harley.

Ashmolean Museum (ăsh mō′ li ån). The first public museum of curiosities in England. It was presented to the University of Oxford in 1677 by Elias Ashmole (1617-92), the antiquarian, who had inherited the greater part of the contents from his friend John Tradescant. Ashmole later gave his library to the University. The museum building was the work of Sir Christopher Wren.

Ashtoreth (ăsh′ to reth). The goddess of fertility and reproduction among the Canaanites and Phœnicians, called by the Babylonians *Ishtar* (Venus), and by the Greeks *Astarte* (*q.v.*). She may possibly be the "queen of heaven" mentioned by Jeremiah (vii, 18, xliv, 17, 25). Formerly she was supposed to be a moongoddess, hence Milton's reference in his *Ode on the Nativity*.

Moonëd Ashtaroth,
Heaven's queen and mother both.

Ashur. *See* ASSHUR.

Asinego (ăs i nē′ gō) (Port.) A young ass, a simpleton.

Thou hast no more brain than I have in mine elbows; an asinego may tutor thee—
SHAKESPEARE: *Troilus and Cressida*, ii, 1.

Asir. *See* ÆSIR.

Asmodeus (ăs mō dē′ us, ăs mō′ di ùs). The "evil demon" who appears in the Apocryphal book of *Tobit*, borrowed (and to some extent transformed) from Aeshma, one of the seven archangels of Persian mythology. The name is probably the Zend *Aeshmo daeva* (the demon Aeshma), and is not connected with the Heb. *samad*, to destroy. The character of Asmodeus is explained in the following passage from *The Testament of Solomon*—

I am called *Asmodeus* among mortals, and my business is to plot against the newly-wedded, so that they may not know one another. And I sever them utterly by many calamities; and I waste away the beauty of virgins, and estrange their hearts.

In *Tobit* Asmodeus falls in love with Sara, daughter of Raguel, and causes the death of seven husbands in succession, each on his bridal night. After her marriage to Tobias, he was driven into Egypt by a charm, made by Tobias of the heart and liver of a fish burnt on perfumed ashes, and being pursued was taken prisoner and bound.

Better pleased
Than Asmodeus with the fishy fume
That drove him, though enamoured, from the spouse
Of Tobit's son, and with a vengeance sent
From Media post to Egypt, there fast bound.
MILTON: *Paradise Lost*, iv, 167.

Le Sage gave the name to the companion of Don Cleofas in his *Devil on Two Sticks*.

Asoka (ăs' ō kà). An Indian king of the Maurya dynasty of Magadha, 263-226 B.C., who was converted to Buddhism by a miracle and became its "nursing father," as Constantine was of Christianity. He is called "the king beloved of the gods."

Aspasia (a spā' zi à). A Milesian woman (fl. 440 B.C.), celebrated for her beauty and talents, who lived at Athens as mistress of Pericles, and whose house became the centre of literary and philosophical society. She was the most celebrated of the Greek Hetæræ, and on the death of Pericles (429 B.C.) lived with the democratic leader, Lysicles.

Aspatia (a spā' shà), in the *Maid's Tragedy*, of Beaumont and Fletcher, is noted for her deep sorrows, her great resignation, and the pathos of her speeches. Amyntor deserts her, women point at her with scorn, she is the jest and by-word of everyone, but she bears it all with patience.

Asphaltic Lake. The Dead Sea, where asphalt abounds both on the surface of the water and on the banks. Asphalt is a bitumen.

There was an asphaltic and Bituminous nature in that Lake before the fire of Gomorrah.
Sir THOS. BROWNE: *Religio Medici*, i, 19.

There is a bituminous, or asphalt, lake in Trinidad.

Asphodel (ăs' fō del). Old-fashioned garden flowers of the natural order Liliaceæ. The name daffodil is a corruption of asphodel. In the language of flowers it means "regret." It was said that the spirits of the dead sustained themselves on the roots of this flower, and the ancients planted them on graves. Pliny and others said that the ghosts beyond Acheron roamed through the meadows of asphodel, in order to reach the waters of Lethe or Oblivion.

Ass. The dark stripe running down the back of an ass, crossed by another at the shoulders, is, according to tradition, the cross that was communicated to the creature when our Lord rode on the back of an ass in His triumphant entry into Jerusalem.

An ass in a lion's skin. A coward who hectors, a fool that apes the wise man. The allusion is to the fable of an ass that put on a lion's hide, but was betrayed when he began to bray.

To make an ass of oneself. To do something very foolish. To expose oneself to ridicule.

Assassins (à săs' inz). A sect of Oriental fanatics of a military and religious character, founded in Persia in 1090 by Hassan ben Sabbah, better known as the *Old Man* (or *Sheikh*) *of the Mountains* (*see under* MOUNTAIN), because the sect migrated to Mount Lebanon and made it its stronghold. This band was the terror of the world for two centuries, and, to the number of 50,000 strong, offered formidable opposition to the Crusaders. Their religion was a compound of Magianism, Judaism, Christianity, and Mohammedanism, and their name is derived from *haschisch* (bang), an intoxicating drink, with which they are said to have "doped" themselves before perpetrating their orgies of massacre. They were finally put down by the Sultan Bibars, about 1272.

Assay (à sā), or *Essay* (through O.Fr. from Lat. *exagium*, to weigh). To try or test; to determine the amount of different metals in an ore, etc.; and, formerly, to taste food or drink before it is offered to a sovereign; hence, *to take the assay* is to taste wine to prove it is not poisoned.

The aphetic form of the word, "say," was common down to the 17th century, and Edmund, in *King Lear* (v, 5), says to Edgar, "Thy tongue, some *say* of breeding breathes"; *i.e.* thy speech gives indication of good breeding—it savours of it.

Assay, as a noun, means a test or trial, as in—
[He] makes vow before his uncle never more
To give the assay of arms against your majesty.
SHAKESPEARE: *Hamlet*, ii, 2.

But for the last three hundred years the spelling *essay* has been adopted (from French) for the noun, in all uses except those connected with the assaying of metals.

Assaye Regiment. *See* REGIMENTAL NICKNAMES.

Assemblage, Nouns of. Long custom and technical usage have ascribed certain words to assemblages of animals, things, or persons. Some of the principal are given here:

Animals, birds, etc.

antelopes: a herd.,
asses: a pace or herd.
badgers: a cete.
bears: a sleuth.
bees: a swarm, a grist.,
birds: a flock, flight, congregation, volery.
bitterns: a sedge or siege.
boars: a sounder.
bucks: a brace or leash.
buffaloes: a herd.
cattle: a drove or herd.
chickens: a brood.
choughs: a chattering.
coots: a covert.
cranes: a herd, sedge, or siege.
cubs: a litter.
curlews: a herd.
deer: a herd.
ducks: (in flight) a team.
elk: a gang.
ferrets: a fesnyng.
fishes: a shoal, draught, haul, run, or catch.
flies: a swarm.
foxes: a skulk.
geese: (in flight) a skein; (on the ground), a gaggle.
gnats: a swarm or cloud.
goats: a herd or tribe.
goldfinches: a charm.
grouse: (a single brood), a covey; (several broods), a pack.
hares: a down or husk.
hawks: a cast.
hens: a brood.
herons: a sedge or siege.
herrings: a shoal.
hounds: a pack or mute.
kangaroos: a troop.
kine: a drove.
kittens: a kindle.
larks: an exaltation.
leopards: a leap.
lions: a pride.
mares: a stud.
monkeys: a troop.
nightingales: a watch.
oxen: a yoke, drove, team, or herd.
partridges: a covey.
peacocks: a muster.
pheasants: a nye or nide.
pigeons: a flock or flight.
pilchards: a shoal.
plovers: a wing or congregation.
porpoises: a school.
pups: a litter.
quails: a bevy.
rooks: a building or clamour
seals: a herd or pod.
sheep: a flock.
swans: a herd or bevy.
swifts: a flock.
swine: a sounder or drift.
whales: a school, gam, or pod.
wolves: a pack, rout, or herd.
woodcock: a fall.

Things

aeroplanes: a flight, squadron.
arrows: a sheaf.
bells: a peal.
boats: a flotilla.
bowls: a set.
bread: a batch.
cards: a pack, a deck (Am.).
cars: a fleet.
eggs: a clutch.
flowers: a bouquet or nosegay.
golf-clubs: a set.
guns: (sporting), a pair.
grapes: a cluster or bunch.
onions: a rope.
pearls: a rope or string.
rags: a bundle.
sails: an outfit.
ships: a fleet or squadron.
stars: a cluster or constellation.
steps: a flight.
trees: a clump.

Persons

actors: a company, cast, or troupe.
angels: a host.
baseball team: a nine.
beaters: a squad.
bishops: a bench.
cricket team: an eleven.
dancers: a troupe.
football: (Association), an eleven; (Rugby), a fifteen.
girls: a bevy.
labourers: a gang.
magistrates: a bench.
minstrels: a troupe.
musicians, a band, an orchestra.
police: a posse.
rowing: an eight, a four, a pair.
runners: a field.
sailors: a crew.
savages: a horde.
servants: a staff.
worshippers: a congregation.

Asshur. The chief god of the Assyrian pantheon, perhaps derived from the Babylonian god of heaven, Anu. His symbol was the winged circle in which was frequently enclosed a draped male figure carrying three horns on the head and with one hand stretched forth, sometimes with a bow in the hand. His wife was Belit (*i.e.* the Lady, *par excellence*), who has been identified with the Ishtar (*see* ASHTORETH) of Nineveh.

Assiento Treaties (Sp. *asiénto*, agreement). Contracts entered into by Spain with Portugal, France, and England to supply her South American colonies with Negro slaves. England joined in 1713, after the peace of Utrecht, and kept the disgraceful monopoly (with a few breaks) till 1750.

Assumption, Feast of the. In the R.C. Church the principal feast day of the Virgin Mary, observed on August 15th. On November 1st,

1950, Pope Pius XII declared *ex cathedra* that thenceforth it would be a dogma of the Church that at the death of the Virgin her body was preserved from corruption, and that shortly afterwards it was assumed (Lat. *assumere*, to take to) into heaven and reunited to her soul.

Assurance. Audacity, brazen self-confidence. "His assurance is quite unbearable."

Assurance provides for the contingence of a certainty, *e.g.* life assurance is a financial provision for the certain fact of death. Insurance provides against what may or may not happen, *e.g.* burglary, fire.

Astarte (à star' ti). The Greek name for Ashtoreth (*q.v.*), sometimes thought to have been a moon-goddess. Hence Milton's allusion:—

> With these in troop
> Came Astoreth, whom the Phœnicians called
> Astartë, queen of heaven, with crescent horns.
>> *Paradise Lost*, i, 437.

Byron gave the name to the lady beloved by Manfred in his drama, *Manfred*. It has been suggested that Astarte was drawn from the poet's sister, Augusta (Mrs. Leigh).

Astolat (ăs' tō lăt). This town, mentioned in the Arthurian legends, is generally identified with Guildford, in Surrey, though there can be no certainty.

The Lily Maid of Astolat. Elaine (*q.v.*).

Astoreth. *See* ASHTORETH.

Astræa (ăs trē' à). Equity, innocence. During the Golden Age this goddess dwelt on earth, but when sin began to prevail, she reluctantly left it, and was metamorphosed into the constellation *Virgo*.

> When hard-hearted interest first began
> To poison earth, Astræa left the plain.
>> THOMSON: *Castle of Indolence*, I, x.

Pope gave the name to Mrs. Aphra Behn (1640-89), playwright and novelist, author of the once-popular novel *Oroonoko*.

Sir John Davies (1569-1626) wrote a series of twenty-six acrostics, entitled *Hymns to Astraea*, in honour of Queen Elizabeth.

Astral Body. In theosophical parlance, the phantasmal or spiritual appearance of the physical human form, that is existent both before and after the death of the material body, though during life it is not usually separated from it; also the "kamarupa" or body of desires, which retains a finite life in the astral world after bodily death.

Astral spirits. The spirits of the dead that occupy the stars and the stellar regions, or astral world. According to the occultists, each star has its special spirit; and Paracelsus maintained

that every man had his attendant star, which received him at death, and took charge of him till the great resurrection.

Astrology. The ancient and mediæval so-called "science" that professed to foretell events by studying the position of the stars and discovering their occult influence on human affairs. It is one of the most ancient superstitions; it prevailed from earliest times among the Chaldeans, Egyptians, Etruscans, Hindus, Chinese, etc., and had a powerful influence in the Europe of the Middle Ages. *Natural Astrology*—*i.e.* the branch that dealt with meteorological phenomena and with time, tides, eclipses, the fixing of Easter, etc.—was the forerunner of the science of Astronomy; what is now known as "astrology" was formerly differentiated from this as *Judicial Astrology*, and dealt with star-divination and the occult planetary and sidereal influences upon human affairs. *See* HOUSES, ASTROLOGICAL; HOROSCOPE; MICROCOSM.

Astronomers Royal. (1) Flamsteed, 1675; (2) Halley, 1719; (3) Bradley, 1742; (4) Bliss, 1762; (5) Maskelyne, who originated the Nautical Almanack, 1765; (6) Pond, 1811; (7) Airy, 1835; (8) Christie, 1881; (9) Sir F. W. Dyson, 1910; (10) Sir H.S. Jones 1933

Asur (ăs' ŭr). The national god of the ancient Assyrians; the supreme god over all the gods. *See* ASSHUR.

Asurbanipal. *See* SARDANAPALUS.

Asylum means, literally, a place where pillage is forbidden (Gr. *a*, not, *sulon*, right of pillage). The ancients set apart certain places of refuge, where the vilest criminals were protected, from both private and public assaults.

Asynja (ăs in' yà). The goddesses of Asgard; the feminine counterparts of the Æsir.

At Home. *See* HOME.

Atalanta's Race (ăt à lăn' tà). Atalanta, in Greek legend, was a daughter of Iasus and Clymene. She took part in the Calydonian hunt and, being very swift of foot, refused to marry unless the suitor should first defeat her in a race. Milanion overcame her at last by dropping, one after another, during the race, three golden apples that had been given him for the purpose by Venus. Atalanta was not proof against the temptation to pick them up, and so lost the race and became a wife. In the Bœotian form of the legend Hippomenes takes the place of Milanion.

Ate (ā' tē). In Greek mythology, the goddess of vengeance and mischief; she was driven out of heaven, and took refuge among the sons of men.

With Atë by his side come hot from hell. . . .
Cry "Havoc" and let slip the dogs of war.
                    SHAKESPEARE: *Julius Cæsar*, iii, 1.

In Spenser's *Faerie Queene* (IV, i, iv, ix, etc.), the name is given to a lying and slanderous hag, the companion of Duessa.

Atheists. During World War II Father W. T. Cummings, an American army chaplain at Bataan, in one of his sermons used the phrase, "there are no atheists in foxholes," meaning that no one can deny the existence of God in the face of imminent death.

Athenæum (ăth ė nē' ŭm). A famous academy or university situated on the Capitoline Hill at Rome, and founded by Hadrian about A.D. 133. So called in honour of Athene. As now used the name usually denotes a literary or scientific institution.

The Athenæum Club in London was established in 1824; the review of this name (now merged in the *Spectator*) was founded by James Silk Buckingham in 1828.

Athene (à thē' ne). The goddess of wisdom and of the arts and sciences in Greek mythology: the counterpart of the Roman Minerva (*q.v.*).

Athens. When the goddess of wisdom disputed with the sea-god which of them should give name to Athens, the gods decided that it should be called by the name of that deity which bestowed on man the most useful boon. Athene (the goddess of wisdom) created the olive tree, Poseidon created the horse. The vote was given in favour of the olive tree, and the city was called Athens. An olive branch was the symbol of *peace*, and was also the highest prize of the victor in the Olympic games. The horse, on the other hand, was the symbol of *war*.

Athens of the New World. Boston.

Athenian Bee. Plato (429-327 B.C.), a native of Athens, was so called because, according to tradition, when in his cradle a swarm of bees alighted on his mouth, and in consequence his words flowed with the sweetness of honey. The same tale is told of St. Ambrose, and others. *See* BEE. Xenophon (444-359 B.C.) is also called "the Bee of Athens," or " the Athenian Bee."

Atlantean Shoulders. Shoulders able to bear a great weight, like those of Atlas (*q.v.*).
          Sage he stood,
With Atlantean shoulders, fit to bear
The weight of mightiest monarchies.
                    MILTON: *Paradise Lost*, ii, 305.

Atlantes (ăt lăn' tēz). Figures of men, used in architecture as pillars. So called from Atlas (*q.v.*). Female figures are called Caryatides (*q.v.*). *See also* TELAMONES.

Atlantic Charter. President Roosevelt and Winston Churchill after meeting at sea during the 1939-45 War made a declaration of their common principles, August 14th 1941, known as the Atlantic Charter. They declared, among other things, that the U.S. and Great Britain desired no aggrandizement, that they wished all peoples to live under their chosen form of Government and to have access to those raw materials necessary to their economic prosperity, that they hoped for improved labour standards and social security for all, and that when peace came they wished all men to live free from fear and from want. Finally, they urged general disarmament at the end of hostilities.

Atlantic Ocean. The ocean is so called either from the Atlas mountains, the great range in north-west Africa which, to the ancients, seemed to overlook the whole ocean, or from Atlantis (*q.v.*).

Atlantic Wall. The name given by the Germans in World War II to their defences built up around the west coast of France to resist the expected Allied landings.

Atlantis. A mythical island of great extent which was anciently supposed to have existed in the Atlantic Ocean. It is first mentioned by Plato (in the *Timœus* and *Critias*), and Solon was told of it by an Egyptian priest, who said that it had been overwhelmed by an earthquake and sunk beneath the sea 9,000 years before his time. *Cp.* LEMURIA; LYONESSE.

Atlas (ăt' làs)". In Greek mythology, one of the Titans condemned by Zeus for his share in the War of the Titans to uphold the heavens on his shoulders. He was stationed on the Atlas mountains in Africa, and the tale is merely a poetical way of saying that they prop up the heavens, because they are so lofty.
Bid Atlas, propping heaven, as poets feign,
His subterranean wonders spread!
                    THOMSON: *Autumn*, 797.

A book of maps is so called because the figure of Atlas with the world on his back was employed by Mercator on the title-page of his collection of maps in the 16th century. In the paper trade *Atlas* is a standard size of drawing-paper measuring 26 × 34 in.

Atli. *See* ETZEL.

Atman (ăt' màn), in Buddhist philosophy, is the noumenon of one's own self. Not the Ego, but the ego divested of all that is objective; the "spark of heavenly flame." In the Upanishads the Atman is regarded as the sole reality.
The unseen and unperceivable, which was formerly called the soul, was now called the self, Atman. Nothing

could be predicated of it except that it was, that it perceived and thought, and that it must be blessed.

MAX MULLER.

Atomic Energy and the Atomic Bomb. All matter consists of atoms, and science asserts that each atom is composed of three types of particle, the proton, the electron and the neutron; the first possesses a positive electric charge, the second a negative charge of equal value, the neutron has no such charge. The protons, neutrons and some of the electrons form a nucleus around which the remainder of the electrons revolve. The binding force of the nucleus is not the same for every element. When the nucleus of one atom of Uranium 235 is split up energy is released, due to the formation of an element with a lower binding force. In addition neutrons are emitted which, in their turn, split up other atoms. If the whole process expands in this way it is called a chain reaction, and if sufficient material is available a terrific explosion results.

Atomic theory. The doctrine that all elemental bodies consist of aggregations of *atoms* (*i.e.* the smallest indivisible particles of the element in question), not united fortuitously, but according to fixed proportions. The four laws of Dalton are—constant proportion, reciprocal proportion, multiple proportion, and compound proportion.

Atossa (atos′ ā). Sarah, Duchess of Marlborough (1660-1744), so called by Pope (*Moral Essays*, ii), was the friend of Lady Mary Wortley Montagu, whom he calls *Sappho*. Herodotus says that Atossa, the mother of Xerxes, was a follower of Sappho.

A-trip. The anchor is *a-trip* when it has just been drawn from the ground in a perpendicular direction. A sail is *a-trip* when it has been hoisted from the cap, and is ready for trimming.

Atropos (ăt′ rō pos). In Greek mythology the eldest of the Three Fates, and the one who severs the thread of human life.

Attaint (etymologically the same word as *attain*, through Fr. from Lat. *ad*, to, *tangere*, to touch). An old term in chivalry, meaning to strike the helmet and shield of an antagonist so firmly with the lance, held in a direct line, as either to break the lance or overthrow the person struck. Hence, to convict, condemn; hence, to condemn one convicted of treason to loss of honours and death. The later development of the word was affected by its fanciful association with *taint*.

Attic. The Attic Bee, Sophocles (495-405 B.C.), the tragic poet, a native of Athens; so called from the great sweetness of his compositions. *See also* ATHENIAN BEE.

Atticus (ăt′ i kus). The most elegant and finished scholar of the Romans, and a bookseller (109-32 B.C.). His admirable taste and sound judgment were so highly thought of that even Cicero submitted several of his treatises to him.

Attorney (a ter′ ni) (Fr. *atourner*, to attorn, or turn over to another). One who acts as agent for another, especially in legal matters. The work of an attorney is now undertaken by a solicitor, and the term is only used in "Power of Attorney" described below. A solicitor is one who solicits or petitions in Courts of Equity through counsel. At one time solicitors belonged to Courts of Equity, and attorneys to the other courts.

From and after Act 36, 37 Vict, lxvi, 87, "all persons admitted as solicitors, attorneys, or proctors . . . empowered to practise in any court, the jurisdiction of which is hereby transferred to the High Court of Justice, or the Court of Appeal, shall be called Solicitors of the Supreme Court." (1873.)

Power of Attorney. Legal authority given to another to collect rents, pay wages, invest money, or to act in matters stated in the instrument, according to his own judgment. In such cases *quod aliquis facit per aliquem, facit per se*.

Warrant of Attorney. The legal instrument which confers on another the "Power of Attorney."

The **Attorney-General** is the chief law officer of the Government and head of the Bar. He conducts cases on behalf of the Crown, advises the various departments of State on legal matters, and, if necessary, justifies such advice and action in Parliament.

Au courant (ō koo′ ron) (Fr.), "acquainted with" (literally, in the current [of events]). To keep one *au courant* of everything that passes, is to keep one familiar with, or informed of, passing events.

Au fait (Fr.). Skilful, thorough master of; as, He is quite *au fait* in those matters, *i.e.* quite master of them or conversant with them.

Au pied de la lettre (Fr.). *Literatim et verbatim*; according to the strict letter of the text.

Arthur is but a boy, and a wild, enthusiastic young fellow whose opinions one must not take *au pied de la lettre*.

THACKERAY: *Pendennis*, i, 11.

Au revoir (Fr.). "Good-bye for the present." Literally, *till seeing you again.*

Aubaine. *See* DROIT D'AUBAINE.

Aubry's Dog. *See* DOG.

Auburn (aw′ bern). It is supposed that this hamlet described by Goldsmith in *The Deserted Village* was Lissoy, County Westmeath, Ireland.

Audley. We will John Audley it. A theatrical phrase meaning to abridge, or bring to a conclusion, a play in progress. It is said that in the 18th century a travelling showman named Shuter used to lengthen out his performance till a goodly number of newcomers were waiting for admission to the next house. An assistant would then call out, "Is John Audley here?" and the play was brought to an end as soon as possible.

Audrey. In Shakespeare's *As You Like It*, an awkward country wench, who jilted William for Touchstone. *See also* TAWDRY.

Augury (aw' gū ri) (probably from Lat. *avis*, a bird, and *garrire*, to talk), means properly the function of an augur, *i.e.* a religious official among the Romans who professed to foretell future events from omens derived chiefly from the actions of birds. The augur, having taken his stand on the Capitoline Hill, marked out with his wand the space of the heavens to be the field of observation, and divided it from top to bottom. If the birds appeared on the left of the division the augury was unlucky, but if on the right it was favourable.

This form of divination may have been due to the earliest sailors, who, if they got out of sight of land, would watch the flight of birds for indications of the shore. *Cp.* INAUGURATE; SINISTER.

August. This month was once called *sextilis*, as it was the sixth from March, with which the year used to open, but it was changed to *Augustus* in compliment to Augustus (63 B.C.-A.D. 14), the first Roman Emperor, whose "lucky month" it was. *Cp.* JULY. It was the month in which he entered upon his first consulship, celebrated three triumphs, received the oath of allegiance from the legions which occupied the Janiculum, reduced Egypt, and put an end to the civil wars.

The old Dutch name for August was *Oostmaand* (harvest-month); the old Saxon *Weodmonath* (weed-month), where weed signifies vegetation in general. In the French Republican·calendar it was called *Thermidor* (hot-month, July 19th to August 17th).

Augustus. A title conferred in 27 B.C. upon Caius Julius Cæsar Octavianus, the first Roman Emperor, meaning *reverend*, or *venerable*, and probably in origin *consecrated by augury*. In the reign of Diocletian (284-313) the two emperors each bore the title, and the two viceroys that of *Cæsar*. Prior to that time Hadrian limited the latter to the heir presumptive.

Augustus was the name given to Philippe II of France (1165-1223) and to Sigismund II of Poland (1520-72) both of whom were born in the month of August.

Augusta. The Roman name for the town that occupied the site of the City of London.

Augustan Age. The most fruitful and splendid time of Latin literature, so called from the Emperor Augustus. Horace, Ovid, Propertius, Tibullus, Virgil, etc., flourished in his reign, from 27 B.C. to A.D. 14.

Augustan History. A series of histories of the Roman Empire from Hadrian to Numerianus (117-285), of unknown authorship and date, but ascribed to Ælius Spartianus, Julius Capitolinus, Ælius Lampridius, Vulcatius Gallicanus, Trebellius Pollio, and Flavius Vopiscus.

Augustine, The Second. Thomas Aquinas, the *Angelic Doctor* (*q.v.*).

Auld Brig and New Brig. Robert Burns thus refers to the bridges over the river Ayr.

Auld Hornie. After the establishment of Christianity, the heathen deities were degraded by the Church into fallen angels; and Pan, with his horns, crooked nose, goat's beard, pointed ears, and goat's feet, was transformed to his Satanic majesty, and called Old Horney.

> O thou, whatever title suit thee,
> Auld Hornie, Satan, Nick, or Clootie.
> BURNS.

Auld Reekie. Edinburgh old town; so called because it generally appeared to be capped by a cloud of "reek" or smoke.

Aulic Council (Lat. *aula*, a court). The council of the Kaiser in the Holy Roman Empire, from which there was no appeal. It was instituted in 1501, and came to an end with the extinction of the Empire in 1806, though the name was afterwards given to the Emperor of Austria's Council of State.

Aulis (aw' lis). A harbour in Bœotia where the Greek fleet is said to have assembled before sailing against Troy. The goddess Artemis becalmed the vessels because Agamemnon had once killed a stag in the grove sacred to her, and it was declared that she could be propitiated only by the sacrifice of Agamemnon's daughter Iphigenia. The story is the subject of an opera (1774) by Gluck.

Aums-ace. *See* AMBSAS.

Aunt Sally. A game in which sticks or cudgels are thrown at a wooden head mounted on a pole, the object being to hit the nose of the figure, or break the pipe stuck in its mouth. The word *aunt* was anciently applied to any old woman; thus, in Shakespeare, Puck speaks of

> The wisest aunt telling the saddest tale.
> *Midsummer Night's Dream*, ii, 1.

Aureole. Strictly speaking the same as the *vesica piscis* (*q.v.*), *i.e.* an elliptical halo of light or colour surrounding the whole figure in early paintings of the Saviour and sometimes of the saints. Now, however, frequently used as though synonymous with *nimbus* (*q.v.*). Du Cange informs us that the aureole of nuns is *white*, of martyrs *red*, and of doctors *green*.

Aurora (aw rôr′ á). Early morning. According to Grecian mythology, the goddess Aurora, called by Homer "rosy-fingered," sets out before the sun, and is the pioneer of his rising.

> The Orator hath yoked
> The Hours, like young Aurora, to his car.
>   WORDSWORTH: *Prelude*, vii, 501.

Aurora's tears. The morning dew.

Aurora borealis. The electrical lights occasionally seen in the northern part of the sky; also called "Northern Lights," and "Merry Dancers." *See* DERWENTWATER. The similar phenomenon that occurs in the south and round the South Pole is known as the *Aurora Australis*.

Ausone, Chateau (aw ōn). A very fine claret, so called because the vineyard is reputed to be on the site of a villa built by the poet Ausonius (4th century A.D.) at Lucaniacum (St. Emilion).

Ausonia (aw sō′ ni á). An ancient name of Italy; so called from Auson, son of Ulysses, and father of the Ausones.

> England, with all thy faults, I love thee still . . .
> I would not yet exchange thy sullen skies,
> And fields without a flower for warmer France
> With all her vines; nor for Ausonia's groves
> Of golden fruitage, and her myrtle bowers.
>   COWPER: *The Task*, ii, 206-15.

Auspices (aw′ spi sēz). In ancient Rome the *auspex* (pl. *auspices*, from *avis*, a bird and *specere*, to observe) was one who observed the flight of birds and interpreted the omens. *Cp.* AUGURY.

Only the chief in command was allowed to take the auspices of war, and if a subordinate gained a victory, he was said to win it "under the good auspices" of his superior. Hence our modern use of the term.

Aussie (aw′ si, os′ i). This was a familiar name given to the Australian troops during and after World War I. Among themselves a common colloquial epithet was "digger."

Auster (Gr. *austeros*, hot, dry). A wind pernicious to flowers and health. In Italy one of the South winds was so called; its modern name is the *Sirocco*. In England it is a damp wind, generally bringing wet weather.

> Whan the wode wexeth rody of rosene floures, in the
> first somer sesoun, thorugh the brethe of the winde
> Zephirus that wexeth warm, yif the cloudy wind Auster
> blowe felliche, than goth awey the fairnesse of thornes.
>   CHAUCER: *Boethius*, II, iii.

Austin Friars. *See* AUGUSTINIAN FRIARS. The narrow lane in the City of London of this name is so called because it is on part of the site of an Augustinian priory, the church of which remained until 1941 when it was destroyed by an aerial bomb.

Australia. The States of Australia have their own familiar names: —

South Australia, the Wheat State.
Queensland, Bananaland.
Victoria, the Cabbage Patch.
New South Wales, Ma State.
Northern Territory, Land of the White Ant.

Among the cities, Perth is called The Swan City; Adelaide, The City of the Churches; Melbourne, City of the Cabbage Garden.

Autarchy and **Autarky** (aw′ tar ki). These homonyms have widely different meanings. *Autarchy* is despotism, self-government, absolute dictatorship; *autarky* means self-sufficiency, independence, especially in the economic sphere.

Aut Cæsar aut nullus (awt sē′ sar awt nul us) (Lat. either a Cæsar or a nobody). Everything or nothing; all or not at all. Cæsar used to say, "he would sooner be first in a village than second at Rome." The phrase was used as a motto by Cæsar Borgia (1478-1507), the natural son of Pope Alexander VI.

Authentic Doctor. A title bestowed on the scholastic philosopher, Gregory of Rimini (d.1358).

Authorized Version, The. *See* BIBLE, THE ENGLISH.

Autocrat of the Breakfast Table. A name given to Oliver Wendell Holmes, who wrote a series of essays under this title for the first twelve numbers of the *Atlantic Monthly* in 1857. They were published in volume form the following year.

Auto da Fe (aw′ tō da fā) (Port. an act of faith). An assembly of the Spanish Inquisition for the examination of heretics, or for the carrying into execution of the sentences imposed by it. Those who persisted in their heresy were delivered to the secular arm and usually burnt. The reason why inquisitors *burnt* their victims was, because they were forbidden to "shed blood"; a tergiversation based on the axiom of the Roman Catholic Church, *Ecclesia non novit sanguinem* (The Church is untainted with blood).

Autolycus (aw tol′ i kús). In Greek mythology, son of Mercury, and the craftiest of thieves. He stole the flocks of his neighbours, and changed their marks; but Sisyphus outwitted him by marking his sheep under their feet. Autolycus, delighted with this device, became friends with Sisyphus. Shakespeare uses his name for the rascally pedlar in *The Winter's Tale*, and says:—

My father named me Autolycus; who being, as I am, littered [*i.e.* born] under Mercury, was likewise a snapper-up of unconsidered trifles.

Winter's Tale, iv, 2.

Autumn. The third season of the year; *astronomically*, from September 21st to December 21st, but *popularly* comprising (in England) August, September, and October.

Figuratively the word may mean the fruits of autumn, as in Milton's:—

Raised of grassy turf
Their table was, and mossy seats had round,
And on her ample square, from side to side,
All autumn piled.

Paradise Lost, v, 391.

or, a season of maturity or decay, as in Shelley's:—

His limbs were lean; his scattered hair,
Sered by the autumn of strange suffering,
Sung dirges in the wind.

Alastor, 248.

He is come to his autumn. A colloquialism, which may mean that he has entered on his period of (natural or induced) decay.

Avalon (ăv' à lon). A Celtic word meaning "the island of apples," and in Celtic mythology applied to the Island of Blessed Souls, an earthly paradise set in the western seas. In the Arthurian legends it is the abode and burial-place of Arthur, who was carried hither by Morgan le Fay. Its identification with Glastonbury (*q.v.*) rests on etymological confusion. Ogier le Dane and Overon also held their courts at Avalon.

Avant-garde (ă' von gard) (Fr.). The advanced guard of an army, usually nowadays cut down to *vanguard*. The term is also applied to ulta-modern and experimental young artists and writers.

Avatar (Sans. *avatara*, descent; hence, incarnation of a god). In Hindu mythology, the advent to earth of a deity in a visible form. The ten avataras of Vishnu are by far the most celebrated. The 1st advent (the Matsya), in the form of a fish; 2nd, (the Kurma), in that of a tortoise; 3rd (the Varaha), of a boar; 4th (the Narasinha), of a monster, half man and half lion; 5th (the Vamana), in the form of a dwarf; 6th (Parashurama), in human form, as Rama with the axe; 7th (Ramachandra), again as Rama; 8th, as Krishna (*q.v.*); 9th, as Buddha. These are all past. The 10th advent will occur at the end of four ages, and will be in the form of a white horse (Kalki) with wings, to destroy the earth.

The word is used metaphorically to denote a manifestation or embodiment of some idea or phase:—

I would take the last years of Queen Anne's reign as the zenith, or palmy state, of Whiggism, in its divinest avatar of common sense.

COLERIDGE: *Table-talk*.

Ave (ā' vi, a' vā). Latin for "Hail!"

Ave Maria (Lat. Hail, Mary!). The first two words of the angel's salutation to the Virgin Mary (*Luke* i, 28). In the Roman Catholic Church the phrase is applied to an invocation to the Virgin beginning with those words; and also to the smaller beads of a rosary, the larger ones being termed *paternosters*.

Avenger of Blood, The. The man who, in the Jewish polity, had the right of taking vengeance on him who had slain one of his kinsmen (*Josh*. xx, 5, etc.). The Avenger in Hebrew is called *goel*.

Cities of refuge were appointed for the protection of homicides, and of those who had caused another's death by accident. (*Num*. xxxv, 12). The Koran sanctions the Jewish custom.

Avesta (a ves' tà). The Zoroastrian and Parsee Bible, dating in its present form from the last quarter of the 4th century, A.D., collected from the ancient writings, sermons, etc., of Zoroaster (fl. before 800 B.C.), oral traditions, etc. It is only a fragment, and consists of (1) the Yasna, the chief liturgical portion, which includes *Gathas*, or hymns; (2) the Vispered, another liturgical work; (3) the Vendidad, which, like our Pentateuch, contains the laws; (4) the Yashts, dealing with stories of the different gods; together with prayers and other fragments.

The books are sometimes erroneously called the Zend-Avesta; this is a topsy-turvy misunderstanding of the term "Avesta-Zend," which means simply "text and commentary."

Avignon Popes (à vē' nyon). In 1309 Pope Clement V left Rome and transferred the papal court to Avignon, where the popes remained for seventy years of strife and confusion. The Avignon popes were:

Clement V	1305-1314	Innocent VI	1352-1362
John XXII	1316-1334	Urban V	1362-1370
Benedict XII	1334-1342	Gregory XI	1370-1378
Clement VI	1342-1352		

A vinculo matrimonii (ā ving' kū lō măt ri mō ni ī) (Lat.). A total divorce from marriage ties. A divorce a *mensa et thoro* (*i.e.* from table and bed—from bed and board) is partial, because the parties may, if they choose, come together again; but a divorce a *vinculo matrimonii* is granted in cases in which the "marriage" was never legal owing to a pre-contract (bigamy), consanguinity, or affinity.

Avoid Extremes. A traditional saying of Pittacus of Mitylene (652-569 B.C.), one of the seven Wise Men of Greece. It is echoed in many writers and literatures. Compare the advice given by Phœbus to Phaethon when he was preparing to drive the chariot of the sun:—

Medio tutissimus ibis (You will go more safely in the middle).—OVID: *Met*, ii, 137.

Avoirdupois (ăv′ ĕr dū poiz). Fr. *avoir, aver* or *avier*, goods in general, and *poise* = *poids* (weight). Not the verb, but the noun *avoir*. Properly *avoir de poids* (goods having weight), goods sold by weight. There is an obsolete English word *aver*, meaning goods in general, hence also cattle; whence such compounds as *aver-corn, aver-penny, aver-silver* and *aver-land*.

Axe. To hang up one's axe. To retire from business, to give over a useless project. The allusion is to the battle-axe, formerly devoted to the gods and hung up when fighting was over. *See* ASK.

He has an axe to grind. Some selfish motive in the background; some personal interest to answer. Franklin tells of a man who wanted to grind his axe, but had no time to turn the grindstone. Going to the yard where he saw young Franklin, he asked the boy to show him how the machine worked, kept praising him till his axe was ground, and then laughed at him for his pains.

Axis. The term used by the Fascist states of Central Europe, in the sense of an alliance.

It was first used by Mussolini, in 1936 in a speech in which he declared the German-Italian agreement to be "an axis round which all European states animated by the will to collaboration and peace can also assemble."

Ayah (ī′ ya). Now an Anglo-Indian word, but originally Portuguese. A native Hindu nurse or lady's maid.

Ayeshah (ī yesh′ a). Mohammed's second and favourite wife. He married her when she was only nine years old, and died in her arms. She was born about 611 and died about 678.

Aymon, The Four Sons of (ā′ mon). Aymon is a semi-mythical hero, and was father of Reynaud (or Rinaldo, *q.v.*), Guiscard, Alard, and Richard, all of whom were knighted by Charlemagne. The earliest version was probably compiled by Huon de Villeneuve from earlier chansons in the 13th century. The brothers, and their famous horse Bayard (*q.v.*), appear in many poems and romances, including Tasso's *Jerusalem Delivered*, Pulci's *Morgante Maggiore*, Boiardo's *Orlando Inna-morato*, Ariosto's *Orlando Furioso*, etc., and the story formed the basis of a number of French chap-books.

Ayrshire Poet. Robert Burns (1759-96), who was born at Alloway near the town of Ayr.

Azazel (á zăz′ el). In *Lev.* xvi we read that among other ceremonies the high priest, on the Day of Atonement, cast lots on two goats; one lot was *for the Lord,* and the other lot *for Azazel*. Milton uses the name for the standard-bearer of the rebel angels (*Paradise Lost*, i, 534). In Mohammedan legend, Azazel is a jinn of the desert; when God commanded the angels to worship Adam, Azazel replied, "Why should the son of fire fall down before a son of clay?" and God cast him out of heaven. His name was then changed to *Eblis* (*q.v.*), which means "despair."

Azaziel (á zāz′ i el). In Byron's *Heaven and Earth,* a seraph who fell in love with Anah, a granddaughter of Cain. When the flood came, he carried her under his wing to another planet.

Azrael (ăz′ rāl). In Mohammedan legend, the angel that watches over the dying, and takes the soul from the body; the angel of death. He will be the last to die, but will do so at the second trump of the archangel. *See* ADAM.

The Wings of Azrael. The approach of death; the signs of death coming on the dying.

Azrafil. *See* ISRAFIL.

Aztecs (ăz′ teks). A branch of the Nahuatl Indians who came (probably) from the northwest and settled in the valley of Mexico about the 11th or 12th century, and ultimately subjugated the aborigines. A wealthy and highly civilized people renowned for their building. Their power was brought to an end by the Spaniards under Cortes between 1519 and 1530.

Azure (ăzh′ ūr, ā′ zūr). Heraldic term for the colour blue. Represented in royal arms by the planet Jupiter, in noblemen's by the sapphire. The ground of the old shield of France was azure. Emblem of fidelity and truth. Represented in heraldic devices by horizontal lines. Ultimately Arabic or Persian, and connected with "lapis *lazuli*," for which the word "azure" used to stand. Also used as a synonym for the clear, blue sky.

B

B. The form of the Roman capital "B" can be traced through early Greek to Phœnician and Egyptian hieratic; the small "b" is derived from the cursive form of the capital. The letter is called in Hebrew *beth* (a house); in Egyptian hieroglyphics it was represented by the crane.

B in *Roman notation* stands for 300; with a *line above*, it denotes 3,000.

Marked with a B. In the Middle Ages, and as late as the 17th century (especially in America), this letter was branded on the forehead of convicted blasphemers. In France *être marqué au "b"* means to be either one-eyed, hump-backed, or lame (*borgne, bossu, boiteux*); hence, a poor, miserable sort of creature.

Not to know B from a battledore, or **from a bull's foot.** To be quite illiterate, not to know even one's letters. Conversely, *I know B from a bull's foot*, means "I'm a sharp, knowing person; you can't catch *me!*" *Cp.* HAWK and HANDSAW.

B. and S. Brandy and soda.

B.C. In dates an abbreviation for "Before Christ," before the Christian era.

Marked with B.C. When a soldier disgraced himself by insubordination he was formerly marked with "B.C." (bad character) before he was drummed out of the regiment.

Baal. A Semitic word meaning *proprietor* or *possessor*, primarily the title of a god as lord of a place (*e.g. Baal-peor*, lord of Peor), or as possessor of some distinctive characteristic or attribute (*e.g. Baal-zebub*, or *Beelzebub, q.v.*). The worship of the Baals—for each village community had its own—was firmly established in Canaan at the time of the Israelites' incursion; the latter adopted many of the Canaanitish rites, and grafted them on to their own worship of Jahwe (Jehovah), Jahwe becoming—especially when worshipped at the "high places"—merely the national Baal. It was this form of worship that Hosea and other prophets denounced as heathenism. Bel (*q.v.*) is the Assyrian form of the name. *See also* BELPHEGOR.

Babel. A perfect Babel. A thorough confusion. "A Babel of sounds." A confused uproar, in which nothing can be heard but hubbub.. The allusion is to the confusion of tongues at Babel (*Gen.* xi).

Babes in the Wood. *See* CHILDREN. The phrase has been humorously applied to (1) simple trustful folks, never suspicious, and easily gulled; (2) insurrectionary hordes that infested the mountains of Wicklow and the woods of Enniscorthy towards the close of the 18th century; and (3) men in the stocks or in the pillory.

Babies in the Eyes. Love in the expression of the eyes. Love is the little babe Cupid, and hence the conceit, originating from the miniature image of oneself in the pupil of another's eyes.

In each of her two crystal eyes
Smileth a naked boy [Cupid].
LORD SURREY.

She clung about his neck, gave him ten kisses,
Toyed with his locks, looked babies in his eyes.
HEYWOOD: *Love's Mistress.*

Babylon (băb′ i lŏn). **The Modern Babylon.** So London is sometimes called, on account of its wealth, luxury, and dissipation; also (with allusion to Babel) because of the many nationalities that meet, and languages that are spoken there.

The hanging gardens of Babylon. *See* HANGING.

The whore of Babylon. An epithet bestowed on the Roman Catholic Church by the early Puritans and some of their descendants. The allusion is to *Rev.* xvii-xix. (*Cp.* SCARLET WOMAN.) In the book of the *Revelation* Babylon stands for Rome, the capital of the world, the embodiment of luxury, vice, splendour, tyranny, and all that the early Church knew was against the spirit of Christ.

Babylonian Captivity. The seventy years that the Jews were captives in Babylon. They were made captives by Nebuchadnezzar, and released by Cyrus (536 B.C.).

Baca, The Valley of (ba′ ka). An unidentified place mentioned in *Ps.* lxxxiv, 6, meaning the Valley of Weeping, and so translated in the Revised Version. Baca trees were either mulberry trees or balsams.

Bacbuc (băk′ bŭc). A Chaldean or Assyrian word for an earthenware pitcher, cruse, or bottle, taken by Rabelais as the name of the Oracle of the Holy Bottle (and of its priestess), to which Pantagruel and his companions made a famous voyage. The question to be proposed was whether or not Panurge ought to marry. The Holy Bottle answered with a click like the noise made by a glass snapping. Bacbuc told Panurge the noise meant *trinc* (drink), and that was the response, the most direct and positive ever given by the oracle. Panurge might interpret it as he liked, the obscurity would always save the oracle. *See* ORACLE.

Bacchus (băk' ŭs). In Roman mythology, the god of wine, the Dionysus of the Greeks, son of Zeus and Semele. He is represented in early art as a bearded man and completely clad, but after the time of Praxiteles as a beautiful youth with black eyes, golden locks, flowing with curls about his shoulders, and filleted with ivy. In peace his robe was purple, in war he was covered with a panther's skin. His chariot was drawn by panthers.

In the famous statue in Rome he has a bunch of grapes in his hand and a panther at his feet. Pliny tells us that, after his conquest of India, Bacchus entered Thebes in a chariot drawn by elephants, and, according to some accounts, he married Ariadne after Theseus had deserted her in Naxos.

The name "Bacchus" is a corruption of Gr. *Iacchus* (from *Iache*, a shout), and was originally merely an epithet of Dionysus as the noisy or rowdy god.

> As jolly Bacchus, god of pleasure,
> Charmed the wide world with drink and dances,
> And all his thousand airy fancies.
> PARNELL.

Bacchanalia. The triennial festivals held at night in Rome in honour of Bacchus, called in Greece *Dionysia*, Dionysus being the Greek equivalent of Bacchus. In Rome, and in later times in Greece, they were characterized by drunkenness, debauchery, and licentiousness of all kinds; but originally they were very different and were of greater importance than any other ancient festival on account of their connexion with the origin and development of the drama; for in Attica, at the Dionysia choragic literary contests were held, and from these both tragedy and comedy originated. Hence *bacchanalian*, drunken. The terms are now applied to any drunken and convivial orgy on the grand scale.

Bacchanals (băk' à nălz) (*see also* BAG o' NAILS), *Bacchants*, *Bacchantes*. Priests and priestesses, or male and female votaries, of Bacchus; hence, a drunken royster.

Bachelor. A man who has not been married. This is a word whose ultimate etymology is unknown; it is from O.Fr. *bacheler*, which is from a late Latin word *baccalaris*. This last may be merely a translation of the French word, as it is only of rare and very late occurrence, but it may be allied to *baccalarius*, a late Latin adjective applied to farm labourers, the history of which is very doubtful.

In the Prologue to the *Canterbury Tales* (1, 80), Chaucer uses the word in its old sense of a knight not old enough to display his own banner, and so following that of another:

> With him ther was his sone, a young Squyer,
> A lovyere, and a lusty bacheler.

Taxes on bachelors. By an Act of 1694 a tax was imposed on unmarried male persons above the age of twenty-five, varying in amount from £12 10s. to 1s. according to the taxpayer's status. It was repealed in 1706. In 1785 bachelors' servants were subjected to a higher tax than those of other persons. In the graduated Income Tax designed by Pitt in 1799 the rate for bachelors was higher than for married men. In the existing Income Tax system a bachelor pays at a higher rate than a married man by having no allowances for wife, children, etc.

Bachelor of Arts. A student who has taken the university degree below that of Master.

Bachelor of Salamanca. The last novel of Le Sage (published in 1736); the hero is a bachelor of arts, Don Cherubin de la Ronda; he is placed in different situations of life, and associates with all classes of society.

Bachelor's buttons. Several flowers are so called. Red batchelor's buttons, the double red campion; yellow, the upright crowfoot; white, the white ranunculus, or white campion.

> The similitude these flowers have to the jagged cloath buttons anciently worne . . . gave occasion . . . to call them Bachelor's Buttons.
> <div align="right">GERARD: <i>Herbal.</i></div>

Or the phrase may come from a custom sometimes observed by countrymen of carrying the flower in their pockets to know how they stand with their sweethearts. If the flower dies, it is a bad omen; but if it does not fade, they may hope for the best.

Back, To. To support with money, influence, or encouragement; as to "back a friend"; to lay money on a horse in a race, "backing" it to win or for a place.

A commercial term, meaning to *endorse*. When a merchant backs or endorses a bill, he guarantees its value.

Falstaff says to the Prince:—

You care not who sees your back. Call you that backing of your friends? A plague upon such backing!
1 *Henry IV*, ii, 4.

Back-of-beyond. A phrase originating in Australia to describe the wide inland spaces, the *great Outback*. The phrase **backblock** is found in 1850, referring to those vast territories divided up by the government into blocks for settlement.

Back the oars, or **back water,** is to row backwards, that the boat may move the reverse of its ordinary direction.

Laid on one's back. Laid up with chronic ill-health; helpless.

Thrown on his back. Completely beaten. A figure taken from wrestling.

To back out. To withdraw from an engagement, bargain, etc.; to retreat from a difficult position.

To back the field. To bet on all the horses bar one.

To back the sails. So to arrange them that the ship's way may be checked.

To back up. To uphold, to support. As one who stands at your back to support you. An advance by the batsman not taking strike at cricket in order to be ready to take a quick run if the striker makes an opportunity.

To break the back of. To finish the hardest part of one's work.

To get one's back up. To be irritated. The allusion is to a cat, which sets its back up when attacked by a dog or other animal.

To go back on one's word. To withdraw what one has said; to refuse to perform what one has promised. **To go back on a person** is to betray him.

To have one's back to the wall. To act on the defensive against odds. One beset with foes tries to get his back against a wall that he may not be attacked by foes behind.

To take a back seat. To withdraw from a position one has occupied or attempted to occupy; to retire into obscurity, usually as a confession of failure.

Backbite, To. To slander behind one's back.

To be prynces in pryde and pouerte to despise
To backbite, and to bosten and bere fals witnesse.
Piers Plowman.

He that backbiteth not with his tongue.
Psalm xv, 3.

Backfire. An explosion in the exhaust of a motor-car. In prairie or forest fires the term is applied to a fire deliberately started and controlled which is driven towards the dangerous conflagration so that the two burn themselves out.

Backgammon. The A.S. *bac gamen* (back game), so called because the pieces (in certain circumstances) are taken up and obliged to go back to enter at the table again.

Back-hander. A blow with the back of the hand. Also one who takes *back* the decanter in order to *hand* himself another glass before the decanter is passed on.

I'll take a back-hander, as Clive don't seem to drink.
THACKERAY: *The Newcomes*, ch. xliii.

A back-handed compliment: a compliment which is so phrased as to imply an insult.

Backstairs influence. Private or unrecognized influence, especially at Court. Royal palaces have more than one staircase, and those who sought the sovereign upon private matters would use one in an unobtrusive position; it was, therefore, highly desirable to conciliate the servants or underlings in charge of the "back stairs."

Hence, *backstairs gossip*, tittle-tattle obtained from servants; *backstairs plots*, or *politics*, underground or clandestine intrigue.

Backward blessing. A curse. To say the Lord's Prayer backwards was to invoke the devil.

Backwater. This means properly a pool or creek of still water fed indirectly by a river or stream. It has come to mean figuratively any state in which one is isolated from the active flow of life.

Bacon. To baste your bacon. To strike or scourge one. Bacon is the outside portion of the sides of pork, and may be considered generally as the part which would receive a blow.

Falstaff's remark to the travellers at Gads-hill, "On, bacons, on!" (1 *Henry IV*, ii, 2) is an allusion to the fact that formerly swine's flesh formed the staple food of English rustics; hence such terms as *bacon-brains* and *chaw-bacon* for a clownish blockhead.

To bring home the bacon. To bring back the prize; to succeed. This phrase may have originated in reference to the contest for the Dunmow flitch, or to the sport of catching a greased pig at country fairs.

Baconian Philosophy. A system of philosophy based on principles laid down by Francis Bacon, Lord Verulam, in the 2nd book of his *Novum Organum*. It is also called inductive philosophy.

Baconian Theory. The theory that Lord Bacon wrote the plays attributed to Shakespeare.

Bacon's Brazen Head. *See* BRAZEN HEAD.

Bactrian Sage. Zoroaster, or Zarathrustra, the founder of the Perso-Iranian religion, who is supposed to have flourished in Bactria (the modern Balkh) before 800 B.C.

Bad. Among rulers surnamed "The Bad" are William I, King of Sicily from 1154 to 1166, Albert, Landgrave of Thuringia and Margrave of Meissen (d. 1314), and Charles II, King of Navarre (1332-87).

Bad blood. Vindictiveness, ill-feeling; hence, *to make bad blood*, or *to stir up bad blood*, to create or renew ill-feeling and a vindictive spirit.

You are in my bad books. *See* BLACK BOOKS.

Bad debts. Debts not likely to be paid.

Bad egg. A disreputable character; a thoroughly bad fellow.

Bad form. Not in good taste.

The Bad Lands. In America, the *Mauvaises Terres* of the early French settlers west of Missouri; extensive tracts of sterile, alkali hills, rocky, desolate, and almost destitute of vegetation, in South Dakota.

A bad lot. A person of bad moral character, or one commercially unsound. Also a commercial project or stock of worthless value. Perhaps from auctioneering slang, meaning a lot which no one will bid for.

A bad shot. A wrong guess. A sporting phrase; a bad shot is one which does not bring down the bird shot at, one that misses the mark.

He is gone to the bad. Has become a ruined man, or a depraved character. He is mixing with bad companions, has acquired bad habits, or is (usually implying "through his own fault") in bad circumstances.

To the bad. On the wrong side of the account; in arrears.

Badger, A. A hawker, huckster, or itinerant dealer, especially in corn, but also in butter, eggs, fish, etc. The word is still in use in some dialects: its derivation is not certainly known, but it is not in any way connected with a badge worn. Fuller derived it from Lat. *bajulare*, to carry, but there is no substantiation for this. The modern hawker's licence dates from the licences that badgers had to obtain from a Justice under Act 5 and 6 Edw. VI, c. 14, §7.

Under Dec. 17, 1565, we read of "Certain persons upon Humber side who . . . buy great quantities of corn, two of whom were authorised badgers."
State Papers (Domestic Series).

To badger. To tease, annoy, or persistently importune, in allusion to badger-baiting. A badger was kennelled in a tub, where dogs were set upon him to worry him out. When dragged from his tub the poor beast was allowed to retire to it till he recovered from the attack. This process was repeated several times.

It is a vulgar error that the legs of a badger are shorter on one side than on the other.
I think that Titus Oates was as uneven as a badger.
MACAULAY.

Drawing a badger, is drawing him out of his tub by means of dogs.

In the U.S.A. **badger** is the slang name of an inhabitant of Wisconsin.

Badinguet (ba′ din gā). A nickname given to Napoleon III. It is said to be the name of the workman whose clothes he wore when he contrived to escape from the fortress of Ham, in 1846.

If Badinguet and Bismarck have a row together let them settle it between them with their fists, instead of troubling hundreds of thousands of men who . . . have no wish to fight.
ZOLA: *The Downfall*, ch. ii.

Napoleon's adherents were known as *Badingueux.*

Badminton (băd′ min tòn). The country seat of the Dukes of Beaufort in Gloucestershire. It has given its name to a drink and a game. The drink is a claret-cup made of claret, sugar, spices, soda-water, and ice. In pugilistic parlance blood, which is sometimes called "claret" (*q.v.*), is also sometimes called "badminton," from the colour.

The game badminton is a predecessor of, and is similar to, lawn tennis; it is played with shuttlecocks instead of balls.

Badoura (ba doo′ rà). "The most beautiful woman ever seen upon earth," heroine of the story of Camaralzaman and Badoura in the *Arabian Nights.*

Baedeker (bā′dė ker). **Starred in Baedeker.** For many years tourists the world over have flocked to places of interest, red guide-book in hand. Karl Baedeker (1801-59) brought out his first guide-book (to Holland, Belgium and the Rhine) by arrangement with Mr. John Murray in 1839. In subsequent years he and his agents wrote exhaustive guide-works of almost every part of the world. Baedeker inaugurated the somewhat invidious and not always reliable system of marking with one or more stars objects and places of interest according to their historic or aesthetic importance.

Baffle. Originally a punishment meted out to a recreant or traitorous knight by which he was degraded and thoroughly disgraced, part of which seems to have consisted in hanging him or his effigy by the heels from a tree and loudly proclaiming his misdeeds. *See* Spenser's *Faerie Queene*, VI, vii, 26:—

> Letting him arise like abject thrall
> He gan to him object his haynous crime,
> And to revile, and rate, and recreant call,
> And lastly to despoyle of knightly bannerall.
> And after all, for greater infamie,
> He by the heeles he hung upon a tree,
> And baffuld so, that all which passed by,
> The picture of his punishment might see,
> And by the like ensample warned bee.
> How ever they through treason doe trespasse.

Bag and Baggage, as "Get away with you, bag and baggage," *i.e.* get away, and carry with you all your belongings. Originally a military phrase signifying the whole property and stores of an army and of the soldiers composing it. Hence **the bag and baggage policy**. In 1876 Gladstone, speaking on the Eastern question, said, "Let the Turks now carry away their abuses in the only possible manner, namely, by carrying away themselves. . . . One and all, *bag and baggage*, shall, I hope, clear out from the province they have desolated and profaned." *See also* BAGGAGE.

A bag of bones. Very emaciated; generally "A mere bag of bones."

Bag o' Nails. Corruption of *Bacchanals*. A not uncommon inn-sign, *The Devil and the Bag o' Nails*, represents Pan, with his cloven hoofs and his horns, accompanied by satyrs.

A bag of tricks, or the whole bag of tricks. The whole lot, the entire collection. This is an allusion to the conjuror's bag in which he carries the various properties and impedimenta for performing his tricks.

The bottom of the bag. The last expedient, having emptied every other one out of one's bag; a trump card held in reserve.

In the bag. As good as certain.

To be left holding the bag. To have one's comrades decamp or withdraw leaving one with the entire onus of what was originally a group responsibility.

To empty the bag. To tell the whole matter and conceal nothing (Fr. *vider le sac*, to expose all to view).

To give the bag, now means the same as **to give the sack** (*see* SACK), but it seems originally to have had the reverse meaning; a servant or employee leaving without having given notice was said to have given his master "the bag."

To let the cat out of the bag. *See* under CAT.

To bag. Secure for oneself; probably an extension of the sporting use of the word, meaning, to put into one's bag what one has shot, caught, or trapped. Hence, **a good bag**, a large catch of game, fish, or other animals sought after by sportsmen.

Bag-man, A. A commercial traveller, who carries a bag with samples to show to those whose custom he solicits. In former times commercial travellers used to ride a horse with saddle-bags sometimes so large as almost to conceal the rider.

Bags I. *See* FAINS.

Bags. Slang for "trousers," which may be taken as the bags of the body. When the pattern was very staring and "loud," they once were called *howling-bags*.

Oxford bags are wide-bottomed flannel trousers.

Bags of mystery. Slang for sausages or saveloys; the allusion is obvious.

Baga de Secretis. Records in the Record Office of trials for high treason and other State offences from the reign of Edward IV to the close of the reign of George III. These records contain the proceedings in the trials of Anne Boleyn, Sir Walter Raleigh, Guy Fawkes, the regicides, and of the risings of 1715 and 1745.

Baggage, as applied to a worthless or a flirtatious woman, dates from the days when soldiers' wives taken on foreign service with the regiment travelled with the regimental stores and baggage.

Bail (Fr. *bailler*, to deliver up). Security given for the temporary release of an accused person pending his trial or the completion of his trial; also the person or persons giving such security. *See also* LEG-BAIL.

Common bail, or bail below. A bail given to the sheriff to guarantee the appearance of the defendant in court at any day and time the court demands.

Special bail, or bail above. A bail which includes, besides the guarantee of the defendant's appearance, an undertaking to satisfy all claims made on him.

Bail up! The Australian bushranger's equivalent for the highwayman's "Stand and deliver!"

Bailiwick (bā' li wik). The county in which a sheriff, as bailiff of the King, exercises jurisdiction; or the liberty of some lord "who has an exclusive authority within its limits to act as the sheriff does in the county."

> The sheriff of the shire, whose peculiar office it is to walke continuallye up and downe his balywick as ye would have a marshall.
> SPENSER: *State of Ireland*, 1597.

Out of one's bailiwick, far from home, on strange ground.

Baily's Beads. *See* BEAD.

Bain Marie (băn má rē). The French name for a double saucepan like a glue-pot. The term is sometimes used in English kitchens. It appears earlier (as in Mrs. Glasse's *Cookery Book*, 1796) under its Latin name, *Balneum Mariœ*, hence the "St. Mary's bath" of Ben Jonson's *Alchemist*, II, iii. The name is supposed to be due to the gentleness of this method of heating.

Bairam (bī' răm). The name given to two great Mohammedan feasts. The Lesser begins on the new moon of the month Shawwal, at the termination of the fast of Ramadan, and lasts three days. The Greater ('Idul'-Kabir) is celebrated on the tenth day of the twelfth month (Dhul Hijja), lasts for four days, and forms the concluding ceremony of the pilgrimage to Mecca. It comes seventy days after the Lesser Bairam.

Bajadere. *See* BAYADERE.

Bajan, Bajanella. *See* BEJAN.

Bajazet (băj' à zet). Sultan of the Turks from 1389 to 1403, he was a great warrior, among his other victories being that of Nicopolis in 1396 when he defeated the allied armies of the Hungarians, Poles, and French. But he was himself beaten by Timur at Ankara (1402) and held prisoner by him until his death. There is no warrant whatsoever for the story that Timur carried him about in an iron cage, but the story inspired both Marlowe and Rowe to some of their finest writing.

Baked Meats, or Bake-meats. Meat pies. "The funeral baked meats did coldly furnish forth the marriage tables" (*Hamlet*, i, 2); *i.e.* the hot meat pies served at the funeral and not eaten, were served cold at the marriage banquet.

Baker, The. Louis XVI was called "the Baker," the queen was called "the baker's wife" (or *La Boulangère*), and the dauphin the "shop boy"; because they gave bread to the mob of starving men and women who came to Versailles on October 6th, 1789.

The return of the baker, his wife, and the shop-boy to Paris [after the king was brought from Versailles] had not had the expected effect. Flour and bread were still scarce.—A. DUMAS: *The Countess de Charnty*, ch. ix.

Baker's dozen. Thirteen for twelve. When a heavy penalty was inflicted for short weight, bakers used to give a surplus number of loaves, called the *inbread*, to avoid all risk of incurring the fine. The 13th was the "vantage loaf."

Bakha. The sacred bull of Hermonthis in Egypt. He changed colour every hour of the day, and is supposed to have been an incarnation of Menthu, the Egyptian personification of the heat of the sun.

Baksheesh (băk' shēsh). A Persian word for a gratuity. These gifts are insolently and persistently demanded throughout the Near East by beggars, camel-men, servants and all sorts of officials more as a claim than a gratuity.

I was to give the men, too, a *"baksheish,"* that is a present of money, which is usually made upon the conclusion of any sort of treaty.—KINGLAKE: *Eothen*.

Balafré, Le (băl' a frā) (Fr. the gashed). Henri, second Duke of Guise (1550-88). In the Battle of Dormans he received a sword-cut which left a frightful scar on his face. Henri's son, François, third Duke of Guise, also earned—and was awarded—the same title; and it was given by Scott (in *Quentin Durward*) to Ludovic Lesly, an archer of the Scottish Guard.

Balan (bā' làn). The name of a strong and courageous giant in many old romances. In *Fierabras* (*q.v.*) the "Sowdan of Babylon," father of Fierabras, ultimately conquered by Charlemagne. In the Arthurian cycle, brother of Balin (*q.v.*).

Balance, The. "Libra," an ancient zodiacal constellation between Scorpio and Virgo; also the 7th sign of the zodiac, which now contains the constellation Virgo, and which the sun enters a few days before the autumnal equinox.

According to Persian mythology, at the Last Day a huge balance, as big as the vault of heaven, will be displayed; one scale pan will be called that of light, and the other that of darkness. In the former all good will be placed, in the latter all evil; and everyone will receive his award according to the verdict of the balance.

In commercial parlance one's *balance* is the total money remaining over after all assets are realized and all liabilities discharged. Hence the phrases:—

He has a good balance at his banker's. His credit side shows a large balance in his favour.

To strike a balance. To calculate the exact difference, if any, between the debit and credit side of an account.

Balance of trade. The money-value difference between the exports and imports of a nation.

Balance of power. Such an adjustment of power among sovereign States as results in no one nation having such a preponderance as could enable it to endanger the independence of the rest.

Baldheaded. To go for someone bald-headed, that is without restraint or compunction, probably dates from the days when men wore wigs, and any energetic action required that the wig should be thrown aside and the owner go into the fray unencumbered.

Baldachin (bol' dà kin). The dais or canopy under which, in Roman Catholic processions, the Holy Sacrament is carried: also the canopy above an altar. It is the Ital. *baldacchino*, so called from Baldacco (Ital. for Bagdad), where the cloth was originally made.

Balder (bol' der). Son of Odin and Frigga; the Scandinavian god of light, who dwelt at Breidhablik, one of the mansions of Asgard. He is the central figure of many myths, the chief being connected with his death. He is said to have been slain by his rival Hodhr while fighting for possession of the beautiful Nanna. Another legend tells that Frigga bound all things by oath not to harm him, but accidentally omitted the mistletoe, with a twig of which Balder was slain. His death was the prelude to the final overthrow of the gods.

Balderdash. A word of uncertain origin, formerly meaning froth, also a mixture of incongruous liquors (such as wine and beer or beer and milk), but now denoting nonsensical talk, ridiculous poetry, jumbled ideas, etc. It may be connected with the Dan. *balder*, noise, clatter; but in view of the earlier senses of the word this is, at least, doubtful.

Bale. When bale is highest, boot is nighest. An old Icelandic proverb that appears in Heywood and many other English writers. It means, when things have come to the worst they must needs mend. *Bale* means "evil," and is common to most Teutonic languages; *boot* (*q.v.*) is the M.E. *bote*, relief, remedy.

Bale out. The literal meaning of this phrase is to ladle out with buckets, as when one empties the water out of a small boat. Among flying men "to bale out" means to descend from an aeroplane by parachute when some emergency necessitating this arises, and in the army to get out of a tank in a hurry when it is hit.

Balfour of Burley, John. Leader of the Covenanters in Scott's *Old Mortality.* His prototype in real life was John Balfour of Kinloch. Scott seems to have confused him with John, Lord Balfour of Burleigh, who died in 1688 and was not a Covenanter.

Balin (băl'in). Brother to Balan in the Arthurian romances. They were devoted to each other, but they accidentally met in single combat and slew one another, neither knowing until just before death who was his opponent. At their request they were buried in one grave by Merlin. The story is told in Malory, Bk. ii. Tennyson gives a much altered version in the *Idylls of the King.*

Balios. *See* HORSE.

Balisarda. *See* SWORD.

Balistraria (băl is trâr' i à) (mediæval Lat.). Narrow apertures in the form of a cross in the walls of ancient castles, through which crossbow-men discharged their arrows.

Balk (bawk). Originally a ridge or mound on the ground (O.E. *balca*), then the ridge between two furrows left in ploughing, the word came to be figuratively applied to any obstacle, stumbling-block, or check on one's actions; as in billiards, the balk (or *baulk*) is the part of the table behind the *baulk-line* from which one has to play when, in certain circumstances, one's freedom is checked. So, also, to *balk* is to place obstacles in the way of.

Balker. One who from an eminence on shore directs fishermen where shoals of herrings have gathered together. Probably from the Dutch *balken*, to shout, and connected with the O.E. *bælcan*, with the same meaning.

Balkis (bol' kis). The Mohammedan name for the Queen of Sheba, who visited Solomon.

Ball. "Ball," the spherical body, is a Middle English and Old Teutonic word; "ball," the dancing assembly, is from O.Fr. *baler*, to dance, from late Lat. *ballare*. The two are in no way connected.

To keep the ball a-rolling. To continue without intermission. To keep the fun, or the conversation, etc., alive; to keep the matter going. A metaphor taken from several games played with balls.

To have the ball at your feet. To have a great opportunity. A metaphor from football.

To take the ball before the bound. To anticipate an opportunity; to be over-hasty. A metaphor from cricket.

The ball is with you. It is your turn now.

A ball of fortune. One tossed like a ball, from pillar to post; one who has experienced many vicissitudes of fortune.

To open the ball. To lead off the first dance at a ball.

To strike the ball under the line. To fail in one's object. The allusion is to tennis, in which a line is stretched in the middle of the court, and the players standing on each side have to send the ball *over* the line.

Ball-game. The game of baseball.

"Play ball!". Phrase used by the umpire in baseball to indicate that the game may begin.

Ballad. Originally a song to dance-music, or a song sung while dancing. It is from late Lat. *ballare*, to dance (as "ball," the dance), through Provençal *balada*, and O.Fr. *balade*.

Let me make the ballads, and who will may make the laws. Andrew Fletcher of Saltoun, in Scotland, wrote to the Marquis of Montrose, "I knew a very wise man of Sir Christopher Musgrave's sentiment. He believed, if a man were permitted to make all the ballads, he need not care who should make the laws" (1703).

Ballade (bàl ad'). This is an artificial verse-form originating with the Provençal troubadours. In its normal type it consists of three stanzas of eight lines, followed by a verse of four lines known as the Envoi. The principal rules for the ballade are: The same set of rhymes in the same order they occupy in the first stanza must repeat throughout the whole of the verses. No word used as a rhyme must be used again for that purpose throughout the ballade. Each stanza and the Envoi must close with the refrain; the Envoi always taking the same rhymes as the last half of the preceding verse. Only three rhymes are permissible. The sequence of the rhymes is usually:— a, b, a, b, b, c, b, c, for each verse and b, c, b, c, for the Envoi.

Ballet. A theatrical representation of some adventure, intrigue, or emotional phase by pantomime and dancing. Baltazarini, director of music to Catherine de Medici, is said to have been the inventor of ballets as presented in modern times: for long they were an integral part of Italian opera.

Balliol College, Oxford, founded in 1263, by Sir John de Baliol (father of Baliol, King of Scotland) and his wife, Devorguilla.

Balloon. The balloon was invented by Jacques Etienne Montgolfier (1745-1799). The first ascent was made in 1783, the balloon being caused to rise by hot air. In 1825 Charles Green went up in the first gas-filled balloon. During the siege of Paris, in 1871, fifty-four balloons were dispatched carrying 2,500,000 letters. In World War I captive balloons were largely used by both sides to observe the enemy's movements and dispositions. A barrage of captive balloons was used in both World Wars as a defence of cities against enemy aircraft.

Ballot. This method of voting is so called because it was originally by the use of small balls secretly put into a box, as is still done in clubs, etc. Voting for Parliamentary elections was first carried out by ballot in 1870 (the Ballot Act was two years later) and the method then introduced has since obtained. The names of candidates are printed in alphabetical order on a voting paper, the elector marks a cross against his choice, and the folded paper is then slipped into a sealed box.

Ballyhoo (băl i hoo')· The word is said to come from Ballyhooly, a village in Co. Cork, but in its present sense its origin is in the U.S.A. Ballyhoo means noisy demonstration to attract attention, exaggerated publicity, or extravagant advertisement.

Balm (Fr. *baume*; a contraction of *balsam*). An aromatic, resinous gum exuding from certain trees, and used in perfumery and medicine; hence, a soothing remedy or alleviating agency.

Is there no balm in Gilead? (*Jer.* viii, 22). Is there no remedy, no consolation? "Balm" in this passage is the Geneva Bible's translation of the Heb. *sori*, which probably means mastic, the resin yielded by the mastic tree, *Pistacia Lentiscus*, which was formerly an ingredient used in many medicines. In Wyclif's Bible the word is translated "gumme," and in Cover-dale's "triacle." See TREACLE.

The gold-coloured resin now known as "Balm of Gilead" is that from the *Balso-modendron Gileadense*, an entirely different tree.

Baltic Sea. Scandinavia used to be known as *Baltia*. There is a Lithuanian word, *baltas*, meaning "white," from which the name may be derived; but it may also be from Scand *balta*, a strait or *belt*, and the Baltic would then be the sea of the "belts."

Baltic, The, in commercial parlance is the familiar name of the *Baltic Mercantile and Shipping Exchange*, which was founded in the 17th century. It deals with chartering of ships, freights, marine insurance, etc., all over the world.

Bamberg Bible, The. See BIBLE, SPECIALLY NAMED.

Bambino (băm bē' nō). An image of the infant Jesus, swaddled. The word is Italian, meaning an infant.

Bambocciades (băm boch' i ădz). Pictures of scenes in low life, such as country wakes, penny weddings, and so on, so called from the Ital. *bamboccio*, a cripple, a nickname given to Pieter van Laar (*c.* 1613-*c.* 1674), a noted Dutch painter of such scenes. See MICHAEL-ANGELO DES BAMBOCHES.

Bamboozle. To cheat by cunning, or daze with tricks. It is a slang term of uncertain origin which came into use about the end of the 17th century.

All the people upon earth, excepting those two or three worthy gentlemen, are imposed upon, cheated, bubbled, abused, bamboozled.

ADDISON: *The Drummer.*

Ban (A.S. *bannan,* to summon, O.Teut. to proclaim). Originally meaning to summon, the verb came to mean to imprecate, to anathematize, to pronounce a curse upon; and the noun from being a general proclamation was applied specifically to an ecclesiastical curse or denunciation, a formal prohibition, a sentence of outlawry, etc. Banish and BANNS (*q.v.*), are from the same root.

Ban, King. In the Arthurian legends, father of Sir Launcelot du Lac. He died of grief when his castle was taken and burnt through the treachery of his seneschal.

Banagher, That beats (băn ′à her). Wonderfully inconsistent and absurd—exceedingly ridiculous. Banagher is a town in Ireland, on the Shannon, in Offaly. It formerly sent two members to Parliament, and was a famous pocket borough. When a member spoke of a family borough where every voter was a man employed by the lord, it was not unusual to reply, "Well, that beats Banagher."

Grose, however, gives another explanation. According to him Banagher (or Banaghan) was an Irish minstrel famous for telling wonderful stories of the Munchausen kind.

"Well," says he, "to gratify them I will. So just a morsel. But, Jack, this beats Bannagher."—W. B. YEATS: *Fairy Tales of the Irish Peasantry,* p. 196.

Banat (băn′ ăt). A territory under a *ban* (Persian for lord, master), particularly certain districts of Hungary and Croatia. The word was brought into Europe by the Avars, a Ural-Altaic people allied to the Huns, who appeared on the Danube and settled in Dacia in the latter half of the 6th century.

Banbury. A town in Oxfordshire, proverbially famous for its Puritans, its "cheese-paring," its cakes, and its cross. Hence a *Banbury man* is a Puritan or bigot. The term is common in Elizabethan literature: Zeal-of-the-land-busy, in Jonson's *Bartholomew Fair,* is described as a "Banbury man." and Braithwaite's lines in *Drunken Barnabee's Journal* (1638) are well known:

In my progresse travelling Northward,
Taking my farewell o'th Southward,
To *Banbery* came I, O prophane one!
Where I saw a Puritane one,

Hanging of his Cat on Monday,
For killing of a Mouse on Sonday.

Banbury cake is a sort of spiced, pastry turnover, once made exclusively at Banbury.

Banbury Cross was removed by the Puritans as a heathenish memorial in 1646, but the present one was placed on the site in its stead in 1858.

Banco (băng′ kō). A commercial term denoting bank money of account as distinguished from currency; it is used principally in exchange business, and in cases where there is an appreciable difference between the actual and the nominal value of money.

In banco. A late Latin legal phrase, meaning "on the bench"; it is applied to sittings of the Superior Court of Common Law in its own bench or court, and not on circuit, or at *Nisi Prius* (*q.v.*).

Bandana or **Bandanna** (băn dăn′ à). An Indian word (*bandhnu,* a mode of dyeing) now usually restricted to handkerchiefs of either silk or cotton having a dark ground of Turkey red or blue, with white or yellow spots.

Bandbox, He looks as if he were just out of a. He is so neat and precise, so carefully got up in his dress and person, that he looks like some company dress, carefully kept in a bandbox, a cardboard box for millinery formerly used by parsons for keeping their clerical bands (*q.v.*) in.

Neat as a bandbox. Neat as clothes folded and put by in a bandbox.

The Bandbox Plot. Rapin (*History of England,* iv, 297) tells us that a bandbox was sent to the lord-treasurer, in Queen Anne's reign, with three pistols charged and cocked, the triggers being tied to a pack-thread fastened to the lid. When the lid was lifted, the pistols would go off and shoot the person who opened the lid. He adds that Dean Swift happened to be by at the time the box arrived, and seeing the pack-thread, cut it, thereby saving the life of the lord-treasurer.

Two ink-horn tops your Whigs did fill
With gunpowder and lead;
Which with two serpents made of quill,
You in a bandbox laid;
A tinder-box there was beside,
Which had a trigger to it.
To which the very string was ty'd
That was designed to do it.

Plot upon Plot (about 1713).

Bandicoot. To bandicoot is an Australian phrase meaning to steal vegetables—often by removing the roots—as with potatoes and carrots—and leaving the tops standing in the ground so that the theft is not noticed.

Bandwagon. To climb on the bandwagon is to show support for a popular movement or cause with intent to reap easy material benefit. It was customary in the U.S.A., particularly the Southern States, for a band to play through the streets on a wagon to advertise a forthcoming meeting, political or otherwise. At election time local leaders would show their support of a candidate by climbing on the wagon and riding with the band.

Bandy. I am not going to bandy words with you — *i.e.* to wrangle. The metaphor is from the Irish game bandy (the precursor of hockey), in which each player has a stick with a crook at the end to strike a wooden or other hard ball. The ball is bandied from side to side, each party trying to beat it home to the opposite goal. The derivation of the word is quite uncertain. It was earlier a term in tennis, as is shown by the passage in Webster's *Vittoria Corombona* (iv, 4), where the conspirators regret that the handle of the racket of the man to be murdered had not been poisoned —

That while he had been bandying at tennis,
He might have sworn himself to hell, and strook
His soul into the hazard.

Bane really means ruin, death, or destruction (A.S. *bana*, a murderer); and "I will be his bane" means I will ruin or murder him. Bane is, therefore, a mortal injury.

My bane and antidote are both before it.
This [sword] in a moment brings me to an end.
But this [Plato] assures me I shall never die.
ADDISON: *Cato.*

Bangers (băng' erz). One of the many slang terms for sausages.

Banian, Banyan (băn' yản) (Sanskrit *vanij*, a merchant). This was the name applied to a caste of Hindu traders, who wore a particular dress, were strict in their observance of fasts, and abstained from eating any kind of flesh. It is from this circumstance that sailors speak of **Banyan Days** (*q.v.*).

The word is also used to describe a sort of loose house-coat worn by Anglo-Indians.

Bank. The original meaning was "bench" or "shelf"; in Italy the word (*banco*) was applied specially to a tradesman's counter, and hence to a money-changer's bench or table, which gives the modern meaning of an establishment which deals in money, investments, etc.

Bank of a river. Stand with your back to the source, and face to the sea or outlet: the *left* bank is on your left, and *right* bank on your right hand.

Bankside. Part of the borough of Southwark on the right bank of the Thames, between Blackfriars and Waterloo Bridges. In Shakespeare's time it was noted for its theatres, its prison, and its brothels. Hence, **Sisters of the Bank**, an old term for prostitutes.

Come I will send for a whole coach or two of Bankside ladies, and we will be jovial. — RANDOLPH: *The Muses' Looking Glass*, II, iv.

Bankrupt. In Italy, when a moneylender was unable to continue business, his bench or counter (see BANK) was broken up, and he himself was spoken of as a *bancorotto* — *i.e.* a bankrupt. This is said to be the origin of our term.

Banks's Horse. A horse trained to do all manner of tricks, called Marocco, and belonging to one Banks about the end of the reign of Queen Elizabeth. One of his exploits is said to have been the ascent of St. Paul's steeple. A favourite story of the time is of an apprentice who called his master to see the spectacle. "Away, you fool," said the shopkeeper; "what need I go to see a horse on the top when I can see so many asses at the bottom!" When Banks went to Paris in 1601 he was packed off to prison, as the city authorities and the Church suspected that Marocco's tricks were performed by black magic.

Bannatyne Club. A literary club, named after George Bannatyne (d. about 1608), to whose industry we owe the preservation of much early Scottish poetry. It was instituted in 1823 by Sir Walter Scott, and had for its object the publication of rare works illustrative of Scottish history, poetry, and general literature. The club was dissolved in 1859.

Banner of the Prophet, The. What purports to be the actual standard of Mohammed is preserved in the Eyab mosque of Constantinople. It is called *Sin'aqu'sh-sharif* and is 12 feet in length. It is made of four layers of silk, the topmost being green, embroidered with gold. In times of peace the banner is guarded in the hall of the "noble vestment," as the dress worn by the Prophet is styled. In the same hall are preserved many other relics including the stirrup, the sabre, and the bow of Mohammed.

Banner of France, The sacred, was the *Oriflamme* (*q.v.*).

Banners in churches. These are suspended as thank offerings to God. Those in St. George's Chapel, Windsor, Henry VII's Chapel, Westminster, etc., are to indicate that the knight whose banner is hung up avows himself devoted to God's service.

Banneret. One who leads his vassals to battle under his own banner. Also an order of knighthood formerly conferred on the field of battle for deeds of valour. The first knight-banneret to be made seems to have been John de Copeland, who, in 1346, captured King David Bruce at Neville's Cross. The order was allowed to become extinct soon after the first creation of baronets, in 1611.

Banns of Marriage. The publication in the parish church for three successive Sundays of an intended marriage. It is made after the Second Lesson of the Morning Service. To announce the intention is called "Publishing the banns," from the words "I publish the banns of marriage between . . ." The word is from the same root as BAN (*q.v.*).

To forbid the banns. To object formally to the proposed marriage.

And a better fate did poor Maria deserve than to have a banns forbidden by the curate of the parish who published them.—STERNE: *Sentimental Journey.*

Banquet used at one time to have, besides its present meaning, the meaning of dessert. Thus, in the *Pennyless Pilgrimage* (1618) John Taylor, the Water Poet, says: "Our first and second course being three-score dishes at one boord, and after that, always a banquet." The word is from Ital. *banco* (*see* BANK), a bench or table; at which one sits for a meal, hence "bad manners at table."

Banshee. The domestic spirit of certain Irish or Highland Scottish families, supposed to take an interest in its welfare, and to wail at the death of one of the family. The word is the Old Irish *ben side*, a woman of the elves or fairies.

Bantam. A little bantam cock. A plucky little fellow that will not be bullied by a person bigger than himself. The bantam cock will encounter a dunghill cock five times his own weight, and is therefore said to "have a great soul in a little body." The bantam originally came from Bantam, in Java.

Banzai. The Japanese victory cry, meaning " Ten thousand years."

Baphomet. An imaginary idol or symbol, which the Templars were said to worship in their mysterious rites. The word is a corruption of Mahomet, (Fr. *Baphomet*; O.Sp. *Matomat.*)

Baptism. This sacrament of the Christian Church dates back in one form or another to pre-apostolic times.

Baptism for the dead was the baptism of a living person instead of and for the sake of one who had died unbaptized.

Baptism of blood was martyrdom for the sake of Christ and supplied the place of the sacrament if the martyr was unbaptized.

Baptism of desire is the virtue or grace of baptism acquired by one who dies earnestly desiring baptism before he can receive it.

Baptism of fire is really martyrdom, but the phrase was misapplied by Napoleon III to one who went under fire in battle for the first time.

Bar. The whole body of barristers; as *bench* means the whole body of judges. The bar is the partition separating the seats of the benchers from the rest of the hall, and, like the rood-screen of a church, which separates the chancel from the rest of the building, is due to the old idea that the laity form an inferior order of beings.

To be called to the bar. To be admitted a barrister. Students having attained a certain status used to be called from the body of the hall within the bar, to take part in the proceedings of the court. To disbar means to expel a barrister from his profession.

To be called within the bar. To be appointed King's Counsel.

Trial at Bar. By full court of judges in the Queen's Bench division. These trials are for very difficult causes, before special juries, and occupy the attention of the four judges in the superior court, instead of at *Nisi Prius*.

At the bar. The prisoner at the bar, the prisoner in the dock before the judge.

Bar, excepting. In racing phrase a man will bet "Two to one, bar one," that is, two to one against any horse in the field with one exception. The word means "barring out," shutting out, debarring, as in Shakespeare's:—

Nay, but I bar to-night: you shall not gage me by what we do to-night.—*Merchant of Venice*, ii, 2.

Bar. An honourable ordinary, in heraldry, consisting of two parallel horizontal lines drawn across the shield and containing a fifth part of the field.

A barre . . . is drawne overthwart the escochon . . . : it containeth the fifth part of the Field.
GWILLIM: *Heraldry.*

Bar sinister. A phrase popularly used to imply bastardy, though the heraldic sign intended is a *bend sinister* (*q.v.*).

Barathron, or **Barathrum.** A deep ditch behind the Acropolis of Athens into which malefactors were thrown; somewhat in the same way as criminals at Rome were cast from the Tarpeian Rock. Sometimes used figuratively, as in Massinger's *New Way to Pay Old Debts*, where Sir Giles Overreach calls Greedy a "barathrum of the shambles" (iii, 2), meaning that he was a sink into which any kind of food or offal could be thrown.

Mercury: Why, Jupiter will put you all into a sack together, and toss you into Barathrum, terrible Barathrum.
Carion: Barathrum? What's Barathrum?
Mer.: Why, Barathrum is Pluto's boggards [privy]: you must be all thrown into Barathrum.
> RANDOLPH: *Hey for Honesty*, v, 1 (c.1630).

Barb (Lat. *barba*, a beard). Used in early times in England for the beard of a man, and so for similar appendages such as the feathers under the beak of a hawk; but its first English use was for a curved-back instrument such as a fish-hook (which has one backward curve, or *barb*), or an arrow (which has two). The *barb* of an arrow is, then, the metal point having two iron "feathers," which stick out so as to hinder extraction, and does not denote the feather on the upper part of the shaft.

Barb. A Barbary steed, noted for docility, speed, endurance, and spirit, formerly also called a Barbary, as in Ben Jonson's:—

You must . . . be seen on your barbary often, or leaping over stools for the credit of your back.
> *Silent Women*, IV, 1.

Cp. also BARBARY ROAN.

Barbarian. The Greeks and Romans called all foreigners *barbarians* (babblers; men who spoke a language not understood by them); the word was probably merely imitative of unintelligible speech, but may have been an actual word in some outlandish tongue.

If then I know not the meaning of the voice [*words*], I shall be to him that speaketh a barbarian, and he that speaketh will be a barbarian unto me.
> 1 *Cor.* xiv, 11.

Barbarossa (bar bà ros' à). (*Red-beard*, similar to *Rufus*). The surname of Frederick I of Germany (1121-90). *Khaireddin Barbarossa*, the famous corsair, became Bey of Algiers in 1518, and in 1537 was appointed high admiral of the Turkish fleet. With Francis I he captured Nice in 1543; he died at Constantinople three years later.

Barbary Roan, the favourite horse of Richard II. *See* HORSE.

O, how it yearned my heart when I beheld
In London streets that coronation day,
When Bolingbroke rode on roan Barbary!
That horse that thou [Rich. II] so often hast bestrid,
That horse that I so carefully have dressed.
> SHAKESPEARE: *Richard* II, v, 5.

Cp. BARBED STEED.

Barbason (bar' bà son). A fiend mentioned by Shakespeare in the *Merry Wives of Windsor*, ii, 2, and in *Henry V*, ii, 1.

Amaimon sounds well, Lucifer well, Barbason well, yet they are . . . the names of fiends.—*Merry Wives.*

The name seems to have been obtained from Scot's *Discoverie of Witchcraft* (1584),

where we are told of "Marbas, alias Barbas," who—

is a great president, and appeareth in the forme of a mightie lion; but at the commandment of a conjuror cummeth up in a likenes of a man, and answereth fullie as touching anie thing which is hidden or secret.

Barbecue (bar' be kū) (Sp. *barbacoa*, a wooden framework set on posts). A term used in America formerly for a wooden bedstead, and also for a kind of large gridiron upon which an animal could be roasted whole. Hence, an animal, such as a hog, so roasted; also the feast at which it is eaten, and the process of roasting it.

Oldfield, with more than harpy throat subdued,
Cries, " Send me, ye gods, a whole hog barbecued!"
> POPE: *Satires*, ii, 25.

Barbed Steed. A horse in armour. *Barbed* should properly be *barded*; it is from the Fr. *barde*, horse-armour. Horses' "bards" were the metal coverings for the breast and flanks.

And now, instead of mounting barbèd steeds
To fright the souls of fearful adversaries,
He capers nimbly in a lady's chamber,
To the lascivious pleasing of a lute.
> SHAKESPEARE: *Richard III*, i, 1.

Barber. Every barber knows that.
Omnibus notum tonsoribus.
> HORACE: 1 *Satires*, vii, 3.

In ancient Rome, as in modern England, the barber's shop was a centre for the dissemination of scandal, and the talk of the town.

Barber Poet. Jacques Jasmin (1798-1864), a Provencal poet, who was also known as "the last of the Troubadours," was so called. He was a barber.

Barber's pole. This pole, painted spirally with two stripes of red and white, and displayed outside barber's shops as a sign, is a relic of the days when the callings of barber and surgeon were combined; it is symbolical of the winding of a bandage round the arm previous to bloodletting. The gilt knob at its end represents the brass basin which is sometimes actually suspended on the pole. The basin has a curved gap cut in it to fit the throat, and was used for lathering customers before shaving them. The Barber-Surgeons' Company was founded in 1461 and was re-incorporated in 1540. In 1745 it was decided that the business or trades of barber and surgeon were really independent of each other and the two branches were separated; but the ancient company, or guild, was allowed to retain its charter. The last barber-surgeon in London is said to have been one Middleditch, of Great Suffolk Street in the Borough, who died 1821.

To this year (1541), (says Wornum) . . . belongs the Barber-Surgeons' picture of Henry (VIII) granting a charter to the Corporation. The barbers and surgeons of London, originally constituting one company, had been separated, but were again, in the 32 Henry VIII, combined into a single society, and it was the ceremony of presenting them with a new charter which is commemorated by Holbein's picture, now in their hall in Monkwell Street.

Barber of Seville. The comedy by this name (*Le Barbier de Séville*) was written by Beaumarchais and produced in Paris in 1775. In it appeared for the first time the famous character of Figaro. In 1780 Paisiello produced an opera bouffe on the same lines, but this was eclipsed in 1816 by the appearance of Rossini's *Barbiere di Siviglia*, with words by Sterbini. On its first appearance it was hissed but it has since maintained its place as one of the most popular operas ever written.

Barcelona (bar se lō′ na) A fichu, piece of velvet for the neck, or small necktie, made at Barcelona, and common in England in the early 19th century. Also a neckcloth of some bright colour, as red with yellow spots.
Now on this handkerchief so starch and white
She pinned a Barcelona black and tight.
PETER PINDAR: Portfolio (Dinah).

Barchester. An imaginary cathedral town (said to be Salisbury), in the county of Barsetshire; the setting of the Barchester Novels by Anthony Trollope (1815-82). These are: *The Warden*, 1855; *Barchester Towers*, 1857; *Doctor Thorne*, 1858; *Framley Parsonage*, 1861; *The Small House at Allington* (1864); and *Last Chronicle of Barset*, 1867.

Barcochebah or **Barchochebas** (Shimeon) (bar koch′ e ba). An heroic leader of the Jews against the Romans A.D. 132. He took Jerusalem in 132, and was proclaimed king, many of the Jews believing him to be the Messiah, but in 135 he was overthrown with great slaughter. Jerusalem was laid in ruins, and he himself slain. It is said that he gave himself out to be the "Star out of Jacob" mentioned in *Numb*. xxiv, 17. (Bar Cochba in *Hebrew* means "Son of a star.")

Bard. The minstrel of the ancient Celtic peoples, the Gauls, British, Welsh, Irish, and Scots; they celebrated the deeds of gods and heroes, incited to battle, sang at royal and other festivities, and frequently acted as heralds. The oldest bardic compositions that have been preserved are of the 5th century.

Bard of Avon. William Shakespeare (1564-1616), who was born and buried at Stratford-upon-Avon.

Bard of Ayrshire. Robert Burns (1759-96), a native of Ayrshire.

Bard of Hope. Thomas Campbell (1777-1844), author of *The Pleasures of Hope*.

Bard of the Imagination. Mark Akenside (1721-70), author of *Pleasures of the Imagination*.

Bard of Memory. Samuel Rogers (1763-1855), author of *The Pleasures of Memory*.

Bard of Olney. William Cowper (1731-1800), who resided at Olney, in Bucks, for many years.

Bard of Prose. Boccaccio (1313-75), author of the *Decameron*.
The Bard of Prose, creative spirit! he
Of the Hundred Tales of Love.
BYRON: Childe Harold, IV, lvi.

Bard of Rydal Mount. William Wordsworth (1770-1850); so called because Rydal Mount was his mountain home.

Bard of Twickenham. Alexander Pope (1688-1744), who resided at Twickenham.

Bardolph (bar′ dolf). One of Falstaff's inferior officers. Falstaff calls him "the knight of the burning lamp," because his nose was so red, and his face so "full of meteors." He is a low-bred, drunken swaggerer, without principle, and poor as a church mouse. (*Merry Wives*; *Henry IV*, 1, 2.)

Barefaced. The present meaning, *audacious, shameless, impudent*, is a depreciation of its earlier sense, which was merely *open* or *unconcealed*. A "bare face" is, of course, one that is beardless, one the features of which are in no way hidden. The French equivalent is *à visage découvert*, with uncovered face.

Barefooted. Certain friars and nuns (some of whom use sandals instead of shoes), particularly the reformed section of the Order of Carmelites (White Friars) that was founded by St. Theresa in the 16th century. These are known as the *Discalced Carmelites* (Lat. *calceus*, a shoe). The practice is defended by the command of our Lord to His disciples: "Carry neither purse, nor scrip, nor shoes" (*Luke* x. 4). The Jews and Romans used to put off their shoes in mourning and public calamities, by way of humiliation.

Bargain. Into the bargain. In addition thereto; besides what was bargained for.

To make the best of a bad bargain. To bear bad luck, or bad circumstances with equanimity.

To stand to a bargain. To abide by it; the Lat. *stare conventis, conditionibus stare, pactis stare*, etc.

Barisal Guns. A name given to certain mysterious booming sounds heard in many parts of the world as well as Barisal (Bengal), generally on or near water. They resemble the sound of distant cannon, and are probably of subterranean origin. At Seneca Lake, New York, they are known as *Lake guns*, on the coast of Holland and Belgium as *mistpoeffers*, and in Italy as *bombiti, baturlio marina*, etc.

Bark. Dogs in their wild state never bark; they howl, whine, and growl, but do not bark. Barking is an acquired habit.

Barking dogs seldom bite. Huffing, bouncing, hectoring fellows rarely possess cool courage. Similar proverbs are found in Latin, French, Italian, and German.

To bark at the moon. To rail uselessly, especially at those in high places, as a dog thinks to frighten the moon by baying at it. There is a superstition that when a dog does this it portends death or ill-luck.

I'd rather be a dog, and bay the moon,
Than such a Roman.
SHAKESPEARE: *Julius Cæsar*, iv, 3.

His bark is worse than his bite. He scolds and abuses roundly, but does not bear malice, or do mischief.

To bark up the wrong tree. To waste energy, to be on the wrong scent. The phrase comes from raccoon hunting. This sport always takes place in the dark, with dogs which are supposed to mark the tree where the raccoon has taken refuge, and bark until the hunter arrives. But even dogs can mistake the tree in the dark, and often bark up the wrong one.

Barlaam and Josaphat (bar' lăm, jos' ả făt). An Eastern romance telling how Barlaam, an ascetic monk of the desert of Sinai, converted Josaphat, son of a Hindu king, to Christianity. Probably written in the first half of the 7th century, it seems to have been put into its final form by St. John of Damascus, a Syrian monk of the 8th century; it became immensely popular in the Middle Ages, and includes (among many other stories) the Story of the Three Caskets, which was used by Shakespeare in the *Merchant of Venice*. A poetical version was written by von Ems (13th cent.).

Barley. To cry barley. To ask for truce (in children's games). Probably a corruption of *parley*, from Fr. *parler*, to speak. In Scots, to **have a barley** is to have a break, to pause for a moment's rest.

Barmecide's Feast (bar me sīd). An illusion: particularly one containing a great disappointment. The reference is to the Story of the Barber's Sixth Brother in the *Arabian Nights*. A prince of the great Barmecide family in Bagdad, wishing to have some sport, asked Schacabac, a poor, starving wretch, to dinner, and set before him a series of empty plates. "How do you like

your soup?" asked the merchant. "Excellently well," replied Schacabac. "Did you ever see whiter bread?" "Never, honourable sir," was the civil answer. Illusory wine was later offered him, but Schacabac excused himself by pretending to be drunk already, and knocked the Barmecide down. The latter saw the humour of the situation, forgave Schacabac, and provided him with food to his heart's content.

Barmy. Mad, crazy. Sometimes spelled "balmy," but properly as above, as from "barm," froth, ferment. Burns has: —

Just now I've taen the fit o' rhyme,
My barmie noddle's working prime.
To James Smith, 19.

Hence, in prison slang **to put on the barmy stick** is to feign insanity; and the "Barmy Ward" is the infirmary in which the insane, real or feigned, are confined.

Barnabas. St. Barnabas' Day, June 11th. St. Barnabas was a fellow-labourer of St. Paul. His symbol is a rake, because June 11th is the time of hay harvest.

Barnacle. A species of wild goose allied to the brent goose, also the popular name of the Cirripedes, especially those which are attached by a stalk to floating balks of timber, the bottoms of ships, etc. In mediæval times it was thought that the two were different forms of the same animal (much as are the frog and the tadpole), and as late as 1636 Gerard speaks of "broken pieces of old ships on which is found certain spume or froth, which in time breedeth into shells, and the fish which is hatched therefrom is in shape and habit like a bird."

The origin of this extraordinary belief is very obscure, but it is probably due to the accident of the identity of the name coupled with the presence in the shell-fish of the long feathery cirri which protrude from the shells and, when in the water, are very suggestive of plumage. In England the name was first attached to the bird. It is thought to be a diminutive of the M.E. *bernake*, a species of wild goose. The name of the shell-fish, on the other hand, may be from a diminutive (*pernacula*) of the Lat. *perna*, a mussel or similar shell-fish, though no such diminutive has been traced. With an identity of name it was, perhaps, natural to look for an identity of nature in the two creatures.

The name is given figuratively to close and constant companions, hangers on, or sycophants; also to placemen who stick to their offices but do little work, like the barnacles which stick to the bottoms of ships but impede their progress.

Barnacles. Spectacles; especially those of a heavy or clumsy make or appearance. A slang term, from their supposed resemblance in shape to the twitches or "barnacles" formerly used by farriers to keep under restraint unruly horses during the process of bleeding, shoeing, etc. This instrument consisted of two branches joined at one end by a hinge, and was employed to grip the horse's nose. The word is probably a diminutive of the O.Fr. *bernac*, a kind of muzzle for horses.

Barn-burners. Destroyers, who, like the Dutchman of story, would burn down their barns to rid themselves of the rats.

Barnstormer. A slang term for a strolling player, and hence for any second-rate actor, especially one whose style is of an exaggerated declamatory kind. From the custom of itinerant troupes of actors giving their shows in village barns when better accommodation was not forthcoming.

Baron is from late Lat. *baro* (through O.Fr. *barun*), and meant originally "a man," especially opposed to something else, as a freeman to a slave, a husband to a wife, etc., and also in relation to someone else, as "the king's man." From the former comes the legal and heraldic use of the word in the phrase *baron and feme*, husband and wife: from the latter the more common use, the king's "man" or "baron" being his vassal holding tenure of the king by military or other service. To-day a baron is a member of the lowest order of nobility; he is addressed as "Lord," and by the Sovereign as "Our right trusty and well beloved." The premier English barony is that of De Ros, dating from 1264.

The War of the Barons was the insurrection of the barons, under Simon de Montfort against the arbitrary government of Henry III, 1263-65. Drayton's poem *The Barons' Wars* was published in 1603.

Baron Bung. Mine host, master of the beer bung.

Baron Munchausen. *See* MUNCHAUSEN.

Baron of beef. Two sirloins left uncut at the backbone. The *baron* is the backpart of the ox, called in Danish, the *rug*. Jocosely, but wrongly, said to be a pun upon *baron* and *sir* loin.

Baronet. An hereditary titled order of commoners, ranking next below barons and next above knights, using (like the latter) the title "Sir" before the Christian name, and the contraction "Bt." after the surname. The degree, as it now exists, was instituted by James I, and the title was sold for £1,000 to gentlemen possessing not less than £1,000 per annum, for the plantation of Ulster, in allusion to which the Red Hand of Ulster (*see under* HAND) is the badge of Baronets of England, the United Kingdom, and of Great Britain, also of the old Baronets of Ireland (created prior to the Union in 1800).

The premier baronetcy is that of Bacon of Redgrave, originally conferred in 1611 on Nicholas, half-brother of Sir Francis Bacon, Viscount St. Albans.

Barrack. To barrack, is to jeer or shout rude commentaries at the players of games. The word came into use about 1880 in Australia where barracking is considered a legitimate and natural hazard with which, for instance, first-class cricketers have to contend.

Barracks. Soldiers' quarters of a permanent nature. The word was introduced in the 17th century from Ital. *baracca*, a tent, through Fr. *baraque*, a barrack.

Barrage (bǎ′ razh) (Fr.). The original meaning of this word was an artificial dam or bar across a river to deepen the water on one side of it, as the great barrage on the Nile at Assouan. But from World War I the term is applied to a curtain of projectiles from artillery which is ranged to fall in front of advancing troops, or to keep off raiding aircraft, or to shield offensive operations, etc. cp. BALLOON.

Barratry. A legal term denoting (1) the offence of vexatiously exciting or maintaining lawsuits, and (2)—the commoner use—fraud or criminal negligence on the part of the master or crew of a ship to the detriment of the owners. Like many of our legal terms, it is from Old French.

Barrell's Blues. The 4th Foot; so called from the colour of their facings, and William Barrell, colonel of the regiment (1734-9). Now called "The King's Own (Royal Lancaster Regiment)." They were called "Lions" from their badge, the Lion of England.

Barricade. To block up a street, passage, etc. The term rose in France in 1588, when Henri de Guise returned to Paris in defiance of the king's order. The king sent for his Swiss Guards, and the Parisians tore up the pavement, threw chains across the streets, and piled up barrels (Fr. *barriques*) filled with earth and stones, behind which they shot down the Swiss.

The day of the Barricades—

(1) May 12th, 1588, when the people forced Henry III to flee from Paris.

(2) August 5th, 1648, the beginning of the Fronde (*q.v.*).

(3) July 27th, 1830, the first day of *la grande semaine* which drove Charles X from the throne.

(4) February 24th, 1848, which resulted in the abdication of Louis Philippe.

(5) June 25th, 1848, when the Archbishop of Paris, was shot in his attempt to quell the insurrection.

(6) December 2nd, 1851, the day of the *coup d'état*, when Louis Napoleon made his appeal to the people for re-election to the Presidency for ten years.

Barrister. One admitted to plead at the bar; one who has been "called to the bar." *See* BAR. They are of two degrees, the lower order being called simply "barristers," or formerly "outer" or "utter" barristers; the higher "King's Counsel." Until 1880 there was a superior order known as "Serjeants-at-Law" (*q.v.*). The King's Counsel (K.C.) is a senior, and when raised to this position he is said to "take silk," being privileged to wear a silk gown and, on special occasions, a full-bottomed wig. The junior counsel, or barristers, wear a plain stuff gown and a short wig.

A Revising Barrister. One appointed to revise the lists of electors for members of parliament.

A Vacation Barrister. Formerly one newly called to the bar, who for three years had to attend in "Long Vacation." The practice (and consequently the term) is now obsolete.

Barristers' Bags. *See* LAWYERS.

Barristers' gowns. "Utter barristers wear a stuff or bombazine gown, and the puckered material between the shoulders of the gown is all that is now left of the purse into which, in early days, the successful litigant . . . dropped his . . . pecuniary tribute . . . for services rendered" (*Notes and Queries*, March 11th, 1893, p. 124). The fact is that the counsel was supposed to appear merely as a friend of the litigant. Even now he cannot recover his fees by legal process.

Barry Cornwall, poet. The *nom de plume* of Bryan Waller Proctor (1787-1874). Writer of once-popular songs.

Bartholomew, St. The symbol of this saint is a knife, in allusion to the knife with which he was flayed alive. He is commemorated on August 24th, and is said to have been martyred in Armenia, A.D. 44.

Bartholomew doll. A tawdry, over-dressed woman; like one of the flashy, bespangled dolls offered for sale at Bartholomew Fair.

Bartholomew Fair. A fair held for centuries from its institution in 1133 at Smithfield, London, on St. Bartholomew's Day: after the change of the calendar in 1752 it was held on September 3rd. While it lasted the Fair was the centre of London life; Elizabethan and Restoration playwrights and story-tellers are full of its amusements and dissipations. Besides the refreshment stalls, loaded with roast pork and cakes, there were innumerable side-shows:

Here's that will challenge all the fairs
Come buy my nuts and damsons, and Burgamy pears!

Here's the *Woman of Baylon, the Devil and the Pope,*
And here's the little girl, just going on the rope!
Here's *Dives and Lazarus, and* the *World's Creation;*
Here's the Tall Dutchwoman, the like's not in the nation.
Here is the booths where the high Dutch maid is,
Here are the bears that dance like any ladies;
Tat, tat, tat, tat, says little penny trumpet;
Here's Jacob Hall, that does so jump it, jump it;
Sound trumpet, sound, for silver spoon and fork,
Come, here's your dainty pig and pork!
Wit and Drollery (1682).

Not even the Puritans were able to put down the riotings of Bartholomew Fair, and it went on in ever increasing disrepute until 1840, when it was removed to Islington. This was its death, and in 1855 it disappeared from utter neglect and inanition. Ben Jonson wrote a comedy satirizing the Puritans under this name.

Base Tenure. Originally, tenure not by *military*, but by *base*, service, such as a serf or villein might give: later, a tenure in fee-simple that was determinate on the fulfilment of some contingent qualification.

Base of operations. In military parlance, the protected place from which operations are conducted, where magazines of all sorts are formed, and upon which (in case of reverse) the army can fall back.

Basic English. A fundamental selection of 850 English words designed by C. K. Ogden as a common first step in the teaching of English and as an auxiliary language. The name comes from the initials of the words British, American, Scientific, International, Commercial.

Basil (băz′ il) (Gr. *basilikos*, royal). An aromatic plant so called because it was thought to have been used in making royal perfume. The story of Isabella who placed her murdered lover's head in a pot and planted basil on top, which she watered with her tears, was taken by Keats from Boccaccio's *Decameron*, V, 5.

Basilian Monks. Monks of the Order of St. Basil, who lived in the 4th century. It is said that the Order has produced 14 popes, 1,805 bishops, 3,010 abbots, and 11,085 martyrs.

Basilica (bà zil′ i kà) (Gr. *basilikos*, royal). Originally a royal palace, but afterwards (in Rome) a large building with nave, aisles, and an apse at one end, used as a court of justice and for public meetings. By the early Christians they were easily adapted for purposes of worship; the church of St. John Lateran at Rome was an ancient basilica.

Basilisco (bă zil is ′kō). A cowardly, bragging knight in Kyd's tragedy, *Solyman and Perseda* (1588). Shakespeare (*King John*, i, 1) makes the Bastard say to his mother, who asks him why he boasted of his ill-birth, "Knight, knight, good mother, Basilisco-like"—*i.e.* my boasting has made me a knight. In the earlier play Basilisco, speaking of his name, adds, "Knight, good fellow, knight, knight!" and is answered, "Knave, good fellow, knave, knave!"

Basilisk (băz′ i lisk). The king of serpents (Gr. *basileus*, a king), a fabulous reptile, also called a *cockatrice* (*q.v.*), and alleged to be hatched by a serpent from a cock's egg; supposed to have the power of "looking anyone dead on whom it fixed its eyes."

> The Basiliske . . .
> From powerful eyes close venim doth convay
> Into the lookers hart, and killeth farre away.
> SPENSER: *Faerie Queene*, IV, vii, 37.

Also the name of a large brass cannon in use in Elizabethan times.

> Thou hast talk'd
> Of sallies and retires, of trenches, tents,
> Of palisadoes, frontiers, parapets,
> Of basilisks, of cannon.
> SHAKESPEARE: 1 *Henry IV*, ii, 3.

Bass (băs). The inner bark of the limetree, or linden, properly called *bast*, a Teutonic word the ultimate origin of which is unknown. It is used by gardeners for packing, tying up plants, protecting trees, etc.; also for making mats, light baskets, hats, and (in Russia) shoes, while in parts of Central Europe a cloth is woven from it.

Bast. *See* BUBASTIS.

Bastard. An illegitimate child; a French word, from the Old French and Provençal *bast*, a pack-saddle. The pack-saddles were used by muleteers as beds; hence, as *bantling* (*q.v.*) is a "bench-begotten" child, so is *bastard*, literally, one begotten on a pack-saddle bed.

The name was formerly given to a sweetened Spanish wine (white or brown) made of the bastard muscadine grape.

Baste. I'll baste your jacket for you, *i.e.* cane you. **I'll give you a thorough basting,** *i.e.* beating. (A word of uncertain origin).

Bastille (băs tēl′) means simply a building (O.Fr. *bastir*, now *bâtir*, to build). The famous state prison in Paris was commenced by Charles V as a royal château in 1370, and it was first used as a prison by Louis XI. It was seized and sacked by the mob in the French Revolution, July 14th, 1789, and on the first anniversary its final demolition was begun and the Place de la Bastille laid out on its site. July 14th is the national holiday in France.

Bat. Harlequin's lath wand (Fr. *batte*, a wooden sword).

Off his own bat. By his own exertions; on his own account. A cricketer's phrase, meaning runs won by a single player.

To carry out one's bat (in cricket). Not to be "out" when the time for drawing the stumps has arrived.

Parliament of Bats. *See* CLUB PARLIAMENT.

To get along at a great bat. Here the word means *beat*, *pace*, rate of speed.

To have bats in the belfry. To be crazy in the head, bats in this case being the nocturnal creatures.

Batman. A military officer's soldier-servant; but properly a soldier in charge of a *bat-horse* (or pack-horse) and its load. From Fr. *bat*, a pack-saddle (O.Fr. *bast*; *see* BASTARD).

Batavia (bȧ tā′ vi ȧ). The Netherlands; so called from the Batavi, a German tribe which in Roman times inhabited the modern Holland.

Bate me an Ace. *See* BOLTON.

Bath. Knights of the Bath. This name is derived from the ceremony of bathing, which used to be practised at the inauguration of a knight, as a symbol of purity. The last knights created in this ancient form were at the coronation of Charles II in 1661. The Order was revived by George I, in 1725, and remodelled by the Prince Regent in 1815. G.C.B. stands for *Grand Cross of the Bath* (the first class); K.C.B. *Knight Commander of the Bath* (the second class); C.B. *Companion of the Bath* (the third class).

Bath metal. An alloy like pinchbeck (*q.v.*) consisting of about sixteen parts copper and five of zinc.

Bathia (băth′ i ȧ). The name given in the Talmud to the daughter of Pharaoh who found Moses in the ark of bulrushes.

Bath-kol (băth kol′) (daughter of the voice). A sort of divination common among the ancient Jews after the gift of prophecy had ceased. When an appeal was made to Bath-kol, the first words uttered after the appeal were considered oracular. *See* Ray's *Three Physico-Theological Discourses*, iii, 1693.

Bathos (bā′ thos) (Gr. *bathos*, depth). A ludicrous descent from grandiloquence to commonplace.

> The Taste of the Bathos is implanted by Nature itself in the soul of man.—POPE: *Bathos: Art o Sinking*, ii (1727).

A good example is the well-known couplet given by Pope:

> And, thou, Dalhousie, the great god of war,
> Lieutenant-general to the earl of Mar.
> *Ibid.*, ix.

Bathsheba (băth′ shė bȧ). In Dryden's *Absalom and Achitophel*, intended for the Duchess of Portsmouth, a favourite of Charles II.

The allusion is to the wife of Uriah the Hittite, beloved by David (2 *Sam.* xi).

Bathyllus (băth' i lŭs). A beautiful boy of Samos, greatly beloved by Polycrates the tyrant, and by the poet Anacreon. (Horace: *Epistle* xiv, 9.)

Batiste (bà tēst'). A kind of cambric (*q.v.*), so called from Baptiste of Cambrai, who first manufactured it in the 13th century.

Baton de commandement (băt' òn de kom and' mon) (Fr. literally "commander's truncheon"). The name given by archæologists to a kind of rod, usually of reindeer horn, pierced with one or more round holes, and sometimes embellished with carvings. It belongs to the Magdalenian age; but its use or purpose is quite unknown.

Batrachomyomachia (bă' trak ō mī' ō mā kyà). A storm in a puddle; much ado about nothing. The word is the name of a mock heroic Greek epic, supposed to be by Pigres of Caria, but formerly attributed to Homer. It tells, as its name imports, of a *Battle between the Frogs and Mice*.

Batta (băt' à). An Anglo-Indian term for perquisites. Properly, an extra allowance to troops when in the field or on special service. Sometimes spelt *batty*.

He would rather live on half-pay in a garrison that could boast of a fives-court than vegetate on full batta where there was none.—G. R. GLEIG: *Thomas Munro*, vol. i, ch. iv, p. 287.

Battle. A pitched battle. A battle which has been planned, and the ground pitched on or chosen beforehand.

Battle royal. A certain number of cocks, say sixteen, are pitted together; the eight victors are then pitted, then the four, and last of all the two; and the winner is victor of the battle royal. Metaphorically, the term is applied to any contest of wits, etc.

A close battle. Originally a naval fight at "close quarters," in which opposing ships engage each other side by side.

Line of battle. The formation of the ships in a naval engagement. A *line of battle ship* was a capital ship fit to take part in a main attack. *Frigates* did not join in a general engagement.

Half the battle. Half determines the battle. Thus, "The first stroke is half the battle," that is, the way in which the battle is begun determines what the end will be.

Trial by battle. The submission of a legal suit to a combat between the litigants, under the notion that God would defend the right.

Wager of battle. One of the forms of ordeal or appeal to the judgment of God, in the old Norman courts of the kingdom. It consisted of a personal combat between the plaintiff and the defendant, in the presence of the court itself. Abolished by 59 Geo. III, c. 46 (1819).

Battle above the Clouds. *See* CLOUDS.

Battle bowler. This was a nickname given in World War I to the steel helmet or "tin hat" worn at the front. Used again 1939-45, when it was also called a "tin topee."

Battle of the Books. A satire by Swift (written 1697, published 1704), on the literary squabble as to the comparative value of ancient and modern authors. In the battle the ancient books fight against the modern books in St. James's Library. *See* BOYLE CONTROVERSY.

Battle of Britain. The prolonged aerial operations over Southern England and the Channel, August-September 1940, in which the German Luftwaffe endeavoured to seize superiority in the air from the R.A.F. (as a necessary prelude to the invasion of Britain) and was defeated.

Battledore. Originally the wooden bat used in washing linen. The etymology of the word is not at all certain, but there is an old Provençal *batedor*, meaning a washing-beetle.

Battledore book. A name sometimes formerly given to a horn-book (*q.v.*), because of its shape. Hence, perhaps, the phrase "Not to know B from a battledore." *See* B.

Battue (bă tū). A French word meaning literally "a beating," used in English as a sporting term to signify a regular butchery of game, the "guns" being collected at a certain spot over which the birds are driven by the beaters who "beat" the bushes, etc., for the purpose. Hence, a wholesale slaughter, especially of unarmed people.

Batty. *See* BATTA.

Baturlio marina. *See* BARISAL GUNS.

Baubee. *See* BAWBEE.

Bauble. A fool should never hold a bauble in his hand. "Tis a foolish bird that fouls its own nest." The bauble was a short stick, ornamented with ass's ears, carried by licensed fools. (O.Fr. *babel*, or *baubel*, a child's toy; perhaps confused with the M.E. *babyll* or *babulle*, a stick with a thong, from *bablyn*, to waver or oscillate.)

If every fool held a bauble, fuel would be dear. The proverb indicates that the world contains a vast number of fools.

To deserve the bauble. To be so foolish as to be qualified to carry the fool's emblem of office.

Baucis. See PHILEMON.

Bauld Wullie. See BELTED WILL.

Baulk. See BALK.

Baviad, The (băv′ i ăd). A merciless satire by Gifford on the Della Cruscan poetry, published 1794, and republished the following year with a second part called *The Mœviad*. Bavius and Mævius were two minor poets pilloried by Virgil (*Eclogue*, iii, 9).

He may with foxes plough, and milk he-goats,
Who praise Bavius or on Mævius dotes.

And their names are still used for inferior versifiers.

May some choice patron bless each grey goose quill,
May every Bavius have his Bufo still.
POPE: *Prologue to Satires*, 249.

Bavieca. The Cid's horse.

Bavius. See BAVIAD.

Bawtry. Like the saddler of Bawtry, who was hanged for leaving his liquor (Yorkshire proverb). It was customary for criminals on their way to execution to stop at a certain tavern in York for a "parting draught." The saddler of Bawtry refused to accept the liquor and was hanged. If he had stopped a few minutes at the tavern, his reprieve, which was on the road, would have arrived in time to save his life.

Baxterians. Followers of Richard Baxter (1615-91), a noted English Nonconformist. His chief doctrines were—(1) That Christ died in a spiritual sense for the elect, and in a general sense for all; (2) that there is no such thing as reprobation; (3) that even saints may fall from grace. He thus tried to effect a compromise between the "heretical" opinions of the Arminians and the Calvinists.

Bay. The shrub was anciently supposed to be a preservative against lightning, because it was the tree of Apollo. Hence, according to Pliny, Tiberius and other Roman emperors wore a wreath of bay as an amulet, especially in thunder-storms.

Reach the bays—
I'll tie a garland here about his head;
'Twill keep my boy from lightning.
WEBSTER: *Vittoria Corumbona*, v, 1.

The bay being sacred to Apollo is accounted for by the legend that he fell in love with, and was rejected by, the beautiful Daphne, daughter of the river-god Peneos, in Thessaly, who had resolved to pass her life in perpetual virginity. She fled from him and sought the protection of her father, who changed her into the bay-tree, whereupon Apollo declared that henceforth he would wear bay leaves instead of the oak, and that all who sought his favour should follow his example.

The withering of a bay-tree was supposed to be the omen of a death. Holinshed refers to this superstition:—

In this yeare [1399] in a manner throughout all the realme of England, old baie trees withered, and, afterwards, contrarie to all mens thinking, grew greene againe; a strange sight, and supposed to impart some unknown event.—III, 496, 2, 66.

Shakespeare makes use of this note in his *Richard II*, ii, 4:—

'Tis thought the king is dead. We'll not stay—
The bay-trees in our country are withered.

In another sense Bay is a reddish-brown colour, generally used of horses. The word is the Fr. *bai*, from Lat. *badius*, a term used by Varro in his list of colours appropriate to horses. Bayard (*q.v.*) means "bay-coloured."

Bay at the moon, To. See BARK.

Bay salt. Coarse-grained salt, formerly obtained by slow evaporation of sea-water and used for curing meat, etc. Perhaps so called because originally imported from the shores of the *Bay* of Biscay. "Bay," in this case, does not signify the colour.

Bay Psalm Book. A metrical version of the Psalms published by Stephen Daye at Cambridge, Massachusetts, in 1680. One of the first printed works of the New World, and now highly prized. "What the Gutenberg Bible is to Europe, the *Bay Psalm Book* is to the United States"—A. E. Newton. In 1947 a copy changed hands at auction for $151,000.00.

Bay State, The. Massachusetts. In Colonial days its full title was "The Colony of Massachusetts Bay": hence the name.

Bayadere (bā ya′ dâr). A Hindu dancing girl employed both for religious dances and for private amusement. The word is a French corruption of the Portuguese *bailadeira*, a female dancer.

Bayard (bā′ yard). A horse of incredible swiftness, given by Charlemagne to the four sons of Aymon. See AYMON. If only one of the sons mounted, the horse was of the ordinary size; but if all four mounted, his body became elongated to the requisite length. He is introduced in Boiardo's *Orlando Innamorato*; Ariosto's *Orlando Furioso*, and elsewhere, and legend relates that he is still alive and can be heard neighing in the Ardennes on Midsummer Day. The name is used for any valuable or wonderful horse, and means a "high bay-coloured horse."

Bayardo. The famous steed of Rinaldo (*q.v.*), which once belonged to Amadis of Gaul. See HORSE.

Bayes (bāz). A character in the *Rehearsal*, by the Duke of Buckingham (1671), designed to satirize Dryden. The name refers to the laureateship.

Dead men may rise again, like Bayes's troops, or the savages in the Fantocini. In the *Rehearsal* a battle is fought between foot-soldiers and great hobby-horses. At last Drawcansir kills all on both sides. Smith then asks how they are to go off, to which Bayes replies, "As they came on—upon their legs"; upon which they all jump up alive again.

Bayeux Tapestry (bī' yer). A strip of linen 231 ft. long and 20 in. wide on which is represented in tapestry the mission of Harold to William, Duke of Normandy (William the Conqueror), and all the incidents of his history from then till his death at Hastings in 1066. It is preserved at Bayeux, and is supposed to be the work of Matilda, wife of William the Conqueror.

In the tapestry, the Saxons fight on foot with javelin and battle-axe, and bear shields with the British characteristic of a boss in the centre. The men are moustached.

The Normans are on horseback, with long shields and pennoned lances. The men are not only shaven, but most of them have a complete tonsure on the back of the head, whence the spies said to Harold, "There are more priests in the Norman army than men in Harold's."

Bayonet (bā' ō nét). A stabbing weapon fixed to a rifle for shock action by infantry. Its name is said to be taken from Bayonne where it was first made. The bayonet is mentioned in the memoirs of Puysegur, in 1647; it was introduced into the English army in 1672. In its original form it was a plug bayonet, fitted into the barrel of the musket, and had therefore to be removed before the gun could be fired.

Bayonets. A synonym of "rank and file," that is, privates and corporals of infantry. As, "the number of bayonets was 25,000."

It is on the bayonets that a Quartermaster-General relies for his working and fatigue parties.—HOWITT: *Hist. of Eng.* (year 1854, p. 260).

Bayou State (bī' yoo). The State of Mississippi; so called from its numerous bayous. A bayou is a creek, or sluggish and marshy overflow of a river or lake. The word may be of native American origin, but is probably a corruption of Fr. *boyau*, gut.

Bazooka. American one-man, short-range anti-tank weapon (1941-45). The name became freely applied to the British and German weapons of the same nature (P.I.A.T.—projectile infantry anti-tank—and *Panzerfaust*).

To be bazookaed. To be in a tank struck by such a projectile.

Beachcomber. One who, devoid of other means of existence, subsists on what flotsam and jetsam he can find on the seashore. The word originated in New Zealand, where it is found in print by 1844; an earlier form (1827) was *beach ranger*, analogous to *Bushranger* (*q.v.*).

Bead. From A.S. *-bed* (in *gebed*), a prayer, *biddan*, to pray. "Bead," thus originally meant simply "a prayer"; but as prayers were "told" (*i.e.* account kept of them) on a "paternoster," the word came to be transferred to the small globular perforated body a number of which, threaded on a string, composed this paternoster or "rosary."

To count one's beads. To say one's prayers. See ROSARY.

To draw a bead on. See DRAW.

To pray without one's beads. To be out of one's reckoning.

St. Martin's beads. Flash jewellery. St. Martin-le-Grand was at one time a noted place for sham jewellery.

Bead-house. An almshouse for beadsmen.

Bead-roll. A list of persons to be prayed for; hence, also, any list.

Beak. Slang for a police magistrate, but formerly (16th and 17th cent.) for a constable. Various fanciful derivations have been suggested, but the etymology of the word is unknown.

Beaker. A drinking-glass; a rummer; a wide-mouthed glass vessel with a lip, used in scientific experiments. A much-travelled word, having come to us by way of the Scandinavian *bikkar*, a cup (Dut. *beker*; Ger. *becher*), from Greek *bikos*, a wine-jar, which was of Eastern origin. Our *pitcher* is really the same word.

O for a beaker full of the warm South,
Full of the true, the blushful Hippocrene.
KEATS: *Ode to a Nightingale.*

Bean. Every bean has its black. *Nemo sine vitiis nascitur* (Everyone has his faults). The bean has a black eye. (*Ogni grano ha la sua semola.*)

He has found the bean in the cake. He has got a prize in the lottery, has come to some unexpected good fortune. The allusion is to twelfth cakes in which a bean is buried. When the cake is cut up and distributed, he who gets the bean is the twelfth-night king. See BEAN-KING.

Jack and the bean-stalk. See JACK.

Old bean. A slang expression of good-natured familiarity that became very common early in the 20th century.

Bean-feast. Much the same as wayz-goose (*q.v.*). A feast given by an employer to those he employs. Probably so called because either beans or a bean-goose used to be a favourite dish on such occasions.

Bean-goose. A migratory bird which appears in England in the autumn; so named from a mark on its bill like a horse-bean. It is next in size to the greylag-goose.

Bean-king. *Rey de Habas*, the child appointed to play the part of king on twelfth-night. Twelfth-night was sometimes known as *the Bean-king's festival*.

Beans. Slang for property, money; also for a sovereign, and (formerly) a guinea. In this sense it is probably the O.Fr. cant, *biens*, meaning property; but in such phrases as *not worth a bean*, the allusion is to the bean's small value.

Like a beane [alms-money] in a monkeshood.
                                        COLGRAVE.

Full of beans. Said of a fresh and spirited horse; hence, in good form; full of health and spirits.

Without a bean. Penniless, "broke."

To spill the beans. To give away a secret; to let the cat out of the bag.

Bear. In the phraseology of the Stock Exchange, a speculator for a fall. (*Cp.* BULL.)

Thus, **to operate for a bear,** or **to bear the market,** is to use every effort to depress prices, so as to buy cheap and make a profit on the rise. Such a transaction is known as a **Bear account.**

The term is of some antiquity, and was current at least as early as the South Sea Bubble, in the 18th century. Its probable origin will be found in the proverb, "Selling the skin before you have caught the bear." One who sold stocks in this way was formerly called a *bearskin jobber*.

The Bear. Albert, margrave of Brandenburg (1106-70). He was so called from his heraldic device.

The bloody bear, in Dryden's *The Hind and the Panther*, means the Independents.

The bloody bear, an independent beast,
Unlicked to form, in groans her hate expressed.
                                        Pt. i, 35, 36.

In mediæval times it was popularly supposed that bear-cubs were born as shapeless masses of flesh and fur, and had to be literally "licked into shape" by their mothers. Hence the reference in the above quotation, and the phrase "*to lick into shape*" (*q.v.*).

The Great Bear, and **Little Bear.** These constellations were so named by the Greeks, and their word, *arktos*, a bear, is still kept in the names Arcturus (the bear-ward, *ourcs*, guardian) and Arctic (*q.v.*). The Sanskrit name for the Great Bear is from the verb *rakh.* to be bright, and it has been suggested that the Greeks named it *arktos* as a result of confusion between the two words. *Cp.* CHARLES'S WAIN; NORTHERN WAGONER.

The wind-shaked surge, with high and monstrous mane,
Seems to cast water on the burning bear
And quench the guards of th' ever-fixed pole.
                            SHAKESPEARE: *Othello*, ii, 1.

The guards referred to in the above extract are β and γ of Ursa Minor. They are so named, not from any supposed guarding that they do, but from the Sp. *guardare*, to behold, because of the great assistance they were to mariners in navigation.

The classical fable is that Calisto, a nymph of Diana, had two sons by Jupiter, which Juno changed into bears, and Jupiter converted into constellations.

'Twas here we saw Calisto's star retire
Beneath the waves, unawed by Juno's ire.
                            CAMOËNS: *Lusiad*, Bk. v.

The Northern Bear. In political cartoons, etc., Russia is depicted as a bear.

A bridled bear. A young nobleman under the control of a travelling tutor. *See* BEAR-LEADER.

The bear and ragged staff. A crest of the Nevilles and later Earls of Warwick, often used as a public-house sign. The first earl is said to have been Arth or Arthgal, of the Round Table, whose cognizance was a *bear*, *arth* meaning a bear (Lat. *ursa*). Morvid, the second earl, overcame, in single combat, a mighty giant, who came against him with a club consisting of a tree pulled up by the roots, but stripped of its branches. In remembrance of his victory over the giant he added "the ragged staff."

Bear-leader. A common expression in the 18th century denoting a travelling tutor who escorted a young nobleman, or youth of wealth and fashion, on the "Grand Tour." From the old custom of leading muzzled bears about the streets, and making them show off in order to attract notice and money. This practice was made illegal only in 1925.

Bear! (said *Dr. Pangloss* to his pupil). Under favour young gentleman, I am the bear-leader, being appointed your tutor.—G. COLMAN: *Heir-at-Law.*

Bear, To. Come, bear a hand! Come and render help. Bring a hand, or bring your hand to bear on the work going on.

To bear arms. To do military service; to be entitled to heraldic coat of arms and crest.

To bear away (nautical). To keep away from the wind.

To bear one company. To be one's companion.

His faithful dog shall bear him company.
                    POPE: *Essay on Man*, epistle i, 112.

To bear down. To overpower.

To bear down upon (nautical). To approach from the weather side.

Bear in mind. Remember; do not forget. Carry in your recollection.

To bear out. To corroborate, to confirm.

To bear up. To support; to keep the spirits up.

To bear with. To show forbearance; to endure with complacency.

To bear the bell. *See* BELL.

Beard. Among the Jews, Turks, and Eastern nations generally the beard has long been regarded as a sign of manly dignity. To cut it off wilfully was a deadly insult, and the Jews were strictly forbidden to cut it off ceremonially, though shaving it was a sign of mourning. No greater insult could be offered a man than to pluck or even touch his beard, hence the phrase **to beard one,** to defy him, to contradict him flatly, to insult him. By touching or swearing by one's own beard one's good faith was assured.

The dyeing of beards is mentioned by Strabo, and Bottom the Weaver satirizes the custom when he undertakes to play Pyramus, and asks, "What beard were I best to play it in?"

I will discharge it in either your straw-colour beard, your orange-tawny beard, your purple-ingrain beard, or your French-crown-colour beard (your perfect yellow).
Midsummer Night's Dream, i, 2.

Beards are encouraged in the Royal Navy, but not permitted in the other Services, though in World War II the Army turned a blind eye to the beards of some individuals performing unusually hazardous duty behind the enemy's lines.

To beard the lion in his den. To defy personally or face to face.

To make one's beard. To have one wholly at your mercy, as a barber has when holding a man's beard to dress it, or shaving the chin of a customer. So, to be able to do what you like with one, to outwit or delude him.

Though they preye Argus, with his hundred yën,
To be my warde-cors, as he can best,
In feith, he shal nat kepe me but me lest;
Yet coude I make his berd, so moot I thee.
CHAUCER: *Wife of Bath's Prologue*, 358.

I told him to his beard. I told him to his face, regardless of consequences; I spoke to him openly and fearlessly.

Maugre his beard. In spite of him.

"'Tis merry in hall when beards wag all" — *i.e.* when feasting goes on.

Then was the minstrel's harp with rapture heard;
The song of ancient days gave huge delight;
With pleasure too did wag the minstrel's beard,
For Plenty courted him to drink and bite.
PETER PINDAR: *Elegy to Scotland.*

To laugh at a man's beard. To attempt to make a fool of him — to deceive by ridiculous exaggeration.

"By the prophet! but he laughs at our beards," exclaimed the Pacha angrily. "These are foolish lies." — MARRYAT: *Pacha of Many Tales.*

To laugh in one's beard. To laugh up one's sleeve, that is, surreptitiously.

To lie in one's beard. To accuse someone of so doing is to stress the severity of the accusation (Elizabethan).

Bearded women. St. Paula the Bearded, a Spanish saint of uncertain date of whom it is said that when being pursued by a man she fled to a crucifix and at once a beard and moustache appeared on her face, thus disguising her and saving her from her would-be ravisher. A somewhat similar story is told of St. Wilgefortis, a mythical saint supposed to have been one of seven daughters born at a birth to a king of Portugal; also of the English saint, St. Uncumber.

Many bearded women are recorded in history; among them may be mentioned: —

Bartel Grætjë, of Stuttgart, born 1562.

Charles XII had in his army a woman whose beard was a yard and a half long. She was taken prisoner at the battle of Pultawa, and presented to the Czar, 1724.

Mlle Bois de Chêne, born at Geneva in 1834, and exhibited in London in 1852-3; she had a profuse head of hair, a strong black beard, large whiskers, and thick hair on her arms and back.

Julia Pastrana, found among the Digger Indians of Mexico, was exhibited in London in 1857; died, 1862, at Moscow; was embalmed by Professor Suckaloff; and the embalmed body was exhibited in London.

Bearings. I'll bring him to his bearings. I'll bring him to his senses, put him on the right track. Bearings is a term in navigation signifying the direction in which an object is seen. Thus to keep one's bearings is to keep on the right course, in the right direction.

To lose one's bearings. To become bewildered; to get perplexed as to which is the right road.

To take the bearings. To ascertain the relative position of some object.

Béarnais, Le. Henry IV of France (1553-1610); so called from *Le Béarn*, his native province.

Beast. The Number of the Beast. *See* NUMBER.

Beast of Belsen. In World War II the name applied to Joseph Kramer, commandant of the notorious Belsen Concentration Camp.

Beat (A.S. *beatan*). The first sense of the word was that of striking; that of overcoming or defeating followed on as a natural extension. A track, line, or appointed range. A walk often trodden or beaten by the feet, as **a policeman's beat.** The word means a beaten path.

Not in my beat. Not in my line; not in the range of my talents or inclination.

Off his beat. Not on duty; not in his appointed walk; not his speciality or line.

Off his own beat his opinions were of no value.
EMERSON: *English Traits*, ch. i.

On his beat. In his appointed walk; on duty.

Out of his beat. In his wrong walk; out of his proper sphere.

Dead beat. So completely beaten or worsted as to have no leg to stand on. Like a dead man with no fight left in him; quite tired out.

Dead beat escapement (of a watch). One in which there is no reverse motion of the escape-wheel.

That beats Banagher. *See* BANAGHER: TERMAGANT.

To beat about. A nautical phrase, meaning to tack against the wind.

To beat about the bush. To approach a matter cautiously or in a roundabout way; to shilly-shally; perhaps because one goes carefully when beating a bush to find if any game is lurking within.

To beat an alarm. To give notice of danger by beat of drum.

To beat a retreat (Fr. *battre en retraite*); *to beat to arms*; *to beat a charge.* Military terms similar to the above.

To beat down. To make a seller abate his price.

To beat or drum a thing into one. To repeat as a drummer repeats his strokes on a drum.

To beat hollow, or to a mummy, a frazzle, to ribbons, a jelly, etc. To beat wholly, utterly, completely.

Beati Possidentes (bē a' tī pos i den' tēz). Blessed are those who have (for they shall receive). "Possession is nine points of the law."

Beatific Vision. The sight of God, or of the blessed in the realms of heaven, especially that granted to the soul at the instant of death. *See Is.* vi, 1-4, and Acts vii, 55, 56.

Beatification (bē ăt i fi kā' shùn). In the R.C. Church this is a solemn act by which a deceased person is formally declared by the Pope to be one of the blessed departed and therefore a proper subject for a mass and office in his honour, generally with some local restriction. Beatification is usually, though not necessarily, a step to canonization.

Beatitude (bē ăt'it tūd). In theology this is the perfect good which completely satisfies all desire.

The Beatitudes are the eight blessings pronounced by Our Lord at the opening of the Sermon on the Mount (*Matt.* v. 3-11).

Beatrice. Celebrated by Dante in the *Vita Nuova* and the *Divina Commedia*, this girl was born 1266 and died in 1290, under twenty-four years old. She was a native of Florence, of the Portinari family, and married Simone de' Bardi in 1287. Dante married Gemma Donati about two years after Beatrice's death.

Beau (bō). The French word, which means "fine," or "beautiful," has, in England, often been prefixed to the name of a man of fashion, or a fop as an epithet of distinction. The following are well known:—

Beau Brummel. George Bryan Brummel (1778-1840).

Beau D'Orsay. Count D'Orsay (1801-52), called by Byron *Jeune Cupidon.*

Beau Feilding. Robert Feilding (d. 1712), called "Handsome Feilding" by Charles II. He died in Scotland Yard, London, after having been convicted of bigamously marrying the Duchess of Cleveland, a former mistress of Charles II. He figures as Orlando in Steele's *Tatler* (Nos. 50 and 51).

Beau Hewitt. The model for "Sir Fopling Flutter," hero of Etheredge's *Man of Mode.*

Beau Nash. Richard Nash (1674-1762). Son of a Welsh gentleman, a notorious diner-out. He undertook the management of the rooms at Bath, and conducted the public balls with a splendour and decorum never before witnessed.

Beau Didapper, in Fielding's *Joseph Andrews*, and **Beau Tibbs,** noted for his finery, vanity, and poverty in Goldsmith's *Citizen of the World,* may also be mentioned.

In America the word *beau* is applied to a girl's favourite admirer, or lover.

Beau ideal. Properly, the ideal Beautiful, the abstract idea of beauty, *idéal*, in the French, being the adjective, and *beau*, the substantive: but in English the parts played by the words are usually transposed, and thus have come to mean the ideal type or model of anything in its most consummate perfection.

Beau monde. The fashionable world; people who make up the coterie of fashion.

Beau trap. An old slang expression for a loose paving-stone under which water lodged, and which squirted up filth when trodden on, to the annoyance of the smartly dressed.

Beauclerc (bō' klĕrk) (*good scholar*). Applied to Henry I (1068-1135), who had clerk-like accomplishments, very rare in the times in which he lived.

Beaumontague or **Beaumontage.** Material used for filling in accidental holes in wood- or metal-work, repairing cracks, disguising bad joinery, etc. Said to be so called from the celebrated French geologist, Elie de Beaumont (1798-1874), who also gave his name to **beaumonlite,** a silicate of copper.

Beauseant (bō sā' ón). The battle-cry of the Knights Templar. *See* TEMPLAR.

Beautiful Parricide. Beatrice Cenci, daughter of Francesco Cenci, a dissipated and passionate Roman nobleman. With her brothers, she plotted the death of her father because of his unmitigated cruelty to his wife and children. She was executed in 1599, and at the trial her counsel, with the view of still further gaining popular sympathy for his client, accused the father, probably without foundation, of having attempted to commit incest with her. Her story has been a favourite theme in poetry and art; Shelley's tragedy *The Cenci* is particularly noteworthy.

Beauty. Beauty is but skin deep.

O formose puer, nimium ne crede colori.
VIRGIL: *Ecloques*, ii.

(O my pretty boy, trust not too much to your pretty looks.)

Beauty and the Beast. The hero and heroine of the well-known fairy tale in which Beauty saved the life of her father by consenting to live with the Beast; and the Beast, being disenchanted by Beauty's love, became a handsome prince, and married her.

The story is found in Straparola's *Piacevoli Notti* (1550), and it is from this collection that Mme le Prince de Beaumont probably obtained it when it became popular through her French version (1757). It is the basis of Grétry's opera *Zémire et Azor* (1771).

The story of a handsome and wealthy prince being compelled by enchantment to assume the appearance and character of a loathsome beast or formidable dragon until released by the pure love of one who does not suspect the disguise, is of great antiquity and takes various forms. Sometimes, as in the story of Lamia, and the old ballads *Kempion* and *The Laidley Worm of Spindlestoneheugh*, it is the woman—the "Loathly Lady" of the romances— who is enchanted into the form of a serpent and is only released by the kiss of a true knight.

Beauty sleep. Sleep taken before midnight. Those who habitually go to bed, especially during youth, after midnight, are supposed to become pale and more or less haggard.

Beaux Esprits (bō zā sprē) (Fr.). Men of wit or genius (singular, *Un bel esprit*, a wit, a genius).

Beaux yeux (bō zyĕr´) (Fr.). Beautiful eyes or attractive looks. "I will do it for your *beaux yeux*" (because you are so pretty, or because your eyes are so attractive).

Bed. The great bed of Ware. A bed eleven feet square, and capable of holding twelve persons. It dates from the last quarter of the 16th century. In 1931 it came into the possession of the Victoria and Albert Museum.

Although the sheet were big enough for the bed of Ware in England.—SHAKESPEARE: *Twelfth Night*, iii, 2.

As you make your bed you must lie on it. Everyone must bear the consequences of his own acts.

To bed out. To plant what are called "bedding-out plants" in a flower-bed. Bedding out plants are reared in pots, generally in a hothouse, and are transferred into garden-beds early in the summer. Such plants as geraniums, marguerites, fuchsias, pentstemons, petunias, verbenas, lobelias, calceolarias, etc., are meant.

To make the bed. To arrange it and make it fit for use. In America this sense of "make" is more common than it is with us. "Your room is made," arranged in due order.

You got out of bed the wrong way, or **with the left leg foremost.** Said of a person who is patchy and ill-tempered. It was an ancient superstition that it was unlucky to set the left foot on the ground first on getting out of bed. The same superstition applies to putting on the left shoe first, a "fancy" not yet wholly exploded. Augustus Cæsar was very superstitious in this respect.

Bed of justice. *See* LIT.

A bed of roses. A situation of ease and pleasure.

A bed of thorns. A situation of great anxiety and apprehension.

In the twinkling of a bed-post or **bed-staff.** As quickly as possible. In old bed-frames it is said that posts were placed in brackets at the two sides of the bedstead for keeping the bed-clothes from rolling off; there was also in some cases a staff used to beat the bed and clean it. In the reign of Edward I, Sir John Chichester had a mock skirmish with his servant (Sir John with his rapier and the servant with the bed-staff), in which the servant was accidentally killed. Wright, in his *Domestic Manners*, shows us a chambermaid of the 17th century using a bed-staff to beat up the bedding. "Twinkling" is from A.S. *twinclian*, a frequentative verb connected with *twiccan*, to twitch, and connotes rapid or tremulous movement.

I'll do it instantly, in the twinkling of a bed-staff.
SHADWELL: *Virtuoso*, i, 1 (1676).

The phrase is probably due to the older and more readily understandable one, *in the twinkling of an eye*, in the smallest thinkable fraction of time:—

We shall all be changed in a moment, in the twinkling of an eye, at the last trump.—1 *Cor.* xv, 51, 52.

Bedchamber Question. In May, 1839, Lord Melbourne's Whig ministry resigned, and when Sir Robert Peel formed a government he intimated to Queen Victoria that he would expect the Whig ladies of the bedchamber to be replaced by Tories. The Queen refused to accede to this request, and persisting in her refusal, called Lord Melbourne to her aid. A new Whig ministry was formed, which lasted until 1841, by which time the Prince Consort was able to smooth over the difficulty when a Tory government was formed.

Bedel, or **Bedell** (bē' dĕl). Old forms of the word *beadle* (*q.v.*), still used at Oxford and Cambridge in place of the modern spelling for the officer who carries the mace before the Vice-Chancellor and performs a few other duties. At Oxford there are four, called *bedels*; at Cambridge there are two, called *bedells*, or *esquire-bedells*.

Beder (bē' der). A village between Medina and Mecca famous for the first victory gained by Mohammed over the Koreshites (624 A.D.). In the battle he is said to have been assisted by 3,000 angels, led by Gabriel, mounted on his horse Haizum.

Bedlam. A lunatic asylum or madhouse; a contraction for *Bethlehem*, the name of a religious house in London, converted into a hospital for lunatics. St. Mary of Bethlehem was the first English and the second European lunatic asylum. Founded in Bishopsgate, London, in 1247, it became a madhouse in 1403. In 1676 it was transferred to Moorfields, near where Liverpool-St. Station now stands, and was one of the sights of London, where, for twopence, anyone might wander in and gaze at the poor distracted wretches behind their bars and bait them with foolish and cruel questions. It was a holiday resort and place for

assignations, one of the disgraces of 17th-century London.

All that I can say of Bedlam is this; 'tis an alms-house for madmen, a showing room for harlots, a sure market for lechers, a dry walk for loiterers.
WARD'S *London Spy* (1698).

In 1815 Bedlam was moved to St. George's Fields, Lambeth, and in 1926 to the country, near Beckenham, Kent.

Bedlamite. A madman, a fool, an inhabitant of Bedlam. *See* ABRAM-MAN.

Bedlam, Tom o'. *See* TOM.

Bednall Green. *See* BEGGAR'S DAUGHTER.

Bedouins (bed' ou inz). French (and thence English) form of an Arabic word meaning "a dweller in the desert," given indiscriminately by Europeans to the nomadic tribes of Arabia and Syria, and applied in journalistic jargon to gipsies, or the homeless poor of the streets. In this use it is merely a further extension of the term "street Arab," which means the same thing.

Bed-rock. American slang for one's last shilling. A miner's term for the hard basis rock which is reached when the mine is exhausted. "I'm come down to the bedrock," *i.e.* my last dollar.

Bedroll (western U.S.A.). A tarpaulin in which a cowboy keeps his blankets and possessions. Once he has thrown it on to the cook's chuck-wagon he owes complete allegiance to the outfit.

Bee. Legend has it that Jupiter was nourished by bees in infancy, and Pindar is said to have been nourished by bees with honey instead of milk.

The Greeks consecrated bees to the moon. With the Romans a flight of bees was considered a bad omen. Appian (*Civil War*, Bk. ii) says a swarm of bees lighted on the altar and prognosticated the fatal issue of the battle of Pharsalia.

The coins of Ephesus had a bee on the reverse.

When Plato was an infant, bees settled on his lips when he was asleep, indicating that he would become famous for his honeyed words.

And as when Plato did i' the cradle thrive,
Bees to his lips brought honey from their hive.
W. BROWNE: *Britannia's Pastorals*, ii.

The same story is told of Sophocles, Pindar, St. Chrysostom, and others, including St. Ambrose, who is represented with a beehive.

The Bee was the emblem of Napoleon I.

The name **bee** is given, particularly in America, to a social gathering for some useful work, the allusion being to the social and industrious character of bees. The name of the object of the gathering generally precedes the word, as a *spelling-bee* (for a competition in spelling), *apple-bees*, *husking-bees*, etc. It is an old Devonshire custom, carried across the Atlantic in Stuart times, but the *name* appears to have originated in America.

See also ANIMALS IN SYMBOLISM.

The Athenian Bee. *See* ATHENIAN.

Bee-line. The shortest distance between two given points; such as a bee is supposed to take in making for its hive. *Air-line* is another term for the same thing.

To have your head full of bees, or to have a bee in your bonnet. To be cranky; to have an idiosyncrasy; to be full of devices, crotchets, fancies, inventions, and dreamy theories. The connexion between bees and the soul was once generally maintained: hence Mohammed admits bees to Paradise. Porphyry says of fountains, "they are adapted to the numphs, or those souls which the ancient called bees." *Cp.* MAGGOT.

Beef. This word, from the O.Fr. *boef* (mod. Fr. *bœuf*), an ox, is, like *mutton* (Fr. *mouton*), a reminder of the time when, in the years following the Norman Conquest, the Saxon was the down-trodden servant of the conquerors: the Normans had the cooked meat, and when set before them used the word they were accustomed to; the Saxon was the herdsman, and while the beast was under his charge called it by its Saxon name.

Beefeaters. The popular name of the Yeomen of the Guard in the royal household, appointed, in 1485, by Henry VII, to form part of the royal train at banquets and on other grand occasions; also of the Yeomen Extraordinary of the Guard, who were appointed as Warders of the Tower of London by Edward VI, and wear the same Tudor-period costume as the Yeomen of the Guard themselves.

There is no evidence whatever for the old guess that the word is connected with the French *buffet*, and signifies "an attendant at the royal buffet, or sideboard"; on the contrary, every indication goes to show that it means exactly what it says, viz. "eaters of beef." That "eater" was formerly used as a synonym for "servant" is clear, not only from the fact that the O.E. *hláf-œta* (literally, "loaf-eater") meant "a menial servant," but also from the passage in Ben Jonson's *Silent Woman* iii, 2, (1609) where Morose, calling for his servants, shouts,

Bar my doors! bar my doors! Where are all my eaters? My mouths, now? Bar up my doors, you varlets!

Sir. S. D. Scott, in his *The British Army* (i, 513), quotes an early use of the word from a letter of Prince Rupert's dated 1645, and shows (p. 517) that the large daily allowance of beef provided for their table makes the words in their literal meaning quite appropriate.

There is plenty of evidence to show that in the 17th century there was little doubt of the meaning of the word: *e.g.* Cartwright's *The Ordinary*, ii, 1 (1651):—

Those goodly Juments of the guard would fight
(As they eat beef) after six stone a day.

Beelzebub. The name should toe spelt *Beelzebul* (or, rather, *Baalzebul*, *see* BAAL), and means "lord of the high house"; but, as this title was ambiguous and might have been taken as referring to Solomon's Temple, the late Jews changed it to *Beelzebub*, which has the meaning "lord of flies." Beelzebub was the particular Baal worshipped originally in Ekron and afterwards far and wide in Palestine and the adjacent countries. To the Jews he came to be the chief representative of the false gods, and he took an important place in their hierarchy of demons. He is referred to in *Matt.* xii, 24, as "the prince of the devils," and hence Milton places him next in rank to Satan.

One next himself in power, and next in crime,
Long after known in Palestine, and named
Beelzebub.   *Paradise Lost*, i, 79.

Beeswing. The second crust, or film, composed of shining scales of mucilage, which forms in good port and some other wines after long keeping, and which bears some resemblance to the wings of bees. Unlike the "crust" which forms on the bottle, it is not detrimental if it passes into the decanter at decanting.

Beetle, To. To overhang, to threaten, to jut over. The word seems to have been first used by Shakespeare:

Or to the dreadful summit of the din,
That beetles o'er his base into the sea.
Hamlet, i, 4.

It is formed from the adjective, *beetle-browed*, having prominent or shaggy eyebrows; and it is not the case, as has sometimes been stated, that the adjective was formed from the verb. The derivation of *beetle* in this use is not quite certain, but it probably refers to the tufted antennae which, in some beetles, stand straight out from the head.

Befana (be fa' na). The good fairy of Italian children, who is supposed to fill their stockings with toys when they go to bed on Twelfth Night. Someone enters the children's bedroom for the purpose, and the wakeful youngsters cry out, "*Ecco la Befana.*" According to legend,

Befana was too busy with house affairs to look after the Magi when they went to offer their gifts, and said she would wait to see them on their return; but they went another way, and Befana, every Twelfth Night, watches to see them. The name is a corruption of *Epiphania*.

Before the Lights. *See* LIGHTS.

Before the Mast. *See* MAST.

Beg. A Turkish chief or governor. *See* BEY.

Beg the Question, To. To assume a proposition which, in reality, involves the conclusion. Thus, to say that parallel lines will never meet because they are parallel, is simply to assume as a fact the very thing you profess to prove. The phrase is the common English equivalent of the Latin term, *petitio principii*.

Beggar. A beggar may sing before a pick-pocket. *Cantabit vacuus coram latrone viator* (*Juvenal*, x, 22). A beggar may sing in the presence of thieves because he has nothing in his pocket to lose.

Beggar of Bednall Green. *See* BESSEE, THE BEGGAR'S DAUGHTER.

Beggars cannot be choosers. Beggars must take what is given them, and not dictate to the giver what they like best. They must accept and be thankful.

Beggars' barm. The thick foam which collects on the surface of ponds, brooks, and other pieces of water where the current meets stoppage. It looks like barm or yeast, but, being unfit for use, is only beggarly barm at best.

Beggars' bullets. Stones.

To go by beggar's bush, or **Go home by beggar's bush**—*i.e.* to go to ruin. Beggar's bush is the name of a tree which once stood on the left hand of the London road from Huntingdon to Caxton; so called because it was a noted rendezvous for beggars. These punning phrases and proverbs are very common.

Set a beggar on horseback, and he'll ride to the de'il. There is no one so proud and arrogant as a beggar who has suddenly grown rich.

> Such is the sad effect of wealth—rank pride—
> Mount but a beggar, how the rogue will ride!
> PETER PINDAR: Epistle to Lord Lonsdale.

The proverb is common to many languages.

Beghards (be gardz). A monastic fraternity which rose in the Low Countries in the 12th century, so called from Lambert le Begue, a priest of Liége, who also founded a sisterhood. They took no vows, and were free to leave the society when they liked. In the 17th century, those who survived the persecutions of the Popes and Inquisition joined the Tertiarii of the Franciscans. *See* BEGUINES.

Beglerbed. *See* BASHAW.

Begorra. An Irish form of the English minced oath "begad," for "By God."

Beguine (bé gēn'). A popular Martinique and South American dance, or music for this dance, in bolero rhythm. This rhythm inspired Cole Porter's success of the 1930s, "Begin the Beguine."

Beguines (bā gēn). A sisterhood founded in the 12th century by Lambert le Begue (*see* BEGHARDS). The Beguines were at liberty to quit the cloister and to marry; they formerly flourished in the Low Countries, Germany, France, and Italy; and there are still communities with this name in Belgium. The cap called a *béguin* was named from this sisterhood.

Begum. A lady, princess, or woman of high rank in India; the wife of a ruler (fern, of *Beg*, *see* BEY).

Behemoth (be hē' moth). The animal described under this name in *Job* xl, 15 *et seq.*, is, if an actual animal were intended, almost certainly the hippopotamus; but modern scholarship rather tends to the opinion that the reference is purely mythological. The English poet Thomson, apparently took it to be the rhinoceros:

> Behold! in plaited mail,
> Behemoth rears his head.
> The Seasons: Summer, 709.

The word is sometimes pronounced Be'hemoth; but Milton, like Thomson, places the accent on the second syllable.

> Scarce from his mold
> Behemoth, biggest born of earth, upheaved
> His vastness.
> Paradise Lost, vii, 471.

Behmenists (bā' men ists). A sect of theosophical mystics, so called from Jacob Behmen, or Böhme (1575-1624), their founder. The first Behmenist sect in England was founded under the name of *Philadelphists* by a certain Jane Leade, in 1697.

Behram (bē' ràm). The most holy kind of fire, according to Parseeism (*q.v.*). *See also* GUEBRES.

Bejan (bē' jàn). A freshman or greenhorn. This term was introduced into some of the Scottish Universities from the University of Paris, and is a corruption of Fr. *bec jaune*, yellow beak, with allusion to a nestling or unfledged bird. At Aberdeen a woman student is called a *banjanella* or *bejanella*.

In France *béjaune* is still the name for the repast that the freshman is supposed to provide for his new companions.

Bel. The name of two Assyrio-Babylonian gods; it is the same word as Baal (*q.v.*). The story of Bel and the Dragon, in which we are told how Daniel convinced the king that Bel was not an actual living deity but only an image, was formerly part of the *Book of Daniel*, but is now relegated to the Apocrypha.

Bel Esprit (bel es prē) (Fr.). Literally, fine mind, means, in English, a vivacious wit; one of quick and lively parts, ready at repartee (pl. *beaux esprits*).

Belch, Sir Toby. A reckless, roistering, jolly fellow: from the knight of that name in Shakespeare's *Twelfth Night*.

Belcher. A pocket-handkerchief—properly, one with white spots on a blue ground; so called from Jim Belcher (1781-1811), the pugilist, who adopted it. The Belcher ring was a massive gold affair, sometimes set with a precious stone.

Belfry. A military tower, pushed by besiegers against the wall of a besieged city, that missiles may be thrown more easily against the defenders. (From O.Fr. *berfrei*, *berfroi*, Mid. High Ger. *bercfrit*—*berc*, shelter, *fride*, peace—a protecting tower.) A church steeple is called a belfry from its resemblance to these towers, and not because bells are hung in it.

Belial (bē′ li ál) (Heb.). The worthless or lawless one, *i.e.* the devil.

What concord hath Christ with Belial?

                         2 Cor. vi, 15.

Milton, in his pandemonium, makes him a very high and distinguished prince of darkness.

Belial came last—than whom a spirit more lewd
Fell not from heaven, or more gross to love
Vice for itself.

                Paradise Lost, bk. i, 490.

Sons of Belial. Lawless, worthless, rebellious people.

Now the sons of Eli were sons of Belial.

                        1 Sam. ii, 12.

Belisarius (bel i sâr′ i us). **Belisarius begging for an obolus.** Belisarius (d. 565), the greatest of Justinian's generals, being accused of conspiring against the life of the emperor, was deprived of all his property. The tale is that his eyes were put out, and that when living as a beggar in Constantinople he fastened a bag to his roadside hut, with the inscription, "Give an obolus to poor old Belisarius."

This tradition is of no historic value.

Belit. *See* ASSHUR.

Bell, Acton, Currer, and Ellis. These were the names under which Anne, Charlotte, and Emily Brontë wrote their novels.

Bell. As the bell clinks, so the fool thinks, or, As the fool thinks, so the bell clinks. The tale says when Whittington ran away from his master, and had got as far as Highgate Hill, he was hungry, tired, and wished to return. Bow

Bells began to ring, and Whittington fancied they said, "Turn again, Whittington, Lord Mayor of London." The bells clinked in response to the boy's thoughts.

Passing bell. The hallowed bell which used to be rung when persons were *in extremis*, to scare away evil spirits which were supposed to lurk about the dying ready to pounce on the soul while *passing* from the body. It is a very ancient custom, and the Athenians used to beat on brazen kettles at the moment of a decease to scare away the Furies. A secondary object was to announce to the neighbourhood the fact that all good Christians might offer up a prayer for the safe *passage* of the soul into Paradise. The bell rung at a funeral is sometimes improperly called the "passing bell."

The Koran says that bells hang on the trees of Paradise, and are set in motion by wind from the throne of God, as often as the blessed wish for music.

Bells as musical
As those that, on the golden-shafted trees
Of Eden, shook by the eternal breeze.

           T. MOORE: *Lalla Rookh*, pt. i.

Ringing the hallowed bell. Consecrated bells were believed to be able to disperse storms and pestilence, drive away devils (*see* PASSING BELL, *above*), and extinguish fire. In France in quite recent times it was by no means unusual to ring church bells to ward off the effects of lightning, and as lately as 1852 it is said that the Bishop of Malta ordered the church bells to be rung for an hour to "lay a gale of wind."

Funera plango, fulgura frango, sabbata pango,
Excito lentos, dissipo ventos, paco cruentos.

          A Helpe to Discourse (1668).
(Death's tale I tell, the winds dispel, ill-feeling quell,
The slothful shake, the storm-clouds break, the Sabbath wake.)

The legend on the Münster bell, cast at Basle in 1486, known as Schiller's bell because it furnished him with the idea for his *Lied von der Glocke*, reads:

Vivos ⊥ Voco ⊥ Mortuos ⊥ Plango ⊥ Fulgura ⊥ Frango.

Ringing the bells backwards, is ringing a muffled peal. *Backwards* is often used to denote "in a reverse manner," as, "I hear you are grown rich—" "Yes, backwards," meaning "quite the reverse." A muffled peal is a peal of sorrow, not of joy, and was formerly sometimes employed as a tocsin, or notice of danger.

Sound as a bell. Quite sound. A cracked bell is useless.

Blinde Fortune did so happily contrive,
That we as sound as bells did safe arive
At Dover.

          Taylor's Workes, ii, 22 (1630).

Tolling the bell for church. The "church-going bell," as Cowper called it (*Alexander Selkirk*) was in pre-Reformation days rung, not as an invitation to church, but as an Ave Bell, to invite worshippers to a preparatory Prayer to the Virgin.

Bell-the-Cat. Archibald Douglas, fifth Earl of Angus (d. 1514), was so called. James III made favourites of architects and masons. One mason, named Cochrane, he created Earl of Mar. The Scottish nobles held a council in the church of Lauder for the purpose of putting down these upstarts, when Lord Gray asked, "Who will bell the cat?" "That will I," said Douglas, and he fearlessly put to death, in the king's presence, the obnoxious minions. The allusion is to the fable of the cunning old mouse (given in *Piers Plowman* and elsewhere), who suggested that they should hang a bell on the cat's neck to give notice to all mice of her approach. "Excellent," said a wise young mouse, "but who is to undertake the job?"

Bell-wavering. Vacillating, swaying from side to side like a bell. A man whose mind jangles out of tune from delirium, drunkenness, or temporary insanity, is said to have his wits gone bell-wavering.

Bellwether of the flock. A jocose and rather deprecatory term applied to the leader of a party. The allusion is to the wether or sheep which leads the flock with a bell fastened to its neck.

Belladonna (bel à don′ à). The Deadly Nightshade. The name is Italian, and means "beautiful lady"; it is not certainly known why it should have been given to the plant. One account says that it is from a practice once common among ladies of touching their eyes with it to make the pupils large and lustrous; but another has it that it is from its having been used by an Italian poisoner, named Leucota, to poison beautiful women. It is used today by ophthalmic surgeons in order to enlarge the pupil so that they may more easily examine the inside of the eye.

Bellarmine (bel′ ar mīn). A large Flemish gotch, or stone beer-jug, originally made in Flanders in ridicule of Cardinal Bellarmine (1542-1621), the great persecutor of the Protestants there. It carried a rude likeness of the cardinal. *Cp.* GREYBEARD.

Belle (bel) (Fr.). A beauty. **The Belle of the ball.** The most beautiful woman in the room.

La belle France. A common French phrase applied to France, as "Merrie England" is to our own country.

Belles lettres (bel letr). Polite literature; poetry, and standard literary works which are not scientific or technical: the study or pursuit of such literature. The term—which is French —has given birth to the very ugly words *bellettrist* and *bellettristic*.

Bellerophon (be ler′ ō fon). The Joseph of Greek mythology; Antæa, the wife of Prœtus, being the "Potiphar's wife" who tempted him, and afterwards falsely accused him. Her husband, Prœtus, sent Bellerophon with a letter to Iobates, the King of Lycia, his wife's father, recounting the charge, and praying that the bearer might be put to death. Iobates, unwilling to slay him himself, gave him many hazardous tasks (including the killing of the Chimæra, *q.v.*), but as he was successful in all of them Iobates made him his heir. Later Bellerophon is fabled to have attempted to fly to heaven on the winged horse Pegasus, but Zeus sent a gadfly to sting the horse, and the rider was thrown.

Bellerophon has frequently been used for the name of a ship in the British Navy. The most famous took part in the Battle of the Nile, Trafalgar, etc., and was the vessel in which Napoleon surrendered himself to the British and which brought him to England. It was corrupted by sailors, etc., to "Billy Ruffian," "Bully-ruffran," "Belly-ruffron," etc.

Why, she and the Belly-ruffron seem to have pretty well shared and shared alike.—Captain MARRYAT: *Poor Jack*, ch. xiii.

Bellerus (bĕ lē′ rŭs). The name of a giant invented by Milton by way of accounting for "Bellerium," the old Roman name for the Land's End district of Cornwall:

Sleep'st by the fable of Bellerus old.
MILTON: *Lycidas*, 160.

Milton had originally written "Corineus" (*q.v.*), a name already well known in British legend.

Bellona. In Roman mythology, the goddess of war and wife (or sometimes sister) of Mars. She was probably in origin a Sabine deity.

Belly. The belly and its members. The fable of Menenius Agrippa to the Roman people when they seceded to the *Sacred Mount*: "Once on a time the members refused to work for the lazy belly; but, as the supply of food was thus stopped, they found there was a necessary and mutual dependence between them." The fable is given by Æsop and by Plutarch, whence Shakespeare introduces it in his *Coriolanus*, i, 1.

The belly has no ears. A hungry man will not listen to advice or arguments. The Romans had the same proverb, *Venter non habet aures*; and in French, *Ventre affamé n'a point d'oreilles.*

Belomancy (bel' ō măn si) (Gr). Divination by arrows. Labels being attached to a given number of arrows, the archers let them fly, and the advice on the label of the arrow which flies farthest is accepted and acted on. Sir Thomas Browne describes a method of belomancy in *Pseudodoxia Epidemica*, v, 23, and says that it—

hath been in request with Scythians, Alanes, Germans, with the Africans and Turks of Algier.

Beloved Disciple. St. John. (*John* xiii, 23, etc.)

Beloved Physician. St. Luke. (*Col.* iv, 14.)

Belphœbe (bel fē' bi). The huntress-goddess in Spenser's *Faerie Queene*, daughter of Chrysogone and sister of Amoret, typifies Queen Elizabeth as a model of chastity. She was of the Diana and Minerva type; cold as an icicle, passionless, immovable, and, like a moonbeam, light without warmth.

Belt. To hit below the belt. To strike unfairly. It is prohibited in the Queensberry rules of prize fighting to hit below the waist-belt.

Belted Will. Lord William Howard (1563-1640), a Border chief, son of the fourth Duke of Norfolk, and warden of the western marches. He was so called by Scott. To his contemporaries he was known as "Bould Wullie." His wife was called "Bessie with the braid apron."

Beltane (bel' tān). In Scotland, old Mayday, the beginning of summer; also the festival that was held on that day, a survival of the ancient heathen festival inaugurating the summer, at which the Druids lit two "bel-fires" between which the cattle were driven, either preparatory to sacrifice or to protect them against disease. The word is Gaelic, and means literally "the blaze-kindling."

Belvedere (bel' vė dēr). A sort of pleasure house built on an eminence in a garden, from which one can survey the surrounding prospect, or a look-out on the top of a house. The word is Italian, and means a *fine sight.*

Benares (ben âr' ēz). The holy city of the Hindus, being to them what Mecca is to the Moslems. It was founded about 1200 B.C. and was for many years a Buddhist centre, being conquered by the Mohammedans in 1193. It is celebrated for its temples and shrines to which pilgrims go from all India.

Benbow. A name almost typical of a brave sailor, from John Benbow (1653-1702), a noted English Admiral. It is told of him that in an engagement with the French near St. Martha, on the Spanish coast, in 1701, his legs and thighs were shivered into splinters by a chain-shot, but, supported in a wooden frame, he remained on the quarter deck till morning, when Du Casse bore away. Almeyda, the Portuguese governor of India, in his engagement with the united fleet of Cambaya and Egypt, had his legs and thighs shattered in a similar manner; but, instead of retreating, had himself bound to the ship's mast, where he "waved his sword to cheer on the combatants," till he died from loss of blood.

Whirled by the cannon's rage, in shivers torn,
His thighs far shattered o'er the waves are borne;
Bound to the mast the god-like hero stands,
Waves his proud sword and cheers his woeful bands;
Though winds and seas their wonted aid deny,
To yield he knows not but he knows to die.
CAMOËNS: *Lusiad*, Bk. x.

Somewhat similar stories are told of Cynægiros and Jaafer (*qq.v.*).

Bench. Originally the same word as BANK, it means, properly, a long wooden seat, hence the official seat of judges in Court, bishops in the House of Lords, aldermen in the council chamber, etc.; hence, by extension judges, bishops, etc., collectively, the court or place where they administer justice or sit officially, the dignity of holding such an official status, etc. Hence **Bench of bishops.** The whole body of prelates, who sit in the House of Lords.

To be raised to the bench. To be made a judge.

To be raised to the Episcopal bench. To be made a bishop.

King's (or **Queen's**) **Bench.** *See* KING'S.

Bench and Bar. Judges and barristers. *See* BAR; BARRISTER.

Benchers. Senior members of the Inns of Court. They exercise the functions of calling students to the bar (*q.v.*). and have powers of expulsion.

Bendemeer (ben' de mēr). A river that flows near the ruins of Chilminar or Istachar, in the province of Chusistan, in Persia.

There's a bower of roses by Bendemeer's stream,
And the nightingale sings round it all the day long.
MOORE: *Lalla Rookh*, I.

Bender. A sixpenny-piece; perhaps because it can be bent without much difficulty. Also (in schoolboy slang) a "licking" with the cane, the culprit being in a bent position. In Scotland it is an old term for a hard drinker, and in the United States it is still given to a drinking bout.

Benedicite (ben e dīs' i ti). The 2nd pers. pl. imperative of the Latin verb, *benedicere*, meaning "bless you," or "may you be blessed." In the first given sense it is the opening word of many old graces ("Bless ye the Lord," etc.); hence, a grace, or a blessing.

The second sense accounts for its use as an interjection or expression of astonishment, as in Chaucer's

> The god of love, A benedicite,
> How myghty and how great a lord is he!
> > *Knight's Tale*, 927.

Benedick. A sworn bachelor caught in the snares of matrimony: from Benedick in Shakespeare's *Much Ado about Nothing*.

> Let our worthy Cantab be bachelor or Benedick, what concern is it of ours.—Mrs. EDWARDS: A *Girton Girl*, ch. xv.

Benedick and Benedict are used indiscriminately, but the distinction should be observed.

Benedict. A bachelor, not necessarily one pledged to celibacy, but simply a man of marriageable age, not married. St. Benedict was a most uncompromising stickler for celibacy.

> Is it not a pun? There is an old saying, "Needles and pins; when a man marries his trouble begins." If so, the unmarried man is *benedictus*.—*Life in the West* (1843).

Benedictine. A liqueur made at the Benedictine monastery at Fécamp, France.

Benedictines. Monks who follow the rule of St. Benedict. They recite the Divine Office at the canonical hours, and are at other times employed in study, teaching or manual labour. They are known as the "Black Monks" (the Dominicans being the *Black Friars*). The Order was founded by St. Benedict at Subiaco and Monte Cassino, Italy, about 530, and its members have from the earliest times been renowned for their learning. A similar order for nuns was founded by St. Scholastica, sister of St. Benedict.

Benefice. Under the Romans certain grants of lands made to veteran soldiers were called *beneficia*, and in feudal times an estate held for life in return for military or other service *ex mero beneficio* of the donor was called "a benefice." When the popes assumed the power of the feudal lords with reference to ecclesiastical patronage the name was retained for a "living."

Benefit of Clergy. Originally, the privilege of exemption from trial by a secular court enjoyed by the clergy if arrested for felony. In time it comprehended not only the ordained clergy, but all who, being able to write and read, were capable of entering into holy orders. It seems to have been based on the text, "Touch not mine anointed, and do my prophets no harm" (1 *Chron.* xvi, 22), and it was finally abolished in the reign of George IV (1827). *Cp.* NECK-VERSE.

Benevolence. A means of raising money by forced loans and without the instrumentality of Parliament, first resorted to in 1473 by Edward IV. It seems to have been used for the last time by James I in 1614, but it was not declared illegal till the passing of the Bill of Rights in 1689.

Bengal Tigers. The old 17th Foot, whose badge, a royal tiger, was granted them for their services in India (1802-23). Now the Leicester Regiment and known simply as "The Tigers."

Benjamin. The pet, the youngest; in allusion to Benjamin, the youngest son of Jacob (*Gen.* xxxv, 18). Also (in early- and mid-19th cent.), an overcoat; so called from a tailor of the name, and rendered popular by its association with Joseph's "coat of many colours."

Benjamin's mess. The largest share. The allusion is to the banquet given by Joseph, viceroy of Egypt, to his brethren. "Benjamin's mess was five times so much as any of theirs" (*Gen.* xliii, 34).

Benjamin tree. A tree of the Styrax family that yields benzoin, of which the name is a corruption, and so used by Ben Jonson in *Cynthia's Revels* (V, ii), where the Perfumer says:—

> Taste, smell; I assure you, sir, pure benjamin, the only spirited scent that ever awaked a Neapolitan nostril.

Benthos (ben′ thos). This is a new word in English, coming directly from a Greek word meaning the sea-bottom. It is now applied particularly to the bottom of deep oceans and to the minute aquatic organisms that live down there.

Beowulf (bā′ ō wulf). The hero of the ancient Anglo-Saxon epic poem of the same name, of unknown date and authorship, but certainly written before the coming of the Saxons to England, and modified subsequent to the introduction of Christianity.

The scene is laid in Denmark or Sweden: the hall (Heorot) of King Hrothgar is raided nightly by Grendel (*q.v.*), whom Beowulf mortally wounds after a fierce fight. Grendel's dam comes next night to avenge his death. Beowulf pursues her to her lair under the water and ultimately slays her with a magic sword. Beowulf in time becomes king, and fifty years later meets his death in combat with a dragon, the guardian of an immense hoard, the faithful Wiglaf being his only follower at the end.

The epic as we know it dates from the 8th century, but it probably represents a gradual growth which existed in many successive versions. In any case, it is not only the oldest epic in English, but the oldest in the whole Teutanic group of languages.

Berenice. The sister-wife of Ptolemy Euergetes, king of Egypt (247-222 B.C.). She vowed to sacrifice her hair to the gods, if her husband returned home the vanquisher of Asia. She suspended her hair in the temple of Arsinoe at Zephyrium, but it was stolen the first night, and Conon of Samos told the king that the winds had wafted it to heaven, where it still forms the seven stars near the tail of Leo, called *Coma Berenices*. The story has been used as the subject of many great works, particularly Racine's tragedy and an opera by Handel.

Bergomask (ber' gō mask). A rustic dance (*see Midsummer Night's Dream*, v, 1); so called from Bergamo, a Venetian province, the inhabitants of which were noted for their clownishness. Also, a clown.

Berkshire (bark' shĕr). From the A.S. *Berrocshyre*, either from its abundance of *berroc* (box-trees), or the *bare-oak-shire*, from a polled oak common in Windsor Forest, where the Britons used to hold meetings

Berlin. An old-fashioned four-wheeled carriage with a hooded seat behind. It was introduced into England by a German officer about 1670.

Berlin Decree. A decree issued at Berlin by Napoleon I in November, 1806, forbidding any of the nations of Europe to trade with Great Britain, proclaiming her to be in a state of blockade, declaring all British property forfeit, and all British subjects on French soil prisoners of war.

Bermoothes (bĕr mō ooth' ēz). The name of the island in *The Tempest*, feigned by Shakespeare to be enchanted and inhabited by witches and devils.

From the still-vexed Bermoothës, there she's hid.
The Tempest, i, 2.

Shakespeare almost certainly had the recently discovered Bermudas in his mind.

Bermudas (bĕr mū' dàz). The Bermudas was an old name for a district of London—thought to have been the narrow alleys in the neighbourhood of Covent Garden, St. Martin's Lane, and the Strand—which was an Alsatia (*q.v.*), where the residents had certain privileges against arrest. Hence, **to live in the Bermudas**, to skulk in some out-of-the-way place for cheapness or safety.

Bernardine. A monk of the Order of St. Bernard of Clairvaux; a Cistercian (*q.v.*).

Bernardo del Carpio. A semi-mythical Spanish hero of the 9th century, and a favourite subject of the minstrels, and of Lope de Vega who wrote many plays around his exploits.

He is credited with having defeated Roland at Roncesvalles.

Bernesque Poetry. Serio-comic poetry; so called from Francesco Berni (1498-1535), of Tuscany, who greatly excelled in it. Byron's *Beppo* is a good example of English bernesque; and concerning it Byron wrote to John Murray, his publisher:—

Whistlecraft is my immediate model, but Berni is the father of that kind of writing.

Berserker. In Scandinavian mythology, a wild, ferocious, warlike being who was at times possessed of supernatural strength and fury. The origin of the name is doubtful; one account says that it was that of the grandson of the eight-handed Starkader and the beautiful Alfhilde, who was called *bœr-serce* (bare of mail) because he went into battle unharnessed. Hence, any man with the fighting fever on him.

Another disregards this altogether and holds that the name means simply "men who have assumed the form of bears." It is used in English both as an adjective denoting excessive fury and a noun denoting one possessed of such.

Berth. He has tumbled into a nice berth. A nice situation or fortune. The place in which a ship is anchored is called its berth, and the sailors call it a *good* or *bad* berth as they think it favourable or otherwise. The space also allotted to a seaman for his hammock is called his berth.

To give a wide berth. Not to come near a person; to keep a person at a distance; literally, to give a ship plenty of room to swing at anchor.

Bertha, Frau. A German impersonation of the Epiphany, corresponding to the Italian Befana (*q.v.*). She is a white lady, who steals softly into nurseries and rocks infants asleep, but is the terror of all naughty children. Her feet are very large, and she has an iron nose.

Berthe au Grand Pied (bert ō gron pē ā). Mother of Charlemagne, and great-grand-daughter of Charles Martel; so called because she had a club-foot. She died at an advanced age in 783.

Bertram, Count of Rousillon, beloved by Helena, the hero of Shakespeare's *All's Well that Ends Well*.

I cannot reconcile my heart to Bertram, a man noble without generosity, and young without truth; who marries Helena as a coward, and leaves her as a profligate.— Dr. JOHNSON.

Besaile. A word formerly used in England for a great-grandfather, it is the French *bisaieul*.

Writ of besaile. An old legal term meaning:—

A writ that lies for the heire, where his great grandfather was seized the day that he died, or died seised of Land in fee-simple, and a stranger enters the day of the death of the great grandfather, or abates after his death, the heire shall have writ against such a disseisor or abator.—*Termes de la Ley* (1641).

Besant. *See* BEZANT.

Beside the Cushion, an odd phrase first used by Judge Jeffreys in the sense of "beside the question," "not to the point." Any cogent point raised by some wretch in his own defence was ruthlessly swept away as "beside the cushion."

Besom. To hang out the besom. To have a fling when your wife is gone on a visit. To be a quasi bachelor once more. *Cp.* the French colloquialism, *rôtir le balai.*

(Literally, "to roast the besom") which means "to live a fast life" or "to go on the razzle-dazzle."

Bess, Good Queen. Queen Elizabeth I (1533-1603).

Bess of Hardwick. Elizabeth Talbot, Countess of Shrewsbury (1518-1608), to whose charge, in 1569, Mary Queen of Scots was committed. The countess treated the captive queen with great harshness, being jealous of the earl her husband. Bess of Hardwick married four times: Robert Barlow (when she was only fourteen); Sir William Cavendish; Sir William St. Loe, Captain of Queen Elizabeth's Guard; and lastly, George, sixth Earl of Shrewsbury. She built Hardwick Hall, and founded the wealth and dignity of the Cavendish family.

Best. At best or **At the very best.** Looking at the matter in the most favourable light. Making every allowance.

Man is a short-sighted creature at best—DEFOE: *Colonel Jack.*

At one's best. At the highest or best point attainable by the person referred to.

For the best. With the best of motives; with the view of obtaining the best results.

I must make the best of my way home. It is getting late and I must use my utmost diligence to get home as soon as possible.

To best somebody. To get the better of him; to outwit him and so have the advantage.

To have the best of it, or, **To have the best of the bargain.** To have the advantage or best of a transaction.

To make the best of the matter. To submit to ill-luck with the best grace in your power.

See also BETTER.

Bestiaries or **Bestials.** Books very popular in the 11th, 12th, and 13th centuries, containing accounts of the supposed habits and peculiarities of animals, which, with the legendary lore connected with them, served as texts for devotional homilies. They were founded on the old *Physiologi,* and those in

English were, for the most part, translations of Continental originals. The *Bestiaires* of Philippe de Thaon, Guillaume le Clerc, and *Le Bestiaire d'Amour,* by Richard de Fournival, were among the most popular.

Bête Noire (bāt nwar) (Fr. black beast). The thorn in the side, the bitter in the cup, the spoke in the wheel, the black sheep, the object of aversion. A black sheep has always been considered an eyesore in a flock, and its wool is really less valuable. In times of superstition it was looked on as bearing the devil's mark.

The Dutch sale of tin is the *bête noire* of the Cornish miners.—*The Times.*

Bethlehemites. An order of reformed Dominicans, the friars of which wore a star upon the breast in memory of the Star of Bethlehem, introduced into England about 1257. Also a branch of the Augustinians, founded in Guatemala in 1653 by Peter Betancus, a native of the Canaries, for spreading the Gospel and serving the sick in Spanish America. Its members wore a shield on the right shoulder, on which was shown the manger of Bethlehem.

Bethlemenites. Followers of John Huss, so called because he used to preach in the church called Bethlehem of Prague.

Bethnal Green. *See* BEGGAR'S DAUGHTER.

Betrothal. An engagement is nowadays considered a more or less private affair which may or may not be made the occasion of celebrations. It was formerly—and still is on the Continent—a ceremony of more public importance. Canon law recognizes betrothal as a formal ceremony consisting of an exchange of rings (hence the English engagement ring), a kiss (not unknown in England either), and the joining of hands in the presence of witnesses. In France all this had to be done in the presence of the parish priest. It was also usual for the parties to break a coin and each keep a portion. This ceremony was binding, though the engagement could be broken by mutual consent. The Church, however, reserved to itself the right to excommunicate either party who, without cause or agreement with the other, broke it off. In England the Civil Law came down in the same sense when, in 1735, an Act was passed enabling an aggrieved party to bring an action at common law for breach of promise.

Betrothed, The. Curiously enough, this title was chosen independently of one another by two great writers who published historical novels in the same year, 1825. Sir Walter Scott's *Betrothed* is a tale of the Crusaders and Wales;

Manzoni's *Betrothed* (*I Promessi Sposi*) is about Milan in the 17th century.

Better. Better off. In easier circumstances.

For better for worse. For ever. From the English marriage service, expressive of an indissoluble union.

My better half. A jocose way of saying my wife. As the twain are one, each is half. Horace calls his friend *animœ dimidium meœ* (*Odes* 1, iii, 8).

To be better than his word. To do more than he promised.

To think better of the matter. To give it further consideration; to form a more correct opinion respecting it.

Between. Between hay and grass. Neither one thing nor yet another; a hobbledehoy, neither a man nor yet a boy.

Between cup and lip. *See* SLIP.

Between Scylla and Charybdis. *See* CHARYBDIS.

Between two fires. Between two dangers. Troops caught between fire from opposite sides

Between two stools you fall to the ground. The allusion is to a practical joke played at sea, in which two stools are set side by side, and it is arranged that the victim shall unexpectedly fall between them. Compare:—

> Like a man to double business bound,
> I stand in pause where I shall first begin,
> And both neglect.
>   SHAKESPEARE: *Hamlet*, ii, 3.

He who hunts two hares leaves one and loses the other.

Simul sorbere ac flare non possum.

Between you and me. In confidence be it spoken. Sometimes, **Between you and me and the gatepost** (or **bed-post**). These phrases, for the most part, indicate that some illnatured remark or slander is about to be made of a third person, but occasionally they refer to some offer or private affair. **Between ourselves** is another form of the same phrase.

Betwixt. Betwixt and between. Neither one nor the other, but somewhere between the two. Thus, grey is neither white nor black, but betwixt and between the two.

Betwixt wind and water. A nautical phrase denoting that part of the hull that is below the water-line except when the ship heels over under pressure of the wind. It was a most dangerous place for a man-of-war to be shot in; hence a "knock-out" blow is often said to have caught the victim betwixt wind and water.

Sir Bevis of Hamtown. A mediæval chivalric romance, slightly connected with the Charlemagne cycle, which (in the English version) tells how the father of Bevis was slain by the mother, and how, on Bevis trying to avenge the murder, she sold him into slavery to Eastern merchants. After many adventures he converts and carries off Josian, daughter of the Soldan, returns to England, gets his revenge, and all ends happily. "Ham-town" is generally taken as meaning "Southampton," but it is really a corruption of *Antona*, for in the original Italian version the hero is called "Beuves d'Antone," which, in the French, became "Beuves d'Hantone." Drayton tells the story in his *Polyolbion*, Song ii, lines 260-384.

Bevoriskius (be vôr is' ki ús), whose *Commentary on the Generations of Adam* is referred to by Sterne in the *Sentimental Journey*, was Johan van Beverwyck (1594-1647), a Dutch medical writer and author of a large number of books.

Bevy. A throng or company of ladies, roebucks, quails, or larks. The word is the Italian *bevu*, a drink, but it is not known how it acquired its present meaning. It may be because timid, gregarious animals, in self-defence, go down to a river to drink in companies.

> And upon her deck what a bevy of human flowers—
> young women, how lovely!—young men, how noble!—
>   DE QUINCEY: *Dream-fugue*.

Bezaliel (be zā' el). In Dryden's *Absalom and Achitophel* is meant for Henry Somerset, 3rd Marquis of Worcester and 1st Duke of Beaufort (1629-1700). He was an adherent of Charles II.

> Bezaliel with each grace and virtue fraught,
> Serene his looks, serene his life and thought;
> On whom so largely Nature heaped her store,
> There scarce remained for arts to give him more.
>   Pt. ii, 947.

Bezant (be zănt') (from *Byzantium*, the old name of Constantinople). A gold coin of greatly varying value struck at Constantinople by the Byzantine Emperors. It was current in England till the time of Edward III. In *heraldry*, the name is given to a plain gold roundel borne as a charge, and supposed to indicate that the bearer had been a Crusader.

Bezoar (bă' zōr). A stone from the stomach or gall-bladder of an animal, set as a jewel and believed to be an antidote against poison.

Bezonian (be zō' ni àn). A new recruit; applied originally in derision to young soldiers sent from Spain to Italy, who landed both ill-accoutred and in want of everything (Ital. *besogni*, from *bisogno*, need; Fr. *besoin*). "Under which king, bezonian? Speak or die" (*2 Hen. IV*, v, 3). Choose your leader or take the consequences.

> Great men oft die by vile bezonians.
>   SHAKESPEARE: *2 Henry VI*, iv, 1.

Bias (bī′ ǎs). The weight in bowls which makes them deviate from the straight line; hence any favourite idea or pursuit, or whatever predisposes the mind in a particular direction.

Bowls are not now loaded, but the bias depends on the shape of the bowls. They are flattened on one side, and therefore roll obliquely.

Your stomach makes your fabric roll
Just as the bias rules the bowl.
PRIOR: *Alma*, iii.

Bible, The English. The principal versions of the English Bible in chronological order are: —

Wyclif's Bible. The name given to two translations of the Vulgate, one completed in 1380 and the other a few years later, in neither of which was Wyclif concerned as a translator. Nicholas of Hereford made the first version as far as *Baruch* iii, 20; who was responsible for the remainder is unknown. The second version has been ascribed to John Purvey, a follower of Wyclif. The Bible of 1380 was the first complete version in English; as a whole it remained unprinted until 1850, when the monumental edition of the two versions by Forshall and Madden appeared, but in 1810 an edition of the New Testament was published by H. H. Baber, an assistant librarian at the British Museum.

Tyndale's Bible. This consists of the New Testament (printed at Cologne, 1525), the Pentateuch (Marburg, Hesse, 1530 or 1531), *Jonah*, Old Testament lessons appointed to be read in place of the Epistles, and a MS. translation of the Old Testament to the end of *Chronicles* which was afterwards used in Matthew's Bible (*q.v.*). His revisions of the New Testament were issued in 1534 and 1535. Tyndale's principal authority was Erasmus's edition of the Greek Testament, but he also used Erasmus's Latin translation of the same, the Vulgate, and Luther's German version. Tyndale's version fixed the style and tone of the English Bible, and subsequent Protestant versions of the books on which he worked should—with one or two minor exceptions—be looked upon as revisions of his, and not as independent translations.

Coverdale's Bible. The first complete English Bible to be printed, published in 1535 as a translation out of Douche (*i.e.* German) and Latin by Myles Coverdale. It consists of Tyndale's translation of the Pentateuch and New Testament, with translations from the Vulgate, a Latin version (1527-8) by the Italian Catholic theologian, Sanctes Peginus, Luther's German version (1534) and the Swiss-German version of Zwingli and Leo Juda (Zurich, 1527-9). The first edition was printed at Antwerp, but the second (Southwark, 1537) was the first Bible printed in England. Matthew's Bible (*q.v.*) is largely based on Cover-dale's. *See* BUG BIBLE *below.*

Matthew's Bible. A pronouncedly Protestant version published in 1537 as having been "truly and purely translated into English by Thomas Matthew," which was a pseudonym, adopted for purposes of safety, of John Rogers, an assistant of Tyndale. It was probably printed at Antwerp, and the text is made up of the Pentateuch from Tyndale's version together with his hitherto unprinted translation of *Joshua* to 2 *Chronicles* inclusive and his revised edition of the New Testament, with Coverdale's version of the rest of the Old Testament and the Apocrypha. It was quickly superseded by the Great Bible (*q.v.*), but it is of importance as it formed the starting-point for the revisions which culminated in the Authorized Version. *See* BUG BIBLE *below.*

The Great Bible. Coverdale's revision of his own Bible of 1535 (*see* COVERDALE'S BIBLE *above*), collated with Tyndale's and Matthew's, printed in Paris by Regnault, and published by Grafton and Whitchurch in 1539. It is a large folio, and a splendid specimen of typography. It is sometimes called "Cromwell's Bible," as it was undertaken at his direction, and it was made compulsory for all parish churches to purchase a copy. The Prayer Book version of the Psalms comes from I the November, 1540, edition of the Great Bible. *See also* CRANMER'S BIBLE.

Cranmer's Bible. The name given to the Great Bible (*q.v.*) of 1540. It, and later issues, contained a prologue by Cranmer, and on the wood-cut title-page (by Holbein) Henry VIII is shown seated while Cranmer and Cromwell distribute copies to the people.

Cromwell's Bible. The Great Bible (*q.v.*) of 1539. The title-page (*see* CRANMER'S BIBLE *above*) includes a portrait of Thomas Cromwell.

The Bishops' Bible. A version made at the instigation of Archbishop Parker (hence also called "Matthew Parker's Bible"), to which most of the Anglican bishops were contributors. It was a revision of the Great Bible (*q.v.*), first appeared in 1568, and by 1602 had reached its eighteenth edition. It is this edition that forms the basis of our Authorized Version. *See* TREACLE BIBLE *below.*

The Geneva Bible. A revision of great importance in the history of the English Bible, undertaken by English exiles at Geneva during

the Marian persecutions and first published in
1560. It was the work of William Whittingham,
assisted by Anthony Gilby and Thomas Sampson.
Whittingham had previously(1557) published
a translation of the New Testament. The
Genevan version was the first English Bible to
be printed in roman type instead of black letter,
the first in which the chapters are divided into
verses (taken by Whittingham from Robert
Stephen's Greek-Latin Testament of 1537), and
the first in which italics are used for explanatory and connective words and phrases (taken
from Beza's New Testament of 1556). It was
immensely popular; from 1560 to 1616 no year
passed without a new edition, and at least two
hundred are known. In every edition the word
"breeches" occurs in *Gen.* iii, 7; hence the
Geneva Bible is popularly known as the
"Breeches Bible" (*q.v.*). *See* GOOSE BIBLE,
PLACE-MAKERS' BIBLE, *below.*

The Authorized Version. This, the version
in general use in England, was made by a body
of scholars working at the command of King
James I (hence sometimes called "King James's
Bible") from 1604 to 1611, and was published
in 1611. The modern "Authorized Version" is,
however, by no means an exact reprint of that
authorized by King James; a large number of
typographical errors which occurred in the first
edition have been corrected, the orthography,
punctuation, etc., has been modernized, and
the use of italics, capital letters, etc., varied.
The Bishops' Bible (*q.v.*) was used as the basis
of the text, but Tyndale's, Matthew's, Coverdale's,
and the Geneva translations were also followed
when they agreed better with the original.

King James's Bible. The Authorized Version
(*q.v.*).

Matthew Parker's Bible. The Bishops'
Bible (*q.v.*).

There have been several versions of the
scriptures in modern English, of which the
following are noteworthy:

The New Testament in Modern Speech,
translated from the Greek by R. F. Weymouth,
1903.

A new translation of the Bible by James
Moffat (N.T., 1913; O.T., 1924).

A new translation from the Vulgate by R. A.
Knox, 1944.

SPECIALLY NAMED EDITIONS OF THE BIBLE.
The following Bibles are named either from
typographical errors or archaic words that they
contain, or from some special circumstance in
connexion with them:—

Adulterous Bible. The "Wicked Bible" (*q.v.*).

Affinity Bible, of 1923, which contains a
table of affinity with the error: "A man may not
marry his grandmother's wife."

Bedell's Bible. A translation of the Authorized Version into Irish carried out under the
direction of Bedell (d. 1642), Bishop of Kilmore
and Ardagh.

The Breeches Bible. The Genevan Bible
(*see above*) was popularly so called because in it
Gen. iii, 7, was rendered, "The eyes of them
bothe were opened . . . and they sowed figge-tree
leaves together, and made themselves breeches."
This reading occurs in every edition of the
Genevan Bible, but not in any other version,
though it is given in the then unprinted Wyclif
MS. ("ya swiden ye levis of a fige tre and madin
brechis"), and also in the translation of the
Pentateuch given in Caxton's edition of Voragine's
Golden Legend (1483).

The Brother's Bible. The "Kralitz Bible"
(*q.v.*).

The Bug Bible. Coverdale's Bible (*q.v.*), of
1535, is so called because *Ps.* xci, 5, is translated,
"Thou shalt not nede to be afrayed for eny
bugges by night." The same reading occurs in
Matthew's Bible (*q.v.*) and its reprints; the
Authorized and Revised Versions both read
"terror."

The Ferrara Bible. The first Spanish edition
of the Old Testament, translated from the
Hebrew in 1553 for the use of the Spanish Jews.
A second edition was published in the same
year for Christians.

The Fool Bible. During the reign of Charles I
an edition of the Bible was printed in which the
text of Psalm xliv, 1 read "The fool hath said in
his heart there is a God." For this mistake the
printers were fined £3,000 and all copies were
suppressed.

Forgotten Sins Bible, of 1638. *Luke* vii, 47
reads "Her sins which are many are forgotten."

The Forty-two Line Bible. The "Mazarin
Bible" (*q.v.*).

The Goose Bible. The editions of the
Genevan Bible (*q.v.*) printed at Dort; the Dort
press had a goose as its device.

The Gutenberg Bible. The "Mazarin
Bible" (*q.v.*).

The He Bible. In the two earliest editions of
the Authorized Version (both 1611) in the first
(now known as "the He Bible") *Ruth* iii, 15,
reads: "and *he* went into the city"; the other
(known as "the She Bible") has the variant
"*she.*" "He" is the correct translation of the

Hebrew, but nearly all modern editions—with the exception of the Revised Version—perpetuate the confusion and print "she."

The Idle Bible. An edition of 1809, in which "the idole shepherd" (*Zech.* xi, 17) is printed "the idle shepherd." In the Revised Version the translation is "the worthless shepherd."

Incunabula Bible. The date on the title-page reads 1495 instead of 1594.

The Leda Bible. The third edition (second folio) of the Bishops' Bible (*q.v.*), published in 1572, and so called because the decoration to the initial at the *Epistle to the Hebrews* is a startling and incongruous woodcut of Jupiter visiting Leda in the guise of a swan. This, and several other decorations in the New Testament of this edition, were from an edition of Ovid's *Metamorphoses*; they created such a storm of protest that they were never afterwards used.

The Lions Bible. A Bible issued in 1804 contains a great number of printers' errors of which the following are typical: *Numbers*, xxxv, 18, "The murderer shall surely be put together" instead of "to death"; 1 *Kings* viii, 19, "but thy son that shall come forth out of thy lions" instead of "loins"; *Galatians* v, 17, "For the flesh lusteth after the Spirit" instead of "against the Spirit".

The Mazarin Bible. The first printed Bible (an edition of the Vulgate), and the first known book to be printed from movable type. It contains no date, but was printed probably in 1455, and was certainly on sale by the middle of 1456. It was printed at Mainz, probably by Fust and Schoeffer, but as it was for long credited to Gutenberg—and it is not yet agreed that he was not responsible—it is frequently called the **Gutenberg Bible.** By bibliographers it is usually known as the *Forty-two Line Bible* (it having 42 lines to the page), to differentiate it from the Bamberg Bible of 36 lines. Its popular name is due to the fact that the copy discovered in the Mazarin Library, Paris, in 1760, was the first to be known and described. A copy of Vol. I in unusually fine state and contemporary binding fetched a record price of £21,000 at auction in London, in 1947.

The Old Cracow Bible. The "Leopolita Bible" (*q.v.*).

The Ostrog Bible. The first complete Slavonic edition; printed at Ostrog, Volhynia, Russia, in 1581.

Pfister's Bible. The "Thirty-six Line Bible" (*q.v.*).

The Place-makers' Bible. The second edition of the Geneva Bible (*q.v.*), 1562; so called from a printer's error in *Matt*, v, 9, "Blessed are the placemakers [peacemakers], for they shall be called the children of God." It has also been called the "Whig Bible."

The Printers' Bible. An edition of about 1702 which makes David pathetically complain that "printers [princes] have persecuted me without a cause" (*Ps.* cxix, 161).

The Proof Bible (Probe-Bibel). The revised version of the first impression of Luther's German Bible. A final revised edition appeared in 1892.

The Rosin Bible. The Douai Bible (*q.v.*). 1609, is sometimes so called, because it has in *Jer.* viii, 22: "Is there noe rosin in Galaad." The Authorized Version translates the word by "balm," but gives "rosin" in the margin as an alternative. *Cp.* Treacle Bible *below*.

Schelhorn's Bible. A name sometimes given to the "Thirty-six Line Bible" (*q.v.*).

The September Bible. Luther's German translation of the New Testament, published anonymously at Wittenberg in September, 1522.

Sting Bible, of 1746. *Mark* vii, 35 reads "the sting of his tongue" instead of "string."

The Thirty-six Line Bible. A Latin Bible of 36 lines to the column, probably printed by A. Pfister at Bamberg in 1460. It is also known as the Bamberg, and Pfister's, Bible, and sometimes as Schelhorn's, as it was first described by the German bibliographer J. G. Schelhorn, in 1760.

The To-remain Bible. In a Bible printed at Cambridge in 1805 *Gal.* iv, 29, reads: "Persecuted him that was born after the spirit to remain, even so it is now." The words "to remain" were added in error by the compositor, the editor having answered a proofreader's query as to the comma after "spirit" with the pencilled reply "to remain" in the margin. The mistake was repeated in the first 8vo edition published by the Bible Society (1805), and again in their 12mo edition dated 1819.

The Treacle Bible. A popular name for the Bishops' Bible (*q.v.*), 1568, because in it, *Jer.* viii, 22, reads: "Is there no tryacle in Gilead, is there no phisition there?" *Cp.* Rosin Bible *above*. In the same Bible "tryacle" is also given for "balm" in *Jer.* xlvi, 11, and *Ezek.* xxvii, 17. Coverdale's Bible (1535) also uses the word "triacle." *See* Treacle.

The Unrighteous Bible. An edition printed at Cambridge in 1653, containing the printer's error, "Know ye not that the unrighteous shall inherit [for *shall not inherit*] the Kingdom of

God?" (1 *Cor.* vi, 9). The same edition gave *Rom.* vi, 13, as: "Neither yield ye your members as instruments of righteousness unto sin," in place of "*unrighteousness.*" This is also sometimes known as the "Wicked Bible."

The Vinegar Bible. An edition printed at Oxford in 1717 in which the chapter heading to *Luke* xx is given as "The parable of the Vinegar" (instead of "Vineyard").

The Whig Bible. Another name for the "Place-makers' Bible" (*q.v.*).

The Wicked Bible. So called because the word *not* is omitted in the seventh commandment, making it, "Thou shalt commit adultery." Printed at London by Barker and Lucas, 1632. The "Unrighteous Bible" (*q.v.*) is also sometimes called by this name.

The Zurich Bible. A German version of 1530 composed of Luther's translation of the New Testament and portions of the Old, with the remainder and the Apocrypha by other translators

STATISTICS OF THE BIBLE. The following statistics are those given in the *Introduction to the Critical Study and Knowledge of the Bible*, by Thos. Hartwell Horne, D.D., first published in 1818. They apply to the English Authorized Version.

	O.T.	N.T.	Total.
Books	39	27	66
Chapters	929	260	1,189
Verses	23,214	7,959	31,173
Words	593,493	181,253	774,746
Letters	2,728,100	838,380	3,566,480

Apocrypha. Books, 14; chapters, 183; verses, 6,031; words, 125,185; letters, 1,063,876.

	O.T.	N.T.
Middle book	Proverbs.	2 Thess.
Middle chapter	Job xxix.	Rom. xiii and xiv.
Middle verse	2 Chron. xx, 17 & 18.	Acts xvii, 17.
Shortest verse	1 Chron. i, 25.	John xi, 35.
Shortest chapter	Psalm cxvii.	
Longest chapter	Psalm cxix.	

Ezra vii, 21, contains all the letters of the alphabet except j.

2 Kings xix, and Isaiah xxxvii, are exactly alike.

The last two verses of 2 Chron. and the opening verses of Ezra are alike.

Ezra ii, and Nehemiah vii, are alike.

The word *and* occurs in the O.T. 35,543 times, and in the N.T. 10,684 times.

The word *Jehovah* occurs 6,855 times, and *Lord* 1,855 times.

About 30 books are mentioned in the Bible, but not included in the canon.

Biblia Pauperum (*the poor man's Bible*). A picture-book, widely used by the illiterate in the Middle Ages in place of the Bible. It was designed to illustrate the leading events in the salvation of man, and later MSS. as a rule had a Latin inscription to each picture. These *biblia* were among the earliest books to be printed, and they remained popular long after the invention of movable type. See MIRROR OF HUMAN SALVATION.

Bibliomancy. Divination by means of the Bible. See SORTES BIBLICÆ.

Bibliomania. A love of books pursued to the point of unreason or madness. There is a legend that Don Vicente, a Spanish scholar, committed murder to obtain possession of what he thought was a unique book.

Bibliophilia is a devotion to books and the collecting of them, that stops short of bibliomania.

Bibulus (bib' ū lŭs). Colleague of Julius Cæsar, a mere cipher in office, whence his name has become proverbial for one in office who is a mere *fainéant*.

Bickerstaff, Isaac. A name assumed by Dean Swift in a satirical pamphlet against Partridge, the almanack-maker. This produced a paper war so diverting that Steele issued the *Tatler* under the editorial name of "Isaac Bickerstaff, Esq., Astrologer" (1709). Later there was an actual Isaac Bickerstaffe, a playwright, born in Ireland in 1735.

Bicorn (bī' kôrn). A mythical beast, fabled by the early French romancers to grow very fat and well-favoured through living on good and enduring husbands. It was the antitype to Chichevache (*q.v.*).

Chichevache (or *lean cow*) was said to live on good women; and a world of sarcasm was conveyed in always representing Chichevache as very poor,—all ribs, in fact—her food being so scarce as to keep her in a wretched state of famine. Bycorne, on the contrary, was a monster who lived on good men; and he was always bursting with fatness; like a prize pig.—SIDNEY LANIER: *Shakespere and his Forerunners*, ch. vi.

Bi-corn (two-horns) contains an allusion to the horned cuckold.

Bid. The modern verb, "to bid," may be from either of the two Anglo-Saxon verbs, (1) *béodan*, meaning to stretch out, offer, present, and hence to inform, proclaim, command, or (2) *biddan*, meaning to importune, beg, pray, and hence also, command. The two words have now become very confused, but the four following examples are from (1), *béodan*:—

To bid fair. To seem likely; as "He bids fair to do well"; "It bids fair to be a fine day."

To bid for (votes). To promise to support in Parliament certain measures, in order to obtain votes.

To bid against one. To offer or promise a higher price for an article at auction.

I bid him defiance. I offer him defiance; I defy him.

The examples next given are derived from (2), *biddan*:—

I bid you good night. I wish you good night, or I pray that you may have a good night. "Bid him welcome."

Neither bid him God speed.—2 *John* 10, 11.

To bid one's beads. To tell off one's prayers by beads. *See* BEADS.

To bid the (marriage) banns. To ask if anyone objects to the marriage of the persons named. "*Si quis*" (*q.v.*).

To bid to the wedding. In the New Testament is to ask to the wedding feast.

Bidding-prayer (A.S. *biddan*; *see* BID). This term, now commonly applied to a prayer for the souls of benefactors said before the sermon, is due to its having been forgotten after the Reformation that when the priest was telling the congregation who or what to remember in "bidding their prayers" he was using the verb in its old sense of "pray," *i.e.* "praying their prayers." Hence, in Elizabeth's time the "bidding of prayers" came to signify "the directing" or "enjoyning" of prayers; and hence the modern meaning.

Biddy (*i.e.* Bridget). A generic name for an Irish servant-maid, as Mike is for an Irish labourer. These generic names were once very common: for example, Tom Tug, a waterman; Jack Pudding, a buffoon; Cousin Jonathan, a citizen of the United States; Cousin Michel, a German; John Bull, an Englishman; Colin Tompon, a Swiss; Nic Frog, a Dutchman; Mossoo, a Frenchman; John Chinaman, and many others.

In Arbuthnot's *John Bull* Nic Frog is certainly a Dutchman; and Frogs are called "Dutch Nightingales." As the French have the reputation of feeding on frogs the word has been transferred to them, but, properly, Nic Frog is a Dutchman.

Bifrost (Icel. *bifa*, tremble, *rost*, path). In Scandinavian mythology, the bridge between heaven and earth, Asgard and Midgard; the rainbow may be considered to be this bridge, and its various colours are the reflections of its precious stones.

The keeper of the bridge is Heimdall (*q.v.*).

Big. To look big. To assume a consequential air.

To look as big as bull beef. To look stout and hearty, as if fed on bull beef. Bull beef was formerly recommended for making men strong and muscular.

To talk big. To boast or brag.

Big Ben. The name given to the large bell in the Clock Tower (or St. Stephen's Tower) at the Houses of Parliament. It weighs $13\frac{1}{2}$ tons, and is named after Sir Benjamin Hall, Chief Commissioner of Works in 1856, when it was cast.

Big Bertha. A gun of large calibre used by the Germans to shell Paris from a range of 75 miles, during the 1914-18 War. It was so named by the French in allusion to Frau Bertha Krupp, of armament fame.

Big-endians. In Shift's *Gulliver's Travels*, a party in the empire of Lilliput, who made it a matter of conscience to break their eggs at the *big end*; they were looked on as heretics by the orthodox party, who broke theirs at the *little end*. The *Big-endians* typify the Catholics, and the *Little-endians* (*q.v.*) the Protestants.

Big Gooseberry Season, The. The "silly season," the dead season, when newspapers are glad of any subject to fill their columns; monster gooseberries will do for such a purpose.

Big House, an American slang term for prison.

Big-wig. A person in authority, a "nob." Of course, the term arises from the custom of judges, bishops, and so on, wearing large wigs. Bishops no longer wear them.

Bigamy (big' à mi). Though many plots and stories have been worked up on the theme of supposed bigamous marriages, the Law is very plain and outspoken on the matter. If a spouse has not been heard of for seven years or more before a second marriage, the prosecution has to prove that the prisoner had good cause to believe that the real spouse was alive; if he or she is able to convince the Court that there was every reason to believe the missing spouse dead, even though seven years had not elapsed since the last communication, the prisoner is entitled to a verdict of Not Guilty. The maximum punishment is seven years' penal servitude.

Bight (bīt). **To hook the bight**—*i.e.* to get entangled. A nautical phrase; the bight is the bend or doubled part of a rope, and when the fluke of one anchor gets into the "bight" of another's cable it is "hooked."

Bilbo (bil' bō). A rapier or sword. So called from Bilbao, in Spain, once famous for its finely tempered blades. Falstaff says to Ford:

I suffered the pangs of three several deaths; first, an intolerable fright, to be detected . . . next, to be compassed, like a good bilbo . . . hilt to point, heel to head; and then . . . —*Merry Wives*, iii, 5.

Bile. It rouses my bile. It makes me angry or indignant. In Latin, *biliosus* (a bilious man) meant a choleric one. According to the ancient theory, bile is one of the humours of the body, black bile is indicative of melancholy, and when excited abnormally bile was supposed to produce choler or rage.

It raised my bile
To see him so reflect their grief aside,
HOOD: *Plea of Midsummer Fairies*, stanza 54.

Bilge-water. Stale dregs; bad beer; any nauseating drink. Slang from the sea; the bilge is the lowest part of a ship, and, as the rain or sea-water which trickles down to this part is hard to get at, it is apt to become foul and very offensive.

In slang *bilge* is any worthless or sickly sentimental stuff.

Bilk. Originally a word used in cribbage, meaning to spoil your adversary's score, to *balk* him; perhaps the two words are mere variants. The usual meaning now is to cheat, to obtain goods and decamp without paying for them; especially to give a cabman less than his fare, and, when remonstrated with, give a false name and address.

Bill. The nose, also called the beak. Hence, "Billy" is slang for a pocket-handkerchief.

Lastly came Winter, clothed all in frize,
  Chattering his teeth for cold that did him chill;
Whilst on his hoary beard his breath did freeze,
And the dull drops that from his purpled bill,
As from a limbeck did adown distill.
SPENSER: *Faerie Queene*, VII, vii, 31.

Bill, A. The draft of an Act of Parliament, When a Bill is passed and has received the royal sanction it becomes an Act.

Bill of exchange. An order transferring a named sum of money at a given date from the debtor ("drawee") to the creditor ("drawer"). The drawee having signed the bill becomes the "acceptor," and the document is then negotiable in commercial circles just as is money itself.

We discovered, many of us for the first time, that the machinery of commerce was moved by bills of exchange. I have some of them—wretched, crinkled, scrawled over, blotched, frowsy—and yet these wretched little scraps of paper moved great ships, laden with thousands of tons of precious cargo, from one end of the world to the other. What was the motive power behind them? The honour of commercial men.—LLOYD GEORGE: *Speech to London Welshmen*, Sept. 19th, 1914.

Bill of fare. A list of the dishes provided, or which may be ordered, at a restaurant, etc.; a menu.

Bill of health. A document, duly signed by the proper authorities, to certify that when the ship set sail no infectious disorder existed in the place. This is a *clean* bill of health, and the term is frequently used figuratively.

A foul bill of health is a document to show that the place was suffering from some infection when the ship set sail. If a captain cannot show a *clean bill*, he is supposed to have a foul one.

Bill of Pains and Penalties. A legislative Act imposing punishment (less than capital) upon a person charged with treason or other high crimes. It is like a Bill of Attainder (*q.v.*), differing from it in that the punishment is never capital and the children are not affected.

Bill of quantities. An abstract of the probable cost of a building, etc.

Bill of Rights. The declaration delivered to the Prince of Orange (William III) on his election to the British throne, and accepted by him, confirming the rights and privileges of the people. (Feb. 13th, 1689.)

Bill of sale. When a person borrows money and delivers goods as security, he gives the lender a "bill of sale," that is, permission to sell the goods if the money is not returned on a stated day.

Bills receivable. Promissory notes, bills of exchange, or other acceptances held by a person to whom the money stated is payable.

Billabong (Austr.). A dried-up water course, from *billa*, a creek, and *bong*, to die.

Billies and Charlies. Bogus medieval metal objects cast in lead or cock-metal (an alloy of lead and copper) and artificially aged with acid. Between 1847 and 1858 William Smith and Charles Eaton produced these objects literally by the thousand and planted them or had them planted on sites being excavated in and around London. Finally exposed as forgeries, the objects are affectionally known by the names of their manufacturers and today command a market as ingenious curiosities.

Billingsgate. The site of an old passage through that part of the city wall that protected London on the river side: so called from the Billings, who were the royal race of the Varini, an ancient tribe mentioned by Tacitus. Billingsgate has been the site of a fish-market for many centuries, and its porters, etc., were famous for their foul and abusive language at least three hundred years ago.

Parnassus spoke the cant of Billingsgate.
DRYDEN: *Art of Poetry*, c, 1.

To talk Billingsgate. To slang; to use foul, abusive language; to scold in a vulgar, coarse style.

You are no better than a Billingsgate fish-fag.
You are as rude and ill-mannered as the women
of Billingsgate fish-market.

Billingsgate pheasant. A red herring; a
bloater.

Billy. A policeman's staff, which is a little
bill or billet.

A pocket-handkerchief (*see* BILL). "A blue
billy" is a handkerchief with blue ground and
white spots.

The tin in which originally Australian
station-hands made tea and did most of their
cooking. The word probably comes from *billa*,
a creek—hence water.

Billy Barlow. A street droll, a merry-andrew;
so called from a half-idiot of the name, who fancied himself some great personage. He was well
known in the East of London in the early half
of last century, and died in Whitechapel workhouse. Some of his sayings were really witty,
and some of his attitudes really droll.

Billy and Charlie. *See* FORGERIES.

Billy boy. A bluff-bowed, North Country
coasting vessel of river-barge build.

Billy goat. A male goat. From this came
the term once common for a tufted beard—a
"billy"—or goatee.

Bimini. A legendary island of the Bahamas
where the fountain of youth gave everlasting
life to all who drank of it. From this legend
there is an island named Bimini or Bemini.

Binary Arithmetic (bī' na ri). Arithmetic in
which the base of the notation is 2 instead of
10, a method suggested for certain uses by
Leibnitz. The unit followed by a *cipher* signifies
two, by another *unit* it signifies three, by *two*
ciphers it signifies four, and so on. Thus, 10
signifies 2, 100 signifies 4; while 11 signifies 3. etc.

Binary Theory. A theory which supposes
that all acids are a compound of hydrogen with
a simple or compound radicle, and all salts are
similar compounds in which a metal takes the
place of hydrogen.

Bingham's Dandies. *See* REGIMENTAL
NICKNAMES.

Bird. This is the Middle English and Anglo-
Saxon *brid* (occasionally *byrde* in M.E.), which
meant only the young of feathered flying
animals, *foul, foule*, or *fowel* being the M.E.
corresponding to the modern *bird*.

An endearing name for a girl.
And by my word, your bonnie bird
In danger shall not tarry;
So, though the waves are raging white,
I'll row you o'er the ferry.
CAMPBELL: *Lord Ullin's Daughter*.

This use of the word is connected with *burd*
(*q.v.*), a poetic word for a maiden (*cf.* Bride)
which has long been obsolete, except in ballads.
In modern slang "bird" has by no means the
same significance as it is a rather contemptuous
term for a young woman.

Bird is also a familiar term for the shuttlecock
used in Badminton.

**A bird in the hand is worth two in the
bush; a pound in the purse is worth two in the
book.** Possession is better than expectation.

It is found in several languages:
Italian: E meglio aver oggi un uovo, che
domani una gallina.
French: Un, Tiens vaut, ce dit-on, mieux
que deux Tu l'auras.
L'un est sur, l'autre ne l'est pas.
                              La Fontaine, v, iii.
German: Ein vogel in der hand ist besser als
zehn über land.
Besser ein spatz in der hand, als ein storch
auf dem dache.
Latin: Certa amittimus dum incerta
petimus (*Plautus*).
On the other side we have "Qui ne s'aventure,
n'a ni cheval ni mule." "Nothing venture, nothing
gain." "Use a sprat to catch a mackerel." "Chi
non s'arrischia non guadagna."

A bird of ill-omen. A person who is
regarded as unlucky; one who is in the habit of
bringing ill news. The phrase dates from the
time of augury (*q.v.*) in Greece and Rome, and
even to-day many look upon owls, crows, and
ravens as unlucky birds, swallows and storks as
lucky ones.

Ravens, by their acute sense of smell, can
locate dead and decaying bodies at a great
distance; hence, perhaps, they indicate death.
Owls screech when bad weather is at hand, and
as foul weather often precedes sickness, so the
owl is looked on as a funeral bird.

A bird of passage. A person who shifts from
place to place; a temporary visitant, like a
cuckoo, the swallow, starling, etc.

A little bird told me so. From *Eccles*. x, 20;
"Curse not the king, no not in thy thought, . . .
for a bird of the air shall carry the voice, and
that which hath wings shall tell the matter."

Birds of a feather flock together. Persons
associate with those of a similar taste and
station as themselves. Hence, *of that feather*,
of that sort.
I am not of that feather to shake off
My friend, when he must need me.
SHAKESPEARE: *Timon of Athens*, i, 1.

Fine feathers make fine birds. *See* FEATHER.

Old birds are not to be caught with chaff. Experience teaches wisdom.

One beats the bush, another takes the bird. The workman does the work, master makes the money. *See* BEAT.

The Arabian bird. The phœnix (*q.v.*).

The bird of Juno. The peacock. Minerva's bird is either the cock or the owl; that of Venus is the dove.

The bird of Washington. The American or bald-headed eagle.

The well-known bald-headed eagle, sometimes called the Bird of Washington.—WOOD.

Thou has kept well the bird in thy bosom. Thou hast remained faithful to thy allegiance or faith. The expression was used of Sir Ralph Percy (slain in the battle of Hedgeley Moor in 1464) to express his having preserved unstained his fidelity to the House of Lancaster.

'Tis the early bird that catches the worm. It's the energetic man who never misses an opportunity who succeeds.

To get the bird. To be hissed; to meet with a hostile reception. *See* BIG BIRD.

To kill two birds with one stone. To effect two objects with one outlay of trouble.

Birdie. A hole at golf which the player has completed in one stroke less than par (the official figure). Two strokes less is an *eagle*.

BIRDS PROTECTED BY SUPERSTITIONS:

Choughs were protected in Cornwall, because the soul of King Arthur was fabled to have migrated into a chough.

The Hawk was held sacred by the Egyptians, because it was the form assumed by Ra or Horus; and the **Ibis** because it was said that the god Thoth escaped from the pursuit of Typhon disguised as an Ibis.

Mother Carey's Chickens, or Storm Petrels, are protected by sailors, from a superstition that they are the living forms of the souls of deceased sailors.

The Robin is protected, both on account of Christian tradition and nursery legend. *See* ROBIN REDBREAST.

The Stork is a sacred bird in Sweden, from the legend that it flew round the cross, crying *Styrka, Styrka,* when Jesus was crucified. *See* STORK.

Swans are superstitiously protected in Ireland from the legend of the Fionnuala (daughter of Lir), who was metamorphosed into a swan and condemned to wander in lakes and rivers till Christianity was introduced. Moore wrote a poem on the subject.

Birdcage Walk (St. James's Park, London); so called from an aviary that used to be there for the amusement of Charles II.

Birnam Wood (ber' năm). Birnam is a hill in Perthshire, 11 miles north-west of Perth, and formerly part of the royal forest known as Birnam Wood.

Birthday Suit. He was in his birthday suit. Quite nude, as when born.

Birthstones. *See* PRECIOUS STONES.

Bis (Lat., twice). French and Italian audiences at theatres, concerts, etc., use this word as English audiences use "Encore."

Bis dat, qui cito dat (he gives twice who gives promptly)—*i.e.* prompt relief will do as much good as twice the sum at a future period (*Publius Syrus Proverbs*).

Biscuit. The French form of the Lat, *bis coctum, i.e.* twice baked. In English it was formerly spelt as pronounced—*bisket*—the irrational adoption of the foreign spelling without the foreign pronunciation is comparatively modern.

In pottery, earthenware or porcelain, after it has been hardened in the fire, but has not yet been glazed, is so called. Porcelain groups so prepared at Sèvres, and neither coloured nor glazed, were made fashionable in the 1750s by Mme de Pompadour, who had a great liking for them.

Bise (bēz). A keen dry wind from the north, sometimes with a bit of east in it, that is prevalent in Switzerland and the neighbouring parts.

The Bise blew cold.

ROGERS: *Italy*, pt. 1, div. ii, stanza 4.

Bishop (A.S. *biscop*, from Lat. *episcopus*, and Gr. *episkopos*, an inspector or overseer). One of the higher order of the Christian priesthood who presides over a diocese (either actually or formally) and has the power of ordaining and confirming in addition to the rights and duties of the inferior clergy.

The name is given to one of the men in chess (formerly called the "archer"), to the ladybird (*see* BISHOP BARNABEE *below*), and to a drink made by pouring red wine (such as claret or burgundy), either hot or cold, on ripe bitter oranges, the liquor being sugared and spiced to taste. Similar drinks are *Cardinal*, which is made by using *white* wine instead of red, and *Pope*, which is made by using *tokay*.

See also BOY BISHOP.

The bishop hath put his foot in it. Said of milk or porridge that is burnt, or of meat overroasted. Tyndale says, "If the porage be burned to, or the meate ouer rosted, we saye the byshope hath put his fote in the potte," and explains it thus, "because the bishopes burn who they lust." Such food is also said to be *bishopped*.

To bishop. There are two verbs, "to bishop," both from proper names. One is obsolete and meant to murder by drowning: it is from a man of this name who, in 1831, drowned a little boy in Bethnal Green and sold his body to the surgeons for dissection. The other is slang, and means to conceal a horse's age by "faking" his teeth.

Bishop Barker. An Australian term used around Sydney for the largest glass of beer available, named from Frederick Barker (1808-82), Bishop of Sydney (consecrated 1854) who was a very tall man.

Bishop Barnabee. The May-bug, ladybird, etc. There is an old Sussex rhyme:—

Bishop, Bishop Barnabee,
Tell me when my wedding shall be;
If it be to-morrow day,
Ope your wings and fly away.

Bishop in Partibus. *See* IN PARTIBUS.

The Bishops' Bible. *See* BIBLE, THE ENGLISH.

Bissextile (bi seks' til). Leap-year (*q.v.*). We add a day to February in leap-year, but the Romans counted February 24th twice. Now, February 24th was called by them "*dies bissextus*" (*sexto calendas Martias*), the sextile or sixth day before March 1st; and this day being reckoned twice (*bis*) in leap-year, which was called "*annus bissextus.*"

Bistro. A small, unpretentious restaurant in France where a cheap meal may be obtained quickly. Derived from the Russian word "bistro," meaning "quick". When the Russian army entered Paris in 1815, the troops wanted large meals at a low price and were always in a hurry; whenever they entered a restaurant they shouted "Bistro! bistro!" and the French adopted the word.

Bit. A piece, a morsel. Really the same word as *bite* (A.S. *bitan*), meaning a piece bitten off, hence a piece generally; it is the substantive of *bite*, as *morsel* (Fr. *morceau*) is of *mordre*.

Also used for a piece of money, as a "threepenny-bit," a "two-shilling bit," etc.

Bit is old thieves' slang for money generally, and a coiner is known as a "bit-maker"; but in Spanish North America and the West Indies it was the name of a small silver coin representing a portion, or "bit," of the dollar. In U.S.A. a "bit" is 12½ cents, half a quarter.

In the 1920s **bit** was a contemptuous phrase for someone's girl, short for "bit of fluff."

Bit (*of a horse*). **To take the bit in** (*or between*) **one's teeth.** To be obstinately self-willed; to make up one's mind not to yield. When a horse has a mind to run away, he catches the bit "between his teeth," and the driver has no longer control over him.

Bitt. To bitt the cable is to fasten it round the "bitt" or frame made for the purpose, and placed in the fore part of the vessel.

Bitter End, The. À *outrance*; with relentless hostility; also applied to affliction, as, "she bore it to the bitter end," meaning to the last stroke of adverse fortune. "Bitter end" in this phrase is a sea term meaning the end of a rope, or that part of the cable which is "abaft the bitts." When there is no windlass the cables are fastened to bitts, that is, wooden posts fixed in pairs on the deck; and when a rope is payed out until all of it is let out and no more remains, the end at the bitts—hence the *bitter* end, as opposed to the other end—is reached. In Captain Smith's *Seaman's Grammar* (1627) we read:—

A Bitter is but the turne of a Cable about the Bits, and veare it out by little and little. And the Bitters end, is that part of the Cable doth stay within boord.

However, we read in *Prov.* v, 4, "Her end is bitter as wormwood," which may share the origin of the modern use of this phrase.

Bittock. A little bit; -ock as a diminutive is preserved in bull-ock, hill-ock, butt-ock, etc. "A mile and a bittock" is a mile and a little bit.

Black for mourning was a Roman custom; (*Juvenal*, x, 245) borrowed from the Egyptians. Mutes at funerals who wore black cloaks, were sometimes known as the *blacks*, and sometimes as the Black Guards. *Cp.* BLACKGUARDS.

I do pray ye
To give me leave to live a little longer.
You stand about me like my Blacks.
BEAUMONT and FLETCHER: *Monsieur Thomas*, iii, 1.

In several of the Oriental nations it is a badge of servitude, slavery, and low birth. Our word *blackguard* (*q.v.*) seems to point to this meaning, and the Lat. *niger*, black, also meant *bad*, *unpropitious*. *See under* COLOURS for its symbolism, etc.

Black as a crow, etc. Among the many common similes used in connexion with "black" are black as a crow, a raven, a raven's wing, ink, hell, hades, death, the grave, your hat, a thundercloud, Egypt's night, a Newgate knocker (*q.v.*), ebony, a wolf's mouth, a coal-pit, coal, pitch, soot, etc. Most of these are self-explanatory.

Beaten black and blue. So that the skin is black and blue with the marks of the beating.

Black in the face. Extremely angry. The face is discoloured with passion or distress.

Mr. Winkle pulled . . . till he was black in the face.—DICKENS: *Pickwick Papers*.

He swore himself black in the face.—*Peter Pindar* (*Wolcott*).

I must have it in black and white, *i.e.* in plain writing; the paper being white and the ink black.

O, he has basted me rarely, sumptuously! but I have it here in black and white [*pulls out the warrant*], for his black and blue shall pay him.

JONSON: *Every Man in His Humour*, iv, 2.

To say black's his eye, *i.e.* to vituperate, to blame. The expression, **Black's the white of his eye,** is a modern variation. To say the eye is black or evil, is to accuse a person of an evil heart or great ignorance.

I can say black's your eye though it be grey. I have connived at this.—BEAUMONT and FLETCHER: *Love's Cure*, ii, 1.

To swear black is white, To swear to any falsehood no matter how patent it is.

Black and Tans. Members of the irregular force enlisted in 1920 for service in Ireland as auxiliaries to the Royal Irish Constabulary. So called because their original uniform was the army khaki with the black leather accoutrements of the R.I.C.

Black Act. An Act passed in 1722 (9 Geo. I, c. 22) imposing the death penalty for certain offences against the Game Laws, and specially directed against the Waltham deer-stealers, who blackened their faces and, under the name of *Blacks*, committed depredations in Epping Forest. This Act was repealed in 1827.

Black Art. The art practised by conjurors, wizards, and others who professed to have deal-ings with the devil; so called from the idea that necromancy (*q.v.*) was connected with the Lat. *niger*, black.

Wi' deils, they say, L——d safe's! colleaguin'
At some black art.

BURNS: *On Grose's Peregrinations*.

Black-balled. Not admitted to a club, or suchlike; the candidate proposed is not accepted as a member. In voting by ballot, those who accepted the person proposed used to drop a white or red ball into the box, but those who would exclude the candidate dropped into it a black one.

Black books. To be in my black books. In bad odour; in disgrace; out of favour. A *black book* is a book recording the names of those who are in disgrace or have merited punish-ment. Amherst, in his *Terræ Filius, or the Secret History of the Universities of Oxford* (1726), speaks of the Proctor's black book, and tells us that no one can proceed to a degree whose name is found there.

Black cap. A small square of black cloth. This is worn by a judge when he passes sentence of death on a prisoner; it is part of the judge's full dress, and is also worn on November 9th, when the new Lord Mayor takes the oath at the Law Courts. Covering the head was a sign of mourning among the Israelites, Greeks, Romans, and Anglo-Saxons. *Cp.* 2 *Sam.* xv, 30.

Black Cattle. Negro slaves. *Cp.* BLACKBIRDS, and *see* BLACK OX.

Black Country, The. The crowded manu-facturing district of the Midlands of which Birmingham is the centre. It includes Wolver-hampton, Walsall, Redditch, etc., and has been blackened by its many coal and iron mines, and smoking factory shafts.

Black Death. A plague which ravaged Europe in 1348-51; it was a putrid typhus, in which the body rapidly turned black. It reached England in 1349, and is said to have carried off twenty-five millions (one fourth of the popula-tion) in Europe alone, while in Asia and Africa the mortality was even greater.

Black Diamonds. Coals. Coals and diamonds are both forms of carbon.

Blackfellows. The name given to the aborigines of Australia. Their complexion is not really black, but a dark coffee colour.

Black Flag. The pirate's flag; the "Jolly Roger."

Pirates of the Chinese Sea who opposed the French in Tonquin were known as "the Black Flags," as also were the troops of the Caliph of Bagdad because his banner—that of the Abbasides—was *black*, while that of the Fatimites was *green* and the Ommiades *white*. It is said that the black curtain which hung before the door of Ayeshah, Mohammed's favourite wife, was taken for a national flag, and is still regarded by Mussulmans as the most precious of relics. It is never unfolded except as a decla-ration of war.

A black flag is run up over a prison immedi-ately after an execution has taken place within its walls.

Blackfoot. A Scottish term for a match-maker, or an intermediary in love affairs; if he chanced to play the traitor he was called a *white-foot*.

In the first half of the 19th century the name was given to one of the Irish agrarian secret societies:—

And the Blackfoot who courted each foeman's approach,
Faith! 'tis hot-foot he'd fly from the stout Father Roach.
LOVER.

Blackfeet. The popular name of two North American Indian tribes, one an Algonquin nation calling themselves the *Siksika*, and coming originally from the Upper Missouri district, the other, the *Sihasapa*.

Black Friars. The Dominican friars; so called from their black cloaks. The district of this name in the City of London is the site of a large monastery of Dominicans who used to possess rights of sanctuary, etc.

Black Friday. December 6th, 1745, the day on which the news arrived in London that the Pretender had reached Derby; also May 10th, 1886, when widespread panic was caused by Overend, Gurney and Co., the brokers, suspending payment.

Blackguards. The origin of this term, which for many years has been applied to low and worthless characters generally, and especially to roughs of the criminal classes, is not certainly known. It may be from the link-boys and torch-bearers at funerals, who were called by this name, or from the scullions and kitchen-knaves of the royal household who, during progresses, etc., had charge of the pots and pans and accompanied the wagons containing these, or from an actual body, or guard, of soldiers wearing a black uniform. The following extract from a proclamation of May 7th, 1683, in the Lord Steward's office would seem to bear out the second suggestion:—

Whereas . . . a sort of vicious, idle, and master-less boyes and rogues, commonly called the Black guard, with divers other lewd and loose fellows . . . do usually haunt and follow the court. . . . Wee do hereby strictly charge . . . all those so called, . . . with all other loose, idle . . . men . . . who have intruded themselves into his Majesty's court and stables . . . to depart upon pain of imprisonment.

Black Hand. A lawless secret society, formerly active in the U.S.A.; most of the members were Italians.

Black jack. A large leather gotch, or can, for beer and ale, so called from the outside being tarred.

He hath not pledged one cup, but looked most wickedly
Upon good Malaga; flies to the black-jack still,
And sticks to small drink like a water-rat.
MIDDLETON: *The Witch*, i, 1.
Fill, fill the goblet full with sack!
I mean our tall black-jerkin Jack.

Whose hide is proof 'gainst rabble Rout
And will keep all ill weather out.
ROBT. HEATH: *Song in a Siege* (1650).

In Cornwall the miners call blende or sulphide of zinc. "Black Jack," the occurrence of which is considered by them a favourable indication. Hence the saying, **Black Jack rides a good horse,** the blende rides upon a lode of good ore.

A blackjack is a small club weighted at the end, much used by gangsters for knocking people unconscious.

The name Black Jack was given to the American general John Alexander Logan (1826-86) on account of his dark complexion and hair. It was also given to General Pershing (1860-1948) who commanded the Americans in World War I.

Blacklead. *See* MISNOMERS.

Black-leg. An old name for a swindler, especially in cards and races; now used almost solely for a non-union workman, one who works for less than trade-union wages, or one who continues to work during a strike.

Black letter. The Gothic or German type which, in the early days of printing, was the type in commonest use. The term came into use about 1600, because of its heavy, black appearance in comparison with roman type.

Black letter day. An unlucky day; one to be recalled with regret. The Romans marked their unlucky days with a piece of black charcoal, and their lucky ones with white chalk, but the allusion here is to the old liturgical calendars in which the saints' days and festivals are distinguished by being printed in red.

Black list. A list of persons in disgrace, or who have incurred censure or punishment; a list of bankrupts for the private guidance of the mercantile community. *See* BLACK BOOKS.

Blackmail (blăk' māl). "Mail" here is the Old English and Scottish word meaning rent, tax, or tribute. In Scotland *mails* and *duties* are rents of an estate in money or otherwise. Blackmail was originally a tribute paid by the Border farmers to freebooters in return for protection or for immunity from molestation. Hence the modern signification—any payment extorted by intimidation or pressure.

Black market. A phrase that came into use during World War II, to describe illicit dealing in rationed goods.

Black Mass. This is the name given to the sacrilegious mass said by diabolists in which the Devil was invoked in place of God and various obscene rites performed in ridicule of the proper ceremony.

Black Monday. Easter Monday, April 14th, 1360. Edward III was with his army lying before Paris, and the day was so dark, with mist and hail, so bitterly cold and so windy, that many of his horses and men died. Monday after Easter holidays is called "Black Monday," in allusion to this fatal day. Launcelot says:

> It was not for nothing that my nose fell a-bleeding on Black Monday last, at six o'clock i' the morning.
> SHAKESPEARE: *Merchant of Venice*, ii, 5.

As a matter of fact April 14th, 1360, was a Tuesday; moreover Easter fell on the previous week in that year.

February 27th, 1865, was so called in Melbourne from a terrible sirocco from the NNW, which produced dreadful havoc between Sandhurst and Castlemain. School-boys give the name to the first Monday after the holidays are over, when lessons begin again.

Black Monks. The Benedictines (*q.v.*).

Black-out. From the day war was declared against Germany (Sept. 3, 1939) to the day hostilities ceased (May 8, 1945) it was obligatory throughout Great Britain to shield windows at night so that no slightest gleam of light should be visible from without. By this means enemy raiding aircraft were deprived of the help of landmarks and were literally left in the dark as to where there were towns or villages.

Black Parliament. This is the name often given to the Parliament that was opened in Nov., 1529, for the purpose of furthering Henry VIII's seizing and consolidating his thefts of Church property. During the six and a half years of its existence it carried out the king's arbitrary orders with a servility no parliament has shown before or since.

Black Rod. The short title of a Court official, who is styled fully "Gentleman Usher of the Black Rod," so called from his staff of office—a black wand surmounted by a golden lion. He is the Chief Gentleman Usher of the Lord Chamberlain's Department, and also Usher to the House of Lords and the Chapter of the Garter.

Black Rood of Scotland. The "piece of the true cross" or *rood*, set in an ebony crucifix, which St. Margaret, the wife of King Malcolm Canmore, left to the Scottish nation at her death in 1093. It fell into the hands of the English at the battle of Neville's Cross (1346), and was deposited in St. Cuthbert's shrine at Durham Cathedral, but was lost at the Reformation.

Black Sea, The. Formerly called the Euxine (*q.v.*), this sea probably was given its present name by the Turks who, accustomed to the Ægean with its many islands and harbours, were terrified by the dangers of this larger stretch of water which was destitute of shelter and was liable to sudden and violent storms and thick fogs.

Black sheep. A disgrace to the family or community; a *mauvais sujet*. Black sheep are looked on with dislike by some shepherds, and are not so valuable as white ones. *Cp.* BÊTE NOIRE.

Black Shirts. The black shirt was the distinguishing garment worn by the Italian Fascists and adopted in England by their imitators.

Blacksmith. A smith who works in black metal (such as iron), as distinguished from a whitesmith, who works in tin or other white metal. *See* HARMONIOUS, LEARNED.

Black velvet. A drink composed of champagne and Guinness stout in equal parts. It was the favourite drink of the Iron Chancellor, Bismarck.

Black Watch. Originally companies employed about 1725 by the English government to watch the Islands of Scotland, They dressed in a "black" or dark tartan. They were enrolled in the regular army as the 42nd regiment under the Earl of Crawford, in 1737. Their tartan is still called "The Black Watch Tartan." The regiment is now officially "The Royal Highlanders," but is still called "The Black Watch." They are easily recognized by the small bunch of red feathers, known as the red hackle, which they wear on their bonnets in lieu of a regimental badge.

Blade. A knowing blade, a sharp fellow: **a regular blade,** a buck or fop. As applied to a man the word originally carried the sense of a somewhat bullying bravado, a fierce and swaggering man, and he was probably named from the sword that he carried.

Bladud (blā' dŭd). A mythical king of England, father of King Lear. He built the city of Bath, and dedicated the medicinal springs to Minerva. Bladud studied magic, and, attempting to fly, fell into the temple of Apollo and was dashed to pieces. (*Geoffrey of Monmouth*.)

Blanch, To. A method of testing the quality of money paid in taxes to the King, invented by Roger of Salisbury in the reign of Henry I. 44 shillings' worth of silver coin was taken at random from the amount being paid. The Master of the Assaye then melted a pound's weight of it and the impurities were skimmed off. If the resulting mass was then light, the tax-payer had to throw in enough pennies to balance the scale.

Blank cartridge. Cartridge with powder only, that is, without shot, bullet, or ball. Used in drill and in saluting. Figuratively, empty threats.

Blank cheque. A cheque duly signed, but without specifying any sum of money; the amount to be filled in by the payee.

To give a blank cheque is, figuratively, to give *carte blanche* (*q.v.*).

Blank verse. Rhymeless verse in continuous decasyllables with iambic or trochaic rhythm, first used in English by the Earl of Surrey in his version of the *Æneid*, about 1540. There is other unrhymed verse, but it is not usual to extend to such poems as Collins's *Ode to Evening*, Whitman's *Leaves of Grass*, or the *vers libre* of to-day, the name blank verse.

Blanket. The wrong side of the blanket. An illegitimate child is said to come of the wrong side of the blanket.

A wet blanket. A discouragement; a marplot or spoil-sport. A person is a wet blanket who discourages a proposed scheme. "Treated with a wet blanket," discouraged. "A wet blanket influence," etc. A wet blanket is used to smother fire, or to prevent one escaping from a fire from being burnt.

Blanketeers. The name given to a body of some 5,000 working men out of employment who assembled on St. Peter's Field, Manchester, March 10th, 1817, and provided themselves with blankets intending to march to London, to lay before the Prince Regent a petition of grievances. Only six got as far as Ashbourne Bridge, when the expedition collapsed.

In more recent times journalists have applied the name to similar bodies of unemployed, both in Great Britain and in America.

Blarney. Soft, wheedling speeches to gain some end; flattery, or lying, with unblushing effrontery. Blarney is a village near Cork. Legend has it that Cormack Macarthy held its castle in 1602, and concluded an armistice with Carew, the Lord President, on condition of surrendering the fort to the English garrison. Day after day his lordship looked for the fulfilment of the terms, but received nothing but soft speeches, till he became the laughing-stock of Elizabeth's ministers, and the dupe of the Lord of Blarney.

To kiss the Blarney Stone. In the wall of the castle at Blarney, about twenty feet from the top and difficult of access, is a triangular stone containing this inscription: "Cormac Mac Carthy *fortis me fieri fecit*, A.D. 1446." Tradition says that to whomsoever can kiss this is given the power of being able to obtain all his desires by cajolery. As it is almost impossible to reach, a substitute has been provided by the custodians of the castle, and it is said that this is in every way as efficacious as the original.

Among the criminal classes of America "to blarney" means to pick locks.

Blasé. Surfeited with pleasure. A man *blasé* is one who has had his fill of all the pleasures of life and has no longer any appetite for any of them. The word comes from the French *blaser*, to exhaust with enjoyment.

Blasphemy (blăs' fĕ mi). The Greek from which this word comes means "evil speaking" but in English the term is limited to any impious or profane speaking of God or of sacred things. In Law blasphemy is constituted by the publication of anything ridiculing or insulting Christianity, or the Bible, or God in the shape of any Person of the Holy Trinity. At one time the courts held that unorthodox arguments constituted blasphemy. In 1930 a Bill was introduced to make prosecutions for blasphemy illegal, but it was dropped.

Blasphemous Balfour. Sir James Balfour, the Scottish judge, was so called because of his apostasy. He died in 1583. He served, deserted, and profited by all parties.

Blast. To strike by lightning; to cause to wither. The "blasted oak." This is the sense in which the word is used as an expletive.

> If it [the ghost] assume my noble father's person,
> I'll cross it, though it blast me.
>
> SHAKESPEARE: *Hamlet*, i, 1.

The use of Blast! as an imprecation goes back to at least Stuart times; as an imprecatory adjective—"a blasted rascal"—it is employed even by the elegant Chesterfield.

In full blast. In full swing; "all out." As one might say, "The speakers at Hyde Park on Saturday were in full blast." A metaphor from the blast furnace in full operation.

Blaze. A white mark in the forehead of a horse, and hence a white mark on a tree made by chipping off a piece of bark and used to serve as an indication of a path, etc. The word is not connected with the *blaze* of a fire, but is from Icel. *blesi*, a white star on the forehead of a horse, and is connected with Ger. *blasz*, pale.

To blaze a path. To notch trees as a clue. Trees so notched are called in America "blazed trees," and the white wood shown by the notch is called a blaze.

To blaze abroad. To noise abroad. "Blaze" here is the Icel. *blasa*, to blow, from O.Teut. *blœsan*, to blow, and is probably ultimately the same as Lat. *flare*. Dutch *blazen* and Ger. *blasen* are cognate words. *See* BLAZON.

He began to publish it much and to blaze abroad the matter.—*Mark* i, 45.

Blazer. A brightly coloured jacket, used in boating, cricket, and other summer sports. Originally applied to those of the Lady Margaret crew (Camb.), whose boat jackets are the brightest possible scarlet.

A blazer is the red flannel boating jacket worn by the Lady Margaret, St. John's College, Cambridge, Boat Club.—*Daily News*, August 22nd, 1889.

Bleed. To make a man bleed is to make him pay dearly for something; to victimize him. Money is the life-blood of commerce.

It makes my heart bleed. It makes me very sorrowful.

Take your own will; my very heart bleeds for thee.
FLETCHER: *Queen of Corinth*, ii, 3.

Bleeding Heart, Order of the. One of the many semi-religious orders instituted in the Middle Ages in honour of the Virgin Mary, whose "heart was pierced with many sorrows."

Bleeding of a dead body. It was at one time believed that, at the approach of a murderer, the blood of the murdered body gushed out. If in a dead body the slightest change was observable in the eyes, mouth, feet, or hands, the murderer was supposed to be present. The notion still survives in some places.

Bleeding the monkey. The same as *Sucking the Monkey*. *See* MONKEY.

Blefuscu (ble fŭs' kū). An island in Swift's *Gulliver's Travels*, (*q.v.*). In describing it Swift satirized France.

Blemmyes (blem' iz). An ancient nomadic Ethiopian tribe mentioned by Roman writers as inhabiting Nubia and Upper Egypt. They were fabled to have no head, their eyes and mouth being placed in the breast. *Cp.* ACEPHALITES; CAORA.

Blenheim Palace (blen' im). The mansion near Woodstock, Oxfordshire, given by the nation to the Duke of Marlborough, for his victory over the French at Blenheim, Bavaria, in 1704.

When Europe freed confessed the saving power
Of Marlborough's hand, Britain, who sent him forth,
Chief of confederate hosts, to fight the cause
Of liberty and justice, grateful raised
This palace, sacred to the leader's fame.
LORD GEO. LYTTELTON: *Blenheim*.

The building was completed in 1716, and the architect was Sir John Vanbrugh, for whom the epitaph was written:—

Lie heavy on him, Earth, for he
Laid many a heavy load on thee.

And of all his buildings Blenheim was probably the heaviest.

The Palace has given its name to a small dog, the *Blenheim Spaniel*, a variety of King Charles's Spaniel, and to a golden-coloured apple, the *Blenheim Orange*.

Bless. He has not a sixpence to bless himself with, *i.e.* in his possession; wherewith to make himself happy. This expression may perhaps be traced to the time when coins were marked with a deeply indented cross; silver is still used by gipsy fortune-tellers and so on for crossing one's palm for good luck.

Blessing. Among Greek and R.C. ecclesiastics the thumb and first two fingers, representing the Trinity, are used in ceremonial blessing in the name of the Father, and of the Son, and of the Holy Ghost. The thumb, being strong, represents the *Father*; the long or second finger, *Jesus Christ*; and the first finger, the *Holy Ghost*, which proceedeth from the Father and the Son.

Blighter. Slightly contemptuous but good-natured slang for a man, a fellow; generally with the implication that he is a bit of a scamp or, at the moment, somewhat obnoxious.

Blighty. Soldiers' slang for England or the homeland—came into popular use during World War I, but was well known to soldiers who had served in India long before. It is the Urdu Vilayati or Bilati, an adjective meaning provincial, removed at some distance; hence adopted by the military for England.

Blimey. One of the numerous class of mild oaths or expletives whose real meaning is little understood by those who use them. This is a corruption of "blind me!"

Blind. A pretence; something ostensible to conceal a covert design. The metaphor is from window-blinds, which prevent outsiders from seeing into a room.

As an adjective *blind* is one of the many euphemisms for "drunk"—short for "blind drunk," *i.e.* so drunk as to be unable to distinguish things clearly.

Landlady, count the lawin,
The day is near the dawin;
Ye're a' blind drunk, boys,
And I'm but jolly fou.

In engineering a tube, valve or aperture of which one end which would be expected to be open is in fact closed, either as called for in the design or unintentionally through faulty workmanship, is described as blind.

Blind as a bat. A bat is not blind, but if disturbed and forced into the sunlight it cannot see, and blunders about. It sees best in the dusk.

Blind as a beetle. Beetles are not blind, but the dor-beetle or hedge-chafer, in its rapid flight, will occasionally bump against one as if it could not see.

Blind as a mole. Moles are not blind, but as they work underground, their eyes are very small. There is a mole found in the south of Europe, the eyes of which are covered by membranes, and probably this is the animal to which Aristotle refers when he says, "the mole is blind."

Blind as an owl. Owls are not blind, but being night birds, they see better in partial darkness than in the full light of day.

Blind leaders of the blind. Those who give advice to others in need of it, but who are, themselves, unfitted to do so. The allusion is to *Matt*, xv, 14.

To go it blind. To enter upon some undertaking without sufficient forethought, inquiry, or preparation.

When the devil is blind. A circumlocution for "never." For similar phrases *see* NEVER.

You came on his blind side. His soft or tender-hearted side. Said of persons who wheedle some favour out of another. He yielded because he was not wide awake to his own interest.

Blind alley, A. A *cul de sac*, an alley with no outlet. It is blind because it has no "eye" or passage through it.

Blindman's buff. A very old-established name for an old and well-known children's game. "Buff" here is short for "buffet," and is an allusion to the three buffs or pats which the "blind man" gets when he has caught a player.

Blindman's holiday. The hour of dusk, when it is too dark to work, and too soon to light candles. The phrase was in common use at least as early as Elizabethan times.

What will not blind Cupid doe in the night, which is his blindman's holiday.
T. NASHE: *Lenten Stuffe* (1599).

Blindmen's Dinner, The. A dinner unpaid for, the landlord being made the victim. Eulenspiegel (*q.v.*) being asked for alms by twelve blind men, said, "Go to the inn; eat, drink, and be merry, my men; and here are twenty florins to pay the bill." The blind men thanked him;

each supposing one of the others had received the money. Reaching the inn, they told the landlord of their luck, and were at once provided with food and drink to the amount of twenty florins. On asking for payment, they all said, "Let him who received the money pay for the dinner"; but none had received a penny.

Blindworm. *See* MISNOMERS.

Blind spot. This is a small area not sensitive to light, situated on the retina where the optic nerve enters. The term is used figuratively to describe some area in one's discernment where judgment and understanding are lacking.

Block. To block a Bill. In parliamentary language means to postpone or prevent the passage of a Bill by giving notice of opposition, and thus preventing its being taken after half-past twelve at night.

A chip of the old block. *See* CHIP.

To cut blocks with a razor. *See* CUT.

Blockhead. A stupid person; one without brains. The allusion is to a wig-maker's dummy or *tête à perruque*, on which he fits his wigs.

Your wit will not so soon out as another man's will; 'tis strongly wedged up in a blockhead.
SHAKESPEARE: *Coriolanus*, ii, 3.

Blockhousers. The oldest Negro Regiment in the U.S. Army, nicknamed from its gallant assault on a blockhouse in the Spanish-American War.

Blood. In figurative use, *blood*, being treated as the typical component of the body inherited from parents and ancestors, came to denote members of a family or race as distinguished from other families and races, hence family descent generally, and hence one of noble or gentle birth, which latter degenerated into a buck, or aristocratic rowdy.

The gallants of those days pretty much resembled the bloods of ours.
GOLDSMITH: *Reverie at the Boar's Head Tavern.*

A blood horse. A thoroughbred; a horse of good parentage or stock.

A prince of the blood. One of the Royal Family. *See* BLOOD ROYAL.

Bad blood. Anger, quarrels; as, *It stirs up bad blood*. It provokes to illfeeling and contention.

Blood and iron policy—*i.e.* war policy. No explanation needed.

Blood is thicker than water. Relationship has a claim which is generally acknowledged. It is better to seek kindness from a kinsman than from a stranger. Water soon evaporates and leaves no mark behind; not so blood. So the interest we take in a stranger is thinner and more evanescent than that which we take in a blood relation. The proverb occurs in Ray's Collection (1672) and is probably many years older.

Blood money. Money paid to a person for giving such evidence as shall lead to the conviction of another; money paid to the next of kin to induce him to forgo his "right" of seeking blood for blood, or (formerly) as compensation for the murder of his relative; money paid to a person for betraying another, as Judas was paid blood-money for his betrayal of the Saviour.

Blood relation. One in direct descent from the same father or mother; one of the same family stock.

In cold blood. Deliberately; not in the excitement of passion or of battle.

It makes one's blood boil. It provokes indignation and anger.

It runs in the blood. It is inherited or exists in the family or race.

It runs in the blood of our family.—SHERIDAN: *The Rivals*, iv, 2.

Laws written in blood. Demades said that the laws of Draco were written in blood, because every offence was punishable by death.

My own flesh and blood. My own children, brothers, sisters, or other near kindred.

Blood, toil, tears and sweat. The words used by Winston Churchill in his speech to the House of Commons, 13 May, 1940, on becoming Prime Minister. "I would say to the House as I have said to those who have joined this government, I have nothing to offer but blood, toil, tears and sweat." In his *Anatomie of the World* John Donne says, "Mollifie it with thy teares, or sweat, or blood."

Young blood. Fresh members; as, "To bring young blood into the concern." The term with the article, "a young blood," signifies a young rip, a wealthy young aristocrat of convivial habits.

Blood Royal. The royal family or race; also called simply "the blood," as "a prince of the blood."

Bloodhound. Figuratively, one who follows up an enemy with pertinacity. Bloodhounds used to be employed for tracking wounded game by the blood spilt; subsequently they were employed for tracking criminals and slaves who had made their escape, and were hunters of blood, not hunters *by* blood. The most noted breeds are the African, Cuban, and English.

Bloodstone. See HELIOTROPE.

Bloodsucker. An animal like the leech, or the fabled vampire which voraciously sucks blood and which, if allowed, will rob a person

of all vitality. Hence, a sponger, a parasite, or one intent upon another's material ruin.

See REGIMENTAL NICKNAMES.

Bloody. Several fanciful derivations have been found for this expletive, once considered more vulgar than recent usage suggests. The most romantic of these was that the word is a corruption of "By our Lady"; another school of thought imagined that it came from an association of ideas with "bloods" or aristocratic rowdies. There is little doubt, however, that its original meaning was, as it implies, "covered with blood." Partly owing to its unpleasant, violent, and lurid associations, it easily became applied as an intensive in a general way.

It was bloody hot walking to-day.—SWIFT: *Journal to Stella*, letter xxii.

As a title the adjective has been bestowed on Otto II, Emperor of the Holy Roman Empire, 973-983, and the English Queen Mary (1553-58) has been called "Bloody Mary" on account of the religious persecutions which took place in her reign.

Bloody-bones. A hobgoblin; generally "Raw-head and Bloody-Bones."

Bloody Eleventh. See REGIMENTAL NICKNAMES.

Bloody hand. A term in old Forest Law denoting a man whose hand was bloody, and was therefore presumed to be the person guilty of killing the deer shot or otherwise slain. In *heraldry*, the "bloody hand" is the badge of a baronet, and the armorial device of Ulster. In both uses it is derived from the O'Neils. See RED HAND, and HAND, THE RED.

Bloody Mars. A local English name for a variety of wheat. It is a corruption of the French *blé de Mars*, March grain.

Bloody-nose. The popular name of the common wayside beetle, *Timarcha lœvigata*, which can emit a reddish liquid from its joints when disturbed.

Bloody Pots, The. See KIRK OF SKULLS.

Bloody Thursday. The Thursday in the first week in Lent used to be so called.

Bloody Wedding. The massacre of St. Bartholomew in 1572 is so called because it took place during the marriage feast of Henri (afterwards Henri IV) and Marguerite (daughter of Catherine de' Medici).

Bloom, Leopold. See ULYSSES.

Bloomers. A female costume consisting of a short skirt and loose trousers gathered closely round the ankles, so called from Mrs. Amelia Bloomer, of New York, who tried in 1849 to introduce the fashion. Nowadays "bloomers" is usually applied only to the trousers portion of the outfit.

Blooming. A meaningless euphemism for the slang epithet "bloody."

Blouse. A short smock-frock of a blue colour worn commonly by French workmen. *Bleu* is French argot for *manteau*.

> A garment called *bliaut* or *bliaus*, which appears to have been another name for a surcoat. . . . In this *bliaus* we may discover the modern French *blouse*, a . . . smock-frock.
> PLANCHÉ: *British Costume*.

The word is more commonly used for a woman's light bodice worn with a skirt.

Blow. The English spelling *blow* represents three words of different origin, viz.—

(1) To move as a current of air, to send a current of air from the mouth, etc., from the A.S. *blawan*, cognate with the Mod. Ger. *blähen* and Lat. *flare*.

(2) To blossom, to flourish, from A.S. *blowan*, cognate with *bloom*, Ger. *bluhen*, and Lat. *florera*; and

(3) A stroke with the first, etc., which is most likely from an old Dutch word, *blau*, to strike.

In the following phrases, etc., the numbers refer to the group to which each belongs.

A blow out (1). A "tuck in," or feast which swells out the paunch. Also applied to the sudden flattening of a pneumatic tyre when the inner tube is punctured.

At one blow (3). By one stroke.

To blow one's top (1). To lose one's temper.

Blown (1), in the phrase "fly-blown," is a legacy from pre-scientific days, when naturalists thought that maggots were actually blown on to the meat by blow-flies.

Blown (1). Phrase applied to an internal combustion engine in which the fuel is forced into the cylinders with the aid of a supercharger, or blower.

It will soon blow over (1). It will soon be no longer talked about; it will soon come to an end, as a gale or storm blows over or ceases.

I will blow him up sky high (1). Give him a good scolding. The metaphor is from blasting by gunpowder.

The first blow is half the battle (3). Well begun is half done. Pythagoras used to say, "The beginning is half the whole." "*Incipe*: *Dimidium facti est cœposse*" (Ausonius). "*Dimidium facti, qui cœpit, habet*" (Horace). "*Ce n'est que le premier pas qui coûte.*"

To blow a cloud (1). To smoke a cigar, pipe, etc. This term was in use in Queen Elizabeth's reign.

To blow a trumpet (1). To sound a trumpet.
> But when the blast of war blows in our ears,
> Let us be tigers in our fierce deportment.
> *Henry V*, iii, 1.

To blow great guns (1). Said of a wind which blows so violently that its noise resembles the roar of artillery.

To blow hot and cold (1). To be inconsistent. The allusion is to the fable of a traveller who was entertained by a satyr. Being cold, the traveller blew his fingers to warm them, and afterwards blew his hot broth to cool it. The satyr, in great indignation, turned him out of doors, because he blew both hot and cold with the same breath.

To blow off steam (1). To get rid of superfluous temper. The allusion is to the forcible escape of superfluous steam no longer required.

To blow the gaff (1). To let out a secret; to inform against a companion; to "peach." Here *gaff* is a variant of *gab* (*q.v.*).

To blow up (1). To inflate, as a bladder; to explode, to burst into fragments; to censure severely. See *I will blow him up*, above.

Without striking a blow. Without coming to a contest.

Blower. A common term in the Army for wireless and telephone apparatus. Also term in motor sport used for a supercharger; a supercharged engine is said to be "blown."

Blowzy. Coarse, red-faced, bloated; applied to women. The word is allied to blush, blaze, etc.
> A face made blowzy by cold and damp.
> GEORGE ELIOT: *Silas Marner*.

Blubber (M.E. *bloberen*, probably of imitative origin). To cry like a child, with noise and slavering; *cp. slobber, slaver*.
> I play the boy, and blubber in thy bosom.
> OTWAY: *Venice Preserved*, i, 1.

The word is also used attributively, as in blubber-lips, blubber-cheeks, fat flabby cheeks, like whale's blubber.

Bluchers (bloo' kerz). Half boots; so called after Field-Marshal von Blücher (1742-1819).

Blue or *Azure* is the symbol of Divine eternity and human immortality. Consequently, it is a mortuary colour—hence its use in covering the coffins of young persons. When used for the garment of an angel, it signifies faith and fidelity. As the dress of the Virgin, it indicates modesty. In *blazonry*, it signifies chastity, loyalty, fidelity, and a spotless reputation, and seems frequently to represent silver; thus we have the *Blue Boar* of Richard III, the *Blue Lion* of the Earl of Mortimer, the *Blue Swan* of Henry IV, the *Blue Dragon*, etc.

The *Covenanters* wore blue as their badge, in opposition to the scarlet of royalty. They based their choice on *Numb*. xv, 38, "Speak unto the children of Israel, and bid them that they make them fringes in the borders of their garments . . . and that they put upon the fringe . . . a *ribband of blue*."

See COLOURS for its symbolisms.

A blue, or a "staunch blue," descriptive of political opinions, for the most part means a Tory, for in most counties the Conservative colour is blue. *See* BLUE-COAT SCHOOL; BLUE STOCKING.

Also, at Oxford and Cambridge, a man who has been chosen to represent his 'Varsity in rowing, cricket, etc. Some sports, such as hockey and lacrosse, come in a lower category, and for these a "half blue" is awarded.

A dark blue. An Oxford man or Harrow boy.

A light blue. A Cambridge man or Eton boy.

The Oxford Blues. *See* REGIMENTAL NICK-NAMES.

True blue will never stain. A really noble heart will never disgrace itself. The reference is to blue aprons and blouses worn by butchers, which do not show blood-stains.

To look blue. To be depressed.

He was blue in the face. He had made too great an effort; was breathless and exhausted either bodily or with suppressed anger or emotion.

A priest of the blue bag. A cant name for a barrister. *See* LAWYER'S BAG.

Bluebeard. A bogy, a merciless tyrant, in Charles Perrault's *Contes du Temps* (1697). The tale of Bluebeard (Chevalier Raoul) is known to every child, but many have speculated on the original of this despot. Some say it was a satire on Henry VIII, of wife-killing notoriety. Dr. C. Taylor thinks it is a type of the castle lords in the days of knight-errantry. Holinshed calls Giles de Retz, Marquis de Laval, the original Bluebeard; he lived at Machecoul, in Brittany, was accused of murdering six of his seven wives, and was ultimately strangled and burnt in 1440.

Campbell has a Bluebeard story in his *Tales of the Western Highlands*, called *The Widow and her Daughters*; it is found also in Strapola's *Nights*, the *Pentamerone*, and elsewhere. *Cp.* the *Story of the Third Calender* in the *Arabian Nights*.

Bluebeard's key. When the blood stain of this key was rubbed out on one side, it appeared on the opposite side; so prodigality being overcome will appear in the form of meanness; and friends, over-fond, will often become enemies.

Blue billy. A blue neckcloth with white spots. *See* BILLY.

Blue Bird of Happiness. This is an idea elaborated from Maeterlinck's play of that name, first produced in London in 1910. It tells the story of a boy and girl seeking "the blue bird" which typifies happiness. This fancy of Maeterlinck's introduced for a time the phrase into English.

Blue blood. High or noble birth or descent; it is a Spanish phrase, and refers to the fact that the veins shown in the skin of the pure-blooded Spanish aristocrat, whose race had suffered no Moorish or other admixture, were more blue than those of persons of mixed, and therefore inferior, ancestry.

Blue Boar. A public-house sign; the cognisance of Richard III. In Leicester is a lane in the parish of St. Nicholas, called the *Blue Boar Lane*, because Richard slept there the night before the battle of Bosworth Field.

The bristly boar, in infant gore,
Wallows beneath the thorny shade.
                              GRAY: *The Bard*.

Blue Bonnets, or **Blue Caps.** The Highlanders of Scotland, or the Scots generally. So called from the blue woollen cap at one time in very general use in Scotland, and still far from uncommon.

He is there, too, . . . and a thousand blue caps more.
                              1 *Henry IV*, ii, 4.

Blue Books. In England, parliamentary reports and official publications presented by the Crown to both Houses of Parliament. Each volume is in folio, and is covered with a blue wrapper.

Short Acts of Parliament, etc., even without a wrapper, come under the same designation.

The official colour of Spain is *red*, of Italy *green*, of France *yellow*, of Germany and Portugal, *white*.

In America the "Blue Books" (like our "Red Books") contain lists of those persons who hold government appointments.

Blue bottle. A constable, a policeman; also, formerly, an almsman, or anyone whose distinctive dress was blue.

You proud varlets, you need not be ashamed to wear blue when your master is one of your fellows.
                              DEKKER: *The Honest Whore* (1602).

Shakespeare makes Doll Tearsheet denounce the beadle as a "blue-bottle rogue."

I'll have you soundly swinged for this, you blue-bottle rogue. — SHAKESPEARE: 2 *Henry IV*, v, 4.

Blue-eyed Maid. Minerva, the goddess of wisdom, is so called by Homer.

Now Prudence gently pulled the poet's ear,
And thus the daughter of the Blue-eyed Maid,
In flattery's soothing sounds, divinely said,
"O Peter, eldest-born of Phœbus, hear."
PETER PINDAR: *A Falling Minister.*

Blue fish, The. The shark, technically called
Carcharias glaucus, the upper parts of which are
blue. This should be distinguished from *blue
fish,* an edible fish found in American waters.

Blue gown. A harlot. Formerly a blue gown
was a dress of ignominy for a prostitute who had
been arrested and placed in the House of
Correction.

The bedesmen, to whom the kings of Scotland distributed certain alms, were also known
as *blue gowns,* because their dress was a cloak or
gown of coarse blue cloth. The number of these
bedesmen was equal to that of the king's years,
so that an extra one was added at every returning
birthday. These paupers were privileged to ask
alms through the whole realm of Scotland. *See*
GABERLUNZIE.

Blue laws. This is a phrase used in U.S.A. to
describe laws which interfere with personal
freedom, tastes and habits, such as sumptuary
laws and those regulating private morals. The
name was first given to several laws of this kind
said to have been imposed in the colonies
of Connecticut and New Haven in the early
18th century.

Blue-light Federalists. A name given to
those Americans who were believed to have
made friendly ("blue-light") signals to British
ships in the war of 1812.

Bluemantle. One of the four English
Pursuivants (*q.v.*) attached to the College of
Arms, or Heralds' College, so called from his
official robe.

Blue Monday. The Monday before Lent,
spent in dissipation. It is said that dissipation
gives everything a blue tinge. Hence "blue"
means tipsy.

Blue moon. Once in a blue moon. Very
rarely indeed.

Blue Peter. A flag with a blue ground and
white square in the centre, hoisted as a signal
that the ship is about to sail. It takes its name
from a "repeater", a naval flag hoisted to indicate
that a signal has not been read and should be
repeated, this flag having been used with that
meaning originally.

To hoist the blue Peter. To leave.
"When are you going to sail?"
"I cannot justly say. Our ship's bound for America
next voyage . . . but I've got to go to the Isle of Man first
. . . And I may have to hoist the blue Peter any day."
Mrs. GASKELL: *Mary Barton,* ch. xiii.

Blue Ribbon. The blue ribbon is the
Garter, the badge of the highest and most
coveted Order of Knighthood in the gift of the
British Crown; hence the term is used to denote
the highest honour attainable in any profession,
walk of life, etc. The blue ribbon of the Church
is the Archbishopric of Canterbury, that in law
is the office of Lord Chancellor. *See* CORDON
BLEU.

Blue stocking. A female pedant. In 1400 a
society of ladies and gentlemen was formed at
Venice, distinguished by the colour of their
stockings, and called *della calza.* It lasted till
1590, when it appeared in Paris and was the
rage among the lady *savants.* From France it
came to England in 1780, when Mrs. Montague
displayed the badge of the Bas-bleu club at her
evening assemblies. Mr. Benjamin Stillingfleet
was a constant attendant of the *soirées.* The last
of the clique was Miss Monckton, afterwards
Countess of Cork, who died 1840, but the
name has survived.

Blues. A traditional form of American
Negro folk-song, of obscure origin, but expressive
of the unhappiness of slaves in the Deep South.
Usually consists of 12 bars, made up of three
4-bar phrases in 4/4 time. Both the words and
accompaniment (which form an antiphonal)
should be improvised, though many famous
Blues have been written down; the subject
matter is usually love, the troubles which have
beset the singer, or a nostalgic longing for
home. The best-known Blues singer was Bessie
Smith (d. 1936).

Bluff, To. In Poker and other card-games, to
stake on a bad hand. This is a dodge resorted to
by players to lead an adversary to throw up his
cards and forfeit his stake rather than risk them
against the "bluffer."

So, by extension, to bluff is to deceive by
pretence. **To call someone's bluff** is to unmask
his deception.

Bluff Harry or **Hal.** Henry VIII, so called
from his bluff and burly manners (1491-1547).

Blunderbore. A nursery-tale giant, brother
of Cormoran, who put Jack the Giant Killer
to bed and intended to kill him; but Jack
thrust a billet of wood into the bed, and crept
under the bedstead. Blunderbore came with
his club and broke the billet to pieces, but
was much amazed at seeing Jack next morning
at breakfast-time. When his astonishment was
abated he asked Jack how he had slept.
"Pretty well," said the Cornish hero, "but
once or twice I fancied a mouse tickled me

with its tail." This increased the giant's surprise. Hasty pudding being provided for breakfast, Jack stowed away such huge stores in a bag concealed within his dress that the giant could not keep pace with him. Jack cut the bag open to relieve "the gorge," and the giant, to affect the same relief, cut his throat and thus killed himself.

Blunderbuss. A short gun with a large bore. (Dut. *donderbus*, a thunder-tube.)

Blunt. Ready money; a slang term, the origin of which is unknown.

To get a Signora to warble a song,
You must fork out the blunt with a haymaker's prong!
HOOD: *A Tale of a Trumpet.*

Blurb. A paragraph printed on the dust-wrapper or in the preliminary leaves of a book purporting to tell what the book is about, written by the publisher and usually of a laudatory nature. The phrase was coined by Gelett Burgess, the American novelist (1866-1951), about the year 1900, when he defined it as "self-praise: to make a noise like a publisher."

Blurt Out, To. To tell something from impulse which should not have been told. To speak incautiously, or without due reflection. Florio makes the distinction, to "flurt with one's fingers, and blurt with one's mouth."

Blush. At first blush, at first sight, on the first glance. The word comes from the Old English *blusch*, a gleam, a glimpse, a momentary view. This sense of the word dropped out of use in the 16th century, except in the above phrase.

To hide a blisful blusch of the bright sunne.
Sir Gawayne and the Green Knight.
At the first blush we thought they had been shippes come from France.—*Hakluyt's Voyages,* III.

Boadicea (bō à dis ē′ à). Much has been written about this heroic queen of the ancient Britons. She was the wife of Prasutagus, king of the Iceni, on whose death the Romans seized the territory, scourged the widow and ill-treated the daughters. Enfuriated and crying for vengeance, Boadicea raised a revolt of the Iceni and Trinobantes, burned Camulodunum and Londinium (Colchester and London) but was eventually defeated (A.D. 62) by Suetonius Paulinus. Rather than fall into the hands of the Romans she took poison and died.

Boanerges (bō à nĕr ′jēz). A name given to James and John, the sons of Zebedee, because they wanted to call down "fire from heaven" to consume the Samaritans for not "receiving" the Lord Jesus. It is said in the Bible to signify "sons of thunder," but "sons of

tumult" would probably be nearer its meaning (*Luke* ix, 54; *see Mark* iii, 17).

Boar, The. Richard III. *See* BLUE BOAR.

The wretched, bloody, and usurping boar
That spoiled your summer fields and fruitful vines:
. . . This foul swine . . . lies now . . .
Near to the town of Leicester, as we learn.
SHAKESPEARE: *Richard III,* v. 3.

Buddha and the boar. A Hindu legend relates that Buddha died from eating boar's flesh dried. The third avatar of Vishnu was in the form of a boar, and in the legend "dried boar's flesh" probably typifies esoteric knowledge prepared for popular use. None but Buddha himself must take the responsibility of giving out occult secrets, and he died while preparing for the general esoteric knowledge.

The bristled Baptist boar. So Dryden denominates the Anabaptists in his *Hind and Panther.*

The bristled Baptist boar, impure as he [*the ape*],
But whitened with the foam of sanctity,
With fat pollutions filled the sacred place,
And mountains levelled in his furious race.
Pt. i, 43.

Boar's Head. The Old English custom of serving this as a Christmas dish is said to derive from Scandinavian mythology. Freyr, the god of peace and plenty, used to ride on the boar Gullinbursti; his festival was held at Yuletide (*winter solstice*), when a boar was sacrificed to his honour.

The head was carried into the banqueting hall, decked with bays and rosemary on a gold or silver dish, to a flourish of trumpets and the songs of the minstrels. Many of these carols are still extant (*see* CAROL), and the following is the first verse of that sung before Prince Henry at St. John's College. Oxford, at Christmas, 1607:—

The Boar is dead,
So, here is his head;
    What man could have done more
Than his head off to strike,
Meleager like
And bring it as I do before?

The Boar's Head Tavern. Made immortal by Shakespeare, this used to stand in East-cheap, on the site of the present statue of William IV. The sign was the cognisance of the Gordons, the progenitor of which clan slew, in the forest of Huntley, a wild boar, the terror of all the Merse (1093).

Board. In all its many senses, this word is ultimately the same as the A.S. *bord,* a board, plank, or table; but the verb, *to board,* meaning to attack and enter a ship by force, hence to embark on a ship, and figuratively to accost or approach a person, is short for Fr. *aborde*, from *aborder*, which itself is from the same word, *bord*, as meaning the side of a ship. In *starboard, larboard, on board* and *overboard* the sense "the side of a ship" is still evident.

> I'll board her, though she chide as loud
> As thunder.
>
> *Taming of the Shrew*, i, 2.

Boast of England, The. A name given to "Tom Thumb" or "Tom-a-lin" by Richard Johnson, who in 1599 published a "history of this ever-renowned soldier, the Red Rose Knight, surnamed The Boast of England, showing his honourable victories in foreign countries, with his strange fortunes in Faëry Land, and how he married the fair Angliterra, daughter of Prester John. . . ."

Boatswain. (bō′ zàn). The officer who has charge of the boats, sails, rigging, anchors, cordage, cables, and colours. Swain is the old Scand. *sveinn*, a boy, servant, attendant; hence the use of the word in poetry for a shepherd and a sweetheart.

> The merry Bosun from his side
> His whistle takes.
>
> DRYDEN: *Albion and Albanius*.

Boaz. *See* JACHIN.

Bob. Slang for a shilling. The origin of the word is unknown. It dates from about 1800.

Bob. A term used in campanology denoting certain changes in the long peals rung on bells. A *bob minor* is rung on six bells, a *bob triple* on seven, a *bob major* on eight, a *bob royal* on ten, and a *bob maximus* on twelve.

To give the bob to anyone. To deceive, to balk. Here *bob* is from M.E. *bobben*, O.Fr. *bober*, to befool.

> With that, turning his backe, he smiled in his sleeve, to see howe kindely hee had given her the bobbe.—
> GREENE: *Menaphon* (1589).

To bob for apples or cherries is to try and catch them in the mouth while they swing backwards and forwards. *Bob* here means to move up and down buoyantly; hence, the word also means "to curtsy," as in the Scottish song, **If it isn't weel bobbit we'll bob it again**, signifying, if it is not well done we'll do it again.

To bob for eels is to fish for them with a *bob*, which is a bunch of lobworms like a small mop. Fletcher uses the word in this sense:—

> What, dost thou think I fish without a bait, wench?
> I bob for fools: he is mine own, 1 have him.
> I told thee what would tickle him like a trout;
> And, as I cast it, so I caught him daintily.
>
> *Rule a Wife and Have a Wife*, ii, 4.

To bob means also to thump, and a *bob* is a blow.

> He that a fool doth very wisely hit,
> Doth very foolishly, although he smart,
> Not to seem senseless of the bob.
>
> *As You Like It*, ii, 7.

Bear a bob. Be brisk. The allusion is to bobbing for apples, which requires great agility and quickness.

A bob wig. A wig in which the bottom locks are turned up into bobs or short curls.

Bobbed hair is hair that has been cut short—docked—like a bobtailed horse's tail.

Bob's your uncle. In other words, "That'll be all right; you needn't bother any more." The origin of the phrase is unknown; it was certainly in use in the 1880s, but no satisfactory explanation of who "Bob" was has been brought forward.

Pretty bobbish. Pretty well (in spirits and health), from *bob*, as in the phrase *bear a bob* above.

Bobby. A policeman; this slang word is derived from Sir *Robert* Peel, and became popular through his having in 1828 remodelled the Metropolitan Police Force. *Cp.* PEELER.

Bobby-sox. Ankle-length socks affected by teen-age girls in the U.S.A. in the early 1940s; hence the noun **Bobby-soxers**, young women who achieved notoriety by unruly demonstrations at the public appearances of fashionable crooners.

Bobadil. A military braggart of the first water. Captain Bobadil is a character in Ben Jonson's *Every Man in his Humour*. This name was probably suggested by Bobadilla, first governor of Cuba, who sent Columbus home in chains.

Bobbery, as **Kicking up a bobbery,** making a squabble or tumult, kicking up a shindy. It is much used in India, and most probably comes from Hind. *bapre*, "Oh, father!" a common exclamation of surprise.

Boccus, King. *See* SIDRAC.

Bodkin. A word of uncertain origin, originally signifying a small dagger. In the early years of Elizabeth's reign it was applied to the stiletto worn by ladies in the hair. In the *Seven Champions*, Castria took her silver bodkin from her hair, and stabbed to death first her sister and then herself, and it is probably with this meaning that Shakespeare used the word in the well-known passage from *Hamlet*, "When he himself might his quietus make with a bare bodkin."

To ride bodkin. To ride in a carriage between two others, the accommodation being only for two. There is no ground for the suggestion that *bodkin* in this sense is a contraction of *bodykin*, a little body. The allusion to something so slender that it can be squeezed in anywhere is obvious.

> If you can bodkin the sweet creature into the coach.
> GIBBON.

> There is hardly room between Jos and Miss Sharp, who are on the front seat, Mr. Osborne sitting bodkin opposite, between Captain Dobbin and Amelia.
> THACKERAY: *Vanity Fair.*

Bodle. A Scotch copper coin, worth about the sixth of a penny; said to be so called from Bothwell, a mint-master.

> Fair play, he car'd na deils a boddle.
> BURNS: *Tam o' Shanter,* 110.

To care not a bodle is equivalent to our English phrase, "Not to care a farthing."

Bodleian Library (bod lē′ an) (Oxford). So called because it was restored by Sir Thomas Bodley in 1597. It was originally established in 1455 and formally opened in 1488, but it fell into neglect in the course of the next century. It is now, in size and importance, second only to the library of the British Museum, and is one of the five libraries to which a copy of all copyright books must be sent.

Body (A.S. *bodig*).

A compound body, in old chemical phraseology, is one which has two or more *simple* bodies or *elements* in its composition, as water.

A regular body, in geometry, means one of the five regular solids, called "Platonic" because first suggested by Plato. *See* PLATONIC BODIES.

The heavenly bodies. The sun, moon, stars, and so on.

The seven bodies (of alchemists). The seven metals supposed to correspond with the seven "planets."

Planets.		Metals.
1. Apollo, or the Sun	..	Gold.
2. Diana, or the Moon	..	Silver.
3. Mercury	..	Quicksilver.
4. Venus	..	Copper.
5. Mars	..	Iron.
6. Jupiter	..	Tin.
7. Saturn	..	Lead.

To body forth. To give mental shape to an ideal form.

> Imagination bodies forth
> The forms of things unknown.
> SHAKESPEARE: *Midsummer Night's Dream,* v, 1.

To keep body and soul together. To sustain life; from the notion that the soul gives life. The Latin *anima,* and the Greek *psyche,* mean both soul and life; and, according to Homeric mythology and the common theory of "ghosts," the departed soul retains the shape and semblance of the body. *See* ASTRAL BODY.

Body colour. Paint containing body or consistency. Water-colours are made opaque by mixing with white lead.

Body politic. A whole nation considered as a political corporation; the state. In Lat., *totum corpus reipublicœ.*

Body-snatcher. One who snatches or purloins bodies, newly buried, to sell them to surgeons for dissection. The first instance on record was in 1777, when the body of Mrs. Jane Sainsbury was "resurrected" from the burial ground near Gray's Inn Lane. The "resurrection men" (*q.v.*) were imprisoned for six months.

By a play on the words, a bum-bailiff was so called, because his duty was to snatch or capture the body of a delinquent.

Bœotia (bē ō′ shä). The ancient name for a district in central Greece, probably so called because of its abundance of cattle, but, according to fable, because Cadmus was conducted by an ox (Gr. *bous*) to the spot where he built Thebes.

Bœotian (bē ō′ shàn). A rude, unlettered person, a dull blockhead. The ancient Bœotians loved agricultural and pastoral pursuits, so the Athenians used to say they were dull and thick as their own atmosphere; yet Hesiod, Pindar, Corinna, Plutarch, Pelopidas, and Epaminondas, were all Bœotians.

Bœotian ears. Ears unable to appreciate music or rhetoric.

> Well, friend, I assure thee thou hast not got Bœotian ears [*because you can appreciate the beauties of my sermons*].—LE SAGE: *Gil Blas,* vii, 3.

Boethius (bō ē′ thi ùs). Interest in this Roman author (A.D. *c.* 475-*c.* 524) chiefly arises from the fact that his *De Consolatione Philosòphiae* was translated by King Alfred and by Chaucer, who mentions him in the *Canterbury Tales.*

Boffin. A nickname given in the R.A.F. during World War II to research scientists or "backroom boys" (*q.v.*).

Bogus. An adjective applied to anything spurious, sham, or fraudulent, as *bogus currency, bogus transactions.* The word came from America, and is by some connected with *bogy*; but there are other suggestions. One is that it is from an Italian named *Borghese* who, about 1837, was remarkably successful in amassing a fortune in the Western States by means of forged bills, fictitious cheques, etc.; another, that ten years before this the name was given to an apparatus for coining false money; while Lowell (*Biglow Papers*) says, "I more than suspect the word to be a corruption of the French *bagasse*."

Bogy. A hobgoblin; a person or object of terror; a bugbear. The word appeared only in the early 19th century, and is probably connected with the Scottish *bogle*, and so with the obsolete *bug*.

Colonel Bogy. A name given in golf to an imaginary player whose score for each hole is settled by the committee of the particular club and is supposed to be the lowest that a good average player could do it in. *Beating Bogy* or *the Colonel*, is playing the hole in a less number of strokes.

During World War I troops on the march were forbidden to sing a catchy song entitled *Colonel Bogy* as the words they substituted for the real one's were not considered edifying.

Bohea (bō hē'). A type of tea much favoured in the 18th century. The name is a corruption of Wu-i, the hills in China upon whose slopes it is grown.

Bohemia, The Queen of. This old public-house sign is in honour of Elizabeth, daughter of James I, who was married to Frederick, elector palatine, for whom Bohemia was raised into a separate kingdom. It is through her that the Hanoverians succeeded to the throne of Great Britain.

Bohemian. A slang term applied to literary men and artists of loose and irregular habits, living by what they can pick up by their wits. Originally the name was applied to the gipsies, from the belief that before they appeared in western Europe they had been denizens of Bohemia, or because the first that arrived in France came by way of Bohemia (1427). When they presented themselves before the gates of Paris they were not allowed to enter the city, but were lodged at La Chapelle, St. Denis. The French nickname for gipsies is *cagoux* (unsociables).

Boiling-point. He was at boiling-point. Very angry indeed. Properly the point of heat at which water, under ordinary conditions, boils (212° Fahrenheit, 100° Centigrade, 80° Réaumur).

Bold. Bold as Beauchamp. It is said that Thomas Beauchamp, Earl of Warwick, with one squire and six archers, overthrew 100 armed men at Hogges, in Normandy, in 1346.

This exploit is not more incredible than that attributed to Captal-de-Buch, who, with forty followers, cleared Meux of the insurgents called *La Jacquerie*, 7,000 of whom were slain

by this little band, or trampled to death in the narrow streets as they fled panic-struck (1358).

Bold as brass. Downright impudent; without modesty. Similarly we say "brazenfaced."

I make bold to say. I take the liberty of saying; I venture to say.

Bolerium Promontory (bol ē' ri úm). Land's End; the Bellerium (*see* BELLERUS) of the Romans.

Bolero (bo lâr' ō). A Spanish dance; so called from the name of the inventor.

Bolingbroke (bōl' ing bruk). Henry IV of England; so called from Bolingbroke, in Lincolnshire, where he was born (1367-1413).

Bollandists. Editors of the *Acta Sanctorum* begun by John Bollandus, Dutch Jesuit martyrologist (1596-1665); the first two volumes were published in 1643; these contain the saints commemorated in January. The work is not yet finished, but the sixty-first folio volume was published in 1875.

Bollen. Swollen. The past participle of the obsolete English verb, *bell*, to swell. Hence "joints bolne-big" (*Golding*), and "bolne in pride" (*Phaer*). The seed capsule or pod of flax or cotton is called a "boll."

> The barley was in the ear, and the flax was boiled.
> *Exod.* ix, 31.

Bologna Stone (bo lon' yà). A sulphate of baryta found in masses near Bologna. After being heated, powdered, and exposed to the light it becomes phosphorescent.

Bolognese School. There were three periods to the Bolognese School in painting—the Early, the Roman, and the Eclectic. The first was founded by Marco Zoppo, in the 15th century, and its best exponent was Francia. The second was founded in the 16th century by Bagnacavallo, and its chief exponents were Primaticio, Tibaldi, and Nicolo dell' Abate. The third was founded by the Carracci, at the close of the 16th century, and its best masters have been Domenichino, Lanfranco, Guido, Schidone, Guercino, and Albani.

Boloney (bȯ lō' ni). Originally meaning a Bologna sausage, the word is now used to describe something pretentious but useless and worthless. "Bunk" and "hooey" are employed in this same way.

Bolshevik (bol' she vik) or (less correctly) **Bolshevist.** Properly, a member of the Russian revolutionary party that seized power under Lenin in 1917, declared war on capitalism and the bourgeoisie in all lands, and aimed at the establishment of supreme rule by the proletariat. The Bolshevik government was so called because it professed to act in the name of the majority (*bolshe* is the comparative of the adjective *bolshoi*, big, large, and *bolsheviki* = majority).

Bolt. Originally meaning a short thick arrow with a blunt head, is an Anglo-Saxon word, and must not be confused with the old word *bolt* (O.Fr. *bulter*, connected with Lat. *burra*, a coarse cloth) meaning a sieve, or to sieve. This latter word is almost obsolete, but is used by Browning:—

> The curious few
> Who care to sift a business to the bran
> Nor coarsely bolt it like the simpler sort.
>
> *Ring and the Book*, i, 923.

From meaning an arrow *bolt* came to be applied to the door fastening, which is of a similar shape, and these meanings (a missile capable of swift movement, and a fastening) have given rise to combinations and phrases of very separated meaning, as will be seen from the following

Bolt upright. Straight as an arrow.

> Winsinge she was, as is a jolly colt,
> Long as a mast, and upright as a bolt.
>
> CHAUCER: *Miller's Tale*, 77.

The fool's bolt is soon spent. A foolish archer shoots all his arrows so heedlessly that tie leaves himself no resources in case of need.

The horse bolted. The horse shot off like a bolt or arrow.

To bolt out the truth. To blurt it out; also **to bolt out**, to exclude or shut out by bolting the door.

A bolt from the blue. A sudden and wholly unexpected catastrophe or event, like a "thunderbolt" from the blue sky, or flash of lightning without warning and wholly unexpected. Here "bolt" is used for lightning, though, of course, in strict language, a meteorite, not a flash of lightning, is a thunderbolt.

> Namque Diespiter
> Igni corusco nubila dividens,
> Plerumque, per purum tenantes
> Egit equos volucremque currum. . . .
>
> Horace: 1 *Ode* xxxiv, 5, etc.

Bolt in tun. In heraldry, a bird-bolt, in pale, piercing through a tun, often used as a public-house sign. The punning crest of Serjeant Bolton, who died 1787, was "on a wreath a tun erect proper, transpierced by an arrow fesseways or." Another family of the same name has for crest "a tun with a bird-bolt through it proper." A third, harping on the same string, has "a bolt gules in a tun or." The device was adopted as a public-house sign in honour of some family who own it as a coat of arms.

Bolus. Properly, a rather large-sized pill; so called from a Greek word meaning a roundish lump of clay.

Bomb. A metal shell filled with an explosive. From the Gr. *bombos*, any deep, especially humming, noise (ultimately the same word as *boom*).

King Bomba. A nickname given to Ferdinand II, King of Naples, in consequence of his cruel bombardment of Messina in 1848, in which the slaughter and destruction of property was most wanton.

Bomba II was the nickname given to his son Francis II for bombarding Palermo in 1860. He was also called *Bombalino* (Little Bomba).

Bombshell. A word used figuratively in much the same way as *bolt* in *a bolt from the blue*.

Bombast literally means the produce of the bombyx, or silk-worm (Gr. *bombux*); formerly applied to cottonwool used for padding, and hence to inflated language.

> We have received your letters full of love. . . .
> And in our maiden council rated them . . .
> As bombast and as lining to the time.
>
> SHAKESPEARE: *Love's Labour's Lost*, v, 2.

Bombiti. See BARISAL GUNS.

Bon Gaultier Ballads (bon gol' tyèr). Parodies of contemporary poetry by W. E. Aytoun and Sir Theodore Martin. They first appeared in *Tait's*, *Fraser's*, and *Blackwood's Magazines* in the 'forties, and were published in volume form in 1885.

Bon mot (bong mō) (Fr.). A good or witty saying; a pun; a clever repartee.

Bon ton (Fr.). Good manners or manners accredited by good society.

Bon vivant (Fr.). A free liver; one who indulges in the "good things of the table." *Bon viveur* means much the same, but is rather stronger, suggesting one who makes a pursuit of other pleasures besides those of the table.

Bona Fide (bō' nà fī' dì) (Lat.). Without subterfuge or deception; really and truly. Literally, *in good faith*. **To produce bona fides** is to produce credentials, to give proof that someone is what he appears to be or can perform that which he says he can.

Bonanza (bon ǎn' zà). This is a Spanish and Portuguese word meaning fair weather at sea, and prosperity generally. It found its way into English through the miners on the Pacific coast of N. America who applied it to any very rich body of ore in a mine. The silver deposits of the Comstock Mine in Nevada were thus called the Bonanza Mines.

Bona-roba (bō' nà rō' ba). (from Ital. *buona roba*, good stuff, fine gown, fine woman). A courtesan; so called from the smartness of her robes or dresses.

We knew where the bona-robas were.
2 Henry IV, iii, 2.

Bonduca (bon dū′ ka). One of the many forms of the name of the British Queen, which in Latin was frequently (and in English is now usually) written *Boadicea* (*q.v.*). Fletcher wrote a fine tragedy with this name (1616), the principal characters being Caractacus and Bonduca.

Bone. Old thieves' slang for "good," "excellent." From the Fr. *bon*. The lozenge-shaped mark chalked by tramps and vagabonds on the walls of houses where they have been well received is known among the fraternity as a "bone."

Also slang for dice and counters used at cards; and the man who rattles or plays the bones in a negro minstrel show is known as "Uncle Bones."

Bone, To. To filch, as, *I boned it.* Shakespeare (2 *Henry VI*, i, 3) says, "By these ten bones, my lord . . ." meaning the ten fingers; and (*Hamlet*, iii, 2) calls the fingers "pickers and stealers." So "to bone" may mean to finger, that is, "to pick and steal."

Other suggested explanations of the origin of the term are that it is in allusion to the way in which a dog makes off with a bone, and that it is a corruption of the slang "bonnet" (*q.v.*).

You thought that I was buried deep
Quite decent-like and chary,
But from her grave in Mary-bone,
They've come and boned your Mary!
HOOD: *Mary's Ghost.*

A bone of contention. A disputed point; a point not yet settled. The metaphor is taken from two dogs fighting for a bone.

Bred in the bone. A part of one's nature. "What's bred in the bone will come out in the flesh." A natural propensity cannot be repressed.

To have a bone to pick with someone. To have an unpleasant matter to discuss and settle. This is another allusion from the kennel. Two dogs and one bone invariably forms an excellent basis for a fight.

To make no bones about the matter. To do it, say it, etc., without hesitation; to offer no opposition, present no difficulty or scruple. Dice are called "bones," and the Fr. *flatter le dé* (to mince the matter) is the opposite of our expression. To make no bones of a thing is not to flatter, or "make much of," or humour the dice in order to show favour. Hence, *without more bones.* Without further scruple or objection.

Bone-lace. Lace woven on bobbins made of trotter-bones.

Bone-shaker. An "antediluvian," dilapidated four-wheel cab; also an early type of bicycle in use before rubber tyres, chain drive, spring saddles, etc., were thought of.

Boney (bō′ ni). "If you aren't a good boy Boney will catch you" was an old threat of the short-tempered nurse, Boney being Napoleon Bonaparte, whose threatened invasion of England was a real scare in the early 19th century.

Bonfire. Originally a *bone-fire*, that is, a fire made of *bones*; *see* the *Festyvall* of 1493, printed by Wynkyn de Worde in 1515: "In the worship of St. John, the people . . . made three manner of fires: one was of clean bones and no wood, and that is called a bonefire; another of clean wood and no bones, and that is called a wood-fire . . . and the third is made of wood and bones, and is called 'St. John's fire'"; and:—

In some parts of Lincolnshire . . . they make fires in the public streets . . . with bones of oxen, sheep, etc . . . heaped together . . . hence came the origin of bon-fires.— LELAND (1552).

Bonhomie (bon′ o mē) (Fr.). Kindness, good nature; free and easy manners; the quality of being "a good fellow."

The other redeeming qualities of the Meccan are his courage, his bonhomie, his manly suavity of manners.— R. F. BURTON, *El-Medinah.*

Bonhomme. A French peasant. *See* JACQUES BONHOMME.

Bonnet. A player at a gaming-table, or bidder at an auction, to lure others to play or bid, so called because he blinds the eyes of his dupes, just as if he had struck their bonnet over their eyes.

Braid bonnet. The old Scottish cap, made of milled woollen, without seam or lining.

Glengarry bonnet. The Highland bonnet, which rises to a point in front.

He has a green bonnet. Has failed in trade. In France it used to be customary, even in the 17th century, for bankrupts to wear a green *bonnet* (cloth cap).

He has a bee in his bonnet. *See* BEE.

Bonnet lairds. Local magnates or petty squires of Scotland, who wore the braid bonnet, like the common people.

Bonnet-piece. A gold coin of James V of Scotland, the king's head on which wears a bonnet.

Bonnet Rouge. The red cap of Liberty worn by the leaders of the French revolution. It is the emblem of Red Republicanism.

Bonnie Dundee. John Graham, of Claverhouse, Viscount Dundee. Born about 1649, he became a noted soldier in the Stuart cause, and was killed at the Battle of Killiecrankie in 1689.

Bonny-clabber. Sour buttermilk used as a drink. (Irish, *bainne*, milk; *claba*, thick or thickened.)

> It is against my freehold, my inheritance,
> My Magna Charta, cor *lœtificat*,
> To drink such balderdash or bonny-clabber!
> Give me good wine!
>   BEN JONSON: *The New Inn*, I, i.

Bonus. Something "extra"; something over and above what was expected, due, or earned; something "to the good" (Lat. *bonus*, good). An extra dividend paid to shareholders out of surplus profits is called a bonus; so is the portion of profits distributed to certain insurance-policy-holders; and also—as was the custom in the case of Civil Servants and others—a payment made to clerks, workmen, etc., over and above that stipulated for to meet some special contingency that had been un-provided for when the rate was fixed.

Bonze. The name given by Europeans to the Buddhist clergy of the Far East, particularly of Japan. In China the name is given to the priests of the Fohists.

Booby. A spiritless fool, who suffers himself to be imposed upon.

> Ye bread-and-butter rogues, do ye run from me?
> An my side would give me leave, I would so hunt ye,
> Ye porridge-gutted slaves, ye veal-broth boobies!
> BEAUMONT and FLETCHER:
>   *Humorous Lieutenant*, iii, 7.

The player who comes in last in whist-drives, etc.; the lowest boy in the class.

Also a species of Gannet, whose chief characteristic is that it is so tame that it can often be taken by hand.

Booby-prize. The prize—often one of a humorous or worthless kind—given to the "booby" at card parties, children's parties, etc., *i.e.* to the player who makes the lowest score.

Booby trap. A trap set to discomfit an unsuspecting victim.—*e.g.* among children, placing a book on top of a door to fall on whoever opens the door; in war, attaching an explosive charge to the door so that whoever opens it will be killed.

Boogie-woogie (boo' gi woo' gi). A style of piano playing. The left hand maintains a heavy repetitive pattern over which the right hand improvises at will. Probably developed in the Middle West by jazz musicians early in the 20th century, and later given its name by the negro pianist Cou-Cou Davenport, from "Boogie," the devil, or all the troubles in life.

Boojum. *See* SNARK.

Book (A.S. *boc*; Dan. *beuke*; Ger. *buche*, a beech-tree). Beech-bark was employed for carving names before the invention of printing.

> Here on my trunk's surviving frame,
> Carved many a long-forgotten name. . . .
> As love's own altar, honour me:
> Spare, woodman, spare the beechen tree.
>   CAMPBELL: *Beech Tree's Petition*.

In betting the *book* is the record of bets made by the *bookmaker* with different people on different horses.

In whist, bridge, etc., the *book* is the first six tricks taken by either side. The whole pack of cards is sometimes called a "book"—short for "the Devil's picture-book."

Bell, book and candle. *See* BELL.

Beware of a man of one book. Never attempt to controvert the statement of anyone in his own special subject. A shepherd who cannot read will know more about sheep than the wisest bookworm. This caution is given by St. Thomas Aquinas.

On the books. On the list of a club, the list of candidates, the list of voters, or any official list. At Cambridge University they say "on the boards."

Out of my books. Not in favour; no longer on my list of friends.

The Battle of the Books. The Boyle controversy (*q.v.*).

That does not suit my book. Does not accord with my arrangements. The reference is to betting-books, in which the bets are formally entered.

The Book of Books. The Bible; also called simply "the Book," or "the good Book."

The Book of Life, or **of Fate.** In Bible language, a register of the names of those who are to inherit eternal life (*Phil.* iv, 3; *Rev.* xx, 12).

To book it. To take down an order; to make a memorandum; to enter in a book.

To speak by the book. To speak with meticulous exactness. To speak *literatim*, according to what is in the book.

To speak like a book. To speak with great precision and accuracy; to be full of information. Often used of a pedant.

To take one's name off the books. To withdraw from a club. In the passive voice it means to be excluded, or no longer admissible to enjoy the benefits of the institution. *See* ON THE BOOKS, above.

Book-binding. A craft practised since the early Middle Ages when books had become made up of leaves instead of being in a long roll. Most styles of binding are known by the names of their practitioners, but there are others which are known either from the type of design or the name of the patron commissioning them, *e.g.*:—

Aldine. A simple design including a few graceful arabesques, the style in which the Venetian printer Aldus Manutius (fl. 1494-1515) had his wares bound for the general public.

Blind-tooled. A binding on which the ornament is colourless, *i.e.* the tools are pressed direct on to the leather without gold.

Canevari. A style combining gilt arabesques with a cameo, usually of some classical subject, impressed in the centre in blind. Generally ascribed to the Italian Demetrio Canevari, first half 16th century.

Cathedrale. Bindings executed during the second quarter of the 19th century. Under the influence of the Gothic Revival in France and England, the designs resemble the tracery of church windows, hence *reliures à la cathedrale.*

Club. Highly ornamental bindings executed at the "Club Bindery," the private workshop organized by the Grolier Club, New York, during the first decade of the 20th century.

Cottage. A style peculiar to England in the later 17th century; the frame-work in the gilt design includes at top and bottom a triangle resembling a low gable. Associated with the name of Samuel Mearne, a stationer who (though not himself a binder) was binder by appointment to Charles II.

Dentette. (Fr.) "Lace" style, so called from the fact that the design in gilt was of an intricacy and delicacy which resembled lace. Associated particularly with the Padeloup family of binders in France, first half 18th century.

Dos à Dos (Fr.). Back to back. Two books share three boards between them and open on opposite sides. Popular in the 17th century for binding books in pairs, such as the Old and New Testaments.

Fanfare (Fr., pomp.). Very rich bindings with an intricate pattern in gold over the whole, working out to the edges from a small oval in the centre which was either left plain or contained the coat of arms of the owner. Particularly brilliant exponent was the French binder Nicolas Eve, late 16th century.

Grolier. Bindings in the Italian arabesque style done for the French statesman and bibliophile Jean de Grolier (1479-1565). They all bear on the upper cover the lettering *J. Grolerii et amicorum.*

Harleian. A style of binding used upon the great collection of Robert Harley, first Earl of Oxford (1661-1724). Usually red leather, with an ornate diamond-shaped pattern in the centre, surrounded by a broad rectangular border.

Little Gidding. Nicholas Ferrar set up an English Protestant Nunnery at Little Gidding (Huntingdon) in 1625, at which binding was practised by all the inmates. Many bindings, particularly embroidered ones, are ascribed to them, but without any certainty.

Lyonese. An intricate pattern of strapwork in gold is supplemented and heightened by staining the leather or inlaying it with another colour. As these bindings, which date from the second half of the 16th century, are mostly found on books printed at Lyons, they are so called, though it is not certain that they were done there.

Macabre. Bindings executed for Henry III of France after the death of the Princesse de Clèves, and using tears, skulls and bones tooled in silver to express his grief.

Pointillé. In this style all gilt lines are broken into a series of little dots to give a shimmering brilliance. The best exponent was the French binder Le Gascon, mid-17th century.

Roxburghe. Quarter bound in brown leather with crimson paper sides, the style chosen by the Roxburghe Club, an association of wealthy and noble bibliophiles at the beginning of the 19th century.

Sombre. Bindings in black leather tooled entirely in blind, a style affected in the 17th century in England for religious works.

Wotton. Bindings executed for Thomas Wotton, called the English Grolier because, copying the French collector, he had *Thomae Wottoni et amicorum* stamped on his books. Mid-16th century.

Full bound. Bound fully in leather.

Half bound. Leather back and corners, with cloth or paper sides.

Quarter bound. Leather back with cloth or paper sides.

Booking office. In coaching days, when accommodation in the stage coaches was very limited, the traveller had to enter his name in a book kept in the office of the coaching inn, and wait his turn for a place in the coach. For the first few years after the introduction of railways all tickets were written out and entered up in their books by the clerks in the booking offices.

Book-keeper. Clerk who keeps the accounts in merchant's offices, etc.

Book-keeping is the system of keeping debtor and creditor accounts in books provided for the purpose, either by single or by double entry. In the first named each debit or credit is entered only once into the ledger, either as a debit or credit item, under the customer's or salesman's name; in double entry, each item is entered twice into the ledger, once on the debit and once on the credit side.

Waste book. A book in which items are not posted under heads, but as each transaction occurred.

Day book. A book in which are set down the debits and credits which occur day by day. These are ultimately "posted" in the ledger (*q.v.*).

Bookmaker. A professional betting man who makes a "book" (*see above*) on horse-races, etc. Also called a *bookie*.

Bookworm. One always poring over books; so called in allusion to the maggot that eats holes in books, and lives both in and on their leaves.

Boom (boom). A sudden and great demand of a thing, with a corresponding rise in its price. This usage of the word seems to have arisen in America, probably with allusion to the suddenness and rush with which the shares "go off," the same word being used for the rush of a ship under press of sail. The word arises from the sound of booming or rushing water, and the sound made by the bittern is known as *booming*.

The boom was something wonderful. Everybody bought, everybody sold.—MARK TWAIN: *Life on the Mississippi*, ch. 57.

It is also used of a period of rising prices and prosperity, general or particular.

Also a spar on board ship, or the chained line of spars, balks of timber, etc., used as a barrier to protect harbours, is the Dutch *boom*, meaning a tree or pole, our *beam*.

Boon Companion. A convivial or congenial companion. A *bon vivant* is one fond of good living. "Who leads a good life is sure to live well." (Fr. *bon*, good.)

Boondoggling. An expression used in the early 1930s to denote useless spending, usually referring to the spending of money by the U.S. government to combat the depression.

Boot. An instrument of torture made of four pieces of narrow board nailed together, of a length to fit the leg. The leg being placed therein, wedges were inserted till the victim confessed or fainted.

All your empirics could never do the like cure upon the gout as the rack in England or your Scotch boots.— MARSTON: *The Malcontent*.

I measure five feet ten inches without my boots. The meaning is obvious but there is also an allusion to the chopine (*q.v.*) or high-heeled boot, worn at one time to increase the stature.

The boot is on the other foot. The case is altered; you and I have changed places, and whereas before *I* appeared to be in the wrong *you* are now shown to be.

The order of the boot. "The sack"; notice of dismissal from one's employment.

To go to bed in his boots. To be very tipsy.

To have one's heart in one's boots. To be utterly despondent.

I will give you that to boot, *i.e.* in addition. The A.S. *bōt* (Gothic *bota*) means advantage, good, profit; as in Milton's "Alas, what boots it with uncessant care" (*Lycidas*), Alas, what profit is it . . . ?

It also meant compensation paid for injury; reparation. *Cp.* HOUSE-BOTE.

As anyone shall be more powerful . . . or higher in degree, shall he the more deeply make boot for sin, and pay for every misdeed.

Laws of King Ethelred.

Boots. A servant at inns, etc., whose duty it is to clean the boots. Dickens has a Christmas Tale (1855) called *The Boots of the Holly-tree Inn*.

The bishop with the shortest period of service in the House of Lords, whose duty it is to read prayers, is colloquially known as the "Boots," perhaps because he walks into the House in a dead man's shoes or boots, *i.e.* he was not there till some bishop died and left a vacancy.

Booty. The spoils of war.

Playing booty. A trick of dishonest jockeys —appearing to use every effort to come in first, but really determined to lose the race.

Mr. Kemble [in the *Iron Chest*] gave a slight touch of the jockey, and "played booty." He seemed to do justice to the play, but really ruined its success.

George Colman the Younger.

Booze. To drink steadily and continually. Though regarded as slang, this is the M.E. *bousen*, to drink deeply, probably connected with Dut. *buizen*, and Ger. *bousen*, to drink to excess. Spenser uses the word in his description of Gluttony:—

Still as he rode, he somewhat still did eat,
And in his hand did beare a bouzing can,
Of which he supt so oft, that on his seat
His drunken corse he scarse upholden can.

Faerie Queene, I, iv, 22.

Borak or **Al Borak** (bôr′ ak) (the lightning). The animal brought by Gabriel to carry Mohammed to the seventh heaven, and itself received into Paradise. It had the face of a man, but the cheeks of a horse; its eyes were like jacinths, but brilliant as the stars; it had the wings of an eagle, spoke with the voice of a man, and glittered all over with radiant light.

Bordar. In Anglo-Saxon England, a villein of the lowest rank who did menial service for his lord in return for his cottage; the *bordars*, or *bordarii*, were the labourers, and the word is the Med. Lat. *bordarius*, a cottager.

Border, The. The frontier of England and Scotland, which, from the 11th to the 15th century, was the field of constant forays, and a most fertile source of ill blood between North and South Britain.

> March, march, Ettrick and Teviotdale.
> Why the deil dinna ye march forward in order?
> March, march, Eskdale and Liddesdale—
> All the Blue Bonnets are bound for the border.
> SCOTT: *The Monastery.*

Border Minstrel. Sir Walter Scott (1771-1832). because he sang of the border.

Border States, The. The five "slave" states (Delaware, Maryland, Virginia, Kentucky, and Missouri) which lay next to the "free states" were so called in the American Civil War, 1861-65.

Bore. A person who bestows his tediousness on you, one who wearies you with his prate, his company, or his solicitations.

The derivation of the word is uncertain; in the 18th century it was used as an equivalent for *ennui*; hence, for one who suffers from *ennui*, and afterwards for that which, or one who, causes *ennui*.

In racing terminology *to bore* is to ride so that another horse is thrust or pushed off the course, a sense in which it is also used of boats in rowing; in pugilistic language it is to force one's opponent on to the ropes of the ring by sheer weight.

Bore of the Severn. In the Severn and other river estuaries certain winds cause a bore, or great tidal wave that rushes up the channel with violence and noise. In England it is best known in the Severn, Trent, Wye, and Solway Firth, but bores also occur in the Ganges, Indus, and Brahmapootra, in which last the wave rises to some 12 feet.

Boreas (bôr′ ē ăs). In Greek mythology, the god of the north wind, and the north wind itself. He was the son of Astræus, a Titan, and Eros, the morning, and lived in a cave of Mount Hæmus, in Thrace.

Hence *boreal*, of or pertaining to the north.

> In radiant streams,
> Bright over Europe, bursts the Boreal morn.
> THOMSON: *Autumn*, 98.

Born. Born in the purple (a translation of Gr. *porphyrogenitus*). The infant of royal parents in opposition to one **born in the gutter**, or the child of beggars. This refers to the chamber lined with porphyry by one of the Byzantine empresses for her accouchement, and has nothing to do with the purple robes of royalty.

Born with a silver spoon in one's mouth. Born to good luck; born with hereditary wealth. The reference is to the usual gift of a silver spoon by the godfather or godmother of a child. The lucky child does not need to wait for the gift, for it is born with it in its mouth or inherits it at birth. A phrase with a similar meaning is **born under a lucky star;** this, of course, is from astrology.

In all my born days. Ever since I was born; in all my experience.

Not born yesterday. Not to be taken in; worldly wise.

Poets are born, not made. One can never be a poet by mere training or education if one has been born without the "divine afflatus." A translation of the Latin phrase *Poeta nascitur non fit*, of which an extension is *Nascimur poetæ fimus oratores*, we are born poets, we are made orators.

Borrow. Originally a noun (A.S. *borg*) meaning a pledge or security, the modern sense of the verb depended on the actual giving in pledge of something as security for the loan; a security is not now essential in a borrowing transaction, but the idea that the loan is the property of the lender and must be returned some day is always present. The noun sense is seen in the old oath *St. George to borowe*, which is short for "I take St. George as pledge," or "as witness"; also in:

> Ye may retain as borrows my two priests.—SCOTT: *Ivanhoe*, ch. xxxiii.

Borrowed or **borrowing days.** The last three days of March are said to be "borrowed from April," as is shown by the proverb in Ray's *Collection*—"March borrows three days of April, and they are ill." The following is an old rhyme on the same topic:—

> March said to Aperill,
> I see 3 hoggs [*hoggets, sheep*] upon a hill:
> And if you'll lend me dayes 3
> I'll find a way to make them dee [*die*].
> The first o' them was wind and weet,
> The second o' them was snaw and sleet,
> The third o' them, was sic a freeze
> It froze the birds' nebs to the trees,
> But when the Borrowed Days were gane
> The 3 silly hoggs came hirpling [*limping*] hame.

February also (in Scotland) has its "borrowed" days. They are the 12th, 13th and 14th, which are said to be borrowed from January. If these prove stormy the year will be favoured with good weather; but if fine, the year will be foul and unfavourable. They are called by the Scots *Faoilteach*, and hence *faoilteach* means execrable weather.

Borrowed time, to live on. To continue to live after every reasonable presumption is that one should be dead, *i.e.* living on time borrowed from Death.

Borstall (A.S. *beork*, a hill, and *steall*, place, or *stigol*, stile). A narrow roadway up the steep ascent of hills or downs. The word has given the name to the village of Borstal, near Rochester (Kent), and hence to the *Borstal system*, a method of treating youthful offenders against the law by technical instruction and education in order to prevent their drifting into the criminal classes. The first reformatory of this kind was instituted at Borstal in 1902.

Bosey (Austr.). A cricket term for a googly (*q.v.*) and so called from the English bowler B. J. T. Bosanquet who toured Australia in 1903-04. The term was also applied to a single bomb dropped from a plane, in World War II.

Bosh. A Persian word meaning worthless. It was popularized by James Morier in his novel *Ayesha* (1834), and other eastern romances.

I always like to read old Darwin's *Love of the Plants*: bosh as it is in a scientific point of view.
                                KINGSLEY: *Two Years Ago*, ch. x.

Bosom Friend. A very dear friend. Nathan says, "It lay in his bosom, and was unto him as a daughter" (2 *Sam*. xii, 3). Bosom friend, *ami de cœur*. St. John is represented in the New Testament as the "bosom friend" of Jesus.

Bosporus (bos´pôr ŭs) (incorrectly written **Bosphorus**) is a Greek compound meaning "the ford of the ox," or "Oxford." Legend says that Zeus greatly loved Io; he changed her into a white cow or heifer from fear of Hera, to flee from whom Io swam across the strait, which was thence called *bos poros*, the passage of the cow. Hera discovered the trick, and sent a gadfly to torment Io, who was made to wander, in a state of frenzy, from land to land. The wanderings of Io were a favourite subject of story with the ancients. Ultimately, the persecuted Argive princess found rest on the banks of the Nile.

Boss, a master, is the Dut. *baas,* head of the household. Hence the great man, chief, an overseer.

The word was originally more widely used in the United States than in England, it having been attached to political leaders, financial magnates, etc., who—generally by dubious methods—seek to obtain a preponderating influence.

Boss-eyed. Slang for having one eye injured, or a bad squint, or for having only one eye in all. Hence, **boss one's shot,** to miss one's aim, as a person with a defective eye might be expected to do; and *a boss*, a bad shot. **Boss-backed,** a good old word for "hump-backed," is in no way connected with this. *Boss* here is a protuberance or prominence, like the bosses on a bridle or a shield.

Boston Tea-party. An incident leading up to the American War of Independence. The British Parliament had passed laws which favoured the London East India Company at the expense of American traders. Three cargoes of tea which arrived at Boston Harbour in 1773, shortly after the legislation, were thrown overboard as a protest by a party of colonists dressed as Indians. This act of defiance is known as the Boston Tea-party.

Botanomancy (bot´ ăn ō măn´ si) Divination by leaves. One method was by writing sentences on leaves which were exposed to the wind, the answer being gathered from those which were left; another was through the crackling made by the leaves of various plants when thrown on the fire or crushed in the hands.

Botany Bay. An extensive inlet in New South Wales, discovered by Captain Cook in 1770. It was the first place of his landing upon Australian soil, and Cook himself thus named it on account of the great variety of new plants found there. Botany Bay was wrongly applied as a name of the convict settlement established in 1788 at Sydney Cove. In contemporary parlance the name was applied not only to New South Wales but even to the whole of Australia.

Bo-tree. The pipal tree, or *Ficus religiosa*, of India, allied to the banyan, and so called from Pali *Bodhi*, perfect knowledge, because it is under one of these trees that Gautama attained enlightenment and so became the Buddha. At the ruined city of Anuradhapura in Ceylon is a bo-tree that is said to have grown from a cutting sent by King Asoka in 288 B.C.

Bottle. The accepted commercial size of a wine bottle is one holding $26\frac{2}{3}$ fluid ounces per reputed quart. Large bottles are named as follows:—

Magnum	...	holding	2	ordinary	bottles.
Double-magnum or Jeroboam		"	4	"	"
Rehoboam	..	"	6	"	"
Methuselah	..	"	8	"	"
Salmanazar	..	"	12	"	"
Balthazar	..	"	16	"	"
Nebuchadnezzar		"	20	"	"

Brought up on the bottle. Said of a baby which is artificially fed instead of being nursed at the breast.

Looking for a needle in a bottle of hay, or **in a haystack.** Looking for a very small article amidst a mass of other things. Bottle is a diminutive of the Fr. *botte*, a bundle; as *botte de foin*, a bundle of hay.

> Methinks I have a great desire to a bottle of hay.
> *Midsummer Night's Dream*, iv, 1.

To bottle up one's feelings, emotions, etc. To suppress them; to hold them well under control.

Bottle-washer. Chief agent; the principal man employed by another; a factotum. The full phrase—which usually is applied more or less sarcastically—is "chief cook and bottle-washer."

Bottled moonshine. Social and benevolent schemes, such as Utopia, Coleridge's Pantisocracy, the dreams of Owen, Fourier, St. Simon, the New Republic, and so on.

The idea was probably suggested by Swift's Laputan philosopher, in *Gulliver's Travels*, who

> Had been eight years upon a project of extracting sunbeams out of cucumbers, which were to be put into phials hermetically sealed, and let out to warm the air in raw inclement summers.

Bottom. In nautical language the keel of a ship, that part of the hull which is below the waves; hence, the hull itself, and hence extended to mean the whole ship, especially in such phrases as *goods imported in British bottoms* or *in foreign bottoms*.

A vessel is said to have a *full bottom* when the lower half of the hull is so disposed as to allow large stowage, and a *sharp bottom* when it is capable of speed.

At the bottom. At the base or foot.

> Pride is at the bottom of all great mistakes.
> RUSKIN: *True and Beautiful*, p. 426.

From the bottom of my heart. Without reservation.

> If one of the parties . . . be content to forgive from the bottom of his heart all that the other hath trespassed against him.—*Prayer Book*.

He was at the bottom of it. He really instigated it, or prompted it.

To get to the bottom of the matter. To ascertain the entire truth; to bolt a matter to its bran.

To knock the bottom out of anything. *See* KNOCK.

To touch bottom. To reach the lowest depth.

A horse of good bottom means of good stamina, good foundation.

Bottom the Weaver. A man who fancies he can do everything, and do it better than anyone else. Shakespeare has drawn him as profoundly ignorant, brawny, mock heroic, and with an overflow of self-conceit. He is in one part of *Midsummer Night's Dream* represented with an ass's head, and Titania, queen of the fairies, under a spell, caresses him as an Adonis.

The name is very appropriate, as one meaning of *bottom* is a ball of thread used in weaving, etc. Thus in Clark's *Heraldry* we read, "The coat of Badland is *argent*, three bottoms in fess *gules*, the thread *or*."

Bottomless Pit, The. Hell is so called in the book of *Revelation*, xx, 1. The expression had previously been used by Coverdale in *Job* xxxvi, 16.

William Pitt was humorously called *the bottomless Pitt*, in allusion to his remarkable thinness.

Bottomry. A nautical term implying a contract by which in return for money advanced to the owners a ship, or *bottom* (*q.v.*), is, in a manner, mortgaged. If the vessel is lost the lender is not repaid; but if it completes its voyage he receives both principal and interest.

Boudicca. The preferred form of Boadicea (*q.v.*).

Boudoir. Properly speaking, a room for sulking in (Fr. *bouder*, to sulk). When the word was introduced into England in the last quarter of the 18th century it was as often applied to a man's sanctum as to a woman's retiring room; now, however, it is used only for a private apartment where a lady may retire, receive her intimate friends, etc.

Bought and Sold, or **Bought, Sold, and Done For.** Ruined, done for, outwitted.

> Jocky of Norfolk, be not too bold,
> For Diccon, thy master, is bought and sold.
> *Richard III*, v, 3.

> It would make a man mad as a buck to be so bought and sold.—*Comedy of Errors*, iii, 1.

Bouillabaisse (boo' ya bās). A soup, for which Marseilles is celebrated, made of fish boiled with herbs in water or white wine.

Boulangism (boo lonj' izm). This was a sort of political frenzy that swept over France in 1886-87. General Boulanger (1837-91) was a smart soldier who, in 1886, was appointed minister of war. By genuine reforms in the army, but more by a spectacular display of his handsome person on a fine horse at reviews, he won the hearts and stirred the imagination of the Paris mob, who cried that he was the one man in France to retrieve the glories lost in the disastrous Franco-Prussian war. But Boulanger was really a man of straw, played on by all the reactionary parties in France, and after sweeping the country in a wave of patriotism and xenophobia, the Boulangist movement died out from lack of any man to lead it. Boulanger fled to exile, and eventually committed suicide in Brussels.

Bounce. Brag, swagger; boastful and mendacious exaggeration.

> He speaks plain cannon, fire, and smoke, and bounce.
> SHAKESPEARE: *King John*, ii, 2.

On the bounce. Ostentatiously swaggering. Trying to effect some object "on the bounce" is trying to attain one's end through making an impression that is unwarrantable.

Bounds, Beating the. An old custom, still kept up in a few English parishes, of going round the parish boundaries on Holy Thursday, or Ascension Day. The school-children, accompanied by the clergymen and parish officers, walked through their parish from end to end; the boys were switched with willow wands all along the lines of boundary, the idea being; to teach them to know the bounds of their parish.

Many practical jokes were played even during the first quarter of the nineteenth century, to make the boys remember the delimitations: such as "pumping them," pouring water clandestinely on them from house windows, beating them with thin rods, etc.

Beating the bounds was called in Scotland *Riding the marches* (bounds), and in England the day is sometimes called *gang-day*.

Bounder. To call a man a bounder was to stigmatize him as a vulgar, ill-mannered cad, an outsider, one who did not behave himself, especially where women are concerned.

Bounty. *See* QUEEN ANNE'S BOUNTY.

Bounty. The Mutiny of the. Much has been written and acted on the theme of this famous tragedy. In 1788 Captain William Bligh was sent in command of H.M.S. *Bounty* to the Society Islands to collect vegetable products with a view to propagating them in the W. Indies. In April, 1789, his crew mutinied and Bligh, with 18 loyal sailors, was set adrift in an open boat, ultimately landing in Timor, near Java. Meanwhile the crew of the *Bounty* reached Tahiti, whence nine of them, accompanied by some native men and women, sailed to the uninhabited Pitcairn Island where they settled. Ten years later only one of the men, John Adams, was alive, but there were several women and children from whom the present inhabitants are descended.

Bouquet. French for nosegay, bunch of flowers. The word is used in English also for the flavour or aroma of wine, a jewelled spray, and a large flight of rockets or of pheasants which have been driven by the beaters.

Bourbon (boor' bon). The Bourbon Kings of France were Henry IV, Louis XIII, XIV, XV, and XVI (1589-1793), Louis XVIII and Charles X (1814-30). The family is so named from the seigniory of Bourbon, in the Bourbonnais, in Central France, and is a branch of the Capet stock, through the marriage of Beatrix, heiress of the Bourbons, to Robert, Count of Clermont, sixth son of Louis IX, in 1272. Henry IV was tenth in descent from Louis IX and the twentieth king to succeed him.

Bourbons also reigned over Naples and the two Sicilies, and the present royal house of Spain is Bourbon, being descended from Philippe, Duke of Anjou, a grandson of Louis XIV, who became King of Spain in 1700.

It was said of the Bourbons that they forgot nothing and learned nothing.

In U.S.A. the term Bourbon is used for whisky made from Indian corn, sometimes with rye or malt added. The name comes from Bourbon (*pron.* ber' bun) County, Kentucky, where the whisky was originally made.

Bourgeois (Fr.). Our burgess; a member of the class between the "gentlemen" and the peasantry. It includes merchants, shopkeepers, and the so-called "middle class."

In typography, *bourgeois* (pronounced burjois') is the name of a size of type between long primer and brevier.

Bourgeoisie (Fr.). The merchants, manufacturers, and master-tradesmen considered as a class.

> The Commons of England, the Tiers-Etat of France, the bourgeoisie of the Continent generally, are the descendants of this class [artisans] generally.
> MILL: *Political Economy*.

In recent years, particularly since the Russian Revolution, when this class was held to be chiefly responsible for the continuance of privilege and for all sorts of abuses during the old regime and the early part of the new, the word *bourgeoisie* has been applied more particularly to the unimaginative, conventional and narrow-minded section of the middle classes.

Boustrophedon (boo strof' e don). A method of writing found in early Greek inscriptions in which the lines run alternately from right to left and left to right, like the path of oxen in ploughing. (Gr. *boustrepho*, ox-turning.)

Bouts-rimés (boo rē' mā) (Fr. rhymed-endings). A parlour game which, in the 18th century, had a considerable vogue in literary circles as a test of skill. A list of words that rhyme with one another is drawn up; this is handed to the competitors, and they have to make a poem to the rhymes, each rhyme-word being kept in its place on the list.

Bovey Coal. A lignite found at Bovey Tracy, in Devonshire.

Bow (bō) (A.S. *boga*; connected with the O.Teut, *beguan*, to bend.)

Bow (bou). The fore-end of a boat or ship. (A.S. *bog* or *boh*, connected with Dan, *boug*, Icel. *bogr*, a shoulder.)

Bow-wow Word (bou wou). A word in imitation of the sound made, as hiss, cackle, murmur, cuckoo, etc. Hence *the bow-wow school*, a term applied in ridicule to philologists who sought to derive speech and language from the sounds made by animals. The terms were first used by Max Müller.

Bowden (bou' den). **Not every man can be vicar of Bowden.** Not everyone can occupy the first place. Bowden is one of the best livings in Cheshire.

Bowdlerize (bou' dler īz). To expurgate a book. Thomas Bowdler, in 1818, gave to the world an edition of Shakespeare's works "in which nothing is added to the original text; but those words and expressions are omitted which cannot with propriety be read aloud in a family." This was in ten volumes. Bowdler subsequently treated Gibbon's *Decline and Fall* in the same way. Hence the words Bowdlerist, Bowdlerizer, Bowdlerism, etc.

Bower. A lady's private room. (A.S. *bur*, a chamber.)

But come to my bower, my Glasgerion,
　When all men are at rest;
As I am a ladie true of my promise,
　Thou shalt bee a welcome guest.
　　　　　　From the ballad *Glasgerion.*

Hence, *bower-woman*, a lady's maid and companion.

Bower, the term used in euchre, is an entirely different word. It is *bauer*, a peasant or knave.

But the hands that were played
　By that heathen Chinee,
And the points that he made,
　Were quite frightful to see—
Till at last he put down a right bower
Which the same Nye had dealt unto me.
　BRET HARTE: *Plain Language from Truthful James.*

The *right bower* is the knave of trumps; the *left bower* is the other knave of the same colour.

Bower of Bliss. In Spenser's *Faerie Queene* (Bk. II) the enchanted home of Acrasia.

Bowie Knife. James Bowie (pron. Boo-ee)

was a Southerner who for some years from 1818 smuggled negro slaves with the great pirate Jean Lafitte. In 1827 he was present at a duel on a sandbar in the Mississippi near Natchez which ended in a general melée in which six of the seconds and spectators were killed and fifteen wounded. Bowie killed one Major Norris Wright with a knife he had made from a black-smith's rasp—10 to 15 inches long, with one sharp edge and curving to a point. This knife attracted so much attention that Bowie sent it to a cutler in Philadelphia, who marketed copies as the Bowie-knife. Bowie moved to Texas where, in the revolution against Mexico, he was killed with Davy Crockett by General Santa Anna after the fall of the Alamo on March 6th, 1836.

Bowing (bou' ing). We uncover the head when we wish to salute anyone with respect; but the Jews, Turks, Siamese, etc., uncover their feet. The reason is this: With us the chief act of investure is crowning or placing a cap on the head; but in the East it is putting on the slippers.

Bowler Hat. This stiff, felt hat—known in America as a Derby hat—was the invention of a London hatter. The *Daily News* for August 8th, 1868, says: "Mr. Bowler, of 15 St. Swithin's Lane has, by a very simple contrivance invented a hat that is completely ventilated whilst, at the same time, the head is relieved of the pressure experienced in wearing hats of the ordinary description." The last words apply to the hot and heavy top hats until then in universal use.

Bowling, Tom (bō ling). The type of a model sailor; from the character of that name in Smollett's *Roderick Random.*

The Tom Bowling referred to in Dibdin's famous sea-song was Captain Thomas Dibdin, brother of Charles Dibdin (1768-1833), who wrote the song, and father of Thomas Frognall Dibdin, the bibliomaniac.

Here a sheer hulk lies poor Tom Bowling,
　The darling of the crew.

Bowls. They who play bowls must expect to meet with rubbers. Those who touch pitch must expect to defile their fingers. Those who enter upon affairs of chance, adventure, or dangerous hazard must make up their minds to encounter crosses, losses, or difficulties. The *rubber* is the final game which decides who is the winner.

Bowyer God. The "archer god," usually Cupid, but in his translation of the *Iliad* Bryant (I, v, 156) applies the epithet to Apollo.

Box. I've got into the wrong box. I am out of my element, or in the wrong place. Lord

Lyttelton used to say that whenever he went to Vauxhall and heard the mirth of his neighbours, he used to fancy pleasure was in every box but his own. Wherever he went for happiness, he somehow always got into the wrong box.

Box and Cox has become a phrase which can only be explained by the story. Box and Cox were two lodgers who, unknown to each other, occupied the same room, one being out at work all day, the other all night.

Box-cars. In throwing dice, in the U.S.A., a double six is known as a box-cars; from its resemblance to freight cars, or goods wagons.

Box Days. In the Scottish Court of Session, two days in spring and autumn, and one at Christmas, during vacation, in which pleadings may be filed. This custom was established in 1690, for the purpose of expediting business. Each judge has a private box with a slit, into which informations may be placed on box days, and the judge, who alone has the key, examines the papers in private.

Boxing-Day. *See* CHRISTMAS BOX.

Boxing weights.—

Flyweight,	112 lb. and under.
Bantam,	118 lb. "
Feather,	126 lb. "
Light,	135 lb. "
Welter,	147 lb. "
Middle,	160 lb. "
Light heavy,	175 lb. "
Heavy,	all over 175 lb.

Boxers. A secret society in China which took a prominent part in the rising against foreigners in 1900 and was suppressed by joint European action. The Chinese name was *Gee Ho Chuan*, signifying "righteousness, harmony, and fists," and implying training as in athletics, for the purpose of developing righteousness and harmony.

Boy Scouts were started in Great Britain by General Baden-Powell in 1908, with the purpose of training lads to be good citizens with high ideals of honour, thoughtfulness for others, cleanliness, obedience and self-reliance. The movement spread to other countries and in 1950 had a membership of over five million young people. Scouts are graded according to age into three classes; Wolf Cubs, 8 to 11; Scouts, 11 and upwards; Rover Scouts over 17. *See also* GIRL GUIDES.

Boycott. To boycott a person is to refuse to deal with him, to take any notice of him, or even to sell to him. The term arose in 1881, when Captain Boycott, an Irish landlord, was thus ostracized by the Irish agrarian insurgents.

One word as to the way in which a man should be boycotted. When any man has taken a farm from which a tenant has been evicted, or is a grabber, let everyone in the parish turn his back on him; have no communication with him; have no dealings with him. You need never say an unkind word to him; but never say anything at all to him. If you must meet him in fair, walk away from him silently. Do him no violence, but have no dealings with him. Let every man's door be closed against him; and make him feel himself a stranger and a castaway in his own neighbourhood.—J. DILLON, M.P.: *Speech to the Land League* (February 26th, 1881).

Boyle Controversy. A book-battle between Charles Boyle, fourth Earl of Orrery, and the famous Bentley, respecting the *Epistles of Phalaris*, which were edited by Boyle in 1695. Two years later Bentley published his celebrated *Dissertation*, showing that the epistles (*see* PHALARIS) were spurious, and in 1699 published another rejoinder, utterly annihilating the Boyle partisans. Swift's *Battle of the Books* (*q.v.*) was one result of the controversy.

Boyle's law. The volume of a gas is inversely proportional to the pressure if the temperature remains constant. If we double the pressure on a gas, its volume is reduced to one-half; if we quadruple the pressure, it will be reduced to one-fourth; and so on; so called from the Hon. Robert Boyle (1627-91).

Boyle Lectures. A course of eight sermons on natural and revealed religion delivered annually at St. Mary-le-Bow Church, London. They were instituted by the Hon. Robert Boyle, and began in 1692, the year after his death.

Boz. Charles Dickens (1812-70). "Boz, my signature in the *Morning Chronicle*," he tells us, "was the nickname of a pet child, a younger brother, whom I had dubbed Moses, in honour of the *Vicar of Wakefield*, which, being pronounced *Boses*, got shortened into *Boz*."

Bradamante (brăd′ à mănt). The sister of Rinaldo in *Orlando Furioso* and *Innamorato*. She is represented as a wonderful Christian Amazon, possessed of an irresistible spear which unhorsed every knight it struck.

Bradbury. A £1-note, as issued by the Treasury 1914-28, bearing the signature of J.S. Bradbury (subsequently Baron Bradbury), who was at that time Permanent Secretary to the Treasury.

Bradshaw's Guide was started in 1839 by George Bradshaw (1801-53) printer, in Manchester. The *Monthly Guide* was first issued in December, 1841, and consisted of thirty-two pages, giving tables of forty-three lines of English railway.

Brag. A game at cards; so called because the players brag of their cards to induce the company to make bets. The principal sport of the game is occasioned by any player *bragging* that he holds a better hand than the rest of the party, which is declared by saying "I brag," and staking a sum of money on the issue. (*Hovle*.)

Braggadocio (brăg á dō' si ō). A braggart; one who is valiant with his tongue but a great coward at heart *Cp.* ERYTHYNUS. The character is from Spenser's *Faerie Queene*, and a type of the "Intemperance of the Tongue." After a time, like the jackdaw in borrowed plumes, Braggadocio is stripped of all his glories: his shield is claimed by Sir Marinell; his lady is proved by the golden girdle to be the false Florimel; his horse is claimed by Sir Guyon; Talus shaves off his beard and scourges his squire; and the pretender sneaks off amidst the jeers of everyone. It is thought that the poet had the Duke d'Alençon, a suitor of Queen Elizabeth, in his eye when he drew this character (*Faerie Queene*, ii, 3; iii, 5, 8, 10; iv, 2,4; v, 3; etc.).

Brahma (bra'má). In Hinduism Brahma, properly speaking, is the Absolute, or God conceived as entirely impersonal; this theological abstraction was later endowed with personality, and became the Creator of the universe, the first in the divine Triad, of which the other partners were Vishnu, the maintainer, and Siva (or Shiva), the destroyer. As such the Brahmins claim Brahma as the founder of their religious system.

> Whate'er in India, holds the sacred name
> Of piety or lore, the Brahmins claim;
> In wildest rituals, vain and painful, lost,
> Brahma, their founder, as a god they boast.
> CAMOËNS: *Lusiad*, Bk. vii.

Brahmin. A worshipper of Brahma, the highest caste in the system of Hinduism, and of the priestly order. *See* CASTE.

Brahmo Somaj (Sanskrit, "the Society of Believers in the One God"). A monotheistic sect of Brahmins, founded in 1818 in Calcutta by Ramohun Roy (*c*. 1777-1833), a wealthy and well-educated Brahmin who wished to purify his religion and found a National Church which should be free from idolatry and superstition. In 1844 the Church was reorganized by Debendro Nath Tagore, and since that time its reforming zeal and influence has gained it many adherents.

Brains Trust. Originally a name applied by James M. Kieran of the *New York Times* to the advisers of Franklin Roosevelt in his election campaign. Later applied to the group of college professors who advised him in administering the New Deal. In England the name was given to a popular radio programme in which well-known public figures aired their views on questions submitted by listeners.

Brain-wave. A sudden inspiration; "a happy thought."

Brand. The merchant's or excise mark branded on the article itself, the vessel which contains the article, the wrapper which covers it, the cork of the bottle, etc., to guarantee its being genuine, etc.

Brandan, St., or **Brendan.** A semi-legendary Irish saint, said to have died and been buried at Clonfert (at the age of about 94), in 577, where he was abbot over 3,000 monks.

He is best known on account of the very popular mediæval story of his voyage in search of the Earthly Paradise, which was supposed to be situated on an island in mid-Atlantic. The voyage lasted for seven years, and the story is crowded with marvellous incidents, the very birds and beasts he encountered being Christians and observing the fasts and festivals of the Church!

> And we came to the Isle of a Saint who had sailed
> with St. Brendan of yore,
> He had lived ever since on the Isle and his winters
> were fifteen score.
> TENNYSON: *Voyage of Maeldune*.

Brandenburg. Confession of Brandenburg. A formulary or confession of faith drawn up in the city of Brandenburg in 1610, by order of the elector, with the view of reconciling the tenets of Luther with those of Calvin, and to put an end to the disputes occasioned by the Confession of Augsburg.

Brandon. An obsolete form of *brand*, a torch. *Dominica de brandonibus* (St. Valentine's Day), when boys used to carry about brandons (Cupid's torches).

Brandy is a spirit distilled from the fermented juice of the grape, and may be made wherever wine is made. The most famous are those made in the Cognac and Armagnac districts of France.

Brass. Impudence, effrontery. **As bold as brass,** with barefaced effrontery. **Brass** is also a slang term for money.

A church **brass** is a funeral effigy made in latten and fastened down to a tombstone forming part of the floor of a church. Such effigies are mostly of the 14th and 15th centuries and are decorative in design. Rubbings can be made most successfully with cobbler's wax on coarse paper.

The Man of Brass. Talus, the work of Vulcan. He traversed Crete to prevent strangers from setting foot on the island, threw rocks at the Argonauts to prevent their landing, and used to make himself red-hot, and then hug intruders to death.

Brass Hat. A soldier's name for a staff officer, or an officer of high rank. It dates from the South African War (1899-1902), and refers to the gold oak leaves with which such officers' hats were ornamented on the brim.

To get down to brass tacks. To get down to the essentials, or the tacks which hold the structure together.

Brassbounder. A premium apprentice on a merchant ship.

Brat. A child, especially in contempt. The origin of the word is unknown, but it may be from the Welsh *breth*, swaddling clothes, or Gaelic *brat*, an apron.

> O Israel! O household of the Lord!
> O Abraham's brats! O brood of blessed seed!
> GASCOIGNE: *De Profundis.*

Brave. A fighting man, among the American Indians, was so called

Alonso IV, of Portugal (1290-1357) was so called.

Bravery. Finery is the Fr. *braverie*. The French for courage is *bravoure*.

> What woman in the city do I name
> When that I say the city woman bears
> The cost of princes on unworthy shoulders?
> Who can come in and say that I mean her? . . .
> Or what is he of basest function
> That says his bravery is not of my cost?
> *As You Like It*, ii, 7.

Brawn. The test of the brawn's head. A little boy one day came to the court of King Arthur, and, drawing his wand over a boar's head, declared, "There's never a cuckold's knife can carve this head of brawn." No knight in the court except Sir Cradock was able to accomplish the feat. (Percy's *Reliques.*)

Bray. *See* VICAR.

Brazen Age. The age of war and violence. It followed the silver age.

> To this next came in course the brazen age,
> A warlike offspring, prompt to bloody rage,
> Not impious yet. Hard steel succeeded then,
> And stubborn as the metal were the men.
> DRYDEN: *Metamorphoses*, i.

Brazen-faced. Bold (in a bad sense), without shame.

> What a brazen-faced varlet art thou!
> SHAKESPEARE: *King Lear*, ii, 2.

Brazen head. The legend of the wonderful head of brass that could speak and was omniscient is common property to early romances, and is of Eastern origin. In *Valentine and Orson*, for instance, we hear of a gigantic head kept in the

castle of the giant Ferragus (*q.v.*). of Portugal. It told those who consulted it whatever they required to know, past, present, or to come; but the most famous in English legend is that fabled to have been made by the great Roger Bacon.

It was said if Bacon heard it speak he would succeed in his projects; if not, he would fail. His familiar, Miles, was set to watch, and while Bacon slept the Head spoke thrice: "Time is"; half an hour later it said, "Time was." In another half-hour it said, "Time's past," fell down, and was broken to atoms. Byron refers to this legend.

> Like Friar Bacon's brazen head, I've spoken,
> "Time is," "Time was," "Time's past."

References to Bacon's Brazen Head are frequent in literature. Most notable is Robert Greene's *Honorable History of Friar Bacon and Friar Bungay*, 1594. Among other allusions may be mentioned:

> Bacon trembled for his brazen head.
> POPE: *Dunciad*, iii, 104.
> Quoth he, "My head's not made of brass,
> As Friar Bacon's noddle was."
> BUTLER: *Hudibras*, ii, 2.

See also SPEAKING HEADS.

Brazen out, To. To stick to an assertion knowing it to be wrong; to outface in a shameless manner; to disregard public opinion.

Breach of Promise. A contract to marry is as binding in English law as any other contract, and if it is broken the party breaking it is liable to pay damages. The woman who breaks an engagement is just as liable in law as a man. In actions for breach of promise of marriage the plaintiff is entitled to the recovery of any pecuniary loss, such as the cost of a trousseau, and such sentimental or punitive damages as the jury may consider appropriate. *See* BETROTHAL.

Breaches, meaning *creeks* or *small bays*, is to be found in *Judges* v, 17. Deborah, complaining of the tribes who refused to assist her in her war with Sisera, says that Asher remained "in his breaches," that is, creeks on the seashore.

> Spenser uses the word in the same way: —
> The heedful Boateman strongly forth did stretch
> His brawnie armes, and all his body straine,
> That th' utmost sandy breach they shortly fetch.
> *Faerie Queene*, II, xii, 21.

In Coverdale's version of the Bible the passage is rendered

> Asser sat in the haven of the see, and taried in his porcions.

Bread. Cast thy bread upon the waters: for thou shalt find it after many days (*Eccles.* xi, 1). When the Nile overflows its banks the weeds perish and the soil is disintegrated. The rice-seed being cast into the water takes root, and is found in due time growing in healthful vigour.

To break bread. To partake of food. Common in Scripture language.

Upon the first day of the week, when the disciples came together to break bread, Paul preached to them.— *Acts* xx, 7.

Breaking of bread. The Eucharist.

They continued . . . in breaking of bread, and in prayer.—*Acts* ii, 42 and 46.

To know which side one's bread is buttered. To be mindful of one's own interest.

Break, To. To bankrupt (*q.v.*).

To break a bond. To dishonour it.

To break a butterfly on a wheel. To employ superabundant effort in the accomplishment of a small matter.

Satire or sense, alas! can Sporus feel,
Who breaks a butterfly upon a wheel.
POPE: *Epistle to Dr. Arbuthnot*, 307-8.

To break a matter to a person. To be the first to impart it, and to do so cautiously and piecemeal.

To break bread. *See* BREAD.

To break cover. To start forth from a hiding-place.

To break down. To lose all control of one's feelings; to collapse, to become hysterical. A *break-down* is a temporary collapse in health; it is also the name given to a wild kind of negro dance.

To break faith. To violate one's word or pledge; to act traitorously.

To break ground. To commence a new project. As a settler does.

To break in. To interpose a remark. To train a horse to the saddle or to harness, or to train any animal or person to a desired way of life.

To break one's fast. To take food after long abstinence; to eat one's breakfast after the night's fast.

To break one's neck. To dislocate the bones of one's neck.

To break the ice. To prepare the way; to cause the stiffness and reserve of intercourse with a stranger to relax; to impart to another bit by bit distressing news or a delicate subject.

To break your back. To make you bankrupt; to reduce you to a state of impotence. The metaphor is from carrying burdens on the back.

To break up. To discontinue classes at the end of term time and go home; to separate. Also, to become rapidly decrepit or infirm. "Old So-and-so is breaking up; he's not long for this world."

To break with someone. To cease from intercourse.

If thou dost love fair Hero, cherish it;
And I will break with her, and with her father,
And thou shalt have her.
Much Ado, i, 1.

To get a break. To have an unexpected chance; to have an opportunity of advancing oneself in business, etc.

To make a break may mean either to make a complete change, or it may imply the committing of some social error, an unfortunate mistake.

To run up a score in billiards or snooker.

Break. A short solo improvisation in jazz music.

Breakers Ahead. Hidden danger at hand. Breakers in the open sea always announce sunken rocks, sand banks, etc.

Breaking a Stick. Part of the marriage ceremony of certain North American Indians, as breaking a wineglass is part of the marriage ceremony of the Jews.

In one of Raphael's pictures we see an unsuccessful suitor of the Virgin Mary breaking his stick. This alludes to the legend that the several suitors were each to bring an almond stick, which was to be laid up in the sanctuary over-night, and the owner of the stick which budded was to be accounted the suitor which God approved of. It was thus that Joseph became the husband of Mary.

In Florence is a picture in which the rejected suitors break their sticks on Joseph's back.

Breast. To make a clean breast of it. To make a full confession, concealing nothing.

Breath. All in a breath. Without taking breath (Lat. *continenti spiritu*).

It takes one's breath away. The news is so astounding it causes one to hold one's breath with surprise.

Out of breath. Panting from exertion; temporarily short of breath.

Save your breath to cool your porridge. Don't talk to me, it is only wasting your breath.

You might have saved your breath to cool your porridge.—Mrs. GASKELL: *Libbie Marsh* (Era 111).

To catch one's breath. To check suddenly the free act of breathing.

"I see her," replied I, catching my breath with joy.
Capt. MARRYAT: *Peter Simple*.

To hold one's breath. Voluntarily to cease breathing for a time.

To take breath. To cease for a little time from some exertion in order to recover from exhaustion of breath.

Under one's breath. In a whisper or undertone of voice.

To breathe one's last. To die.

Breeches. To wear the breeches. Said of a woman who usurps the prerogative of her husband. Similar to **The grey mare is the better horse.** *See* GREY.

Breeches Bible, The. *See* BIBLE, SPECIALLY NAMED.

Breeches buoy. A pair of short canvas breeches forming a cradle in which, by means of a pulley and rope, people can be conveyed from ship to ship or ship to shore.

Breeze, meaning a light gale or strongish wind (and, figuratively, a slight quarrel) is from the Fr. *brise*, and Span. *brisa*, the north-east wind. *Breeze*, the small ashes and cinders used in burning bricks, and nowadays worked up into breeze-blocks for building, is the Fr. *braise*, older form *brese*, meaning glowing embers, or burning charcoal, and is connected with Swed. *brasa*, fire, and our *brazier*. *Breeze* in *breeze-fly* is A.S. *briosa*. So the three words, *breeze*, are in no way connected.

The breeze-fly. The gad-fly; called from its sting (A.S. *briosa*; Gothic, *bry*, a sting).

Breezy. A breezy person is one who is open, jovial, perhaps inclined to be a little boisterous.

Brehon Laws (brē′ hon). This is the English name for an ancient legal system which prevailed in Ireland from about the 7th century. They cover every phase of Irish life and furnish an interesting picture of the country in those early days.

Brendan, St. *See* BRANDAN.

Bren-gun. The World War II equivalent of a Lewis (*q.v.*) machine-gun. It was originally made in Brno, Czechoslovakia, and then manufactured in Enfield, England. The word "bren" is a blend of Brno and Enfield.

Brentford. Like the two kings of Brentford smelling at one nosegay. Said of persons who were once rivals, but have become reconciled. The allusion is to *The Rehearsal* (1672), by the Duke of Buckingham. "The two kings of Brentford enter hand in hand," and the actors, to heighten the absurdity, used to make them enter " smelling at one nosegay " (act ii, sc. 2).

Bretwalda (bret′ wol′ dà). The name given to Egbert and certain other early English kings who exercised a supremacy—often rather shadowy—over the kings of the other English states. *See* HEPTARCHY. It means "ruler" or "overlord of the Brets" or "Britons."

The office of Bretwalda, a kind of elective chieftainship, of all Britain, was held by several Northumbrian kings, in succession.

EARLE: *English Tongue*, p. 26.

Brevet Rank (brev′ ét). Titular rank without the pay that usually goes with it. A brevet major had the title of major, but the pay of captain, or whatever his *substantive* rank happened to be. (Fr. *brevet*, dim. of *bref*, a letter, a document.)

Breviary (brē′ vi àr i). A book containing the daily "Divine Office," which those in orders in the Roman Catholic Church are bound to recite. The Office consists of psalms, collects, readings from Scripture, and the life of some saint or saints.

Brew. Brew me a glass of grog, *i.e.* mix one for me. *Brew me a cup of tea, i.e.* make one for me. *The tea is set to brew, i.e.* to draw. The general meaning of the word is to boil or mix; the restricted meaning is to make malt liquor.

Brewer. The Brewer of Ghent, Jakob van Artevelde (d. 1345); a popular Flemish leader who, though by birth an aristocrat, was a member of the Guild of Brewers.

Brian Boru, or Boroma (brī′ àn bo roo′, bo ro′ ma). This great Irish chieftain was king of Munster in 978 and became chief king of all Ireland in 1002. On Good Friday, 1014, his forces defeated the Danes at the battle of Clontarf, but Brian, who was too old to fight, being almost eighty, was killed in his tent.

Briareus (brī âr′ ē ús), or Ægeon. A giant with fifty heads and a hundred hands. Homer says the gods called him Briareus, but men called him Ægeon (*Iliad*, i, 403). He was the offspring of Heaven and Earth and was of the race of the Titans, with whom he fought in the war against Zeus.

He [Ajax] hath the joints of every thing, but every thing so out of joint that he is a gouty Briareus, many hands and no use, or purblind Argus, all eyes and no sight.—
SHAKESPEARE: *Troilus and Cressida*, i, 2.

The Briareus of languages. Cardinal Mezzofanti (1774-1849), who is said to have spoken fifty-eight different tongues. Byron called him "a walking polyglot; a monster of languages; a Briareus of parts of speech."

Bold Briareus. Handel (1685-1759), so called by Pope:—

Strong in new arms, lo! giant Handel stands,
Like bold Briareus, with a hundred hands;
To stir, to rouse, to shake the soul he comes,
And Jove's own thunders follow Mars's drums.
POPE: *Dunciad*, iv, 65.

Briar-root Pipe. A tobacco-pipe made from the root-wood of the large heath (*bruyère*), which grows in the south of France.

Bribery and Corruption is a phrase often used rather loosely in English. In English law a bribe is a gift or other material inducement held out to a person to betray a trust or duty.

Bribing at an election is a very serious offence, of which briber and bribed are held to be equally guilty. The payment of secret commissions to induce business is forbidden by the Prevention of Corruption Act of 1906. The servant or agent asking for such a bribe is equally punishable with the briber, the maximum punishment being a fine of £500 with or without imprisonment for a maximum of two years.

Bric-à-brac. Odds and ends of curiosities. In French, a *marchand de bric-à-brac* is a seller of rubbish, as old nails, old screws, old hinges, and other odds and ends of small value; but we employ the phrase for odds and ends of vertu. *Bricoler* in archaic French means *Faire toute espèce de métier*, to be Jack of all trades. *Brac* is the ricochet of *bric*, as fiddle-faddle and scores of other double words in English. Littré says that it is formed on the model of *de bric et de broc*, by hook or by crook.

Brick. A regular brick. A jolly good fellow; perhaps because a brick is solid, four-square, plain, and reliable.

> A fellow like nobody else, and in fine, a brick.—
> GEORGE ELIOT: *Daniel Deronda*, Bk. ii, ch. 16.

Bride. The bridal wreath is a relic of the *corona nuptialis* used by the Greeks and Romans to indicate triumph.

Bride-ale. *See* CHURCH-ALE. It is from this word that we get the adjective *bridal*.

Bride cake. A relic of the Roman *confarreatio*, a mode of marriage practised by the highest class in Rome. It was performed before ten witnesses by the Pontifex Maximus, and the contracting parties mutually partook of a cake made of salt, water, and flour (*far*). Only those born in such wedlock were eligible for the high sacred offices.

Bride or wedding favours represent the true lover's knot, and symbolize union.

Bride of the Sea. Venice; so called from the ancient ceremony of the wedding of the sea by the Doge, who threw a ring into the Adriatic, saying, "We wed thee, O sea, in token of perpetual domination." This took place each year on Ascension Day, and was enjoined upon the Venetians in 1177 by Pope Alexander III, who gave the Doge a gold ring from his own finger in token of the victory achieved by the Venetian fleet at Istria over Frederick Barbarossa, in defence of the pope's quarrel. At the same time his Holiness desired that the doges should throw a similar one into the sea on each succeeding Ascension Day, in commemoration of the event. *See* BUCENTAUR.

Bridegroom. In O.E. this word was *bride-gome* (A.S. *bryd-guma*), from Gothic *guma*, a man. In M.E. times the *-gome* became corrupted into *grome*, and owing to this confusion and the long loss of the archaic *guma*, the word became connected with *grom*, or *grome*, a lad (which gives our *groom*), and hence the modern *bridegroom*.

Bridewell. A generic term for a house of correction, or prison, so called from the City Bridewell, in Blackfriars, which was built as a hospital on the site of a former royal palace over a holy well of medical water, called St. Bride's (Bridget's) Well. After the Reformation, Bridewell was made a penitentiary for unruly apprentices and vagrants. It was demolished in 1863.

> At my first entrance it seemed to me rather a Prince's Palace than a House of Correction, till gazing round me, I saw in a large room a parcel of ill-looking mortals stripped to their shirts like haymakers, pounding hemp. . . . From thence we turned to the women's apartment, who we found were shut up as close as nuns. But like so many slaves they were under the care and direction of an overseer who walked about with a very flexible weapon of offence to correct such hempen journey-women as were unhappily troubled with the spirit of idleness.—NED WARD: *The London Spy*.

Bridge. A variety of whist, said to have originated in Russia, in which one of the hands ("dummy") is exposed. **Auction Bridge** is a modification of bridge, in which there are greater opportunities for gambling.

Contract Bridge is a development of Auction Bridge in which the pair of partners cannot score the tricks they win towards making a game unless they have previously contracted to do so. To win a game one of the pairs must score 100 points for tricks as contracted, the value of the tricks being reckoned in points according to whatever suit is trumps. The further ramifications of Contract Bridge call for a modern "Hoyle" rather than a modern "Brewer."

Bridge of Jehennam. Another name for Al-Sirat (*q.v.*).

Bridge of Sighs. Over this bridge, which connects the palace of the doge with the state prisons of Venice, prisoners were conveyed from the judgment-hall to the place of execution.

> I stood in Venice on the Bridge of Sighs,
> A palace and a prison on each hand.
> BYRON: *Childe Harold's Pilgrimage*, iv, 1.

A bridge over the Cam at St. John's College, Cambridge, which resembles the Venetian original, is called by the same name.

Waterloo Bridge, in London, used, some years ago, when suicides were frequent there, to be called *The Bridge of Sighs*, and Hood gave the name to one of his most moving poems:—

One more Unfortunate,
   Weary of breath,
Rashly importunate,
   Gone to her death!

Bridle. To bite on the bridle is to suffer great hardships. Horses bite on the bridle when trying, against odds, to get their own way.

Bridle road or way. A way for a riding-horse, but not for a horse and cart.

To bridle up. In Fr. *se rengorger*, to draw in the chin and toss the head back in scorn or pride. The metaphor is to a horse pulled up suddenly and sharply.

Bridport. Stabbed with a Bridport dagger, *i.e.* hanged. Bridport, in Dorsetshire, was once famous for its hempen goods, and monopolized the manufacture of ropes, cables, and tackling for the British navy. The hangman's rope being made at Bridport gave birth to the proverb.—Fuller: *Worthies.*

Brief. In legal parlance, a summary of the relevant facts and points of law given to a counsel in charge of a case. Hence, a *briefless barrister,* a barrister with no briefs, and therefore no clients.

Brief is also the name given to a papal letter of less serious or important character than a bull (*q.v.*); and, in the paper trade, to foolscap ruled with a marginal line, and either thirty-six or forty-two transverse lines, also to the size of a foolscap sheet when folded in half.

Brig, brigantine (brig, brig′ ån tēn). The terms applied to two smaller types of sailing vessel. A brig was a two-masted craft with both masts square-rigged; the brigantine, also two-masted, had the fore-mast square-rigged and the main-mast fore-and-aft rigged.

Brigade of Guards. See HOUSEHOLD TROOPS.

Brigand. A French word, from the Ital. *brigante*, pres. part. of *brigare*, to quarrel. In England *brigands* were originally light-armed, irregular troops, like the Bashi-Bazouks, and, like them, were addicted to marauding. The *Free Companies* of France were brigands.

In course of time the Ital. *brigante* came to mean a robber or pirate; hence the use of *brigandine*, later *brigantine*, for a sailing vessel, and also *brig* (*q.v.*).

Brilliant. A form of cutting of precious stones introduced by Vincenzo Peruzzi at Venice in the late 17th century. Most diamonds are now brilliant-cut, and the word "brilliant" commonly means a diamond cut in this way. In a perfect brilliant there are 58 facets.

Brilliant Madman, The. Charles XII of Sweden. (1682, 1697-1718).

Macedonia's madman or the Swede.
                    JOHNSON: *Vanity of Human Wishes.*

Bring. To bring about. To cause a thing to be done.

To bring down the house. To cause rapturous applause in a theatre.

To bring into play. To cause to act, to set in motion.

To bring round. To restore to consciousness or health; to cause one to recover (from a fit, etc.).

To bring to. To restore to consciousness; to resuscitate. There are other meanings.

"I'll bring her to," said the driver, with a brutal grin; "I'll give her something better than camphor."
                    MRS. STOWE: *Uncle Tom's Cabin.*

To bring to bear. To cause to happen successfully.

To bring to book. To detect one in a mistake.

To bring to pass. To cause to happen.

Brinvilliers, Marquise de (brin vē′ yā), a noted French poisoner. She was born about 1630 and was executed in Paris in 1676. Having ruined her husband, the Marquis, and squandered his fortune, she became the lover of the Seigneur de Sainte Croix, who instructed her in the use of a virulent poison, supposed to have been aqua tofana. With this she poisoned her father and other members of her family in order to obtain possession of the family lands and wealth. Her crimes came to light when she accidentally poisoned Sainte Croix, in 1672.

Briny. I'm on the briny. The sea, which is salt like brine.

Brioche (brē′ osh). A kind of sponge-cake made with flour, butter, and eggs. When Marie Antoinette was talking about the bread riots of Paris during October 5th and 6th, 1789, the Duchesse de Polignac naïvely exclaimed, "How is it that these silly people are so clamorous for *bread*, when they can buy such nice brioches for a few sous?" It is said that our own Princess Charlotte avowed "that she would for her part *rather eat beef than starve*," and wondered that the people should be so obstinate as to insist upon having bread when it was so scarce.

Brisbane Line. In World War II a defensive position running from north of Brisbane to north of Adelaide, to which it was intended to retire if the Japanese invaded Australia in 1942.

Brissotins. A nickname given to the advocates of reform in the French Revolution, because they were "led by the nose" by Jean Pierre Brissot. The party was subsequently called the Girondists (*q.v.*).

Bristol Board. A stiff drawing-paper with a smooth surface, or a fine quality of cardboard composed of two or more sheets pasted together, the substance of board being governed by the number of sheets. Said to have been first made at Bristol.

Bristol Boy, The. Thomas Chatterton (1752-70), who was born at Bristol, and there composed his *Rowley Poems. See* ROWLEY.

> The marvellous boy.
> The sleepless soul that perished in his pride.
>   WORDSWORTH: *Resolution and Independence.*

Bristol cream is a particularly fine rich brand of sherry. *See* BRISTOL MILK.

Britain. The derivation of this word is not certainly known, but its first recorded use is by the Greeks, who probably obtained it through the Greek colony at Massilia (Marseilles). *Itan,* or *etan,* in Basque signifies a district or country; the root appears in many names, *e.g.* Aqu*itan*ia, Lus*itan*ia, Maure*tan*ia.

Another suggestion is that it is from the Cymric-Celtic root, *brith,* meaning "to paint," with allusion to woad-painting of their bodies by the aborigines.

Great Britain consists of "Britannia prima" (England), "Britannia secunda" (Wales), and "North Britain" (Scotland), united under one sway. The term first came into use in 1604, when James I was proclaimed "King of Great Britain."

Greater Britain. The whole British Empire, *i.e.* Great Britain, the Dominions and Colonies.

Britannia. The first known representation of Britannia as a female figure sitting on a globe, leaning with one arm on a shield, and grasping a spear in the other hand, is on a Roman coin of Antoninus Pius, who died A.D. 161. The figure reappeared on our copper coin in the reign of Charles II, 1665, and the model was Frances Stewart, afterwards created Duchess of Richmond. The engraver was Philip Roetier, 1665.

> The King's new medall, where in little, there is Mrs. Stewart's face . . . and a pretty thing it is, that he should choose her face to represent Britannia by.—*Pepys's Diary.*

British Council. This was established in 1934 for the purpose of encouraging British cultural interests abroad, including the formation of schools, the introduction of foreign students to this country, and the projection of a knowledge of all aspects of British life and thought through the press, films, distribution of literature, exhibitions, lectures, concerts and plays. The British Council is financed by Parliament, on a Foreign Office vote.

British Empire, Order of the. This order was instituted in 1917 with two divisions, military and civil. It is conferred for services rendered to the Empire, whether at home or abroad and is given to women equally with men. There are five classes: Knight Grand Cross (G.B.E.); Knight Commander (K.B.E.); Commander (C.B.E.); Officer (O.B.E.); and member (M.B.E.). In the case of women D.B.E. (D = dame) takes the place of K.B.E.

Britisher, A. An American term for a Briton, a native of the British Isles, often with a derogatory implication.

Brittany, The Damsel of. Eleanor, daughter of Geoffrey, second son of Henry II of England, and Constance, daughter of Conan IV of Brittany. At the death of Prince Arthur (1203) she was heiress to the English throne, but John confined her in Bristol castle, where she died in 1241.

Broach. To broach a new subject. To start one in conversation. The allusion is to beer barrels, which are tapped by means of a peg called a *broach.* So "to broach a subject" is to introduce it, to bring it to light, as beer is drawn from the cask after the latter has been *broached.*

> I did broach this business to your highness.
>   *Henry VIII,* ii, 4.

Broad Arrow. The representation of an arrowhead placed on Government stores, and also upon the uniform of convicts. It was introduced by Henry, Earl of Romney, who was Master General of the Ordnance, 1693-1702 and employed his own cognisance of a pheon, or broad arrow.

Broadcasting. This is the term used to describe the sending out of wireless programmes of news, music, etc., to be received by those who have the necessary apparatus to listen in. The first transmitting station for entertainment and educational purposes began broadcasting in 1920. In May, 1922, the Marconi Co. began a programme of speech and music from Marconi House, London (2LO). In October of the same year the British Broadcasting Company came into being, and in 1926 this became the British Broadcasting Corporation (B.B.C.) with a royal charter. In 1950 the number of licences issued amounted to nearly twelve million.

Broadcloth. The best cloth for men's clothes. So called from its great breadth. It required two weavers, side by side, to fling the shuttle across it. Originally two yards wide, now about fifty-four inches; but the word is now used to signify a fine, plain-wove, black cloth.

> An honest man, close-button'd to the chin,
> Broadcloth without, and a warm heart within.
> COWPER: *Epistle to Joseph Hill.*

Broadside. A large sheet of paper printed on one side only; strictly, the whole should be in one type and one measure, *i.e.* must not be divided into columns. It is also called a *broadsheet.*

> Van Citters gives the best account of the trial. I have seen a broadside which confirms his narrative.
> MACAULAY: *History.*

In naval language, a *broadside* means the whole side of a ship; and to "open a broadside on the enemy" is to discharge all the guns on one side at the same moment.

Brobdingnag. In Swift's *Gulliver's Travels,* the country of giants, to whom Gulliver was a pigmy "not half so big as a round little worm plucked from the lazy finger of a maid." Hence the adjective, *Brobdingnagian,* colossal.

Brogue. An Irish word, *brog,* a shoe, connected with A.S. *broc,* breeches. A *brogue* is properly, a stout coarse shoe of rough hide; and secondarily hose, trousers. The use of *brogue* for the dialect or manner of speaking may be from this—*i.e.* "brogue" is the speech of those who wear "brogues".

Broken Music. In Elizabethan England this term meant (*a*) part, or concerted music, *i.e.* music performed on instruments of different classes, such as the "consorts" given in Morley's *Consort Lessons* (1599), which are written for the treble lute, cithern, pandora, flute, treble viol, and bass viol, and (*b*) music played by a string orchestra, the term in this sense probably originating from harps, lutes, and such other stringed instruments as were played without a bow, not being able to sustain a long note. It is in this sense that Bacon uses the term:—

> Dancing to song is a thing of great state and pleasure. I understand it that the song be in quire, placed aloft and accompanied with some broken music.—*Essays: Of Masques and Triumphs.*

Shakespeare two or three times makes verbal play with the term:—

> *Pand.:* What music is this?
> *Serv.:* I do but partly know, sir; it is music in parts. . . .
> *Pand.:* . . . Fair Prince, here is good broken music.
> *Paris.:* You have broke it, cousin; and by my life, you shall make it whole again.
> *Troilus and Cressida,* iii. 1.

Broker. This word meant originally a man who broached wine, and then sold it; hence, one who buys to sell again, a retailer, a second-hand dealer, a middleman. The word is formed in the same way as *tapster,* one who *taps* a cask. In modern use some restricting word is generally

prefixed: as bill-broker, cotton-broker, ship-broker, stock-broker, etc.

Bromide. A person given to making trite remarks; later, the remark itself. It was first used in this sense by Gelett Burgess (1866-1951) in his novel *Are You a Bromide?* 1906.

Bronco (western U.S.A.). A wild or semi-wild horse (Sp. *bronco,* rough). A **Bronco-buster** is a highly-skilled horse-breaker specializing in the training of such animals.

Brontes (bron' tēz). A blacksmith personified; in Greek mythology, one of the Cyclops. The name signifies *Thunder.*

Bronx cheer. The American term for a derisive sound made with the tongue between the lips, known in England as a "raspberry."

Broom. The small wild shrub with yellow flowers (Latin *planta genista*) from which the English royal dynasty, the Plantagenets, took their name. The founder of the dynasty, Geoffrey of Anjou (father of Henry II) is said to have worn a sprig of it in his hat. The name was officially adopted by Richard of York (father of Richard III) about 1460.

Broom. A broom is hung at the masthead of ships about to be sold—to be "swept away." The idea is popularly taken from Admiral van Tromp (*see* PENNANT); but probably this allusion is more witty than true. The custom of hanging up something special to attract notice is very common; thus an old piece of carpet from a window indicates household furniture for sale; a wisp of straw indicates oysters for sale; a bush means wine for sale, etc., etc.

Brother. A fellow-member of a religious order. *Friar,* from Lat. *frater,* and Fr. *frère,* is really the same word.

Also used as the official title of certain members of livery companies, of the members (always known as "Elder Brethren") of Trinity House (*q.v.*), and the official mode of address of one barrister to another.

Brother used attributively with another substantive denotes a fellow-member of the same calling, order, corporation, etc. Thus *brother birch,* a fellow-schoolmaster, *brother-blade,* a fellow-soldier or companion in arms, *brother bung,* a fellow licensed victualler, *brother mason,* a fellow freemason, etc., etc.

Browbeat. To beat or put a man down with sternness, arrogance, insolence, etc.; from knitting the brows and frowning on one's opponent.

Brown. A copper coin, a penny; so called from its colour. Similarly a sovereign is a "yellow boy."

To be done brown. To be deceived, taken in; to be "roasted." This is one of many similar expressions connected with cooking. *See* COOKING.

Browned off. This is a slang phrase that came into general use during World War II, meaning "fed up," bored or disillusioned. Various derivations of the phrase have been suggested, but none of them appears satisfactory.

Brown Bill. A kind of halbert used by English foot-soldiers before muskets were employed. They were staff weapons, with heads like bill-hooks but furnished with spikes at the top and back. The *brown* probably refers to the rusty condition in which they were kept; though, on the other hand, it may stand for *burnished* (Dut. *brun*, shining), as in the old phrases "my bonnie brown sword," "brown as glass," etc. Keeping the weapons *bright*, however, is a modern fashion; our forefathers preferred the honour of blood stains. In the following extract the term denotes the soldiers themselves:—

> Lo, with a band of bowmen and of pikes,
> Brown bills and targetiers.
>
> MARLOWE: *Edward II*, 1, 1324.

Brown Bomber. Joe Louis (*b.* 1914), undefeated heavyweight champion of the world from 1937 until his retirement in 1949. On his return in 1950 he was defeated by Ezzard Charles. He began his professional career in 1934, winning 27 fights, all but four by knock-outs. He won the heavyweight title from Jim Braddock and successfully defended it more than 22 times before joining up in the U.S. army. Louis is possibly the greatest heavyweight boxer ever known. The phrase applied to him springs from his being a Negro and (presumably) from the lethal power of his punches.

Brown study. Absence of mind; apparent thought, but real vacuity. The corresponding French expression explains it—*sombre rêverie*. *Sombre* and *brun* both mean sad, melancholy, gloomy, dull.

> Invention flags, his brain grows muddy,
> And black despair succeeds brown study.
>
> CONGREVE: *An Impossible Thing.*

Brownie. The house spirit in Scottish superstition. He is called in England Robin Goodfellow. At night he is supposed to busy himself in doing little jobs for the family over which he presides. Farms are his favourite abode. Brownies are brown or tawny spirits, in opposition to fairies, which are fair or elegant ones. *See also* GIRL GUIDE.

It is not long since every family of considerable substance was haunted by a spirit they called Browny,

which did several sorts of work; and this was the reason why they gave him offerings . . . on what they called "Browny's stone."—MARTIN: *Scotland.*

Brownists. Followers of Robert Brown, of Rutlandshire, a vigorous Puritan controversialist in the time of Queen Elizabeth. The later "Independents" held pretty well the same religious tenets as the Brownists. Sir Andrew Aguecheek says:—

> I'd as lief be a Brownist as a politician.
>
> SHAKESPEARE: *Twelfth Night*, iii, 2.

Bruin (broo' in). In Butler's *Hudibras*, one of the leaders arrayed against the hero. His prototype in real life was Talgol, a Newgate butcher who obtained a captaincy for valour at Naseby. He marched next to Orsin (Joshua Gosling, landlord of the bear-gardens at Southwark).

Sir Bruin. The bear in the famous German beast-epic, *Reynard the Fox.*

Brumby. An Australian wild horse. The origin of the word is obscure.

Brummagem (brŭm' à jem). Worthless or very inferior metal articles made in imitation of better ones. The word is a local form of the name *Birmingham*, which is the great mart and manufactory of gilt toys, cheap jewellery, imitation gems, and the like.

Brunhild (broon' hild). Daughter of the King of Issland (*i.e.* Isalaland, in the Low Countries), beloved by Günther, one of the two great chieftains in the *Nibelungenlied*. She was to be carried off by force, and Günther asked his friend Siegfried to help him. Siegfried contrived the matter by snatching from her the talisman which was her protector, but she never forgave him for his treachery.

Brunswicker. *See* BLACK BRUNSWICKERS.

Brunt. To bear the brunt. To bear the worst of the heat, and collision. The "brunt of a battle" is the hottest part of the fight. *Cp.* FIRE-BRAND.

Brush. The tail of a fox or squirrel, which is brush-like and bushy.

He brushed by me. He just touched me as he went quickly past. Hence also *brush*, a slight skirmish.

To brush up. To renovate or revive; to bring again into use what has been neglected as, "I must brush up my French."

Brut (brut). A rhyming chronicle of British history beginning with the mythical *Brut*, or *Brute* (*q.v.*), and so named from him. Wace's *Le Roman de Brut*, of *Brut d'Angleterre*, written in French about 1150, is a rhythmical version of Geoffrey of Monmouth's *History* with

additional legends. It is here that first mention
is made of Arthur's Round Table. Wace's work
formed the basis of Layamon's *Brut* (early
13th cent.), a versified history of England from
the fall of Troy to A.D. 689 Layamon's poem
contains 32,250 lines; Wace's rather over 14,000.
See ARTHUR.

Brute or **Brutus** (broot). In the mythological
history of England, the first king of the Britons
was son of Sylvius (grandson of Ascanius and
great-grandson of Æneas). Having inadvertently killed his father, he first took refuge in
Greece and then in Britain. In remembrance
of Troy, he called the capital of his kingdom
Troy-novant (*q.v.*), now London.

Brutum fulmen (broo' tum fŭl' men) (Lat.).
A noisy but harmless threatening; an innocuous
thunderbolt.

The phrase is from Pliny's "*Bruta fulmina et
vana, ut quœ nulla veniant ratione naturæ*"
(II, xliii, 113) — Thunderbolts that strike blindly
and harmlessly, being traceable to no natural
cause.

The Actors do not value themselves upon the Clap,
but regard it as a mere *Brutum fulmen*, or empty Noise,
when it has not the sound of the Oaken Plant in it. —
ADDISON: *Spectator* (November 29th, 1711).

Brutus, Junius (broo' tus joo' ni ŭs). In legend,
the first consul of Rome, fabled to have held office
about 509 B.C. He condemned to death his own
two sons for joining a conspiracy to restore to the
throne the banished Tarquin. He was —

The public father who the private quelled,
And on the dread tribunal sternly sat.
                  THOMSON: *Winter.*

Brutus, Marcus (85-42 B.C.). Cæsar's friend,
who joined the conspirators to murder him
because he made himself a king.

And thou, unhappy Brutus, kind of heart,
Whose steady arm, by awful virtue urged,
Lifted the Roman steel against thy friend.
        THOMSON: *Winter,* 324-6.

Et tu, Brute. Thou, too, Brutus! The reference
is to the exclamation of Julius Cæsar when
he saw that his old friend was one of the
conspirators engaged in stabbing him to death.

Bub. Drink; particularly strong beer.

Drunk with Helicon's waters and double-brewed
bub. — PRIOR: *To a Person who wrote ill.*

Bubastis. Greek name of Bast, or Pasht, the
Diana of Egyptian mythology; she was daughter
of Isis and sister of Horus, and her sacred
animal was the cat. *See* CAT.

Bubble, or **Bubble Scheme.** A project or
scheme of no sterling worth and of very ephemeral
duration — as worthless and frail as a bubble. The
word was in common use in the 18th century to
denote a swindle. *See* MISSISSIPPI; SOUTH SEA.

The Bubble Act. An Act of George I,
passed in 1719, its object being to punish the
promoters of bubble schemes. It was repealed
in 1825.

Bubble and squeak. Cold boiled potatoes
and greens fried up together, sometimes with
bits of cold meat as well. They first bubbled in
water when boiled, and afterwards hissed or
squeaked in the frying-pan.

Bucca (bŭk' à). A goblin of the wind, supposed by the ancient inhabitants of Cornwall to
foretell shipwrecks; also a sprite fabled to live in
the tin-mines.

Buccaneer (bŭk a nēr'). Properly, a seller of
smoke-dried meat, from the Brazilian word
boucan, a gridiron or frame on which flesh was
barbecued, which was adopted in France, and
boucanier formed from it. *Boucanier* was first
applied to the French settlers in Hayti, whose
business it was to hunt animals for their skins
and who frequently combined with this business that of a marauder and pirate. *Buccaneer*
thus became applied to any desperate, lawless,
piratical adventurer.

Bucentaur (bū sen' tôr). The name of the
Venetian state-galley employed by the Doge
when he went on Ascension Day to wed the
Adriatic. The word is Gr. *bous*, ox, and *centauros*,
centaur; and the original galley was probably
ornamented with a man-headed ox.

The spouseless Adriatic mourns her lord
And, annual marriage now no more renew'd,
The Bucentaur lies rotting unrestored,
Neglected garment of her widowhood.
        BYRON: *Childe Harold,* iv, 9.

The last *Bucentaur*, third of the name, was
destroyed by the French in 1798. *See* BRIDE OF
THE SEA.

Bucephalos (*bull-headed*). A horse. Strictly
speaking, the favourite charger of Alexander
the Great.

Buchanites. A sect of fanatics who appeared
in the west of Scotland in 1783. They were
named after Mrs. or Lucky Buchan, their
founder, who called herself "Friend Mother in
the Lord," claiming to be the woman mentioned
in *Rev.* xii, and maintaining that the Rev. Hugh
White, a convert, was the "man-child."

I never heard of alewife that turned preacher, except
Luckie Buchan in the West.
        SCOTT: *St. Ronan's Well,* c. ii.

Buck. A dandy; a gay and spirited fellow; a
fast young man.

A most tremendous buck he was, as he sat there
serene, in state, driving his greys.
        THACKERAY: *Vanity Fair,* ch. vi.

The word is also American slang for a dollar.

Buck-basket. A linen-basket. To buck is to wash clothes in lye. When Cade says his mother was "descended from the Lacies," two men overhear him, and say, "She was a pedlar's daughter, but not being able to travel with her furred pack, she washes bucks here at home" (2 *Henry VI*, iv, 2). The word is probably connected with Ger. *beuche*, clothes steeped in lye, and Fr. *buer*, to steep in lye; and perhaps with A.S. *buc*, a pitcher.

To give the bucket, to get the bucket. To give (or receive) notice of dismissal from employment. Here *bucket* is synonymous with *sack* (*q.v.*).

To kick the bucket. To die. *Bucket* here is a beam or yoke (O.Fr. *buquet*, Fr. *trébuchet*, a balance), and in East Anglia the big frame in which a newly slaughtered pig is suspended by the heels is still called a "bucket." An alternative theory is offered that the bucket was a pail kicked away by a suicide, who stood on it the better to hang himself.

Buckhorn. *See* STOCKFISH.

Buckhorse. A severe blow or slap on the face. So called from John Smith, a pugilist of about 1740, whose nickname it was. "Buckhorse" was so insensible to pain that, for a small sum, he would allow anyone to strike him on the side of the face with all his force.

Buckle, I can't buckle to. I can't give my mind to work. The allusion is to buckling on one's armour or belt.

To cut the buckle. To caper about, to heel and toe it in dancing. In jigs the two feet buckle or twist into each other with great rapidity.

Throth, it wouldn't lave a laugh in you to see the parson dancin' down the road on his way home, and the ministher and methodist praicher cuttin' the buckle as they went along.—W. B. YEATS: *Fairy Tales of the Irish Peasantry*, p. 98.

To talk buckle. To talk about marriage.

Buckler. *See* SHIELDS.

Buckram. A strong coarse kind of cloth stiffened with gum; perhaps so called (like *Astrakhan*, from the Eastern city) from Bokhara. In the Middle Ages the name was that of a valuable fabric that came from the East.

Buckshee (buk' shē). This word undoubtedly comes from baksheesh (*q.v.*) though in its new usage it means something given away free, something thrown in gratis.

Buck-tooth. A large projecting front-tooth; formerly also called a *butter-tooth*.

Buckwheat. A corruption of *beech-wheat* (A.S. *boc*, beech; *see* BUCKINGHAM), so called because its seeds are triangular, like beech-mast.

The botanical name is *Fagopyrum* (beech-wheat).

> The buckwheat
> Whitened broad acres, sweetening with its flowers
> The August wind.
>   BRYANT: *The Fountain*, stanza 7.

Buddha (bŭd' à) (Sanskrit, "the Enlightened"). The title given to Prince Siddhartha or Gautama (*q.v.*), also called (from the name of his tribe, the Sakhyas) Sakya muni, the founder of Buddhism, who lived from about 623 B.C. to 543 B.C.

Buddhism. The system of religion inaugurated by the Buddha in India in the 6th century B.C. The general outline of the system is that the world is a transient reflex of deity; that the soul is a "vital spark" of deity; and that it will be bound to matter till its "wearer" has, by divine contemplation, so purged and purified it that it is fit to be absorbed into the divine essence.

The four sublime verities of Buddhism are as follows:—

(1) Pain exists.

(2) The cause of pain is "birth sin." The Buddhist supposes that man has passed through many previous existences, and all of the heaped-up sins accumulated in these previous states constitute man's "birth-sin."

(3) Pain is ended only by Nirvana.

(4) The way that leads to Nirvana is—right faith, right judgment, right language, right purpose, right practice, right obedience, right memory, and right meditation (eight in all).

The abstract nature of the religion, together with the overgrowth of its monastic system and the superior vitality and energy of Brahminism, caused it to decline in India itself; but it spread rapidly in the surrounding countries and took so permanent a hold that it is computed that at the present time it has some 140 million adherents, of whom $10\frac{3}{4}$ millions are in India, and the rest principally in Ceylon, Tibet, China, and Japan.

Esoteric Buddhism. *See* THEOSOPHY.

Budgeree (bŭj' ėr rē). An Aboriginal Australian word meaning excellent, especially good.

Budget. The statement which the Chancellor of the Exchequer lays annually before the House of Commons, respecting the national income and expenditure, taxes, and salaries. The word is the old Fr. *bougette*, a wallet, and the present use arose from the custom of bringing to the House the papers pertaining to these matters in a leather bag, and laying them on the table. Hence, *to budget*, to prepare a budget or estimate.

A budget of news. A bagful of news, a large stock of news.

Cry budget. A watchword or shibboleth; short for Mumbudget (*q.v.*). Slender says to Shallow:—

We have a nay-word how to know one another. I come to her in white and cry *mum*: she cries *budget*: and by that we know one another.

SHAKESPEARE: *Merry Wives of Windsor*, v, 2.

Buff. Properly, soft, stout leather prepared from the skin of the *buffalo*; hence, any light-coloured leather; and hence the figurative use, the bare skin. "To stand in buff" is to stand without clothing in one's bare skin. "To strip to the buff" is to strip to the skin.

To stand buff. To stand firm, without flinching. Here *buff* means a blow or buffet. *Cp.* BLINDMAN'S BUFF.

And for the good old cause stood buff,
'Gainst many a bitter kick and cuff.
BUTLER: *Hudibras's Epitaph.*

I must even stand buff and outface him. — FIELDING.

The phrase also occurs as **to stand bluff.** Sheridan, in his *School for Scandal*, ii, 3, says: —

That he should have stood bluff to old bachelor so long, and sink into a husband at last.

Here the allusion is probably nautical; a "bluff shore" is one with a bold and almost perpendicular front.

Buffs. *See* REGIMENTAL NICKNAMES.

Buffalo Bill. This was the name made famous by William Frederick Cody (1846-1917), one of the world's greatest showmen. He was born in Iowa and when little more than a boy was a rider of the Pony Express (*q.v.*). In 1861 he became a scout and guide for the U.S. army, and fought in the Civil War. In 1867 he made a contract to supply the labourers constructing the Kansas Pacific railway with buffalo meat, hence his sobriquet. Later on he was fighting once more in the Indian wars and single-handed killed Yellowhand, the Cheyenne chief. In 1883 he organized his Wild West show, which he brought to Europe for the first time in 1887. He paid various visits after this and toured the Continent in 1910. He died at Denver. It is no exaggeration to say that his show, with its Indians, cowboys, sharp-shooters and rough-riders has never been surpassed.

Buffer. A chap, a silly old fellow. In M.E. *buffer* meant a stutterer, and the word is used in *Is.* xxii, 4, in Wyclif's version, where the Authorized Version reads, "And the tongue of the stammerers shall be ready to speak plainly."

Buffoon. Properly, one who puffs out his cheeks, and makes a ridiculous explosion by causing them suddenly to collapse (Ital. *buffone*, from *buffare*, to puff out the cheeks, hence, to jest).

Bug. An old word for goblin, sprite, bogy; probably from Welsh *bwg*, a ghost. The word is used in Coverdale's Bible, which is hence known as the "Bug Bible" (*see* BIBLE, SPECIALLY NAMED), and survives in *bogle*, *bogy*, and in *bugaboo*, a monster or goblin, introduced into the tales of the old Italian romancers, and *bugbear*, a scarecrow, or sort of hobgoblin in the form of a bear.

For all that here on earth we dreadfull hold,
Be but as bugs to fearen babes withall.
SPENSER: *Faerie Queene*, II, xii, 25.

Warwick was a bug that feared us all.
SHAKESPEARE: 3 *Henry IV*, v, 3.

To the world no bugbear is so great
As want of figure and a small estate.
POPE: *Satires*, iii, 67-68.

Making believe
At desperate doings with a bauble-sword
And other bugaboo-and-baby-work.
BROWNING: *Ring and the Book*, v, 949.

In common usage the word **bug** is applied to almost any kind of insect or germ, though more especially to a beetle or an insect that creeps or crawls. Colloquially it can be used to refer to any mental infection, such as "he has the money bug" of one whose sole interest is making money.

Buhl. An incorrect form of Boulle (*q.v.*).

Bulbul. An Eastern bird of the thrush family, noted for its beautiful singing; hence applied to the nightingale.

Bull. A blunder, or inadvertent contradiction of terms, for which the Irish are proverbial. *The British Apollo* (No. 22, 1708) says the term is derived from one Obadiah Bull, an Irish lawyer of London, in the reign of Henry VII, whose blundering in this way was notorious, but there is no corroboration of this story, which must be put down as *ben trovato*. There was a M.E. verb *bull*, to befool, to cheat, and there is the O.Fr. *boule* or *bole*, fraud, trickery; the word may be connected with one of these.

Slang for a five-shilling piece. "Half a bull" is half a crown. Possibly from *bulla* (*see* POPE'S BULL *below*); but, as *bull's eye* was an older slang term for the same thing, this is doubtful. Hood, in one of his comic sketches, speaks of a crier who, being apprehended, "swallowed three hogs (shillings) and a bull." It is also short for bull's eye (*q.v.*).

"Bull" is also a slang term in the British Army for excessive requirements of cleanliness and neatness, needless polishing of equipment, etc.

In Stock Exchange phraseology, a bull is a speculative purchase for a rise; also a buyer who does this, the reverse of a *bear* (*q.v.*). A bull-account is a speculation made in the hope that the stock purchased will rise before the day of settlement.

The terms "bull" and "bear" are broadly used on the Stock Exchange to describe an optimist or pessimist in share-dealing, and were already used in that sense in the early 18th century.

In astronomy, the English name of the northern constellation (Lat. *Taurus*) which contains Aldebaran and the Pleiades; also the sign of the zodiac that the sun enters about April 22nd and leaves a month later. It is between Aries and Gemini.

The Pope's bull. An edict or mandate issued by the Pope, so called from the heavy leaden seal (Lat. *bulla*) appended to the document. *See* GOLDEN BULL.

Bull is also the name given to a drink made from the swillings of empty spirit-casks. *See* BULLING THE BARREL.

A bull in a china shop. A maladroit hand interfering with a delicate business; one who produces reckless destruction.

To take the bull by the horns. To attack or encounter a threatened danger fearlessly: to go forth boldly to meet a difficulty.

Bull-baiting. Bull- and bear-baiting were popular sports in Tudor and Stuart England. The beasts were tethered and set upon by dogs specially trained for this "sport." In his Diary for June 16th, 1670, John Evelyn describes what he calls "a rude and dirty pastime." Baiting was not prohibited in England until 1835.

Bull's-eye. The inner disk or centre of a target.

To make a bull's-eye, or **to score a bull.** To gain some signal advantage; a successful *coup*. To fire or shoot an arrow right into the centre disk of the target.

A black globular sweetmeat with whitish streaks, usually strongly flavoured with peppermint.

Also, a small cloud suddenly appearing, seemingly in violent motion, and expanding till it covers the entire vault of heaven, producing a tumult of wind and rain (1 *Kings* xviii, 44).

Also, a thick disk or boss of glass. Hence, a *bull's-eye lantern*, also called a *bull's-eye*.

Bull sessions. In U.S.A. this phrase is applied to long talks, among men only, about life in general or some particular problem.

Bulldog. A man of relentless, savage disposition is sometimes so called. A "bulldog courage" is one that flinches from no danger. The "bulldog" was the dog formerly used in bull-baiting.

In University slang the "bulldogs" or "bullers" are the two myrmidons (*q.v.*) of the proctor, who attend his heels like dogs, and are ready to spring on any offending undergraduate.

Boys of the bulldog breed. Britons especially with reference to their pugnacity. The phrase comes from the song, "Sons of the sea, all British born," that was immensely popular at the close of the 19th century.

Bullet. Every bullet has its billet. Nothing happens by chance, and no act is altogether without some effect.

Bulletin. An official report of an officer to his superior, or of medical attendants respecting the health of persons of notoriety. The word is borrowed from the French, who took it from the Ital. *bulletino*, a passport or lottery ticket, from *bulla* (*see* POPE'S BULL *above*). because they were authenticated by an official *bulla* or seal.

News bulletin is the term used for the periodical broadcasts of news by radio, etc.

Bulling the barrel. Pouring water into a rum cask, when it is nearly empty, to prevent its leaking. The water, which gets impregnated with the spirit and is frequently drunk, is called *bull*.

Seamen talk of *bulling the teapot* (making a second brew), *bulling the coffee*, etc.

Bullion. Gold or silver in the mass as distinguished from manufactured articles or coined money; also, a fringe made of gold or silver wire. The word is from the Fr. *bouillon*, boiling, and seems to refer to the "boiling," or melting, of the metal before it can be utilized.

Bully. To overbear with words. A *bully* is a blustering menacer. The original meaning of the noun was "sweetheart," as in—

I kiss his dirty shoe, and from heart-string
I love the lovely bully.
                          SHAKESPEARE: *Henry V*, iv, 1.

It is probably to be derived from Dut. *boel*, a lover; and the later meaning may have been influenced by Dut. *bul*. a bull, also a clown, and *bulderen*, to bluster.

Bum. An old word, now almost restricted to schoolboy slang, for the buttocks, posterior. It is an American term for a vagrant; hence a slang word describing any worthless fellow.

Bum-bailiff. The Fr. *pousse-cul* seems to favour the notion that *bum*-bailiff is no corruption. These officers, who made an arrest for debt by touching the debtor on the back, are frequently referred to as *bums*.

Scout me for him at the corner of the orchard, like a bum-bailiff.—*Shakespeare: Twelfth Night*, iii, 4.

Bum-boat. A small wide boat to carry provisions to vessels lying off shore. Also called "dirt-boats," being used for removing filth from ships lying in the Thames.

Bumble. A beadle. So called from the officious, overbearing beadle in Dickens's

Oliver Twist; hence *bumbledom*, fussy officialism, especially on the part of the parish officers; also parochial officials collectively.

Bummaree. A class of middlemen or fish-jobbers in Billingsgate Market, whose business is *bummareeing, i.e.* buying parcels of fish from the salesmen, and then retailing them. The etymology of the word is unknown, but it has been suggested that it is a corruption of *bonne marée*, good fresh fish, *marée* being a French term for all kinds of fresh sea-fish.

Bumper. A full glass, generally connected with a "toast." It may be so called because the surface of the wine "bumps up" in the middle, but it is more likely from the notion that it is a "bumping" or "thumping," *i.e.* a large glass.

Bumpkin. A loutish person. Dut. *boomken*, a little tree, a small block; hence, a blockhead.

Bumptious. Arrogant, full of mighty airs and graces; apt to take offence at presumed slights. A humorous formation from *bump*, probably modelled on *presumptuous*.

Bun. A tail. *See* BUNNY.

Bun. "Hot cross buns" on Good Friday were supposed to be made of the dough kneaded for the host, and were marked with the cross accordingly. As they are said to keep for twelve months without turning mouldy, some persons still hang up one or more in their house as a "charm against evil."

It may be remarked that the Greeks offered to Apollo, Diana, Hecate, and the Moon, cakes with "horns." Such a cake was called a *bous*, and (it is said) never grew mouldy. The round bun represented the full moon, and the "cross" symbolized the four quarters.

> Good Friday comes this month: the old woman runs
> With one a penny, two a penny "hot cross buns".
> Whose virtue is, if you believe what's said,
> They'll not grow mouldy like the common bread.
> *Poor Robin's Almanack*, 1733.

Buna. The German name for synthetic rubber developed during World War II. It was made by the polymerization of butadrene.

Bunce. A slang term for money; particularly for something extra or unexpected in the way of profit. Thought to be a corruption of *bonus* (*q.v.*).

Bunch of Fives. Slang for the hand or fist.

Bundle of sticks. Æsop, in one of his fables, shows that sticks one by one may be readily broken; not so when several are bound together in a bundle. The lesson taught is that "Union gives strength."

The symbol was adopted by, and gave its name to the political system of Fascism, from Lat. *fasces*, a bundle of sticks.

Bundling. The curious and now obsolete New England custom of engaged couples going to bed together fully dressed and thus spending the night. It was a recognized proceeding to which no suggestion of impropriety was attached.

> Stopping occasionally in the villages to eat pumpkin pies, dance at country frolics, and bundle with the Yankee lasses.—WASHINGTON IRVING: *Knickerbocker*.

The same custom existed in Wales.

Bung. A cant term for a publican; also for a toper. "Away, . . . you filthy bung," says Doll to Pistol (2 *Henry IV*, ii, 4).

Bung up. Close up, as a bung closes a cask.

Bungalow. Originally, the house of a European in India, generally of one floor only with a verandah all round it, and the roof thatched to keep off the hot rays of the sun. A *dak-bungalow* is a caravansary or house built by the Government for the use of travellers. (Hindustani, *bangla*, of Bengal.)

Bunkum, Claptrap A representative at Washington being asked why he made such a flowery and angry speech, so wholly uncalled for, made answer, "I was not speaking to the House, but to Buncombe," which he represented (North Carolina).

> When a critter talks for talk's sake, jist to have a speech in the paper to send to home, and not for any other airthly puppus but electioneering, our folks call it bunkum.—HALIBURTON: *Sam Slick*.

Bunny. A rabbit. So called from the provincial word *bun*, a tail, especially of a hare, which is said to "cock her bun." Bunny, a diminutive of bun, applied to a rabbit, means the animal with the "little tail."

Bunting. In Somersetshire *bunting* means sifting flour. Sieves were at one time made of a strong gauzy woollen cloth, which was tough and capable of resisting wear. It has been suggested that this material was found suitable for flags, and that the name for the stuff of which they are now made is due to this.

A "bunt-mill" is a machine for sifting corn.

Bunyan, Paul. A legendary hero of the lumber camps of the north-western U.S.A. His feats—such as cutting the Grand Canyon of the Colorado by dragging his pick behind him—are told and retold with embellishments by the lumbermen; some of them were collected in a curious volume titled, *Paul Bunyan Comes West*.

Burden of a Song. A line repeated at intervals so as to constitute a refrain or chorus. It is the Fr. *bourdon*, the big drone of a bagpipe, or double-diapason of an organ, used in forte parts and choruses.

Burden of Isaiah. "The burden of Babylon, which Isaiah the son of Amoz did see." *Burden*, here, is a literal translation of the Heb. *massa* (rendered in the Vulgate by *onus*), which means "lifting up" either a burden or the voice; hence "utterance," hence a prophecy announcing a calamity, or a denunciation of hardships on those against whom the burden is uttered.

The burden of proof. The obligation to prove something.

The burden of proof is on the party holding the affirmative [because no one can prove a negative, except by *reductio ad absurdum*].

GREENLEAF: *On Evidence*, vol. i, pt. 2, ch. iii.

Bureaucracy. A system of government in which the business is carried on in bureaux or departments. Hence, *bureaucrat*, the head of a department in a bureaucracy. The Fr. *bureau* means not only the office of a public functionary, but also the whole staff of officers attached to the department.

As a word of reproach, bureaucracy means the senseless and soulless application of rules and regulations.

Burglary means, in English law, breaking into a house by night with intent to commit a felony. In Common Law "night" means between sunset and sunrise, but by the Larceny Act of 1861, it is limited to the hours between 9 p.m. and 6 a.m. This Act makes it equally burglary to break out of a house at night after having committed a felony in it. When committed by day these offences are known as housebreaking and are viewed somewhat differently by the Law.

Burgundy. A name loosely applied in England to dark red wine of more than usual alcoholic strength, but really wine (both red and white) from the province of Burgundy, grown between Dijon and Chasne, south of Beaune.

Burgundy pitch. *See* MISNOMERS.

Burial of an Ass. No burial at all, just thrown on a refuse-heap.

He shall be buried with the burial of an ass, drawn and cast forth beyond the gates of Jerusalem.

Jer. xxii, 19.

Burke. To murder by smothering. So called from William Burke, an Irish navvy, who, with his accomplice William Hare, used to suffocate his victims and sell the bodies to surgeons for dissection. Hanged at Edinburgh, 1829.

To burke a question. To smother it in its birth. *The publication was burked*, suppressed before it was circulated.

Burlaw. *See* BYRLAW.

Burleigh. As significant as the shake of Lord Burleigh's head. In Sheridan's *Critic* is introduced a mock tragedy called *The Spanish Armada*. Lord Burleigh is supposed to be too full of state affairs to utter a word; he shakes his head, and Puff explains what the shake means.

Burler. *See* BIRLER.

Burlesque. Father of burlesque poetry. Hipponax of Ephesus (6th cent. B.C.).

Burma Road, The. This great highway was constructed to open up the western interior of China by communication with the sea. It was made in 1937-39, for a distance of 770 miles from Lashio to Kunming, in Yunnan. During the war it was the chief highway for war supplies to China until the Japanese cut it in 1941. It was recaptured in 1945. Lorries do the entire trip in seven days, and by means of the extension being made and planned, will be able to penetrate far into the country.

Burn. His money burns a hole in his pocket. He cannot keep it in his pocket, or forbear spending it.

You cannot burn the candle at both ends. You cannot do two opposite things at one and the same time; you cannot exhaust your energies in one direction, and yet reserve them unimpaired for something else. If you go to bed late you cannot get up early.

Bursa (Gr., a hide). So the citadel of Carthage was called. The tale is that when Dido came to Africa she bought of the natives "as much land as could be encompassed by a bull's hide." The agreement was made, and Dido cut the hide into thongs, so as to enclose a space sufficient for a citadel. *Cp.* DONCASTER.

The following is a similar story: The Yakutsks granted to the Russian explorers as much land as they could encompass with a cow's hide; but the Russians, cutting the hide into strips, obtained land enough for the port and town of Yakutsk.

The Indians have a somewhat similar tradition. The fifth incarnation of Vishnu was in the form of a dwarf called Vamen. Vamen obtained permission to have as much land as he could measure in three paces to build a hut on. The request was laughed at but freely granted; whereupon the dwarf grew so prodigiously that, with three paces, he strode over the whole world.

Burst. To inform against an accomplice. Slang variety of "split" (turn king's evidence, impeach). The person who does this *splits* or breaks up the whole concern.

I'm bursting to tell you so-and-so. I'm all agog to tell you; I can't rest till I've told you.

On the burst. See BUST.

Burton. Gone for a Burton. It is now difficult to ascertain the origin of this phrase which, starting among flying men in World War II, has now taken its place in the language. It probably suggests that the missing airman has gone for a pint of Burton ale or stout. Its meaning is always sinister, implying that whoever has gone for a Burton has crashed or come to grief in some way.

Bury the Hatchet. Let bygones be bygones. The "Great Spirit" commanded the North American Indians, when they smoked their calumet or peace-pipe, to bury their hatchets, scalping-knives, and war-clubs, that all thought of hostility might be put out of sight.

Buried was the bloody hatchet;
Buried was the dreadful war-club;
Buried were all warlike weapons,
And the war-cry was forgotten;
Then was peace among the nations.
LONGFELLOW: *Hiawatha*, xiii.

Burying at cross roads. See CROSS-ROADS.

Bus. A contraction of *omnibus* (*q.v.*). The word is used by airmen and motorists in a humorous, almost affectionate, way for their conveyances.

Busman's holiday. There is a story that in old horse-bus days a driver spent his holiday travelling to and on a bus driven by one of his pals. From this has arisen the phrase, which means occupying one's spare and free time in carrying on with one's usual work, in other words, a holiday in name only.

Busby. A frizzled wig; also the tall cap of a hussar, artilleryman, etc., which hangs from the top over the right shoulder. It is not known what the word is derived from; Doctor Busby, master of Westminster School from 1638 to 1695, did not wear a frizzled wig, but a close cap, somewhat like a Welsh wig. See WIG.

Bush. One beats the bush, but another has the hare. See BEAT THE BUSH.

Bush. An Australian term for wild, wooded country, derived from the Dutch *bosch*. The word was imported from South Africa before 1820, and gave rise to a whole vocabulary— *bushman, bush telegraph, bush ranger*, etc.

Bushmen (Dut. *Boschjesman*). Natives of South Africa who live in the "bush"; the aborigines of the Cape; dwellers in the Australian "bush"; bush farmers.

Bushmen . . . are the only nomads in the country. They never cultivate the soil, nor rear any domestic animal save wretched dogs.
LIVINGSTONE: *Travels*, ch. ii.

Bush-shanty (Austr.). A hut selling illegal liquor, often in the gold-rush areas. Hence *to shanty* is to pub-crawl.

Bushwhacker (Austr.). One who lives in the bush. (U.S.A.) a deserter in the Civil War who looted behind the lines.

Bushed. An Australian word meaning "lost." It has wandered so far from its original connotation of "bush" that we find such a phrase as "a small ship became bushed in the great Van Dieman Gulf." BARRATT, *Coast of Adventure*, 1944.

Bush telegraph. In early Australian slang, one who informed the *bushrangers* (*q.v.*) of police movements; now widespread to indicate any unofficial and mysterious source of information.

Business. A.S. *bisigness*, from *bisigian*, to occupy, to worry, to fatigue. In theatrical parlance "business" or "biz" means byplay. Thus, Hamlet trifling with Ophelia's fan, Lord Dundreary's hop, and so on, are the special "business" of the actor of the part. As a rule, the "business" is invented by the actor who creates the part, and it is handed down by tradition.

Business to-morrow. When the Spartans seized upon Thebes they placed Archias over the garrison. Pelopidas, with eleven others, banded together to put Archias to the sword. A letter containing full details of the plot was given to the Spartan polemarch at the banquet table; but Archias thrust the letter under his cushion, saying, "Business to-morrow." But long ere that sun arose he was numbered with the dead.

The business end. The end of the tool, etc., with which the work is done. The "business end of a tin-tack" is its point; of a revolver, its muzzle; and so on.

To do someone's business for him. To ruin him, to settle him for ever; kill him.

Busiris (bū sī' ris). A mythical king of Egypt who, in order to avert a famine, used to sacrifice to the gods all strangers who set foot on his shores. Hercules was seized by him; and would have fallen a victim, but he broke his chain, and slew the inhospitable king.

Busker. There is an old verb *to busk*, meaning to improvise, and it is from this that the word *busker* is derived, to describe a street or beach singer or performer.

Buss. To kiss. The word is obsolete; it is probably onomatopœic in origin, but *cp.* Lat. *basium*, Ital. *bacio*, Sp. *beso*, and Fr. *baiser*.

> Yon towers, whose wanton tops do buss the clouds,
> Must kiss their own feet.
>   SHAKESPEARE: *Troilus and Cressida*, iv, 5.

Bust. A frolic; a drunken debauch. The word is a vulgarization of *burst* (*q.v.*).

Busted. Done for; exploded.

To go on the bust. To go on the spree; to paint the town red.

Buster. Anything of large or unusual size or capacity: a "whacking great lie."

To come a buster. To come a cropper; to meet with a serious set-back or fall.

In Australia a **Southerly Buster** is a heavy gale from the south, striking the east coast of Australia and New Zealand.

Busybody. A busybody was originally an arrangement of mirrors set outside a window to enable those within to see anyone approaching from either end of the street.

Butcher. A title given to many soldiers and others noted for their bloodthirstiness. Achmed Pasha was called *djezzar* (the butcher), and is said to have whipped off the heads of his seven wives.

The Bloody Butcher. The Duke of Cumberland (1721-65), second son of George II. So called from his barbarities in suppressing the rebellion of the Young Pretender.

The Royalist Butcher. Blaise de Montluc (1502-77), a Marshal of France, distinguished for his cruelties to the Protestants in the reign of Charles IX.

Butter. This word is sometimes used figuratively for flattery, soft soap, "wiping down" with winning words. *Punch* expressively calls it "the milk of human kindness churned into butter." (A.S. *butere*, Lat. *butyrum*, Gr. *boutyron*, *i.e.* *bouturos*, cow-cheese, as distinguished from goat- or ewe-butter.)

Buttered ale. A beverage made of ale or beer mixed with butter, sugar, and cinnamon.

He knows which side his bread is buttered. He knows his own interest.

> I know what's what, I know on which side
> My bread is butter'd.
>   FORD: *The Ladies Triall* (1638).

He looks as if butter would not melt in his mouth. He seems suspiciously amiable. He looks quite harmless and expressly made to be played upon. Yet beware, and "touch not a cat but a glove."

> She smiles and languishes, you'd think that butter would not melt in her mouth.—THACKERAY: *Pendennis*, lx.

Soft or **fair words butter no parsnips.** Saying " 'Be thou fed,' will not feed a hungry man." Mere words will not find salt to our porridge, or butter to our parsnips.

> Fair words butter no cabbage.
>   WYCHERLEY: *Plain Dealer*, v, 3 (1674).
> Fine words, says our homely old proverb, butter no parsnips.—LOWELL.

To butter one's bread on both sides. To be wastefully extravagant and luxurious; also, to run with the hare and hunt with the hounds, to gain advantages from two sides at once.

Buttercups. So called because they were once supposed to increase the butter of milk. No doubt those cows give the best milk that pasture in fields where buttercups abound, not because these flowers produce butter, but because they grow only on sound, dry, old pastures, which afford the best food. Miller, in his *Gardener's Dictionary*, says they were so called "under the notion that the yellow colour of butter is owing to these plants."

Butter-fingers. Said of a person who lets things fall out of his hand. His fingers are slippery, and things slip from them as if they were greased with butter. Often heard on the cricket field.

> I never was a butter-fingers, though a bad batter.
>   H. KINGSLEY.

Butterfly. A light, flippant, objectless young person who flutters from pleasure to pleasure. One who is in good form when all is bright and when every prospect pleases, but is "done for" when the clouds gather.

In the cab-trade the name used to be given to those drivers who took to the occupation only in summer-time, and at the best of the season.

> The feeling of the regular drivers against these "butterflies" is very strong.
>   *Nineteenth Century* (March, 1893, p. 177).

Butterfly kiss. A kiss with one's eyelashes, that is, stroking the cheek with one's eyelashes.

Button. The two buttons on the back of a coat, in the fall of the back, are a survival of the buttons on the back of riding-coats and military frocks of the 18th century, occasionally used to button back the coat-tails.

A decoy in an auction-room is colloquially known as a *button*, because he "buttons" or ties the unwary to bargains offered for sale. The button fastens or fixes what else would slip away.

Buttons. A page, whose jacket in front is remarkable for a display of small round buttons, as close as they can be inserted, from chin to waist.

> The titter of an electric bell brought a large fat buttons, with a stage effect of being dressed to look small.—HOWELL: *Hazard of New Fortunes*, ch. vii.

To press the button. To set in motion, literally or figuratively, generally by simple means as the pressing of a button will start electrically-driven machinery or apparatus.

Mediation was ready to come into operation by any method that Germany thought possible if only Germany would "press the button" in the interests of peace.— Sir EDW. GREY to the British Ambassador at Berlin, July 29th, 1914.

To take by the button. To buttonhole. *See below.*

Buttonhole. A flower or nosegay worn in the buttonhole of a coat.

To buttonhole a person. To detain him in conversation; to apprehend, as, "to take fortune by the button." The allusion is to a custom, now discontinued, of holding a person by the button or buttonhole in conversation. The French have the same locution: *Serrer le bouton (à quelqu'un).*

He went about buttonholing and boring everyone.
           H. KINGSLEY: *Mathilde.*

Buy. To buy in. To collect stock by purchase; to withhold the sale of something offered at auction, because the bidding has not reached the "reserve price." On the Stock Exchange *buying in* is the term used when, a seller having sold stock that he is unable to deliver, the buyer purchases the stock himself in the market and charges the extra cost, if any, to the original seller.

To buy off. To give a person money to drop a claim, put an end to contention, or throw up a partnership.

To buy out. To redeem or ransom.

Not being able to buy out his life . . .
Dies ere the weary sun set.
      SHAKESPEARE: *Comedy of Errors,* i, 2.

Buzz. A rumour, a whispered report.

Yes, that, on every dream,
Each buzz, each fancy . . .
He may enguard his dotage.
      SHAKESPEARE: *King Lear,* i, 4.

Buzzard. In Dryden's *Hind and Panther* is meant for Dr. Burnet, whose figure was lusty.

Buzzard called hawk by courtesy. It is a euphemism—a brevet rank—a complimentary title.

The noble Buzzard ever pleased me best;
Of small renown, 'tis true; for, not to lie
We call him but a hawk by courtesy.
      DRYDEN: *Hind and Panther,* iii, 1221.

Between hawk and buzzard. Not quite the master or mistress nor quite a servant. Applied to "bear-leaders" (*q.v.*), governesses, and other grown-up persons who used to be allowed to come down to dessert, but not to the dinner-table.

By-and-by now means a little time hence, but when the Bible was translated it meant instantly. "When persecution ariseth . . . by-and-by he is offended" (*Matt,* xiii, 12); rendered in *Mark* iv, 17, by the word "immediately." Our *presently* means in a little time or soon, but formerly it meant "at present," "at once," and in this sense it is not uncommonly still used in U.S.A.

By and large. Taking one thing with another, speaking generally. This is really a nautical phrase. When a vessel was close-hauled, order might be given to sail "by and large," that is, slightly off the wind, or easier for the helmsman and less likely for the vessel to be taken aback under his steering.

By-laws. Local laws. From *by,* a borough. *See* BYRLAW. Properly, laws by a town council, and bearing only on the borough or company over which it has jurisdiction.

By-line. A journalist's signature. When a newspaper reporter progresses from anonymous to signed articles, he is said to have got a by-line.

By-the-by. *En passant,* laterally connected with the main subject. "By-play" is side or secondary play; "by-roads and streets" are those which branch out of the main thoroughfare. The first "by" means *passing from one to another,* as in the phrase "Day by day." Thus "By-the-by" is passing from the main subject to a *by* or secondary one.

By-the-way. An introduction to an incidental remark thrown in, and tending the same way as the discourse itself.

Byrsa. *See* Bursa.

Byzantine (bi zăn′ tīn). Another name for the *bezant* (*q.v.*).

Byzantine art (from Byzantium, the ancient name of Constantinople). That symbolical system which was developed by the early Greek or Byzantine artists out of the Christian symbolism. Its chief features are the circle, dome, and round arch; and its chief symbols the lily, cross, vesica, and nimbus. St. Sophia, at Constantinople, and St. Mark, at Venice, are excellent examples of Byzantine architecture and decoration; and the Roman Catholic Cathedral at Westminster is a development of the same.

Byzantine Empire. The Eastern or Greek Empire, which lasted from the separation of the Eastern and Western Empires on the death of Theodosius in A.D. 395, till the capture of Constantinople by the Turks in 1453.

C

C. The form of the letter is a rounding of the Gr. *gamma* (Γ), which was a modification of the Phœnician sign for *gimel*, a camel. It originally corresponded with Gr. *gamma*, as its place in the alphabet would lead one to suppose.

When the French *c* has a mark under it, thus ç, called a cedilla, it is to be pronounced as an *s*.

There is more than one poem written of which every word begins with C. There is one by Hamconius, called *"Certamen catholicum cum Calvinistis,"* and another by Henry Harder. *See* ALLITERATION.

Ça ira (it will go). The name, and refrain, of a popular patriotic song in France which became the *Carillon National* of the French Revolution (1790). It went to the tune of the *Carillon National*, which Marie Antoinette was for ever strumming on her harpsichord.

As a rallying cry it was borrowed from Benjamin Franklin, who used to say, in reference to the American revolution, *"Ah! ah! ça ira, ça ira!"* ('twill be sure to do).

The refrain of the French revolutionary version was:—
Ah! ça ira, ça ira, ça ira,
Les aristocrates à la lanterne.

Cab. A contraction of *cabriolet*, a small, one-horse carriage, so called from Ital. *capriola*, a caper, the leap of a kid, from the lightness of the carriage when compared with the contemporary cumbersome vehicles. Cabs were introduced in London about 1823.

Cabal. A junto (*q.v.*) or council of intriguers. One of the Ministries of Charles II was called a "cabal" (1670), because the initial letters of its members formed the word: Clifford, Ashley, Buckingham, Arlington, and Lauderdale. This accident may have popularized the word, but it was in use in England many years before this, and is the Hebrew *qabbalah*. *See* CABBALA.

These ministers were emphatically called the Cabal, and they soon made the appellation so infamous that it has never since . . . been used except as a term of reproach.—MACAULAY: *England*, I, ii.

Cabala, Cabalist. *See* CABBALA.

Caballero. A Spanish knight or gentleman (literally, one who rides a horse, *caballo*); also a grave and stately dance, so called from the ballad to the music of which it was danced. The ballad begins—
Esta noche le mataron al caballero.

Cabbala. The doctrine of a type of Jewish mysticism which emerged in Spain and Provence in the 13th century. It owes much to the Gnostics, conceiving the Godhead as a dynamic system of ten spheres. Interference with the system resulted in sin. Every act of man was therefore aimed at the redemption and unification of God. The most important Kabbalistic work is the *Zohar*. The word is the Heb. *gabbalah*, accepted tradition.

Cabbalist. In the Middle Ages the cabbalists were chiefly occupied in concocting and deciphering charms, mystical anagrams, etc., by unintelligible combinations of certain letters, words, and numbers; in search for the philosopher's stone; in prognostications, attempted or pretended intercourse with the dead, and suchlike fantasies.

Cabinet Ministers. In British politics, a deliberative committee of the principal members of the Government, who are privileged to consult and advise the sovereign (originally in his private *cabinet*, or chamber), and who lead, and are responsible to, Parliament. The number of members has varied from a dozen to as many as twenty-two, but it always contains the chief officers of state, viz. the Prime Minister, the First Lord of the Treasury (these offices are often combined), the Lord High Chancellor, Lord President of the Council, Lord Privy Seal, Chancellor of the Exchequer, the First Lord of the Admiralty, the Secretaries for Home Affairs, Foreign Affairs, the Colonies, Dominions, Scotland, War, and Air, the President of the Board of Trade, and the Ministers of Labour, Fuel, Education, Health, and Agriculture. Of the other Ministers the following are sometimes included in the Cabinet: the Chancellor of the Duchy of Lancaster, the Postmaster-General,

Ministers of Supply, Food, Pensions, Works, Town and Country Planning, National Insurance, Civil Aviation, Information.

Cabiri (ka bī' ri). The Phœnician name for the seven planets collectively; also mystic and minor divinities worshipped in Asia Minor, Greece, and the islands. (Phœn. *kabir*, powerful.)

Cabochon (ka bō shong). A term applied to a precious stone, cut in a rounded shape, without facets. Garnets, sapphires, and rubies are the stones most commonly cut *en cabochon*.

Caboodle (kà boodl'). **The whole caboodle**, the whole lot. The origin of the word is obscure, but it may come from the Dutch *boedel*, possession, household goods, property. In this sense it has long been a common term among New England long-shoremen.

Caboose (kà boos'). On American railroads, a wagon used for transporting workmen or the train crew.

Cachet (kăsh' ā) (Fr.). A seal; hence, a distinguishing mark, a stamp of individuality.

Cacodæmon (kăk ō dē' mon). An evil spirit (Gr. *kakos daimon*). Astrologers give this name to the Twelfth House of Heaven, from which only evil prognostics proceed.

Hie thee to hell for shame, and leave the world,
Thou cacodemon.
SHAKESPEARE: *Richard III*, i, 3.

Cacoethes (kăk ō ēth' ēz) (Gr.). A "bad habit."

As soon as he came to town, the political *Cacoethes* began to break out upon him with greater violence, because it had been suppressed.
SWIFT: *Life of Steele*.

Cacoethes loquendi. A passion for making speeches or for talking.

Cacoethes scribendi. The love of rushing into print; a mania for authorship.

Tenet insanabile multos
Scribendi cacoethes.
The incurable itch for scribbling infects many.
Juv. VII, 51.

Cad. A low, vulgar ill-mannered fellow; also, before the term fell into its present disrepute, an omnibus conductor. The word is, like the Scots *caddie* (*q.v.*), probably from cadet (*q.v.*).

Caddie. This means now almost solely the boy or man who carries a golfer's clubs on the links (and, now and then, gives the tyro advice). It is another form of *cadet* (*q.v.*), and was formerly in common use in Scotland for errand boys, odd-job men, chairmen, etc.

All Edinburgh men and boys know that when sedan-chairs were discontinued, the old cadies sank into ruinous poverty, and became synonymous with roughs. The word was brought to London by James Hannay, who frequently used it. — M. PRINGLE.

Caddy in **tea-caddy** is a Malay word (*kati*), and properly denotes a weight of 1 lb. 5 oz. 2 dr., that is used in China and the East Indies.

Cader Idris (kă' der id' ris). *Cader* in Welsh is "chair," and *Idris* is the name of one of the old Welsh giants. The legend is that anyone who passes the night sitting in this "chair" will be either a poet or a madman.

Cadet is a student at the Royal Military College at Sandhurst, with which Woolwich Academy was amalgamated in 1946, or in one of H.M. training ships. From these places the boys are sent (after passing certain examinations) into the army as ensigns or second lieutenants, and into the navy as midshipmen.

Cadi (kā' di). Arabic for a town magistrate or inferior judge.

Cadmus. In Greek mythology, the son of Agenor, king of Phœnicia, and Telephassa; founder of Thebes (Bœotia) and the introducer of the alphabet into Greece. (*Cp.* PALAMEDES.) The name is Semitic for "the man of the East." Legend says that, having slain the dragon which guarded the fountain of Dirce, in Bœotia, he sowed its teeth, and a number of armed men sprang up surrounding Cadmus with intent to kill him. By the counsel of Athene, he threw a precious stone among them, who, striving for it, killed one another.

Cadmean letters. The sixteen simple Greek letters said, in Greek mythology, to have been introduced by Cadmus (*q.v.*) from Phœnicia. The Cadmeans were those who in pre-Trojan times occupied the country afterwards called Bœotia. Hence the Greek tragedians often called the Thebans Cadmeans.

Cadmean victory. A victory purchased with great loss. The allusion is to the armed men who sprang out of the ground from the teeth of the dragon sown by Cadmus (*q.v.*), who fell foul of each other, only five escaping death.

Cadre (kad' er; kad' ri). (Fr., frame.) In military parlance a skeleton of trained or key men, so arranged that the addition of untrained personnel will yield a full-size efficient unit.

Caerleon (kâr' lē' ón). The Isca Silurum of the Romans; a town on the Usk, in Wales, about 3 miles N.E. of Newport. It is the traditional residence of King Arthur, where he lived in splendid state, surrounded by hundreds of knights, twelve of whom he selected as Knights of the Round Table.

Cæsar (sē' zàr). The cognomen of Caius Julius Cæsar was assumed by all the male members of his dynasty as a part of the imperial dignity, and after them by the successive emperors. After the death of Hadrian (138) the title was assigned to those who had been nominated by the emperors as their successors and had been associated with them in ruling. The titles *Kaiser and Tsar* are both forms of *Cæsar*.

> Thou art an emperor, Cæsar, keisar, and Pheezar.
> SHAKESPEARE: *Merry Wives of Windsor*, i, 3.
> No bending knees shall call thee Cæsar now.
> SHAKESPEARE: *3 Henry VI*, iii, 1.

Cæsarian operation. The extraction of a child from the womb by cutting the abdomen; so called because Julius Cæsar was thus brought into the world.

Caftan (kăf' tàn). A garment worn in Turkey and other Eastern countries. It is a sort of under-tunic or vest tied by a girdle at the waist. *Cp.* GABERDINE.

> Picturesque merchants and their customers, no longer in the big trousers of Egypt, but [in] the long caftans and abas of Syria.
> B. TAYLOR: *Lands of the Saracen*, ch. ix.

Cagliostro (kă lyos' trō). Count Alessandro di Cagliostro was the assumed name of the notorious Italian adventurer and impostor, Giuseppe Balsamo (1743-95), of Palermo. He played a prominent part in the affair of the Diamond Necklace (*q.v.*), and among his many frauds was the offer of everlasting youth to all who would pay him for his secret.

Cagot (ka' gō). A sort of gipsy race living in the Middle Ages in Gascony and Béarn, supposed to be descendants of the Visigoths, and shunned as something loathsome. *Cp.* CAQUEUX; COLLIBERTS. In modern French, a hypocrite or an ultra-devout person is called a *cagot*. From this use of the word came *cagoule*, meaning a penitent's hood or cowl, and from this, again, the sinister *cagoulards* took their name—French political plotters hiding their infamy beneath masks and hoods.

Cainites (kā' nītz). An heretical sect of the 2nd century. They renounced the New Testament in favour of *The Gospel of Judas*, which justified the false disciple and the crucifixion of Jesus; and they maintained that heaven and earth were created by the evil principle, and that Cain with his descendants were the persecuted party.

Caird (kârd). This is a North Country and Scottish name for a tramp, a tinker, a Gipsy or even a jockey. It comes from the Gaelic *ceard*, a smith, brazier.

To go like hot cakes. To be a great success; to sell well.

To take the cake. To carry off the prize. The reference is to the negro **cake walk**, the prize for which was a cake. It consists of walking round the prize cake in pairs, while umpires decide which pair walk the most gracefully. From this a dance developed which was popular in the early part of the 20th century before the serious introduction of Jazz.

In ancient Greece a cake was the award of the toper who held out the longest; and in Ireland the best dancer in a dancing competition was rewarded, at one time, by a cake.

> A churn-dish stuck into the earth supported on its flat end a cake, which was to become the prize of the best dancer. . . . At length the competitors yielded their claims to a young man . . . who taking the cake, placed it gallantly in the lap of a pretty girl to whom . . . he was about to be married.—BARTLETT and COYNE: *Scenery and Antiquities of Ireland*, vol. ii, p. 64.

You cannot eat your cake and have it too. You cannot spend your money and yet keep it. You cannot serve God and Mammon.

Calainos (kà lī' nos). The most ancient of Spanish ballads. Calainos the Moor asked a damsel to wife; she consented, on condition that he should bring her the heads of the three paladins of Charlemagne—Rinaldo, Roland, and Oliver. Calainos went to Paris and challenged the paladins. First Sir Baldwin, the youngest knight, accepted the challenge and was overthrown; then his uncle Roland went against the Moor and smote him.

Calamanco (kă l à măng' kō). A Low German word of uncertain origin denoting a glossy woollen fabric, sometimes striped or variegated. The word has been applied attributively to a cat, in which connexion it means striped or tortoiseshell.

Calatrava, Order of (kăl à tra' va). A Spanish military Order of Knighthood founded by Sancho III of Castile in 1158 to commemorate the capture of the fortress of Calatrava from the Moors in 1147. The first knights were the keepers of the fortress; their badge is a red cross, fleury, and is worn on the left breast of a white mantle.

Calceolaria (kăl sē ō lâr' i à). Little-shoe flowers; so called from their resemblance to fairy slippers (Lat. *calceoluo*.)

Calculate is from the Lat. *calculi* (pebbles), used by the Romans for counters. In the abacus (*q.v.*), the round balls were called *calculi*. The Greeks voted by pebbles dropped into an urn—a method adopted both in ancient Egypt and Syria; counting these pebbles was "calculating" the number of voters.

I calculate. A peculiarity of expression common in the western states of North America. In the southern states the phrase is "I reckon," in the middle states "I expect," and in New England "I guess." All were imported from the Mother Country by early settlers.

Your aunt sets two tables, I calculate; don't she?
SUSAN WARNER: *Queechy*, ch. xix.

The calculator. A number of mathematical geniuses have been awarded this title; among them are:—

Alfragan, the Arabian astronomer. Died 830.

Jedediah Buxton (1707-72), of Elmton, in Derbyshire; a farm labourer of no education who exhibited in London in 1754.

George Bidder and Zerah Colburn (1804-40), who exhibited publicly.

Inaudi exhibited "his astounding powers of calculating" at Paris in 1880; his additions and subtractions, contrary to the usual procedure, were left to right.

Buxton, being asked "How many cubical eighths-of-an-inch there are in a body whose three sides are 23,145,786 yards, 5,642,732 yards, and 54,965 yards?" replied correctly without setting down a figure.

Colburn, being asked the square root of 106,929 and the cube root of 268,336,125, replied before the audience had set the figures down.

PRICE: *Parallel History*, vol. ii, p. 570.

Caledonia. Scotland; the ancient Roman name, now used only in poetry and in a few special connexions, such as the Caledonian Railway, the Caledonian Canal, the Caledonian Ball, etc.

Not thus, in ancient days of Caledon,
Was thy voice mute amid the festal crowd.
SCOTT.

O Caledonia, stern and wild,
Meet nurse for a poetic child.
SCOTT: *Lay of the Last Minstrel.*

Calembour (ka lem boor') (Fr.). A pun, a jest. From Wigand von Theben, a priest of *Kahlenberg* in Lower Austria, who was introduced in *Eulenspiegel* (*q.v.*), and other German talcs. He was noted for his jests, puns, and witticisms; and in the French translations appeared as the Abbé de Calembourg, or Calembour.

Calendar.

The Julian Calendar. *See* JULIAN.

The Gregorian Calendar. A modification of the Julian, introduced in 1582 by Pope Gregory XIII, and adopted in Great Britain in 1752. This is called "the New Style." *See* GREGORIAN YEAR.

The Mohammedan Calendar, used in Moslem countries, dates from July 16th, 622, the day of the Hegira (*q.v.*). It consists of 12 lunar months of 29 days 12 hours, 44 minutes each; consequently the Mohammedan year consists of only 354 or 355 days. A cycle is 30 years.

The French Revolutionary Calendar, adopted on October 5th, 1793, retrospectively as from September 22nd, 1792, and in force in France till January 1st, 1806, consisted of 12 months of 30 days each, with 5 intercalary days, called Sansculotides (*q.v.*) at the end. It was devised by Gilbert Romme (1750-95), the names of the months having been given by the poet, Fabre d'Eglantine (1755-94).

The Newgate Calendar. *See* NEWGATE.

To kill the fatted calf. To welcome with the best of everything. The phrase is taken from the parable of the prodigal son (*Luke* xv, 30).

Calf-love. Youthful fancy, immature love as opposed to a lasting attachment.

"It's a girl's fancy just, a kind of calf-love."
Mrs. GASKELL: *Sylvia's Lovers.*

Calf-skin. Fools and jesters used to wear a calf-skin coat buttoned down the back. In allusion to this custom, Faulconbridge says insolently to the Archduke of Austria, who had acted most basely to Richard Cœur-de-Lion:—

Thou wear a lion's hide! Doff it, for shame,
And hang a calf-skin on those recreant limbs.
SHAKESPEARE: *King John*, iii, 1.

Caliban (kăl' i băn). Rude, uncouth, unknown. The allusion is to Shakespeare's Caliban (*The Tempest*), the deformed, half-human son of a devil and a witch, slave to Prospero. In this character it has been said that Shakespeare had not only invented a *new creation*, but also a *new language*.

Coleridge says, "In him [Caliban], as in some brute animals, this advance to the intellectual faculties, without the moral sense, is marked by the appearance of vice."

Caligula (kà lig' ū là). Roman emperor (A.D. 37-41); so called because, when he was with the army as a boy, he wore a military sandal called a *caliga*, which had no upper leather, and was used only by the common soldiers.

Caligula was a voluptuous brute whose cruelty and excesses amounted almost to madness. Hence Horace Walpole coined the word *Caligulism.* Speaking of Frederick, Prince of Wales, he says:—

—Alas! it would be endless to tell you all his Caligulisms.—*Letter to France*, November 29th, 1745.

Calipash and Calipee (kăl i păsh', kăl i pē'). These are apparently fancy terms (though the former may come from the word Carapace) to describe choice portions of the turtle. Calipash is the fatty, dull-greenish substance belonging to the upper shield; calipee is the light-yellow, fatty stuff belonging to the lower shield. Only epicures and aldermen can tell the difference.

Cut off the bottom shell, then cutoff the meat that grows to it (which is the callepy or fowl).
Mrs. RAFFALD: *English Housekeeping* (1769).

Caliph (kā' lif). A title given to the successors of Mohammed (Arab. *Khalifah*, a successor; *khalafa*, to succeed). Among the Saracens a caliph is one vested with supreme dignity. The caliphate of Bagdad reached its highest splendour under Haroun al-Raschid, in the 9th century. For the last 200 years the appellation has been swallowed up in the titles of *Shah, Sultan, Emir,* etc. The last Sultan of Turkey claimed the title in a vain attempt to impose his authority on all Moslem lands; it is still used of rulers of Mohammedan States in their capacity as successors of Mohammed.

Calisto and Arcas (kå lis′ tō, ar′ kås). Calisto was an Arcadian nymph metamorphosed into a she-bear by Jupiter. Her son Arcas having met her in the chase, would have killed her, but Jupiter converted him into a he-bear, and placed them both in the heavens, where they are recognized as the Great and Little Bear.

Calixtines (kå liks′ tīnz). A religious sect of Bohemians in the 15th century; so called from *Calix* (the chalice), which they insisted should be given to the laity in the sacrament of the Lord's Supper, as well as the bread or wafer. They were also called Utraquists (*q.v.*).

Call. A "divine" summons or invitation, as "a call to the ministry."

A curtain call. An invitation to an actor to appear before the curtain, and receive the applause of the audience.

A call to the Bar. The admission of a law student to the privileges of a barrister. *See* BAR.

The call of God. An invitation, exhortation, or warning, by the dispensations of Providence (*Isa.* xxii, 12); divine influence on the mind to do or avoid something (*Heb.* iii, 1).

To call. To invite: as, the trumpet calls.
> If honour calls, where'er she points the way,
> The sons of honour follow and obey.
> CHURCHILL: The Farewell.

In U.S.A. **to call** means somewhat ambiguously "to telephone." "He called me" may mean "he summoned me" or "he telephoned me."

To call in question. To doubt the truth of a statement; to challenge the truth of a statement. "*In dubium vocare.*"

To be called (or **sent**) **to one's account.** To be removed by death. To be called to the judgment seat of God to give an account of one's deeds, whether they be good, or whether they be evil.
> Cut off even in the blossoms of my sin,
> Unhouseled, disappointed, unaneled,
> No reckoning made, but sent to my account
> With all my imperfections on my head;
> O horrible! O horrible! most horrible.
> SHAKESPEARE: Hamlet, i, 5.

To call to arms. To summon to prepare for battle. "*Ad arma vocare.*"

To call to mind. To recollect, to remember.

Calligraphy. The art of handwriting. The finest calligraphy in western civilization is the *Cancelleresca Corsiva* or Cursive Chancellery hand used by the Apostolic Secretaries in the 15th century, the hand on which italic type is based. To-day it is applied generally to the art of the scribe preparing manuscripts such as rolls of honour or professional presentations. A handwriting which is based on a good model and has any artistic pretentions is called a calligraphic hand.

Calliope (kå lī ō pi) (Gr., beautiful voice). Chief of the nine Muses (*q.v.*); the muse of epic or heroic poetry, and of poetic inspiration and eloquence. Her emblems are a stylus and wax tablets.

The word is also applied to a steam-organ composed of steam-whistles making a raucous blare.

Callippic Period (kå lip′ ik). An intended correction of the Metonic Cycle (*q.v.*) by Callippus, the Greek astronomer of the 4th century B.C. To remedy the defect in the Metonic Cycle Callippus quadrupled the period of Meton, making his Cycle one of seventy-six years, and deducted a day at the end of it, by which means he calculated that the new and full moons would be brought round to the same day and hour. His calculation, however, is not absolutely accurate, as there is one whole day lost every 553 years.

Calumet (kăl′ u met). This name for the tobacco-pipe of the North American Indians, used as a symbol of peace and amity, is the Norman form of Fr. *chalumeau* (from Lat. *calamus,* a reed), and was given by the French-Canadians to certain plants used by the natives as pipe-stems, and hence to the pipe itself.

The calumet, or "pipe of peace," is about two and a half feet long, the bowl is made of highly polished red marble, and the stem is a reed, which is decorated with eagles' quills, women's hair, and so on.

To present the calumet to a stranger is a mark of hospitality and goodwill; to refuse the offer is an act of hostile defiance.
> Giche Manito, the mighty,
> Smoked the calumet, the Peace-Pipe
> As a signal to the nations.
> LONGFELLOW: Hiawatha, i.

Calvary. The Latin translation of the Gr. *golgotha* (*q.v.*), which is a transliteration of the Hebrew word for "a skull." The name given to the place of our Lord's crucifixion. Legend has it that the skull of Adam was preserved here, but the name is probably due to some real or fancied resemblance in the configuration of the ground to the shape of a skull.

The actual site of Calvary has not been determined, though there is strong evidence in favour of the traditional site, which is occupied by the Church of the Holy Sepulchre. Another position which has strong claims is an eminence above the grotto of Jeremiah, outside the present wall and not far from the Damascus Gate on the north side of Jerusalem.

A Calvary. A representation of the successive scenes of the Passion of Christ in a series of pictures, etc., in a church. The shrine containing the representations.

A Calvary cross. A Latin cross mounted on three steps (or grises).

Calvary clover. A common trefoil, *Medicago echinus*, said to have sprung up in the track made by Pilate when he went to the cross to see his "title affixed" (Jesus of Nazareth, king of the Jews). Each of the three leaves has a little carmine spot in the centre; in the daytime they form a sort of cross; and in the flowering season the plant bears a little yellow flower, like a "crown of thorns." Julian tells us that each of the three leaves had in his time a white cross in the centre, and that the centre cross lasts visible longer than the others.

Calves. The inhabitants of the Isle of Wight were sometimes so called from a tradition that a calf once got its head firmly wedged in a wooden pale, and, instead of breaking up the pale, the farm-man cut off the calf's head.

His calves are gone to grass. Said of a spindle-legged man. And another mocking taunt is, "Veal will be dear, because there are no calves."

Calves' Head Club. Instituted in ridicule of Charles I, and apparently first mentioned in a tract (given in the *Harleian Miscellany*) of 1703 by Benjamin Bridgwater, stating that it first met in 1693. It lasted till about 1735. The annual banquet was held on January 30th, and consisted of calves' heads dressed in sundry ways to represent Charles and his courtiers; a cod's head, to represent Charles, independent of his kingly office; a pike with little ones in its mouth, an emblem of tyranny; a boar's head with an apple in its mouth to represent the king preying on his subjects, etc. After the banquet, the *Icon Basilike* was burnt, and the parting cup "To those worthy patriots who killed the tyrant," was drunk.

Calvinism. One of the sternest and most uncompromising sects of Christianity, and a joyless seriousness is often to be found among those who follow its tenets. This frequently evinces itself in a rigid Sabbatarianism and a suspicion of the theatre and other forms of art.

The five chief points of Calvinism are:

(1) Predestination, or particular election.

(2) Irresistible grace.

(3) Original sin, or the total depravity of the natural man, which renders it morally impossible to believe and turn to God of his own free will.

(4) Particular redemption.

(5) Final perseverance of the saints.

Calydon (kăl' i don). In classical geography, a city in Ætolia, Greece, near the forest which was the scene of the legendary hunt of the Calydonian boar (*see* BOAR). Also, in Arthurian legend, the name given to a forest in the northern portion of England.

Calypso (kȧ lip' sō). In classical mythology, the queen of the island Ogygia on which Ulysses was wrecked. She kept him there for seven years, and promised him perpetual youth and immortality if he would remain with her for ever. Ogygia is generally identified with Gozo, near Malta.

A calypso is a type of popular song evolved by the Negroes of the West Indies.

Cam and Isis. The universities of Cambridge and Oxford; so called from the rivers on which they stand.

May you, my Cam and Isis, preach it long,
"The right divine of kings to govern wrong."
POPE: *Dunciad*, iv, 187.

Cama. The god of young love in Hindu mythology. His wife is Rati (*voluptuousness*), and he is represented as riding on a sparrow, holding in his hand a bow of flowers and five arrows (*i.e.* the five senses).

Over hills with peaky tops engrail'd,
And many a tract of palm and rice,
The throne of Indian Cama slowly sail'd
A summer fann'd with spice.
TENNYSON: *The Palace of Art.*

Camargo (kȧ mar' gō). Marie-Anne Cuppi (1710-1770). The greatest dancer of the 18th century, flourished in France; from her the modern Society in London devoted to the Ballet Jakes takes its name.

Camber. In British legend, the second son of Brute (*q.v.*). Wales fell to his portion; which is one way of accounting for its ancient name of Cambria.

Cambria (kăm' bri a). The ancient name of Wales, the land of the Cimbri or Cymry.

Cambria's fatal day.—GRAY: *Bard.*
The Cambrian mountains, like far clouds,
That skirt the blue horizon, dusky rise.
THOMSON: *Spring*, 961-62.

Cambric. A kind of very fine white linen cloth, so named from Cambrai (Flem. *Kameryk*), in Flanders, where for long it was the chief manufacture.

He hath ribands of all the colours i' the rainbow;
inkles, caddisses, cambricks, and lawns.
SHAKESPEARE: *Winter's Tale*, iv, 3.

Camden Society. An historical society
founded in 1838 for the publication of early
historic and literary remains connected with
English history, and so named in honour of
William Camden (1551-1623), the antiquary.
In 1897 it amalgamated with the Royal Historical
Society, and its long series of publications was
transferred to that body.

Camel. The name of Mohammed's favourite
camel was Al Kaswa. The mosque at Koba covers
the spot where it knelt when Mohammed fled
from Mecca. He considered the kneeling of the
camel as a sign sent by God, and remained at
Koba in safety for four days. The swiftest of his
camels was Al Adha, who is fabled to have
performed the whole journey from Jerusalem
to Mecca in four bounds, and, in consequence,
to have had a place in heaven allotted him with
Al Borak (*q.v.*), Balaam's ass, Tobit's dog, and
the dog of the seven sleepers.

To break the camel's back. To pile on one
thing after another till at last the limit is reached
and a catastrophe or break-down caused. The
proverb is "It is the last straw that breaks the
camel's back." *See* STRAW.

**It is easier for a camel to go through the
eye of a needle, than for a rich man to enter
into the kingdom of God** (*see* EYE). In the
Koran we find a similar expression: "The impious
shall find the gates of heaven shut; nor shall he
enter till a camel shall pass through the eye of a
needle." In the Rabbinical writings is a passage
which goes to prove that the word *camel* should
not be changed into *cable*, as Theophylact suggests: "Perhaps thou art one of the Pampedithians,
who can make an elephant pass through the
eye of a needle."

It is as hard to come, as for a camel
To thread the postern of a needle's eye.
SHAKESPEARE: *Richard II*, v, 5.

Some think to avoid a difficulty by rendering
Matt. xix, 24, "It is easier for a *cable* to go
through the eye of a needle . . .", but the word
is κάμηλον and the whole force of the passage
rests on the "impossibility" of the thing, as it is
distinctly stated in *Mark* x, 24. "How hard is it
for them that trust in [their] riches, ἐπὶ τοῖς
χρήμασιν . . ." It is impossible by the virtue of
money or by bribes to enter the kingdom of
heaven.

Camelot (kăm' e lot). In British fable, the
legendary spot where King Arthur held his
court. It has been tentatively located at various

places—in Somerset, near Winchester (*q.v.*), in
Wales, and even in Scotland.

Hanmer, referring to *King Lear*, ii, 2, says
Camelot is Queen Camel, Somersetshire, in
the vicinity of which "are many large moors
where are bred great quantities of geese, so that
many other places are from hence supplied
with quills and feathers." Kent says to the Duke
of Cornwall:—

Goose, if I had you upon Sarum Plain,
I'd drive ye cackling home to Camelot.

It seems, however, far more probable that
Kent refers to Camelford, in Cornwall, where
the Duke of Cornwall resided, in his castle of
Tintagel. He says, "If I had you on Salisbury
Plain [where geese abound], I would drive you
home to Tintagel, on the river Camel." Though
the Camelot of Shakespeare is Tintagel or
Camelford, yet the Camelot of King Arthur
may be Queen Camel; and indeed visitors are
still pointed to certain large entrenchments at
South Cadbury (Cadbury Castle) called by the
inhabitants "King Arthur's Palace."

Cameo (căm' i ō). An ornamental carving
in relief on a precious or semi-precious stone. It
is the opposite of *intaglio*, which is an incised
carving. Onyx and sardonyx, with their layers of
light and dark, were much used by the cameo
cutters of Greece and Rome, and have always
been the favourite stones for these ornaments.
However, amethysts, turquoises and most gems
have at some time been cut as cameos. In the
nineteenth century, cameos were cut in shells,
coral, and jet. *Cameos* (1900) by Cyril Davenport,
F.S.A., gives further information.

Cameronian Regiment. The 26th Infantry,
which had its origin in a body of Cameronians
(*q.v.*), in the Revolution of 1688. Now the 1st
Battalion of the Scottish Rifles; the 2nd Battalion
is the old No. 90.

Camilla (kà mil' à). In Roman legend a
virgin queen of the Volscians. Virgil (*Æneid*,
vii, 809) says she was so swift that she could run
over a field of corn without bending a single
blade, or make her way over the sea without
even wetting her feet.

Not so when swift Camilla scours the plain,
Flies o'er the unbending corn and skims along the main.
POPE: *Essay on criticism*, 372.

Camisarde or **Camisado** (kăm' i sard, kăm
i sa' dō). A night attack; so called because the
attacking party wore a *camise* or camisard over
their armour, both to conceal it, and that they
might the better recognize each other in the dark.

Camisards. In French history, the Protestant
insurgents of the Cevennes, who resisted the

violence of the dragonnades, long after the revocation of the edict of Nantes (1685), and so called from the white shirts (*camisards*) worn by the peasants. Their leader was Jean Cavalier (1681-1740), afterwards Governor of Jersey.

Camisole. A loose jacket worn by women when dressed in *négligé*; an underbodice worn immediately beneath a blouse.

Camlan, Battle of. In Arthurian legend the battle which put an end to the Knights of the Round Table, and at which Arthur received his death wound from the hand of his nephew Modred, who was also slain. It took place about A.D. 537, but its site (traditionally placed in Cornwall) is as conjectural as that of Camelot (*q.v.*).

Cammock. As crooked as a cammock. The cammock is a crooked staff, or a stick with a crook at the head, like a hockey stick or shinty club; also, a piece of timber bent for the knee of a ship. The word is probably of Gaulish origin; it is found in Middle English, and there are Gaelic, Welsh, Irish, and Manx variants.

Though the cammock, the more it is bowed the better it serveth; yet the bow, the more it is bent and occupied the weaker it waxeth.—LYLY: *Euphues.*

Camorra (kȧ mor' ȧ). A lawless, secret society of Italy organized early in the 19th century. It claimed the right of settling disputes, etc., and was so named from the blouse (Ital. *camorra*) worn by its members, the *Camorrists.*

Campania (kăm pā' ni ȧ) (Lat., level country). The ancient geographical name for the district south-east of the Tiber, containing the towns of Cumæ, Capua, Baiæ, Puteoli, Herculaneum, Pompeii, etc.

Disdainful of Campania's gentle plains.
THOMOSON: *Summer.*

Campaspe (kăm păs' pe). A beautiful woman, the favourite concubine of Alexander the Great. Apellas, it is said, modelled his Venus Anadyomene from her.

Cupid and my Campaspe play'd
At Cards for kisses, Cupid paid.
LYLY: *Song from "Campaspe."*

Campbellites. Followers of John McLeod Campbell (1800-72), who taught the universality of the atonement, for which, in 1830, he was ejected by the General Assembly of the Church of Scotland.

In the United States the name is sometimes given to the *Disciples of Christ*, a body founded by Thomas and Alexander Campbell in Pennsylvania in 1809. They reject creeds, practise immersion and weekly communion, and uphold Christian union on the foundation of the Bible alone. They are also known as Christians.

Campeador. The Cid (*q.v.*).

Camp-followers. The old-time armies, which lived on the country, moved in leisurely fashion and laid up in winter quarters, were accompanied by a number of civilian followers such as washerwomen and sutlers who sold liquors and provisions, etc. These were called camp-followers.

In the moment of failure (at Bannockburn) the sight of a body of camp-followers whom they mistook for reinforcements to the enemy, spread panic through the English host.
J. R. GREEN: *Short History.*

Canaille (ka nī') (Fr., a pack of dogs). The mob, the rabble; a contemptuous name for the populace generally.

To keep the sovereign canaille from intruding on the retirement of the poor king of the French.
BURKE.

Canard (kăn' ar) (Fr., a duck). A hoax, a ridiculously extravagant report. Littré says that the term comes from an old expression, *vendre un canard à moitié*, to half-sell a duck. As this is no sale at all it came to mean "to take in," "to make a fool of." Another explanation is that a certain Cornelissen, to try the gullibility of the public, reported in the papers that he had twenty ducks, one of which he cut up and threw to the nineteen, who devoured it greedily. He then cut up another, then a third, and so on till the nineteenth was gobbled up by the survivor—a wonderful proof of duck voracity.

Canary. Wine from these islands was very popular in the 16th and 17th centuries.

Host: Farewell, my hearts, I will to my honest knight Falstaff, and drink canary with him.
Merry Wives of Windsor, iii, 2.

Cancan. A fast and extremely dexterous dance, sometimes accompanied by extravagant and often indecent postures, and originally performed in the casinos of Paris. The most famous example is in Offenbach's opera *Orpheus in the Underworld*.

They were going through a quadrille with all those supplementary gestures introduced by the great Rigolboche, a notorious *danseuse*, to whom the notorious cancan owes its origin.
A. EGMONT HAKE: *Paris Originals* (1878).

Cancel. A leaf printed and inserted in a book to replace that which was originally printed, because of last minute corrections or errors detected after printing. In bibliographical terminology the new leaf being inserted is called the *cancellans* and that which it replaces is the *cancellanda*.

Cancer. One of the twelve signs of the zodiac (the Crab). It appears when the sun has reached its highest northern limit, and begins to go backward towards the south; but, like a crab, the return is sideways (June 21st to July 23rd).

According to fable, Juno sent Cancer against Hercules when he combated the Hydra of Lerna. It bit the hero's foot, but Hercules killed the creature, and Juno took it up to heaven.

Candaules (kăn daw' lēz). King of Lydia about 710 to 668 B.C. Legend relates that he exposed the charms of his wife to Gyges (*q.v.*).

Candid Camera. An unseen camera which is used to photograph an unsuspecting subject. Candid camera shots, which are often ridiculous, are much used in pictorial journalism.

Candidate (Lat. *candidates*, clothed in white). One who seeks or is proposed for some office, appointment, etc. Those who solicited the office of consul, quæstor, prætor, etc., among the Romans, arrayed themselves in a loose white robe. It was loose that they might show the people their scars, and white in sign of fidelity and humility.

Candide (kan' dēd). The hero of Voltaire's philosophical novel, *Candide, ou l'Optimisme* (1759). All sorts of misfortunes are heaped upon him, and he bears them with unfailing optimism, in the belief that all's for the best in the best of all possible worlds.

He is not fit to hold the candle to him. He is very inferior. The allusion is to link-boys who held candles in theatres and other places of night amusement.

Some say, compared to Buononcini
That Mynheer Handel's but a ninny;
Others aver that he to Handel
Is scarcely fit to hold a candle.
BYRON: *Feuds between Handel and Buononcini.*

Candlemas Day. February 2nd, the feast of the Purification of the Virgin Mary, when Christ was presented by her in the Temple; one of the quarter days in Scotland. In Catholic churches all the candles which will be needed in the church during the year are consecrated on this day; they symbolize Jesus Christ, called "the light of the world," and "a light to lighten the Gentiles." The Romans had a custom of burning candles to scare away evil spirits.

If Candlemas Day be dry and fair,
The half o' winter's come and mair;
If Candlemas Day be wet and foul,
The half o' winter was gane at Youl.
Scotch Proverb.

The badger peeps out of his hole on Candlemas Day, and, if he finds snow, walks abroad; but if he sees the sun shining he draws back into his hole.
German Proverb.

Canephorus (kà nef' ôr ùs) (pi. *canephori*). A sculptured figure of a youth or maiden bearing a basket on the head. In ancient Greece the canephori bore the sacred things necessary at the feasts of the gods.

Canicular Days (Lat. *canicula*, dim. of *canis*, a dog). The dog-days (*q.v.*).

Canicular period. The ancient Egyptian cycle of 1461 years or 1460 Julian years, also called a *Sothic period*, (*q.v.*), during which it was supposed that any given day had passed through all the seasons of the year.

Canker. The briar or dog-rose.
Put down Richard, that sweet lovely rose.
And plant this thorn, this canker, Bolingbroke.
SHAKESPEARE: 1 *Henry IV*, i, 3.
Also a caterpillar that destroys leaves, buds, etc.
As killing as the canker to the rose.
MILTON: *Lycidas.*

Cannæ. The place where Hannibal defeated the Romans under Varro and L. Æmilius Paulus with great slaughter in 216 B.C., by means of withdrawing his centre and so enveloping the enemy—one of the most difficult manœuvres in war to perform. Any fatal battle that is the turning point of a great general's prosperity may be called his Cannæ. Thus Moscow was the Cannæ of Napoleon.

Cannibal. A word applied to those who eat human flesh. It is the Sp. *Canibales*, a corruption of *Caribes*, *i.e.* the Caribs, inhabitants of the Antilles, some of whom, when discovered by Columbus, were said to be man-eaters.
The natives live in great fear of the canibals [i.e. Caribals, or people of Cariba].—COLUMBUS.

Cannon. This term in billiards is a corruption of *carom*, which is short for Fr. *carambole*, the red ball (*caramboler*, to touch the red ball). A cannon is a stroke by which the player's ball touches one of the other balls in such a way as to glance off and strike the remaining ball.

Canny. See CA' CANNY.

Canoe. Like *cannibal*, *canoe* is one of the very few words we get from native West Indian. This is a Haitian word, *canoa*, and was brought to Europe by the Spaniards. It originally meant a boat hollowed out of a tree-trunk.

Paddle your own canoe. Mind your own business. The caution was given by President Lincoln, but it is an older saying and was used by Capt. Marryat (*Settlers in Canada*, ch. viii) in 1844. Sarah Bolton's poem in *Harper's Magazine* for May, 1854, popularized it:—
Voyage upon life's sea,
To yourself be true,

And, whate'er your lot may be,
Paddle your own canoe.

Canon. From Lat. and Gr. *canon*, a carpenter's
rule, a rule, hence a standard (as "the canons
of criticism"), a model, an ordinance, as in
Shakespeare's:—

Or that the Everlasting had not fixed
His canon 'gainst self-slaughter.
Hamlet, i, 2.

The canon. Canon law (*q.v.*).

Self-love which is the most inhibited sin in the canon.
All's Well that Ends Well, i, 1.

In music, from the same derivation, a composition written strictly according to rule, for
two or three voices which sing exactly the same
melody one a few beats after the other, either at the
same or a different pitch—as *Three Blind Mice*.

Also, the body of the books in the Bible
which are accepted by the Christian Church
generally as genuine and inspired; the whole
Bible from *Genesis* to *Revelation*, excluding the
Apocrypha. Called also the *sacred canon* and
the *Canonical Books*.

The Church dignitary known as a *Canon* is
a capitular member of a cathedral or collegiate
church, usually living in the precincts, and observing the statutable rule or canon of the body
to which he is attached. The canons, with the
dean at their head, constitute the governing
body, or *chapter*, of the cathedral.

Canon law. A collection of ecclesiastical
laws which serve as the rule of church government. The professors or students of canon law
are known as *canonists*.

Doubt not, worthy senators! to vindicate the sacred
honour and judgment of Moses your predecessor, from
the shallow commenting of scholastics and canonists.—
MILTON: *Doctrine of Divorce, Introd.*

Canonical dress. The distinctive or appropriate costume worn by the clergy according to
the direction of the canon. Bishops, deans, and
archdeacons, for instance, wear canonical hats.
This distinctive dress is sometimes called simply
"canonicals"; Macaulay speaks of "an ecclesiastic
in full canonicals." The same name is given
also to the special robes of other professions,
and to special parts of such robes, such as the
pouch on the gown of an M.D., originally
designed for carrying drugs; the *lamb-skin* on a
B.A. hood, in imitation of the *toga Candida* of
the Romans; the *tippet* on a barrister's gown,
meant for a wallet to carry briefs in; and the
proctors' and pro-proctors' *tippet*, for papers—a
sort of sabretache.

Canonical hours. The different parts of the
Divine Office which follow and are named
after the hours of the day. They are seven—viz.

matins, prime, tierce, sext, nones, vespers, and
compline. Prime, tierce, sext, and nones are
the first, third, sixth, and ninth hours of the day,
counting from six in the morning. Compline is
a corruption of *completorium* (that which completes the services of the day). The reason why
there are seven canonical hours is that David
says, "Seven times a day do I praise thee"
(*Ps.* cxix, 164).

In England the phrase means more especially the time of the day within which persons
can be legally married, *i.e.* from eight in the
morning to six p.m.

Canonical obedience. The obedience due by
the inferior to the superior clergy. Thus bishops
owe canonical obedience to the archbishop of
the same province.

Canopus (kà nō′ pus). A seaport in ancient
Egypt, 15 miles N.E. of Alexandria. Also the
name of the bright star in the southern constellation *Argo navis*. Except for Sirius this is the
brightest star in the heavens.

We drank the Libyan sun to sleep, and lit
Lamps which out-burn'd Canopus.
TENNYSON: *Dream of Fair Women.*

Canopic vases. Vases used by the Egyptian
priests for holding the viscera of bodies embalmed, four being provided for each body. So
called from Canopus, in Egypt, where they
were first used.

Canopy properly means a *gnat curtain*.
Herodotus tells us (ii, 95) that the fishermen of
the Nile used to lift their nets on a pole, and
form thereby a rude sort of tent under which
they slept securely, as gnats will not pass
through the meshes of a net. Subsequently the
hangings of a bed were so called, and lastly the
canopy borne over kings. (Gr. *konops*, a gnat.)

Cant. A whining manner of speech; class
phraseology, especially of a pseudo-religious
nature (Lat. *canto*, to sing, whence "chant"). It
seems to have been first used of the whining
manner of speech of beggars, who were known
as "the canting crew" (*q.v.*). In Harman's
*Caveat, or Warning, for Common Cursetors,
vulgarly called Vagabonds* (1567), we read:—

As far as I can learne or understand by the examination
of a number of them, their language—which they terme
peddelars Frenche or Canting—began but within these
xxx yeeres.

And one of the examples of "canting" that
he gives begins:—

Bene Lightmans to thy quarromes, in what tipken
hast thou lypped in this darkemans, whether in a
Iybbege or in the strummel? (Good-morrow to thy body,
in what house hast thou lain in all night, whether in a
bed or in the straw?)

The term was in familiar use in the time of Ben Jonson, signifying "professional slang," and "to use professional slang."

> The doctor here . . .
> When he discourses of dissection
> Of *vena cava* and of *vena porta* . . .
> What does he else but cant? Or if he run
> To his judicial astrology,
> And trowl the *trine*, the *quartile*, and the *sextile* . . .
> Does he not cant?
> > BEN JONSON: *The Staple of News, IV*, iv (1625).

Cant also means insincerity or conventionality in speech or thought.

> Rid your mind of cant.
> > Dr. JOHNSON.

From this it is extended to include any assumption or affectation of enthusiasm for high thoughts or aims.

Canting crew. Beggars, gipsies, thieves, and vagabonds, who use "cant" (*q.v.*). In 1696 "E. B. Gent," published the first English Slang Dictionary, with the title "A New Dictionary of the Terms, Ancient and Modern, of the Canting Crew in its several Tribes."

Cantabrian Surge. The Bay of Biscay. So called from the Cantabri who dwelt about the Biscayan shore. Suetonius tells us that a thunderbolt fell in the Cantabrian Lake (Spain) "in which twelve axes were found." (*Galba*, viii.)

> She her thundering army leads
> To Calpé [Gibraltar] . . . or the rough
> Cantabrian Surge.
> > AKENSIDE: *Hymn to the Naiades*.

Canteen means properly a wine-cellar (Ital. *cantina*, a cellar). Then a refreshment house in a barrack for the use of the soldiers, whence it has now come to be applied to a communal restaurant for members of a large firm, etc. Then a vessel for holding liquid refreshment, carried by soldiers on the march; and finally a complete outfit of cutlery.

Canter. An easy gallop; originally called a *Canterbury pace* or *gallop*, from the ambling gait adopted by mounted pilgrims to the shrine of St. Thomas à Becket at Canterbury.

Canterbury Tales. Chaucer set it forth that he was in company with a party of pilgrims going to Canterbury to pay their devotions at the shrine of Thomas à Becket. The party assembled at an inn in Southwark, called the Tabard, and there agreed to tell one tale each, both in going and returning. He who told the best tale was to be treated with a supper on the homeward journey. The work is incomplete, and we have none of the tales told on the way home.

Canucks (ka nŭks′). The name given in the U.S.A. to Canadians generally, but in Canada itself to Canadians of French descent. The origin is uncertain, but it has been suggested that it is a corruption of *Connaught*, a name originally applied by the French Canadians to Irish immigrants.

Canvas means cloth made of hemp (Lat. *cannabis*, hemp). **To canvas a subject** is to strain it through a hemp strainer, to sift it; and to **canvas a borough** is to solicit the votes.

Cap. The word is used figuratively by Shakespeare for the top, the summit (of excellence, etc.); as in *They wear themselves in the cap of the time* (*All's Well*, ii, 1), *i.e.* "They are the ornaments of the age"; *a very riband in the cap of youth* (*Hamlet*, iv, 7); *Thou art the cap of all the fools alive* (*Timon*, iv, 3); *on fortune's cap we are not the very button* (*Hamlet*, ii, 2); etc.

Cap and gown. The full academical costume of a university student, tutor, or master, worn at lectures, examinations, and after "hall" (dinner).

> Is it a cap and gown affair?
> > C. BEDE: *Verdant Green*.

Cap in hand. Submissively. To wait on a man cap in hand is to wait on him like a servant, ready to do his bidding.

Fool's cap. A conical cap with feather and bells, such as licensed fools used to wear. For the paper so called, *see* FOOLSCAP.

John Knox cap. An early form of the trencher, mortar-board, or college cap (*q.v.*), worn at the Scottish Universities.

Phrygian cap. Cap of liberty (*q.v.*).

Square cap. A trencher or mortar-board, like the college cap (*q.v.*).

Trencher cap, or **mortar-board.** A cap with a square board, generally covered with black cloth, and a tassel, worn with academical dress; a college cap (*q.v.*).

A feather in one's cap. An achievement to be proud of; something creditable.

I must put on my thinking cap. I must think about the matter before I give a final answer. The allusion is to the official cap of a judge, formerly donned when passing any sentence, but now only when passing sentence of death.

If the cap fits, wear it. If the remark applies to you, apply it yourself. Hats and caps differ very slightly in size and appearance, but everyone knows his own when he puts it on.

Setting her cap at him. Trying to catch him for a sweetheart or a husband. In the days when ladies habitually wore caps they would naturally put on the most becoming, to attract the attention and admiration of the favoured gentleman.

To cap. To take off, or touch, one's cap to, in token of respect; also to excel.

Well, that caps the globe. — C. Brontë: *Jane Eyre.*

To cap a story. To go one better; after a good story has been told to follow it up with a better one of the same kind.

To cap verses. Having the metre fixed and the last letter of the previous line given, to add a line beginning with that letter, thus:

The way was long, the wind was cold (D)
Dogs with their tongues their wounds do heal (L).
Like words congealed in northern air (R).
Regions Cæsar never knew (W).
With all a poet's ecstasy (Y).
You may deride my awkward pace, etc., etc.

There are parlour games of capping names, proverbs, etc., in the same way, as: Plato, Otway, Young, Goldsmith, etc., "Rome was not built in a day," "Ye are the salt of the earth," "Hunger is the best sauce," "Example is better than precept," "Time and tide wait for no man," etc.

To cap it all. To surpass what has gone before; to make things even worse.

To gain the cap. To obtain a bow from another out of respect.

Such gains the cap of him that makes them fine,
But keeps his book uncrossed.
                            Shakespeare: *Cymbeline*, iii, 3.

To pull caps. To quarrel like two women, who pull each other's caps. An obsolete phrase, used only of women. In a description of a rowdy party in 18th-century Bath we read: —

At length they fairly proceeded to pulling caps, and everything seemed to presage a general battle . . . they suddenly-desisted, and gathered up their caps, ruffles, and handkerchiefs.

Smollett: *Humphrey Clinker: Letter* xix.

To send the cap round. To make a collection. This is from the custom of street musicians, acrobats, etc., of sending a cap round among the onlookers to collect their pennies.

Wearing the cap and bells. Said of a person who is the butt of the company, or one who excites laughter at his own expense. The reference is to licensed jesters formerly attached to noblemen's establishments. *See* Cap and Bells *above.* Their headgear was a cap with bells.

One is bound to speak the truth . . . whether he mounts the cap and bells or a shovel hat [like a bishop]. — Thackeray.

To be capped. A player who has represented England, Scotland, Ireland, or Wales in an international match at any of the major field sports may wear a cap bearing the national emblem. Hence the phrase: He was capped for England.

Capability Brown. Lancelot Brown (1715-83) landscape gardener and architect, one of the founders of the modern or English style of landscape gardening. He received this name because he habitually assured prospective employers that their land held "great capabilities."

Cap-à-pie (kăp à pē). From head to foot; usually with reference to arming or accoutring. From O.Fr. *cap à pie* (Mod.Fr. *de pied en cap*).

Armed at all points exactly cap-a-pie.
                            Shakespeare: *Hamlet*, i, 2.
I am courtier, cap-a-pé.
                            Shakespeare: *Winter's Tale*, iv, 3.

Cape. The Cape. Cape of Good Hope Province.

Cape cart. This is the name given to a two-wheeled, hooded, horse-drawn cart originally used in Cape Colony and S. Africa generally.

Cape gooseberry. Although it takes its name from the Cape, this plant originally came from S. America and its botanical name is *Physalis peruviana.* It is much prized for its decorative bladder-like calyx.

Spirit of the Cape. *See* Adamastor.

Cape of Storms. *See* Storms.

Capel Court. A lane adjacent to the Stock Exchange in London where dealers congregate to do business: hence used sometimes for the Stock Exchange itself. Hence also *Capel Courtier,* a humorous term for a professional stock-dealer. So called from Sir William Capel, Lord Mayor in 1504.

Caper. The weather is so foul not even a Caper would venture out. A Manx proverb. A Caper is a fisherman of Cape Clear in Ireland, who will venture out in almost any weather.

To cut capers. To spring upwards in dancing, and rapidly interlace one foot with the other; figuratively, to act in an unusual manner with the object of attracting notice. **Caper** here is from Ital. *capra*, a she-goat, the allusion being to the erratic way in which goats will jump about.

Cut your capers! Be off with you!

I'll make him cut his capers, *i.e.* rue his conduct.

Caper Merchant. A dancing-master who cuts "capers."

Capet. Hugh Capet, the founder of the Capetian dynasty of France, is said to have been so named from the *cappa*, or monk's hood, which he wore as lay abbot of St. Martin de Tours. The Capetians reigned over France till 1328, when they were succeeded by the House of Valois; but *Capet* was considered the family name of the kings, hence, Louis XVI was arraigned before the National Convention under the name of Louis Capet.

Capital. Money or money's worth available for production.

His capital is continually going from him [the merchant] in some shape and returning to him in another.
ADAM SMITH: *Wealth of Nations*, Bk. ii, ch. 1.

Active capital. Ready money or property readily convertible into it.

Circulating capital. Wages, or raw material. This sort of capital is not available a second time for the same purpose.

Fixed capital. Land, buildings, and machinery, which are only gradually consumed.

To make capital out of. To turn to account: thus, in politics, one party is always ready to make political capital out of the errors of the other.

Capitano, El Gran (el grăn kăp i ta′ nō) (*i.e.* the Great Captain). The name given to the famous Spanish general Gonsalvo de Cordova (1453-1515), through whose efforts Granada and Castile were united.

Capitulary (kăp it′ ū làr i). A collection of ordinances or laws, especially those of the Frankish kings. The laws were known as *capitulars* because they were passed by a chapter (*q.v.*).

Capon (kā′ pon). Properly, a castrated cock; but the name has been given to various fish, perhaps originally in a humorous way by friars who wished to evade the Friday fast and so eased their consciences by changing the name of the fish, and calling a chicken a *fish out of the coop*.

Capon is also an obsolete term for a love-letter, after the Fr. *poulet*, which means not only a chicken but also a love-letter, or a sheet of fancy notepaper. Thus Henri IV, consulting with Sully about his marriage, says: "My niece of Guise would please me best, though report says maliciously that she loves poulets in paper better than in a fricassee."

Boyet . . . break-up this capon [*i.e.* open this love-letter].
SHAKESPEARE: *Love's Labour's Lost*, iv, 1.

Capricorn (kăp′ ri kôrn). Called by Thomson, in his *Winter*, "the centaur archer." Anciently, the winter solstice occurred on the entry of the sun into Capricorn, *i.e.* the Goat: but the stars, having advanced a whole sign to the east, the winter solstice now falls at the sun's entrance into Sagittarius (the centaur archer), so that the poet is strictly right, though we commonly retain the ancient classical manner of speaking. Capricorn is the tenth, or, strictly speaking, the eleventh, sign of the zodiac (December 21-January 20).

According to classical mythology, Capricorn was Pan, who, from fear of the great Typhon, changed himself into a goat, and was made by Jupiter one of the signs of the zodiac.

Captain. The Great Captain. *See* CAPITANO, EL GRAN.

A led captain. An obsequious person, who dances attendance on the master and mistress of a house, for which service he has a knife and fork at the dinner table.

Captain Armstrong. A name for a cheating jockey—one who pulls a horse with a *strong arm*, and so prevents his winning.

Captain Cauf's Tail. In Yorkshire, the commander-in-chief of the mummers who used to go round from house to house on Plough Monday (*q.v.*). He was most fantastically dressed, with a cockade and many coloured ribbons; and he always had a genuine calf's (cauf's) tail affixed behind.

Captain Copperthorne's Crew. All masters and no men.

Capuchin (kăp′ ū chin). A friar of the Franciscan Order (*q.v.*) of the new rule of 1525; so called from the *capuce* or pointed cowl.

Capulet (kăp′ ū let). A noble house in Verona, the rival of that of Montague; Juliet is of the former, and Romeo of the latter. Lady Capulet is the beau-ideal of a proud Italian matron of the 15th century (Shakespeare: *Romeo and Juliet*). The expression so familiar, "the tomb of all the Capulets," is from Burke; he uses it in his reflections on the *Revolution in France* (vol. iii, p. 349), and again in his *Letter to Matthew Smith*, where he says:—

'I would rather sleep in the southern corner of a country churchyard than in the tomb of the Capulets.

Caqueux (ka kė). A sort of gipsy race in Brittany, similar to the Cagots of Gascony, and Colliberts of Poitou.

Carabas (kăr′ a ba). **He is a Marquis of Carabas.** An ultra-conservative nobleman, of unbounded pretensions and vanity, who would restore the lavish foolery of the reign of Louis XIV; one with Fortunatus's purse, which was never empty. The character is taken from Perrault's tale of *Puss in Boots*, where he is Puss's master.

Prêtres que nous vengeons
Levez la dîme et partageons;
Et toi, peuple animal,
Porte encor le bât féodal. . . .
Chapeau bas! Chapeau bas!
Gloire au marquis de Carabas!
Béranger (1816).

The Marquis of Carabas in Disraeli's *Vivian Grey* is intended for the Marquis of Clanricarde.

Carabinier. *See* CARBINEER.

Caracalla (kăr′ a kăl′ à). Aurelius Antoninus, Roman Emperor, 211-17, was so called because he adopted the Gaulish *caracalla* in preference to the Roman toga. It was a large, close-fitting, hooded mantle, reaching to the heels, and slit up before and behind to the waist. *Cp.* CURMANTLE.

Carack. *See* CARRACK.

Caradoc (kà răd' ok). A Knight of the Round Table, noted for being the husband of the only lady in the queen's train who could wear "the mantle of matrimonial fidelity." He appears (as Craddocke) in the old ballad *The Boy and the Mantle* (given in Percy's *Reliques*): —

Craddocke called forth his ladye,
And bade her come in;
Saith, Winne this mantle, ladye,
With a little dinne.

Also, in history, the British chief whom the Romans called Caractacus (lived about A.D. 50).

Caran d'Ache (kă ràn dash'). This was the pseudonym of Emanuel Poiré (1858-1909), a well-known French caricaturist. He was famous in his time as an illustrator of military subjects, and his biting cartoons and caricatures appeared in various papers and magazines.

Carat. A measure of weight, about $\frac{1}{147}$ of an ounce, used for precious stones; also a proportional measure of $\frac{1}{24}$th used to describe the fineness of gold, thus, gold of 22 carats has 22 parts pure gold and 2 parts alloy. The Arabic *qirat*, meaning the seed of the locust tree, the weight of which represented the Roman *siliqua*, was $\frac{1}{24}$th of the golden *solidus* of Constantine, which was $\frac{1}{6}$th of an ounce. It is from these fractions that it has come about that a carat is a twenty-fourth part. The name may come from the Arabic, or from Greek κεράτιον, seed of the locust-tree. *See* GOLD.

Caraway (kăr' à wā). The flavouring of cakes with caraway seeds was once more common than is now the case. Cakes so flavoured were called caraways, hence Shallow's invitation to Falstaff: —

Nay, you shall see my orchard, where in an arbour we will eat a last year's pippin of my own braffing, with a dish of caraways.

2 *Henry IV*, v, 3.

Carbonari (kar bo na' rē) (singular, *carbonaro*). This name, assumed by a secret political society in Italy (organized 1808-14), means *charcoal burners*. Their place of muster they called a "hut"; its inside, "the place for selling charcoal"; and the outside, the "forest." Their political opponents they called "wolves." Their object was to convert the kingdom of Naples into a republic. The name was later applied to other secret political societies.

Carcass. The shell of a house before the floors are laid and walls plastered; the skeleton of a ship, a wreck, etc. The body of a dead animal, so called from Fr. *carcasse*, Lat. *carcosium*.

The Goodwins, I think they call the place; a very dangerous flat and fatal, where the carcases of many a tall ship lie buried.

SHAKESPEARE: *Merchant of Venice*, iii, 1.

The name was also given to an obsolete type of incendiary shell projected from a mortar.

Charlestown, . . . having been fired by a carcass from Copp's Hill, sent up dense columns of smoke.

LESSING: *United States*.

Card. Slang for a queer fellow, an eccentric, a "character."

You're a shaky old card; and you can't be in love with this Lizzie.

DICKENS: *Our Mutual Friend*, Bk. iii, ch. i.

Cards. It is said that there never was a good hand at whist containing four clubs. Such a hand is called "The Devil's Four-poster."

In Spain, spades used to be *columbines*; clubs, *rabbits*; diamonds, *pinks*; and hearts, *roses*. The present name for spades is *espados* (swords); of clubs, *bastos* (cudgels); of diamonds, *dineros* (square pieces of money used for paying wages); of hearts, *copas* (chalices).

The French for spade is *pique* (pikemen or soldiers); for club, *trèfle* (clover, or husbandmen); of diamonds, *carreaux* (building tiles, or flagstones); of hearts, *cœur*.

The English spade is the French form of a pike, and the Spanish name; the club is the French trefoil, and the Spanish name.

Court cards. *See* COURT.

Cardigan (car' di gàn). This is a knitted woollen over-waistcoat, with or without sleeves, and it takes its name from the 7th Earl of Cardigan, who commanded the Light Brigade and led it in the famous charge at Balaclava. The garment appears to have been first worn by our men in the bitter cold of the Crimean winter.

Cardinal. The Lat. *cardo* means a hinge; its adjective, *cardinalis* (from which we get "cardinal"), meant originally "pertaining to a hinge," hence "that on which something turns or depends," hence "the principal, the chief." Hence, in Rome a "cardinal church" (*ecclesia cardinalis*) was a principal or parish church as distinguished from an oratory attached to such, and the chief priest (*presbyter cardinalis*) was the "cardinal," the body (or "College") of cardinals forming the Council of the Pope, and electing the Pope from their own number. This did not become a stabilized regulation till after the third Lateran Council (1173), since when the College of Cardinals has consisted of six cardinal bishops, fifty cardinal priests, and fourteen cardinal deacons.

The cardinal's red hat was made part of the official vestments by Innocent IV (1245) "in token of their being ready to lay down their life for the gospel."

Cardinal humours. An obsolete medical term for the four principal "humours" of the body, viz. blood, phlegm, yellow bile, and black bile.

Cardinal numbers. The natural, primitive numbers, which answer the question "how many?" such as 1, 2, 3, etc. 1st, 2nd, 3rd, etc., are *ordinal* numbers.

Cardinal points of the compass. Due north, west, east, and south. So called because they are the points on which the intermediate ones, such as NE., NW., NNE., etc., hinge or hang. (Lat. *cardo*, a hinge.)

The poles, being the points upon which the earth turns, were called in Latin *cardines* (*cardo*, a hinge, *see* CARDINAL *above*), and the *cardinal points* are those which lie in the direction of the poles and of sunrise and sunset. Thus, also, the winds that blow due east, west, north, and south are known as the *cardinal winds*. It is probably from the fact that the cardinal points are *four* in number that the cardinal humours, virtues, etc., are also *four*.

Cardinal virtues. Justice, prudence, temperance, and fortitude, on which all other virtues hang or depend. A term of the Schoolmen, to distinguish the "natural" virtues from the "theological" virtues (faith, hope, and charity).

Care. Care killed the cat. It is said that "a cat has nine lives," yet care would wear them all out.

Hang sorrow! care'll kill a cat.
BEN JONSON: *Every Man in his Humour*, i, 3.

Caricatures mean sketches "overloaded"; hence, exaggerated drawings. (Ital. *caricatura*, from *caricare*, to load or burden.)

Carillons (ka ril′ yonz), in France, are chimes or tunes played on bells; but in England the suites of bells that play the tunes. The word is the O.Fr. *quarignon*, from late Lat. *quatrinio*, a chime played on four bells; carillons were formerly rung on four bells; nowadays the number is usually eight, but the "bob maximus" (*see* BOB) is rung on twelve.

Carle Sunday; Carlings. *See* CARE SUNDAY.

Carlists (kar′ lists). Don Carlos (1788-1855) was the second son of Charles IV of Spain, and on the death of his brother, Ferdinand VII would have become king of Spain had not the Salic Law been set aside and Ferdinand's daughter Isabella declared Queen. He set up his claim to the throne, the Church sided with

him, and for years Spain was rent by factious war between the Carlists and the queen's party. The Carlist activities did not really cease until the death of Don Carlos II, in 1909. The last pretender died childless in 1936, and the following year the party was merged by General Franco in his Falange.

Carlovingians (kar lo ving′ giànz) or *Carolingians*. So called from Carolus Magnus, or Charlemagne. They were descended from Frankish lords in Austria in the 7th century, and furnished the second royal dynasty in France (751-987), a dynasty of German Emperors (752-911), and of Italian kings (774-961).

Carmagnole (kar ma nyōl). Originally the name of a kind of jacket worn in France in the 18th century, and introduced there from Carmagnola, in Piedmont, where it was the dress of the workmen. It was adopted by the Revolutionists, and the name thus came to be applied to them, to the soldiers of the first Republic, and to a song and a wild kind of dance that became immensely popular and was almost invariably used at the executions of 1792 and 1793. The first verse of the song is:—

> Madame Veto avait promis
> De faire égorger tout Paris,
> Madame Veto avait promis
> De faire égorger tout Paris.
> Mais son coup a manqué
> Grace á nos canonnié:
> Dansons la carmagnole, Vive le son, vive le son,
> Dansons la carmagnole, Vive le son du canon.

Madame Veto was the people's name for Queen Marie Antoinette, as she was supposed to have inspired the king's unfortunate use of the veto.

The word was subsequently applied to other revolutionary songs, such as *Ça ira*, the *Marseillaise*, the *Chant du départ*; also to the speeches in favour of the execution of Louis XVI, called by Barère, *des Carmagnoles*.

Carmelites (kar′ me lītz). Mendicant friars, the first rule of whose Order is said to have been given by John, patriarch of Jerusalem, A.D. 400, and to have been formed from the records of the prophet Elijah's life on Mount Carmel. Also called White Friars, from their white cloaks. *See* BAREFOOTED.

Carmen Sylva (kar′ men sil′ và). This was the pen-name of Queen Elizabeth of Rumania (1843-1916). She was a woman of cultivated tastes, a musician, painter, and writer of poems and stories.

Carney. To wheedle, to caress, to coax. An old dialect word of unknown origin.

Carnival. The season immediately preceding Lent, ending on Shrove Tuesday, and a period in many Roman Catholic countries devoted to amusement; hence, revelry, riotous amusement. From the Lat. *caro, carnis,* flesh, *levare,* to remove, signifying the abstinence from meat during Lent. The earlier word, *carnilevamen,* was altered in Italian to *carnevale,* as though connected with *vale,* farewell—farewell to flesh.

Carol (from O.Fr. *carole,* which is probably from Lat. *choraula,* a dance). The earliest meaning of the word in English is a round dance, hence a song that accompanied the dance, hence a light and joyous hymn, a meaning which came to be applied specially to, and latterly almost confined to, such a hymn in honour of the Nativity and sung at Christmas time by wandering minstrels. The earliest extant English Christmas carol dates from the 13th century, and was originally written in Anglo-Saxon; a translation of the first verse is here given. The first printed collection of Christmas carols came from the press of Wynkyn de Worde in 1521; it included the Boar's Head Carol, which is still sung at Queen's College, Oxford. For another example, *see* BOAR'S HEAD.

> Lordlings, listen to our lay—
> We have come from far away
>   To seek Christmas;
> In this mansion we are told
> He his yearly feast doth hold;
>   'Tis to-day!
> May joy come from God above,
> To all those who Christmas love.

Carolingians. *See* CARLOVINGIANS.

Carouse (ka rouz′). To drink deeply, to make merry with drinking; hence a drinking bout. The word is the German *garaus,* meaning literally "right out" or "completely"; it was used specially of completely emptying a bumper to someone's health.

The word *rouse,* a bumper, as in Shakespeare's:—

> The king doth wake to-night, and takes his rouse.
>   *Hamlet,* i, 4.

probably arose from the similarity of sound between "to drink carouse" and "to drink a rouse."

Carpathian Wizard. Proteus, who lived in the island of Carpathus (now Scarpanto), between Rhodes and Crete, who could transform himself into any shape he pleased. He is represented as carrying a sort of crook in his hand, because he was an ocean shepherd and had to manage a flock of sea-calves.

> By the Carpathian wizard's book.
>   MILTON: *Comus,* 872.

Carpe Diem (kar′ pā dī′ em). Enjoy yourself while you have the opportunity. Seize the present day. "*Dum vivimus, vivamus.*"

> Carpe diem quam minimum credula postere.
>   HORACE: *Odes,* I, xi, 8.
> Seize the present, trust to-morrow e'en as little as you may.—CONNINGTON.

Carpet. The magic carpet. The carpet which, to all appearances, was worthless, but which, if anyone sat thereon, would transport him instantaneously to the place he wished to go, is one of the stock properties of Eastern wonder-tales and romance. It is sometimes termed *Prince Housain's carpet,* because of the popularity of the *Story of Prince Ahmed* in the *Arabian Nights,* where it supplies one of the principal incidents; but the chief magic carpet is that of King Solomon, which, according to the Mohammedan legend related in the Koran, was of green silk. His throne was placed on it when he travelled, and it was large enough for all his forces to stand upon, the men and women on his right hand, and the spirits on his left. When all were arranged in order, Solomon told the wind where he wished to go, and the carpet, with all its contents, rose in the air and alighted at the place indicated. In order to screen the party from the sun, the birds of the air with outspread wings formed a canopy over the whole party.

Carpet-bagger. The name given in the U.S.A. to the Northern political adventurers, who sought a career in the Southern States after the Civil War of 1865. Their only "property qualification" was in the personal baggage they brought with them, and they were looked upon with great suspicion. In U.S.A. members of Congress and the State legislatures almost invariably reside in the district which they represent.

Carrack. A large merchant ship which, in Elizabethan times, carried the valuable cargoes from the Spice Islands and the Far East to Portugal, and could readily be fitted out as a man-of-war.

> "And now hath Sathanas," seith he, "a tayl
> Brodder than of a carrik is the sayl."
>   CHAUCER: *Somnour's Prologue,* 23.

Carriage. This used to mean, that which is carried, luggage; also the supports or mount of a piece of ordnance.

> And after those days we took up our carriages, and went up to Jerusalem.—*Acts* xxi, 15.

In *Num.* iv, 24, where the text gives "burdens," the marginal rendering is "carriage," and the usage is not at all uncommon in the English of that date.

Carriage company. Persons who go visiting in their private carriage.

> Seeing a great deal of carriage company.—*Thackeray.*

Carronade (kăr o nād′). A short gun of large calibre like a mortar, having no trunnions and so differing from howitzers, first made in 1779 at the Carron foundry, Scotland. Carronades are fastened to their carriages by a loop underneath, and were chiefly used on ships, to enable heavy shot to be thrown at close quarters.

Carry. Carry arms! Carry swords! Military commands directing that the rifle or drawn sword is to be held in a vertical position in the right hand and against the right shoulder.

Carry coals. *See* COALS.

To carry everything before one. To be beyond competition; to carry off all the prizes; to be a successful competitor in any form of examination or sport.

To carry fire in one hand and water in the other. To say one thing and mean another; to flatter, to deceive; to lull suspicion in order the better to work mischief.

Altera manu fert aquam, altera ignem,
Altera manu fert lapideum, altera panem ostentat.
Plautus.

In one hand he carried water, in the other fire; in one hand he bears a stone, in the other he shows a piece of bread.

To carry on. (1) To continue an activity from the point already reached, particularly in military parlance. (2) To make a scene, lose one's temper—"he carried on something dreadful."

To carry out or **through.** To continue a project to its completion.

To carry one's bat. Said of a cricketer who is "not out" at the close of the game. Hence, figuratively, to outlast one's opponents, to succeed in one's undertaking.

Carry swords! *See* CARRY ARMS!

To carry the day. To win the contest; to carry off the honours of the day.

To carry weight. In horse racing, to equalize the weight of two or more riders by adding to the lighter ones, till both (or all) the riders are made of uniform weight.

He carries weight! he rides a race!
'Tis for a thousand pounds.
COWPER: *John Gilpin.*

Also, to have influence.

Cart. To put the cart before the horse is to reverse the right order or allocation of things.

This methinkes is playnely to sett the carte before the horse.—*The Babees Book* (Early English Tract Society, p. xxiii).

The phrase has its counterpart in other languages:—

French: Mettre la charette avant les bœufs.
Latin: Currus bovem trahit
    Præpostere.
Greek: Hysteron proteron.
German: Die pferde hinter den wagen spannen.
Italian: Metter il carro innanzi ai buoi.

Carte. Carte blanche (Fr.). A paper with only the signature written on it, so that the person to whom it is given may write his terms knowing that they will be accepted. Literally, a blank paper. It was originally a military phrase, referring to unconditional surrender; but it is now used entirely in a figurative sense, conferring absolute freedom of action on one to whom it is given.

Carte de visite (Fr.). A visiting card; a photographic likeness on a card, originally intended to be used as a visiting card. The idea was started in 1857, but it never "caught on," as such, although the small size of photograph became very popular.

Cartel (kar tel′). This is a word with several meanings. Originally it was applied only to a written agreement between opponents in a war arranging the exchange of prisoners. From that it was extended to include the ship used for such an exchange. It has since come to mean a working arrangement between rival commercial concerns in one or more countries to regulate the price of the commodity they are interested in, invariably at the expense of the community.

Cartesian Philosophy (kar tē zhán). The philosophical system of René Descartes (1596-1650), a founder of modern philosophy. The basis of his system is *cogito ergo sum. See* COGITO. Thought must proceed from soul, and therefore man is not wholly material; that soul must be from some Being not material, and that Being is God. As for physical phenomena, they must be the result of motion excited by God, and these motions he termed *vortices.*

Carthage of the North (kar′ thaj). This was the name given to Lübeck, when it was the head of the Hanseatic League.

Carthaginem esse delendam. *See* DELENDA EST CARTHAGO.

Carthaginian faith. Treachery. *See* PUNICA FIDES.

Carthusians. An order of monks, founded about 1086 by St. Bruno, of Cologne, who, with six companions, retired to the solitude of La Grande Chartreuse, thirteen miles northeast of Grenoble, and there built his famous monastery. In 1902 the monks were evicted by order of the French government, and in the following year their buildings and property were sold, the monks themselves settling at the Certosa (Charterhouse) near Lucca.

The first English Charterhouse was established in 1178; the monks of the London Charterhouse were among the staunchest opponents of Henry VIII. In 1833 the Carthusians were re-established in the Charterhouse at Parkminster, Sussex. *See* CHARTREUSE.

Cartoon. Originally a design drawn on *cartone* (pasteboard) to serve as a model for a work of art, such as a fresco or tapestry. Now applied to a caricature or political sketch.

Caryatides (kăr i ăt′ idz). Figures of women in Greek costume, used in architecture to support entablatures. Caryæ, in Laconia, sided with the Persians at Thermopylæ; in consequence of which the victorious Greeks destroyed the city, slew the men, and made the women slaves. Praxiteles, to perpetuate the disgrace, employed figures of these women, instead of columns. *Cp.* ATLANTES, CANEPHORUS.

Casabianca, Louis (kăs à bi ăng′ kà). Captain of the French man-of-war, *L'Orient*. At the battle of Aboukir, having first secured the safety of his crew, he blew up his ship, to prevent it falling into the hands of the English. His little son, Giacomo Jocante, refusing to leave him, perished with his father. Mrs. Hemans made a ballad on the incident.

Case. The case is altered. *See* PLOWDEN.

To case. To skin an animal; to deprive it of its "case." *See* FIRST CATCH YOUR HARE, *s.v.* CATCH.

Case-hardened. Impenetrable to all sense of honour or shame. The allusion is to steel hardened by carbonizing the surface.

Cashier. To dismiss an officer from the army, to discard from society. (Dut. *casseren*, Fr. *casser*, to break; Ital. *cassare*, to blot out.)

> The ruling rogue, who dreads to be cashiered,
> Contrives, as he is hated, to be feared.
> SWIFT: *Epistle to Mr. Gay*, 137.

Cashmere. *See* KERSEYMERE.

Casino (kà sē′ nō). Originally, a little *casa* or room near a theatre where persons might retire, after the play was over, for dancing or music.

Cask. A vessel for the storing of wine in bulk. Some local names for casks are as follows:—

Arroba, Spain; *basil*, Portugal; *barile*, Italy; *barrique*, France; *Breute*, Switzerland; *Dreiling*, *Eimer*, or *Fuder*, Austria; *Oxhoft*, Hamburg; *bochonok*, Russia.

Casket Homer. *See* HOMER.

Casket Letters, The. Letters supposed to have been written between Mary Queen of Scots and Bothwell, at least one of which was held to prove the complicity of the Queen in the murder of her husband, Darnley. They were kept in a casket which fell into the hands of the Earl of Morton (1567); they were examined and used as evidence (though denounced as forgeries by the Queen—who was never allowed to see them), and they disappeared after the execution of the Regent, the Earl of Gowrie (1584), in whose custody they had last been. They have never been recovered, and their authenticity is still a matter of dispute.

Cassandra (kà săn′ drà). A prophetess. In Greek legend the daughter of Priam and Hecuba, gifted with the power of prophecy; but Apollo, whose advances she had refused, brought it to pass that no one believed her predictions, although they were invariably correct. She appears in Shakespeare's *Troilus and Cressida*.

Cassation. The Court of Cassation, in France, is the highest Court of Appeal, the Court which can *casser* (quash) the judgment of other Courts.

Cassi. Inhabitants of what is now the Cassio hundred, Hertfordshire, referred to by Cæsar, in his *Commentaries*. The name can still be traced in Cassiobury Park, Watford.

Cassiopeia (kăs i ō pē′ à). In Greek mythology, the wife of Cepheus, King of Ethiopia, and mother of Andromeda (*q.v.*). In consequence of her boasting of her beauty, she was sent to the heavens as the constellation Cassiopeia, the chief stars of which form the outline of a woman seated in a chair and holding up both arms in supplication.

> That starred Ethiop queen that strove
> To set her beauty's praise above
> The sea-nymphs and their powers offended.
> MILTON: *Il Penseroso*.

Cassiterides (kăs i ter′ i dēz). The tin islands, generally supposed to be the Scilly Islands and Cornwall; but possibly the isles in Vigo Bay are meant. It is said that the Veneti procured tin from Cornwall, and carried it to these islands, keeping its source a profound secret. The Phœnicians were the chief customers of the Veneti.

Cast. A cast of the eye. A squint. One meaning of the word cast is to twist or warp. Thus, a fabric is said to "cast" when it warps; the seamen speak of "casting," or turning the head of a ship on the tack it is to sail. We also speak of a "casting vote" (*q.v.*).

> My goode bowe clene cast [twisted] on one side.
> ASCHAM: *Toxophilus*.

Cast down. Dejected. (Lat. *dejectus*.)

To cast about. To deliberate, to consider, as, "I am casting about me how I am to meet the expenses." A sporting phrase. Dogs, when they have lost scent, "cast for it," *i.e.* spread out and search in different directions to recover it.

To cast in one's lot. To share the good or bad fortune of another.

To cast pearls before swine. To give what is precious to those who are unable to understand its value: a biblical phrase (*see Matt.* vii, 6). If pearls were cast to swine, the swine would trample them under foot.

Casting vote. The vote of the presiding officer when the votes of the assembly are equal. This final vote casts, turns, or determines the question.

Castaly (kăs' tȧ li). A fountain of Parnassus sacred to the Muses. Its waters had the power of inspiring with the gift of poetry those who drank of them.

> What was the great Parnassus' self to Thee,
> Mount Skiddaw? In his natural sovereignty
> Our British Hill is nobler far; he shrouds
> His double front among Atlantic clouds,
> And pours forth streams more sweet than Castaly.
>   WORDSWORTH: *Miscellaneous Sonnets*, v.

Caste (Port. *casta*, race). One of the hereditary classes of society in India; hence any hereditary or exclusive class, or the class system generally. The four Hindu castes are *Brahmins* (the priestly order), *Shatriya* (soldiers and rulers), *Vaisya* (husbandmen and merchants), *Sudra* (agricultural labourers and mechanics). The first issued from the mouth of Brahma, the second from his arms, the third from his thighs, and the fourth from his feet. Below these come thirty-six inferior classes, to whom the Vedas are sealed, and who are held cursed in this world and without hope in the next.

Castle. Castle in the air. A visionary project, day-dream, splendid imagining which has no real existence. In fairy tales we often have these castles built at a word, and vanishing as soon, like that built for Aladdin by the Genie of the Lamp. Also called *Castles in Spain*; the French call them *Chateaux d'Espagne* or *Chateaux en Asie*. See CHATEAU.

Castle of Bungay. In Camden's *Britannia* (1607) the following lines are attributed to Lord Bigod of Bungay or the borders of Suffolk and Norfolk: —

> Were I in my Castle of Bungay
> Upon the river of Waveney,
> I would ne care for the King of Cockney.

The events referred to belong to the reign of Stephen or Henry II. The French have a proverb: *Je ne voudrais pas être roi, si j' étais prévot de Bar-sur-Aube*, I should not care to be king if I were Provost of Bar-sur-Aube (the most

lucrative and honourable of all the provostships of France). A similar idea is expressed in the words —

> And often to our comfort we shall find,
> The sharded beetle in a safer hold
> Than is the full-winged eagle.
>   SHAKESPEARE: *Cymbeline*, iii, 3.

Almost to the same effect Pope says: —

> And more true joy Marcellus exiled feels,
> Than Cæsar with a senate at his heels.
>   *Essay on Man*, iv, 257.

Castle Terabil (or "Terrible") in Arthurian legends stood in Launceston. It had a steep keep environed with a triple wall. Sometimes called Dunheved Castle.

Castor and Pollux (kas' tŏr, pol' uks). In Roman mythology, the twin sons of Jupiter and Leda. Jupiter is said to have visited Leda in the form of a swan; she produced two eggs, from one of which sprang Castor and Clytemnestra, and from the other Pollux and Helen. Castor and Pollux, also known as the Dioscuri (*q.v.*), had many adventures, were worshipped as gods, and were finally placed among the constellations.

Their names used to be given by sailors to the St. Elmo's Fire or Corposant (*q.v.*). If only one flame showed itself, the Romans called it *Helen*, and said that it portended that the worst of the storm was yet to come; but two or more luminous flames they called *Castor and Pollux*, and said that they boded the termination of the storm.

Casus belli (kā' sūs bel' ī). (Lat.). A ground for war; an occurrence warranting international hostilities.

M. Cambon asked me what we should say about the violation of the neutrality of Belgium. I said that was a much more important matter; we were considering what statement we should make in Parliament to-morrow — in effect, whether we should declare violation of Belgian neutrality to be a *casus belli*. — Sir EDW. GREY to the British Ambassador at Paris, August 2nd, 1914.

Cat. Called a "familiar," from the mediæval superstition that Satan's favourite form was a black cat. Hence witches were said to have a cat as their familiar. The superstition may have arisen from the classical legend of Galinthias who was turned into a cat and became a priestess of Hecate.

In ancient Rome the cat was a symbol of liberty. The goddess of Liberty was represented as holding a cup in one hand, a broken sceptre in the other, and with a cat lying at her feet. No animal is so great an enemy to all constraint as a cat.

In Egypt the cat was sacred to Isis, or the moon. It was held in great veneration, and was worshipped with great ceremony as a symbol of the moon, not only because it is more active after sunset, but from the dilatation and contraction of its pupil, symbolical of waxing and waning. The goddess Bast (see BUBASTIS), representative of the life-giving solar heat, was portrayed as having the head of a cat, probably because that animal likes to bask in the sun. Diodorus tells us that whoever killed a cat, even by accident, was by the Egyptians punished by death, and according to ancient tradition, Diana assumed the form of a cat, and thus excited the fury of the giants.

The male, or Tom, cat was formerly—and in Scotland still is—known as a Gib cat; the female as a Doe cat. The word "cat" has other connotations, *e.g.* a spiteful woman; hence a spiteful remark is said to be "catty." In early days "cat" was a slang term for a harlot.

CAT PROVERBS AND SAYINGS

A cat has nine lives. A cat is more tenacious of life than many animals. It is a careful, sly, and suspicious beast, and—in the wild state—is strong, hardy, and ferocious; also, after a fall, it generally lights upon its feet without injury, the foot and toes being well padded.

Tyb.: What wouldst thou have with me?
Mer.: Good king of cats, nothing but one of your nine lives.
SHAKESPEARE: *Romeo and Juliet*, iii, 1.
A cat has nine lives, and a woman has nine cats' lives.—FULLER: *Gnomologia.*

A cat may look at a king. An impertinent remark by an inferior, meaning, "I am as good as you." There was a political pamphlet published with this title in 1652.

Cheshire cat. *See* TO GRIN LIKE A CHESHIRE CAT *below.*

It is still a diversion in Scotland to hang up a cat in a small cask or firkin, half filled with soot; and then a parcel of clowns on horseback try to beat out the ends of it, in order to show their dexterity in escaping before the contents fall upon them.
Vol. I, p. 155 (Edn. of 1794).

It is raining cats and dogs. Very heavily.
I know Sir John would go, though he was sure it would rain cats and dogs.
SWIFT: *Polite Conversation*, ii.

Like a cat on hot bricks. Very uneasy; not at all "at home" in the situation, whatever it may be.

Not room to swing a cat. Swinging cats as a mark for sportsmen was at one time a favourite amusement. There were several varieties of this diversion. *See* HANG ME IN A BOTTLE *above*, and TO FIGHT LIKE KILKENNY CATS *below*. It is probable that the custom of tormenting cats by the ignorant arose from their supposed connexion with witches.

Mrs. Crupp had indignantly assured him that there wasn't room to swing a cat there; but as Mr. Dick justly observed to me, . . . "You know, Trotwood, I don't want to swing a cat, I never do swing a cat. Therefore what does that signify to *me!*"
DICKENS: *David Copperfield*, ch. xxxv.

Smollett had previously used the phrase in *Humphrey Clinker, Lett*, xxxvi; and it is quite possible that *cat* was originally *cot*, the phrase being a sailor's expression, and the allusion to a swung hammock or cot.

Sick as a cat. Cats are very subject to vomiting. Hence one is said *to cat*, or to *shoot the cat* in vomiting.

To grin like a Cheshire cat. An old simile, popularized by Lewis Carroll:—
"Please would you tell me," said Alice a little timidly, . . . "why your cat grins like that?" "It's a Cheshire cat," said the Duchess, "and that's why."—*Alice in Wonderland* (1865), ch. vi.

The phrase has never been satisfactorily accounted for, but it has been said that cheese was formerly sold in Cheshire moulded like a cat that looked as though it was grinning. The humorous explanation is that the cats there know that Cheshire is a County Palatine (*q.v.*), and that the idea is so funny that they are perpetually amused at it!

To let the cat out of the bag. To disclose a secret. It was formerly a trick among country folk to substitute a cat for a sucking-pig, and bring it in a bag to market. If any greenhorn chose to buy a "pig in a poke" without examination, all very well; but if he opened the sack, "he let the cat out of the bag," and the trick was disclosed.

When the cat's away the mice will play. Advantage will be taken of the absence of the person in authority. An old proverb, found in many languages. It is given in Ray's Collection.

CAT NAMES, PHRASES, ETC.

Cat and Fiddle. Several fanciful derivations have been found for this inn sign. There can be little doubt that it comes from the nursery rhyme, with a possible reference to the once popular game of tip-cat or trap-ball, and the fiddle for a dance that were provided as attractions for customers. It is worth mentioning that the *Dunciad* (i, 224) refers in contempt to Cibber as "the *Bear* and Fiddle of the town."

Cat and Kittens. A public-house sign, alluding to the range of pewter-pots of various sizes that were so called. Stealing these pots was termed "cat and kitten sneaking."

Cat and Mouse Act. *To play cat and mouse* with one is "to have him on a string"; while he is in your power to pretend constantly to let him go, but not actually to do so. During the Suffragette agitation at the beginning of the 20th century an Act was passed in 1912 with the object of rendering nugatory the tactics of imprisoned suffragettes who went on "hunger-strike." Under this Act such "hunger-strikers" could be set at liberty, but were liable to re-arrest as soon as they were sufficiently recovered to undergo the remainder of their sentence. This unenlightened Act was not particularly successful.

Cat-call. A kind of whistle used at theatres by the audience to express displeasure or impatience. A hideous noise like the *call* or *waul* of a *cat*.

I was very much surprised with the great consort of cat-calls ... to see so many persons of quality of both sexes assembled together in a kind of caterwauling.
Spectator, No. 361.

Cat-eyed. Able to see in the dark.

Cat ice. Very thin, almost transparent ice from which the water that was underneath has receded; so slight as to be unable to bear a cat.

Cat-lap. A contemptuous name for tea, or other "soft" drink such as a cat could swallow; a non-alcoholic liquor.

A more accomplished old woman never drank cat-lap.—SCOTT: *Redgauntlet*, ch. xii.

Cat o' mountain. The wild-cat; also the leopard, or panther; hence a wild, savage sort of man.

Cat-nap. To snatch a few minutes sleep in a chair or in a car, between one's appointments or activities, from the propensity of cats for dozing off wherever they are and in any position.

Cat-o'-nine-tails. A whip with nine lashes, used for punishing offenders, briefly called *a cat*. Popular superstition says that it has *nine* tails because a flogging by a "trinity of trinities" would be both more sacred and more efficacious. Lilburn was scourged, in 1637, with a whip having only three lashes, but there were twenty knots in each tail, and, as he received a lash every three paces between the Fleet and Old Palace Yard, Cook says that 60,000 stripes were inflicted. Titus Oates was scourged, in the reign of James II, with a cat having six lashes, and, between Newgate and Tyburn, received as many as 17,000 lashes. Thrashing in the British army and navy is no longer employed, but a modified form of it is still, though rarely, used as a civil punishment for crimes committed with violence.

Cat Stane. The name given to certain monoliths in Scotland (there is one near Kirkliston, Linlithgow), so called from Celtic *cath*, a battle, because they mark the site of some battle. They are not Druidical stones.

Cat's-brains. This curious name is given to a geological formation of sandstone veined with chalk. It is a phrase frequently met with in old agricultural deeds and surveys.

Cat's cradle. A game played with a piece of twine by two children. The suggestion that the name is a corruption of *cratch-cradle*, or the manger cradle in which the infant Saviour was laid (cratch is the Fr. *crèche*, a rack or manger), is unsupported by any evidence.

Cat's eye. A gem which possesses chatoyancy, or a changeable lustre. The true, or precious, cat's eye is a variety of chrysoberyl. The semi-precious cat's eye is a kind of quartz.

To live under the cat's foot. To be under petticoat government; to be henpecked. A mouse under the paw of a cat lives but by sufferance and at the cat's pleasure.

To be made a cat's paw of, *i.e.* the tool of another, the medium of doing another's dirty work. The allusion is to the fable of the monkey who wanted to get some roasted chestnuts from the fire, and used the paw of his friend, the cat, for the purpose.

I had no intention of becoming a cat's paw to draw European chestnuts out of the fire.—Com. RODGERS.

At sea, light air during a calm causing a ripple on the water, and indicating a storm, is called by sailors a *cat's paw*, and seamen affirm that the frolics of a cat indicate a gale.

Cat's whisker. In the old-fashioned crystal wireless sets this was the name given to the fine wire that made contact with the crystal.

Catacomb (kăt′ à cōm). A subterranean gallery for the burial of the dead, especially those at Rome. The origin of the name is unknown, but it does not appear to have been used till about the 5th century of our era (though the catacombs themselves were in existence, and used for burial, long before), and then only in connexion with one cemetery, that of St. Sebastian, on the Appian Way. This was called the Cœmeterium Catacumbas, or, shortly, *Catacumbas*, which name in course of time was applied equally to similar cemeteries. *Catacumbas* was probably, therefore, a place-name, denoting the site of this particular cemetery.

Cataian (kà̇t ā′ yan). A native of Cathay or China; hence, a thief, liar, or scoundrel, because the Chinese had the reputation of being such.

I will not believe such a Cataian, though the priest of the town commended him for a true man.
SHAKESPEARE: *Merry Wives*, ii, 1.

Catalogue raisonné (rā′ zò nā). A catalogue of books, paintings, etc., classed according to their subjects and often with explanatory notes or comments..

Catamaran (kăt å má răn'). A scraggy old woman, a vixen; so called by a play on the first syllable. It properly means a raft consisting of three logs lashed together with ropes; used on the coasts of Coromandel and Madras.

No, you old catamaran, though you pretend you never read novels. . . .
THACKERAY: *Lovel the Widower*, ch. i.

Catastrophe (kå tăs' trō fi) (Gr. *kata*, downwards, *strephein*, to turn). A turning upside down. Originally used of the change which produces the *dénouement* of a drama, which is usually a "turning upside down" of the beginning of the plot.

All the actors must enter to complete and make up the catastrophe of this great piece.
Sir T. BROWNE: *Religio Medici*.

Pat, he comes, like the catastrophe of the old comedy.—*King Lear*, i, 2.

Catch. Catch as catch can. Get by hook or crook all you can; a phrase from the child's game of this name, or from the method of wrestling so called, in which the wrestlers are allowed to get a grip anyhow or anywhere.

All must catch that catch can.
JOHNSON: *Rambler*, No. 197.

Catch me at it. Most certainly I shall never do what you say.

"Catch me going to London!" exclaimed Vixen.
Miss BRADDON. *Vixen*.

To be caught napping. To suffer some disadvantage while off one's guard. Pheasants, hares, and other animals are sometimes surprised "napping."

To catch on. To make its way; to become popular. As in

One can never tell what sort of song will catch on with the public, but the one that does is a little gold mine.

You'll catch it. You'll get severely punished. Here "it" stands for the undefined punishment, such as a whipping, a scolding, or other unpleasant consequence.

Catchpenny. A worthless article puffed up to catch the pennies of those who are foolish enough to buy it.

Catchpole. A constable; a law officer whose business it was to apprehend criminals. This is nothing to do with a *pole* or staff, nor with *poll*, the head, but is mediæval Lat. *chassipullus*, one who hunts or chases fowls (*pullus*, a fowl).

Catchword. A popular cry, a word or a phrase adopted by any party for political or other purposes. "Three acres and a cow," "Your food will cost you more," are good examples.

In printing, the first word on a page which is printed at the foot of the preceding page is known as the *catchword*; The first book so printed was a *Tacitus*, by John de Spira, 1469.

Printers also use the same name for the main words in a dictionary; *i.e.* those at the start of each article, printed in bold type so as to catch the eye.

In theatrical parlance, the cue, *i.e.* the last word or so of an actor's speech, is called the *catchword*.

Catechumen (kăt e kū' men). One taught by word of mouth (Gr. *katecheein*, to din into the ears). Those about to be baptized in the Early Church were first taught by word of mouth, and then catechized on their religious faith and duties.

Caterans, or **Catherans** (kăt' e ránz). Highland Scottish freebooters; the word occurs in Scottish romances and ballads.

Caterpillar. Caterpillar Club. An unofficial club started by the Irvin Parachute Company, during the 1939-45 war, who presented a small gold caterpillar pin to any R.A.F. airman who had baled out in action, on his supplying the number of the parachute which had saved his life. A similar organization known as the *Goldfish Club* existed for those who had been forced to use their rubber dinghies.

Caterpillar traction. This is a device for moving a heavy load over soft ground where wheels will sink. Round the wheels passes an endless band of linked plates which so forms a track along which the vehicle progresses. The device is much used for agricultural vehicles and for tanks and other military vehicles.

Catgut. Cord of various thicknesses, made from the intestines of animals (usually sheep, but never cats), and used for strings of musical instruments and racquets for ball games. Why it should have been called *cat*-gut has never been satisfactorily explained, but it may be a corruption of *kit-gut*, *kit* being an old word for a small fiddle. In support of this we have the following from Cartwright's *The Ordinary* (1634):—

Hearsay: Do you not hear her guts already squeak
 Like kit-strings?
Slicer: They must come to that within
 This two or three years: by that time she'll be
 True perfect cat.   *Act* i, 2.
Here's a tune indeed! pish,
I had rather hear one ballad sung i' the nose now
Than all these simpering tunes played upon cat's-guts
And sung by little kitlings.
MIDDLETON: *Women Beware Women*, iii, 2.

Shakespeare, however, definitely gives catgut its true origin:—

Now, divine air! Now is his soul ravished! Is it not
strange that sheep's guts should hale souls out of men's
bodies? Well, a horn for my money, when all's done.—
Much Ado, ii, 3.

Catgut scraper. A fiddler.

Catharine, St. St. Catharine was a virgin
of royal descent in Alexandria, who publicly
confessed the Christian faith at a sacrificial
feast appointed by the Emperor Maximinus, for
which confession she was put to death by torture
by means of a wheel like that of a chaff-cutter.
Hence

Catharine wheel, a sort of firework; in the
form of a wheel which is driven round by the
recoil from the explosion of the various squibs
of which it is composed.

Catharine-wheel window. A wheel-window,
sometimes called a rose-window, with radiating
divisions.

The Order of St. Catharine. A Russian
order founded for ladies of the nobility by Peter
the Great after his naval victory of Åland in
1714, and so named in compliment to his wife,
Catharine.

To braid St. Catharine's tresses. To live a
virgin.

Thou art too fair to be left to braid St. Catharine's
tresses.—LONGFELLOW: *Evangeline*.

Catharine Théot (tā′ ō). This French
visionary was somewhat like our Joanna
Southcott, calling herself The Mother of God
and changing her name to Theos (God). In the
height of the Revolution she preached the
worship of the Supreme Being and announced
that Robespierre was the forerunner of The
Word. Robespierre himself believed in her, and
she called him her well-beloved son and chief
prophet. She was guillotined in 1795, being
just seventy years of age.

Cathay (kȧ thā′). Marco Polo's name for a
country in Eastern Asia, roughly identical with
Northern China; from *Ki-tah*, the name of the
ruling race in those parts in the 10th century.

Better fifty years of Europe than a cycle of Cathay.
TENNYSON: *Locksley Hall*.

Catherine. *See* CATHARINE.

Catholic. The word (Gr. *katholikos*,
general, universal) means general, universal,
comprehensive—a sense which is seen in such
a sentence as Wordsworth's:—

Creed and test
Vanish before the unreserved embrace
Of catholic humanity.
Ecclesiastical Sonnets, III, xxxvi.

Hence from the Church point of view, it
distinguishes first the whole body of Christians
as apart from "Jews, heretics, and infidels":

secondly, a member of a Church which claims
the Apostolic Succession and direct descent
from the earliest body of Christians; and
thirdly, a member of the Roman Catholic
Church, *i.e.* the Western or Latin branch of the
ancient Catholic (or *universal*) Church.

Alphonso I, King of Asturias, 739-757, was
surnamed *The Catholic* on account of his zeal
in erecting and endowing monasteries and
churches. *See* CATHOLIC KING.

A man of catholic tastes is one who is interested in a wide variety of subjects.

Catholic Church. The entire body of
Christians considered as a whole, as distin-
guished from the Churches and sects into
which it has divided. At the Reformation the
Western Church was called by the Reformers the
Roman Catholic Church, and the Established
Church of England was called the "Protestant
Church," or the "Reformed National Church."
Many members of the Anglican Church still
consider and call themselves Catholics.

Catholic and Apostolic Church. The
name given to the followers of Edward Irving
(1792-1834), and to the Church founded by
him in 1829. Also called Irvingites.

Catholic Epistles. Those Epistles in the
New Testament not addressed to any particular
church or individual; the *general* epistles, viz.
those of James, Peter, and Jude, and the first of
John; 2 John is addressed to a "lady," and 3 John
to Gaius, and these are usually included.

**Catholic King, or His Most Catholic
Majesty.** A title given by the Pope to Ferdinand,
King of Aragon (1474-1516), for expelling the
Moors from Spain, and thereafter used as the
appellation of the kings of Spain. *Cp*. RELIGIOUS.

Catholic League. A confederacy of Catholics
formed in 1614 to counter-balance the Evangelic
League of Bohemia. The two Leagues kept
Germany in perpetual disturbance, and ultimately led to the Thirty Years War (1618-48).

Catholicon (kȧ thol′ i kòn). A panacea, a
universal remedy.

Meanwhile, permit me to recommend,
As the matter admits of no delay,
My wonderful catholicon.
LONGFELLOW: *The Golden Legend*, i.

Catholicos (kȧ thol′ i kòs). The head of the
Assyrian Nestorians. Now called the Patriarch
of Armenia.

Cato (kā′ tō). **He is a Cato.** A man of simple
life, severe morals, self-denying habits, strict
justice, brusque manners, blunt of speech, and
of undoubted patriotism, like the Roman censor
of that name (234-149 B.C.).

Cato Street Conspiracy. A scheme entertained by Arthur Thistlewood (1770-1820) and other conspirators to overthrow the Government by assassinating the Cabinet Ministers (February 1820). So called from Cato Street (now Horace Street), Edgware Road, where their meetings were held.

Catsup. *See* KETCHUP.

Caucasian (kaw kā' shȧn). This is the term employed to designate the white or European race of mankind. It originated with Blumenfeld (1752-1840) who, in 1775, selected a Georgian skull as the perfect type—a view that has since proved wrong. The term is, however, still retained in modern ethnology, though with certain reservations.

Caucus (kaw' kŭs). An American word, first recorded as having been used in Boston about 1750, introduced into English political slang and popularized by Joseph Chamberlain about 1878. In America it means a meeting of some division, large or small, of a political or legislative body, for the purpose of agreeing upon a united course of action in the main assembly. In England it is applied opprobriously to an inner committee or organization which seeks to manage affairs behind the backs of its party. The origin of the word is unknown, but it may be connected with the Algonquin word *cau-cau-as-u*, one who advises.

In all these places is a severall commander, which they call *Werowance*, except the *Chickahamanians*, who are governed by the priests and their Assistants, or their Elders called *caw-cawwassoughes*.—Capt. JOHN SMITH'S *"Travels in Virginia"; 6th Voyage* (1606).

Caudine Forks (kaw' dīn). A narrow pass in the mountains near Capua, now called the Valley of Arpaia. It was here that the Roman army, under the consuls T. Veturius Calvinus and Sp. Postumius, fell into the hands of the Samnites (321 B.C.), and were made to pass under the yoke.

Hard as it was to abandon an enterprise so very dear to him . . . he did not hesitate to take the more prudent course of passing under (*sic*) the Caudine Forks of the Monroe doctrine, and leave Maximilian and the French bondholders to their fate.

    Standard, November 17th, 1866.

Caught Napping. *See under* CATCH.

Caul. In the Middle Ages and down to the 17th century this word was used for a net confining a woman's hair, now called a snood:—

Her head with ringlets of her hair is crowned,
And in a golden caul the curls are bound.
    DRYDEN: *Aeneid* vii.

It was also used to describe any membrane enclosing the viscera, *e.g.* The caul that is above the liver, *Ex.* xxxix, 13.

The membrane on the head of some newborn infants is called the caul and is supposed to be a charm against death by drowning.

To be born with a caul was with the Romans tantamount to our phrase, "To be born with a silver spoon in one's mouth," meaning "born to good luck."

You were born with a caul on your head.
    BEN JONSON: *Alchemist*, i. 1.

Cauld-lad, The, of Hilton Hall. A house-spirit, who moved about the furniture during the night. Being resolved to banish him, the inmates left for him a green cloak and hood, before the kitchen-fire, which so delighted him that he never troubled the house any more; but sometimes he might be heard singing:—

Here's a cloak, and here's a hood,
The cauld-lad of Hilton will do no more good.

Causa causans (kaw' zȧ kaw' zănz). The initiating cause; the primary cause.

Causa causata. The cause which owes its existence to the *causa causans*; the secondary cause.

Causa vera (*u*) The immediate predecessor of an effect; (*b*) a cause verifiable by independent evidence. (Mill.)

In theology God is the *causa causans*, and creation the *causa causata*. The presence of the sun above the horizon is the *causa vera* of daylight, and his withdrawal below the horizon is the *causa vera* of night.

Cause, The. A mission; the object or project.

To make common cause. To work for the same object. Here "cause" is the legal term, meaning *pro* or *con*, as it may be, the cause or side of the question advocated.

Cause célèbre (Fr.). Any famous law case or trial.

Aristotelian causes are these four:

(1) **The Efficient Cause.** That which immediately produces the effect.

(2) **The Material Cause.** The matter on which (1) works.

(3) **The Formal Cause.** The Essence of "Form" (= group of attributes) introduced into the matter by the efficient cause.

(4) **The Final** or **Ultimate Cause.** The purpose or end for which the thing exists or the causal change takes place. But God is called the ultimate Final Cause, since, according to Aristotle, all things tend, so far as they can, to realize some Divine attribute.

God is also called **The First Cause,** or the Cause Causeless, beyond which even imagination cannot go.

Causerie (kō' zĕr i). Gossip, small-talk; in journalism a chatty kind of essay or article, a set of gossipy paragraphs. (Fr. *causer*, to chat.)

Cavalier. A horseman; whence a knight, a gentleman (Span. *caballero*, *b* and *v* being interchangeable in that language.)

Cavaliers. Adherents of Charles I. Those of the opposing Parliament party were called *Roundheads*.

Cavaliere servente (kăv a lyēr′ i sĕr ven′ te) (Ital.). A cavalier in attendance; especially a man who devotes himself to running about after a married woman; much the same as a *cicisbeo* (*q.v.*).

> An English lady asked of an Italian,
> What were the actual and official duties
> Of the strange thing some women set a value on
> Which hovers oft about some married beauties,
> Call'd "cavalier servente"? a Pygmalion
> Whose statues warm (I fear, alas! too true 't is)
> Beneath his art. The dame, press'd to disclose them
> Said—"Lady, I beseech you to *suppose them*."
> BYRON: *Don Juan*, IX, li.

Cave of Adullam. *See* ADULLAMITES.

Caveat (kā′ vē ăt). Lat., "let him beware"; a notice directing the recipient to refrain from some act pending the decision of the Court. **Hence, to enter a caveat.** To give legal notice that the opponent is not to proceed with the suit in hand until the party giving the notice has been heard; to give a warning or admonition.

Caveat emptor. Lat., "let the purchaser beware"; *i.e.* the buyer must keep his eyes open, for the bargain he agrees to is binding. The full legal maximum is:—

> Caveat emptor, quia ignorare non debuit quod jus alienum emit—Let a purchaser beware, for he ought not to be ignorant of the nature of the property which he is buying from another party.

Cavel. A parcel or allotment of land; originally, a lot (that is cast). From Dut. *kavel*, a lot, whence *kaveln*, to assign by lot.

Cavendish (kăv′ en dish). It is not now known who was the Cavendish who gave his name to this tobacco, which is sometimes called Negro-head. Sweetened with syrup or molasses, it is a softened tobacco pressed into quadrangular cakes. It is used for smoking or chewing.

Caviare (kăv i âr). The roe of the sturgeon, pickled, salted, and prepared for use as a relish. Caviare is an acquired taste and, as a rule, it is not appreciated by people until they have got used to it; hence Shakespeare's *caviare to the general* (*Hamlet*, ii, 2), above the taste or comprehension of ordinary people.

> He [Cobbett] must, I think, be caviare to the Whigs.
> HAZLITT: *Table-talk*.

Caxon. A worn-out wig; also a big cauliflower wig, worn out or not. It has been suggested that the word is from the personal name Caxon.

> People scarce could decide on its phiz,
> Which looked wisest—the caxon or jowl.
> PETER PINDAR: *The Portfolio*.

Caxton, William. Father of English printing, hence his name is widely applied to branded articles in the printing and paper trades. Born in the Weald of Kent, he learnt his printing in Cologne and Bruges. He set up shop at the Sign of the Red Pale in the shadow of Westminster Abbey about 1476 and died about 1491, by which time he had printed about a hundred books.

Cayuse. An Indian pony. The Cayuses were a Red Indian tribe. Since about 1880 the word has meant "a horse of little value."

Cean (sē′ ăn). **The Cean poet.** Simonides, of Ceos.

> The Cean and the Teian muse.
> BYRON: *Don Juan* (Song: *The Isles of Greece*).

Cecilia, St. (se sil′ i à). A Roman who underwent martyrdom in the 3rd century. She is the patron saint of the blind, being herself blind; she is also patroness of musicians, and "inventor of the organ."

> At length divine Cecilia came,
> Inventress of the vocal frame.
> DRYDEN: *Alexander's Feast*.

According to tradition an angel fell in love with her for her musical skill. Her husband saw the heavenly visitant, who gave to both a crown of martyrdom which he brought from Paradise.

St. Cecilia's Day is November 22nd, on which the Worshipful Company of Musicians, a Livery Company of London, meet and go in procession for divine service in St. Paul's Cathedral.

Cecil's Fast. A dinner of fish. William Cecil, Lord Burghley, chief minister to Queen Elizabeth for nearly forty years, introduced a Bill to enjoin the eating of fish on certain days in order to restore the fish trade.

Ceiling. This is the term applied to the maximum height to which an aeroplane can climb. The phrase has also been extended to mean the highest prices that can be reached for any article. Also used in aeronautical circles to denote the height of the cloud base above ground level. **Ceiling zero** means that the clouds or mist are down to the ground itself, or so near it as to make the taking-off or landing of aircraft impracticable except by instruments.

Celarent. *See* SYLLOGISM.

Celestial City. Heaven is so called by John Bunyan in his *Pilgrim's Progress*.

Celestial Empire, China; a translation of the Chinese *Tien Chao*, literally "heavenly dynasty," alluding to the belief that the old

Emperors were in direct descent from the gods. Hence the Chinese themselves are sometimes spoken of as *Celestials.*

Celestines. An order of reformed Benedictine monks, founded about 1254 by Pietro di Murrone who, in 1294, became Pope as Celestine V.

Celt (selt, kelt). A piece of stone, ground artificially into a wedge-like shape, with a cutting edge. Used before the employment of bronze and iron, for knives, hatchets, and chisels.

Celtic (sel′ tik, kel′ tik). Applied to the peoples and languages of the great branch of the Aryans which includes the Irish, Manx, Welsh, ancient Cornish, Breton, and Scottish Gaels. Anciently the term was applied by the Greeks and Romans to the peoples of Western Europe generally, but when Cæsar wrote of the Celtæ he referred to the people of middle Gaul only. The word *Celt* probably means a warrior; fable accounts for it by the story of Celtina, daughter of Britannus, who had a son by Hercules, named Celtus, who became the progenitor of the Celts.

Cemetery properly means a sleeping-place (Gr. *koimeterion,* a dormitory). The Persians call their cemeteries "The Cities of the Silent."

Cenci. *See* BEAUTIFUL PARRICIDE.

Cenomanni (sen ō ma′ ni). The name given to the inhabitants of Norfolk, Suffolk, and Cambridge by Cæsar in his *Commentaries.*

Centaur. Mythological beast, half horse and half man. Centaurs are said to have dwelt in ancient Thessaly; a myth the origin of which is probably to be found in the expert horsemanship of the original inhabitants. *See* IXION. The Thessalian centaurs were invited to a marriage feast, and, being intoxicated, behaved with great rudeness to the women. The Lapithæ took the women's part, fell on the centaurs, and drove them out of the country.

Cento (Lat., a patchwork). Poetry made up of lines borrowed from established authors. It was an art freely practised in the decadent period of Greece and Rome, and Ausonius, who has a nuptial idyll composed from verses selected from Virgil, composed rules governing their manufacture. Among well-known examples are the *Homerocentones,* the *Cento Virgilianus* by Proba Falconia (4th cent.), and the hymns made by Metellus out of the Odes of Horace. Of modern centos the following portion of a Shakespearean cento that appeared in English, November, 1919, may serve as an example:—

Let fame that all hunt after in their lives
Among the buzzing pleased multitude

For present comfort and for future good,
Taint not thy mind: nor let thy soul contrive
With all the fierce endeavour of your wit
To woo a maid in way of marriage,
As it is common for the younger sort,
The lunatic, the lover, and the poet:
Thus bad begins, and worse remains behind.
I see a man's life is a tedious one,
For it appears, by manifest proceeding,
There's nothing serious in mortality.
Life's but a walking shadow, a poor player,
And one man in his time plays many parts,
As an unperfect actor on the stage.

Centre Party. In politics, the party occupying a place between two extremes: the *left centre* is the more radical wing, and the *right centre* the more conservative. In the French Revolution *the Centre* of the Legislative Assembly included the friends of order.

In the Fenian rebellion, 1866, the chief movers were called *Head Centres,* and their subordinates *Centres.*

Centurion (sen tū′ ri on) (Lat. *centum,* a hundred). A Roman officer who had the command of 100 men. There were sixty centurions, of varying ranks, to a legion, the chief being the first centurion of the first maniple of the first cohort; his title was Primus pilus prior, or Primipilus. The centurion's emblem of office was a vine-staff.

Cephalus and Procris (sef′ a lŭs, prok′ ris). Cephalus was husband of Procris, who, out of jealousy, deserted him. He went in search of her, and rested awhile under a tree. Procris, knowing of his whereabouts, crept through some bushes to ascertain if a rival was with him; and he, hearing the noise and thinking it to be made by some wild beast, hurled his javelin into the bushes and slew her. When the unhappy man discovered what he had done, he slew himself in anguish of spirit with the same javelin.

Pyramus: Not Shafalus to Proems was so true.
Thisbe: As Shafalus to Procrus, I to you.
SHAKESPEARE: *Midsummer Night's Dream,* v. 1.

Cepheus (sē′ fūs). A northern constellation; named from Cepheus, King of Ethiopia, husband of Cassiopeia and father of Andromeda.

Cerberus (sĕr′ bĕ rus). A grim, watchful keeper, house-porter, guardian, etc. Cerberus, according to Roman mythology, is the three-headed dog that keeps the entrance of the infernal regions. Hercules dragged the monster to earth, and then let him go again. Orpheus lulled Cerberus to sleep with his lyre; and the Sibyl who conducted Æneas through the Inferno, also threw the dog into a profound sleep with a cake seasoned with poppies and honey. *See under* SOP.

The origin of the fable of Cerberus may be found in the custom of the ancient Egyptians of guarding graves with dogs.

Ceremonious, The. Pedro IV of Aragon (1336-87) was so surnamed.

Ceremony (Lat. *cærimonia*). By way of accounting for this word, which is probably connected with Sanskrit *karman*, a religious action, a rite, Livy tells that when the Romans fled before Brennus, one Albinus, who was carrying his wife and children in a cart to a place of safety, overtook at Janiculum the Vestal virgins bending under their load, took them up and conveyed them to Cære, in Etruria. Here they remained, and continued to perform their sacred rites, which were consequently called "Cære-monia."

Master of the Ceremonies. A Court official, first appointed by James I, to superintend the reception of ambassadors and strangers of rank, and to prescribe the formalities to be observed in levees and other grand public functions. The title is now given to one whose duty it is to see that all goes smoothly at balls and suchlike social gatherings: frequently abbreviated to "M.C."

Don't stand on ceremony. Feel at home, be natural, don't be formal.

Ceres (sē' rēs). The Roman name of *Mother Earth*, the protectress of agriculture and of all the fruits of the earth; later identified with the Greek Demeter.

Cess. A tax, contracted from assessment ("sess"); as a "church-cess." In Ireland the word is used sometimes as a contraction of success, meaning luck, as "bad cess to you!"

Out of all cess. Beyond all estimation or valuation.

The poor jade is wrung in the withers out of all cess.—
SHAKESPEARE: 1 *Henry IV*, ii, 1.

C'est magnifique. *C'est magnifique, mais ce n'est pas la guerre.* "It is magnificent, but it is not war." The criticism on the charge of the Light Brigade at Balaclava (Oct. 25th, 1854), made on the field at the time, by the French General Bosquet to A. H. Layard.

Cestui que vie. This and the two following are old Anglo-French legal terms (*cestui* = he, or him). The person for whose life any lands or hereditaments may be held.

Cestui que use, the person to whose use anyone is infeoffed of lands or tenements.

Cestui que trust, the person for whose benefit a trust has been created.

Cestus (ses' tus). The girdle of Venus, made by her husband Vulcan; but when she

wantoned with Mars it fell off, and was left on the "Acidalian Mount." It was of magical power to move to ardent love. By a poetical fiction all women of irresistible attraction are supposed to be wearers of Aphrodite's girdle, or the cestus.

The word was also applied to the Roman boxing-glove, composed of leather bands wound round the hand and wrist, and often loaded with iron.

Chacun a son goût (shăk'ùn a son goo). "Everyone has (*a*) his taste"; or, "Everyone to (*à*) his taste." The former is French, the latter is English-French for *à chacun son goût* or *chacum* (*à*) *son goût*. The phrase is much more common with us than it is in France, where we meet with the phrases—*Chacun a sa chacunerie* (everyone has his idiosyncrasy), and *chacun a sa marotte* (everyone has his hobby). In Latin *sua cuique voluptas*, every man has his own pleasures.

Chaff. An old bird is not to be caught with chaff. An experienced man, or one with his wits about him, is not to be deluded by humbug. The reference is to throwing chaff instead of bird-seed to allure birds.

Chair, The. The office of chief magistrate in a corporate town; the office of a professor, etc., as "The chair of poetry, in Oxford, is now vacant." The word is furthermore applied to the president of a committee or public meeting. Hence the chairman himself. When debaters call out "Chair," they mean that the chairman is not properly supported, and his words not obeyed as they ought to be. Another form of the same expression is, "Pray support the Chair."

Below the chair. Said of one who has not yet reached the presidential position, as of an alderman who has not yet served the mayoralty.

Passed the chair. One who has served the chief office.

To take the chair. To become the chairman or president of a public meeting. The chairman is placed in some conspicuous place, like the Speaker of the House of Commons, and his decision is absolutely final in all points of doubt. Usually the persons present nominate and elect their own chairman; but in some cases there is an *ex officio* chairman.

As a slang expression, **to be in the chair** may mean to be host or to be called on to pay for a round of drinks.

Chair of St. Peter. The office of the Pope of Rome, founded by St. Peter, the apostle; but

St. Peter's Chair means the Catholic festival held in commemoration of the two episcopates founded by the apostle, one at Rome, and the other at Antioch (January 18th and February 22nd).

Chalk. Chalk it up. Put it to his credit.

I cannot make chalk of one and cheese of the other. I must treat both alike; I must show no favouritism.

I know the difference between chalk and cheese. Between what is worthless and what is valuable, between a counterfeit and a real article. Of course, the resemblance of chalk to cheese has something to do with the saying, and the alliteration helps to popularize it.

I beat him by a long chalk. Thoroughly. In allusion to the ancient custom of making merit marks with chalk, before lead pencils were so common.

Walk your chalk. Get you gone. Lodgings wanted for the royal retinue used to be taken arbitrarily by the marshal and sergeant-chamberlain, the inhabitants were sent to the right about, and the houses selected were notified by a chalk mark. When Marie de' Medicis, in 1638, came to England, Sieur de Labat was employed to mark "all sorts of houses commodious for her retinue in Colchester." The phrase is "Walk, you're chalked," corrupted into *Walk your chalk*.

At one time it was customary for a landlord to give the tenant notice to quit by chalking the door.

The prisoner has cut his stick, and walked his chalk, and is off to London.—C. KINGSLEY: *Two Years Ago*, i.

Challenge. This meant originally an accusation or charge, and secondarily a claim, a defiance. It comes through French from the Lat. *calumnia*, a false accusation, and is thus etymologically the same word as "calumny."

Challenging a jury. This may be to object to all the jurors from some informality in the way they have been "arrayed" or empanelled, or to one or more of the jurors, from some real or supposed disqualification or bias of judgment. In the first case it is a **challenge to the array**, and this must be based on some default of the sheriff, or his officer who arrayed the panel.

If any member of the jury is thought not qualified to serve, or if he is supposed to be biased, he may be challenged. In capital cases a prisoner may challenge persons without assigning any reason, and in cases of treason as many as thirty-five.

Chambre (shom' brâ). From French *chambre*, a room. Used of wine which has been warmed to raise it from cellar temperature to the temperature of the room in which it is to be served, which for red wine is ideal.

Chambre Ardente (shombr ar dont') (Fr.). In French history, the name given to certain Courts of Justice held under the *ancien régime*, for trying exceptional cases, such as charges of heresy, poisoning, etc. They were usually held at night, and both then and when held in the daytime were lighted by torches. These courts were devised by Cardinal Lorraine. The first was held in the reign of François I, for trying heretics. Brinvilliers and her associates were tried in a darkened court in 1680.

The same name is given to the room or hall in which a lying-in-state takes place, because it is usually furnished with lighted candles.

Chameleon. You are a chameleon, *i.e.* very changeable — shifting according to the opinions of others, as the chameleon, to a very limited extent, can change its hue to that of contiguous objects.

As the chameleon, who is known
To have no colours of its own,
But borrows from his neighbour's hue,
His white or black, his green or blue.
                 PRIOR.

Champ de Mars (shon dĕ mars). Clovis and the early Frank kings held meetings in March when feudal gifts and fees were paid and homage received. It was this ancient custom that was seized upon in the French Revolution when, in the summer of 1790, an enormous amphitheatre was dug by the Paris citizens, and the Federation of Freedom sworn at the altar of the Fatherland.

Napoleon I gave the name of **Champ de Mai** to the assembly he called together on May 1st, 1815, when he proclaimed the result of the plebiscite ratifying the liberal *Acte additionnel* on his return from Elba.

Champak (chăm' păk). An Indian magnolia (*Michelia Champaca*). The wood is sacred to Buddha, and the strongly scented golden flowers are worn in the black hair of Indian women.

The Champak odours fail.
       SHELLEY: *Lines to an Indian Air*.

Champion of England. A person whose office it is to ride up Westminster Hall on a Coronation Day, and challenge anyone who disputes the right of succession. The office was established by William the Conqueror, and was given to Marmion and his male descendants, with the manor of "broad Scrivelsby." De Ludlow received the office and manor through the female line; and at the Coronation of Richard II Sir John Dymoke succeeded through the female line also. Since then the office has continued in the Dymoke family, but the actual riding and challenge has been discontinued since the coronation of George IV. Instead, the Champion bears the sovereign's standard at the coronation.

Chance. See MAIN·CHANCE.

To chance your arm, or your luck. To run a risk in the hope of "bringing it off" and obtaining a profit or advantage of some sort.

Chancel means a lattice screen. In the Roman law courts the lawyers were cut off from the public by such a screen (Lat. *cancellus*).

Chancel of a church. That part of a church which contains the altar, and the seats set apart for the choir. It is generally raised a step or more above the floor of the nave.

Chancellery. "The chancelleries of Europe" is a favourite journalistic phrase. The word *chancellery* is applied to the office attached to an embassy or consulate, where dispatches are drafted and written, incoming dispatches decoded and considered, and all the embassy clerical work carried through.

Chancellor. A petty officer (*cancelarius*) in the Roman law courts stationed at the chancel (*q.v.*) as usher of the court. In the Eastern Empire he was a secretary or notary, subsequently invested with judicial functions. The office was introduced into England by Edward the Confessor, and under the Norman kings the chancellor was made official secretary of all important legal documents. In France the chancellor was the royal notary, president of the councils, and keeper of the Great Seal.

Chancellor, Dancing. See DANCING.

The Lord Chancellor, or the **Lord High Chancellor.** The highest judicial functionary of Britain, who ranks above all peers, except princes of the blood and the Archbishop of Canterbury. He is "Keeper of the Great Seal," is called "Keeper of His (or Her) Majesty's Conscience," and presides on the Woolsack in the House of Lords, and in the Chancery Division of the Supreme Court.

Chancellor of the Exchequer. The minister of finance in the Cabinet; the highest financial official of State in the kingdom.

Chancery. One of the three divisions of the High Court of Justice. It is concerned with Equity and is presided over by the Lord Chancellor. All its work is done in London.

Change. Ringing the changes. Repeating the same thing in different ways. The allusion is to bell-ringing. For the sharper's meaning of the term, *see* RINGING.

To know how many changes can be rung on a peal, multiply the number of bells in the peal by the number of changes that can be rung on a peal consisting of one bell less, thus: 1 bell no change; 2 bells, 1 by 2 = 2 changes; 3 bells, 2 by 3 = 6 changes; 4 bells, 6 by 4 = 24 changes; 5 bells, 24 by 5 = 120 changes; 6 bells, 720 changes, etc.

Changeling. A peevish, sickly child. The notion used to be that the fairies took a healthy child, and left in its place one of their starveling elves which never thrived.

> The king doth keep his revels here to-night:
> Take heed the queen come not within his sight;
> For Oberon is passing fell and wrath,
> Because that she as her attendant hath
> A lovely boy, stolen from an Indian king:
> She never had so sweet a changeling.
> SHAKESPEARE: *Midsummer Night's Dream*, ii, 1.

Chant du départ (shon dū dā par). After the *Marseillaise*, this was the most celebrated song of the French Revolution. It was written by M. J. Chenier, for a public festival, 1794, to commemorate the taking of the Bastille. The music is by Méhul. A mother, an old man, a child, a wife, a girl, and three warriors sing a verse in turn, and the sentiment of each is, "We give up our claims on the men of France for the good of the Republic." *Cp.* CARMAGNOLE.

> La république nous appelle,
> Sachons vaincre ou sachons périr;
> Un Français doit vivre pour elle,
> Pour elle un Français doit mourir.

Chanticleer. The cock, in the tale of *Reynard the Fox*, and in Chaucer's *Nonne Prestes Tale*; also in Rostand's well-known play of this name produced in Paris in 1910. (Fr. *chanter-clair*, to sing *clairment*, *i.e.* distinctly.)

> My lungs began to crow like chanticleer.
> SHAKESPEARE: *As You Like It*, ii, 7.

Chantrey Bequest. When Sir Francis Leggatt Chantrey (1781-1841), the sculptor, died he left a sum yielding about £3,000 a year to the Royal Academy, of which the President was to receive £300, the secretary £50, and the remainder was to be devoted to the purchase for the nation of works of art executed in Great Britain.

Chaonian Bird (kā ō' ni àn). This is the poetic name for a dove, and takes its origin from the legend that the dove bore the oracles of Chaonia.

Chaonian food. Acorns. So called from the oak trees of Chaonia or Dodona. Some think *beech-mast* is meant, and tell us that the bells of the oracle were hung on beech-trees, not on oaks.

Chap. A man, properly a merchant. A chapman (O.E. *ceap-mann*) is a merchantman or tradesman. "If you want to buy, I'm your chap." A good chap-man or chap became in time a good fellow. Hence, *A good sort of chap, a clever chap*, etc.

An awkward customer is an analogous phrase.

Chap-book. A cheap little book containing tales, ballads, lives, etc., sold by chapmen.

Chaps are wide leather overalls worn by American cowboys over their trousers to protect their legs from injury, colloquially abbreviated from the Sp. *chaparejos*/leather breeches.

Chapeau bras (shăp ō bra). A soft three-cornered fiat silk hat which could be folded and carried under the arm (Fr. *chapeau*, hat, *bras*, arm). It was used in France with the court dress of the 18th century.

Chapel. Originally, a chest containing relics, or the shrine thereof, so called from the *capella* (little cloak or cope) of St. Martin, which was preserved by the Frankish kings as a sacred relic. The place in which it was kept when not in the field was called the *chapelle*, and the keeper thereof the *chapelain*. Hence, the name came to be attached to a sanctuary, or a private place of worship other than a parish or cathedral church; and is also used for a place of worship not connected with the State, as a Methodist Chapel, a Baptist Chapel, etc.

In printing-house parlance a *chapel* is an association of journeymen (compositors, machinemen, etc.), who meet periodically to discuss matters of common interest connected with their work, to decide upon the course of action to be taken in cases of disputes or differences between themselves and their employers, etc. The chairman is known as the "father of the chapel." The origin of the term is obscure; an accepted but far from certain derivation traces it back to the early days of printing, when presses were set up in the chapels attached to abbeys, as those of Caxton in Westminster Abbey. *Cp.* MONK; FRIAR.

Chapel of ease. A place of worship for the use of parishioners residing at a distance from the parish church.

Chaperon (shăp′ e rōn). A married or elderly woman who attends a young unmarried girl in public places and acts as her guide, adviser, and, when necessary, protector. So called from the Spanish hood worn by duennas in former times.

To chaperon. To accompany a young unmarried woman *in loco parentis*, when she appears in public or in society.

Char (char). This is a common abbreviation for "charwoman," a woman who chars or chares, *i.e.* works by the hour or day at house-cleaning. The word comes from O.E. *cerr, cerran*, meaning to turn. It has come back to England from U.S.A. in the form of "chore," a monotonous but necessary task, household or otherwise.

The Army slang word "char," meaning tea appears to come from the Hind, *cha*, with various Indian and Chinese words of similar sound, all meaning tea.

Character. An oddity. One who has a distinctive peculiarity of manner: Sam Weller is a character, so is Pickwick.

In character. In harmony with personality or habitual behaviour.

Out of character. Not in harmony with a person's actions, writings, profession, age, or status in society.

Chare Thursday. Another form of *Shear* or *Shere Thursday*; the same as *Maundy Thursday* (*q.v.*).

Charge, To. To make an attack or onset in battle.

Curate in charge. A curate placed by a bishop in charge of a parish where there is no incumbent, or where the incumbent is suspended.

To charge oneself with. To take upon oneself the onus of a given task.

To charge a person. To accuse him formally of a crime or misdemeanour. It must be answered before the appropriate court or authority.

To give charge over. To set one in authority over.

I gave my brother Hanani.... charge over Jerusalem.—*Neh.* vii, 2.

To give in charge. To hand over a person to the charge of a policeman.

To have in charge. To have the care of something.

To return to the charge. To renew the attack.

To take in charge. To "take up" a person given in charge; to take upon oneself the responsibility of something; to make an arrest.

Chargé d'Affaires. The proxy of an ambassador, or the diplomatic agent where none higher has been appointed.

Charing Cross. The original "Charing Cross" was erected in the centre of the ancient village of Charing, which stood midway between the cities of London and Westminster, by Edward I to commemorate his Queen, Eleanor, because it was there that her coffin was halted for the last time on its progress from Harby, Notts, where the Queen died, to Westminster, where she was buried.

The present cross is a copy (made to scale) by E. M. Barry, R.A., of the original one that was demolished by the Puritans in 1647, and that stood on the south side of Trafalgar Square on the site now occupied by the equestrian statue of Charles I. It was erected in 1865 in the courtyard of Charing Cross Station.

Chariot. According to Greek mythology, the chariot was invented by Erichthonius to conceal his feet, which were those of a dragon.

Chariots or cars. That of

ADMETUS was drawn by lions and wild boars.
BACCHUS by panthers.
CERES by winged dragons.
CYBELE by lions.
DIANA by stags.
JUNO by peacocks.
NEPTUNE by sea-horses.
PLUTO by black horses.
The SUN by seven horses (the seven days of the week).
VENUS by doves.

Charity. Charity begins at home. "Let them learn first to show piety at home" (1 *Tim.* v, 4).

Cold as charity. An ironic allusion to unsympathetic benevolence.

Charivari (shǎ ri va′ ri). The clatter made with pots and pans, whistling, bawling, hissing, and so on. Our concert of "marrow-bones and cleavers"; the German *Katzenmusik*, got up to salute with ridicule unequal marriages. The name was taken as that of a satirical journal founded in Paris by Charles Philipon in 1832, and hence in 1841 *Punch* adopted as its sub-title *The London Charivari*.

Charlatan (shar′ là tàn). This word comes originally from the Italian *ciarlare*, to prate, to chatter, to babble. It is usually applied to one who sells quack remedies and covers his ignorance in a torrent of high-sounding and often meaningless words.

Saltimbancoes, Quacksalvers, and Charlatans deceive the people in lower degrees.—SIR T. BROWNE, *Vulgar Errors*, 1646.

Charlatans and impostors have always thriven on the ignorance and credulity of mankind, and it is to draw a fine distinction in roguery to differentiate between them. A charlatan, however, is one who, such as a quack or astrologer, claims to possess special knowledge of medicine or more abstruse matters; the

imposter pretends to be something or someone he really is not.

It is difficult to make choice among the charlatans of history. Nostradamus (1503-66) was an astrologer and physician who, in 1555, brought out a book of prophecies so vague in their terms that whether they were fulfilled or not is mere matter of conjecture. John Partridge (1644-1715) was a good example of the English breed, rendered forever a laughing-stock by Swift's skit on his astrological achievements. Cagliostro (Joseph Balsamo, 1743-95) was rather an impostor than a charlatan, though he shined in either category. Perhaps the most striking example of modern charlatanry was Sequoa, a white man posing as Red Indian, who toured Britain about 1890, in a coach with attendant Redskins and a brass band, drawing teeth "painlessly" (all squeals drowned by the band) and supplying an "Indian oil" to cure all manner of aches and pains.

Charlemagne (sharl′ mān) (742-814). Charles the Great became king of the Franks in 771, and in 800 founded the Holy Roman Empire. He ruled over nearly all western Europe and was noted for his work as a lawgiver, administrator, protector of the Church and promoter of education.

Charlemagne and his Paladins are the centre of a great series of chivalric romances. (*See* PALADINS, LA SOYENSE.) We are told that the great emperor was eight feet in height, and of correspondingly enormous strength, so that with his hands alone he could bend three horseshoes at once. He was buried at Aix la Chapelle (Aachen), but according to legend he waits, crowned and armed, in Oldenburg, Hesse, for the day when Antichrist shall appear; he will then go forth to battle and rescue Christendom. Another legend says that in years of plenty he crosses the Rhine on a golden bridge, to bless the cornfields and vineyards.

Charles. An ill-omened name for rulers:

England: Charles I was beheaded by his subjects. (*See also below.*)

Charles II lived long in exile. (*See also below.*)

Charles Edward, the Young Pretender, died in poverty in Rome.

France: Charles II, the Fat, reigned wretchedly, was deposed, and died a beggarly dependant on the stinting bounty of the Archbishop of Metz.

Charles III, the Simple, died a prisoner in the castle of Péronne.

Charles IV, the Fair, reigned six years, married thrice, but buried all his children except one daughter, who was forbidden by the Salic law to succeed to the crown.

Charles VI lived and died an idiot or madman.

Charles VII starved himself to death, partly through fear of being poisoned and partly because of a painful and incurable abscess in his mouth.

Charles VIII accidentally smashed his head against the lintel of a doorway in the Château Amboise, and died in agony, leaving no issue.

Charles IX died at the age of twenty-four, harrowed in conscience for the part he had taken in the "Massacre of St. Bartholomew."

Charles X spent a quarter of a century in exile, and less than six years after he succeeded to the throne, fled for his life and died in exile.

Charles le Téméraire, of Burgundy, lost his life at Nancy, where he was utterly defeated by the Swiss.

Naples: Charles I saw the French massacred in the "Sicilian Vespers," and experienced only disasters.

Charles II, the Lame, was in captivity at his father's death.

Charles III, his grandson, was assassinated.

Charles I of England. When Bernini's bust of Charles I was brought home, the King was sitting in the garden of Chelsea Palace. He ordered the bust to be uncovered, and at the moment a hawk with a bird in its beak flew by, and a drop of blood fell on the throat of the bust. The bust was ultimately destroyed when the palace was burnt down.

The bronze statue of Charles I looking down Whitehall has an interesting history. It was modelled by Le Soeur and cast in 1639. After the execution of the King his statue was taken down by order of Parliament and sold to a brazier named Rivers, on the express condition that it should be melted down. But Rivers buried the statue, though he turned a pretty penny by selling bronze knives, forks, etc., which were alleged to be made from the "martyred" king's statue. On the Restoration he dug up the figure, and in 1674 it was placed on a new pedestal on its present site.

Charleston. A fox-trot popular c. 1925-27. It originated among the American Negroes. It is also the name of a cotton-trading seaport in South Carolina the population of which is half Negro.

Charm. Deriving from the Latin *carmen*, a song, a charm is an incantation that is alleged to work magic, though the word is usually applied to some object that averts ill luck or brings good. Volumes have been written about charms, for since the earliest dawn of intelligence mankind has sought to propitiate the beneficent powers or placate the malevolent ones. There are still all kinds of charms in use, often half-ashamedly—touching wood to avert bad luck, avoiding the number 13, first-footing at the New Year, and so forth; these are but a few relics of more credulous days. A good selection of charms is to be found described in Brand's *Antiquities.*

Chartreuse. A greenish or yellowish liqueur, made of brandy, and various aromatic herbs.

When the monks returned to La Chartreuse after their expulsion during the French Revolution they found the place in ruins and all their property alienated. To supply the wants of the community they concocted and sold the liqueur and before long were making a large revenue. This has always been spent on the maintenance of Carthusian houses, though the greater proportion of it has been devoted to charity. The recipe has now been sold and the production of the liqueur commercialized. *See* CARTHUSIANS.

Charybdis (kả rib′ dis). A whirlpool on the coast of Sicily. Scylla and Charybdis are employed to signify two equal dangers. Thus Horace says an author trying to avoid Scylla, drifts into Charybdis, *i.e.* seeking to avoid one fault, falls into another.

The Homeric account says that Charybdis dwelt under an immense fig-tree on the rock, and that thrice every day he swallowed the waters of the sea and thrice threw them up again; but later legends have it that he stole the oxen of Hercules, was killed by lightning, and changed into the gulf.

Thus when I shun Scylla, your father. I fall into Charybdis, your mother.—SHAKESPEARE: *Merchant of Venice*, iii, 5.

Chase. A small, unenclosed deer-forest held, for the most part, by a private individual, and protected only by common law. Forests are *royal* prerogatives, protected by the "Forest Laws."

An iron frame used by printers for holding sufficient type for one side of a sheet, where it is held tight by quoins, or small wedges of wood, is also called a *chase.* Here the word is the French *chasse,* from Lat. *capsa,* a case: the other *chase* given above is O.Fr. *chacier,* from Lat. *captiare,* to chase, itself from *capere,* to take.

Chasidim (chăs′ i dim). After the Babylonish captivity the Jews were divided into two groups— those who accepted and those who rejected the Persian innovation. The former were called *chasidim* (pietists), and the latter *zadikim* (the upright ones).

Chastity Girdle. A padded, metal appliance in the shape of a belt that a man could fasten around his wife in such a way as to preclude possibility of unfaithfulness during his prolonged absence. It is said to have come into vogue in the times of the Crusades when men set forth on protracted journeys and campaigns. One or two examples only are to be found in museums.

Chasuble (chăz' ū bél). This is one of the most richly ornamented ecclesiastical garments, some of the older examples being embroidered with exquisite workmanship. The chasuble is the principal vestment worn by the priest when saying Mass. It is supposed to represent the seamless coat of Christ, and is a rectangular, sleeveless garment, with a hole for the head in the middle, thus hanging down both back and front to between the hips and knees.

> And ye, louely ladyes, with youre longe fyngres,
> That ye han silke and sendal to sowe, what tyme is,
> Chesibles for chapelleynes cherches to honoure.
> PIERS PLOWMAN.

Château (shă tō). French for castle, mansion, country seat, and hence, an estate in the country.

The wines of the Bordeaux district of France are all named after the château of the estate on which they are grown. A Château-bottled wine is one bottled on the estate by the proprietor, which he only does in years when he is satisfied with the quality.

Château en Espagne, a castle in the air (*q.v.*).

Chatelaine (shăt' e lān). Originally the mistress of a château, a chatelaine now usually signifies a brooch or clasp from which a variety of objects hang on short chains. They are the things which the mistress of the castle was likely to use—keys, a watch, scissors, knives and trinkets. Chatelaines have been made in gold, silver, enamel, and cut steel, and in imitations of these materials. Since 1900 they have been little used, and their use during the century before was a fashionable affectation. In 1947 a fashion for so-called chatelaines arose in the U.S.A. These were ornaments formed of two or more brooches, preferably old and valuable, pinned across the corsage and joined by chains.

Chatterbox. A talkative person. Shakespeare speaks of the clack-dish. "His use was to put a ducat in her clack-dish" (*Measure for Measure*, iii, 2)—*i.e.* the box or dish used by beggars for collecting alms, which the holder clatters to attract attention. We find also chatter-basket in old writers, referring to the child's rattle.

Chatterpie. A familiar name for the magpie; also used figuratively for a chatterbox (*q.v.*).

Chauvinism (shō' vin izm). Blind and pugnacious patriotism of an exaggerated kind; unreasoning jingoism. Nicholas Chauvin, a soldier of the French Republic and Empire, was madly devoted to Napoleon and his cause. He was introduced as a type of exaggerated bellicose patriotism into quite a number of plays (Scribe's *Le Soldat laboureur*, Cogniard's *La Cocarde tricoleur*, 1831, Bayard and Dumanoir's *Les Aides de camps*. Charet's *Consent Chauvin*, are some of them), and his name was quickly adopted on both sides of the Channel.

Chawbacon. A contemptuous name for an uncouth rustic, supposed to eat no meat but bacon.

Che sara, sara (chā sa ra', sa ra'). What shall be, will be. The motto of the Russells (Bedford).

> What doctrine call ye this, *Che sera, sera*:
> What will be, shall be?
> MARLOWE: *Dr. Faustus*, i, 48.

Cheap as a Sardinian. A Roman phrase referring to the great crowds of Sardinian prisoners brought to Rome by Tiberius Gracchus, and offered for sale at almost any price.

Cheap jack. A travelling vendor of small wares, who is usually ready to "cheapen" his goods, *i.e.* take less for them than the price he first named.

Cheapside bargain. A weak pun, meaning that the article was bought cheap or under its market value. Cheapside, is on the south side of the *Cheap* (or *Chepe*), one of the principal market-places of Old London, so called from A.S. *ceapian*, to buy, *cypan*, to sell, *ceap*, a price or sale.

Cheater. Originally an *Escheator* or officer of the king's exchequer appointed to receive dues and taxes. The present use of the word shows how these officers were wont to fleece the people. *Cp.* CATCHPOLE; also the New Testament word "publicans," or collectors of the Roman tax in Judæa, etc.

Checkmate. A term in chess meaning to place your adversary's king in such a position that, had it been any other piece, it could not escape capture. Figuratively, "to checkmate" means to foil or outwit another; "check-mated," outmanœuvred. The term is from the Arabic *shah mat*, the king is dead, the phrase having been introduced into Old Spanish and Portuguese as *xaque mate*.

Checks. To hand in one's checks. *See* HAND.

Cheek. Cheek by jowl. Side by side, close together. Cheek is the A.S. *ceace*, and jowl is from A.S. *ceafl*, jaw, which became in M.E. *chowl*, and was confused with M.E. *cholle*, from A.S. *ceolur*, throat.

I'll go with thee, cheek by jowl.—SHAKESPEARE: *Midsummer Night's Dream*, iii, 2.

To cheek, or **to give cheek.** To be insolent, to be saucy.

None of your cheek. None of your insolence. We say a man is very **cheeky,** meaning that he is saucy and presumptuous.

Cheese. Tusser in his *Five Hundred Points of Good Husbandry* (1573) says that a cheese, to be perfect, should not be like (1) Gehazi, *i.e.* dead white, like a leper; (2) not like Lot's wife, all salt; (3) not like Argus, full of eyes; (4) not like Tom Piper, "hoven and puffed," like the cheeks of a piper; (5) not like Crispin, leathery; (6) not like Lazarus, poor; (7) not like Esau, hairy; (8) not like Mary Magdalene, full of whey or maudlin; (9) not like the Gentiles, full of maggots or gentils; and (10) not like a bishop, made of burnt milk; this last is a reference to the old phrase, *the bishop hath put his foot in it. See* BISHOP.

A green cheese. An unripe cheese; also a cheese that is eaten fresh (like a cream cheese) and is not kept to mature.

Big cheese. (Slang). The boss, or person of importance.

The moon made of green cheese. *See* MOON.

'Tis an old rat that won't eat cheese. It must be a wondrously toothless man that is inaccessible to flattery; he must be very old indeed who can abandon his favourite indulgence; only a very cunning rat knows that cheese is a mere bait.

Cheesemongers. An old popular name (before the Peninsular War) for the 1st Lifeguards; either because up to that time they had never served overseas, or (traditionally) because when the regiment was remodelled in 1788 certain commissions were refused on the ground that the ranks were composed of tradesmen instead of, as formerly, gentlemen. It is said that at Waterloo the commanding officer, when leading the regiment to a charge, cried, "Come on, you damned cheesemongers!" since when the name was accepted as a compliment rather than a reproach.

Cheese-toaster. A sword; also called a "toasting-fork," etc.

Put up thy sword betime;
Or I'll so maul you and your toasting-iron
That you shall think the devil is come from hell
SHAKESPEARE: *King John*, iv, 3.

The sight of the blade, which glistened by moonlight in his face, checked, in some sort, the ardour of his assailant, who desired he would lay aside his toaster, and take a bout with him at equal arms.—SMOLLETT: *Peregrine Pickle*, ch. xxiv.

Chef d'Œuvre (Fr., literally, a chief work). A masterpiece.

Chemosh (kē' mosh). The national god of the Moabites; very little is known of his cult, but human beings were sacrificed to him in times of crisis.

Next, Chemos, the obscene dread of Moab's sons,
From Aroer to Nebo, and the wild
Of southmost Abarim.
MILTON: *Paradise Lost*, i, 406-8.

Chequers (chek' ėrz). A public-house sign. The arms of Fitzwarren, the head of which house, in the days of the Henrys, was invested with the power of licensing vintners and publicans, may have helped to popularize this sign, which indicated that the house was duly licensed; but it has been found on houses in Pompeii, and probably referred to some game, like draughts, which might be indulged in on the premises. Gayton, in his *Notes on Don Quixote* (p. 340), in speaking of our public-house signs, refers to our notices of "billiards, kettle-noddy-boards, tables, truncks, shovel-boards, fox-and-geese, and the like." Also, payment of doles, etc., used to be made at certain public-houses, and a chequer-board was provided for the purpose. In such cases the sign indicated the house where the parish authorities met for that and other purposes.

Chequers, the country seat of the Prime Minister of England for the time being, was presented to the nation for this purpose by Sir Arthur and Lady Lee (Lord and Lady Lee of Fareham) in 1917, and was first officially occupied by the then Prime Minister (Mr. David Lloyd George) in January, 1921. It is a Tudor mansion, standing in a large and well-wooded estate in the Chilterns, about three miles from Princes Risborough.

Cheronean (kē rō nē' ȧn). **The Cheronean Sage.** Plutarch, who was born at Chæronea, in Bœotia (A.D. 46-120).

Cherry. Cherry-breeches or **cherry-pickers.** Familiar names for the 11th Hussars. *See* CHERUBIMS.

Cherry trees and the cuckoo. The cherry tree is strangely mixed up with the cuckoo in many cuckoo stories, because of the tradition that the cuckoo must eat three good meals of cherries before he is allowed to cease singing.

Cuckoo, cuckoo, cherry-tree,
Good bird, prithee, tell to me
How many years I am to see.

The answer is gathered from the number of times the cuckoo repeats its cry.

The whole tree or **not a cherry on it.** "*Aut Cæsar aut nullus.*" All in all or none at all.

To make two bites of a cherry. To divide something too small to be worth dividing; to take two spells over a piece of work that should be done in one.

Cherubims. The name once given popularly to the 11th Hussars. It seems inevitable that "Cherry bums" should be applied to men with cherry-pink uniform breeches.

Cheshire Cat. To grin like a Cheshire cat. *See* CAT.

Chess. "The game of the kings"; the word *chess* being the modern English representative of Persian *shah* (*see* CHECKMATE), a king. This word in Arabic was pronounced *shag*, which gave rise to the late Lat. *scaccus*, whence the O.Fr. *eschec*, Mod.Fr. *échecs*, and E. *chess*. Derivatives in other languages are *scacco* (Ital.), *jaque* (Span.), *xaque* (Port.), *schach* (Ger.).

Chestnut. A stale joke. The term is said to have been popularized in America by a Boston actor named Warren, who, on a certain apposite occasion, quoted from *The Broken Sword*, a forgotten melodrama by William Dimond, first produced in 1816 at Covent Garden. Captain Xavier, a principal character, is for ever repeating the same yarns, with variations. He was telling about one of his exploits connected with a cork-tree, when Pablo corrected him, "A chestnut-tree, you mean, captain." "Bah!" replied the captain, "I say a cork-tree." "A chestnut-tree," insisted Pablo. " I must know better than you," said the captain; "it was a cork-tree, I say." " A chestnut," persisted Pablo. " I have heard you tell the joke twenty-seven times, and I am sure it was a chestnut."

Chestnut Sunday. A Sunday in spring, generally that immediately before or after Ascension Day, is so called in the London district, because about that time the chestnut avenue at Hampton Court bursts into bloom.

Cheval (she văl) (Fr., a horse).

Cheval de bataille (Fr., literally "horse of battle"). One's strong argument; one's favourite subject.

Cheval glass. A large, swinging mirror, long enough to reflect the whole of the figure; so called from the "horse," or framework, which supports it.

Chevalier de St. George. *See* CAVALIER.

Chevalier d'industrie. A man who lives by his wits and calls himself a gentleman; an adventurer, swindler.

Be cautiously upon your guard against the infinite number of fine-dressed and fine-spoken chevaliers d'industrie and avanturiers, which swarm at Paris.— CHESTERFIELD: *Letters to his Son,* cxc (April 26th, 1750).

Cheveril (chev'ér il). **He has a cheveril conscience.** An accommodating one; one that will easily stretch like cheveril or kid leather.

Oh, here's a wit of cheveril, that stretches from an inch narrow to an ell broad!—SHAKESPEARE: *Romeo and Juliet,* ii, 4.

Your soft cheveril conscience would receive,
If you might please to stretch it.
SHAKESPEARE: *Henry VIII,* ii, 3.

Chevy Chase. There had long been a rivalry between the families of Percy and Douglas, which showed itself by incessant raids into each other's territory. Percy of Northumberland one day vowed he would hunt for three days in the Scottish border, without condescending to ask leave of Earl Douglas. The Scots warden said in his anger, "Tell this vaunter he shall find one day more than sufficient." The ballad called *Chevy Chase* mixes up this hunt with the battle of Otterburn, which, Dr. Percy justly observes, was "a very different event."

Chian Painter, The. *See* APELLES.

Chiaroscuro (kyar os koo' rō). A style of painting to represent only two colours, now called "black and white"; also the production of the effects of light and shade in drawings, paintings, etc.

Chiar-oscuro . . . is the art of representing light in shadow and shadow in light, so that the parts represented in shadow shall still have the clearness and warmth of those in light; and those in light, the depth and softness of those in shadow.—*Chambers's Encyclopædia,* ii, p. 171.

Chic (shik). A French word of uncertain origin meaning the knack of being able to do anything well. In English the word is applied more especially to good taste in dressing, to smartness and style, to being "just right" in appearance.

The word may be connected with German *schick*, skill, tact, but this is by no means certain.

Chichivache (chich' e vash). A fabulous animal that lived only on good women, and was hence all skin and bone, because its food was so extremely scarce; the antitype to Bicorn (*q.v.*). Chaucer introduced the word into English from French; but in doing so he changed *chichifache* (thin or ugly face) into *chichivache* (lean or meagre-looking cow), and hence the animal was pictured as a kind of bovine monstrosity.

O noble wyves, ful of heigh prudence,
Let noon humilitie your tonges nayle:
Ne lat no clerk have cause or diligence
To write of you a story of such mervayle
As of Griseldes, pacient and kynde,
Lest Chichivache you swolwe in hir entraile.
                    CHAUCER: *Envoy to the Clerk's Tale.*

Lydgate wrote a poem entitled *Bycorne and Chichevache.*

Curses like chickens come home to roost. *See* CURSES.

Don't count your chickens before they are hatched. Don't anticipate profits before they come. One of Æsop's fables describes a market woman saying she would get so much for her eggs, with the money she would buy a goose; the goose in time would bring her so much, with which she would buy a cow, and so on; but in her excitement she kicked over her basket and all her eggs were broken. "Don't crow till you are out of the wood" has a similar meaning. *Cp.* ALNASCHAR'S DREAM.

She's no chicken. She's not so young as she used to be.

Chicken-hearted or **chicken-livered.** Cowardly. Young fowls are remarkably timid, and run to the wing of the hen upon the slightest cause of alarm.

Child. At one time this was a provincial term for a female infant, and was the correlative of boy.

Mercy on 's! A barne, a very pretty barne. A boy or a child, I wonder? — SHAKESPEARE: *Winter's Tale,* iii, 3.

Child of God. In the Anglican and Catholic Church, one who has been baptized; others consider the phrase to mean one converted by special grace and adopted into the holy family of God's Church.

In my baptism, wherein I was made a member of Christ, the child of God, and an inheritor of the Kingdom of Heaven. — *Church Catechism.*

Childe. In *Childe Harold, Childe Roland, Childe Tristam,* etc., "Childe" is a title of honour, like the Spanish "infante" and "infanta." In the time of chivalry, noble youths who were candidates for knighthood were, during their time of probation, called *infans, valets, damoysels, bacheliers,* and *childe.*

Childe Harold. Byron's poem depicts a man sated of the world, who roams from place to place to flee from himself. The "Childe" is, in fact, Lord Byron himself, who was only twenty-one when he began, and twenty-eight when he finished the poem. In canto i (1809), he visited Portugal and Spain; in canto ii (1810), Turkey in Europe; in canto iii (1816), Belgium and Switzerland; and in canto iv (1817), Venice, Rome, and Florence.

The children or **babes in the wood.** The foundation of this ballad, which is told in Percy's *Reliques,* appears again in a crude melodrama of 1599 by Robert Farrington, entitled *Two Lamentable Tragedies: the one of the Murder of Maister Beech, a chandler in Thames Streete, the other of a young child murthered in a wood by two ruffins with the consent of his unkle.* It is not known which is the earlier, the play or the ballad. The story is, shortly, as follows: — The master of Wayland Hall, Norfolk, left a little son and daughter to the care of his wife's brother; both were to have money, but if the children died first the uncle was to inherit. After twelve months the uncle hired two ruffians to murder the babes; one of the ruffians relented and killed his fellow, leaving the children in a wood; they died during the night, and "Robin Redbreast" covered them over with leaves. All things went ill with the wicked uncle; his sons died, his barns were fired, his cattle died, and he himself perished in gaol. After seven years the ruffian was taken up for highway robbery, and confessed the whole affair.

Children. Three hundred and sixty-five at a birth. It is said that a Countess of Henneberg accused a beggar of adultery because she carried twins, whereupon the beggar prayed that the countess might carry as many children as there are days in the year. According to the legend, this happened on Good Friday, 1276. All the males were named John, and all the females Elizabeth. The countess was forty-two at the time.

Chiliasts (kī' li ästs) (Gr. *chilias,* a thousand). Those who believe that Christ will return to this earth and reign a thousand years in the midst of His saints. Originally a Judaistic theory, it became a heresy in the early Christian Church, and though it was condemned by St. Damasus, who was Pope from 366 to 384, it was not extirpated. Article xli of the English Church, as published in 1553, further condemned Chiliasm; this Article was omitted in 1562. *Millenarians* is another name for the Chiliasts.

Chillingham Cattle. A breed of cattle preserved in the Northumberland park of the Earl of Tankerville, supposed to be the last remnant of the wild oxen of Britain.

Chillon (shē' yong). **Prisoner of Chillon.** François de Bonnivard (d. about 1570), a Genevan prelate and politician. Byron makes him one of six brothers, all of whom suffered for their opinions. The father and two sons died on the battlefield; one was burnt at the stake; three were incarcerated in the dungeon of

Chillon, on the edge of the Lake of Geneva— of these, two died, and François, who had been imprisoned for "republican principles" by the Duke-Bishop of Savoy, was set at liberty by "the Béarnais" after four years' imprisonment.

Chilo. One of the "Seven Sages of Greece" (*q.v.*).

Chiltern Hundreds. There are three, viz. Stoke, Desborough, and Burnham, Bucks. At one time the Chilterns, between Bedford and Hertford, etc., were much frequented by robbers, so a steward was appointed by the Crown to put them down. The necessity has long since ceased, but the office remains; and, since 1740, when a Member of Parliament wishes to vacate his seat, one way of doing so is by applying for the stewardship of the Chiltern Hundreds; for no member of Parliament may resign his seat, but if he accepts an office of profit under the Crown he is obliged to be re-elected if he wishes to remain a member. The Stewardship of the Manor of Northstead (Yorks) is used in the same way. The gift of both is in the hands of the Chancellor of the Exchequer; it was refused to a member for Reading in 1842.

The Stewardships of Old Sarum (Wilts), East Hendred (Berks), Poynings (Sussex), Hempholwic (Yorks), were formerly used for the same purpose, as were (till 1838) the Escheatorships of Munster and Ulster.

Chimæra (kī mē' rà) (Gr. *chimaira*, a she-goat). A fabulous monster of Greek mythology, described by Homer as a monster with a goat's body, a lion's head, and a dragon's tail. It was born in Lycia, and was slain by Bellerophon. Hence the term is used in English for an illusory fancy, a wild, incongruous scheme.

Chimney Money or **Hearth Money.** A yearly tax of two shillings on every fireplace in England and Wales: first levied in 1663 and abolished in 1689.

Chimneypot hat. The cylindrical black silk hat, usually known as the top-hat or silk hat.

China Clay. A mineral, obtained largely from Cornwall, used in the manufacture of porcelain, and by papermakers to obtain finish and consistency, also for coating art and chromo papers.

Chinaman. A left-hander's googly, a cricketing term (*see* GOOGLY).

Chinatown. A part of any city where the population is Chinese, the most famous being in the United States.

Chindit (chin' dit). Stylized lions characteristic of Burmese and Malayan sculpture and religious architecture. Adopted as the insignia of the troops operating in the Malay jungle behind the Japanese lines under Brigadier Wingate in the 1939-45 war, who hence were familiarly known as *Chindits*.

Chintz. A plural word that has erroneously become singular. The Hindi *chint* (from Sanskrit *chitra*, variegated) was the name given in the 17th century to the painted and stained calico imported from the East; but as the plural (*chints*) was more common in commercial use than the singular it came to be taken for a singular, and was written *chince* or *chinse* and finally *chintz*.

Chip. A carpenter is known by his chips. A man is known to be a carpenter by the chips in his workshop, so the profession or taste of other men may be known by their manners or mode of speech.

A chip of the old block. A son or child of the same stuff as his father. The chip is the same wood as the block. Burke applied the words to William Pitt.

To have a chip on one's shoulder. To be seeking a quarrel. A person who is always ready to take offence is said to go about with a chip on his shoulder.

Chippie. A knee-length frock worn in the red-light district of New Orleans; hence the U.S. phrase for a prostitute; can be used as a phrase of back-handed affection, as with the Blues singer Bertha "Chippie" Hill.

Chiron (kī' ron). The centaur who taught Achilles and many other heroes music, medicine, and hunting. Jupiter placed him in heaven among the stars as Sagittarius (*the Archer*).

In the *Inferno* Dante gives the name to the keeper of the lake of boiling blood, in the seventh circle of hell.

Chirping Cup. A merry-making glass or cup of liquor. Wine that maketh glad the heart of man, or makes him sing for joy.

> A chirping cup is my matin song,
> And my vesper bell is my bowl; Ding dong!
> *A Friar of Orders Grey.*
>
> The chirping and moderate bottle.
> BEN JONSON.
> He takes his chirping pint, and cracks his jokes.
> POPE: *Moral Essays*, iii.

Chivalry (shiv' àl ri). This is a general term for all things pertaining to the romance of the old days of knighthood. The word is of similar origin to *cavalry*, coming from Fr. *cheval*, a horse, and *chevalier*, a horseman. Chivalry embodied the Middle Age conception of the ideal life, where valour, courtesy, generosity and dexterity in arms were the summit of any man's attainment.

For him behoveth to be of soch chiualrie and so aventurouse that he com by hymselfe and enquere after the seint Graal that my feire doughter kepeth.
Merlin (E.E.T.S., iii).

A great literature arose out of chivalry—the Roland epics, those of Charlemagne, and Arthur. It was, perhaps, prophetic of the fate of chivalry itself that in every case these great epics end in tragedy:

The paladins of Charlemagne were all scattered by the battle of Roncesvalles.

The champions of Dietrich were all assassinated at the instigation of Chriemhild, the bride of Etzel, King of the Huns.

The Knights of the Round Table were all extirpated in the fatal battle of Camlan.

The flower of chivalry. *See* FLOWER.

Chivy. To chase or urge someone on; also a chase in the game of "Prisoners' Base." One boy "sets a chivy" by leaving his base, when one of the opposite side chases him, and if he succeeds in touching him before he reaches "home," the boy touched becomes a prisoner. The word is a variant spelling of *chevy*, from *Chevy Chase* (*q.v.*).

Chivy or **chivvy.** Slang for the face. An example of rhyming slang (*q.v.*). Here the full term to rhyme with *face* is *Chevy Chase*.

Chloe (klō' é). The shepherdess beloved by Daphnis in the pastoral romance of Longus, entitled *Daphnis and Chloe*, and hence a generic name among romance writers and pastoral poets for a rustic maiden—not always of the artless variety.

In Pope's *Moral Essays* (ii) Chloe is intended for Lady Suffolk, mistress of George II. "Content to dwell in decencies for ever"; and Prior uses the name for Mrs. Centlivre.

Chock-full. Chock-a-block. Absolutely full; no room for any more. It is a very old expression in English, dating back at least to Chaucer's time, though, apparently, not used by him. It does not seem to have any etymological connexion with *choke* (as though meaning "full enough to choke one"); but this spelling—as well as *chuck*—has been in common use.

Ayr was holding some grand market; streets and inn had been chokefull during the sunny hours.—CARLYLE, in *Froude's Jane W, Carlyle*, vol. i, letter lxxxvii.

Chocolate. The produce of the cocoa-berry was introduced into England from Central America in the early 16th century as a drink; it was sold in the London coffee-houses from the middle of the 17th century. The *Cocoa Tree* was one of the most famous coffee-houses of the early 18th century.

Choice. Choice spirit. A specially select or excellent person, a leader in some particular capacity. From Antony's speaking of Cæsar and Brutus as—

The choice and master spirit of this age.
SHAKESPEARE: *Julius Cæsar*, iii,1.

Of two evils choose the less. The proverb is given in John Heywood's collection (1546), but it is a good deal earlier, and occurs in Chaucer's *Troilus and Criseyde* (ii, 470) as—

Of harmes two, the lesse is for to chese.

Thomas à Kempis (*Imit. Christi*, iii, 12) has—

De duobus malis minus est semper eligendum (Of two evils the less is always to be chosen).

which is an echo of Cicero's

Ex malis eligere minima oportere (Of evil one should select the least).—*De Officiis*, iii, 1.

Choker. Formerly a broad neck-cloth, worn in full dress, and by waiters and clergymen; now a high, stiff collar or a necklace worn tight round the neck.

Chop. The various modern uses of *chop* represent two or three different words. *To chop*, meaning to cut a piece off with a sudden blow, is a variant spelling of *chap*, a cleft in the skin, and *to chap*, to open in long slits or cracks. From this we get:—

Chops of the Channel. The short broken motion of the waves, experienced in crossing the English Channel; also the place where such motion occurs. In this use, however, the word may be *chops*, the jaw (*see below*), because the Chops of the Channel is an old and well-understood term for the entrance to the Channel from the Atlantic.

Chop house. An eating-house where chops and steaks are served.

I dine at the *Chop-House* three days a week, where the good company wonders they never *see* you of late.—STEELE: *Spectator*, No. 308 (22 Feb., 1712).

In the three following phrases *chop* comes from the same root as *chap* in *chapman* (*q.v.*), and signifies to barter, exchange, or sell.

To chop and change. To barter by rule of thumb; to fluctuate, to vary continuously.

To chop an article also means to dispose of it arbitrarily, even at a loss.

To chop logic. To bandy words; to altercate. Bacon says, "Let not the council chop with the judge."

How now, how now, chop logic! What is this?
"Proud," and "I thank you," and "I thank you not,"
And yet "not proud."
SHAKESPEARE: *Romeo and Juliet*, iii, 5.

The wind chops about. Shifts from point to point suddenly. Hence, *choppy*, said of a variable wind, and of the rough sea produced by such; and *to chop round*—

How the House of Lords and House of Commons chopped round.—THACKERAY: *The Four Georges* (George I).

Chop, the face, and **chops,** the jaws or mouth, is a variant spelling of *chap* (as in *Bath chap,* the lower part of a pig's face, cured). From this come.

Chop-fallen, or **chap-fallen.** Crestfallen; down in the mouth.

Down in the chops. Down in the mouth; in a melancholy state; with the mouth drawn down.

To lick one's chops. To relish in anticipation.

Finally, in the slang phrase **first chop,** meaning excellent, the word is the Hindi *chhap,* a print or stamp, used in India and China by English residents for an official seal, also for a passport or permit; and a Chinese custom-house is known as a chop-house.

Chopsticks. The two thin sticks of wood or ivory that the Chinese use to eat with. They attain marvellous dexterity in the use of these implements, and the word is a rendering of Chin, *k'wai-tsze,* meaning "the quick ones." In pidgin English (*q.v.*) *chop* means "quick."

Choriambic Metre. Horace gives us a great variety, but the main feature in all is the prevalence of the choriambus ($-\smile\smile-$). Specimen translations in two of these metres are subjoined:

(1) Horace, 1 *Odes,* viii.

$-\smile\smile-|\smile--$

$-\smile|--|-\smile\smile-|-\smile\smile-|\smile--$

Lydia, why on Stanley,
By the great gods, tell me, I pray, ruinous love you centre?
Once he was strong and manly,
Never seen now, patient of toil Mars' sunny camp to enter.   *E. C. B.*

(2) The other specimen is 1 *Odes,* xii.

$--|-\smile\smile-|\smile--$

$--|-\smile\smile-|-\smile\smile-|\smile--$

When you, with an approving smile,
Praise those delicate arms, Lydy, of Telephus,
Ah me! how you stir up my bile!
Heart-sick that for a boy you should forsake me thus.   *E. C. B.*

Chouans (shoo' ong). French insurgents of the Royalist party during the Revolution. Jean Cottereau was their leader, nicknamed *Chouan* (a corruption of Fr. *chat-huant,* a screech-owl), because he was accustomed to warn his companions of danger by imitating the screech of an owl. Cottereau (killed 1794) was followed by George Cadoudal (executed 1804). *See also* COMPANIONS OF JEHU; VENDÉE.

Chouse (chouz). This is a rather odd word, meaning to cheat or swindle. It has an interesting origin, coming from the Turkish *cha'ush,* an interpreter, messenger, etc. The interpreter of the Turkish embassy in England in 1609 defrauded his government of £4,000, and the notoriety of the swindle caused the word *chiaus* or *chouse* to be adopted.

Dapper.   What do you think of me,
               That I am a Chiause?
Face.   What's that?
Dapper.   The Turk was here—
               As one would say, do you think
               I am a Turk.
           BEN JONSON: *Alchemist,* i. 2.

You shall chouse him out of horses, clothes, and money, and I'll wink at it.—DRYDEN: *Wild Gallant,* ii, 1.

Chriss-cross, or **Christ-cross, Row.** The alphabet in a hornbook, which had a cross like the Maltese cross (✠) at the beginning and end.

Sir Ralph.   I wonder, wench, how I thy name might
             know.
Mall.   Why, you may find it, sir, in th' Christcross
             row.
Sir Ralph.   Be my schoolmistress, teach me how to
             spell it.
Mall.   No, faith, I care not greatly, if I tell it;
             My name is Mary Barnes.
   PORTER: *Two Angry Women of Abington,* v, 1 (1599).

The word appears as *Christ-cross, criss-cross,* etc., and Shakespeare shortened it to *cross-row:*—

He hearkens after prophecies and dreams;
And from the cross-row plucks the letter G,
And says a wizard told him that by G
His issue disinherited should be.
                Richard III, I, i.

As the Maltese cross was also sometimes used in place of XII to mark that hour on clocks the word has occasionally been used for noon:—

The feskewe of the Diall is upon the Chriss-crosse of Noone.—*The Puritan Widow,* iv, 2 (*Anon,* 1607).

Christendom. All Christian countries generally; formerly it also meant the state or condition of being a Christian. Thus, in Shakespeare's *King John,* the young prince says:—

By my Christendom!
So I were out of prison and kept sheep,
I should be merry as the day is long.
                Act iv, sc. 1.

Christian. A follower of Christ. So called first at Antioch (*Acts* xi, 26). Also, the hero of Bunyan's allegory, *Pilgrim's Progress.* He flees from the City of Destruction, and journeys to the Celestial City. He starts with a heavy burden on his back, but it falls off when he stands at the foot of the cross.

Christian Brothers. A secret society formed in London in the early 16th century to distribute the New Testament in English. The name is now better known as that of the teaching congregation of laymen, founded in 1684 by St. John Baptist de la Salle.

Most Christian Doctor. John Charlier de Gerson (1363-1429).

Most Christian King. The style of the King of France since 1469, when it was conferred on

Louis XI by Pope Paul II. Previously to that the title had been given in the 8th century to Pepin le Bref by Pope Stephen III (714-68), and again in the 9th century to Charles le Chauve.

Cp. RELIGIOUS.

Christiana (kris ti an' à). The wife of Christian in Pt. ii of Bunyan's *Pilgrim's Progress*, who journeyed with her children and Mercy from the City of Destruction some time after her husband.

Christinos. Supporters of the Queen-Regent Christina during the Carlist wars in Spain, 1833-40.

Christmas. December 25th is Christmas Day. In England, from the 7th to as late as the 13th century, the year was reckoned from Christmas Day; but in the 12th century the Anglican Church began the year on March 25th, a practice which was adopted by civilians at the beginning of the 14th century, and which remained in force till the reformation of the calendar in 1752. Thus, the civil, ecclesiastical, and legal year, which was used in all public documents, began on Christmas Day till the end of the 13th century, but the historical year had, for a very long time before then, begun on January 1st.

Christmas cards. These are of comparatively recent origin, the earliest having, it is said, been designed in 1844 by W. C. T. Dobson, R.A., a painter of pretty works of that nature.

Christmas decorations. The great feast of Saturn was held in December, when the people decorated the temples with such green things as they could find. The Christian custom is the same transferred to Him who was born in Bethlehem on Christmas Day. The holly or holy-tree is called Christ's-thorn in Germany and Scandinavia, from its use in church decorations and its putting forth its berries about Christmas time. The early Christians gave an emblematic turn to the custom, referring to the "righteous branch," and justifying the custom from *Isaiah* lx, 13—"The glory of Lebanon shall come unto thee; the fir-tree, the pine-tree, and the box together, to beautify the place of my sanctuary."

The custom of having a Christmas tree decorated with candles and hung with presents came to England with the craze for German things that followed Queen Victoria's marriage to Prince Albert of Saxe-Coburg-Gotha in 1840. Santa Claus (whose name has not even yet become anglicized) with his reindeer had been unknown until then.

Christopher, St. Legend relates that St. Christopher was a giant who one day carried a child over a brook, and said, "Chylde, thou hast put me in grete peryll. I might bere no greater burden." To which the child answered, "Marvel thou nothing, for thou hast borne all the world upon thee, and its sins likewise." This is an allegory: Christopher means *Christ-bearer*; the *child* was Christ, and the *river* was the river of death.

Chronogram. A sentence or inscription in which certain letters stand for a date or epoch. In this double Chronogram upon the year 1642, (one part in Latin and the other in the English of that Latin) the capitals in each produce the total of 1642.

JV DeVs IaM propItIVs sIs regI regnoqVe hVIC VnIVerso.

O goD noVV sheVV faVoVr to the kIng anD thIs VVhoLe LanD.

VDVIMIIVIIVVICVIV	1642.
DVVVVVVIDIVVLLD	1642.

Chrysippus. *Nisi Chrysippus fuisset, Porticus non esset.* Chrysippus of Soli was a disciple of Zeno the Stoic and Cleanthes, his successor. He did for the Stoics what St. Paul did for Christianity—that is, he explained the system, showed by plausible reasoning its truth, and how it was based on a solid foundation. Stoicism was founded by Zeno; but if Chrysippus had not advocated it, it would never have taken root.

Chum. A crony, a familiar companion, properly a bedfellow. The word first appeared in the 17th century; its origin has not been ascertained.

To chum in with. To be on very intimate and friendly terms with.

Church. This is the A.S. *circe*, or *cirice*, which comes through W.Ger. *kirika*, from Gr. *kuriakon*, a church, the neuter of the adjective *kuriakos*, meaning of, or belonging to, the Lord.

The Anglican Church. Since the Reformation the English branch of the Protestant Church which, since 1532, has been known as the "Established Church of England," because established by Act of Parliament. It disavows the authority of the Pope, and rejects certain dogmas and rules of the Roman Church.

The Catholic Church. The Western Church called itself so when it separated from the Eastern Church. It is also called the Roman Catholic Church, to distinguish it from the Anglican Church or Anglican Catholic Church, a branch of the Western Church.

The Established Church. The State Church, the Church officially recognized and adopted by any country. In England it is Episcopalian (*see* ANGLICAN CHURCH *above*), in Scotland

Presbyterian, but in Wales, since the disestablishment of the Church of England in Wales by Act of Parliament in 1920, there is no Established Church.

Church of North America (Episcopalian) established November 1784, when Bishop Seabury, chosen by the Churches of Connecticut, was consecrated in Scotland. The first convention was held at Philadelphia in 1787.

Church of Scotland. See PRESBYTERIAN, which became the established religion of Scotland on the abolition of Episcopacy in 1638. The head of the Church is the Moderator, and it is regulated by four Courts: the General Assembly, Synod, Presbytery, and Kirk Sessions.

The Church Invisible. Those who are known to God alone as His sons and daughters by adoption and grace. See CHURCH VISIBLE.

There is . . . a Church visible and a Church invisible: the latter consists of those spiritual persons who fulfil the notion of the Ideal Church—the former is the Church as it exists in any particular age, embracing within it all who profess Christianity.—F. W. ROBERTSON: Sermons (series IV, ii).

The Church Militant. The Church as consisting of the whole body of believers, who are said to be "waging the war of faith" against "the world, the flesh, and the devil." It is therefore militant, or in warfare.

To church a woman. To read the appointed service when a woman comes to church after a confinement to return thanks to God for her "safe deliverance" and restored health.

To go into the Church. To take holy orders.

Churchwarden. A long clay pipe, such as churchwardens used to smoke a century or so ago when they met together in the parish tavern, after they had made up their accounts in the vestry, or been elected to office at the Easter meeting.

Churchyard cough. A deep, chesty cough which sounds like a presage of death.

Churrigueresque (chu rig er esk'). Overornate, as applied to architecture. The word, frequently used by Richard Ford (1796-1858) in his writings on Spain, derives from Jose Churriguera (1650-1723), a Spanish architect of the baroque school.

Cicero (sis' er ō). The great Roman orator, philosopher, and statesman (106-43 B.C.), Marcus Tullius, said by Plutarch to have been called Cicero from Lat. cicer (a wart or vetch), because he had "a flat excrescence on the tip of his nose."

Cicerone. A guide to point out objects of interest to strangers. So called from the great orator Cicero, in the same way as Paul was called

by the men of Lystra "Mercurius, because he was the chief speaker."

Cicisbeo (chich is bā' ō). A dangler about women; the professed gallant of a married woman. Cp. CAVALIERE SERVENTE. Also the knot of silk or ribbon which is attached to fans, walking-sticks, umbrellas, etc. Cicisbeism, the practice of dangling about women.

Cid (sid). A corruption of seyyid, Arabic for lord. The title given to Roderigo or Ruy Diaz de Bivar (born about 1040, died 1099), also called El Campeador, the national hero of Spain and champion of Christianity against the Moors. His exploits, real and legendary, form the basis of many Spanish romances and chronicles, as well as Corneille's tragedy, Le Cid (1636).

Cid Hamet Benengeli. The supposititious author upon whom Cervantes fathered The Adventures of Don Quixote.

Of the two bad cassocks I am worth . . . I would have given the latter of them as freely as even Cid Hamet offered his . . . to have stood by.—STERNE.

Cigars and Cigarettes. The word cigar comes from cicada, the Spanish cigar-shaped beetle. The natives of Cuba were already smoking tobacco in this form when the white men first invaded their country. Cigars as we know them were introduced into U.S.A. by General Putnam, in 1762, on his return from the capture of Havana by the Earl of Albemarle, and this fashion of smoking soon spread to Europe. Cheroots (from the Tamil shuruttu, a roll) are made from tobacco grown in S. India or the Philippines, and are merely rolled, with the ends cut square.

Cigarettes originated in Spain (Borrow called them paper cigars, and the Spanish call them cigarillos, little cigars), and at first were rolled by the smoker as he needed them. It was not until the late 19th century that they were sold rolled and in packets. Even readymade cigarettes in Spain to-day are designed to be untwisted at the ends and re-rolled before smoking.

Cimmerian Darkness (sī mēr' i an). Homer (possibly from some story as to the Arctic night) supposes the Cimmerians to dwell in a land "beyond the ocean stream," where the sun never shone. (Odys., xi, 14.)

I carried am into waste wildernesse,
Waste wildernes, amongst Cymerian shades,
Where endles paines and hideous heavinesse,
Is round about me heapt in darksome glades.
                 SPENSER: Virgil's Gnat.
In dark Cimmerian desert ever dwell.
                 MILTON: L'Allegro.

The Cimmerians were known in post-Homeric times as an historical people on the shores of the Black Sea, whence the name Crimea.

Cinch (sinch). This word, which comes from the Spanish, is the term used in western U.S.A. for the strong leather or canvas girth of a saddle or pack. From that it came to mean a tight grip; and by an easy transition a sure thing, a safe proposition.

Cinderella (sin der rel' à). Heroine of a fairy tale of very ancient, probably Eastern, origin, that was mentioned in German literature in the 16th century and was popularized by Perrault's *Contes de ma mère l'oye* (1697). Cinderella is drudge of the house, dirty with housework, while her elder sisters go to fine balls. At length a fairy enables her to go to the prince's ball; the prince falls in love with her, and she is discovered by means of a glass slipper which she drops, and which will fit no foot but her own.

The *glass* slipper is a mistranslation of *pantoufle en vair* (a fur, or sable, slipper), not *en verre*. Sable was worn only by kings and princes, so the fairy gave royal slippers to her favourite.

Cinquecento (ching' kwė chen' tō). The Italian name for the sixteenth century (1501-1600), applied as an epithet to art and literature with much the same significance as Renaissance or Elizabethan. It was the revival of the classical or antique, but is generally understood as a derogatory term, implying debased or inferior art.

Cinter (sin' ter). This is frequently confused with the word "centre," though it comes from the same original as the French *ceinture*, a girdle. A cinter, or cintre, is the wooden shape on which an arch is built.

Cipher. This word comes from the Arabic *cifr*, meaning zero, naught. Through various ways it has come to be used for a message so set forth on paper as to be comprehensible only to one acquainted with that particular and secret system of writing. The simplest cipher is that once employed by Julius Cæsar, who used certain letters in place of the right ones, *e.g. d* for *a, e* for *b*, and so on through the alphabet. Later ciphers used numbers or invented characters to replace letters. In more recent years the most complicated systems of ciphering have come into use by spies, diplomatic observers, etc., but experts claim that no cipher has yet been invented that cannot be "broken down" by close study and the application of certain recognized methods.

Circe (sĕr' si). A sorceress in Greek mythology, who lived in the island of Ææa. When Ulysses landed there, Circe turned his companions into swine, but Ulysses resisted this metamorphosis

by virtue of a herb called *moly* (*q.v.*), given him by Mercury.

> Who knows not Circe,
> The daughter of the Sun, whose charmed cup
> Whoever tasted lost his upright shape,
> And downward fell into a grovelling swine?
> MILTON: Comus, 50-53.

Circle. Great circle. Navigation, whether on the sea or in the air, is principally done with the aid of a great circle. This is a line on the earth's surface which lies in a plane through the centre of the earth, or any circle on the earth's surface which divides the world into two equal parts. The shortest line between any two points on the earth's surface is on a great circle, hence the ascertaining of great circles is of the utmost importance in nautical or aerial navigation.

Circuit. The journey made through the counties of Great Britain by the judges twice a year. There are six circuits in England, two in Wales, and three in Scotland. Those in England are called the South-Eastern, Midland, Northern, North Eastern, Oxford, and Western Circuit; those of Wales, the North Wales and Chester, and the South Wales Division; and those of Scotland, the Southern, Western, and Northern.

Circumlocution Office. A term applied in ridicule by Dickens in *Little Dorrit* to our public offices, because each person tries to shuffle off every act to someone else; and before anything is done it has to pass through so many departments and so much time elapses that it is hardly worth having bothered about it.

> Whatever was required to be done, the Circumlocution Office was beforehand with all the public departments in the art of perceiving—How not to do it.—DICKENS: *Little Dorrit*, ch. x.

Cist (kist) (Gr. *kiste*, Lat. *cista*). A chest or box. Generally used as a coffer for the remains of the dead. The Greek and Roman cist was a deep cylindrical basket made of wickerwork. The basket into which voters cast their tablets was called a "cist"; but the mystic cist used in the rites of Ceres was latterly made of bronze. *Cp.* KIST OF WHISTLES.

Cistercians. A monastic order, founded at Cistercium or Citeaux by Robert, abbot of Molême, in Burgundy, in 1098, as a branch of the Benedictines; the monks are known also as *Bernardines*, owing to the patronage of St. Bernard of Clairvaux about 1200. In 1664 the order was reformed on an excessively strict basis by Jean le Boutillier de Rance.

Citadel (Ital. *citadella*, a little city). In fortification, a small strong fort, constructed either within the place fortified, or at its most inaccessible spot, to give refuge for the garrison, that it may prolong the defence after the place has fallen, or hold out for the best terms of capitulation. Citadels generally command the interior of the place, and are useful, therefore, for overawing a population which might otherwise strive to shorten a siege.

Citizen King, The. Louis Philippe of France. So called because he was elected King of the French (not king of France) by the citizens of Paris. (Born 1773, reigned 1830-48, died 1850.)

City. Strictly speaking, a large town with a corporation and cathedral; but any large town is so called in ordinary speech. In the Bible it means a town having walls and gates.

The eldest son of the first man [Cain] builded a city (Gen. iv, 17)—not, of course, a Nineveh or a Babylon, but still a city.—RAWLINSON: *Origin of Nations*, pt. i, ch. i.

The City of a Hundred Towers. Pavia, in Italy; famous for its towers and steeples.

The City College. An old irony. Newgate.

The City of Bells. Strasburg.

The City of Brotherly Love. A somewhat ironical, but quite etymological, nickname of Philadelphia (Gr. *Philadelphia means* "brotherly love").

The City of David. Jerusalem. So called in compliment to King David (2 *Sam*. v, 7, 9).

The City of Destruction. In Bunyan's *Pilgrim's Progress*, the world of the unconverted.

The City of God. The Church, or whole body of believers; the kingdom of Christ, in contradistinction to the City of Destruction (*q.v.*). The phrase is that of St. Augustine; one of his chief works bearing the title, *De Civitate Dei*.

The City of Lanterns. A supposititious city in Lucian's *Veræ Historiæ*, situate somewhere beyond the zodiac. *Cp.* LANTERN-LAND.

The City of Legions. Caerleon-on-Usk, where King Arthur held his court.

The City of Lilies. Florence.

The City of Magnificent Distances. Washington, D.C., famous for its wide avenues and splendid vistas.

The City of Palaces. Agrippa, in the reign of Augustus, converted Rome from "a city of brick huts to one of marble palaces."

Marmoream se relinquere quam latericiam accepisset. —SUETONIUS: *Aug. xxix.*

Calcutta is called the "City of Palaces."

City of Refuge. Moses, at the command of God, set apart three cities on the east of Jordan, and Joshua added three others on the west, whither any person might flee for refuge who had killed a human creature inadvertently. The three on the east of Jordan were Bezer, Ramoth,

and Golan; the three on the west were Hebron, Shechem, and Kedesh (*Deut.* iv, 43; *Josh.* xx, 1-8).

By Mohammedans, Medina, in Arabia, where Mohammed took refuge when driven by conspirators from Mecca, is known as "the City of Refuge." He entered it, not as a fugitive, but in triumph 622 A.D. Also called the *City of the Prophet*.

The City of the Seven Hills. Rome, built on seven hills (*Urbs septacollis*). The hills are the Aventine, Cælian, Capitoline, Esquiline, Palatine, Quirinal, and Viminal.

The AVENTINE HILL was given to the people. It was deemed unlucky, because here Remus was slain. It was also called "Collis Dianæ," from the Temple of Diana which stood there.

The CÆLIAN HILL was given to Cælius Vibenna, the Tuscan, who came to the help of the Romans in the Sabine war.

The CAPITOLINE HILL or "Mons Tarpeius," also called "Mons Saturni," on which stood the great castle or capitol of Rome. It contained the Temple of Jupiter Capitolinus.

The ESQUILINE HILL was given by Augustus to Mecænas, who built thereon a magnificent mansion.

The PALATINE HILL was the largest of the seven. Here Romulus held his court, whence the word "palace" (*palatium*).

The QUIRINAL HILL was where the Quirés or Curés settled. It was also called "Cabalinus," from two marble statues of a horse, one of which was the work of Phidias, the other of Praxiteles.

The VIMINAL HILL was so called from the number of osiers (*vimines*) which grew there. It contained the Temple of Jupiter Viminalis.

The City of the Sun. Baalbec, Rhodes, and Heliopolis, which had the sun for tutelary deity, were so called. It is also the name of a treatise on the Ideal Republic by the Dominican friar Campanella (1568-1639), similar to the *Republic* of Plato, *Utopia* of Sir Thomas More, and *Atlantis* of Bacon.

The City of the Three Kings. Cologne; the reputed burial-place of the Magi (*q.v.*).

The City of the Tribes. Galway; because it was anciently the home of the thirteen "tribes" or chief families, who settled there in 1232 with Richard de Burgh.

The City of the Violated Treaty. Limerick; because of the way in which the Pacification of Limerick (1691) was broken by England.

The City of the Violet Crown. Athens is so called by Aristophanes (ἰοστέφανος)—*Equites*, 1323 and 1329; and *Acharnians*, 637. Macaulay refers to Athens as the "violet-crowned city." Ion (a violet) was a representative king of Athens, whose four sons gave names to the four Athenian classes; and Greece, in Asia Minor, was called Ionia. Athens was the city of "Ion crowned its king" or "of the Violet crowned."

Civil war. War between citizens (*civiles*). In English history the term is applied to the war between Charles I and his Parliament; but the War of the Roses was a civil war also. In America, the War of Secession (1861-65).

Civis Romanus sum (siv′ is rō mā′ nus sŭm). "I am a Roman citizen," a plea which sufficed to arrest arbitrary condemnation, bonds, and scourging. Hence, when the centurion commanded Paul "to be examined by scourging," he asked, "Is it lawful for you to *scourge* a Roman citizen, and *uncondemned?*" (1) No Roman citizen could be condemned unheard; (2) by the Valerian Law he could not be bound; (3) by the Sempronian Law it was forbidden to *scourge* him, or to beat him with rods. *See also* Acts xvi, 37, etc.

The phrase later gained an English fame from the peroration of Palmerston's greatest speech, in 1850: "As the Roman, in days of old, held himself free from indignity when he could say *Civis Romanus sum*, so also a British subject, in whatever land he may be, shall feel confident that the watchful eye and the strong arm of England will protect him against injustice and wrong."

Civvie Street (siv′ i). In the 1939-45 War this was the term by which men in the Services referred to civilian life.

Clabber Napper's Hole. Near Gravesend; said to be named after a freebooter; but more likely the Celtic *Caerber l'arber* (water-town lower camp).

Clack Dish. A dish or basin with a movable lid. Some two or three centuries ago beggars used to proclaim their want by clacking the lid of a wooden dish.

> Can you think, I get my living by a bell and clack-dish?
> .... How's that?
> Why, begging, sir.
> MIDDLETON: *Family of Love* (1608).

Clam. A bivalve mollusc like an oyster, which burrows in sand or mud. In America especially clams are esteemed as a delicacy. They are gathered only when the tide is out, hence the saying, "Happy as a clam at high tide." The word is also used as slang for the mouth, and for a close-mouthed person.

Close as a clam. Mean, close-fisted; from the difficulty with which a clam is made to open its shell and give up all it has worth having.

Clan. The system whereby the head of the family, or clan, had entire jurisdiction over its members is said to have arisen in Scotland in the early 11th century. The legal power and hereditary jurisdiction of the head of a clan was abolished in 1747, following the '45 rebellion. Nevertheless the heads of certain clans, notably McLeod, still exercise considerable authority over their members and hold punctiliously attended gatherings. The phrase **a gathering of the clans** has been taken into slang use to imply any coming together of like-minded persons, usually for convivial purposes.

Clan-na-Gael, The (klăn nå gāl′). An Irish Fenian organization founded in Philadelphia in 1881, and known in secret as the "United Brotherhood"; its avowed object being to secure "the complete and absolute independence of Ireland from Great Britain, and the complete severance of all political connexion between the two countries, to be effected by unceasing preparation for armed insurrection in Ireland."

Clapboard. From Ger. *klappholz* (*holz*, wood), meaning small pieces of split oak used by coopers for cask staves. In the U.S.A. a roofing board, made thin at one edge and overlapping the next one, a weatherboard.

In England the word was formerly used by coopers in the same way as in Germany, and also for wainscoting.

Clapperclaw. To jangle, to claw or scratch; to abuse, revile; originally meaning to claw with a clapper of some sort.

> Now they are clapper-clawing one another; I'll go look on.—SHAKESPEARE: *Troilus and Cressida*, v. 4.

Clapper-dudgeons. Abram-men (*q.v.*), beggars from birth. The *clapper* is the tongue of a bell, and in cant language the human tongue. *Dudgeon* is the hilt of a dagger; and perhaps the original meaning is one who knocks his *clap dish* (or CLACK DISH, *q.v.*) with a dudgeon.

Clap-trap. Something introduced to win applause; something really worthless, but sure to take with the groundlings. A *trap* to catch applause.

Clare, Order of St. A religious order of women, the second that St. Francis instituted. It was founded in 1212, and took its name from its first abbess, Clara of Assisi. The nuns are called Minoresses and Poor Clares, or Nuns of the order of St. Francis. *See* FRANCISCANS.

Clarenceux King-of-Arms (klăr′ en sū). The second in rank of the three English Kings-of-Arms (*q.v.*) attached to the Heralds' College (*q.v.*). His jurisdiction extends over the counties east, west, and south of the Trent. The name was taken in honour of the Duke of Clarence, third son of Edward III.

Clarendon. The Constitutions of Clarendon. Laws made by a general council of nobles and prelates, held at Clarendon, in Wiltshire, in 1164, to check the power of the Church, and restrain the prerogatives of ecclesiastics. These famous ordinances, sixteen in number, define the limits of the patronage and jurisdiction of the Pope in these realms.

Clarendon type. A bold-faced, condensed type.

Claret. The English name for the red wines of Bordeaux, originally the yellowish or light red wines as distinguished from the white wines. The name—which is not used in France—is the O.Fr. *clairet*, diminutive of *clair*, from Lat. *clarus*, clear. The *colour* receives its name from the *wine*, not vice versa.

Claret cup. A drink made of claret, brandy, lemon, borage, sugar, ice, and carbonated water.

To broach one's claret, or to tap one's claret jug. To give one a bloody nose.

Classics. The best authors. The Romans were divided by Servius into five classes. Any citizen who belonged to the highest class was called *classicus*, all the rest were said to be *infra classem* (unclassed). From this the best authors were termed *classici auctores* (classic authors), *i.e.* authors of the best or first class. The high esteem in which Greek and Latin were held at the revival of letters obtained for these authors the name of classic, emphatically; and when other first-rate works are intended some distinctive name is added, as the English, French, Spanish, etc., classics.

Classic Races. The five chief horse-races in England, all for three-year-olds, are: The One Thousand Guineas, for fillies only, and the Two Thousand Guineas, for fillies and colts, both run at Newmarket. The Oaks, for fillies only, and the Derby, for Fillies and colts, both run at Epsom. The St. Leger, for fillies and colts, run at Doncaster.

Claude Lorraine (*i.e.* of Lorraine). This incorrect form is generally used in English for the name of Claude Gelée (1600-82), the French landscape painter, born at Chamagne, in Lorraine.

Claw. The sharp, hooked nail of bird or beast, or the foot of an animal armed with claws. *To claw* is to lay one's hands upon things; to clutch, to tear or scratch as with claws; formerly it also meant to stroke, to tickle; hence to please, flatter, or praise. Thus *Claw me I will claw thee*, means, "praise me, and I will praise you," or, "scratch my back, and I'll scratch yours."

Laugh when I am merry, and claw no man in his humour.—SHAKESPEARE: *Much Ado*, i, 3.

Claw-backs. Flatterers. Bishop Jewel speaks of "the Pope's claw-backs."

Clay, Feet of. An unexpected flaw in the character of an admired person. The phrase arises from the image in Nebuchadnezzar's dream, (*Daniel* ii, 31, 32) of which the head was of gold, the breast and arms of silver, the belly and thighs of brass, the legs of iron, and the feet of iron and clay.

Claymore. The two-edged sword anciently used by Scottish Highlanders; from Gaelic *claidheamh* (a sword), and *mor* (great).

I've told thee how the Southrons fell
Beneath the broad claymore.
    AYTOUN: *Execution of Montrose*.

Clean. Free from blame or fault.

Create in me a clean heart, O God, and renew a right spirit within me.—*Psalm* li, 10.

Used adverbially, it means entirely, wholly; as, "you have grown clean out of knowledge," *i.e.* wholly beyond recognition.

Contricioun hadde clene forgeten to crye and to wepe.
    PIERS PLOWMAN, xx.

The people . . . passed clean over Jordan.
    Joshua iii, 17.

A clean tongue. Not abusive, not profane, not foul.

Cleanliness is next to godliness. An old saying, quoted by John Wesley (*Sermon* xcii, *On Dress*), Matthew Henry, and others. The origin is said to be found in the writings of Phinehas ben Yair, an ancient Hebrew rabbi.

To clean down. To sweep down, to swill down.

To clean out. To purify, to make tidy. Also, to win another's money till his pocket is quite empty; to impoverish him of everything. De Quincey says that Richard Bentley, after his lawsuit with Dr. Colbatch, "must have been pretty well cleaned out."

To clean up. To wash up, to put in order; to wash oneself.

To have clean hands. To be quite clear of some stated evil. Hence *to keep the hands clean*, not to be involved in wrong-doing; and "clean-handed";—

He that hath clean hands and a pure heart.
    Psalm xxiv, 4.

To live a clean life. To live blameless and undefiled.

To make a clean breast of it. To make a full and unreserved confession.

To show a clean bill of health. *See* BILL.

To show a clean pair of heels. To make one's escape by superior speed, to run away. Here "clean" means free from obstruction.

Clean and unclean animals. Among the ancient Jews (*see Lev.* xi) those animals which chew the cud and part the hoof were clean, and might be eaten. Hares and rabbits could not be eaten because (although they chew the cud) they do not part the hoof. Pigs and camels were unclean, because (although they part the hoof) they do not chew the cud. Birds of prey were accounted unclean. Fish with fins and scales were accounted fit food for man.

According to Pythagoras, who taught the doctrine of the transmigration of the soul, it was lawful for man to eat only those animals into which the human soul never entered, and those into which the human soul did enter were unclean or not fit for human food. This notion existed long before the time of Pythagoras, who learnt it in Egypt.

Clear (verb). **To be quite cleared out.** To have spent all one's money; to have not a farthing left. *Cleared out* means, my purse or pocket is cleared out of money.

To clear away. To remove, to melt away, to disappear.

To clear for action. The same as "to clear the decks." *See below.*

To clear off. To make oneself scarce, to remove oneself or something else.

To clear out. To eject; to empty out, to make tidy.

To clear the air. To remove the clouds, mists, and impurities; figuratively, to remove the misunderstandings or ambiguities of a situation, argument, etc.

To clear the court. To remove all strangers, or persons not officially concerned in the suit.

To clear the decks. To prepare for action by removing everything not required; playfully used of eating everything eatable on the dinner-table, etc.

To clear the dishes. To empty them of their contents.

To clear the land. A nautical phrase meaning to have good sea room.

To clear the room. To remove from it every thing or person not required.

To clear the table. To remove what has been placed on it.

To clear up. To become fine after rain or cloudiness; to make manifest; to elucidate what was obscure; to tidy up.

Clear (the adjective). Used adverbially, *clear* has much the same force as the adverb *clean* (*q.v.*)—wholly, entirely; as, "He is gone clear away," "Clear out of sight."

A clear day. An entire, complete day. "The bonds must be left three clear days for examination," means that they must be left for three days not counting the first or the last.

A clear head. A mind that is capable of understanding things clearly.

A clear statement. A straightforward and intelligible statement.

A clear style (of writing). A lucid method of expressing one's thoughts.

A clear voice. A voice of pure intonation, neither husky, mouthy, nor throaty.

Clear grit. The right spirit, real pluck; also the genuine article, the real thing. Originally a piece of American slang.

In Canadian politics the name *Clear-grits* was given in the early 80s of last century to the Radicals.

Clearing house. The office or house where bankers do their "clearing," that is, the exchanging of bills and cheques and the payment of balances, etc. Also, the house where the business of dividing among the different railway companies the proceeds of traffic passing over several lines for one covering payment was carried through. In London, the bankers' clearing house has been in Lombard Street since 1775. Each bank sends to it daily all the bills and cheques not drawn on its own firm; these are sorted and distributed to their respective houses, and the balance is settled by transfer tickets.

A "clearing banker" is a banker who has the *entrée* of the clearing house.

London has become the clearing-house of the whole world, the place where international debts are exchanged against each other. And something like 5,000 million pounds'-worth of checks and bills pass that clearing yearly.—A. C. PERRY: *Elements of Political Economy*, p. 363.

Cleave. Two quite distinct words, the one meaning to *stick to*, and the other to *part from* or to *part asunder*. A man "shall cleave to his wife" (*Matt.* xix, 5). As one that "cleaveth wood" (*Ps.* cxli, 7). The former is the A.S. *clifian*, to stick to, and the latter is *cleofan*, to split.

Clench and **Clinch.** The latter is a variant of the former, which is the M.E. *clenchen*, from A.S. (*be-*)*clencan*, to hold fast. In many uses the two words are practically synonymous, meaning to grasp firmly, to fasten firmly together, to make firm; but *clench* is used in such phrases as "he clenched his fists," "he clenched his nerves bravely to endure the pain," "to clench one's teeth"; while *clinch* is used in the more material senses, such as to turn the point of a nail in order to make it fast, and also in the phrase "to clinch an argument." In business, "to clinch a deal" is to ratify it, to make it certain.

That was a clincher. That argument was not to be gainsaid; that remark drove the matter home, and fixed it.

Cleopatra (klē ō păt′ rà). (69-30 B.C.). She was Queen of Egypt, being joint ruler with and wife of her brother Ptolemy Dionysius. In 48 B.C. she was ousted from the throne but in 47 was reinstated by Julius Cæsar, who was captivated by her charms. In 41 Mark Antony fell under her spell and repudiated his wife Octavia for her sake. Fighting with Octavian, Mark Antony was defeated at Actium and committed suicide. Cleopatra also killed herself by means of the bite of an asp.

Cleopatra's Needle. The obelisk so called, now in London on the Thames Embankment, was brought there in 1878 from Alexandria, whither it and its fellow (now in Central Park, New York) had been moved from Heliopolis by Augustus about 12 B.C. It has no connexion with Cleopatra, and it has carved on it hieroglyphics that tell of its erection by Thothmes III, a Pharaoh of the 18th dynasty who lived many centuries before her time.

Clergy. Ultimately from Gr. *kleros*, a lot or inheritance, with reference to *Deut.* xviii, 2, and *Acts* i, 17; thus, the men of God's lot or inheritance. In St. Peter's first epistle (ch. v, 3) the Church is called "God's heritage" or lot. In the Old Testament the tribe of Levi is called the "lot or heritage of the Lord."

Benefit of Clergy See BENEFIT.

Clerical Titles. *Clerk.* As in ancient times the clergyman was about the only person who could write and read, the word *clerical*, as used in "clerical error," came to signify an orthographical error. As the respondent in church was able to read, he received the name of *clerk*, and the assistants in writing, etc., are so termed in business. (Lat. *clericus*, a clergyman.)

Curate. One who has the cure of souls. As the cure of the parish used to be virtually entrusted to the clerical stipendiary, the word *curate* was appropriated to this assistant.

Parson. The same word as *person*. As Blackstone says, a parson is "*persona ecclesiæ*, one that hath full rights of the parochial church."

Though we write "parson" differently, yet 'tis but "person"; that is the individual person set apart for the service of such a church, and 'tis in Latin *persona*, and *personatus* is a parsonage. Indeed with the canon lawyers, *personatus* is any dignity or preferment in the church. — SELDEN: *Table-talk.*

Rector. One who has the parsonage and great tithes. The man who rules or guides the parish. (Lat., a ruler.)

Vicar. One who does the "duty" of a parish for the person who receives the tithes. (Lat. *vicarius*, a deputy.) *Incumbents* and *Perpetual Curates* are now termed Vicars.

The French *curé* equals our vicar, and their *vicaire* our curate.

Clerical vestments. *White.* Emblem of purity, worn on all feasts, saints' days, and sacramental occasions.

Red. The colour of blood and of fire, worn on the days of martyrs, and on Whit Sunday, when the Holy Ghost came down like tongues of fire.

Green. Worn only on days which are neither feasts nor fasts.

Purple. The colour of mourning, worn on Advent Sundays, in Lent, and on Ember days.

Black. Worn on Good Friday, and when masses are said for the dead.

Clerkenwell (klark′ én wel). At the holy well in this district the parish clerks of London used to assemble yearly to play some sacred piece.

Client. In ancient Rome a *client* was a plebian under the patronage of a patrician, who was therefore his *patron*. The client performed certain services, and the patron was obliged to protect his life and interests. The word in English means a person who employs the services of a legal adviser to protect his interests.

Climacteric (klī măk′ tér ik). It was once believed by astrologers that the 7th and 9th years, with their multiples, especially the *odd* multiples (21, 27, 35, 45, 49, 63, and 81), were critical points in life; these were called the *Climacteric Years* and were presided over by Saturn, the malevolent planet. 63, which is produced by multiplying 7 and 9 together, was termed the *Grand Climacteric*, which few persons succeeded in out-living.

There are two years, the seventh and the ninth, that commonly bring great changes in a man's life, and great dangers; wherefore 63, that contains both these numbers multiplied together, comes not without heaps of dangers.— *Levinus Lemnius.*

Climax means a *ladder* (Gr.), and is the rhetorical figure in which the sense rises gradually in a series of images, each exceeding its predecessor in force or dignity. Popularly, but erroneously, the word is used to denote the last step in the gradation, the point of highest development.

Clinch, Clincher. *See* CLENCH.

Clinker-built, said of a ship whose planks overlap each other, and are riveted together. The opposite to clinker-built is carvel-built (*q.v.*).

Clio (klī' ō) was one of the nine Muses, the inventress of historical and heroic poetry.

Addison adopted the name as a pseudonym, and many of his papers in the *Spectator* are signed by one of the four letters in this word, probably the initial letters where they were written—of Chelsea, London, Islington, Office. *Cp.* NOTARIKON.

Clipper. A fast sailing-ship; in Smyth's *Sailor's Word Book* (1867) said to be "formerly applied to the sharp-built raking schooners of America, and latterly to Australian passenger-ships."

The name is now applied almost exclusively to a transatlantic flying-boat.

She's a clipper. Said of a stylish or beautiful woman.

Cliquot (klē' kō). A nickname of Frederick William IV of Prussia (1795-1861), so called from his fondness for champagne.

Cloacina (klō a sī' nà). Goddess of sewers. (Lat. *cloaca*, a sewer.)

Then Cloacina, goddess of the tide,
Whose sable streams beneath the city glide,
Indulged the modish flame: the town she roved,
A mortal scavenger she saw, she loved.
GAY: Trivia, ii.

Cloak and Sword Plays. Swashbuckling plays, full of fighting and adventure. The name comes from the Spanish comedies of the 16th century dramatists, Lope de Vega and Calderon—the *Commedia de capa y espada*; but whereas with them it signified merely a drama of domestic intrigue and was named from the rank of the chief characters, in France—and, through French influence, in England—it was applied as above.

Clock. The tale about St. Paul's clock striking thirteen is given in Walcott's *Memorials of Westminster*, and refers to John Hatfield, who died 1770, aged 102. He was a soldier in the reign of William III, and was accused before a court-martial of falling asleep on duty upon Windsor Terrace. In proof of his innocence he asserted that he heard St. Paul's clock strike thirteen, which statement was confirmed by several witnesses.

A strange incident is related concerning the striking of Big Ben. On the morning of Thursday, March 14th, 1861, "the inhabitants of Westminster were roused by repeated strokes of the new great bell, and most persons supposed it was for the death of a member of the royal family. It proved, however, to be due to some derangement of the clock, for at four and five o'clock ten and twelve strokes were struck

instead of the proper number." It was within twenty-four hours of this that the Duchess of Kent (Queen Victoria's mother) was declared by her physicians to be dying, and early on the 16th she was dead.

Clodhopper. A rustic, a farmer's labourer, who hops or walks amongst the clods. Infantry are called "clodhoppers" or "footsloggers," because they have to walk.

Clog Almanac. A primitive almanac or calendar, originally made of a four-square "clog," or log of wood; the sharp edges were divided by notches into three months each, every week being marked by a bigger notch. The faces contained the saints' days, the festivals, the phases of the moon, and so on, sometimes in Runic characters, whence the "clog" was also called a "Runic staff." They are not uncommon, and specimens may be seen in the British Museum, the Bodleian, the Ashmolean, and other places at home and abroad.

Clogs are also wooden shoes.

Cloister. He retired into a cloister, a monastery. Almost all monasteries have a cloister or covered walk, which generally occupies three sides of a quadrangle. Hence *cloistered*, confined, withdrawn from the world in the manner of a recluse:—

I cannot praise a fugitive, and cloistered virtue, unexercised and unbreathed, that never sallies out and sees her adversary, but slinks out of the race where that immortal garland is to be run for, not without dust and heat.—MILTON: *Areopagitica*.

Cloth, The. This word was formerly applied to the customary garb of any trade, and is akin in usage to the word *livery*. About the 17th century it became restricted to the clergy; the clerical office; thus we say "having respect for the cloth."

Cloth-yard. A measure for cloth, differing slightly from the yard of to-day.

Cloth-yard shaft. An arrow a cloth-yard in length.

Clotho. One of the Three Fates in classic mythology. She presided over birth, and drew from her distaff the thread of life; Atropos presided over death and cut the thread of life; and Lachesis spun the fate of life between birth and death. (Gr. *klotho*, to draw thread from a distaff.)

Cloud. A dark spot on the forehead of a horse between the eyes. A white spot is called a star, and an elongated star is a blaze. *See* BLAZE.

Agrippa. He [Antony] has a cloud on his face.
Enobarbus. He were the worse for that were he a horse.
SHAKESPEARE: Antony and Cleopatra, iii, 2.

Every cloud has a silver lining. There is some redeeming brightness in the darkest prospect; "while there is life there is hope."

He is in the clouds. In dreamland; entertaining visionary notions and so having no distinct idea about the matter in question.

He is under a cloud. Under suspicion, in disrepute.

Cloven Foot. To show the cloven foot, *i.e.* to show a knavish intention; a base motive. The allusion is to Satan, represented with the legs and feet of a goat; and, however he might disguise himself, he could never conceal his cloven feet. *See* BAG O' NAILS; CLOOTIE.

Clover. He's in clover. In luck, in prosperous circumstances, in a good situation. The allusion is to cattle feeding in clover fields.

Clown. It is probable that the circus clown, in his baggy costume and whitened face with grotesque red lips and odd little tuft of black hair, is a relic of the devil as he appeared in the medieval miracle plays. He has come to us, with his drolleries and antics, through a succession of fools and jesters. Of the many famous clowns that have amused generations of children and grown-ups, two figures are outstanding— Joseph Grimaldi (1779-1837) and, in recent times, the Swiss Grock (Charles Adrien Wettach). *See* HARLEQUIN.

Club. In England the club has played an important part in social life, especially during the 18th century. John Aubrey (1626-97) says "we now use the word clubbe for a sodality in a taverne." Clubs came into vogue in the reign of Queen Anne, as we see from the *Tatler* and *Spectator*. Some of them were political, such as the "October," the "Saturday," and the "Green Ribbon," at which adherents or opponents of the ministry of the day forgathered. But the social clubs where cultured men could meet and exchange conversation had their parent in Dr. Johnson whose Ivy Lane Club (founded in 1749) and Literary Club (1763) gathered many of the leading men of the day and set a standard for the times. For many years clubs met in taverns and coffee-houses, and it was not until the Regency that they began to occupy their own premises. In the first quarter of the 19th century a great number came into existence, some, such as Watiers, being solely gambling centres. The first ladies' club was the Alexandra (1883) to which no man—not even the Prince of Wales—was allowed admittance. Among the principal London clubs are the following, with their dates of foundation:—

Army and Navy, 1838.	Lansdowne, 1935.
Athenæum, 1824.	Lyceum, 1904.
Bath, 1894.	M.C.C., 1787.
Beefsteak, 1876	Marlborough, 1868.
Boodle's, 1763.	National Liberal, 1882.
Brooks's, 1764.	Reform, 1832.
Carlton, 1832.	Royal Aero, 1901.
Cavalry, 1890.	Royal Automobile, 1897.
Conservative, 1840.	Savage, 1857.
Constitutional, 1883.	Savile, 1868.
Devonshire, 1875.	Thatched House, 1869.
Garrick, 1831.	Travellers, 1819.
Guards, 1813.	Turf, 1868.
Junior Army & Navy, 1911.	United Services, 1815.
Junior Carlton, 1864.	White's, 1693.

In France clubs assumed great political importance at the time of the Revolution. They dated from about 1782. The Club des Cordeliers numbered Danton and Desmoulins among its members. The most famous was the Club des Jacobins. From these two the Mountain party emerged. They disappeared with the coming of the Directory in 1799.

Clue. I have not yet got the clue; to give a clue, *i.e.* a hint. A clue is a ball of thread (A.S. *cleowen*). The only mode of finding the way out of the Cretan labyrinth was by a skein of thread, which, being followed, led the right way.

Clumsy. A Scandinavian word, meaning originally "numbed with cold," and so "awkward," "unhandy." Piers Plowman has "thou clomsest for cold," and Wyclif has with clomsid handis" (*Jer.* xlvii, 3).

Clym of the Clough. A noted archer and outlaw, supposed to have lived shortly before Robin Hood, who, with Adam Bell and William of Cloudesly, forms the subject of one of the ballads in Percy's *Reliques*, the three becoming as famous in the north of England as Robin Hood and Little John in the midland counties. Their place of resort was in Engle-wood Forest, near Carlisle. Clym of the Clough means Clement of the Cliff. He is mentioned in Ben Jonson's *Alchemist* (I, ii, 46).

Clytie. In classical mythology, an ocean nymph, in love with Apollo. Meeting with no return, she was changed into the heliotrope, or sunflower, which, traditionally, still turns to the sun, following him through his daily course.

Cnidian Venus, The. The exquisite statue of Venus by Praxiteles, formerly in her temple at Cnidus. It is known through the antique reproduction now in the Vatican.

Coach. When railways replaced the old forms of road travel in the 30s and 40s of the last century, they took over the old coaching terms familiar to all who travelled about the country.

Carriage, coach, driver, guard, "Right, away!" are all words reminiscent of old coaching days.

It is from this association that a private tutor, or the trainer of an athletic team is coach, for it is his task to get his pupil or team trained as fast as possible.

A slow coach. A dullard, an unprogressive person.

What a dull, old-fashioned chap thou be'st . . . but thou wert always a slow-coach.—MRS. GASKELL: *Cibbie Marsh* (Era 2).

To dine in the coach. In the captain's private room. The *coach* or *couch* of one of the old, large-sized men-of-war was a small apartment near the stern, the floor being formed of the aftmost part of the quarterdeck, and the roof by the poop.

Coal. To blow the coals. To fan dissensions, to excite smouldering animosity into open hostility, as dull coals are blown into a blaze with a pair of bellows.

To call, or **haul, over the coals.** To bring to task for shortcomings; to scold. At one time the Jews were "bled" whenever the kings or barons wanted money; and one very common torture, if they resisted, was to haul them over the coals of a slow fire, to give them a "roasting." In Scott's *Ivanhoe*, Front-de-Bœuf threatens to haul Isaac over the coals.

To carry coals. To be put upon. "Gregory, o' my word, we'll not carry coals"—*i.e.* submit to be "put upon" (*Romeo and Juliet*, i, 1). So in *Every Man out of his Humour*, "Here comes one that will carry coals, *ergo*, will hold my dog." The allusion is to the dirty, laborious occupation of charcoal carriers.

To carry coals to Newcastle. To do what is superfluous; to take something where it is already plentiful. The French say, "*Porter de l'eau à la rivière*" (to carry water to the river).

To heap coals of fire on one's head. To melt down one's animosity by deeds of kindness; to repay bad treatment with good.

If thine enemy be hungry, give him bread to eat; and if he be thirsty, give him water to drink; for thou shalt heap coals of fire upon his head.—*Prov.* xxv, 21, 22.

Coaling, in theatrical slang, means telling phrases and speeches, as, "My part is full of 'coaling lines.'" Possibly from *cole* (*q.v.*), money, such a part being a profitable one.

Coalition Government. A government formed by various parties by mutual consent to waive differences of policy and opinion in face of more serious considerations. Examples are those under Fox and North in 1783, of Whigs and Peelites in 1852, of Conservatives and Liberal-Unionists in 1895. In 1915 H. H. Asquith formed a coalition of Unionists and Liberals to carry through the World War I, and this was re-formed by Lloyd George in 1916, lasting until 1922. In 1931 Ramsay MacDonald formed a National Government to deal with the crisis of the Gold Standard. In 1940 Winston Churchill formed a Coalition Government to carry on the World War II, and this lasted until 1945 when, at the General Election, Labour was returned to power with an overwhelming majority.

Coast, To. To free-wheel down a hill on a bicycle, etc.; to come down the hill without working the pedals, or—of motor-cycles and cars—with the engine cut off. The term was originally American or Canadian, an ice-covered slope down which one slides on a sledge being called a *coast*, and hence the action of sliding being termed *coasting*.

Coasting trade. Trade between ports of the same country carried on by coasting vessels.

The coast is clear. There is no likelihood of interference. It was originally a smuggling term, implying that no coastguards were about.

Coat. Cut your coat according to your cloth. Curtail your expenses to the amount of your income; live within your means. *Si non possis quod velis, velis id quod possis.*

To baste someone's coat. To dust his jacket: to beat him.

To wear the king's coat. To be a soldier.

Turning one's coat for luck. It was an ancient superstition that this was a charm against evil spirits. *See* TURNCOAT.

William found

A means for our deliverance: "Turn your cloaks," Quoth hee, "for Pucke is busy in these oakes." RICHARD CORBETT (1582-1635): *Iter Borealë*.

Coat of Arms. Originally, a surcoat worn by knights over their armour, decorated with devices by which the wearer could be described and recognized; hence the heraldic device of a family. The practice of bearing on the armour or its covering some distinguishing mark is of very ancient date. It was introduced into England by the Crusaders who in the Holy Land were forced to cover their armour with cloth to ward off the fierce sun; at that time its rules and customs were codified, and "heraldry" was brought almost to a science.

Cob. A short-legged, stout variety of horse, rather larger than a pony, from thirteen to nearly fifteen hands high. The word means big, stout. It also meant a tuft or head (from *cop*), hence eminent, large, powerful. The "*cob of* *the county*" is the great boss thereof. **A rich cob** is a plutocrat. Hence also a male, as a cob-swan.

Riding horses run between fifteen and sixteen hands in height, and carriage horses, between sixteen and seventeen hands.

Cobalt. From the Ger. *Kobold*, a gnome, the demon of mines. This metal, from which a deep blue pigment is made, was so called by miners partly because it was thought to be useless and partly because the arsenic and sulphur with which it was found in combination had bad effects both on their health and on the silver ores. Its presence was consequently attributed to the ill offices of the mine demon.

Cobber (Austr.). A friend or companion; possibly from the old Suffolk *to cob*, to form a friendship.

Cobber Kain—Flying Officer E. J. Kain, D.F.C., was the first New Zealand air ace; he was killed on active service in June 1940.

Cobbler. A drink made of wine (sherry), sugar, lemon, and ice. It is sipped up through a straw. *See* COBBLER'S PUNCH.

This wonderful invention, sir, . . . is called cobbler —Sherry cobbler, when you name it long; cobbler when you name it short.—DICKENS: *Martin Chuzzlewit*, xvii.

Cobbler's punch. Gin and water, with a little treacle and vinegar.

Cobbler's toast. Schoolboys' bread and butter, toasted on the dry side and eaten hot.

Cobweb. The net spun by a spider to catch its prey. *Cob*, or *cop*, is an old word for a spider, so called from its round, stubby body; it is found in the A.S. *attorcoppa*, poisonous spider.

Cochineal (koch' i nēl). A red dye used for colouring materials and also food. It is made from the insect of the same name, which acquires its colour from feeding on the cactus. Cochineal was brought to Europe by the Spaniards, soon after the conquest of Mexico, in 1518.

Cock (noun). In classical mythology the cock was dedicated to Apollo, the sun-god, because it gives notice of the rising of the sun. It was dedicated to Mercury, because it summons men to business by its crowing. And to Æsculapius, because "early to bed and early to rise, makes a man healthy."

According to Mohammedan legend the Prophet found in the first heaven a cock of such enormous size that its crest touched the second heaven. The crowing of this celestial bird arouses every living creature from sleep except man. The Moslem doctors say that Allah lends a willing ear to him who reads the Koran, to him who prays for pardon, and to the cock whose chant is divine melody. When this cock ceases to crow, the day of judgment will be at hand.

Peter Le Neve affirms that a cock was the warlike ensign of the Goths, and therefore used in Gothic churches for ornament.

The weathercock is a very old symbol of vigilance. From its position at the top of steeple or tower it can be seen far and wide. As the cock heralds the coming day, so does the weathercock tell the wise man what the weather will likely be.

A cock and bull story. A long, rambling, idle, or incredible yarn; a canard. There are various so-called explanations of the origin of the term, but the most likely is that it is connected with the old fables in which cocks, bulls, and other animals discoursed in human language on things in general. In Bentley's *Boyle Lecture* (1692) occurs the passage:—

That cocks and bulls might discourse, and hinds and panthers hold conferences about religion.

The "hind and panther" allusion is an obvious reference to Dryden's poem (published five years before), and it is possible that the "cocks and bulls" would have had some meaning that was as well known to contemporaries but has been long since forgotten. See also the closing chapter of Sterne's *Tristram Shandy*; the last words in the book are:—

L—d! said my mother, what is all this story about? —A COCK and a BULL, said *Yorick*—And one of the best of its kind, I ever heard.

The French equivalents are *faire un coq à l'âne* and *un conte de ma mère l'oie* (a mother goose tale), and it is worth noting that in Scotland a satire or lampoon and also a rambling, disconnected story used to be called a *cockalane*, direct from the Fr. *coq à l'âne*.

A cock of hay or haycock. A small heap of hay thrown up temporarily. (Ger. *kocke*, a heap of hay; Norw. *kok*, a heap.)

Cock of the walk. The dominant bully or master spirit. The place where barndoor fowls are fed is *the walk*, and if there is more than one cock, they will fight for the supremacy of this domain.

Every cock crows on its own dunghill, or **Ilka cock crows on its ain midden.** It is easy to brag of your deeds in your own castle when safe from danger and not likely to be put to the proof.

Nourish a cock, but offer it not in sacrifice. This is the eighteenth Symbolic Saying in the Protreptics of Iamblichus. The cock was sacred to Minerva, and also to the sun and moon, and it would be impious to offer a sacrilegious offering to the gods. What is already consecrated to God cannot be employed in sacrifice.

The red cock will crow in his house. His house will be set on fire.

"We'll see if the red cock craw not in his bonnie barnyard ae morning." "What does she mean?" said Mannering. . . . "Fire-raising," answered the . . . dominie. — SCOTT: *Guy Mannering*, ch. iii.

To cry cock. To claim the victory; to assert oneself to be the superior. As a "cock of the walk" (*q.v.*) is the chief or ruler of the whole walk, so to cry cock is to claim this cockship.

Cock-crow. The Hebrews divided the night into four watches: (1) The "beginning of the watches" or "even" (*Lam.* ii, 19); (2) "The middle watch" or "midnight" (*Judges* vii, 19); (3) "The cock-crowing"; (4) "The morning watch" or "dawning" (*Exod.* xiv, 24).

Ye know not when the master of the house cometh, at even, or at midnight, or at the cock-crowing, or in the morning.—*Mark* xiii, 35.

The Romans divided the day into sixteen parts, each one hour and a half, beginning at midnight. The third of these divisions (3 a.m.) they called *gallicinium*, the time when cocks begin to crow; the next was *conticinium*, when they ceased to crow; and fifth was *diluculum*, dawn.

If the Romans sounded the hour on a trumpet three times it would explain the diversity of the Gospels: "Before the cock crow" (*John* xiii, 38, *Luke* xxii, 34, and *Matt.* xxvi, 34); but "Before the cock crow *twice*" (*Mark* xiv, 30)—that is, before the trumpet has finished sounding.

Cock-eye. A squint. Cock-eyed, having a squint; cross-eyed. There seems to be no connexion between this and the Irish and Gaelic *caog*, a squint; it may mean that such an eye has to be *cocked*, as the trigger of a gun is cocked, before it can do its work effectively; or it may be from the verb *to cock* in the sense of "turning up"—as in *to cock the nose*.

Cock-eyed is also slang for nonsensical.

Cock-fighting was introduced into Britain by the Romans. It was a favourite sport both with the Greeks and with the Romans.

In the 12th century it was the sport of schoolboys on Shrove Tuesday. The cockpit at Whitehall was added by Henry VIII, and the "royal diversion," as it was called, was very popular with James I and Charles II. Cock-fighting was made illegal in Britain in 1849; it continued in New York until the 1870s.

That beats cock-fighting. That is most improbable and extraordinary. The allusion is to the extravagant tales told of fighting-cocks.

That cock won't fight. That dodge won't answer; that tale won't wash. The allusion is to a bet being made on a favourite cock, which, when pitted, refuses to fight.

To live like fighting-cocks. To live in luxury. Fighting-cocks used to be high fed in order to aggravate their pugnacity and increase their powers of endurance.

Cock-horse. To ride a cock-horse. A cockhorse is really a hobby-horse, but the phrase means to sit astride a person's foot or knee while he jogs it up and down.

Cock Lane Ghost. A tale of terror without truth; an imaginary tale of horrors. In Cock Lane, Smithfield (1762), certain knockings were heard, which Mr. Parsons, the owner, declared proceeded from the ghost of Fanny Kent, who died suddenly, and Parsons wished people to suppose that she had been murdered by her husband. All London was agog with this story. Royalty and the nobility made up parties to go to Cock Lane to hear the ghost; Dr. Johnson and other men of learning and repute investigated the alleged phenomena; but in the end it was found that the knockings were produced by Parsons's daughter (a girl twelve years of age) rapping on a board which she took into her bed. Parsons was condemned to stand in the pillory. *Cp.* STOCKWELL GHOST.

Cock-pit. The arena in which game-cocks were set to fight; also the name of a 17th-century theatre built about 1618 on the site of a cock-pit in Drury Lane; and of that of the after part of the orlop deck of an old man-of-war, formerly used as quarters for the junior officers and as a sick-bay in time of war.

Captain Hardy, some fifty minutes after he had left the cock-pit, returned; and, again taking the hand of his dying friend and commander, congratulated him on having gained a complete victory.—SOUTHEY: *Life of Nelson*, ch. ix.

In aeroplanes the space where the pilot sits is called the cockpit.

The judicial committee of the Privy Council was also so called, because the council-room is built on the old cock-pit of Whitehall palace.

Great consultations at the cockpit about battles, duels, victories, and what not.—*Poor Robin's Almanack*, 1730.

Cockshut, or **Cockshut time.** Twilight; the time when the *cockshut, i.e.* a large net employed to catch woodcocks, used to be spread. The net was so called from being used in a glade through which the woodcocks might *shoot* or dart.

Let me never draw a sword again,
Nor prosper in the twilight, cockshut light
When I would fleece the wealthy passenger . . .
If I, the next time that I meet the slave,
Cut not the nose from off the coward's face.
        Arden of Feversham, iii, 2 (1592).

See also Shakespeare's *Richard III*, v. 3.

Cockshy. A free fling or "shy" at something. The allusion is to the once popular Shrove-Tuesday sport of shying or casting stones or sticks at cocks.

The phrase became popular in military circles during the World War II to imply an ill-considered, ill-prepared attempt at something.

Cock sure. As sure as a cock: meaning either "with all the assurance (brazen-faced impudence) of a game-cock," or "as sure as the cock is to crow in the morning," or even "with the security and certainty of the action of a cock, or tap, in preventing the waste of liquor."

Shakespeare employs the phrase in the sense of "sure as the cock of a firelock."

We steal as in a castle, cock-sure. — 1 *Henry IV*, ii, 1.

And the phrase "Sure as a gun" seems to favour the latter explanation.

Cock (verb). In the following phrases, all of which connote assertiveness, obtrusiveness, or aggressiveness in some degree, the allusion is to game-cocks, whose strutting about, swaggering, and ostentatious pugnacity is proverbial.

To cock the ears. To prick up the ears, or turn them as a horse does when he listens to a strange sound.

To cock your eye. To shut one eye and look with the other in a somewhat impertinent manner; to glance at questioningly. *Cp.* COCK-EYE.

Cocked hat. A hat with the brim turned, like that of a bishop, dean, etc. It is also applied to the *chapeau bras* (*q.v.*) and the military full-dress hat, pointed before and behind, and rising to a point at the crown, the *chapeau à cornes*. "Cock" in this phrase means to turn; *cocked*, turned up.

Knocked into a cocked hat. In the game of ninepins, three pins were set up in the form of a triangle, and when all the pins except these three were knocked down, the set was technically said to be "knocked into a cocked hat." In modern colloquial usage, to knock someone into a cocked hat is to beat him in a contest of skill, etc.

Cockade. A badge worn on the head-dress of menservants of Royalty and of those holding His Majesty's commission, such as naval and military officers, diplomatists, lord-lieutenants, high sheriffs, etc. The English cockade is black and circular in shape with a projecting fan at the top, except for naval officers, for whom the shape is oval without the fan. This form of cockade was introduced from Hanover by George I; under Charles I the cockade had been scarlet, but Charles II changed it to white, and thus the *white cockade* became the badge of the Pretenders, William III adopting an orange cockade (as Prince of Orange). From Fr. *cocarde*, a plume, rosette, or bunch of ribbons, originally worn by Croatian soldiers serving in the French army, and used to fix the flaps of the hat in a cocked position.

To mount the cockade. To become a soldier.

Cockaigne, Land of (kok ān′). An imaginary land of idleness and luxury, famous in mediæval story, and the subject of more than one poem, one of which, an early translation of a 13th-century French work, is given in Ellis's *Specimens of Early English Poets*. In this "the houses were made of barley sugar and cakes, the streets were paved with pastry, and the shops supplied goods for nothing."

London has been so called (*see* COCKNEY), but Boileau applies the name to Paris.

Allied to the Ger. *kuchen*, a cake. Scotland is called the "land of cakes."

Cockatoo. Old Australian slang for a convict serving his sentence on Cockatoo Island, Sydney, which began to be used for that purpose in 1839. Also used of small farmers in Australia who were described as "just picking up the grains of a livelihood like cockatoos do maize."

Cockatrice. A fabulous and heraldic monster with the wings of a fowl, tail of a dragon, and head of a cock. So called because it was said to be produced from a cock's egg hatched by a serpent. According to legend, the very look of this monster would cause instant death. In consequence of the *crest* with which the head is crowned, the creature is called a basilisk (*q.v.*). Isaiah says, "The weaned child shall put his hand on the cockatrice' den" (xi, 8), to signify that the most obnoxious animal should not hurt the most feeble of God's creatures.

Figuratively, it means an insidious, treacherous person bent on mischief.

They will kill one another by the look, like cockatrices. —SHAKESPEARE: *Twelfth Night*, iii, 4.

Cockle. A bivalve mollusc, the shell of which was worn by pilgrims in their hats (*see* COCKLE HAT). The polished side of the shell was scratched with some crude drawing of the Virgin, the Crucifixion, or some other subject connected with the pilgrimage. Being blessed by the priest, the shells were considered amulets against spiritual foes, and might be used as drinking vessels.

To warm the cockles of one's heart. Said of anything that pleases one immensely and gives one a gratifying sensation, such as does a glass of really good port. (Lat. *cochleæ cordis*, the ventricles of the heart.)

Cockney. This is the M.E. *cokeney*, meaning "a cock's egg" (*-ey* = A.S. *æg*, an egg), *i.e.* a small egg with no yolk that is occasionally laid by hens; hence applied originally to a foolish, spoilt, cockered child:—

I made thee a wanton and thou hast made me a fool, I brought thee up like a cockney and thou hast handled me like a cock's-comb, I made more of thee than became a father and thou less of me than beseemed a child.
LYLY: *Euphues* (1578).

From this the word came to signify a foolish or effeminate person; hence, by the country-dwellers—the majority of the population—it was applied to townsmen generally, and finally became restricted to its present meaning, one born within sound of Bow Bells, London; one possessing London peculiarities of speech, etc.; one who, hence, is—or is supposed to be—wholly ignorant of country sports, country life, farm animals, plants, and so on.

As Frenchmen love to be bold, Flemings to be drunk. Welchmen to be called Britons, and Irishmen to be costermongers; so cockneys, especially she cockneys, love not aqua-vitæ when 'tis good for them.—DEKKER and WEBSTER: *Westward Hoe*, ii, 2, (1607).

Shakespeare uses the word for a squeamish woman:—

Cry to it, nuncle, as the cockney did to the eels, when she put them into the paste alive.—*King Lear*, ii, 4.

Cocktail. An aperitif, or short drink taken before a meal, concocted of spirits (usually gin), bitters, flavouring, etc. There are many varieties of cocktail, most of them of U.S.A. origin. Champagne cocktail is champagne flavoured with Angostura bitters and brandy; soda cocktail is soda-water, sugar, and bitters.

Did ye iver try a brandy cocktail, Cornel?—THACKERAY: *The Newcomes*, xiii.

Cocky. Bumptious, overbearing, conceited, and dogmatic; like a little bantam cock.

Coconut. Milk in the coconut. *See* MILK.

Cocqcigrues. At the coming of the Cocqci-grues. More correctly Coquecigrues (kok' sē groo). These are fabulous animals of French legend, and they have now become labels for an idle story. In French the above phrase—*à la venue des coquecigrues* is equivalent to saying Never.

"That is one of the seven things," said the fairy Bedonebyasyoudid, "I am forbidden to tell till the coming of the Cocqcigrues."—C. KINGSLEY: *The Water Babies*, ch. vi.

Cocytus (ko sī' tŭs). One of the five rivers of hell. The word means the "river of lamentation." The unburied were doomed to wander about its banks for 100 years. It flows into the river Acheron.

Cocytus, named of lamentation loud
Heard on the rueful stream.
MILTON: *Paradise Lost*, ii, 579.

Codger. A familiar and somewhat disrespectful term applied to an elderly man, generally one with some minor eccentricities. Originally a mean, stingy old chap: probably a variant of *cadger* (*q.v.*).

Cœur de Lion (kĕr de lē' on). Richard I of England; called the lion-hearted from the prodigies of personal valour performed by him in the Holy Land. (1157, 1189-99.)

The traditional stage pronunciation of this is kôr de lī' on.

Coffee. The Turkish word is *qahwah*, which is pronounced *kahveh* and is applied to the infusion only, not to the plant or its berries.

Coffee was introduced into England in 1641; the first coffee-house in this country was opened at Oxford in 1650, and the first in London dates from the following year.

It was an old custom in the Ardennes to take ten cups of coffee after dinner, and each cup had its special name. (1) Café, (2) Gloria, (3) Pousse Café, (4) Goutte, (5) Regoutte, (6) Surgoutte, (7) Rincette, (8) Re-rincette, (9) Sur-rincette, and (10) Coup de l'étrier.

Gloria is coffee with a small glass of brandy in lieu of milk; those following it have an ever-increasing quantity of alcohol; and the last is the "stirrup cup."

Pousse café is now a common term for a liqueur after coffee.

Coffin. A raised crust, like the lid of a basket. Hence Shakespeare speaks of a "custard coffin" (*Taming of the Shrew*, iv, 3). (Gr. *kophinos*, a basket.)

Of the paste a coffin will I rear.
SHAKESPEARE: *Titus Andronicus*, v. 2.

To drive a nail into one's coffin. To do anything that would tend to cut short one's life; to put a spoke in one's wheel.

Care to our coffin adds a nail, no doubt;
But every grin so merry draws one out.
PETER PINDAR: *Expostulatory Odes*, xv.

Cogito, ergo sum. The axiom formulated by Descartes (1596-1650) as the starting-place of his system of philosophy: it means "I think, therefore I am." Descartes, at the beginning, provisionally doubted everything, but he could not doubt the existence of the *ego*, for the mere fact that I doubt presupposes the existence of the I; in other words, the *doubt* could not exist without the I to doubt.

He [Descartes] stopped at the famous formula, "I think, therefore I am." Yet a little consideration will show this formula to be full of snares and verbal entanglements. In the first place, the "therefore" has no business there. The "I am" is assumed in the "I think," which is simply another way of saying "I am thinking."

And, in the second place, "I think" is not one simple proposition, but three distinct assertions rolled into one. The first of these is "something called I exists"; the second is, "something called thought exists"; and the third is, "the thought is the result of the action of the I."

Now, it will be obvious to you, that the only one of these three propositions which can stand the Cartesian test of certainty is the second.—HUXLEY: *Descartes' Discourse on Method.*

Coin. Paid in his own coin. Tit for tat.

To coin money. To make money with rapidity and ease.

See ANGEL, BAWBEE, CAROLUS, CROSS AND PILE, CROWN, DOLLAR, FARTHING, FLORIN, GROAT, GUINEA, MANCUS, PENNY, PIECES OF EIGHT, SHILLING, SOVEREIGN, etc.

Colcannon (kŏl kăn' ŏn). Potatoes and cabbage pounded together and then fried in butter (Irish). "Col" is cole or cale, *i.e.* cabbage.

About 1774 Isaac Sparks, the Irish comedian, founded in Long Acre a Colcannon Club.—*The Athenæum*, January 20th, 1875.

Cold. Done in cold blood. (Fr. *sang froid.*) Not in the heat of temper; deliberately, and with premeditation. The allusion is to the ancient notion that the blood grew hot and cold, and this difference of temperature ruled the temper.

Cold-blooded animals. As a rule, all invertebrate animals, and all fishes and reptiles, are cold-blooded, the temperature of their blood being about equal to the medium in which they live.

To have cold feet is to be timorous or cowardly. An expression originating in the U.S.A. in the 1890s.

To show or **give one the cold shoulder** is to assume a distant manner towards a person, to indicate that you wish to cut him.

Cold war. The term applied to the state of tension between two countries when all the elements of war are present without a recourse to actual fighting.

Coldbrand. *See* COLBRONDE.

Cole. An old canting term for money. *Cp.* COALING.

My lusty rustic, learn and be instructed. Cole is, in the language of the witty, money; the *ready*, the *rhino*.—SHADWELL: *Squire of Alsatia*, IV, xvi (1688).

To post or **tip the cole.** To pay or put down the cash.

If he don't tip the cole without more ado, give him a taste of the pump, that's all.—HARRISON AINSWORTH: *Jack Sheppard.*

Cole, King. A legendary British king, described in the nursery rhyme as "a merry old soul" fond of his pipe, fond of his glass, and fond of his "fiddlers three." Robert of Gloucester says he was father of St. Helena (and consequently grandfather of the Emperor

Constantine); and Colchester has been said to have been named after him, though it is more probable that the town is named from Lat. *colonia.*

Colettines. *See* FRANCISCANS.

Coliseum. *See* COLOSSEUM.

Collar. Against the collar. Somewhat fatiguing. When a horse travels uphill the collar distresses his neck, so foot travellers often find the last mile or so "against the collar," or distressing.

In collar. In harness. The allusion is to a horse's collar, which is put on when about to go to work.

Out of collar. Out of work, out of a place.

To collar. To seize (a person) by the collar; to steal; to appropriate without leave; to acquire (of possessions).

To collar the cole. To steal the money. *See* COLE.

To slip the collar. To escape from restraint; to draw back from a task begun.

To work up to the collar. To work tooth and nail; not to shirk the work in hand. A horse that lets his collar lie loose on his neck without bearing on it does not draw the vehicle at all, but leaves another to do the real work.

Collectivism. The opposite of Individualism. A system in which the government would be the sole employer, the sole landlord, and the sole paymaster. Private property would be abolished, the land, mines, railways, etc., would be nationalized; everyone would be obliged to work for his living, and the State obliged to find the work.

College. The Lat. *collegium*, meaning colleagueship or partnership, hence a body of colleagues, a fraternity. In English the word has a very wide range, as, College of the Apostles, College of Physicians, College of Surgeons, Heralds' College, College of Justice, etc.; and on the Continent we have College of Foreign Affairs, College of War, College of Cardinals, etc.

In old slang a prison was known as a *college*, and the prisoners as *collegiates*. Newgate was "New College," and *to take one's final at New College* was to be hanged. The King's Bench Prison was "King's College," and so on.

Collins (kol' inz). A word sometimes applied to the "bread-and-butter letter" one writes after staying at another person's house. In *Pride and Prejudice* Mr. Collins appears as a bore and snob of the first water; after a protracted and unwanted visit at the Bennetts' his parting words are: "Depend upon it, you will speedily receive from me a letter of thanks for this as well as for every other mark of your regard during my stay in Hertfordshire."

Tom Collins. *See* TOM.

Cologne (ko lōn). **The three kings of Cologne.** The three Wise Men of the East, the Magi (*q.v.*), Caspar, Melchior, and Balthazar, whose bones, according to mediæval legend, were deposited in Cologne Cathedral.

Eau de Cologne. *See* EAU DE COLOGNE.

Colombier. A standard size of drawing and plate papers measuring $23\frac{1}{2}$ by $34\frac{1}{2}$ inches. The name is derived from an ancient watermark of a dove (Fr. *colombe*), the emblem of the Holy Ghost.

Colonel. Regiments in the British Army have two Colonels: (i) Honorary Colonel, a courtesy title accepted by a member of the Royal Family, elder statesman or member of the peerage associated with the territory from which the regiment is raised; (ii) Colonel, a senior officer, usually of General rank, who has served in the Regiment, and who becomes its titular head and its spokesman *vis-à-vis* the War Office. The commanding officer of a battalion is a lieutenant-colonel.

Colonnade. The. *See* CYNIC TUB.

Colophon. The statement containing information about the date, place, printer, and edition which, in the early days of printing, was given at the end of the book but which now appears on the title page. From Gr. *kolophon*, the top or summit, a word which, according to Strabo, is from Colophon, a city of Ionia, the inhabitants of which were such excellent horsemen that they would turn the scale of battle to the side on which they fought; hence *To add a colophon* means "to supply the finishing stroke."

The volume was uninjured . . . from title-page to colophon.—SCOTT: *The Antiquary*.

The term is now loosely applied to a printer's or publisher's house device.

Colorado (U.S.A.). The river (and hence the State) was so named by the Spanish explorers from its *coloured* (*i.e.* reddish) appearance.

Colorado beetle. This beetle, which is the terror of the potato-grower, for it will devastate whole fields, was first observed in the Rocky Mountain regions in 1859. It has since spread over large areas of America and has made its way at times into Europe, despite the most stringent precautions taken by the governments of the countries threatened.

Colosseum (kol o sē' ŭm). The great Flavian amphitheatre of ancient Rome, said to be so named from the colossal statue of Nero that stood close by in the Via Sacra. It was begun by Vespasian in A.D. 72, and for 400 years was the scene of the gladiatorial contests. The ruins remaining are still colossal and extensive, but quite two-thirds of the original building have been taken away at different times and used for building material.

Byron, adapting the exclamation of the 8th-century pilgrims (and adopting a bad spelling), says:—

> While stands the Coliseum, Rome shall stand:
> When falls the Coliseum, Rome shall fall;
> And when Rome falls—the world.
> *Childe Harold*, IV, cxlv.

The name has since been applied to other amphitheatres and places of amusement. *Cp.* PALLADIUM.

Colossus or **Colossos** (ko los' ŭs) (Lat. and Gr. for a gigantic statue). The Colossus of Rhodes, completed probably about 280 B.C., was a representation of the sun-god, Helios, and commemorated the successful defence of Rhodes against Demetrius Poliorcetes in 304 B.C. It was one of the Seven Wonders of the World; it stood 105 ft. high, and is said to have been made by the Rhodian sculptor Chares, a pupil of Lysippus from the warlike engines abandoned by Demetrius. The story that it was built striding across the harbour and that ships could pass full sail, between its legs, rose in the 16th century, and has nothing to support it; neither Strabo nor Pliny makes mention of it, though both describe the statue minutely. Tickell out-Herods Herod in the following lines:—

> So, near proud Rhodes, across the raging flood,
> Stupendous form! the vast Colossus stood,
> While at one foot the thronging galleys ride,
> A whole hour's sail scarce reached the further side;
> Betwixt his brazen thighs, in loose array,
> Ten thousand streamers on the billows play.
> *On the Prospect of Peace.*

> He doth bestride the narrow world
> Like a Colossus.
> SHAKESPEARE: *Julius Cæsar*, i, 2.

Colour. PHRASES.

I should like to see the colour of your money. I should like to have some proof that you have any; I should like to receive payment.

Off colour. Not up to the mark; run down; seedy; tainted.

To change colour. To blush; especially to look awkward and perplexed when found out in some deceit or meanness.

To come off with flying colours. To be completely triumphant, to win "hands down." The allusion is to a victorious fleet sailing into port with all the flags flying at the mastheads.

To come out in one's true colours. To reveal one's proper character, divested of all that is meretricious.

To describe (a matter) in very black colours. To see it with a jaundiced eye, and describe it accordingly; to describe it under the bias of strong prejudice.

To desert one's colours. To become a turncoat; to turn tail. The allusion is to the military flag.

To get one's colours. To be rewarded for athletic achievement by the privilege of wearing some special garment, (as cap and blazer in cricket) decorated with or composed of one's school or college colours. *See* CAPPED, FLANNELS.

To paint in bright or **lively colours.** To see or describe things in *couleur de rose*.

To put a false colour on a matter. To misinterpret it, or put a false construction on it.

To sail under false colours. To act hypocritically; to try to attain your object by appearing to be other than you are. The term is a nautical one, and refers to the practice of pirates approaching their unsuspecting prey with false colours at the mast.

To see things in their true colours. To see them as they really are.

Under colour of. Under pretence of; under the alleged authority of.

Wearing his colours. Taking his part; being strongly attached to him. The idea is from livery.

With colours nailed to the mast. Holding out to the bitter end. If the colours are nailed to the mast they cannot be lowered in sign of defeat or submission.

With the colours. Said of a soldier who is on the active strength of a regiment, as opposed to one in the reserve.

Colours. TECHNICAL TERMS.

Complementary colours. Colours which, in combination, produce white light. The colour transmitted is always complementary to the one reflected.

Fast colours. Colours which do not wash out in water.

Fundamental colours. The seven colours of the spectrum: Violet, indigo, blue, green, yellow, orange, and red.

Primary, or **simple colours.** Colours which cannot be produced by mixing other colours. Those generally accepted as primary are red, yellow, and blue, but violet is sometimes substituted for the last named.

Secondary colours. Those which result from the mixture of two or more primary colours, such as orange, green, and purple.

Regimental colours. The flags peculiar to Regiments, once carried into battle, on which they are entitled to embroider their battle-honours— the names of actions in which they distinguished themselves, and associated with the unit by permission of the King. These flags are now laid up on the outbreak of war in the Cathedral or great church of the territory from which the Regiment is raised. The Royal Regiment of Artillery has no colours, regarding its guns with special veneration instead (to allow one's guns to be captured by the enemy being the same disgrace as having one's colours captured). The Regimental colours of Napoleon's Army were the famous eagle standards, copied from the eagles of the Roman legions; the capture of a Napoleonic eagle was such an unusual feat that Regiments which did so (such as the Scots Greys) usually incorporated the eagle into their Regimental device.

Colours. IN SYMBOLISM, ECCLESIASTICAL USE, etc.

Black:
In *blazonry*, sable, signifying prudence, wisdom, and constancy; it is engraved by perpendicular and horizontal lines crossing each other at right angles.
In *art*, signifying evil, falsehood, and error.
In *Church decoration* it is used for Good Friday.
As *a mortuary colour*, signifying grief, despair, death. (In the Catholic Church violet may be substituted for black).
In *metals* it is represented by lead.
In *precious stones* it is represented by the diamond.
In *planets* it stands for Saturn.

Blue:
Hope, love of divine works; (in dresses) divine contemplation, piety, sincerity.
In *blazonry*, azure, signifying chastity, loyalty, fidelity; it is engraved by horizontal lines.
In *art* (as an angel's robe) it signifies fidelity and faith; (as the robe of the Virgin Mary), modesty and (in the Catholic Church) humility and expiation.
In *Church decoration*, blue and green were used indifferently for ordinary Sundays in the pre-Reformation Church.
As *a mortuary colour* it signifies eternity (applied to Deity), immortality (applied to man).
In *metals* it is represented by tin.
In *precious stones* it is represented by sapphire.
In *planets* it stands for Jupiter.

Pale Blue:
Peace, Christian prudence, love of good works, a serene conscience.

Green:
Faith, gladness, immortality, the resurrection of the just; (in dresses) the gladness of the faithful.
In *blazonry*, vert, signifying love, joy, abundance; it is engraved from left to right.

In art, signifying hope, joy, youth, spring (among the Greeks and Moors it signifies victory).

In Church decoration it signifies God's bounty, mirth, gladness, the resurrection; used for weekdays and Sundays after Trinity.

In metals it is represented by copper.

In precious stones it is represented by the emerald.

In planets it stands for Venus.

Pale Green:

Baptism.

Purple:

Justice, royalty.

In blazonry, purpure, signifying temperance; it is engraved by lines slanting from right to left.

In art. signifying royalty.

In Church decoration it is used for Ash Wednesday and Holy Saturday.

In metals it is represented by quicksilver.

In precious stones it is represented by amethyst.

In planets it stands for Mercury.

Red:

Martyrdom for faith, charity; (in dresses) divine love. Innocent III says of martyrs and apostles, *"Hi et illi sunt flores rosarum et lilia convallium."* (*De Sacr. alto Myst.*, i, 64.)

In blazonry, gules; blood-red is called sanguine. The former signifies magnanimity, and the latter, fortitude; it is engraved by perpendicular lines.

In Church decoration it is used for martyrs and for Whit Sunday.

In metals it is represented by iron (the metal of war).

In precious stones it is represented by the ruby.

In planets it stands for Mars.

White:

In blazonry, argent; signifying purity, truth, innocence; in engravings *argent* is left blank.

In art, priests, Magi, and Druids are arrayed in white. Jesus after the resurrection should be draped in white.

In Church decoration it is used for festivals of Our Lord, for Maundy Thursday, and for all Saints except Martyrs.

As a mortuary colour it indicates hope.

In metals it is represented by silver.

In precious stones it is represented by the pearl.

In planets it stands for Diana or the Moon.

Yellow:

In blazonry, or; signifying faith, constancy, wisdom, glory; in engravings it is shown by dots.

In modern art, signifying jealousy, inconstancy, incontinence. In France the doors of traitors used to be daubed with yellow, and in some countries Jews were obliged to dress in yellow. In Spain the executioner is dressed in red and yellow.

In Christian art Judas is arrayed in yellow; but St. Peter is also arrayed in golden yellow.

In metals it is represented by gold.

In precious stones it is represented by the topaz.

In planets it stands for Apollo or the Sun.

Violet, Brown, or Grey

are used in *Church decoration* for Advent and Lent; and in other symbolism *violet* usually stands for penitence, and *grey* for tribulation.

Colour-blindness. Incapacity of discerning one colour from another. The term was introduced by Sir David Brewster; formerly it was known as *Daltonism*, because it was first

described by John Dalton (1766-1844), the scientist (who himself suffered from it), in 1794. It is of three sorts: (1) inability to discern any colours, so that everything is either black or white, shade or light; (2) inability to distinguish between primary colours, as red, blue, and yellow; or secondary colours, as green, purple, and orange; and (3) inability to distinguish between such composite colours as browns, greys, and neutral tints. Except in this one respect, the colour-blind may have excellent vision.

Colt. A person new to office; an awkward young fellow who needs "breaking in"; specifically, in legal use, a barrister who attended a sergeant-at-law at his induction.

I accompanied the newly made Chief Baron as his colt.—POLLOCK.

In cricket a Colt team is made up of a club's most promising young players.

The word is used as an abbreviation for "Colt's Revolver," patented by Col. Sam Colt (U.S.A.) in 1835; and it is also an old nautical term for a piece of knotted rope 18 inches long for the special benefit of ship boys; a cat-o'-nine- tails.

To colt. Obsolete slang for to befool, gull, cheat.

Harebrain: We are fools, tame fools!
Bellamore: Come, let's go seek him.
He shall be hanged before he colt us so basely.
BEAUMONT and FLETCHER: *Wit Without Money*, iii, 2.

The verb is still used in provincial dialects for making a newcomer pay his footing.

Colt's-tooth. The love of youthful pleasure. Chaucer uses the word "coltish" for skittish, and his Wife of Bath says:—

He was, I trowe, a twenty winter old,
And I was fourty, if I shal seye sooth;
But yet I hadde alwey a coltes tooth.
Prologue: 602.

Horses have colt's teeth at three years old, a period of their life when their passions are strongest.

Well, said, Lord Sands;
Your colt's-tooth is not cast yet.
SHAKESPEARE: *Henry VIII*, i, 3.

Her merry dancing-days are done;
She has a colt's-tooth still, I warrant.
KING: *Orpheus and Eurydice*.

Columbine. A stock character in old Italian comedy, where she first appeared about 1560, and thence transplanted to English pantomime. She was the daughter of Pantaloon (*q.v*), and the sweetheart of Harlequin (*q.v.*), and, like him, was supposed to be invisible to mortal eyes. Columbina in Italian is a pet name for a lady-love, and means dove-like.

Column. The Column of Marcus Aurelius. Erected at Rome in memory of the Emperor Marcus Aurelius Antoninus. Like that of Trajan (*q.v.*), this column is covered externally with spiral bas-reliefs representing the wars carried on by the emperor. It is a Roman Doric column of marble on a square pedestal, and (omitting the statue) is 95 ft. in height.

Sixtus V caused the original statue of this column to be replaced, in 1589 by a figure of St. Paul.

The Column at Boulogne, or The Column of the Grand Army; a marble Doric column, 176 ft. high, surmounted by a bronze statue of Napoleon I, to commemorate the camp of Boulogne, formed 1804-5 with the intention of invading England.

The Duke of York's Column, in London, at the top of the Waterloo Steps leading from Waterloo Place into the Mall. Erected in 1830-3 in memory of Frederick, Duke of York, second son of George III, who died in 1827. It is of the Tuscan order, was designed by R. Wyatt, and is made of Aberdeen granite. It is 124 ft. in height; it contains a winding staircase to the platform, and on the summit is a statue of the duke by Sir R. Westmacott.

Columns, or **Pillars, of Hercules.** *See* PILLAR.

The Column of July. Erected in Paris in 1840, on the spot where the Bastille stood, to commemorate the revolution of July, 1830, when Charles X abdicated. It is a bronze Corinthian column, 13 ft. in diameter, and 154 ft. in height, and is surmounted by a gilded statue of Liberty.

London's Column. *See* MONUMENT.

The Nelson Column. In Trafalgar Square, London; was erected in 1843. The four lions, by Landseer, were added in 1867. It is a Corinthian column of Devonshire granite on a square base, copied from a column in the temple of Mars Ultor (the avenging god of war) at Rome; it stands 145 ft. high, the statue surmounting it (by E. H. Baily, R.A.) being 17 ft. high. The following reliefs in bronze are on the sides of the pedestal:— (*North*) the battle of the Nile, where Nelson was wounded; (*south*) Nelson's death at the battle of Trafalgar; (*east*) the bombardment of Copenhagen; and (*west*) the battle of St. Vincent.

Column of the Place Vendôme. Paris, 1806-10; made of marble encased with bronze, and erected in honour of Napoleon I. The spiral outside represents in bas-relief the battles of Napoleon I, ending with Austerlitz in 1805. It is 142 ft. in height and is an imitation of Trajan's Column. In 1871 the statue of Napoleon, which surmounted it, was hurled to the ground by the Communards, but in 1874 a statue of Liberty was substituted.

Trajan's Column. At Rome; made of marble A.D. 114, by Apollodorus. It is a Roman Doric column of marble, 127½ ft. in height, on a square pedestal, and has inside a spiral staircase of 185 steps lighted by 40 windows. It was surmounted by a statue of the Emperor Trajan, but Sixtus V supplanted the original statue by that of St. Peter. The spiral outside represents in bas-relief the battles of the emperor.

Coma Berenices. *See* BERENICE.

Comazant (kom' à zănt). Another name for Corposant (*q.v.*).

Comb. A crabtree comb. Slang for a cudgel. To smooth your hair with a crabtree comb, is to give the head a knock with a stick.

To comb your noddle with a three-legged stool (*Taming of the Shrew*, i, 1) is to beat you about the head with a stool. Many stools, such as those used by milkmaids, are still made with three legs; and these handy weapons seem to have been used at one time pretty freely, especially by angry women.

Come. A come down. Loss of prestige or position.

Come February, Michaelmas, etc. A colloquialism for "next February," etc.

> Come Lammas-eve at night shall she be fourteen.
>   SHAKESPEARE: *Romeo and Juliet*, i, 3.

Come home. Return to your house; to touch one's feelings or interest.

> I doe now publish my Essayes: which, of all my other workes, have been most currant: for that, as it seems, they come home to men's businesse and bosomes.—BACON: *Epistle Dedicatory to the Essays*, 1625.

Come inside. A humorously scornful remark at one time made to one who was talking nonsense or behaving in a foolish manner. The allusion is to a picture in *Punch* showing a lunatic looking over the wall of an asylum at an angler fishing; and, when he hears that the latter has been there all day without getting a bite and proposes still to remain, the lunatic feelingly invites him to "come inside" to the asylum.

Come out. Said of a young woman after she has been presented at Court, or has entered into society as a "grown up" person. She "comes out into society."

If the worst comes to the worst. *See* WORST.

Marry come up. *See* MARRY.

To come a cropper. *See* CROPPER.

To come down a peg. *See* PEG.

To come down handsome. To pay a good price, reward, subscription, etc.

To come down upon one. To reproach, to punish severely, to make a peremptory demand.

To come it strong. To lay it on thick; to exaggerate or overdo. *See* DRAW IT MILD.

To come off. To occur, to take place, as "my holiday didn't come off after all."

To come off with honours. To proceed to the end successfully.

To come over one. To wheedle one to do or give something; to cheat or overreach one; to conquer or get one's own way.

To come round. *See* COMING.

To come short. Not to be sufficient. "To come short of" means to miss or fail of attaining.

To come the old soldier over one. To attempt to intimidate or bully one by an assumption of authority.

To come to. To amount to, to obtain possession. "It will not come to much." To regain consciousness after a fainting-fit, etc.

To come to blows. To start fighting.

To come to grief, to hand. *See* GRIEF; HAND.

To come to pass. To happen, to befall, to come about.

What thou hast spoken is come to pass.—*Jer.* xxxii, 24.

It came to pass in those days that there went out a decree.—*Luke* ii, 1.

To come to stay. An expression used of something which possesses permanent qualities.

To come to the hammer, the point, the scratch. *See* HAMMER; POINT; SCRATCH.

To come under. To fall under; to be classed under.

To come up smiling. To laugh at discomfiture or punishment; to emerge from disaster unruffled.

To come up to. To equal, to obtain the same number of marks, to amount to the same quantity.

What's to come of it? What's to come of him? A contracted form of *become*.

To come of a good stock is to be descended from a good family.

He is coming round. Recovering from sickness; recovering from a fit of the sulks; returning to friendship; **he is coming round to my way of thinking,** he is beginning to think as I do.

Comedy means a village song (Gr. *komē-ōdē*), referring to the village merry-makings, in which songs still take a conspicuous place. The Greeks had certain festal processions of great licentiousness, held in honour of Dionysus, in the suburbs of their cities, and termed *komoi* or village revels. On these occasions an ode was generally sung, and this ode was the foundation of Greek comedy. *Cp.* TRAGEDY.

The Father of Comedy. Aristophanes (about 450-380 B.C.), the Athenian-dramatist.

Commandment. The ten commandments. A common piece of slang in Elizabethan days for the ten fingers or nails.

Could I come near your beauty with my nails
I'd set my ten commandments in your face.
                SHAKESPEARE: *2 Henry VI*, i, 3.

The eleventh commandment. An ironical expression, signifying "Thou shalt not be found out."

Commando (kŏ man' dō). This word was originally used in the South African War, being the term used by the Boers to designate a mobile body of armed men. In World War II it was used as the name of the volunteer body of special troops trained for hazardous assault tasks. The word has since been again extended to mean a member of such a body, one of a commando.

Comme il faut (kom ēl fō) (Fr.). As it should be; quite proper; quite according to etiquette or rule.

It never can have been *comme il faut* in any age or nation for a man of note . . . to be continually asking for money.—MACAULAY: in Trevelyan's *Life*, vol. ii, ch. xiv.

Commendam (kom en' dăm). **A living in commendam** is a living temporarily held by someone until an incumbent is appointed. The term was specially applied to a bishop who, when accepting the bishopric, had to give up all his preferments, but to whom such preferments were *commended* by the Crown till they could be properly transferred. This practice was abolished by Act of Parliament in 1836.

Commissar (kom' i sar). An official in the U.S.S.R. who has charge of a separate branch of government administration. The Council of People's Commissars is composed of the chairman, his deputy, and people's commissars for Foreign Affairs, Armed Forces, Foreign Trade, Posts, Finance, etc. They are responsible to the Supreme Council of the U.S.S.R.

Committee. A committee of the whole house, in Parliamentary language, is when the Speaker leaves the chair and all the members form a committee, where anyone may speak once or more than once. In such cases the chair is occupied by the Chairman of Committees, elected with each new Parliament.

A **joint committee** is a committee nominated partly by the House of Lords and partly by the House of Commons.

A **standing committee** is a committee which continues to the end of the current session. To this committee are referred all questions which fall within the scope of its appointment.

Commodore. A corruption of "commander" (Fr. *commandeur*; Dut. *kommandeur*). A naval officer ranking above a captain and below a rear-admiral, ranking with brigadier in the army. By courtesy the title is given to the senior captain when two or more ships are in company; also to the president of a yacht club.

In the United States Navy the office has been abolished since 1899, but the title was retained as a retiring rank for captains.

Common. Short for common land, which is public property. A common cannot be enclosed and denied to the use of the public without an Act of Parliament. Until the late 18th and early 19th centuries every village in England had its common lands, divided into strips of which each villager had the use of one or more to cultivate for his own use. When the crops had been taken in from these, the whole area was thrown open for the common grazing of cattle, etc. By various Acts of Parliament these common lands were taken from the villagers and enclosed by larger farmers, etc., only the less fertile portions being left uncultivated and given over to the common grazing purposes of the community. In Scotland an Act of 1695 gave power to divide the common land among the persons who had right thereon.

Common Prayer. The Book of Common Prayer. The book used by the Established Church of England in "divine service." Common, in this case, means *united*, or *general*.

The first complete English Book of Common Prayer (known as the First Prayer-book of Edward VI) appeared in 1549; this was revised in 1552 and 1559; slight alterations were made at the Hampton Court Conference (1604), and it received its final form, except for some very minor changes after the Savoy Conference of 1662.

In 1927 a revised Prayer Book was accepted by the Houses of Convocation and the Church Assembly. It was, however, rejected by the House of Commons on the grounds that the proposed changes weakened the Protestant character of the book.

Common sense. Natural intelligence; good, sound, practical sense; general sagacity. Formerly the expression denoted a supposed internal sense held to be common to all five senses, or one that acted as a bond or connecting medium for them.

Commoner. The Great Commoner. The elder William Pitt (1708-78), afterwards Earl of Chatham.

Commons. To put someone on short commons. To stint him, to give him scanty meals. In the University of Cambridge the food provided for each student at breakfast was called his *commons*; hence food in general or meals.

To come into commons. To enter a society in which the members have a common or general dinner table. To be removed from the society is to be *discommonsed*:—

He [Dryden] was in trouble [at Cambridge] on July 19th, 1652, when he was discommonsed and gated for a fortnight for disobedience and contumacy.— SAINTSBURY: *Dryden*, ch. i.

Commonwealths, Ideal. The most famous ideal, or imaginary, Commonwealths are those sketched by Plato in the *Republic* (from which all the others derive), by Cicero in his *De Republica*, by St. Augustine in his *De Civitate Dei* (*The City of God*), by Dante in his *De Monarchia*, by Sir Thomas More in *Utopia* (1516), by Bacon in the *New Atlantis* (a fragment, 1616), by Campanella, a Dominican friar (about 1630), and by Samuel Butler in *Erewhon* (1872).

To these some would add Johnson's *Rasselas* (1759), Lytton's *Coming Race* (1871), Bellamy's *Looking Backward* (1888), Wm. Morris's *News from Nowhere* (1891), H. G. Wells's *In the Days of the Comet* (1906) and *The World Set Free* (1914).

Communist. An adherent of communism.

Communism means a self-supporting society distinguished by common labour, common property, and common means of intelligence and recreation.—G. J. HOLYOAKE: in *"The Labour World,"* No. 11, 1890.

Companion Ladder. The ladder leading from the poop to the main deck, also the staircase from the deck to a cabin.

Companions of Jehu. The *Chouans* (*q.v.*) were so called, from a fanciful analogy between their self-imposed task and that appointed to Jehu, on being set over the kingdom of Israel. Jehu was to cut off Ahab and Jezebel, with all their house, and all the priests of Baal. The Chouans were to cut off all who assassinated Louis XVI, and see that his brother (*Jehu*) was placed on the throne.

Complex. A combination of memories and wishes which exercise an influence on the personality.

Inferiority complex. A term applied to a supposed feeling of inferiority in persons who appear over-conscious of their own shortcomings.

To have a complex about something. To have a strong feeling either for or against something; to be over-concerned about it.

Compline (kom' plin). The last of the seven R.C. canonical hours, said about 8 or 9 p.m., and so called because it *completes* the series of the daily prayers or hours. From M.E. and O.Fr. *complie*, Lat. *completa* (hora).

In ecclesiastical Lat. *vesperinus*, from *vesper*, means evening service, and *completinus* seems to be formed on the same model.

Comrades. Literally, those who sleep in the same *chamber* (*camera*). It is a Spanish military term derived from the custom of dividing soldiers into chambers, and the early form of the word in English is *camerade*.

Comus (kō' mus). In Milton's masque of this name, the god of sensual pleasure, son of Bacchus and Circe. The name is from the Gr. *komos*, carousal.

In the masque the elder brother is meant for Viscount Brackley, the younger brother is Thomas Egerton, and the lady is Lady Alice Egerton, children of the Earl of Bridgewater, at whose castle in Ludlow it was first presented in 1634.

Con amore (kon a môr' i) (Ital.). With heart and soul; as, "He did it *con amore*"—*i.e.* lovingly, with delight, and therefore in good earnest.

Con spirito (Ital.). With quickness and vivacity. A musical term.

Conan (kō' nan). The Thersites of *Fingal* (in Macpherson's *Ossian*); brave even to rashness.

Blow for blow or **claw for claw, as Conan said.** Conan made a vow never to take a blow without returning it; when he descended into the infernal regions, the arch fiend gave him a cuff, which Conan instantly returned, saying "Claw for claw."

Concert Pitch. The degree of sharpness or flatness adopted by musicians acting in concert, that all the instruments may be in accord. In England "concert pitch" is usually slightly higher than the pitch at which instruments are generally tuned.

Hence the figurative use of the term: **to screw oneself up to concert pitch** is to make oneself absolutely ready, prepared for any emergency or anything one may have to do.

Conchy. *See* CONSCIENTIOUS OBJECTOR.

Concierge (kon' se ârj) (Fr.). The door-porter of a public building, an hotel, or a house divided into flats, etc.

Conciergerie (Fr.). The office or room of a concierge, a porter's lodge; a state prison. During the Revolution it was the prison where the chief victims were confined prior to execution.

Conclave. Literally, a set of rooms, all of which can be opened by one key (Lat. *con clavis*). The word is applied to the little cells erected for the cardinals who meet to choose a new Pope; hence, the assembly of cardinals for this purpose; hence, any private assembly for discussion. The conclave of cardinals dates back to 1271. Some days after the death of a Pope the cardinals assembled in Rome enter the conclave apartments of the Vatican and are there locked in in such stringent seclusion that no contact whatsoever occurs between them and the outside world. Votes are taken morning and evening until one candidate has secured a two-thirds majority of the votes. He is then acclaimed Pope.

Shakespeare used the word for the body of cardinals itself.—

And once more in my arms I bid him [Cardinal Campeius] welcome,
And thank the holy conclave for their loves.
Henry VIII, ii, 2.

Concordat (kon kôr' dăt). An agreement made between a ruler and the Pope; as the Concordat of 1801 between Napoleon and Pius VII; the Concordat of 1516 between François I and Leo X to abolish the "pragmatic sanction"; and the Germanic Concordat of 1448 between Frederick III and Nicholas V. In 1929 a concordat between the Papacy and the Italian government established the Vatican State.

Condominium (con dō min' i ùm). This is a political phrase to describe the joint government or sovereignty of two or more powers over a region or country. An example of this is the condominium of the New Hebrides shared by Britain and France.

Confederate States. The eleven States which seceded from the Union in the American Civil War (1861-66)—viz. Georgia, North and South Carolina, Virginia, Tennessee, Alabama, Louisiana, Arkansas, Mississippi, Florida, Texas. They were all readmitted into the Union between 1866 and 1870.

Confederation of the Rhine. Sixteen German provinces in 1806 dissolved their connexion with Germany, and allied themselves with France. It was dissolved in 1813.

Confession, Seal of. Confession is a collective term for the whole administration of the R.C. sacrament of penance. The priest who bears the penitent's confession is bound under the most binding vows not to divulge anything he hears in the confessional, nor can he be forced to reveal in the witness-box of a court of law any information he may have thus obtained.

Confusion Worse Confounded. Disorder made worse than before.

With ruin upon ruin, rout on rout,
Confusion worse confounded.
MILTON: *Paradise Lost*, ii, line 996.

Congé (kon jā') (Fr., *leave*). "To give a person his congé" is to dismiss him from your service. "To take one's congé" is to give notice to friends of your departure. This is done by leaving a card at the friend's house with the letters P.P.C. (*pour prendre congé*, to take leave) inscribed on the left-hand corner.

Congé d'elire (Fr., leave to elect). A royal warrant given to the dean and chapter of a diocese to elect the person nominated by the Crown to their vacant see.

Congregationalists. Those Protestant Dissenters who maintain that each congregation is an independent community, and has a right to make its own laws and choose its own minister. They derive from the Puritans and Independents of the time of Queen Elizabeth.

Congress (kon' gres). In its particular sense this word is applied to the supreme legislative body of the U.S.A., composed of the Senate and the House of Representatives (96 senators and 435 representatives). Senators are elected for 6 years, representatives for 2 years. The President can veto any legislation passed by Congress, but if it be passed again by a two-thirds majority it becomes law.

The Indian National Congress was founded in 1885, but after various vicissitudes was reformed by Gandhi in 1920 for the purpose of winning the independence of India. This was gained in 1947 with the formation of the Republic of India, and Dominion of Pakistan.

Congreves. Predecessors of Lucifer matches, also invented by Sir Wm. Congreve. The splints were first dipped in sulphur, and then tipped with chlorate of potash paste, in which gum was substituted for sugar, and there was added a small quantity of sulphide of antimony. The match was ignited by being drawn through a fold of sandpaper with pressure. *Cp.* PROMETHEANS; LUCIFERS.

Conjuring Cap. I mast put on my conjuring cap—*i.e.* your question requires deliberate thought, and I must reflect on it. Tradition says that Eric XIV, King of Sweden (1560-77), was a great believer in magic, and had an "enchanted cap" by means of which he pretended to exercise power over the elements. When a storm arose, his subjects used to say "The king has got on his conjuring cap."

Conker (cong' kĕr). This is a children's name for a horse-chestnut, and is possibly derived from the French *conque*,, a shell. Schoolboys thread the chestnuts on a string and then play conkers by each taking his turn at striking his opponent's conker with his own until one or other is destroyed.

Another curious slang use of this word is *conk*, meaning a nose, hence *conky* a big- or beak-nosed person.

The phrase **to conk out,** meaning to break down, to cease to fire (of a motor) is probably onomatopoeic.

Connecticut (kȯ net' i kŭt), is the Mohegan dialect word *Quonaughicut*, meaning "long tidal river."

Conqueror. The title was applied to the following:—

Alexander the Great. *The conqueror of the world*. (356-323 B.C.).

Alfonso I, of Portugal. (About 1109-1185.)

Aurungzebe the Great. The most powerful of the Moguls. (1619, 1659-1707.)

James I of Aragon. (1206, 1213-76.)

Mohammed II, Sultan of Turkey. (1430-81.)

Othman or Osman I. Founder of the Turkish power. (1259, 1299-1326.)

Francisco Pizarro. *Conquistador*. So called because he conquered Peru. (1475-1541.)

William, Duke of Normandy. So called because he obtained England by conquest. (1027, 1066-87.)

Conqueror's nose. A prominent straight nose, rising at the bridge. Charlemagne had such a nose, so had Henry the Fowler (Heinrich I of Germany); Rudolf I of Germany; Friedrich I of Hohenzollern, famous for reducing to order his unruly barons by blowing up their castles (1382-1440); our own "Iron Duke"; Bismarck, the Iron Chancellor of Prussia, etc.

Conquest, The. The accession of William I to the crown of England (1066).

Conscience. Conscience clause. A clause in an Act of Parliament to relieve persons with conscientious scruples from certain requirements in it. It generally has reference to religious matters, but it came into wider prominence in connexion with the Compulsory Vaccination Act of 1898.

Conscience money. Money paid anonymously to Government by persons who have defrauded the revenue, or who have understated their income to the income-tax assessors. The sum is advertised in the *Gazette*.

Have you the conscience to [demand such a price]? Can your conscience allow you to [demand such a price]?

In all conscience. As, "And enough too, in all conscience." Meaning that the demand made is as much as conscience would tolerate without accusing the person of actual dishonesty; to the verge of that fine line which separates honesty from dishonesty.

My conscience! An oath. I swear by my conscience.

To make a matter of conscience of it. To treat it according to the dictates of conscience, to deal with it conscientiously.

To speak one's conscience. To speak one's own mind, give one's own private thoughts or opinions.

By my troth, I will speak my conscience of the king.—SHAKESPEARE: *Henry V*, i, 4.

Conscientious objector. One who takes advantage of a *conscience clause* (*q.v.*), and so does not have to comply with some particular requirement of the law in question. The name used to be applied specially to those who would swear legally that they had a conscientious objection to vaccination.

In the two World Wars the term was applied to those who obtained exemption from military service on grounds of conscience. These were also known as *Conchies* and *C.O.s*.

Conscript Fathers. In Lat. *Patres Conscripti*. The Roman senate. Romulus instituted a senate consisting of a hundred elders, called *Patres* (Fathers). After the Sabines joined the State, another hundred were added. Tarquinius Priscus, the fifth king, added a third hundred, called *Patres Minorum Gentium*. When Tarquinius Superbus, the seventh and last king of Rome, was banished, several of the senate followed him, and the vacancies were filled up by Junius Brutus, the first consul. The new members were enrolled in the senatorial register, and called *Conscripti*; the entire body was then addressed as *Patres* [*et*] *Conscripti* or *Patres, Conscripti*.

Consentes Dii. The twelve chief Roman deities—

Jupiter, Apollo, Mars, Neptune, Mercury, and Vulcan.

Juno, Vesta, Minerva, Ceres, Diana, and Venus.

Ennius puts them into two hexameter verses:—
Juno, Vesta, Minerva, Ceres, Diana, Venus, Mars, Mercurius, Jovi', Neptunus, Vulcanus, Apollo.

Called "*consentes*," says Varro,
Quia in consilium Jovis adhibebantur.—*De Lingua Latina*, vii, 28.

Consenting Stars. Stars forming configurations for good or evil. In *Judges* v, 20, we read that "the stars in their courses fought against Sisera," *i.e.* formed unlucky or malignant configurations.

. . . . Scourge the bad revolting stars
That have consented unto Henry's death.
SHAKESPEARE: 1 *Henry VI*, i, 1.

Conservative. One who wishes to preserve the union of Church and State, and not radically to alter the constitution. The word was first used in this sense in January, 1830, by J. Wilson Croker in the *Quarterly Review*—"We have always been conscientiously attached to what is called the Tory, and which might with more propriety be called the Conservative, party" (p. 276).

Canning, ten years previously, had used the word in much the same way in a speech delivered at Liverpool in March, 1820.

Consistory. An ecclesiastical court. In the Church of Rome it is the assembly in council of the Pope and cardinals; in England it is a diocesan court, presided over by the chancellor of the diocese.

Constable (Lat. *comes-stabuli*) means "Master of the Horse" (with which office, however, it now has no connexion in Britain). *Cp.* MARSHAL. The *Constable of France* was the title of the principal officer of the household of the early Frankish kings, and from being the head groom of the stable he ultimately became commander-in-chief of the army, supreme judge of all military matters and matters pertaining to chivalry, etc. The office was abolished in 1627.

Constable is also a term for the governor of a fortress, as the Constable of the Tower of London.

The Constable of England, or **Lord High Constable,** was a similar official in existence before 1066, but since 1521 the title has been granted only temporarily, for the purposes of Coronations.

The Lord High Constable of Scotland was an office instituted about 1147 by David I. Conferred by Robert Bruce in 1321 on Sir Gilbert Hay, created Earl of Erroll, heritably, in which family the office still remains.

Drink the constable. *See* MOROCCO.

To overrun or **outrun the constable.** To get into debt; to spend more than one's income; to talk about what you do not understand.

Quoth Hudibras, Friend Ralph, thou hast
Outrun the constable at last;

For thou hast fallen on a new
Dispute, as senseless as untrue.
BUTLER: Hudibras, i, 3.

Who's to pay the constable? Who is to pay the score?

Constituent Assembly. The first of the national assemblies of the French Revolution; so called because its chief work was the drawing up of a new constitution for France. It sat from 1788 to 1791.

After the chaos resultant on the World War II a National Constituent Assembly of 522 deputies was elected in France, according to the constitution promulgated in October, 1945.

Constitution. The fundamental laws of a state; the way in which a state is organized or constituted—despotic, aristocratic, democratic, monarchic, oligarchic, etc.

To give a nation a constitution. To give it fixed laws, and to limit the powers of the nominal ruler or head of the state, so that the people are not subject to arbitrary government or caprice. A despotism or autocracy is solely under the unrestricted will of the despot or autocrat.

Apostolic Constitutions. A doctrinal code relating to the Church, the duties of Christians, etc., contained in eight books of doubtful date, possibly as early as the 3rd century, but certainly later than the time of the Apostles, to whom at one time they were attributed.

Consummatum est (kon sŭm' ā tum est) (Lat.). It is finished: the last words of our Lord on the cross (*John* xix, 30).

> *Meph.*: O, what will I not do to obtain his soul?
> *Faust.*: Consummatum est; this bill is ended,
> And Faustus hath bequeathed his soul to Lucifer.
MARLOWE: Doctor Faustus, v, 74.

Contemplate. To meditate or reflect upon; to consider attentively. The word takes us back to the ancient Roman augurs, for the *templum* (whence our *temple*) was that part of the heavens which he wished to consult. Having mentally divided it into two parts from top to bottom, he watched to see what would occur; and this watching of the *templum* was called *contemplating*.

Contempt of Court. Refusing to conform to the rules of the law courts. *Consequential* contempt is that which tends to obstruct the business or lower the dignity of the court by indirection. *Direct* contempt is an open insult or resistance to the judge or others officially employed in the court.

Contemptibles, The Old. The original Expeditionary Force of 160,000 men that left England in August, 1914, to join the French and Belgians against Germany. The soldiers gave themselves this name as a compliment, from an army order that was said to have been given at Aix on August 19th by the Kaiser to his generals.

> It is my royal and imperial command that you exterminate the treacherous English, and walk over General French's contemptible little army.

It is only fair to add that this "order" is almost certainly apocryphal.

Contenement (kon ten' e ment). A word used in Magna Charta, the exact meaning of which is not ascertainable, but which probably denotes the lands and chattels connected with a tenement; whatever befits the social position of a person, as the arms of a gentleman, the merchandise of a trader, the ploughs and wagons of a peasant, etc.

> In every case the contenement (a word expressive of chattels necessary to each man's station) was exempted from seizure.—HALLAM: *Middle Ages*, Pt. ii, ch. viii.

Continental. Not worth a Continental. Worthless. No more valuable than the bank-notes issued by the American Continental Congress during the War of Independence and until the adoption of the Constitution, which were backed by no reserves whatever.

Continental System. A name given to Napoleon's plan for shutting out Great Britain from all commerce with the continent of Europe. He forbade under pain of war any nation of Europe to receive British exports, or to send imports to any of the British dominions. It began November 21st, 1806.

Contingent. The quota of troops furnished by each of several contracting powers, according to agreement. The word properly means something happening by chance; hence we call a fortuitous event a contingency.

Continuity Man, Girl. The technique of cinematography allows of a play, etc., being photographed in scenes and incidents not necessarily in sequence. Each scene, etc., is, moreover, "shot" many times. It is therefore essential that the greatest care be taken to see that every detail of costume, scenery, etc., is correct when one scene or incident is "shot" several times. With poor continuity an actress may be wearing a ring when she sits down to dinner, and later in the same meal be found without one. It is the task of the continuity man or girl to see that such a mistake is averted.

Contra (Lat.). Against; generally in the phrase *pro and contra* or *pro* and *con*. (*q.v.*). In bookkeeping a *contra* is an entry on the right-hand, or credit side, of the ledger. *See* PER CONTRA.

A contra-account is one kept by a firm which both buys from and sells to the same client, so that the transactions cancel out as paper entries.

Contra bonos mores (Lat.). Not in accordance with good manners; not *comme il faut* (*q.v.*).

Contretemps (Fr.). A mischance, something inopportune. Literally, "out of time."

Conventicle. The word was applied originally by the early Christians to their meeting-places, but it was soon used contemptuously by their opponents, and it thus acquired a bad or derisive sense, such as a clandestine meeting with a sinister intention; a private meeting of monks to protest against the election of a proposed abbot, for instance, was called a conventicle. It now means a religious meeting, or meeting-place, of Dissenters, a chapel (*q.v.*).

Conventicle Act. An Act passed in 1664 declaring that a meeting of more than five persons held for religious worship and not in accordance with the Book of Common Prayer was a seditious assembly. It was repealed by the Toleration Act (1689).

Convention, The. Two Parliaments were so called: one in 1660, because it was not held by the order of the king, but was convened by General Monk; and that convened on January 22nd, 1689, to confer the crown on William and Mary.

In the U.S.A. a convention is a meeting of a number of persons, as delegates, for any common purpose. The meeting held by a political party for the purpose of selecting a candidate for the presidential election is called a National Convention. In the French Revolution the National Convention was the sovereign assembly convened by the Constituent Assembly. It governed France from Sept. 1792, to Oct., 1795.

Convey. A polite term for *steal*. Thieves are, by a similar euphemism, called *conveyers*. (Lat. *con-veho*, to carry away.)

> Convey, the wise it call, Steal! foh! a fico for the phrase.—SHAKESPEARE: *Merry Wives of Windsor*, i, 3.
>
> Bolingbroke: Go, some of you, convey him to the Tower.
> *Rich. II*: O, good! "Convey." Conveyers are ye all,
> That rise thus nimbly by a true king's fall.
> *Richard II*, iv, 4.

Cooing and Billing, like Philip and Mary on a shilling. The reference is to coins struck in 1555, in which Mary and her consort are placed face to face, and not cheek by jowl, the usual way.

> Still amorous, and fond, and billing,
> Like Philip and Mary on a shilling.
> *Hudibras*, Pt. iii, 1.

Cook, Cooking. Terms belonging to cuisine applied to man under different circumstances:

Sometimes he is well *basted*; he *boils* with rage, is *baked* with heat, and *burns* with love or jealousy. Sometimes he is *buttered* and well buttered; he is often *cut up*, *devoured* with a flame, and *done brown*. We *dress his jacket* for him; sometimes he is *eaten up* with care; sometimes he is *fried*. We *cook his goose* for him, and sometimes he makes a goose of himself. We make a *hash* of him, and at times he makes a hash of something else. He gets into *hot water*, and sometimes into a *mess*. Is made into *mince-meat*, makes mincemeat of his money, and is often in a *pickle*. We are often asked to *toast* him, sometimes he gets well *roasted*, is sometimes *set on fire*, put into a *stew*, or is in a *stew* no one knows why.

A "soft" is *half-baked*, one severely handled is well *peppered*, to falsify accounts is to *cook* or *salt* them, wit is *Attic salt*, and an exaggerated statement must be taken *cum grano salis*.

A pert young person is a *sauce box*, a shy lover is a *spoon*, a rich father has to *fork out*, and is sometimes *dished* of his money.

A conceited man does not think small *beer* (or small potatoes) of himself, and one's mouth is called a *potato-trap*. A simpleton is a *cake*, a *gudgeon*, and a *pigeon*. Some are *cool as a cucumber*, others *hot as a quail*. A chubby child is a little *dumpling*. A woman may be a *duck*; a courtesan was called a *mutton* or *laced mutton*, and a large, coarse hand is a *mutton fist*. A greedy person is a *pig*, a fat one is a *sausage*, and a shy one, if not a sheep, is certainly *sheepish*; while a Lubin casts *sheep's eyes* at his lady-love. A coward is *chicken*-hearted, a fat person is *crummy*, and a cross one is *crusty*, while an aristocrat belongs to the *upper crust* of society. A Yeoman of the Guard is a *beef-eater*, a soldier a *red herring*, or a *lobster*, and a stingy, ill-tempered old man is a *crab*. A walking advertiser between two boards is a *sandwichman*. An alderman in his chain is a *turkey hung with sausages*. Two persons resembling each other are like as *two peas*. A chit is a mere *sprat*, a delicate maiden a *tit-bit*, and a colourless countenance is is called a *whey-face*. Anything unexpectedly easy is a *piece of cake*.

What's cooking? What is in hand, what's doing.

Cook your goose. *See* GOOSE.

Cooked. *The books have been cooked*. The ledger and other trade books have been tampered with, in order to show a false balance.

Cool hundred, thousand (or any other sum). The whole of the sum named. Cool, in this case, is merely an emphatic; it may have originally had reference to the calmness and deliberation with which the sum was counted out and the total made up.

He had lost a cool hundred, and would no longer play.—FIELDING: *Tom Jones*, VIII, xii.

Coop. U.S. slang for prison.

To fly the coop is to escape from prison.

Cooper. Half stout and half porter. The term arose from the old practice at breweries of allowing the coopers a daily portion of stout and porter. As they did not like to drink porter after stout, they mixed the two together.

Cop. To catch, lay hold of, capture. To "get copped" is to get caught by the police, whence *cop* and *copper* (*q.v.*), a policeman. Perhaps connected with Lat. *capere*, to take, etc.

A fair cop is applied to the case of a criminal caught *in flagrante delicto*.

The word is used for catching almost anything, as punishment at school, or even an illness, fever, or cold:—

They thought I was sleepin', ye know,
And they sed as I'd copped it o' Jim;
Well, it come like a bit of a blow,
For I watched by the deathbed of him.
SIMS: *Dagonet Ballads* (*The Last Letter*).

The East Anglian word to *cop* meaning to throw or toss (whence *cop-halfpenny*, a name for chuck-farthing) is not connected with this.

Copenhagen (kō pén hā′ gén). This was the name of the horse ridden by the Duke of Wellington at Waterloo "from four in the morning till twelve at night." He was a rich chestnut, 15 hands high. Pensioned off in the paddocks of Stratfieldsaye, Copenhagen lived to the age of twenty-seven; his skeleton is in the United Services Museum, Whitehall.

Copernicanism. The doctrine that the earth moves round the sun, in opposition to the doctrine that the sun moves round the earth; so called after Nicolas Copernicus (1473-1543), the Prussian astronomer. *Cp.* PTOLEMAIC SYSTEM.

Whereas it has come to the knowledge of the Holy Congregation that that false Pythagorean doctrine altogether opposed to Holy Scripture, on the mobility of the earth and the immobility of the sun, taught by Nicholas Copernicus. . . . This congregation has decreed that the said book of Copernicus be suspended until it be corrected.—*Decree of the Holy Congregation of the Index*, 1616.

Cophetua (ko fet′ ū à). An imaginary king of Africa, of great wealth, who "disdained all womankind," and concerning whom a ballad is given in Percy's *Reliques*. One day he saw a beggar-girl from his window, and fell in love with her. He asked her name; it was Penelophon, called by Shakespeare Zenelophon (*Love's Labour's Lost*, iv, 1). They lived together long and happily, and at death were universally lamented.

King Cophetua loved the beggar-maid.
SHAKESPEARE: *Romeo and Juliet*, ii, 1.

Copper. Among the old alchemists copper was the symbol of Venus.

The name is given to the large vessel used for laundry purposes, cooking, etc., which was formerly made of copper but is now more usually of iron; also to pence, halfpence, farthings, cents, etc., although nowadays they are made of bronze; true copper coinage has not been minted in England since 1860.

In slang a **copper** is a policeman, *i.e.* one who "cops," or catches, offenders.

Copper captain. A "Brummagem," or sham, captain; a man who "swanks about" with the title but has no right to it. Michael Perez is so called in *Rule a Wife and have a Wife*, by Beaumont and Fletcher.

To this copper-captain was confided the command of the troops.—W. IRVING: *Knickerbocker*.

Copper Nose. Oliver Cromwell; also called "Ruby Nose," "Nosey," and "Nose Almighty," no doubt from some scorbutic tendency which showed itself in a big red nose.

Copper-nose Harry. Henry VIII. When Henry VIII had spent all the money left him by his miserly father, he minted an inferior silver coin, in which the copper alloy soon showed itself on the more prominent parts, especially the nose of the face; and hence the people soon called the king "Old Copper-nose."

Copperheads. Secret foes. Copperheads are poisonous snakes of North America (*Trigonocephalus contortrix*), which, unlike the rattlesnakes, give no warning of their attack. The name was applied by the early colonists to the Indians, then to the Dutch (*see* Washington Irving's *History of New York*), and, finally, in the Civil War to the pro-Southerners among the Northerners, the covert friends of the Confederates.

Copus (kō′ pùs). University slang for a drink made of beer, wine, and spice heated together, and served in a "loving-cup." Variously accounted for as being dog-Latin for *cupellon Hippocratis* (a cup of hippocras), or short for *episcopus*, in which case it would be the same as the drink "bishop." (*q.v.*).

Copy. A printer's term for original MS., typescript, or printed matter that is to be set up in type.

That's a mere copy of your countenance. Not your real wish or meaning, but merely one you choose to present to me.

Copyhold estate. Land held by a tenant by virtue of a copy of the roll made by the steward of the manor from the court-roll kept in the manor-house. It was ended by legislation in 1925.

Copyright. The exclusive right of multiplying for sale copies of works of literature, art, etc., or substantial parts thereof, allowed to the author or his assignees. The first copyright Act in England is that of 1709; modifications and additions to it were made at various times, and in 1842 a new Act was passed granting copyright for forty-two years after publication or until the expiration of seven years from the death of the author, whichever should be the longer.

The question of international copyright was settled by the Berne Convention of 1908, to which all countries subscribed except U.S.A., Russia, and China. To carry out the articles of the convention so far as Great Britain was concerned the Copyright Act of 1911 was passed, by which protection was granted for 50 years from the death of the author or the publication of the work, whichever date was the later. In U.S.A. protection of copyright can be secured only by the complete production of the work in U.S.A. It lasts for 28 years, with right to renew for another similar period.

The Act of 1911 deals also with the copyright in photographs, engravings, architectural designs, musical compositions, gramophone records, etc.

A copy of every copyright book has to be presented to the British Museum and, on application being made, to the Bodleian, the Cambridge University Library, the Advocates' Library at Edinburgh, Trinity College, Dublin, and the National Library of Wales at Aberystwyth. Before the Act of 1842 Sion College, Glasgow, Aberdeen, and St. Andrews Universities, and King's Inns, Dublin, also had compulsory presentation copies.

Coq à l'âne. See COCK, A COCK AND BULL STORY.

Corah (kôr' a), in Dryden's *Absalom and Achitophel* (*q.v.*), is meant for Titus Oates. See *Numb.* xvi.

Sunk were his eyes, his voice was harsh and loud;
Sure signs he neither choleric was, nor proud;
His long chin proved his wit; his saint-like grace
A church vermilion, and a Moses' face.
His memory, miraculously great,
Could plots, exceeding man's belief, repeat.
DRYDEN: *Absalom and Achitophel*, i, 646.

Coral. The Romans used to hang beads of red coral on the cradles and round the necks of infants, to "preserve and fasten their teeth,"

and save them from "the falling sickness." It was considered by soothsayers as a charm against lightning, whirlwind, shipwreck, and fire. Paracelsus says it should be worn round the neck of children as a preservative "against fits, sorcery, charms, and poison," and Norse legend says that it is fashioned beneath the waves by Marmendill. The *bells* on an infant's coral are a Roman Catholic addition, the object being to frighten away evil spirits by their jingle.

Coral is good to be hanged about the neck of children . . . to preserve them from the falling sickness. It has also some special sympathy with nature, for the best coral . . . will turn pale and wan if the party that wears it be sick, and it comes to its former colour again as they recover.—SIR HUGH PLATT: *Jewel-House of Art and Nature* (1594).

Coram judice (kôr' am joo' di si) (Lat.). Under consideration; still before the judge.

Cordelia (kôr dē' li à). The youngest of Lear's three daughters, and the only one that loved him. She appears in Holinshed's *Chronicle* (whence Shakespeare drew most of his facts) as "Cordeilla," as "Cordell" in the *Mirour for Magistrates* (1555) and as "Cordella" in the older play of *Leir* (1594). The form "Cordelia" seems to appear for the first time in Spenser's *Faerie Queene* (ii, 10). See LEAR, KING.

Cordelia's gift. A "voice ever soft, gentle, and low; an excellent thing in woman." Shakespeare: *King Lear*, v, 3.

It is her voice that he hears prevailing over the those [*sic*] of the rest of the company, . . . for she has not Cordelia's gift.—MISS BROUGHTON: *Dr. Cupid.*

Cordon (Fr.). A ribbon or cord: especially the ribbon of an order of chivalry; also, a line of sentries or military posts enclosing some position; hence, an encircling line.

Cordon bleu. A knight of the ancient order of the *St. Esprit* (Holy Ghost); so called because the decoration is suspended on a blue ribbon. It was at one time the highest order in the kingdom of France.

The title is also given, as a compliment, to a good cook.

Un grand cordon. A member of the French *Légion d'Honneur*. The cross is attached to a *grand* (broad) ribbon.

Un repas de cordon bleu. A well-cooked and well-appointed dinner. The commandeur de Souvé, Comte d'Olonne, and some others, who were *cordons bleus* (*i.e.* knights of St. Esprit), met together as a sort of club, and were noted for their excellent dinners. Hence, when anyone has dined well he said, "*Bien, c'est un vrai repas de cordon bleu.*"

Corduroy. A corded fabric, originally made of silk, and worn by the kings of France in the chase (Fr. *corde du roy*). It is also a coarse, thick, ribbed cotton stuff, capable of standing hard wear.

Corduroys. Trousers made of corduroy. Brown corduroy trousers were worn by officers of the British 8th Army in the Western Desert, 1940-2, not, as many have thought, as an affectation, but because this material stood up to wear in the sand better than battle-dress serge, and was less chafing in the heat.

Corineus. A mythical hero in the suite of Brute, who conquered the giant Goemagot (Gogmagog), for which achievement the whole western horn of England was allotted him. He called it Corinea, and the people Corineans, from his own name. *See* BELLERUS.

> In meed of these great conquests by them got,
> Corineus had that province utmost west
> To him assyned for his worthy lot,
> Which of his name and memorable gest,
> He called Cornwall.
> > SPENSER: *Faerie Queene*, ii, 10.

Corinth. Non cuivis homini contingit adire Corinthum. A tag from Horace (Ep. I, xvii), quoted of some difficult attainment that can be achieved only by good fortune or great wealth. Professor Corrington translates it:—

> You know the proverb, "Corinth town is fair,
> But 'tis not every man that can get there."

Gellius, in his *Noctes Atticæ*, i, 8, says that Horace refers to Laïs (*q.v.*), who sold her favours at so high a price that not everyone could afford to purchase them; but Horace says, "To please princes is no little praise, for it falls not to every man's lot to go to Corinth." That is, it is as hard to please princes as it is to get to Corinth, perhaps because of the expense, and perhaps because it is situated between two seas, and hence called Bimâris Corinthus.

Corinthian. A licentious libertine. The loose-living of Corinth was proverbial both in Greece and in Rome.

In the Regency the term was applied to a hard-living group of sportsmen whose time was largely spent in practising pugilism and horse-racing. The sporting rake in Pierce Egan's *Life in London* (1821) was known as "Corinthian Tom"; in Shakespeare's day a "Corinthian" was the "fast man" of the period. *Cp.* EPHESIAN.

> I am no proud Jack, like Falstaff; but a Corinthian, a lad of mettle, a good boy.—1 *Henry IV*, ii, 4.

The only survival of the term to-day is in the Corinthian amateur football club.

Corinthian Order. The most richly decorated of the five orders of Greek architecture. The shaft is fluted, and the capital is bell-shaped and adorned with acanthus leaves. *See* ACANTHUS.

Corinthian brass. An alloy made of a variety of metals (said to be gold, silver, and copper) melted at the conflagration of Corinth in 146 B.C., when the city was burnt to the ground by the consul Mummius. Vases and other ornaments, made by the Romans of this metal, were of greater value than if they had been silver or gold.

> I think it may be of Corinthian brass,
> Which was a mixture of all metals, but
> The brazen uppermost.
> > BYRON: *Don Juan*, vi, 56.

Corked. Properly used of a bottle of wine which has not been opened; generally used in place of "corky"—*i.e.* the wine itself has become tainted through the cork being a bad one.

Corker. That's a corker. That's a tremendous example of whatever is in question—a story, a ball in cricket, or anything you wish.

Cormoran. The Cornish giant, who in the nursery tale, fell into a pit dug by Jack the Giant-killer. For this doughty achievement Jack received a belt from King Arthur, with this inscription—

> This is the valiant Cornish man
> That slew the giant Cormoran.
> > *Jack the Giant-killer.*

Corn. There's corn in Egypt. There is abundance; there is a plentiful supply. The reference is to the Bible story of Joseph in Egypt (*Ex.* xlii, 2).

Cornage. A rent in feudal times fixed with relation to the number of horned cattle in the tenant's possession. In Littleton's *Tenures* (1574) it was mistakenly said to be "a kind of tenure in grand serjeanty," the service being to blow a horn when an invasion of the Scots was imminent. Until the true meaning of the term was given in the Oxford Dictionary this was the explanation always given.

Corner. The condition of the market with respect to a commodity which has been largely bought up, in order to create a virtual monopoly and enhance its market price; as a corner in pork, etc. The idea is that the goods are piled and hidden in a corner out of sight.

> The price of bread rose like a rocket, and speculators wished to corner what little wheat there was.—*New York Weekly Times* (June 13, 1894).

To make a corner. To combine in order to control the price of a given article, and thus secure enormous profits.

Corner-stone. A large stone laid at the base of a building to strengthen the two walls forming a right angle; in ancient buildings they were sometimes as much as 20 feet long and 8 feet thick. In figurative use, Christ is called (*Eph.* ii, 20) the chief corner-stone because He united the Jews and Gentiles into one family; and daughters are called cornerstones (*Ps.* cxliv, 12) because, as wives and mothers, they unite together two families.

Why should we make an ambiguous word the corner-stone of moral philosophy?—JOWETT: *Plato*, iv, 30.

Cornish. Cornish hug. A hug to overthrow you. The Cornish men were famous wrestlers, and tried to throttle their antagonist with a particular grip or embrace called the Cornish hug.

The Cornish are Masters of the Art of Wrestling. . . . Their Hugg is a cunning close with their fellow-combatant; the fruits whereof is his fair fall, or foil at the least. It is figuratively appliable to the deceitful dealing of such who secretly design their overthrow, whom they openly embrace.—FULLER: *Worthies* (1661).

Cornish language. This member of the Brythonic branch of the Celtic languages became virtually extinct nearly 200 years ago. It is supposed that Dolly Pentreath (Dorothy Jeffery, 1685-1777) was the last to speak Cornish as a native language. It is still spoken as an acquired language by a few cultured Cornishmen and there is a certain literature available.

Cornish names.
By Tre, Pol, and Pen.
You shall know the Cornishmen.

Thus, *Tre* (a town) gives Trefry, Tregengon, Tregony, Tregothnan, Trelawy, Tremayne, Trevannion, Treveddoe, Trewithen, etc.

Pol (a head) gives Polkerris Point, Polperro, Polwheel, etc.

Pen (a top) gives Penkevil, Penrice, Penrose, Pentire, etc.

Cornubian Shore. Cornwall, famous for its tin mines.

. . . from the bleak Cornubian shore
Dispense the mineral treasure, which of old
Sidonian pilots sought.
AKENSIDE: *Hymn to the Naiads.*

Cornwall. The county is probably named from Celtic *corn, cornu,* a horn, with reference to the configuration of the promontory. For the legendary explanation of the name, *see* CORINEUS.

Corny. U.S. slang for anything, such as music, which is affectedly and spuriously sweet. It is also used of anything of poor quality or hackneyed.

Coronach (kor´ ō nach). Lamentation for the dead, as anciently practised in Ireland and Celtic Scotland. (Gael. *comh ranach,* crying together.) Pennant says it was called by the Irish *hululoo.*

Coroner. Properly, the crown officer (Lat. *corona,* crown). In Saxon times it was his duty to collect the Crown revenues; next, to take charge of Crown pleas; but at present his duties are almost entirely confined to searching into cases of sudden or suspicious death. The coroner also holds inquiries, or inquests, on treasure trove. *Crowner* was formerly a correct way of pronouncing the word, hence Shakespeare's—

But is this law?
Ay, marry, is't; crowner's quest law.
Hamlet, v, 1.

Coronet. A crown inferior to the royal crown. A *duke's* coronet is adorned with strawberry leaves above the band; that of a *marquis* with strawberry leaves alternating with pearls; that of an *earl* has pearls elevated on stalks, alternating with leaves above the band; that of a *viscount* has a string of pearls above the band, but no leaves; that of a *baron* has only six pearls.

Corporation. A *municipal corporation* is a body of men elected for the local government of a city or town, consisting of the mayor, aldermen, and councillors. The word is facetiously applied to a large paunch, from the tendency of civic magnates to indulge in well-provided feasts and thus acquire generous figures.

Corposant. The St. Elmo's Fire (*q.v.*) or "Castor and Pollux" of the Romans; the ball of fire which is sometimes seen playing round the masts of ships in a storm. So called from Span. *corpo santo,* holy body. Sometimes known as *comazant.*

Corps legislatif (kôr´ lej is là tēf´). At various periods of modern French history this phrase has been used for the lower house of the legislature. In 1799 Napoleon substituted a *Corps legislatif* and a tribunal for the two councils of the Directory. In 1807 there was a *c.l.* and a *conseil d'état;* in 1849 a *c.l.* was formed with 750 deputies; and under Napoleon III the legislative power was vested in the Emperor, the Senate and the *Corps legislatif.*

Corps Diplomatique (Fr.). A diplomatic body; the foreign representatives at a Court collectively.

Corpus (kôr´ pùs) (Lat., a body). The whole body or substance; especially the complete collection of writings on one subject or by one person, as the *Corpus poetarum Latinorum,* the *Corpus historicum medii œvi,* etc.

Also, short for Corpus Christi College.

Corpus Christi. A festival of the Church, kept on the Thursday after Trinity Sunday, in honour of the Blessed Sacrament. It was instituted by Urban IV in 1264, and was the regular time for the performance of religious dramas by the trade guilds. In England many of the Corpus Christi plays of York, Coventry, and Chester are extant.

Corpus Christi College at Cambridge was founded in 1352, and the College of the same name at Oxford in 1516.

Corpus delicti (Lat.). The material thing in respect to which a crime has been committed; thus a murdered body or a portion of the stolen property would be a "corpus delicti."

Corpuscular Philosophy. The theory promulgated by Robert Boyle which sought to account for all natural phenomena by the position and motion of corpuscles. *Cp.* ATOMIC PHILOSOPHY.

Corrector. *See* ALEXANDER THE CORRECTOR.

Corroboree. The name of a dance indulged in by Australian aborigines on festal or warlike occasions; hence any hilarious or slightly riotous assembly. The word belongs to the language of the natives of Port Jackson, (Sydney), New South Wales.

Corruption of Blood. Loss of title and entailed estates in consequence of treason, by which a man's *blood* is *attainted* and his issue suffers.

Corsair (kôr' sâr) means properly "one who gives chase." Applied to the pirates of the northern coast of Africa. (Ital. *corso*, a chase; Fr. *corsaire*; Lat. *cursus*.)

Byron's poem in heroic couplets, *The Corsair*, was written in 1813.

Corsican (kôr' si kàn). For many years this was the derogatory epithet applied to Napoleon, as Consul and Emperor, in allusion to his place of birth. It was often expanded to "the Corsican upstart" by the Colonel Blimps of the day.

Cortes (kôr' tez). The Spanish or Portuguese parliament. The word means "court officers."

Cortina (kôr'tī nà) (Lat., cauldron). The tripod of Apollo, which was in the form of a cauldron; hence, any tripod used for religious purposes in the worship of the ancient Romans.

Corvinus (kôr vī' nus). Matthias I, King of Hungary, 1458-90, younger son of Janos Hunyady, was so called from the raven (Lat. *corvus*) on his shield. He was one of the greatest of all book collectors, and for his superb library some of the earliest gilt-tooled bindings were executed. They may be recognized by the raven introduced into the design, and are among the highest prizes of bibliophily.

Marcus Valerius is also said to have been so called because, in a single combat with a gigantic Gaul during the Gallic war, a raven flew into the Gaul's face and so harassed him that he could neither defend himself nor attack his adversary.

Corycian Cave (kor is' i àn). A cave on Mount Parnassus; so called from the nymph Corycia. The Muses are sometimes in poetry called Corycides or the Corycian Nymphs.

> The immortal Muse
> To your calm habitations, to the cave
> Corycian . . . will guide his footsteps.
>   AKENSIDE: *Hymn to the Naiads.*

Corydon (kor' i don). A conventional name for a rustic, a shepherd; a brainless, love-sick fellow; from the shepherd in Virgil's *Eclogue* VII, and in Theocritus.

Coryphæus (kôr i fē' us). The leader and speaker of the chorus in Greek dramas; hence, figuratively, the leader generally, the most active member of a board, company, expedition, etc. At Oxford University the assistant of the Choragus (*q.v.*) is called the Coryphæus.

> In the year 1626, Dr. William Heather, desirous to ensure the study and practice of music at Oxford in future ages, established the offices of Professor, Choragus, and Coryphæus, and endowed them with modest stipends.—*Grove's Dictionary of Music.*

Coryphée. A ballet-dancer; strictly speaking, the leader of the ballet.

Cosmopolite (kos mop' ō līt) (Gr. *cosmospolites*). A citizen of the world. One who has no partiality to any one country as his abiding place; one who looks on the whole world with "an equal eye."

Coss, Rule of. An old name for algebra (also called the *Cossic Art*); from Ital. *regola di cosa*, *cosa* being an unknown quantity, or a "thing." *See* WHETSTONE OF WITTE.

Cosset. A pet; especially a pet lamb brought up in the house. Hence, *to cosset*, to make a pet of, to fondle, caress. Probably from A.S. *cot-sœta*, a dweller in a cottage.

Costa Brava (kos' ta bra' va). The precipitous coast of Spain lying on the Mediterranean between Port Bou and San Feliu de Guixols.

Costard. A large, ribbed apple, and, metaphorically, a man's head. *Cp.* COSTER-MONGER.

> Take him over the costard with the hilts of thy sword.—SHAKESPEARE: *Richard III*, i, 4.

Shakespeare gives the name to a clown in *Love's Labour's Lost*, who apes the court wit of the period, but misapplies and miscalls like Mrs. Malaprop or Dogberry.

Costermonger. A seller of eatables about the streets, properly an apple-seller; from *costard* (q.v.), and *monger*, a trader; A.S. *mangian*, to trade; a word still retained in iron-monger, cheese-monger, fish-monger, etc. It is usually abbreviated to *coster* and is often applied generically to a Cockney of the East End.

Côte (kōt) (Fr., coast).

Côte d'Azur. The Mediterranean coast of France between Menton and Cannes, so named in 1887 by the poet Stephen Liegeard.

Côte d'Or. The department of France of which Dijon is the chief town. It is famous for its vineyards, for within its boundaries the whole of the best Burgundy is produced. The area extends south from Dijon, embracing Gevrey, Chambolle, Vougeot, Vosne, Nuits, Aloxe-Corton, Beaune, Pommard, Volnay, Meursault, Santenay, and ends at Chasne.

Côtes-du-Rhône. The name given collectively to the wines grown in the Rhône valley, below Lyons, of which the most famous are Chateauneuf-du-Pape, and Hermitage.

Coterie (kōt' e rē). A French word originally signifying something like our "guild," a society where each paid his *quota*, but now applied to an exclusive set or clique, especially one composed of persons of similar tastes, aims, prejudices, etc.

Cotillon (ko til' yon). Originally a brisk dance by four or eight persons, in which the ladies held up their gowns and showed their under-petticoats (Fr. *cotillon*, a petticoat). Later the dance became a very elaborate one with many added figures; but it is very rarely seen in modern ball-rooms.

Cotswold. You are as long a-coming as Cotswold barley. The Cotswold Hills, in Gloucestershire, are very cold and bleak, exposed to the winds, and very backward in vegetation, but they yield a good late supply of barley.

Cotswold lion. An ironical name for a sheep, for which Cotswold hills are famous.

Then will he look as fierce as a Cotsold lion.
UDALL: *Roister Doister*, IV, vi (c. 1566).

Cottage. This word, now applied to any small dwelling in the country, is found in law in the 13th century as signifying a small house without land.

Cottage Countess, The. Sarah Hoggins, of Shropshire, daughter of a small farmer, who, in 1791, married Henry Cecil, nephew and heir presumptive of the 9th Earl of Exeter. At the time he had no courtesy title and was a plain "Mr." He was living under the name of John Jones, and was separated from his wife, from whom he subsequently obtained a divorce and an Act of Parliament to legitimatize the children of his second wife. Sarah Hoggins was seventeen at the time of her marriage, and "John Jones" was thirty. They were married by licence in the parish church of Bolas Magna, Salop and lived there for two years until his succession to the peerage made her a Countess. She died in 1797, four years before her husband's elevation to the Marquessate. Tennyson's poem, *The Lord of Burleigh*, is founded on this episode.

Cottage loaf. A loaf of bread in two round lumps, a smaller on top of a larger, and baked with a good crust.

Cotton. A cotton king. A rich Manchester cotton manufacturer, a king in wealth, style of living, equipage, number of employees, etc. Many county families had this origin.

To cotton to a person. To cling to or take a fancy to a person. To stick to a person as cotton sticks to our clothes.

To cotton on. To catch on, to grasp a line of thought.

Cottonian Library. The remarkable library founded by the noted antiquary Sir Robert Bruce Cotton (1571-1631), It was augmented by his son and grandson, and having been secured for the nation by statute in 1700, was eventually deposited in the British Museum on the foundation of that institution in 1753. It is particularly rich in early MSS.

Cottys (kot' is). One of the three hundred-handed giants, son of Uranus (Heaven) and Gaea (Earth). His two brothers were Briareus and Gyges. *See* HUNDRED-HANDED.

Cotytto (ko tī' tō). The Thracian goddess of immodesty, worshipped at Athens with licentious rites. *See* BAPTES.

Hail! goddess of nocturnal sport,
Dark-veiled Cotytto.
MILTON: *Comus* 129,130.

Where are they, Cotytto or Venus,
Astarte or Ashtaroth, where?
SWINBURNE: *Dolores*.

Couleur de rose (koo lĕr de rōs) (Fr., rose-coloured). Highly coloured; too favourably considered; overdrawn with romantic embellishments, like objects viewed through glass tinted with rose pink.

Council, Privy, Œcumenical, etc. *See these words.*

Count. A title of honour, used on the Continent and equivalent to English *earl* (A.S. *eorl*, a warrior), of which *countess* is still the feminine and the title of the wife or widow of an earl. *Count* is from Lat. *comitem*, accusative of *comes*, a companion, which was a military title, as *Comes Littoris Saxonici*, Count of the Saxon Shore, the Roman general responsible for the south-eastern coasts of Britain.

Count, To. From O.Fr. *conter*, Lat. *computare* (*putare*, to think), to compute, to reckon.

To be counted out is said of a boxer who, after being knocked down, fails to regain his feet during the ten seconds counted out loud by the referee. **Count me out.** Do not reckon me in on this.

To count upon. To rely with confidence on someone or something; to reckon on.

To count without your host. *See* RECKON.

Countenance, To. To sanction; to support. Approval or disapproval is shown by the countenance. The Scripture speaks of "the light of God's countenance," *i.e.* the smile of approbation; and to "hide His face" (or countenance) is to manifest displeasure.

To keep in countenance. To encourage, or prevent someone losing his countenance or feeling dismayed.

To keep one's countenance. To refrain from smiling or expressing one's thoughts by the face.

Out of countenance. Ashamed, confounded. With the countenance fallen or cast down.

To put one out of countenance is to make one ashamed or disconcerted. To "discountenance" is to set your face against something done or propounded.

Counter. Under the counter is a phrase that came into use during World War II in connection with dishonest tradesmen who, when commodities were in short supply, kept out of sight under the counter sufficient quantities to sell to favoured customers, often at enhanced prices.

Counter-caster. One who keeps accounts, or casts up accounts by counters. Thus, at the opening of *Othello*, Iago in contempt calls Cassio "a great arithmetician," and "this counter-caster"; and in *The Winter's Tale*, the Clown says: "Fifteen hundred shorn; what comes the wool to? I cannot do 't without counters" (iv, 3).

Counter-jumper. A contemptuous epithet applied by the ignorant to a shop assistant, who may be supposed to have to jump over the counter to go from one part of the shop to another.

Counterpane. A corruption of *counterpoint*, from the Lat. *culcita puncta*, a stitched quilt. This, in French, became *courte-pointe*, corrupted into *contre-pointe*, *counterpoint*, where point is pronounced "poyn," corrupted into "pane."

Countess. *See* COUNT; COTTAGE COUNTESS.

Country. Black Country. *See* BLACK.

Country dance. A corruption of the Fr. *contre danse*; *i.e.* a dance where the partners face each other, as in Sir Roger de Coverley.

Father of his country. *See* FATHER.

To appeal, or go, to the country. To dissolve Parliament in order to ascertain the wish of the country by a new election of representatives.

County. A shire; originally the district ruled by a count. The name is also officially applied to *county boroughs, i.e.* towns with more than 50,000 inhabitants which, under the Local Government Act of 1888, rank as administrative counties. For various names of divisions of counties, *see* HUNDRED.

County family. A family belonging to the nobility or gentry with an ancestral seat in the county.

County palatine. Properly, the dominion of an earl palatine (*see* PALATINATE), a county over which the count had royal privileges. Cheshire and Lancashire are the only Counties Palatine in England now; but formerly Durham, Pembroke, Hexhamshire, and the Isle of Ely had this rank.

Coup (koo) (Fr.). Properly a blow or stroke, but used both in French and English in a large number of ways, as for a clap of thunder, a draught of liquids, a piece of play in a game (a move in chess, etc.), a stroke of policy or of luck, a trick, etc.

A good coup. A good hit or haul.

Coup d'essai. A trial-piece; a piece of work serving for practice.

Coup d'état. A state stroke, and the term is applied to one of those bold measures taken by Government to prevent a supposed or actual danger; as when a large body of men are arrested suddenly for fear they should overturn the Government.

The famous *coup d'état*, by which Louis Napoleon became possessed of absolute power, took place on December 2nd, 1851.

Coup de grâce. The finishing stroke; the stroke of mercy. When a criminal was tortured by the wheel or otherwise, the executioner gave him a *coup de grâce*, or blow on the head or breast, to put him out of his misery.

Coup de main. A sudden stroke, a stratagem whereby something is effected suddenly; a *coup*.

It appears more like a line of march than a body intended for a *coup de main*, as there are with it bullocks and baggage of different kinds. —WELLINGTON: *Dispatches*, vol. i, p. 25.

Coup d'œil. A view, glance, prospect; the effect of things at the first glance; literally "a stroke of the eye."

Coup de pied de l'âne. Literally, a kick from the ass's hoof; figuratively, a blow given to a vanquished or fallen man; a cowardly blow; an insult offered to one who has not the power of returning or avenging it. The allusion is to the fable of the sick lion kicked by the ass.

Coup de soleil. A sunstroke, any malady produced by exposure to the sun.

Coup de théâtre. An unforeseen or unexpected turn in a drama producing a sensational effect; a piece of clap-trap, something planned for effect. Burke throwing down the dagger in the House of Commons (*see* DAGGER SCENE) intended a *coup de théâtre*.

Coup manqué. A false stroke, a miss, a failure.

Shoot dead, or don't aim at all; but never make a *coup manqué.*—OUIDA: *Under Two Flags*, ch. xx.

Coupon. In commercial phraseology, a coupon is a certificate of interest which is to be cut off (Fr. *couper*) from a bond and presented for payment. It bears on its face the date and amount of interest to be paid.

In times when rationing has been necessary the word has been employed for the detachable portions of a ration-book required to buy clothing, etc.

In political phraseology *the coupon* was the official recognition given by Lloyd George and Bonar Law to parliamentary candidates who proclaimed their allegiance to the coalition programme at the General Election of December, 1918. Hence, *couponeer*, a politician who accepted the "coupon."

Court. From Lat. *cohors, cohortem*, originally a coop or sheepfold. It was on the Latium hills that the ancient Latins raised their *cors* or *cohors*, small enclosures with hurdles for sheep, etc. Subsequently, as many men as could be cooped or folded together were called a *cohort*. The cattle-yard, being the nucleus of the farm, became the centre of a lot of farm cottages, then of a hamlet, town, fortified place, and lastly of a royal residence.

Court cards. A corruption of **coat card,** so called because these cards bear the representation of a clothed or *coated* figure, and not because the king, queen, and knave may be considered to belong to a Court.

The king of clubs may originally have represented the arms of the Pope; of spades, the king of France; of diamonds, the King of Spain; and of hearts, the King of England. The French kings in cards are called David (spades), Alexander (clubs), Cæsar (diamonds), and Charles (hearts)—representing the Jewish, Greek, Roman, and Frankish empires. The queens or dames are Argine—*i.e.* Juno (hearts), Judith (clubs), Rachel (diamonds), and Pallas (spades)—representing royalty, fortitude, piety, and wisdom. They were likenesses of Marie d'Anjou, the queen of Charles VII; Isabeau, the queen-mother; Agnes Sorel, the king's mistress; and Jeanne d'Arc, the dame of spades, or war.

Court Circular. The information concerning the movements and doings of Royalty and the Court generally, supplied to the newspapers by the Court Newsman. He gives reports of levees, drawing-rooms, state balls, royal concerts, meetings of the cabinet ministers, deputations to ministers, and so on. George III, in 1803, introduced the custom to prevent misstatements on these subjects.

Court cupboard. A movable buffet to hold flagons, cans, cups, and beakers.

Away with the joint-stools, remove the court-cupboard, look to the plate.—SHAKESPEARE: *Romeo and Juliet*, i, 5.

Court fools. *See* FOOLS.

Court holy water. An obsolete Elizabethan term for fair speeches, which look like promises of favour, but end in nothing.

O nuncle, court holy-water in a dry house is better than this rain-water out o' door.—SHAKESPEARE: *King Lear*, iii, 2.

In Florio's Italian Dictionary (1598) *Mantellizzare* is translated by "to flatter or fawne upon, to court one with faire words or give court holywater."

Court-leet. *See* LEET.

Court martial. A court convened as circumstances may require to try a person subject to military law. In Great Britain such courts were instituted in consequence of the Mutiny Act of 1690.

Court plaster. The plaster of which the court ladies made their patches. These patches, worn on the face, were cut into all sorts of fanciful shapes, some even patching their faces with a coach and four, a ship in full sail, a chateau, etc. This ridiculous fashion was in vogue in the reign of Charles I; and in Queen Anne's time was employed as a political badge.

Your black patches you wear variously,
Some cut like stars, some in half-moons, some lozenges.

BEAUMONT AND FLETCHER: *Elder Brother*, iii, 2.

Court of Arches. *See* ARCHES.

Court of love. A judicial court for deciding affairs of the heart, established in Provence during the days of the Troubadours. The following is a case submitted to their judgment: A lady listened to one admirer, squeezed the hand of another, and touched with her toe the foot of a third. Query: Which of these three was the favoured suitor?

Court of Pie-powder. *See* PIE-POWDER.

Court of Session. The supreme civil tribunal in Scotland. It dates from 1532, and represents the united powers of the Session of James I of Scotland, the Daily Council of James IV, and the Lords Auditors of Parliament. Since 1830 it has consisted of an Inner and an Outer House; the total number of judges is thirteen, including the Lord President (or Lord Justice General) and the Lord Justice Clerk.

Out of court. Not admissible evidence within the terms of reference of the trial being conducted by the Court in question.

To settle out of court. A case, almost invariably involving damages, which is settled by the respective litigants' solicitors, before it is called to court, agreeing on a sum to be paid by the litigant who admits himself to be in the wrong.

Courtepy. *See* PEA-JACKET.

Courtesy. (kĕr' tĕ si) Civility, politeness. It was at the courts of princes and great feudatories that all in attendance practised the refinements of the age in which they lived. The word originally meant the manners of the court.

Courtesy titles. Titles assumed or granted by social custom, but not of any legal value. The courtesy title of the eldest son of a duke is *marquis*; of a marquis is *earl*; of an earl is *viscount*. Younger sons of peers are by courtesy called *lord* or *honourable*, and the daughters are *lady* or *honourable*. These titles do not give the holders the right to sit in the House of Lords.

Cousin. Blackstone says that Henry IV, being related or allied to every earl in the kingdom, artfully and constantly acknowledged the connexion in all public acts. The usage has descended to his successors, and in British royal writs and commissions an *earl* is still styled "Our right trusty and well-beloved cousin," a *marquis* "Our right trusty and entirely-beloved cousin," and a *duke* "Our right trusty and right-entirely-beloved cousin."

The word is also used by sovereigns in addressing one another formally; and in Italy it was a very high honour to be nominated by the king a "Cousin of the King."

Cousin Betsy, or **Betty.** A half-witted person, a "Bess of Bedlam" (*q.v.*).

[None] can say Foster's wronged him of a penny, or gave short measure to a child or a cousin Betsy.—MRS GASKELL.

To call cousins. This formerly meant to claim relationship—

He is half-brother to this Witword by a former wife, who was sister to my Lady Wishfort, my wife's mother; if you marry Millamant you must call cousins too.— CONGREVE: *Way of the World*, i, 5.

Couvade. The name given by anthropologists to the custom prevalent among some primitive races by which the father of a newly born infant makes a pretence of going through the same experiences as the mother, lies up for a time, abstains from certain foods, etc., as though he, too, were physically affected by the birth (from Fr. *couver*, to hatch). The custom has been observed by travellers in Guiana and other parts of South America, among some African tribes, in parts of China, Borneo, etc., and it was noted by the ancients as occurring in Corsica and among the Celtiberians.

Covent Garden. A corruption of *Convent* Garden; the garden and burial ground attached to the convent of Westminster, and turned into a fruit and flower market in the reign of Charles II. At the dissolution of the monasteries the site was granted to the Duke of Somerset; on his attainder in 1552 it passed to the Earl of Bedford, to whose descendants it belonged till 1914, when it was sold by the 11th Duke.

Covent Garden has various claims to fame. During the 17th and 18th centuries it was the centre of the rowdier element of London's social life, the stamping-ground of the Mohocks and other semi-fashionable ruffians. Its coffee-houses and taverns were favourite resorts of such men of parts as Dryden, Otway, Steele, Fielding, Foote, Garrick, etc. The vegetable market was opened in the early 17th century, but was not properly organized until 1828.

Covent Garden Theatre was opened by Rich, the harlequin, in 1732 with Congreve's *Way of the World*. After Rich's death it was sold to George Colman the elder, who, in 1777, brought out *She Stoops to Conquer*. The house has been twice burned down (1808 and 1856); in 1847 it started a famous career as The Royal Italian Opera House, and in the years that have followed it has become one of the greatest opera-houses in Europe.

Coventry. Coventry Mysteries. Miracle plays supposed to have been acted at Corpus Christi (*q.v.*) at Coventry till 1591. They were published in 1841 for the Shakespeare Society; but, though called *Ludus Coventriœ* by Sir Robert Bruce Cotton's librarian in the time of James I, it is doubtful whether they had any special connexion with the town.

To send one to Coventry. To take no notice of him; to make him feel that he is in disgrace by having no dealings with him. *Cp.* BOYCOTT. It is said that the citizens of Coventry had at one time so great a dislike to soldiers that a woman seen speaking to one was instantly tabooed; hence, when a soldier was sent to Coventry he was cut off from all social intercourse.

Hutton, in his *History of Birmingham*, gives a different version. He says that Coventry was a stronghold of the Parliamentary party in the Civil Wars, and that troublesome and refractory Royalist prisoners were sent there for safe custody.

Cover. To break cover. To start from the covert or temporary lair. The usual earth-holes of a fox being blocked the night before a hunt, the creature makes some gorse-bush or other cover its temporary resting-place, and as soon as it quits it the hunt begins.

Coverley. Sir Roger de Coverley. A member of an hypothetical club in the *Spectator*, "who lived in Soho Square when he was in town." Sir Roger is the type of an English squire in the reign of Queen Anne.

Who can be insensible to his unpretending virtues and amiable weaknesses; his modesty, generosity, hospitality, and eccentric whims; the respect for his neighbours, and the affection of his domestics?—HAZLITT.

The well-known country dance was known by this name (or, rather, as *Roger of Coverly*) many years before Addison's time.

Cow. The cow that nourished Ymir with four streams of milk was called Audhumla.

The whiter the cow, the surer is it to go to the altar. The richer the prey, the more likely is it to be seized.

The system of impropriations grew so rapidly that, in the course of three centuries, more than a third part of all the benefices in England became such, and those the richest, for the whiter the cow, the surer was it to go to the altar.—BLUNT: *Reformation in England*, p. 63.

Cowboy. Today the term universally used for the cattleman of the American West. Its earliest known use is quite different: it was a name adopted by a group of guerillas operating in New York State during the Revolutionary War. Its next use was by a gang of wild riders under the leadership of one Ewen Cameron who specialized in beating up Mexicans soon after Texas became an independent State, in 1835.

Cow-lick. A tuft of hair on the forehead that cannot be made to lie in the same direction as the rest of the hair.

This term must have been adopted from a comparison with that part of a . . . cow's hide where the hairs, having different directions, meet and form a projecting ridge, supposed to be occasioned by the animals licking themselves.—BROCHETT: *Glossary of North Country Words*.

Cowpuncher. A recent synonym for cowboy, derived from the metal-tipped pole with which cattle are driven when being loaded on rail.

Coward. Ultimately from Lat. *cauda*, a tail, the allusion seems to be either from an animal "turning tail" when frightened, or from its cowering with its tail between its legs.

In the French version of *Reynard the Fox* the Hare is called *Coart*, which may refer either to his timidity or to the conspicuousness of his tail (O.Fr. *coe*) as it runs away.

A beast *cowarded*, in *heraldry*, is one drawn with its tail between its legs.

Cowper Justice. Cupar Justice (*q.v.*).

Cowper-Temple Clause. Clause 14 of the Education Act of 1870 (so called from its author, W. Cowper-Temple (1811-88), which regulated religious teaching in public elementary schools. It enacted that "in any school provided by a School Board, no religious catechism or religious formulary which is distinctive of any particular denomination, shall be taught."

Coxcomb. An empty-headed, vain person. The ancient licensed jesters were so called because they wore a cock's comb in their caps.

Coxcombs, an ever empty race.
Are trumpets of their own disgrace.
GAY: *Fables*, xix.

Coxswain (cok'son). The helmsman; originally the *swain* or *servant* of a *cock* (see COCKBOAT). The old spelling of the word was *Cockswain*.

Crack. First-rate, excellent, quite at the top of its class; something that is "cracked up" (*see below*), as a crack regiment, a crack hand of cards, a crack shot, etc. Formerly the word was used substantively for a lively young fellow, a wag:—

Indeed, la! 'tis a noble child; a crack, madam.
SHAKESPEARE: *Coriolanus*, i, 3.

A gude crack. In Scottish dialect, a good chat or conversation, also a good talker.

Wi' merry sangs, an' friendly cracks,
I wat they did na weary;
And unco tales, an' funnie jokes—
Their sports were cheap an' cheery.
BURNS: *Halloween*.

To be a gude crack . . . was essential to the trade of a "puir body" of the more esteemed class.—SCOTT: *Antiquary* (Introduction).

Crack-brained. Eccentric; slightly mad.

Cracked pipkins are discovered by their sound. Ignorance is betrayed by speech.

They bid you talk—my honest song
Bids you for ever hold your tongue;
Silence with some is wisdom most profound—
Cracked pipkins are discovered by the sound.
PETER PINDAR: *Lord B. and his Motions*.

In a crack. Instantly. In a snap of the fingers, in the time taken by a crack or shot.

> Do pray undo the bolt a little faster—
> They're on the stair just now, and in a crack
> Will all be here.
> BYRON: *Don Juan*, I, cxxxvii.

To crack a bottle. In this phrase the word means to open and drink:—

> They went to a tavern and there they dined,
> And bottles cracked most merrilie.
> *Bold Pedlar and Robin Hood.*

> You'll crack a quart together. Ha, will you not, Master Bardolph.—*2 Henry IV*, v. 3.

> Dear Tom, this brown jug that now foams with mild ale,
> From which I now drink to sweet Nan of the Vale,
> Was once Toby Filpot's, a thirsty old soul
> As e'er cracked a bottle, or fathomed a bowl.
> O'KEEFE: *Poor Soldier.*

To crack a crib. To break into a house as a thief. *See* CRIB. Hence, *cracksman*, a burglar.

To crack up. To praise highly, to eulogize.

> We find them cracking up the country they belong to, no matter how absurd may be the boast.—JAS. PAYN: *By Proxy*, ch. i.

It also means to break down in health or mind; or to crash an aeroplane or motor car.

Cracker. A word used in several senses:

A small firework (U.S.A., 'fire-cracker).

A bon-bon containing sweets or toys with an appropriate motto, in use at Christmas.

A flaky, unsweetened water biscuit; in the U.S.A. the word is applied to any kind of biscuit.

Poor white folk in the Southern U.S.A., and back-country folk generally. This is an early 19th-century term, arising from the long whips they cracked at their horse teams.

Crackers. 20th-century slang phrase for mentally unbalanced.

Cracksman. A burglar. *See* TO CRACK A CRIB *above*.

Cradle-holding. A name given to land held by Borough English (*q.v.*).

Craft. Skill, ability, trade (A.S. *crœft*). A **craftsman** is a mechanic. A handicraft is manual skill, *i.e.* mechanical skill; *leechcraft* is skill in medicine (A.S., *lœce*, a physician); and before *crafty* adopted its bad sense it meant merely skilful, ingenious.

Small craft. Such vessels as schooners, sloops, cutters, and so on.

The Craft is the word usually employed by Freemasons to describe their fraternity.

Cram. To tell what is not true. A **crammer**, an untruth. The allusion is to stuffing a person with useless rubbish. It is, perhaps, in this connexion that working at high pressure for an examination is termed **to cram**.

Crambo. A game which consists in someone setting a line which another is to rhyme to, but no one word of the first line must occur in the second. The word is of uncertain origin, but possibly it comes from the billiards term *carambole*.

> Get the maids to crambo of an evening and learn the knack of rhyming.—CONGREVE: *Love for Love*, i, 1.

Dumb crambo is a somewhat similar game, but there the words are expressed in pantomime or dumb show.

Crank. In Elizabethan thieves' slang, an Abram-man (*q.v.*); so called from Ger. *krank* (sickly). It was formerly used of a leaky ship, and is still employed in the U.S.A. in the sense of weak or sickly. Nowadays a **crank** is a person with a mental twist, an eccentric person, and the name is obviously an extension of the mechanical crank, which is a bent axle or handle designed to convert lineal into rotary motion, or to impart motion to a wheel.

Cranmer's Bible. *See* BIBLE, THE ENGLISH.

Crannock. An Irish measure which, in the days of Edward II, contained either eight or sixteen pecks. *Curnock* is another form of the word: this was a dry measure of varying capacity, but usually 3 bushels for wheat, 4 bushels for corn, and from 10 to 15 bushels for coal, lime, etc.

Craps. The American term for dice, a most popular form of gambling in U.S.A. When New Orleans was a French city, about 1800, Bernard Marigny introduced dice-playing from France. He was a Creole and as such was known as a "Johnny Crapaud." Dice-throwing was associated with him and thus became "Johnny Crapaud's game" shortened into "craps." Marigny named a street in the Vieux Carré of New Orleans "Craps Street," but in 1850 it was rechristened "Burgundy Street."

Les anciens crapauds prenderont Sara. One of the cryptic "prophecies" of Nostradamus (1503-66). Sara is *Aras* reversed, and when the French under Louis XIV took Arras from the Spaniards, this verse was remembered.

Crape. A saint in crape is twice a saint in awn. (Pope: *Ep. to Cobham*, 136.) Crape (a sort of bombazine, or alpaca) is the stuff of which cheap clerical gowns used to be made, "lawn" refers to the lawn sleeves of a bishop. Crape was also the material used for mourning dresses, etc. It is said to have been first made by St. Badorn, Queen of France, c. 680.

Cravat (krȧ văt'). This neckcloth was introduced into France in the 17th century by Croatian soldiers, or, as they called themselves, Cravates (O.Slav. *khruvat*). The Croats guarded the Turkish frontiers of Austria, and when France organized a regiment on the model of the Croats, their linen neckcloths were imitated, and the regiment was called "The Royal Cravat."

Crawler (Austr.). A convict who escaped with the connivance of the overseer, allowing himself to be re-captured in order that the overseer might collect the reward. In this sense it is found in *The Adventures of Philip Rashleigh* (1825) and it thus considerably antedates the modern use as a sycophant.

Crawley. Crooked as Crawley or **Crawley brook,** a river in Bedfordshire. That part called the brook, which runs into the Ouse, is so crooked that a boat would have to go eighty miles in order to make a direct progress of eighteen. (Fuller: *Worthies*.)

Creaking Doors Hang the Longest. Delicate persons often outlive the more robust.

Creature. Wine, whisky or other spirits. The use of the word is a facetious adaptation of the passage "Every creature of God is good," 1 *Tim.* iv, 4, used in the defence of wine as a legitimate drink.

> I find my master took too much of the creature last night, and now is angling for a quarrel.— DRYDEN: *Amphitryon*, iii, 1.

Creature-comforts. Food and other things necessary for the comfort of the body. Man being supposed to consist of body and soul, the body is the creature, but the soul is the "vital spark of heavenly flame."

Crédit Mobilier (krä' dē mō bil' yā). A joint-stock company, founded Paris 1852, licensed to indulge in any form of trading for profits.

Credo (krē' dō). A statement of belief. *Credo quia impossibile* (Lat.), I believe it because it is impossible. A paradox ascribed to St. Augustine, but founded on a passage in Tertullian's *De Carne Christi*, IV:—

> Credibile est, quia ineptum est . . . . certum est quia impossibile.

Crème de la Crème (krām de la krām) (Fr.). Literally, "cream of the cream"; used figuratively for the very choicest part of something which itself is very choice.

Cremorne Gardens (kre môrn'). These pleasure gardens were in Chelsea, on the site now largely occupied by the Lots Road Power Station. The Gardens were opened in 1845 and for some years furnished the gayer side of London with much the same fare that Vauxhall had previously supplied. Spectacular balloon ascents were made from there; a mediæval tournament was got up; and every night there was dancing to be had, with all the other attractions of shady paths, flickering lamps, and attractive girls. Eventually the Gardens became such a centre of rowdiness that the neighbourhood revolted, and they were closed for good in 1877. Their memory is preserved in some of Whistler's Nocturnes.

Creole (krē' ōl). A person of European parentage born in the West Indies or central America—a term of 16th-century Spanish origin (from *criollo*. W. Indian corruption of Sp. *Criadillo*, from *criado*=bred, brought up). Used by the French of white residents (whether Fr. or Sp.) in Louisiana. The Empress Josephine was a Creole from Martinique.

Crescent. Tradition says that "Philip, the father of Alexander, meeting with great difficulties in the siege of Byzantium, set the workmen to undermine the walls, but a crescent moon discovered the design, which miscarried; consequently the Byzantines erected a statue to Diana, and the crescent became the symbol of the state."

Another legend is that Othman, the Sultan, saw in a vision a crescent moon, which kept increasing till its horns extended from east to west, and he adopted the crescent of his dream for his standard, adding the motto, "*Donec repleat orbem*."

Cressida (kres' i dà), **Cressid.** Daughter of Calchas, a priest, beloved by Troilus (*q.v.*). They vowed eternal fidelity to each other, and as pledges of their vow Troilus gave the maiden a sleeve, and Cressid gave the Trojan prince a glove. Scarce had the vow been made when an exchange of prisoners was agreed to. Diomed gave up three Trojan princes, and was to receive Cressid in lieu thereof. Cressid vowed to remain constant, and Troilus swore to rescue her. She was led off to the Grecian's tent, and soon gave all her affections to Diomed—nay, even bade him wear the sleeve that Troilus had given her in token of his love.

> As false
> As air, as water, wind, or sandy earth,
> As fox to lamb, as wolf to heifer's calf,
> Pard to the hind, or step-dame to her son;
> "Yea," let them say, to stick the heart of falsehood,
> "As false as Cressid."
>
> *Troilus and Cressida*, iii, 2.

Crestfallen. Dispirited. The allusion is to fighting cocks, whose crest falls in defeat and rises rigid and of a deep-red colour in victory.

> Shall I seem crest-fallen in my father's sight?
> SHAKESPEARE: *Richard II*, i, 1.

Crete (krēt). **Hound of Crete.** A bloodhound.
Coupe le gorge, that's the word. I thee defy again,
O hound of Crete. SHAKESPEARE: *Henry V*, ii, 1.

The Infamy of Crete. The Minotaur (*q.v*).
There lay stretched
The infamy of Crete, detested brood
Of the feigned heifer.
                    DANTE: *Hell*, xii (Cary's translation).

Cretinism (kret' in izm). Mental imbecility.
accompanied by goitre. So called from the
Crétins of the Alps. The word is a corruption of
Christian (*Chrétien*), because, being baptized,
and only idiots, they were "washed from original sin," and incapable of actual sin. Similarly,
idiots are called *innocents*. (Fr. *crétin*.)

Crewel Garters. Garters made of worsted
or yarn.
Ha! ha! look, he wears cruel garters.
                    SHAKESPEARE: *King Lear*, ii, 4.

The resemblance in sound between *crewe*
(the derivation of which is unknown) and *cruel*
formerly gave rise to many puns, *e.g.* —
Wearing of silk, why art thou so cruel?
                    Woman's a Weathercock (1612).

Crib. Thieves' slang for a house or dwelling,
as "Stocking Crib" (a hosier's shop), "Thimble
Crib" (a silversmith's); also slang for a petty
theft, and for a translation from Latin, Greek,
etc., surreptitiously used by schoolboys in doing
their lessons. **To crib** is to pilfer or purloin, and
to copy someone else's work without acknowledging it, to plagiarize.

The word originally denoted a manger with
bars; hence its application to a child's cot.

To crack a crib. *See* CRACK.

Cricket. The earliest mention of the game
appears to be the reference in the Guild Merchant
Book of Guildford, dated 1598, when John
Denwick of Guldeford, being then about
fifty-nine years of age, deposed that he had known
a certain parcel of land "for the space of Fyfty
years and more," and that "hee and several of
his fellowes did runne and play there at Creckett
and other plaies" when he was a scholar at the
Guildford Free School. This would take the
game back to the end of Henry VIII's reign, and
it was certainly a Wykehamist game in the days
of Elizabeth.

In 1700 two stumps were used 24 inches
apart and 12 inches high, with long bails atop.
A middle stump was added by the Hambledon
Club in 1775. The height of the stumps was
raised to 28 inches in 1929. The length of run
is 22 yards.

The first cricket club was the Hambledon,
which practically came to an end in 1791, but
existed in name till 1825.

The Marylebone Cricket Club (M.C.C.),
which is regarded as the governing body of the
game, was founded in 1787. Its ground was
originally on the site now occupied by Dorset
Square; in 1811 the groundsman, Thomas
Lord, moved it to Regent's Park, and in 1814 to
its present position in St. John's Wood, known
after him as Lord's Cricket Ground.

The word *cricket* is probably from A.S. *cric*,
cryec, a staff, and is thus connected with *crutch*.

It's not cricket. It's not done in a fair and
sportsmanlike way.

Crikey (krī' ki). An exclamation; a mild
oath; originally a euphemistic modification of
Christ.

Crillon (krē' yon). **Where wert thou, Crillon?**
Crillon, surnamed *the Brave*, in his old age
went to church, and listened intently to the
story of the Crucifixion. In the middle of the
narrative he grew excited, and, unable to contain himself, cried out, "*Où étais-tu, Crillon?*"
One of the finest hotels in Paris, in the Place de
la Concorde, is named from this hero; it was
the German Headquarters during the occupation, 1940-44.

Crillon (1541-1615) was one of the greatest
captains of the 16th century. He fought at the
battle of Ivry (1590), and was entitled by Henri
IV "*le brave des braves.*"
Henri IV, after the battle of Argives (1589), wrote to
Crillon: "*Prend-toi, brave Crillon, nous avons vaincu à
Arques, et tu n'y étais pas.*" This letter has become
proverbial.

Crimp. A decoy; especially one of those
riverside pests who purport to supply ships with
sailors, but who are in league with public-houses
and low-class lodging-houses, into which they
decoy the sailors and relieve them of their
money under one pretence or another.

Crinoline (krin' ō lēn). The word comes
from Latin *crinis*, hair, and *linum*, linen, and
originally meant the stiff horsehair and linen
material used to swell out the skirts of women's
dresses. When enormous skirts became fashionable, about 1856, cages of steel or whalebone
were worn to keep them spread to their full
extent, and these were called crinolines.
The crinoline reached its largest spread about
1866, and then quickly subsided, to be replaced
by the bustle.

Cripplegate. This district in the City of
London was so called before the Conquest
from the number of cripples who resorted
thither to beg, because of the parish church of
St. Giles (*q.v.*), the patron of cripples (*Stow*).
Churches dedicated to this saint are common

in the suburbs of large towns, as St. Giles of Norwich, Cambridge, Salisbury, etc.

Crishna. *See* KRISHNA.

Crisis properly means the "ability to judge." Hippocrates said that all diseases had their periods, when the humours of the body ebbed and flowed like the tide of the sea. These tidal days he called *critical days*, and the tide itself a *crisis*, because it was on these days the physician could determine whether the disorder was taking a good or a bad turn. The seventh and all its multiples were critical days of a favourable character. (Gr. *krinein*, to decide or determine.)

Criss-cross Row. *See* CHRISS-CROSS.

Critic. A judge; an arbiter. (Gr. *krinein*, to judge, to determine.)

A captious, malignant critic is called a Zoilus (*q.v.*).

"And what of this new book the whole world makes such a rout about?" "Oh, it is out of all plumb, my lord; quite an irregular thing! not one of the angles at the four corners is a right angle. I had my rule and compasses in my pocket." "Excellent critic!"

"And for the epic poem your lordship bade me look at, upon taking the length, breadth, height, and depth of it, and trying them at home upon an exact scale of Bossu's [Bossut's], 'tis out, my lord, in every one of its dimensions." "Admirable connoisseur!"—STERNE: *Tristram Shandy*, vol. iii, ch. xii.

The abbé Charles Bossut (1730-1814) was a noted mathematician and geometer.

Croak, To. In slang this means to die, the term probably coming from the hoarse death rattle or croak of the expiring breath. A hedge doctor, or wandering quack is known as a *Crocus*, or one who makes his patients croak.

Croaker. A raven, so called from its croak; one who takes a desponding view of things. Goldsmith, in his *Good-natured Man*, has a character so named.

Crocodile. A symbol of deity among the Egyptians, because, says Plutarch, it is the only aquatic animal which has its eyes covered with a thin transparent membrane, by reason of which it sees and is not seen, as God sees all, Himself not being seen. To this he subsequently adds another reason, saying, "The Egyptians worship God symbolically in the crocodile, that being the only animal without a tongue, like the Divine Logos, which standeth not in need of speech." (*De Iside et Osiride*, vol. ii, p. 381.)

Achilles Tatius says, "The number of its teeth equals the number of days in a year." Another tradition is that, during the seven days held sacred to Apis, the crocodile will harm no one.

Crocodile tears. Hypocritical tears. The tale is, that crocodiles moan and sigh like a person

in deep distress, to allure travellers to the spot, and even shed tears over their prey while in the act of devouring it.

> As the mournful crocodile
> With sorrow snares relenting passengers.
> SHAKESPEARE: *2 Henry VI*, iii, 1.

Crœsus (krē′ sūs). **Rich as Crœsus.** Crœsus, King of Lydia (560-546 B.C.), was so rich and powerful that all the wise men of Greece were drawn to his court, and his name became proverbial for wealth.

Crofters. Small holders in the Highlands of Scotland; also Cottars (*cf.* Burns, *Cottar's Saturday Night*).

Crone. From Old North Fr. *carone*, a worn-out horse, which gives in Mod. Fr. *carogne*, a contemptuous word for an old woman. It is from Lat. *caro*, flesh, and is so connected with *carrion*. *Crone* was also applied to an old ewe, and in this case is direct from Mid. Dutch, *kronie*, *karonie*, an old sheep, which has the same origin as *carone*.

> Take up the bastard; take 't up, I say; give 't to thy crone.—SHAKESPEARE: *Winter's Tale*, ii, 3.

Cronian Sea. The north polar sea: so called from Cronos. Pliny says "*A Thule unius diei navigatione mare concretum, a nonnullis cronium appellatur.*" (*Nat. Hist.*, iv, 16.)

> As when two polar winds blowing adverse
> Upon the Cronian sea.
> MILTON: *Paradise Lost*, x, 290.

Cronos or **Cronus** (krō′ nos). *See* KRONOS.

Crony. A familiar friend. *An old crony* is an intimate of times gone by. The word was originally (17th cent.) University slang, and seems to have no connexion with *crone* (*q.v.*); it may be from Gr. *kronios*, long-lasting (*kronos*, time), meaning a long-lasting friend.

Crook. By hook or **crook.** *See* HOOK.

To crook the elbow, or **finger.** The American equivalent to the English elbow-lifting, *i.e.* having a drink, especially drinking as a habit.

Crooning. A competent musical critic describes crooning thus: "A reprehensible form of singing that established itself in light entertainment music about the 1930s . . . The principle of crooning is to use as little voice as possible and instead to make a sentimental appeal by prolonged moaning somewhere near the written notes, but preferably never actually on those notes. The smallest vocal equipment is sufficient for the purpose of crooning, one of its admirers' delusions being that it does not become wholly satisfactory until it is amplified by a microphone." (Eric Blom).

Crop Up or **Out.** To rise out of, to appear at the surface. A mining term. Strata which rise to the surface are said to *crop out.* We also say, such and such a subject *crops up* from time to time—*i.e.* rises to the surface; such and such a thing *crops out* of what you were saying—*i.e.* is *apropos* thereof.

Share-cropper (U.S.A.). Under-privileged classes in the Southern States who work on the cotton plantations and take a share of the crops in lieu of wages.

Croquet (krō′ ki). This once popular garden game takes its name from the French *croc,* a hook, as the early croquet mallets were shaped like hockey-sticks. It came into fashion in Britain about 1856.

Crore. In India, a hundred lacs of rupees.

Cross. The cross is not solely a Christian symbol, originating with the crucifixion of the Redeemer. In Carthage it was used for ornamental purposes; runic crosses were set up by the Scandinavians as boundary marks, and were erected over the graves of kings and heroes; Cicero tells us (*De Divinatione,* ii, 27, and 80, 81) that the augur's staff with which they marked out the heaven was a cross; the Egyptians employed the same as a sacred symbol, and two buns marked with the cross were discovered at Herculaneum. It was a sacred symbol among the Aztecs long before the landing of Cortes; in Cozumel it was an object of worship; in Tabasco it symbolized the god of rain; and in Palinque it is sculptured on the walls with a child held up adoring it. It was one of the emblems of Quetzalcoatl, as lord of the four cardinal points, and the four winds that blow therefrom.

The cross of the crucifixion is legendarily said to have been made of four sorts of wood (palm, cedar, olive, and cypress), to signify the four quarters of the globe.

Ligna crucis palma, cedrus, cupressus, oliva.

In his *Monasteries of the Levant* (1848) Curzon gives the legend that Solomon cut down a cedar and buried it on the spot where the pool of Bethesda stood later. A few days before the crucifixion, this cedar floated to the surface of the pool, and was employed as the upright of the Saviour's cross.

It is said that Constantine, on his march to Rome, saw a luminous cross in the sky, in the shape and with the motto *In hoc vinces,* by this [sign] conquer. In the night before the battle of Saxa Rubra (312) a vision appeared to the Emperor in his sleep, commanding him to inscribe the cross and the motto on the shields of his soldiers. He obeyed the voice of the vision, and prevailed. The monogram is ΧΡιστος (Christ). *See* Gibbon's *Decline and Fall,* ch. xx.

This may be called a standing legend; for, besides St. Andrew's cross, and the Dannebrog (*q.v.*), there is the story concerning Don Alonzo before the battle of Ourique in 1139, when the figure of a cross appeared in the eastern sky; Christ, suspended on it, promised the Christian king a complete victory, and the Moors were totally routed. This legend is commemorated by Alonzo's device, in a field argent five escutcheons azure, in the form of a cross, each escutcheon being charged with five bezants, in memory of the five wounds of Christ. *See* LABARUM.

In heraldry, as many as 285 varieties of cross have been recognized, but the twelve in ordinary use, and from which the others are derived, are:—(1) The ordinary cross; (2) the cross humetté, or couped; (3) the cross urdé, or pointed; (4) the cross potent; (5) the cross crosslet; (6) the cross botonné, or treflé; (7) the cross moline; (8) the cross potence; (9) the cross fleury; (10) the cross patté; (11) the Maltese cross (or eight-pointed cross); (12) the cross cleché and fitché.

As a mystic symbol the number of crosses may be reduced to four;

The Greek cross found on Assyrian tablets, Egyptian and Persian monuments, and on Etruscan pottery.

The Latin cross or *crux immissa.* This symbol is found on coins, monuments, and medals long before the Christian era.

The tau cross or *crux commissa.* Very ancient indeed, and supposed to be a phallic emblem.

The tau cross with a handle, or *crux ansata,* is common to several Egyptian deities, as Isis, Osiris, etc.; and is the emblem of immortality and life generally. The circle signifies the eternal preserver of the world, and the T is the monogram of Thoth, the Egyptian Mercury, meaning wisdom. *See* CROSS.

The Invention of the Cross. A church festival held on May 3rd, in commemoration of the discovery (Lat. *invenire,* to discover) of the Cross (326) by St. Helena (*q.v.*). At her direction, after a long and difficult search in the neighbourhood of the Holy Sepulchre (which had been over-built with heathen temples), the remains of the three buried crosses were found. These were applied to a sick woman, and that which effected her cure was declared to be the True Cross. The Empress had this enclosed in a silver shrine (after having carried a large piece to Rome),

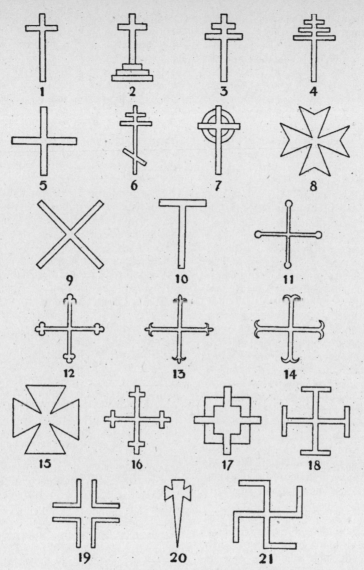

Crosses.—1. Latin. 2. Calvary. 3. Patriarchal, Archiepiscopal, Lorraine. 4. Papal. 5. Greek. 6. Russian. 7. Celtic. 8. Maltese. 9. St. Andrew's. 10. Tau. 11. Pommé. 12. Botonné. 13. Fleury. 14. Moline. 15. Patté. 16. Crosslet. 17. Quadrate. 18. Potent. 19. Voided and couped. 20. Patté fiché. 21. Fylfot, Swastika.

and deposited in a church that was built on the spot for the purpose.

The Cross of Lorraine, with two bars, was adopted as the emblem of the Free French during World War II.

The Red Cross on a white ground, sometimes called the Cross of Geneva, is the Swiss flag reversed, and indicates the neutrality of hospitals and ambulances.

Everyone must bear his own cross. His own burden or troubles. The allusion is to the law that the person condemned to be crucified was to carry his cross to the place of execution.

Hot cross buns. *See* BUN.

On the cross. Not "on the square," not straightforward. To get anything "on the cross" is to get it unfairly or dishonestly.

The judgment of the cross. An ordeal instituted in the reign of Charlemagne. The plaintiff and defendant were required to cross their arms upon their breast, and he who could hold out the longest gained the suit.

To cross it off or **out.** To cancel it by running your pen across it.

To cross swords. To fight a duel; metaphorically, to meet someone in argument or debate.

To cross the hand. Gypsy fortune-tellers always bid their dupe to "cross their hand with a bit of silver." This, they say, is for luck. The silver remained with the owner of the crossed hand. The sign of the cross warded off witches and all other evil spirits, and, as fortune-telling belongs to the black arts, the palm is signed with a cross to keep off the wiles of the devil. "You need fear no evil, though I am a fortune-teller, if by the sign of the cross you exorcise the evil spirit."

To cross the line—*i.e.* the equator. To pass to the other side of the equator. It is still the custom on board ship to indulge in horseplay when crossing the line, and those who are doing so for the first time are usually subjected to humorous indignities.

Cross and Ball. The orb of royalty is a sphere or ball surmounted by a cross, an emblem of empire introduced in representations of our Saviour. The cross stands *above* the ball, to signify that the spiritual power is above the temporal.

Cross-bench. Seats set at right angles to the rest of the seats in the House of Commons and the House of Lords, and intended for those members who are independent of any recognized party. Hence, *cross-bencher*, an independent, and the *cross-bench mind*, an unbiased or neutral mind.

Crossbill. The red plumage and the curious bill (the horny sheaths of which cross each other obliquely) of this bird are accounted for by a mediæval fable which says that these distinctive marks were bestowed on the bird by the Saviour at the Crucifixion, as a reward for its having attempted to pull the nails from the Cross with its beak. Schwenckfeld in 1603 (*Theriotrópheum Silesiœ*) gave the fable in the Latin verses of Johannes Major; but it would be better known to English readers through Longfellow's "Legend of the Crossbill" from the German of Julius Mosen.

Cross-biting. Cheating; properly, cheating one who has been trying to cheat you—biting in return. Hence, *cross-biter*, a swindler. *Laurence Crossbiter* is the name given to one of the rogues in *Cock Lorell's Bote (q.v.).*

Cross-bones. *See* SKULL AND CROSS-BONES.

Cross questions and crooked answers. A parlour game which consists in giving ludicrous or irrelevant answers to simple questions. Hence, the phrase is used of one who is "hedging," or trying by his answers to conceal the truth when he is being questioned.

Cross-roads. All (except suicides) who were excluded from holy rites were piously buried at the foot of the cross erected on the public road, as the place next in sanctity to consecrated ground. Suicides were ignominiously buried on the highway, generally at a crossing, with a stake driven through their body.

> Our orthodox coroner doubtless will find it a felo-de-se,
> And the stake and the cross-road, fool, if you will,
> does it matter to me?   TENNYSON: *Despair.*

Cross-row. Short for CHRISS-CROSS ROW.

Crossword puzzle. A puzzle in which words must be discovered to fill in, letter by letter, the squares into which a rectangular diagram is divided. Clues are furnished and most of the letters form parts of two words, one reading across and the other down the rectangle. There have long been simple puzzles of this nature, but the more ingenious crossword was invented in U.S.A., about 1923, and immediately welcomed in Britain.

Cross, meaning irritable, bad tempered.

Cross-grained. Patchy, ill-tempered, self-willed. Wood must be worked with the grain; when the grain crosses we get a knot or curling, which is hard to work uniform.

Cross-patch. A disagreeable, ill-tempered person, male or female. Patch (*q.v.*) is an old name for a fool, and with the meaning "fellow" it is common enough in Shakespeare, as a "scurvy patch," a "soldier's patch," "What patch is made our porter?" "a crew of patches," etc.

> Cross-patch, draw the latch,
>> Sit by the fire and spin;
> Take a cup, and drink it up,
>> Then call your neighbours in.
>> *Old Nursery Rhyme.*

Crow. A crow symbolizes contention, discord, strife.

As the crow flies. The shortest route between two given places. The crow flies straight to its destination. *Cp.* BEE-LINE.

To crow over one. To exult over a vanquished or abased person. The allusion is to cocks, who always crow when they have gained a victory.

To eat crow. To be forced to do something extremely disagreeable. The expression arose from an incident during an armistice in the war between Britain and the U.S.A. in 1812. A New Englander, having crossed the British lines by mistake, while out hunting, brought down a crow. A British officer, who heard the shot, determined to punish him. He was himself unarmed, but gained possession of the American's gun by praising his marksmanship and asking to see his weapon. Covering the huntsman with his own gun, the soldier declared that he was guilty of trespass and ordered him to take a bite out of the crow. The American was forced to obey. However, when the soldier returned the gun and told him to go, the American in his turn covered the soldier and compelled him to eat the remainder of the crow.

Crow's Nest. The "look out"—originally a barrel fixed to the masthead of an old-fashioned whaling-ship.

Crowd, Croud, or Crouth. An ancient Celtic species of fiddle with from three to six strings (Welsh *crwth*). Hence *crowder*, a player on a *crowd*. The last noted player on this instrument was John Morgan, who died in 1720.

> Harke how the minstrels gin to shrill aloud
> Their merry musick that resounds from far
> The pipe, the tabor, and the trembling croud,
> That well agree withouten breach or jar.
>> SPENSER: *Epithalamion.*

I never heard the olde song of *Percy and Duglas*, that I found not my heart mooved more then with a trumpet: and yet is it sung but by some blinde Crouder, with no rougher voyce, then rude stile.—SIDNEY: *Apologie for Poetrie.*

Crown. In heraldry, nine crowns are recognized: The oriental, the triumphal or imperial, the diadem, the obsidional crown, the civic, the crown vallery, the mural crown, the naval, and the crown celestial.

Among the Romans of the Republic and Empire crowns of various patterns formed marks of distinction for different services; the principal ones were:—

The blockade crown (*corona obsidionalis*), presented to the general who liberated a beleaguered army. This was made of grass and wild flowers gathered from the spot.

A *camp crown* (*corona castrenses*) was given to him who first forced his way into the enemy's camp. It was made of gold, and decorated with palisades.

A *civic crown* to one who saved a *civis* or Roman citizen in battle. It was of oak leaves, and bore the inscription, H.O.C.S.—*i.e. hostem occidit, civem servavit* (*a foe he slew, a citizen saved*).

A *mural crown* was given to that man who first scaled the wall of a besieged town. It was made of gold and decorated with battlements.

A *naval crown*, of gold, decorated with the beaks of ships, was given to him who won a naval victory.

An *olive crown* was given to those who distinguished themselves in battle in some way not specially mentioned.

An *ovation crown* (*corona ovatio*) was by the Romans given to a general in the case of a lesser victory. It was made of myrtle.

A *triumphal crown* was by the Romans given to the general who obtained a triumph. It was made of laurel or bay leaves. Sometimes a massive gold crown was given to a victorious general. *See* LAUREL.

The iron crown of Lombardy is the crown of the ancient Longobardic kings. It was used at the coronation of Agilulph, King of Lombardy, in 591, and among others that have since been crowned with it are Charlemagne, as King of Italy (774), Henry of Luxemburg (the Emperor Henry VII), as King of Lombardy (1311), Frederick IV (1452), Charles V (1530), and in 1805 Napoleon put it on his head with his own hands.

In 1866, at the conclusion of peace, it was restored by Austria to Italy and was replaced in the cathedral at Monza, where Charlemagne had been crowned, and whence it had been taken in 1859. The crown is so called from a narrow band of iron about three-eighths of an inch broad, and one-tenth of an inch in thickness, within it, said to be beaten out of one of the nails used at the Crucifixion. According to tradition, the nail was given to Constantine by his mother, St. Helena, who discovered the cross. The outer circlet is of beaten gold, and set with precious stones.

Crowns of Egypt. *See* EGYPT.

The crown, in English coinage, is a five-shilling piece, and is so named from the French *denier à la couronne*, a gold coin issued by Philip of Valois (1339) bearing a large crown on the obverse. The English crown was a gold coin of about $43\frac{1}{2}$ grs. till the end of Elizabeth's reign, except for a silver crown which was issued in the last coinage of Henry VIII and one other of Edward VI.

In the paper trade, **crown** is a standard size of printing paper measuring 15 by 20 inches; so called from an ancient watermark.

Crowner. An old pronunciation of "coroner" (*q.v.*), perhaps with the suggestion that he is an officer of the Crown.

The crowner hath sat on her, and finds it Christian burial.—*Hamlet*, v.1.

Crucial (kroo′ shǎl). **A crucial test.** A very severe and undeniable one. The allusion is to a fancy of Lord Bacon, who said that two different diseases or sciences might run parallel for a time, but would ultimately cross each other: thus, the plague might for a time resemble other diseases, but when the *bubo* or boil appeared, the plague would assume its specific character. Hence the phrases *instantia crucis* (a crucial or unmistakable symptom), a crucial experiment, example, question, etc. *Cp.* CRUX.

Cruel, The. Pedro, King of Castile (1334, 1350-69).

Cruel garters. *See* CREWEL.

Cruet. In common parlance this word is used in the plural to mean the salt, pepper, and mustard usually placed on the table for meals. A cruet is really a small bottle and is used specifically for each of the small bottles in which the water and wine for the eucharist and the ablutions of the Mass are served upon the altar.

Cruiser. Cruiser weight is the same as light-heavy weight. *See* BOXING.

Cruller. In the U.S.A. a sweet cake or biscuit in the form of strips or twists or rings, which has been fried in deep fat.

Crummy. In obsolete slang, expressive of something desirable, as *that's crummy*, that's good; also meaning plump, well developed, as *she's a crummy woman*, a fine, handsome woman. Among soldiers, however, the word has always meant lousy, infested with lice, and this is now the only meaning attached to the word.

Crusade (kroo sād). A war undertaken in late mediæval times by Christians against the Turks and Saracens for the recovery of the Holy Land and, nominally at least, for the honour of the Cross. Each nation had its special colour, which, says Matthew Paris (i, 446), was *red* for France; *white* for England; *green* for Flanders; for Italy it was *blue* or *azure*; for Spain, *gules*; for Scotland, *a St. Andrew's cross*; for the Knights Templars, *red on white*.

There were eight principal crusades:—

1. A crusade proclaimed by Urban II, in 1095. Two columns led by Peter the Hermit and Walter the Pennyless, set out in 1096 and were destroyed. A second expedition under Hugh the Great (father of Hugh Capet, later king of France), Raymond Count of Toulouse, Robert Duke of Normandy, and Godfrey de Bouillon, was successful and ended by achieving the proclamation of Godfrey as King of Jerusalem, 1099.

2. An unsuccessful expedition, promoted by St. Bernard, under the leadership of the Emperor Conrad III and Louis VII of France, 1147-49.

3. Jerusalem and Ascalon having been lost in 1187, a crusade for their recovery was preached by Gregory VIII, and Frederick Barbarossa set out in 1189; Philip II Augustus, King of France and Richard I of England started the following year. A stalemate was reached and the crusade abandoned in 1192.

4. A crusade was preached by Fulke of Neuilly in 1198. It was led by Baldwin of Flanders and the Doge of Venice. Constantinople was captured and Baldwin was elected Emperor in 1202.

5. In 1217 an unsuccessful expedition set out under Andrew, King of Hungary, to return in 1221.

6. The Emperor Frederick II set out in 1228, and the following year was crowned King of Jerusalem.

7. Following the loss of the Holy Land in 1244, St. Louis (Louis IX of France) set out in 1248. He was captured by the Saracens in 1250; a ten years' truce was declared and Louis returned to France.

8. Louis and Prince Edward (afterwards Edward I) of England set out in 1270. St. Louis died on August 25, and the crusade ended with a twenty years' truce in 1272.

The Children's Crusade, consisting of a body of 30,000 boys and girls between the ages of ten and sixteen, led by a shepherd boy, Stephen, set out from Vendôme to capture Jerusalem in 1212. The King of France, parents and priests had all forbidden their departure, but they got to Marseilles where they were embarked for Palestine. Some perished at sea and the rest were sold through the treachery of the ship-owners as slaves to Barbary. There were two other contingents, from the Germanies, one of which lost half its numbers while crossing the Mont Cenis, the remainder being kidnapped or dying of want and weariness; the other crossed the St. Gothard, reached Brindisi, and were sold as slaves to the Moors.

Crush. To crush a bottle—*i.e.* drink one. Milton has *crush the sweet poison* (*Comus*, 47). The idea is that of crushing the grapes. Shakespeare has also *burst* a bottle in the same sense (Induction of *Taming of the Shrew*). *See* CRACK.

Come and crush a cup of wine.
SHAKESPEARE: *Romeo and Juliet*, i, 2.

To have a crush on someone, meaning to have a very passing infatuation for someone—a schoolgirl's phrase and emotion.

Crust. The upper crust (of society). The aristocracy; the upper ten-thousand. The phrase was first used in *Sam Slick*. The upper crust was at one time the part of the loaf placed before the most honoured guests. Thus, in Wynkyn de Worde's *Boke of Keruinge* (carving) we have these directions: "Then take a lofe in your lyfte hande, and pare ye lofe rounde about; then cut the ouer-cruste to your souerayne . . ."

Crusted port. When port is first bottled its fermentation is not complete; in time it precipitates argol on the sides of the bottle, where it forms a crust. Crusted port, therefore, is port which has completed its fermentation. A splash of whitewash is usually dabbed on the bottle so that it will be kept the right way up, for careless movement would cause the crust to slip and spoil the wine.

Crusting. An American hunting term for taking big game in winter when the ice of ponds, rivers and lakes will bear the weight of a man but not that of a moose or deer.

Crusty. Ill-tempered, apt to take offence; cross, peevish. In Shakespeare's play Achilles addresses the bitter Thersites with:—

How now, thou core of envy!
Thou crusty batch of nature, what's the news?
Troilus and Cressida, v, i.

Crux. A knotty point, a difficulty. *Instantia crucis* means a crucial test (*q.v.*), or the point where two similar diseases *crossed* and showed a special feature. It does not refer to the cross, an instrument of punishment; but to the crossing of two lines, called also a *node* or knot; hence a trouble or difficulty. *Quœ te mala crux agitat?* (Plautus); What evil cross distresses you?—*i.e.* what difficulty, what trouble are you under?

Crux pectoralis. The cross which bishops of the Church of Rome suspend over their breast. *See also* CROSS.

Cry. For names of the distinctive cries of animals, *see* ANIMALS.

A far cry. A long way; a very considerable distance; used both of space and of time, as, "it is a far cry from David to Disraeli," but they both were Jews, "it's a far cry from Clapham to Kamschatka." Sir Walter Scott several times uses the phrase, "It's a far cry to Lochow (Lochawe)," and he tells us that this was a proverbial expression among the Campbells,

meaning that their ancient hereditary dominions lay beyond the reach of an invading enemy.—*Legend of Montrose*: ch. xii.

In full cry. In full pursuit. A phrase from hunting, with allusion to a yelping pack of hounds in chase.

It's no good crying over spilt milk. It's useless bewailing the past.

To cry cave (kā' vi). To give warning (Lat. *cave*, beware); used by schoolboys when a master comes in sight.

To cry off. To get out of a bargain; to refuse to carry out one's promise.

To cry stinking fish. To belittle one's own endeavours, offerings, etc. "To cry" here is to offer for sale by shouting one's wares in the street.

To cry up. To praise loudly and publicly.

To cry wolf. *See* WOLF.

Crypto-Catholic. A person who is secretly a Catholic but for some ulterior motive conceals the fact and poses as a Protestant. The term is also applied (Crypto-Communist, -Fascist, etc.) to one who secretly works for the cause of his party though outwardly appearing to have no connection with it.

Crystal Gazing, or, as it is sometimes termed, Scrying, is a very ancient form of divination. It is alleged that certain people can, by gazing fixedly and deeply into a polished crystal ball, see what is about to happen or what is actually happening at some distant place. It is said that scenes are enacted and places are recognizable as clearly as in the view-finder of a camera. Crystal gazing has been, and, indeed, still is, a practice that lends itself to the skill of impostors, and from a psychic standard it is not to be encouraged.

Crystal Palace. This was one of the glories of the Victorian era. The original Crystal Palace, built entirely of glass and iron, was erected in Hyde Park to house the 1851 Great Exhibition. When the exhibition closed the building was moved (1854) to Sydenham where it was re-erected with some alterations and the addition of two towers which for many years were visible for many miles around. Exhibitions, concerts, and other events took place in the Palace, which became national property in 1911. The whole building was entirely destroyed by fire in November, 1936.

The crystalline sphere. According to Ptolemy, the ninth orb, identified by some with "the waters which were above the firmament" (*Gen.* i, 7); it was placed between the "primum mobile" and the firmament or sphere of the fixed stars and was held to have a shivering movement that interfered with the regular motion of the stars.

> They pass the planets seven, and pass the fixed
> And that crystalline sphere, whose balance weighs
> The trepidation talked.
>
> MILTON: *Paradise Lost*, iii, 481.

Cub. An ill-mannered lout. The cub of a bear is said to have no shape until its dam has licked it into form.

> A bear's a savage beast, of all
> Most ugly and unnatural;
> Whelped without form until the dam
> Has licked it into shape and frame.
>
> BUTLER: *Hudibras*, i, 3.

Cubbing, or **Cub-hunting.** This is the term employed to describe the preliminary training given to young foxhounds before regular hunting begins. Fox cubs have not the craftiness nor staying power of the older beast, and thus furnish better sport for young hounds and young riders.

Cuba. The Roman deity who kept guard over infants in their cribs and sent them to sleep. Lat. *cubo*, to lie down in bed.

Cubism (kū′ bizm). The doctrine of an early-20th-century school of painters who depict surfaces, figures, tints, light and shade, etc., on canvas by means of a multiplicity of cubes. The name was given to this school, somewhat disparagingly, by Henri Matisse, in 1908. It was a form of art wholly devoid of representation and divorced from realism, excluding any attempt to depict actual appearances and spurning all the accepted canons of art. Picasso was its great exponent; Braque, Leger, and Derain explored its possibilities in many of their works.

Cubit (kū′ bit). An ancient measure of length, the word coming from the Latin *cubitum*, the elbow. Approximately it applied to the length from the elbow to the tip of the longest finger. The Hebrews had two cubits, the ordinary cubit as above, measuring about 22 in. and a longer one used by Ezekiel for measuring the Temple. The most ancient cubit was the Egyptian, which measured 20·64 in. and was divided into seven palms. It was employed in the design and building of the Pyramids, and measuring sticks have been found proving the use of this measure for at least three centuries before Christ. The Roman cubit measured 17·4 in.

Cuckold. The husband of an adulterous wife; so called from *cuckoo*, the chief characteristic of this bird being to deposit its eggs in other birds' nests. Johnson says "it was usual to alarm a husband at the approach of an adulterer by calling out 'Cuckoo,' which by mistake was applied in time to the person warned." Greene calls the cuckoo "the cuckold's quirister" (*Quip for an Upstart Courtier*, 1592), and the Romans used to call an adulterer a "cuckoo," as "*Te cuculum uxor ex lustris rapit*" (Plautus: *Asinaria*, v, 3). *Cp.* ACTÆON; HORN; *and see quotation under* LADY'S SMOCK.

Cuckoo. There are many old folk rhymes about this bird; one says:—

> In April the cuckoo shows his bill;
> In May he sings all day;
> In June he alters his tune;
> In July away he'll fly;
> In August go he must.

Other sayings are:—

Turn your money when you hear the cuckoo, and you'll have money in your purse till he come again.

And—

The cuckoo sings from St. Tiburtius' Day (April 14th) to St. John's Day (June 24th).

Cuckoo oats and woodcock hay make a farmer run away. If the spring is so backward that oats cannot be sown till the cuckoo is heard (*i.e.* April), or if the autumn is so wet that the aftermath of hay cannot be got in till woodcock shooting (middle of November), the farmer must be a great sufferer.

Cuckoo-spit. A frothy exudation deposited on plants by certain insects, especially the frog-hopper (*Aphrophora spumaris*), for the purpose of protecting the larvæ. So called from an erroneous popular notion that the froth was spat out by cuckoos.

> It must be likewise understood with some restriction what hath been affirmed by *Isidore*, and yet delivered by many, that Cicades are bred out of Cuccow spittle or Woodsear; that is, that spumous, frothy dew or exudation, or both, found upon Plants, especially about the joints of Lavender and Rosemary, observable with us about the latter end of May.— SIR THOMAS BROWNE: *Pseud. Epidemica*, v, 3.

Cuddy, an abbreviation of Cuthbert, is the North Country and Scottish familiar name for a donkey, as elsewhere he is called Neddy or Jack.

Cudgel. To cudgel one's brains. To make a painful effort to remember or understand something. The idea is from taking a stick to beat a dull boy under the notion that dullness is the result of temper or inattention.

> Cudgel thy brains no more about it; for your dull ass will not mend his pace with beating.— SHAKESPEARE: *Hamlet*, v, 1.

To take up the cudgels. To maintain an argument or position. To fight, as with a cudgel, for one's own way.

Cue (kū). The tail of a sentence (Fr. *queue*), the catchword which indicates when another actor is to speak; a hint.

> When my cue comes, call me, and I will answer.— A *Midsummer Night's Dream*, iv, 1.

To give the cue. To give the hint.

In another sense *cue* means a person's frame of mind—in a good or bad skin.

My uncle was in thoroughly good cue.
DICKENS: *Pickwick Papers.*

Cuerp. *See* QUERPO.

Cui bono? (kwī bō′ nō). Who is benefited thereby? To whom is it a gain? A common, but quite erroneous, meaning attached to the words is, What good will it do? For what good purpose? It was the question of the Roman judge L. Cassius Pedanius. *See* Ciccro, *Rosc. Am.*, xxx, 84.

Cato, that great and grave philosopher, did commonly demand, when any new project was propounded unto him, *cui bono*, what good will ensue in case the same is effected?—FULLER: *Worthies* (The Design, i.).

Cul de Sac (kul de săk) (Fr.). A blind alley, or road blocked up at one end like a sack. Figuratively, an argument, etc., that leads to nothing.

Cullinan Diamond (kú lin′ án). The largest diamond ever known. It was discovered in 1905 at the Premier Mine in South Africa, and when found weighed 3,025¾ carats (about 1 lb. 6 oz.), as against the 186 1/16 carats of the famous Koh-i-Nor (*q.v.*) in its uncut state. It was purchased by the South African Government for £150,000 and presented to Edward VII, and now forms part of the Crown Jewels, its estimated value being over £1,000,000. It was cut into a number of stones, of which the two largest weigh over 516 and 309 carats respectively. It was named from the manager of the mine at the time of its discovery.

Cully. A fop, a fool, a dupe. Perhaps a contracted form of *cullion*, a despicable creature (Ital. *coglione*). Shakespeare uses the word two or three times, as "Away, base cullions!" (*2 Henry VI*, i, 3), and again in *Taming of the Shrew*, iv, 2—"And makes a god of such a cullion." *Cp.* GULL.

You base cullion, you.
BEN JONSON: *Every Man in his Humour*, iii, 2.

Culver (kŭl′ vėr). A dove or pigeon; from A.S. *culfre*, which is probably an English word and unconnected with Lat. *columba*. Hence culver-house, a dovecote.

On liquid wing,
The sounding culver shoots.
THOMSON: *Spring.* 452.

Culverin (kŭl′ vĕr in). A long, slender piece of artillery employed in the 16th century. It was 5¼ in. bore and fired a projectile of 18 lb. Queen Elizabeth's "Pocket Pistol" in Dover Castle is a culverin. So called from Lat. *colubrinus* (Fr. *coulevrine*), snake-like.

Culverkeys (kŭl′ vėr kēz). An old popular name for various plants, such as the bluebell, columbine, squill, etc., the flowers of which have some resemblance to a bunch of keys (O.E. *culfre*, a dove).

Cumberland Poets, or Lake Poets. One or other of these terms used often to be applied to the poets Wordsworth (1770-1850), Southey (1774-1843), and Coleridge (1772-1834) who lived about the the lakes of Cumberland. According to Jeffrey, of the *Edinburgh Review*, they combined the sentimentality of Rousseau with the simplicity of Kotzebue and the homeliness of Cowper.

Cunctator (kŭngk tā tôr) (Lat., *the delayer*). Quintus Fabius Maximus (d. 203 B.C.), the Roman general who baffled Hannibal by avoiding direct engagements, and wearing him out by marches, countermarches, and skirmishes from a distance. This was the policy by which Duguesclin forced the English to abandon their French possessions in the reign of Charles V. *Cp.* FABIAN.

Cuneiform Letters (kū nē′ i fôrm). Letters like wedges (Lat. *cuneus*, a wedge). They form the writing of ancient Persia, Babylonia, Assyria, etc., and, dating from about 3800 B.C. to the early years of the Christian era, are the most ancient specimens of writing known to us. Cuneiform inscriptions first attracted interest in Europe in the early 17th century, but no deciphering was successful until 1802 (by Grotefend, of Hanover).

Cunning. This is a word to which various meanings are attached and on which several phrases depend. It originally comes from the same word as does "ken," to know, and was applied to someone who *knew* things. As Wyclif's bible translates *Genesis* ii, 9:

A tree of kunnynge of good and euil.

By an extension of this came the meaning of skill:—

If I forget thee, O Jerusalem, let my right hand forget her cunning.—*Psalm* cxxxvii.

The word had, however, already begun to infer a knowledge of occult and evil matters:—

We take cunning for a sinister and crooked wisdom.—
BACON: *Cunning.*

and a Cunning Man, or Woman, was merely another name for a wizard, or witch. Hence it grew to mean sly and crafty, the sense in which it is commonly used now.

The American usage, in the sense of charming, or pretty or engaging, was customary there by the mid-19th century.

Cunobelin (kū′ nō bel′ in). Cunobelinus, King of the Catuvellauni (A.D. 5-40), and the father of Caractacus. His name is preserved, in modified form, in Cymbeline, and in "Cunobelin's gold-mines," the local name for the dene-holes in the chalk beds of Little Thurrock, Essex, which were traditionally used by Cunobelin for hiding.

Cup. A mixture of strong ale with sugar, spice, and a lemon, properly served up hot in a silver cup. Sometimes a roasted orange takes the place of a lemon. If wine is added, the cup is called *bishop* (*q.v.*); if brandy is added, the beverage is called *cardinal*.

Cider cup, claret cup, etc., are drinks made of cider, claret, etc., with sugar, fruit, and herbs.

Cup Final. *See* ASSOCIATION FOOTBALL CUP.

He was in his cups. Intoxicated. *Inter pocula, inter vina.* (Horace: 3 *Odes*, vi, 20.)

Let this cup pass from me. Let this trouble or affliction be taken away, that I may not be compelled to undergo it; this cup is "full of the wine of God's fury," let me not be compelled to drink it. The reference is to Christ's agony in the garden (*Matt*, xxvi, 39).

My cup runs over. My blessings overflow. Here cup signifies portion or blessing.
My cup runneth over . . . goodness and mercy shall follow me all the days of my life.—*Ps*. xxiii, 5, 6.

There's many a slip' twixt the cup and the lip.

We must drink the cup. We must bear the burden awarded to us, the sorrow which falls to our lot.

Not my cup of tea. A phrase meaning, it does not suit me, this is not the sort of thing I want.

Cupper. A comfortable colloquial abbreviation of "a cup of tea." "Come in and have a nice cupper," *i.e.* "Come in and have a nice cup of tea."

Cups as sports trophies. An engraved (usually silver) cup is a common form of trophy. One of the oldest is the Waterloo Cup for coursing, which originated in 1836 and owes its name to the fact that its leading promoter was landlord of the Waterloo Hotel, Liverpool.

The Davis Cup for an international lawn tennis championship was presented by Dwight Davis in 1900. Another tennis trophy is the Wightman Cup, given by Mrs. George Wightman, in 1923, for competition between teams of women players from U.S.A. and Great Britain.

The America Cup, for an international yacht race, was originally named the Queen's Cup, and was offered by the Royal Yacht Squadron in 1851. In 1857 it was won by an American yacht

and has since been called the America Cup. For many years Sir Thomas Lipton built yachts in an endeavour to win back the Cup but it has remained in American hands.

The Ryder Cup for international golf matches was presented by Samuel Ryder in 1927, though up to the present only the British and American professional teams have competed for it—no other country being able to produce a team of sufficiently high standard. The Walker Cup was given in 1922 by an American, George H. Walker, for a golf match to be played twice a year between teams of amateurs of Great Britain and U.S.A. The Curtis Cup, given in 1923 by two American lady champions, the Misses Margaret and Harriot Curtis, is for a golf match between teams of ladies of Great Britain and the U.S.A.

See also ASSOCIATION FOOTBALL CUP.

Cupid. The god of love in Roman mythology (Lat. *cupido*, desire, passion), identified with the Greek Eros; son of Mercury and Venus. He is usually represented as a beautiful winged boy, blindfolded, and carrying a bow and arrows, and one legend says that he whets with blood the grindstone on which he sharpens his arrows.
Ferus et Cupido,
Semper ardentes acuens sagittas.
HORACE: 2 *Odes*, viii, 14, 15.

Cupid and Psyche (sī' ki). An episode in the *Golden Ass* (*q.v.*) of Apuleius. It is an allegory representing the progress of the soul to perfection. William Morris retells the story in his *Earthly Paradise* (*May*), as also does Walter Pater in *Marius the Epicurean*. *See* PSYCHE.

Cur. A mongrel or worthless dog; hence, a fawning, mean-spirited fellow. The word is from Scandinavian *kurra*, to snarl, to grumble, and is first used in England with "dog"—*kur-dogge*, a growling or snarling dog.
Like a wylde Bull, that being at a bay
Is bayted of a mastiffe, and a hound,
And a curre-dog.
SPENSER: *Faerie Queene*, VI, v, 19.
What would you have, you curs,
That like nor peace nor war?
SHAKESPEARE: *Coriolanus*, i, 1.

Curate. *See* CLERICAL TITLES.

Curate's egg. Among the catch-phrases that *Punch* has introduced into the English language, "Good in parts, like the curate's egg" is, perhaps, the most commonly used. The illustrated joke showed a nervous young curate, at his bishop's breakfast table. He has been asked by his lordship whether his egg is to his liking; terrified to say that it is bad, he stammers out that "it's good in parts."

Curfew (kěr' fū). The custom of ringing a bell every evening as a signal to put out fires and go to bed. The word comes from the Fr. *couvre feu*, and shows its Norman origin. William the Conqueror instituted the curfew in England in 1068, fixing the hour at eight in the evening. The word is now extended to mean the period commonly ordered by all occupying armies in time of war or civil commotion when civilians must stay within doors.

The curfew tolls the knell of parting day.
GRAY'S *Elegy*.

Curmudgeon (kĕr mŭj' ón). A grasping, miserly churl. Concerning this word Johnson says in his dictionary: "It is a vitious manner of pronouncing *cœur méchant*, Fr., an unknown correspondent," meaning that this suggestion was supplied by some correspondent unknown. By a ridiculous blunder, Ash (1775) copied it into his dictionary as "from Fr. *cœur*, unknown, *méchant*, correspondent"! The actual etymology of the word has not been traced.

Currant. A corruption of *Corinth*, whence currants were imported probably in the 16th century. Originally called "raisins of Corauntz," *Corauntz* being Anglo-French for Corinth.

Currency. A word applied in early Australia to the wide variety of coins then in circulation, as apart from English gold coins, which were called sterling. The word assumed the connotation of "Australian," and in novels of the mid-19th century the word "uncurrency" is found in the sense of "un-Australian."

Current. The drift of the current is the rate per hour at which the current runs.

The setting of the current is that point of the compass towards which the waters of the current run.

Curry Favour. A corruption of the M.E. *to curry favel*, to rub down Favel: *Favel* (or *Fauvel*) being the name of the horse in the 14th-century French satire *Roman de Fauvel*, which was a kind of counterpart to the more famous romance, *Reynard the Fox*. Fauvel, the fallow-coloured horse, takes the place of Reynard, and symbolizes cunning or duplicity; hence, to curry, or stroke down, Favel, was to enlist the services of duplicity, and so, to seek to obtain by insincere flattery or officious courtesy.

Curse. Curses, like chickens, come home to roost. Curses fall on the head of the curser, as chickens which stray during the day return to their roost at night.

Cursing by bell, book, and candle. *See* BELL.

Not worth a curse. I don't care a curse (or **cuss**). Here "curse" is the O.E. *cresse* or *cerse*, Mod. E. *cress*, *i.e.* something quite valueless.

Similarly, the Lat. *nihil* (*nihilum*) is *ne hilum*, not (worth) the black eye of a bean. Other phrases are "not a straw," "not a pin," "not a rap," "not a bit," "not a jot," "not a pin's point," "not a button."

Wisdom and witt nowe is not worthe a kerse.
LANGLAND: *Piers Plowman*.

The curse of Cain. One who is always on the move and has no abiding place is said to be "cursed with the curse of Cain." The allusion is to God's judgment on Cain after he had slain his brother Abel: —

And now art thou cursed from the earth, ... a fugitive and a vagabond shalt thou be in the earth.—
Gen. iv, 11-12.

The curse of Scotland. The nine of diamonds. It may refer to the arms of Dalrymple, Earl of Stair—viz. or, on a saltire argent, nine lozenges of the first. The earl was justly held in abhorrence for the massacre of Glencoe, and he was also detested in Scotland for his share in bringing about the Union with England in 1707. The phrase seems to be first recorded in the early 18th century, for in Houston's *Memoirs* (1715-47) we are told that Lord Justice Clerk Ormistone became universally hated in Scotland, where they called him the Curse of Scotland; and when the ladies were at cards playing the Nine of Diamonds (commonly called the Curse of Scotland) they called it the Justice Clerk.

Other attempts at accounting for the nickname are: (1) The nine of diamonds in the game of *Pope Joan* is called the Pope, the Antichrist of the Scottish reformers. (2) In the game of *comette*, introduced by Queen Mary, it is the great winning card, and the game was the curse of Scotland because it was the ruin of many families. (3) The word "curse" is a corruption of *cross*, and the nine of diamonds is so arranged as to form a St. Andrew's Cross; but as there is no evidence that the St. Andrew's Cross was ever looked upon in Scotland as a curse, and as also the nine of hearts would do as well, this explanation must be abandoned. (4) Some say it was the card on which the "Butcher Duke" wrote his cruel order after the Battle of Culloden; but this took place in 1746, which would seem to make it too late for the reference given above.

Grose says of the nine of diamonds: "Diamonds ... imply royalty ... and every ninth King of Scotland has been observed for many ages to be a tyrant and a curse to the country."—*Tour Thro' Scotland*, 1789.

Cursitor (kĕrs' i tòr). In the procedure of the old Courts of Chancery, which was revised in the mid-19th century, the issue of writs by the court was done by 24 cursitors, who between them covered all the counties in England and Wales. The word comes from the Latin *cursor*, a runner, and refers to the long journeys they had to perform when issuing the writs. Cursitor Street, Chancery Lane, takes its name from the office of the cursitors, built by Sir Nicholas Bacon (1509-79), father of the great chancellor.

Curtain. Curtain lecture. The nagging of a wife after she and her husband are in bed. *See* CAUDLE LECTURE.

> Besides what endless brawls by wives are bred,
> The curtain lecture makes a mournful bed.
> DRYDEN.

Curtain raiser. *See* LEVER DE RIDEAU.

To ring down the curtain. To bring a matter to an end. A theatrical term. When the play is over, the bell rings and the curtain comes down.

The last words of Rabelais are said to have been, "Ring down the curtain, the farce is played out."

Curtana (kĕr tā′ nȧ). The sword of mercy borne before the English kings at their coronation; it has no point and is hence *shortened* (O.Fr. *curt*, Lat. *curtus*). It is called the sword of Edward the Confessor, which, having no point, was the emblem of mercy. The royal sword of England was so called to the reign of Henry III.

> But when Curtana will not do the deed
> You lay the pointless clergy-weapon by,
> And to the laws, your sword of justice fly.
> DRYDEN: *Hind and Panther*, Pt. ii, 419.

Cushcow Lady. A Yorkshire name for the ladybird (*q.v.*).

Cushion. Cushion dance. A lively dance in which kissing while kneeling on a cushion was a prominent feature; popular in early Stuart times.

> In our court in Queen Elizabeth's time, gravity and state was kept up; in King James's time things were pretty well; but in King Charles's time there has been nothing but Trench-more and the cushion dance, *omnium gatherum*, tolly polly, *hoyte cum toyte.*—SELDEN'S *"Table Talk" (King of England)*.

The dance survived in rural districts until comparatively recent times, and is probably still practised. John Clare (1793-1864), the peasant poet of Northamptonshire, mentions it in his *May-Day Ballad*:—

> And then comes the cushion, the girls they all shriek,
> And fly to the door from the old fiddler's squeak;
> But the doors they are fastened, so all must kneel down,
> And take the rude kiss from th' unmannerly clown.

Cuss. A fellow, usually used with an epithet as in the case of "customer" (*q.v.*). Presumably from "curse" which in 19th-century U.S. was found used in the same way.

Cussedness. Perversity; malice prepense; an evil temper. In this sense the word seems to have been originally an Americanism; the M.E. word *cursydnesse* meant sheer wickedness.

Custard Coffin. *See* COFFIN.

Customer. Slang for a man or a fellow in a general way; usually with some qualification, as, *an ugly customer, a rum customer*, a person better left alone, as he is likely to show fight if interfered with. *Cp.* CARD.

Custos Rotulorum (*keeper of the rolls*). The chief civil officer or principal justice of the peace of a county, to whose custody are committed the records or rolls of the sessions.

Cut. Cut and come again. Take a cut from the joint, and come for another if you like; a colloquial expression for "there's plenty of it, have as much as you like." It is used by Swift in *Polite Conversation*, ii.

Cut and dried. Already prepared. "He had a speech all cut and dried." The allusion is to timber, cut, dried, and fit for use.

> Sets of phrases, cut and dry,
> Evermore thy tongue supply.
> SWIFT: *Betty the Grizette*.

Cut and run. Be off as quickly as possible. A sea phrase, meaning cut your cable and run before the wind.

Cut neither nails nor hair at sea. Petronius says:—

> Non licere cuiquam mortalium in nave neque unges neque capillos deponere, nisi cum pelago ventus irascitur.

The cuttings of the nails and hair were votive offerings to Proserpine, and it would excite the jealousy of Neptune to make offerings to another in his own special kingdom.

Cut no ice. Be of no account, make no impression, presumably borrowed from figure skating.

To cut a swath. To make an impression. An American colloquialism usually used in the negative. A swath is the amount of grass or crop cut down with one sweep of a scythe.

Cut out of whole cloth. Entirely false. Suggested probably by the mendacious claims of tailors' advertisements.

The cut of his jib. The contour or expression of his face. A sailor's phrase. The cut of a jib or foresail of a ship indicates her character, hence a sailor says of a suspicious vessel, he "does not like the cut of her jib."

Cut off with a shilling. Disinherited. Blackstone tells us that the Romans set aside those testaments which passed by the natural heirs unnoticed; but if any legacy was left, no matter how small, it proved the testator's intention. English law has no such provision, but the notion at one time prevailed that the name of the heir should appear in the will; and if he was bequeathed "a shilling," that the testator had not forgotten him, but disinherited him intentionally.

His life was cut short. He died prematurely. The allusion is to Atropos, one of the three Parcæ, cutting the thread of life spun by her sister Clotho.

To cut. To renounce acquaintance. There are four sorts of cut—

(1) The *cut direct* is to stare an acquaintance in the face and pretend not to know him.

(2) The *cut indirect*, to look another way, and pretend not to see him.

(3) The *cut sublime*, to admire the top of some tall edifice or the clouds of heaven till the person cut has passed by.

(4) The *cut infernal*, to stoop and adjust your boots till he has gone past.

To cut a dash. To make a show; to get oneself looked at and talked about for a showy or striking appearance. "Dashing" means *striking—i.e.* showy, as a "dashing fellow," a "dashing equipage."

To cut blocks with a razor. To do something astounding by insignificant means; to do something more eccentric than expedient, to "make pin-cushions of sunbeams" (Swift). The tale is that Accius Nævius, a Roman augur, opposed king Tarquin the Elder, who wished to double the number of senators. Tarquin sneered at his pretensions of augury, and asked if he could do what was then in his thoughts. "Undoubtedly," replied Nævius; and Tarquin with a laugh said, "Why, I was thinking whether I could cut through this whetstone with a razor." "Cut boldly," cried Nævius, and the whetstone was cleft in two. This story forms the subject of the *Bon Gaultier Ballads*, and Goldsmith refers to it in his *Retaliation*—

In short, 'twas his [Burke's] fate, unemployed or in place, sir,
To eat mutton cold, and cut blocks with a razor.

To cut capers. *See* CAPERS.

To cut one's comb. *See* COMB.

To cut short is to shorten. "Cut short all intermission" (*Macbeth*, iv, 3).

To cut it short (cp. AUDLEY) means to bring to an end what you are doing or saying.

To cut the ground from under one, or from under his feet. To leave an adversary no ground to stand on, by disproving all his arguments.

To cut the knot. To break through an obstacle. The reference is to the Gordian knot (*q.v.*) shown to Alexander, with the assurance that whoever loosed it would be made ruler of all Asia; whereupon the Macedonian cut it in two with his sword, and claimed to have fulfilled the prophecy.

To cut the painter. *See* PAINTER.

To cut up rough. To be disagreeable or quarrelsome about anything.

Cut-off. The American equivalent of the English short cut.

Cut out. Left in the lurch; superseded. In cards, when there are too many for a game (say whist), it is customary for the players to cut out after a rubber, in order that another player may have a turn. This is done by the players cutting the cards on the table, when the lowest turn-up gives place to the new hand.

He is cut out for a sailor. His natural propensities are suited for the vocation. The allusion is to cutting out cloth, etc., for specific purposes.

Cute. An American colloquialism for smart, pretty, attractive. It is a contraction of "acute," and is found in Nathan Bailey's dictionary of 1721.

Cuthbert. A name given during World War I to fit and healthy men of military age who, particularly in Government offices, were not "combed out" to go into the Army; also, of course, to one who actually avoided military service. It was coined by "Poy," the cartoonist of the *Evening News*, who represented these civilians as frightened-looking rabbits.

St. Cuthbert's beads. See BEAD.

St. Cuthbert's duck. The eider duck; so called because it breeds in the Farne Islands, St. Cuthbert's headquarters, and figures in the legends of the saint.

St. Cuthbert's Stone, and Well. A granite rock in Cumberland, and a spring of water close by.

Cuthbert Bede was the pen-name of the Rev. Edward Bradley (1827-89), author of *Verdant Green* (*q.v.*) and other pieces of Victorian humour.

Cutler's Poetry. Mere jingles or rhymes. Knives had, at one time, a distich inscribed on the blade by means of aqua fortis.

Whose posy was
For all the world like cutler's poetry
Upon a knife.
SHAKESPEARE: *Merchant of Venice*, v, 1.

Cutpurse. Now called "pickpocket." The two words are of historical value. When purses were worn suspended from a girdle, thieves cut the string by which the purse was attached; but when pockets were adopted, and purses were no longer hung on the girdle, the thief was no longer a cutpurse, but became a pickpocket.

To have an open ear, a quick eye, and a nimble hand, is necessary for a cutpurse.—SHAKESPEARE: *Winter's Tale*, iv, 3.

Cutter. A single-masted, deep-keeled and fore-and-aft rigged sailing vessel. The term is also applied to a light-armed naval vessel—a revenue cutter—used to prevent smuggling, etc.

Cutter's law. Not to see a fellow want while we have cash in our purse. Cutter's law means the law of purse-cutters, robbers, brigands, and highwaymen.

I must put you in cash with some of your old uncle's broad-pieces. This is cutter's law; we must not see a pretty fellow want, if we have cash ourselves.—SCOTT: *Old Mortality*, ch. ix.

Cwt. is C. *centum*, wt. *weight*, meaning hundred-weight. *Cp.* DWT.

Cyanean Rocks, The (sī ān' i an). The Symplegades, two movable rocks at the entrance of the Euxine, *i.e.* where the Bosphorus and Black Sea meet. They were said to close together when a vessel attempted to sail between them, and thus crush it to pieces. Cyanean means *blue-coloured*, and Symplegades means *dashers together*.

Cycle. A period or series of events or numbers which recur everlastingly in precisely the same order.

Cycle of the moon, called "Meton's Cycle," from Meton, who discovered it, is a period of nineteen years, at the expiration of which time the phases of the moon repeat themselves on the same days as they did nineteen years previously. *See* CALLIPPIC PERIOD.

Cycle of the sun. A period of twenty-eight years, at the expiration of which time the Sunday letters recur and proceed in the same order as they did twenty-eight years previously. In other words, the days of the month fall again on the same days of the week.

The Platonic cycle or **great year.** That space of time which, according to ancient astronomers, elapses before all the stars and constellations return to their former positions in respect to the equinoxes. Tycho Brahë calculated this period at 25,816 years, and Riccioli at 25,920.

Cut out more work than can be done
In Plato's year, but finish none.
BUTLER: *Hudibras*, iii, 1.

Cyclops (sī' klops) (Gr., circular-eye). One of a group of giants that, according to legend, inhabited Thrace. They had only one eye each, and that in the centre of their forehead, and their work was to forge iron for Vulcan. They were probably Pelasgians, who worked in quarries, and attached a lantern to their forehead to give them light underground. *Cp.* ARIMASPIANS.

Cyclopean Masonry (sī klō' pian). The old Pelasgic ruins of Greece, Asia Minor, and Italy, such as the Gallery of Tiryns, the Gate of Lions at Mycenæ, the Treasury of Athens, and the Tombs of Phoroneus and Danaos. They are composed of huge blocks fitted together without mortar, with marvellous nicety, and are fabled to be the work of the Cyclops (*q.v.*). The term is also applied to similar structures in many parts of the world.

Cynic (sin' ik). The ancient school of Greek philosophers known as the *Cynics* was founded by Antisthenes, a pupil of Socrates, and made famous by his pupil, Diogenes. They were ostentatiously contemptuous of ease, luxury, or wealth, and were given their name because Antisthenes held his school in the Gymnasium, *Cynosarges* (white dog), so called because a white dog once carried away part of a victim which was there being offered to Hercules. The effigy over Diogenes's pillar was a dog, with this inscription:—

"Say, dog, I pray, what guard you in that tomb?"
"A dog."—"His name?"—"Diogenes."—"From far?"
"Sinope."—"What! who made a tub his home?"
"The same; now dead, amongst the stars a star."

Cynic Tub, The. The tub from which Diogenes lectured. Similarly we speak of the "Porch" (*q.v.*), meaning Stoic philosophy; the "Garden" (*q.v.*), Epicurean philosophy; the "Academy" (*q.v.*), Platonic philosophy; and the "Colonade," meaning Aristotelian philosophy.

[They] fetch their doctrines from the Cynic tub.
MILTON: *Comus*, line 708.

Cynosure (sin' ō shur). The Pole star; hence, the observed of all observers. Greek for *dog's tail*, and applied to the constellation called *Ursa Minor*. As seamen guide their ships by the north star, and observe it well, the word "cynosure" is used for whatever attracts attention, as "The cynosure of neighbouring eyes" (*Milton*), especially for guidance in some doubtful matter.

Cynthia (sin' thi à). The moon; a surname of Artemis or Diana. The Roman Diana, who represented the moon, was called Cynthia from Mount Cynthus in Delos, where she was born.

And from embattled clouds emerging slow,
Cynthia came riding on her silver car.
BEATTIE: *Minstrel.*

Pope, speaking of the inconstant character of woman, "matter too soft a lasting mark to bear," says—

Come, then, the colours and the ground prepare!
Dip in the rainbow, trick her off in air;
Choose a firm cloud, before it fall, and in it
Catch, ere she change, the Cynthia of this minute.
Epistle, ii, 17-20.

By Elizabethan poets—Spenser, Phineas Fletcher, Raleigh, Ben Jonson, and others—

the name was one of the many that was applied to Queen Elizabeth.

Cypress. A funeral tree; dedicated by the Romans to Pluto, because when once cut it never grows again. It is said that its wood was formerly employed for making coffins; hence Shakespeare's "In sad cypress let me be laid" (*Twelfth Night*, ii, 4).

Cypresse garlands are of great account at funeralls amongst the gentiler sort, but rosemary and bayes are used by the commons both at funeralls and weddings. They are plants which fade not a good while after they are gathered . . . and intimate that the remembrance of the present solemnity might not dye presently. — COLES: *Introduction to the Knowledge of Plants.*

Cyprian (sip′ ri ạn). Cyprus was formerly famous for the worship of Venus; hence the adjective has been applied to lewd or profligate persons and prostitutes.

A Night Charge at Bow Street Office; with other matters worth knowing, respecting the unfortunate CYPRIAN, the feeling COACHMAN, and the generous MAGISTRATE. — PIERCE EGAN: *Life in London,* Bk. ii, ch. ii.

Cyprian brass, or *œs Cyprium,* copper. Pliny (Bk. xxxiv, c, ii) says, "*in Cypro enim prima œris inventio fuit.*"

Cyrano de Bergerac (sē ra′ nō de bâr zhėr ak). Cyrano is mostly known as the eponymous hero of Rostand's play, which appeared in 1897 with Coquelin in the title-role. The real Cyrano de Bergerac (1619-55) was a novelist and dramatist, as well as a soldier and duelist — the latter largely on account of his great nose. His best-known book was *Comic Histories of the States and Empires of the Moon,* 1656.

Czechoslovakia (che′ kō slō vǎk′ yà). The name of the republic formed after World War I by the union of Bohemia, Moravia, Silesia, Slovakia, and part of Ruthenia, under the presidency of Thomas Masaryk (1850-1937). The capital city is Prague. After appealing in vain to the Western powers for help, it was overrun by Nazi Germany in 1938 regained its freedom in 1945 but fell into Communist hands in 1948

D

D. This letter is the outline of a rude archway or door. It is called in Phœnician and Hebrew *daleth* (a door) and in Gr. *delta* (*q.v.*). In Egyptian hieroglyphics it is a man's hand.

D. or **d.** indicating a penny or pence, is the initial of the Lat. *denarius* (*q.v.*).

As a Roman numeral **D** stands for 500, and represents the second half of CIↃ, the ancient Tuscan sign for one thousand. **D** with a dash over it (D̄) is 5,000.

Da Capo (D.C.). (Ital.) A musical term meaning, from the beginning—that is, finish with a repetition of the first strain.

Dab. Clever, skilled; as "a dab-hand at it." The origin is unknown, but it has been suggested that it is a contraction of the Lat. *adeptus*, an adept. "Dabster" is another form.

> An Eton stripling, training for the law,
> A dunce at learning, but a dab at taw [marbles].
> ANON.: *Logic; or, The Biter Bit.*

Dabbat (*Dabbatu 'l-arz*). In Mohammedan mythology the monster (literally "reptile of the earth") that shall arise at the last day and cry that mankind has not believed in the Divine revelations.

By some it is identified with the Beast of the Apocalypse. (*Rev.* xix, 19; xx, 10.)

Dacia (dā′ si à). A Roman province in part of what is now Hungary.

Dacoit (dà koit′). This is an Urdu word meaning a robber. It is applied to the bands of robbers and pirates who infest the forests and rivers of Burma, and to organized bands of robbers in India. In Indian law dacoity means robbery with violence by not less than five men.

Dactyls. Mythical beings connected with the worship of Cybele, in Crete, to whom is ascribed the discovery of iron. Their number was originally three—the Smelter, the Hammer, and the Anvil; but was afterwards increased to five males and five females, whence their name Dactyls or Fingers.

In prosody a dactyl is a foot of three syllables, the first long and the others short (¯ ˘ ˘) —again from the similarity to the joists of a finger.

Dad or **Daddy.** A child's word (common to many languages) for "father"; for example:

Gaelic, *daidein*; Welsh, *tad*; Cornish, *tat*; Latin, *tata, tatula* (papa); Greek, *tata, tetta,* used by youths to an elder; Sanskrit, *tata*; Lap. *dadda*.

Daddy Long-legs. A crane-fly, applied also to the long-legged spiders called "harvest-men."

Dadaism (da′ da izm). A school of art, painting, and writing that had its beginning in New York and Zürich in 1916, arising from indignation and despair at the catastrophe of World War I and increasing with the ensuing peace. The artists endeavoured to free themselves from *all* previous artistic conventions in an iconoclastic attack on what they considered cultural shams. The movement died about 1922 and was succeeded by Surrealism (*q.v.*). The name Dadaism was derived from the French phrase *aller à dada*, ride a cock-horse, and was chosen at random from a dictionary. Its principal exponents were Tristan Tzara, Max Ernst, Picabia.

Dædalus (dē′ dà lus). A Greek who formed the Cretan labyrinth, and made for himself wings, by means of which he flew from Crete across the Archipelago. He is said to have invented the saw, the axe, the gimlet, etc., and his name is perpetuated in our *dœdal*, skilful, fertile of invention, *dœdalian*, labyrinthine or ingenious, etc. *Cp.* ICARUS.

Daffodil. Legend says that the daffodil, or "Lent Lily," was once white; but Persephone, who had wreathed her head with them and fallen asleep, was captured by Pluto, at whose touch the white flowers turned to a golden yellow. Ever since the flower has been planted on graves. Theophilus and Pliny tell us that they grow on the banks of Acheron and that the spirits of the dead delight in the flower, called by them the Asphodel. In England it used to be called the Affodil. (French, *asphodile*; Lat., *asphodelus*; Gr. *asphodelos*.)

An attempt was made in the 20th century in Britain to introduce it as the national emblem of Wales because the leek was considered vulgar.

> Flour of daffodil is a cure for madness.—*Med. MS. Lincoln Cathedral*, f. 282.

Dagger or **Long Cross** (†), used for reference to a note after the asterisk (*), is a Roman Catholic character, originally employed in church books, prayers of exorcism, at benedictions, and so on, to remind the priest where to make the sign of the cross. This sign is sometimes called an obelisk—that is, "a spit." (Gr., *obelos*, a spit.)

In the arms of the City of London, the dagger commemorates Sir William Walworth's dagger, with which he slew Wat Tyler in 1381. Before this time the cognizance of the City was the sword of St. Paul.

> Brave Walworth, knight, lord mayor, that slew
>   Rebellious Tyler in his alarmes;
> The king, therefore, did give him in lieu
>   The dagger to the city armes.
> *Fourth year of Richard II* (1381). *Fishmongers' Hall.*

Dagger-scene in the House of Commons. Edmund Burke, during the French Revolution, threw down a dagger on the floor of the House, exclaiming as he did so: "There's French fraternity for you! Such is the weapon which French Jacobins would plunge into the heart of our beloved king." Sheridan spoilt the dramatic effect, and set the House in a roar by his remark: "The gentleman, I see, has brought his knife with him, but where is his fork? *Cf.* COUP DE THÉÂTRE.

Daggle-tail or **Draggle-tail.** A slovenly woman, the bottom of whose dress trails in the dirt. *Dag* (of uncertain origin) means loose ends, mire or dirt; whence *dag-locks*, the soiled locks of a sheep's fleece, and *dag-wool*, refuse wool.

Dago (dā' gō). A disparaging epithet applied to a Spaniard, Portuguese, or Italian generally. The word originated in Louisiana where a man of Spanish parentage was popularly called Diego.

Dagonet, Sir. The fool of King Arthur in the Arthurian legends; he was knighted by the king himself.

> I remember at Mile End Green, when I lay at Clement's Inn, I was then Sir Dagonet in Arthur's show.—*2 Henry IV*, iii, 2. (Justice Shallow).

"Dagonet" was the name under which G. R. Sims (1847-1922) wrote weekly articles in the *Referee* which were very popular in their day.

Daguerreotype (dȧ gâr' ō tīp). A photographic process invented by L. J. M. Daguerre (1789-1851) and J. N. Niepce (*d.*1833). The process, which was introduced in 1839, consisted in exposing in a camera a plate of silvered copper on which a film of silvered iodide had been formed by iodine vapour. It was the first photographic process to yield a technically good result.

Dahlia (dā' lyȧ). This plant, bearing strikingly beautiful flowers, was discovered in Mexico by Humboldt in 1789; he sent specimens to Europe, and in 1791 it was named in honour of Andrew Dahl, the Swedish botanist and pupil of Linnæus. It was cultivated in France in 1802, and two years later in England.

Daibutsu (dī but' soo). The great bronze Buddha at Kamakura, formerly the capital of Nippon (Japan). It is in a sitting posture, and is 50 ft. high and 97 ft. in circumference; the face is 8 ft. long and the thumbs a yard round.

> Above the old songs turned to ashes and pain,
> Under which Death enshrouds the idols and trees
>   with mist of sigh,
> (Where are Kamakura's rising days and life of old?)
> With heart heightened to hush, the Daibutsu for
>   ever sits.   *Yone Noguchi.*

Daikoku (da ē' kō ku). One of the seven gods of Good Fortune in the Japanese pantheon; he is invoked specially by artisans.

Dais. The raised floor at the head of a dining-room, designed for the high, or principal, table, but originally the high table itself; from late Lat. *discus*, a table. The word was also used (as it still is in French) for a canopy, especially the canopy over the high table. Hence, *Sous le dais*, in the midst of grandeur.

Daisy. Ophelia gives the queen a daisy to signify "that her light and fickle love ought not to expect constancy in her husband." So the daisy is explained by Greene to mean a *Quip for an upstart courtier.*

The word is *Day's eye* (A.S. *dœges eage*), and the flower is so called because it closes its pinky lashes and goes to sleep when the sun sets, but in the morning expands its petals to the light. *Cp,* VIOLET.

> That well by reason men calle it maie,
> The daisie, or else the eie of daie.
>   CHAUCER: *Legend of Good Women (Prol.).*

Daisy-roots. Legend says that these, like dwarf-elder berries, stunt the growth, a superstition which probably arose from the notion that everything had the property of bestowing its own speciality on others. *Cp.* FERN SEED.

> She robbed dwarf-elders of their fragrant fruit
> And fed him early with the daisy root,
> Whence through his veins the powerful juices ran,
> And formed the beauteous *miniature* of man.
>   TICKELL: *Kensington Gardens.*

Dak-bungalow. *See* BUNGALOW.

Dalai-Lama. *See* LAMA.

Dalkey, King of. A burlesque officer, like the Mayor of Garratt (*q.v.*). Dalkey is a small island in St. George's Channel, near Kingstown, to the south of Dublin Bay.

Dalmatica or **Dalmatic** (dăl măt'i ka). A vestment open in front, reaching to the knees, worn by Catholic bishops and deacons over the *alb* or *stole*. It is in imitation of the regal vest of Dalmatia, and was imported into Rome by the Emperor Commodus.

A similar robe is worn by kings at coronations and other great solemnities.

Daltonism. *See* COLOUR-BLINDNESS.

Dam. The female parent of animals such as the horse, sheep, etc.; the counterpart of "sire"; when used of human beings the word has always a very opprobious significance. It is another form of *dame*. *See* THE DEVIL AND HIS DAM.

Damascening (dăm à sēn' ing). Producing upon steel a blue tinge and ornamental figures, sometimes inlaid with gold and silver, as in Damascus blades; so called from Damascus, which was celebrated in the Middle Ages for this class of ornamental art.

Damask. Linens and silks first made at Damascus, imitated by the French and Flemish. Introduced into England by refugee Flemish weavers about 1570. The *damask rose* was brought to England from Southern Europe by Dr. Linacre, physican to Henry VIII, about 1540.

Damiens' Bed of Steel (dăm' i enz). Robert François Damiens, in 1757, attempted the life of Louis XV. As a punishment, and to strike terror into the hearts of all regicides, he was chained to an iron bed that was heated, his right hand was burned in a slow fire, his flesh was torn with pincers and the wounds dressed with molten lead, boiling wax, oil, and resin, and he was ultimately torn to pieces by wild horses.

> The uplifted axe, the agonizing wheel,
> Luke's iron crown, and Damiens' bed of steel.
> GOLDSMITH: *The Traveller* (1768).

Damn. Not worth a damn. Worthless; not even worth cursing. The derivation of the phrase from the Indian coin, a *dam* (96 to the penny) has no foundation in fact. Goldsmith, in his *Citizen of the World*, uses the expression, "Not that I care three damns." Another vague imprecation, said to have been commonly used by the great Duke of Wellington, is Not *a twopenny damn*.

To damn with faint praise. To praise in such measured terms as to deprive the praise of any real value.

> Damn with faint praise, assent with civil leer,
> And, without sneering, teach the rest to sneer.
> POPE: *Epistle to Arbuthnot.*

Damocles's Sword. Impending evil or danger. Damocles, a sycophant of Dionysius the Elder, of Syracuse, was invited by the tyrant to try the felicity he so much envied. Accepting, he was set down to a sumptuous banquet, but overhead was a sword suspended by a hair. Damocles was afraid to stir, and the banquet was a tantalizing torment to him.

Damon and Pythias. A type of inseparable friends. They were Syracusans of the first half of the 4th century B.C.: Pythias being condemned to death by Dionysius the tyrant, obtained leave to go home to arrange his affairs after Damon had agreed to take his place and be executed should Pythias not return. Pythias being delayed, Damon was led to execution, but his friend arrived just in time to save him. Dionysius was so struck with this honourable friendship that he pardoned both of them.

Damsel. Its usual meaning is a virgin, a maiden, often a waiting-maid. From the old French *damoisele*, the feminine form of *damoisel*, a squire; this is from Med. Lat. *domicellus*, a contracted form of *dominicellus*, the diminutive of *dominus*, lord. (*Cp.* DONZEL.) In mediæval France the *domicellus* or *damoiseau* was the son of a king, prince, knight, or lord before he entered the order of knighthood; the king's bodyguards were called his *damoiseaux* or *damsels*. Froissart styles Richard II *le jeune damoisel Richart*, and Louis VII (*Le Jeune*) was called the *royal damsel*.

Damson. Originally called the *Damascene plum*, from *Damascus*, it having been imported from Syria.

Dan. A title of honour meaning *Sir* or *Master* (Lat. *dominus*, *cp.* Span, *don*), common with the old poets, as Dan Phœbus, Dan Cupid, Dan Neptune, Dan Chaucer, etc. (*Cp.* DOM.)

> Dan Chaucer, well of English undefiled,
> On Fame's eternal beadroll worthy to be filed.
> SPENSER: *Faerie Queene*, IV, ii, 32.

From Dan to Beersheba. From one end of the kingdom to the other; all over the world; everywhere. The phrase is Scriptural, Dan being the most northern and Beersheba the most southern cities of the Holy Land. We have a similar expression, "From Land's End to John o' Groats."

Danace (dăn' ās). An ancient Persian coin, worth rather more than the Greek *obolus* (*q.v.*), and sometimes, among the Greeks, placed in the mouth of the dead to pay their passage across the ferry of the Lower World.

Danaë (dăn' à ē). An Argive princess, daughter of Acrisius, King of Argos. He, told that his daughter's son would put him to death, resolved that Danaë should never marry, and accordingly locked her up in an inaccessible tower. Zeus foiled the king by changing himself into a shower of gold, under which guise he readily found access to the fair prisoner, and she thus became the mother of Perseus.

Danaides (dăn ā′ i dēz). The fifty daughters of Danaus, King of Argos. They married the fifty sons of Ægyptus, and all but Hypermnestra, wife of Lynceus, at the command of their father murdered their husbands on their wedding night. They were punished in Hades by having to draw water everlastingly in sieves from a deep well.

Dance of Death. An allegorical representation of Death leading all sorts and conditions of men in a dance to the grave, originating in Germany in the 14th century as a kind of morality play, quickly becoming popular in France and England, and surviving later principally by means of pictorial art. There is a series of woodcuts, said to be by Hans Holbein (1538), representing Death dancing after all sorts of persons, beginning with Adam and Eve. He is beside the judge on his bench, the priest in the pulpit, the nun in her cell, the doctor in his study, the bride, and the beggar, the king and the infant; but he is "swallowed up at last."

On the north side of Old St. Paul's was a cloister, on the walls of which was painted, at the cost of John Carpenter, town clerk of London (15th century), a "Dance of Death," or "Death leading all the estate, with speeches of Death, and answers," by John Lydgate. The Death-Dance in the Dominican Convent of Basle was retouched by Holbein.

Dances, National. When Handel was asked to point out the peculiar taste of the different nations of Europe in dancing, he ascribed the *minuet* to the French, the *saraband* to the Spaniard, the *arietta* to the Italian, and the *hornpipe* and the *morris-dance* to the English. To these might be added the *reel* to the Scots, and the *jig* to the Irish.

Astronomical dances, invented by the Egyptians, designed to represent the movements of the heavenly bodies.

The Bacchic dances were of three sorts: grave (like our minuet), gay (like our gavotte), and mixed (like our minuet and gavotte combined).

The dance Champêtre, invented by Pan, quick and lively. The dancers (in the open air) wore wreaths of oak and garlands of flowers.

Children's dances, in Lacedemonia, in honour of Diana. The children were nude; and their movements were grave, modest, and graceful.

Corybantic dances, in honour of Bacchus, accompanied with timbrels, fifes, flutes, and a tumultuous noise produced by the clashing of swords and spears against brazen bucklers.

Funereal dances, in Athens, slow, solemn dances in which the priests took part. The performers wore long white robes, and carried cypress slips in their hands.

Hymeneal dances were lively and joyous. The dancers were crowned with flowers.

Jewish dances. David danced in certain religious processions (2 *Sam.* vi, 14). The people sang and danced before the golden calf *(Exod.* xxxii, 19). And in the book of *Psalms* (cl, 4) we read, "Praise Him with the timbrel and dance." Miriam the, sister of Moses, after the passage of the Red Sea, was followed by all the women with timbrels and dances *(Exod.* xv, 20).

Of the Lapithœ, invented by Pirithous. These were exhibited after some famous victory, and were designed to imitate the combats of the Centaurs and Lapithœ. These dances were both difficult and dangerous.

May-day dances at Rome. At daybreak lads and lasses went out to gather "May" and other flowers for themselves and their elders; and the day was spent in dances and festivities.

Military dances. The oldest of all dances executed with swords, javelins, and bucklers. Said to be invented by Minerva to celebrate the victory of the gods over the Titans.

Nuptial dances. A Roman pantomimic performance resembling the dances of our Harlequin and Columbine.

Pyrrhic dance. See PYRRHIC.

Salic dances, instituted by Numa Pompilius in honour of Mars. They were executed by twelve priests selected from the highest of the nobility, and the dances were performed in the temple while sacrifices were being made and hymns sung to the god.

Dancing Chancellor, The. Sir Christopher Hatton (1540-91) was so called, because he first attracted Queen Elizabeth's notice by his graceful dancing in a masque at Court. He was Lord High Chancellor from 1587 till his death.

> His bushy beard, and shoestrings green,
> His high-crowned hat and satin doublet,
> Moved the stout heart of England's queen,
> Though Pope and Spaniard could not trouble it.
>   GRAY: *A Long Story.*

Dandelion (dăn′ de lī on). The leaves of the plant have jagged, tooth-like edges; hence its name, which is a form of the M.E. *dent de lyoun*, from Fr. *dent de lion*, lion tooth. Its Lat. name is *Taraxacum dens leonis.*

Dander. Is your dander up or **riz?** Is your anger excited? Are you in a rage? This is generally considered to be an Americanism, but it is of uncertain origin, and as a synonym for *anger* has been a common dialect word in several English counties. In the present sense it is more likely that it is one of the words (like *waffle*, and *hook* for a point of land) imported into America by the early Dutch colonists, from *donder*, thunder; the Dutch *op donderen* is to burst into a sudden rage.

He was as spunky as thunder, and when a Quaker gets his dander up, it's like a Northwester.
SEBAR SMITH: *Letters of Major Jack Downing* (1830).

Dandy. A coxcomb; a fop. The term seems to have originated in Scotland in the late 18th century, and may be merely the name *Andrew*, or a corruption of *dandiprat* (*q.v.*) or of the earlier *Jack-a-dandy*.

In paper-making the *dandy*, or *dauby-roller*, is the cylinder of wire gauze which comes into contact with paper while on the machine in a wet and elementary stage. It impresses the watermark, and also the ribs in "laid" papers.

Dane-geld. A tribute paid by the English to stop the ravages of the Danes in the late 10th and early 11th centuries.

Dannebrog or **Danebrog** (dăn′ e brog). The national flag of Denmark (*brog* is Old Danish for cloth). The tradition is that Waldemar II of Denmark saw in the heavens a fiery cross which betokened his victory over the Esthonians (1219). This story is very similar to that of Constantine (*see* under CROSS) and of St. Andrew's Cross.

Dannocks. Hedging-gloves. The word is said to be a corruption of *Doornick*, the Flemish name of Tournay, where they may have been originally manufactured. *Cp.* DORNICK.

Dansker (dăn′ sker). A Dane. Denmark used to be called Danskë. Hence Polonius says to Reynaldo, "Inquire me first what Danskers are in Paris." (*Hamlet*, ii, 1.)

Dante and Beatrice (dăn′ te, bē′ à tris, bā à trē′ chi). Beatrice Portinari was only eight years old when the poet first saw her. His abiding love for her was pure as it was tender. Beatrice married a nobleman, named Simone de Bardi, and died young, in 1290. Dante married Gemma, of the powerful house of Donati. In the *Divina Commedia* the poet is conducted first by Virgil (who represents human reason) through hell and purgatory; then by the spirit of Beatrice (who represents the wisdom of faith); and finally by St. Bernard (who represents the wisdom from on high).

Dantesque (dăn′ tesk). Dante-like—that is, a minute lifelike representation of horrors, whether by words, as in the poet, or in visible form, as in Doré's illustrations of the *Inferno*.

Daphne (dăf′ ni). Daughter of a river-god, loved by Apollo. She fled from the amorous god, and escaped by being changed into a laurel, thenceforth the favourite tree of the sun-god.

> Nay, lady, sit. If I but wave this wand.
> Your nerves are all chain'd up in alabaster,
> And you a statue, or, as Daphne was,
> Root-bound, that fled Apollo.
> > MILTON: *Comus*, 678.

Daphnis (dăf′ nis). In Greek mythology, a Sicilian shepherd who invented pastoral poetry. He was a son of Mercury and a Sicilian nymph, was protected by Diana, and was taught by Pan and the Muses.

The lover of Chloe (*q.v.*) in the Greek pastoral romance of Longus, in the 4th century. Daphnis was the model of Allan Ramsay's *Gentle Shepherd*, and the tale is the basis of St. Pierre's *Paul and Virginia*.

Dapple. The name given in Smollett's translation of *Don Quixote* to Sancho Panza's donkey (in the original it has no name). The word is probably connected with Icel. *depill*, a spot, and means blotched, speckled in patches. A *dapple-grey* horse is one of a light grey shaded with a deeper hue; a *dapple-bay* is a light bay spotted with bay of a deeper colour.

Darby and Joan. The type of loving, old-fashioned, virtuous couples. The names belong to a ballad written by Henry Woodfall, and the characters are said to be John Darby, of Bartholomew Close, who died 1730, and his wife, "As chaste as a picture cut in alabaster. You might sooner move a Scythian rock than shoot fire into her bosom." Woodfall served his apprenticeship to John Darby; but another account localizes the couple in the West Riding of Yorkshire.

The French equivalent is *C'est St. Roch et son chien*.

Darbyites (dar′ bi ītz). A name sometimes given to the Plymouth Brethren (*q.v.*), from John Nelson Darby (1800-82), the founder.

Dardanelles (dar dà nelz). The entrance to the Straits of Gallipoli, commanded by the two forts of Sestos and Abydos, built by the Sultan Mahomet IV in 1659, and taking their name from the adjacent town of Dardanus. The British fleet passed through the Straits in 1807 and 1853; but the campaign to force the Straits in 1915 was unsuccessful.

Daric. An ancient Persian gold coin, probably so called from *dara*, a king (*see* DARIUS), much in the same way as our *sovereign*, but perhaps from Assyrian *dariku*, weight. Its value is put at about 23s. There was also a silver daric, worth one twentieth of the gold.

Darius (dà rī′ ùs). A Greek form of Persian *dara*, a king, or of Sanskrit *darj*, the maintainer. Gushtasp, or Kishtasp assumed the title on ascending the throne in 521 B.C., and is generally known as Darius the Great.

Legend relates that seven Persian princes agreed that he should be king whose horse neighed first; and the horse of Darius was the first to neigh.

It is said that Darius III (Codomanus), the last king of Persia, who was conquered by Alexander the Great (331 B.C.), when Alexander succeeded to the throne, sent to him for the tribute of golden eggs, but the Macedonian answered, "The bird which laid them is flown to the other world, where Darius must seek them." The Persian king then sent him a bat and ball, in ridicule of his youth; but Alexander told the messengers, with the bat he would beat the ball of power from their master's hand. Lastly, Darius sent him a bitter melon as emblem of the grief in store for him; but the Macedonian declared that he would make the Shah eat his own fruit.

Dark. A dark horse. A racing term for a horse of good pretensions, but of which nothing is positively known by the general public. The epithet is applied to a person whose abilities are untried or whose probable course of action is unknown.

A leap in the dark. A step the consequences of which cannot be foreseen. Thomas Hobbes is reported to have said on his death-bed, "Now am I about to take my last voyage—a great leap in the dark." Hallam considered this term to apply to the period lasting from A.D. 475 to about the middle of the 12th century; in 1868 Lord Derby applied the words to the Reform Bill.

The Dark Ages. The earlier centuries of the Middle Ages (*q.v.*); so called because of the intellectual darkness thought to be characteristic of the period.

The dark Continent. Africa; concerning which the world was so long "in the dark," and which, also, is the land of dark races.

The darkest hour is that before the dawn. When things have come to their worst, they must mend. In Lat., *Post nubila Phœbus.*

To darken one's door. To cross one's threshold: almost entirely used only in a threatening way, as "Don't you dare to darken my door again!"

Darkie. A former colloquial name for an American Negro, found as early as 1775.

Darley Arabian. In 1704 Thomas Darley sent from Aleppo to his father Richard Darley, of Aldby Park, Yorks, an Arab horse of the best Maneghi breed. From this thoroughbred stallion came a famous breed of race-horses, including Eclipse (*q.v.*) who was Darley Arabian's great-grandson.

It is interesting to note that the entire thoroughbred race throughout the world is descended from three Arabs, of which Darley Arabian was one. The others were Byerley Turk, the charger of Capt. Byerley at the Battle of the Boyne, and Godolphin Arabian, brought to England in 1730 by Edward Coke, from whose hands he passed into the possession of the Earl of Godolphin.

D'Artagnan (dar ta nyón). The hero of Dumas's novels *The Three Musketeers, Twenty Years After,* etc., was a real man—Charles de Baatz, Seigneur d'Artagnan, a Gascon gentleman who was born at Lupiac in 1611. He rose to be captain in Louis XIV's Mousquetaires and eventually became general of brigade. He was killed at the siege of Maestricht, in 1673. Dumas and his collaborator Maquet worked up the story from the *Memoires de M. D'Artagnan,* written by Courtilz de Sandras and published in Cologne, 1701-02.

Darwinian Theory. Charles Darwin (1809-82) published in 1859 *Origin of Species,* to prove that the numerous species now existing on the earth sprang originally from one or at most a few primal forms; and that the present diversity is due to special development and natural selection. In recent times the Darwinian theory has undergone very considerable modification but it is still the basis of scientific research. *See* EVOLUTION.

Dash. *One* dash under a word in MS. means that the part so marked must be printed in italics; *two* dashes means small capitals; *three* dashes, large capitals.

Cut a dash. *See* CUT.

Date. Not up to date. Not in the latest fashion, behind the times.

To have a date. To have an appointment, more particularly with someone of the opposite sex.

Datum Line (dā' tùm). A term used in surveying and engineering to describe a line from which all heights and depths are measured. The datum line upon which the Ordnance Survey maps of Great Britain are based was, until 1921, the mean sea-level at Liverpool; since that date it has been the mean sea-level at Newlyn, Cornwall.

Daughter. The daughter of Peneus. The bay-tree was so called because it grew in greatest perfection on the banks of the River Peneus.

The daughter of the horseleech. One very exigent; one for ever sponging on another. *Prov.* xxx, 15.

The horseleech hath two daughters, crying, Give, Give.

The scavenger's daughter. *See* SCAVENGER.

Dauphin (daw' fin). The heir of the French crown under the Valois and Bourbon dynasties. Guy VIII, Count of Vienne, was the first so styled, because he wore a *dolphin* as his cognizance. The title descended in the family till 1349, when Humbert III ceded his seigneurie, the Dauphiné, to Philippe VI (de Valois), one condition being that the heir of France assumed the title of *le dauphin*. The first French prince so called was Jean, who succeeded Philippe; and the last was the Duc d'Angoulême, son of Charles X, who renounced the title in 1830.

Grand Dauphin. Louis, Duc de Bourgogne (1661-1711), eldest son of Louis XIV, for whose use was published the Delphin Classics (*q.v.*).

Second or **Little Dauphin.** Louis, son of the Grand Dauphin (1682-1712).

Davenport (dăv′ ẽn pôrt). This word, which owes its origin to the name of some now-forgotten craftsman, is applied to two different articles of furniture; one kind of davenport is a small desk with drawers on each side; the other is a large upholstered sofa or settee that can also be made up into a bed.

David. In Dryden's *Absalom and Achitophel* (*q.v.*), represents Charles II.

Once more the godlike David was restored
And willing nations knew their lawful lord.

David and Jonathan. A type of inseparable friends. Similar examples of friendship were Pylades and Orestes (*q.v.*); Damon and Pythias (*q.v.*); etc.

I am distressed for thee, my brother Jonathan. Very pleasant hast thou been to me. Thy love to me was wonderful, passing the love of women.—2 *Sam.* i, 26.

Davidians, Davists. *See* Familists.

Davis Cup. A silver trophy for an international Lawn Tennis team championship, presented by the American politician, Dwight F. Davis (1875-1945) in 1900. Its holders have been:—

1903-06	Great Britain
1907-11	Australasia
1912	Great Britain
1913	U.S.A.
1914-19	Australasia
1920-26	U.S.A.
1927-32	France
1933-36	Great Britain
1937-38	U.S.A.
1939-45	Australia
1946-49	U.S.A.
1950	Australia
1952	Australia

Davy Jones. A sailor's name for the supposed evil spirit of the sea.

He's gone to Davy Jones's locker. The nautical way of saying that a messmate is dead and has been buried at sea. It has been conjectured that Jones is a corruption of Jonah the prophet who was thrown into the sea.

This same Davy Jones, according to the mythology of sailors, is the fiend that presides over all the evil spirits of the deep, and is seen in various shapes . . . warning the devoted wretch of death and woe.—Smollett: *Peregrine Pickle*, xiii.

Day. When it begins. (1) With *sunset*: The Jews in their "sacred year," and the Church—hence the eve of feast-days; the ancient Britons "*non dierum numerum, ut nos, sed noctium computant*," says Tacitus—hence "se'n-night" and "fort'night"; the Athenians, Chinese, Mohammedans, etc., (2) With *sunrise*: The Babylonians, Syrians, Persians, and modern Greeks. (3) With *noon*: The ancient Egyptians and modern astronomers. (4) With *midnight*: The English, French, Dutch, Germans, Spanish, Portuguese, Americans, etc.

A day after the fair. Too late; the fair you came to see is over.

Day in, day out. All day long and every day.

Every dog has its day. *See* Dog.

I have had my day. My prime of life is over;

Old Joe, sir . . . was a bit of a favourite . . . once; but he has had his day.—Dickens: *Dombey and Son.*

Day of the Barricades, Dupes. *See these words.*

Daylight. Toast-masters used to cry out, "Gentlemen, no daylights nor heeltaps." This meant that the wineglass was to be full to the brim so that light could not be seen between the edge of the glass and the top of the wine; and that every drop of it must be drunk. *See* Heeltap.

Daylight Saving. A system of advancing the clock by an hour on some specified day in the Spring, and putting back the hands one hour on a specified day in autumn. By this device greater advantage can be taken of the longer evenings of summertime. The originator was William Willett (1856-1915) a London builder who advocated the scheme for some years but died before it was adopted (as a war measure) in 1916. By an Act of 1925 Daylight Saving started the third week in April and ended the first week in October, but since the outbreak of World War II the dates have varied from year to year.

In 1941 a system of Double Summer Time was introduced, the clock being set back yet another hour (*i.e.* two hours in advance of G.M.T.) during the height of summer, approx. April to August.

Daylights. Pugilists' slang for the eyes.

To beat the living daylights out of him, to heavily chastise. **To let daylight into him,** to pierce a man with sword or bullet.

Dayspring. The dawn.

The dayspring from on high hath visited us.—*Luke* i, 78.

Daystar. The morning star. Hence the emblem of hope or better prospects.

Again o'er the vine-covered regions of France,
See the day-star of Liberty rise.—WILSON: *Noctes.*

De die in diem (dē dī′ ē in dī′ em) (Lat.). From day to day continuously, till the business is completed.

The Ministry have elected to go on *de die in diem.*—*Newspaper paragraph.*

De facto (Lat.). Actually, in reality; in opposition to **de jure**, lawfully or rightfully. Thus John was *de facto* king, but Arthur was so *de jure*. A legal axiom says: "*De jure Judices, de facto Juratores, respondent*"; Judges look to the law, juries to the facts.

De jure. *See* DE FACTO, *above.*

De mortuis nil nisi bonum (dē môr′ tū is nil nī′ sī bō′ num) (Lat.). Of the dead speak kindly or not at all. "Speak not evil of the dead" was one of the maxims of Chilo (*q.v.*).

De novo (dē nō′ vō) (Lat.). Afresh; over again from the beginning.

De profundis (dē prō fŭn′ dis) (Lat.). Out of the deep; hence, a bitter cry of wretchedness. *Ps.* cxxx is so called from the first two words in the Latin version. It forms part of the Roman Catholic burial service.

These words were chosen as the title of Oscar Wilde's apologia, published posthumously in 1905.

De rigueur (dĕ rigĕr′) (Fr.). According to strict etiquette; quite *comme il faut*, in the height of fashion.

De trop (dĕ trō) (Fr.). One too many; when a person's presence is not wished for, that person is *de trop.*

Dead. Dead as a door-nail. The door-nail is either one of the heavy-headed nails with which large outer doors used to be studded, or the knob on which the knocker strikes. As this is frequently knocked on the head, it cannot be supposed to have much life left in it. The expression is found in *Piers Plowman.*

Come thou and thy five men, and if I do not leave you all as dead as a door-nail, I pray God I may never eat grass more.—SHAKESPEARE: *2 Henry VI*, iv, 10.

Other well-known similes are "Dead as a shotten herring," "as the nail in a coffin," "as mutton," and Chaucer's "as stoon [stone]."

Let the dead bury the dead. (*Matt*, viii, 22). Let bygones be bygones. Don't rake up old and dead grievances.

Let me entreat you to let the dead bury the dead, to cast behind you every recollection of bygone evils, and to cherish, to love, to sustain one another through all the vicissitudes of human affairs in the times that are to come.—GLADSTONE: *Home Rule Bill* (February 13th, 1893).

Dead beat. Exhausted. In the U.S.A. the word is used as a noun, a worthless fellow.

Dead drunk. So intoxicated as to be wholly powerless.

Dead-eye. A block of wood with three holes through it, for the lanyards of rigging to reeve through, without sheaves, and with a groove round it for an iron strap. An old name for them is "dead men's eyes."

Dead heat. A race in which two (or more) leading competitors reach the goal at the same time, thus making it necessary to run the race over again. *See* HEAT.

To work a dead horse. To perform work already paid for; to pay off a debt.

Dead languages. Languages no longer spoken; such as Latin and Sanskrit.

Dead letter. A law no longer acted upon. Also a letter which cannot be delivered by the postal authorities because the address is incorrect, or the person addressed cannot be found.

Dead-letter Office. *See* BLIND DEPARTMENT, *and* DEAD LETTER *above.*

Deadline. A final demarcation of time, *i.e.* the last hour or minute when a newspaper can go to press.

Dead lock. A lock which has no spring catch. Metaphorically, a state of things so entangled that there seems to be no practical solution.

Dead Man's Hand. In electric railways the accelerator lever contains a spring so contrived that if the motor-man for any reason takes his hand off it the power is automatically cut off.

In the western States of U.S.A. a Dead Man's Hand is a combination of aces and eights in the game of Poker, and it is so called because when the famous sheriff Wild Bill Hicock was shot at Deadwood, S. Dakota, he held such cards in his hand.

Dead men. Empty bottles.

Down among the dead men let me lie. Let me get so intoxicated as to slip from my chair, and lie under the table with the empty bottles.

Dead men's shoes. *See* SHOE.

Dead reckoning. A calculation of the ship's place without any observation of the heavenly bodies. An approximation made by consulting the log, compass, chronometer, the direction, wind, and so on.

Dead right. Entirely right.

Dead ropes. Those which are fixed or do not run on blocks.

Dead Sea. The salt lake in Palestine, in the ancient Vale of Siddim; so called by the Romans (*Mare Mortuum*), also *Lacus Asphaltites*. The water is limpid, and of a bluish-green colour; it supports no life other than microbes and a few very low organisms. It is about 46 miles long by 10 miles broad; its surface is about 1,300 ft. below sea-level, and it attains a depth of nearly 1,300 ft. The percentage of salt in the ocean generally is about three or four, but of the Dead Sea it is twenty-six or more.

Dead Sea fruit. *See* APPLES OF SODOM.

To be at a dead set. To be set fast, so as not to be able to move. The allusion is to machinery.

Dead weight. The weight of something without life; a burden that does nothing towards easing its own weight; a person who encumbers us and renders no assistance. *Cp.* DEAD LIFT.

Deaf. Deaf as an adder. "They are like the deaf adder that stoppeth her ear; which will not hearken to the voice of charmers, charming never so wisely." (*Ps.* lviii, 4, 5). In the East, if a viper entered the house, the charmer was sent for, who enticed the serpent and put it into a bag. According to tradition, the viper tried to stop its ears when the charmer uttered his incantation, by applying one ear to the ground and twisting its tail into the other.

In the United States deaf adder is one of the names of the copperhead (*q.v.*).

Deaf as a post. Quite deaf; or so inattentive as not to hear what is said. One might as well speak to a gatepost or log of wood.

Deal. This is a word to which several meanings are attached. It can mean a business transaction; the distribution of a pack of cards; pinewood or fir wood; a plank of this wood measuring not less than 6 ft. long, 7 in. across, and 3 in. thick; a lot, a quantity; a share.

To deal with is to be concerned with, or to handle, or to do business with.

To deal out is to hand out in shares, esp. cards in a game.

Dean. (Lat. *decanus*, one set over ten.) The ecclesiastical dignitary who presides over the chapter (*q.v.*) of a cathedral or collegiate church, this having formerly consisted of ten canons (*q.v.*). In ecclesiastical use there are also deans not having chapters (such as the Deans of Westminster and Windsor, and the Bishop of London is *ex officio* Dean of the Province of Canterbury. **Rural deans** are subsidiary officers of archdeacons.

The title "Dean" is also borne by certain resident Fellows at English Universities who have special functions; by the head of Christ Church, Oxford; and, in Scotland, by the President of the Faculty of Advocates (*Dean of Faculty*), and certain magistrates (*Dean of Guild*). In the U.S.A., a dean is an administrative officer of a college or university, who supervises a school, a faculty, or a body of Students, e.g. Dean of Women, Dean of the Graduate School.

The chief or senior of any group of men may be called a dean, as dean of the diplomatic corps.

Dear. Dear bought and far brought, or **felt.** A gentle reproof for some extravagant purchase of luxury.

My dearest foe. As "my dearest friend" is one with whom I am on the greatest terms of friendship, so "my dearest foe" is one with whom I am on the greatest terms of enmity.

> Would I had met my dearest foe in heaven,
> Or ever I had seen that day, Horatio.
> SHAKESPEARE: *Hamlet*, i, 2.

Oh, dear me! A very common exclamation; there is no foundation for the suggestion that it is a corruption of the Ital. *O Dio mio!* (Oh, my God!); it is more likely to have originated as a euphemism for the English "*Oh, damn me!*"

Death. Milton makes Death keeper, with Sin, of Hell-gate.

> The other shape
> (If shape it might be called that shape had none
> Distinguishable in member, joint or limb;
> Or substance might be called that shadow seemed;)
> The likeness of a kingly crown had on.
> MILTON: *Paradise Lost*, ii, 666-673.

At death's door. On the point of death; very dangerously ill.

Black death. *See* BLACK.

Death from Strange Causes.

Æschylus was killed by the fall of a tortoise on his bald head from the claws of an eagle in the air. Valerius Maximus, ix, 12, and Pliny, *History*, vii, 7.

Agathocles, tyrant of Sicily, was killed by a toothpick at the age of ninety-five.

Anacreon was choked by a grape-stone. Pliny, *History*, vii, 7.

Bacon died of a cold contracted when stuffing a fowl with snow to see whether by this means it would "keep."

Robert Burton (of the *Anatomy of Melancholy*) died on the very day that he himself had astrologically predicted.

Chalchas, the soothsayer, died of laughter at the thought of having outlived the predicted hour of his death.

Charles VIII, of France, conducting his queen into a tennis-court, struck his head against the lintel, and it caused his death.

Fabius, the Roman prætor, was choked by a single goat-hair in the milk which he was drinking. Pliny, *History*, vii, 7.

Frederick Lewis, Prince of Wales, son of George II, died from the blow of a cricket-ball.

Gabrielle (*La belle*), the mistress of Henri IV, died from eating an orange.

Lepidus (*Quintus Æmilius*), going out of his house, struck his great toe against the threshold and expired.

Louis VI met with his death from a pig running under his horse and causing it to stumble.

Otway, the poet, in a starving condition, had a guinea given him, with which he bought a loaf of bread, and died while swallowing the first mouthful.

Philomenes died of laughter at seeing an ass eating the figs provided for his own dessert. Valerius Maximus.

George, *Duke of Clarence*, brother of Edward IV, was drowned in a butt of malmsey. *See* MALMSEY.

Saufeius (*Appius*) was choked to death supping up the white of an under-boiled egg. Pliny, *History*, vii, 33.

Death-watch. Any species of *Anobium*, a genus of wood-boring beetles, that make a clicking sound, once supposed to presage death.

Death's-head Moth. *Acherontia atropos*, is so called from the markings on the back of the thorax, which closely resemble a skull. It is also called the Hawk Moth.

Debonair (de bon âr') (*Le Débonnaire*). Louis I of France (778, 814-40), also called *The Pious*, son and successor of Charlemagne; a man of courteous manners, cheerful temper, but effeminate and deficient in moral energy.

Debt of Nature. To pay the debt of Nature. To die. Life is a loan, not a gift, and the debt is paid off by death.

The slender debt to Nature's quickly paid.
QUARLES: *Emblems.*

Decameron (de kăm' e rŏn). The collection of 100 tales by Boccaccio (1353) represented as having been told in ten days (Gr. *deka*, ten, *hemera*, day) during the plague at Florence in 1348. The storytellers were also ten (seven ladies and three gentlemen), and they each told a tale on each day.

Decathlon. An athletic contest in the modern Olympic games, consisting of ten events: 100 metres race, long jump, putting the shot, high jump, 400 metres race, 110 metres hurdles, discus, pole vault, throwing the javelin, and 1,500 metres race.

December (Lat., *the tenth month*). So it was when the year began in March with the vernal equinox; but since January and February have been inserted before it, the term is etymologically incorrect.

The old Dutch name was *Winter-maand* (winter-month); the old Saxon, *Mid-winter-monath* (midwinter-month); whereas June was *Mid-sumor-monath*. Christian Saxons called December *Se ura geóla* (the anti-yule). In the French Republican calendar it was called *Frimaire* (hoar-frost month, from November 22nd to December 20th).

The Man of December. Napoleon III (1808-73). He was made President of the French Republic December 11th, 1848; made his coup *d'état* December 2nd, 1851; and became Emperor December 2nd, 1852.

Deck. A pack of cards, or that part of the pack which is left after the hands have been dealt. The term was used in England until the 19th century; it is now in use in the U.S.A.

But whilst he thought to steal the single ten,
The king was slyly fingered from the deck.
3 *Henry VI*, v, 1.

Clear the decks. Get everything out of the way that is not essential; get ready to set to work. A sea term. Decks are cleared before action.

To sweep the deck. To clear off all the stakes. *See above.*

To deck is to decorate or adorn. (Dut. *dekken*, to cover; perhaps connected with A.S. *theccan*, to thatch.)

I thought thy bride-bed to have decked, sweet maid,
And not have strewed thy grave.
SHAKESPEARE: *Hamlet*, v, 1.

Deckle Edge. The feathery edge occurring round the borders of a sheet of handmade or mould-made paper, due to the *deckle* or frame of the mould. It can be imitated in machine-made papers.

Décolleté (dā kol' e tā). The French for a "dress cut low about the bosom."

Decoration Day or **Memorial Day.** May 30th; set apart in the United States for decorating the graves of those who fell in the Civil War (1861-5).

Decoy Duck. A bait or lure; a duck taught to allure others into a net, and employed for this purpose.

Decuman Gate. A Roman military term. The principal entrance to a camp, situated on the side farthest from the enemy, and so called because it was guarded by the 10th cohort of each legion (*decimus*, tenth).

Dedaliab. *See* DÆDALUS.

Dedalus, Stephen (dēd' á lùs). The young man whose literary and moral development is described in James Joyce's *Portrait of the Artist* *as a Young Man*. He also appears as a character in *Ulysses*.

Dee, Dr. John Dee (1527-1608) was a famous astrologer; he was patronized by Queen Elizabeth, and was a man of vast knowledge, whose library, museum, and mathematical instruments were valued at £2,000. On one occasion the populace broke into his house and destroyed the greater part of his valuable collection, under the notion that Dee held intercourse with the devil. He ultimately died a pauper, at the advanced age of eighty-one and was buried at Mortlake. He professed to be able to raise the dead, and had a magic mirror, a piece of solid pink-tinted glass about the size of an orange, in which persons were told they could see their friends in distant lands and how they were occupied. It was afterwards in Horace Walpole's collection at Strawberry Hill, and is now in the British Museum.

Deed Poll (dēd pōl). A deed drawn by one party, and so called because such deeds were formerly written on parchment with a polled or straight edge, in distinction to the indentures, which had an indented or wavy edge. It is by deed poll that one changes one's name or executes any deed that does not concern another party.

Deer. Supposed by poets to shed tears. The drops, however, which fall from their eyes are not tears, but an oily secretion from the so-called tear-pits.

> A poor sequestered stag . . .
> Did come to languish. . . and the big round tears
> Coursed one another down his innocent nose
> In piteous chase.   As You Like It, ii, 2.

Deerslayer. The first of the Leather-stocking Novels (*q.v.*) by Fenimore Cooper, and one of the names given to the hero Natty Bumpo.

Default. Judgment by default is when the defendant does not appear in court on the day appointed. The judge gives sentence in favour of the plaintiff, not because the plaintiff is right, but from the default of the defendant.

Defeat. "What though the field be lost? all is not lost." (Milton: *Paradise Lost*, i, lines 105-6.)

"All is lost but honour" (*Tout est perdu fors l'honneur*). A saying founded on a letter written by François I to his mother after the Battle of Pavia in 1525.

Defender of the Faith. A title (Lat. *fideli defensor*) given by Pope Leo X to Henry VIII of England, in 1521, for a Latin treatise *On the Seven Sacraments*. Many previous kings, and even subjects, had been termed "defenders of the Catholic faith," "defenders of the Church," and so on, but no one had borne it as a title.

> God bless the king! I mean the "faith's defender!"
> God bless—no harm in blessing—the Pretender.
> But who Pretender is, or who is king—
> God bless us all! that's quite another thing.
>   JOHN BYRON (1692-1763).

Richard II, in a writ to the sheriffs, uses these words: "*Ecclesia cujus nos defensor sumus*," and Henry VII, in the Black Book, was styled " Defender of the Faith."

Deficient. A *deficient* number is one of which the sum of all its divisors is less than itself, as 10, the divisors of which are 1, 2, 5 = 8, which is less than 10.

Deficit, Madame. Marie Antoinette; so called because she was always demanding money of her ministers, and never had any. According to the Revolutionary song:—

> La Boulangère a des écus,
> Qui ne lui content guère.
> See BAKER.

Degrees, Songs of. Another name for the Gradual Psalms (*q.v.*).

Dei Gratia (dē ī grā′ shà) (Lat.). By the grace of God. Introduced into English charters in 1106. It appears as "D.G." on English coins, *Cp.* GRACELESS FLORIN.

From the time of Offa, King of Mercia (A.D. 780), we find occasionally the same or some similar assumption as, *Dei dono, Christo donante*, etc.

From about 676 to 1170 the Archbishop of Canterbury and some other ecclesiastical dignitaries used the same style; the Archbishop is now *divina providentia*.

Dei Judicium (dē ī joo dish′ i um) (Lat.). The judgment of God; so the judgment by ordeals was called, because it was taken as certain that God would deal rightly with the appellants.

Deidamia (dē ī dā′ mia). When Achilles (*q.v.*) was concealed in the island of Scyrus dressed as a woman he met this daughter of Lycomedes, and she became by him the mother of Pyrrhus or Neoptolemus.

Deities. The more important deities of classical, Teutonic, and Scandinavian mythology are given as entries in this work; the present list is only intended to include collective names and the gods of a few special localities, functions, etc.

Air: Ariel; Elves. *See* ELF.
Caves or Caverns: Hill-people, Pixies.
Corn: Ceres (Gr., Demēter).
Domestic Life: Vesta.
Eloquence: Mercury (Gr., Hermes).
Evening: Vesper.

Fairies: (q.v.)

Fates, The: Three in number (Gr., Parcæ, Moiræ, Keres; Scand., Norns).

Fire: Vulcan (Gr., Hephaistŏs), Vesta, Mulciber.

Furies, The: Three in number (Gr., Eumenides, Erinnyes).

Gardens: Príāpus; Vertumnus with his wife Pomōna.

Graces, The: Three in number (Gr., Charītes).

Hades: Pluto, with his wife Proserpine (Gr., Aidēs and Persephŏne).

Hills: Pixies; Trolls. There are also Wood Trolls and Water Trolls.

Home Spirits (q.v.): Penātes, Lares.

Hunting: Diana (Gr., Artêmis).

Justice: Themis, Astræa, Nemesis.

Love: Cupid (Gr., Eros).

Marriage: Hymen.

Medicine: Æsculāpius.

Morning: Aurora (Gr., Eōs).

Mountains: Orēads, from the Gr., ὄρος, a mountain; Trolls.

Ocean: Oceanides. *See* SEA, below.

Poetry and Music: Apollo, the nine Muses *(q.v.)*.

Rainbow: Iris.

Riches: Plutus.

Rivers and Streams: Fluviäles (Gr., Potamēides; Naiads; Nymphs.)

Sea, The: Neptune (Gr., Pŏseidon), his son Triton, Nixies, Mermaids, Nereids.

Shepherds and their *Flocks:* Pan, the Satyrs.

Springs, Lakes, Brooks, etc.: Nēreides or Naiads. *See* RIVERS, above.

Time: Saturn (Gr., Chrŏnos).

Trees: See WOODS, below.

War: Mars (Gr., Arēs), Bellōna, Thor.

Water-nymphs: Naiads, Undine.

Winds: Æŏlus.

Wine: Bacchus (Gr., Dionysùs).

Wisdom: Minerva (Gr., Pallas, Athēnē, or Pallas-Athēnē).

Woods: Dryads (A Hamadryad presides over some particular tree), Wood-Trolls.

Youth: Hēbē.

Delaware (del' à wâr). The name of a State, river, and bay in the United States; so called from Thomas West, Baron De la Warr (1577-1618), first Governor of Virginia, in 1611.

Delectable Mountains. In Bunyan's *Pilgrim's Progress,* a range of mountains from which the "Celestial City" may be seen. They are in Immanuel's land, and are covered with sheep, for which Immanuel had died.

Delenda est Carthago (dè len' dà est kar' thà gō), Lat. "Carthage must be destroyed." The words with which Cato the Elder concluded every speech in the Senate when Carthage was such a menace to the power of Rome. They are now proverbial, and mean, "That which stands in the way of our greatness must be removed at all hazards."

Delft, or more correctly *Delf.* A common sort of pottery made at Delft in Holland, a town noted from the 16th to the 18th centuries for its very excellent pottery.

Delirium. From the Lat. *lira* (the ridge left by the plough), hence the verb *de-lirare,* to make an irregular ridge in ploughing. *Delirus* was one who couldn't plough a straight furrow, hence a crazy, doting person, one whose mind wandered from the subject in hand; and *delirium* is the state of such a person. *Cp.* PREVARICATION.

Della Cruscans (del' a krŭs' kànz) or *Della Cruscan School.* A school of poetry started by some young Englishmen at Florence in the latter part of the 18th century. Their silly, sentimental affectations, which appeared in the *World* and the *Oracle,* created for a time quite a furore, but were mercilessly gibbeted in the *Baviad* and *Mæviad* of Gifford (1794 and 1795). The clique took its name from the famous Accademia della Crusca (literally, Academy of Chaff) which was founded in Florence in 1582 with the object of purifying the Italian language—sifting away its "chaff"—and which in 1611 published an important dictionary.

Delos. A floating island, according to Greek legend, ultimately made fast to the bottom of the sea by Poseidon. Apollo having become possessor of it by exchange, made it his favourite retreat. It is the smallest of the Cyclades.

Delphi or **Delphos.** A town of Phocis, at the foot of Mount Parnassus (the modern Kastri), famous for a temple of Apollo and for an oracle which was silenced only in the 4th century A.D. by Theodosius, and was celebrated in every age and country.

Delphi was looked upon by the ancients as the "navel of the earth," and in the temple was kept a white stone bound with a red ribbon, to represent the navel and umbilical cord.

In the *Winter's Tale* (the same play in which he gives Bohemia a seacoast) Shakespeare makes Delphos an island.

Delta. A tract of alluvial land enclosed by the mouth of a river. The name, from the Greek letter Δ, *delta,* was originally given to the area of the mouths of the Nile, which was of triangular shape: it has since been applied to similar formations, such as the deltas of the Danube, Rhine, Ganges, Indus, Mississippi, etc.

Deluge. The Bible story of Noah's Flood has its counterpart in several mythologies and folk lores. In Babylonia it appears in the 11th tablet of the Gilgamesh Epic but on a higher level of civilization, for Utnapishtim (Noah) takes into the ark with him craftsmen and treasure.

Apollodorus tells the story of Deucalion and Pyrrha (*q.v.*). Of this story there are several versions, in one of which Deucalion is replaced by Ogyges.

One of the Indian deluge stories tells how Manu was warned by a fish, which towed the boat he made and brought it to safety.

In all these stories it is observable that, as in the case of Noah, the survivors' first act was to render thanks to the god who had preserved their lives.

Somewhat similar deluge stories are found in China, Burma, New Guinea, Polynesia and both the American continents.

See also AFTER ME THE DELUGE.

Demerit (dē mer' it) has reversed its original meaning (Lat. *dēmērere*, to merit, to deserve). The *de-* was originally intensive, as in "demand," "de-scribe," "de-claim," etc., but in mediæval Latin it came to be regarded as privative, and in English the word hence had both a good and a bad sense, of which the latter is now the only one remaining.

My demerits [deserts]
May speak unbonneted.
                                                    Othello, i, 2.

Demesne. *See* MANOR.

Demeter (de mē' ter). One of the great Olympian deities of ancient Greece, identified with the Roman Ceres (*q.v.*). She was the goddess of fruits, crops, and vegetation generally, and the protectress of marriage. Persephone (Proserpine) was her daughter.

Demijohn (dem' i jon). A glass vessel with a large body and small neck, enclosed in wickerwork like a Florence flask, and containing more than a bottle. The word is from the Fr. *dame-jeanne*, "Madame Jane," which has been thought to be a corruption of *Damaghan*, a town in Persia. There is, however, no support for this; it is more likely that the word is simply a popular name—"Dame Jane"—like "Bellarmine" (*q.v.*), but it is possible that it is from the Lat. *de mediana*, of middle size, or even *dimidium*, half.

Demi-monde (dem' i mond). Female society only half acknowledged, as *le beau monde* is Society. The term was first used by Dumas *fils*, and has been sometimes incorrectly applied to fashionable courtesans.

[Dumas'] *demi-monde* is the link between good and bad society . . . the world of compromised women, a social limbo, the inmates of which . . . are perpetually struggling to emerge into the paradise of honourable and respectable ladies.—*Fraser's Magazine*, 1885.

Demi-rep (dem' i rep). A woman whose character has been blown upon, one "whom everybody knows to be what nobody calls her" (*Fielding*). A contraction of *demi-reputation*.

Democracy. A form of Government in which the sovereign power is in the hands of the people, and exercised by them directly or indirectly: also, a State so governed, and the body of the people, especially the non-privileged classes. (Gr. *demoskratia*, the rule of the people.)

Democrats. Advocates of government by the people. A term adopted by the French revolutionists to distinguish themselves from the *aristocrats*. Adopted by the pro-slavery Southern States in the U.S.A., now a political party more of the Republicans.

Demogorgon (dem ō gor' gon). A terrible deity, whose very name was capable of producing the most horrible effects. He is first mentioned by the 4th-century Christian writer, Lactantius, who, in so doing is believed to have broken the spell of a mystery, for *Demogorgon* is supposed to be identical with the infernal Power of the ancients, the very mention of whose name brought death and disaster, to whom reference is made by Lucan and others:—

Must I call your master to my aid,
At whose dread name the trembling furies quake,
Hell stands abashed, and earth's foundations shake?
                        ROWE: *Lucan's Pharsalia*, vi.

Hence Milton speaks of "the dreaded name of Demogorgon" (*Paradise Lost*, ii, 956). According to Ariosto Demogorgon was a king of the elves and fays who lived on the Himalayas, and once in five years summoned all his subjects before him to give an account of their stewardship. Spenser (*Faerie Queene*, iv, ii, 47) says that he dwells in the deep abyss with the three fatal sisters.

Demon (Austr.). A convict serving his sentence of transportation in Van Diemen's Land (Tasmania).

Demons, Prince of. Asmodeus (*q.v.*), also called "The Demon of Matrimonial Unhappiness."

Demy (de mī'). A size of paper between royal and crown, measuring $17\frac{1}{2}$ by $22\frac{1}{2}$ in. in printing papers, and $15\frac{1}{2}$ by 20 in. in writing papers. It is from Fr. *demi* (half), probably meaning "half imperial."

A **Demy** of Magdalen College, Oxford, is a foundation scholar, whose allowance or "commons" was originally *half* that of a Fellow.

Den. God ye good den! An abbreviated form of the old salutation "God give you *good even*(ing)."

Nurse: God ye good morrow, gentlemen
Mer: God ye good den, fair gentlewoman.
                SHAKESPEARE: *Romeo and Juliet*, ii, 4.

Denarius (den âr′ i ùs). A Roman silver coin equal in value to ten ases (*deni-ases*), or about 8½ d. The word was used in France and England for the inferior coins, whether silver or copper, and for ready money generally. The initial "d." for penny (£ s. d.) is from *denarius*.

The denarius . . . shown to our Lord . . . was the tribute-money payable by the Jews to the Roman emperor, and must not be confounded with the tribute paid to the Temple.—MADDEN: *Jewish Coinage*, ch. xi.

Denarius Dei (Lat., God's penny). An earnest of a bargain, which was given to the church or poor.

Denarii St. Petri. Peter's pence (*q.v.*).

Denizen. A person who lives *in* a country as opposed to foreigners who live *outside* (Lat. *de-intus*, from within, through O.Fr. *deinzein*). In English law the word means a made citizen— *i.e.* an alien who has been naturalized by letters patent.

A denizen is a kind of middle state, between an alien and a natural-born subject, and partakes of both.— BLACKSTONE: *Commentaries*, Bk. i, ch. x.

Denmark. According to the *Roman de Rose*, Denmark means the country of Danaos, who settled here with a colony after the siege of Troy, as Brutus is said by the same sort of name-legend to have settled in Britain. Saxo-Germanicus, with equal absurdity, makes Dan, the son of Humble, the first king, to account for the name of the country.

The true origin of the word is from the march, or boundary of the Danes.

Denys, St. (dé né′). The apostle to the Gauls and patron saint of France. He is said to have been beheaded at Paris in 272, and, according to tradition, carried his head, after martyrdom, for six miles in his hands and laid it on the spot where stands the cathedral bearing his name. The tale may have taken its rise from an ancient painting of the incident, in which the artist placed the head between the martyr's hands so that the trunk might be recognized.

Depart. Literally, to part thoroughly; to separate effectually. The marriage service in the old prayer-books had "till death us depart," which has been corrupted into "till death us do part."

"Depart" is sound English for "part asunder," which was altered to "do part" in 1661, at the pressing request of the Puritans, who knew as little of the history of their national language as they did of that of their national Church.—J. H. BLUNT: *Annotated Book of Common Prayer*.

Department. France is divided into departments, as Great Britain and Ireland are divided into counties or shires. From 1768 it was divided into *governments*, of which thirty-two were grand and eight *petit*. In 1790, by a decree of the Constituent Assembly, it was mapped out *de novo* into eighty-three departments. In 1804 the number of departments was increased to 107, and in 1812 to 130. In 1815 the territory was reduced to eighty-six departments, and continued so till 1860, when Savoy and Nice were added. The present number is ninety, including Corsica and the provinces of Alsace and Lorraine.

Depot. The American term for a railway station, in use since the first introduction of railways into that country.

Derby (dĕr′ bi). The American term for the hat known as the Bowler (*q.v.*) in England. The Brown Derby is a well-known restaurant in Hollywood, shaped like a hat, frequented by the film colony.

Derby Scheme (dar′ bi). As a compromise with conscription the Government introduced a scheme in 1915 (when the Earl of Derby was at the War Office) of voluntary enlistment for men between 18 and 41, who would be called to the colours in age groups. It did not succeed, and conscription was introduced in January, 1916.

Derby Stakes (dar′ bi). Started by Edward Stanley, the twelfth Earl of Derby, in 1780, the year after his establishment of the Oaks stakes (*q.v.*).

Derrick. A temporary crane to remove goods from the hold of a vessel, etc.; so called from Derrick, the Tyburn hangman early in the 17th century. The name was first given to the gibbet; hence, from the similarity in shape, to the crane.

He rides circuit with the devil, and Derrick must be his host, and Tyborne the inn at which he will light.— DEKKER: *Bellman of London* (1608).

Derwentwater. Lord Derwentwater's lights. A local name for the Aurora Borealis; James, Earl of Derwentwater, was beheaded for rebellion February 24th, 1716, and it is said that the northern lights were unusually brilliant that night.

Desert Rats. Sobriquet of the 7th Armoured Division which, already in the Western Desert before the outbreak of war in 1939, served in the Eighth Army throughout the North African campaigns. Afterwards served in N.W. Europe. Its divisional sign was a red desert rat on a black ground. The 4th Armoured Brigade, also of long standing in the desert, used a black rat on a white ground. The name was given contemptuously by Mussolini but adopted with pride and pleasure.

Dessert means simply the cloth removed (Fr. *desservir*, to clear the table); and dessert is that which comes after the cloth is removed.

Destruction. Prince of Destruction. Tamerlane or Timour the Tartar (1333-1405), the terror of the East. He was conqueror of Persia and a great part of India, and was threatening China when he died.

Desultory. Those who rode two or more horses in the circus of Rome, and used to leap from one to the other, were called *desultores* (*de*, and *saltire*, to leap); hence *desultor* came in Latin to mean one inconstant, or who went from one thing to another; and desultory means the manner of a desultor.

Deucalion's Flood. The Deluge, of Greek legend. Deucalion was son of Prometheus and Clymene, and was king of Phthia, in Thessaly. When Zeus sent the deluge Deucalion built a ship, and he and his wife, Pyrrha, were the only mortals saved. The ship at last rested on Mount Parnassus, and Deucalion was told by the oracle at Themis that to restore the human race he must cast the bones of his mother behind him. His interpretation of this was the stones of his mother Earth, so the two cast these as directed and those thrown by Deucalion became men, and those thrown by his wife became women.

Deuce. The two, in games with cards, dice, etc. (Fr. *deux*). The three is called "Tray" (Fr. *trois*; Lat. *tres*).

The deuce is in you. You are a very demon.

What the deuce is the matter? What in the world is amiss?

Deus. Deus ex machina. The intervention of some unlikely event, in order to extricate one from difficulties. Literally, it means "a god (let down upon the stage) from the machine," the "machine" being part of the furniture of the stage in an ancient Greek theatre.

Deva. Chester, or the Dee.

> Nor yet where Deva spreads her wizard stream.
>   MILTON: *Lycidas*.

Devil. Represented with a cloven foot, because by the Rabbinical writers he is called *seirizzim* (a goat). As the goat is a type of uncleanness, the prince of unclean spirits is aptly represented under this emblem.

In his *Divina Commedia* Dante gives the following names to the various devils:—

Alichino, the allurer; *Barbariccia*, the malicious; *Calcobrina*, the grace-scorner; *Caynazzo*, the snarler; *Ciriato Sannuto*, the tusked boar; *Dragnignazzo*, the fell dragon; *Farfarello*, the scandalmonger; *Graffiacane*, the doggish; *Libicocco*, the ill-tempered; *Rubicante*, the red with rage; *Scarmiglione*, the baneful.

In legal parlance a *devil* is a leader's assistant

(also a barrister) who gets up the facts of a brief, with the laws bearing on it, and summarize the case for the pleader.

Cheating the devil. Mincing an oath; doing evil for gain, and giving part of the profits to the Church, etc. In a literal sense, cheating the devil is by no means unusual in monkish traditions. Thus the "Devils' Bridge," over the Fall of the Reuss, in the canton of the Uri, Switzerland, is a single arch over a cataract. It is said that Satan knocked down several bridges, but promised the abbot, Giraldus of Einsiedeln, to let this one stand, provided he would give him the first living thing that crossed it. The abbot agreed, and threw across it a loaf of bread, which a hungry dog ran after, and "the rocks re-echoed with peals of laughter to see the devil thus defeated." (Longfellow: *Golden Legend*, v.)

Rabelais says that a farmer once bargained with the devil for each to have on alternate years what grew under and over the soil. The canny farmer sowed carrots and turnips when it was his turn to have the under-soil share, and wheat and barley the year following. (*Pantagruel*, Bk. iv, ch. xlvi.)

Give the devil his due. Give even a bad man or one hated like the devil the credit he deserves.

> *Poins*: Jack, how agrees the devil and thee about thy soul, that thou soldest him on Good Friday last, for a cup of Madeira, and a cold capon's leg?
> *Prince*: Sir John stands to his word, the devil shall have his bargain; for he was never yet a breaker of proverbs, he will give the devil his due.
>   1 *Henry IV*, i, 2.

Go to the devil. The obvious meaning of this phrase is, to go to ruin. In the 17th century, however, wits used to make a play on the applicability of the phrase to the Devil Tavern, Temple Bar, one of the most famous taverns in the City, and a haunt of lawyers from the neighbouring Temple. The sign of the tavern was the Devil pulling St. Dunstan's nose. The Devil was a favourite resort of Ben Jonson, and numerous references to it appear in Elizabethan and Stuart literature.

> *Bloodhound*: As you come by Temple Bar make a step to th' Devil.
> *Tim.*: To the Devil, father?
> *Sim.*: My master means the sign of the Devil; and he cannot hurt you, fool; there's a saint holds him by the nose.
>   W. ROWLEY: *A Match at Midnight*, 1633.

He needs a long spoon who sups with the devil. *See* SPOON.

Here's the very devil to pay. Here's a pretty kettle of fish. I'm in a pretty mess; this is confusion worse confounded. *Cp.* THE DEVIL TO PAY *below*.

Talk of the devil and he's sure to appear. Said of a person who has been the subject of conversation, and who unexpectedly makes his appearance. An older proverb still is: "Talk of the Dule and he'll put out his horns"; but the modern euphemism is: "Talk of an angel and you'll hear the fluttering of its wings."

Forthwith the devil did appear,
For name him, and he's always near.
PRIOR: *Hans Carvel.*

Tell the truth and shame the devil. A very old saying, of obvious meaning.

Glendower: I can teach you, cousin, to command the devil.

Hotspur: And I can teach thee, coz, to shame the devil

By telling truth: tell truth and shame the devil.
SHAKESPEAR: 1 *Henry IV,* iii, 1.

The devil and his dam. The devil and something even worse. Dam (*q.v.*) here may mean either *mother* (the usual meaning), or *wife.* Quotations may be adduced in support of either of these interpretations, and it is to be noted that frequently (*cp. Paradise Lost,* ii) there is no differentiation. Also, Rabbinical tradition relates that Lilith was the wife of Adam, but was such a vixen that Adam could not live with her, and she became the devil's dam. We also read that Belphegor "came to earth to seek him out a dam."

In many mythologies the devil is typified by an animal; the Irish and others call him a *black cat*; the Jews speak of him as a *dragon* (which idea is carried out in our George and the Dragon); the Japanese call him a species of *fox*; others say he is a *goat,* a *camel,* etc., and Dante associates him with *dragons, swine,* and *dogs.* In all which cases dam for mother is not inappropriate.

The devil's door. A small door in the north wall of some old churches, which used to be opened at baptisms and communions to "let the devil out." The north used to be known as "the devil's side." where Satan and his legion lurked to catch the unwary.

The devil sick would be a monk.
When the Devil was sick, the devil a monk would be;
When the Devil got well, the devil a monk was he.

Said of those persons who in times of sickness or danger make pious resolutions, but forget them when danger is past and health recovered. The lines are found as an interpolation in Urquhart and Motteux's translation of Rabelais (Bk. iv, ch. xxiv). A correct translation of what Rabelais actually wrote is:—

"There's a rare rogue for you," said Eusthenes, "there's a rogue, a rogue and a half. This makes good the Lombard's proverb, 'Passato el Pericolo, gabbato el Santo'" [when the danger is passed, the Saint is mocked].

The devil to pay and no pitch hot. The "devil" is a seam between the garboard-strake and the keel, and to "pay" is to cover with pitch (O.Fr. *payer,* to pitch, whence Fr. *poix*; see PAY). In former times, when vessels were often careened for repairs, it was difficult to calk and pay this seam before the tide turned. Hence the locution, the ship is careened, the devil is exposed, but there is no hot pitch ready, and the tide will turn before the work can be done.

To hold a candle to the devil. *See* CANDLE.

To kindle a fire for the devil. To offer sacrifice, to do what is really sinful, under the delusion that you are doing God's service.

To lead one the devil's own dance. To give him endless trouble; to lead him right astray.

To play the very devil with something. To muddle and mar it in such a way as to spoil it utterly.

To pull the devil by the tail. To struggle constantly against adversity.

To say the devil's paternoster. To grumble; to rail at providence.

To whip the devil round the stump. An American phrase meaning to enjoy the fruits of evil-doing without having to suffer the penalty; to dodge a difficulty dishonestly but successfully.

The Devil's Current. Part of the current of the Bosporus is so called, from its great rapidity.

Devil's Den. A cromlech in a valley, near Marlborough. It now consists of two large uprights and an impost. The third upright has fallen.

The Devil's Dyke. A ravine in the South Downs, Brighton. The legend is, that St. Cuthman, walking on the downs, prided himself on having Christianized the surrounding country, and having built a nunnery where the dyke-house now stands. Presently the devil appeared and told him all his labour was vain, for he would swamp the whole country before morning. St. Cuthman went to the nunnery and told the abbess to keep the sisters in prayer till after midnight, and then illuminate the windows. The devil came at sunset with mattock and spade, and began cutting a dyke into the sea, but was seized with rheumatic pains all over his body. He flung down his mattock and spade, and the cocks, mistaking the illuminated windows for sunrise, began to crow; whereupon the devil fled in alarm, leaving his work not half done.

The same name is given to a prehistoric earthwork in Cambridgeshire, stretching across Newmarket Heath from Rech to Cowledge.

The Devil's Frying-pan. A Cornish tin-mine worked by the Romans.

The Devil's Hole. A name of the Peak Cavern, in Derbyshire.

The Devil's Nostrils. Two vast caverns separated by a huge pillar of natural rock in the mainland of the Zetland Islands.

The Devil's Punch Bowl. A deep combe on the S.W. side of Hindhead Hill, two miles N. of Haslemere, in Surrey. A similar dell in Mangerton Mountain, near Killarney, has the same name.

The Devil's Throat. Cromer Bay. So called from its danger to navigation.

The Devil's Tower. A great rectangular granite obelisk, over 600 feet in height, in the Black Hills, Dakota, U.S.A.

IN COMMON TERMS AND NAMES.

Devil and bag o' nails. *See* BAG O' NAILS.

Devil dodger. A sly hypocrite; a ranting preacher.

Devil may care. Wildly reckless; also a reckless fellow.

Devil on two sticks. The English name of Le Sage's novel *Le diable boiteux* (1707), in which Asmodeus (*q.v.*) plays an important part. It was dramatized by Foote in 1768. *See also* DIABOLO.

Devil's apple. The mandrake; also the thorn apple.

Devil's bedpost. In card games, the four of clubs. *Cp.* DEVIL'S FOUR-POSTER *below*.

Devil's Bible. *See* DEVIL'S BOOKS *below*.

Devil's bird. A Scots name for the yellow bunting; from its note, *deil*.

Devil's bones. Dice, which are made of bones and lead to ruin.

Devil's books, or Devil's picture-book. Playing cards. A Presbyterian phrase, used in reproof of the term King's Books, applied to a pack of cards, from the Fr. *livre des quatre rois* (the book of the four kings). Also called the *Devil's Bible*.

Devil's candle. So the Arabs call the mandrake, from its shining appearance at night.

Devil's candlestick. The common stinkhorn fungus; *Phallus impudicus*; also called the *devil's horn* and the *devil's stinkpot*.

Devil's coach-horse. A large rove-beetle, *Goerius olens*.

Devil's coach-wheel. The corn crowfoot.

Devil's daughter. A shrew. *Cp.* DEVIL'S DAUGHTER'S PORTION *in* PHRASES *above*.

Devil's dozen. Thirteen; twelve, and one over for the devil. *Cp.* BAKER'S DOZEN.

Devil's dust. The flock made from old rags torn up by a machine called the "devil"; also the shoddy made from this.

Does it beseem thee to weave cloth of devil's dust instead of pure wool?—CARLYLE (1840).

De Vinne, Theodore Low (1828-1914). A famous American printer who brought about great improvements in American typography. His principal work was *The Practice of Typography*, 1900-4.

Devonshire. English legend accounts for the name (which is really from that of the ancient Celtic inhabitants, the Damnonii) by saying that it is from Debon, one of the heroes who came with Brutus from Troy. When Brutus allotted out the island, this portion became *Debon's share*.

In mede of these great conquests by them got
  Corineus had that province utmost west . . .
And Debon's share was that is Devonshire.
      SPENSER: *Faerie Queene*, II, x, 12.

The Devonshire Poet. O. Jones, a journeyman wool-comber, who lived at the close of the 18th century. Other Devonshire poets are John Gay (1685-1732) of Barnstaple and Edward Capern (1819-94), called "The rural Postman of Bideford."

Dexter (deks' tér). A Latin word meaning "to the right, on the right-hand side"; hence *dextrous* originally signified "right-handed." In Heraldry the term *dexter* is applied to that side of the shield which is to the right of the person bearing it upon the arm, hence it indicates the *left* side of the shield as seen by the spectator, either when viewed as an actual shield or when seen depicted.

Diable, Le. Olivier Le Dain, the tool of Louis XI, and once the king's barber. So called because he was as much feared as the devil himself and even more disliked. He was hanged in 1484, after the death of the king.

Diabolo. An old game that was revived about 1907, in which the players have each two sticks connected with a cord on which they spin, and pass from one to the other, a reel-shaped top. It used to be called the "devil on two sticks," the top being the "devil."

Diadem (dī' à dem). In ancient times the headband or fillet worn by kings as a badge of royalty was called a diadem; it was made of silk or linen and was tied at the back, with the ends falling on the neck. The diadem of Bacchus was a broad band which might be unfolded to make a veil. The Emperor Constantine was the first to wear a diadem of jewels, and from his time rows of pearls and precious stones have made up the royal and imperial diadems.

To him who wears the regal diadem.
Paradise Lost.

Mont Blanc is the monarch of mountains
    They crown'd him long ago
On a throne of rocks, in a robe of clouds,
    With a diadem of snow.
BYRON: *Manfred*, i, 1.

Dialectics. Logic in general; the art of disputation; the investigation of truth by analysis; that strictly logical discussion which leads to reliable results. Gr. *dialegein*, to speak thoroughly.

Kant used the word to signify the critical analysis of knowledge based on science, and Hegel for the philosophic process of reconciling the contradictions of experience in a higher synthesis.

The following questions from John of Salisbury are fair specimens of the dialectics of the Schoolmen (*q.v.*):—

When a person buys a whole cloak, does the cowl belong to his purchase?

When a hog is driven to market with a rope round its neck, does the man or the rope take him.

Diamond. A corruption of *adamant* (*q.v.*). So called because the diamond, which cuts other substances, can be cut or polished with no substance but itself (Gr. *a damao*, what cannot be subdued).

In Spenser's *Faerie Queene* (Bk. iv), Diamond is one of the three sons of Agapë. He was slain by Cambalo.

Diamond is the playing area in the game of Baseball.

A diamond of the first water. A specially fine diamond, one of the greatest value for its size. The colour or lustre of a diamond is called its "water."

A rough diamond. An uncultivated genius; a person of excellent parts, but without society manners.

As for Warrington, that rough diamond had not had the polish of a dancing-master, and he did not know how to waltz.—THACKERAY.

Black diamonds. *See* BLACK.

Diamond cut diamond. Cunning outwitting cunning; a hard bargain over-reached. A diamond is so hard that it can only be ground by diamond dust, or by rubbing one against another.

Diamond Jim. Jim Brady, an American railway magnate who liked to cover his person with diamonds of great size in the form of rings, buttons, tie pins, etc.

The diamond jousts. Jousts instituted by King Arthur, "who by that name had named them, since a diamond was the prize." The story, as embroidered by Tennyson in his *Lancelot and Elaine* from Malory (Bk. xviii, ch. 9-20) is that Arthur found nine diamonds from the crown of a slain knight and offered them as the prize of nine jousts in successive years.

Diamond Pitt. Thomas Pitt (1653-1726), owner of the famous Pitt Diamond (*q.v.*), and grandfather of the Earl of Chatham, was so known.

Diana (dī ăn′ a). An ancient Italian and Roman divinity, later identified with the Olympian goddess Artemis, who was daughter of Zeus and Leto, and twin-sister of Apollo. She was the goddess of the moon and of hunting, protectress of women, and—in earlier times at least—the great mother goddess or Nature goddess. *Cp.* SELENE. The temple of Diana at Ephesus, one of the Seven Wonders of the World (*q.v.*), built by Dinochares, was set on fire by Herostratos, for the sake of perpetuating his name. The Ionians decreed that anyone who mentioned his name should be put to death, but this very decree gave it immortality. The temple was discovered in 1872.

Diana of Ephesus. This statue, a cone surmounted by a bust covered with breasts, we are told, fell from heaven. If so, it was an aerolite; but Minucius (2nd cent, A.D.), who says he saw it, describes it as a wooden statue, and Pliny, a contemporary, tells us it was made of ebony. Probably the real "image" was a meteorite, and in the course of time a wooden one was substituted.

The palladium of Troy, the most ancient image of Athena at Athens, the statues of Artemis at Tauris and Cybele at Pessinus, the sacred shield of the Romans, and the shrine of our Lady of Loretto, are examples of objects of religious veneration which were said to have been sent from heaven.

Diana's Worshippers. Midnight revellers. So called because they return home by moonlight, and so, figuratively, put themselves under the protection of Diana (*q.v.*).

Diapason (dī á pā′ son). The word is Greek (short for *dia pason chordon* through all the chords) and means an harmonious

combination of notes; hence harmony itself.
Dryden says:—

> From harmony, from heavenly harmony
>   The universal frame began;
> From harmony to harmony .
>   Thro' all the compass of the notes it ran,
>   The diapason closing full in man.
> *Song for St. Cecilia's Day.*

According to the Pythagorean system, the world is a piece of harmony and man the full chord. *Cp.* MICROCOSM.

Diaper (dī' à pĕr). A sort of variegated white cloth, so called from Gr. *dia*, through, *aspros*, white, white in places. The name is not connected with *Ypres*, nor with *jasper*.

It is usually a repeated pattern of squares or lozenges, and in this sense is used in heraldry for a pattern on the field or an ordinary of other than heraldic bearings. A more homely usage of the word applies it to a baby's "nappy."

Diavolo, Fra. Michele Pozza, an insurgent of Calabria (1760-1806), round whom Scribe wrote a libretto for Auber's comic opera (1830).

Dibs. Money. *Cp.* Tips, gifts to schoolboys.

The knuckle-bones of sheep used for gambling purposes are called dibbs; and Locke speaks of stones used for the same game, which he calls *dibstones*.

Dicers' Oaths. False as dicers' oaths. Worthless or untrustworthy, as when a gambler swears never to touch dice again. (*Hamlet*, iii, 4.)

Dichotomy (dik ot' ō mi). This comes from a Greek word meaning a cutting in two, and it is applied in biology and logic to a continuous division into pairs usually of opposite characteristics. A good example of dichotomy in all its senses is the mistletoe, the main stem of which divides into two, each part of which divides again into two, and so on to the little berries which appear in twos.

Dick. Richard; from *Ric*, short for the Anglo-Norman *Ricard*; the diminutive "Dicky" is also common.

> Jockey of Norfolk [Lord Howard], be not too bold,
> For Dickon [*or* Dicky], thy master, is bought and sold,
> *Richard III*, v, 3.
>   (Dickson is Richard III)

Dickens. *Dickens*, in **What the dickens**, is probably a euphemism for the devil, or Old *Nick*, and is nothing to do with Charles Dickens. In Low German we find its equivalent, *De duks!* Mrs. Page says:—

> I cannot tell what the dickens his name is.—*Merry Wives of Windsor*, iii, 2.

Dickey. In George III's time, a flannel petticoat.

> A hundred instances I soon could pick ye—
>   Without a cap we view the fair,

> The bosom heaving alto bare,
> The hips ashamed, forsooth, to wear a dicky.
> PETER PINDAR: *Lord Auckland's Triumph.*

It was afterwards applied to what were called false shirts—*i.e.* a starched shirt front worn over a flannel shirt; also to any other article of dress pretending to be what it isn't; and to leather aprons, children's bibs, the rumble behind a carriage, etc.

Dictys Cretensis. Reputed author of an eye-witness account in Latin of the siege of Troy. It was well known in the Middle Ages and formed the basis of many stories.

Didactic Poetry. Poetry which uses the beauties of expression, imagination, sentiment, etc., for teaching some moral lesson, as Pope's *Essay on Man*, or the principle of some art or science, as Virgil's *Georgics*, Garth's *Dispensary*, or Darwin's *Botanic Garden*. (Gr. *didasko*, I teach.)

Diddle. To cheat in a small way, as "I diddled him out of . . ." Edgar Allan Poe wrote an essay on "Diddling Considered as one of the Exact Sciences."

> A certain portion of the human race
> Has certainly a taste for being diddled.
> HOOD: *A Black Job.*

Jeremy Diddler. An adept at raising money on false pretences. From Kenny's farce called *Raising the Wind*.

Diderick. *See* DIETRICH.

Dido. The name given by Virgil to Elissa, founder and queen of Carthage. She fell in love with Æneas, driven by a storm to her shores, who, after abiding awhile at Carthage, was compelled by Mercury to leave the hospitable queen. Elissa, in grief, burnt herself to death on a funeral pile. (*Æneid*, i, 494-iii, 650.) Dido is really the Phœnician name of Astarte (Artemis), goddess of the moon and protectress of the citadel of Carthage.

It was Porson who said he could rhyme on any subject; and being asked to rhyme upon the three Latin gerunds, which, in the old Eton Latin grammar, are called *-di*, *-do*, *-dum*, gave this couplet:—

> When Dido found Æneas would not come,
> She mourned in silence, and was Di-do dum(b).

Didoes, To cut up. (U.S.A. 19th-century slang), to make merry, rag about.

Didymus (did' i mùs). This being the Greek word for a twin it was applied to St. Thomas (*q.v.*) as the name Thomas means, in Aramaic, a twin.

Die. The die is cast. The step is taken, and I cannot draw back. So said Julius Cæsar when he crossed the Rubicon—*jacta alea esto*, let the die be cast!

> I have set my life upon the cast,
> And I will stand the hazard of the die.
> *Richard III*, v, 4.

Never say die. Never despair; never give up.

Whom the gods love die young. This is from Menander—*Hon hoi theoi philousin apothneskei neos.* Demosthenes has a similar apophthegm. Plautus has the line, *Quem di diligunt adolescens moritur* (*Bacch.* IV, vii, 18).

Die-hards. In political phraseology *Die-hards* are the crusted members of any party who stick to their long-held theories through thick and thin, regardless of the changes that time or a newly awakened conscience may bring; those who would rather "die in the last ditch" than admit the possibility of their having been short-sighted.

Die Hards, The. *See* REGIMENTAL NICK-NAMES.

Diego, San (săn dī ē′ gō, dē ā′ gō). A modification of Santiago (St James), champion of the red cross, and patron saint of Spain.

Dietrich of Bern (dē′ trik). The name given by the German minnesingers to Theodoric the Great (454-526), king of the Ostrogoths (Bern = Verona). He appears in many Middle High German poems, especially the *Nibelungenlied*, where he is one of the liegemen of King Etzel.

Dieu (dyĕ). **Dieu et mon droit** (God and my right). The parole of Richard I at the battle of Gisors (1198), meaning that he was no vassal of France, but owed his royalty to God alone. The French were signally beaten, but the battle-word does not seem to have been adopted as the royal motto of England till the time of Henry VI.

Dieu-donné. Name given to Louis XIV in his infancy.

Difference. When Ophelia is distributing flowers (*Hamlet*, iv, 5) and says: "You must wear your rue with a difference," she is using the word in the heraldic sense and means "you must wear it as though it were marked in such a way as will slightly change the usual meaning of the plant," which was a symbol of repentance ("herb of grace"); or, on the assumption that she was offering the flower to the queen, Ophelia may have implied that they were both to wear rue: the one as the affianced of Hamlet, eldest son of the late king; the other as the wife of Claudius his brother, and the cadet branch.

In heraldry, *Differences or marks of cadency* indicate the various branches of a family.

The eldest son, during the lifetime of his father, bears a *label*, *i.e.* a bar or fillet, having three pendants broader at the bottom than at the top. The second son bears a *crescent*. The third, a *mullet* (*i.e.* a star with five points). The fourth, a *martlet*. The fifth, an *annulet*. The sixth, a *fleur-de-lis*. The seventh, a *rose*. The eighth, a *cross-moline*. The ninth, a *double quatre foil*.

To difference is to make different by the superimposition of a further symbol.

Diggings. Lodgings, rooms, apartments. A word imported from California and its gold diggings.

> My friend here wants to take diggings; and as you were complaining that you would get someone to go halves with you, I thought I had better bring you together.—SIR ARTHUR CONAN DOYLE: *A Study in Scarlet*, ch. 1.

Digits. The first nine numerals; so called from the habit of counting as far as ten on the fingers. (Lat. *digitus*, a finger.)

In astronomy, the word signifies the twelfth part of the diameter of the sun or moon; it is used principally in expressing the magnitude of an eclipse.

Dii Penates (dī′ i pe nā′ tēz) (Lat.). House-hold gods; now used colloquially for articles about the house that are specially prized. *Cp.* LARES.

Dilemma. The horns of a dilemma. A difficulty of such a nature that whatever way you attack it you encounter an equal amount of disagreeables. Macbeth, after the murder of Duncan, was "on the horns of a dilemma." If he allowed Banquo to live, he had reason to believe that Banquo would supplant him; if, on the other hand, he resolved to keep the crown for which "he had 'filed his hands," he must "step further in blood," and cut Banquo off.

"Lemma" means art assumption, a thing taken for granted (Gr. *lambanein*, to take). "Dilemma" is a double lemma, a two-edged sword, or a bull which will toss you whichever horn you lay hold of, called by the Schoolmen *argumentum cornutum*.

> A young rhetorician said to an old sophist, "Teach me to plead, and I will pay you when I gain a cause." He never had a cause till his old tutor master sued for payment; and he argued, "If I gain the cause I shall not pay you, because the judge will say I am not to pay; and if I lose my cause I shall not be required to pay, according to the terms of our agreement." To this the master replied, "Not so; if you gain your cause you must pay me according to the terms of our agreement; and if you lose your cause the judge will condemn you to pay me."

Dilettante (di lĕ tăn′ ti) (Ital.; pl. *dilettanti*). An amateur of the fine arts; a would-be connoisseur; frequently applied to a trifling pretender to knowledge of some art or science.

Diligence. A four-wheeled stage-coach, drawn by four or more horses, common in France before the introduction of railroads. The word is the same as the noun from *diligent*, which formerly meant speed, dispatch, as in Shakespeare's "If your diligence be not speedy I shall be there before you" (*King Lear*, i, 5).

Dime (U.S.A.). A ten-cent piece.

Dime novel (U.S.A.). Cheap publication of a lurid nature, originally costing a dime.

Dimetæ (dim' e tē). The ancient inhabitants of Carmarthenshire, Pembrokeshire, and Cardiganshire.

Dimity (dim' i ti). Stout cotton cloth woven with raised patterns. It has been said to be so called from Damietta, in Egypt, but is really from the Gr. *di-mitos* (double-thread). *Cp.* SAMITE.

Dingbats. An Australian colloquial term for delirium tremens.

Ding-dong. A ding-dong battle. A fight in good earnest. *Ding-dong* is an onomatopœic word, reproducing the sound of a bell; and here the suggestion is that the blows fell regularly and unfalteringly, like the hammer-strokes of a bell.

Dint. By dint of war; by dint of argument; by dint of hard work. Dint means a blow or striking (A.S. *dynt*); whence perseverance, power exerted, force; it also means the indentation made by a blow.

Diogenes (dī oj' e nēz). A noted Greek cynic philosopher (about 412-323 B.C.), who, according to Seneca, lived in a tub. Alexander the Great so admired him that he said, "If I were not Alexander I would wish to be Diogenes."

> The whole world was not half so wide
> To Alexander, when he cried
> Because he had but one to subdue,
> As was a paltry narrow tub to
> Diogenes.   BUTLER: *Hudibras*, i, 3.

Diogenes was also the surname of Romanus IV, Emperor of the East, 1067-71.

Diomedes (dī ō mē' dēz) or **Diomed.** In Greek legend, a hero of the siege of Troy, among the Greeks second only to Achilles in bravery. With Odysseus he removed the Palladium from the citadel of Troy. He appears as the lover of Cressida in Boccaccio's *Filostrato* and in later works.

Dionysus (dī ō nī' sus). The Greek name of Bacchus (*q.v.*).

Dioscuri. Castor and Pollux (*q.v.*). Gr. *Dios kouros*, sons of Zeus.

The horses of the Dioscuri. Cyllaros and Harpagos. *See* HORSE.

Dip. The dip of the horizon is the apparent slope of the horizon as seen by an observer standing above sea level. This slope is due to the convexity of the earth.

Dip of the needle is the inclination of a compass needle vertically. At the magnetic poles this is 90° and at the magnetic equator 0°.

To dip the flag is to lower it for a moment and then hoist again, as a form of salute.

To dip the headlights of a car is to lower them and turn them on again.

To go for a dip. To go bathing. This is a very old English phrase.

Dip. A cheap and common kind of candle, made by dipping into melted tallow the cotton which forms the wick.

Dipping (U.S.A.). The name given in Virginia and N. Carolina to the habit, there once prevalent, of chewing snuff.

Diphthera (dif' thē rà) (Gr.). A piece of prepared hide or leather; specifically, the skin of the goat Amalthea, on which Jove wrote the destiny of man. **Diphtheria** is an infectious disease of the throat; so called from its tendency to form a false membrane.

Diploma (dip lō' mà) (Gr.). Literally, something folded. Diplomas used to be written on parchment, folded, and sealed. The word is applied to licences given to graduates to assume a degree, to clergymen, to physicians, etc.; and also to the credentials of an ambassador, etc., authorizing him to represent his Government; whence *diplomacy*, the negotiations, privileges, tact, etc., of a *diplomatist*.

Diplomatics. The name formerly (and sometimes still) given to the science of palæography—that is, deciphering and investigating old charters, diplomas, titles, etc. Papebroch, the Bollandist, originated the study in 1675; but Mabillon, another Bollandist, reduced it to a science in his *De re Diplomatica*, 1681. Toustain and Tassin further developed it in their treatise entitled *Nouveau Traité de Diplomatique*, 1750-60.

Diptych (Gr. *diptuchos*, folded in two). A register folded into two leaves, opening like a book. The Romans kept in a book of this sort the names of their magistrates, and Catholics employed the word for the registers in which were written the names of those who were to be specially commemorated when oblations were made for the dead. The name is also given to altar pieces and other paintings that fold together in the middle on a hinge.

Dircæan Swan. Pindar; so called from Dirce, a fountain in the neighbourhood of

Thebes, the poet's birthplace (518-442 B.C.). The fountain is named from Dirce, who was put to death by the sons of Antiope for her brutal treatment of their mother, and was changed into the spring by Bacchus.

Direct Action. A method of attaining, or attempting to attain, political ends by non-political means (such as striking or withdrawing labour).

Direct tax. One collected *directly* from the owner of property subject to the tax, as the income-tax. *Indirect taxes* are taxes upon marketable commodities, such as tea and sugar, the tax on which is added to the article, and is thus paid by the purchaser indirectly.

Dirleton. Doubting with Dirleton, and resolving those doubts with Stewart. Doubting and answering those doubts, but doubting still. It is a Scottish phrase; and the allusion is to the *Doubts and Questions in the Law* (1698), by Sir John Nisbet of Dirleton, the Lord President, and Sir James Stewart's *Dirleton's Doubts and Questions . . . Resolved and Answered* (1715). Of the former work Lord Chancellor Hard-wicke remarked, "His *Doubts* are better than most people's *certainties*."

Dirt. The origin of this word is Teutonic and we find its equivalent in the Icelandic *drit*, meaning excrement. In modern usage the sense has been extended to include loose or packed soil, alluvial earth, gravel, etc., and, figuratively, obscenity of any kind, especially in language.

Pay dirt. Soil containing gold or diamonds, whichever is being sought.

Dirt cheap. Very low-priced.

Throw plenty of dirt and some will be sure to stick. Scandal always leaves a trail behind; find plenty of fault, and some of it will be believed. In Lat., *Fortiter calumniari, aliquid adhœrēbit*.

To eat dirt. To put up with insults and mortification.

Dis. The Roman name of the Greek Pluto (*q.v.*).

> Proserpine gathering flowers,
> Herself a fairer flower, by gloomy Dis
> Was gathered.
> MILTON: *Paradise Lost*, iv, 270.

Disastrous Peace, The (*La Paix Malheureuse*). A name given to the Treaty of Câteau Cambrésis (1559), which followed the battle of Gravelines. It was signed by France, Spain, and England, and by it France ceded the Low Countries to Spain, and Savoy, Corsica, and 200 forts to Italy. But she retained Calais.

Discalced. *See* BAREFOOTED.

Discharge Bible, The. *See* BIBLE, SPECIALLY NAMED.

Disciples of Christ. *See* CAMPBELLITES.

Discipline, A. A scourge used for penitential purposes.

> Before the cross and altar a lamp was still burning, . . . and on the floor lay a small discipline or penitential scourge of small cord and wire, the lashes of which were stained with recent blood.—SCOTT: *The Talisman*, ch. iv.

This is a transferred sense of one of the ecclesiastical uses of the word—the mortification of the flesh by penance.

Discord. Literally, severance of hearts (Lat. *discorda*). It is the opposite of *concord*, the coming together of hearts. In music, it means disagreement of sounds, as when a note is followed by or played with another which is disagreeable to a musical ear.

The apple of discord. *See* APPLE.

Discount. At a discount. Not in demand; little valued; less esteemed than formerly; below par. (Lat. *dis-computare*, to depreciate.)

Disestablishment. The governmental act of withdrawing a Church from its position or privileges in relation to the State. The Irish Church was disestablished by an Act of Parliament in 1869; that of Wales in 1920.

Dispansation (Lat. *dispensatio*, from *dis-* and *pendere*, to weigh). The system which God chooses to *dispense* or establish between Himself and man. The dispensation of *Adam* was that between Adam and God; the dispensation of *Abraham*, and that of *Moses*, were those imparted to these holy men; the *Gospel* dispensation is that explained in the Gospels.

A dispensation from the Pope. Permission to *dispense* with something enjoined; a licence to do what is forbidden, or to omit what is commanded by the law of the Church, as distinct from the moral law.

Displaced Persons, a phrase that arose in World War II when it was applied to the millions of homeless and uprooted people in Germany who had either been imported there by the German government as slaves when their homes were overrun and destroyed or who had lost their homes in the ravages caused by the Russian invasion. Colloquially known as "Displaced persons" since their rehabilitation presented such appalling problems to the soldiers first charged with the task.

Distaff. The staff from which the flax was drawn in spinning; hence, figuratively, woman's work, and a woman herself, the allusion being to the old custom of women, who spun from morning to night. *Cp.* SPINSTER.

> I blush that we should owe our lives to such
> A king of distaffs!
>
> BYRON: *Sardanapalus*, II, i.

Distemper. An undue mixture (Lat. *distemperare*, to mix amiss). In medicine a distemper arises from the redundancy of certain secretions or morbid humours. The distemper in dogs is an undue quantity of secretions manifested by a running from the eyes and nose.

Dithyrambic (dith·i răm' bik) (Gr. *dithyrambo*, a choric hymn). Dithyrambic poetry was originally a wild, impetuous kind of Dorian lyric in honour of Bacchus, traditionally ascribed to the invention of Arion of Lesbos (about 620 B.C.), who has hence been called the father of dithyrambic poetry.

Dittany (dit' à ni). This plant (*Origanum dictamnus*), so named from Dicte in Crete, where it grew in profusion, was anciently credited with many medicinal virtues, especially in enabling arrows to be drawn from wounds and curing such wounds. In Tasso's *Jerusalem Delivered* (Bk. ix) Godfrey is healed in this way.

> Stags and hinds, when deeply wounded with darts, arrows, and bolts, if they do but meet the herb called dittany, which is common in Candia, and eat a little of it, presently the shafts come out, and all is well again; even as kind Venus cured her beloved by-blow Æneas.—
> *Rabelais* (*Urquhart and Motteux*): Bk. iv, ch. lxii.

Ditto (dit' ō) (Ital. *detto*, said; from Lat. *dictum*). That which has been said before; the same or a similar thing. The word is often, in writing, contracted to *do.*

A suit of dittoes. Coat, waistcoat, and trousers all alike, or all ditto (the same).

To say ditto. To endorse somebody else's expressed opinion.

Divan (Tur. and Pers.). Primarily, a collection of sheets; hence, a collection of poems, a register (and the registrar) of accounts, the office where accounts are kept, a council or tribunal, a long seat or bench covered with cushions, a court of justice, and a custom house (whence *douane*). The word, in its ramifications and extensions, is somewhat like our *board* (*q.v.*); in England its chief meanings are (1) a comfortable sofa, (2) a bed without head-board or foot-board, and formerly (3) a public smoking-saloon.

Dive. A low resort. The phrase, of 19th-century U.S.A. origin, spread to common use in England in the 20th century.

Divide. When the members in the House of Commons interrupt a speaker by crying out *divide*, they mean, bring the debate to an end and put the motion to the vote—*i.e.* let the ayes divide from the noes, one going into one lobby, and the others into the other.

Divide and govern (Lat. *divide et impera*). A maxim of Machiavelli (1469-1527) meaning that if you divide a nation into parties, or set your enemies at loggerheads, you can have your own way. Coke, in his *Institutes* (pt. iv, cap. i) speaks of the maxim as "that exploded adage."

> Every city or house divided against itself shall not stand.—*Matt*, xii, 25.

Divination (div i nā' shùn). There are numerous species of divination referred to in the Bible. The following are the most notable, and to most of these there are many other allusions in the Bible beside those indicated.

> JUDICIAL ASTROLOGY (*Dan.* ii, 2).
> WITCHCRAFT (1 *Sam.* xxviii).
> ENCHANTMENT (2 *Kings* xxi, 6).
> CASTING LOTS (*Josh*, xviii, 6).
> By NECROMANCY (1 *Sam.* xxviii, 12).
> By RHABDOMANCY or rods (*Hos.* iv, 12).
> By TERAPHIM or household idols (Gen. xxxi; 1 *Sam.* xv, 23, R.V.).
> By HEPATOSCOPY or inspecting the liver of animals (*Ezek.* xxi, 21, 26).
> By DREAMS and their interpretations (*Gen.* xxxvii, 10).
> Divination by fire, air, and water; thunder, lightning, and meteors; etc.
> The *Urim and Thummin* was a prophetic breastplate worn by the High Priest.
> (Consult: *Gen.* xxxvii, 5-11; xl, xli; 1 *Sam.* xxviii, 12; 2 *Chron.* xxxiii, 6; *Prov.* xvi, 33; *Ezek.* xxi, 21; *Hos.* iii, 4, 5, etc.)

Divine, The. Theophrastus, the name of the Greek philosopher (390-287 B.C.), means "the Divine Speaker," an epithet bestowed on him by Aristotle, on account of which he changed his name from Tyrtamus.

Hypatia (*c.* 370-415), who presided over the Neoplatonic School at Alexandria, was known as "the Divine Pagan."

Jean de Ruysbroek (*see* ECSTATIC DOCTOR) was also called "the Divine Doctor."

A name given to Michael Angelo (1475-1564) was "the Divine Madman."

Ariosto (1474-1533), Italian poet, Raphael (1483-1520), the painter, Luis de Morales (1509-86), a Spanish religious painter, and Ferdinand de Herrera (1534-67), the Spanish lyric poet, were all known as "the Divine."

The Divine Plant. Vervain. *See* HERBA SACRA.

The divine right of kings. The notion that kings reign by direct ordinance of God, quite apart from the will of the people. This phrase was much used in the 17th century on account of the pretensions of the Stuart kings; and the idea arose from the Old Testament, where kings are called "God's anointed," because they were God's vicars on earth, when the Jews changed their theocracy for a monarchy.

The right divine of kings to govern wrong.
POPE; *Dunciad*, iv, 188.

Divining rod. A forked branch of hazel, one prong of which is held in either hand. The inclination of the rod, when controlled by a qualified person, called a *diviner*, is said to indicate by its movements the presence of water-springs, precious metal, oil, etc.

Divining, or *dowsing* (*see* DOWSE), as it is also called, has been the subject of numerous scientific investigations, and while these have shown that the claims of diviners can in many cases be substantiated, there is still no satisfactory scientific explanation of the phenomenon. This method of discovering hidden treasure naturally lends itself to the exploitation of the fraudulent and the "gulling" of the credulous.

Division. The sign ÷ for division was brought into use by John Pell (1611-85), the noted Cambridge mathematician who became Professor of Mathematics at Amsterdam in 1643.

In its military sense a *division* is the largest formation in an army which has a constant establishment, so designed as to be self-contained with its own services. Invented by Napoleon. In the British army it totals 15,000 men.

Divorcement. A bill of divorcement is a phrase going back to the days of the old divorce procedure. Before the Divorce Act of 1857 divorce could be granted only by the ecclesiastical courts of the various dioceses. Even then remarriage by either of the parties was prohibited, except a special Bill was taken to Parliament and passed after debate—a procedure so expensive that few could afford it.

Dixie Land. The Southern States of the U.S.A. The name, according to one story, originated in the "dix," or ten-dollar bank-note of Louisiana. When times were prosperous, these bills circulated so freely that Louisiana was called the "land of dixies." It has also been said to have got its name from "Mason and *Dixon's* Line" (*q.v.*), which formed the boundary between the slave-holding and the "free" States. The explanation given below is the most likely to be correct:—

When slavery existed in New York, one DIXIE owned a large tract of land on Manhattan Island, and a large number of slaves. The increase of the slaves and of the abolition sentiment caused an emigration of the slaves to more thorough and secure slave sections, and the negroes who were thus sent off (many being born there) naturally looked back to their old houses, where they had lived in clover, with feelings of regret, as they could not imagine any place like DIXIE'S. Hence it became synonymous with an ideal locality combining ease, comfort, and material happiness of every description.—
Charlestown Courier: June 11th, 1885.

A song of this name, by Albert Pike, was adopted as the marching song of the Southern armies:—

Advance the flag of Dixie!
    Hurrah! Hurrah!
For Dixie's land we'll take our stand
    To live and die for Dixie.

Dixie, the soldier's name for a large cooking kettle, is the Hindi *degshi*, a pot, vessel.

Do. A contraction of *ditto* (*q.v.*).

Do. A verb, and auxiliary, that forms part of countless phrases and lends itself to almost countless uses. Its chief modern significations are:—

(Transitive) To put, as in *To do to death*; to bestow, cause to befall, etc., as *It did him no harm, To do a good turn*; to perform, perpetrate, execute, etc., as *To do one's work, Thou shalt do no murder, What will he do with it? All is done and finished.*

(Intransitive) To exert actively, to act in some way, as *Let us do or die, I have done with you, How do you do? I'm doing very well, thank you, That will do.*

(Causal and Auxiliary). Used instead of a verb just used, as *He plays as well as you do.* Periphrastically as an auxiliary of the Pres. and Past Indicative and the Imperative, used for the sake of emphasis, euphony, or clarity, also in negative and interrogative sentences: *I DO wish you would let me alone, Not a word did he say, Billiards and drinking do make the money fly, Do you like jazz? I do not care for it. Do tell me where you've been! Don't stop!*

Do as you would be done by. Behave to others as you would have them behave to you.

To do away with. To abolish, put an end to, destroy entirely.

To do for. To act for or manage for. *A man ought to do well for his children*; a landlady *does for* her lodgers. Also, to ruin, destroy, wear out. *I'll do for him.* I'll ruin him utterly, or even, I'll kill him; *taken in and done for*, cheated and fleeced; *this watch is about done for*, it's nearly worn out.

To do it on one's head. Said of doing something with consummate ease; a rather scornful expression. "I bet you couldn't walk a mile in seven minutes"; "Pooh! I could do it on my head!"

To do one proud. To flatter him; to treat him in an exceptionally lavish and hospitable way.

To do oneself proud, or **well.** To give oneself a treat.

To do the grand, amiable, etc. To act (usually with some ostentation) in the manner indicated by the adjective.

To do up. To repair, put in order. "This chair wants doing up," *i.e.* renovating. Also, to make tidy, to put up or fasten a parcel, and to wear out, tire. "I'm quite done up," I'm worn out, exhausted. *Cp.* DUP.

To do without so-and-so. To deny oneself it, to manage without it.

To have to do with. To have dealings or intercourse with, to have relation to. "That has nothing to do with the case."

Well to do. In good circumstances, well off, well provided for.

Dobbin. A steady old horse, a child's horse.

Dobby, a silly old man, also a house-elf similar to a brownie. All these are one and the same word, an adaptation of *Robin*, diminutive of *Robert*.

Sober Dobbin lifts his clumsy heel.
                    BLOOMFIELD: *Farmer's Boy* (Winter).

The dobbie elves lived in the house, were very thin and shaggy, very kind to servants and children, and did many a little service when people had their hands full.

The Dobby's walk was within the inhabited domains of the Hall.—SCOTT: *Peveril of the Peak,* ch. x.

Docetes. An early Gnostic heretical sect, which maintained that Jesus Christ was divine only, and that His visible form, the crucifixion, the resurrection, etc., were merely illusions. (The word is Greek, and means *phantomists*.)

Dock Brief. In English law anyone accused of an offence and brought to trial is entitled to defend himself or be defended by counsel. When a prisoner in the dock pleads inability to employ counsel, the presiding judge can instruct a barrister present in court to undertake the defence, a small fee for this being paid by the court.

Doctor. A name given to various adulterated or falsified articles because they are "doctored," *i.e.* treated in some way that strengthens them or otherwise makes them capable of being passed off as something better than they actually are. Thus a mixture of milk, water, nutmeg, and rum is called *Doctor*; the two former ingredients being "doctored" by the two latter.

Brown sherry is so called by licensed victuallers because it is concocted from a thin wine with the addition of unfermented juice and some spirituous liquor.

In nautical slang the ship's cook is known as "the doctor," because he is supposed to "doctor" the food; and a seventh son used to be so dubbed from the popular superstition that he was endowed with power to cure agues, the king's evil, and other diseases.

Doctored dice. Loaded dice; dice which are so "doctored" as to make them turn up winning numbers; also called simply *doctors*.

"The whole antechamber is full, my lord—knights and squires, doctors and dicers."

"The dicers with their doctors in their pockets, I presume."—SCOTT: *Peveril of the Peak,* ch. xxviii.

Doctor Fell.

I do not like thee, Dr. Fell,
The reason why I cannot tell;
But this I know, I know full well,
I do not like thee, Dr. Fell.

These well-known lines are by the "facetious" Tom Brown (1663-1704), and the person referred to was Dr. John Fell, Dean of Christ Church (1625-86), who expelled him, but said he would remit the sentence if Brown translated the thirty-third Epigram of Martial:

Non amo te, Zabidi, nec possum dicere quare;
Hoc tantum possum dicere non amo te.

The above is the translation, which is said to have been given impromptu.

It was this Dr. Fell who in 1667 presented to the University of Oxford a complete type-foundry containing punches and matrices of a large number of founts—Arabic, Syriac, Coptic and other learned alphabets, as well as the celebrated "Fell" Roman.

To doctor the accounts. To falsify them. The allusion is to drugging wine, beer, etc., and to adulteration generally.

To doctor the wine. To drug it, or strengthen it with brandy; to make weak wine stronger, and "sick" wine more palatable. The fermentation of cheap wines is increased by fermentable sugar. As such wines fail in aroma, connoisseurs smell at their wine.

To have a cat doctored. A colloquialism for having a young tom-cat "cut," or castrated.

To put the doctor on a man. To cheat him. The allusion to "doctored dice" is obvious.

Who shall decide when doctors disagree? When authorities differ, the question *sub judice* must be left undecided. (POPE: *Moral Essays,* ep. iii, line 1.)

Doctors of Learning, Piety, etc.

Admirable Doctor: Roger Bacon (1214-92).

Angelic Doctor: St. Thomas Aquinas (1224-74).

Divine Doctor: John Ruysbroek (1294-1381)

Invincible Doctor: William Occam (1276-1347)

Irrefragable Doctor: Alexander of Hales (*d.* 1245).

Mellifluous Doctor: St. Bernard of Clairvaux (1091-1153).

Seraphic Doctor: St. Bonaventura (1221-74).

Subtle Doctor: Duns Scotus (1265-1308).

Wonderful Doctor: Roger Bacon (1214-92).

Documentary film. A film devised and produced for the sole purpose of giving a realistic and accurate picture of some aspect of everyday life or work.

Doddypoll. A blockhead, a silly ass. *Poll*, of course, is the head; and *doddy* is the modern *dotty*, silly, from the verb *to dote*, to be foolish or silly. There is an Elizabethan romantic comedy (about 1595) called The *Wisdom of Doctor Doddypoll*, thought by some to be by George Peele.

Dodger. A "knowing fellow". One who knows all the tricks and ways of London life, and profits by such knowledge.

(U.S.A.) A hard cake, or biscuit.

The Artful Dodger. The sobriquet of John Dawkins, a young thief in Dickens's *Oliver Twist*.

Dodman. A snail; the word is still in use in Norfolk. Fairfax, in his *Bulk and Selvedge* (1674), speaks of "a snayl or dodman."

> Doddiman, doddiman, put out your horn,
> Here comes a thief to steal your corn.
> *Norfolk rhyme*

Hodmandod is another variation of the same word.

Dodona (do dō' nà). A famous oracle in the village of Dodona in Epiros, and the most ancient of Greece. It was dedicated to Zeus, and the oracles were delivered from the tops of oak and other trees, the rustling of the wind in the branches being interpreted by the priests. Also, brazen vessels and plates were suspended from the branches, and these, being struck together when the wind blew, gave various sounds from which responses were concocted. Hence the Greek phrase *Kalkos Dodones* (brass of Dodona), meaning a babbler, or one who talks an infinite deal of nothing.

Doe. John Doe and Richard Roe. Any plaintiff and defendant in an action of ejectment. They were sham names used at one time to save certain "niceties of law"; but the clumsy device was abolished in 1852. Any mere imaginary persons, or men of straw. The names "John o' Noakes" and "Tom Styles" are similarly used.

Doeg (dō' eg). In Dryden's *Absalom and Achitophel* (*q.v.*), is meant for Elkanah Settle, a poet who wrote satires upon Dryden, but was no match for his great rival.

Doff is do-off, as "Doff your hat." So *Don* is do-on, as "Don your clothes." *Dup* is do-up, as "Dup the door" (*q.v.*).

> Doff thy harness, youth . . .
> And tempt not yet the brushes of the war.
> *Troilus and Cressida*, v, 3.

Dog. This article is subdivided into five parts:
1. Dogs in Phrases and Colloquialisms.
2. Dogs of note in the Classics and in legend.
3. Dogs famous in History, Literature, Fiction, etc.
4. Dogs in Symbolism and Metaphor.
5. Dog—or dog's—in combination.

(1) IN PHRASES AND COLLOQUIALISMS.

A black dog has walked over him. Said of a sullen person. Horace tells us that the sight of a black dog with its pups was an unlucky omen, and the devil has been frequently symbolized by a black dog.

A cat and dog life. See CAT (To live a, etc.).

A dead dog. Something utterly worthless. A Biblical phrase (*see* 1 *Sam*. xxiv, 14, "After whom is the king of Israel come out? After a dead dog?") *Cp. also* IS THY SERVANT, etc., *below*.

A dirty dog. One morally filthy; one who talks and acts nastily. In the East the dog is still held in abhorrence, as the scavenger of the streets. "Him that dieth in the city shall the dogs eat" (1 *Kings* xiv, 11).

A dog in the manger. A churlish fellow, who will not use what is wanted by another, nor yet let the other have it to use. The allusion is to the well-known fable of a dog that fixed his place in a manger, would not allow an ox to come near the hay and would not eat it himself.

A living dog is better than a dead lion. The meanest thing with life in it is better than the noblest without. The saying is from *Eccles*. ix, 4. The Italians say "A live ass is worth more than a dead doctor."

A dog's age. A very long time.

Dogs howl at death. A widespread superstition.

> In the rabbinical book it saith
> The dogs howl when, with icy breath,
> Great Sammael, the angel of death,
> Takes thro' the town his flight.
> LONGFELLOW: *Golden Legend*, iii.

Every dog has his day. You may crow over me to-day, but my turn will come by and by. In Latin *Hodie mihi, cras tibi*, "To-day to me, tomorrow to thee." "*Nunc mihi, nunc tibi, benigna*" (*fortuna*), fortune visits every man once; she favours me now, but she will favour you in your turn.

> Thus every dog at last will have his day—
> He who this morning smiled, at night may sorrow;
> The grub to-day's a butterfly to-morrow.
> PETER PINDAR: *Odes of Condolence*.

He who has a mind to beat his dog will easily find a stick. If you want to abuse a person, you will easily find something to blame. Dean

Swift says, "If you want to throw a stone, every lane will furnish one."

Is thy servant a dog, that he should do this thing? Said in contempt when one is asked to do something derogatory or beneath him. The phrase is (slightly altered) from 2 *Kings* viii, 13.

Sydney Smith, when asked if it was true that he was about to sit to Landseer, the animal painter, for his portrait, replied, "What! is thy servant *a dog* that he should do this thing?"

It was the story of the dog and the shadow. A case of one who gives up the substance for its shadow. The allusion is to the well-known fable of the dog who dropped his bone into the stream because he opened his mouth to seize the reflection of it.

Lazy as Lawrence's, or **Ludlam's dog.** *See* LAZY.

Let sleeping dogs lie; don't wake a sleeping dog. Let well alone; if some contemplated course of action is likely to cause trouble or land you in difficulties you had better avoid it.

It is nought good a sleping hound to wake,
Nor yeve a wight a cause to devyne.
CHAUCER: *Troilus and Criseyde*, iii, 764.

Love me love my dog. If you love me you must put up with my defects.

Not to have a word to throw at a dog. Said of one who is sullen or sulky.

Cel.: Why, cousin! why, Rosalind! Cupid have mercy! Not a word?
Ros.: Not one to throw at a dog.
As You Like It, i, 3.

Old dogs will not learn new tricks. People in old age do not readily conform to new ways.

St. Roch and his dog. Emblematic of inseparable companions; like "a man and his shadow." One is never seen without the other. *See* ROCH, ST.

Sick as a dog. Very sick. We also say "Sick as a cat." *See* CAT. The Bible speaks of dogs returning to their vomit (*Prov.* xxvi, 11; 2 *Pet.* ii, 22).

The dogs of war. The horrors of war, especially famine, sword, and fire.

And Cæsar's spirit, ranging for revenge,
With Até by his side, come hot from hell,
Shall in these confines, with a monarch's voice,
Cry "Havoc," and let slip the dogs of war.
Julius Cæsar, iii, 1.

The hair of the dog that bit you. It used to be considered that the best cure for a "thick head" was another drink; it is, perhaps, a matter for trial and error. The allusion is to an ancient notion that the burnt hair of a dog is an antidote to its bite. *Similia similibus curantur.*

The more I see of men the more I love dogs. A misanthropic saying, the meaning of which is obvious. It is probably French in origin—*Plus je vois les hommes, plus j'admire les chiens.*

There are more ways of killing a dog than by hanging. There is more than one way of achieving your object. The proverb is found in Ray's *Collection* (1742).

Throw it to the dogs. Throw it away, it is useless and worthless.

Throw physic to the dogs! I'll none of it.
Macbeth, v, 3.

To blush like a dog, or **like a blue** or **black dog.** Not to blush at all.

To call off the dogs. To desist from some pursuit or inquiry; to break up a disagreeable conversation. In the chase, if the dogs are on the wrong track, the huntsman calls them off.

To die like a dog. To have a shameful, or a miserable, end.

To go to the dogs. To go to utter ruin, morally or materially; to become impoverished.

To lead a dog's life. To be bothered and harried from pillar to post, never to be left in peace.

To put on the dog. To behave in a conceited or bumptious manner.

To rain cats and dogs. *See* CAT (*It is raining*, etc.).

To wake a sleeping dog. *See* LET SLEEPING DOGS LIE, *above*.

(2) DOGS OF NOTE IN THE CLASSICS AND IN LEGEND.

Geryon's dogs. Gargittios and Orthos. The latter was the brother of Cerberus, but had one head less. Hercules killed both these monsters.

Icarius's dog. Mæra (*the glistener*). *See* ICARIUS.

Orion's dogs. Arctophonos (*bear-killer*), and Ptoophagos (the *glutton* of *Ptoon*, in Bœotia).

Procris's dog. Lælaps. *See* PROCRIS.

Ulysses's dog. Argos; he recognized his master after his return from Troy, and died of joy.

Cuchullain's hound. Luath (*q.v.*).

Fingal's dog. Bran (*q.v.*).

King Arthur's favourite hound. Cavall.

Llewelyn's greyhound. Beth Gelert (*q.v.*).

Mauthe dog. (*See* MAUTHE.)

Montargis, Dog of. Aubry's dog. (*See above.*)

Roderick the Goth's dog. Theron.

Seven Sleepers, Dog of the. Katmir who, according to Mohammedan tradition, was admitted to heaven. He accompanied the seven noble youths who fell asleep for 309 years to the cavern in which they were walled up, and remained standing for the whole time, neither moving, eating, drinking, nor sleeping.

Tristran's dog. Hodain, or Leon.

(3) DOGS FAMOUS IN HISTORY, LITERATURE, FICTION, ETC.

Boatswain. Byron's favourite dog; the poet wrote an epitaph on him and he was buried in the garden of Newstead Abbey.

Bounce. Alexander Pope's dog.

Boy. Prince Rupert's dog; he was killed at the battle of Marston Moor.

Brutus. Landseer's greyhound; jocularly called "The Invader of the Larder."

Dash. Charles Lamb's dog.

Diamond. The little dog belonging to Sir Isaac Newton. One winter's morning he upset a candle on his master's desk, by which papers containing minutes of many years' experiments were destroyed. On perceiving this terrible catastrophe Newton exclaimed: "Oh, Diamond, Diamond, thou little knowest the mischief thou hast done!" and at once set to work to repair the loss.

Flush. Elizabeth Barrett Browning's dog.

Geist. One of Matthew Arnold's dachshunds. He wrote the poem *Geist's Grave* in memory of him.

Giallo. Walter Savage Landor's dog.

Hamlet. A black greyhound belonging to Sir Walter Scott.

Kaiser. Another of Matthew Arnold's dachshunds. (*See* GEIST *above*). In his poem, *Kaiser Dead*, the poet mentions also Toss, Rover, and Max.

Lufra. The hound of Douglas, in Scott's *Lady of the Lake.*

Maida. Sir Walter Scott's favourite deerhound.

Mathe. Richard II's greyhound. It deserted the king and attached itself to Bolingbroke.

Toby. Punch's famous dog; named after the dog that followed Tobit in his journeys, a favourite in mediæval biblical stories and plays.

(4) IN SYMBOLISM AND METAPHOR.

Dogs, in mediæval art, symbolize fidelity. A dog is represented as lying at the feet of St. Bernard, St. Benignus, and St. Wendelin; as licking the wounds of St. Roch; as carrying a lighted torch in representations of St. Dominic.

Dogs in effigy. In funeral monuments a dog is often sculptured at the foot of the central effigy; this has no symbolical significance, it is usually a memento of the dead person's pet.

The Thracian dog. Zoilus (4th cent, B.C.), the carping critic of ancient Greece.

Like curs, our critics haunt the poet's feast,
And feed on scraps refused by every guest;

From the old Thracian dog they learned the way
To snarl in want, and grumble o'er their prey.
PITT: *To Mr. Spence.*

(5) IN COMBINATION.

Dog-, or dog's-, in combinations is used (besides in its literal sense as in dog-biscuit, dog-collar) for

(*a*) denoting the male of certain animals, as dog-ape, dog-fox, dog-otter.

(*b*) denoting inferior plants, or those which are worthless as food for man, as dog-brier, dog-cabbage, dog-leek, dog-lichen, dog-mercury, dog-parsley, dog-violets (which have no perfume), dog-wheat. *Cp.* DOG-GRASS, DOG-ROSE *below.*

(*c*) expressing spuriousness or some mongrel quality, as dog's-logic, dog-Latin (*q.v.*).

Dogsbody. An undistinguished and unskilled individual, required for menial tasks.

Dog-cheap. Extremely cheap; "dirt-cheap."

Dog-days. Days of great heat. The term comes from the Romans, who called the six or eight hottest weeks of the summer *caniculares dies*. According to their theory, the dog-star Sirius, rising with the sun, added to its heat, and the dog-days (about July 3rd to August 11th) bore the combined heat of the dog-star and the sun. *See* DOG-STAR.

Dogs'-ears. The corners of pages crumpled and folded down.

Dogs'-eared. Pages so crumpled and turned down. The ears of many dogs turn down and seem quite limp.

Dog fight, a skirmish between fighter planes.

Dog house. In the dog house. In disgrace, as a dog confined to his kennel. Usually applied to a husband who has been misbehaving and whose wife treats him with disdain.

Dog-star. Sirius, the brightest star in the firmament, whose influence was anciently supposed to cause great heat; pestilence, etc. *See* DOG-DAYS.

Dog-vane. A nautical term for a small vane placed on the weather gunwale to show the direction of the wind. Sailors also apply it to a cockade.

Dog-watch. The two short watches on board ship, one from four to six, and the other from six to eight in the evening, introduced to prevent the same men always keeping watch at the same time. *See* WATCH.

Doggo. To lie doggo. To get into hiding and remain there; to keep oneself secluded.

Dog-goned. An American euphemism for the oath "God-damned."

But when that choir got up to sing,
    I couldn't catch a word;
They sung the most doggonedest thing
    A body ever heard!
           WILL CARLETON: *Farm Ballad.*

Dog Tags. American identity discs (World War II).

Dog-tired. Exhausted, usually after exercise; and wanting only to curl up like a dog and go to sleep.

Dogaressa. The wife of a doge (*q.v.*).

Dogberry. An ignorant, self-satisfied, overbearing, but good-natured night-constable in Shakespeare's *Much Ado About Nothing*; hence, an officious and ignorant Jack in office.

Doge (dāj) (Lat. *dux*, a duke or leader). The chief magistrate in Venice while it was a Republic. The first doge was Paolo Anafesto (Paoluccio), 697, and the last, Luigi Manin (1789). *See* BRIDE OF THE SEA.

For six hundred years . . . her [Venice's] government was an elective monarchy, her . . . doge possessing, in early times at least, as much independent authority as any other European sovereign.—RUSKIN: *Stones of Venice*, vol. I, ch. i.

The chief magistrate of Genoa was called a doge from 1339 (Simon Boccanegra) down to 1797, when the government was abolished by the French.

Doggerel (dog' ėr ėl). This is an old word, with no obvious connexion with *dog*. It was originally applied to a loose, irregular measure in burlesque poetry, such as that of Butler's *Hudibras*, and it is in this sense that Chaucer uses the word:—

"Now such a rym the devel I beteche!
This may wel be rym dogerel," quod he.
           Prol. to Tale of Melibeus.

The word is now applied only to verse of a mean and paltry nature, lacking both sense and rhythm.

Dogie (dō'gi, *not* dog'i). In the western U.S.A. the term for an undersized calf. At round-up time all calves that had lost their mothers were called "dough-guts," and this became contracted into "dogie."

Doh, or **Do** (dō). The first or tonic note of the solfeggio system of music.

Do, re, mi, fa, sotl, la (Ital.); *ut, re, mi, fa, sol, la* (Fr.). The latter are borrowed from a hymn by Paulus Piaconus, addressed to St. John, which Guido of Arezzo, in the 11th century, used in teaching singing:

Ut queant laxis, *Re*-sonare fibris,
Mi-ra gestorum *Fa*-muli tuorum,
Sol-ve pollutis *La*-biis reatum.
           Sancte Joannes.

Ut-tered be thy wondrous story,
Re-prehensive though I be,
Me make mindful of thy glory,
Fa-mous son of Zacharee;
Sol-ace to my spirit bring,
La-bouring they praise to sing.   E.C.B.
See ARETINIAN SYLLABLES.

Doily. A small cloth used to cover dessert plates, or a mat or napkin on which to stand plates, glasses, bottles, etc. In the 17th century the word was an adjective denoting a cheap woollen material; thus Dryden speaks of "doyley petticoats," and Steele, in No. 102 of the *Tatler*, speaks of his "doiley suit." The Doyleys, from which the stuff was named, were linen-drapers in the Strand, from the late 17th century to 1850.

Doldrums, The. A condition of depression, slackness, or inactivity; hence applied by sailors to a region where ships are likely to be becalmed, especially that part of the ocean near the equator noted for calms, squalls, and baffling winds, between the NE. and SE. trade winds.

But from the bluff-head, where I watched to-day,
I saw her in the doldrums.
        BYRON: *The Island*, canto ii, stanza 21.

In the doldrums. In the dumps.

Dole (Lat. *dolor*, grief, sorrow). Lamentation.
  What if . . .
He now be dealing dole among his foes,
And over heaps of slaughtered walk his way?
        MILTON; *Samson Agonistes*, 1529.

To make dole. To lament, to mourn.

Yonder they lie; the poor old man, their father, making such pitiful dole over them that all the beholders take his part with weeping.—*As You Like It*, i, 2.

Dole (A.S. *dal*, a portion, *dœl*, deal). A portion allotted; a charitable gift, alms. The word was later usually applied to the weekly payment, made for a limited period to certain classes of unemployed from funds contributed by workers, employers, and the State.

Happy man be his dole. May his share or lot be that of a happy or fortunate man.

Your father and my uncle have made motions: if it be my luck, so; if not, happy man be his dole!—*Merry Wives*, iii, 4.

Dollar. The sign $, is probably a modification of the figure 8 as it appeared on the old Spanish "pieces of eight," which were of the same value as the dollar.

The word is a variant of *thaler* (Low Ger. *dahler*; Dan. *daler*), and means "a valley", (our *dale*). The counts of Schlick, at the close of the 15th century, extracted from the mines at *Joachim's thal* (Joachim's valley) silver which they coined into ounce-pieces. These pieces, called *Joachim's thalers*, gained such high repute that they became a standard coin. Other coins being made like them were called *thalers* only. The American dollar equals 100 cents, in English money about 7s. 2d. It was adopted as the monetary unit of the U.S.A. in 1785 but was not coined until 1792.

Dolmen (dol' men). The name given in France to cromlechs (*q.v.*), particularly those of Brittany (Breton *tol*, a table, *men*, stone). They are often called by the rural population devils' tables, fairies' tables, and so on.

The Constantine Dolmen, Cornwall, is 33 ft. long, 14½ deep, and 18½ across. It is calculated to weigh 750 tons, and is poised on the points of two natural rocks.

Dolphin. *Cp.* DAUPHIN. The dolphin is noted for its changes of colour when taken out of the water.

> Parting day
> Dies like the dolphin, whom each pang imbues
> With a new colour as it gasps away.
> The last still loveliest.
> <div align="right">BYRON: <i>Childe Harold,</i> iv, 29.</div>

D.O.M., inscribed on bottles of Benedictine liqueur, among other places, stands for *Deo optimo maximo*, To God the best and greatest.

Dom (Lat. *dominus*). A title applied in the Middle Ages to the Pope, and at a somewhat later period to other Church dignitaries. It is now restricted to priests and choir monks of the Benedictine Order, and to some few other monastic orders. The Sp. *don*. Port, *dom*, and M.E. *dan* (as in *Dan Chaucer*) are the same word.

Domiciliary Visit (dom i sil' yà ri). An official visit paid by the police or other authorities to a private dwelling in order to search for incriminating papers, etc. In Britain a magistrate's warrant must be obtained before a domiciliary visit can be made.

Dominations. *See* DOMINIONS.

Dominic, St. (1170-1221), who preached with great vehemence against the Albigenses, was called by the Pope "Inquisitor-General," and was canonized by Gregory IX. He is represented with a sparrow at his side, and a dog carrying in its mouth a burning torch. The devil, it is said, appeared to the saint in the form of a sparrow, and the dog refers to the story that his mother, during her pregnancy, dreamt that she had given birth to a dog, spotted with black and white spots, which lighted the world with a burning torch.

Dominical Letters. The letters which denote the Sunday or *dies dominica*. The first seven letters of the alphabet are employed; if

January 1st is a Sunday the dominical letter for the year will be A, if the 2nd is a Sunday it will be B, if the 3rd, C, and so on. In Leap years there are two dominical letters, one for the period up to February 29th, and the other for the rest of the year.

Dominicans. An order of preaching friars, instituted by St. Dominic in 1215, and introduced into England (at Oxford) in 1221. They were formerly called in England *Black Friars*, from their black dress, and in France *Jacobins*, because their mother-establishment in Paris was in the Rue St. Jacques. They have always been one of the intellectual pillars of the Church, largely on account of their most distinguished member, St. Thomas Aquinas. They were also called "Hounds of the Lord," *Domini canes*.

Dominions. The sixth of the nine orders in the mediæval hierarchy of the angels. *See* ANGEL. They are symbolized in art by an ensign, and are also known as "Dominations."

The word is also applied to the self-governing possessions of the British Crown. The word was first given in this sense to the Dominion of Canada, which was formed by the federation of the Canadian provinces in 1867.

The other British Dominions are: The Commonwealth of Australia, 1900; The Dominion of New Zealand, 1907; The Union of South Africa, 1909; the Republic of India, 1947; the Dominion of Pakistan, 1947; the Dominion of Ceylon, 1948. In 1925 a Secretaryship of State for Dominion Affairs was created, to deal with business connected with the Dominions, as well as the affairs of Southern Rhodesia and the S. African territories of Basuto-land, Bechuanaland, and Swaziland. The Dominions are represented in London by High Commissioners.

Domino (dom' i nō) (Ital.). Originally a hooded cloak worn by canons; hence a disguise worn at masquerades consisting of a hooded garment, then the hood only, and finally the half mask covering an inch or two above and below the eyes, worn as a disguise.

The name came to be applied to the game probably through a custom of calling *faire domino* when winning with the last piece— much as the French still say *faire capot* (*capot* also means "hood"); in the Navy and Army the last lash of a flogging was known as *the domino*.

Don is do-on, as "Don your bonnet." *See* DOFF, DUP.

Then up he rose, and donned his clothes,
And dupp'd the chamber door.

Hamlet, iv, 5.

Don. A man of mark, an aristocrat. At the universities the masters and fellows are termed *dons*. The word is the Spanish form of Lat. dominus. *Cp.* DAN, DOM.

Don Juan (don joo' an). Don Juan Tenorio, the hero of a large number of plays and poems, as well as of Mozart's opera, *Don Giovanni*, round whom numerous legends have collected, was the son of a leading family of Seville in the 14th century, and killed the commandant of Ulloa after seducing his daughter. To put an end to his debaucheries the Franciscan monks enticed him to their monastery and killed him, telling the people that he had been carried off to hell by the statue of the commandant, which was in the grounds.

His name has passed into a synonym for a rake, roué, or aristocratic libertine, and in Mozart's opera (1787) Don Giovanni's valet, Leporello, says his master had "in Italy 700 mistresses, in Germany 800, in Turkey and France 91, in Spain 1,003." His dissolute life was dramatized by Gabriel Tellez in the 17th century, by Molière, Corneille, Shadwell, Grabbe (German), Dumas, and others, and in the 20th century by Bataille, and Rostand.

In Byron's well-known poem (1819-24), when Juan was sixteen years old he got into trouble with Donna Julia, and was sent by his mother, then a widow, on his travels. His adventures in the Isles of Greece, at the Russian Court, in England, etc., form the story of the poem, which, though it extends to sixteen cantos, is incomplete.

Don Quixote (don kwik' zot). The hero of the great romance of that name by Miguel de Cervantes Saavedra (1547-1616). It was published at Madrid, Part I in 1605, Part II in 1615. Don Quixote is a gaunt country gentleman of La Mancha, gentle and dignified, affectionate and simple-minded, but so crazed by reading books of knight-errantry that he believes himself called upon to redress the wrongs of the whole world, and actually goes forth to avenge the oppressed and run atilt with their oppressors. Hence, a **quixotic** man is a dreamy, unpractical, but essentially good, man—one with a "bee in his bonnet."

Donatists. Followers of Donatus, a Numidian bishop of the 4th century who, on puritanical grounds, opposed Cecilianus. Their chief dogma is that the outward Church is nothing, "for the letter killeth, it is the spirit that giveth life." St. Augustine of Hippo vigorously combated their heresies.

Doncaster. The "City on the river Don." Celt. *Don*, that which spreads. Sigebert, monk of Gemblours, in 1100, derived the name from *Thong-ceaster*, the "castle of the thong," and says that Hengist and Horsa purchased of the British king as much land as they could encompass with a leather thong, which they cut into strips, and so encompassed the land occupied by the city.

Donkey. An ass. The word is of comparatively recent origin, being first recorded about 1782 (*Hickey's Memoirs*, ii, 276), and seems at first to have rhymed with "monkey." It is a diminutive, and may be connected with *dun*, in reference to its tint. "Dun," in "Dun in the mire" was a familiar name for a horse, and the "donkey" is a smaller, or more diminutive beast of burden. For the tradition concerning the "cross" on the donkey's back, *see* ASS.

Not for donkey's years. Not for a long time. The allusion is to the old tradition that one never sees a dead donkey.

Donnybrook Fair. This fair, held in August from the time of King John, till 1855, was noted for its bacchanalian orgies and light-hearted rioting. Hence it is proverbial for a disorderly gathering or a regular rumpus. The village was a mile and a half south-east of Dublin, and is now one of its suburbs.

Donzel. A squire or young man of good birth not yet knighted. This is an anglicized form of Ital. *doncello*, from late Lat. *domicellus*. *See* DAMSEL.

He is esquire to a knight-errant, donzel to the damsels.—BUTLER: *Characters*.

Doodle. To draw designs, patterns, sketches, etc., aimlessly and absent-mindedly while occupied in conversation, listening, and the like. Psychologists profess to find considerable significance in the drawings thus made.

Though the habit has existed for many centuries the word was brought into prominence as a result of the film *Mr. Deeds goes to Town*, 1936.

Doodle-bug. This was a name popularly given to the pilotless aeroplane bombs, also known as VI and "Flying Bombs," showered on the southern portions of Britain by the Germans in 1944.

Doom (A.S. *dom*). The original meaning was law, or judgment, that which is set up, as a statute: hence, **the crack of doom,** the signal for the final judgment. The book of judgments compiled by King Alfred was known as the *dom-boc*. This word is sometimes used to designate the frescoes, etc., found in old churches depicting the Day of Judgment, *e.g.* the Wenhaston Doom.

Door. The Anglo-Saxon *dor* (fem. *duru*). The word in many other languages is similar; thus, Dan. *dor*, Icel. *dyrr*, Gr. *thura*, Lat. *fores*, Ger. *thüre*.

Dead as a door-nail. *See* DEAD.

Door-money. Payment taken at the doors for admission to an entertainment, etc.

He laid the charge at my door. He accused me of doing it.

Indoors. Inside the house; also used attributively, as, *an indoor servant*.

Next door to it. Within an ace of it (*see* ACE); very like it; next-door neighbour to it.

Out of doors. Outside the house; in the open air.

Dope. Properly, some thick or semi fluid liquid used for food or as a lubricant (Dut. *doopen*, to dip). The name was applied to a varnish used for aeroplane wings, the odour of which in some cases had a stupefying effect upon the workers. Hence it came to be used for noxious drugs, such as cocaine; and confirmed drug-takers have since been called *dope-fiends*. *Dope* is also used, figuratively, for flattery, or words that are intended to lead one into a false sense of security, power, etc.; also for information.

Dorcas Society. A woman's circle for making clothing for the poor. So called from Dorcas, in *Acts* ix, 39, who made "coats and garments" for widows.

Dorian, Doric. Pertaining to Doris, one of the divisions of ancient Greece, or to its inhabitants, a simple, pastoral people.

Dorian mode. The scale represented by the white keys on a pianoforte, beginning with D. A simple, solemn form of music, the first of the authentic Church modes.

Doric dialect. The dialect spoken by the natives of Doris, in Greece. It was broad and hard. Hence, any broad dialect such as that of rustics. Robert Burns's verses are an example of British Doric.

Doric Order. The oldest, strongest, and simplest of the Grecian orders of architecture. The Greek Doric is simpler than the Roman imitation. The former stands on the pavement without fillet or other ornament, and the flutes are not scalloped. The Roman column is

placed on a plinth, has fillets, and the flutings, both top and bottom, are scalloped.

The Doric Land. Greece, Doris being a part of Greece.

> Through all the bounds
> Of Doric land.
>
> MILTON: *Paradise Lost*, Bk. i, 519.

The Doric reed. Pastoral poetry. Everything Doric was very plain, but cheerful, chaste, and solid.

> The Doric reed once more
> Well pleased, I tune.
>
> THOMSON: *Autumn*, 3.

Dorigen (dôr' i jen). The heroine of Chaucer's *Franklin's Tale*, which was taken from Boccaccio's *Decameron* (X, v), the original being in the Hindu *Vetala Panchavinsati*.

Dorinda, in the verses of the Earl of Dorset, is Catherine Sedley, Countess of Dorchester, mistress of James II.

Doris. *See* NEREIDS.

Dormer Window. The window of an attic standing out from the slope of the roof; properly, the window of a bedroom. (O.Fr. *dormeor*, a dormitory.)

Dorothea, St. (dor ō thē' à). A martyr under Diocletian about 303. She is represented with a rose-branch in her hand, a wreath of roses on her head, and roses with fruit by her side; The legend is that Theophilus, the judge's secretary, scoffingly said to her, as she was going to execution, "Send me some fruit and roses, Dorothea, when you get to Paradise." Immediately after her execution, a young angel brought him a basket of apples and roses, saying, "From Dorothea in Paradise," and vanished. The story forms the basis of Massinger's tragedy, *The Virgin Martyr* (1620).

Doss. Slang for a sleep; also for a bed or a place where one sleeps—a *doss-house*, *dossing-ken*. The word dates from the 18th century, and is probably connected with the old *dorse*, a back (Lat. *dorsum*, Fr. *dos*). Hence also *dosser*, one who sleeps in a common lodging-house.

Dot. *See* I.

Dot and carry one. An infant just beginning to toddle; one who limps in walking; a person who has one leg longer than the other.

Dotterel. A doting old fool; an old man easily cajoled. So called from the bird; a species of plover, which is easily approached and caught.

Double (Lat. *duplus*, twofold). One's double is one's *alter ego* (*q.v.*). The word is applied to such pairs as the Corsican brothers, the Dromio brothers, and the brothers Antipholus.

Double-bank. A phrase used in Britain in reference to two or more cars or cyclists abreast on a road; in Australia it is applied to two people riding one horse.

To double-cross. To betray or cheat an associate, more especially an associate in an already shady undertaking.

A double first. In the first class both of the classical and mathematical final examinations, Oxford; or of the classical and mathematical triposes, Cambridge. Now, a first class in any two final examinations.

Double dealing. Professing one thing and doing another inconsistent with that promise.

Doable Dutch. Gibberish, jargon, of a foreign tongue not understood by the hearer. Dutch is a synonym for foreign; and double implies something excessive, in a twofold degree.

Double-edged. Able to cut ehher way; used metaphorically of an argument which makes both for and against the person employing it, or which has a double meaning.

"Your Delphic sword," the panther then replied,
"Is double-edged and cuts on either side."
DRYDEN; *Hind and Panther*, pt. iii, 191.

Double entendre. An incorrect English version of the French *double entente*, a word which secretly expresses a rude or coarse covert meaning, generally of an indelicate character. *Entendre* is the infinitive mood of the French verb, and is never used as a noun.

Double time. A military phrase, applied to orderly running on the march, etc. It is quick march, the rate of progress (officially 165 steps of 33 in., *i.e.* $453\frac{1}{4}$ ft., to the minute) being *double* that of the ordinary walking pace. *See* TO DOUBLE UP *below*.

Double-tongued. Making contrary declarations on the same subject at different times; deceitful; insincere.

Be grave, not double-tongued.—1 *Tim.* iii, 8.

To double back. To turn back on one's course.

To double up. To fold together. "To double up the fist" is to fold the fingers together so as to make the hand into a fist. "To double a person up" is to strike him in the wind, so as to make him double up with pain.

In military phraseology, "Double up there!" is an order to hurry, to "get a move on," run. Also to put two people in the space normally allocated to one if accommodation is temporarily short. *See* DOUBLE TIME *above*.

Double summer time. *See* DAYLIGHT SAVING.

Double take. An acting trick. It consists in looking away from the person who has addressed a remark to you, and then looking back at him quickly when the purport of the remark sinks in.

To work double tides. To work extra hard, with all one's might.

Doubting Castle. The castle of the giant Despair, in which Christian and Hopeful were incarcerated, but from which they escaped by means of the key called "Promise." (BUNYAN: *Pilgrim's Progress.*)

Doubting Thomas. *See* THOMAS, ST.

Douceur (Fr.). A gratuity for service rendered or promised; a tip.

Doughboy (U.S.A.). First, doughcake baked for sailors, then the buttons on their coats; then buttons on infantry uniforms (civil war), thence infantry man.

Doughface (U.S.A.). Inhabitant of the Northern States who was in favour of maintaining slavery in the South.

Douglas. The Scottish family name is from the river Douglas in Lanarkshire, which is the Celtic *dhu glaise*, black stream, a name in use also in Ireland, the Isle of Man, etc., and in Lancashire corrupted to *Diggles*. Legend explains it by inventing an unknown knight who came to the assistance of some Scottish king. After the battle the king asked who was the "Du-glass" chieftain, his deliverer, and received for answer *Sholto Du-glass*, which is said to be good Gaelic for "Behold the dark-grey man you inquired for."

"I will not yield him an inch of way, had he in his body the soul of every Douglas that has lived since the time of the Dark Gray Man."—SCOTT: *The Abbot*, ch. xxviii.

Dout. A contraction of *do-out*, as don is of *do-on*, doff of *do-off*, and dup of *do-up*. In some southern counties they still say *dout the candle* and *dout the fire*, and call extinguisher *douters*.

The dram of eale
Doth all the noble substance dout.
Hamlet, i, 4.

Dove. The name means "the diver-bird"; perhaps from its habit of ducking the head. So also Lat. *columba* is the Gr. *kolumbis* (a diver).

In Christian art the dove symbolizes the Holy Ghost, and the seven rays proceeding from it the seven gifts of the Holy Ghost. It also symbolizes the soul, and as such is sometimes represented coming out of the mouth of saints at death.

A dove bearing a ring is an attribute of St. Agnes; St. David is shown with a dove on his shoulder; St. Dunstan and St. Gregory the Great with one at the ear; St. Enurchus with one on his head; and St. Remigius with the dove bringing him holy chrism.

The clergy of the Church of England are allegorized as doves in Dryden's *Hind and Panther*, part iii, 947, 998-1002.

Dove's dung. In 2 *Kings* vi, 25, we are told that during the siege of Samaria "there was a great famine . . . and . . . an ass's head was sold for fourscore pieces of silver, and the fourth part of a cab of dove's dung for five pieces of silver." "Ass's head" and "dove's dung" are both undoubtedly incorrect, the true rendering probably being "a homer of lentils" and "pods of the carob (or locust) tree," the Hebrew for which expressions could easily be misread for the Hebrew of the others. Locust pods are still commonly sold in the East for food, and it is thought that they are the "husks" referred to in the parable of the Prodigal Son.

Dover. In the professional slang of English cooks a *resurrection pie* or any *réchauffé* is called a *dover* (do over again).

A jack of Dover. *See* JACK.

When Dover and Calais meet Never.

Merry Dun of Dover. *See* MERRY.

Dovetail. Metaphorically, to fit on or fit in nicely; to correspond. In carpentry it means the fitting one board into another by a tenon in the shape of a dove's tail, or wedge reversed.

Dower. Gifts by a husband to his wife before marriage. That portion of a man's estate which the wife enjoys for life after her husband's death. Most large estates have a **Dower house** to which the widow retires, leaving the big house to the heir who has inherited the estate.

Dowlas, Mr. (dou' làs). A generic name for a linendraper, who sells dowlas, a coarse linen cloth, so called from Daoulas, in Brittany, where it was manufactured.

Mrs. Quickly: I bought you a dozen of shirts to your back.

Falstaff: Dowlas, filthy dowlas: I have given them away to bakers' wives, and they have made bolsters of them.

Mrs. Quickly: Now, as I am true woman, holland of eight shillings an ell.   1 *Henry IV*, iii, 3.

Down. Down and out. Said of one who has not only come right down in the world but has, apparently, not the slightest chance of getting up again.

Down in the mouth. Out of spirits: disheartened. When persons are very sad and low spirited, the corners of the mouth are drawn down. **Down in the jib** is a nautical phrase of the same meaning.

Down on his luck. In ill luck; short of cash and credit.

Down on the nail. *See* NAIL.

Down with (so-and-so)! Away with! A cry of rage and exasperation, like the Fr. *à bas*.

He is very much run down. Very out of sorts; in need of a thorough rest and overhauling, like a clock that has *run down*.

Ups and downs. The twists and turns of fortune; one's successes and reverses.

Fraudulent transactions have their downs as well as their ups.—DICKENS: *Martin Chuzzlewit*, ch. xvi.

Down-easter. An American from New England.

Down-town. Business district of an American city, so called from New York where financial houses are concentrated in the southern tip of Manhattan Island.

Downing Street. A name often given to the heads of the British Government collectively.

No. 10 was given in 1735 by George II to Sir Robert Walpole as the official residence of the Prime Minister, and it is there that the meetings of the Cabinet are usually held. The house retains its old façade but has been altered inside from time to time. No. 11 is the official residence of the Chancellor of the Exchequer; No. 12 is the Government Whips' office. The street was named in honour of Sir George Downing (*c.* 1623-84), a noted Parliamentarian and ambassador, who served under both Cromwell and Charles II.

Downright. Thoroughly, from top to bottom, throughout; "downright honest," "downright mad"; outspoken; fixed in opinions; utter, as a "downright shame."

Downy. An old slang word long since in disuse.

Dowse (*see also* DOUSE). To search for water, etc., with a divining-rod (*q.v.*), which is also called a *dowsing-rod*, and the practitioners of the art *dowsers*. The origin of the term is disputed, but as the art was introduced from Germany (in the 16th cent.) it may be connected with Ger. *deuten*, to declare or interpret.

Doxology (doks ol' ō ji). This comes from a Greek word meaning a hymn of praise to God. The Greater Doxology is the hymn *Gloria in Excelsis Deo* at the Eucharist. The Lesser Doxology is the *Gloria Patri* (Glory be to the Father, etc.) sung at the end of each psalm in the liturgy. The hymn "Praise God from whom all blessings flow" is also known as the Doxology.

Dozen. Twelve: the word is all that is left (in English) of the Latin *duodecim*, twelve, the *-en* representing the Latin suffix *-ena*. A *long dozen* is thirteen. *See* BAKER'S DOZEN.

To talk nineteen to the dozen. To talk at a tremendous rate, or with excessive vehemence.

Draconian Code (drȧ kō′ ni ȧn). One very severe. Draco was an Athenian law-maker of the 7th cent. B.C., and the first to produce a written code of laws for Athens. As nearly every violation of his laws was a capital offence, Demades the orator said that "Draco's code was written in blood."

(Military.) A body of men of any size sent to a unit or formation for service, presumably having the same origin as a draft or cheque, since it fully or partially fills the requirement for which the unit has indented.

Dragon. The Greek word *drakon* comes from a verb meaning "to see," to "look at," and more remotely "to watch" and "to flash."

A dragon is a fabulous winged crocodile, usually represented as of large size, with a serpent's tail; whence the words serpent and dragon are sometimes interchangeable. The word was used in the Middle Ages as the symbol of sin in general and paganism in particular, the metaphor being derived from *Rev.* xii. 9, where Satan is termed "the great dragon" and *Ps.* xci. 13, where it is said that the saints "shall trample the dragon under their feet." Hence, in Christian art the dragon symbolizes Satan or sin, as when represented at the feet of Christ and the Virgin Mary; and St. John the Evangelist is sometimes represented holding a chalice, from which a dragon is issuing.

Among the many saints who are usually pictured with dragons may be mentioned St. Michael, St. George, St. Margaret, Pope Sylvester, St. Samson (Archbishop of Dol), St. Donatus, St. Clement of Metz; St. Romain of Rouen, who destroyed the huge dragon, La Gargouille, which ravaged the Seine; St. Philip the Apostle, who killed another at Hierapolis, in Phrygia; St. Martha, who slew the terrible dragon, Tarasque, at Aix-la-Chapelle; St. Florent, who killed a dragon which haunted the Loire; St. Cado, St. Maudet, and St. Pol. who did similar feats in Brittany; and St. Keyne of Cornwall.

In classical legend the idea of *watching* is retained in the story of the dragon who guards the golden apples in the garden of the Hesperides.

Among the ancient Britons and Welsh the dragon was the national symbol on the war standard; hence the term, Pendragon (*q.v.*) for the *dux bellorum*, or leader in war (*pen* = head or chief).

Dragon's Blood. A picturesque name given to no more awesome substance than the red resinous exudation from the fruits of a number of palms. It was formerly used as an astringent in medicine, and is still employed as a colouring matter for varnishes.

In German mythology, when Siegfried was told to bathe in the blood of a dragon in order to make him immune from injury, a linden leaf fell on him as he was doing so and covered a small place on his body that thus remained vulnerable. From this legend the name 'Dragon's Blood' has been applied to a cheap red Rhine wine. There is a possible connexion between this story and the term "dragon's blood" applied to a powder used in printing which, applied to a block for processing, prevents the etching of that portion thus covered.

The Chinese dragon. In China, a five-clawed dragon is introduced into pictures and embroidered on state dresses as an amulet.

To sow dragons' teeth. To foment contentions; to stir up strife or war; especially to do something that is intended to put an end to strife but which brings it about later. The Philistines "sowed dragons' teeth" when they took Samson, bound him, and put out his eyes; the ancient Britons did the same when they massacred the Danes on St. Bryce's Day, as also did the Germans when they robbed France of Alsace Lorraine.

The reference is to the classical story of Cadmus, who slew the dragon that guarded the well of Ares and sowed some of its teeth, from which sprang up the men called Sparti, or the Sown-men, who all killed each other except five, who became the ancestors of the Thebans. Those teeth which Cadmus did not sow came to the possession of Æetes, King of Colchis; one of the tasks he enjoined on Jason was to sow them and slay the armed warriors that rose therefrom.

Dragon's Hill. A site in Berkshire where one legend has it that St. George killed the dragon. A bare place is shown on the hill, where nothing will grow, for there the blood of the dragon ran out.

In Saxon annals we are told that Cerdic, founder of the West Saxon kingdom, slew there Naud (or Natanleod, the people's refuge), the pen-dragon, with 5,000 men.

Dragonades. A series of religious persecutions by Louis XIV, prior to the revocation of the Edict of Nantes, which drove many thousand Protestants out of France. Their object was to root out "heresy"; if the heretics would not recant, they had *dragoons* (hence the name) billeted on them, who were given a free hand to treat them in any way they liked. The origin of this name for a type of mounted soldier is obscure. In 1554 Marshal Brissac armed some of his horsemen with short carbines on the muzzles of which were engraved dragons spouting fire, and some ascribe the term to these. More likely, however, is the theory that the word comes from the *dragon*, or standard, borne by a mounted regiment formed in the French army in 1585.

Dramatic unities. The three dramatic unities, viz. the rules governing the so-called "classical" dramas, are founded on Renaissance misconceptions of passages in Aristotle's *Poetics*, and are hence sometimes, though very incorrectly, styled the *Aristotelean Unities*. They are, that in dramas there should be (1) Unity of Action, (2) Unity of Time, and (3) Unity of Place. Aristotle lays stress on (1), meaning that an organic unity, or a logical connexion between the successive incidents, is necessary; but (2) was deduced by Castelvetro (1505-71), the 16th-century Italian scholar and critic, from the passage in the *Poetics* where Aristotle, in comparing Epic Poetry and Tragedy, says that the former has no limits in time but the latter

endeavours, as far as possible, to confine itself to a single revolution of the sun, or but slightly to exceed this limit

—a passage which was merely an incidental reference to a contemporary custom and was never intended as the enunciation of an inviolable law of the drama. Having thus arrived at the Unity of Time, (3) the Unity of Place followed almost perforce, though there is not even a hint of it in Aristotle.

The theory of the Three Unities was formulated in Italy nearly a century before it was taken up in France (Cintio, Robortelli, Maggi, and Scaliger being the principal exponents), where it became, after much argument, the corner-stone of the literary drama. The principle had little success in England—despite the later championship of Dryden (see his *Essay on Dramatic Poesy*), Addison (as exemplified in his *Cato*), and others. It was not till Corneille's triumph with *Le Cid* (1636) that the convention of the Three Unities can be said to have been finally adopted. It is almost unnecessary to add that Shakespeare, and every great dramatist not bound by a self-imposed tradition, was with Aristotle in holding that so

long as the Unity of Action is observed the others do not matter. Ben Jonson's *The Alchemist* (1610) is, perhaps, the best example of the small class of English plays in which the Unities of Place and Time have been purposely adhered to.

Dramatis Personæ (drăm′ á tis pĕr sō′ nē). The characters of a drama, novel, or (by extension), of an actual transaction.

Drat. A variant of *Od rot!* "Od" (*q.v.*) being a minced form of "God," and the vowel showing the same modification as in "Gad!" or "Gadzooks!"

Draupnir (drawp′ nēr). Odin's magic ring, from which every ninth night dropped eight rings equal in size and beauty to itself. It was fashioned by the dwarfs.

Draw. A drawn game, battle, etc. One in which the result is in doubt, neither side having achieved success: perhaps so called from a battle in which the troops on both sides are *drawn off*, neither side claiming the victory.

A good draw. A first-rate attraction— "Performing elephants are always 'a good draw' at circuses." The noun also may mean a drawn game, or the result of drawing lots, etc.

Hanged, drawn, and quartered. Strictly speaking, the phrase should read *Drawn, hanged, and quartered*; for the allusion is to the sentence formerly passed on those convicted of high treason, which was that they should be *drawn* to the place of execution on a hurdle or at a horse's tail instead of being carried or allowed to walk, then hanged, and then quartered.

Later, drawing, or disembowelling, the criminal was added to the punishment after the hanging and before the quartering, and it was sometimes supposed that the "drawn" in the phrase referred to this process instead of to the earlier one. Thus the sentence on Sir William Wallace was that he should be drawn (*detrahatur*) from the Palace of Westminster to the Tower, then hanged (*suspendatur*), then disembowelled or drawn (*devaletur*), then beheaded and quartered (*decolletur et decapitetur*).

Lord Ellenborough used to say to those condemned, "You are drawn on hurdles to the place of execution, where you are to be hanged, but *not* till you are dead; for, while still living, your body is to be taken down, your bowels torn out and burnt before your face; your head is then cut off, and your body divided into four quarters— *Gentleman's Magazine*, 1803.

To draw a bead on somebody. To take aim at him with a rifle or revolver. The "bead" referred to is the foresight.

To draw a badger. *See* BADGER.

To draw a furrow. To plough or draw a plough through a field so as to make a furrow.

To draw a person out. To entice a person to speak on any subject, to obtain information, to encourage one too shy to talk.

To draw amiss. To take the wrong direction. A hunting term, *to draw* meaning to follow scent.

To draw blank. To meet with failure in one's pursuit. The allusion is to sportsmen "drawing" a covert and finding no game. *To draw a blank* refers to having no luck in a lottery, sweepstake, etc. To fail in a search.

To draw stumps. To mark the final close of a game of cricket the stumps are drawn from the ground and taken away.

To draw the line. To set a definite limit beyond which one refuses to go; to impose a restriction on one's behaviour from fear of going too far. "He was utterly unprincipled, but he drew the line at blackmail," *i.e.* he would stop short at blackmail.

To draw a bow at a venture; to draw the long bow. *See* BOW.

Drawback. Something to set against the profits or advantages of a concern. In commerce, it is duty charged on goods paid back again when the goods are exported.

It is only on goods into which dutiable commodities have entered in large proportion and obvious ways that drawbacks are allowed.—H. GEORGE: *Protection or Free Trade?* ch. ix.

In common parlance a *drawback* is an inconvenience in something otherwise desirable.

Drawcansir. A burlesque tyrant in Buckingham's *Rehearsal* (1671); hence, a blustering braggart. The character was a caricature of Dryden's Almanzor (*Conquest of Granada*). Drawcansir's opening speech (he has only three) is:—

He that dares drink, and for that drink dares die,
And, knowing this, dares yet drink on, am I.
Rehearsal, iv, 1.

which parodies Almanzor's:—

He who dares love, and for that love must die,
And, knowing this, dares yet love on, am I,
Conquest of Granada, IV, iii.

Cp. BAYES; BOBADIL.

Drawing-room. This was originally a room into which the women withdrew after dinner, leaving the men to remain at table drinking. When this custom fell into desuetude the drawing-room became a room for entertainment and conversation as distinct from the dining-room reserved for meals. In the Victorian suburban villa the drawing-room was a sort of state apartment, rarely entered and yet more rarely used. The word is also applied to a levee where ladies are presented to the sovereign.

Drawlatch. An old name for a robber, a housebreaker; *i.e.* one who entered by drawing up the latch with the string provided for the purpose and stole all he could carry away with him.

Dreams, The Gates of. There are two, viz. that of ivory and that of horn. Dreams which delude pass through the Ivory Gate, those which come true pass through the Gate of Horn.

That children dream not the first half-year; that men dream not in some countries, with many more, are unto me sick men's dreams; dreams out of the ivory gate, and visions before midnight.—SIR THOMAS BROWNE: *On Dreams.*

This fancy depends upon two puns: ivory in Greek is *elephas,* and the verb *elephairo* means "to cheat with empty hopes"; the Greek for horn is *keras,* and the verb *karanoo* means "to accomplish."

The Immortal Dreamer. John Bunyan (1628-88).

Dreng. An ancient Northumbrian term (from Danish) for a free tenant who held his land by a tenure dating from before the Conquest. It occurs in Domesday Book.

Dresser. In theatrical parlance this is the person who looks after dresses, and prepares for the stage an actor or actress. In furniture a dresser is a large stand with shelves for holding dishes, plates, etc., and drawers for cutlery and silver.

Dreyfusard, Dreyfusite. An advocate of the innocence of Capt. Alfred Dreyfus (1859-1935), a French artillery officer of Jewish descent, who was convicted in 1894 on a charge of having betrayed military secrets, degraded and sent to Devil's Island. In 1899 the first trial was annulled. He was brought back to France, retried, and again condemned, but shortly afterwards pardoned, though it was not until 1914 that he was finally and completely rehabilitated.

Drink. Drink-money. A "tip"; a small gratuity to be spent on drinking the health of the giver; a *pourboire* (Fr., for drink).

In the drink. In the sea, in the water, a service colloquial term of World War II.

The big drink. An American expression for any large stretch of water, such as the Atlantic (*cp.* HERRING-POND) or Lake Superior.

In airman's slang to be **ditched in the drink** is to make a forced landing on water, esp. the sea.

It is meat and drink to me. It is something that is almost essential to my well-being or happiness; something very much to be desired.

It is meat and drink to me to see a clown.
As You Like It, v, 1.

One must drink as one brews. One must take the consequences of his actions; "as one makes his bed so must he lie in it."

I am grieved it should be said he is my brother, and take these courses: well, as he brews, so shall he drink.
—JONSON: *Every Man in his Humour*, ii, 1.

To drink at Freeman's Quay. To get one's drink at someone else's expense. It is said that at one time all porters and carmen calling at Freeman's Quay, near London Bridge, had a pot of beer given them gratis, but the explanation is scarcely necessary and probably untrue.

To drink deep. To drink heavily, to excess, or habitually. Shakespeare uses the expression metaphorically:—

Cant.: If it pass against us,
We lose the better half of our possession; . . .
And to the coffers of the king beside,
A thousand pounds by the year. Thus runs the bill.
Ely: This would drink deep.
Cant.: 'Twould drink the cup and all.
Henry V, i, 1.

To drink like a fish. To drink abundantly or excessively. Many fish swim with their mouths open, thus appearing to be continually drinking. The expression is found in Beaumont and Fletcher.

To drink the cup of sorrow, etc. *See* CUP.

To drink the waters. To take medicinal waters, especially at a spa.

Drive. He is driving pigs, or **driving pigs to market.** Said of one who is snoring, because the grunt of a pig resembles the snore of a sleeper.

To drive a good bargain. To exact more than is quite equitable.

Heaven would no bargain for its blessings drive.—
DRYDEN: *Astrœa Redux*, i, 137.

To drive a quill. *See* QUILLDRIVERS.

To drive a roaring trade. To do a brisk business.

What are you driving at? What do you want to prove? What do you want me to infer?

Dromio (drō′ mi ō). **The brothers Dromio.** Two brothers exactly alike, who served two brothers exactly alike, and the mistakes of masters and men form the fun of Shakespeare's *Comedy of Errors*, based on the *Menœchmi* of Plautus.

Drone. The male of the bee, which does no work but lives on the labours of the worker-bees; hence, a sluggard; an idle person who lives on the work or means of another.

The three lower pipes of a bagpipe are called the drones, because they produce an unchanging, monotonous bass humming like that of a bee.

Drop. A drop in one's eye. Not exactly intoxicated, but having had quite enough.

We are na fou, we're nae that fou,
But just a drappie in our e'e!
BURNS: *Willie Brew'd a Peck o' Maut.*

A drop in the ocean. An infinitesimal quantity; something that scarcely counts or matters in comparison with the whole.

A drop of the cratur. *See* CREATURE.

A dropping fire. An irregular fusillade from small-arms, machine guns, etc.

To drop across. To encounter accidentally or casually.

To drop an acquaintance. To allow acquaintanceship to lapse.

To drop in. To make a casual call, not invited; to pay an informal visit.

To get the drop on someone. To have him in your power, probably from the early method of pistol shooting whereby the weapon was raised high and then lowered, or dropped, towards its target.

To drop off. "Friends drop off," fall away gradually. "To drop off to sleep," to fall asleep (especially in weariness or sickness).

To take a drop. A euphemism for taking what the drinker chooses to call by that term. It may be anything from a sip to a Dutchman's draught.

To take one's drops. To drink spirits in private.

Drown. Drowning men catch at straws. Persons in desperate circumstances cling in hope to trifles wholly inadequate to rescue or even help them.

Drug. *See* DOPE. **A drug in the market.** Something not called for, which no one will buy.

Druid (droo′ id). A member of the ancient Gaulish and British order of priests, teachers of religion, magicians, or sorcerers. The word is the Lat. *druidœ* or *druides* (always plural), which was borrowed from the Old Irish *drui* and Gaelic *draoi*. The druidic cult presents many difficulties, and practically our only literary sources of knowledge of it are Pliny and the Commentaries of Cæsar, whence we learn that the rites of the Druids were conducted in oak-groves and that they regarded the oak and the mistletoe with peculiar veneration; that they studied the stars and nature generally; that they believed in the transmigration of souls, and dealt in "magic." Their distinguishing badge was a serpent's egg (*see below*), to which very powerful properties were credited. The order seems to have been highly organized, and according to Strabo every chief had his druid, and every chief druid was allowed a guard of thirty men.

In Butler's *Hudibras* (III, i) there is an allusion to the

Money by the Druids borrowed,
In t'other world to be restored.

This refers to a legend recorded by one Patricius (? St. Patrick) to the effect that the Druids were wont to borrow money to be repaid in the life to come. His words are "*Druidæ pecuniam mutuo accipiebant in posteriore vita reddituri.*"

On account of the inferred connexion between the Druids and the bards the name is still kept in use by the Welsh Eisteddfods, and it is with this sense that Collins employed it in his eulogy on Thomson:—

In yonder grave a Druid lies.

United Ancient Order of Druids. A secret benefit society founded in London in 1781 and introduced to U.S.A. in 1883. It now has lodges, or "groves" as they are called, in many parts of the world.

Drum. A popular name in the 18th century— and later—for a crowded evening party, so called from its resemblance in noise to the drumming up of recruits. The more riotous of these parties were called *drum-majors*.

This is a riotous assembly of fashionable people, of both sexes, at a private house, consisting of some hundreds, not unaptly stiled a drum, from the noise and emptiness of the entertainment.—SMOLLETT: *Advice, a Satire* (1746).

To drum up. To get together unexpectedly or in an emergency, as "to drum up a meal."

Drum ecclesiastic. The pulpit cushion, often vigorously thumped by what are termed "rousing preachers."

When Gospel trumpeter, surrounded
With long-eared rout, to battle sounded;
And pulpit, drum ecclesiastic,
Was beat with fist instead of a stick.
BUTLER: *Hudibras*, I, i.

Drum-head court-martial. One held in haste; a court-martial summoned on the field round the drum to deal summarily with an offender.

Drumsticks. Legs, especially very thin ones, or the legs of a cooked fowl.

Drunk. Drunk as a fiddler. The reference is to the fiddler at wakes, fairs, and on board ship, who used to be paid in liquor for playing to the dancers.

Drunk as a lord. In the late 18th century and early 19th the habit of gross drinking was at its height and a man of fashion was judged—or prided himself—on the number of bottles of port he could drink at a sitting. Few dinners ended without placing the guests under the table in a hopeless state of intoxication; hence the expression.

Drunkard's cloak. A tub with holes for the arms to pass through, used in the 17th century for drunkards and scolds by way of punishment.

Drunken Parliament, The. The Parliament assembled at Edinburgh, January 1st, 1661, of which Burnet says the members "were almost perpetually drunk."

Drury Lane. This famous London street (and, consequently, the theatre) is named from Drury House, built in the time of Henry VIII by Sir William Drury. It stood on a site about in the middle of the present Aldwych.

The first Drury Lane Theatre was opened on April 8, 1663, and nine years later was burned down. Its successor was designed by Wren, and this was replaced in 1794 by a third theatre, which was destroyed by fire in 1809. The present building was designed by Wyatt and opened in 1812. It was on its boards that Edmund Kean achieved his first great triumph, as Shylock, in 1814.

Druses. A people and sect of Syria, living about the mountains of Lebanon and Anti-Libanus. Their faith is a mixture of the Pentateuch, the Gospel, the Koran, and Sufism. They offer up their devotions in both mosques and churches, worship the images of saints, and yet observe the fast of Ramadan. Their name is probably from that of their first apostle, Ismail Darazi, or Durzi (11th century A.D.).

Dry. Thirsty. Hence to drink is to "wet your whistle" (*i.e.* throat); and malt liquor is called "heavy wet."

Dry goods. Merchandise such as cloth, stuffs, silks, laces, and drapery in general, as opposed to groceries.

Dry lodgings. An old expression for sleeping accommodation without board. Gentlemen who took their meals at clubs lived in "dry lodgings."

Dry rot is a diseased condition of timber due to the ravages of certain species of fungi. The affected parts crumble away to a brownish powder upon exposure to a dry atmosphere. Dry rot cannot develop in wood to which air currents have free access, hence the necessity of having air-bricks in an outside wall beneath the floor level.

Dry shave. A shave without soaping the face; to scrape the face with a piece of iron hoop; to scratch the face; to box it and bruise it. The fellow will get a dry shave.
> PETER PINDAR: *Great Cry and Little Wool*, Ep. 1.
> I'll shave her, like a punished soldier, dry.
> PETER PINDAR: *The Lousiad,* canto ii.

Dry wine. Opposed to sweet or fruity wine. In sweet wine some of the sugar is not yet decomposed; in *dry* wine all the sugar has been converted into alcohol. In the same way we speak of a *dry biscuit* as opposed to a sweet biscuit.

Not dry behind the ears. As innocent as a new-born child. When young animals are born, the last place to become dry after birth is the small depression behind each ear.

Dryad (drī′ ăd). In classical mythology, a tree-nymph (Gr. *drus*, a tree) who was supposed to live in the trees and die when the trees died. Eurydice, the wife of Orpheus the poet, was a dryad. Also called *hamadryads* (Gr. *hama*, with).

Dualism (dū′ à lizm). A system of philosophy which refers all things that exist to two ultimate principles, such as Descartes' Thought (*res cogitans*) and Extension (*res extensa*), or — in the theological sense — good and evil. In modern philosophy it is opposed to monism (*q.v.*), and insists that the creator and creation, mind and body, are distinct entities.

Dub. To make a knight by striking him on the shoulder with a sword; to give the accolade. The word probably comes from the Old French *aduber*, to equip with arms, to invest with armour, though it has undoubtedly got mixed with the other Old French word *dober*, to strike.

Dub up. Pay down the money; "fork out!" Another form of *dup* (*q.v.*), do up.

Ducat (dŭk′ ăt). A piece of money first coined in 1140 by Roger II of Sicily as Duke of the duchy (*ducato*) of Apulia. This was a silver coin. In 1284 the Venetians struck a gold coin with the legend *Sit tibi, Christe, datus, quem tu regis, iste ducatus* (may this duchy which you rule be devoted to you, O Christ), and through this the name, already in use, gained wider currency. The ducat mentioned by Shakespeare in *The Merchant of Venice* is the Spanish coin, valued at about 6s. 8d.

Duce (doo′ chā). This title, meaning in Italian a leader, was adopted by the Fascist dictator Benito Mussolini (1883-1945) on his assumption of power in 1922. "Duce! Duce!" was the cry of the crowds stirred almost to frenzy by his impassioned oratory.

Duchess. The wife or widow of a duke; in slang use contracted to *dutch*, and applied to the wife of a coster, as in the song "My old dutch."

Duck. A contraction of duck's egg (*see below*).

A lame duck. A stock-jobber or dealer who will not, or· cannot, pay his losses. He has to "waddle out of the alley like a lame duck."
> "I don't like the looks of Mr. Sedley's affairs . . . He's been dabbling on his own account I fear . . . and unless I see Amelia's ten thousand down you don't marry her. I'll have no lame duck's daughter in my family."—
> THACKERAY: *Vanity Fair*, ch. xiii.

Ducks and drakes. The ricocheting or rebounding of a stone thrown from the hand to skim along the surface of a pond or river. **To play ducks and drakes with one's money** is to throw it away carelessly and just on amusement, or for the sake of watching it go and making a splash.
> What figured slates are best to make
> On watery surface duck and drake.
> BUTLER: *Hudibras*, ii, 3.

Dud. Something or somebody that is useless or a failure. The word became very common in World War I, when it was applied to shells that did not explode, inefficient officers, unworkable pieces of mechanism, etc. Its origin is not known. Dut. *dood* means dead, but no connexion between this and *dud* has been traced.

Dude (dūd). A masher. One who renders himself conspicuous by affectation of dress, manners, and speech. The word was invented in America about 1883, and soon became popular in London.
> I should just as soon expect to see Mercutio smoke a cigarette, as to find him ambling about the stage with the mincing manners of a dude.—JEFFERSON: *Century Magazine*, January, 1890.

Dude Ranch. Ranch in the Western States of America especially organized as a holiday camp for inexperienced horsemen.

Dudman and Ramhead. When Dudman and Ramhead meet. Never. Dudman and Ramhead (now spelt Ramehead) are two forelands on the Cornish coast, about twenty miles apart. *See* NEVER.

Duds. A word in use for five hundred years at least, signifying clothes of some sort; formerly coarse cloaks, but in modern use slang for any clothes, usually with a disparaging implication. Its origin is unknown.

Duenna (dū en ′à). The female of the Spanish *don* (*q.v.*); strictly, the chief lady in waiting on the Queen of Spain, but, in common parlance, a woman who is half companion and half governess, in charge of the younger female members of a Spanish or Portuguese family; hence, in England, a chaperon—especially one who takes her duties very seriously.

> There is no duenna so rigidly prudent and inexorably. decorous as a superannuated coquette.—
> W. IRVING: *Sketch-book* (*Spectre Bridegroom*).

Duessa (dū es′ à) (*Double-mind* or *Falsehood*). In Spenser's *Faerie Queene* (Bk. I) the "scarlet woman," typifying the Roman Catholic Church, and (Bk. V) Mary Queen of Scots. She was the daughter of Deceit and Shame, and assumed divers disguises to beguile the Red Cross Knight.

Duffer. A stupid, foolish, incompetent person, one of slow wit; the origin of the word is not clear, but *duff* is old thieves' slang for "to fake," and as a counterfeit coin was called a *duffer* the name may have been transferred to persons who, similarly, were "no good."

Dug-out. (1) a canoe cut out of a solid tree trunk. (2) An artificial cave in war or peace. (3) A retired officer brought back into service.

Duke (Lat. *dux*, leader). The title belonging to the highest rank of nobility in England. The first English dukedom to be created was that bestowed by Edward III on his eldest son, the Black Prince, in 1338, when he was raised from Earl of Cornwall to Duke of Cornwall. The title is very rarely conferred; and except for royal dukes, since 1874 (Duke of Westminster) it has been conferred only on the Earl of Fife, who was created Duke of Fife on his marriage with Princess Louise (1889). On his death in 1912 his daughter, Princess Arthur of Connaught, became Duchess of Fife in her own right, by special remainder. There are four royal and twenty-six noble dukedoms.

Duke Combe. William Combe (1741-1820), author of *The Tours of Dr. Syntax*, etc., was so called, because of the splendour of his dress, the profusion of his table, and the magnificence of his deportment, in the days of his prosperity. Having spent all his money he turned author, but passed the last fifteen years of his life in the King's Bench Prison.

The Duke of Exeter's daughter. A rack in the Tower of London, so called from a minister of Henry VI, who sought to introduce its use into England (1447).

The Great Duke. The Duke of Wellington (1769-1852), also called "the Iron Duke," a name later given to a famous battleship (1913).

Dukeries. A district in Nottinghamshire, so called from the number of noble residences in the vicinity, including Welbeck Abbey (Duke of Portland), Clumber (Duke of New-castle), Thoresby (Earl Manvers), etc.

Dulcarnon (dŭl kar′ non). The horns of a dilemma (or *Syllogismum cornutum*); at my wits' end; a puzzling question. From an Arabic word meaning "the possessor of two horns." The 47th proposition of the First Book of Euclid is called the Dulcarnon, as the 5th is the Pons Asinorum, because the two squares which contain the right angle roughly represent horns. Chaucer uses the words in *Troilus and Criseyde*, Bk. iii, 931, 933.

To be in Dulcarnon. To be in a quandary, or on the horns of a dilemma.

To send me to Dulcarnon. To daze with puzzles.

Dulce Domum (dŭl′ si dō′ mŭm). A school holiday song: the words mean—*not*, as often supposed, "sweet home," but—"the sweet (sound of the word) 'home'." The song originated at Winchester, and is said to have been written by a boy who was confined for misconduct during the Whitsun holidays, "as report says, tied to a pillar." On the evening preceding the Whitsun holidays, the master, scholars, and choristers still walk in procession round the pillar, chanting the six stanzas of the song. The music is by John Reading (d. 1692), organist of Winchester Cathedral, who also composed the Adeste Fideles (*q.v.*).

> Dulce domum resonemus.
> Let us make the sweet song of home to resound.

Dulce est desipere in loco (dŭl′ si est dè sip′ è ri in lō′ kō). It is delightful to play the fool occasionally; it is nice to throw aside one's dignity and relax at the proper time (Horace: 4 *Odes*, xii, 28).

Dulce et decorum est pro patria mori. (dŭl. si et de kôr′ um est prō pǎt′ ri à môr′ ī). It is sweet and becoming to die on our country's behalf, or to die for one's country (Horace: 3 *Odes*, ii, 13).

Dulcimer (dŭl′ si mer). In *Dan.* iii, 5, etc., this word is used to translate a Hebrew word rendered in Greek by *symphonia*, which was applied to a kind of bagpipe. In modern use a dulcimer is a hollow triangular box strung with wires of varying lengths, which are struck with a little rod held in each hand.

Dulcinea (dŭl sin′ ē à). A lady-love. Taken from the name of the lady to whom Don Quixote paid his knightly homage. Her real name was Aldonza Lorenzo, but the knight dubbed her Dulcinea del Toboso.

Sancho Panza says she was "a stout-built sturdy wench, who could pitch the bar as well as any young fellow in the parish."

Dulcinists (dŭl' si nists). Heretics who followed the teaching of Dulcin or Dolcinus, who taught that God reigned from the beginning to the coming of Messiah; and that Christ reigned from His ascension to the 14th century, when He gave up His dominion to the Holy Ghost. Dulcin was burnt by order of Clement IV (1307). There is a reference to Dulcin in Dante's *Inferno* (xxviii, 55).

Dulia. *See* LATRIA.

Dumb-bell. Originally, an apparatus for developing the muscles, similar to that which sets church bells in motion. It consisted of a flywheel with a weight attached, which the gymnast had to raise. The present dumb-bell, which answers a similar purpose, has been given the same name.

Dumb waiter. A piece of dining-room furniture, fitted with shelves, to hold glasses, dishes, and plate. So called because it answers all the purposes of a waiter, and is not possessed of a tongue.

Dummy. In bridge or in three-handed whist the exposed hand is called dummy. Double-dummy bridge is bridge played by only two players but with the usual four hands."

Dump. Although this is a fairly modern colloquialism it is really an old word, coming from the Middle English *dumpen*, to cast down.

The modern usage of the word is, to unload roughly, to toss on to a refuse heap, to throw quantities of goods on a foreign market, usually at a loss.

The noun, a *dump*, besides meaning a refuse heap, is more generally applied to a military or other deposit of supplies for storage, or waiting for future use.

The word is also used for various "dumpy" objects of little value, such as leaden disks, and small coins such as one that was current in Australia in the early 19th century and was made by cutting a portion out of a Spanish dollar. Hence, *not worth a dump*. The word is probably a back formation from *dumpy*, short and thick.

> Death saw two players playing cards,
> But the game was not worth a dump.
>   HOOD: *Death's Ramble*, stanza 14.

Dumps. To be in or **down in the dumps.** Out of spirits; Gay's Third Pastoral is *Wednesday, or the Dumps*.

Why, how now, daughter Katharine? In your dumps?—*Taming of the Shrew*, ii, 1.

In Elizabethan times the name was given to any plaintive tone, and also to a slow and mournful sort of dance.

> They would have handled me a new way;
> The devil's dump had been danced then.
>   BEAUMONT AND FLETCHER: *the pilgrim*, v, 4.

Dun. One who importunes for payment of a bill. The tradition is that it refers to Joe Dun, bailiff of Lincoln in the reign of Henry VII. The *British Apollo* (1708) said he was so active and dexterous in collecting bad debts that when anyone became "slow to pay" the neighbours used to say to the creditors, "Dun him" (send Dun after him).

An Universitie dunne . . . is an inferior creditor of some ten shillings or downewards, contracted for horse hire, or perchance drinke, too weake to be put in suite.—EARLE: *Microcosmographia* (1628).

Dun Cow. The savage beast slain by Guy of Warwick (*q.v.*). A huge tusk, probably that of an elephant, is still shown at Harwich Castle as one of the horns of the dun cow.

The fable is that it belonged to a giant, and was kept on Mitchell (Middle) Fold, Shropshire. Its milk was inexhaustible; but one day an old woman who had filled her pail, wanted to fill her sieve also. This so enraged the cow that she broke loose from the fold and wandered to Dunsmore heath, where she was slain.

Dunce. A dolt; a stupid person. The word is taken from *Duns* Scotus (about 1265-1308), so called from his birthplace, Dunse, in Scotland, the learned schoolman. His followers were called Dunsers or Scotists (*q.v.*). Tyndal says, when they saw that their hair-splitting divinity was giving way to modern theology, "the old barking curs raged in every pulpit" against the classics and new notions, so that the name indicated an opponent to progress, to learning, and hence a dunce.

> He knew what's what, and that's as high
> As metaphysic wit can fly. . . .
> A second Thomas, or at once
> To name them all, another Dunse.
>   BUTLER: *Hudibras*, i, 1.

Duns Scotus was buried at Cologne; his epitaph reads:—

> Scotia me genuit, Anglia me suscepit,
> Gallia me docuit, Colonia me tenet.

The Parliament of Dunces. Convened by Henry IV at Coventry, in 1404, and so called because all lawyers were excluded from it. Also known as the Lawless, and Unlearned, Parliament.

Dunderhead. A blockhead, or, rather, a muddle-headed person. The history of the word is obscure: *dunder* may be connected with the Scottish *donnered*, or merely be modelled on *blunder*. It appears in early-17th-century works.

Dungarees (dŭng' gà rēz). This comes from a Hindustani word, *dungri*, meaning a kind of coarse cotton cloth. It is applied to an overall suit of coarse (usually blue) cloth.

Dunk, To. (U.S.A.). To dip bread, toast, or doughnuts in one's coffee.

Dunkers. *See* TUNKERS.

Dunmow (dŭn' mō). **To eat Dunmow bacon.** To live in conjugal amity, without even wishing the marriage knot to be less firmly tied. The allusion is to a custom said to have been instituted by Juga, a noble lady, in 1111, and restored by Robert de Fitzwalter in 1244; which was, that

any person from any part of England going to Dunmow, in Essex, and humbly kneeling on two stones at the church door, may claim a gammon of bacon, if he can swear that for twelve months and a day he has never had a household brawl or wished himself unmarried.

Between 1244 and 1772 eight claimants were admitted to eat the flitch. Their names merit immortality:

1445. Richard Wright, labourer, Bauburgh, near Norwich.

1467. Steven Samuel, of Little Ayston, Essex.

1510. Thomas Ley, fuller, Coggeshall, Essex.

1701. William and Jane Parsley, butcher, Much-Easton, Essex. Same year, John and Ann Reynolds, Hatfield Regis.

1751. Thomas Shakeshaft, woolcomber, Weathersfield, Essex.

1763. *Names not recorded.*

1772. John and Susan Gilder, Tarling, Essex.

Allusions to the custom are very frequent in 17th- and 18th-century literature; and in the last years of the 19th century it was revived. A travesty of the old ceremony.

Dunscore. The saut lairds o' Dunscore. Gentlefolk who have a name but no money. The tale is that the "puir wee lairds of Dunscore" (a parish near Dumfries) clubbed together to buy a stone of salt, which was doled out to the subscribers in small spoonfuls, that no one should get more than his due quota.

Duns Scotus. *See* DUNCE.

Dunstable (dŭn' stàbl). Bailey, as if he actually believed it, gives the etymology of this word *Duns' stable*; adding Duns or "Dunus was a robber in the reign of Henry I, who made it dangerous for travellers to pass that way." It is Celtic *dun*, a hill-fortress, and *staple*, an emporium or market (from late Lat. or O.Fr.).

Dunsterforce. The name given to the men sent to Baku in 1918 under the command of Maj.-Gen. L. C. Dunsterville (1865-1946), who had been a schoolfellow of Rudyard Kipling and the hero of *Stalky & Co.* The purpose of this expedition was to prevent the Turks and Germans reaching Baku and its oil wells. Dunsterforce held the town successfully and prevented the enemy from reaching the Caspian Sea, the whole affair making a very gallant adventure.

Duodecimo (dū ō des' i mō). A book whose sheets are folded into twelve leaves each (Lat. *duodecim*, twelve), often called "twelvemo," from the contraction 12mo. The book is naturally a small one, hence the expression is sometimes applied to other things of small size, such as a dwarf. *Cp.* DECIMO-SEXTO.

Duration. In World Wars I and II the engagement of men called to the colours in Britain was "for the duration of the emergency," which meant that their services could be retained until the King signed an Order declaring the state of emergency to be at an end. Hence the phrase became synonymous with "a long time," or a time in the far distant future.

Durbar (dĕr' bar). The word comes from the Persian *der*, a door, and *bar*, admittance, and is properly used in India for the court, council, or council-chamber of a native ruler. It is also used for an official reception on a large scale, or for a state ceremony such as the magnificent durbar for the proclamation of George V as Emperor of India, in 1911.

Durden, Dame. A generic term for a good, old-fashioned housewife. In the old song she kept five serving girls to carry the milking pails, and five serving men to use the spade and flail; and of course the five men loved the five maids.

'Twas Moll and Bet, and Doll and Kate, and Dorothy Draggletail;
And John and Dick, and Joe and Jack, and Humphrey with his flail.   ANON.

Dust. Slang for money; probably in allusion to the moralist's contention that money is worthless.

Down with the dust! Out with the money; dub up! The expression is at least three hundred years old, and it is said that Swift once took for the text of a charity sermon, "He who giveth to the poor, lendeth to the Lord." Having thrice repeated his text, he added: "Now, brethren, if you like the security, *down with your dust.*" That ended his sermon!

I'll dust your jacket for you. Give you a good beating; also used with *doublet, trousers*, etc., in place of jacket. *See* quotation from Smollett, *under* DOUSE IN THE CHOPS.

To bite the dust. *See* BITE.

To kiss or **lick the dust.** *See* KISS.

To raise a dust, to kick up a dust. To make a commotion or disturbance.

To shake the dust from one's feet. To show extreme dislike of a place, and to leave it with the firm intention of never returning. The allusion is to the Eastern custom.

And whosoever shall not receive you or hear your words, when ye depart out of that house or city, shake off the dust of your feet.—*Matt.* x, 14.

But the Jews . . . raised persecution against Paul and Barnabas, and expelled them out of their coasts. But they shook off the dust of their feet against them, and came unto Iconium.—*Acts* xiii, 50, 51.

Duty means what is due or owing, a debt which should be paid. In this sense it is applied to the tax or impost charged by government on certain goods when imported from foreign countries. Obedience is the debt of citizens to rulers for protection, and service is the debt of persons employed for wages received.

Strictly considered, all duty is owed originally to God only; but . . . duties to God may be distributed . . . into duties towards self, towards manhood, and towards God.—GREGORY: *Christian Ethics*, I, i.

England expects that every man will do his duty. Nelson's signal to his fleet just before the battle of Trafalgar (1805).

Dwarf. Dwarfs have figured in the legends and mythology of nearly every race, and Pliny gives particulars of whole races of them, possibly following travellers' reports of African pigmies. Among the Teutonic and Scandinavian peoples dwarfs held an important place in mythology. They generally dwelt in rocks, caves, and recesses of the earth, were the guardians of its mineral wealth and precious stones, and were very skilful in the working of these. They had their own king, as a rule were not inimical to man, but could on occasion be intensely vindictive and mischievous.

In England diminutive persons—dwarfs—were popular down to the 18th century as court favourites or household pets; and in later times they have frequently been exhibited as curiosities at circuses, etc.

Among those recorded in legend or history (with their reputed heights) the following are, perhaps, the most famous:—

ALBERICH (*q.v.*), the dwarf of the *Nibelungenlied*.

ANDROMEDA and CONOPAS, each 2 ft. 4 in. Dwarfs of Julia, niece of Augustus.

BEBE, or Nicholas Ferry, 2 ft. 9 in. A native of France (1714-37). He had a brother and sister, both dwarfs.

BORUWLASKI (*Count Joseph*), 3 ft. 3 in. at the age of thirty (d. 1837).

BUCKINGER (*Matthew*), a German, born 1674. He was born without hands, legs, or feet. Facsimiles of his writing are amongst the Harleian MSS.

CHE-MAH (a Chinaman), 2 ft. 1 in., weight 52 lb. Exhibited in London in 1880.

COLOBRI (*Prince*) of Sleswig, 2 ft. 1 in., weight 25 lb. at the age of 25 (1851).

CONOPAS. *See* ANDROMEDA *above*.

COPPERNIN, the dwarf of the Princess of Wales, mother of George III. The last court dwarf in England.

CRACHAMI (*Caroline*). Born at Palermo; 1 ft. 8 in. at death. (1814-24.) Exhibited in Bond Street, London, 1824.

DECKER or DUCKER (*John*), 2 ft. 6 in. An Englishman (1610).

FAIRY QUEEN (*The*), 1 ft. 4 in., weight 4 lb. Exhibited in Regent Street, London, 1850. Her feet were less than two inches.

GIBSON (*Richard*), a good portrait painter (1615-90). His wife's maiden name was Anne Shepherd. Each measured 3 ft. 10 in. Waller sang their praises:—

Design or chance makes others wive,
But Nature did this match contrive,

HUDSON (*Sir Jeffrey*). Born at Oakham, Rutlandshire; 3 ft. 9 in. at the age of thirty (1619-78); he figures in Scott's *Peveril of the Peak*.

JARVIS (*John*), 2 ft. Page of honour to Queen Mary (1508-56).

LOLKES (*Wybrand*), 2 ft. 3 in., weight 57 lb. Exhibited at Astley's in 1790.

LUCIUS, 2 ft., weight 17 lb. The dwarf of the Emperor Augustus.

MAGRI, COUNT PRIMO. *See* WARREN *below*.

MARINE (*Lizzie*), 2 ft. 9 in., weight 45 lb.

MIDGETS, THE. Lucia Zarate, the elder sister, 1 ft. 8 in., weight 4¾ lb. at the age of eighteen. Her sister was a little taller. Exhibited in London, 1881.

MILLER (*Miss*), of Virginia, 2 ft. 2 in.

MITE (*General*), 1 ft. 9 in. (weight 9 lb.) at the age of seventeen. Exhibited in London, 1881.

NUTT, COMMODORE. *See* TOM THUMB *below*.

PAAP (*Simon*). A Dutch dwarf, 2 ft. 4 in., weight 27 lb.

SAWYER (*A. L.*), 2 ft. 6½ in., weight 39 lb. Editor in 1883, etc., of the *Democrat*, a paper of considerable repute in Florida.

STOBERIN (*C. H.*), of Nuremberg, 2 ft. 11 in. at the age of twenty.

STOCKER (*Nannette*), 2 ft. 9 in. Exhibited in London in 1815.

STRASSE DAVIT Family. Man 1 ft. 8 in.; woman, 1 ft. 6 in.; child, at age of seventeen, only 6 in. Embalmed in the chemical library of Rastadt.

TERESIA (*Madame*). A Corsican, 2 ft. 10 in., weight 27 lb. Exhibited in London 1773.

TOM THUMB (*General*), whose name was Charles S. Stratton, born at Bridgeport in Connecticut, U.S., (1838-83). Exhibited first in London in 1844. In 1863 he married Lavinia Warren, and was then 31 in. in height, she being 32 in., and 21 years old. They visited England in the following year with their dwarf son, Commodore Nutt.

WANMER (*Lucy*), 2 ft. 6 in., weight 45 lb. Exhibited in London, 1801, at the age of forty-five.

WARREN (*Lavinia*). *See* TOM THUMB *above*. In 1885 she married another dwarf, Count Primo Magri, who was 2 ft. 8 in.

WORMBERG (*John*), 2 ft. 7 in. at the age of thirty-eight (Hanoverian period).

XIT was the dwarf of Edward VI.

ZARATE. *See* MIDGETS *above*.

Dyed in the Wool. Thorough-going, 100 percent. (16th-century origin).

Dying Sayings (real or traditional):

ADAMS (*President*): "Independence for ever."

ADAMS (*John Q.*): "It is the last of earth. I am content."

ADDISON: "See in what peace a Christian can die."

ALBERT (*Prince Consort*): "I have such sweet thoughts." *or* "I have had wealth, rank, and power; but, if these were all I had, how wretched I should be!"

ALEXANDER I (of Russia): "Que vous devez être fatiguée" (to his wife Elizabeth).

ALEXANDER II (of Russia): "I am sweeping through the gates, washed in the blood of the Lamb."

ALFIERI: "Clasp my hand, dear friend, I am dying."

ANAXAGORAS (the philosopher, who kept a school, being asked if he wished for anything, replied): "Give the boys a holiday."

ANGELO (*Michael*): "My soul I resign to God, my body to the earth, my worldly goods to my next of kin."

ANTOINETTE. (*See* MARIE.)

ANTONY (of Padua): "I see my God. He calls me to Him."

ARCHIMEDES (being ordered by a Roman soldier to follow him, replied): "Wait till I have finished my problem."

AUGUSTUS (to his friends): "Do you think I have played my part pretty well through the farce of life?"

BACON (*Francis*): "My name and memory I leave to men's charitable speeches, to foreign nations and to the next age."

BAILLY: "Yes! But it is with cold." (This he said on his way to the guillotine, when one said to him, "Why, how you tremble.")

BEARD (*Dr. G. M.*, 1883): "I should like to record the thoughts of a dying man for the benefit of science, but it is impossible."

BEAUMONT (*Cardinal*): "What! is there no escaping death?"

BECKET (*Thomas à*): "I confide my soul and the cause of the Church to God, to the Virgin Mary, to the patron saints of the Church, and to St. Dennis." (As he went to the altar in Canterbury Cathedral, where he was assassinated.)

BEDE (*The Venerable*): (Having dictated the last sentence of his translation of St. John's Gospel, and being told by the Scribe that the sentence was now written) "It is well; you have said the truth: it is indeed."

BEECHER (*Henry Ward*): "Now comes the mystery."

BEETHOVEN (who was deaf): "I shall hear in heaven."

BERRY (*Madame de*): "Is not this dying with courage and true greatness?"

BLOOD (*Colonel*): "I do not fear death."

BOILEAU: "It is a great consolation to a poet on the point of death that he has never written a line injurious to good morals."

BOLEYN (*Anne*): "The executioner is, I believe, very expert; and my neck is very slender."

BROUGHTON (*Bishop*): "Let the earth be filled with His glory."

BURKE: "God bless you."

BURNS: "Don't let the awkward squad fire over my grave."

BYRON: "I must sleep now."

CÆSAR: "Et tu, Brute?" (To Brutus, his most intimate friend, when he stabbed him.)

CAMERON (*Colonel James*): "Scots, follow me!" (He was killed at Bull Run, July 21st, 1861.)

CASTLEREAGH: "Bankhead, let me fall into your arms. It is all over." (Said to his doctor.)

CATESBY (one of the conspirators in the Gunpowder Plot): "Stand by me, Tom, and we will die together."

CATO THE YOUNGER (on seeing that the sword's point was sharp and before thrusting it into his body): "Now I am master of myself."

CHARLEMAGNE: "Lord, into Thy hands I commend my spirit." *Cp.* COLUMBUS, LADY JANE GREY, and TASSO.

CHARLES I (just before he laid his head on the block, to Juxon, Archbishop of Canterbury): "Remember."

CHARLES II: "I have been a most unconscionable time a-dying; but I hope you will excuse it." (To James): "Do not, do not let poor Nelly starve."

CHARLES VIII (*of France*): "I hope never again to commit a mortal sin, nor even a venial one, if I can help it."

CHARLES IX (of France, in whose reign occurred the Massacre of St. Bartholomew): "Nurse, nurse, what murder! what blood! O! I have done wrong: God pardon me."

CHESTERFIELD (*Lord*): "Give Dayrolles a chair."

CHRYSOSTOM: "Glory to God for all things. Amen."

CICERO (to his assassins): "Strike!"

COKE (*Sir Edward*): "Thy kingdom come; Thy will be done."

COLIGNY: "Honour these grey hairs, young man." (To the German who assassinated him.)

COLUMBUS: "Lord, into Thy hands I commend my spirit." *Cp.* CHARLEMAGNE and TASSO.

COPERNICUS: "Now, O Lord, set Thy servant free." (*See Luke* ii, 29.)

CRANMER: "That unworthy hand! That unworthy hand!" (As he held in the flames his right hand which had signed his apostasy.)

CROME (*John*): "O Hobbema, Hobbema, how I have loved you."

CROMWELL: "My design is to make what haste I can to be gone."

CUVIER (to the nurse who was applying leeches): "Nurse, it was I who discovered that leeches have red blood."

DANTON (to the executioner): "Be sure you show the mob my head. It will be a long time ere they see its like."

DARWIN: "I am not in the least afraid to die."

DEMONAX (the philosopher): "You may go home, the show is over" (*Lucian*). *Cp.* RABELAIS.

DERBY (*Earl of*): "Douglas, I would give all my lands to save thee."

DIDEROT: "The first step towards philosophy is incredulity."

DOUGLAS (*Earl*): "Fight on, my merry men."

EDWARD I: "Carry my bones before you on your march, for the rebels will not be able to endure the sight of me, alive or dead."

EDWARDS (*Jonathan*): "Trust in God, and you need not fear."

ELDON (*Lord*): "It matters not where I am going whether the weather be cold or hot."

ELIZABETH (*Queen*): "All my possessions for a moment of time."

ELLIOTT (*Ebenezer*): "A strange sight, sir, an old man unwilling to die."

ELPHEGE (*Archbishop of Canterbury*): "You urge me in vain. I am not the man to provide Christian flesh for Pagan teeth, by robbing my flock to enrich their enemy."

ENGHIEN (*Duc d'*): "I die for my king and for France." (Shot by order of Napoleon I in 1804).

EPAMINONDAS (wounded; on being told that the Thebans were victorious): "Then I die happy." *Cp.* WOLFE.

ETTY: "Wonderful! Wonderful this death!"

FONTENELLE: "I suffer nothing, but I feel a sort of difficulty in living longer."

FOX (C. J.): "It don't signify, my dearest, dearest Liz." (To his wife).

FOX (George, the Quaker): "Never heed! the Lord's power is over all weakness and death."

FREDERICK V (of Denmark): "There is not a drop of blood on my hands." Cp. PERICLES.

GAINSBOROUGH: "We are all going to heaven and Van Dyck is of the company." Cp. CROME.

GARTH (Sir Samuel): "Dear gentlemen, let me die a natural death" (to his physicians; Garth was a doctor himself!).

GASTON DE FOIX: "I am a dead man! Lord, have mercy upon me!"

GEORGE IV: "Wally, what is this? It is death, my boy. They have deceived me." (Said to his page, Sir Walthen Waller.)

GOETHE: "Light! more light!"

GRANT (General): "I want nobody distressed on my account."

GRATTON: "I am perfectly resigned. I am surrounded by my family. I have served my country. I have reliance upon God and I am not afraid of the Devil."

GREELEY (Horace): "It is done."

GREGORY VII: "I have loved justice and hated iniquity, therefore I die in exile." (He had retired to Salerno after his disputes with the Emperor, Henry IV.)

GREY (Lady Jane): "Lord, into Thy hands I commend my spirit." Cp. CHARLEMAGNE.

GUSTAVUS ADOLPHUS: "I am sped, brother. Save thyself."

HALE (Capt. Nathan, hanged by the British Army in America for espionage): "I regret that I have but one life to give for my country."

HANNIBAL: "Let us now relieve the Romans of their fears by the death of a feeble old man."

HAVELOCK (Sir Henry): "Come, my son, and see how a Christian can die."

HAYDN died singing "God preserve the emperor!"

HAZLITT: "I have led a happy life."

HENRY II: "Now let the world go as it will; I care for nothing more." (When told that his favourite son John was one of those who were conspiring against him.)

HENRY VIII: "All is lost! Monks, monks, monks!"

HERBERT (George): "Now, Lord, receive my soul."

HOBBES: "I am taking a fearful leap in the dark."

HOFER (Andreas): "I will not kneel. Fire!" (Spoken to the soldiers commissioned to shoot him.)

HOLLAND (Lord): "If Mr. Selwyn calls, let him in: if I am alive I shall be very glad to see him, and if I am dead he will be very glad to see me."

HUMBOLDT: "How grand these rays! They seem to beckon earth to heaven."

HUNTER (Dr. William): "If I had strength to hold a pen, I would write down how easy and pleasant a thing it is to die."

HUSS (John) (to an old woman thrusting another faggot on the pile to burn him): "Sancta simplicitas!"

JACKSON ("Stonewall"): "Let us pass over the river, and rest under the shade of the trees."

JAMES V (of Scotland): "It [the crown of Scotland] came with a lass and will go with a lass." (This he said when told that the queen had given birth to a daughter—the future Mary Queen of Scots.)

JEFFERSON (of America): "I resign my spirit to God, my daughter to my country."

JEROME (of Prague): "Thou knowest, Lord, that I have loved the truth."

JOAN OF ARC: "Jesus! Jesus! Jesus! Blessed be God."

JOHNSON (Dr.): "God bless you, my dear." (To Miss Morris).

JULIAN (called the "Apostate"): "Vicisti, O Galilee" ("Thou hast conquered; O Galilæan").

KEATS: "Severn—I—lift me up—I am dying—I shall die easy; don't be frightened—be firm, and thank God it has come."

KEN (John) (Bishop): "God's will be done."

KNOX: (John): "Now it is come."

LAMB (Charles): "My bed-fellows are cramp and cough—we three all in one bed."

LAMBERT (the Martyr): "None but Christ! None but Christ!" (As he was pitched into the flames.)

LATIMER: "Be of good cheer, Master Ridley; we shall this day kindle such a candle in England, as, I trust in God, shall never be extinguished" (to Ridley, at the stake).

LAUD (Archbishop): "No one can be more willing to send me out of life than I am desirous to go."

LAWRENCE (Sir Henry): "Let there be no fuss about me, let me be buried with the men."

LEICESTER (Earl of): "By the arm of St. James, it is time to die."

LEOPOLD I (Kaiser): "Let me die to the sound of sweet music." Cp. MIRABEAU.

LOCKE (John): "Oh! the depth of the riches of the goodness and knowledge of God. Cease now." (To Lady Masham, who was reading to him some of the Psalms.)

LOUIS IX: "I will enter now into the house of the Lord."

LOUIS XIV: "Why weep you? Did you think I should live for ever? I thought dying had been harder."

LOUIS XVI (on the scaffold): "Frenchmen, I die guiltless of the crimes imputed to me. Pray God my blood fall not on France!"

MACAULAY: "I shall retire early; I am very tired."

MACHIAVELLI: "I love my country more than my soul."

MALESHERBES (to the priest): "Hold your tongue! your wretched chatter disgusts me."

MARGARET (of Scotland, wife of Louis XI of France): "Fie de la vie! qu'on ne m'en parle plus."

MARIE ANTOINETTE: "Farewell, my children, for ever. I am going to your father."

MARTINEAU (Harriet): "I see no reason why the existence of Harriet Martineau should be perpetuated."

MARY (Queen of England): "You will find the word Calais written on my heart."

MARY II (to Archbishop Tillotson, who had paused in reading a prayer): "My Lord, why do you not go on? I am not afraid to die."

MELANCHTHON (in reply to the question. "Do you want anything?"): "Nothing but heaven."

MIRABEAU: "Let me fall asleep to the sound of delicious music." Cp. LEOPOLD.

MOHAMMED: "O Allah! Pardon my sins. Yes, I come."

MONICA (St.): "In peace I will sleep with Him and take my rest." (St. Augustine: Confessions.)

MONMOUTH (Duke of): "There are six guineas for you and do not hack me as you did my Lord Russell."

MONTAGU (Lady Mary Wortley): "It has all been very interesting."

MOODY (the evangelist): "I see earth receding: Heaven is opening; God is calling me."

MOORE (Sir John): "I hope my country will do me justice."

MORE (*Sir Thomas*): "See me safe up [i.e. on ascending the scaffold]; for my coming down, let me shift for myself."

MOZART: "You spoke of a refreshment, Emile; take my last notes, and let me hear once more my solace and delight."

MURAT (*King of Naples*): "Soldiers, save my face; aim at my heart. Farewell." (Said to the men detailed to shoot him.)

NAPOLEON I: "Mon Dieu! La Nation Française. Tête d'armée."

NAPOLEON III: "Were you at Sedan?" (To Dr. Conneau.)

NELSON: "I thank God I have done my duty. Kiss me, Hardy."

NERO: "Qualis artifex pereo." ("What an artist the world is losing in me!").

NEWTON: "I don't know what I may seem to the world. But as to myself I seem to have been only like a boy playing on the seashore and diverting myself in now and then finding a smoother pebble or prettier shell than ordinary, whilst the great ocean of truth lay all undiscovered before me."

PALMER (*John, the actor*): "There is another and a better world." (Said on the stage. It is a line in the part he was playing—*The Stranger*.)

PALMERSTON: "Die, my dear doctor! that's the *last* thing I shall do."

PASCAL: "My God, forsake me not."

PERICLES: "I have never caused any citizen to put on mourning on my account." *Cp.* FREDERICK V.

PETERS (*Hugh, the regicide*): "Friend, you do not well to trample on a dying man." (To his executioner.)

PITT (*William, the Younger*): "Alas, my country! How I leave my country!"

PLATO: "I thank the guiding providence and fortune of my life, first, that I was born a man and a Greek, not a barbarian not a brute; and next, that I happened to live in the age of Socrates."

POE (*Edgar Allan*): "Lord, help my soul!"

POMPADOUR (*Mme de*): "Stay a little longer, M. le Curé, and we will go together."

PONIATOWSKI (after the bridge over the Pliesse was blown up): "Gentlemen, it behoves us now to die with honour."

POPE: "Friendship itself is but a part of virtue."

QUIN (*the actor*): "I could wish this tragic scene were over, but I hope to go through it with becoming dignity."

RABELAIS: "Let down the curtain, the farce is over." *Cp.* DEMONAX. Also, "I am going to seek the great perhaps."

RALEIGH: "It matters little how the head lies." (Said on the scaffold where he was beheaded.)

RENAN: "We perish, we disappear, but the march of time goes on for ever."

REYNOLDS (*Sir Joshua*): "I know that all things on earth must have an end, and now I am come to mine."

RHODES (*C. J.*): "So little done, so much to do."

RICHARD I: "Youth, I forgive thee!" (Said to Bertrand de Gourdon, who shot him with an arrow at Chalus.) Then to his attendants he added, "Take off his chains, give him 100 shillings, and let him go."

RICHARD III: "Treason! treason!" (At Bosworth, where his best men deserted him and joined Richmond, afterwards Henry VII.)

ROCHEJAQUELEIN (the Vendean hero): "We go to meet the foe. If I advance, follow me; if I retreat, slay me; if I fail, avenge me."

ROLAND (*Madame*, on her way to the guillotine): "O liberty! What crimes are committed in thy name!"

ROSCOMMON (*Earl of*):
"My, God, my Father, and my Friend,
Do not forsake me at my end."
(Quoting from his own translation of the *Dies Iræ*.)

RUSSELL (*Lord*; executed 1683): "The bitterness of death is now past."

SALADIN: "When I am buried, carry my winding-sheet on the point of a spear, and say these words: Behold the spoils which Saladin carries with him! Of all his victories, realms, and riches, nothing remains to him but this." *Cp.* SEVERUS.

SCARRON: "Ah, my children, you cannot cry for me so much as I have made you laugh."

SCHILLER: "Many things are growing plain and clear to my understanding."

SCOTT (*Sir Walter*): "God bless you all, I feel myself again." (To his family.)

SERVETUS (at the stake): "Christ, Son of the eternal God, have mercy upon me." (Calvin insisted on his saying, "the eternal Son of God" but he would not, and was burnt to death.)

SEVERUS: "I have been everything, and everything is nothing. A little urn will contain all that remains of one for whom the whole world was too little." *Cp.* SALADIN.

SHERIDAN: "I am absolutely undone."

SIDNEY (*Sir Philip*) (To his brother Robert): "Govern your will and affections by the will and word of your Creator: in me beholding the end of this world with all her vanities."

SIWARD (the Dane): "Lift me up that I may die standing, not lying down like a cow." *Cp.* VESPASIAN.

SOCRATES: "Crito, we owe a cock to Æsculapius."

STAËL (*Madame de*): "I have loved God, my father, and liberty."

STEPHEN (the first Christian martyr): "Lord, lay not this sin to their charge."

TALMA: "The worst is, I cannot see." (But his last word was) "Voltaire."

TASSO: "Lord, into Thy hands I commend my spirit." Also recorded of CHARLEMAGNE, LADY JANE GREY, COLUMBUS, and others.

TAYLOR (*General Zachary*): "I have tried to do my duty, and am not afraid to die. I am ready."

TAYLOR (*the "Water-Poet"*): "How sweet it is to rest!"

TENTERDEN (*Lord Chief Justice*): "Gentlemen of the jury, you may retire."

THERAMENES (the Athenian condemned by Critias to drink hemlock, said as he drank the poison): "To the health of the fair Critias."

THISTLEWOOD (*executed for high treason*, 1820): "I shall soon know the grand secret."

THOREAU: "I leave this world without a regret."

THURLOW (*Lord*): "I'll be shot if I don't believe I'm dying."

TYNDALE: "Lord, open the eyes of the King of England" (*i.e.* Henry VIII).

VANE (*Sir Harry*): "It is a bad cause which cannot bear the words of a dying man."

VESPASIAN: "A king should die standing" (*See* SIWARD); but his last words were, "Ut puto, deus fio" i.e. "I suppose I am now becoming a god," referring to the apotheosization of Cæsars after death.

VICTORIA (*Queen*): "Oh, that peace may come" (referring to the war in South Africa then in progress).

VOLTAIRE: "Do let me die in peace."

WASHINGTON: "It is well. I die hard, but am not afraid to go."

WEBSTER (Daniel): "Life, life! Death, death! How curious it is!"

WESLEY (Charles): "I shall be satisfied with Thy likeness—satisfied."

WESLEY (John): "The best of all is, God is with us."

WILBERFORCE (His father said to him, "So He giveth His beloved sleep"; to which Wilberforce replied): "Yes, and sweet indeed is the rest which Christ giveth." (Saying this, he never spoke again.)

WILLIAM (of Nassau): "O God, have mercy upon me, and upon this poor nation." (This was just before he was shot by Balthasar Gerard.)

WILSON (the ornithologist): "Bury me where the birds will sing over my grave."

WISHART: "I fear not this fire" (at the stake).

WOLCOT ("Peter Pindar"): "Give me back my youth!"

WOLFE (General): "What! do they run already? Then I die happy." Cp. EPAMINONDAS.

WOLSEY (Cardinal): "Had I but served my God with half the zeal that I have served my king, He would not have left me in my grey hairs."

WORDSWORTH: "God bless you! Is that you, Dora?"

ZISKA (John): "Make my skin into drum-heads for the Bohemian cause."

Many of these sayings, like all other history, belong to the region of Phrase and Fable.

Dymphna (dimf′ nà). The tutelar saint of the insane. She is said to have been the daughter of an Irish prince of the 7th century, and was murdered at Gheel, in Belgium, by her own father, because she resisted his incestuous passion. Gheel has long been a centre for the treatment of the mentally afflicted.

Dysmas (dis′ măs). The traditional name of the Penitent Thief, who suffered with Christ at the Crucifixion. His relics are claimed by Bologna, and in some calendars he is commemorated on March 25th. In the apocryphal Gospel of Nicodemus he is called *Dimas* (and elsewhere *Titus*), and the Impenitent Thief *Gestas*.

E

E. This letter is the representative of the hieroglyphic fretwork, ⊓, and of the Phœnician and Hebrew sign for a window, called in Hebrew *he*.

In *Logic*, E denotes a universal negative proposition, and is thus the opposite of A (*q.v.*).

The following legend is sometimes seen engraved under the two tables of the Ten Commandments in churches:—

PRSVR Y PRFCT MN
VR. KP THS PRCPTS TN
The vowel E
Supplies the key.

E.G., *e.g.* (Lat. *exempli gratia*). By way of example; for instance.

E pluribus unum (ē ploo′ ri bus ū′ nŭm) (Lat.). One unity composed of many parts. The motto of the United States of America; taken from *Moretum* (line 103), a Latin poem attributed to Virgil.

Eager Beaver. American expression, in World War II, for a recruit so over-zealous that he would volunteer for jobs on every possible occasion. Subsequently passed into civilian use.

Eagle. Thy youth is renewed like the eagle's (*Ps.* ciii, 5). This refers to the ancient superstition that every ten years the eagle soars into the "fiery region," and plunges thence into the sea, where, moulting its feathers, it acquires new life. *Cp.* PHŒNIX.

She saw where he upstarted brave
Out of the well . . .
As eagle fresh out of the ocean wave,
Where he hath lefte his plumes all hory gray,
And decks himself with fethers youthly gay.
SPENSER: *Faerie Queene*, I, xi, 34.

In Christian art the eagle is emblematic of St. John the Evangelist, St. Augustine, St. Gregory the Great and St. Prisca. Emblematically or in heraldry the eagle is a charge of great honour. It was called the Bird of Jove by the Romans, and borne on their army standards. France (under the Empires), Austria, Prussia and Russia adopted it as a royal or imperial emblem.

The American Eagle, with outspread wings—spread-eagle—is specifically the emblem of the U.S.A. It is sometimes erroneously called the Bald Eagle, though it is really the white-headed

eagle of N. America, *Haliaetus leucocephalus*. The U.S. coin called an eagle is a gold coin of the value of 10 dollars. An earlier coin known as an eagle was found in Ireland in the first years of Edward I, about 1272—again because of the bird impressed upon it.

Ear (A.S. *eare*). If your ears burn someone is talking about you. This is a very old superstition; Pliny says, "When our ears do glow and tingle, some do talk of us in our absence." In *Much Ado About Nothing* (iii, 1), Beatrice says when Ursula and Hero had been talking of her, "What fire is in mine ears?" Sir Thomas Browne ascribes the conceit to guardian angels, who touch the right ear if the talk is favourable and the left if otherwise. This is done to cheer or warn.

One ear tingles; some there be
That are snarling now at me.
HERRICK: *Hesperides*.

About one's ears. Causing trouble. The allusion is to a hornet's nest buzzing about one's head; thus, to bring the house about one's ears is to set the whole family against him.

Bow down thine ear. Condescend to hear or listen (*Ps.* xxxi, 2).

By ear. To sing or play *by ear* means to sing or play without reading the musical notes, depending on the ear only.

Give ear to. Listen to; give attention to.

I am all ear. All attention.

I was all ear,
And took in strains that might create a soul
Under the ribs of death.
MILTON: *Comus*, 574.

I'll send you off with a flea in your ear. See FLEA.

In at one ear, and out of the other. Forgotten as soon as heard.

the sermon . . . of Dame Resoun . . .
It toke no sojour in myn hede.
For alle yede out at oon er
That in at that other she did lere.
Romaunt of the Rose, 5148 (c. 1400).

Lend me your ears. Pay attention to what I am about to say.

Friends, Romans, countrymen, lend me your ears;
I come to bury Cæsar, not to praise him.
Julius Cæsar, iii, 2.

Little pitchers have large ears. *See* PITCHER.

Mine ears hast thou bored. Thou hast accepted me as thy bond-slave for life. If a Hebrew servant declined to go free after six years' service, the master was to bore his ear with an awl, in token of his voluntary servitude for life (*Exod.* xxi, 6).

No ear. A bad ear for music; "ear-blind" or "sound-blind."

To come to the ears of. To come to someone's knowledge, especially by hearsay.

To get the wrong sow by the ear. *See* SOW.

To fall together by the ears. *See* FALL.

To have itching ears. To enjoy scandal-mongering, hearing news or current gossip. (2 *Tim.* iv, 3.)

To prick up one's ears. To listen attentively to something not expected, as horses prick up their ears at a sudden sound.

> Like unbacked colts, they pricked their ears,
> SHAKESPEARE: *Tempest*, iv, 1.

To set people together by the ears. To create ill-will among them; to set them quarrelling and, metaphorically, pulling each other's ears, as dogs do when fighting.

> When civil dudgeon first grew high,
> And men fell out, they knew not why;
> When hard words, jealousies, and fears,
> Set folks together by the ears.
> BUTLER: *Hudibras* (opening lines).

To tickle the ears. To gratify the ear either by pleasing sounds or flattering words.

To turn a deaf ear. To refuse to listen; to refuse to accede to a request.

Walls have ears. *See* WALL.

Within earshot. Within hearing.

Ear-marked. Marked so as to be recognized; figuratively, marked or set aside for some special purpose. The allusion is to setting owner's marks on the ears of cattle and sheep.

> The late president [Balmaceda] took on board a large quantity of silver, which had been ear-marked for a particular purpose.—*Newspaper paragraph*, Sept. 4, 1891.

Earl (A.S. *eorl*, a man of position, in opposition to *ceorl*, a churl or freeman of the lowest rank; *cp.* Dan. *jarl*). The third in dignity in the British peerage, ranking next below Marquess (*q.v.*). In Anglo-Saxon times, it was a title of the highest dignity and eminence, and was even applied to sovereign princes. Earl Godwin was a ruler of enormous power, as also were the earls created by the Norman kings. *Cp.* VISCOUNT. William the Conqueror, tried to introduce the word Count, but did not succeed, although the wife of an earl is still called a *countess*.

An earl's coronet has eight silver balls mounted on gold rays which reach to the top of the cap, with small strawberry leaves alternating between them.

> The sheriff is called in Latin vice-comés, as being the deputy of the earl or comés, to whom the custody of the shire is said to have been committed.—BLACK-STONE: *Commentaries*, I, ix.

Earl Marshal. A high officer of state who presides over the College of Arms, grants armorial bearings, and is responsible for the arrangement of State ceremonials, processions, etc. Since 1483 the office has been hereditary in the line of the Dukes of Norfolk.

Earl of Mar's Grey Breeks. The 21st Foot (the Royal Scots Fusiliers) are so called because they wore *grey breeches* when the Earl of Mar was their colonel (1678-86).

Earthquakes. According to Indian mythology, the world rests on the head of a great elephant, "Muha-pudma," and when, for the sake of rest, the huge monster refreshes itself by moving its head, an earthquake is produced.

The lamas say that the earth is placed on the back of a gigantic frog, and when the frog stretches its limbs or moves its head, it shakes the earth. Other Eastern mythologists place the earth on the back of a tortoise.

Greek and Roman mythologists ascribe earthquakes to the restlessness of the giants which Jupiter buried under high mountains. Thus Virgil (*Æneid*, iii, 578) ascribes the eruption of Etna to the giant Enceladus.

Earwig. A.S. *ear-wicga*, ear-beetle; so called from the erroneous notion that these insects are apt to get into our ears, and so penetrate the brain.

Metaphorically, one who whispers all the news and scandal going, in order to curry favour; a flatterer.

> Court earwigs banish from your ears.
> *Political Ballads* (1688).

Ease. From O.Fr. *eise*, Mod.Fr. *aise*.

At ease. Without pain or anxiety.

Chapel of ease. *See* CHAPEL.

Ease her! An order given on a small steamer to reduce speed. The next order, is generally "Back her!" and then "Stop her!"

Ill at ease. Uneasy, not comfortable, anxious.

Stand at ease! An infantry drill command for a position less rigid than *attention*, with the feet apart and hands joined behind the back. It is intermediate between *attention* and *stand easy!* in which complete freedom (short of moving away) is allowable.

East. The custom of **turning to the east** when the creed is repeated is to express the belief that Christ is the Dayspring and Sun of Righteousness. The altar is placed at the east end of the church to remind us of Christ, the Dayspring and Resurrection; and persons are buried with their feet to the East to signify that they died in the hope of the Resurrection.

The ancient Greeks always buried their dead with the face *upwards*, looking towards heaven; and the feet turned to the east or the rising sun, to indicate that the deceased was on his way to Elysium, and not to the region of night. (Diogenes Laertius: *Life of Solon*, in Greek.)

East is East and West is West. A phrase from Rudyard Kipling emphasizing the divergence of views on ethics and life in general between the Oriental and Western races—a dichotomy that appears to admit of no compromise.

> Oh, East is East, and West is West and never the twain shall meet,
> Till Earth and Sky stand presently at God's great Judgment Seat;
> But there is neither East nor West, Border, nor Breed nor Birth,
> When two strong men stand face to face, though they come from the ends of the Earth.
> *The Ballad of East and West.*

Far East, China, Japan, etc.

Middle East, Iran, Irak, etc.

Near East, Turkey, Syria, Palestine, Asia Minor, etc.

Eastern Shore, The. Maryland between the Atlantic Ocean and Delaware Bay.

Easter. The name was adopted for the Christian Paschal festival from A.S. *eastre*, a heathen festival held at the vernal equinox in honour of the Teutonic goddess of dawn, called by Bede *Eostre* (cognate with Lat. *aurora* and Sanskrit *ushas*, dawn). On the introduction of Christianity it was natural for the name of the heathen festival to be transferred to the Christian, the two falling about the same time.

Easter Sunday is the first Sunday after the Paschal full moon, *i.e.* the full moon that occurs on the day of the vernal equinox (March 21st) or on any of the next 28 days. Consequently, Easter Sunday cannot be earlier than March 22nd, or later than April 25th. This was fixed by the Council of Nicæa, A.D. 325.

It was formerly a common belief that the sun danced on Easter Day.

> But oh, she dances such a way,
> No sun upon an Easter day
> Is half so fine a sight.
> SIR JOHN SUCKLING: *Ballad upon a Wedding.*

Sir Thomas Browne combats the superstition:—

> We shall not, I hope, disparage the Resurrection of our Redeemer, if we say the Sun doth not dance on Easter day. And though we would willingly assent unto

any sympathetical exultation, yet cannot conceive therein any more than a Tropical expression.—*Pseudodoxia Epidemica*, V, xxii.

Easter eggs, or **Pasch eggs,** are symbolical of creation, or the re-creation of spring. The practice of presenting them at Easter came into England from Germany in the 19th century. It probably derives from the old ecclesiastical prohibition of eating eggs during Lent, but allowing them again at Easter. In modern times the Germans have favoured the rabbit as an Easter symbol.

> Bless, Lord, we beseech thee, this Thy creature of eggs, that it may become a wholesome sustenance to Thy faithful servants, eating it in thankfulness to Thee, on account of the resurrection of our Lord.—POPE PAUL V: *Ritual.*

Easterlings. An old name (first used in the 16th century) for any foreigner coming to England from the East; but specially applied to the merchants from the Hanse towns of northern Germany.

Eat. To eat together was, in the East, a sure pledge of protection. A man once prostrated himself before a Persian grandee and implored protection from the rabble. The nobleman gave him the remainder of a peach which he was eating, and when the incensed multitude arrived, and declared that the man had slain the only son of the nobleman, the heart-broken father replied, "We have eaten together; go in peace," and would not allow the murderer to be punished.

Let us eat and drink, for to-morrow we die. *Is.* xxii, 13. A traditional saying of the Egyptians who, at their banquets, exhibited a skeleton to the guests to remind them of the brevity of human life.

To eat a man's salt. *See* SALT.

To eat coke, humble pie, the leek. *See these words.*

To eat dog. An Indian custom at councils of importance. Later when white men took exception, they were permitted to avoid offence by placing a silver dollar on the dish and passing it: the next man took the dollar and ate the dog. Hence the expression in American politics *to eat dog for another.*

To eat its head off. Said of an animal (usually a horse) that eats more than he is worth, or whose work does not pay for the cost of keeping.

To eat one out of house and home. To eat so much that one will have to part with house and home in order to pay for it. It is the complaint of hostess Quickly to the Lord Chief

Justice when he asks for "what sum" she had arrested Sir John Falstaff. She explains the phrase by "he hath put all my substance into that fat belly of his." (2 *Henry IV*, ii, 1.)

To eat one's heart out. To fret or worry unreasonably; to allow grief or vexation to predominate over the mind, tincture all one's ideas, and absorb all other emotions.

To eat one's terms. To be studying for the bar. Students are required to dine in the Hall of an Inn of Court at least three times in each of the twelve terms before they are "called" to the bar.

To eat one's words. To retract in a humiliating manner; to unsay what you have said.

To eat well. To have a good appetite. But "It eats well" means that what is eaten is agreeable or flavorous. To "eat badly" is to eat without appetite or too little.

Eau de Cologne. A perfumed spirit, originally prepared at Cologne. It was invented by an Italian chemist, Johann Maria Farina, who settled in Cologne in 1709. The usual recipe prescribes twelve drops of each of the essential oils, Bergamot, citron, neroli, orange, and rosemary, with one dram of Malabar cardomoms and a gallon of rectified spirits, which are distilled together.

Eau de vie (ō de vē) (Fr., water of life). Brandy. A translation of the Latin *aqua vitæ* (*q.v.*). This is a curious perversion of the Spanish *acqua di vite* (water or juice of the vine), rendered by the monks into *aqua vitæ* instead of *aqua vitis*, and confounding the juice of the grape with the alchemists' elixir of life. The same error is perpetuated in the Italian *acqua vite*.

Eavesdropper. One who listens stealthily to conversation. The eavesdrop or eavesdrip was the space of ground liable to receive the water dripping from the eaves of a house. An eavesdropper is one who places himself in the eaves-drip to overhear what is said in the house.

Under our tents I'll play the eavesdropper,
To hear if any mean to shrink from me.
Richard III, v, 3.

Ecce homo (ek' si hō' mō) (Lat., Behold the man). The name given to many paintings of Our Lord crowned with thorns and bound with ropes, as He was shown to the people by Pilate, who said to them, *"Ecce homo!"* (*John* xix, 5), notably those by Correggio, Titian, Guido Reni, Van Dyck, Rembrandt, Poussin, and Albrecht Dürer. In 1865 Sir John Seeley published a survey of the life and work of Christ with the title "Ecce Homo."

Ecce signum (ek' si sig' nŭm). See it, in proof. Behold the proof.

I am eight times thrust through the doublet, four through the hose; my buckler cut through and through; my sword hacked like a handsaw—ecce signum!—
1 Henry IV, ii, 4.

Eccentric. Deviating from the centre (Lat. *ex centrum*); hence irregular, not according to rule. Originally applied to those planets which apparently wander round the earth, like comets, the earth not being in the centre of their orbit.

In geometry the term is applied to two circles, one within the other, with different centres; in mechanics it is a wheel with its axle not coaxial with the exact centre of the wheel. In general speech eccentric means out of the ordinary, odd, unconventional, abnormal, and an eccentric is a person with these characteristics.

Ecclesiastes (e klē' si ăs' tēz). One of the books in the Old Testament, arranged next to Proverbs, formerly ascribed to Solomon, because it says (verse 1), "The words of the Preacher, the son of David, king in Jerusalem," but now generally assigned to an unnamed author of the 3rd century B.C., writing after Malachi but before the time of the Maccabees. The Hebrew name is *Koheleth*, which means "the Preacher."

Ecclesiastical. The father of ecclesiastical history. Eusebius of Cæsarea (about 264-340).

Ecclesiasticus. One of the books of the Old Testament Apocrypha, traditionally (and probably correctly) ascribed to a Palestinian sage named Ben Sirah, or Jesus, the Son of Sirach. In the Talmud it is quoted as *Ben Sira*, and in the Septuagint its name is *The Wisdom of Jesus, the Son of Sirach*. It was probably written early in the 2nd century B.C. It was given its present name by early Greek Christians because, in their opinion, it was the chief of the apocryphal books, designated by them *Ecclesiastici Libri* (books to be read in churches), to distinguish them from the canonical Scriptures.

Echidna (e kid' nă). A monster of classical mythology, half woman, half serpent. She was mother of the Chimæra, the many-headed dog Orthos, the hundred-headed dragon of the Hesperides, the Colchian dragon, the Sphinx, Cerberos, Scylla, the Gorgons, the Lernæan hydra, the vulture that gnawed away the liver of Prometheus, and the Nemean lion.

Spenser makes her the mother of the Blatant Beast (*q.v.*).:—

Echidna is a Monster direfull dred,
  Whom Gods doe hate, and heavens abhor to see;
So hideous is her shape, so huge her hed,
  That even the hellish fiends affrighted bee
At sight thereof, and from her presence flee:
  Yet did her face and former parts professe
A faire young Mayden full of comely glee;
But all her hinder parts did plaine expresse
  A monstrous Dragon, full of fearefull ugliness.
                              Faerie Queene, VI, vi, 10.

In zoology an echidna is a porcupine ant-eater found in Australia and New Guinea, allied to the platypus.

Echo (ek' ō). The Romans say that Echo was a nymph in love with Narcissus, but her love not being returned, she pined away till only her voice remained.

Sweet Echo, sweetest nymph, that liv'st unseen
  Within thy airy shell,
By slow Meander's margent green . . .
Canst thou not tell me of a gentle pair
That likest thy Narcissus are?
                              MILTON: *Comus,* 230.

To applaud to the echo. To applaud vigorously—so loudly as to produce an echo.

Eckhardt (ek' hart). **A faithful Eckhardt, who warneth everyone.** Eckhardt, in German legends, appears on the evening of Maundy Thursday to warn all persons to go home, that they may not be injured by the headless bodies and two-legged horses which traverse the streets on that night.

Eclectics (ek lek' tiks). The name given to those who do not attach themselves to any special school (especially philosophers and painters), but pick and choose from various systems, selecting and harmonizing those doctrines, methods, etc., which suit them (Gr. *ek-legein,* to choose, select). Certain Greek philosophers of the 1st and 2nd centuries B.C. were styled Eclectics; and there is the Eclectic school of painters, *i.e.* the Italians of the 17th century who followed the great masters.

Eclipse, one of the most famous of English race-horses. The great-grandson of Darley Arabian (*q.v.*) he was foaled April 1st, 1764, ran his first race May 3rd, 1769, and from then until October, 1770, ran in eighteen races, never being beaten. His skeleton is preserved in the Royal Veterinary College, London. **The Eclipse Stakes** is a race for horses of three years and upwards, run at Sandown Park. It was inaugurated in 1884.

Eclipses were considered by the ancient Greeks and Romans as bad omens. Nicias, the Athenian general, was so terrified by an eclipse

of the moon, that he durst not defend himself from the Syracusans; in consequence of which his whole army was cut to pieces, and he himself was put to death.

The Romans would never hold a public assembly during an eclipse. Some of their poets feign that an eclipse of the moon is because she is on a visit to Endymion.

A very general notion was and still is common among backward races that the sun or moon has been devoured by some monster and hence the custom of beating drums and kettles to scare away the monster. The Chinese, Laps, Persians, and some others call the evil beast a dragon. The East Indians say it is a black griffin.

The notion of the ancient Mexicans was that eclipses were caused by sun and moon quarrels.

Ecliptic (e klip' tik). The track in the heavens along which the sun appears to perform its annual march. It lies in the middle of the Zodiac (*q.v.*) and is, of course, a purely imaginary line produced by the earth's motion about the sun.

Economy. Literally, "household management" (Lat. *œconomia,* from Gr. *oikos,* house nemein, to deal out).

There are many British proverbs and sayings teaching the value of economy:—

"No alchemy like frugality"; "ever save, ever have"; "a pin a day is a groat a year"; "take care of the pence, and the pounds will take care of themselves"; "many a mickle makes a muckle"; "frae saving, comes having"; "a penny saved is a penny gained"; "little and often fills the purse"; and there is Mr. Micawber's wise saying:—

Annual income twenty pounds, annual expenditure nineteen nineteen six, result happiness. Annual income twenty pounds, annual expenditure twenty pounds ought and six, result misery.—DICKENS: *David Copperfield,* ch. xii.

The Christian economy. The religious system based on the teachings of Jesus Christ as recorded in the New Testament.

The economy of nature. The laws of nature, whereby the greatest amount of good is obtained; or the laws by which the affairs of nature are regulated and disposed; the system and interior management of the animal and vegetable kingdoms, etc.

Animal . . . economy, according to which animal affairs are regulated and disposed.—SHAFTESBURY: *Characteristics.*

The Mosaic economy. The religious system revealed by God to Moses and set forth in the Old Testament.

Political economy. Science of the production, distribution, and management of wealth, especially as dealing with the principles whereby the revenues and resources of a nation are made the most of.

Ecstasy (Gr. *ek*, out, *stasis*, a standing). Literally, a condition in which one stands out of one's mind, loses one's wits, or is "beside oneself." St. Paul refers to this when he says he was caught up to the third heaven and heard unutterable words, "whether in the body, or out of the body, I cannot tell" (2 *Cor.* xii, 2-4). St. John also says he was "in the spirit"—*i.e.* in an ecstasy—when he saw the apocalyptic vision (*Rev.* i, 10). The belief that the soul left the body at times was very general in former ages, and there was a class of diviners among the ancient Greeks called **Ecstatici**, who used to lie in trances, and when they came to themselves gave strange accounts of what they had seen while they were "out of the body."

Ecstatic Doctor, The. Jean de Ruysbroek, the mystic (1294-1381).

Ectoplasm (ĕk' tŏ plăsm) (Gr. *ectos*, outside; *plasma*, form). In biology this is an external modified layer of protoplasm, but it has acquired a wider sense in its spiritualistic meaning of the tangible emanation from a medium employed in materialization.

Eden. Paradise, the country and garden in which Adam and Eve were placed by God (*Gen.* ii, 15) but lost by their disobedience. The word means *delight, pleasure.*

Eden Hall. The luck of Eden Hall. An enamelled drinking-glass, made probably in Venice in the 10th century, in the possession of the Musgrave family at Eden Hall, Cumberland, and traditionally supposed to be endowed with fortune-bringing properties. The tale is that it was taken from St. Cuthbert's Well in the garden, when the fairies left this glass by the well while they danced. The superstition is—

If that glass shall break or fall,
Farewell the luck of Eden Hall.

With the break-up of the estate in 1920 the cup was sold.

Edge (A.S. *ecg*). **It is dangerous to play with edged tools.** It is dangerous to tamper with mischief or anything that may bring you into trouble.

Not to put too fine an edge on it. Not to mince the matter; to speak plainly.

To be on edge. To be very eager or impatient.

To edge away. To move away very gradually, as a ship moves from the edge of the shore.

To edge on. *See* EGG ON.

To fall by the edge of the sword. By a cut from the sword; to be slain in battle.

To have the edge on someone. To have an advantage.

To set one's teeth on edge. To give one the horrors; to induce a tingling or grating sensation in one's teeth, as from acids or harsh noises.

In those days they shall say no more, the fathers have eaten a sour grape, and the children's teeth are set on edge.—*Jer.*, xxxi, 29.

I had rather hear a brazen canstick turned,
Or a dry wheel grate on the axle-tree;
And that would set my teeth nothing on edge,
Nothing so much as mincing poetry.
1 *Henry IV*, iii, 1.

Edinburgh. Edwin's burgh; the fort built by Edwin, king of Northumbria (616-33). Dunedin (Gaelic *dun*, a fortress) and Edina are poetical forms.

Effendi (e fen' di). A Turkish title, equivalent to the English "Mr." or "Esq." but always following the name. It is given to emirs, men of learning, the imams of mosques, etc.

Effigy. To burn or **hang one in effigy.** To burn or hang the representation of a person, instead of the person himself, in order to show popular hatred, dislike, or contempt. From earliest times and in all countries magic has been worked by treating an effigy as one would fain treat the original. In France the public executioner used to hang the effigy of the criminal when the criminal himself could not be found.

Égalité (ā găl' itā). Philippe, Duc d'Orléans (b. 1747, guillotined 1793), father of Louis-Philippe, King of the French, assumed the name when he renounced his title and voted for the death of Louis XVI. The motto of the revolutionary party, with which he sided, was "Liberty, fraternity, and equality (*égalité*)."

A bad egg. A bad speculation; a "bad-lot"; a person or thing that does not come up to expectations.

Don't put all your eggs in one basket. Don't venture all you have in one speculation; don't put all your property in one bank. The allusion is obvious.

Like as two eggs. Exactly alike.

They say we are almost as like as eggs.—*Winter's Tale*, i. 2.

Show him an egg, and instantly the whole air is full of feathers. Said of a very sanguine man, because he is "counting his chickens before they are hatched."

Sure as eggs is eggs. Professor de Morgan suggested that this is a corruption of the logician's formula, "*x* is *x*."

Teach your grandmother to suck eggs. Attempt to teach your elders.

The mundane egg. The Phœnicians, Egyptians, Hindus, Japanese, and many other ancient nations maintained that the world was egg-shaped, and was hatched from an egg made by the Creator; and in some mythologies a bird is represented as laying the mundane egg on the primordial waters.

Anciently this idea was attributed to Orpheus, hence the "mundane egg" is also called the *Orphic egg*.

> The opinion of the oval figure of the earth is ascrib'd to Orpheus and his disciples; and the doctrine of the mundane egg is so peculiarly his, that 'tis called by Proclus the Orphick egg.—BURNET: *The Sacred Theory of the Earth* (1684).

To egg on. To incite, to urge on. Here *egg* is simply another form of *edge*—to edge on, *i.e.* to drive one nearer and nearer to the edge until the plunge is taken.

To tread upon eggs. To walk gingerly, as if walking over eggs, which are easily broken.

Egg-trot, or **Egg-wife's trot.** A cautious, jog-trot pace, like that of a housewife riding to market with eggs in her panniers.

Egil. Brother of Weland, the Vulcan of Northern mythology. Egil was a great archer, and in the Saga of Thidrik there is a tale told of him the exact counterpart of the famous story about William Tell and the apple. *See* TELL.

Eglantine. In the romance of Valentine and Orson, daughter of King Pepin, and bride of her cousin Valentine. She soon died.

Madame Eglantine. The prioress in Chaucer's *Canterbury Tales.* Good-natured, wholly ignorant of the world, vain of her courtly manners, and noted for her partiality to lap-dogs, her delicate oath, "by seint Eloy," her "entuning the service swetely in her nose," and her speaking French "after the scole of Stratford atte Bowe."

Ego (Lat., "I"). In various philosophical systems *ego* is used of the conscious thinking subject and *non-ego* of the object. The term *ego* was introduced into philosophy by Descartes, who employed it to denote the whole man, body and mind. Fichte later used the term *the absolute ego,* meaning thereby

> the non-individual being, neither subject nor object, which posits the world of individual egos and non-egos.

In psycho-analysis the *ego* is that part of the mind that perceives and takes cognisance of external reality and adjusts responses to it. *See* ID.

Egoism. The theory in Ethics which places man's *summum bonum* in self. The correlative of altruism, or the theory which places our own greatest happiness in making others happy.

Egoism is selfishness pure, altruism is selfish benevolence. Hence *egoist,* one who upholds and practises this theory.

> To say that each individual shall reap the benefits brought to him by his own powers . . . is to enunciate egoism as an ultimate principle of conduct.—SPENCER: *Data of Ethics,* p. 189.

Egotism. The too frequent use of the word I; the habit of talking about oneself, or of parading one's own doings. **Egotist,** one addicted to egotism.

Egypt, in Dryden's satire of *Absalom and Achitophel,* means France.

> Egypt and Tyrus [Holland] intercept your trade,
> And Jebusites [Papists] your sacred rites invade.
> Pt. i, 705-6.

Crowns of Egypt. Ancient Egypt was divided into two parts, Upper Egypt, or the South Land, and Lower Egypt, or the Northern Land, the kings styling themselves *suten bat,* kings of the north and south. As ruler of the two countries each king wore the crown made up of the White Crown of the South and the Red Crown of the North, and it is from this crown, named Pschent, that they can be distinguished in hieroglyphics or on monuments.

Eight. Behind the eight ball. In a dangerous position, from which it is impossible to escape. The phrase comes from the game of Kelly pool, in one variety of which all the balls must be pocketed in a certain order, except the black ball, numbered eight. If another ball touches the eight ball, the player is penalized. Therefore, if the eight ball is in front of the one which he intends to pocket, he is in a hazardous position.

One over the eight, a euphemism for slightly drunk.

Eikon Basilike (ī 'kon băz il' i ki) (Gr., royal likeness). *EIKΩN BAΣIΛIKH; the Pourtraicture of His Sacred Majestie in His Solitudes and Sufferings,* was published in 1649 and purported to set forth the private meditations, prayers, and thoughts of Charles I on the political situation during and before his imprisonment. Its authorship was at first attributed by Royalists to the king himself, and so late as 1824 this theory was supported by Christopher Wordsworth, Master of Trinity College, Cambridge. At the time of the Restoration John Gauden (1605-62) claimed authorship of it when putting up for the bishopric of Worcester; but who actually wrote it is still an open question.

El Dorado (el dôr a' dō) (Sp., the gilded). Originally, the name given to the supposed king of Manoa, the fabulous city of enormous wealth as located by the early explorers on the

Amazon. He was said to be covered with oil and then powdered with gold-dust, an operation performed from time to time so that he was permanently, and literally, gilded. Many expeditions, both from Spain and England (two of which were led by Sir Walter Raleigh) tried to discover this king, and the name was later transferred to his supposed territory. Hence any extraordinarily rich region, or vast accumulation of gold, precious stones, or similar wealth.

Elagabalus (el à găb' à lus). A Syro-Phœnician sun-god, worshipped in Rome and represented under the form of a huge conical stone. The Roman emperor, originally Varius Avitus Bassanius (A.D. 205-22), son of a cousin of Caracalla but put forward as a son of Caracalla himself, was so called because in childhood he had been a priest of Elagabalus (or Heliogabalus). Of all the Roman emperors none exceeded him in debauchery. His cruelties were so hideous and his personal habits so loathsome that there can be no doubt of his insanity. He reigned about four years (A.D. 218-22), and was put to death by the prætorians.

Elaine. The "lily maid of Astolat" (*q.v.*), who in Tennyson's *Lancelot and Elaine* (*Idylls o, the King*), in which he follows Malory (Bk. xviii, ch. 9-20), loved Sir Lancelot "with that love which was her doom." *See* DIAMOND JOUSTS.

Elbow. *See* ELL.

A knight of the elbow. A gambler.

At one's elbow. Close at hand.

Elbow grease. Hard manual labour, especially rubbing and scrubbing. A humorous expression that was in use at least three hundred years ago. We say "*Elbow grease* is the best furniture oil."

Elbow room. Sufficient space for the work in hand.

Out at elbows. Shabbily dressed, "down at heel."

To elbow one's way in. To push one's way through a crowd; to get a place by hook or crook.

To elbow out; to be elbowed out. To supersede: to be ousted by a rival.

To lift the elbow. To drink; usually said of an habitual drinker.

Up to one's elbow. Very busy, full of work. Work piled up to one's elbows.

Elden Hole. Elden Hole needs filling. A reproof given to great braggarts. Elden Hole is a deep chasm in the Derbyshire Peak, long reputed to be bottomless. *See* Scott's *Peveril of the Peak*, ch. iii.

Elder Brethren. *See* TRINITY HOUSE.

Elder-tree. A tree of evil associations in popular legend, and, according to mediæval fable, that on which Judas Iscariot hanged himself, the mushroom-like excrescences on the bark still being known as *Judas's* (or *Jew's*) *ears.*

Sir John Maundeville, speaking (1364) of the Pool of Siloe. says, "Fast by is the elder-tree on which Judas hanged himself . . . when he sold and betrayed our Lord." Shakespeare, in *Love's Labour's Lost*, v. 2, says, "Judas was hanged on an elder."

> Judas he japed
> With Jewen silver,
> And sithen on an eller
> Hanged hymselve.
> *Vision of Piers Plowman: Passus* I.

See also FIG-TREE; JUDAS TREE.

A pleasant, old-fashioned country wine is made from elderberries.

Eleanor Crosses. The crosses erected by Edward I to commemorate his queen, Eleanor, whose body was brought from Nottinghamshire to Westminster for burial. At each of the following places, where the body rested, a cross was set up: Lincoln, Grantham, Stamford, Geddington, Northampton, Stony Stratford, Waltham, West Cheap (Cheapside). Of these only the crosses at Geddington, Northampton and Waltham now exist.

See CHARING CROSS.

Eleatic Philosophy. Founded by Xenophanes of Elea (about 530 B.C.). who, in opposition to the current Greek system founded on polytheism and anthropomorphism, taught the unity and unchangeableness of the Divine. Through Parmenides and Zeno in the 5th century the school exercised great influence on Plato.

Elecampane. A composite plant (*Inula helenium*), the candied roots of which (like ginger) are used as a sweetmeat, and which was formerly fabled to have magical properties, such as curing wounds, conferring immortality, etc. Pliny tells us it sprang from Helen's tears.

> Here, take this essence of elecampane;
> Rise up, Sir George, and fight again.
> *Miracle Play of St. George.*

Electra. One of the Pleiades (*q.v.*), mother of Dardanus, the mythical ancestor of the Trojans. She is known as "the Lost Pleiad," for it is said that she disappeared a little before the Trojan war, that she might be saved the mortification of seeing the ruin of her beloved city. She showed herself occasionally to mortal eye, but always in the guise of a comet. *See Od.*, v, and *Il.*, xviii.

Electra, the sister of Orestes, figures in the *Oresteia* of Aeschylus and two other dramas, both entitled *Electra*, by Sophocles and Euripedes. The daughter of Agamemnon and Clytemnestra, she incited Orestes to kill their mother in revenge for the latter's murder of Agamemnon on his return from Troy. In modern psychology an Electra complex is a girl's attraction towards her father accompanied with hostility towards her mother.

Electricity (Gr. *elektron*, amber), Thales (600 B.C.) observed that amber when rubbed attracted light substances, and this observation followed out has led to the present science of electricity.

Electuary (e lek' tū ǎr i). Coming from a Greek word meaning to lick up, this term is applied in pharmacy to medicines sweetened with honey or syrup, and originally meant to be licked off the spoon by the patient.

Elegant Extracts. The 85th Foot, remodelled in 1813 after the numerous courts-martial which then occurred. The officers of the regiment were removed, and officers drafted from other regiments were substituted in their places. The 85th is now called the "Second Battalion of the Shropshire Light Infantry." The first battalion is the old 23rd.

At Cambridge, in the good old times, men who were too good to be plucked and not good enough for the poll, but who were yet allowed to pass, were nicknamed the *Elegant Extracts*. There was a similar limbo in the honour list, called the Gulf (*q.v.*), in allusion to the "great gulf fixed." Both nicknames come from the late-18th-century liking for anthologies called "Elegant Extracts."

Elegiacs. Verse consisting of alternate hexameters (*q.v.*) and pentameters (*q.v.*), so called because it was the metre in which the elegies of the Greeks and Romans were usually written. In Latin it was commonly used by Ovid, Catullus, Tibullus, and others; the following is a good specimen of English elegiacs:—

> Man with inviolate caverns, impregnable holds in
>   his nature,
> Depths no storm can pierce, pierced with a shaft of
>   the sun:
> Man that is galled with his confines, and burdened
>   yet more with his vastness,
> Born too great for his ends, never at peace with his goal.
> SIR WM. WATSON: *Hymn to the Sea* (1899).

Element. In modern scientific parlance an *element* is a substance which resists analysis or splitting up into different substances. There are 96 of these. But in ancient and mediæval philosophy an *element* was one of the simple substances of which all things were held to be composed, Aristotle, following Empedocles of Sicily (c. 450 B.C.), taught that there were four, viz. fire, air, water, and earth; but later a fifth, the *quinta essentia*, or *quintessence*, which was supposed to be common to the four and to unify them, was added.

> Does not our life consist of the four elements?
> *Twelfth Night*, ii, 3.

The word is often applied loosely and figuratively, and is used to describe the resistance wire and former of a resistance type of electric heater; also to denote one of the electrodes of a primary or secondary cell. In *military* parlance it is used to describe portions of a unit or formation detached from their parent unit.

In one's element. In one's usual surroundings, within one's ordinary range of activity, enjoying oneself thoroughly. The allusion is to the natural abode of any animals, as the air to birds, water to fish.

> Ferguson was in his element . . . with the malevolent activity and dexterity of an evil spirit, he ran from outlaw to outlaw, chattered in every ear, and stirred up in every bosom savage animosities and wild' desires,—MACAULAY: *History of England*, ch. v.

The elements. Atmospheric powers; the winds, storms, etc.

> Rumble they bellyful! Spit, fire! spout, rain!
> Nor rain, wind, thunder, fire, are my daughters:
> I tax not you, you elements, with unkindness;
> I never gave you kingdom, call'd you children,
> You owe me no subscription: then, let fall
> Your horrible pleasure.
> *King Lear*, iii, 2.

Elephant. Elephants have been used by oriental potentates for state ceremonies or as engines of war from time immemorial. When the Romans first saw elephants, in the army of Pyrrhus, they called them "Leuconian oxen"; their horses refused to face the great beasts and galloped back, causing panic among the infantry. In 250 B.C. Caecilius Metellus vanquished Hasdrubal at Panormus and captured 120 elephants which were taken in strong rafts across the sea to adorn the proconsul's triumph.

A white elephant. Some possession the expense or responsibility of which is more than it is worth. The allusion is to the story of a King of Siam who used to make a present of a white elephant to courtiers whom he wished to ruin.

King of the White Elephant. The proudest title borne by the old kings of Ava and Siam. In Ava the white elephant bore the title of "lord," and had a minister of high rank to superintend his household.

Only an elephant can bear an elephant's load. An Indian proverb: Only a great man can do the work of a great man; also, the burden is more than I can bear; it is a load fit for an elephant.

Elephant and Castle. A public-house sign at Newington that has given its name to a railway station and to a district in South London. The sign is the crest of the Cutlers' Company, who owned the site and into whose trade the use of ivory entered largely. In ancient times war elephants bore fortified "castles" on their backs from which bowmen and armed knights penetrated into the enemy's ranks.

Eleusinian Mysteries. The religious rites in honour of Demeter or Ceres, performed originally at Eleusis, Attica, but later at Athens as part of the state religion. There were Greater and Lesser Eleusinia, the former being celebrated between harvest and seedtime and the latter in early spring. Little is known about the details, but the rites included sea bathing, processions, religious dramas, etc., and the initiated attained thereby a happy life beyond the grave

Elevation of the Host. This is the term used for the raising of the Host and the Chalice after consecration in the Mass, for the adoration of the faithful.

Eleven. This is the A.S. *endlesfon*, from a Teutonic *ainlif*, the ain- representing "one," and the suffix being cognate with the Lithuanian *-lika* (and probably with Lat. *linquere*, to leave, *liqui*, left) in *wenolika*, eleven, the meaning being that there is still one left to be counted after counting ten (the fingers of the two hands).

At the eleventh hour. Just in time; from the parable in *Matt*, xx, 1-16.

The Eleven Thousand Virgins. *See* URSULA.

Elf. Originally a dwarfish being of Teutonic mythology, possessed of magical powers which it used either for the benefit or to the detriment of mankind. Later the name was restricted to a malignant kind of imp, and later still to those airy creatures that dance on the grass in the full moon, have fair golden hair, sweet musical voices, magic harps, etc.

> Spenser relates (*Faerie Queene*, II, x, 70):—
> How first Prometheus did create
> A man, of many partes from beasts derived . . .
> That man so made he called Elfe, to weet
> Quick, the first authour of all Elfin kind.

Spenser's remark that *elf* means "quick" is, of course, an invention; as also is the amusing one (mentioned with disapproval by Johnson, s.v. GOBLIN) that *Elf* and *Goblin* are derived from "Guelf and Ghibelline"; the word is A.S. *ælf*, from Icel. ālfr, and Teut. *alp*, a nightmare.

Elgin Marbles (el' gin). The 7th Earl of Elgin (1766-1841) was envoy to the Sublime Porte (Turkey) from 1799 to 1803, and on visits to Greece—at that time a Turkish possession— he observed that from neglect and depredations many Classical sculptures, etc., were in danger of destruction. At his own expense he made a collection of statuary and sculpture (including several works of Phidias) from the Parthenon and the Erechtheion and brought them to England. In 1812 he sold them to the British Government for £35,000, which was half what he had paid for their removal. He also brought casts of various objects left *in situ*, and a comparison of these casts with the originals as preserved to-day reveals considerable damage in the century that has elapsed, and justifies Elgin's removal of what was brought to England.

Elia (ē' lyà). A *nom de plume* adopted by Charles Lamb (1775-1834).

The adoption of this signature was purely accidental Lamb's first contribution to the *London Magazine* was a description of the old South-Sea House, where he had passed a few months' novitiate as a clerk, . . . and remembering the name of a gay light-hearted foreigner, who fluttered there at the time, substituted his name for his own.—TALFOURD.

Elijah's Melons. Certain stones on Mount Carmel are so called.

The story is that the owner of the land refused to supply the wants of the prophet, and consequently his melons were transformed into stones.—STANLEY; *Sinai and Palestine*.

Eliot, George. The pseudonym of Mary Ann Evans (1819-80). Her first novel appearing under this name was *Scenes of Clerical Life*, 1858.

Elissa (el is' à). Step-sister of Medina and Perissa, and mistress of Hudibras in Spenser's *Faerie Queene* (II, ii).

By Virgil, Ovid, etc. Dido, Queen of Carthage, was sometimes called "Elissa."

Elixir of Life. The supposed potion of the alchemists that would prolong life indefinitely. It was imagined sometimes as a dry drug, sometimes as a fluid. *Elixir* (Arabic, a powder for sprinkling on wounds) also meant among alchemists the philosopher's stone, the tincture for transmuting metals, etc., and the name is now given to any sovereign remedy for disease—especially one of a "quack" character.

Elizabeth. The name is originally Hebrew and means "the oath of God," *i.e.* the oath in memory of the covenant made with Abraham. Among its large number of variants are: Eliza, Elsie, Elsabin (Scandinavian), Elspeth, Lizzy, Elisabet, Elisabetta, Elisavetta, Elise, Isabel,

Isabeau, Isa, Lescinska (Russian), Betty, Betsy, Bettina, Bess, Bessy, Beth, etc.

St. Elizabeth of Hungary. Patron saint of queens, being herself a queen. She died in 1231 at the age of 24, and her day is November 19th. For the story of the conversion of flowers into bread, *see* MELON.

Elizabethan. Belonging to, or having the characteristics of the period of Queen Elizabeth (1558-1603), used especially of literature, architecture, costume and the like. The period was one of great vitality, which resulted in a high level of accomplishment in all the arts, especially in poetry and the drama.

Ell. An old measure of length which, like *foot*, was taken from a part of the body, viz. the forearm. The word (A.S. *eln*) is from a Teutonic word *alina*, the forearm to the tip of the middle finger, which also gives *elbow* (*q.v.*) and is cognate with Lat. *ulna*. The ell was of various lengths. The English ell was 45 inches, the Scots ell only 37 inches, while the Flemish ell was three-quarters of a yard, and a French ell a yard and a half.

Elohim. The plural form of the Heb. *eloah*, God, sometimes used to denote heathen gods collectively (Chemosh, Dagon, Baal, etc.), but more frequently used as a singular denoting one god, or God Himself. In 1 *Sam.* xxviii, 13, where the witch of Endor tells Saul "I saw gods [Heb. *elohim*] ascending out of the earth," this is an exceptional use of the word, and would seem to imply spirits of the departed, rather than gods. *See next article.*

Elohistic and Jehovistic Scriptures. Elohim and Jehovah. (*Jakveh or Yahve*) are two of the most usual of the many names given by the ancient Hebrews to the Deity, and the fact that they are both used with interchangeable senses in the Pentateuch gave rise to the theory, widely held by Hebraists and biblical critics, that these books were written at two widely different periods; the Elohistic paragraphs, being more simple, more primitive, more narrative, and more pastoral, being held to be the older; while the later Jehovistic paragraphs, which indicate a knowledge of geography and history, seem to exalt the priestly office, and are altogether of a more elaborate character, were subsequently enwoven with these. *See* JEHOVAH.

Eloquent. The old man eloquent. Isocrates (436-338 B.C.), the Greek orator. When he heard that Grecian liberty was extinguished by the battle of Chæronea, he died of grief.

That dishonest victory
At Chæronea, fatal to liberty,
Killed with report that old man eloquent.
        MILTON: *Sonnets* (*To Lady Margaret Ley*).

The eloquent doctor. Peter Aureolus (14th century), Archbishop of Aix, a schoolman.

Elsinore. The castle at which the action of Shakespeare's *Hamlet* takes place. It is actually the Castle Kronstadt, north of Copenhagen. The modern Danish name is Helsingör.

Elysium (e liz' i ùm). The abode of the blessed in Greek mythology; hence the Elysian Fields, the Paradise or Happy Land of the Greek poets. *Elysian* means happy, delightful.

O'er which were shadowy cast Elysian gleams.
        THOMSON: *Castle of Indolence*, i, 44.
Would take the prisoned soul,
And lap it in Elysium.
        MILTON: *Comus*, 261-2.

Elzevir (el' ze vēr). An edition of a classic author, published and printed by the family of Elzevir over the period from 1583 to about 1710. Louis, founder of the family, settled in Leyden about 1580; in 1583 he printed *J. Drusii Ebraicum quaestionum*, and in 1592 published at his own risk a Eutropius, by P. Merula. Louis and his descendants carried on the press at Leyden until 1654, when it was moved to Amsterdam. After some years it was split up, a few Elzevir volumes being published in Utrecht (1667-72), and Abraham, the last of the family, being university printer at Leyden, 1681-1712. Many Elzevir editions bear no other typographical mark than the words *Apud Elzeverios*, or *Ex Officina Elzeveriana*. The total number of works bearing the name of Elzevir is 1213, of which 968 are in Latin, 44 in Greek, 126 in French and 75 in other languages.

Embargo (em bar' gō). **To lay an embargo on.** To prohibit, to forbid. The word comes from the Spanish *embargar*, to detain, and is especially applied to the prohibition of foreign ships to enter or leave a port, or undertake any commercial transaction, also to the seizure of a ship, goods, etc., for the use of the State.

Embarras de Richesse (om ba ra' de rē shes') (Fr.). A perplexing amount of wealth, or too great an abundance of anything; more matter than can conveniently be employed. The phrase was used as the title of a play by the Abbé d'Allainval (1753).

Emblem. A symbolical figure; a picture with a hidden meaning which is "cast into" (Gr. *em*, in, *ballein*, to cast) the visible device. Thus, a *balance* is an emblem of justice, *white* of purity, a *sceptre* of sovereignty.

Some of the most common and simple emblems of the Christian Church are:—

A *chalice*. The eucharist.

The *circle inscribed in an equilateral triangle*. or *the triangle in a circle*. To denote the co-equality and co-eternity of the Trinity.

A *cross*. The Christian's life and conflict; the death of Christ for man's redemption.

A *crown*. The reward of the perseverance of the saints.

A *dove*. The Holy Ghost.

A *hand from the clouds*. To denote God the Father.

A *lamb, fish, pelican*, etc. The Lord Jesus Christ.

A *phœnix*. The resurrection.

Emblematical poems. Poems consisting of lines of different lengths so that when printed or written the outline of the poem on the page can be made to represent the object of the verse. Thus, George Herbert in the *Temple* prints a poem on the *Altar* that is shaped like an altar, and one on *Easter Wings* like wings. George Puttenham in his *Arte of English Poesie* (1589) gives a chapter on this form of word-torture (which he calls "Proportion in Figure"), giving examples of eggs, crosses, pillars, pyramids, etc., and it was gibbeted by Ben Jonson, Dryden, Addison, and others.

As for altars and pyramids in poetry, he has outdone all men that way; for he has made a gridiron and a frying-pan in verse, that besides the likeness in shape, the very tone and sound of the words did perfectly represent the noise that is made by these utensils.—SAMUEL BUTLER: *Character of a Small Poet*.

Emelye (em' e li). The sister-in-law of "Duke Theseus," beloved by the two knights, Palamon and Arcyte, the former of whom had her to wife.

Emerald. According to Eastern tradition, if a serpent fixes its eyes upon an emerald it becomes blind (Ahmed ben Abdalaziz; *Treatise on Jewels*). Other properties were also given to it, and in *The Lover's Complaint* (usually printed as though by Shakespeare) the author speaks of:—

The deep-green emerald, in whose fresh regard
Weak sights their sickly radiance do amend.

The Emerald Isle. Ireland. This term was first used by Dr. Drennan (1754-1820), in the poem called *Erin*. Of course, it refers to the bright-green verdure of the island.

Nor one feeling of vengeance presume to defile
The cause or the men of the Emerald Isle.
E. J. DRENNAN: *Erin*.

Emeritus (e mer' i tŭs). Deriving from the Latin *emereri*, to serve but one's time, the word is now used of a professor, minister, etc., who is retired from his office by reason of age or illness but retained on the rolls with full honour.

Emeute (e mūt') (Fr.). A seditious rising or small riot. Literally, a moving-out (Lat. *e-moveo*).

Emilie (em' i lē). The "divine Emilie," to whom Voltaire wrote verses, was the Marquise du Châtelet, with whom he lived at Cirey for some ten years, between 1735 and 1749.

Emperor. A title applied to sovereigns of the highest class. It was first used in this sense by Julius Cæsar in 58 B.C. and was assumed by all his successors, the last Roman Emperor of the West was Augustulus, A.D. 475; the last emperor of the East was Constantine, A.D. 1453. In 800 Charlemagne revived the Empire and as the Holy Roman Empire it lasted until 1806; the Emperors of Austria retaining the title until the fall of Austria in 1918.

In 1804 Napoleon crowned himself Emperor of the French; the First Empire fell in 1815, and the Second Empire under Napoleon III lasted from 1853 until 1870.

In 1870 William I, King of Prussia, was declared Emperor of Germany (Kaiser) and that empire lasted until the abdication of William II, in 1918.

Ivan the Terrible was called Tsar, or Emperor of Moscow in 1533, but it was Peter the Great who established the Tsardom of Russia in 1689. The Russian Empire as an autocracy lasted until 1917.

Victor Emanuel III, King of Italy, was declared Emperor of Abyssinia in 1936; eight years later he and his family were deposed and exiled from Italy.

The British sovereigns were Emperors of India from 1876 until the partition of the continent into the Republic of India and Dominion of Pakistan, in 1947.

Outside Europe: Brazil was an empire 1821-89; Mexico, 1822-3 and 1864-7; Haiti, 1804-6. The term Emperor has also been applied loosely to the sovereigns of China, Japan, Mongolia, Ethiopia and Manchuria.

Emperor. A standard size of drawing paper measuring 48 by 72 inches. This is the largest sheet made by hand.

Emperor, not for myself, but for my people. The maxim of Hadrian, the Roman Emperor (117-138).

The Emperor of Believers. Omar l (581-644), father-in-law of Mohammed, and second caliph of the Mussulmans.

Empire City, The. New York, the great commercial city of the United States. New York

State, on account of its leading position in wealth, population, etc., is called the **Empire State**. Hence the name of the tallest skyscraper in the city.

Empire Style. The style of furniture, costume, etc., that came into vogue during the Consulate and Empire of Napoleon, lasting approximately from 1800 until 1820. The Empire style followed on after the pseudo-classical fervour of the Revolution, but was itself largely inspired by Napoleon's wish to embellish his court with something of the splendour of imperial Rome. The campaign in Egypt added certain Egyptian touches, such as the introduction of the sphinx, into its style of ornamentation. In architecture the Empire style was largely an imitation of the Roman; in furniture there was a certain massiveness and angularity, and a great use of metal (chiefly bronze) appliqué ornament. Though Napoleon himself observed the utmost simplicity the court costume was rich and ornate, especially in the military and civil uniforms. Women's fashions changed constantly, but the high-waisted Grecian style remained a constant motif.

Empirics. An ancient Greek school of medicine founded by Serapion of Alexandria, who contended that it is not necessary to obtain a knowledge of the nature and functions of the body in order to treat diseases, but that experience is the surest and best guide (Gr. *empeiros*, experienced, from *peira*, trial). They were opposed to the Dogmatic School founded by Hippocrates, which made certain dogmas or theoretical principles the basis of practice. Hence any quack or pretender to medical skill is called an *empiric*:

> We must not
> So stain our judgment, or corrupt our hope,
> To prostitute our past-cure malady
> To empirics.
>
> *All's Well That Ends Well*, ii, 1.

Empyrean (em pi rē' ån). According to Ptolemy, there are five heavens, the last of which is pure elemental fire and the seat of deity; this fifth heaven is called the empyrean (Gr. *empuros*, fiery); hence, in Christian angelology, the abode of God and the angels. *See* HEAVEN.

> Now had the Almighty Father from above,
> From the pure empyrean where He sits
> High throned above all height, bent down his eye.
>
> MILTON; *Paradise Lost*, iii, 56.

En bloc (ong blok) (Fr.). The whole lot together; *en masse*.

En garçon (ong gar' song) (Fr.). As a bachelor. "To take me *en garçon*," without ceremony, as a bachelor fares in ordinary life.

En grande toilette; en grande tenue (ong gron twa let) (Fr.). In full dress; dressed for a great occasion.

En masse (ong măs) (Fr.). The whole lot just as it stands; the whole.

En papillotes (Fr.). In a state of undress; literally, in curl-papers. Cutlets with frills on them are *en papillotes*.

En famille (ong fa mē) (Fr.). In the privacy of one's own home.

En passant (ong păs' ong) (Fr.). By the way. A remark made *en passant* is one dropped in, almost an aside.

En pension (ong pon' si on) (Fr.). *Pension* is payment for board and lodging; hence, a boarding-house. "To live *en pension*" is to live at a boarding-house or at an hotel, etc., for a charge that includes board and lodging.

En rapport (ong ra pôr) (Fr.). In harmony with; in sympathetic lines with.

En route (ong root). On the way; on the road or journey.

Encomium (en kō' mi úm). From a Greek word meaning a eulogy or panegyric in honour of a victor in the Bacchic games; hence, praise, eulogy, especially of a formal nature. The encomium was sung in the procession which marched from *kome to kome*, *i.e.* village to village.

Encore (ong kôr). A good example of "English French" (*q.v.*); our use of this word is unknown to the French, who say *bis* (twice) if they wish a thing to be repeated. *Encore une tasse* is "another cup," *encore une fois* "once again."

Encyclopedia (en sī klō pē' di à). A book giving clear information on all branches of knowledge or on some particular art or science. One of the earliest known is that of Pliny the Elder (A.D. 23-79) entitled *Naturalis historia* in 37 books, dealing mainly with geography, medicine and art. For many generations this served as a compendium of all that could be or needed to be known. In 1360 Bartholomew de Granville wrote *De proprietatibus rerum*, in 19 books, starting with an article on God and ending with a list of birds' eggs. In 1704 John Harris (*c.* 1667-1719) produced a *Lexicon technicum or an Universal Dictionary of Arts and Sciences*, but this was soon overshadowed by the work of Ephraim Chambers (*d.* 1740) who, in 1728, brought out his *Cyclopedia . . . a Universal Dictionary of Arts and Sciences*, in two volumes. With additions and supplements this was reprinted throughout the 18th century. The *Encyclopædia Britannica* was first published in Edinburgh, in three volumes, 1768-71, and went through many editions, each much larger than its predecessor, until the 11th (1908) which was issued, but not owned by Cambridge University. In 1920 the *Britannica* passed into American hands, and subsequent editions have been issued by them.

The French *Encyclopédie ou Dictionnaire raisonné des sciences*, etc., appeared in 28 folio volumes (11 of which were of plates) between 1751 and 1765, with supplements, and an index which was published in 1780. It was edited by Diderot, assisted by d'Alembert, and many of the leading men of letters (hence called Encyclopedists) contributed to it. Its frank and objective attitude towards the problems of the times, towards science and religion, made it a potent weapon in the service of the philosophic doctrines that were influential causes of the Revolution.

End. A rope's end. A short length of rope bound at the end with thread, and used for punishing the refractory.

At my wits' end. At a standstill how to proceed farther; nonplussed.

He is no end of a fellow. A capital chap; a most agreeable companion.

Odds and ends. Fragments, remnants, odd ends of miscellaneous articles; bits and pieces of trifling value.

The end justifies the means. A false doctrine, frequently condemned by various popes, which teaches that evil means may be employed to produce a good effect. The true doctrine is that an act is vitiated by any defect in the act itself; not even the smallest sin may be committed that good may come.

> The End must justifie the means:
> He only Sins who Ill intends:
> Since therefore 'tis to Combat Evil;
> 'Tis lawful to employ the Devil.
> PRIOR: *Hans Carvel*.

The ends of the earth. The remotest parts of the earth, the regions farthest from civilization.

To be one's end. The cause or agent of his death.

> This apoplexie will be his end.
> 2 *Henry IV*, iv, 4.

To begin at the wrong end. To attempt to do something unmethodically.

To burn the candle at both ends. *See* BURN.

To come to the end of one's tether. *See* TETHER.

To go off the deep end. To get unnecessarily excited.

To have it at my finger's end. *See* FINGER.

To make ends meet. To make one's income cover expenses; to keep out of debt.

To put an end to. To terminate or cause to terminate.

To the bitter end. *See* BITTER.

West end, East end. The quarter or part of a town west or east of the central part. In London, and many other large towns, the West End is the fashionable quarter and the East End the part where the population lives that do the work.

End of the world, The. According to rabbinical legend, the world is to last six thousand years. The reasons assigned are (1) because the name *Yahweh* contains six letters; (2) because the Hebrew letter *m* occurs six times in the book of *Genesis*; (3) because the patriarch Enoch, who was taken to heaven without dying, was the sixth generation from Adam (Seth, Enos, Cainan, Mahalaleel, Jared, Enoch); (4) because God created the world in six days; (5) because six contains three binaries—the first 2000 years were for the law of nature, the next 2000 years the written law, and the last 2000 the law of grace.

End papers. The two leaves front and back of a book, one of which is pasted down on to the inside of the cover and the other is a flyleaf; they may be coloured or marbled.

Endymion (en dim' i on). In Greek mythology, a beautiful youth, sometimes said to be a king and sometimes a shepherd, who, as he slept on Mount Latmus, so moved the cold heart of Selene, the Moon goddess, that she came down and kissed him and lay at his side. He woke to find her gone, but the dreams which she gave him were such that he begged Zeus to give him immortality and allow him to sleep perpetually on Mount Latmus. Other accounts say that Selene herself bound him by enchantment so that she might come and kiss him whenever she liked. Keats used the story as the framework of his long allegory, *Endymion* (1817), and it forms the basis of Lyly's comedy, *Endimion, the Man in the Moone* (1585).

> The moon sleeps with Endymion,
> And would not be awaked.
> *Merchant of Venice*, v, 1.

Enfant terrible (ong fong te rēbl) (Fr.). Literally, a terrible child. An embarrassing person, one who says or does awkward things at inconvenient times.

Enfilade (en fi lād) (Fr.). means literally to spin out; to put thread in (a needle), as *enfiler une aiguille*; to string beads by putting them on a thread, as *enfiler des perles*. Bullets being compared to thread, we get the meaning to fire them through opposing ranks as thread through a needle; hence, to scour or rake with shot from the flank.

England. The name comes from the *Angles* (land of the Angles), who migrated from the east of the Elbe to Schleswig (between the Jutes and the Saxons), and passed over in great numbers to Britain during the 5th century; but Verstegan (1605) has a story that Egbert was "chiefly moved" to call his kingdom England "in respect of Pope Gregory's changing the name of *Engelisce* into *Angellyke*." And this "may have moved our kings upon their best gold coins to set the image of an angel."

Little Englander. One who would rather see England small, contented, and as self-contained as possible than have her the head of a world-wide Empire, the possession of which might be a source of trouble and danger to her; the opposite to an Imperialist. The term was in use during the S. African War of 1899-1902.

English. The language of the people of England; also the people themselves. *Middle English* is the language as used from about 1150 to 1500; *Old English*, also called somewhat incorrectly *Anglo-Saxon*, is that in use before 1150.

In typography, *English* was the name given to a large size of type, two points (*i.e.* one-thirty-sixth of an inch) larger than pica and four points smaller than great primer.

Plain English. Plain, unmistakable terms. To tell a person *in plain English* what you think of him is to give your very candid opinion without any beating about the bush.

The King's (or **Queen's**) **English.** English as it should be spoken. The term is found in Shakespeare (*Merry Wives*, i, 4), but it is older, and was evidently common. **Queene's English** occurs in Nash's *Strange Newes of the Intercepting Certaine Letters* (1593), and "thou clipst the Kinge's English" in Dekker's *Satiromastix* (1602).

These fine English clerkes will saih thei speake in their mother tongue, if a manne should charge them for counterfeityng the Kinges Englishe.—WILSON: *Arte of Rhetoricke* (1553).

To put on English (U.S.A.). In billiards, to apply spin to the ball.

Englishman. The national nickname of an Englishman is "John Bull" (*q.v.*). The old French nickname for him was "Goddam."

Ennius (en' i ůs). The earliest of the great epic poets of Rome (about 239-169 B.C.), and chief founder of Latin literature.

The English Ennius. Layamon (fl. *c.* 1200), who made a late Anglo-Saxon paraphrase of Wace's *Roman de Brut*, has been so called, but the title is usually given to Chaucer.

The French Ennius. Guillaume de Lorris (about 1235-65), author of the *Romance of the Rose*. Sometimes Jehen de Meung (about 1260-1318), who wrote a continuation of the romance, is so called.

The Spanish Ennius. Juan de Mena (d. 1456), born at Cordova.

Enow. The representative of the inflexional plural of the A.S. adjective *genogh* (mod. *enough*), and still called by Johnson in his Dictionary (1755) "the plural of enough." It was used for numbers reckoned by tale, as: There are chairs enow, nails enow, men enow, etc.; but now *enough* does duty for both words, and *enow* is archaic.

Ensign (en' sěn).

The British Navy. The Union Jack (*q.v.*). The *white* ensign (Royal Navy) is the banner of St. George with the Jack cantoned in the first quarter; the *red* ensign is that of the merchant navy; the *blue*, that of the Navy reserve. *See* FLAG.

U.S.A. The Stars and Stripes.

In the British Army an ensign was formerly an officer to whom was entrusted the bearing of the regimental colours. It was the lowest commissioned rank, and in 1871 it was abolished, that of second lieutenant being substituted though the rank is still retained in the Footguards. In Shakespearean times the word was twisted into "ancient" or "auncient." In the U.S. Navy ensign is the lowest commissioned rank; it was instituted in 1862 when the rank of passed midshipman was abolished.

Entail (en' tāl). An estate in which the rights of the owner are *cut down* (Fr. *tailler*, to cut) by his being deprived of the power of alienating them and so barring the rights of his issue.

To cut off the entail is to put an end to the limitation of an inheritance to a particular line or class of heirs.

Entente cordiale (on tont' kôr di al') (Fr.). A cordial understanding between nations; not amounting to an alliance, but something more than a *rapprochement*. The term is not new, but is now usually applied to the *entente* between England and France that was arranged largely by the personal endeavours of Edward VII in 1906.

If Guizot remains in office Normanby must be recalled, as the only chance of a renewal of the *entente cordiale*.—*Greville's Diary, p.* 189 (1847).

Enthusiast. Literally, one who is possessed or inspired by a God (Gr. *en theos*). *Inspired* is very similar, being the Lat. *in spirare*, to breathe in (the god-like essence). In the 17th and 18th centuries the word *enthusiasm* was applied disparagingly to emotional religion. It is, according to Locke, "founded neither on reason nor divine revelation, but rises from the conceits of a warmed or over-weening brain."

Entrée (on' trā). In full-course dinners a made dish served between the fish and the joint; from this it has come to mean almost any made dish of meat or poultry.

To have entrée. To have the right or privilege of admission.

Entremets (on' tré mā) are served between the roast and the dessert; in other words they are the sweet course, which in the U.S.A. is known as dessert.

Entre nous (Fr.). Between you and me, in confidence.

Eolian Harp. *See* ÆOLIAN

Eolithic Age, The (ē ō lith' ik). The name given by palæontologists to the earliest part of the Stone Age (Gr. *eos*, dawn, *lithos*, a stone), which is characterized by the rudest stone implements.

Eolus. *See* ÆOLUS

Eon. *See* ÆON.

Epact (ē' păkt) (Gr. *epagein*, to intercalate). The excess of the solar over the lunar year, the former consisting of 365 days, and the latter of 354, or eleven days fewer. The epact of any year is the number of days from the last new moon of the old year to the 1st of the following January. It was formerly used in determining the date of Easter. *See* Tables at beginning of Prayer Book.

Epaulette (ep' aw let). A shoulder ornament worn by officers of the Royal Navy above the rank of sub-lieutenant, when in full dress. Epaulettes ceased to be worn in the Army in 1855. Officers of the U.S. Navy above the rank of ensign wear epaulettes, but since 1872 in the army they are worn by generals only.

Ephialtes. A giant, brother of Otus (*q.v.*), who was deprived of his left eye by Apollo, and of his right eye by Hercules.

Ephors. Spartan magistrates, five in number, annually elected from the ruling caste. They exercised control even over the kings and senate.

Epic. A poem of dramatic character dealing by means of narration with the history, real or fictitious, of some notable action or series of actions carried out under heroic or supernatural guidance. Epic poetry may be divided into two main classes: (*a*) the popular or national epic, including such works as the Greek *Iliad* and *Odyssey*, the Sanskrit *Mahabharata*, and the Teutonic *Niebelungenlied*: and (*b*) the literary or artificial epic, of which the *Æneid*, Ariosto's *Orlando Furioso*, Tasso's *Gerusalemme Liberata*, and Milton's *Paradise Lost* are examples.

Father of Epic Poetry. Homer.

Epicurus (ep i kū' rus). The Greek philosopher (*c.* 340-270 B.C.) who founded the Epicurean school. His axiom was that "happiness or enjoyment is the *summum bonum* of life." His disciples corrupted his doctrine into "Good living is the object we should all seek."

Hence, *epicure*, one devoted to the pleasures of the table; *epicurean*, pertaining to good eating and drinking, etc.

> Epicurean cooks
> Sharpen with cloyless sauce his appetite.
> *Antony and Cleopatra*, ii, 1.

Epigoni. *See* THEBES (*The Seven against Thebes*).

Epigram (ep' i grăm). This was originally a simple inscription attached to religious offerings, etc., but even in Classic times it came to mean any short piece of verse conveying a single idea with neatness and grace, though usually with a sting in its tail:

> Treason doth never prosper; what's the reason?
> For if it prosper, none dare call it treason.
> SIR JOHN HARINGTON, 1618.

> You beat your pate, and fancy wit will come:
> Knock as you please, there's nobody at home.
> ALEXANDER POPE.

> The Devil having nothing else to do
>   Went off to tempt My Lady Poltagrue.
> My Lady, tempted by a private whim,
>   To his extreme annoyance, tempted him.
> HILAIRE BELLOC.

> Sir, I admit your general rule,
> That every poet is a fool:
> But you yourself may serve to show it,
> That every fool is not a poet.
> MATTHEW PRIOR.

Epimenides (e pi men' i dēz). A Cretan poet and philosopher of the 7th century B.C. who, according to Pliny (*Natural History*), fell asleep in a cave when a boy, and did not wake for fifty-seven years, when he found himself endowed with miraculous wisdom. *Cp.* RIP VAN WINKLE.

Epiphany (e pif' à ni) (Gr. *epiphaneia*, an appearance, manifestation). The time of appearance, meaning the period when the star appeared to the wise men of the East. January 6th is the Feast of the Epiphany in commemoration of this.

Episode (Gr., coming in besides—*i.e.* adventitious). Originally, the parts in dialogue which were interpolated between the choric songs in Greek tragedy; hence, an adventitious tale introduced into the main story that can be naturally connected with the framework but which has not necessarily anything to do with it.

In music, an intermediate passage in a fugue, whereby the subject is for a time suspended.

Epistle (e pis' ĕl). This word, akin in origin to *apostle*, comes from a Greek verb meaning to send to, and is properly applied to a letter sent to a person at a distance. In modern usage a long and somewhat wordy letter is facetiously called an epistle. The word is more generally applied to the letters sent by the apostles to the various churches in which they were interested. There are thirteen from St. Paul, one from St. James, two from St. Peter, three from St. John, one from St. Jude and the epistle to the Hebrews of unknown authorship.

The epistle side of an altar is to the celebrant's right as he faces it.

Epitaph (ep' i taf). In its strict meaning this is an inscription on a tomb, but it is frequently extended to include any brief and strikingly apt commemoration of a dead person:

Si monumentum requiris circumspice.
Sir Christopher Wren's epitaph in St. Paul's.
Fuller's Earth.
        Thomas Fuller's epitaph on himself, 1661.
Life is a jest, and all things show it
I thought so once, and now I know it.
        John Gay's epitaph on himself, 1732.
Here a pretty baby lies
Sung asleep with lullabies;
Pray be silent, and not stir
Th' easy earth that covers her.
        Robert Herrick, upon a child.
His foe was folly and his weapon wit.
Epitaph on W. S. Gilbert by "Anthony Hope" Hawkins.

Epoch (ē' pok) (Gr., a stoppage, pause). A definite point of time; also the period that dates from such, the sequence of events that spring from it. The word is used with much the same sense as "era"; we speak of both the "Epoch" and the "Era" of the Reformation, for instance.

Epsom Races. Horse races instituted in the early 17th century and held on Epsom Downs for four days in May. The second day (Wednesday) is "Derby day" (*q.v.*), and on the fourth the "Oaks" (*q.v.*) is run.

There are other races held at Epsom besides the great four-day races—for instance, the City and Suburban and the Great Metropolitan (both handicap races).

Epsom salts. Magnesium sulphate; used medicinally as a purgative, etc., and so called because it was originally (from 1618) obtained by the evaporation of the water of a mineral spring in the vicinity of Epsom, Surrey.

Equality. The sign of equality in mathematics, two parallel lines ($=$), was invented by Robert Recorde, who died 1558.

As he said, nothing is more equal than parallel lines.

Equation of Time. The difference between mean and apparent time—*i.e.* the difference between the time as shown by a perfect clock and that indicated by a sundial. The greatest difference is at the beginning of November, when the sun is somewhat more than sixteen minutes slow. There are days in December, April, June, and September when the sun and the clocks agree.

Equipage (ek' wi păj). To *equip* means to arm or furnish, and *equipage* is the furniture of a military man or body of troops. Hence *camp equipage* (all things necessary for an encampment); *field equipage* (all things necessary for the field of battle); *tea equipage* (a complete tea-service); a *prince's equipage*, and so on. The word was often used for carriage and horses.

Era. A series of years beginning from some epoch or starting-point as:—

		B.C.
The Era of the Greek Olympiads	.	776
"	the Foundation of Rome	753
"	Nabonassar	747
"	Alexander the Great	324
"	the Selcucidæ	312
"	Julian	45
"	Abraham starts from Oct. 1, 2016 B.C.	
"	Actium starts from Jan. 1, 30 B.C.	
"	American Independence, July 4, A.D. 1776.	
"	Armenia, July 9, A.D. 552.	
"	Augustus, 27 B.C.	
"	Diocletian, Aug. 29, A.D. 284.	
"	Tyre, Oct. 19, 125 B.C.	
"	the Chinese, 2697 B.C.	
"	the French Republic, Sept. 22, A.D. 1792.	
"	the Hegira, July 16, A.D. 622. (The flight of Mohammed from Mecca.)	
"	the Maccabees, 166 B.C.	
"	Yezdegird (Persian), June 16, A.D. 632.	

The Christian Era begins theoretically from the birth of Christ, though the actual Nativity was probably in 4 B.C.

Erastians. The followers of Thomas Lieber (1524-83), a German heretic who wrote a work on excommunication in which he advocated the imposition of restrictions on ecclesiastical jurisdiction. His name was Grecized into *Erastus* (*i.e.* the lovely, or beloved). *Erastianism,* *i.e.* state supremacy or interference in ecclesiastical affairs, is named from him. The Church of England is sometimes called "Erastian," because the State controls its ritual and temporalities, and the sovereign, as the "head" of it, appoints bishops and other dignitaries.

Erato. One of the nine Muses (*q.v.*); the muse of erotic poetry; usually represented holding or playing a lyre.

Erewhon (ēr' won, âr' e won). The name of the ideal commonwealth in Samuel Butler's philosophical novel of the same name (1872). It is an anagram of "Nowhere." *Cp.* COMMONWEALTH, IDEAL.

Erin. Ireland (*q.v.*).

Erin go bragh! Ireland for ever. *See* MAVOURNIN.

Erinyes (e rin' yēz). In Greek mythology, daughters of Ge (Earth), avengers of wrong; the Furies. *See* EUMENIDES; FURIES.

Ermine (ĕr' min). This is another name for the stoat, *Putorius erminea*, which has a brown coat in summer and a white one in winter, with a black tip to the tail. The word ermine is applied chiefly to the fur, which in its white state is used for the robes of judges and peers, and women's cloaks. It is one of the furs in heraldry, being represented by a number of small arrowheads beneath three dots, all black and symmetrically arranged on a white field. There are two other furs, variations of this: *ermines* (ĕr' minz) which is the reverse of ermine, being white spots on a black field; and *erminois* (ĕr' min ois), black spots on a gold (or) field. It is unheraldic to wear fur on a fur.

Ermine Street. One of the most ancient roads in Britain; originally running from Colchester by way of Godmanchester and Lincoln to York, but later connected by the Romans with London, in the south, and the Wall of Hadrian in the north. The origin of the name is obscure, but it is not Roman. It may be connected with Old Teutonic *irmin*, mighty, large. The most important of the other so-called "Roman roads" in Britain are *Watling Street, Icknield Street*, and the *Fosse Way* (*qq.v.*).

Eros. The Greek god of love, the youngest of all the gods; equivalent to the Roman Cupid (*q.v.*). The name is also given to the bronze winged archer surmounting the memorial to the 7th Earl of Shaftesbury, in the centre of Piccadilly Circus, London. The memorial was designed and the figure executed by Sir Alfred Gilbert (1854-1934) and unveiled in 1893.

Ersatz (âr'zats). A German word meaning artificial, something substituted for a natural product. In a wider application it includes anything of the nature of an inferior imitation or substitute.

Erse. The native language of the West Highlanders of Scotland. The word, which is now nearly obsolete, is a variant of *Irish*, and was applied by the Lowlanders to the Highland Gaelic. In the 18th century Scots was often called Erse, without distinction of Highland and Lowland; and Irish was spoken of as Irish Gaelic.

Erudite. Most erudite of the Romans. Marcus Terentius Varro (116-27 B.C.), a man of vast and varied erudition in almost every department of literature.

Erythynus (e rith' i nûs). **Have no doings with the Erythynus,** *i.e.* "don't trust a braggart." The Erythynus is mentioned by Pliny (ix, 77) as a red fish with a white belly, and Pythagoras used it as a symbol of a braggadocio, who fable says is white-livered.

Escapist (es kāp' ist.). The term applied by psycho-analysts to one who shirks unpleasant realities by withdrawing into a world of fantasy, or by concentrating on other and pleasanter activities or subjects for thought.

Esoteric (Gr.). Those within, as opposed to *exoteric*, those without. The term originated with Pythagoras, who stood behind a curtain when he gave his lectures. Those who were allowed to attend the lectures, but not to see his face, he called his *exoteric disciples*; but those who were allowed to enter the veil, his *esoteric*.

Aristotle adopted the same terms; those who attended his evening lectures, which were of a popular character, he called his *exoterics*; and those who attended his more abstruse morning lectures, his *esoterics*.

Esoteric Buddhism. *See* THEOSOPHY.

Esprit de corps (es' prē de kôr) (Fr.). The spirit of pride in the society with which you are associated, and regard for its traditions and institutions.

Esquire (Lat. *scutiger*, a shield-bearer). One who carried the *escu* or shield of a knight.

According to a dictum of the College of Heralds:—

The following persons are legally "Esquires":—The sons of peers, the sons of baronets, the sons of knights, the eldest sons of the younger sons of peers, and their eldest sons in perpetuity, the eldest son of the eldest son of a knight, and his eldest son in perpetuity, the kings of arms, the heralds of arms, officers of the Army or Navy of the rank of captain and upwards, sheriffs of Counties for life, J.P.'s of counties whilst in commission, serjeants-at-law, Queen's [King's] counsel, serjeants-at-arms, Companions of the Orders of Knighthood, certain principal officers in the Royal household, deputy lieutenants, commissioners of the Court of Bankruptcy, masters of the Supreme Court, those whom the Sovereign, in any commission or warrant, styles esquire, and any person who, in virtue of his office, takes precedence of esquires."

To these, doctors of law, barristers, physicians and graduates of the universities not in holy orders are often added; but the general use of the suffix has robbed it of all distinction. It is never used in America, and rarely in the overseas parts of the Empire.

Essays. Lord Bacon's essays were the first in English that bore the name.

To write just treatises requireth leisure in the writer and leisure in the reader . . . which is the cause which hath made me choose to write certain brief notes . . . which I have called essays. The word is late, but the thing is ancient.—*Suppressed Dedication to Prince Henry.*

Estate (O.Fr. *estat*, Lat. *status* from *stare*, to stand). **Estates of the realm.** The powers that have the administration of affairs in their hands, that on which the realm stands. The three estates of Britain are the Lords Spiritual, the Lords Temporal, and the Commons; popularly speaking, the public press is termed the "fourth estate" (*q.v.*). It is a mistake to call the three estates of England the Sovereign, the Lords, and the Commons.

The king and the three estates of the realm assembled in parliament.—*Collect for Nov. 5.*

Est-il-possible (ā tēl pos ēbl). A nickname of Prince George of Denmark (1653-1708), the consort of Queen Anne. The story goes that when he was told of the abdication of his father-in-law, James II, all he did was to exclaim, "Est-il possible?" and when told, further, of the several noblemen who had fallen away from him, "Est-il possible?" exhausted his indignation.

Estotiland (es tōt' i land). An imaginary tract of land near the Arctic Circle in North America, said to have been discovered by John Scalve, a Pole. It is mentioned, and shown, in Peter Heylin's *Microcosmos* (1622).

The snow
From cold Estotiland.
MILTON: *Paradise Lost*, x, 685.

Estramaçon (es tre mà son) (Fr.). A blow or cut with a sword, hence also "estramaçonner".

Estrich. The old name for the ostrich (q.v.).

Eternal, The. God.

The Eternal City. Rome. The epithet occurs in Ovid, Tibullus, etc., and in many official documents of the Empire; also Virgil (*Æneid*, i, 79) makes Jupiter tell Venus he

would give to the Romans *imperium sine fine* (an eternal empire).

Etesian Wind (e tē' zhàn). A Mediterranean wind which rises annually (Gr. *etos*, a year) about the dog-days, and blows forty days together in the same direction. It is gentle and mild.

Deem not, good Porteus, that in this my song
I mean to harrow up thy humble mind,
And stay that voice in London known so long;
For balm and softness, an Etesian wind.
PETER PINDAR: *Nil Admirare.*

Ethiopia (ē thi ō' pya). This very ancient name has been revived in modern times as the official designation of Abyssinia. From the 11th century B.C. until the 4th century A.D. Ethiopia was an independent state, often of considerable power, as when in the 8th century B.C. it conquered Egypt and for two hundred years imposed its rulers upon her. In the 4th century A.D. Ethiopia was ravaged by Abyssinia, and in the 6th century its place was taken by the Christian state of Nubia. Tradition has it that the Queen of Sheba was an Ethiopian, and from her Menelik and the sovereigns of Abyssinia claim descent. Candace was the hereditary title of the Queens of Meroe, in Upper Nubia. The monarch of Ethiopia styles himself Emperor, King of Kings, Conquering Lion of the Tribe of Judah, Elect of God. The country was conquered and overrun by the Italians in 1936, but liberated in 1945. The ancient Ethiopian language of the Church and literature is Geeze (gēz), of the Semitic group.

From earliest times the Ethiopians have been proverbial for their blackness:

Can the Ethiopian change his skin, or the leopard his spots?—*Jer.* xiii, 23.

Her beauty hangs upon the cheek of night
As a rich jewel in an Ethiop's ear.
Romeo and Juliet, i, 5.

Ethnophrones (Gr. *ethnos-phren*, heathen-minded). A sect of heretics of the 7th century, who combined such pagan practices as divination, augury, astrology, etc., with Christianity.

Ethon. The eagle or vulture that gnawed the liver of Prometheus.

Etiquette. The usages of polite society. The word means a ticket or card, and refers to the ancient custom of delivering a card of directions and regulations to be observed by all those who attended court. In French the word originally meant a soldier's billet.

Etiquette . . . had its original application to those ceremonial and formal observances practised at Court. . . . The term came afterwards . . . to signify certain formal methods used in the transactions between Sovereign States.—BURKE: *Works*, vol. viii, p. 329.

Etna (et' nà). The highest active volcano in Europe. It stands over the Straits of Messina, 10,750 ft. high, covering an area of 460 sq. miles, and is ever active from some of its 200 minor cones. Serious eruptions occurred in 1923 and 1928, yet many towns and villages live within its continual menace. In Sicily Etna is known as Monte Gibello. Virgil (*Æneid*, iii, 578, etc.) ascribes its eruption to the restlessness of Enceladus, a hundred-headed giant, who lies buried under the mountain, where also the Greek and Latin poets placed the forges of Vulcan and the smithy of the Cyclops.

Etruscans (e trŭs' kànz). These ancient and mysterious people lived in the region of Italy now corresponding more or less to Tuscany. The many monuments in their old lands have never been deciphered, and very little is known of their language. Their art is of high quality, and they have never been excelled in the making of gold jewellery. Of recent years it has been discovered that the Etruscans were Orientals, coming from Asia Minor originally, perhaps from Lydia but certainly from between the Hellespont and Syria.

Etzel. The name given in German heroic legend to Attila (d. A.D. 453), King of the Huns, a monarch ruling over three kingdoms and more than thirty principalities.

Eucharist. The consecrated Elements in Holy Communion. (Gr. *eucharistos*, grateful). Literally, a thank-offering. Our Lord said, "Do this in remembrance of me"—*i.e.* out of gratitude to me. *Cp.* IMPANATION.

Euclid (ū' klid). Many generations of schoolboys knew geometry only as "Euclid," for the teaching of that branch of mathematics was based on the *Elements* of Eucleides, a Greek geometer who lived in Alexandria about 300 B.C. Of his 15 books some have been lost and others mutilated by commentators and transcribers. Euclid's methods have been discarded in modern teaching mainly because they ignore measurement and constructive movement.

Eucrates (ū krā' tēz). **More shifts than Eucrates.** Eucrates, the miller, was one of the archons of Athens, noted for his shifts and excuses for neglecting the duties of the office.

Eudoxians (ū doks' i ànz). Heretics, whose founder was Eudoxius, patriarch of Antioch in the 4th century. They maintained that the Son had a will independent of the Father, and that sometimes their wills were at variance.

Eugenius (ū jē' ni us). The friend and counsellor of Yorick in Sterne's *Tristram Shandy* is intended for John Hall Stevenson (1718-85), the disreputable author of *Crazy Tales*, and a relative of Sterne's.

Eumæus (ū mē' ùs). The slave and swineherd of Ulysses; hence, a swineherd.

> This second Eumæus strode hastily down the forest glade, driving before him ... the whole herd of his inharmonious charges.—SCOTT.

Eumenides (ū men' i dēz) (Gr., the good-tempered ones). A name given by the Greeks to the Furies, as it would have been ominous and bad policy to call them by their right name, *Erinyes* (*q.v.*).

Euphemism (ū' fe mizm). Word or phrase substituted, to soften an offensive expression. Pope refers to the use of euphemisms in his lines.

> To rest, the cushion and soft dean invite,
> Who never mentions hell to ears polite.
> > *Moral Essays*, epist. iv, 149.

"His Satanic majesty"; "light-fingered gentry"; "a gentleman on his travels" (*one transported*); "an obliquity of vision" (*a squint*) are common examples.

Eureka (ū rē' kà) (Gr., more correctly *Heureka*, I have found it). An exclamation of delight at having made a discovery; originally that of Archimedes, the Syracusan philosopher, when he discovered how to test the purity of Hiero's crown. The tale is, that Hiero delivered a certain weight of gold to a smith to be made into a votive crown, but, suspecting that the gold had been alloyed with an inferior metal, asked Archimedes to test it. The philosopher did not know how to proceed, but in stepping into his bath, which was quite full, observed that some of the water ran over. It immediately struck him that a body must remove its own bulk of water when it is immersed; silver is lighter than gold, therefore a pound-weight of silver will be more bulky than a pound-weight of gold, and would consequently remove more water. In this way he found that the crown was deficient in gold; and Vitruvius says:

> When the idea flashed across his mind, the philosopher jumped out of the bath exclaiming, "Heureka! heureka!" and, without waiting to dress himself, ran home to try the experiment.

"Eureka!" is the motto of California, in allusion to the gold discovered there.

Eurus (ū' rùs). The east wind; connected with Gr. *eos* and Lat. *aurora*, the dawn.

> While southern gales or western oceans roll,
> And Eurus steals his ice-winds from the pole.
> > DARWIN: *Economy of Vegetation*, canto vi.

Eurydice (ū rid′ i si). In Greek mythology the wife of Orpheus, killed by a serpent on her wedding night. Orpheus went down to the infernal regions to seek her, and was promised she would return on condition that he looked not back till she had reached the upper world. When the poet got to the confines of his journey, he turned his head to see if Eurydice were following, and she was instantly caught back again into Hades.

Restore, restore Eurydice to life;
Oh, take the husband or return the wife.
POPE: *Ode on St. Cecilia's Day.*

Eustathians (ū stā thi anz). The followers of Eustathius, Bishop of Sebaste, in Armenia, who was deposed by the council of Gangra in 380.

Euterpe (ū tĕr′ pi). One of the nine Muses (*q.v.*); the inventor of the double flute; the muse of Dionysiac music; patroness of joy and pleasure, and of flute-players.

Eutychians (ū tik′ yānz). Heretics of the 5th century, violently opposed to the Nestorians. They maintained that Jesus Christ was entirely God previous to the incarnation, and entirely man during His sojourn on earth, and were thus the forerunners of the Monophysites (*q.v.*). The founder was Eutyches, an abbot of Constantinople, excommunicated in 448.

Euxine Sea (ūks′ īn). The Greek name for the Black Sea (*q.v.*), meaning the "hospitable." It was originally called by that people *Axeinos*, inhospitable, on account of its stormy character and rocky shores; but this name was changed euphemistically, as it was never thought wise to give a derogatory (even though true) name to any force of nature. *Cp.* ERINYES and EUMENIDES.

Evangelists. The four Evangelists, Matthew, Mark, Luke, and John, are usually represented in art as follows:—

Matthew. With a pen in his hand, and a scroll before him, looking over his left shoulder at an angel.

Mark. Seated writing, and by his side a couchant winged lion.

Luke. With a pen, looking in deep thought over a scroll, and near him a cow or ox chewing the cud. He is also frequently shown as painting a picture, from the tradition that he painted a portrait of the Virgin.

John. A young man of great delicacy, with an eagle in the background to denote sublimity.

The more ancient symbols were—for Matthew, a *man's face*; for Mark, *a lion*; for Luke, *an ox*; and for John, *a flying eagle*; in allusion to the four living creatures before the throne of God, described in the Book of Revelation: "The first . . . was like a lion, and the second . . . like a calf, and the third . . . had a face as a man, and the fourth . . . was like a flying eagle" (iv, 7).

Another explanation is that Matthew is symbolized by a *man*, because he begins his gospel with the humanity of Jesus, as a descendant of David; Mark by a *lion*, because he begins his gospel with the scenes of John the Baptist and Jesus in the Wilderness; Luke by a *calf*, because he begins his gospel with the priest sacrificing in the temple; and John by an *eagle*, because he soars high, and begins his gospel with the divinity of the Logos. The four symbols are those of Ezekiel's cherubim.

Irenæus says: "The lion signifies the royalty of Christ; the calf His sacerdotal office; the man's face His incarnation; and the eagle the grace of the Holy Ghost."

In the event. "In the event of his being elected," means *in case*, or provided he is elected; if the result is that he is elected.

Ever and Anon. From time to time. *See* ANON.

Ever-Victorious Army, The. A force of Chinese, officered by Europeans and Americans, raised in 1861, and placed under the command of Gordon. *See* CHINESE GORDON. By 1864 it had stamped out the Taeping rebellion, which had broken out in 1851.

Everyman. The central character in the most famous 15th-century English morality play (*q.v.*) of the same name, which is considered by some to be a translation from a Dutch original (*c.* 1495), by others to have been the original. Everyman is summoned by Death and invites all his acquaintances (such as Kindred, Good Deeds, Goods, Knowledge, Beauty, Strength, etc.) to accompany him on his journey, but of them all only Good Deeds will go with him. The play in a German translation became world famous between the two world wars on account of Max Reinhardt's lavish production of it upon the steps of the cathedral at successive Salzburg festivals.

The **Everyman Library** was started by Dents, London, in 1906 with 50 titles of which the first was Boswell's Johnson. By the end of 1951 the library included 990 titles.

Evidence, In. Before the eyes of the people; to the front; actually present (Lat.). Evidence, meaning testimony in proof of something, has a large number of varieties, as:—

Circumstantial evidence. That based on corroborative incidents.

Demonstrative evidence. That which can be proved without leaving a doubt.

Direct evidence. That of an eye-witness.

External evidence. That derived from history or tradition.

Internal evidence. That derived from conformity with what is known.

Material evidence. That which is essential in order to carry proof.

Moral evidence. That which accords with general experience.

Presumptive evidence. That which is highly probable.

Prima facie evidence. That which seems likely, unless it can be explained away.

King's evidence. That of an accessory against his accomplices, under the promise of pardon.

Self evidence. That derived from the senses: manifest and indubitable.

Evil Eye. The alleged faculty of causing material harm by means of a glance; in rural England it is called "overlooking." From its Latin name, *fascinum*, comes the word "fascination." The evil eye is a form of witchcraft, owing its origin to the presumption that the human eye is capable of operating at a distance. In southern European countries the baleful effect of the evil eye is counteracted by closing the fist except for the forefinger and little finger, which are extended. This is a gesture of primeval antiquity. Virgil speaks of an evil eye making cattle lean.

Nescio quis teneros oculus mihi fascinat agnos.
Ecl. iii, 103.

Evil May Day. The name given to the serious rioting made on May 1st, 1517, by the London apprentices, who fell on the French residents. The insurrection forms the basis of the anonymous Elizabethan play, *Sir Thomas More.*

The Evil One. The Devil.

Evil Principle. *See* AHRIMAN.

Of two evils, choose the least. *See* CHOICE.

Ewe-lamb. A single possession greatly prized; in allusion to the story told in 2 *Sam.* xii, 1-14.

Ex (Lat.). From, out of, after, or by reason of; it forms part of many adverbial phrases, of which those in common use in English are given below. As a prefix *ex*, when joined to the name of some office or dignity denotes a former holder of that office, or the holder immediately before the present holder. *An ex-president* is some former holder of the office; *the ex-president* is the same as "the late president," the one just before the present one.

Ex libris. Literally, "from the (collection of) books." The phrase is written in the books or printed on the bookplate, and is followed by the name of the owner in the genitive. Hence, a bookplate is often called an *ex libris.*

Ex parte. Proceeding only from one of the parties; hence, prejudiced. An ex-parte statement is a one-sided or partial statement, a statement made by one side without modification from the other.

Ex post facto. From what is done afterwards; retrospective. An *ex post facto* law is a law made to meet and punish a crime after the offence has been committed.

Ex professo. Avowedly; expressly.

I have never written *ex professo* on the subject. GLADSTONE: *Nineteenth Century,* Nov., 1885.

Ex proprio motu. Of his (or its) own accord; voluntarily.

Ex uno omnes. From the instance deduced you may infer the nature of the rest. A general inference from a particular example; if one oak bears acorns, all oaks will.

Exaltation. In astrology, a planet was said to be in its "exaltation" when it was in that sign of the zodiac in which it was supposed to exercise its strongest influence. Thus the exaltation of Venus is in Pisces, and her "dejection" in Virgo.

And thus, god woot, Mercurie is desolate
In Pisces, wher Venus is exaltat.
CHAUCER: *Wife of Bath's Prologue,* 703.

Exaltation of the Cross. A feast held in the Roman Catholic Church on September 14th (Holy Cross Day), in commemoration of the victory over the Persians in 627, when Heraclius recovered and restored to Calvary the cross that had been carried away by Khosroes the Persian.

Excalibur (eks kăl′ i bĕr). The name of Arthur's sword (O.Fr. *Escalibor*), called by Geoffrey of Monmouth *Caliburn,* and in the *Mabinogion Caledvwlch.* There was a sword called *Caladbolg,* famous in Irish legend, which is thought to have meant "hard-belly," *i.e.* capable of consuming anything; this and the name *Excalibur* are probably connected.

By virtue of being the one knight who could pull Excalibur from a stone in which it had been magically fixed Arthur was acclaimed as "the right born king of all England." After his last battle, when the king lay sore wounded, it was returned at his command by Sir Bedivere to the Lady of the Lake. *See* Malory, Bk. xxi, ch. v, and Tennyson's *Passing of Arthur* (*Idylls of the King*).

Excelsior (Lat., higher). Aim at higher things still. It is the motto of the United States, and has been made popular by Longfellow's poem so named.

Exception. The exception proves the rule.
Without a rule, there could be no exception;
the very fact of an exception proves there must
be a rule.

To take exception. To feel offended; to find
fault with.

Exchequer. Court of Exchequer. In the sub-
division of the court in the reign of Edward I, the
Exchequer acquired a separate and independent
position. Its special duty was to order the revenues
of the Crown and recover the king's debts. It
was called the *Scaccarium*, from Lat. *scaccum*,
a chess-board, because a chequered cloth was
used on the table of the court. Foss, in his *Lives
of the Judges* (1848-57), says:—

All round the table was a standing ledge four
fingers broad, covered with a cloth bought in the Easter
Term, and this cloth was "black rowed with strekes
about a span," like a chess-board. On the spaces of this
cloth counters were arranged, marked for checking
computations.

The Chancellor of the Exchequer is an
office that originated under Henry III. Now a
leading member of the Cabinet, he presents
the Budget to the House of Commons and is
responsible for the collecting and spending of
the national revenue.

Excise. Literally, a piece cut off (Lat. *excido*).
It is a toll or duty levied on articles of home
consumption.

Taxes on commodities are either on production
within the country, or on importation into it, or on
conveyance or sale within it; and are classed respectively
as excise, customs, or tolls.—MILL: *Political Economy*,
Bk. v. ch. iii, p. 562.

In his Dictionary Dr. Johnson defined excise
as "A hateful tax levied upon commodities."

Excommunication. An ecclesiastical censure
by which a person is deprived of the communion
of the Church. Excommunicants lose the right
of attending divine service and receiving the
sacraments; they have no share in indulgences
or in public prayers or Masses. If clerics they
are forbidden to administer the sacraments.
Formal sentence is ordinarily required, but
in certain cases excommunication is incurred
at once by the commission of a forbidden act,
ipso facto.

The practice of excommunication was
no doubt derived from the Jewish practice at
the time of Christ, which entailed exclusion
from religious and social intercourse (*cp.
Luke* vi, 22); *cp.* INTERDICT; BELL, BOOK AND
CANDLE.

From the same word-origin, a prisoner
could be held *ex communicado, i.e.* no one
whatsoever could talk to him.

Exeat (Lat., he may go out). Permission
granted by a bishop to a priest to leave his diocese.
In the universities, permission to a student to
be out of College for one or more nights, as
opposed to an *absit* permitting his absence
during the inside of a day.

Exempli gratia (Lat.). For the sake of example:
abbreviated to "*e.g.*" when used as the introduction to an example.

Exequatur. An official recognition of a
person in authorizing him to exercise his power;
formerly, the authoritative recognition of a
papal bull by a bishop, sovereign, etc. The word
is Latin, and means, "he may exercise" (the
function to which he has been appointed.).

Exeter. *See also* EXTER.

The Duke of Exeter's daughter. *See* DUKE.

The Exeter Book. A MS. collection of
Anglo-Saxon poetry presented about 1060 by
Bishop Leofric to Exeter Cathedral, and still
preserved in the library there. It includes poems
and "riddles" by Cynewulf (8th century), the
legends of St. Guthlac and St. Juliana,
"Widsith," "The Wanderer," "The Complaint
of Deor," etc.

The **Exon** or **Exeter Domesday** (*q.v.*) is also
sometimes called the "Exeter Book."

Exhibition. A scholarship, *i.e.* a fixed sum
spread over a definite period given by a school
or university, etc., as a result of an examination,
for the purpose of assisting in defraying the cost
of education. The word was formerly used for
maintenance generally, pecuniary support, an
allowance of meat and drink.

They have founded six exhibitions of £15 each per
annum, to continue for two years and a half.—TAYLOR:
The University of Dublin, ch. v.

Exhibitionism. In psycho-pathology this is
an act of sexual gratification obtained by publicly
exhibiting some part of the body normally
clothed. In a less marked form exhibitionism
takes the shape of performing acts likely to
attract attention; in a yet milder form, to mere
showing-off.

Existentialism (eks is ten' shăl izm). A
philosophical theory originating with Soren
Kierkegaard (1815-55) and current for a time in
France after World War II, largely owing to
the teaching of Jean-Paul Sartre. Man, say the
Existentialists, can be free only through the full
consciousness of his illogical position in a universe that has little relation to himself and is in
itself meaningless.

Exit (Lat., he goes out). A stage direction
showing when an actor is to leave the stage;

hence, the departure of an actor from the stage and departure generally, especially from life; also a door, passage, or way out.

> All the world's a stage,
> And all the men and women merely players:
> They have their exits and their entrances.
> <div align="right"><i>As You Like It</i>, ii, 7.</div>

Exodus (Gr. *ex odos*, a journey out). The second book of the Old Testament, which relates the departure of the Israelites from Egypt under the guidance of Moses; hence, a going out generally, especially a transference of population on a considerable scale, as *the exodus from Ireland*, meaning the departure of the Irish in large numbers for America; and the expulsion of colonists from Nova Scotia in 1755.

Exon. One of the four officers in command of the Yeomen of the Guard; the acting officer who resides at the court; an exempt. The word is an Anglicized pronunciation of the Fr. *exempt*, this having been the title of a junior officer (next below an ensign) in the Life Guards.

Exon (short for Lat, *Exoniensis*, of *Exonia*, *i.e.* Exeter) is the signature of the Bishop of Exeter. *See* EPISCOPAL SIGNATURES.

Exon Domesday. A magnificent MS. on 532 folio vellum leaves, long preserved among the muniments at Exeter Cathedral, containing the survey of Wilts, Dorset, Somerset, Devon, and Cornwall. In 1816 it was published by Sir Henry Ellis as a Supplement to Domesday Book (*q.v.*).

Exoteric. *See* ESOTERIC.

Experimental Philosophy. Science founded on experiments or data, in contradistinction to moral and mathematical sciences; also called *natural philosophy*.

Experto crede (Lat.). Believe one who has had experience in the matter. The phrase is used to add significance or weight to a warning.

Exposé (Fr.). A formal exposition; also, an exposure of something discreditable.

Extradition. The return of a criminal to stand trial, on request of the country in which his crimes are committed to the country to which he has fled. The first extradition treaty was signed between England and France in 1843.

Extreme Unction. One of the seven sacraments of the Catholic Church, founded on *James* v, 14, "Is any sick among you? let him call for the elders of the Church; and let them pray over him, anointing him with oil in the name of the Lord."

Eye. A sheet in the wind's eye. An early stage of intoxication.

A sight for sore eyes. A proverbial expression used of something that is very welcome, pleasant, and unexpected.

Eyes to the blind. A staff; perhaps in allusion to that given to Tiresias (*q.v.*) by Athene, to serve him for the eyes of which she had deprived him.

In my mind's eye. In my perceptive thought.

In the wind's eye. Directly opposed to the wind.

In the twinkling of an eye. Immediately, very soon.

My eye! or **Oh, my eye!** an exclamation of astonishment. *See* ALL MY EYE.

One-eyed. An expression of contempt; as, "I've never been in such a one-eyed town," *i.e.* such a poverty-stricken, mean, or unpleasing town.

One-eyed peoples. *See* ARIMASPIANS; CYCLOPS.

One might see that with half an eye. Easily; at a mere glance.

The eye of a needle. The words of Christ in *Matt*. xix, 24:—

> It is easier for a camel to go through the eye of a needle, than for a rich man to enter into the kingdom of God.

enshrine a proverbial saying, and there is no need to suppose that by "the eye of a needle" was intended the small arched entrance through the wall of a city, nor is there any evidence that such a gateway had any such name in Biblical times. *See* CAMEL. A similar Eastern proverb occurs at *Matt*. xxiii, 24:—

> Ye blind guides, which strain at a gnat and swallow a camel;

and "In Media a camel can dance on a bushel," meaning that there all things are possible, is another ancient Eastern saying.

The Eye of Greece. Athens.

> Athens, the eye of Greece, mother of arts.
> <div align="right">MILTON: <i>Paradise Regained</i>, iv, 240.</div>

The Eye of the Baltic. Gottland, in the Baltic.

The eye of the storm. An opening between the storm clouds. *Cp.* BULL'S EYE.

To cast sheep's eyes at one. *See* SHEEP.

To cry one's eyes out. To cry immoderately or excessively.

To have, or **keep, an eye on.** To keep strict watch on the person or thing referred to.

To have an eye to. To keep constantly in view; to act from motives of policy. *See* MAIN CHANCE.

To make eyes at. To look amorously or lovingly at.

To make someone open his eyes. To surprise him very much, and make him stare with wonder or admiration.

To pipe your eye. *See* PIPE.

To see eye to eye. To be of precisely the same opinion; to think both alike.

Up to the eyes. Wholly, completely; *as up to the eyes in work*, very fully occupied, *mortgaged up to the eyes*, to the last penny obtainable.

Eye-opener. Something that furnishes enlightenment, also, a strong, mixed drink, especially a morning pick-me-up.

Eye-service. Unwilling service; the kind that is only done when under the eye of one's master.

Servants, be obedient to them that are your masters . . . not with eye service, as men pleasers; but as the servants of Christ.—*Eph.* vi, 5, 6.

Eye-teeth. The canine teeth; so called because their roots extend upwards nearly to the orbits of the eyes.

He has cut his eye-teeth. *See* TOOTH.

To draw one's eye-teeth. To take the conceit out of a person; to fleece one without mercy;

Eye-wash. Flattery; soft sawder; fulsome adulation given for the purpose of blinding one to the real state of affairs.

Eyre (âr). **Justices in Eyre.** The ancient itinerant judges who, from about 1100 to 1285, used to ride on circuit from county to county holding courts. *Eyre* is from late Lat. *iterare*, to journey, Lat. *iter*, a journey.

F

F. The first letter in the Runic futhorc (*q.v.*), but the sixth in the Phœnician and Latin alphabets, and their derivatives. The Egyptian hieroglyph represented a horned asp, and the Phœnician and Semitic character a peg.

Double F (Ff or **ff)** as an initial in a few personal names, as *Ffoulkes, ffrench*, etc., is a mistaken use in *print* of the mediæval or Old English capital F (**ℱ**) as it appears *written* in engrossed leases, etc. In script the old capital *F* looked very much like two small f's entwined, and it so appears in all old documents, and in many modern legal ones, not only in the case of personal names but of all words beginning with a capital *F*. Its modern use is an affectation.

F is written on his face. The letter F used to be branded near the nose, on the left cheek of felons, on their being admitted to "benefit of clergy." The same was used for brawling in church. The custom was abolished by law in 1822.

F.A.N.Y. (British). First Aid Nursing Yeomanry, founded 1909. The first women to serve with the British Army besides regular nurses. In 1916 they began to drive ambulance convoys, and transport duties replaced their previous medical duties. Retained after 1918. Called out during the General Strike 1926. Active again on transport work, 1939-45.

F.E.R.T. *See* ANNUNCIATION, ORDER OF THE.

F.F.V. First Families of Virginia, a snobbish term used in the 19th century by descendants of the first settlers.

F.O.B. Free on board; meaning that the shipper, from the time of shipment, is free from all risk. Also prices are quoted as, for instance, "F.O.B. Detroit" where the goods have to make a long and expensive journey from the place of manufacture to their purchaser.

Fabius (fā' bi ùs). *See* CUNCTATOR, *and* FABIAN SOCIETY, *below.*

The American Fabius. George Washington (1732-99), whose military policy was similar to that of Fabius. He wearied out the English troops by harassing them, without coming to a pitched battle.

Fabian Society (fā' bi àn). An association of socialists founded in January, 1884, by a small group of "intellectuals," which included George Bernard Shaw (1856-1950) and Sidney Webb (1859-1947) among others. As announced in its prospectus, it

aims at "the reorganization of society by the emancipation of land and industrial capital from individual and class ownership and the vesting of them in the community for the general benefit" . . . and at "the transfer to the community of the administration of such industrial capital as can conveniently be managed socially."

The name is derived from Quintus Fabius (275-203 B.C.), surnamed "Cunctator" (*q.v.*), the Roman general, who won his way against Hannibal by wariness not by violence, by caution, not by defiance.

Fables. *See* ÆSOP; PILPAY. La Fontaine (1621-95) has been called the French Æsop, and John Gay (1685-1732) the English.

Fabliaux (fab' lē ō). Metrical tales, for the most part comic and satirical, and intended primarily for recitation by the Trouvères, or early poets north of the Loire, in the twelfth and thirteenth centuries. The word is used very widely, for it includes not only such tales as *Reynard the Fox*, but all sorts of familiar incidents of knavery and intrigue, legends, family traditions, and caricatures, especially of women.

Face. A colloquialism for cheek, impudence, self-confidence, etc., as "He has face enough for anything," *i.e.* cheek or assurance enough. The use is quite an old one:

I admire thy impudence; I could never have had the face to have wheedled the poor knight so. — ETHEREGE: *She Would if She Could*, I, i (1668).

Face to face. In the immediate presence of each other; two or more persons facing each other.

On the face of it. To all appearance; in the literal sense of the words.

That puts a new face on the matter. Said when fresh evidence has been produced, or something has happened which sets the case in a new light and makes it look different.

To draw a long face. To look dissatisfied or sorrowful, in which case the mouth is drawn down at the corners, the eyes are dejected, and the face has an elongated appearance.

To face down. To withstand with boldness and effrontery.

To face the music. To stand up boldly and meet a crisis without faltering.

To fly in the face of. To oppose violently and unreasonably: to set at defiance rashly.

To have two faces, or **to keep two faces under one hood.** To be double-faced; to pretend to be very religious, and yet live an evil life.

To look a person in the face, or **full in the face.** To meet with a steady gaze; implying lack of fear, or, sometimes, a spirit of defiance.

To lose face. To be lowered in the esteem of others through an affront to one's dignity—a matter of the utmost importance in the Far East.

To put a bold, or **a good, face on the matter.** To make the best of a bad matter; to bear up under something disagreeable.

To save one's face. Narrowly to avoid almost inevitable disgrace, disaster, or discomfiture.

To shut the door in one's face. To put an end to the negotiations, or whatever is in hand.

Face-lifting. A method of enhancing beauty or concealing the marks of age by an operation in which the skin of the face is tightened and wrinkles removed.

Faced. With a facing, lining of the cuffs, etc.; used of an inferior article bearing the surface of a superior one, as when cotton-velvet has a silk surface.

Bare-faced. *See* BAREFACED.

Shame-faced. Having shame expressed in the face. *Cp.* SHAMEFAST.

Face-card or **Faced-card.** A court card, a card with a face on it.

Facile princeps. By far the best; admittedly first.

Facilis descensus Averno. *See* AVERNUS.

Factotum (Lat. *facere totum*, to do everything required). One who does for his employer all sorts of services. Sometimes called a *Johannes Factotum.* Formerly the term meant a "Jack-of-all-trades," and it is in this sense that Greene used it in his famous reference to Shakespeare:—

There is an upstart Crow, beautified with our feathers, that with his *Tygers heart wrapt in a Players hide*, supposes he is as well able to bumbast out a blanke verse as the best of you: but being an absolute *Johannes fac totum*, is in his owne conceit the onely Shake-scene in a countrie.—*Green's Groatsworth of Wit* (1592).

Fad. A hobby, a temporary fancy, a whim. Perhaps a contraction of faddle in "fiddle-faddle."

Fade. To fade in, to fade out. Phrases applied in cinematography to the operation of causing a picture to appear or disappear

gradually; and similarly in broadcasting, it describes the fading of sound into silence.

In golf, a ball so struck that towards the end of its flight it drifts towards the right is said to have a bit of fade.

Faërie (fā' ĕr i). The land of the fays or faeries. The chief fay realms are Avalon, an island somewhere in the ocean; Oberon's dominions, situated "in wilderness among the holtis hairy"; and a realm somewhere in the middle of the earth, where was Pari Banou's palace.

For learnëd Colin [Spenser] lays his pipes to gage.
And is to Faëry gone a pilgrimage,
DRAYTON: *Eclogue*, iii.

Faerie Queene, The (fâr i kwēn). An allegorical romance of chivalry by Edmund Spenser, originally intended to have been in 12 books, each of which was to have portrayed one of the 12 moral virtues. Only six books of twelve cantos each, and part of a seventh, were written (I to III published in 1590, IV to VI in 1596, and the remaining fragments in 1611). It details the adventures of various knights, who personify different virtues, and belong to the court of Gloriana, the Faerie Queene, who sometimes typifies Queen Elizabeth.

Fag. Slang for a cigarette. The origin of the word is not known. **Fag-end.** The stub of a cigarette.

In public schools a fag is a small boy who waits upon a bigger one. The system was already established at Eton and Winchester in the 16th century. Dr. Arnold (1795-1842) the famous headmaster of Rugby, described it as "the power given by the supreme authorities of the School to the Sixth Form to be exercised by them over the lower boys for the sake of securing a regular government among the boys themselves and avoiding the evil of anarchy." *Tom Brown's School Days* and many volumes of reminiscences reveal the system at its best and worst.

Faggot. A bundle of sticks.

In mediæval times heretics were often burned at the stake with faggots, hence an embroidered representation of a faggot was worn on the arm by those who had recanted their "heretical" opinions. It was designed to show what they merited but had narrowly escaped.

Faggot votes. Votes obtained by the nominal transfer of properly to a person whose income was not otherwise sufficient to qualify him for being a voter.

The "faggot" was a bundle of property divided into small lots for the purpose stated above.

Lord Lonsdale had conveyed to him a certain property, on which he was to vote in that borough, as, what was familiarly called a faggot vote.—SIR F. BURDETT: *Parl. Debates*, 1817.

The culinary *faggot*, deriving from the Latin *ficatum*, the liver of a pig fattened on figs, is a dish of liver chopped and seasoned with herbs before baking.

Faience. Majolica. So called from Faenza, where, in 1299, it was first manufactured. It is termed majolica because the first specimens the Italians saw came from Majorca.

Faint. Faint heart ne'er won fair lady. An old proverb, with obvious meaning. It occurs in Phineas Fletcher's *Britain's Ida* (ca. v, st. 1), 1628, but is probably a good deal older.

Fair. As PERSONAL EPITHETS.

Edwy, or Eadwig, King of Wessex (938-58).

Charles IV, King of France, *le Bel* (1294, 1322-8).

Philippe IV of France, *le Bel* (1268, 1285-1314).

Fair Geraldine. *See* GERALDINE.

The Fair-haired. Harold I, King of Norway (reigned 872-930).

Fair Maid of Anjou. Lady Edith Plantagenet (fl. 1200), who married David. Prince Royal of Scotland.

Fair Maid of Brittany. Eleanor (d. 1241), granddaughter of Henry II, and, after the death of Arthur (1203), the rightful sovereign of England. Her uncle, the usurper King John, imprisoned her in Bristol Castle, which she left to enter a nunnery at Amesbury. Her father, Geoffrey, John's elder brother, was Count of Brittany.

Fair Maid of Kent. Joan (1328-85), Countess of Salisbury, wife of the Black Prince, and only daughter of Edmund Plantagenet, Earl of Kent. She had been twice married ere she gave her hand to the prince.

Fair Maid of Norway. Margaret (1283-90), daughter of Eric II of Norway, and granddaughter of Alexander III of Scotland. On his death she was recognized by the states of Scotland as successor to the throne. She set out for her kingdom, but died at sea from seasickness.

Fair Maid of Perth. Katie Glover, heroine of Scott's novel of the same name, is supposed to have lived in the early 15th century, but is not a definite historical character, though her house is still shown at Perth.

Fair Rosamond. *See* ROSAMOND.

A day after the fair. Too late for the fun; wise after the event. Here *fair* is (through French) from Lat. *feria*, a holiday, and is quite unconnected with the adjective *fair*, which is the A.S. *fæger*.

Fair and square. Honestly, justly, with straightforwardness.

Fair game. A worthy subject of banter; one who exposes himself to ridicule and may be fairly made a butt of.

Fair Trade. An old euphemism for smuggling.

In politics the phrase signifies reciprocity of protection or free trade; that is, free trade to those nations that grant free trade to us.

In a fair way. On the right tack.

Fairway. The clear run from hole to hole on a golf-course, etc.

The fair sex. Women generally; the phrase was modelled on the French *le beau sexe*.

Fair Isle. One of the Shetlands where a special pattern of knitting is done.

Fairy. The names of the principal fairies and of groups of similar sprites known to fable and legend are given throughout the DICTIONARY.

Fairies of nursery mythology wear a red conical cap; a mantle of green cloth, inlaid with wild flowers; green pantaloons, buttoned with bobs of silk; and silver shoon. Some accounts add that they carry quivers of adderslough, and bows made of the ribs of a man buried where "three lairds' lands meet"; that their arrows are made of bog-reed, tipped with white flints, and dipped in the dew of hemlock; and that they ride on steeds whose hoofs would not "dash the dew from the cup of a harebell."

> Fairies small Two foot tall,
> With caps red On their head
> Dance a round On the ground.
> JASPER FISHER: *Song from Fuimus Troes* (1633).

Fairy rings. Circles of rank or withered grass, often seen in lawns, meadows, and grass-plots, and popularly supposed to be produced by fairies dancing on the spot. In sober truth, these rings are simply an agaric or fungus below the surface, which has seeded circularly, as many plants do. Where the ring is brown and almost bare, the "spawn" has enveloped the roots and thus prevented their absorbing moisture; but where the grass is rank the "spawn" itself has died, and served as manure to the young grass.

> You demi-puppets, that
> By moonshine do the green-sour ringlets make,
> Whereof the ewe not bites.
> SHAKESPEARE: *Tempest*, v, 1.

Fairy sparks. The phosphoric light from decaying wood, fish, and other substances. Thought at one time to be lights prepared for the fairies at their revels.

Fait accompli (fā tá kom′ plē) (Fr.). An accomplished fact, something already done; a scheme which has been already carried out; often used in the sense of stealing a march on some other party.

I pointed out to Herr von Jagow that this *fait accompli* of the violation of the Belgian frontier rendered, as he would readily understand, the situation exceedingly grave.—*Sir Edward Goschen, Ambassador in Berlin, to Sir Edward Grey*, 8 Aug., 1914.

Faith. Act of faith. *See* AUTO DA FE.

Defender of the Faith. *See* DEFENDER.

In good faith. *"Bona fide"; "de bonne foi"*; with no ulterior motive.

To pin one's faith to. *See* PIN.

Faithful, in Bunyan's *Pilgrim's Progress*, is seized at Vanity Fair, burnt to death, and taken to heaven in a chariot of fire. A Puritan used to be called *Brother Faithful*. The active disciples of any cult are called *the faithful*.

Commander of the Faithful. The Caliph is so called by Mohammedans.

Father of the faithful. Abraham (*Rom*. iv; *Gal*. iii, 6-9).

Most Faithful King, The. The appellation by which the kings of Portugal used to be addressed by the Vatican. *Cp*. RELIGIOUS.

Fake. A fraud or swindle; also verb, as "to fake antiques," "to fake the accounts," *i.e.* to "cook" them, falsify them. The word is old thieves' slang from Dutch or German, and was originally *feague*. *Feaguing* a horse was making it look younger or stronger for purposes of sale, *Cp*. TO BISHOP.

Fakir (fā' kēr). Properly, a Mohammedan religious beggar or mendicant. Fakirs wear coarse black or brown dresses, and a black turban over which a red handkerchief is tied, and perform menial offices connected with burials, the cleaning of mosques, and so on. The use of the word has been extended to include both Moslem and Hindu holy men, often distinguished by their ascetisicm and indifference to pain or discomfort.

Fall. In music, a sinking of tone, a cadence.

That strain again! it had a dying fall:
O! it came o'er my ear like the sweet sound
That breathes upon a bank of violets,
Stealing and giving odour.
SHAKESPEARE: *Twelfth Night*, i, 1.

The strains decay,
And melt a way.
In a dying, dying fall.
POPE: *St. Cecilia's Day*.

In the fall. In the autumn, at the fall of the leaf. Though now commonly classed as an Americanism the term was formerly in good use in England, and is found in the works of Drayton, Middleton, Raleigh, and other Elizabethans.

What crowds of patients the town doctor kills,
Or how, last fall, he raised the weekly bills.
DRYDEN: *Juvenal*.

The Fall of man. The degeneracy of the human race in consequence of the disobedience of Adam.

Fall line. The point at which rivers begin to fall on their way to the sea. It is a term of American geology, but its implications are largely sociological, the fall line determining the location of cities and influencing the lives of those inhabiting the area, who are known as Fall Liners. For example, in the Southern States of U.S.A. the fall line runs through Virginia, down to Georgia and turns across to the Mississippi, producing circumstances and problems of national importance.

To ride for a fall. *See* RIDE.

To try a fall. To wrestle, when each tries to "fall" or throw the other.

I am given, sir . . . to understand that your younger brother, Orlando, hath a disposition to come in disguised against me to try a fall.—*As You Like It*, i, 1.

See also FALLING-BANDS.

To fall away. To lose flesh; to degenerate; to quit a party, as "his adherents fell away one by one."

To fall back upon. To have recourse to.

To fall flat. To lie prostrate or procumbent; to fail to interest, as "the last act fell flat."

To fall from. To violate, as "to fall from his word"; to tumble or slip off, as "to fall from a horse"; to abandon or go away from, as "to fall from grace," to relapse into sin.

To fall in. To take one's place with others; to concur with, as "he fell in with my views"— that is, his views or ideas fell into line with my views or ideas. *Cp*. FALL OUT.

To fall in love with. To become enamoured of.

To fall in with. To meet accidentally; to come across. This is a Latin phrase, *in aliquam casu incidere*.

To fall out. To quarrel; also, to happen. *Cp*. FALL IN.

Three children sliding on the ice
Upon a summer's day:
As it fell out they all fell in.
The rest they ran away.
PORSON: *Mother Goose*.

See ye fall not out by the way.—*Gen*. xlv, 24.

To leave the ranks; hence, to take one's departure, to desert some cause.

To fall short of. To be deficient of a supply. To fall short of the mark is a figure taken from archery, quoits, etc., where the missile falls to the ground before reaching the mark.

To fall sick. To be unwell. A Latin phrase. *In morbum incidere*. *Cp*. FALLING SICKNESS.

To fall through. To fail of being carried out or accomplished.

To fall together by the ears. To fight and scratch each other; to contend in strife. *See* EAR.

To fall under. To incur, as, "to fall under the reproach of carelessness"; to be submitted to, as, "to fall under consideration."

To fall upon. To attack, as "to fall upon the rear"; to throw oneself on, as, "he fell on his sword,"; to happen on, as, "On what day does Easter fall?"

To fall upon one's feet. To find oneself unexpectedly lucky; to find oneself in a situation where everything seems to go right. Evidently from the old theory that a cat always falls on its feet and is able to get away unhurt.

Falling sickness. Epilepsy, in which the patient falls suddenly to the ground. Shakespeare plays on the term:—

And honest Casca, we have the falling-sickness.
Brutus: He hath the falling-sickness.
Cassius: No, Cæsar hath it not: but you, and I,
                      Julius Cæsar, i, 2.

Falling stars. Meteors. Mohammedans believe them to be firebrands flung by good angels against evil spirits when they approach too near the gates of heaven. A wish wished as a star falls is supposed to come true.

Fallow. Fallow land is land ploughed and harrowed but left unsown. The word is A.S. *fælging*, connected with *fælga*, harrows for breaking crops, and is nothing to do with the *fallow* of *fallow deer*. Fallow in this sense means "reddish yellow," and is the A.S. *fealu*, which is related to Dut. *vaal*, Ger. *fahl*, and Lat. *palidus*, pale.

False. False colours. *See* COLOUR.

Falstaff (fawl' staf). A fat, sensual, boastful, and mendacious knight; full of wit and humour; he was the boon companion of Henry, Prince of Wales. (1 and 2 *Henry IV*, and *Merry Wives of Windsor*.) Hence, *Falstaffian*, possessing Falstaff's characteristics.

Falutin' *See* HIGH FALUTIN'

Fame. Temple of Fame. A Pantheon (*q.v.*) where monuments to the famous dead of a nation are erected and their memories honoured. Hence, *he will have a niche in the Temple of Fame*, he has done something that will cause his people to honour him and keep his memory green.

The temple of fame is the shortest passage to riches and preferment.—*Letters of Junius: Letter* lix.

Familiar, or **Familiar spirit** (Lat. *famulus*, a servant). A spirit slave, sometimes in human form, sometimes appearing as a cat, dog, raven, or other dumb creature, petted by a "witch," and supposed to be her demon in disguise.

Away with him! he has a familiar under his tongue.—*2 Henry VI*, iv, 7.

Familiarity. Familiarity breeds contempt. The proverb appears in English at least as early as the mid-16th century (Udall), and was well known in Latin.

Fan. Used from about 1900 as an abbreviation of *fanatic* (*q.v.*), an ardent admirer or devotee. Admiring letters written to the object of such devotion are known as **fan mail.**

Fanatic. Literally one who is possessed of the enthusiasm or madness of the temple, *i.e.* engendered by over-indulgence in religious observances (Lat. *fanum*, a temple—the Eng. *fane*). Among the Romans there were certain persons who attended the temples and fell into strange fits, in which they were credited with being able to see the spirits of the past and to foretell the events of the future.

      Earth's fanatics make
Too frequently heaven's saints.
      MRS. BROWNING: *Aurora Leigh*, ii, 448.

Fancy. Love—*i.e.* the passion of the *fantasy* or imagination.

    Tell me where is fancy bred,
    Or in the heart or in the head.
              Merchant of Venice, iii, 2.

The fancy. In early 19th-century sporting parlance a collective name for prize-fighters.

Fancy-man. Originally a *cavaliere servente* (*q.v.*) or *cicisbeo* (*q.v.*); one selected by a married woman to escort her to theatres, etc., to ride about with her, and to amuse her. It is now more usually applied to a harlot's *souteneur*.

Fancy-sick. Love-sick.

All fancy-sick she is, and pale of cheer.
          Midsummer Night's Dream, iii, 9.

Fanny Adams. *Sweet Fanny Adams*, meaning "nothing at all," though (especially by its initials alone) with a somewhat ambiguous connotation, is a phrase with a tragic origin. In 1810 a girl Fanny Adams was murdered at Alton, Hants, and her body cut up and thrown into the river Wey. With gruesome humour the Navy took up her name as a synonym for tinned mutton, and *Sweet Fanny Adams* became a phrase for anything worthless or, in fact, for nothing at all.

Fantom. An old spelling of PHANTOM (*q.v.*).

Far. A far cry. *See* CRY.

Far and away. Beyond comparison; as, "far and away the best," some person or thing beyond all rivalry.

Far and wide. To a good distance in every direction. "To spread the news far and wide," to blazon it everywhere.

Far-fetched. Not closely connected; strained, as, "a far-fetched simile," a "far-fetched allusion."

The passion for long, involved sentences . . . and far-fetched conceits . . . passed away, and a clearer and less ornate style became popular.—LECKY: *England in the Eighteenth Century*, vol. i, ch. 1.

Far from it. Not in the least; by no means; quite the contrary. If the answer to "Was he sober at the time?" is "Far from it," the implication is that he was in a considerably advanced state of intoxication.

Far gone. Deeply affected: as, "far gone in love."

Farce. A grotesque and exaggerated kind of comedy, full of ludicrous incidents and expressions. The word is the Old French *farce*, stuffing (from Lat. *farcire*, to stuff), hence an interlude stuffed into or inserted in the main piece, such interludes always being of a racy, exaggerated comic character.

Farce is that in poetry which grotesque is in a picture. The persons and action of a farce are all unnatural, and the manners false, that is inconsisting with the characters of mankind.—DRYDEN: *Parallel of Poetry and Painting*.

The following couplet was written by Garrick on the self-knighted Sir John Hill (d. 1775) a quack whose adventures would make a book in themselves. He had written a farce in which Garrick played, and which was a failure:—

For physic and farces his equal there scarce is,
His farces are physic, his physic a farce is.

Fare. (A.S. *faran*, to go, to travel; connected with Lat. *portare*, to carry.) The noun formerly denoted a journey for which a sum was paid; but now the sum itself, and, by extension, the person who pays it. In certain English dialects, *e.g.* Suffolk, the verb *fare* is used in its original sense of "to go," also as an auxiliary with much the same sense as "to do,"

Farewell. Good-bye; adieu. It was originally addressed to one about to start on a journey, expressing the wish that the *fare* would be a good one.

Farrago (fä ra′ gō). **A farrago of nonsense.** A confused heap of nonsense. *Farrago* (Lat.) is properly a mixture of *far* (meal) with other ingredients for the use of cattle.

A farrago
Or a made dish in Court: a thing of nothing.
BEN JONSON: *Magnetick Lady*, i, 1.
Yet do I carry everywhere with me such a confounded farrago of doubts, fears, hopes, wishes.—SHERIDAN: *Rivals*, ii, 1.

Farthing. A fourth part. Silver penny pieces used to be divided into four parts thus, ⊕. One of these quarters was a *feorthing* or fourth part.

I don't care for it a brass farthing. James II debased all the coinage, and issued, amongst other worthless coins, brass pence, halfpence, and farthings.

Fascinate. Literally, to cast a spell by means of the eye (Lat. *fascinum*, a spell). The allusion is to the ancient notion of bewitching by the power of the eye: *Cp.* EVIL EYE.

None of the affections have been noted to fascinate and bewitch, but love and envy.—BACON: *Essays; Of Envy*.

Fascinator. An opera cloak was thus termed in the 18th century; an evening-wear head veil.

Fascism (făsh′ izm, făs′ izm). A political movement, originating in Italy, that takes its name from the old Roman *fasces*, a bundle of sticks borne by lictors as an emblem of office. Its leader was Benito Mussolini (1883-1945), who took advantage of the discontent felt in Italy after World War I to form a quasi-military party, to combat communism. In 1922 the Fascists "marched on Rome," overthrew the existing government and replaced it by a government under Mussolini, with the king as a figurehead. Thenceforward Italy was a Fascist country until her defeat in 1943.

Fascism is strictly authoritarian and as such has its followers and imitators in other countries and societies. As evolved by Mussolini it was a technique for obtaining power, for exacting a ruthless militarism and rejecting all appeal to ethics. Struggles between races are beneficial, said Mussolini: "War is to the man what maternity is to the woman. . . . I find peace depressing and the negation of the fundamental values of man." Fascism denies democracy; the liberty of the individual is abolished in favour of the state; the inequality of men and races is proclaimed as immutable and even beneficial. "Credere, obbedire, combattere" (To have faith, to obey, to fight) is the final slogan.

Fashion. In a fashion or **after a fashion.** "In a sort of a way"; as, "he spoke French after a fashion."

Fast. The adjective was used figuratively of a person of either sex who is addicted to pleasure and dissipation; of a young man or woman who "goes the pace,"

To play fast and loose. To run with the hare and hunt with the hounds; to blow both hot and cold; to say one thing and do another. The allusion is probably to an old cheating game that used to be practised at fairs. A belt was folded, and the player was asked to prick it with a skewer, so as to pin it *fast* to the table; having so done, the adversary took the two ends, and *loosed* it or drew it away, showing that it had not been pierced at all.

He forced his neck into a noose,
To show his play at fast and loose;

And when he chanced t'escape, mistook,
For art and subtlety, his luck.
BUTLER: *Hudibras*, iii, 2,

Fasti (făs' tī). Working days; when, in Rome, the law-courts were open. Holy days (*dies non*), when the law-courts were not open, were, by the Romans, called *ne-fasti*.

The *Fasti* were listed in calendars, and the registers of events occurring during the year of office of a pair of consuls was called *fasti consulares*; hence, any chronological list of events or office-holders became known as *fasti*, and hence such titles as *Fasti Academœi Mariscallanœ Aberdonenses*, selections from the records of the Marischal College, Aberdeen.

Fasting. In its literal meaning this is a complete abstention from food and drink, but the word is more usually applied to an extreme limitation of diet. In this sense its therapeutical value has been proved in various forms of disease. Fasting has, however, been adopted more as a religious exercise from the earliest times. Celts, Mexicans, Peruvians, Assyrians, Egyptians, Hebrews, and Mohammedans have alike used it as a means of penance or purification. Contemplatives and men of the stature of Mahatma Gandhi have found it helpful. Fasting plays an important part in Christian Church discipline; with more or less strictness the 40 days of Lenten fasting are observed throughout the Christian world.

In more recent times fasting (under the epithet of hunger-striking) has been practised, by political and other prisoners as a method of calling attention to alleged injustices.

Fat. In printer's slang is composition that does not entail a lot of setting, and hence can be done quickly. **A bit of fat.** An unexpected stroke of luck; also, the best part of anything, especially, among actors, a good part in a play.

Fat-head. A silly fool, a dolt.

The fat is in the fire. Something has been let out inadvertently which will cause a "regular flare up"; it's all over, all's up with it. The allusion is to frying; if the grease is spilt into the fire, the coals smoke and blaze so as to spoil the food.

The Fat:—
Alfonzo II of Portugal (1212-23).
Charles II of France, *le Gros* (832, 884-8).
Louis VI of France, *le Gros* (1078, 1108-37).

Fata (fä' tà) (Ital., a fairy). Female supernatural beings introduced in Italian mediæval romance, usually under the sway of Demogorgon (*q.v.*).

Fata Morgana. A sort of mirage in which objects are reflected in the sea, and sometimes on a kind of aerial screen high above it, occasionally seen in the neighbourhood of the Straits of Messina, so named from Morgan le Fay (*q.v.*) who was fabled by the Norman settlers in England to dwell in Calabria.

Fatal Gifts.
See CADMUS, HARMONIA, NECKLACE, NESSUS, NIBELUNGEN HOARD, OPAL, TOLOSA, etc.

Fate. The cruel fates. The Greeks and Romans supposed there were three Parcæ or Fates, who arbitrarily controlled the birth, life, and death of every man. They were Clotho (who held the distaff), Lachesis (who spun the thread of life), and Atropos (who cut it off when life was ended); called "cruel" because they paid no regard to the wishes of anyone.

Father. The name is given as a title to Catholic priests; also to the senior member of a body or profession, as the *Father of the House of Commons*, the *Father of the Bench*, and to the originator or first leader of some movement, school, etc., as the *Father of Comedy* (Aristophanes), the *Father of English Song* (Cædmon). In ancient Rome the title was given to the senators (*cp.* PATRICIAN; CONSCRIPT FATHERS), and in ecclesiastical history to the early Church writers and doctors.

To father a thing on one. To impute it to him; to assert that he was the originator of it.

Father of his Country. Cicero was so entitled by the Roman senate. They offered the same title to Marius, but he refused to accept it.

Several of the Cæsars were so called—Julius, after quelling the insurrection of Spain; Augustus, etc.

Cosimo de' Medici (1389-1464).

George Washington, the first President of the United States (1732-99).

Andrea Doria (1468-1560). Inscribed on the base of his statue by his countrymen of Genoa.

Andronicus Palæologus II assumed the title (about 1260-1332).

Victor Emmanuel II (1820-78) first king of Italy, was popularly called Father of his Country in allusion to his unnumbered progeny of bastard children.

Fathers of the Church. All those writers of the first twelve centuries whose works on Christian doctrine are considered of weight and worthy of respect. But the term is more strictly applied to those teachers of the first twelve, and especially of the first six centuries who added notable holiness and complete orthodoxy to their learning. The chief are:—

1st century, Clement of Rome; 2nd cent., Cyril of Jerusalem, Ignatius of Antioch, Justin, Irenaeus, Polycarp; 3rd cent., Cyprian, Dionysius; 4th cent., Hilary, Ephraem the Syrian, Optatus, Epiphanius; 5th cent., Peter Chrysologus, Pope Leo the Great, Cyril of Alexandria, Vincent of Lerins; 6th cent., Caesarius of Arles; 7th cent., Isidore; 8th cent. John the Damascene, Venerable Bede; 11th cent., Peter Damian; 12th cent., Anselm, Bernard.

Fatima (făt′ i mā); The last of Bluebeard's wives. See BLUEBEARD. She was saved from death by the timely arrival of her brother with a party of friends. Mohammed's daughter was called Fatima.

Fatted Calf. See CALF.

Fault. In geology, the break or displacement of a stratum of rock.

At fault. Not on the right track. Hounds are at fault when the fox has jumped upon a wall, crossed a river, cut through a flock of sheep, or doubled like a hare, because the scent, i.e. the track, is broken.

To a fault. In excess; as, kind to a fault. Excess of every good is more or less evil.

To find fault. To blame; to express disapprobation.

Fauna (faw′ nà). The animals of a country at any given period. The term was first used by Linnæus in the title of his Fauna Suecica (1746), a companion volume to his Flora Suecica of the preceding year, and is the name of a Roman rural goddess, sister of Faunus.

Nor less the place of curious plant he knows—
He both his Flora and his Fauna shows.
CRABBE: Borough.

Faust (foust). The hero of Marlowe's Tragical History of Dr. Faustus (about 1589) and Goethe's Faust (1790-1833) is founded on Dr. Johann Faust, or Faustus, a magician and astrologer, who was born in Wurtemberg and died about 1538.

The idea of making a pact with the devil for worldly reasons is of Jewish origin and dates back to the time of Christ. All subsequent legends of necromancers became crystallized round the person of Faustus. In 1587 he appeared for the first time as the central figure in The History of Dr. Faustus, the Notorious Magician and Master of the Black Art (published at Frankfort-on-Main), which immediately became popular and was soon translated into English, French, and other languages.

The basis of the legend is that, in return for twenty-four years of further life during which he is to have every pleasure and all knowledge at his command, Faust sells his soul to the devil, and the climax is reached when, at the close of the period, the devil claims him for his own.

The story of Faust has struck the fancy of composers. Spohr's opera Faust, 1816; Wagner's Overture Faust, 1839; Berlioz's Damnation de Faust, 1846; Gounod's opera, 1859; Boito's Mefistophele, 1868; Zollner's opera Faust, 1887. In addition to these are numerous musical compositions, ballets, etc.

There was another Faust of whom stories used to be told in the 16th century. This was Johann Fust or Faust (d. c. 1466), a German money-lender, who formed a partnership with the printer Gutenberg in 1450. On the termination of this in 1455 Fust demanded the repayment of the capital he had put into the business, and in default of this seized all Gutenberg's types and plant. With this Fust started business on his own account, with his son-in-law Peter Schoffer as manager. Gutenberg was obliged to carry on his business with inferior types and presses.

Faux pas (fō pa) (Fr.). A "false step"; a breach of manners or moral conduct.

The fact is, his Lordship, who hadn't it seems,
Form'd the slightest idea, not ev'n in his dreams,
That the pair had been wedded according to law,
Conceived that his daughter had made a faux pas.
BARHAM (INGOLDSBY): Some account of a New Play.

Favonius (fō vō′ ni ús). The Latin name for the tephyr or west wind. It means the wind favourable to vegetation.

If to the torrid Zone her way she bend,
Her the coole breathing of Favonius lend,
Thither command the birds to bring their quires,
That Zone is temp'rate.
HABBINGTON: Castara: To the Spring (1634).

Favour. Ribbons made into a bow are called favours from being bestowed by ladies on the successful champions of tournaments (Cp. TRUE-LOVERS' KNOT.)

Here, Fluellen; wear thou this favour for me, and stick it in thy cap.—SHAKESPEARE: Henry V, iv, 7.

To curry favour. See CURRY.

Favourites. False curls on the temples; a curl of hair on the temples plastered with some cosmetic; whiskers made to meet the mouth.

Yet tell me, sire, don't you as nice appear
With your false calves, bardash, and fav'rites here? MRS. CENTLIVRE: The Platonic Lady; Epilogue (1721).

Fay. See FAIRY.

Morgan le Fay. See MORGAN.

Fearless (Fr., Sans peur). Jean, Duke of Burgundy (1371-1419). Cp. BAYARD.

Feast. A day set apart for the commemoration of some event or mystery in the life of Our

Lord, His mother, or some event of religious importance. Feasts are either immovable or movable.

The chief immovable feasts in the Christian calendar are the four quarter-days—viz. the Annunciation or Lady Day (March 25th), the Nativity of John the Baptist (June 24th), Michaelmas Day (September 29th), and Christmas Day (December 25th). Others are the Circumcision (January 1st), Epiphany (January 6th), All Saints' (November 1st), and the several Apostles' days.

The movable feasts depend upon Easter Sunday. They are—

Palm Sunday. The Sunday next before Easter Sunday.

Good Friday. The Friday next before Easter Sunday.

Ash Wednesday. The first day of Lent, 40 days before Easter.

Sexagesima Sunday. Sixty days before Easter Sunday.

Ascension Day or Holy Thursday. Fortieth day after Easter Sunday.

Pentecost or Whit Sunday. The seventh Sunday after Easter Sunday.

Trinity Sunday. The Sunday next after Pentecost.

Feast of Reason. Conversation on and discussion of learned and congenial subjects.

There St. John mingles with my friendly bowl
The feast of reason and the flow of soul.
POPE: Imitations of Horace, ii, 1.

Feasts of Reason. See REASON, GODDESS OF.

Feather. A broken feather in one's wing. A scandal connected with one.

A feather in your cap. An honour to you. The allusion is to the very general custom in Asia and among the American Indians of adding a feather to the headgear for every enemy slain. The ancient Lycians, and many others had a similar custom, and it is still usual for the sportsman who kills the first woodcock to pluck out a feather and stick it in his cap.

The custom, in one form or another, seems to be almost universal; in Hungary, at one time, none might wear a feather but he who had slain a Turk, and it will be remembered that when Gordon quelled the Taiping rebellion he was honoured by the Chinese Government with the "yellow jacket and peacock's feather."

Birds of a feather flock together. See BIRD.

Fine feathers make fine birds. Said sarcastically of an overdressed person who does not live up to his (or her) clothes.

In full feather. Flush of money. In allusion to birds not on the moult.

Tarred and feathered. See TAR.

Tickled with a feather. Easily moved to laughter. "Pleased with a rattle, tickled with a straw" (POPE: Essay on Man), is more usual.

To feather one's nest well. To provide for one's own interests; to secure one's own financial well-being. The phrase is commonly used with a somewhat disapproving implication.

To smooth one's ruffled feathers. To recover one's equanimity after an insult, etc.

Featherweight. Something of extreme lightness in comparison with others of its kind. The term is applied to a jockey weighing not more than 4 st. 7 lb. or to a boxer weighing not more than 9 st. In the paper trade the name is given to very light antique, laid, or wove book papers. They are manufactured mainly from esparto, and are very loosely woven.

Feature (Lat. facere, to make) formerly meant, the "make" or general appearance of anything. Spenser speaks of God's "secret understanding of our feature"—i.e. make or structure. It now means principally that part which is most conspicuous or important. Thus we speak of the chief feature of a painting, a garden, a book, etc.; a moving picture is said to feature such and such a popular favourite or incident.

February. The month of purification amongst the ancient Romans. (Lat. februo, to purify by sacrifice.)

Candlemas Day (q.v.), February 2nd, is the feast of the Purification of the Virgin Mary. It is said, if the weather is fine and frosty at the close of January and beginning of February, we may look for more winter to come than we have seen up to that time.

Si sol splendescat Maria Purificante,
Major erit glacies post festum quam fuit ante.
SIR T. BROWNE: Vulgar Errors.

The Dutch used to term the month Spokkelmaand (vegetation-month); the ancient Saxons, Sprote-cal (from the sprouting of potwort or kele); they changed it subsequently to Sol-monath (from the returning sun). In the French Republican calendar it was called Pluviose (rain-month, January 20th to February 20th). See also FILL-DYKE.

Federal. The modern usage of this term in the U.S.A. relates to the central government of the country as distinct from the governments of the various component States. In this sense the Federal Bureau of Investigation (F.B.I.) is an organization of the Department of Justice of the U.S. Government which investigates offences against the laws of the U.S.A., especially such crimes as bank robberies, espionage, blackmail, etc. Its agents are known familiarly as G-men (Government men) and are all specially selected for intrepidity as criminal-hunters.

Federalist. The party in America which in 1787 was in favour of adopting the constitution of that year. Besides Washington, it was led by Alexander Hamilton and John Adams, who later became enemies. The party controlled the government until 1801. It was also the name of a newspaper during this period which provided a model of good prose.

Federal States. The name given in the American War of Secession (1861-65) to those northern states which combined against the eleven southern or Confederate states (*q.v.*).

Fee. This is an Anglo-French word, from Old High Ger. *fehu*, wages, money, property, cattle, and is connected with the A.S. *feoh*, cattle, goods, money. So in Lat. *pecunia*, money, from *pecus*, cattle. Capital is *capita*, heads (of cattle), and chattels is a mere variant.

At a pin's fee. *See* PIN.

To hold in fee. To hold as one's lawful and absolute possession.

> Once did she hold the gorgeous east in fee:
> And was the safeguard of the west.
>   WORDSWORTH: *The Venetian Republic.*

Fehmgericht. *See* VEHMGERICHT.

Felix the Cat, hero of early animated cartoons, appeared in 1921, in a production by Pat Sullivan. Throughout his many adventures Felix the black cat kept on walking, and thus originated a once-familiar catch-phrase.

Fell, Dr. *See* DOCTOR. FELL.

Fell's Pointer. U.S.A. 18th century. A resident of the dockside area of Baltimore.

Fellow-traveller. A person in sympathy with a political party but not a member of that party; used most often of Communist sympathizers. The term (Rus. *poputchik*) was coined by Leon Trotsky.

"He is but one of a reputed short list of seven fellow-travellers under threat of expulsion."—Comment in *Time and Tide*, May 1st, 1948, on the Labour Party's expulsion of one of its members.

Felo de se (fē' lō dē sē). The act of a suicide when he commits self-murder; also, the self-murderer himself. Murder is felony, and a man who murders himself commits this felony—*felo de se.*

Feme-covert (fem kŭv' ert). A married woman, *i.e.* a woman who is under the *cover*, authority, or protection of her husband. The word is the Anglo-French and Old French form of Mod. Fr. *femme*

couverte, and *couverte* is still used in fortification, etc., with the sense "protected."

Feme-sole (fem sōl). A single woman. **Feme-sole merchant,** a woman, married or single, who carries on a trade on her own account.

Feminine ending. An extra unaccented syllable at the end of a line of verse, *e.g.* in lines 1 and 3 of the following:—

> With rue my heart is laden
>   For golden friends I had,
> For many a rose-lipt maiden
>   And many a light-foot lad.
>   A. E. HOUSMAN.

Femynye (fem' i ni). A mediæval designation for the kingdom of the Amazons. Gower terms Penthesilea "queen of Feminee."

> He [Theseus] conquered al the regne of Femynye,
> That whylom was y-claped Scithia;
> And weddede the quene Ipolita.
>   CHAUCER: *Knight's Tale*, 8.

Fence. Slang term for a receiver of stolen goods.

To sit on the fence. To take care not to commit oneself; to hedge. The characteristic attitude of "Mr. Facing-Both-Ways."

Fennel. Fennel was anciently supposed to be an aphrodisiac, thus "to eat conger and fennel" (two hot things together) was provocative of sexual licence. Hence Falstaff's remark about Poins:—

He plays at quoits well, and eats conger and fennel, and drinks off candles' ends for flap-dragons, and rides the wild mare with the boys.—2 *Henry IV*, ii, 4.

It was also emblematical of flattery, and may have been included among the herbs distributed by Ophelia (*Hamlet* iv, 5) for this reason.

> Fenel is for flaterers,
>   An evil thing it is sure:
> But I have alwa'es meant truely,
>   With constant heart most pure.
> A *Nosegay alwaies Sweet* (in "A Handful of Pleasant Delights," 1584).

Uppon a banke, bordring by, grew women's weedes Fenell I meane for flatterers, fit generally for that sexe.
    GREENE: *A Quip for an Upstart Courtier* (1592).

The herb was also credited with being able to clear the sight, and was said to be the favourite food of serpents, with the juice of which they restore their sight when dim.

Fenrir or **Fenris** (fen' rĕr). In Scandinavian mythology the wolf of Loki (*q.v.*). He was the brother of Hel (*q.v.*), and when he gaped one jaw touched earth and the other heaven. In the *Ragnarok* he swallows the sun and conquers Odin; but being conquered by Vidar, he was cast into Niflheim, where Loki was confined.

Feræ Naturæ (fer' ē nā tū' rē) (Lat., of savage nature). The legal term for animals living in a wild state, as distinguished from those which are domesticated.

Women are not comprised in our Laws of Friendship: they are *Feræ Naturæ.*—DRYDEN: *The Mock Astrologer,* iv.

Ferdinand the Bull, whose adventures were related in a Walt Disney film of 1939, first appeared in a book by Munro Leaf. His delight in the smell of flowers became for a time proverbial.

Ferragus. The giant of Portugal in *Valentine and Orson* (*q.v.*). The great "Brazen Head" (*q.v.*), that told those who consulted it whatever they required to know, was kept in his castle.

Ferrara. *See* ANDREA FERRARA.

Ferrara Bible, The. *See* BIBLE, SPECIALLY NAMED.

Ferrex and Porrex. Two sons of Gorboduc, a mythical British king, who divided his kingdom between them. Porrex drove his brother from Britain, and when Ferrex returned with an army he was slain, but Porrex was shortly after put to death by his mother. The story is told in Geoffrey of Monmouth's *Historia Regum Britanniæ,* and it forms the basis of the first regular English tragedy, *Gorboduc,* or *Ferrex and Porrex,* written by Thomas Norton and Thomas Sackville, Lord Buckhurst, and acted in 1561.

Fesse. *See* HERALDRY.

Fetch. A wraith—the disembodied ghost of a living person; hence *fetch-light,* or *fetch-candle,* a light appearing at night and supposed to foretell the death of someone. Fetches most commonly appear to distant friends and relations, at the very instant preceding the death of those they represent.

Fetches. Excuses, tricks, artifices.

Deny to speak with me? They are sick? they are weary?
They have travelled all the night? Mere fetches.
                    King Lear, ii, 4.

Fetish (fet′ ish). The name given by the early Portuguese travellers to amulets and other objects supposed to have supernatural powers, used by the natives on the Guinea Coast; from Port, *feitço,* sorcery, charm (Lat. *factitius,* artificial). Hence, an idol, and object of devotion. Fetishism is found in all primitive nations, taking the form of a belief that the services of a spirit may be appropriated by the possession of its material emblem. In psychopathology the word is used to designate a condition or perversion in which sexual gratification is obtained from other than the genital areas of the body, or from some object that has become thus emotionally charged.

Feud (fūd). A word of two very different meanings. In its more usual sense a feud is a continuous, bitter quarrel between individuals, families, or parties. Feuds have never played much part in the English manner of life. *See* VENDETTA. In its other sense a feud is a fief, or land held in fee (*q.v.*).

Feudal System, The. A system founded on the tenure of feuds or fiefs, given in compensation for military service to the lord of the tenants. It was introduced into England by William the Conqueror, who made himself owner of the whole country and allowed the nobles to hold it from him by payment of homage and military and other service. The nobles in turn had vassals bound to them by similar obligations.

Feuilleton (fė yė tong) (Fr., from feuille, a leaf). The part of French newspapers devoted to tales, light literature, etc.; hence, in England a serial story in a newspaper, or the "magazine page."

Fey (fā). Epithet applied when a person suddenly breaks into a state of light-heartedness. This was formerly supposed to be an indication of an early approaching death. The word is the A.S. *fœge* (on the point of death, or doomed to die).

FFI. *Forces Françaises de l'Interieure.* Frenchmen within France who continued the struggle against Germany after the fall of their country in 1940. They were first armed by Britain and their co-operation with British parachute agents was co-ordinated and directed by an organization at the War Office. Later the United States also co-operated through their OSS (*q.v.*). These Frenchmen were familiarly known as *Maquis* (*q.v.*). As soon as the allied invasion landed in June 1944 they came into the open as a civilian army.

Fiasco. A failure. In Italy they cry *Ola, ola, fiasco!* to an unpopular singer.

In Italian *fiasco* means a flask, and it is uncertain how it became, in Venetian slang, to mean a failure, an attempt that comes to nothing.

Fiat (fī′ át) (Lat., let it be done). **I give my fiat to that proposal.** I consent to it. A fiat in law is an order of the court directing that something stated be done.

Fiat experimentum in corpore vili. *See* CORPUS VILE.

Fiat justitia ruat cœlum. *See* PISO'S JUSTICE.

Fib. An attendant on Queen Mab in Drayton's *Nymphidia.* Fib, meaning a falsehood, is the Latin *fabula,* a fable.

Fiddle (A.S. *fithele;* perhaps connected with mediæval Lat. *vitula* or *vidula,* whence *violin*). A violin or stringed instrument of that nature. In Stock Exchange slang a *fiddle* is one-sixteenth of a pound—1s. 3d.

Fit as a fiddle. In fine condition, perfect trim or order.

He was first fiddle. Chief man, the most distinguished of the company. The allusion is to the leader of concerts, who leads with a fiddle.

To play second fiddle. To take a subordinate part.

To fiddle about. To trifle, fritter away one's time, mess about, play at doing things instead of doing them. To fiddle with one's fingers is to move them about as a fiddler moves his fingers up and down the fiddle-strings.

To fiddle. To manipulate accounts, etc., to one's own advantage, or to the advantage of the parties concerned. "He fiddled it," might indicate that he covered up a deficiency in the accounts.

Fiddle-de-dee! An exclamation signifying what you say is nonsense.

All the return he ever had ... was a word, too common, I regret to say, in female lips, viz., fiddle-de-dee. — DE QUINCEY: *Secret Societies.*

Fiddle-faddle. To busy oneself with nothing; to dawdle; to talk nonsense.

Ye may as easily
Outrun a cloud, driven by a northern blast,
As fiddle-faddle so.
        JOHN FORD: *The Broken Heart,* i, 3. (1633).

Fiddler. Slang for a sixpence; also for a farthing.

Drunk as a fiddler. *See* DRUNK.

Fiddlesticks! An exclamation signifying what you say is not worth attention; much the same as *fiddle-de-dee* (*q.v.*).

The devil rides on a fiddlestick. *See* DEVIL (PHRASES).

Fidei Defensor. *See* DEFENDER OF THE FAITH.

FIDO. Fog Investigation and Dispersal Operation. A method of dispersing fog on airfields by ejecting burning petrol from jets along the runways, developed in Britain during World War II.

Fie! An exclamation indicating that what is reproved is indelicate or undesirable. It is an old word, and is found in many languages; it seems to be an instinctive sound uttered on experiencing something disagreeable.

No word ne wryteth he
Of thilke wikke ensample of Canacee,
That lovede hir owne brother sinfully;
Of swiche cursed stories I sey "fy."
        CHAUCER: *Man of Lawes Prologue,* 77.

Field. In huntsman's language, the field means all the riders.

In heraldry, the entire surface of the shield.

In military language, the place where a battle is fought, or is about to be fought; the battle itself, or the campaign.

In sportsmen's language it means all the horses of any one race.

In the field. A competitor for a prize. A term in horse-racing, as, "So-and-so was in the field." Also in war, as, "the French were in the field already."

To take the field. To make the opening moves in a campaign; to move the army preparatory to battle.

Field-day. A day of particular excitement or importance. A military term, meaning a day when troops have manœuvres or field practice.

Field of Blood. Aceldama (*q.v.*).

Field of fire. (Mil.). That part of the terrain before infantry or machine guns which their weapons can cover — *i.e.* which is not interrupted by woods, buildings, or the contours of the ground.

Field of force. A term used in physics to denote the range within which a force, such as magnetism, is, effective.

Field of vision or **view.** The space in a telescope, microscope, etc., within which the object is visible

Fierabras, Sir (fi' ér à bràs). One of Charlemagne's paladins, and a leading figure in many of the romances. He was the son of Balan (*q.v.*), King of Spain, and for height of stature, breadth of shoulder, and hardness of muscle he never had an equal. His pride was laid low by Olivier, he became a Christian, was accepted by Charlemagne as a paladin, and ended his days in the odour of sanctity. *See* BALAN.

Fiery Cross, The. A signal anciently sent round the Scottish clans in the Highlands summoning them to assemble for battle. It was symbolical of fire and sword, and consisted of a cross the ends of which had been burnt and then dipped in the blood of some animal slain for the purpose — a relic of Gaelic rites. See Scott's *Lady of the Lake,* canto iii, for an account of it.

The Ku Klux Klan adopted this symbol when it arose after the American Civil War.

Fifth. Fifth column. Persons in a country who, whether as individuals or as members of an organization, are ready to give help to an enemy. The origin of the phrase is attributed to General Mola who, in the Spanish Civil War (1936-39), said that he had four columns encircling Madrid and a fifth column working for him in the city.

Fifty-four Forty or **Fight.** A slogan used in the U.S.A. presidential election of 1846. For some years there had been a dispute with Britain as to the northern boundary of the U.S.A. in the far west. The U.S.A. claimed that their territory should extend as far north as the southern border of Russian Alaska, which was 54° 40′ N.; Great Britain rejected this, and in 1818 it was agreed that the disputed territory should be jointly administered for ten years, which was later extended indefinitely. In 1846 the question was brought forward again in the U.S.A. as an issue in the election. Shortly afterwards, the new President Polk came to an amicable agreement that U.S. territorial claims should end on the 49th parallel.

Fig. Most phrases that include the word *fig* have reference to the fruit as being an object of trifling value; but in

In full fig, meaning "in full dress," *figged out,* "dressed up," etc., the word is a variant of *feague* (*see* FAKE).

I don't care a fig for you; not worth a fig. Nothing at all. Here fig is either an example of something comparatively worthless or the Spanish *fico*—adopted as English by the Elizabethans—a gesture of contempt made by thrusting the thumb between the first and second fingers, much as we say, "I don't care that for you," snapping the fingers at the same time. *See* THUMB (*To bite one's thumb*).

A fig for Peter.

2 *Henry VI*, ii, 9.

The figo for thy friendship.

Henry V, iii, 6.

Fig leaf. The leaf of the fig tree or the banyan, according to the Bible story (*Gen.* iii, 7) used by Adam and Eve to cover their nakedness after the Fall. In the days of Victorian prudery tin fig leaves were fitted to statuary in the museums, Crystal Palace, etc.

Figaro (fig′ à rō). A type of cunning dexterity, and intrigue. The character is in the *Barbier de Séville* (1775) and *Mariage de Figaro* (1784), by Beaumarchais. In the former he is a barber, and in the latter a valet; but in both he outwits everyone. There are several operas founded on these dramas, as Mozart's *Nozze di Figaro*, Paisiello's *Il Barbiere di Siviglia*, and Rossini's *Il Barbiere di Siviglia*.

Fight. He that fights and runs away May live to fight another day. An old saw found in many languages. Demosthenes, being reproached for fleeing from Philip of Macedon at Chæronea, replied, "A man that runs away may fight again."

He that fights and runs away
May turn and fight another day;
But he that is in battle slain
Can never rise to fight again.

These lines occur in James Ray's *Complete History of the Rebellion,* 1749. A similar sentiment is expressed in *Hudibras,* iii, 3:

For those that fly may fight again,
Which he can never do that's slain.

Fighting French, or **La France Combattante,** included all Frenchmen at home and abroad who joined together to collaborate with the Allied Nations in their war against Germany. After the fall of France, in 1940, General de Gaulle gathered round him such French troops, etc., as had escaped from France and formed them into a body called the Free French, with the cross of Lorraine for their emblem. On July 14th, 1942, this name was changed to The Fighting French. Not only did French troops fight side by side with the Allies in Africa, Italy, and wherever else there was fighting to be done, but in France itself they worked and fought behind the lines, organizing resistance and making themselves an annoyance and terror to the German occupying authorities.

One of the greatest deeds of this body was the march of General Le Clerc with his column from Lake Chad across the Sahara to join the British 8th Army in Libya. Strengthened and made into an armoured division Le Clerc's men fought thenceforward throughout the war and were given the honour of being the first formation to enter Paris, 23rd August, 1944.

Figure. From Lat. *fingere,* to shape or fashion; not etymologically connected with Eng. *finger,* though the primitive method of calculating was doubtless by means of the fingers. For Roman figures, etc., *see* NUMERALS.

A figure of fun. Of droll appearance, whether from untidiness, quaintness, or other peculiarity. "A pretty figure" is a rather stronger expression.

Figure-head. A figure on the head or projecting cutwater of a sailing ship, which has ornamental value but is of no practical use; hence a nominal leader who has no real authority but whose social or other position inspires confidence.

Filch. To steal or purloin. A piece of 16th-century thieves' slang of uncertain origin. *File* (*q.v.*) was used in much the same sense, but there is no evidence of etymological connexion.

With cunning hast thou filched my daughter's heart.
Midsummer Night's Dream, i, 2.

A *filch* or *filchman* was a staff with a hook at the end, for plucking clothes from hedges, articles from shop windows, etc.

File. Old slang for a rapscallion or worthless person; also for a pick-pocket. It comes from the same original as the word *vile,* though in the sense in which it is sometimes used, as meaning a hard-headed, heartless person, it seems to have been connected with the hard, rasping tool, a file.

In single file. Single line; one behind another. (Fr. *file*, a row.).

Rank and file. Soldiers and non-commissioned officers as apart from commissioned officers; hence, the followers in or private members of a movement as apart from its leaders. *Rank* refers to men standing abreast, *file* to men standing behind each other.

Filibuster (fil' i bŭs ter). A piratical adventurer, a buccaneer (*q.v.*). The word is through Span, *filibustero* from Dut. *vrijbuiter*, a freebooter.

To filibuster. In U.S.A. politics, to manœuvre to frustrate the passing of a bill. It is based on the right of a member of Congress not to be interrupted so long as he holds the floor of the House. The member may recite or talk about any subject under the sun until the time available for passing the bill is exhausted.

Filioque Controversy (fil i ō' kwė). An argument that long disturbed the Eastern and Western Churches, and the difference of opinion concerning which still forms one of the principal barriers to their fusion. The point was: Did the Holy Ghost proceed from the Father *and* the Son (*Filio-que*), or from the Father only? The Western Church maintains the former, and the Eastern the latter dogma. The *filio-que* was recognized by the Council of Toledo, 589.

The gist of the argument is this: If the Son is one with the Father, whatever proceeds from the Father must proceed from the Son also. This is technically called "The Procession of the Holy Ghost."

Fill-dyke. The month of February, when the rain and melted snow fills the ditches to overflowing.

February fill-dyke, be it black or be it white [wet or snowy];
But if it be white it's better to like. *Old Proverb.*

Filter (Lat. *feltrum*, felt; *filtrum*, a strainer). Literally, to run through felt, as jelly is strained through flannel. The Romans strained the juice of their grapes through felt into the wine-vat, after which it was put into the casks.

Fin de siècle (Fr., end of the century). It has come to mean decadent with particular reference to the 19th century.

Finance. By devious routes this word comes from the late Latin *finis*, a settlement of a debt, or the winding up of a dispute by the payment of ransom. Hence, revenue derived from fines or subsidies and, in the plural, available money resources. Thus we say, "My finances are

exhausted," meaning I have no more funds or available money.

Financial year. The annual period for which accounts are made up. The Finance Act is the name given to the annual Act of Parliament that legalizes the proposals contained in the Budget. The financial year of the British Government ends on the 31st of March.

Find. Findings keepings! An exclamation made when one has accidentally found something that does not belong to him, and implying that it is now the finder's property. This old saying is very faulty law.

Fine. Fine as fivepence. An old alliterative saying meaning splendidly dressed or turned out.

Fine feathers make fine birds. *See* FEATHER.

In fine. To sum up; to come to a conclusion; in short.

One of these fine days. Some time or other; at some indefinite (and often problematical) date in the future.

The fine arts. Those arts which chiefly depend on a delicate or fine imagination, as music, painting, poetry, and sculpture, as opposed to the *useful arts*, *i.e.* those which are practised for their utility and not for their own sake, as the arts of weaving, metal-working, and so on.

Fingal (fing' gàl). The great Gaelic semi-mythological hero, father of Ossian (*q.v.*), who was purported by Macpherson to have been the original author of the long epic poem *Fingal* (1762), which narrates the hero's adventures.

Finger (A.S. *finger*). The old names for the fingers are:—

A.S. *thuma*, the thumb.

Towcher (the finger that touches), *foreman*, or *pointer*. This was called by the Anglo-Saxons the *scite-finger*, *i.e.* the shooting finger, and is now commonly known as the index finger, because it is the one used in pointing.

Long-man or *long finger*.

Lech-man or *ring-finger*. The former means "medical finger," and the latter is a Roman expression, "*digitus annularis*." Called by the Anglo-Saxons the *gold-finger*. This finger between the long and little finger was used by the Romans as a ring-finger, from the belief that a nerve ran through it to the heart. Hence the Greeks and Romans used to call it the *medical* finger, and used it for stirring mixtures, under the notion that nothing noxious could touch it without its giving instant warning to the heart. It is still a general notion in parts of England that it is bad to rub salve or scratch the skin with any but the ring finger.

At last he put on her medical finger a pretty, handsome gold ring, whereinto was enchased a precious toadstone of Beausse.—RABELAIS: *Pantagruel*, iii, 17.

Little-man or *little finger*. Called by the Anglo-Saxons the *ear-finger*, because it can, from its diminutive size, be most easily introduced into the orifice of the ear.

The fingers each had their special significance in alchemy, and Ben Jonson says—

The thumb, in chiromancy, we give to Venus;
The fore-finger to Jove; the midst to Saturn;
The ring to Sol; the least to Mercury.
Alchemist, i, 2.

Blessing with the fingers. *See* BLESSING.

Cry, baby, cry; put your finger in your eye, etc. This nursery rhyme seems to be referred to in *Comedy of Errors*, ii, 2:—

No longer will I be fool,
To put the finger in the eye and weep.

Fingers were made before forks. The saying is used (especially at mealtimes) when one wants to convey that ceremony is unnecessary. It makes an interesting commentary on this self-evident statement that forks were not introduced into England until about 1620, before which period fingers were used.

His fingers are all thumbs. Said of a person awkward in the use of his hands.

To keep one's fingers crossed. To hope for success, to try to ensure against disaster. From the superstition that making the sign of the cross will avert bad luck.

Lifting the little finger. Tippling. In holding a tankard or glass, many persons stick out or lift up the little finger.

My little finger told me that. The same as "A little bird told me that" (*see* BIRD), meaning, I know it, though you did not expect it. The expression is in Molière's *Malade Imaginaire*.

By the pricking of my thumbs,
Something wicked this way comes.
Macbeth, iv, 1.

The popular belief was that an itching or tingling foretold some change or other.

To have a finger in the pie. To assist or mix oneself officiously in any matter. Said usually in contempt, or censoriously.

To lay, or **put, one's finger upon.** To point out precisely the meaning, cause, etc.; to detect with complete accuracy.

To twist someone round one's little finger. To do just what one likes with him, to be master of his actions.

Finger-print. An impression taken in ink of the whorls of lines on the finger. In no two persons are they alike, and they never change through the entire life of any individual; hence,

they are of very great value as a means of identifying criminals.

Though the individuality of finger-prints had long been known, the publication of Sir Francis Galton's *Finger Prints* (1893) and *Finger Print Directory* (1895) drew attention to the facts. The full value of finger-prints was developed by Sir Edward Henry who devised a numerical formula for classifying the impressions. The Henry system has been widely adopted by the police organizations of the world.

Fir-tree. Atys was metamorphosed into a fir-tree by Cybele, as he was about to lay violent hands on himself. (OVID: *Metamorphoses*, x, 2.)

Fir-cone. This forms the tip of the thyrsus (*q.v.*) of Bacchus because the juice of the fir-tree (*turpentine*) used to be mixed by the Greeks with new wine to make it keep.

Fire. (A.S. *fyr*; Gr. *pur*.)

Fire away! Say on; say what you have to say. The allusion is to firing a gun; as, You are primed up to the muzzle with something you want to say; fire away and discharge your thoughts.

I have myself passed through the fire; I have smelt the smell of fire. I have had experience in trouble, and am all the better for it. The allusion is to the refining of gold, which is passed through the fire and so purged of all its dross.

I will go through fire and water to serve you; *i.e.* through any difficulties or any test. The reference may be to the ordeals of fire and water which were common methods of trial in Anglo-Saxon times.

No smoke without fire. To every scandal there is some foundation. Every effect is the result of some cause.

The Great Fire of London (1666) broke out at Master Farryner's, the king's baker, in Pudding Lane (the Monument now marks the spot) and after three days and nights was arrested at Pie Corner, Smithfield, and at the Temple, Fleet Street. St. Paul's Cathedral, eighty-nine other churches, 13,200 houses were burnt down, and 373 acres within the walls and 64 acres without were devastated. In the City itself only 75 acres 3 roods remained unconsumed.

To fire up. To become indignantly angry; to flare up, get unduly and suddenly excited.

We do not fire first, gentlemen. According to tradition this very chivalrous reply was made to Lord Charles Hay (in command of the Guards) at the opening of the battle of Fontenoy (1745) by the French Marquis d'Auteroche after the former had advanced from the British lines and invited the French commander to order his men to fire. The story is told by the historian Espagnac as well as by Voltaire, but it is almost certainly *ben trovato,* and is not borne out by the description of the battle written a few days after the encounter by Lord Charles to his father, the Marquis of Tweeddale.

Fire-brand. An incendiary; one who incites to rebellion; like a blazing brand which sets on fire all it touches.

Our fire-brand brother, Paris, burns us all.
Troilus and Cressida, ii, 2.

Fire-drake or **Fire-dragon.** A fiery serpent, an ignis-fatuus of large proportions, superstitiously believed to be a flying dragon keeping guard over hid treasures.

There is a fellow somewhat near the door, he should be a brazier by his face, for, o' my conscience, twenty of the dog-days now reign in 's nose. . . . That fire-drake did I hit three times on the head.—*King Henry VIII,* v, 3.

Fire-eaters. Persons ready to quarrel for anything. The allusion is to the jugglers who "eat" flaming tow, pour molten lead down their throats, and hold red-hot metal between their teeth. Richardson, in the 17th century; Signora Josephine Girardelli (the original Salamander), in the early part of the 19th century; and Chaubert, a Frenchman, of the present century, were the most noted of these exhibitors.

At first hand. By one's own knowledge or personal observation.

First Fleet. The first convoy of ships taking convicts to Australia in 1788. The second fleet arrived in 1790. To have been a *first fleeter* became a matter of some pride, and the expression was in use as late as 1848.

First floor. In England the first floor is the story next above the ground-floor, or entrance floor; but in America it is the ground floor itself.

First-fruits. The first profitable results of labour. In husbandry, the first corn that is cut at harvest, which, by the ancient Hebrews, was offered to Jehovah. We also use the word figuratively, as, the first-fruits of sin, the first-fruits of repentance.

First light. Roughly, dawn. Used in World War II to signify the earliest time at which infantry can see to make their way forward; *first tank light,* about half an hour later, is the earliest time that a tank, closed down for battle, can see to move. The phrases *last light* and *last tank light* are used at the end of the day.

Fish. The fish was used as a symbol of Christ by the early Christians because the letters of its Greek name—Ichthus (*q.v.*)—

formed a monogram of the words Jesus Christ, Son of God, Saviour.

Ivory and mother-o'-pearl counters used in card games, some of which are more or less fish-shaped are so called, not from their shape, but from Fr. *fiche,* a peg, a card-counter. *La fiche de consolation* (a little piece of comfort or consolation) is the name given in some games to the points allowed for the rubber.

Fish day (Fr. *jour. maigre*). A day when persons in the Roman Catholic Church are forbidden to eat meat without ecclesiastical permission; viz. all Fridays and ember days, Ash Wednesday, the Wednesdays of Lent, the vigils of Pentecost, Assumption, All Saints, and Christmas.

Fish-wife. A woman who hawks fish about the streets.

Fish-wives are renowned for their powers of vituperation; hence the term is applied to any blatant, scolding woman.

A fish out of water. Said of a person who is out of his usual environment and so feels awkward and in the way; also of one who is without his usual occupation and is restless in consequence.

A pretty kettle of fish. *See* KETTLE.

I have other fish to fry. I am busy and cannot attend to anything else just now.

Neither fish, flesh, nor fowl; or **neither fish, flesh, nor good red herring.** Suitable to no class of people; neither one thing nor another. Not fish (food for the monk), not flesh (food for the people generally), nor yet red herring (food for paupers).

To drink like a fish. *See* DRINK.

To fish for compliments. To try to obtain praise usually by putting leading questions.

To fish in troubled waters. To scramble for personal advantage in times of rebellion, war, etc.; to try to make a calamity a means to personal profit.

Five. The pentad, one of the mystic numbers, being the sum of $2 + 3$, the first *even* and first *odd* compound. Unity is God alone, *i.e.* without creation. Two is diversity, and three (being $1 + 2$) is the compound of unity and diversity, or the two principles in operation since creation, and representing all the powers of nature.

Bunch of fives. Pugilistic slang for the fist.

Five fingers. A fisherman's name for the star-fish.

The Five Nations. A description applied by Kipling to the British Empire—the Old Country, with Canada, Australia, South Africa, and India.

In American history the term refers to the five confederated Indian tribes inhabiting the present State of New York, viz. the Mohawks, Oneidas, Onondagas, Cayugas, and Senecas. Known also as the Iroquois Confederacy.

The Five Points. *See* CALVINISM.

Five senses. The five senses are feeling, hearing, seeing, smelling, tasting.

The five wits. Common sense, imagination, fantasy, estimation, and memory. Common sense is the outcome of the five senses; imagination is the "wit" of the mind; fantasy is imagination united with judgment; estimation estimates the absolute, such as time, space, locality, and so on; and memory is the "wit" of recalling past events.

> Four of his five wits went halting off.
> *Much Ado*, i, 1.

> These are the five witts removyng inwardly:
> First, "Common witte," and then "Ymagination,"
> "Fantasy," and "Estimation" truely.
> And "Memory."
> STEPHEN HAWES: *The Passe-tyme of Plesure* (1515)

Also used to mean the five senses.

> Alone and warming her five wits
> The white owl in the belfry sits.—TENNYSON.

Fiver. A five-pound note. A "tenner" is a ten-pound note.

Fix. In a fix. In an awkward predicament.

Fixed stars. Stars whose relative position to other stars is always the same, as distinguished from planets, which shift their relative positions.

Flags. The following national flags are described as though flying from a mast on the reader's left-hand side.

Argentine: 3 horizontal stripes, blue, white, blue.

Austria: 3 horizontal stripes, red, white, red.

Belgium: 3 vertical stripes, black, yellow, red.

Brazil: Green, with yellow lozenge in centre bearing a blue sphere with white band and stars.

British Empire: *See* UNION JACK.

Chile: 2 horizontal bands, white and red; in top left corner a white star on a blue square.

China: Red with blue square in left corner bearing a white sun.

Czechoslovakia: 2 horizontal stripes, red and white, with blue triangle in top left corner.

Denmark: Red with white cross from edge to edge.

Egypt: Green with white crescent and 35-pointed stars.

Eire: 3 vertical stripes, green, white, orange.

Ethiopia: 3 horizontal stripes, green, yellow, red.

Finland: White field with a blue cross.

France: 3 vertical stripes, blue, white, red.

Germany: 3 horizontal stripes, black, red, gold.

Greece: 9 horizontal stripes, blue and white, with white cross on a blue ground in top left corner.

Hungary: 3 horizontal stripes, red, "white, green.

Iceland: Blue, with a white-bordered cross from edge to edge.

India, Republic of: 3 horizontal stripes, saffron, white, green.

Iran: White bordered with green at top and red at bottom with arms of lion and sun in centre.

Iraq: 3 horizontal bars, black, white, green, with a red triangle bearing 2 white stars, in left corner.

Italy: 3 vertical stripes, green, white, red.

Japan: White, charged with red rising sun and 16 rays reaching to the edge.

Mexico: 3 vertical stripes, green, white, red.

Netherlands: 3 horizontal stripes, red, white, blue.

Norway: Red with a white-bordered blue cross to edges.

Pakistan: Green with white border, charged with white crescent and star.

Peru: 3 vertical stripes, red, white, red.

Poland: Flag divided horizontally, white and red.

Portugal: Flag divided vertically green and red.

Rumania: vertical stripes, blue, yellow, red.

Siam: 5 horizontal stripes, red, white, blue, white, red.

Spain: 3 horizontal stripes, red, yellow, red.

Sweden: Blue with yellow cross to edges.

Switzerland: Red field with white cross charged on it.

Turkey: Red with white crescent with star in its centre.

U.S.A.: *See* STARS AND STRIPES.

U.S.S.R.: Red with yellow hammer and sickle surmounted by a 5-pointed star, all in the top left corner.

Yugoslavia: 3 horizontal stripes blue, white, red.

On railways and elsewhere a **red flag** is used for signalling Danger; a **green flag** for Go ahead, or Proceed with Caution.

A **black flag** is the emblem of piracy or of no quarter. *See* BLACK.

The Red Flag is the symbol of international Socialism, red having been traditionally recognized as the colour of social revolutionary movements ever since the French Revolution. *The Red Flag* is a Socialist anthem written by Jim Connell and set to several tunes.

A **white flag** is the flag of truce or surrender, hence **to hang out the white flag** is to sue for quarter, to give in.

A **yellow flag** signals contagious disease on board ship, and all vessels in quarantine or having contagious disease aboard are obliged to fly it.

To flag down. To stop someone: from motor racing, in which the stewards wave a flag at the winner or at any driver they require to stop or to warn to proceed with caution.

The flag of distress. A flag hoisted at the masthead in reverse position to signal that trouble of some sort is on board.

To hang the flag half-mast high is in token of mourning or distress.

Flagellants (flă jel' ants). The Latin *flagellum* means a scourge, and this name is given to groups of fanatical persons who performed and administered exaggerated physical penances in public. They appeared in several places and times during the Middle Ages, particularly in Italy in 1260, and again in 1348 when the movement spread further afield in Europe. Although individuals such as St. Vincent Ferrer made use of the flagellant movements for legitimate religious purposes, the

Church has never encouraged the practice of public flagellation and has definitely condemned any excesses in this direction.

Flagellum Dei (Lat., the scourge of God). Attila was so called. *See* SCOURGE OF GOD.

Flak. The German abbreviation, adopted into English, of *Flugabwehrkanone*, meaning antiaircraft gun or gunfire.

Flam. Flattery for an object; blarney; humbug.
They told me what a tine thing it was to be an Englishman, and about liberty and property . . . I find it was a flam.—GODWIN: *Caleb Williams*, vol. ii, ch. v.

Flamboyant Architecture. A florid style which prevailed in France in the 15th and 16th centuries. So called from its flame-like tracery. The flamboyant architects of the decline, says Ruskin, were
"nothing but skilful masons, with more or less love of the picturesque, and redundance of undisciplined imagination, flaming itself away in wild and rich traceries, and crowded bosses of grotesque figure sculpture."

Flame. A sweetheart. "An old flame," a quondam sweetheart.

Flaming. Superb, captivating, ostentatious. The Fr. *flambant*, originally applied to those persons who dressed themselves in rich dresses "flaming" with gold and silver thread.

Flaming swords. Swords with a wavy or *flamboyant* edge, used now only for state purposes. The Dukes of Burgundy carried swords of this sort, and they were worn in our country till the accession of William III.

Flaminian Way. The great northern road of ancient Italy, constructed by C. Flaminius in 220 B.C. It led from the Flaminian gate of Rome to Ariminium (Rimini).

Flanders. Flanders' Babies. Cheap wooden jointed dolls common in the early 19th century.

Flanders Mare, The. So Henry VIII called Anne of Cleves, his fourth wife whom he married in January, 1540, and divorced in July of the same year. She died at Chelsea in 1557.

Flanders Poppies. The name given to the red artificial poppies sold in the streets on Remembrance Day for the benefit of ex-service men. The connexion with poppies comes from a poem by John McCrae, which appeared in *Punch*, December 8th, 1915:—
If ye break faith with us who die
We shall not sleep, though poppies grow
In Flanders fields.

Flaneur (Fr.). A lounger, gossiper. From *flaner*, to saunter about.

Flannels. To be awarded one's flannels. To gain one's cricket colours at Eton.

Flap-dragons. An old name for our "snap-dragon," *i.e.* raisins soaked in spirit, lighted, and floating in a bowl of spiritous liquor. Gallants used to drink flap-dragons to the health of their mistresses, and would frequently have lighted candle-ends floating in the liquor to heighten the effect. Hence:—
He drinks off candles' ends for flap-dragons.—2 *Henry IV*, ii, 4.

Flap-jack. A cake baked on a griddle or in a shallow pan, and so called from the practice of tossing it into the air when it was done on one side, and catching it flat with the brown side uppermost.
We'll have flesh for holidays, fish for fasting-days, and more o'er puddings and flap-jacks.—*Pericles*, ii, 1.

In the 20th century the word has been applied to a woman's flat powder compact.

Flapper. In the early years of this century a familiar term for a young girl in her teens. The hair was worn long and plaited in a pigtail, tied with a large bow, which may have suggested a flapper.

Flash. Showy, smart, "swagger"; as a *flash wedding*, a *flash hotel*. In Australia the term *flash* or *flashy* is applied "to anyone who is proud and has nothing to be proud of," J. KIRBY: *Old Times in the Bush of Australia*, 1895.

Also counterfeit, sham, fraudulent. **Flash notes** are forged notes; a **flash man** is a thief or the companion of thieves.

A mere flash in the pan. All sound and fury, signifying nothing; like the attempt to discharge an old flint-lock gun that ends with a flash in the lock-pan, the gun itself "hanging fire."

Flat. One who is not sharp.

Flat-foot. U.S.A. slang for a policeman. In English slang he is a **flattie.**

To be caught flat-footed. To be caught unprepared, as a football player who is tackled by an opponent before he has been able to advance.

To come out flat-footed. To state one's beliefs positively, as though firmly planted on one's feet.

Flat top. British and American name for aircraft-carrier (World War II).

Flat as a flounder. I knocked him down flat as a flounder. A flounder is one of the flatfish.

Flat as a pancake. Quite flat.

Flatterer. Vitellius (A.D. 15-69), Roman Emperor for a short while in 69. He was a sycophant of Nero's, and his name became a synonym for a flatterer (Tacitus, *Ann.*, vi, 32).

When flatterers meet, the devil goes to dinner. Flattery is so pernicious, so fills the heart with pride and conceit, so perverts the judgment and disturbs the balance of the mind, that Satan himself could do no greater mischief, so he goes to dinner and leaves the leaven of wickedness to operate its own mischief.

> Porteus, there is a proverb thou shouldst read:
> "When flatterers meet, the devil goes to dinner."
> PETER PINDAR: *Nil Admirari.*

Flea. A flea's jump. It has been estimated that if a man, in proportion to his weight, could jump as high as a flea, he could clear St. Paul's Cathedral with ease.

Aristophanes, in the *Clouds,* says that Socrates and Chærephon tried to measure how many times its own length a flea jumped. They took in wax the size of a flea's foot; then, on the principle of *ex pede Herculem,* calculated the length of its body. Having found this, and measured the distance of the flea's jump from the hand of Socrates to Chærephon, the knotty problem was resolved by simple multiplication.

A more flea-bite. A thing of no moment.

Great fleas have lesser fleas. No matter what our station in life, we all have some "hangers on."

> Hobbes clearly proves that every creature
> Lives in a state of war by nature;
> So naturalists observe a flea
> Has smaller fleas that on him prey,
> And these have smaller still to bite 'em,
> And so proceed *ad infinitum.*
> SWIFT: *Poetry; a Rhapsody.*

Fleeced. Cheated of one's money; sheared like a sheep.

Fleet, The. Fleet Marriages. Clandestine marriages, at one time performed without banns or licence by needy chaplains, in the Fleet Prison, London. As many as thirty marriages a day were sometimes celebrated in this disgraceful manner; and Malcolm tells us that 2,954 were registered in the four months ending with February 12th, 1705. The practice was suppressed and declared null and void in 1774.

Fleet Prison. The most notorious of the old debtors' prisons, the Fleet Prison stood on the site now occupied by the Memorial Hall, Farringdon Street. Its history was as dismal as the building itself. Originally used for prisoners committed by the Star Chamber, on the abolition of that court it became a prison for debtors, bankrupts, and persons charged with contempt of court. It was in charge of a warden, who bought the job and reimbursed himself from the exorbitant fees he charged prisoners for board, lodging, and innumerable privileges they never received. Every day a prisoner took it in turns to beg from passers-by, standing in a barred cage opening on the street. The prison was burned down in the Great Fire (1666) and

again by the Gordon Rioters in 1780. It was rebuilt again but in 1844 the prisoners were removed to the Queen's Bench Prison, and in 1864 the place was pulled down. *See* LIBERTIES OF THE FLEET, *under* LIBERTY.

Fleet Street. Now synonymous with journalism and newspaperdom, Fleet Street in London was a famous thoroughfare centuries before the first newspaper was published there at the close of the 18th century. It takes its name from the old Fleet River, which ran from Hampstead through Hockley-in-the-Hole to Saffron Hill, near where it joined the Hole Bourne (whence *Holborn*), flowing on with it under what is now Farringdon Street and New Bridge Street to fall into the Thames at Black-friars. It was navigable for coal-boats, etc., as far as Holborn Bridge (near the present Viaduct), but latterly became so foul that in 1764 it was arched over, and it is now used as a sewer. From earliest days there was a bridge (the Fleet Bridge) across the river at the modern Ludgate Circus.

Flemish School. A school of painting established by the brothers Van Eyck, in the 15th century. The chief *early* masters were Memling, Weyden, Matsys, and Mabuse. Of the *second* period, Rubens and Van Dyck, Snyders, and the younger Teniers.

Fleur-de-lis, -lys, or **-luce** (flĕr de lē, loos) (Fr., lily-flower). The name of several varieties of iris, and also of the heraldic lily, which is here shown and which was borne as a charge on the old French royal coat-of-arms.

In the reign of Louis VII (1137-80) the national standard was thickly charged with flowers. In 1365 the number was reduced by Charles VI to *three* (the mystical church number). Guillim, in his *Display of Heraldrie,* 1611, says the device is "Three toads erect, saltant"; in allusion to which Nostradamus, in the 16th century, calls Frenchmen *crapauds.* The *fleur-de-lis* was chosen by Flavio Gioja to mark the north point of the compass, out of compliment to the King of Naples, who was of French descent. Gioja was an early-14th-century Italian navigator to whom has been (incorrectly) ascribed the invention of the mariner's compass (*q.v.*).

Flibbertigibbet. One of the five fiends that possessed "poor Tom" in *King Lear.* Shakespeare got the name from Harsnet's *Declaration of Egregious Popish Impostures* (1603), where we are told of forty fiends which the Jesuits cast out, and among the number was "Fliberdigibet," a name which had previously been used by Latimer and others for a mischievous gossip. Elsewhere the name is apparently a synonym for Puck.

Flick. A cinematograph film; **to go to the flicks**, to go to the pictures.

Flimsy (flim′ zi). A newspaper journalist's term for newspaper copy, or a telegram. It arises from the thin paper (often used with a sheet of carbon paper to take a copy) on which the reporters and others write up their matter for the press. *Flimsy* is also used for a £5 bank note.

Fling. I must have a fling at . . . Throw a stone at something. To attack with words, especially sarcastically. To make a haphazard venture. Allusion is to hurling stones from slings.

To have his fling. To sow his wild oats. The Scots have a proverb:—

Let him tak' his fling and find oot his ain wecht (weight).

meaning, give him a free hand and he'll soon find his level.

Flint. To skin a flint. *See* SKIN.

Flirt. A coquette. The word is from the verb, flirt, as, "to flirt a fan," *i.e.* to open it, or wave it, with a sharp, sudden motion. The fan being used for coquetting, those who coquetted were called "flirts." In Dr. Johnson's day a *flirt*, according to his *Dictionary*, was "a pert hussey"; and he gives an account of one in No. 84 of *The Rambler*, which, in some few particulars, resembles the modern article.

Flittermouse. A bat (*cp.* Ger. *Fledermaus*). An earlier name was *flinder mouse*.

Then came . . . the flyndermows and the wezel and ther cam moo than xx whiche wolde not have comen yf the foxe had loste the feeld.—CAXTON: *Reynard the Fox*, xli.

Floor. I floored him. Knocked him down on the floor; hence figuratively, to overcome, beat, or surpass.

Flora's Dial. A fanciful or imaginary dial supposed to be formed by flowers which open or close at stated hours.

Florentine Diamond. One of the large and famous diamonds in the world, weighing 133 carats. It formed part of the Austrian crown jewels, and previously belonged to Charles, Duke of Burgundy. Tradition relates that it was picked up by a peasant and sold for half a crown.

Florid Architecture. The later stages of the pointed style in England (about 1480-1537), often called the Tudor, remarkable for its florid character, or profusion of ornament.

Florida. In 1512 Ponce de Leon sailed from France to the West in search of "the Fountain of Youth." He first saw land on Easter Day, which was then popularly called in Spain *pascua florida*, flowery Easter, and on that account called the new possession "Florida."

Florimel (flor′ i mel). A character in Spenser's *Faerie Queens* typifying the complete charm of womanhood.

Florin. An English silver coin representing 2s., first issued in 1849 as a tentative introduction of a decimal coinage, being one-tenth of a pound. Camden informs us that Edward III issued gold florins worth 6s., in 1337. The word is generally supposed to be derived from Florence; but as the coin had a lily on one side, probably it is connected with the Lat. *flos*, a flower. *Cp.* GRACELESS FLORIN.

Flotsam and Jetsam. Wreckage found in the sea or on the shore. "Flotsam," goods found *floating* on the sea; "jetsam," things thrown out of a ship to lighten it. (O.Fr. *floter*, to float; Fr. *jeter*, to throw out). *Cp.* LAGAN.

Flowers and Trees.

(1) Dedicated to heathen gods:

The Cornel cherry-tree to Apollo.

″	Cypress	″	Pluto.
″	Dittany	″	The Moon.
″	Laurel	″	Apollo.
″	Lily	″	Juno.
″	Maidenhair	″	Pluto.
″	Myrtle	″	Venus.
″	Narcissus	″	Ceres.
″	Oak	″	Jupiter.
″	Olive	″	Minerva.
″	Poppy	″	Ceres.
″	Vine	″	Bacchus.

(2) Dedicated to saints:

Canterbury Bells	to	St. Augustine of England.
Crocus	″	St. Valentine.
Crown Imperial	″	Edward the Confessor.
Daisy	″	St. Margaret.
Herb Christophe	″	St. Christopher.
Lady's-smock	″	The Virgin Mary.
Rose	″	Mary Magdalene.
St. John's-wort	″	St. John.
St. Barnaby's Thistle	″	St. Barnabas.

(3) National emblems:

Leek	emblem	of Wales.
Lily (*Fleur-de-lys*)	″	Bourbon France.
″ (*Giglio bianco*)	″	Florence.
″ white	″	the Ghibelline badge.
″ red	″	badge of the Guelphs.
Linden	″	Prussia.
Mignonette	″	Saxony.
Pomegranate	″	Spain.
Rose	″	England.
″ red, Lancastrians; white, Yorkists.		
Shamrock	emblem	of Ireland.
Thistle	″	Scotland.
Violet	″	Athens.
Sugar Maple.	″	Canada.

(4) Symbols:

Box	a symbol	of the resurrection.
Cedars	″	the faithful.
Corn-ears	″	the Holy Communion
Dates	″	the faithful.
Grapes	″	this is my blood.

Holly	"	the resurrection.
Ivy	"	the resurrection.
Lily	"	purity.
Olive	"	peace.
Orange-blossom	"	virginity.
Palm	"	victory.
Rose	"	incorruption.
Vine	"	Christ our Life.
Yew	"	death.

N.B.—The laurel, oak, olive, myrtle, rosemary, cypress, and amaranth are all funereal plants.

Flowers in Christian Traditions. Many plants and flowers, such as the aspen, elder, passion-flower, etc., play their part in Christian tradition.

The following are said to owe their stained blossoms to the blood which trickled from the cross:—

The *red anemone*; the *arum*; the *purple orchis*; the crimson-spotted leaves of the *roodselken* (a French tradition); the spotted *persicaria*, snake-weed.

Flowery Kingdom, The. China; a translation of the Chinese *Hwa-kwo*.

Flower of Chivalry. A name given to several knights of spotless reputation, *e.g.*—

Sir William Douglas, Knight of Liddesdale (slain 1353).

Bayard (*le chevalier sans peur et sans reproche*) (1475?-1524).

Sir Philip Sidney (1554-86),

Flower of Kings (Lat. *Flos regum*). King Arthur was so called by John of Exeter, who was Bishop of Winchester and died 1268.

Fluff. To bungle, to foozle, to do something carelessly and unskilfully. In theatrical parlance an actor fluffs a part when he loses or has not learned his words.

A little bit of fluff. Edwardian slang for a girl, especially a lively one of the fluffy variety.

Fluke. A lucky chance, a stroke or action that accidentally meets with success, as in billiards when one plays for one thing and gets another. Hence an advantage gained by luck more than by skill or judgment.

Flummery. Flattering nonsense, palaver. In Wales it is a food made of oatmeal steeped in water and kept till it has become sour. In Cheshire and Lancashire it is the prepared skin of oatmeal mixed with honey, ale, or milk; pap; blanc-mange. (Welsh, *llymry*, wash-brew, from *llym*, sour or sharp.)

Flummux, To. To bamboozle; to deceive; to be in a quandary. "I am regularly flummuxed"—*i.e.* perplexed. It is probably the Old English provincial word *flummocks*, to maul or mangle, or *flummock*, bewilderment, also untidiness or an untidy person.

Flunk. To fail in examinations or a test completely; found in U.S.A. by mid-19th century.

Flunkey. A male livery servant, a footman, lackey. The word usually has a contemptuous implication and suggests snobbery and toadyism; hence *flunkeydom*, *flunkeyish*, etc., pertaining to toadies. Probably a Scottish form of *flanker*, *i.e.* one who runs at the side (of carriages, etc.). *Cp.* Fr. *flanquer*, to run at the side of.

Flurry. The death-struggle of a whale after harpooning.

Flush. In cards, a whole hand of one suit.

Flush of money. Full of money. Similarly a *flush of water* means a sudden and full flow of water (Lat. *flux-us*).

To flush game. A gun dog is said to flush game when he disturbs them and they take to the air.

Flute. The Magic Flute. an opera by Mozart (*Die Zauberflöte*), The "flute" was bestowed by the powers of darkness, and had the power of inspiring love. Tamino and Pamina are guided by it through all worldly dangers to the knowledge of Divine Truth.

Flutter. Colloquial term for a small gamble.

Flutter the Dovecotes, To. To disturb the equanimity of a society. The phrase occurs in *Coriolanus* (v, 6).

Fly. An insect (plural *flies*): For the theatrical use, *see* FLYMAN.

It is said that no fly was ever seen in Solomon's temple; and according to Mohammedan legend, all flies shall perish except one, and that is the bee-fly.

The god or **lord of flies.** In the temple of Actium the Greeks used annually to sacrifice an ox to Zeus, who, in this capacity, was sur-named Apomyios, the averter of flies. Pliny tells us that at Rome sacrifice was offered to flies in the temple of Hercules Victor, and the Syrians offered sacrifice to the same insects. *See* ACHOR; BEELZEBUB.

Flies in amber. *See* AMBER.

Fly. Perspicacious in an unpleasant way, unlikely to be caught.

The fly in the ointment. The trifling cause that spoils everything; a biblical phrase.

Dead flies cause the ointment of the apothecary to send forth a stinking savour; so doth a little folly him that is in reputation for wisdom and honour.—*Eccles.* x, 1.

There are no flies on him. *He's* all right; he's very alert; you won't catch him napping.

To fly a kite. *See* KITE.

To fly in one's face. To get into a passion with a person; to insult; as a hawk, when irritated, flies in the face of its master.

To fly in the face of danger. To run in a fool-hardy manner into danger, as a hen flies in the face of a dog or cat.

To fly in the face of providence. To act rashly, and throw away good opportunities; to court danger.

To fly out at. To burst or break into a passion.

Fly-boy. The boy in a printing-office who lifts the printed sheets off the press; so called because he catches the sheets as they fly from the tympan immediately the frisket is opened.

Fly-by-night. One who defrauds his creditors by decamping at night-time; also the early name of a sedan-chair, and later of a horsed vehicle (hence FLY, a cab).

To come off with flying colours is to succeed triumphantly, as a ship coming out of action with all her colours flying.

Flying Dutchman. In the superstitions of seamen a spectral ship that is supposed to haunt the southern seas round the Cape of Good Hope. She is only to be seen in stormy weather and bodes no good to those who pass her. There are various stories to account for this mysterious and ghostly craft; that worked out by Wagner in his opera *Der Fliegende Hollander* (1843) was partly suggested by Heinrich Heine. Captain Marryat's novel *The Phantom Ship* (1839) tells of Philip Vanderdecken's successful but disastrous search for his father, the captain of the *Flying Dutchman*.

Fo'c's'le. *See* FORECASTLE.

Fogy or **Fogey. An old fogy.** A man of advanced years and somewhat antiquated ideas. A disrespectful but good-humoured description. Several fanciful derivations have been found for this word, but its origin is unknown.

Foil. That which sets off something to advantage. The allusion is to the metallic leaf used by jewellers to set off precious stones. (Fr. *feuille*; Lat. *folium*; Gr. *phullon*, a leaf.)

> I'll be your foil, Laertes. In mine ignorance
> Your skill shall, like a star i' the darkest night,
> Stick fiery off indeed.   *Hamlet*, v, 2.

Folio. Properly, a ream or sheet in its standard size; but when used of books it denotes a book whose sheets have been folded once only, so that each sheet makes two leaves; hence, a book of large size. Demy folio = $11\frac{1}{4} \times 17\frac{1}{2}$ in., crown folio = 10×15 in., and so forth. It is from the Ital. *un libro in foglio*, through the Fr. *in-folio*.

Folio so-and-so, in mercantile books, means page so-and-so, and sometimes the two pages which lie exposed at the same time, one con-

taining the credit and the other the debit of one and the same account. So called because ledgers, etc., are made in folio.

Printers call a page of MS. or printed matter a *folio* regardless of size.

In conveyances, MSS., typewritten documents, etc., seventy-two words, and in Parliamentary proceedings ninety words, make a folio.

Folkland. *See* BOCKLAND.

Folk-lore. The study or knowledge of the superstitions, mythology, legends, customs, traditions, sayings, etc., of a people. The word was coined in 1846 by W. J. Thoms (1803-85), editor of the *Athenæum*.

Follow. Follow-my-leader. A parlour game in which each player must exactly imitate the actions of the leader, or pay a forfeit.

Follow your nose, go straight on.

He who follows truth too closely will have dirt kicked in his face. Be not too strict to pry into abuse.

To follow suit. To do as the person before you has done. A phrase from card-playing.

Follower. In addition to its proper meaning of one who follows a leader, the word was used in Victorian days to designate a maid-servant's young man.

> Mrs. Marker . . . offers eighteen guineas . . .
> Five servants kept . . . No followers.
>   DICKENS: *Nicholas Nickleby*.

Folly. A fantastic or foolishly extravagant country seat, built for amusement or vainglory. *Fisher's Folly*, a large and beautiful house in Bishopsgate, with pleasure-gardens, bowling-green, and hothouses, built by Jasper Fisher, one of the six clerks of Chancery and a Justice of the Peace, is an historical example. Queen Elizabeth lodged there; in 1620 it was acquired by the Earl of Devonshire, and its site is now occupied by Devonshire Square.

> Kirby's castle, and Fisher's folly,
> Spinola's pleasure, and Megse's glory.
>   STOW: *Survey* (1603).

Font or **Fount.** A complete set of type of the same body and face, with all the points, accents, figures, fractions, signs, etc., that ordinarily occur in printed books and papers. A complete fount (which, of course, includes *italics*) comprises 275 separate pieces of type, not including the special characters needed in almanacs, astronomical and medical works, etc. The word is French, *fonte*, from *fondre* (to melt or cast). *Cp.* TYPE; LETTER.

The food of the gods. *See* AMBROSIA; NECTAR.

To become food for the worms, or **for the fishes.** To be dead and buried, or to be drowned.

Fool. We have many old phrases in which this word plays the chief part; among those which need no explanation are: **A fool and his money are soon parted; Fortune favours fools; There's no fool like an old fool;** etc. Others that may be mentioned are:—

A fool's paradise. To be in a fool's paradise is to be in a state of contentment or happiness that rests only on unreal, fanciful foundations.

As the fool thinks, so the bell clinks. A foolish person believes what he desires.

Every man hath a fool in his sleeve. No one is always wise; there is something of the fool about everyone.

At forty every man is a fool or **his own physician.** Said by Plutarch (*Treatise on the Preservation of Health*) to have been a saying of Tiberius. It implies that by the age of 40 a man ought to have learnt enough about his own constitution to be able to keep himself in health.

The wisest fool in Christendom. James I was so called by Henry IV of France, who learnt the phrase of Sully.

To be a fool for one's pains. To have worked ineffectively; to have had no reward for one's labours.

To fool about or **around.** To play the fool; to hang around in an aimless way.

To fool away one's time, money, etc. To squander it, fritter it away.

To make a fool of someone. To mislead him.

Young men think old men fools, old men know young men are. An old saying quoted by Camden in his *Remains* (1605, p. 228) as by a certain Dr. Metcalfe. It occurs also in Chapman's *All Fools*, v, 2 (acted 1599).

Court fools. From mediæval times till the 17th century licensed fools or jesters were commonly kept at court, and frequently in the retinue of wealthy nobles. Thus we are told, that the regent Morton had a fool, Patrick Bonny; Holbein painted Sir Thomas More's jester, Patison, in his picture of the chancellor; and as late as 1728 Swift wrote an epitaph on Dickie Pearce, the fool of the Earl of Suffolk, who died at the age of 63 and is buried in Berkeley Churchyard, Gloucestershire. Dagonet, the fool of King Arthur, is also remembered.

Among the most celebrated court fools are:— Rayère, of Henry I; Scogan, of Edward IV; Thomas Killigrew, called "King Charles's jester" (1611-82); Archie Armstrong (d. 1672), and Thomas Derrie, jesters in the court of James I.

James Geddes, to Mary Queen of Scots; his predecessor was Jenny Colquhoun.

Patch, the court fool of Elizabeth, wife of Henry VII.

Will Somers (d. 1560), Henry VIII's jester, and Patche, presented to that monarch by Cardinal Wolsey; and Robert Grene, jester in the court of Queen Elizabeth.

The fools of Charles V of France were Mitton and Thévenin de St. Léger; Haincelin Coq belonged to Charles VI, and Guillaume Louel to Charles VII. Triboulet was the jester of Louis XII and François I (1487-1536); Brusquet, of whom Brantôme says "he never had his equal in repartee," of Henri II; Sibilot and Chicot, of Henri III and IV; and l' Angély, of Louis XIII.

In *chess* the French name for the "bishop" is *fou* (*i.e.* fool), and they used to represent it in a fool's dress; hence, Regnier says: *Les fous sont aux échecs les plus proches des Rois* (14 *Sat.*). *Fou* is said to be a corruption of an eastern word for an elephant (*see* Thomas Hyde's *De Ludis Orientalium*, i, 4, 1689), and on old boards the places occupied by our "bishops" were occupied by elephants.

Foolscap. A standard size of printing paper measuring $13\frac{1}{2} \times 17$ in. and of writing paper measuring $13\frac{1}{4} \times 16\frac{1}{2}$ in. The name is derived from an ancient watermark, of which the first known specimen occurs in 1540.

Foot. The foot as a measure of length ($= 12$ in., $\frac{1}{3}$ of a yard, or $\cdot 3047075$ of a metre) is common to practically all nations and periods, and has never varied much more than does the length of men's feet, from which the name was taken.

In prosody, the term denotes a division in verse which consists of a certain number of syllables (or pauses) one of which is stressed. Here the term, which comes from Greece, refers to beating time with the foot.

At one's feet. "To cast oneself at someone's feet" is to be entirely submissive to him, to throw oneself on his mercy.

Best foot foremost. Use all possible dispatch. To "set on foot" is to set going. If you have various powers of motion, set your best foremost.

Nay, but make haste; the better foot before.
King John, iv, 2.

Enter a house right foot foremost (*Petronius*). It is unlucky to enter a house or to leave one's chamber left foot foremost. Augustus was very superstitious on this point. Pythagoras taught that it is necessary to put the shoe on the right foot first. Iamblichus tells us this symbolized that man's first duty is reverence to the gods.

First foot. *See* FIRST.

How are your poor feet? An old street-cry said to have originated at the Great Exhibition of London in 1851. Tramping about the galleries broke down all but trained athletes.

I have not yet got my foot in. I am not yet familiar and easy with the work. The allusion is to the preliminary exercises in Roman foot-races. While the signal was waited for, the candidates made essays of jumping, running, and posturing, to excite a suitable warmth and make their limbs supple. This was "getting their foot in" for the race. *Cp.* HAND.

To foot it. To walk the distance instead of riding it; also to dance.

> Lo how finely the graces can it foote to the Instrument. They dauncen deftly, and singen soote in their meriment.
>
> SPENSER: *Shepherd's Calendar*; April.

To foot the bill. To pay it; to promise to pay the account by signing one's name at the foot of the bill.

To have one's foot on another's neck. To have him at your mercy; to tyrannize over, or domineer over him completely. *See Josh*, x, 24.

To measure another's foot by your own last. To apply your personal standards to the conduct or actions of another; to judge people by yourself.

To put one's foot down. To make a firm stand, to refuse or insist upon a thing firmly and finally.

To set a man on his feet. To start him off in business, etc., especially after he has "come a cropper."

To show the cloven foot. To betray an evil intention. The devil is represented with a cloven hoof.

To trample under foot. To oppress, or outrage; to treat with the greatest contempt and discourtesy.

With one foot in the grave. In a dying state.

You have put your foot in it nicely. You have got yourself into a pretty mess. As the famous Irish bull has it, "Every time I open my mouth I put my foot in it."

Footloose. Unfettered, a 17th-century expression. It survives to-day in the phrase "footloose and fancy free."

He is on good footing with the world. He stands well with the world.

To pay your footing. To give money for drink when you first enter on a trade. Entry money for being allowed to put your foot in the premises occupied by fellow-craftsmen. *Cp.* GARNISH.

Footmen. *See* RUNNING FOOTMEN.

Footnotes. Notes placed at the bottom of a page.

Footlights. To appear before the footlights. To appear on the stage, where a row of lights is placed in front along the floor to lighten it up.

Fop's Alley. An old name for a promenade in a theatre, especially the central passage between the stalls, right and left in the opera-house.

Forbidden Fruit, The. Figuratively, unlawful sexual indulgence. According to Mohammedan tradition the forbidden fruit partaken of by Eve and Adam was the banyan or Indian fig. *See* FIG LEAF.

Fore. A cry of warning used by golfers before driving.

To the fore. In the front rank; eminent.

To come to the fore. To stand out prominently; to distinguish oneself; to stand forth.

Fore-and-aft. All over the ship; lengthwise, in opposition to "athwartships" or across the line of the keel.

Foreclose. To put an end to. A legal term, meaning to close before the time specified.

When a mortgager has failed to pay a debt the mortgagee may bring an action to foreclose, and the court will then hold that if the mortgager does not redeem within a certain time the mortgagee shall become owner of the property.

Forefather's Day. *See* PILGRIM FATHERS.

Forehand. In the 17th century forehanded meant provident, thrifty. To-day it survives only in games, denoting a stroke in which the player takes a ball on his natural side—*i.e.* right side for a right-handed player, as opposed to *backhand*.

Foreshortening. This is a technical term in perspective drawing. In a portrait, for example, an arm represented as pointing at full length towards the observer occupies less space than if it were shown as pointing to one side; yet the perspective must clearly indicate that the full length of the arm is the same.

> He forbids the fore-shortenings, because they make the parts appear little.—DRYDEN.

Foreign correspondent. A newspaper correspondent living in foreign parts, not a correspondent who is a foreigner. Until *The Times* newspaper originated the system of sending specially equipped men to reside abroad and send news regularly, all foreign news was sent by casual and amateur correspondents whose own political views gave a distinctive colour to the news—or the presentation of it—they transmitted.

Forgeries. Broadly speaking, a forgery is an attempt to pass off as genuine some piece of spurious work or writing. It is not always easy to distinguish a forgery and an imposture; strictly, perhaps, the Rowley poems are impostures, rather than forgeries.

The Ireland Forgeries. One of the most famous of literary forgers was William Henry Ireland (1777-1835), the son of a bookseller and amateur antiquarian. When only 17 young Ireland produced a number of seemingly ancient leases and other documents purporting to be in the handwriting of William Shakespeare, among them being a love-letter to Ann Hathaway, enclosing a lock of hair. Emboldened by the credulity with which his impostures were accepted, he next came out with two new "Shakespeare" plays—*Vortigern* and *Henry II*. Ignoring the protests of Kemble, who was suspicious from the outset, Sheridan produced *Vortigern* at Drury Lane in 1796. During the rehearsals Mrs. Siddons and Mrs. Palmer resigned their roles and refused to be associated with so palpable a fraud. On the opening night the theatre was packed with an audience that grew increasingly critical as the play went on; and when Kemble spoke in his part, "When this solemn mockery is o'er," the house yelled and hissed until the curtain fell—on the first and last performance of *Vortigern*. Meanwhile Malone and other critics had studied the *Miscellaneous Papers* said to be Shakespeare's and had declared them forgeries—eventually extorting a confession from Ireland late in that same year, 1796.

Fork. Old thieves' slang for a finger; hence **to fork out,** to produce and hand over, to pay up.

A forked cap. A bishop's mitre; so called by John Skelton (early 16th cent.). It is cleft or forked.

Fingers were made before forks. See FINGERS.

The forks. The gallows (Lat. *furca*). The word also meant a kind of yoke, with two arms stretching over the shoulders, to which the criminal's hands were tied. The punishment was of three degrees of severity: (1) The *furca ignominiosa*; (2) the *furca pœnālis*; and (3) the *furca capitālis*. The first was for slight offences, and consisted in carrying the *furca* on the shoulders, more or less weighted. The second consisted in carrying the *furca* and being

scourged. The third was being scourged to death. The word *furcifer* meant what we call a gallows-bird or vile fellow.

The Caudine Forks. See CAUDINE.

Form. Good or bad form is conformity—or otherwise—with the unwritten laws and conventionalities of society.

We'll eat the dinner and have a dance together or we shall transgress all form.—STEELE: *Tender Husband*, v. 1.

Forma pauperis (fôr' ma paw' pèr is) (Lat. plea of poverty). *To sue in forma pauperis.* When a person has just cause of a suit, but is so poor that he cannot raise the money necessary to enter it, the judge will assign him lawyers and counsel without the usual fees.

Fortiter in re (fôrt' i tẽr in rē) (Lat.). Firmness in doing what is to be done; an unflinching resolution to persevere to the end. See SUAVITER IN MODO.

Fortunatus (fôr tū nā' tùs). A hero of mediæval legend (from Eastern sources) who possessed an inexhaustible purse, a wishing cap, etc. He appears in a German *Volksbuch* of 1509, Hans Sachs dramatized the story in 1553, and at Christmas, 1599, Dekker's *Pleasant Comedy of Old Fortunatus* was played before Queen Elizabeth.

You have found Fortunatns's purse. Are in luck's way.

Fortune. Fortune favours the brave. The expression is found in Terence—*Fortes fortuna adjuvat* (*Phormio*, i, 4); also in Virgil—*Audentes fortuna juvat* (*Æn.* x, 284), and many other classic writers.

Fortunate Islands. An ancient name for the Canary Islands; also, for any imaginary lands set in distant seas, like the "Islands of the Blest."

Their place of birth alone is mute
To sounds that echo farther west
Than your sire's Islands of the Blest.
BYRON: *The Isles of Greece* (*Don Juan*, iii).

Forty. A number of frequent occurrence in Scripture, and hence formerly treated as, in a manner, sacrosanct. Moses was forty days in the mount; Elijah was forty days fed by ravens; the rain of the flood fell forty days, and another forty days expired before Noah opened the window of the ark; forty days was the period of embalming; Nineveh had forty days to repent; Our Lord fasted forty days; He was seen forty days after His resurrection, etc.

St. Swithin betokens forty days' rain or dry weather; a quarantine extends to forty days; forty days, in the Old English law, was the limit for the payment of the fine for manslaughter; the privilege of sanctuary was for forty days; the widow was allowed to remain in her husband's house for forty days after his decease; a knight enjoined forty days' service of his tenant; a stranger, at the expiration of forty days, was compelled to be enrolled in some tithing; Members of Parliament were protected from arrest forty days after the prorogation of the House, and forty days before the House was convened; a new-made burgess had to forfeit forty pence unless he built a house within forty days, etc. etc.

Fool or **physician at forty.** *See* FOOL.

Forty stripes save one. The Jews were forbidden by the Mosaic law to inflict more than forty stripes on an offender, and for fear of breaking the law they stopped short of the number. If the scourge contained three lashes, thirteen strokes would equal "forty save one."

The Thirty-nine Articles of the Anglican Church used sometimes to be called "the forty stripes save one" by theological students.

Forty winks. A short nap.

The Forty Immortals (or simply **the Forty**). The members of the French Academy, who number forty.

The Hungry Forties. *See* HUNGRY.

The roaring forties. The Atlantic Ocean between 40° and 50° north latitude; well known for its rough and stormy character.

Forty-niners. Prospectors for gold, who rushed to California following the discovery of gold there in 1848. Best remembered to-day, perhaps, in the song *Clementine*.

Forty-two Line Bible, The. *See* BIBLE, SPECIALLY NAMED.

Fosse, The, or **Fosse-way.** One of the four principal highways made by the Romans in England. It leads from Axminster through Bath, Cirencester, Leicester, and Lincoln, and had a fosse or ditch on each side of it. *Cp.* ERMINE STREET.

Fou. Scots expression for drunk. It is a variant of *full*.

> The clachan yill had made me canty.
> I was na fou, but just had plenty.
>   BURNS: *Death and Dr. Hornbook.*

Fount of type. *See* FONT; LETTER; TYPE.

Fountain pen. This apparently modern invention is really of considerable antiquity. In the anonymous "Diary of a Journey to Paris in 1657-58" under date July 11th, 1657 there is reference to a man who "makes pens of silver in which he puts ink, which does not get dry, and without having to take any, one can write a half-quire of paper at a sitting." In 1721 there is an advertisement in a Welsh almanac, "Inkhorns. Fountain pens, the best sort of Holman's ink powder, and red and black led pencils."

Fountain of Youth. In popular folk-tales, a fountain supposed to possess the power of restoring youth. Expeditions were fitted out in search of it, and at one time it was supposed to be in one of the Bahama Islands.

Four. Four Freedoms. Franklin Roosevelt, during World War II, declared as one of the aims of the democratic nations that when the war was over all the peoples of earth might live in freedom from fear, and from want, and with freedom of speech and of worship.

The History of the Four Kings (**Livre des Quatre Rois**). A pack of cards. In a French pack the four kings are Charlemagne, David, Alexander, and Cæsar.

Four Letters, The. *See* TETRAGRAMMATON.

Four Sons of Aymon. *See* AYMON.

Fourth dimension. The three dimensions of space universally recognized are length, breadth, and height; three in number because we can draw three lines, but no more, all at right angles to one another. A piece of line has only one dimension—length; a region of a surface has two—length and breadth; a solid body in space has three. After the mathematician has applied Algebra to Geometry he can increase the number of his variables without altering the character of his equations; and retaining for convenience his geometrical vocabulary he constructs what he calls an algebraic geometry of as many dimensions as he pleases. A four-dimensional body may be thought of as bearing the same relation to one in the three-dimensional space which we perceive as volume does to area, or area to length. The measurement of time introduces a fourth variable into everyday life; but to say that for that reason time *is* the fourth dimension of space, and is somehow at right angles to every line that we can draw is a confusion of language. It is safe to say that in mathematical operations time is sometimes found to be behaving very like a fourth, spatial dimension.

Fourth of July. *See* INDEPENDENCE DAY.

Fourteen, in its connexion with Henri IV and Louis XIV, The following are curious and strange coincidences:—

HENRI IV:

14 letters in the name Henri-de-Bourbon. He was the 14th king of France and Navarre on the extinction of the family of Navarre. He was born on Dec. 14, 1553, the

sum of which year amounts to 14; he was assassinated on May 14, 1610; and lived 4 times 14 years, 14 weeks, and 4 times 14 days.

14 May, 1552, was born Marguerite de Valois his first wife.

14 May, 1588, the Parisians rose in revolt against him because he was a "heretic."

14 March, 1590, he won the great battle of Ivry.

14 May, 1590, was organized a grand ecclesiastical and military demonstration against him, which drove him from the faubourgs of Paris.

14 Nov., 1590, the Sixteen took an oath tő die rather than submit to a "heretic" king.

It was Gregory XIV who issued a Bull excluding Henri from the throne.

14 Nov., 1592, the Paris parlement registered the papal Bull.

14 Dec., 1599, the Duke of Savoy was reconciled to Henri IV.

14 Sept., 1606, was baptized the dauphin (afterwards Louis XIII) son of Henri IV.

14 May, 1610, Henry was assassinated by Ravaillac.

LOUIS XIV:

14th of the name. He mounted the throne 1643, the sum of which figures equals 14. He died 1715, the sum of which figures also equals 14. He reigned 77 years, the sum of which two figures equals 14. He was born 1638, died 1715, which added together equals 3353, the sum of which figure comes to 14.

Fourteen Points. Conditions laid down by President Woodrow Wilson (1856-1924) as those on which the Allies were prepared to make peace with Germany. He outlined them in a speech to Congress on January 11th, 1918, and at the end of the war they were accepted as the basis for the peace. They included the evacuation by Germany of all allied territory, the restoration of Poland, freedom of the seas, reduction of armaments, and open diplomacy.

Fox. As a name for the Old English broadsword *fox* probably refers to a maker's mark of a dog, wolf, or fox. The swords were manufactured by Julian del Rei of Toledo, whose trade-mark was a little dog, mistaken for a fox.

O signieur Dew, thou diest on point of fox,
Except, O signieur, thou do give to me
Egregious ransom.—*Henry V*, iv, 4.

I had a sword, ay, the flower of Smithfield for a sword, a right fox i' faith.—PORTER: *Two Angry Women of Abington* (1599).

To fox. To steal or cheat; keep an eye on somebody without seeming so to do. A dog, a fox, and a weasel sleep, as they say, "with one eye open."

Foxed. A print or page of a book stained with reddish brown marks is said to be "foxed," because of its colour.

Foxed was also an expression widely used in military parlance during World War II for "bewildered."

Fox-hole. A small slit trench for one or more men.

A fox's sleep. A sleep with one eye. Assumed indifference to what is going on. *See above.*

A wise fox will never rob his neighbour's hen-roost. It would soon be found out, so he goes farther from home where he is not known.

Every fox must pay his skin to the furrier. The crafty shall be taken in their own wiliness.

Reynard the Fox. *See* REYNARD.

The fox and the grapes. "It's a case of the fox and the grapes" is said of one who wants something badly but cannot obtain it, and so tries to create the impression that he doesn't want it at all. The allusion is to one of Æsop's fables. *See* GRAPES.

Fox-fire. The phosphoric light, without heat, which plays round decaying matter. It is the Fr. *faux*, or "false fire," and was first found in 1485.

Foxglove. The flower is named from the animal and the glove. The reason for the second half is obvious from the finger-stall appearance of the flower, but it is not known how the fox came to be associated with it. It belongs to the botanical genus *Digitalis*, or finger-shaped. The leaves of this genus contain several powerful principles which are highly valuable in the treatment of heart disease.

Fox-trot. A modern ball-room dance. It was introduced from America in the first half of the 20th century. A horse's *fox-trot* is the short steps it takes when changing from a trot to a walk.

Fra Diavolo (fra dē av′ ō lō). Auber's opera of this name (1830) is founded on the exploits of Michele Pozza (1760-1806), a celebrated brigand and renegade monk, who evaded pursuit for many years amidst the mountains of Calabria.

France. *See* FRANK.

Francesca da Rimini (frän ches′ kȧ da rim′ i ni). Daughter of Guido da Polenta, Lord of Ravenna. Her story is told in Dante's *Inferno* (canto v). She was married to Giovanni Malatesta, Lord of Rimini, but her guilty love for his younger brother, Paolo, was discovered, and both were put to death by him about 1289. Stephen Phillips has a play (1900), and Silvio Pellico a tragedy, on the subject.

Franciscans (frăn sis′ kȧnz). The friars minor founded by St. Francis of Assisi in 1209. They form one Order of Friars Minor, divided into three distinct and independent branches, of which one is known simply as Friars Minor, another as Friars Minor Conventual and the third as Friars Minor Capuchin. The Order had 64 houses in England at the time of the Reformation, being known as Grey Friars, from the indeterminate colour of their habit; which is now brown. The Friars Minor observe the unmitigated rule of St. Francis, with its insistence on poverty, abstinence, and preaching; Friars Minor Conventual have a modified rule with regard to the holding of property, and wear a black tunic with a white cord. The Capuchins, initiated in 1525, have the strictest rules of any, subsisting largely on the begging of the lay brothers. The Recollects, or Cordeliers, and Observants were formerly divisions of the Order, and were amalgamated with the Friars Minor by Leo XIII in 1897.

The *Order of Franciscan Nuns* was founded in 1212 by St. Clare; they are hence known as the *Clares* or *Poor Clares*; also *Minoresses*. Various reformations have taken place in the Order, giving rise to the *Colettines*, *Grey Sisters*, *Capuchin Nuns*, *Sisters of the Annunciation*, *Conceptionists*, and the *Urbanists*, the last named observing a modified rule and being permitted to hold property.

Frangipane, frangipani (frăn' ji pān, frăn ji pa' ni). The name is supposed to come from the Marquis Frangipani, a soldier under Louis XIV. It is applied to a kind of pastry cake filled with cream, almonds, and sugar; also to a perfume made from, or imitating the smell of, the flower of a West Indian tree *Plumeria rubra*, or red jasmine.

Frank. One belonging to the Teutonic nations that conquered Gaul in the 6th century (whence the name *France*). By the Turks, Arabs, etc., of the Levant the name is given to any of the inhabitants of the western parts of Europe, as the English, Germans, Spaniards, French, etc.

Frankelin's Tale (*Chaucer*). *See* DORIGEN.

Frankenstein (frăng kĕn stīn). The young student in Mary Wollstonecraft Shelley's romance of that name (1818). He made a soulless monster out of corpses from churchyards and dissecting-rooms, and endued it with life by galvanism. The tale shows how the creature longed for sympathy, but was shunned by everyone and became the instrument of dreadful retribution on the student who usurped the prerogative of the Creator.

Frankfurter. A small smoked sausage of beef and pork, somewhat akin to the saveloy.

Frankincense (frăngk' in sens). The literal meaning of this is pure, or true incense. It is a fragrant gum exuded from several trees of the genus *Boswellia*, abundant on the Somali coast and in South Arabia. The ceremonial use of frankincense was practised by the Egyptians, Persians, Babylonians, Hebrews, Greeks, and Romans, and the gum is an ingredient of modern incense used liturgically.

Frater (frā' ter). The refectory or dining-room of a monastery, where the brothers (Lat. *fratres*) met together for meals. Also called the *fratry*.

In old vagabonds' slang a *frater* was much the same as an Abram-man (*q.v.*).

A Frater goeth wyth a Lisence to beg for some Spittlehouse or Hospital. Their pray is comonly upon poore women as they go and come to the markets.— AWDELEY: *Fraternity of Vacabondes* (1575).

Fraternity, The. A term highwaymen used to apply to themselves as a body. It implied a friendship and union among themselves that by no means existed, for like all rogues, highwaymen were very jealous of one another.

Fraticelli (frāt i chel' ē) (*Little Brethren*). A sect of renegade and licentious monks which appeared about the close of the 13th century and threw off all subjection to the Pope, whom they denounced as an apostate. They had wholly disappeared by the 15th century.

Frazzle (U.S.A.). A frayed edge, hence **worn to a frazzle**, reduced to a state of nerviness.

Free. A free and easy. A social gathering where persons meet together without formality to chat and smoke. **In a free and easy way**; with an entire absence of ceremony.

A free fight. A fight in which all engage, rules being disregarded.

Free on board. Said of goods delivered on board ship, or into the conveyance, at the seller's expense; generally contracted to F.O.B.

I'm free to confess. There's nothing to prevent me admitting. . . .

To have a free hand. *See* HAND.

To make free with. To take liberties with; to treat whatever it is as one's own.

Free French. *See* FIGHTING FRENCH.

Free lance. *See* LANCE.

Free Trade. The system by which goods are allowed to enter one country from another country without paying customs duty for the protection of home producers. For many years it was held that the prosperity of Britain depended upon leaving the ports open to the shipping and goods of all the world. In 1932 Great Britain abandoned Free Trade by imposing a general tariff on imported goods.

The Apostle of Free Trade. Richard Cobden (1804-65), who established the Anti-Corn Law League in 1838.

Freebooter. A pirate, an adventurer who makes his living by plundering; literally, one who obtains his booty free (Dut. *vrij*, free, *buit*, booty).

Freehold. An estate held in fee-simple or fee-tail; one on which no duty or service is owing to any lord but the sovereign. *Cp.* Copy-hold.

Freeman of Bucks. A cuckold. The allusion is to the buck's horn. *See* Horns.

Freemasonry. In its curious and characteristic ritual Freemasonry traces its origins to the building of Solomon's Temple. Without accepting or rejecting this theory, however, it can be taken as a fact that it has existed for many centuries as a secret society. In mediæval days operative, *i.e.* actual stone-masons, banded together with secret pass-words, signs and tests, and Masonic students find material for research in the marks engraved on fashioned stones in cathedrals and certain ancient buildings. Freemasonry as we know it was already flourishing in the 17th century, and although Sir Christopher Wren's association with the Craft has not been established, it is likely. Elias Ashmole describes his own initiation in 1682. The mother Grand Lodge of England was founded in London in 1717 and took under its aegis the many small lodges that were working up and down the country. Even the extremely ancient York lodge, which has given its name to most of the Masonic rites of the Continent and U.S.A., acknowledged its authority. From this first Grand Lodge of England derive all Masonic lodges of whatever kind throughout the world.

In Britain Masonry has three degrees, the first is called Entered Apprentice; the second, Fellow Craft, the third, Master Mason. Royal Arch masonry is an adjunct to these, and is peculiar to Britain. Mark Masonry is a comparatively modern addition to the fraternity. In the U.S.A. the first regular lodge was founded at Boston in 1733, though there are minutes extant of a lodge in Philadelphia in 1730. The ritual side of Freemasonry has appealed to American more than it has to British masons, and many degrees are worked in U.S.A. with elaborate ritual and mysteries. In addition to the three degrees of British masonry there are the Cryptic Degrees of Royal and Select Masters; the Chivalric Rite, with three degrees

of Knights Red Cross, Temple and of Malta; and the 33 degrees of the Ancient and Accepted Scottish Rite. The various Grand Orients of the Continent (all disowned by the Grand Lodge of England on account of their political activities) were founded at different times and work modifications of the Scottish Rite. The part played by masonic lodges in the French Revolution is still obscure; Philippe Egalité was head of the Grand Orient but repudiated it during the Terror. Napoleon was reported to have been initiated at Malta in 1798; he certainly favoured masonry and during the Empire Cambacérès, Murat, and Joseph Bonaparte were successive Grand Masters. Freemasonry has been condemned by the Holy See not only for being a secret society but for its alleged subversive aims—aims that may be cherished by Continental Masons but which are quite unknown to their British and American brethren.

The Lady Freemason. Women are not admitted into freemasonry, but the story goes that a lady was initiated in the early 18th century. She was the Hon. Elizabeth St. Leger, daughter of Lord Doneraile, who hid herself in an empty clock-case when the lodge was held in her father's house, and witnessed the proceedings. She was discovered, and compelled to submit to initiation as a member of the craft.

Freezing-point. The temperature at which a liquid becomes solid; if mentioned without qualification, 32° Fahrenheit (0° Centigrade), the freezing-point of water is meant. For other liquids the name is added as the freezing-point of milk, sulphuric ether, quicksilver, and so on. In Centigrade and Réaumur's instruments zero marks the freezing-point. The zero of Fahrenheit's thermometer is 32° below the freezing-point of water, being the lowest temperature observed by him in the winter of 1709.

French. French Cream. Brandy; from the custom (which came from France) of taking a cup of coffee with brandy in it instead of cream after dinner.

Done like a Frenchman, turn and turn again (1 *Henry VI*, iii, 4). The French were frequently ridiculed as a fickle, wavering nation. Dr. Johnson says he once read a treatise the object of which was to show that a weathercock is a satire on the word *Gallus* (a Gaul or cock).

Fresco (fres' kō). A method of painting upon fresh mortar. The plaster must be fresh to absorb the colour, and since it dries rapidly, the artist must work with great dexterity and speed. The wall must be free of saltpetre, and only such colours can be used as are not affected by lime—many brilliant greens, reds and yellow being thus ruled out. Frescoes should not be confused with wall paintings such as Leonardo's famous Last Supper at Santa Maria delle Grazie, Milan.

Freshman. An undergraduate of a university in his first term.

Freyja (frā′ yà). In Scandinavian mythology the sister of Freyr and wife of Odin, who deserted her because she loved finery better than her husband. She is the fairest of the goddesses, goddess of love and also of the dead. She presides over marriages, and, besides being the Venus, may be called the Juno of Asgard. She is also known as *Frea, Frija, Frigg, Frige*, etc., and it is from her that our *Friday* is named.

Friar (Lat. *frater*, a brother). A religious, especially one belonging to one of the four great orders, *i.e.* Franciscans, Dominicans, Augustinians, and Carmelites. *See these names.*

In printer's slang a *friar* is a part of the sheet which has failed to receive the ink properly, and is therefore paler than the rest. As Caxton set up his press in Westminster Abbey, it is but natural that monks and friars should give foundation to some of the printer's slang. *Cp.* MONK.

Curtal Friar. *See* CURTAL.

Friar John. A prominent character in Rabelais's *Gargantua and Pantagruel*, a tall, lean, wide-mouthed, long-nosed friar of Seville.

In the original he is called "Friar John *des Entommeures*": Urquhart mistakenly translated this as "of the Funnels"; "of the Trenchermen" is the best equivalent (*entamer*, to broach, to carve, with reference to a hearty appetite). *Entonnoirs* are "funnels"; and as this word has been used as slang for the throat perhaps that accounts for the mistake.

Friar Tuck. Chaplain and steward of Robin Hood.

In this our spacious isle I think there is not one
But he hath heard some talk of Hood and Little John;
Of Tuck, the merry friar, which many a sermon made
In praise of Robin Hood, his outlaws, and their trade.
DRAYTON: *Polyolbion*, xxvi, 311-16.

Friar's Heel. The outstanding upright stone at Stonehenge, formerly supposed by some to stand in the central axis of the avenue, is so called. Geoffrey of Monmouth says the devil bought the stones of an old woman in Ireland, wrapped them up in a wyth, and brought them to Salisbury Plain. Just before he got to Mount Ambre the wyth broke, and one of the stones fell into the Avon, the rest were carried to the plain. After the fiend had fixed them in the ground, he cried out, "No man will ever find out how these stones came here." A friar replied, "That's more than thou canst tell," whereupon the foul fiend threw one of the stones at him and struck him on the heel. The stone stuck in the ground and remains so to the present hour.

Friars Major (*Fratres majores*). The Dominicans.

Friars Minor (*Fratres minores*). The Franciscans.

Friar's Tale. In the *Canterbury* Tales a tale throwing discredit on Summoners. Chaucer obtained it from the Latin collection, *Promptuarium Exemplorum*.

Friday. The sixth day of the week was the *dies Veneris* in ancient Rome, *i.e.* the day dedicated to Venus. The northern nations adopted the Roman system of nomenclature, and the sixth day was dedicated to their nearest equivalent to Venus, who was Frigg or Freyja (*q.v.*); hence the name *Friday* (A.S. *frige-dœg*). In France the Latin name was kept, and Friday is *Vendredi*.

Friday was regarded by the Norsemen as the luckiest day of the week: among Christians generally it has been regarded as the unluckiest, because it was the day of Our Lord's crucifixion, and is a fast-day in the Catholic Church. Mohammedans (among whom Friday is the Sabbath) say that Adam was created on a Friday, and legend has it that it was on a Friday that Adam and Eve ate the forbidden fruit, and on a Friday that they died. Among the Buddhists and Brahmins it is also held to be unlucky; and the old Romans called it *nefastus*, from the utter overthrow of their army at Gallia Narbonensis. In England the proverb is that "a Friday moon brings foul weather," but it is not, apparently, unlucky to be born on this day, for, according to the old rhyme, "Friday's child is loving and giving."

Black Friday. *See* BLACK.

Good Friday. *See* GOOD.

He who laughs on Friday will weep on Sunday. Sorrow follows in the wake of joy. The line is taken from Racine's comedy, *Les Plaideurs*.

Man Friday. The young savage found by Robinson Crusoe on a Friday, and kept as his servant and companion on the desert island; hence, a faithful and willing attendant, ready to turn his hand to anything.

Never cut your nails on a Friday. "Cut them on Friday you cut them for sorrow." *See* NAIL-PARING.

Friend. A Quaker (*q.v.*), *i.e.* a member of the Society of Friends; also, one's second in a duel, as "Captain B. acted as his friend." In the law courts counsel refer to each other as "my learned friend," though they may be entire strangers, just as in the House of Commons one member speaks of another as "my honourable friend."

A friend in need is a friend indeed. The Latin saying (from Ennius) is, *Amicus certus in re incerta cernitur*, a sure friend is made known when (one is) in difficulty.

A friendly suit, or **action.** An action at law brought, not with the object of obtaining a conviction or damages, but to discover the law on some debatable point, to get a legal and authoritative decision putting some fact on record.

Friendship. The classical examples of lasting friendship between man and man are Achilles and Patroclus, Pylades and Orestes, Damon and Pythias, and Nisus and Euryalus. *See these names.* To these should be added David and Jonathan.

Frigg, or **Frigga.** *See* FREYJA.

Frills. "Airs and graces"; as, **to put on frills,** to give oneself airs.

Fringe. The fringes on the garments of the Jewish priests were accounted sacred, and were touched by the common people as a charm. Hence the desire of the woman who had the issue of blood to touch the fringe of Our Lord's garment. (*Matt*, ix, 20-22.)

Frippery. Rubbish of a tawdry character; worthless finery; foolish levity. A *friperer* or *fripperer* was one who dealt in old clothes (*cp.* Fr. *friperie*, old clothes, cast-off furniture, etc.).

Old clothes, cast dresses, tattered rags,
Whose works are e'en the frippery of wit.
BEN JONSON: *Epig.* I, lvi.

Also, a shop where odds and ends, old clothes, and so on are dealt in. Hence Shakespeare's:—

We know what belongs to a frippery.
Tempest, iv, 1.

Fritz. Frederick the Great of Prussia (1712, 1740-86) was known as *Old Fritz*. In World War I the men in the trenches commonly hailed any prisoner or German in the enemy lines as *Fritz*.

Froebel (frer' b ĕl). The name given to a system of teaching young children devised by F. W. A. Froebel (1782-1852), a German

schoolmaster. The main part of his system has been put into practice in kindergartens where children's senses are developed by means of clay-modelling, work with colour-brushes, mat-plaiting, etc., as well as the care of animals, flowers, and suchlike.

Frog. A frog and mouse agreed to settle by single combat their claims to a marsh; but, while they fought, a kite carried them both off. (Æsop: *Fables*, clxviii.)

Old Æsop's fable, where he told
What fate unto the mouse and frog befel.
CARY: *Dante*, cxxiii.

In Ovid's *Metamorphoses* (vi, 4) we are told that the Lycian shepherds were changed into frogs for mocking Latona.

As when those hinds that were transformed to frogs
Railed at Latona's twin-born progeny.
MILTON: *Sonnet*, vii.

Frenchmen, properly *Parisians*, have been nicknamed Frogs or Froggies (*grenouilles*) from their ancient heraldic device (*see* FLEUR-DE-LIS), which was three frogs or three toads. *Qu'en disent les grenouilles?*—What do the frogs (people of Paris) say?—was in 1791 a common court phrase at Versailles. There was a point in the pleasantry when Paris was a quagmire, called *Lutetia* (mud-land). *See* CRAPAUD. Further point is given to the nickname by the fact that the back legs of the edible frog (*Rana esculenta*) form a delicacy in French cuisine that awakened much contemptuous humour in the less exquisite English.

Frogmen. In World War II strong swimmers dressed in rubber suits with paddles on their feet resembling frogs legs, who entered enemy harbours by night and attached explosives to shipping and installations. Since the war they have sometimes been used in salvage operations.

Frog's march. Carrying an obstreperous prisoner, face downwards, by his four limbs.

It may be fun to you, but it is death to the frogs. A caution, telling one that one's sport should not be at the expense of other people's happiness. The allusion is to Æsop's fable of a boy stoning frogs for his amusement.

A frog in the throat. A temporary loss of voice.

Frost Saints. *See* ICE SAINTS.

Frozen Words. Everyone knows the incident of the "frozen horn" related by Munchausen, also how Pantagruel and his friends, on the confines of the Frozen Sea, heard the uproar of a battle, which had been frozen the preceding winter, released by a thaw (Rabelais: Bk. iv, ch. 56). The joke appears to have been well known to the ancient Greeks, for Antiphanes applies it to the discourses of Plato: "As the cold of certain cities is so intense that it freezes the very words we utter, which remain congealed till the heat of summer thaws them, so the mind of youth is so thoughtless that the wisdom of Plato lies there frozen, as it were, till it is thawed by the ripened judgment of mature age" (Plutarch's *Morals*).

Frying-pan. Out of the frying-pan into the fire. In trying to extricate yourself from one evil, you fall into a greater. The Greeks used to say, "Out of the smoke into the flame"; and the French say, *"Tomber de la poêle dans la braise."*

Fuchsia (fū′ shà). A genus of highly ornamental shrubs coming from Mexico and the Andes, though two species are found in New Zealand. They were so named in 1703, in honour of the German botanist Leonhard Fuchs (1501-66). The best-known varieties in this country are derived from the Chilian species *Fuchsia macrostemma*.

Fuel. Adding fuel to fire. Saying or doing something to increase the anger of a person already angry.

Führer (fū′ rĕr). The title, meaning in German "leader," assumed by Adolf Hitler when he acceded to the supreme power in Germany on the death of Hindenburg in 1934.

Fulbright Scholar. Public Law 584 (of the 79th Congress of the United States) declared that moneys accruing from the disposal of surplus U.S.A. war stores at the end of World War II should be left in the countries where they accumulated and used to pay the expenses of exchange scholarships and professorships. Those benefiting from the scheme are known as "Fulbright scholars" after Senator Fulbright, of Arkansas, who promoted this enlightened and successful bill.

Fulhams, or **Fullams.** An Elizabethan name for loaded dice. Dice made with a cavity were called gourds; those made to throw the high numbers were high fullams or gourds, and those made to throw the low numbers were low fullams or gourds.

> For gourd and fullam holds
> And "high" and "low" beguile the rich and poor.
> *Merry Wives of Windsor,* i, 3.
> Have their fulhams at command,
> Brought up to do their feats at hand.
> BUTLER: *Upon Gaming.*

The name was probably from Fulham, which was notorious as the resort of crooks and rogues of every description.

Full. Full dress. The dress worn on occasions of ceremony; court dress, uniform, academicals, evening dress, etc., as the case may be. A **full-dress debate** is one for which preparation and arrangements have been made, as opposed to one arising casually.

Full house. A term in the game of poker for a hand holding three of one kind and two of another, *e.g.* 3 tens and 2 sixes.

Full of beans. *See* BEAN.

In full cry. Said of hounds that have caught the scent, and give tongue in chorus; hence, hurrying in full pursuit.

In full fig. *See* FIG.

In full swing. Fully at work; very busy; in full operation.

Fum, or **Fung-hwang.** The phœnix (*q.v.*) of Chinese legend, one of the four symbolical animals presiding over the destinies of China.

It originated from fire, was born in the Hill of the Sun's Halo, and has its body inscribed with the five cardinal virtues. It is this curious creature that is embroidered on the dresses of certain mandarins.

Fum. *See* GEORGE, ST.

Fume. In a fume. In ill temper, especially from impatience.

Fun. To make fun of. To make a butt of; to ridicule; to play pranks on one.

Like fun. Thoroughly, energetically, with delight.

> On'y look at the dimmercrats, see what they've done,
> Jest simply by stickin' together like fun.
> LOWELL: *Biglow Papers* (First series, iv, st. 5).

Fund. The Funds, or **The Public Funds.** Money lent at interest to Government on Government security.

Fundamentalism. A religious movement that arose in U.S.A. about 1919. It opposed all theories of evolution and anthropology, teaching that God transcends all the laws of nature, and that He manifests Himself by exceptional and extraordinary activities. Belief in the literal meaning of the Scriptures is an essential tenet. In 1925 a professor of science was convicted of violating the State laws of Tennessee by teaching evolution, and this incident aroused interest and controversy far beyond the religious circles of U.S.A. The Fundamentalist attitude was largely set forth by William Jennings Bryan, who insisted that the theory of evolution was a denial of Bible teaching and hence a doctrine inimical to Christianity.

Funeral (Late Lat. *funeralis*, adj. from *funus*, a burial). *Funus* is connected with *fumus*

(Sanskrit *dhu-mas*), smoke, and the word seems to have referred to the ancient practice of disposing of the dead by cremation. Funerals among the Romans took place at night by torchlight, that magistrates and priests might not be made ceremonially unclean by seeing a corpse, and so be prevented from performing their sacred duties.

Most of our funeral customs are derived from the Romans; as dressing in black, walking in procession, carrying insignia on the bier, raising a mound over the grave, called *tumulus* (whence our *tomb*), etc. In Roman funerals, too, the undertaker, attended by lictors dressed in black, marched with the corpse, and, as master of the ceremonies, assigned to each follower his proper place in the procession. The Greeks crowned the dead body with flowers, and placed flowers on the tomb also; and the Romans decked the funeral couch with leaves and flowers, and spread flowers, wreaths, and fillets on the tomb of friends. In England the *Passing Bell* or the *Soul Bell* used to be tolled from the parish church when a parishioner was dying, and there are many references to it in literature. At the funeral the bell would be tolled at intervals as many times as the dead person's age in years.

Public games were held both in Greece and Rome in honour of departed heroes. Examples of this custom are numerous; as the games instituted by Hercules at the death of Pelops, those held by Achilles in honour of Patroclus (*Iliad*, Bk. xxiii), those held by Æneas in honour of his father Anchises (*Æneid*, Bk. v), etc.; and the custom of giving a feast at funerals came to us from the Romans, who not only feasted the friends of the deceased, but also distributed meat to the persons employed.

> Thrift thrift, Horatio! the funeral baked meats
> Did coldly furnish forth the marriage tables.
> *Hamlet*, i, 2.

Fung-hwang. See FUM.

Funk. To be in a funk, or **a blue funk,** may be the Walloon "*In de fonk zun*," literally to "be in the smoke." Colloquially to be in a state of trepidation from uncertainty or apprehension of evil. It first appeared in England at Oxford in the first half of the 18th century.

Funny Bone. A pun on the word *humerus*, the Latin (and hence scientific) name for the upper bone of the arm. It is the inner condyle of this, or, to speak untechnically, the knob, or *enlarged end* of the bone terminating where the ulnar nerve is exposed at the elbow. A knock on this bone at the elbow produces a painful sensation.

Furbelow. A corruption of *falbalas* (*q.v.*).

Furcam et Flagellum (fĕr' kăm et flă jel' ŭm) (Lat., gallows and whip). The meanest of all servile tenures, the bondman being at the lord's mercy, both life and limb. *Cp.* FORKS.

Furies, The. The Roman name (*Furiæ*) for the Greek Erinyes (*q.v.*), said by Hesiod to have been the daughters of Ge (the earth) and to have sprung from the blood of Uranus, and by other accounts to be daughters of night and darkness. They were three in number, Tisiphone (the Avenger of blood), Alecto (Implacable), and Megæra (Disputatious).

The Furies of the Guillotine. Another name for the *tricoteuses* (*q.v.*)

Futhorc (fu' thôrk). The ancient Runic alphabet of the Anglo-Saxons and other Teutons; so called, on the same principle as the A B C, from its first six letters, viz., *f, u, th, o, r, k*.

Futurism. An art movement which originated in Turin in 1910 under the influence of F. T. Marinetti. Its adherents sought to introduce into painting a "poetry of motion" whereby, for example, the painted gesture should become actually "a dynamic condition." The Futurists tried to indicate not only the state of mind of the painter but also that of the figures in the picture. The original Futurists included Marinetti, Boccioni, Carra, Russolo, and Severini. Their first exhibitions were held in Paris, 1911, and London, 1912.

Fylfot. A mystic sign or emblem, known also as the *swastika* and *gammadion*, and in heraldry as the *cross cramponee*, used (especially in Byzantine architecture and among the North American Indians) as an ornament, and as of religious import. It has been found at Hissarlik, on ancient Etruscan tombs, Celtic monuments, Buddhist inscriptions, Greek coins, etc., and has been thought to have represented the power of the sun, of the four winds, of lightning, and so on. Its shape is that of a right-angled cross, the arms of which are of equal length, with an additional piece at the extremity of each, fixed at a right-angle, each addition being of the same length and in the same direction. It is used nowadays in jewellery as an emblem of luck.

The name *fylfot* was adopted by antiquaries from a MS. of the 15th century, and is probably *fill foot*, signifying a device to fill the foot of a stained window. *See* SWASTIKA.

G

G. This letter is a modification of the Latin C (which was a rounding of the Greek *gamma*, Γ); until the 3rd century B.C. the *g* and *k* sounds were represented by the same letter, C. In the Hebrew and old Phœnician alphabets G is the outline of a camel's head and neck. Heb. *gimel*, a camel.

G.C.B. *See* BATH.

G.I. In World War II, American enlisted men called themselves G.I.s. It is actually an abbreviation of Government Issue, a term attached to all their clothing, equipment, etc. After speaking for some time of G.I. shirts, G.I. blankets, and G.I. haircuts, the soldiers began to apply the term to themselves.

G-man, short for Government Man, an agent of the U.S. Federal Bureau of Investigation. *See* FEDERAL.

G.O.M. The initial letters of "Grand Old Man," a nickname of honour given to W. E. Gladstone (1809-98) in his later years. Lord Rosebery first used the expression in 1882.

Gab. The gift of the gab or **gob.** Fluency of speech, also the gift of boasting, connected with *gabble*, and perhaps with *gab*, the mouth.

> There was a man named Job
> Lived in the land of Uz,
> He had a good gift of the gob,
> The same thing happen us.
> *Book of Job: ascribed to Zachary Boyd* (d. 1653).

Gaberdine (găb′ er dēn). A long, coarse cloak or gown, especially as worn in the Middle Ages by Jews and almsmen. The word is the Spanish *gabardina*, a frock worn by pilgrims.

> You call me misbeliever, cut-throat dog,
> And spit upon my Jewish gabardine.
> *Merchant of Venice*, i, 3.

Gaberlunzie (găb′ er lŭnzi, găb′ er lŭn yi), A mendicant; or one of the king's bedesmen, who were licensed beggars. The name has also been given to the wallet carried by a *gaberlunzie-man*. Its derivation is unknown.

Gabriel (gā′ bri el) (*i.e.* man of God). One of the archangels of Hebrew mythology, sometimes regarded as the angel of death, the prince of fire and thunder, but more frequently as one of God's chief messengers, and traditionally said to be the only angel that can speak Syriac

and Chaldee. The Mohammedans call him the chief of the four favoured angels, and the spirit of truth. Milton makes him chief of the angelic guards placed over Paradise.

> Betwixt these rocky pillars Gabriel sat,
> Chief of the angelic guards.
> *Paradise Lost*, iv, 549.

In the *Talmud* Gabriel appears as the destroyer of the hosts of Sennacherib, as the man who showed Joseph the way (*Gen.* xxxvii, 15), and as one of the angels who buried Moses (*Deut.* xxxiv, 6).

It was Gabriel who (we are told in the Koran) took Mohammed to heaven on Alborak and revealed to him his "prophetic lore." In the Old Testament Gabriel is said to have explained to Daniel certain visions; in the New Testament he announced to Zacharias the future birth of John the Baptist, and appeared to Mary, the mother of Jesus (*Luke* i, 26, etc.).

Gad-fly. Not the *roving* but the *goading* fly (A.S. *gad*, a goad).

Gadget (găj′ et). An expressive word introduced into general use during World War I, popularized, apparently, by the R.A.F. where it was used for almost any little tool or appliance.

Gadshill (gădz hil). About 3 miles N.W. of Rochester. Famous for the attack of Sir John Falstaff and three of his knavish companions on a party of four travellers, whom they robbed of their purses (1 *Henry IV*, ii, 4), and also as the home of Charles Dickens, who died there in 1870.

Gadshill is also the name of one of the thievish companions of Sir John Falstaff.

Gad-steel. Flemish steel. So called because it is wrought in *gads*, or small bars (A.S. *gad*, a small bar; Icel. *gaddr*, a spike).

> I will go get a leaf of brass,
> And with a gad of steel will write these words.
> *Titus Andronicus*, iv, 1.

Gaelic (gă′ lik). The language of the Gaelic branch of the Celtic race which, in Greek and Roman times, occupied much of Central Europe. The name is now applied only to the Celtic language spoken in the Scottish Highlands. In the 18th century this was called Erse.

Gaff. Slang for humbug; also for a cheap public entertainment or a low-class music-hall.

Gaffer. An old country fellow; a boss or foreman; a corruption of "grandfather." *Cp.* GAMMER.

If I had but a thousand a year, Gaffer Green,
If I had but a thousand a year.
Gaffer Green and Robin Rough.

Gag. In theatrical parlance, an interpolation. When Hamlet directs the players to say no more "than is set down" (iii, 2) he cautions them against gagging; also a joke.

Gag-man. One who is employed to supply jokes for films or radio programmes.

To apply the gag. Said of applying the closure in the House of Commons. Here *gag* is something forced into the mouth to prevent speech.

Gala Day (gā′ là). A festive day; a day when people put on their best attire. (Ital. *gala*, finery.)

Galahad, Sir (găl′ a hăd). In the Arthurian legends the purest and noblest knight of the Round Table. He is a late addition and was invented by Walter Map in his *Quest of the San Graal.* He was the son of Lancelot and Elaine: at the institution of the Round Table one seat (the *Siege Perilous*) was left unoccupied, and could be occupied only by the knight who could succeed in the Quest. When Sir Galahad sat there it was discovered that it had been left for him. *Vide* Malory's *Morte d'Arthur*, Tennyson's *The Holy Grail*, etc.

Galatea (găl à tē′ a). A sea-nymph, beloved by Polypheme, but herself in love with Acis. Acis was crushed under a huge rock by the jealous giant, and Galatea threw herself into the sea, where she joined her sister nymphs. Handel has an opera entitled *Acis and Galatea* (1732). The Galatea beloved by Pygmalion (*q.v.*) was a different person.

Galaxy, The (găl′ àk si). The "Milky Way." A long white luminous track of stars which seems to encompass the heavens like a girdle. According to modern astronomical theory the Galaxy is a vast collection of stars set in a curiously flattened shape something like a double convex lens. It is because our Sun—and we ourselves in the planetary system with it—is in the midst of this Galaxy that the mass of stars appears so dense when we are looking lengthwise through it, whereas when we look out sideways, so to speak, we see the constellations of the heavens separately. It is supposed that the whole vast Galactic system revolves round a centre somewhere in the constellation of Sagittarius, 30,000 light years (a light year is six million million miles) from the Sun.

According to classic fable, it is the path to the palace of Zeus or Jupiter. (Gr. *gala*, *galaktos*, milk.)

Through all her courts
The vacant city slept; the busy winds,
That keep no certain intervals of rest,
Moved not; meanwhile the galaxy displayed
Her fires, that like mysterious pulses beat,
Aloft;—momentous but uneasy bliss!
WORDSWORTH: *Vandracour and Julia*, 94.

Galimatias (găl i mā′ shàs). Nonsense; unmeaning gibberish. The word first appeared in France in the 16th century, but its origin is unknown; perhaps it is connected with *gallimaufry* (*q.v.*). In his translation of Rabelais Urquhart heads ch. ii of Bk. I a "Galimatias of Extravagant Conceits found in an Ancient Monument."

Gall (gawl). Bile; the very bitter fluid secreted by the liver; hence used figuratively as a symbol for anything of extreme bitterness; colloquially, impudence.

Gall and wormwood. Extremely disagreeable and annoying.

And I said, My strength and my hope is perished from the Lord: Remembering my affliction and my misery, the wormwood and the gall.—*Lam.* iii, 18, 19.

The gall of bitterness. The bitterest grief; extreme affliction. The ancients taught that grief and joy were subject to the gall as affection was to the heart, knowledge to the kidneys, and the gall of bitterness means the bitter centre of bitterness, as the heart of heart means the innermost recesses of the heart or affections. In the *Acts* it is used to signify "the sinfulness of sin," which leads to the bitterest grief.

I perceive thou art in the gall of bitterness, and in the bond of iniquity.—*Acts* viii, 23.

Gallant. The meaning of this word varies with its pronunciation. As găl′ ànt it is an adjective meaning brave, grand, fine, chivalrous; as gàl ănt′ it describes the cavalier or admirer of women, a flirt, or the adjective and verb implying this.

Gallery. To play to the gallery. To work for popularity. As an actor who sacrifices his author for popular applause.

The instant we begin to think about success and the effect of our work—to play with one eye on the gallery—we lose power, and touch, and everything else.—KIPLING: *The Light that Failed.*

Galley Halfpence. Silver coin brought over by merchants ("galley-men") from Genoa, who used the Galley Wharf, Thames Street. These halfpence were larger than our own, and their use was forbidden in England early in the 15th century.

Gallia (găl' i à). France; the Latin name for Gaul.

Gallia Braccata (*trousered Gaul*). Gallia Narbonensis—South-western Gaul, from the Pyrenees to the Alps—was so called from the "braccæ," or trousers, which the natives wore in common with the Scythians and Persians.

Gallia Comata. That part of Gaul which belonged to the Roman emperor, and was governed by legates (*legati*), was so called from the long hair (*coma*) worn by the inhabitants flowing over their shoulders.

Gallicism (găl' i sizm). A phrase or sentence constructed after the French idiom; as, "when you *shall have returned* home you will find a letter on your table." In *Matt.* xv, 32, is a Gallicism: "I have compassion on the multitude, because *they continue* with me now three days, and have nothing to eat." *Cp. Mark* viii, 2.

Gallimaufry (găl i maw' fri). A medley; any confused jumble of things; but strictly speaking, a hotch-potch made up of all the scraps of the larder. (Fr. *galimafrée*, the origin of which is unknown, though it is probably related to *galimatias*).

> He woos both high and low, both rich and poor,
> Both young and old, one with another, Ford;
> He loves the galimaufry [all sorts].
> *Merry Wives*, ii, 1.

Gallo-Belgicus (găl ō bel' ji kús). An annual register in Latin for European circulation, first published in 1598.

> It is believed,
> And told for news with as much diligence
> As if 'twere writ in Gallo-Belgicus.
> THOMAS MAY: *The Heir*, 1615.

Galloglass (găl' ō glas). An armed servitor (or foot-soldier) of an ancient Irish chief. O.Ir. and Gael, *gall*, a stranger, *oglach*, a warrior.

> The Galloglass are pycked and scelected men of great and mightie bodies, crewel without compassion.
> —JOHN DYMMOK: *Treatice of Ireland* (1600).

Galloway (găl' ō wā). A horse less than fifteen hands high, of the breed which originally came from Galloway in Scotland.

> Thrust him downstairs! Know we not Galloway nags?—2 *Henry IV*, ii, 4.

Gallup Poll (găl' úp pōl). A method devised by Dr. George Gallup for ascertaining the trend of public opinion by interrogating a cross-section of the population. Trained interviewers question a very small sample of the public, which is carefully chosen with regard to its composition of men or women, geographical distribution, age groups and social position. For the British Parliamentary election of 1945 the interviewers spoke to 1,809 persons out of the 25,000,000 voters. These were so scientifically selected that the Gallup Poll forecast was less than 1 per cent. wrong when the actual voting figures were made known. On the other hand, their forecast was as wrong as that of everyone else at the American Presidential election of 1948.

Galore (gà lôr'). One of our words from Old Irish *go leor*, to a sufficiency; hence, in abundance, and abundance itself.

> For his Poll he had trinkets and gold galore,
> Besides of prize-money quite a store.
> *Jack Robinson* (A *Sailor's Song*).

Galosh (gà losh'). The word comes to us from the Span, *galocha* (wooden shoes); Ger. *galosche*; Fr. *galoche*, which is probably from Gr. *kalopous*, a shoe-maker's last.

The word was originally applied to a kind of clog or patten worn as a protection against wet in days when silk or cloth shoes were common. It is in this sense that writers so remote as Langland use the word:—

> . . . the kynde of a knyght that Cometh to be doubed,
> To geten hus gilte spores and galoches y-couped.
> *Piers Plowman*, xxi, 12.

The modern galoshes are rubber overshoes, and are sometimes spelled *goloshes*.

Galway Jury (gawl' wā). An enlightened, independent jury. The expression has its birth in certain trials held in Ireland in 1635 upon the right of the king to the counties of Ireland. Leitrim, Roscommon, Sligo, and Mayo gave judgment in favour of the Crown, but Galway opposed it; whereupon the sheriff was fined £1,000, and each of the jurors £4,000.

Gama, Vasco da (văs' kō da ga' ma). One of the greatest of the early Portuguese navigators (d. 1524), and the first European to double the Cape of Good Hope. He is the hero of Camoëns's *Lusiad* (1572),

> Gama, captain of the venturous band,
> Of bold emprise, and born for high command,
> Whose martial fires, with prudence close allied,
> Ensured the smiles of fortune on his side.

Game. Certain wild animals and birds, legally protected, preserved, and pursued for sport, such as hares, pheasants, partridges, grouse, heath-game, etc. *See* SPORTING SEASON.

The game is not worth the candle. *See* CANDLE.

The game is up. The scheme, endeavour, etc., has come to nothing; everything has failed.

He's a game 'un! He's got some pluck; he's "a plucked 'un." Another allusion to game-cocks.

He's at his little games again, or **at the same old game.** He's at his old tricks; he's gone back to his old habits or practices.

To have the game in one's hands. To have such an advantage that success is assured; to hold the winning cards.

To play a waiting game. To bide one's time, knowing that that is the best way of winning; to adopt Fabian tactics (*q.v.*).

To play the game. To act in a straightforward, honourable manner; to keep to the rules.

This they all with a joyful mind
Bear through life like a torch in flame,
And falling, fling to the host behind—
"Play up! Play up! and play the game!"
SIR H. NEWBOLT: Vitae Lampada.

Game Laws. A survival of the forest laws, imposed by William the Conqueror. Game licences were first issued in 1784. The seasons during which certain game might be shot were set out in the Game Act of William IV, 1831.

Game leg. A lame leg. In this instance *game* is a dialect form of the Celtic *cam*, meaning crooked. It is of comparatively modern usage.

Gammy is also used in this sense.

Gammadion (ga mā' di ón). The *fylfot* (*q.v.*), or swastika, so called because it resembles four Greek capital gammas (Γ) set at right angles.

Gammer. A rustic term for an old woman; a corruption of *grandmother*, with an intermediate form "granmer." *Cp.* GAFFER.

Gammon. This word comes from the same original as *game* and *gamble*, but in Victorian slang it meant to impose upon, delude, cheat; and sometimes, to play a game upon. As an exclamation it meant "Nonsense, you're pulling my leg!"

A landsman said, "I twig the chap—he's been upon the Mill,
And 'cause he gammons so the flats, ve calls him Veeping Bill."
Ingoldsby Legends.

Gammon, the buttock or thigh of a hog salted and cured, is the Fr. *jambon*, O.Fr. *gambon*, from *gambe*, the leg.

Gamut (găm' ŭt). Originally, the first or lowest note in Guido of Arezzo's scale, corresponding to G on the lowest line of the modern bass stave; later, the whole series of notes recognized by musicians; hence, the whole range or compass.

It is *gamma ut*; *gamma* (the third letter of the Greek alphabet) was used by Guido to mark the first or lowest note in the mediæval scale; and *ut* is the first word in the mnemonic stanza, *Ut queant laxis resonare fibris*, etc. (*see* DOH), containing the names of the hexachord. *Gamma ut*, or G *ut*, was added to the scale in the 11th century.

Ganelon. A type of black-hearted treachery, figuring in Dante's *Inferno* and grouped by Chaucer (*Nun's Priest's Tale*, 407) with Judas Iscariot and "Greek Sinon, that broghtest Troye al outrely to sorwe." He was Count of Mayence, one of Charlemagne's paladins. Jealousy of Roland made him a traitor; and in order to destroy his rival, he planned with Marsillus, the Moorish king, the attack of Roncesvalles.

Ganesha (găn' esh á). The god of wisdom in Hindu mythology, lord of the Ganas, or lesser deities. He was the son of Siva, is propitiated at the commencement of important work, at the beginning of sacred writings, etc.

Gang. A gang of saws. A number of circular power-driven saws mounted together so that they can reduce a tree trunk to planks at a single operation.

Gang agley, To (Scot.). To go wrong. The verb to *glee*, or *gley*, means to look asquint, sideways.

The best-laid schemes of mice and men
Gang aft agley. BURNS: To a Mouse.

Gang-day. The day when boys *gang* round the parish to beat its bounds. *See* BOUNDS.

Ganges, The (găn' jēz). So named from *ganga* or *gunga*, a river; as in *Kishenganga*, the black river; *Neelganga*, the blue river; *Naraingunga*, the river of Naranyana or Vishnu, etc. The Ganges is the *Borra Ganga*, or great river.

Those who through the curse, have fallen from heaven, having performed ablution in this stream, become free from sin; cleansed from sin by this water, and restored to happiness, they shall enter heaven and return again to the gods.—*The Ramayana* (section xxxv).

Gangway. Originally, the boarded way (hence sometimes called the *gang-board*, gang, an alley) in the old galleys made for the rowers to pass from stem to stern, and where the mast was laid when it was unshipped; now, the board with a railing at each side by which passengers walk into or out of a ship.

As we were putting off the boat they laid hold of the gangboard and unhooked it off the boat's stern.—COOK: *Second Voyage*, Bk. iii, ch. iv.

Below the gangway. In the House of Commons, on the farther side of the passage-way between the seats which separate the Ministry from the rest of the Members. To sit "below the gangway" is to sit amongst the general members, and not among the Ministers or ex-Ministers and leaders of the Opposition.

Ganymede (găn' i mēd). In Greek mythology, the cup-bearer of Zeus, successor to Hebe, and the type of youthful male beauty. Originally a Trojan youth, he was taken up to Olympus and made immortal. Hence, a cupbearer generally.

> Nature waits upon thee still,
> And thy verdant cup does fill;
> 'Tis fill'd wherever thou dost tread
> Nature's self's thy Ganymede.
>> COWLEY: *The Grasshopper* (*Anacreontics*).

Gaora (gā ôr′ a). According to Hakluyt this was a tract of land inhabited by people without heads, with eyes in their shoulders and their mouths in their breasts. *See* BLEMMYES.

Garcia (gar′ si à). **To take a message to Garcia** is to be resourceful and courageous, to be able to accept responsibility and carry one's task through to the end. The phrase originated in the exploit of Lieut. Andrew Rowan who, in the Spanish-American War of 1898, made his way through the Spanish blockade into Cuba, made contact with General Calixto Garcia, chief of the Cuban insurgent forces, and carried news from him back to Washington.

Garcias. The soul of Pedro Garcias. Money. The story is that two scholars of Salamanca discovered a tombstone with this inscription: "Here lies the soul of the licentiate Pedro Garcias"; and on searching found a purse with a hundred golden ducats. (*Gil Bias*, Preface.)

Garden. Garden City. A name given alike to Norwich and to Chicago; also, as a general name, to model suburbs and townships that have been planned with a special view to the provision of open spaces, and wide roads.

The Garden or **Garden Sect.** The disciples of Epicurus, who taught in his own private garden.

The Garden of Eden. *See* EDEN. The name as applied to Mesopotamia, with its vast sandy deserts, is nowadays somewhat ironical; but it is traditionally supposed to be its "original site."

Gardy loo. The cry of warning formerly given by Edinburgh housewives when about to throw the contents of the slop-pail out of the window into the street below. It is a corruption of Fr. *garde l'eau*, beware of the water.

> At ten o'clock at night the whole cargo is flung out of a back window that looks into some street or lane, and the maid calls "Gardy loo" to the passengers.— SMOLLETT: *Humphrey Clinker.*

Gargamelle (gar′ gà mel). In Rabelais's satire, daughter of the king of the Parpaillons (*butterflies*), wife of Grangousier, and mother of Gargantua (*q.v.*). On the day that she gave birth to him she ate sixteen quarters, two bushels, three pecks, and a pipkin of *dirt*, the mere remains left in the tripe which she had for supper.

She is said to be meant either for Anne of Brittany, or Catherine de Foix, Queen of Navarre.

Gargantua (gar găn′ tū à). A giant of mediæval (perhaps Celtic) legend famous for his enormous appetite (Sp. *garganta*, gullet), adopted by Rabelais in his great satire (1532), and made the father of Pantagruel. One of his exploits was to swallow five pilgrims with their slaves and all in a salad. He is the subject of a number of chap-books, and became proverbial as a voracious and insatiable guzzler.

> You must borrow me Gargantua's mouth first [before I can utter so long a word]; 'tis a word too great for any mouth of this age's size.—*As You Like It*, iii, 2.

Gargouille (gar goo ēl′). The great dragon that lived in the Seine, ravaged Rouen, and was slain by St. Romanus, Bishop of Rouen, in the 7th century.

Gargoyle (gar′ goil). A spout for rain-water in Gothic architecture, projecting from the wall so that the water falls clear, and usually carved into some fantastic shape, such as a dragon's head, through which the water flows. So named from Fr. *gargouille*, the throat, gullet.

Garibaldi (gär i bol′ di). The red shirt made famous by Garibaldi and his men in their deliverance of Italy in 1860 had a very simple origin. It was in Montevideo, in 1843, where Garibaldi was raising an Italian legion, that a number of red woollen shirts came on the market owing to the difficulty of export due to the war with Argentina. The Uruguay government bought them up cheaply and handed them over to Garibaldi for his men. When the Italian Legion came over to Europe in 1848 they brought their red shirts with them, thus furnishing Italy with her long-treasured symbol of freedom.

The Garibaldi biscuit, in which currants are mixed in the pastry, was a form of food much favoured by the General on his farm in Caprera.

Garland. The primary use of this word, meaning a wreath of flowers either worn or festooned around some object, has been extended to include a collection of pieces in prose or verse, a sort of choice anthology.

> What I now offer to your Lordship is a collection of Poetry, a kind of Garland of Good Will.—PRIOR'S dedication to his *Poems.*

Garlic. The old superstition that garlic can destroy the magnetic power of the loadstone has the sanction of Pliny, Solinus, Ptolemy, Plutarch, Albertus, Mathiolus, Rueus, Rulandus, Renodæus, Langius, and others. Sir Thomas Browne places it among *Vulgar Errors* (Bk. ii, ch. 3).

Martin Rulandus saith that Onions and Garlick . . . hinder the attractive power [of the magnet] and rob it of its virtue of drawing iron, to which Renodæus agrees; but this is all lies.—W. SALMON: *The Complete English Physician*, ch. xxv (1693).

Garnish. In old prison slang, the entrance-money, to be spent in drink, demanded by jailbirds of new-comers. *Garnish* means embellishment, extra decoration to dress, etc.; hence, it was applied by prisoners to fetters, and the garnish-money was money given for the "honour" of wearing them. The custom became obsolete with the reform of prisons.

In its original meaning to *garnish* was to *warn*, and it is in this sense that the word is now used legally. John X (called the garnishee) is garnished or warned not to pay a sum he owes to Henry Y as Henry Y owes money to George Z but is disputing the debt.

Garraway's. A noted coffee-house in Change Alley, Cornhill, which existed for over 200 years and was founded by Thomas Garway, a tobacconist and coffee merchant in the 16th century. Here the promoters of the South Sea Bubble met. Sales were held periodically, and tea was introduced to England in 1657, selling at from 16s. to 50s. a pound. Garraway's was closed and the house demolished in 1874.

Garrotte (Span, *garrote*, a stick). A Spanish method of execution by fastening a cord round the neck of the criminal and twisting it with a *stick* till strangulation ensued. In 1851 General Lopez was garrotted for attempting to gain possession of Cuba; and about that time the term was first applied to the practice of London thieves and roughs who strangled their victim while an accomplice rifled his pockets.

Garter. The Most Noble Order of the Garter. The highest order of knighthood in Great Britain and in the world, traditionally instituted by King Edward III about 1348, re-constituted in 1805 and 1831. The popular legend is that Joan, Countess of Salisbury, accidentally slipped her garter at a court ball. It was picked up by the king, who gallantly diverted the attention of the guests from the lady by binding the blue band round his own knee, saying as he did so, *"Honi' soit qui mal y pense"* (Evil—or shame—be to him who thinks evil of it) (*q.v.*). The order is limited to the Sovereign, and other members of the Royal Family, with twenty-five Knights, and such foreign royalties as may be admitted by statute. The only Ladies of the Garter are the Sovereign's Queen and his eldest daughter when she is heir apparent to the throne; and until, in 1912, Viscount Grey

(then Sir Edward Grey) was admitted to the order, no commoner for centuries had been able to put "K.G." after his name.

Each knight is allotted a stall in St. George's Chapel, Windsor. The habits and insignia are the garter, mantle, surcoat, hood, star, collar, and George—a jewelled figure representing St. George and the Dragon.

Wearing the garters of a pretty girl either on the hat or knee was a common custom with our forefathers. Brides usually wore on their legs a host of gay ribbons, to be distributed after the marriage ceremony amongst the bridegroom's friends; and the piper at the wedding dance never failed to tie a piece of the bride's garter round his pipe.

Magic garters. In the old romances, etc., garters made of the strips of a young hare's skin saturated with motherwort. Those who wore them excelled in speed.

Prick the garter. An old swindling game, better known as "Fast and loose." *See under* FAST.

Garvies. Sprats; perhaps so called from Inch-garvie, the island in the Firth of Forth that supports the central pier of the Forth Bridge.

Gas mask. A popular name for any contrivance designed to preserve the wearer from inhaling poison gas. In World War I (when gas was first used) the gas mask went through various forms from a sort of greasy felt domino to a box respirator strapped on the chest. In World War II there were several kinds of respirator—for infants, for small children, civilians, civilians on national duty, and for the Services; all of which differed only in the period for which they were effective.

Gat. American slang term for an automatic pistol, much used during the prohibition era of gangsters. It is a wrongly applied contraction of Gatling, from the first machine-gun invented by Richard Gordon Gatling during the American Civil War.

Gat-tooth. Chaucer's "Wife of Bath" was *gat-toothed* (*see Prol. to Cant. Tales*, 468, and *Wife of Bath's Prol.* 603); this probably means that her teeth were set wide apart, with *gats*, *i.e.* openings or gaps between them; but some editors have thought it is *goat-toothed* (A.S. *gat*), *i.e.* lascivious, like a goat.

Gate. Gate money. Money paid at the door or gate for admission to an enclosure where some entertainment or contest, etc., is to take place.

Gate-posts. The post on which a gate hangs is called the hanging-post; that against which it shuts is called the banging-post.

Gath (găth). In Dryden's *Absalom and Achitophel* (*q.v.*), this means Brussels, where Charles II long resided while in exile.

Gathering is a common phrase among Dissenters to describe any sort of religious or social assembly.

Bibliographically, it is any number of leaves which may be put together and joined into a section of the book by being sewn through.

Gatling Gun. An early form of automatic weapon invented in the U.S.A. in 1867. It had a large number of barrels, the projectiles in which could be discharged in rapid succession. It preceded all types of weapons constructed on the principle of discharging numerous projectiles rapidly through the same barrel, as a machine gun.

Gauche (gōsh) (Fr., the left hand). Awkward.

Gaucherie. Behaviour not according to the received forms of society; awkward and untoward ways.

Gaucho (gou' chō). A cowboy of the S. American pampas, of mixed Indian and Spanish descent. The word is also applied to an itinerant minstrel of the Argentine pampas, who goes from village to village with horse and guitar.

Gaudy-day (gaw' di) (Lat. *gaudium*, joy). A holiday, a feast-day; especially an annual celebration of some event, such as the foundation of a college.

Gaul (gawl). In classical geography, the country inhabited by the Gauls, hence, in modern use, France. *Cisalpine Gaul* lay south and east of the Alps, in what is now northern Italy. *Transalpine Gaul* was north and northwest of the Alps, and included Narbonensis, Aquitania, Lugdunensis, and Belgica. It was inhabited by Franks, Germans, Burgundians, Celts and others, as well as Gauls.

Insulting Gaul has roused the world to war.
THOMSON: *Autumn.*
Shall haughty Gaul invasion threat?—BURNS.

Gaunt. John of Gaunt (1340-99), third son of Edward III; so called from Ghent, in Flanders, the place of his birth.

Gauntlet. To run the gauntlet. To be attacked on all sides, to be severely criticized. The word came into English at the time of the Thirty Years' War as *gantlope*, meaning the passage between two files of soldiers, and is the Swedish *gata*, a way, passage (*cp.* GAT-TOOTH *above*), and *lopp* (connected with our *leap*), a course. The reference is to a punishment formerly common among soldiers and sailors; the company or crew, provided with rope ends,

were drawn up in two rows facing each other, and the delinquent had to run between them, while every man dealt him as severe a chastisement as he could.

To throw down the gauntlet. To challenge. The custom in the Middle Ages, when one knight challenged another, was for the challenger to throw his gauntlet on the ground, and if the challenge was accepted the person to whom it was thrown picked it up.

Gautama (gaw ta' ma). The family name of Buddha (*q.v.*). His personal name was Siddhattha, his father's name Suddhodana, and his mother's Maya. *Buddha* means "The Enlightened," "The One Who Knows," and he assumed this title at about the age of 36, when, after seven years of seclusion and spiritual struggle, he believed himself to have attained to perfect truth.

Gauvaine. Gawain (*q.v.*).

Gawain (gȧ wān). One of the most famous of the Arthurian knights, nephew of King Arthur, and probably the original hero of the Grail quest. He appears in the Welsh *Triads* and the *Mabinogion* as Gwalchmei, and in the Arthurian cycle is the centre of many episodes and poems. The Middle English poem (about 1360), *Sir Gawain and the Green Knight*, is a romance telling how Gawain beheads the Green Knight in single combat.

Gay. A gay deceiver. A Lothario (*q.v.*); a libertine.

Gaze. To stand at gaze. To stand in doubt what to do. A term in forestry. When a stag first hears the hounds it stands dazed, looking all round, and in doubt what to do. Heralds call a stag which is represented full-faced, a "stag at gaze."

As the poor frightened deer, that stands at gaze,
Wildly determining which way to fly.
Rape of Lucrece, 1149.

Gaze-hound. *See* LYME-HOUND.

Gazebo (gȧ zē' bō). A humorous Latin future tense applied to the English *gaze*, to describe a summer-house with an extensive prospect. The word is also used for a balcony, window, or any other vantage spot whence a good view can be obtained.

Gazette. A newspaper. The first newspapers were issued in Venice by the Government, and came out in manuscript once a month, during the war of 1563 between the Venetians and Turks. The intelligence was read publicly in certain places, and the fee for hearing it read was one *gazetta* (a Venetian coin, somewhat less than a farthing in value).

The first official English newspaper, called *The Oxford Gazette*, was published in 1642, at Oxford, where the Court was held. On the removal of the Court to London, the name was changed to *The London Gazette*. This name was revived in 1665, during the Great Fire. Now the official *Gazette*, published every Tuesday and Friday, contains announcements of pensions, promotions, bankruptcies, dissolutions of partnerships, etc.

Gazetteer. A geographical and topographical index or dictionary; so called because the name of one of the earliest in English (L. Eachard's, 1693) was *The Gazetteer's or Newsman's Interpreter*, i.e. it was intended for the use of journalists, those who wrote for the Gazettes.

Gear. In machinery, the wheels, chains, belts, etc., that communicate motion to the working parts are called the gear or *gearing* (Sax. *gearwa*, clothing). The term is more particularly applied to a toothed wheel or a series of toothed wheels for the transmission of motion from one machine to another, or from one part of a machine to another. *High gear* is said of an arrangement of wheels, etc., whereby the driving part moves slowly in relation to the driven part; *Low gear* is the reverse of this, the driving part moving relatively more quickly than the driven; *Differential gear* is a combination of toothed gear wheels connecting two axles but allowing them to revolve at different speeds. *Gear* is also applied to all forms of equipment, as, for example, *sports gear*.

Gehenna (ge hen' à) (Heb.). The place of eternal torment. Strictly speaking, it means simply the Valley of Hinnom (*Ge-Hinnom*), where sacrifices to Baal and Moloch were offered (*Jer.* xix, 6, etc.), and where refuse of all sorts was subsequently cast, for the consumption of which fires were kept constantly burning.

> And made his grove
> The pleasant valley of Hinnom, Tophet thence
> And black Gehenna called, the type of hell.
> MILTON: *Paradise Lost*, Bk. i, 403.

Gelert (gel' ẽrt). Llewelyn's dog. *See* BETH GELERT.

Gemara (ge ma' rà) (Aramaic, complement). The second part of the Talmud (*q.v.*), consisting of annotations, discussions, and amplifications of the *Mishna*, which is the first part. The *Mishna* is the interpretation of the written law, the *Gemara* the interpretation of the *Mishna*. There is the Babylonian *Gemara* and the Jerusalem *Gemara*. The former, which is the more complete, is by the academies of Babylon, and was completed about A.D. 500;

the latter; by those of Palestine, completed towards the close of the 4th or during the 5th century A.D.

Gemini (jem' i ni). A zodiacal sign. *See* THE TWINS.

Gendarmes (zhon' darm). "Men at arms," the armed police of France. The term was first applied to those who marched in the train of knights; subsequently to the cavalry; in the time of Louis XIV to a body of horse charged with the preservation of order; after the Revolution to a military police chosen from old soldiers of good character; and now to the ordinary police.

Gender Words. These are words which, prefixed to the noun, indicate an animal's sex: —

Bull, cow: Elephant, rhinoceros, seal, whale.

Dog, bitch: ape, fox (the bitch is usually called a vixen), otter, wolf.

Buck, doe: hare, rabbit, deer.

He, she: general gender words for quadrupeds.

Cock, hen: gender words for most birds.

In many cases a different word is used for each of the sexes, *e.g.:* —

Boar, sow; cockerel, pullet; colt, filly; drake, duck; drone, bee; gander, goose; hart, roe; ram, ewe; stag, hind; stallion, mare; steer, heifer; ram, wether; tup, dam.

Generalissimo. The supreme commander, especially of a force drawn from two or more nations, or of a combined military and naval force. The title is said to have been coined by Cardinal Richelieu on taking supreme command of the French armies in Italy, in 1629. Called *Tagus* among the ancient Thessalians, *Brennus* among the ancient Gauls, *Pendragon* among the ancient Welsh or Celts.

In modern times the title has been applied to Marshal Foch (1851-1929) who was appointed generalissimo of the Allied forces in France in 1918; to Joseph Stalin (b. 1879) who was made marshal and generalissimo of the Soviet forces in 1943; to General Franco (b. 1882) who proclaimed himself generalissimo of the Spanish army in 1939; to Marshal Chiang Kai-Shek, President of the Nationalist Republic of China, and leader of the Chinese armies against the Japanese and internal foes.

Generous. Generous as Hatim. An Arabian expression. Hatim was a Bedouin chief famous for his warlike deeds and boundless generosity. His son was contemporary with Mohammed.

> Let Zal and Rustum bluster as they will,
> Or Hatim call to Supper—heed not you.
> FITZGERALD: *Rubáiyát of Omar Khayyám*, x.

Geneva (je nē′ và). *See* GIN.

Geneva Convention. Henri Dunant, a Swiss, published an account of the sufferings of the wounded at the battle of Solferino in 1859. From this sprang (1) the International Red Cross, and (2) an international convention, 1864, governing the treatment of wounded. At a conference in London in 1872 Dunant suggested a code for the treatment of prisoners of war which was adopted by all civilized nations.

Geneva courage. Pot valour; the braggadocio which is the effect of having drunk too much gin (*q.v.*), or *geneva*. *Cp.* DUTCH COURAGE.

Geneva Cross. *See* RED CROSS.

Geneva doctrines. Calvinism. Calvin, in 1541, was invited to take up his residence in Geneva as the public teacher of theology. From this period Geneva was for many years the centre of education for the Protestant youths of Europe.

Geneviève, St. (je nà vēv) (422-512). Patroness of the city of Paris. Her day is January 3rd, and she is represented in art with the keys of Paris at her girdle, a devil blowing out her candle, and an angel relighting it, or as restoring sight to her blind mother, or guarding her father's sheep. She was born at Nanterre, and was influential in averting a threatened attack on Paris by Attila, the Hun.

Genius (pl. **Genii**). In Roman mythology the tutelary spirit that attended one from his cradle to his grave, governed his fortunes, determined his character, and so on. The Eastern genii (sing. genie) were entirely different from the Roman, not attendant spirits, but fallen angels, dwelling in Dijin-nistan, under the dominion of Eblis; the Roman were very similar to the guardian angels spoken of in *Matt.* xviii, 10; and in this sense Mephistopheles is spoken of as the *evil genius* (the "familiar") of Faust. The Romans maintained that two genii attended every man from birth to death—one good and the other evil. Good luck was brought about by the agency of "his good genius," and ill luck by that of his "evil genius."

The *genius loci* was the tutelary deity of a place.

The word is from the Lat. *gignere*, to beget (Gr. *gignesthai*, to be born), from the notion that birth and life were due to these *dii genitales*. Hence it is used for birth-wit or innate talent; hence propensity, nature, inner man.

Genocide (jen′ ō sīd). A word invented by Prof. Raphael Lemkin, of Duke University, U.S.A., and used in the drafting of the official indictment of war criminals in 1945. It comes from the Greek *genos*, race; and Latin *caedere*, to kill. It is defined as acts intended to destroy, in whole or in-part, national, ethnical, racial, or religious groups. On 9th December, 1948, it was declared by the United Nations General Assembly to be a crime in international law.

Genre Painter (zhon′ rė). A painter of domestic, rural, or village scenes, such as *A Village Wedding*, *The Young Recruit*, *Blind Man's Buff*, *The Village Politician*, etc. In the drama, Victor Hugo introduced the genre system in lieu of the stilted, unnatural style of Louis XIV's era.

We call those "genre" canvases, whereon are painted idylls of the fireside, the roadside, and the farm; pictures of real life.—E. C. STEDMAN; *Poets of America*, ch. iv.

Gens (jenz) (Lat. pl. *gentes*). A clan or sept in ancient Rome; a number of families deriving from a common ancestor, having the same name, religion, etc.

Gens braccata (Lat.). Trousered people. The Romans wore no trousers ("breeches") like the Gauls, Scythians, and Persians. *Cp.* GALLIA BRACCATA.

Gens togata. *See* TOGA.

Gentle. Belonging to a family of position; well born; having the manners of genteel persons.

We must be gentle, now we are gentlemen.— *Winter's Tale*, v, 2.

The word is from Lat. *gentilis*, of the same family or *gens*, through O.Fr. *gentil*, high-born.

Gentleman (formed on the model of Fr. *gentilhomme*). Properly, a man entitled to bear arms but not of the nobility; hence, one of gentle birth, of some position in society, and with the manners, bearing, and behaviour appropriate to one in such a position.

Be it spoken (with all reverent reservation of duty) the King who hath power to make Esquires, Knights, Baronets, Barons, Viscounts, Earls, Marquesses, and Dukes, *cannot make a Gentleman*, for Gentilitie is a matter of race, and of blood, and of descent, from Gentle and noble parents and ancestors, which no Kings can give to any, but to such as they beget.—EDMOND HOWES.

Juliana Berners, in her *Boke of St. Albans* (1486), in the treatise "Blasyng of Armys," has a curious use of the word:—

Of the offspring of the gentilman Jafeth came Habraham, Moyses, Aron, and the profettys: and also the kyng of the right lyne of Mary, of whom that gentilman Jhesus was borne very god and man: after his manhode kyng of the londe of Judea of Jues, gentilman by is modre Mary prynce of Cote armure.

In the *York Mysteries* also (about 1440) we read, "Ther schall a gentilman, Jesu, unjustely be judged."

A gentleman at large. A man of means, who does not have to work for his living, and is free to come and go as he pleases. Formerly the term denoted a gentleman attached to the court but having no special duties.

A gentleman of fortune. A pirate, an adventurer (a euphemistic phrase).

A gentleman of the four outs. A vulgar upstart, with-*out* manners, with-*out* wit, with-*out* money, and-with-*out* credit. There are variants of the phrase, and sometimes the *outs* are increased to five:—

Out of money, and out of clothes,
Out at the heels, and out at the toes,
Out of credit—but, don't forget,
Never *out of* but aye *in* debt!

A gentleman's gentleman. A manservant, especially a valet.

Fag.: My master shall know this—and if *he* don't call him out *I* will.
Lucy: Ha! ha! ha! You gentlemen's gentlemen are so hasty!　　SHERIDAN: *The Rivals*, II, ii.

Gentlemen at Arms, The Honourable Corps of The Bodyguard of the Sovereign (formerly called *Gentlemen Pensioners*), acting in conjunction with the Yeomen of the Guard (*q.v.*). It consists of 40 retired officers of ranks from general to major of the Regular Army and Marines, and has a Captain, Lieutenant, Standard Bearer, Clerk of the Cheque & Adjutant, and a Harbinger.

The gentleman in black velvet. It was in these words that the 18th-century Jacobites used to toast the mole that made the molehill that caused William III's horse to stumble and so brought about his death.

The Old Gentleman. The Devil; Old Nick. Also a special card in a prepared pack, used for tricks or cheating.

To put a churl upon a gentleman. To drink beer just after drinking wine.

Geomancy (jē' ō măn si) (Gr. *ge*, the earth; *manteia*, prophecy). Divining by the earth. Diviners in the 16th century made deductions from the patterns made by earth thrown into the air and allowed to fall on some flat surface, and drew on the earth their magic circles, figures, lines, etc.

Geopolitics (jē ō pol' i tiks). Theories relating to a nation's political dependence on physical environment and its geographical position. The chief developers of these theories were Sir Halford Mackinder, Father Walsh (U.S.A.), and Karl Haushofer in Germany. The Nazis seized on the teachings of the last-named and distorted them to support their demand for *lebensraum*.

George. St. George. The patron saint of England since about the time of the institution of the Order of the Garter (*c.* 1348), when he was "adopted" by Edward III. He is commemorated on April 23rd.

St. George had been popular in England from the time of the early Crusades, for he was said to have come to the assistance of the Crusaders at Antioch (1089), and many of the Normans (under Robert, son of William the Conqueror) then took him as their patron.

St. George suffered martyrdom near Lydda before the 4th century. There are various versions of his *Acta*, one saying that he was a tribune and that he was asked to come and subdue a dragon that infested a pond at Silene, Libya, and fed on the dwellers in the neighbourhood. St. George came, rescued a princess (Sabra) whom the dragon was about to make its prey, and slew the monster.

That St. George is an historical character is beyond all reasonable doubt; but no connexion whatever can be established between this martyr and the Arian bishop George of Cappadocia, as Gibbon and others have suggested.

The legend of St. George and the dragon is simply an allegorical expression of the triumph of the Christian hero over evil, which St. John the Divine beheld under the image of a dragon. Similarly, St. Michael, St. Margaret, St. Silvester, and St. Martha are all depicted as slaying dragons; the Saviour and the Virgin as treading them under their feet; St. John the Evangelist as charming a winged dragon from a poisoned chalice given him to drink; and Bunyan avails himself of the same figure when he makes Christian prevail against Apollyon.

The legend forms the subject of an old ballad given in Percy's *Reliques*, in which St. George was the son of Lord Albert of Coventry.

St. George he was for England, St. Denis was for France. This refers to the war-cries of the two nations—that of England was "St. George!" that of France, "Montjoye St. Denis!"

Our ancient word of courage, fair "St. George",
Inspire us with the spleen of fiery dragons.
　　　　　　　　　Richard III, v, 3.

St. George's Cross. Red on a white background.

George IV was the only English king whose manner of life dubbed him with nicknames. As Prince Regent he was known as "Prinny," "Prince Florizel" (the name under which he corresponded with Mrs. Robinson); "The First Gentleman of Europe," "The Adonis of fifty" (for writing this Leigh Hunt was sent to prison in 1813). As king he was called, among less offensive titles, "Fum the Fourth." Byron writes (*Don Juan*, xi, 78):—

And where is Fum the Fourth, our royal bird?

George Cross and Medal. The George Cross is second only to the Victoria Cross. It consists of a plain silver cross, with a medallion showing St. George and the Dragon in the centre. The words "For Gallantry" appear round the medallion, and in the angle of each limb of the cross is the royal cipher. It hangs from a dark blue ribbon. The George Cross was founded in 1940, primarily for civilians, and is awarded only for acts of the greatest heroism or the most conspicuous courage in circumstances of extreme danger. The George Medal (red ribbon with five narrow blue stripes) is awarded in similar circumstances to the Cross where services are not so outstanding as to merit the higher award.

Geraint (ge rānt' ge rīnt'). In Arthurian legend, a tributary prince of Devon, and one of the knights of the Round Table. In the *Mabinogion* story he is the son of Erbin, as he is in the French original, Chrestien de Troyes' *Eric et Enide*, from which Tennyson drew his *Geraint and Enid* in the *Idylls of the King.*

Geraldine (je' răl dēn). **The Fair Geraldine.** Lady Elizabeth Fitzgerald (d. 1589) is so called in the Earl of Surrey's poems. She was the youngest daughter of the Earl of Kildare.

Geranium. The Turks say this was a common mallow changed by the touch of Mohammed's garment.

The word is Gr. *geranos*, a crane; and the wild plant is called "Crane's Bill," from the resemblance of the fruit to the bill of a crane.

Gerda, or **Gerdhr** (gĕr' dà). In Scandinavian mythology (the *Skirnismal*), a young giantess, wife of Frey, and daughter of the frost giant Gymer. She is so beautiful that the brightness of her naked arms illumines both air and sea.

Geriatrics (jĕ ri ăt' riks). The study of old age, medically and socially. The word comes from the Greek *geron*, an old man.

German or **germane.** Pertaining to, nearly related to, as *cousins-german* (first cousins), *germane to the subject* (bearing on or pertinent to the subject). This word has no connexion with the German nation, but is Lat., *germanus*, of the same germ or stock.

Those that are germane to him, though removed fifty times, shall all come under the hangman.— *Winter's Tale*, iv, 3.

Germany. The English name for the German *Deutschland* (Fr. *Allemagne*) is the Lat. *Germania*, the source of which is not certain; it is thought to be the form given by the Romans to the Celtic or Gaulish name for the Teutons; in which case it may be connected either with Celt, *gair*, neighbour, *gavim*, war-cry, or *ger*, spear.

Geoffrey of Monmouth, recording popular eponymic legends, says that Ebrancus, a mythological descendant of Brute (*q.v.*) and founder of York (*Eboracum*), had twenty sons and thirty daughters. All the sons, except the eldest, settled in Germany, which was therefore called the land of the *germans* or brothers. Spenser, speaking of "Ebranck," says:—

An happy man in his first days he was,
  And happy father of fair progeny;
For all so many weeks as the year has
  So many children he did multiply!
  Of which were twenty sons, which did apply
Their minds to praise and chivalrous desire.
  Those germans did subdue all Germany,
Of whom it hight.   *Faerie Queene*, II, x, 22.

German comb. The four fingers and thumb. The Germans were the last nation to adopt periwigs; and while the French were never seen without a comb in one hand, the Germans adjusted their hair by running their fingers through it.

He apparelled himself according to the season, and afterwards combed his head with an Alman comb.— RABELAIS: Bk. i, 21.

German silver. A silvery-looking alloy of copper, zinc, and nickel. It was first made in Europe at Hildburghausen, in Germany, in the early 19th century, but had been used by the Chinese time out of mind.

Geronimo (je ron' i mō). The name taken by Goyathlay (One who Yawns), an Apache chieftain who led a sensational Indian campaign against the Whites in 1885-6. He was captured by General Cook, escaped, was recaptured, and imprisoned for some time. He later became a member of the Dutch Reformed Church, and wrote his memoirs, 1906.

Gerrymander (jer i măn' dĕr). So to divide a county or nation into representative districts as to give one special political party undue advantage over others. The word is derived from Elbridge Gerry (1744-1814), who adopted the scheme in Massachusetts in 1812 when he was governor. Gilbert Stuart, the artist, looking at the map of the new distribution, with a little invention converted it into a salamander. "No, no!" said Russell, when shown it, "not a Sala-mander, Stuart, call it a Gerry-mander."

Hence, to hocus-pocus statistics, election results, etc., so as to make them appear to give other than their true result, or so as to affect the balance.

Geryon (ger' i on). In Greek mythology, a monster with three bodies and three heads, whose oxen ate human flesh, and were guarded by Orthros, a two-headed dog. Hercules slew both Geryon and the dog.

Gesta Romanorum (jes' ta rō má nôr' ùm). A pseudo-devotional compilation of popular tales in Latin (many from Oriental sources), each with an arbitrary "moral" attached for the use of preachers, assigned—in its collected form—to about the end of the 14th century. The name, meaning "The Acts of the Romans," is merely fanciful. It was first printed at Utrecht about 1472, and the earliest English edition is that of Wynkyn de Worde about 1510, but long before this the people had, through the pulpit, come to know it, and many English poets, from Chaucer to William Morris, have laid it under contribution. Shakespeare drew the plot of *Pericles* from the *Gesta Romanorum*, as well as the incident of the three caskets in the *Merchant of Venice*.

Gestapo (ge sta' pō). A word made up from the German *Geheime Staatspolizei*, the political police who acquired such sinister fame in Nazi Germany. It was organized by Heinrich Himmler as an independent supreme Reich authority, beyond all judicial or administrative control, and to it was committed the execution of all punitive or repressive measures of the government.

Gestas (jes' tăs). The traditional name of the impenitent thief. *See* DYSMAS.

Get. With its past and past participle *got*, one of the hardest-worked words in the English language; the following example from a mid-Victorian writer shows some of its uses—and abuses:—

I got on horseback within ten minutes after I got your letter. When I got to Canterbury I got a chaise for town; but I got wet through, and have got such a cold that I shall not get rid of in a hurry. I got to the Treasury about noon, but first of all got shaved and dressed. I soon got into the secret of getting a memorial before the Board, but I could not get an answer then; however, I got intelligence from a messenger that I should get one next morning. As soon as I got back to my inn, I got my supper, and then got to bed. When I got up next morning, I got my breakfast, and, having got dressed, I got out in time to get an answer to my memorial. As soon as I got it, I got into a chaise, and got back to Canterbury by three, and got home for tea. I have got nothing for you, and so adieu.

For phrases such as **To get out of bed the wrong side, To get the mitten, To get the wind up,** etc., see the main word in the phrase.

How are you getting on? How do things fare with you? How are you prospering?

To get at. To tamper with, bribe, influence to a wrong end; especially used in horse-racing.

To get by. To get along all right, just satisfactorily.

To get down to it. To set about your work or whatever it is you have in hand in down-right earnest.

To get off. To escape; also (of a girl) to become engaged to be married, or to make acquaintanceship with a man.

To get there. To succeed; to "arrive"; attain one's object.

To get up. To rise from one's bed. To learn, as "I must get up my history." To organize and arrange, as "We will get up a bazaar."

To get well on, or **well oiled.** To become intoxicated.

Who are you getting at? Who are you trying to take a rise out of? Whose leg are you trying to pull? A question usually asked sarcastically by the intended butt.

Gethsemane (geth sem' à ni). The *Orchis maculata*, supposed in legendary story to be spotted by the blood of Christ.

Gewgaw. A showy trifle. The word may be an imitation of Fr. *jou-jou*, a baby word for a toy (*jouer*, to play), or it may be from *givegove*, a M.E. reduplication of *give*.

Ghost. To give up the ghost. To die. The idea is that life is independent of the body, and is due to the habitation of the ghost or spirit in the material body.

Man dieth, and wasteth away: yea, man giveth up the ghost, and where is he?—*Job* xiv, 10.

The ghost of a chance. The least likelihood. "He has not the ghost of a chance of being elected," not the shadow of a probability.

Ghost-word. A term invented by Skeat (*Philol. Soc. Transactions*, 1886) to denote words that have no real existence but are due to the blunders of scribes, printers, or editors, etc. Like ghosts we may seem to see them, or may fancy that they exist; but they have no real entity. We cannot grasp them. When we would do so, they disappear. *Acre-fight* and *slughorn* (*q.v.*) are examples.

Intrusive letters that have no etymological right in a word but have been inserted through false analogy with words similarly pronounced (like the *gh* in *sprightly* or the *h* in *aghast*) are sometimes called **ghost-letters**.

Ghost writer. The anonymous author who writes speeches, articles, or even books—

especially autobiographies—for which another and better-known person gets the credit.

Giants, *i.e.* persons well above the average height and size, are by no means uncommon as "sports" or "freaks of nature"; but the widespread belief in pre-existing races or individual instances of giants among primitive peoples is due partly to the ingrained idea that the present generation is invariably a degeneration— "There were giants in the earth in those days" (*Gen.* vi, 4)—and partly to the existence from remote antiquity of cyclopæan buildings, gigantic sarcophagi, etc., and to the discovery from time to time in pre-scientific days of the bones of extinct monsters which were taken to be those of men. Among instances of the latter may be mentioned the following:—

A skeleton discovered at Lucerne in 1577 19 ft. in height. Dr. Plater is our authority for this measurement.

"Teutobochus," whose remains were discovered near the Rhone in 1613. They occupied a tomb 30 ft. long. The bones of another gigantic skeleton were exposed by the action of the Rhone in 1456. If this was a human skeleton, the height of the living man must have been 30 ft.

Pliny records that an earthquake in Crete exposed the bones of a giant 46 cubits (*i.e.* roughly 75 ft.) in height; he called this the skeleton of Orion, others held it to be that of Otus.

Antæus is said by Plutarch to have been 60 cubits (about 90 ft.) in height. He furthermore adds that the grave of the giant was opened by Serbonius.

The "monster Polypheme." It is said that his skeleton was discovered at Trapani, in Sicily, in the 14th century. If this skeleton was that of a man, he must have been 300 ft. in height.

Giants of the Bible.

ANAK. The eponymous progenitor of the Anakim (*see. below*). The Hebrew spies said they were mere grasshoppers in comparison with these giants. (*Josh*, xv, 14; *Judges* i, 20; and *Numb*, xiii, 33).

GOLIATH of Gath (I *Sam*. xvii, etc.). His height is given as 6 cubits and a span: the cubit varied and might be anything from about 18 in. to 21 in., and a span was about 9 in.; this would give Goliath a height of between 9 ft. 9 in. and 11 ft. 3 in.

OG, King of Bashan (*Josh*, xii, 4, *Deut*. iii, 8, iv, 47, etc.), was "of the remnant of the Rephaim." According to tradition, he lived 3,000 years and walked beside the Ark during the Flood. One of his bones formed a bridge over a river. His bed (*Deut*. iii, 11) was 9 cubits by 4 cubits.

The ANAKIM and REPHAIM were tribes of reputed giants inhabiting the territory on both sides of the Jordan before the coming of the Israelites. The NEPHILIM, the offspring of the sons of God and the daughters of men (*Gen*. vi, 4), a mythological race of semi-divine heroes, were also giants.

The giants of Greek mythology were, for the most part, sons of Tartarus and Ge. When they attempted to storm heaven, they were hurled to earth by the aid of Hercules, and buried under Mount Etna. Those of Scandinavian mythology were evil genii, dwelling in Jotunheim (*giant-land*), who had terrible and superhuman powers, could appear and disappear, reduce and extend their stature at will, etc.

Many names of ancient giants will be found in their appropriate places in this Dictionary.

Giants of Later Tradition.

ANDRONICUS II was 10 ft. in height. He was grandson of Alexius Comnenus. Nicetas asserts that he had seen him.

CHARLEMAGNE was nearly 8 ft. in height, and was so strong he could squeeze together three horseshoes with his hands.

ELEAZER was 7 cubits (nearly 11 ft.). Vitellus sent this giant to Rome; he is mentioned by Josephus.

Goliath was 6 cubits and a span.

GABARA, the Arabian giant, was 9 ft. 9 in. This Arabian giant is mentioned by Pliny, who says he was the tallest man seen in the days of Claudius.

HARDRADA (*Harold*) was nearly 8 ft. in height ("5 ells of Norway"), and was called "the Norway giant."

MAXIMINUS I was 8 ft. 6 in. in height. Roman emperor from about 235 to 238.

OSEN (*Heinrich*) was 7 ft. 6 in. in height at the age of 27, and weighed above 37 st. He was born in Norway.

PORUS was 5 cubits in height (about $7\frac{1}{2}$ ft.). He was an Indian king who fought against Alexander the Great near the Hydaspes. (*Quintus Curtius*: *De rebus gestis Alexandri Magni*.)

Josephus speaks of a Jew 10 ft. 2 in.

Becanus asserts that he had seen a man nearly 10 ft. high, and a woman fully 10 ft.

Gasper Bauhin speaks of a Swiss 8 ft. in height.

Del Rio tells us he himself saw a Piedmontese in 1572 more than 9 ft. in height.

A Mr. Warren (in *Notes and Queries*, August 14th, 1875) said that his father knew a woman 9 ft. in height, and adds "her head touched the ceiling of a good-sized room."

Vanderbrook says he saw in the Congo a black man 9 ft. high.

A giant was exhibited at Rouen in the early part of the 18th century 17 ft. 10 in. (!) in height.

Gorapus, the surgeon, tells us of a Swedish giantess, who, at the age of 9, was over 10 ft. in height.

Turner, the naturalist, tells us he *saw* in Brazil a giant 12 ft. in height.

M. Thevet published, in 1575, an account of a South American giant, the skeleton of which he measured. It was 11 ft. 5 in.

Giants of Modern Times.

BAMFORD (*Edward*) was 7 ft. 4 in. He died in 1768, and was buried in St. Dunstan's churchyard.

BATES (*Captain*) was 7 ft. $11\frac{1}{2}$ in. He was a native of Kentucky, and was exhibited in London in 1871.

His wife, Anne Hannen Swan, a native of Nova Scotia, was the same height.

BLACKER (*Henry*) was 7 ft. 4 in. and most symmetrical. He was born at Cuckfield, in Sussex, in 1724, and was called "The British Giant."

BRADLEY (*William*) was 7 ft. 9 in. in height. He was born in 1787, and died 1820. His birth is duly registered in the parish church of Market Weighton, in Yorkshire, and his right hand is preserved in the museum of the College of Surgeons.

BRICE (*M. J.*) exhibited under the name of Anak, was 7 ft. 8 in. in height at the age of 26. He was born in 1840 at Ramonchamp, in the Vosges, and visited England 1862-5. His arms had a stretch of $95\frac{1}{2}$ in.

BRUSTED (*Von*) was 8 ft. in height. This Norwegian giant was exhibited in London in 1880.

BUSBY (*John*) was 7 ft. 9 in. in height, and his brother was about the same. They were natives of Darfield, in Yorkshire.

CHANG, the Chinese giant, was 8 ft. 2 in. in height. He was exhibited in London in 1865-6, and again in 1880.

COTTER (*Patrick*) was 8 ft. 7½ in. in height. This Irish giant died at Clifton, Bristol, in 1802. A cast of his hand is preserved in the museum of the College of Surgeons.

DANIEL, the porter of Oliver Cromwell, was a man of gigantic stature.

ELEIZEGUE (*Joachim*) was 7 ft. 10 in. in height. He was a Spaniard, and exhibited in the Cosmorama Regent Street, London, in the mid-19th century.

EVANS (*William*) was 8 ft. at death. He was a porter of Charles I, and died in 1632.

FRANK (*Big*) was 7 ft. 8 in. in height. He was Francis Sheridan, an Irishman, and died in 1870.

FRENZ (*Louis*) was 7 ft. 4 in, in height. He was called "the French giant," and his left hand is preserved in the museum of the College of Surgeons.

GILLY was 8 ft. This Swedish giant was exhibited in the early part of the 10th century.

GORDON (*Alice*) was 7 ft. in height. She was a native of Essex, and died in 1737, at the age of 19.

HALE (*Robert*) was 7 ft. 6 in. in height. He was born at Somerton, in Norfolk, and was called "the Norfolk giant" (1820-62).

HOLMES (*Benjamin*) was 7 ft. 6 in. in height. He was a Northumberland man, and was made sword-bearer to the Corporation of Worcester. He died in 1892.

LOUISHKIN. A Russian giant of 8 ft. 5 in.; drum-major of the Imperial Guards.

MCDONALD (*James*) was 7 ft. 6 in. in height. Born in Cork, Ireland, and died in 1760.

MCDONALD (*Samuel*) was 6 ft. 10 in. in height. This Scot was usually called "Big Sam." He was the Prince of Wales's footman, and died in 1802.

MAGRATH (*Cornelius*) was 7 ft. 10 in. in height at the age of 16. He was an orphan reared by Bishop Berkeley, and died at the age of 20 (1740-60).

MELLON (*Edmund*) was 7 ft. 6 in. in height at the age of 19. He was born at Port Leicester, in Ireland (1665-84).

MIDDLETON (*John*) was 9 ft. 3 in. in height. (*Cp.* GABARA, *above.*) "His hand was 17 inches long and 8½ broad." He was born at Hale, Lancashire, in the reign of James I. (*Dr. Plott: Natural History of Staffordshire,* p. 295.)

MILLER (*Maximilian Christopher*) was 8 ft. in height. His hand measured 12 in., and his forefinger was 9 in. long. This Saxon giant died in London at the age of 60 (1674-1734).

MURPHY was 8 ft. 10 in. in height. An Irish giant of the late 18th century. He died at Marseilles.

O'BRIEN, or CHARLES BYRNE, was 8 ft. 4 in. in height. The skeleton of this Irish giant is preserved in the College of Surgeons. He died in Cockspur Street, London (1761-83).

O'BRIEN (*Patrick*), was 8 ft. 7 in. in height. He died August 3, 1804, aged 39.

RIECHART (*J. N.*) was 8 ft. 4 in. in height. He was a native of Friedberg, and both his father and mother were of gigantic stature.

SALMERON (*Martin*) was 7 ft. 4 in. in height. He was called "The Mexican Giant."

SAM (*Big*). *See* MCDONALD.

SHERIDAN. *See* FRANK.

Swan (*Anne Hannen*). *See* BATES.

TOLLER (*James*) was 8 ft. at the age of 24. He died in February, 1819.

In the museum of Trinity College, Dublin, is a human skeleton 8 ft. 6 in. in height.

Thomas Hall, of Willingham, was 3 ft. 9 in. at the age of 3.

Giaour (jou' ér). Among Mohammedans, one who is not an adherent of their faith, especially a Christian; generally used with a contemptuous or insulting implication. The word is a variant of Guebre (*q.v.*).

The city won for Allah from the Giaour,
The Giaour from Othman's race again may wrest.
          BYRON: *Childe Harold,* c. ii, st. 77.

Gib Cat (jib kăt). A tom-cat. The male cat used to be called Gilbert. Tibert or Tybalt (*q.v.*) is the French form of Gilbert, and hence Chaucer, or whoever it was that translated that part of the *Romance of the Rose,* renders "Thibert le Cas" by "Gibbe, our Cat" (line 6204). Generally used of a castrated cat.

I am as melancholy as a gib cat or a lugged bear.—1 *Henry IV,* i, 2.

Gibberish (jib' er ish). Unmeaning talk; words without meaning; formerly, the lingo of rogues and gipsies. Johnson says in his *Dictionary*—

As it was anciently written *gebrish* it is probably derived from the chymical cant [*i.e.* the mystical language of the alchemists], and originally implied the jargon of *Gebir* and his tribe.

Geber, the Arabian, was by far the greatest alchemist of the 11th century, and wrote several treatises in mystical jargon. Friar Bacon, in 1282, furnishes a specimen of this gibberish. He is giving the prescription for making gunpowder, and says:—

Sed tamen salis-petræ
LURU MONE CAP URBE
Et sulphuris.

The second line is merely an anagram of *Carbonum pulvere* (pulverized charcoal).

Gibeonite (gib' i on īt). A slave's slave, a workman's labourer, a farmer's understrapper, or Jack-of-all-work. The Gibeonites were made "hewers of wood and drawers of water" to the Israelites (*Josh,* ix, 27).

Gibraltar (jib rol' tàr). The "Calpe" and "Pillars of Hercules" of the ancients, The modern name is a corruption of *Gebel-al-Tarik,* the Hill of Tarik, Tarik being a Saracen leader who, under the orders of Mousa, landed at Calpe in 710, utterly defeated Roderick, the Gothic King of Spain, and built a castle on the rock. It was taken from the Moors in 1462; in 1704 a combined force of English and Dutch took the place, since when it has remained in British hands. The Spaniards and French beseiged it in 1704-5, the Spaniards in 1727, and the Spaniards and French in 1779-83, when it was held by Lord Heathfield.

Gibson Girl. A type of feminine beauty characteristic of its period depicted by Charles Dana Gibson (1867-1944) in several popular series of black-and-white drawings, dating from 1896. His delineations of the American girl enjoyed an enormous vogue, culminating in the series entitled *The Education of Mr. Pipp* which appeared in *Colliers Weekly* (1899) and formed the basis of a play of that name. The Gibson girl, who was depicted in various poses and occupations, was tall, bending forward somewhat from the waist, her individuality accentuated by the period costume of sweeping skirts and large hats.

Gifford Lectureships founded in the universities of Edinburgh, Glasgow, Aberdeen, and St. Andrews in 1885 by a bequest of Adam Lord Gifford. Their subject is Natural Theology, without reference to creed or sect.

Gift-horse. Don't look a gift-horse in the mouth.

When a present is made, do not inquire too minutely into its intrinsic value. The proverb has its counterpart in many languages.

Giglet. Formerly a light, wanton woman, the word is still in common use in the West of England for a giddy, romping, tomboy girl; and in Salop a flighty person is called a "giggle."

> If this be
> The recompense of striving to preserve
> A wanton gigglet honest, very shortly
> 'Twill make all mankind panders.
> MASSINGER: *The Fatal Dowry*, III, i (1619).

Gigman. A quite respectable person (in contempt); hence *gigmanity*, smug respectability, a word invented by Carlyle. A witness in the trial for murder of John Thurtell (1823) said, "I always thought him [Thurtell] a respectable man." And being asked by the judge why he thought so, replied, "He kept a gig."

Gigolo (jig' ō lō). A French slang term for a prostitute's bully, but more commonly applied to a lounge lizard, a fellow who hires himself out as a dancing-partner or male escort to wealthy women.

Gilbertian (gil bĕr' ti ån). A term applied to anything humorously topsy-turvy, any situation such as those W. S. Gilbert (1836-1911) depicted in the Gilbert and Sullivan operas. Of these perhaps the *Mikado* (1885) furnishes the best examples.

Gilbertines (gil' bĕr tīnz). An English religious order founded in the 12th century by St. Gilbert of Sempringham, Lincolnshire. The monks observed the rule of the Augustinians and the nuns that of the Benedictines.

Gild. To gild the pill. It was the custom of old-time doctors—quacks and genuine—to make their nauseous pills more attractive, at least to the sight, by gilding them over a thin coating of sugar. Hence the phrase means to make an unattractive thing at least appear desirable.

Gilded Chamber, The. A familiar name for the House of Lords.

Giles. A mildly humorous generic name for a farmer; the "farmer's boy" in Bloomfield's poem was so called.

Giles, St. Patron saint of cripples. The tradition is that Childeric, king of France, accidentally wounded the hermit in the knee when hunting; and the hermit, that he might the better mortify the flesh, refusing to be cured remained a cripple for life.

His day is September 1st, and his symbol a hind, in allusion to the "heaven directed hind" which went daily to his cave near the mouth of the Rhone to give him milk. He is sometimes represented as an old man with an arrow in his knee and a hind by his side.

Churches dedicated to St. Giles were usually situated in the outskirts of a city, and originally without the walls, cripples and beggars not being permitted to pass the gates. *See* CRIPPLE-GATE.

Giles of Antwerp. Giles Coignet, the Flemish painter (1530-1600).

Gills. Humorous slang for the mouth.

Blue about the gills. Down in the mouth; depressed looking.

Rosy, or red about the gills. Flushed with liquor.

White in the gills. Showing unmistakable signs of fear or terror—sometimes of sickness.

Gillie. A Gaelic word for a Highland manservant or attendant, especially one who waits on a sportsman fishing or hunting.

Gillyflower (jil i flou' ér). Not the *July-flower*, but Fr. *giroflée*, from *girofle* (a clove), called by Chaucer "gylofre." The common stock, the wallflower, the rocket, the clove pink, and several other plants are so called. (Gr. *karuophullon*; Lat. *caryophyllum*.)

> The fairest flowers o' the season
> Are our carnations and streaked gillyflowers.
> *Winter's Tale*, iv, 2.

Gilpin, John (gil' pin), of Cowper's famous ballad (1782) is a caricature of a Mr. Beyer, an eminent linendraper at the end of Paternoster

Row, where it joins Cheapside. He died in 1791, at the age of 98. It was Lady Austin who told the adventure to our domestic poet, to divert him from his melancholy. The marriage adventure of Commodore Trunnion in *Peregrine Pickle* is very similar to the wedding-day adventure of John Gilpin.

> John Gilpin was a citizen
> Of credit and renown;
> A trainband captain eke was he
> Of famous London town.

Gilt-edge Investments. A phrase introduced in the last quarter of the 19th century to denote securities of the most reliable character, such as Consols and other Government and Colonial stock, first mortgages, debentures, and shares in first-rate companies, etc.

Gimlet-eyed (gim' let), keen-eyed, very sharp-sighted, given to watching or peering into things. A *gimlet-eye* is occasionally applied to a squint.

Gimmer. A jointed hinge; in Somersetshire, *gimmace*. These words, as also *gimmal*, are variants of *gemel*, a ring formed of two interlaced rings, from Lat. *gemellus*, the diminutive of *geminus*, a twin.

> Their poor jades
> Lob down their heads, dropping the hides and hips . . .
> And in their pale dull mouths the gimmal bit
> Lies foul with chew'd grass, still and motionless.
> *Henry V*, iv, 2.

Gimmick (gim' ik). The first use of this word in U.S.A. slang was to describe some device by which a conjurer or fair-ground showman worked his trick. In later usage it is applied to some distinctive quirk or trick associated with a film or radio star.

Gin. A contraction of *Geneva*, the older name of the spirit, from Fr. *genièvre* (O.Fr. *genèvre*), juniper, the berries of which were at one time used to flavour the extract of malt in the manufacture of gin.

Gin-sling. A long drink composed mainly of gin and lemon. It has been attributed to John Collins, famous bar-tender of Limmer's Hotel in London, but it dates from before his time and is found in the U.S.A. by 1800.

Ginevra (jin ev' ra). A young Italian bride who hid in a trunk with a spring-lock. The lid fell upon her, and she was not discovered till the body had become a skeleton.

Gingerbread. Tawdry wares, showy but worthless. The allusion is to the gingerbread cakes fashioned like men, animals, etc., and profusely decorated with gold leaf or Dutch leaf, which looked like gold, commonly sold at fairs up to the middle of the 19th century.

To take the gilt off the gingerbread. To destroy the illusion; to appropriate all the fun or profit and leave the dull base behind.

Gingerly. Cautiously, with hesitating, mincing, or faltering steps. The word is over 400 years old in English; it has nothing to do with ginger, but is probably from O.Fr. *gensour*, comparative of *gent*, delicate, dainty.

> They spend their goods . . . upon their dansing minions, that mins it fel gingerlie, God wot, tripping like gotes, that an egge would not brek under their feet.—
> STUBBES: *Anatomy of Abuses*, II, i, (1583).

Gingham (ging' am). A playful equivalent of umbrella; properly, a cotton or linen fabric dyed usually in stripes or checks; so called from a Malay word *ginggang* (that came to us through Dutch), meaning stripe.

Gipsy. A member of a dark-skinned nomadic race which first appeared in England about the beginning of the 16th century, and, as they were thought to have come from Egypt, were named *Egyptians*, which soon became corrupted to *Gypcians*, and so to its present form. They call themselves *Romany* (from Gipsy *rom*, a man, husband), which is also the name of their language—a debased Hindi dialect with large additions of words from Persian, Armenian, and many European languages.

The name of the largest group of European gipsies is *Atzigan*; this, in Turkey and Greece, became *Tshingian*, in the Balkans and Roumania *Tsigan*, in Hungary *Czigany*, in Germany *Zigeuner*, in Italy *Zingari*, in Portugal *Cigano*, and in Spain *Gitano*. The original name is said to mean "dark man." *See also* BOHEMIAN.

Serious study of the Gipsies, their origin, history, language, etc., has been carried out by George Borrow, R. Hindes-Groome, B. Vesey-Fitzgerald, and others.

Giralda. The name given to the great square tower of the cathedral at Seville (formerly a Moorish minaret), which is surmounted by a statue of Faith, so pivoted as to turn with the wind. *Giralda* is a Spanish word, and means a weather-vane.

Gird. To gird up the loins. To prepare for hard work or a journey. The Jews wore a girdle only when at work or on a journey. Even to the present day, Eastern people who wear loose dresses gird them about the loins.

Girdle. A good name is better than a golden girdle. A good reputation is better than money. It used to be customary to carry money in the belt, or in a purse suspended from it, and a girdle of gold meant a "purse of gold."

Children under the girdle. Not yet born.

He has a large mouth but small girdle. Great expenses but small means.

He has undone her girdle. Taken her for his wife. The Roman bride wore a chaplet of flowers on her head, and a girdle of sheep's wool about her waist. A part of the marriage ceremony was for the bridegroom to loose this.

If he be angry, he knows how to turn his girdle (*Much Ado About Nothing*, v, 1). He knows how to prepare himself to fight. Before wrestlers engaged in combat, they turned the buckle of their girdle behind them. Thus, Sir Ralph Winwood writes to Mr. Secretary Cecil:

I said, "What I spake was not to make him angry." He replied, "If I were angry, I might turn the buckle of my girdle behind me."—Dec. 17, 1602.

The girdle of Venus. *See* CESTUS.

To put a girdle round the earth. To travel or go round it. Puck says, "I'll put a girdle round about the earth in forty minutes." (*Midsummer Night's Dream*, ii, 2.)

Girl. This word is not present in Anglo-Saxon, but appears in Middle English (13th cent.), and its etymology has given rise to a host of guesses. It was formerly applicable to a child of either sex (a boy was sometimes distinguished as a "knave-girl"), and is nowadays applied to an unmarried woman of almost any age. It is probably a diminutive of some lost word cognate with Pomeranian *goer* and Old Low German *gor*, a child. It appears nearly 70 times in Shakespeare, but only twice in the Authorized Version (*Joel* iii, 3; *Zech*. viii, 5).

Girl Guides. The opposite number to the Boy Scouts and organized in 1910 by General Baden-Powell and his sister, Miss Agnes Baden-Powell. The training is essentially the same as that of the Scouts and is based on similar promises and laws. There are three sections: Brownies, aged 8 to 11; Guides, 11 to 16; and Rangers for girls over 16 years of age.

In U.S.A., where they were organized in 1921, they are called Girl Scouts.

Girondists, or **The Gironde.** The moderate republicans in the French Revolution (1791-93). So called from the department of Gironde, which chose for the Legislative Assembly men who greatly distinguished themselves for their oratory, and formed a political party. They were subsequently joined by Brissot (and were hence sometimes called the *Brissotins*), Condorcet, and the adherents of Roland.

They were the ruling party in 1792 but were overthrown in the Convention by the Mountain in 1793 and many of their leaders were executed, including Brissot, Vergniaud, Gensonné, Ducos and Sillery.

Gis. A corruption of Jesus or J. H. S. Ophelia says, "By Gis and by St. Charity" (*Hamlet*, iv, 5).

Gitano. *See* GIPSY.

Give. For phrases such as **Give the devil his due, Give a dog a bad name and hang him, To give one beans,** etc., see the principal noun.

A given name. In American usage a **given name** is a first, or Christian name.

A give-away is a revealing or betraying circumstance.

To give and take. To be fair; in intercourse with others to practise forbearance and consideration. In horse-racing a **give and take plate** is a prize for a race in which the runners which exceed a standard height carry more, and those that come short of it less, than the standard weight.

To give away. To hand the bride in marriage to the bridegroom, to act the part of the bride's father. Also, to let out a secret, inadvertently or on purpose; to betray an accomplice.

To give in. To confess oneself beaten, to yield.

To give it anyone, to give it him hot. To scold or thrash a person. As "I gave it him right and left." "I'll give it you when I catch you."

To give oneself away. To betray oneself by some thoughtless action or remark; to damage one's own cause by carelessly letting something out.

To give what for. To administer a sound thrashing.

To give way. To break down; to yield.

Gizzard. The strong, muscular second stomach of birds, where the food is ground, attributed humorously to man in some phrases.

That stuck in his gizzard. Annoyed him, was more than he could stomach, or digest.

Glacis. The sloping bank on the outer edge of the covered way in old fortifications.

Glad. To give **the glad eye.** *See* EYE.

Glad rags. A demoded slang term for evening dress.

Gladiators. Those who fought in the ring in Rome, originally criminals who thus had the choice of death or liberty. They first appeared at the funeral ceremonies of the Romans in 263 B.C.; they were introduced into festivals about 215 B.C. Such combats were suppressed in the Eastern Empire by Constantine in A.D. 325 and in the West by Theodoric in A.D. 500.

Glamorgan (glà môr' gàn). Geoffrey of Monmouth says that Cundah and Morgan, the sons of Gonorill and Regan, usurped the crown at the death of Cordellia. The former resolved to reign alone, chased Morgan into Wales, and slew him at the foot of a hill, hence called Gla-Morgan or Glyn-Morgan, valley of Morgan. (*See* Spenser: *Faerie Queene* II, x, 33.) The name is really Welsh for "the district by the side of the sea" (*gwlad*, district, *mor*, the sea, *gant*, side).

Glass. Glass breaker. A wine-bibber. In the early part of the 19th century it was by no means unusual with topers to break off the stand of their wineglass, so that they might not be able to set it down, but were compelled to drink it clean off, without heel-taps.

Glass House. Army slang for a military prison. It was originally applied to the military prison at North Camp, Aldershot, which had a glass roof.

Those who live in glass houses should not throw stones. Those who are open to criticism should be very careful how they criticize others. An old proverb found in varying forms from the time of Chaucer at least (*Troylus and Cresseide*, Bk. ii). *Cp. also Matt*, vii, 1-4.

Glass slipper (of Cinderella). *See* CIN-DERELLA.

Glasse, Mrs. Hannah. A name immortalized by the reputed saying in a cookery book, "First catch your hare" (*which see under* CATCH).

Glassite. A Sandemanian (*q.v.*).

Glastonbury. An ancient town in Somerset, dating from Roman times, and famous in the Arthurian and Grail cycles as the place to which Joseph of Arimathea came, and as the burial place of King Arthur (*see* AVALON). It was here that Joseph planted his staff—the famous *Glastonbury Thorn*—which took root and burst into leaf every Christmas Eve. This name is now given to a variety of Cratægus, or hawthorn, which flowers about old Christmas Day, and is fabled to have sprung from Joseph's staff.

The name, A.S. *Glœstingaburh*, means "the city of Glæstings." Its origin, says Professor Freeman,

lurks in a grotesque shape, in that legend of Glæsting and his sow, a manifestly English legend, which either William of Malmesbury himself or some interpolator at Glastonbury has strangely thrust into the midst of the British legends. Glæsting's lost sow leads him by a long journey to an apple-tree by the old church; pleased with the land, he takes his family, the Glæstingas, to dwell there.—*English Towns*, p. 95.

Glaucus (glaw' kús). The name of a number of heroes in classical legend, including:

(1) A fisherman of Bœotia, who became a sea-god endowed with the gift of prophecy and instructed Apollo in the art of soothsaying. Milton alludes to him in *Comus* (1. 895), and Spenser mentions him in the *Faerie Queene* (IV, xi, 13):

And Glaucus, that wise soothsayer understood

and Keats gives his name to the old magician whom Endymion met in Neptune's hall beneath the sea (*Endymion*, Bk. iii). *See also* SCYLLA.

(2) A son of Sisyphus who would not allow his horses to breed; the goddess of Love so infuriated them that they killed him. Hence, the name is given to one who is so overfond of horses that he is ruined by them.

(3) A commander of the Lycians in the War of Troy (*Iliad*, Bk. vi,) who was connected by ties of ancient family friendship with his enemy, Diomed. When they met in battle they not only refrained from fighting but exchanged arms in token of amity. As the armour of the Lycian was of gold, and that of the Greek of brass, it was like bartering precious stones for French paste. Hence the phrase A Glaucus swap.

Gleipnir (glīp' nér) (Old Norse, the fetter). In Scandinavian legend, the chain by which the wolf Fenrir was bound. It was extremely light, and made of the noise made by the footfalls of a cat, the roots of the mountains, the sinews of bears, the breath of fishes, the beards of women, and the spittle of birds. When the chain breaks, the wolf will be free and the end of the world will be at hand.

Glencoe. The massacre of Glencoe. The treacherous massacre of the Macdonalds of Glencoe on February 13th, 1692. Pardon had been offered to all Jacobites who submitted on or before December 31st, 1691. Mac-Ian, chief of the Macdonalds of Glencoe, delayed till the last minute, and, on account of the state of the roads, did not make his submission before January 6th. The Master of Stair (Sir John Dalrymple) obtained the king's permission "to extirpate the set of thieves." Accordingly, on February 1st, 120 soldiers, led by a Captain Campbell, marched to Glencoe, told the clan they were come as friends, and lived peaceably among them for twelve days; but on the morning of the 13th, the glenmen, to the number of thirty-eight, were scandalously murdered, their huts set on fire, and their flocks and herds driven off as plunder. Thomas Campbell and Scott have written poems, and Talfourd a play on the subject.

Global (glō' bál). A word that came into use in World War II, meaning world-wide, extending to every part of the globe.

Gloria (glôr' i a). A cup of coffee with brandy in it instead of milk; also, a mixture of silk and wool used for covering umbrellas, etc.

Gloria in Excelsis (glôr i a in ek sel' sis). The doxology, "Glory be to the Father," etc., so called because it begins with the words sung by the angels at Bethlehem. The first verse is said to be by St. Basil, and the latter portion is ascribed to Telesphorus, 139 A.D. During the Arian controversy it ran thus: "Glory be to the Father by the Son, and in the Holy Ghost."

Gloriana (glôr i an' à). Spenser's name in his *Faerie Queene* for the typification of Queen Elizabeth I. She held an annual feast for twelve days, during which time adventurers appeared before her to undertake whatever task she chose to impose upon them. On one occasion twelve knights presented themselves before her, and their exploits form the scheme of Spenser's allegory of which only six and a half books remain.

Glory, glorious. Hand of Glory. In folk lore, a dead man's hand, preferably one cut from the body of a man who has been hanged, soaked in oil and used as a magic torch by thieves. Robert Graves points out that Hand of Glory is a translation of the French *main de gloire*, a corruption of *mandragore*, the plant man-dragora, whose roots had a similar magic value to thieves. *See* HAND.

Glory-hole. A small room, cupboard, etc., where all sorts of rubbish and odds and ends are heaped.

Glory be to the Father. *See* GLORIA IN EXCELSIS.

Glorious John. John Dryden, the poet (1631-1701). George Borrow gave this name to the publisher John Murray (1778-1843).

Glorious First of June. June 1st, 1794, when Lord Howe, who commanded the Channel fleet, gained a decisive victory over the French off Cape Ushant.

Glorious Uncertainty of the Law, The. The toast at a dinner given to the judges and counsel in Serjeant's Hall. The occasion was the elevation of Lord Mansfield to the peerage and to the Lord Chief Justiceship (1756), and was somewhat prophetic of the legal decisions and innovations that were to follow.

Gloucester (glos' těr). The Celtic name of the town was *Caer Glou* (bright city); the Romans Latinized this to *Glevum colonia*; the Saxons restored the old *Glou*, and added *ceaster*, to signify it had been a Roman camp.

Glove. In the days of chivalry it was customary for knights to wear a lady's glove in their helmets, and to defend it with their life.

One ware on his headpiece his ladies sleve, and another bare on hys helme the glove of his dearlynge.— HALL: *Chronicle, Henry IV.*

On ceremonial occasions gloves are not worn in the presence of royalty, because one is to stand unarmed, with the helmet off the head and gauntlets off the hands, to show that there is no hostile intention.

Gloves used to be worn by the clergy to indicate that their hands are clean and not open to bribes; and in an assize without a criminal, the sheriff presents the judge with a pair of white gloves. Anciently, judges were not allowed to wear gloves on the bench; so to give a judge a pair of gloves symbolized that he need not take his seat. But, on the contrary, bishops were sometimes given gloves as a symbol of accession to their See. The Glovers Company of London was founded in 1556.

Hand in glove. Sworn friends; on most intimate terms; close companions, like glove and hand.

He bit his glove. He resolved on mortal revenge. On the Border, to bite the glove was considered a pledge of deadly vengeance.

Stern Rutherford right little said,
But bit his glove and shook his head.
                SCOTT: *Lay of the Last Minstrel.*

Here I throw down my glove. I challenge you. In allusion to an ancient custom of a challenger throwing his glove or gauntlet at the feet of the person challenged, and bidding him to pick it up. *To take up the glove* means to accept the challenge.

I will throw my glove to Death itself, that there's no maculation in thy heart.—*Troilus and Cressida*, iv, 4.

Gnome (nōm). According to the Rosicrucian system, a misshapen elemental spirit, dwelling in the bowels of the earth, and guarding the mines and quarries. The word seems to have been first used (perhaps invented) by Paracelsus, and to be Gr. *ge-nomos*, earth-dweller. *Cp.* SALAMANDER.

The four elements are inhabited by spirits called sylphs, gnomes, nymphs, and salamanders. The gnomes or demons of the earth, delight in mischief.—POPE: *Pref. Letter to the Rape of the Lock.*

Gnostics (nos' tiks). The *knowers*, opposed to *believers*, various sects in the first six centuries of the Christian era, which tried to accommodate Christianity to the speculations of Pythagoras, Plato, and other Greek and Oriental philosophers. They taught that knowledge, rather than mere faith, is the true key of salvation. In the Gnostic creed Christ is esteemed merely as an eon or divine attribute personified, like Mind, Truth, Logos, Church, etc., the whole of which eons made up this divine pleroma or fullness.

Go. A go. A fix, a scrape; as in **here's a go** or **here's a pretty go**—here's a mess or awkward state of affairs. Also a share, portion, or tot, as **a go of gin**.

A go-between. One who acts as an intermediary; one who interposes between two parties.

All the go. All the fashion, quite in vogue.

Her *carte* is hung in the West-end shops,
  With her name in full on the white below;
And all day long there's a big crowd stops
  To look at the lady who's "all the go".
SIMS: *Ballads of Babylon* ("Beauty and the Beast)".

Go as you please. Not bound by any rules; do as you like; unceremonious.

Go it! An exclamation of encouragement, sometimes ironical.

Go it alone. From the game of euchre, to play single-handed.

I'll go through fire and water to serve you. *See* FIRE.

I've gone and done it! or **I've been and gone and done it!** There! I've done the very thing I oughtn't to have done!

It is no go. It is not workable.

That goes without saying. The French say: *Cela va sans dire*. That is a self-evident fact; well understood or indisputable.

To give one the go-by. To pass without notice.

To go ahead. To prosper, make rapid progress towards success; to start.

To go back on one's word. To fail to keep one's promise.

To go by the board, the whole hog, to the wall, with the stream, etc. In these and many similar phrases see under the principal word.

To go for a man. To attack him, either physically or in argument, etc.

To go farther and fare worse. To take more pains and trouble and yet find oneself in a worse position.

To go hard with one. To prove a troublesome matter. "It will go hard with me before I give up the attempt," *i.e.* I won't give it up until I have tried every means to success, no matter how difficult, dangerous, or painful it may be.

To go in for. To follow as a pursuit or occupation.

To go the whole hog. *See* HOG.

To go it. To be fast, extravagant, headstrong in one's behaviour and habits. **To go it blind** is to act without stopping to deliberate. In poker, if a player chooses to "go it blind," he doubles the *ante* before looking at his cards.

To go off one's head, nut, onion, rocker, etc. Completely to lose control of oneself; to go mad, either temporarily or permanently; to go out of one's mind.

To go on all fours. *See* ALL FOURS.

To go to grass. To succumb, give in. From the putting out of race-horses or hunters to grass when they are too old for racing or hunting.

To go to the wall. *See* WALL.

To go under. To become ruined; to fail utterly, lose caste.

Also to pass as, to be known as; as "He goes under the name of 'Mr. Taylor,' but we all know he is really 'Herr Schneider.' "

Go-backs. Would-be settlers in the Far West who returned East discouraged and spread gloomy rumours about the difficulties they had encountered.

Go-getter. An enterprising, ambitious person.

Goat. From very early times the *goat* has been connected with the idea of sin (*cp.* SCAPE-GOAT) and associated with devil-lore. It is an old superstition in England and Scotland that a goat is never seen during the whole of a twenty-four hours, because once every day it pays a visit to the devil to have its beard combed. Formerly the devil himself was frequently depicted as a goat; and the animal is also a type of lust and lechery.

To get one's goat. An old Americanism for annoying one, making him wild.

Gobbler. A turkey-cock is so called from its cry.

Gobelin Tapestry (go' be lin). So called from the Gobelins, a French family of dyers founded by Jean Gobelin (d. 1476); their tapestry works were taken over by Louis XIV as a royal establishment about 1670, and are still in the Faubourg St. Marcel, Paris. Part of the buildings were burned down by the Communards in 1871.

Goblin. A familiar demon, dwelling, according to popular belief, in private houses and chinks of trees; and in many parts miners attribute those strange noises heard in mines to them. The word is the Fr. *gobelin*, probably a diminutive of the surname *Gobel*, but perhaps connected with Gr. *kobalos*, an impudent rogue, a mischievous sprite, or with the Ger. *kobold* (*q.v.*).

God. A word common, in slightly varying forms, to all Teutonic languages, probably from a Sanskrit root, *ghu*—to worship; it is in no way connected with *good*.

It was Voltaire who said, *"Si Dieu n'existait pas, il faudrait l'inventer."*

Greek and Roman gods were divided into *Dii Majores* and *Dii Minores*, the greater and the lesser. The Dii Majores were twelve¹ in number:—

LATIN.	GREEK.
JUPITER (*King*)	ZEUS.
Apollo (*the sun*)	Apollōn.
Mars (*war*)	Arēs.
Mercury (*messenger*)	Hermēs
Neptune (*ocean*)	Poseidon.
Vulcan (*smith*)	Hephaistos.
JUNO (*Queen*)	HERA.
Cerēs (*tillage*)	Demēter.
Diana (*moon, hunting*)	Artĕmis.
Minerva (*wisdom*)	Athēne.
Venus (*love and beauty*)	Aphroditē.
Vesta (*home-life*)	Hestia.

Their blood was *ichor*, their food was *ambrosia*, their drink *nectar*.

Four other deities are often referred to:—

Bacchus (*wine*)	Dionysos.
Cupid (*love*)	Eros.
Pluto (*the underworld*)	Plutōn.
Saturn (*time*)	Kronos.

Of these Proserpine (*Latin*) and Persephone (*Greek*) was the wife of Pluto, Cybele was the wife of Saturn, and Rhea of Kronos.

In Hesiod's time the number of gods was thirty thousand, and that none might be omitted the Greeks observed a Feast of the Unknown Gods.

> Some thirty thousand gods on earth we find
> Subjects of Zeus, and guardians of mankind.
> *Hesiod*, i, 250.

God helps those who help themselves. In French, *Aide-toi, le ciel t'aidera. (La Fontaine,* vi, 18.); and among the *Fragments* of Euripides is:—

> Bestir yourself, and then call on the gods,
> For heaven assists the man that laboureth.
> No. 435.

God made the country, and man made the town. Cowper in *The Task* (The Sofa 749). *Cp.* Cowley's "God the first garden made, and the first city Cain" (*On Gardens*). Varro says in *De Re Rustica, Divina Natura dedit agros; ars humana œdificavit urbes.*

God save the Queen. *See* NATIONAL ANTHEM.

God sides with the strongest. Fortune favours the strong. Napoleon I said, *Le bon Dieu est toujours du côté des gros bataillons,* God is always on the side of the big battalions, but the phrase is far older than his day. Tacitus (*Hist.* iv, 17) has *Deos fortioribus adesse,* the gods are on the side of the strongest; the Comte de Bussy, writing to the Count of Limoges, used it in 1677, as also did Voltaire in his *Epistle à M. le Riche,* February 6th, 1770.

Whom God would destroy He first makes mad. A translation of the Latin version (*Quos Deus vult perdere, prius dementat*) of one of the *Fragments* of Euripides. *Cp.* also *Stultum facit fortuna quem vult perdere* (Publius Syrus, No. 612). He whom Fortune would ruin she robs of his wits.

Whom the gods love die young. The Lat. *Quem Di diligunt, adolescens moritur* (Plautus: *Bacchides,* IV, vii, 18). Byron says:—

> Heaven gives its favourites early death.
> *Childe Harold*, iv, 102.

God's Acre. A churchyard or cemetery.

Godless Florin. *See* GRACELESS FLORIN.

Goddam or **Godon** (gŏ dăm', gŏ don'). A name given by the French to the English at least as early as the 15th century, on account of the favourite oath of the English soldiers which was looked upon almost as a shibboleth. Joan of Arc is reported to have used the word on a number of occasions in contemptuous reference to her enemies.

Godfather. To stand godfather. To pay the reckoning, godfathers being often chosen for the sake of the present they are expected to make to the child at christening or in their wills.

Godchild. One for whom a person stands sponsor in baptism. A godson or a goddaughter.

Godiva, Lady (gŏ dī' và). Patroness of Coventry. In 1040, Leofric, Earl of Mercia and Lord of Coventry, imposed certain exactions on his tenants, which his lady besought him to remove; he said he would do so if she would ride naked through the town. Lady Godiva took him at his word, and the Earl faithfully kept his promise.

The legend is recorded by Roger of Wendover (d. 1236), in *Flores Historiarum,* and this was adapted by Rapin in his *History of England,* 1732 into the story as commonly known. An addition of the time of Charles II asserts that everyone kept indoors at the time, but a certain tailor peeped through his window to see the lady pass and was struck blind in consequence. He has ever since been called "Peeping Tom of Coventry." Since 1678 the incident of Lady Godiva's ride has been annually commemorated at Coventry by a procession in which "Lady Godiva" plays a leading part.

Godolphin Barb. *See* DARLEY ARABIAN.

Goel (gō' el). The name among the ancient Jews for one who redeemed back to the family property that a member of it had sold; as this was usually done by the next of kin, on whom also devolved the duty of the avenger of blood, the name was later applied specially to the avenger of blood.

Goemot or **Goemagot** (gō' mot, gō em' à got). Names given in Geoffrey of Monmouth's *Chronicles* (I, xvi), Spenser's *Faerie Queene* (II, x, 10), etc., to Gog Magog (*q.v.*).

Gog and **Magog.** In English legend, the sole survivors of a monstrous brood, the offspring of the thirty-three infamous daughters of the Emperor Diocletian, who murdered their husbands. Being set adrift in a ship they reached Albion, where they fell in with a number of demons. Their descendants, a race of giants, were extirpated by Brute and his companions, with the exception of Gog and Magog, who were brought in chains to London and were made to do duty as porters at the royal palace, on the site of the Guildhall, where their effigies were placed at least since the reign of Henry V. The old giants were destroyed in the Great Fire, and were replaced by figures fourteen feet high, carved in 1708 by Richard Saunders and were subsequently destroyed in the wreck of Guildhall in an air raid in 1940. Formerly wickerwork models were carried in the Lord Mayors' Shows.

In the Bible Magog is spoken of as a son of Japhet (*Gen.* x, 2), in the *Revelation* Gog and Magog symbolize all future enemies of the kingdom of God, and in *Ezekiel* Gog is a prince of Magog, a terrible ruler of a country in the north, probably Scythia or Armenia. By rabbinical writers of the 7th century A.D. Gog was identified with Antichrist.

Gogmagog Hill. The higher of two hills, some three miles south-east of Cambridge. The legend is that Gogmagog fell in love with the nymph Granta, but she would have nothing to say to the huge giant, and he was metamorphosed into the hill. (DRAYTON: *Polyolbion*, xxi.)

Goggles. A very ancient word coming, through the old English *gogelen*, to look asquint, from the Celtic *gog*, a nod, a shaking of the head. The word is now applied to spectacles, but until Victorian days it was used to describe any rolling of the eyes or squinting.

> Such sight have they that see with goggling eyes.
> SIR P. SIDNEY: *Arcadia*.

> He goggled his eyes and groped in his money-pocket. — HORACE WALPOLE: *Letters*.

Golconda (gol kon' dà). An ancient kingdom and city in India (west of Hyderabad), famous and powerful up to the early 17th century. The name is emblematic of great wealth, particularly of diamonds; but there never were diamond mines in Golconda, the stones were only cut and polished there.

Gold. By the ancient alchemists, gold represented the sun, and silver the moon. In heraldry gold (called "or") is depicted by dots.

In Great Britain every article in gold is compared with a given standard of pure gold, which is supposed to be divided into twenty-four parts called *carats* (*q.v.*); gold equal to the standard is said to be twenty-four carats fine. Manufactured articles are never made of pure gold, but the quality of alloy used has to be stated. Sovereigns (and most wedding rings) contain two parts of alloy to every twenty-two of gold, and are said to be twenty-two carats fine. Thus, 20 lb. troy of standard gold were coined into 934 sovereigns and 1 half-sovereign; 1 oz. troy was therefore worth £3 17s. $10\frac{1}{2}$d. (£46 14s. 6d. per lb.), and 1 oz. of pure gold, on the same basis, £4 4s. $11\frac{1}{2}$d. Since 1915 the market price of gold has, however, exceeded these figures. The best gold watch-cases contain six parts of silver or copper to eighteen of gold, and are therefore eighteen carats fine; cheaper gold articles may contain nine, twelve, or even fifteen parts of alloy.

A gold brick. An American phrase descriptive of any form of swindling. It originated in the gold-rush days when a cheat would sell his dupe an alleged—or even a real—gold brick, in the latter case substituting a sham one before making his get-away. In World War II, **gold-bricking** was synonymous with idling, shirking, or getting a comrade to do one's job.

All he touches turns to gold. All his ventures succeed; he is invariably fortunate. The allusion is to the legend of Midas (*q.v.*).

All that glisters is not gold (Shakespeare: *Merchant of Venice*, ii, 7). Do not be deceived by appearances.

> All thing which that schineth as the gold
> Nis not gold as that I have herd it told.
> CHAUCER: *Canon's Yeoman's Tale*, 243.

> Not all that tempts your wand'ring eyes
> And heedless hearts, is lawful prize;
> Nor all that glisters gold.
> GRAY: *Ode on Death of a Favourite Cat.*

Healing gold. Gold given to a king for "healing" the king's evil, which was done by a touch.

Golden Age. An age in the history of peoples when everything was as it should be, or when the nation was at its summit of power, glory, and reputation; the best age, as the golden age of innocence, the golden age of literature. Ancient chronologers divided the time between Creation and the birth of Christ into ages; Hesiod describes five. *See* AGE.

The "Golden Ages" of the various nations are usually given as follows: —

ASSYRIA. From the reign of Esarhaddon, third son of Sennacherib, to the fall of Nineveh (about 700 to 600 B.C.).

CHALDÆO-BABYLONIAN EMPIRE. From the reign of Nabopolassar to that of Belshazzar (about 606-538 B.C.).

CHINA. The reign of Tae-tsong (618-26), and the era of the Tâng dynasty (626-84).

EGYPT. The reigns of Sethos I and Rameses II (about 1350-1273 B.C.), the XIXth Dynasty.

MEDIA. The reign of Cyaxares (about 634-594 B.C.).

PERSIA. From the reign of Khosru, or Chosroes, I, to that of Khosru II (about A.D. 531-628).

ENGLAND. The reign of Elizabeth I (1558-1603).

FRANCE. Part of the reigns of Louis XIV and XV (1640-1740).

GERMANY. The reign of Charles V (1519-58).

PORTUGAL. From John I to the close of Sebastian's reign (1383-1578).

PRUSSIA. The reign of Frederick the Great (1740-86).

RUSSIA. The reign of Peter the Great (1672-1725).

SPAIN. The reign of Ferdinand and Isabella, when the crowns of Castile and Aragon were united (1474-1516).

SWEDEN. From Gustavus Vasa to the close of the reign of Gustavus Adolphus (1523-1632).

Golden Apples. *See* APPLE OF DISCORD; ATALANTA'S RACE; HESPERIDES.

Golden Ass, The. A satirical romance by Apuleius, written in the 2nd century, and called the *golden* because of its excellency. It tells the adventures of Lucian, a young man who, being accidentally metamorphosed into an ass while sojourning in Thessaly, fell into the hands of robbers, eunuchs, magistrates, and so on, by whom he was ill-treated; but ultimately he recovered his human form. It contains the story of Cupid and Psyche — the latest born of the myths.

Golden Bull, The. An edict by the Emperor Charles IV, issued at the Diet of Nuremberg in 1356, for the purpose of fixing how the German emperors were to be elected. It was sealed with a golden *bulla*. *See* BULL.

To worship the golden calf. To bow down to money, to abandon one's principles for the sake of gain. The reference is to the golden calf made by Aaron when Moses was absent on Mt. Sinai. For their sin in worshipping the calf the Israelites paid dearly (*Exodus*, xxxii).

Golden Fleece, The. The old Greek story is that Ino persuaded her husband, Athamas, that his son Phryxus was the cause of a famine which desolated the land. Phryxus was thereupon ordered to be sacrificed, but, being apprised of this, he made his escape over sea on the winged ram, Chrysomallus, which had a golden fleece. When he arrived at Colchis, he sacrificed the ram to Zeus, and gave the fleece to King Æetes, who hung it on a sacred oak. It later formed the quest of Jason's celebrated Argonautic expedition, and was stolen by him. *See* ARGO; JASON.

Australia has been called "The Land of the Golden Fleece," because of the quantity of wool produced there.

Golden Gate, The. The name given by Sir Francis Drake to the strait connecting San Francisco Bay with the Pacific. San Francisco is hence called *The City of the Golden Gate*.

Golden Horn, The. The inlet of the Bosporus on which Istanbul is situated. So called from its curved shape and great beauty.

Golden Legend, The. (Lat. *Legenda aurea*.) A collection of so-called lives of the saints made by Jacques de Voragine in the 13th century; valuable for the picture it gives of mediæval manners, customs, and thought. Jortin says that the "lives" were written by young students of religious houses to exercise their talents by accommodating the narratives of heathen writers to Christian saints.

Longfellow's *The Golden Legend* (1851) is based on a story by Hartmann von der Aue, a German minnesinger of the 12th century.

Golden number. The number of the year in the Metonic Cycle (*q.v.*). As this consists of nineteen years it may be any number from 1 to 19, and in the ancient Roman and Alexandrian calendars this number was marked in gold, hence the name. The rule for finding the golden number is: —

Add one to the number of years and divide by nineteen; the quotient gives the number of cycles since 1 B.C. and the remainder the golden number, 19 being the golden number when there is no remainder.

It is used in determining the Epact and the date of Easter.

Golden Roses. An ornament made of gold in imitation of a spray of roses, one rose containing a receptacle into which is poured balsam and musk. The rose is solemnly blessed by the Pope on Laetare Sunday, and is conferred from time to time on sovereigns and others, churches and cities distinguished for their services to the Church. The last to receive it was Queen Elizabeth of the Belgians in 1925. That presented by Pius IX to the Empress Eugenie in 1856 is preserved in Farnborough Abbey.

Golden Rule, The. "Do as you would be done by."

Whatsoever ye would that men should do to you, do ye even so to them: for this is the law and the prophets.—*Matt.* vii, 12.

Golden shower or **Shower of gold.** A bribe, money. The allusion is to the classical tale of Zeus and Danaë. *See* DANAË.

Golden State, The. California; so called from the gold fever of 1849.

Golden Verses. Greek verses containing the moral rules of Pythagoras, usually thought to have been composed by some of his scholars. He enjoins, among other things, obedience to God and one's rulers, deliberation before action, fortitude, and temperance in exercise and diet. He also suggests making a critical review each night of the actions of that day.

Golden Wedding. The fiftieth anniversary of wedding, husband and wife being both alive.

A good name is better than a golden girdle. *See* GIRDLE.

The golden bowl is broken. Death. A biblical allusion:—

Or ever the silver cord be loosed, or the golden bowl be broken, or the pitcher be broken at the fountain, or the wheel broken at the cistern; then shall the dust return to the earth as it was; and the spirit shall return unto God who gave it.—*Eccles.* xii, 6, 7.

The golden section of a line. Its division into two such parts that the area of the rectangle contained by the smaller segment and the whole line equals that of the square on the larger segment. (*Euclid,* ii. 11.)

Goldfish Club. World War II. It is similar to the Caterpillar Club (*q.v.*) and is for those who had ditched their aeroplanes and taken to the rubber dinghy. A cloth insignia was presented.

Golgotha (gol' goth à). The place outside Jerusalem where Christ was crucified. The word is Aramaic and means "a skull," and according to Jerome and others the place was so called from a tradition that Adam's skull had been found there. The more likely reason is that it designated a bare hill or rising ground, having some fancied resemblance to a bald skull.

Golgotha seems not entirely unconnected with the hill of Gareb, and the locality of Goath, mentioned in *Jer.* xxxi, 39, on the north-west of the city. I am inclined to fix the place where Jesus was crucified . . . on the mounds which command the valley of Hinnom, above Birket-Mamila.—RENAN: *Life of Jesus,* ch. xxv.

Golgotha, at the University church, Cambridge, was the gallery in which the "heads of the houses" sat; so called because it was the place of skulls or heads. It has been more wittily than truly said that Golgotha was the place of empty skulls.

Goliath (gō lī' àth). The Philistine giant, slain by the stripling David with a small stone hurled from a sling. (1 *Sam.* xvii, 23-54.)

Golosh. *See* GALOSH.

Gombeen Man. A village usurer; a money-lender. The word is of Irish extraction.

They suppose that the tenants can have no other supply of capital than from the gombeen man.—EGMONT HAKE: *Free Trade in Capital.*

Gomerell (gom' ér él), a Scottish word for a stupid senseless person, a blockhead.

Gondola (gon' dō là). A long, narrow Venetian boat. Also the carriage attached to an airship in which the passengers are carried.

Goneril (gon' er il). One of Lear's three daughters. Having received her moiety of Lear's kingdom, the unnatural daughter first abridged the old man's retinue, then gave him to understand that his company was troublesome. In Holinshed she appears as "Gonorilla." *Cp.* CORDELIA.

Gonfalon or **Gonfanon** (gon' fà lon). An ensign or standard. A *gonfalonier* was a magistrate in certain of the old Italian republics that had a gonfalon.

Ten thousand thousand ensigns high advanced,
Standards and gonfalons, 'twixt van and rear
Stream in the air, and for distinction serve
Of hierarchies, of orders, and degrees.
                    MILTON: *Paradise Lost,* v. 589.

Gonnella's Horse (gò nel' à). Gonnella, the domestic jester of the Duke of Ferrara, rode on a horse all skin and bone. The jests of Gonnella are in print.

His horse was as lean as Gonnella's, which (as the Duke said) "Osso atque pellis totus erat" (Plautus).—CERVANTES: *Don Quixote.*

Gonsalez (gon sa' lez). Fernan Gonsalez, the hero of many Spanish ballads, lived in the 10th century. His life was twice saved by his wife Sancha, daughter of Garcias, King of Navarre.

Gonville and Caius. *See* CAIUS.

Good. The Good. Among the many who earned—or were given—this appellation are:—

Alfonso VIII (or IX) of Leon, "The Noble and Good" (1158-1214).

Haco I, King of Norway (about 920-960).

Jean II of France, *le Bon* (1319, 1350-64).

Jean III, Duke of Brittany (1286, 1312-41).

Philip the Good, Duke of Burgundy (1396, 1419-67).

René, called *The Good King René*, Duke of Anjou, Count of Provence, Duke of Lorraine, and King of Sicily (1409-80).

The Prince Consort, *Albert the Good* (1819-61), husband of Queen Victoria.

Good Friday. The Friday preceding Easter Day, held as the anniversary of the Crucifixion. "Good" here means *holy*; Christmas, as well as Shrove Tuesday, used to be called "the good tide."

Born on Good Friday. According to old superstition, those born on Christmas Day or Good Friday have the power of seeing and commanding spirits.

Good Parliament, The. Edward III's Parliament of 1376; so called because of the severity with which it pursued the unpopular party of the Duke of Lancaster.

Good Regent. James Stewart, Earl of Moray (d. 1570), a natural son of James V and half-brother of Mary Queen of Scots. He was appointed Regent of Scotland after the imprisonment of Queen Mary.

Good and all, For. Not tentatively, not in pretence, nor yet temporarily, but *bona fide*, and altogether.

The good woman never died after this, till she came to die for good and all.—L'ESTRANGE: *Fables*.

Good-bye. A contraction of *God be with you*. Similar to the French adieu, which is *à Dieu* (I commend you to God).

Goodfellow. *See* ROBIN GOODFELLOW.

Goodman. A husband or master. In *Matt*, xxiv, 43, "If the goodman of the house had known in what watch the thief would come, he would have watched."

There's nae luck about the house
When our gudeman's awa.—*Mickle*.

Goodman of Ballengeich. The assumed name of James V of Scotland when he made his disguised visits through the country districts around Edinburgh and Stirling, after the fashion of Haroun-al-Raschid, Louis XI, etc.

Goodman's Croft. The name given in Scotland to a strip of ground or corner of a field left untilled, in the belief that unless some such place were left, the spirit of evil would damage the crop. Here *Goodman* is a propitiatory euphemism for the devil.

Goods. I carry all my goods with me (*Omnia mea mecum porto*). Said by Bias, one of the seven sages, when Priene was besieged and the inhabitants were preparing for flight.

That fellow's the goods. He's all right, just the man for the job.

"He's got the goods on you!" He's got evidence against you.

To deliver the goods. Said of one who fulfills his promises or who comes up to expectations.

Goody. A depreciative, meaning weakly, moral and religious. In French, *bon homme* is used in a similar way.

The word is also a rustic variant of *goodwife*, the mistress of a household (*cp.* GOODMAN), and is sometimes used as a title, like "Gammer" (*q.v.*), as "Goody Blake," "Goody Dobson."

A goody is something especially nice to eat, a sweet, jam tart, or curranty bun.

Goody-goody. Affectedly, or even hypocritically, pious, but with no strength of mind or independence of spirit.

Goody Two-shoes. This nursery tale first appeared in 1765. It was written for John Newbery (1713-67), the originator of children's books, probably by Oliver Goldsmith.

Googly. A cricket term for a ball bowled so as to break a different way from the way it swerves.

Goose. A foolish or ignorant person is called a *goose* because of the alleged stupidity of this bird; a tailor's smoothing-iron is so called because its handle resembles the neck of a goose. Note that the plural of the iron is *gooses*, not *geese*.

Come in, tailor; here you may roast your goose.—
Macbeth, ii, 3.

Goose fair. A fair formerly held in many English towns about the time of Michaelmas (*q.v.*), when geese were plentiful. That still held at Nottingham was the most important.

Goose month. The lying-in month for women.

His geese are swans. He sees things in too rosy a light, is too pleased with his own doings and his own possessions.

Goose step. A form of military marching in which the legs are moved only from the hips, the knees being kept rigid, each leg being swung as high as possible. It was never popular in the British army, where it was introduced as a form of recruit drill in the late 18th century. In a modified form it still exists in the slow march. The goose step (*Stechschritt*) in its most exaggerated form has been a full-dress and processional march in the German army since the days of Frederick the Great. When the Axis flourished it was introduced into the Italian army (*il passo di oca*) but it was soon ridiculed into desuetude.

Goose-trap. A late-18th-century American colloquialism for a swindle.

He can't say Bo! to a goose. *See* Bo.

He killed the goose that laid the golden eggs. He grasped at what was more than his due, and lost what he had. The Greek fable says a countryman had a goose that laid golden eggs; thinking to make himself rich, he killed the goose to get the whole stock of eggs at once, but lost everything.

He's cooked his goose. He's done for himself, he's made a fatal mistake, ruined his chances, "dished" himself. The phrase is of 19th-century origin, though how it arose cannot now be traced.

If they come here we'll cook their goose,
The Pope and Cardinal Wiseman.
Street ballad of 1851, the time of the "Papal Aggression."

Mother Goose. Famous as giving the name to *Mother Goose's Nursery Rhymes*, which first seems to have been used in *Songs for the Nursery: or Mother Goose's Melodies for Children*, published by T. Fleet in Boston, Mass., in 1719. The rhymes were free adaptations of Perrault's *Contes de ma mère l'oye* ("Tales of my Mother Goose") which appeared in 1697.

The Goose and Gridiron. A public-house sign, properly the coat of arms of the Company of Musicians—viz. a *swan* with expanded wings, within a *double tressure* [the gridiron], counter, flory, argent. Perverted into a goose striking the bars of a gridiron with its foot; also called "The Swan and Harp."

In the United States the name is humorously applied to the national coat-of-arms—the American eagle with a gridiron-like shield on its breast.

The old woman is plucking her goose. A children's way of saying "it is snowing."

The royal game of goose. The game referred to by Goldsmith (*Deserted Village*, 232) as being present in the ale-house—

The pictures placed for ornament and use,
The twelve good rules, the royal game of goose—

was a game of compartments through which the player progressed according to the cast of the dice. At certain divisions a goose was depicted, and if the player fell into one of these he doubled the number of his last throw and moved forward accordingly.

The "twelve good rules" was a broadside showing a rough cut of the execution of Charles I with the following "rules" printed below:—

1. Urge no healths; 2. Profane no divine ordinances; 3. Touch no state matters; 4. Reveal no secrets; 5. Pick no quarrels; 6. Make no comparisons; 7. Maintain no ill opinions; 8. Keep no bad company; 9. Encourage no vice; 10. Make no long meals; 11. Repeat no grievances; 12. Lay no wagers.

These were said to have been "found in the study of King Charles the First, of Blessed Memory," and in the 18th century were frequently framed and displayed in taverns.

Gooseberry. Gooseberry fool. A dish made of gooseberries scalded and pounded with cream.

The word *fool* is from the French *fouler*, to press or crush.

Let anything come in the shape of fodder or eatinge stuffe, it is wellcome, whether it be Sawsedge, or Custard, or Flawne, or Foole.—JOHN TAYLOR: *The Great Eater*, 1610.

To play, or be gooseberry. To act as chaperon; to be an unwanted third when lovers are together. The origin of the phrase is obscure, but it has been suggested that it arose from the charity of the chaperon occupying herself in picking gooseberries while the lovers were more romantically occupied.

Goosebridge. Go to Goosebridge. "Rule a wife and have a wife." Boccaccio (ix, 9) tells us that a man who had married a shrew asked Solomon what he should do to make her more submissive; and the wise king answered, "Go to Goosebridge." Returning home, deeply perplexed, he came to a bridge which a muleteer was trying to induce a mule to cross. The beast resisted, but the stronger will of his master at length prevailed. The man asked the name of the bridge, and was told it was "Goosebridge."

Gopher (gō′ fér). A native of Minnesota, U.S.A. The word probably comes from the prairie rodent of that name.

Gopher wood, the wood of which Noah made his ark (*Gen.* vi, 14). There has been much discussion as to what wood is really meant, but it is now considered that it is that of the cypress.

Gordian Knot (gôr′ di án). A great difficulty. Gordius, a peasant, being chosen king of Phrygia, dedicated his wagon to Jupiter, and fastened the yoke to a beam with a rope of bark so ingeniously that no one could untie it. Alexander was told that "whoever undid the knot would reign over the whole East." "Well then," said the conqueror, "it is thus I perform the task," and, so saying, he cut the knot in twain with his sword. Thus: **To cut the Gordian knot** is to get out of a difficult or awkward position by one decisive step; to solve a problem by a single brilliant stroke.

Such praise the Macedonian got
For having rudely cut the Gordian knot.
WALLER: *To the King*.

Turn him to any cause of policy,
The Gordian knot of it he will unloose,
Familiar as his garter.
Henry V, i, 1.

Gordon Riots. Riots in 1780, headed by Lord George Gordon, to compel the House of Commons to repeal the bill passed in 1778 for the relief of Roman Catholics. Gordon was of unsound mind, and died in 1793, a proselyte to Judaism. Dickens has given a very vivid description of the Gordon Riots in *Barnaby Rudge*.

Gore. A triangular piece of material, or of land, from the low Latin *gora*. *Cp*. Kensington Gore, and the Gore, New York (late 18th century).

Gorgon (gôr′ gon). Anything unusually hideous, particularly a hideous or terrifying woman. In classical mythology there were three Gorgons, with serpents on their heads instead of hair; Medusa was the chief, and the only one that was mortal; but so hideous was her face that whoever set eyes on it was instantly turned into stone. She was slain by Perseus, and her head placed on the shield of Minerva.

What was that snaky-headed Gorgon shield
That wise Minerva wore, unconquered virgin,
Wherewith she freezed her foes to congealed stone?
But rigid looks of chaste austerity,
And noble grace, that dashed brute violence
With sudden adoration and blank awe.
MILTON: *Comus*, 458.

Gorgonzola (gôr gŏn zō′ la). A town in Italy some 12 miles north-east of Milan and chiefly famous for the cheese once made there. This is of a Stilton nature, made from the whole milk of cows and mottled or veined with a penicillium which is the principal ripening agent. It is usually exported with a thin, clay-like coat made of gypsum and lard or tallow.

Gospel. This is an Anglo-Saxon compound word, "god spell," good news. It is employed to describe collectively the lives of Christ as narrated by the evangelists in the New Testament; it signifies the message of redemption set forth in those books; it is used as a term for the entire Christian system of religion; and it is applied to any doctrine or teaching set forth for some specific purpose.

The first four books of the New Testament, known as the Gospels, are ascribed to Matthew, Mark, Luke, and John. The first three of these are called "synoptic," as they follow the same lines and have, broadly speaking, the same point of view. The fourth Gospel was written some thirty years later than the others. Critics are still uncertain as to the real authorship of the Gospels.

Gospel according to . . . The chief teaching of [so-and-so]. *The Gospel according to Mammon* is the making and collecting of money.

The Gospel of Nicodemus, or "The Acts of Pilate" is an apocryphal book compiled about the 5th century. It gives an elaborate and fanciful description of the trial, death and resurrection of Our Lord; names the two thieves (Dismas and Gestas); Pilate's wife (Procla); the centurion (Longinus), etc., and ends with the conversion of Annas, Caiaphas, and the Sanhedrin.

The Gospel of Peter is an apocryphal book first mentioned in the year 191. Only a fragment remains, and it departs from the canonical gospels in several particulars.

The Gospel of Thomas is a Gnostic apocryphal book full of stories of crude prodigies and puerile fancies.

The gospel of wealth. The hypothesis that wealth is the great end and aim of man, the one thing needful.

The Gospel side of the altar is to the left of the celebrant facing the altar.

Gossamer. According to legend, this delicate thread is the ravelling of the Virgin Mary's winding-sheet, which fell to earth on her ascension to heaven. It is said to be *God's seam*, *i.e.* God's thread. Actually, the name is from M.E. *gossomer*, literally *goose-summer*, or St. Martin's summer (early November), when geese are eaten and gossamer is prevalent.

Gossip. A tattler; a sponsor at baptism, a corruption of *God-sibb*, a kinsman in the Lord. (A.S. *sibb*, relationship, whence *sibman*, kinsman; *he is our sib*, is still used.)

'Tis not a maid, for she hath had gossips [sponsors for her child]; yet 'tis a maid, for she is her master's servant, and serves for wages.—*Two Gentlemen of Verona*. iii, 1.

Goth. One of an ancient tribe of Teutons which swept down upon and devastated large portions of southern Europe in the 3rd to 5th centuries, establishing kingdoms in Italy, southern France, and Spain. They were looked on by the civilized Romans as merely destroying barbarians; hence the name came to be applied to any rude, uncultured, destructive people.

The last of the Goths. *See* RODERICK.

Gotham (gō′ thăm). **Wise Men of Gotham**—fools, wiseacres. The village of Gotham, in Nottinghamshire, was for centuries proverbial for the folly of its inhabitants, and many tales have been fathered on them, one of which is their joining hands round a thornbush to shut in a cuckoo. *Cp*. COGGESHALL.

It is said that King John intended to make a progress through this town with the view of purchasing a castle and grounds. The townsmen had no desire to be saddled with this expense, and therefore when the royal messengers appeared, wherever they went they saw the people occupied in some idiotic pursuit. The king being told of it, abandoned his intention, and the "wise men" of the village cunningly remarked, "More fools pass through Gotham than remain in it."

A collection of popular tales of stupidity was published in the reign of Henry VIII as *Merie Tales of the Mad Men of Gotam, gathered together by A. B. of Phisike, Doctour.* This "A. B." has been supposed to be Andrew Boorde (*c.* 1490-1549), physician and traveller.

Most nations have fixed upon some locality as their limbus of fools; thus we have Phrygia as the fools' home of Asia Minor, Abdera of the Thracians, Bœotia of the Greeks, Nazareth of the ancient Jews, Swabia of the modern Germans, and so on.

Gothamites. Inhabitants of New York. The term was in use by 1800. The name of Gotham was given to New York by Washington Irving in his *Salmagundi,* 1807.

Gothic Architecture. A style prevalent in Western Europe from the 12th to the 16th centuries, characterized by the pointed arch, clustered columns, etc. The name has nothing to do with the Goths, but was bestowed in contempt by the architects of the Renaissance period on mediæval architecture, which they termed clumsy, fit only for barbarians or Goths.

St. Louis . . . built the Ste. Chapelle of Paris, . . . the most precious piece of Gothic in Northern Europe.—RUSKIN: *Fors Clavigera,* vol. i.

A revival in England of Gothic architecture and ornament, was started by wealthy *dilettanti* such as Horace Walpole in the 18th century. It was further popularized by Ruskin and Sir Walter Scott, and took a concrete form in the architecture of the Catholic A. W. Pugin (1812-52).

Gourmand and **Gourmet** (goor' mond, goor' mā) (Fr.). The *gourmand* is one whose chief pleasure is eating; but a *gourmet* is a connoisseur of food and wines. The *gourmand* regards quantity more than quality, the *gourmet* quality more than quantity. *See* APICIUS.

In former times [in France] *gourmand* meant a judge of eating, and *gourmet* a judge of wine . . . *Gourmet* is now universally understood to refer to eating, and not to drinking.—HAMERTON: *French and English,* Pt. v, ch. iv.

Gout. The disease is so called from the Fr. *goutte,* a drop, because it was once thought to proceed from a "drop of acrid matter in the joints."

Goven. St. Goven's Bell. *See* INCHCAPE.

Government Stroke. Early Australian slang for taking a long time over very little work; still a common expression in that country.

Gowan (gou' an). A Scotch word for various field flowers, especially the common daisy, sometimes called the *ewe-gowan,* apparently from the ewe, as being frequent in pastures fed on by sheep.

Grab. To clutch or seize. *He grabbed him, i.e.* he caught him.

Land grabber. A common expression in Ireland during the last two decades of the 19th century, to signify one who takes the farm or land of an evicted tenant. The corresponding phrase in the 18th century was *Land Pirate.*

Grace. A courtesy title used in addressing or speaking of dukes, duchesses, and archbishops. "His Grace the Duke of Devonshire," "My Lord Archbishop, may it please Your Grace," etc.

Act of grace. A pardon; a general pardon granted by Act of Parliament, especially that of 1690, when William III pardoned political offenders; and that of 1784, when the estates forfeited for high treason in connexion with "the '45" were restored.

Grace before (or **after**) **meat.** A short prayer asking a blessing on, or giving thanks for, one's food. Here the word (which used to be plural) is a relic of the old phrase *to do graces* or *to give graces,* meaning to render thanks (Fr. *rendre graces,* Lat. *gratias agere*), as in Chaucer's

They weren right glad and joyeful, and answereden ful mekely and benignely, yeldinge graces and thankinges to hir lord Melibee. *Tale of Melibeus,* §71.

Grace cup or **Loving cup.** This is a large tankard or goblet from which the last draught at a banquet is drunk, the cup being passed from guest to guest. The name is also applied to a strong brew, as at Oxford, of beer flavoured with lemon-peel, nutmeg and sugar, and very brown toast.

Grace days, or **Days of grace.** The three days over and above the time stated in a commercial bill. Thus, if a bill is drawn on June 20th, and is payable in one month, it is due on July 20th, but three "days of grace" are added, bringing the date to July 23rd.

Grace, Herb of. *See* HERB OF GRACE.

Grace notes are musical embellishments, vocal or instrumental, not essential to the harmony or melody of a piece. They used to be much more common in music for the viol and harpsichord than they are for modern instruments, and it was not unusual for a virtuoso to introduce them at his own discretion.

The three Graces. In classical mythology, the goddesses who bestowed beauty and charm and were themselves the embodiment of both. They were the sisters Aglaia, Thalia, and Euphrosyne.

> They are the daughters of sky-ruling Jove,
> By him begot of faire Eurynome, . . .
> The first of them hight mylde Euphrosyne,
> Next faire Aglaia, last Thalia merry;
> Sweete Goddesses all three, which me in mirth do cherry.
>
> SPENSER: *Faerie Queene*, VI, x, 22.

Andrea Appiani (1754-1817), the Italian fresco artist, was known as *the Painter of the Graces*.

Time of grace. *See* SPORTING SEASONS.

To get into one's good graces. To insinuate oneself into the favour of.

To fall from grace. Apart from a theological implication, this means to relapse from a moral position one has attained.

Year of Grace. The year of Our Lord, Anno Domini. In University language it is the year allowed to a Fellow who has been given a College living, at the end of which he must resign either his fellowship or the living.

Graceless or **Godless florin.** The first issue of the English florin (1849), called "Graceless" because the letters D.G. ("by God's grace") were omitted, and "Godless" because of the omission of F.D. ("Defender of the Faith").

It happened that Richard Lalor Sheil (1791-1851), master of the Mint at the time, was a Catholic, and the suspicion was aroused that the omission was made on religious grounds. The florins were called in and re-cast, and Mr. Sheil left the Mint the following year on his appointment as minister to Florence.

Grade. In American usage this word is used for the more common English *gradient* for the rate of ascent or descent of a road or railway track, also for the hill itself. A *grade-crossing* is usually known in Britain as a *level crossing*.

To make the grade, to rise to the occasion, to have it in one to do what has to be done; from the analogy of a locomotive succeeding in drawing its load up a steep gradient.

Gradual. An antiphon sung between the Epistle and the Gospel, as the deacon ascends the *steps* (late Lat. *graduales*) of the altar. Also, a book containing the musical portions of the service at mass—the *graduals, introits, kyries, gloria in excelsis, credo*, etc.

Græmes, The (grāmz). A clan of freebooters who inhabited the Debatable Land (*q.v.*),

and were transported to Ireland at the beginning of the 17th century.

Graft. Illicit profit or commission. Of U.S.A. origin, the word is now world wide. It seems to have come into use in the 1890s.

Grahame's Dyke. A popular name for the remains of the old Roman wall between the firths of Clyde and Forth, the Wall of Antoninus.

Grail, The Holy. The cup or chalice traditionally used by Christ at the Last Supper, and the centre round which a huge *corpus* of mediæval legend, romance, and allegory revolves.

According to one account, Joseph of Arimathæa preserved the Grail, and received into it some of the blood of the Saviour at the Crucifixion. He brought it to England, but it disappeared. According to others, it was brought by angels from heaven and entrusted to a body of knights who guarded it on top of a mountain. When approached by anyone of not perfect purity it disappeared from sight, and its quest became the source of most of the adventures of the Knights of the Round Table. *But see also* PERCEFOREST.

The mass of literature concerning the Grail cycle, both ancient and modern, is enormous; the chief sources of the principal groups of legends are—the *Peredur* (Welsh, given in the *Mabinogion*), which is the most archaic form of the Quest story; Wolfram's *Parzifal* (about 1210), the best example of the story as transformed by ecclesiastical influence; the 13th-century French *Percival le Gallois* (founded on earlier English and Celtic legends which had no connexion with the Grail), showing Percival in his later rôle as an ascetic hero (translated by Dr. Sebastian Evans, 1893, as *The High History of the Holy Grail*); and the *Quête du St. Graal*, which, in its English dress, forms Bks. 13-18 of *Malory's Morte d'Arthur*. *See* FISHERMAN, KING; GALAHAD; PERCIVAL.

It was the French poet, Robert le Boron (fl. about 1215), who, in his *Joseph d'Arimathie* or *Le Saint Graal*, first definitely attached the history of the Grail to the Arthurian cycle.

The framework of Tennyson's *Holy Grail* (1869, *Idylls of the King*), in which the poet expressed his "strong feeling as to the Reality of the Unseen," is taken from Malory.

Grain. A knave in grain. A thoroughgoing knave, a knave all through. An old phrase which comes from dyeing. The brilliant crimson dye obtained from the kermes and cochineal insects used to be thought to come from some seed, or grain; it was of a very durable and lasting nature, dyed the thing completely and finally, through and through. Hence also the word *ingrained*, as in "an ingrained [*i.e.* ineradicable] habit."

> How the red roses flush up in her cheeks,
> And the pure snow with goodly vermeil stain
> Like crimson dyed in grain!
> > SPENSER: *Epithalamion*, 226.
> 'Tis ingrain, sir; 'twill endure wind and weather.—
> SHAKESPEARE: *Twelfth Night*, i, 5.

To go against the grain. Against one's inclination. The allusion is to wood, which cannot be easily planed the wrong way of the grain.

> Your minds,
> Pre-occupied with what you rather must do
> Than what you should, made you against the grain
> To voice him consul.—*Coriolanus*, ii, 3.

With a grain of salt. *See* SALT.

Gramercy. Thank you very much; from O.Fr. *grant*, great, *merci*, reward, the full meaning of the exclamation being "May God reward you greatly." When Gobbo says to Bassanio, "God bless your worship!" he replies, "Gramercy. Wouldst thou aught with me?" (*Merchant of Venice*, ii, 2.)

The Scourge of Grammar. So Pope, in the *Dunciad* (iii, 149), called Giles Jacob (1686-1744), a very minor poet, who, in his *Register of the Poets*, made an unprovoked attack on Pope's friend, Gay.

Prince of Grammarians. Apollonius of Alexandria (2nd cent. B.C.), so called by Priscian.

Le Grand Bâtârd. Antoine de Bourgogne (d. 1504), a natural son of Philip the Good, famous for his deeds of prowess.

Le Grand Condé. Louis II of Bourbon, Prince de Condé, one of France's greatest military commanders (1621-86). The funeral oration pronounced at his death was Bossuet's finest composition.

Le Grand Corneille. Pierre Corneille, the French dramatist (1606-84).

Le Grand Dauphin. Louis, son of Louis XIV (1661-1711).

La Grande Mademoiselle. The Duchesse de Montpensier (1627-93), daughter of Gaston, Due d'Orléans, and cousin of Louis XIV.

Le Grand Monarque. Louis XIV, King of France (1638-1715).

Le Grand Pan. Voltaire (1694-1778).

Monsieur le Grand. The Grand Equerry of France in the reign of Louis XIV, etc.

Grand.

Grand Alliance. Signed May 12th, 1689, between Germany and the States General, subsequently also by England, Spain, and Savoy, to prevent the union of France and Spain.

Grand Guignol. *See* GUIGNOL.

Grand Lama. *See* LAMA.

Grandee. In Spain, a nobleman of the highest rank, who has the privilege of remaining covered in the king's presence.

Grandison, Sir Charles, the hero of Samuel Richardson's *History of Sir Charles Grandison*, published in 1753. Sir Charles is the beau-ideal of a perfect hero, the union of a good Christian and a proper English gentleman, aptly described by Sir Walter Scott as "a faultless monster that the world ne'er saw." It has been suggested that Richardson's model for this character was the worthy Robert Nelson (1665-1715), a religious writer and eminent non-juror.

Grandison Cromwell. The nickname given by Mirabeau to Lafayette (1757-1834), implying that he had all the ambition of a Cromwell, but wanted to appear before men as a Sir Charles Grandison.

Grandmontines. An order of Benedictine hermits founded by St. Stephen of Muret about 1100, with its mother house at Grandmont, Normandy. They came to England soon after the foundation and established three houses, one of which, at Craswall, Herefordshire (fl. *c.* 1222-1464) is one of the loneliest and most interesting monastic ruins in England.

Grange. Properly the *granum* (granary) or farm of a monastery, where the corn was kept in store. In Lincolnshire and the northern counties the name is applied to any lone farm; houses attached to monasteries where rent was paid in grain were also called granges.

> Till thou return, the Court I will exchange
> For some poor cottage, or some country grange
> > DRAYTON: *Lady Geraldine to Earl of Surrey*.

Tennyson's poem, *Mariana*, was suggested by the line in Shakespeare's *Measure for Measure* (iii, 1):—

> There, at the moated grange resides this dejected Mariana.

The word came into more common use in Victorian times when new and largish houses were being built in the country and often magniloquently called The Grange.

In U.S.A. **The Grange** is a nation-wide association for promoting the interests of agriculture.

Grangousier. In Rabelais's satire, *Gargantua and Pantagruel*, a king of Utopia, who married in "the vigour of his old age," Gargamelle, daughter of the king of the Parpaillons, and became the father of Gargantua (*q.v.*). Some say he is meant for Louis XII, but Motteux thinks the "academy figure" of this old Priam was John d'Albret, King of Navarre.

Granite. Granite City, The. Aberdeen.

Granite Redoubt. The grenadiers of the Consular Guard were so called at the battle of Marengo in 1800, because when the French had given way they formed into a square, stood like stone against the Austrians, and stopped all further advance.

Granite State, The. New Hampshire is so called, because the mountainous parts are chiefly granite.

Granny-knot. An ill-tied reef knot which breaks down when any strain is placed upon it.

Grape. The grapes are sour. You disparage it because it is beyond your reach. The allusion is to Æsop's well-known fable of the fox which tried in vain to get at some grapes, but when he found they were beyond his reach went away saying, "I see they are sour."

Grape shot. A form of projectile at one time much used with smooth-bore guns. It consisted of a large number of cast-iron bullets packed in layers between thin iron plates and then arranged in tiers (usually three), the whole being held together by an iron bolt passing through the centre of the plates. When fired the shot broke up and distributed the bullets in showers. The well-known phrase "A whiff of grape shot" occurs in Carlyle's *French Revolution* (III, vii, 7).

Grape-sugar. Another name for glucose (dextrose), a fermentable sugar, less sweet than cane-sugar, and obtained from dried grapes and other fruits as well as being made chemically. It is used in the manufacture of jams, beer, etc.

Grapevine telegraph. The intangible and un-traceable means whereby rumours—as often as not false—are conveyed around by whisperings, etc.

Grass. Not to let the grass grow under one's feet. To be very active and energetic.

A grass hand is a compositor who fills a temporary vacancy; hence *to grass*, to take only temporary jobs as a compositor.

Grass widow. Formerly, an unmarried woman who has had a child; but now, a wife temporarily parted from her husband; also, by extension, a divorced woman. The word has nothing to do with *grace* widow (a widow by courtesy). The phrase *grass widower* is used in the same sense.

Grasshopper. Considered as the sign of a grocer because it was the crest of Sir Thomas

Gresham, merchant grocer. The Royal Exchange, founded by him, used to be profusely decorated with grasshoppers, and the brass one on the eastern part of the present building escaped the fires of 1666 and 1838.

Grattan's Parliament. The free Irish Parliament established in Dublin in 1782, when Henry Grattan (1746-1820) obtained the repeal of Poynings' Law (*q.v.*). It lasted till the coming into force of the Act of Union, January 1st, 1801.

Grave. Solemn, sedate, and serious in look and manner. This is Lat. *gravis*, heavy, grave; but "grave," a place of interment, is A.S. *græf*, a pit; *graf-an*, to dig.

Close as the grave. Very secret indeed.

It's enough to make him turn in his grave. Said when something happens to which the deceased person would have strongly objected.

Someone is walking over my grave. An exclamation made when one is seized with an involuntary convulsive shuddering.

With one foot in the grave. At the very verge of death. The expression was used by Julian, who said he would "learn something even if he had one foot in the grave." The parallel Greek phrase is, "With one foot in the ferryboat," meaning Charon's.

Gray-back. Confederate soldier in the American Civil War. So called from the colour of the Confederate army uniform.

Grease. Slang for money, especially that given as a bribe; "palm-oil."

Like greased lightning. Very quick indeed.

To grease one's palm or **fist.** To give a bribe.

> Grease my fist with a tester or two, and ye shall find it in your pennyworth.—QUARLES: *The Virgin Widow*, iv, 1, p. 40.

> S.: You must oyl it first.
> C.: I understand you—
> Greaze him i' the fist.
> CARTWRIGHT: *Ordinary* (1651).

To grease the wheels. To make things run smoothly, pass off without a hitch; usually by the application of a little money.

Great, The. The term is usually applied to the following:—

ABBAS I, Shah of Persia. (1557, 1585-1628).
ALBERTUS MAGNUS, the schoolman. (d. 1280.)
ALEXANDER, of Macedon. (356, 340-323 B.C.).
ALFONSO III, King of Asturias and Leon. (884, 866-912.)
ALFRED, of England. (849, 871-901).
ST. BASIL, Bishop of Cæsarea. (4th cent.)
CANUTE, of England and Denmark. (995, 1014-1035.)
CASIMIR III, of Poland. (1309, 1333-1370.)
CHARLES, King of the Franks and Emperor of the Romans, called *Charlemagne*. (764-814.)

CHARLES III, Duke of Lorraine. (1543-1608).
CHARLES EMMANUEL I, Duke of Savoy. (1562-1630.)
CLOVIS, King of the Franks. (466-511.)
CONDÉ. *See* LOUIS II, *below.*
CONSTANTINE I, Emperor of Rome. (272, 306-337.)
CYRUS, founder of the Persian Empire. (d. 529 B.C.)
DARIUS, King of Persia. (d. 485 B.C.)
DOUGLAS (*Archibald, the great Earl of Angus,* also called *Bell-the-Cat* [*q.v.*]).
FERDINAND I, of Castile and Leon (Reigned 1034-1065.)
FREDERICK WILLIAM, Elector of Brandenburg, surnamed *The Great Elector.* (1620-1688.)
FREDERICK II, of Prussia. (1712, 1740-1786.)
GREGORY I, Pope. (544, 590-604.)
GUSTAVUS ADOLPHUS, of Sweden. (1594, 1611-1632.)
HENRY IV, of France. (1553, 1589-1610.)
HEROD I, King of Judea. (73-3 B.C.)
JOHN I, of Portugal. (1357, 1385-1433.)
JUSTINIAN I, Emperor of the East. (483, 527-565.)
LEO I, Pope. (440-461.)
LEO I, Emperor of the East. (457-474.)
LEOPOLD I, of Germany. (1640-1705.)
LEWIS I, of Hungary. (1326, 1342-1383.)
LOUIS II, DE BOURBON, Prince of Condé, Duc d'Enghien (1621-1686), always known as *The Great Condé.*
LOUIS XIV, called *Le Grand Monarque.* (1638, 1643-1714.)
MAXIMILIAN, Duke of Bavaria, victor of Prague. (1573-1651.)
COSMO DE' MEDICI, first Grand Duke of Tuscany. (1519, 1537-1574.)
GONZALES PEDRO DE MENDOZA, *great Cardinal of Spain,* statesman and scholar. (1428-1495.)
MOHAMMED II, Sultan of the Turks. (1430, 1451-1481.)
NICHOLAS I, Pope (from 858-867.)
OTHO I, Emperor of the Romans. (912, 936-973.)
PETER I, of Russia. (1672, 1689-1725.)
PIERRE III, of Aragon. (1239, 1276-1285.)
SANCHO III, King of Navarre. (About 965-1035.)
SAPOR III, King of Persia. (d. 380.)
SFORZA (*Giacomo*), the Italian general. (1369-1424.)
SIGISMUND II, King of Poland. (1467, 1506-1548.)
THEODORIC, King of the Ostrogoths. (454, 475-526.)
THEODOSIUS I, Emperor. (346, 378-395.)
MATTEO VISCONTI, Lord of Milan. (1252, 1295-1323.)
VLADIMIR, Grand Duke of Russia. (973-1015.)
WALDEMAR I, of Denmark. (1131, 1157-1182.)

Great Divide. The Rocky Mountains.

Great Elector, The. Frederick William, Elector of Brandenburg (1620-88).

Great Go. At the universities, a familiar term for the final examinations for the B.A. degree; at Oxford usually shortened to *Greats.* *Cp.* LITTLE GO.

Great Harry. The name popularly given to the *Henry Grace de Dieu,* the first double-decked warship in the English navy. Built in 1512, and named after Henry VIII, she was a three-master of about 1,000 tons, carried 72 guns and sailed with a crew of 700 men. She was burned accidentally at Woolwich, in 1533.

Great Head. Malcolm III, of Scotland; also called *Canmore,* which means the same thing. (Reigned 1057-1093.)

Great Lakes. The five American inland seas—Lakes Erie, Huron, Michigan, Ontario, and Superior.

Great Mogul. The title of the chief of the Mogul Empire (*q.v.*).

Great Scott or Scot! An exclamation of surprise, wonder, admiration, indignation, etc. It seems to have originated in America about the late 60s of last century, perhaps in memory of General Winfield Scott (1786-1866) a popular figure in the mid-19th century after his victorious campaign in Mexico in 1847.

In England the expression is sometimes humorously extended to "Great Scotland Yard!"

Great Unknown, The. Sir Walter Scott, who published *Waverley* (1814), and the subsequent novels as "by the author of Waverley," anonymously. It was not till 1827 that he admitted the authorship, though it was already pretty well known.

The Great White Way. The name formerly applied to Broadway, the theatrical district of New York City.

Greatheart, Mr. The guide of Christiana and her family to the Celestial City in Bunyan's *Pilgrim's Progress,* part II.

Grecian. *See* BLUE-COAT SCHOOL.

Grecian bend. An affectation in walking with the body stooped slightly forward, assumed by English women in 1868.

A Grecian nose or **profile** is one where the line of the nose continues that of the forehead without a dip.

Greco, El (grek' ō), or **The Greek.** A Cretan named Domenico Theotocopuli, who studied under Titian and Michelangelo, and moved to Spain about 1570. He was the foremost painter of the Castilian school in the 16th century.

Greegrees. The name given on the West Coast of Africa to amulets, charms, fetishes, etc.

A greegree man. One who sells these.

Greek. A merry Greek. In *Troilus and Cressida* (i, 2) Shakespeare makes Pandarus, bantering Helen for her love to Troilus, say, "I think Helen loves him better than Paris"; to which Cressida, whose wit is to parry and pervert, replies, "Then she's a merry Greek indeed," insinuating that she was a "woman of pleasure." *See* GRIG.

All Greek to me. Quite unintelligible; an unknown tongue or language. Casca says, "For mine own part, it was all Greek to me." (*Julius Cæsar,* 1, 2.)

Greek Church. A name often given inaccurately to the Eastern or Orthodox Church (*q.v.*)

of which the Greek Church is only an auto-cephalous unit, recognized as independent by the Patriarch of Constantinople in 1850. It is governed by a synod under the presidency of the Archbishop of Athens, and does not differ in any point of doctrine from its parent the Orthodox Church.

Greek Cross. *See* CROSS.

Greek fire. A combustible composition used for setting fire to an enemy's ships, fortifications, etc., of nitre, sulphur, and naphtha. Tow steeped in the mixture was hurled in a blazing state through tubes, or tied to arrows. The invention is ascribed to Callinicos, of Heliop-olis, A.D. 668, and it was used by the Greeks at Constantinople.

Greek gift. A treacherous gift. The reference is to the Wooden Horse of Troy (*q.v.*), or to Virgil's *Timeo Danaos et dona ferentes* (*Æneid*, ii, 49), "I fear the Greeks, even when they offer gifts."

Greek trust. No trust at all. "*Græca fides*" was with the Romans no faith at all.

Green. Young, fresh, as *green cheese*, cream cheese, which is eaten fresh; *a green old age*, an old age in which the faculties are not impaired and the spirits are still youthful; *green goose*, a young or mid-summer goose.

If you would fat green geese, shut them up when they are about a month old.—MORTIMER: *Husbandry.*

Immature in age or judgment, inexperienced, young.

My salad days
When I was green in judgment!
Antony and Cleopatra, i, 5.
The text is old, the orator too green.
Venus and Adonis, 806.

Simple, raw, easily imposed upon; the characteristic greenhorn (*q.v.*).

"He is so jolly green," said Charley.—DICKENS: *Oliver Twist*, ch. ix.

For its symbolism, etc., *see* COLOURS.

The wearing of the green. An Irish patriotic and revolutionary song, dating from 1798. Green (*cp.* EMERALD ISLE) was the emblematic colour adopted by Irish Nationalists.

They're hanging men and women for the wearing of the green.

Green belt. A stretch of country around a city or large town that has been set aside to be kept open and free from all building except within certain limits.

Green-eyed monster, The. So Shakespeare called jealousy:—

Iago: O! beware, my lord, of jealousy;
It is the green-ey'd monster which doth mock
The meat it feeds on. *Othello*, iii, 3.

A greenish complexion was formerly held to be indicative of jealousy; and as cats, lions, tigers, and all the green-eyed tribe "mock the meat they feed on," so jealousy mocks its victim by loving and loathing it at the same time.

Green fingers, said of a successful gardener whose fingers are supposed to have a sort of magic touch that makes whatever he plants grow and flourish.

Green hands. A nautical phrase for inferior sailors. *See* ABLE-BODIED SEAMAN, *and cp.* GREENHORN *below*.

The Green Knight. In the old romance, *Valentine and Orson*, a Pagan who demanded Fezon in marriage but, overcome by Orson, resigned his claim.

Green Man. This common public-house sign probably represents either a Jack-in-the-Green (*q.v.*), or a game-keeper, who used at one time to be dressed in green.

But the "Green Man" shall I pass by unsung,
Which mine own James upon his sign-post hung?
His sign, his image—for he once was seen
A squire's attendant, clad in keeper's green.
CRABBE: *Borough*.

The public-house sign, *The Green Man and Still*, is probably from the arms of the Distillers' Company, the supporters of which were two Indians, which, by the sign-painters, were depicted as clad in green boughs like a "green man" or Jack-in-the-Green.

On a golf course **the green-man** is the club servant who is responsible for the putting greens.

Green Mountain Boys. Men of Vermont, U.S.A.—a term in use since 1775. Vermont, or Vert Mont, so called from its forest-covered mountains, was formed from the states of New Hampshire and New York in 1777, largely through the action of its farmers who agitated for an independent state of their own, and were called the Green Mountain Boys.

Green Ribbon Day in Ireland is March 17th, St. Patrick's Day, when the shamrock and green ribbon are worn as the national badge.

Green room. The common waiting-room beyond the stage at a theatre for the performers; so called because at one time the walls were coloured green to relieve the eyes affected by the glare of the stage lights.

Green sickness, the old name for chlorosis, a form of anaemia now very rare but once common in adolescent girls. It was characterized by a greenish pallor.

Green wax. In old legal practice an estreat (certified extract from an official record) formerly delivered to the sheriff by the Exchequer for levy. It was under the seal of the court, which was impressed upon green wax.

Greenbacks. A legal tender note in the United States, first issued in 1862, during the Civil War, as a war-revenue measure; so called because the back is printed in green.

Greengage. A variety of plum introduced into England from France (with others) by Sir William Gage of Hengrave, Suffolk, about 1725, and named in honour of him. Called by the French "Reine Claude," out of compliment to the daughter of Anne de Bretagne and Louis XII, generally called *la bonne reine* (1499-1524).

Greenhorn. A novice at any trade, profession, sport, etc., a simpleton, a youngster. *Cp.* GREEN HAND; GREENER.

Greensleeves. A very popular ballad in Elizabethan days, first published in 1581, given *in extenso* in Clement Robinson's *Handefull of Pleasant Delites* (1584), and twice mentioned by Shakespeare (*Merry Wives*, ii, 1, and v, 5.). The air goes back to Elizabethan times, and was used for many ballads. During the Civil Wars it was a party tune to which the Cavaliers sang political ballads. Pepys (April 23rd, 1660) mentions it under the title of *The Blacksmith*, by which it was sometimes known.

Greenlander. A native of Greenland, which was originally so called (*Gronland*) by the Norsemen in the 10th century with the idea that if only they gave the country a good name it would induce settlers to go there! Facetiously applied to a greenhorn.

Greenwich. So named by Danish settlers; it means "the green place on the bay" (*wich, vig*), or place situated on the coast or near the mouth of a river; as Sandwich, Lerwick, Schleswig.

Greenwich time. Mean time for the meridian of Greenwich, *i.e.* the system of time in which noon occurs at the moment of passage of the mean sun over the meridian of Greenwich. It is the standard time adopted by astronomers; Greenwich noon is in legal use throughout Great Britain, Ireland, France, Belgium, Spain, Portugal, the Faröe Islands, Gibraltar, Algeria, St. Thomas and Princes Isles, the Ivory Coast, Dahomey, and Morocco.

Since 1883 the system of Standard Time by zones has been accepted by all civilized nations. Standard Time differs from Greenwich Mean Time by an integral number of hours, either slow or fast. Mid-European Time, is, for example, one hour fast of Greenwich Time; Pacific Time is 9 hours slow; *i.e.* noon at Greenwich is 3 a.m. of the same day in British Columbia.

Gregorian. Gregorian Calendar. *See* CALENDAR.

Gregorian chant. Plain-song, a mediæval system of church music, so called because it was introduced into the service by Gregory the Great (600).

Gregorian Epoch. The epoch or day on which the Gregorian calendar commenced in October, 1582.

Gregorian telescope. The first form of the reflecting telescope, invented by James Gregory (1638-75), professor of mathematics at St. Andrews (1663).

Gregorian tree. The gallows; so named from Gregory Brandon and his son, Robert (who was popularly known as "Young Gregory") hangmen from the time of James I to 1649. Sir William Segar, Garter Knight of Arms, granted a coat of arms to Gregory Brandon. *See* HANGMEN.

This trembles under the black rod, and he
Doth fear his fate from the Gregorian tree.
            Mercutius Pragmaticus (1641).

Gregorian Year. The civil year, according to the correction introduced by Pope Gregory XIII in 1582. *See* CALENDAR. The equinox which occurred on March 25th in the time of Julius Cæsar, fell on March 11th in the year 1582. This was because the Julian calculation of $365\frac{1}{4}$ days to a year was 11 min. 10 sec. too much. Gregory suppressed ten days in October, so as to make the equinox fall on March 21, 1583, as it did at the Council of Nice, and, by some simple arrangements, prevented the recurrence in future of a similar error.

The New Style, as it was called, was adopted in England in 1752, when Wednesday, September 2nd, was followed by Thursday, September 14th.

This has given rise to a double computation, as Lady Day, March 25th, Old Lady Day, April 6th; Midsummer Day, June 24th, Old Midsummer Day, July 6th; Michaelmas Day, September 29th, Old Michaelmas Day, October 11th; Christmas Day, December 25th, Old Christmas Day, January 6th.

Until 1752 the legal new year in Britain began on March 25th, though New Year's Day was popularly reckoned as January 1st. It was, therefore, customary to put for all dates between January 1st and March 25th the two years involved: *e.g.* January 31st, 1721 in popular reckoning would be written or printed as

January 31st, 1720/21, that is, 1720 legally but popularly and actually 1721.

Gremlin (grem' lin). One of a tribe of imaginary elves, whom the R.A.F. in World War II blamed for all inexplicable failures, mechanical or otherwise, in aeroplanes.

Grenadier. Originally a soldier whose duty in battle was to throw grenades, *i.e.* explosive shells, weighing from two to six pounds. There were some four or five tall, picked men, chosen for this purpose from each company; later each regiment had a special company of them; and when, in the 18th century, the use of grenades was discontinued (not to be revived until World War I), the name was retained for the company composed of the tallest and finest men. In the British Army it now survives only in the Grenadier Guards, the First regiment of Foot Guards (3 battalions), noted for their height, fine physique, traditions, and discipline.

Grendel. The mythical, half-human monster in *Beowulf* (*q.v.*), who nightly raided the king's hall and slew the sleepers; he was slain by Beowulf.

Gresham, Sir Thomas. *See* CLEOPATRA AND HER PEARL; GRASSHOPPER.

To dine with Sir Thomas Gresham. *See* DINE.

Grève (grāv). **Place de Grève.** The Tyburn of old Paris, where for centuries public executions took place. The present Hôtel de Ville occupies part of the site, and what is left of the *Place* is now called the *Place de l'Hôtel de Ville.* The word *grève* means the strand of a river or the shore of the sea, and the *Place* is on the bank of the Seine.

Who has e'er been to Paris must needs know the Grève,
The fatal retreat of th' unfortunate brave,
Where honour and justice most oddly contribute
To ease Hero's pains by a halter or gibbet.
PRIOR: *The Thief and the Cordelier.*

Grey. Greys, The. The Royal Scots Greys (2nd Dragoons) were raised in 1678. It is now uncertain whether their name comes from their grey horses or their uniform, which was also grey. The horses survived the uniform, but both have now gone, as the regiment is mechanized.

Greybeard. An old man—generally a doddering old fellow; also an earthen pot for holding spirits; a large stone jar. *Cp.* BELLARMINE.

Grey Cloak. A City of London alderman who has passed the chair; so called because his official robe is furred with grey amis.

Grey Eminence. The name given to François Leclerc du Tremolay (1577-1638), or Père Joseph, as he was called, the Capuchin

agent and trusty counsellor of Cardinal Richelieu. He owed his sobriquet to the fact that his influence and his policy inspired the Cardinal's actions, and that he was, as it were, a shadowy cardinal in the background.

Grey Friars. Franciscans (*q.v.*). Black Friars are Dominicans, and White Friars Carmelites.

Grey goose feather, or **wing.** "The grey goose wing was the death of him," the arrow which is winged with grey goose feathers.

Grey mare. *See* MARE.

Grey matter, a pseudo-scientific euphemism for the brain, for common sense. The active part of the brain is composed of a greyish tissue which contains the nerve-endings.

Greyhound. Juliana Berners, in the *Boke of St. Albans* (1486) gives the following as "the propreteïs of a goode Grehound":—

A greyhounde shoulde be heded like a snake, And necked like a Drake; Foted like a Kat, Tayled like a Rat; Syded like a Teme, Chyned like a Beme.

"Syded like a teme" probably means both sides alike, a plough-team being meant.

Greyhound. The Greyhound as a public-house sign is in honour of Henry VII, whose badge it was; it is still the badge (in silver) of the King's Messengers.

Gridiron. This is emblematic of St. Lawrence whose feast is celebrated on August 10. One unsubstantiated legend says that he was roasted on a gridiron; another that he was bound to an iron chair and thus roasted alive. All that is certainly known of him is that he was martyred in the year 258 and is buried in the church dedicated to him outside the walls of Rome. The church of St. Lawrence Jewry in the City of London has a gilt gridiron for a vane.

Grief. To come to grief. To meet with disaster; to be ruined; to fail in business.

Griffin. A mythical monster, also called *Griffon, Gryphon,* etc., fabled to be the offspring of the lion and eagle. Its legs and all from the shoulder to the head are like an eagle, the rest of the body is that of a lion. This creature was sacred to the sun, and kept guard over hidden treasures. *See* ARIMASPIANS.

[The Griffin is] an Emblem of valour and magnanimity, as being compounded of the Eagle and Lion, the noblest Animals in their kinds; and so is it applicable unto Princes, Presidents, Generals, and all heroick Commanders; and so is it also born in the Coat-arms of many noble Families of *Europe.*—SIR THOMAS BROWNE: *Pseudodoxia Epidemica,* III, xi.

The Londoners' familiar name for the figure on the monument placed on the site of Temple Bar is *The Griffin.*

Among Anglo-Indians a newcomer, a greenhorn (*q.v.*) is called a *griffin*; and the residue of a contract feast, taken away by the contractor, half the buyer's and half the seller's, is known in the trade as *griffins*.

A **griffon** is a small, rough-haired terrier used in France for hunting.

Grig. Merry as a grig. A grig is a cricket, or grasshopper; but it is by no means certain that the animal is referred to in this phrase (which is at least as old as the mid-sixteenth century); for *grig* here may be a corruption of *Greek*, "merry as a Greek," which dates from about the same time. Shakespeare has: "Then she's a merry Greek"; and again, "Cressid 'mongst the merry Greeks" (*Troilus and Cressida*, i, 2; iv, 4); and among the Romans *Græcari* signified "to play the reveller."

Grim. The giant in Bunyan's *Pilgrim's Progress* (pt. ii), who tried to stop pilgrims on their way to the Celestial City, but was slain by Mr. Greatheart *See also* CRIMODY. GRIM'S DYKE.

Grimalkin. An old she-cat, especially a wicked-or eerie-looking one: from *grey* and *Malkin* (*q.v.*). Shakespeare makes the Witch in *Macbeth* say, "I come, Graymalkin." The cat was supposed to be a witch and was the companion of witches.

Grimm's Law. The law of the permutation of consonants in the principal Aryan languages, first formulated by Jacob L. Grimm, the German philologist, in 1822. Thus, what is *p* in Greek, Latin, or Sanskrit, becomes *f* in Gothic, and *b* or *f* in the Old High German; what is *t* in Greek, Latin, or Sanskrit becomes *th* in Gothic, and *d* in Old High German; etc. Thus changing *p* into *f*, and *t* into *th*, "pater" becomes "father." Grimm's Law has, naturally, much greater philological importance than this example shows.

Grimsby (Lincolnshire). Founded, according to the old legend, by Grim, the fisherman who saved the life of Havelok (*q.v.*), son of the king of Denmark. Grim was laden with gifts by the royal parent, and returned to Lincolnshire, where he built the town whose ancient seal still contains the names of "Gryme" and "Habloc."

Grin. To grin like a Cheshire cat. *See* CAT.

You must grin and bear it. Resistance is hopeless; you may make a face, if you like, but you cannot help yourself.

Grind. To work up for an examination.

To grind one down. To reduce the price asked; to lower wages.

To take a grind. To take a constitutional; to cram into the smallest space the greatest amount of physical exercise. This is the physical grind. The literary grind is a turn at hard study.

Grinders. The double teeth which grind the food put into the mouth. The preacher speaks of old age as the time when "the grinders cease because they are few" (*Eccles*. xii, 3).

To take a grinder. An obsolete gesture of obloquy and insult, performed by applying the left thumb to the nose and revolving the right hand round it, as if working a hand-organ or coffee-mill; done when someone had tried to practise on your credulity, or to impose upon your good faith.

Grisilda or **Griselda** (gri zil' dà, gri zel' dà). The model of enduring patience and obedience, often spoken of as "Patient Grisel." She was the heroine of the last tale in Boccaccio's *Decameron*, obtained by him from an old French story, *Parement des Femmes*; it was translated from Boccaccio by Petrarch, and thence used by Chaucer for his *Clerk's Tale* in the *Canterbury Tales*.

The synopsis of the story is:—

The Marquis of Saluzzo, having been prevailed upon by his subjects to marry, in order to please himself in the affair, made a choice of a countryman's daughter [viz., Griselda], by whom he had two children which he pretended to put to death. Afterwards, feigning that he was weary of his wife, and had taken another, he had his own daughter brought home, as if he had espoused her, whilst his wife was sent away destitute. At length, being convinced of her patience, he brought her home again, presenting her children, now grown up, and ever afterwards loved and honoured her as his lady.

The trials to which the flinty-hearted marquis subjected his innocent wife are almost as unbelievable as the fortitude with which she is credited to have borne them, and perhaps it is just as well that, as Chaucer says in his own "Envoy" to the *Clerk's Tale*:—

Grisilde is dead, and eke her pacience,
And both at once buried in Italie.

Grist. All's grist that comes to my mill. All is appropriated that comes to me; I can make advantage out of anything; all is made use of that comes in my way. Grist is that quantity of corn which is to be ground at one time.

To bring grist to the mill. To bring profitable business or gain; to furnish supplies.

Grit. *See* CLEAR GRIT, *s.v.* CLEAR.

Grizel (griz' el). A variant—like *Grissel*—of *Griselda* (*q.v.*). Octavia, wife of Mark Antony and sister of Augustus Cæsar, is called the "patient Grizel" of Roman story.

For patience she will prove a second Grissel.
Taming of the Shrew, ii, 1.

Groaning Chair. A rustic name for a chair in which a woman sits after her confinement to receive congratulations. Similarly "groaning cake" and "groaning cheese" (called in some dialects *kenno*, because its making was kept a secret) are the cake and cheese which used to be provided in "Goose month" (*q.v.*), and "groaning malt" was a strong ale brewed for the occasion.

For a nurse, the child to dandle,
Sugar, soap, spiced pots and candle,
A groaning chair and eke a cradle.
Poor Robin's Almanack, 1676.

You half-faced groat. A 16th-century colloquialism for "You worthless fellow." The debased groats issued in the reign of Henry VIII had the king's head in profile, but those in the reign of Henry VII had the king's head with the full face. *See King John*, i, 1.

Thou half-faced groat! You thick-cheeked chitty-face!
MUNDAY: *The Downfall of Robert, Earle of Huntingdon*, (1598).

Groats. Husked oat or wheat, fragments rather larger than grits (A.S. *grut*, coarse meal).

Blood without groats is nothing. Family without fortune is worthless. The allusion is perhaps to black pudding, which consists chiefly of blood and groats formed into a sausage.

Grog. Any spirits, but especially rum, diluted with water. Admiral Vernon, who was nicknamed **Old Grog** by his sailors because he walked the deck in rough weather in a *grogram cloak*, was the first to dilute the rum on board ship, hence the name. **Six-water grog** is one part rum to six parts of water.

Grog-blossoms. Blotches or pimples on the face produced by over-indulgence in drink.

Grogram (grog' ràm). A coarse kind of taffeta made of silk and mohair or silk and wool, stiffened with gum. A corruption of the Fr. *gros-grain*.

Gossips in grief and grograms clad.
PRAED: *The Troubadour*, c. i, st. 5.

The blood of the Grograms. *See* BLOOD.

Grommet. *See* GRUMMET.

Grongar Hill, on the right bank of the Towy in Carmarthenshire, was rendered famous by the poem of that name by John Dyer (*c.* 1700-58). Although a native of a nearby village, Llangathen, most of his life was spent in Lincolnshire where he held various livings. His descriptions of Grongar Hill and its neighbourhood have a peculiar fascination.

Groom of the Stole. *See* STOLE.

Groove. To get into a groove. To get into a narrow, undeviating course of life or habit, to become restricted in outlook and ways.

To be in the groove. To be in the right mood, to be doing something successfully. A phrase originating from the accurate reproduction of music by a needle set in the grooves of a gramophone record.

Gross. The French word *gros*, big, bulky, corpulent, coarse, which in English has developed many meanings not present in French. Thus, a *gross* is twelve dozen; a *great gross*, twelve gross; *gross weight* is the entire weight without deductions; *gross average* is the general average. A *villein in gross* was a villein the entire property of his master, and not attached to the land; a *common in gross* is one which is entirely personal property, and does not belong to the manor. *Cp.* ADVOWSON IN GROSS.

Grotesque. Literally, in "Grotto style." The chambers of ancient buildings revealed in mediæval times in Rome were called *grottoes*, and as the walls of these were frequently decorated with fanciful ornaments and *outré* designs, the word *grotesque* (*grotesco*) came to be applied to similar ornamentation.

Ground. Ground floor. The story level with the ground outside; or, in a basement-house, the floor above the basement. In U.S.A. known as the first floor.

Ground swell. A long, deep rolling or swell of the sea, caused by a recent or distant storm, or by an earthquake.

To break ground. To be the first to commence a project, etc.; to take the first step in an undertaking.

To gain ground. To make progress; to be improving one's position.

To have the ground cut from under one's feet. To see what one has relied on for support suddenly removed.

To hold one's ground. To maintain one's authority, popularity, etc.; not to budge from one's position.

To lose ground. To become less popular or less successful; to drift away from the object aimed at.

To shift one's ground. To try a different plan; to change one's argument or the basis of one's reasoning.

To stand one's ground. Not to yield or give way; to stick to one's colours; to have the courage of one's opinion.

Ground hog. The wood-chuck or N. American marmot.

Ground-hog Day. Candlemas (February 2nd), from the saying that the ground hog first appears from his hibernation on that day.

Groundlings. Those who occupied the cheapest portion of an Elizabethan theatre, *i.e.* the pit, which was the bare ground in front of the stage, without any seats. The actor who to-day "plays to the gallery" in Elizabethan times

Split the ears of the groundlings.
Hamlet, iii, 2.

Gruel (groo' ĕl). To take one's gruel, to accept one's punishment, to take what's coming to one.

He had a gruelling, he was punished severely (in boxing, etc.).

A gruelling time, gruelling heat, etc. Exhausting, over-powering.

Grummet. The cabin-boy on board ship; the youth whose duty it was to take in the top-sails, or top the yard for furling the sails or sling-ing the yards. The name is also given to a ring of rope made by laying a single strand, and to a powder-wad.

Grundy. What will Mrs. Grundy say? What will our strait-laced neighbours say? The phrase is from Tom Morton's *Speed the Plough* (1798). In the first scene Mrs. Ashfield shows herself very jealous of neighbour Grundy, and farmer Ashfield says to her: "Be quiet, wull ye? Always sing, dinging Dame Grundy into my ears. What will Mrs. Grundy zay? What will Mrs. Grundy think? . . ."

Gruyère Cheese (groo' yâr). A kind of cheese made in the Jura district of Switzerland and France, taking its name from the district of Gruyère in Canton Fribourg. The curd is pressed in large, shallow cylindrical moulds, and while still in the mould is well salted for at least a month. The cheese is of a pale yellow colour and is characterized by an abundance of large air-bubbles.

Gryll. Let Gryll be Gryll, and have his hoggish mind (Spenser: *Faerie Queene*, II, xii, 87). Don't attempt to wash a blackamoor white; the leopard will never change his spots. Gryll is the Gr. *grullos*, a hog. When Sir Guyon disen-chanted the forms in the Bower of Bliss (*q.v.*) some were exceedingly angry, and Gryll, who had been metamorphosed by Acrasia into a hog, abused him most roundly.

Guano (gwa' nō). A fertilizing substance found on many small islands off the western coast of South America and other places. It is composed of the droppings of the immense flocks of sea-birds that resort to these rocky islets, and is found in beds as much as 60 ft. in depth. It is valuable as containing much ammonium oxalate with urates, and phosphates.

Guard. To be off one's guard. To be careless or heedless.

To put one on his guard. To "give him the tip," show him where the danger lies.

A guardroom is the place where military offenders are detained; and a **guardship** is a ship stationed in a port or harbour for its defence.

Guards, The. *See* HOUSEHOLD TROOPS.

Guards of the Pole. *See* BEAR, THE GREAT.

Gudrun (gud' run). The heroine of the great popular German epic poem, *Gudrun*, or *Kudrun*, written about 1210, and founded on a passage in the prose Edda (*q.v.*).

Gudule or **Gudila, St.** (gu dūl'). Patron saint of Brussels, daughter of Count Witger, died 712. She is represented with a lantern, from a tradition that she was one day going to the church of St. Morgelle with a lantern, which went out, but the holy virgin lighted it again with her prayers. Her feast day is January 8th.

Guebres or **Ghebers** (gā' bĕrz). Followers of the ancient Persian religion, reformed by Zoroaster; fire-worshippers; Parsees. The name, which was bestowed upon them by their Arabian conquerors, is now applied to fire-worshippers generally.

Guelphs and **Ghibellines** (gwelfs, gib' e lēnz). Two great parties whose conflicts made so much of the history of Italy and Germany in the 12th, 13th, and 14th centuries. The Guelphs were the papal and popular party in Italy; their name is the Italian form of *Welfe*, as "Ghibelline" is that of *Waiblingen*, and the origin of these two words is this: At the battle of Weinsburg, in Suabia (1140), Conrad, Duke of Franconia, rallied his followers with the war-cry *Waiblingen* (his family estate), while Henry the Lion, Duke of Saxony, used the cry of *Welfe* (the family name). The Ghibellines supported in Italy the side of the German emperors; the Guelphs opposed it, and supported the cause of the Pope.

The reigning dynasty in Great Britain, the royal House of Windsor, is, through the ducal House of Brunswick, descended from the Guelphs.

Gucnever. *See* GUINEVER.

Guerilla War (ge ril' à). A petty war carried on by bodies of irregular troops acting inde-pendently of each other. From Span. *guerilla*, diminutive of *guerra*, war. The word is applied to the armed bands of peasants, and to individuals, who carry on irregular war on their own account, especially at such time as their government is contending with invading armies.

Guerinists (ger' i nists). An early 17th-century sect of French Illuminati (*q.v.*), founded by Peter Guérin. They were Antinomians, and claimed a special revelation of the Way to Perfection.

Guerino Meschino [*the Wretched*]. An Italian romance, half chivalric and half allegorical, first printed in Padua in 1473. Guerino was the son of Millon, King of Albania. On the day of his birth his father was dethroned, and the child was rescued by a Greek slave, and called Meschino. When he grew up he fell in love with the Princess Elizena, sister of the Greek Emperor, at Constantinople.

Guernsey Lily. *See* MISNOMERS.

Guess. The modern American use of the verb, meaning to think, to suppose, to be pretty sure, was good colloquial English before America was colonized. Shakespeare has:—

Bed.: Ascend, brave Talbot; we will follow thee.
Tal.: Not all together: better far, I guess,
That we do make our entrance several ways.
                                1 *Henry VI*, ii, 1.
and Spenser:—
But now is time, I gesse, homeward to go.
                Shepherd's Calendar: June, 117.

Gueux, Les (lā gĕr). The league of Flemish nobles organized in 1565 to resist the introduction of the Spanish Inquisition into the Netherlands by Philip II of Spain. The word means "ragamuffins" or "beggars"; and the origin of its application is said to be that when the Duchess of Parma made inquiry about them of Count Berlaymont, he told her they were "the scum and offscouring of the people" (*les gueux*). The party took the name in defiance, and dressed like beggars, substituting a fox's tail for a feather, etc.

Guignol (gē' nyol). The principal character in a popular French puppet-show (very like our "Punch and Judy") dating from the 18th century. As the performance comprised *macabre* and gruesome incidents the name came to be attached to short plays of this nature; hence *Grand Guignol*, a series of such plays, or the theatre in which they are performed.

Guildhall. Properly, the meeting-place of a trade guild, *i.e.* an association of persons exercising the same trade or craft, formed for the protection and promotion of their common interests. In London the guilds became of importance in the 14th century, and as it came

about that the Corporation was formed almost entirely from among their members their Hall was used as the Town Hall or headquarters of the Corporation, as it still is to-day. Here are the Court of Common Council, the Court of Aldermen, the Chamberlain's Court, the police court presided over by an alderman, the Corporation Art Gallery, Museum, etc.

Portions of the London Guildhall were badly damaged in the air-raids of 1940-41, the Council Chamber and the roof of the great hall being entirely destroyed.

The ancient guilds are to-day represented by the Livery Companies (*q.v.*).

Guillemites. *See* WILLIAM OF MALEVAL, ST.

Guillotine (gil' ō tēn). So named from Joseph Ignace Guillotin (1738-1814), a French physician, who proposed its adoption to prevent unnecessary pain.

It was introduced April 25th, 1792, and is still used in France. A previous instrument invented by Antoine Louis (1723-92), a French surgeon, was called a Louisette. The Maiden (*q.v.*) was a similar instrument.

In English Parliamentary phraseology the terms "guillotine," "to guillotine," "to apply the guillotine," signify the curtailment of a debate by fixing beforehand when the vote on the various parts of a Bill must be taken.

Guinea. A gold coin current in England from 1663 to 1817, originally made of gold from Guinea in West Africa and intended for use in the Guinea trade. The earliest issues bore a small elephant beneath the head of the king. The nominal value was originally 20s.; from 1717 it was legal tender for 21s., but its actual value varied, and in 1695, owing to the bad condition of silver coin, was as high as 30s.

It is still the custom for professional fees, subscriptions, the price of race-horses, pictures, and other luxuries, to be paid in guineas, though there is no such coin current. *See* SPADE GUINEA.

Guinea fowl. So called because it was brought to us from the coast of Guinea, where it is very common.

Guinea-hen. An Elizabethan synonym for a prostitute.
    Ere .... I would drown myself for the love of a Guinea-hen, I would change my humanity with a baboon.—*Othello*, i, 3.

Guinever (gwin 'e vēr) (Geoffrey of Monmouth's *Guanhumara*, the Welsh *Gwenhwyvar*, meaning "the white ghost"). In the Arthurian legends, the wife of King Arthur. According to

Malory she was the daughter of Leodegrance, king of the land of Cameliard. She entertained a guilty passion for Sir Launcelot of the Lake, one of the knights of the Round Table, but during the absence of King Arthur in his expedition against Leo, king of the Romans, she was seduced by Modred, her husband's nephew, who had usurped the kingdom. Arthur hastened back, Guinever fled, and a desperate battle was fought, in which Modred was slain and Arthur mortally wounded. Guinever took the veil at Almesbury, where later she died. She was buried at Glastonbury, and has left her name as a synonym for a beautiful, faithless, but repentant wife.

Gule (gūl). **The Gule of August.** August 1st, Lammas Day, a quarter day in Scotland, and half quarter day in England. The word is probably the Welsh *gwyl* (Lat. *vigilia*), a festival.

Gules (gūlz). The heraldic term for red. In engraving it is shown by perpendicular parallel lines. From mediæval Latin *gulæ*, ermine dyed red.

> With man's blood paint the ground, gules, gules.
> *Timon of Athens*, iv, 3.
> And threw warm gules on Madeline's fair breast.
> KEATS: *Eve of St. Agnes*.

Gulf Stream. The great, warm ocean current which flows out of the Gulf of Mexico (whence its name) and, passing by the eastern coast of the United States, is, near the banks of Newfoundland, deflected across the Atlantic to modify the climate of Western Europe as far north as Spitzbergen and Nova Zembla. It washes the shores of the British Isles.

Gulistan (Pers., the garden of roses). The famous collection of moral sentences by Sadi (about 1190-1291), the most celebrated of Persian poets, except, perhaps, Omar Khayyam. It consists of sections on kings, dervishes, contentment, love, youth, old age, social duties, etc., with many stories and philosophical sayings.

Gull. A well-known Elizabethan synonym for one who is easily duped, especially a highborn gentleman (*cp.* BEJAN). Dekker wrote his *Gull's Hornbook* (1609) as a kind of guide to the behaviour of contemporary gallants.

> The most notorious geck and gull
> That e'er invention played on.
> SHAKESPEARE: *Twelfth Night*, v, 1.

Gulliver's Travels (gŭl' i ver). This, the best known of the works of Jonathan Swift (1667-1745) was published in 1726. It consists of four travels of Captain Lemuel Gulliver. The first is to Lilliput, a country of tiny men and women some six inches high; the second is to Brobdingnag, a land of giants as big in comparison to Gulliver as he was to the Lilliputians. His third voyage took him to Laputa, the flying island inhabited by scientific quacks. Lastly Gulliver found himself in the country of the Houyhnhnms (pronounced whin' imz), a race of horses endowed with human reason and bearing rule over the race of men called Yahoos. Frequently looked upon as a mere children's book, it is in reality a biting social and political satire.

> Whether we read it, as children do, for the story, or as historians, for the political allusions, or as men of the world, for the satire and philosophy, we have to acknowledge that it is one of the wonderful and unique books of the world's literature.—EDMUND GOSSE: *History of English Literature*.

Gully-raker. In early Australian slang, one who combs wild country and appropriates any unbranded cattle he finds there.

Gumbo. A thick vegetable soup eaten in the U.S.A.

Gummed. He frets like gummed velvet or **gummed taffety.** Velvet and taffeta were sometimes stiffened with gum to make them "sit better," but, being very stiff, they fretted out quickly.

Gumption. Common sense, the wit to turn things to account, capability. The derivation and origin of the word are unknown.

Gum-shoes. The American name for the English galoshes.

Gun. This word was formerly used for some large, stone-throwing engine of war besides the firearm, but it is not certain that the first-mentioned use was the earlier. In *The House of Fame* (iii, 553) Chaucer speaks of the trumpet sounding:—

> As swifte as pelet out of gonne
> Whan fire is in the poudre ronne.

and in the *Legend of Good Women* (*Cleopatra*, 58) he seems to use the word in reference to the ballista:—

> With grisly soune out gooth the grete gonne,
> And hertely they hurtelen al attones,
> And fro the toppe down cometh the grete stones.

The word is a shortened form of the old Scandinavian female name, *Gunnildr* (*gunnr* is Icelandic for war, and *hildr* for battle); and it may have been given first to the ballista and then, when cannon came into use, transferred to the firearm. The bestowing of female names on arms is not uncommon; there are the famous "Mons Meg," "Queen Elizabeth's pocket-pistol," as well as the "Big Bertha" of World War I—the long-range gun that bombarded Paris, so called in honour of Bertha

Krupp, wife of the head of the great armament factory at Essen.

To stick to one's guns. To maintain one's position, argument, etc., in spite of opposition.

To gun for someone. To set out deliberately to get a person and do him a mischief.

To give it the gun. In R.A.F. parlance during World War II, to open the throttle of an aeroplane suddenly and hard.

Gun cotton. A highly explosive compound, prepared by saturating cotton or other cellulose material with nitric and sulphuric acids.

Gun-man. A desperado armed with a revolver and prepared to use it in the most reckless manner. A term of American origin.

Gun money. Base money issued in Ireland by James II, made from old brass cannon, with a small admixture of silver.

Gun room. A room in the afterpart of a lower gun-deck for the accommodation of junior officers.

Gun-runner. One who unlawfully smuggles guns into a country for belligerent purposes. The word is formed on the model of *blockade-runner*.

Gunnar. The Norse form of *Gunther* (*q.v.*).

Gunpowder Plot. The project of a few Roman Catholics to destroy James I with the Lords and Commons when he opened Parliament, on November 5th, 1605.

It was to be done by exploding barrels of gunpowder placed in cellars adjacent to the chamber, and Guy Fawkes, a convert to Catholicism, was deputed to fire the train. Had the plot succeeded, and king and Parliament been destroyed, Prince Charles and his sister were to have been made captive, and a Catholic rising attempted in the Midlands. One of the Catholic peers was, however, warned to keep away from Parliament that day; he communicated his news to the authorities; the cellars were searched and Guy Fawkes taken, the night of November 4th.

The ceremony of searching the vaults of the Houses before the annual opening of Parliament is a legacy of the Gunpowder Plot.

Gunther (gun′ ter). In the Nibelungen saga, a Burgundian king, brother of Kriemhild (= Gudrun), the wife of Sigurd (= Siegfried). He resolved to wed the martial queen Brunhild (*q.v.*), who had made a vow to marry only the man who could ride through the flames that encircled her castle. Gunther failed (*see* GRANI), but Siegfried did so in his likeness and remained with the Queen for three nights,

his sword being between them all the time. Gunther then married Brunhild, but later Kriemhild told Brunhild that it was Siegfried who had ridden through the fire; jealousy sprang up between the families, Siegfried was slain at Brunhild's desire, and she killed herself, her dying wish being to be burnt on a pile with Siegfried at her side, his sword between them. Gunther was slain by Atli because he refused to reveal where he had hidden the hoard of the Nibelungs. Gundicarius, a Burgundian king who, with his whole tribe, perished by the sword of the Huns in 437, is supposed to be the historical character round whom these legends collected.

Gurgoyle. *See* GARGOYLE.

Gurney Light. *See* BUDE.

Guru (goo′ roo). A Sanskrit word meaning venerable; it is now applied to a Hindu spiritual teacher and leader.

Guthlac, St., (gŭth′ lăk) of Crowland, Lincolnshire, is represented in Christian art as a hermit punishing demons with a scourge, or consoled by angels while demons torment him. He was a member of the royal family of Mercia in the 7th century.

Guthrum (gŭth′ rŭm). **Silver of Guthrum's Lane.** Fine silver was at one time so called, because the chief gold and silver smiths of London resided there in the 13th and 14th centuries. The street, which is now called *Gutter Lane*, and runs from Cheapside into Gresham Street, was originally *Gudrun's* or *Goderun's Lane*. The hall of the Goldsmiths' Company is still in this locality.

Guy. An effigy of a man, stuffed with combustibles and supposed to represent Guy Fawkes, carried round in procession and finally burnt on November 5th, in memory of Gunpowder Plot (*q.v.*); hence, any dowdy, fantastic figure, a "fright." In American usage the word, as applied to a person, has a much wider significance, and can mean almost anyone.

Guy's Hospital. Founded in 1722 by Thomas Guy (*c.* 1645-1724), bookseller, and philanthropist. He amassed an immense fortune in 1720 by speculations in the South Sea Stock. and gave £238,292 to found and endow the hospital which is situated in Southwark.

Gwynn, Eleanor or **Nell** (1650-87) was a popular London actress, She first became known when selling oranges at the Theatre Royal, Drury Lane, and in 1665 she appeared as Cydaria in Dryden's *Indian Emperor*. She was an illiterate girl but excellent company and soon won the favour of Charles II by whom she had a son, Charles Beauclerk (1670-1726) who was created Duke of St. Albans in 1684. Nell Gwynn left the stage in 1682, but she never lost the king's favour, and one of his dying wishes was that she should be looked after.

Gyges (gī' jēz). A king of Lydia of the 7th century B.C., who founded a new dynasty, warred against Asurbanipal of Assyria, and is memorable in legend for his ring and his prodigious wealth.

According to Plato, Gyges descended into a chasm of the earth, where he found a brazen horse; opening the sides of the animal, he found the carcass of a man, from whose finger he drew a brazen ring which rendered him invisible.

> Why, did you think that you had Gyges ring,
> Or the herb that gives invisibility [fern-seed]?
> BEAUMONT AND FLETCHER: *Fair Maid of the Inn*, i, 1.

It was by the aid of the ring that Gyges obtained possession of the wife of Candaules (*q.v.*) and, through her, of his kingdom.

Gymnosophists (jim nos' o fists). A sect of ancient Hindu philosophers who went about with naked feet and almost without clothing. They lived in woods, subsisted on roots, and never married. They believed in the transmigration of souls. (Gr. *gumnos*, naked; *sophistes*, sage).

Gyp (jip). The name at Cambridge (and at Durham) for a college servant, who acts as valet to two or more undergraduates, the counterpart of the Oxford *scout*. He differs from a bedmaker, inasmuch as he does not make beds; but he runs on errands, waits at table, wakes men for morning chapel, brushes their clothes, and so on. The word is probably from *gippo*, a 17th-century term for a scullion.

Gypped. Many of the creeks and rivers in the cattle country of the U.S.A. contain so much gypsum, or alkali salts, that anyone drinking immoderately therefrom suffers a stomach attack, and is referred to as "gypped." The phrase now in general use denoting to have been "had" or "done down" probably descends from this origin.

Gyromancy. A kind of divination performed by walking round in a circle or ring until one fell from dizziness, the direction of the fall being of significance.

Gytrash. A north-of-England spirit, which, in the form of horse, mule, or large dog, haunts solitary ways, and sometimes comes upon the belated travellers.

> I remembered certain of Bessie's tales, wherein figured a . . . spirit called a Gytrash.—CHARLOTTE BRONTË: *Jane Eyre*, xii.

H

H. The form of our capital **H** is through the Roman and Greek directly from the Phœnician (Semitic) letter *Heth* or *Kheth*, which, having two cross-bars instead of one, represented a fence. The corresponding Egyptian hieroglyph was a sieve, and the Anglo-Saxon rune is called *hœgel*, hail.

H.M.S. Her *or* His Majesty's service *or* ship, as H.M.S. *Wellington.*

Habeas Corpus (hā' bē ås kôr' pùs). The Habeas Corpus Act was passed in 1679, and defined a provision of similar character in Magna Charta, to which also it added certain details. Its chief purpose was to prohibit any judge, under severe penalties, from refusing to issue to a prisoner a Writ of Habeas Corpus by which the jailer was obliged to produce the prisoner in court in person and to certify the cause of imprisonment, thus preventing people being imprisoned on mere suspicion, and making it illegal for one to be left in prison an indefinite time without trial.

It further provides that every accused person shall have the question of his guilt decided by a jury of twelve, and not by a Government agent or nominee; that no prisoner can be tried a second time on the same charge; that every prisoner may insist on being examined within twenty days of his arrest, and tried at the next session; and that no one may be sent to prison beyond the seas, either within or without the British Dominions.

Habeas Corpus means "[I hear] that you have the body"; these being the opening words of the writ.

The Habeas Corpus Act has been suspended in times of political and social disturbance, and its provisions have been more than once amended and extended.

A Habeas Corpus Act was passed in Ireland in 1782, and in Scotland its place is taken by the *Wrongous Imprisonment Act* of 1701.

Haberdasher. The word is probably connected with O.Fr. *hapertas*, a word of unknown origin denoting some kind of fabric; but Prof. Weekley makes what he calls the "dubious" conjecture that it is from O.Fr. *avoir* (*aveir*), goods, property (as in *avoirdupois*), and Fr. and Provençal *ais*, a shop-board.

> To match this saint there was another,
> As busy and perverse a brother,
> An haberdasher of small wares
> In politics and state affairs.
>
> BUTLER: *Hudibras*, iii, 2.

The Haberdashers is one of the twelve great London livery companies, It was founded in the 15th century as the Merchant Haberdashers' Company. The Hall, destroyed by enemy action in 1940, was built by Christopher Wren.

Habsburg or **Hapsburg** (habz' běrg) is a contraction of *Habichts-burg* (Hawk's Castle); so called from the castle on the right bank of the Aar, built in the 11th century by Werner, Bishop of Strasburg, whose nephew (Werner II) was the first to assume the title of "Count of Habsburg." His great-grandson, Albrecht II, assumed the title of "Landgraf of Sundgau." His grandson, Albrecht IV, in the 13th century, laid the foundation of the greatness of the House, the original male line of which became extinct on the death of Charles VI in 1740. The late imperial family of Austria were the Habsburg-Lorraines, springing from the marriage of Maria Theresa, daughter of Charles VI, with Francis I, Duke of Lorraine, in 1736.

Hack. Short for *hackney* (*q.v.*), a horse let out for hire; hence, one whose services are for hire, especially a literary drudge, compiler, fur-bisher-up of better men's work. Goldsmith, who well knew from his own experience what the life was, wrote an "Epitaph" on one:—

> Here lies poor Ned Purdon, from misery freed,
> Who long was a bookseller's hack;
> He led such a damnable life in this world,
> I don't think he'll wish to come back.

Hackell's Coit. A vast stone said to weigh about 30 tons, near Stanton Drew, Somerset; so called from a tradition that it was a quoit or coit thrown by Sir John Hautville. In Wiltshire three huge stones near Kennet are called the *Devil's coits.*

Hackney. Originally (14th cent.) the name given to a class of medium-sized horses, distinguishing them from war-horses. They were used for ordinary riding, and later the name was applied to a horse let out for hire—whence **hackney carriage** and **hackney writer** or **hack** (*q.v.*).

The knights are well horsed, and the common people and others on litell *hakeneys* and geldynges.—*Froissart.*

The name of the London borough of Hackney has no connection whatever with the foregoing. There is some doubt as to its actual derivation; the earliest mention of the place is in a patent of Edward IV.

Haddock. According to tradition, it was a haddock in whose mouth St. Peter found the piece of money, the *stater* or shekel (*Matt.* xvii, 27), and the two marks on the fish's neck are said to be impressions of the finger and thumb of the apostle. It is a pretty story, but haddocks cannot live in the fresh water of the Lake of Gennesaret. *Cp.* JOHN DORY.

O superstitious dainty, Peter's fish,
How com'st thou here to make so goodly dish?
METELLUS· *Dialogues* (1693).

Hades (hā′ dēz). In Homer, the name of the god (Pluto) who reigns over the dead; but in later classical mythology the abode of the departed spirits, a place of gloom but not necessarily a place of punishment and torture. As the state or abode of the dead it corresponds to the Hebrew *Sheol*, a word which, in the Authorized Version, has frequently been translated by the misleading *Hell*. Hence *Hades* is sometimes vulgarly used as a euphemism for *Hell*.

The word is usually derived from Gr. a, privative, and *idein*, to see, *i.e.* the unseen: but this derivation is not at all certain. *Cp.* INFERNO.

Hadith (hā′ dith) (Ar., *a saying or tradition*). The traditions about the prophet Mohammed's sayings and doings. This compilation, which was made in the 10th century by the Moslem jurists Moshim and Bokhari, forms a supplement to the Koran as the Talmud to the Jewish Scriptures. The Hadith was not allowed originally to be committed to writing, but the danger of the traditions being perverted or forgotten led to their being placed on record.

Hadrian's Wall, a Roman rampart that runs for $73\frac{1}{2}$ miles between Wallsend-on-Tyne and Bowness on the Solway Firth. It was erected about A.D. 122 by the Emperor Hadrian to keep back the Pictish tribes of North Britain, and was repaired by Severus in 208. The wall was 20 ft. high and 8 ft. thick, with strong points every mile or so, and towers between. To the south of the wall is a parallel *vallum* or ditch with three ramparts, all of earthworks. Excavations

and research have been made at various points, notably at the ancient Borco-vicus, near the present Housesteads.

Hæmony (hē′mò ni). The name invented by Milton (*Comus*, 638) for a mythical plant which is of "sovereign use gainst all enchantments, mildew, blast, or damp, or ghastly Furies' apparition." The reference is probably to *Hœmonia*, an old name for Thessaly, a country specially endowed with mystical associations by the ancient Greeks, but Coleridge rather fancifully says the word is *hœma-oinos* (blood-wine), and refers to the blood of Jesus Christ, which destroys all evil. The leaf, says Milton, "had prickles on it," but "it bore a bright golden flower." With this explanation the *prickles* become the crown of thorns, the *flower* the fruits of salvation.

Hafiz (ha′ fiz). A Persian poet (fl. 14th cent.), and one of the greatest poets of the world. His *ghazels* (*i.e.* songs, odes) tell of love and wine, nightingales, flowers, the instability of all things human, of Allah and the Prophet, etc.; and his tomb at Shiraz is still the resort of pilgrims. The name *Hafiz* is Arabic for "one who knows the Koran and Hadith (*q.v.*) by heart."

Hag. A witch or sorceress; originally, an evil spirit, demon, harpy. (A.S. *hœgtesse*, a witch or hag.)

How now, you secret, black, and midnight hags?
Macbeth, iv, 1.

Hagen (ha′ gen). In the *Nibelungenlied* and the old Norse sagas (where he is called Hogni), a Burgundian knight, liegeman to the king, Gunther (*q.v.*), in some accounts his brother and in others a distant kinsman.

Haggadah (hàga′ dà). The portion of the Mid-rash (*q.v.*) which contains rabbinical interpretations of the historical and legendary, ethical, parabolic, and speculative parts of the Hebrew Scriptures: the portion devoted to law, practice, and doctrine is called the *Halachah*. They were commenced in the 2nd century A.D. and completed by the 11th.

Hagganah (hǎg à na′), the Jewish defence force raised in Palestine during the British mandate (1923-48), for defensive and aggressive action towards establishing the country as a Jewish commonwealth.

Hague, The (hāg), is the English form of the Dutch's *Gravenhage* or *Den Haag*, the capital of the Netherlands. The Hague Tribunal is an international court of Justice established at the suggestion of Tsar Nicholas II in 1899, when 16 powers signed the agreement by which each power nominates four members to serve for six years. Many international cases have been referred to the Court, including one about the sovereignty of Greenland, in 1932, which was adjudicated to Denmark.

Ha-ha. A ditch or sunk fence serving the purpose of a hedge without breaking the prospect.

Haidee (hī' dē). A beautiful Greek girl in Byron's *Don Juan* who died of love when parted from him.

Hail. Health, an exclamation of welcome, like the Lat *salve*. It is from the Icel. *heill*, hale, healthy, and represents the A.S. greeting *wes hal* (may you) be in whole (or good) health. *Hail*, the frozen rain, is A.S. *hagol*.

All hail, Macbeth! Hail to thee, thane of Glamis.
Macbeth, i, 3.

To hail an omnibus or a cab is to accost the driver in order to stop or hire the vehicle.

Hainault (hā' nolt). A province in Belgium. Also a forest in Essex which ceased to exist in the 19th century, though the name survives. The Fairlop oak (*q.v.*) was here.

Hair. One single tuft is left on the shaven crown of a Mussulman, for Mohammed to grasp hold of when drawing the deceased to Paradise.

And each scalp had a single long tuft of hair.
BYRON: *Siege of Corinth.*

The scalp-lock of the North American Indians, left on the otherwise bald head, is for a conquering enemy to seize when he tears off the scalp.

The ancients believed that till a lock of hair is devoted to Proserpine, she refuses to release the soul from the dying body. When Dido mounted the funeral pile, she lingered in suffering till Juno sent Iris to cut off a lock of her hair; Thanatos did the same for Alcestis, when she gave her life for her husband; and in all sacrifices a forelock was first cut off from the head of the victim as an offering to the black queen.

It was an old idea that a person with red hair could not be trusted, from the tradition that Judas had red hair.

Rosalind: His very hair is of the dissembling colour.
Celia: Somewhat browner than Judas's.—*As You Like It*, iii, 4.

A man with black hair but a red beard was the worst of all. The old rhyme says:—

A red beard and a black head.
Catch him with a good trick and take him dead.

See also RED-HAIRED PERSONS.

Byron says, in *The Prisoner of Chillon*:—
My hair is grey, but not with years,
Nor grew it white

In a single night,
As men's have grown from sudden fears.

and it is a well-authenticated fact that this can take, and has taken, place. It is told that Ludovico Sforza became grey in a single night; Charles I, also, while he was on his trial; and Marie Antoinette grew grey from grief during her imprisonment.

Hair shirt, a garment of coarse haircloth (made from horsehair and wool or cotton) worn next the skin by ascetics and penitents.

Hair-spring is a fine, spiral spring in a clock or watch for regulating the movement of the balance.

Hair trigger, a trigger that allows the firing mechanism of a rifle or revolver to be operated by a very slight pressure. Invented in the 16th century.

To make one's hair stand on end. To terrify. Dr. Andrews, of Beresford Chapel, Walworth, who attended an execution says: "When the executioner put the cords on the criminal's wrists, his hair, though long and lanky, of a weak iron-grey, rose gradually and stood perfectly upright, and so remained for some time, and then fell gradually down again."

Fear came upon me and trembling, . . . [and] the hair of my flesh stood up.—*Job* iv, 14, 15.

To split hairs. To argue over petty points, make fine, cavilling distinctions, quibble over trifles.

To tear one's hair. To show signs of extreme anguish, grief, or vexation.

Hair-breadth 'scape. A very narrow escape from some danger or evil. In measurement the forty-eighth part of an inch is called a "hair-breadth."

Wherein I spake of most disastrous chances
Of moving accidents by flood and field.
Of hair-breadth 'scapes i' th' imminent deadly breach.   *Othello*, i, 3.

Hair Stane. A hoar-stone (*q.v.*) is so called in Scotland.

Hajar al-Aswad (hä' jar al ăs' wăd). The famous black stone in the north-east corner of the Kaaba; it is an irregular oval, about 7 in. in breadth, and is surrounded with a circle of gold. The legend is that when Abraham wished to build the Kaaba, the stones came to him of their own accord, and the patriarch commanded all the faithful to kiss this one.

The stone is probably an aerolite, and it was worshipped long before Mohammed's day, for in the 2nd century A.D. Maximus Tyrius spoke of the Arabians paying homage to it, and Persian legend states that it was an emblem of Saturn.

Hajji Baba (hăj′ i ba′ ba), the title of the strange story told by J. J. Morier (*c.* 1780-1849) which has become a classic of its kind. Morier was born in Syria and spent much of his life in the East. In 1824 he published this remarkable romance of Persia in which Hajji Baba, a barber and a delightful rogue of the Gil Bias genus, narrated his adventures shady and amusing. So true to life was the story that the Persian government took pains to prove that it was not an authentic account of a real person but the work of a devil-inspired Ferangi.

Halcyon Days (hăl′ si on). A time of happiness and prosperity. Halcyon is the Greek for a kingfisher, compounded of *hals* (the sea) and *kuo* (to brood on). The ancient Sicilians believed that the kingfisher laid its eggs and incubated for fourteen days, before the winter solstice, on the surface of the sea, during which time the waves of the sea were always unruffled.

Amidst our arms as quiet you shall be
As halcyon brooding on a winter's sea. DRYDEN
The peaceful king fishers are met together
About the deck and prophesie calm weather.
                                        WILD: *Iter Boreale.*

Half. Half and half. A mixture of two liquors, especially porter and ale, in equal quantities.

Half is more than the whole. This is what Hesiod said to his brother Perseus, when he wished him to settle a dispute without going to law. He meant "half of the estate without the expense of law will be better than the whole after the lawyers have had their pickings." The remark, however, has a very wide signification.

Unhappy they to whom God has not revealed,
By a strong light which must their sense control.
That half a great estate's more than the whole.
            COWLEY: *Essays in Verse and Prose,* iv.

Half-seas over. Midway between one condition and another: now usually applied to a person slightly drunk.

I am half-seas o'er to death.—DRYDEN.

I have just left the Right Worshipful and his Myrmidons about a Sneaker of Five Gallons. The whole Magistracy was pretty well disguised before I gave 'em the Slip. Our Friend the Alderman was half Seas over.—*Spectator,* No. 616 (Nov. 5th, 1714).

My better half. *See* BETTER.

Not half. Not half bad means "not at all bad"; pretty good, indeed; better than I had expected; but **Not half!** has a more ironical meaning, and means something like *"Rather! I should think so!"*

To do a thing by halves. To do it in a slapdash manner, very imperfectly.

To go halves. To share something equally with another.

Half-deck. An old sailing-ship term: the quarters of the second mate, carpenters, coopers, boatswain, and all secondary officers. *Quarterdeck,* the quarters of the captain and superior officers. In a gun-decked ship *half-deck* is below the *spar-deck,* and extends from the main-mast to the cabin bulkheads.

Half-mast high. The position of a flag flying from the middle of the flagstaff in token of respect to a dead person.

Halgaver (hăl′ gȧ vĕr). **Summoned before the mayor of Halgaver.** The mayor of Halgaver is an imaginary person, and the threat is given to those who have committed no offence against the laws, but are simply untidy and slovenly. Halgaver is a moor in Cornwall, near Bodmin, famous for an annual carnival held there in the middle of July. Charles II was so pleased with the diversions when he passed through the place on his way to Scilly that he became a member of the "self-constituted" corporation. The mayor of Garratt (*q.v.*) is a similar "magnate."

Halifax, Nova Scotia, was so called by the Hon. Edward Cornwallis, the governor, in compliment to his patron, the Earl of Halifax (1749).

Hall Mark. The official mark stamped on gold and silver articles after they have been assayed, so called because the assaying or testing and the stamping was done at the Goldsmiths' Hall. The hall mark includes (1) the standard mark, (2) the assay office, or "hall" mark, (3) the date letter, and sometimes (4) the duty mark. With it is found (5) the maker's mark.

(1) The standard mark. For gold, a *crown* in England and a *thistle* in Scotland, for 22- and 18-carat gold. In Ireland, a *crowned harp* for 22-carat, *three feathers* for 20-carat and a *unicorn's head* for 18-carat. Lower standards of gold have the number of carats in figures, without the device.

For silver, a *lion passant* in England, a *thistle* in Edinburgh, a *thistle* plus a *lion rampant* in Glasgow, *a crowned harp* in Dublin.

(2) The Assay Office mark.

London—a leopard's head (*q.v.*).

Sheffield—a York Rose for gold, a crown for silver.

Chester—three sheaves and a sword.

Edinburgh—a castle.

Glasgow—the city arms: a tree, a bird, a bell, and a salmon with a ring in its mouth.

Dublin—Hibernia.

Marks of Assay Offices now closed, and dates of closing:—

Exeter, 1882—a castle.

Newcastle, 1883—three castles.

Norwich, 1701—castle over lion.

York, 1856—five lions on a cross.

(3) The date letter. A letter of the alphabet indicates the date of an article. The London Assay Office uses 20 letters of the alphabet, Glasgow 26 and most of the others 25. The letter is changed each year, and at the beginning of each new cycle a new type-face is adopted and the shape of the letters' frame is changed. Given the date letter and the Assay Office mark, the date of manufacture of an article may be easily discovered on referring to a table.

(4) The duty mark. Articles on which duty has been paid are stamped with the head of the reigning sovereign.

(5) The maker's mark. A device or set of initials which the maker has registered at the Assay Office, and which he stamps on goods which he intends to send for hall marking.

Hallel (hăl' el). A Jewish hymn of praise sung at the four great festivals, consisting of *Ps.* cxiii to cxviii both included. *Ps.* cxxxvi was called the Great Hallel. And sometimes the Songs of Degrees (*see* GRADUAL PSALMS) sung standing on the fifteen steps of the inner court seem to be so called (*i.e.* cxx to cxxxvii both included).

Hallelujah is the Heb. *halelu-Jah*, "Praise ye Jehovah."

Halloween (hăl ō ēn'). October 31st, which in the old Celtic calendar was the last day of the year, its night being the time when all the witches and warlocks were abroad and held their wicked revels. On the introduction of Christianity it was taken over as the Eve of All Hallows, or All Saints, and—especially in Scotland and the north of England—it is still devoted to all sorts of games in which the old superstitions can be traced. *See* Burns's poem *Hallowe'en*.

Halo. In Christian art the same as a nimbus (*q.v.*). The luminous circle round the sun or moon caused by the refraction of light through a mist is also called a halo. The word is from Gr. *halos*, originally a circular threshing-floor.

Ham Actor. A bad actor, especially one who over-acts or performs his part in a stiff and stilted fashion. The origin of the term is uncertain; it may arise from the delusion such bad actors often entertain that they can perform that most difficult of parts—Hamlet.

Hamiltonian System. A method of teaching foreign languages by inter-linear translations, suggested by James Hamilton (1769-1831).

Hamlet. It's Hamlet without the Prince. Said when the person who was to have taken the principal place at some function is absent. The allusion, of course, is to Shakespeare's *Tragedie of Hamlet, Prince of Denmark*, which would lose all its meaning if the part of the Prince were omitted.

The play is based on a crude story told by the 13th-century Saxo Grammaticus (a Danish chronicler) in his *Historia Danica* (first printed 1514), which found a place in Pierre de Belleforest's *Histoires Tragiques* (1570), a French miscellany of translated legend and romance. This formed the groundwork of the lost pre-Shakespearean play—the so-called *Ur-Hamlet* (Ger. *Ur*, original)—which Shakespeare transformed into a great dramatic masterpiece.

Hammer. In personal appellatives:—

Pierre d'Ailly (1350-1425), *Le Marteau* (hammer) des *Hérétiques*, president of the council that condemned John Huss.

St. Augustine (354-430) is called by Hakewell "that renowned pillar of truth and hammer of heresies."

John Faber (1478-1541), the German controversialist, was surnamed *Malleus Hereticorum*, from the title of one of his works.

St. Hilary, Bishop of Poitiers (d. 368), was known as "The Hammer of the Arians."

Charles Martel (*q.v.*).

Edward I (1239-1307), "Longshanks," was called "The Hammer of the Scots." On his tomb in Westminster Abbey is the inscription *"Edwardus longus Scotorum Malleus hic est."*

The second name of Judas *Maccabeus*, the son of Mattathias the Hasmonean, is thought by some to denote that he was a "Hammer" or "Hammerer," because *Makkébeth* is Hebrew for a certain kind of hammer.

Hammer and Sickle. Since 1923, the emblems of the U.S.S.R., symbolic of productive work in the factory and on the land.

Gone to the hammer. Applied to goods sent to a sale by auction; the auctioneer giving a rap with a small hammer when a lot is sold, to intimate that there is an end to the bidding, hence *to sell under the hammer*.

To hammer away at anything. To go at it doggedly; to persevere.

Hammercloth. The cloth that covers the driver's seat, or "box," in an old-fashioned coach. It may be connected with Dan. *hammel*, a swingle-bar, or with *hammock*, the seat which the cloth covers being formed of straps or webbing stretched between two crutches like a sailor's hammock.

Hammock or **Hummock.** A small round hill, usually wooded.

Hanaper (hăn′ ȧ pĕr). *Hanap* was the mediæval name for a goblet or wine-cup, and the *hanaper* (connected with *hamper*) was the wickerwork case that surrounded it. Hence the name was given to any round wicker basket and especially to one in which documents that had passed the Great Seal were kept in the Court of Chancery. The office where the Chancellor carried on his business—the Exchequer, or a branch thereof—thus came to be known as the *Hanaper*, and its officials as Comptrollers, Clerks, etc., of the Hanaper. In England these were abolished in 1842, but for many years in Ireland the official title of the Permanent Secretary to the Chancery Division and to the Lord Chancellor remained "Clerk of the Crown and Hanaper."

Hancock. John Hancock (1737-93) was an American statesman and the first to sign the Declaration of Independence, beneath which document his signature stands out boldly. *To put your John Hancock* to a deed, etc., was an old American phrase for signing it.

Hand. A symbol of fortitude in Egypt, of fidelity in Rome. Two hands symbolize concord; by a closed hand Zeno represented dialectics, and by an open hand eloquence.

In early art the Deity was frequently represented by a hand extended from the clouds; sometimes the hand was open, with rays issuing from the fingers, but generally it was in the act of benediction, *i.e.* with two fingers raised.

In card-games the word is used for the game itself, for an individual player (as "a good *hand* at whist") or the cards held by him.

> A saint in heaven would grieve to see such "hand"
> Cut up by one who will not understand.
> CRABBE: *Borough.*

Also for style of workmanship, handwriting, etc. ("he writes a good *hand*").

Operatives at a factory are called *hands*. As a measure of length *a hand* = four inches. Horses are measured up the fore leg to the shoulder, and are called 14, 15, 16 (as it may be), hands high.

Hand gallop. A slow and easy gallop, in which the horse is kept well in hand.

Hand paper. A particular sort of paper well known in the Record Office, and so called from its water-mark, which goes back to the 15th century.

A bird in hand. *See* BIRD.

A note of hand. A promise to pay made in writing and duly signed.

An old hand at it. One who is experienced at it.

A poor hand. An unskilful one. "He is but a poor hand at it," *i.e.* he is not skilful at the work.

All hands. The nautical term for the whole of the crew.

At first or **second hand.** As the original (*first*) purchaser, owner, hearer, etc., or (*second*) as one deriving, learning, etc., through another party.

At hand. Conveniently near. "Near at hand," quite close by.

Cap in hand. Suppliantly, humbly; as, "To come cap in hand." *See* CAP.

From hand to hand. From one person to another.

Hand in hand. In friendly fashion; unitedly.

Hand over hand. To go or to come up hand over hand, is to travel with great rapidity, as climbing a rope or a ladder, or as one vessel overtakes another. Sailors in hauling a rope put one hand over the other alternately as fast as they can. In French, *Main sur main.*

Hands up! The order given by captors when taking prisoners. The hands are to be held stretched high above the head to preclude any possibility of resistance or the use of revolvers, etc.

He is my right hand. My principal assistant, my best and most trustworthy man.

In hand. Under control, in possession; also, under progress.

In one's own hands. In one's sole control, ownership, management, responsibility, etc.

Kings have long hands. *See* KING.

Laying on of hands. *See* TO LAY HANDS ON, *below.*

Many hands make light work. An old proverb (given in Ray's *Collection*, 1742) enshrining the wisdom of a fair division of labour. The Romans had a similar saying, *Multorum manibus magnum levatur onus*, by the hands of many a great work is lightened.

Offhand. In a casual, unceremonious fashion, curt, rude; extempore.

Off one's hands. No longer under one's responsibilities. If something—or somebody—is left on one's hands one has to take entire responsibility.

On the other hand. A phrase used in the presentation of a case meaning "from *that* point of view," as opposed to the point of view already mentioned.

Out of hand. At once; done with, over.

We will proclaim you out of hand.

3 Henry VI, iv, 7.

And, were these inward wars once out of hand,
We would, dear lords, unto the Holy Land.

2 Henry IV, iii, 1.

Also with the meaning "beyond control"; as, "these children are quite out of hand."

The hand that rocks the cradle rules the world. The line is from the poem "What Rules the World?" by the American poet, William Ross Wallace (1819-81):—

They say that man is mighty,
   He governs land and sea,
He wields a mighty sceptre
   O'er lesser powers that be;
But a mightier power and stronger
   Man from his throne has hurled,
And the hand that rocks the cradle
   Is the hand that rules the world.

To ask or **give the hand of so-and-so.** To ask or give her hand in marriage.

To bear a hand. To come and help.

To change hands. To pass from a possessor to someone else.

To come to hand. To be received; to come under one's notice.

To come to one's hand. It is easy to do.

To get one's hand in. To become familiar with the work in hand.

To get the upper hand. To obtain the mastery.

To give one's hand upon something. To take one's oath on it; to pledge one's honour to keep the promise.

To hand down to posterity. To leave for future generations.

To have a free hand. To be able to do as one thinks best without referring the matter to one's superiors; to be quite uncontrolled by outside influences.

To have a hand in the matter. To have a finger in the pie.

My hands are full. I am fully occupied; I have as much work to do as I can manage.

To lay hands on. To apprehend; to lay hold of.

Lay hands on the villain.

Taming of the Shrew, v, 1.

In ecclesiastical use the **laying on of hands**, or *imposition of hands*, is the laying on, or the touch, as in signing the cross, of a bishop's hands in ordination or confirmation.

Among the Romans a hand laid on the head of a person indicated the right of property. Thus if a person laid claim to a slave, he laid his hand upon him in the presence of the prætor.

To lend a hand. To help; to give assistance.

To live from hand to mouth. To live without any provision for the morrow.

To play one's own hand. To look after Number One; to act entirely for one's own advantage.

To play into someone's hands. Unwittingly or carelessly to act so that the other party gets the best of it; to do just what will help him and not advance your own cause.

To serve someone hand and foot. To be at his beck and call; to be his slave.

To shake hands. To salute by giving a hand received into your own a shake; to bid adieu.

Fortune and Antony part here; even here
Do we shake hands.

Antony arid Cleopatra, iv, 10.

The custom of shaking hands in confirmation of a bargain has been common to all nations and all ages. In feudal times the vassal put his hands in the hands of his overlord on taking the oath of fidelity and homage.

To take something off one's hands. To relieve one of something troublesome.

To wash one's hands of a thing. To have nothing to do with it after having been concerned in the matter; to abandon it entirely. The allusion is to Pilate's washing his hands at the trial of Jesus.

When Pilate saw that he could prevail nothing, but that rather a tumult was made, he took water, and washed his hands before the multitude, saying, I am innocent of the blood of this just person; see ye to it.— Matt. xxvii, 24.

To win hands down. To be victor without the slightest difficulty. The allusion is to horse-racing; if the jockey wins with his hands down it shows that he has not had to worry himself—he has had a "walk-over."

With a heavy hand. Oppressively; without sparing.

It is a damned and a bloody work;
The graceless action of a heavy hand,
If that it be the work of any hand.

King John, iv, 3.

Handicap. A game at cards not unlike loo, but with this difference—the winner of one trick has to put in a double stake, the winner of two tricks a triple stake, and so on. Thus: if six persons are playing, and the general stake is 1s., and A gains three tricks, he gains 6s., and has to "hand i' the cap" or pool 3s. for the next deal. Suppose A gains two tricks and B one, then A gains 4s. and B 2s., and A has to stake 3s. and B 2s. for the next deal.

In common parlance a handicap is a difficulty—physical or otherwise—under which a person labours; a short-sighted man is handicapped without his spectacles.

Handicap, in racing, is the adjudging of various weights to horses differing in age, power, or speed, in order to place them all, as far as possible, on an equality. In golf it is a certain number of strokes allowed to a player to allow him a reasonable chance of scoring par at any game. If two unequal players challenge each other at chess, the superior gives up a piece, and this is his handicap. So called from the custom of drawing lots out of a hat or cap.

The Winner's Handicap. The winning horses of previous races being pitted together are first handicapped according to their respective merits: the horse that has won three races has to carry a greater weight than the horse that has won only two, and this latter more than its competitor who is winner of a single race only.

Handirons. *See* ANDIRONS.

Handle. A handle to one's name. Some title, as "lord," "sir," "doctor."

To fly off the handle. To fly into a rage, or lose one's head, as the head of an axe might fly dangerously off its shaft.

Handsel (A.S. *handselen*, delivery into the hand). A gift for luck; earnest-money; the first money received in a day. Hence *Handsel Monday*, the first Monday of the year, when little gifts used to be given before our Boxing Day (*q.v.*) took its place. To "handsel a sword" is to use it for the first time; to "handsel a coat," to wear it for the first time, etc.

Handsome. Handsome is as handsome does. It is one's *actions* that count, not merely one's appearance or promises. The proverb is in Ray's *Collection* (1742), and is also given by Goldsmith in *The Vicar of Wakefield* (ch. i).

To do the handsome towards one, to act handsomely. To be liberal, generous.

Handwriting on the Wall. An announcement of some coming calamity, or the imminent fulfilment of some doom. The allusion is to the handwriting on Belshazzar's palace wall announcing the loss of his kingdom (*Dan.* v).

Hang. Hang it all! I'll be hanged! Exclamations of astonishment or annoyance; mild imprecations, a mincing form of "damned."

Hanged, drawn, and quartered. *See* DRAWN.

To get the hang of a thing. To understand the drift or connexion; to acquire the knack.

To hang about. To loaf, loiter. In America *to hang around* is more usual.

To hang back. To hesitate to proceed.

To hang by a thread. To be in a very precarious position. The allusion is to the sword of Damocles (*q.v.*).

To hang fire. To fail in an expected result. The allusion is to a gun or pistol which fails to go off.

To hang a jury. To reduce them to disagreement so that they cannot bring in a verdict.

To hang on by the eyelids is to maintain one's position only with the greatest difficulty or by the slightest of holds.

Where do you hang out? Where are you living or lodging ? The phrase may arise from the old custom of shopkeepers and others hanging a sign outside their residence and places of business. Inn signs and barbers' poles are among the few survivals of this custom.
"I say, old boy, where do you hang out?" Mr. Pickwick replied that he was at present suspended at the George and Vulture.—DICKENS: *Pickwick Papers*, ch. xxx.

Hangdog look. A guilty, shame-faced look.

Hanging Gardens of Babylon. A square garden (according to Diodorus Siculus), 400 ft. each way, rising in a series of terraces from the river in the northern part of Babylon, and provided with earth to a sufficient depth to accommodate trees of a great size. These famous gardens were one of the Seven Wonders of the World, and according to tradition were constructed by Nebuchadnezzar, to gratify his wife Amytis, who felt weary of the flat plains of Babylon, and longed for something to remind her of her native Median hills.

Hangmen and Executioners.
The best known to history are:—
BULL, the earliest hangman whose name survives (about 1593).
JOCK SUTHERLAND.
DERRICK, who cut off the head of Essex in 1601.
GREGORY BRANDON (about 1648), and ROBERT BRANDON, his son, who executed Charles I. These were known as "the two Gregories" (*see* GREGORIAN TREE).
SQUIRE DUN, mentioned in *Hudibras* (Pt. iii, c. 2).
JACK KETCH (1678) executed Lord Russell and the Duke of Monmouth. His name became a general term to denote a hangman.
ROSE, the butcher (1686).
EDWARD DENNIS (1780). introduced in Dickens's *Barnaby Rudge*.
THOMAS CHESHIRE, nicknamed "Old Cheese."
WILLIAM CALCRAFT (1800-79) was appointed official hangman in 1829 and was pensioned off in 1874.
WILLIAM MARWOOD (1820-83) is known in the profession for having invented the "long drop."
Of French executioners, the most celebrated are Capeluche, headsman of Paris during the terrible days of the Armagnacs and Burgundians; and the two brothers Sanson, who worked the guillotine during the first French Revolution.

The fee given to the executioner at Tyburn used to be $13\frac{1}{2}$d., with $1\frac{1}{2}$d. for the rope.

For half of thirteen-pence ha'penny wages
I would have cleared all the town cages,
And you should have been rid of all the stages
I and my gallows groan.
The Hangman's Last Will and Testament (*Rump Songe*).

Noblemen who were to be beheaded were expected to give the executioner from £7 to £10 for cutting off their head; and it is still the case that any peer who comes to the halter can claim the privilege of being suspended by a silken rope.

Hanger. A short sword or dagger that hung from the girdle; also the girdle itself.

Men's swords in hangers hang fast by their side.—
J. TAYLOR (1630).

Hankey Pankey. Jugglery, fraud. The word is probably a variation of Hocus Pocus.

Hanse Towns (hăn′ sė). The maritime cities of Germany, which belonged to the Hanseatic League (*q.v.*).

The Hanse towns of Lübeck, Bremen, and Hamburg are commonwealths even now (1877).—FREEMAN: *General Sketch*, ch. x, p. 174.

Hanseatic League (hănz iăt′ ik). The confederacy, first established in 1239, between certain cities of Northern Germany for their mutual prosperity and protection. The diet which used to be held every three years was called the *Hansa* (Old High German for *Association*), and the members of it *Hansards*. The league in its prosperity comprised eighty-five towns; it declined rapidly in the Thirty Years War; in 1669 only six cities were represented; and the last three members of the league (Hamburg, Lübeck, and Bremen) joined the German Customs Union in 1889.

Hansom. A light two-wheeled cab, very popular in London before the introduction of taxi-cabs early in this century. It was invented in 1834 by J. Aloysius Hansom (1803-82), the architect of Birmingham Town Hall. The original vehicle had two very large wheels with sunk axle-trees and a seat for the driver by the side of the passenger. Subsequent improvements reduced the size of the wheels, placed the driver in a dickey at the back, and provided a pair of double doors in front of the passenger with sliding glass folding panels lowered from the roof by the driver.

Happy. Happy as a clam. *See* CLAM.

Happy dispatch. *See* HARA-KIRI.

Happy family. The name given in travelling menageries to a collection of all sorts of animals of different and antagonistic habits living together peaceably. It is now more generally associated with a children's card game.

Happy-go-lucky. Thoughtless, indifferent, care-free.

Happy is the nation that has no history. The old proverb says in other words what Gibbon remarked in the *Decline and Fall*, ch. iii:—

History is, indeed, little more than the register of the crimes, follies, and misfortunes of mankind.

Montesquieu said much the same:—

Heureux les peuples dont l'histoire est ennuyeux.

Hara-kiri (ha ra ki′ ri) (Jap. *hara*, the belly, *kiri* to cut). A method of suicide by disembowelling practised by Japanese military officials, daimios, etc., when in serious disgrace or liable to be sentenced to death, or when their honour is irretrievably impugned. The first recorded instance of *hara-kiri*, or *Happy Dispatch*, as it is also called, is that of Tametomo, brother of Sutoku, an ex-Emperor in the 12th century, after a defeat at which most of his followers were slain.

Harbinger. One who looks out for lodgings, etc.; a courier; hence, a forerunner, a messenger. (O.H.Ger. *hari*, an army, *bergan*, to lodge.)

I'll be myself the harbinger, and make joyful
The hearing of my wife with your approach.
Macbeth, i, 4.

Hard. Hard and fast. Strict, unalterable. A "hard and fast rule" is one that must be rigidly adhered to and cannot be relaxed for anyone. Originally a nautical phrase, used of a ship run aground.

Hard-boiled, an expressive term for one who is toughened by experience, a person with no illusions or sentimentalities.

Hard cash. Money; especially actual money—as opposed to cheques or promises— "down on the nail"; formerly coin as distinguished from bank-notes.

Hard hit. Seriously damaged by monetary losses; as "He was hard hit in the slump after the war"; also, badly smitten with love.

Hard labour. Enforced labour added to the punishment of criminals receiving a sentence of six months or over. It used to consist largely of working the treadmill, stone-breaking, oakum picking, etc.

Hard tack, ship's biscuit, coarse, hard bread.

Hard of hearing. Unable to hear properly; rather deaf.

Hard up. Short of money. Originally a nautical phrase; when a vessel was hard put to it by stress of weather the order *Hard up the helm!* was given, and the tiller was put up as far as possible to windward so as to turn the ship's head away from the wind. So, when a man is "hard up" he has to weather the storm as best he may.

Hardshell. A term used in American politics for an "out-and-outer," one prepared, and anxious, to "go the whole hog." In 1853 a *hardshell* in the Southern States was for the Execution of the Fugitive Slave law, while *soft-shells* were for the maintenance of national harmony at all costs.

Hardy. Brave or daring, hence the phrase, *hardi comme un lion.*

Among those who have been surnamed "The Hardy" are:—

William Douglas, defender of Berwick (d. 1302);

Philippe III of France (1245, 1270-85); and Philippe II, Duke of Burgundy (1342, 1363-82).

Hare. It is unlucky for a hare to cross your path, because witches were said to transform themselves into hares.

A witch is a kind of hare
And marks the weather
As the hare doth.
BEN JONSON: *Sad Shepherd*, ii, 2.

In the North, until comparatively recently, if a fisherman on his way to the boats chanced to meet a woman, parson, or hare, he turned back, being convinced that he would have no luck that day.

The superstitious is fond in observation, servile in feare.... This man dares not stirre forth till his breast be crossed, and his face sprinkled: if but an hare crosse him the way, he returnes.—BP. HALL: *Characters* (1608).

According to mediæval "science," the hare was a most melancholy beast, and ate wild succory in the hope of curing itself; its flesh, of course, was supposed to generate melancholy in any who partook of it.

Fal.: 'Sblood, I am as melancholy as a gib cat, or a lugged bear.
Prince: Or an old lion, or a lover's lute.
Fal.: Yea, or the drone of a Lincolnshire bagpipe.
Prince: What sayest thou to a hare, or the melancholy of Moor-ditch?   1 *Henry IV*, i, 2.

Another superstition was that hares are sexless, or that they change their sex every year.

Snakes that cast their coats for new,
Cameleons that alter hue,
Hares that yearly sexes change.
FLETCHER: *Faithful Shepherd*, iii, 1.

And among the Hindus the hare is sacred to the moon because, as they affirm, the outline of a hare is distinctly visible in the full disk.

Mad as a March hare. Hares are unusually shy and wild in March, which is their rutting season.

Erasmus says "Mad as a marsh hare," and adds, "hares are wilder in marshes from the absence of hedges and cover."

The hare and the tortoise. An allusion to the well-known fable of the race between the hare and the tortoise, won by the latter; and the moral, "Slow and steady wins the race."

To hold with the hare and run with the hounds. To play a double and deceitful game, to be a traitor in the camp. To run with the hounds as if intent to catch the hare, all the while being the secret friend of poor Wat. In the American Civil War these double-dealers were called Copperheads (*q.v.*).

To kiss the hare's foot. To be too late for anything, to be a day after the fair. The hare has gone by, and left its footprint for you to salute. A similar phrase is *To kiss the post.*

Hare-brained. Mad as a March hare, giddy, foolhardy.

Let's leave this town; for they [the English] are hairbrained slaves,
And hunger will enforce them to be more eager.
1 *Henry VI*, i, 2.

Probably from this, in World War II arose the term **a hare** to denote a baseless idea which, if pursued, would lead to nothing.

Harefoot. The surname given to Harold I, youngest son of Canute (1035-40).

Hare-lip. A cleft lip; so called from its resemblance to the upper lip of a hare. It was fabled to be caused at birth by an elf or malicious fairy.

This is the foul fiend Flibbertigibbet. He begins at curfew, and walks till the first cock. He . . . squints the eye and makes the hare-lip.—*King Lear*, iii, 4.

Hare-stone. Another form of *Hoar-stone* (*q.v.*).

Harem (hâr' em). The name given by Mohammedans to those apartments (and the occupants) which are appropriated exclusively to the female members of a family. The word is Arab. *haram*, from *harama*, be prohibited.

Harleian (har lē' an). Robert Harley, Earl of Oxford (1661-1724) and his son Edward, the second earl (1689-1741) were great collectors of manuscripts, scarce tracts, etc. Their library was purchased by the nation in 1753 and deposited in the British Museum, and the *Harleian MSS.* are amongst its most valuable literary and historical possessions. The *Harleian Miscellany* (10 vols., first published 1744-46) contains reprints of nearly 700 tracts, etc., mostly of the 16th and 17th centuries; and since 1870 the Harleian Society has published numerous volumes of Registers, Heralds' Visitations, and Pedigrees.

Harlem, New York City, was named after their home town of Haarlem by the early Dutch settlers. It is now the uptown section of New York and is the metropolis of the Negro population of the city.

Harlequin (har′ le kwin). In the British pantomime, a mischievous fellow supposed to be invisible to all eyes but those of his faithful Columbine (*q.v.*). His office is to dance through the world and frustrate all the knavish tricks of the Clown, who is supposed to be in love with Columbine. He wears a tight-fitting spangled or parti-coloured dress and is usually masked. He derives from *Arlecchino*, a stock character of Italian comedy (like Pantaloon and Scaramouch), whose name was in origin probably that of a sprite or hobgoblin. One of the demons in Dante is named "Alichino," and another devil of mediæval demonology was "Hennequin."

The old Christmas pantomime or harlequinade is essentially a British entertainment, first introduced by John Weaver (1673-1760), a dancing-master of Shrewsbury, in 1702.

> What Momus was of old to Jove
> The same a harlequin is now.
> The former was buffoon above,
> The latter is a Punch below.
> SWIFT: *The Puppet Show.*

The prince of Harlequins was John Rich (1681-1761).

Harlequin. So Charles Quint (1500-58) was called by François I of France.

Harlot. Popular etymology used to trace this word to Arlotta, mother of William the Conqueror, but it is O.Fr. *herlot* and Ital. *arlotto*, a base fellow, vagabond, and was formerly applied to males as well as females. Hence Chaucer speaks of "a sturdy harlot . . . that was her hostes man."

> He was a gentil harlot, and a kinde;
> A bettre felaw shulde man no wher finde.
> *Canterbury Tales*, prol. 649.
> The harlot king is quite beyond mine arm.
> *Winter's Tale*, ii, 3.

The earliest sense of the word may have been "camp-follower," and if so it represents O.H. Ger. *hari*, war, and *lotter* (A.S. *loddere*), a beggar, wastrel.

Harm. Harm set, harm get. Those who lay traps for others get caught themselves. Haman was hanged on his own gallows. Our Lord says, "They that take the sword shall perish with the sword" (*Matt.* xxvi, 52).

Harmattan (har măt′ àn). A wind which blows periodically from the interior parts of Africa towards the Atlantic. It prevails in December, January, and February, and is generally accompanied with fog, but is so dry as to wither vegetation and cause human skin to peel off.

Harmonia (har mō′ ni à). **Harmonia's Necklace.** An unlucky possession, something that brings evil to all who possess it. Harmonia was the daughter of Mars and Venus. On her marriage with King Cadmus, she received a necklace which proved fatal to all who possessed it. *Cp.* FATAL GIFTS.

On the same occasion Vulcan, to avenge the infidelity of her mother, made the bride a present of a robe dyed in all sorts of crimes, which infused wickedness *and* impiety into all her offspring. Both Harmonia and Cadmus, having suffered many misfortunes, and seen their children a sorrow to them, were changed into serpents.

Medea, in a fit of jealousy, sent Creusa a wedding robe, which burnt her to death.

Harmonists. A sect founded in Würtemberg by George and Frederick Rapp about 1780. They emigrated to the U.S.A. in 1815 (Indiana, later Pittsburg, Pa.). They are now extinct and little is known of their tenets, except that they held property in common and regarded marriage as a purely civil contract.

Harness. Out of harness. Not in practice, retired. A horse out of harness is one not at work.

Haro (hă′ rō). **To cry out haro to anyone.** To denounce his misdeeds, to follow him with hue and cry. "Ha rou" was the ancient Norman hue and cry, and the exclamation made by those who wanted assistance, their person or property being in danger.

In the Channel Isles, *Haro!* said to have been originally *Ha! ho! à l'aide, mon prince!·*is a protest still in vogue when one's property is endangered, and is still a form of legal appeal. It is supposed to have been an appeal to Rollo, Duke of Normandy.

Haroun al Raschid (hà roon′ ăl răsh′ id). Calif of Bagdad, of the Abbasside line (763-809). The adventures and stories connected with him form a large part of the *Arabian Nights Entertainments* (*q.v.*).

Harp. The cognizance of Ireland. According to tradition, one of the early kings of Ireland was named David, and this king took the harp of the Psalmist as his badge. But King John, to distinguish his Irish coins from the English, had them marked with a triangle, either in allusion to St. Patrick's explanation of the Trinity, *or* to signify that he was king of England, Ireland, and France, and the harp may have originated from this. Henry VII was the first to adopt it as the Irish device, and James I to place it in the third quarter of the royal achievement of Great Britain.

To harp for ever on the same string. To reiterate, to return continually to one point or argument.

Still harping on my daughter.—*Hamlet*, ii, 1.

Harpagon (ar på gong). A miser, the chief character in Molière's *L'Avare*, 1668.

Harpocrates (har pok' rå tēz). The Greek form of the Egyptian Hcru-P-Khart (Horus the Child), who is figured as a youth with one finger pointing to his mouth. He was adopted by them as the god of silence.

I assured my mistress she might make herself perfectly easy on that score for I was the Harpocrates of trusty valets.—*Gil Bias*, iv, 2.

Harpsichord (harp' si kôrd). The most important of the stringed instruments with keyboards before the invention of the pianoforte. The strings are plucked by quills of leather plectra inserted in "jacks" or uprights, which are caused to pass the strings when the keys are depressed. The harpsichord was universally used in the 16th to 18th centuries. As a distinctive instrument and not merely a crude piano it has been reintroduced for the performance of music originally composed for it.

Harpy. In classical mythology, a winged monster with the head and breasts of a woman, very fierce, starved-looking, and loathsome, living in an atmosphere of filth and stench, and contaminating everything it came near. Homer mentions but *one* harpy, Hesiod gives *two*, and later writers *three*. Their names, Ocypeta (*rapid*), Celeno (*blackness*), and Aello (*storm*), indicate that these monsters were personifications of whirlwinds and storms.

Harridan (hăr' i dån). A haggard old beldame. So called from the Fr. *haridelle*, a worn-out jade of a horse.

Harris, Mrs. The fictitious crony of Sarah Gamp (*q.v.*), to whom the latter referred for the corroboration of all her statements (*Martin Chuzzlewit*).

Old Harry. A familiar name for the devil; Old Scratch. Probably from the personal name (*cp. Old Nick*), but perhaps with some allusion to the word *harry*, meaning to plunder, harass, lay waste, from which comes the old *liarrow*, as in the title of the 14th-century *estrif*, or miracle-play, *The Harrowing of Hell*.

Hart. In Christian art, the emblem of solitude and purity of life. It was the attribute of St. Hubert, St. Julian, and St. Eustace. It was also the type of piety and religious aspiration (*Ps.* xlii, 1). *Cp.* HIND.

Hart of grease. A hunter's phrase for a fat venison; a stag full of the pasture, called by Jaques "a fat and greasy citizen" (As *You Like It*, ii, 1).

Hart royal. A male red deer, when the crown of the antler has made its appearance, and the creature has been hunted by a king.

The White Hart, or **Hind,** with a golden chain, in public-house signs, is the badge of Richard II, which was worn by his adherents. It was adopted from his mother, Joan of Kent, whose cognizance it was.

Harum Scarum (hâr' ùm skâr' ùm). Giddy, hare-brained; or a person so constituted. From the old *hare* (*cp.* HARRY) to harass, and *scare*; perhaps with the additional allusion to the "madness of a March *hare*."

Who's there? I s'pose young harum-scarum.
Cambridge Facetiæ: Collegian and Porter.

Haruspex (pl. *haruspices*). Officials among the Etruscans and ancient Romans who interpreted the will of the gods by inspecting the entrails of animals offered in sacrifice (O.Lat. *haruga*, a victim; *specio*, I inspect). Cato said, "I wonder how one haruspex can keep from laughing when he sees another."

Harvard University. The senior University in the U.S.A., situated at Cambridge, Mass., and founded in 1636 by the general court of the colony in Massachusetts Bay. In 1638 it was named after John Harvard (1607-1638), who had left to it his library and half his estate.

Harvest Moon. The full moon nearest the autumnal equinox, which rises for several days nearly at sunset, and at about the same time.

Hash. A mess, a muddle; as, "a pretty hash he made of it."

Hassan-Ben-Sabah (hăs' ăn ben sa' ba). The Old Man of the Mountain, founder of the sect of the Assassins (*q.v.*).

Hassock. A footstool, properly one made of coarse grass (A.S. *hassuc*), or sedge (Welsh *hesg*).

Hassocks should be gotten in the fens, and laid at the foot of the said bank . . . where need required.—
DUGDALE: *Imbanking*, p. 322.

Hat. How Lord Kingsale acquired the right of wearing his hat in the royal presence is this: King John and Philip II of France agreed to settle a dispute respecting the duchy of Normandy by single combat. John de Courcy, conqueror of Ulster and founder of the Kingsale family, was the English champion, and no sooner appeared than the French champion put spurs to his horse and fled. The king asked the earl what reward should be given him, and he replied, "Titles and lands I want not, of these I have enough; but in remembrance of this day I beg the boon, for myself and successors, to remain covered in the presence of your highness and all future sovereigns of the realm." So runs the story.

The privilege was at one time more extensive; Motley informs us that all the Spanish grandees had the privilege of being covered in the presence of the reigning monarch; and to this day, in England, any peer of the realm has the right to sit in a court of justice with his hat on.

In the House of Commons, whilst a division is proceeding a member may speak on a point of order arising out of or during the division, but if he does so he must speak sitting and with his head covered.

It was a point of principle with the early Quakers not to remove the hat as a mark of respect but to remain covered, even in the presence of royalty. The story goes that on one occasion William Penn came into the room where Charles II was standing and kept his hat on; whereupon Charles removed his own hat. "Friend Charles," said Penn, "why dost thou uncover thy head?" "Friend Penn," answered Charles with a smile, "it is the custom here that only one person wears his hat in the king's presence."

Hat-trick. A cricket phrase for taking three wickets with three successive balls. A bowler who did this used to be entitled to a new hat at the expense, of his club.

A white hat. A white hat used to be emblematical of radical proclivities, because the Radical reformer, "Orator" Henry Hunt (1773-1835) wore one during the Wellington and Peel administration.

Street arabs used to accost a person wearing a white hat with the question, "Who stole the donkey?" and a companion would answer, "Him wi' the white hat on."

Never wear a brown hat in Friesland. When at Rome do as Rome does. In Friesland (a province of the Netherlands) the inhabitants used to cover the head first with a knitted cap, a high silk skull-cap, a metal turban, and over all a huge flaunting bonnet. A traveller once passed through the province with a common brown wide-awake, and was hustled by the workmen, jeered at by the women, pelted by the boys, and sneered at by the magnates.

To eat one's hat. Indicative of strong emphasis. "I'd eat my hat first," "I'd be hanged first."

"If I knew as little of life as that, I'd eat my hat and swallow the buckle whole," said the clerical gentleman.— DICKENS: *Pickwick Papers*, ch. xlii.

To hang up one's hat in a house. To make oneself at home; to become one of the family.

Hatches. Put on the hatches. Figuratively, shut the door. (A.S. *hæce*, a gate; *cp. haca*, a bar or bolt.)

To throw the hatchet. To exaggerate heavily, tell falsehoods. In allusion to an ancient game where hatchets were thrown at a mark, like quoits. It means the same as drawing the longbow (*q.v.*).

Hatto (hăt' ō). A 10th-century archbishop of Mainz, a noted statesman and councillor of Otho the Great, proverbial for his perfidy, who, according to tradition (preserved in the *Magdeburg Centuries*), was devoured by mice. The story says that in 970 there was a great famine in Germany, and Hatto, that there might be better store for the rich, assembled the poor in a barn, and burnt them to death, saying: "They are like mice, only good to devour the corn." By and by an army of mice came against the archbishop, who, to escape the plague, removed to a tower on the Rhine; but hither came the mouse-army by hundreds and thousands, and ate him up. The tower is still called Mouse-tower (*q.v.*).

Many similar legends, or versions of the same legend, are told of the mediæval Rhineland.

Count Graaf raised a tower in the midst of the Rhine, and if any boat attempted to evade payment of toll, the warders shot the crew with crossbows. One year a famine prevailed, and the count made a corner in wheat and "profiteered" grossly; but an army of rats, pressed by hunger, invaded his tower, and falling on the old baron, worried him to death and then devoured him.

Widerolf, bishop of Strasburg (in 997), was devoured by mice because he suppressed the convent of Seltzen, on the Rhine.

Bishop Adolf of Cologne was devoured by mice or rats in 1112.

Freiherr von Güttingen collected the poor in a great barn, and burnt them to death; and being invaded by rats and mice, ran to his castle of Güttingen. The vermin, however, pursued him and ate him clean to the bones, after which his castle sank to the bottom of the lake, "where it may still be seen."

A similar tale is recorded in the chronicles of William of Mulsburg, Bk. ii; and *cp*. PIED PIPER.

Havelok the Dane (hăv' lok). A hero of mediæval romance. He was the orphan son of

Birkabegn, king of Denmark, was exposed at sea through the treachery of his guardians, and the raft drifted to the coast of Lincolnshire. Here a fisherman named Grim found the young prince, and brought him up as his own son. In due time he became king of Denmark and of part of England; Grim was suitably rewarded, and with the money founded the town of Grimsby (*q.v.*).

Haver-cakes. Oaten cakes (Scand. *hafre*; Ger. *hafer*, oats).

Haversack. Strictly speaking, a bag to carry oats in. *See* HAVER-CAKES. It now means any small canvas bag for rations, etc., slung from the shoulder; a gunner's leather-case for carrying charges.

Havre, Le (le avr). A contraction of *Le havre* (the haven, harbour) *de notre Dame de grâce*.

Hawcubites (haw' kū bītz). Street bullies in the reign of Queen Anne. It was their delight to molest and ill-treat the old watchmen, women, children, and feeble old men who chanced to be in the streets after sunset. The succession of these London pests after the Restoration was: The Muns, the Tityre Tus, the Hectors, the Scourers, the Nickers, then the Hawcubites (1711-14), and then the Mohocks—most dreaded of all.

> From Mohock and from Hawcubite,
> Good Lord deliver me,
> Who wander through the streets at nighte,
> Committing cruelty.
> They slash our sons with bloody knives,
> And on our daughters fall:
> And, if they murder not our wives,
> We have good luck withal.

The name Hawcubite is probably a combination of *Mohawk* and *Jacobite*.

Hawk.

(1) Different parts of a hawk:

Arms. The legs from the thigh to the foot
Beak. The upper and crooked part of the bill.
Beams. The long feathers of the wings.
Clap. The nether part of the bill.
Feathers summed and unsummed. Feathers full *or* not full grown.
Flags. The next to the principals.
Glut. The slimy substance in the pannel.
Gorge. The crow or crop.
Haglurs. The spots on the feathers.
Mails. The breast feathers.
Nares. The two little holes on the top of the beak.
Pannel. The pipe next to the fundament.
Pendent feathers. Those behind the toes.
Petty singles. The toes.
Pounces. The claws.
Principal feathers. The two longest.
Sails. The wings.
Sear or *sere.* The yellow part under the eyes.
Train. The tail.

(2) Different sorts of hawk:

Gerfalcon. A Gerfalcon (esp. the Tercel, or male) is for a king.
Falcon or *Tercel gentle.* For a prince.
Falcon of the rock. For a duke.
Falcon peregrine. For an earl.
Bastard hawk. For a baron.
Sacre and a *sacret.* For a knight.
Lanare and *Lanret.* For a squire.
Merlin. For a lady.
Hoby. For a young man.
Goshawk. For a yeoman.
Tercel. For a poor man.
Sparrow hawk. For a priest.
Musket. For a holy-water clerk.
Kestrel. For a knave or servant.

Dame Juliana Berners.

The "Sore-hawk" is a hawk of the first year: so called from the French, *sor* or *saure*, brownish-yellow.

(3) The dress of a hawk:

Bewits. The leathers with the hawk-bells, buttoned to the bird's legs.
Creanse. A packthread or thin twine fastened to the leash in disciplining a hawk.
Hood. A cover for the head, to keep the hawk in the dark. A *rufter hood* is a wide one, open behind, *To unstrike the hood* is to draw the strings so that the hood may be in readiness to be pulled off.
Jesses. The little straps by which the leash is fastened to the legs.
Leash. The leather thong for holding the hawk.

(4) Terms used in falconry:

Casting. Something given to a hawk to cleanse her gorge.
Cawking. Treading.
Cowering. When young hawks, in obedience to their elders, quiver and shake their wings.
Crabbing. Fighting with each other when they stand too near.
Hack. The place where a hawk's meat is laid.
Imping. Repairing a hawk's wing by engrafting a new feather.
Inke or *Ink.* The breast and neck of a bird that a hawk preys on.
Intermewing. The time of changing the coat.
Lure. A figure of a fowl made of leather and feathers.
Make. An old staunch hawk that sets an example to young ones.
Mantling. Stretching first one wing and then the other over the legs.
Mew. The place where hawks sit when moulting.
Muting. The dung of hawks.
Pelf or *pill.* What a hawk leaves of her prey.
Pelt. The dead body of a fowl killed by a hawk.
Perch. The resting-place of a hawk when off the falconer's wrist.
Plumage. Small feathers given to a hawk to make her cast.
Quarry. The fowl or game that a hawk flies at.
Rangle. Gravel given to a hawk to bring down her stomach.
Sharp set. Hungry.
Tiring. Giving a hawk a leg or wing of a fowl to pull at.

The peregrine when full grown is called a **blue-hawk**.

The hawk was the symbol of **Ra** or **Horus**, the sun-god of the Egyptians.

See BIRDS (protected by superstitions).

Hawthorn. The symbol of "Good Hope" in the language of flowers, because it shows that winter is over and spring at hand. The Athenian girls used to crown themselves with hawthorn flowers at weddings, and the marriage-torch was made of hawthorn. The Romans considered it a charm against sorcery, and placed leaves of it on the cradles of newborn infants.

The hawthorn was chosen by Henry VII for his device, because the crown of Richard III was discovered in a hawthorn bush at Bosworth.

Hay, Hagh, or **Haugh** (all pron. hā). An enclosed estate; rich pasture-land, especially a royal park; as Bilhagh (*Billa-haugh*), Beskwood- or Bestwood-hay, Lindeby-hay, Welleyhay or Wel-hay. These were "special reserves" of game for royalty alone.

A bottle of hay. *See* BOTTLE.

Between hay and grass. Too late for one and too soon for the other.

Neither hay nor grass. That hobbledehoy state when a youth is neither boy nor man.

Make hay while the sun shines. Strike while the iron is hot; take time by the forelock; one to-day is worth two to-morrows.

Hayseed. An American colloquial term for a countryman, a rustic.

Haywire. To go haywire is to run riot, to behave in an uncontrolled manner. This American phrase probably arises from the difficulty of handling the coils of wire used for binding bundles of hay; if such a coil is unfastened unskilfully it springs out in great loops that quickly become entangled and unmanageable.

Hay, Antic. The hay was an old English country dance, somewhat of the nature of a reel, with winding, sinuous movements around other dancers or bushes, etc., when danced in the open.

My men like satyrs grazing on the lawn
Shall with their goat feet dance the antic hay.
MARLOWE: *Edward II*, i, 1.

Haysugge. *See* ISAAC.

Hayward, an official in the old English village whose duty it was to look after the hedges and boundaries and impound any cattle found straying.

I haue an horne and be haywarde and liggen oute
a nyghtes
And keep my com in my croft fro pykers and theeves.
Piers Plowman (C), vi. 16.

Hazazel. The scapegoat. *See* AZAZEL.

Haze. To bully (first used at sea). "It is very expressive to a sailor, and means to punish by hardwork." R. H. DANA: *Two Years Before the Mast*, 1840.

He Bible, The. *See* BIBLE, SPECIALLY NAMED.

Head. Cattle are counted by the *head*; labourers by *hands*, as "How many hands do you employ?"; soldiers by their *arms*, as "So many rifles, bayonets," etc.; guests at dinner by the *cover*, as "Covers for ten," etc.

Human beings are, in some circumstances, counted as "heads, as, for instance, in contracting for meals the caterer will take the job at so much "a head"—*i.e.* for each person.

Head and shoulders. A phrase of sundry shades of meaning. Thus "head and shoulders taller" means considerably taller; "to turn one out head and shoulders" means to drive one out forcibly and without ceremony.

Heads I win, tails you lose. Descriptive of a one-sided arrangement.

Heads or tails. Guess whether the coin tossed up will come down with head-side uppermost or not. The side not bearing the head has various devices, which are all included in the word tail, meaning opposite to the head. The ancient Romans used to play this game, but said, "Heads or ships."

He has quite turned her head. He has so completely enchanted her that she is unable to take a reasonable view of the situation.

He has a head on his shoulders. He is a clever fellow, with brains in his head.

He has quite lost his head. He is so excited and confused that he does not know the right thing to do.

I can make neither head nor tail of it. I cannot understand it at all. A gambling phrase.

Off one's head. Deranged; delirious; extremely excited.

Over head and ears. *See* EAR.

To come to a head. To ripen, to reach a crisis. The allusion is to the ripening, or coming to a head, of a suppurating boil or ulcer.

To head off. To intercept; get ahead of and force to turn back.

To hit the nail on the head. To guess aright; to do the right thing. The allusion is obvious. The French say, *Vous avez frappé au but* (You have hit the mark); the Italians have the phrase, *Avete dato in brocca* (You have hit the pitcher), alluding to a game where a pitcher stood in the place of Aunt Sally (*q.v.*). The Lat. *Rein acu tetigisti* (You have touched the thing with a needle), refers to the custom of probing sores.

To keep one's head above water. To avoid bankruptcy.

To make head, or **headway.** To get on, to struggle effectually against something.

To take it into one's head. To conceive a notion.

Heady. Wilful; also, affecting the head, as "The wine or beer is heady."

Health. Drinking healths. This custom, of immemorial antiquity, William of Malmesbury says, took its rise from the death of young King Edward the Martyr (979), who was traitorously stabbed in the back while drinking a cup of wine presented to him by his mother Elfrida. According to Rabelais the giant, Gab-bara, was "the first inventor of the drinking of healths." He was an ancestor of Gargantua.

It was well known to the ancients. The Greeks handed the cup to the person toasted and said, "This to thee." Our holding out the wineglass is a relic of this Greek custom.

The Romans had a curious fashion of drinking the health of a mistress, which was to drink a bumper to each letter of her name. Hudibras satirizes this custom, which he calls "spelling names with beer-glasses" (ii, 1). In Plautus, we read of a man drinking to his mistress with these words: *Bene vos, bene nos, bene te, bene me, bene nostrum etiam Stephanium* (Here's to you, here's to us all, here's to thee, here's to me, here's to our dear——). (*Stich*, v, 4.) Martial, Ovid, Horace, etc., refer to the same custom.

The Saxons were great health-drinkers, and Geoffrey of Monmouth (Bk. vi, 12) says that Hengist invited King Vortigern to a banquet to see his new levies. After the meats were removed, Rowena, the beautiful daughter of Hengist, entered with a golden cup full of wine, and, making obeisance, said, "*Lauerd kining, wacht heil*" (Lord King, your health). The king then drank and replied, *Drinc heil* (Here's to you). See WASSAIL.

Heap. Struck all of a heap. Struck with astonishment.

Hear, hear! An exclamation used to call attention to the words of a speaker, usually with approbation. Until the late 17th century such approval was shown by a loud humming among the hearers, and "Hear him!" was used to silence interrupters and remind others of the duty of attending to what was being said. In the Parliament of 1689 the Whigs greeted every speech by one of their own party with shouts of "Hear, hear him!" to drown any Tory interjections, and from this the phrase grew to its present significance.

Hearse. Originally a framework shaped like an ancient harrow (O.Fr. *herce*, a harrow),

holding candles and placed over a bier or coffin. These frames at a later period were covered with a canopy, and lastly were mounted on wheels and became the modern carriage for the dead.

Heart. In Christian art the *heart* is an attribute of St. Teresa.

The flaming heart is the symbol of charity, and an attribute of St. Augustine, denoting the fervency of his devotion. The heart of the Saviour is frequently so represented.

The Bleeding Heart. *See* BLEEDING.

A heart to heart talk. A confidential talk in private; generally one in which good advice is offered, or a warning or reprimand given.

After my own heart. Just what I like; in accordance with my wish.

From the bottom of one's heart. Fervently; with absolute sincerity.

His heart is in the right place. He is kind and sympathetic in spite, perhaps, of appearances. He is perfectly well disposed.

His heart sank into his boots. In Latin, *Cor illi in genua decidit.* In French, *Avoir la peur au ventre.* The last two phrases are very expressive: Fear makes the knees shake, and it gives one a stomach ache; but the English phrase suggests that his heart or spirits sank as low as possible short of absolutely deserting him.

His heart was in his mouth. That choky feeling in the throat which arises from fear, conscious guilt, shyness, etc.

In one's heart of heart. In the farthest, innermost, most secure recesses of one's heart.

> Give me that man
> That is not passion's slave, and I will wear him
> In my heart's core, ay, in my heart of heart.
> *Hamlet*, ii, 2.

The phrase is often heard as "heart of *hearts*," but this, as will be seen from Shakespeare's very clear reference to the "heart's core," is incorrect. *Cp.* also:—

> Even the very middle of my heart
> Is warmed.
> *Cymbeline*, ii, 6.

Out of heart. Despondent; without sanguine hope.

Set your heart at rest. Be quite easy about the matter.

Take heart. Be of good courage. Moral courage at one time was supposed to reside in the heart, physical courage in the stomach, wisdom in the head, affection in the reins or kidneys, melancholy in the bile, spirit in the blood, etc.

To break one's heart. To waste away or die of disappointment. "Broken-hearted," hopelessly distressed. It is not impossible to die "of a broken heart," but it is never caused through grief.

To eat one's heart out. To brood over some trouble to such an extent that one wears oneself out with the worry of it; to suffer from hopeless disappointment in expectations.

To learn by heart. *See* LEARN.

To lose one's heart to. To fall in love with somebody.

To set one's heart upon. Earnestly to desire it.

To take to heart. To feel deeply pained at something which has occurred; to appreciate fully the implications of.

To wear one's heart upon one's sleeve. To expose one's secret intentions to general notice; the reference being to the custom of tying your lady's favour to your sleeve, and thus exposing the secret of the heart. Iago says:—

When my outward action doth demonstrate
The native act and figure of my heart
In compliment extern, 'tis not long after
But I will wear my heart upon my sleeve
For daws to peck at: I am not what I am.
         Othello, i, 6.

With all my heart, or **with my whole heart and soul.** With all the energy and enthusiasm of which I am capable.

With heart and hand. With enthusiastic energy.

Heartbreaker. A flirt. Also a particular kind of curl. A loose ringlet worn over the shoulders, or a curl over the temples.

Heart of Midlothian. The old jail, the Tolbooth of Edinburgh, taken down in 1817. Sir Walter Scott has a novel so entitled.

Heartsease (harts' ēz). The *viola tricolor*. It has a host of fancy names; as the "Butterfly flower," "Kiss me quick," a "Kiss behind the garden gate," "Love in idleness" (*q.v.*), "Pansy," Three faces under one hood," the "Variegated violet," "Herba Trinitatis," etc.

Hearth Money. *See* CHIMNEY MONEY.

Heat. One course in a race; that part of a race run as "instalment" of the main event. One, two, or more heats make a race. A *dead heat* is a heat in which two or more competitors are tied for the first place.

Feigned Zeal, you saw, set out with speedier pace,
But the last heat Plain Dealing won the race.
    DRYDEN: *Albion and Albanius; Epilogue.*

To turn the heat on. To subject to a severe cross-examination, to grill.

Heaven (A.S. *heofon*). The word properly denotes the abode of the Deity and His angels— "heaven is My throne" (*Is.* lxvi, 1, and *Matt.* v, 34)— but it is also used in the Bible and elsewhere for the air, the upper heights as "the fowls of heaven," "the dew of heaven," "the clouds of heaven"; "the cities are walled up to heaven" (*Deut.* i, 28); and a tower whose top should "reach unto heaven" (*Gen.* xi, 4); the starry firmament, as, "Let there be lights in the firmament of heaven" (*Gen.* i, 14).

In the Ptolemaic system (*q.v.*) the heavens were the successive spheres of space enclosing the central earth at different distances and revolving round it at different speeds. The first seven were those of the so-called Planets, *viz.* the Moon, Mercury, Venus, the Sun, Mars, Jupiter, and Saturn; the eighth was the firmament of heaven containing all the fixed stars; the ninth was the crystalline sphere, invented by Hipparchus (2nd cent. B.C.), to account for the precession of the equinoxes. These were known as *The Nine Heavens* (*see* NINE SPHERES); the tenth—added much later—was the primum mobile.

The Seven Heavens (of the Mohammedans). *The first heaven* is of pure silver, and here the stars, each with its angel warder, are hung out like lamps on golden chains. It is the abode of Adam and Eve.

The second heaven is of pure gold and is the domain of John the Baptist and Jesus.

The third heaven is of pearl, and is allotted to Joseph. Here Azrael, the angel of death, is stationed, and is for ever writing in a large book or blotting words out. The former are the names of persons born, the latter those of the newly dead.

The fourth heaven is of white gold, and is Enoch's. Here dwells the Angel of Tears, whose height is "500 days' journey," and he sheds ceaseless tears for the sins of man.

The fifth heaven is of silver and is Aaron's. Here dwells the Avenging Angel, who presides over elemental fire.

The sixth heaven is composed of ruby and garnet, and is presided over by Moses. Here dwells the Guardian Angel of heaven and earth, half-snow and half-fire.

The seventh heaven is formed of divine light beyond the power of tongue to describe, and is ruled by Abraham. Each inhabitant is bigger than the whole earth, and has 70,000 heads, each head 70,000 mouths, each mouth 70,000 tongues and each tongue speaks 70,000 languages, all for ever employed in chanting the praises of the Most High.

To be in the seventh heaven. Supremely happy. The Cabbalists maintained that there are seven heavens, each rising in happiness above the other, the seventh being the abode of God and the highest class of angels. *See also* PARADISE.

Heavy. Heavy man. In theatrical parlance, an actor who plays foil to the hero, such as the king in *Hamlet*; Iago is another "heavy man's" part as foil to Othello.

Heavy water is the name given to deuterium oxide, a liquid similar to ordinary water but about 10 per cent denser. It is largely used in experiments in nuclear physics and its properties and possible uses are still being investigated.

Heavies, The. *See* REGIMENTAL NICKNAMES.

Hebe (hē' bi). Goddess of youth, and cupbearer to the celestial gods. She had the power of restoring the aged to youth and beauty (Greek mythology).

> Wreathed smiles
> Such as hang on Hebe's cheek,
> And love to live in dimple sleek.
> MILTON: *L'Allegro*.

Hecate (hek' à ti). One of the Titans of Greek mythology, and the only one that retained her power under the rule of Zeus. She was the daughter of Perses and Asteria, and became a deity of the lower world after taking part in the search for Proserpine. She taught witchcraft and sorcery, and was a goddess of the dead, and as she combined the attributes of, and became identified with, Selene, Artemis, and Persephone, she was represented as a triple goddess and was sometimes described as having three heads—one of a horse, one of a dog, and one of a lion. Her offerings consisted of dogs, honey, and black lambs, which were sacrificed to her at cross-roads. Shakespeare refers to the triple character of this goddess:

> And we fairies that do run
> By the triple Hecate's team.
> *Midsummer Night's Dream*, v, 2.

Hecatomb (hek' à tom). In Greek antiquities, a sacrifice consisting of a hundred head of oxen (*hekaton*, a hundred); hence, a large number. Keats speaks of "hecatombs of vows," Shelley of "hecatombs of broken hearts," etc.

It is said that Pythagoras, who, we know, would never take life, offered up 100 oxen to the gods when he discovered that the square of the hypotenuse of a right-angled triangle equals the sum of the squares of the other two sides. This is the 47th proposition of Bk. i of "Euclid," called the Dulcarnon (*q.v.*).

Hector (hek' tòr). Eldest son of Priam, the noblest and most magnanimous of all the Trojan chieftains in Homer's *Iliad*. After holding out for ten years, he was slain by Achilles, who lashed him to his chariot, and dragged the dead body in triumph thrice round the walls of Troy. The *Iliad* concludes with the funeral obsequies of Hector and Patroclus.

In modern times his name has somewhat deteriorated, for it is used to-day for a swaggering bully, and "to hector" means to browbeat, bully, bluster.

Hecuba (hek' ū bà). Second wife of Priam, and mother of nineteen children, including Hector. When Troy was taken by the Greeks she fell to the lot of Ulysses. She was afterwards metamorphosed into a dog, and threw herself into the sea. Her story has furnished a host of Greek tragedies.

> I have heard my grandsire say full oft,
> Extremity of griefs would make men mad;
> And I have read that Hecuba of Troy
> Ran mad through sorrow.
> *Titus Andronicus*, iv, 1.

Hedge. To hedge, in betting, is to protect oneself against loss by cross bets; to prevaricate,

> He [Godolphin] began to think . . . that he had betted too deep . . . and that it was time to hedge.—MACAULAY: *England*, vol. iv, ch. xvii.

The word is used attributively for persons of low origin, vagabonds who ply their trade in the open, under—or between—the hedges, etc.; hence for many low and mean things, as *hedge-priest*, a poor or vagabond parson; *hedge-writer*, a Grub Street author; *hedge-marriage*, a clandestine one, etc.; *hedge-born swain*, a person of mean, or illegitimate, birth (1 *Henry VI*, iv, 1); *hedge-school*, a school kept in the open air, at one time common in Ireland; etc.

Hedonism. The doctrine of Aristippus, that pleasure or happiness is the chief good and chief end of man (Gr. *hedone*, pleasure).

Heebie-jeebies (hē' bi jē' biz), an American slang term descriptive of intense nervousness, the jitters.

Heel. In American slang usage a *heel* is a cad, a despicable fellow with no sense of decency or honour.

A heeler is the hanger-on of a political boss.

Heeled, in Western U.S.A. means supplied with all necessities, particularly money and firearms.

Achilles' heel. *See* ACHILLES.

Down, or **out at heels.** In a sad plight, in decayed circumstances, like a beggar whose boots are worn out at the heels.

> A good man's fortune may grow out at heels.
> *King Lear*, ii, 2.

To cool or **kick one's heels.** To be kept waiting a long time, especially after an appointment has been given one.

To lift up the heel against. To spurn, physically or figuratively; to treat with contumely or contempt: to oppose, to become an enemy.

Yea, mine own familiar friend, in whom I trusted, which did eat of my bread, hath lifted his heel against me.—*Ps.* xli, 9.

To take to one's heels. To run off.

Bumpers all round, and no heel-taps. The bumpers are to be drained to the bottom of the glass.

Heep, Uriah. An abject toady and a malignant hypocrite, making great play of being "'umble," but in the end falling a victim to his own malice.—DICKENS: *David Copperfield.*

Hegemony (he gem' o ni). **The hegemony of nations.** The leadership. (Gr. *hegemonia*, from ago, to lead.)

Hegira (hej' i ra, hē jī' ra) (Arab, *hejira*, the departure). The epoch of the flight of Mohammed from Mecca to Medina when he was expelled by the magistrates, July 15th, 622. The Mohammedan calendar starts from this event.

Heimdall (hīm' dal). One of the gods of Scandinavian mythology, son of the nine virgins, daughters of Ægir, and in many attributes identical with Tiw.

Heir-apparent. The actual heir who will succeed if he outlive the present holder of the crown, estate, etc., as distinguished from **heir-presumptive**, whose succession may be broken by the birth of someone nearer akin to the holder. Thus, in the time of Queen Victoria, the Princess Royal was heir-presumptive until the Prince of Wales, afterwards Edward VII, was born and became heir apparent. At the death of his predecessor the heir-apparent becomes **heir-at-law**.

Hel. The name in late Scandinavian mythology of the queen of the dead; also of her place of abode, which was the home of the spirits of those who had died in their beds as distinguished from Valhalla, the abode of heroes slain in battle.

Heldenbuch (hel' den buk) (Ger., *Book of Heroes*). The name given to the collection of songs, sagas, etc., recounting the traditions and myths of Dietrich of Bern. Much of it is ascribed to Wolfram von Eschenbach.

Helen. The type of female beauty. She was the daughter of Zeus and Leda, and wife of Menelaos, king of Sparta. She eloped with Paris, and thus brought about the siege and destruction of Troy.

For which men all the life they here enjoy
Still fight, as for the Helens of their Troy.

SIR FULKE GREVILLE, LORD BROOKE: *Treatie of Humane Learning.*

She moves a goddess and she looks a queen.
POPE : *Homer's Iliad,* iii.

St. Helen's fire. The St. Elmo's Fire, or Corpozant (*q.v.*), occasionally seen on the masts of ships, etc. If the flame is single, foul weather is said to be at hand; but if two or more flames appear, the weather will improve. *See* CASTOR AND POLLUX.

Helena (hel' en à). The type of a lovely woman, patient and hopeful, strong in feeling, and sustained through trials by her enduring and heroic faith. (*All's Well that Ends Well.*)

Helena, St. Mother of Constantine the Great. She is represented in royal robes, wearing an imperial crown, because she was empress. Sometimes she carries in her hand a model of the Holy Sepulchre, an edifice raised by her in the East; sometimes she bears a large cross, typical of her alleged discovery of Our Lord's Cross (*see Invention of the Cross, under* CROSS); sometimes she also bears the three nails by which the Saviour was affixed to the cross. She died about 328, and is commemorated on August 18th.

The island of St. Helena (săn' tà lē' nà) in the South Atlantic, discovered by the Portuguese on St. Helena's Day, 1501, was the place of exile of Napoleon from 1815 until his death in 1821.

Helicopter (hel' i kop t ėr). A flying-machine that can raise itself vertically by means of horizontally revolving propellers. The uses of these aircraft have not yet been fully explored and developed.

Heliopolis (hel i op' ō lis, hē' li op' ō lis), the City of the Sun, a Greek form of (1) Baalbek, in Syria; and (2) of An, in ancient Egypt, noted for its temple of Actis, which may be the Beth Shemesh, or Temple of the Sun, referred to in *Jer.* xliii, 13. It is now a pleasant residential suburb of Cairo.

Helios (hē' li os). The Greek sun-god, who rode to his palace in Colchis every night in a golden boat furnished with wings. He is called Hyperion by Homer, and, in later times, Apollo.

Heliotrope (hel' i ō trōp, hē' li ō trōp). Apollo loved Clytie (*q.v.*), but forsook her for her sister Leucothoe. On discovering this, Clytie pined away; and Apollo changed her at death to a flower, which, always turning towards the sun, is called heliotrope. (Gr. "turn-to-sun.")

The bloodstone, a greenish quartz with veins and spots of red, used to be called "heliotrope," the story being that if thrown into a bucket of water it turned the rays of the sun to blood-colour. This stone also had the power of rendering its bearer invisible.

No hope had they of crevice where to hide,
Or heliotrope to charm them out of view.
DANTE: *Inferno*, xxvi.

Hell. This word occurs twenty-one times in the Authorized Version of the New Testament. In nine instances the Greek word is *Hades*; in eight instances it is *Gehenna*; and in one it is *Tartarus*.

According to the Koran, Hell has seven portals leading into seven divisions (*Surah* xv, 44).

True Buddhism admits of no Hell, properly so called (*cp.* NIRVANA), but certain of the more superstitious acknowledge as many as 136 places of punishment after death, where the dead are sent according to their degree of demerit.

Classic authors tell us that the Inferno is encompassed by five rivers: Acheron, Cocytus, Styx, Phlegethon, and Lethe. Acheron, from the Gr. *achos-reo*, grief-flowing; Cocytus, from the Gr. *kokuo*, to weep, supposed to be a flood of tears; Styx, from the Gr. *stugeo*, to loathe; Phlegethon, from the Gr. *phlego*, to burn; and Lethe, from the Gr. *lethe*, oblivion. *See also* INFERNO.

Hell is paved with good intentions. This occurs as a saying of Dr. Johnson (Boswell's *Life*, ann. 1775), but it is a good deal older than his day. It is given by George Herbert (*Jacula Prudentum*) (1633) as "Hell is full of good meanings and wishes."

It was hell broken loose. Said of a state of anarchy or disorder.

Why, here you have the awfulest of crimes
For nothing! Hell broke loose on a butterfly!
A dragon born of rose-dew and the moon!
BROWNING: *Ring and the Book*, iv, 1601.

The road to hell is easy. *Facilis descensus Averno. See* AVERNUS.

The Vicar of Hell. *See* VICAR.

To give one hell. To make things very unpleasant for oneself.

To Hell or **Connaught.** This phrase, usually attributed to Cromwell, and common to the whole of Ireland, rose thus: during the Commonwealth all the native Irish were dispossessed of their lands in the other three provinces and ordered to settle in Connaught, under pain of death.

To lead apes in hell. *See* APE.

Hellenes (hel' ēnz). "This word had in Palestine three several meanings: sometimes it designated the pagans; sometimes the Jews, speaking Greek and dwelling among the pagans; and sometimes proselytes of the gate, that is, men of pagan origin converted to Judaism, but not circumcised" (*John* vii, 35, xii, 20; *Acts* xiv, 1, xvii, 4, xviii, 4, xxi, 28). (Renan: *Life of Jesus*, xiv.)

The Greeks were called *Hellenes*, from Hellen, son of Deucalion and Pyrrha, their legendary ancestor; the name has descended to the modern Greeks, and their ruler is not "King of Greece," but "King of the Hellenes." The ancient Greeks called their country "Hellas"; it was the Romans who applied to it the name "Græcia," which, among the inhabitants themselves, referred only to Epirus.

Hellenic. The common dialect of the Greek writers after the age of Alexander. It was based on the Attic.

Hellenistic. The dialect of the Greek language used by the Jews. It was full of Oriental idioms and metaphors.

Hellenists. Those Jews who used the Greek or Hellenic language; also a Greek scholar.

Hellespont (hel' es pont). The "sea of Helle"; so called because Helle, the sister of Phryxus, was drowned there. She was fleeing with her brother through the air to Colchis on the golden ram to escape from Ino, her mother-in-law, who most cruelly oppressed her, but turning giddy, she fell into the sea. It is the ancient name of the Dardanelles and is celebrated in the legend of Hero and Leander (*q.v.*).

Helmet. The helmets of Saragossa were most in repute in the days of chivalry.

Mohammed's helmet. Mohammed wore a double helmet; the exterior one was called *al mawashah* (the wreathed garland).

The helmet of Perseus rendered the wearer invisible. This was the "helmet of Hades," which, with the winged sandals and magic wallet, he took from certain nymphs who held them in possession; but after he had slain Medusa he restored them again, and presented the Gorgon's head to Athene (Minerva), who placed it in the middle of her ægis.

The pointed helmet in the bas-reliefs from the earliest palace of Nimroud appears to have been the most ancient. . . . Several were discovered in the ruins. They were iron, and the rings which ornamented the lower part . . . were inlaid with copper.—LAYARD: *Nineveh and its Remains*, vol. ii, Pt. ii, ch. iv.

In heraldry, the helmet, resting on the chief of the shield, and bearing the crest, indicates rank.

Gold, with six bars, or with the visor raised (in full face), for royalty;

Steel, with gold bars, varying in number (in profile), for a nobleman;

Steel, without bars, and with visor open (in profile), for a knight or baronet;

Steel, with visor closed (in profile), for a squire or gentleman.

Helot (hel′ ŏt). A slave in ancient Sparta; hence, a slave or serf. The Spartans used to make a helot drunk as an object-lesson to the youths of the evils of intemperance. Dr. Johnson said of one of his old acquaintances:—

> He is a man of good principles; and there would be no danger that a young gentleman should catch his manner; for it is so very bad, that it must be avoided. In that respect he would be like the drunken Helot.— Boswell's *Life*: ann. 1779.

Helter-skelter. Higgledy-piggledy; in hurry and confusion. A jingling expression, more or less imitating the clatter of swiftly moving feet; post-haste, as Shakespeare uses the expression (2 *Henry IV*, v, 3) :—

> Sir John I am thy Pistol and thy friend,
> And helter-skelter have I rode to thee,
> And tidings do I bring.

Helvetia (hel vē′ sha). Switzerland. So called from the Helvetii, a powerful Celtic people who dwelt thereabouts.

Hemp. When hempe is spun England is done.

Lord Bacon says he heard the prophecy when he was a child, and he interpreted it thus: Hempe is composed of the initial letters of Henry, Edward, Mary, Philip, and Elizabeth. At the close of the last reign "England was done," for the sovereign no longer styled himself "King of England," but "King of Great Britain and Ireland." *See* NOTARIKON.

Hen. A grey hen. A stone bottle for holding liquor. Large and small pewter pots mixed together are called "hen and chickens."

> A dirty leather wallet lay near the sleeper, . . . also a grey-hen which had contained some sort of strong liquor.— EMMA ROBINSON: *Whitefriars*, ch. viii.

A whistling maid and a crowing hen is fit for neither God nor men. A whistling maid means a witch, who whistles like the Lapland witches to call up the winds; they were supposed to be in league with the devil. The crowing of a hen was supposed to forebode a death. The usual interpretation is that masculine qualities in women are undesirable.

Hen-pecked. A man who tamely submits to the lectures and nagging of his wife is said to be "hen-pecked."

Henchman. A faithful follower. Originally a squire or attendant, especially one who looked after the horses (A.S. *hengest,* horse, and *man*).

> I do but beg a little changeling boy
> To be my henchman.
> A *Midsummer Night's Dream,* ii, 1.

Hep, an American slang phrase of uncertain origin meaning "aware of, informed of, wise to."

Hep-cat, one who is fond of and moved by fast and noisy music.

Hephaestos (hē fes′ tos). The Greek Vulcan.

Heptameron, The. A collection of Italian and mediæval stories written by—or at any rate ascribed to—Marguerite of Angoulême, Queen of Navarre (1492-1549), and published posthumously in 1558. They were supposed to have been related in seven days, hence the title (Gr. *hepta,* seven, *hemera,* day; *cp.* DECAMERON; HEXAMERON).

Heptarchy (Gr., seven governments). The Saxon Heptarchy was the division of England into seven parts, each of which had a separate ruler: as Kent, Sussex, Wessex, Essex, East Anglia, Mercia, and Northumbria. It flourished in various periods from the 6th to the 9th centuries under a Bretwalda (*q.v.*), but seldom consisted of exactly seven members, and the names and divisions were constantly changing.

Hera (hē′ rå). The Greek Juno, the wife of Zeus. (The word means "chosen one," *haireo.*)

Heraldry. The herald (O.Fr. *heralt, heraut*) was an officer whose duty it was to proclaim war or peace, carry challenges to battle, and messages between sovereigns, etc.; nowadays war or peace is still proclaimed by the heralds, but their chief duty as court functionaries is to superintend state ceremonies such as coronations, installations, etc., and also to grant arms, trace genealogies, attend to matters of precedence, honours, etc.

Edward III appointed two heraldic kings-at-arms for south and north—Surroy and Norroy—in 1340. The English College of Heralds was incorporated by Richard III in 1483-84. It consists of three kings of arms, and four pursuivants, under the Earl Marshal, which office is hereditary in the line of the Dukes of Norfolk.

The three kings of arms are Garter (blue), Clarenceux, and Norroy (purple).

The six heralds are styled Somerset, Richmond, Lancaster, Windsor, Chester, and York.

The four pursuivants are Rouge Dragon, Blue Mantle, Portcullis, and Rouge Croix.

Garter King of Arms is so called from his special duty to attend at the solemnities of election, investiture, and installation of Knights of the Garter; he is Principal King of Arms for all England.

Clarenceux King of Arms. So called from the Duke of Clarence, brother of Edward IV. His jurisdiction extends over England south of the Trent.

Norroy King of Arms has similar jurisdiction to Clarenceux, only on the north side of the Trent.

The "Bath King of Arms" is not a member of the Heralds' College, and is concerned only with the Order of the Bath.

The Scottish and Irish officers of Arms are, unlike those of England, directly under the Government, and are not connected with the Earl Marshal or Garter.

In *Scotland* the heraldic college consists of *Lyon King of Arms*, three heralds (*Albany, Ross*, and *Rothesay*), and three pursuivants (*Garrick, March*, and *Unicorn*).

In *Ireland* it consists of *Ulster King of Arms*, two heralds (*Dublin* and *Cork*), and one pursuivant (*Athlone*).

In *Blazonry*, the *coat of arms* represents the knight himself from whom the bearer is descended.

The *shield* represents his body, and the *helmet* his head.

The *flourish* is his mantle.

The *motto* is the ground or moral pretension on which he stands.

The *supporters* are the pages, designated by the emblems of bears, lions, and so on.

There are nine *points* on the *shield* or *escutcheon*, distinguished by the first nine letters of the alphabet—three at top, A, B, C; three down the middle, D, E, F; and three at the bottom, G, H, I. The first three are *chiefs*; the middle three are the *collar point, fess point*, and *nombril* or *navel point*; the bottom three are the *base* points.

It should be noted that in heraldry the shield is taken as being held before the wearer; hence the *dexter*, or right side is the left side of the shield as it appears on paper.

The *tinctures* or *colours* used in heraldry are known by distinctive names, also sometimes by equivalents among the planets and precious stones. They are:—

Gold: or, Sol, topaz.
Silver: argent, Luna, pearl.
Red: gules, Mars, ruby.
Blue: azure, Jupiter, sapphire.
Black: sable, Saturn, diamond.

Green: vert, Venus, emerald.
Purple: purpure, Mercury, amethyst.

Besides these there are the different furs, as *ermine, vair*, and their arrangements as *erminois, erminites, pean, potent, verry*, etc.

Marshalling is the science of bringing together the arms of several families in one escutcheon.

The following are the main terms used in heraldry:—

Bend, a diagonal stripe.

Bordure, an edge of a different colour round the whole shield.

Chevron, a bent stripe, as worn by noncommissioned officers in the army, but the point upwards.

Cinquefoil, a five-petalled formalised flower.

Couchant, lying down.

Counter-passant, moving in opposite directions.

Couped, cut off straight at the stem or neck.

Coward, coué, with tail hanging between the legs.

Displayed, (of birds) with wings and talons outspread.

Dormant, sleeping.

Endorse, a very narrow vertical stripe, *see* Pale.

Erased, with nothing below the stem or neck, which ends roughly as opposed to the sharp edge of *couped*.

Fesse, a horizontal stripe across the middle of the shield.

File, a horizontal bar from which normally depend one or more smaller bars called *labels*.

Gardant, full-faced.

Hauriant, standing on its tail (of fishes).

Issuant, rising from the top or bottom of an ordinary.

Lodged, reposing (of stags, etc.).

Martlet, a swallow, with no feet.

Mullet, a star of a stated number of points.

Naiant, swimming (of fishes).

Nascent, rising out of the middle of an ordinary.

Pale, a wide vertical stripe down the centre of the shield.

Pallet, a narrow vertical stripe; *see* Pile.

Passant, walking, the face in profile (emblematic of resolution).

Passant gardant, walking, with full face (emblematic of resolution and prudence).

Passant regardant, walking and looking behind.

Pile, a narrow triangle.

Rampant, rearing, with face in profile (emblematic of magnanimity).

Rampant gardant, erect on the hind legs; full face (emblematic of prudence).

Rampant regardant, erect on the hind legs; side face looking behind (emblematic of circumspection).

Regardant, looking back (emblematic of circumspection).

Salient, springing (emblematic of valour).

Sejant, seated (emblematic of counsel).

Statant, standing still.

Trippant, running (of stags, etc.).

Volant, flying.

Herb. Herb of grace. Rue is so called probably because (owing to its extreme bitterness) it is the symbol of repentance.

> Here did she fall a tear; here in this place,
> I'll set a bank of rue, sour herb of grace;
> Rue, even for ruth, here shortly shall be seen,
> In the remembrance of a weeping queen.
>
> *Richard II,* iii, 4.

Jeremy Taylor, quoting from the *Flagellum Dæmonum,* a form of exorcism by Father Jerome Mengus (used in exorcizing Martha Brosser in 1599), says:—

> First, they are to try the devil by holy water, incense, sulphur, rue, which from thence, as we suppose, came to be called "herb of grace,"—and especially, St. John's wort, which therefore they call "devil's flight," with which if they cannot cast the devil out, yet they may do good to the patient.—*A Disuasive from Popery,* I, ii, 9 (1664).

Herb Trinity. The popular name for the pansy (*q.v.*), *Viola tricolor*; also called "Three-faces-under-a-hood"; the markings of the pansy account for both names. *Cp.* HEARTSEASE.

Herculaneum (hĕr kū lā′ ni ŭm), one of the ancient towns on the Bay of Naples destroyed in the eruption of A.D. 79. But whereas Pompeii was buried in ashes, Herculaneum was overwhelmed with molten lava and its remains have had to be hewn with difficulty from this rock. The architectural remains are inferior to those of Pompeii but the works of art are superior.

Hercules (hĕr′ kū lēz). A hero of ancient Greek myth, who was possessed of superhuman physical strength and vigour. He is represented as brawny, muscular, short-necked, and of huge proportions. The Pythian told him if he would serve Eurystheus for twelve years he should become immortal; accordingly he bound himself to the Argive king, who imposed upon him twelve tasks of great difficulty and danger:

(1) To slay the Nemean lion.

(2) To kill the Lernean hydra.

(3) To catch and retain the Arcadian stag.

(4) To destroy the Erymanthian boar.

(5) To cleanse the stables of King Augeas.

(6) To destroy the cannibal birds of the Lake Stymphalis.

(7) To take captive the Cretan bull.

(8) To catch the horses of the Thracian Diomedes.

(9) To get possession of the girdle of Hip-polyta, Queen of the Amazons.

(10) To take captive the oxen of the monster Geryon.

(11) To get possession of the apples of the Hesperides.

(12) To bring up from the infernal regions the three-headed dog Cerberus.

After death Hercules took his place in the heavens as a constellation, and is still to be seen between Lyra and Corona Borealis.

The Attic Hercules. Theseus, who went about like Hercules, destroying robbers and achieving wondrous exploits.

Hercules' choice. Immortality the reward of toil in preference to pleasure. Xenophon tells us that when Hercules was a youth he was accosted by Virtue and Pleasure, and asked to choose between them. Pleasure promised him all carnal delights, but Virtue promised immortality. Hercules gave his hand to the latter, and, after a life of toil, was received amongst the gods.

Hercules' horse. Arion, given him by Adrastos. It had the power of speech, and its feet on the right side were those of a man.

Hercules' Pillars. *See* PILLARS.

Herculean knot (hĕr kū lē′ ăn). A snaky complication on the rod or caduceus of Mercury, adopted by the Grecian brides as the fastening of their woollen girdles, which only the bridegroom was allowed to untie. As he did so he invoked Juno to render his marriage as fruitful as that of Hercules, whose numerous wives all had families. Amongst his wives were the fifty daughters of Thestius, all of whom conceived in one night. *See* KNOT.

Heretic. From a Greek word meaning "one who chooses," hence *heresy* means simply "a choice." A heretic is one who chooses his own creed instead of adopting one set forth by authority.

The principal heretical sects of the first six centuries were:—

FIRST CENTURY: The *Simonians* (from Simon Magus), *Cerinthians* (Cerinthus), *Ebionites* (Ebion), and *Nicolaitans* (Nicholas, deacon of Antioch).

SECOND CENTURY: The *Basilidians* (Basilides), *Carpocratians* (Carpocraies), *Valentinians* (Valentinus), *Gnostics* (Knowing Ones), *Nazarenes*, *Millenarians*, *Cainites* (Cain), *Sethians* (Seth), *Quartodecimans* (who kept Easter on the fourteenth day of the first month), *Cerdonians* (Cerdon), *Marcionites* (Marcion), *Montanists* (Montanus), *Alogians* (who denied the "Word"), *Artotyrites* (*q.v.*), and *Angelics* (who worshipped angels).

Tatianists belong to the 3rd or 4th century. The Tatian of the 2nd century was a Platonic philosopher who wrote *Discourses* in good Greek; Tatian the heretic lived in the 3rd or 4th century, and wrote very bad Greek. The two men were widely different in every respect, and the authority of the heretic for "four gospels" is of no worth.

THIRD CENTURY: The *Patri-passians*, *Arabaci*, *Aquarians*, *Novatians*, *Origenists* (followers of Origen), *Melchisedechians* (who believed Melchisedec was the Messiah), *Sabelliano* (from Sabellius), and *Manicheans* (followers of Mani).

FOURTH CENTURY: The *Arians* (from Arius), *Colluthians* (Colluthus), *Macedonians*, *Agnetæ*, *Apollinarians* (Apollinaris), *Timotheans* (Timothy, the apostle), *Collyridians* (who offered cakes to the Virgin Mary), *Seleucians* (Seleucius), *Priscillians* (Priscillian), *Anthropomorphites* (who ascribed to God a human form), *Jovinianists* (Jovinian), *Messalians*, and *Bonosians* (Bonosus).

FIFTH CENTURY: The *Pelagians* (Pelagius), *Nestorians* (Nestorius), *Eutychians* (Eutychus), *Theo-paschites* (who said all the three persons of the Trinity suffered on the cross).

SIXTH CENTURY: The *Predestinarians*, *Incorruptibilists* (who maintained that the body of Christ was incorruptible), the new *Agnoetæ* (who maintained that Christ did not know when the day of judgment would take place), and the *Monothelites* (who maintained that Christ had but one will).

Heriot (her' i ŏt). The ancient right of the lord of a manor to the best beast or chattel of a deceased copyhold tenant. The word is compounded of the Sax. *here* (army), *geatwe* (equipments), because originally it was military furniture, such as armour, arms, and horses paid to the lord of the fee.

Hermæ. *See* HERMES.

Hermaphrodite (her măf' rō dīt). A person or animal with indeterminate sexual organs, or with these organs being of both sexes; a flower containing both the male and female organs of reproduction. The word is derived from the fable of Hermaphroditus, son of Hermes and Aphrodite. The nymph Salmacis became enamoured of him, and prayed that she might be so closely united that "the twain might become one flesh." Her prayer being heard, the nymph and boy became one body. (Ovid: *Metamorphoses*, iv, 347.)

Though hermaphroditism in human beings to the extent of the combination in one person of certain characteristics of the two sexes is not unknown, a *true* hermaphrodite is rare, and the so-called examples are almost invariably merely cases of the malformation of the reproductive organs.

The Jewish Talmud contains several references to hermaphrodites; they are recognized in English law, and an old French law allowed them great latitude. The ancient Athenians commanded that they should be put to death. The Hindus and Chinese enact that every hermaphrodite should choose one sex and keep to it. According to fable, all persons who bathed in the fountain Salmăcis, in Carïa, became hermaphrodites.

Hermes. The Greek Mercury, whose busts, known as *Hermæ*, were affixed to stone pillars and set up as boundary marks at street corners, and so on. The Romans used them also for garden decorations.

Among alchemists Hermes was the usual name for quicksilver or mercury (*q.v.*).

See Milton's *Paradise Lost*, iii, 603.

Hermetically sealed. Closed securely; from sealing a vessel *hermetically, i.e.* as a chemist, a disciple of Hermes Trismegistus, would, by heating the neck of the vessel till it is soft, and then twisting it till the aperture is closed up.

Hero. No man is a hero to his valet. An old saying. Plutarch has the idea both in his *De Iside* and *Regum et Imperatorum Apothegmata*. And Montaigne in his *Essays* (Bk. iii, ch. ii) amplifies the idea—

Tel a esté miraculeux au monde, auquel sa femme et son valet n'ont rien veu seulement de remarquable; peu d'hommes ont esté admirez par leur domestiques. (Such an one has been, as it were, miraculous in the world in whom his wife and valet have seen nothing even remarkable; few men have been admired by their servants.)

Cp. the Latin saying frequently quoted by Bacon, *Verior fama e domesticis emanat* (Truer fame comes from one's servants), and *Matt*, xiii, 57—

A prophet is not without honour save in . . . his own house.

Heroic age. That age of a nation which comes between the purely mythical period and the historic. This is the age when the sons of the gods were said to take unto themselves the daughters of men, and the offspring partake of the twofold character.

Heroic size in sculpture denotes a stature superior to ordinary life, but not colossal.

Heroic verse. That verse in which epic poetry is generally written. In Greek and Latin it is hexameter verse, in English it is ten-syllable iambic verse, either in rhymes or not; in Italian it is the *ottava rima*. So called because it is employed to celebrate heroic exploits.

Hero and Leander. The old Greek tale is that Hero, a priestess of Venus, fell in love with Leander, who swam across the Hellespont every night to visit her. One night he was drowned, and heart-broken Hero drowned herself in the same sea. The story is told in one of the poems of Musæus, and in Marlowe and Chapman's *Hero and Leander*.

Lord Byron and Lieutenant Ekenhead repeated the experiment of Leander in 1810 and accomplished it in 1 hour 10 minutes. The distance, allowing for drifting, would be about four miles. In *Don Juan* Byron says of his hero:—

> A better swimmer you could scarce see ever,
> He could, perhaps, have pass'd the Hellespont,
> As once (a feat on which ourselves we prided)
> Leander, Mr. Ekenhead, and I did.
>> *Canto*, II, cv.

Herod (her' od). **To out-herod Herod.** To outdo in wickedness, violence, or rant, the worst of tyrants. Herod, who destroyed the babes of Bethlehem (*Matt.* ii, 16), was made (in the ancient mysteries) a ranting, roaring tyrant; the extravagance of his rant being the measure of his bloody-mindedness. *Cp.* PILATE.

> Oh, it offends me to the soul to hear a robustious, periwig-pated fellow tear a passion to tatters, to very rags, to split the ears of the groundlings . . . it out-herods Herod.—*Hamlet*, iii, 2.

Herrenvolk (hâr én fōk), a German word, meaning broadly "master race," used in the Nazi philosophy to describe the superiority of the German peoples.

Herring. A shotten herring. One that has shot off or ejected its spawn, and hence is worthless.

> Go thy ways, old Jack; die when thou wilt. If manhood, good manhood, be not forgot upon the face of the earth, then am I a shotten herring. There live not three good men unhanged in England, and one of them is fat and grows old.—I *Henry IV*, ii, 4.

Drawing a red herring across the path. Trying to divert attention from the main question by some side issue. A red herring (*i.e.* one dried, smoked, and salted) drawn across a fox's

path destroys the scent and sets the dogs at fault.

Herring-bone (in building). Courses of stone laid angularly, thus: ⋖⋖⋖. Also applied to strutting placed between thin joists to increase their strength.

In needlework an embroidery stitch, or alternatively a kind of cross-stitch used to fasten down heavy material.

Hershey Bar (hēr' shi). In the U.S.A. a Hershey Bar is a trade-marked form of sweetmeat; in U.S. army slang the term was applied to the gold narrow bar worn by troops on the left sleeve to indicate that they had done six months' overseas service.

Hertha. *See* NERTHUS.

Hesperia (hes pēr' i à) (Gr., western). Italy was so called by the Greeks, because it was to them the "Western Land"; and afterwards the Romans, for a similar reason, transferred the name to Spain.

Hesperides (hes per' i dēz). Three sisters who guarded the golden apples which Hera received as a marriage gift. They were assisted by the dragon Ladon. Hercules, as the last of his "twelve labours," slew the dragon and carried some of the apples to Eurystheus.

Many poets call the place where these golden apples grew the "garden of the Hesperides." Shakespeare (*Love's Labour's Lost*, iv, 3) speaks of "climbing trees in the Hesperides." (*See Comus*, lines 402-6.)

> Show thee the tree, leafed with refined gold,
> Whereon the fearful dragon held his seat.
> That watched the garden called Hesperides.
> ROBERT GREENE: *Friar Bacon and Friar Bungay* (1589).

Hesperus (hes' per ús). The evening star, because it sets in the west. *See* HESPERIA.

> Ere twice in murk and occidental damp
> Moist Hesperus hath quenched his sleepy lamp.
>> *All's Well that Ends Well*, ii, 1.

The Wreck of the Hesperus, a ballad once learned by every child at school, written by H. W. Longfellow in 1842, and based upon an actual disaster at sea.

Hessian. A coarse, strong cloth made from jute or hemp originally made in Hesse in Germany. Hessian boots were first worn by troops in Germany and became fashionable in England in the 19th century.

Hexameter (hek zăm' e těr). The metre in which the Greek and Latin epics were written, and which has been imitated in English in such poems as Longfellow's *Evangeline*, Clough's *Bothie*, Kingsley's *Andromeda* (probably the best), etc.

The line consists, says Professor Saintsbury (*Manual of English Prosody*, iv, 1):—

of six feet, dactyls or spondees at choice for the first four, but normally always a dactyl in the fifth and always a spondee in the sixth—the latter foot being by special licence sometimes allowed in the fifth also (in which case the line is called spondaic), but never a dactyl in the sixth. To this metre, and to the attempts to imitate it in English, the term should be strictly confined, and never applied to the Alexandrine or iambic trimeter.

Verse consisting of alternate hexameters and pentameters (*q.v.*) is known as elegiac (*q.v.*). Coleridge illustrates this in his:—

In the hexameter rises the fountain's silvery column;
In the pentameter aye falling in melody back.

The Authorized Version of the Bible furnishes a number of examples of "accidental" hexameter lines; the following are well known:—

How art thou fallen from Heaven, O Lucifer son of the Morning.

Why do the heathen rage and the people imagine a vain thing?

God is gone up with a shout, the Lord with the sound of the trumpet.

Hiawatha. The Iroquois name of a hero of miraculous birth who came (under a variety of names) among the North American Indian tribes to bring peace and goodwill to man. In Longfellow's poem (1855) he is an Ojibway, son of Mudjekeewis (the west wind) and Wenonah. He represents the progress of civilization among the American Indians. He married Minnehaha "Laughing Water." When the white man landed and taught the Indians the faith of Jesus, Hiawatha exhorted them to receive the words of wisdom, to reverence the missionaries who had come so far to see them.

Hibernia (hī bĕr' ni a). The Latin name for Ireland, and hence still used in poetry. It is a variant of the old Celtic *Erin*.

Hic Jacets. Tombstones, so called from the first two words of their Latin inscriptions: "Here lies . . ."

By the cold *Hic Jacets* of the dead.
TENNYSON: *Idylls of the King* (Vivien).

Old Hickory. General Andrew Jackson (1767-1845), President of the United States, 1829-37. He was first called "Tough," from his great powers of endurance, then "Tough as hickory," and lastly, "Old Hickory."

Hidalgo (hi dăl' gō). The title in Spain of the lower nobility. The word is from Lat. *filius de aliquo*, son of someone, or, as we should say, the son of a "somebody." In Portuguese it is *Fidalgo*.

Hide of Land. The term applied in Anglo-Saxon times to a portion of land that was sufficient to support a family; usually from 60 to 100 acres, but no fixed number. A hide of good arable land was smaller than a hide of inferior quality.

Hieroglyphs (hī ér ō glifs). The name applied to the picture characters which the Egyptians used in writing. The Egyptians called them, "words of the gods," and coming to us through the Greek, *hiero* means sacred, *glyph*, what is carved. For many years these inscribed symbols of beasts and birds, men and women, were undecipherable, but in 1822 a French archæologist, J. F. Champollion, pieced together an alphabet from the three-language inscription on the Rosetta Stone (*q.v.*) and from those small beginnings the decipherment of hieroglyphic inscriptions has enabled scholars to elucidate the whole history of Egyptian civilization.

Higgledy-piggledy. In great confusion; at sixes and sevens; perhaps with reference to a higgler or pedlar whose stores are all huddled together. *Higgledy* would then mean after the fashion of a higgler's basket; *piggledy* is a ricochet word suggested by this.

High. High-ball, the American term for a drink of whiskey diluted with water, soda-water or ginger ale and served in a tall glass with ice.

High-brow. A self-consciously cultured person; especially one who, in his own estimation at least, is intellectually superior. The terms *low-brow* and *middle-brow* have developed from this.

High Church. The name given to one of the three great schools in the Anglican Church, distinguished by its maintenance of sacerdotal claims and assertions of the efficacy of the sacraments.

High days. Festivals. **On high days and holidays.** Here "high" means grand or great.

High falutin. Oratorical bombast, affected pomposity, tall talk. The word is perhaps a variant of *high-flown*.

High seas. All the sea which is not the property of a particular country. The sea up to three miles out from the coast belongs to the country, and is called "territorial waters." High seas, like high-ways, means for public use. In both cases the word *high* means "chief," "principal."

High tea. A meal served about the usual teatime which includes besides tea, fish, cold meats, pastry, etc. It is common in Scotland and the North of England, and generally in agricultural communities.

A well understood "high tea" should have cold roast beef at the top of the table, a cold Yorkshire pie at the bottom, a mighty ham in the middle. The side dishes

will comprise soused mackerel, pickled salmon (in due season), sausages and potatoes, etc., etc. Rivers of tea, coffee, and ale, with dry and buttered toast, sally-lunns, scones, muffins and crumpets, jams and marmalade.—
Daily Telegraph, May 9th, 1893.

High words. Angry words.

Highgate. A North London suburb, so called from a gate set up there about 400 years ago to receive tolls for the bishop of London, when the old miry road from Gray's Inn Lane to Barnet was turned through the bishop's park. The village being perched on a hill explains the first part of the name.

Highlands. That part of Scotland lying north of the line approximately Dumbarton to Stonehaven. Stirling is known as "the gateway to the Highlands"; in the wars between Scotland and England, in possession of this strong point carried immense advantage.

Highland Mary. The most shadowy of Robert Burns's sweethearts, but the one to whom he addressed some of his finest poetry, including "My Highland Lassie, O," "Highland Mary" ("Ye banks and braes and streams around the castle o' Montgomery"), "Thou Ling'ring Star," and—perhaps—"Will ye go to the Indies, my Mary?"

She is said to have been a daughter of Archibald Campbell, a Clyde sailor, and to have died young about 1784 or 1786.

Highness. A title of honour (used with a possessive pronoun) given to royalties and a few others of exalted rank. In England the title *Royal Highness* was formerly given to the Sovereign, his consort, his sons and daughters, brothers and sisters, paternal uncles and aunts, grandsons and granddaughters being the children of sons, and great-grandchildren being the children of an eldest son of any Prince of Wales; but by the proclamation of June 17th, 1917 (when the style, the House of Windsor, was adopted), the title *Royal Highness* was confined in future to children of the Sovereign and to grandchildren in the male line.

James I was the first King of England to be styled "Your Royal Highness"; Oliver Cromwell and his wife were both called "Your Highness."

Serene Highness was a title of many of the members of the former German Imperial, Royal, and Ducal Houses.

Hijacker (hī' jăk ėr). In American slang a bandit who preys on such criminals as bootleggers by robbing them of their ill-gotten booty; a parasite on rogues.

Hike. To hike is an old English dialect word meaning to walk a long distance; it is now used in the sense of going on a cross-country tramp organized by a club or undertaken by a smaller party of two or three.

To hitch-hike is to travel from one place to another by getting lifts from cars and lorries.

Hilary Term (hil' à ri), in the Law Courts, begins on the day after Plough Monday (*q.v.*) and ends the Wednesday before Easter. It is so called in honour of St. Hilary, whose day is January 13th.

Hildebrand (hil' de brănd). The Nestor of German romance. His story is told in the *Hildebrandslied*, an Old High German poem, and he also appears in the *Nibelungenlied*, *Dietrich von Bern*, etc. Like Maugis among the heroes of Charlemagne, he was a magician as well as champion.

The name is, however, more commonly associated with the great pope St. Gregory VII (*c.* 1020-85) who was elected to the papal chair in 1073. He curbed the temporal power and reformed the Church from top to bottom, enforced celibacy among the clergy, put down simony, and promoted piety. His uncompromising forcefulness made him many enemies and gained him few friends. He was canonized in 1728, his feast day being May 25th.

Hill. Hill-billy, an American phrase descriptive of a countryman from the hilly or mountainous districts. The hill-billy is a distinctive type, whose music and literature are being increasingly studied.

Hill folk. So Scott calls the Cameronian Scottish Covenanters, who met clandestinely among the hills. Sometimes the Covenanters generally are so called.

A class of beings in Scandinavian tradition between the elves and the human race were known as "hill folk" or "hill people." They were supposed to dwell in caves and small hills, and to be bent on receiving the benefits of man's redemption.

Hills. Prayers were offered on the tops of high hills, and temples built on "high places," from the notion that the gods could better hear prayers on such places, as they were nearer heaven. It will be remembered that Balak (*Num.* xxiii, xxiv) took Balaam to the top of Peor and other high places when Balaam wished to consult God. We often read of "idols on every high hill" (*Ezek.* vi, 13). *Cp.* HIGH PLACES.

Old as the hills. Very old indeed.

Hind. Emblematic of St. Giles, because "a heaven-directed hind went daily to give him milk in the desert, near the mouth of the Rhone." *Cp.* HART.

The hind of Sertorius. Sertorius was invited by the Lusitanians to defend them against the Romans. He had a tame white hind, which he taught to follow him, and from which he pretended to receive the instructions of Diana. By this artifice, says Plutarch, he imposed on the superstition of the people.

The milk-white hind, in Dryden's *Hind and the Panther,* means the Roman Catholic Church, milk-white because "infallible." The panther, full of the spots of error, is the Church of England.

Without unspotted, innocent within,
She feared no danger, for she knew no sin.
Part i, 3, 4.

Hindustan (hin doo stań). India; properly, the country watered by the river Indus, *i.e.* the country known by the ancients as "India." From Pers. *hindu,* water, *stan,* district or region. The suffix is common in the East, as Afghanistan, Baluchistan, Gulistan (the district of roses), Kafiristan (the country of the unbelievers), etc. *See* INDIA.

Hindustan Regiment. *See* REGIMENTAL NICKNAMES.

Hinny. *See* MULE.

Hipped. Melancholy, low-spirited, suffering from a "fit of the blues." **The hip** was formerly a common expression for morbid depression (now superseded by *the pip*); it is an abbreviation of *hypochondria.*

Hip! Hip! Hurrah! The old fanciful explanation of the origin of this cry is that *hip* is a notarikon (*q.v.*), composed of the initials *Hierosolyma est Perdita,* and that when the German knights headed a Jew-hunt in the Middle Ages, they ran shouting "Hip! Hip!" as much as to say "Jerusalem is destroyed."

Hurrah (*q.v.*) was derived from Slavonic *hu-raj* (to Paradise), so that *Hip! hip! hurrah!* would mean "Jerusalem is lost to the infidel, and we are on the road to Paradise." These etymons may be taken for what they are worth! The older English form of this cry was Huzza!

Hippocampus (hip' ō kăm' pŭs) (Gr. *hippos,* horse; *kampos,* sea monster). A seahorse, having the head and forequarters resembling those of a horse, with the tail and hindquarters of a fish or dolphin. It was the steed of Neptune (*q.v.*).

Hippocras (hip' ō krăs). A cordial of the late Middle Ages and down to Stuart times made of Lisbon and Canary wines, bruised spices, and sugar; so called from being passed through Hippocrates' sleeve (*q.v.*).

When these [*i.e.* other wines] have had their course which nature yeeldeth, sundrie sorts of artificial stuffe as ypocras and wormewood wine, must in like maner succeed in their turnes. —*Harrison's Description of England,* II, vi (1577).

Hippocrates (hip ok' rà tēz). A Greek physician who lived from *c.* 460-377 B.C., and is commonly called the Father of Medicine. He was member of the famous family of priest-physicians, the Asclepiadae, and was an acute and indefatigable observer, practising as both physician and surgeon. More than seventy of his essays are extant. In the Middle Ages he was called "Ypocras" or "Hippocras." Thus:

Well knew he the old Esculapius,
And Deiscorides, and eek Rufus,
Old Ypocras, Haly, and Galien.
CHAUCER: *Canterbury Tales* (*Prologue,* 431).

Hippocrates' sleeve. A woollen bag of a square piece of flannel, having the opposite corners joined, so as to make it triangular. Used by chemists for straining syrups, decoctions, etc., and anciently by vintners, whence the name of Hippocras (*q.v.*).

Hippocratic oath. A code of ethics governing the profession and sworn to by physicians upon taking a doctor's degree. The oath relates particularly to the inviolability of secrecy concerning any communication made by a patient in the course of consultation, and enjoins the absolute integrity essential in dealing with problems arising from a patient's confession or revelation.

Hippogriff (hip' ō grif) (Gr. *hippos,* a horse; *gryphos,* a griffin). The winged horse, whose father was a griffin and mother a filly. A symbol of love (Ariosto: *Orlando Furioso,* iv, 18, 19).

So saying, he caught him up, and without wing
Of hippogrif, bore through the air sublime,
Over the wilderness and o'er the plain.
MILTON: *Paradise Regained,* iv, 541-3.

Hippolyta (hip ol' i tà). Queen of the Amazons, and daughter of Mars. Shakespeare has introduced the character in his *A Midsummer Night's Dream,* where he betroths her to Theseus, Duke of Athens. In classic fable it is her sister Antiope who married Theseus, although some writers justify Shakespeare's account. Hippolyta was famous for a girdle given her by her father, and it was one of the twelve labours of Hercules to possess himself of this prize.

Hippolytus (hip ol' it ŭs). Son of Theseus, King of Athens. He was dragged to death by wild horses, and restored to life by Esculapius.

Hippomenes (hip om' en ēz). The name given in Bœotian legend to the Greek prince who ran a race with Atalanta (q.v.) for her hand in marriage. He had three golden apples, which he dropped one by one, and which the lady stopped to pick up. By this delay she lost the race.

Hiroshima (hi rō shē′ mȧ), a Japanese army base and a city of 343,000 inhabitants, was the target of the first atomic bomb to be dropped in warfare, August 6th, 1945. The flash of the explosion was seen 170 miles away, and a column of black smoke rose over the city to a height of 40,000 feet. The entire business section of Hiroshima disappeared, 60,000 persons were killed, 100,000 injured, and twice that number made homeless.

Hispania (his păn′ yȧ). Spain. So called from the Phænician word *Sapan*, or *Span*, the skin of the marten (or perhaps rabbit), which was procured from Spain in great quantities.

Hispaniola (his păn yō′ lȧ), the old name for the island of Haiti. When Columbus discovered the island on his first voyage, 1492, he named it Española, or Little Spain, which in the maps was Latinized as above. It was not until 1844, when the island was divided politically into Haiti and the Dominican Republic, that the old name completely disappeared.

History. The Father of History. Herodotus, the Greek historian (5th cent. B.C.). So called by Cicero.

The Father of Ecclesiastical History. Euse-bius of Cæsarea (about 264-340):

Father of French History. André Duchesne (1584-1640).

Father of Historic Painting. Polygnotus of Thaos (fl. 463-435. B.C.)

Happy is the nation that has no history. *See* HAPPY.

Histrionic, pertaining to the drama or to theatrical matters, is from the Lat. *histrio*, a stage-player. *History* is quite another word, being the Greek *historia*, *histor*, a judge, allied to *histamai*, to know.

Hit. A great hit. A piece of good luck. From the game *hit and miss*, or the game of backgammon, where "two hits equal a gammon."

To hit it off. To describe a thing tersely and epigrammatically; to make a sketch truthfully and quickly.

To hit it off together. To agree together, or suit each other.

To hit the nail on the head. *See* HEAD.

To make a hit. To meet with great approval; to succeed unexpectedly in an adventure or speculation.

Hitch. Hitch your wagon to a star. Aim high; don't be content with low aspirations.

The phrase is from Emerson's essay *Civilization*. Young expressed much the same idea in his *Night Thoughts* (viii): —

Too low they build who build beneath the stars.

There is some hitch. Some impediment. A horse is said to have a hitch in his gait when he is lame.

Hitlerism, a generic term for the whole doctrine and practice of Fascism, exemplified in the regime of Adolf Hitler (1889-1945).

Hittites built up one of the ancient civilizations of the world. Little is known of their origin; they first appear in eastern Asia Minor where their superior knowledge of implements and weapons of the early copper-age culture enabled them to master all their foes. They also bred and harnessed the horse—one of the earliest people to do so. The Hittites were well established by the 3rd millennium B.C.; they overturned the first dynasty of Babylon in 1925 B.C. and in one form or another flourished until about 700 B.C. when Carchemish, their main city fell to the Assyrians.

Hoarstone. A stone marking out the boundary of an estate, properly an old, grey, lichen-covered stone. They are also called "Hour-stones" and (in Scotland) "Hare Stanes," and have been erroneously taken for Druidical remains.

Hob and nob. *See* HOB-NOB.

Hobble Skirts. This women's fashion of skirts so tight round the ankles that the wearer was impeded in walking—much as a horse is hobbled—was at its height in 1912 and was gone by 1914.

Hobby. A favourite pursuit; a personal pastime that interests or amuses one.

There are two words *hobby*, and they are apt to be confused. The earlier, meaning a medium-sized horse, is the M.E. *hobyn* (*cp.* *Dobbin* as a name for a horse), the later, a small species of falcon, is the O.F. *hobé* or *hobet*, from **Lat.** *hobetus*, a falcon. It is from the first that our "hobby," a pursuit, comes. It is through **hobby-horse**, a light frame of wickerwork, appropriately draped, in which someone performed ridiculous gambols in the old morris dances, and later applied to a child's plaything consisting of a stick across which he straddled, with a horse's head on one end.

To ride a hobby-horse was to play an infantile game of which one soon tired; and now implies to dwell to excess on a pet theory; the transition is shown in a sentence in one of Wesley's sermons (No. lxxxiii): —

Every one has (to use the cant term of the day) his hobby-horse!

Hobgoblin (hob gob′ lin). An impish, ugly, and mischievous sprite, particularly Puck or Robin Goodfellow (*q.v.*). The word is a variant of *Rob-Goblin—i.e.* the goblin Robin, just as Hodge is the nickname of Roger.

> Those that Hobgoblin call you, and sweet Puck,
> You do their work, and they shall have good luck.
> *A Midsummer Night's Dream*, ii, 1.

Hob-nob. A corruption of *hab nab*, meaning "have or not have," hence hit or miss, at random; and, secondarily, give or take, whence also an open defiance.

> The citizens in their rage shot habbe or nabbe [hit or miss] at random.—HOLINSHED: *History of Ireland*.
> He writes of the weather hab nab and as the toy takes him, chequers the year with foul and fair.—*Quack Astrologer* (1673).
> He is a devil in private brawls . . . hob nob is his word, give 't or take 't.—*Twelfth Night*, iii, 4.
> Not of Jack Straw, with his rebellious crew,
> That set king, realm and laws at hab or nab [defiance].
> SIR J. HARINGTON: *Epigram*, iv.

To hobnob or **hob and nob together.** To be on intimate terms of good-fellowship, hold close and friendly conversation with, etc.; especially to drink together as cronies—probably with the meaning of "give and take."

> "Have another glass!" "With you Hob and nob," returned the sergeant. "The top of mine to the foot of yours—the foot of yours to the top of mine—Ring once, ring twice—the best tune on the Musical Glasses! Your health."—DICKENS: *Great Expectations*, ch. v.

Hobo (hō′ bō). Late-19th-century American for a tramp, vagrant.

Hock. German white wine, so called from Hockheim, on the River Main. It used to be called hoccamore.

> Restored the fainting high and mighty
> With brandy, wine, and aqua-vitæ;
> And made 'em stoutly overcome
> With Bacrack, Hoccamore, and Mum.
> BUTLER: *Hudibras*, III, iii, 297.

The earlier English name was *Rhenish*.

There are several colloquial uses of this word hock. In American slang **to hock** is to pawn and a **hock-shop** a pawnbroker's.

Hockey cake. The cake given out to the harvesters when the hock cart (*q.v.*) reached home. *Hockey* is the old name in the eastern counties for the harvest-home feast.

Hock-day or **Hock Tuesday.** The second Tuesday after Easter Day, long held as a festival in England; it was the time for paying church dues, and landlords received an annual tribute called **Hock-money**, for allowing their tenants and serfs to commemorate it. Its origin is unknown; but the old idea that it commemorates the massacre of the Danes in 1002 does not seem to be tenable, as this took place in November.

> Hoke Monday was for the men and Hock Tuesday for the women. On both days the men and women alternately, with great merryment, obstructed the public road with ropes, and pulled passengers to them, from whom they exacted money to be laid out in pious uses.—BRAND: *Antiquities*, vol. i, p. 187.

Hockey. A game of Indian origin in which each player has a hooked stick with which to strike the ball. Hockey is simply the diminutive of *hook*.

Hocus Pocus (hō′ kŭs pō′ kŭs). The words formerly uttered by conjurers when performing a trick; hence the trick or deception itself, also the juggler himself.

The phrase dates from the early 17th century, and is the opening of a ridiculous string of mock Latin used by some well-known performer (*Hocus pocus, toutus talontus, vade celerita jubes*), the first two words of which may have been intended as a parody of *Hoc est corpus*, the words of consecration in the Mass, while the whole was reeled off merely to occupy the attention of the audience.

Our word *hoax* is probably a contraction of *hocus pocus*, which also supplies the verb *to hocus*, to cheat, bamboozle, tamper with.

Hodge-podge. A medley, a mixed dish of "bits and pieces all cooked together." The word is a corruption of *hotch-pot* (*q.v.*).

Hoe-cake (U.S.A.). Flat cake originally baked on a hoe held over a coal fire.

Hog. Properly a male swine, castrated, and—as it is raised solely for slaughter—killed young. The origin of the word is not certain, but it may originally have referred to age more than to any specific animal. Thus, boars of the second year, sheep between the time of their being weaned and shorn, colts, and bullocks a year old, were all called *hogs* or *hoggets*, which name was specially applied to a sheep after its first shearing. A boar three years old is a "hog-steer."

In slang use a *hog* is a gluttonous, greedy, or unmannered person; motorists who, caring nothing for the rights or convenience of other travellers, drive in a selfish and reckless manner wanting the whole road to themselves are called *road-hogs*.

To go the whole hog. To do the thing completely and thoroughly, without compromise or reservation; to go the whole way. William Cowper says (*Hypocrisy Detected*, 1779) that the Moslem divines sought to ascertain which part of the hog was forbidden as food by the Prophet. Unable to come to a decision, each thought excepted the portion of the meat he most preferred, and as the tastes of the worthy imams differed:

> The conscience freed from every clog.
> Mohammedans eat up the hog.

A more probable origin of the phrase is that a *hog* was old slang for a shilling—*to go the whole hog* was to spend the whole shilling at one go, to spare nothing.

Formerly, any small silver coin, a shilling or sixpence, or (in the U.S.A.) a ten-cent piece, was contemptuously styled a *hog*.

In U.S.A. the phrase came into popularity during Andrew Jackson's campaign for the Presidency, in 1828. Hence the expression *whole-hogger*, one who will see the thing through to the bitter end, and "damn the consequences." At the time of Joseph Chamberlain's agitation on behalf of Protection (1903, *et seq.*) those who advocated a complete tariff of protective duties regardless of possible reciprocity were called the *whole-hoggers*.

Hogen Mogen (hō′ gen mō′ gen). Holland or the Netherlands; so called from *Hooge en Mogende* (high and mighty), the Dutch style of addressing the States-General.

> But I have sent him for a token
>   To your low country Hogen-Mogen.
>   BUTLER: *Hudibras*, III, i, 1440.

Hogmanay (hog mà nā′). The name given in Scotland to the last day of the year, also to an entertainment or present given on that day. It is from the French, and probably represents the O.Fr. *aiguillanneuf*, which has been (somewhat doubtfully) explained as standing for *au guy l'an neuf*, "(good luck) to the mistletoe of the new year."

It is still the custom in parts of Scotland for persons to go from door to door on New Year's Eve asking in rude rhymes for cakes or money; and in Galloway the chief features are "taking the cream off the water," wonderful luck being attached to a draught thereof; and "the first foot" (*q.v.*) or giving something to drink to the first person who enters the house.

Hogshead. A large cask containing approximately 52½ gallons; also, the measure of this, apart from the cask. The word dates from the 14th century and is composed of *hog* and *head*, and not of *ox* and *hide*, or of any of the other fancy etymologies that have been proposed. The reason for the name is obscure; but *cp.* the name of a Low German measure for beer, *bullenkop*, bull's head.

Hoi Polloi (hoi pol′ oi) (Gr., the many). The masses of the people, the majority.

> If by the people you understand the multitude, the *hoi polloi*, 'tis no matter what they think; they are sometimes

in the right, sometimes in the wrong; their judgment is a mere lottery.—DRYDEN: *Essay on Dramatic Poesy* (1668).

At the Universities the poll-men, *i.e.* those who take a degree without honours, are colloquially known as the *hoi polloi*.

Hoity-toity. A reduplicated word (like *harum-scarum, mingle-mangle, hugger-mugger*, etc.), probably formed from the obsolete verb *hoit*, to romp about noisily. It is used as an adjective, meaning "stuck up," haughty, or petulant; as a noun, meaning a good romp or frolic; and as an interjection expressing disapproval or contempt of one's airs, assumptions, etc.

> "I do not speak on your account, Mrs. Honour" [said Mrs. Western's maid], "for you are a civilized young woman; and when you have seen a little more of the world, I should not be ashamed to walk with you in St. James Park." "Hoity toity!" cries Honour, "Madam is in her airs, I protest."—FIELDING: *Tom Jones*. Bk. vii, ch. viii.

See also the quotation from Selden given under CUSHION DANCE, where *hoyte-cum-toyte* is used of rowdy behaviour.

Hokey-pokey (hō′ ki pō′ ki), the name given to cheap ice-cream as sold in the street. The name comes from hocus-pocus (*q.v.*) but the connexion is not obvious. Also a ludicrous dance popular during the 1940s in English dance-halls.

Hokum (hō′ kùm), an American colloquialism (also deriving from hocus-pocus) for any device employed to create a poignant effect or stimulate easy sentimentality.

Holborn. This London name, originally that of the northern portion of the Fleet stream, is not a corruption of Old Bourne, as Stow asserts, but of Holeburne, the *burne* or stream in the *hole* or hollow. It is spelt Holeburne in *Domesday Book*, i, 127a; and in documents connected with the nunnery of St. Mary, Clerkenwell (during the reign of Richard II).

Hold. Hold hard! Stop; go easy; keep a firm hold, seat, or footing, as there is danger else of being overthrown. A caution given when a sudden change of *vis inertiæ* is about to occur.

Hold off! Keep at a distance.

Hold the fort! Maintain your position at all costs. Immortalized as a phrase from its use by General Sherman, who signalled it to General Corse from the top of Kenesaw in 1864 during the American Civil War.

To cry hold. To give the order to stop; in the old tournaments, when the umpires wished to stop the contest they cried out "Hold!"

> Lay on Macduff,
> And damn'd be him that first cries, "Hold, enough!"
>   *Macbeth*, v, 8.

To hold the candle to one, a candle to the devil. *See* CANDLE.

To hold forth. To speak in public; to harangue; to declaim. An author holds forth certain opinions or ideas in his book, *i.e.* exhibits them or holds them out to view. A speaker does the same in an oratorical display.

Hold your horses! Be patient, wait a moment; hold up for a while whatever you are doing.

To hold good. To be valid, or applicable. We say "such and such a proverb is very true, but it does not hold good in every case," *i.e.* it does not always apply.

To hold in. To restrain. The allusion is to horses reined up tightly.

To hold in esteem. To regard with esteem.

To hold one in hand or **in play.** To divert one's attention, or to amuse in order to get some advantage.

To hold one's own. To maintain one's own opinion, position, way, etc.

To hold one's tongue. To keep silence. In Coverdale's Bible (1535), where the Authorized Version has "But Jesus held his peace" (*Matt.* xxvi, 63) the reading is "Jesus helde his tonge."

To hold out. To endure, persist; not to succumb.

To hold over. To keep back, retain in reserve, defer.

To hold up. To stop, as a highwayman does, with the object of robbing. In this connexion the order, "Hold up your hands!" or "Hold 'em up!" means that the victim must hold them above his head to make sure that he is not reaching for a weapon.

To hold water. To bear close inspection; to endure a trial; generally used negatively, as "That statement of yours won't hold water," *i.e.* it will prove false as soon as it is examined. A vessel that will hold water is sound.

Hole. A better 'ole. Any situation that is preferable to that occupied at present. The phrase dates from World War I when it originated from a drawing by the humorist Bruce Bairnsfather, depicting "Old Bill" taking cover in a wet and muddy shell-hole and rebutting the complaints of his companion with the remark "If you know a better 'ole, go to it."

Fox-hole. World War II. A phrase of U.S.A. origin for a small slit-trench to hold one man.

In a hole. In an awkward predicament; in a difficulty or a position from which it is not easy to extricate oneself.

Holger Danske (hoi' ger dăn' sk ė). The national hero of Denmark. *See* OGIER THE DANE.

Holiday. Give the boys a holiday. This custom of marking some specially noteworthy event is of great antiquity; it is said that Anaxagoras, on his death-bed, being asked what honour should be conferred upon him, replied, "Give the boys a holiday."

Holiday speeches. Fine or well-turned speeches or phrases; complimentary speeches. We have also "holiday manners," "holiday clothes," meaning the best we have.

> With many holiday and lady terms
> He questioned me.
> 1 *Henry IV*, i, 3.

Holland. The country gets its name from the well-wooded (*holt*, wood) land around Dordrecht, to which it was originally applied; the district in South Lincolnshire is called "Holland" from *holl* (*adj.*), lying in a hollow, *i.e.* low-lying land.

Holland, the cloth, is so called because it was originally manufactured in, and imported from, Holland; its full name was *holland cloth*.

Hollands, or properly **Hollands gin,** is the Dut. *Hollandsch geneveer*.

Hollow. I beat him hollow. Completely, thoroughly. *Hollow* is, perhaps, here a corruption of *wholly*.

Holly. The custom of decking the interiors of churches and houses with holly at Christmastime is of great antiquity, and was probably employed by the early Christians at Rome in imitation of its use by the Romans in the great festival of the Saturnalia, which occurred at the same season of the year.

Hollyhock is the A.S. *holihoc*, the *holy mallow*, *i.e.* the marsh-mallow. It is a mistake to derive the second syllable from *oak*.

Holmes. *See* SHERLOCK HOLMES.

Holy. Holy Alliance. A league formed by Russia, Austria, and Prussia in 1815 to regulate the affairs of Europe after the fall of Napoleon "by the principles of Christian charity"—meaning that every endeavour would be made to stabilize the existing dynasties and to resist all change. It lasted until 1830, and was joined by all the European sovereigns except George III, the Sultan of Turkey and the Pope.

Holy Boys, The. *See* REGIMENTAL NICKNAMES.

Holy City. That city which the religious consider most especially connected with their faith, thus:

> *Allahabad* is the Holy City of the Moslems of India.
> *Benares* of the Hindus.

Cuzco of the ancient Incas.

Fez of the Western Arabs.

Jerusalem of the Jews and Christians.

Kairwan, near Tunis contains the Okbar Mosque in which is the tomb of the prophet's barber.

Mecca and *Medina* as the places of the birth and burial of Mohammed.

Moscow and *Kief* of the Russians, the latter being the cradle of Christianity in Russia.

Holy Coat. *See* TRÈVES.

Holy Cross (or **Holy Rood**) **Day.** September 14th, the day of the Feast of the Exaltation of the Cross, called by the Anglo-Saxons "Rood-mass-day," commemorating the return of the true Cross to Jerusalem by the Emperor Heraclius in 627, after retaking it from the Persians who had carried it off thirteen years before.

It was on this day that the Jews in Rome used to be compelled to go to church, and listen to a sermon—a custom done away with about 1840 by Pope Gregory XVI. *See* Browning's *Holy Cross Day* (1855).

Holy Family. The infant Saviour and his attendants, as Joseph, Mary, Elizabeth, Anne the mother of Mary, and John the Baptist. All five figures are not always introduced in pictures of the "Holy Family."

Holy Ghost, The. The third Person of the Trinity, the Divine Spirit; represented in art as a dove.

The seven gifts of the Holy Ghost are: (1) counsel, (2) the fear of the Lord, (3) fortitude, (4) piety, (5) understanding, (6) wisdom, and (7) knowledge.

Holy Land, The.

(1) Christians call Palestine the Holy Land, because it was the site of Christ's birth, ministry, and death.

(2) Mohammedans call Mecca the Holy Land, because Mohammed was born there.

(3) The Chinese Buddhists call India the Holy Land, because it was the native land of Sakya-muni, the Buddha (*q.v.*).

(4) The Greeks considered Elis as Holy Land, from the temple of Olympian Zeus and the sacred festival held there every four years.

Holy League, The. A combination formed by Pope Julius II in 1511 with Venice, Maximilian of Germany, Ferdinand III of Spain, and various Italian princes, to drive the French out of Italy.

Other leagues have been called by the same name, particularly that formed in the reign of Henri III of France (1576), under the auspices of Henri de Guise, "for the defence of the Holy Catholic Church against the encroachments of the reformers," *i.e.* for annihilating the Huguenots.

Holy Maid of Kent, The. Elizabeth Barton (*c.* 1506-34) who incited the Roman Catholics to resist the Reformation, and imagined that she acted under inspiration. Having announced the doom and speedy death of Henry VIII for his marriage with Anne Boleyn, she was hanged at Tyburn in 1534.

Holy Office, The. *See* INQUISITION.

Holy of Holies. The innermost apartment of the Jewish temple, in which the ark of the covenant was kept, and into which only the high priest was allowed to enter, and that but once a year on the Day of Atonement. Hence, a private apartment, a *sanctum sanctorum* (*q.v.*).

Holy Roman Empire, The. The name given to the confederation of Central European States that subsisted, either in fact or in theory, from A.D. 800, when Charlemagne was crowned Emperor of the West, until 1806. It was first called "Holy" by Barbarossa, in allusion both to its reputed divine appointment, and to the inter-dependence of Empire and Church; it comprised the German-speaking peoples of Central Europe, and was ruled by an elected Emperor, who claimed to be the representative of the ancient Roman Emperors.

After the defeat of Austerlitz the Habsburg Emperor lost even the semblance of authority over the greater part of the Empire, and the constitution of this ancient estate ceased to exist even in name. At Napoleon's bidding Francis II published an Act (1806) declaring himself Emperor of Austria and abdicating from the throne of an outworn and dishonoured fiction—the Holy Roman Empire—which was justly stigmatized by a contemporary as being neither Holy, nor Roman, nor an Empire.

Holy Rood Day. *See* HOLY CROSS DAY.

Holy Thursday. An old name in England for Ascension Day (*q.v.*), *i.e.* the Thursday but one before Whitsun. By Roman Catholics and others Maundy Thursday (*q.v.*), *i.e.* the Thursday before Good Friday, is called "Holy Thursday." *See also* IN CÆNA DOMINI.

Holy Saturday. *See* HOLY WEEK.

Holy War. A war in which religious fanaticism plays, or purports to play, a considerable part. The Crusades, the Thirty Years War, the wars against the Albigenses, etc., were so called.

The *Jehad* or Holy War of the Moslems, is a call to the whole Islamic world to take arms against the Unbelievers.

John Bunyan's *Holy War,* published in 1682, tells the story of the assault of the armies of

Satan against the citadel of Mansoul; despite many excellences it lacks the spontaneity and naivety of *Pilgrim's Progress*.

Holy Water. Water blessed by a priest or bishop for sacramental purposes. Its principal use is at the *Asperges*, or aspersing of the congregation before High Mass, but it is employed in nearly every blessing which the Church gives.

Holy Week. The last week in Lent. It begins on Palm Sunday; the fourth day is called "Spy Wednesday" (an allusion to Judas Iscariot's spying on Jesus preparatory to betraying him); the fifth is "Maundy Thursday" (*q.v.*); the sixth is "Good Friday"; and the last "Holy Saturday" or the "Great Sabbath."

Holy Week has been called *Hebdomada Muta* (Silent Week); *Hebdomada Inofficiosa* (Vacant Week); *Hebdomada Penitentialis*; *Hebdomada Indulgentiæ*; *Hebdomada Luctuosa*; *Hebdomada Nigra*; and *Hebdomada Ultima*.

Holy Writ. The Bible.

> Trifles light as air
> Are to the jealous confirmations strong
> As proofs of holy writ.
>   *Othello*, III, 3.

Homburg. A soft felt hat popularized by Edward VII. It was originally made in Homburg in Prussia where the King "took the waters."

Home. At home. At one's own house and prepared to receive visitors. An *at home* is a more or less informal reception for which arrangements have been made. *To be at home to somebody* is to be ready and willing to receive him; *to be at home with a subject* is to be familiar with it, quite conversant with it.

Home, sweet home. This popular English song first appeared in the opera *Clari, the Maid of Milan* (Covent Garden, 1823). The words were by John Howard Payne (an American), and the music by Sir Henry Bishop, who professed to have founded it on a Sicilian air.

One's long home. The grave.

Man goeth to his long home, and the mourners go about the streets.—*Eccles.* xii, 5.

To come home to one. To reach one's heart; to become thoroughly understood or realized.

I doe now publish my Essayes; which, of all my other workes, have been most Currant: For that, as it seems they come home, to Mens Businesse, and Bosomes.—BACON: *Epistle Dedicatorie to the "Essayes"* (1625).

To come home to roost. Usually said of a lie, fault, hidden sin, etc., which eventually rebounds to the discomfiture of its originator.

To make oneself at home. To dispense with ceremony in another person's house, to act as though one were at home.

Homer (hō' mèr). The name given to the entirely unknown poet—or group of poets

perhaps—to whom is assigned the authorship of the *Iliad* (*q.v.*) and the *Odyssey* (*q.v.*), the greatest monuments of ancient or modern epic poetry.

Some writers have considered Homer to have been a mythical figure, but modern scholarship tends to regard the epics as actually the work of a blind poet Homer who lived some time between 1200 and 850 B.C.

No doubt was ever entertained by the ancients respecting the personality of Homer. Pindar, Aristotle, Plato, and others, all assumed this fact; nor did they even doubt that the *Iliad* and *Odyssey* were the work of one mind.—R. W. BROWNE: *Historical Classical Literature*.

Homer's birthplace is unknown. The old rhyme, founded on an epigram preserved by Aulus Gellius, says:—

> Seven cities warred for Homer being dead,
> Who living had no roof to shroud his head.
>   HEYWOOD: *Hierarchie of the Blessed Angels* (1635).

the "seven cities" being Smyrna, Rhodes, Colophon, Salamis, Chios, Argos, and Athens. *See* SCIO'S.

Among the many names and epithets that have been bestowed on him are Melesigenes the Man of Chios (*see* CHIOS); the Blind Old Man; and Mæonides (*q.v.*). He is spoken of as *Mæonius senex*, and his poems as *Mæoniæ chartæ* or *Mæonia carmina*.

Milton has been called the English Homer, Ossian the Gaelic Homer, Plato the Homer of philosophers; Byron called Fielding the prose Homer of human nature; and Dryden (*Essay on Dramatic Poesy*) says:—

Shakespeare was the Homer, or father of our dramatic poets; Jonson was the Virgil, the pattern of elaborate writing; I admire him but I love Shakespeare.

Homœopathy (hō mi op' à thi) (Gr. *homoios pathos*, like disease). The plan of curing a disease by minute doses of a medicine which would in healthy persons produce the disease. The theory was first formulated and practised by Samuel Hahnemann (1755-1843), a German physician.

Honey. An expression of endearment (with allusion to sweetness), formerly common, but now largely confined to the North of England.

> Him thinketh verraily that he may see
> Noë's flood come walwing as the see
> To drenchen Alisoun, his hony dere.
>   CHAUCER: *Miller's Tale*, 429.

Honeydew. A sweet substance found on the leaves of lime-trees and some other plants. Bees and ants are fond of it. It is probably the excretion of the aphis, and gets its popular name from its great sweetness coupled with its dew-like appearance.

> Some framed faire lookes, glancing like evening lights,
> Others sweet words, dropping like honny dew.
>   SPENSER : *Faerie Queene*, II, v, 33.

Honeymoon. The first month after marriage, especially that part of it spent away from home. It appears to have been an ancient custom to drink a dilution of honey for thirty days after marriage—*i.e.* a moon's age, hence the name. Attila is said to have drunk so liberally of this potion that he died of suffocation in A.D. 453.

Honeysuckle. *See* MISNOMERS.

Hong Merchants. Those Chinese merchants who, under licence from the government of China, held the monopoly of trade with Europeans until 1842, when the restriction was abolished by the Treaty of Nanking. The Chinese applied the word *hong* to the foreign factories situated at Canton.

Honi soit qui mal y pense (on' ē swa kē măl ē pons). The motto of the Most Noble Order of the Garter (*q.v.*). The common rendering of the motto as "Evil be to him who evil thinks" has little meaning. A better rendering is, "Shame to him who thinks evil of it."

Honky-tonk (hong' ki tongk), an American slang term for a brothel, a disreputable nightclub or low roadhouse.

Honour. In feudal law, a superior seigniory, on which other lordships or manors depended by the performance of customary services. At bridge, the *honours* are the five highest trump cards—ace, king, queen, knave, and ten.

An affair of honour. A dispute to be settled by a duel. Duels were generally provoked by offences against the arbitrary rules of etiquette, courtesy, or feeling, called the laws "of honour"; and, as these offences were not recognizable in the law courts, they were settled by private combat.

Debts of honour. Debts contracted by betting or gambling, so called because these debts cannot be enforced as such by law.

Honours of war. The privilege allowed to an enemy, on capitulation, of being permitted to retain his offensive arms. This is the highest honour a victor can pay a vanquished foe. Sometimes the troops so treated are allowed to march with all their arms, drums beating, and colours flying.

Laws of honour. Certain arbitrary rules which the fashionable world tacitly admits; they wholly regard deportment, and have nothing to do with moral offences. Breaches of this code are punished by expulsion or suspension from society, "sending to Coventry" (*q.v.*).

Legion of Honour. *See* LEGION.

Point of honour. An obligation which is binding because its violation would offend some conscientious scruple or notion of self-respect.

Word of honour. A gage which cannot be violated without placing the breaker of it beyond the pale of respectability and good society.

Honourable. A title of honour accorded in the United Kingdom to the younger sons of earls and the children of viscounts, of barons and life peers, to maids of honour, the Lord Provost of Glasgow, justices of the High Court except lords justices and justices of appeal. In the House of Commons one member speaks of another as "the honourable member for—". In U.S.A. *honourable* is a courtesy title applied to persons of distinction in legal or civic life. *See also* RIGHT HONOURABLE.

Hooch, an American slang term for whisky or crude raw spirits, often made surreptitiously or obtained illegally. The word comes from the Alaskan Indian *hoochinoo*, a crude distilled liquor.

Hood. The hood (or cowl) **does not make the monk.** It is a man's way of life, not what he professes to be, that really matters; from the Latin *Cueullus non facit monachum.*

> *Escalus:* Signior Lucio, did not you say you knew that Friar Lodowick to be a dishonest person?
> *Lucio: Cucullus non facit monachum:* honest in nothing, but in his clothes; and one that hath spoke most villainous speeches of the duke.—*Measure for Measure*, v, 1.

> They should be good men; their affairs are righteous
> But all hoods make not monks.
> *Henry VIII*, iii. 1.

The origin of the phrase is probably to be found in these lines from St. Anselm's *Carmen de Contemptu Mundi* (11th cent.):—

> Non tonsura facit monachum, non horrida vestis;
> Sed virtus animi, perpetuusque rigor.

Hood, Robin. *See* ROBIN HOOD.

Hoodlum (American slang). A rough hooligan. The word was originally confined to the particular variety native to San Francisco.

Hoo-doo, originating from Voodoo (*q.v.*), this term is applied to any person or object that is supposed to bring bad luck.

Hoo-ey, an exclamation of incredulity— nonsense! absurd!

Hook. Above your hook. Beyond your comprehension; beyond your mark. The allusion is perhaps to hat-pegs placed in rows, the higher rows being beyond the reach of small statures.

By hook or crook. Either rightfully or wrongfully; somehow; one way or another.

There is more than one attempted explanation of the phrase; it is probable, however, that it derives from an old manorial custom which authorized tenants to take as much firewood from the hedges, etc., as could be cut with a crook or bill-hook, and as much low timber as could be reached down from the boughs by a shepherd's crook.

> Dynmure Wood was ever open and common to the . . . inhabitants of Bodmin . . . to bear away upon their backs a burden of lop, crop, hook, crook, and bag wood.—*Bodmin Register* (1525).

He is off the hooks. Done for, laid on the shelf, superseded, dead. The bent pieces of iron on which the hinges of a gate rest and turn are called *hooks*.

Hook, line, and sinker. To swallow a tale, hook, line, and sinker is to be extremely gullible, like the hungry fish that swallows not only the baited hook, but the lead weight and some of the line as well.

Hooky. To play hooky is to play truant, especially from school.

Hooligan. A violent young rough. The term originated in the last years of the 19th century from the name of one of this class. From it is derived the substantive *hooliganism*.

> The original *Hooligans* were a spirited Irish family of that name whose proceedings enlivened the drab monotony of life in Southwark towards the end of the 19th century. The word is younger than the Australian *larrikin*, of doubtful origin, but older than Fr. *apache.*—ERNEST WEEKLEY: *Romance of Words* (1912).

Hooped Pots. Drinking pots at one time were marked with bands, or hoops, set at equal distances, so that when two or more drank from the same tankard no one should take more than his share. Jack Cade promises his followers that "seven halfpenny loaves shall be sold for a penny; the three-hooped pot shall have ten hoops; and I will make it felony to drink small beer." (2 *Henry VI*, iv, 2.)

> I beleeve hoopes in quart pots were invented to that ende, that every man should take his hoope, and no more.—NASH: *Pierce Pennilesse* (1592).

Hoosegow (hooz' gou), in American slang, a gaol. The word comes from the Mexican-Spanish *juzgado*, a court of justice.

Hoosier (hoo' zhér), an inhabitant of the State of Indiana, the Hoosier State. The origin of the name is now unknown, it is doubtless that of some forgotten local magnate or character.

Hope. *See* PANDORA'S BOX.

Thomas Campbell (1777-1844) was known as *The Bard of Hope*, on account of his poem, "The Pleasures of Hope" (1799).

Horace. The Roman lyric poet, born 65 B.C., died 8 B.C.

Horace of England. George, Duke of Buckingham, preposterously declared Cowley to be the Pindar, Horace, and Virgil of England.

Ben Jonson was nicknamed Horace by Dekker in the so-called "War of the Theatres."

Horace of France. Jean Macrinus or Salmon (1490-1557); and Pierre Jean de Béranger (1780-1857), also called the French Burns.

Horace of Spain. The brothers Lupercio (1559-1613) and Bartolme Argensola (1562-1631).

Horn. Astolpho's horn. Logistilla gave Astolpho at parting a horn that had the virtue of being able to appal and put to flight the boldest knight or most savage beast. (ARIOSTO: *Orlando Furioso*, Bk. viii.)

Cape Horn. So named by Schouten, a Dutch mariner, who first doubled it (1616). He was a native of Hoorn, in north Holland, and named the cape after his native place.

The Horn gate. *See* DREAMS, GATES OF.

Horn of fidelity. Morgan le Fay sent a horn to King Arthur, which had the following "virtue":—No lady could drink out of it who was not "to her husband true"; all others who attempted to drink were sure to spill what it contained. This horn was carried to King Mark, and "his queene with a hundred ladies more" tried the experiment, but only four managed to "drinke cleane." Ariosto's *enchanted cup* possessed a similar spell.

Horn of plenty. Amalthea's horn (*q.v.*), the cornucopia, an emblem of plenty.

Ceres is drawn with a ram's horn in her left arm, filled with fruits and flowers; sometimes they are being poured on the earth, and sometimes they are piled high in the horn as in a basket. Diodorus (iii, 68) says the horn is one from the head of the goat by which Jupiter was suckled.

King Horn. *See under* KING.

Moses' Horns. *See* MOSES.

Horn with horn or **horn under horn.** The promiscuous feeding of bulls and cows, or, in fact, all horned beasts that are allowed to run together on the same common.

The horns of a dilemma. *See* DILEMMA.

To come (or **be squeezed**) **out at the little end of the horn.** To come off badly in some affair; get the worst of it; fail conspicuously.

To draw in one's horns. To retrench, to curtail one's expenditure; to retract, or mitigate, a pronounced opinion; to restrain pride. The allusion is to the snail.

To the horns of the altar. *Usque ad aras amicus.* Your friend even to the horns of the altar—*i.e.* through thick and thin. In swearing, the ancient Romans held the horns of the altar, and one who did so in testimony of friendship could not break his oath without calling on himself the vengeance of the angry gods.

The altar in Solomon's temple had a projection at each of the four corners called "horns"; these were regarded as specially sacred, and probably typified the great might of God (*cp. above*).

To wear the horns. To be a cuckold. This old term is possibly connected with the chase. In the rutting season one stag selects several females, who constitute his harem, till another stag contests the prize with him. If beaten he is without associates till he finds a stag feebler than himself, who is made to submit to similar terms. As stags are horned, and have their mates taken from them by their fellows, the application is palpable.

Another explanation (*see* N.E.D.) is that it is due

to the practice formerly prevalent of planting or engrafting the spurs of a castrated cock on the root of the excised comb, where they grew and became horns, sometimes of several inches long.

In support of this it is noteworthy that *hahnrei*, the German equivalent for *cuckold*, originally signified a capon.

To show one's horns. To let one's evil intentions appear. The allusion, like that in "to show the cloven hoof," is to the Devil—"Old Hornie."

To take the bull by the horns. *See* BULL.

Auld Hornie. The devil, so called in Scotland. The allusion is to the horns with which Satan is generally represented.

O thou! whatever title suits thee,
Auld Hornie, Satan, Nick, or Clootie.
BURNS: *Address to the Deil.*

Horn-book. A thin board of oak about nine inches long and five or six wide, on which were printed the alphabet, the nine digits, and sometimes the Lord's Prayer, the Creed, and the Angelic Salutation. Horn-books were in use in elementary schools for the poor when books were scarce and expensive, and survived well into the 18th century. They had a handle, and were covered in front with a sheet of thin horn; the back was often ornamented with a rude sketch of St. George and the Dragon. *See* CHRISS-CROSS ROW.

Thee will I sing, in comely wainscot bound,
And golden verge inclosing thee around;
The faithful horn before, from age to age
Preserving thy invulnerable page;
Behind, thy patron saint in armour shines,
With sword and lance to guard the sacred lines.
TICKELL: *The Horn Book.*

Their books of stature small they took in hand

Which with pellucid horn secured are
To save from finger wet the letters fair.
SHENSTONE: *Schoolmistress.*

Death and Doctor Hornbook. In this satire by Robert Burns "Doctor Hornbook" stands for John Wilson the apothecary, whom the poet met at the Tarbolton Masonic Lodge.

Horner, Little Jack. *See* JACK.

Hornpipe. The dance is so called because it used to be danced to the *pib-corn* or *hornpipe*, an instrument consisting of a pipe each end of which was made of horn. In his *Dictionary* Johnson mistakenly said that it was "danced commonly to *a horn*."

Hornswoggle, To. U.S.A. slang meaning to cheat. Variants are *honeyfackle, honeyfoggle*.

Horoscope. The figure or diagram of the twelve houses of heaven, showing the positions of the planets at a given time. The horoscope is used by astrologers for calculating nativities and working out the answers to various horary questions. *See* HOUSES, ASTROLOGICAL. The word (Greek) means the "hour-scrutinized," because it is the disposition of the heavens at the exact hour of birth which is examined.

Hors de combat (ôr de kom' ba) (Fr., out of battle). Incapable of taking any further part in the fight.

He (*i.e.* Cobbett) levels his antagonists, he lays his friends low, and puts his own party *hors de combat.*—HAZLITT: *Table Talk.*

Hors d'œuvre (ôr dĕvr) (Fr., outside the work). A relish served at the beginning of a dinner as a whet to the appetite, not as an integral part of the meal. In French the expression is also used in architecture for an outbuilding or outwork, and as a literary term for a digression or interpolated episode.

Horse. A dark horse. A horse whose merits as a racer are not known to the general public; hence, a person who keeps his true capabilities to himself till he can produce them to the best advantage.

A horse of another colour. A different affair altogether.

As strong as a horse. Very strong. *Horse* is often used with intensive effect; as, *to work,* or *to eat, like a horse.*

A Trojan horse. A deception, a concealed danger. *See* WOODEN HORSE OF TROY.

Don't look a gift-horse in the mouth. *See* GIFT-HORSE.

Hold your horses. Don't be in such a hurry; keep your temper.

One man may steal a horse, while another may not look over the hedge. Some people are specially privileged, and can take liberties, or commit crimes, etc., with impunity, while others get punished for very trivial offences. An old proverb; given by Heywood (1546).

Riding the wooden horse. Being strapped to a wooden contrivance shaped something like a horse's back and flogged. An old form of military punishment.

Straight from the horse's mouth. Direct from the highest authority, which can not be questioned. The only certain way of discovering the age of a horse is by examining its lower jaw.

'Tis a good horse that never stumbles. Everyone makes mistakes sometimes; Homer sometimes nods.

To back the wrong horse. To make an error in judgment, and suffer for it. A phrase from the Turf. Speaking in the House of Lords (January 19th, 1897), Lord Salisbury said:—

I consider that both parties have been mistaken in their policy towards the Turkish Empire; they staked their money on the wrong horse at the time of the Crimean War.

To be on one's high horse, to ride the high horse. To be overbearing and arrogant; to give oneself airs. Formerly people of high rank rode on tall horses or chargers.

To ride on the horse with ten toes. To walk; to ride on Shanks's mare (q.v.).

You can take a horse to the water but you cannot make him drink. There is always *some* point at which it is impossible to get an obstinate man to proceed farther in the desired direction. The proverb is an old one, and is found in Heywood (1846).

The fifteen points of a good horse—

A good horse sholde have three propyrtees of a man, three of a woman, three of a foxe, three of a hare, and three of an asse

Of a man. Bolde, prowde, and hardye.

Of a woman. Fayre-breasted, faire of haire, and easy to move.

Of a foxe. A fair taylle, short eers, with a good trotte.

Of a hare. A grate eye, a dry head, and well rennynge.

Of an asse. A bygge chynn, a flat legge, and a good hoof.—*Wynkyn de Worde* (1496).

Famous Horses of Myth and History

In classical mythology the names given by various poets to the horses of Helios, the Sun, are:—

Actæon (effulgence); *Æthon* (fiery red); *Amethea* (no loiterer); *Bronte* (thunder); *Erythreos* (red producer); *Lampos* (shining like a lamp; one of the noontide horses); *Phlegon* (the burning one; noontide); and *Purocis* (fiery hot; also noontide).

Pluto's horses were: *Abaster* (away from the stars); *Abatos* (inaccessible); *Aeton* (swift as an eagle); and *Nonios*; and Aurora's: *Abraxas* (q.v.), *Eöos* (dawn), and *Phæthon* (the shining one).

Alborak. See Borak, below.

Alfana ("mare"). Gradasso's horse, in *Orlando Furioso.*

Aquiline ("like an eagle"). Raymond's steed, bred on the banks of the Tagus. (Tasso: *Jerusalem Delivered.*)

Arion ("martial"). Hercules' horse, given to Adrastus. The horse of Neptune, brought out of the earth by striking it with his trident; its right feet were those of a man, it spoke with a human voice, and ran with incredible swiftness.

Arundel. The horse of Bevis of Hamtown, or Southampton. The word means "swift as a swallow" (Fr. *hirondelle*).

Baiardo (the same name as *Bayard* below). Rinaldo's horse, of a bright bay colour, once the property of Amadis of Gaul. According to tradition it is still alive, but flees at the approach of man, so that it can never be caught. (*Orlando Furioso.*)

Balios (Gr. "swift"). One of the horses given by Neptune to Peleus. It afterwards belonged to Achilles. Like Xanthos, its sire was the west wind, and its dam Swift-foot the harpy.

Barbary. See Roan Barbary.

Bavieca. The Cid's horse. He survived his master two years and a half, during which time no one was allowed to mount him; and when he died he was buried before the gate of the monastery at Valencia, and two elms were planted to mark the site.

Bayard ("bay coloured"). The horse of the four sons of Aymon, which grew larger or smaller as one or more of the four sons mounted it. According to tradition, one of the footprints may still be seen in the forest of Soignes, and another on a rock near Dinant.

Black Agnes. The palfrey of Mary Queen of Scots, given her by her brother Moray, and named after Agnes of Dunbar.

Black Bess. The famous mare ridden by the highwayman Dick Turpin, which, tradition says, carried him from London to York.

Black Saladin. Warwick's famous horse, which was coal-black. Its sire was Malech, and according to tradition, when the race of Malech failed, the race of Warwick would fail also. And it was so.

Borak (Al). The mare which conveyed Mohammed from earth to the seventh heaven. It was milk-white, had the wings of an eagle, and a human face, with horse's cheeks. Every pace she took was equal to the farthest range of human sight. The word is Arabic for "the lightning."

Brigadore or *Brigliadore* ("golden bridle"). Sir Guyon's horse, in Spenser's *Faerie Queene* (V, ii, etc.). It had a distinguishing black spot in its mouth, like a horseshoe.

Orlando's famous charger, second only to Bajardo in swiftness and wonderful power's, had the same name—*Brigliadoro*.

Bucephalus ("ox-head"). The celebrated charger of Alexander the Great. Alexander was the only person who could mount him, and he always knelt down to take up his master. He was thirty years old at death, and Alexander built a city for his mausoleum, which he called Bucephala.

Carman. The Chevalier Bayard's horse, given him by the Duke of Lorraine. It was a Persian horse from Kerman or Carmen (Laristan).

Celer ("swift"). The horse of the Roman Emperor Verus. It was fed on almonds and raisins, covered with royal purple, and stalled in the imperial palace.

Cerus. The horse of Adrastus, swifter than the wind (*Pausanias*). The word means "fit."

Copenhagen. Wellington's charger at Waterloo. It died in 1835 at the age of twenty-seven. *Cp. Marengo.*

Cyllaros. Named from Cylla, in Troas, a celebrated horse of Castor or Pollux.

Dapple. Sancho Panza's ass in *Don Quixote*. So called from its colour.

Dinos ("the marvel"). Diomed's horse.

Ethon ("fiery"). One of the horses of Hector.

Fadda. Mohammed's white mule.

Ferrant d'Espagne ("the Spanish traveller"). The horse of Oliver, one of Charlemagne's paladins.

Galathe ("cream-coloured"). One of Hector's horses.

Grani ("grey-coloured"). Siegfried's horse, of marvellous swiftness.

Grizzle. Dr. Syntax's horse, all skin and bone; in Combe's *Tour of Dr. Syntax*, etc. (1812).

Haizum. The horse of the archangel Gabriel. (Koran.)

Harpagus ("one that carries off rapidly"). One of the horses of Castor and Pollux.

Hippocampus. One of Neptune's horses. It had only two legs, the hinder quarter being that of a dragon or fish.

Hrimfaxi. The horse of Night, from whose bit fall the "rime-drops" which every night bedew the earth. (Scandinavian mythology.)

Incitatus ("spurred-on"). The horse of the Roman Emperor Caligula, made priest and consul. It had an ivory manger, and drank wine out of a golden pail.

Kantaka. The white horse of Prince Gautama, the Buddha (*q.v.*).

Lampon ("the bright one"). One of the horses of Diomed.

Lamri. King Arthur's mare. The word means "the curvetter."

Marengo. The white stallion which Napoleon rode at Waterloo. It is represented in Vernet's picture of *Napoleon Crossing the Alps*. *Cp.* COPENHAGEN.

Malech. See Black Saladin above.

Marocco. Banks's performing horse, famous in the late Elizabethan period, and frequently mentioned by the dramatists. Its shoes were of silver, and one of its exploits was to mount the steeple of old St. Paul's.

The Pale Horse. Death. *Rev.* vi, 8.

Pegasus ("born near the *pege* or source of the ocean"). The winged horse of Apollo and the Muses. Perseus rode him when he rescued Andromeda.

Phallas ("stallion"). The horse of Heraclius.

Phrenicos ("intelligent"). The horse of Hiero of Syracuse, that won the Olympic prize for single horses in the seventy-third Olympiad.

Podarge ("swift-foot"). One of the horses of Hector.

Roan Barbary. The favourite horse of Richard II.

> When Bolingbroke rode on Roan Barbary
> That horse that thou so often hast bestrid.
> *Richard II*, v, 5.

Rosabelle. The favourite palfrey of Mary Queen of Scots.

Rosinante ("formerly a hack"). Don Quixote's horse, all skin and bone.

Saladin. See Black Saladin above.

Savoy. The favourite black horse of Charles VIII of France; so called from the Duke of Savoy who gave it him. It had but one eye, and "was mean in stature."

Shibdiz. The Persian Bucephalus, fleeter than the wind. It was the charger of Chosroes II of Persia.

Sleipnir. Odin's grey horse, which had eight legs and could traverse either land or sea. The horse typifies the wind which blows over land and water from eight principal points.

Sorrel. The horse of William III, which stumbled by catching his foot in a mole-heap.

This accident ultimately caused the king's death. *Sorrel*, like *Savoy*, was blind of one eye, and "mean of stature."

Strymon. The horse immolated by Xerxes before he invaded Greece. Named from the river Strymon, in Thrace, from which vicinity it came.

Tachebrune. The horse of Ogier the Dane.

Trebizond. The grey horse of Guarinos, one of the French knights taken at Roncesvalles.

Vegliantino ("the little vigilant one"). The famous steed of Orlando, called in French romance *Veillantif*, Orlando there appearing as Roland.

White Surrey. The favourite horse of Richard III.

Saddle White Surrey for the field to-morrow.
Richard III, v, 3.

Xanthus ("golden-hued"). One of the horses of Achilles, who announced to the hero his approaching death when unjustly chidden by him. Its sire was *Zephyros*, and dam *Podarge*.

USED EMBLEMATICALLY.

In Christian art, the horse is held to represent courage and generosity. It is an attribute of St. Martin, St. Maurice, St. George, and St. Victor, all of whom are represented on horseback. St. Léon is represented on horseback, in pontifical robes, blessing the people.

In the catacombs, where the horse is a not uncommon emblem, it probably typifies the transitoriness of life. Sometimes a palm-wreath is placed above its head.

The inn-sign of **The White Horse** in its various forms comes from the heraldic device of the House of Hanover, a white horse courant. During the reigns of the two first Georges a number of country inns and taverns exchanged their Stuart signs of Royal Oak, Rose, etc., to emblems better fitting the new times and dynasty.

Horse-chestnut. In his *Herball* (1597) Gerarde tells us that the tree is so called—

For that the people of the East countries do with the fruit thereof cure their horses of the cough . . . and such like diseases.

Another explanation is that when a slip is cut off obliquely close to a joint, it presents a miniature of a horse's hock and foot, shoe and nails. (*Cp.* HORSE-VETCH.) But the use of *horse-*attributively to denote something that is inferior, coarse, or unrefined, is quite common.

Horse-laugh. A coarse, vulgar laugh.

Horse-play. Rough play.

Horse-power. The standard theoretical unit of rate of work, equal to the raising of 33,000 lb.

one foot high in one minute. This was fixed by Watt, who, when experimenting to find some settled way of indicating the power exerted by his steam-engine, found that a strong dray horse working at a gin for eight hours a day averaged 22,000 foot-pounds per minute. He increased this by 50 per cent., and this, ever since, has been 1 horse-power.

Horse sense. Practical common sense; the term originated in western U.S.A.

It is lucky to pick up a horseshoe. This is from the old notion that a horseshoe nailed to the house door was a protection against witches. Lord Nelson had one nailed to the mast of the ship *Victory*.

The legend is that the devil one day asked St. Dunstan, who was noted for his skill in shoeing horses, to shoe his "single hoof." Dunstan, knowing who his customer was, tied him tightly to the wall and proceeded with his job, but purposely put the devil to so much pain that he roared for mercy. Dunstan at last consented to release his captive on condition that he would never enter a place where he saw a horseshoe displayed.

In 1251 Walter le Brun, farrier, in the Strand, London, was to have a piece of land in the parish of St. Clements, to place there a forge, for which he was to pay the parish six horseshoes, which rent was paid to the Exchequer every year, and was for some centuries rendered to the Exchequer by the Lord Mayor and citizens of London, to whom subsequently the piece of ground was granted.

Horse-wrangler, a western American term for a breaker-in and herder of horses.

Hortus Siccus (hôr' tus sik' us) (Lat., a dry garden). A collection of plants dried and arranged in a book.

Horus (hôr' us). One of the major gods of the ancient Egyptians, a blending of Horus the Elder, the sun-god (corresponding to the Greek Apollo), and Horus the Child (*see* HARPOCRATES), the son of Osiris and Isis. He was represented in hieroglyphics by a hawk, which bird was sacred to him, or as a hawk-headed man; and his emblem was the winged sun-disk. In many of the myths he is hardly distinguishable from Ra.

Hospital (Lat. *hospitale*, *hospitium*, from *hospes*, a guest), Originally a hospice, or hostel for the reception of pilgrims, the word came to be applied to a charitable institution for the aged and infirm (as in *Greenwich Hospital*, *Chelsea Hospital*), to similar institutions for the education of the young (as in *Christ's Hospital*), and so, finally, to its present usual sense, a place where the sick and wounded are cared for, and where medical students gain their experience in the treatment of disease, etc. The words *hostel* and *hotel* are "doublets" of *hospital*. Another common variation is *hospice*.

Host. The consecrated bread of the Eucharist is so called in the Latin Church because it is regarded as a real victim consisting of flesh, blood, and spirit, offered up in sacrifice; so called from *hostia*, the Latin word for a lamb when offered up in sacrifice (a larger animal was *victima*). At the Benediction it is exposed for adoration or carried in procession in a transparent vessel called a "monstrance."

Host as an army, a multitude. At the breaking up of the Roman Empire the first duty of every subject was to follow his lord into the field, and the proclamation was *bannire in hostem* (to order out against the foe), which soon came to signify "to order out for military service," and *hostem facere* came to mean "to perform military service." *Hostis* (military service) next came to mean the *army* that went against the foe, whence this word *host. Host,* one who entertains guests, is from Lat. *hospes*, a guest.

Hot. A phrase used in jazz music to describe a piece played with great spirit; when the players are carried away by the music they "get hot."

Hot air. Empty talk, boasting, threats, etc.; bombast. Hence, a *hot-air merchant*, one whose "vaporizings" are "full of sound and fury, signifying nothing"; a declamatory windbag.

Hot-pot. A dish of mutton or beef with sliced potatoes cooked in an oven in a tight-lidded pot. A favourite dish in the North of England.

Like hot cakes. Very rapidly; as in "The goods sold like hot cakes."

Not so hot, a slang phrase meaning not so good, not very satisfactory.

To blow hot and cold. *See* BLOW.

To get into hot water. To get into difficulties, or in a state of trouble and anxiety.

Hotch-pot. This word is used with the same significance as *hotch-potch* (*q.v.*), but it also has a legal use, which descends from Norman times in England, and is, apparently, the earlier. It meant the amalgamating of landed property that had belonged to a person dying intestate for the purpose of dividing the whole between the heirs in equal, or legal, shares.

It was also applied to such cases as the following:—

Suppose a father has advanced money to one child, at his death this child receives such sum as, added to the loan, will make his share equal to that of the other members of the family. If not content, he must bring into *hotch-pot* the money that was advanced, and the whole is then divided amongst all the children according to the terms of the will.

Hotch-potch (Fr. *hochepot; hocher*, to shake together, and *pot*). A hodge-podge (*q.v.*); a mixed dish; a confused mixture or jumble; a thick broth containing meat and vegetables.

Hotspur. A fiery person who has no control over his temper. Harry Percy (1364-1403), son of the first Earl of Northumberland (*see* 1 *Henry IV*), was so called. The 14th Earl of Derby (1799-1869) several times Prime Minister, was sometimes called the "*Hotspur of debate,*" though he was more generally known as the "Rupert of debate."

Hound. To hound a person is to persecute him, or rather to set on persons to annoy him, as hounds are let from the slips at a hare or stag.

Hour. A bad quarter of an hour. *See* QUART D'HEURE.

At the eleventh hour. Just in time not to be too late; only just in time to obtain some benefit. The allusion is to the parable of labourers hired for the vineyard (*Matt.* xx).

My hour is not yet come. The time for action has not yet arrived; properly, the hour of my death is not yet fully come. The allusion is to the belief that the hour of one's death is preordained.

When Jesus knew that his hour was come.—*John* xiii, 1.

In an evil hour. Acting under an unfortunate impulse. In astrology we have our lucky and unlucky hours.

In the small hours of the morning. One, two, and three, after midnight.

To keep good hours. To return home early every night; to go to bed betimes. Also, to be punctual in attending to one's work.

Houri (hoo' ri). One of the black-eyed damsels of the Mohammedan Paradise, possessed of perpetual youth and beauty, whose virginity is renewable at pleasure; hence, in English use, any dark-eyed and attractive beauty.

Every believer will have seventy-two of these *houris* in Paradise, and, according to the Koran, his intercourse with them will be fruitful or otherwise, according to his wish. If an offspring is desired, it will grow to full estate in an hour.

House. A house of call. Some house, frequently a public-house, that one makes a point of visiting or using regularly; a house where workers in a particular trade meet when out of employment, and where they may be engaged.

A house of correction. A jail governed by a keeper. Originally it was a place where vagrants were made to work, and offenders were kept in ward for the correction of small offences.

House of office, a Stuart term for a privy.

House to house. Performed at every house, one after another; as, "a house-to-house canvass."

Like a house afire. Very rapidly. The phrase alludes to the rapidity with which the old wooden houses with their straw-thatched roofs, were burned down once they caught fire.

The House. A familiar name for Christ Church, Oxford, the London Stock Exchange, and the deliberative bodies in various forms of government:

House of Lords, the peers of the United Kingdom.

House of Commons, the elected representatives of the British people, and those of Canada.

House of Representatives, the lower legislative chamber in U.S.A., Australia, New Zealand.

House of Assembly, South Africa.

The House of . . . denotes a royal or noble family with the ancestors and branches, as the *House of Windsor* (the British Royal Family), the *House of Stuart,* the *House of Brunswick,* etc.; also a commercial establishment or firm as the *House of Tellson,* the banking firm in Dickens's *Tale of Two Cities,* the *House of Cassell,* the publishers, etc.

The House of God. Not solely a church, or a temple made with hands, but any place sanctified by God's presence. Thus, Jacob in the wilderness, where he saw the ladder set up leading from earth to heaven, said, "This is none but the house of God, and this is the gate of heaven" (*Gen.* xxviii, 17).

To eat one out of house and home. *See* EAT.

To keep house. To maintain an establishment. "To go into housekeeping" is to start a private establishment.

To keep a good house. To supply a bountiful table.

To keep open house. To give free entertainment to all who choose to come.

Houses, Astrological. In judicial astrology the whole heaven is divided into twelve portions by means of great circles crossing the north and south points of the horizon, through which the heavenly bodies pass every twenty-four hours. Each of these divisions is called a *house;* and in casting a horoscope (*q.v.*) the whole is divided into two parts (beginning from the east), six above and six below the horizon. The eastern ones are called the *ascendant,* because they are about to rise; the other six are the *descendant,* because they have already passed the zenith. The twelve houses each have their special functions—(1) the house of life; (2) fortune and riches; (3) brethren; (4) parents and relatives; (5) children; (6) health; (7) marriage; (8) death; (9) religion; (10) dignities; (11) friends and benefactors; (12) enemies.

Three houses were assigned to each of the four ages of the person whose horoscope was to be cast, and his lot in life was governed by the ascendancy or descendancy of these at the various periods, and by the stars which ruled in the particular "houses."

Household, The. Specifically, the immediate members of the Royal Family but more particularly the retinue of court officials, servants, and attendants attached to the sovereign's and other royal households. The principal officials of the sovereign's household are the Lord Chamberlain, Lord Steward, Master of the Horse, Treasurer of the Household, all of whom are personally appointed. The higher members of the Household in Scotland are mostly hereditary.

Household gods. The Lares and Penates (*q.v.*), who presided over the dwellings and domestic concerns of the ancient Romans; hence, in modern use, the valued possessions of home, all those things that go to endear it to one.

Bearing a nation with all its household gods into exile.
       LONGFELLOW: *Evangeline.*

Housel (hou' zel). To give the Sacrament (A.S. *husel;* connected with Goth. *hunsl.* sacrifice). *Cp.* UNANELED.

Children were christened, and men houseled and assoyled through all the land, except such as were in the bill of excommunication by name expressed.—
HOLINSHED: *Chronicle.*

Houssain (hu sān'). Brother of Prince Ahmed in one of the *Arabian Nights* stories. He possessed a piece of carpet or tapestry of such wonderful power that he had only to sit upon it, and it would transport him in a moment to any place to which he desired to go.

Houyhnhnms (*whinims*, or *whinhims*). A race of horses endowed with reason and all the finer characteristics of man, introduced with caustically satirical effect by Swift in his *Gulliver's Travels*. The name was the author's invention, coined in imitation of the "whinny" of a horse.

> Nay, would kind Jove my organ so dispose
> To hymn harmonious Houyhnhnms through the nose
> I'd call thee Houhnhnm, that high-sounding name;
> Thy children's noses all should twang the same.
> POPE: *Mary Gulliver to Capt. Lemuel Gulliver; an Epistle.*

Hoyle. According to Hoyle. According to the best usage, or the highest authority. Edmond Hoyle, who wrote in 1742 *A Short Treatise on the Game of Whist*, was for many years quoted as an authority in all disputes over games of whist.

Hrimfaxi. *See* HORSE.

Hub. The nave of a wheel; a boss; the centre of any form of activity.

In the U.S.A. *The Hub* is Boston, Mass.

> Boston State-house is the hub of the solar system.—
> HOLMES: *Autocrat of the Breakfast Table*, ch. vi, p. 143.

Hubba Hubba. An exclamation of enthusiasm of American origin which came into wide prevalence during World War II. Like all such expressions its origin is obscure, though it has been ingeniously traced back to an old English expression: "Hubba—a cry given to warn fishermen of the approach of pilchards."

Hubert, St. Patron saint of huntsmen (d. 727). He was the son of Bertrand, Duc d'Aquitaine, and cousin of King Pepin. Hubert was so fond of the chase that he neglected his religious duties for his favourite amusement, till one day a stag bearing a crucifix menaced him with eternal perdition unless he reformed. Upon this he entered the cloister, became in time Bishop of Liége, and the apostle of Ardennes and Brabant. Those who were descended of his race were supposed to possess the power of curing the bite of mad dogs.

In art he is represented as a bishop with a miniature stag resting on the book in his hand, or as a huntsman kneeling to the miraculous crucifix borne by the stag. His feast day is November 3rd.

Hudibras (hū' di brās). A satirical poem in three parts and nine cantos (published 1663-78) by Samuel Butler, so named from its hero, who is said to be a caricature of Sir Samuel Luke, a patron of Butler. The *Grub Street Journal* (1731) maintains it was Colonel Rolle, of Devonshire, with whom the poet lodged for some time, and adds that the name is derived from Hugh de Bras, the patron saint of the county. Hudibras represents the Presbyterian party, and his squire the Independents.

> 'Tis sung there is a valiant Mameluke,
> In foreign land ycleped—.
> BUTLER: *Hudibras*, i, 1.

Zachary Grey's notes to *Hudibras* seem to prove conclusively that Sir Samuel Luke is referred to—a not too-honest man of doubtful loyalties.

There are two characters of this name in Spenser's *Faerie Queene*: (1) the lover of Elissa (II, ii), typifying rashness, and (2) a, legendary king of Britain (II, x, 25).

Hue and Cry. The old legal name for the official outcry made when calling for assistance "with horn and with voice," in the pursuit of a criminal escaping from justice (O.Fr. *huer*, to shout). Persons failing to respond when the "hue and cry" was raised were liable to penalties; hence, a clamour or outcry, a cry, of alarm.

> But now by this, with noyse of late uprore,
> The hue and cry was raysed all about.
> SPENSER: *Faerie Queene*, VI, xi, 46.

Hug. To hug the shore. In the case of a ship, to keep as close to the shore as is compatible with the vessel's safety.

To hug the wind. To keep a ship close hauled.

Hugger-mugger. One of a large class of reduplicated words (*i.e. namby-pamby, skimble-skamble, flip-flap*, etc.) of uncertain origin, but probably an extension of *hug*. Clandestinely, secretly; also, in an untidy, disorderly manner.

The king in *Hamlet* says of Polonius: "We have done but greenly in hugger-mugger to inter him"—*i.e.* to smuggle him into the grave clandestinely and without ceremony.

North, in his *Plutarch*, says: "Antonius thought that his body should be honourably buried, and not in hugger-mugger" (clandestinely).

Ralpho says:—

> While I, in hugger-mugger hid,
> Have noted all they said and did.
> BUTLER: *Hudibras*, iii, 3.

In modern speech we say—*He lives in a hugger-mugger sort of way; the rooms were all hugger-mugger* (disorderly).

Huguenot (hū' ge not). The French Protestants (Calvinists) of the 16th and 17th centuries. The name was first applied to the revolutionaries of Geneva by the adherents of the Duke of Savoy, about 1560, and is probably an adaptation of the Ger. *eidgenossen*, confederates.

Philippe de Mornay (1549-1623), the great supporter of the French Protestants, was nicknamed "the Huguenot Pope."

Huitzilopochtli. *See* MEXITL.

Hulda (hŭl' dà). The old German goddess of marriage and fecundity, who sent bride-grooms to maidens and children to the married. The name means "the Benignant."

Hulda is making her bed. It snows.

Hulking. A great hulking fellow. A great overgrown one. A hulk is a large, unwieldy ship, or the body of a superannuated one, that looks very clumsy as it lies ashore. Shakespeare says—referring to Falstaff:—

Harry Monmouth's brawn, the hulk Sir John
Is prisoner to your son.—2 *Henry IV*, i, 1.

Hull, Hell, and Halifax. An old beggars' and vagabonds' "prayer," quoted by Taylor, the Water Poet (early 17th cent.), was:

From Hull, Hell, and Halifax,
Good Lord, deliver us.

"Hell" was probably the least feared as being farthest from them; Hull was to be avoided because it was so well governed that beggars had little chance of getting anything without doing hard labour for it; and Halifax, because anyone caught stealing cloth in that town was beheaded without further ado.

Hullabaloo (hŭl à bà loo'). Uproar. The word is fairly modern (middle of the 17th cent.); it is of uncertain origin, but is probably a reduplicated word formed on *holloa!* or *hullo!* *Cp.* HURLY-BURLY.

Hulled (U.S.A.). Made a prisoner after capitulating, from the surrender of General Hull at Detroit, August 16th, 1812.

Hulsean Lectures (hŭl' sē àn). Instituted by the Rev. John Hulse (1708-90), of Cheshire, in 1777. Some four or six sermons on Christian evidences are preached annually at Great St. Mary's, Cambridge, by the Hulsean Lecturer, who, till 1860, was entitled the Christian Advocate. Hulse also bequeathed estates to the University as an endowment for a Hulsean Professor of Divinity, and for certain Hulsean prizes.

Hum and Haw, To. To hesitate to give a positive answer; to hesitate in making a speech. To introduce *hum* and *haw* between words which ought to follow each other freely.

Huma (hū' mà). A fabulous Oriental bird which never alights, but is always on the wing. It is said that every head which it overshadows will wear a crown. The bird suspended over the throne of Tippoo Sahib at Seringapatam repre-sented this poetical fancy.

Humanitarians (hū măn i târ' i ànz). A name that used to be given to certain Arian heretics who believed that Jesus Christ was only man. The disciples of St. Simon were so called also, because they maintained the perfectibility of human nature without the aid of grace.

Nowadays the term is usually applied to philanthropists whose object is the welfare of humanity at large.

Humanities or **Humanity Studies.** Gram-mar, rhetoric, and poetry, with Greek and Latin (*literæ humaniores*); in contradistinction to divinity (*literæ divinæ*).

The humanities . . , is used to designate those studies which are considered the most specially adapted for training . . . true humanity in every man.—TRENCH: *Study of Words*, Lect. iii.

A degree, L.H.D., Litterarum Humaniorum Doctor (Doctor of Humane Letters), is given at some of the American universities.

Humanity Martin. Richard Martin (1754-1834) one of the founders of the Royal Society for the Prevention of Cruelty to Animals. He secured the passage of several laws making cruelty to certain animals illegal.

Humber. The legendary king of the Huns who are fabled to have invaded Britain about 1000 B.C.; he was defeated in a great battle by Locrine, and his body was cast into the river Abus, which was forthwith renamed the Humber. (*Geoffrey of Monmouth*.)

Their chieftain Humber named was aright
Unto the mighty streame him to betake,
Where he an end of battell and of life did make.
    SPENSER: *Faerie Queene*, II, x, 16.

Humble. Humble bee. A corruption of the Ger. *hummel bee*, the buzzing bee. Sometimes called the Dumble-dor. Also Bumble-bee, from its booming drone.

Humble cow. A cow without horns.

To eat humble pie. To come down from a position you have assumed; to be obliged to take "a lower room." Here "humble" is a pun on *umble*, the umbles being the heart, liver, and entrails of the deer, the huntsman's perquisites. When the lord and his household dined the venison pasty was served on the dais, but the *umbles* were made into a pie for the huntsman and his fellows, who took the lower seats.

Humbug. A hoax or imposition; also (as verb) to hoax, cajole, impose upon. The word is of unknown origin, but was new in the middle of the 18th century, and the Earl of Orrery, writing in the *Connoisseur* in 1754, called it a—

New-coined expression, which is only to be found in the nonsensical vocabulary and sounds absurd and disagree-able whenever it is pronounced.

Humhum. (U.S.A.) A thin cambric material.

Humour. As good humour, ill or **bad humour.** etc. According to an ancient theory, there are four principal humours in the body: phlegm, blood, choler, and black bile. As any one of these predominates it determines the temper of the mind and body; hence the expressions sanguine, choleric, phlegmatic, and melancholic humours. A just balance made a good compound called "good humour"; a preponderance of any one of the four made a bad compound called an ill or evil humour. *See* Ben Jonson's *Every Man Out of His Humour* (*Prologue*).

Humpty Dumpty. A little deformed dwarf, "humpty" and "dumpty." There used to be a drink of this name, composed of ale boiled with brandy; and it is also applied—in allusion to the old nursery rhyme—to an egg, and to anything that is, or may be, irretrievably shattered.

Hunch, a colloquial term—originally American—for a premonition, a shrewd guess.

Hundred. An English county division dating from pre-Conquest times, and supposed to be so called either because it comprised exactly one hundred hides of land, or one hundred families, grouped together for civil and military purposes, these families being collectively responsible to the authorities in case of crime within the "hundred."

Northumberland, Cumberland, Westmorland, and Durham were divided into "wards" (*q.v.*).

Yorkshire, Lincolnshire, and Notts, into "wapentakes" (*q.v.*). Yorkshire has also three special divisions called "ridings" (*q.v.*).

Kent was divided into five "lathes" (*q.v.*), with subordinate hundreds.

Sussex into six "rapes" (*q.v.*), with subordinate hundreds.

It will be all the same a hundred years hence. An exclamation of resignation—it doesn't much matter *what* happens. It is an old saying, and occurs in Ray's *Collection*, 1742. A similar one is:—

A thousand pounds and a bottle of hay
Is all one thing at Doom's-day.—*Ray*.

The Hundred Days. The days between March 20th, 1815, when Napoleon reached the Tuil-eries, after his escape from Elba, and June 28th, the date of the second restoration of Louis XVIII. These hundred days were noted for five things:

The additional Act to the constitutions of the empire, April 22;
The Coalition;
The Champ de Mai, June 1;
The battle of Waterloo, June 18;
The second abdication of Napoleon in favour of his son, June 22.

Napoleon left Elba February 26th; landed near Cannes March 1st, entered Paris March 20th, and signed his abdication June 22nd.

The address of the prefect of Paris to Louis XVIII on his second restoration begins: "A hundred days, sire, have elapsed since the fatal moment when your Majesty was forced to quit your capital in the midst of tears." This is the origin of the phrase.

The Hundred-eyed. Argus, in Greek and Latin fable. Juno appointed him guardian of Io (the cow), but Jupiter caused him to be put to death; whereupon Juno transplanted his eyes into the tail of her peacock.

The Hundred-handed. Three of the sons of Uranus, viz. Ægæon or Briareus, Kottos, and Gyges or Gyes. After the war between Zeus and the Titans, when the latter were overcome and hurled into Tartarus, the Hundred-handed ones were set to keep watch and ward over them.

Sometimes Cerberus (*q.v.*) is so called, because from his three necks sprang writhing snakes instead of hair.

The Hundred Years War. The long series of wars between France and England, beginning in the reign of Edward III, 1337, and ending in that of Henry VI, 1453.

The first battle was a naval action off Sluys, and the last the fight at Castillon. It originated in English claims to the French Crown and resulted in the English being expelled from the whole of France, except Calais.

Hungary Water. Made of rosemary flowers and spirit, said to be so called because the receipt was given by a hermit to a Queen of Hungary.

Hunky, Hunky dory (hŭng' ki, hŭng' ki dôr' i), American slang for all's right, satisfactory.

Hunt. Like Hunt's dog, he would neither go to church nor stay at home. A Shropshire saying. The story is that one Hunt, a labouring man, kept a mastiff, which, on being shut up while his master went to church, howled and barked so as to disturb the whole congregation; whereupon Hunt thought he would take him to church the next Sunday, but the dog positively refused to enter. The proverb is applied to a self-willed person, who will neither be led nor driven.

Hunter, Mr. and Mrs. Leo Hunter. Characters in *Pickwick Papers* who hunt up the celebrities, or "lions," to grace their parties and bring them renown and reputation.

The hunter's moon. The month or moon following the "harvest moon" (*q.v.*). Hunting does not begin until after harvest.

The mighty hunter. Nimrod is so called (*Gen.* x, 9). The meaning seems to be a conqueror. Jeremiah says, "I [the Lord] will send for many hunters [warriors], and they shall hunt [chase] them [the Jews] from every mountain . . . and out of the holes of the rocks" (xvi, 16).

> Proud Nimrod first the bloody chase began—
> A mighty hunter, and his prey was man.
> > POPE: *Windsor Castle.*

Hunters and Runners of classic renown:—

ACASTUS, who took part in the famous Calydonian hunt (a wild boar).

ACTÆON, the famous huntsman who was transformed by Diana into a stag, because he chanced to see her bathing.

ADONIS, beloved by Venus, slain by a wild boar while hunting.

ADRASTUS, who was saved at the siege of Thebes by the speed of his horse Arion, given him by Hercules.

ATALANTA, who promised to marry the man who could outstrip her in running.

CAMILLA, the swiftest-footed of all the companions of Diana.

LADAS, the swiftest-footed of all the runners of Alexander the Great.

MELEAGER, who took part in the great Calydonian boar-hunt.

ORION, the great and famous hunter, changed into the constellation, so conspicuous in November.

PHEIDIPPIDES, who ran 135 miles in two days.

Huntingdonians. Members of "the Countess of Huntingdon's Connexion," a sect of Calvinistic Methodists founded in 1748 by Selina, widow of the ninth Earl of Huntingdon, and George Whitefield, who had become her chaplain. The churches founded by the Countess, numbering some 38, are mostly affiliated with the Congregational Union.

Hurdy-gurdy. A stringed musical instrument, like a rude guitar, the music of which is produced by the friction of a rosined wheel on the strings, which are stopped by means of keys. It had nothing whatever to do with the modern barrel-organ or piano-organ of the streets.

Hurly-burly. Uproar, tumult, especially of battle. A reduplication of *hurly*. *Cp.* HULLA-BALOO.

> Now day began to break, and the army to fall again into good order, and all the hurly-burly to cease.— *North's Plutarch, Antonius* (1579).

> When the hurly-burly's done,
> When the battle's lost and won.
> > The Witches, in *Macbeth*, i, 1.

In the *Garden of Eloquence* (1577) the word given as a specimen of onomatopœia.

Hurrah. A later (17th cent.) form of the earlier *huzza*, an imitative sound expressing joy, enthusiasm, pleasure at victory, etc. The word may be connected with the Low Ger. *hurra*, in which case it was probably introduced by soldiers about the time of the Thirty Years War.

The Norman battle-cry was "Ha Rollo!" or "Ha Rou!"

Hurricane (hŭr′ i kán). An 18th-century term for a large private party or rout; so called from its hurry, bustle, and noise. *Cp.* DRUM.

> There is a squeeze, a fuss, a drum, a rout, and lastly a hurricane, when the whole house is full from top to bottom.—*Mrs. Barbauld* (1779).

The word is West Indian, and was introduced through Spanish; it means a very violent storm of wind.

Hurry. An imitative word, probably connected with *hurl* (as in *hurly-burly*), which first appears in Shakespeare:—

> She spied the hunted boar,
> Whose frothy mouth . . .
> A second fear through all her sinews spread,
> Which madly hurries her she knows not whither.
> > *Venus and Adonis*, 904.

Husband. The word is Anglo-Saxon, from *hus*, house, and Old Norse *bondi*, a freeholder or yeoman, from *bua*, to dwell; hence the word is literally, a house-owner in his capacity as head of the household, and so came to be applied to a man joined to a woman in marriage, who was, naturally, the head of his household. When Sir John Paston, writing to his mother in 1475, said—

> I purpose to leeffe alle heer, and come home to you and be your hisbonde and balyff,

he was proposing to come and manage her household for her. We use the word in the same sense in such phrases as **To husband one's resources.**

Similarly a ship's husband is an official responsible for seeing that all the equipment, etc., necessary for going to sea is placed on board a ship before sailing, that all the regulations relating to the voyage are fulfilled, and that the captain is sufficiently furnished with money, etc., for carrying on business when in foreign or other ports.

Thomas Tusser was in error when he derived the word from "houseband," as in the following distich:—

> The name of the husband, what is it to say?
> Of wife and of *house*-hold the *band* and the stay.
> > *Five Hundred Points of Good Husbandry* (1557).

Husbandry is merely the occupation of the (original) *husband*, *i.e.* the management of the household and what pertains thereto; it became restricted later to farm-management, and the *husband* became the *husbandman*.

I commit into your hands
The husbandry and manage of my house.
> *Merchant of Venice*, iii, 4.

Hush. Hush-hush, a term that came into use in World War I to describe very secret operations, designs, or inventions.

Hush-money. Money given as a bribe for silence or "hushing" a matter up.

Husky. In American usage this word is applied to a big, burly, strong man. As an abbreviation for the word *Eskimo* it is the name used for an Eskimo sledge dog.

Hussar (hu zar'). An Hungarian word (*huszar*), which is ultimately from the same Greek word that gives us our *corsair*. It was applied in the time of Matthias Corvinus (mid-15th cent.), to a body of light horsemen, and was hence adopted in various European armies to denote light cavalry.

Hussites (hŭs' ītz). Followers of John Huss, the Bohemian reformer, in the 15th century. *Cp.* BETHLEMENITES.

Hussy (hŭz' i). Nowadays a word of contempt implying an ill-behaved girl, a "jade" or "minx," it is no other than the honourable appellation *housewife* (pron. "hussif"). Just as *wench* has come down in the world, so has *hussy* been degraded.

Hutin (oo' tan). **Louis le Hutin.** Louis X (1289, 1314-16) was so nicknamed. It means "the quarreller," "the stubborn or headstrong one," and it is uncertain why the name was given to this insignificant king of France.

Hutkin. A word in some dialects for a cover for a sore finger, made by cutting off the finger of an old glove; called also, a *hut*, *hutch*, and *hutchkin*.

Huzza! An exclamation of joy or applause; the forerunner of *Hurrah!* (*q.v.*). The word has no etymology, being merely an extension of an involuntary vocable, such as *Chut!* or *Pshaw!*

Hyacinth (hī' a sinth). According to Greek fable, the son of Amyclas, a Spartan king. The lad was beloved by Apollo and Zephyr, and as he preferred the sun-god, Zephyr drove Apollo's quoit at his head, and killed him. The blood became a flower, and the petals are inscribed with the signature A I, meaning *woe*. (Virgil: *Eclogues*, iii, 106).

> The hyacinth bewrays the doleful "A I,"
> And culls the tribute of Apollo'a sigh.
> Still on its bloom the mournful flower retains
> The lovely blue that dyed the stripling's veins.
> > CAMOËNS: *Lusiad*, ix.

Hyades (hī' a dēz) (Gr. *huein*, to rain). Seven nymphs placed among the stars, in the constellation Taurus, which threaten rain when they rise with the sun. The fable is that they wept the death of their brother Hyas so bitterly that Zeus, out of compassion, took them to heaven.

> The seaman sees the Hyades
> Gather an army of Cimmerian clouds . . .
> All-fearful folds his sails, and sounds the main,
> Lifting his prayers to the heavens for aid
> Against the terror of the winds and waves.
> > MARLOWE: 1 *Tamburlaine*, III, ii.

Hybla (hib' là). A city and mountain in Sicily, famous for its honey. *Cp.* HYMETTUS.

> For your words, they rob the Hybla bees
> And leave them honeyless.
> *Ant.*: Not stingless too.
> *Bru.*: O, yes, and soundless too;
> For you have stol'n their buzzing, Antony,
> And very wisely threat before you sting.
> > *Julius Cæsar*, v, 1.

Hydra (hī' drà). A monster of the Lernean marshes, in Argolis. It has nine heads, and it was one of the twelve labours of Hercules to kill it. As soon as he struck off one of its heads, two shot up in its place; hence *hydra-headed* applies to a difficulty which goes on increasing as it is combated.

Hyena (hī ē' nà). Held in veneration by the ancient Egyptians, It is fabled that a certain stone, called the "hyænia," is found in the eye of the creature, and Pliny asserts (*Nat. Hist.*, xxxvii, 60) that when placed under the tongue it imparts the gift of prophecy.

> The skilful Lapidarists of Germany affirm that this beast hath a stone in his eye (or rather his head) called Hyæna or Hyænius.—TOPSELL: *Four-footed Beasts* (1607).

Hygeia (hī jē' à). Goddess of health in Greek mythology, and the daughter of Æsculapius (*q.v.*). Her symbol was a serpent drinking from a cup in her hand.

Hymen (hī' men). Properly, a marriage song of the ancient Greeks; later personified as the god of marriage, represented as a youth carrying a torch and veil—a more mature Eros, or Cupid.

Hyperbole (hī pĕr' bō li). The rhetorical figure of speech which consists of exaggeration or extravagance in statement for the purpose of giving effect but not intended to be taken *au pied de la lettre*—*e.g.* "the waves were mountains high."

> Hyperboles are of two kinds; either such as are employed in description, or such as are suggested by the warmth of passion.—LINDLEY MURRAY: *English Grammar*, I, p. 510.

Hyperion (hī pĕr' i on). In Greek mythology, one of the Titans, son of Uranus and Ge, and father of Helios, Selene, and Eos (the Sun,

Moon, and Dawn). The name is sometimes given by poëts to the sun itself, but not by Keats in his wonderful "poetical fragment" of this name (1820).

Hypermnestra (hī pĕrm nes' trȧ). Wife of Lynceus and the only one of the fifty daughters of Danaos who did not murder her husband on their bridal night. *See* DANAIDES.

Hypnotism (hip' nō tizm). The art of producing trance-sleep, or the state of being hypnotized. Dr. James Braid of Manchester gave it this name (1843), after first having called it *neuro-hypnotism*, an inducing to sleep of the nerves (Gr.).

The method, discovered by Mr. Braid, of producing this state . . . appropriately designated . . . hypnotism consists in the maintenance of a fixed gaze for several minutes . . . on a bright object placed somewhat above [the line of sight], at so short a distance [as to produce pain].—CARPENTER: *Principles of Mental Physiology*, ii, i.

Hypochondria (hī pō kon' dri ȧ) (Gr. *hypo, chrondros*, under the cartilage—*i.e.* the spaces on each side of the epigastric region) A morbid depression of spirits for which there is no known or defined cause, so called because it was supposed to be caused by some derangement in these parts, which were held to be the seat of melancholy.

Hypocrite (hip' ō krit). **Prince of hypocrites.** Tiberius Cæsar (42 B.C., A.D. 14 to 37) was so called because he affected a great regard for decency, but indulged in the most detestable lust and cruelty.

Abdallah Ibn Obba and his partisans were called The Hypocrites by Mohammed, because they feigned to be friends, but were in reality foes.

Hypocrites' Isle. *See* CHANEPH.

Hypodorian Mode. *See* ÆOLIAN.

Hyssop (his' ŏp). David says (*Ps.* li, 7): "Purge me with hyssop, and I shall be clean." The reference is to the custom of ceremonially sprinkling the unclean with a bunch of hyssop (marjorum or the thorny caper) dipped in water in which had been mixed the ashes of a red heifer. This was done as they left the Court of the Gentiles to enter the Court of the Women (*Numb*, xix, 17, 18).

Hysteron Proteron (his' tĕr on prȯ' tĕr on), from the Greek meaning "hinder foremost," is a term used in logic and rhetoric to describe a figure of speech in which the word that should come last is placed first, or the second of two consecutive propositions is stated first, *e.g.* "Let us die, and rush into the midst of the fray."

I

I. The ninth letter of the alphabet, also of the futhorc (*q.v.*), representing the Greek *iota* and Semitic *yod*. The written (and printed) *i* and *j* were for long interchangeable; it was only in the 19th century that in dictionaries, etc., they were treated as separate letters (in Johnson's Dictionary, for instance, *iambic* comes between *iamb* and *jangle*), and hence in many series—such as the signatures of sheets in a book, hallmarks on plate, etc.—either I or J is omitted. *Cp.* U.

The dot on the small *i* is not originally part of the letter, but was introduced about the 11th century as a diacritic in cases where two *i*'s came together (*e.g. filii*) to distinguish between these and *u*.

To dot the i's and cross the t's. To be meticulous, particularly about things of apparently little consequence, to clinch an agreement.

Iambic (ī ăm′ bik). An *iamb*, or *iambus*, is a metrical foot consisting of a short syllable followed by a long one, as *away*, *deduce*, or an unaccented followed by an accented, as *be gone! Iambic* verse is verse based on iambs, as, for instance, the Alexandrine measure, which consists of six iambuses:—

> I think the thoughts you think; and if I have the knack
> Of fitting thoughts to words, you peradventure lack,
> Envy me not the chance, yourselves more fortunate!
> BROWNING: *Fifine at the Fair*, lxxvi.

Father of Iambic verse, Archilochos of Paros (fl. *c.* 700 B.C.).

Ianthe (ī ăn′ thi), a Cretan girl who, as told in Ovid's *Metamorphoses*, ix, 5, married Iphis, who had been transformed for the purpose, from a girl into a young man. The Ianthe to whom Lord Byron dedicated his *Childe Harold*, was Lady Charlotte Harley, born 1801, and only eleven years old at the time. Shelley gave the name to his infant daughter.

Iberia (ī bēr′ i à), Spain; the country of the Iberus, the ancient name of the river Ebro. The Iberians were the prehistoric, non-Aryan inhabitants of the peninsula, probably of African origin. The Spanish Basques are their nearest modern representatives.

Iberia's Pilot. Christopher Columbus (1446?-1507).

> Launched with Iberia's pilot from the steep,
> To worlds unknown, and isles beyond the deep.
> CAMPBELL: *The Pleasures of Hope*, ii.

Ibid. (ib′ id). A contraction of Lat. *ibidem*, in the same place.

Ibis (ī′ bis). A sacred bird of the ancient Egyptians, specially connected with the god Thoth, who in the guise of an Ibis escaped the pursuit of Typhon. Its white plumage symbolized the light of the sun, and its black neck the shadow of the moon, its body a heart, and its legs a triangle. It was said that it drank only the purest of water, and that the bird was so fond of Egypt that it would pine to death if transported elsewhere. The practical reason for the protection of the Ibis—for it was a crime to kill it— was that it devoured crocodiles' eggs, serpents and all sorts of noxious reptiles and insects. *Cp.* ICHNEUMON.

Iblis. *See* EBLIS.

Ibraham (ib′ rà him). The Abraham of the Koran.

Icarius (i kâr′ i ùs). In Greek legend an Athenian who was taught the cultivation of the vine by Dionysus (Bacchus). He was slain by some peasants who had become intoxicated with wine he had given them, and who thought they had been poisoned. They buried the body under a tree; his daughter Erigone, searching for her father, was directed to the spot by the howling of his dog Mœra, and when she discovered the body she hanged herself for grief. Icarius became the constellation *Boötes*, Erigone the constellation *Virgo*, and Mœra the star *Procyon*, which rises in July, a little before the dog-star.

Icarus (ik′ à rus). Son of Dædalus (*q.v.*). He flew with his father from Crete; but the sun melted the wax with which his wings were fastened on, and he fell into the sea. Those waters of the Ægean were thenceforward called the Icarian Sea.

Ice. Ice age. There have been several glacial epochs, but what is commonly known by that name was the earlier part of the existing geological period, the Pleistocene, when a considerable portion of the northern hemisphere was overwhelmed by ice caps or ice sheets. Ice covered large areas of northwestern Europe, Canada, and the U.S.A., and as it melted the included stones were spread out in vast sheets of irregular deposits. Man was contemporary with at least the latter periods of the Ice Age, his remains having been found in England and France together with the mammoth and reindeer in beds earlier than the last glacial deposits. Science has as yet found no satisfactory explanation of the causes of the Ice Age.

To break the ice. To broach a disagreeable subject; to open the way, take the first step, make the plunge

[We] An' if you break the ice, and do this feat. . . .
Will not so graceless be, to be ingrate.
Taming of the Shrew, i, 2.

To skate over thin ice. To take unnecessary risks, especially in conversation or argument; to touch on dangerous subjects very lightly.

Iceberg. A mass of ice, broken from a glacier which ends in the sea, and floated about the ocean by the currents. The magnitude of some icebergs is considerable. One seen off the Cape of Good Hope was two miles in circumference, and a hundred and fifty feet high. For every cubic foot above water there must be at least eight cubic feet below; their weight must be enormous, and the danger to shipping — witness the *Titanic* disaster of April, 1912 — is very great.

Ich Dien (ik dēn). According to a Welsh tradition, Edward I promised to provide Wales with a prince "who could speak no word of English," and when his second son Edward (afterwards Edward II) was born at Carnarvon he presented him to the assembly, saying in Welsh *Eich dyn* (behold the man). The words are actually German, meaning "I serve," and are erroneously said to have been adopted as the Prince of Wales's motto by the Black Prince, together with the three white ostrich plumes, from John, King of Bohemia, who fell at the Battle of Crecy, 1346.

Ichabod (ik' à bod). A son of Phinehas, born just after the death of his father and grandfather (1 *Sam.* iv, 21). The name (Heb. I-kab-hoth) means "where is the glory?" It is usually popularly translated by "the glory has departed."

Ichthus (ik' thùs). Greek for "fish," which in primitive times was used as a symbol of Christ because the word is formed of the initial letters *Iesous CHristos, THeou Uios, Soter,*

Jesus Christ, Son of God, Saviour. This notarica is found on many seals, rings, urns, and tombstones belonging to the early times of Christianity, and was supposed to be a "charm" of mystical efficacy.

Icon or Ikon (ī' kon), from the Greek *eikon,* an image or likeness, is a representation in the form of painting, low-relief sculpture or mosaic of some sacred personage in the Eastern Church. Excepting the face and hands, the whole is often covered with an embossed metal plaque representing the figure and drapery. Icons are greatly venerated by the Russian peasantry.

Iconoclasts (Gr., "image breakers"). Reformers who rose in the Eastern Church in the 8th century, and were specially opposed to the employment of pictures, statues, emblems, and all visible representations of sacred objects. The crusade against these things began in 726 with the Emperor Leo III (the Isaurian), and continued for one hundred and twenty years under Constantine Copronymus, Leo the Armenian, Theophilus, and other Byzantine Emperors, who are known as the Iconoclast Emperors.

Id, in Freudian psychology is the whole reservoir of impulsive reactions that forms the mind, of which the ego is a superficial layer. It is the totality of impulses or instincts comprising the true unconscious mind.

Ideal Republics. *See* COMMONWEALTHS.

Idealism. Subjective idealism, taught by Fichte (1762-1814), supposes the object (say a tree) and the image of it on the mind are one. Or rather, that there is no object outside the mental idea.

Objective idealism, taught by Schelling (1775-1854), supposes that the tree and the image thereof on the mind are distinct from each other.

Absolute idealism, taught by Hegel (1770-1831), supposes there is no such thing as phenomena; that mind, through the senses, creates its own world. In fact, that there is no real, but all is ideal.

Personal idealism, as expounded by William James (1842-1910), lays special emphasis on the authority of the will and the initiative of the self in experience, as opposed to the tendency of absolute idealism to minimize the working of the individual soul.

Idealists. They may be divided into two distinct sections —

(1) Those who follow Plato, who taught that before creation there existed certain types or

ideal models, of which *ideas* created objects are the visible images, Malebranche, Kant, Schelling, Hegel, etc., were of this school.

(2) Those who maintain that all phenomena are only subjective—that is, mental cognizances only within ourselves, and what we see and what we hear are only brain impressions. Of this school were Berkeley, Hume, Fichte, and many others.

Ides (īdz). In the Roman calendar the 15th of March, May, July, and October, and the 13th of all the other months; always eight days after the Nones.

Beware the Ides of March. Said as a warning of impending and certain danger. The allusion is the warning received by Julius Cæsar before his assassination:—

Furthermore, there was a certain soothsayer that had given Cæsar warning long time afore, to take heed of the day of the Ides of March (which is the fifteenth of the month), for on that day he should be in great danger. That day being come, Cæsar going into the Senate-house and speaking merrily unto the soothsayer, told him, "The Ides of March be come"; "So be they," softly answered the soothsayer, "but yet are they not past."— PLUTARCH: *Julius Cæsar* (*North's trans.*).

See also Julius Cæsar, i, 2, iii, 1, etc.

Idiot. Originally—in Greece—a private person, one not engaged in any public office, hence an uneducated, ignorant person. Jeremy Taylor says, "Humility is a duty in great ones, as well as in idiots" (private persons). The Greeks have the expressions, "a priest or an idiot" (layman), "a poet or an idiot" (prose-writer). In 1 *Cor.* xiv, 16, where the Authorized Version has "how shall he who occupieth the place of the unlearned say Amen . . . ?" Wyclif's version reads " . . . who fillith the place of an idyot, how schal he seie amen . . . ?"

Idomeneus (ī dom' in ūs). King of Crete, an ally of the Greeks at Troy. After the city was burnt he made a vow to sacrifice whatever he first encountered, if the gods granted him a safe return to his kingdom. It was his own son that he first met; he offered him up to fulfil his vow, but a plague followed, and the king was banished from Crete as a murderer. (*Iliad.*) *Cp.* IPHIGENIA.

Iduna or Idun (i dū' nà, i dūn'). In Scandinavian mythology, daughter of the dwarf Svald, and wife of Bragi. She was guardian of the golden apples which the gods tasted as often as they wished to renew their youth.

Ifs and Ans.

If ifs and ans
Were pots and pans
Where would be the tinker?

An old-fashioned jingle to describe wishful thinking. The "ans"—often erroneously written "ands"—is merely the old "an" for "if."

Ignatius, St. (ig nā' shùs). According to tradition, St. Ignatius was the little child whom our Saviour set in the midst of His disciples for their example. He was a convert of St. John the Evangelist, was consecrated Bishop of Antioch by St. Peter, and is said to have been thrown to the beasts in the amphitheatre by Trajan, about 107. He is commemorated on February 1st, and is represented in art accompanied by lions, or chained and exposed to them, in allusion to his martyrdom.

Ignis Fatuus (ig' nis făt' ū ùs). The "Will o' the wisp" or "Friar's lanthorn" (*q.v.*), a flame-like phosphorescence flitting over marshy ground (due to the spontaneous combustion of gases from decaying vegetable matter), and deluding people who attempt to follow it: hence, any delusive aim or object, or some Utopian scheme that is utterly impracticable. The name means "a foolish fire"; it is also called "Jack o' Lantern," "Spunkie," "Walking Fire," and "Fair Maid of Ireland."

When thou rannest up Gadshill in the night to catch my horse, if I did not think thou hadst been an *ignis fatuus* or a ball of wildfire, there's no purchase in money.— 1 *Henry IV*, iii, 3.

According to a Russian superstition, these wandering fires are the spirits of still-born children which flit between heaven and the Inferno.

Ignoramus (ig nôr ā' mus). One who ignores the knowledge of something; one really unacquainted with it. It is an ancient law term. The grand jury used to write *Ignoramus* on the back of indictments "not found" or not to be sent into court. Hence *ignore*.

Igraine (i grān). Wife of Gorlois (*q.v.*), Duke of Tintagel, in Cornwall, and mother of King Arthur. His father, Uther Pendragon, married Igraine thirteen days after her husband was slain.

Ihram (i răm). The ceremonial garb of Mohammedan pilgrims to Mecca; also, the ceremony of assuming it.

We prepared to perform the ceremony of *Al-Ihram* (assuming the pilgrim garb) . . . we donned the attire, which is nothing but two new cotton cloths, each six feet long by three and a half broad, white with narrow red stripes and fringes. . . . One of these sheets, technically armed the *Rida*, is thrown over the back, and, exposing the arm and shoulder, is knotted at the right side in the style of *Wishah*. The *Izar* is wrapped round the loins from waist to knee, and, knotted or tucked in at the middle, supports itself.— BURTON: *Pilgrimage to Al-Madinah and Mecca*, xxvi.

I.H.S.—*i.e.* the Greek *IHΣ*, meaning *IHΣovs* (Jesus), the long e (H) being mistaken for a capital H, and the dash perverted into a cross. The letters being thus obtained, St. Bernardine of Siena, in 1347, applied them to *Jesus Hominum Salvator* (Jesus, the Saviour of men), another application being *In hac salus* (safety in this *i.e.* the Cross).

Iliad (il' i ȧd) (Gr. *Ilias*, gen. *Iliad-os*, the land of Ilium). The tale of the siege of Troy, or Ilium, an epic poem attributed to Homer (*q.v.*), in twenty-four books. Menelaus, King of Sparta, received as his guest Paris, a son of Priam, King of Troy, who ran away with Helen, wife of Menelaus. Menelaus induced the Greeks to lay siege to Troy to avenge the perfidy, and the siege lasted ten years. The poem begins in the tenth year with a quarrel between Agamemnon, King of Mycenæ and commander-in-chief of the allied Greeks, and Achilles, the hero who had retired from the army in ill temper. The Trojans now prevail, and Achilles sends his friend Patroclus to oppose them, but Patroclus is slain. Achilles, in a desperate rage, rushes into the battle, and slays Hector, the commander of the Trojan army. The poem ends with the funeral rites of Hector.

The French Iliad. The *Romance of the Rose* (*see* ROSE) has been so called. Similarly, the *Nibelungenlied* (*q.v.*) and the *Lusiad* (*q.v.*) have been called respectively the *German* and *Portuguese Iliad.*

Ilk (A.S. *ilca*, the same). Only used— correctly—in the phrase **of that ilk**, when the surname of the person spoken of is the same as the name of his estate; *Bethune of that ilk* means "Bethune of Bethune." It is a mistake to use the phrase "All that ilk" to signify all of that name or family.

Illegitimates. An old Australian slang phrase applied to early settlers who came to the country voluntarily, and not for "legal" reasons—*i.e.* as convicts.

Illinois. Originally the name of a confederacy of North American Indian tribes who were allied to the French. *Illini* means "man," and the French substituted their plural termination *-ois* for the Indian *-uk.*

Illinois nut. The pecan.

Ill-starred. Unlucky; fated to be unfortunate. Othello says of Desdemona, "O ill-starred wench!" The allusion is to the astrological dogma that the stars influence the fortunes of mankind.

Illuminated Doctor. Raymond Lully (1254-1315), the Spanish scholastic philosopher; also Johann Tauler (1294-1361), the German mystic.

Illuminati. The baptised were at one time so called, because a lighted candle was given them to hold as a symbol that they were illuminated by the Holy Ghost.

The name has been given to, or adopted by, several sects and secret societies professing to have superior enlightenment, especially to a republican society of deists, founded by Adam Weishaupt (1748-1830) at Ingoldstadt in Bavaria in 1776, having for its object the establishment of a religion consistent with "sound reason."

Among others to whom the name has been applied are the Hesychasts; the Alombrados, a Spanish sect founded about 1575 by the Carmelite, Catherine de Jesus, and John of Willelpando, the members of which rejected the sacraments; the French Guerinists; the Rosicrucians (*q.v.*); and in the U.S.A. to the Jeffersonians, and (by them) to the Princetonians and opponents of Freemasonry.

Illuminator, The. The surname given to St. Gregory of Armenia (257-331), the apostle of Christianity among the Armenians.

Ilokano (ē lō ka' nō), an Indonesian language spoken in Luzon; but the term is also in use since World War II to describe a sort of lingua franca composed of Malay, English, and Spanish, common in the Philippines and adjacent islands of Malaysia.

Image-breakers, The. *See* ICONOCLASTS.

Imaum or **Imam** (i' măm, i măm'). A member of the priestly body of the Mohammedans. He recites the prayers and leads the devotions of the congregation. The Sultan of Turkey as "head of the Moslems" was an Imaum, and the title is also given to the Sultan of Muscat and to the heads of the four orthodox Moslem sects. The word means *teacher* or *guide. Cp.* ULEMA.

Imbroglio (im brō lyō) (Ital.). A complicated plot; a misunderstanding of a complicated nature.

Immaculate Conception. This dogma, that the Virgin Mary was conceived without original sin, was first broached by St. Bernard, was stoutly maintained by Duns Scotus and his disciples, but was not declared by the Roman Catholic Church to be an article of faith till 1854. It was proclaimed by Pius IX in the bull *Ineffabilis Deus* in these words:—

That the most blessed Virgin Mary, in the first moment of her conception, by a special grace and privilege of Almighty God, in virtue of the merits of Christ, was preserved immaculate from all stain of original sin.

The Feast of the Immaculate Conception is celebrated on December 8th, and is a holiday of obligation (*q.v.*).

Immolate (im′ ō lāt). To sacrifice; literally, "put meal on one" (Lat. *immolare*, to sprinkle with meal). The reference is to the ancient Roman custom of sprinkling wine and fragments of the sacred cake (*mola salsa*) on the head of a victim to be offered in sacrifice.

Immortal. The Immortal. Yông-Tching (1723-36), third of the Manchu dynasty of China, assumed the title.

The Immortal Tinker. John Bunyan (1628-88), a tinker by trade.

The Immortals. The forty members of the French Academy; also the name given to a body of 10,000 foot-soldiers, which constituted the bodyguard of the ancient Persian kings, and to other highly trained troops.

In the British Army the 76th Foot were called "The Immortals," because so many were wounded, but not killed, in India (1788-1806). This regiment, with the old 33rd, now forms the two battalions of the West Riding regiment.

Imp. A graft (A.S. *impian*), a shoot; hence offspring, and a child. In hawking, "to imp a feather" was to engraft or add a new feather for a broken one. The needles employed for the purpose were called "imping needles."

The noun "imp," child, did not formerly connote mischievousness as it now does; Thomas Cromwell, writing to Henry VIII, speaks of "that noble imp your son."

Let us pray for . . . the king's most excellent majesty and for . . . his beloved son Edward, our prince, that most angelic imp.—*Pathway to prayer.*

Milton calls the serpent "fittest imp of fraud" (*Paradise Lost*, ix, 89).

Lincoln Imp. *See* LINCOLN.

Imperial. From the Lat. *imperialis, imperium*, the word really means anything to do with an empire or emperor. Following are some of its special and particular applications:—

A standard size of printing paper measuring between 22 × 30 in. and 22 × 32 in. Also of writing paper measuring 22 × 30 in.

In Russia there used to be current a gold coin, value 15 roubles, called an "imperial."

A tuft of hair on the chin, all the rest of the beard and all the whiskers being shaved off. So called from the Emperor Napoleon III (1808-73), who set the fashion.

Imperial Conference. The origin of this goes back to Queen Victoria's Jubilee (1887) when the prime ministers of the various dominions were in London and met together to confer. Similar conferences were held in 1897, 1902, 1907, 1911, and since World War I it has met every few years in London or elsewhere.

The Imperial Service Order was instituted by Edward VII in 1902 for Civil Servants with long and meritorious records.

Imperialism, coming from the Latin *imperium* is applied in modern times to the belief in the expansion and development of an empire, more especially the British Empire. It came into use in the latter part of the 19th century, since when the word has gradually come to acquire a somewhat derogatory meaning, suggestive of jingoism.

Imposition. A task given in schools, etc., as a punishment. The word is taken from the verb *impose*, as the task is imposed. In the sense of a *deception* it means to "put a trick on a person," hence, the expression "to put on one," etc.

Imposition of hands. The bishop laying his hand on persons confirmed or ordained (*Acts* vi, viii, xix). *See* TO LAY HANDS ON *under* HAND.

Impossibilities (phrases).
Gathering grapes from thistles.
Fetching water in a sieve.
Washing a blackamoor white.
Catching wind in cabbage nets.
Flaying eels by the tail.
Making cheese of chalk.
Squaring the circle.
Turning base metal into gold.
Making a silk purse of a sow's ear.
　　(And hundreds more).

Impressionist. An important school in the history of painting. As the name implies, it desired to capture the impression of colour of transitory and volatile nature rather than its form. The first phase—the study of light—was headed by Edouard Manet (1832-83); the second, which specialized in "*peinture claire*"—an endeavour to eliminate grey and black from the palette and achieve the effects of light by dabs of pure juxtaposed colour—by Claude Monet (1840-1926).

Imprimatur (im pri mā′ tŭr). An official licence to print a book, especially a licence from the ecclesiastical authorities of the Catholic Church, or—where censorship exists—from the official censor. The word is the 3rd sing. pres. subj. of Lat. *imprimere*, "let it be printed."

What advantage is it to be a man, over it is to be a boy at school, if we have only escaped the ferula, to come under the fescue of an Imprimatur? If serious and elaborate writings, as if they were no more than the theme of a grammar-lad under his pedagogue, must not be uttered without the cursory eyes of a temporizing and extemporizing licenser?—MILTON: *Areopagitica*.

Impropriation. Profits of ecclesiastical property in the hands of a layman, who is called the *impropriator*. *Appropriation* is the term used when the profits of a benefice are in the hands of a college or spiritual corporation.

In commendam (in kom en' dâm) (Lat., in trust). The holding of church preferment for a time, on the recommendation of the Crown, till a suitable person can be provided. Thus a benefice-holder who has become a bishop and is allowed to hold his living for a time is said to hold it *in commendam*.

In esse (in es' i). In actual existence (Lat. *esse*, to be), as opposed to *in posse*, in potentiality. Thus a living child is "in esse," but before birth is only "in posse."

In extenso (in eks ten' sō) (Lat.). At full length, word for word, without abridgment.

In extremis (in eks trē' mis) (Lat.). At the very point of death; *in articulo mortis*.

In flagrante delicto (in flâ grän' te de lik' to). Red-handed; in the very fact (Lat., while the offence is flagrant).

In gremio legis (in grē' mi ō lē' jis) (Lat.). Under the protection of (literally, at the breast of) the law.

In loco parentis (in lō' kō pa ren' tis). (Lat.). In the position of being in a parent's place.

In medias res (in mē' di ǎs rēz) (Lat.). In the middle of the subject. In novels and epic poetry, the author generally begins *in medias re*, and explains the preceding events as the tale unfolds. In history, on the other hand, the author begins *ab ovo* (*q.v.*).

In memoriam (in me môr' i ǎm) (Lat.). In memory of.

In petto (in pet' ō) (Ital.). Held in reserve, kept back, something done privately, and not announced to the general public. (Lat. *in pectore*, in the breast.)

Cardinals in petto. Cardinals chosen by the Pope, but not yet publicly announced. Their names are *in pectore* (of the Pope).

In posse. See IN ESSE.

In propria persona (in prop' ri a pěr sō' nà) (Lat.). Personally, and not by deputy or agents.

In re (in rē) (Lat.). In the matter of; on the subject of; as *In re* Jones *v.* Robinson. But **in rem**, against the property or thing referred to.

In situ (in sī' tū) (Lat.). In its original place.

I at first mistook it for a rock *in situ*, and took out my compass to observe the direction of its cleavage.—DARWIN: *Voyage in the Beagle*, ix.

In statu quo (in stǎt' ū kwō) or *In statu quo ante* (Lat.). In the condition things were before the change took place. Thus, two nations arming for war may agree to lay down arms on condition that all things be restored to the same state as they were before they took up arms.

In toto (in tō' tō) (Lat.). Entirely, altogether.

In vacuo (in vǎk' ū ō) (Lat.). In a vacuum—*i.e.* in a space from which, nominally all, and really almost all, the air has been taken away.

In vino veritas (Lat.). See VINO.

Inaugurate. To install into some office with appropriate ceremonies, to open or introduce formally. From Lat. *inaugurare*, which meant first to take omens from the flight of birds by augury (*q.v.*), and then to consecrate or install after taking such omens.

Inbread. See BAKER'S DOZEN:

Inca (ing' kà). A king or royal prince of the ancient Peruvians. Of this dynasty Manco Capac was the founder (*c.* A.D. 1240) and Atahualpa, murdered by the Spaniards in 1533, the last. The Inca Empire covered a wide area extending from Quito southwards into northern Chile, and from the Pacific seaboard to beyond the Andes, a region over 2,000 miles long and 500 miles wide, with its capital at Cuzco. The Incas were skilful agriculturists, and maintained an enlightened social and economic regime that has not been seen in S. America since their time.

The Inca was a war-chief, elected by the Council to carry out its decision.—BRINTON: *The American Race* (*South American Tribes*), pt. i, ch. ii, p. 211.

Incog.—*i.e.* **Incognito** (in kog' ni tō) (Ital.). Under an assumed name or title. When a royal person travels, and does not wish to be treated with royal ceremony, he assumes some inferior title for the nonce, and travels *incog*.

Income Tax. From the days of the Revolution of 1688 English statesmen have taken steps in one direction or another to introduce a tax on incomes. The first workable tax of this nature was devised by William Pitt, in 1799, to finance the war with France. A tax of 10 per cent. was put on all incomes over £200, with a modified charge for those between that sum and £60, beneath which all were exempt. This tax was dropped in 1802 but the next year a new Income Tax was introduced on practically the same system of schedules, etc., as is still in force. Though aiming at only 5 per cent. of the Income, this tax yielded as much as the earlier tax. The new tax was dropped in 1815, but it was renewed by Peel in 1842, with an exemption limit of £150 (in 1853 lowered to £100) at a rate varying between 6d. and 8d. in the £. In 1874-75 this sank so low as 2d. in the £. In the South African war the Income Tax rose to 1s.; in World War I to 6s. and in World War II to 10s. Since World War I a surtax has been charged in addition to the standard rate of Income Tax on incomes over £2,000.

In 1944 a system of Pay As You Earn (P.A.Y.E.) was introduced which facilitated the payment and collection of Income Tax by making the employer deduct the tax from the employee's wages.

Incorruptible, The. Robespierre. *See* SEA-GREEN.

Incubus (ing' kū bŭs). A nightmare, anything that weighs heavily on the mind. In mediæval times it denoted an evil spirit who was supposed to consort with women in their sleep. (Lat. *incubo*, nightmare, from *incubare*, to lie on.)

Merlin was the son of no mortal father, but of an Incubus; one of a class of beings not absolutely wicked, but far from good, who inhabit the regions of the air.— BULLFINCH: *Age of Chivalry*, pt. i, ch. iii.

Indenture (in den' chŭr). A written contract, specially one between an apprentice and his master; so called because the identical documents held by each party had their edges indented in such a manner that they would fit precisely into each other.

Independence Day. July 4th, which is kept as a national holiday in the United States of America, because the declaration by the American States, declaring the colonies free and independent and absolved from all allegiance to Great Britain, was signed on that day (1776).

Index. The "Roman Index" includes the *Index Librorum Prohibitorum* and the *Index Expurgatorius*. The former contains a list of such books as are absolutely forbidden to be read by Catholics. The latter contains such books as are forbidden till certain parts are omitted or amended. Rules for the guidance of the compilers were formulated by the Council of Trent (1563), and the first *Index* was published under Pius IV in 1564. The lists are made out by a board of cardinals (*Congregation of the Index*). Besides the Protestant Bibles, and the works of such schismatics as Arius and Calvin, we find in the lists the following well-known names:—

Of English authors: Addison, Bacon, Chaucer, Gibbon, Goldsmith, Hallam, Andrew Lang, Locke, J. S. Mill, Milton, Robertson, Whately, etc., and even some children's tales.

Of French authors: Arnauld, Descartes, Dumas, Fenélon, Hugo, Malebranche, Montaigne, Pascal, Renan, Taine, Voltaire, etc.

Of Italian authors: Dante, d'Annunzio, Guicciardini, Sismondi.

India. The independence of India was created by a Bill introduced on July 4th, 1947 and given the Royal Assent on the 19th of the same month. On August 15th British India became two dominions—India and Pakistan, the first mainly Hindu and the second almost entirely Moslem. Each has its own legislature and Governor General. Each independent state was left to decide for itself to which of the two dominions it would belong.

India is so named from Indus (the river), in Sanskrit *Sindhu*, in Persic *Hindu* (the water). *Hindustan* is the *stan* or "country" of the river *Hindus*.

India paper. A creamy-coloured printing-paper originally made in China and Japan from vegetable fibre, and used for taking off the finest proofs of engraved plates; hence **India proof**, the proof of an engraving on India paper, before lettering.

The *India paper* (or *Oxford India paper*) used for printing Bibles and high-class "thin paper" and "pocket" editions, is a very thin, tough and opaque imitation of this.

Indian. American Indians. When Columbus landed on one of the Bahamas he thought that he had reached India, and in this belief gave the natives the name of Indians. Nowadays, in order to avoid ambiguity, the American Indians are known by ethnologists as **Amerinds**.

Indian file. One after the other, singly. The American Indians, when they go on an expedition, march one by one. The one behind carefully steps in the footprints of the one before, and the last man of the file is supposed to obliterate the footprints. Thus, neither the track nor the number of invaders can be traced.

Indian summer. The autumnal summer, occurring as a rule in the early part of October. It is often the finest and mildest part of the whole year, especially in North America.

The gilding of the Indian summer mellowed the pastures far and wide. The russet woods stood ripe to be stript, but were yet full of leaf. The purple of heath-bloom, faded but not withered, tinged the hills. . . . Fieldhead gardens bore the seal of gentle decay; . . . its time of flowers and even of fruit was over.—C. BRONTË: *Shirley*, ch. xxvii.

Indo-European, a term invented by Thomas Young the Egyptologist in 1813 and later adopted by scientists to describe the race and language from which the main Indian and European peoples sprang. Anthropologists have devoted to the subject much study as yet inconclusive; philologists have classified the Indo-European languages in such broad groups as Greek; Latin; Celtic; Teutonic; Sanskrit and Iranian; Armenian; Slavonic; Albanian.

Indonesia (in dō nē' zhà), a term that includes the islands of the Malay Archipelago and such islands as Sumatra, Java, Borneo, the Celebes, the Lesser Sunda Islands, the Moluccas, the Philippines.

Induction (Lat., the act of leading in). When a clergyman is inducted to a living he is led to the church door, and the ring which forms the handle is placed in his hand. The door being opened, he is next led into the church, and the fact is announced to the parish by tolling the bell.

Indulgence. In Catholic theology the remission before God of the temporal punish ment due for those sins of which the guilt has been forgiven in the sacrament of Penance. The competent ecclesiastical authority grants such indulgences out of the Treasury of the Church (q.v.); they are either plenary or partial; partial remitting a part only of such punishment due for sin at any given moment, the proportion being expressed in terms of time (e.g. thirty days, seven years). The precise meaning of these terms has never been defined, but they date back to the ancient penitential discipline of the Church. In the Middle Ages indulgences were of high commercial value, and it was the sale of them that first roused the ire of Luther and prepared the way for the Reformation.

Industrial Revolution is the term applied to the social and economic changes that took place in Britain from the late 18th to the mid-19th century, when the introduction of machinery in manufacture and railways for transport entirely revolutionized the methods of living and the location of industries throughout the country.

Ineffable. See AFFABLE.

Infallibility. The doctrine that the Pope, when speaking *ex cathedra* (q.v.) on a question of faith or morals, is free from error did not become an accepted dogma of the Church until the Vatican Council of 1870. The promulgation of the dogma, after having been agreed to by the council (many members dissenting or abstaining from voting), was publicly read by Pius IX at St. Peter's.

Infallibility does not involve inspiration or universal inerrability; the Pope does not originate new doctrines infallibly, his infallibility preserves him from making errors in defining truths of doctrines or morals.

Infant. Literally, one who is unable to speak (Lat. *infans*, ultimately from *in*, negative, and *fari*, to speak. *Cp.* INFAMOUS *above*). Used as a synonym of "childe," as in *Childe Harold* (q.v.), meaning a knight or youth of gentle birth, the word was once of common occurrence. Thus, as in the following passage, Spenser frequently refers to Prince Arthur in this way: —

The Infant harkened wisely to her tale,
And wondered much at Cupid's judg'ment wise.
Faerie Queene, VI, viii, 25.

Infanta. Any princess of the blood royal, except an heiress of the crown, was so called in Spain and in Portugal.

Infante. All the sons of the sovereigns of Spain bore this title; as did those of Portugal, except the crown prince, who was called in Spain the Prince of Asturias.

Infantry. Foot soldiers. This is the same word as *infant* (q.v.); it is the Italian *infanteria*, a foot soldier, from *infanta*, a youth; hence, one who is too inexperienced to serve in the cavalry.

Inferiority Complex. A psycho-analytical term for a complex resulting from a sense of inferiority dating from childhood. Over-compensation for that feeling produces, it is suggested, an exaggerated or even abnormal desire for success, power, and accomplishment, and frequently a conceited and pushing attitude.

Inferno (in fĕr' nō). We have Dante's notion of the infernal regions in his *Inferno*; Homer's in the *Odyssey*, Bk. xi; Virgil's in the *Æneid*, Bk. vi; Spenser's in the *Faerie Queene*, Bk. ii, canto 7; Ariosto's in *Orlando Furioso*, Bk. xvii; Tasso's in *Jerusalem Delivered*, Bk. iv.; Milton's in *Paradise Lost*; Fénelon's in *Télémaque*, Bk. xviii; and Beckford's in his romance of *Vathek*. See HELL: HADES.

Informer. Readers of *Pickwick Papers* and other novels of the period will find references to police informers. Before the organization of the police and detective forces a thriving trade used to be driven by a certain class of persons who frequented the streets and public places on the look-out for anyone committing minor illegal acts, which they reported to the authorities for a small fee.

Infra dig. Not befitting one's position and Public character. Short for Lat. *infra dignitatem*, beneath (one's) dignity.

Infralapsarian. The same as a SUBLAPSARIAN (*q.v.*).

Inhibition, in psychology, is an unconscious force forbidding what would otherwise be an impulse or urge.

Injunction. A writ forbidding a person to encroach on another's privileges; as, to sell a book which is only a colourable copy of another author's book; or to infringe a patent; or to perform a play based on a novel without permission of the novelist; or to publish a book the rights of which are reserved. Injunctions are of two sorts—temporary and perpetual. The first is limited "till the coming on of the defendant's answer"; the latter is based on the merits of the case, and is of perpetual force.

Ink. From Lat. *encaustum* (Gr. *enkaustos*, burnt in), the name given to the purple fluid used by the Roman emperors for writing with.

Inkhorn terms. A common term in Elizabethan times for pedantic expressions which smell of the lamp. The inkhorn was the receptacle for ink which pedants and pedagogues wore fastened to the clothing.

> I know them that thinke rhetorique to stand wholie upon darke wordes, and hee that can catch an ynke home terme by the taile, him they coumpt to be a fine Englishman.—WILSON: *Arte of Rhetorique* (1553).

Shakespeare uses the phrase, an "Inkhorn mate" (1 *Henry VI*, iii, 1).

Ink-slinger (U.S.A., ink-jerker). A contemptuous name for a writer, especially for a newspaper journalist.

Inn. The word is Anglo-Saxon, and meant originally an ordinary dwelling-house, residence, or lodging. Hence Clifford's Inn, once the mansion of De Clifford; Lincoln's Inn, the abode of the Earls of Lincoln; Gray's Inn, that of the Lords Gray, etc.

> Now, whenas Phœbus, with his fiery waine,
> Unto his inne began to draw apace.
> SPENSER: *Faerie Queene*, VI, iii, 29.

Innocent, An. An idiot or born fool was formerly so called. *Cp.* BENET.

> Although he be in body deformed, in minde foolish, an innocent borne, a begger by misfortune, yet doth he deserve a better than thy selfe.—LYLY: *Euphues* (1579).

Innuendo (in ū en' dō). An implied or covert hint of blame, a suggestion that one dare not make openly, so it is made indirectly, as by a nod; originally a law term, meaning the person nodded to or indirectly referred to (Lat., *in-nuo*, to nod to).

Ino. *See* LEUCOTHEA.

Inoculation. Originally, the horticultural practice of grafting a *bud* (Lat., *oculus*) into an inferior plant, in order to produce flowers or fruits of better quality; hence, introducing into the body infectious matter which produces a mild form of the disease against which this treatment is counted on to render one immune.

Inquisition. A court instituted to inquire into offences against the Roman Catholic religion, and fully established by Gregory IX in 1229. Torture, as a means of extracting recantations or evidence, was first authorized by Innocent IV in 1252, and those found guilty were handed over to the secular arm to be dealt with according to the secular laws of the land. The Inquisition was generally administered by the Dominicans, from which Order came the notorious Torquemada (1420-98), who was Inquisitor-General 1483-94. It was most active in southern Europe, particularly in Spain, where it flourished from 1237 to 1820. It was suppressed in France in 1772. The Inquisition now known as the Holy Office occupies itself with the protection of faith and morals and among other activities examines and, where it considers necessary, prohibits books dangerous to the faithful.

Insane Root, The. A plant which is not positively identified, but which was probably henbane or hemlock, supposed to deprive of his senses anyone who took it. Banquo says of the witches:—

> Were such things here as we do speak about?
> Or have we eaten on the insane root
> That takes the reason prisoner?
> *Macbeth*, i, 3.

There were many plants to which similar properties were, rightly or wrongly, attributed, such as the mandrake, belladonna (deadly nightshade), poppy, etc.; and *cp.* MOLY.

Inscription (*on coins*). *See* LEGEND.

Inspired Idiot, The. Oliver Goldsmith (1728-1774) was so called by Horace Walpole.

Institutes. A digest of the elements of a subject, especially of law. The most celebrated is the *Institutes of Justinian*, completed in A.D. 533 at the order of the Emperor. It was based on the earlier *Institutes of Gaius*, and was intended as an introduction to the Pandects (*q.v.*). Other *Institutes* are those of Florentius, Callistratus, Paulus, Ulpiant, and Marcian.

Insulin (in' su lin), a specific discovered by Sir F. G. Banting (1891-1941). It is extracted from the pancreatic glands of oxen and its function is to reduce the sugar in the blood; for this reason it is used in the treatment of diabetes.

Insult. Literally, to leap on (the prostrate body of a foe); hence, to treat with contumely

(Lat. *insultare*, *saltus*, a leap). Terence says, *Insultare fores calcibus* (*Eunuchus*, ii. 2, 54). It will be remembered that the priests of Baal, to show their indignation against their gods, "leaped upon the altar which they had made" (1 *Kings* xviii, 26). *Cp.* DESULTORY.

Intaglio (in ta' lyō) (Ital.). A design cut into a gem, like a crest or initials in a stamp. The design does not stand out in relief, as in a cameo (*q.v.*), but is hollowed in.

Intelligence Quotient, commonly abbreviated to I.Q., is the ratio, expressed as a percentage, of a person's mental age to his actual age, the former being the age for which he scores 100 per cent. when tested by the Binet or some similar system. The Binet Tests consist in testing a child's intelligence by asking standard questions adapted to the intelligence of a normal child of that age.

Intelligentsia (in tel i jen' si à). A Russian term for the educated and cultured classes, which has acquired in English a somewhat derogatory sense.

Intercalary (in tĕr kăl' à ri) (Lat. *inter*, between, *calare*, to proclaim solemnly). An intercalary day is a day thrust in between two others, as February 29th in leap year; so called because, among the Romans, this was a subject for solemn proclamation. *Cp.* CALENDS.

Interdict (in' tĕr dikt). In the Roman Catholic Church an Interdict is a sentence of excommunication directed against a place and/or its inhabitants; if the place only is under the interdict the sacraments cannot be administered there, burials with religious ceremonies are prohibited, and all church communion is in abeyance. The most remarkable instances are:—

586. The Bishop of Bayeux laid an interdict on all the churches of Rouen, in consequence of the murder of the Bishop Prétextat.

1081. Poland was laid under an interdict by Gregory VII, because Boleslas II had murdered Stanislaus at the altar.

1180. Scotland was put under a similar ban by Pope Alexander III.

1200. France was interdicted by Innocent III, because Philippe Auguste refused to marry Ingelburge, who had been betrothed to him.

1209. England was under similar sentence for six years (Innocent III), in the reign of King John.

Interest (Lat. *interesse*, to be a concern to). The *interest* on money is the sum which a borrower agrees to pay a lender for its use.

Simple interest is interest on the principal, or money lent, only; compound interest is interest on the principal plus the interest as it accrues.

In an interesting condition. Said of a woman who is expecting to become a mother. The phrase came into use in the 18th century.

Interloper. One who "runs" between traders and upsets their business by interfering with their actual or supposed rights. The word came into English through the Dutch trade in the 16th century, and the *lope* is a dialect form of *leap* confused with Dut. *loopen*, to run (as in *elope*).

Intrigue (in trēg'). From the Latin *tricae*, trifles, whence the verb *intrico*, to entangle. In its more common use the word means an underhand plot, a piece of crafty manœuvring, or a liaison. Within the 20th century, however, it has come to be used as a transitive verb meaning to rouse the interest of, to awaken curiosity, as one may talk of an intriguing play, or a situation that intrigued one. In the 17th and 18th centuries this connotation was not at all rare.

Introvert. The psychological term for an introspective person who instinctively seeks to alter his conception of external realities to make them correspond more closely with his own desires. An introvert is interested mainly in his own mental processes and in the way in which he is regarded by others; he is thus retiring in manner and usually shy.

Invalides (an' và lēd). *Hôtel des Invalides*. The great institution founded by Louis XIV at Paris in 1670 for disabled and superannuated soldiers. It contains large numbers of military trophies, statues, paintings, etc., and a museum of artillery and mediæval and renaissance armour.

The central feature of the church of the Invalides is the tomb of Napoleon, whose body was brought hither from St. Helena in 1840. Close by are the tombs of his son, the Duke of Reichstadt (L'Aiglon) and Marshal Foch (1851-1929). Others buried there are Marshal Turenne (1611-75); General Bertrand (1773-1844); Marshals Duroc (1772-1813) and Grouchy (1766-1847); General Kléber (1753-1800); Joseph Bonaparte, King of Naples and Spain (1768-1844); and Jerome Bonaparte, King of Westphalia (1784-1860).

Inventions. The following are some of the most important inventions in the history of civilized man. No date can be given to the most useful invention of all, that of the wheel (involving the use of rollers and pulleys) for in Europe and Asia Minor it dates back to prehistoric times. Yet in America and in early Egypt the pulley was unknown.

Lever and screw: Archimedes (*c.* 287-212, B.C.)

Printing: from movable type, China, A.D. 1041; in Europe, 1440.

Gunpowder (in the Western world): the monk Berthold Schwartz, 1313.

Logarithms: J. Napier, 1614; J. Burgi, 1620.

Steam engine: Piston, Newcommen, 1698.
　　　　　　Condenser, Watt, 1769.
　　　　　　Locomotive, Trevethick, 1804.
　　　　　　Turbine, Parsons, 1884.

Spinning jenny: Arkwright, 1769.

Gas illumination: Murdoch, 1792.

Electricity: Leyden Jar, 1745.
　　　　　　Electro-magnetic induction, Faraday, 1831.

Steel: Bessemer process, 1856.

Anæsthetics: Humphrey Davy, 1799.
　　　　　　Chloroform, Simpson, 1847.

Wireless: receiving and transmitting apparatus, Marconi, 1895.

Internal combustion engine: Gottlieb, 1883.

Aeroplane: Wright Brothers, 1903.

Radiography: Röntgen Rays, 1895.

Photography: J. N. Niepce, 1817, Daguerre, 1839.

Atomic energy: splitting of the atom by Cockroft and Walton, 1932.

Invention of the Cross. *See* CROSS.

Inventors. A curious instance of the *sin of* invention is mentioned in the *Bridge of Allan Reporter*, February, 1803:—

It is told of Mr. Ferguson's grandfather, that he invented a pair of fanners for cleaning grain, and for this proof of superior ingenuity he was summoned before the Kirk Session, and reproved for trying to place the handiwork of man above the time-honoured practice of cleaning the grain on windy days, when the current was blowing briskly through the open doors of the barn.

It is extraordinary how many inventors have been "hoist with their own petard"; the following list—in which some entries will no doubt be found that belong to the realm of fable—is by no means complete:—

Bastille. Hugues Aubriot, Provost of Paris, who built the Bastille, was the first person confined therein. The charge against him was heresy.

Brazen Bull. Perillos of Athens made a brazen bull for Phalaris, Tyrant of Agrigentum, intended for the execution of criminals, who were shut up in the bull, fires being lighted below the belly. Phalaris admired the invention, and tested it on Perillos himself, who was the first person baked to death in the horrible monster.

Cannon. Thomas Montacute, 4th Earl of Salisbury was the first to use cannon, and was the first Englishman killed by a cannon ball, at Tourelles, 1428.

Catherine Wheel. The inventor of St. Catherine's Wheel, a diabolical machine consisting of four wheels turning different ways, and each wheel armed with saws, knives, and teeth, was killed by his own machine; for when St. Catherine was bound on the wheel, she fell off, and the machine flew to pieces. One of the pieces struck the inventor, and other pieces struck several of the men employed to work it, all of whom were killed. (*Metaphrastes*.)

Eddystone. Henry Winstanley erected the first Eddystone lighthouse. It was a wooden polygon, 100 feet high, on a stone base; but it was washed away by a storm in 1703, and the architect perished in his own edifice.

Gallows and *Gibbet*. We are told in the book of *Esther* that Haman devised a gallows 50 cubits high on which to hang Mordecai, by way of commencing the extirpation of the Jews; but the favourite of Ahasuerus was himself hanged thereon. We have a repetition of this incident in the case of Enguerrand de Marigni, Minister of Finance to Philippe the Fair, who was hung on the gibbet which he had caused to be erected at Montfaucon for the execution of certain felons; and four of his successors in office underwent the same fate.

Guillotine. J. B. V. Guillotin, M.D., of Lyons, was guillotined, but it is an error to credit him with the invention of the instrument. The inventor was Dr. Joseph Agnace Guillotin.

Iron Cage. The Bishop of Verdun, who invented the Iron Cage, too small to allow the person confined in it to stand upright or lie at full length, was the first to be shut up in one; and Cardinal La Balue, who recommended them to Louis XI, was himself confined in one for ten years.

Iron Shroud. Ludovico Sforza, who invented the Iron Shroud, was the first to suffer death by this horrible torture.

Maiden. The Regent Morton of Scotland, who invented the Maiden (*q.v.*), was the first to be beheaded thereby.

Ostracism. Clisthenes introduced the custom of Ostracism (*q.v.*), and was the first to be banished thereby.

The *Perrière* was a piece of mediæval artillery for throwing stones of 3,000 lb. in weight; and the inventor fell a victim to his own invention by the accidental discharge of a perrière against a wall.

Sanctuary. Eutropius induced the Emperor Arcadius to abolish the benefit of sanctuary; but a few days afterwards he committed some offence and fled for safety to the nearest church. St. Chrysostom told him he had fallen into his own net, and he was put to death. (*Life of St. Chrysostom.*)

Turret-ship. Cowper Coles, inventor of the Turret-ship, perished in the *Captain* off Finisterre September 7th, 1870.

Witch-finding. Matthew Hopkins, the witch-finder, was himself tried by his own tests, and put to death as a wizard in 1647.

Invisibility, according to fable, might be obtained in a multitude of ways. For example:—

Alberich's cloak, "Tarnkappe," which Siegfried got possession of, rendered him invisible. (*Nibelungenlied.*)

A *dead hand.* It was believed that a candle placed in a dead man's hand gives no light to any but those who use it. *See* HAND.

The *helmet* of Perseus and the helmet that Pluto gave to the Cyclops (*Orci Galea*) both rendered the wearers invisible.

Jack the Giant-killer had a cloak of invisibility as well as a cap of knowledge.

Otnit's ring. The ring of Otnit, King of Lombardy, according to the *Heldenbuch,* possessed a similar charm.

Reynard's wonderful ring had three colours, one of which (green) caused the wearer to become invisible. (*Reynard the Fox, q.v.*)

See also FERN SEED; GYGES' RING; HELIOTROPE.

The Druids were supposed to possess the power of making themselves invisible by producing a magic mist; and this spell, the *faeth fiadha,* appears in the stories of St. Patrick and other early British saints.

Invulnerability. There are many fabulous instances of this having been acquired. According to ancient Greek legend, a dip in the river Styx rendered Achilles invulnerable, and Medea rendered Jason, with whom she had fallen in love, proof against wounds and fire by anointing him with the Promethean unguent.

Siegfried was rendered invulnerable by anointing his body with dragon's blood. (*Nibelungenlied.*)

Ionic (ī on' ik). **Ionic Architecture.** So called from Ionia, where it took its rise. The capitals are decorated with volutes, and the cornice with dentils. The shaft is fluted; the entablature either plain or embellished.

The people of Tonia formed (heir order of architecture on the model of a young woman dressed in her hair, and of an easy, elegant shape; whereas the Doric had been formed on the model of a robust, strong man.—*Vitruvius.*

Ionic School. The school of philosophy that arose in Ionia in the 6th century B.C., and which formed the starting-point of the whole of Greek philosophy. It included Thales, Anaximander, Anaximenes, Heraclitus, and Anaxagoras; and the great advance they made was the recognition that matter, motion, and physical causation were themselves manifestations of the Absolute Reality. They also tried to show that all created things spring from one universal physical cause; Thales said it was water, Anaximenes thought it was air, Anaxagoras that it was atoms, Heraclitus maintained that it was fire or caloric while Anaximander insisted that the elements of all things are eternal, for *ex nihilo nihil fit.*

Iota. See I, JOT.

IOU, *i.e.* "I owe you." The memorandum of a debt given by the borrower to the lender. It requires no stamp unless it specifies a day of payment, when it becomes a *bill,* and must be stamped.

Iphigenia (if i jen ē' a, if i je nī' à). In classical legend, the daughter of Agamemnon and Clytemnestra. One account says that her father, having offended Artemis by killing her favourite stag, vowed to sacrifice to the angry goddess the most beautiful thing that came into his possession in the next twelve months; this was an infant daughter. The father deferred the sacrifice till the fleet of the combined Greeks that was proceeding to Troy reached Aulis and Iphigenia had grown to womanhood. The Calchas told him that the fleet would be windbound till he had fulfilled his vow; accordingly the king prepared to sacrifice his daughter, but Artemis at the last moment snatched her from the altar and carried her to heaven, substituting a hind in her place. Euripides, Æschylus, and Sophocles all wrote tragedies on Iphigenia. *Cp.* IDOMENEUS.

Ipse dixit (ip' se diks' it) (Lat., he himself said so). A mere assertion, wholly unsupported. "It is his *ipse dixit*'" implies that there is no guarantee that what he says is so.

Ipso facto (Lat., by the very fact). Irrespective of all external considerations of right or wrong; absolutely. It sometimes means the act itself carries the consequences (as excommunication without the actual sentence being pronounced).

By burning the Pope's bull, Luther *ipso facto* [by the very deed itself] denied the Pope's supremacy. Heresy carries excommunication *ipso facto*.

I.R.A. The Irish Republican Army, which opposed the Crown forces, the Royal Irish Constabulary, the "Black and Tans," etc., in the rebellion that preceded the grant of dominion status in 1921.

Irak (ē răk'). The name given at different times to varying portions of Mesopotamia (*q.v.*), Babylonia, and the surrounding country. It is now the official name of that portion of the country ruled by the king of Irak with his capital at Bagdad.

Iran (ē ran'), since March, 1935, the official Persian name of modern Persia, though in 1949 it was announced that foreigners might use the name of Persia. The Iranian languages, including Zend and Old Persian, form a branch of the great Indo-European family.

Ireland. Called by the natives Erin, *i.e.* *Erin-nis*, or *Iar-innis* (west island).

By the Welsh, Yver-den (west valley).

By Apuleius, Hibernia, which is *Iernia*, a corruption of *Iar-inni-a*.

By Juvenal (ii, 260), Juverna or Juberna, the same as *Ierna* or *Iernia*.

By Claudian, Ouernia, the same.

By moderns, Ireland, which is *Iar-en-land* (land of the west).

After many struggles throughout the 19th century Ireland was given Home Rule (*q.v.*) in 1914, though the Act was not put into operation until 1920. After much unrest the country was divided into Eire and Northern Ireland in 1921, the former being a sovereign democratic State with a constitution (remodelled in 1937), while Northern Ireland consisting of the counties of Antrim, Armagh, Down, Fermanagh, Londonderry and Tyrone, and the boroughs of Belfast and Londonderry, remains an integral part of the British Empire, with a parliament of its own, returning 12 members to the House of Commons in Westminster.

The fair maid of Ireland. Ignis fatuus (*q.v.*).

He had read in former times of a Going Fire, called "Ignis Fatuus." the fire of destiny; by some, "Will with the Wisp," or "Jack with the Lantern"; and likewise, by some simple country people, "The Fair Maid of Ireland," which used to lead wandering travellers out of their way.—*The Seven Champions of Christendom*, i, 7.

The three great saints of Ireland. St. Patrick, St. Columba, and St. Bridget.

Iris (ī' ris). Goddess of the rainbow, or the rainbow itself. In classical mythology she is called the messenger of the gods when they intended *discord*, and the rainbow is the bridge or road let down from heaven for her accommodation. When the gods meant *peace* they sent Mercury.

I'll have an Iris that shall find thee out.
2 *Henry VI*, iii, 2.

Besides being poetically applied to the rainbow the name, in English, is given to the coloured membrane surrounding the pupil of the eye, and to a family of plants (Iridaceæ) having large, bright-coloured flowers and tuberous roots.

Iron. The Iron Age. An archæological term denoting the cultural phase conditioned by the discovery of the use of iron for edged tools, weapons, etc. Iron was known as a curiosity by the builders of the pyramids, but it was not until 1000 B.C. that iron-working became general in the Mediterranean basin. Its gradual development from the bronze age precursors is traceable at Hallstatt, and its fuller development at La Tene; these places give their names to the first and second periods of the early Iron Age.

The era between the death of Charlemagne and the close of the Carlovingian dynasty (728-987) is sometimes so called from its almost ceaseless wars. It is sometimes called the *leaden* age for its worthlessness, and the *dark* age for its barrenness of learned men. *See* also AGE.

Iron-arm. François de la Noue (1531-91), the Huguenot soldier, *Bras de Fer*, was so called. Fierabras (*q.v.*). is another form of the same.

The Iron Cross. A Prussian military decoration (an iron Maltese cross, edged with silver). It was instituted by Frederick William III in 1813 during the struggle against Napoleon, and was remodelled by William I in 1870, with three grades, in civil and military divisions. In World War I some 3,000,000 Iron Crosses were awarded; there are no figures for World War II.

Iron Curtain. A phrase used to describe the almost impenetrable secrecy with which all happenings in the U.S.S.R. or countries dominated by Russia are concealed from the rest of the world. The phrase was first used by Count Schwerin von Krosigk, the German statesman, in 1945.

The Iron Maiden of Nuremberg. A mediæval instrument of torture used in Germany for "heretics," traitors, parricides, etc. It was a box big enough to admit a man, with folding-doors, the whole studded with sharp iron spikes. When the doors were closed on him these spikes were forced into the body of the victim, who was left there to die in horrible torture.

Iron rations. Bully beef; tinned meat. Also emergency rations (*q.v.*).

Shooting-iron. Slang for a small firearm, especially a pistol or revolver.

To rule with a rod of iron. To rule tyrannically.

Ironside. Edmund II (about 989-1016), King of the West Saxons from April to November, 1016, was so called, from his iron armour.

Nestor Ironside. Sir Richard Steele assumed the name in *The Guardian*.

Ironsides. The soldiers that served under Cromwell were so called, especially after the battle of Marston Moor (1644), where they displayed an iron resolution. The name had first been applied only to a special regiment of stalwarts.

Iron-tooth. Frederick II, Elector of Brandenburg (1440-1470).

Too many irons in the fire. More affairs in hand than you can properly attend to. The allusion is to a smithy where the smith has a number of irons heating to red heat.

In irons. In fetters. A square-rigged sailing vessel is said to be in irons when the yards are so braced that some sails being full of wind and others aback, the vessel is temporarily unmanageable.

Strike while the iron is hot. Don't miss a good opportunity; seize time by the forelock; make hay while the sun shines.

Irony (ī' ron i). A dissembling (Gr. *eiron*, a dissembler, *eironeia*); hence, subtle sarcasm, language having a meaning different from the ostensible one but understood correctly by the initiated. Socratic irony is an assumption of ignorance, as a means of leading on and eventually confuting an opponent.

The irony of fate. A strange fatality which has brought about something quite the reverse of what might have been expected.

By the irony of fate the Ten Hours Bill was carried in the very session when Lord Ashley, having changed his views on the Corn Laws, felt it his duty to resign his seat in Parliament. — *The Leisure Hour*, 1887.

Iroquois (ir' ō kwa). The name given by the French to the five (later six) confederate tribes of North American Indians, viz. the Mohawks, Oneidas, Onondagas, Cayugas, Senecas, and sixth the Tuscaroras, added in 1712, forming "The Six Nations of the Iroquois Confederacy."

Irresistible. Alexander the Great went to consult the Delphic oracle before he started on his expedition against Persia. He chanced, however, to arrive on a day when no responses were made. Nothing daunted, he went in search of the Pythia, and when she refused to attend, took her to the temple by force. "Son," said the priestess, "thou art irresistible." "Enough," cried Alexander; "I accept your words as an answer."

Irus (ī' rus). The beggar of gigantic stature, who waited on the suitors of Penelope. Ulysses, on his return, felled him to the ground with a single blow, and flung his corpse out of doors.

Poorer than Irus. A Greek proverb, adopted by the Romans and the French, alluding to the beggar referred to above.

Irvingites. Members of the Catholic Apostolic Church founded about 1829 by Edward Irving, a Presbyterian minister and a friend of the Carlyles. Irving claimed to revive the college of the Apostles, and established a complex hierarchy with such symbolical titles as "Angel," "Prophet," etc. In their early days they claimed to have manifested the gift of tongues.

Isaac. A hedge-sparrow; a dialect form of *haysugge*, or *haysuck*, an obsolete name for the bird (used by Chaucer). The name meant a *sucker* (small thing) that lived in a *hay* or hedge; a corruption of Chaucer's word, *heisuagge*.

Isabelle. The *colour* so called is the yellow of soiled calico. A yellow-dun horse is, in France, *un cheval isabelle.* According to Isaac D'Israeli (*Curiosities of Literature*) Isabel of Austria, daughter of Philip II, at the siege of Ostend vowed not to change her linen till the place was taken. As the siege lasted three years, we may suppose that it was somewhat soiled by three years' wear.

Another story, equally unwarranted, attaches it to Isabella of Castile, who, we are told, made a vow to the Virgin not to change her linen till Granada fell into her hands.

There is, however, no reason for accepting these very fanciful derivations. The word appears in an extant list of Queen Elizabeth's clothes of July, 1600 ("one rounde gowne of Isabella-colour satten").

Isaiah (ī zī' à). Great controversy has raged round the ascribed author of this book. It seems certain that he was a man of rank and influence, between 735 B.C. and the invasion of Sennacherib in 701. His great task was to warn the Hebrews of the impending Assyrian invasion and recall them to the true worship of Jahveh. In its English version the book of Isaiah contains some of the finest writing in the language.

Ishbosheth (ish bō′ sheth), in Dryden's *Absalom and Achitophel*, is meant for Richard Cromwell. His father, Oliver, is Saul.

The actual Ishbosheth (man of shame) was the son of Saul, who was proclaimed King of Israel at his father's death (*see* 2 *Sam*. iv), and was almost immediately superseded by David.

Ishtar (ish′ tar). The Babylonian goddess of love and war (Gr. *Astarte*), corresponding to the Phœnician Ashtoreth (*q.v.*), except that while the latter was identified with the moon Ishtar was more frequently identified with the planet Venus. She was the wife of Bel.

Isiac Tablet (*i.e.* tablet of Isis). A spurious Egyptian monument sold by a soldier to Cardinal Bembo in 1527, and preserved at Turin. It is of copper, and on it are represented most of the Egyptian deities in the mysteries of Isis. It was said to have been found at the siege of Rome in 1525.

Isis (ī′ sis). The principal goddess of ancient Egypt, sister and wife of Osiris, and mother of Horus. She was identified with the moon (Osiris being a sun-god), and the cow was sacred to her, its horns representing the crescent moon.

Her chief temples were at Abydos, Busiris, and Philæ; she is represented as a queen, her head being surmounted by horns and the solar disk or by the double crown. Proclus mentions a statue of her which bore the inscription—

I am that which is, has been, and shall be. My veil no one has lifted. The fruit I bore was the Sun—

hence **to lift the veil of Isis** is to pierce to the heart of a great mystery.

She was identified with Io, Aphrodite, and others by the Greeks; with Selene, Ceres, Venus, Juno, etc., by the Romans; and the Phœnicians confused her with Ashtoreth. Her worship as a nature goddess was very popular among the later Greeks and with the Romans of republican times. Milton, in *Paradise Lost* (I, 478), places her among the fallen angels.

Isis, River. *See* THAMES.

Islam (iz lam′). The Mohammedan religion, the whole body of Mohammedans, the true Mohammedan faith. The Moslems say every child is born in Islam, and would continue in the true faith if not led astray. The word means *resignation* or *submission to the will of God*.

Islam consists of five duties:—

(1) Bearing witness that there is but one God.
(2) Reciting daily prayers.
(3) Giving the appointed and legal alms.
(4) Observing the Ramazan (a month's fast).
(5) Making a pilgrimage to Mecca at least once in a lifetime.

Islands of the Blest. *See* FORTUNATE ISLANDS.

Isle of Dogs. A peninsula on the left bank of the Thames between the Limehouse and Blackwall reaches, opposite Greenwich. It is said to be so called because it was here that Edward III kept his greyhounds; but another explanation is that it is a corruption of *Isle of Ducks*, from the number of wild fowl anciently inhabiting the marshes.

Ismene. In Greek legend, daughter of Œdipus and Jocasta. Antigone was buried alive by the order of King Creon, for burying her brother Polynices, slain in combat by his brother Eteocles. Ismene declared that she had aided her sister, and requested to be allowed to share the same punishment.

Isocrates (ī sok′ rà tēz), was one of the great orators of Athens and was distinguished as a teacher of eloquence. He died 338 B.C.

The French Isocrates. Esprit Fléchier (1632-1710), Bishop of Nismes, specially famous for his funeral orations.

Isolationism. A nationalistic philosophy opposed to political co-operation with any other nation or group of nations; the term is especially applied to a school of thought in U.S.A. which repudiates any foreign alliances, friendships, connexions or commitments.

Israel (iz rāl), in Dryden's *Absalom and Achitophel* (*q.v.*), stands for England.

Israfel (is′ rà fel). The angel of music of the Mohammedans. He possesses the most melodious voice of all God's creatures, and is to sound the Resurrection Trump which will ravish the ears of the saints in paradise. Israfel, Gabriel, and Michael were the three angels that, according to the Koran, warned Abraham of Sodom's destruction.

In Heaven a spirit doth dwell
  Whose heart-strings are a lute;
None sing so wildly well
As the angel Israfel,
And the giddy Stars (so legends tell),
Ceasing their hymns, attend the spell
  Of his voice, all mute.   E. A. POE: *Israfel*.

Issachar (is′ à kar), in Dryden's satire of *Absalom and Achitophel* (*q.v.*), means Thomas Thynne (1648-82), of Longleat, known as "Tom of Ten Thousand."

Issei (ē′ sā). A Japanese word meaning "first born" or "first generation," applied to a person of Japanese ancestry, born in Japan, but taking up residence in U.S.A., though retaining allegiance to Japan. A Japanese born in U.S.A. and loyal to that country is called a Nisei.

Issue. The point of law in debate or in question. "At issue," under dispute.

To join issue. To take opposite views of a question, or opposite sides in a suit.

To join issues. To leave a suit to the decision of the court because the parties interested cannot agree.

Istar. *See* ISHTAR.

Isthmian Games (is' mi an). Games consisting of chariot races, running, wrestling, boxing, etc., held by the ancient Greeks in the Isthmus of Corinth every alternate spring, the first and third of each Olympiad. Epsom races, and other big sporting events, have been called our "Isthmian games" in allusion to these.

Istanbul (is tĕn bul') the name by which old Constantinople, until 1923 the capital of the Turkish Empire, is now known.

Isumbras. *See* ISENBRAS.

It. I'm it! I'm a person of some importance.

In for it. About "to catch it"; on the point of being in trouble.

In such phrases as this, and as **to come it strong, to rough it**, etc., **it** is the definite object of the transitive or intransitive verb.

It, is used in U.S.A. as "He" is in England to denote the child who must catch the others at tag, or find them at hide-and-seek. The word was also used at one time as a humorous euphemism for sex appeal.

Italian hand. I see his fine Italian hand in this may be said of a picture in which the beholder can discern the work of a particular artist through certain characteristics of his which appear. Or it may be remarked of an intrigue, in which the characteristics of a particular plotter are apparent. The Italian hand was originally the cancelleresca type of handwriting, used by the Apostolic Secretaries, and distinguishable by its grace and fineness from the Gothic styles of Northern Europe.

Italic. Pertaining to Italy, especially ancient Italy and the parts other than Rome.

Italic type or italics (the type in which the letters, instead of being erect—as in roman— slope from left to right, *thus*) was first used by Aldo Manuzio in 1501 in an edition of Virgil, and was dedicated by him to Italy—hence its name. It has been said that italic type was based on the beautiful handwriting of the poet Petrarch. Francesco of Bologna cast it.

The words italicized in the Bible have no corresponding words in the original. The translators supplied these words to render the sense of the passage more full and clear.

Italic School of Philosophy. The Pythagorean (6th cent. B.C.), so called because Pythagoras taught in Italy.

Italic version. An early Latin version of the Bible, prepared from the Septuagint. It preceded the Vulgate, or the version by St. Jerome.

Itch, To. Properly, to have an irritation of the skin which gives one a desire to scratch the part affected; hence, figuratively, to feel a constant teasing desire for something. The figure of speech enters into many phrases; as, *to itch* or *to have an itch for gold*, to have a longing desire for wealth; *an itching palm* means the same:—

Let me tell you, Cassius, you yourself
Are much condemned to have an itching palm.
Julius Cæsar, iv, 3.

Similarly, **to have itching ears,** is to be very desirous for news or novelty:—

The time will come when they will not endure the sound doctrine; but, having itching ears, will heap to themselves teachers after their own lusts.—2 *Tim.* iv, 3 (R.V.)

Ithuriel (ith ū' ri él). The angel who, with Zephon (*q.v.*), was, in Milton's *Paradise Lost*, commissioned by Gabriel to search for Satan, after he had effected his entrance into Paradise. The name is Rabbinical, and means "the discovery of God."

Ithuriel and Zephon, with winged speed
Search through this garden; leave unsearched no nook.
Paradise Lost, Bk. iv, 788.

He was armed with a spear, the slightest touch of which exposed deceit.

Him [*i.e.* Satan], thus intent Ithuriel with his spear
Touched lightly; for no falsehood can endure
Touch of celestial temper, but returns
Of force to its own likeness.
Paradise Lost, iv, 810.

Itinerary. The account of a route followed by a traveller. The Itinerary of Antoninus marks out all the main roads of the Roman Empire, and the stations of the Roman army. The Itinerary of Peutinger (*Tabula Peutingeriana*) is also an invaluable document of ancient geography, executed A.D. 383, in the reign of Theodosius the Great, and hence called sometimes the *Theodosian Table*.

Ivan (ī' van). The Russian form of John, called *Juan* in Spain, *Giovanni* in Italian.

Ivan the Terrible. Ivan IV of Russia (1530, 1533-84), infamous for his cruelties, but a man of great energy. He first adopted the title of Tsar.

Ivanhoe (ī' van hō). Sir Walter Scott took the name of his hero from the village of Ivanhoe, or Ivinghoe, in Bucks; a line in an old rhymed proverb—"Tring, Wing, and Ivanhoe"—attracted his attention.

Ivanovitch (ē văn′ ō vich). The national impersonation of the Russians as a people, as *John Bull* is of the English,

Ivory. Ivory Gate. *See* DREAMS, GATES OF.

Ivory shoulder. *See* PELOPS.

Ivory tower. A place of refuge from the world and its strivings and posturings. The phrase is a symbol first used by Sainte-Beuve as *un tour d'ivoire*.

Ivories. Teeth; also dice, keys of the piano, billiard balls, dominoes, etc.

Ivy (A.S., *ifig*). Dedicated to Bacchus from the notion that it is a preventive of drunkenness. But whether the Dionysian ivy is the same plant as that which we call *ivy* is doubtful, as it was famous for its golden berries, and was termed *chryso-carpos*. An ivy wreath was the prize of the Isthmian games, until it was superseded by a pine garland.

In Christian symbolism *ivy* typifies the everlasting life, from its remaining continually green.

Ixion. In Greek legend, a king of the Lapithæ who was bound to a revolving wheel of fire in the Infernal regions, either for his impious presumption in trying to imitate the thunder of heaven, or for boasting of the favours of Hera, Zeus having sent a cloud to him in the form of Hera, and the cloud having become by him the mother of the Centaurs (*q.v.*).

J

J. The tenth letter of the alphabet; a modern letter, only differentiated from *I* (*q.v.*), the consonantal functions of which it took, in the 17th century, and not completely separated till the 19th. There is no roman J or j in the 1611 Authorized Version of the Bible. In the Roman system of numeration it was (and in medical prescriptions still is) used in place of i as the final figure in a series—iij, vij, etc., for iii, vii.

Jabberwocky (jăb′ er wok′ i), the eponymous central figure of a strange, almost gibberish poem in Lewis Carroll's *Through the Looking-glass*. It contains many significant "portmanteau words," as subsequently explained to Alice by Humpty Dumpty.

Jack. A personal name, probably a diminutive of *John*, but confused with the French *Jacques* (*q.v.*). *Jack* is also the siang term in Australia for a policeman.

Before you can say Jack Robinson. Immediately. Grose says that the saying had its birth from a very volatile gentleman of that name, who used to pay flying visits to his neighbours, and was no sooner announced than he was off again; Halliwell says (*Archaic Dictionary*, 1846):—

> The following lines from "an old play" are elsewhere given as the original phrase—
> A warke it ys as easie to be done
>   As tys to saye *Jacke! robys on*.

But the "old play" has never been identified, and both these accounts are palpably *ben trovato*. The phrase was in use in the 18th century, and is to be found in Fanny Burney's *Evelina* (1778), II, xxxvii.

"Before you could say Jack Robinson" was the refrain of an immensely popular song sung by Thomas Hudson at the Cyder Cellars in the early 19th century.

Jack of all trades and master of none. One who can turn his hand to anything is not usually an expert in any one branch. *Jack of all trades* is a contemptuous expression—more grandiloquently he is a sciolist.

Jack-a-dandy. A term of endearment for a smart, bright little fellow;

> Smart she is, and handy, O!
> Sweet as sugar-candy, O! . . .
> And I'm her Jack-a-dandy, O!

Jackanapes. A pert, vulgar, apish little fellow; a prig. Jackanapes must, however, have been in use before it became a nickname, and it is uncertain whether the -*napes* is connected originally with *ape* or with *Naples*, *Jackanapes* being a *Jack* (monkey) of (imported from) *Naples*, just as *fustian-a-napes* was fustian from Naples. There is an early 15th-century record of monkeys being sent to England from Italy; and by the 16th century, at all events, *Jackanapes* was in use as a proper name for a tame ape.

> I will teach a scurvy jackanape priest to meddle or make.—*Merry Wives of Windsor*, i, 4.

Jackass. An unmitigated fool.

Jackdaw. A prating nuisance.

Jack-knife. Phrases from the similitude of a jack-knife in which the big blade doubles up into the handle.

(i) In logging, where two logs jam end to end and hold up the rest;

(ii) In swimming a form of fancy dive.

Jack-pot. In poker, a pot which cannot be opened until a player has a pair of jacks, or better.

Jackstones. A game played with six small stones or specially shaped pieces of metal, and a rubber ball.

Jackstraws. The American name for the game of spillikins.

Jackass, Jack-baker (a kind of owl), **Jack** or **dog fox, Jack hare, Jack rat, Jack shark, Jack snipe**; a young pike is called a *Jack*, so also were the male birds used in falconry.

Jack-in-the hedge, Jack-go-to-bed-at-noon, Jack-jump-about, and **Jack-in-the-bush,** are names of various common wild flowers. **Jack-in-the-pulpit,** a North American woodland plant, *Arisaema triphyllum*, with an upright club-shaped spike, or spadix within an over-arching green or purple sheath.

Jack-curlew. The whimbrel, a small species of curlew.

Jack-in-a-bottle. The long-tailed tit-mouse, or bottle-tit; so called from the shape of its nest.

Jack-rabbit. A large prairie-hare of North America; shortened from **Jackass-rabbit,** a name given to it on account of its very long ears and legs.

Jack Amend-All. One of the nicknames given to Jack Cade (killed 1450), the leader of "Cade's Rebellion." He promised to remedy all abuses.

Jack and the Beanstalk. A nursery tale found among all sorts of races from Icelanders to Zulus.

Jack and Jill. It has been suggested that the well-known nursery rhyme is a relic of a Norse myth, the two children are said to have been kidnapped by the moon while drawing water, and they are still to be seen with the bucket hanging from a pole resting on their shoulders.

An otherwise unknown comedy *Jack and Jill* is mentioned in the Revels Accounts as having been played at court in 1567-8. *Jill*, or *Gill*, is an abbreviation of *Gillian*, for *Juliana*.

Jack Horner. A very fanciful explanation of the old nursery rhyme "Little Jack Horner" is that Jack was steward to the Abbot of Glastonbury at the time of the Dissolution of the Monasteries, and that he, by a subterfuge, became possessed of the deeds of the Manor of Mells, which is in the neighbourhood and which is still owned by his descendants of the same name. Some say that these deeds with others were sent to Henry VIII concealed, for safety, in a pasty; that "Jack Horner" was the bearer; and that on the way, he lifted the crust and extracted this "plum."

Jack of Newbury. John Winchcombe alias Smallwood (d. 1520), a wealthy clothier in the reign of Henry VIII. He was the hero of many chap-books, and is said to have kept 100 looms in his own house at Newbury, while legend relates that he equipped at his own expense 100 to 200 of his men to aid the king against the Scots in Flodden Field.

Jack the Ripper. An unknown person who committed a series of murders on prostitutes in the East End of London in 1888-89. He gave himself the name, and the mystery surrounding his crimes made it very widely known.

The first murder was April 2nd, 1888; the next was August 7th; the third was August 31st; the fourth was September 8th; the fifth was September 30th, when two women were murdered; the sixth was November 9th; the seventh was December 20th, in a builder's yard; the eighth was July 17th, 1889, at Whitechapel; the ninth was September 17th.

Jack Straw. The name (or nickname) of one of the leaders in the Peasants' Revolt of 1381. There is an allusion to him in Chaucer's *Nun's Prologue* (1386), and the name soon came to signify a man of straw, a worthless sort of person.

It shall be but the weight of a strawe, or the weight of Jack Strawe more.—THOS. NASH: *Nashe's Lenten Stuffe* (1598).

Jacky Howe (Austr.). A short-sleeved shirt worn by shearers, called after Jack Howe, whose 320 sheep sheared in eight hours—a feat performed in Queensland about 1900—still holds the world's record.

Jack-snip. A botching tailor.

Jack Sprat. A dwarf; as if sprats were dwarf mackerels. Children, by a similar metaphor, are called small fry.

Jack Tar. A common sailor, whose hands and clothes are tarred by the ship's tackling.

Jack-o'-lantern. A will-o'-the-wisp. *See* IGNIS FATUUS.

Jack Frost. The personification of frost or frosty weather.

Jack-in-the-box. A toy consisting of a box out of which, when the lid is raised, a figure springs.

A very large number of appliances and parts of appliances are called by this name; such as the **jack**, **bottle-jack**, or **roasting-jack**, used for turning the meat when roasting before an open fire; the **jack** used for lifting heavy weights; the rough stool or wooden horse used for sawing timber on; etc. Other instances of this use are:—

Boot-jack. An instrument for drawing off boots.

Jack-block. A block attached to the topgallant-tie of a ship.

Jack-in-the-basket. The cap or basket on the top of a pole to indicate the place of a sand-bank at sea, etc.

Jack-roll. The cylinder round which the rope of a well coils.

Jack-screw. A large screw rotating in a threaded socket, used for lifting heavy weights.

Lifting-jack. A machine for lifting the axle-tree of a vehicle when the wheels are cleaned or the tires require attention.

Smoke-jack. An apparatus in a chimney-flue for turning a spit. It is made to revolve by the upward current of smoke and air.

The JACK is also applied to the small flag flown at the bow in ships (*cp.* UNION JACK); a small drinking vessel made of waxed leather, the large one being called a *black jack* (*q.v.*), and to an inferior kind of armour consisting of a leather surcoat worn over the hauberk, from the 14th to the 17th century. It was formed by overlapping pieces of steel fastened by one edge upon canvas, coated over with cloth or velvet, and was worn by the peasantry of the English borders in their skirmishes with moss-troopers, etc. North, in his translation of *Plutarch* (1579; *Life of Crassus*), applies the word to the armour of the Parthians:—

For himself [*i.e.* Crassus] and his men with weak and light staves, brake upon them that were armed with curaces of steel, or stiff leather jacks.

And the "jack" at bowls is so called because it is very small in comparison with the bowls themselves.

Jack plane, Jack saw. A plane or saw to do rough work before the finer instruments are used.

Jack rafter. A rafter in a hipped roof, shorter than a full-sized one.

Jack rib. An inferior rib in an arch, being shorter than the rest.

Jack timbers. Timbers in a building shorter than the rest.

Jack towel. A long towel hung on a roller.

Jackal. A toady. One who does the dirty work of another. It was once thought that the jackals hunted in troops to provide the lion with prey, hence they were called the "lion's providers." No doubt the lion will at times avail himself of the jackal's assistance by appropriating prey started by these "hunters," but it would be folly to suppose that the jackal acted on the principle of *vos non vobis. See* LION'S PROVIDER.

Jackeroo, a name used in Australia in the first half of the 19th century to describe a young Englishman newly arrived to learn farming. It was said by some to be derived from the Queensland *tchaceroo,* the shrike, noted for its garrulity. Later the name was applied simply to a station hand. **Jilleroo,** a feminine adaptation of Jackeroo, used for land girls in Australia during World War II.

Jacket. Diminutive of *jack,* a surcoat (whence the armour.

The skin of a potato is called its "jacket." Potatoes brought to table unpeeled are said to be "with their jackets on."

To dust one's jacket, or to give one a good jacketing. *See* DUST.

Jacksonian Professor. The professor of natural and experimental philosophy at Cambridge. The professorship was founded in 1782 by the Rev. Richard Jackson (1700-82), a fellow of Trinity.

Jacob. Jacob's ladder. The ladder seen by the patriarch Jacob in a vision (*Gen.* xxviii, 12). *Jacob* is, on this account, a cant name for a ladder, and steep and high flights of steps going up cliffs, etc., are often called *Jacob's ladders,* as is a flaw in a stocking where only the weft threads are left, giving a ladder-like appearance. There is a garden flower also so called.

Jacobins. The Dominicans were so called in France from the "Rue St. Jacques," Paris, where they first established themselves in 1219; and the French Revolutionary club (known as the "Society of Friends of the Constitution" when founded at Versailles in 1789) took the name because, on their removal to Paris, they met in the hall of an ex-convent of Jacobins, in the Rue St. Honoré. The Jacobins were at first constitutional monarchists, with Mirabeau as one of their leading members. After the king's flight to Varennes in 1791 there was a schism in the party and the main body became extreme republicans, swayed by Robespierre, St. Just, Marat, and Couthon. During the Terror they had unrivalled power, but the fall of Robespierre in 1794 brought their reign to an end and in November of that year the club was suppressed. Their badge was the Phrygian Cap of Liberty.

Jacobites (jăk′ ō bītz). The supporters of the right of James II and his descendants to the throne of Great Britain and Ireland. They came into existence after the flight of James II in 1688, and were strong in Scotland and the North of England. They were responsible for two risings, in 1715 and 1745, the latter marking the virtual end of Jacobitism as a political force. The last male descendant of James II, Henry Cardinal of York, died in 1807; a certain number of sentimental adherents to the lost cause are still to be found here and there.

Jacobites. An Oriental sect of Monophysites, so called from Jacobus Baradæus, Bishop of Edessa, in Syria, in the 6th century. The Jacobite Church comprises three Patriarchates, viz., those of Alexandria, Antioch, and Armenia.

Jacobus (jà kō′ bus). The unofficial name of a gold coin of the value of from 20s. to 24s., struck in the reign of James I.

Jacquard Loom (jăk′ ard). So called from Jos. Marie Jacquard (1752-1834), of Lyons, its inventor. It is a machine for weaving figures upon silks and muslins.

Jacques (zhak) (Fr.). A generic name for the poor artisan class in France (*see* JACQUERIE, LA, *below*), so called from the *jaque,* a rough kind of waistcoat, sleeved, and coming almost to the knees, that they used to wear.

Jaques, il me faut troubler ton somme;
  Dans le village, un gros huissier
  Rude et court, suivi du messier:
C'est pour l'impôt, las! mon pauvre homme,
  Lève-toi, Jacques, lève-toi,
  Voici venir l'huissier du roi.

Béranger (1831).

Jade. The fact that in mediæval times this ornamental stone was supposed, if applied to the side, to act as a preservative against colic is enshrined in its name, for *jade* is from the Spanish *piedra de ijada*, stone of the side; and its other name, *nephrite*, is from Gr. *nephros*, kidney. Among the North American Indians it is still worn as an amulet against the bite of venomous snakes, and to cure the gravel, epilepsy, etc.

Jade. A worthless horse. An old woman (used in contempt). A young woman (not necessarily contemptuous).

Jains. A sect of dissenter from Hinduism of great antiquity, its known history going back beyond 477 B.C. Its differences from Hinduism are theological and too abstruse for expression in brief. Jains being largely traders the sect is wealthy though comparatively small in size and influence.

Jalopy (jàl ō′ pi or jà lop′ i), an American colloquial term for an old, decrepit automobile.

Jam. Used in a slang way for something really nice, especially if unexpected; something delightful, tip-top.

There must have been a charming climate in Paradise and [the] connubial bliss [there] . . . was real jam.—SAM SLICK: *Human Nature.*

Jam session. A meeting of jazz musicians improvising spontaneously, without rehearsal.

Jamboree (jăm bò rē′), originally meaning a noisy merry-making, this word is now more usually applied to a large rally of Boy Scouts, usually of an international scope.

James. A sovereign; a jacobus (*q.v.*); also called a "jimmy." *Half a jimmy* is half a sovereign.

James, Jesse (1847-82) was one of the most notorious of the American bandits of his time. In 1867 he organized a band of bank and train robbers who perpetrated a number of infamous murders and crimes of the most daring nature. A reward of $10,000 was put on his head and two members of his own band shot him in his home at St. Joseph, Missouri.

James, St. The Apostle St. James the Great is the patron saint of Spain. Legend states that after his death in Palestine his body was placed in a boat with sails set, and that next day it reached the Spanish coast; at Padron, near Compostella, they used to show a huge stone as the veritable boat. According to another legend, it was the *relics* of St. James that were miraculously conveyed to Spain in a ship of marble from Jerusalem, where he was bishop. A knight saw the ship sailing into port, his horse took fright, and plunged with its rider into the sea.

The knight saved himself by "boarding the marble vessel," but his clothes were found to be entirely covered with scallop shells.

The saint's body was discovered in 840 by divine revelation to Bishop Theodomirus, and a church was built at Compostella for its shrine.

St. James is commemorated on July 25th, and is represented in art sometimes with the sword by which he was beheaded, and sometimes attired as a pilgrim, with his cloak covered with shells.

The Court of St. James's. The British court, to which foreign ambassadors are officially accredited. St. James's Palace, Pall Mall, stands on the site of a 12th-century leper hospital dedicated to St. James the Less. The Palace was a royal residence from 1698 until 1837, and since then has been used for levees and drawing-rooms.

Jameson Raid, a coup d'etat attempted in S. Africa by Dr. L. S. Jameson in 1895. With the connivance of Cecil Rhodes he organized a force of some 500 men to invade the Transvaal simultaneously with a rising of Uitlanders in Johannesburg. Jameson crossed the Bechuanaland border but was met by a Boer force at Doornkop and compelled to surrender. The Boers handed the invaders over to the British authorities and Jameson and others were tried for treason and sentenced to various terms of imprisonment.

Jamshid (jăm shid′). In Persian legend, the fourth king of the Pishdadian Dynasty, *i.e.* the earliest, who is fabled to have reigned for 700 years and to have had the Deevs, or Genii, as his slaves. He possessed a seven-ringed golden cup, typical of the seven heavens, the seven planets, the seven seas, etc., which was full of the elixir of life; it was hidden by the genii and was said to have been discovered while digging the foundations of Persepolis.

Jane. A small Genoese silver coin; so called from Fr. *Genes*, Genoa.

Because I could not give her many a jane.
SPENSER: *Faerie Queene*, III, vii, 58.

In American slang a *jane* is a derogatory term for a woman.

Jansenists (jăn′ sen ists). A sect of Christians, who held the doctrines of Cornelius Jansen, (1585-1638), Bishop of Ypres. Jansen professed to have formulated the teaching of Augustine, which resembled Calvinism in many respects. He taught the doctrines of "irresistible grace," "original sin," and the "utter helplessness of the natural man to turn to God." Louis XIV took part against them, and they were put down by

Pope Clement XI, in 1705, in the famous bull Unigenitus (*q.v.*).

Januarius, St. (jăn ū âr′ i ús). The patron saint of Naples, a bishop of Benevento who was martyred during the Diocletian persecution, 304. He is commemorated on September 19th, and his head and two vials of his blood are preserved in the cathedral at Naples. This congealed blood is said to liquefy several times a year.

January. The month dedicated by the Romans to Janus (*q.v.*), who presided over the entrance to the year and, having two faces, could look back to the year past and forward on the current year.

The Dutch used to call this month *Lauw-maand* (frosty-month); the Saxons, *Wulf-monath*, because wolves were very troublesome then from the great scarcity of food. After the introduction of Christianity, the name was changed to *Se œftera geola* (the after-yule); it was also called *Forma monath* (first month). In the French Republican calendar it was called *Nivose* (snow-month, December 20th to January 20th).

It's a case of January and May. Said when an old man marries a young girl. The allusion is to the Merchant's Tale in Chaucer's *Canterbury Tales*, in which May, a lovely girl, married January, a Lombard baron sixty years of age.

Janus (jā′ nús). The ancient Roman deity who kept the gate of heaven; hence the guardian of gates and doors. He was represented with two faces, one in front and one behind, and the doors of his temple in Rome were thrown open in times of war and closed in times of peace. The name is used allusively both with reference to the double-facedness and to war. Thus Milton says of the Cherubim:—

> Four faces each
> Had, like a double Janus.
> *Paradise Lost*, xi, 129.

And Tennyson—

> State-policy and church-policy are conjoint,
> But Janus-faces looking diverse ways.
> *Queen Mary*, III, ii.

While Dante says of the Roman eagle that it—

> composed the world to such a peace,
> That of his temple Janus barr'd the door.
> *Paradiso*, vi, 83 (*Cary's tr.*).

Japanese Vellum. An extremely costly hand-beaten Japanese paper manufactured from the inner bark of the mulberry tree.

Jarkman. Sixteenth-century slang for an Abram-man (*q.v.*), especially one who was able to forge passes, licences, etc. *Jark* was rogues' cant for a seal, whence also a licence of the Bethlehem Hospital to beg.

Jarnac. Coup de Jarnac. A treacherous and unexpected attack; so called from Guy Chabot, Sieur de Jarnac, who, in a duel with La

Châteigneraie, on July 10th, 1547, in the presence of Henri II, first "hamstrung" his opponent and then, when he was helpless, slew him.

Jason (jā′ són). The hero of Greek legend who led the Argonauts (*q.v.*) in the quest for the Golden Fleece. He was the son of Æson, king of Ioclus, was brought up by the centaur, Chiron, and when he demanded his kingdom from his half-brother, Pelias, who had deprived him of it, was told he could have it in return for the Golden Fleece. Jason thereupon gathered together the chief heroes of Greece and set sail in the *Argo*. After many tests and trials he, through the help of Medea (*q.v.*), was successful. He married Medea, but later deserted her, and, according to one account, he killed himself with grief, according to another was crushed to death by the keel of his old ship, *Argo*, while resting beneath it.

Jaundice (Fr. *jaune*, yellow). A *jaundiced eye*. A prejudiced eye which sees only faults. It was a popular belief that to the eye of a person who had the jaundice everything looked of a yellow tinge.

> All seems infected that th' infected spy,
> As all seems yellow to the jaundiced eye.
> POPE: *Essay on Criticism*, ii, 359.

Jaw. To jaw, to annoy with words, to jabber, wrangle, or abuse.

A break-jaw word; a jaw-breaker. A very long word, or one hard to pronounce.

Jay. Old slang for a frivolous person, a wanton.

> This jay of Italy . . . hath betrayed him.—*Cymbeline*, iii, 4.

Jay hawker. In older American slang, a bandit.

Jaywalker. One who crosses a street regardless of traffic regulations.

Jazz (jăz). The folk-music of the American Negro. Originating in the cotton-fields, it was developed in New Orleans and thence spread up the Mississippi in the river boats to Chicago. Now world-wide, this type of music, originally and sometimes still the expression of a naturally musical people, is too often confused with insipid dance tunes.

Buddy Bolden, one of the greatest trumpet-players, was playing in New Orleans in the 1880s. The music started up the river in 1915, and in March, 1916, Bert Kelly's "Jazz Band" (the first to be so called) was engaged by the Boosters' Club, of Chicago, scored an immediate success, and started jazz on its conquering career.

The origin of the name is uncertain. One account is that it is an adaptation of the name of one *Razz*, who was a band conductor in New Orleans about 1904; another that it has long been a common word to the Negro and on the Barbary coast, and means simply "to mess 'em up and slap it on thick," and another that it was the spontaneous production of a brainwave on the part of Bert Kelly.

Je ne sais quoi (zhe ne sā kwa) (Fr., I know not what). An indescribable something; as "There was a *je ne sais quoi* about him which made us dislike him at first sight."

Jedwood Justice. Putting an obnoxious person to death first, and trying him afterwards. This sort of justice was dealt to moss-troopers. Same as *Jedburgh justice, Jeddart justice.* We have also "Cupar justice" and "Abingdon law."

Jedwood justice—hang in haste and try at leisure.—SCOTT: *Fair Maid of Perth*, ch. xxxii.

Jeep (jēp). A small all-purpose car developed by the U.S.A. during World War II. Its 4-wheel drive and high and low gear-boxes gave it astonishing cross-country performances. Its value to the Allied armed forces was inestimable. The experimental models were called Beeps, Peeps and Blitz Buggies, but the name Jeep had been coined and had stuck by early 1941.

Jehovah (je hō′ và). The name JEHOVAH itself is an instance of the extreme sanctity with which the name of God was invested, for this is a disguised form of the name. This word JHVH, the sacred tetragrammaton (*q.v.*), was too sacred to use, so the scribes added the vowels of *Adonai*, thereby indicating that the reader was to say *Adonai* instead of JHVH. At the time of the Renaissance these vowels and consonants were taken for the sacred name itself and hence *Jehovah* or *Yahwe*.

Jehovistic. *See* ELOHISTIC.

Jehovah's Witnesses, a sect of religious pacifists who refuse to acknowledge the authority of the State when it crosses their religious views or doctrines.

Jehu (jē′ hū). A coachman, especially one who drives at a rattling pace.

The watchman told, saying, . . . The driving is like the driving of Jehu the son of Nimshi; for he driveth furiously.—2 *Kings* ix, 20.

Jekyll (jek′ il). **Dr. Jekyll and Mr. Hyde.** Two phases of one man. Jekyll is the "would do good," Hyde is "the evil that is present." The phrase comes from R. L. Stevenson's *The Strange Case of Dr. Jekyll and Mr. Hyde*, first published in 1886.

Jellyby, Mrs. (jel′ i bi). The type of the enthusiastic, unthinking philanthropist who forgets that charity should begin at home. Dickens, *Bleak House.*

Jemmy (the diminutive or pet form of *James*). Slang for a number of different things, as a burglar's crowbar; a sheep's head, boiled or baked, said to be so called from the tradition that James IV of Scotland breakfasted on a sheep's head just before the battle of Flodden Field (September 9th, 1513); also, a greatcoat; and—as an adjective—spruce, dandified. *See* JEMMY JESSAMY.

She presently returned with a pot of porter and a dish of sheep's heads; which gave occasion to several pleasant witticisms on the part of Mr. Sikes, founded upon the singular coincidence of jemmies, being a cant name, common to them, and also to an ingenious instrument much used in his profession.—DICKENS: *Oliver Twist*, ch. xx.

Jemmy Dawson. *See* DAWSON.

Jemmy Jessamy. A Jack-a-dandy; a lady's fondling, "sweet as sugar-candy."

This was very different language to that she had been in the habit of hearing from her Jemmy Jessamy adorers.—THACKERAY: *Barry Lyndon*, ch. xiii.

Jenny Wren. The sweetheart of Robin Red-breast in the old nursery rhyme.

Robin promised Jenny, if she would be his wife, she should "feed on cherry-pie and drink currant-wine"; and he says:—

"I'll dress you like a goldfinch,
Or any peacock gay;
So, dearest Jen, if you'll be mine,
Let us appoint the day."

Jenny replies:—

"Cherry-pie is very nice,
And so is currant wine;
But I must wear my plain brown gown
And never go too fine."

Jeopardy (jep′ ar di). Hazard, danger. It originally signified an even chance, hence an uncertain chance, something hazardous. It has since been extended to mean exposure to the risk of death, loss, or injury. The word is French in derivation—*jeu*, game; *parti*, divided.

Jeremiah (jer e mī′ à). **The British Jeremiah.** Gibbon so calls Gildas (fl. 6th cent.), author of *Lamentations over the Destruction of Britain.*

Jeremiad (jer e mī′ àd). A pitiful tale, a tale of woe to produce compassion; so called from the "Lamentations" of the prophet Jeremiah.

Jericho (jer′ i kō). Used in a number of phrases for the sake of giving verbal definition to some altogether indefinite place. The reason for fixing on this particular town is possibly to be found in 2 *Sam.* x, 5, and 1 *Chron.* xix, 5.

Jerkin. A short coat or jacket, formerly made of leather; a close waistcoat.

A plague of opinion, one may wear it on both sides, like a leather jerkin.—*Troilus and Cressida*, iii, 3.

Jerkwater. An early American term for a small train on a branch railway line.

Jerome, St. (jer′ ōm). A father of the Western Church, and translator of the Vulgate (*q.v.*). He was born about 340, and died at Bethlehem in 420. He is generally represented as an aged man in a cardinal's dress, writing or studying, with a lion seated beside him. His feast is kept on September 30th.

Jeronimo (jĕ ron′ imō). The chief character in the *Spanish Tragedy* by Thomas Kyd (acted about 1590). On finding his application to the king ill-timed, he says to himself, "Go by, Jeronimo," which tickled the fancy of the audience so that it became for a time a street jest, and was introduced into many contemporary plays, as in Shakespeare's *Taming of the Shrew* (*Induction*), Jonson's *Every Man in his Humour* (1, v), Dekker's *Shoemaker's Holiday* (II, i), etc. *See also* GERONIMO.

Jerrican. (World War II). A 4½-gallon petrol or water container which would stand rough handling and stack easily, developed by the Germans for the Afrika Korps. Borrowed by the British in Libya (hence its name), it became the standard unit of fuel replenishment throughout the Allied armies.

Jerry. In World War I this was an army nickname for a German, or Germans collectively.

Jerry-built. Unsubstantial. A "jerry-builder" is a speculative builder who runs up cheap, unsubstantial houses, using materials of the commonest kind. The name is probably in some way connected with *Jeremiah*.

Jerusalem. Julian the Apostate, the Roman Emperor (d. 363), with the intention of pleasing the Jews and humbling the Christians, said that he would rebuild the temple and city, but was mortally wounded before the foundation was laid, and his work set at naught by "an earthquake, a whirlwind, or a fiery eruption" (*see* Gibbon's *Decline and Fall*, ch. xxiii).

Much has been made of this by early Christian writers, who dwell on the prohibition and curse pronounced against those who should attempt to rebuild the city, and the fate of Julian is pointed out as an example of Divine wrath.

Jerusalem, in Dryden's *Absalom and Achitophel* (*q.v.*), means London (Pt. i, v. 86, etc.).

The New Jerusalem. The paradise of Christians, in allusion to *Rev.* xxi.

Jerusalem artichoke. Jerusalem is here a corruption of Ital. *Girasole*. Girasole is the sunflower, which this vegetable resembles both in leaf and stem.

Jerusalem Chamber. The Chapter-house of Westminster Abbey. Henry IV died there, March 20th, 1413.

> It hath been prophesied to me many years,
> I should not die but in Jerusalem.
> 2 Henry IV, iv, 5.

Pope Silvester II was told the same thing, and he died as he was saying Mass in a church so called. (Bacon; *Tusculum*.)

The Lower House of Convocation usually meets in the Jerusalem Chamber.

Jerusalem Cross. A cross potent. *See* POTENT.

Jess (through Fr. from Lat. *jactus*, a cast, throw). A short strap of leather tied about the legs of a hawk to hold it on the fist. Hence, metaphorically, a bond of affection, etc.

> If I prove her haggard,
> Though I that her jesses were my dear heart-strings,
> I'd whistle her off.   *Othello*, iii, 3.

Jessamy Bride. The fancy name given by Goldsmith to Mary Horneck when he fell in love with her in 1769. *Cp.* JEMMY JESSAMY.

Jesse, or **Jesse Tree** (jĕs′ i). A genealogical tree, usually represented as a vine or as a large brass candlestick with many branches, tracing the ancestry of Christ, called a "rod out of the stem of Jesse" (*Is.* xi. 1). Jesse is himself sometimes represented in a recumbent position with the vine rising out of his loins; hence a stained-glass window representing him thus with a tree shooting from him containing the pedigree of Jesus is called a *Jesse window*.

Jesters. *See* COURT FOOLS, *under* FOOLS.

Jesuit (jez′ ū it). The popular name of members of the Society of Jesus, founded by St. Ignatius Loyola in 1533, who, when asked what name he would give his order, replied, "We are a little battalion of Jesus." The order was founded to combat the Reformation and to propagate the faith among the heathen, but through its discipline, organization, and methods of secrecy, it acquired such political power that it came into conflict with both the civil and religious authorities; it was driven from France in 1594, from England in 1579, from Venice in 1607, from Spain in 1767, from Naples in 1768; in 1773 it was altogether suppressed by Pope Clement XIV, but was revived in 1814.

Owing to the casuistical principles maintained by many of its leaders and attributed to the order as a whole the name *Jesuit* has acquired a very opprobrious signification in both Protestant and Roman Catholic countries, and a *Jesuit*, or *Jesuitical person* means (secondarily) a deceiver, prevaricator, one who "lies like truth," or palters in a double sense, that "keeps the word of promise to our ear, and breaks it to our hope."

Jesuit's bark. *See* PERUVIAN.

Jetsam or **Jetson** (jet' sàm). Goods cast into the sea to lighten a ship (Fr. *Jeter*, to cast out). *See* FLOTSAM: LIGAN.

Jettatura (yet à too' rà). The Italian phrase for the evil eye, a superstition that certain persons have the power, by looking at one, to cast a malevolent spell. This can be countered only by various gestures, chief among which is the extending of the clenched fist with the index and little fingers stuck out like horns. The superstition and all connected with it is of extreme antiquity.

Jeu d'esprit (je des prē) (Fr.). A witticism.

Jeu de mot (je de mō) (Fr.). A pun; a play on some word or phrase.

Jeunesse Dorée (je nes' dôr ā) (Fr.). The "gilded youth" of a nation; that is, the rich and fashionable young unmarried men.

There were three of the *jeunesse dorée*, and, as such, were pretty well known to the ladies who promenade the grand circle.—T. TERREL: *Lady Delmar*, ix.

Jew. In Dryden's *Absalom and Achitophel* (*q.v.*) the *Jews* stand for those English who were loyal to Charles II, called David.

Jew's-harp. It is not known how or why this very simple musical instrument got its name (known from the 16th cent.); it has no special connexion with the Jews, and is not like a harp.

It was called by Bacon *jeutrompe*, by Beaumont and Fletcher, *jew-trump*, and in Hakluyt's *Voyages* (1595), *jew's-harp*.

Jew's ear. A fungus that grows on the Judas-tree (*q.v.*); its name is due to a mistranslation of its Latin name, *Auricula Judæ*, *i.e.* Judas's ear.

Jewels have (or had) in the popular belief special significations in various ways. For instance, each month was supposed to be under the influence of some precious stone—

January	..	Garnet	.. Constancy.
February	..	Amethyst	.. Sincerity.
March	..	Bloodstone	.. Courage.
April	..	Diamond	.. Innocence.
May	..	Emerald	.. Success in love.
June	..	Agate	.. Health and long life.
July	..	Cornelian	.. Content.
August	..	Sardonyx	.. Conjugal fidelity.
September	..	Sapphire	.. Antidote to madness.
October	..	Opal	.. Hope.
November	..	Topaz	.. Fidelity.
December	..	Turquoise	.. Prosperity.

The signs of the zodiac were represented by—

Aries	.. Ruby.	Libra	.. .. Jacinth.
Taurus	.. Topaz.	Scorpio	.. .. Agate.
Gemini	.. Carbuncle.	Sagittarius	.. .. Amethyst.
Cancer	.. Emerald.	Capricornus	.. .. Beryl.
Leo.	.. Sapphire.	Aquarius	.. .. Onyx.
Virgo	.. Diamond.	Pisces	.. .. Jasper.

And among heralds and astrologists jewels represented special tinctures or planets, as the topaz "or" (*gold*), and *Sol*, the sun; the pearl or crystal, "argent" (*silver*), and the moon; the ruby, "gules" (*red*), and the planet Mars; the sapphire, "azure" (*blue*), and Jupiter; the diamond, "sable" (*black*), and Saturn; the emerald, "vert" (*green*), and Venus; the amethyst "purpure" (*purple*), and Mercury.

These are my jewels! *See* TREASURES.

Jezebel (jez' é b él). **A painted Jezebel.** A flaunting woman of bold spirit but loose morals; so called from Jezebel, wife of Ahab, King of Israel (*see* 2 *Kings*, ix, 31).

Jib. A triangular sail borne in front of the foremast. It has the bowsprit for a base in small vessels, and the jib-boom in larger ones, and exerts an important effect, when the wind is abeam, in throwing the ship's head to leeward. The **jib-boom** is an extension of the bowsprit by the addition of a spar projecting beyond it. Sometimes the boom is further extended by another spar called the *flying jib-boom*. The *jib-topsail* is a light sail flying from the extreme forward end of the flying jib-boom, and set about half-way between the mast and the boom.

The cut of his jib. A sailor's phrase, meaning the expression of a person's face. Sailors recognize vessels at sea by the cut of the jibs, and in certain dialects the *jib* means the lower lip. Thus, *to hang the jib* is to look ill-tempered, or annoyed.

To jib. To start aside, to back out; a "jibbing horse" is one that is easily startled. It is probably from the sea-term, to *gybe*, *i.e.* to change tacks by bearing away before the wind.

Jiffy. In a jiffy. In a minute; in a brace of shakes; before you can say "Jack Robinson." The origin of the word is unknown, but it is met with as early as the late 18th century.

Jig, from *gigue*. A short piece of music much in vogue in olden times, of a very lively character, either six-eight or twelve-eight time, and used for dance-tunes. It consists of two parts, each of eight bars. Also the dance itself.

You jig, you amble, and you lisp.—*Hamlet*, iii, 1.

The jig is up. Your trickery is discovered. "Jig" was old slang for a joke or trick.

Jill. A generic name for a lass, a sweetheart. *See* JACK AND JILL *under* JACK.

Jilleroo. *See* JACKAROO.

Jim Crow. A popular Negro song and dance of last century; introduced by T. D. Rice, the original "nigger minstrel," at Washington in 1835, and brought to the Adelphi, London, in the following year. A renegade or turncoat was called a "Jim Crow," from the burden of the song:—

Wheel about and turn about
And do jis so,
Ebry time I wheel about
I jump Jim Crow.

Jim Crow cars. Railway coaches set apart for the sole use of Negroes.

Jim Crow regulations. Any rules which prohibit Negroes from associating with or enjoying the same privileges as white people.

Jingo (jing′ gō). A word from the unmeaning jargon of the 17th-century conjurers (*cp.* HOCUS-POCUS), probably substituted for *God*, in the same way as *Gosh*, *Golly* etc., are. In Motteux's translation of Rabelais (1694), where the original reads *par Dieu* (Bk. iv, lvi), the English rendering is "By jingo"; but there is a possibility that the word is Basque *Jinko* or *Jainko*, God, and was introduced by sailors.

Hey, Jingo! What the de'il's the matter?
Do mermaids swim in Dartford water?
               SWIFT: *Actæon or The Original Horn Fair.*

The modern meaning of the word, a blustering so-called "patriot" who is itching to go to war on the slightest provocation—a *Chauvinist* in France—is from a music-hall song by G. W. Hunt, which was popular in 1878 when the country was supposed to be on the verge of intervening in the Russo-Turkish War on behalf of the Turks:—

We don't want to fight; but, by Jingo, if we do,
We've got the ships, we've got the men, and got the money too.

The Russophobes became known as the *Jingoes,* and a noisy, war-mongering policy has been labelled *Jingoism* ever since.

Jinks (jingks). **High jinks.** The present use of the phrase expresses the idea of pranks, fun, and jollity.

The frolicsome company had begun to practise the ancient and now forgotten pastime of *High Jinks.* The game was played in several different ways. Most frequently the dice were thrown by the company, and those upon whom the lot fell were obliged to assume and maintain for a time a certain fictitious character, or to repeat a certain number of fescennine verses in a particular order. If they departed from the character assigned . . . they incurred forfeits, which were compounded for by swallowing an additional bumper.—SCOTT: *Guy Mannering,* xxxvi.

Jinn (jin). Demons of Arabian mythology, according to fable created from fire two thousand years before Adam was made of earth, and said to be governed by a race of kings named Suleyman, one of whom "built the pyramids." Their chief abode is the mountain Kâf, and they assume the forms of serpents, dogs, cats, monsters, or even human beings, and become invisible at pleasure. The evil jin are hideously ugly, but the good are exquisitely beautiful. The word is plural; its singular is *jinnee.*

Jinx (jingks). A colloquial term in U.S.A. for a person or thing supposed to bring ill luck.

Jitney (jit′ ni). An American term for an automobile plying for hire or hired to carry passengers. The name comes from the slang word for a five-cent piece—a jitney—as this was the fare originally charged for each passenger.

Jitters. An American phrase for nervousness, apprehensiveness; hence *jittery* is nervous, jumpy.

Jitterbug is one whose responses to the rhythm of swing music take the form of violent and unexpected dance movements, making him (or her) dance in an unpredictable, often acrobatic fashion.

Jiujitsu, Jujitsu (joo jit′ soo). The Japanese art of self-defence. It is based on leverage applied to the assailant's limbs which are forced into unnatural positions, called locks, to which there is no key; the victim must either give in or have the limb broken. The neck, body and hip joints are all susceptible to such attack, the spine can be injured and the hips dislocated.

Jive. A canting name for the livelier and debased forms of jazz music, largely accomplished by uninspired improvisations of short phrases. The adepts have developed a vocabulary of their own, known as *jive-talk.*

Joachim, St. (jo′ a kim). The father of the Virgin Mary. Generally represented as an old man carrying in a basket two turtledoves, in allusion to the offering made for the purification of his daughter. His wife was St. Anne.

Job (jōb). The personification of poverty and patience, in allusion to the patriarch whose history is given in the Bible.

I am as poor as Job, my lord, but not so patient.—2 *Henry IV,* i, 2.

In the Koran Job's wife is said to have been either Rahmeh, daughter of Ephraim, son of Joseph, or Makhir, daughter of Manasses; and the tradition is recorded that Job, at the command of God, struck the earth with his foot from the dunghill where he lay, and instantly there welled up a spring of water with which his wife washed his sores, and they were miraculously healed.

Job's comforter. One who means to sympathize with you in your grief, but says that you brought it on yourself; thus in reality adding weight to your sorrow.

Job (job). A piece of chance work; a public work or office not for the public benefit, but for the profit of the person employed; a misfortune, an untoward event; a "jab"; also, among printers, all kinds of work not included in the term "book-work" or newspapers.

A bad job. An unfortunate happening; a bad speculation.

A job lot. A lot of miscellaneous goods.

A ministerial job. Sheridan says:— "Whenever any emolument, profit, salary, or honour is conferred on any person not deserving it—that is a job; if from private friendship, personal attachment, or any view except the interest of the public, anyone is appointed to any public office . . . that is a job."

> No cheek is known to blush, or heart to throb,
> Save when they lose a question or a job.
> POPE: *Essay on Criticism*, i, 104,

Jockey. Properly, "a little Jack" (*q.v.*). So in Scotch, "Ilka Jeanie has her Jockie."

All fellows, Jockey and the laird (man and master). (*Scots proverb.*)

To jockey. To deceive in trade; to cheat; to indulge in sharp practice.

Jockey of Norfolk. Sir John Howard (*c.* 1430-85), the first Howard to be Duke of Norfolk, and a firm adherent of Richard III. On the night before the battle of Bosworth, where he was slain, he found in his tent the warning couplet:

> Jockey of Norfolk, be not too bold,
> For Dickon thy master, is bought and sold.

Joe. The American equivalent of the British "Tommy," an enlisted soldier. The full phrase is G.I. Joe, the initials standing for "Government Issue," as stamped on all U.S.A. military equipment.

Joe in Australian usage was formerly a term of the greatest insult. Charles Joseph Latrobe was governor of Victoria in 1851 and set the police to checking up every gold-miner to see that he had a licence. Hence "Joe!" was a warning cry at the approach of the Law.

Joe Miller. *See* MILLER.

Joey. A groat; so called from Joseph Hume (1777-1855), M.P. for Kilkenny at the time, who, about 1835, strongly recommended the coinage of groats for the sake of paying short cab-fares, etc. In Australia a young kangaroo is called a *joey*.

Joggis or **Jogges.** *See* JOUGS.

John. The English form of Lat. and Gr. *Johannes*, from Heb. *Jochanan*, meaning "God is gracious." The feminine form, *Johanna*, or *Joanna*, is nearer the original. The French equivalent of "John" is *Jean* (formerly *Jehan*), the Italian *Giovanni*, Russian *Ivan*, Gaelic *Ian*, Irish, *Sean* or *Shaun*, German *Johann* or *Johannes*, which is contracted to *Jan*, *Jahn*, and *Hans*.

For many centuries John has been one of the most popular of masculine names in England—probably because it is that of St. John the Evangelist, St. John the Baptist and many other saints.

There have been twenty-three Popes of this name, nearly all of whom were bad, unfortunate, or mere nonentities; England has had one King John (also unfortunate). The most famous "Johns" of history are probably *John of Gaunt* (1340-99), the fourth son of Edward III, and *Don John of Austria* (1547-78), illegitimate son of the Emperor Charles V, celebrated as a military leader, for his naval victory over the Turks at Lepanto (1571), and as Governor of the Netherlands.

The principal SAINTS of the name are:—

St. John the Evangelist or the Divine. His day is December 27th, and he is usually represented bearing a chalice from which a serpent issues, in allusion to his driving the poison from a cup presented to him to drink. Tradition says that he took the Virgin Mary to Ephesus after the Crucifixion, that in the persecution of Domitian (96) he was plunged into a cauldron of boiling oil, but was delivered unharmed, and was afterwards banished to the isle of Patmos (where he is said to have written the Book of Revelation), but shortly returned to Ephesus, where he died.

St. John the Baptist. Patron saint of missionaries, because he was sent "to prepare the way of the Lord." His day is June 24th, and he is represented in a coat of sheepskin (in allusion to his life in the desert), either holding a rude wooden cross, with a pennon bearing the words, *Ecce Agnus Dei*, or with a book on which a lamb is seated; or holding in his right hand a lamb surrounded by a halo, and bearing a cross on the right foot.

St. John of the Cross. Founder of the Discalced Carmelites (1568). A friend and co-worker with St. Teresa in the reform of the Carmelites, he is now better known for his mystical writings *The Dark Night of the Soul*, *Spiritual Canticles*, etc. St. John of the Cross was one of the greatest mystics the Christian Church has known. He died in 1591 and was canonized in 1726, his feast day being November 24th.

St. John Damascene. One of the Fathers of the Church. He was born at Damascus, opposed the Iconoclasts (*q.v.*), and died about 770. He is commemorated on March 27th.

John-a-Droynes. An Elizabethan term for a country bumpkin. There is a foolish character in Whetstone's *Promos and Cassandra* (1578), who, being seized by informers, stands dazed, and suffers himself to be quietly cheated out of his money. In *Superbiœ Flagellum*, by John Taylor, the Water Poet (1621), we read of "Jack and Jill, and John a Drones his issue," the meaning evidently being "the rag, tag, and bobtail."

John Anderson, my Jo. Burns's well-known poem is founded on an 18th-century song which, in its turn, was a parody of a mid-16th century anti-Roman Catholic song in ridicule of the Sacraments of the Church. The whole is given in the *Percy Folio MS*. The first verse is:—

John Anderson, my Jo, cum in as ye gae by,
And ye sall get a sheip's heid weel baken in a pye;
Weel baken in a pye, and the haggis in a pat:
John Anderson, my Jo, cum in, and ye's get that.

Jo is an old Scottish word for a sweetheart.

John-a-Nokes and John-a-Stiles. Names formerly given, instead of the very impersonal "A and B," to fictitious persons in an imaginary action at law: hence either name may stand for "just anybody." *Cp.* DOE.

Poets gyve names to men they write of, which argueth a conceite of an actuall truth, and so, not being true, prooves a falshood. And doth the Lawyer lye then, when under the names of *John a stile* and *John a noakes*, hee puts his case?—SIR PHILIP SIDNEY: *An Apologie for Poetrie* (1595).

John Audley. *See* AUDLEY.

John Brown (1800-59). An American abolitionist who led a body of men to free Negro slaves at Harper's Ferry, Virginia, October 16th, 1859. The famous Union song of the Civil War, "John Brown's Body," made him a legend.

John Bull. The national nickname for an Englishman, represented as a bluff, kind-hearted, bull-headed farmer. The character is from Dr. John Arbuthnot's satire *The History of John Bull*, which was originally published in 1712 as *Law in a Bottomless Pit*. "John Bull" is the Englishman, the Frenchman is termed *Lewis Baboon*, the Dutchman *Nicholas Frog*, etc.

John dory (dôr ′i). A golden yellow fish, the *Zeus faber*, common in the Mediterranean and round the south-western coasts of England. Its name was *dory* (Fr. *dorée*, golden) long before the *John* was added; this was probably a humorous amplification—from the name of some real or imaginary person—with, perhaps, a side allusion to Fr., *jaune*, yellow.

There is a tradition that it was from this fish (*but see* HADDOCK) that St. Peter took the stater or shekel. Hence it is called in French *le poisson de St. Pierre*, and in Gascon, the *golden* or *sacred cock*, meaning St. Peter's cock. Like the haddock, it has an oval black spot on each side,

said to be the finger-marks of St. Peter, when he held the fish to extract the coin.

John Roberts. Obsolete slang for a very large tankard, supposed to hold enough drink for any ordinary drinker to last through Saturday and Sunday. This measure was introduced into Wales in 1886 to compensate topers for the Sunday closing, and derived its name from John Roberts, M.P., author of the Sunday Closing Act.

John Tamson's man. A henpecked husband; one ordered here, there, and everywhere. Tamson—*i.e.* spiritless, a *Tame-son*.

John with the Leaden Sword. John of Lancaster, Duke of Bedford (1389-1435), third son of Henry IV, who acted as regent in France from 1422 to 1429, was so called by Earl Douglas.

Johnny. A superfine, dandified youth, was known as a *Johnny* in the latter part of last century, but from earlier times it has been applied indiscriminately to the British bourgeois. Byron, February 23rd, 1824, writes to Murray his publisher respecting an earthquake:—

If you had but seen the *English Johnnies*, who had never been out of a cockney workshop before . . . [running away . . .].

Johnny-cake. An American name for a cake made of maize-meal, formerly much esteemed as a delicacy. It is said to be a corruption of *journey*-cake.

Johnny Raw. A nervous novice, a newly enlisted soldier; an adult apprentice in the ship trade.

Johnny Reb. In the American Civil War a Federal name for a Confederate soldier—from the Northern point of view, a rebel.

Joint, in U.S.A. slang originally meant a sordid place where illicit spirits could be bought and drunk, opium smoked, etc. From that it has come to be applied, disparagingly, to any place of common resort, restaurant, etc.

To case a joint. To inspect a place with a view to committing robbery there.

Jolly. A sailor's nickname for a marine, a militiaman being a *tame jolly*.

To stand and be still to the Birken'ead drill is a damn tough bullet to chew.
An' they done it, the Jollies,—'Er Majesty's Jollies—soldier an' sailor too!
            KIPLING: *Soldier an' Sailor Too*.

The noun is also slang for a man who bids at auction with no intention of buying, but merely to force up the price.

As an adjective and adverb, *jolly* frequently has an intensive, approving, or ironical effect:—

All was jolly quiet at Ephesus before St. Paul came thither.—JOHN TRAPP: *Commentary* (1656).

'Tis likely you'll prove a jolly surly groom.
            Taming of the Shrew, iii, 2.

Jolly-boat. A small boat usually hoisted at the stern of a ship. *Jolly* here is probably connected with the Danish *jolle*, Dut. *jol*, and our *yawl*.

A jolly good fellow. A very social and popular person. When toasts are drunk "with musical honours" the chorus usually is—

For he's a jolly good fellow [three times].
  And so say all of us,
With a hip, hip, hip, hooray!

The Jolly Roger. *See* ROGER.

Jongleur (zhong' gler). A mediæval minstrel who recited verses, while accompanying himself on a musical instrument. Jongleurs formed a branch of the Troubadours—a force which permeated culture throughout Europe. Petrarch compared the function of the Jongleur in the spread of literature and education to that of the book-publisher.

Jordan almond. Here *Jordan* has nothing to do with the river (*cp.* JERUSALEM ARTICHOKE), but is a corruption of Fr. *jardin*, garden. The Jordan almond is a fine variety which comes chiefly from Malaga.

Jordan passed. Death over. The Jordan separated the wilderness [of the world] from the Promised Land, and thus came to be regarded almost as the Christian "Styx" (*q.v.*).

Jorum. A large drinking-bowl, intended specially for punch. The name is thought to be connected with King *Joram* (*cp.* JEROBOAM), who "brought with him vessels of silver, and vessels of gold, and vessels of brass" (2 *Sam.* viii, 10).

Josaphat. An Indian prince converted by the hermit Barlaam. *See* BARLAAM AND JOSAPHAT.

Joseph. One not to be seduced from his continency by the severest temptation is sometimes so called. The reference is to Joseph in Potiphar's house (*Gen.* xxxix). *Cp.* BELLEROPHON.

A great-coat used to be known by the same name, in allusion to Joseph, who left his garment, or upper coat, behind him.

Joseph, St. Husband of the Virgin Mary, and the reputed father of Jesus. He is patron saint of carpenters, because he was of that craft.

In art Joseph is represented as an aged man with a budding staff in his hand. His day is March 19th.

Joseph of Arimathea. The rich Jew, probably a member of the Sanhedrin, who believed in Christ but feared to confess it, and, after the Crucifixion, begged the body of the Saviour and deposited it in his own tomb (*see Matt.* xxvii, 57-60, *Mark* xv, 42). Legend relates that he was imprisoned for 42 years, during which time he was kept alive miraculously by the Holy Grail (*see* GRAIL), and that on his release by

Vespasian, about 63 A.D., he brought the Grail and the spear with which Longinus wounded the crucified Saviour, to Britain, and there founded the abbey of Glastonbury (*q.v.*), whence he commenced the conversion of Britain.

The origin of these legends is to be found in a group of apocryphal writings of which the *Evangelium Nicodemi* is the chief; these were worked upon at Glastonbury between the 8th and 11th centuries, were further embellished by Robert de Borron in the 13th, the latter version (by way of Walter Map) being woven, by Malory into his *Morte d'Arthur*.

Josh. An American slang term meaning to chaff, to banter or tease.

Joshua tree. The *Yucca brevifolia*, a spiky-leaved tree growing in the desert areas of the southwestern regions of the U.S.A. and in Mexico.

Joss. An idol or house-god of the Chinese; every family has its joss. A temple is called a *joss-house*, and a *joss-stick* is a stick of scented wood which is burnt as incense in a joss-house.

Jot. A very little, the least quantity possible. The iota [*i*] (see I) is the smallest letter of the Greek alphabet, called the Lacedemonian letter.

Heven and erthe shal soner passe away then one iote of goddis worde shal passe unfulfilled.—GEO. JOY: *An Apology to W. Tindale* (1535).

This bond doth give thee here no jot of blood.
  Merchant of Venice, iv, 1.

Jot or tittle. A tiny amount. The jot is i or iota, and the tittle, from Lat. *titulus*, is the mark, or dot over the i.

Jotunheim (jō' tùn hīm). Giant land. The home or region of the Scandinavian giants or *Jotunn*.

Jongs (joogz). The Scottish pillory, or, more properly, an iron ring or collar fastened by a short chain to a wall, and used as a pillory. Jamieson says, "They punish delinquents, making them stand in 'jogges,' as they call their pillories."

Jourdain, Monsieur. The type of the bourgeois placed by wealth in the ranks of gentlemen, who makes himself ridiculous by his endeavours to acquire their accomplishments. He is chiefly remembered from the delight he felt when he discovered that whereas some men wrote poetry, he had been speaking prose all his life without knowing it. The character is from Molière's comedy *Le Bourgeois Gentilhomme* (1670).

Journal (O.Fr., from Lat. *diurnalis*, diurnal, *dies*, a day).

Applied to newspapers, the word strictly means a daily paper; but the extension of the term to weekly and other periodicals is sanctioned by custom.

Jove (jōv). Another name of Jupiter (*q.v.*), the later being *Jovis pater*, father Jove. The Titans made war against Jove, and tried to dethrone him.

Milton, in *Paradise Lost*, makes Jove one of the fallen angels (i, 512).

Jovial (jō' vi al). Merry and sociable, like those born under the planet Jupiter, which astrologers considered the happiest of the natal stars.

Our jovial star reigned at his birth.
Cymbeline, v, 4.

Joy-ride. A ride in a motor-car, especially when it is driven fast and somewhat recklessly and more particularly still when it is done without the owner's knowledge or permission.

Joy stick. The control column of an aeroplane or glider, which is linked to the elevators and ailerons to control them.

Jubilee. In Jewish history the year of *jubilee* was every fiftieth year, which was held sacred in commemoration of the deliverance from Egypt. In this year the fields were allowed to lie fallow, land that had passed out of the possession of those to whom it originally belonged was restored to them, and all who had been obliged to let themselves out for hire were released from bondage. The year of jubilee was proclaimed with trumpets of ram's horn, and takes its name from *jobil*, a ram's horn. (*See Lev.* xxv, 11-34, 39-54; and xxvii, 16-24).

Hence any fiftieth anniversary, especially one kept with great rejoicings, is called a *Jubilee*, and the name has been applied to other outbursts of joy or seasons of festivity, such as the *Shakespeare Jubilee*, which was held at Stratford-on-Avon in September, 1769, and the *Protestant Jubilee*, celebrated in Germany in 1617 at the centenary of the Reformation.

King George III held a *Jubilee* on October 25th, 1809, that being the day before he *commenced* the fiftieth year of his reign; and Queen Victoria celebrated hers on June 21st, 1887, two days after she had *completed* her fiftieth year on the throne. Ten years later Queen Victoria kept her *Diamond Jubilee* as a thanksgiving for sixty years of queenhood, and a reign the length of which exceeded that of any of her predecessors. The only other English monarchs to have *Jubilees* were Henry III (who reigned for 56 years and 6 weeks), and Edward III (51 years and nearly 5 months). On May 6th, 1935, George V celebrated the *Silver Jubilee* (twenty-five years) of his accession to the throne.

In the Catholic Church Pope Boniface VIII instituted a *Jubilee* or Holy Year in 1300 for the purpose of granting indulgences, and ordered it to be observed every hundred years. Clement VI reduced the interval to fifty years, Urban IV to thirty, Sixtus IV to the present interval of twenty-five. There was a Jubilee in 1950. It is only on the occasion of a Jubilee that the Porta Santa (Holy Door) in St. Peter's, Rome, is opened.

Judas. Judas Iscariot, who betrayed his Master.

Judas kiss. A deceitful act of courtesy or simulated affection. Judas betrayed his Master with a kiss (*Matt.* xxvi, 49).

So Judas kissed his Master,
And cried, "All hail!" whenas he meant *all harm*.
3 Henry VI, v, 7.

Jude, St. Represented in art with a club or staff, and a carpenter's square, in allusion to his trade. His day is celebrated with that of St. Simon on October 28th.

Judge. Judge's black cap. *See* BLACK CAP.

Judges' robes. In the criminal courts, where the judges represent the sovereign, they appear in full court dress, and wear a scarlet robe; but in nisi prius courts the judge sits merely to balance the law between civilians, and therefore appears in his judicial undress, or violet gown.

Judge Lynch. In the U.S.A., a lynching, or the personification of lynch law.

Judicial Committee. A committee of the Privy Council and the final court of appeal in the British Empire, except in Great Britain itself. Constituted by an Act of 1833, it hears appeals from the courts of law throughout the Empire; the members being the Lord Chancellor and persons who hold or have held high judicial office in Great Britain or the Overseas Dominions. They do not deliver a judgment but state that they will advise His Majesty to allow or disallow an appeal. However, most members of the Commonwealth have now abolished appeal to the Privy Council.

Jug-band. A jazz band in the Deep South, in which one of the players blew a trombone or cornet into a large whiskey jug, so producing a deep resonant beat.

Jugged hare. Hare stewed in a jug or jar.

To be jugged. To be put in prison.

Juggernaut or **Jagganath.** A Hindu god, "Lord of the World," having his temple at Puri, in Orissa. The legend, as told in the *Ayeen-Akbery*, is that a learned Brahman was sent to look out a site for a temple. The Brahman wandered about for many days, and then saw a crow dive into the water; he then washed and made obeisance to the element. This was selected as the site of the temple. While the temple was a-building the king, Indica Dhumna, was told in a dream that the true form of Vishnu should be revealed to him in the morning. When the king went to see the temple he beheld a log of wood in the water, and this log he accepted as the realization of his dream, enshrining it in the temple.

Jagganath is regarded as the remover of sin. His image is on view three days in the year: the first day is the Bathing Festival, when the god is washed; he is then supposed to have a cold for ten days, at the end of which he is again brought out and taken in his car to the nearest temple; a week later the car is pulled back amid the rejoicings of the multitude at his recovery. It was on the final day that fanatical devotees used to throw themselves to be crushed beneath the wheels of the enormous, decorated machine, in the idea that they would thus obtain immediate admission to Paradise. Hence the phrase *the car of Juggernaut* is used of customs, institutions, etc., beneath which people are ruthlessly and unnecessarily crushed.

Juggler (Lat. *joculator*, a player). In the Middle Ages, jugglers accompanied the minstrels and troubadours, and added to their musical talents sleight of hand, antics, and feats of prowess to amuse the company assembled. In time the music was dropped, and tricks became the staple of wandering performers.

Juke Box. An American term for a gramophone or automatic musical box that plays a selection of pieces when a coin is inserted.

Julep. A long drink flavoured with mint; a great favourite in the Southern States of the U.S.A.

Julian. Pertaining to Julius Cæsar (100-44 B.C.), particularly with reference to the Calendar (*i.e.* the "Old Style") instituted by him in 46 B.C. (the *Julian Year* consisting of $365\frac{1}{4}$ days), which was in general use in Western Europe until it was corrected by Gregory XIII in 1582, in England until 1752, and until 1918 in use in Russia. To allow for the odd quarter day Cæsar ordained that every fourth year should contain 366 days, the additional day being introduced after the 6th of the calends of March, *i.e.* February 24th. Cæsar also divided the months into the number of days they at present contain, and July (*q.v.*) is named in his honour.

July. The seventh month, named by Mark Antony, in honour of Julius Cæsar, who was born in it. It was previously called *Quintilis*, as it was the fifth month of the Roman year; its Anglo-Saxon name was *litha se æfterra* (lithe,-mild).

The old Dutch name for it was *Hooy-maand* (hay-month); the old Saxon, *Mædd-monath* (because the cattle were turned into the meadows to feed), and *Lida æftevr* (the second mild or genial month). In the French Republican calendar it was called *Messidor* (harvest-month, June 19th to July 18th).

Until the late 18th century, *July* was accented on the first syllable; why the change took place no one seems to know.

> Her lips were red; and one was thin,
> Compar'd to that was next her chin
>   (Some bee had stung it newly):
> But, Dick, her eyes so guard her face,
> I durst no more upon them gaze
>   Than on the sun in July.
>   SUCKLING: *Ballad Upon a Wedding* (1646).

And even as late as 1798 Wordsworth wrote:—

> In March, December, and in July,
> 'Tis all the same with Harry Gill;
> The neighbours tell, and tell you truly,
> His teeth they chatter, chatter still.
>   *Goody Blake and Harry Gill.*

Jumbo. The name of an exceptionally large African elephant which, after giving rides to many thousands of children in the London Zoo, was sold, in 1882, to Barnum's Greatest Show on Earth. He weighed $6\frac{1}{2}$ tons. He was accidentally killed by a railway engine in 1885, but his name is still synonymous with the idea of an elephant in children's minds.

Jump. To fit or unite with like a graft; as, *our inventions meet and jump in one*. Hence exactly, precisely.

> Good advice is easily followed when it jumps with our own ... inclinations.—LOCKHART: *Sir Walter Scott*, ch. x.

In jazz when the music is of an exciting and lively tempo it is said to *jump*.

To jump at an offer. To accept eagerly.

To jump over the broomstick. To marry in an informal way. A "brom" is the bit of a bridle; to "jump the brom" is to skip over the marriage restraint, and "broomstick" is a mere corruption.

To jump the gun. To start ahead of time, as a nervous competitor in a race, who starts before the gun is fired.

Jumper. Originally a coarse canvas or hard-material sort of shirt reaching to the hips, and worn by sailors and other heavy labourers. The use of the word for the woollen garment worn by women is of fairly recent growth. It is from the obsolete *jump*, a short coat worn by men two hundred years ago, connected with Fr. *jupe*, and *jupon*, a petticoat.

June. The sixth month, named from the Roman *Junius* gens. Ovid says, *Junius a juvenum nomine dictus*. (*Fasti*, v, 78.)

The old Dutch name was *Zomer-maand* (summer-month); the old Saxon, *Sere-monath* (dry-month), and *Lida-œrra* (joy time). In the French Republican calendar the month was called *Prairial* (meadow-month, May 20th to June 18th).

Junk. Salt meat supplied to vessels for long voyages (*cp.* HARNESS CASK), so called because it is hard and tough as old rope-ends, which may have got the name *junk* from the rush-like shore plant, *Juncus maritimus*. Junk is often called "salt horse." The word is more usually applied to cast-off broken things, valueless odds and ends of lumber.

Junk shop. A shop where such stuff is sold.

Junket (jung' ket). Curdled cream with spice, etc.; any dainty. So called because it was originally made in a rush basket (Ital. *giuncata*, from Lat. *juncus*, a rush).

> You know there wants no junkets at the feast.
> *Taming of the Shrew*, ii, 2.

Junketing. Feasting, merrymaking.

> But great is song
> Used to great ends . . . for song
> Is duer unto freedom, force and growth
> Of spirit than to Junketing and love.
> TENNYSON: *Princess*, Pt. iv.

Juno (joo' nō). In Roman mythology the "venerable ox-eyed" wife of Jupiter, and queen of heaven. She is identified with the Greek Hera, was the special protectress of marriage and of woman, and was represented as a war goddess.

Junonian Bird. The peacock, dedicated to the goddess-queen.

Junta (jŭn' tä). In Spain a council or legislative assembly other than the Cortes (*q.v.*), which may be summoned either for the whole country, for one of its separate parts, or for some special object only. The most famous was that called together by Napoleon in 1808.

> I had also audience of the King, to whom I deliver'd two Memorials since, in His Majesty's name of *Great Britain*, that a particular Junta of some of the Council of State and War might be appointed to determine the business.—*Howell's Letters*, Bk. i, sect, iii, 10 (*Madrid*, Jan. 5th, 1622).

Jupiter (joo' pi ter). The supreme deity of Roman mythology, corresponding to the Greek Zeus (*see* JOVE), son of Cronos, or Saturn (whom he dethroned) and Rhea. He was the special protector of Rome, and as Jupiter Capitolinus—his temple being on the Capitoline Hill—presided over the Roman games. He determined the course of all human affairs and made known the future to man through signs in the heavens, the flight of birds (*see* AUGURY), etc.

As Jupiter was lord of heaven and prince of light, *white* was the colour sacred to him; hence among the mediæval alchemists *Jupiter* designated tin. In heraldry Jupiter stands for *azure*, the blue of the heavens.

His statue by Phidias (taken to Constantinople by Theodosius I and there destroyed by fire in A.D. 475) was one of the Seven Wonders of the World.

Jurassic Rocks (joo răs' ik). The group of limestone rocks embracing the strata between the top of the Rhætic Beds and the base of the Purbeckian Rocks, thus including the Lias and Oolites. So named from the Swiss *Jura*, where they are typically developed.

Jus. Latin for law.

Jus civile (Lat.). Civil law.

Jus divinum (Lat.). Divine law.

Jus gentium (Lat.). International law.

Just, The. Among rulers and others who have been given this surname are:—

Aristides, the Athenian (d. 468 B.C.).

Baharam, styled *Shah Endeb*, fifth of the Sassanidæ (276-96).

Casimir II, King of Poland (1117, 1177-94).

Ferdinand I, King of Aragon (1373, 1412-16).

Haroun al-Raschid. The most renowned of the Abbasside califs, and the hero of several of the *Arabian Nights* stories (765, 786-808).

James II, King of Aragon (1261-1327).

Khosru or Chosroes I of Persia (531-79), called by the Arabs *Malk al Adel* (the Just King).

Pedro I of Portugal (1320, 1357-67).

Juste milieu (zhust mē lye) (Fr.). The golden mean.

> The Church of England is the *juste milieu*.
> LADY BLOOMFIELD: *Reminiscences*, II, p. 18 (1883).

Justice. *See* JEDWOOD JUSTICE.

Justices in Eyre. *See* EYRE.

Poetic justice. That ideal justice which poets exercise in making the good happy, and the bad unsuccessful in their evil schemes.

Juvenal (joo' ve năl) (Lat., from *juvenis*), A youth; common in Shakespeare, thus:—

> The juvenal, the prince your master, whose chin is not yet fledged.—*2 Henry IV*, i, 2.

Juveniles. In theatrical parlance, those actors who play young men's parts; in the journalistic and book-trade, periodicals or books intended for the young.

K

K. The eleventh letter of the alphabet, representing the Greek *kappa*, and Hebrew *kaph*. The Egyptian hieroglyphic for *k* was a bowl. The Romans, after the C was given the K sound, gave up the use of the letter, except in abbreviated forms of a few words from Greek; thus, false accusers were branded on the forehead with a K (*kalumnia*), and the Carians, Cretans, and Cilicians were known as *the three bad K's*.

K is the recognized abbreviation of *Knight* in a large number of British Orders (but the abbreviation of "Knight" *per se* is *Kt.*).

In order of precedence these are:

K.G. Knight of the Garter.
K.T., K.P. Knight of the Thistle, Knight of St. Patrick.
K.C.B. Knight Commander of the Bath.
K.C.S.I.   "   "   "   Star of India.
K.C.M.G.   "   "   "   St. Michael & St. George.
K.C.I.E.   "   "   "   Indian Empire.
K.C.V.O. "   "   "   Victorian Order.
K.B.E.   "   "   "   British Empire.
Kt. Knight Bachelor.

Kabbalah. *See* CABBALA.

Ka me, ka thee. You scratch my back and I'll scratch yours; one good turn deserves another; do me a service, and I will give you a helping hand when you require one. It is an old proverb, and appears in Heywood's collection (1546).

Kaaba (ka' bà) (Arabic, *kabah*, a square house). A shrine of Mecca, said to have been built by Ishmael and Abraham on the spot where Adam first worshipped after his expulsion from Paradise. The building which stands in the centre of the court is about 50 ft. high; its peculiar sanctity is due to the Black Stone, which is built into the N.E. corner. This stone, about 6 in. in diameter, is kissed by every pilgrim. The present Kaaba was built in 1626; it is covered with a cloth of black brocade that is replaced with considerable ceremony every year.

Kaffir (kăf'ir) (Arabic, *Kafir*, an infidel). A name formerly given to Hottentots who rejected the Moslem faith, also to the natives of *Kafiristan* ("the country of the infidels"), in northern Afghanistan; but now restricted to the Bantu races of South Africa, especially the Xosa tribe.

Kaffirs, Kaffir market. The Stock Exchange names for shares in South African mines, and for the market in which they are dealt.

Kailyard School. A school of writers, who took their subjects from Scottish humble life; it flourished in the 'nineties of last century, and included such writers as Ian Maclaren, J. J. Bell, S. R. Crockett, and J. M. Barrie. The name is due to the motto—"There grows a bonnie brier bush in our kailyard"—used by Ian Maclaren for his *Beside the Bonnie Brier Bush* (1894).

Kaintuck. Louisiana French corruption of Kentucky. It was a term of opprobrium applied in the late 18th and early 19th centuries to Kentuckians and in particular to inhabitants of the American States in general; New Orleans dreaded the incursions of barbarous traders and riverboat crews who swarmed into the city to drink and fight and generally disrupt the life of peaceful citizens. Today the phrase has lost its bite and can be used as a term of affection.

Kaiser (kī' zer). The German form of *Cæsar*; the title formerly used by the head of the Holy Roman Empire, and by the Emperors of Germany and Austria. It was Diocletian who (about 284) ordained that *Cæsar* should be the title of the Emperor of the West, and it is thence that the modern *Kaiser* takes its rise.

Kali (ka' lē). The Hindu goddess after whom Calcutta receives its name, Kali-ghat, the steps of Kali, *i.e.* those by which her worshippers descended from the bank to the waters of the Ganges. She was the wife of Siva (*q.v.*), was the acme of bloodthirstiness, many human sacrifices being made to her, and it was to her that the Thugs sacrificed their victims. Her idol is black, besmeared with blood; she has red eyes, four arms with blood-stained hands, matted hair, huge fang-like teeth, and a protruding tongue that drips with blood. She wears a necklace of skulls, ear-rings of corpses, and is girdled with serpents.

Kalki. *See* AVATAR.

Kalmar. The Union of Kalmar. A treaty made on July 12th, 1397, uniting the kingdoms of Norway, Sweden and Denmark. This union lasted till it was dissolved by Gustavus Vasa in 1523.

Kalmucks—*i.e.* *Khalmuiku* (apostates) from Buddhism. A race of nomadic Mongols, extending from western China to the valley of the Volga, and adhering to a debased form of Buddhism.

Kalyb (kă' lib). The "Lady of the Woods," who stole St. George from his nurse, brought him up as her own child, and endowed him with gifts. St. George enclosed her in a rock, where she was torn to pieces by spirits. (*Seven Champions of Christendom*, Pt. i.)

Kamerad (ka' mĕ rad). (Ger., comrade, mate.) A word used by the Germans in World War I as an appeal for quarter. It is now used in English with the meaning "I surrender."

Kami (ka' mē). A god or divinity in *Shinto*, the native religion of Japan; also the title given to daimios and governors, about equal to our "lord."

Kamikaze (ka mi ka zi) (World War II) Japanese word meaning "divine wind" and applied to suicide squadrons and suicide resistance.

Karma (kar' má) (Sans., action, fate). In Buddhist philosophy, the name given to the results of action, especially the cumulative results of a person's deeds in one stage of his existence as controlling his destiny in the next.

Among Theosophists the word has a rather wider meaning, viz. the unbroken sequence of cause and effect; each effect being, in its turn, the cause of a subsequent effect. It is a Sanskrit word, meaning "action" or "sequence."

Karmathians (kar mā 'thi ánz). A Mohammedan sect which rose in Irak in the 9th century. Its founder was Karmat, a labourer who professed to be a prophet; they were communistic pantheists and rejected the forms and ceremonies of the Koran, which they regarded as a purely allegorical work.

Karttikeya (kar ti kē' yà). The Hindu Mars, and god of war. He is shown riding on a peacock, with a bow in one hand and an arrow in the other, and is known also as *Skanda* and *Kumara*.

Kaswa, Al. (kăs' wà). Mohammed's favourite camel, which fell on its knees in adoration when the prophet delivered the last clause of the Koran to the assembled multitude at Mecca.

Katerfelto (kăt er fel' tō). A generic name for a quack or charlatan, Gustavus Katerfelto was a celebrated quack who became famous during the influenza epidemic of 1782, when he exhibited in London his solar microscope and created immense excitement by showing the infusoria of muddy water. The doctor used to aver that he was the greatest philosopher since the time of Sir Isaac Newton. He was a tall man, dressed in a long, black gown and square cap, and died in 1799.

> Katerfelto with his hair on end,
> At his own wonders wondering for his bread.
> COWPER: *Task; The Winter Evening* (1782).

Keblah (keb' la). The point towards which Mohammedans turn when they worship, *i.e.* the Kaaba (*q.v.*) at Mecca; also the niche or slab (called the *mihrab*) on the interior wall of a mosque indicating this direction.

Kedar's Tents (kē' dà). This world. Kedar was a son of Ishmael (*Gen.* xxv, 15), and was the ancestor of an important tribe of nomadic Arabs. The phrase means houses in the wilderness of this world, and comes from *Ps.* cxx, 5: "Woe is me, that I sojourn in Mesech, that I dwell in the tents of Kedar."

Kedgeree (kej'' er ē) (Hindi, *khichri*). In India a stew of rice, vegetables, eggs, butter, etc.; but in England a dish of re-cooked fish with boiled rice, eggs, sauce, etc., is so called.

Keel. Keel-hauling or **-haling**. Metaphorically, a long, troublesome, and vexatious examination or repetition of annoyances from one in authority. The term comes from a practice that was formerly common in the Dutch and many other navies of tying delinquents to a yardarm with weights on their feet, and dragging them by a rope under the keel of a ship, in at one side and out at the other. The result was often fatal.

Keening. A weird lamentation for the dead, common in Galway. The coffin is carried to the burying place, and while it is carried three times round, the mourners go to the graves of their nearest kinsfolk and "keen." The word is Ir. *cacoine*, from *caoinim*, to weep.

Keep. One's *keep* is the amount that it takes to maintain one; heard in such phrases as **You're not worth your keep.** The *keep* of a mediæval castle was the main tower or stronghold, the donjon.

Keep your breath to cool your porridge. Look after your own affairs, and do not put your spoke in another person's wheel.

To keep a stiff upper lip. To preserve a resolute appearance; not to give way to grief.

To keep at arm's length. To prevent another from being too familiar.

To keep body and soul together. *See* BODY.

To keep company with. A phrase formerly commonly used to describe a friendship preliminary to courtship.

To keep down. To prevent another from rising to an independent position; to keep in subjection; also to keep expenses low.

To keep up. To continue, as, "to keep up a discussion"; to maintain, as, "to keep up one's courage," "to keep up appearances"; to continue *pari passu*, as "Keep up with the rest."

Keeping-room. In 18th-century American parlance, the second-best room in the house.

Kehama (ke ha′ mà). The Hindu rajah in Southey's epic, *The Curse of Kehama* (1810), who obtains and sports with supernatural powers

Kells, The Book of. Kells is an ancient Irish town in county Meath, once the residence of the kings of Ireland and the see of a bishop until 1300. Among its antiquities, but now preserved in Trinity College, Dublin, is the finest extant early Irish illuminated MS. of the Gospels, dating from the 8th century.

Kelly. As game as Ned Kelly. An Australian phrase referring to a noted desperado, who became something of a folk-hero. Ned Kelly (1854-80), after enormous depredations, was captured in a suit of armour made by himself, and hanged at Melbourne.

Kelmscott Press, was a private printing press founded in 1890 by William Morris in a cottage adjoining his residence, Kelmscott House, Hammersmith, with the assistance of Emery Walker and Sidney Cockerell. The object was to return to the finest principles of printing in the 15th century.

Kenelm, St. An English saint, son of Kenwulf, King of Wessex in the early 9th century. He was only seven years old when, by his sister's order, he was murdered at Clente-in-Cowbage, Gloucestershire. The murder, says Roger of Wendover, was miraculously notified at Rome by a white dove, which alighted on the altar of St. Peter's, bearing in its beak a scroll with these words:—

In Clent cow pasture, under a thorn,
Of head bereft, lies Kenelm king-born.

St. Kenelm's feast day is July 17th.

Kenna. *See* KENSINGTON GARDEN.

Kenne. A stone that by mediæval naturalists was fabled to be formed in the eye of the stag. It was used as an antidote to poison. *Cp.* HYENA.

Kennel. A dog's shelter; from Lat. *canis* (a dog), Ital. *canile*; but *kennel*, a gutter, is, like *channe* and *canal*, from Lat. *canalis*, a pipe (our *cane*) through which water was conveyed.

Kensington Garden. A mock-heroic poem by Thomas Tickell (pub. 1722) peopling Kensington Gardens, which a few years before had been laid out, with fairies. The gardens were the royal domain of Oberon, and the hero is Albion, son of "Albion's royal blood," who was stolen thence by a fairy named Milkah. He later fell in love with Kenna, daughter of Oberon, and after many adventures and a war caused by Oberon's opposition they were married and "lived happy ever after."

Kent (Lat. *Cantium*), the territory of the Kantii or Cantii; Old British, *Kant*, a corner or headland. In the reign of Queen Elizabeth Kent was so notorious for highway robbery that the word signified a "nest of thieves."

Some bookes are arrogant and impudent;
So are most thieves in Christendome and Kent.
        TAYLOR, *the Water Poet* (1630).

"Kent" and "Christendom" have been verbally associated from very early times, partly, no doubt, because of the alliteration, partly, perhaps, because it was to Kent that St. Augustine first brought Christianity.

Kentish Fire. Rapturous applause, or three times three and one more. The expression originated with the protracted cheers given in Kent to the No-Popery orators in 1828-29. Lord Winchilsea, who proposed the health of the Earl of Roden on August 15th, 1834, said: "Let it be given with the 'Kentish Fire.'"

Kentishmen's Tails. *See* TAILS.

Kent's Cavern, a mile or so out of Torquay, is a limestone cave in which a great number of bones and flint implements have been discovered. There appear to have been two different periods of occupation in prehistoric times, and the objects found in the cave throw important light on the civilization of those ages.

Kentucky Derby. One of the classic races in U.S.A., run since 1875 at Churchill Downs, Louisville, Ky. It is a mile and a half, for three-year-olds.

Kentucky Pill. A bullet.

Kepler's Laws. Astronomical laws first enunciated by Johann Kepler (1571-1630). They formed the basis of Newton's work, and are the starting-point of modern astronomy. They are:—

(1) That the orbit of a planet is an ellipse, the sun being in one of the foci.

(2) That every planet so moves that the line drawn from it to the sun describes equal areas in equal times.

(3) That the squares of the times of the planetary revolutions are as the cubes of their mean distances from the sun.

Kernel. *The kernel of the matter;* its gist, true import; the core or central part of it. The word is the A.S. *cyrnel,* diminutive of *corn.*

Kersey. A coarse cloth, usually ribbed, and woven from long wool; said to be so named from Kersey, in Suffolk, where it was originally made. Shakespeare uses the word figuratively ("russet yeas and honest kersey noes," *Love's Labour's Lost,* v, 2), with the meaning plain or homely.

Kerseymere. A twilled fine woollen cloth of a particular make, formerly called *cassimere,* a variation of *cashmere,* its present name being due to confusion with *kersey* (*see above*).

Cashmere, a fine woollen material, is so called because it is made from hair of the goats of *Kashmir.*

Kerton. *See* EXTER.

Kestrel. A hawk of a base breed, hence a worthless fellow.

No thought of honour ever did assay
His baser brest; but in his kestrell kynd
A pleasant veine of glory he did find . . .
        SPENSER: *Faerie Queene,* II, iii, 4.

Ketch. *See* JACK KETCH, under JACK.

Ketchup. A sauce made from mushrooms, tomatoes, etc., which originally, with its name, came from the Far East.

Soy comes in Tubbs from Jappan, and the best ketchup from Tonquin; yet good of both sorts are made and sold very cheap in China.—LOCKYER: *Trade with India* (1711).

The word is from Chinese, through Malay, *kechap.*

Kettle. Old thieves' slang for a watch; a **tin kettle** is a silver watch and a **red kettle** a gold one.

A kettle of fish. An old Border name for a kind of *fête champêtre,* or picnic by the riverside in which newly caught salmon is the chief dish. Having thickened some water with salt to the consistency of brine, the salmon is put therein and boiled; and when fit for eating, the company partake in gipsy fashion. The discomfort of this sort of picnic probably gave rise to the phrase "A pretty kettle of fish," meaning an awkward state of affairs, a mess, a muddle.

The surgeon . . . was now come to acquaint Mr. Towouse that his guest was in such extreme danger of his life, that he scarce saw any hopes of his recovery. "Here's a pretty kettle of fish," cried Mrs. Tow-wouse, "you have brought upon us! We are like to have a funeral at our own expense."—FIELDING: *Joseph Andrews,* I, xii.

Kettledrum. A drum made of a thin hemispherical shell of brass or copper with a parchment top.

Also, an obsolete name for an afternoon tea-party, so called because it was on a somewhat

smaller scale than the regular "drum" (*q.v.*), and also in playful allusion to the presence of the tea *kettle.*

Kevin, St. (kev' in). An Irish saint of the 6th century, of whom legend relates that, like St. Senanus, he retired to an island where he vowed no woman should ever land. A girl named Kathleen followed him, but the saint hurled her from a rock, and her ghost never left the place while he lived. A rock at Glendalough (Wicklow) is shown as the bed of St. Kevin. Moore has a poem on this tradition (*Irish Melodies,* iv).

Kex. The dry, hollow stem of umbelliferous plants, like the hemlock. Tennyson says in *The Princess,* "Though the rough kex break the starred mosaic." Nothing breaks a pavement like the growth of grass or lichen through it.

Key. Metaphorically, that which explains or solves some difficulty, problem, etc., as *the key to a cipher,* the means of interpreting it, *the key to a "roman à clef,"* the list showing whom the fictional characters represent in actual life. Also, a place which commands a large area of land or sea, as Gibraltar is the key **to the Mediterranean,** and, in the Peninsular War, Ciudad Rodrigo (taken by Wellington, 1812) was known as the **key to Spain.**

In music the lowest note of a scale is the **keynote,** and gives its name to the scale, or **key,** itself: hence the figurative phrases *in key, out of key,* in or out of harmony with.

St. Peter's keys. The cross-keys on the papal arms symbolizing:

The power of the keys. The supreme ecclesiastical authority claimed by the pope as successor of St. Peter. The phrase is derived from *St. Matt.* xvi, 19:—

And I will give unto thee the keys of the kingdom of heaven: and whatsoever thou shalt bind on earth shall be bound in heaven: and whatsoever thou shalt loose on earth shall be loosed in heaven.

The Gold Key. The office of Groom of the Stole (*see* STOLE), the holder of which had a golden key as his emblem.

The queen's keys. An old legal phrase for the crowbars, hammers, etc., used to force an entrance so that a warrant could be executed.

At the ceremony of locking up the Tower of London at night, the keys are brought to the main guard house, where the sentry demands, "Who goes there?" "Keys," is the answer. "Whose keys?" "Queen Elizabeth's keys." "Advance Queen Elizabeth's keys, and all's well."

To have the key of the street. To be locked out of doors; to be turned out of one's home.

Keys of stables and cowhouses are not infrequently, even at the present day, attached to a stone with a hole through it with a piece of horn attached to the handle. This is a relic of an ancient superstition. The *halig*, or holy stone, was looked upon as a talisman which kept off the fiendish Mara (nightmare); and the horn was supposed to ensure the protection of the god Pan.

The Cross Keys as a public-house sign has an ecclesiastical origin (*see. St. Peter's keys, above*). St. Peter is always represented in art with two keys in his hand; they are consequently the insignia of the papacy, and are borne saltire-wise, one of gold and the other of silver. They also form the arms of the Archbishop of York; the Bishop of Winchester bears two keys and sword in saltire, and the bishops of St. Asaph, Gloucester, Exeter, and Peterborough bear two keys in saltire. The *cross-keys* are also the emblem of St. Servatius, St. Hippolytus, St. Geneviève, St. Petronilla, St. Osyth, St. Martha, and St. Germanus of Paris.

Key-cold. Deadly cold, lifeless. A key, on account of its coldness, is still sometimes employed to stop bleeding at the nose.

Poor key-cold figure of a holy king!
Pale ashes of the house of Lancaster!
Thou bloodless remnant of that royal blood
Richard III, i, 2.

Keys, The House of. The representative branch of the Legislature, or Tynwald, of the Isle of Man, which consists of two branches, viz. the Governor and Council, and this House. Since 1866 the twenty-four members of the House of Keys have been popularly elected every seven years; previous to that date the House was self-elected, vacancies being filled by the House presenting to the governor "two of the eldest and worthiest men of the isle," one of which the governor nominated.

The governor and his council consists of the governor, the bishop, the attorney-general, two deemsters (or judges), members appointed by the governor and four members appointed by the House of Keys.

The Keystone State. Pennsylvania; so called from its position and importance.

Keystone Comedies. Early film comedies at Hollywood made between 1916 and about 1926 by the Keystone Company, featuring Mack Sennett.

Khaki (ka' ki). A Hindu word, meaning *dusty*, or *dust-coloured*, from *khak*, dust. Khaki was first used by British troops at the time of the Indian Mutiny, when it was adopted as the uniform for an irregular corps of Guides, raised at Meerut, hence called the *Khaki Risala*

(*Risala* = squadron). In 1882 the War Office discussed the question of adopting it as the general active service uniform, but, though certain regiments wore it then, and in the Omdurman campaign in Egypt sixteen years later, on the North-West Frontier, etc., it was not generally introduced until the Boer War of 1899-1902.

Khalifa (ka lē' fà). An Arabic word meaning "successor" and the title adopted by Abdullah el Tashi, the successor in 1885 of the Mahdi (*q.v.*). Much was heard of the Khalifa in late Victorian days, for it was against him that the British expedition went under Lord Kitchener in 1898, when his power was broken at the battle of Omdurman.

Khamsin. *See* KAMSIN.

Khedive (ke dēv'). The title by which, from 1867 to 1914, the ruler of Egypt, as viceroy of the Sultan of Turkey, was known. The word is Turkish (from Persian) and means a prince, or viceroy.

In 1914 Egypt was a semi-independent tributary state of Turkey, occupied by British troops. The then Khedive, Abbas II, joined the Central Powers, and was deposed, a British Protectorate being declared. The title then disappeared, and the new ruler, Hussein Kamil, became King of Egypt.

Kibitzer (kib' it zér). An American colloquial term to describe, originally, a spectator at a card game who looks over the players' shoulders and as often as not gives unwanted advice. The word is of Yiddish-German derivation.

Kiblah. *See* KEBLAH.

Kibosh (kī' bosh). **To put the kibosh on.** To put an end to; dispose of. Mr. Charles Funk received the following explanation of its origin from Mr. Padraic Colum: " 'Kibosh,' I believe, means the cap of death' and it is always used in that sense—'He put the kibosh on it.' In Irish it could be written 'cie bais'—the last word pronounced 'bosh,' the genitive of 'bas,' death."

Kick. Slang for a sixpence, but only in compounds. "Two-and-a-kick" is two shillings and sixpence.

He's not got a kick left in him. He's done for, "down and out." The phrase is from pugilism.

More kicks than ha'pence. More abuse than profit. Called "monkey's allowance" in allusion to monkeys led about to collect ha'pence by exhibiting "their parts." The poor brutes get the kicks if they do their parts in an unsatisfactory manner, but the master gets the ha'pence collected.

Quite the kick. Quite a dandy. The Italians call a dandy a *chic*. The French *chic* means knack, as *avoir le chic*, to have the knack of doing a thing smartly.

> I cocked my hat and twirled my stick,
> And the girls they called me quite the kick.
> *George Colman the Younger.*

To get the kick out. To be summarily dismissed; given the sack or "the Order of the Boot."

To kick one's heels. *See* HEEL.

Kick-off, in football, the start or resumption of a game by kicking the ball from the centre of the field.

To kick the bucket. *See* BUCKET.

To kick up a dust, a row, etc. To create a disturbance. The phrase "to kick up the dust" explains the other phrases.

Kickshaws. Made dishes, odds and ends, and dainty trifles of small value. Formerly written "kickshose." (Fr. *quelque chose.*)

> Some pigeons, Davy, a couple of short-legged hens, joint of mutton, and any pretty little tiny kickshaws.—2 *Henry IV,* v, 1.

Kid. A faggot or bundle of firewood. **To kid** is to bind up faggots. In the parish register of Kneesal church there is the following item: "Leading kids to church, 2s. 6d.," that is, carting faggots to church.

Kid. A young child; in allusion to kid, the young of the goat, a very playful and frisky little animal.

The verb **to kid,** means to make a fool of.

Kidd, Captain. A famous pirate about whom many stories and legends have arisen. Originally commissioned with letters of marque, he was disowned by his employers and turned pirate. He was hanged at Execution Dock, Tilbury, in 1701.

Kiddies, The. *See* REGIMENTAL NICKNAMES.

Kidnapping is a slang word imported into the language in the 17th century. "Nabbing" a "kid," or a child was the popular term for the abominable offence of stealing young children and selling them to sea captains and others who bore them off to work on the plantations in America. The most notorious instance of kidnapping in modern times was the stealing and murder of Colonel Lindbergh's infant son in 1932.

Kidney. Temperament, disposition; stamp.

Men of another kidney or of the same kidney. The *reins* or *kidneys* were even by the Jews supposed to be the seat of the affections.

Kill. To kill two birds with one stone. *See* BIRD.

Killed by Kindness. It is said that Draco, the Athenian legislator, met with his death

from his popularity, being smothered in the theatre of Ægina by the number of caps and cloaks showered on him by the spectators (590 B.C.). Thomas Heywood wrote a play called *A Woman Killed with Kindness* (1603).

Killing. Irresistible, overpowering, fascinating, or bewitching; so as to compel admiration and notice.

> Those eyes were made so killing.
> POPE: *Rape of the Lock*, v, 64.

A killing pace. Too hot or strong to last; exceptionally great; exhausting.

Killing no murder. A pamphlet published in Holland and sent over to England in 1657 advising the assassination of Oliver Cromwell. It purported to be by one William Allen, a Jesuit, and has frequently been attributed to Silas Titus (later made a colonel and Groom of the Bedchamber by Charles II), but it was actually by Col. Edward Sexby, a Leveller, who had gone over to the Royalists, and who, in 1657, narrowly failed in an attempt to murder Cromwell.

The texts on the title-page are:—

> And all the People of the Land rejoiced: and the City was quiet, after that they had slain Athaliah with the Sword.—2 *Chron.* xxiii, 21.

> Now after the time that Amaziah did turn away from following the Lord, they made a conspiracy against him in Jerusalem, and he fled to Lachish; but they sent to Lachish after him, and slew him there.—2 *Chron.* xxv, 27.

Kilroy. (World War II.) The phrase "Kilroy was here" was found written up wherever the Americans (particularly Air Transport Command) had been, somewhat like "Chad" (*q.v.*) in Britain. Various theories have been put forward as to its origin—one being that a certain Kilroy was inspector in a shipyard at Quincy, Mass., and wrote the words in chalk on equipment to indicate that he had inspected it—but it seems more likely that the phrase grew by accident. Imitations such as "Clem" did not become so fashionable.

Kilter. Out of kilter. Out of order.

Kin, Kind.

> King: But now, my cousin Hamlet, and my son—
> Ham.: A little more than kin, and less than kind.
> *Hamlet,* i, 2.

Kin or **kinsman** is a relative by marriage or blood more distant than father and son.

Kind means of the same sort of genus, as man-kind or man-genus.

Hamlet says he is more than *kin* to Claudius (as he was stepson), but still he is not of the same *kind*, the same class, He is not a bird of the same feather as the king.

Kindergarten (kin' dėr gar' tėn) meaning in German a children's garden, is the term applied to schools in which very young children are taught by the use of objects, games and songs. The system was initiated in Germany by Friederich Froebel (1782-1852) in 1840.

King. The A.S. *cyning*, from *cyn*, a nation or people, and the suffix -*ing*, meaning "of," as "son of," "chief of," etc. In Anglo-Saxon times the king was elected by the Witenagemot, and was therefore the *choice of the nation*.

King Alfred, H.M.S. The name given to the shore station at which officers of the Royal Navy are trained.

King of Kings. In the Prayer Book the term, of course, refers to the Deity, but it has been assumed by many Eastern rulers, especially by the sovereigns of Abyssinia.

King of the King. Cardinal Richelieu (1585-1642) was so called, because of his influence over Louis XIII of France.

The King of the Border. A nickname of Adam Scott of Tushielaw (executed 1529), a famous border outlaw and chief.

The King of Dunces. In his first version of the *Dunciad* (1712), Pope gave this place of honour to Lewis Theobald (1688-1744); but in the edition of 1742 Colley Cibber (1671-1757) was put to reign in his stead.

The King of Men. A title given both to Zeus and Agamemnon.

The King of Painters. A title assumed by Parrhasius, the painter, a contemporary of Zeuxis (400 B.C.). Plutarch says he wore a purple robe and a golden crown.

The King of Rome. A title conferred by Napoleon I on his son François Charles Joseph Napoleon, Duke of Reichstadt (1811-32), on the day of his birth. He was called *L'Aiglon* (the young eagle) by Edmond Rostand in his play.

The King of Waters. The river Amazon, in South America.

The King of the World. The title (in Hindi *Shah Jehan*) assumed by Khorrum Shah, third son of Selim Jehan Ghir, and fifth of the Mogul emperors of Delhi (reigned 1628-58).

King's Cave. Opposite to Campbelton; so called because it was here that King Robert Bruce and his retinue lodged when they landed on the mainland from the Isle of Arran.

King's Crag. Fife, in Scotland. So called because Alexander III of Scotland was killed there (1286).

As he was riding in the dusk of the evening along the sea-coast of Fife, betwixt Burnt-island and King-horn, he approached too near the brink of the precipice, and his horse, starting or stumbling, he was thrown over the rock and killed on the spot. . . . The people of the country still

point out the very spot where it happened, and which is called "The King's Crag." — SCOTT: *Tales of a Grandfather*, vi.

King's Cross. Up to the accession of George IV this London locality was called "Battle Bridge" and had an infamous notoriety. The name was changed in 1821, when the neighbourhood was being developed by speculating builders. A battle is said to have been fought on this site between King Alfred and the Danes, but it is mostly a matter of legend, no facts having yet been discovered to substantiate the story. There was never any cross here, only a singularly bad statue of George IV which was taken down in 1842.

King of Arms. The official title of the chief heralds. In England there are three kings of arms, Garter, Clarenceux, and Norroy and Ulster; in Scotland there is the Lord Lyon King of Arms. The Order of the Bath has its own Bath King of Arms, instituted in 1725. In Ireland the office of Ulster King of Arms is now associated with the Norroy King of Arms in England.

King Charles's head. A phrase applied to an obsession, a fixed fancy. It comes from Mr. Dick, the harmless half-wit in *David Copperfield*, who, whatever he wrote or said always got round to the subject of King Charles's head, about which he was composing a memorial — he could not keep it out of his thoughts.

King Charles's Spaniel. A small black-and-tan spaniel with a rounded head, short muzzle, full, rather protruding eyes. This variety came into favour at the Restoration, but the colour of the dogs at that time was liver and white.

King Cotton. Cotton, the staple of the Southern States of America, and one of the chief articles of manufacture in England. The expression was first used by James H. Hammond in the United States Senate in 1858.

King's County in the province of Leinster in Eire is now called Offaly, and Queen's County is now Leix.

King's Cup Air Race was instituted in 1922 for a cup presented by George V. It is a handicap air race open only to British and Empire pilots flying British or Dominion aeroplanes. The winner in 1950 was E. Day, at a speed of 138 m.p.h.

King James's Bible. *See* BIBLE, THE ENGLISH.

King Log and King Stork. *See* LOG.

King's (or **Queen's**) **Messenger** is an official of the British Foreign Office whose duty it is to carry personally confidential messages from London to any embassy or legation abroad. He carries as his badge of office a silver greyhound, and though he naturally receives courtesies and help in the countries across which he travels, he enjoys no diplomatic immunities or privileges save that of passing through the customs the "diplomatic bag" he is carrying.

King-maker, The. Richard Neville, Earl of Warwick (1420-71); so called because, when he sided with Henry VI, Henry was king, but when he sided with Edward IV, Henry was deposed and Edward crowned. He was killed at the battle of Barnet. He was first called "the king-maker" by John Major in his *History of Greater Britain, England and Scotland*, 1521.

King's (or Queen's) Bench. The Supreme Court of Common Law; so called because at one time the sovereign presided in this court, and the court followed the sovereign when he moved from one place to another. Originally called the *Aula Regia*, it is now a division of the High Court of Judicature.

King-pin, in skittles, etc., the pin in the centre when all the pins are in place, or the pin at the front apex. Figuratively the word is used to describe the principal person in a company, cast, etc.

King Horn. The hero of a French metrical romance of the 13th century, and the original of our *Horne Childe*, generally called *The Geste of Kyng Horn*. The nominal author is a certain *Mestre Thomas*.

Like a king. When Porus, the Indian prince, was taken prisoner, Alexander asked him how he expected to be treated. "Like a king," he replied; and Alexander made him his friend.

Pray aid of the king (or **queen**). When someone, under the belief that he has a right to the land, claims rent of the king's tenants, they appeal to the sovereign, or "pray aid of the king."

The books of the four kings. A pack of cards.

After supper were brought in the books of the four kings.—RABELAIS: *Gargantua and Pantagruel*, i, 22.

The king of beasts. The lion.

The King of Terrors. Death.

The king of the forest. The oak, which not only braves the storm, but fosters the growth of tender parasites under its arms.

The king's cheese goes half in paring. A king's income is half consumed by the numerous calls on his purse.

The King's English. *See* ENGLISH.

The Three Kings of Cologne. The Magi (*q.v.*).

King's (or Queen's) Counsel. In England a member of the Bar appointed by the Crown on the nomination of the Lord Chancellor, in Scotland on the recommendation of the Lord Justice-General. A K.C. wears a silk gown and is thus often called a silk. He takes precedence over the junior Bar, and in a case must have a junior barrister with him.

King's Evil. Scrofula; so called from a notion which prevailed from the reign of Edward the Confessor to that of Queen Anne that it could be cured by the royal touch. The Jacobites considered that the power did not descend to William III and Anne because the "divine" hereditary right was not fully possessed by them, but the office remained in our Prayer-Book till 1719. Prince Charles Edward, when he claimed to be Prince of Wales, touched a female child for the disease in 1745. One of the last persons touched in England was Dr. Johnson, in 1712, when less than three years old, by Queen Anne. The practice was introduced by Henry VII of presenting the person "touched" with a small gold or silver coin, called a touch-piece. The one presented to Dr. Johnson has St. George and the Dragon on one side and a ship on the other; the legend of the former is *Soli deo gloria,* and of the latter *Anna D: G.M.B.R.F: ET.H.REG.* (Anne, by the Grace of God, of Great Britain, France, and Ireland Queen).

We are told that Charles II touched 92,107 persons. The smallest number in one year was 2,983, in 1669; and the largest number was in 1684, when many were trampled to death. (*See* Macaulay's *History of England,* ch. xiv.) John Brown, a royal surgeon, had to superintend the ceremony.

Cp. Macbeth, iv, 3:—
Malcolm: Comes the king forth, I pray you?
Doctor: Ay, sir; there are a crew of wretched souls
That stay his cure; their malady convinces
The great assay of art; but, at his touch
Such sanctity hath heaven given his hand,
They presently amend.

The French kings laid claim to the same divine power from the time of Clovis, A.D. 481, and on Easter Sunday, 1686, Louis XIV touched 1,600 persons, using these words: *Le roy te touche, Dieu te guerisse.*

Days fatal to Kings. Much foolish superstition has been circulated respecting certain days supposed to be "fatal" to the crowned heads of Great Britain. The following notes will help the reader to discriminate truth from fiction:—

Of the sovereigns who have died since 1066 *Sunday* has been the last day of the reign of seven, *Monday, Tuesday* and *Thursday* that of six each, *Friday* and *Wednesday* of five, and *Saturday* of four.

Sunday: Henry I, Edward III, Henry VI, James I, William III, Anne, George I.

Monday: Stephen, Richard II, Henry IV, Henry V, Richard III, George V.

Tuesday: Richard I, Edward II, Charles I, James II, William IV, Victoria.

Wednesday: John, Henry III, Edward IV, Edward V, George VI.

Thursday: William I, William II, Henry II, Edward VI, Mary I, Elizabeth.

Friday: Edward I, Henry VIII, Charles II, Mary II, Edward VII.

Saturday: Henry VII, George II, George III, George IV.

Kingdom Come. Death, the grave, execution, the next world.

And forty pounds be theirs, a pretty sum,
For sending such a rogue to kingdom come.
　　　　　　　PETER PINDAR: *Subjects for Painters.*

Kingsale. The premier baron of Ireland, Lord Kingsale, is one of the two British subjects who claim the right of wearing a hat in the presence of royalty. *See* HAT.

Kingston Bridge. A card bent so that when the pack is cut it is cut at this card.

Kingston-on-Thames. Named *King's stone* from a large square block of stone near the town hall, on which the early Anglo-Saxon monarchs knelt when they were appointed to the kingly office: Edward the Elder, Athelstan, Edmund, Ethelred, Edred, Edwy, and Edward the Martyr received on this stone the royal unction. The stone is now enclosed.

Kingstown (Eire), by the Irish called Dunleary. The name was changed in 1821 out of compliment to George IV, who visited Ireland that year, and left Dunleary harbour for his return home on September 5th.

Kinless Loons. The judges whom Cromwell sent into Scotland were so termed, because they had no relations in the country and so were free from temptation to nepotism. They tried the accused on the merits of the case.

Kiosk (kē' osk). A Turkish summer-house or pavilion supported by pillars which were usually covered with vines or flowering creepers and often enclosed a fountain. In England and western Europe the name is given to bandstands, pavilions for the sale of refreshments, etc., and to small enclosed stalls for the sale of newspapers in the street; booths for public telephones, etc.

Kirk of Skulls. Gamrie Church, in Banffshire; so called because the skulls and other bones of the Norsemen who fell in the neighbouring field, the *Bloody Pots,* were built into its walls.

Kirke's Lambs. *See* REGIMENTAL NICKNAMES.

Kismet (kis'met). Fate, destiny; or the fulfilment of destiny; from Turk, *quismat,* portion, lot (*qasama,* to divide).

Kiss. A very ancient and widely spread mode of salutation, frequently mentioned in the Bible, both as an expression of reverence and adoration and as a greeting or farewell between friends. Esau embraced Jacob, "fell on his neck and kissed him" (*Gen.* xxxiii, 4), the repentant woman kissed the feet of Christ (*Luke* vii, 45), and the disciples from Ephesus "fell on Paul's neck and kissed him" (*Acts* xx, 37). But kissing between the sexes was unknown among the ancient Hebrews, and while the cheeks, forehead, beard, hands, and feet might be kissed the lips might not, the passage in the Bible (*Prov.* xxiv, 26, *see* marginal note in Revised Version) that seems to contradict this being a mistranslation. "Kiss the Son, lest He be angry" (*Ps.* ii, 12), means worship the Son of God. This is the only reference in the Bible to the Kiss of Homage.

The old custom of "kissing the bride" comes from the Salisbury rubric concerning the Pax (*q.v.*).

In billiards (and also bowls) a *kiss* is a very slight touch of one moving ball on another, especially a second touch, accidental or designed; and the name also used to be given to a little drop of sealing-wax accidentally let fall beside the seal.

Kiss the place to make it well. Said to be a relic of the custom of sucking poison from wounds. St. Martin of Tours, when he was at Paris, observed at the city gates a leper full of sores; and, going up to him, he kissed the sores, whereupon the leper was instantly made whole (Sulpicius Severus: *Dialogues*). Similar stories are told of St. Mayeul, and quite a number of saints.

Who ran to help me, when I fell,
And would some pretty story tell,
Or kiss the place to make it well?
　　　　　　　ANN TAYLOR: *My Mother.*

To kiss the book. To kiss the Bible, or the New Testament, after taking an oath; the kiss of confirmation or promise to act in accordance with the words of the oath and a public acknowledgment that you adore and fear to offend, by breaking your oath, the God whose book you reverence.

In the English Courts, the Houses of Parliament, etc., non-Christians and others who have scruples are now permitted to affirm without going through this ceremony.

Kist of Whistles. A church-organ (Scotch). *Kist* is the same word as *cist* (*q.v.*), a chest.

Kit. From Dut. *kitte*, a wooden receptacle made of hooped staves; hence that which contains the necessaries, tools, etc., of a workman; and hence the articles themselves collectively.

Kit-cat Club. A club formed about the beginning of the 18th century by the leading Whigs of the day, and held in the house of Christopher Catt, a pastrycook of Shire Lane, which used to run north from Temple Bar to Carey Street (its site is now covered by the Law Courts). Christopher Catt's mutton pies, which were eaten at the club, were also called *kit-cats*, and in the *Spectator* (No. IX) we are told that it was from these the club got its name.

Steele, Addison, Congreve, Garth, Vanbrugh, Manwaring, Stepney, Walpole, and Pulteney were of it; so was Lord Dorset and the present Duke. Manwaring . . . was the ruling man in all conversation . . . Lord Stanhope and the Earl of Essex were also members. . . . Each member gave his [picture].—*Pope to Spence.*

Sir Godfrey Kneller painted forty-two portraits of the club members for Jacob Tonson, the secretary, whose villa was at Barn Elms, where latterly the club was held. In order to accommodate the paintings to the height of the club-room, he was obliged to make them three-quarter lengths (28 in. by 36 in.), hence a three-quarter portrait is still called a *kit-cat*. The set of portraits is now in the National Portrait Gallery, London.

Kit's Coty House. A great cromlech, $3\frac{1}{2}$ m. N.W. of Maidstone on the Rochester road, consisting of a vast block of sandstone resting on three other blocks. It is near the ancient battlefield of Aylesford, where the Saxons under Hengist and Horsa fought the Britons, whose chieftain was, according to the Chronicles, named Catigern, and some authorities derive the name from him. The dolmen is undoubtedly much older than his day, and the name may be British for "the tomb in the woods" (Wel. *coed*, a wood).

Kite. In lawyer's slang, a junior counsel who is allotted at an assize court to advocate the cause of a prisoner who is without other defence.

In R.A.F. slang, any aircraft.

In Stock Exchange slang, a worthless bill.

To fly the kite. To "raise the wind" by questionable methods, such as by sending begging letters to persons of charitable reputation or by means of worthless bills.

Kiwanis (ki wa' nis). An organization founded in U.S.A. in 1915 aiming to improve business ethics and provide leadership for raising the level of business and professional ideals. There are many Kiwanis clubs in U.S.A. and Canada.

Kiwi (kē' wē). A New Zealand bird incapable of flight. In flying circles the word is applied to a man of the ground staff at an aerodrome. In Australia it is often used to denote a New Zealander.

Klondike (klon' dīk). A river and district of Yukon Territory in Canada. In 1896 placer gold was discovered in the creeks that flow into the river and for some years much gold was produced. The famous Gold Rush took place 1897-98.

Knave (A.S. *cnafa*, Ger. *knabe*). Originally merely a boy or male-child, then a male servant or one in low condition and finally—its present sense—an unprincipled and dishonourable rascal.

The tyme is come, a knave-child she ber;
Mauricius at the font-stoon they him calle.
　　　　CHAUCER: *Man of Lawe's Tale*, 722.
And sche bare a knave child that was to reulynge alle folkis in an yrun gherde (*Auth. Ver.*—And she brought forth a man child, who was to rule all nations with a rod of iron). *Wyclif's Bible. Rev.* xii, 5.

In cards the *knave* (or *jack*), the lowest court card of each suit, is the common soldier or servant of the royalties.

Knee. Knee tribute. Adoration or reverence, by prostration or bending the knee. *Cp.* LIP-SERVICE.

Coming to receive from us
Knee-tribute yet unpaid, prostration vile.
　　　　MILTON: *Paradise Lost*, v, 782.

Weak-kneed. Irresolute, not thorough; as, *a weak-kneed Christian*, a Laodicean, neither hot nor cold.

Kneph. Another name of the Egyptian god Amen-Ra (*q.v.*).

Knickerbockers, or **Knickers.** Loose-fitting breeches, gathered in below the knee, and worn by boys, cyclists, sportsmen, tourists, etc., and by women as an undergarment. So named from George Cruikshank's illustrations of *Knickerbocker's History of New York*, a burlesque published in 1809 by Washington Irving, where the Dutch worthies are drawn with very loose knee-breeches. The name *Knickerbacker* is found among the old Dutch inhabitants of New York a century and more earlier; it probably signified a *baker* of *knickers*, *i.e.* clay marbles.

Knight (A.S. *cniht*). Originally meaning merely a boy or servant, the word came to denote a man of gentle birth who, after serving at court or in the retinue of some lord as a page and esquire, was admitted with appropriate ceremonies to an honourable degree of military rank and given the right to bear arms.

The Knight, or Knight Bachelor, of to-day is a commoner who is the possessor of a personal and non-hereditary dignity conferred by the sovereign, carrying with it the prefix "Sir" and a place in the Table of Precedence next above County Court Judges and next below Knight Commanders of the Order of the British Empire. The wife of a Knight is usually entitled "Lady" or "Dame," but this, as in the case of Baronets, is a matter of courtesy only, not of right.

There are nine *Orders of Knighthood* in the British Empire, viz. (in the following order of precedence) the Garter, the Thistle, St. Patrick, the Bath, the Star of India, St. Michael and St. George, the Indian Empire, the Royal Victorian Order, and the British Empire. After these come the Knights Bachelor, who are members of no Order and who do not constitute an order. *Bachelor* here is Fr. *bas chevalier*, signifying "lower than the Knight of an order."

The word *knight* is used in various slang or jocular phrases denoting a member of some trade or profession, follower of some calling or occupation, etc. Thus we have *Knight of the blade*, a roystering bully, *Knight of the cleaver*, a butcher, *Knight of the cue*, a billiard player, *Knight of the needle*, a tailor, *Knight of the pestle*, a druggist, *Knight of the road*, a footpad, *Knight of the spigot*, a tapster, *Knight of the wheel*, a cyclist, etc., etc.

Knight Baronet. The title originally given to Baronets (*q.v.*) when the degree was instituted by James I in 1611.

Knights of Columbus. A Roman Catholic fraternal and philanthropic society in U.S.A., founded in 1882 with the aim of uniting lay-men of the Church in corporate religious and civic unity and usefulness.

Knight errant. A mediæval knight, especially a hero of those long romances satirized by Cervantes in *Don Quixote*, who wandered about the world in quest of adventure and in search of opportunities of rescuing damsels in distress and performing other chivalrous deeds.

It seemed unto him [Don Quixote] very requisite and behooveful . . . that he himself should become a knight-errant, and go throughout the world, with his horse and armour, to seek adventures, and practise in person all that he had read was used by knights of yore; revenging all kinds of injuries, and offering himself to occasions and dangers, which, being once happily achieved, might gain him eternal renown.—CERVANTES: *Don Quixote* (*Shelton's tr.* 1612).

The Knight of the Rueful Countenance. *Don Quixote* (*q.v.*).

Knight of the Shire. The old name for one of the two gentlemen of the rank of knight who represented a county or shire in the English Parliament; a member elected by a county, in contradistinction to a borough member.

Knight of the square flag. A knight banneret, in allusion to cutting off the points of his pennon when he was raised to this rank on the battlefield.

The Knight of the Swan. Lohengrin (*q.v.*).

Knight service. The tenure of land, under the feudal system, on the condition of rendering military service to the Crown.

Knight's fee. The amount of land for which, under the feudal system, the services of a knight were due to the Crown. There was no fixed unit, some were larger than others; William the Conqueror created 60,000 such fees when he came to England, and in his time all who had £20 a year in lands or income were compelled to be knights.

Knights of Labour. An organization of working men, founded at Philadelphia in 1869. At first secret, it later emerged to play an important part in the American Trade Union movement. Its objects were to regulate wages, hours of work, etc., and to control strikes. It secured the establishment of Labour Day (*q.v.*) as a national holiday. In the early 20th century it ceased to exist, being unable to compete with the more powerful American Federation of Labour (founded 1886).

Knights of the Round Table. *See* ROUND TABLE.

Knights of Windsor. A small order of knights, originally founded by Edward III in 1349 as the "Poor Knights of the Order of the Garter." It was at first formed of 26 veterans, but since the time of Charles I the numbers have been fixed at 13 for the Royal Foundation and 5 for the Lower (since abolished) with a Governor. The members are retired meritorious military officers. They are granted apartments in Windsor Castle and pensions ranging from £50 to £130 a year. They must be in residence for at least nine months in the year, must attend St. George's Chapel on saints' days, and occasionally act as guards of honour. Their present uniform was assigned by William IV, who made their title the "Military Knights of Windsor"; and their early connexion with the Order of the Garter is still retained in many ways, as, for instance, every K.G. on appointment has to give a sum of money for distribution among them, and the Sovereign appoints members in his capacity as head of the Order of the Garter.

Knock, To. Slang for to create a great impression, to be irresistible; as in Albert Chevalier's song, "Knocked 'em in the Old Kent Road" (1892), *i.e.* astonished the inhabitants, filled them with admiration.

To knock about or around. To wander about town "seeing life" and enjoying oneself.

A knock-about turn. A music-hall term for a noisy, boisterous act in which (usually) a couple of red-nosed comedians indulge in violent horseplay.

Knock-kneed. With the knees turned inwards so that they knock together in walking.

To be knocked into a cocked hat, or **into the middle of next week.** To be thoroughly beaten. *See* COCKED.

To get the knock (or **the nasty knock**). To have a blow (actual or figurative) that finishes one off.

To knock the bottom or the stuffing out of anything. To confound, bring to naught, especially to show that some argument or theory is invalid and "won't hold water."

To knock under. To acknowledge oneself defeated, in argument or otherwise, to knuckle under. Perhaps from the old custom of a disputant who gets the worst of it tapping the under side of the table or from the habit, in hard-drinking days, of subsiding under the table.

> He that flinches his Glass, and to Drink is not able,
> Let him quarrel no more, but knock under the table.
> *Gentleman's Journal: March,* 1691-2.

Knock-out. Primarily, a disabling blow, especially (in pugilism) one out of guard on the point of the chin, which puts the receiver to sleep and so finishes the fight. Hence, a complete surprise is "a fair knock-out."

In the auction room a *knock-out* is a sale at which a ring of dealers combine to keep prices artificially low, so that they obtain the goods and afterwards sell them among themselves, dividing the profits.

Knockers. Goblins, or kobolds (*q.v.*), who dwell in mines, and indicate rich veins of ore by their presence. In Cardiganshire and elsewhere miners attribute the strange noises so frequently heard in mines to these spirits.

Knot. (Lat. *nodus,* Fr. *nœud,* Dan. *knude,* Dut. *knot,* A.S. *cnotta,* allied to *knit.*)

He has tied a knot with his tongue he cannot untie with his teeth. He has got married. He has tied the marriage-knot (*q.v.*) by saying, "I take thee for my wedded wife," etc., but it is not to be untied so easily.

True lovers' knot. Sir Thomas Browne thinks the knot owes its origin to the *nodus Herculanus,* a snaky complication in the

caduceus or rod of Mercury, in which form the woollen girdle of the Greek brides was fastened (*Pseudodoxia Epidemica,* V, xxii).

To seek for a knot in a rush. Seeking for something that does not exist. Not a very wise phrase, seeing there are *jointed* rushes, probably not known when the proverb was first current.

Knotgrass. This grass, *Polygonum aviculare,* was formerly supposed, if taken in an infusion, to stop growth.

> Get you gone, you dwarf;
> You minimus, of hindering knotgrass made.
> *Midsummer Night's Dream,* iii, 2.
> The child's a fatherless child; and say they should put him into a straight pair of gaskins (breeches), 'twere worse than knot-grass; he would never grow after it.—
> BEAUMONT AND FLETCHER: *Knight of the Burning Pestle,* ii, 2.

Knout (Russ., *knut,* probably connected with *knot*). A long, hard leather thong or a knotted bunch of thongs formerly used in Russia for corporal punishment on prisoners; hence, a symbol of supremely autocratic rule.

Know Nothings. An American Party which, in 1856, ruled New Orleans in an era of despotic corruption. They were opposed to the Catholic Church and to the absorption of foreigners into the American body politic. Their name came from their stock reply to any awkward question: "I know nothing in our principles contrary to the Constitution."

Know Thyself. The admonition of the oracle of Apollo at Delphi; also attributed (by Diogeneus Laertius, i, 40) to Thales, also to Solon the Athenian lawgiver, Socrates, Pythagoras, and others.

Knuckle. To knuckle under. To acknowledge oneself beaten, to sue for pardon; in allusion to the old custom of striking the under side of a table with the knuckles when defeated in an argument. *Cp.* TO KNOCK UNDER.

To knuckle down to. To submit to.

To knuckle down to it. To work away at it, heart and soul; to do one's best.

Kobold (kob' ōld). A house-spirit in German superstition; similar to our Robin Goodfellow, and the Scots brownie. Also a gnome who works in the mines and forests.

Kochlani (kok la' ni). Arabian horses of royal stock, of which genealogies have been preserved for more than 2,000 years. It is said that they are the offspring of Solomon's stud. (*Niebuhr.*)

Koheleth. *See* ECCLESIASTES.

Koh-i-Nur (kō i nôr) (Pers., mountain of light). A large diamond which, since 1849, has been among the British Crown Jewels. It is said to have been known 2,000 years ago, but its authentic history starts in·1304, when it was wrested by the Sultan, Al-eddin, from the Rajah of Malwa. From his line it passed in 1526 to Humaiun, the son of Sultan Baber, and thence to Aurungzebe (d. 1707), the Mogul Emperor, who used it for the eye of a peacock in his famous peacock throne at Delhi. In 1739 it passed into the hands of Nadir Shah, who called it the Koh-i-nur. It next went to the monarchs of Afghanistan, and when Shah Sujah was deposed he gave it to Runjit Singh, of the Punjab, as the price of his assistance towards the recovery of the throne of Cabul. After Runjit's death (1839) it was kept in the treasury at Lahore, and when the Punjab was annexed to the British Crown, in 1849, it was, by stipulation, presented to Queen Victoria. At this time it weighed $186\frac{1}{16}$ carats, but after its acquisition it was cut down to $106\frac{1}{16}$ carats. There is a tradition that it always brings ill luck to its possessor.

Kohl or **Kohol** (kōl). Finely powdered antimony, used by women in Persia and the East to blacken the inside of their eyelids.

> And others mix the Kohol's jetty dye
> To give that long, dark languish to the eye.
> THOMAS MOORE: *Lalla Rookh*, Pt. i.

Korah. *See* ASAPH.

Koran (ko răn'), or, with the article, *Al Koran*. The bible or sacred book of the Mohammedans, containing the religious, social, civil, commercial, military, and legal code of Islam. The Koran, which contains 114 chapters, or *Surahs*, is said to have been communicated to the prophet at Mecca and Medina by the angel Gabriel, with the sound of bells. It is written in Arabic and was compiled from Mohammed's own lips.

Korrigans (kor' i gănz). Nine fays of Breton folklore, who can predict future events, assume any shape they like, move quick as thought from place to place, and cure diseases or wounds.

Kosher (kō' sher). A Hebrew word denoting that which is permitted by, or fulfils the requirements of, the law; applied usually to food—especially to meat which has been slaughtered and prepared in the prescribed manner.

Kratim. The dog of the Seven Sleepers. More correctly called Katmir or Ketmir (*q.v.*).

Kremlin, The. A gigantic pile of buildings in Moscow of every style of architecture: Arabesque, Gothic, Greek, Italian, Chinese, etc., enclosed by battlemented and many-towered

walls $1\frac{1}{2}$ miles in circuit. It contains palaces and cathedrals, churches, convents, museums and barracks, arcades and shops, the great bell, and, before the Revolution, the Russian treasury, government offices, the ancient palace of the patriarch, a throne-room, etc. It was built by two Italians, Marco and Pietro Antonio, for Ivan III in 1485 to 1495, but the Great Palace, as well as many other buildings, dates only from the middle of the 19th century, previous palaces, etc., having been destroyed at various times. There had been previously a wooden fortress on the spot. As the seat of government of the U.S.S.R. the word "Kremlin" is often used symbolically of that government, just as the Vatican is for the Papacy, or Quai D'Orsay for the French government.

The name is from Russ. *kreml*, a citadel, and other towns beside Moscow possess kremlins, but none on this scale.

Kreuzer (kroit' zer). A small copper coin in Southern Germany and Austria, formerly of silver and marked with a cross (Ger. *kreuz*, Lat. *crux*). It is worth (nominally) one-third of a penny.

Kreig-spiel. *See* WAR GAME.

Kriemhild (krēm' hild). The legendary heroine of the Nibelungenlied (*q.v.*), a woman of unrivalled beauty, daughter of the Burgundian, King Gibich, and sister of Gunther, Gernot, and Giselher. She first married Siegfried (*q.v.*), and next Etzel (Attila), king of the Huns.

Krishna (krish' na) (*the black one*). One of the greatest of the Hindu deities, the god of fire, lightning, storms, the heavens, and the sun, usually regarded as the eighth avatar (*q.v.*) of Vishnu. One story relates that Kansa, demonking of Mathura, having committed great ravages, Brahma prayed to Vishnu to relieve the world of its distress; whereupon Vishnu plucked off two hairs, one white and the other black, and promised they should revenge the wrongs of the demon-king. The black hair became Krishna.

Another myth says that Krishna was the son of Vasudeva and Devaki, and when he was born among the Yadavas at Mathura, between Delhi and Agra, his uncle, King Kansa, who had been warned by heaven that this nephew was to slay him, sought to kill Krishna, who was, however, smuggled away. He was brought up by shepherds, and later killed his uncle and became King of the Yadavas in his stead. He was the Apollo of India and the idol of women. His story is told in the Bhagavadghita and Bhagavatapurana.

Kronos or **Cronus** (krō' nos). One of the Titans of Greek mythology, son of Uranus and Ge, father (by Rhea) of Hestia, Demeter, Hera, Hades, Poseidon, and Zeus. He dethroned his father as ruler of the world, and was in turn dethroned by his son, Zeus. By the Romans he was identified with Saturn (*q.v.*).

Ku Klux Klan (kū klŭks klăn). A secret society in the southern U.S.A. that was founded in Pulaski, Tenn., in 1865, at the close of the Civil War. It was originally a social club with a fanciful ritual and uniform that easily terrified the Negroes. The organization rapidly increased in numbers and, together with a similar society known as the White Camelias (1867) it overawed the whole black population of the South until 1870. Its policy for securing white supremacy was carried to the most extreme lengths and its murders and terrorism grew so numerous and formidable that in 1871 an Act of Congress was passed suppressing it.

The Ku Klux Klan was fully organized, the whole of the South forming its Invisible Empire under a Grand Wizard. Each State was a Realm under a Grand Dragon; a number of counties made a Dominion ruled by a Grand Titan; each county was a Province under a Grand Giant, the Provinces themselves being divided into Dens, each under a Grand Cyclops. Private members were called Ghouls and the minor officials had fantastic titles such as Furies, Goblins, Night Hawks, etc.

In 1915 the Knights of the Ku Klux Klan came into existence at Atlanta, Georgia, and in the hysteria following World War I the movement swept the South. It admitted to membership only native-born, white, Gentile, Protestant Americans and from 1922 until 1925 it controlled elections and politics in several of the Southern States. But its violent views defeated its own ends and by 1927 the society was moribund.

Kudos (kü' dos) (Gr., renown). A slang or colloquial phrase for credit, fame, glory.

Kultur (kul tur'). The German system of intellectual, moral, æsthetic, economic, and political progress, which is characterized by the subordination of the individual to the State, and through the power of which it was hoped that "kultur" would be imposed on the rest of the world.

It does not mean the same as English *culture*, which is translated by *bildung*.

Kulturkampf. In German history, the long and bitter struggle (Ger. *kampf*) which took place in the 'seventies of last century between Bismarck and the Vatican, with the idea of ensuring the unity of the new Empire and protecting the authority of its government against outside interference. Many laws were passed against the Catholic hierarchy, but political complications very soon brought about the repeal of the more oppressive, and the Catholics were left practically in their old position.

Kuomintang (kwō' min' tăng'). A Chinese political party formed by Sun Yat-sen in 1912 on the foundation of the Chinese Republic. A combination of several political groups, it came into power in 1927 under the leadership of General Chiang Kai-shek. The three Chinese words mean "nation," "people," "party" and may be translated as "National Party."

Kyrie Eleison (ki ri e e lī' son) (Gr., "Lord have mercy"). The short petition used in the liturgies of the Eastern and Western Churches, as a response at the beginning of the Mass and in the Anglican Communion Service. Also, the musical setting for this.

Kyrle Society, The (kĕrl). Founded 1877 for decorating the walls of hospitals, school-rooms, mission-rooms, cottages, etc.; for the cultivation of small open spaces, window gardening, the love of flowers, etc.; and improving the artistic taste of the poorer classes. It was named in memory of John Kyrle (1637-1724), Pope's "Man of Ross." *See* ROSS.

L

L. This letter, the twelfth of the alphabet, in Phœnician and Hebrew represents an ox-goad, *lamed*, and in the Egyptian hieroglyphic a lioness.

L, for a pound sterling, is the Lat. *libra*, a pound. In the Roman notation it stands for 50, and with a line drawn above the letter, for 50,000.

La Belle Sauvage (la bel sō vazh'). The site on the north side of Ludgate Hill occupied by the House of Cassell from 1852 until May 11th, 1941, when the whole area was demolished in an air raid. It took its name from the inn that stood there, noted for the dramatic performances that took place in its courtyard in the 16th and early 17th centuries, and as the starting-place for coaches to the eastern counties in the 18th century, and until the advent of railways. As early as 1530 it appears as "The Belle Savage," and in 1555 as "'la Bell Savage' otherwise 'le Bell Savoy.'" The inn would seem to have been originally called "The Bell," or "The Bell on the Hoop" (the latter was common as part of inn names) and, at some early date, to have been owned by one "Savage"; for, in a deed enrolled in the Close Rolls of 1453 John Frensh confirms to his mother Joan Frensh

all that tenement or inn with its appurtenance called Savages ynn, alias vocat "le Belle on the Hope," in the parish of St. Bridget in Fleet Street.

(Fleet Street at that time extended up Ludgate Hill as far as the Old Bailey).

La Mancha, the Knight of (la man' chà). Don Quixote de la Mancha, the hero of Cervantes' romance *Don Quixote*. La Mancha, an old province of Spain, is now a part of Ciudad Real.

La-di-da (la' dė da'). A yea-nay sort of fellow, with no backbone; an affected fop with a drawl in his voice. Also used adjectivally, as "in a la-di-da" sort of way.

The phrase was popularized by a song sung by the once-famous Arthur Lloyd, the refrain of which was:—

La-di-da, la-di-do, I'm the pet of all the ladies,
The darlings like to flirt with Captain La-di-da-di-do.

Labarum (lăb' à rum). The standard borne before the Roman emperors. It consisted of a gilded spear, with an eagle on the top, while from a cross-staff hung a splendid purple streamer, with a gold fringe, adorned with precious stones. Constantine substituted a crown for the eagle, and inscribed in the midst the mysterious monogram. *See* CROSS.

Labour Party. One of the great political parties of Great Britain. It was founded in 1900 for the express purpose of securing the representation of the working classes in Parliament. At the General Election of 1906 29 out of 50 candidates were successful; in 1924 the first Labour government was formed under Ramsay MacDonald, though it lasted only 9 months.

In 1929 Labour came once again into power; forming a coalition with the Tories in 1931 and itself giving way to a Tory government in 1935. After World War II Labour swept the country in the General Election of 1945, was returned again in 1950 with a majority over all the other parties, and gave way to a Tory government in October 1951.

Labour Day is a legal holiday in the U.S.A. and some provinces of Canada. It is held on the first Monday in September "in honour of the labouring class."

Labyrinth (lăb' i rinth). A Greek word of unknown (but probably Egyptian) origin, denoting a mass of buildings or garden walks, so complicated as to puzzle strangers to extricate themselves; a maze. The maze at Hampton Court, formed of high hedges, is a labyrinth on a small scale. The chief labyrinths of antiquity are:—

(1) The Egyptian, by Petesuchis or Tithoes, near the Lake Mœris. It had 3,000 apartments, half of which were underground (1800 B.C.).—*Pliny*, xxxvi, 13; and *Pomponius Mela*, i, 9.

(2) The Cretan, by Dædalus, for imprisoning the Minotaur. The only means of finding a way out of it was by help of a skein of thread. (*See Virgil: Æneid*, v.)

(3) The Cretan conduit, which had 1,000 branches or turnings.

(4) The Lemnian, by the architects Smilis, Rholus, and Theodorus. It had 150 columns, so nicely adjusted that a child could turn them. Vestiges of this labyrinth were still in existence in the time of Pliny.

(5) The labyrinth of Clusium, made by Lars Porsena, King of Etruria, for his tomb.

(6) The Samian, by Theodorus (540 B.C.). Referred to by Pliny; by Herodotus, ii, 145; by Strabo, x; and by Diodorus Siculus, i.

(7) The labyrinth at Woodstock, built by Henry II to protect Fair Rosamund.

Lac of Rupees. One hundred thousand rupees. The nominal value of the Indian rupee is 2s., and at this rate of exchange a lac of rupees is equivalent to £10,000. Its value varies, however, according to the market value of silver.

Laches (lăsh' iz). A legal term, from the Old French *laschesse*, meaning negligence, especially any inexcusable delay in making a claim.

Lachesis (lăk' e sis). The Fate who spins life's thread, working into the woof the events destined to occur. *See* FATE.

Lackadaisical. Affectedly languid, pensive, sentimental. The word is an extension of the old *lackadaisy*, which, in its turn, is an extended form of *lackaday!* or *alackaday!* an exclamation of regret, sorrow, or grief.

Laconic (là con' ik). Pertaining to Laconia or Sparta; hence very concise and pithy, for the Spartans were noted for their brusque and sententious speech. When Philip of Macedon wrote to the Spartan magistrates, "If I enter Laconia, I will level Lacedæmon to the ground," the ephors sent back the single word, "If." Cæsar's dispatch *Veni, vidi, vici* (*q.v.*) and Sir Charles Napier's apocryphal "Peccavi" (*q.v.*) are well-known examples of laconicisms.

Lacrosse (la kros). A ball game originally played by N. American Indians and now the national game of Canada. The ball is of rubber; it is caught in a net-like racket and thrown through a goal. The playing space between the goals varies from 100 to 150 yards; the goal posts at either end are 6 ft. apart and 6 ft. high. There are twelve players on a side, and the object of the game is to score goals by kicking, striking or carrying the ball on the crosse, in which lies the great art of the game.

Ladas (lā' dăs). Alexander's messenger, noted for his swiftness of foot, mentioned by Catullus, Martial, and others.

Ladon (lā' don). The name of the dragon which guarded the apples of the Hesperides (*q.v.*), also of one of the dogs of Actæon.

Ladrones (la' drōnz). The island of thieves; so called, in 1519, by Magellan, on account of the thievish habits of the aborigines.

Lady. Literally "the bread-maker," as *lord* (*q.v.*) is "the bread-guarder." A S. *hlœfdige*, from *hlaf*, loaf, and a supposed noun *dige*, a kneader, connected with Gothic *deigan*, to knead. The original meaning was simply the female head of the family, the "house-wife."

Ladybird, Ladyfly, or **Ladycow.** The small red coleopterous insect of the genus *Coccinella* with black spots, called also Bishop Barnaby (*q.v.*), and, in Yorkshire, the Cushcow Lady.

Lady Bountiful. The benevolent lady of a village. The character is from Farquhar's *Beaux Stratagem* (1707).

Lady Day. March 25th, to commemorate the Annunciation of Our Lady, the Virgin Mary. It used to be called "St. Mary's Day in Lent" to distinguish it from other festivals in honour of the Virgin, which were also, properly speaking, "Lady Days." Until 1752 Lady Day was the legal beginning of the year, and dates between January 1st and that day were shown with the two years, *e.g.* January 29th, 1648/9, *i.e.* January 29th, 1649.

Lady-killer. A male flirt; a great favourite with the ladies or one who devotes himself to their conquest.

Lady Margaret Professor. The holder of the Chair of Divinity, founded in 1502, at Cambridge by Lady Margaret Beaufort (1443-1509), the mother of Henry VII, who also founded Christ's (1505) and St. John's Colleges (1508).

The Lady of England and Normandy. The Empress Maud, or Matilda (1102-67), daughter of Henry I of England, and wife of the Emperor Henry V of Germany. The title of *Domina Anglorum* was conferred upon her by the Council of Winchester, April 7th, 1141. (Rymer: *Fœdera,* i.)

Charlotte M. Tucker (1823-93), a writer for children, used the signature "A.L.O.E.," meaning "A Lady of England."

The Lady of the Lake. In the Arthurian legends, Vivien, the mistress of Merlin. She lived in the midst of an imaginary lake surrounded by knights and damsels. *See* LANCELOT.

In Scott's poem of this name (1810) the lady is Ellen Douglas, who lived with her father near Loch Katrine.

The Lady of the Lamp. A name given to Florence Nightingale (1820-1910) because she went the rounds of the hospital wards in Scutari during the Crimea war, carrying a lighted lamp.

Our Lady of Mercy. A Spanish order of knighthood, instituted in 1218 by James I of Aragon, for the deliverance of Christian captives amongst the Moors. Within the first six years, as many as 400 captives were rescued by these knights.

The Ladies' Mile. A stretch of the road on the north side of the Serpentine, Hyde Park, much favoured in Victorian days by "equestriennes."

The Coaching and Four-in-Hand Clubs held their meets there in spring.

Lag. An old English slang term for a convict, especially one under sentence of transportation. An *old lag* was a phrase used in Australia to describe a convict who had served his sentence, or a ticket-of-leave man.

Lagniappe (lăn yăp'). A phrase from the Southern States of U.S.A. meaning a sort of token gift given to a customer with his purchase, by way of compliment or as good measure. The word comes from the Am.-Spanish *la ñapa*, the gift.

Laid. The term used in the paper trade for the ribbed appearance in papers, due to manufacture on a mould or by a dandy on which the wires are *laid* side by side instead of being *woven* transversely.

Lais (lā' is). The name of two celebrated Greek courtezans; the earlier was the most beautiful woman of Corinth, and lived at the time of the Peloponnesan War. The beauty of Lais the Second so excited the jealousy of the Thessalonian women that they pricked her to death with their bodkins. She was the contemporary and rival of Phryne and sat to Apelles as a model. Demosthenes tells us that Lais sold her favours for 10,000 (Attic) drachmæ (about £300).

Laissez faire (lā zā fâr) (Fr., let alone). The principle of allowing things to look after themselves, especially the policy of non-interference by Government in commercial affairs. The phrase comes from the motto of the mid-18th century "Physiocratic" school of French economists, *Laissez faire, laissez passer* (let us alone, let us have free circulation for our goods), who wished to have all customs duties abolished and thus anticipated the later Free-traders.

Lake Dwellings. Prehistoric human dwellings on certain lakes in Switzerland, Ireland, etc., built on piles at their shallow edges. The remains found in various examples show that they date from the Neolithic and early metallic periods.

Lakin. By'r lakin. An oath, meaning "By our Ladykin," or Little Lady, where little does not refer to size, but is equivalent to *dear*.

> By'r lakin, a parlous [perilous] fear.—*A Midsummer Night's Dream*, iii, 1.

Laksmi or **Lakshmi.** One of the consorts of the Hindu god Vishnu, and mother of Kama (*q.v.*). She is goddess of beauty, wealth, and pleasure, and the Ramayana describes her as springing from the foam of the sea.

Lama. The Tibetan word *blama* (*b* silent) for a Buddhist priest or monk. The Grand Lama or Dalai Lama (the Sacred Lama) was the ruler of Tibet, under the more or less nominal suzerainty of China. In 1910 he fled to India before an invading Chinese army, was deposed, and Tibet has since been in an unsettled state. The Teshu, or Tashi, Lama is the chief lama of Mongolia. The religion of both Mongolia and Tibet is called Lamaism and is a corrupt form of Buddhism. The priests are housed in great monasteries known as lamaseries.

Lamb. In Christian art, an emblem of the Redeemer, in allusion to *John* i, 29, "Behold the Lamb of God, which taketh away the sin of the world."

It is also the attribute of St. Agnes, St. Geneviève, St. Catherine, and St. Regina. John the Baptist either carries a lamb or is accompanied by one. It is also introduced symbolically to represent any of the "types" of Christ; as Abraham, Moses, and so on.

Lambert Daniel (1770-1809). Lambert was the most corpulent man of whom there is any record. In the year 1793, when he was 23 years of age, he weighed thirty-two stone, and at his death no less than fifty-two and three-quarters stone. From 1791 until 1805 he was keeper of Leicester Gaol, after which he came to London, where he exhibited himself "to select company."

Lambert's Day, St. September 17th. St. Lambert, a native of Maestricht, lived in the 7th century.

> Be ready, as your lives shall answer it,
> At Coventry, upon St. Lambert's day.
> > *Richard II*, i, 1.

Lambeth. A London district on the South side of the River.

Lambeth Palace. The official residence of the archbishops of Canterbury since 1197. The palace was built by Hubert Walter, Archbishop of Canterbury, 1193-1205. The followers of Wat Tyler raided the palace on June 14th, 1381, destroyed many valuable books and papers and ended by beheading the archbishop, John of Sudbury. The library and chapel were damaged in an air-raid in 1941.

Lamia (lā' mi a). A female phantom, whose name was used by the Greeks and Romans as a bugbear to children. She was a Libyan queen beloved by Jupiter, but robbed of her offspring by the jealous Juno; and in consequence she vowed vengeance against all children, whom she delighted to entice and devour.

> . . . a troop of nice wantons, fair women, that like to Lamiæ had faces like angels, eies like stars, brestes like the golden front in the Hesperides, but from the middle downwards their shapes like serpents.—GREENE: *A Quip for an Upstart Courtier* (1592).

Witches in the Middle Ages were called *Lamiœ*, and Keats's poem *Lamia* (1820), which relates how a bride when recognized returned to her original serpent form, represents one of the many superstitions connected with the race. Keats's story came (through Burton) from Philostratus' *De Vita Apollonii*, Bk. iv. In Burton's rendering, the sage Apollonius, on the wedding night—

found her out to be a serpent, a lamia . . . When she saw herself descried, she wept, and desired Apollonius to be silent, but he would not be moved, and thereupon she, plate, house, and all that was in it, vanished in an instant; many thousands took notice of this fact, for it was done in the midst of Greece.—*Anatomy of Melancholy*, Pt. iii, sect. ii, memb. i, subsect. i.

Lammas Day (lăm′ as). August 1st; one of the regular quarter days in Scotland, and in England the day on which, in Anglo-Saxon times, the first-fruits were offered. So called from A.S. *hlafmœsse*, the loaf-mass. *See also* LLEW LLAW GYFFES.

At latter Lammas. A humorous way of saying "Never."

Lamourette's Kiss (la moo ret′). A term used in France (*baiser Lamourette*) to denote an insincere or ephemeral reconciliation. On July 7th, 1792, the Abbé Lamourette induced the different factions of the Legislative Assembly to lay aside their differences and give the kiss of peace; but the reconciliation was unsound and very short-lived.

Lamp. The Lamp of Heaven. The moon. Milton calls the stars "lamps."

Why shouldst thou . . .
In thy dark lantern thus close up the stars,
That Nature hung in heaven, and filled their lamps
With everlasting oil, to give due light
To the misled and lonely traveller?
Comus, 200-204.

Sepulchral lamps. The Romans are said to have preserved lamps in some of their sepulchres for centuries, and many legends are told of their never dying. In the papacy of Paul III (1534-40) one was found in the tomb of Tullia (Cicero's daughter), which had been shut up for 1,550 years, and at the dissolution of the monasteries a lamp was found which is said to have been burning 1,200 years. Two are preserved in Leyden museum.

Nor can thy flame immortal burn
Like monumental fires within an urn.
T. STANLEY (1625-78).

It smells of the lamp. Said of a literary composition that bears manifest signs of midnight study; one that is over-laboured. In Lat. *olet lucernam*.

Lampadion (lăm pā′ di on). The received name of a lively, petulant courtesan, in the later Greek comedy.

Lampoon. A sarcastic or scurrilous personal satire, so called from Fr. *lampons*, let us drink, which formed part of the refrain of a 17th-century French drinking song.

These personal and scandalous libels, carried to excess in the reign of Charles II, acquired the name of lampoons from the burden sung to them: "Lampone, lampone, camerada lampone"—Guzzler, guzzler, my fellow guzzler.

Lancastrian (lăn kăs′ tri ăn). An adherent of the Lancastrian line of kings, or one of these kings (Henry IV, V, VI), who were descended from John of Gaunt, Duke of Lancaster third son of Edward III, as opposed to the *Yorkists*, who sprang from Edmund, Duke of York, Edward III's fourth son. The Lancastrian badge was the red rose and the Yorkist the white.

Lance. An attribute in Christian art of St. Matthew and St. Thomas, the apostles; also of St. Longinus, St. George, St. Adalbert, St. Barbara, St. Michael, and several others.

A free lance. One who acts on his own judgment, and not from party motives; a journalist who is not definitely attached to, or on the salaried staff of, any one paper.

The reference is to the Free Companies of the Middle Ages, called in Italy *condottieri* and in France *compagnies grandes*, which were free and willing to sell themselves to any master and any cause, good or bad.

Lance-corporal. A private soldier acting as a corporal, usually as a first step to being promoted to that rank. Similarly, a **lance-sergeant** is a corporal who performs the duties of a sergeant on probation.

Lancelot du Lac. One of the earliest romances of the Round Table (1494).

Sir Lancelot was the son of King Ban of Brittany, but was stolen in infancy by Vivienne, the Lady of the Lake (*q.v.*); she plunged with the babe into the lake (whence the cognomen of *du Lac*), and when her *protégé* was grown into man's estate, presented him to King Arthur. Sir Lancelot went in search of the Grail (*q.v.*), and twice caught sight of it. Though always represented in the Arthurian romances as the model of chivalry, bravery, and fidelity, Sir Lancelot was the adulterous lover of Guinevere, wife of King Arthur, his friend, and it was through this love that the war, which resulted in the disruption of the Round Table and the death of Arthur, took place.

Land. The Land of Beulah (*Is.* lxii, 4). In *Pilgrim's Progress* it is that land of heavenly joy where the pilgrims tarry till they are summoned to enter the Celestial City.

The Land of Nod. To go to the land of Nod is to go to bed. There are many similar puns, and more in French than in English.

The Land of Promise, or **the Promised Land.** Canaan, which God promised to give to Abraham for his obedience. *See Ex.* xii, 25, *Deut.* ix, 28, etc.

The Land of Steady Habits. A name given to the State of Connecticut, which was the original stronghold of Presbyterianism in America and the home of the notorious Blue Laws (*q.v.*).

Land-lubber. An awkward or inexpert sailor on board ship.

Land-slide. Used metaphorically of a crushing defeat at the polls, or of a complete reversal of the votes.

Landau (lăn dō). A four-wheeled carriage, the top of which may be thrown back; first made at Landau, in Bavaria, in the 18th century.

Landscape. A country scene, or a picture representing this. The word comes from Dutch *scape* being connected with our *shape*, and the A.S. *scap-an*, to shape, to give a form to. The old word in English was *Landskip*.

Father of landscape gardening. André Le-nôtre (1613-1700).

Landwehr (lănd' vār), in Germany and Switzerland, troops composed of men in civil life who have had an army training and are liable to be called to the colours in times of national emergency.

Lane. 'Tis a long lane that has no turning. Every calamity has an ending.

> Hope peeps from a cloud on our squad,
> Whose beams have been long in deep mourning;
> 'Tis a lane, let me tell you, my lad,
> Very long that has never a turning.
> PETER PINDAR : *Great Cry and Little Wool*, epist. 1.

Lang Syne (*Scots*, long since). In the olden time, in days gone by.

Auld Lang Syne, usually attributed to Robert Burns, is really a new version by him of a very much older song: in Watson's Collection (1711) it is attributed to Francis Sempill (d. 1682), but it is probably even older. Burns says in a letter to Thomson, "It is the old song of the olden times, which has never been in print. . . . I took it down from an old man's singing," and in another letter, "Light be the turf on the heaven-inspired poet who composed this glorious fragment."

Language. Language was given to men to conceal their thoughts. *See* SPEECH.

The three primitive languages. The Persians say that Arabic, Persian, and Turkish are three primitive languages. Legend has it that the serpent that seduced Eve spoke Arabic, the most suasive language in the world; that Adam and Eve spoke Persian, the most poetic of all languages; and that the angel Gabriel spoke Turkish, the most menacing.

Langue d'oc; langue d'oïl (lang dok; lang do il). The former is the old Provençal language, spoken on the south of the River Loire; the latter Northern French, spoken in the Middle Ages on the north of that river, the original of modern French. So called because our "yes" was in Provençal *oc* (from Latin *hoc illud*) and in the northern speech *oïl* (*oui*).

Lansquenet. *See* LANCE-KNIGHT.

Lantedo. *See* ADELANTADO.

Laocoon (lā ok' ō on). A son of Priam and priest of Apollo of Troy, famous for the tragic fate of himself and his two sons, who were crushed to death by serpents while he was sacrificing to Poseidon, in consequence of his having offended Apollo. The group representing these three in their death agony, now in the Vatican, was discovered in 1506, on the Esquiline Hill (Rome). It is a single block of marble, and is attributed to Agesandrus, Athenodorus, and Polydorus of the School of Rhodes in the 2nd century B.C. It has been restored.

Lessing called his treatise on the limits of poetry and the plastic arts (1766) *Laocoon* because he uses the famous group as the peg on which to hang his dissertation.

> Since I have, as it were, set out from the Laocoon, and several times return to it, I have wished to give it a share also in the title.—*Preface*.

Laodamia (lā ō dăm ī' à). The wife of Protesilaus, who was slain before Troy. She begged to be allowed to converse with her dead husband for only three hours, and her request was granted; when the respite was over, she voluntarily accompanied the dead hero to the shades. Wordsworth has a poem on the subject (1815).

Laodicean (lā ō di sē' àn). One indifferent to religion, caring little or nothing about the matter, like the Christians of that church, mentioned in the book of *Revelation* (iii, 14-18).

Lapithæ (lăp' i thē). A people of Thessaly, noted in Greek legend for their defeat of the Centaurs at the marriage-feast of Hippodamia, when the latter were driven out of Pelion. The contest was represented on the Parthenon, the

Theseum at Athens, the Temple of Apollo at Basso, and on numberless vases.

Lapsus Linguæ (lăp′ sŭs ling′ gwē) (Lat.). A slip of the tongue, a mistake in uttering a word, an imprudent word inadvertently spoken.

We have also adopted the Latin phrases *lapsus calami* (a slip of the pen), and *lapsus memoriæ* (a slip of the memory).

Larder. A place for keeping bacon (Lat. *laridum*), from O.Fr. *lardier* or *lardoir*, a store-room for bacon. This shows that swine were the chief animals salted and preserved in olden times.

The Douglas Larder. The English garrison and all its provisions in Douglas Castle, Lanark, seized by "the Good" Lord James Douglas, in 1307.

He caused all the barrels containing flour, meat, wheat, and malt to be knocked in pieces, and their contents mixed on the floor; then he staved the great hogsheads of wine and ale, and mixed the liquor with the stores; and last of all, he killed the prisoners, and flung the dead bodies among this disgusting heap, which his men called, in derision of the English, "The Douglas Larder."—SCOTT: *Tales of a Grandfather*, iii.

Robin Hood's Larder. *See* OAKS.

Wallace's Larder is very similar to Douglas's. It consisted of the dead bodies of the garrison of Ardrossan, in Ayrshire, cast into the dungeon keep. The castle was surprised by Wallace in the reign of Edward I.

Lares and Penates. Used as a collective expression for home, and for those personal belongings that make home homely and individual. In ancient Rome the *lares* (sing. *lar*) were the household gods, usually deified ancestors or heroes; the *penates* were also guardian deities of the household (and the State), but were more in the nature of personifications of the natural powers, their duty being to bring wealth and plenty rather than to protect and ward off danger. The *Lar familiaris* was the spirit of the founder of the house, which never left it, but accompanied his descendants in all their changes.

Large. A vulgarism for excess, as **That's all very fine and large,** that's a trifle steep, "coming it a bit thick," etc.; *To talk large*, to brag, "swank" in conversation, talk big; *a large order*, an exaggerated claim or statement, a difficult undertaking.

To sail large. A nautical phrase for to sail with the wind not straight astern, but "abaft the beam."

Set at large. At liberty. It is a French phrase; *prendre la large* is to stand out to sea, or occupy the main ocean, so as to be free to move. Similarly, to be set at large is to be placed free in the wide world.

Lark. A spree or frolic. The word is a modern adaptation (about 1800) of the dialectal *lake*, sport, from M.E. *laik*, play, and A.S. *lac*, contest. *Skylark*, as in *skylarking* about, etc., is a still more modern extension. Hood plays on the two words—for the name of the bird, the old *laverock*, A.S. *laferce*, is in no way connected with this—in his well-known lines:

So, Pallas, take thine owl away
And let us have a lark instead!

When the sky falls we shall catch larks. *See* SKY.

Larvæ. A name among the ancient Romans for malignant spirits and ghosts. The *larva* or ghost of Caligula was often seen (according to Suetonius) in his palace.

[Fear] sometimes representeth strange apparitions, as their fathers and grandfathers ghosts, risen out of their graves, and in their winding-sheets: and to others it sometimes sheweth Larves, Hobgoblins, Robbin-good-fellowes, and such other Bug-beares and Chimeraes.—*Florio's Montaigne*, I, xvii.

Lascar. An East Indian sailor employed on European vessels. The natives of the East Indies call camp-followers *lascars*. (Hindu *lashkar*, a soldier.)

Last. Last Light. *See* FIRST LIGHT.

Last Man, The. Charles I was so called by the Parliamentarians, meaning that he would be the last king of Great Britain. His son, Charles II, was called *The Son of the Last Man*.

Last of the Barons, The. Another name given to Warwick, the King-maker (*q.v.*).

Last of the Romans. A title, or sobriquet, given to a number of historical characters, among whom are—

Marcus Junius Brutus (85-42 B.C.), one of the murderers of Cæsar.

Caius Cassius Longinus (d. 42 B.C.), so called by Brutus.

Stilicho, the Roman general under Theodosius.

Aetius, the general who defended the Gauls against the Franks and other barbarians, and defeated Attila near Châlons in 451. So called by Procopius.

François Joseph Terasse Desbillons (1711-89), a French Jesuit; so called from the elegance and purity of his Latin.

Pope called Congreve *Ultimus Romanorum*, and the same title was conferred on Dr. Johnson, Horace Walpole, and C. J. Fox.

Last of the Saxons, The. King Harold (1022-66), who was defeated and slain at the Battle of Hastings.

Last Supper. Leonardo da Vinci's famous picture of this was painted on a wall of the refectory of the convent of Santa Maria delle Grazie, Milan, in 1494-97. The artist varied the normal tempera with a formula of his own which was not a success, hence the painting wore badly with time. Although the refectory was reduced to ruins by Allied bombs in August, 1943, the wall on which the Last Supper is painted remained practically unharmed—the picture itself quite undamaged. It is now hermetically sealed behind glass and thermostatically controlled to prevent further deterioration.

La Tene (la tān), or The Shallows is a site at the eastern end of the Lake of Neuchatel, Switzerland, where extensive remains of the Second Iron Age have been found. It was discovered when the level of the lake was lowered, and a number of weapons, ornaments, pieces of jewellery, etc., from about 550 B.C. until the Christian era were brought to light.

Lateran (lăt′ e rán). The ancient palace of the Laterani, which was appropriated by Nero and later given by the Emperor Constantine to the popes. Fable derives the name from *lateo*, to hide, and *rana*, a frog, and accounts for it by saying that Nero once vomited a frog covered with blood, which he believed to be his own progeny, and had it hidden in a vault. The palace built on its site was called the "Lateran," or the palace of the *hidden frog*.

Lateran Council. Name given to each of the five œcumenical councils held in the Lateran Church at Rome. They are (1) 1123; held under Calixtus II; it confirmed the Concordat of Worms; (2) 1139, when Innocent II condemned Anacletus II and Arnold of Brescia; (3) 1179, under Alexander III; it was concerned with the election of popes; (4) 1215, when Innocent III condemned the Albigenses; and (5) 1512-17, under Julius II and Leo X, when the Canons of the Council of Pisa were abrogated.

The locality in Rome so called contains the Lateran palace, the Piazza, and the Basilica of St. John Lateran. The Basilica is the Pope's cathedral church. The palace (once a residence of the popes) is now a museum.

Lathe. An old division of a county, containing a number of hundreds. The term is now confined to Kent, which is divided into five *lathes*. In Sussex similar county divisions are called *rapes*.

Spenser, in his *Description of Ireland* (1596), uses *lathe* or *lath* for the division of a hundred:—

If all that tything failed, then all that lath was charged for that tything; and if the lath failed, then all that hundred was demanded for them [*i.e.* turbulent fellows], and if the hundred, then the shire.

Latin. The language spoken by the ancient inhabitants of Latium, in Italy, and by the ancient Romans. Alba Longa was head of the Latin League, and, as Rome was a colony of Alba Longa, it is plain to see how the Roman tongue was Latin.

The tale is that the name *Latium* is from *lateo*, to lie hid, and was so called because Saturn lay hid there, when he was driven out of heaven by the gods.

According to Roman tradition the Latini were the aborigines, and Romulus and Remus were descended from Lavinia, daughter of their king, Latinus (*q.v.*).

The earliest known specimen of the Latin language is an inscription of the 5th century B.C., or even earlier, found in the Forum in 1899 on a pyramidal stone. This, unfortunately, was broken and the upper half missing; as the lines were written alternately from the bottom upwards and the top downwards, the meaning of the inscription cannot be ascertained.

The fragment of a hymn of the Arval Brethren, formerly thought to be very ancient, dates only from the early part of the 3rd cent. A.D. The *hymn* itself, of which this is a corrupt form, is of very great antiquity, but the tablet is comparatively modern. It was discovered in 1778 in the grove of the *Dea Dia*, five miles from Rome on the Via Campana.

Classical Latin. The Latin of the best authors of the Golden or Augustan Age (about 75 B.C. to A.D. 145), as Livy, Tacitus, and Cicero (prose), Horace, Virgil, and Ovid (poets).

Late Latin. The period which followed the Augustan Age, to about A.D. 600; it includes the Church Fathers.

Low Latin. Mediæval Latin, mainly early French, Italian, Spanish, and so on.

Middle, or **Mediæval, Latin.** Latin from the 6th to the 16th century, both inclusive. In this Latin, prepositions frequently supply the cases of nouns.

The Latin cross. Formed thus: †. The Greek cross has four equal arms, thus: +.

The Latin races. The peoples the basis of whose language is Latin; *i.e.* the Italians, Spanish, Portuguese, French, Rumanians, etc.

Latium. See LATIN.

Latona (là tō′ nà). The Roman name of the Greek Leto, mother by Jupiter of Apollo and Diana. Milton, in one of his sonnets, refers to the legend that when she knelt with her infants in arms by a fountain in Delos to quench her thirst, some Lycian clowns insulted her and were turned into frogs.

As when those hinds that were transformed to frogs
Railed at Latona's twin-born progeny,
Which after held the sun and moon in fee.

Latria and **Dulia** (lăt′ ri a, dū′ li a). Greek words adopted by the Roman Catholics; the former to express that supreme reverence and adoration which is offered to God alone; and the latter, that secondary reverence and adoration which is offered to saints. *Latria* is from the Greek suffix *-latreia*, worship, as in our ido*latry*; *dulia* is the reverence of a *doulos* or slave. **Hyperdulia** is the special reverence paid to the Virgin Mary.

Latter-day Saints. *See* MORMONISM.

Lattice. *See* RED LATTICE.

Laugh. He laughs best that laughs last. A game's not finished till it's won. In Ray's *Collection* (1742) is "Better the last smile than the first laughter," and the French have the proverb *Il rit bien qui rit le dernier.*

It's no laughing matter. It's really serious; it's no subject for merriment.

Laughing-stock. A butt for jokes.

Launcelot. *See* LANCELOT.

Laura. The girl of this name immortalized by Petrarch is generally held to have been Laure de Noves, who was born at Avignon in 1308, was married in 1325 to Hugues de Sede, and died of the plague in 1348, the mother of eleven children. It was Petrarch's first sight of her, in the church of St. Clara, Avignon, on April 6th, 1327 (exactly 21 years before her death) that, he says, made him a poet.

Laura (Gr. *laura*), an alley. An aggregation of separate cells under the control of a superior. In monasteries the monks live under one roof; in lauras they live each in his own cell apart; but on certain occasions they assemble and meet together, sometimes for a meal, and sometimes for a religious service.

Laureate, Poet. *See* POET LAUREATE.

Laurel. The Greeks gave a wreath of laurels to the victor in the Pythian games, but the victor in the Olympic games had a wreath of wild olives, in the Nemean games a wreath of green parsley, and in the Isthmian games a wreath of dry parsley or green pine-leaves.

The ancients believed that laurel communicated the spirit of prophecy and poetry. Hence the custom of crowning the pythoness and poets, and of putting laurel leaves under one's pillow to acquire inspiration. Another superstition was that the bay laurel was antagonistic to the stroke of lightning; but Sir Thomas Browne, in his *Vulgar Errors*, tells us that Vico-mereatus proves from personal knowledge that this is by no means true.

Laurel, in modern times, is a symbol of victory and peace, and of excellence in literature and the arts. St. Gudule, in Christian art, carries a laurel crown.

Lavender. The earliest form of the word is Med. Lat. *livendula*, and it is probably, like our *livid*, from *livere*, to make bluish; as, however, the plant has for centuries been used by laundresses for scenting linen, and in connexion with the bath, later forms of the word are associated with *lavare*, to wash. The modern botanical name is *Lavandula*. It is a token of affection.

> He from his lass him lavender hath sent,
> Showing his love and doth requital crave.
> DRAYTON: *Eclogue.*

Lavinia (lăv in' i à). Daughter of Latinus (*q.v.*), betrothed to Turnus, King of the Rutuli. When Æneas landed in Italy, Latinus made an alliance with the Trojan hero, and promised to give him Lavinia to wife. This brought on a war between Turnus and Æneas, which was decided by single combat, in which Æneas was victor (Virgil: *Æneid*, vi.).

Shakespeare gives the name to the daughter of Titus Andronicus in the play of that name.

Law. In-laws. A way of referring to one's relations by marriage—mother-in-law, sisters-in-law, etc. *In-law* is short for in *Canon law*, the reference being to the degrees of affinity within which marriage is allowed or prohibited.

Law-calf. A bookseller's term for a special kind of binding in plain sheep or calf used largely for law-books.

> Gentlemen who had no briefs to show carried under their arms goodly octavos, with a red label behind, and that underdone-pie-crust-coloured cover, which is technically known as "law calf."—DICKENS: *Pickwick Papers*, ch. xxxiv.

Law Latin. The debased Latin used in legal documents. *Cp.* DOG LATIN.

Law Lords. Members of the House of Lords who are qualified to deal with the judicial business of the House, *i.e.* the Lord High Chancellor, the Lord Chief Justice, the Master of the Rolls, the Lords of Appeal in Ordinary, and such peers as are holding or have held high judicial office.

Possession is nine points of the law. *See* NINE.

Quips of the law. *See* CEPOLA.

The laws of the Medes and Persians. Unalterable laws.

> Now, O king . . . sign the writing, that it be not changed, according to the law of the Medes and Persians which altereth not.—*Dan.* vi, 8.

To have the law of one. To take legal proceedings against him.

To lay down the law. To speak in a dictatorial manner; to give directions or order in an offensive and high-handed way.

To take the law into one's own hands. To try to secure satisfaction by force; to punish, reward, etc., entirely on one's own responsibility without obtaining the necessary authority.

Lawn. Fine, thin cambric, used for the rochets of Anglican bishops, ladies' handkerchiefs, etc. So called from *Laon* (O.Fr. *Lan*), a town in the Aisne department of France, which used to be famous for its linen factories.

Man of lawn. A bishop.

Lawn-market. The higher end of the High Street, Edinburgh, and the old place for executions; hence, **to go up the Lawn-market,** in Scots parlance, means to go to be hanged.

Up the Lawn-market, down the West Bow,
Up the lang ladder, down the short low.
Schoolboy Rhyme (Scotland).

Lawn-tennis. The game of tennis greatly simplified and played on an open lawn. It was introduced in England in 1877 and has acquired universal popularity. *See* TENNIS.

Lawrence, St. The patron saint of curriers, who was broiled to death on a gridiron. He was deacon to Sixtus I and was charged with the care of the poor, the orphans, and the widows. In the persecution of Valerian (258), being summoned to deliver up the treasures of the church, he produced the poor, etc., under his charge, and said to the prætor, "These are the church's treasures." He is generally represented as holding a gridiron, and is commemorated on August 10th.

The phrase **Lazy as Lawrence** is said to take its origin from the story that when being roasted over a slow fire he asked to be turned, "for," said he, "that side is quite done." This expression of Christian fortitude was interpreted by his torturers as evidence of the height of laziness, the martyr being too indolent even to wriggle.

Lay. Pertaining to the people, or laity (Lat. *laicus*) as distinguished from the clergy. Thus, a *lay brother* is one who, though not in holy orders, is received into a monastery and is bound by its vows.

A **layman** is, properly speaking, anyone not in holy orders; but the term is also used by professional men—especially doctors and lawyers— to denote one not of their particular profession.

Lay figures. Wooden figures with free joints, used by artists chiefly for the study of how drapery falls. The word was earlier *layman*, from Dut. *leeman*, a contraction of *ledenman, i.e. led* (now *lid*), a joint, and *man*, man. Horace Walpole uses layman (1762), but *lay figure* had taken its place by the end of the 18th century.

Lay (the verb). **To lay about one.** To strike out lustily on all sides.

He'll lay about him to-day.—*Troilus and Cressida*, i, 2.

To lay it on thick. To flatter or over-praise.

To lay out. (*a*) To disburse.

(*b*) To display goods; place in convenient order what is required for wear.

(*c*) To prepare a corpse for the coffin, by placing the limbs in order, and dressing the body in its grave-clothes.

To lay to one's charge. To attribute an offence to a person.

And he [Stephen] kneeled down, and cried with a loud voice, Lord lay not this sin to their charge.—*Acts*, vii, 60. The phrase occurs again in the Bible, *e.g. Deut.* xxi, 8; *Rom.* viii, 33, etc.

Laylock. Ancient rustic name for lilac.

Lazar House or **Lazaretto.** A house for lazars, or poor persons affected with contagious diseases. So called from the beggar Lazarus (*q.v.*).

Lazarillo de Tormes (lăz á ril′ yo de tôrm′ ez). A romance, something in the *Gil Blas* style, satirizing all classes of society. Lazarillo, a light, jovial, audacious manservant, sees his masters in their undress, and exposes their foibles. It was by Diego Hurtado de Mendoza, general and statesman of Spain, and was published in 1553.

Lazarus (lăz′ á rus). Any poor beggar; so called from the Lazarus of the parable, who was laid daily at the rich man's gate (*Luke* xvi).

Lazy-bones. A lazy fellow, a regular idler. The expression is some hundreds of years old.

Go tell the Labourers, that the lazie bones
That will not worke, must seeke the beggars gaines.
NICHOLAS BRETON: *Pasquil's Madcap* (1600).

Lazy man's load. One too heavy to be carried; so called because lazy people, to save themselves the trouble of coming a second time, are apt to overload themselves.

Lazzaroni. *See* LAZARONE.

L'état c'est moi (lă ta sā mwa) (Fr., I am the State). The reply traditionally ascribed to Louis XIV when the President of the Parlement of Paris offered objections "in the interests of the State" to the king's fiscal demands. This was in 1655, when Louis was only 17 years of age; on this principle he acted with tolerable consistency throughout his long reign.

Le roi (La reine) le ueut (Fr., The king (queen) wills it). The form of royal assent to Bills submitted to the Crown. The dissent is expressed by *Le roi (La reine) s'avisera* (the king (queen) will give it his consideration).

Leach. *See* LEECH.

Lead (led) was, by the ancient alchemists, called Saturn.

The *lead*, or *blacklead*, of a *lead* pencil contains no lead at all, but is composed of plumbago or graphite, an almost pure carbon with a touch of iron. It was so named in the 16th century, when it was thought to be or to contain the metal.

Leads, The. Famous prison in Venice, in which Casanova was incarcerated and from which he escaped.

Lead (lēd) (the verb.) (A.S. *lædan*).

Leader. The first violin of an orchestra, the first cornet of a military band, etc., is called the **leader**.

Leading article, or **Leader.** A newspaper article by the editor or a special writer. So called because it takes the lead or chief place in the summary of current topics, and expresses the policy of the paper.

Leading counsel in a case, the senior counsel on a circuit.

Leading lady or **man.** The actress or actor who takes the chief rôle in a play.

Leading note (*music*). The seventh of the diatonic scale, which *leads* to the octave, only half a tone higher.

Leading question. A question so worded as to suggest an answer. "Was he not dressed in a black coat?" leads to the answer "Yes." In cross examining a witness, leading questions are permitted, because the chief object of a cross-examination is to obtain contradictions.

Leaf. Before the invention of paper one of the substances employed for writing upon was the leaves of certain plants. The reverse and obverse pages of a book are still called leaves; and the double page of a ledger is termed a "folio," from *folium*, a leaf. *Cp.* the derivation of paper itself, from *papyrus*, and *book*, from *boc*, a beech-tree. There are still extant many ancient MSS. written on palm or other leaves.

To take a leaf out of my book. To imitate me; to do as I do. The allusion is to literary plagiarisms.

To turn over a new leaf. To amend one's ways, to start afresh.

League. The Holy League. Several leagues are so denominated. The three following are the most important: 1511, by Pope Julius II; Ferdinand the Catholic, Henry VIII, the Venetians, and the Swiss against Louis XII; and that of 1576, founded at Péronne for the maintenance of the Catholic Faith and the exclusion of Protestant princes from the throne of France. This league was organized by the Guises to keep Henri IV from the throne. The struggle that ensued formed the subject of Voltaire's epic known first as *La Ligue* and subsequently as *La Henriade*, 1724.

The League of Nations. A league, having headquarters at Geneva, formed after the close of World War I, largely through the exertions of Woodrow Wilson, President of the United States 1913-21, whose action was, however, repudiated by the United States. At one time or another some 44 nations were members of the League. The League was founded on a Covenant and a Charter of XXVI Articles, the High Contracting Parties agreeing to the Covenant in order to promote International Co-operation and to achieve International Peace and Security, by the acceptance of obligations not to resort to War. The final session of the League was on April 18th, 1946, the United Nations having come into existence on the 24th October, 1945.

Leak. To leak out. To come clandestinely to public knowledge. As a liquid leaks out of an unsound vessel, so the secret oozes out unawares.

Leaning Tower. The campanile or bell-tower of the cathedral of Pisa stands apart from the cathedral itself. It is 181 ft. high, $57\frac{1}{2}$ ft. in diameter at the base, and leans about 14 ft. from the perpendicular. It was begun in 11/4 and the sinking commenced during construction. Galileo availed himself of the overhanging tower to make his experiments in gravitation. At Caerphilly, Glamorganshire, there is a tower which leans 11ft. in 80. This was caused by an attempt to blow it up with gunpowder during the Civil Wars.

The Leaning Tower of Pisa continues to stand because the vertical line drawn through its centre of gravity passes within its base.—GANOT: *Physics*.

Leap Year. A year of 366 days, a *bissextile* year (*q.v.*); *i.e.* in the Julian and Gregorian calendars any year whose date is exactly divisible by four except those which are divisible by 100 but not by 400. Thus 1900 (though exactly divisible by 4) was not a leap year, but 2000 will be.

In ordinary years the day of the month which falls on Monday this year will fall on Tuesday next year, and Wednesday the year after; but the fourth year will leap over Thursday to Friday. This is because a day is added to February, the reason being that the astronomical year (*i.e.* the time that it takes the earth to go round the sun) is approximately $365\frac{1}{4}$ days (365·2422), the difference between ·25 and ·2422 being righted by the loss of the three days in 400 years.

It is an old saying that during leap year the ladies may propose, and, if not accepted, claim a silk gown. The origin of this cannot now be traced; there is, however, an Act of the Scottish parliament, passed in 1288, which says "it is statut and ordaint that during the rein of hir

maist blissit Megeste, for ilke year known as
lepe yeare, olk mayden ladye of bothe highe
and lowe estait shall hae liberte to bespeke ye
man she like, albeit he refuses to taik hir to be
his lawful wyfe, he shall be mulcted in ye sum
of ane pundis or less, as his estait may be;
except and awis gif he can make it appeare that
he is betrothit ane ither woman he then shall
be free." A few years later than this a somewhat similar law was passed in France. In the
15th century the custom was legalized in both
Genoa and Florence.

Lear, King. A legendary king of Britain
whose story is told by Shakespeare. In his old
age he divided his kingdom between Goneril
and Regan, two of his daughters, who professed
great love for him. These two daughters drove
the old man mad by their unnatural conduct,
while the third, Cordelia (*q.v.*), who had been
left portionless, succoured him and came with
an army to dethrone her two sisters, but was
captured and slain in prison. King Lear died
over her body.

Camden tells a similar story of Ina, King of
the West Saxons. The story of King Lear is
given in the *Gesta Romanorum* (of a Roman
emperor), in the old romance of *Perceforest*, and
by Geoffrey of Monmouth in his *Chronicles*,
whence Holinshed, Shakespeare's immediate
source, transcribed it. Spenser introduced the
same story into his *Faerie Queene* (II, x). *See* LIR.

Learn. To learn a person a thing, or **to
do something** is now a provincialism, but was
formerly quite good English. Thus, in the Prayer
Book version of the *Psalms* we have "Lead me
forth in thy truth and learn me," and "such as
are gentle them shall he learn his way" (xxv, 4, 8);
and other examples of this use of *learn* as an active
verb will be found at *Ps.* cxix, 66 and cxxxii, 13.

The red plague rid you
For learning me your language.
Tempest, i, 2.

To learn by heart. To commit to memory, to
learn word for word. The phrase is a translation
of the Fr. *apprendre par cœur*; which is, however, a mistranslation of the L. *apprehendere per
chorum*. In mediæval Latin *chorus* was a school
class, where lessons were largely learned by
repeating aloud the actual words of the teacher.

Learned (lĕrn' ed). Colman, king of
Hungary (1095-1114), was called *The Learned*.
Cp. BEAUCLERC.

Leather. Nothing like leather. The story is
that a town in danger of a siege called together
a council of the chief inhabitants to know what

defence they recommended. A mason suggested
a strong wall, a shipbuilder advised "wooden
walls," and when others had spoken, a currier
arose and said, "There's nothing like leather."

Another version is, "Nothing like leather to administer
a thrashing."

Leatherstocking Novels. The novels by
Fenimore Cooper in which Natty Bumpo,
nicknamed *Leatherstocking* and *Hawkeye*, is a
leading character. They are *The Pioneers*
(1823), *The Last of the Mohicans* (1826),
The Prairie (1826), *The Pathfinder* (1840), and
The Deerslayer (1841). "Leatherstocking" was a
hardy backwoodsman, a type of North American
pioneer.

Leave in the lurch. *See* LURCH.

Lebensraum (lā bĕnz roum'). A German
phrase (room for living) somewhat akin to Land
Hunger (*q.v.*). It is applied especially to the
additional territory required by a nation for the
expansion of its trade and the settlement of
a population growing too numerous to be
sustained in the mother country.

Leda. In Greek mythology, the mother by
Zeus (who is fabled to have come to her in the
shape of a swan) of two eggs, from one of which
came Castor and Clytemnestra, and from the
other Pollux and Helen.

Leda Bible, The. *See* BIBLE, SPECIALLY
NAMED.

Lee. In nautical language, the side or quarter
opposite to that against which the wind blows;
the sheltered side, the side away from the windward or weather side. From A.S. *hleo, hleow*, a
covering or shelter.

Lee shore. The shore under the lee of a
ship, or that towards which the wind blows.

Lee side. *See* LEEWARD.

Lee tide. A tide running in the same
direction as the wind blows; if in the opposite
direction it is called *a tide under the lee*.

Leeward (loo' ard). Toward the lee (*q.v.*), or
that part towards which the wind blows; *windward* is in the opposite direction, viz., in the
teeth of the wind. *See* A-WEATHER; LEE.

Leech. One skilled in medicine or "leechcraft"; the word, which is now obsolete, is
the A.S. *lœce*, one who relieves pain, from
lacnian, to heal. The blood-sucking worm,
the *leech*, gets its name probably from the
same word, *the healer*.

And straightway sent, with carefull diligence,
To fetch a leach the which had great insight
In that disease.
SPENSER: *Faerie Queene*, I, x, 23.

Leech-finger. *See* MEDICINAL FINGER.

Leek. The national emblem of Wales. The story is that St. David, patron saint of the Welsh, on one occasion caused his countrymen under King Cadwallader to distinguish themselves from their Saxon foes by wearing a leek in their caps.

Shakespeare makes out that the Welsh wore leeks at the battle of Poitiers, for Fluellen says:—

If your majesty is remembered of it, the Welshmen did goot service in a garden where leeks grow, wearing leeks in their Monmouth caps, which, your majesty know, to this hour is an honourable padge of the service; and I do believe your majesty takes no scorn to wear the leek upon St. Tavy's Day.—*Henry V*, iv, 7.

To eat the leek. To be compelled to eat your own words, or retract what you have said. Fluellen (in *Henry V*) is taunted by Pistol for wearing a leek in his hat. "Hence," says Pistol, "I am qualmish at the smell of leek." Fluellen replies, "I beseech you . . . at my desire . . . to eat this leek." The ancient answers, "Not for Cadwallader and all his goats." Then the peppery Welshman beats him, nor desists till Pistol has swallowed the entire abhorrence.

Lees. There are lees to every wine. The best things have some defect. A French proverb.

Doubt is the lees of thought.
BOKER: *Doubt*, etc., i, 11.

Settling on the lees. Making the best of a bad job; settling down on what is left, after having squandered the main part of one's fortune.

Leet or **Court-leet.** A manor court for petty offences, held once a year; the day on which it was held. The word is probably connected with A.S. *lathe* (*q.v.*), a division of a county.

Who has a breast so pure,
But some uncleanly apprehensions
Keep leets and law-days and in session sit
With meditations lawful?
Othello, iii, 3.

Left. The *left* side of anything is frequently considered to be unlucky, of bad omen (*cp.* AUGURY; SINISTER), the *right* the reverse.

In politics the *left* is the opposition, the party which, in a legislative assembly, sits on the left of the Speaker or President. The *left wing* of a party is composed of its extremists, the "irreconcilables. The term *leftist* has been used since *c.* 1930 to denote a person of Socialist or Communist tendencies.

A left-handed compliment. A compliment which insinuates a reproach.

A left-handed marriage. A morganatic marriage (*q.v.*), in which the husband gave his *left* hand to the bride instead of the right, when saying, "I take thee for my wedded wife."

A left-handed oath. An oath not intended to be binding.

Leg. In many phrases, *e.g.* "to find one's legs," "to put one's best leg foremost," *leg* is interchangeable with *foot* (*q.v.*).

Leg and leg. Equal, or nearly so, in a race, game, etc. *Cp.* NECK AND NECK.

On its last legs. Moribund; obsolete; ready to fall out of cognisance.

Show a leg, there! Jump out of bed and be sharp about it! A phrase from the Navy.

To give a leg up. To render timely assistance, "to help a lame dog over a stile," Originally from horsemanship—to help one into the saddle.

To have good sea legs. To be a good sailor; to be able to stand the motion of the ship without getting sea sick.

Leg-pulling, in England, means teasing or chaffing (*see* PULL), in U.S.A. it means toadying, intriguing, or blackmailing.

To stand on one's own legs. To be independent, to be earning one's own living. Of course, the allusion is to being nursed, and standing "alone."

Without a leg to stand on. Having no excuse; divested of all support; with no chance of success.

Legal tender. Money which, by the law of the particular country, a creditor is bound to accept in discharge of a debt. In England the tender of gold, Treasury notes, and Bank of England notes (except for £10 and upwards) is legal up to any amount, with the one exception that a creditor of the Bank of England cannot be compelled to receive his money in Bank of England notes. Silver is not legal tender for sums over forty shillings, nor bronze for sums over one shilling.

Legem Pone (lē′ jem pō ne). Old slang for money paid down on the nail, ready money; from the opening words of the first of the psalms appointed to be read on the twenty-fifth morning of the month—*Legem pone mihi, Domine, viam justificationum tuarum* (Teach me, O Lord, the way of thy statutes, *Ps.* cxix, 33). March 25th is the first pay-day of the year, and thus the phrase became associated with cash down.

Use *legem pone* to pay at thy day,
But use not *oremus* for often delay.
TUSSER: *Good Husbandry* (1557).

Oremus (let us pray) occurs frequently in the Roman Catholic liturgy. Its application to a debtor who is suing for further time is obvious.

Legend. Literally and originally, "something to be read" (Lat. *lagenda*, from *legere*, to read); hence the narratives of the lives of saints and martyrs were so termed from their being read, especially at matins, and after dinner in the refectories. Exaggeration and a love for the wonderful so predominated in these readings, that the word came to signify a traditional story, especially one popularly regarded as true, a fable, a myth.

In Numismatics the legend is the inscription impressed in letters on a coin or medal. Formerly the words on the obverse only (*i.e.* round the head of the sovereign) were called the legend, the words on the reverse being the inscription; but this distinction is no longer recognized by numismatists. It is also properly applied to the title on a map or under a picture.

Leglen-girth. To cast a leglen-girth. To have made a *faux pas*, particularly by having an illegitimate child; to have one's reputation blown upon. *Leglen* is Scottish for a milk-pail, and a *leglen-girth* is its lowest hoop.

Leicester. The town gets its name from Lat. *Legionis castra*, the camp of the legion, it having been the headquarters of a legion during the Roman occupation of Britain. *Caerleon*, in Wales, *Leon*, Spain, and *Ledjun*, in Palestine, owe their names to the same cause.

Leicester Square (London). So called from the family mansion of the Sydneys, Earls of Leicester, which stood on the north-east side in the 17th century.

Leipzig Fairs. These were sample fairs to which commercial agents used to flock from all parts of the world. The Spring Fair opened the first week in March, the Autumn Fair the last week in August, and each lasted three weeks. All sorts of wares including pottery, textiles, glass, machinery, books, etc., were on sale.

Leitmotiv (līt' mō tēf'). This is a German word meaning the leading motive, and is applied in music to a theme associated with a personage, etc., in an opera or similar work which is quoted at appropriate times and worked up symphonically. The term has got into general usage to describe any phrase or turn of thought or speech that continually recurs with a certain association.

Lemmings are one of the curiosities of nature, and their blind instinct is the origin of several fables. The lemming is a mouse-like rodent, some five inches long, that lives in the grass and bushes in the higher lands of the great mountain ranges of Scandinavia. Lemmings multiply at such a rate that every three or four years they make a vast migration, coming down the mountain slopes, swimming rivers and lakes, but always descending. As they pass on

their way, devastating the countryside, they are harassed by man, birds of prey and beasts, but undeterred they push in their millions ever onwards and downwards until they reach the sea, into which they plunge and are drowned.

Various theories have been advanced to account for their behaviour. It would seem that lemmings are obeying a blind instinct, inherited maybe from Miocene days when the Baltic and North Sea were dry land which could offer a refuge for their overcrowded, teeming hosts.

Lemnos. The island where Vulcan fell when Jupiter flung him out of heaven. One myth connected with Lemnos tells how the women of the island, in revenge for their ill-treatment, murdered all the men. The Argonauts (*q.v.*) were received with great favour by the women, and as a result of their few months' stay the island was repopulated: the queen, Hypsipyle, became the mother of twins by Jason.

Lemures (lem' ū rēz). The name given by the Romans to the spirits of the dead, especially spectres which wandered about at night-time to terrify the living. *Cp.* LARVÆ. (Ovid: *Fasti.* v.)

> The lars and lemures moan with midnight plaint.
> MILTON: *Ode on the Nativity.*

Lemuria (le mū' ri à). The name given to a lost land that is supposed to have connected Madagascar with India and Sumatra in prehistoric times. *See* W. Scott Elliott's *The Lost Lemuria* (1904). *Cp.* ATLANTIS.

Lend Lease. On March 11th, 1942, President Roosevelt signed the Lend-Lease Act whereby U.S.A. was committed to lend or lease military equipment, stores, food, etc., to the governments of the powers fighting Fascism in the name of democracy. Fifteen powers in addition to the twenty Latin-American Republics benefited by Lend-Lease, and over £1,000,000,000 was expended by U.S.A. It was ended by President Truman on the conclusion of hostilities in 1945.

Leningrad (len' in grăd). The present name of what was once known as St. Petersburg, the capital city of Tsarist Russia. It was founded by Peter the Great in 1703; the name was changed to Petrograd in 1914, and to Leningrad in 1924.

Lens (Lat., a lentil or bean). Glasses used in optical instruments are so called because the double convex one, which may be termed the perfect lens, is of a bean shape.

Lent (A.S. *lencten*). *Lenctentid* (spring tide) was the Saxon name for March, because in this month there is a manifest lengthening of the days. As the chief part of the great fast, from Ash

Wednesday to Easter, falls in March, this period received the name of the *Lencten-fæsten*, or Lent.

The fast of thirty-six days was introduced in the 4th century. Felix III (483-492) added four days in 487, to make it correspond with Our Lord's fast in the wilderness.

Lent lily. The daffodil, which blooms in Lent.

Lenten. Frugal, stinted, as food in Lent. Shakespeare has "lenten entertainment" (*Hamlet*, ii, 2); "a lenten answer" (*Twelfth Night*, i, 5); "a lenten pye" (*Romeo and Juliet*, ii, 4).

> And with a lenten salad cooled her blood.
>   DRYDEN: *Hind and Panther*, iii, **27**.

Leonidas of Modern Greece (lē on' i dăs). Marco Bozzaris, who with 1,200 men put to rout 4,000 Turco-Albanians, at Kerpenisi, but was killed in the attack (1823). He was buried at Missolonghi.

Leonine (lē' ō nīn). Lion-like; also, relating to one of the popes named *Leo*, as **the Leonine City,** the part of Rome surrounding the Vatican, which was fortified by Leo IV in the 9th century.

Leonine contract. A one-sided agreement; so called in allusion to the fable of *The Lion and his Fellow-Hunters. Cp.* GLAUCUS SWOP, *under* GLAUCUS.

Leonine verses. Latin hexameters, or alternate hexameters and pentameters, rhyming at the middle and end of each respective line. These fancies were common in the 12th century, and are said to have been popularized by and so called from Leoninus, a canon of the church of St. Victor, in Paris; but there are many such lines in the classic poets, particularly Ovid. In English verse, any metre which rhymes middle and end may be called Leonine verse.

Leopard. So called because it was thought in mediæval times to be a cross between the lion (*leo*), or lioness, and the *pard*, which was the name given to a panther that had no white specks on it.

References to the impossibility of a leopard changing its spots are frequent; the allusion is to *Jeremiah*, xiii, 23.

> Lions make leopards tame.
> Yea; but not change his spots.
>   *Richard II*, i, 1.

In Christian art the leopard represents that beast spoken of in *Revelation* xiii, 1-8, with seven heads and ten horns; six of the heads bear a nimbus, but the seventh, being "wounded to death," lost its power, and consequently is bare.

> And the beast which I saw was like unto a leopard, and his feet were as the feet of a bear, and his mouth as the mouth of a lion.—*Rev.* xiii, 2.

The lions in the coat of arms of England. *See* LION.

The leopard's head, or King's Mark, on silver is really a lion's head. It is called a leopard, because the O.Fr. heraldic term *Leopart* means a lion passant guardant.

Leopolita Bible. *See* BIBLE, SPECIALLY NAMED.

Leprachaun (lep 'rå kawn). The fairy shoemaker of Ireland; so called because he is always seen working at a single shoe (*leith*, half, *brog*, a shoe or brogue). Another of his peculiarities is that he has a purse that never contains more than a single shilling.

> Do you not catch the tiny clamour,
> Busy click of an elfin hammer,
> Voice of the Leprachaun singing shrill,
> As he merrily plies his trade?
>   W. B. YEATS: *Fairy and Folk Tales*.

He is also called lubrican, cluricaune (*q.v.*), etc. In Dekker and Middleton's *Honest Whore* (Pt. II, III, i) Hippolito speaks of Bryan, the Irish footman, as "your Irish lubrican."

Lesbian (lez' by ån). Pertaining to Lesbos, one of the islands of the Greek Archipelago, or to Sappho, the famous poetess of Lesbos, and to the homosexual practices attributed to her.

The Lesbian Poets. Terpander, Alcæus, Arion, and Sappho, all of Lesbos.

Let, to permit, is the A.S. *læt-an*, to suffer or permit; but *let*, to hinder, now obsolete or archaic, is the verb *lett-an*. From this comes a *let* in ball games such as lawn-tennis, where a point is played again because there has been a hindrance.

> Oftentimes I purposed to come unto you, but was let hitherto.—*Rom.* i, 13.

> Yf any man had rathere bestowe thys tyme upon hys owne occupatyon . . . he is not letted nor prohibited.—MORE: *Utopia*, II, iv.

Letter. The name of a character used to represent a sound, and of a missive or written message. Through O.Fr. *lettre*, from Lat. *littera*, a letter of the alphabet, the plural of which (*litteræ*) denoted an epistle. The plural, with the meaning literature, learning, erudition (as in *man of letters*, *republic of letters*, etc.), dates in English from at least the time of King Alfred, and is seen in Cicero's *otium literatum*, lettered ease.

The number of letters in the English alphabet is 26, but in a fount of type 206 characters are required; these are made up of Roman lower case (*i.e.* small letters), capitals, and small capitals; included are the diphthongs (Æ, æ, etc.) and ligatures (ff, fi, fl, ffi, ffl), the remaining characters being the accented letters, *i.e.* those with the grave ('), acute ('), circumflex (^), diæresis (¨), or tilde (~), and the "cedilla *c*" (ç). To these characters must be added the figures, fractions, points (, !, etc.), brackets, reference marks (*, §, etc.), and commercial and mathematical signs (£, %, +, etc.) in common use. *Cp.* TYPOGRAPHICAL SIGNS; FONT.

The proportionate use of the letters of the alphabet is given as follows:—

E .. 1,000	H .. 540	F .. 236	K .. 88
T .. 770	R .. 528	W .. 190	J .. 55
A .. 728	D .. 392	Y .. 184	Q .. 50
I .. 704	L .. 360	P .. 168	X .. 46
S .. 680	U .. 296	G .. 168	Z .. 22
O .. 672	C .. 280	B .. 158	
N .. 670	M .. 272	V .. 120	

Consonants, 5,977. Vowels, 3,400.

Another "fount-scheme" gives a rather different order, viz. e, t, a, o, i, n, s, r, h, d, l, u, c, m, f, w, y, p, g, b, v, k, j, q, x, fi, ff, fl, z, ffi, ffl, "e" accounts for 7.83 per cent. of the fount, "z" for 0.17, and the first twelve characters here given for 50 per cent. of the whole. The least wanted character is the italic capital Ç, of which it has been calculated that only five are necessary for a million type.

As initials the order of frequency is very different, the proportion being:—

S .. 1,194	M .. 439	W .. 272	Q .. 58
C .. 937	F .. 388	G .. 266	K .. 47
P .. 804	I .. 377	U .. 228	Y .. 23
A .. 574	E .. 340	O .. 206	Z .. 18
T .. 571	H .. 308	V .. 172	X .. 4
D .. 505	L .. 298	N .. 153	
B .. 463	R .. 291	J .. 69	

See also TYPE; FONT.

Letter of credence, or **letters credential,** formal documents with which a diplomatic agent is furnished accrediting him on his appointment to a post at the seat of a foreign government.

Letter of Credit. A letter written by a merchant or banker to another, requesting him to credit the bearer with certain sums of money. *Circular Notes* are letters of credit carried by travellers.

Letter of Licence. An instrument in writing made by a creditor, allowing a debtor longer time for the payment of his debt.

Leucadia or **Leucas** (lū kā′ di a). One of the Ionian Islands, now known as Santa Maura. Here is the promontory from which Sappho threw herself into the sea when she found her love for Phaon was in vain.

Haste, Sappho, haste, from high Leucadia throw
Thy wretched weight, nor dread the deeps below!
There injured lovers, leaping from above,
Their flames extinguish, and forget to love.
                    POPE: *Sappho to Phaon.*

Leucothea (lū kōth′ ē a) (*The White Goddess*). So Ino, the mortal daughter of Cadmus and wife of Athamas, was called after she became a sea goddess. Athamas in a fit of madness slew one of her sons; she threw herself into the sea with the other, imploring assistance of the gods, who deified both of them. Her son, Melicertes, then renamed Palæmon, was called by the Romans Portunus, or Portumnus, and became the protecting genius of harbours.

Levant (le vănt′). **He has levanted**—*i.e.* made off, decamped. A *levanter* is an absconder, especially one who makes a bet, and runs away without paying his bet if he loses. From Span. *levantar el campo*, or *la casa*, to break up the camp or house.

Levant and Ponent Winds. The east wind is the Levant, and the west wind the Ponent. The former is from Lat. *levare*, to raise (sunrise), and the latter from *ponere*, to set (sunset).

Forth rush the Levant and the Ponent winds.
                    MILTON: *Paradise Lost*, x, 704.

Levant, the region, strictly speaking, means the eastern shore of the Mediterranean; but is often applied to the whole East.

Levant and Couchant (lev′ ánt, kou′ chánt). Applied in legal phraseology to cattle which have strayed into another's field, and have been there long enough to lie down and sleep. The owner of the field can demand compensation for such intrusion. (Lat. *levantes et cubantes*, rising up and going to bed.)

Levee (le′ vi) (Fr., *lit.*, a rising, *i.e.* from bed). An official reception of men only by the sovereign or his representative, held usually in the afternoon.

It was customary for the queens of France to receive at the hour of their *levée*—*i.e.* while making their toilet—the visits of certain noblemen. The court physicians, messengers from the king, the queen's secretary, and some few others demanded admission as a right, so ten or more persons were often in the dressing-room while the queen was making her toilet and sipping her coffee.

In the Southern U.S.A. the word *levee* is used for an earth or masonry embankment for preventing the overflowing of a river.

Levée en masse (Fr.). A patriotic rising of a whole nation to defend their country.

Level. Level-headed. Shrewd, business-like, characterized by common sense; said of one who "has his head screwed on the right way."

Levellers. In English history, a body of ultra-Republicans in the time of Charles I and the Commonwealth, who wanted all men to be placed on a level, particularly with respect to their eligibility to office. John Lilburne was one of the leaders of the sect, which was active from 1647 to 1649, when it was suppressed.

In Irish history the name was given to the 18th century agrarian agitators, afterwards called Whiteboys (q.v.). Their first offences were levelling the hedges of enclosed commons; but their programme developed into a demand for the general redress of all agrarian grievances.

Lever de Rideau (lev' ā de rē' dō) (Fr., curtain-raiser). A short sketch performed on the stage before drawing up the curtain on the real play of the evening.

Leviathan (le vī' à thàn). The name (Hebrew for "that which gathers itself together in folds," Cp. Is. xxvii, 1) given in the Bible to a sea-serpent, though in Job xli, 1, it is possible that the reference is to the crocodile. Cp. BEHEMOTH.

The name is applied to a ship of great size from the reference in Ps. civ, 25, 26—

This great and wide sea, wherein are things creeping innumerable, both small and great beasts. There go the ships; there is that leviathan, whom thou hast made to play therein.

But this is a mistranslation of the Hebrew, the correct rendering being—according to Dr. Cheyne—

... There dragons move along; (yea), Leviathan whom thou didst appoint ruler therein.

Hobbes took the name as the title for his treatise on "the Matter, Forme, and Power of a Commonwealth Ecclesiasticall and Civil" (1651), and applied it to the Commonwealth as a political organism. He says:—

I have set forth the nature of man, (whose Pride and other Passions have compelled him to submit himselfe to Government;) together with the great power of his Governour, whom I compared to Leviathan, taking that comparison out of the two last verses of the one and fortieth of Job; where God having set forth the great power of Leviathan, calleth him King of the Proud.— Leviathan; Pt. ii, ch. xxviii.

The Leviathan of Literature. Dr. Johnson (1709-84).

Levitation is a term applied to the phenomenon of heavy bodies rising and floating in the air. It is frequently mentioned in the Hindu scriptures and other writings, and it is a not-uncommon attribute of Catholic saints. Joseph of Cupertino (1603-66) was the subject of such frequent levitation that he was forbidden by his superiors to attend choir and performed his devotions in a special chapel where his levitation would cause no distraction to other worshippers. D. D. Home was alleged by Sir W. Crookes to have had this power or gift. Scientific research has not yet found an explanation.

Levites (lē' vīts). In Dryden's Absalom and Achitophel (q.v.), the Dissenting clergy who were expelled by the Act of Conformity.

Lex non scripta (leks non skrip' ta) (Lat., unwritten law). The common law, as distinguished from the statute or written law. Common law does not derive its force from being recorded, and though its several provisions have been compiled and printed, the compilations are not statutes, but simply remembrancers.

Liar. Liars should have good memories. This old proverb, which is found in many languages and was quoted by St. Jerome in the 4th century, has been traced to Quintillian's Mendacem memorem esse oportet. "It is fitting that a liar should be a man of good memory" (Institutes, IV, ii, 91). It occurs in Taverner's translation of Erasmus's Proverbs (1539)—

A lyer ought not to be forgetfull.

And Montaigne says (Essayes, I, ix):—

It is not without reason, men say, that he who hath not a good and readie memorie, should never meddle with telling of lies, and feare to become a liar.

Libel (Lat. libellus, a little book). A writing of a defamatory nature, one which contains malicious statements ridiculing someone or calculated to bring him into disrepute, etc.; a lampoon, a satire. Originally a plaintiff's statement of his case, which usually "defames" the defendant, was called a "libel," for it made a "little book."

Malicious intention is not necessary to make a written or printed statement libellous if it reflects on the character of another and is published without lawful justification or excuse, and the use of the name of a real person in a work of fiction has been held to constitute a libel.

In legal phraseology a libel is the written statement commencing a suit, containing the plaintiff's allegations.

Liber (Lat., a book).,

Liber Albus (Lat., the white book). A compilation of the laws and customs of the City of London, made in 1419, by John Carpenter, town clerk.

Liber Niger. The Black Book of the Exchequer, compiled by Gervase of Tilbury, in the reign of Henry II. It is a roll of the military tenants.

Liberal. A political term introduced in the early 19th century from Spain and France (where it denoted "advanced" or revolutionary politicians), and employed in 1815 by Byron, Leigh Hunt, and others as the title of a periodical representing their views in politics, religion, and literature. It was originally bestowed upon the advanced Whigs as a term of reproach.

But when the moderate Whigs formed a coalition with the Tories and the advanced Whigs with the Radicals, it was adopted by the latter party; it came into general use about 1831, when the Reform Bill, in Lord Grey's Ministry, gave it prominence.

Influenced in a great degree by the philosophy and the politics of the Continent, they [the Whigs] endeavoured to substitute cosmopolitan for national principles, and they baptized the new scheme of politics with the plausible name of "Liberalism."—DISRAELI, June 24, 1872.

Liberate. At a press conference in May, 1944, President Roosevelt said that the Allied campaigns in Europe were a liberation, not an invasion. This gave rise to a sarcastic use of the verb "to liberate" as a synonym for "to loot."

Liberator, The. The Peruvians so call Simon Bolivar (1783-1830), who established the independence of Peru. Daniel O'Connell (1775-1847) was also so called, because he led the agitation which resulted in the repeal of the Penal Laws and the Emancipation of the Irish Roman Catholics.

Liberator was the name associated with a famous financial crash at the close of last century. In 1868 Jabez Balfour promoted the Liberator Building Society in which a great number of small investors embarked their entire capital. The crash came in 1892, owing to the systematic fraud whereby Balfour had applied the funds to all manner of wild speculation. Balfour, at the time M.P. for Burnley, was sentenced to 14 years penal servitude.

Liberator of the World. So Benjamin Franklin (1706-90) has been called.

Libertarians. *See* AGENT.

Libertine. A debauchee, a dissolute person; one who puts no restraint on his personal indulgence.

A libertine, in earlier use, was a speculative freethinker in matters of religion and in the theory of morals . . . but [it has come] to signify a profligate.—TRENCH: *On the Study of Words*, lecture iii.

In the New Testament the word is used to mean a freedman (Lat. *Libertinus*).

Then there arose certain of the synagogue, which is called the synagogue of the Libertines, . . . disputing with Stephen.—*Acts* vi, 9.

There was a sect of heretics in Holland, about 1525, who maintained that nothing is sinful but to those who think it sinful, and that perfect innocence is to live without doubt.

Liberty means "to do what one likes." (Lat. *liber*, free.)

Civil liberty. The liberty of a subject to conduct his own affairs as he thinks proper, provided he neither infringes on the equal liberty of others, nor offends against the good morals or laws under which he is living.

Moral liberty. Such freedom as is essential to render a person responsible for what he does, or what he omits to do.

Natural liberty. Unrestricted freedom to exercise all natural functions in their proper places; the state of being subject only to the laws of nature.

Political liberty. The freedom of a nation from any unjust abridgment of its rights and independence; the right to participate in political elections and civil offices, and to have a voice in the administration of the laws under which one lives.

Religious liberty. Freedom in religious opinions, and in both private and public worship, provided such freedom in no wise interferes with the equal liberty of others.

The liberty of the press. The right to publish what one pleases, subject only to penalty if the publication is mischievous, hurtful, or libellous to the state or individuals.

Cap of Liberty. *See* CAP.

Liberty Enlightening the World. The colossal statue standing on Bedloe's (or Liberty) Island, at the entrance of New York Harbour, presented to the American people by France in commemoration of the centenary of the American Declaration of Independence, and inaugurated in 1886. It is of bronze, 155 ft. in height (standing on a pedestal 135 ft. high), and represents a woman, draped, and holding a lighted torch in her upraised hand. It is the work of the Alsatian sculptor, Auguste Bartholdi (1834-1904).

The statue of Liberty, placed over the entrance of the Palais Royal, Paris, was modelled from Mme Tallien.

Libido (li bē' dō). A term used by Freud to designate "the energy of those instincts which have to do with all that may be comprised under the word 'Love'." More simply, it is applied to the innate impelling force of sex urge.

Libra (Lat., the balance). The seventh sign of the Zodiac (and the name of one of the ancient constellations), which the sun enters about September 22nd and leaves about October 22nd. At this time the day and night being weighed would be found equal.

Library. Before the invention of paper the thin rind between the solid wood and the outside bark of certain trees was used for writing on; this was in Lat. called *liber*, which came in time to signify also a "book." Hence our *library*, the place for books; *librarian*, the keeper of books; and the French *livre*, a book.

Libya. The north of Africa between Egypt and the Atlantic Ocean. It was the Greek name for Africa in general. The Romans used the word sometimes as synonymous with Africa, and sometimes for the fringe containing Carthage.

Libya was occupied by the Italians in 1911-12, and by the Treaty of Ouchy (1912) the sovereignty of the province was transferred from Turkey to Italy. The Italians began its colonization, and so late as 1938 some 16,000 emigrants left Genoa for the province. In 1942-43 the Germans and Italians were driven from Libya in the British advance from El Alamein. In 1949 the General Assembly of the United Nations decreed that Libya should become an independent state by January 1st, 1952. On this date Libya became a kingdom under Sayed Mohammed Idris.

Lich. A dead body (A.S. *lie*; Ger. *leiche*).

Lich-fowls. Birds that feed on carrion, as night-ravens, etc.

Lich-gate. The shed or covered place at the entrance of churchyards, intended to afford shelter to the coffin and mourners, while they wait for the clergyman to conduct the cortège into the church.

Lich-owl. The screech-owl, superstitiously supposed to foretell death.

Lich-wake or **Lyke-wake.** The funeral feast or the waking of a corpse, *i.e.* watching it all night.

In a pastoral written by Ælfric in 998 for Wilfsige, Bishop of Sherborne, the attendance of the clergy at lyke-wakes is forbidden.

Lich-way. The path by which a funeral is conveyed to church, which not infrequently deviates from the ordinary road. It was long supposed that wherever a dead body passed became a public thoroughfare.

Lick. I licked him. I flogged or beat him. A **licking** is a thrashing, or—in games—a defeat, as *I gave him a good licking at billiards*.

A lick and a promise. To give a lick and a promise to a piece of work is to do it in a hasty and superficial way—as a cat might give its dirty face one quick lick of its tongue with a promise of more cleaning later.

To go at a great lick. To run, ride, etc., at great speed; to put on a spurt.

To lick into shape. To make presentable; to give a good appearance, decent manners, etc., to. In allusion to the tradition that the cubs of bears are cast shapeless, and remain so till the dam has licked them into proper form. *See* BEAR.

> So watchful Bruin forms, with plastic care,
> Each growing lump, and brings it to a bear.
> PoPE: *Dunciad*, i, 101.

To lick one's lips. To give evident signs of the enjoyment of anticipation.

Lickspittle. A toady, the meanest of sycophants.

Lictors. Binders (Lat. *ligo*, to bind or tie). These Roman officers were so called because they bound the hands and feet of criminals before they executed the sentence of the law.

Lidice (lid'i si). Once a mining village in Czechoslovakia. In 1942 the German authorities asserted that the inhabitants had helped the patriots who had assassinated the atrocious Reinhard Heydrich, Nazi governor of Bohemia. All the adult inhabitants of Lidice were shot and the children taken away none have ever known where; the village was then utterly rased to the ground. This example of German ferocity aroused such indignation throughout the civilized world that in U.S.A., Mexico, and elsewhere a number of towns and villages were renamed Lidice in its memory.

Lido (lē' dō). An outdoor bathing-pool, usually with a place for sunbathing and often with accommodation for concerts or other amusements. The name is taken from the sandy island called the Lido, facing the Adriatic outside Venice, and a fashionable bathing resort.

Lie. A falsehood (A.S. *lyge*, from *leogan*, to lie).

A lie hath no feet. Because it cannot stand alone. In fact, a lie wants twenty others to support it, and even then is in constant danger of tripping. *Cp.* LIAR (*Liars should have good memories*).

A white lie. A conventional lie, such as telling a caller that Mrs. A. or Mrs. B. is not at home, meaning not "at home" to that particular caller.

It is said that Dean Swift called on a friend, and was told "master is not at home." The friend called on the dean, and Swift, opening the window, shouted, "Not at home." When the friend expostulated, Swift said, "I believed your footman when he said his master was not at home; surely you can believe the master himself when he tells you he is not at home."

Lie detector. An American invention which records the heart-beats of a man under questioning. It has been found that a human being cannot tell a lie without the pulse of his heart increasing, and this increase of pulsation is recorded. In some States of the Union the findings of this machine are accepted as legal evidence.

The Father of lies. Satan (*John* viii, 44).

Lie (A.S. *licgan*, to 'bide or rest).
Lie heavy on him, earth, for he
Laid many a heavy load on thee.

This is part of Dr. Evan's epitaph on Sir John Vanbrugh (1664-1726), the dramatist, herald, and architect. The "heavy loads" referred to were Blenheim, Greenwich Hospital (which he finished), Castle Howard in Yorkshire, and other massive buildings.

To lie in. To be confined in childbirth.

To lie in state. Said of a corpse of a royal or distinguished person that is displayed to the general public.

To lie low. To conceal oneself or one's intentions.
All this while Brer Rabbit lay low.—JOEL CHANDLER HARRIS: *Uncle Remus*.

To lie over. To be deferred; as, this question must lie over till next sessions.

Liege (lēj). The word means one bound, a bondsman (O.Fr. *lige*, connected with O.H.-Ger. *ledig*, free); hence, vassals were called *liege-men*—*i.e.* men bound to serve their lord, or *liege lord*.
Unarmed and bareheaded, on his knees, and with his hands placed between those of his lord, he [the military tenant] repeated these words: "Hear, my lord, I have become your liegeman of life and limb, and earthly worship; and faith and truth I will bear to you to live and die.—LINGARD: *History of England*, vol. ii, ch. 1.

Lieutenant (in the British Navy and Army, lef ten' ånt; American usage, loo ten' ånt), is the Latin *locum-tenens*, through the French. A *Lieutenant-Colonel* is the colonel's deputy. The *Lord-Lieutenant* of Ireland was the representative of the Crown in that country.

Life (A.S. *lif*). **Drawn from life.** Drawn or described from some existing person or object.

For life. As long as life continues.

For the life of me. True as I am alive. Even if my life depended on it. A strong asseveration, originally "under pain of losing my life."
Nor could I, for the life of me, see how the creation of the world had anything to do with what I was talking about.—GOLDSMITH: *Vicar of Wakefield*.

Large as life. Of the same size as the object represented.

On my life. I will answer for it by my life.

People of high life. The upper ten, the *haut monde*.

To bear a charmed life. To escape accidents in a marvellous manner.

To know life. To be well versed in the niceties of social intercourse, good breeding, manners, etc.; to be up to all the dodges by which one may be imposed upon.

To see life. To "knock about" town, where life may be seen at its fullest; to move in smart or fast society.

To the life. In exact imitation. "Done to the life."

Life Guards. The two senior cavalry regiments of the Household Troops (*q.v.*), the members of which are not less than six feet high; hence, a fine, tall, manly fellow is called "a regular Life Guardsman."

Life preserver. A buoyant jacket, belt, or other appliance, to support the human body in water; also a loaded staff or knuckle-duster for self-defence.

Air-lift. Organized manœuvre to transport a quantity of troops or stores to a destination by air. The *Berlin air-lift*, to victual the British and American zones of the city after the Russian embargo on all land transport, began June 28th, 1948 and ended May 12th, 1949, having made in all 195,530 flights and carried 1,414,000 tons of food, coal and other stores.

Lifter. A thief. We still call one who plunders shops a "shop-lifter."
Is he so young a man, and so old a lifter?
Troilus and Cressida, i, 2.

Lifting. In Scotland, the raising of the coffin on to the shoulders of the bearers. Certain ceremonies preceded the funeral.
At the first service were offered meat and ale; at the second, shortbread and whisky; at the third, seed-cake and wine; at the fourth, currant-bun and rum; at the last, sugar-biscuits and brandy.

Lifting the little finger. See FINGER.

Ligan. See LAGAN.

Light. The A.S. of this word in both senses, *i.e.* illumination and smallness of weight, is *leoht*, but in the former sense it is connected with Ger. *licht*, Lat. *lux*, and Gr. *leukos* (white), and in the latter with Ger. *leicht*, Gr. *elachus* (not heavy), and Sansk. *laghu*. The verb *to light*, to dismount, to settle after flight, is A.S. *lihtan*, from the last mentioned *leoht*, originally meaning to lighten, or relieve of a burden.

Light Infantry. In the British Army, infantry carrying less equipment than normal and trained to move at high speed in manœuvring round the flanks of an enemy. They were introduced into the British Army by Sir John Moore (1761-1809). The regiments so designated still march at a high speed, with short paces and with arms trailed instead of carried at the slope.

Light troops. A term formerly applied to light cavalry, *i.e.* lancers and hussars, who are neither such large men as the "Heavies," nor yet so heavily equipped.

The light of Thy countenance. God's smile of approbation and love.

Lift up the light of Thy countenance on us.—*Ps.* iv, 6.

The light of the age. Maimonides or Rabbi Moses ben Maimon, of Cordova (1135-1204).

To bring to light. To discover and expose.

The duke yet would have dark deeds darkly answered; he would never bring them to light; would he were returned!—*Measure for Measure*, iii, 2.

To light upon. To discover by accident; to come across by a lucky chance. Thus, Dr. Johnson wrote to Mrs. Thrale "How did you light on your specifick for the tooth-ach?"

To make light of. To treat as of no importance; to take little notice of.

Behold, I have prepared my dinner: my oxen and my fatlings are killed, and all things are ready; come unto the marriage.

But they made light of it, and went their ways, one to his farm, another to his merchandise.—*Matt.* xxii, 4, 5.

To throw or **shed light upon.** To elucidate, to explain.

Lighthouse. *See* PHAROS.

Light year. This is a term used by scientists as a unit in measuring stellar distances. Light travels at the rate of 186,000 miles a second; a light year, or the distance travelled by light in a year, is, therefore, 5,876,068,880,000 miles.

Lightning. Hamilcar (d. 228 B.C.), the Carthaginian general, was called "Barca," the Phœnician for "lightning" (Heb. *Barak*), both on account of the rapidity of his march and for the severity of his attacks.

Chain lightning. Two or more flashes of lightning repeated without intermission.

Forked lightning. Zig-zag lightning.

Globular lightning. A meteoric ball (of fire), which sometimes falls on the earth and flies off with an explosion.

Lightning conductor. A metal rod raised above a building with one end in the earth, to carry off the lightning and prevent its injuring the building.

Lightning preservers. The most approved classical preservatives against lightning were the eagle, the sea-calf, and the laurel. Jupiter chose the first, Augustus Cæsar the second, and Tiberius the third. (*Columella*, x; *Sueton.* in *Vit. Aug.*, xc.; ditto in *Vit. Tib.*, lxix). *Cp.* HOUSE-LEEK.

Bodies scathed and persons struck dead by lightning were said to be incorruptible; and anyone so distinguished was held by the ancients in great honour. (J. C. Bullenger: *De Terrae Motu*, etc., v, 11.)

Lilburne. If no one else were alive, John would quarrel with Lilburne. John Lilburne (1614-57) was a contentious Leveller (*q.v.*) in the Commonwealth; so rancorous against rank that he could never satisfy himself that any two persons were exactly on the same level.

Is John departed? and is Lilburne gone?
Farewell to both—to Lilburne and to John.
Yet, being gone, take this advice from me.
Let them not both in one grave buried be.
Here lay ye John, lay Lilburne thereabout;
For if they both should meet, they would fall out.
                              Epigrammatic Epitaph.

Lilith (lil' ith). A Semitic (in origin probably Babylonian) demon supposed to haunt wildernesses in stormy weather, and to be specially dangerous to children and pregnant women. She is referred to in *Is.* xxxiv, 14, as the "screech-owl" (Revised Version, "night monster," and in margin "Lilith"); and the Talmudists give the name to a wife that Adam is fabled to have had before Eve, who, refusing to submit to him, left Paradise for a region of the air, and still haunts the night. Superstitious Jews put in the chamber occupied by their wife four coins inscribed with the names of Adam and Eve and the words "Avaunt thee, Lilith!" Goethe introduced her in his *Faust*, and Rossetti in his *Eden Bower* adapted the Adamitic story, making the Serpent the instrument of Lilith's vengeance. *See* THE DEVIL AND HIS DAM *under* DEVIL, and *Cp.* LAMIA.

Lilli Marlene. A song composed by Norbert Schultze, in 1938, and sung by the Swedish singer Lala Anderson. It was broadcast by the German radio on the capture of Belgrade, 1941, and became a favourite song of the Afrika Korps. From them it was caught up by the British 8th Army. In 1944 a documentary film, *The True Story of Lilli Marlene* appeared, featuring Lala Anderson herself.

Lilliput. The country of pigmies ("Lilliputians") to whom Captain Lemuel Gulliver was a giant. (Swift: *Gulliver's Travels*.)

Lily, The. There is a tradition that the lily sprang from the repentant tears of Eve as she went forth from Paradise.

In Christian art, the lily is an emblem of chastity, innocence, and purity. In pictures of the Annunciation, Gabriel is sometimes represented as carrying a lily-branch, while a vase containing a lily stands before the Virgin, who is kneeling in prayer. St. Joseph holds a lily-branch in his hand, indicating that his wife Mary was a virgin.

Lily of France. The device of Clovis was three black toads (*see* CRAPAUD); but the story goes that an aged hermit of Joye-en-valle saw a miraculous light stream one night into his cell, and an angel appeared to him holding an azure shield of wonderful beauty, emblazoned with three gold lilies that shone like stars, which the hermit was commanded to give to Queen Clotilde; she gave it to her royal husband, whose arms were everywhere victorious, and the device was thereupon adopted as the emblem of France. (*See Les Petits Bollandistes*, vol. vi, p. 426.). It is said the people were commonly called *Liliarts*, and the kingdom *Lilium* in the time of Philippe le Bel, Charles VIII, and Louis XII. *See* FLEUR-DE-LYS.

Florence is "The City of Lilies."

By "the lily in the field" in *Matt.* vi, 28, which is said to surpass Solomon in all his glory, is meant simply the wild lily, probably a species of iris. Our "lily of the valley"—with which this is sometimes confused—is one of the genus *Convallaria*, a very different plant.

To paint the lily. *See* PAINT.

Limb. Slang for a mischievous rascal, a young imp; it is short for the older *Limb of the devil*, where the word implies "agent" or "scion." Dryden called Fletcher "a limb of Shakespeare."

Limbo (Lat., border, fringe, edge). The borders of hell; the portion assigned by the Schoolmen to those departed spirits to whom the benefits of redemption did not apply through no fault of their own.

The Paradise of Fools. As fools or idiots are not responsible for their works, the old Schoolmen held that they are not punished in purgatory and cannot be received into heaven, so they go to a special "Paradise of Fools."

> Then might you see
> Cowls, hoods, and habits, with their wearers tossed
> And fluttered into rags; then relics, beads,
> Indulgences, dispenses, pardons, bulls,
> The sport of winds. All these, upwhirled aloft,
> Into a Limbo large and broad, since called
> The Paradise of Fools.
>
> MILTON: *Paradise Lost*, iii, 489.

Cp. FOOL'S PARADISE *under* FOOL.

Limehouse. At one time descriptive of violent abuse of one's political opponents: so called out of compliment to a speech by Lloyd George at Limehouse, London, on July 30th, 1909, when he poured forth scorn and abuse on dukes, landlords, financial magnates, etc.

Lime-light. A vivid light, giving off little heat, produced by the combustion of oxygen and hydrogen on a surface of lime. It is also called Drummond Light, after Thomas Drummond (1797-1840), who invented it in 1826. It was

tried at the South Foreland lighthouse in 1861. But its main use developed in the theatre, where it could be used to throw a powerful beam upon one player to the exclusion of others on the stage. Hence the phrase **to be in the lime-light**, to be in the full glare of public attention.

Limerick. A nonsense verse in the metre, popularized by Edward Lear in his *Book of Nonsense* (1846), of which the following is an example:—

> There was a young lady of Wilts,
> Who walked up to Scotland on stilts;
>   When they said it was shocking
>   To show so much stocking,
> She answered, "Then what about kilts?"

The name was not given till much later, and comes from the chorus, "We'll all come up, come up to Limerick," which was interposed after each verse as it was improvised and sung by a convivial party.

Limey (līʹ mi). In American and Australian slang this means a British sailor or ship, or just a Briton. It comes from the old system of taking steps to prevent scurvy by making the crew take lime water.

Limp. A word formed of the initials of Louis (XIV), James (II), his wife Mary of Modena, and the Prince (of Wales), and used as a Jacobite toast in the time of William III. *Cp.* NOTARIKON.

Lincoln College (Oxford). Founded by Richard Fleming, Bishop of Lincoln, in 1427, and completed by Thomas Rotherham, Bishop of Lincoln (afterwards Archbishop of York and Lord Chancellor), in 1479.

Lincoln Imp. A grotesque carving, having long ears and only one leg, in the Angel Choir of Lincoln Cathedral.

The devil looking over Lincoln. *See* DEVIL.

Lincoln's Inn. One of the four Inns of Court (*q.v.*), in London. Henry Lacy, Earl of Lincoln, built a mansion here in the 14th century on ground which had belonged to the Black Friars, but was granted to him by Edward I. A Bishop of Chichester, in the reign of Henry VII, granted leases here to certain students of law.

Lindabrides (lin dȧ brīʹ dēz). A heroine in *The Mirror of Knighthood*, whose name at one time was a synonym for a kept mistress.

Linden. The German name (largely used in England) for lime trees. *Unter den Linden* ("under the limes") is the name of the principal street in Berlin. It is about 1;100 yd. in length.

Baucis (*see* PHILEMON) was converted into a linden tree.

Line. All along the line. In every particular, as in such phrases as—

The accuracy of the statement is contested all along the line by persons on the spot.

Crossing the line. Sailing across the Equator. Advantage is usually taken of this for all sorts of sports aboard ship, playing great practical jokes on those who have never crossed the Line before. The custom was at its prime in the old sailing-ship days, A sailor crudely dressed as Father Neptune, accompanied by a yet cruder Amphitrite appeared over the ship's side, followed by yet others, naked to the waist and painted with red ochre or the like. The neophytes were then seized, lathered with some horrible compound and while still struggling were forcibly shaved with a piece of rusty hoop iron. This was the usual procedure, accompanied by much horseplay and licence.

Line of direction. The line in which a body moves, a force acts, or motion is communicated, In order that a body may stand without falling, a line let down from the centre of gravity must fall within the base on which the object stands. Thus the leaning tower of Pisa does not fall, because this rule is preserved.

Line of life. In palmistry, the crease in the left hand beginning above the web of the thumb, and running towards or up to the wrist.

The nearer it approaches the wrist the longer will be the life, according to palmists. If long and deeply marked, it indicates long life with very little trouble; if crossed or cut with other marks, it indicates sickness.

The thin red line. British infantrymen in action. The old 93rd Highlanders were so described at the battle of Balaclava by W. H. Russell, because they did not take the trouble to form into square; their regimental magazine is named *The Thin Red Line.*

To read between the lines. To discern the secret meaning. One method of cryptography is to write so that the hidden message is revealed only when alternate lines are read.

What line are you in? What trade or profession are you of? Commercial travellers use the word frequently to signify the sort of goods which they have to dispose of; as, one travels "in the hardware line," another "in the drapery line," or "grocery line," etc.

Line-up. A phrase with a variety of meanings; a parade of persons, especially criminals, for inspection or recognition; an arrangement of players at the start of a game; the deploying of opposing forces before a battle.

To shoot a line. An R.A.F. phrase meaning to exaggerate, to tell a tall story.

Lingo. Talk, language, especially some peculiar or technical phraseology; from *lingua*, tongue.

Lingua Franca (ling' gwa frăng' ká). A species of Italian mixed with French, Greek, Arabic, etc., spoken on the coasts of the Mediterranean. Also, any jumble of different languages.

Lining of the Pocket. Money.

My money is spent: Can I be content
With, pockets deprived of their lining?
The Lady's Decoy, or Man Midwife's Defence, 1738, p. 4.

When the great court tailor wished to obtain the patronage of Beau Brummel, he made him a present of a dress-coat lined with bank-notes. Brummel wrote a letter of thanks, stating that he quite approved of the coat, and he especially admired the lining.

Linnæan System (lin ē' án). The artificial classification adopted by the great Swedish naturalist Linnæus (1707-78), who arranged his three kingdoms of animals, vegetables, and minerals into classes, orders, genera, species, and varieties, according to certain characteristics.

Linne, The Heir of (lin). The hero of an old ballad, given in Percy's *Reliques*, which tells how he wasted his substance in riotous living, and, having spent all, sold his estates to his steward, reserving only a poor lodge in a lonely glen. When no one would lend him money, he retired to the lodge, where was dangling a rope with a running noose. He put it round his neck and sprang aloft, but he fell to the ground, and when he came to espied two chests of beaten gold, and a third full of white money, over which was written—

Once more, my sonne, I sette thee clere;
Amend thy life and follies past;
For but thou amend thee of thy life,
That rope must be thy end at last.

The heir of Linne now returned to his old hall, where he was refused the loan of forty pence by his quondam steward; one of the guests remarked that he ought to have lent it, as he had bought the estate cheap enough. "Cheap call you it?" said the steward; "why, he shall have it back for 100 marks less." "Done," said the heir of Linne, and recovered his estates.

Lion. As an agnomen.

Alp Arslan, son of Togrul Beg, the Perso-Turkish monarch (reigned 1063-72) was surnamed *The Valiant Lion.*

Ali Pasha, called *The Lion of Janina*, overthrown in 1822 by Ibrahim Pasha. (1741, 1788-1822.)

Arioch (fifth of the dynasty of Ninu, the Assyrian), called Arioch Ellasar—*i.e.* Arioch

Melech al Asser, *the Lion King of Assyria*. (1927-1897 B.C.)

Damelowiez, Prince of Haliez, who founded Lemberg (*Lion City*) in 1259.

Gustavus Adolphus, called *The Lion of the North*. (1594, 1611-32.)

Hamza, called *The Lion of God and His Prophet*. So Gabriel told Mohammed that his uncle was enregistered in heaven.

Henry, Duke of Bavaria and Saxony, was called *The Lion* for his daring courage. (1129-95.)

Louis VIII of France was called *The Lion* because he was born under the sign Leo. (1187, 1223-26.)

Richard I. Cœur de Lion (*Lion's heart*), so called for his bravery. (1157, 1189-99.)

William of Scotland, so called because he chose a red lion *rampant* for his cognizance. (Reigned 1165-1214).

See LION OF GOD *below*.

A lion is emblem of the tribe of Judah; Christ is called "the lion of the tribe of Judah."

Judah is a lion's whelp: . . . he couched as a lion, and as an old lion; who shall rouse him up?—*Gen.* xlix, 9.

Among the titles of the Emperor of Abyssinia are Conquering Lion of the Tribe of Judah, Elect of God, King of the Kings of Ethiopia.

The Lion in Story and Legend

Cybele is represented as riding in a chariot drawn by two tame lions.

Pracriti, the goddess of nature among the Hindus, is represented in a similar manner.

Hippomenes and *Atalanta* (fond lovers) were metamorphosed into lions by Cybele.

Hercules is said to have worn over his shoulders the hide of the Nemean lion (*see* NEMEAN), and the personification of Terror is also arrayed in a lion's hide.

The story of Androcles and the lion (*see* ANDROCLES) has many parallels, the most famous of which are those related of St. Jerome and St. Gerasimus:—

While St. Jerome was lecturing one day, a lion entered the schoolroom, and lifted up one of its paws. All the disciples fled; but Jerome, seeing that the paw was wounded, drew out of it a thorn and dressed the wound. The lion, out of gratitude, showed a wish to stay with its benefactor. Hence the saint is represented as accompanied by a lion.

St. Gerasimus, says the story, saw, on the banks of the Jordan, a lion coming to him, limping on three feet. When it reached the saint it held up to him the right paw, from which Gerasimus extracted a large thorn. The grateful beast attached itself to the saint, and followed him about as a dog.

Half a score of such tales are told by the Bollandists in the *Acta Sanctorum*; and in more recent times a similar one was told of Sir George Davis, an English consul at Florence at the beginning of the 19th century. One day he went to see the lions of the great Duke of Tuscany. There was one which the keepers could not tame; but no sooner did Sir George appear than it manifested every symptom of joy. Sir George entered its cage, when the lion leaped on his shoulder, licked his face, wagged its tail, and fawned on him like a dog. Sir George told the great duke that he had brought up the creature; but as it grew older it became dangerous, and he sold it to a Barbary captain. The duke said that he had bought it of the very same man, and the mystery was solved.

Sir Iwain de Galles, a hero of romance, was attended by a lion, which, in gratitude to the knight who had delivered it from a serpent with which it had been engaged in deadly combat, ever after became his faithful servant, approaching the knight with tears, and rising on its hind-feet like a dog.

Sir Geoffrey de Latour was aided by a lion against the Saracens; but the faithful brute was drowned in attempting to follow the vessel in which the knight had embarked on his departure from the Holy Land.

The lion will not touch the true prince (1 *Henry IV*, ii, 4). This is an old superstition, and has been given a Christian significance, the "true prince" being the Messiah, It is applied to any prince of blood royal, supposed at one time to be hedged around with a sort of divinity.

Fetch the Numidian lion I brought over;
If she be sprung from royal blood, the lion
He'll do her reverence, else . . .
He'll tear her all to pieces.
FLETCHER: *The Mad Lover*, iv, 5.

The lion in Heraldry

Ever since 1164, when it was adopted as a device by Philip I, Duke of Flanders, the lion has figured largely and in an amazing variety of positions as an heraldic emblem, and, as a consequence, in public-house signs. The earliest and most important attitude of the heraldic lion is *rampant* (the device of Scotland), but it is also shown as *passant, passant gardant* (as in the shield of England), *salient, sejant*, etc., and even *dormant. For these terms see* HERALDRY.

The lions in the arms of England. They are three lions passant gardant, *i.e.* walking and showing the full face. The first was that of

Rollo, Duke of Normandy, and the second represented the country of Maine, which was added to Normandy. These were the two lions borne by William the Conqueror and his descendants. Henry II added a third lion to represent the Duchy of Aquitaine, which came to him through his wife Eleanor. Any lion not rampant is called a *lion leopardé*, and the French heralds call the lion passant a *leopard*; accordingly Napoleon said to his soldiers, "Let us drive these leopards (the English) into the sea."

Since 1603 the royal arms have been supported as now by (dexter) the English lion and (sinister) the Scottish unicorn (see UNICORN); but prior to the accession of James I the sinister supporter was a family badge. Edward III, with whom supporters began, had a lion and eagle; Henry IV, an antelope and swan; Henry V, a lion and antelope; Edward IV, a lion and bull; Richard III, a lion and boar; Henry VII, a lion and dragon; Elizabeth, Mary, and Henry VIII, a lion and greyhound.

The lion in the arms of Scotland is derived from the arms of the ancient Earls of Northumberland and Huntingdon, from whom some of the Scottish monarchs were descended. The *tressure* is referred to the reign of Achaius (d. about 819), who made a league with Charlemagne, "who did augment his arms with a double trace formed with Floure-de-lyces, signifying thereby that the lion henceforth should be defended by the ayde of Frenche-men." (Holinshed: *Chronicles*.)

Sir Walter Scott says:—

William, King of Scotland, having chosen for his armorial bearing a Red Lion *rampant*, acquired the name of William the Lion; and this rampant lion still constitutes the arms of Scotland; and the president of the heraldic court . . . is called Lord Lion King-at-Arms.— *Tales of a Grandfather*, iv.

A lion at the feet of crusaders or **martyrs,** in effigy, signifies that they died for their cause.

The Lion of St. Mark, or *of Venice*. A winged lion *sejant*, holding an open book with the inscription *Pax tibi, Marce, Evangelista Meus*. A sword-point rises above the book on the dexter side, and the whole is encircled by an aureola.

Among other distinctive lions that appear in blazonry and on the signs of inns, etc., may be mentioned:—

Blue, the badge of the Earl of Mortimer, also of Denmark.

Crowned, the badge of Henry VIII.

Golden, the badge of Henry I, and also of Percy, Duke of Northumberland.

Rampant, with the tail between its legs and turned over its back, the badge of Edward IV as Earl of March.

Red, of Scotland; also the badge of John of Gaunt, Duke of Lancaster, who assumed this badge as a token of his claim to the throne of Castile.

Sleeping, the device of Richard I.

Statant gardant (*i.e.* standing and showing a full face), the device of the Duke of Norfolk.

White, the device of the Duke of Norfolk; also of the Earl of Surrey, Earl of Mortimer, and the Fitz-Hammonds.

Lions. The lions of a place are sights worth seeing, or the celebrities; so called from the ancient custom of showing strangers, as chief of London sights, the lions at the Tower. The Tower menagerie was abolished in 1834.

Lion's Head. In fountains the water is often made to issue from the mouth of a lion. This is a very ancient custom. The Egyptians thus symbolized the inundation of the Nile, which happens when the sun is in Leo (July 28th to August 23rd), and the Greeks and Romans adopted the device for their fountains.

To place one's head in the lion's mouth. To expose oneself needlessly and foolhardily to danger.

Lion's Provider. A jackal; a foil to another man's wit, a humble friend who plays into your hand to show you to best advantage. The jackal (*q.v.*) feeds on the lion's leavings, and is said to yell to advise the lion that it has roused up his prey, serving the lion in much the same way as a dog serves a sportsman.

> . . . the poor jackals are less foul,
> As being the brave lion's keen providers,
> Than human insects catering for spiders
> BYRON: *Don Juan*, ix, 27.

Lion's share. The larger part: all or nearly all. In *Æsop's Fables*, several beasts joined the lion in a hunt; but, when the spoil was divided, the lion claimed one quarter in right of his prerogative, one for his superior courage, one for his dam and cubs, "and as for the fourth, let who will dispute it with me." Awed by his frown, the other beasts yielded and silently withdrew. *Cp*. MONTGOMERY.

Lionize a person, To, is either to show him the *lions*, or chief objects of attraction, or to make a lion of him by fêting him and making a fuss about him.

Lip. Lip homage or **service.** Verbal devotion. Honouring with the lips while the heart takes no part nor lot in the matter. *See Matt*, xv, 8; *Is.* xxix, 13.

To bite one's lip. To express vexation and annoyance, or to suppress some unwanted emotion as laughter or anger.

To carry a stiff upper lip. To be self-reliant; to bear oneself courageously in face of difficulties or danger.

To curl the lip. To express contempt or disgust with the mouth.

To hang the lip. To drop the under lip in sullenness or contempt. Thus in *Troilus and Cressida* (iii, 1) Helen explains why her brother Troilus is not abroad by saying, "He hangs the lip at something."

A foolish hanging of thy nether lip.— 1 *Henry IV*, i, 4.

To shoot out the lip. To show scorn.

All they that see me laugh me to scorn. They shoot out the lip; they shake the head . . .—*Ps.* xxii, 7.

Liqueur (li kū' ėr). An aromatic and usually sweetened drink combined with various flavourings to give a distinctive character. Liqueurs generally consist of equal portions of alcohol and syrup made from cane sugar mixed with essences and herbs. Some of the most renowned liqueurs originated in monasteries, and the secret of their recipe has been and still is jealously guarded. Among the chief of these are the green and yellow Chartreuse, now made at Tarragona by paid servants and lay brothers. The great profits help to keep up the monasteries and maintain considerable charities. Benedictine, although made on the site of the great monastery of Fécamp, has nothing whatever to do with the monastic order—it is an ordinary commercial product.

Liquidate. In the sinister slang introduced by Fascism, this means to kill, to get out of the way by murder.

Lisbon. Camoëns, in the *Lusiad*, derives the name from *Ulyssippo* (Ulysses' polis or city), and says that it was founded by Ulysses; but it is in fact the old Phœnican *Olisippo*, the walled town. The root *Hippo* appears as the name of more than one ancient African city, also in Orippo, Lacippo, and other Spanish towns.

Lismahago (lis mȧ hā' gō). A proud but poor, and very conceited, Scots captain, in Smollett's *Humphrey Clinker*. Fond of disputation, jealous of honour, and brimful of national pride, he marries Miss Tabitha Bramble.

Lit de Justice (lē de zhus tēs). Properly the, seat occupied by the French king when he attended the deliberations of his *parlement*; hence, the session itself, any arbitrary edict. As the members derived their power from the king, when the king was present their power returned to the fountain-head, and the king was arbitrary. What he then proposed could not be controverted, and had the force of law. The last *lit de justice* was held by Louis XVI in 1787.

Little. Little by little. Gradually; a little at a time.

Many a little makes a mickle. The real Scottish proverb is: "A wheen o 'mickles mak's a muckle," where mickle means *little*, and muckle *much*; but the Anglo-Saxon *micel* or *mycel* means "much," so that, if the Scots proverb is accepted, we must give a forced meaning to the word "mickle."

Little Britain. The name given in the old romances to Armorica, now Brittany; also called Benwic.

The street in the City of London of this name was first so called in the time of Queen Elizabeth; previously it was known as *Britten* or *Brettone Street*, and is said to have been so called because the Dukes of Brittany had had a mansion on this site. The old name of the northern part of Little Britain was *Duke Street*.

Little Englanders. An opprobrious name which became popular about the time of the last Boer War for those who upheld the doctrine that the English should concern themselves with England only, and were opposed to any extension of the Empire.

Little Entente was the name given to some of the Near Eastern countries before World War II. Czechoslovakia, Yugoslavia, and Rumania signed formal treaties of alliance in 1920 and again in 1929, one of the chief objects being to prevent the restoration of the Hapsburgs to the throne of Hungary.

Little John. A semi-legendary character in the Robin Hood cycle, a big stalwart fellow, first named John Little (or John Nailor), who encountered Robin Hood, and gave him a sound thrashing, after which he was rechristened, and Robin stood godfather.

"This infant was called John Little," quoth he;
"Which, name shall be changed anon.
The words we'll transpose, so wherever he goes,
His name shall be called Little John".
RITSON: *Robin Hood*, xxi.

Little Mary. *See* MARY.

Little Masters. A name applied to certain designers who worked for engravers, etc., in the 16th and 17th centuries, because their designs were on a small scale, fit for copper or wood. The most famous are Jost Amman, Hans Burgmair (who made drawings in wood illustrative of the triumph of the Emperor Maximilian), Albert Altdorfer, and Heinrich Aldegraver.

Albert Dürer and Lucas van Leyden made the art renowned and popular.

Little Parliament, The. Another name for the Barebones Parliament (*q.v.*).

Little Red Ridinghood. This nursery tale is, with slight alterations, common to Sweden, Germany, and France. It comes to us from the French *Le Petit Chaperon Rouge*, in Charles Perrault's *Contes des Temps*, and was probably derived from Italy. The *finale*, which tells of the arrival of a huntsman who slits open the wolf and restores little Red Ridinghood and her grandmother to life, is a German addition.

Little Rhody. The State of Rhode Island, U.S.A.

Liturgy. The Greek word from which this comes means *public service*, or *worship of the gods*, and the arranging of the dancing and singing on public festivals, the equipping and manning of ships, etc. In the Church of England it means the religious forms prescribed in the Book of Common Prayer.

Liver. The liver was anciently supposed to be the seat of love; hence, when Longaville reads the verses, Biron says, in an aside, "This is the liver-vein, which makes flesh a deity" (*Love's Labour's Lost*, iv, 3); and in *The Merry Wives of Windsor* (ii, 1) Pistol speaks of Falstaff as loving Ford's wife "with liver burning hot."

Another superstition concerning this organ was that the liver of a coward contained no blood; hence such expressions as **white-livered, lily-livered,** and Sir Toby's remark in *Twelfth Night* (ii, 2): —

For Andrew, if he were opened, and you find so much blood in his liver as will clog the foot of a flea, I'll eat the rest of the anatomy.

In the auspices taken by the Greeks and Romans before battle, if the liver of the animals sacrificed was healthy and blood-red, the omen was favourable; but if pale, it augured defeat.

Liverpool. There have been many guesses at the origin of this place-name (which was first recorded about 1190, as *Leverpol*), the most probable deriving it from Welsh *Llyr-pwl*, the sea-pool, though both the Norse *hlithar polir,* the pool of the slape, and Eng. *lither* (stagnant) *pool* have something to recommend them.

It was in the 17th century that antiquarians invented the *liver*, a mythical bird, to account for the name. They evolved it from the bird in the arms of the city, which was intended for an heraldic representation of the eagle of St. John the Evangelist.

A native of Liverpool is called a **Liverpudlian** or a **Dicky Sam**.

Livery. What is delivered. The clothes of a manservant delivered to him by his master. The stables to which your horse is delivered for keep. Splendid dresses were formerly given to all the members of royal households; barons and knights gave uniforms to their retainers, and even a duke's son, serving as a page, was clothed in the *livery* of the prince he served.

What livery is we know well enough; it is the allowance of horse-meate to keepe horses at lively; the which word, I guess, is derived of delivering forth their nightly food. — *Spenser on Ireland.*

The colours of the livery of menservants should be those of the field and principal charge of the armorial shield; hence the royal livery is scarlet trimmed with gold.

Liverymen. The freemen of the London livery companies are so called because they were entitled to wear the livery of their respective companies.

Livy. Livy of France, The. Juan de Mariana (1537-1624).

Livy of Portugal, The. João de Barros, the chief of the Portuguese historians (1496-1570).

Lizard. Supposed, at one time, to be venomous, and hence a "lizard's leg" was an ingredient of the witches' cauldron in *Macbeth.*

Poison be their drink! . . .
Their chiefest prospect murdering basilisks!
Their softest touch as smart as lizard's stings!
2 Henry VI, iii, 2.

Lizard Point (Cornwall). Gaelic, "the point of the high (*ard*) fort (*lis*)." *Ard* appears in a large number of place names — *Ardrossan* (the little high point), *Ardwick* (the high town), the *Ardennes* (high valleys), etc., and *Lis* in *Lismore, Liskeard, Ballylesson* (the town of the little fort), etc.

Lounge lizard. A phrase current in the 1920s to describe a young man who spent his time, or, often made his living, by dancing and waiting upon elderly women.

Llew Llaw Gyffes, or the Lion with the Steady Hand, a hero of the type of Hercules, was worshipped in ancient Britain and until the 19th century in some parts of Wales. His death on the first Sunday in August, was celebrated by a feast called Lugh-mass, sometimes confounded with Lammas.

Lloyd's. An association of underwriters, merchants, shipowners, brokers, etc., principally dealing with ocean-borne commerce, marine insurance, and the publication of shipping intelligence. So called because the society was founded (1689) in Tower Street, and moved (1691) to a coffee-house kept in Lombard Street by one Edward Lloyd. In 1774 the offices, or *Lloyd's Rooms*, were removed to the Royal Exchange; in 1928 to Leadenhall Street.

Load Line is another name for the Plimsoll Mark (*q.v.*) that is carried amidships by every vessel of the Merchant Navy. It shows the maximum depth to which she may be loaded in salt water, in fresh water, at different times of the year, in different oceans, etc.

Loaf. In sacred art a loaf held in the hand is an attribute of St. Philip the Apostle, St. Osyth, St. Joanna, St. Nicholas, St. Godfrey, and of many other saints noted for their charity to the poor.

With an eye to the loaves and fishes. With a view to the material benefits to be derived. The allusion is to the Gospel story of the crowd following Christ, not for the spiritual doctrines He taught, but for the loaves and fishes distributed by Him amongst them.

Jesus answered them and said, Verily, verily, I say unto you, Ye seek Me, not because ye saw the miracles, but because ye did eat of the loaves, and were filled.— John vi, 26,

Loafer. One who idles away his time, or saunters about as though he had all his life to do it in; a lazy "do-nothing." The word was originally American slang (about 1830), and was probably German—either a mispronunciation of *lover*, or from *laufen*, to run, go, move.

Loathly Lady. A stock character of the old romances who is so hideous that everyone is deterred from marrying her. When, however, she at last finds a husband her ugliness—the effect of enchantment—disappears, and she becomes a model of beauty. Her story—a very common one, in which sometimes the enchanted beauty has to assume the shape of a serpent or some hideous monster—is the feminine counterpart of that of "Beauty and the Beast" (*q.v.*).

Lobby. A vestibule or corridor, usually giving access to several apartments, from Med. Lat. *lobia*, a word used in the monasteries for the passages (connected with *lodge*). In the Houses of Parliament the name is given to the corridors ("Division Lobbies") to which members of the Commons go to vote, and also to the large anteroom to which the public are admitted. The latter gives us the verb **to lobby**, to solicit the vote of a member or to seek to influence members, and the noun **lobbyist**, one who does this.

Loblolly. A sailors' term for spoon-victuals, pap, water-gruel, and so on.

Loblolly boy. A surgeon's mate in the Navy, a lad not yet out of his spoon-meat.

Loblolly-boy is a person on board a man-of-war who attends the surgeon and his mates, but knows as much

about the business of a seaman as the author of this poem.—*The Patent* (1776).

Lobsters. Soldiers used to be popularly called lobsters, because they were "turned red" when enlisted into the service. But the term was originally applied to a troop of horse soldiers in the Great Rebellion, clad in armour which covered them as a shell.

Sir William Waller received from London (in 1643) a fresh regiment of 500 horse, under the command of Sir Arthur Haslerig, which were so prodigiously armed that they were called, by the king's party "the regiment of lobsters," because of their bright iron shells with which they were covered, being perfect cuirassiers, and were the first seen so armed on either side.—CLARENDON: *History of the Rebellion*, iii, 91.

Local, in colloquial parlance, means the nearest or the most frequented public house.

Local option is the choice allowed to a town, county, or other locality to decide what course it shall take on a given question, specifically the sale of liquor. In 1913 Carlisle was given local option in this sense, in each area the electors having the decision as to whether or not intoxicating liquor should be sold.

Lochinvar (lok in var'), being in love with a lady at Netherby Hall, persuaded her to dance one last dance. She was condemned to marry a "laggard in love and a dastard in war," but her young chevalier swung her into his saddle and made off with her, before the "bridegroom" and his servants could recover from their astonishment. (Scott: *Marmion*.)

Loch Ness Monster. In April, 1933, a motorist driving along the shore of Loch Ness, Scotland, saw at some distance from the land what seemed a strange object, subsequently described as being 30 ft. long, with two humps, a snake-like head at the end of a long neck, and two flippers about the middle of the body. It was "seen" by others, and a brisk tourist trade began to centre around its movements. Public interest and excitement were worked up by newspaper reports, and the question of an official investigation was raised in Parliament, but negatived. A well-known circus proprietor offered £20,000 for the monster, but it resisted all baits and allurements. From time to time fresh evidences of its presence have been reported, but scientists have found few details to arouse their interest. The popular theory is that the creature is a diplodoccus or some prehistoric survival, but scientists preserve an open mind on the existence or nature of the Loch Ness Monster.

Locksley Hall. Tennyson's poem of this name (1842) deals with an imaginary place and an imaginary hero. The Lord of Locksley Hall fell in love with his cousin Amy; she married a rich clown, and he, indignant at this, declared he would wed a savage; he changed his mind, however, and decided, "Better fifty years of Europe than a cycle of Cathay."

In 1886 Tennyson published *Locksley Hall Sixty Years After*, another dramatic poem.

Locksmith's Daughter. A key.

Lock, Stock, and Barrel. The whole of anything. The lock, stock, and barrel of a gun is the complete firearm.

Locrine (lok rīn'). Father of Sabrina, and eldest son of the mythical Brutus, King of ancient Britain. On the death of his father he became king of Loegria. (Geoffrey: *Brit. Hist.*, ii, 5.)

Virgin daughter of Locrine,
Sprung from old Anchises' line.
     MILTON: *Comus*, 942-3.

An anonymous tragedy, based on Holinshed and Geoffrey of Monmouth, was published under this name in 1595. As the words "Newly set foorth, overseene and corrected, By W. S." appear on the title-page, it was at one time ascribed to Shakespeare. It has also been ascribed to Marlowe, Greene, and Peele—the weight of evidence being rather in favour of the last named.

Locum tenens (lō' kum tē' nens) (Lat.). One (especially a doctor) acting temporarily for another.

Locus. Latin for a place.

Locus delicti. The place where a crime was committed.

Locus in quo (Lat.). The place in question, the spot mentioned.

Locus pœnitentiæ (Lat.). Place for repentance—that is, the licence of drawing back from a bargain, which can be done before any act has been committed to confirm it. In the interview between Esau and his father Isaac, St. Paul says that the former "found no place for repentance, though he sought it carefully with tears" (*Heb.* xii, 17)—*i.e.* no means whereby Isaac could break his bargain with Jacob.

Locus sigilli (Lat.). The place where the seal is to be set; usually abbreviated in documents to "L.S."

Locus standi (Lat.). Recognized position, acknowledged right or claim, especially in courts of law. We say such-and-such a one has no *locus standi* in society.

Locusta (lō kūs' tà). A woman who murders those she professes to nurse, or those whom it is her duty to take care of. Locusta lived in the early days of the Roman Empire, poisoned Claudius and Britannicus, and attempted to destroy Nero; bat, being found out, she was put to death.

Lode. Originally a ditch that guides or leads, water into a river or sewer, from A.S. *lad*, way, course (connected with *to lead*); hence, in mines, the vein that leads or guides to ore.

Lodestar. The North Star or Pole Star; the *leading-star* by which mariners are guided (*see* LODE).

Your eyes are lodestars.—*Midsummer Night's Dream*, i, 1.

Lodestone, Loadstone. The magnet or stone that guides.

Loegria or **Logres** (lo eg' ri à, lō' gres). England is so called by Geoffrey of Monmouth, from Locrine (*q.v.*).

His [Brute's] three sons divide the land by consent;
Locrine had the middle part, Loegra.—MILTON: *History of England*, Bk. i.

Thus Cambria to her right, what would herself restore,
And rather than to lose Loegria, looks for more.
     DRAYTON: *Polyolbion*, iv.

Log. Instrument for measuring the velocity of a ship in motion. In its simplest form it is a flat piece of wood, some six inches in radius, in the shape of a quadrant, and made so that it will float perpendicularly. To this is fastened the log-line, knotted at intervals. *See* KNOT.

Log-book. On board ship, the journal in which the "logs" are entered. It contains also all general transactions pertaining to the ship and its crew, such as the strength and course of the winds, everything worthy of note.

Log-cabin Campaign (U.S.A.). Political campaign in 1840, in which Gen. W. H. Harrison is said to have lived in a log-cabin and subsisted mainly on hard cider.

Log-rolling. Applied in politics to the "give and take" principle, by which one party will further certain interests of another in return for assistance given in passing their own measures; in literary circles it means mutual admiration. The mutual admirers are called "log-rollers," and the allusion (originally American) is to neighbours who assist a new settler to roll away the logs of his "clearing."

Logs. An early Australian name for prison, changed with time and circumstances to *The Bricks*.

Loganberry. A cross between the raspberry and blackberry; so called from Judge Logan, of California, who was the first to cultivate it.

Loggerheads. Fall to loggerheads: to squabbling and fisticuffs. The word is used by Shakespeare. *Logger* was the name given to the heavy wooden clog fastened to the legs of grazing horses to prevent their straying.

Logres, Logria. *See* LOEGRIA.

Logris. Same as Locrine (*q.v.*).

Lohengrin (lō′ en grin). A son of Percival, in German legend, attached to the Grail Cycle, and Knight of the Swan. He appears at the close of Wolfram von Eschenbach's *Parzival* (about 1210), and in other German romances, where he is the deliverer of Elsa, Princess of Brabant, who has been dispossessed by Tetramund and Ortrud. He arrives at Antwerp in a skiff drawn by a swan, champions Elsa, and becomes her husband on the sole condition that she shall not ask his name or lineage. She is prevailed upon to do so on the marriage-night, and he, by his vows to the Grail, is obliged, to disclose his identity, but at the same time disappears. The swan returns for him, and he goes; but not before retransforming the swan into Elsa's brother Gottfried, who, by, the wiles of the sorceress Ortrud, had been obliged to assume that form. Wagner's opera of this name was composed in 1847.

Loins. Gird up your loins. Brace yourself for vigorous action, or energetic endurance. The Jews wore loose garments, which they girded about their loins when they travellèd or worked.

Gird up the loins of your mind.—1 *Pet.* i, 13.

My little finger shall be thicker than my father's loins (1 *Kings* xii, 10). My lightest tax shall be heavier than the most oppressive tax of my predecessor. The arrogant answer of Rehoboam to the deputation which waited on him to entreat an alleviation of "the yoke" laid on them by Solomon. The reply caused the revolt of all the tribes, except those of Judah and Benjamin.

Loki (lō′ ki). The god of strife and spirit of evil in Norse mythology, son of the giant Firbauti and Laufey, or Nal, the friend of the enemy of the gods, and father of the Midgard Serpent, Fenrir, and Hel. It was he who artfully contrived the death of Balder (*q.v.*). He was finally chained to a rock with ten chains, and— according to one legend—will so continue till the Twilight of the Gods, when he will break his bonds; the heavens will disappear, the earth be swallowed up by the sea, fire shall consume the elements, and even Odin, with all his kindred deities, shall perish. Another story has it that he was freed at Ragnarok, and that he and Heimdall fought till both were slain.

Lollards. The early German reformers and the followers of Wyclif were so called. An ingenious derivation is given by Bailey, who suggests the Latin word *lolium* (darnel), because these reformers were deemed "tares in God's wheat-field," but the name is from Mid. Dut. *lollaerd*, a mutterer, one who mumbles over prayers and hymns.

Gregory XI, in one of his bulls against Wyclif, urged the clergy to extirpate this *lolium*.

London. The origin of the name is uncertain, but it first appears in *Tacitus* (Lib. XIV, ch. xxxiii, 61 A.D.):

At Suetonius mira constantia medios inter hostes Londinium perrexit, cognomento quidem coloniæ non insigne, sed copia negotiatorum et commeatum maxime celebre.

Stow, following Geoffrey of Monmouth, says that it was originally called Troynoyant (*q.v.*), and that Cæsar's "cittie of the Trino-bantes" meant London. By later Latin writers it was frequently called "Londinium Augusta."

The first syllable may represent Welsh *lli*, water, and the second be the Celtic *dun*, a hill-fort—the fort on the water; *lon-* may equally well be Celtic *lon*, a marsh, or *llwyn*, a grove, while another authority says that it is Welsh *llong*, a ship—the City of Ships.

Francis Crossley derives the name from *Luan-dun* (Celtic), City of the Moon, and tradition says there was once a temple to Diana (the Moon) where St. Paul's now stands; but he says that Greenwich (*q.v.*) is *Grianwich* (City of the Sun), also Celtic. It would fill a page to give a list of guesses made at the derivation of the word London.

London Bridge. There was a bridge over the Thames in the 10th century. There was a new one of wood in 1014. The stone bridge (1176-1209) was by Peter of Colechurch. The present London Bridge, constructed of granite, was begun in 1824, and finished in seven years. It was built some 50 yards west of the old bridge, which started from Fish Street Hill. It was designed by Sir John Rennie, and cost £1,458,000. Till 1750 London Bridge was the only bridge crossing the Thames in London.

London Regiment consists of two regular battalions of the City of London Regiment (Royal Fusiliers) and a number of territorial battalions including the London Rifle Brigade, Kensingtons, Artists Rifles, London Scottish, etc.

London Stone. The ancient Roman stone now fixed for security in the wall of St. Swithin's church, facing Cannon Street station, and guarded by an iron grille. It has two inscriptions, one in Latin and one in English. The latter runs thus:—

London stone. Commonly believed to be a Roman work, long placed about xxxv feet hence towards the south-west, and afterwards built into the wall of this church, was, for more carefvl protection and transmission to future ages, better secured by the churchwardens in the year of OVR LORD MDCCCLXIX.

It is supposed to have been the central milliarium (*milestone*) of Roman London, similar to that in the Forum of Rome, from which the high roads radiated and were measured.

Londonderry. This Northern Ireland county took its prefix of "London" when, in 1609, much of the land was made over to the corporation of London. The capital city, long known as Derry, was besieged for 15 weeks by James II in 1689 and its citizens were reduced to great distress before the relieving fleet broke the boom across the harbour, June 30th, 1689.

Lone Star State. The state of Texas, U.S.A.

Long. For **Long chalks, dozen, odds,** etc., *see* these words.

Long Meg and her daughters. In the neighbourhood of Penrith, Cumberland, is a circle of 67 (Camden says 77) stones, some of them 10 ft. high, ranged in a circle. Some seventeen paces off, on the south side, is a single stone, 15 ft, high, called *Long Meg*, the shorter ones being called *her daughters*.

This, and the Robrick stones in Oxfordshire, are supposed to have been erected at the investiture of some Danish kings, like the Kingstoler in Denmark and the Moresteen in Sweden.—CAMDEN: *Britannia*.

Long Parliament. The parliament that sat 12 years and 5 months, from November 2nd, 1640, to April 20th, 1653, when it was dissolved by Cromwell. A fragment of it called "The Rump" (*q.v.*), continued till the Restoration, in 1660.

Long Range Desert Patrol. A British military organization of volunteers in World War II who, in N. Africa, penetrated behind the enemy's lines to do as much damage as possible. Their most celebrated exploit was the raid on Field Marshal Rommel's headquarters, carried out by a small group under Lieut-Col. Keyes, who was posthumously awarded the V.C.

Long-Sword (*Longue épée*). The surname of William, the first Duke of Normandy (d. 943). He was the great-great-grandfather of William the Conqueror, and so a direct ancestor of our reigning House. The name was also given to William, third Earl of Salisbury (d. 1226), a natural son of Henry II and (according to a late tradition) Fair Rosamund.

He enjoyed many honours and was one of those who advised John to seal Magna Charta.

Cut and long tail. One and another, all of every description. The phrase had its origin in the practice of cutting the tails of certain dogs and horses, and leaving others in their natural state, so that cut and long tail horses or dogs included all the species, Master Slender says he will maintain Anne Page like a gentlewoman. "Ah!" says he—

That I will, come cut and long tail under the degree of a squire [*i.e.* as well as any man can who is not a squire].—SHAKESPEARE: *Merry Wives of Windsor*, iii, 4.

Long words. "Honorificabilitudinitatibus," (*q.v.*) has often been called the longest word in the English language; "quadradimensionality" is almost as long, and "antidisestablishmentarianism" beats it by one letter.

While there is some limit to the coining of polysyllabic words by the conglomeration of prefixes, combining forms, and suffixes (*e.g.* "deanthropomorphization," "inanthropomorphizability"), there is little to the length to which chemists will go in the nomenclature of compounds, and none at all to that indulged in by facetious romancers like Rabelais, the author of *Croquemitaine*. The chemists furnish us with such concatenations (for they are scarcely *words*) as " nitrophenylenediamine," and "tetramethyldiamidobenzhydrols"; but the worst in this sort are far surpassed by the nonsense words found in Urquhart and Motteux's translation of Rabelais. The following comes from chapter xv of Bk. IV:—

He was grown quite esperruquanchurelubelouzeririeliced down to his very heel . . . (J. M. Cohen in Penguin Classics: . . . bruisedblueandcontused . . .)

The longest place-name in Britain is that of a village in Anglesea, Llanfairpwllgwyngyllgogerychwyrndrobwllllandyssiliogogogoch (usually called Llanfairpwll). In the postal directory the first twenty letters only are given as a sufficient address for practical purposes, but the full name contains 59 letters. The meaning is, "The church of St. Mary in a hollow of white hazel, near to the rapid whirlpool, and to St. Tisilio church, near to a red cave."

The longest English surname is said to be Featherstonehaugh, often pronounced făn'-shaw.

The longest English monosyllables are probably "stretched" and "screeched."

The German language lends itself to very extensive agglomerations of syllables, but the following official title of a North Bohemian official—Lebensmittelzuschusseinstellungs kommissionsvorsitzenderstellvertreter," *i.e.*

Deputy-President of the Food-Rationing-Winding-up-Commission—would be hard to beat.

Longchamps (long shong). The racecourse at the end of the Bois de Boulogne, Paris. An abbey formerly stood there, and it was long celebrated for the promenade of smartly dressed Parisians which took place on the Wednesday, Thursday, and Friday of Holy Week.

The custom dates from the time when all who could do so went to the abbey to hear the Ténèbres sung in Holy Week; and it survives as an excellent opportunity to display the latest spring fashions.

Longevity (lon jev' i ti). The oldest man of modern times was Thomas Carn, if we may rely on the parish register of St. Leonard's, Shoreditch, where it is recorded that he died in the reign of Queen Elizabeth, aged 207. He was born in 1381, in the reign of Richard II, lived in the reigns of ten sovereigns, and died in 1588. Henry Jenkins was only 160 when he died in 1670 and remembered going (when he was a boy of twelve) with a load of arrows, to be used in the battle of Flodden Field. Thomas Parr died in 1635 at the age of 152. William Wakley (according to the register of St. Andrew's Church, Shifnal, Salop) was at least 124 when he died. He was baptized at Idsal 1590, and buried at Adbaston, November 28th, 1714, and he lived in the reigns of eight sovereigns. Mary Yates, of Lizard Common, Shifnal, married her third husband at the age of 92, and died in 1776, at the age of 127.

Look. To look black, blue, daggers, a gift-horse, etc., *see* these words.

Look before you leap. Consider well before you act.

> And look before you ere you leap,
> For, as you sow, you're like to reap.
>
> BUTLER: *Hudibras*, canto ii, Pt. ii, 502.

It is unlucky to break a looking-glass. The nature of the ill-luck varies; thus, if a maiden, she will never marry; if a married woman, it betokens a death, etc. This superstition arose from the use made of mirrors in former times by magicians. If in their operations the mirror used was broken, the magician was obliged to give over his operation, and the unlucky inquirer could receive no answer.

Looping the Loop. The airman's term for the evolution which consists of describing a perpendicular circle in the air; at the top of the circle, or "loop," the airman and the aeroplane are, of course, upside down. The term comes from a kind of switchback that used to be popular at fairs, etc., in which a rapidly moving car or bicycle performed a similar evolution on a perpendicular circular track.

Loose. Figuratively—of lax morals; dissolute, dissipated.

> Drummond . . . was a loose and profane man: but a sense of honour which his two kinsmen wanted restrained him from a public apostasy.—MACAULAY: *Hist. of Eng.*, ch. vi.

A loose fish. See FISH.

At a loose end. Without employment, or uncertain what to do next.

Having a tile loose. See TILE.

On the loose. Dissolute (which is *dis-solutus*). *Living on the loose* is leading a dissolute life.

To play fast and loose. See FAST.

Loose-strife. The name of this plant is an instance of erroneous translation. The Greeks called it *lusimachion*, from the personal name *Lusimachos*, and this was treated as though it were *lusi-*, from *luein*, to loose, and *mache*, strife. Pliny refers the name to one of Alexander's generals, said to have discovered its virtues, but the mistake obtained such currency that the author of *Flora Domestica* tells us that the Romans put these flowers under the yokes of oxen to keep them from quarrelling with each other; for (says he) the plant keeps off flies and gnats and thus relieves horses and oxen from a great source of irritation. Similarly in Fletcher's *Faithful Shepherdess* (II, ii), we read—

> Yellow Lysimachus, to give sweet rest,
> To the faint shepherd, killing, where it comes,
> All busy gnats, and every fly that hums.

Lope. See SLOPE.

Lord. A nobleman, a peer of the realm; formerly (and in some connexions still), a ruler, a master, the holder of a manor.

The word is a contraction of A.S. *hlaford*, *hlaf*, loaf, and modern *ward*, *i.e.* the bread-guardian, or *-keeper*, the head of the household (*cp.* LADY); all members of the House of Lords are Lords (the Archbishops and Bishops being Lords Spiritual, and the lay peers Lords Temporal); and the word is given as a courtesy title as a prefix to the Christian and surname of the younger sons of dukes and marquises, and to the eldest sons of viscounts and earls when the fathers hold subordinate titles as barons, and as a title of honour to certain official personages, as the Lord Chief Justice and other Judges, the Lord Mayor, Lord Advocate, Lord Rector, etc. A baron is called by his title of peerage (either a surname or territorial designation), prefixed by the title "Lord," as "Lord Dawson.," "Lord Islington," and it may also be substituted in other than strictly ceremonial use for "Marquis," "Earl," or "Viscount," the *of* being dropped, as "Lord Salisbury" (for "the Marquis of Salisbury"), "Lord Derby" ("The Earl of Derby"), etc.; this cannot be done in the case of dukes.

Lords and ladies. The popular name of the wild arum, *Arum maculatum*.

My Lord. The correct form to use in addressing Judges of the Supreme Court (usually slurred to "M'Lud"), also the respectful form of address to bishops, noblemen under the rank of a Duke, Lord Mayors, Lord Provosts, and the Lord Advocate.

The Lord knows who, what, where, etc. Flippant expressions used to denote one's own entire ignorance of the matter.

> Great families of yesterday we show,
> And lords, whose parents were the Lord knows who.
> DEFOE: *The True-Born Englishman*, 374.
> Ask where's the north? At York, 'tis on the Tweed;
> In Scotland, at the Orcades; and there,
> At Greenland, Zembla, or the Lord knows where.
> POPE: *Essay on Man*, ii, 217.

The Lord's Day. Sunday.

To live like a lord. To fare luxuriously, live like a fighting-cock (*q.v.*).

To lord it, or **lord it over.** To play the lord; to rule tyrannically, to domineer.

> Yon grey towers that still
> Rise up as if to lord it over air.
> WORDSWORTH: *The Punishment of Death*, Sonn. i.

When our Lord falls in our Lady's lap. When Easter Sunday falls on the same date as Lady Day (March 25th). This is said to bode ill for England. In the 19th century the combination occurred only twice (1883 and 1894); in the 20th its sole occurrence was in 1951.

Lord's Cricket Ground. The headquarters of the Marylebone Cricket Club (M.C.C.) and of cricket generally, is at St. John's Wood, London. Its founder, Thomas Lord (1757-1832), was groundsman at the White Conduit Club, London, in 1780. In 1797 he started a cricket ground of his own on the site of what is now Dorset Square, moving the turf in 1811 to a new site near Regent's Canal whence, in 1814, he transferred it to the present position.

Lorel. A worthless person; a rogue or black-guard. The word is from *loren*, the past part. of the old verb *leese*, to lose, and is chiefly remembered through "Cock Lorell". *See* COCK LORELL'S BOTE.

> Here I set before the good Reader the leud, lousey language of these lewtering Luskes and lasy Lorrels, wherewith they bye and sell the common people as they pas through the countrey. Whych language they terme Peddelar's Frenche.—*Harman's Caveat* (1567).

Lorelei (lo' rĕ lī). The name of a steep rock on the right bank of the Rhine, near St. Goar, some 430 ft. high. It is noted for its remarkable echo and is the traditional haunt of a siren who lures boatmen to their death. Heine and others have written poems on it, and Max Bruch made it the subject of an opera (*Die Lorelei*) produced in 1864. Mendelssohn began an uncompleted opera with the same title in 1847.

Loss. To be at a loss. To be unable to decide. To be puzzled or embarrassed. As: "I am at a loss for the proper word."

Lost Tribes. The term used for that portion of the Hebrew race that disappeared from North Palestine about 140 years before the dispersion of the Jews. This disappearance has caused much speculation, especially among those who look forward to a restoration of the Hebrews as foretold in the O.T. In 1649 John Sadler suggested that the English were of Israelitish origin. This suggestion was developed by Richard Brothers, the half-crazy enthusiast who declared himself Prince of the Hebrews and Ruler of the World (1792). The theory has since been developed by other writers.

Lothario (lo thâr' i ō). **A gay Lothario.** A gay libertine, a seducer of women, a debauchee. The character is from Rowe's tragedy *The Fair Penitent* (1703), which is founded on Massinger's *Fatal Dowry*, though Rowe probably got the name from Davenant's *Cruel Brother* (1630), where is a similar character with the same name.

> Is this that haughty, gallant, gay Lothario?
> *Fair Penitent*, v, 1.

Lothian (lōth' i an) (Scotland). So named, according to tradition, from King Lot, or Lothus, Llew, the second son of Arthur, also called Lothus. He was the father of Modred, leader of the rebellious army that fought at Camlan, 537 A.D.

Lotus (lō' tus). A name given to many plants, *e.g.* by the Egyptians to various species of water-lily, by the Hindus and Chinese to the Nelumbo (a water-bean, *Nymphœaceœ speciosum*), their "sacred lotus," and by the Greeks to *Zizyphus Lotus*, a north African shrub of the natural order Rhamneæ, the fruit of which was used for food.

According to Mohammed a lotus-tree stands in the seventh heaven, on the right hand of the throne of God, and the Egyptians pictured God sitting on a lotus above the watery mud. Jamblichus says the leaves and fruit of the lotus-tree being *round* represent "the motion of intellect"; its towering up through mud symbolizes the eminency of divine intellect over matter; and the Deity sitting on it implies His intellectual sovereignty. (*Myster. Egypt.*, sec. 7, cap. ii, p. 151.)

The classic myth is that *Lotis*, a daughter of Neptune, fleeing from Priapus was changed into a tree, which was called *Lotus* after her, while another story goes that *Dryope* of Œchalia was one day carrying her infant son, when she plucked a lotus flower for his amusement, and was instantaneously transformed into a lotus.

Lotus-eaters or **Lotophagi**, in Homeric legend, are a people who ate of the lotus-tree (thought to be intended for *Zizyphus Lotus, see above*), the effect of which was to make them forgot their friends and homes, and to lose all desire of returning to their native country, their only wish being to live in idleness in Lotus-land (*Odyssey*, xi). Hence, a *lotus-eater* is one living in ease and luxury.

Louis, St. (Louis IX of France, 1215, 1226-70), is usually represented as holding the Saviour's crown of thorns and the cross; sometimes, however, he is pictured with a pilgrim's staff, and sometimes with the standard of the cross, the allusion in all cases being to his crusades. He was canonized in 1297, his feast day being August 25th.

Louisette. *See* GUILLOTINE.

Louisiana (loo ēz 'i ăn à). U.S.A. So named in compliment to Louis XIV of France. The name originally applied to the French possessions in the Mississippi Valley.

The Louisiana Purchase was the acquisition by the U.S. Government in 1803 of New Orleans and a vast tract of territory extending westward from the Mississippi to the Rockies, and northward from the Gulf of Mexico to the Canadian border, from the French under Napoleon (then First Consul) for the sum of $15,000,000.

Lounge Lizard. *See* LIZARD.

Lourdes (loord). A famous scene of pilgrimage, situated in the south-west of France. In 1858 Bernadette Soubirous, a simple peasant girl, claimed that the Virgin Mary had appeared to her on eighteen occasions. Investigation failed to shake her narrative, and a spring with miraculous healing properties that appeared at the same time began to draw invalids from all parts of the world. Lourdes became the greatest sanctuary in Christendom and is resorted to by thousands, sick and well, every year.

Louver or **Louvre.** The tower or turret of mediæval buildings, originally designed for a sort of chimney to let out the smoke by means of *louvre boards, i.e.* narrow sloping and overlapping boards which, while allowing smoke to emerge, prevented the entrance of rain. *Louvre* is the old Fr. *lover* or *lovier*, probably from Old High Ger. *lauba*, whence our *lodge*.

Louvre (loo' vrė). The former royal palace of the French kings in Paris.

Dagobert is said to have built here a hunting-seat, but the present buildings were begun by Francis I in 1541. Since the French Revolution the greater part of the Louvre has been used for the national museum and art gallery.

He'll make your Paris Louvre shake for it.
Henry V, ii, 4.

Love. The word is connected with Sanskrit *lubh*, to desire (Lat. *lubet*, it pleases), and was *lufu* in A.S.

A labour of love. Work undertaken for the love of the thing, without regard to pay.

Love and lordship never like fellowship. Neither lovers nor princes can brook a rival.

Love in a cottage. A marriage for love without sufficient means to maintain one's social status. "When poverty comes in at the door, love flies out of the window."

Love in a hut, with water and a crust,
Is—Love, forgive us!—cinders, ashes, dust;
Love in a palace is, perhaps, at last
More grievous torment than a hermit's fast.
KEATS: *Lamia*, Pt. ii.

Love me, love my dog. If you love anyone, you will like all that belongs to him. St. Bernard quotes this proverb in Latin, *Qui me amat, amat et canem meam.*

Love's Girdle. *See* CESTUS.

Not for love or money. Unobtainable, either for payment or for entreaties.

There is no love lost between so and so. The persons referred to have no love for each other. Formerly the phrase was used in exactly the opposite sense—it was *all* love between them, and none of it went a-missing. In the old ballad *The Babes in the Wood* we have—

No love between these two was lost
Each was to other kind.

To play for love. To play without stakes, for nothing.

Love-lock. A small curl worn by women, plastered to the temples; sometimes called a *beau* or *bow* catcher. A man's "love-lock" is called a *bell-rope*. At the latter end of the 16th century the love-lock was a long lock of hair hanging in front of the shoulders, curled and decorated with bows and ribbons.

Love-powders or **Potions** were drugs to excite lust. Once these love-charms were generally believed in; thus, Brabantio accuses Othello of having bewitched Desdemona with "drugs to waken motion"; and Lady Grey was accused of having bewitched Edward IV "by strange potions and amorous charms" (*Fabian*, p. 495).

Love-in-Idleness. One of the numerous names of the pansy or heartsease (*q.v.*). Fable has it that it was originally white, but was changed to purple by Cupid.

> Yet marked I where the bolt of Cupid fell,
> It fell upon a little Western flower.
> Before, milk-white, now purple with love's wound;
> The maidens call it Love-in-idleness.
> *Midsummer Night's Dream*, ii, 1.

Love's Labour's Lost. The exact form of the title of this, probably the first of Shakespeare's plays (1588), cannot be ascertained, but the above is the generally accepted form, the first "s" denoting the possessive, and the second the contraction of "is." On the title-page of the first quarto it is given as "A Pleasant Conceited Comedie called, Loves labors lost," with no apostrophes; the running head-line of this edition, however, is "Love's Labour's Lost," while the title given to the play in the first folio (1623) is "Loves Labour's Lost." Other variants are Mere's "Love labors lost" and Robert Tofte's "Loves Labour Lost" (both 1598), Sir Walter Cope's "Loves Labore lost" (1604), Drummond of Hawthornden's "Loves Labors Lost" (1606), and Dryden's "Love's labour lost" (1672).

Lovel, the Dog. See RAT; CAT, etc.

Lovelace. The principal male character of Richardson's novel *Clarissa Harlowe* (1748). He is a selfish voluptuary, a man of fashion, whose sole ambition is to seduce young women, and he is—like Lothario (*q.v.*)—often taken as the type of a libertine. Crabbe calls him "rich, proud, and crafty; handsome, brave, and gay."

Low. To lay low is transitive, and means to overthrow or to kill; **to lie low** is intransitive, and means to be abased, or dead, and (in slang use) to bide one's time, to do nothing at the moment.

In low water. Financially embarrassed; or, in a bad state of health. The phrase comes from seafaring men; *cp.* "stranded," "left high and dry."

Low-bell. A bell formerly used in night-fowling. The birds were first roused from their slumber by its tinkling, and then dazzled by a *low* (Sc. for "a blaze" or "flame") so as to be easily caught. The word *low-bell* was, however, in earlier use for any small bell, such as a sheep-bell, without any connexion with lights or fowling.

The sound of the low-bell makes the birds lie close, so that they dare not stir whilst you are pitching the net: for the sound thereof is dreadful to them; but the sight of the fire, much more terrible, makes them fly up, so that they become instantly entangled in the net.—*British Sportsman* (1792).

Low Church. The popular name given to the evangelical party in the Church of England which maintains the essential Protestantism of that institution, adheres to the doctrinal and devotional formulas of the Book of Common Prayer, and regards the Bible as the ultimate rule of faith.

Low Sunday. The Sunday next after Easter.

The popular English name of Low Sunday has probably arisen from the contrast between the joys of Easter and the first return to ordinary Sunday services. On this Sunday, or sometimes on the fourth Sunday after Easter, it was the custom, in primitive days, for those who had been baptized the year before to keep an anniversary of their baptism, which was called the Annotine Easter, although the actual anniversary of the previous Easter might fall on another day.—*Blunt's Annotated Book of Common Prayer.*

Lower case. The printer's name for the small letters (minuscules) of a fount of type, as opposed to the capitals; these are, in a type-setter's "case," on a *lower* level than the others.

Lower Empire. The later Roman, especially the Western Empire, from about the foundation of the Eastern Empire in 364 to the fall of Constantinople in 1453.

Lower House, The. The second of any two legislative chambers; in England, the House of Commons.

Loyal. Only one regiment of all the British army is so called, and that is the Loyal North Lancashire. It was so called in 1793, and probably had some allusion to the French revolutionists.

Loyola, St. Ignatius (ig nā' shŭs loi ō' lä) (1491-1556). Founder of the Society of Jesus (the order of Jesuits), is depicted in art with the sacred monogram I.H.S. on his breast, or as contemplating it, surrounded by glory in the skies, in allusion to his claim that he had a miraculous knowledge of the mystery of the Trinity vouchsafed to him. He was a son of the Spanish ducal house of Loyola, and after being severely wounded at the siege of Pampeluna (1521) left the army and dedicated himself to the service of the Virgin. The society of Jesus (*see* JESUITS), which he projected in 1534, was confirmed by Paul III in 1540.

Luath (loo' ath). The name of Burns's favourite dog, and that which he gave to the poor man's dog representing the peasantry in his poem *The Twa Dogs*. Burns got the name

from Macpherson's *Ossian*, where it is borne by
Cuchullin's dog.

A ploughman's collie,
A rhyming, ranting, raving billie,
Wha for his friend and comrade had him,
And in his freaks had Luath ca'd him
After some dog in Highland sang
Was made lang syne—Lord knows how lang.
BURNS: *The Twa Dogs.*

Lucasta (lū kăs' tà), to whom Richard
Lovelace sang (1649), was Lucy Sacheverell,
called by him *lux casta, i.e.* Chaste Lucy.

Luce. The full-grown pike (*Esox lucius*), from
Gr. *lukos,* a wolf, meaning the wolf of fishes.

Shakespeare plays upon the words *luce* and
louse (*Merry Wives,* I, i) at the expense of
Justice Shallow, who stands for his old enemy,
Sir Thomas Lucy. According to Ferne's *Blazon
of Gentry* (1586) the arms of the Lucy family
were "Gules, three lucies hariant, argent," but
Dugdale (*Warwickshire,* 1656) gives a representation of a quartering of the Lucy arms where
the "dozen white luces" are shown.

They may give the dozen white luces in their coat.—
Merry Wives, i, 1.

Luce was also formerly used as a contraction
of *fleur-de-lys* (*q.v.*). The French messenger says
to the Regent Bedford—

Cropped are the flower de luces in your arms;
Of England's coat one-half is cut away.
1 *Henry VI,* i, 1.

Referring of course to the loss of France.

Lucifer (loo' si fĕr). Venus, as the morning
star. When she *follows* the sun and is an
evening star, she is called *Hesperus.*

Isaiah applied the epithet "Day-star" to the
king of Babylon who proudly boasted he would
ascend to the heavens and make himself equal
to God, but who was fated to be cast down to
the uttermost recesses of the pit. This epithet
was translated into "Lucifer"—

Take up this proverb against the king of Babylon,
and say, . . . How art thou fallen, from heaven, O Lucifer,
son of the morning!—*Is.* xiv, 4, 12.

By St. Jerome and other Fathers the name
was applied to Satan. Hence poets feign that
Satan, before he was driven out of heaven for
his pride, was called Lucifer, and Milton, in
Paradise Lost, gives this name to the demon of
"Sinful Pride," and hence, too, the phrase
Proud as Lucifer.

Lucifer-match, or **Lucifer.** The name
given by the inventor to one of the earliest
forms (about 1832) of matches tipped with
a combustible substance and ignited by friction, an improvement on the Congreves
and Prometheans (*qq.v.*); hence, any match
igniting by friction.

Luciferians. A sect of the 4th century, who
refused to hold any communion with the
Arians, who had renounced their "errors" and
been readmitted into the Church. So called
from Lucifer, Bishop of Cagliari, in Sardinia,
their leader.

Lucius. One of the mythical kings of
Britain, placed as the great-great-grandson of
Cymbeline (*q.v.*), and fabled as the first Christian
king. He is supposed to have died about 192.
See PUDENS.

Luck. Accidental good fortune. (Dut., *luk*;
Ger. *glück,* verb *glücken,* to succeed, to prosper.)

Down on one's luck. Short of cash and
credit.

Luck or **lucky penny.** A trifle returned to a
purchaser for good luck; also a penny with a
hole in it, supposed to ensure good luck.

Not in luck's way. Not unexpectedly
promoted, enriched, or otherwise benefited.

Lucky. In Scotland a term of familiar but
respectful endearment for any elderly woman;
often used of the landlady of an ale-house.

A lucky dip, or **bag.** A tub or other receptacle
in which are placed a number of articles
covered with bran or the like. Much in request
at bazaars and so on, where the visitors pay so
much for a "dip" and take what they get.

A lucky stone. A stone with a natural hole
through it. *Cp.* LUCK PENNY.

To cut one's lucky (old slang). To decamp
or make off quickly: to "cut one's stick" (*q.v.*).
As *luck* means chance, the phrase may signify,
"I must give up my chance and be off."

To strike lucky. *See* STRIKE.

Lucullus sups with Lucullus (lŭk ŭl' ŭs).
Said of a glutton who gormandizes alone.
Lucullus was a rich Roman, noted for his magnificence and self-indulgence. Sometimes
above £1,700 was expended on a single meal,
and Horace tells us he had 5,000 rich purple
robes in his house. On one occasion a very
superb supper was prepared, and when asked
who were to be his guests the "rich fool"
replied, "Lucullus will sup to-night with Lucullus"
(110-57 B.C.).

Lucus a non lucendo (lū' kŭs ā non loo
sen' dō). An etymological contradiction; a
phrase used of etymologists who accounted for
words by deriving them from their opposites. It
means literally "a grove (called *lucus*) from not
being lucent" (*lux,* light, *luceo,* to shine). It was
the Roman grammarian Honoratus Maurus
Servius (fl. end of 4th cent, A.D.) who provided
this famous etymology. In the same way *ludus,*

a school, may be said to come from *ludere*, to play, and our word *linen*, from *lining*, because it is used for linings.

One *Tryphiodorus . . .* composed an Epick Poem . . . of four and twenty books, having entirely banished the letter A from his first Book, which was called *Alpha* (as *Lucus a non Lucendo*) because there was not an *Alpha* in it.—ADDISON: *Spectator*, No. 59.

Lucy, St. Patron saint for those afflicted in the eyes. She is supposed to have lived in Syracuse and to have suffered martyrdom there about 303. One legend relates that a nobleman wanted to marry her for the beauty of her eyes; so she tore them out and gave them to him, saying, "Now let me live to God." Hence she is represented in art carrying a palm branch and a platter with two eyes on it. Her day is December 13th.

Lud's Town. London; so called from King Lud.

And on the gates of Lud's town set your heads.
SHAKESPEARE: *Cymbeline*, iv, 2.

Luddites. Discontented workmen who, from 1811 to 1816, went about the manufacturing districts (especially Nottingham) breaking machines, under the impression that machinery threw men out of work. So called from Ned Lud, of Leicestershire, who forced his way into a house, and broke two stocking-frames, whence the leader of these rioters was called *General Lud*.

In the winter of 1811 the terrible pressure of this transition from handicraft to machinery was seen in the Luddite, or machine-breaking, riots which broke out over the northern and midland counties; and which were only suppressed by military force.—J.R. GREEN: *Short History*, x, § iv.

Ludgate. One of the gates in the old City walls of London standing (till 1760) on Ludgate Hill, a few yards above the Old Bailey. It was probably on the site of a gate in the later Roman wall, but its first mention (as *Ludgata*) occurs in the early 12th century. Suggestions have been made that the true origin of the name is to be found in *Floodgate* (or *Fleetgate*, *cp. Fleet Street*, which at one time extended to Ludgate), or in A.S. *leode*, people, nation (*cp.* the *Porto del populi* of Rome).

Ludgate was used as a free prison in 1373, but soon lost that privilege. A romantic story is told of Sir Stephen Forster, who was Lord Mayor in 1454. He had been a prisoner at Ludgate, and begged at the gate, where he was seen by a rich widow, who bought his liberty, took him into her service, and afterwards married him. To commemorate this, Sir Stephen enlarged the prison accommodation, and added a chapel. The old gate was taken down and rebuilt in 1586. The new-built gate was destroyed in the Great Fire of London, and the next gate (used also as a prison for debtors) was pulled down in 1760.

Stow says:

King Lud, repairing the city, called it after his name *Lud's town*: the strong gate which he built in the west part he likewise named Lud-gate. In the year 1260 the gate was beautiful with images of Lud and other kings. Those images, in the reign of Edward VI, had their heads smitten off . . . Queen Mary did set new heads on their old bodies again.
Survey of London.

[Lud] Built that gate of which his name is hight,
By which he lies entombëd solemnly.
Spencer: *Faërie Queene*, ii, x, 46.

The statue of Queen Elizabeth I formerly on old Lud Gate is now built into the façade of St. Dunstan's Church, Fleet Street.

Ludlum. *See* LAZY.

Luez. *See* LUZ.

Luff. The weather-gauge; the part of a vessel towards the wind. (Dut. *loef*, a weather-gauge.)

Luff! Put the tiller on the lee-side. This is done to make the ship sail nearer the wind.

A ship is said to **spring her luff** when she yields to the helm by sailing nearer the wind.

Lumber. Formerly a pawnbroker's shop (from *Lombard, q.v.*). Thus Lady Murray (*Lives of the Baillies*, 1749) writes: "They put all the little plate they had in the lumber, which is pawning it, till the ships came home."

From its use as applied to old broken boards and bits of wood the word was extended to mean timber sawn and split, especially when the trees have been felled and sawn *in situ*.

Lump. If you don't like it, you may lump it. Whether you like to do it or not, no matter; you must take it without choice; it must be done.

Lumpkin, Tony (Goldsmith's *She Stoops to Conquer*). A sheepish, mischievous, idle, cunning lout, "with the vices of a man and the follies of a boy."

Lunar Month. From new moon to new moon, *i.e.* the time taken by the moon to revolve round the earth, about $29\frac{1}{2}$ days. Popularly, the lunar month is 28 days. In the Jewish and Mohammedan calendars, the lunar month commences at sunset of the day when the new moon is first seen after sunset, and varies in length, being sometimes 29 and sometimes 30 days. **Lunar Year.** Twelve lunar months, *i.e.* about $354\frac{1}{3}$ days.

Lunatics. Literally, moon-struck persons. The Romans believed that the mind was affected by the moon, and that "lunatics" grew more and more frenzied as the moon increased to its full.

The various mental derangements . . . which have been attributed to the influence of the moon, have given to this day the name *lunatics* to persons suffering from serious mental disorders.—CROZIER: *Popular Errors*, ch. iv.

Lunch, Luncheon. *Lunch* was originally a variant of *lump*, meaning a piece or slice of bread, etc. The *-eon* is a later extension, perhaps representing *-ing* ("Noonings and intermealiary Lunchings," Brome's *Mad Couple*, about 1650), but affected by the suffix of *nuncheon*. This *-eon* has now been dropped except as an affectation of gentility.

Luni (loo' nē). The ancient Etruscan town of Luna some 70 miles from Genoa. The quarries nearby furnish a beautiful white marble which takes its name from the place "marmo lunese" and the whole district is called La Lunigiana.

Lupercal, The (lū pĕr kăl). In ancient Rome, an annual festival held on the spot where Romulus and Remus were suckled by the wolf (*lupus*), on February 15th, in honour of Lupercus, the Lycæan Pan (so called because he protected the flocks from wolves). It was on one of these occasions that Antony thrice offered Julius Cæsar the crown, and Cæsar refused, saying, "Jupiter alone is king of Rome."

> You all did see that on the Lupercal,
> I thrice presented him a kingly crown,
> Which he did thrice refuse.
>
> *Julius Cæsar*, iii, 2.

Lurch. To leave in the lurch. To leave a person in a difficulty. In cribbage one is *left in the lurch* when his adversary has run out his score of sixty-one holes before he himself has turned the corner (or pegged his thirty-first) hole. In some card-games it is a *slam*, that is, when one side wins the entire game before the other has scored a point.

Lush. Beer and other intoxicating drinks. The word is well over a century old, and is of uncertain origin. Up to about 1895 there was a convivial society of actors called "The City of Lushington," which met in the Harp Tavern, Russell Street, and claimed to have been in existence for 150 years. *Lush* may have come from the name of this club, though it is just as likely that the club took its name from the *lush*—for which it was famous.

Lusitania (loo si tăn' yȧ). The Cunard liner that was torpedoed and sunk by a German submarine off the Old Head of Kinsale on May 7th, 1915, with the loss of 1198 lives. The sinking of the *Lusitania* was notorious as the first of many subsequent examples of German atrocities. The Germans struck a medal to celebrate this feat.

Lustral (lŭs' trȧl). Properly, pertaining to the *Lustrum* (*q.v.*); hence, purificatory, as *lustral water*, the water used in Christian as well as many pagan rites for aspersing worshippers. In Rome the priest used a small olive or laurel branch for sprinkling infants and the people.

Lusus. Pliny (iii, 1) tells us that Lusus was the companion of Bacchus in his travels, and settled a colony in Portugal; whence the country was termed *Lusitania*, and the inhabitants *Lusians*, or *the sons of Lusus*.

Lutestring. A glossy silk fabric; the French *lustrine* (from *lustre*).

Speaking in lutestring. Flash, highly polished oratory. The expression was used more than once by Junius. Shakespeare has "taffeta phrases and silken terms precise." We call inflated speech "fustian" (*q.v.*) or "bombast" (*q.v.*); say a man talks *stuff*; term a book or speech made up of other men's brains, *shoddy* (*q.v.*); sailors call telling a story "spinning a yarn," etc, etc.

Lutetia (Lat. *lutum*, mud). The ancient name of Paris, which, in Roman times, was merely a collection of mud hovels. Cæsar called it *Lutetia Parisiorum* (the mud-town of the Parisii), which gives the present name *Paris*.

Lutin. A goblin in the folklore of Normandy; similar to the house-spirits of Germany. The name was formerly *netun*, and is said to come from the Roman sea-god *Neptune*. When the *lutin* assumes the form of a horse ready equipped it is called *Le Cheval Bayard*.

To lutin. To twist hair into elf-locks. These mischievous urchins are said to tangle the mane of a horse or head of a child so that the hair must be cut off.

Lutine Bell (loo' tēn). H.M.S. *Lutine*, a French warship that had been captured and put into service by the British, sailed from Yarmouth for Holland on October 9th, 1799, with bullion and specie to the value of some £500,000. That same night she was wrecked on a sandbank off the Zuyder Zee, with the loss of every soul on board save one, who died as soon as rescued. It was a black day for Lloyd's underwriters. In 1858 some £50,000 was salvaged, and among other things the *Lutine*'s bell and rudder were brought back to England. The latter was made into the official chair for Lloyd's chairman and a secretary's desk; the bell was hung up at Lloyd's and is rung once whenever a total wreck is reported, and twice when an overdue ship is reported.

Lycanthropy (lī kăn' thrō pi). The insanity afflicting a person who imagines himself to be some kind of animal and exhibits the tastes, voice, etc., of that animal; formerly the name given by the ancients to those who imagined themselves to be wolves (Gr. *lukos*, wolf, *anthropos*, man). The *werewolf* (*q.v.*) has sometimes been called a *lycanthrope*; and *lycanthropy* was sometimes applied to the form of witchcraft by which witches transformed themselves into wolves.

Lycaon (lī kā' on). In classical mythology, a king of Arcadia, who, desirous of testing the divine knowledge of Jove, served up human flesh on his table; for which the god changed him into a wolf. His daughter, Callisto, was changed into the constellation the Bear, which is sometimes called *Lycaonis Arotos*.

Lycidas (lis' i dǎs). The name under which Milton celebrated the untimely death of Edward King, Fellow of Christ's College, Cambridge, who was drowned in his passage from Chester to Ireland, August 10th, 1637. He was the son of Sir John King, Secretary for Ireland.

Lycopodium (lī kō pō' di ŭm). A genus of perennial plants comprising the club-mosses, so called from their fanciful resemblance to a wolf's foot (Gr. *lukos*, wolf, *pous*, *podos*, foot); the powder from the spore-cases of some of these is used in surgery as an absorbent and also—as it is highly inflammable—for stage-lightning.

Lyddite (lid' īt). A high-explosive composed mainly of picric acid; so called from Lydd, in Kent, where are situated the artillery ranges on which it was first tested in 1888.

Lydford Law. Punish first and try afterwards. Lydford, in the county of Devon, was a fortified town, where were held the courts of the Duchy of Cornwall. Offenders against the stannary laws were confined before trial in a dungeon so loathsome and dreary that they frequently died before they could be brought to trial. *Cp.* CUPAR JUSTICE.

Lydia (lid' i à). The ancient name of a district in the middle of Asia Minor which was an important centre of early civilization and exerted much influence on Greece. Gyges (716 B.C.) was one of its most famous rulers, and the Empire flourished until its overthrow by the Persians under Cyrus (546 B.C.).

Lynceus (lin' sūs). One of the Argonauts (*q.v.*). He was so sharp-sighted that he could see through the earth, and distinguish objects nine miles off.

Non possis oculo quantum contendere Lynceus.
HORACE: 1 *Epistle*, i, 28.

Lynch Law (linch). Mob-law, law administered by private persons. The origin of the term is unknown; none of the suggested derivations

from James Lynch or Justice Lynch having any foundation in fact.

The term is first recorded in 1817, and is certainly American in origin, though there is an old northern English dialect word *linch*, meaning to beat or maltreat.

In the U.S.A. the drastic justice of Lynch Law—usually true justice, it must be observed—was effective where the civil law failed in clearing the West of outlaws, cattle-thieves, and rogues in general.

Lynx (lingks). The animal proverbial for its piercing eyesight is a fabulous beast, half dog and half panther, but not like either in character. The cat-like animal now called a lynx is not remarkable for keen-sightedness. The word is probably related to Gr. *lussein*, to see. *Cp.* LYNCEUS.

Oh, I must needs o' the sudden prove a lynx
And look the heart, that stone-wall, through and through
Such an eye, God's may be,—not yours nor mine.
BROWNING: *The Ring and the Book*, xi, 917.

Lyonesse (lī on es'). "That sweet land of Lyonesse"—a tract of land fabled to stretch between the Land's End and the Scilly Isles, now submerged full "forty fathoms under water." Arthur came from this mythical country.

Faery damsels met in forest wide
By knights of Logres, or of Lyones,
Lancelot, or Pelleas, or Pellenore.
MILTON: *Paradise Regained*, ii, 359.

Lyre (līr). That of Terpander and Olympus had only three strings; the Scythian lyre had five; that of Simonides had eight; and that of Timotheus had twelve. It was played either with the fingers or with a plectrum. The lyre is called by poets a "shell," because the cords of the lyre used by Orpheus, Amphion, and Apollo were stretched on the shell of a tortoise. Hercules used boxwood.

Amphion built Thebes with the music of his lyre, for the very stones moved of their own accord into walls and houses.

Arion charmed the dolphins by the music of his lyre, and when the bard was thrown overboard one of them carried him safely to Tænarus.

Hercules was taught music by Linus. One day, being reproved, the strong man broke the head of his master with his own lyre.

Orpheus charmed savage beasts, and even the infernal gods, with the music of his lyre, or—as some have it, lute.

M

M. The thirteenth letter of the English alphabet (the twelfth of the ancient Roman, and twentieth of the *futhorc*), M in the Phœnician character represented the wavy appearance of water, and is called in Hebrew *mem* (water). The Egyptian hieroglyphic represented the owl. In English M is always sounded, except in words from Greek in which it is followed by *n*, as *mnemonics, Mnason* (Acts xxi, 16).

In Roman numerals M stands for 1,000 (Lat. *mille*): MCMLII = one thousand, nine hundred and fifty-two.

Persons convicted of manslaughter, and admitted to the benefit of clergy, used to be branded with an M. It was burnt on the brawn of the left thumb.

What is your name? N or **M.** (Church Catechism.) *See* N.

M, to represent the human face. Add two dots for the eyes, thus, .M. These dots being equal to O's, we get OMO (*homo*) Latin for man.

> Who reads the name,
> For *man* upon his forehead, there the M
> Had traced most plainly.
> DANTE: *Purgatory*, xxiii.

MS. (pl. MSS.). Manuscript; applied to literary works either in handwriting or typescript. (Lat. *manuscriptum*, that which is written by the hand.)

Mab (perhaps the Welsh *mab*, a baby). The "fairies' midwife"—*i.e.* employed by the fairies as midwife to deliver man's brain of dreams. Thus when Romeo says, "I dreamed a dream to-night," Mercutio replies, "Oh, then, I see Queen Mab hath been with you," When Mab is called "queen," it does not mean sovereign, for Titania as wife of King Oberon was Queen of Faery, but simply female. A.S. *quén* or *cwén* (modern *quean*) meant neither more nor less than *woman*; so "elf-queen," and the Danish *ellequinde*, mean *female elf*, and not "queen of the elves."

Excellent descriptions of Mab are given by Shakespeare (*Romeo and Juliet*, i, 4), by Ben Jonson, by Herrick, and by Drayton in *Nymphidea*.

Macaber (or **Macabre**), **the Dance.** *See* DANCE OF DEATH.

Macadamize (mà kǎd′ à mīz). A method of road-making introduced about 1820 by John L. Macadam (1756-1836), consisting of layers of broken stones of nearly uniform size, each layer being separately crushed into position by traffic, or (later) by a heavy roller.

Macaire, Robert (mà kâr′). The typical villain of French comedy; from the play of this name (a sequel to *L'Auberge des Adrets*) by Frédéric Lemaître and Benjamin Antier (1834): Macaire is—
le type de la perversité, de l'impudence, de la friponnerie audacieuse, le héros fanfaron du vol et de l'assassinat.

"Macaire" was the name of the murderer of Aubrey de Montdidier in the old French legend; he was brought to justice by the sagacity of Aubrey's dog, the Dog of Montargis. *See* DOG.

Macaroni (mǎk′ à rō ni). A coxcomb (Ital. *un maccherone*, see next entry). The word is derived from the Macaroni Club, instituted in London about 1760 by a set of flashy men who had travelled in Italy, and introduced at Almack's subscription table the new-fangled Italian food, *macaroni*. The Macaronies were the most exquisite fops; vicious, insolent, fond of gambling, drinking, and duelling, they were (about 1773) the curse of Vauxhall Gardens.

An American regiment raised in Maryland during the War of Independence was called The Macaronies from its showy uniform.

Macaronic Latin. Dog Latin (*q.v.*), modern words with Latin endings, or a mixture of Latin and some modern language. From the Italian *macheroni* (macaroni), a mixture of coarse meal, eggs, and cheese. The law pleadings of G. Steevens, as *Daniel* v. *Dishclout* and *Bullum* v. *Boatum*, are excellent examples.

Macbeth (màc beth′). The story of Shakespeare's tragedy (written 1605-6, acted certainly in 1610 and probably four years earlier, and first printed in the First Folio, 1623) is taken from Holinshed, who copied it from the *History of Scotland*, by Hector Boece (1527).

History states that Macbeth slew Duncan at Bothgowan, near Elgin, in 1039, and not, as Shakespeare says, at his castle of Inverness; the attack was made because Duncan had usurped the throne, to which Macbeth had the better claim. As a king Macbeth proved a very just and equitable prince, but the partisans of Malcolm got head, and succeeded in deposing Macbeth, who was slain in 1056, at Lumphanan. He was thane of Cromarty [Glamis] and afterwards of Moray [Cawdor].—LARDNER: *Cabinet Cyclopædia.*

Ambition is the dominant trait in the character of Lady Macbeth, and to gain her ends she hesitates at nothing. Her masterful mind sways the weaker Macbeth to "the mood of what she liked or loathed." She is a Medea, or Catherine de' Medici, or Cæsar Borgia in female form.

The real name of Lady Macbeth was Graoch, and instead of being urged to the murder of Duncan through ambition, she was goaded by deadly injuries. She was, in fact, the granddaughter of Kenneth IV, killed in 1003, fighting against Malcolm II.—LARDNER: *Cabinet Cyclopædia*, vol. i, p. 17.

Maccabæus (măk à bē' us). The surname given to Judas (the central figure in the struggle for Jewish independence, about 170-160 B.C.), third son of Mattathias, the Hasmonæan, and hence to his family or clan. It has generally been supposed that the name is connected with Heb. *Makkébeth*, hammer (Judas being the *Hammerer* of the Syrians just as Charles *Martel* was of the Saracens), but this view is open to many weighty objections, and the origin of the name is wholly obscure.

Maccabees, The. The family of Jewish heroes, descended from Mattathias the Hasmonæan (*see above*) and his five sons, John, Simon, Judas, Eleazar, and Jonathan, which delivered its race from the persecutions of the Syrian king Antiochus Epiphanes (175-164 B.C.), and established a line of priest-kings which lasted till supplanted by Herod in 40 B.C. Their exploits are told in the two *Books of the Maccabees*, the last books in the Apocrypha.

Macduff (mac dūf'). The thane of Fife in *Macbeth* (*q.v.*). His castle of Kennoway was surprised by Macbeth, and his wife and babes "savagely slaughtered." Macduff vowed vengeance and joined the army of Siward, to dethrone the tyrant. On reaching the royal castle of Dunsinane they fought, and Macbeth was slain.

History states that Macbeth was defeated at Dunsinane, but escaped from the battle and was slain at Lumphanan in 1056.—LARDNER: *Cabinet Cyclopædia*, vol. i, p. 17.

Mace. Originally a club armed with iron, and used in war; now a staff of office pertaining to certain dignitaries, as the Speaker of the House of Commons, Lord Mayors and Mayors, etc. Both sword and mace are symbols of dignity,

suited to the times when men went about in armour, and sovereigns needed champions to vindicate their rights.

Macedon (măs' e dŏn). **Macedon is not worthy of thee,** is what Philip said to his son Alexander, after his achievement with the horse Bucephalus, which he subdued to his will, though only eighteen years of age.

Macedonian Madman, The. *See* MADMAN.

Macedonians. A religious sect, so named from Macedonius, an Arian patriarch of Constantinople, in the 4th century. They denied the divinity of the Holy Ghost, and that the essence of the Son is the same in kind with that of the Father.

MacFarlane's Geese. The proverb is that "MacFarlane's geese like their play better than their meat." The wild geese of Inch-Tavoe (Loch Lomond) used to be called *MacFarlane's Geese* because the MacFarlanes had a house on the island, and it is said that the geese never returned after the destruction of that house. One day James VI visited the chieftain, and was highly amused by the gambols of the geese, but the one served at table was so tough that the king exclaimed, "MacFarlane's geese like their play better than their meat."

MacGregor (mà greg' òr). The motto of the MacGregors is, "E'en do and spair nocht," said to have been given them in the 12th century by a king of Scotland. While the king was hunting he was attacked by a wild boar; when Sir Malcolm requested permission to encounter the creature, "E'en do," said the king, "and spair nocht." Whereupon the strong baronet tore up an oak sapling and dispatched the enraged animal. For this defence the king gave Sir Malcolm permission to use the said motto, and, in place of a Scotch fir, to adopt for crest *an oak-tree eradicate, proper.*

Another motto of the MacGregors is *Sriogal mo dhream, i.e.* "Royal is my tribe."

The MacGregors furnish the only instance of a race being forbidden to bear its family name. It was proscribed by James VI owing to the treachery of the family, who then took the name of Murray. Charles II restored them to their estates and name in 1661, but under William and Mary the law of proscription again came into force, and it was not till 1822 that Sir John Murray, as he then was, obtained by royal licence the right to resume the ancient name of his family, MacGregor.

Machiavelli, Niccolo (nik ō lō' ma kyà vel' i) (1469-1527). The celebrated Florentine statesman, and author of *Il Principe*, an exposition of unscrupulous statecraft, whose name has long been used as an epithet or synonym for an intriguer or for an unscrupulous politician, while political cunning and overreaching by diplomacy and intrigue are known as *Machiavellianism* or *Machiavellism*. The general trend of *Il Principe* is to show that rulers may resort to any treachery and artifice to uphold their arbitrary power, and whatever dishonourable acts princes may indulge in are fully set off by the insubordination of their subjects.

Macintosh. Cloth waterproofed with rubber by a process patented in 1823 by Charles Macintosh (1766-1843); also a coat made of this.

Mackerel Sky. A sky dappled with detached rounded masses of white cloud, something like the markings of a mackerel.

To throw a sprat to catch a mackerel. *See* SPRAT.

Mackworth's Inn. *See* BARNARD'S INN.

Macmillanites. A religious sect of Scotland, who in 1743 seceded from the Cameronians because they wished to adhere more strictly to the principles of the Reformation in Scotland; so named from John Macmillan (1670-1753), their leader. They called themselves the "Reformed Presbytery."

Macrocosm (Gr., the *great world*), in opposition to the microcosm, the *little world*. The ancients looked upon the universe as a living creature, and the followers of Paracelsus considered man a miniature representation of the universe. The one was termed the Macrocosm, the other the Microcosm (*q.v.*).

Mad. Mad as a hatter. The original "mad hatter" was Robert Crab, who set up at Chesham in the 17th century; he was eccentric, and finally gave all his goods to the poor. Degrees of insanity were common in the hat trade owing to the effects of mercurio nitrate used in treating felt. The phrase is found in Thackeray's *Pendennis*, ch. X, 1849, and was popularized by Lewis Carroll in *Alice in Wonderland*, 1865.

Madame. The wife of Philippe Duc d'Orléans, brother of Louis XIV, was so styled; other ladies were only Madame This or That.

Madame la Duchesse. Wife of Henri Jules de Bourbon (1627-93), eldest son of the Prince de Condé.

Mademoiselle. The daughter of Philippe, Duc de Chartres, grandson of Philippe, Duc d'Orléans, brother of Louis XIV.

La Grande Mademoiselle. The Duchesse de Montpensier, cousin to Louis XIV, and daughter of Gaston, Duc d'Orléans.

Madge. A popular name for the barn owl.
'Sdeins, an I swallow this, I'll ne'er draw my sword in the sight of Fleet-street again while I live; I'll sit in a barn wiih madge-howlet, and catch mice first. — BEN JONSON: *Every Man in his Humour*, ii, 1.

Madoc (măd' ok). A legendary Welsh prince, youngest son of Owain Gwyneth, king of North Wales, who died in 1169. According to tradition he sailed to America, and established a colony on the southern branches of the Missouri. About the same time the Aztecs forsook Aztlan, under the guidance of Yuhidthiton, and founded the empire called Mexico, in honour of Mexitli, their tutelary god. Southey's poem, *Madoc* (1805), harmonizes these two events.

Madonna (Ital., my lady). A title specially applied to the Virgin Mary.

Mæcenas (mē sē' năs). A patron of letters; so called from C. Cilnius Mæcenas (d. 8 B.C.), a Roman statesman in the reign of Augustus, who kept open house for all men of letters, and was the special friend and patron of Horace and Virgil. Nicholas Rowe so called the Earl of Halifax on his installation to the Order of the Garter (1714).

The last English Mæcenas. Samuel Rogers (1763-1855), poet and banker.

Maelström (māl' strom) (Norw., whirling stream). A dangerous whirlpool off the coast of Norway, between the islands of Moskenaso and Varo (in the Lofoten Islands), where the water is pushed and jostled a good deal, and where, when the wind and tide are contrary, it is not safe for small boats to venture.

It was anciently thought that it was a subterranean abyss, penetrating the globe, and communicating with the Gulf of Bothnia.

The name is given to other whirlpools, and also, figuratively, to any turbulent or overwhelming situation.

Mæonides (mē on' i dēz), or **The Mæonian Poet.** Homer (*q.v.*), either because he was the son of Mæon, or because he was born in Mæonia (Asia Minor).

Mæra. The dog of Icarius (*q.v.*).

Mæviad. *See* BAVIAD.

Mae West (mā west). The name given by flying men in World War II to the inflatable life-preserver vest or jacket worn when there was a possibility of their being forced into the sea. The name was given in compliment to the figure and charms of the famous film star.

Maffick. To celebrate an event, especially an occasion of national rejoicing, with wild and extravagant exuberance. From the uproarious scenes and unrestrained exultation that took place in London on the night of May 18th, 1900, when the news of the relief of Mafeking (besieged by the Boers since the previous November) became known.

Mafia (mă fē' a). In Sicily, those who take part in active hostility to the law, viz. the greater part of the population. *Mafia* is often erroneously stated to denote an organized secret society.

Mag. A contraction of magpie. **What a mag you are!** You chatter like a magpie. A prating person is called "a mag."

Not a mag to bless myself with. Not a half-penny.

Maga (mā' gà). A familiar name for *Blackwood's Magazine*.

Magazine. A place for stores (Arab, *makhzan*, a storehouse). This meaning is still retained for military and some other purposes; but the word now commonly denotes a periodical publication containing contributions by various authors. How this came about is seen from the *Introduction* to the *Gentleman's Magazine* (1731)—the first to use the word in this way:—

This Consideration has induced several Gentlemen to promote a Monthly Collection to treasure up, as in a Magazine, the most remarkable Pieces on the Subjects above mention'd.

Magdalene (măg' dà lēn). An asylum for the reclaiming of prostitutes; so called from Mary Magdalene or Mary of Magdala, "out of whom He had cast seven devils" (*Mark* xvi, 9).

Magdalen College, Oxford (1458) and **Magdalene College, Cambridge** (1542), are pronounced mawd' lin.

Magdalenian (măg é lē' nyàn). The name given to a late period of the Stone Age, during which the climate was cold and reindeer, bison, and wild horses roamed over all Europe. It was at this time that the mammoth became extinct. Stone Age man attained his highest degree of civilization in the Magdalenian period, the finest examples of which are found in the district of La Madeleine, Dordogne, France.

Magdeburg Centuries. The first great work of Protestant divines on the history of the Christian Church. It was begun at Magdeburg by Matthias Flacius, in 1552, and published at Basle (13 volumes), 1560-74. As each century occupies a volume, the thirteen volumes complete the history to 1300.

Magellan, Straits of (mà jel' àn). So called after Fernão de Magelhaes (*c.* 1480-1521), the Portuguese navigator, and first circumnavigator of the globe, who discovered them in 1520.

Magenta (mà jen' tà). A brilliant red aniline dye derived from coal-tar, named in commemoration of the bloody battle of Magenta, when the Austrians were defeated by the French and Sardinians. This was just before the dye was discovered, in 1859.

Maggot. There was an old idea that whimsical or crotchety persons had maggots in their brains—

Are you not mad, my friend? What time o' th' moon is't?
Have not you maggots in your brains?
    FLETCHER: *Women Pleased*, iii, 4 (1620).

Hence we have the adjective *maggoty*, whimsical, full of fancies. Fanciful dance tunes used to be called *maggots*, as in *The Dancing Master* (1716) there are many such titles as "Barker's maggots," "Cary's maggots," "Draper's maggots," etc., and in 1685 Samuel Wesley father of John and Charles Wesley, published a volume with the title *Maggots; or Poems on Several Subjects*.

Magi (mā' jī) (Lat.; pl. of *magus*). Literally "wise men"; specifically, the Three Wise Men of the East who brought gifts to the infant Saviour. Tradition calls them Melchior, Gaspar, and Balthazar, three kings of the East. The first offered gold, the emblem of royalty; the second, frankincense, in token of divinity; and the third, myrrh, in prophetic allusion to the persecution unto death which awaited the "Man of Sorrows."

MELCHIOR means "king of light."
GASPAR, or CASPAR, means "the white one."
BALTHAZAR means "the lord of treasures."

Mediæval legend calls them the Three Kings of Cologne, and the Cathedral there claims their relics. They are commemorated on January 2nd, 3rd, and 4th, and particularly at the Feast of the Epiphany.

Among the ancient Medes and Persians the Magi were members of a priestly caste credited with great occult powers, and in Camoëns' *Lusiad* the term denotes the Indian Brahmins. Ammianus Marcellinus says that the Persian *magi* derived their knowledge from the Brahmins of India (i, 23), and Arianus expressly calls the Brahmins "magi" (i, 7).

Maginot Line (ma' zhi no). A zone of fortifications, mostly of concrete, with impregnable gun-positions, shelters, etc., built along the eastern frontier of France between 1929 and 1934, and named after André Maginot (1877-1932), Minister of War, who was responsible for their construction. The line extended from the Swiss border to that of Belgium, and for long it deluded the French into the belief that it would make a German invasion impossible. This might have been true, had the Germans not entered France through Belgium in 1940, turning the Maginot Line, which thus served no purpose whatever.

Magna Charta. The *Great Charter* of English liberty extorted from King John, 1215.

It contained (in its final form) 37 clauses, and is directed principally against abuses of the power of the Crown and to guaranteeing that no subject should be kept in prison without trial and judgment by his peers.

Magnanimous, The. Alfonso V of Aragon (1385, 1416-58).

Chosroes or Khosru, King of Persia, twenty-first of the Sassanides, surnamed *Noushirwan* (the Magnanimous) (531-579).

Magnet. The loadstone; so called from Magnesia, in Lydia, where the ore was said to abound. Milton uses the adjective for the substantive in the line "As the magnetic hardest iron draws" (*Paradise Regained*, ii, 168).

Magnetic Mountain. A mountain of mediæval legend which drew out all the nails of any ship that approached within its influence. It is referred to in Mandeville's Travels and in many stories, such as the tale of the Third Calender and one of the voyages of Sinbad the Sailor in the *Arabian Nights*.

Magnificat. The hymn of the Virgin (*Luke* i, 46-55) beginning "My soul doth magnify the Lord" (*Magnificat anima mea Dominum*), used as part of the daily service of the Church since the beginning of the sixth century, and at Evening Prayer in England for over 800 years.

C'est magnifique, mais ce n'est pas la guerre. A magnificent gesture, but not real warfare. Admirable, but not according to rule. The comment on the field made by the French General Bosquet to A. H. Layard on the charge of the Light Brigade at Balaclava. It has frequently been attributed to Marshal Canrobert.

Magnolia (măg nō' li à). A genus of North American flowering trees so called from Pierre Magnol (1638-1715), professor of botany at Montpellier.

Magnum (măg' num). A wine bottle, double the size of the ordinary bottle—holding two quarts or thereabouts. *Cp.* JEROBOAM.

Magnum opus. The chief or most important of one's literary works.

My magnum opus, the "Life of Dr. Johnson" . . . is to be published on Monday, 16th May.—BOSWELL: *Letter to Rev. W. Temple*, 1791.

Magpie. Formerly "maggot-pie," *maggot* representing *Margaret* (*cp. Robin* redbreast, *Tom*-tit, and the old *Phyllyp*-sparrow), and *pie* being *pied*, in allusion to its white and black plumage.

Augurs and understood relations have
(By magotpies, and choughs, and rooks) brought forth
The secret'st man of blood.
Macbeth, iii, 4.

The magpie has generally been regarded as an uncanny bird: in Sweden it is connected with witchcraft, in Devonshire if a peasant sees one he spits over his shoulder three times to avert ill luck, and in Scotland magpies flying near the windows of a house foretell the early death of one of its inmates.

The following rhyme about the number of magpies seen in the course of a walk is old and well known:—

One's sorrow, two's mirth,
Three's a wedding, four's a birth,
Five's a christening, six a dearth,
Seven's heaven, eight is hell,
And nine's the devil his ane sel.'

In target-shooting the score made by a shot striking the outermost division but one is called a *magpie* because it was customarily signalled by a black and white flag; and formerly bishops were humorously or derisively called magpies because of their black and white vestments.

Lawyers, as Vultures, had soared up and down;
Prelates, like Magpies, in the Air had flown.
Howell's Letters: Lines to the Knowing Reader (1645).

Magus. *See* SIMON MAGUS.

Magyar (mà jar'). The dominant race in Hungary. Magyars are not of Aryan stock but of the Finno-Ugrian peoples, who invaded Hungary about the end of the 9th century and settled there. The Hungarian language is one of the most difficult to master in Europe.

Mahabharata (ma ha ba ra' tà). One of the two great epic poems of ancient India (*cp.* RAMAYANA), about eight times as long as the *Iliad* and *Odyssey* together. Its main story is the war between descendants of Kuru and Pandu, but there are an immense number of episodes.

Maha-pudma. *See* TORTOISE.

Maharajah (ma ha ra' ja) (Sansk., "great king"). The title of certain native rulers of India whose territories are very extensive. The wife of a Maharajah is a *Maharanee*.

Mahâtma (mà hăt′ mà) (Sansk., "great soul"). Max Müller tells us that:—

Mahâtma is a well-known Sanskrit word applied to men who have retired from the world, who, by means of a long ascetic discipline, have subdued the passions of the flesh, and gained a reputation for sanctity and knowledge. That these men are able to perform most startling feats, and to suffer the most terrible tortures, is perfectly true.—*Nineteenth Century*, May, 1893.

By the Esoteric Buddhists the name is given to adepts of the highest order, a community of whom is supposed to exist in Tibet, and by Theosophists to one who has reached perfection spiritually, intellectually, and physically. As his knowledge is perfect he can produce effects which, to the ordinary man, appear miraculous.

The title was later associated with Mohandas Gandhi, the Hindu leader of revolt against British rule in India. A preacher and unceasing practiser of the doctrine of nonviolence, by his life of pure simplicity and his intercessory fasts—often carried to the verge of death—he acquired an immense influence over Indians of all creeds and races. Gandhi was assassinated by a fanatical Hindu at the age of 78, on January 30th, 1948.

Mah-jongg (ma jong′). A Chinese game played with dominoes made of ivory and bamboo. There are usually four players at a table, each acting for himself. The dominoes, which number 136, are arranged in three suits, and there are four sets of each. One consists of three honours—red, white, and green; another represents the four winds, north, south, east, and west; the third consists of three sets of nine dominoes named characters, circles, and bamboos. The object of each player is to obtain the highest scoring hand, known as Mah-jongg.

Mahomet. *See* MOHAMMED.

Mahoun, Mahound. Names of contempt for Mohammed, a Moslem, a Moor, particularly in romances of the Crusades. The name is sometimes used as a synonym for "the Devil."

Oft-times by Termagant and Mahound swore.
SPENSER: *Faerie Queene*, VI, vii, 47.

Maid. Maid Marian. A female character in the old May games and morris dances, in the former usually being Queen of the May. In the later Robin Hood ballads she became attached to the cycle as the outlaw's sweetheart, probably through the performance of Robin Hood plays at May-day festivities. The part of Maid Marian both in the games and the dance was frequently taken by a man dressed as a woman.

[The Courtier] must, if the least spot of morphew come on his face, have his oyle of tartar, his *lac virginis*, his camphir dissolved in verjuice, to make the foole as faire, for sooth, as if he were to playe Maid Marian in a May-game or moris-dance.—GREENE: *Quip for an Upstart Courtier* (1592).

Maid of Athens. The girl immortalized by Byron, was Theresa Macri.

Maid of Norway. Margaret (1283-90), daughter of Eric II and Margaret of Norway. On the death of Alexander III of Scotland (1285), her maternal grandfather, she was acknowledged Queen of Scotland, and was betrothed to Edward, son of Edward I of England, but she died on her passage to Scotland.

Maid of Orleans. Joan of Arc (1412-31), who raised the siege of Orleans in 1429. She was canonized in 1920, her feast day being May 8th.

Maiden. A machine resembling the guillotine, used in Scotland in the 16th and 17th centuries for beheading criminals, and introduced there by the Regent Morton for the purpose of beheading the laird of Pennycuik. It was also called "the widow."

Maiden or **Virgin Queen.** Elizabeth I, Queen of England, who never married. (1533, 1558-1603.)

Maiden Town. A town never taken by the enemy (*cp.* MAIDEN ASSIZE *above*). Also, specifically, Edinburgh, from tradition that the maiden daughters of a Pictish king were sent there for protection during an intestine war.

Mail Order. The carrying on of business by post, that is of receiving orders and cash by post and sending on the goods purchased by the customer also by post, grew to enormous dimensions in U.S.A. where, in great agricultural areas, it was the only method whereby people could obtain other than the mere necessaries of life.

Main chance, The. Profit or money, probably from the game called hazard, in which the first throw of the dice is called the *main*, which must be between four and nine, the player then throwing his *chance*, which determines the main.

To have an eye to the main chance. To keep in view the money or advantage to be made out of an enterprise.

Main Street. The principal thoroughfare in many of the smaller towns and cities of U.S.A. The novel of this name, by Sinclair Lewis (1920) epitomized the social and cultural life of these towns, and gave the phrase a significance of its own.

Maintenance (Fr. *main, tenir*, to hold in the hand, maintain). Means of support or sustenance: in legal phraseology, officious intermeddling in litigation with which one has rightfully nothing whatever to do. *Cp.* CHAMPERTY. Actions for maintenance are rare, but damages can be recovered for this abuse of legal process.

Maize. American superstition had it that if a damsel found a blood-red ear of maize, she would have a suitor before the year was over.

Even the blood-red ear to Evangeline brought not her lover.

LONGFELLOW: *Evangeline.*

Majesty. Henry VIII was the first English sovereign who was styled "His Majesty," though it was not till the time of the Stuarts that this form of address had become stereotyped, and in the Dedication to James I prefixed to the Authorized Version of the Bible (1611) the King is addressed both in this way and as "Your Highness."

The Lord of Heaven and earth blesse your Majestie with many and happy dayes, that as his Heavenly hand hath enriched your Highnesse with many singular and extraordinary Graces, etc.

Henry IV was "His Grace"; Henry VI, "His Excellent Grace"; Edward IV, "High and Mighty Prince"; Henry VII, "His Grace" and "His Highness"; Henry VIII, in the earlier part of his reign, was styled "His Highness." "His Sacred Majesty" was a title assumed by subsequent sovereigns, but was afterwards changed to "Most Excellent Majesty." "His Catholic Majesty" was the king of Spain, and "His Most Christian Majesty" the king of France.

In heraldry, an eagle crowned and holding a sceptre is said to be "an eagle in his majesty."

Majolica Ware. A pottery originally made in the island of Majorca or Majolica. *See* FAIENCE.

Major-General. A rank in the British Army above that of Brigadier and below that of Lieutenant-General. The distinguishing badge is a crossed sword and baton with one star. The rank was first instituted by Cromwell in 1655, after his quarrel with the Parliament; each major-general was to govern a military district with civil and military powers. As such the scheme was in force until 1657, when the civil side was dropped and the rank became purely military.

Majority. He has joined the majority. He is dead. Blair says, in his *Grave*, "'Tis long since Death had the majority."

Make. In America this word is much more frequently used with the meaning put ready for use than it is with us; we have the phrase *to make the bed*, and Shakespeare has *make the door* (*see* DOOR), but in the States such phrases as *Have you made my room?* (*i.e.* put it tidy), are

common. *To make good, to make one's pile, to make a place* (*i.e.* to arrive there), are among the many Americanisms in which this word is used. *To make a die of it*, to die, is another.

Why, Tom, you don't mean to make a die of it?— R. M. BIRD: *Nick of the Woods* (1837).

On the make. Looking after one's own personal advantage; intent on the "main chance."

To make it. To succeed in catching a train, keeping an appointment, etc.

To make away with. To put or take out of the way, run off with; to squander; also to murder; *to make away with oneself* is to commit suicide.

To make believe. To pretend; to play a game at.

We will make believe that there are fairies in the world. KINGSLEY: *Water Babies*, ch. ii.

Make-believe is also used as a noun.

To make good. To fulfil one's promises or to come up to expectations, to succeed.

Whether or not the new woman Mayor would "make good" was of real interest to the country at large.—*Evening Post* (*New York*), Sept. 14th, 1911.

Also to replace, repair, or compensate for; as, "My car was damaged through your carelessness, so now you'll have to make it good."

Makeshift. A temporary arrangement during an emergency.

Make-up. The general use of this term as noun and verb to describe face cosmetics and their application is of theatrical origin, being employed to describe the materials used by an actor for painting his face and otherwise transforming his appearance to suit a character on the stage; the manner in which he is *made up*; hence, in colloquial use, the sum of one's characteristics, idiosyncrasies, etc. In *printing* the *make-up* is the arrangement of the printed matter in columns, pages, etc.

Malakoff (măl' a kof). This fortification, which was carried by storm by the French, September 8th, 1855 was named from a drunken Russian sailor who lived at Sebastopol, and, being dismissed the dockyards in which he had been employed, opened a liquor-shop on the hill outside the town. His old friends gathered round, other houses sprang up, and "Malakoff," as it came to be called, was ultimately fortified.

Malaprop, Mrs. (măl' à prop). The famous character in Sheridan's *The Rivals*. Noted for her blunders in the use of words (Fr. *mal à propos*). "As headstrong as an *allegory* on the banks of the Nile" is one of her grotesque misapplications; and she has given us the word *malapropism* to denote such mistakes.

Malaysia (mả lā′ zyà). The collective name given to the whole Malay Archipelago, as opposed to Malaya, which is applied to the southern and greater portion of the Malay Peninsula. Amongst other islands Malaysia includes the Sunda Islands, the Moluccas, Borneo, and the Philippines.

Malbrouk or **Marlbrough.** The old French song, *"Malbrouk s'en va-t-en guerre"* (Marlborough is off to the wars), is said to date from 1709, when the Duke of Marlborough was winning his battles in Flanders, but it did not become popular till it was applied to Charles Churchill, 3rd Duke of Marlborough, at the time of his failure against Cherbourg (1758), and was further popularized by its becoming a favourite of Marie Antoinette about 1780, and by its being introduced by Beaumarchais into *Le Mariage de Figaro* (1784). The air, however (the same as our "We won't go home till morning"), is of far older date, was well known in Egypt and the East, and is said to have been sung by the Crusaders. According to a tradition recorded by Châteaubriand, the air came from the Arabs, and the tale is a legend of Mambron, a crusader.

> Malbrouk s'en va-t-en guerre,
> Mironton, mironton, mirontaine;
> Malbrouk s'en va-t-en guerre,
> Nul sait quand reviendra.
> Il reviendra z'à pâques —
> Mironton, mironton, mirontaine . . .
> Ou à la Trinitè.

Male. Applied in the vegetable kingdom to certain plants which were supposed to have some masculine property or appearance, as the *male fern* (*Nephrodium filix-mas*), the fronds of which cluster in a kind of crown; and to precious stones—particularly sapphires—that are remarkable for their depth or brilliance of colour.

Malice. In addition to its common meaning malice is a term in English law to designate either actual ill-will formed against another in the mind of the person charged with malice or the doing of some deliberate act so injurious to another that the law will imply evil intent—this is commonly known as malice prepense, or malice aforethought. Malicious damage is a legal term meaning damage done to property wilfully and purposely; malicious prosecution means the preferring a criminal prosecution or the presentation of a bankruptcy petition maliciously and without reasonable cause.

Malkin (mol′ kin). An old diminutive of Matilda; formerly used as a generic term for a kitchen-wench or untidy slut; also for a cat (*see* GRIMALKIN), and for a scarecrow or grotesque puppet.

> All tongues speak of him . . .
> The kitchen malkin pins
> Her richest lochram 'bout her reechy neck,
> Clambering the walls to eye him.
> *Coriolanus*, ii, 1.

The name was also sometimes given to the Queen of the May (*see* MAID MARIAN):—

> Put on the shape of order and humanity.
> Or you must marry Malkin, the May lady.
> BEAUMONT AND FLETCHER: *Monsieur Thomas*, ii, 2.

Mall, The (măl). A broad promenade in St. James's Park, London, so called because the game of *Pall-mall* (*q.v.*) used to be played there. The *mall* was the mallet with which the ball was struck.

> Noe persons shall after play carry their malls out of St. James's Parke without leave of the said keeper.—
> *Order Book of General Monk* (1662).

Malta. After a varied and eventful history this island became a British possession in 1814 since when it has been almost impregnably fortified as a naval base, commanding the Mediterranean and the approaches to the Suez Canal. For its resistance and suffering under aerial bombardment the island was awarded the George Cross in 1942.

Malta, Knights of, or *Hospitallers of St. John of Jerusalem.* Some time after the first crusade (1042), some Neapolitan merchants built at Jerusalem a hospital for sick pilgrims and a church which they dedicated to St. John; these they committed to the charge of certain knights, called *Hospitallers of St. John.* In 1310 these Hospitallers, having developed into a military Order, took the island of Rhodes, and changed their title into *Knights of Rhodes.* In 1522 they were expelled by the Turks, and took up their residence in Malta, which was ruled by the Grand Master until the island was taken by the French in 1798. The Order is now extinct as a sovereign body, but maintains a lingering existence in Italy, Germany, France, etc., and in Malta, where it still confers titles of "Marquis" and "Count." See HOSPITALLERS.

Maltese Cross. Made thus: ✠. Originally the badge of the Knights of Malta, formed of four barbed arrow-heads with their points meeting in the centre. In modified and elaborated forms it is the badge of many well-known Orders, etc., as the British Victoria Cross and Order of Merit, and the German Iron Cross.

Maltese terrier. An ancient breed of lap-dog, somewhat resembling a Skye terrier though not really a terrier at all. In colour it is pure white, though occasionally marked with fawn; the face and sides are clothed with long, silky hair and the highly-plumed tail usually curves over the back.

Malthusian Doctrine was that population in creases more than the means of subsistence does, so that in time, if no check is put upon the increase of population, many must starve or all be ill fed. It was promulgated by T. R. Malthus (1766-1835), especially in his *Essay on Population* (1798). Applied to individual nations, such as Britain, it intimated that something must be done to check the increase of population, as all the land would not suffice to feed its inhabitants.

Malum (mā' lùm), in Latin, means *an apple*; and *malus, mala, malum* means *evil*. Southey, in his *Commonplace Book*, quotes a witty etymon given by Nicolson and Burn, making the noun derived from the adjective, in allusion, possibly, to the apple eaten by Eve; and there is the schoolboy joke showing how *malo* repeated four times can be translated into a tolerable and fairly lengthy quatrain: —

Malo, I would rather be
Malo, Up an apple tree
Malo, Than a bad man
Malo, In adversity.

Malvern Hills (mawl' věrn). A range of hills or downs extending for some nine miles between Worcestershire and Herefordshire. Worcester Beacon and Hereford Beacon are both nearly 1,400 ft. high; from the former can be seen fifteen counties, the cathedrals of Hereford, Worcester, and Gloucester and five abbeys.

On a May morwenynge on Malverne hilles
Me befel a ferly, of fairye me thogte.
I was wery for-wandred, and wente me to reste
Under a brood bank by a bournes syde,
And as I lay and lenede, and loked on the watres
I slombred into a slepyng, it sweyed so murye.
LANGLAND: *Piers Plowman*.

Mambrino (măm brē nō). A pagan king of old romance, introduced by Ariosto into *Orlando Furioso*. He had a helmet of pure gold which rendered the wearer invulnerable, and was taken possession of by Rinaldo. This is frequently referred to in *Don Quixote*, and we read that when the barber was caught in a shower and clapped his brazen basin on his head, Don Quixote insisted that this was the enchanted helmet of the Moorish king.

Mammet, or **Maumet**. An idol; hence a puppet or doll (as in *Romeo and Juliet*, iii, 5, and 1 *Henry IV*, ii, 3). The word is a corruption of *Mahomet*. Mohammedanism being the most prominent non-Christian religion with which Christendom was acquainted before the Reformation, it became a generic word to designate any false faith; even idolatry is called *mammetry*; and in a 14th-century MS. Bible (first edited by A. C. Paues, 1904) 1 *John v*, 21, reads —

My smale children, kepe ye you from mawmetes and symulacris.

Mammon (măm' on). The god of this world. The word in Syriac means riches, and it occurs in the Bible (*Matt*, vi, 24, *Luke* xvi, 13): "Ye cannot serve God and mammon." Spenser (*Faerie Queene*, II, vii) and Milton (who identifies him with Vulcan or Mulciber, *Paradise Lost*, i, 738-51) both make Mammon the personification of the evils of wealth and miserliness.

Mammon led them on—
Mammon, the least erected Spirit that fell
From Heaven; for even in Heaven his looks and thoughts
Were always downward bent, admiring more
The riches of Heaven's pavement, trodden gold.
Than aught divine or holy.
MILTON: *Paradise Lost*, i, 678.

Mammoth Cave. In Edmonson county, Kentucky; the largest known in the world, discovered in 1809. It comprises a large number of chambers, with connecting passages said to total 150 miles, and covers an area of nearly 10 miles in diameter.

Man. Man in the Moon, Man of Blood, Brass, December, Sin, Straw, War, etc. *See these words*.

Man about town. A fashionable idler.

Man Friday. *See* FRIDAY.

Man-Mountain. *See* QUINBUS FLESTRIN.

Man of letters. An author, a literary scholar.

Man of the world. One "knowing" in world-craft; no greenhorn. Charles Macklin brought out a comedy (1704), and Henry Mackenzie a novel (1773) with the title.

Man of war. A warship in the navy of a government; though the name is masculine, always spoken of as "she." Formerly the term was used to denote a fighting man ("the Lord is a man of war," *Ex*. xv, 3).

The name of the "Man of War Rock," in the Scilly Islands, is a corruption of Cornish *men* (or *maen*) *an vawr*, meaning "big rock."

The popular name of the marine hydrozoan, *Physalia pelagica*, is the *Portuguese man of war*, or, simply, *man of war*.

Man-of-war bird. The frigate-bird.

The Threefold Man. According to Diogenes Laertios, the body was composed of (1) a mortal part; (2) a divine and ethereal part, called the *phren*; and (3) an aerial and vaporous part, called the *thumos*.

According to the Romans, man has a three-fold soul, which at the dissolution of the body resolves itself into (1) the *Manes*; (2) the *Anima* or Spirit; (3) the *Umbra*. The Manes went either to Elysium or Tartarus; the Anima returned to the gods; but the Umbra hovered about the body as unwilling to quit it.

According to the Jews, man consists of body, soul, and spirit.

Man, Isle of. The origin of the name is doubtful, but it may be O. Celt. *man*, a place. The *Old English Chronicle* calls it *Mon ege* (Mona's Isle), Orderic (about 1100) *Insula Man*; while Cæsar called it *Mona*, Pliny *Monapia*, and Ptolemy *Monarina*. To Bede the island was *Mevaniæ Insulæ*, and Nennius gives it its current Latin name as well as its native name—*Eubonia, id est Manau*, The Manx form is *Eilan Mhannin*.

Mancha, La (la man' cha) was a province of Spain almost identical with the modern province of Ciudad Real. It is celebrated as the country of Don Quixote. It is a land of arid steppes and wide expanses of heath and waste, and is the least populated area of Spain.

Manchester. The name—which is given in Domesday Book as *Mamecestre*, and in the *Old English Chronicle* as *Mameceaster*—is of doubtful origin, but the *mam-* is probably Celtic *mam*, rounded, breast-like, in which case the word would be a Latin and Celtic hybrid denoting "the camp by the round bill." A native of Manchester is a Mancunian, from *Mancunium*, the mediæval Latin name of the city.

Mandamus (Lat., we command). A writ of Queen's Bench, commanding the person or corporation, etc., named to do what the writ directs. So called from the opening word.

Mandarin is not a Chinese word, but one given by the Portuguese colonists at Macao to the officials called by the natives *Kwan*. It is from Malay and Hindi *mantri*, counsellor, from Sansk. *mantra*, counsel (*man*, to think).

The word is sometimes used derisively for over-pompous officials, as, "The mandarins of our Foreign Office."

The manderin orange is probably so called from the resemblance of its colour to that of a mandarin's robe.

The nine ranks of mandarins were distinguished by the button in their cap:—1, ruby; 2, coral; 3, sapphire; 4, an opaque blue stone; 5, crystal; 6, an opaque white shell; 7, wrought gold; 8, plain gold; and 9, silver.

The whole body of Chinese mandarins consists of twenty-seven members. They are appointed for (1) imperial birth; (2) long service; (3) illustrious deeds; (4) knowledge; (5) ability; (6) zeal; (7) nobility; and (8) aristocratic birth.—GUTZLAY.

Mandate (Lat. *mandatum, mandare*, to command). An authoritative charge or command; in law, a contract of bailment by which the mandatory undertakes to perform gratuitously a duty regarding property committed to him. After World War I it was decided by the victorious Powers that the former extra-European colonies and possessions of Germany and Turkey should be governed under *mandate* by one or other of the Powers. Thus, the German colonies in West Africa and parts of the Turkish possessions in Palestine and Mesopotamia became *mandatory spheres* under Great Britain.

Mandrake. The root of the mandrake, of mandragora, often divides in two, and presents a rude appearance of a man. In ancient times human figures were cut out of the root, and wonderful virtues ascribed to them, such as the production of fecundity in women (*Gen.* xxx, 14-16). It was also thought that mandrakes could not be uprooted without producing fatal effects, so a cord used to be fixed to the root, and round a dog's neck, and the dog being chased drew out the mandrake and died. Another fallacy was that a small dose made a person vain of his beauty, and a large one made him an idiot; and yet another that when the mandrake is uprooted it utters a scream, in explanation of which Thomas Newton, in his *Herball to the Bible*, says, "It is supposed to be a creature having life, engendered under the earth of the seed of some dead person put to death for murder."

Shrieks like mandrakes, torn out of the earth.
Romeo and Juliet, iv, 3.

Mandrakes called love-apples. From the old notion that they were aphrodisiacs. Hence Venus is called *Mandragoritis*, and the Emperor Julian, in his epistles, tells Calixenes that he drank its juice nightly as a love-potion.

He has eaten mandrake. Said of a very indolent and sleepy man, from the narcotic and stupefying properties of the plant, well known to the ancients.

Give me to drink mandragora . . .
That I might sleep out this great gap of time
My Antony is away.
Antony and Cleopatra, i, 5.

Not poppy, nor mandragora
Nor all the drowsy syrops of the world,
Shall ever medicine thee to that sweet sleep
Which thou owedst yesterday.
Othello, iii, 3.

Manfred. Count Manfred, the hero of Byron's dramatic poem of this name (1817), sold himself to the Prince of Darkness, was wholly without human sympathies, and lived in splendid solitude among the Alps. He loved the Lady Astarte (*q.v.*), who died, but Manfred went to the hall of Arimanes to see her, and was told that he would die the following day. The next day the Spirit of his Destiny came to summon him; the proud count scornfully dismissed it, and died.

Mani (ma′ nē). The moon, in Scandinavian mythology, the son of Mundilfœri (*q.v.*), taken to heaven by the gods to drive the moon-car. He is followed by a wolf, which, when time shall be no more, will devour both Mani and his sister Sol.

Manitou (măn′ i too). The Great Spirit of the American Indians. The word is Algonkin, and means either the Great Good Spirit or the Great Evil Spirit.

Manna (*Ex.* xvi, 15), popularly said to be a corrupt form of *man-hu* (What is this?). The marginal reading gives — "When the children of Israel saw it [the small round thing like hoar-frost on the ground], they said to one another, What is this? for they wist not what it was."

And the house of Israel, called the name thereof manna; and it was like coriander seed, white; and the taste of it was like wafers made with honey.

The word is more probably the Egyptian *mennu*, a waxy exudation of the tamarisk (*Tamarix gallica*).

Manningtree (Essex). Noted for its Whitsun fair, where an ox was roasted whole. Shakespeare makes Prince Henry call Falstaff "a roasted Manningtree ox; with the pudding in his belly" (1 *Henry IV*, ii, 4).

Manoa (mà nō′ à). The fabulous capital of El Dorado (*q.v.*), the houses of which city were said to be roofed with gold.

Manon Lescaut (mă nong les kō). A novel by the Abbé Prevost (1733). It is the history of a young man, the Chevalier des Grieux, possessed of many brilliant and some estimable qualities, who being intoxicated by a fatal attachment to Manon, a girl who prefers luxury to faithful love, sets his love against the claims of society.

Manor. *Demesne* (*i.e.* "domain") land is that near the demesne or dwelling (*domus*) of the lord, and which he kept for his own use. *Manor* land was all that remained (*maneo*), and was let to tenants for money or service; originally, a barony held by a lord and subject to the jurisdiction of his court-baron.

In some manors there was *common land* also, *i.e.* land belonging in common to two or more persons, to the whole village, or to certain natives of the village.

Lord of the manor. The person of corporation in whom the rights of a manor are vested.

Mansard Roof, also called the *curb roof*. A roof in which the rafters, instead of forming a ∧, are broken on each side into an elbow, the lower rafters being nearly vertical and the upper much inclined. It was devised by François Mansard (1598-1666), the French architect, to give height to attics. Mansard's nephew, Jules Hardouin Mansard (1645-1708) was the architect of the palace of Versailles, and the magnificent dome of the Invalides, among many great works of French architecture.

Mansion. The Latin *mansio* (from *manere*, to remain, dwell) was simply a tent pitched on the march, hence sometimes a "day's journey" (*Pliny*, xii, 14). Subsequently the word was applied to a roadside house for the accommodation of strangers (Suetonius: *Tit.* 10).

Mansion House, now the name of the official residence of a Lord Mayor. It was formerly used of any important dwelling, especially the houses of lords of the manor and of high ecclesiatics.

Mantalini, Madame (măn ta lin′ i). A fashionable milliner in Dickens's *Nicholas Nickleby*, near Cavendish Square. Her husband, whose original name was "Muntle," noted for his white teeth, minced oaths, and gorgeous morning gown, lives on his wife's earnings, and ultimately goes to "the demnition bow-wows."

Mantle of Fidelity. The old ballad "The Boy and the Mantle," in Percy's *Reliques*, tells how a little boy showed King Arthur a curious mantle, "which would become no wife that was not leal." Queen Guinever tried it, but it changed from green to red, and red to black, and seemed rent into shreds. Sir Kay's lady tried it, but fared no better; others followed, but only Sir Cradock's wife could wear it. The theme is a very common one in old story, and was used by Spenser in the incident of Florimel's girdle.

Manure (Fr. *main-œuvre*). Literally "hand-work," hence tillage by manual labour, hence the dressing applied to lands. Milton uses the word in its original sense in *Paradise Lost*, iv, 628: —

You flowery arbours. . . . with branches overgrown
That mock our scant manuring.

And in xi, 28, says that the repentant tears of Adam brought forth better fruits than all the trees of Paradise that his hands "manured" in the days of innocence.

Manx cat. A tailless species of cat found in the Isle of Man.

Many a little makes a mickle. Little and often fills the purse. *See* LITTLE.

Many men, many minds, *i.e.* as many opinions as there are persons to give them; an adaptation of Terence's *Quot homines tot sententiæ* (*Phormio*, II, iv, 14).

Too many for me or **One too many for me.** More than a match. *Il est trop fort pour moi.*
The Irishman is cunning enough; but we shall be too many for him.—MRS. EDGEWORTH.

Maori (mou' ri). The aboriginal Polynesian inhabitants of New Zealand; a native word meaning *indigenous.*

Maple Leaf. The emblem of Canada.

Maquis (ma' kē). The thick scrub in Corsica to which bandits retire and resist by arms any attempt to apprehend them. A bandit so on the run is called a *maquisard. See also* F.F.I.

Marabou. A large stork or heron of western Africa, so called from Arab. *murabit,* a hermit, because among the Arabs these birds were held to be sacred. Its feathers are used by ladies for headgear, neck-wraps, etc.

Marabouts. A priestly order of Morocco (Arab. *murabit,* a hermit) which, in 1075, founded a dynasty and ruled over Morocco and part of Spain till it was put an end to by the Almohads in the 12th century.

Marais, Le. *See* PLAIN.

Maranatha (Syriac, *the Lord will come—i.e.* to execute judgment). A word which, with *Anathema* (*q.v.*), occurs in 1 *Cor.* xvi, 22, has been erroneously taken as a form of anathematizing among the Jews; hence, used for a terrible curse.

Marathon Race (măr' à thon). A long-distance running race, named after the Battle of Marathon (490 B.C.) the result of which was announced at Athens by a courier, sometimes called Pheidippides, who fell dead on his arrival. The race, properly of 26 miles, 385 yards, is one of the events at the modern Olympic games. The record (1948) was held by K. Son, of Japan, who in 1936 ran the course in 2 hours, 29 mins., 19·2 secs.

Maravedi or **Marvedie** (mar à ve' di). A very small Spanish copper coin, worth less than a farthing and long obsolete. There are frequent references to it in Elizabethan and 17th-century literature. In the 11th and 12th centuries there was a Portuguese gold coin of the same name, equivalent to about 14s.

Marbles. *See* ARUNDELIAN; ELGIN.

March. The month is so called from "Mars," the Roman war-god and patron deity.
The old Dutch name for it was *Lent-maand* (lengthening-month), because the days sensibly lengthen; the old Saxon name was *Hreth-monath* (rough month, from its boisterous winds); the name was subsequently changed to *Length-monath* (lengthening month); it was also called *Hlyd-monath* (boisterous month); In the French Republican calendar it was called *Ventose* (windy month, February 20th to March 20th).

A bushel of March dust is worth a king's ransom. Because we want plenty of dry, windy weather in March to ensure good crops. The fine for murder used to be proportioned to the rank of the person killed. The lowest was £10, and the highest £60; the former was the ransom of a churl, and the latter of a king.

He may be a rogue, but he's no fool on the march. Though his honesty may be in question he is a useful sort of person to have about.

March borrows three days from April. *See* BORROWED DAYS.

Mad as a March hare. *See* HARE.

To steal a march on. *See* STEAL.

March table. British military term denoting a direction setting out the order in which the elements of a convoy should proceed, the exact minute at which each should pass a given starting point, and the average speed at which each should proceed.

Marching Watch. The guard of civilians enrolled in London during the Middle Ages to keep order in the streets on the Vigils of St. Peter and St. John the Baptist during the festivities then held; used also of the festivities themselves. Henry VIII approved of the pageants, etc., and on one occasion, to encourage them, took his queen, Katharine of Aragon, to witness the proceedings at "the King's Heade in Cheape." The custom fell into abeyance in 1527 on account of the sweating sickness, but was revived a few years later.

Marches. The A.S. *mearc,* a mark, by way of Fr. *marche,* a frontier. The boundaries between England and Wales, and between England and Scotland, were called "marches," and the word is the origin of our *marquis,* the lord of the march.
The word is still applied in the sense that a boundary is shared, e.g. Kent marches with Sussex, that is, the two counties are contiguous.

Riding the marches—*i.e.* beating the bounds of the parish (Scots). *See* BOUNDS, BEATING THE.

Marchington (Staffordshire). Famous for a crumbling short cake. Hence the saying that one of crusty temper is "as short as Marchington wake-cake."

Marchioness, The. The half-starved girl-of-all-work in Dickens's *Old Curiosity Shop*. As she has no name of her own Dick Swiveller gives her that of "Sophronia Sphynx," and eventually marries her.

Marchpane (march' pān). The old name for the confection of almonds, sugar, etc., that we call *marzipan*, this being the German form of the original Ital. *marzapane*, and adopted by us in the 19th century in preference to our own well-established word, because we imported the stuff largely from Germany.

First Serv.: Away with the joint-stools, remove the court-cupboard, look to the plate. Good thou, save me a piece of marchpane.—*Romeo and Juliet*, i, 5.

Mardi Gras (mar dē gra') (Fr., "fat Tuesday"). The last day of the Lent carnival in France, Shrove Tuesday, which is celebrated with all sorts of festivities. In Paris a fat ox used to be paraded through the principal streets, crowned with a fillet, and accompanied by mock priests and a band of tin instruments in imitation of a Roman sacrificial procession.

Mare. The Cromlech at Gorwell, Dorsetshire, is called the White Mare; the barrows near Hambleton, the Grey Mare.

Away the mare. Off with the blue devils, good-bye to care. This mare is the incubus called the nightmare.

To cry the mare (Herefordshire and Shropshire). In harvesting, when the ingathering is complete, a few blades of corn left for the purpose have their tops tied together. The reapers then place themselves at a certain distance, and fling their sickles at the "mare." He who succeeds in cutting the knot cries out "I have her!" "What have you?" "A mare." "Whose is she?" The name of some farmer whose field has been reaped is here mentioned. "Where will you send her?" The name of some farmer whose corn is not yet harvested is here given, and then all the reapers give a final shout.

Mare (mâr' i). The Latin word for *sea*. *Mare clausum* is a sea that is closed by a certain Power or Powers to the unrestricted trade of other nations. *Mare liberum* is a free and open sea. In 1635 John Selden (1584-1654) published a treatise entitled *Mare Clausum*. *Mare nostrum*, "our sea" was a term applied by Italian Fascists to the Mediterranean at the height of their imperial ambitions.

Margaret. A country name for the magpie (*q.v.*); also for the daisy, or marguerite, so called from its pearly whiteness, *marguerite* being Old French for a pearl.

Margaret, St. The chosen type of female innocence and meekness, represented as a young woman of great beauty, bearing the martyr's palm and crown, or with the dragon as an attribute. Sometimes she is delineated as coming from the dragon's mouth, for legend says that the monster swallowed her, but on her making the sign of the cross he suffered her to quit his maw.

Another legend has it that Olybrius, governor of Antioch, captivated by her beauty, wanted to marry her, and, as she rejected him with scorn, threw her into a dungeon, where the devil came to her in the form of a dragon. She held up the cross, and the dragon fled.

St. Margaret, whose feast is held on July 20th, is the patron saint of the ancient borough of Lynn Regis, and on the corporation seal she is represented as standing on a dragon and wounding it with the cross. The inscription is "SVB . MARGARETA . TERITUR . DRACO . STAT . CRUCE . LÆTA."

Margarine (there are two pronunciations of this; mar' jà rēn, mar' gà rēn). It is a well-known butter substitute made of a great variety of vegetable and animal fats and oils. It takes its name from the Greek *margaron*, a pearl.

Margin. In many old books a commentary was printed in the margin (as in our Bible of the present day); hence the word was often used for a commentary itself, as in Shakespeare's—

His face's own margent did quote such amazes.
Love's Labour's Lost, ii, 1.
I knew you must be edified by the margent.
Hamlet, v, 2.

Marguerite des Marguerites (*the pearl of pearls*). So Francis called his sister, Marguerite de Valois (1492-1549), authoress of the *Heptameron*. She married twice; first, the Duc d'Alençon, and then Henri d'Albret, king of Navarre, and was known for her Protestant leanings.

Sylvius de la Haye published (1547) a collection of her poems with the title *Marguerites de la marguerite des princesses*, etc.

Marian Year. The method of reckoning March 25th, the Feast of the Annunciation of Our Lady, as the first day of the year. This was employed until the reform of the calendar in 1752, and still exists as more or less the beginning of the financial year.

Marigold. The plant *Calendula officinalis* and its bright yellow flower are so called in honour of the Virgin Mary.

This riddle, Cuddy, if thou canst, explain . . .
What flower is that which bears the Virgin's name,
The richest metal added to the same?
              GAY: *Pastoral.*

In 17th-century slang a marigold (or "mary-gold") meant a sovereign.

Marimba (mà rim' bà). A musical instrument formed of strips of wood struck by hammers or sticks. It is of African origin but it has been improved upon and popularized in Central America, where it got its present name.

Marine. The female Marine. Hannah Snell, of Worcester (1723-92), who (according to tradition), passing herself off as a Marine, took part in the attack on Pondicherry. It is said that she ultimately opened a public-house in Wapping, but retained her male attire.

Mariner's compass. Traditionally claimed by the Chinese to have been in use as early as 2364 B.C., but first recorded as being used for sea travel by a Chinese writer of about A.D. 800. It was introduced to Europe by Marco Polo, but it is probable that it was known—as the result of independent discovery—in the 12th century. See FLEUR-DE-LIS.

Marjoram (mar' jôr àm). **As a pig loves marjoram.** Not at all. "How did you like so-and-so?" "Well, as a pig loves marjoram." Lucretius tells us (vi, 974), *Amaricinum fugitat sus,* swine shun marjoram; but it is not at all certain that the Latin *amaricus* is identical with our *marjoram.*

Mark. A man of mark. A notable or famous man; one who has "made his mark" in some walk of life.

Mark time! Move the feet alternately as in marching, but without advancing or retreating from the spot.

Mark is also a British military term denoting a version or issue of a piece of equipment. The first issue of a new weapon, for example, is Mark I, which continues until any alteration or improvement, however small, is made in the design. Subsequent issues are known as Mark II until any further alteration is made, and so on.

To make one's mark. To distinguish oneself. To write one's name (or make one's mark) on the page of history.

In olden times persons who could not write "made their mark" as they do now, but we find in ancient documents words such as these: "This (grant) is signed with the sign of the cross for its greater assurance (or) greater inviolability," and after the sign follows the name of the donor.

To toe the mark. To line up abreast of the others; so, to "fall in" and do one's duty.

Up to the mark. Generally used in the negative; as, "Not quite up to the mark," not good enough, not up to the standard fixed by the assay office for gold and silver articles; not quite well.

Mark, as a name.

Mark, King. A king of Cornwall in the Arthurian romances, Sir Tristram's uncle. He lived at Tintagel, and is principally remembered for his treachery and cowardice, and as the husband of Isolde the Fair, who was passionately enamoured of his nephew, Tristram (*q.v.*).

Mark Twain. The pseudonym of the American novelist and humorist, Samuel L. Clemens (1835-1910) who adopted it from the Mississippi river pilots' cry, "Mark twain!" When taking soundings.

St. Mark's Eve. An old custom in North-country villages is for people to sit in the church porch on this day (April 24th) from 11 at night to 1 in the morning for three years running, and the third time they will see the ghosts of those who are to die that year pass into the church.

Poor Robin's Almanack for 1770 refers to another superstition:—

On St. Mark's Eve, at twelve o'clock,
The fair maid will watch her smock,
To find her husband in the dark,
By praying unto good St. Mark.

Keats has an unfinished poem on the subject, and he also refers to it in *Cap and Bells* (lvi) :—

Look in the Almanack—Moore never lies—
April the twenty-fourth,—this coming day
Now breathing its new bloom upon the skies,
Will end in St. Mark's Eve; you must away,
For on that eve alone can you the maid convey.

Market-penny. A toll surreptitiously exacted by servants sent out to buy goods for their master; secret commission on goods obtained for an employer.

Marlborough (mawl' brò). **Statutes of Marlborough.** Laws passed in 1267 by a parliament held in Marlborough Castle. They reaffirmed in more formal fashion the Provisions of Westminster of a few years earlier.

Marmion (mar' mi òn). A romantic poem by Scott (pubd. 1808), telling the story of Lord Marmion, an entirely fictional character, who lived in the Border Country in the time of Henry VIII and James IV of Scotland. He was slain at the battle of Flodden.

Maro (mâr' ō). Virgil (70-19 B.C.), whose full name was Publius Virgilius Maro; born on the banks of the river Mincio, at the village of Andes, near Mantua.

Marocco or **Morocco.** The name of Banks's horse (*q.v.*).

Maronites (măr′ ō nītz). A nation and Church of Arabic-speaking Syrian Christians, united to the Roman Catholic Church but still retaining the Syrian liturgy and many of their peculiarities. They descend from a sect of Monothelites of the 8th century, and are so called from their chief seat, the monastery of Maron, on the slopes of Lebanon, which was named from Maron (Syriac, "my lord," or "master"), Patriarch of Antioch in the 6th century.

Maroon (mà roon′). To set a person on an inhospitable shore and leave him there (a practice common with pirates and buccaneers); a corruption of *Cimarron*, a word applied by Spaniards to anything unruly, whether man or beast. As a noun the word denotes runaway slaves or their descendants who live in the wilds of Dutch Guiana, Brazil, etc. Those of Jamaica are the offspring of runaways from the old plantations or from Cuba, to whom, in 1738, the British Government granted a tract of land, on which they built two towns.

Maroon, the firework that explodes like a cannon going off, is so called from Fr. *marron*, a chestnut, probably with reference to the popping of chestnuts when being roasted.

In World War I air-raid warnings and all-clear signals were made by means of maroons.

In the U.S.A. the term was also applied to a hunting or fishing expedition in the form of a prolonged picnic lasting several days.

Marplot. An officious person who defeats some design by gratuitous meddling. The name is given to a silly, cowardly, inquisitive Paul Pry, in *The Busybody* (1710), by Mrs. Centlivre. Similarly we have Shakespeare's "Sir Oliver *Mar-text*," the clergyman in *As You Like It*, and "Sir Martin *Mar-All*, the hero of the Duke of Newcastle's comedy of that name, which was founded on Molière's *L'Etourdi*.

Marprelate Controversy. The name given to the vituperative paper war of about 1589, in which the Puritan pamphleteers attacked the Church of England under the pseudonym "Martin Marprelate." Thomas Cooper, Bishop of Winchester, defended the Church, and the chief of the "Martinists" were probably Udall, Throckmorton, Penry, and Barrow. Udall died in prison (1592); Penry and Barrow were executed in 1593. Some thirty pamphlets are known to have been published in this controversy.

Marque. *See* LETTER OF.

Marquess or **Marquis** (O.Fr. *marchis*, warden of the marches). A title of nobility, in England ranking next below that of Duke (*q.v.*). It was first conferred on Richard II's favourite, Robert de Vere, Earl of Oxford, who was created Marquess of Dublin in 1385. A marquess is addressed as "The Most Honourable the Marquess of—", his younger sons and daughters bear the honorary titles of Lord and Lady.

Marriage. Marriage knot, The. The bond of marriage effected by the legal marriage service. The Latin phrase is *nodus Herculeus*, and part of the marriage service was for the bridegroom to loosen (*solvere*) the bride's girdle, not to *tie* it. In the Hindu marriage ceremony the bridegroom hangs a ribbon on the bride's neck and ties it in a knot. Before the knot is tied the bride's father may refuse consent unless better terms are offered, but immediately the knot is tied the marriage is indissoluble. The Parsees bind the hands of the bridegroom with a seven-fold cord, seven being a sacred number. The ancient Carthaginians tied the thumbs of the betrothed with a leather lace.

The practice of throwing rice (*see* RICE) is also Indian.

Marriages are made in heaven. This does not mean that persons in heaven "marry and are given in marriage," but that the partners joined in marriage on earth were foreordained to be so united. E. Hall (1499-1547) says, "Consider the old proverbe to be true that saieth: Marriage is destinie," *Cp.* "Hanging and wiving, etc." *under* HANG.

Married women take their husband's surname. This was a Roman custom. Thus Julia, Octavia, etc., married to Pompey, Cicero, etc., would be called Julia of Pompey, Octavia of Cicero. Our married women are named in the same way, omitting "of."

Mars. The Roman god of war; identified in certain aspects with the Greek Ares. He was also the patron of husbandmen.

The planet of this name was so called from early times because of its reddish tinge, and under it, says the *Compost of Ptholomeus*, "is borne theves and robbers . . . nyght walkers and quarell pykers, bosters, mockers, and skoffers; and these men of Mars causeth warre, and murther, and batayle. They wyll be gladly smythes or workers of yron . . . lyers, gret swerers. . . . He is red and angry . . . a great walker, and a maker of swordes and knyves, and a sheder of mannes blode . . . and good to be a barboure and a blode letter, and to drawe tethe."

Among the alchemists Mars designated iron, and in Camoën's *Lusiad* typified divine fortitude. As Bacchus, the evil demon, is the guardian power of Mohammedanism, so Mars is the guardian of Christianity.

The Mars of Portugal. Alfonso de Albuquerque, Viceroy of India (1452-1515).

See also MARTIANS.

Marseillaise (*Eng.* mar se lāz', *Fr.* mar sā yāz'). The hymn of the French revolution. Claude Joseph Rouget de Lisle (1760-1835), an artillery officer in garrison at Strasbourg, composed both the words and the music (April 24th, 1792). On July 30th, 1792, the Marseilles volunteers entered Paris singing the song; and the Parisians, enchanted with it, called it the *Hymne des Marseillais.*

Marshal (A.S. *mere,* mare, *scealc,* servant; O.Fr. *mareschal*). Originally one who tended horses, either as a groom or farrier; now the title of high officials about the Court, in the armed forces, etc. In the Army Field-Marshal (*q.v.*) is the highest rank; in the Royal Air Force Marshal of the R.A.F., Air Chief Marshal, Air Marshal, and Air Vice-Marshal, correspond to Field-Marshal, General, Lieutenant-General, and Major-General respectively. The military rank of Marshal of France was revived by Napoleon I, who gave the baton to a number of his most able generals. No Marshals were created after 1870 until 1916 when the title was given to General Joffre (1852-1931). Generals Foch (1851-1929), Lyautey (1854-1934), and Pétain (1856-1951) were also Marshals of France.

Marshall Plan. This was a plan for aiding the stricken European states after World War II. On June 5th, 1947, G. C. Marshall, Secretary of State for the U.S.A., called upon the countries of Europe to work out a programme of reconstruction for which he promised American assistance "so far as it may be practicable." After consultation together most of the powers concerned, with the exception of Russia and the eastern European states under her tutelage, agreed to participate and on April 3rd, 1948 the scheme came into force by Congress passing a Foreign Aid Bill of $3,800,000,000. Britain ceased to receive Marshall Aid in 1950.

Marshalsea Prison. An old prison in Southwark, London (demolished in 1849), so called because it was formerly governed by a *Knight Marshal, i.e.* an official of the Royal Household who took cognizance of offences committed within the royal verge and who presided over the *Marshalsea Court* (amalgamated with the Queen's Bench in 1842). It was the Marshal of this prison who was beheaded by the rebels under Wat Tyler in 1381.

Martel (mar' tel). The surname given to Charles; son of Pépin d'Héristal (about 690-791), probably because of his victory over the Saracens, who had invaded France under Abd-el-Rahman in 732. It is said that Charles "knocked down the foe, and crushed them beneath his axe, as a *martel* or hammer crushes what it strikes." Another suggestion is that he was so called because his patron saint (and the patron saint of Tours, near which he gained his great victory) was *St. Martellus* (or *Martin*).

Martello Towers. Round towers about forty feet in height, of great strength, and situated on a coast or river-bank. Many of them were built on the south-eastern coasts of England about 1804, to repel the threatened Napoleonic invasion; and they took their name from *Mortella* (Corsica), where a tower from which these were designed had proved, in 1794, extremely difficult to capture.

Mar-text. *See* MARPLOT.

Martha, St., patron saint of good housewives, is represented in art in homely costume, bearing at her girdle a bunch of keys, and holding a ladle or pot of water in her hand. Like St. Margaret, she is accompanied by a dragon bound, for she is said to have destroyed one that ravaged the neighbourhood of Marseilles, but she has not the palm and crown of martyrdom. She is commemorated on July 29th, and is patron of Tarascon.

Martha's Vineyard. An island, some 100 sq. miles in area, off the S.E. coast of Massachusetts. It was discovered in 1602 by Bartholomew Gosnold, the discoverer of Cape Cod and the adjacent coasts, and so named by him. Martha's Vineyard is now a popular summer resort with a population, in 1940, of over 5,000.

Martian Laws. Laws traditionally said to have been compiled by Martia, wife of Guithelin, great-grandson of Mulmutius, who established in England the Mulmutine Laws (*q.v.*). Alfred translated both these codes into Saxon-English.

> Guynteline . . . whose queen, . . . to show her upright mind,
> To wise Malmutius' laws her Martian first did frame.
> DRAYTON: *Polyolbion,* viii.

Martians (mar' shánz). The hypothetical inhabitants of the planet Mars. This planet has an atmosphere of much less density than that of the earth, but it has clouds and seasonal changes which have led some observers to presume that there is vegetation of a sort. From this it was an easy step to imagine life on its surface and in 1898 H. G. Wells wrote *The War of the Worlds* in which he recounted the adventures and horrors of a war between the fabulous men of Mars and the dwellers on Earth.

Martin. One of the swallow tribe; probably so called from the Christian name *Martin* (St. Martin's bird is the *goose*), but possibly because it appears in England about March (*the Martian* month) and disappears about Martinmas.

In *Reynard the Fox* (*q.v.*) *Martin* is the Ape; Rukenaw was his wife, Fubrumpe his son, and Byteluys and Hattenette his two daughters; and in Dryden's *Hind and the Panther*, an allegory, Martin means the Lutheran party; so called by a pun on the name of Martin Luther.

Martin, St. The patron saint of innkeepers and drunkards, usually shown in art as a young mounted soldier dividing his cloak with a beggar. He was born of heathen parents but was converted in Rome, and became Bishop of Tours in 371, dying at Caudes forty years later. His day is November 11th, the day of the Roman *Vinalia*, or Feast of Bacchus; hence his purely accidental patronage (as above), and hence also the phrase *Martin drunk*.

The usual illustration of St. Martin is in allusion to the legend that when he was a military tribune stationed at Amiens he once, in midwinter, divided his cloak with a naked beggar, who craved alms of him before the city gates. At night, the story says, Christ Himself appeared to the soldier, arrayed in this very garment.

Martinmas. The feast of St. Martin, November 11th. *His Martinmas will come, as it does to every hog*—i.e. all must die. November was the great slaughtering time of the Anglo-Saxons, when oxen, sheep, and hogs, whose food was exhausted, were killed and salted. Thus the proverb intimates that our day of death will come as surely as that of a hog at St. Martin's-tide.

Martinet. A strict disciplinarian; so called from the Marquis de Martinet, colonel commanding Louis XIV's own regiment of infantry. All young noblemen were obliged, by direction of the king, to command a platoon in this unit before purchasing command of an infantry regiment, and Martinet's own system for inculcating in these wild young men the principles of military discipline earned him immortal fame. He was slain at the siege of Doesbourg, in 1672 (Voltaire, *Louis XIV*, c. 10).

Martyr (Gr.), simply means a witness, but is applied to one who witnesses a good confession with his blood.

The Martyr King. Charles I of England, beheaded January 30th, 1649.

Martyr to science. A title conferred on anyone who loses his health or life through his devotion to science; especially Claude Louis, Count Berthollet (1748-1822), who tested in his own person the effects of carbolic acid on the human frame, and died under the experiment.

Marvedie. *See* MARAVEDI.

Mary. As *the Virgin*, she is represented in art with flowing hair, emblematical of her virginity.

As *Mater Dolorosa*, she is represented as somewhat elderly, clad in mourning, head draped, and weeping over the dead body of Christ.

As *Our Lady of Dolours*, she is represented as seated, her breast being pierced with seven swords, emblematic of her seven sorrows.

As *Our Lady of Mercy*, she is represented with arms extended, spreading out her mantle, and gathering sinners beneath it.

As *The glorified Madonna*, she is represented as bearing a crown and sceptre, or a ball and cross, in rich robes and surrounded by angels.

Her seven joys. The Annunciation, Visitation, Nativity, Epiphany, Finding in the Temple, Resurrection, Ascension.

Her seven sorrows. Simeon's Prophecy, the Flight into Egypt, Christ Missed, the Betrayal, the Crucifixion, the Taking Down from the Cross, and the Entombment.

Little Mary. A euphemism for the stomach; from the play of that name by J. M. Barrie (1903).

The four Marys. Mary Beaton (or *Bethune*), Mary Livingston (or *Leuson*), Mary Fleming (or *Flemyng*), and Mary Seaton (or *Seyton*); called the "Queen's Marys," that is, the ladies of the same age as Mary, afterwards Queen of Scots, and her companions. Mary Carmichael was not one of the four, although introduced in the well-known ballad.

> Yestre'en the queen had four Marys,
>   This night she'll hae but three:
> There was Mary Beaton, and Mary Seaton,
>   Mary Carmichael, and me.

Mary of Arnhem. Name used by Helen Sensburg in Nazi propaganda broadcasts to British troops in North-west Europe, 1944-45. Her melting voice made her programmes very popular with the British, but without the results for which she hoped.

Mary, Highland. *See* HIGHLAND MARY.

Mary Magdalene, St. Patron saint of penitents, being herself the model penitent of Gospel history. Her feast is July 22nd.

In art she is represented either as young and beautiful, with a profusion of hair, and holding a box of ointment, or as a penitent, in a sequestered place, reading before a cross or skull.

Mary Queen of Scots. Shakespeare being under the patronage of Queen Elizabeth, and knowing her jealousy, would not, of course, praise openly her rival queen; but in the *Midsummer Night's Dream* (ii, 1) composed in 1592, five years after the execution of Mary, he wrote these exquisite lines:—

> Thou rememberest
> Since once I sat upon a promontory,
> And heard a *mermaid* on a *dolphin's* back
> Uttering such dulcet and harmonious breath
> That the *rude sea* grew civil at her song;
> And *certain stars* shot *madly from their spheres*.
> To hear the sea-maid's music.
>
> *Act* ii, 1.

These have been conjectured to refer to the ill-fated queen on the following grounds:—
Mermaid and *sea-maid*, Mary; on the *dolphin's* back, she married the *Dolphin* or *Dauphin* of France; *the rude sea grew civil*, the Scottish rebels; *certain stars*, the Earl of Northumberland, the Earl of Westmoreland, and the Duke of Norfolk; *shot madly from their spheres*, that is, revolted from Queen Elizabeth, bewitched by the *sea-maid's* sweetness.

Maryland (U.S.A.) was so named in compliment to Henrietta Maria, Queen of Charles I. In the Latin charter it is called *Terra Mariæ*.

Marylebone (London) is not a corruption of *Marie la bonne*, but "Mary on the bourne," *i.e.* the Tyburn (*q.v.*), as Holborn is "Old Bourne."

Mascot. A person or thing that is supposed to bring good luck (*cp.* JETTATURA). The word is French slang (perhaps connected with Provençal *masco*, a sorcerer), and was popularized in England by Audran's opera, *La Mascotte*, 1880.

> Ces envoyés du paradis,
> Sont des Mascottes, mes amis,
> Heureux celui que le ciel dote d'une Mascotte.
>
> *La Mascotte.*

Masher. An old-fashioned term for a "nut" or dude (*q.v.*); an exquisite; a lardy-dardy swell. This sort of thing used to be called "crushing" or killing, and, as mashing is crushing, the synonym was substituted about 1880. A lady-killer, a crusher, a masher, all mean the same thing.

Mask, The Man in the Iron. A mysterious individual held for over forty years as a State prisoner by Louis XIV at Pignerol and other prisons, ultimately dying in the Bastille, Nov. 19th, 1703; with, his identity still undisclosed. His name was given as "Marchiali" when he was buried; but despite the numerous conjectures and wide research that have been made, no one to this day knows for certain who he was. One name put forward is that of General du Bulonde, who, in 1691, raised the siege of Cuneo against the orders of Catinat. In 1891 Capt. Bazeriès published in *Le Temps* translations of some cipher dispatches, apparently showing that this is the solution.

Other persons who have been suggested are:—

A twin brother of Louis XIV; or, perhaps, an elder brother, whose father is given as Cardinal Mazarin or the Duke of Buckingham.

Louis, Duc de Vermandois, natural son of Louis XIV by De la Vallière, who was imprisoned for life because he gave the Dauphin a box on the ears.

It is now considered probable that he was Count Girolamo Mattioli, Minister to the Duke of Mantua, who had acted treacherously towards Louis in refusing to give up the fortress of Casale—the key of Italy—after signing a treaty promising to do so, and in consequence was lured on to French soil, captured, and imprisoned at Pignerol.

Among the less likely names that have been put forward are the Duke of Monmouth, Avedick (an Armenian patriarch), Fouquet (the disgraced Minister of Finance), the Duc de Beaufort (who disappeared at the siege of Candia in 1669), and Mattioli's secretary, Jean de Gonzague.

Masochism (măs' ō kizm). A psychological term for the condition in which sexual gratification depends on the subject's self-humiliation and self-inflicted physical pain. It takes its name from Leopold von Sacher-Masoch (1836-95) the Austrian novelist who first described this aberration.

Mason and Dixon's Line. The southern boundary line which separated the free state of Pennsylvania from what were at one time the slave states of Maryland and Virginia. It lies in 39° 43' 26" north latitude, and was fixed by Charles Mason and Jeremiah Dixon, English astronomers and surveyors (1763-67).

Mass (măs, mas). The R.C. name for the Eucharist. There are several kinds of Mass, the principal being High Mass, or *Missa solemnis* in which the celebrant is assisted by a deacon and subdeacon—it requires the presence of a choir, a number of acolytes or servers, and the use of incense; Sung Mass, said and sung by the celebrant alone; Low Mass, which is said by the celebrant alone in four tones of voice; clear, medium, low, and inaudible (secret). There is also Pontifical Mass, sung by a cardinal, bishop in his own diocese, or abbot in his own abbey, with a very full ritual, three assistants and at least nine acolytes.

Mass observation is a British trade-mark name for a system of obtaining information as to popular sentiment and opinion similar to the Gallup Poll (*q.v.*).

Massachusetts (măs à choo' sets) (U.S.A.). So called from the tribe of Indians of that name. Its origin is not clear; one suggestion is that it means "the Blue Mountains," and another that it is *massa*, great, *wadehuash*, mountains, *et*, near, *i.e.* near-the-great-mountain.

Massacre of the Innocents. The slaughter of the male children of Bethlehem "from two years old and under," when Jesus was born (*Matt.* ii, 16). This was done at the command of Herod the Great in order to cut off "the babe" who was destined to become "King of the Jews."

In parliamentary phraseology, the phrase denotes the withdrawal at the close of a session of the bills which there has been no time to consider and pass.

Old Masters. The great painters (especially of Italy and the Low Countries) who worked from the 13th century to about the end of the 16th, or a little later. Also their paintings.

Mastic. A kind of chewing-gum made of the resin of *Pistachia Lentiscus*, a tree of the Levant and other Eastern parts, formerly much used in medicine. It was said to promote appetite, and therefore only increased the misery of a hungry man.

> Like the starved wretch that hungry mastic chews,
> But cheats himself and fosters his disease.
> WEST: *Triumphs of the Gout* (*Lucian*).

Matador (măt' à dôr). In Spanish bull-fights the star or leader of each team, who has to play the bull alone and finally kill it.

In the game of ombre, *Spadille* (the ace of spades), *Manille* (the seven of trumps), and *Basto* (the ace of clubs) are called "Matadors."

> Now move to war her sable Matadores . . .
> Spadillo first, unconquerable lord,
> Led off two captive trumps, and swept the board,
> As many more Manillo forced to yield.
> And marched a victor from the verdant field.
> Him Basto followed . . ."
> POPE: *Rape of the Lock*, canto iii.

In the game of dominoes of this name the double-blank and all the "stones" that of themselves make seven (6-1, 5-2, and 4-3) are "matadors," and can be played at any time.

Mate. A man does not get his hands out of the tar by becoming second mate. In long-past days of sailing-ships the second mate was expected to put his hands into the tar bucket for tarring the rigging, like the men below him. The first mate was exempt from this dirty work.

Maté (măt' ā). Paraguay tea, made from the leaves of the Brazilian holly (*Ilex Paraguayensis*), is so called from the vessel in which it is infused. The vessels are generally hollow gourds.

Materialism. The doctrines of a *Materialist*, who maintains that there is nothing in the universe but matter, that mind is a phenomenon of matter, and that there is no ground for assuming a spiritual First Cause; as against the orthodox doctrine that the soul is distinct from the body, and is a portion of the Divine essence breathed into the body. Materialism is opposed to Idealism; in the ancient world its chief exponents were Epicurus and Lucretius, in modern times the 18th-century French philosophers, Helvétius, d'Holbach, and Lamettrie.

Materialize. A word used in psychical research to describe the assumption of bodily form of psychical phenomena. The principles governing materialization are as yet unknown, and little progress has been made in discovering them.

Matriculate means to enrol oneself in a society (Lat. *matricula*, a roll or register). The University is called our *alma mater* (propitious mother). The students are her *alumni* (foster-children), and become so by being enrolled in a register after certain forms and examinations.

In common parlance it used to mean to pass the entrance examination that permits one to be entered as a student at a university. Many, however, sat for the matriculation examinations who had no intention of proceeding to a university. It has now been abolished.

Matsya. *See* AVATAR.

Matter-of-fact. Unvarnished truth; prosaic, unimaginative, as a "matter-of-fact swain."

Matthew, St. Represented in art (1) as an evangelist—an old man with long beard—an angel generally standing near him dictating his Gospel; (2) As an apostle, in which capacity he bears a purse, in reference to his calling as a publican; sometimes he carries a spear, sometimes a carpenter's rule or square. His symbol is an angel, or a man's face (*see* EVANGELISTS), and he is commemorated on September 21st.

Legend has it that St. Matthew preached for 15 years in Judæa after the Ascension, and then carried the Gospel to Ethiopia, where he was martyred.

In the last of Matthew. At the last gasp, on one's last legs. This is a German expression, and arose thus: a Catholic priest said in his sermon that Protestantism was in the last of Matthew, and, being asked what he meant, replied, "The last five words of the Gospel of St. Matthew are these: 'The end of this dispensation.' " He quoted the Latin version; ours is less correctly translated "the end of the *world*."

Matthew Parker's Bible: Matthew's Bible. *See* BIBLE, THE ENGLISH.

Maudlin. Stupidly sentimental. *Maudlin drunk* is the drunkenness which is sentimental and inclined to tears. *Maudlin slip-slop* is sentimental chit-chat. The word is derived from Mary *Magdalen*, who is drawn by ancient painters with a lackadaisical face, and eyes swollen with weeping.

Maul of Monks, The. Thomas Cromwell (1485-1540), visitor-general of English monasteries, many of which he summarily suppressed.

Maumet, Maumetry. *See* MAMMET.

Maundrel. A foolish, vapouring gossip. The Scots say, "Haud your tongue, maundrel." As a verb it means to babble, to prate, as in delirium, in sleep, or intoxication. The term is said to be from Sir John *Mandeville*, 14th-century traveller in the Far East, the account of whose adventures (earliest MS., 1371) is full of strange stories and unverified events.

Maundy Thursday. The day before Good Friday is so called from the first words of the antiphon for that day being *Mandatum novum do vobis*, a new commandment I give unto you (*St. John* xiii, 34), with which the ceremony of the washing of the feet begins. This is still carried out in R.C. cathedral churches and monasteries. In the monasteries it was the custom to wash the feet of as many poor people as there were monks, and for centuries in England the sovereign, as a token of humility, did the same. Mention is made in the Wardrobe Book of Edward I of money being given on Easter Eve to thirteen poor people whose feet the Queen had washed; the custom is said to have been kept up as late as the time of James II, but now the distribution of money (*see* MAUNDS) is all that is left of it.

The word has been incorrectly derived from *maund* (a basket), because on the day before the great fast Catholics brought out their broken food in *maunds* to distribute to the poor. This custom in many places gave birth to a fair, as the Tombland Fair of Norwich, held on the plain before the Cathedral Close.

Mauritania (maw ri tā' nyà). Morocco and Algiers, the land of the ancient Mauri or Moors. The kingdom of Mauritania was annexed to the Roman Empire in A.D. 42, and was finally disintegrated when overrun by the Vandals in 429.

Mausoleum. Originally the name of the tomb of Mausolus, King of Caria, to whom Artemisia (his wife) erected at Halicarnassus a splendid sepulchral monument (353 B.C.). Parts of this sepulchre, which was one of the Seven Wonders of the World, are now in the British Museum. The name is now applied to any sepulchral monument of great size or architectural quality.

The chief mausoleums are: that of Augustus; of Hadrian, *i.e.* the castle of St. Angelo, at Rome; that erected in France to Henry II by Catherine de' Medicis; that of St. Peter the Martyr in the church of St. Eustatius, by G. Balduccio in the 14th century.

Mauthe Dog. A ghostly black spaniel that for many years haunted Peel Castle, in the Isle of Man. It used to enter the guardroom as soon as candles were lighted, and leave it at daybreak. While this spectre dog was present the soldiers forbore all oaths and profane talk. One day a drunken trooper entered the guardhouse alone out of bravado, but lost his speech and died in three days.

Mauvais, mauvaise (mō vā, mo vāz). French, bad.

Mauvais ton. Bad manners. Ill-breeding, vulgar ways.

Mauvaise honte. Bad or silly shame. Bashfulness, sheepishness.

Mauvaise plaisanterie. A rude or ill-mannered jest; a jest in bad taste.

Maverick. A wanderer; unbranded cattle. Samuel A. Maverick, a Texas lawyer, took over some cattle for a debt sometime before the Civil War. The Negro whom he left in charge of them failed to brand the calves and let them wander. In 1855 Maverick sold the herd to a neighbour, Beauregard, who by the terms of the deal was to have all cattle, branded and unbranded, on Maverick's range. Beauregard started a round-up and his riders spread far and wide, claiming any unbranded animal as "a Maverick."

Mawworm (maw' wĕrm). A hypocritical pretender to sanctity, a pious humbug. From the character of this name in Isaac Bickerstaffe's *The Hypocrite* (1769).

Maximum and **Minimum** (Lat.). The *greatest* and the *least* amount; as, the maximum profits or exports and the minimum profits or exports; the maximum and minimum price of corn during the year. The terms are also employed in mathematics, etc.; a *maximum and minimum thermometer* is one that indicates the highest and lowest temperatures during a specified period.

May. The Anglo-Saxons called this month *thrimilce*, because then cows can be milked three times a day; the present name is the Latin *Maius* from *Maia*, the goddess of growth and increase, connected with *major*.

The old Dutch name was *Blou-maand* (blossoming month). In the French Republican calendar the month was called *Floréal* (the time of flowers, April 20th to May 20th).

Here we go gathering nuts in May. *See* NUTS.

It's a case of January and May. *See* JANUARY.

May-day. Polydore Virgil says that the Roman youths used to go into the fields and spend the calends of May in dancing and singing in honour of Flora, goddess of fruits and flowers. The English consecrated May-day to Robin Hood and Maid Marian, because the favourite outlaw died on that day, and villagers used to set up Maypoles (*q.v.*), and spend the day in archery, morris dancing, and other amusements.

The old custom of singing the *Hymnus Eucharisticus* on the top of Wolsey's Tower, Oxford, as the clock strikes five on May Morning is still kept up by the choristers of Magdalen. This is a relic of the requiem mass that, before the Reformation, was sung at this spot and time for the repose of the soul of Henry VII. The opening lines of the hymn are:—

Te Deum Patrem colimus,
Te laudibus prosequimur;
Qui corpus cibo reficis,
Cœlesti mentem gratia.

Evil May Day. *See* EVIL.

Maypole, Queen, etc. Dancing round the Maypole on May Day, "going a-Maying," electing a May Queen, and lighting bonfires, are all remnants of nature-worship, and may be traced to the most ancient times. The chimney-sweeps used to lead about a Jack-i'-the-green. and the custom is not yet quite extinct, especially in country towns.

Any very tall, ungainly woman is sometimes called a "Maypole," a term which was bestowed as a nickname on the Duchess of Kendal, one of George I's mistresses.

Maya Civilization. The Mayas were an American Indian race who possessed an advanced civilization at the time of the Spanish conquest of Central America. The oldest dated monument approximates to A.D. 50, when the race centre was in the neighbourhood of Yucatan. A general decay in art and the building of the great pyramidal temples set in in the 15th century and the Maya civilization was gradually absorbed into the Aztec of S. Mexico. Little progress has been made in the decipherment of the Maya inscriptions and the history and mode of life of this ancient people is still largely conjectural.

Mayduke Cherries. So called from Médoc, a district of France, whence the cherries first came to us.

Mayflower. The name of the ship that took the Pilgrim Fathers (*q.v.*) from Plymouth to Massachusetts in 1620. It was about 180 tons. An unauthenticated theory is that the timbers of the old *Mayflower* form part of a barn at Jordans, Bucks.

Mayonnaise. A sauce made with pepper, salt, oil, vinegar, and the yolk of an egg beaten up together. When the Duc de Richelieu captured Mahon, Minorca, in 1756, he demanded food on landing; in the absence of a prepared meal, he himself took whatever he could find and beat it up together—hence the original form *mahonnaise*.

Mayor. The chief magistrate of a city, elected by the citizens, and holding office for twelve months.

The chief magistrate of London is The Right Hon. the Lord Mayor, one of the Privy Council.

Since 1389 the magistracy of York has been headed by a Lord Mayor, and the other English towns in which the chief magistrate is Lord Mayor are Birmingham, Liverpool, Manchester, Leeds, Sheffield, Bristol, Hull, Bradford and Newcastle-on-Tyne.

At the Conquest the sovereign appointed the chief magistrates of cities. That of London was called the Port-Reeve, but Henry II changed the word to the Norman *maire* (our mayor). John made the office annual; and Edward III (in 1354) conferred the title of "The Right Hon. the Lord Mayor of London."

The first Lord Mayor's Show was in 1458, when Sir John Norman went by water in state, to be sworn in at Westminster; and the cap and sword were given by Richard II to Sir William Walworth, for killing Wat Tyler.

Mayor of Garratt. *See* GARRATT.

Mayor of the Palace (*Maire du Palais*). The superintendent of the king's household, and steward of the royal *leudes* (companies) of France, before the accession of the Carlovingian dynasty.

Mazarin, Cardinal Jules (1602-61), was an Italian-born French stateman, trained by and successor to Cardinal Richelieu, and minister to the Queen-Regent during the minority of Louis XIV.

Mazarine Bible, The. *See* BIBLE, SPECIALLY NAMED.

Mazarin Library. The first public Library in Paris. The great Cardinal Mazarin left his collection of 40,000 books to the city on his death in 1661, and himself composed the rules for its conduct.

Mazarinades. Pamphlets in prose or verse published against Cardinal Mazarin by supporters of the Fronde (the armed opposition to Louis XIV during his minority, 1648-53).

Mazeppa, Ivan (må zep' à) (1644-1709). The hero of Byron's poem was born of a noble Polish family in Podolia, became a page in the court of John Casimir, King of Poland, but intrigued with Theresia, the young wife of a Podolian count, who had the young page lashed naked to a wild horse, and turned adrift. The horse dropped dead in the Ukraine, where Mazeppa was released and cared for by Cossacks. He became secretary to the hetman, and at his death was appointed his successor. Peter I created him Prince of the Ukraine, but in the wars with Sweden Mazeppa deserted to Charles XII and fought against Russia at Pultowa. After the loss of this battle, Mazeppa fled to Valentia, and then to Bender, where he committed suicide. Byron makes Mazeppa tell his tale to Charles after the battle of Pultowa.

Adah Isaacs Menken (1835-68) was famous for her equestrian performance in the stage version of *Mazeppa* at Astley's, in 1844.

Mazer (mā' zer). A large drinking vessel originally made of maple-wood, and so called from O.Fr. *masere*, O.H. Ger. *masar*, a knot in wood, maple wood.

> A mazer wrought of the maple ware.
> SPENSER: *Shepheard's Calendar* (August).

Mazikeen or **Shedeem** (măz' i kēn). A species of beings in Jewish mythology resembling the Arabian jinn (*q.v.*), and said to be the agents of magic and enchantment. When Adam fell, says the Talmud, he was excommunicated for 130 years, during which time he begat demons and spectres, for, it is written "Adam lived 130 years and (*i.e.* before he) begat children in his own image" (*Gen.* v, 3). (*Rabbi Jeremiah ben Eliezar.*)

> And the Mazikeen shall not come nigh thy tents. —
> Ps. xci, 5 (Chaldee version).

McCoy. The real McCoy. Something excellent; something genuine. From an early 20th-century American prize-fighter known as "Kid McCoy," whose fame was so great that other less able fighters adopted his name to gain some of his glory. There were many McCoys but only one "real" one.

Mealy-mouthed is the Greek *meli-muthos* (honey-speech), and means velvet-tongued, afraid of giving offence, hypocritical, "smarmy."

Meander (mē ăn' der). To wind, to saunter about at random; so called from the Mænder, a winding river of Phrygia. The term is also applied to an ornamental pattern of winding lines, used as a border on pottery, wall decorations, etc.

Means Test. By the 1934 revision of the Unemployment Act, the claimant for insurance benefit was called upon to undergo an inquisition, known as the Means Test, and furnish information as to the total amount of money coming into the household from any source whatsoever, thus laying before the officials the private affairs of every member of his family. The purpose of this was, of course, to safeguard public funds and ensure that the minimum relief should be furnished, but its application was felt by the unemployed to attach an odious stigma to an already unfortunate situation. The Means Test was abolished by the Labour Government in the National Insurance Act that came into force in 1948.

Measure (O.Fr. *mesure*, Lat. *mensura*, *metiri*, to measure). **Beyond measure**, or **out of all measure**. Beyond all reasonable degree; exceedingly, excessively.

> Thus out of measure sad. — *Much Ado About Nothing*, i, 3.

To measure one's length on the ground. To fall flat on the ground; to be knocked down.

> If you will measure your lubber's length, tarry. —
> *King Lear*, i, 4.

To measure other people's corn by one's own bushel. *See* BUSHEL.

To measure strength. To wrestle together; to fight, to contest.

To measure swords. To try whether or not one is strong enough or sufficiently equally matched to contend against another. The phrase is from duelling, in which the seconds measure the swords to see that both are of one length.

> So we measured swords and parted. — *As You Like It*, v, 4.

To take the measure of one's foot. To ascertain how far a person will venture; to make a shrewd guess of another's character. The allusion is to "*Ex pede Herculem.*"

Measure for Measure. The plot of Shakespeare's play (acted 1604, first printed 1623) is founded on Whetstone's *Promos and Cassandra* (1582), which was taken from the 85th tale in Cinthio's *Hecatommithi* (1565). Promos is called by Shakespeare, "Lord Angelo"; and Cassandra is "Isabella." Her brother, called by Shakespeare "Claudio," is named Andrugio in the story.

Meat, Bread. These words tell a tale; for both can connote food in general. The Italians and Asiatics eat little animal food, and with them the word *bread* stands for food; so also with the poor, whose chief diet it is; but the English once consumed meat very plentifully, and this word, which simply means food, almost exclusively implies animal food. In the banquet given to Joseph's brethren, the viceroy commanded the servants "to set on *bread*" (*Gen.* xliii, 31). In *Ps.* civ, 27, it is said of fishes, creeping things, and crocodiles, that God giveth them their *meat* in due season.

Mecca. The birthplace of Mohammed in Arabia. It is one of the two holy cities, the other being Medina. Derivatively it means "a place one longs to visit."

Mecklenburg Declaration. The first declaration of independence in the U.S.A., made at Mecklenburg, N. Carolina, on May 20th, 1775.

Medal of Honor. A U.S.A. medal awarded by Congress to soldiers, sailors, and marines who have shown conspicuous gallantry in the face of the enemy and have risked their lives beyond any call that duty may have made upon their services.

Medea (me dē′ à). In Greek legend, a sorceress, daughter of Ǽtes, King of Colchis. She married Jason, the leader of the Argonauts, whom she aided to obtain the golden fleece, and was the mother of Medus, whom the Greeks regarded as the ancestor of the Medes. *See* HARMONIA.

Medea's kettle or **cauldron.** A means of restoring lost youth. Medea cut an old ram to pieces, threw the pieces into her cauldron, and a young lamb came forth. The daughters of Pelias thought to restore their father to youth in the same way; but Medea refused to utter the magic words, and the old man ceased to live.

> Get thee Medea's kettle and be boiled anew.—
> CONGREVE: *Love for Love*, iv.

Medici (med′ i chi). A great and powerful family that ruled in Florence from the 15th to the 18th centuries. It was founded by Giovanni Medici, a banker, whose son, Cosimo (1389-1464), was famous as a patron of art and learning. His grandson, Lorenzo the Magnificent (1448-92), was one of the outstanding figures of the Renaissance.

From Lorenzo, brother of Cosimo the Elder, came the line of Grand Dukes of Tuscany. The first of these, and founder of the line, was Lorenzo's great-grandson Cosimo (1519-1574) who was regarded by many as the original of Machiavelli's *Prince.* The Medici family gave three Popes to the Church, Leo X (1475-1521; pope 1513-21) in whose reign the Reformation began under Martin Luther; Leo XI who reigned as Pope only a few months in 1605; and Clement VII (1478-1534; pope 1523-34) who refused to grant Henry VIII a divorce from Catherine of Aragon.

Medicine. From the Lat. *medicina*, which meant both the physician's art and his laboratory, and also a medicament. The alchemists applied the word to the philosopher's stone, and the elixir of life; hence Shakespeare's

> How much unlike art thou, Mark Antony!
> Yet, coming from him, that great medicine hath
> With his tinct gilded thee.
> *Antony and Cleopatra*, i, 5.

And the word was—and is—frequently used in a figurative sense, as—

> The miserable have no other medicine
> But only hope.
> *Measure for Measure*, iii, 1.

Among the North American Indians *medicine* is a spell, charm, or fetish, and sometimes even Manitou (*q.v.*) himself, hence *Medicine-man*, a witch-doctor or magician.

The Father of Medicine. Aretæus of Cappadocia, who lived at the close of the first and beginning of the second centuries, and Hippocrates of Cos (460-377 B.C.) are both so called.

Medina (me dī′ nà). In Spenser's *Faerie Queene* (II, ii) the typification of "the golden mean" (Lat. *medium*). She was step-sister of Perissa (*excess*) and Elissa (*deficiency*), who could never agree upon any subject.

The Arabian city of *Medina* (mė dē′ nà) is the second holy city of the Mohammedans, called "Yathrib" before Mohammed fled thither from Mecca, but afterwards Medina-al-Nabi (the city of the prophet), whence its present name. In Spain there are four or five Medinas, *Medina-Sidonia* was so called by the Moors because it was believed to be on the site of the city Asidur, which was founded by Phœnicians from Sidon.

Mediterranean. The midland sea; the sea in the middle of the (Roman) earth (Lat. *medius*, middle, *terra*, land).

Medusa (me dū' zȧ). The chief of the Gorgons, (*q.v.*) of Greek mythology. Legend says that she was a beautiful maiden, specially famous for her hair; but that she violated the temple of Athene, who thereupon transformed her hair into serpents and made her face so terrible that all who looked on it were turned to stone. Perseus, assisted by Athene (who lent him her shield wherein he looked only on the *reflection* of Medusa during his attack), struck off her head, and by its means rescued Andromeda *(q.v.)* from the monster. Medusa was the mother by Poseidon of Chrysaor and Pegasus. The story of Perseus is well told in Charles Kingsley's *Heroes*.

Meerschaum (mēr' shawm) (Ger., sea-froth). This mineral (used for making tobacco-pipes), from having been found on the seashore in rounded white lumps, was ignorantly supposed to be sea-froth petrified; but it is a compound of silica, magnesia, lime, water, and carbonic acid. When first dug it lathers like soap, and is used as a soap by the Tartars.

Meg. Formerly slang for a guinea, but now signifying a halfpenny. *Cp.* MAG.

No, no; Meggs are Guineas; Smelts are half guineas.—SHADWELL: *Squire of Alsatia*, I, i (1688).

Mons Meg. A great 15th-century piece of artillery in Edinburgh Castle, made at Mons, in Flanders. It was considered a palladium by the Scotch. *Cp.* LONG MEG.

Roaring Meg. Formerly any large gun that made a great noise when let off was so called, as Mons Meg herself and a cannon given by the Fishmongers of London, and used in 1689. Burton says: "Music is a roaring Meg against melancholy."

Drowning the noise of their consciences . . . by ringing their greatest Bells, discharging their roaring-megs.—TRAPP: *Comment on Job* (1656).

Mein Kampf (mīn kămf). The political and half mystical thesis in which Adolf Hitler embodied his social and racial theories; his doctrine of anti-Semitism; and his call for revenge for the disasters of 1918 and the revision of the Versailles treaty. He wrote *My Struggle*—as the title may be translated—while undergoing a sentence of imprisonment at Landsberg-am-Lech for his part in the abortive "Beer Hall Putsch" of 1923; it was published in 1925 and as he increased in power so did *Mein Kampf* become increasingly the Nazi bible.

Meiosis (mī ō' sis). This word, coming from the Greek and meaning "lessening" is applied to the ironical form of speech in which a negative is used for the affirmation of its contrary, as "no small quantity" meaning "a considerable quantity," or "not so bad," meaning "quite good." It is also known as litotes.

Meistersingers (mī' ster sing' erz). Burgher poets of Germany, who attempted, in the 14th to 16th centuries, to revive the national minstrelsy of the *Minnesingers* (*q.v.*), which had fallen into decay. Hans Sachs, the cobbler (1494-1576), was the most celebrated.

Die Meistersinger von Nürnberg. An opera by Wagner (1868) in which he satirized his critics.

Melampod (mel' ȧm pod). Black hellebore; so called from Melampus, a famous soothsayer and physician of Greek legend, who with it cured the daughters of Prætus of their melancholy (Virgil: *Georgics*, iii, 550).

My seely sheep, like well below.
 They need not melampode;
For they been hale enough I trow,
 And liken their abode.
      SPENSER: *Eclogue*, vii.

Melancholy Lowness of spirits, supposed at one time to arise from a redundance of black bile (Gr. *melas chole*).

Melancholy Jacques. So Jean Jacques Rousseau (1712-78) was called for his morbid sensibilities and unhappy spirit. The expression is from *As You Like It*, ii, 1.

Melanchthon (me lăngk' thon) is the Greek for *Schwarzerde* (black earth), the real name of this reformer (1497-1560). Similarly, *Œcolam-padius* is the Greek version of the German name *Hauschein*, and *Desiderius Erasmus* is one Latin and one Greek rendering of the name *Gheraerd Gheraerd*.

Melba. Péche Melba, a confection of fruit (usually peach), cream and icecream. **Melba toast,** narrow slices of thin toast. These take their name from Dame Nellie Melba (1861-1931) the great Australian operatic soprano.

Melibœus or **Melibe** (mel i bē' us, mel' i bi). The central figure in Chaucer's prose *Tale of Melibœus* (*Canterbury Tales*), which is a translation of a French rendering of Albertano da Brescia's Latin *Liber Consolationis et Concilii*. Melibœus is a wealthy young man, married to Prudens. One day, when gone "into the fields to play," enemies beat his wife and left his daughter for dead. Melibœus resolved upon vengeance, but his wife persuaded him to call together his enemies, and he told them he forgave them "to this effect and to this ende, that God of His endeles mercy wole at the tyme of oure deyinge forgive us oure giltes that we have trespassed to Him in this wreeched world."

Melibœan Dye. A rich purple. Melibœa, in Thessaly, was famous for the *ostrum*, a fish used in dyeing purple.

A military vest of purple flowed.
Lovelier than Meliboœan.
MILTON: Paradise Lost, xi, 242.

Melicertes (mel i sĕr' tēz). Son of Ino, a sea deity of Greek legend (*see* LEUCOTHEA). Athamas imagined his wife to be a lioness, and her two sons to be lion's cubs. In his frenzy he slew one of the boys, and drove the other (named Melicertes) with his mother into the sea. The mother became a sea goddess, and the boy the god of harbours.

Melisande (mel' i sănd). The same as Melusina (*q.v.*).

Melodrama. Properly (and in the early 19th cent.) a drama in which song and music were introduced (Gr. *melos*, song), an opera. These pieces were usually of a sensational character, and now—the musical portions having been gradually dropped—the word denotes a lurid, sensational play, highly emotional, and with a happy ending in which the villain gets all he so richly deserves.

Melon. The Mohammedans say that the eating of a melon produces a thousand good works. There are certain stones on Mount Carmel called *Stone Melons*. The tradition is that Elijah saw a peasant carrying melons, and asked him for one. The man said they were not melons but stones, and Elijah instantly converted them into stones.

A like story is told of St. Elizabeth of Hungary. She gave so bountifully to the poor as to cripple her own household. One day her husband met her with her lap full of something, and demanded of her what she was carrying. "Only flowers, my lord," said Elizabeth, and to save the lie God converted the loaves into flowers.

Melpomene (mel pom' e ni). The muse of tragedy.

Up then Melpomene, thou mournfullest Muse of mine.
Such cause of mourning never hadst afore.
SPENSER: Shepherd's Calendar, November.

Memento mori (me men' tō môr' ī) (Lat., remember you must die). An emblem of mortality, such as a skull; something to put us in mind of the shortness and uncertainty of life.

I make as good use of it [Bardolph's face] as many a man doth of a death's head or a memento mori.—*Henry IV*, iii, 3.

Memnon. The Oriental or Ethiopian prince who, in the Trojan War, went to the assistance of his uncle Priam and was slain by Achilles, His mother Eos (the Dawn) was inconsolable for his death, and wept for him every morning.

The Greeks called the statue of Amenophis III, in Thebes, that of Memnon. When first struck by the rays of the rising sun it is said to have produced a sound like the snapping asunder of a cord. Poetically, when Eos kissed her son at daybreak, the hero acknowledged the salutation with a musical murmur.

Memnon's sister, in *Il Penseroso*, is perhaps the Himera, mentioned by Dictys Cretensis; but Milton is supposed to have invented her, because it might be presumed that any sister of the black but comely Memnon would be likewise.

Black, but such as in esteem
Prince Memnon's sister might beseem.
Il Penseroso, 18.

Probably all that is meant is this: Black so delicate and beautiful that it might beseem a sister of Memnon the son of Aurora or the early day-dawn.

The legend given by Dictys Cretensis (Bk. vi) is that Himera, on hearing of her brother's death, set out to secure his remains, and encountered at Paphos a troop laden with booty, and carrying Memnon's ashes in an urn. Pallas, the leader of the troop, offered to give her either the urn or the booty, and she chose the urn.

Memory. The Bard of Memory. Samuel Rogers (1763-1855), the banker-poet; author of *The Pleasures of Memory* (1792).

Memorial Day, also known as Decoration Day, May 30th, observed in U.S.A. since the Civil War to commemorate the soldiers and sailors who fell in action. In some of the Southern States April 26th, May 10th or June 3rd are kept as Memorial Day.

Mendelism. The theory of heredity promulgated by Gregor Johann Mendel (1822-84), the Austrian scientist and Abbot of Brünn, showing that the characters of the parents of cross-bred offspring reappear in certain proportions in successive generations according to definite laws. **Mendel's Law** was discovered by him in 1865 through experiments with peas.

Mendicant Orders, or **Begging Friars.** The orders of the Franciscans (*Grey Friars*), Augustines (*Austin Friars*), Carmelites (*White Friars*), and Dominicans (*Black Friars*).

Menechmians (me nek' mi ánz). Persons exactly like each other; so called from the *Menœchmi* of Plautus, the basis of Shakespeare's *Comedy of Errors*, in which not only the two Dromios are exactly like each other, but Antipholus of Ephesus is the facsimile of his brother, Antipholus of Syracuse.

Menelaus (men e lā' ùs). Son of Atreus, brother of Agamemnon, and husband of Helen, through whose desertion of him was brought about the Trojan War. He was the King of Sparta or of Lacedæmon.

Menevia (me nē' vi a). A form of the old name, *Mynyw*, of St. David's (Wales). Its present name is from Dewi, or David, the founder of the episcopal see in the 6th century.

Meng-tse. The fourth of the sacred books of China; so called from the name of its author (d. about 290 B.C.), Latinized into Mencius. It was written in the 4th century B.C. Confucius or Kung-fu-tse wrote the other three; viz. Ta-heo (*School of Adults*), Chong-yong (*The Golden Mean*), and Lun-yu (or *Book of Maxims*).

Mother of Meng. A Chinese expression, meaning "an admirable teacher." Meng's father died soon after the birth of the sage, and he was brought up by his mother.

Menippus (men ip' ùs), the cynic, was born at Gadara, Syria, in the 3rd century B.C. He was called by Lucian "the greatest snarler and snapper of all the old dogs" (*cynics*).

Varro wrote the *Satyræ Menippeæ*, and in imitation of it a political pamphlet, in verse and prose, designed to expose the perfidious intentions of Spain in regard to France, and the criminal ambition of the Guise family, was published in 1593 as *The Menippean Satire*. The authors were Pierre Leroy (d. 1593), Pithou (1539-96), Passerat (1534-1602), and Rapin, the poet (1540-1608).

Mennonites. Followers of Simon Menno (1492-1559), a native of Friesland, who modified the fanatical views of the Anabaptists. The sect still survives, in the United States as well as in Holland and Germany.

Mensheviks (men' she viks). A Russian word for a minority party. After the Russian Revolution of November, 1917, the less radical socialists who were in opposition to the more violent Bolshevik government, took this name.

Mentor. A guide, a wise and faithful counsellor; so called from Mentor, a friend of Ulysses, whose form Minerva assumed when she accompanied Telemachos in his search for his father.

Menu or **Manu** (mē' nū). In Hindu philosophy, one of a class of Demiurges of whom the first is identified with Brahma. Brahma divided himself into male and female, these produced *Viraj*, from whom sprang the first *Menu*, a kind of secondary creator. He gave rise to ten *Prajapatis* ("lords of all living"); from these came seven *Menus*, each presiding over a certain period, the seventh of these being *Menu Vaivasvata* ("the sun-born") who is now reigning and who is looked upon as the creator of the living races of beings. To him are ascribed the *Laws of Menu*, now called the *Manavadharmashastra*, a section of the Vedas containing a code of civil and religious law compiled by the Manavans.

Meo periculo (mē ō per ik' ū lō) (Lat. at my own risk). On my responsibility; I being bond.

Mephibosheth (me fib' ō sheth), in Dryden's *Absalom and Achitophel*, Pt. ii, (*q.v.*) is meant for Samuel Pordage (d. 1691), a poetaster.

Mephistopheles (mef is tof' e lēz). A manufactured name (possibly from three Greek words meaning "not loving the light") of a devil or familiar spirit which first appears in the late mediæval Faust legend; he is well known as the sneering, jeering, leering tempter in Goethe's *Faust*. He is mentioned by Shakespeare (*Merry Wives*, i, 1) and Fletcher as *Mephostophilus*, and in Marlowe's *Faustus* as *Mephostopilis*.

Mercator's Projection is Mercator's chart or map for nautical purposes. The meridian lines are at right angles to the parallels of latitude. It is so called because it was devised by Gerhard Kremer (= merchant, pedlar) (1512-94), whose surname Latinized is *Mercator*.

Merchant Adventurers were a guild of traders originally established in Brabant in 1296. Henry VII granted a patent for the Adventurers in England in 1505 and they were incorporated in 1564.

Merchant of Venice. The interwoven stories of Shakespeare's comedy (written 1598, published 1600) are drawn from mediæval legends the germs of which are found in the *Gesta Romanorum*. The tale of the bond is ch. xlviii, and that of the caskets is ch. xcix. Much of the plot is also given in the 14th century *Il Pecorone* of Ser Giovanni; but Shakespeare could not read Italian, there was no translation in his day, and it is more than doubtful whether he ever saw or was aware of it.

Mercury (mėr' kū ri). The Roman equivalent of the Greek Hermes (*q.v.*), son of Maia and Jupiter, to whom he acted as messenger. He was the god of science and commerce, the patron of travellers and also of rogues, vagabonds, and thieves. Hence, the name of the god is used to denote both a messenger and a thief: —

Delay leads impotent and snail-pac'd beggary.
Then fiery expedition be my wing,
Jove's Mercury, and herald for a king.
Richard III, iv, 3.

My father named me Autolycus; who being, as I am, littered under Mercury, was likewise a snapper-up of unconsidered trifles.—*Winter's Tale*, iv, 2.

Mercury is represented as a young man with winged hat and winged sandals (*talaria*), bearing the *caduceus* (*q.v.*), and sometimes a purse.

Posts with a marble head of Mercury on them used to be erected where two or more roads met, to point out the way. (*Juvenal*, viii, 53.)

In astrology, Mercury "signifieth subtill men, ingenious, inconstant: rymers, poets, advocates, orators, phylosophers, arithmeticians, and busie fellowes," and the alchemists credited it with great powers and used it for a large number of purposes. See Ben Jonson's masque, *Mercury Vindicated*.

Mercurial (mer kū′ ri ἀl). Light-hearted, gay, volatile; because such were supposed by the astrologers to be born under the planet Mercury.

Mercy. The seven corporal works of mercy are:—
(1) To tend the sick.
(2) To feed the hungry.
(3) To give drink to the thirsty.
(4) To clothe the naked.
(5) To house the homeless.
(6) To visit the fatherless and the afflicted.
(7) To bury the dead.

Matt, xxv, 35-40.

Merciless (or **Unmerciful**) **Parliament, The** (from February 3rd to June 3rd, 1388). A junto of fourteen tools of Thomas, Duke of Gloucester, which assumed royal prerogatives, and attempted to depose Richard II.

Meridian. Sometimes applied, especially in Scotland, to a noonday dram of spirits.

He received from the hand of the waiter the meridian, which was placed ready at the bar.—SCOTT: *Redgauntlet*, ch. i.

Merit, Order of. This is a British order for distinguished service in all callings. It was founded by Edward VII in 1902, with two classes, civil and military. The Order is limited to 24 members—men and women—and confers no precedence; it is designated by the letters O.M., following the first class of the Order of the Bath and precedes all letters designating membership of other Orders. The badge is a red and blue cross pattee, with a blue medallion in the centre surrounded by a laurel wreath, and bears the words "For Merit"; the ribbon is blue and crimson. Crossed swords are added to the badge for military members.

Merlin. The historical Merlin was a Welsh or British bard, born towards the close of the 5th century, to whom a number of poems have been very doubtfully attributed. He is said to have become bard to King Arthur, and to have lost his reason and perished on the banks of the river after a terrible battle between the Britons and their Romanized compatriots about 570.

His story has been mingled with that of the enchanter Merlin of the Arthurian romances, which, however, proceeds on different lines. This Prince of Enchanters was the son of a damsel seduced by a fiend, but was baptized by Blaise, and so rescued from the power of Satan. He became an adept in necromancy, but was beguiled by the enchantress Nimue, who shut him up in a rock, and later Vivien, the Lady of the Lake, entangled him in a thorn-bush by means of spells, and there he still sleeps, though his voice may sometimes be heard.

He first appears in Nennius (as Ambrosius); Geoffrey of Monmouth wrote the *Vita Merlini* (about 1145); this was worked upon by Wace and Robert de Borron, and formed the basis of the English prose romance *Merlin*, and of most of the Merlin episodes in the Arthurian cycle. *See also* Spenser's *Faerie Queene* (III, iii), and Tennyson's *Idylls*.

Now, though a Mechanist, whose skill
Shames the degenerate grasp of modern science,
Grave Merlin (and belike the more
For practising occult and perilous lore)
Was subject to a freakish will
That sapped good thoughts, or scared them with defiance.

WORDSWORTH: *The Egyptian Maid*.

The English Merlin. William Lilly (1602-81), the astrologer, who published two tracts under the name of "Merlinus Anglicus" and was the most famous charlatan of his day.

Mermaid. The popular stories of the mermaid, a fabulous marine creature half woman and half fish—allied to the Siren (*q.v.*) of classical mythology—probably arose from sailors' accounts of the dugong, a cetacean whose head has a rude approach to the human outline. The mother while suckling her young holds it to her breast with one flipper, as a woman holds her infant in her arm. If disturbed she suddenly dives under water, and tosses up her fish-like tail.

In Elizabethan plays the term is often used for a courtesan. *See* Massinger's *Old Law*, iv, 1, Shakespeare's *Comedy of Errors*, iii, 2, etc.

Merope (mer′ ō pe). One of the Pleiades; dimmer than the rest, because, according to Greek legend, she married a mortal. She was the mother of Glaucus.

Merovingian Dynasty (mer ō ving′ gi ἀn). The dynasty of Merovius, a Latin form of *Merwig* (great warrior), who is said to have ruled over the Franks in the 5th century. The dynasty rose to power under Clovis (d. 511), and gradually gave way before the Mayors of the Palace (*q.v.*), until in 751 the Merovingians were deposed by Pepin the Short, grandson of Pepin of Heristal.

Merrie England. *See* MERRY.

Merrow (Irish, *muirrúhgach*). A mermaid, believed by Irish fishermen to forebode a coming storm.

It was rather annoying to Jack that, though living in a place where the merrows were as plenty as lobsters, he never could get a right view of one.—W. B. YEATS: *Fairy and Folk Tales*, p. 63.

Merrows are of human shape above but from the waist like a fish. The females are attractive, but the, males have green teeth, green hair, pig's eyes, and red noses. Fishermen dread to meet them.

Merry. The original meaning is *pleasing, delightful*; hence, *giving pleasure*; hence *mirthful, joyous*.

The old phrase *Merrie England* (*Merry London*, etc.) merely signified that these places were pleasant and delightful, not necessarily bubbling over with merriment; and so with *the merry month of May*.

Thou Saint George shalt called bee,
Saint George of mery England, the signe of victoree.
SPENSER: *Faerie Queene*, i, x, 61.
Thus all through merry Islington
These gambols did he play.
COWPER: *John Gilpin*.

The phrase *merry men*, meaning the companions at arms of a knight or outlaw (especially Robin Hood), is really for *merry meinie*. *See* MEINIE.

Merrythought. The furcula or wishing-bone in the breast of a fowl; sometimes broken by two persons, when the one who holds the larger portion has his wish, as it is said.

'Tis merry in hall, when beards wag all (2 *Henry IV*, v, 3). It is a sure sign of mirth when the beards of the guests shake with laughter.

To make merry. To be jovial, festive; **to make merry over**, to treat with amusement or ridicule, to make fun of.

Merveilleuse (mâr vī yers) (Fr., marvellous). The sword of Doolin of Mayence (*q.v.*). It was so sharp that when placed edge downwards it would cut through a slab of wood without the use of force.

The term is also applied to the dress worn by the fops and ladies of the Directory period in France, who were noted for their extravagance and aping of classical Greek modes.

Mesa. Spanish and Mexican term for grassy table-land.

Meschino. *See* GUERINO MESCHINO.

Mesmerism (mez' měr izm). So called from Friedrich Anton Mesmer (1733-1815), of Meersburg, Baden, who introduced his theory of "animal magnetism" into Paris, in 1778. It is the basis or forerunner of hypnotism, the therapeutic employment of which is being increasingly studied by the medical and psychiatric professions.

Mesopotamia (mes ō pot ām' i à) (Gr., the land between the rivers, *i.e.* the Euphrates and Tigris). The territory bounded by Kurdistan on the N. and NE., the Persian Gulf on the S. and SE., Persia on the E., and Syria and the Arabian Desert on the W. Since World War I—as a consequence of which it was freed from Turkish rule and constituted a separate kingdom—its name has been changed to *Irak* (*q.v.*), or *Iraq*.

Mess. The usual meaning to-day is a dirty, untidy state of things, a muddle, a difficulty (*to get into a mess*); but the word originally signified a portion of food (Lat. *missum*, *mittere*, to send; *cp.* Fr. *mets*, viands, Ital. *messo*, a course of a meal); thence it came to mean mixed food—especially for an animal—and so a confusion, medley, jumble.

Another meaning was a small group of persons (usually four) who at banquets sat together and were served from the same dishes. This use gave rise not only to the army and navy *mess* (used also at the Inns of Court), but to the Elizabethans using it in place of "four" or "a group of four." Thus, Lyly says, "Foure makes a messe, and we have a messe of masters." (*Mother Bombie*, ii, 1), and Shakespeare calls the four sons of Henry his "mess of sons" (2 *Henry VI*, i, 4); and says (*Love's Labour's Lost*, iv, 3), "You three fools lacked me . . . to make up the mess."

Messiah (me sī' à), from the Hebrew *mashiach*, one anointed. It is the title of an expected leader of the Jews who shall deliver the nation from its enemies and reign in permanent triumph and peace. Equivalent to the Greek word Christ, it is applied by Christians to Jesus. *Messiah* (incorrectly *The Messiah*) is the title of an oratorio by Handel, first produced in Dublin in 1742.

Mestizo. Spanish-Mexican phrase for a half-breed.

Metals. Metals used to be divided into two classes—*Noble*, and *Base*. The *Noble*, or *Perfect, Metals* were gold and silver, because they were the only two known that could be not changed or "destroyed" by fire; the remainder were *Base*, or *Imperfect*.

The seven metals in alchemy.
Gold, Apollo or the sun.
Silver, Diana or the moon.

Quicksilver, Mercury.
Copper, Venus.
Iron, Mars.
Tin, Jupiter.
Lead, Saturn.

The only metals used in heraldry are *or*
(gold) and *argent* (silver).

Metamorphic Rocks (met à môr ′fik).
Sedimentary or eruptive rocks whose original
character has been more or less altered by
changes beneath the surface of the earth. These
include gneiss, mica-schist, clay-slate, marble,
and the like, which have become more or less
crystalline.

Metaphysics (met à fiz′ iks) (Gr., after-
physics, so called because the disciples of
Aristotle held that matter or nature should be
studied before mind). The science of metaphysics is the consideration of things in the
abstract—that is, divested of their accidents,
relations, and matter; the philosophy of being
and knowing; the theoretical principles forming
the basis of any particular science; the philosophy
of mind.

Methodists. A name given (1729) by a
student of Christ Church to the brothers
Wesley and their friends, who used to assemble
on given evenings for religious conversation,
because of the methodical way in which they
observed their principles. The word was in use
many centuries earlier for those (especially
physicians) who attached great importance to
method, and the name was at one time applied
to the Jesuits, because they were the first to give
systematic representations of the method of
polemics. Theophilus Gale (1628-78) speaks of
a religious sect called "the New Methodists"
(*Court of the Gentiles*).

Primitive Methodists. A secession from
the Methodists, led by Hugh Bourne in 1810.
They adopted this name because they reverted
to the original methods of preaching of the
Wesleys.

Methuselah (me′ thū zè là). **Old as
Methuselah.** Very old indeed, almost incredi-
bly old. He is the oldest man mentioned in the
Bible, where we are told (*Gen*, v, 27) that he
died at the age of 969.

Metonymy (me ton′ i mi). The use of the
name of one thing for another, as "the Bench"
for the magistrates or judges sitting in court,
"a silk" for a King's Counsel, "the bottle" for
alcoholic liquor. The word is Greek, meaning a
change of name.

Metropolitan. A prelate who has suffragan
bishops subject to him. The two metropolitans
of England are the archbishops of Canterbury
and York, and the two of Ireland the archbishops
of Armagh and Dublin. The word does not
mean the prelate of the metropolis (Gr. *meter*,
mother, *polis*, city) in a secular sense, but the
prelate of a "mother city" in an ecclesiastical
sense—*i.e.* a city which is the mother or ruler
of other cities. Thus, the Bishop of London is
not a metropolitan, but the Archbishop of
Canterbury is *metropolitanus et primus totius
Angliæ*, and the Archbishop of York *primus et
metropolitans Angliæ*.

In the Greek Church a metropolitan ranks
next below a patriarch and next above an
archbishop.

Mews. Stables, but properly a cage for
hawks when moulting (O.F. *mue*, Lat. *mūtāre*,
to change). The word has acquired its present
meaning because (in the 17th cent.) the royal
stables were built upon the site (now occupied
by the National Gallery) where formerly the
king's hawks were kept; and the name was transferred from the establishment for hawks to that
of horses.

Mexitl, or **Mextli** (meks′ itl). The principal
god of the ancient Mexicans (whence the
name of their country), to whom enormous
sacrifices, running into many thousands of
human beings, were offered at a time. Also
called *Huitzilopochtli*.

Mezzotint, or **Mezzo tinto** (Ital., medium
tint). A process of engraving in which a copper
plate is uniformly roughened so as to print at
deep black, lights and half-lights being then
produced by scraping away the burr; also a print
from this, which is usually a good imitation of
an Indian-ink drawing.

Micah Rood's Apples. Apples with a spot of
red in the heart. The story is that Micah Rood
was a prosperous farmer at Franklin, Pa. In
1693 a pedlar with jewellery called at his
house, and next day was found murdered under
an apple-tree in Rood's orchard. The crime was
never brought home to the farmer, but next
autumn all the apples of the fatal tree bore inside
a red blood-spot, called "Micah Rood's Curse,"
and the farmer died soon afterwards.

Michael, St. The great prince of all the
angels and leader of the celestial armies.

And there was war in heaven: Michael and his
angels fought against the dragon; and the dragon fought
and his angels, and prevailed not.—*Rev.* xii, 7, 8.

Go, Michael, of celestial armies prince,
And thou, in military prowess next,
Gabriel; lead forth to battle these my sons

Invincible; lead forth my armed Saints
By thousands and by millions ranged for fight.
MILTON: *Paradise Lost*, vi, 44.

His day ("St. Michael and All Angels") is Sept. 29th (*see* MICHAELMAS), and in the Roman Catholic Church he is also commemorated on May 8th, in honour of his apparition in 492 to a herdsman of Monte Gargano. In the Middle Ages he was looked on as the presiding spirit of the planet Mercury, and bringer to man of the gift of prudence.

The planet Mercury, whose place
Is nearest to the sun in space,
　Is my allotted sphere;
And with celestial ardour swift
I bear upon my hands the gift
　Of heavenly *prudence* here.
LONGFELLOW: *Golden Legend, The Miracle play*, iii.

In art St. Michael is depicted as a beautiful young man with severe countenance, winged, and clad in either white or armour, bearing a lance and shield, with which he combats a dragon. In the final judgment he is represented with scales, in which he weighs the souls of the risen dead.

Michaelmas Day. September 29th, the Festival of St. Michael and All Angels (*see* MICHAEL, *above*), one of the quarter-days when rents are due, and the day when magistrates are elected.

The custom of eating goose at Michaelmas (*see also* ST. MARTIN'S GOOSE) is many centuries old, and probably arose solely because geese were plentiful and in good condition at this season, and we are told that tenants formerly presented their landlords with one to keep in their good graces. The popular story, however, is that Queen Elizabeth, on her way to Tilbury Fort on September 29th, 1588, dined at the seat of Sir Neville Umfreyville, and partook of geese, afterwards calling for a bumper of Burgundy, and giving as a toast, "Death to the Spanish Armada!" Scarcely had she spoken when a messenger announced the destruction of the fleet by a storm. The queen demanded a second bumper, and said, "Henceforth shall a goose commemorate this great victory." This tale is marred by the awkward circumstances that the fleet was dispersed by the winds in July, and the thanksgiving sermon for the victory was preached at St. Paul's on August 20th. Gascoigne, who died 1577, refers to the custom of goose-eating at Michaelmas as common:—

At Christmas a capon, at Michaelmas a goose,
And somewhat else at New Yere's tide, for feare the
lease flies loose.

Mickey Finn. A draught or powder slipped into liquor to render the drinker unconscious.

The term comes from a notorious figure in 19th century Chicago.

Mickey Mouse, one of the most famous and popular characters of Walt Disney's animated cartoons. *Steamboat Willie* (1928) starring Mickey Mouse was the first animated cartoon in colours.

Microcosm (mī krō kozm) (Gr., little world). So man is called by Paracelsus. The ancients considered the world (*see* MACROCOSM) as a living being; the sun and moon being its *two eyes*, the earth its *body*, the ether its *intellect*, and the sky its *wings*. When man was looked on as the world in miniature, it was thought that the movements of the world and of man corresponded, and if one could be ascertained, the other could be easily inferred; hence arose the system of astrology, which professed to interpret the events of a man's life by the corresponding movements, etc., of the stars.

Micronesia (mī krō nē' zhà). The name given to the groups of small Pacific islands north of the Equator and east of the Philippines, including the Marianas, the Caroline and the Marshall islands.

Midas (mī' dăs). A legendary king of Phrygia who requested of the gods that everything he touched might be turned to gold. His request was granted, but as his food became gold the moment he touched it, he prayed the gods to take their favour back. He was then ordered to bathe in the Pactolus, and the river ever after rolled over golden sands.

Another story told of him is, that when appointed to judge a musical contest between Apollo and Pan, he gave judgment in favour of the satyr; whereupon Apollo in contempt gave the king a pair of ass's ears. Midas hid them under his Phrygian cap; but his barber discovered them, and, not daring to mention the matter, dug a hole and relieved his mind by whispering in it "Midas has ass's ears," then covering it up again. Budæus gives a different version. He says that Midas kept spies to tell him everything that transpired throughout his kingdom, and the proverb "kings have long arms" was changed to "Midas has long ears."

A parallel of this tale is told of Portzmach, king of a part of Brittany. He had all the barbers of his kingdom put to death, lest they should announce to the public that he had the ears of a horse. An intimate friend was found willing to shave him, after swearing profound secrecy; but not able to contain himself, he confided his secret to the sands of a river bank. The reeds of this river were used for pan-pipes and haut-bois, which repeated the words "Portzmach—King Portzmach has horse's ears."

Middle. Middle Ages. The period from about 476·(the fall of·the Roman Empire) to 1453 (the capture of Constantinople by·the Turks). It varies a little with almost every nation; in France it is usually dated from Clovis to Louis XI (481 to 1461); in England, from the Heptarchy to the accession of Henry VII (409 to 1485). The earlier part of this time (to about 1200) is usually referred to as the Dark Ages (*q.v.*).

Middle Kingdom is the Chinese term for China proper, the eighteen inner provinces; anciently for the Chinese Empire as being situated in the centre of the world. The Middle Empire in Egyptian history is the great period from 2200 to 1690 B.C. comprising the XI to the XIV Dynasties.

Midgard. In Scandinavian mythology, the abode of the first pair, from whom sprang the human race. It was made of the eyebrows of Ymer, and was joined to Asgard by the rainbow bridge called Bifrost.

> Asgard is the abode of the celestials.
> Utgard is the abode of the giants.
> Midgard is between the two—better than Utgard, but inferior to Asgard.

Mid-Lent Sunday. The fourth Sunday in Lent. It is called *dominica refectionis* (Refection Sunday), because the first lesson is the banquet given by Joseph to his brethren, and the gospel of the day is the miraculous feeding of the five thousand. It is the day on which simnel cakes (*q.v.*) are eaten, and it is also called Mothering Sunday (*q.v.*).

Midnight Oil. Late hours.

Burning the midnight oil. Sitting up late, especially when engaged on literary work.

Smells of the midnight oil. *See* IT SMELLS OF THE LAMP *under* LAMP.

Midrash (mid´ rash). The rabbinical investigation into and interpretation of the Old Testament writings, which began when the Temple at Jerusalem was destroyed and was committed to writing in a large number of commentaries between the 2nd and 11th centuries A.D. The three ancient *Midrashim* (*Mechiltha*, *Sifre*, and *Sifra*—first half of the 2nd century) contain both the Halachah and the Haggadah (*q.v.*).

Midsummer. The week or so round about the summer solstice (June 21st). **Midsummer Day** is June 24th, St. John the Baptist's Day, and one of the quarter days.

Midsummer ale. Festivities which used to take place in rural districts at this season. Here *Ale* has the same extended meaning as in "Church-ale" (*q.v.*).

Midsummer madness. Olivia says to Malvolio, "Why, this is very midsummer madness" (*Twelfth Night*, iii, 4). The reference is to the rabies of dogs, which was supposed to be brought on by midsummer heat. People who were a bit inclined to be mad used to be said *to have but a mile to midsummer.*

Midsummer Night's Dream, A. Shakespeare's comedy (acted 1595, first printed 1600) is indebted to Chaucer's *Knight's Tale* for the Athenian setting, and to Ovid's *Metamorphoses* for the Pyramus and Thisbe interlude; but its airy grace and the ingenious inter-weaving of the four separate threads are all Shakespeare's own.

Midway Islands are a cluster of islands in the North Pacific, about 1200 miles NW. of Hawaii and forming part of that Territory. The Japanese suffered a heavy naval defeat near the islands in June, 1942.

Midwife (A.S., *mid*, with; *wif*, woman). The nurse who is *with* the mother in her labour.

Mikado (mik à ´dō) (Jap. *mi*, exalted; *kado*, gate or door). The title of the Emperor of Japan (*cp.* SHOGUN).

Milan (mi lăn´). The English form of Milano, the capital city of Lombardy, in Latin *Mediolanum*, in the middle of the plain, *i.e.* the Plain of Lombardy. In the Middle Ages Milan was famous for its steel, used for making swords, chain armour, etc.

The edict of Milan. Proclaimed, by Constantine, after the conquest of Italy (313), to secure to Christians the restitution of their civil and religious rights.

The Milan Decree. A decree made by Napoleon, dated "Milan, Dec. 27th, 1807," declaring "the whole British Empire to be in a state of blockade, and forbidding all countries either from trading with Great Britain or from even using an article of British, manufacture."

> This decree was killing the goose which laid the golden eggs, for England was the best customer of the very countries thus restricted from dealing with her.

Milanion. *See* ATALANTA'S RACE.

Mile. A measure of length; in the British Empire and the United States, 1,760 yd.; so called from Lat. *mille*, a thousand, the Roman lineal measure being 1,000 paces, or about 1,680 yds. The old Irish and Scottish miles were a good deal longer than the standard English, that in Ireland (still in use in country parts) being 2,240 yd.

The *Nautical* or *Geographical Mile*, is supposed to be one minute of a great circle of the earth; but as the earth is not a true sphere the length of a minute is variable, so a mean length—6,080 ft. (2,026 yd. 2 ft.)—has been fixed by the British Admiralty. The Geographical Mile varies slightly with different nations, so there is a further *International Geographical Mile*, which is invariable at one-fifteenth of a degree of the earth's equator, equal to about 4·61 statute miles of 5,280 ft.

Milesians. Properly, the inhabitants of Miletus; but the name has been given to the ancient Irish because of the legend that two sons of Milesius, a fabulous king of Spain, conquered the country and repeopled it after exterminating the Firbolgs—the aborigines.

My family, by my father's side, are all the true ould Milesians, and related to the O'Flahertys, and O'Shaughnesses, and the M'Lauchlins, the O'Donnaghans, O'Callaghans, O'Geogaghans, and all the thick blood of the nation; and I myself am an O'Brallaghan, which is the ouldest of them all.—
MACKLIN: *Love à la Mode.*

Milk, To. Slang for to get money out of somebody in an underhand way; also, to plunder one's creditors, and (in mining) to exhaust the veins of ore after selling the mine.

A land of milk and honey. One abounding in all good things, or of extraordinary fertility. *Joel* iii, 18, speaks of "the mountains flowing with milk and honey." Figuratively used to denote the blessings of heaven.

Jerusalem the golden,
With milk and honey blest.

Milk teeth. The first, temporary, teeth of a child.

The milk of human kindness. Sympathy, compassion. The phrase is from *Macbeth*, i, 5

. . . . yet I do fear thy nature
It is too full o' th' milk of human kindness.

To cry over spilt milk. *See* CRY.

Milksop. An effeminate person; one without energy, one under petticoat government. The allusion is to young, helpless children, who are fed on pap.

Milky Way. A great circle of stars entirely surrounding the heavens, apparently so crowded together that they look to the naked eye like a "way" or stream of faint "milky" light. *See* GALAXY.

A broad and ample road, whose dust is gold
And pavement stars, as stars to thee appear,
Seen in the galaxy—that Milky Way,
Thick, nightly, as a circling zone, thou seest
Powdered with stars.

MILTON: *Paradise Lost*, vii, 577, etc.

Mill. To fight, or a fight. It is the same word as the mill that grinds flour (from Lat. *molere*, to grind). Grinding was anciently performed by pulverizing with a stone or pounding with the hand. *To mill* is to beat with the fist, as persons used to beat corn with a stone.

To mill about is to move aimlessly in a circle, like a herd of cattle.

The mills of God grind slowly. Retribution may be delayed, but it is sure to overtake the wicked. The *Adagia* of Erasmus puts it, *Sero molunt deorum molæ*, and the sentiment is to be found in many authors, ancient and modern.

The mills of God grind slowly, yet they grind exceeding small;
Though with patience He stands waiting, with exactness He grinds all.

LONGFELLOW: *Retribution.*

Millennium (mi len' i um). A thousand years (Lat., *mille annus*). In *Rev.* xx, 2, it is said that an angel bound Satan a thousand years, and in verse 4 we are told of certain martyrs who will come to life again, and "reign with Christ a thousand years." "This," says St. John, "is the first resurrection"; and this is what is meant by the millennium.

Millenarians, or Chiliasts, is the name applied to an early Christian sect who held this opinion strongly. In the 19th century belief in this doctrine was revived by various sects such as the Plymouth Brethren.

Millerites. Followers of William Miller of Massachusetts (1782-1849) who in 1831 preached that the end of the world would come in 1843—now called Adventists.

Milliner. A corruption of *Milaner*; so called from Milan, in Italy, which at one time gave the law to Europe in all matters of taste, dress, and elegance.

Nowadays one nearly always means a woman when one speaks of a milliner, but it was not always so; Ben Jonson, in *Every Man in his Humour*, i, 3, speaks of a "milliner's wife," and the French have still *une modiste* and *un modiste.*

Man-Milliner. An effeminate fellow, or one who busies himself over trifles.

The Morning Herald sheds tears of joy over the fashionable virtues of the rising generation, and finds that we shall make better man-milliners, better lacqueys, and better courtiers than ever.—HAZLITT: *Political Essays* (1814).

Millstone. Hard as the nether millstone. Unfeeling, obdurate. The lower or "nether" of the two millstones is firmly fixed and very hard; the upper stone revolves round it on a shaft, and the corn, running down a tube inserted in the upper stone, is ground by the motion of the upper stone upon the lower one.

Milo (mī' lō). A celebrated Greek athlete of Crotona (*q.v.*) in the late 6th cent. B.C. It is said that he carried through the stadium at Olympia a heifer four years old, and ate the whole of it afterwards. When old he attempted to tear in two an oak-tree, but the parts closed upon his hands, and while held fast he was devoured by wolves.

Milton. "Milton," says Dryden, in the preface to his *Fables*, "was the poetical son of Spenser. . . . Milton has acknowledged to me that Spenser was his original."

Milton of Germany. Friedrich G. Klopstock (1724-1803), author of *The Messiah* (1773). Coleridge says he is "a very German Milton indeed."

Mimosa (mi mō' zà). Niebuhr says the Mimosa "droops its branches whenever anyone approaches it, seeming to salute those who retire under its shade." The name reflects this notion, as the plant was thought to *mimic* the motions of animals, as does the Sensitive Plant.

Mince Pies at Christmas time are said to have been emblematical of the manger in which our Saviour was laid. The paste over the "offering" was made in form of a *cratch* or *hay-rack*. Southey speaks of—

Old bridges dangerously narrow, and angles in them like the corners of an English mince-pie, for the foot-passengers to take shelter in.—*Esprinella's Letters* III. 384 (1807).

Mince pies. Rhyming slang for "the eyes."

To make mincemeat of. Utterly to demolish; to shatter to pieces. Mincemeat is meat minced, *i.e.* cut up very fine.

Mincing Lane (London). Called in the 13th century *Menechinelane, Monechenlane*, etc., and in the time of Henry VIII *Mynchyn Lane*. The name is from A.S. *mynechenn*, a nun (fem. of *munuc*, monk), and the street is probably so called from the tenements held there by the nuns of St. Helen's, in Bishopsgate Street. Mincing Lane is the centre of the tea trade, for which it is often used as a generic term.

Mind. Mind your own business; mind your eye, etc. *See these words.*

Minerva (mi něr' và). The Roman goddess of wisdom and patroness of the arts and trades, fabled to have sprung, with a tremendous battle-cry, fully armed from the head of Jupiter. She is identified with the Greek Athene, and was one of the three chief deities, the others being Jupiter and Juno. She is represented as grave and majestic, clad in a helmet and with drapery over a coat of mail, and bearing the ægis on her breast. The most famous statue of this goddess was by Phidias, and was anciently one of the Seven Wonders of the World.

The Minerva Press. A printing establishment in Leadenhall Street, London, famous in the late 18th century for its trashy, ultra-sentimental novels, which were characterized by complicated plots, and the labyrinths of difficulties into which the hero and heroine got involved before they could be married.

Miniature. Originally, a rubrication or a small painting in an illuminated MS., which was done with *minium* or red lead. Hence, the word came to express any small portrait or picture on vellum or ivory; but it is in no way connected with the Latin *minor* or *minimus*.

Minimalist is a term applied in Russian politics to a less radical member of the Social Revolutionary party.

Minims (Lat. *Fratres Minimi*, least of the brethren). A term of self-abasement assumed by a mendicant order founded by St. Francis of Paula, in 1453; they went bare-footed, and wore a coarse, black woollen stuff, fastened with a woollen girdle, which they never put off, day or night. The order of St. Francis of Assisi had already engrossed the "humble" title of *Fratres Minores* (inferior brothers). The superior of the minims is called *corrector*.

Minister. Literally, an inferior person, in opposition to *magister*, a superior. One is connected with the Latin *minus*, and the other with *magis*. Our Lord says, "Whosoever will be great among you, let him be your minister," where the antithesis is well preserved; and Gibbon mentions—

a multitude of cooks, and inferior ministers, employed in the service of the kitchens.—*Decline and Fall*, ch. xxxi.

The minister of a church is a man who *serves* the parish or congregation; and the minister of the Crown is the sovereign's or state's servant.

Florimond de Remond, speaking of Albert Babinot, one of the disciples of Calvin, says, "He was a student of the Institutes, read at the hall of the Equity school in Poitiers, and was called *la Ministerie*." Calvin, in allusion thereto, used to call him "Mr. Minister," whence not only Babinot but all the other clergy of the Calvinistic Church were called *ministers*.

Minnehaha (min e ha' ha) (*Laughing-water*). The lovely daughter of the old arrow-maker of the Dacotahs, and wife of Hiawatha in Longfellow's poem. She died of famine.

Minnesingers (min' e sing erz). Minstrels. The lyric poets of 12th- to 14th-century Germany were so called, because the subject of their lyrics was *minne-sang* (love-ditty). The chief *minnesingers* were Heinrich von Ofterdingen, Wolfram von Eschenbach, Walther von der

Vogelweide, and (the earliest) Heinrich von Veldeke. All of them were men of noble birth, and they were succeeded by the Meistersingers (q.v.).

Minoan. See MINOS.

Minories (min' ôr iz) (London). So called from the Abbey of the *Minoresses* of St. Mary of the Order of St. Clare which, till the Dissolution of the Monasteries, stood on the site.

Minorities, or **Minors.** See FRANCISCANS.

Minos (mī' nos). A legendary king and lawgiver of Crete, made at death supreme judge of the lower world, before whom all the dead appeared to give an account of their stewardship, and to receive the reward of their deeds. He was the husband of Pasiphæ and the owner of the labyrinth constructed by Dædalus. From his name we have the adjective *Minoan*, pertaining to Crete: the *Minoan period* is the Cretan bronze age, roughly about 2500-1200 B.C.

Minotaur (min' ō tôr). A mythical monster with the head of a bull and the body of a man, fabled to have been the offspring of Pasiphæ and a bull that was sent to her by Poseidon. Minos kept it in his labyrinth and fed it on human flesh, 7 youths and 7 maidens being sent as tribute from Athens every year for the purpose. Theseus slew this monster.

Minstrel. Originally, one who had some official duty to perform (Lat. *ministerialis*), but quite early in the Middle Ages restricted to one whose duty it was to entertain his employer with music, story-telling, juggling, etc.; hence a travelling gleeman and entertainer.

Mint. The name of the herb is from Lat. *menth* (Gr. *mintha*), so called from Minthe, daughter of Cocytus, and a favourite of Pluto. This nymph was metamorphosed by Pluto's wife (Proserpine) out of jealousy, into the herb called after her name. The fable means that mint is a capital medicine. Minthe was a favourite of Pluto, or death, that is, was sick and on the point of death; but was changed into the herb mint, that is, was cured thereby.

> Could Pluto's queen, with jealous fury storm
> And Minthe to a fragrant herb transform?
> OVID.

The Mint, a place where money is coined, gets its name from A.S. *mynet*, representing Lat. *moneta*, money.

Minute. A minute of time (one-sixtieth part of an hour) is so called from the mediæval Latin *pars minuta prima*, which, in the old system of sexagesimal fractions, denoted *one-sixtieth* part of the unit. In the same way, in Geometry, etc., a minute is *one-sixtieth* part of a degree.

A **minute** of a speech, meeting, etc., is a rough draft taken down in *minute* or small writing, to be afterwards *engrossed*, or written larger. It is from the Fr. *minute*.

Minute-men. Men who are ready to turn out and fight at a minute's notice. The expression was first generally used in connexion with the Connecticut farmers who fought against the British in 1775.

Miocene (mī' ō sēn). The geological period immediately preceding the Pliocene, when the mastodon, dinotherium, protohippus and other creatures flourished.

Miramolin. The title in the Middle Ages of the Emperor of Morocco.

Merlin's magic mirror, given by Merlin to King Ryence. It informed the king of treason, secret plots, and projected invasions. (Spenser: *Faerie Queene*, iii, 2.)

Reynard's wonderful mirror. This mirror existed only in the brain of Master Fox; he told the queen lion that whoever looked in it could see what was done a mile off. The wood of the frame was not subject to decay, being made of the same block as King Crampart's magic horse. (*Reynard the Fox*, ch. xii.)

Mirza (měr' zà) (Pers., royal prince). The term is used in two ways by the Persians; when *prefixed* to a surname it is simply a title of honour: but when *annexed* to the surname, it means a prince of the blood royal.

Miscreant means a false believer. (Fr., *miscréance*.) A term first applied to the Mohammedans, who, in return, call Christians *infidels*, and associate with the word all that we mean by "miscreants."

Mise (mēz) (O.Fr., expenses), means an honorarium, especially that given by the people of Wales to a new Prince of Wales on his entrance upon his principality, or by the people of the county palatine of Chester on change of an Earl (the Prince of Wales is Earl of Chester). At Chester a mise-book is kept, in which every town and village is rated to this honorarium.

Littleton (*Dict.*) says the usual sum is £500.

Mise en scène (Fr., setting on stage). The stage setting of a play, including the scenery, properties, etc., and the general arrangement of the piece. Also used metaphorically.

Miserere (miz e rē' re). The fifty-first psalm is so called because its opening words are *Miserere mei Deus* (Have mercy upon me, O God. See NECK-VERSE). One of the evening services of Lent is called *miserere*, because this penitential psalm is sung, after which a sermon is delivered. The under side of a folding seat in choir-stalls is called a *miserere*, or, more properly, a *misericord*; when turned up it forms a ledge-seat sufficient to rest the aged in a kneeling position.

Misers. The most renowned are:—

Baron Aguilar or Ephraim Lopes Pereira d'Aguilar (1740-1802), born at Vienna and died at Islington, worth £200,000.

Daniel Dancer (1716-94). His sister lived with him, and was a similar character, but died before him, and he left his wealth to the widow of Sir Henry Tempest, who nursed him in his last illness.

Sir Harvey Elwes, who died worth £250,000, but never spent more than £110 a year. His sister-in-law inherited £100,000, but actually starved herself to death, and her son *John* (1714-89), M.P., an eminent brewer in Southwark, never bought any clothes, never suffered his shoes to be cleaned, and grudged every penny spent in food.

Thomas Guy, founder of Guy's Hospital (*q.v.*).

William Jennings (1701-97), a neighbour and friend of Elwes, died worth £200,000. *See* HARPAGON.

Mishna (mish' nå) (Heb., repetition or instruction). The collection of moral precepts, traditions, etc., forming the basis of the Talmud; the second or oral law (*see* GEMARA). It is divided into six parts: (1) agriculture; (2) Sabbaths, fasts, and festivals; (3) marriage and divorce; (4) civil and penal laws; (5) sacrifices; (6) holy persons and things.

Misnomers. In English nomenclature we have many words and short phrases that can be called "misnomers"; some of these have arisen through pure ignorance (and when once a useful word has been adopted and taken to our bosoms nothing—not even conviction of etymological errors—will eradicate it), some through confusion of ideas or the taking of one thing for another, and some through the changes that time brings about. *Catgut*, for instance, was in all probability, at one time made from the intestines of a *cat*, and now that sheep, horses, asses, etc., but never *cats*, are used for the purpose the name still remains.

A large number of these "misnomers" will be found scattered throughout this book (*see especially* CLEOPATRA'S NEEDLE, GERMAN SILVER, HONEYDEW, HUMBLE PIE, INDIANS (AMERICAN), JERUSALEM ARTICHOKE, MEERSCHAUM, MOTHER OF PEARL, POMPEY'S PILLAR, SAND-BLIND, SLUGHORN, VENTRILOQUISM, WOLF'S-BANE, and WORMWOOD); and we give a few more below:—

Black beetles are neither black nor beetles; their alternative name, *cockroach*, is from the Span. *cucaracha*.

Blacklead is plumbago or graphite, a form of carbon, and has no lead in its composition. *See under* LEAD.

Blind worms are no more blind than *moles* are; they have very quick and brilliant eyes, though somewhat small.

Brazilian grass does not come from Brazil or even grow in Brazil, nor is it a grass. It consists of strips of a palm-leaf (*Chamærops argentea*), and is chiefly imported from Cuba.

Burgundy pitch is not pitch, nor is it manufactured or exported from Burgundy. The best is a resinous substance prepared from common frankincense, and brought from Hamburg: but by far the larger quantity is a mixture of resin and palm oil.

China, as a name for porcelain, gives rise to the contradictory expressions British china, Sèvres china, Dresden china, Dutch china, Chelsea china, etc.; like wooden or iron milestones, brass shoe-horns, coppers for our bronze coinage, etc.

Dutch clocks are not of Dutch but German (*Deutsch*) manufacture.

Elements. Fire, air, earth, and water, still often called "the four elements," are not elements at all.

Forlorn hope (*q.v.*) is not etymologically connected with *hope*, though the term is usually employed in connexion with almost hopeless enterprises. The actual derivation is the Dutch *verloren houp*, a lost troop.

Galvanized iron is not galvanized. It is simply iron coated with zinc, and this is done by dipping the iron into molten zinc.

Guernsey lily (*Nerine* or *Imbrofia sarniensis*) is not a native of Guernsey but of Japan and South Africa. It was discovered by Kæmpfer in Japan, and the ship which was bringing specimens of the new plant to Europe was wrecked on the coast of Guernsey; some of the bulbs that were washed ashore took root and germinated, hence the misnomer.

Guinea-pigs (*q.v.*) have no connexion with the pig family, nor do they come from Guinea.

Honeysuckle. So named because of the old but entirely erroneous idea that bees extracted honey therefrom. The honeysuckle is useless to the bee.

Indian ink comes from China, not from India.

Rice paper is not made from rice, but from the pith of the Formosan plant, *Aralia papyrifera*, or hollow plant, so called because it is hollow when the pith has been pushed out.

Running the gauntlet (*see* GAUNTLET) has nothing to do with gauntlets (gloves), though these may be used in the process.

Salt of lemon is in reality potassium acid oxalate, or potassium quadroxalate.

Silver paper, in which chocolates, etc., are sometimes wrapped, is not, of course, made from silver. It is usually composed of tin-foil.

Slow-worm. Not so called because it is *slow*; the first syllable is corrupted from *slay* and it was called the *slay-worm* (= serpent) from the idea that this perfectly harmless creature was venomous.

Titmouse. Nothing to do with *mouse*, though the erroneous plural *titmice*—has now probably come to stay. The second syllable represents A.S. *mase*, used of several small birds. *Tit* is Scandinavian, and also implies "small," as in *titbit*.

Tonquin beans. A geographical blunder, for they are the seeds, the *Dipteryx odorata*, from Tonka, in Guiana, not Tonquin, in Asia.

Turkeys do not come from Turkey, but North America, through Spain, or India. The French call them "dindon," *i.e. d'Inde* or *coq d'Inde*, a term equally incorrect.

Turkey rhubarb neither grows in Turkey, nor is it imported from Turkey. It grows in the great mountain chain between Tartary and Siberia, and is a Russian monopoly.

Turkish baths are not of Turkish origin though they were introduced from the Near East, popularly associated with Turkish rule and customs. The correct name of Hammam was commonly used in England in the 17th century, and for many years there was a Hummum's Hotel in Covent Garden on the site of a 17th-century Turkish Bath.

Whalebone is no bone at all, nor does it possess any properties of bone. It is a substance attached to the upper jaw of the whale, and serves to strain the algæ and small life from the water which the creature takes up in large mouthfuls.

Misprision. (Fr. *mépris*). Concealment, neglect of; in law, an offence bordering on a capital offence.

Misprision of felony. Neglecting to reveal a felony when known.

Misprision of treason. Neglecting to disclose or purposely concealing a treasonable design.

Misrule, Feast of. *See* KING OF MISRULE.

Miss, Mistress, Mrs. (masteress, lady-master). Miss used to be written Mis, and is the first syllable of Mistress; Mrs. is the contraction of *mistress*, called Mis'ess. So late as the reign of George II unmarried women used to be styled Mrs., as, Mrs. Lepel, Mrs. Bellenden, Mrs. Blount, all unmarried women. (*See* Pope's *Letters*.)

Mistress was originally an honourable term for a sweetheart or lover—"Mistress mine, where are you roaming". It has since come to mean a woman who lives with a man as his wife but without being so.

The mistress of the night. The tuberose is so called because it emits its strongest fragrance after sunset.

In the language of flowers, the tuberose signifies "the pleasures of love."

The mistress of the world. Ancient Rome was so called, because all the known world gave her allegiance.

Miss. To fail to hit, or—in such phrases as **I miss you now you are gone**—to lack, to feel the want of.

A miss is as good as a mile. A failure is a failure be it ever so little, and is no more be it ever so great; a narrow escape is an escape. An old form of the phrase was *An inch in a miss is as good as an ell*.

The missing link. A popular term for the hypothetical being that is supposed, according to the theory of evolution, to bridge the gap between man and the anthropoid apes. Haeckel held it to be *Pithecanthropus erectus*; but scientists are not agreed, either on this or on the number of "missing links" there may be. Professor Woodward, in a lecture on the Rhodesian skull discovered at Broken Hill in 1921, said—

The Rhodesian man was one of the links in the chain of which many species would be found. It would be a long time before a connecting series of missing links would be discovered which would be convincing.

Mississippi Bubble. The French "South Sea Scheme," and equally disastrous. It was projected by the Scots financier, John Law (1671-1729), and had for its object the payment of the National Debt of France, which amounted to 208 millions sterling, on being granted the exclusive trade of Louisiana, on the banks of the Mississippi. Inaugurated in 1717, it was taken up by the French Government, and in 1719 the shares were selling at forty times their original value. But in 1720 the "bubble" burst, France was almost ruined, Law fled to Russia, and his estates were confiscated.

Missouri (mis oo' ri, miz oo' rà). **I'm from Missouri** is equivalent to "I'm hard-headed and you have to show me" or "I won't believe anything without proof." First used in a speech in 1899 by Willard D. Vandiver, Congressman from Missouri.

Missouri Compromise. An arrangement whereby Missouri was in 1820 admitted to the Union as a Slave State, but that at the same time there should be no slavery in the state north of 36° 30'.

Mistletoe (mis' ĕl tō) (A.S. *mistiltan; mist*, being both basil and mistletoe, and *tan*, a twig). The plant grows as a parasite on various trees, especially the apple tree, and was held in great veneration by the Druids when found on the oak. Shakespeare calls it "the *baleful* mistletoe" (*Titus Andronicus*, ii, 3), perhaps in allusion to the Scandinavian legend that it was with an arrow made of mistletoe that Balder (*q.v.*) was slain, but probably with reference either to the popular but erroneous notion that mistletoe berries are poisonous, or to the connexion of the plant with the human sacrifices of the Druids. It is in all probability for this latter reason that mistletoe is rigorously excluded from church decorations.

Kissing under the mistletoe. An English Christmas-time custom, dating back at least to the early 17th century. The correct procedure, now rarely observed, is that as the young man kisses a girl under the mistletoe he should pluck a berry, and that when the last berry is gone there should be no more kissing.

Marwell Old Hall, once the residence of the Seymours and afterwards of the Dacre family, has a similar tradition attached to it.

Mistpoeffers. *See* BARISAL GUNS.

Mistral, The. A violent north-west wind blowing down the Gulf of Lyons; felt particularly at Marseilles and the south-east of France.

Mistress. *See* MISS.

Mithra or **Mithras** (mith' rà). The god of light of the ancient Persians, one of their chief deities, and the ruler of the universe. Sometimes used as a synonym for the sun. The word means *friend*, and this deity is so called because he befriends man in this life, and protects him against evil spirits after death. He is represented as a young man with a Phrygian cap, a tunic, a mantle on his left shoulder, and plunging a sword into the neck of a bull (*see Thebais*, i).

The Mithraic rites—

have been maintained by a constant tradition, with their penances and tests of the courage of the candidate for admission, through the Secret Societies of the Middle Ages and the Rosicrucians, down to the modern faint reflex of the latter, the Freemasons.—KNIGHT: *Symbolical Language.*

Sir Thomas More called the Supreme Being of his *Utopia* "Mithra."

Mittimus (mit' i mús) (Lat., we send). A command in writing to a jailer, to keep the person named in safe custody. Also a writ for removing a record from one court to another. So called from the first word of the writ.

Mitton. The Chapter of Mitton. So the battle of Mitton was called, because so many priests took part therein. It was fought in 1319, and the Scots defeated the forces of the Archbishop of York.

Mnemonics (ne mon' iks). The art of improving the memory by artificial aids and methods. Such methods usually depend on the association of ideas and are chiefly based on the principles of localization and analogy. The word comes from the Greek *mnemonikos*, of memory.

Mnemosyne (ne mos' i ni). Goddess of memory and mother by Zeus of the nine Muses of Greek mythology. She was the daughter of Heaven and Earth (Uranus and Ge).

> To the Immortals every one
> A portion was assigned of all that is;
> But chief Mnemosyne did Maia's son
> Clothe in the light of his loud melodies.
>   SHELLEY: *Homer's Hymn to Mercury*, lxxiii.

Moabite Stone, The. An ancient *stele*, bearing the oldest extant Semitic inscription, now in the Louvre, Paris. The inscription, consisting of thirty-four lines in Hebrew-Phœnician characters, gives an account of the war of Mesha, King of Moab, who reigned about 850 B.C., against Omri, Ahab, and other kings of Israel (*see* 2 *Kings*, iii). Mesha sacrificed his eldest son on the city wall in view of the invading Israelites. The stone was discovered by F. Klein at Dibhan in 1868, and is 3 ft. 10 in. high, 2 ft. broad and $14\frac{1}{2}$ in. thick. The Arabs resented its removal, and splintered it into fragments, but it has been restored.

Moaning Minnie. World War II term for a six-barrelled German mortar, so named from the rising shriek it gave when the six projectiles were simultaneously released. The name was also given popularly to the air-raid warning siren.

Mob. A contraction of the Latin *mobile vulgus* (the fickle crowd). The term was first applied to the people by the members of the

Green-ribbon Club, in the reign of Charles II. (*Northern Examiner*, p. 574.)

In subsequent years the word was applied to an organized criminal gang.

Mockery. "It will be a delusion, a mockery, and a snare." Thomas, Lord Denman, observed this in his judgment on the case of The Queen *v.* O'Connell (1844).

Mock-up. Phrase originating in World War II for a model or any full-size working model. (2) American phrase for panels mounted with models of aircraft parts used by the A.A.F. for instructional purposes.

Modality, in scholastic philosophy, means the *mode* in which anything exists. Kant divides our judgment into three modalities: (1) *Problematic*, touching possible events; (2) *Assertoric*, touching real events; (3) *Apodictic*, touching necessary events.

Modernism. A movement in the Catholic Church which sought to interpret the ancient teachings of the Church in the light of the scientific knowledge of modern times. It was condemned by Pope Pius X in 1907 in the encyclical *Pascendi*, which stigmatized it as the "synthesis of all heresies."

Modus operandi (Lat.). The mode of operation; the way in which a thing is done or should be done. **Modus vivendi** (Lat., way of living). A mutual arrangement whereby persons not at the time being on friendly terms can be induced to live together in harmony. The term may be applied to individuals, to societies, or to peoples.

Mofussil (East Indies). The subordinate divisions of a district; the rural divisions of a district; the rural districts as apart from the chief city or seat of government, which is called the *sudder*; provincial.

To tell a man that fatal charges have been laid against him, and refuse him an opportunity for explanation, this is not even Mofussil justice.—*The Times.*

Mogul (mō' gŭl). **The Mogul Empire.** The Mohammedan-Tartar Empire in India which began in 1526 with Baber, great-grandson of Timur, or Tamerlane, and split up after the death of Aurungzebe in 1707, the power passing to the British and the Mahrattas. The Emperor was known as the *Great* or *Grand Mogul*; besides those mentioned, Akbar, Jahangir, and Shah Jehan are the most noteworthy.

Mogul cards. The best-quality playing-cards were so called because the wrapper, or the "duty-card" (cards are subject to excise duty) was decorated with a representation of the Great Mogul. Inferior cards were called

"Harrys," "Highlanders," and "Merry Andrews" for a similar reason.

Mohair (mō' hâr) (Probably the Arabic *mukhayyar*, goat's-hair cloth). It is the hair of the Angora goat, introduced into Spain by the Moors, and thence brought into Germany.

Mohammed, Mahomet (Arab., "the praised one"). The titular name of the founder of Islam (*q.v.*) or Mohammedanism (born at Mecca about 570, died at Medina, 632), which was adopted by him about the time of the Hegira to apply to himself the Messianic prophecies in the Old Testament (*Haggai* ii, 7, and elsewhere). His original name is given both as Kotham and Halabi.

Angel of. When Mohammed was transported to heaven, he says: "I saw there an angel, the most gigantic of all created beings. It had 70,000 heads, each had 70,000 faces, each face had 70,000 mouths, each mouth had 70,000 tongues, and each tongue spoke 70,000 languages; all were employed in singing God's praises." This must not, of course, be taken as a definition of belief, but as a mode of Oriental emphasis.

Banner of. Sanjaksherif, kept in the Eyab mosque, at Constantinople.

Bible of. The Koran.

Camel (*swiftest*). Adha.

Cave. The cave in which Gabriel appeared to Mohammed (610) was in the mountain of Hirâ, near Mecca.

Coffin. Legend used to have it that Mohammed's coffin is suspended in mid-air at Medina without any support.

Sp'ritual men are too transcendent . . .
To hang, like Mahomet, in the air,
Or St. Ignatius at his prayer,
By pure geometry.
          BUTLER: *Hudibras*, III, ii, 602.

Daughter (*favourite*), Fatima.

Dove. Mohammed had a dove which he fed with wheat out of his ear. When it was hungry it used to light on the prophet's shoulder, and thrust its bill into his ear to find its meal. Mohammed thus induced the Arabs to believe that he was divinely inspired.

Was Mahomet inspired with a dove?
          1 *Henry VI*, i, 2.

Father. Abdallah, of the tribe of Koreish. He died a little before or a little after the birth of Mohammed.

Father-in-law (father of Ayesha), Abu-Bekr. He succeeded Mohammed and was the first calif.

Flight from Mecca (called the Hegira), A.D. 622. He retired to Medina.

Hegira. See above. Flight.

Horse. Al Borak (*The Lightning*). It conveyed the prophet to the seventh heaven.

Miracles. Several are traditionally mentioned, but many of the True Believers hold that he performed no miracle. That of the moon is best known.

Habib the Wise asked Mohammed to prove his mission by cleaving the moon in two. Mohammed raised his hands towards heaven, and in a loud voice summoned the moon to do Habib's bidding. Accordingly, it descended to the top of the Kaaba (*q.v.*), made seven circuits, and, coming to the prophet, entered his right sleeve and came out of the left. It then entered the collar of his robe, and descended to the skirt, clove itself into two plaits, one of which appeared in the east of the skies and the other in the west; and the two parts ultimately reunited and resumed their usual form.

Mother of. Amina, of the tribe of Koreish. She died when Mohammed was six years old.

Paradise of. The ten animals admitted to the Moslem's paradise are:—

(1) The dog Kratim, which accompanied the Seven Sleepers.

(2) Balaam's ass, which spoke with the voice of a man to reprove the disobedient prophet.

(3) Solomon's ant, of which he said, "Go to the ant, thou sluggard . . ."

(4) Jonah's whale.

(5) The ram caught in the thicket, and offered in sacrifice in lieu of Isaac.

(6) The calf of Abraham.

(7) The camel of Saleb.

(8) The cuckoo of Bilkis.

(9) The ox of Moses.

(10) Mohammed's horse, Al Borak.

Stepping-stone. The stone upon which the prophet placed his foot when he mounted Al Borak on his ascent to heaven. It rose as the beast rose, but Mohammed, putting his hand upon it, forbade it to follow him, whereupon it remained suspended in mid-air, where the True Believer, if he has faith enough, may still behold it.

Tribe. On both sides, the Koreish.

Uncle, who took charge of Mohammed at the death of his grandfather, Abu Tâlib.

Wives. Ten in number, viz. (1) Kadija, a rich widow of the tribe of Koreish, who had been twice married already, and was forty years of age. For twenty-five years she was his only wife, but at her death he married nine others, all of whom survived him.

The nine wives. (1) Ayesha, daughter of Abu Bekr, only nine years old on her wedding-day. This was his youngest and favourite wife.

(2) Sauda, widow of Sokram, and nurse to his daughter Fatima.

(3) Hafsa, a widow twenty-eight years old, who also had a son. She was daughter of Omeya.

(4) Zeinab, wife of Zaid, but divorced in order that the prophet might take her to wife.

(5) Barra, wife of a young Arab and daughter of Al Hareth, chief of an Arab tribe. She was a captive.

(6) Rehana, daughter of Simeon, and a Jewish captive.

(7) Safiya, the espoused wife of Kenana. Kenana was put to death. Safiya outlived the prophet forty years.

(8) Omm Habiba—*i.e.* mother of Habiba; the widow of Abu Sofian.

(9) Maimuna, fifty-one years old, and a widow, who survived all his other wives.

Also ten or fifteen concubines, chief of whom was Mariyeh, mother of Ibrahim, the prophet's only son, who died when fifteen months old.

Year of Deputations, A.D. 630, the 8th of the Hegira.

If the mountain will not come to Mohammed, Mohammed must go to the mountain. When Mohammed introduced his system to the Arabs, they asked for miraculous proofs. He then ordered Mount Safa to come to him, and as it did not move, he said, "God is merciful. Had it obeyed my words, it would have fallen on us to our destruction. I will therefore go to the mountain, and thank God that He has had mercy on a stiffnecked generation." The phrase is often used of one who, not being able to get his own way, bows before the inevitable.

Moira. Fate, or Necessity, supreme even over the gods of Olympus.

Molinism (mol' i nizm). The system of grace and election taught by Louis Molina, the Spanish Jesuit (1535-1600).

The Pope's great self—Innocent by name . . .
'Twas he who first bade leave those souls in peace.
Those Jansenists, renicknamed Molinists. . . .
"Leave them alone," bade he, "those Molinists!
Who may have other light than we perceive,
Or why is it the whole world hates them thus?"
BROWNING: *The Ring and the Book,* I, 300-17.

His doctrine was that grace is a free gift to all, but that the consent of the will must be present before that grace can be effective.

Moll, Molly. Moll Cutpurse. *See* CUTPURSE.

Take away this bottle, it has Moll Thomson's mark on it. Moll Thomson is M.T. (*empty*).

Molly coddle. A pampered creature, afraid that the winds of heaven should visit him too roughly.

Molly Maguires. An Irish secret society organized in 1843. Stout, active young Irishmen dressed up in women's clothes and otherwise disguised themselves to surprise those employed to enforce the payment of rents. Their victims were ducked in bog-holes, and many were beaten most unmercifully.

A similar secret society in the mining districts of Pennsylvania was (about 1877) known by the same name.

The judge who tried the murderer was elected by the Molly Maguires; the jurors who assisted him were themselves Molly Maguires. A score of Molly Maguires came forward to swear that the assassin was sixty miles from the spot on which he had been seen to fire at William Dunn . . . and the jurors returned a verdict of Not Guilty.—
W. HEPWORTH DIXON: *New America*, ii, 28.

Molly Mog. This celebrated beauty was an innkeeper's daughter, at Oakingham, Berks. She was the toast of the gay sparks of the first half of the 18th century, and died unmarried in 1766, at the age of sixty-seven. Gay has a ballad on this *Fair Maid of the Inn*, in which the "swain" alluded to is Mr. Standen, of Arborfield, who died in 1730. It is said that Molly's sister Sally was the greater beauty. A portrait of Gay still hangs in the inn.

Molmutius or **Mulmutius**. *See* MULMUTINE LAWS.

Moloch (mō′ lok). Any influence which demands from us the sacrifice of what we hold most dear. Thus, *war* is a Moloch, *king mob* is a Moloch, the *guillotine* was the Moloch of the French Revolution, etc. The allusion is to the god of the Ammonites, to whom children were "made to pass through the fire" in sacrifice (*see* 2 *Kings*, xxiii, 10). Milton says he was worshipped in Rabba, in Argob, and Basan, to the stream of utmost Arnon. (*Paradise Lost*, i, 392-398.)

Molotov. The name of Vyacheslav Mikhailovich Molotov, the Russian diplomat, was adopted in World War II in several ways:—

Molotov breadbasket. A canister of incendiary bombs which, on being launched from a plane, opened and showered the bombs over a wide area.

Molotov cocktail. A home-made anti-tank bomb, invented and first used by the Finns against the Russians (1940) and developed in England as one of the weapons of the Home Guard. It consisted of a bottle filled with inflammable and glutinous liquid, with a slow match protruding from the top. When thrown at a tank the bottle burst, the liquid ignited and spread over the plating of the tank.

Moly (mō′ li). The mythical herb given, according to Homer, by Hermes to Ulysses as an antidote against the sorceries of Circe.

Black was the root, but milky white the flower,
Moly the name, to mortals hard to find.
Pope's Odyssey, x, 365.
That moly
That Hermes once to wise Ulysses gave.
MILTON: *Comus*, 655.

The name is given to a number of plants, especially of the *Allium* (garlic) family, as the wild garlic, the Indian moly, the moly of Hungary, serpents moly, the yellow moly, Spanish purple moly, Spanish silver-capped moly, and Dioscorides' moly.

They all Flower in May, except "the sweet moly of Montpelier," which blossoms in September.

Momus (mō′ mus). One who carps at everything. Momus, the sleepy god of the Greeks, son of Nox (Night), was always railing and carping.

Momus, being asked to pass judgment on the relative merits of Neptune, Vulcan, and Minerva, railed at them all. He said the horns of a bull ought to have been placed in the shoulders, where they would have been of much greater force; as for man, he said Jupiter ought to have made him with a window in his breast, whereby his real thoughts might be revealed.

Hence Byron's—
Were Momus' lattice in our breasts . . .
Werner, iii, 1.

Monday. The second day of the week; called by the Anglo-Saxons Monandæg, *i.e.* the day of the Moon.

That Monday feeling. Disinclination to return to work after the week-end break.

Mongrel Parliament. The Parliament that met at Oxford in 1681 and passed the Exclusion Bill.

Monism (mō′ nizm). The doctrine of the oneness of mind and matter, God and the universe. It ignores all that is supernatural, any dualism of mind and matter, God and creation; and there can be no opposition between God and the world, as unity cannot be in opposition to itself. Monism teaches that "all are but parts of one stupendous whole, whose body nature is, and God the soul"; hence, whatever is, only conforms to the cosmical laws of the universal ALL.

Haeckel explained it thus in 1866: "Monism (the correlative of Dualism) denotes a unitary conception, in opposition to a supernatural one. Mind can never exist without matter, nor matter without mind." As God is the same "yesterday, to-day, and for ever," creation must be the same, or God would not be unchangeable.

Monitor. So the Romans called the nursery teacher. The *Military Monitor* was an officer to tell young soldiers of the faults committed against the service. The *House Monitor* was a slave to call the family of a morning, etc.

A shallow-draught ironclad with a flat deck, sharp stern, and one or more movable turrets, was so called. They were first used in the American War of Secession, and were so named by the inventor, Captain Ericsson, because they were to be "severe monitors" to the leaders of the Southern rebellion.

The word is also used to designate a broadcasting official employed to listen in to foreign (esp. enemy) radio transmissions in order to analyse the news announced and to study propaganda. In normal circumstances the duties of a monitor include checking the quality of transmissions.

Monk. The word *monk* is often employed loosely and incorrectly for any religious living in community or belonging to an order. In the Western Church only members of the following orders are monks: Benedictines, Cistercians, Carthusians, and four smaller orders. Members of the great orders of Dominicans, Franciscans, Carmelites, and Augustinians are friars.

In printing, a black smear or blotch made by leaving too much ink on the part. Caxton set up his printing-press in the *scriptorium* of Westminster Abbey (*see* CHAPEL); and the association gave rise to the slang expressions *monk* and *friar* (*q.v.*) for black and white defects.

Monk Lewis. Matthew Gregory Lewis (1775-1818) is so called from his highly coloured "Gothic" novel *Ambrosio, or the Monk* (1795).

Monkey. Slang for £500 or (in America) $500; also for a mortgage (sometimes extended to *a monkey with a long tail*), and among sailors the vessel which contains the full allowance of grog for one mess. A child, especially an active, meddlesome one, is often called "a little monkey"—for obvious reasons.

Monkey's allowance. More kicks than halfpence. The allusion is to the monkeys formerly carried about for show; they picked up the halfpence, but carried them to the master, who kept kicking or ill-treating the poor creatures to urge them to incessant tricks.

Monkey board. In the old-fashioned horsed knifeboard omnibuses, the step on which the conductor stood, and on which he often skipped about like a monkey.

Monkey jacket. A short coat worn by seamen; so called because it has "no more tail than a monkey," or, more strictly speaking, an ape.

Monkey puzzle. The Chilean pine, *Araucaria imbricata*, whose twisted and prickly branches puzzle even a monkey to climb.

Monkey tricks. Mischievous, illnatured, or deceitful actions.

To get one's monkey up. To be riled or enraged; monkeys are extremely irritable and easily provoked.

To monkey with or **about.** To tamper with or play mischievous tricks. *To monkey with the cards* is to try to arrange them so that the deal will not be fair; *to monkey with the milk* is to add water to it and then sell it as pure and unadulterated.

Monkey suit, in the U.S.A. services, is the term applied to full dress uniform, also to an aviator's overalls. The phrase is often used for men's formal dress on important occasions.

Monmouth. The town at the mouth of the Monnow, surname of Henry V of England, who was born there.

Monmouth cap. A soldier's cap.

> The soldiers that the Monmouth wear,
> On castles' tops their ensigns rear.

The best caps were formerly made at Monmouth, where the cappers' chapel doth still remain.—FULLER: *Worthies of Wales,* p. 50.

Monmouth Street (London) takes its name from the unfortunate son of Charles II, executed for rebellion in 1685. Later Dudley Street, St. Giles, and now forming part of Shaftesbury Avenue close to Soho Square, where the Duke of Monmouth had his town house, it was formerly noted for its secondhand clothes shops; hence the expression *Monmouth Street finery* for tawdry, pretentious clothes.

> [At the Venetian carnival] you may put on whate'er
> You like by way of doublet, cape, or cloak.
> Such as in Monmouth-street, or in Rag Fair
> Would rig you out in seriousness or joke.
> BYRON: *Beppo,* v.

Monotheism (mon' ō thē izm) (Gr. *monos theos,* one God). The doctrine that there is but one God.

The only large monotheism known to historic times is that of Mahomet.—GLADSTONE, in *Contemporary Review,* June, 1876.

Monroe Doctrine (mùn rō'). The doctrine first promulgated in 1823 by James Monroe (President of the U.S.A., 1817-25), to the effect that the American States are never to entangle themselves in the broils of the Old World, nor to suffer it to interfere in the affairs of the New; and they are to account any attempt on the part of the Old World to plant their systems of government in any part of North America not at the time in European occupation dangerous to American peace and safety. The capture of Manila and the cession of the Philippine Islands to the United States in 1898, and still more the part the States took in the two World Wars has abrogated a large part of this famous Doctrine.

Mons Meg. *See* MEG.

Monsieur. The eldest brother of the king of France was formerly so called, especially Philippe, Duc d'Orléans, brother to Louis XIV (1640-1701).

Monsieur de Paris. The public executioner or Jack Ketch of France.

Riccardo de Albertes was a personal friend of all the "Messieurs de Paris," who served the Republic. He attended all capital executions. — *Newspaper Paragraph*, January 25th, 1893.

Monsieur le Grand. The Great Equerry of France.

The Peace of Monsieur. The peace that the Huguenots, the Politiques, and the Duke d'Alençon ("Monsieur") obliged Henri III of France to sign in 1576. By it the Huguenots and the Duke gained great concessions.

Monsignor (mon sē' nyôr) (pl. *monsignori*). A title pertaining to all prelates in the R.C. Church, which includes all prelates of the Roman court, active or honorary. Used with the surname, as Monsignor So-and-so it does away with the barbarism of speaking of Bishop So-and-so, which is as incorrect as calling the Duke of Marlborough "Duke Churchill."

Monsoon (Arab. *mausim*, time, season). A periodical wind; especially that which blows off S.W. Asia and the Indian Ocean from the south-west from April to October, and from the north-east during the rest of the year.

Mont (Fr., hill). The technical term in palmistry for the eminences at the roots of the fingers.

That at the root of the
thumb is the Mont de Mars.
index finger is the Mont de Jupiter.
long finger is the Mont de Saturne.
ring finger is the Mont de Soleil.
little finger is the Mont de Venus.
The one between the thumb and index finger is called the Mont de Mercure and the one opposite the Mont de Lune.

Mont de Piété. A pawnshop in France; first instituted as *monti di pieta* (charity loans) under Leo X (reigned 1513-21), at Rome, by charitable persons who wished to rescue the poor from usurious moneylenders. They advanced small sums of money on the security of pledges, at a rate of interest barely sufficient

to cover the working expenses of the institution. Both the name and system were introduced into France and Spain. Public granaries for the sale of corn are called in Italian *Monti frumentarii*. "Monte" means a public or state loan; hence also a "bank."

Montage (mon' tazh). In cinematography the final arrangement and assembling of photos to make a continuous film; also the art of film-cutting.

Montagnards. *See* MOUNTAIN, THE.

Monteith (mon tēth). A scalloped basin to cool and wash glasses in; a sort of punch-bowl, made of silver or pewter, with a movable rim scalloped at the top; so called, according to Anthony Wood, in 1683 from "a fantastical Scot called 'Monsieur Monteigh' who at that time or a little before wore the bottome of his coate so notched ⌣ ⌣ ⌣ ⌣."

New things produce new names, and thus Monteith
Has by one vessel saved his name from death. — KING.

Montgomery (mŭn gŭm' er i). A Norman name, not Welsh. The town was founded by a Norman named Baldwin, and was in Welsh called *Trefaldwyn*, "house of Baldwin": in 1086 it was taken by Roger Montgomery, Earl of Shrewsbury, Count of the Marches to William the Conqueror, and it was given his name — which is a French place-name, the *Hill of Gomerie*.

Montgomery's division, all on one side. This is a French proverb, and refers to the Free Companies of the 16th century, of which a Montgomery was a noted chief. The booty he took he kept himself.

Month. One of the twelve portions into which the year is divided. Anciently a new month started on the day of the new moon, or the day after; hence the name (A.S. *monath*), which is connected with *moon*. *See* LUNAR MONTH; and, for the months themselves *see* their names throughout this DICTIONARY.

The old mnemonic for remembering the number of days in each month runs —

Thirty days hath September,
April, June, and November,
February eight-and-twenty all alone
And all the rest have thirty-one,
Unless that Leap Year doth combine
And give to February twenty-nine.

This, with slight variations, is to be found in Grafton's *Chronicles* (1590), the play *The Return from Parnassus* (1606), etc. In Harrison's *Description of England* (prefixed to Holinshed's *Chronicle*, 1577) is the Latin version: —

Junius, Aprilis, Septémq; Novemq; tricenos,
Unum plus reliqui, Februs tenet octo vicenos.
At si bissextus fuerit superadditur unus.

A month of Sundays. An indefinite long time; never. *See* NEVER.

Monument. The fluted Roman-Doric column of Portland stone (202 ft. high) built by Sir Christopher Wren to commemorate the Great Fire of London in 1666 is known as The Monument. It stands near the north end of London Bridge, about the spot where the fire started.

The old inscription (effaced in 1831) maintained that the fire had been caused—

by ye treachery and malice of ye popish faction, in order to ye carrying on their horrid plott for extirpating the Protestant religion, and old English liberty, and the introducing popery and slavery.

and it was this that made Pope refer to it as—

London's column, pointing at the skies
Like a tall bully, lifts the head, and lies.

Moral Essays, III, 339.

When looking at monuments and effigies, etc., in our churches, it may be useful to remember the following points which must not, however, be taken as invariable rules:—

Founders of chapels, etc., lie with their monument built into the wall.

Figures with their hands on their breasts, and chalices, represent *priests*.

Figures with crozier, mitre, and pontificals, represent *prelates*.

Figures with armour represent *knights*.

Figures with legs crossed represent either *crusaders* or *married men*, but those with a scallop shell are certainly *crusaders*.

Female figures with a mantle and large ring represent *nuns*.

In the age of chivalry the woman was placed on the man's right hand; but when chivalry declined she was placed on his left hand.

It may usually be taken that inscriptions in Latin, cut in capitals, are of the first twelve centuries; those in Lombardic capitals and French, of the 13th; those in Old English text, of the 14th; while those in the English language and Roman characters are subsequent to the 14th century.

Tablets against the wall came in with the Reformation; and brasses are for the most part subsequent to the 13th century.

Monumental City. Baltimore, Maryland, is so called because it abounds in monuments; witness the obelisk, the 104 churches, etc.

Moon. The word is probably connected with the Sanskrit root *me-*, to measure (because time was measured by it). It is common to all Teutonic languages (Goth, *mena*, O.Frisian

mona, O.Norm. *mane*, A.S. *mona*, etc.), and is almost invariably masculine. In the Edda the *son* of Mundilfœri is Mani (moon), and *daughter* Sôl (*sun*); so it is still with the Lithuanians and Arabians, and so was it with the ancient Slavs, Mexicans, Hindus, etc., and the Germans to this day have *Frau Sonne* (Mrs. Sun) and *Herr Mond* (Mr. Moon).

The Moon is represented in five different phases: (1) new; (2) full; (3) crescent or descrescent; (4) half; and (5) gibbous, or more than half. In pictures of the Assumption it is shown as a crescent under Our Lady's feet; in the Crucifixion it is eclipsed, and placed on one side of the cross, the sun being on the other; in the Creation and Last Judgment it is also introduced by artists.

In classical mythology the moon was known as *Hecate* before she had risen and after she had set; as *Astarte* when crescent; as *Diana* or *Cynthia* (she who "hunts the clouds") when in the open vault of heaven; as *Phœbe* when looked upon as the sister of the sun (*i.e. Phœbus*); and was personified as *Selene* or *Luna*, the lover of the sleeping *Endymion*, *i.e.* moonlight on the fields (*see these names*).

The moon is called *triform*, because it presents itself to us either *round*, or *waxing* with horns towards the east, or *waning* with horns towards the west.

One legend connected with the moon was that there was treasured everything wasted on earth, such as misspent time and wealth, broken vows, unanswered prayers, fruitless tears, abortive attempts, unfulfilled desires and intentions, etc. In Ariosto's *Orlando Furioso* Astolpho found on his visit to the Moon (Bk. xviii and xxxiv, 70) that bribes were hung on gold and silver hooks; princes' favours were kept in bellows; wasted talent was kept in vases, each marked with the proper name, etc.; and in *The Rape of the Lock* (canto v) Pope tells us that when the Lock disappeared—

Some thought it mounted to the lunar sphere,
Since all things lost on earth are treasured there,
There heroes' wits are kept in pond'rous vases,
And beaux' in snuff-boxes and tweezer-cases.
There broken vows and death-bed alms are found
And lovers' hearts with ends of ribbon bound,
The courtier's promises, and sick man's prayers,
The smiles of harlots, and the tears of heirs
Cages for gnats, and chains to yoke a flea.
Dried butterflies, and tomes of casuistry.

Hence the phrase, *the limbus of the moon*.

I know no more about it than the man in the moon. I know nothing at all about the matter.

Moonlight flit. A clandestine removal of one's furniture during the night, to avoid paying one's rent or having the furniture seized in payment thereof.

Moon-rakers. A nickname of people of Wiltshire. The absurd story offered to account for the name is that in the "good old times" they were noted smugglers, and one night, seeing the coastguard on the watch, they sank some smuggled whisky in the sea. When the coast was clear they employed rakes to recover their goods, when the coastguard reappeared and asked what they were doing. Pointing to the reflection of the moon in the water, they replied, "We are trying to rake out that cream cheese yonder."

Moon's men. Thieves and highwaymen who ply their trade by night.

The fortune of us that are but Moon's-men doth ebb and flow like the sea.—1 *Henry IV*, i, 2.

Moonstone. A variety of feldspar, so called on account of the play of light which it exhibits. It contains bluish white spots, which, when held to the light, present a silvery play of colour not unlike that of the moon.

Once in a blue moon. *See* BLUE MOON.

The cycle of the moon. *See* CYCLE.

The Island of the Moon. Madagascar is so named by the natives.

The limbus of the moon. *See above.*

The man in the moon. Some say it is a man leaning on a fork, on which he is carrying a bundle of sticks picked up on a Sunday. The origin of this fable is from *Numb.* xv, 32-36. Some add a dog also; thus the prologue in *Midsummer Night's Dream* says, "This man with lantern, dog, and bush of thorns, presenteth moonshine"; Chaucer says "he stole the bush" (*Test. of Cresseide*). Another tradition says that the man is Cain, with his dog and thorn bush; the thorn bush being emblematical of the thorns and briars of the fall, and the dog being the "foul fiend." Some poets make out the "man" to be Endymion, taken to the moon by Diana.

The Mountains of the Moon means simply White Mountains. The Arabs call a white horse "moon-coloured."

To aim or **level at the moon.** To be very ambitious; to aim in shooting at the moon.

To cast beyond the moon. *See* CAST.

To cry for the moon. To crave for what is wholly beyond one's reach. The allusion is to foolish children who want the moon for a plaything. The French say, "He wants to take the moon between his teeth" (*Il veut prendre la lune avec les dents*), alluding to the old proverb about "the moon," and a "green cheese."

You would have me believe that the moon is made of green cheese—*i.e.* the most absurd thing imaginable.

You may as soon persuade some Country Peasants, that the Moon is made of Green-Cheese (as we say) as that 'tis bigger than his Cart-wheel.—WILKINS: *New World*, i (1638).

Moonlighting. Riding after cattle by night in Australia.

Moonshine. A U.S.A. colloquial term for illicitly distilled liquor.

Moor. The word comes from Gr. and Lat. *Mauros*, an inhabitant of Mauretania (*q.v.*). In the Middle Ages, the Europeans called all Mohammedans *Moors*, in the same manner as the Eastern nations called all inhabitants of Europe *Franks*, Camoëns, in the *Lusiad* (Bk. viii), gives the name to the Indians.

Moor-slayer or **Mata-moros.** A name given to St. James, the patron saint of Spain, because, as the legends say, in encounters with the Moors he came on his white horse to the aid of the Christians.

Moot. In Anglo-Saxon times, the assembly of freemen in a township, tithing, etc. *Cp.* WITENAGEMOT. In legal circles the name is given to the students' debates on supposed cases which formerly took place on the halls of Inns of Court. The benchers and the barristers, as well as the students, took an active part. In a few towns, *e.g.* Aldeburgh, Suffolk, the town hall is still called the Moot Hall.

Hence, **moot case** or **moot point,** a doubtful or unsettled question, a case that is open to debate.

Morality Play. An allegorical dramatic form, in vogue from the 14th to the 16th centuries in which the vices and virtues were personified and the victory of the last clearly established. One of the best known morality plays was *Everyman*, a 15th-century English play translated from the Dutch *Elkerlijk*.

Moratorium (mor à tôr' i ŭm) (Lat. *morari*, to delay). A legal permission to defer for a stated time the payment of a bond, debt, or other obligation. This is done to enable the debtor to pull himself round by borrowing money, selling effects, or otherwise raising funds to satisfy obligations. The device was adopted in 1891 in South America during the panic caused by the Baring Brothers' default of some twenty millions sterling, and the word came into popular use during World War I, and afterwards in connexion with the inability of Germany to pay to date the stated amount due as reparations under the Treaty of Versailles.

In Great Britain, on Aug. 6th, 1914, a moratorium was proclaimed giving the banks power to retain certain sums credited to them and putting off the payment of Bills of Exchange and other debts for a month; this was later extended to Oct. 4th, and a partial renewal to assist certain interests was allowed to Nov. 4th.

Moravians (mo rā' vi ǎnz). A religious community tracing its origin to John Huss (*see* BOHEMIAN BRETHREN), expelled by persecution from Bohemia and Moravia in the 17th century. They are often called *The Bohemian Brethren*.

More. More or less. Approximately; in round numbers; as "It is ten miles, more or less, from here to there," *i.e.* it's about ten miles.

The more one has, the more he desires. In French, *Plus il en a, plus il en veut.* In Latin, *Quo plus habent, eo plus cupiunt.*

> My more having would be a source
> To make me hunger more.
> *Macbeth*, iv, 3.

The more the merrier, the fewer the better cheer, or **fare.** The proverb is found in Ray's *Collection* (1742), and in Heywood's (1548).

To be no more. To exist no longer; to be dead.

> Cassius is no more.
> *Julius Cæsar.*

Morgan le Fay (môr' gàn le fā). The fairy sister of King Arthur; one of the principal characters in Arthurian romance and in Celtic legend generally; also known as *Morgaine* and (especially in *Orlando Furioso*) as *Morgana* (*see* FATA MORGANA).

In the Arthurian legends it was Morgan le Fay who revealed to the King the intrigues of Lancelot and Guinevere. She gave him a cup containing a magic draught, and Arthur had no sooner drunk it than his eyes were opened to the perfidy of his wife and friend.

In *Orlando Furioso* she is represented as living at the bottom of a lake, and dispensing her treasures to whom she liked; and in *Orlando Innamorato*, she first appears as "Lady Fortune," but subsequently assumes her witch-like attributes. In Tasso her three daughters, Morganetta, Nivetta, and Carvilia, are introduced.

In the romance of *Ogier the Dane* Morgan le Fay receives Ogier in the Isle of Avalon when he is over one hundred years old, restores him to youth, and becomes his bride.

Morganatic Marriage (môr gàn ǎt' ik). A marriage between a man of high (usually royal) rank and a woman of inferior station, by virtue of which she does not acquire the husband's rank and neither she nor the children of the marriage are entitled to inherit his title or possessions; often called a "left handed marriage" (*q.v.*) because the custom is for the man to pledge his troth with his left hand instead of the right. George William, Duke of Zell, married Eleanora d'Esmiers in this way, and she took the name and title of Lady of Harburg; her daughter was Sophia Dorothea, the wife of George I. An instance of a morganatic marriage in the British Royal Family is that of George, Duke of Cambridge (1819-1904), cousin of Queen Victoria, who married morganatically in 1840. His children took the surname Fitz-George.

The word comes from the mediæval Latin phrase *matrimonium ad morganaticam*, the last word representing the O.H.Ger. *morgan geba*, morning-gift, from husband to wife on the morning after the consummation of the marriage, hence the wife's only claim to her husband's possessions.

Morgane: Morganetta. *See* MORGAN LE FAY.

Morgiana (môr ji ǎn' à). The clever, faithful, female slave of Ali Baba, who pries into the forty jars, and discovers that every jar, but one contains a man. She takes oil from the only one containing it, and, having made it boiling hot, pours enough into each jar to kill the thief concealed there. At last she kills the captain of the gang, and marries her master's son. (*Arabian Nights; Ali Baba and the Forty Thieves.*)

Morgue (môrg). A mortuary, a building, especially that in Paris, where the bodies of persons found dead are exposed to view so that people may come and identify them. The origin of the name is unknown; it does not seem to be connected in any way with *mors*, death, and is probably the same word as *morgue*, meaning of stately or haughty mien. It was formerly applied to prison vestibules, where new criminals were placed to be scrutinized, that the prison officials might become familiar with their faces and general appearance.

> On me conduit donc au petit chastelet, ou du guichet estant passé dans la morgue, un homme gros, court, et carré, vint à moy. — ASSOUCY: *La Prison de M. Dassouch* (1674), p. 35.

> Morgue. Endroit ou l'on tient quelque temps ceux que l'on ecroue, afin que les guichetiers puissent les reconnaitre ensuite. — *Fleming and Tibbins*, vol. ii, p. 688.

Morgue la Faye. The form taken by the name Morgan le Fay (*q.v.*) in *Ogier the Dane*.

Morley, Mrs. The name under which Queen Anne corresponded with "Mrs. Freeman" (Sarah Churchill, Duchess of Marlborough).

Mormonism. The religious and social system of the Mormons, or Latter-day Saints; largely connected in the minds of most people with the practice of polygamy, which became part of the Mormon code in 1852, but is now a diminishing—if not vanished—quantity. Hence the phrase a *regular Mormon,* for a flighty person who cannot keep to one wife or sweetheart.

The fraternity takes its name from *The Book of Mormon,* or *Golden Bible,* which is alleged to have been written on golden plates by the angel Mormon, but was possibly abstracted from a romance (1811) by the Rev. Solomon Spaulding (1761-1816). Joseph Smith (1805-44), adapted this and claimed it as a direct revelation. Smith was born in Sharon, Windsor county, Vermont, and founded the denomination in 1830. He was cited thirty-nine times into courts of law, and was at last assassinated by a gang of ruffians while in prison at Carthage, ill. His successor was Brigham Young (1801-77), a carpenter, who led the "Saints," driven from home by force, to the valley of the Salt Lake, 1,500 miles distant, generally called Utah, but by the Mormons themselves *Deseret* (Bee-country), the New Jerusalem, where they have been settled, despite many disputes with the United States Government, since 1848.

The Mormons accept the Bible as well as the *Book of Mormon* as authoritative, they hold the doctrines of repentance and faith (putting a curious construction on the latter); and they believe in baptism, the Eucharist, the physical resurrection of the dead, and in the Second Coming, when Christ will have the seat of His power in Utah. Marriage may be either for time or for eternity; in the latter case consummation is unnecessary, for the man and the wife or wives he has taken in this way will spend the whole of the afterlife together; in the former case the rite is gone through solely that the community may be increased and multiplied.

Morning. The first glass of whisky drunk by Scottish fishermen in salutation to the dawn. One fisherman will say to another, "Hae ye had your morning, Tam?"

Morning Star, The. Byron's name for Mary Chaworth, his charming neighbour at Newstead, with whom he was in love early in his life.

Morpheus (môr' fūs). Ovid's name for the son of Sleep, and god of dreams; so called from Gr. *morphe,* form, because he gives these airy nothings their form and fashion. Hence the name of the narcotic, *morphine,* or *morphia.*

Morrice, Gil (or **Childe**). The hero of an old Scottish ballad, a natural son of an earl and the wife of Lord Barnard, and brought up "in

the gude grene wode." Lord Barnard, thinking the Childe to be his wife's lover, slew him with a broad-sword, and setting his head on a spear gave it to "the meanest man in a' his train" to carry to the lady. When she saw it she said to the baron, "Wi' that same spear, O pierce my heart, and put me out o' pain"; but the baron replied, "Enouch of blood by me's bin spilt, sair, sair I rew the deid," adding—

I'll ay lament for Gil Morice,
  As gin he were mine ain;
I'll neir forget the dreiry day
  On which the youth was slain.
                    Percy's Reliques, ser. iii, 1.

Percy says this pathetic tale suggested to Home the plot of his tragedy, *Douglas.*

Morse Code. A system of sending messages by telegraph, heliograph, flags, etc., invented in 1835 by the American S. F. B. Morse (1791-1872). Each letter, figure, and punctuation mark is represented by dots, dashes, or a combination of them; thus dot, dash (. —) stands for *a,* dash, dot, dot, dot (— . . .) for *b,* a single dot for *e,* four dots and a dash (. . . . —) for 4, etc. The first message in Morse code was sent May 24th, 1844, from Washington to New York, reading, "What hath God wrought?" In visual signalling a short flash or a rapid dip of the flag corresponds with the dot, and a long or slow with the dash.

Mortal. A mortal sin. A "deadly" sin, one which deserves everlasting punishment; opposed to *venial.*

Earth trembled from her entrails, . . . some sad drops
Wept at completing of the mortal Sin
Original; while Adam took no thought.
            MILTON: *Paradise Lost,* ix, 1003.

In slang and colloquial speech the word is used to express something very great—as "He's in a mortal funk," "There was a mortal lot of people there," or as an emphatic expletive—"You can do any mortal thing you like."

Mortar. Originally a short gun with a large bore for throwing bombs. Said to have been used at Naples in 1435; first made in England in 1543. To-day mortars take the form of a long smooth-bored pipe which throws a bomb with a high trajectory with extreme accuracy.

Mortar-board. A college cap surmounted by a square "board" covered with black cloth. The word is possibly connected with Fr. *mortier,* the cap worn by the ancient kings of France, and still used officially by the chief justice or president of the court of justice, but is more likely an allusion to the small square board on which a bricklayer carries his mortar—frequently balanced on his head.

Morte d'Arthur, Le (môrt dar' th ėr) (*see* Arthurian romances), was compiled by Sir Thomas Malory from French originals, and printed by Caxton in 1485. It contains—

The Prophecies of Merlin.
The Quest of the St. Graal.
The Romance of Sir Lancelot of the Lake.
The History of Sir Tristram; etc., etc.

Tennyson's *Morte d'Arthur* gives a poetic version of some of these poems, not always following the originals and rarely preserving their mediæval atmosphere.

Morther. *See* MAUTHER.

Mortimer. Fable has it that this family name derives from an ancestor in crusading times, noted for his exploits on the shores of the Dead Sea (*De Mortuo Mari*). Fact, however, is not so romantic. *De Mortemer* was one of William the Conqueror's knights and is mentioned in the Roll of Battle Abbey; he was tenant in chief of *Mortemer*, a township in Normandy.

Mortmain (môrt' mān) (O.Fr., Lat. *mortua manus*, dead hand). A term applied to land that was held inalienably by ecclesiastical or other corporations, In the 13th century it was common for persons to make over their land to the Church and then to receive it back as tenants, thus escaping their feudal obligations to the king. In 1279 the *Statute of Mortmain* prohibiting grants of land to the "dead hand" of the Church was passed.

Morton's Fork. John Morton (c. 1420-1500), Cardinal Archbishop of Canterbury, introduced a plan for increasing the royal revenues, in the time of Henry VII, so arranged that nobody should escape. Those who were rich were forced to contribute on the ground that they could well afford it, those who lived without display on the ground that their economies must mean that they were saving money.

Moses. The horns of Moses' face. Moses is conventionally represented with horns, owing to a blunder in translation. In *Ex.* xxxiv, 29, 30, where we are told that when Moses came down from Mount Sinai "the skin of his face shone," the Hebrew for this *shining* may be translated either as "sent forth *beams*" or "sent forth *horns*"; and the Vulgate took the latter as correct, rendering the passage—*quod cornuta esset facies sua. Cp. Hab.* iii, 4, "His brightness was as the light; He had horns [*rays of light*] coming out of His hand."

Michael Angelo followed the earlier painters in depicting Moses with horns.

Moses' rod. The divining-rod (*q.v.*) is some-times so called, after the rod with which Moses worked wonders before Pharaoh (*Ex.* vii, 9), or the rod with which he smote the rock to bring forth water (*Ex.* xvii, 6).

Moslem or **Muslim** (moz' lem, mŭz' lim). A Mohammedan, the pres. part. of Arab. *aslama*, to be safe or at rest, whence Islam (*q.v.*). The Arabic plural *Moslemin* is sometimes used, but *Moslems* is more common, and in English more correct.

Mother. Properly a female parent (Sansk. *mātr*, Gr. *mètèr*, Lat. *mater*, A.S. *mōdor*, Ger. *mutter*, Fr. *mère*, etc.); hence, figuratively, the source or origin of anything, the head or headquarters of a religious or other community, etc.

Mother Ann, Bunch, Goose, Shipton, etc. *See* these names.

Mother Carey's chickens. Stormy petrels. Mother Carey is *mata cara*, dear mother. The French call these birds *oiseaux de Notre Dame* or *aves Sanctæ Mariæ. See* Captain Marryat's *Poor Jack*, where the superstition is fully related.

Mother Carey's Goose. The great black petrel or fulmar of the Pacific.

Mother Carey is plucking her goose. It is snowing. *Cp.* HULDA. Sailors call falling snow *Mother Carey's chickens.*

Mother Church. The Church considered as the central fact, the head, the last court of appeal in all matters pertaining to conscience or religion. St. John Lateran, at Rome (*see* LATERAN), is known as the Mother and Head of all Churches. Also, the principal or oldest church in a country or district; the cathedral of a diocese.

Mother country. One's native country; or the country whence one's ancestors have come to settle. England is the *Mother country* of Australia, New Zealand, Canada, etc. The German term is *Fatherland*.

Mother's Day. In U.S.A. the second Sunday in May is observed as an occasion for each person to remember his mother by some act of grateful affection. In schools Mother's Day is observed on the Friday preceding the above date.

Mothering Sunday. Mid-Lent Sunday, a great holiday, when the Pope blesses the golden rose, children go home to their mothers to feast on "mothering cakes," and "simnel cakes" (*q.v.*) are eaten. It is said that the day received its appellation from the ancient custom of visiting the "mother church" on that day; but to school-children it always meant a holiday, when they went home to spend the day with their mother or parents.

Mother Earth. When Junius Brutus (after the death of Lucretia) formed one of the deputation to Delphi to ask the Oracle which of the three would succeed Tarquin, the response was, "He who should first kiss his mother." Junius instantly threw himself on the ground, exclaiming, "Thus, then, I kiss thee, Mother Earth," and he was elected consul.

Mother-of-pearl. The inner iridescent layers of the shells of many bivalve molluscs, especially that of the pearl oyster.

The Mother of Believers. Among Mohammedans, Ayeshah, the second and favourite wife of Mohammed, who was called the "Father of Believers."

The Mother of Cities (*Amu-al-Bulud*). Balkh is so called.

Mother of Presidents. The State of Virginia.

Does your mother know you're out? A jeering remark addressed to a presumptuous youth or to a simpleton. The phrase is the title of a comic poem published in the *Mirror*, April 28th, 1838. It became a catch phrase both in England and in America, and occurs in the *Ingoldsby Legends*, "Misadventures at Margate."

Tied to one's mother's apron-strings. *See* APRON.

Motion. The laws of motion, according to Galileo and Newton.

(1) If no force acts on a body in motion, it will continue to move uniformly in a straight line.

(2) If force acts on a body, it will produce a change of motion proportionate to the force, and in the same direction (as that in which the force acts).

(3) When one body exerts force on another, that *other* body reacts on it with equal force.

Motley. Men of motley. Licensed fools; so called because of their dress.

Motley is the only wear.

As You Like It, ii, 7.

Motu proprio (mō' tū prop' ri ō) (Lai.). Of one's own motion; of one's own accord. Always applied to a rescript drawn up and issued by the pope on his own initiative without the advice of others, and signed by him.

Mountain. Mountain ash. *See* ROWAN-TREE.

Mountain dew. Scotch whisky; formerly that from illicit stills hidden away in the mountains.

If the mountain will not come to Mohammed, etc. *See* MOHAMMED.

The mountain (*La Montagne*). The extreme democratic party in the French Revolution, the members of which were known as *Les Montagnards* because they seated themselves on the highest benches of the hall in which the National Convention met. Their leaders were Danton and Robespierre, Marat, St. André, Legendre, Camille Desmoulins, Carnot, St. Just, and Collot d'Herbois, the men who introduced the "Reign of Terror." Extreme Radicals in France are still called *Montagnards*.

The mountain in labour. A mighty effort made for a small effect. The allusion is to the celebrated line "*Parturiunt montes, nascetur ridiculus mus* (*Ars Poetica*, 139), which Horace took from a Greek proverb preserved by Athenæus.

The story is that the Egyptian King Tachos sustained a long war against Artaxerxes Ochus, and sent to the Lacedemonians for aid. King Agesilaus went with a contingent, but when the Egyptians saw a little, illdressed lame man, they said: "*Parturiebat mons; formidavat Jupiter; ille vero murem peperit.*" ("The mountain laboured, Jupiter stood aghast, and a mouse ran out.") Agesilaus replied, "You call me a mouse, but I will soon show you I am a lion."

Creech translates Horace, "The travailing mountain yields a silly mouse", and Bolleau, "*La montagne en travail enfante une souris.*"

The Old Man of the Mountains (*Sheikh-al-Jebal*). Hassan ben Sabbah, the founder of the Assassins (*q.v.*), who made his stronghold in the mountain fastnesses of Lebanon. He died in 1124, and in 1256 his dynasty, and nearly all the Assassins, were exterminated by the Tartar prince, Hulaku.

To make mountains of molehills. To make a difficulty of trifles. *Arcem ex cloaca facere.* The corresponding French proverb is, *Faire d'un mouche un éléphant.*

Mountebank (mount'e bãngk). A vendor of quack medicines at fairs, etc., who attracts the crowd by doing juggling feats or other antics from the tail of a cart or other raised platform; hence, any charlatan or self-advertising pretender. The *bank* or bench was the counter on which shopkeepers displayed their goods, and street-vendors used to *mount* on their *bank* to patter to the public. The Italian word, from which ours comes, is *montambanco*, and the French *saltimbanque.*

Mourning (môrn' ing). *Black.* To express the privation of light and joy, the midnight gloom of sorrow for the loss sustained. The colour of mourning in Europe; also in ancient Greece and the Roman Empire.

Black and white striped. To express sorrow and hope. The mourning of the South Sea Islanders.

Greyish brown. The colour of the earth, to which the dead return; used for mourning in Ethiopia.

Pale brown. The colour of withered leaves. The mourning of Persia.

Sky blue. To express the assured hope that the deceased has gone to heaven; used in Syria, Armenia, etc.

Deep blue. The colour of mourning in Bokhara, also that of the Romans of the Republic.

Purple and violet. To express royalty, "kings and priests to God." The colour of mourning for cardinals and the kings of France; in Turkey the colour is violet.

White. Emblem of "white-handed hope." Used by the ladies of ancient Rome and Sparta, also in Spain till the end of the 15th century. Henry VIII wore white for Anne Boleyn.

Yellow. The sear and yellow leaf. The colour of mourning in Egypt and in Burma, where also it is the colour of the monastic order. In Brittany, widows' caps among the *paysannes* are yellow. Anne Boleyn wore yellow mourning for Catherine of Aragon. Some say yellow is in token of exaltation. *See also* BLACK CAP.

Mournival. *See* GLEEK.

Mouse. The soul was often supposed in olden times to make its way at death through the mouth of man in the form of some animal, sometimes a pigeon, sometimes a mouse or rat. A red mouse indicated a pure soul; a black mouse, a soul blackened by pollution; a pigeon or dove, a saintly soul.

Exorcists used to drive out evil spirits from the human body, and Harsnet gives several instances of such expulsions in his *Popular Impositions* (1604).

Mouse Tower, The. A mediæval watchtower on the Rhine, near Bingen, so called because of the tradition that Archbishop Hatto (*q.v.*) was there devoured by mice. The tower, however, was built by Bishop Siegfried, two hundred years after the death of Hatto, as a toll-house for collecting the duties upon all goods which passed by. The German *maut* means "toll," (mouse is *maus*), and the similarity of the words together with the great unpopularity of the toll on corn gave rise to the tradition.

Mouth. Down in the mouth. *See* DOWN.

His mouth was made. He was trained or reduced to obedience, like a horse trained to the bit.

At first, of course, the fireworker showed fight . . . but in the end "his mouth was made," his paces formed, and he became a very serviceable and willing animal.— LE FANU : *House in the Churchyard*, ch. xcix.

That makes my mouth water. The fragrance of appetizing food excites the salivary glands.

The phrase means—that makes me long for or desire it.

Hold your mouth! A rougher equivalent of "hold your tongue!"; keep silent.

To laugh on the wrong side of one's mouth. *See* LAUGH.

To mouth one's words. To talk affectedly or pompously; to declaim.

He mouths a sentence as curs mouth a bone.
                    CHURCHILL: *The Rosciad*, 322.

To open one's mouth wide. To name too high a price; to strain after too big a prize.

Moutons (moo′ tong). **Revenons à nos moutons** (Fr.). Literally "Let us come back to our sheep," but used to express "let us return to the subject." The phrase is taken from the 14th-century French comedy *La Farce de Maître Pathelin*, or *l'Avocat Pathelin* (line 1282), in which a woollen-draper charges a shepherd with ill-treating his sheep. In telling his story he kept for ever running away from his subject; and to throw discredit on the defendant's attorney (Pathelin), accused him of stealing a piece of cloth. The judge had to pull him up every moment, with "*Mais, mon ami, revenons à nos moutons.*" The phrase is frequently quoted by Rabelais. *See* PATELIN: SANS SOUCI.

Move. Give me where to stand, and I will move the world. So said Archimedes of Syracuse; and the instrument he would have used is the lever.

Mow (mō). The three *mows* in English are altogether different words, though spelt alike. *Mow*, a heap of hay, etc. ("the barley-mow") is A.S. *mūga*, connected with Icel. *müge*, a swath. *Mow* to cut down grass, corn, and so on, is A.S. *māwan*, connected with Ger. *mähen*, Gr. *amân*, and Lat. *mēlere*, to reap; and *Mow* a grimace (in "mops and mows," *q.v.*) is Fr. *moue*, a pout or grimace.

Much. The miller's son in the Robin Hood stories. In the morris-dances he played the part of the Fool, and his great feat was to bang the head of the gaping spectators with a bladder of peas.

Much Ado about Nothing. Shakespeare's comedy, named from a proverbial saying of the time, and with only the slightest relevance to the plot, was probably written in 1599, and was published in 1600.

The story first appears (about 1550) in Bandello's *Novelle* (No. xxii), where the slandered heroine is Fenicia, and a French translation of this was given in Belleforest's *Les Histoires Tragiques* (1559), with which

Shakespeare was well acquainted. Ariosto also, calling the injured bride Ginevra and her lover Ariodante, used the story in his *Orlando Furioso* (canto v), and it appears again in Spenser's *Faerie Queene* (II, iv), where Claribell is the name of the heroine. A lost play called *A Historie of Ariodante and Ginevra* was given at Court by the boys of Merchant Taylors' School in 1583; this may have formed the groundwork of Shakespeare's comedy, but many of the episodes—especially those in which Dogberry and the rustic watchmen are concerned—bear all the marks of originality.

Mufti (mŭf′ ti). An Arabic word meaning an official expounder of the Koran and Mohammedan law; but used in English to denote *civil*, as distinguished from *military* or official costume. Our meaning dates from the early 19th century, and probably arose from the resemblance that the flowered dressing-gown and tasselled smoking-cap worn by officers at that time when in their quarters off duty bore to the stage get-up of an Eastern mufti.

Mug. This word, used as slang for a face, is of obscure origin, possibly coming from the gypsy meaning a simpleton or muff. **To mug up,** meaning to study hard for a specific purpose, *e.g.* to pass an examination, is an old university phrase; it has been suggested that it comes from the theatre where an actor, while making up his face or "mug," would hurriedly con over his words.

Mug-house. An ale-house was so called in the 18th century where some hundred persons assembled in a large tap-room to drink, sing, and spout. One of the number was made chairman. Ale was served to the guests in their own mugs, and the place where the mug was to stand was chalked on the table.

Muggins. Slang for a fool or simpleton—a *Juggins* is the same thing; also for a pettifogging magnate, a village leader. Muggins is a surname, and those bearing it sometimes like to hear it pronounced mū′ ginz.

Mugwump (mŭg′ wŭmp). An Algonquin word meaning a chief; in Eliot's Indian Bible the word "centurion" in the *Acts* is rendered *mugwump*. It is now applied in the United States to independent members of the Republican party, those who refuse to follow the dictum of a caucus, and all political Pharisees whose party vote cannot be relied on.

"I suppose I am a political mugwump," said the Englishman. "Not yet," replied Mr. Reed. "You will be when you have returned to your allegiance."—*The Liverpool Echo,* July 19th, 1886.

Mulatto (mū lăt′ ō) (Span., from *mulo*, a mule). The offspring of a negress by a white man; loosely applied to any halfbreed. *Cp.* CREOLE.

Mulberry. Fable has it that the fruit was originally white, and became blood-red from the blood of Pyramus and Thisbe (*see* PYRAMUS). The botanical name is Morus, from the Greek *moros* (a fool); so called, we are told in the *Hortus Anglicus*, because "it is reputed the wisest of all flowers, as it never buds till the cold weather is past and gone." Ludovic Sforza, who prided himself on his prudence, chose a mulberry-tree for his device, and was called "*Il Moro.*"

In the *Seven Champions* (Pt. i, ch. iv) Eglantine, daughter of the King of Thessaly, was transformed into a mulberry-tree.

Here we go round the mulberry bush. An old game in which children take hands and dance round in a ring, singing a song of which this is the refrain.

In World War II **Mulberry** was the code name given to the engineering feat of making a pre-fabricated port and towing it across to the Normandy coast to make possible the supply of the Allied armies in France in 1944. Submersible sections of concrete formed a breakwater and quay alongside which the transports were tied up for the stores to be unloaded. The name was chosen because at the time it was the next in rotation on the British Admiralty's list of names available for war ships.

Mulciber (mŭl′ si ber). A name of Vulcan (*q.v.*) among the Romans; it means *the softener,* because he softened metals.

> Round about him [Mammon] lay on every side
> Great heaps of gold that never could he spent:
> Of which some were rude ore, not purified
> Of Mulciber's devouring element.
> SPENSER: *Faerie Queene,* II, vii, 5.

Mule. The offspring of a male ass and a mare; hence, a hybrid between other animals (or plants), as a *mule canary*, a cross between a canary and a goldfinch. The offspring of a stallion and a she-ass is not, properly speaking, a mule, but a *hinny.*

Very stubborn or obstinate people are sometimes called *mules*, in allusion to the well-known characteristic of the beast; and the *spinning-mule* was so called because it was—

> a kind of mixture of machinery between the warp-machine of Mr. Arkwright and the woof-machine or hand-jenny of Mr. Hargrave.—*Encyc. Britannica,* 1797.

Mulmutine Laws (mŭl′ mŭ tīn). The code of Dunvallo Mulmutius, the sixteenth legendary King of the Britons (about 400 B.C.), son of

Cloten, King of Cornwall. It is said to have been translated by Gildas from British into Latin, and to have formed the basis of King Alfred's code, which obtained in England till the Conquest. (Holinshed: *History of England*, iii, 1.)

Mulmutius made out laws,
Who was the first of Britain which did put
His brows within a golden crown, and called
Himself a king,
Cymbeline, iii, 1.

Multipliers. So alchemists, who pretended to multiply gold and silver, were called. An Act was passed (2 Henry IV, c. iv) making the "art of multiplication" felony. In the *Canterbury Tales*, the Canon's Yeoman (*see Prologue* to his *Tale*) says he was reduced to poverty by alchemy, adding: "Lo, such advantage is't to multiply."

Multitude, Nouns of. Dame Juliana Berners, in her *Booke of St. Albans* (1486), says, in designating companies we must not use the names of multitudes promiscuously, and examples her remark thus:—

"We say a *congregacyon* of people, a *hoost* of men, a *felyshyppynge* of yeomen, and a *bevy* of ladyes; we must speak of a *herde* of dere, swannys, cranys, or wrenys, a *sege* of herons or bytourys, a *muster* of pecockes, a *wutche* of nyghtyngales, a *fllyghte* of doves, a *claterynge* of choughes, a *pryde* of lyons, a *slewthe* of beeres, a *gagle* of geys, a *skulke* of foxes, a *sculle* of frerys, a *pontificalitye* of prestys, and a *superfluyte* of nonnes.—*Booke of St. Albans* (1486).

She adds, that a strict regard to these niceties better distinguishes "gentylmen from ungentylmen," than regard to the rules of grammar, or even to the moral law. (*See* ASSEMBLAGE, NOUNS OF.)

Multum in parvo (mŭl 'tŭm in par' vō) (Lat.). Much "information" condensed into few words or into a small compass.

Mum. A strong beer made in Brunswick; said to be so called from Christian Mumme, by whom it was first brewed in the late 15th century.

Mum's the word. Keep what is told you a profound secret. *See* MUMCHANCE.

Seal up your lips, and give no words but—mum.
2 *Henry VI*, i 2.

Mumchance. Silence. Mumchance was a game of chance with dice, in which silence was indispensable. *Mum* is connected with *mumble* (Ger. *mummeln*; Dan. *mumle*, to mumble). *Cp.* MUMBUDGET.

And fro "mumchance," howe'er the *chance* may fall.
You must be *mum* for fear of spoiling all.
Machiavell's Dogg.

Mumbo Jumbo (mŭm' bō jŭm' bō). The name given by Europeans (possibly from some lost native word) to a bogy or grotesque idol venerated by certain African tribes; hence, any object of blind and unreasoning worship.

Mungo Park in his *Travels in Africa* says that Mumbo Jumbo is not an idol, any more than the American *Lynch*, but merely one disguised to punish unruly wives. It not infrequently happens that a house which contains many wives becomes unbearable. In such a case, either the husband or an agent disguises himself as "Mumbo Jumbo" and comes at dusk with a following, making the most hideous noises possible. When the women have been sufficiently scared, "Mumbo" seizes the chief offender, ties her to a tree, and scourges her, amidst the derision of all present.

Mummer. A contemptuous name for an actor; from the parties that formerly went from house to house at Christmas-time *mumming*, *i.e.* giving a performance of St. George and the Dragon and the like, in dumb-show.

Peel'd, patch'd, and piebald, linsey-woolsey brothers.
Grave mummers! sleeveless some, and shirtless others.
POPE: *Dunciad*, III, 115.

Mummy is the Arabic *mum*, wax used for embalming; from the custom of anointing the body with wax and wrapping it in cerecloth.

Mumping day. St. Thomas's Day, December 21st, is so called in some parts of the country, because on this day the poor used to go about begging, or, as it was called, "a-gooding," that is, getting gifts to procure *good things* for Christmas.

In Lincolnshire the name used to be applied to Boxing Day (*q.v.*); in Warwickshire the term used was "going a-corning," *i.e.* getting gifts of corn.

Mumpsimus. Robert Graves, in *Impenetrability*, gives this word as an example of the practice of making new words by declaration. With the meaning, "an erroneous doctrinal view obstinately adhered to," mumpsimus was put into currency by Henry VIII in a speech from the throne in 1545. He remarked, "Some be too stiff in their old mumpsimus, others be too busy and curious in their sumpsimus." He referred to a familiar story in the jest-books of a priest who always read in the Mass "quod in ore mumpsimus" instead of "sumpsimus," as his Missal was incorrectly copied. When his mistake was pointed out, he said that he had read it with an *m* for forty years, "and I will not change my old mumpsimus for your new sumpsimus." The word no longer has its doctrinal meaning, and is now used to mean "an established manuscript-reading that, though obviously incorrect, is retained blindly by old-fashioned scholars."

Munchausen, Baron (mŭn' chou zen). A traveller who meets with the most marvellous adventures, the hero of a collection of stories by Rudolph Erich Raspe, published in English in 1785. The incidents were compiled from various sources, including the adventures of an actual Hieronymus Karl Friedrich von Münchhausen (1720-97), a German officer in the Russian army, noted for his marvellous stories, Bebel's *Facetiæ*, Castiglione's *Cortegiano*, Bildermann's *Utopia*, etc. The book is a satire either on Baron de Tott, or on Bruce, whose *Travels in Abyssinia* were looked upon as mythical when they first appeared.

Mundane Egg. See EGG.

Mundungus (mŭn dŭng' gŭs). Bad tobacco; originally offal, or refuse, from Span, *mondongo*, black pudding.

In Sterne's *Sentimental Journey* (1768) the word is used as a name for Samuel Sharp, a surgeon, who published *Letters* from *Italy*: and Smollett, who published *Travels through France and Italy* (1766), "one continual snarl," was called "Smelfungus."

Mungo, St. (mŭng' gŏ). An alternative name for St. Kentigern (*q.v.*).

A superior kind of shoddy, made from second-hand woollens, is known as *mungo*.

Munich Pact or Agreement. The pact signed by Germany, France, Great Britain, and Italy on September 29th, 1938, whereby the Sudetenland of Czechoslovakia was ceded to Germany. From this unfortunate act of appeasement the phrase has come to mean any dishonourable appeasement.

Muscadins (mŭs' kà dinz). Parisian exquisites who aped those of London about the time of the French Revolution. They wore top-boots with thick soles, knee-breeches, a dress-coat with long tails, and a high stiff collar, and carried a thick cudgel called a *constitution*. It was thought "John Bullish" to assume a huskiness of voice, a discourtesy of manners, and a swaggering vulgarity of speech and behaviour.

> Cockneys of London, Muscadins of Paris.
> BYRON: *Don Juan*, viii. 124.

Muses. In Greek mythology the nine daughters of Zeus and Mnemosyne; originally goddesses of memory only, but later identified with individual arts and sciences. The paintings of Herculaneum show all nine in their respective attributes. They are:—

Calliope: the chief of the Muses..
Clio: heroic exploits and history.
Euterpe: Dionysiac music and the double flute.
Thalia: gaiety, pastoral life, and comedy.
Melpomene: song, harmony, and tragedy.
Terpsichore: choral dance and song.
Erato: the lyre and erotic poetry.
Polyhymnia: the inspired and stately hymn.
Urania: celestial phenomena and astronomy.
See these names.

Museum. Literally, a home or seat of the Muses. The first building to have this name was the university erected at Alexandria by Ptolemy Soter about 300 B.C.

Mushroom. Slang for an umbrella, on account of the similarity in shape; and as mushrooms are of a very rapid growth, applied figuratively to almost anything that "springs up in the night," as a new, quickly built suburb, an upstart family, and so on. In 1787 Bentham said—somewhat unjustly—"Sheffield is an oak; Birmingham is a mushroom."

To mushroom. To expand into a mushroom shape; said especially of certain soft-nosed rifle-bullets used in big-game shooting, or of a dense cloud of smoke that spreads out high in the sky.

Music. Father of modern music. Mozart (1756-91) has been so called.

Father of Greek music. Terpander (fl. 676 B.C.).

The prince of music. Giovanni Pierluigi da Palestrina (1524-94).

Music hath charms, etc. The opening line of Congreve's *Mourning Bride*.

> Music hath charms to soothe a savage breast,
> To soften rocks, or bend a knotted oak.

The allusion is to Orpheus (*q.v.*), who—

> With his lute made trees,
> And the mountain tops that freeze,
> Bow themselves when he did sing.
> *Henry VIII*, iii, 1.

And the lines are among those most frequently misquoted in the whole of English poetry, the words "a savage breast" being turned into "the savage beast." James Bramston, in his *Man of Taste* (1733), wittily substituted for the second line, "And therefore proper at a sheriff's feast."

Muslim. See MOSLEM.

Muslin. So called from Mosul, in Asia, where it was first manufactured (Fr. *mousseline*, Ital. *mussolino*).

Mustang (U.S.A.). A wild horse.

Mustard. So called because originally *must*, new wine (Lat. *mustus*, fresh, new) was used in mixing the paste. Fable, however, alleges that the name arose because in 1382 Philip the Bold, Duke of Burgundy, granted to the town of Dijon, noted for its mustard, armorial bearings with the motto MOULT ME TARDE '*Multum ardeo*, I ardently desire'. The arms and motto, engraved on the principal gate, were adopted as a trade-mark by the mustard merchants, and got shortened into Moult-tarde (to burn much).

Mustard, ground and sifted to a flour, is said to have been the invention of an old Durham woman named Clements, who came to London in 1720 with her concoction, which pleased the palate of George I and hence became popular.

After meat, mustard. Expressive of the sentiment that something that would have been welcome a little earlier has arrived too late, I have now no longer need of it. *C'est de la moutarde après dîner.*

Mussulman. A Mohammedan, a Moslem (*q.v.*). The plural is Mussulmans.

Mutantur. *See* TEMPORA MUTANTUR.

Mute, To stand. An old legal term for a prisoner who, when arraigned for treason or felony, refused to plead or gave irrelevant answers.

Mutton (Fr. *mouton*, a sheep). In old slang, a prostitute, frequently extended to *laced mutton*.

Speed: Ay, sir: I, a lost mutton, gave your letter to her, a laced mutton; and she, a laced mutton, gave me, a lost mutton, nothing for my labour.—SHAKESPEARE: *Two Gentlemen of Verona*, i, 1.

The old lecher hath gotten holy mutton to him, a Nunne, my lord.—GREENE: *Friar Bacon*.

It was with this suggestion that Rochester wrote his mock epitaph on Charles II:—

Here lies our mutton-eating king,
    Whose word no man relies on;
He never *said* a foolish thing,
    And never *did* a wise one.

Mutual Friends. Can people have mutual friends? Strictly speaking *not*; but since Dickens adopted the solecism in the title of his novel, *Our Mutual Friend* (1864), many people have objected to the correct term, *common friends*. *Mutual* implies reciprocity from one to the other (Lat. *mutare*, to change); the friendship between two friends should be mutual, but this mutuality cannot be extended to a third party.

A mutual flame was quickly caught,
    Was quickly, too, revealed;
For neither bosom lodged a thought
    Which virtue keeps concealed.
                        Edwin and Emma.

Mynheer (mīn hēr'). The Dutch equivalent for "Mr."; hence, sometimes used for a Dutchman.

'Tis thus I spend my moments here,
And wish myself a Dutch mynheer.
                        COWPER: *To Lady Austin*.

Myrrha. The mother of Adonis, in Greek legend. She is fabled to have had an unnatural love for her own father, and to have been changed into a myrtle tree.

Myrtle. If you look at a leaf of myrtle in a strong light, you will see that it is pierced with innumerable little punctures. According to fable, Phædra, wife of Theseus, fell in love with Hippolytus, her stepson; and when Hippolytus went to the arena to exercise his horses, Phædra repaired to a myrtle-tree in Trœzen to await his return, and beguiled the time by piercing the leaves with a hairpin. The punctures referred to are an abiding memento of this legend.

In *Orlando Furioso* Astolpho is changed into a myrtle-tree by Acrisia. *See also* MYRRHA *above*.

The ancient Jews believed that the eating of myrtle leaves conferred the power of detecting witches; and it was a superstition that if the leaves crackled in the hands the person beloved would prove faithful.

The myrtle which dropped blood. Æneas (*Æneid*, Bk. iii) is represented as tearing up the myrtle which dropped blood. Polydorus tells us that the barbarous inhabitants of the country pierced the myrtle (then a living being) with spears and arrows. The body of the myrtle took root and grew into the bleeding tree.

Mystery. In English two totally distinct words have been confused here: *mystery*, the archaic term for a handicraft, as *in the art and mystery of printing*, is the same as the French *métier* (trade, craft, profession), and is the M.E. *mistere*, from mediæval Lat. *misterium, ministerium*, ministry.

Mystery, meaning something beyond human comprehension, is (through French) from the Lat. *mysterium* and Gr. *mustes*, from *muen*, to close the eyes or lips. It is from this sense that the old miracle-plays, mediæval dramas in which the characters and story were drawn from sacred history, were called *Mysteries*, though, as they were frequently presented by members of some single guild, or *mystery* in the handicraft sense, even here the words were confused and opening made for many puns.

The three greater mysteries. In ecclesiastical language, the Trinity, Original Sin, and the Incarnation.

N

N. The fourteenth letter of our alphabet; represented in Egyptian hieroglyph by a water-line (∿). It was called *nun* (a fish) in Phœnician, whence the Greek *nu*.

N, a numeral. Gr. v = 50, but, v = 50,000. N (Lat.) = 90, or 900, but $\bar{N}$ = 90,000, or 900,000.

n. The sign ~ (*tilde*) over an "n" indicates that the letter is to be pronounced as though followed by a "y," as *cañon* = *canyon*. It is used thus almost solely in words from Spanish. In Portuguese the accent (called *til*) is placed over vowels to Indicate that they have a nasal value.

nth, or nth plus one. The expression is taken from the index of a mathematical formula, where n stands for any number, and $n+1$, one more than any number. Hence, *n-dimensional*, having an indefinite number of dimensions, *n-tuple* (on the analogy of *quadruple*, *quintuple*, etc.), having an indefinite number of duplications.

N or M. The answer given to the first question in the Church of England Catechism; and it means that here the person being catechized gives his or her *name* or *names*. Lat. *nomen vel nomina*. The abbreviation for the plural *nomina* was—as usual—the doubled initial (*cp*. "LL.D." for Doctor of Laws); and this, when printed (as it was in old Prayer Books) in black-letter and close together, ℜℜ came to be taken for ℳ.

In the same way the N. in the marriage-service ("I M. take thee N. to my wedded wife") merely indicates that the *name* is to be spoken in each case; but the M. and N. in the publication of banns ("I publish the Banns of Marriage between M. of —— and N. of ——") stand for *maritus*, bridegroom, and *nupta*, bride.

Nab. Colloquial for to seize suddenly, without warning. (*Cp*. Norw. and Swed. *nappa*, Dan., *nappe*). Hence *nabman*, a sheriff's officer or police-constable.

Ay, but so be if a man's nabbed, you know.
GOLDSMITH: *The Good-natured Man*.

Naboth's Vineyard (nā′ both). The possession of another coveted by one able to possess himself of it. (1 *Kings* xxi.)

Nabu. *See* NEBO.

Nadir (năd′ ir). An Arabic word, signifying that point in the heavens which is directly opposite to the zenith, *i.e.* directly under our feet; hence, figuratively, the lowest depths of degradation. *See also* ZENITH.

Nævius. *See* ACCIUS NÆVIUS.

Nag, Nagging. Constant fault-finding. (A.S. *gnag-an*, to gnaw, bite.) We call a slight but constant pain, like a toothache, a *nagging pain*.

Naiad (nī′ ăd). Nymph of lake, fountain, river, or stream in classical mythology.

You nymphs, call'd Naiads, of the wand'ring brooks,
With your sedg'd crowds, and ever-harmless looks,
Leave your crisp channels, and on this green land
Answer your summons: Juno does command.
Tempest iv. 1

Nail. The nails with which Our Lord was fastened to the cross were, in the Middle Ages, objects of great reverence. Sir John Mandeville says, "He had two in his hondes, and two in his feet; and of on of theise the emperour of Constantynoble made a brydille to his hors, to bere him in bataylle; and throghe vertue thereof he overcam his enemyes" (c. vii). Fifteen are shown as relics. *See* IRON CROWN.

In ancient Rome a nail was driven into the wall of the temple of Jupiter every 13th September. This was originally done to tally the year, but subsequently it became a religious ceremony for warding off calamities and plagues from the city. Originally the nail was driven by the *prœtor maximus*, subsequently by one of the consuls, and lastly by the dictator (*see Livy*, vii, 3).

A somewhat similar ceremony took place in Germany in World War I when patriotic Germans drove nails into a large wooden statue of Field-Marshal Hindenburg, buying each nail in support of a national fund.

For want of a nail. "For want of a nail, the shoe is lost; for want of a shoe, the horse is lost; and for want of a horse, the rider is lost." (Herbert: *Jacula Prudentum*.)

Hard as nails. Stern, hard-hearted, unsympathetic; able to stand hard blows like nails. The phrase is used with both a physical and a figurative sense; a man in perfect training is "as hard as nails," and bigotry, straitlacedness, rigid puritanical Pharisaism, make people "hard as nails."

I know I'm as hard as nails already; I don't want to get more so.—EDNA LYALL: *Donovan*, ch. xxiii.

I nailed him (or **it**). I pinned him, meaning I secured him. *Is.* (xxii, 23) says, "I will fasten him as a nail in a sure place."

On the nail. At once; without hesitation; as, "to pay down on the nail."

In O'Keefe's *Recollections* we are told that in the centre of Limerick Exchange is a pillar with a circular plate of copper about 3 ft. in diameter, called *The Nail*, on which the earnest of all Stock Exchange bargains has to be paid; there were four pillars called *Nails* and used for a similar purpose at Bristol; and at the Liverpool Exchange there was a plate of copper called *The Nail* on which bargains were settled. But the phrase cannot come from any such source, as it was common in England by the 16th century, long before Exchanges were in existence. *Cp.* SUPERNACULUM.

To drive a nail into one's coffin. *See* COFFIN.

To hit the nail on the head. To come to a right conclusion. In Latin, *Rem tenes.*

Tooth and nail. *See* TOOTH.

With colours nailed to the mast. *See* COLOURS.

Nail-paring. Superstitious people are very particular as to the day on which they cut their nails. The old rhyme is:—

Cut them on Monday, you cut them for health;
Cut them on Tuesday, you cut them for wealth;
Cut them on Wednesday, you cut them for news;
Cut them on Thursday, a new pair of shoes;
Cut them on Friday, you cut them for sorrow;
Cut them on Saturday, you see your true love tomorrow;
Cut them on Sunday, your safety seek
The devil will have you the rest of the week.

Another rhyme conveys an even stronger warning on the danger of nail-cutting on a Sunday:—

A man had better ne'er be born
As have his nails on a Sunday shorn.

Nain Rouge (nān roozh) (Fr., red dwarf). A lutin or house spirit of Normandy, kind to fishermen. There is another called *Le petit homme rouge* (the little red man).

Naked. A.S. *nacod*, a common Teutonic word, connected with Lat. *nudus*, nude. Destitute of covering; hence, figuratively, defenceless, exposed; without extraneous assistance, as *with the naked eye, i.e.* without a telescope or other optical aid.

Naked boy, or **lady.** The meadow saffron (*Colchicum autumnale*); so called because, like the almond, peach, etc., the flowers come out before the leaves. It is poetically called "the leafless orphan of the year," the flowers being orphaned or destitute of foliage.

The naked truth. The plain, unvarnished truth; truth without trimmings. The fable says that Truth and Falsehood went bathing; Falsehood came first out of the water, and dressed herself in Truth's garments. Truth, unwilling to take those of Falsehood, went naked.

Namby-pamby. Wishy-washy; insipid, weakly sentimental; said especially of authors. It was the nickname of Ambrose Philips (1671-1749), bestowed upon him by Harry Carey, the dramatist, for his verses addressed to Lord Carteret's children, and was adopted by Pope.

Name.

What's in a name? That which we call a rose,
By any other name would smell as sweet.
Romeo and Juliet, ii, 2.

In the name of. In reliance upon; or by the authority of.

To call a person names. To blackguard him by calling him nicknames, or hurling opprobrious epithets at him.

Sticks and stones
May break my bones,
But names can never hurt me.
Old Rhyme.

To take God's name in vain. To use it profanely, thoughtlessly, or irreverently.

Thou shalt not take the name of the Lord thy God in vain.—*Exod.* xx, 7.

Among all primitive peoples, and the ancient Hebrews were no exception, the *name* of a deity is regarded as his manifestation, and is treated with the greatest respect and veneration; and among savage tribes there is a widespread feeling of the danger of disclosing one's name, because this would enable an enemy by magic means to work one some deadly injury; the Greeks were particularly careful to disguise or reverse uncomplimentary names (*see* ERINYES; EUMENIDES; EUXINE).

Nancy, Miss. An effeminate, foppish youth. The celebrated actress, "Mrs." Anne Oldfield (*see* NARCISSA) was nicknamed "Miss Nancy."

Nancy Boy is applied to a homosexual.

Nankeen. So called from Nankin, in China. It is the natural yellow colour of Nankin cotton.

Nantes (nănts). **Edict of Nantes.** The decree of Henri IV of France, published from Nantes in 1598, securing freedom of religion to all Protestants. Louis XIV revoked it in 1685.

Nap. The doze or short sleep gets its name from A.S. *hnœppian,* to sleep lightly: the surface of cloth is probably so called from Mid. Dutch *noppe*; and *Nap*, the card game, is so called in honour of Napoleon III.

To catch one napping. *See* CATCH.

Napier's Bones (nā′ pēr). The little slips of bone or ivory invented in 1615 by John Napier of Merchiston (1550-1617). He had, the previous year, invented logarithms, and by the use of these on his strips of ivory, he shortened the labour of trigonometrical calculations. By shifting these rods the result required is obtained.

Napoleon Bonaparte. For all his many glaring faults and ambitions, Napoleon was one of the greatest men modern civilization has produced. Within the short space of 15 years his campaigns and victories changed the aspect of Europe and made him the master of kings and peoples from Spain to the borders of Russia. His influence is felt to this day in the **Code Napoleon**, the code of laws prepared under his direction, which forms the substance of the laws of France and Belgium and in importance is only second to the code of Justinian. Equality in the eyes of the Law, justice, and common sense may be called its keynotes.

Napoleon III. Few men have had so many nicknames.

MAN OF DECEMBER, so called because his *coup d'état* was December 2nd, 1851, and he was made emperor December 2nd, 1852.

MAN OF SEDAN, and, by a pun, *M. Sedantaire*. It was at Sedan he surrendered his sword to William I. King of Prussia (1870).

MAN OF SILENCE, from his great taciturnity.

COMTE D'ARENENBERG, the name and title he assumed when he escaped from the fortress of Ham.

BADINGUET, the name of the mason who changed clothes with him when he escaped from Ham. The emperor's partisans were called *Badingueux*, those of the empress were *Montijoyeaux*.

BOUSTRAPA is a compound of Bou[logne], Stra-[sbourg], and Pa[ris] the places of his noted escapades.

RANTIPOLE, harum-scarum, half-foot and half-madman.

There are some curious numerical coincidences connected with Napoleon III and Eugénie. The last complete year of their reign was 1869. (In 1870 Napoleon was dethroned and exiled.)

Now, if to the year of coronation (1852), you add either the birth of Napoleon, or the birth of Eugénie, or the capitulation of Paris, or the date of marriage, the sum will always be 1869. For example:—

1852 {Coronation.}	1852	1852	1852
1} Birth 8{ of 0{Napo- 8} leon.	1} Birth 8{ of 2{Eugé- 6} nie.	1} Date 8{ of 5{ mar- 3} riage.	1}Capit- 8{ulat'n 7{ of 1} Paris.
1869	1869	1869	1869

And if to the year of *marriage* (1853) these dates are added, they will give 1870, the fatal year.

Naraka (nar′ à kà). The hell of Hindu mythology. It has twenty-eight divisions, in some of which the victims are mangled by ravens and owls; in others they are doomed to swallow cakes boiling hot, or walk over burning sands.

Narcissa (nar sis′ à), in the *Night Thoughts*, was Elizabeth Lee, Dr. Young's stepdaughter.

In Pope's *Moral Essays* "Narcissa" stands for the actress, Anne Oldfield (1683-1730). When she died her remains lay in state attended by two noblemen. She was buried in Westminster Abbey in a very fine Brussels lace head-dress, a holland shift, with a tucker and double-ruffles of the same lace, new kid gloves, etc.

"Odious! In woollen? 'Twould a saint provoke!"
Were the last words that poor Narcissa spoke.
POPE: *Moral Essays*, i, 246.

"In woollen" is an allusion to a law enacted for the benefit of the wool trade, that all shrouds were to be made of wool.

Narcissus (nar sis′ us). The son of Cephisus in Greek mythology; a beautiful youth who saw his reflection in a fountain, and thought it the presiding nymph of the place. He tried to reach it, and jumped into the fountain, where he died. The nymphs came to take up the body that they might pay it funeral honours, but found only a flower, which they called by his name. (Ovid's *Metamorphoses*, iii, 346, etc.)

Plutarch says the plant is called Narcissus from the Greek *narke* (numbness), and that it is properly *narcosis*, meaning the plant which produces numbness or palsy.

Echo fell in love with Narcissus.

Sweet Echo, sweetest nymph that liv'st unseen . . .
Canst thou not tell me of a gentle pair,
That likest thy Narcissus are?
MILTON: *Comus*, 235.

Narcissism is the psychoanalytical term for sexual excitement through admiration of one's own body.

Nark. A police spy or informer; from a Romany word *nak*, a nose, on the analogy of Nosey Parker.

Nary. U.S.A. colloquial expression for "never" or "never a"; as in "They take everything, and nary dollar do you get." *Nary a red* is "never a red cent."

National Anthem. It is said by some that both the words and music of "God save the Queen," the British national anthem, were composed by Dr. John Bull (d. 1628), organist at Antwerp cathedral 1617-28, where the original MS. is still preserved. Others attribute them to Henry Carey, author of *Sally in our Alley*. The words, "Send her victorious," etc., look like a Jacobite song, and Sir John Sinclair tells us he saw that verse cut in an old glass tankard, the property of P. Murray Threipland, of Fingask Castle, whose predecessors were staunch Jacobites.

No doubt the words have often been altered. The air and opening words were probably suggested by the *Domine Salvum* of the Catholic Church. In 1605 the lines, "Frustrate their knavish tricks," etc., were perhaps added in reference to Gunpowder Plot; and in 1740 Henry Carey reset both words and music for the Mercers' Company on the birthday of George II.

The National Anthems or principal patriotic songs of the leading nations follow:—

Argentine: *Oid mortales, el grito sagrado Libertad.*

Australia: *Advance Australia.*

Austria: (Republic) *Österreichische Bundeshymne.*

Belgium: The *Brabançonne (q.v.).*

Brazil: *Ouviram do Yspiranga as margens placidas.*

Canada: *The Maple Leaf Forever.* (French) *O Canada terre de nos aieux.*

Chile: *Duke patria.*

Denmark: *The Song of the Danebrog (see* DANEBROG*); Kong Christian stod ved hoïen Mast, Rög og Damp* (King Christian stood beside the lofty mast, In mist and smoke).

France: The *Marseillaise (q.v.).*

Germany: *Deutschland über alles* (Germany over all).

Greece: *Se gnorizo apo ten kopsi tu spati' iu ten tromere.*

Holland: *Wien Neerlandsch bloed in de aders vloeit, Van vreemde smetten vrij : . .* (Let him in whose veins flows the blood of the Netherlands, free from an alien strain . . .)

Italy: Garibaldi's Hymn.

Mexico: *Mexicanos al grito guerra.*

New Zealand: *God defend New Zealand.*

Norway: *Ja, vi elsker dette Landet som del stiger frem* (Yes, we love our country, just as it is).

Peru: *Somos libros, seamos lo siempre.*

Portugal: *Heiros do mar.*

Russia: (1917-44) The Internationale; (since 1944) *Gymn Sovietskogo Soiusa.*

Scotland: *Scots wha hae wi' Wallace bled.*

South Africa: *Die Stem van Suid-Afrika.*

Spain: *Marcha grandera.*

Sweden: *Du gamla du friska, du fjellhog Nord, Du tysta, du glädjerika sköna!* (Thou ancient, free, and mountainous North! Thou silent, joyous, and beautiful North!)

Switzerland: *Rufst du, mein Vaterland. Sieh uns mit Herz und Hand, All dir geweiht!* (Thou call'st, my Fatherland! Behold us, heart and hand, all devoted to thee!)

The United States: *The Star-spangled Banner.* *See* STARS AND STRIPES.

Wales: *Mae hen wlad fy nhadau* (Land of my fathers); also *Men of Harlech.*

National Colours. (*See* COLOURS.)

National Debt. Money borrowed by a Government, on the security of the taxes, which are pledged to the lenders for the payment of interest. The portion of our National Debt which is converted into bonds or annuities is known as the *Funded Debt*, and the portion that is repayable at a stated time or on demand as the *Floating Debt*.

The National Debt in William III's reign was £15,730,439.

At the commencement of the American war, £128,583,635.

At the dose thereof, £249,851,628.

At the close of the French war, £840,850,491.

The existence of National Debts is almost entirely due to wars, as the following figures will show in the case of the British Debt.

Just before the Revolution of 1688 it stood at £664,263; the Revolution added nearly £16,000,000; the Marlborough campaigns in Queen Anne's reign added nearly £38,000,000, the American War, in George III's, £121,000,000, and the Napoleonic Wars (1793-1816) over £600,000,000, bringing the total debt in 1816 to £900,436,000. At Queen Victoria's accession (1837) this had been reduced to £788,000,000; the Crimean War added £33,000,000, and thereafter reductions were made annually (with only five exceptions) till 1899, the year of the outbreak of the Boer War, when the Debt stood at £628,021,572. This war added over £160,000,000, but from 1904 to the outbreak of World War I reductions were made annually (with one exception), so that in 1914 the Debt was £651,270,091. On March 31st, 1951, the British National Debt stood at £26,000,000,000.

National Guard. Military forces raised in each State but partly trained, equipped and quartered by the U.S.A. Federal government. When called up by the President these forces become an integral part of the armed forces.

Nations, Battle of the. A name given to the great battle of Leipzig in the Napoleonic wars (Oct. 16th-19th, 1813), when the French under Napoleon were defeated by the coalition armies, consisting of the Prussians, Russians, Austrians, and Swedes.

Native (Lat., *nativus*, produced by birth, natural). In feudal times, one born a serf. After the Conquest, the natives were the serfs of the Normans. Wat Tyler said to Richard II:

The first peticion was that he scholde make alle men fre thro Ynglonde and quiete, so that there scholde not be eny native man after that time.—HIGDEN: *Polychronicon*, viii, 457.

Legally, a person is a native of the place of his parents' domicile, wherever he himself may have happened to be born.

Oysters raised in artificial beds are called *natives*, though they may be, and frequently are, imported. This is because artificially reared oysters are the best, and for centuries the best oysters were those actually taken from British waters. It is a case of the transference of a convenient name.

Nativity, The. Christmas Day, the day set apart in honour of the Nativity or Birth of Christ.

Natter, To. To talk aimlessly, foolishly or without sense. It is a Scots word of long standing, probably deriving from the Icelandic *knetta*, to grumble.

Nature. In a state of nature. Nude or naked.

Natural. A born idiot; one on whom education can make no impression. As nature made him, so he remains.

A natural child. One not born in lawful wedlock. The Romans called the children of concubines *naturales*, children according to nature, and not according to law.

Cui pater est populus, pater est sibi nullus omnes;
Cui pater est populus non habet ille patrem.—OVID.

In Music a **natural** is a white key on the pianoforte, etc., as distinguished from a black key. In musical notation the sign ♮ is employed to counteract the following note from a sharp or flat in the signature.

Natural Philosophy. *See* EXPERIMENTAL.

Naught, Nought. These are merely variants of the same word, *naught* representing A.S. *na whil* and *nought, no whit*. In most senses they are interchangeable; but nowadays *naught* is the more common form, except for the name of the cipher, which is usually *nought*.

Naught was formerly applied to things that were bad or worthless, as in 2 *Kings* ii, 19, "The water is naught and the ground barren," and it is with this sense that Jeremiah (xxiv, 2) speaks of "naughty figs":—

One basket had very good figs, even like the figs that are first ripe. . . . The other basket had very naughty figs which could not be eaten.

The Revised Version did away with the old "naughty" and substituted "bad"; and in the next verse, where the Authorized calls the figs "evil," the Douai Version has:—

The good figges, exceeding good, and the naughtie figges, exceeding naught; which can not be eaten because they are naught.

Nausicaa (naw sik ā′ a). The Greek heroine whose story is told in the Odyssey. She was the daughter of Alcinous, king of the Phæacians, and the shipwrecked Odysseus found her playing at ball with her maidens on the shore. Pitying his plight she conducted him to her father, by whom he was entertained.

Nautical Mile. *See* MILE.

Navaho (năv′ à hō). The largest tribal group of N. American Indians in the U.S.A. Their reservations are in New Mexico and Arizona, where they retain much of their traditional way of life and eschew contact with the white men. The Navahos belong to the southern division of the Athapascan stock, to which belong the Apache tribes.

Nazaræans or **Nazarenes** (năz′ à rēnz). A sect of Jewish Christians, who believed Christ to be the Messiah, that He was born of the Holy Ghost, and that He possessed a Divine nature, but who, nevertheless, conformed to the Mosaic rites and ceremonies.

Nazarene. A native of Nazareth; Our Lord is so called (*John* xviii, 5, 7; *Acts* xxiv, 5), though He was born in Bethlehem.

Can any good thing come out of Nazareth? (*John* i, 46). A general insinuation against any family or place of ill repute. Can any great man come from such an insignificant village as Nazareth?

Nazi (nat′ zi, naz′ i). the shortened form of *National-Sozialist*, the name given to the party of Adolf Hitler and its members.

Ne plus ultra (nē plŭs ŭl′ trà) (Lat., nothing further, *i.e.* perfection). The most perfect state to which a thing can be brought. *See* PLUS ULTRA.

Neanderthal Man (ni ăn′ dĕr tal). A palæolithic race inhabiting Europe during the Mousterian period. It was first revealed by the discovery of a human burial in a grotto of the Neanderthal ravine near Dusseldorf, in 1856. Its fossil remains have since been found in widely scattered caves.

Near, meaning *mean*, is rather a curious play on the word *close* (close-fisted). What is "close by" is near.

Nebuchadnezzar (neb ū kăd nez′ àr). This name which is now firmly fixed in English, is a mistake, for it is a misrendering in the Hebrew of Daniel (and consequently in English and other translations) of the

Babylonian *Nabu-kudur-usur*, and should be *Nebuchadrezzar*, as indeed it is given in *Jer.* xxi, 2, etc. The French call him *Nabuchodonosor*, or *Nabuchodoroser*, which are nearer the Greek transliteration. The name means *Nebo protects the crown. See* NEBO.

Nebuchadnezzar was the greatest king of Assyria, and reigned for forty-three years (604-561 B.C.). He restored his country to its former prosperity and importance, practically rebuilt Babylon, restored the temple of Bel, erected a new palace, embanked the Euphrates, and probably built the celebrated Hanging Gardens. His name became the centre of many legends, and of the story related by Daniel (iv, 29-33) that he was one day walking—

in the palace of the kingdom of Babylon and said, "Is not this great Babylon that I have built . . . by the might of my power, and for the honour of my majesty?" And "the same hour . . . he was driven from men, and did eat grass as oxen, and his body was wet with the dew of heaven, till his hairs were grown like eagles' feathers, and his nails like birds' claws."

This is an allusion to the suspension of his interest in public affairs, which lasted, as his inscription records, for four years.

Necessitarians. *See* AGENT.

Necessity. Necessity knows no law. These were the words used by Dr. von Bethmann-Hollweg, the German Imperial Chancellor, in the Reichstag on August 4th, 1914, as a justification for the German infringement of Belgian neutrality:—

Gentlemen, we are now in a state of necessity (*Notwehr*), and necessity (*Not*) knows no law. Our troops have occupied Luxemburg and perhaps have already entered Belgian territory.

To quote Milton—

So spake the Fiend, and with necessity,
The tyrant's plea excused his devilish deeds.
Paradise Lost, iv, 393.

The phrase is, of course, not original. Cromwell used it in a speech to Parliament on September 12th, 1654, but to very different purpose:—

Necessity hath no law. Feigned necessities, imaginary necessities, are the greatest cozenage men can put upon the Providence of God, and make pretences to break known rules by.

It is common to most languages. Publius Syrus has *Necessitas dat legem, non ipsa accipit* (Necessity gives the law, but does not herself accept it), and the Latin proverb *Necessitas non habet legem* appears in *Piers Plowman* (14th century) as "Neede hath no lawe."

To make a virtue of necessity. To "grin and bear it"; what can't be cured must be endured."

Thanne is it wisdom, as it thinketh me
To maken vertu of necessitee.
CHAUCER: *Knight's Tale*, 3041.

Are you content to be our general?
To make a virtue of necessity
And live, as we do, in this wilderness?
Two Gentlemen of Verona, iv, 1.

Quintilian has *laudem virtutis necessitati damus*: St. Jerome (epistle 54, section 6), *Fac de necessitate virtutem*. In the *Roman de la Rose*, line 14058, we find *S'il ne fait de necessite virtu*, and Boccaccio has *Si come savia fatta della necessita*.

Neck. Slang for brazen impudence, colossal cheek.

Neck and neck. Very near in merit; very close competitors. A phrase used in horse races, when two or more horses run each other very closely.

Neck of woods. (U.S.A.). A settlement in the forest.

Stiff-necked. Obstinate and self-willed. In the *Psalms* we read: "Speak not with a stiff neck" (lxxv, 5); and *Jer.* xvii, 23, "They obeyed not, but made their necks stiff"; and Isaiah (xlviii, 4) says: "Thy neck is an iron sinew." The allusion is to a wilful horse, ox, or ass, which will not answer to the reins.

To get it in the neck. To be completely defeated, thoroughly castigated, soundly rated, etc. The phrase is an Americanism, from the picturesque expression of one who has just been "through it"—*I got it where the chicken got the axe*—which, of course, is "in the neck."

To stick one's neck out. To expose oneself to being hurt, as a chicken might stick out its neck for the axe.

Necking. The now common phrase for mild amorous play should be distinguished from the meaning of the word in the Western States of the U.S.A. There necking is to tie a restless animal by the neck to a tame one in order to render it more tractable.

Neck-tie party. (U.S.A.). A hanging, particularly by lynch law (*q.v.*).

Necklace. A necklace of coral or white bryony beads used to be worn by children to aid their teething. Necklaces of hyoscyamus or henbane-root have been recommended for the same purpose.

The fatal necklace. Cadmus received on his wedding-day the present of a necklace, which proved fatal to everyone who possessed it. Some say that Vulcan, and others that Europa, gave it to him. Harmonia's necklace (*q.v.*) was a similar fatal gift.

Necromancy (nek' rō măn' si). Prophesying by calling up the dead, as the witch of Endor called up Samuel (1 *Sam.* xxviii, 7 ff.) (Gr. *nekros*, the dead; *manteia*, prophecy.)

Nectar (Gr.). The drink of the gods of classical mythology. Like their food, *Ambrosia*, it conferred immortality. Hence the name of the *nectarine*, so called because it is "as sweet as nectar."

Needham. You are on the high-road to Needham—to ruin or poverty. The pun is on the *need*, and there is no reference to Needham in Suffolk. *Cp.* LAND OF NOD.

Negative. The answer is in the negative. The circumlocutory Parliament way of enouncing the monosyllable *No*.

Negus (nē' gus). The drink—port or sherry, with hot water, sugar, and spices—is so called from a Colonel Francis Negus (d. 1732), who first concocted it.

The supreme ruler of Abyssinia is entitled *the Negus*, from the native *n'gus*, meaning crowned.

Nemesis (nem' é sis). The Greek goddess who allotted to men their exact share of good, or bad fortune, and was responsible for seeing that everyone got his due and deserts; the personification of divine retribution. Hence, retributive justice generally, as **the Nemesis of nations**, the fate which, sooner or later, has overtaken every great nation of the ancient and modern world.

And though circuitous and obscure
The feet of Nemesis how sure!
   SIR WILLIAM WATSON: *Europe at the Play.*

Nemo me impune lacessit (nē' mō mē im pū ni lá ses' it) (Lat.). No one injures me with impunity. The motto of the Order of the Thistle (*q.v.*).

Neolithic Age, The (nē ō lith' ik) (Gr. *neos*, new, *lithos*, a stone). The later Stone Age of Europe, the earlier being called the Palæolithic (Gr. *palaios*, ancient). Stone implements of the Neolithic age are polished, more highly finished, and more various than those of the Palæolithic, and are found in kitchen-middens and tombs, with the remains of recent and extinct animals, and sometimes with bronze implements. Neolithic man knew something of agriculture, kept domestic animals, used boats, and caught fish.

Nepenthe or **Nepenthes** (ne pen' thé) (Gr. *ne*, not, *penthos*, grief). An Egyptian drug mentioned in the *Odyssey* (iv, 228) that was fabled to drive away care and make persons forget their woes. Polydamna, wife of Thonis, king of Egypt, gave it to Helen, daughter of Jove and Leda.

That nepenthes which the wife of Thone
In Egypt gave the Jove-born Helena.
   MILTON: *Comus*, 695-6.

Nephew (Fr. *neveu*, Lat. *nepos*). Both in Latin and in archaic English the word means a grandchild, or descendant. Hence, in the Authorized Version of 1 *Tim.* v, 4, we read—"If a widow have children or nephews," but in the Revised "grandchildren." Propertius has it, *Me inter seros laudabit Roma nepotes* (posterity).

Niece (Lat. *neptis*) also means a granddaughter or female descendant. *See* NEPOTISM.

Nepotism (Lat. *nepos*, a nephew or kinsman). An unjustifiable elevation of one's own relations to places of wealth and trust at one's disposal.

Neptune (nep' tūn). The Roman god of the sea, corresponding with the Greek Poseidon (*q.v.*), hence used allusively for the sea itself. Neptune is represented as an elderly man of stately mien, bearded, carrying a trident, and sometimes astride a dolphin or a horse. *See* HIPPOCAMPUS.

. . . great Neptune with this threeforkt mace,
That rules the Seas, and makes them rise or fall;
His dewy lockes did drop with brine apace,
Under his Diademe imperiall.
   SPENSER. *Fuerie Queene*, IV, xi, 11.

Neptunian or **Neptunist.** The name given to certain 18th-century geologists, who held the opinion of Werner (1750-1817), that all the great rocks of the earth were once held in solution in water, and were deposited as sediment. The *Vulcanists* or *Plutonians* ascribed them to the agency of fire.

Nereus (nē' rūs). A sea-god of Greek mythology, represented as a very old man. He was the father of the fifty Nereids (*q.v.*), and his special dominion was the Ægean Sea.

Nereids were the sea-nymphs of Greek mythology, the fifty daughters of Nereus and "grey-eyed" Doris. The best known are Amphitrite, Thetis, and Galatea; Milton refers to another, Panope—in *Lycidas* (line 99)—

The air was calm, and on the level brine
Sleek Panope with all her sisters played.

And the names of all will be found in Spenser's *Faerie Queene*, Bk. iv, c. xi, verses 48-57.

Neri. *See* BIANCHI.

Nero, A. Any bloody-minded man, relentless tyrant, or evil-doer of extraordinary savagery; from the depraved and infamous Roman Emperor, C. Claudius Nero (A.D. 54-68), who set fire to Rome to see, it is said, "what Troy would have looked like when it was in flames," and is reported to have fiddled as he watched the conflagration.

Nero of the North. Christian II of Denmark (1481-1559), also called "The Cruel." He massacred the Swedish nobility at Stockholm in 1520, and thus prepared the way for Gustavus Vasa and Swedish freedom.

Nerthus or **Hertha.** The name given by Tacitus to a German or Scandinavian goddess of fertility, or "Mother Earth," who was worshipped on the island of Rugen. She roughly corresponds with the classical Cybele; and is probably confused with the Scandinavian god *Njorthr* or *Niordhr*, the protector of sailors and fishermen. *Nerthus* and *Njorthr* alike mean "benefactor."

Nest-egg. Money laid by. The allusion is to the custom of placing an egg in a hen's nest to induce her to lay her eggs there. If a person has saved a little money, it serves as an inducement to him to increase his store.

Nestor. King of Pylos, in Greece; the oldest and most experienced of the chieftains who went to the siege of Troy. Hence the name is frequently applied as an epithet to the oldest and wisest man of a class or company. Samuel Rogers, for instance, who lived to be 92, was called "the Nestor of English poets."

Net. On the Old Boy net. To arrange something through a friend (originally, someone known at school) instead of through the usual channels — a British military expression in World War II.

Never. There are numerous locutions to express this idea; as —
At the coming of the Coquecigrues (RABELAIS: *Pantagruel*).
At the Latter Lammas.
On the Greek Calends.
In the reign of Queen Dick.
On St. Tib's Eve.
In a month of five Sundays.
When two Fridays or three Sundays come together.
When Dover and Calais meet.
When Dudman and Ramehead meet.
When the world grows honest.
When the Yellow River runs clear.

Never Never Land. Originally a phrase applied to the whole of the Australian "Out Back," but since the publication of *We of the Never Never* by Mrs. Aeneas Gunn (1908) restricted to the Northern Territory. It was used by J. M. Barrie in *Peter Pan* (1904).

New. New Deal. The name given to President Roosevelt's policy, announced in his first presidential campaign (1932) when he said "we are going to think less about the producer and more about the consumer . . . and bring about a more equitable distribution of the national income." The New Deal took shape in the National Industrial Recovery Act which empowered the President to lay down codes regulating industry, child labour, minimum wages and maximum hours. In 1935 these codes were judged unconstitutional by the U.S. Supreme Court.

Newfangled. Applied to anything of a quite new or different fashion; a novelty. The older word was *newfangle* —
Men loven of propre kinde newfangelnesse
As briddes doon that men in cages fede . . .
So newfangel ben they of hir mete,
And loven novelryes of propre kinde.
CHAUCER: *Squire's Tale*, 602, 610.
M.E. *fangel*, from A.S. *fang*, past part. of *fōn*, to take, meaning "always ready to take, or grasp at, some new thing."

New Theology. An interpretation of Christian teaching based on broader views than that of the older fundamental reading of the Bible. It was first expounded in 1907 by R. J. Campbell, at the time Congregational minister at the City Temple. He later entered the Church of England.

New Thought. A general term for a system of therapeutics based on the theory that the mental and physical problems of life should be met, regulated and controlled by the suggestion of right thoughts. This system has nothing in common with Christian Science, auto-suggestion or psycho-therapy.

New World. America: the Eastern Hemisphere is called the Old World.

New Year's Day. January 1st. The Romans began their year in March; hence *September, October, November, December* for the 7th, 8th, 9th, and 10th months. Since the introduction of the Christian era, Christmas Day, Lady Day, Easter Day, March 1st and March 25th have in turns been considered as New Year's Day; but at the reform of the calendar in the 16th century (*see* CALENDAR), January 1st was accepted by practically all Christian peoples.

In England the civil and legal year began on March 25th till after the alteration of the style, in 1752, when it was fixed, like the historic year, to January 1st. In Scotland the segal year was changed to January 1st as far back as 1600.

Newcastle upon Tyne was so called (*Noef-Chastel-sur-Tine*, or *Novum Castellum*) from the castle built there by Robert, son of the Conqueror, in 1080, to defend the neighbourhood from the Scots. Previous names were, in Roman times, *Pons Ælii*, and, by the Anglo-Saxons, *Munechecaster* (Monks' castle).

Newcastle was the first coal port in the world and the first charter granted to the town for the digging of coal was given by Henry III in 1239.

To carry coals to Newcastle. *See* COAL.

New England. The name given collectively to the north-eastern States of the U.S.A.—Connecticut, Massachusetts, Rhode Island,

Vermont, New Hampshire and Maine. The name was given by Captain John Smith to what was then part of "North Virginia," granted to the Plymouth Company by James I, in 1606. Between 1643 and 1684 the New England Confederation of the colonies of Massachussetts Bay, Plymouth, Connecticut, and New Haven was in force to secure a united defence against the Dutch and the Indians.

Newgate. According to Stow this was first built in the city wall of London in the time of Henry I, but excavations have shown that there was a Roman gate here, about 31 ft. in width. It may have fallen into disuse, and have been repaired by Henry I, the present name being given at the time.

New Jerusalem. The city of heaven foretold in *Rev.* xxi, "coming down from God out of heaven, prepared as a bride adorned for her husband."

New South Wales is the oldest state in the Commonwealth of Australia. It was so named in 1770 by Captain Cook from its fancied resemblance from the sea to the northern shores of the Bristol Channel. The famous penal settlement of Botany Bay was founded there in 1787, five miles south of the present city of Sydney, itself named after Thomas Townshend, 1st Viscount Sydney, at that time secretary of state in charge of colonial affairs.

New York. The first settlements here were made on Manhattan Island by the Dutch in 1614. Manhattan Island was bought from the Indians for cloth and trinkets to the total value of about £5. Under the name of New Amsterdam it was held by the Dutch until 1644. In that year the whole of the Atlantic seaboard was granted by Charles II to his brother James, Duke of York. Col. Richard Nicolls sailed there at once with four ships and 30 soldiers, and overcoming the gallant resistance of the Dutch governor, Peter Stuyvesant, captured the place and renamed it after his patron, New York. It has thus no connection with the English city of York.

N

News. The letters E W used to be prefixed to
S

newspapers to show that they obtained information from the four quarters of the world, and the supposition that our word *news* is thence derived is at least ingenious; the old-fashioned way of spelling the word, *newes*, is alone fatal to the conceit. Fr. *nouvelles* is the real source.

News is conveyed by letter, word or mouth
And comes to us from North, East, West and South.
Witt's Recreations.

The word is now nearly always construed as singular ("the news *is* very good this morning"), but it was formerly treated as a plural, and in the *Letters of Queen Victoria* the Queen, and most of her correspondents, followed that rule:—

The news from Austria are very sad, and make one very anxious.—*To the King of the Belgians*, 20 Aug., 1861.

Newscast. The American term for the radio broadcast of news.

Newt. *See* NICKNAMES.

Newtonian Philosophy. The astronomical system that in the late 17th century displaced the Copernican (*see* COPERNICANISM), together with the theory of universal gravitation. So called after Sir Isaac Newton (1642-1727), who established the former and discovered the latter.

Nature and Nature's laws lay hid in night
God said. "Let Newton be," and all was light.
POPE.

Next of Kin. The legal term for a person's nearest relative, more especially where estate is left by an intestate. In English law the next of kin in priority is:

Husband or wife; children; father or mother (equally if both alive); brothers and sisters; half brothers and sisters; grandparents; uncles and aunts; half uncles and aunts; the Crown.

Next Friend, in law, is an adult who brings an action in a court of law on behalf of a minor.

Nibelungenlied, The (nē be lung' en lēd). A Middle High German poem, the greatest monument of early German literature, founded on old Scandinavian legends contained in the *Volsunga Saga* and the *Edda*, and written in its present form by an anonymous South German of the early part of the 13th century.

Nibelung was a mythical king of a race of Scandinavian dwarfs dwelling in *Nibelheim* (*i.e.* "the home of darkness, or mist"). These *Nibelungs*, or *Nibelungers*, were the possessors of the wonderful "Hoard" of gold and precious stones guarded by the dwarf Alberich; and their name passed to later holders of the Hoard, Siegfried's following and the Burgundians being in turn called "the Nibelungs."

Siegfried, the hero of the first part of the poem, became possessed of the Hoard and gave it to Kriemhild as her marriage portion. After his murder Kriemhild carried it to Worms, where it was seized by Hagen and Gunther. They buried it in the Rhine, intending later to enjoy it; but they were both slain for refusing to reveal its whereabouts, and the Hoard remains for ever in the keeping of the Rhine Maidens. The second part of the Nibelungenlied tells of the marriage of the widow Kriemhild with King

Etzel (Attila), the visit of the Burgundians to the court of the Hunnish king, and the death of all the principal characters, including Gunther, Hagen, and Kriemhild.

Nic Frog. *See* FROG.

Nicholas, St. One of the most popular saints in Christendom, especially in the East. He is the patron saint of Russia, of Aberdeen, of parish clerks, of scholars (who used to be called *clerks*), of pawnbrokers (because of the three bags of gold—transformed to the three gold balls—that he gave to the daughters of a poor man to save them from earning their dowers in a disreputable way), of little boys (because he once restored to life three little boys who had been cut up and pickled in a salting-tub to serve for bacon), and is invoked by sailors (because he allayed a storm during a voyage to the Holy Land) and against fire. Finally, he is the original of Santa Claus (*q.v.*).

Little is known of his life, but he is said to have been Bishop of Myra (Lycia) in the early 4th century, and one story relates that he was present at the Council of Nice (325) and there buffeted Arius on the jaw. His day is December 6th, and he is represented in episcopal robes with either three purses of gold, three gold balls, or three small boys, in allusion to one or other of the above legends.

Nick. Slang for to pilfer; and, in the 18th century, for to break windows by throwing coppers at them:—

> His scattered pence the flying Nicker flings,
> And with the copper shower the casement rings.
> GAY: Trivia, iii.

He nicked it. Won, hit, accomplished it. A nick is a winning throw of dice in the old game of "hazard."

In the nick of time. Just at the right moment. The allusion is to tallies marked with nicks or notches. *Cp.* PRICK OF NOON.

Old Nick. The Devil. The term was in use in the 17th century, and is perhaps connected with the German *Nickel*, a goblin (*see* NICKEL), or in some forgotten way with St. Nicholas. Butler's derivation from Nicholas Machiavelli is, of course, poetical licence:—

> Nick Machiavel had ne'er a trick
> (Though he gives name to our old Nick)
> But was below the least of these.
> Hudibras, iii, 1.

Nicker, or **Nix.** In Scandinavian folklore, a water-wraith, or kelpie, inhabiting sea, lake, river, and waterfall. They are sometimes represented as half-child, half-horse, the hoofs being reversed, and sometimes as old men sitting on rocks wringing the water from their hair. The female nicker is a *nixy*.

Another tribe of water-fairies are the Nixes, who frequently assume the appearance of beautiful maidens.— DYER: *Folk-lore of Plants*, ch. vii.

Nickname. Originally *an eke-name, eke* being an adverb meaning "also," A.S. *eac*, connected with *iecan*, to supply deficiencies in or to make up for. A *newt* in the same way was originally "an eft" or "an evt"; "v" and "u" being formerly interchangeable gave us "neut," or "newt."

The "eke" of a beehive is the piece added to the bottom to enlarge the hive.

National Nicknames:

For an American of the United States, "Brother Jonathan." For America as a national entity, "Uncle Sam."

For a Dutchman, "Nic Frog" and "Mynheer Closh."

For an Englishman, "John Bull."

For a Frenchman, "Crapaud," "Johnny" or "Jean," "Robert Macaire."

For French Canadians, "Jean Baptiste."

For French reformers, "Brissotins."

For French peasantry, "Jacques Bon-homme."

For a German, "Cousin Michael" or "Michel"; "Hun"; "Jerry": "Fritz."

For an Irishman, "Paddy."

For an Italian, "Antonio," or "Tony."

For a Scot, "Sandy" or "Mac."

For a Spaniard or Portuguese, "Dago" (Diego).

For a Welshman, "Taffy."

Nicotine (nik' ō tēn). So named from *Nico-tiana*, the Latin name of the tobacco-plant, given to it in honour of Jean Nicot (*c.* 1530-1600), Lord of Viliemain, who was French ambassador in Madrid and introduced tobacco into France in 1560.

Nightcap. A drink before going to bed.

Nightingale. The Greek legend is that Tereus, King of Thrace, fetched Philomela to visit his wife, Procne, who was her sister; but when he reached the "solitudes of Heleas" he dishonoured her, and cut out her tongue that she might not reveal his conduct. Tereus told his wife that Philomela was dead, but Philomela made her story known by weaving it into a peplus, which she sent to Procne. Procne, in revenge, cut up her own son and served it to Tereus, and as soon as the king discovered it he pursued his wife, who fled to Philomela; whereupon the gods changed all three into birds; Tercus became the *hawk*, his wife, the *swallow*, and Philomela the *nightingale*, which is still called Philomel (*lit.* lover of song) by the poets.

> Youths and maidens most poetical. . . .
> Full of meek sympathy must heave their sighs
> O'er Philomela's pity-pleading strains.
> COLERIDGE: The Nightingale.

The Swedish Nightingale. The operatic singer, Jenny Lind (1820-87), afterwards Mme. Goldschmidt. She was a native of Stockholm.

Nightmare. A sensation in sleep as if something heavy were sitting on one's breast; formerly supposed to be caused by a monster (*see* INCUBUS) who actually did this; it was not unfrequently called the *night-hag*, or the *riding of the witch*. The second syllable is the A.S. *mare* (old Norse *mara*), an incubus, and appears again in the French equivalent *cauchemar*, "the fiend that tramples." The word is now more often employed to describe a frightening dream, a night terror.

Nightmare of Europe, The. Napoleon Bonaparte was so called.

Nihilism (nī' hil izm) (Lat. *nihil*, nothing). An extreme form of Socialism, the prelude to Bolshevism (*see* BOLSHEVIST), which took form in Russia in the 50s of last century, and was specially active in the 70s, and later, under Bakounin. It aimed at the complete overthrow of law, order, and all existing institutions, with the idea of re-forming the world *de novo*.

The name was given by the novelist, Ivan Turgenieff (1818-83).

Nil admirari (Lat.). To be stolidly indifferent. Neither to wonder at anything nor yet to admire anything. The tag is from Horace (*Ep.* I, vi, 1):—

Nil admirari prope res est una, Numici,
Solaque, quæ possit facere et servare beatum.
(Not to admire, Numicius, is the best—
The only way to make and keep men blest.)
Connington.

Nil desperandum. Never say die; never give up in despair; another tag from Horace (*Carmen*, I, vii, 27):—

Nil desperandum Teucro duce et auspice Teucro
(There is naught to be despaired of when we are under
Teucer's leadership and auspices).

Nile. The Egyptians used to say that the rising of the Nile was caused by the tears of Isis. The feast of Isis was celebrated at the anniversary of the death of Osiris, when Isis was supposed to mourn for her husband.

The hero of the Nile. Horatio, Lord Nelson (1758-1805).

Nimbus (nim' bŭs) (Lat., a cloud). In Christian art a halo of light placed round the head of an eminent personage. There are three forms: (1) *Vesica piscis*, or fish form (*cp.* ICHTHUS), used in representations of Christ and occasionally of the Virgin Mary, extending round the whole figure; (2) a circular halo; (3) radiated like a star or sun. The enrichments are: (1) for Our Lord, a cross; (2) for the Virgin, a circlet of stars; (3) for angels, a circlet of small rays, and an outer circle of quatrefoils; (4) the same for saints and martyrs, but with the name often inscribed round the circumference; (5) for the Deity the rays diverge in a triangular direction. Nimbi of a square form signify that the persons so represented were living when they were painted.

The nimbus was used by heathen nations long before painters introduced it into sacred pictures of saints, the Trinity, and the Virgin Mary. Proserpine was represented with a nimbus; the Roman emperors were also decorated in the same manner, because they were *divi*.

Nimini-pimini (nim' i ni pim' i ni). Affected simplicity. Lady Emily, in General Burgoyne's *The Heiress*, III, ii (1786), tells Miss Alscrip to stand before a glass and keep pronouncing *nimini-pimini*—"The lips cannot fail to take the right plie."

The conceit was borrowed by Dickens in *Little Dorrit*, where Mrs. General tells Amy Dorrit—

Papa gives a pretty form to the lips. *Papa, patatoes, poultry, prunes,* and *prism* are all very good words for the lips, especially *prunes* and *prism*.

The form miminy-piminy is also in use:—

A miminy-piminy, *Je-ne-sais-quoi* young man.—
W. S. GILBERT: *Patience*, II.

Nincompoop (nin' kóm poop). A poor thing of a man. Said to be a corruption of the Latin *non compos* (*mentis*), but of this there is no evidence. The last syllable is probably connected with Dut. *poep*, a fool.

Nine. Nine, five, and three are mystical numbers—the *diapason* (*q.v.*), *diapente*, and *diatrion* of the Greeks. Nine consists of a trinity of trinities. According to the Pythagoreans man is a full chord, or eight notes, and Deity comes next. Three, being the trinity, represents a perfect *unity*; twice three is the perfect *dual*; and thrice three is the perfect *plural*. This explains why nine is a mystical number.

From the earliest times the number nine has been regarded as of peculiar significance. Deucalion's ark, made by the advice of Prometheus, was tossed about for *nine* days, when it stranded on the top of Mount Parnassus. There were the *nine* Muses (*q.v.*), frequently referred to as merely "the Nine"—

Descend, ye Nine! Descend and sing
The breathing instruments inspire.
POPE: *Ode on St. Cecilia's Day.*

There were **nine Gallicenæ** or virgin priestesses of the ancient Gallic oracle; and Lars Porsena swore by the *nine* gods—

Lars Porsena of Clusium
By the nine gods he swore
That the great house of Tarquin
Should suffer wrong no more.
MACAULAY: *Lays of Ancient Rome (Horatius,* i).

who were Juno, Minerva, and Tinia (*the three chief*), Vulcan, Mars, Saturn, Hercules, Summanus, and Vedius; while the *nine* of the Sabines were Hercules, Romulus, Esculapius, Bacchus, Æneas, Vesta, Santa, Fortuna, and Fides.

Niobe's children lay *nine* days in their blood before they were buried; the Hydra had *nine* heads; at the *Lemuria*, held by the Romans on May 9th, 11th, and 13th, persons haunted threw black beans over their heads, pronouncing nine times the words: "Avaunt, ye spectres, from this house!" and the exorcism was complete (*see* Ovid's *Fasti*).

There were *nine* rivers of hell, or, according to some accounts the Styx encompassed the infernal regions in *nine* circles; and Milton makes the gates of hell "thrice three-fold; three folds are brass, three iron, three of adamantine rock." They had nine folds, nine plates, and nine linings. (*Paradise Lost*, ii, 645).

Vulcan, when kicked from Olympus, was *nine* days falling to the island of Lemnos; and when the fallen angels were cast out of heaven, Milton says "*Nine* days they fell" (*Paradise Lost*, vi. 871).

In the early Ptolemaic system of astronomy, before the Primum Mobile (*q.v.*) was added, there were *nine* spheres; hence Milton, in his *Arcades*, speaks of the "celestial syrens' harmony that sit upon the *nine* enfolded spheres." They were those of the Moon, Mercury, Venus, the Sun, Mars, Jupiter, Saturn, and the Firmament or that of the fixed stars, and the Crystalline Sphere. In Scandinavian mythology there were *nine* earths, Hel (*q.v.*) being the goddess of the ninth; there were *nine* worlds in Niflheim, and Odin's ring dropped eight other rings (*nine* rings of mystical import) every *ninth* night.

In folk-lore *nine* appears many times. The Abracadabra was worn *nine* days, and then flung into a river; in order to see the fairies one is directed to put "*nine* grains of wheat on a four-leaved clover"; *nine* knots are made on black wool as a charm for a sprained ankle; if a servant finds *nine* green peas in a peascod, she lays it on the lintel of the kitchen door, and the first man that enters in is to be her cavalier; to see *nine* magpies is most unlucky; a cat has *nine* lives (*see also* CAT O' NINE TAILS); and the *nine* of Diamonds is known as the Curse of Scotland (*q.v.*).

The weird sisters in *Macbeth* sang, as they danced round the cauldron, "Thrice to thine, and thrice to mine, and thrice again to make up *nine*"; and then declared "the charm wound up";

and we drink a *Three-times-three* to those most highly honoured.

Leases are sometimes granted for 999 years, that is *three* times *three-three-three*. Even now they run for ninety-nine years, the dual of a trinity of trinities.

See also the *Nine Points of the Law*, in PHRASES, *below*, and the *Nine Worthies*, under WORTHIES.

There are *nine* orders of angels (*see* ANGELS); in Heraldry there are *nine* marks of cadency and *nine* different crowns recognized; and among ecclesiastical architects there are *nine* crosses, viz., altar, processional, roods on lofts, reliquary crosses, consecration, marking, pectoral, spire crosses, and crosses pendent over altars.

Dressed up to the nines. To perfection from head to foot.

Nine-tail bruiser. Prison slang for the cat-o'-nine-tails (*q.v.*).

Nine times out of ten. Far more often than not; in a great preponderance.

Possession is nine points of the law. It is every advantage a person can have short of actual right. The "nine points of the law" have been given as—

(1) A good deal of money; (2) a good deal of patience; (3) a good cause; (4) a good lawyer; (5) a good counsel; (6) good witnesses; (7) a good jury; (8) a good judge; and (9) good luck.

Niobe. The personification of maternal sorrow. According to Grecian fable. Niobe, the daughter of Tantalus and wife of Amphion, King of Thebes, was the mother of twelve children, and taunted Latona because she had only two— Apollo and Diana. Latona commanded her children to avenge the insult, and they caused all the sons and daughters of Niobe to die. Niobe was inconsolable, wept herself to death, and was changed into a stone, from which ran water, "Like Niobs, all ears" (*Hamlet*, i, 2).

Nip. Nip of whisky, etc. Short for **Nipperkin.** A small wine and beer measure containing about half a pint, or a little under; now frequently called "a nip."

His hawk-economy won't thank him for't
Which stops his petty nipperkin of port.
PETER PINDAR: *Hair Powder.*

The traditional Devon and Cornish song *The Barley Mow* starts with drinking the health out of the "jolly brown bowl," and at each chorus increases the size of the receptacle until in the sixteenth and last we have—

We'll drink it out of the ocean, my boys,
Here's a health to the barley-mow!
The ocean, the river, the well, the pipe, the hogshead, the half-hogshead, the anker, the half-anker, the gallon, the half-gallon, the pottle, the quart, the pint,

the half a pint, the quarter-pint, the nipperkin, *and* the jolly brown bowl!

Nip and tuck. A neck-and-neck race; a close fight.

Number Nip. Another name for Rübezahl (*q.v.*).

To nip in the bud. To destroy before it has had time to develop; usually said of bad habits, tendency to sin, etc. Shakespeare has—

The third day comes a frost, a killing frost;
And, when he thinks, good easy man, full surely
His greatness is a-ripening, *nips his root,*
And then he falls, as I do.

Henry VIII, iii, 2.

Nipper. Slang for a small boy.

Nippon (ni pon′). The Japanese name of Japan.

Nirvana (ner van′ à) (Sansk., a blowing out, or extinction). Annihilation, or rather the final deliverance of the soul from transmigration (*see* BUDDHISM).

Nisei (nē′ sā). A person born in the U.S.A. of Japanese descent but a loyal American.

Nisroch (nis′ rok). The Assyrian god in whose temple Sennacherib was worshipping when he was slain (2 *Kings* xix, 37). Nothing is known of the god, and the name is probably a corruption either of Asur or of Nusku, a god connected with Nebo (*q.v.*).

Nitwit. A slow-witted person, one who is irresponsible and is liable to say or do foolish and irrelevant things.

Nix. *See* NICKER. The word is also slang for "nothing." "You can't get him to work for nix," *i.e.* without paying him. In this sense it is from Ger. *nichts,* nothing.

Nizam (nī zăm′). A title of sovereignty in Hyderabad (India), contracted from *Nizam-ul-mulk* (regulator of the state), the style adopted by Asaf Jan, who obtained possession of the Deccan in 1713.

Njorthr. *See* NERTHUS.

No. No dice (U.S.A.). Nothing doing.

No Man's Land. The name applied to the area between hostile entrenched lines or to any space contested by both sides and belonging to neither.

Noah's Ark. A name given by sailors to a white band of cloud spanning the sky like a rainbow and in shape something like the hull of a ship. If east and west expect dry weather, if north and south expect wet.

Noah's Wife. According to legend she was unwilling to go into the ark, and the quarrel between the patriarch and his wife forms a prominent feature of *Noah's Flood,* in the Chester and Townley Mysteries.

Hastow nought herd, quod Nicholas, also
The sorwe of Noe with his felawshipe
Er that he mighte gete his wyf to shipe?

CHAUCER: *Miller's Tale,* 352.

Nob. Slang for the head (probably from *knob*); also for a person of rank and position (contraction of *noble* or *nobility*). *Cp.* SNOB.

Nobel Prizes. Prizes established by the will of Alfred Bernard Nobel (1833-96), the Swedish chemist and inventor of dynamite, etc., to encourage work in the cause of humanity. There are five prizes given annually, each of about £7,000, as follows: (1) for the most noteworthy work in *physics,* (2) in *chemistry,* (3) in *medicine* or *physiology,* (4) in *idealistic literature,* and (5) in the furtherance of universal peace. W. C. Röntgen, Mme. Curie, A. Carrel, Rudyard Kipling, Maeterlinck, Hauptmann, Rabindranath Tagore, Romain Rolland, Elihu Root, Woodrow Wilson, F. G. Banting, W. B. Yeats, Albert Einstein, Sir A. Fleming, Luigi Pirandello, Sinclair Lewis, G. B. Shaw, Pearl Buck, Sir Norman Angell, The Society of Friends (Quakers), T. S. Eliot, Earl Russell, Mr. Ralph Bunche, are among those to whom the prizes have been awarded.

Noblesse oblige (nō bles′ ō blēzh) (Fr.). Noble birth imposes the obligation of high-minded principles and noble actions.

Nod. A nod is as good as a wink to a blind horse. However obvious a hint or suggestion may be it is useless if the other person is unable to see it.

The Land of Nod. *See* LAND.

Noel (nō′ el). In English (also written *Nowell*), a Christmas carol, or the shout of joy in a carol; in French, Christmas Day. The word is Provençal *nadal,* from Lat. *natalem,* natal.

Nowells, nowells, nowells!
Sing all we may,
Because that Christ, the King,
Was born this blessed day.—*Old Carol.*

Nolens volens (nō′ lenz vō′ lenz). Whether willing or not. Two Latin participles meaning "being unwilling (or) willing." *Cp.* WILLY-NILLY.

Noli me tangere (nol′ i me tăn′ jer i) (Lat., touch me not). The words Christ used to Mary Magdalene after His resurrection (*John* xx, 17), and given as a name to a plant of the genus *Impatiens.* The seed-vessels consist of one cell in five divisions, and when the seed is ripe each of these, on being touched, suddenly folds itself into a spiral form and leaps from the stalk. *See* Darwin's *Loves of the Plants,* ii, 3.

Noll. Old Noll. Oliver Cromwell was so called by the Royalists. Noll is a familiar form of *Oliver.*

Nolle prosequi (nol' i prō sek' wi) (Lat., to be unwilling to prosecute). A petition from a plaintiff to stay a suit. *Cp.* NON PROS.

Nolo episcopari (nō' lō ep isk ō pâ' ri) (Lat., I am unwilling to be made a bishop). The formal reply supposed to be returned to the royal offer of a bishopric. Chamberlayne says (*Present State of England,* 1669) that in former times the person about to be elected modestly refused the office twice, and if he did so a third time his refusal was accepted.

Nom. Nom de guerre is French for a "war name," but really means an assumed name. It was customary at one time for everyone who entered the French army to assume a name; this was especially the case in the times of chivalry, when knights were known by the device on their shields.

Nom de plume. English-French for "pen name," or pseudonym, the name assumed by a writer, cartoonist, etc., who does not choose to give his own to the public; as *Currer Bell* (Charlotte Brontë), *Fiona McLeod* (William Sharp), *Henry Seton Merriman* (Hugh Stowell Scott), etc. Occasionally, as in the case of *Voltaire* (François Marie Arouet) and *De Stendhal* (Marie Henri Beyle), the assumed name quite replaces the true name.

Nominalist (nom' i nal ist). The schoolmen's name for one who—following William of Occam—denied the objective existence of abstract ideas; also, the name of a sect founded by Roscelin, Canon of Compiègne (1040-1120), who maintained that if the Father, Son, and Holy Ghost are *one God*, they cannot be three distinct *persons*, but must be simply three *names* of the same being; just as father, son, and husband are three distinct names of one and the same man under different conditions. Abélard, Hobbes, Locke, Bishop Berkeley, Condillac, and Dugald Stewart are noted Nominalists. *Cp.* REALISTS.

Non. The Latin negative, *not*; adopted in English, and very widely employed, as a prefix of negation, *e.g.* in *non-abstainer, non-conformist, non-existent, non-resident, nonsense, nonsuit,* etc.

Non sequitur (Lat., it does not follow). A conclusion which does not follow from the premises stated; an inconsequent statement, such as Artemus Ward's—

I met a man in Oregon who hadn't any teeth—not a tooth in his head,—yet that man could play on the bass drum better than any man I ever met.

Nonconformists. In England, members of Protestant bodies who do *not conform* to the doctrines of the Church of England (also called *Dissenters*); especially the 2,000 clergy who, in 1662, left the Church rather than submit to the conditions of the Act of Uniformity— *i.e.* "unfeigned assent to all and everything contained in the Book of Common Prayer."

Nonjurors. Those clergymen who refused to take the oath of allegiance to the new government after the Revolution (1690). They were Archbishop Sancroft with eight bishops, and four hundred clergymen, all of whom were ejected from their livings. The non-juring bishops ordained clergy and kept up the "succession" until the death of the last "bishop" in 1805. *Cp.* SEVEN BISHOPS, THE.

Nonplus (Lat., no more). A quandary: a state of perplexity when "no more" can be said on the subject. When a man is *nonplussed* or has *come to a nonplus* in an argument, it means that he is unable to deny or controvert what is advanced against him. *To nonplus* a person is to put him into such a fix.

Norfolk Island. A South Pacific island belonging to Australia. It was discovered by Captain Cook in 1774 and was for many years a penal settlement for the most desperate convicts who had to be segregated from the other penal transportees in Australia. In 1856 Norfolk Island was colonized by the people from Pitcairn Island who were descended from the mutineers of the *Bounty* (*q.v.*).

Norman French. The Old French dialect spoken in Normandy at the time of the conquest of England and spoken by the dominant class in the latter country for some two centuries after the conquest. Vestiges of it remain in the formal words of the royal assent given to Bills that have passed through Parliament—"La Reine le veult"—and in the "Fitz" (*fils*, son) that precedes certain family surnames.

Norns, The. The three giant goddesses who, in Scandinavian mythology, presided over the fates of both men and gods.

Norrisian Professor (nor is' i an). A Professor of Divinity in Cambridge University. This professorship was founded in 1760 by John Norris (1734-77), of Whitton, Norfolk. The four divinity professors are Lady Margaret's, the Regius, the Norrisian, and the Hulsean.

Norroy (*i.e.* north roy, or king). The third king of arms is so called, because his office is on the north side of the river Trent; that of the south side is called Clarenceux (*q.v.*).

North-east Passage, The. A way to India from Europe round the north extremity of Asia.

It had been often attempted even in the 16th century. Hence Beaumont and Fletcher:

That everlasting cassock, that has worn
As many servants our as the North-east Passage
Has consumed sailors.

The Woman's Prize, ii, 2.

North Pole. For two or three centuries men tried to reach the North Pole, and many were the speculations as to what would be found when they got there. It was not until April 6th, 1909, that the American sailor and explorer Robert Edwin Peary (1856-1920) reached the Pole, by that time known to be the central point of the shallow Arctic basin wherein lies the Arctic Ocean, of which the surface near the Pole is floating and moving ice. In May, 1933, the North Pole was claimed by the Russians as a Soviet possession and four years later they established a Polar station there, under Prof. Otto Schmidt.

North-west Passage. The name given to an assumed passage to China and the Orient round the north of the American continent. Attempts to find it were made in the 16th and 17th century by such sailors as the Cabots, Frobisher, Gilbert, Davis, Hudson, and Baffin. In the 19th century the quest was followed by Ross, Parry, and Sir John Franklin who lost his life and the lives of his crew in the attempt. It was not until 1903-05 that Roald Amundsen made the complete voyage.

The Northern Gate of the Sun. The sign of Cancer, or summer solstice; so called because it marks the northern tropic.

The Northern Lights. The Aurora Borealis (*q.v.*).

The Northern Wagoner. The genius presiding over the Great Bear, or Charles's Wain (*q.v.*), which contains seven large stars.

By this the northern wagoner has set
His sevenfold team behind the stedfast star [*the polestar*].

SPENSER: *Faerie Queene*, I, ii, 1.

Dryden calls the Great Bear *the Northern Car*, and similarly the crown in Ariadne has been called *the Northern Crown*.

Nose. A nose of wax. *See* WAX.

As plain as the nose on your face. Extremely obvious, patent to all.

Led by the nose. Said of a person who has no volition of his own but follows with docility the guidance of a stronger character. In another sense it appears in *Isaiah* xxxvii, 29:—"Because thy rage against me . . . is come up into mine ears, therefore will I put my hook in thy nose . . . and will turn thee back. . . ." Horses, asses, etc., led by bit and bridle, are led by the nose.

Hence Iago says of Othello, he was "led by the nose as asses are" (i, 3). But buffaloes, camels, and bears are actually led by a ring inserted in their nostrils.

Though authority be a stubborn bear, yet he is often led by the nose with gold.—*Winter's Tale*, iv, 4.

Nose tax. It is said that in the 9th century the Danes imposed a poll tax in Ireland, and that this was called the "Nose Tax," because those who neglected to pay were punished by having their noses slit.

On the nose. An American expression meaning exactly on time. It originated in the broadcasting studio, where the producer, when signalling to the performers, puts his finger on his nose when the programme is running to schedule time.

The Pope's nose. The rump of a fowl, which is also called the parson's nose. The phrase is said to have originated during the years following James II's reign, when anti-Catholic feeling was high.

To count noses. A horse-dealer counts horses by the *nose*, as cattle are counted by the *head*; hence, the expression is sometimes ironically used of numbering votes, as in the Division lobbies.

To cut off your nose to spite your face, or **to be revenged on your face.** To act out of pique in such a way as to injure yourself.

To follow one's nose. To go straight ahead; to proceed without deviating from the path.

Juan, following honour and his nose,
Rush'd where the thickest fire announced most foes.

BYRON: *Don Juan*, VIII, xxxii.

To keep one's nose to the grindstone. To keep hard at work. Tools, such as scythes, chisels, etc., are constantly sharpened on a stone or with a grindstone.

Be to the poor like onie whunstane,
And haud their noses lo the grunstane.

BURNS: *Dedication to Gavin Hamilton*.

To pay through the nose. To pay an excessive price, or at an exorbitant rate. There may be some connexion between this old phrase, "rhino" (*q.v.*), slang for money, and Gr. *rhinos*, the nose; or there may be an allusion to nose-bleeding and being *bled* for money.

To poke or **thrust one's nose in.** Officiously to intermeddle with other people's affairs; to intrude where one is not wanted.

To put one's nose out of joint. To supplant a person in another's good graces; to upset one's plans; to humiliate a conceited person.

To turn up one's nose. To express contempt. When a person sneers he turns up the nose by curling the upper lip.

Under one's very nose. Right before one; in full view.

Nosey. Very inquisitive; given to overmuch poking of the nose into other people's business. One who does this is often called a **Nosey Parker**, an epithet of unknown origin.

The Duke of Wellington was familiarly called "Nosey" by the soldiery. His "commander's face" with its strongly accentuated aquiline nose, was a very distinguishing feature of the Iron Duke. The nickname was also given to Oliver Cromwell. *See* COPPER-NOSE.

Nostradamus, Michel (nos' trä dä' müs). A French astrologer (1503-66) who published an annual "Almanack" as well as the famous *Centuries* (1555) containing prophecies which, though the book suffered papal condemnation in 1781, still occasion controversy from time to time. His prophecies are couched in most ambiguous language, hence the saying *as good a prophet as Nostradamus—i.e.* so obscure that none can make out your meaning.

Nostrum (nos' trüm) (Lat., our own). A term applied to a quack medicine, the ingredients of which are supposed to be a secret of the compounders; also, figuratively, to any political or other scheme that savours of the charlatan.

Notables. An assembly of nobles or notable men, in French history, selected by the king to form a parliament. They were convened in 1626 by Richelieu, and not again till 1787 when Louis XVI called them together with the view of relieving the nation of some of its pecuniary embarrassments. The last time they ever assembled was November 6th, 1788.

Notarikon (nō târ' i kon). A cabalistic word (Gr. *notarikon*, Lat. *notarius*, a shorthand-writer) denoting the old Jewish art of using each letter in a word to form another word, or using the initials of the words in a sentence to form another word, etc., as *Cabal* itself (*q.v.*) was fabled to have been formed from Clifford, Ashley, Buckingham, Arlington, and Lauderdale, and as the term *Ichthus* (*q.v.*) was applied to the Saviour. Other instances will be found under A.E.I.O.U.; CLIO; HEMPE; LIMP; and SMECTYMNUUS; *cp. also* HIP.

Notch. Out of all notch. *See* SCOTCH.

Note-sharer (U.S.A.). A bill discounter, usurer.

Nothing. Mere nothings. Trifles; unimportant things or events.

> You shapeless nothing in a dish,
> You that are but almost a fish—
>   COWPER: *The Poet, the Oyster*, etc.

Next to nothing. A very little. As "It will cost next to nothing," "He eats next to nothing."

Nothing doing! A slang expression, generally implying that you are disappointed in your expectations, or refuse some request.

Nothing venture, nothing have. If you daren't throw a sprat you mustn't expect to catch a mackerel; don't be afraid of taking a risk now and then. A very old proverb.

Out of nothing one can get nothing; the Latin *Ex nihilo nihil fit—i.e.* every effect must have a cause. It was the dictum by which Xenophanes, founder of the Eleatic School (*q.v.*), postulated his theory of the eternity of matter. Persius (*Satires*, iii, 84) has *De nihilo nihilum, in nihilum nil posse reverti*, From nothing nothing, and into nothing can nothing return.

We now use the phrase as equivalent to "You cannot get blood from a stone," or expect good work from one who has no brains.

That's nothing to you, or to do with you. It's none of your business.

There's nothing for it but . . . There's no alternative; take it or leave it.

To come to nothing. To turn out a failure; to result in naught.

To make nothing of. To fail to understand; not to succeed in some operation.

Novatians (nō vā' shánz). Followers of Novatianus, a presbyter of Rome in the 3rd century. They differed little from the orthodox Catholics, but maintained that the Church had no power to allow one who had lapsed to be readmitted.

Novella (nō vel' lá). A short story of the kind contained in Boccaccio's *Decameron*. These *novelle* were immensely popular in the 16th and 17th centuries and were the forerunners of the long novel that later developed from them, as also of the short story of more recent times.

November (Lat. *novem*, nine). The ninth month in the ancient Roman calendar, when the year began in March, now the eleventh. The old Dutch name was *Slaght-maand* (slaughter-month, the time when the beasts were slain and salted down for winter use); the old Saxon, *Wind-monath* (wind-month, when the fishermen drew their boats ashore, and gave over fishing till the next spring); it was also called *Blot-monath*—the same as *Slaght-maand*. In the French Republican calendar it was called *Brumaire* (fog-month, October 22nd to November 21st).

Novena (nō vē' nà). In R.C. devotions a prayer for some special object or occasion extended over a period of nine days. Various reasons have been adduced for the choice of nine days, but at root the custom seems to have been taken over from Roman paganism.

Nowell. See NOEL.

Noyades (nwa' yad) (Fr., drownings). A means of execution adopted by Carrier at Nantes, in the French Revolution (1793-4). Prisoners to be "removed" were first bound and then stowed in the hold of a vessel which had a movable bottom. This was sent to the middle of the Loire, the vessel was scuttled, and the victims drowned. Nero, at the suggestion of Anicetus, attempted to drown his mother in the same manner.

Nude. Naked. Rabelais (IV, xxix) says that a person without clothing is dressed in "grey and cold" of a comical cut, being "nothing before, nothing behind, and sleeves of the same." King Shrovetide, monarch of Sneak Island, was so arrayed.

Nullification (U.S.A.). In a political sense this term is said to have first been used by Thomas Jefferson in 1798. In 1832 South Carolina said they would *nullify* tariffs by not allowing duty to be collected at Charleston; hence those who set State rights above Federal Law are called *nullifiers*.

Numbers, Numerals. Pythagoras looked on numbers as influential principles; in his system—

1 was Unity, and represented Deity, which has no parts.
2 was Diversity, and therefore disorder; the principle of strife and all evil.
3 was Perfect Harmony, or the union of unity and diversity.
4 was Perfection; it is the first square ($2 \times 2 = 4$).
5 was the prevailing number in Nature and Art.
6 was Justice.
7 was the climacteric number in all diseases; called the *Medical Number*. See CLIMACTERIC.

With the ancient Romans 2 was the most fatal of all the numbers; they dedicated the second month to Pluto, and the second day of the month to the Manes.

In old ecclesiastical symbolism the numbers from 1 to 13 were held to denote the following:—

1 The Unity of God.
2 The hypostatic union of Christ, both God and man.
3 The Trinity.
4 The number of the Evangelists.
5 The wounds of the Redeemer: two in the hands, two in the feet, one in the side.
6 The creative week.
7 The gifts of the Holy Ghost (*Rev.* i, 12), and the seven times Christ spoke on the cross.
8 The number of beatitudes (*Matt.* v, 3-11).
9 The nine orders of angels.
10 The number of the Commandments.
11 The number of the Apostles who remained faithful.
12 The original college.
13 The final number after the conversion of Paul.

Apocalyptic number, 666. See NUMBER OF THE BEAST *below*.

Cyclic number. A number the final digit of whose square is the same, 5 (25) and 6 (36) are examples.

Golden number. See GOLDEN.

His days are numbered. They are drawing to a close; he is near death.

God hath numbered thy kingdom, and finished it.—*Dan.* v, 26.

Irrational number. A definite number not expressible in a definite number of digits, as the root of a number that cannot be exactly extracted.

Medical number. In the Pythagorean system (*see above*), 7.

Number of the Beast, The. 666; a mystical number of unknown meaning but referring to some man mentioned by St. John.

Let him that hath understanding count the number of the beast; for it is the number of a man; and his number is Six hundred threescore and six.—*Rev.* xiii, 18.

One of the most plausible suggestions is that it refers to Neron Cæsar, which in Hebrew characters with numerical value gives 666, whereas Nero, without the final "n," as in Latin, gives 616 (n = 50), the number given in many early MSS., according to Irenaeus.

Among the Cabalists every letter represented a number, and one's number was the sum of these equivalents to the letters in one's name. If, as is probable, the *Revelation* was written in Hebrew, the number would suit either Nero, Hadrian, or Trajan—all persecutors; if in Greek, it would fit Caligula or *Lateionos, i.e.* the Roman Empire; but almost any name in any language can be twisted into this number, and it has been applied to many persons assumed to have been Antichrist, or Apostates, Diocletian, Evanthas, Julian the Apostate, Luther, Mohammed, Paul V, Silvester II, Napoleon Bonaparte, Charles Bradlaugh, William II of Germany, and several others; as well as to certain phrases supposed to be descriptive of "the Man of Sin," as Vicar-General of God, Kakos Odegos (bad guide), Abinu Kadescha Papa (our holy father the pope), *e.g.*—

M	a	o	m	e	t	i	s
40,	1,	70,	40,	5,	300,	10,	200 = 666
L	a	t	e	i	n	o	s
30,	1,	300,	5,	10,	50,	70,	200 = 666

One suggestion is that St. John chose the number 666 because it just fell short of the holy number 7 in every particular; was straining at every point to get there, but never could, See *also* MYSTERIUM.

Odd numbers. See ODD.

Your number's up. You are in a very serious position or, sometimes, about to die. A soldier's phrase; in the American army a soldier who has just been killed or has died is said to have "lost his mess number." An older phrase used in the British Navy was "to lose the number of his mess."

Numerals. All our numerals and ordinals up to a million (with one exception) are Anglo Saxon. The one exception is *Second*, which is French. The Anglo-Saxon word was *other*, as First, Other, Third, etc., but as this was ambiguous the Fr. *seconde* was early adopted. Million is from Lat. *mille*, a thousand.

The primitive method of counting was by the fingers (*cp.* DIGIT); thus in the Roman system of numeration the first four were simply i, ii, iii, iiii; five was the outline of the hand simplified into a v; the next four figures were the two combined, thus, vi, vii, viii, viiii; and ten was a double v, thus, x. At a later period iiii and viiii were expressed by one less than five (i-v) and one less less than ten (i-x); nineteen was ten-plus-nine (x + ix), etc. *See also* ARABIC FIGURES.

Nuremberg (nū'. rem bĕrg). One of the principal cities of Bavaria (in German Nuernberg), with a long and honorable history, among other things famous as the home of Albrecht Dürer. After 1933 the Nazi party held its annual September conventions there, and in 1935 the infamous *Nuremberg Laws* were promulgated, dividing the people of Germany into three classes: Aryans (with full civic rights); Jews (with no rights); and mixed Aryans and Jews (who might acquire Aryan rights by marrying Germans). As the centre of Nazi Germany Nuremberg was chosen as the venue for the trial of the 23 chief Nazi leaders which opened November 21st, 1945 and concluded October 1st, 1946, when 3 were acquitted, 11 were condemned to death and the remainder sentenced to various terms of imprisonment.

Nursery. A room set apart for the use of young children (Lat. *nutrire*, to nourish); hence, a garden for rearing plants (tended by a *nursery-man*).

In horse-racing, *Nurseries* are races for two-year-olds; and figuratively the word is used of any place or school of training for the professions, etc.

Under William Rufus the Chancery became a nursery of clever and unscrupulous churchmen.—FREEMAN: *The Norman Conquest*, V, 135.

Nut. Slang for the head; perhaps so called from its resemblance to a nut.

Also slang for a swell young man about town, a dude (in this sense frequently written— and pronounced—with an initial *k*, *knut*); from a music-hall song of the early 20th century, sung by Basil Hallam, "I'm Gilbert the Filbert, the colonel of the K-nuts."

A hard nut to crack. A difficult question to answer; a hard problem to solve.

Here we go gathering nuts in May. This burden of the old children's game is a perversion of "Here we go gathering *knots* of may," referring to the old custom of gathering knots of flowers on May-day, or, to use the ordinary phrase, "to go a-maying." There are no nuts to be gathered in May.

Off one's nut. Crazy, daft.

To be off one's nut, to be nuts. Crazy, demented. Hence, **Nut house.** A lunatic asylum.

The "Iliad" in a nutshell. Pliny (vii, 21) tells us that the *Iliad* was copied in so small a hand that the whole work could lie in a walnut shell; his authority is Cicero (*Apud Gellium*, ix, 421).

> Whilst they (as Homer's *Iliad* in a nut)
> A world of wonders in one closet shut.
> *On the Tradescants' Monument, Lambeth Churchyard*.

Huet, Bishop of Avranches (d. 1721), proved by experiment that a parchment 27 by 21 centimetres would contain the entire *Iliad*, and that such a parchment would go into a common-sized nut; he wrote eighty verses of the *Iliad* (which contains in all 501,930 letters) on a single line of a page similar to this DICTIONARY. This would be 19,000 verses to the page, or 2,000 more than the *Iliad* contains.

In the Harleian MSS. (530) is an account of Peter Bales, a clerk of the Court of Chancery about 1590, who wrote out the whole Bible so small that he in-closed it in a walnut shell of English growth. Lalanne describes, in his *Curiosités Bibliographiques*, an edition of Rochefoucault's *Maximes*, published by Didot in 1829, on pages one inch square, each page containing 26 lines, and each line 44 letters. Charles Toppan, of New York, engraved on a plate one-eighth of an inch square 12,000 letters; the *Iliad* would occupy 42 such plates engraved on both sides. George P. Marsh says, in his *Lectures*, he has seen the entire Koran in a parchment roll four inches wide and half an inch in diameter.

Nutmeg State. The nickname of Connecticut. The story is that the inhabitants at one time manufactured wooden nutmegs for export.

O

O. The fifteenth letter of our alphabet, the fourteenth of the ancient Roman, and the sixteenth of the Phœnician and Semitic — in which it was called "the eye." Its name in Anglo-Saxon was *oedel*, home.

A headless man had a letter [o] to write,
He who read it [*naught*] had lost his sight.
The dumb repeated it [*naught*] word for word,
And deaf was the man who listened and heard [*naught*].

Dr. Whewell.

The Fifteen O's, or the O's of St. Bridget. Fifteen meditations on the Passion, composed by St. Bridget. Each begins with *O Jesu*, or a similar invocation.

The Seven O's, or the Great O's of Advent. The seven antiphons to the Magnificat sung during the week preceding Christmas. They commence respectively with *O Sapientia, O Adonai, O Radix Jesse, O Clavis David, O Oriens Splendor, O Rex gentium*, and *O Emmanuel*. They are sometimes called *The Christmas O's*.

O'. An Irish patronymic. (Gael, *ogha*, Ir. *oa*, a descendant.)

O' in *tam-o'-shanter, what's o'clock? cat-o'-nine-tails*, etc., stands for *of*; but in such phrases as *He comes home late o' night, I go to church o' Sundays*, it represents M.E. *on*.

O.K. All correct, all right; a reassuring affirmative that, coming from the U.S.A. to England has spread colloquially throughout several European languages. It derives probably from the Choctaw *oke*, meaning, "It is so." Andrew Jackson (1767-1845), who was notoriously illiterate, used the phrase. In the presidential campaign of 1828 Jackson's opponents asserted that he derived the abbreviation from his own spelling "orl korrect."

Oaf. A corruption of *ouph* (elf). A foolish lout or dolt is so called from the notion that idiots are changelings, left by the fairies in place of the stolen ones.

This guiltless oaf his vacancy of sense
Supplied, and amply too, by innocence.

BYRON: *Verses found in a Summer-house.*

Then ye returned to your trinkets; then ye contented your souls
With the flannelled fools at the wicket, or the muddied oafs at the goals.

RUDYARD KIPLING: *The Islanders.*

Oak. The oak was in ancient times sacred to the god of thunder because these trees are said to be more likely to be struck by lightning than any other. Among the Druids the oak was held in the greatest veneration.

Some Famous Oaks:

The *Abbot's Oak*, near Woburn Abbey, is so called because the Woburn abbot was hanged on one of its branches, in 1537, by order of Henry VIII.

The *Bull Oak*, Wedgenock Park, was growing at the time of the Conquest.

Cowthorpe Oak, near Wetherby, in Yorkshire, will hold seventy persons in its hollow. It is said to be over 1,600 years old.

The *Ellerslie Oak*, near Paisley, is reported to have sheltered Sir William Wallace and 300 of his men.

Fairlop Oak, in Hainault Forest, was 36 ft. in circumference a yard from the ground. It was blown down in 1820.

Owen Glendower's Oak, at Shelton, near Shrewsbury, was in full growth in 1403, for in this tree Owen Glendower witnessed the great battle between Henry IV and Henry Percy. Six or eight persons can stand in the hollow of its trunk. Its girth is $40\frac{1}{4}$ ft.

The *Major Oak*, Sherwood Forest, Edwinstowe, according to tradition, was a full-grown tree in the reign of King John. The hollow of the trunk will hold fifteen persons, but a new bark has considerably diminished the opening. Its girth is 37 or 38 ft., and the head covers a circumference of 240 ft.

The *Parliament Oak*, Clipston, in Sherwood Forest, was the tree under which Edward I, in 1282, held his parliament. He was hunting when a messenger came to tell him of the revolt of the Welsh. He hastily convened his nobles under the oak, and it was resolved to march at once against Llewelyn, who was slain. It was standing until early in this century.

The *Oak of the Partisans*, in Parcy Forest, St. Ouen, in the department of the Vosges, is 107 ft. in height. At the beginning of this century it was 706 years old.

Queen's Oak, Huntingfield, Suffolk, is so named because near this tree Queen Elizabeth I shot a buck.

The *Reformation Oak*, on Mousehold Heath, near Norwich, is where the rebel Ket held his court in 1549, and when the rebellion was stamped out nine of the ringleaders were hanged on this tree.

Robin Hood's Larder is an oak in Sherwood Forest. The tradition is that Robin Hood used its hollow trunk as a hiding-place for the deer he had slain. Late in the last century some schoolgirls boiled their kettle in it, and burnt down a large part of the tree, but every effort was made to preserve what remained.

The Royal Oak. See OAK-APPLE DAY.

Sir Philip Sydney's Oak, near Penshurst, was planted at his birth in 1554, and was commemorated by Ben Jonson and Waller.

The *Swilcar Oak*, in Needwood Forest, Staffordshire, is between 600 and 700 years old.

William the Conqueror's Oak, in Windsor Great Park, is 38 feet in girth.

The *Winfarthing Oak* is said to have been 700 years old at the time of the Conquest.

Oakley, Annie. An expert American markswoman (1860-1926), who in Buffalo Bill's Wild West Show, using a playing card as a target, centred a shot in each of the pips. From this performance of hers, and the resemblance of the card to a punched ticket, springs the American use of the name "Annie Oakley" to mean a complimentary ticket to a show, a meal ticket, or a pass on a railway.

Oaks, The. One of the "classic" horse-races; it is for three-year-old fillies, and is run at Epsom shortly before or after the Derby (*q.v.*). So called by the twelfth Earl of Derby, who established the race in 1779, from an estate of his near Epsom named "The Oaks."

Oannes (ō ăn' ēz). A Babylonian god having a fish's body and a human head and feet. In the daytime he lived with men to instruct them in the arts and sciences, but at night retired to the depths of the Persian Gulf. He has been identified with Ea of the cuneiform inscriptions.

Oar. To put your oar into my boat. To interfere with my affairs. "Paddle your own canoe, and don't put your oar into my boat."

Oasis (ō ā' sis) (Coptic, *ouahe*, from *ouih*, to dwell). A fertile spot in the midst of a desert country, especially in the deserts of Africa where wells of water or small lakes are to be found, and vegetation is pretty abundant. Hence a sudden cessation of pain, or a sudden

pleasure in the midst of monotonous existence, is sometimes called "a perfect oasis."

Oats. He has sown his wild oats. He has left off his gay habits and is become steady. The reference is to the folly of sowing wild, *i.e.* bad, grain instead of good; but it is worth noting that in Denmark the thick vapours which rise just before the land bursts into vegetation are called *Lokkens havre* (Loki's wild oats), and when the fine weather succeeds, the Danes say, "*Loki has sown his wild oats.*"

Obadiah (ō be dī' à). A slang name for a Quaker.

Obeah, Obi (ō 'be à). The belief in and practice of obeah, *i.e.*, a kind of sorcery or witchcraft prevalent in West Africa and formerly in the West Indies. *Obeah* is a native word, and signifies something put into the ground, to bring about sickness, death, or other disaster.

Obelisk. A tapering pillar stone, originally erected by the Egyptians, who placed them in pairs before temple portals. They were usually monoliths of pink syenite, with a base width one-tenth of the height and a copper-sheathed, pyramidal apex. Each of the obelisk's four faces bore incised hieroglyphs. The best known in England is Cleopatra's Needle, placed on the Victoria Embankment, London, in 1878, its partner being set up in Central Park, New York. These granite obelisks were erected in Heliopolis by Thothmes III, about 1475 B.C., and removed to Alexandria by Augustus Cæsar in 12 B.C.

The tallest of all obelisks is at Rome, taken there from Heliopolis by the Emperor Caligula and erected in the circus that is now the Piazza of St. Peter's. Although weighing some 320 tons, it was moved bodily on rollers by Pope Sixtus V, in 1586—an astonishing engineering feat, considering the appliances then available. The task was so tricky that spectators were forbidden to utter a sound on pain of death. But at a critical moment, when the immense weight of stone appeared to be straining the ropes to breaking point, one of the workmen, a sailor from San Remo, called "Acqua alle fune"—Water on the ropes—and saved the situation at the risk of his life.

The Obelisk of Luxor, in the Place de la Concorde, Paris, came from Thebes and was presented to Louis Philippe, in 1831, by the then Khedive of Egypt. Its hieroglyphs record the deeds of Rameses II (13th century, B.C.).

Oberammergau. *See* PASSION PLAY.

Obermann (ō' bĕr măn). The impersonation of high moral worth without talent, and the tortures endured by the consciousness of this defect. From Senancour's psychological romance of this name (1804), in which Obermann, the hero, is a dreamer perpetually trying to escape from the actual.

Oberon (ō' bĕr on). King of the Fairies, husband of Titania. Shakespeare introduces them in his *Midsummer Night's Dream*. The name is probably connected with Alberich (*q.v.*), the king of the elves.

He first appears in the mediæval French romance, *Huon de Bordeaux*, where he is a son of Julius Cæsar and Morgan le Fay. He was only three feet high, but of angelic face, and was lord and king of Mommur. At his birth the fairies bestowed their gifts—one was insight into men's thoughts, and another was the power of transporting himself to any place instantaneously; and in the fullness of time legions of angels conveyed his soul to Paradise.

Obi. *See* OBEAH.

Obiter dictum (ob' i tér dik' tŭm) (Lat.). An incidental remark, an opinion expressed by a judge, but not judicially. An *obiter dictum* has no authority beyond that of deference to the wisdom, experience, and honesty of the person who utters it; but a judicial sentence is the verdict of a judge bound under oath to pronounce judgment only according to law and evidence.

Object; Objective. *See* SUBJECT.

Oblong (U.S.A.). A late 19th-century slang term for a bank note.

Obverse. That side of a coin or medal which contains the principal device. Thus, the obverse of our coins is the side which contains the sovereign's head; the other side is the "reverse."

Occam's Razor. *Entia non sunt multiplicanda* (entities are not to be multiplied). With this axiom, which means that all unnecessary facts or constituents in the subject being analysed are to be eliminated, Occam dissected every question as with a razor.

William of Occam, the *Doctor Singularis et Invincibilis* (d. 1347), was a scholastic philosopher, famous as the great advocate and reviver of nominalism (*q.v.*).

Occasion. A lame old hag in Spenser's *Faerie Queene* (II, iv), mother of Furor, and symbolical of the cause of anger.

To improve the occasion. To draw a moral lesson from some event which has occurred.

Occult Sciences (Lat. *occultus*, related to *celāre*, to hide). Magic, alchemy, and astrology; so called because they were hidden mysteries.

Oceana (ō sē' á na). A philosophical treatise on the principles of government by James Harrington (1656). *See* COMMONWEALTHS, IDEAL.

Octavo (ok tā' vō). A book in which each sheet of paper is folded into eight leaves (16 pages); contracted thus—8vo. (Ital. *un' ottavo*, Fr. *in octavo*, Lat. *octo*, eight.) An octavo can be of almost any size, dependent entirely on the size of the sheets before folding.

October. The eighth month of the ancient Roman calendar (Lat. *octo*, eight) when the year began in March; the tenth of ours. The old Dutch name was *Wyn-maand*; the Anglo-Saxon, *Winmonath* (wine-month, or the time of vintage); also *Teo-monath* (tenth-month) and *Winter-fylleth* (winter full-moon). In the French Republican calendar it was *Vendémiaire* (time of vintage, September 22nd to October 21st).

A tankard of October. A tankard of the best and strongest ale, brewed in October.

October Club. A club of extreme Tories founded in 1710, with the password "October"—easily remembered "by a country gentleman who loved his ale." In the last years of Queen Anne's reign the October Club was a staunch supporter of the Jacobites.

Od. *See* ODYLE.

Odal. *See* UDAL.

Odd. There's luck in odd numbers. This is a very ancient fancy. According to the Pythagorean system, "all nature is a harmony," man is a full chord; and all beyond is Deity, so that *nine* represents Deity. A major chord consists of a fundamental or tonic, its major third, and its just fifth. As the odd numbers are the fundamental notes of nature, the last being Deity, it will be easy to see how they came to be considered the great or lucky numbers. *Cp.* DIAPASON; NUMBER.

Good luck lies in odd numbers. . . . They say, there is divinity in odd numbers, either in nativity, chance, or death—*Merry Wives of Windsor*, v, 1.

The odd numbers 1, 3, 5, 7, 9 (*which see*) seem to play a far more important part than the even numbers. *One* is Deity, *three* the Trinity, *five* the chief division, *seven* is the sacred number, and *nine* is three times three, the great climacteric.

Numero Dens impare gaudet (the god delights in odd numbers—*Virgil, Eclogues*, viii, 75). Three indicates the "beginning, middle, and end." The Godhead has three persons; so in classic mythology Hecate had threefold power; Jove's symbol was a triple thunderbolt, Neptune's a sea-trident, Pluto's a three-headed dog; the Fates were three, the Furies three, the Graces three, the Horæ three; the Muses three-times-three. There are seven notes, nine planets, nine orders of angels, seven days a week, thirteen lunar months, or 365 days a year, etc.; five senses, five fingers on the hand and toes on the foot, five continents, etc.

At odds. At variance.

Odin (ō' din). The Scandinavian name of the god called by the Anglo-Saxons Woden (*q.v.*). Odin was god of wisdom, poetry, war, and agriculture. He was god of the dead, also, and presided over banquets of those slain in battle. *See* VALHALLA. He became the *All-wise* by drinking of Mimir's fountain, but purchased the distinction at the cost of one eye, and is often represented as a one-eyed man wearing a hat and carrying a staff. His remaining eye is the Sun.

Odium theologicum (ō' di úm thē ō loj' i kúm) (Lat.). The bitter hatred of rival theologians. No wars so sanguinary as holy wars; no persecutions so relentless as religious persecutions; no hatred so bitter as theological hatred.

Odor lucri (ō' dôr lū' krī) (Lat.). The sweets of gain; the delights of money-making.

Odour. In good odour; in bad odour. In favour, out of favour; in good repute, in bad repute.

The odour of sanctity. In the Middle Ages it was held that a sweet and delightful odour was given off by the bodies of saintly persons at their death, and also when their bodies, if "translated," were disinterred. Hence the phrase, *he died in the odour of sanctity, i.e.* he died a saint. The Swedenborgians say that when the celestial angels are present at a deathbed, what is then cadaverous excites a sensation of what is aromatic.

There is an "odour of iniquity" as well as an "odour of sanctity," and Shakespeare has a strong passage on the odour of impiety. Antiochus and his wicked daughter were killed by lightning, and the poet says: —

> A fire from heaven came and shrivelled up
> Their bodies, e'en to loathing; for they so stunk
> That all those eyes adored them ere their fall
> Scorned now their hand should give them burial.
> *Pericles*, ii, 4.

Od's, used in oaths, as: —

Od's bodikins! or *Odsbody!* means "God's body."

Od's pittikins! God's pity.

Od's plessed will! (*Merry Wives of Windsor*, i, 1.)

Od rot 'em! See DRAT.

Od-zounds! God's wounds.

Odyle (od' īl). The name formerly given to the hypothetical force which emanates from a medium to produce the phenomena connected with mesmerism, spirit-rapping, table-turning, and so on. Baron von Reichenbach (1788-1869) called it *Od force*, and taught that it pervaded all nature, especially heat, light, crystals, magnets, etc., and was developed in chemical action; and also that it streamed from the fingers of specially sensitive persons.

> That od-force of German Riechenbach
> Which still from female finger-lips burns blue.
> MRS. BROWNING: *Aurora Leigh*, vii, 295.

Odyssey (od' i si). The epic poem of Homer which records the adventures of *Odysseus* (Ulysses) on his home-voyage from Troy. The word is an adjective formed out of the hero's name, and means the *things* or *adventures* of Ulysses.

Œcumenical Councils (ē kū men' ik àl). Ecclesiastical councils whose findings are — or were — recognized as applying to the whole of the Christian world (Gr. *oikoumenikos*, the inhabited — *ge*, earth being understood), and the members of which were drawn from the whole Church. They are: —

Nicæa, 325, 787; Constantinople, 381, 553, 680-1, 869; Ephesus, 431; Chalcedon, 451; Lateran, 1123, 1139, 1179, 1215, 1512-17; Lyons, 1245,1274; Vienne, 1311-13; Constance, 1414-18; Basle-Ferrara-Florence, 1431-43; Trent, 1545-1563; Vatican, 1869 (adjourned 1870 and still unfinished).

Of these the Church of England recognizes only six: —

Nicæa, 325, against the Arians.
Constantinople, 381, against "heretics."
Ephesus, 431, against the Nestorians and Pelagians.
Chalcedon, 451, when Athanasius was restored.
Constantinople, 553, against Origen.
Constantinople, 680, against the Monothelites.

Œdipus (ē' di pús) was the son of Laius, King of Corinth, and of Jocasta his wife. To avert the fulfilment of a prophecy Œdipus was exposed on the mountains as an infant and taken in and reared by the shepherds. When grown to manhood he unwittingly slew his father; then, having solved the riddle of the Sphinx, he became King of Thebes, thereby gaining the hand in marriage of Jocasta, his mother, of whose relationship to himself they were both ignorant. When the facts came to light Jocasta hanged herself and Œdipus tore out his own eyes.

An Œdipus complex is the psychoanalytical term for the sexual desire (usually unrecognized by himself) of a son for his mother and conversely an equally unrecognized jealous hatred of his father.

Off (Lat. *ab*, from, away). The house is a *mile* off—*i.e.* is "away" or "from" us a mile. The word preceding off defines its scope. To be "*well* off" is to be away or on the way towards well-being; to be *badly* off is to be away or on the way to the bad.

The **off-side** of horses when in pairs is that to the *right* hand of the coachman (*cp.* NEAR); and a "Soccer" football referee signals *Off-side* and awards a free kick when a player has kicked the ball—there being none of his opponents except the goal-keeper between himself and his opponents' goal—unless he himself has taken the ball there. The off-side rules vary with the different varieties of football.

, An act of behaviour, a thing, a person, etc., is said to be *a bit off* when it is not quite up to the mark—it is a bit "off colour" (*see* COLOUR); and a girl is said "to get off with a man" when she sets out to attract him and succeeds.

Office, The Holy. The Inquisition (*q.v.*).

Og, King of Bashan, according to Rabbinical mythology was an antediluvian giant, saved from the flood by climbing on the roof of the ark. After the passage of the Red Sea, Moses first conquered Sihon, and then advanced against the giant Og (whose bedstead, made of iron, was above 15 ft. long and nearly 7 ft. broad (*Deut*, iii, 11). The legend says that Og plucked up a mountain to hurl at the Israelites, but he got so entangled with his burden that Moses was able to kill him without much difficulty.

In Dryden's *Absalom and Achitophel* (*q.v.*), Og stands for Thomas Shadwell (*see* MAC-FLECKNOE). He was very large and fat.

Ogham (og' ăm). The alphabet in use among the ancient Irish and British nations. There were twenty characters, each of which was composed of any number of thin strokes from one to five, which were arranged and grouped above, below, or across a horizontal line.

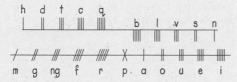

The word is connected with *Ogmius*, the name, according to Lucian, of a Gaulish god who presided over speech.

Ogier the Dane (ō' ji ĕr). One of the great heroes of mediæval romance; a paladin of Charlemagne, and son of Geoffrey, King of Denmark, of which country (as Holger Danske) he is still the national hero. Fairies attended at his birth, and bestowed upon him divers gifts. Among these fairies was Morgan le Fay (*q.v.*), who when the knight was a hundred years old embarked him for Avalon, "hard by the terrestrial paradise." On reaching the island he entered the castle, where he found a horse sitting at a banquet-table. The horse, who had once been a mighty prince, conducted him to Morgan le Fay, who gave him a ring which removed all infirmities and restored him to ripe manhood, and a crown which made him forget his country and past life, and introduced him to King Arthur. Two hundred years rolled on, and France was invaded by the Paynims. Morgan le Fay now sent Ogier to defend "*le bon pays de France*"; and when he had routed the invaders she took him back to Avalon, where he remains until the time for him to reappear on this earth of ours has arrived. William Morris gives a rendering of the romance in his *Earthly Paradise* (*August*).

Ogres of nursery story are giants of very malignant disposition, who live on human flesh. The word was first used (and probably invented) by Perrault in his *Contes* (1697), and is thought to be made up from *Orcus*, a name of Pluto, the god of Hades.

Ogygia (ō jij' i a). *See* CALYPSO.

Oi Polloi, properly *Hoi Polloi* (*q.v.*). The commonalty, the many. In University slang the "poll men," or those who take degrees without "honours."

Oil. Oil of palms. *See* PALM-OIL.

To pour oil on troubled waters. To soothe by gentle words; to bring about a state of calm after great anger or excitement, etc., by tact and diplomacy.

The allusion is to the well-known fact that during a storm at sea the force of the waves striking against a ship is very much lessened by pouring out oil. In Bede's *Ecclesiastical History* (735) it is said that St. Aidan gave a young priest who was to convoy a maiden destined for the bride of King Oswin a cruse of oil to pour on the sea if the waves became stormy. A storm did arise, and the priest, pouring the oil on the waves, actually reduced them to a calm.

To strike oil. To make a happy hit or valuable discovery. The phrase refers to hitting upon or discovering a bed of petroleum or mineral oil.

Old. Used in slang and colloquial talk as a term of endearment or friendship, as in *My* *dear old chap, my old man* (*i.e.* my husband); as a general disparagement, as in *Old cat, old fogy, old geezer, old stick-in-the-mud*; and as a common intensive, as in Shakespeare's "Here will be an old abusing of God's patience and the king's English," and in the modern *Any old thing will do*.

For names such as Old Grog, Harry, Noll, Rowley, Scratch, Tom, etc., *see these words*.

Old and Bold. *See* REGIMENTAL NICKNAMES.

Old Braggs. The Gloucestershire Regiment, the 28th Foot, raised in 1694. The name is derived from General Philip Bragg, who was colonel of the regiment from 1734 to 1759.

Old Contemptibles. The British Expeditionary Force that crossed to France in 1914 and fought in the battle and retreat from Mons. The phrase originated in the alleged comment of the Kaiser about "the contemptible British army."

Old Cracow Bible. *See* BIBLE, SPECIALLY NAMED.

Old Dominion. Virginia. Every Act of Parliament up to the Declaration of Independence designated Virginia "the Colony and Dominion of Virginia." Captain John Smith, in his *History of Virginia* (1629), calls this "colony and dominion" *Ould Virginia*, in contradistinction to *New England*, and other British settlements.

Old Dozen. *See* REGIMENTAL NICKNAMES.

Old Fogs. *See* REGIMENTAL NICKNAMES.

Old Glory. The United States Flag. *See* STARS AND STRIPES.

Old Guard. The Imperial Guard created by Napoleon in 1804 and composed of picked men, the flower of the French army. Devoted to the Emperor, with a magnificent uniform including a huge bearskin hat, with better pay and rationing than the rest of the army, the Old Guard were to be relied upon in any desperate strait of battle, and it was they who made the last charge of the French at Waterloo. Figuratively the phrase Old Guard is used for the stalwarts of any party or movement.

Old Hickory. The nickname of General Andrew Jackson (1767-1845), 7th President of the U.S.A.; it arose from the staunchness and strength of his character.

Old King Cole. *See* COLE.

Old Lady of Threadneedle Street. *See* THREADNEEDLE.

Old Man Eloquent. Isocrates; so called by Milton. When he heard of the result of the

battle of Chæronea, which was fatal to Grecian liberty, he died of grief.

That dishonest victory
At Chæronea, fatal to liberty,
Killed with report that Old Man Eloquent
MILTON: *Sonnets.*

This name was also applied to John Quincy Adams (1767-1848), 6th President of the U.S.A., 1825-29.

Old Man of the Mountain. Hassan-ben-Sabah, the sheikh Al Jebal, and founder of the sect called Assassins (*q.v.*).

Old Man of the Sea. In the *Arabian Nights* story of *Sinbad the Sailor*, the Old Man of the Sea hoisted himself on the shoulders of Sinbad and clung there for many days and nights, much to the discomfort of Sinbad, who finally released himself by making the Old Man drunk. Hence, any burden, figurative or actual, of which it is impossible to free oneself without the greatest exertions is spoken of as an Old Man of the Sea.

Old Rough and Ready. General Zachary Taylor (1784-1850), 12th President of the U.S.A., 1849-50.

Old School Tie. Literally a necktie of the colours of the wearer's public school, but more often used figuratively in a pejorative sense as a symbol of the class distinction allegedly assumed by those who went to a public school.

Old Style—New Style. Terms used in chronology; the *Old Style* being the Julian Calendar (*q.v.*), and the *New Style* the Gregorian (*q.v.*). *See also* CALENDAR.

Old World. So Europe, Asia, and Africa are called when compared with North and South America (the New World).

Oligarchy (ol′ i gar ki) (Gr. *oligos*, the few; *archē*, rule). A government in which the supreme power is vested in a small number of families or a few members of a class.

Olio (ō′ li ō) (Span, *olla*, a stew, or the pot in which it is cooked, from Lat. *olla*, a pot). In Spain a mixture of meat, vegetables, spices, etc., boiled together and highly seasoned; hence, any hotchpotch of various ingredients, as a miscellaneous collection of verses, drawings, pieces of music, etc.

Olive. In ancient Greece the olive was sacred to Pallas Athene, in allusion to the story (*see* ATHENS) that at the naming of Athens she presented it with an olive tree. It was the symbol of peace, and also an emblem of fecundity, brides wearing or carrying an olive garland as ours do a wreath of orange blossom. A crown of olive was the highest distinction of a citizen

who had deserved well of his country, and was
the highest prize in the Olympic Games.

In the O.T. the subsiding of the Flood was
demonstrated to Noah by the return of a dove
bearing an olive leaf in her beak (*Gen.* viii, 11).

To hold out the olive branch. To make
overtures for peace; in allusion to the olive
being an ancient symbol of peace. In some of
Numa's medals the king is represented holding
an olive twig, indicative of a peaceful reign.

Olive branches. A facetious term for
children in relation to their parents; the allusion
is to "Thy wife shall be as a fruitful vine . . . thy
children like olive plants round about thy
table" (*Ps.* cxxviii, 3).

> The wife and olive branches of one Mr. Kenwigs.—
> DICKENS: *Nicholas Nickleby*, xiv.

Oliver. Charlemagne's favourite paladin,
who, with Roland, rode by his side. He was the
son of Regnier, Duke of Genoa (another of the
paladins), and brother of the beautiful Aude.
His sword was called *Hauteclaire*, and his horse
Ferrant d'Espagne.

A Roland for an Oliver. *See* ROLAND.

Olympia. The ancient name of a valley in
Elis, Peloponnesus, so called because here
were held the famous games in honour of the
Olympian Zeus (*see below*). In the valley was
built the Altis, an enclosure of about 500 ft. by
600 ft., which contained, besides the temple
of Zeus, the Herœum, the Metroum, etc., the
Stadium, with gymnasia, baths, etc. Hence,
the name has been given to large buildings (more
particularly the great halls and amphitheatre
near Hammersmith, London) in which sporting
events, spectacles, exhibitions, and so on can
be presented under cover.

Olympiad. Among the ancient Greeks, a
period of four years, being the interval between
the celebrations of the Olympic Games (*q.v.*).
The first Olympiad began in 776 B.C., and the
last (the 23rd) in A.D. 393.

Olympian Zeus or **Jove.** A statue by
Phidias, one of the "Seven Wonders of the
World." Pausanias (vii, 2) says when the sculptor
placed it in the temple at Olympia (433 B.C.),
he prayed the god to indicate whether he was
satisfied with it, and immediately a thunderbolt
fell on the floor of the temple without doing the
slightest harm.

It was a chryselephantine statue, *i.e.* made
of ivory and gold, and though seated on a
throne, was 60 ft. in height. The left hand
rested on a sceptre, and the right palm held a
statue of Victory in solid gold. The robes were

of gold, and so were the four lions which
supported the footstool. The throne was of
cedar, embellished with ebony, ivory, gold, and
precious stones.

It was removed to Constantinople in the 5th
century A.D.; and perished in the great fire of 475.

Olympic Games. The greatest of the four
sacred festivals of the ancient Greeks, held at
Olympia (*q.v.*) every fourth year, in the month
of July. The festival began with sacrifices and
included racing, wrestling, and all kinds of
contests, ending on the fifth day with processions, sacrifices, and banquets to the victors—
who were garlanded with olive leaves.

The Olympic Games were revived in 1896,
the first meeting being held at Athens in that
year. These were followed at four-yearly intervals:
1900 (Paris), 1904 (St. Louis), 1908 (London),
1912 (Stockholm), 1920 (Antwerp), 1924
(Paris), 1928 (Amsterdam), 1932 (Los Angeles),
1936 (Berlin), 1948 (London), 1952 (Helsinki).
The games in 1916, 1940, and 1944 were not
held on account of World Wars I and II.

Olympus. The home of the gods of ancient
Greece, where Zeus held his court, a mountain
about 9,800 ft. high on the confines of
Macedonia and Thessaly. The name is used
for any pantheon, as "Odin, Thor, Balder, and
the rest of the Northern Olympus."

Om. Among the Brahmans, the mystic
equivalent for the name of the Deity; it has
been adopted by modern occultists to denote
absolute goodness and truth or the spiritual
essence.

Omar Khayyam (ō′ mar kī yăm′), Persian
poet, astronomer, and mathematician, lived at
Nishapur, where he died about the age of 50 in
A.D. 1123. He was known chiefly for his work
on algebra until Edward Fitzgerald published a
poetical translation of his poems in 1859. Little
notice of this was taken, however, until the
early '90s when the Rubaiyat took Britain and
America by storm. It is frankly hedonistic in
tone, but touched with a melancholy that
attunes with eastern and western pessimism
alike. Fitzgerald never pretended that his work
was other than a free version of the original; he
made several revisions, but did not improve on
his first text.

Ombre (om′ b ér). A card-game, introduced
into England from Spain in the 17th century,
and very popular till it was supplanted by
quadrille, about 1730. It was usually played
by three persons, and the eights, nines, and tens
of each suit were left out. Prior has an epigram

on the game; he was playing with two ladies, and Fortune gave him "success in every suit but hearts." Pope immortalized the game in his *Rape of the Lock*.

Omega (ō 'meg à). The last letter of the Greek alphabet. *See* ALPHA.

Omelet (om' lĕt). **You can't make omelets without breaking eggs.** Said by way of warning to one who is trying to "get something for nothing"—to accomplish some desired object without being willing to take the necessary trouble or make the necessary sacrifice. The phrase is a translation of the French *On ne saurait faire une omelette sans casser des œufs*.

Omen (ō' men). Some phenomenon or unusual event taken as a prognostication either of good or evil; a prophetic sign or augury. The Latin word was adopted in the 16th century; its origin is unknown, but it is thought to be connected with *audire*, to hear. Some well-known examples of accepting omens, apparently evil, as of good augury, are:—

Leotychides II, of Sparta, was told by his augurs that his projected expedition would fail, because a viper had got entangled in the handle of the city key. "Not so," he replied. "The key caught the viper."

When Julius Cæsar landed at Adrumetum he happened to trip and fall on hit face. This would have been considered a fatal omen by his army; but, with admirable presence of mind, he exclaimed, "Thus I take possession of thee, O Africa!" Told of Scipio also.

When William the Conqueror leaped upon the English shore he fell on his face and a great cry went forth that it was an ill-omen; but the duke exclaimed: "I have taken seisin of this land with both my hands."

Omnibus (om' ni bùs) (dative pl. of Lat. *omnis*, all, for all). The name was first applied to the public vehicle in France in 1828. In the following year it was adopted by Shillibeer for the vehicles which he started on the Paddington (now Marylebone) Road, London. The plural is *omnibuses*, and the word is generally abbreviated to *bus*, without any initial apostrophe—just as *cabriolet* became *cab*, not *cab'*.

Omnium (om' ni ùm) (Lat., of all). The particulars *of all* the items, or the assignment *of all* the securities, of a government loan.

On dit (ong dē) (Fr., they say). A rumour, a report, a bit of gossip. "There is an *on dit* that the prince is to marry soon."

One. The word has a good many indefinite applications, as a person or thing of the kind implied or already mentioned (*I like those hats*; *I must buy one*), an unspecified person (*One doesn't do that sort of thing*), someone or something, anyone or anything.

There is One above is a reference to the Deity; *the Evil One* is the Devil.

By one and one. Singly, one at a time; entirely by oneself.

He was one too many for me. He was a little bit too clever, he outwitted me.

Number one. Oneself; hence, to take care of number one, to look after oneself, to seek one's own interest; to be selfish.

One and all. Everybody individually and jointly. The phrase is the motto of Cornishmen.

One-horse. Third-rate, petty, insignificant; as, *a one-horse show*, *a one-horse town*, etc. The phrase is of American origin, and the allusion was to a town so poor and idle that one horse was enough for all its transportation.

One of these days. At some unspecified time in the future, generally the rather remote and uncertain future.

To go one better than he did. To do a little more, etc., than he did. The phrase is from card-playing; at poker if one wishes to continue betting one has to "go" at least "one better," *i.e.* raise the stake.

Oneida Community, The. *See* PERFECTIONISTS.

Onomatopeia (on ō măt ō pē' â). The grammatical term for forming a word by imitating the sound associated with the object designated, or for a word that appears to suggest its nature or qualities. "Cuckoo" and "tingle" are examples of onomatopeia. The word itself comes from the Greek for "making of words."

Onus (ō' nus) (Lat.). The burden, the responsibility; as, "The whole *onus* must rest on your own shoulders."

Onus probandi (Lat., the burden of proving). The obligation of proving some proposition, accusation, etc.; as, "The *onus probandi* rests with the accuser."

Onyx (on 'iks) is Greek for a finger-nail; so called because the colour of an onyx resembles that of the finger-nail.

Oom Paul. "Uncle" Paul, the name familiarly applied to Paul Kruger (1825-1902), President of the Transvaal Republic and inspirer of the Dutch resistance to the British rule in South Africa.

Opal (Gr. *opallios*, probably from Sansk. *upala*, a gem). This semi-precious stone—a vitreous form of hydrous silica—is well known for its play of iridescent colours, and has long been considered to bring ill luck. Alphonso XII of Spain (1874-85) is said to have had one that seemed to be fatal. On his wedding-day he presented it in a ring to his wife, and her death occurred soon afterwards. Before the funeral he gave the ring to his sister, who died a few days later. The king then presented it to his sister-in-law, and she died within three months. Alphonso, astounded at these fatalities, resolved to wear the ring himself, and within a very short time he too was dead. The Queen Regent then suspended it from the neck of the Virgin of Almudena of Madrid.

> Not an opal
> Wrapped in a bay-leaf in my left fist,
> To charm their eyes with.
> > BEN JONSON: *New Inn*, i, 6.

Open door. In political parlance the principle of admitting all nations to a share in a country's trade, etc. The phrase is also applied to any loophole being left for the possibility of negotiation between contending parties, nations, etc.

Opera. A production for the stage composed of music and drama. The dialogue is mostly in verse and is sung to orchestral accompaniment; lyrics are an important element and in older operas a ballet was often included. The rise of opera began about 1582, but it was not until the first opera house was opened in Venice, in 1637, that it became popular as a form of entertainment. Alessandro Scarlatti (1659-1725) established the aria as a legitimate form of expressing soliloquy, and introduced the recitativo. In England Henry Purcell (*c.* 1658-95) was the father of opera, writing some 42 musical works for the stage, some of them, such as *Dido and Æneas* (1689) being full operas. In 1930 the British Government allocated a yearly sum of £17,000 for subsidizing opera in London and the provinces.

Operetta is a very light opera with spoken dialogue, such as the Gilbert and Sullivan works.

Operations. In World War II operations were given code-names by which they could be known, for reasons of convenience and security. These should be differentiated from names, such as FIDO and PLUTO, which were made up of initials and had a special meaning; these will be found under their separate headings. Among the most important Allied operations were:—

Anvil. American and French landing in Southern France.

Capital. The investing of North and Central Burma by Admiral Lord Mountbatten and General Stilwell.

Crossroads. First atom bomb test at Bikini, May 1946.

Dynamo. British evacuation from Dunkirk.

Eclipse. First plan for Allied occupation of Germany.

Epsom. Major British operation south of Caen to break out of the beachhead, June 1944.

Goldflake. Large-scale switch of British and Canadian troops from the Italian front to that in Northwest Europe, February 1945.

Neptune. Naval name for the operations against North-west France, 1944.

Overlord. Allied invasion of North-west Europe, 1944. First known as *Roundup.*

Torch. Allied invasion of North-west Africa, 1942.

Operations, Base of, Line of. *See* BASE.

Opinicus (op in' i kŭs). A fabulous monster, composed of dragon, camel, and lion, used in heraldry. It forms the crest of the Barber Surgeons of London. The name seems to be a corruption of *Ophincus*, the classical name of the constellation, the serpent (Gr. *ophis*).

Opium-eater. Thomas De Quincey (1785-1859), author of *The Confessions of an English Opium-Eater* (1821).

Opposition. The constitutional term for whichever of the great political parties is not in power. In the House of Commons the Opposition sits on the benches on the Speaker's left, on the front bench being the leaders who are, generally, ministers-elect waiting for a change of Government. The Leader of the Opposition, elected by his Party, receives an official salary from the State of £2,000 a year.

Optime (op' ti mē). In Cambridge phraseology a graduate in the second or third division of the Mathematical Tripos, the former being *Senior Optimes* and the latter *Junior Optimes*. The term comes from the Latin phrase formerly used—*Optime disputasti* (You have disputed very well). The class above the Optimes is composed of Wranglers (*q.v.*).

Optimism. The doctrine that "whatever is, is right," that everything which happens is for the best. It was originally set forth by Leibnitz (1646-1716) from the postulate of the omnipotence of God, and is cleverly travestied by Voltaire in his *Candide, ou l'Optimisme* (1759), where Dr. Pangloss continually harps on the maxim that "all is for the best in this best of all possible worlds."

Opus (ō' pus) (Lat. a work). *See* MAGNUM OPUS.

Oracle (Lat. *oraculum*, from *orāre*, to speak, to pray). The answer of a god or inspired priest to an inquiry respecting the future; the deity giving responses; the place where the deity could be consulted, etc.; hence, a person whose utterances are regarded as profoundly wise, an infallible, dogmatical person—

> I am Sir Oracle,
> And when I ope my lips let no dog bark.
> > *Merchant of Venice*, i, 1.

In ancient Greece oracles were extremely numerous, and very expensive to those who consulted them. The most famous were the—

Oracle of APOLLO, at Delphi, the priestess of which was called the Pythoness; at Delos, and at Claros.

Oracle of DIANA, at Colchis; of ESCULAPIUS, at Epidaurus, and another in Rome.

Oracle of HERCULES, at Athens, and another at Gades.

Oracle of JUPITER, at Dodona (the most noted); another at Ammon, in Libya; another in Crete.

Oracle of MARS, in Thrace; MINERVA, in Mycenæ; PAN, in Arcadia.

Oracle of TRIPHONIUS, in Bœotia, where only men made the responses.

Oracle of VENUS, at Paphos, another at Aphaca, and many others.

In most of the temples women, sitting on a tripod, made the responses, many of which were either ambiguous or so obscure as to be misleading: to this day, our word *oracular* is still used of obscure as well as of authoritative pronouncements.

The difficulty of making head or tail of oracles is well illustrated by the following classic examples:—

When Crœsus consulted the Delphic oracle respecting a projected war, he received for answer, "*Crœsus Halyn penetrans magnum, pervertet opum vim*" (When Crœsus passes over the river Halys, he will overthrow the strength of an empire). Crœsus supposed the oracle meant he would overthrow the enemy's empire, but it was his own that he destroyed.

Pyrrhus, being about to make war against Rome, was told by the oracle: "*Aio te, Æacide, Romanos vincere posse*" (I say, Pyrrhus, that you the Romans can conquer), which may mean either *You, Pyrrhus, can overthrow the Romans*, or *Pyrrhus, the Romans can overthrow you*.

Another prince, consulting the oracle on a similar occasion, received for answer, "*Ibis redibis nunquam per bella peribis*" (You shall go you shall return never you shall perish by the war), the interpretation of which depends on the position of the comma; it may be *You shall return, you shall never perish in the war*, or *You shall return never, you shall perish in the war*, which latter was the fact.

Philip of Macedon sent to ask the oracle of Delphi if his Persian expedition would prove successful, and received for answer—

The ready victim crowned for death
Before the altar stands.

Philip took it for granted that the "ready victim" was the King of Persia, but it was Philip himself.

When the Greeks sent to Delphi to know if they would succeed against the Persians, they were told—

Seed-time and harvest, weeping sires shall tell
How thousands fought at Salamis and fell.

But whether the Greeks or the Persians were to be "the weeping sires," no indication was given, nor whether the thousands "about to fall" were to be Greeks or Persians.

When Maxentius was about to encounter Constantine, he consulted the guardians of the Sibylline Books as to the fate of the battle, and the prophetess told him, "*Illo die hostem Romanorum esse periturum*," but whether Maxentius or Constantine was "the enemy of the Roman people" the oracle left undecided.

In the Bible we have a similar equivoque: When Ahab, King of Israel, was about to wage war on the king of Syria, and asked Micaiah if Ramoth-Gilead would fall into his hands, the prophet replied, "Go, for the Lord will deliver the city into the hands of the king" (1 *Kings* xxii, 15, 35).

The Oracle of the Holy Bottle. The oracle to which Rabelais (Bks. iv and v) sent Panurge and a large party to obtain an answer to a question which had been put to sibyl and poet, monk and fool, philosopher and witch, judge and fortune-teller: "whether Panurge should marry or not?" The oracle was situated at Bacbuc (*q.v.*), "near Cathay in Upper Egypt," and the story has been interpreted as a satire on the Church. The celibacy of the clergy was for long a moot point, and the "Holy Bottle" or cup to the laity was one of the moving causes of the schisms from the Church. The crew setting sail for the Bottle refers to Anthony, Duke of Vendôme, afterwards king of Navarre, setting out in search of religious truth.

Orange. This distinctive epithet of the ultra-Protestants of Northern Ireland and of Ulster-men generally, it is said, became attached to them because in 1795 two members of the famous "Orange Lodge" of Freemasons (which had been revived in Belfast about 1780) were active in raising the Orange Lodges (*see below*), an armed force of Protestant volunteers—hence called "Orange boys"—in defence of civil and religious liberty.

The Orange Lodge was named in honour of William of Orange (William III), the Protestant opposer of James II in the "Glorious Revolution" of 1689, and the victor at the Battle of the Boyne (1690).

Orange Lodges or Clubs are referred to in print as early as 1769. Thirty years later the Orangemen were a very powerful society, having a "grand lodge" extending over the entire province of Ulster and through all the centres of Protestantism in Ireland.

Orangemen. A name given to the members of an Orange Lodge; originating in their respect for the memory of William III of the House of Orange.

Orange blossom. The conventional decoration for the bride at a wedding, introduced as a custom into England iron France about 1820. The *orange* is said to indicate the hope of fruitfulness, as few trees are more prolific, while the *white blossoms* are symbolical of innocence.

Hence the phrase, **to go gathering orange blossoms**, to look for a wife.

Orange Free State. This province of the Union of South Africa originated in 1824 when some Dutch farmers from Cape Colony settled across the Orange River. They had trouble with the Basutos, but they held on and in 1854 formed a republic with this name. In 1899 the Orange Free State joined the Transvaal in making war on Great Britain and it was consequently annexed in 1900. In 1907 it was given responsible government and three years later it joined the Union.

Orange Peel. A nickname given to Sir Robert Peel when Chief Secretary for Ireland (1812-18), on account of his strong anti-Catholic proclivities.

Orator. Orator Henley. John Henley (1692-1756), who for about thirty years delivered lectures on theological, political, and literary subjects.

Orator Hunt. Henry Hunt (1773-1835), a politician and radical reformer was so named. He presided at the famous "Peterloo" meeting (*q.v.*) and as M.P. for Preston (1830-33) presented the first petition to Parliament in favour of woman's rights.

Oratorio is sacred story or drama set to music, in which solo voices, chorus, and instrumental music are employed. In 1574 St. Philip Neri introduced the acting and singing of sacred dramas in his Oratory at Rome, and it is from this that the term comes. Oratorio has appealed to many of the greatest composers of the past, outstanding among them being Handel.

Orc. A sea-monster fabled by Ariosto, Drayton, Sylvester, etc., to devour men and women. The name was sometimes used for the whale. Milton speaks of the Mount of Paradise being "pushed by the hornéd flood":—

Down the great river to the opening Gulf,
And there take root, an island salt and bare,
The haunt of seals, and orcs, and sea-mews' clang.
Paradise Lost, xi, 833.

Orchard properly means a garden-yard. *Hortyard* was one of the old spellings, and in this form its connexion with Lat. *hortus*, a garden, is clear.

The hortyard entering [he] admires the fair
And pleasant fruits. GEORGE SANDYS.

Ordeal (A.S. *ordel*, related to *adædan*, to deal, allot, judge). The ancient Anglo-Saxon and Teutonic practice of referring disputed questions of criminality to supernatural decision, by subjecting the suspected person to physical tests by fire, boiling water, battle, etc.; hence, figuratively, an experience testing endurance, patience, courage, etc.

This method of "trial" was based on the belief that God would defend the right, even by miracle if needful. All ordeals, except the ordeal of battle, were abolished in England by law in the early 13th century.

In **Ordeal of battle** the accused person was obliged to fight anyone who charged him with guilt. This ordeal was allowed only to persons of rank.

Ordeal of fire was also for persons of rank only. The accused had to hold in his hand a piece of red-hot iron, or to walk blindfold and barefoot among nine red-hot plough-shares laid at unequal distances. If he escaped uninjured he was accounted innocent, otherwise not. This might be performed by deputy.

Ordeal of hot water was for the common people. The accused was required to plunge his arm up to the elbow in boiling water, and was pronounced guilty if the skin was injured in the experiment. **Ordeal of cold water.** The accused, being bound, was tossed into a river; if he *sank* he was acquitted, but if he *floated* he was accounted guilty. This ordeal remained in use for the trial of witches to comparatively recent times.

The **Ordeal of the Eucharist** was for priests, it was supposed that the elements would choke him if taken by a guilty man.

In the **Ordeal of the Corsned** (*q.v.*) consecrated bread and cheese was similarly given. Godwin, Earl of Kent, is said to have been choked when, being accused of the murder of the king's brother, he submitted to this ordeal.

Order! When members of the House of Commons and other debaters call out *Order!* they mean that the person speaking is in some way breaking the rule or *order* of the assembly, and has to be *called to order*.

Architectural orders. *See* ARCHITECTURE.

Holy orders. A clergyman is said to be *in holy orders* because he belongs to one of the *orders* or ranks of the Church. In the Church of England these are three, viz., Deacon, Priest, and Bishop; in the Roman Catholic Church there is a fourth, that of Sub-deacon.

In ecclesiastical use the term also denotes a fraternity of monks or friars (as the *Franciscan Order*), and also the Rule by which the fraternity is governed.

The order of the day. In the House of Commons the ordinary public business of each day as classified as consisting of notices of motions and orders of the day. A motion becomes an order of the day as soon as the debate on it has been adjourned by order of the House to a particular day. *See* QUESTION.

Ordinary. In Law an ordinary is one who has an "ordinary or regular jurisdiction" in his own right, and not by depute. Thus a judge who has authority to take cognizance of causes in his own right is an ordinary. A bishop is an ordinary in his own diocese, because he has authority to take cognizance of ecclesiastical matters therein; an archbishop is the ordinary of his province, having authority in his own right to receive appeals therein from inferior jurisdictions. The chaplain of Newgate was also called the ordinary thereof.

A meal prepared at an inn at a fixed rate for all comers is called an "ordinary"; hence, also, the inn itself: —

'Tis almost dinner; I know they stay for you at the ordinary.—BEAUMONT AND FLETCHER: *Scornful Lady*, iv, 1.

And in Heraldry the "ordinary" is a simple charge, such as the chief, pale, fesse, bend, bar, chevron, cross, or saltire.

Oregon Trail. This started as a number of paths that left the Missouri River at almost any good crossing point between Independence, Missouri, and Omaha, Nebraska. The various feeders met on the banks of the Platte River in Nebraska, at a point somewhat east of the present Kearney. At this point they merged with the Mormon Trail as far as Fort Laramie. There the Cherokee Trail, often used by migrants from the south, joined the united Oregon-Mormon Trail. The goal and true end of the Trail was at Fort Vancouver, or at the point opposite to it at the mouth of the Willamette. Many people from the Middle West, and the Eastern States, as well as immigrants from Europe used it as it was the safest overland route to the gold-fields of California.

Orgies (ôr′ jez). Drunken revels, riotous feasts; hence, figuratively, wild or licentious extravagance. So called from the Gr. *orgia*, the secret, nocturnal festivals in honour of Bacchus (*q.v.*).

Orgoglio (ôr gō′ lyō) (Ital., Arrogant Pride, or Man of Sin). In Spenser's *Faerie Queene* (I, vii, and viii), a hideous giant as tall as three men, son of Earth and Wind.

He typifies the tyrannical power of the Church of Rome; in slaying him Arthur first cut off his *left arm*—i.e. Bohemia was first cut off from the Church of Rome; then the giant's *right leg*—i.e. England, when Orgoglio fell to earth, and was easily dispatched.

Orientation. The placing of the east window of a church due east (Lat. *oriens*), that is, so that the rising sun may shine on the altar. Anciently, churches were built with their axes pointing to the rising sun on the saint's day; so that a church dedicated to St. John was not parallel to one dedicated to St. Peter, but in the building of modern churches the saint's day is not, as a rule, regarded.

Figuratively, orientation is the correct placing of one's ideas, mental processes, etc., in relation with themselves and with current thought—the ascertainment of one's "bearings."

Oriflamme (ôr′ i flăm) (Fr., "flame of gold"). The ancient banner of the kings of France, first used as a national banner in 1119. It was a crimson flag cut into three "vandykes" to represent "tongues of fire," with a silken tassel between each, and was carried on a gilt staff (*un glaive tout doré où est attachè une bannière vermeille*). This celebrated standard was the banner of St. Denis; but when the Counts of Vexin became possessed of the abbey it passed into their hands. In 1082 Philippe I united Vexin to the crown, and the sacred Oriflamme fell to the king. It was carried to the field after the battle of Agincourt, in 1415. The romance writers say that "mescreans" (infidels) were blinded by merely looking on it. In the *Roman de Garin* the Saracens cry, "If we only set eyes on it we are all dead men"; and Froissart records that it was no sooner unfurled at Rosbecq than the fog cleared away from the French, leaving their enemies in misty darkness.

In the 15th century the Oriflamme was succeeded by the blue standard powdered with fleurs-de-lis, and the last heard of the original Oriflamme is a mention in the inventory of the Abbey of St. Denis dated 1534.

Original Sin. *See* SIN.

Orion (o rī′ ón). A giant hunter of Greek mythology, noted for his beauty. He was blinded by Œnopion, but Vulcan sent Cedalion to be his guide, and his sight was restored by exposing his eyeballs to the sun. Being slain by Diana, he was made one of the constellations, and is supposed to be attended with stormy weather. His wife was named Sidē, and his dogs Arctophonus and Ptoophagus.

With fierce winds Orion armed
Hath vexed the Red-Sea coast.
MILTON: *Paradise Lost*, I, 305.

The constellation Orion is the clearest defined in the northern winter sky. Below the "shoulder" stars, Betelgeuse and Bellatrix, are the three stars forming the "sword," close to which is the nebula. The "feet," Rugel and Salph, point to Sirius, the brightest star in the heavens.

Orkneys. The name is probably connected with the old *orc* (*q.v.*), a whale, and either Gaelic *innis* or Norse *ey*, an island—"the isles of whales." For centuries the Orkneys were a jarldom of Norway or Denmark, and it was not till 1590 that the latter renounced its claim to sovereignty. They had passed to the Scottish crown in 1468 after having been in the possession of the Earls of Angus for nearly 250 years.

Orlando. The Italian form of "Roland" (*q.v.*), one of the great heroes of mediæval romance, and the most celebrated of Charlemagne's paladins. He appears under this name in the romances mentioned below, and in other works.

Orlando Furioso (Orlando mad). An epic poem in 45 cantos, by Ariosto (published 1515-33). Orlando's madness is caused by the faithlessness of Angelica, but the main subject of the work is the siege of Paris by Agramant the Moor, when the Saracens were overthrown.

The epic is full of anachronisms. We have Charlemagne and his paladins joined by King Edward of England, Richard Earl of Warwick, Henry Duke of Clarence, and the Dukes of York and Gloucester (Bk. vi). Cannon are employed by Cymosco, King of Friza (Bk. iv), and also in the siege of Paris (Bk. vi). We have the Moors established in Spain, whereas they were not invited over by the Saracens for nearly 300 years after Charlemagne's death. In Bk. xvii the late mediæval Prester John (*q.v.*) appears, and in the last three books Constantine the Great, who died 337.

There are English translations by Sir John Harrington (1591), John Hoole (1783), and W. S. Rose (1823-31).

About 1589 a play (printed 1594) by Robert Greene entitled *The History of Orlando Furioso* was produced. In this version Orlando marries Angelica.

Orlando Innamorato (Orlando in love). A romance in verse by Boiardo telling the love of Roland (*q.v.*) and Angelica. Boiardo died in 1494, not having finished the work, and Ariosto wrote his *Orlando Furioso* (*see above*) as a sequel to it. In 1541 Berni turned it into burlesque.

Orleans, The House of. There are several younger sons of the great French family of Bourbon who bore this title, but the main branch stems from Philip, son of Louis XIII, who married Henrietta, the daughter of the English King Charles I. By his second wife Philip had a son Philip (1674-1723) known as the Regent Orleans as he acted in that capacity to Louis XV in his minority. His great-grandson became notorious for his career in the French Revolution when he assumed the name of Philippe Egalité and voted for the death of his kinsman Louis XVI. He was guillotined in 1793, at the age of 46. His son, after many vicissitudes, became King of the French in 1830, but was deposed and sought refuge in England in 1848. In 1883 the older branch of the Bourbon family became extinct and since that date the Orleans family are the "legitimate" claimants to the throne of France.

Orosius (o rō' si ŭs). A Latin writer of the early 5th century A.D., whose *General History*, from the Creation to A.D. 417, is frequently referred to by historians and was translated into Anglo-Saxon by Alfred the Great. Orosius was a native of Tarragona, in Spain, and a friend of St. Augustine's.

Orpheus (ôr' fūs). A Thracian poet of Greek legend (son of Apollo and Calliope), who could move even inanimate things by his music—a power that was also claimed for the Scandinavian Odin. When his wife Eurydice (*q.v.*) died he went into the infernal regions, and so charmed Pluto that she was released on the condition that Orpheus would not look back till they reached the earth. He was just about to place his foot on the earth when he turned round, and Eurydice vanished from him in an instant.

> Orpheus' self may . . . hear
> Such strains as would have won the ear
> Of Pluto to have quite set free
> His half-regained Eurydice.
> MILTON: *L'Allegro*, 145-50.

The prolonged grief of Orpheus at his second loss so enraged the Thracian women that in one of their Bacchanalian orgies they tore him to pieces. The fragments of his body were collected by the Muses and buried at the foot of Mount Olympus, but his head had been thrown into the river Hebrus, whither it was carried into the sea, and so to Lesbos, where it was separately interred.

> What could the Muse herself that Orpheus bore,
> The Muse herself, for her enchanting son,
> Whom universal nature did lament,
> When, by the rout that made the hideous roar
> His gory visage down the stream was sent,
> Down the swift Hebrus to the Lesbian shore?
> MILTON: *Lycidas*, 58.

Orson. Twin brother of Valentine in the old romance. *Valentine and Orson* (*q.v.*). The twins were born in a wood near Orleans, and Orson (Fr. *ourson*, a little bear) was carried off by a bear, which suckled him with her cubs. When he grew up he was the terror of France, and was called the *Wild Man of the Forest*. He was reclaimed by Valentine, overthrew the Green

Knight, and married Fezon, the daughter of Duke Savary of Aquitaine.

Orthodox. The Orthodox Church. *See* GREEK CHURCH.

Orthodox Sunday, in the Eastern Church, is the First Sunday in Lent, to commemorate the restoration of images in 843.

Orts. Crumbs; refuse. (Low Ger. *ort—i.e.* what is left after eating.)

I shall not eat your orts—*i.e.* your leavings.
Let him have time a beggar's orts to crave.
Rape of Lucrece, 985.

Ortus (ôr' tŭ). *Ortus a quercu, non a salice.* Latin for "sprung from an oak, and not from a willow"—*i.e.* stubborn stuff; one that cannot bend to circumstances.

Oscar. A gold-plated figurine awarded annually by the American Academy of Motion Pictures and Sciences for the best film-acting, writing, or production of the year. In 1931 the present executive secretary of the Academy, Mrs. Margaret Herrick, joined as librarian; on seeing the then nameless gold statue for the first time she exclaimed "it reminds me of my Uncle Oscar"—the name stuck.

Osiris (ō sī' ris). One of the chief gods of Egyptian mythology: judge of the dead, ruler of the kingdom of ghosts, the Creator, the god of the Nile, and the constant foe of his brother (or son), Set, the principle of evil. He was the husband of Isis (*q.v.*), and represents the setting sun (*cp.* RA). He was slain, but came to life again and was revenged by Horus and Thoth.

The name means *Many-eyed*. Osiris was usually depicted as a mummy wearing the crown of Upper Egypt, but sometimes as an ox.

Ossian (Oisin) (os' i an). The legendary Gaelic bard and warrior of about the end of the 3rd century, son of Finn (Fingal), and reputed author of *Ossian's Poems*, published 1760-63, by James Macpherson, who professed that he had translated them from MSS. collected in the Highlands. A great controversy as to the authenticity of the supposed originals was aroused; the question has not yet been finally settled, but it is generally agreed that Macpherson, while compiling from ancient sources, was the principal author of the poems as published. The poems are full of Celtic glamour and charm, but are marred by bombast.

Ostend Manifesto. A declaration made in 1857 by the Ministers of the United States in England, France, and Spain, "that Cuba must belong to the United States." Notwithstanding this, until 1898 the island belonged to Spain,

when, as one of the results of the Spanish American War, it was freed and was for four years under the military rule of the United States. In 1902 Cuba was formed into an autonomous republic.

Ostracism (os' trà sizm) (Gr. *ostrakon*, an earthen vessel). Black-balling, boycotting, expelling; exclusion from society or common privileges, etc. The word arose from the ancient Greek custom of banishing one whose power was a danger to the state, the voting for which was done by the people recording their votes on tiles or potsherds. The custom of ostracizing is widespread. St. Paul exhorts Christians to "come out from" idolaters (2 *Cor.* vi, 17); and the Jews ostracized the Samaritans. The Catholic Church anathematizes and interdicts.

Ostrich. At one time the ostrich was fabled, when hunted, to run a certain distance and then thrust its head into the sand, thinking, because it cannot see, that it cannot be seen (*cp.* CROCODILES); this supposed habit is the source of many allusions, *e.g.*—
Whole nations, fooled by falsehood, fear, or pride,
Their ostrich-heads in self-illusion hide,
MOORE: *Sceptic.*

Another source of literary allusion to the bird is its habit of eating indigestible things such as stones and metals to assist the functions of the gizzard—
Ah, villain! thou wilt betray me, and get a thousand crowns of the king by carrying my head to him; but I'll make thee eat iron like an ostrich, and swallow my sword like a great pin, ere thou and I part.—2 *Henry VI*, iv. 10.

Hence, **ostrich-stomachs,** stomachs that will digest anything.

Othello (o thel' ō). Shakespeare's tragedy (written and performed in 1604, first printed 1622) is founded on a tale in Cithio's *Hecatommithi* (1565)—*Un Capitano Moro* (decad. iii, Nov. vii).

Otium cum dignitate (ō' ti ŭm kŭm dig ni tā' ti) (Lat., leisure with dignity). Retirement after a person has given up business and has saved enough to live upon in comfort. The words were taken as a motto by Cicero.
Otium cum dignitate is to be had with £500 a year as well as with 5,000.—POPE: *Letters* (Wks., vol. x, p. 110).

Ottava Rima (o ta' và rē' mà). A stanza of eight ten-syllabled lines, rhyming *a b a b a b c c*, used by Keats in his *Isabella*, Byron in *Don Juan*, etc. It was originally Italian and was employed by Tasso (the lines were eleven-syllabled), Ariosto, and many others.

Ottoman Empire. The Turkish Empire, so called from Othman, or Osman, I, the founder, about 1300, of the dynasty. Our *ottoman*, a kind of sofa having some resemblance to an oriental couch, is, of course, the same word.

Oubliette (oo bli et'). Traditionally a secret dungeon in a mediæval castle or monastery, only accessible from a hole in the roof. It used to be supposed that certain prisoners or refractory monks or nuns were incarcerated in these oubliettes and on occasions sealed up in them. The real use of these cells is a debated point with archæologists.

Ouija (wē' jà). A device employed by spiritualists for receiving spirit messages. It consists of a small piece of wood on wheels, placed on a board marked with the letters of the alphabet and certain commonly-used words. When the fingers of the communicators are placed on the ouija board it moves from letter to letter and thus spells out sentences. The word is a combination of Fr. *oui* and German *ja*, both meaning "yes."

Ovation. An enthusiastic display of popular favour, so called from the ancient Roman *ovatio* or minor triumph, in which the general after a bloodless victory or one over slaves entered the city on horseback or on foot, instead of in a chariot as in the greater triumph, and was crowned with myrtle instead of with gold.

Overlander. From the 1870s any Australian riding through the interior of the country, because the hope of survival if in trouble was to get to the Overland Telegraph Line (Adelaide to Darwin), cut it, and wait for the repair gang. It later came into general use to describe drovers as well as travellers, *c.f.* Banjo Patterson, *Saltbush Bill, King of the Overland, c.* 1890.

Overture (Fr. *ouvert*, O.F. *overt*, past part. of *ouvrir*, to open). An opening, a preliminary proposal; a piece of music for the opening of an opera. **To make overtures** is to be the first to make an advance, as with a view to acquaintanceship, some business deal, or a reconciliation.

Owain (o wān'). The hero of a 12th-century legend. *The Descent of Owain*, written by Henry of Saltrey, an English Benedictine monk. Owain (the name is a form of Welsh *Owen*) was an Irish knight of Stephen's court who, by way of penance for a wicked life, entered and passed through St. Patrick's Purgatory.

Owl, the emblem of Athens, where owls abounded. As Athene (Minerva) and Athenæ (Athens) are the same word, the owl was given to Minerva for her symbol also.

The Greeks had a proverb, **To send owls to Athens,** which meant the same as our *To carry coals to Newcastle* (*q.v.*). *See also* MADGE.

I live too near a wood to be scared by an owl. I am too old to be frightened by a bogy.

Like an owl in an ivy-bush. Having a sapient, vacant look, as some persons have when in their cups; having a stupid vacant stare. Owls are proverbial for their judge-like solemnity; ivy is the favourite plant of Bacchus, and was supposed to be the favourite haunt of owls.

> Good ivy, say to us what birds hast thou?
> None but the owlet that cries "How how!"
> *Carol* (time Henry VI).

Gray, in his *Elegy*, and numerous other poets bracket the two:—

> From yonder ivy-mantled tower
> The moping owl doth to the moon complain.

Owl light. Dusk; the gloaming, "blind man's holiday." Fr. *Entre chien et loup*.

Ox. One of the four figures which made up Ezekiel's cherub (i, 10). It is the emblem of the priesthood, and was assigned to St. Luke (*q.v.*) as his symbol because he begins his gospel with the Jewish priest sacrificing in the Temple.

In early art the ox is usually given as the emblem of St. Frideswide, St. Leonard, St. Sylvester, St. Medard, St. Julietta, and St. Blandina.

Oxgang. An Anglo-Saxon land measure of no very definite quantity, but as much as an ox could *gang* over or cultivate. Also called a *bovate*. The Latin *jugum* was a similar term, which Varro defines *"Quod juncti boves uno die exarāre possunt."*

Eight oxgangs made a carucate. If an oxgang were as much as one ox could cultivate, its average would be about fifteen acres.

Oxford. Oxford bags. Wide-bottomed flannel trousers fashionable in Oxford in the 1920s.

Oxford Blues. The Royal Horse Guards were so called in 1690 because of their blue facings.

Oxford frame. A picture frame made so that the wooden sides cross each other at the corners and project an inch or two; much used for photographs of college groups and so on.

Oxford Group or **Buchmanites.** A religious group named after its founder, Frank Buchman, and in no way connected with Oxford. In main its principles are Christian fellowship, public confession of sins, group "sharings" of spiritual experiences, and dependence on divine guidance in the everyday affairs of life.

Oxford Movement. A successful effort to arouse the Church of England from a period of inertia and indifference that had lasted through much of the 18th century. It was begun in 1833 at Oxford by Dr. Keble and carried on there by

Hurrell Froude, Dr. Pusey, Isaac Williams, Charles Marriott, J. H. Newman, F. W. Faber, J. D. Dalgairns, and W. G. Ward (the last four afterwards went over to the Church of Rome). The Movement insisted on the Catholic character of the Church of England and the resulting necessity for a reformation in its faith and worship. The Movement was condemned by the Church authorities and after the secession of some of its leaders it may be said to have ended, but the results were very great; the Church was transformed and its life renewed, a large and powerful Anglo-Catholic party being formed. *See* TRACTS FOR THE TIMES.

Oxymoron (oks i môr' on). A rhetorical figure in which effect is produced by apparent self-contradictions, such as "More haste less speed," "Cruel to be kind." The word is the Gr. for pointedly foolish.

Oyer and terminer (oi 'ĕr, tĕr' min ĕr). An Anglo-French legal phrase meaning "to hear and determine." *Commissions* or *Writs of oyer and terminer* as issued to judges on circuit twice a year in every county directing them to hold courts for the trial of offences.

Oyez! Oyez! Oyez! (ō yes') (O.Fr., *hear ye!*), The call made by a public crier, court officer. etc., to attract attention when a proclamation is about to be read out. Sometimes written *O yes !*

> Fame with her loud'st O yes!
> Cries, "This is he."
> > SHAKESPEARE: *Troilus and Cressida*, iv, 5.
> But when the Crier cried "O Yes!" the people cried
> "O No!"—BARHAM: *Misadventures at Margate*.

Never eat an oyster unless there's an R in the month. Good advice; which limits the eating of oysters to the months from September to April inclusive. The legal close-time for oysters in England and Scotland, however, extends only from June 15th to Aug. 4th, thus freeing all May and parts of June and August.

Oz. The abbreviation for an ounce is the 15th-century contraction of Ital. *onza*. The "z" here does not play the same part as that in "viz." (*q.v.*). *See also* WIZARD OF OZ.

P

P. The sixteenth letter in the English alphabet; called *pe*, "mouth," by the Phœnicians and ancient Hebrews, and represented in Egyptian hieroglyph by a shutter.

In the 16th century Placentius, a Dominican monk, wrote a poem of 253 hexameter verses called *Pugna Porcorum*, every word of which begins with the letter *p*. It opens thus:—

Plaudite, Porcelli, porcorum pigra propago—

which may be translated—

Praise Paul's prize pig's prolific progeny

The Four P's. A "merry interlude" by John Heywood, written about 1540. The four principal characters are "a Palmer, a Pardoner, a Poticary (apothecary), and a Pedlar."

The five P's. William Oxberry (1784-1824) was so called, because he was Printer, Poet, Publisher, Publican, and Player.

P.C. The Roman *patres conscripti. See* CONSCRIPT FATHERS.

P., P.P., P.P.P. (in music). P = piano, pp = pianissimo, and ppp = pianississimo. Sometimes pp means *piu piano* (more softly).

So f = forte, ff = fortissimo, and fff = fortississimo.

P.P.C. *See* CONGÉ.

P.S. (Lat., *post-scriptum*). Written afterwards—*i.e.* after the letter or book was finished.

P's and Q's. Mind your P's and Q's. Be very circumspect in your behaviour.

Several explanations have been suggested, but none seems to be wholly satisfactory. One is that it was an admonition to children learning the alphabet—and still more so to printers' apprentices sorting type—because of the similar appearance of these tailed letters; another that in old-time bar-parlours in the accounts that were scored up for beer "P" stood for "pints" and "Q" for "quarts," and of course the customer when settling up would find it necessary "to mind his P's and Q's," or he would pay too much; and yet another—from France—is that in the reign of Louis XIV, when huge wigs were worn, and bows were made with great formality, two things were specially required: a "step" with the feet, and a low bend of the body. In the latter the wig would be very apt to get deranged, and even to fall off. The caution, therefore, of the French dancing-master to his pupils was, "Mind your P's (*i.e. pieds*, feet) and Q's (*i.e. queues*, wigs)."

Pace (pā′ si). From the Latin *pax*, meaning peace or pardon, this word is used in the sense of "with the permission of" when preceding the mention of some person who disagrees with what is being said or done.

Pacific Ocean. So named by Magellan in 1520, because there he enjoyed calm weather and a placid sea after the stormy and tempestuous passage of the adjoining straits.

The Pacific.

Amadeus VIII, Duke of Savoy (1383, 1391-1439; d. 1451). He was an anti-pope, as Felix V, from 1440 to 1449.

Frederick III, Emperor of Germany (1415, 1440-93).

Olaf III of Norway (1030-93).

Pack (U.S.A.). To carry, as *to pack a gun*. "We packed the hams and shoulders to camp" (1857).

Packing a jury. Selecting on a jury persons whose verdict may be relied on from proclivity, far more than from evidence.

To pack up. Slang for to take one's departure; to have no more to do with the matter; also to die.

To send one packing. To dismiss him summarily and without ceremony.

Packstaff. *See* PIKESTAFF.

Paddington Fair. A public execution. Tyburn, where executions formerly took place, is in the parish of Paddington. Public executions were abolished in England in 1868.

Paddock. Cold as a paddock. A paddock is a toad or frog; and we have the corresponding phrases "cold as a toad," and "cold as a frog."

Here a little child I stand,
Heaving up my either hand;
Cold as Paddocks though they be,
Here I lift them up to Thee,
For a Benizon to fall
On our meat and on us all.
HERRICK: *Grace for a Child.*

Paddy, Paddywhack. An Irishman; from Patrick (Ir. *Padraig*). In slang both terms are used for a loss of temper, a rage on a small scale; and the latter also denotes the gristle in roast meat.

Padre (pa' drā). The name given by soldiers and sailors to a chaplain. It is Spanish and Portuguese for "father," and was adopted in the British Army in India from the natives, who had learned the term from the Portuguese.

Padua (păd' ū à) was long supposed by the Scottish to be the chief school of necromancy; hence Scott says of the Earl of Gowrie—

He learned the art that none may name
In Padua, far beyond the sea.
Lay of the Last Minstrel.

Paduasoy (păd' ū a soi). A silk stuff, the French *pou-* or *pout-de-soie*, introduced into England in the 17th century and for 150 years or so called *poudesoy* or *poodesoy*. The material had no connexion with Padua, but there was a "say" or serge manufactured there which was known as *Padua say*, and the name *Paduasoy* is due to confusion with this.

Pæan (pē' àn). The name, according to Homer, of the physician to the gods. It was used in the phrase *Io Pæan* as the invocation in the hymn to Apollo, and later in hymns of thanksgiving to other deities; hence *pæan* has come to mean any song of praise or thanksgiving, any shout of triumph or exultation.

Io pæans let us sing,
To physicke's and to poesie's king.
LYLY: *Midas*, v, 3.

Pagan (pā' gàn). The long held idea that this word—which etymologically means a villager, a rustic (Lat. *paganus*)—acquired its present meaning because the Christian Church first established itself in the cities, the village dwellers continuing to be heathen, has been shown by recent research to be incorrect. The name arose from a Roman military colloquialism. *Paganus* (rustic) was the soldier's contemptuous name for a civilian or for an incompetent soldier, and when the early Christians called themselves *miles Christi* (soldiers of Christ) they adopted the soldier-slang, *paganus*, for those who were not "soldiers of Christ." *See* the last note but one to ch. xxi of Gibbon's *Decline and Fall*.

Pageant. A performance, usually in the open air, of a series of dramatic scenes representing outstanding events in the history of a town or building. The fashion for pageants was inaugurated in England by the Sherborne Pageant of 1905. Outstanding pageants were those of Bury St. Edmunds (1907), Oxford (1907), Winchester (1908), Chelsea (1908), Dover (1908). One of the principal producers of pageants was Louis N. Parker (1852-1944).

Pagoda (pà gō' dà). A Buddhist temple or sacred tower in India, China, etc., especially a slender, storied tower built over the relics of a saint. The word is Portuguese, and was formed by them in the 16th century on some now unknown native word which may have been the Persian *but-kadah*, idol-house, or some form of *bhagavat*, holy.

Paint. To paint the lily. To indulge in hyperbolical praise, to exaggerate the beauties, good points, etc., of the subject to a very considerable extent.

To gild refined gold, to paint the lily,
To throw a perfume on the violet, . . .
Is wasteful and ridiculous excess.
King John, iv, 2.

To paint the town red. To have a gay, noisy time; to cause some disturbance in town by having a noisy spree. Possibly from the frequent firing of towns by Indians on the warpath.

Painting. It is said that Apelles, being at a loss to delineate the foam of Alexander's horse, dashed his brush at the picture in despair, and did by accident what he could not accomplish by art.

This story is related of many other artists, and the incident is said actually to have occurred to Michael Angelo when painting the interior of the dome of St. Peter's at Rome.

Many legends are told of pictures so painted that the objects depicted have been taken for the things themselves. It is said, for instance, that Apelles painted Alexander's horse so realistically that a living horse mistook it and began to neigh. Velasquez painted a Spanish admiral so true to life that Philip IV mistook the painting for the man and reproved it severely for not being with the fleet. Zeuxis painted some grapes so well that birds flew at them to peck them. Quentin Matsys painted a fly on a man's leg so inimitably that Mandyn, the artist, tried to brush it off with his handkerchief. Parrhasios, of Ephesus, painted a curtain so well that Zeuxis was deceived by it, and told him to draw it aside that he might see the picture behind it; and Myron, the Greek sculptor, is said to have fashioned a cow so true to nature that a bull mistook it for a living animal.

Painter. The rope by which a ship's boat can be tied to the ship, a buoy, mooring-post, etc. The word is probably an extended sense of the 14th-century *peyntour*, the rope which held the anchor to the ship's side (now called the *shank-painter*), which was from Fr. *pendre*, Lat. *pendere*, to hang.

Pair Off. When two members of Parliament of opposite parties agree to absent themselves, so that when a vote is taken the absence of one neutralizes the missing vote of the other, they are said to *pair off*. In the House of Commons this is usually arranged by the Whips.

Paix (pā). **La Paix des Dames.** The treaty concluded at Cambray, in 1529, between Francis I and Charles V of Germany; so called because it was brought about by Louise of Savoy (mother of the French king) and Margaret, the emperor's aunt.

Pakeha. Any resident in New Zealand who is not a Maori. Thought by some to be a Maori word, it is more probably a native corruption of an unpleasant term of abuse used by early whaling crews.

Pakistan. The name of the present Dominion was coined by Chaudhrie Rahmat Ali in 1933 to represent the units which should be included when the time came: P-Punjab; A-Afghan border states; K-Kashmir; S-Sind; TAN for Baluchistan.

Pal. A gipsy word meaning a brother or mate.

Palace originally meant a dwelling on the Palatine Hill (*See* PALATINATE) of Rome, where Augustus and, later, Tiberius and Nero built their mansions. The word was hence transferred to other royal and imperial residences; then to similar buildings, such as *Blenheim Palace*, *Dalkeith Palace*, and to the official residence of a bishop; and finally to a place of amusement as the *Crystal Palace*, the *People's Palace*, and—in irony—to a *gin palace*.

In parts of Devonshire cellars for fish, storehouses cut in the rock, etc., are called *palaces* or *pallaces*; but this may be from the old word *palis*, a space enclosed by a palisade.

All that cellar and the chambers over the same, and the little pallace and landing-place adjoining the River Dart.—*Lease granted by the Corporation of Totnes in* 1703.

Paladin (păl' á din). Properly, an officer of, or one connected with, the palace (*q.v.*), palatine (*q.v.*); usually confined in romance to the Twelve Peers of Charlemagne's court, and hence applied to any renowned hero or knight-errant.

The most noted of Charlemagne's paladins were Allory de l'Estoc; Astolfo; Basin de Genevois; Fierambras or Ferumbras; Florismart; Ganelon, the traitor; Geoffroy, Seigneur de Bordelois, and Geoffroy de Frises; Guerin, Duc de Lorraine; Guillaume de l'Estoc, brother of Allory; Guy de Bourgogne; Hoël, Comte de Nantes; Lambert, Prince de Bruxelles; Malagigi; Nami or Nayme de Bavière; Ogier the Dane; Oliver (*q.v.*); Otuël; Richard, Duc de Normandie; Rinaldo; Riol du Mans; Roland (*q.v.*), otherwise Orlando; Samson, Duc de Bourgogne; and Thiry or Theiry d'Ardaine. Of these, twelve at a time seemed to have formed a special bodyguard to the king.

Palæolithic Age (pā li ō lith' ik) (Gr. *palaios*, old, *lithos*, a stone). The earlier of the two periods into which the Stone Age of Europe is divided (*cp*. NEOLITHIC).

Palais Rose. The first of many international conferences after World War II was held in the rose-decorated chamber of a Parisian mansion. The monotonous reiteration by the Russian delegate of "No" to every suggestion put forward gave origin to the phrase "Another Palais Rose" to describe an abortive conference.

Palamon and Arcite (păl' á mon, ar sī' tè). Two young Theban knights of romance whose story (borrowed from Boccaccio's *Le Teseide*) is told by Chaucer in his *Knight's Tale*, by Fletcher and (probably) Shakespeare in *The Two Noble Kinsmen* (1634) and elsewhere. Both were in love with Emilia, sister-in-law to the Duke of Athens, in whose hands they were prisoners. In time they obtained their liberty, and the Duke appointed a tournament, promising Emilia to the victor. Arcite prayed to Mars to grant him victory, Palamon prayed to Venus to grant him Emilia. Arcite won the victory, but, being thrown from his horse, died; and Palamon, though not the winner, won the prize.

Pale, The English. The name given in the 15th century to that part of Ireland which had been colonized in the 12th century by Henry II, viz., the districts of Cork, Dublin, Drogheda, Waterford, and Wexford. It was only in these districts that the English law prevailed, hence the phrases, **Within the pale,** and **Outside the pale.** By the 16th century the English Pale had so much contracted that it embraced only the district about 20 miles round Dublin.

Paleface. A name for a white man attributed to the North American Indians as if translated from a term in their languages. Its popularity is largely due to the novels of Fenimore Cooper; but the term became notorious through an earlier connexion with an incident that occurred in 1799. A junior officer named Sterrett, serving on the *Constellation* frigate, wrote home "we would put a man to death for even looking pale on this ship." This letter was published in a Philadelphia paper on March 13th; by early April the affair had become magnified to the point where it was said that Sterrett himself had killed a man for looking pale.

Pales (pā′ lēz). The Roman god of shepherds and their flocks. *See* PALATINATE *above*.

Palimpsest (păl′ imp sest) (Gr. *palin*, again, *psestos*, scraped). A parchment on which the original writing has been effaced and something else has been written. When parchment was scarce the scribes used to erase what was written on it and use it again. As sometimes; they did not rub it out entirely, many works that would otherwise have been lost have been recovered. Thus Cicero's *De Republica*, which was partially erased to make room for a commentary of St. Augustine on the Psalms; has been restored.

Palindrome (păl′ in drōm) (Gr. *palin dromo*, to run back again). A word or line which reads backwards and forwards alike, as M*adam*, also *Roma tibi subito motibus ibit amor*. They had also been called *Sotadics*, from their reputed inventor, Sotades, a scurrilous Greek poet of the 3rd century B.C.

Probably the longest palindrome in English is —

Dog as a devil deified
Deified lived as a god —

and another well known is Napoleon's reputed saying —

Able was I ere I saw Elba.

A good palindrome is attributed to Adam who thus introduced himself to Eve:

Madam, I'm Adam.

The following Greek palindrome is very celebrated: —

ΝΙΨΟΝΑΝΟΜΗΜΑΤΑΜΗΜΟΝΑΝΟΨΙΝ

i.e. wash my transgressions, not only my face. It appears as the legend round many fonts, notably that in the basilica of St. Sophia, Constantinople, those at St. Stephen d'Egres, Paris, and St. Menin's Abbey, Orleans; and, in England, round the fonts of St. Martin's, Lud-gate Hill, St. Mary's, Nottingham, at Dulwich College; and in churches at Worlingworth (Suffolk), Harlow (Essex), Knapton (Norfolk), and Hadleigh (Suffolk).

Palinode (păl′ i nōd) (Gr., a singing again). A song or discourse recanting a previous one; such as that of Stesichorus to Helen after he had been struck blind for singing evil of her, or Horace's *Ode* (Bk. I, xvi), which ends —

. . . nunc ego inhibits
Mutare quero tristia, dum mihi
fias recentatis amica
obprobriis animumque reddas.

It was a favourite form of versification among Jacobean poets, and the best known is that of Francis Quarles (1592-1644) in which man's life is likened to all the delights of nature, all of which fade, and man too dies.

Isaac Watts (1674-1748) has a palinode in which he retracts the praise bestowed upon Queen Anne. In the first part of her reign he wrote a laudatory poem to the queen, but he says that the latter part deluded his hopes and proved him a false prophet.

Pall (pawl). The covering thrown over a coffin is the Latin *pallium*, a square piece of cloth used by the Romans to throw over their shoulders, or to cover them in bed; hence a coverlet.

Pall, the long sweeping robe worn by sovereigns at their coronation, by the Pope, archbishops, etc., is the Roman *palla*, which was only worn by princes and women of honest fame. This differed greatly from the *pallium* (*q.v.*), which was worn by freemen and slaves, soldiers, and philosophers.

Sometimes let gorgeous Tragedy
In sceptred pall come sweeping by.
             MILTON: *Il Penseroso*.

Pall-bearers. The custom of appointing men of mark for pall-bearers came to us from the Romans. Julius Cæsar had magistrates for his pall-bearers; Augustus Cæsar had senators; Germanicus had tribunes and centurions; Æmilis L. Paulus had the chief men of Macedonia who happened to be at Rome at that time; but the poor were carried on a plain bier on men's shoulders.

Pall Mall (păl măl). This fine thoroughfare in the West End of London has been so called since the early 18th century because it is the place where formerly the game of Palle malle (Ital. *palla*, ball, *maglia*, mallet) was played. When first built, about 1690, it was named Catherine Street, in honour of Catherine of Braganza. "Pale malle," says Cotgrave —

is a game wherein a round boxball is struck with a mallet through a high arch of iron. He that can do this most frequently wins.

The game was fashionable in the reign of Charles II, and the walk called the Mall in St. James's Park was appropriated to it for the king and his court.

In town let me live then; in town let me die,
For in truth I can't relish the country, not I.
If one must have a villa in summer to dwell,
O, give me the sweet shady side of Pall Mall!
       CHAS. MORRIS (d. 1832): *The Contrast*.

Palladian. An architectural term for a heavy, classic style based on the work of the Italian architect Andrea Palladio (1518-80). It was introduced into England by Inigo Jones, and the Banqueting Hall, Whitehall, is an example of his Palladian work.

Palladium (på lā′ di ŭm). In classical story, the colossal wooden statue of Pallas in the citadel of Troy, which was said to have fallen from heaven, and on the preservation of which it was believed that the safety of the city depended. It was carried away by the Greeks, and the city burnt to the ground; and later it was said to have been taken to Rome.

Hence, the word is now figuratively applied to anything on which the safety of a people, etc., is supposed to depend.

The liberty of the press is the palladium of all the civil, political, and religious rights of an English man.— *Letters of Junius: Dedication*.

See also ABATON; ANCILE; EDEN HALL.

The rare metallic element found associated with platinum and gold was named *palladium* by its discoverer, Wollaston (1803) from the newly discovered asteroid, *Pallas*; and the same name has been given to a place of amusement in London, apparently through the mistaken idea that the ancient Palladium, like the Colosseum (*q.v.*), was something akin to a circus.

Pallas. A name of Minerva (*q.v.*), sometimes called *Pallas Minerva*. According to fable, Pallas was one of the Titans, and was killed by Minerva, who flayed him, and used his skin for armour. More likely the word is either from *pallo*, to brandish, the compound implying "Minerva who brandishes the spear," or simply *pallax*, virgin.

Palm. The well-known tropical and subtropical tree gets its name from the Latin *palma*, which was a transferred use of *palma*, the palm of the hand, applied to the tree because of the spread-hand or open fan-like appearance of the fronds. The English *palm* (of the hand) represents M.E. (and Fr.) *paume*.

The palm tree is said to grow faster for being weighed down. Hence it is the symbol of resolution overcoming calamity. It is believed by Orientals to have sprung from the residue of the clay of which Adam was formed.

Palm oil. Bribes, or rather money for bribes, fees, etc.

In Ireland the machinery of a political movement will not work unless there is plenty of palm-oil to prevent friction.—*Irish Seditions from 1792 to 1880*, p. 39.

The rich may escape with whole skins, but those without "palm-oil" have scant mercy.—*Nineteenth Century*, Aug., 1892, p. 312.

Palm Sunday. The Sunday next before Easter. So called in memory of Christ's triumphant entry into Jerusalem, when the multitude strewed the way with palm branches and leaves (*John* xii, 12-19).

To palm off. To pass off fraudulently. The allusion is to jugglers, who conceal in the palm of their hand what they pretend to dispose of in some other way.

You may palm upon us new for old.—DRYDEN.

Palmetto State. The State of South Carolina. The palmetto is a fan-leafed palm.

Paludament (pa lū′ då ment). A distinctive mantle worn by a Roman general in the time of war. This was the "scarlet robe" in which Christ was invested. (*Matt.* xxvii, 28.)

They flung on him an old scarlet paludamentum— some cast-off war-cloak with its purple laticlave from the Prætorian wardrobe.—FARRAR: *Life of Christ*, ch. lx.

Pam (păm). The knave of clubs in certain card-games, also the name of a card-game; short for *pamphile*, French for the knave of clubs.

This word is sometimes given as an instance of Johnson's weakness in etymology. He says it is "probably from *palm*, victory; as *trump* from *triumph*."

Pam was the usual nickname of the great Victorian statesman Viscount Palmerston (1784-1865).

Pampas (păm′ pås). Treeless plains, some 2,000 miles long and from 300 to 500 broad, in South America. They cover an area of 750,000 sq. miles. It is the Spanish form of Peruvian *bamba*, meaning *flats* or *plains*.

Pampero, The (păm pē′ ro). A dry, northwest wind that blows in the summer season from the Andes across the pampas to the sea-coast.

Pamphlet. A small unbound book of a few sheets stitched together, usually on some subject of merely temporary interest; so called from O.Fr. *Pamphilet*, the name of a 12th-century erotic Latin poem which was very popular in the Middle Ages.

This word has been the subject of much etymological guesswork. One "authority" derived it from a supposed Pamphila, a Greek lady, whose chief work was said to be a commonplace book of anecdotes, epitomes, notes, etc.; Johnson suggested *par-un-filet* (held "by a thread")—*i.e.* stitched, but not bound, while another "derivation is *paginæ filatæ* (pages tacked together).

Pan (Gr., all, everything). The god of pastures, forests, flocks, and herds of Greek mythology; also the personification of deity displayed in creation and pervading all things. He is represented with lower part of a goat and the upper part of a man; his lustful nature symbolized the spermatic principle of the world; the leopard's skin that he wore indicated the immense variety of created things; and his character of "blameless" symbolized that wisdom which governs the world.

Universal Pan,
Knit with the Graces and the Hours in dance,
Led on the eternal spring.
        MILTON: *Paradise Lost*, iv, 266.

Legend has it that at the time of the Crucifixion, just when the veil of the Temple was rent in twain, a cry swept across the ocean in the hearing of many, "Great Pan is Dead," and that at the same time the responses of the oracles ceased for ever. *See* E. B. Browning's poem of this name.

Pan-pipes. A wind instrument of great antiquity, consisting of a series of pipes of graduated length, across the upper ends of which the player blows, obtaining a scale of thin, reedy notes. Pan-pipes are associated by name and picture with the rural god Pan who, according to Greek legend, invented them and played them to the nymphs and dryads of the mountainside.

Panacea (păn á sē' á) (Gr., all-healing). A universal cure. Panacea was the daughter of Æsculapius (god of medicine), and the medicine that cures is the daughter or child of the healing art.

In the Middle Ages the search for the panacea was one of the alchemists' self-imposed tasks; and fable tells of many panaceas, such as the Promethean unguent which rendered the body invulnerable, Aladdin's ring, the balsam of Fierabras (*q.v.*), and Prince Ahmed's apple (*see* APPLE). *Cp. also* ACHILLES' SPEAR; MEDEA'S KETTLE; etc.

Panache (pan ash'). The literal meaning of this French word is a plume of feathers flying in the wind as from the crest of a helmet. Figuratively, however, "panache" is applied to one's courage or spirit, to keeping one's end up. It is in this sense familiar to those who have read or seen *Cyrano de Bergerac*.

Panama Hat. A light, broad-brimmed hat made of the young leaves of *Carludovica palmata*, a palm-like tree indigenous to Central America.

Pancake. A thin, flat "cake" made in a frying-pan. These pancakes were made from the necessity in the past, when conditions of fasting were more strict, of using up eggs and fat before the beginning of Lent. Shrove Tuesday (*q.v.*), a special day for these, came to be called **Pancake Day**, and the Shrove-bell the **Pancake Bell**.

Pandarus (păn' dà rus). A Lycian leader and ally of the Trojans in Greek legend. Owing to his later connexion with the story of Troilus and

Cressida, he was taken over by the romance writers of the Middle Ages as a procurer. *See* PANDER.

Pandemonium (păn de mō' ni ům) (Gr., all the demons). A wild, unrestrained uproar, a tumultuous assembly. The word was first used by Milton as the name of the principal city in Hell. It was formed on the analogy of *Pantheon* (*q.v.*).

The rest were all
Far to the inland retired, about the walls
Of Pandemonium city and proud seat
Of Lucifer.
        Paradise Lost, x, 424 (*see also* i, 756).

Pander. To pander to one's vices is to act as an agent to them, and such an agent is termed a pander from *Pandarus*, who procures for Troilus (*q.v.*) the love of Cressida. In *Much Ado About Nothing* it is said that Troilus was "the first employer of pandars" (v, 2).

Let all pitiful goers-between be called to the , world's end after my name, call them all "Pandars." Let all constant men be "Troiluses," all false women be "Cressids," and all brokers-between, "Pandars." Say, Amen.—
SHAKESPEARE: *Troilus and Cressida*, iii, 2.

Pandora's Box (păn dôr' à). A present which seems valuable, but which is in reality a curse; like that of Midas (*q.v.*), who found his very food became gold, and so uneatable.

Prometheus made an image and stole fire from heaven to endow it with life. In revenge, Jupiter told Vulcan to make the first woman, who was named Pandora (*i.e.* the All-gifted), because each of the gods gave her some power which was to bring about the ruin of man. Jupiter gave her a box which she was to present to him who married her. Prometheus distrusted Jove and his gifts, but Epimetheus, his brother, married the beautiful Pandora, and—against advice—accepted the gift of the god. Immediately be opened the box all the evils flew forth, and have ever since continued to afflict the world. According to some accounts the last thing that flew out was Hope; but others say that Hope alone remained.

Pangloss, Dr. (păn' gloss) (Gr., all tongues). The pedantic old tutor to the hero in Voltaire's *Candide, ou l'Optimisme* (1759). His great point was his incurable and misleading optimism; it did him no good and brought him all sorts of misfortune, but to the end he reiterated "all is for the best in this best of all possible worlds." This was an attack upon the current theories of J. J. Rousseau.

Panhandle. In the United States a narrow strip of territory belonging to one State which runs between two others, such as the Texas Panhandle, the Panhandle of Idaho, etc. West Virginia is known as **the Panhandle State.**

Panic. The word comes from the god Pan (*q.v.*), because sounds heard by night in the mountains and valleys, which gave rise to sudden and groundless fear, were attributed to him. There are various legends accounting for the name; one is that Bacchus, in his eastern expeditions, was opposed by an army far superior to his own, and Pan advised him to command all his men at dead of night to raise a simultaneous shout. This was rolled from mountain to mountain by innumerable echoes, and the enemy, thinking they were surrounded on all sides, took to sudden flight. *Cp. Judges* vii, 18-21.

Panopticon (păn op′ ti kŏn). The Royal Panopticon of Science and Art, in Leicester Square, was opened in 1852-53 as a place of popular instruction and a home for the sciences and music. It was built in the Moorish style and awakened great admiration. It failed in its original intention, however, and after being closed some years was reopened in 1858 as a place of entertainment, under the name of The Alhambra. For many years this was one of the landmarks of London.

Pantagruel (păn tà groo′ el). The principal character in Rabelais' great satire *The History of Gargantua and Pantagruel* (the first part published in 1532, the last posthumously in 1565), King of the Dipsodes, son of Gargantua (*q.v.*), and by some identified with Henri II of France. He was the last of the giants, and Rabelais says he got his name from the Greek *panta*, all, and Arab, *gruel*, thirsty, because he was born during the drought which lasted thirty and six months, three weeks, four days, thirteen hours, and a little more, in that year of grace noted for having "three Thursdays in one week." He was covered with hair at birth, "like a young bear," and was so strong that though he was chained in his cradle with four great iron chains, like those used in ships of the largest size, he stamped out the bottom, which was made of weavers' beams, and, when loosed by the servants, broke his bonds into five hundred thousand pieces with one blow of his infant fist. When he grew to manhood he knew all languages, all sciences, and all knowledge of every sort, out-Solomoning Solomon in wisdom. His immortal achievement was his voyage from Utopia in quest of the "oracle of the Holy Bottle" (*q.v.*).

Wouldst thou not issue forth . . .
To be the third part in this earthy cell
Of the brave acts of good Pantagruel.
RABELAIS: *To the Spirit of the Queen of Navarre.*

Pantagruelism. Coarse and boisterous buffoonery and humour, especially with a serious purpose—like that for which Pantagruel was famous.

Pantaloon. The breeches, trousers, or underdrawers of various kinds (now often called *pants*) get their name from Pantaloon, a Venetian character in 16th-century Italian comedy, a lean and foolish old man dressed in loose trousers and slippers. His name is said to have come from San Pantaleone (a patron saint of physicians and very popular in Venice), and he was adopted by the later harlequinades and pantomimes as the butt of the clown's jokes.

The sixth age shifts
Into the lean and slipper'd pantaloon,
With spectacles on nose and pouch on side,
His youthful hose well sav'd, a world too wide
For his shrunk shank; and his big manly voice,
Turning again toward childish treble, pipes
And whistles in his sound.
As You Like It, ii, 7.

Playing Pantaloon. Playing second fiddle; being the cat's-paw of another, servilely imitating.

Pantheism (păn′ thē izm). The doctrine that God is everything and everything is God; a monistic theory elaborated by Spinoza, who, by his doctrine of the Infinite Substance, sought to overcome the opposition between mind and matter, body and soul.

Pantheon (păn′ thē on). A temple dedicated to all the gods (Gr. *pan*, all, *theos*, god); specifically, that erected at Rome by Agrippa, son-in-law to Augustus. It is circular, nearly 150 ft. in diameter, and of the same total height; in the centre of the dome roof is a space open to the sky. Since the early 7th century, as Santa Maria Rotunda, it has been used as a Christian church. Among the national heroes buried there are Raffaele, Victor Emmanuel II, and Humbert I.

The Pantheon at Paris was originally the church of St. Geneviève, started by Louis XV and completed in 1790. In 1791 the Convention changed its name to the Pantheon and decreed that men who had deserved well of their country should be buried there. Among them are Rousseau, Voltaire, and Victor Hugo.

Panther (earlier **Panthera**). In mediæval times this animal was supposed to be friendly to all beasts except the dragon, and to attract them by a peculiarly sweet odour it exhaled. Swinburne, in *Laus Veneris*, makes use of this tradition, but gives it a rather different significance:—

As one who hidden in deep sedge and reeds
Smells the rare scent made where a panther feeds,

And tracking ever slotwise the warm smell
Is snapped upon by the warm mouth and bleeds,
His head far down the hot sweet mouth of her—
So one tracks love, whose breath is deadlier.

In the old *Physiologus* the panther was the type of Christ, but later, when the savage nature of the beast was more widely known, it became symbolical of evil and hypocritical flattery; hence Lyly's comparison (in *Euphues, the Anatomy of Wit*) of the beauty of women to a delicate bait with a deadly hook, a sweet panther with a devouring paunch, a sour poison in a silver pot.

The mediæval idea is reflected in (or perhaps arose from) the name, which is probably of Oriental origin but was taken from Gr. *panther*, all beasts.

In *Reynard the Fox* (*q.v.*) Reynard affirms that he sent the queen a comb made of panther's bone, "more lustrous than the rainbow, more odoriferous than any perfume, a charm against every ill, and a universal panacea."

Pantisocracy (păn ti sok' rà si) (Gr., all of equal power). The name given by Coleridge to the communistic, Utopian society that he, with Southey, George Burnett, and others intended (about 1794) to form on the banks of the Susquehannah River. The scheme came to nothing owing chiefly to the absence of funds.

All are not moralists, like Southey, when
He prated to the world of "Pantisocrasy."
BYRON: *Don Juan*, iii, 93.

Pantofles, or **Pantables** (păn' toflz, păn' tàb lz). Slippers, especially loose ones worn by Orientals.

Pantomime (păn' tō mīm). According to etymology this should be all dumb show, but the word was commonly applied to an adaptation of the old Commedia dell'arte that lasted down to the 19th century. The principal characters are Harlequin (*q.v.*) and Columbine, who never speak, and Clown and Pantaloon, who keep a constant fire of joke and repartee. This once popular pantomime has since devolved into a Christmas theatrical entertainment, usually based on a nursery tale, *e.g. Cinderella, Mother Goose,* or even *Robinson Crusoe,* enlivened by catchy songs, pretty girls, and considerable buffooning.

Panurge (Gr. *pan,* all, *ergos,* worker, the "all-doer," *i.e.* the rogue, he who will "do anything or anyone"). The roguish companion of Pantagruel, and one of the principal characters in Rabelais' satire, He was a desperate rake, was always in debt, had a dodge for every scheme, knew everything and something more, was a boon companion of the mirthfullest temper

and most licentious bias; but was timid of danger, and a desperate coward. Panurge consulted lots, dreams, a sibyl, etc., and, lastly, the Oracle of the Holy Bottle; and to every one of the obscure answers Panurge received, whether it seemed to point to "Yes" or to "No," he invariably found insuperable objections.

Some "commentators" on Rabelais have identified Panurge with Calvin, others with Cardinal Lorraine; and this part of the satire seems to be an echo of the great Reformation controversy on the celibacy of the clergy.

Papal States or States of the Church, were the Italian territories under the temporal sovereignty of the Popes until 1860 when, with the exception of the city of Rome and a few outlying possessions, the States were incorporated in the Kingdom of Italy. In 1870, with the withdrawal of the French garrison that had alone enabled the enfeebled Papal government to exist, the Italians entered Rome and the Pope made himself a voluntary "prisoner" in the Vatican. In 1929 the Lateran Treaty was signed between the Holy See and Mussolini's Italian government whereby *de jure* and *de facto* sovereignty was accorded to the Papal authorities in the Vatican City, which includes the Palace, the church and piazza of St. Peter's, and contiguous buildings to the extent of a little under a square mile, with a population of some 600 souls. The Pope's country seat at Castel Gandolfo is also included in the Vatican City.

Paper. So called from the *papyrus,* the giant water reed from which the Egyptians manufactured a material for writing on.

Not worth the paper it's written on. Said of an utterly worthless statement, promise, etc.

The Paper King. John Law, the projector of the Mississippi Scheme (*q.v.*).

To paper a house. In theatrical phraseology, to fill the theatre with "deadheads," or non-paying spectators, admitted by paper orders.

To send in (or **to receive**) **one's papers.** To resign one's appointment, commission, etc., *or* to receive one's dismissal.

Paphian (pā' fi án). Relating to Venus, or rather to Paphos, a city of Cyprus, where Venus was worshipped; a Cyprian; a prostitute.

Papier mâché (păp' yer măsh' ā). Pulped paper mixed with glue, or layers of paper glued together and while pliable moulded to form various articles and ornaments. When dry the material becomes hard and strong. Lacquered, and often inlaid with mother o' pearl, papier maché articles were greatly in vogue in early and mid-Victorian times. In 1772 Henry Clay, of Birmingham, used it in coach-building; in 1845 it was first employed for architectural mouldings, etc.

Papyrus. *See* PAPER. The written scrolls of the ancient Egyptians are called *papyri*, because they were written on this.

Paraclete (păr' à klēt). The advocate; one *called* to aid or support another; from the Gr. *para-kalein*, to call to. The word is used as a title of the Holy Ghost, the Comforter.

O source of uncreated Light,
The Father's promised Paraclete!
    DRYDEN: *Veni, Creator Spiritus.*

Paradise. The Greeks borrowed this word from the Persians, among whom it denoted the enclosed and extensive parks and pleasure grounds of the Persian kings. The Septuagint translators adopted it for the garden of Eden, and in the New Testament and by early Christian writers it was applied to Heaven, the abode of the blessed dead.

A fool's paradise. *See* FOOL.

Paradise and the Peri. *See* PERI.

Paradise Lost. Milton's epic poem was published in 12 books in 1667. It tells the story—

Of Man's first disobedience and the fruit
Of that forbidden tree whose mortal taste
Brought death into the World, and all our woe
With loss of Eden.

Satan rouses the panic-stricken host of fallen angels with tidings of a rumour current in Heaven of a new world about to be created. He calls a council to deliberate what should be done, and they agree to send him to search for this new world. Seating himself on the Tree of Life, Satan overhears Adam and Eve talking about the prohibition made by God, and at once resolves upon the nature of his attack. He takes the form of a mist, and, entering the serpent, induces Eve to eat of the forbidden fruit. Adam eats "that he may perish with the woman whom he loved." Satan returns to Hell to tell his triumph, and Michael is sent to lead the guilty pair out of the Garden.

Milton borrowed largely from the epic of Du Bartas (1544-90), entitled *The Week of Creation* which was translated into almost every European language; and he was indebted to St. Avitus (d. 523), who wrote in Latin hexameters *The Creation, The Fall*, and *The Expulsion from Paradise*, for his description of Paradise (Bk. i), of Satan (Bk. ii), and other parts.

In 1671 *Paradise Regained* (in four books) was published. The subject is the Temptation. Eve, being tempted, fell, and lost Paradise;

Jesus, being tempted, resisted, and regained Paradise.

The Earthly Paradise. In mediæval times it was a popular belief that paradise, a land—or island—where everything was beautiful and restful, and where death and decay were unknown, still existed somewhere on earth and was to be found for the searching. It was usually located far away to the east; Cosmas (7th century) placed it beyond the ocean east of China, in 9th-century maps it is shown in China itself, and the fictitious letter of Prester John to the Emperor Emmanuel Comnenus states that it was within three days' journey of his own territory—a "fact" that is corroborated by Mandeville. The Hereford map (13th century) shows it as a circular island near India, from which it is separated not only by the sea, but also by a battlemented wall. *Cp.* BRANDAN, ST.

Parallel. None but himself can be his parallel. Wholly without a peer. The line occurs in Lewis Theobald's *The Double Falsehood* (1727), iii, 1, a play which Theobald tried to palm off on the literary world as by Shakespeare. There are many similar sentences; for example:—

And but herself admits no parallel.
    MASSINGER: *Duke of Millaine*, iii, 4 (1662).
None but himself can parallel.
    Anagram on John Lilburn (1658).

Paraphernalia (păr à fĕr nā' lyà). Literally, all that a woman can claim at the death of her husband beyond her jointure (Gr. *para*, beside, *pherne*, dowry). In the Roman law her paraphernalia included the furniture of her chamber, her wearing apparel, her jewels, etc. Hence personal attire, fittings generally, anything for show or decoration.

Parasite (păr' à sīt) (Gr. *para sitos*, eating at another's cost). A plant or animal that lives on another; hence a hanger-on, one who fawns and flatters for the sake of what he can get out of it—a "sponger."

Parcheesi (par chē' zi). A game resembling backgammon, played mostly in U.S.A.

Parchment. So called from Pergamum, in Mysia, Asia Minor, where it was used for the purpose of writing when Ptolemy prohibited the exportation of papyrus from Egypt.

Pardon Bell. The Angelus bell. So called because of the indulgence once given for reciting certain prayers forming the Angelus (*q.v.*).

Pardoner's Tale, in Chaucer's *Canterbury Tales*, is that of *Death and the Rioters*, which comes from an Oriental source through the Italian *Cento Novelle Antiche*.

A pardoner was a cleric licensed to preach and collect money for a definite object such as a crusade or the building of a church, for contributing to which an indulgence was attached.

Pariah. A member of the lowest caste of Hindu in Southern India, from a native word meaning "a drummer," because it was these who beat the drums at certain festivals.

Europeans often extend the term to those of no caste at all, hence it is applied to outcasts generally, the lowest of the low.

> There was no worst
> Of degradation spared Fifine; ordained from first
> To last, in body and soul, for one life-long debauch,
> The Pariah of the North, the European Nautch!
> BROWNING: *Fifine at the Fair*, xxxi.

Parian. A name given to a fine statuary porcelain manufactured in the mid-19th century, and used for small figures, vases, chessmen, jewellery, etc.

Parian Chronicle. One of the Arundelian Marbles (*q.v.*), found in the island of Paros, and bearing an inscription which contains a chronological register of the chief events in the mythology and history of ancient Greece during a series of 1,318 years, beginning with the reign of Cecrops (about 1580 B.C.), and ending with the archonship of Diognetus (264 B.C.), of which nearly the last hundred years is now lost.

Paris (păr' is). In Greek legend, the son of Priam, King of Troy, and Hecuba; and through his abduction of Helen (*q.v.*) the cause of the siege of Troy. Before his birth Hecuba dreamed that she was to bring forth a firebrand, and, as this was interpreted to mean that the unborn child would bring destruction to his house, the infant Paris was exposed on Mount Ida. He was, however, brought up by a shepherd, and grew to perfection of beautiful manhood. When the golden Apple of Discord (*see under* APPLE) was thrown on the table of the gods it was Paris who had to judge between the rival claims of Hera (Juno), Aphrodite (Venus), and Athene (Minerva); each goddess offered him bribes — the first power, the second the most beautiful of women, and the third martial glory. He awarded the Apple and the title of "Fairest" to Aphrodite, who in return assisted him to carry off Helen, for whom he deserted his wife, Œnone, daughter of the river-god, Cebren. At Troy Paris earned the contempt of all by his cowardice, and he was fatally wounded with a poisoned arrow by Philoctetes at the taking of the city.

Paris (păr' is), the capital of France. So called from the ancient Celtic tribe, the *Parisii*, whose capital — the modern *Paris* — was known to the Romans as *Lutetia Parisiorum*, the mud-town of the Parisii. *See* LUTETIA. Rabelais gives a whimsical derivation of the name. He tells (I, xvii) how Gargantua played a disgusting practical joke on the Parisians who came to stare at him, and the men said it was a sport "par ris" (to be laughed at); wherefore the city was called Par-'is.

The heraldic device of the city of Paris is a ship. As Sauval says, *"L'ile de la cité est faite comme un grand navire enforcé dans la vase, et échoué au fil de l'eau vers le milieu de la Seine."* This form of a ship struck the heraldic authorities, who, in the latter half of the Middle Ages, emblazoned it in the shield of the city.

Plaster of Paris. Gypsum, especially calcined gypsum used for making statuary casts, keeping broken limbs rigid for setting, etc. It is found in large quantities in the quarries of Montmartre, near Paris.

Parlement. Under the old *régime* in France, the sovereign court of justice where councillors were allowed to plead, and where justice was administered in the king's name. The Paris Parlement received appeals from all inferior tribunals, but its own judgments were final. It took cognizance of all offences against the crown, the peers, the bishops, the corporations, and all high officers of state; and, though it had no legislative power, had to *register* the royal edicts before they could become law. The Parlements were abolished by the Constituent Assembly in, 1790.

Parliamentary language, *i.e.* restrained and seemly language such as is required of any member speaking in Parliament, is now applied to a civil and courteous mode of addressing an opponent in an argument.

Parlour. Originally the reception room in a monastery, etc., where the inmates could see and speak to (Fr. *parler*) their friends.

Parlour boarder. A pupil at a boarding-school who lives with the principal and receives extra care and attention. Hence, used of one in a privileged position.

Parlour tricks. Accomplishments that are useful in company, at At Homes, etc., such as singing, witty conversation, and so on.

Parmesan (par' me zān'). A dry, hard cheese, originally made in Parma, Italy, from skim milk and especially suitable for grating.

Parnassus. A mountain near Delphi, Greece, with two summits, one of which was consecrated to Apollo and the Muses, the other to Bacchus. It is said to have been anciently called *Larnassus*, because Deucalion's ark, *larnax*, stranded there after the flood. After the oracle of Delphi was built at its foot it received the name of Parnassus, which Peucerus says is a corruption of *Har Nahas* (hill of divination).

Owing to its connexion with the Muses, Parnassus came to be regarded as the seat of poetry and music, and we still use such phrases as *To climb Parnassus*, meaning "to write poetry."

O, were I on Parnassus hill,
Or had o' Helicon my fill,
That I might catch poetic skill,
To sing how dear I love thee!
BURNS: *Song.*

Parody. Father of Parody. Hipponax of Ephesus (6th century B.C.). *Parody* means an ode which perverts the meaning of another ode. (Gr. *para ode.*)

Parole (pả rōl') (Fr.). A verbal promise given by a soldier that he will not abuse his leave of absence or by a prisoner of war that he will not attempt to escape.

Parolles (pả rōl' ēz). **He was a mere Parolles.** A pretender, a man of words, and a pedant. The allusion is to the faithless, bragging, slandering villain who dubs himself "captain," pretends to knowledge which he has not, and to sentiments he never feels, in Shakespeare's *All's Well that Ends Well.*

I know him a notorious liar,
Think him a great way fool, solely a coward;
Yet these fixed evils sit so fit on him
That they take place. . . .   Act i, 1.

Parsees (par sēz). Guebres descendants of Persians who fled to India during the Mohammedan persecutions of the 7th and 8th centuries, and still adhere to their Zoroastrian religion. *See also* SILENCE (*Towers of Silence*). The word means *People of Pars—i.e.* Persia.

Parsifal. *See* PERCIVAL.

Parsley. He has need now of nothing but a little parsley—*i.e.* he is dead. A Greek saying; the Greeks decked tombs with parsley, because it keeps green a long time.

He was drawn from Fielding's friend, the Rev. William Young, who edited Ainsworth's *Latin Dictionary* (1752).

Part. A portion, piece, or fragment.
For my part. As far as concerns me.
For the most part. Generally, as a rule.
In good part. Favourably.
Part and parcel. An essential part, portion, or element.

"Well, Mr. Squeers," he said, welcoming that worthy with his accustomed smile, of which a sharp look and a thoughtful frown were part and parcel, "how do you do?"—DICKENS: *Nicholas Nickleby.*

Part of speech. A grammatical class of words of a particular character. The old rhyme by which children used to be taught the parts of speech is:—

Three little words you often see
Are ARTICLES, *a, an,* and *the.*
A NOUN'S the name of anything;
As *school* or *garden, hoop* or *swing.*
ADJECTIVES tell the kind of noun;
As *great, small, pretty, white,* or *brown.*
Instead of nouns the PRONOUNS stand;
Her head, *his* face, *our* arms, *your* hand.
VERBS tell of something being done;
To *read, count, sing, laugh, jump,* or *run.*
How things are done the ADVERBS tell;
As *slowly, quickly, ill,* or *well.*
CONJUNCTIONS join the words together;
As, men *and* women, wind *or* weather.
The PREPOSITION stands before
A noun, as *in* or *through* a door.
The INTERJECTION shows surprise;
As, *oh!* how pretty! *ah!* how wise!
The whole are called nine parts of speech,
Which reading, writing, speaking teach.

Part up! Slang for "hand over," as in "If you don't soon part up with the money you owe me there'll be trouble." An extension of the use is the old saying (Tusser, 1573), *A fool and his money are soon parted.*

Till death us do part. *See* DEPART.

To play a part. To perform some duty or pursue some course of action; also, to act deceitfully. The phrase is from the stage, where an actor's *part* is the words or the character assigned to him.

All the world's a stage,
And all the men and women merely players.
They have their exits and their entrances;
And one man in his time plays many parts.
As You Like It, ii, 7.
Why is the Past belied with wicked art,
The Future made to play so false a part?
WORDSWORTH: *The Warning,* 140.

To take part. To assist; to participate.

But Lilia pleased me, for she took no part
In our dispute.
TENNYSON: *The Princess; Conclusion,* 29.

To take the part of. To side with, to support the cause of.

A man of parts. An accomplished man; one who is clever, talented, or of high intellectual ability.

Low in the world, because he scorns its arts.
A man of letters, manners, morals, parts;
Unpatronised, and therefore little known.
COWPER: *Tirocinium,* 672.

Parting cup. *See* STIRRUP CUP.

The parting of the ways. Said of a critical moment when one has to choose between two different courses of action. The allusion, of course, is to a place at which a road branches off in different directions.

For the difficulties in which we find ourselves now, the parting of the ways was in 1853, when the Emperor Nicholas's proposals were rejected.—LORD SALISBURY: *Speech* (Jan. 19th, 1897).

Parthenon (par' thė non). The great temple at Athens to Athene *Parthenos* (*i.e.* the Virgin), many of the sculptured friezes and fragments of pediments of which are now in the British Museum among the Elgin Marbles (*q.v.*). The Temple was begun by the architect Ictinus about 450 B.C., and the embellishment of it was mainly the work of Phidias, whose colossal chryselephantine statue of Athene was its chief treasure.

Particularists. Those who hold the doctrine of *particular* election and redemption, *i.e.* the election and redemption of some, not all, of the human race.

Partridge. Always partridge! *See* PERDRIX.

St. Partridges' Day. September 1st, the first day of partridge shooting.

Parturiunt montes (par tū' ri ent mon' tēz). *Parturiunt montes, nascetur ridiculus mus.* The mountain was in labour, etc. *See under* MOUNTAIN.

Party. Person or persons under consideration. "This is the next party, your worship"—*i.e.* the next case to be examined. "This is the party that stole the things"—the person or persons accused.

If an evil spirit trouble any, one must make a smoke . . . and the party shall be no more vexed—*Tobit* vi, 7,

As a Victorian colloquialism **party** was synonymous with *person*, as—"That dull old party in the corner."

Parvenu (par' ve nū) (Fr., arrived). An upstart; one who has risen from the ranks. The word was made popular in France by Marivaux' *Paysan Parvenu* (1735).

The insolence of the successful *parvenu* is only the necessary continuance of the career of the needy struggler.—THACKERAY: *Pendennis,* II, xxi.

Pasha (pǎsh' a). A Turkish title borne by governors of provinces and certain military and civil officers of high rank. There were three grades of pashas, which were distinguished by the number of horse-tails carried before them and planted in front of their tents. The highest rank were those of *three tails*; the grand vizier was always such a pasha, as also were commanding generals and admirals; generals of division, etc., were pashas of *two tails*; and generals of brigades, rear admirals, and petty provincial governors were pashas of *one tail*.

Pasquinade (pǎs kwin ād'). A lampoon or political squib, having ridicule for its object; so called from Pasquino, an Italian tailor of the 15th century, noted for his caustic wit. Some time after his death, a mutilated statue was dug up, representing Ajax supporting Menelaus, or Menelaus carrying the body of Patroclus, or else a gladiator, and was placed at the end of the Braschi Palace near the Piazza Navona. As it was not clear what the statue represented, and as it stood opposite Pasquin's house, it came to be called "Pasquin." The Romans affixed their political, religious, and personal satires to it, hence the name. At the other end of Rome was an ancient statue of Mars, called *Marforio,* to which were affixed replies to the Pasquinades.

Then the procession started, took the way
From the New Prisons by the Pilgrim's Street
The street of the Governo, Pasquin's Street,
(Where was stuck up, 'mid other epigrams,
A quatrain . . . but of all that, presently!)
    BROWNING: *The Ring and the Book,* xii, 137.

Pass. A pass or **A common pass.** At the Universities, an ordinary degree, without honours. A candidate getting this is called a *passman*.

To pass the buck. To evade responsibility. An American phrase, coming from the game of poker. The "buck," perhaps a piece of buckshot or a bucktail, was passed from one player to another as a reminder that the recipient was to be the next dealer. The earliest recorded use of the phrase is by Mark Twain in 1872.

Passepartout (pas' par too) (Fr., pass everywhere). A master-key; also a simple kind of picture-frame in which the picture is placed between a sheet of cardboard and a piece of glass, the whole being held together by strips of paper pasted over the edges.

Passim (pǎs' im) (Lat., here and there, in many places). A direction often found in annotated books which tells the reader that reference to the matter in hand will be found in many passages in the book mentioned.

Passion, The. The sufferings of Jesus Christ which had their culmination in His death on the cross.

Passion Flower. A plant of the genus *Passiflora,* whose flowers bear a fancied resemblance to the instruments of the Passion. *Cp.* PIKE'S HEAD. It seems to have first got its name in mediæval Spain.

The *leaf* symbolizes the spear.
The five *anthers,* the five wounds.
The *tendrils,* the cords or whips.
The column of the *ovary,* the pillar of the cross.
The *stamens,* the hammers.

The three *styles*, the three nails.

The *fleshy threads* within the flowers, the crown of thorns.

The *calyx*, the glory or nimbus.

The *white* tint, purity.

The *blue* tint, heaven.

It keeps open three days; symbolizing the three years' ministry.

Passion Play. A development of the mediæval mystery play with especial reference to the story of Our Lord's passion and death. The best known survival of such plays, which were common in France in the 14th century, is the Oberammergau Passion Play which takes place every ten years. In 1633 the Black Death swept over the village of Oberammergau; when it abated the inhabitants vowed to enact the scenes of the Passion every ten years. This has been done at the end of every decade with only one or two failures. Though the cast is still chosen exclusively from inhabitants of the village, the play is no longer the simple expression of piety but has become a highly commercial undertaking, in a special theatre with all the embellishments of costume and properties and an audience drawn thither from all parts of the world.

Passover (pas' ō ver). A Jewish festival to commemorate the deliverance of the Israelites, when the angel of death (that slew the first-born of the Egyptians) *passed over* their houses, and spared all who did as Moses commanded them. It is held from the 15th to the 22nd of the first month, Nisan, *i.e.* about April 13th to 20th.

Passport. A safe conduct issued by the authorities of a nation to its citizens, and required to be produced when crossing national frontiers. Passports were in wide use by the 18th century, but by the mid-19th century were almost obsolete. They were re-introduced with the outbreak of World War I in 1914.

Patch. A fool; so called originally from the nickname of Cardinal Wolsey's jester, Sexton, who got this nickname either from Ital. *pazzo*, a fool, or from the motley or patched dress worn by licensed fools.

What a pied ninny's this! thou scurvy patch!
The Tempest, iii, 2.

To patch up a quarrel. To arrange the matter in a not very satisfactory way; a coat that has been torn and then "patched up" is pretty sure to break out again; so is a quarrel.

Patent (through Fr. from Lat. *patentem*, lying open). Open to the perusal of anybody. A thing that is *patented* is protected by letters patent.

Paternoster (păt' ĕr nos'' tĕr) (Lat., Our Father). The Lord's Prayer; from the first two words in the Latin version. Every tenth bead of a rosary is so called, because at that bead the Lord's Prayer is repeated; and the name is also given to a certain kind of fishing tackle, in which hooks and weights to sink them are fixed alternately on the line, somewhat in rosary fashion.

A paternoster-while. Quite a short time; the times it takes one to say a paternoster.

To say the devil's paternoster. *See* DEVIL.

Paternoster Row (London) was probably so named from the rosary or paternoster makers. There is mention as early as 1374 of a Richard Russell, a "paternosterer," who dwelt there, and we read of "one Robert Nikke, a paternoster maker and citizen," in the reign of Henry IV. Another suggestion is that it was so called because funeral processions on their way to St. Paul's began their *pater noster* at the beginning of the Row. For over three centuries Paternoster Row was the home of publishers and booksellers. It was totally destroyed in an air raid at the end of December, 1940.

Pathfinder. One of the names of Natty Bumpo (*q.v.*) in Fenimore Cooper's Leatherstocking Novels (*q.v.*). It was given to the American Major-General John Charles Fremont (1813-90), who conducted four expeditions across the Rocky Mountains.

Pathfinders. In World War II a R.A.F. term for specially skilled pilots and navigators who flew in first and dropped flares to identify the target for the benefit of the attacking force which followed them.

Patient Grisel. *See* GRISELDA.

Patmos (păt' mos). The island of the Sporades in the Ægean Sea (now called *Patmo* or *Patino*) to which St. John retired—or was exiled (*Rev.* i, 9). Hence the name is used allusively for a place of banishment or solitude.

Patois (păt' wa). Dialect peculiarity, provincialism in speech. It is a 13th-century French word of unknown origin.

Patres Conscripti. *See* CONSCRIPT FATHERS.

Patriarch (Gr. *patria*, family, *archein*, to' rule). The head of a tribe or family who rules by paternal right; applied specially (after *Acts* vii, 8) to the twelve sons of Jacob, and to Abraham, Isaac, and Jacob and their forefathers. In one passage (*Acts* ii, 29) David also is spoken of as a patriarch.

In the early Church "Patriarch," first mentioned in the council of Chalcedon, but virtually existing from about the time of the council of Nice, was the title of the highest of

Church officers. He ordained metropolitans, convened councils, received appeals, and was the chief bishop over several countries or provinces, as an archbishop is over several dioceses. It was also the title given by the popes to the archbishops of Lisbon and Venice, in order to make the patriarchal dignity appear distinct from and lower than the papal, and is that of the chief bishop of various Eastern rites, as the Jacobites, Armenians, and Maronites.

In the Orthodox Eastern Church the bishops of Constantinople, Alexandria, Antioch, and Jerusalem are patriarchs. Within a religious order the title is given to the founder, as St. Benedict, St. Francis, and St. Dominic.

Patrician. Properly speaking, one of the *patres* (fathers) or senators of Rome (*see* PATRES CONSCRIPTI), and their descendants. As they held for many years all the honours of the state, the word came to signify the magnates or nobility of a nation, the aristocrats.

Patrick, St. The apostle and patron saint of Ireland (commemorated on March 17th) was not an Irishman, but was born at what is now Dumbarton (about 373), his father, Calpurnius, a deacon and Roman official, having come from "Bannavem Taberniæ," which was probably near the mouth of the Severn. As a boy he was captured in a Pictish raid and sold as a slave in Ireland. He escaped to Gaul about 395, where he studied under St. Martin at Tours before returning to Britain. There he had a supernatural call to preach to the heathen of Ireland, so he was consecrated and in 432 landed at Wicklow. He at first met with strong opposition, but, going north, he converted first the chiefs and people of Ulster, and later those of the rest of Ireland. He founded many churches, including the cathedral and monastery of Armagh, where he held two synods. He is said to have died at Armagh (about 464) and to have been buried either at Down or Saul—though one tradition gives Glastonbury as the place of his death and burial. Downpatrick cathedral claims his supposed grave which is covered with a massive slab of granite, for which Irishmen of every creed subscribed.

St. Patrick left his name to countless places in Great Britain and Ireland, and many legends are told of his miraculous powers—healing the blind, raising the dead, etc. Perhaps the best known tradition is that he cleared Ireland of its vermin.

The story goes that one old serpent resisted him; but he overcame it by cunning. He made a box, and invited the serpent to enter it. The serpent objected, saying it was too small; but St. Patrick insisted it was quite large enough to be comfortable. After a long contention, the serpent got in to prove it was too small, when St. Patrick slammed down the lid, and threw the box into the sea.

In commemoration of this St. Patrick is usually represented banishing the serpents; and with a shamrock leaf, in allusion to the tradition that when explaining the Trinity to the heathen priests on the hill of Tara he used this as a symbol.

Patriots' Day, in U.S.A. the anniversary of the battle of Lexington, April 19th, 1775, the first battle in the War of Independence. It is a public holiday in Massachusetts and Maine.

Patroclus (på trok' lùs). The gentle and amiable friend of Achilles, in Homer's *Iliad*. When Achilles refused to fight in order to annoy Agamemnon, Patroclus appeared in Achilles's armour at the head of the Myrmidons, and was slain by Hector.

Patroon (på troon'). An old term for a landowner in New Jersey and New York when they belonged to the Dutch. The patroon had certain manorial rights and privileges under a government grant.

Patter. To chatter, to clack, also the running talk of cheap Jacks, conjurers, etc., is from *Paternoster* (*q.v.*). When saying Mass the priest recites it in a low, rapid, mechanical way till he comes to the words, "and lead us not into temptation," which he speaks aloud, and the choir responds, "but deliver us from evil." In the Anglican Prayer Book, the priest is directed to say the whole prayer "with a *loud* voice."

Patter, the patter of feet, of rain, etc., is not connected with the above. It is a frequentative of *pat*, to strike gently.

Pattern. From the same root as *patron* (Lat. *pater*, father). As a *patron* ought to be an example, so pattern has come to signify a model.

Paul. St. Paul. Patron saint of preachers and tentmakers (*see Acts* xviii, 3). Originally called Saul, his name, according to tradition, was changed in honour of Sergius Paulus, whom he converted (*Acts* xiii, 6-12).

His symbols are a sword and open book, the former the instrument of his martyrdom, and the latter indicative of the new law propagated by him as the apostle of the Gentiles. He is represented of short stature, with bald head and grey, bushy beard; and legend relates that when he was beheaded at Rome (A.D. 66), after having converted one of Nero's favourite concubines, milk instead of blood flowed from his veins. He is commemorated on June 29th.

A Paul's man. A braggart; a captain out of service, with a long rapier; so called because the Walk down the centre of old St. Paul's, London, was at one time the haunt of stale knights. These loungers were also known as *Paul's Walkers*. Jonson called Bobadil (*q.v.*) a Paul's man, and in his *Every Man out of his Humour* (1599) is a variety of scenes in the interior of St. Paul's.

Pavan or **Pavin** (pa' van). A stately Spanish dance of the 16th and 17th centuries, said to be so called because in it the dancers stalked like peacocks (Lat. *pavones*), the gentlemen with their long robes of office, and the ladies with trains like peacocks' tails. The pavan, like the minuet, ended with a quick movement called the *galliard*, a sort of gavotte.

Pawnee (paw' nee). Anglo-Indian for water (Hind. *pani*, water).

Brandy pawnee. Brandy and water.

Pax (păks) (Lat., peace). The "kiss of peace," which is given at High Mass. It is omitted on Maundy Thursday

Also a sacred utensil used when mass is celebrated by a high dignitary. It is sometimes a crucifix, sometimes a tablet, and sometimes a reliquary, and is handed round to be kissed as a symbolic substitute for the "kiss of peace."

The old custom of "kissing the bride," which took place immediately before the Communion of the newly married couple and still obtains in some churches, is derived from the Salisbury rubric concerning the Pax in the Missa Sponsalium:—

Tunc amoto pallio, surgant ambo sponsus et sponsa; et accipiat sponsus pacem a sacerdote, et ferat sponsæ osculans eam et neminem alium, nec ipse, nec ipsa; sed statim diaconus vel clericus a presbytero pacem accipiens, ferat aliis sicut solitum est.

Pax! The schoolboy's cry of truce.

Pax Britannica. The peace imposed by British rule. The phrase is modelled on the Latin *Pax Romana*, the peace existing between the different members of the Roman empire.

Pay, to discharge a debt, is through O.Fr. *paier*, from the Latin. *pax*, peace, by way of *pacare*, to appease. The nautical *pay*, to cover with hot tar for waterproofing, represents Lat. *picare*, from *pix*, pitch.

Here's the devil to pay, and no pitch hot. *See* DEVIL.

Who's to pay the piper? Who is to pay the score? The phrase may come from the story of the Pied Piper (*q.v.*), who agreed to rid Hamelin city of rats and mice, and when he had done so was refused his pay. An older and more probable derivation goes back to the piper who used to amuse guests at inns or on the green, and expected his payment for the entertainment.

Pay dirt. A mining term for ground which pays for working.

P.A.Y.E. The initials of Pay As You Earn, a system of collecting Income Tax from weekly earnings, introduced in Britain in 1944. The employer is furnished with a guiding table in accordance with which the proper tax is deducted before wages or salary are paid, and he is responsible to the Income Tax authorities for the sum thus collected.

Peace. A Bill of Peace. A Bill intended to secure relief from perpetual litigation. It is brought by one who wishes to establish and perpetuate a right which he claims, but which, from its nature, is controversial.

Peace Ballot. On June 27th, 1935, the League of Nations Union took a national ballot in Britain on certain questions regarding peace and disarmament. 11,640,066 votes were recorded in favour of adherence to the League of Nations, and over ten million voted for a reduction of armaments. The ballot was interpreted by the Axis powers as a sign of weakness indicating the unwillingness of the British people to go to war in any circumstances and this strengthened the determination of Hitler to stand out for his territorial and other demands.

If you want peace, prepare for war. A translation of the Latin proverb, *Si vis pacem, para bellum*. It goes a step farther than the advice given by Polonius to his son (*Hamlet*, I, iii), for you are told, whether you are "in a quarrel" or not, always to bear yourself so that all possible opposers "may beware of thee."

Peace at any price. Lord Palmerston sneered at the Quaker statesman, John Bright, as a "peace-at-any-price man." *Cp.* CONCHY.

Though not a "peace-at-any-price" man. I am not ashamed to say I am a peace-at-almost-any-price man.—
LORD AVEBURY: *The Use of Life*, xi (1849).

Peace in our time. Phrase used by Neville Chamberlain, Prime Minister, on his return from Munich on September 30th, 1938, when he imagined that by giving way to Hitler he had averted war.

The Perpetual Peace. The peace concluded June 24th, 1502, between England and Scotland, whereby Margaret, daughter of Henry VII, was betrothed to James IV; a few years afterwards the battle of Flodden Field was fought. The name has also been given to other treaties, as that between Austria and Switzerland in 1474, and between France and Switzerland in 1516.

To keep the peace. To refrain from disturbing the public peace or doing anything that might result in strife or commotion. Wrongdoers are sometimes **bound over to keep the peace** for a certain time by a magistrate; a specified sum of money is deposited, and if the man commits a breach of the peace during that time he is not only arrested but his deposit is forfeit.

Peach. To inform, to "split"; a contraction of *impeach*. The word is one of those that has degenerated to slang after being in perfectly good use.

The peacock's feather. An emblem of vainglory, and in some Eastern countries a mark of rank.

As a literary term the expression is used of a borrowed ornament of style spatchcocked into the composition; the allusion being to the fable of the jay who decked herself out in peacock's feathers, making herself an object of ridicule.

The peacock's tail is an emblem of an Evil Eye, or an ever-vigilant traitor; hence the feathers are considered unlucky, and the superstitious will not have them in the house. The classical legend is that Argus (*see* ARGUS-EYED), who had 100 eyes, was changed into a peacock by Juno, the eyes forming the beautifully coloured disks in the tail.

Pea-jacket. A rough overcoat worn by seamen, etc.; probably from the Dutch *pig* or *pije*, a coarse thick cloth or felt. The "courtepy," the short (Fr. *court*) jacket worn by Chaucer's "Clerk of Oxenford," is from the same word:—

Ful thredbare was his overest courtepy,
For he had getten him yet no benefyce.
Canterbury Tales: Prologue, 290.

Peal. To **ring a peal** is to ring 5,040 changes on a set of 8 bells; any number of changes less than that is technically called a *touch* or *flourish*. Bells are first *raised*, and then *pealed*.

This society rung . . . a true and complete peal of 5,040 grandsire triples in three hours and fourteen minutes.—*Inscription in Windsor Curfew Tower*.

Pearls. Dioscorides and Pliny mention the belief that pearls are formed by drops of rain falling into the oyster-shells while open; the raindrops thus received being hardened into pearls by some secretions of the animal.

Cardan says (*De Rerum Varietate*, vii, 34) that pearls are polished by being pecked and played with by doves.

The liquid drops of tears that you have shed
Shall come again, transform'd to orient pearl.
Richard III, iv, 4.

Pearls . . . are believed to be the result of an abnormal secretory process caused by an irritation of the mollusk consequent on the intrusion into the shell of some foreign body, as a grain of sand, an egg of the mollusk itself, or perhaps some cercarian parasite.—G. F. KING: *Gems, etc.*, ch. xii.

Cleopatra (*q.v.*) and Sir Thomas Gresham are said to have dissolved pearls in wine by way of making an ostentatious display of wealth, and a similar act of vanity and folly is told by Horace (2 *Satire*, iii, 239). Clodius, son of Æsop the tragedian, drew a pearl of great value from his ear, melted it in vinegar, and drank to the health of Cecilia Metella. This story is referred to by Valerius Maximus, Macrobius, and Pliny. Horace says,

Qui sanior, ac si
Illud idem in rapidum flumen jaceretve cloacam?
How say you? had the act been more insane
To fling it in a river or a drain?
CONINGTON'S *tr.*

Peckish. Hungry, or desirous of something to eat. Of course "peck" refers to fowls, etc., which peck their food.

When shall I feel peckish again.—DISRAELI: *Sybil*, Bk. vi, ch. iii.

Pecker. Keep your pecker up. As the mouth is in the head, *pecker* (the mouth) means the head; and to "keep your pecker up," means to keep your head up, or, more familiarly, "keep your chin up"; "never say die."

Peckham. All holiday at Peckham—*i.e.* no appetite, not peckish; a pun on the word peck, as going to Bedfordshire is a pun on the word bed.

Going, to Peckham. Going to dinner.

Pecos Bill (pe' kos). A cowboy of American legend who performed superhuman prodigies on the frontier in early days. One of his feats was to dig the Rio Grande river.

Pectoral Cross. *See* CRUX PECTORALIS.

Peculiar. A parish or church which was exempt from episcopal jurisdiction, as a royal chapel, etc. Peculiars were abolished in 1849.

The Court of Peculiars. A branch of the Court of Arches which had jurisdiction over the "peculiars" of the archbishop of Canterbury. *See above*.

The Peculiar People. Properly, the Jews— the "Chosen people"; but taken as a title by a sect founded in 1838, the chief characteristic of which is that its members refuse all medical aid and, as a consequence, are frequently in conflict with the authorities. They have a strong belief in the efficacy of prayer; subscribe to no creed and have no recognized preachers or clergy. The name is based on *Titus* ii, 14— "to purify unto himself a peculiar people."

Pecuniary. From *pecus*, cattle, especially sheep. Varo says that sheep were the ancient medium of barter and standard of value. Ancient coin was marked with the image of an ox or sheep.

Pedagogue (Gr. *pais*, boy, *agein*, to lead). A "boy-leader," hence, a schoolmaster—now usually one who is pompous and pedantic. In ancient Greece the *pedagogos* was a slave whose duty it was to attend his master's son whenever he left home.

Pedlar is not a tramp who goes on his feet, as if from the Lat. *pedes*, feet. The name is probably from the *ped*, a hamper without a lid in which are stored fish or other articles to hawk about the streets. In Norwich there is a place called the Ped-market, where women used to expose eggs, butter, cheese, etc., in open hampers.

Peeler. Slang for a policeman; first applied to the Irish Constabulary founded when Sir Robert Peel was Chief Secretary (1812-18), and afterwards, when Peel as Home Secretary introduced the Metropolitan Police Act (1829), to the English policeman. *Cp.* BOBBY. In the 16th century the word was applied to robbers, from *peel* (later *pill*), to plunder, strip of possessions, rob. Holinshed, in his *Scottish Chronicle* (1570), refers to Patrick Dunbar, who "delivered the countrie of these peelers." *Cp.* also Milton's *Paradise Regained*, iv. 136:—

> That people . . . who, once just,
> Frugal, and mild, and temperate, conquered well
> But govern ill the nations under yoke,
> Peeling their provinces, exhausted all
> By lust and rapine.

Peelites was the name given to the Conservative adherents of Sir Robert Peel when he introduced a Bill for the repeal of the Corn Laws in 1846.

Peep-o'-Day Boys. The Irish Protestant faction in Ulster of about 1786; they were precursors of the Orangemen (*q.v.*), and were active from the period mentioned; so called because they used to visit the houses of their Roman Catholic opponents (called *Defenders*) at "peep of day" searching for arms or plunder.

Peeping Tom of Coventry. *See* GODIVA, LADY.

Peers of the Realm. The five orders of Duke, Marquess, Earl, Viscount, and Baron (*see these names*). The word peer is the Latin *pares* (equals), and in feudal times all great vassals were held equal in rank.

The Twelve Peers of Charlemagne. *See* PALADINS.

Peg. A square peg in a round hole. One who is doing (or trying to do) a job for which he is not suited; *e.g.* a bishop refereeing a prize-fight.

To take one down a peg. To take the conceit out of a braggart or pretentious person. The allusion here is not to peg-tankards, but to a ship's colours, which used to be raised and lowered by pegs; the higher the colours are raised the greater the honour, and to take them down a peg would be to award less honour.

> Trepanned your party with intrigue,
> And took your grandees down a peg.
> > BUTLER: *Hudibras*, ii, 2.

> Well, he has come down a peg or two, and he don't like it.—HAGGARD.

Pegasus (peg' á sus). The winged horse on which Bellerophon (*q.v.*) rode against the Chimæra. When the Muses contended with the daughters of Pieros, Helicon rose heavenward with delight; but Pegasus gave it a kick, stopped its ascent, and brought out of the mountain the soul-inspiring waters of Hippocrene; hence, the name is used for the inspiration of poetry.

> Then who so will with vertuous deeds assay
> To mount to heaven, on Pegasus must ride,
> And with sweete Poets verse be glorified.
> > SPENSER: *Ruines of Time*, 425.

> Now, if my Pegasus should not be shod ill,
> This poem will become a moral model.
> > BYRON: *Don Juan*, V, ii.

In World War II the horse, with Bellerophon on his back, in pale blue on a maroon ground, was adopted as the insignia of all British Airborne troops.

Peking Man, The (*Sinanthropos pekinensis*), is the name given to a suppositional primitive man, based on remains found in caves near Pekin in 1927. Bones of some forty individuals were found, showing considerable resemblance to the Pithecanthropos or ape man supposed to have been in some way connected with primitive man, *Homo sapiens*. The date of Pekin man is about 1,000,000 years ago, but whether he was an ancestor of the human race is still a matter of conjecture and dispute among anthropologists.

Pelagians (pe lā jànz). Heretical followers of the British monk Pelagius (a Latinized form of his native Welsh name, *Morgan*, the sea), who in the 4th and early 5th centuries was fiercely opposed by St. Augustine, and was condemned by Pope Zosimus in 418. They denied the doctrine of original sin or the taint of Adam, and maintained that we have power of ourselves to receive or reject the Gospel.

Pelican (pel' i kàn). In Christian art, a symbol of charity; also an emblem of Jesus Christ, by "whose blood we are healed." St. Jerome gives the story of the pelican restoring its young ones destroyed by serpents, and his own salvation by the blood of Christ; and the popular fallacy that pelicans fed their young with their blood arose from the fact that when the parent bird is about to feed its brood, it macerates small fish in the large bag attached to its under bill, then pressing the bag against its breast, transfers the macerated food to the mouths of the young. The correct term for the heraldic representation of the bird in this act is **a pelican in her piety,** *piety* having the classical meaning of filial devotion.

The mediæval *Bestiary* tells us that the pelican is very fond of its brood, but when the young ones begin to grow they rebel against the male bird and provoke his anger, so that he kills them; the mother returns to the nest in three days, sits on the dead birds, pours her blood over them, revives them, and they feed on the blood.

> Than sayd the Pellycane,
> When my byrdis be slayne
> With my bloude I them reuyue [revive]
> Scrypture doth record,
> The same dyd our Lord,
> And rose from deth to lyue.
> SKELTON: *Armoury of Birdis.*

The Pelican State. Louisiana, U.S.A., which has a pelican in its device.

Pelion (pē' li on). **Heaping Pelion upon Ossa.** Adding difficulty to difficulty, embarrassment to embarrassment, etc. When the giants tried to scale heaven, they placed Mount Pelion upon Mount Ossa, two peaks in Thessaly, for a scaling ladder (*Odyssey,* xi, 315).

> I would have you call to mind the strength of the ancient giants, that undertook to lay the high mountain Pelion on the top of Ossa, and set among those the shady Olympus.—*Rabelais:* IV, xxxviii.

Pell-mell. Headlong; in reckless confusion. From the players of pall-mall (*q.v.*), who rushed heedlessly to strike the ball.

Pelleas, Sir (pel' ē ăs). One of the Knights of the Round Table, famed for his great strength. He is introduced into the *Faerie Queene* (VI, xii) as going after the "blatant beast" when it breaks the chain with which it had been bound by Sir Calidore. See also Tennyson's *Pelleas and Ettare.*

P.E.N. The initials of an international association of poets, playwrights, editors, essayists, and novelists. Its principal activity is the organization of annual reunions of literary and artistic men and women in one or other of the European countries.

Pen. An interesting word eytmologically, for it is the Latin *penna,* a feather, both of which words are derived from the Sanskrit root *pet-,* to fly. *Pet-* gave Sansk. *patra* (feather); this became in Lat. *penna* (Eng. *pen*), and in O. Teut. *fethro* (Ger. *feder,* Dut. *veder,* Eng. *feather*). Also, in O.Fr. *penne* meant both *feather* and *pen,* but in Mod.Fr. it is restricted to the long wing- and tail-feathers and to heraldic plumes on crests, while *pen* is *plume.* Thus, the French and English usage has been vice versa, English using *plume* in heraldry, French using *penne,* the English writing implement being named *pen,* and the French *plume.*

Pencil. Originally, a painter's brush, and still used of very fine paint-brushes, from Lat. *penicillum,* a paint-brush, diminutive of *peniculus,* a brush, which itself is a diminutive of *penis,* a tail. When the modern pencil came into use in the early 17th century it was known as a *dry pencil* or a *pencil with black lead.*

Knight of the pencil. A bookmaker; a reporter; also anyone who makes his living by scribbling.

Pendragon (pen drăg' ŏn). A title conferred on several British chiefs in times of great danger, when they were invested with supreme power, especially (in the Arthurian legends) to Uther Pendragon, father of King Arthur. The word is Welsh *pen,* head, and *dragon* (the reference being to the war-chief's dragon standard); and it corresponded to the Roman *dux bellorum.*

A legend recorded by Geoffrey of Monmouth relates that when Aurelius, the British king, was poisoned by Ambron, during the invasion of Pascentius, son of Vortigern, there "appeared a star at Winchester of wonderful magnitude and brightness, darting forth a ray, at the end of which was a globe of fire in form of a dragon, out of whose mouth issued forth two rays, one of which extended to Gaul and the other to Ireland." Uther ordered two golden dragons to be made, one of which he presented to Winchester, and the other he carried with him as his royal standard, whence he received the title "Pendragon."

Penelope (pė nel' ō pi). The wife of Ulysses and mother of Telemachus in Homeric legend. She was a model of all the domestic virtues.

The Web of Penelope. A work "never ending, still beginning"; never done, but ever in hand. Penelope, according to Homer, was pestered by suitors at Ithaca while Ulysses was absent at the siege of Troy. To relieve herself of their importunities, she promised to make a choice of one as soon as she had finished weaving a shroud for her father-in-law. Every night she unravelled what she had done in the day, and so deferred making any choice until Ulysses returned and slew the suitors.

Peninsular War. The war carried on, under the Duke of Wellington, against the French in Portugal and Spain, between 1808 and 1814. It was brought about through the French attack on Spain and Portugal, and, so far as Britain was concerned, was the most important of the Napoleonic Wars. It resulted in the French being driven from the Peninsula.

Penitential Psalms. The seven psalms expressive of contrition—viz. the vi, xxxii, xxxviii, li, cii, cxxx, cxliii. From time immemorial they have all been used at the Ash Wednesday services; the first three at Matins, the 51st at the Commination, and the last three at Evensong.

Pennsylvania Dutch is the name given to the descendants of the settlers from Southwest Germany who took up their abode in Pennsylvania in the mid-18th century. A German dialect is still spoken by them in East Pennsylvania.

Penny (A.S. *pening*). The English bronze coin worth one-twelfth of a shilling—often called a *copper*, because from 1797 to 1860 pennies were made of copper. From Anglo-Saxon times till the reign of Charles II pennies were of silver, and between that time and 1797 none were coined, though copper halfpence and farthings were. Silver pennies are still coined, but only in very small quantities and solely for use as Maundy Money (*q.v.*). The weight of a new penny is one-third of an ounce avoirdupois, and it is legal tender up to twelve pence.

The plural *pennies* is used of the number of coins, and *pence* of value; and the word is sometimes used to denote coins of low value of other nations, such as in *Luke* xx, 24, where it stands for the Roman denarius.

A pretty penny. A considerable sum of money, an unpleasantly large sum.

A penny for your thoughts! Tell me what you are thinking about. Addressed humorously to one in a "brown study." The phrase occurs in Heywood's *Proverbs* (1546).

A penny saved is a penny earned (or **gained,** etc.). An old adage intended to encourage thrift in the young.

In for a penny, in for a pound. Another way of saying "having put your hand to the plough." Once a thing has been started it must be carried through, no matter what difficulties arise or what obstacles have to be overcome—one is in it and there can be no drawing back.

Penny fish. A name given to the John Dory (*q.v.*) because of the round spots on each side left by St. Peter's fingers.

Penny wise and pound foolish. Said of one who is in danger of "spoiling the ship for a ha'porth of tar," like the man who lost his horse from his penny wisdom in saving the expense of shoeing it afresh when one of its shoes was loose; hence, one who is thrifty in small matters and careless over large ones is said to be *penny wise*.

Take care of the pence and the pounds will take care of themselves. An excellent piece of advice, which Chesterfield records in his *Letters to his son* (Feb. 5th, 1750) as having been given by "old Mr. Lowndes, the famous Secretary of the Treasury, in the reigns of King William, Queen Anne, and George I." Chesterfield adds—

To this maxim, which he not only preached, but practised, his two grandsons, at this time, owe the very considerable fortunes that he left them.

The saying was parodied in the *Advice to a Poet*, which goes "Take care of the *sense* and the *sounds* will take care of themselves."

To turn an honest penny. To earn a little money by working for it.

Pennyroyal. The name of this herb (*Mentha pulegium*), a species of mint, is not connected with the coin, but is a corruption of *pulyole ryale*, from the Latin *pulegium*, thyme (so called from *pulex*, a flea, because it was supposed to be harmful to fleas), and Anglo-French *réal*, royal. The French call the herb *pouliot*, from *pou*, a louse.

Pension. Etymologically, that which is *weighed out* (Lat. *pensionem*, payment, from *pendĕre*, to weigh, also to pay, because payment was originally weighed out. *Cp.* our *pound*, both a weight and a piece of money).

Pension, a boarding-house (to live *expension*, *i.e.* as a boarder), though now pronounced and treated as though French, was, in the 17th century, ordinary English; this use arose because *pension* was the term for any regular payment made for services rendered, such as payment for board and lodging.

Pensioner. The counterpart at Cambridge of the Oxford commoner, *i.e.* an undergraduate who pays for his own commons, etc., and is neither a sizar nor on the foundation of a college.

At the Inns of Court the *pensioner* is the officer who collects the periodical payments made by the members for the upkeep of the Inn.

Gentlemen Pensioners. The old name for the members of the Honourable Corps of Gentlemen-at-arms (*q.v.*).

The Pensioner (or **Pensionary**) **Parliament.** That from May 8th, 1661, to Jan. 24th, 1679; convened by Charles II, and so called because of the many pensions it granted to adherents of the king.

Pentacle (pen' tăkl). A five-pointed star, or five-sided figure, used in sorcery as a talisman against witches, etc., and sometimes worn as a folded headdress of fine linen, as a defence against demons in the act of conjuration. It is also called the Wizard's Foot, and Solomon's Seal (*signum Salamonis*), and is supposed to typify the five senses, though, as it resolves itself into three triangles, its efficacy may spring from its being a triple symbol of the Trinity:

And on her head, lest spirits should invade,
A pentacle, for more assurance, laid.
            ROSE: *Orlando Furioso*, iii, 21.

The Holy Pentacles numbered forty-four, of which, seven were consecrated to each of the planets Saturn Jupiter, Mars, and the Sun; five to both Venus and Mercury; and six to the Moon. The divers figures were enclosed in a double circle, containing the name of God in Hebrew, and other mystical words.

Pentagon (pen' tă gon). A vast five-sided building erected in Washington, D.C., to house government officials. It is said to be so great that newcomers who leave their offices never find them again.

Pentameron (pen tăm' er on). A collection of stories written in the Neapolitan dialect in 1672 by Giovanni Battista Basile. It is modelled on the Decameron but consists of five days of ten stories each and was based on—in some instances was the foundation of—French fairy tales.

The Pentameron (1837) of Walter Savage Landor (1775-1864) was a collection of five long imaginary conversations.

Pentameter (pen tăm' e tĕr). In prosody, a line of five feet, dactyls or spondees divided by a cæsura into two parts of two and a half feet each—the line used in alternation with the hexameter (*q.v.*) in Latin elegiac verse. The name is sometimes wrongly applied to the English five-foot iambic line.

In the hexameter rises the fountain's silvery column,
In the pentameter aye falling in melody back.
            COLERIDGE: *Example of Elegiac metre*.

Pentateuch (pen' ta tūk). The first five books of the Old Testament, anciently attributed to Moses. (Gr. *penta*, five, *teuchos*, a tool, book.)

The Samaritan Pentateuch. The Hebrew text as preserved by the Samaritans; it is said to date from 400 B.C.

Pentathlon (pen tăth' lon). An athletic contest of five events, usually the running broad jump, javelin throw, 200-metre race, discus throw, and 1,500-metre flat race.

Pentecost (pen' te kost) (Gr. *pentecoste*, fiftieth). The festival held by the Jews on the fiftieth day after the second day of the Passover; our Whit Sunday, which commemorates the descent of the Holy Spirit on the Apostles on the Day of Pentecost (*Acts* ii).

Penthesilea (pen the sil ē' a). Queen of the Amazons who, in the post-Homeric legends, fought for Troy; she was slain by Achilles. Hence, any strong, commanding woman; Sir Toby Belch, in *Twelfth Night* (ii, 3), calls Maria by this name.

Pent-house. Originally any smaller building with a sloping roof erected against the wall of a house, the word has now become associated chiefly with the dwelling houses built on the roofs of skyscrapers, etc., above the main roof line, but recessed behind the main wall line.

Peony (pē' ō ni). So called, according to fable, from Pæon, the physician who cured the wounds received by the gods in the Trojan war. The seeds were, at one time, worn round the neck as a charm against the powers of darkness.

About an Infant's neck hang Peonie,
It cures Alcydes cruell Maladie.
            Sylvester's Du Bartas, I, iii 712.

Pepperpot. A stew of tripe, dumplings, and vegetables, originating in Philadelphia.

Per contra (pĕr kon' tra) (Lat.). A commercial term for on the opposite side of the account. Used also of arguments, etc. **Per saltum** (Lat., by a leap). A promotion or degree given without going over the ground usually prescribed. Thus, a clergyman on being made a bishop may have the degree of D.D. given him *per saltum—i.e.* without taking the B.D. degree, and waiting the usual period.

Percival, Sir (pĕr' si vàl). The Knight of the Round Table who, according to Malory's *Morte d'Arthur* (and Tennyson's *Idylls of the King*), finally won a sight of the Holy Grail (*q.v.*). He was the son of Sir Pellinore and brother of Sir Lamerocke, but in the earlier French romances—based probably on the Welsh *Mabinogion* and other Celtic originals—he has no connexion with the Grail, but here (as in the English also) he sees the lance dripping blood, and the severed head surrounded by blood in a dish. The French version of the romance is by Chrétien de Troies (12th century), which formed the basis of Sebastian Evans's *The High History of the Holy Graal* (1893). The German version, *Parsifal or Parzi-val*, was written some 50 years later by Wolf-ram von Eschenbach, and it is principally on this version that Wagner drew for his opera, *parsifal* (1882).

Percy. When Malcolm III of Scotland invaded England, and reduced the castle of Alnwick, Robert de Mowbray brought to him the keys of the castle suspended on his lance; and, handing them from the wall, thrust his lance into the king's eye; from which circumstance, the tradition says, he received the name of "Pierce-eye," which has ever since been borne by the Dukes of Northumberland.

This is all a fable. The Percies are descended from a great Norman baron, who came over with William, and who took his name from his castle and estate in Normandy.—SCOTT: *Tales of a Grandfather*, iv.

Perdita (pĕr′ di tá). In *A Winter's Tale*, the daughter of Leontes and Hermione of Sicily. She was abandoned by order of her father, and put in a vessel which drifted to "the sea-coast of Bohemia," where the infant was discovered by a shepherd, who brought her up as his own daughter. In time Florizel, the son and heir of the Bohemian king Polixenes, fell in love with the supposed shepherdess. The match was forbidden by Polixenes, and the young lovers fled to Sicily. Here the story is cleared up, and all ends happily in the restoration of the lost (Fr. *perdu*) Perdita to her parents, and her marriage with Florizel.

Mrs. Robinson, the actress and mistress of George IV when Prince of Wales, was specially successful in the part of Perdita, and she assumed this name, the Prince being known as Florizel.

Père la Chaise (pâr la shāz). This great Parisian cemetery is on the site of a religious settlement founded by the Jesuits in 1626, and later enlarged by Louis XIV's confessor, Père la Chaise. After the Revolution, the grounds were laid out for their present purpose, and were first used in May, 1804.

Peregrine Falcon. A falcon of wide distribution, formerly held in great esteem for hawking, and so called (13th century) because taken when on their passage or *peregrination*, from the breeding place, instead of straight off the nest, as was the case with most other hawks (Lat. *peregrinus*, a foreigner, one coming from foreign parts).

Dame Juliana Bernérs in the *Book of St. Albans* (*see* HAWK) tells us that the peregrine

was for an earl. The hen is the *falcon* of falconers; the cock the tercel.

The word was formerly used as synonymous with *pilgrim*, and (adjectivally) for one travelling abroad.

Perfect. Perfect number. One of which the sum of all its divisors exactly measures itself, as 6, the divisors of which are 1, 2, 3 = 6. These are very scarce; indeed, from 1 to forty million there are only seven, viz. 6, 28, 496, 8,128, 130,816, 2,096,128, and 33,550,336.

Perfume means simply "from smoke" (Lat. *per fumum*), the first perfumes having been obtained by the combustion of aromatic woods and gums. Their original use was in sacrifices, to counteract the offensive odours of the burning flesh.

Paradise and the Peri. The second tale in Moore's *Lalla Rookh*. The Peri laments her expulsion from heaven, and is told she will be readmitted if she will bring to the gate of heaven the "gift most dear to the Almighty." After a number of unavailing offerings she brought a guilty old man, who wept with repentance, and knelt to pray. The Peri offered the *Repentant Tear*, and the gates flew open.

Pericles, Prince of Tyre (per′ i klēz). According to Sir Sidney Lee, the greater portion of this play, which was ascribed to Shakespeare in all the Quartos (1st, 1608), but was not admitted to the collected works before the Third Folio (1664), was by George Wilkins, author of *The Miseries of Inforst Marriage* (1607), etc. The original story was the work of a late Greek romance writer and was extremely popular in mediæval times. The hero was *Apollonius* of Tyre, and under this name the story occurs in the *Gesta Romanorum*, Gower's *Confessio Amantis* (Bk. viii), and elsewhere.

Perillos and the Brazen Bull. *See under* INVENTORS.

Perilous Castle. The castle of "the good" Lord Douglas was so called in the reign of Edward I, because Douglas destroyed several English garrisons stationed there, and vowed to be revenged on anyone who should dare to take possession of it. Scott calls it "Castle Dangerous" (*see* Introduction of *Castle Dangerous*).

Peripatetic School (per i pá tet′ ik). The school or system of philosophy founded by Aristotle, who used to walk about (Gr. *peri*, about, *patein*, to walk) as he taught his disciples in the covered walk of the Lyceum. This colonnade was called the *peripatos*.

Periphrasis (pe rif′ rȧ sis). The rhetorical term for using more words than are necessary in an explanation or description. A fair example is: "Persons prejudicial to the public peace may be assigned by administrative process to definite places of residence," *i.e.* breakers of the law may be sent to gaol.

Perissa (per is′ ȧ). The typification of excessive exuberance of spirits in Spenser's *Faerie Queene* (II, ii). She was the mistress of Sansloy and a step-sister of Elissa (*q.v.*).

> In wine and meats she flowed above the bank,
> And in excess exceeded her own might;
> In sumptuous tire she joyed herself to prank,
> But of her love too lavish.
> *Faerie Queene*, II, ii, 26.

Periwig. *See* PERUKE.

Periwinkle. The plant gets its name from Lat. *Pervinca*, which may mean either to conquer completely or to bind around, but *why* it should have received this name is unknown, though it may earlier have been applied to some climbing plant. In Italy it used to be wreathed round dead infants, and hence its Italian name, *fiore di morto*.

The sea-snail of this name was called in A.S. *pinewinkle*, the first syllable probably being cognate with Lat. *pina*, a mussel, and *winkle* from A.S. *wincel*, a corner, with reference to its much convoluted shell.

Perk. The derivation of the word is unknown, but as it is first met with (14th century) in connexion with the popinjay (parrot) it may have something to do with *perch*, the parrot bearing itself on its perch in a *perky* or jaunty way; and in some instances (*e.g.* "The eagle and the dove pearke not on one branch," Greene's *Perimedes*, and "Cæsar's crowe durst never cry *Ave* but when she was pearked on the Capitoll," Greene's *Pandosto*) it is not always easy to differentiate the two meanings.

To perk up. To get more lively, to feel better.

Perpetual Motion. The term applied to some theoretical force that will move a machine forever of itself—a mirage which holds attractions for some minds much as did the search for the philosophers' stone, the elixir of life, and the fountain of perpetual youth in less enlightened times.

It is quite possible, theoretically, at least, to eliminate all friction, air resistance, and wear and tear, and if this were done a body to which motion had been given would, unless interfered with, retain it for ever; but *only on the condition that it were given no work to do*; once connect the ideal spinning top with a wheel or crank and the spin would inevitably come to an end.

Persepolis (pĕr sep′ ō lis). The capital of the ancient Persian empire. It was situated some 35 miles NE. of Shirar. The palaces and other public buildings were some miles from the city, and were approached by magnificent flights of steps.

Perseus (pĕr′ sūs). In Greek legend, the hero son of Zeus and Danaë (*q.v.*). He and his mother were set adrift in a chest, but were rescued through the intervention of Zeus, and he was brought up by King Polydectes, who, wishing to marry his mother, got rid of him by giving him the almost hopeless task of obtaining the head of Medusa (*q.v.*). He, with the help of the gods, was successful, and with the head (which turned all that looked on it to stone) he rescued Andromeda (*q.v.*), and later metamorphosed Polydectes and his guests to stone.

Before his birth an oracle had foretold that Acrisius, Danaë's father, would be slain by Danaë's son; and this came to pass, for, while taking part in the games at Larissa, Perseus accidentally slew his grandfather with a discus.

Person. From Lat. *persona*, which meant originally a mask worn by actors (perhaps from *per sonare*, to sound through), and later was transferred to the character or personage represented by the actor (*cp.* our *dramatis personœ*), and so to any human being in his definite character, at which stage the word was adopted in English through the O.Fr. *persone*.

Persona grata (Lat.). An acceptable person; one liked.

> The Count [Münster] is not a *persona grata* at court, as the royal family did not relish the course he took in Hanoverian affairs in 1866.—*Truth*, Oct. 22, 1885.

Perth is Celtic for a bush. The county of Perth is the county of bushes.

The Five Articles of Perth. Those passed in 1618 by order of James VI, enjoining the attitude of kneeling to receive the elements; the observance of Christmas, Good Friday, Easter, and Pentecost; the rite of confirmation, etc. They were ratified August 4th, 1621, called *Black Saturday*, and condemned in the General Assembly of Glasgow in 1638.

Peru (per oo′). **From China to Peru.** From one end of the world to the other; world-wide. Equivalent to the biblical "from Dan to Beersheba." The phrase comes from the opening of Johnson's *Vanity of Human Wishes*—

> Let observation with extensive view
> Survey mankind from China to Peru.

Boileau (*Sat.* viii, 3) had previously written:—

De Paris au Pérou, du Japon jusqu'à Rome.

Peruvian Bark, called also **Jesuit's Bark,** because it was introduced into Spain by the Jesuits. "Quinine," from the same tree, is called by the Indians *quinquina*. See CINCHONA.

Peruke (per ūk') (Fr. *perruke*, the origin of which is unknown though the word has been conjecturally derived from Lat. *pilus*, hair). The wigs are first mentioned in the 16th century; in the next century they became very large, and the fashion began to wane in the reign of George III. *Periwig*, which has been further corrupted into *wig*, is a corrupt form of *peruke*.

Petard (pe tard'). **Hoist with his own petard.** Beaten with his own weapons, caught in his own trap; involved in the danger intended for others, as were many designers of instruments of torture. *See list under* INVENTORS. The petard was a thick iron engine of war, filled with gunpowder, and fastened to gates, barricades, and so on, to blow them up. The danger was lest the engineer who fired the petard should be blown up in the explosion.

> Let it work;
> For 'tis the sport, to have the engineer
> Hoist with his own petard; and it shall go hard
> But I will delve one yard below their mines,
> And blow them at the moon.
>
> *Hamlet,* iii, 4.

Pétaud (pā' tō). **'Tis the court of King Pétaud, where everyone is master.** There is no order or discipline at all. This is a French proverb. *Le roi Pétaud* (Lat. *peto*, I beg) was the title of the chief who was elected by the fraternity of beggars in mediæval France, in whose court all were equal.

Peter. St. Peter. The patron saint of fishermen, being himself a fisherman; the "Prince of the Apostles." His feast is kept universally with that of St. Paul on June 29th, and he is usually represented as an old man, bald, but with a flowing beard, dressed in a white mantle and blue tunic, and holding in his hand a book or scroll. His peculiar symbols are the keys, and a sword (*Matt.* xvi, 19 and *John* xviii, 10).

Tradition tells that he confuted Simon Magus, who was at Nero's court as a magician, and that in A.D. 66 he was crucified with his head downwards at his own request, as he said he was not worthy to suffer the same death as Our Lord. The location of his tomb under the high altar of St. Peter's, Rome, was verified in 1950.

St. Peter's fingers. The fingers of a thief. The allusion is to the fish caught by St. Peter with a piece of money in its mouth. They say that a thief has a fish-hook on every finger.

St. Peter's fish. The John Dory (*q.v.*); also, the haddock.

To peter out. To come gradually to an end, to give out. The phrase came from the American mining camps of about '49, but its origin is not known.

To rob Peter to pay Paul. *See* ROB.

Peterloo or **the Manchester Massacre.** The dispersal by the military on August 16th, 1819, of a large crowd of operatives who had assembled at St. Peter's Field, Manchester, to hear "Orator" Hunt speak in favour of Parliamentary Reform. The arrest of Hunt was ordered, but, as this was impossible and riot was feared, the magistrates gave the hussars orders to charge. Some six persons were killed in the charge, many were injured, and the arrest of Hunt (who was given two years' imprisonment) was effected.

The name was founded on *Waterloo,* then fresh in the popular mind.

Petit Sergeanty. *See* SERGEANTY.

Petitio principii (pe tish' yo prin sip' i ī). A begging of the question, or assuming in the premises the question you undertake to prove. In mediæval logic a principium was an essential, self-evident principle from which particular truths were deducible; the assumption of this principle was the *petitio, i.e.* begging, of it. It is the same as "arguing in a circle."

Petitio Principii, as defined by Archbishop Whately, is the fallacy in which the premise either appears manifestly to be the same as the conclusion, or is actually proved from the conclusion, or is such as would naturally and properly so be proved.—J. S. MILL: *System of Logic*, II, p. 389.

Petticoat Government is management by women; in another phrase, wearing the breeches.

Peutingerian Map. A map of the roads of the ancient Roman empire, constructed in the time of Alexander Severus (A.D. 226), discovered in the early 16th century by Conrad Peutinger, of Augsburg.

Pewter. To scour the pewter. To do one's work.

> But if she neatly scour her pewter,
> Give her the money that is due t' her.
>
> KING: *Orpheus and Eurydice.*

Phædria (fē' dri à). The typification in Spenser's *Faerie Queene* (II, vi) of wantonness; she was handmaid to Acrasia the enchantress, and sailed about Idle Lake in a gondola.

Phaeton (fā' ton). In classical myth, the son of Phœbus (the Sun); he undertook to drive his father's chariot, and was upset and thereby caused Libya to be parched into barren sands, and all Africa to be more or less injured, the inhabitants blackened, and vegetation nearly destroyed, and would have set the world on fire had not Zeus transfixed him with a thunderbolt.

Gallop apace, you fiery-footed steeds,
Towards Phœbus' mansion; such a waggoner
As Phæton would whip you to the west,
And bring in cloudy night immediately.
Romeo and Juliet, iii, 2.

The name is given to a light, four-wheeled open carriage usually drawn by two horses.

Phaeton's bird. The swan. Cygnus, son o Apollo, was the friend of Phaeton and lamented his fate so grievously that Apollo changed him into a swan, and placed him among the constellations.

Phalanx (făl' ăngks). The close order of battle in which the heavy-armed troops of a Grecian army were usually drawn up. Hence, any number of people distinguished for firmness and solidity of union.

Phalaris (făl' à ris). **The brazen bull of Phalaris.** *See under* INVENTORS.

The epistles of Phalaris. A series of 148 letters said to have been written by Phalaris, Tyrant of Agrigentum, Sicily, in the 6th century B.C., and edited by Charles Boyle in 1695. Boyle maintained them to be genuine, but Richard Bentley, applying methods of historical criticism, proved that they were forgeries of about the 7th or 8th centuries, A.D. *See* BOYLE CONTROVERSY.

Phallicism or **Phallic Worship** is the term applied to the primitive worship of fertility as symbolized in the phallus, or male generative organ. Phallic emblems are found in most parts of the world, but there is no reason to suppose that obelisks, church spires, and other suggestive objects are the vestiges of phallic worship.

Phantom. A spirit or apparition, an illusory appearance; from M.E. and O.Fr. *fantosme*, Gr. *phantasma* (*phanein*, to show).

The Phantom Ship. The "Flying Dutchman" (*q.v.*).

Phaon (fā' on). In Spenser's *Faerie Queene* (II, iv), a young man ill-treated by Furor, and rescued by Sir Guyon. The tale is designed to show the evil of intemperate revenge. In some editions of the poem *Phedon* is the name, not *Phaon*.

Pharamond (făr' à mond). In the Arthurian romances, a Knight of the Round Table, who is said to have been the first king of France, and to have reigned in the early 5th century. He was the son of Marcomir and father of Clodion.

La Calprenède's novel *Pharamond, ou l'Histoire de France*, was published in 1661.

Pharaoh (fâr' ō). The title or generic appellation of the kings in ancient Egypt. The word originally meant "the great house," and its later use arose much in the same way as, in modern times, "the Holy See" for the Pope, or "the Sublime Porte" for the Sultan of Turkey.

None of the Pharaohs mentioned in the Old Testament has been certainly identified, owing to the great obscurity of the references and the almost entire absence of reliable chronological data.

According to the Talmud, the name of Pharaoh's daughter who brought up Moses was *Bathia*.

In Dryden's satire *Absalom and Achitophel* (*q.v.*) "Pharaoh" stands for Louis XIV of France.

Pharisees (făr' i sēs) (Heb. *perusim*, from *perash*, to separate) means "those who have been set apart," not as a sect but as a school of ascetics who attempted to regulate their lives by the letter of the Law. The opprobrious sense of the word was given it by their enemies, because the Pharisees came to look upon themselves as holier than other men, and refused to hold social intercourse with them. The Talmud mentions the following classes:—

(1) The "Dashers," or "Bandy-legged" (*Nikfi*), who scarcely lifted their feet from the ground in walking, but "dashed them against the stones," that people might think them absorbed in holy thought (*Matt.* xxi, 44).

(2) The "Mortars," who wore a "mortier," or cap, which would not allow them to see the passers-by, that their meditations might not be disturbed. Having eyes, they saw not (*Matt.* viii, 18).

(3) The "Bleeders," who inserted thorns in the borders of their gaberdines to prick their legs in walking.

(4) The "Cryers," or "Inquirers," who went about crying out, "Let me know my duty, and I will do it" (*Matt.* xix, 16-22).

(5) The "Almsgivers," who had a trumpet sounded before them to summon the poor together (*Matt.* vi, 2).

(6) The "Stumblers," or "Bloody-browed" (*Kizai*), who shut their eyes when they went abroad that they might see no women, being "blind leaders of the blind" (*Matt.* xv, 14). Our Lord calls them "blind Pharisees," "fools and blind."

(7) The "Immovables," who stood like statues for hours together, "praying in the market places" (*Matt.* vi, 5).

(8) The "Pestle Pharisees" (*Medinkia*), who kept themselves bent double like the handle of a pestle.

(9) The "Strong-shouldered" (*Shikmi*), who walked with their back bent as if carrying on their shoulders the whole burden of the law.

(10) The "Dyed Pharisees," called by Our Lord "Whited Sepulchres," whose externals of devotion cloaked hypocrisy and moral uncleanliness. (*Talmud of Jerusalem*, *Berakoth*, ix; *Sota*, v, 7; *Talmud o Babylon*, *Sota*, 22 b.)

Pharos (fâr' os). A lighthouse; so called from the lighthouse—one of the Seven Wonders of the World—built by Ptolemy Philadelphus in the island of Pharos, off Alexandria, Egypt. It was 450 feet high, and, according to Josephus, could be seen at the distance of 42 miles. Part was blown down in 793.

Pheasant. The "Phasian bird"; so called from Phasis, a river of Colchis, whence the bird is said to have spread westward.

Phedon (fē' don). An alternative name of Phaon (*q.v.*).

Phenomenon (fe nom' e non) (pl. phenomena) means simply what has appeared (Gr. *phainomai*, to appear). It is used in science to express the visible result of an experiment. In popular language it means a prodigy, and *phenomenal* (as "a phenomenal success") is colloquial for prodigious.

Phenomenal, soon, we hope, to perish, unregretted, is (at least indirectly, through the abuse of *phenomenon*) from Metaphysics; [such words are] at present, enjoying some vogue as slang, and come from regions that to most of us are overhead.—H. W AND F. G. FOWLER: *The King's English*, ch. i (1906).

Philadelphia (fil à del' fi à). The first city of the State of Pennsylvania, was founded in 1582 by William Penn (1644-1718) and others of the Society of Friends, and so named from the Greek *Philadelpheia*, brotherly love. It was also the name of an ancient city in Asia Minor, the seat of one of the Seven Churches (*Rev.* iii, 7).

Philadelphia lawyer. A lawyer of outstanding ability, with a keen scent for the weaknesses in an adversary's case and a thorough knowledge of the intricacies of the law. "You will have to get a Philadelphia lawyer to solve that" is a familiar American phrase. It is said that in 1735, in a case of criminal libel, the only counsel who would undertake the defence was Andrew Hamilton, the famous Philadelphia barrister, who obtained his client's acquittal in face of apparently irrefutable evidence, and charged no fee. In New England there was a saying that three Philadelphia lawyers were a match for the Devil.

Philadelphists. *See* BEHMENISTS.

Philandering (fi lan' der ing). Coquetting with a woman; paying court, and leading her to think you love her, but never declaring your preference. *Philander* literally means "a lover of men" (Gr. *philos*, loving, *andros*, man), but as the word was made into a proper noun and used for a lover by Ariosto in *Orlando Furioso* (followed by Beaumont and Fletcher in *The Laws of Candy*), it obtained its present signification.

In Norton and Sackville's *Gorboduc* (1561) Philander is the name of a staid old counsellor.

Philistines (fil' is tīnz). The ill-behaved and ignorant; persons lacking in liberal culture or of low and materialistic ideas. This meaning of the word is due to Matthew Arnold, who adapted it from *Philister*, the term applied by students at the German universities to the townspeople, the "outsiders." This is said to have arisen at Jena, because, after a "town and gown" row in 1689, which resulted in a number of deaths, the university preacher took for his text "The Philistines be upon thee" (*Judges* xvi).

The people who believe most that our greatness and welfare are proved by our being very rich, and who most give their lives and thoughts to becoming rich, are just the very people whom we call the Phillistines.—M. ARNOLD: *Culture and Anarchy* (1869).

Philoctetes (fil ok tē' tēz). The most famous archer in the Trojan war, to whom Hercules, at death, gave his arrows. In the tenth year of the siege Ulysses commanded that he should be sent for, as an oracle had declared that Troy could not be taken without the arrows of Hercules. Philoctetes accordingly went to Troy, slew Paris, and Troy fell.

The *Philoctetes* of Sophocles is one of the most famous Greek tragedies.

Philomel *See* NIGHTINGALE.

Philopena (fil ō pe' nà). From the German *vielliebchen*, darling, sweetheart. A philopena is a double almond.

One evening we invited him to dine at our table, and we ate a philopena together.—Mrs. MACKIN: *Two Continents* (1898).

The word is also applied to a game in which each of two persons tries to inveigle the other into paying a forfeit.

Philosopher. The sages of Greece used to be called *sophoi* (wisemen), but Pythagoras thought the word too arrogant, and adopted the compound *Philosophie* (lover of wisdom), whence "philosopher," one who courts or loves wisdom.

Marcus Aurelius (121-80) was surnamed *The Philosopher* by Justin Martyr, and the name was also conferred on Leo VI, Emperor of the East (d. 911), and Porphyry, the Neoplatonic opponent of Christianity (d. 305).

The leading philosophers and Schools of Philosophy in Ancient Greece were—

Philosophers of the Academic sect. Plato, Speusippos, Xenocrates, Polemo, Crates, Crantor, Arcesilaos, Carneades, Clitomachos, Philo, and Antiochos.

Philosophers of the Cynic sect. Antisthenes, Diogenes of Sinope, Monimos, Onesicritos,

Crates, Metrocles, Hipparchia, Menippos, and Menedemos of Lampsacos.

Philosophers of the Cyrenaic sect. Aristippos, Hegesias, Anniceris, Theodoros, and Bion. *Philosophers of the Eleac and Eretriac sects.* Phædo, Plisthenes, and Menedemos of Eretria.

Philosophers of the Eleatic sect. Xenophanes, Parmenides, Melissos, Zeno of Tarsos, Leucippos, Democritos, Protagoras, and Anaxarchos.

Philosophers of the Epicurean sect. Epicuros, and a host of disciples.

Philosophers of the Heraclitan sect. Heraclitos; the names of his disciples are unknown.

Philosophers of the Ionic sect. Anaximander, Anaximenes, Anaxagoras, and Archelaos.

Philosophers of the Italic sect. Pythagoras, Empedocles, Epicharmos, Archytas, Alcmæon, Hippasos, Philolaos, and Eudoxos.

Philosophers of the Megaric sect. Euclid, Eubulides, Alexinos, Euphantos, Apollonius Chronosis, Diodoros, Ichthyas, Clinomachos, and Stilpo.

Philosophers of the Peripatetic sect. Aristotle, Theophrastos, Strato, Lyco, Aristo, Critolaos, and Diodoros.

Philosophers of the Sceptic sect. Pyrrho and Timon.

Philosophers of the Socratic sect. Socrates, Xenophon, Æschines, Crito, Simon, Glauco, Simmias, and Cebes.

Philosophers of the Stoic sect. Zeno, Cleanthes, Chrysippos, Zeno the Less, Diogenes of Babylon, Antipater, Panætios, Epictetus, Marcus Aurelius, and Posidonios.

Philosophers' Stone. The hypothetical substance which, according to the mediæval alchemists, would convert all baser metals into gold. Its discovery was the prime object of all the alchemists; and to the wide and unremitting search that went on for it we are indebted for the birth of the science of Chemistry, as well as for many inventions. It was in searching for this treasure that Bötticher stumbled on the manufacture of Dresden porcelain; Roger Bacon on the composition of gunpowder; Geber on the properties of acids; Van Helmont on the nature of gas; and Dr. Glauber on the "salts" which bear his name.

In Ripley's treatise, *The Compound of Alchymy* (*temp.* Edward IV), we are told the twelve stages, or "gates," in the transmutation of metals. These are:—(1) Calcination; (2) Dissolution; (3) Separation; (4) Conjunction; (5) Putrefaction; (6) Congelation; (7) Cibation; (8) Sublimation; (9) Fermentation; (10) Exaltation; (11) Multiplication; and (12) Projection. Of

these the last two were of much the greatest importance; the former consisted in the "augmentation" of the elixir, the latter in the penetration and transfiguration of metals in fusion by casting the powder of the philosophers' stone upon them, which is then called the "powder of projection." According to one legend, Noah was commanded to hang up the true and genuine philosophers' stone in the ark, to give light to every living creature therein; while another related that Deucalion (*q.v.*) had it in a bag over his shoulder, but threw it away and lost it.

Philter (Gr. *philtron*, from *philein*, to love). A draught or charm to incite in another the passion of love. The Thessalian philters were the most renowned, but both the Greeks and Romans used these dangerous potions, which sometimes produced insanity. Lucretius is said to have been driven mad by a love-potion, and Caligula's death is attributed to some philters administered to him by his wife, Cæsonia. Brabantio says to Othello:—

> Thou hast practised on her [Desdemona] with foul charms,
> Abused her delicate youth with drugs or minerals
> That weaken motion.

Phlogiston (flō jis′ ton) (Gr., burnt up). The name used by early chemists to denote the principle of inflammability that was supposed to be a necessary constituent of combustible material. It was introduced by the German chemist Georg Ernst Stahl, in 1702, and belief in the theory lasted for nearly a century.

Phœbe (fē′ bi). A female Titan of classical myth, daughter of Uranus and Ge; also a name of Diana as goddess of the moon.

Phœbus (Gr., the Shining One). An epithet of Apollo, god of the sun. In poetry the name is sometimes used of the sun itself, sometimes of Apollo as the leader of the Muses.

> Blind Melesigenes, thence Homer called,
> Whose poem Phœbus challenged for his own.
>   MILTON: *Paradise Regained*, iv, 260.

Phœnix (fē′ niks). A fabulous Arabian bird, the only one of its kind, that is said to live a certain number of years, at the close of which it makes in Arabia a nest of spices, sings a melodious dirge, flaps its wings to set fire to the pile, burns itself to ashes, and comes forth with new life.

It is to this bird that Shakespeare refers in *Cymbeline* (i, 7):—

> If she be furnished with a mind so rare,
> She is alone the Arabian bird.

He also wrote the beautiful *Phœnix and Turtle*, based on the legendary love and death of this bird and the turtle-dove.

The phœnix was adopted as a sign over chemists' shops through the association of this fabulous bird with alchemy. Paracelsus wrote about it, and several of the alchemists employed it to symbolize their vocation.

Phœnix period or **cycle,** generally supposed to be 500 years; Tacitus tells us it was 500 years; R. Stuart Poole that it was 1,460 Julian years, like the Sothic Cycle; and Lipsius that it was 1,500 years. Now, the phœnix is said to have appeared in Egypt five times: (1) in the reign of Sesostris; (2) in the reign of Amasis; (3) in the reign of Ptolemy Philadelphus; (4) a year or two prior to the death of Tiberius; and (5) in A.D. 334, during the reign of Constantine. The Phœnix Cycle is therefore irregular, the reign or existence of Sesostris being doubtful; Amasis, 566 B.C.; Ptolemy, 266 B.C.; Tiberius, A.D. 34; Constantine, A.D. 334. In corroboration of this suggestion it must be borne in mind that Jesus Christ, who died A.D. 34, is termed *the Phœnix* by monastic writers. Tacitus (*Annales*, vi, 28) mentions the first four of these appearances.

Phonograph. In Britain this word is applied to the old-fashioned sound-reproducing machine with cylindrical records that has now given place to the gramophone. In American the flat-disk gramophone is called a phonograph.

Phony. An American slang term originating about 1930 for something not genuine, bogus. The word probably comes from the "fawney" ring of imitation gold used by confidence-trick men. The period of more or less inactivity that elapsed between the declaration of war in 1939 and the invasion of Norway, Denmark, Belgium, Holland, and France in 1940 was called the "Phony War" by American journalists disappointed of sensational events.

Phrygians (frij' yànz). An early Christian sect, so called from Phrygia, where they abounded. They regarded Montanus as their prophet, and laid claim to the spirit of prophecy.

Phrygian cap. The cap of liberty (*q.v.*).

Phynnodderee, a Manx hobgoblin combining the properties of the Scandinavian troll, the Scottish brownie and the Irish leprechaun. He drives home straying sheep and helps in the harvesting if a storm be brewing.

Physician (Gr. *phusis*, nature).

The Physician finger. The third, *See* MEDICINAL FINGER.

The Beloved Physician. St. Luke (*q.v.*), so called by St. Paul in *Col.* iv, 14.

The Prince of Physicians. Avicenna, the Arabian (980-1037).

Piazza (pi ăt' zà). An Italian word meaning an open place or square in a town. In America the word has come to mean the verandah of a dwelling-house.

Picador (pik' à dôr) (Span.). An agile horseman, who, in bull fights, is armed with a gilt spear (*pica dorado*), with which he pricks the bull to madden him for the combat.

Picards. A sect of fanatics prevalent in Bohemia and the Vaudois in the early 15th century, said to be so called from Picard of Flanders, their founder, who called himself the New Adam, and tried to introduce the custom of living nude, like Adam in Paradise. They were suppressed by Ziska in 1421.

Picaresque (pik à resk'). The term applied to the class of literature that deals sympathetically with the adventures of clever and amusing rogues (Span. *picaresco*, roguish, knavish). The earliest example of the picaresque novel is Mendoza's *Lazarillo de Tormes* (1554). Le Sage's *Gil Blas* (1715) is perhaps the best known. Nash's *Jack Wilton* (1594) is the earliest English example, and others are Defoe's *Moll Flanders* and *Colonel Jack*.

Picayune. In the days of the French occupation of Florida and Louisiana the Spanish half-real ($2\frac{1}{2}$ d.) was known as a picayune, from Fr. *picaillon*, an old Piedmontese coin. The word is now used in America for anything of trifling value or of a contemptible character.

Piccadilly. This well-known London thoroughfare is named from a house that stood near the corner of Sackville Street and, in the early 17th century, was nicknamed *Pickadilly Hall*. One early account (1656) says the house was so called because it was the "outmost or *skirt* house of the Suburbs that way"; another—of the same date—because it was built by one Higgins, a tailor, who made his fortune by selling "piccadilles."

The "piccadille" was originally "the round hem or the several divisions set together about the skirt of a Garment," and was so called because it was pierced (Sp. *picado*) or slashed; thence it came to be applied to the stiff collar that supported the ruff of 17th-century gallants.

Pick-a-back. On the back or shoulders, as a pack is carried. The term dates at least from the early 16th century, but its precise origin, and the force of the *pick-*, are unknown. Other forms of it are *a-pigga-back*, *piggy-back*, *pick-back*, etc.

Pickle. A rod in pickle. One ready to chastise with at any moment; one "preserved" for use.

I'm in a pretty pickle. In a sorry plight, or state of disorder.

> How cam'st thou in this pickle?
>
> *Tempest* v, 1.

Pickwickian. In a Pickwickian sense. Said of words or epithets, usually of a derogatory or insulting kind, that, in the circumstances in which they are employed, are not to be taken as having quite the same force or implication as they naturally would have. The allusion is to the scene in ch. i of *Pickwick Papers* when Mr. Pickwick accused Mr. Blotton of acting in "a vile and calumnious manner," whereupon Mr. Blotton retorted by calling Mr. Pickwick "a humbug." It finally was made to appear that both had used the offensive words only in a Pickwickian sense, and that each had, in fact, the highest regard and esteem for the other.

Picnic. The word came into use in England about 1800 to denote a fashionable party, often but not always in the open air, at which each guest contributed towards the provisions. It is a translation of Fr. *pique-nique* (which had much the same meaning), the origin of which is uncertain.

Picts. The ancient inhabitants of Scotland, of unknown race. They were gradually dispossessed after the coming of the Scots (Goidels) from northern Ireland, about A.D. 500, and after the union of the Pictish kingdom with that of the Scots under Kenneth Mac-Alpin (844) the remnant was driven to the far north-east. The name is probably not native, but was given them by the Romans because they tattooed their bodies (Lat. *picti*, painted).

Picture (Lat. *pictura*, from *pictus*, past part of *pingere*, to paint). A model, or beau-ideal, as. *He is the picture of health*; *A perfect picture of a house*.

Picture Bible. A name given to the *Biblia pauperum* (*q.v.*).

The pictures. A colloquial and convenient way of referring to a cinematograph entertainment.

Picture hat. A woman's hat, with wide drooping brim, such as was worn by many of the sitters to Reynolds and Gainsborough.

Pidgin-English. The semi-English lingua franca used in China and the Far East, consisting, principally of mispronounced English words with certain native grammatical constructions. For instance, the Chinese cannot pronounce *r*, so replace it with *l*—*te-le* for "three," *solly* for "sorry," etc.—and, in Chinese, between a numeral and its noun there is always inserted a word (called the "classifier") and this,

in Pidgin-English, is replaced by piece—*e.g. one piece knifee, two piece hingkichi* (handkerchiefs). *Pidgin* is a corruption of *business*.

Hence, **this is not my pidgin,** this is not my business, it is not strictly my affair.

Pie or **Pi** (pī). A printing term used to describe the mix-up of types (for instance, when dropped) or a jumble of letters when a word or sentence is badly printed. The origin of the word is obscure; possibly it comes from the analogy of the mixed ingredients in a pie, or it may come from the assortment of types used in the old *pie* or pre-Reformation books of rules for finding the prayers, etc., proper for the day.

Piebald. Parti-coloured (especially black and white like a magpie), usually of horses. The word is from *pie*, the magpie (*q.v.*), and *bald*, of which one of the meanings was "streaked with white," as in the "bald-faced stag."

Piece goods are fabrics woven in the proper lengths for certain purposes rather than lengths cut off from a long bolt.

Pied (pē′ ā) Fr., foot. **Pied-a-terre** (pē ā da târ′) (Fr., foot on the ground). A temporary lodging, or a country residence; a footing.

> Mr. Harding, however, did not allow himself to be talked over into giving up his own and only *pied-à-terre* in the High Street.—ANTHONY TROLLOPE: *Bar-chester Towers.*

Pied de la lettre, Au (Fr., to the foot of the letter). Quite literally—close to the letter.

> A wild enthusiastic young fellow, whose opinions one must not take *au pied de la lettre.*—THACKERAY: *Pendennis*, I, xi.

Pied Piper of Hamelin. The legend is that the town of Hamelin (Westphalia) was infested with rats in 1284, that a mysterious Piper, clad in a parti-coloured suit, appeared in the town and offered to rid it of the vermin for a certain sum, that the townspeople accepted the offer, the Pied Piper fulfilled his contract, and that then the payment was withheld. On the following St. John's Day he reappeared, and again played his pipe. This time all the children of the town, in place of the rats, followed him; he led them to a mountain cave where all disappeared save two—one blind, the other dumb, or lame; and one legend adds that the children did not perish in the mountain, but were led over it to Transylvania, where they formed a German colony. The story is familiar from Robert Browning's poem.

> To blow the pipe his lips he wrinkled,
> And green and blue his sharp eyes twinkled . . .
> And ere three notes his pipe had uttered . . .
> Out of the houses rats came tumbling—

Great rats, small rats, lean rats, brawny rats,
Brown rats, black rats, grey rats, tawny rats . . .
And step by step they followed him dancing,
Till they came to the river Weser.

Pierrot (pēr′ ō) (*i.e.* "Little Peter"). A character originally in French mime, representing a man in growth and a child in mind and manners. He is generally the tallest and thinnest man that can be got, has his face and hair covered with white powder or flour, and wears a white gown with very long sleeves and a row of big buttons down the front.

Piers Plowman. *See* VISION OF PIERS PLOWMAN.

Pig (*see also* HOG). The pig was held sacred by the ancient Cretans because Jupiter was suckled by a sow; it was immolated in the mysteries of Eleusis; was sacrificed to Hercules, to Venus, and to the Lares by all those who sought relief from bodily ailments. The sow was sacrificed to Ceres "because it taught men to turn up the earth"; and in Egypt it was slain at grand weddings on account of its fecundity.

In the forefeet of pigs are very small holes which may be seen when the hair has been carefully removed. The tradition is that the legion of devils entered by these apertures. There are also round it some six rings, the whole together not larger than a small spangle; they look as if burnt or branded into the skin, and the tradition is that they are the marks of the devil's claws when he entered the swine (*Mark* v, 11-15).

A pig in a poke. A blind bargain. The reference is to a common trick in days gone by of trying to palm off on a greenhorn a cat for a sucking-pig. If he opened the poke or sack he "let the cat out of the bag," and the trick was disclosed. The French *chat en poche* (from which the saying may have come) refers to the fact, while our proverb regards the trick. *Pocket* is diminutive of *poke*.

Pig-headed. Obstinate, contrary.

Pigs and whistles. Trifles. *To go to pigs and whistles* is to be ruined, to go to the deuce.

I would be nane surprised to hear the morn that the Nebuchadnezzar was a' gane to pigs and whistles, and driven out with the divors bill to the barren pastures of bankruptcy.—GALT: *The Entail*, I, ix.

Pigs in clover. People who have money but don't know how to behave themselves decently. Also, a game consisting of a box divided into recesses into which one has to roll marbles by tilting the box.

When pigs fly. Never. *See also* SOW.

Pigskin. A saddle, the best being made of pigskin. "To throw a leg across a pigskin" is to mount a horse.

Pigtail. In England the word first appeared (17th century) as the name of a tobacco that was twisted into a thin rope; and it was used of the plait of twisted hair worn by sailors till the early 19th century, as it still is used of that worn by schoolgirls.

When the Mongols invaded and conquered China (*c.* 1660) they imposed on the Chinese as a sign of servitude the obligation of wearing their hair in a pigtail. This custom was observed by Chinese of whatever grade or class until the fall of the Empire in 1912, when their freedom from this vassalage was symbolized by the abolition of the pigtail.

Pig-wife. A woman who sells crockery. A *piggin* was a small pail, especially a milk-pail; and a *pig* a small bowl, cup, or mug.

Pigeon. Slang for a dupe, an easily gullible person, a gull (*q.v.*). To pigeon is to cheat or gull one out of his money by almost self-evident hoaxes. Pigeons are very easily caught by snares, and in the sporting world rogues and their dupes are called "rooks and pigeons." Thackeray has a story entitled "Captain Rook and Mr. Pigeon."

To pluck a pigeon. To cheat a gullible person of his money; to fleece a greenhorn.

Flying the pigeons. Stealing coals from a cart or sack between the coal-dealer's yard and the house of the customer.

Pigeon English. An incorrect form of "Pidgin-English" (*q.v.*).

Pigeon-hole. A small compartment for filing papers; hence, a matter that has been put on one side and forgotten is often said to have been *pigeonholed*. In pigeon-lockers a small hole is left for the pigeons to walk in and out.

Pigeon-livered. Timid, easily frightened, like a pigeon.

It cannot be
But I am pigeon-liver'd, and lack gall
To make oppression bitter, or ere this
I should have fatted all the region kites
With this slave's offal.

Hamlet, ii, 2.

Pigeon pair. Boy and girl twins. It was once supposed that pigeons always sit on two eggs which produce a male and a female, and these twin birds live together in love the rest of their lives.

The black pigeons of Dodona. Two black pigeons, we are told, took their flight from Thebes, in Egypt; one flew to Libya, and the other to Dodona (*q.v.*). On the spot where the former alighted, the temple of Jupiter Ammon was erected; in the place where the other settled, the oracle of Jupiter was established, and there the responses were made by the black pigeons that inhabited the surrounding groves. This fable is probably based on a pun upon the word *peleiai*, which usually meant "old women," but in the dialect of the Epirots signified pigeons or doves.

Piggin. *See* PIG-WIFE *above*.

Pigmies. *See* PYGMIES.

Pigwiggen. An elf in Drayton's *Nymphidia* (1627), in love with Queen Mab. He combats the jealous Oberon with great fury.

> Pigwiggen was this Fairy Knight,
> One wond'rous gracious in the sight
> Of fair Queen Mab, which day and night
> He amorously observed.

Pike. The Germans have a tradition that when Christ was crucified all fishes dived under the waters in terror, except the pike, which, out of curiosity, lifted up its head and beheld the whole scene; hence the fancy that in a pike's head all the parts of the Crucifixion are represented, the cross, three nails, and a sword being distinctly recognizable. *Cp.* PASSION-FLOWER.

Pikestaff. Plain as a pikestaff. Quite obvious and unmistakable. The earlier form of the phrase (mid-16th century) was *plain as a pack-staff, i.e.* the staff on which a pedlar carried his pack, which was worn plain and smooth.

> O Lord! what absurdities! as plain as any packstaff.—
> DRYDEN: *Amphitryon*, III, i.

Pilate. Tradition has it that Pontius Pilate's later life was so full of misfortune that, in Caligula's time, he committed suicide in Rome. His body was cast into the Tiber, but evil spirits disturbed the water so much that it was retrieved and taken to Vienne, where it was thrown into the Rhone, eventually coming to rest in the recesses of a lake on Mount Pilatus (*q.v.*) opposite Lucerne. Another legend states that the suicide occurred so that he might escape the sentence of death passed on him by Tiberius because of his having ordered the crucifixion of Christ; and yet another that both he and his wife became penitent, embraced Christianity, and died peaceably in the faith.

Tradition gives the name Claudia Procula, or Procla, to Pilate's wife, and by some she has been identified with the Claudia of 2 *Tim*, iv, 21.

Pilgrim Fathers. The term applied to the English founders of Plymouth Colony, Massachusetts, in 1620. They belonged to the church founded at Leyden by John Robinson. Having obtained a grant of land in New Jersey they came over from Holland and sailed from Plymouth in the *Mayflower* on September 6th, 1620. The party consisted of 78 men and 24 women. By stress of weather they were compelled to land on the coast of Massachusetts on December 21st, far north of the territory granted to them, and here they founded Plymouth Colony.

The Pilgrims is a club founded in their honour in 1902, with two branches, one in London and the other in New York.

Pilgrimage. A journey to a sacred place undertaken as an act of religious devotion, either simply to venerate it or to ask for the fulfilment of some prayer, or as an act of penance. It is not penitential necessarily, nor need it be performed under conditions of physical discomfort or with great solemnity, hence it can be performed by train or motor with as great reverence as if done barefoot. The chief places in the West were Walsingham and Canterbury (England); Four-vière, Puy, and St. Denis (France); Rome, Loretto, and Assisi (Italy); Compostella, Guadalupe, and Montserrat (Spain); Oetting, Zell, Cologne, Trier, and Einsiedeln (Germany).

The Pilgrimage of Grace. The rising on behalf of the Catholics that broke out in Lincolnshire in the autumn of 1536. It quickly assumed large proportions, but was finally extinguished in March, 1537, by the Council of the North, over 70 of the rebels being executed. Robert Aske, the Archbishop of York, Lord Darcy, and the Percys were the principal leaders.

The Pillars of Hercules. The opposite rocks at the entrance of the Mediterranean, one in Spain and the other in Africa. The tale is that they were bound together till Hercules tore them asunder in order to get to Gades (Cadiz). The ancients called them Calpe and Abyla; we call them Gibraltar and Mount Hacho, on which stands the fortress of Ceuta. Macrobius ascribes the feat of making the division to Sesostris (the Egyptian Hercules), Lucan follows the same tradition; and the Phœnicians are said to have set on the opposing rocks two large pyramidal columns to serve as seamarks, one dedicated to Hercules and the other to Astarte.

Pillory (pil' ôr i). Punishment by the pillory was not finally abolished in England till 1837, but since 1815 it had been in force only for perjury. In Delaware, U.S.A., it was a legal punishment down to 1905. In France it was abolished in 1848.

> The following eminent men have been put in the pillory for literary offences:—Leighton, for tracts against Charles I; Lilburn, for circulating the tracts of Dr. Bastwick; Bastwick, for attacking the Church of England;

Wharton the publisher; Prynne, for a satire on the wife of Charles I; Daniel Defoe, for a pamphlet entitled *The Shortest Way with Dissenters*, etc.

Pilot. Through Fr. from Ital. *pilota*, formerly *pedota*, which is probably connected with Gr. *pēdon*, a rudder.

Pilot fish. The small sea-fish, *Naucrates ductor*, so called because it is supposed to pilot the shark to its prey.

The pilot that weathered the storm. William Pitt, son of the first Earl of Chatham. George Canning, in 1802, wrote a song so called in compliment to him, for his having steered his country safely through the European storm stirred up by Napoleon.

Pilpay or **Bidpay** (pil pā'). The name given as that of the author of *Kalilah and Dimnah* (otherwise known as *The Fables of Pilpay*), which is the 8th-century Arabic version of the Sanskrit *Panchatantra*. The word is not a true name, but means "wise man" (Arab. *bidbah*), and was applied to the chief scholar at the court of an Indian prince.

Pimlico (pim' li kō) (London). At one time a district of public gardens much frequented on holidays. It received its name from Ben Pimlico, famous in the late 16th and early 17th centuries for his nut-brown ale, who had a tavern at Hoxton and, later, one in the neighbourhood of Chelsea.

Have at thee, then, my merrie boyes, and beg for old Ben Pimlico's nut-brown ale. —*Newes from Hogsdon* (1598).

Pin. The original *pin* (A.S. *pinn*, connected with *pinnacle*) was a small tapered peg of wood, horn, metal, etc. In various forms pins were used by all peoples of antiquity, and it is a mistake to suppose that pins were invented in the reign of François I, and introduced into England by Catherine Howard, fifth wife of Henry VIII. In 1347, 200 years before the death of François, 12,000 pins were delivered from the royal wardrobe for the use of the Princess Joan.

I don't care a pin, or a pin's point. In the least.

[the Red-cross Knight] not a pin
Does care for look of living creature's eye.
SPENSER: *Faerie Queene*, I, v, 4.

Not worth a pin. Wholly worthless.

Pin money. A woman's allowance of money for her own personal expenditure. At one time pins were a great expense, and in 14th- and 15th-century wills there are often special bequests for the express purpose of buying pins; when they became cheap and common the women spent their allowance on other fancies, but the term *pin money* remained in vogue.

Miss Hoyden: Now, nurse, if he gives me two hundred a year to buy pins, what do you think he'll give me to buy fine petticoats?
Nurse: Ah, my dearest, he deceives thee foully, and he's no better than a rogue for his pains! These Londoners have got a gibberage with 'em would confound a gipsy. That which they call pin-money is to buy their wives everything in the varsal world, down to their very shoe-ties. —VANBRUGH: *The Relapse*, v, 5 (1697).

Pins and needles. The tingling sensation that comes over a limb when it has been numbed, or "asleep."

There's not a pin to choose between them. They're as like as two peas, practically no difference.

To tirl at the pin. *See* TIRL.

Weak on his pins. Weak in his legs, the legs being a man's "pegs" or supporters.

You could have heard a pin drop. Said of a state—especially a sudden state in the midst of din—of complete silence. Leigh Hunt speaks of "a pin-drop silence" (*Rimini*, I, 144).

Pin-table. A popular game depending partly on skill but mostly on chance in which balls are shot up an inclined table and touch various pins when rolling back, scoring points according to the pins they strike. It is usually combined with a penny-in-the-slot machine which deals the players an allotted number of balls.

Pin-up Girl. In World War II the forces used to pin up in their billets, etc., pictures of film stars, actresses, or their own particular girls. The phrase seems to have come into use in the U.S.A. in 1941.

Pinch. A pinch for stale news. A punishment for telling as news what is well known.

At a pinch. In an urgent case; if hard pressed. There are things that one cannot do in the ordinary way, but that one may manage "at a pinch."

To be pinched for money. To be in financial straits, hard up. Hence, to *pinch and scrape*, or *to pinch it*, to economize.

To pinch. Slang for to steal.

Where the shoe pinches. *See* SHOE.

Pinch-hitter. A person who substitutes for another in a crisis. The term is from the game of Baseball where the pinch-hitter—a man who always hits the ball hard—is put in to bat when his team is in desperate straits.

Pinchbeck. An alloy of copper (5 parts) and zinc (1 part), closely resembling gold. So called from Christopher Pinchbeck (1670-1732), a manufacturer of trinkets, watches and jewellery in Fleet Street, London. The term is used figuratively of anything spurious, of deceptive appearance, or low quality.

Pindaric Verse (pin dar′ ik). Irregular verse; a poem of various metres, and of lofty style, in imitation of the odes of Pindar. *Alexander's Feast*, by Dryden, and *The Bard*, by Gray, are examples.

Pine-tree State. Maine, which has forests of these trees, and bears a pine-tree on its coat of arms.

Pink. The flower is so called because the edges of the petals are *pinked* or notched. The verb *to pink* means to pierce or perforate, also to ornament dress material by punching holes in it so that the lining can be seen, scalloping the edges, etc. In the 17th century it was commonly used of stabbing an adversary, especially in a duel.

In the pink. In a first-rate state of health; flourishing (*cp. next*).

The pink of perfection. The flower or very acme of perfection. In the same way Shakespeare (*Romeo and Juliet*, ii, 4) has "the pink of courtesy."

Pious. The Romans called a man who revered his father *pius*; hence Antoninus was called *Pius*, because he requested that his adoptive father (Hadrian) might be ranked among the gods. Æneas was called *Pius* because he rescued his father from the burning city of Troy. The Italian word *pietà* (*q.v.*) has a similar meaning.

The Pious. Ernest I, founder of the House of Gotha. (1601-74.)

Robert, son of Hugues Capet. (971, 996-1031.)

Louis I of France. *See* DEBONAIR.

Eric IX of Sweden. (d. 1161.)

Frederick III, Elector Palatine. (1575-76.)

Pip. The pips on cards and dice were named from the seeds of fruit (earlier *peep*, origin obscure). This is merely an abbreviated form of *pippin*, which denoted the seed long before it denoted apples raised from seed. *To be pipped* is to be blackballed or defeated, the black ball being the "pip."

Piping hot. Hot as water which pipes or sings; hence, new, only just out.

Piping times of peace (Shakespeare, *Richard III*, i, 1). Times when there was no thought of war, and the pastoral pipe instead of the martial trumpet was heard on the village greens.

Put that in your pipe and smoke it. Digest that, if you can. An expression used by one who has given an adversary a severe rebuke.

The pipe of peace. *See* CALUMET.

To pipe one's eye. To snivel, weep.

To put one's pipe out. To spoil his piping; to make him change his key or sing a different tune; to "take his shine out."

Pipeclay. Routine; fossilized military dogmas of no real worth, such as excessive attention to correctness in dress, drill, etc. (*Cp.* RED TAPE.) Pipeclay was at one time largely used by soldiers for whitening their gloves, belts and other accoutrements.

Pipe-laying. (U.S.A.) Swaying the issue in an election by slipping in voters who are not on the electoral roll.

Office of the Clerk of the Pipe. A very ancient office in the Court of Exchequer, where leases of Crown lands, sheriffs' accounts, etc., were made out. It existed in the reign of Henry II, and was abolished in the reign of William IV.

Piper. Piper's news. Stale news; "fiddler's news" (*q.v.*).

The Pied Piper. *See* PIED.

Tom Piper. So the piper is called in the morris dance.

The Piper referred to by Drayton seems to have been a sort of jongleur or *raconteur* of short tales.

> Tom Piper is gone out, and mirth bewailes,
> He never will come in to tell us tales.

Who's to pay the piper? *See* PAY.

Pippin. *See* PIP.

Piqué (pē′ kā). The art of inlaying gold or silver in another material, such as tortoiseshell or ivory.

Pirie's Chair. "The lowest seat o' hell."

> In Pirie's chair you'll sit, I say,
>   The lowest seat o' hell;
> If ye do not amend your ways,
>   It's there that ye must dwell.
>   *Child's English and Scottish Ballads:*
>   *The Courteous Knight.*

Pis-aller (pēs ăl′ ā) (Fr., worst course). A makeshift; something for want of a better; a *dernier ressort*.

Pistol. Formerly *pistolet*; so called from the old *pistolese*, a dagger or hanger for the manufacture of which Pistoia, in Tuscany, was famous.

Pocket pistol. *See* POCKET.

To fire one's pistol in the air. Purposely to refrain from injuring an adversary. The phrase is often used of argument, and refers to the old practice of duellers doing this when they wished to discharge a "debt of honour" without incurring risks.

Pit-a-pat. My heart goes pit-a-pat. Throbs, palpitates. An echoic or a mere ricochet word, of which there are a great many in English— as "fiddle-faddle," "harum-scarum," "ding-dong," etc.

> Anything like the sound of a rat
> Makes my heart go pit-a-pat.
>   BROWNING: *Pied Piper of Hamelin.*

Pitcairn Island, in the South Pacific, was the first home of the mutineers of the *Bounty* (*q.v.*).

Pitch. The black resinous substance gets its name from Lat. *pix*; the verb (to fling, settle, etc.) is the M.E. *pichen, pykken.*

A pitched battle. One for which both sides have made deliberate preparations.

Pitch and pay. Pay up at once. There is a suppressed pun in the phrase: "to pay a ship" is to pitch it.

The word is pitch and pay—trust none.
Henry V, ii, 3.

Pitch and toss. A game in which coins are pitched at a mark, the player getting nearest having the right to toss all the others' coins into the air and take those that come down with heads up. Hence, *to play pitch and toss* with one's money, prospects, etc., is to gamble recklessly, to play ducks and drakes.

The bounding pinnace played a game
Of dreary pitch and toss;
A game that, on the good dry land,
Is apt to bring a loss.
THOS. HOOD: *The Sea Spell.*

To pitch into one. To assail him vigorously; to give it him hot.

Pitcher. From Lat. *picarium* or *bicarium*; the word is a doublet of BEAKER (*q.v.*).

Little pitchers have long ears. Little folk or children hear what is said when you little think it. The ear of a pitcher is the handle, made somewhat in the shape of a man's ear.

Pixie or **Pixy** (pik' si). A sprite or fairy of folklore, especially in Cornwall and Devon, where some hold pixies to be the spirits of infants who have died before baptism. The Pixy monarch has his court like Oberon, and sends his subjects on their several tasks. The word is probably Celtic, but its history is unknown.

Placebo (plăs ē' bō) (Lat., I shall please, *or* be acceptable). Vespers for the dead; because the first antiphon at Vespers of the Office of the Dead began with the words *Placebo Domino in regione vivorum*, I will walk before the Lord in the land of the living (*Ps.* cxvi, 9).

As sycophants and those who wanted to get something out of the relatives of the departed used to make a point of attending this service and singing the *Placebo* the phrase *to sing Placebo* came to mean "to play the flatterer or sycophant"; and Chaucer (who in the *Merchant's Tale* gives this as a name to a parasite) has—

Flatereres been the develes chapelleyns that singen evere *Placebo.—Parson's Tale*, § 40.

Plagiarist (plā' jà rist), one who appropriates another's ideas, etc., in literature, music, and so on, means strictly one who kidnaps a slave (Lat. *plagiarius*). Martial applies the word to the kidnappers of other men's brains.

Plain, The. The Girondists were so called in the French Revolutionary National Convention, because they sat on the level floor or plain of the hall. After their overthrow this part of the House was called the *marais* or swamp, and included such members as were under the control of the Mountain (*q.v.*).

It's all plain sailing. It's perfectly straightforward; there need be no hesitation about the course of action. A nautical phrase which should be written *plane*, not *plain*. **Plane sailing** is the art of determining a ship's position on the assumption that the earth is flat and she is sailing, therefore, on a plane, instead of a spherical surface, which is a simple and easy method of computing distances.

Plains Indians is the name given by ethnographers to the Indian tribes of the central prairie areas of North America from Alberta to Texas—the land, indeed, once ranged over by the American bison or buffalo on which the Plains Indians largely subsisted. The Plains Indians are the Redskins of romance, with their feather bonnets, tepees, and pipes of peace—the Dakotas, Blackfeet, Cheyennes, Comanches, Pawnees, Apaches, and many others.

Planets. The heavenly bodies that revolve round the sun in approximately circular orbits; so called from Gr. (through Lat. and O.Fr.) *planasthai*, to wander, because, to the ancients, they appeared to wander about among the stars instead of having fixed places.

The *primary planets* are Mercury, Venus, the Earth, Mars, Jupiter, Saturn, Neptune, Uranus, and Pluto (disc. in 1930); these are known as the *major planets*, the asteroids between the orbits of Mars and Jupiter being the *minor planets*.

The *secondary planets* are the satellites, or moons, revolving round a primary.

Mercury and Venus are called *Inferior Planets* because their orbits are nearer to the sun than the Earth's; the remaining planets are *Superior Planets*.

Only five of the planets were known to the ancients (the Earth, of course, not being reckoned), viz. Mercury, Venus, Mars, Jupiter, and Saturn; but to these were added the Sun and the Moon, making seven in all. Among the astrologers and alchemists

THE SUN (APOLLO)	represented	Gold.
THE MOON (DIANA)	"	Silver.
MERCURY	"	Quicksilver.

VENUS	”	Copper.
MARS	”	Iron.
JUPITER	”	Tin.
SATURN	”	Lead.

In heraldry the arms of royal personages used to be blazoned by the names of planets (see HERALDRY).

To be born under a lucky (or **unlucky**) **planet.** According to astrology, some planet, at the birth of every individual, presides over his destiny. Some of the planets, like Jupiter, are lucky; and others, like Saturn, are unlucky. *See* HOUSES, ASTROLOGICAL.

Plank, A. Any one portion or principle of a political *platform* (*q.v.*).

To walk the plank. To be put to the supreme test; also, to be about to die. Walking the plank was a mode of disposing of prisoners at sea, much in vogue among pirates in the 17th century.

Plantagenet (plăn tăj' e net), from *planta genista* (broom-plant), the family cognizance first assumed by Geoffrey, Count of Anjou (d. 1151), during a pilgrimage to the Holy Land, as a symbol of humility. By his wife Matilda, daughter of Henry I of England, he was father of Henry II, the founder of the House of Plantagenet.

The House of Plantagenet. Henry II and the English kings descended in the direct male line from him, viz.:—

Henry II	Edward I
Richard I	Edward II
John	Edward III
Henry III	Richard II

They reigned from 1154 to 1399. *Cp.* ANGEVIN.

Plate. In horse-racing, the gold or silver cup forming the prize; hence the race for such a prize.

Selling plate. A race in which owners of starters have to agree beforehand that the winner shall be sold at a previously fixed price.

Plates of meat. Rhyming slang for "feet"; often abbreviated to *plates*.

Platform. The policy or declaration of the policy of a political party, that on which the party stands, each separate principle being called a *plank* of the platform.

In this sense the word is an Americanism dating from rather before the middle of last century; but in earlier Elizabethan times and later it was used of a plan or scheme of Church government and of political action.

Queen Elizabeth, in answer to the *Supplication* of the Puritans (offered to the Parliament in 1586), said she "had examined the platform and accounted it most prejudicial to the religion established, to her crown, her government, and her subjects."

Platonic (plå ton' ik). Pertaining to or ascribed to Plato, the great Greek philosopher (d. about 347 B.C.) who taught a form of Idealism that attributed real Being to general concepts or Ideas and denied the existence of individual things, the world of *sense* being an illusion, the world of *thought* all.

Platonic bodies. An old name for the five regular geometric solids described by Plato— viz. the tetrahedron, hexahedron, octahedron, dodecahedron, and icosahedron, all of which are bounded by like, equal, and regular planes.

Platonic love. Spiritual love between persons of opposite sexes; the friendship of man and woman, without anything sexual about it. The phrase is founded on a passage towards the end of the *Symposium* in which Plato was extolling not the non-sexual love of a man for a woman, but the loving interest that Socrates took in young men—which was pure, and therefore noteworthy in the Greece of the period.

I am convinced, and always was, that Platonic Love is Platonic nonsense.—RICHARDSON: *Pamela*, I, lxxviii.

The Platonic Year. The same as the Platonic Cycle. *See under* CYCLE.

Platonism is characterized by the doctrine of pre-existing eternal ideas, and teaches the immortality and pre-existence of the soul, the dependence of virtue upon discipline, and the trustworthiness of cognition.

Play. "This may be play to you, 'tis death to us." The allusion is to Æsop's fable of the boys throwing stones at some frogs.

As good as a play. Intensely amusing. It is said to have been the remark of Charles I when he attended the debate on Lord Ross's "Divorce Bill."

Played out. Exhausted; out of date; no longer in vogue.

Playing to the gallery, or **to the gods.** Appealing to the less cultured taste attributed to the common people; appealing to sensational rather than artistic taste.

The "gods" in theatrical phrase are the spectators in the uppermost gallery. The ceiling of Drury Lane Theatre—only just above the gallery—was at one time painted in imitation of the sky, with cupids and deities. In French this gallery is nicknamed *paradis*.

Playing possum. *See* POSSUM.

Pleader, Pleading. *See* SPECIAL PLEADING.

Plebeian (ple bē' àn). One of, or appertaining to, the common people; properly a free citizen of Rome, neither patrician nor client. Plebeians were, however, free landowners, and had their own "gentes."

Plebiscite (pleb' i sit). In Roman history, a law enacted by the "comitia" or assembly of tribes; nowadays it means the direct vote of the whole body of citizens of a State on some definite question.

In France, the resolutions adopted in the Revolution by the voice of the people, and the general votes given during the Second Empire—such as the general vote to elect Napoleon III emperor of the French were by plebiscite.

Pledge. To guarantee; to assign as security; hence, in drinking a toast, to give assurance of friendship by the act of drinking.

> Drink to me only with thine eyes,
> And I will pledge with mine.
>   BEN JONSON.

To take the pledge. To bind oneself by a solemn undertaking to abstain from intoxicating liquors; the *pledge* being the guarantee or security—one's pledged word.

Pleiades (plī' a dēz). The cluster of stars in the constellation Taurus, especially the seven larger ones out of the great number that compose the cluster; so called by the Greeks, possibly from *plein*, to sail, because they considered navigation safe at the return of the Pleiades, and never attempted it after those stars disappeared.

The **Pleiades** were the seven daughters of Atlas and Pleione. They were transformed into stars, one of which, Electra (*q.v.*), is invisible, some said out of shame, because she alone married a human being, while others held that she hides herself from grief for the destruction of the city and royal race of Troy. She is known as "the lost Pleiad":—

> One of those forms which flit by us, when we
> Are young, and fix our eyes on every face; . . .
> Whose course and home we know not, nor shall know
> Like the lost Pleiad seen no more below.
>   BYRON: *Beppo*, xiv.

The name **The Pleiad** has frequently been given to groups of seven specially illustrious persons, *e.g.*:—

The Seven Wise Men of Greece (*q.v.*), sometimes called the *Philosophical Pleiad*.

The Pleiad of Alexandria. A group of seven contemporary poets in the 3rd century B.C., viz. Callimachus, Apollonius of Rhodes, Aratus, Philiscus (called *Homer the Younger*), Lycophron, Nicander, and Theocritus.

Charlemagne's Pleiad, the group of scholars with which the Emperor surrounded himself, viz. Charlemagne (who, in this circle, was known as "David"), Alcuin ("Albinus"), Adelard ("Augustine"), Angilbert ("Homer"), Riculfe ("Damætas"), Varnefrid, and Eginhard.

The French Pleiad of the 16th century, who wrote poetry in the metres, style, etc., of the ancient Greeks and Romans. Of these, Ronsard was the leader, the others being Dorat, Du Bellay, Remi Belleau, Jodelle, Baïf, and Ponthus de Thyard.

The second French Pleiad. Seven contemporary poets in the reign of Louis XIII, very inferior to the "first Pleiad." They are Rapin, Commire, Larue, Santeuil, Ménage, Dupérier, and Petit.

Plonk. Also "Red Biddy" or "pinkie". Cheap red wine fortified with methylated spirit. Much drunk by lower types in Australia.

Plough. Another name for the "Great Bear" (*q.v.*).

Plover. Another old synonym for a dupe or "gull" (*q.v.*); also for a courtesan.

To live like a plover. To live on nothing, to live on air. Plovers, however, live on small insects and worms, which they hunt for in newly ploughed fields.

Pluck, meaning courage, determination, was originally pugilistic slang of the late 18th century, and meant much the same as *heart*. A "pug" who was lacking in pluck was a coward, he hadn't the heart for his job; the *pluck* of an animal is the heart, liver, and lungs, that can be removed by one pull or *pluck*. Cp. the expressions bold *heart*, lily-*livered*, a man of another *kidney*, *bowels* of mercy, a *vein* of fun, it raised his *bile*, etc.

A rejected candidate at an examination is said to be *plucked*, because formerly at the Universities, when degrees were conferred and the names were read out before presentation to the Vice-Chancellor, the proctor walked once up and down the room, and anyone who objected might signify his dissent by *plucking* the proctor's gown. This was occasionally done by tradesmen to whom the candidate was in debt.

Plug. Plug song. A song given publicity, *e.g.* on the wireless. *To plug,* in this connexion, is to publicize—sometimes to an extreme degree.

Plug ugly. A rowdy, unpleasant character, a term said to have originated in Baltimore.

Plum. Old slang for a very large sum of money (properly £100,000), or for its possession. Nowadays the figurative use of the word means the very best part of anything, the "pick of the basket," a windfall, or one of the prizes of life, as "The plums (*i.e.* the chief and highly paid positions) of the Civil Service should go by merit, not influence."

Plumes. In borrowed plumes. Assumed merit; airs and graces not merited. The allusion is to the fable of the jackdaw who dressed up in peacock's feathers.

Plump. To give all one's votes to a single candidate, or to vote for only one when one has the right to vote for more. The earlier phrase was **to give a plumber,** or **to vote plump.**

Plus ultra (plŭs ŭl' trá). The motto in the royal arms of Spain. It was once *Ne plus ultra* ("thus far and no farther"), in allusion to the pillars of Hercules, the *ne plus ultra* of the world; but after the discovery of America, and when Charles V inherited the crown of Aragon and Castile, with all the vast American possessions, he struck out *ne*, and assumed the words *plus ultra* for the national motto, the suggestion being that Spain *can* go farther.

Pluto (ploo' tō). The ruler of the infernal regions in Roman mythology, son of Saturn, brother of Jupiter and Neptune, and husband of Proserpine (*q.v.*); hence, the grave, the place where the dead go to before they are admitted into Elysium or sent to Tartarus.

> Brothers, be of good cheer, this night we shall sup with Pluto.—*Leonidas to the three hundred Spartans before the battle of Thermopylæ.*

> Th' infernal powers
> Covering your foe with cloud of deadly night,
> Have borne him hence to Pluto's baleful bowers.
> *SPENSER: Faerie Queene,* I, v, 14.

A *Pluto* of the 20th century is the large, amiable, and stupid dog who is the companion of Mickey Mouse in Walt Disney's animated cartoons.

In World War II *Pluto* was the code name (from the initials of Pipe Line Under The Ocean) given to the pipelines to carry petrol which were laid across the bed of the English Channel from England to France—from Sandown to Cherbourg and from Dungeness to Boulogne. In all, these Pluto lines covered a distance of 770 miles, and consisted of 23,000 tons of lead piping and 5,500 tons of steel piping. Much of this was recovered in 1949.

Plutonian or **Plutonist.** *See* VULCANIST.

Plutonic Rocks. Granites, certain porphyries and other igneous unstratified crystalline rocks, supposed to have been formed at a great depth and pressure, as distinguished from the volcanic rocks, which were formed near the surface.

So called by Lyell from *Pluto*, as the lord of elemental fire.

Plutus (ploo' tus). In Greek mythology, the god of riches. Hence, **Rich as Plutus,** and *plutocrat*, one who exercises influence or possesses power through his wealth. The legend is that he was blinded by Zeus so that his gifts should be equally distributed and not go only to those who merited them.

Plymouth Brethren. A sect of Evangelical Christians that arose at Plymouth about 1830. They have no regular ministry, holding that national churches are too lax and dissenters too sectarian. Sometimes called "Darbyites" (*q.v.*) from John Nelson Darby (1800-82), their founder.

Pocahontas (pok à hon' tás). Daughter of Powhatan, an Indian chief of Virginia, born about 1595. She is said to have rescued Captain John Smith when her father was on the point of killing him. She subsequently married John Rolfe, one of the settlers at Jamestown, was baptized under the name of Rebecca, and in 1616 was brought to England, where she became an object of curiosity and frequent allusion in contemporary literature. She died at Gravesend in 1617.

> The blessed
> Pocahontas, as the historian calls her,
> And great king's daughter of Virginia. . . .
> *BEN JONSON: Staple of News,* II, i (1625).

Pocket. The word is used by airmen to denote a place where a sudden drop or acceleration is experienced, owing to a local variation in air-pressure.

Pocket battleship. A small, heavily armoured warship built in accordance with the limiting terms of a treaty. By the Treaty of Versailles Germany was forbidden to build battleships of over 10,000 tons. In consequence she constructed several formidable battleships which purported to be within this limit, though it was discovered later that they were not.

Pocket borough. A parliamentary borough where the influence of the magnate was so powerful as to be able to control the election of any candidate.

Pocket judgment. A bond under the hand of a debtor, countersigned by the sovereign. It could be enforced without legal process, but for long has fallen into disuse.

Pocket pistol. Colloquial for a flask carried in "self-defence," because we may be unable to get a dram on the road.

Pocket veto. When the President of the U.S.A. refuses to ratify a Bill which has passed both Houses, he is said to *pocket* it.

Pococurante (pō kō kū răn′ ti) (Ital., *poco curante*, caring little). Insouciant, devil-may-care, easy-go-lucky. Hence, *pococurantism*, indifference to matters of importance but concern about trifles. Also used for one who in argument leaves the main gist and rides off on some minor and indifferent point.

Poet. Poet Laureate. A court official, appointed by the Prime Minister, whose duty it is (or was) to compose odes in honour of the sovereign's birthday and in celebration of State occasions of importance.

The first Poet Laureate officially recognized as such was Ben Jonson, but in earlier times there had been an occasional *Versificator Regis*, and Chaucer, Skelton, Spenser, and Daniel were called "Laureates" though not appointed to that office. The following is the complete list of Poets Laureate:—

Ben Jonson, 1619-1637.
Sir William Davenant, 1660-1668.
John Dryden, 1670-1688.
Thomas Shadwell, 1688-1692.
Nahum Tate, 1692-1715.
Nicholas Rowe, 1715-1718.
Laurence Eusden, 1718-1730.
Colley Cibber, 1730-1757.
William Whitehead, 1757-1785.
Thomas Warton, 1785-1790.
Henry James Pye, 1790-1813.
Robert Southey, 1813-1843.
William Wordsworth, 1843-1850.
Alfred Tennyson, 1850-1892.
Alfred Austin, 1896-1913.
Robert Bridges, 1913-1930.
John Masefield, 1930-

The term arose from the ancient custom in the universities of presenting a laurel wreath to graduates in rhetoric and poetry. There were at one time "doctors laureate," "bachelors laureate," etc.; and in France authors of distinction are still at times "crowned" by the Academy.

Poeta nascitur non lit. Poets are born, not made. *See* BORN.

Poets′ Corner, The. The southern end of the south transept of Westminster Abbey, first so called by Oliver Goldsmith because it contained the tomb of Chaucer. Addison had previously (*Spectator*, No. 26, 1711) alluded to it as the "poetical Quarter," in which, he says—

I found there were Poets who had no Monuments, and Monuments which had no Poets.

Besides Chaucer's tomb it contains that of Spenser, and either the tombs of or monuments to Drayton, Ben Jonson, Shakespeare (a statue), Milton (bust), Samuel Butler, Davenant, Cowley, Prior, Gay, Addison, Thomson, Goldsmith, Dryden, Dr. Johnson, Sheridan, Burns, Southey, Coleridge, Campbell, Macaulay, Longfellow, Dickens, Thackeray, Tennyson, Browning, and Hardy.

The term *Poet's Corner* is also facetiously applied to the part of a newspaper in which poetical contributions are printed.

Pogrom. An organized massacre, especially one of those directed against the Jews in Russia in 1905 and later. The word is Russian, and means devastation (*gromit*, to thunder, to destroy unmercifully).

Poilu (pwa′ lū). The popular name for the French private soldier, equivalent to our "Tommy Atkins." It means literally "hairy," but it had been used by Balzac as meaning "brave."

Point. Defined by Euclid as "that which hath no parts." Playfair defines it as "that which has position but not magnitude," and Legendre says it "is a limit terminating a line," which suggests that a point could not exist, even in imagination, without a line, and presupposes that we know what a *line* is.

A point of honour. *See* HONOUR.

A point-to-point race. A race, especially a steeplechase, direct from one point to another; a cross-country race.

Armed at all points. Armed to the teeth; having no parts undefended.

A figure like your Father,
Arm'd at all points exactly, *Cap a Pe*,
Appears before them.
Hamlet, i, 2.

Come to the point! Speak out plainly what you want; don't beat about the bush, but avoid circumlocution and get to the gist of the matter.

In point of fact. A stronger way of saying "As a fact," or "As a matter of fact."

Not to put too fine a point upon it. Not to be over delicate in stating it; the prelude to a blunt though truthful remark.

To give one points. To be able to accord him an advantage and yet beat him; to be considerably better than he.

To make a point of doing something. To treat it as a matter of duty, or to make it a special object. The phrase is a translation of the older French *faire un point de*.

To stretch a point. To exceed what is strictly right. There may be an allusion here to the tagged laces called *points*, formerly used in costume; to "truss a point" was to tie the laces which held the breeches; to "stretch a point" to stretch these laces, so as to adjust the dress to extra growth, or the temporary fullness of good feeding.

Point-blank. Direct. A term in gunnery; when a cannon is so placed that the line of sight is parallel to the axis and horizontal, the discharge is point-blank, and was supposed to go direct, without curve, to an object within a certain distance. In French *point blanc* is the white mark or bull's-eye of a target, to hit which the ball or arrow must not deviate in the least from the exact path.

Now art thou within point-blank of our jurisdiction regal. — *2 Henry VI*, iv, 7.

Point of No Return. The point at or beyond which the pilot of an aircraft is ordered to go on rather than turn back in the event of trouble.

Poison. It is said that poisons had no effect on Mithridates, King of Pontus. This was Mithridates VI (d. 63 B.C.), called the Great, who succeeded his father at the age of eleven, and fortified his constitution by drinking antidotes to poisons which might at any moment be administered to him by persons about the court. *See* MITHRIDATE.

Poisson d'Avril (pwa' son dà vril) (Fr., April fish). The French equivalent for our "April fool" (*q.v.*).

Poke. A bag, pouch, or sack—from which comes our *pocket*, a little poke. The word is rarely used nowadays, except in the phrase **To buy a pig in a poke** (*see* PIG). The word is not connected with the verb *to poke*.

Poke bonnet. A long, straight, projecting bonnet, commonly worn by women in the early 19th century, and still worn by Salvation Army lasses and old-fashioned Quaker women. Why it was so called is not clear—probably because it projects or *pokes* out.

To poke fun at one. To make one a laughing-stock.

Poker Face. An expressionless face characteristic of the good poker-player who assumes it to conceal from his adversaries any idea of what cards he may be holding.

Poland. The Partition of Poland. This country, situated between the leading military powers of Eastern Europe—Russia, Austria, and Prussia—has for the last two centuries been subject to invasion by, and division between, those countries. The first partition between the three was in 1772; the second in 1793; the final partition in 1796. The kingdom was reconstituted under Napoleon's authority, but was annexed to the Russian crown in 1832. It was again set up, as a republic, in 1919, but partitioned between Germany and Russia in 1939. In 1945 it was again reconstituted as a separate state under Russian dominance.

Polish Corridor. The territory given to Poland by the Treaty of Versailles to enable her to have access to the Baltic Sea. It followed roughly the line of the Vistula and reached the sea to the west of Danzig (declared a free city) and the port of Gdynia was built by Poland for her commerce. The Corridor cut off East Prussia from the rest of Germany and was one of the causes of irritation which eventually led to World War II.

Pole. The stake, mast, measure ($16\frac{1}{2}$ ft.), etc., gets its name from Lat. *palus*, a pale or stake; *pole*—the North Pole, magnetic pole, etc.—is from Gr. *polos*, an axis, pivot.

Barber's pole. *See* BARBER.

Polish Off. To finish out of hand. In allusion to articles polished.

I'll polish him off in no time. I'll set him down, give him a drubbing.

To polish off a meal. To eat it quickly, and not keep anyone waiting.

Polixenes (pol ix' e nēz). Father of Florizel and King of Bohemia in Shakespeare's *Winter's Tale* (*q.v.*).

Polka. A round dance said to have been invented about 1830 by a Bohemian servant girl. In a few years it took Europe by storm. The polka is danced in couples in 2-4 time, the characteristic feature being the rest on the second beat.

Poll (pōl) (of Teutonic origin), means the head; hence, the number of persons in a crowd ascertained by counting heads, hence the counting of voters at an election, and such phrases as **to go to the polls**, to stand for election, and **poll tax**, a tax levied on everybody.

The Cambridge term, **the Poll**, meaning students who obtain only a pass degree, *i.e.* a degree without honours, is probably from Gr. *hoi polloi*, the common herd. These students— *poll men*, are said to *go out in the poll*, and to take a *poll degree*.

Pollux (pol' ŭks). In classical mythology the twin brother of Castor (*q.v.*).

Polly. Mary. The change of M for P in pet names is by no means rare; *e.g.*—

Margaret. Maggie or Meggy, becomes Peggie, and Pegg or Peg.

Martha. Matty becomes Patty.

In the case of *Mary*—*Polly* we see another change by no means unusual—that of *r* into *l* or *ll*. Similarly, *Sarah* becomes Sally; *Dorothea*, Dora, becomes Dolly; *Harry*, Hal.

Polonius (pol ō' ni ŭs). A garrulous old courtier, in *Hamlet*, typical of the pompous, sententious old man. He was father of Ophelia, and lord chamberlain to the king of Denmark.

Polony (po lō' ni). A corruption of *Bologna* (*sausage*).

Poltergeist (pol tĕr gīst). A household spirit, well known to spiritualists, remarkable for throwing things about, plucking the bedclothes, making noises, etc. It is a German term—*polter*, noise, *geist*, spirit.

Polt-foot. A club-foot. Ben Jonson calls Vulcan, who was lame, the "polt-footed philosopher."

Venus was content to take the blake Smith (*i.e.*, blacksmith Vulcan) with his powlt foote.—LYLY: *Euphues.*

Polycrates (pol i krā' tēz), Tyrant of Samos, was so fortunate in all things that Amasis, King of Egypt, advised him to chequer his pleasures by relinquishing something he greatly prized. Whereupon Polycrates threw into the sea a beautiful seal, the most valuable of his jewels. A few days afterwards a fine fish was sent him as a present, and in its belly was found the jewel. Amasis, alarmed at this good fortune, broke off his alliance, declaring that sooner or later this good fortune would fail; and not long afterwards Polycrates was shamefully put to death by Orœtes, who had invited him to his court.

Polydore (pol' i dôr). The name assumed by Guiderius in Shakespeare's *Cymbeline*.

Polyhymnia (pol i him' ni à). The Muse of lyric poetry, and inventor of the lyre. *See* MUSES.

Polyphemus (pol i fē' mùs). One of the Cyclops, an enormous giant, with only one eye, and that in the middle of his forehead, who lived in Sicily. When Ulysses landed on the island, this monster made him and twelve of his crew captives; six of them he ate, and then Ulysses contrived to blind him, and escape with the rest of the crew (*cp.* LESTRIGONS). Polyphemus was in love with Galatea, a sea-nymph who had set her heart on the shepherd Acis; Polyphemus, in a fit of jealousy, crushed him beneath a rock.

Poma Alcinoo dare. *See* ALCINOO.

Pomander (pom ăn' dĕr). From the French *pomme d'ambre*, apple of amber, or ambergris. A ball made of perfume, such as ambergris or musk, which was worn or carried in a perforated case in order to ward off infection or counteract bad smells. The cases, usually of gold or silver, were also called "pomanders."

Pomatum (po mā' tùm). Another name for *pomade*, which was so called because it was originally made by macerating over-ripe apples (Fr. *pommes*) in grease.

There is likewise made an ointment with the pulpe of Apples and Swines grease and Rose water, which is used to beautifie the face . . . called in shops *pomatum*, of the Apples whereof it is made.—GERARDE: *Herbal*, III, xcv (1597).

Pommard. A red Burgundy wine, so called from a village of that name in the Côte d'Or, France. The word is sometimes colloquially used for cider, the pun being on *pomme*, apple.

Pommel. The pommel of a sword is the rounded knob terminating the hilt, so called on account of its apple-like shape (Fr. *pomme*, apple); and *to pommel one*, now to pound him with your fists, was originally to beat him with the pommel of your sword.

Pompadour (pom' pa dôr), as a colour, is claret purple, so called from Louis XV's mistress, the Marquise de Pompadour (1721-64).

There is an old song supposed to be an elegy on John Broadwood, a Quaker, which introduces the word:—

Sometimes he wore an old brown coat.
  Sometimes a pompadore,
  Sometimes 'twas buttoned up behind,
  And sometimes down before.

The word is also applied to a fashion of hairdressing in which the hair is raised (often on a pad) in a wave above the forehead.

Pone, from an Indian word meaning something baked; in the Southern U.S.A. it is used for maize bread.

Pongo. In the ancient romance *The Seven Champions of Christendom* he was an amphibious monster of Sicily who preyed on the inhabitants of the island for many years. He was slain by the three sons of St. George.

Pons Asinorum (ponz ăs i nôr' ùm) (Lat., the asses' bridge). The fifth proposition, Bk. i, of Euclid—the first difficult theorem, which dunces rarely get over for the first time without stumbling. It is anything but a "bridge"; it is really *pedica asinorum*, the "dolt's stumbling-block."

Pontiff. The term was formerly applied to any bishop, but now only to the Bishop of Rome—the Pope—*i.e.* the Sovereign Pontiff. It means literally one who has charge of the bridges, as these were in the particular care of the principal college of priests in ancient Rome, the head of which was the Pontifex Maximus (Lat. *pons, pontis*, a bridge).

Pontius Pilate's Body-guard. *See* REGIMENTAL NICKNAMES.

Pony. Slang for £25; also (especially in the U.S.A.) for a translation crib; also for a small beer-glass holding a little under a gill.

In card games the person on the right hand of the dealer, whose duty it is to collect the cards for the dealer, is called the *pony*, from Lat. *pone*, "behind," being behind the dealer.

Pony Express. This was the U.S. government mail system across the continent just before the days of railways and telegraphs. It ran from St. Joseph, Missouri, to the Pacific Coast and was inaugurated in 1860; less than two years later it was superseded by the electric telegraph. Pony Express is a misnomer, as fleet horses were used, ridden for stages of 10 to 15 miles by men who did three stages, or over 30 miles, before passing on the wallet to the next rider. The schedule time for the whole distance was ten days, but Lincoln's inaugural address was taken across the continent in 7 days 17 hours. The fame of the Pony Express rests largely on the hardihood and courage of the riders, who braved storms, landslides, and Indian ambushes to get their mail through on time.

Poor. Poor as a church mouse. In a church there is no cupboard or pantry where even so little a creature as a mouse could find a crumb.

Poor as Job. The allusion is to Job being deprived by Satan of everything he possessed.

Poor as Lazarus. This is the beggar Lazarus, full of sores, who was laid at the rich man's gate, and desired to be fed from the crumbs that fell from Dives' table (*Luke* xvi, 19-31).

Poor man. The blade-bone of a shoulder of mutton is so called in Scotland. In some parts of England it is termed a "poor knight of Windsor," because it holds the same relation to "Sir Loin" as a Windsor knight does to a baronet. Scott (*Bride of Lammermoor*, ch. xix) tells of a laird who, being asked by an English landlord what he would have for dinner, produced the utmost consternation by saying, "I think I could relish a morsel of a poor man."

Poor Richard. The assumed name of Benjamin Franklin in a series of almanacks from 1732 to 1757. They contained maxims and precepts on temperance, economy, cleanliness, chastity, and other virtues; and several ended with the words, "as poor Richard says."

Pope. The word represents the A.S. *papa*, from ecclesiastical Latin, and Gr. *pappas*, the infantile word for *father* (*cp.* modern "papa"); it is not connected with Lat. *popa*, which denoted an inferior Roman (pagan) priest who brought the victim to the altar and felled it with an axe. In the early Church the title was given to many bishops; Leo the Great (440-61) was the first to

use it officially, and in the time of Gregory VII (1073-85) it was, by decree, specially reserved to the Bishop of Rome. *Cp.* PONTIFF.

According to Platina, Sergius II (844-6) was the first pope who changed his name on ascending the papal chair. Some accounts have it that his name was Hogsmouth, others that it was "Peter di Porca," and he changed it out of deference to St. Peter, thinking it arrogant to style himself Peter II.

Gregory the Great (591) was the first pope to adopt the title *Servus Servorum Dei* (the Servant of the Servants of God). It is founded on *Mark* x, 44.

> Fye upon all his jurisdiccions
> And upon those whiche to hym are detters;
> Fye upon his bulles breves and letters
> Wherein he is named *Servus Servorum*.
>   *Rede Me and be nott Wrothe*, v, 13 (1528).

The title *Vicar of Christ*, or *Vicar of God*, was adopted by Innocent III, 1198. *See also* TIARA.

The number of popes is not certain; there are, however, with the election of Pius XII (1939) 262 commonly enumerated. Of these 204 were Italians, 15 Frenchmen, 15 Greeks, 7 Syrians, 6 Germans, 3 Spaniards, 2 Dalmatians, 2 Africans, and 1 each English, Portuguese, Cretan, Thracian, Sardinian, Jew (St. Peter).

The Pope's eye. The tender piece of meat (the lymphatic gland) surrounded by fat in the middle of a leg of mutton. The French call it *Judas's eye*, and the Germans *the priest's tit-bit*.

The Pope's slave. So Cardinal Cajetan (d. 1534) called the Church.

The Red Pope. The Prefect of the Propaganda (*q.v.*).

Pope Joan. A mythical female pope, fabled in the Middle Ages to have succeeded Leo IV (855). The vulgar tale is that Joan conceived a violent passion for the monk Folda and in order to get admission to him assumed the monastic habit. Being clever and popular, she was elected pope, but was discovered through giving birth to a child during her enthronization. The whole story has long since been exploded.

The name was given to a once popular card-game played with an ordinary pack *minus* the eight of diamonds (called the "Pope Joan"); also to a circular revolving tray divided into eight compartments.

Popinjay (pop' in jay). An old name for a parrot (ultimately of Arabic origin; Gr. *papagos*), hence a conceited or empty-headed fop.

> I then, all smarting with my wounds being cold,
> To be so pestered with a popinjay,

Answered neglectingly I know not what,
He should or he should not.
                                    1 *Henry IV*, i, 3.

The Festival of the Popinjay. The first
Sunday in May, when a figure of a popinjay,
decked with parti-coloured feathers and suspended from a pole, served as a target for shooting
practice. He whose ball or arrow brought down
the bird by cutting the string by which it was
hung, received the proud title of "Captain
Popinjay," or "Captain of the Popinjay," for the
rest of the day, and was escorted home in
Trumph.

Poplar. The poplar was consecrated to
Hercules, because he destroyed Kakos in a cavern
of Mount Aventine, which was covered with
poplars. In the moment of triumph the hero
plucked a branch from one of the trees and
bound it round his head. When he descended
to the infernal regions, the heat caused a profuse
perspiration which blanched the under surface
of the leaves, while the smoke of the eternal
flames blackened the upper surface. Hence the
leaves of the poplar are dark on one side and
white on the other.

Poplin. This silk and worsted material, now
made chiefly in Ireland, gets its name from the
old *papal* (Ital. *papalino*) city of Avignon,
because up to the 17th century that was the chief
seat of its manufacture.

Popular Front. A political alliance by all
Left Wing parties (Labour, Liberal, Socialist,
but not necessarily Communist) against reactionary government and especially dictatorship.

Populist. A term applied in U.S.A. to a
member of the People's Party, a political party
formed in 1891 and committed to the expansion of the currency, the restriction of land
ownership, the state control of transport, etc.

Porcelain, from Ital. *porcellana*, "a little
pig," the name given by the early Portuguese
traders, to cowrie-shells, the shape of which is
not unlike a pig's back, and later to Chinese
earthenware, which is white and glossy, like the
inside of these shells.

Pork, pig. The former is Norman, the latter
Saxon. As in the case of most edible domestic
animals the Norman word is used for the meat
and the Saxon for the live animal.

Porphyrogenitus (pôr fi rō jen' i tŭs). A
surname of the Byzantine Emperor, Constantine
VII (911-59). It signifies "born in the purple"
(Gr. *porphuros*, purple, *genetos*, born), and a
son born to a sovereign after his accession is
called a *porphyrogenito*. *Cp.* PURPLE.

Port. The origin of the nautical term, meaning the left-hand side of a ship when looking
forward, is not certain; but it is probably from
port, a harbour. The word has been in use for
over three centuries, and in course of time took
the place of the earlier *larboard* which was so
easily confused with *starboard*. When the steer-
ing-gear was on the starboard (*i.e. steer-board*)
side it was almost a necessity to enter port and
tie up at the harbour with the larboard side
towards the *port*, and this probably accounts for
the name.

In the days when a ship was steered by a
tiller it was necessary to put the tiller to port in
order to make the rudder—and thus the
vessel—go to starboard. Thus it came that "port
the helm" meant really "steer the ship to starboard." To do away with this anomaly, after
World War I the rule was introduced universally
that "Port the helm" should mean "Turn to
port," and "Starboard the helm," to starboard.

A vessel's **port-holes** are so called from Lat.
porta, a door; the harbour is called a *port* from
Lat. *portus*, a haven; the dark red wine gets its
name *port* from *Oporto*, Portugal, whence it is
exported; and *port*, the way of bearing oneself,
etc. (Queen Elizabeth I, says Speed, daunted
the Ambassador of Poland "with her stately port
and majestical deporture") from Lat. *portare*, to
carry.

Any port in a storm. Said when one is in a
difficulty and some not particularly good way
out offers itself; a last resource.

Porteous Riot. At Edinburgh in September,
1736. John Porteous was captain of the city
guard, and, at the execution of a smuggler
named Andrew Wilson, ordered the guards to
fire on the mob, which had become tumultuous; six persons were killed, and eleven
wounded. Porteous was condemned to death,
but reprieved; whereupon the mob burst into
the jail where he was confined, and, dragging
him to the Grassmarket (the usual place of
execution), hanged him by torchlight on a
barber's pole.

Portia (pôr' shà). A rich heiress and "lady
barrister" in Shakespeare's *Merchant of Venice*
(*q.v.*), in love with Bassanio. Her name is often
used allusively for a female advocate.

Portland Vase. A cinerary urn of transparent
dark blue glass, coated with opaque white
glass cut in cameo fashion, found in a tomb
(supposed to be that of Alexander Severus)
near Rome in the 17th century. In 1770 it
was purchased from the Barberini Palace by

Sir William Hamilton for 1,000 guineas, and came afterwards into the possession of the Duke of Portland, one of the trustees of the British Museum, who placed it in that institution for exhibition. In 1845 a lunatic named Lloyd dashed it to pieces, but it was so skilfully repaired that the damage is barely visible. It is ten inches high, and six in diameter at the broadest part.

Portmanteau Word. An artificial word made up of parts of others, and expressive of a combination denoted by those parts—such as *squarson*, a cross between a *squire* and a *parson*. Lewis Carroll invented the term in *Through the Looking-Glass*, ch. vi; *slithy*, he says, means *lithe* and *slimy*, *mimsy* is *flimsy* and *miserable*, etc. So called because there are two meanings "packed up" in the one word.

Portsoken Ward (pôrt sō' ken). The most easterly of the City of London wards—the old *Knighten Guild* (*q.v.*)—lying outside the wall in the parish of St. Botolph, Aldgate. Its name indicates the *soke* or franchise of the city (*not* of the gate). *Port* is an old name for any city, and occurs in *Portreeve*, the chief city officer.

Poseidon (pó sī'don). The god of the sea in Greek mythology, the counterpart of the Roman Neptune (*q.v.*). He was the son of Cronos and Rhea, brother of Zeus and Pluto, and husband of Amphitrite. It was he who, with Apollo, built the walls of Troy, and as the Trojans refused to give him his reward he hated them and took part against them in the Trojan War. Earthquakes were attributed to him, and he was said to have created the first horse.

Poser. Formerly used of an examiner, one who *poses* (*i.e.* "opposes") questions, especially a bishop's examining chaplain and the examiner it Eton for the King's College fellowship. Nowadays the word usually denotes a puzzling question or proposition.

Posh. Onomatopœic slang for smart, swagger, well-turned-out; as, "You're looking very posh to-day," spruce and well groomed.

Posse (pos' i) (Lat., to be able). A body of men—especially constables—who are armed with legal authority.

Possum. To play possum is to lie low, to feign quiescence, to dissemble. The phrase comes from the opossum's habitual attempt to avoid capture by pretending to be dead.

Post. Beaten on the post. Only just beaten; a racing term, the "post" being the winning-post.

Post haste. With great speed or expedition. The allusion is to the old coaching days, when travelling by relays of horses, or with horses placed on the road to expedite the journey, was the rule in cases of urgency.

Post-Impressionism. Name applied to the group of French painters, headed by Cézanne, Gauguin, and Van Gogh, stemming from *Impressionism* (*q.v.*).

To run your head against a post. To go ahead heedlessly and stupidly, or as if you had no eyes.

Poste restante (Fr., remaining post). A department at a post office to which letters may be addressed for callers, and where they will remain (with certain limits) until called for.

Post (Lat.; in compounds). *Post factum* (Lat.). After the act has been committed.

Post hoc, ergo propter hoc (Lat.). *After* this, therefore *because of* this; expressive of the fallacy that a sequence of events is always the result of cause and effect. The swallows come to England in the spring, but do not bring the spring.

Post meridian (Lat.). After noon; usually contracted to "P.M."

> 'Twas post meridian half-past four,
> By signal I from Nancy parted.
> <div align="right">DIBDIN: <i>Sea Songs</i>.</div>

Post mortem (Lat.). After death; as a post-mortem examination for the purpose of ascertaining the cause of death.

Post obit (Lat. *post obitum*, after the death, *i.e.* of the person named in the bond). An agreement to pay for a loan a larger sum of money, together with interest at death.

Posteriori. *See* A POSTERIORI.

Posy properly means a copy of verses presented with a bouquet. It now means the verses without the flowers, as the "posy of a ring," or the flowers without the verses, as a "pretty posy."

> He could make anything in poetry, from the posy of a ring to the chronicle of its most heroic wearer.—STEDMAN: *Victorian Poets* (Landor), p. 47.

Pot. A big pot. An important person, a personage; a leader of his class or group.

A pot of money. A large amount of money; especially a large stake on a horse.

A little pot is soon hot. A small person is quickly "riled." Grumio makes humorous use of the phrase in *The Taming of the Shrew* (iv, 1).

A watched pot never boils. Said as a mild reproof to one who is showing impatience; watching and anxiety won't hasten matters.

Gone to pot. Ruined, gone to the bad. The allusion is to the pot into which bits of already cooked meat are cast prior to their making their last appearance as hash.

The pot calls the kettle black. Said of a person who accuses another of faults similar to those committed by himself.

The pot of hospitality. The pot or cauldron always hanging over the open fire which in Ireland used to be dipped into by anyone who dropped in at meal-times, or required refreshment.

And the "pot of hospitality" was set to boil upon the fire, and there was much mirth and heartiness and entertainment.—*Nineteenth Century*, Oct., 1891, p. 643.

To keep the pot a-boiling. To go on paying one's way and making enough to live on; also, to keep things going briskly, to see that the interest does not flag.

Pot-boiler. Anything done merely for the sake of the money it will bring in—because it will "keep the pot a-boiling," *i.e.* help to provide the means of livelihood; applied specially to work of small merit by artists or literary men.

Pot-hook. The hook over an open fire on which hung the pot. The term was applied to the shaky curves and loops made by the beginner in handwriting.

Come and take pot-luck with me. Come and take a family dinner at my house; we'll all "dip into the pot" and share anything that's going.

Pot valiant. Made courageous by liquor.

Potato. This very common vegetable (*Solanum tuberosum*) was introduced into Ireland (and thence into England) from America by Sir Walter Raleigh about 1584, but the name (from Haitian *batata*) properly belonged to another tuberous plant (*Batata edulis*, of the natural order *Convolvulaceœ*), now known as the *sweet potato*, which was supposed to have aphrodisiac qualities. It is to this latter that Falstaff refers when he says "Let the sky rain potatoes" (*Merry Wives*, v, 5), and there are many allusinos to it in contemporary literature.

To think small potatoes of it. To think very little of it, to account it of very slight worth, or importance.

Poteen (po tēn') (Irish *poitin*, little pot). Whisky that is produced privately in an illicit still, and so escapes duty.

Potent. Cross potent. An heraldic cross, each limb of which has an additional cross-piece like the head of an old-fashioned crutch; so called from Fr. *potence*, a crutch. It is also known as a *Jerusalem cross*.

Potlatch. A North American Indian feast at which gifts are distributed lavishly to the guests, while the hosts destroy much of their own property in a magnificent ostentation of wealth and possessions. It is a social barbarity to refuse an invitation to a potlatch, or, having been to one, to neglect to give a potlatch in return; rivalry in this insensate feast-giving often reduced the givers to ruin.

Potpourri (pō poo' rē) (Fr.). A mixture of dried sweet-smelling flower-petals and herbs preserved in a vase. Also a hotch-potch or olla podrida. In music, a medley of favourite tunes strung together.

Pourri means rotting [flowers], and potpourri, strictly speaking, is the vase containing the sweet mixture.

Pott. A size of printing and writing paper ($15\frac{1}{2} \times 12\frac{1}{2}$ in.); so called from its original watermark, a pot, which really represented the Holy Grail.

Poult (pōlt). A chicken, or the young of the turkey, guinea-fowl, etc. The word is a contraction of *pullet*, from late Lat. *pulla*, a hen, whence *poultry, poulterer*, etc.

Poulter's Measure. In prosody, a metre consisting of alternate Alexandrines and four-teeners, *i e* twelve syllable and fourteen-syllable lines. The name was given to it by Gascoigne (1576) because, it is said, poulterers—then called *poulters*—used sometimes to give twelve to the dozen and sometimes fourteen. It was a common measure in early Elizabethan times; the following specimen is from a poem by Surrey:—

> Good ladies, ye that have your pleasures in exile,
> Step in your foot, come take a place, and mourn with me a while;
> And such as by their lords do set but little price
> Let them sit still, it skills them not what chance come on the dice.

Pound. The unit of weight (Lat. *pondus*, weight); also cash to the value of twenty shillings sterling, because in the Carlovingian period the Roman pound (twelve ounces) of pure silver was coined into 240 silver pennies. The symbols £ and *lb.* are for *libra*, the Latin for a pound.

In for a penny, in for a pound. *See* PENNY.

Pound of flesh. The whole bargain, the exact terms of the agreement, the bond *literatim et verbatim*. The allusion is to Shylock, in *The Merchant of Venice*, who bargained with Antonio for a "pound of flesh," but was foiled in his suit by Portia, who said the bond was expressly a pound of flesh, and therefore (1) the Jew must cut the exact quantity, neither more nor less than a just pound; and (2) in so doing he must not shed a drop of blood.

Poverty. When poverty comes in at the door, love flies out at the window. An old proverb, given in Ray's *Collection* (1742), and appearing in many languages. Keats says much the same in *Lamia* (Pt. ii):—

Love in a hut, with water and a crust,
Is—Love forgive us—cinders, ashes, dust.

Powder. I'll powder your jacket for you. A corruption of Fr. *poudrer*, to dust.

Not worth powder and shot. Not worth the trouble; the thing shot won't pay the cost of the ammunition.

Pow-wow. A consultation. Derived from the North American Indians.

Practical and **Practicable.** These two words are often confused in common usage. Practical means adapted to actual conditions, pertaining to action not theory or speculation. A practical man is one better adapted to doing manual jobs than to speculating about them. A practical joke (rarely a joke to its victim, be it observed) is a piece of humour that depends on some action on the part of the perpetrator, usually to the discomfiture of the subject.

Practicable is applied to something capable of being done, feasible. In theatrical usage a practicable door or window in a piece of stage scenery is one that can be actually opened and shut.

Præmonstratensian. *See* PREMONSTRATENSIAN.

Præmunire (prē mū nī′ rè). A writ charging a sheriff to summon one accused of an indictable offence committed overseas, authorized by the *Statute of Præmunire* (1392); so called from the words *præmunire facias*, cause thou to warn (so and so) that appear in the opening sentence. The Statute was soon used specially to prevent the purchase in Rome of excommunications, etc., and to stop the assertion or maintenance of papal jurisdiction in England and the denial of the ecclesiastical supremacy of the Crown. Offenders could be punished by outlawry, forfeiture of goods, and attachment.

Praetorian Guard (pre ′tôr′ i ȧn). The household troops of the Roman Empire. *Praetor* was the title given to the consul who had supreme command of the army; his bodyguard was the Praetorian Guard.

Pragmatic Sanction. *Sanctio* in Latin means a "decree or ordinance with a penalty attached," or, in other words, a "penal statute." *Pragmaticus* means "relating to state affairs," so that Pragmatic Sanction is a penal statute bearing on some important question of state. The term was first applied by the Romans to those statutes which related to their provinces. The French applied the phrase to certain statutes which limited the jurisdiction of the Pope; but generally it is applied to an ordinance fixing the succession in a certain line.

Pragmatism (Gr. *pragma*, deed). The philosophical doctrine that the only test of the truth of human cognitions or philosophical principles is their practical results, *i.e.* their workableness. It does not admit "absolute" truth, as all truths change their trueness as their practical utility increases or decreases. The word was introduced in this connexion about 1875 by the American logician C. S. Peirce (1839-1914) and was popularized by William James, whose *Pragmatism* was published in 1907.

Prairie Schooner. A large covered wagon, drawn by oxen or mules, used to transport settlers across the North American continent.

Praise the Lord and Pass the Ammunition (World War II). Phrase used by an American Naval chaplain during the Japanese attack on Pearl Harbour, though the actual identity of the chaplain has since been in dispute. Made the subject of a popular song in 1942.

Prajapatis. *See* MENU.

Prayer-wheel. A device used by the Tibetan Buddhists as an aid or substitute for prayer, the use of which is said to be founded on a misinterpretation of the Buddha's instructions to his followers, that they should "turn the wheel of the law"—*i.e.* preach Buddhism incessantly—we should say as a horse in a mill. It consists of a pasteboard cylinder inscribed with—or containing—the mystic formula *Om mani padme hum* (*q.v.*) and other prayers, and each revolution represents one repetition of the prayers.

Pre-Adamites. The name given by Isaac de la Peyrère (1655) to a race of men whom he supposed to have existed before the days of Adam. He held that only the Jews are descended from Adam, and that the Gentiles derive from these "Pre-Adamites."

Prebend (preb′ end) (O.Fr. from late Lat. *prœbenda*, a grant, pension). The stipend given out of the revenues of the college or cathedral to a canon; he who enjoys the prebend is the *prebendary*, though he is sometimes wrongly called the *prebend*.

Precarious (Lat. *precarius*, obtained by prayer) is applied to what depends on our prayers or requests. A *precarious tenure* is one that depends solely on the will of the owner to concede to our prayer; hence uncertain, not to be depended on.

Précieuses, Les (prä sē ĕrz). The intellectual circle that centred about the Hotel de Rambouillet in 17th-century Paris. It may be interpreted as "persons of distinguished merit."

Their affected airs were the subject of Molière's comedy *Les Prècieuses Ridicules*, 1659.

Precious Stones. The ancients divided precious stones into male and female. The darker stones were called the males, and the light ones were called the females. Male sapphires approach indigo in colour, but the female ones are sky-blue. Theophartus mentions the distinction.

The tent shook, for mighty Saul shuddered; and sparkles 'gan dart

From the jewels that woke in his turban, at once with a start,

All its lordly male-sapphires, and rubies courageous at heart.

BROWNING: *Saul*, viii.

Each month, according to the Poles, is under the influence of a precious stone:—

January	. . Garnet	. . *Constancy*.
February	. . Amethyst	. . *Sincerity*.
March	. . . Bloodstone	. *Courage*.
April	. . . Diamond	. . *Innocence*.
May	. . . Emerald	. . *Success in love*.
June	. . . Agate	. . . *Health and long life*.
July	. . . Cornelian	. . *Content*.
August	. . Sardonyx	. *Conjugal felicity*.
September	Chrysolite	. *Antidote to madness*.
October	. . Opal	. . . *Hope*.
November	. Topaz	. . . *Fidelity*.
December	. Turquoise	. *Prosperity*.

In relation to the signs of the Zodiac—

Aries	. . Ruby.	Libra	. . Jacinth.
Taurus	. Topaz.	Scorpio	. Agate.
Gemini	. Carbuncle.	Sagittarius	. Amethyst.
Cancer	. Emerald.	Capricornus	. Beryl.
Leo	. . Sapphire.	Aquarius	. Onyx.
Virgo	. . Diamond.	Pisces	. . Jasper.

In relation to the planets—

Saturn	. . . Turquoise	. . *Lead*.
Jupiter	. . . Cornelian	. . . *Tin*.
Mars	. . . Emerald	. . . *Iron*.
Sun	. . . Diamond	. . . *Gold*.
Venus	. . . Amethyst	. . . *Copper*.
Moon	. . . Crystal	. . . *Silver*.
Mercury	. . Loadstone	. . . *Quicksilver*.

It was an idea of the ancients that precious stones were dewdrops condensed and hardened by the sun.

Precocious means ripened by the sun before it has attained its full growth (Lat. *prœ*, before, *coquere*, to cook); hence, premature; development of mind or body beyond one's age.

Many precocious trees, and such as have their spring in winter, may be found.—BROWN.

Premier. The *Prime Minister*, or *first* minister of the Crown, formerly (17th century) called the *Premier Minister*, from Fr. *Ministre premier*, first minister. The first British prime minister was Sir Robert Walpole (1676-1745), chief political adviser to George I and II.

Première, the feminine of Fr. *premier*, is used in English of the first performance of a play or showing of a cinematograph film.

Premillenarians. *See* SECOND (*Second Adventists*).

Premonstratensian (prē mon strà tcn' sian) or *Norbertine Order*. An order of Augustinians founded by St. Norbert in 1120 in the diocese of Laon, France. A spot was pointed out to him in a vision, and he termed the spot *Pré Montré* or *Pratum Monstratum* (the meadow pointed out). The order possessed thirty-five monasteries in England—where they were known as the White Canons of the rule of St. Augustine—at the time of the Dissolution.

Prepense (prē pens'). **Malice prepense.** Malice designed or deliberate; "malice aforethought" (Lat. *prœ*, before, Fr. *penser*, to think).

Preposterous (Lat. *prœ*, before, *posterus*, coming after). Literally, "putting the cart before the horse"; hence, contrary to reason or common sense.

Your misplacing and preposterous placing is not all one in behaviour of language, for the misplacing is alwaies intollerable, but the preposterous is a pardonable fault, and many times gives a pretie grace unto the speech. We call it by a common saying to *set the* carte before the horse.—PUTTENHAM: *Arte of English Poesie*, Bk, iii, ch. xxii (1589).

Presbyterian Church. A Church governed by elders or presbyters (Gr. *presbuteros*, elder), and ministers, all of equal ecclesiastical rank; especially the United Presbyterian Church of Scotland, which was formed in 1847 by the union of the United Secession and Relief Churches, and which in 1900 united with the Free Church of Scotland.

Presence. *See* REAL PRESENCE.

Press-gang. The name given to the bodies of men who formerly carried out the impressment of those liable to forced service in the Army or Navy. It was almost entirely used to get men for the Navy. Edward III set up a Commission of Empressment, 1355. In 1641 Parliament declared the system illegal, but it was later used by Cromwell to obtain men for his land forces and in the latter half of the 18th century it was used with much harshness and scandal to recruit men for the Navy.

Prester John (*i.e.* John the Presbyter). A fabulous Christian king and priest, supposed in mediæval times to have reigned somewhere in the heart of Asia in the 12th century. He figures in Ariosto (*Orlando Furioso*, Bks. xvii-xix), and has furnished materials for a host of mediæval legends.

I will fetch you a toothpicker now from the farthest inch of Asia; bring you the length of Prester John's foot; fetch you a hair off the great Cham's beard. . . .—*Much Ado About Nothing*, ii, 1.

According to "Sir John Mandeville" he was a lineal descendant of Ogier the Dane (*q.v.*), who penetrated into the north of India with fifteen of his barons, among whom he divided the land. John was made sovereign of Teneduc, and was called *Prester* because he converted the natives. Another tradition says he had seventy kings for his vassals, and was seen by his subjects only three times in a year. So firm was the belief in his existence that Pope Alexander III (d. 1181) sent him letters by a special messenger. The messenger never returned.

Prestige (pres tēzh). This word has a strangely metamorphosed meaning. The Lat. *præstigiœ* means juggling tricks, hence *prestidigitateur* (Fr.), one who juggles with his fingers. We use the word for that favourable impression which results from good antecedents. The history of the change is this: Juggling tricks were once considered a sort of enchantment; to enchant is to charm, and to charm is to win the heart.

Preston and his Mastiffs. To oppose Preston and his mastiffs is to be foolhardy, to resist what is irresistible. Christopher Preston established the Bear Garden at Hockley-in-the-Hole in the time of Charles II, and was killed in 1700 by one of his own bears.

> . . . I'd as good oppose
> Myself to Preston and his mastiffs loose.
> OLDHAM: *III Satire of Juvenal.*

Pretender. The Old Pretender. James Francis Edward Stuart (1688-1766), son of James II.

The Young Pretender. Charles Edward Stuart (1720-88), son of the "Old Pretender." *See* JACOBITES.

Pretext (prē' tekst). A pretence or excuse. From the Latin *prœtexta*, a dress embroidered in the front worn by Roman magistrates, priests, and children of the aristocracy between the age of thirteen and seventeen. The *prœtextatœ* were dramas in which actors personated those who wore the pretexta; hence persons who pretend to be what they are not.

Prevarication. The Latin word *varico* is to straddle, and *prœvaricor*, to go zigzag or crooked. The verb, says Pliny, was first applied to men who ploughed crooked ridges, and afterwards to men who gave crooked answers in the law courts, or deviated from the straight line of truth. *Cp.* DELIRIUM.

Prevent. Precede, anticipate (Lat. *prœvenio*, to go before). And as what goes before us may hinder us, so prevent means to hinder or keep back.

> My eyes prevent the night watches.—*Ps.* cxix, 148.
> Prevent us, O Lord, in all our doings.—*Book of Common Prayer.*

Previous Question. *See* QUESTION.

Priam (prī' ám), King of Troy when that city was sacked by the Greeks, husband of Hecuba, and father of fifty children, the eldest of whom was Hector. When the gates of Troy were thrown open by the Greeks concealed in the wooden horse, Pyrrhus, the son of Achilles, slew the aged Priam.

Priapus (prī ā' pùs). In Greek mythology, the god of reproductive power and fertility (hence of gardens), and protector of shepherds, fishermen, and farmers. He was the son of Dionysus and Aphrodite, and in later times was regarded, as the chief deity of lasciviousness and obscenity. *See* PHALLICISM.

Prick. Shakespeare has, "'Tis now the prick of noon" (*Romeo and Juliet*, ii, 4), in allusion to the mark on the dial—made by pricking or indenting with a sharp instrument—that indicated 12 o'clock.

The annual choosing of sheriffs used to be done by the king, who pricked the names on a list at haphazard. Sheriffs are still "pricked" by the sovereign, but the names are chosen beforehand.

The prick of conscience. Remorse; tormenting reflection on one's misdeeds. In the 14th century Richard of Hampole wrote a devotional treatise with this title.

To prick up one's ears. To pay particular attention; to do one's best to follow what is going on. In allusion to the twitching of a horse's ears when its attention is suddenly attracted.

Pride, meaning ostentation, finery, or that which persons are proud of. Spenser talks of "lofty trees yclad in summer's pride" (verdure). Pope, of a "sword whose ivory sheath (was) inwrought with envious pride" (ornamentation); and in this sense the word is used by Jacques in that celebrated passage—

> Why, who cries out on pride [dress]
> That can therein tax any private party?
> What woman in the city do I name
> When that I say "the city woman bears
> The cost of princes on unworthy shoulders"?
> . . . What is he of baser function
> That says his bravery [finery] is not of my cost?"
> *As You Like It*, ii, 7.

Pride's Purge. The Long Parliament, not proving itself willing to condemn Charles I, was *purged* of its unruly members by Colonel Thomas Pride (d. 1658), who entered the House with a body of soldiers (December 6th, 1648), arrested 47 members; excluded 96 more, and left the House consisting of less than 80 members—the "Rump" (*q.v.*).

Prig. An old cant word (probably a variant of PRICK) for to filch or steal, also for a thief. In the *Winter's Tale* the clown calls Autolycus a "prig that haunts wakes, fairs, and bear-baitings."

Shadwell uses the term for a pert coxcomb, and nowadays it denotes a conceited, formal, or didactic person—one who tries to teach others how to comport themselves, etc., without having any right to do so.

Shamwell: Cheatly will help you to the ready; and thou shalt shine, and be as gay as any spruce prig that ever walked the street.

Belford Senior: Well, adad, you are pleasant men, and have the neatest sayings with you; "ready," and "spruce prig," and abundance of the prettiest witty words.—SHADWELL: *The Squire of Alsatia*, I, i (1688).

Prima Donna (prī' má don' á) (Ital., first lady). The principal female singer in an opera.

Prima facie (Lat.). At first sight. A *prima facie* case is a case or statement which, without minute examination into its merits, seems plausible and correct.

It would be easy to make out a strong *prima facie* case, but I should advise the more cautious policy of *audi al teram partem*.

Primary Colours. See COLOURS.

Prime (Lat. *primus*, first). In the Catholic Church the first canonical hour of the day, beginning at 6 a.m. Milton terms sunrise "that sweet hour of prime" (*Paradise Lost*, v, 170); and the word is used in a general way of the first beginnings of anything, especially of the world itself. *Cp.* Tennyson's "dragons of the prime" (*In Memoriam*, lvi).

Prime Minister. The first minister of the Crown; the Premier (*q.v.*).

Prime Number. The Golden Number; also called simply "the Prime."

Primed. Full and ready to deliver a speech. We say of a man whose head is full of his subject, "He is primed to the muzzle." Also a euphemism for "drunk." The allusion is to firearms.

Primer (prī' mer). Originally the name of the Prayer-book used by laymen in pre-Reformation England; as this was used as a child's first reading-book—generally with the addition of the ABC, etc.—the name was transferred to such books, and so to elementary books on any subject.

Great primer (pron. prim' er). A large-sized type, rather smaller than **As This,** eighteen-point, $4\frac{1}{4}$ lines to the inch.

Long primer. A smaller-sized type, $9\frac{1}{2}$-point, As this; $7\frac{1}{2}$ lines to the inch.

Primero (prim ēr ō). A very popular card-game for about a hundred years after 1530, in which the cards had three times their usual value, four were dealt to each player, the principal groups being flush, prime, and point. *Flush* was the same as in poker, *prime* was one card of each suit, and *point* was reckoned as in piquet.

I left him at primero with the Duke of Suffolk.— *Henry VIII*, i, 2.

Primrose. A curious corruption of the French *primerole*, which is the name of the flower in M.E. This is from the late Lat. *primula*, and the *rose* (as though from *prima rosa*, the first, or earliest, rose) is due to a popular blunder.

Primum mobile (prī' mum mō' bile) (Lat., the first moving thing), in the Ptolemaic system of astronomy, was the ninth (later the tenth) sphere, supposed to revolve round the earth from east to west in twenty-four hours, carrying with it all the other spheres (*q.v.*). Milton refers to it as "that first mov'd" (*Paradise Lost*, iii, 483), and Sir Thomas Browne (*Religio Medici*) uses the phrase, "Beyond the first movable," meaning outside the material creation. According to Ptolemy the *primum mobile* was the boundary of creation, above which came the empyrean (*q.v.*), or seat of God.

The term is figuratively applied to any machine which communicates motion to others; and also to persons and ideas suggestive of complicated systems. Thus, Socrates may be called the *primum mobile* of the Dialectic, Megaric, Cyrenaic, and Cynic systems of philosophy.

Prince (Lat. *princeps*, chief, leader). A royal title which, in England, is now limited to the sons of the sovereign and their sons. *Princess* is similarly limited to the sovereign's daughters and his sons' (but not daughters') daughters.

Crown Prince. The title of the heir-apparent to the throne in some countries, as Sweden, Denmark, and Japan (formerly also in Germany).

Prince Consort. A prince who is the husband of a reigning queen

Prince Imperial. The title of the heir-apparent in the French Empire of 1852-70.

Prince of Asturias. The title of the heir-apparent to the former Spanish throne.

Prince of Piedmont. The heir-apparent to the House of Savoy, former kings of Italy.

Prince of the Church. A cardinal.

Prince of the Peace. The Spanish statesman Manuel de Godoy (1767-1851) was granted this title for having negotiated peace with France in the Treaty of Basel, 1795.

Prince of Wales. *See* WALES.

Prince Rupert's drops. *See* RUPERT.

Princess Royal, the title of an eldest daughter of a British sovereign. On the death of a Princess Royal the eldest daughter of the then reigning monarch automatically receives the title and retains it for life, no matter how many sovereigns with daughters may occupy the throne during her lifetime. George III's daughter Charlotte, Queen of Wurtemberg, was Princess Royal until her death in 1828; neither George IV nor William IV having daughters the title was in abeyance until 1840 when Queen Victoria's daughter, Princess Victoria (later the Empress Frederick of Germany) succeeded to it. She remained Princess Royal until her death in 1901, when King Edward's daughter, Princess Louise, Duchess of Fife, succeeded. On her death in 1931 the title passed to Princess Mary, Countess of Harewood, daughter of George V.

Principalities. Members of one of the nine orders of angels in mediæval angelology. *See* ANGEL.

> In the assembly next upstood
> Nisroch, of Principalities the prime.
> > MILTON : *Paradise Lost*, vi, 447.

Printing. Wood blocks for printing were first used by the Chinese *c.* A.D. 600, and movable type was employed *c.* 1000. In the Western World there is no evidence successfully to refute the claim of Johann Gutenberg (*c.* 1400-68) who set up a press at Mainz *c.* 1450.

Printers' Bible, The. *See* BIBLE, SPECIALLY NAMED.

Printers' marks.

? is ꝗ—that is, the first and last letters of *quœstio* (question).

! is ᴉₒ. *Io* in Latin is the interjection of joy.

¶ is the initial letter of *paragraph* (reversed).

§ the S-mark or section mark.

* is used by the Greek grammarians to arrest attention to something striking (*asterisk* or star).

† is used by the Greek grammarians to indicate something objectionable (*obelisk* or dagger). Both marks are now used to indicate footnotes.

Priori. *See* A PRIORI.

Priscian's Head (prish' àn). **To break Priscian's head** (in Latin, *Diminuere Priscianis caput*). To violate the rules of grammar. Priscian was a great grammarian of the early 6th century, whose name is almost synonymous with grammar.

> And held no sin so deeply red
> As that of breaking Priscian's head
> > BUTLER: *Hudibras*, pt. ii, 2.

Sir Nathaniel: Laus Deo, bone intelligo.

Holofernes: Bone!—*bone for bene:* Priscian a little scratch'd; 'twill serve.
> > *Love's Labour's Lost*, v, 1.

Prisoner of Chillon, The. *See* CHILLON.

Privilege. In a Parliamentary sense this applies to the rights enjoyed by Members as such. Both Houses have the right of committing to prison an offender against their privilege, nor, unless the commitment be for some other offence than contempt, can the civil courts inquire into the matter. Contempts include disobedience to orders of the House, indignities offered to it, assaults, insults or libels on Members, interference with officers of the House or tampering with witnesses. Freedom of speech is a dearly bought and much cherished privilege, as also is freedom from arrest.

Prize Court. A court of law set up in time of war to examine the validity of capture of ships and goods made at sea by the navy.

Prize money is the name given to the net proceeds of the sale of enemy property, etc., thus captured at sea. Prior to 1914 the distribution of prize money was confined to those ships actually making the capture; since that date the whole prize money is paid into a common fund.

The prize ring is the boxing ring in which a prize fight takes place, a prize fight being a boxing match for a money prize or trophy.

Pro. Latin for, on behalf of.

Pro and con (Lat.). For and against. "Con" is a contraction of *contra*. *The pros and cons* of a matter is all that can be said for or against it.

Probate (prō' bāt) (Lat., proved). The probate of a will is the official proving of it, and a copy certified by an officer whose duty it is to attest it. The original is retained in the court registry, and executors cannot act until probate has been obtained.

Proces-verbal (prō sā vâr' bal) (Fr.). A detailed and official statement of some fact; especially a written and authenticated statement of facts in support of a criminal charge.

Procne. *See* NIGHTINGALE.

Proconsul. A magistrate of Ancient Rome who was invested with the power of a consul and charged with the command of an army or the administration of a province. The name is now often applied to a colonial governor or administrator.

Procris (prok' ris). **Unerring as the dart of Procris.** When Procris fled from Cephalus out of shame, Diana gave her a dog (Lælaps) that never failed to secure its prey, and a dart which not only never missed aim, but which always returned of its own accord to the shooter. *See* CEPHALUS.

Procrustes' Bed (prō krus' tēz). Procrustes, in Greek legend, was a robber of Attica, who placed all who fell into his hands upon an iron bed. If they were longer than the bed he cut off the redundant part, if shorter he stretched them till they fitted it; he was slain by Theseus. Hence, any attempt to reduce men to one standard, one way of thinking, or one way of acting, is called placing them on Procrustes' bed.

> Tyrant more cruel than Procrustes old,
> Who to his iron-bed by torture fits
> Their nobler parts, the souls of suffering wits.
> MALLET: *Verbal Criticism.*

Proctor. Literally this is one who manages the affairs of another, the word being a contraction of "procurator." At the universities of Oxford and Cambridge the proctors are two officials whose duties include the maintaining of discipline. Representatives of ecclesiastical bodies in Convocation are called Proctors. **The Queen's Proctor** is a law official entitled to intervene in a divorce or nullity suit where collusion or fraud is suspected.

Procyon (prō' si on). The Lesser Dog-star, *alpha in Canis Minoris.* It is the eighth brightest star in the heavens. *See* ICARIUS.

Prodigal. Festus says the Romans called victims wholly consumed by fire *prodigœ hostiœ* (victims prodigalized), and adds that those who waste their substance are therefore called prodigals. This derivation is incorrect. Prodigal is Lat. *pro-ago* or *prod-igo*, to drive forth, and persons who had spent all their patrimony were "driven forth" to be sold as slaves to their creditors.

The Prodigal. Albert VI, Duke of Austria (1418-63).

Prodigious! *See* DOMINIE SAMPSON.

Prodigy (Lat. *prodigium*, a portent, prophetic sign). *The prodigy of France.* Guillaume Budé (1467-1540); so called by Erasmus.

The Prodigy of Learning. Samuel Hahnemann (1755-1843), the German, was so called by J. Paul Richter.

Profane means literally before or outside the temple (Lat. *pro fanum*); hence *profanus* was applied to those persons who came to the temple and remaining outside and unattached, were not initiated.

Profile (prō' fīl) means shown by a thread (Ital. *profilo*; Lat. *filum*, a thread). A profile is an outline, but especially a view, or drawing or some other representation, of the human face outlined by the median line. The term "profile," for an essay setting forth the outstanding characteristics of an individual—a verbal outline, so to speak—came into use in the 1940s.

Prog. The verb was used in the 16th century for to poke about for anything, especially to forage for food; hence the noun is slang for food, but its origin is unknown. Burke says, "You are the lion, and I have been endeavouring to prog for you."

> So saying, with a smile she left the rogue
> To weave more lines of death, and plan for prog.
> DR. WOLCOT: *Spider and Fly.*

Prog is also university slang for proctor (*q.v.*).

Programme Music is instrumental music based on a literary, historical, or pictorial subject and intended to describe or illustrate this theme musically.

Progress. To report progress, in parliamentary language, is to conclude for the night the business of a bill, and defer the consideration of all subsequent items thereof till the day nominated by the Prime Minister, hence, to put off anything till a more convenient time.

Projection. Powder of projection. A form of the "Philosopher's Stone" (*q.v.*), which was supposed to have the virtue of changing baser metals into gold. A little of this powder, being cast into the molten metal, was to *project* from it pure gold.

Proletariat (prō le târ' i ăt). The class of the community, labourers and wage-earners, who are destitute of property. In ancient Rome the *proletarii* contributed nothing to the state but their *proles*, *i.e.* offspring; they could hold no office, were ineligible for the army, and were useful only as breeders of the race.

Prometheus (prō mē' thūs) (Gr., Forethought). One of the Titans of Greek myth, son of Iapetus and the ocean-nymph Clymene, and famous as a benefactor to man. It is said that Zeus employed him to make men out of mud and water, and that then, in pity for their state, he stole fire from heaven and gave it to them. For this he was chained by Zeus to Mount Caucasus, where an eagle preyed on his liver all day, the liver being renewed at night. He was eventually released by Hercules, who slew the eagle. It was to counterbalance the gift of fire to mankind that Zeus sent Pandora (*q.v.*) to earth with her box of evils.

Promethean. Capable of producing fire; pertaining to Prometheus (*q.v.*). The earliest "safety" matches, made in 1805 by Chancel, a French chemist, who tipped cedar splints with paste of chlorate of potash and sugar, were known as "Prometheans." They were dipped into a little bottle containing asbestos wetted with sulphuric acid, and burst into flame on being withdrawn.

Promethean fire. The vital principle; the fire with which Prometheus quickened into life his clay images.

> I know not where is that Promethean heat
> That can thy light relume.
> *Othello*, v, 2.

The Promethean unguent. Made from a herb on which some of the blood of Prometheus had fallen. Medea gave Jason some of it, and thus rendered his body proof against fire and warlike instruments.

Promised Land or **Land of Promise.** Canaan; so called because God promised Abraham, Isaac, and Jacob that their offspring should possess it.

Proof. A printed sheet to be examined and approved before it is finally printed. The first, or *foul*, proof is that which contains all the compositor's errors; when these are corrected the impression next taken is called a *clean* proof and is submitted to the author; the final impression, which is corrected by the reader, is termed the *press* proof.

Proof prints. The first impressions of an engraving. *India proofs* are those taken off on *India paper*. **Proofs before lettering** are those taken off before any inscription is engraved on the plate. After the proofs the connoisseur's order of value is—(1) prints which have the letters only in outline; (2) those in which the letters are shaded with a black line; (3) those in which some slight ornament is introduced into the letters; (4) those in which the letters are filled up quite black.

Proof spirit. A term applied to spirituous liquors in which 0·495 of the *weight* and 0·5727 of the *volume* is absolute alcohol, and the specific gravity is 0·91984. When the mixture has more alcohol than water it is called *over proof*, and when less it is termed *under proof*.

Propaganda (prop a găn' dà). The Congregation, or College, of the Propaganda (*Congregatio de propaganda fide*) is a committee of cardinals established in Rome by Gregory XV, in 1622, for propagating the Faith throughout the world. Hence the term is applied to any scheme, association, etc., for making proselytes or influencing public opinion in political, social, and international, as well as in religious matters.

Prophet, The. The special title of Mohammed. According to the Koran there have been 200,000 prophets, but only six of them brought new laws or dispensations, viz. Adam, Noah, Abraham, Moses, Jesus, and Mohammed.

The Great or **Major Prophets.** Isaiah, Jeremiah, Ezekiel, and Daniel; so called because their writings are more extensive than the prophecies of the other twelve.

The Minor or **Lesser Prophets.** Hosea, Joel, Amos, Obadiah, Micah, Jonah, Nahum, Habakkuk, Zephaniah, Haggai, Zechariah, and Malachi, whose writings are less extensive than those of the four Great Prophets.

Propositions, in logic, are of four kinds, called A, E, I, O. "A" is a universal affirmative, and "E" a universal negative; "I" a particular affirmative, and "O" a particular negative.

See also SYLLOGISM.

Props. *See* PROPERTY PLOT.

Prorogue (prō rōg') (Lat. *pro-rogo*, to prolong).

The Parliament was prorogued. Dismissed for the holidays, or suspended for a time. If dismissed entirely it is said to be "dissolved."

Proscenium (prō sē' ni ùm). The front part of the stage, between the drop-curtain and orchestra. (Gr. *proskēnion*; Lat. *proscēnium*.)

Proscription. A sort of hue and cry; so called because among the Romans the names of the persons *proscribed* were written out, and the tablets bearing their names were fixed up in the public forum, sometimes with the offer of a reward for those who should aid in bringing them before the court. If the proscribed did not answer the summons, their goods were confiscated and their persons outlawed. In this case the name was engraved on brass or marble, the offence stated, and the tablet placed conspicuously in the market-place.

Prose means straightforward speaking or writing (Lat. *oratio prosa*—*i.e. pro-versa*), in opposition to foot-bound speaking or writing, *oratio vincta* (fettered speech—*i.e.* poetry).

It was Monsieur Jourdain, in Molière's *Le Bourgeois Gentilhomme*, who suddenly discovered that he had been talking prose for twenty years without knowing it.

Proselytes (pros e līts). From Gr. *proselutos*, one who has come to a place; hence, a convert, especially (in its original application) to Judaism. Among the Jews proselytes were of two kinds—viz. "The proselyte of righteousness" and the "stranger that is within thy gate" (*see* HELLENES). The former submitted to circumcision and conformed to the laws of Moses; the latter went no farther than to refrain from offering sacrifice to heathen gods, and from working on the Sabbath.

Proserpina or **Proserpine** (pro sĕr' pi nà, pros'er pīn). The Roman counterpart of the Greek goddess Persephone, queen of the infernal regions and wife of Pluto. As the personification of seasonal changes she passed six months of the year on Olympus, and six in Hades; while at Olympus she was beneficent, but in Hades was stern and terrible. Legend says that as she was amusing herself in the meadows of Sicily Pluto seized her and carried her off in his chariot to the infernal regions for his bride. In her terror she dropped some of the lilies she had been gathering, and they turned to daffodils.

> O Proserpina.
> For the flowers now, that frighted thou let'st fall
> From Dis's waggon! daffodils,
> That come before the swallow dares, and take
> The winds of March with beauty.
>
> *Winter's Tale*, iv, 4.

In later legend Proserpine was the goddess of sleep, and in the myth of *Cupid and Psyche*, by Apuleius, after Psyche had long wandered about searching for her lost Cupid, she is sent to Proserpine for "the casket of divine beauty," which she was not to open till she came into the light of day. Just as she was about to step on earth Psyche thought how much more Cupid would love her if she were divinely beautiful; so she opened the casket and found it contained Sleep, which instantly filled all her limbs with drowsiness, and she slept as it were the sleep of death.

Prospero (pros' pe rō). The rightful Duke of Milan in *The Tempest*, deposed by his brother. Drifted on a desert island, he practised magic, and raised a tempest in which his brother was shipwrecked. Ultimately Prospero *broke his wand*, and his daughter married the son of the King of Naples. *The Tempest* was the last play that Shakespeare wrote, and it is generally thought that Prospero is an allegorical picture of the dramatist bidding farewell to his work.

Protean. *See* PROTEUS.

Protectionist. One who advocates the imposition of import duties, to "protect" home produce or manufactures.

Protestant. A member of a Christian Church upholding the principles of the Reformation, or (loosely) of any Church not in communion with Rome. Originally, one of the party which adhered to Luther who, in 1529, "protested" against the decree of Charles V of Germany, and appealed from the Diet of Spires to a general council.

The Protestant Pope. Clement XIV. He ordered the suppression of the Jesuits (1773) and was one of the most enlightened men who ever sat in the chair of St. Peter.

Proteus (prō' tūs). In Greek legend, Neptune's herdsman, an old man and a prophet, famous for his power of assuming different shapes at will. Hence the phrase, *As many shapes as Proteus*—i.e. full of shifts, aliases, disguises, etc., and the adjective **protean,** readily taking on different aspects, ever-changing.

Proteus lived in a vast cave, and his custom was to tell over his herds of sea-calves at noon, and then to sleep. There was no way of catching him but by stealing upon him at this time and binding him; otherwise he would elude anyone by a rapid change in shape.

Protevangelium (prō te văn jē' li um). The *first* (Gr. *protos*) gospel, applied to an apocryphal gospel which had been attributed to St. James the Less. It has been supposed by some critics that all the gospels were based upon this, although no vestige of it has been discovered. The name is also given to the curse upon the serpent in *Gen*. iii, 15:—

> And I will put enmity between thee and the woman, and between thy seed and her seed; it shall bruise thy head, and thou shalt bruise his heel,

which has been regarded as the earliest utterance of the gospel.

Prothalamion (prō thà l à' mi ún). The term coined by Spenser (from Gr. *thalamos*, a bridal chamber) as a title for his "Spousall Verse" (1596) in honour of the double marriage of Lady Elizabeth and Lady Katherine Somerset, daughters of the Earl of Worcester, to Henry Gilford and William Peter, Esquires. Hence, a song sung in honour of the bride and bridegroom before the wedding.

Protocol (prō' tō kol). The first rough draft or original copy of a dispatch, which is to form the basis of a treaty; from Gr. *proto-koleon*, a sheet glued to the front of a manuscript, or to the case containing it, and bearing an abstract of the contents and purport. Also the ceremonial procedure used in affairs of diplomacy or on state occasions.

Protoplasm (prō' tō plazm) (Gr. *proto*, first, *plasma*, thing moulded). The physical basis of life; the material composing cells, from which all living organisms are developed. It is a viscid, semi-fluid, semi-transparent substance composed of a highly unstable combination of oxygen, hydrogen, carbon, and nitrogen, capable of spontaneous movement, contraction, etc. It can best be seen in the simpler jellyfishes.

Sarcode (Gr. *sarcos*, flesh) is an earlier name of the substance.

Proud, The. Otho IV, Emperor of Germany (1175, 1209-18).

Tarquin II of Rome. *Superbus*. (Reigned 535-10 B.C., d. 496).

Province. From Lat. *provincia*, the name given by the Romans to a territory brought under subjugation, possibly because previously comquered (*pro*, before, *vincere*, to conquer). It is now applied, in the plural, to districts in a country, usually at a distance from the metropolis, whence the special meaning of *provincial*—narrow, unpolished, rude—and to the territory under the ecclesiastical control of an archbishop or metropolitian.

Prudhomme (proo′ dom). The French colloquialism for a man of experience and great prudence, of estimable character and practical good sense. Your *Monsieur Prudhomme* is never a man of genius and originality. The name arises from the character of Joseph Prudhomme in Henri Mounier's sketch thus entitled (1857).

Prunella (pru′ nel a). A dark, smooth, woollen stuff of which clergymen's and barristers' gowns used to be made; probably so termed from its colour—plum, or prune. It is still in use for gaiters and the uppers of boots.

All leather and prunella. *See* LEATHER.

Prussianism. A term given to the overbearing spirit and methods characteristic of Prussians dating from the military despotism that has flourished among them since the days of Frederick the Great (1712-86). It came to full-flower after the Franco-Prussian war of 1870 when Prussia forced herself as a leader among the German states forming the new German Empire. Under the last Kaiser, who was King of Prussia, the spirit of Prussianism led to World War I, and it has taken a second world war and the virtual obliteration of German civilization to break if not to destroy Prussianism.

Prussian blue. So called because it was discovered by a Prussian, viz. Diesbach, a colourman of Berlin, in 1704. It was sometimes called *Berlin* blue. It is hydrated ferric ferrocyanide, and *prussic acid* (hydrocyanic acid) is made from it.

Psalms. Seventy-three psalms are inscribed with David's name, twelve with that of Asaph the singer; eleven go under the name of the Sons of Korah, a family of singers; one (*i.e. Ps.* xc) is attributed to Moses. The whole compilation is divided into five books: Bk. 1, from i to xli; Bk. 2, from xlii to lxxii; Bk. 3, from lxxiii to lxxxix; Bk. 4, from xc to cvi; Bk. 5, from cvii to cl.

The *Book of Psalms*—or much of its contents—was for centuries attributed to David (hence called the *sweet psalmist* of Israel), but it is very doubtful whether he wrote any of them, and it is certain that the majority belong to a later period. The tradition comes from the author of *Chronicles*, and in 2 *Sam.* xxii is a psalm attributed to David that is identical with *Ps.* xviii. Also, the last verse of *Ps.* lxxii ("the prayers of David the son of Jesse are ended") seems to suggest that he was the author up to that point.

In explanation of the confusion between the R.C. and the Protestant psalters it should be noted that Psalms x to cxiii and cxv to cxlvi in the R.C. psalter are numbered one behind those in the A.V. and Prayer Book.

See GRADUAL PSALMS; PENITENTIAL PSALMS, etc.

Pschent (pshent). The royal double crown of ancient Egypt, combining that of Upper Egypt—a high conical white cap terminating in a knob—with the red one of Lower Egypt, the latter being the outermost.

Pseudonym. *See* NOM DE PLUME.

Psyche (sīk′ ē) (Gr., breath; hence, life, or soul itself). In "the latest-born of the myths," *Cupid and Psyche*, an episode in the *Golden Ass* of Apuleius (2nd century A.D.), a beautiful maiden beloved by Cupid, who visited her every night, but left her at sunrise. Cupid bade her never seek to know who he was, but one night curiosity overcame her prudence; she lit the lamp to look at him, a drop of hot oil fell on his shoulder, and he awoke and fled. The abandoned Psyche then wandered far and wide in search of her lover; she became the slave of Venus, who imposed on her heartless tasks and treated her most cruelly; but ultimately she was united to Cupid, and became immortal. The story is told by Walter Pater in *Marius the Epicurean*.

Ptolemaic System (tol e mā′ ik). The system promulgated by Ptolemy, the celebrated astronomer of Alexandria in the 2nd century A.D., to account for the apparent motion of the heavenly bodies. He taught that the earth is fixed in the centre of the universe, and the heavens revolve round it from east to west, carrying with them the sun, planets, and fixed stars, in their respective spheres (*q.v.*), which he imagined as solid coverings (like so many skins of an onion) each revolving at different velocities. This theory, with slight modifications, held the field till the time of Copernicus (16th century).

Public (Lat. *publicus*, earlier *poplicus* from *poplus*, later *populus*, the people). The people generally and collectively; the members generally of a state, nation, or community. Also, a colloquial contraction of "public-house," frequently abbreviated still further to "pub."

> The simple life I can't afford,
> Besides, I do not tike the grub—
> I want a mash and sausage, "scored"—
> Will someone take me to a pub?
>   G. K. CHESTERTON: *Ballade of an Anti-Puritan.*

Public-house signs. Much of a nation's history, and more of its manners and feelings, may be gleaned from its public-house signs. A very large number of them are selected out of compliment to the lord of the manor, either because he is the "great man" of the neighbourhood, or because the proprietor is some servant whom "it delighted the lord to honour." When the name and titles of the lord have been exhausted, we get his cognizance or his favourite pursuit, as the *Bear and Ragged Staff*, the *Fox and Hounds*. As the object of the sign is to speak to the feelings and attract, another fruitful source is either some national hero or great battle; thus we get the *Marquis of Granby* and the *Duke of Wellington*, the *Waterloo* and the *Alma*. The proverbial loyalty of our nation has naturally shown itself in our tavern signs, giving us the *Victoria*, *Prince of Wales*, the *Albert*, the *Crown*, and so on. Literature is not well represented, though Shakespeare and Ben Jonson give their names to a good many houses, and in London there is a *Milton Arms*, a *Macaulay Arms*, a *Sir Richard Steele*, and a *Sir Walter Scott*, as well as *The Miller of Mansfield*, *Pindar of Wakefield*, *Sir John Falstaff*, *Robinson Crusoe*, and *Valentine and Orson*. The *Good Samaritan*, *Noah's Ark*, *Simon the Tanner*, and *Gospel Oak* all have a biblical flavour, and old ecclesiastical manorial rights are responsible for many tavern signs (*see The Three Kings*, below). Myth and legend are represented by houses named *The Apollo*, *Hercules*, *Phœnix*, *King Lud*, *Merlin's Cave*, *Man in the Moon*, *Punch*, *Robin Hood*, *The Moonrakers*, etc.

Some signs indicate a speciality of the house, as the *Bowling Green*, the *Skittles*; some a political bias, as the *Royal Oak*; a number are reminiscent of the old trade guilds, such as the *Coopers'*, *Bricklayers'*, *Carpenters'*, and *Haberdashers' Arms*; and some are an attempt at wit, as the *Five Alls* and *The World Turned Upside Down*. The following list will serve to exemplify the subject:—

The Bag 'o Nails. A corruption of the "Bacchanals."

The Barley Mow (*q.v.*).

The Bear. From the popular sport of bear-baiting.

The Bear and Bacchus, in High Street, Warwick. A corruption of *Bear and Baculus*— i.e. Bear and Ragged Staff, the badge of the Earl of Warwick.

The Bell. In allusion to races, a silver bell having been the winner's prize up to the reign of Charles II.

The Bell Savage. See LA BELLE SAUVAGE.

The Blue Boar. The cognizance of Richard III.

The Boar's Head. The cognizance of the Gordons, etc.

The Bolt-in-Tun. The punning heraldic badge of Prior *Bolton*, last of the clerical rulers of St. Bartholomew's, previous to the Reformation.

The Bull. The cognizance of Richard, Duke of York. The *Black Bull* is the cognizance of the house of Clare.

The Bull and Gate (*q.v.*).

The Bull's Head. The cognizance of Henry VIII.

The Case is Altered. See PLOWDEN.

The Castle. This, being the arms of Spain, signified that Spanish wines were to be obtained within.

The Cat and Fiddle. See CAT.

The Cat and Wheel. A corruption of "St. Catherine's Wheel"; or an announcement that *cat* and balance-*wheels* are provided for the amusement of customers.

The Chequers. (1) in honour of the Stuarts, whose shield was "cheeky," like a Scotch plaid. (2) In commemoration of the licence granted by the Earls of Arundel or Lords Warrenne. (3) An intimation that a room is set apart for merchants and accountants, where they can be private and make up their accounts, or use their "chequers" undisturbed.

The Coach and Horses. A favourite sign of a posting-house or stage-coach house.

The Cock and Bottle. By some said to be a corruption of the "Cork and Bottle," meaning that wine is sold there in bottles.

The Cross Keys. Common in the mediæval ages, and in allusion to St. Peter, or one of the bishops whose cognizance it is—probably the lord of the manor or the patron saint of the parish church. The cross keys are emblems of the papacy, St. Peter, the Bishop of Gloucester, St. Servetus, St. Hippolytus, St. Geneviève, St. Petronilla, St. Osyth, St. Martha, and St. Germanus.

The Devil. The sign of more than one old public-house in the neighbourhood of Fleet Street. It represents St. Dunstan seizing the devil by the nose. *See* DEVIL.

The Dog and Duck, or *The Duck in the Pond.* Indicating that the sport so called could be seen there. A duck was put into water, and a dog set to hunt it; the fun was to see the duck diving and the dog following it under water.

The Red Dragon. The cognizance of Henry VII or the principality of Wales.

The Spread Eagle. The arms of Germany; to indicate that German wines could be obtained within.

The Fox and Goose. To signify that there are arrangements within for playing the Royal Game of Fox and Goose.

St. George and the Dragon. In compliment to the patron saint of England.

The Globe. The royal cognizance of Portugal; intimating that Portuguese wines were stocked.

The Goat and Compasses. See GOAT.

The Black Goats. A public-house sign, High Bridge Lincoln, formerly *The Three Goats*—*i.e.* three gowts (gutters or drains), by which the water from the Swan Pool (a large lake that formerly existed to the west of the city) was conducted into the bed of the Witham.

The Golden Cross. This refers to the ensigns carried by the Crusaders.

The Green Man. The late gamekeeper of the lord of the manor turned publican. At one time these servants were dressed in green.

The Green Man and Still—*i.e.* the herbalist bringing his herbs to be distilled.

The Hare and Hounds. In compliment to the sporting squire or lord of the manor.

The Hole in the Wall. Probably so called because it was approached by a small passage or "hole" between houses standing in front of the tavern.

The Horse and Chains. A favourite sign for an inn at the foot of a hill, signifying that a chain-horse is kept.

The Horse and Groom. Where a stallion was kept for stud purposes.

The Iron Devil. Said to be a corruption of "Hirondelle" (the swallow).

The Three Kings. A mediæval sign, in allusion to the three kings of Cologne the Magi (*q.v.*). Many public-house signs of this period had a reference to ecclesiastical matters, usually because they were church property or on church land, Such, for instance, are *The Mitre, Abbey, Priory,* and *Lamb and Flag.*

The Man with a Load of Mischief. A public-house sign, Oxford Street, nearly opposite to Hanway Yard. It is said to have been painted by Hogarth, and shows a man carrying a woman and a lot of other *impedimenta* on his back.

The Marquis of Granby. In compliment to John Manners (1721-70), eldest son of John, third Duke of Rutland—a bluff, brave soldier, generous, and greatly beloved by his men.

> What conquest now will Britain boast
>   Or where display her banners?
> Alas! in Granby she has lost
>   True courage and good Manners.

The Pig and Tinder Box. See PIG.

The Plum and Feathers (near Stokenchurch, Oxford). A corruption of the "Plume of Feathers," meaning that of the Prince of Wales.

The Queen of Bohemia. In honour of James I's daughter Elizabeth, who married the King of Bohemia.

The Rose. A symbol of England, as the *Thistle* is of Scotland, and the *Shamrock* of Ireland.

The Rose and Crown. One of the "loyal" public-house signs.

The Rose of the Quarter Sessions. A corruption of *La Rose des Quatre Saisons.*

The Salutation and Cat. The "Salutation" (which refers to the angel saluting the Virgin Mary) is the sign of the house, and the "Cat" is added to signify that arrangements are made for playing *cat* or tipcat.

The Saracen's Head. Reminiscent of the Crusades; adopted probably by some Crusader after his return home, or to excite sympathy with these quixotic expeditions.

The Ship and Shovel. Referring to Sir Cloudesley Shovel, a favourite admiral in Queen Anne's reign.

The Seven Stars. An astrological sign of the Middle Ages.

The Three Suns. The cognizance of Edward IV.

The Sun and the Rose. The cognizance of the House of York.

The Swan with Three Necks. See SWAN.

The Swan and the Antelope. The cognizance of Henry V.

The Talbot (*a hound*). The arms of the Talbot family.

The Turk's Head. Like the "Saracen's Head," an allusion to the Crusades.

The Two Chairmen. Not an uncommon sign for small houses in districts (such as Charing Cross and Wardour Street) that were fashionable residential quarters in the 18th century, when sedan chairs were in vogue.

The Unicorn. The Scottish supporter in the royal arms of Great Britain.

The White Hart. The cognizance of Richard II; the *White Lion*, of Edward IV as Earl of March; *the White Swan*, of Henry IV and Edward III.

Puck. A mischievous, tricksy sprite of popular folk-lore, also called Robin Goodfellow, originally an evil demon, but transformed and popularized in his present form by Shakespeare (*Midsummer Night's Dream*), who shows him as a merry wanderer of the night, "rough, knurly limbed, faun-faced, and shock-pated, a very Shetlander among the gossamer-winged" fairies around him.

Pueblo (pweb' lō). The Spanish word for "people" but applied particularly to the farming, peace-loving Indians of New Mexico and Arizona, and to their commensal dwellings of adobe or stone.

Puff. An onomatopœic word, suggestive of the sound made by puffing wind from the mouth. As applied to inflated or exaggerated praise, extravagantly worded advertisements, reviews, etc., it dates at least from the early 17th century, and the implication is that such commendation is really as worthless and transitory as a puff of wind.

In Sheridan's *The Critic* (1779), Puff, who, he himself says, is "a practitioner in panegyric, or, to speak more plainly, a professor of the art of puffing" gives a catalogue of puffs:—

Yes, sir,—puffing is of various sorts, the principal are, the puff direct, the puff preliminary, the puff collateral, the puff collusive and the puff oblique, or puff by implication. These all assume, as circumstances require, the various forms of letter to the editor, occasional anecdote, impartial critique, observation from correspondent, or advertisement from the party. *The Critic*, I, ii.

Puffed up. Conceited; elated with conceit or praise; filled with wind. A *puff* is a tartlet with a very light or puffy crust.

That no one of you be puffed up one against another.—1 *Cor.* iv, 6.

Puff-ball. A fungus of the genus *Lycoperdon*, so called because it is ball-shaped and when it is ripe it bursts and the spores come out in a "puff" of fine powder.

Pukka (pūk' a). A Hindustani word that has crept into common speech meaning substantial, real, *bona fide*, conventional. It has developed a somewhat derogatory implication.

Pulhems. A system for assessing the physical and mental capabilities of a recruit. It was introduced in the Canadian Army in 1943. The word is a mnemonic: P, physical capacity; U, upper limbs; L, locomotion; H, hearing;

E, eyesight; M, mental capacity; S, stability (emotional). In 1948 the system was introduced into the British armed forces, but with two E's, for the Navy and Air Force demanded that the visual acuity of each eye be registered separately.

Pulitzer Prizes for literary work, the drama and music are awarded annually from funds left for the purpose by Joseph Pulitzer (1847-1911) a prominent and wealthy American editor and newspaper proprietor.

Pull. A long pull, a strong pull, and a pull all together—*i.e.* a steady energetic, and systematic co-operation. The reference may be either to a boat, where all the oarsmen pull together with a long and strong pull at the oars; or it may be to the act of hauling with a rope, when a simultaneous strong pull is indispensable.

To pull one's weight. To do the very best one can, exert oneself to the utmost of one's ability. The phrase comes from rowing; an oarsman who does not put all his weight into the stroke tends to become a passenger.

To pull oneself together. To rouse oneself to renewed activity; to shake off depression or inertia.

To pull someone's leg. To delude him in a humorous way, lead him astray by chaff, exaggeration, etc.

To pull the wool over someone's eyes. To deceive or hoodwink; to blind him temporarily to what is going on.

To pull through. To get oneself well out of a difficulty—such as over a serious illness, through a stiff examination, etc. To work in harmony with one view; to co-operate heartily.

Pullman. Properly a well-fitted railway saloon or sleeping-car built at the Pullman Carriage Works, Illinois; so called from the designer, George M. Pullman (1832-97) of Chicago. The word is now applied to other luxurious railway saloons, and to motor-cars.

Pump. To pump someone is to extract information out of him by artful questions; to draw from him all he knows as one draws water from a well by gradual pumping. Ben Jonson, in *A Tale of a Tub* (IV, iii) has "I'll stand aside whilst thou pump'st out of him his business."

Pumpernickel (pŭmp' ĕr nik el). The coarse rye-bread ("brown George") eaten by German peasants, especially in Westphalia. Thackeray applied the term as a satirical nickname to petty German princelings ("His Transparency, the Duke of Pumpernickel") who made a great show with the court officials and etiquette, but whose revenue was almost *nil*.

Punch. The name of this beverage, which was introduced into England from India in the early 17th century, has generally been held to derive from Hindustani *panch*, five, because it has five principal ingredients (viz. spirit, water, spice, sugar, and some acid fruit essence). There are, however, linguistic and phonetic objections to accepting this derivation—as well as the fact that early recipes give anything from three to six principal ingredients, and there was no reason why it should have been named from five—and it is just as likely that it is merely a contraction by sailors engaged in the East Indian trade of *puncheon*, the large cask from which their grog was served.

Punch, Mr. The hero of the popular puppet show, *Punch and Judy*. The name comes from the Italian *Pulcinello*. In the 18th century the suggestion was made that the name was from a popular and ugly low comedian named Puccio d'Aniello, but nothing definite is known of him, and the conjecture is certainly an example of "popular etymology." Another suggestion is that the name is derived from that of Pontius Pilate in the old mystery plays.

The show first appeared in England a little before the accession of Queen Anne, and the story is attributed to Silvio Fiorillo, an Italian comedian of the 17th century. Punch, in a fit of jealousy, strangles his infant child, whereupon his wife, Judy, fetches a bludgeon with which she belabours him till he seizes another bludgeon, beats her to death, and flings the two bodies into the street. A passing police officer enters the house; Punch flees, but is arrested by an officer of the Inquisition and shut up in prison, whence he escapes by means of a golden key. The rest is an allegory, showing how the light-hearted Punch triumphs over (1) Ennui, in the shape of a dog, (2) Disease, in the disguise of a doctor, (3) Death, who is beaten to death, and (4) the Devil himself, who is outwitted.

The satirical humorous weekly paper, *Punch, or the London Charivari*, is, of course, named from "Mr. Punch." It first appeared on July 17th, 1841.

Pleased as Punch. Greatly delighted. Our old friend is always singing with self-satisfaction in his naughty ways, and his evident "pleasure" is contagious to the beholders.

Punctual. No bigger than a point, exact to a point or moment. (Lat. *ad punctum*.) Hence

the angel, describing this earth to Adam, calls it "This spacious earth, this punctual spot"—*i.e.* a spot no bigger than a point (Milton: *Paradise Lost*, viii, 23).

Punctuality is the politeness of kings (*L'exactitude est la politesse des rois*). A favourite maxim of Louis XVIII, but erroneously attributed by Samuel Smiles to Louis XIV.

Pundit (pŭn′ dit). An East Indian scholar, skilled in Sanskrit, and learned in law, divinity, and science. We use the word for a learned person, also for one more stocked with book lore than deep erudition.

Punic Apple (pū′ nik). A pomegranate; so called because it is the pomum or "apple" belonging to the genus *Punica*.

Pup. Slang for *a pupil*, especially an undergraduate studying with a tutor.

As applied to the young of dogs, the word is an abbreviation of *puppy*, which represents Fr. *poupée*, a dressed doll, a plaything.

An empty-headed, impertinent young fellow is frequently called *a young puppy*, hence Douglas Jerrold's epigram—more witty than true—

Dogmatism is only puppyism come to maturity.

Purgatory. The doctrine of Purgatory, according to which the souls of the departed suffer for a time till they are *purged* of their sin, is of ancient standing, and was held in a modified form by the Jews, who believed that the soul of the deceased was allowed for twelve months after death to visit its body and the places or persons it especially loved. This intermediate state they called by various names, as "the bosom of Abraham," "the garden of Eden," "upper Gehenna." The Sabbath was always a free day, and prayer was supposed to benefit those in this intermediate state.

The outline of this doctrine was annexed by the early Fathers, and was considerably strengthened by certain passages in the New Testament, particularly *Rev.* vi, 9-11, and 1 *Pet.* iii, 18 and 19. The first decree on the subject was promulgated by the Council of Florence, in 1439; and in 1562 it was condemned by the Church of England, the XXIInd of the "Articles of Religion" stating that—

The Romish Doctrine concerning Purgatory . . . is a fond thing vainly invented, and grounded upon no warranty of Scripture, but rather repugnant to the Word of God.

Purge. A neo-euphemism in dictator countries for the elimination (usually by murder) of persons suspected of disaffection or in some other way undesirable to party leaders. The most notorious of party purges was the infamous "night of the knives," on June 30th, 1934, when Roehm, a potential rival of Hitler and some 7,000 others were murdered in cold blood within 24 hours. There have been many "purges" in Bolshevist Russia, but the particulars of them have never come to the light of day.

See also PRIDE'S PURGE.

Puritans. Seceders from the Reformed Church in the sixteenth century; so called because, wishing for a more radical purification of religion, they rejected all human traditions and interference in religious matters, acknowledging the sole authority of the "pure Word of God," without "note or comment." Their motto was: "The Bible, the whole Bible, and nothing but the Bible." The English Puritans were sometimes by the Reformers called *Precisionists*, from their preciseness in matters called "indifferent." Andrew Fuller named them *Nonconformists*, because they refused to subscribe to the Act of Uniformity.

The Puritan hated bearbaiting, not because it gave pain to the bear, but because it gave pleasure to the spectators. Indeed he generally contrived to enjoy the double pleasure of tormenting both spectators and bear.— MACAULAY: *History of England*, Bk. i, ch. ii.

Purlieu (pĕr ´lū). The outlying parts of a place, the environs; originally the borders or outskirts of a forest, especially a part which was formerly part of the forest. So called from O.Fr. *pourallé*, a place free from the forest laws. Henry II, Richard I, and John made certain lands forest lands; Henry III allowed certain portions all round to be freed from the restrictions imposed on the royal forests, and the "perambulation" by which this was effected was called *pourallée*, a going through. The *lieu* (as though for "place") was an erroneous addition due to English pronunciation and spelling of the French word.

In the purlieus of this forest stands
A sheepcote fenced about with olive-trees.
As You Like It, iv, 3.

Purple. The colour of ecclesiastical mourning and penitence (hence worn during Lent); also that of the dress of emperors, kings, and prelates; from the Lat. *purpura* which was formed on Gr. *porphyra*, meaning both the shell-fish which yielded Tyrian purple (a species of *Murex*), and the purplish marble, *porphyry*. A priest is said to be raised to the purple when he is made a cardinal, though the cardinalatial colour is actually red. It is one of the tinctures (*purpure*) used in heraldry, and in engravings is shown by lines running diagonally from sinister

to dexter (*i.e.* from right to left as one looks at it). *See* COLOURS.

Purple Heart. A U.S. army medal awarded for wounds received by enemy action while on active service. It consists of a silver heart bearing the effigy of George Washington, suspended from a purple ribbon with white edges.

Purple patches. Highly coloured or florid passages in a literary work which is (generally speaking) otherwise undistinguished. The allusion is to Horace's *De Arte Poetica*, 1, 15:—

Inceptis gravibus plerumque et magna professis,
Purpureus, late qui splendeat, unus et alter
Adsuitur pannus.
(Often to weighty enterprises and such as profess great objects, one or two purple patches are sewed on to make a fine display in the distance.)

Pursuivant (pĕr´ swi vănt). The lowest grade of the officers of arms composing the College of Arms, or Heralds' College, the others, under the Earl Marshal, being (1) the Kings of Arms, and (2) the Heralds.

England has four Pursuivants, viz. *Rouge Croix*, *Bluemantle*, *Rouge Dragon*, and *Portcullis*; Scotland has three, viz. *Carrick*, *March*, and *Unicorn*; and Ireland one, *Athlone*.

Puss. A conventional call-name for a cat; applied also (in the 17th century and since) to hares. Its original is unknown, though it is present in many Teutonic languages. The derivation from Lat. *lepus*, a hare, Frenchified into *le pus*, is of course only humorous.

Puss in Boots. This nursery tale, *Le Chat Botté*, is from Straparola's *Nights* (1530), No. xi, where Constantine's cat procures his master a fine castle and the king's heiress. It was translated from the Italian into French in 1585, and appeared in Perrault's *Les contes de ma Mère l'Oie* (1697), through which medium it reached England. In the story the clever cat secures a fortune and a royal partner for his master, who passes off as the Marquis of Carabas, but is in reality a young miller without a penny in the world.

Pussyfoot. A person with a soft, cat-like, sneaking tread.

Pygmalion (pig mā´ li ón). A sculptor and king of Cyprus in Greek legend, who, though he hated women, fell in love with his own ivory statue of Aphrodite. At his earnest prayer the goddess gave life to the statue and he married it.

The story is told in Ovid's *Metamorphoses*, x, and appeared in English dress in John Marston's *Metamorphosis of Pygmalion's Image* (1598). Morris retold it in *The Earthly Paradise* (*August*), and W. S. Gilbert adapted it in his comedy of *Pygmalion and Galatea* (1871), in which the sculptor is a married man. His wife (Cynisca) was jealous of the animated statue (Galatea), which, after considerable trouble, voluntarily returned to its original state. The name was used figuratively by G. B. Shaw for a play produced in 1912.

Pygmy (pig′ mi). The name used by Homer and other classical writers for a supposed race of dwarfs said to dwell somewhere in Ethiopia; from Gr. *pugme*, the length of the arm from elbow to knuckles. Fable has it that every spring the cranes made war on them and devoured them; they used an axe to cut down corn-stalks; when Hercules went to the country they climbed up his goblet by ladders to drink from it, and while he was asleep two whole armies of them fell upon his right hand, and two upon his left and were rolled up by Hercules in his lion's skin. It is easy to see how Swift has availed himself of this Grecian legend in his *Gulliver's Travels*.

The term is now applied to certain dwarfish races of central Africa (whose existence was first demonstrated late in the 19th century), Malaysia, etc.; also to small members of a class, as the *pygmy hippopotamus*.

Pylades and Orestes (pī′ lá dēz, ō res′ tēz). Two friends in Homeric legend, whose names have become proverbial for friendship, like those of Damon and Pythias, David and Jonathan. Orestes was the son, and Pylades the nephew, of Agamemnon, after whose murder Orestes was put in the care of Pylades' father (Strophius), and the two became fast friends. Pylades assisted Orestes in obtaining vengeance on Ægisthus and Clytemnestra, and afterwards married Electra his friend's sister.

Pylon (pī′ lon). Properly a monumental gateway (Gr. *pulon*), especially of an Egyptian temple; now usually applied to the obelisks that mark out the course in an aerodrome or to the standards for electric cables.

Pyramid (pir′ á mid). There are some 70 pyramids still remaining in Egypt, but those specially called The Pyramids are the three larger in the group of eight known as the Pyramids of Gizeh. Of these the largest, the Great Pyramid, is the tomb of Cheops, a king of the 4th Dynasty, about 4000 B.C. It was 480 ft. in height (now about 30 ft. less), and the length of each base is 755 ft. The Second Pyramid, the tomb of Chephren (also 4th Dynasty) is slightly smaller (472 ft. by 700 ft.); and the Third, the tomb of Menkaura, or Mycerinus (4th Dynasty, about 3630 B.C.), is much smaller (215 ft. by 346 ft.). Each contains entrances, with dipping passages leading to various sepulchral chambers.

Pyramus (pir′ á můs). A Babylonian youth in Classic story (*see* Ovid's *Metamorphoses*, iv), the lover of Thisbe, Thisbe was to meet him at the white mulberry-tree near the tomb of Ninus, but she, scared by a lion, fled and left her veil which the lion besmeared with blood. Pyramus, thinking his lady-love had been devoured, slew himself, and Thisbe coming up soon afterwards, stabbed herself also. The blood of the lovers stained the white fruit of the mulberry-tree into its present colour. The "tedious brief scene" and "very tragical mirth" presented by the rustics in *Midsummer Night's Dream* is a travesty of this legend.

Pyrrha (pi′ rá). The wife of Deucalion (*q.v.*) in Greek legend. They were the sole survivors of the deluge sent by Zeus to destroy the whole human race, and repopulated the world by casting stones behind them which were turned into men.

> Men themselves, the which at first were framed
> Of earthly mould, and form'd of flesh and bone.
> Are now transformed into hardest stone;
> Such as behind their backs (so backward bred)
> Were thrown by Pyrrha and Deucalion.
> SPENSER: *Fairie Queene*, V, Introd., 2.

Pyrrhic Dance (pi′ rik). The famous wardance of the Greeks; so called from its inventor, Pyrrichos, a Dorian. It was a quick dance, performed in full armour to the flute, and its name is still used for a metrical foot of two short, "dancing" syllables. The *Romaika*, still danced in Greece, is a relic of the ancient Pyrrhic dance.

> Ye have the Pyrrhic dance as yet:
> Where is the Pyrrhic phalanx gone?
> BYRON: *The Isles of Greece*.

Pyrrhic victory. A ruinous victory. Pyrrhus, King of Epirus, after his victory over the Romans at Asculum (279 B.C.), when he lost the flower of his army, said to those sent to congratulate him, "One more such victory and Pyrrhus is undone."

Pythagoras (pī thåg′ or ås). The Greek philosopher and mathematician of the 6th century B.C. (born at Samos), to whom was attributed the enunciation of the doctrines of the transmigration of souls and of the harmony of the spheres, and also the proof of the 47th proposition in the 1st book of Euclid, which is hence called the *Pythagorean proposition*. He taught that the sun is a movable sphere, and that it, and the earth, and all the planets revolve round some central point which they called "the fire."

He maintained that the soul has three vehicles: (1) the *ethereal*, which is luminous and celestial, in which the soul resides in a state of bliss in the stars; (2) the *luminous*, which suffers the punishment of sin after death; and (3) the *terrestrial*, which is the vehicle it occupies on this earth.

Pythagoras was noted for his manly beauty and long hair; and many legends are related of him, such as that he distinctly recollected previous existences of his own, having been (1) Æthalides, son of Mercury, (2) Euphorbus the Phrygian, son of Panthous, in which form he ran Patroclus through with a lance, leaving Hector to dispatch the hateful friend of Achilles, (3) Hermotimus, the prophet of Clazomenæ; and (4) a fisherman. To prove his Phrygian existence he was taken to the temple of Hera, in Argos, and asked to point out the shield of the son of Panthous, which he did without hesitation.

Rosalind alludes to this theory (*As You Like It*, iii, 2) when she says: —

I was never so be-rhymed since Pythagoras' time that I was an Irish rat, which I can hardly remember.

It is also elaborated in the scene between Feste and Malvolio in *Twelfth Night*, iv, 2: —

Clown: What is the opinion of Pythagoras concerning wild fowl?

Mal: That the soul of our grandam might haply inhabit a bird.

Clown: What thinkest thou of his opinion?

Mal.: I think nobly of the soul, and no way approve his opinion.

Other legends assert that one of his thighs was of gold, and that he showed it to Abaris, the Hyperborean priest, and exhibited it in the Olympic Games; also that Abaris gave him a dart by which he could be carried through the air and with which he expelled pestilence, lulled storms, and performed other wonderful exploits.

It was also said that Pythagoras used to write on a looking-glass in blood and place it opposite the moon, when the inscription would appear reflected on the moon's disc; and that he tamed a savage Daunian bear by "stroking it gently with his hand," subdued an eagle by the same means, and held absolute dominion over beasts and birds by "the power of his voice" or "influence of his touch."

Python (pī' thon). The monster serpent hatched from the mud of Deucalion's deluge, and slain near Delphi by Apollo.

Pyx (picks). A small metal Vessel in which the Host is carried to sick people. In pre-Reformation England it was a vessel, often in the shape of a dove, suspended above the altar, in which the sacrament was reserved. Only in the churches of Amiens and Valloires is such a pyx now permitted.

Q

Q. The seventeenth letter of the English alphabet, and nineteenth (*koph*) of the Phœnician and Hebrew, where, in numerical notation, it represented 90 (in late Roman, 500). In English *q* is invariably followed by *u* (except occasionally in transliteration of some Arabic words), and it never occurs at the end of a word.

Q in a corner. An old children's game, perhaps the same as our "Puss in the corner"; also something not seen at first, but subsequently brought to notice. The thong to which seals are attached in legal documents is in French called the *queue*; thus we have *lettres scellées sur simple queue* or *sur double queue*, according to whether they bear one or two seals. In documents where the seal is attached to the deed itself, the corner where the seal is placed is called the *queue*, and when the document is sworn to the finger is laid on the *queue*.

In a merry Q (cue). Humour, temper; thus Shakespeare says, "My cue is villainous melancholy" (*King Lear*, i, 2).

Q. The *nom de plume* of Sir Arthur Quiller-Couch (1863-1944), sometime Professor of English Literature at Cambridge, and author of novels (*e.g. Dead Man's Rock*, 1887) and of several anthologies of prose and verse.

Old Q. William Douglas, third Earl of March, and fourth Duke of Queensberry (1724-1810), notorious for his dissolute life and escapades, especially on the turf.

On the strict Q.T. With complete secrecy. "Q.T." stands for "quiet."

To mind one's P's and Q's. See P.

Q.E.D. (Lat. *quod erat demonstrandum*, which was to be demonstrated). Appended to the theorems of Euclid: — Thus have we proved the proposition stated above, as we were required to do.

Quack or **Quack doctor**; once called *quacksalver*. A puffer of salves; an itinerant drugvendor at fairs, who mounted his tailboard and "quacked" forth the praises of his wares to the gaping rustics. Hence, a charlatan.

Saltimbancoes, quacksalvers, and charlatans deceive them in lower degrees. — Sir Thomas Browne: *Pseudodoxia Epidemica*, I, iii.

Quad. The university contraction for *quadrangle*, the college grounds; hence, *to be in quad* is to be confined to your college grounds. The word **quad** is also applied to one of a family of quadruplets. *Cp.* Quod.

Quadragesima Sunday (kwod rà jes' i mà). The first Sunday in Lent; so called because it is, in round numbers, the fortieth day before Easter.

Quadrilateral. The four fortresses of Peschiera and Mantua on the Mincio, with Verona and Legnago on the Adige. Now demolished.

Lambeth Quadrilateral. The 4 points suggested by the Lambeth Conference of 1888 as a basic for Christian re-union: Bible, Apostolic and Nicene Creeds, 2 Sacraments, Episcopate.

Quadrille (kwod ril'). An old card-game played by four persons with an ordinary pack of cards from which the eights, nines, and tens have been withdrawn. It displaced ombre (*q.v.*) in popular favour about 1730, and was followed by whist.

The square dance of the same name was of French origin, and was introduced into England in 1813 by the Duke of Devonshire.

Quadrillion. In English numeration, a million raised to the fourth power, represented by 1 followed by 24 ciphers; in American and French numeration it stands for the fifth power of a thousand, *i.e.* 1 followed by 15 ciphers.

Quadroon (kwod roon'). A person with one-fourth of black blood; the offspring of a mulatto woman by a white man. The mulatto is half-blooded, one parent being white and the other black.

Quadruple. Quadruple Alliance. An international alliance for offensive or defensive purposes of four powers, especially that of Britain, France, Austria, and Holland in 1718, to prevent Spain recovering her Italian possessions, and that of Britain, France, Spain, and Portugal in 1834 as a counter-move to the "Holy Alliance" between Russia, Prussia, and Austria. Another is that of 1674, when Germany, Spain, Denmark, and Holland formed an alliance against France to resist the encroachments of Louis XIV.

Quadruple Treaty. An agreement signed in 1834 between Britain, France, Spain, and Portugal, whereby the succession of Isabella II to the throne of Spain was accepted despite the Salic Law (*q.v.*).

Quai d'Orsay (kā dôr sā). The quay in Paris running along the left bank of the Seine where are situated the departments of Foreign Affairs and other government offices. The name is applied to the French Foreign Office and sometimes to the French Government as a whole.

Quail. The bird was formerly supposed to be of an inordinately amorous disposition, hence its name was given to a courtesan.

> Here's Agamemnon, an honest fellow enough, and one that loves quails.—*Troilus and Cressida*, v, 1.

Quaker. A familiar name for a member of the Society of Friends, a religious body having no definite creed and no regular ministry, founded by George Fox, 1648-50. It appears from the founder's *Journal* that they first obtained the appellation (1650) from the following circumstance:—"Justice Bennet, of Derby," says Fox, "was the first to call us Quakers, because I bade him quake and tremble at the word of the Lord."

> Quakers (that, like lanterns, bear
> Their light within them) will not swear.
> BUTLER: *Hudibras*, ii, 2.

The name had, however, been previously applied to a sect whose adherents shook and trembled with religious emotion.

Quaker City. Philadelphia.

Quarantine (Ital. *quaranta*, forty). The period, originally forty days, that a ship suspected of being infected with some contagious disorder is obliged to lie off port. Now applied to any period of segregation to prevent infection.

In law the term is also applied to the forty days during which a widow who is entitled to a dower may remain in the chief mansion-house of her deceased husband.

To perform quarantine is to ride off port during the time of quarantine.

Quarrel, to engage in contention, to fall out (from O.Fr. *querele*, Lat. *querela*, complaint, *querī*, to complain).

To quarrel over the bishop's cope—over something which cannot possibly do you any good; over goat's wool. A newly appointed Bishop of Bruges entered the town in his cope, which he gave to the people; and the people, to part it among themselves, tore it to shreds, each taking a piece.

To quarrel with your bread and butter. To act contrary to your best interest; to snarl at that which procures your living, like a spoilt child, who shows its ill-temper by throwing its bread and butter to the ground.

Quarry. An object of chase, especially the bird flown at in hawking or the animal pursued by hounds or hunters. Originally the word denoted the entrails, etc., of the deer which were placed on the animal's *skin* after it had been flayed, and given to the hounds as a reward. The word is the O.Fr. *cuirée*, skinned from *cuir* (Lat. *corium*), skin.

> Your castle is surprised; your wife and babes
> Savagely slaughter'd; to relate the manner,
> Were, on the quarry of these murder'd deer
> To add the death of you.
> *Macbeth*, iv, 2.

The place where marble, stone, etc., is dug out is called a *quarry*, from O.Fr. *quarrière*, Lat. *quadrare*, to square, because the stones were *squared* on the spot.

Quart d'heure (kar děr). **Un mauvais quart d'heure** (Fr., a bad quarter of an hour), used of a short, disagreeable experience.

Quarter. The fourth part of anything, as of a year or an hour, or any material thing.

In weights a *quarter* is 28 lb., *i.e.* a fourth of a hundredweight; as a measure of capacity for grain it is 8 bushels, which used to be one-fourth, but is now one-fifth, of a load. In the meat trade a *quarter* of a beast is a fourth part, which includes one of the legs. A *quarter* in the United States coinage is the fourth part of a dollar; and in an heraldic shield the *quarters* are the divisions made by central lines drawn at right angles across the shield, the 1st and 4th quarters being in the *dexter chief* and *sinister base* (*i.e.* left-hand top and right-hand bottom when looking at it), and the 2nd and 3rd in the *sinister chief* and *dexter base*.

Quarters. Residence or place of abode; as **winter quarters**, the place where an army lodges during the winter months; **married quarters**, the accommodation in a barrack area allotted to regular soldiers who live with their wives and families. **Come to my quarters** is a common phrase among bachelors as an invitation to their rooms. In the Southern U.S.A. the word is used for that part of a plantation allotted to the Negroes.

> There shall no leavened bread be seen with thee, neither shall there be leaven seen . . . in all thy quarters.
> *Exod*. xiii, 7.

A district of a town or city is often known as a *quarter*, and in this sense the French use **Quartier Latin**, in Paris, which is the district where artists live and the medical schools are situated.

Quartered. *See* DRAWN AND QUARTERED.

Quarter Days. (1) New Style—Lady Day (March 25th), Midsummer Day (June 24th), Michaelmas Day (September 29th), and Christmas Day (December 25th).

(2) Old Style—Lady Day (April 6th), Old Midsummer Day (July 6th), Old Michaelmas Day (October 11th), and Old Christmas Day (January 6th).

Quarter Days in Scotland— Candlemas Day (February 2nd), Whitsunday (May 15th), Lammas Day (August 1st), and Martinmas Day (November 11th).

Quarterdeck. The upper deck of a ship from the mainmast to the stern. In men-of-war it is used by officers only. Hence, *to behave as though he were on his own quarterdeck*, to behave as though he owned the place.

Quartermaster. In the army, the officer whose duty it is to attend to the *quarters* of the soldiers. He superintends the issue of all stores and equipment.

In the navy, the petty officer who, besides other duties, has charge of the steering of the ship, the signals, stowage, etc.

Quarto. A size of paper made by folding the sheet twice, giving *four* leaves, or eight pages; hence, a book composed of sheets folded thus. *Cp.* FOLIO; OCTAVO. The word is often written "4to."

Quasi (kwā' zī) (Lat., as if). Prefixed to denote that so-and-so is not the real thing, but may be almost accepted in its place; thus a

Quasi contract is not a real contract, but something which has the force of one.

Quasi historical. Apparently historical; more or less so, or pretending to be so and almost succeeding.

Quasi tenant. The tenant of a house sublet.

Quasimodo Sunday (kwā zī mō dō'). The first Sunday after Easter; so called because the "Introit" of the day begins with these words: *Quasi modo geniti infantes* (1 *Pet.* ii, 2). Also called "Low Sunday."

Quasimodo was also the name of the hunchback in Victor Hugo's *Nôtre Dame de Paris*, 1831.

Que sçais-je? (kě sāzh). The motto adopted by Michel-Eyquem de Montaigne (1533-92), the great French essayist, as expressing the sceptical and enquiring nature of his writings.

Queen. A female reigning sovereign, or the consort of a king; from A.S. *cwen*, a woman (which also gives *quean*, a word still sometimes used slightingly or contemptuously of a woman), from an ancient Aryan root that gave the Old Teutonic stem *kwen-*, Zend *genā*, Gr. *guné*, Slavonic *zená*, O.Ir. *ben*, etc., all meaning "woman." In the 4th-century translation of the Bible by Ulfilas we meet with *gens* and *gino* ("wife" and "woman"); and in the Scandinavian languages *karl* and *kone* still mean "man" and "wife." *Cp.* KING; *see* MAB.

Queen Anne. Daughter of James II and Anne Hyde. She reigned over Great Britain from 1702 to 1714, and her name is still used in certain colloquial phrases.

Queen Anne style. The style in buildings, furniture, silver-ware, etc., characteristic of her period. Domestic architecture, for instance, was noted for many angles, gables, and irregularity of windows.

Queen Anne's Bounty. A fund created out of the firstfruits and tenths which were part of the papal exactions before the Reformation. The *firstfruits* are the whole first year's profits of a clerical living, and the *tenths* are the tenth part annually of the profits of a living. Henry VIII annexed both these to the Crown, but Queen Anne formed them into a perpetual fund for the augmentation of poor livings and the building of parsonages. The sum equals about £14,000 a year.

Queen Dowager. The widow of a deceased king.

Queen Mother. The mother of a reigning sovereign.

> If you hold it fit, after the play
> Let his queen mother all alone entreat him
> To show his griefs.
> *Hamlet*, iii, 1.

Queen of the May. *See* MAY.

Queen Regnant. A queen who holds the crown in her own right, in contradistinction to a *Queen Consort*.

Queen's Bench; Queen's Counsel. *See* KING'S.

Queen's College (Oxford), **Queens' College** (Cambridge). Note the position of the apostrophe in each case—an important matter. The Oxford College was founded (1340) by Robert de Eglesfield in honour of Queen Philippa, consort of Edward III, to whom he was confessor. The Cambridge college numbers two Queens as its founders, viz. Margaret of Anjou, consort of Henry VI (1448), and Elizabeth Wood-ville, Edward IV's consort, who refounded the college in 1465.

Queen's Day. November 17th, the day of the accession of Queen Elizabeth I, first publicly celebrated in 1570, and for over three centuries kept as a holiday in Government offices and at Westminster School.

November 17th at Merchant Taylors' School is a holiday also, now called Sir Thomas White's Founder's Day.

Queen's ware. Glazed Wedgwood earthenware of a creamy colour.

Queen's weather. A fine day for a fête; so called because Queen Victoria was, for the most part, fortunate in having fine weather when she appeared in public.

The Queen of Glory. An epithet of the Virgin Mary.

The Queen of Hearts. Elizabeth (1596-1662), daughter of James I, the unfortunate Queen of Bohemia, so called in the Low Countries from her amiable character and engaging manners, even in her lowest estate.

The Queen of Heaven. The Virgin Mary. In ancient times, among the Phœnicians, Astarte; Greeks, Hera; Romans, Juno; Hecate; the Egyptian Isis, etc., were also so called; but as a general title it applied to Diana, or the Moon, also called *Queen of the Night,* and *Queen of the Tides.* In *Jer.* vii, 18, we read: "The children gather wood . . . and the women knead dough to make cakes to the queen of heaven," *i.e.* the Moon.

The Queen of Love. Aphrodite, or Venus.
Poor queen of love in thine own law forlorn
To love a cheek that smiles at thee in scorn!
Venus and Adonis, 251.

Queen Square Hermit. Jeremy Bentham (1748-1832), who lived at No. 1 Queen Square, London. He was the father of the political economists called Utilitarians, whose maxim is, "The greatest happiness of the greatest number."

The White Queen. Mary Queen of Scots; so called because she dressed in *white* mourning for her French husband (Francis II 1544-60).

Queenhithe (London). The hithe or strand for" lading and unlading barges and lighters in the City. Called "queen" from being part of the dowry of Eleanor, Queen of Henry II.

Queer. Colloquial for out of sorts, not up to the mark, also slang for drunk; and thieves' cant for anything base and worthless, especially counterfeit money.

Querno (kwĕr' nō). Camillo Querno, of Apulia, hearing that Leo X (1513-22) was a great patron of poets, went to Rome with a harp in his hand, and sang his *Alexias,* a poem containing 20,000 verses. He was introduced to the Pope as a buffoon, but was promoted to the laurel.
Rome in her Capitol saw Querno sit,
Thronëd on seven hills the Antichrist of wit.
Dunciad, ii.

Querpo (kĕr' pō). **In querpo.** In one's shirtsleeves; in undress (Span, *en cuerpo,* without a cloak).

Boy, my cloak and rapier; if fits not a gentleman of my rank to walk the streets in querpo.—BEAUMONT AND FLETCHER: *Love's Cure,* ii, 1.

Question. When members' of the House of Commons or other debaters call out *Question,* they mean that the person speaking is wandering away from the subject under consideration.

A leading question. *See* LEADING.

An open question. A statement, proposal, doctrine, or supposed fact, respecting which private opinion is allowed. In the House of Commons every member may vote as he likes, regardless of party politics, on an open question.

Out of the question. Not worth discussing, not to be thought of; quite foreign to the subject.

To pop the question. To propose or make an offer of marriage. As this important demand is supposed to be unexpected, the question is said to be "popped."

Questionists. In the examinations for degrees at Cambridge it was customary, at the beginning of the January term, to hold "Acts," and the candidates for the Bachelor's degree were called "Questionists." They were examined by a moderator, and afterwards the fathers of other colleges "questioned" them for three hours in Latin, and the dismissal uttered by the Regius Professor indicated what class you would be placed in, or that respondent was plucked, in which case the words were simply *Descendus domine.*

Queue (kū). French for tail (*cp.* Q IN A CORNER), hence used of a pigtail, or long plait of hair, also for a line of people waiting their turn at a booking-office, theatre, shop, etc.

To queue up. A term that came into prominence during the World Wars, especially in connexion with the food shortage, when hundreds of people had to wait for hours in long lines before they could obtain their "rations" at the butcher's, grocer's, etc.

Qui vive? (Kē vēv) (Fr.) Literally, *Who lives?* but used as a sentry's challenge and so equivalent to our *Who goes there?* which in French would be *Qui va là?*

To be on the qui vive. On the alert; to be quick and sharp; to be on the tiptoe of expectation, like a sentinel. (*See above.*)

Quia Emptores (kwī' à emp tôr' ēz). A statute passed in the reign of Edward I (1290), to insure the lord paramount his fees arising from escheats, marriages, etc. By it freemen were permitted to sell their lands on condition that the purchaser should hold from the chief lord, and it resulted in a great increase of landowners holding direct from the Crown. So called from its opening words.

Quibble. An evasion; a juggling with words; probably a frequentative of the older *quib*, from Lat. *quibus*, a word constantly occurring in legal documents and so associated with the "quirks and quillets of the law."

Quick. Living; hence animated, lively; hence fast, active, brisk (A.S. *cwic*, living, alive). Our expression "Look alive," means "Be brisk."

Quicksand is sand which shifts its place as if it were alive. *See* QUICK.

Quickset is living hawthorn set in a hedge, instead of dead wood, hurdles, and palings. *See* QUICK.

Quicksilver is *argentum vivum* (living silver), silver that moves about like a living thing. (A.S. *cwic seolfor*.)

> Swift as quicksilver
> It courses through the natural gates
> And alleys of the body.
> *Hamlet*, i, 5.

The quick and dead. The living and the dead.

Quickie. In film parlance, a motion picture made cheaply to catch the cheap market and make a quick return on the money invested.

Quid. Slang for a sovereign (or a pound note). It occurs in Shadwell's *Squire of Alsatia* (1688), but its origin is unknown.

In a *quid of tobacco*, meaning a piece for chewing, *quid* is another form, of *cud*.

Quid pro quo (Lat.). Tit for tat; a return given as good as that received; a Roland for an Oliver; an equivalent.

Quid rides (Lat. Why are you laughing?). It is said that Lundy Foot, a Dublin tobacconist, set up his carriage, and that Curran, when asked to furnish him with a motto, suggested this. The witticism is, however, attributed also to H. Callender, who, we are assured, supplied it to one Brandon, a London tobacconist.

> "Rides" in English, one syllable; in Latin it is two.

Quiddity. The essence of a thing, or that which differentiates it from other things—"the Correggiosity of Correggio," "the Freeness of the Free." Hence used of subtle, trifling distinctions, quibbles, or captious argumentation. Schoolmen say *Quid est?* (what is it?) and the reply is, the *Quid* is so and so, the *What* or the nature of the thing is as follows. The latter *quid* being formed into a barbarous Latin noun becomes *Quidditas*. Hence *Quid est?* (what is it?). Answer: *Tails est quidditas* (its essence is as follows).

> He knew . . .
> Where entity and quididty
> (The ghosts of defunct bodies) fly.
> BUTLER: Hudibras, i, 1.

Quidnunc (Lat., What now?). One who is curious to know everything that's going on, or pretends to know it; a self-important newsmonger and gossip. It is the name of the leading character in Murphy's farce *The Upholsterer, or What News?*

Quill-drivers. Writing clerks.

Quillet (kwil' ét). An evasion. This may be an abbreviation of the old word *quillity* (formed on analogy with *quiddity*) meaning a quibble, or it may be from Lat. *quidlibet, i.e.* "anything you choose." A fanciful suggestion is that it came to England from the French law courts, where each separate allegation in the plaintiff's charge, and every distinct plea in the defendant's answer began with *qu'il est*; whence *quillet*, to signify a false charge, or an evasive answer.

> Oh, some authority how to proceed;
> Some tricks, some quillets, how to cheat the devil.
> *Love's Labour Lost*, iv, 3.

Quinapalus (kwin ăp' á lus). A kind of "Mrs. Grundy" or "Mrs. Harris" invented by Feste, the Clown in *Twelfth Night*, when he wished to give some saying the weight of authority. Hence someone "dragged in" when one wishes to clench an argument by some supposed quotation.

> What says Quinapalus: "Better a witty fool, than a foolish wit."—*Twelfth Night*, i, 5.

Quinbus Flestrin (kwin' bus fles' trin). The man-mountain. So the Lilliputians called Gulliver (ch. ii). Gay has an ode to this giant.

> Bards of old of him told,
> When they said Atlas' head
> Propped the skies.
> GAY: *Lilliputian Ode.*

Quincunx (kwin' kŭngks). An arrangement of five things, one in each corner and one in the middle of a square or oblong space. The term is also applied to trees in an orchard so planted that those in one row face the spaces between those in the adjacent rows.

Quinine. *See* CINCHONA.

Quinquagesima Sunday (kwin kwà jes' i mà) (Lat., fiftieth). Shrove Sunday, or the first day of the week which contains Ash Wednesday. It is so called because in round numbers it is the fiftieth day before Easter.

Quins, The. Marie, Emilie, Yvonne, Cecile, and Annette Dionne, the famous quintuplets born May 28th, 1934, to a farmer in Callander, Ontario. There are seven other children in the family. Medical attention and interest was drawn to the phenomenon of their birth and successful rearing. The Quins were wards of King George VI who, with the Queen, received them during the royal visit to Canada in 1939.

Quintain (kwin' tin). **Riding at the quintain** was a form of medieval knightly exercise. A dummy figure—sometimes only a head—was fastened to one end of a pole swinging horizontally on an upright firmly embedded in the ground. The knight, mounted or on foot, tilted at this figure, and unless he impaled it with his spear it would swing away from him and the opposite end of the pole would swing round and give him a smart blow.

Quintessence. The fifth essence. The ancient Greeks said there are four elements or forms in which matter can exist—fire, air, water, and earth (*see* ELEMENTS); the Pythagoreans added a fifth, the fifth essence—quintessence—*ether*, more subtle and pure than fire, and possessed of an orbicular motion, which flew upwards at creation and formed the material basis of the stars. Hence the word stands for the essential principle or the most subtle extract of a body that can be procured. Horace speaks of "kisses which Venus has imbued with the quintessence of her own nectar."

> Swift to their several quarters hasted then
> The cumbrous elements—earth, flood, fire;
> But this ethereal quintessence of heaven
> Flew upward . . . and turned to stars
> Numberless as thou seest.
> > MILTON: *Paradise Lost*, iii, 716.

Quintillion (kwin til' yon). In English, the fifth power of a million, 1 followed by 30 ciphers; in France and the United States the cube of a million, a million multiplied by a thousand four times over, 1 followed by 18 ciphers. *Cp.* BILLION.

Quirinal (kwi' ri nal). The palace in Rome of the former kings of Italy. The term was usually applied emblematically to the Italian kingdom and government as opposed to the Vatican, the seat of Papal authority and ecclesiastical government.

Quirt (U.S.A.). A riding whip with a short stock and a long lash or braided leather. From the Spanish *cuerda*, cord.

Quis. Latin, Who?

Quis custodiet custodes? (Lat.) [The shepherds keep watch over the sheep], but who is there to keep watch over the shepherds? Said when one is not certain of the integrity of one whom one has placed in a position of trust.

Quis separabit? (**Lat.,** Who shall separate us?) The motto adopted by the Most Illustrious Order of St. Patrick when it was founded in 1783.

Quisling (kwiz' ling). Term applied to a traitor and collaborationist in time of enemy occupation. Vidkun Quisling was a Norwegian who, before the invasion of his country by the Germans in 1940, acted as their advance agent and strove for the downfall of his country. He was appointed the puppet premier, but fled at the defeat of Germany and was caught and executed October 24th, 1945.

Quit. (Fr. *quitter*, to leave, to depart). In U.S.A. this word is more commonly used in the sense of to leave a job or a place.

The Quixote of the North. Charles XII of Sweden (1682, 1697-1718), also called *The Madman.*

Quixotic (kwik zot' ik). Having foolish and unpractical ideas of honour, or schemes for the general good, like Don Quixote (*q.v.*).

Quiz. One who banters or chaffs another. The origin of the word—which appeared about 1780—is unknown; but fable accounts for it by saying that a Mr. Daly, manager of a Dublin theatre, laid a wager that he would introduce into the language within twenty-four hours a new word of no meaning. Accordingly, on every wall, or all places accessible, were chalked up the four mystic letters, and all Dublin was inquiring what they meant. The wager was won, and the word remains current in our language.

Since World War II the word has been applied to a test, usually competitive, of general knowledge.

Quo warranto (kwō war ăn' tō). A writ against a defendant (whether an individual or a corporation) who lays claim to something he has no right to; so named because the offender is called upon to show *quo warranto* (*rem*) *usurpavit* (by what right or authority he lays claim to the matter of dispute.

Quoad hoc (kwō' ăd hok) (Lat.). To this extent, with respect to this.

Quod. Slang for prison. Probably the same word as *quad* (*q.v.*), which is a contraction of *quadrangle,* the enclosure in which prisoners are allowed to walk, and where whippings used to be inflicted. The word was in use in the 17th century.

> Flogged and whipped in quod.
> > HUGHES: *Tom Brown's Schooldays.*

Quodlibet (Lat., what you please). Originally a philosophical or theological question proposed for purposes of scholastic debate, hence a nice and knotty point, a subtlety. *Quidlibet* is a form of the same word.

Quondam (kwon' dam) (Lat., former). We say, He is a quondam schoolfellow—former schoolfellow; my quondam friend, the quondam chancellor, etc.

My quondam barber, but "his lordship" now.
DRYDEN.

Quorum (kwôr' um) (Lat., of whom). The lowest number of members of a committee or board, etc., the presence *of whom* is necessary before business may be transacted; formerly, also, certain Justices of the Peace—hence known as Justices of the Quorum—chosen for their special ability, one or more of whom had to be on the Bench at trials before the others could act. Slender calls Justice Shallow justice of the peace and quorum. (*Merry Wives of Windsor*, i, 1.)

Quos ego (kwōs eg' ō). A threat of punishment for disobedience. The words, from Virgil's *Æneid* (1, 135), were uttered by Neptune to the disobedient and rebellious winds, and are sometimes given as an example of aposiopesis, *i.e.* a stopping short for rhetorical effort, "Whom 1—," said Neptune, the "will punish" being left to the imagination.

Neptune had but to appear and utter a *quos ego* for these windbags to collapse, and become the most subservient of salaried public servants.—*Truth*, January, 1886.

Quota (kwō' tà) (Lat.). The allotted portion or share; the rate assigned to each. Thus we say, "Every man is to pay his quota."

R

R. The eighteenth letter of the English alphabet (seventeenth of the Roman) representing the twentieth of the Phœnician and Hebrew. In the ancient Roman numeration it stood for 80. In England it was formerly used as a branding mark for rogues, particularly kidnappers.

It has been called the "snarling letter" or "dog letter," because a dog in snarling utters a sound resembling r-r-r-r-r, r-r-r-r-r, etc. — sometimes preceded by a g.

> Irritata canis quod R R quam plurima dicat.
> *Lucillus.*

In his *English Grammar made for the Benefit of all Strangers* Ben Jonson says—

> R is the dog's letter, and hurreth in the sound; the tongue striking the inner palate, with a trembling about the teeth.

And see the Nurse's remark about R in *Romeo and Juliet*, ii, 4.

R in prescriptions. The ornamental part of this letter is the symbol of Jupiter (♃), under whose special protection all medicines were placed. The letter itself (*Recipe*, take) and its flourish may be thus paraphrased: "Under the good auspices of Jove, the patron of medicines, take the following drugs in the proportions set down." It has been suggested that the symbol is for *Responsum Raphaelis*, from the assertion of Dr. Napier and other physicians of the 17th century, that the angel Raphael imparted the virtues of drugs.

The three R's. Reading, writing, and arithmetic. The phrase is said to have been originated by Sir William Curtis (d. 1829), who gave this as a toast.

> The House is aware that no payment is made except on the "three R's."—MR. CORY, M.P.: in House of Commons, Feb. 28th, 1867.

Ra (ra). The principal deity of ancient Egypt, one of the numerous forms of the sun-god, and the supposed ancestor of all the Pharaohs. He was the protector of men and vanquisher of evil; Nut, the sky, was his father, and it was said of him that every night he fought with the serpent, Apepi. He is usually represented as hawk-headed, and is crowned with the solar disk and uræus. *See* OSIRIS.

Rabbinic (ră bin′ ik). The Hebrew language as used by the rabbis in their ecclesiastical and theological writings. The term is often applied to modern Hebrew. Among the Jews a Rabbinist is one who follows closely the doctrines and precepts of the Talmud and the traditions of the rabbis.

Rabelaisian (răb el ā′ zian). Coarsely and boisterously satirical; grotesque, extravagant, and licentious in language; reminiscent in literary style of the great French satirist François Rabelais (1483-1553).

Dean Swift, Thomas Amory (d. 1788, author of *John Buncle*), and Sterne have all been called "the English Rabelais"—but the title is not very fitting; indeed, the title is a contradiction in terms; Rabelais was so essentially a Frenchman of the Renaissance that it is impossible to think of an English counterpart of any period.

> If we are to seek for an approximation of Aristophanic humour, we shall find it perhaps in Rabelais. Rabelais exhibits a similar disregard for decency, combining the same depth of purpose and largeness of insight with the same coarse fun.—J. A. SYMONDS: *Studies of Greek Poets.*

Races. The principal horse-races in England are run at Newmarket, Doncaster, Epsom, Goodwood, and Ascot (*See* CLASSIC RACES), but there are a large number of other courses where important meetings are held, and the greatest event in the world of steeplechasing—the Grand National—is run at Aintree, near Liverpool

There are seven annual race meetings at Newmarket: (1) The Craven; (2) first spring; (3) second spring; (4) July; (5) first October; (6) second October; (7) the Houghton.

At Doncaster races are held for two days about the middle of May, four days early in September, and two days toward the end of October.

The Epsom meeting (when the Derby, Oaks, Coronation Cup, etc., are run) is held for four days in the first week of June.

Goodwood (four days) starts on the last Tuesday in July, and Ascot (four days) in the middle of June.

The following are the principal English horse-races, with distances and *venue*: —

> Alexandra Cup (Ascot), 2 m. 6 fur. 75 yd.
> Ascot Gold Cup, 2½ m.

Ascot Gold Vase, 2 m.
Ascot Stakes, $2\frac{1}{2}$ m.
The Cambridgeshire (Newmarket), 9 fur.
The Cesarewitch (Newmarket), $2\frac{1}{4}$ m.
Champagne Stakes (Doncaster), 6 fur. 152 yd
Champion Stakes (Newmarket), $1\frac{1}{4}$ m.
Chester Cup, $2\frac{1}{4}$ m. 77 yd.
Chesterfield Cup (Goodwood), 1 m. 2 fur.
Cheveley Park Stakes (Newmarket), 6 fur.
City and Surburban Handicap (Epsom), $1\frac{1}{4}$ m.
Coventry Stakes (Ascot), 5 fur.
Criterion Stakes (Newmarket), 6 fur.
The Derby (Epsom), $1\frac{1}{2}$ m.
Dewhurst Stakes (Newmarket), 7 fur.
Doncaster Cup, 2 m. 2 fur.
Ebor Handicap (York), $1\frac{3}{4}$ m.
Eclipse Stakes (Sandown), $1\frac{1}{4}$ m.
Goodwood Cup, 2 m. 5 fur.
Goodwood Stakes, 2 m. 3 fur.
Grand Military Gold Cup (Sandown), 3 m. 125 yd.
The Grand National (Aintree), 4 m. 856 yd.
Great Metropolitan Handicap (Epsom), $2\frac{1}{4}$ m.
Great Yorkshire Handicap (Doncaster), 1 m. 6 fur. 632 yd.
Jubilee Handicap (Kempton), $1\frac{1}{4}$ m.
July Stakes (Newmarket), 5 fur. 142 yd.
Lincolnshire Handicap (Lincoln), 1 m.
Liverpool Autumn Cup, 1 m. 2 fur.
Liverpool Summer Cup, 1 m. 3 fur.
Manchester Cup, $1\frac{1}{2}$ m.
Manchester November Handicap, $1\frac{1}{2}$ m.
Middle Park Stakes (Newmarket), 6 fur.
New Stakes (Ascot), 5 fur. 136 yd.
Northumberland Plate (Newcastle), 2 m.
The Oaks (Epsom), $1\frac{1}{2}$ m.
The One Thousand Guineas (Newmarket), 1 m.
Portland Handicap (Doncaster), 5 fur.
Prince of Wales's Stakes (Newmarket), $1\frac{1}{2}$ m.
Royal Hunt Cup (Ascot), 7 fur. 166 yd.
The St. Leger (Doncaster), $1\frac{3}{4}$ m. 132 yd.
Stewards' Cup (Goodwood), 6 fur.
The Two Thousand Guineas (Newmarket), 1 m.

Many of the more important of these races will be found entered in their alphabetical places throughout this Dictionary.

Rache (răch). A hound that hunts by scent (A.S. *raecc*, a hound, A.Nor. *brache*, Ger. *bracken*). They were later called "running hounds" and then simply "hounds," and were used in the Middle Ages for stag, wild boar, and buck hunting.

And first I will begin with raches and their nature, and then greyhounds and their nature, and then alaunts and their nature . . . and then I shall devise and tell the sicknesses of hounds and their diseases.—
EDWARD, 2ND DUKE OF YORK: *The Master of Game, Prologue* (about 1410).

Rachel (ra shel'). A French actress whose real name was Elizabeth Felix (1821-58). She was the daughter of poor Jewish pedlars, but going on the stage as a girl she won a great triumph in 1843 in the name part of Racine's *Phèdre*. As Adrienne Lecouvreur, in Scribe's play of that name (1849), she confirmed her position as one of the greatest tragic actresses in Europe. The cosmetics bearing the name

"Rachel" immortalize a Parisian beauty-specialist of the Second Empire.

Rack. A flying scud, drifting clouds. (Icel. *rek*, drift; *recka*, to drive.)

The cloud-capped towers, the gorgeous palaces,
The solemn temples, the great globe itself,
Yea, all which it inherit, shall dissolve,
And . . . leave not a rack behind.
Tempest, iv, 1.

The instrument of torture so called (connected with Ger. *recken*, to strain) was a frame in which a man was fastened and his arms and legs *stretched* till the body was lifted by the tension several inches from the floor. Not infrequently the limbs were forced thereby out of their sockets. Coke says that the rack was first introduced into the Tower by the Duke of Exeter, constable of the Tower, in 1447, whence it was called the "Duke of Exeter's daughter." Its use in England was abolished in 1640.

Rack. The framework for putting plates and other things on; the grating for holding fodder, etc., is probably connected with this.

Rack and ruin. Utter destitution. Here "rack" is a variety of *wrack* and *wreck*.

To lie at rack and manger. To live without thought of the morrow, like cattle or horses whose food is placed before them without themselves taking thought; hence, to live at reckless expense.

When Virtue was a country maide,
And had no skill to set up trade,
She came up with a carrier's jade,
And lay at rack and manger.
Life of Robin Goodfellow (1628).

To rack one's brains. To strain them to find out or recollect something; to puzzle about something.

Rack rent. The actual value or rent of a tenement, and not that modified form on which the rates and taxes are usually levied; an exorbitant rent, one which is "racked" or stretched.

Racket. Noise or confusion. The word is probably imitative, like *crack, bang, splash*, etc.

To stand the racket. To bear the expense; to put up with the consequences.

Racy. Having distinctive or characteristic piquancy. It was first applied to wine, and comes to us from the Spanish and Portuguese *raiz* (root), meaning having a radical or distinct flavour.

Rich, racy verse, in which we See
The soil from which they come, taste, smell, and See.
COWLEY.

The word now generally implies a hint of indecency.

Racy of the soil. Characteristic of the inhabitants, especially the dwellers in the country, workers on the land.

Radar. Term derived from Radio-Detection-and-Ranging, primarily a means of detecting the presence of aircraft by sending out frequencies which are reflected back when they encounter a solid object. Subsequently developed for use by ships navigating in fog. A British invention, made by R. A. W. Watt, telecommunications advisor to the Air Ministry, in 1935. Britain was far ahead of the world at the start of the war, and without this invention could not have won the Battle of Britain in 1940. Two radar stations were lent to France by Britain in 1939, and a courageous Frenchman, René Varin, was dispatched from England to effect their destruction after the fall of France. The United States had some experimental stations, one of which was at Pearl Harbour and plotted the incoming Japanese aircraft, though the report was unfortunately not taken seriously. When in due course the Germans had developed Radar, countermeasures were developed; they took the form of bundles of tin-foil streamers dropped from bomber formations which registered on and confused the enemy's Radar screens. In 1950 Radar frequencies were sent to and reflected back from the Moon.

Radevore (răd′ e vôr). A kind of cloth, probably tapestry, known in the 14th century. It has been suggested (Skeat) that it was named from Vaur, in Languedoc, *ras* (Eng. *rash*, a smooth—*rased*—textile fabric) *de Vor*.

> This woful lady ylern'd had in youthe
> So that she worken and embrowden kouthe,
> And weven in hire stole the radevore
> As hyt of wommen had be y-woved yore.
>   CHAUCER: *Legend of Good Women*, 2351.

Radical. The term was first applied as a party name in 1818 to Henry Hunt, Major Cartwright, and others of the same clique, ultra-Liberals verging on republicanism, who wished to introduce *radical* reform, *i.e.* one that would go to the root (Lat. *radix, radicis*) of the matter, in the electoral system, and not merely to disfranchise and enfranchise a borough or two. Bolingbroke, in his *Discourses on Parties* (1735), says, "Such a remedy might have wrought a *radical cure* of the evil that threatens our constitution." The term is not now used.

Raft (from the Middle English *raff*, abundance, plenty) is applied to express a number of persons or things.

Rag. A tatter, hence a remnant (as "not a rag of decency," "not a rag of evidence"), hence a vagabond or ragamuffin.

> Lash hence these overweening rags of France.
>   *Richard III*, v, 3.

The word was old cant for a farthing, and was also used generally to express scarcity—or absence—of money:—

> Money by me? Heart and good-will you might,
> But surely, master, not a rag of money.
>   *Comedy of Errors*, iv, 4.

In university slang (and now in general slang) **a rag** is a boisterous jollification, in which practical jokes and horseplay have a large share. **To rag** a man is to torment him in a rough and noisy fashion.

Rag-time. Fast syncopated rhythm, usually played by coloured jazz musicians, popular in the first decade of the 20th century. The name has been perpetuated in the celebrated tune *Alexander's Rag-time Band* by Irving Berlin (1912).

Rag water. Whisky (*thieves' jargon*).

Ragamuffin. A *muffin* is a poor thing of a creature, a "regular muff"; so that a *ragamuffin* is a sorry creature in rags.

> I have led my ragamuffins where they are peppered.—
> 1 *Henry IV*, v, 3.

Ragman Roll. The set of documents recording the names of the Scottish barons who paid homage to Edward I on his progress through Scotland in 1291, now in the Public Record Office. The name probably arose from the quantity of seals hanging from it, and it still survives as "rigmarole" (*q.v.*).

Ragout (ra goo′). A seasoned dish; stewed meat and vegetables highly seasoned. Fr. *ragoûter* (*re*, again, *goûter*, to taste) means to coax a sick person's appetite.

Rahu (ra′ hū). The demon that, according to Hindu legend, causes eclipses. He one day quaffed some of the nectar of immortality, but was discovered by the Sun and Moon, who informed against him, and Vishnu cut off his head. As he had already taken some of the nectar into his mouth, the head was immortal, and he ever afterwards hunted the Sun and Moon, which he caught occasionally, causing eclipses.

Rail To sit on the rail. To hedge or to reserve one's decision. A common American phrase, expressive of the same meaning as our "to sit on the fence" (*q.v.*).

Railroad, Railway. The former is the American form of English *railway*.

To railroad (U.S.A.). To hustle someone through (as of school) or out (as of an assembly) with unseemly haste and without reference to the proper formalities.

Rain. To rain cats and dogs. In northern mythology the cat is supposed to have great influence on the weather, and English sailors still say, "The cat has a gale of wind in her tail," when she is unusually frisky. Witches that rode upon the storms were said to assume the form of cats; and the stormy north-west wind is called the *cat's-nose* in the Harz district even at the present day.

The dog is a signal of *wind*, like the wolf, both of which animals were attendants of Odin, the storm god. In old German pictures the wind is figured as the "head of a dog or wolf," from which blasts issue.

So cat may be taken as a symbol of the down-pouring rain, and the *dog* of the strong gusts of wind accompanying a rainstorm.

Lay by something for a rainy day. Save something against evil times.

Rainbow. The old fable has it that if one reaches the spot where a rainbow touches the earth and digs there one will be sure to find a pot of gold. Hence visionaries, wool-gatherers, daydreamers, are sometimes called *rainbow chasers*, because of their habit of hoping for impossible things.

Rainbow Corner. In World War II Messrs. Lyons' Corner House in Shaftesbury Avenue, London, was taken over and turned into a large café and lounge for American service men under this name. It became a general meeting place for Americans in London during the war. The name was a sentimental reference to the earlier Rainbow Division (*q.v.*), plus the rainbow in the insignia of *SHAEF* (*q.v.*).

Rainbow Division. The most famous and finest Division of the American Army sent to Europe in World War I.

Raison d'être (rā' zon dātr) (Fr.). The reason for a thing's existence, its rational ground for being; as "Once crime were abolished there would be no *raison d'être* for the police."

Rajah (ra' ja). Sanskrit for king, cognate with Lat. *rex*. The title of an Indian king or prince, given later to tribal chiefs and comparatively minor dignitaries and rulers; also to Malayan and Japanese chiefs. *Maha-rajah* means the "great-rajah."

Rake. A libertine. A contraction of rakehell, used by Milton and others.

And far away amid their rakehell band,
They speed a lady left all succourless.
FRANCIS QUARLES.

Rally is *re-alligo*, to bind together again. (French *rallier*.) In Spenser it is spelt "re-allie"—

Before they could new counsels re-allie.
Faerie Queene.

Yes, we'll rally round the flag, boys,
We'll rally once again.
G. F. ROOT: *Battle-cry of Freedom.*

In this sense *rally* is also the gathering together of a group or party, as **Scout Rally**, or **Nuremburg Rally** of the Nazis.

A *rally* in lawn-tennis, badminton, etc., is a rapid return of strokes. **To rally,** meaning to banter or chaff is not connected with this word, but from Fr. *railler*, to deride; our *raillery* is really the same word.

Ralph or **Ralpho.** The squire of Hudibras (*q.v.*). The model was Isaac Robinson, a zealous butcher in Moorfields, always contriving some queer art of church government. He represents the Independent party, and Hudibras the Presbyterian.

The name is made to rhyme with either *safe, Alf,* or *half.*

Ram. Formerly, the usual prize at wrestling matches. Thus Chaucer says of his Miller, "At wrastlynge he wolde 'bere' awey the ram." (*Canterbury Tales: Prologue,* 548.)

The ram of the Zodiac. This is the famous Chrysomallion, whose golden fleece was stolen by Jason in his Argonautic expedition. It was transposed to the stars, and made the first sign of the Zodiac.

Rama (ra' ma). The seventh incarnation of Vishnu (*See* AVATAR). Rama performed many wonderful exploits, such as killing giants, demons, and other monsters. He won Sita to wife because he was able to bend the bow of Siva.

Ramachandra. *See* AVATAR.

Ramadan (răm' à dăn). The ninth month of the Mohammedan year, and the Mussulman's Lent or Holy Month (also transliterated Ramazan).

As the Moslem year is calculated on the system of twelve lunar months, Ramazan is liable at times to fall in the hot weather, when abstinence from drinking as well as from food is an extremely uncomfortable and inconvenient obligation. What wonder, then, that the end of the fast is awaited with feverish impatience?—H. M. BATSON: *Commentary on Fitzgerald's "Omar,"* St. xc.

Rama-Yana (ra' ma ya' na) (*i.e.* the deeds of Rama). The history of Rama, the great epic poem of ancient India, ranking with the Mahabharata (*q.v.*), and almost with the *Iliad*. It is ascribed to the poet Valmiki, and, as now known, consists of 24,000 stanzas in seven books.

Rambouillet, Hotel de (răm bwē' yā). The house in Paris where, about 1615, the Marquise de Rambouillet, disgusted with the immoral and puerile tone of the time, founded the *salon* out of which grew the Académie française. Mme de Sévigné, Descartes, Richelieu, Bossuet, and La Rochefoucauld were among the members. They had a language of their own, calling common things by uncommon names, and so on; the women were known as *Les précieuses* and the men as *Esprits doux*. Preciosity, pedantry, and affectation led to the disruption of the coterie which, after having performed a good and lasting service, was finally demolished by the satire of Molière's *Les précieuses ridicules* (1659) and *Les femmes savantes* (1672).

Rambunctious (răm bŭngk' shŭs). Slang term for tiresomely ferocious.

Rampage. On the rampage. Acting in a violently excited or angry manner. The word was originally Scotch, and is probably connected with *ramp*, to storm and rage.

Rampallion (răm păl' yon). A term of contempt; probably a "portmanteau word" of *ramp* and *rapscallion*; in Davenport's *A New Trick to Cheat the Devil* (1639) we have: "And bold rampallion-like, swear and drink drunk."

Away, you scullion! you rampallion! you fustilarian! I'll tickle your catastrophe.—*2 Henry IV*, ii, 1

Rampant. The heraldic term for an animal, especially a lion, shown rearing up with the fore paws in the air; strictly, a *lion rampant* should stand on the sinster hind-leg, with both fore-legs elevated, and the head in profile.

Ranch (ranch). A very extensive cattle farm in North America, where large herds are maintained entirely on pasturage. The word is also applied to the buildings connected with the ranch where the owner and cowboys live.

Dude ranch. A ranch run as a resort, where city-dwellers can spend their holidays attempting to be cowboys.

Ranee or **Rani.** A Hindu queen; the feminine of Rajah (*q.v.*).

Ranelagh (răn' é là). An old London place of amusement on the site that now forms part of the grounds of Chelsea Hospital. It was named after Richard Jones, 1st Earl of Ranelagh, who built a house and laid out gardens here in 1690. From 1742 to 1803 Ranelagh rivalled Vauxhall Gardens for concerts, masquerades, etc. A notable feature was the Rotunda, built in 1742. It was not unlike the Albert Hall in design, and was 185 ft. across with numerous boxes in which refreshments were served, while the brightly lit floor formed a thronged promenade. The Ranelagh Club was established in 1894 in Barns Elm Park, S.W., to provide facilities for polo, tennis, golf, etc.

Range (U.S.A.). Open grazing ground in the Far West.

Rangers. Picked men in the U.S. Army who worked with British Commandos. They were named after Rogers's Rangers, a body of colonial Indian fighters organized by Major Robert Rogers. Their first appearance was on the Dieppe raid in 1942 on which a small party went as armed observers.

Rank. A row, a line (especially of soldiers); also high station, dignity, eminence, as—

The rank is but the guinea's stamp,
The man's the gowd, for a' that!
            BURNS: *Is therefor Honest Poverty?*

Rank and fashion. People of high social standing; the "Upper Ten."

Rank and file. *See* FILE.

Risen from the ranks. Said of a commissioned officer in the army who formerly worked his way up from private soldier—from the ranks. Often called a *ranker*. Hence applied to a self-made man in any walk of life.

Ransom. In origin the same word as *redemption*, from Lat. *redemptionem*, through O.Fr. *rançon*, earlier *redempçon*.

A king's ransom. A large sum of money.

Rap. Not worth a rap. Worth nothing at all. The rap was a base halfpenny, intrinsically worth about half a farthing, circulated in Ireland in 1721, because small coin was so very scarce.

Many counterfeits passed about under the name of raps.—SWIFT: *Drapier's Letters*.

Rape. One of the six divisions into which Sussex is divided; it is said that each has its own river, forest, and castle. *Herepp* is Norwegian for a parish district, and *rape* in Doomsday Book is used for a district under military jurisdiction, but connexion between the two words is doubtful.

Rape of the Lock. Lord Petre, in a thoughtless moment of frolic gallantry, cut off a lock of Arabella Fermor's hair, and this liberty gave rise to the bitter feud between the two families which Alexander Pope worked up into the best heroic-comic poem of the language. The first sketch was published in 1712 in two cantos, and the complete work, including the most happily conceived machinery of sylphs and gnomes, in five cantos in 1714. Pope, under the name of Esdras Barnevelt, apothecary, later pretended that the poem was a covert satire on Queen Anne and the Barrier Treaty.

Say, what strange motive, goddess, could compel
A well-bred lord to assault a gentle belle;
O say, what stranger cause, yet unexplored,
Could make a gentle belle reject a lord.
            Introduction to the Poem.

Raphael (răf' āl). One of the principal angels of Jewish angelology. In the book of *Tobit* we are told how he travelled with Tobias into Media and back again, instructing him on the way how to marry Sara and to drive away the wicked spirit. Milton calls him the "sociable spirit," and the "affable archangel" (*Paradise Lost*, vii, 40), and it was he who was sent by God to advertise Adam of his danger.

> Raphael, the sociable spirit, hath designed
> To travel with Tobias, and secured
> His marriage with the seven-times-wedded maid.
> *Paradise Lost*, v, 221-3.

Raphael is usually distinguished in art by a pilgrim's staff, or carrying a fish, in allusion to his aiding Tobias to capture the fish which performed the miraculous cure of his father's eyesight.

Raphaelesque. In the style of the great Italian painter Raphael (1483-1520), who was specially notable for his supreme excellence in the equable development of all the essential qualities of art—composition, expression, design, and colouring.

Raphael's cartoons. *See* CARTOON.

Rare (U.S.A.). Underdone, as of a steak; or lightly cooked, as of an egg.

Rascal. Originally a collective term for the rabble of an army, the commonalty, the mob, this word was early (14th century) adopted as a term of the chase, and for long almost exclusively denoted the lean, worthless deer of a herd. In the late 16th century it was retransferred to people, and so to its present meaning, a mean rogue, a scamp, a base fellow. Shakespeare says, "Horns! the noblest deer hath them as huge as the rascal"; Palsgrave calls a starveling animal, like the lean kine of Pharaoh, "a rascall refus beest" (1530). The French have *racaille* (riff-raff).

> Come, you thin thing; come, you rascal.—2 *Henry IV*, v, 4.

Rascal counters. Pitiful £ s.d., "filthy lucre." Brutus calls money paltry compared with friendship, etc.

> When Marcus Brutus grows so covetous,
> To lock such rascal counters from his friends
> Be ready, gods, with all your thunderbolts,
> Dash him to pieces.
> *Julius Cæsar*, iv, 5.

Raspberry, To give a. A 20th-century slang expression, used on both sides of the Atlantic, for showing contempt of someone. In action, *to give a raspberry* is to put one's tongue between the closed lips and expel air forcibly with a resulting rude noise. It is otherwise known as the *Bronx cheer*.

Rasselas (răs' e lăs). Prince of Abyssinia, in Dr. Johnson's philosophical romance of that name (1759). He leaves a secluded "Happy Valley," shut off from all contact with the world or with evil, and his adventures in the world outside teach him that the virtuous man is not necessarily a happy one.

"Rasselas" is a mass of sense, and its moral precepts are certainly conveyed in striking and happy language. The mad astronomer who imagined that he possessed the regulation of the weather and the distribution of the seasons, is an original character in romance; and the happy valley in which Rasselas resides is sketched with poetical feeling.—YOUNG.

Rat. The Egyptians and Phrygians deified rats. The people of Bassora and Cambay to the present time forbid their destruction. In Egypt the rat symbolized utter destruction, and also wise judgment, the latter because rats always choose the best bread.

Pliny tells us (VIII, lvii) that the Romans drew presages from these animals, and to see a *white* rat foreboded good fortune. The bucklers at Lanuvium being gnawed by rats presaged ill-fortune, and the battle of the Marses, fought soon after, confirmed this superstition.

As wet as, or like a drowned rat. Soaking wet; looking exceedingly dejected.

I smell a rat. I perceive there is something concealed which is mischievous. The allusion is to a cat *smelling* a rat, while unable to *see* it.

Rats! An exclamation of incredulity, wonder, surprise, etc.

To rat. To forsake a losing side for the stronger party, as rats are said to forsake unseaworthy ships. One who deserts his party, as a "blackleg" during a strike, is sometimes called a rat.

> Averting . . .
> The cup of sorrow from their lips,
> And fly like rats from sinking ships.
> SWIFT: *Epistle to Mr. Nugent.*

Rattening. Destroying or taking away a workman's tools, or otherwise incapacitating him from doing work, with the object of forcing him to join a trade union or to obey its rules. The term used to be common in Yorkshire, but is not heard much nowadays.

Rattler. The term for a train, usually a local one made up of old rolling-stock, which has long been used both in Australia and the U.S.A.

Raven. A bird of ill omen; fabled to forebode death and bring infection and bad luck generally. The former notion arises from its following an army under the expectation of finding dead bodies to *raven* on; the latter notion is a mere offshoot of the former, seeing pestilence kills as fast as the sword.

> The boding raven on her cottage sat,
> And with hoarse croakings warned us of our fate.
> GAY: *Pastorals; The Dirge.*

Jovianus Pontanus relates two skirmishes between ravens and kites near Beneventum, which prognosticated a great battle, and Nicetas speaks of a skirmish between crows and ravens as presaging the irruption of the Scythians into

Thrace. Cicero was forewarned of his death by the fluttering of ravens, and Macaulay relates the legend that a raven entered the chamber of the great orator the very day of his murder and pulled the clothes off his bed. Like many other birds, ravens indicate by their cries the approach of foul weather, but "it is ful unleful to beleve that God sheweth His prevy counsayle to crowes, as Isidore sayth."

Of inspired birds ravens are accounted the most prophetical. Accordingly, in the language of that district, "to have the foresight of a raven" is to this day a proverbial expression.—MACAULAY: *History of St. Kilda*, p. 174.

When a flock of ravens forsakes the woods we may look for famine and mortality, because "ravens bear the characters of Saturn, the author of these calamities, and have a very early perception of the bad disposition of that planet." *See Athenian Oracle*, Supplement, p. 476.

As if the great god Jupiter had nothing else to doe but to dryve about jacke-dawes and ravens.—CARNEADES.

According to Roman legend ravens were once as white as swans and not inferior in size; but one day a raven told Apollo that Coronis, a Thessalian nymph whom he passionately loved, was faithless. The god shot the nymph with his dart; but, hating the tell-tale bird—

He blacked the raven o'er,
And bid him prate in his white plumes no more.
ADDISON: *Translation of Ovid*, Bk. ii.

In Christian art the raven is an emblem of God's Providence, in allusion to the ravens which fed Elijah. St. Oswald holds in his hand a raven with a ring in its mouth; St. Benedict has a raven at his feet; St. Paul the Hermit is drawn with a raven bringing him a loaf of bread, etc.

The fatal raven, consecrated to Odin, the Danish war god, was the emblem on the Danish standard, *Landeyda* (the desolation of the country), and was said to have been woven and embroidered in one noontide by the daughters of Regner Lodbrok, son of Sigurd, that dauntless warrior who chanted his death-song (the *Krakamal*) while being stung to death in a horrible pit filled with deadly serpents. If the Danish arms were destined to defeat, the raven hung his wings; if victory was to attend them, he stood erect and soaring, as if inviting the warriors to follow.

The Danish raven, lured by annual prey,
Hung o'er the land incessant.
THOMSON: *Liberty*, Pt. iv.

The two ravens that sit on the shoulders of Odin are called Huginn and Muninn (*Mind and Memory*).

Ravenstone (Ger. *rabenstein*). The old stone gibbet of Germany; so called from the ravens which are wont to perch on it.

Do you think
I'll honour you so much as save your throat
From the Ravenstone, by choking you myself?
BYRON: *Werner*, ii, 2.

Razzia (răt' zi à). An incursion made by the military into an enemy's country for the purpose of carrying off cattle or slaves, or for enforcing tribute. It is the French form of an Arabic word, and is usually employed in connexion with Algerian and North African affairs.

Razzle-dazzle. A boisterous spree, a jollification.

Re (rē) (Lat.). Respecting; in reference to; as, "*re* Brown," in reference to the case of Brown.

Reach of a river. The part which lies between two points or bends; so called because it *reaches* from point to point.

When he drew near them he would turn from each,
And loudly whistle till he passed the Reach.
CRABBE: *Borough*.

Ready. An elliptical expression for ready money. Goldsmith says, *Æs in presenti perfectum format* ("Ready-money makes a man perfect"). (*Eton Latin Grammar.*)

Lord Strut was not very flush in the "ready."—DR. ARBUTHNOT.

Real Presence. The doctrine that Christ Himself is present in the bread and wine of the Eucharist after consecration. In the Church of England "real" implies that—

The Body of Christ is given, taken, and eaten, in the Supper, only after an heavenly and spiritual manner.—(*Thirty-nine Articles*; No. xxviii.)

In the Roman Catholic and Lutheran Churches "real" implies that the actual Body is present—in the former case by transubstantiation, and in the latter by consubstantiation.

Realism. A form of philosophy which, for example, gathered a school of eminent French writers at the end of the 19th century. The leaders were Zola and Maupassant, and their aim was to describe life as it is and not as people like to think that it is or should be. The brutality and outspokenness of their writings led to an outcry; Anatole France, for example, described Zola's great novel *La Terre* as "a heap of ordure."

Ream (ultimately from Arab. *rizmah*, a bundle). A ream of paper, unless otherwise specified, contains 480 sheets; a "perfect" ream for printing papers contains 516 sheets; a ream of envelope paper contains 504 sheets, and of news, 500 sheets.

An "insides" ream contains 480 sheets all "insides," *i.e.* 20 good or inside quires of 24 sheets; a "mill" ream contains 480 sheets, and consists of 18 "good" or "insides" quires of 24 sheets each, and 2 "outsides" quires of 24 sheets each.

Rearmouse or **Reremouse.** The bat (A.S. *hreremus*, probably the fluttering-mouse, from *hrere-an*, to move or flutter). Of course, the "bat" is not a winged mouse.

Reason. It stands to reason. It is logically manifest ; this is the Latin *constat* (*constare*, literally, to stand together).

The Goddess of Reason. The central figure in an attempt to substitute a religion for Christianity during the French Revolution, which was known as The Feast of Reason. The role was taken by various young women who, in turns, were enthroned and "worshipped" in the cathedral of Notre Dame. Mlle Condeille, of the Opera, was one of the earliest of these "goddesses" (Nov. 10th, 1793); she wore a red Phrygian cap, a white frock, a blue mantle, and tricolour ribbons; her head was filleted with oak-leaves, and in her hand she carried the pike of Jupiter-Peuple. Others were Mme Momoro (wife of the printer), and the actresses Mlle Maillard and Mlle Aubray. The procession was attended by the municipal officers and national guards, while troops of ballet girls carried "torches of truth"; and many apostate clergy stripped themselves of their canonicals, and, wearing red nightcaps, joined in this blasphemous mockery. So did Julien of Toulouse, a. Calvinistic minister. Such Feasts of Reason were held in various towns of France for several years after.

Rebeccaites (re bek' a ītz). Welsh rioters in 1843, who, led by a man in woman's clothes, went about demolishing turnpike gates. The name was taken from *Gen.* xxiv, 60. When Rebecca left her father's house, Laban and his family "blessed her," and said, "Let thy seed possess the gate of those that hate them."

Rebellion, The Great. In English history, the struggle between Parliament (the people) and the Crown, which began in the reign of James I, broke into Civil War in 1642, and culminated in the execution of Charles I (Jan. 29th, 1649).

The revolts in favour of the Stuarts in 1715 and 1745 (*see* FIFTEEN; FORTY-FIVE) have also each been called *The Rebellion*.

Rebus (rē' bús) (Lat., with things). A hieroglyphic riddle, *non verbis sed rebus*. The origin of the word has, somewhat doubtfully, been traced to the lawyers of Paris who, during the carnival, used to satirize the follies of the day in squibs called *De rebus quæ geruntur* (on the current events), and, to avoid libel actions, employed hieroglyphics either wholly or in part.

In heraldry the name is given to punning devices on a coat of arms suggesting the name of the family to whom it belongs; as the broken spear on the shield of Nicholas *Breakspear* (Pope Adrian IV).

Recessional. The music or words, or both accompanying the procession of clergy and choir when they retire after a service. The term is often associated with Rudyard Kipling's well-known verses (1897) beginning:

God of our fathers, known of old—
  Lord of our far-flung battle-line—
Beneath whose awful Hand we hold
  Dominion over palm and pine—
Lord God of Hosts, be with us yet,
Lest we forget, lest we forget!

Recipe, Receipt. *Recipe* is Latin for take, and contracted into ℞ is used in doctors' prescriptions. *See* R.

Reckon. I reckon, in the sense of "I guess" was in use in England by the early 17th century; it is now almost obsolete in Britain but is still widely used in the U.S.A.

Day of reckoning. Settlement day; when one has to pay up one's account or fulfil one's obligation; also used of the Day of Judgment.

Record. That which is *recorded* (originally "got by heart"—Lat. *cor, cordis*, heart); hence the modern meaning, the best performance or most striking event of its kind recorded, especially in such phrases as **to beat the record, to do it in record time,** etc.; also the engraved disk on which music that can be audibly transmitted by means of a gramophone is recorded.

Court of Record. A court whose proceedings are officially recorded and can be produced as evidence.

Off the record. Originally a legal term, whereby a judge directs that improper or irrevelant evidence shall be struck off the record. This since became commonly synonymous with *in confidence, an unofficial expression of views*.

Recusants (rek' ū zánts). The name given in English history to those who refused to attend services of the Church of England. At different times heavy fines and even imprisonment have attached to recusancy. The name was commonly used of Roman Catholics.

Red. One of the primary colours (*q.v.*); in heraldry said to signify magnanimity and fortitude; in ecclesiastical use worn at certain seasons; and in popular folklore the colour of magic.

Red is the colour of magic in every country, and has been so from the very earliest times. The caps of fairies and musicians are well-nigh always red.—YEATS: *Fairy and Folk Tales of the Irish Peasantry*, p. 61.

Nowadays it is more often symbolical of anarchy and revolution—"Red ruin, and the breaking up of laws" (Tennyson: *Guinevere*, 421). In the French Revolution the *Red Republicans* were those extremists who never hesitated to dye their hands in blood in order to accomplish their political object. In Russia red is supposed to be the beautiful colour. *Krása* is beauty; *kranie* is red. This may account for its adoption by the Bolsheviki, but, in general, red is regarded as the colour of liberty. *See* RED FLAG *below*.

Red is the colour of the royal livery; and it is said that this colour—technically called "pink" (*q.v.*)—was adopted by huntsmen because fox-hunting was declared a royal sport by Henry II.

In the old ballads *red* was frequently applied to gold ("the gude red gowd"), and this use still survives in thieves' cant, a gold watch being a *red kettle*, and the chain a *red tackle*. One of the names given by the alchemists to the Philosophers' Stone (*q.v.*) was *the red tincture*, because, with its help, they hoped to transmute the base metals to gold.

Red Book. A directory relating to the court, the nobility, and the "Upper Ten" generally. The *Royal Kalendar*, published from 1767 to 1893, was known by this name, as also Webster's *Royal Red Book*, a similar work, first issued in 1847.

The name is also given to other special works covered in red, as, *e.g.* the old Austro-Hungarian Empire, the official parliamentary papers of which corresponded to our "Blue Books." A book which gave account of the court expenditure in France before the Revolution, and an English manuscript containing the names of those who held lands *per baroniam* in the reign of Henry II, etc.

The Red Book of the Exchequer. *Liber ruber Scaccarii* in the Record Office. It was compiled in the reign of Henry III (1246), and contains the returns of the tenants *in capite* in 1166, who certify how many knights' fees they hold, and the names of those who hold or held them; also the only known fragment of the Pipe Roll of Henry II, copies of the important Inquisition returned into the exchequer in 13 John, and matter from the Pipe Rolls and other sources. It was printed in the Rolls Series (edited by Hubert Hall) in 1896.

Redbreasts. The old Bow Street "runners," police officers combining the duties of informers, detectives, and general agents.

The Bow Street runners ceased out of the land soon after the introduction of the new police. I remember them very well as standing about the door of the office in Bow Street. They had no other uniform than a blue dress-coat, brass buttons . . . and a bright red cloth waist-coat. . . . The slang name for them was "Redbreasts."— DICKENS: *Letters*.

Red Button. In the Chinese Empire a mandarin of the first class wore one of these as a badge of honour in his cap. *Cp.* PANJANDRUM.

An interview was granted to the admiral [Elliot] by Kishen, the imperial commissioner, the third man in the empire, a mandarin of first class and red button.— HOWITT: *History of England*, p. 471 (1841).

Not a red cent. No money at all; "stony-broke." An Americanism; the cent used to be copper, but is now an alloy of copper, tin, and zinc.

Redcoats. British soldiers, from the colour of the uniform formerly universal in line regiments. Cromwell's New Model Army was the first to wear red coats as a uniform. Each regiment was distinguished by the colour of the facings—Blue, Green, Buff, etc., and was known by that name.

The Red Crescent, Lion, Sun. The equivalent in non-Christian countries of the Red Cross (*q.v.*), *i.e.* the military hospital service.

Red Cross. The badge adopted by all civilized nations (except those who use the *Red Crescent*, etc.), in accordance with the Geneva Convention of 1864, as that of military ambulance and hospital services, hospital ships, etc. It is a red Greek Cross on a white ground, and is also called the *Geneva Cross*.

Hence the name of various national societies for the relief of the wounded and sick.

Also, the St. George's Cross (*q.v.*), the basis of the Union Jack, and the old national emblem of England.

The Red Cross Knight in Spenser's *Faerie Queene* (Bk. I) is a personification of St. George, the patron saint of England. He typifies Christian Holiness, and his adventures are an allegory of the Church of England. The Knight is sent by the Queen to destroy a dragon which was ravaging the kingdom of Una's father. With Una he is driven into Wandering Wood, where they encounter Error, and pass the night in Hypocrisy's cell. Here he is deluded by a false vision and, in consequence, abandons Una and goes with Duessa (False-faith) to the palace of Pride. He is persuaded by Duessa to drink of an enchanted fountain, becomes paralysed, and is taken captive by Orgoglio, whereupon Una seeks Arthur's help, and the prince goes to the rescue. He slays Orgoglio, and the Red Cross Knight is taken by Una to the house of Holiness to be healed. On leaving Holiness they journey onwards, and as they draw near the end of their quest the dragon flies at the knight, who has to do battle with it for three whole days before he succeeds in slaying it. The Red Cross Knight and Una are then united in marriage.

The Red Feathers. *See* REGIMENTAL NICKNAMES.

Red Eye (U.S.A.). Cheap whisky.

Red Flag. The emblem of Bolshevism, Communism, and revolution generally. English Communists have a "battle hymn" with this title. The red flag was used during the French Revolution as the symbol of insurrection and terrorism, and in the Roman Empire it signified war and a call to arms.

Red Hackle. *See* REGIMENTAL NICKNAMES.

Red-handed. In the very act; as though with red blood of murder still on his hand.

The Red Hand of Ulster. *See* ULSTER.

Red-haired persons have for centuries had the reputation of being deceitful and unreliable — probably owing to the tradition that Judas Iscariot (*q.v.*) had red hair. The fat of a dead red-haired person used to be in request as an ingredient for poisons (*see* Middleton's *The Witch*, V, ii) and Chapman says that flattery, like the plague —

> Strikes into the brain of man,
> And rageth in his entrails when he can,
> Worse than the poison of a red-hair'd man.
> *Bussy d'Ambois*, iii, ii.

The old rhyme says —

> With a red man rede thy rede;
> With a brown man break thy bread;
> At a pale man draw thy knife;
> From a black man keep thy wife.

See also HAIR.

Red Indians. The North American Indians; so called because of their copper-coloured skin; also called *Redskins* and *red men*.

A red-laced jacket. Old military slang for a flogging.

Red-lattice phrases. Pot-house talk. A red lattice at the doors and windows was formerly the sign that an ale-house was duly licensed; see the page's quip on Bardolph in 2 *Henry IV*, ii, 2 — "'a calls me e'en now, my lord, through a red lattice, and I could discern no part of his face from the window."

> I, I, I myself sometimes leaving the fear of heaven on the left hand . . . am fain to shuffle, to hedge and to lurch; and yet you rogue, will ensconce your rags . . . your red-lattice phrases . . . under the shelter of your honour. — *Merry Wives of Windsor*, ii, 2.

The Red Laws. The civil code of ancient Rome. Juvenal says, *Per lege rubros majoram leges* (*Satires*, xiv, 193). The civil laws, being written in vermilion, were called *rubrica*, and *rubrica vetavit* means, It is forbidden by the civil laws.

> The prætor's laws were inscribed in *white* letters, as Quintilian informs us (xii, 3 "*prætores edicta sua in alba*

proponebant") and imperial rescripts were written in purple.

Red-letter day. A lucky day; a day to be recalled with delight. In almanacs, saints' days and holidays are printed in red ink, other days in black; and only the former have special services in our Prayer Book.

> "It's a great piece of luck, ma'am," said Mrs. Belfield, "that you should happen to come here of a holiday! . . . Why, you know, ma'am, to-day is a red-letter day — " — FANNY BURNEY: *Cecilia*, X, vi.

Red Light District. That quarter of a large city where brothels are located, these houses being frequently indicated by a red light outside.

Red man. A term of the old alchemists, used in conjunction with "white woman" to express the affinity and interaction of chemicals. In the long list of terms that Surface scoffingly gives (Ben Jonson's *The Alchemist*, II, iii) "your red man and your white woman" are mentioned.

The French say that a red man commands the elements, and wrecks off the coast of Brittany those whom he dooms to death. The legend affirms that he appeared to Napoleon and foretold his downfall.

See also RED INDIANS, *above*.

To paint the town red. *See* PAINT.

Red Sea. So called by the Romans (*Mare rubrum*) and by the Greeks, as a translation of the Semitic name, the reason for which is uncertain; also formerly called the "Sedgy Sea," because of the seaweed which collects there.

To see red. To give way to excessive passion or anger; to be violently moved, run amok.

Red snow. Snow reddened by the presence of a minute alga, *Protococcus nivalis*, in large numbers. It is not at all uncommon in arctic and alpine regions, where its sanguine colour formerly caused it to be regarded as a portent of evil.

Red tape. Official formality, or rigid adherence to rules and regulations, carried to excessive lengths; so called because, lawyers and government officials tie their papers together with red tape. Charles Dickens is said to have introduced the expression; but it was the scorn continually poured upon this evil of officialdom by Carlyle that brought it into popular use.

Redemptioner. An immigrant who is obliged to pay back his passage money out of his earnings after landing in the new country.

Reductio ad absurdum. A proof of inference arising from the demonstration that every other hypothesis involves an absurdity. Thus, suppose I want to prove that the direct road from two given places is the shortest, I should say, "It must either be the shortest or not the shortest. If *not* the shortest, then some other road is the direct road; but there cannot be two shortest roads, therefore the direct road must be the shortest."

Reduplicated or **Ricochet Words.** There are probably some hundreds of these words, which usually have an intensifying force, in use in English. The following, from ancient and modern sources, will give some idea of their variety:—chit-chat, click-clack, clitter-clatter, dilly-dally, ding-dong, drip-drop, fal-lal, flim-flam, fiddle-faddle, flip-flap, flip-flop, hanky-panky, harum-scarum, helter-skelter, heyve-keyve, higgledy-piggledy, hob-nob, hodge-podge, hoity-toity, hubble-bubble, hugger-mugger, hurly-burly, mingle-mangle, mish-mash, mixy-maxy, namby-pamby, niddy-noddy, niminy-piminy, nosy-posy, pell-mell, ping-pong, pit-pat, pitter-patter, pribbles and prabbles, random-tandem, randy-dandy, razzle-dazzle, riff-raff, roly-poly, shilly-shally, slip-slop, slish-slosh, tick-tack, tip-top, tittle-tattle, wibble-wobble, wig-wag, wiggle-waggle, wish-wash, wishy-washy.

Reef. He must take in a reef or so. He must reduce his expenses; he must retrench. A reef is that part of a sail which is rolled and tied to reduce the area caught by the wind.

Reefer. An Australian term for one searching for gold. In American slang it is used for a marijuana cigarette, otherwise known as, *i.e.*, *tea* or *gauge*, *muggles*, *muta*. In English a reefer is a short, double-breasted overcoat largely worn in the Navy.

Reel. Right off the reel. Without intermission. A reel is a device for winding rope. A reel of cotton is a certain quantity wound on a bobbin.

We've been travelling best part of twenty-four hours right off the reel.—BOLDREWOOD: *Robbery under Arms*, ch. xxxi.

In the cinematograph world a *reel* is a convenient length of film for winding on one spool and showing at one performance.

The Scottish dance, *reel*, is from Gaelic *righil* or *ruithil*.

Referendum. The submission of a definite political question to the whole electorate for a direct decision by the general vote. This is not done in Great Britain, but is a general rule in Switzerland. After the Great War certain questions, as the apportionment of Schleswig-Holstein and other disputed areas, were submitted to a plebiscite, which is not quite the same thing as a referendum, but is the taking of a general vote as to future policy.

Refresher. An extra fee paid to a barrister in long cases in addition to his retaining fee, originally to remind him of the case entrusted to his charge.

Regan (rē găn). The second of King Lear's unfilial daughters, in Shakespeare's tragedy— "most barbarous, most degenerate." She was married to the Duke of Cornwall.

Regatta (re găt' a). A boat-race, or organized series of boat-races; the name originally given to the races held between Venetian gondoliers, the Italian meaning "strife" or "contention."

Regency. There have been a number of regencies in European history, usually during the minority of a sovereign. In British history the term is usually applied to the period 1811-20 when George Prince of Wales (afterwards George IV) acted as regent because of his father's insanity.

In French history the word refers to the years from 1715 to 1723 when the Duke of Orleans was regent for the minor Louis XV.

Regent's Park (London). This park, formerly called Marylebone Park, covering 472 areas, was originally attached to a palace of Queen Elizabeth 1, but at the beginning of the 17th century much of the land was let on long leases, which fell in early in the 19th century. It was laid out by the architect, John Nash (1752-1835) for the Prince Regent (George IV) and named in honour of him.

Regicides. The name applied in English history to those men who sat in judgment on Charles I, in 1649, and especially the 58 who signed his death warrant. After the Restoration, when some of the regicides were dead and others in flight, 10 were executed and 25 others imprisoned for life. The bodies of Cromwell, Ireton, Bradshaw, and Pride were disinterred, and after a solemn trial for treason were dismembered and exhibited at Temple Bar and other places.

Regimental and Divisional Nicknames. (In addition to the better-known ones mentioned in alphabetical order).

British Army

Assaye Regiment. The 74th Foot, so called because they first distinguished themselves in the battle of Assaye, where 2,000 British and 2,500 Sepoy troops under Wellington defeated 50,000 Mahrattas, in 1803. This regiment is now called "the 2nd Battalion of the Highland Light Infantry." The first battalion was the old No. 71.

Belfast Regiment, The. The old 35th Foot, raised in Belfast in 1701, is now called the 1st battalion of the Royal Sussex, the 2nd battalion being the old 107th.

Bingham's Dandies. The 17th Lancers; so called from their colonel, the Earl of Lucan, formerly Lord Bingham. The uniform was noted for its admirable fit and smartness. Now called "The Duke of Cambridge's Own Lancers."

Black Horse. The 7th Dragoon Guards, or the Princess Royal's Dragoon Guards." Their "facings" are black. Also called "Strawboots," "The Blacks."

Blayney's Bloodhounds. The old 89th Foot; so called because of their unerring certainty, and untiring perseverance in hunting down the Irish rabels in 1798, when the corps was commanded by Lord Blaney.

This regiment was later called "the Second Battalion of the Princess Victoria's Irish Fusiliers." The *first* battalion is the old 87th Foot.

Bloody Eleventh. The Devonshire Regiment, 11th Foot, raised in 1685. At the Battle of Salamanca, in the Peninsular War, the regiment fought so stubbornly that there was hardly a man among them who was not wounded, and from this exploit they got their name.

Bloodsuckers. The 63rd Regiment of Foot are nicknamed "the Bloodsuckers."

Brickdusts. The 53rd Foot; so called from the brickdust-red colour of their facings. Also called *Five-and-thre' pennies*, a play on the number and the old rate of daily pay of the ensigns or subalterns.

Now the 1st battalion of the "King's Shropshire Light Infantry." The 2nd battalion is the old 85th.

Buckmaster's Light Infantry. The 3rd West India Regiment was so called from Buckmaster, the tailor, who used to issue "Light Infantry uniforms" to the officers of the corps without any authority from the Commander-in-Chief.

Buffs. The Royal East Kent Regiment, the 3rd Foot. They were first raised in 1572, but the Buffs actually date from 1664 when the regiment was properly constituted. They take their name from the colour of the equipment. They were originally called the Holland Regiment on account of long service in that country in the 17th century.

The Rothshire Buffs. The old 78th, now the second battalion of the Seaforth Highlanders.

Cross-belts. The 8th King's Royal Irish Hussars, raised by William III, in 1693. The unit fought in Spain in 1710, during one fight practically destroying a Spanish cavalry regiment, whose cross-belts they removed and wore themselves.

Desert Rats. *See* DESERT.

The Devil's Own. The 88th Foot, the Connaught Rangers. So called by General Picton from their bravery in the Peninsular War, 1809-14. Also the Inns of Court Regiment, which was at one time chiefly recruited from among lawyers.

The Die Hards. The Middlesex Regiment, the 57th Foot, which was raised in 1755. At the Battle of Albuera, May 16th, 1811, the regiment was hard pressed; Colonel Inglis (later General Sir William) who was badly wounded, refused to be taken to the rear, but lay where he fell, crying, "Die hard, men, die hard!"

The Dirty Half-Hundred. The 50th Foot (The Queen's Own), so called because during a Peninsular War battle the men wiped their sweaty faces with their black cuffs.

The Dirty Shirts. The 101st Foot (2nd Munster Fusiliers), which fought at Delhi in their shirt-sleeves (1857).

Eliott's Tailors. The 15th (King's) Hussars. In 1759 Lieutenant-Colonel Eliott (later Lord Heath-field, hero of Gibraltar) enlisted a large number of tailors into a cavalry regiment modelled after the Prussian hussars. This regiment so highly distinguished themselves, that George III granted them the honour of being called "the King's."

The Fighting Fifth. The 5th Foot, now the "Northumberland Fusiliers." This sobriquet was given to the regiment during the Peninsular War; it was also known as the "Old and Bold Fifth," and "the Duke of Wellington's Body-guard."

Heavies, The. The heavy cavalry, especially the Dragoon Guards, which consists of men of greater build and height than Lancers and Hussars. The term Heavies or Heavy Artillery was formerly applied to ordnance of any calibre of 6 in. and over, manned by gunners of the Royal Garrison Artillery.

Hindustan Regiment. The old 76th; so called because it first distinguished itself in Hindustan. It is also called the *Seven and Sixpennies*, from its number. Now the 2nd battalion of the West Riding, the 1st being the old No. 33rd.

Holy Boys, The. The Royal Norfolk Regiment, the 9th Foot. The regimental badge is a figure of Britannia, and in the Peninsular War the Spaniards thought this was a representation of the Virgin Mary, hence the nickname. A detachment of the regiment buried Sir John Moore, at Corunna, in 1809, and in full dress all officers still wear a strip of mourning in his memory.

The Immortals. In the British Army the 76th Foot were called "The Immortals," because so many were wounded, but not killed, in India (1788-1806). This regiment, with the old 33rd, now forms the two battalions of the West Riding regiment.

Kiddies, The. The Scots Guards, raised in the reign of Charles I. When James II attempted to overawe the City of London by forming a large camp on Hounslow Heath, the three regiments of Guards then in existence were present, and the Scots Guards, being the junior, gained this disrespectful nickname.

Kirke's Lambs. The Queen's Royal West Surrey Regiment, so called from their colonel, Percy Kirke (*c.* 1646-91). The regiment was originally known as the Tangier Regiment, the badge of which was a Pascal Lamb, the crest of the house of Braganza, in compliment to Queen Catherine, to whom they were a guard of honour in her progress to London. There was an ironical turn to the nickname as "Kirke's Lambs" were notoriously a tough lot.

Lacedæmonians, The (lăs e de mō' ni ánz). An old nickname of the Duke of Cornwall's Light Infantry; because in 1777 their colonel made a long harangue, under heavy fire, on Spartan discipline and the military system of the Lacedæmonians. *See* RED FEATHERS.

Mutton Lancers. The Queen's Royal Regiment (West Surrey), the 2nd Foot; raised in 1661. The nickname comes from the regimental badge—the Pascal Lamb bearing a lance.

Old and Bold. The old 14th Foot the Prince of Wales's Own (West Yorkshire Regiment).

Old Bold. The 1st Battalion Worcestershire Regiment, the old 29th Foot.

Old Bold Fifth. The Northumberland Fusiliers; formerly the 5th Foot.

Old Dozen. The Suffolk Regiment, formerly the 12th Foot.

Old Fogs. The 87th Foot, the Royal Irish Fusiliers, so called from the war-cry "*Fag-an-Bealach*" (Clear the way), pronounced *Faug-a-bollagh*.

Orange Lilies. The nickname of the old 35th Foot, now the Royal Sussex Regiment, raised at Belfast in 1701 by the Earl of Donegal. A firm supporter of William III he chose orange facings for the uniform; the *lilies* represent the white plumes given in recognition of their gallantry at Quebec in 1759, when they routed the Royal Roussillon French Grenadiers.

The Oxford Blues. The Royal Horse Guards were so called in 1690, from the Earl of Oxford their commander and the blue facings. Wellington, in one of his dispatches, writes:—"I have been appointed colonel of the Blues."

Pontius Pilate's Body-guard. The 1st Foot Regiment, now called the Royal Scots, the oldest regiment in the British Army. The fable is that when in the French service as *Le Régiment de Douglas* they had a dispute with the Picardy regiment about the antiquity of their respective corps. The Picardy officers declared they were on duty on the night of the Crucifixion, when the colonel of the 1st Foot replied, "If we had been on guard, we should not have slept at our posts."

The Queen's Bays. The 2nd Dragoon Guards; so called because they are mounted on bay horses: often known, "for short," as *The Queen's*.

The Red Feathers. The Duke of Cornwall's Light Infantry. They cut to pieces General Wayne's brigade in the American War, and the Americans vowed to give them no quarter. So they mounted red feathers that no others might be subjected to this threat. Later they wore red puggarees on Indian service. *See* LACEDÆMONIANS.

Red Hackle. The nickname of "The Black Watch," the regiment officially known as "The Royal Highlanders." They are easily recognized by the small bunch of red feathers, known as the red hackle, which they wear on their bonnets in lieu of a regimental badge.

The Saucy Greens. The 2nd Battalion Worcestershire Regiment, the old 36th Foot.

The Saucy Sixth. The Royal Warwickshires, formerly the 6th Foot.

The Saucy Seventh. The 7th (Queen's Own) Hussars.

Wolfe's Own. The 1st Battalion, the Loyal Regiment, so called for their distinguished service under Wolfe, at Louisburg (1758) and Quebec (1759).

American Army

Infantry Divisions

1st: The Red One. Name given it by the Germans, who saw the red "1" on their shoulder patch. According to legend, the original red "1" was improvised from the cap of an enemy soldier killed by a 1st Division doughboy in World War I when the division earned the right to proclaim itself the first American division (1918) in France, first to fire on the enemy, first to suffer casualties, first to take prisoners, first to stage a major offensive, and first to enter Germany.

2nd: Indian Head. A long-forgotten truck driver of the division in World War I adorned the side of his vehicle with a handsome shield framing an Indian head which was adopted by the division as its shoulder insignia. Hence the name "Indian Division."

3rd: Marne or Rock of the Marne. In World War I because of its impregnable stand against the Germans' last great counter-offensive. The three diagonal stripes in its insignia symbolize its participation in three major battles in 1918.

4th: Ivy. From its insignia. The selection of that design is one of the few known instances of authorized military frivolity. "I-vy" is simply spelling out letter form the Roman numeral for "four."

5th: Red Diamond. From its insignia. The Red Diamond was selected at the suggestion of Major Charles A. Meats that their insignia be the "Ace of Diamonds, less the Ace." Originally there was a white "5" in the centre. This was removed when they reached France.

6th: Sight Seein' Sixth. In World War I the division was in so many engagements and so many long marches that it got this name.

7th: Hourglass. From insignia, a red circle bearing a black hourglass which is formed by a "7" resting on an inverted "7."

8th: Pathfinder. From their insignia, which is a golden arrow through a figure "8" pointing the way. Also called the "Golden Arrow Division."

9th: Hitler's Nemesis. A newspaper at home dubbed them this.

10th: Mountaineers. This division was given the task of dislodging crack German mountain troops from the heights of Mt. Belvedere. It was composed of famous American skiers, climbers, forest rangers, and wild life Servicemen.

24th: Victory. The Filipinos on Leyte greeted them with the "V" sign.

25th: Tropic Lightning. Activated from elements of the Hawaiian Division, Regular Army troops. No other division was so quickly in combat after it was formed.

26th: Yankee. Originally composed of National Guard troops from the New England (Yankee) States.

27th: New York. Division originally composed of New York State National Guard. Sometimes called the "Empire Division." New York is called the Empire State.

28th: Keystone. Troops from Pennsylvania, which is known as the "Keystone State."

29th: Blue and Gray. Organized in World War I from National Guardsmen of New Jersey, Delaware, Virginia, Maryland, and the District of Columbia. Its shoulder patch of blue and grey, the colours of the rival armies in the Civil War, symbolizes unity of former embattled states. They are combined in a monad, the Korean symbol for eternal life.

30th: Old Hickory. Composed after World War I from National Guardsmen of the Carolinas, Georgia, and Tennessee, Andrew Jackson's old stamping grounds. He was known as "Old Hickory,"

31st: Dixie. Originally composed of men of the "Deep South" or "Dixie."

32nd: Red Arrow. On tactical maps the enemies' lines are indicated in red. Their patch is a reminder to those who wear it that the enemy has never stopped them. Another nickname, "Les Terribles," was given them by an admiring French general during World War I, when they earned four battle streamers and were first to crack the Hindenberg line.

33rd: Illinois or **Golden Cross.** The division was originally composed mostly of Illinois troops. Their shoulder patch was a yellow cross on a black circle. The cross was an old symbol for marking government property and the only paint available where they were assembling their equipment was yellow. The insignia was originally to mark equipment. It was officially known as the "Prairie Division" because its personnel came from the prairie states. It was also called the "Money Division" because of the large amount of buried treasure they unearthed.

34th: Red Bull. Its patch is a red bull's skull on an olla, a Mexican water bottle. Inspired by the desert country of the South-west where it trained in World War I.

35th: Santa Fe. So called because the ancestors of its personnel blazed the old Santa Fe trail. Insignia is the original marker used on the trail.

36th: Texas. Personnel was from Oklahoma and Texas. The arrowhead of its insignia represented Oklahoma and the "T" was for Texas.

37th: Buckeye. Composed of Ohio troops. Ohio is known as the "Buckeye State." Insignia is that of the state flag.

38th: Cyclone. Got its name in 1917 at Shelby, Mississippi, when the tent city in which it was bivouacked was levelled by winds. The division struck like a cyclone when it landed in Luzon.

40th: Sunshine. From its insignia, which is symbolic of the Golden West sunshine. Troops were from California, Nevada, and Utah.

41st: Jungleers. It was the first complete division to reach the South-west Pacific and has done more jungle fighting than any other American outfit.

42nd: Rainbow. Nickname originated from the fact that this division was composed of military groups from the district of Columbia and twenty-five states, representing several sections, nationalities, religions, and viewpoints. They blended themselves into one harmonious unit. A major in World War I, noting its various origins, said, "This division will stretch over the land like a rainbow."

43rd: Winged Victory. Received its name on Luzon. It is formed from the name of its commanding general, Maj.-Gen. Leonard F. Wing, and the ultimate goal of the division.

45th: Thunderbird. Included 1,500 American Indians from twenty-eight tribes. Originally the insignia was an old Indian symbol of the swastika, but when Hitler adopted it they changed the division insignia to another traditional Indian symbol, the Thunderbird, sacred bearer of unlimited happiness.

63rd: Blood and Fire. When the division was activated in June following the Casablanca Conference they adopted the conference's resolution, to make their enemies "bleed and burn in expiation of their crimes against humanity," as their symbol.

65th: Battle Axe. Its patch is a white halbert on a blue shield. The halbert, a sharp-pointed battle-axe, was a potent weapon of the 15th-century foot soldier, being suitable either for a powerful cutting smash or for a quick thrust. It is an emblem that signifies both the shock action and the speed of the modern infantry division.

66th: Panther. The black panther on its shoulder patch symbolizes the attributes of a good infantryman: ability to kill, to be aggressive, alert, stealthy, cunning, agile, and strong.

70th: Trailblazers. Their insignia combines an axe, a snowy mountain, and a green fir tree, symbols of the pioneers who blazed the trail to Oregon and the Williamette Valley, where most of their training was accomplished.

76th: Liberty Bell. In World War I their original shoulder patch was a Liberty Bell. In 1919 this was officially changed to the present one: a shield with a white label, an heraldic device indicating the eldest son. The 76th was the first draft division from civilian ranks. Its present nickname is "Onaway," the alert call of the Chippewa Indians in whose hunting grounds they trained.

77th: Statue of Liberty. Their insignia bears the picture of the Statue of Liberty, because most of the personnel in World War I was from New York City.

78th: Lightning. The shoulder patch originated in World War I because the battles of that division were likened by the French to a bolt of lightning, leaving the field blood red.

79th: Cross of Lorraine. Having distinguished itself at Montfaucon in Lorraine, the division selected the Cross of Lorraine, a symbol of triumph, as its insignia.

80th: Blue Ridge. Its insignia symbolizes the three Blue Ridge states, Pennsylvania, Virginia, and West Virginia, from which most of its World War I personnel were drawn.

81st: Wild Cat. Gets its name from Wildcat Creek that flows through Fort Jackson, S.C. It is generally credited as the first to wear the shoulder patch.

84th: Railsplitter. Primarily made up of National Guard units from Illinois, Kentucky, and Indiana, the Lincoln states. They called themselves the Lincoln Division. Their insignia is a red disc with a white axe which splits a rail. In World War II they called themselves the "Railsplitters." The Germans called them the "Hatchet-men."

85th: Custer. The initials on its insignia "CD" stand for Custer Division, because they were activated at Camp Custer, Michigan in World War I.

86th: Blackhawk. Its insignia is a black hawk with wings outspread superimposed on a red shield. On the breast of the hawk is a small red shield with black letters "B H" for its nickname. Its personnel in World War I were drawn from Illinois, Wisconsin, and Minnesota, the territory inhabited by Chief Blackhawk and his tribe. Bird symbolizes keenness, cunning, and tenacity.

87th: Golden Acorn. Their patch is a green field with a golden acorn which symbolizes strength.

88th: Blue Devil. Their patch is a blue four-leaf clover formed from two crossed Arabic numerals, "88."

89th: Rolling W. The "W" on its insignia within a circle forms an "M" when it is inverted, the two letters standing for Middle West, the section of the country from which its personnel were drawn. The circle indicates speed and stability.

90th: Tough 'Ombres. The letter "T" of its insignia, standing for Texas, bisects the letter "O" for Oklahoma. The men of the division say it stands for "Tough 'Ombres."

91st: Powder River. The division has a war-whoop which comes from a World War I incident. When asked where they were from, they yelled, "Powder River—Let 'er buck." Powder River is in Montana, the home state of the division in World War I.

92nd: Buffalo. Insignia is a black buffalo on olive drab background with black border. In the days of hostile Indians a troop of Negroes who were on border patrol killed buffaloes in the winter and used them for clothing. The Indians called them the "Black Buffaloes." The men of this Negro division in World War I were trained at Fort Huachuca in this same locality.

95th: Victory. Their oval blue patch bears a red numeral "9" with a white Roman numeral "V." The "V" also stands for "Victory."

96th: Deadeye. Their name came from their perfect marksmanship while in training.

97th: Trident. Their insignia is a trident, white on a blue field. Neptune's trident represents the coastal states Maine, Vermont, and New Hampshire, from which they came. There is a prong for each state. The blue represents their freshwater lakes, and the white their snowy mountains.

98th: Iroquois. Its patch consists of a shield in the shape of the great seal of the State of New York. The head of the Iroquois Indian chief is in orange. These were the colours of the Dutch House of Nassau, which was responsible for the settlement of New Amsterdam, later New York. The five feathers worn by the Indian represent the Five Nations (Onondagas, Cayugas, Senacas, Mohawks, and Oneidas) who formed the Iroquois Confederacy. The personnel of the division were from New York.

99th: Checkerboard. The blue and white squares resembling a checkerboard were on the coat-of-arms of William Pitt. The home station of the division was Pittsburgh.

102nd: Ozark. A large golden "O" on a field o blue. Within the "O" is the letter "Z," from which is suspended an arc. This represents the word "Ozark." The personnel came from the Ozark Mountain region.

103rd: Cactus. A green Saguaro cactus in a blue base superimposed on a yellow disc was adopted by this Reserve division which had its headquarters in Denver, Colorado. Yellow disc represents the golden sky, while the green cactus growing in the blue sage-covered earth is characteristic of the South-west.

106th: Golden Lion. Their patch represents a golden lion's face on a blue background encircled by white and red borders. The blue represents the infantry, red the supporting artillery, and the lion's face strength and power.

Airborne Divisions

13th: Blackcats. Gets its name from its flaunting of superstition. Its number is "13," it was reactivated on Friday the 13th.

17th: Thunderbolt. From the surprise of their attacks from the air. Also called the "Golden Talon," from its shoulder patch: stretching golden talons on a field of black, representing ability to seize; black suggests darkness under which many operations were carried out.

82nd: All American. In World War I the division was composed of men from every state in the union. Originally an infantry division, when it was reactivated as an airborne division it retained its insignia, adding the word "Airborne" above.

101st: Screaming Eagle. Its white eagle's head with gold beak on a black shield is based on Civil War tradition. The black shield recalls the "Iron Brigade," one regiment of which possessed the famous eagle "Old Abe" which went into battle with them as their screaming mascot.

Regnal Year is the year of a sovereign's reign, accession, *e.g.* regnal year 1 of Elizabeth II dating from the accession began on February 6th, 1952. The regnal year is only used for dating Acts of Parliament.

Regular (U.S.A.). In the early 19th century this meant thorough, well founded. In the 20th century it is more usually applied to people, *e.g. a regular guy*, a straightforward dependable man.

Regulars. All the British military forces serving in the army as a profession, as distinct from the *Auxiliary Forces*, viz. the Special Reserve (which takes the place of the old Militia), and the Territorial Force (*i.e.* Yeomanry and the old Volunteers).

Rehabilitation is a word of wide implications, the most general of which is, perhaps, the restoration to normalcy of one who has suffered in mind or body as a result of war wounds or strain, or who has lost touch with his usual way of life for some length of time through mental or physical illness.

Reign of Terror. The period in the French Revolution from March 1793 until July 1794, when supreme power was in the hands of the Committee of Public Safety, formed by the Jacobins and dominated by Robespierre, St. Just,

and Couthon. In addition to supporters of the old regime, hundreds of revolutionaries themselves perished by the guillotine, drowning, or shooting, as a result of the universal atmosphere of suspicion, mistrust, hatred, and private spite.

Reilly, To lead the life of. To live luxuriously. From a comic song "Is That Mr. Reilly," by Pat Rooney, popular in the U.S.A. in the 1880s. The song described what the hero would do if he "struck it rich."

Rein (connected with *retain*, from Lat. *retinere*, to hold back). The strap attached to the bit, used in guiding horses. **To give the reins.** To let go unrestrained; to give licence.

To take the reins. To assume the guidance of direction.

Relic, Christian. The corpse of a saint or any part thereof; any part of his clothing; or anything intimately connected with him. The veneration of Christian relics goes back to the 2nd century, and a vast amount of legend, exaggeration, and downright fiction has grown up around them since then. Honour may be paid to those relics whose genuineness is morally certain, but the question of their authenticity is one of fact, to be determined by the evidence, and the Church does not guarantee the genuineness of a single specific relic. Many famous relics are almost certainly spurious, but there is no need to presume deliberate fraud. Many of the relics in churches in Rome and elsewhere are in themselves interesting on account of their great antiquity, even if they are not "genuine."

Remember! The last injunction of Charles I, on the scaffold, to Bishop Juxon. It has been interpreted as meaning that Charles, who was at heart a Catholic, felt that his misfortunes were a divine visitation on him for retaining church property confiscated by Henry VIII, and made a vow that if God would restore him to the throne he would restore this property to the Church. He was asking the Bishop to remember this vow, and to see that his son carried it out. Charles II, however, wanted all the money he could get, and the Church lands were never restored.

Remigius, or **Remy, St.** (re mij' i ŭs, re' mi) (438-533), bishop and confessor, is represented as carrying a vessel of holy oil, or in the act of anointing therewith Clovis, who kneels before him. When Clovis presented himself for baptism, Remy said to him, "Sigambrian, henceforward burn what thou has worshipped, and worship what thou hast burned."

Remonstrants. Another name for the Arminians (*q.v.*).

Renaissance (Fr., re-birth). The term applied, broadly, to the movement and period of transition between the mediæval and modern worlds which, beginning with Petrarch and subsequent Italian humanists in the 14th century, was immensely stimulated by the fall of Constantinople (1453), resulting in the dissemination of Greek scholarship and Byzantine art, the invention of printing (about the same time), and the discovery of America (1492). In England this revival first manifested itself in the early years of the 16th century, and affected principally literature and, later, architecture.

All the Renaissance principles of art tended, as I have before often explained, to the setting Beauty above Truth, and seeking for it always at the expense of Truth. And the proper punishment of such pursuit—the punishment which all the laws of the universe rendered inevitable—was, that those who thus pursued beauty should wholly lose sight of beauty.—RUSKIN: *Modern Painters*, IV, xvi, § 12.

Renard (ren' ard). **Une queue de renard.** A mockery. At one time a common practical joke was to fasten a fox's tail behind a person against whom a laugh was designed. Panurge (*q.v.*) never refrained from attaching a fox's tail or the ears of a leveret behind a Master of Arts or Doctor of Divinity, whenever he encountered them. (*Gargantua*, ii, 16.) *See also* REYNARD.

C'est une petite vipère,
Qui n'épargneroit pas son père,
Et qui par nature ou par art
Scait couper la queue au renard.
BEAUCAIRE: *L'Embarras de la Foire*.

Rendezvous. The place to which you are to repair, a meeting, a place of muster or call. Also used as a verb. (Fr. *rendez*, betake; *vous*, yourself.) In British military parlance usually contracted to R.V.

His house is a grand rendezvous of the *élite* of Paris. The Imperial Guard was ordered to rendezvous in the Champs de Mars.

René (re' nā). **Le Bon Roi René** (1408-80). Son of Louis II, Due d'Anjou, Comte de Provence, father of Margaret of Anjou. The last minstrel monarch, just, joyous, and debonair; a friend to chase and tilt, but still more so to poetry and music. He gave in largesse to knights-errant and minstrels (so says Thiebault) more than he received in revenue.

Studying to promote, as far as possible, the immediate mirth and good humour of his subjects . . . he was never mentioned by them excepting as *Le bon Roi René*, a distinction . . . due to him certainly by the qualities of his heart, if not by those of his head.—SCOTT: *Anne of Geierstein*, ch. xxix.

Reno Divorces. Reno is the largest city in the State of Nevada, where the divorce laws are easier than in most of the other States. Seven grounds for absolute divorce are recognized, and a residence of six weeks only is requisite to enable a suit to be brought.

Repertory Company. A theatrical company that produces a number of plays, operas, etc., often at successive performances, or gives, maybe, a week to each. Such companies are becoming established in many smaller towns out of reach of the big centres of population.

Republic of Letters, The. The world of literature; authors generally and their influence. Goldsmith, in *The Citizen of the World*, No. 20 (1760), says it "is a very common expression among Europeans"; it is found in Molière's Le *Mariage Forcé*, Sc. vi (1664).

Republican Queen. Sophia Charlotte (1668-1705), wife of Frederick I of Prussia, was so nicknamed on account of her advanced political views. She was the daughter of George I of Britain, the friend of Leibniz, and a woman of remarkable culture. Charlottenburg was named after her.

Requests, Court of. *See* CONSCIENCE, COURT OF.

Requiem (rē' kwi em). The first word of the prayer *Requiem æternam dona eis, domine, et lux perpetua luceat eis* (Eternal rest give them, O Lord, and let everlasting light shine upon them) used as the introit of a Mass for the Dead (Requiem Mass).

Reremous. *See* REARMOUSE.

Reservation (U.S.A.). A tract of land set aside for occupation solely by Indians.

Resolute. The Resolute Doctor. John Baconthorp (d. 1346), head of the Carmelites in England (1329-33) and commentator on Aristotle.

The Most Resolute Doctor. Guillaume Durandus de St. Pourçain (d. about 1333), a French Dominican philosopher, bishop of Meaux (1326), and author of *Commentaries sur Pierre Lombard* (publ. 1508).

Responsions. *See* SMALLS.

Restoration. Term applied in British history to the recall to the throne, in 1660, of the royal family of Stuart in the person of Charles II, eldest son of Charles I, who was beheaded in 1649. After the austerity imposed on the nation by the Puritan regime of the Commonwealth, the return of the King brought about a reaction that flowered in the drama, literature, and life of the nation. In France the royal house of Bourbon was restored after the fall of Napoleon in 1815.

Louis XVIII was the brother of the late king Louis XVI whose son, dynastically known as Louis XVII, never came to the throne or reached manhood.

Resurrection Men. Grave-robbers, body-snatchers (*q.v.*). The term was first applied to the infamous Burke and Hare, of Edinburgh, who in 1829 were convicted of rifling graves to sell the bodies for dissection by doctors and students at the School of Medicine. They also murdered persons to supply bodies when occa-sion served.

> The body-snatchers, they have come,
>   And made a snatch at me;
> 'Tis very hard them kind of men
>   Won't let a body be.
> The cock it crows—I must be gone—
>   My William, we must part;
> But I'll be yours in death although
>   Sir Astley has my heart.
>   HOOD: *Mary's Ghost.*

The reference is to Sir Astley Cooper (1768-1841), the great surgeon and lecturer on anatomy.

Reveille (re văl' i) (Fr. *réveiller*, to awake). The signal by bugle or beat of drum, notifying soldiers that it is time to rise, and informing the sentries that they may forbear from challenging.

Reverend. An archbishop is *the Most Reverend* (Father in God); a bishop, *the Right Reverend*; a dean, *the Very Reverend*; an archdeacon, *the Venerable*; all the rest of the clergy, *the Reverend.*

Revival of Letters, The. A term applied to the Renaissance (*q.v.*) in so far as the movement reacted on literature. It really commenced earlier—at the close of the Dark Ages (*q.v.*)—but it received its chief impulse from the fall of Constantinople (1453) and the consequent dispersal over Europe of Greek MSS. and Greek scholars.

Revue (re vū'). A theatrical entertainment characterized by songs and music, dancing, and constant change, with a somewhat indefi-nite plot and (hence the name) usually allu-sions to current topics.

> Revue amuses by fun, by satire of passing events, by gorgeous spectacle which delights the child in all of us, by song and dance, by glimpses of drama, by the agility of man and the beauty of woman, above all by the rapid alternation of these elements; its crowning virtue is variety.—A. B. WALKLEY: in *The Times*, Mar. 22nd, 1922.

Rexists. A Belgian political party formed by Léon Degrelle in 1936 advocating Fascist ideals and working hand in hand with the Nazis. It was markedly collaborationist during the German occupation of Belgium and was accordingly suppressed when the country regained its liberty. The name is an adaptation of "Christus Rex," Christ the King, the watchword of a Catholic Young People's Action Society, founded in 1925.

Reynard (rā' nard). A fox. Caxton's form of the name in his translation (from the Dutch) of the *Roman de Renart* (see REYNARD THE FOX, *below*). *Renart* was the Old French form, from Ger. *Reginhart*, a personal name; the Dutch was *Reynaerd* or *Reynaert.*

> Where prowling Reynard trod his nightly round.
>   BLOOMFIELD: *Farmer's Boy.*

Reynard the Fox. A mediæval beast-epic, satirizing contemporary life and events, in which all the characters are animals. Such anthropo-morphic epics were common in mediaeval France.

The germ of the story is found in Æsop's fable, *The Fox and the Lion*; this was built upon by more than one writer, but the *Roman* as we now know it is by a Fleming named *Willem*, of the early 13th century, of which a new and enlarged version was written about 1380 by an unknown author, Caxton having made his translation from a late 15th-century Dutch ver-sion of this, which was probably by Herman Barkhusen.

Reynard's globe of glass. Reynard, in *Reynard the Fox* (see above), said he had sent this invaluable treasure to her majesty the queen as a present; but it never came to hand, inas-much as it had no existence except in the imagination of the fox. It was supposed to reveal what was being done—no matter how far off—and also to afford information on any subject that the person consulting it wished to know. **Your gift was like the globe of glass of Master Reynard.** A great promise, but no performance.

Rhapsody meant originally "songs strung together" (Gr. *rapto*, to sew or string together; *ode*, a song). The term was applied to portions of the *Iliad* and *Odyssey*, which bards recited, as our minstrels sang the deeds of famous heroes.

Rheims-Douai Version, The. *See* DOUAI BIBLE.

Rhetorical Question. The term in Logic for a question to which no considered answer is ex-pected or desired, the question having been asked to produce effect only. An example is the once-popular "Are we downhearted?" only asked to elicit the answer "No."

Rhino (rī' nō). Slang for money; the term was in use as early as the 17th century. *See under* NOSE, *To pay through the nose.*

> Some, as I know,
> Have parted with their ready rhino.
>   *The Seamans' Adieu* (1670).

Rhodes Scholarships. Under the will of Cecil Rhodes (1853-1902) scholarships at Oxford were endowed for foreign and overseas students. By subsequent rearrangement U.S.A. sends 32 annually (4 students from each of 8 regions consisting of 6 States); India 2; 1 from each State or Province of Canada, Australia, and South Africa. Scholarships are also awarded to certain schools in New Zealand, Newfoundland, Rhodesia, Jamaica, Bermuda, Malta, and East Africa. 5 scholarships were allotted to Germany until 1914, and 2 for the period between the wars. The scholarships are worth £400 per annum for a period of 3 years.

Rhodian Bully, The. The Colossus of Rhodes (*q.v.*).

> Yet fain wouldst thou the crouching world bestride,
> Just like the Rhodian bully o'er the tide.
> PETER PINDAR: *The Lusiad*, canto 2.

Rhodian Law, The. The earliest system of marine law known to history; compiled by the Rhodians about 900 B.C.

Rhopalic Verse. Verse consisting of lines in which each successive word has more syllables than the one preceding it (Gr. *rhopalon*, a club, which is much thicker at one end than at the other).

> Rem tibi confeci doctissime, dulcisonorum.
> Spes deus aeternæ-est stationis conciliator.
> Hope ever solaces miserable individuals.
> 1 2 3 4 5

Rhyme. Neither rhyme nor reason. Fit neither for amusement nor instruction. An author took his book to Sir Thomas More, chancellor of Henry VIII, and asked his opinion. Sir Thomas told the author to turn it into rhyme. He did so, and submitted it again to the lord chancellor. "Ay! ay!" said the witty satirist, "that will do, that will do. 'Tis rhyme now, but before it was neither rhyme nor reason."

The lines on his pension, traditionally ascribed to Spenser, are well known: —

> I was promised on a time
> To have reason for my rhyme;
> From that time unto this season,
> I received nor rhyme nor reason.

Rhyming Slang. A kind of slang in which the word intended was replaced by one that rhymed with it, as "Charley Prescott" for *waistcoat*, "plates of meat" for *feet*. When the rhyme is a compound word the rhyming part is almost invariably dropped, leaving one who does not know somewhat in the dark. Thus Chivy (Chevy) Chase rhymes with "face," by dropping "chase" *chivy* remains, and becomes the accepted slang word. Similarly, daisies = *boots*, thus: daisyroots will rhyme with "boots," drop the rhyme and

daisy remains. By the same process *sky* is slang for *pocket*, the compound word which gave birth to it being "sky-rocket." "Christmas," a *railway guard*, as "Ask the Christmas," is, of course, from "Christmas-card"; and "raspberry," *heart*, is "raspberry-tart."

> Then came a knock at the Rory o' More [door]
> Which made my raspberry beat.

Other examples are given under their proper heads.

Ribston Pippin. So called from Ribston, in Yorkshire, where the first pippins, introduced from Normandy about 1707, were planted. It is said that Sir Henry Goodriche planted three pips; two died, and from the third came all the Ribston apple-trees in England.

Rice. The custom of throwing rice after a bride comes from India, rice being, with the Hindus, an emblem of fecundity. The bridegroom throws three handfuls over the bride, and the bride does the same over the bridegroom. *Cp.* MARRIAGE KNOT.

Rice Christians. Converts to Christianity for worldly benefits, such as a supply of rice to Indians. Profession of Christianity born of lucre, not faith.

Rice-paper. See MISNOMERS.

Richard Roe. See DOE.

Richmond. Another Richmond in the field. Said when another unexpected adversary turns up. The reference is to Shakespeare's *Richard III*, v, 4, where the king, speaking of Henry of Richmond (afterwards Henry VII), says —

> I think there be six Richmonds in the field;
> Five have I slain to-day, instead of him —
> A horse! a horse! my kingdom for a horse!

Rick Mould. Fetching the rick mould is a "fiat-catching" trick played during the hay-harvest. The greenhorn is sent to borrow a rick-mould, with strict injunction not to drop it. Something very heavy is put in a sack and hoisted on his back; when he has carried it carefully in the hot sun to the hayfield he gets well laughed at for his pains.

Ricochet (rik' ō shā). The skipping of a flung stone over water ("ducks and drakes"), the bound of a bullet or other projectile after striking; hence, applied to anything repeated over and over again, *e.g.* the fabulous bird that had only one note. Marshal Vauban (1633-1707) invented a *ricochet battery*, the application of which was ricochet firing.

Riddle. Josephus relates how Hiram, King of Tyre, and Solomon had once a contest in riddles, when Solomon won a large sum of money, though he subsequently lost it to Abdemon, one of Hiram's subjects.

Plutarch states that Homer died of chagrin because he could not solve a certain riddle. *See* SPHINX.

Riddle me riddle me ree. *See* REE.

A riddle of claret. Thirteen bottles, a magnum and twelve quarts; said to be so called because in certain old golf clubs magistrates invited to the celebration dinner presented the club with this amount, sending it in a *riddle* or sieve.

Ride. To ride (U.S.A.). To oppress, to pick on and irritate until the person becomes exasperated.

Riding the marshes. *See* BOUNDS, BEATING THE.

To ride abroad with St. George, but at home with St. Michael. Said of a henpecked braggart. St. George is represented as riding on a war charger; St. Michael on a dragon. Abroad a man rides, like St. George, on a horse which he can control and govern; but at home he has "a dragon" to manage, like St. Michael.

To take for a ride. Originally this meant to pull someone's leg or make him the butt of a joke, but it has become a gangster euphemism for murder. The victim is induced or forced to enter a car with one or more companions who, in the course of the ride, murder him. Under the Nazi regime in Germany high officials, generals, etc. (*e.g.* Rommel), were requested to take a car ride with one or two of Hitler's trusties and then given the alternative choice of suicide or being murdered.

Rider. An addition to a manuscript, such as a codicil to a will; an additional clause tacked to a bill in Parliament, *over-riding* the preceding matter when the two come into collision; hence, a corollary or obvious supplement, and, in Euclid, etc., a subsidiary problem.

In American Negro parlance, a *rider* is a lover. The word is found throughout Negro folk music as *easy rider*.

Ridiculous. There is but one step from the sublime to the ridiculous. In his *Age of Reason* (1794), Pt. ii, *note*, Tom Paine said, "The sublime and the ridiculous are often so nearly related that it is difficult to class them separately. One step above the sublime makes the ridiculous, and one step above the ridiculous makes the sublime again."

Napoleon, who was a great admirer of Tom Paine, use to say, " Du sublime au ridicule il n'y a qu'un pas."

Rienzi, Cola di (rē en' zi). A patriot of Rome who incited the people to rise against the Papal and Imperial governments. In May 1347,

he was declared Tribune, but his power was crushed and he fled. In 1354 Pope Innocent VI sent him to Rome once more as a Senator, but while attempting to quell a riot he met his death. In *Rienzi* (1835) Bulwer Lytton tells the story of the Tribune.

Riff-raff. The offscouring of society, perhaps the "refuse and sweepings." *Raff* in Swedish means sweepings, but the old French term *rif et raf* meant one and all, whence the phrase *Il n'a laissé ni rif ni raf* (he has left nothing behind him). Gabriel Harvey (in *Piercer's Supererogation*, 1593) speaks of "the riffe-raffe of the scribbling rascality."

Riffle (U.S.A.). A small rapid, a piece where the current of a stream flows swiftly and the water is disturbed. From this, probably, is evolved the jazz term, a *riff*, which is a short, improvised musical phrase.

Rifle. The firearm gets its name from the spiral grooves (Low Ger. *riffel*, Swed. *refia*) in the bore, which give the bullet a rotatory motion. The verb, *to rifle*, meaning to pillage or plunder, is connected with this through the O.Fr. *rifler*, to graze, scratch, strip, etc.

Rift in the Lute. A small defect which mars the general result.

Unfaith in aught is want of faith in all
  It is the little rift within the lute
  That by-and-by will make the music mute,
And ever widening slowly silence all.
  TENNYSON: *Merlin and Vivien; Vivien's Song.*

Rig. There is more than one word composed of these three letters, but the etymology and division of them are alike uncertain. In the sense of dressing it was originally applied to a ship; a ship that is thoroughly furnished with spars, gear, tackle, and so on is *well rigged*, and its ropes and stays are its *rigging*. Hence, *a good rig out*, a first-rate outfit in clothes, equipment, etc.

In the U.S.A. before the days of motor-cars a *rig* was a carriage or private conveyance.

The word also formerly was used of a strumpet, and a lewd woman was said to be *riggish*. Also, a hoax or dodge; hence a swindle, and the phrase to **rig the market**, to raise or lower prices by underhand methods so that one can make a profit.

To run the rig. To have a bit of fun, or indulge in practical jokes.

He little thought when he set out
  Of running such a rig.
    COWPER: *John Gilpin.*

Rigadoon. A lively dance for two people, said to have been invented towards the close of the 17th century by a dancing-master of Marseilles named *Rigadou*.

Isaac's Rigadoon shall live as long

As Raphael's painting, or as Virgil's song.
JENYNS: Art of Dancing, canto ii.

Right. In politics the Right is the Conservative party, because in the continental chambers the Conservatives sit on the right-hand side of the Speaker, the Liberals, Radicals, and Labour on the left.

It'll all come right in the end. The cry of the optimist when things are going wrong.

In one's right mind. Sane; in a normal state after mental excitement. The phrase comes from *Mark* v, 15 —

And they . . . see him that was possessed with the devil, and had the legion, sitting, and clothed, and in his right mind.

Right foot foremost. It is still considered unlucky to enter a house, or even a room, on the left foot, and in ancient Rome a boy was stationed at the door of a mansion to caution visitors not to cross the threshold with their left foot, which would have been an ill omen.

Right-hand man. An invaluable, or confidential, assistant; originally applied to the cavalryman at the right of the line, whose duties were of great responsibility.

Right Honourable. A prefix to the title of earls, viscounts, barons, and the younger sons of dukes and marquesses. All privy councillors and some lord mayors, Lords Justices of Appeal, and other civic dignitaries are also *Right Honourables*. The corresponding prefix for a marquess is *The Most Honourable*, and for a duke *His Grace*. Younger sons of earls, and all sons of viscounts and barons are *Honourables*, as are justices of the High Court, maids of honour, and certain Colonial and other ministers. Members of Parliament when in the House are usually addressed as "My honourable friend," or "the honourable member for So-and-so."

Righto! or **Right ho!** A colloquial form of cheerful assent; *right you are* is a similar exclamation.

Right of way. The legal right to make use of a certain passage whether high road, by-road, or private road. Private right of way may be claimed by immemorial usage, special permission, or necessity; but a funeral *cortège* or bridal party having passed over a certain field does not give to the public the right of way, as many suppose.

Declaration of Rights. An instrument submitted to William and Mary and accepted by them (February 13th, 1689), setting forth the fundamental principles of the constitution. The chief items are: The Crown cannot levy taxes without the consent of Parliament, nor keep a standing army in times of peace; the Members of Parliament are free to utter their thoughts, and a Parliament is to be convened every year; elections are to be free, trial by jury to be inviolate, the right of petition not to be interfered with, and the Sovereign should take the oath against Transubstantiation and not marry a Roman Catholic.

To put things to rights. To put every article in its proper place.

Rigmarie (rig ma ′rē). An old Scottish coin of low value. The word originated from one of the "billon" coins struck in the reign of Queen Mary, which bore the words *Reg. Maria* as part of the legend.

Billon is mixed metal for coinage, especially silver largely alloyed with copper.

Rigmarole (rig′ mȧ rōl). A rambling, disconnected account, an unending yarn.

You never heard such a rigmarole. . . . He said he thought he was certain he had seen somebody by the rick and it was Tom Bakewell who was the only man he knew who had a grudge against Farmer Blaize and if the object had been a little bigger he would not mind swearing to Tom and would swear to him for he was dead certain it was Tom only what he saw looked smaller and it was pitch-dark at the time . . . etc. — MEREDITH: *Richard Feverel*, ch. xi.

The word is said to be a popular corruption of *Ragman Roll* (*q.v.*); it is recorded from the early 18th century.

Rile. A dialect word, common in Norfolk and other parts for stirring up water to make it muddy; hence, to excite or disturb, and hence the modern colloquial meaning, to vex, annoy, make angry. It comes from O.Fr. *roillier*, to roll or flow (of a stream).

Rimfaxi. *See* HORSE.

Rinaldo. One of the great heroes of mediæval romance (also called Renault of Montauban, Regnault, etc.), a paladin of Charlemagne, cousin of Orlando (*q.v.*), and one of the four sons of Aymon. He was the owner of the famous horse Bayard, and is always painted with the characteristics of a borderer — valiant, ingenious, rapacious, and unscrupulous.

In Tasso's *Jerusalem Delivered* Rinaldo was the Achilles of the Christian army, despising gold and power but craving renown.

In Ariosto's *Orlando Furioso* he appears as the son of the fourth Marquis d'Este, Lord of Mount Auban or Albano, eldest son of Amon or Aymon, nephew of Charlemagne. He was the rival of his cousin Orlando, but Angelica detested him.

Ring. The noun (meaning a circlet) is the A.S. *hring*; the verb (to sound a bell, or as a bell) is from A.S. *hringan*, to clash, ring, connected with Lat. *clangere*, to clang.

A ring worn on the forefinger is supposed to indicate a haughty, bold, and overbearing spirit; on the long finger, prudence, dignity, and discretion; on the marriage finger, love and affection; on the little finger, a masterful spirit. *Cp.* WEDDING FINGER.

The wearing of a wedding-ring by married women is now universal in Christian countries, but the custom varies greatly in detail. It appears to have originated in the betrothal rings given as secular pledges by the Romans. Until the end of the 16th century it was the custom in England to wear the wedding-ring on the third finger of the right hand.

As the forefinger was held to be symbolical of the Holy Ghost, priests used to wear their ring on this in token of their spiritual office. Episcopal rings, worn by cardinals, bishops and abbots are of gold with a stone—cardinals a sapphire, bishops and abbots an amethyst—and are worn upon the third finger of the right hand. The pope wears a similar ring, usually with a cameo, emerald, or ruby. A plain gold ring is put upon the third finger of the right hand of a nun on her profession.

Amongst the Romans, only senators, chief magistrates, and in later times knights, enjoyed the *jus annuli aurei*, the right to wear a ring of gold. The emperors conferred this upon whom they pleased, and Justinian extended the privilege to all Roman citizens.

Rings noted in Fable and History.

Agramant's ring. This enchanted ring was given by Agramant to the dwarf Brunello, from whom it was stolen by Bradamant and given to Melissa. It passed successively into the hands of Rogero and Angelica (who carried it in her mouth) (*Orlando Furioso*, Bk. v).

The ring of Amasis. A ring with the same story as that of Polycrates. *See below.*

Corcud's ring. This magic ring was composed of six metals, and ensured the wearer success in any undertaking in which he chose to embark (*Chinese Tales; Corcud and his Four Sons*).

The Doge's ring. The doge of Venice, on Ascension Day, used to throw a ring into the sea from the ship *Bucentaur* (*q.v.*), to denote that the Adriatic was subject to the republic of Venice as a wife is subject to her husband. *See* DOGE.

The ring of Edward the Confessor. It is said that Edward the Confessor was once asked for alms by an old man, and gave him his ring. In time some English pilgrims went to the Holy Land and happened to meet the same old man, who told them he was John the Evangelist, and gave them the identical ring to take to "Saint" Edward. It was preserved in Westminster Abbey.

The ring of Gyges. See GYGES.

The ring of Innocent. On May 29th, 1205, Innocent III sent John, King of England, four gold rings set with precious stones, and explained that the *rotundity* signifies *eternity*—remember we are passing through time into eternity; the *number* signifies the *four* virtues which make up constancy of mind—viz. justice, fortitude, prudence, and temperance; the *material* signifies "the wisdom from on high," which is as gold purified in the fire; the *green* emerald is emblem of "faith," the *blue* sapphire of "hope," the *red* garnet of "charity," and the *bright* topaz of "good works." (Rymer: *Fœdera*, vol. i, 139.)

Dame Liones' ring, given by her to Sir Gareth during a tournament. It ensured the wearer from losing blood when wounded.

"This ring," said Dame Liones, "increaseth my beauty . . . . That which is green it turns red, and that which is red it turns green. That which is blue it turns white and that which is white it turns blue. Whoever beareth this ring can never lose blood, however wounded."—*History of Prince Arthur*, i, 146.

Luned's ring rendered the wearer invisible. Luned or Lynet gave it to Owain, one of King Arthur's knights.

Take this ring, and put it on thy finger, with the stone inside thy hand, and close thy hand upon it. As long as thou concealest the stone the stone will conceal thee.—*Mabinogion* (*Lady of the Fountain*).

The Ring of the Nibelung. See NIBELUNG.

The ring of Ogier (*q.v.*) was given him by Morgan le Fay. It removed all infirmities, and restored the aged to youth again.

Otnit's ring of invisibility belonged to Otnit, King of Lombardy, and was given to him by the queen-mother when he went to gain the soldan's daughter in marriage. The stone had the virtue of directing the wearer the right road to take in travelling (*The Heldenbuch*).

Polycrates' ring was flung into the sea to propitiate Nemesis, and was found again by the owner inside a fish. *Cp.* KENTIGERN.

Reynard's wonderful ring. This ring, which existed only in the brain of Reynard, had a stone of three colours—red, white, and green. The *red* made the night as clear as the day; the *white* cured all manner of diseases; and the *green* rendered the wearer of the ring invincible (*Reynard the Fox*, ch. xii).

Solomon's ring, among other wonderful things, sealed up the refractory Jinni in jars, and cast them into the Red Sea.

The steel ring, made by Seidel-Beckit, enabled the wearer to read the secrets of another's heart (*Oriental Tales, The Four Talismans*).

The talking ring was given by Tartaro, the Basque Cyclops, to a girl whom he wished to marry. Immediately she put it on, it kept incessantly saying, "You there, and I here." In order to get rid of the nuisance, the girl cut off her finger and threw it and the ring into a pond.

This Basque legend is given in Campbell's *Popular Tales of the West Highlands*, and in Grimm's *Tales* (*The Robber and his Sons*).

Ringleader. The moving spirit, the chief, in some enterprise, especially one of a mutinous character; from the old phrase to *lead the ring*, the *ring* being a group of associated persons.

Ring and the Book, The. A long poem (20,934 lines), by Robert Browning, telling twelve times over, from different points of view, the story of a *cause célèbre* of Italian history (1698). Guido Franceschini, a Florentine nobleman of shattered fortune, marries Pompilia, an heiress, to repair his state. Pompilia is a supposititious child of Pietro, supplied by his wife, Violante, to prevent certain property going to an heir not his own. The bride reveals to Guido this fact, and the first trial occurs to settle the said property. The count treats his bride so brutally that she quits his roof under the protection of Caponsacchi, a young priest, and takes refuge in Rome. Guido follows and has them arrested; a trial ensues, a separation is permitted. Pompilia is sent to a convent and Caponsacchi is suspended for three years. Pompilia's health gives way, and as the birth of a child is expected, she is permitted to leave the convent and live with her putative parents. She pleads for a divorce, but, pending the suit, the child is born. The count, hearing thereof, murders Pietro, Violante, and Pompilia; but, being taken red-handed, is executed.

A ring of bells. A set of bells (from three to twelve) for change ringing, tuned to the diatonic scale.

It has the true ring—has intrinsic merit; bears the mark of real talent. A metaphor taken from the custom of judging genuine money by its "ring" or sound.

Ring off! The expression commonly used on the telephone when one has a wrong connexion or it is desired that the conversation should cease.

Ringing the changes. Properly, producing continual changes on a set of bells without repetition, *changes* being variations—according to certain rules—from the regular striking order.

Figuratively the phrase has two meanings:

(1) to try every way of doing a thing, to "run a thing to death," work it for all it's worth, etc., as in—

I have likewise seen an Hymn in Hexameters to the Virgin *Mary* which filled a whole Book tho' it consisted but of the eight following Words:

Tot, tibi, sunt, Virgo, dotes, quot, sidera, Cœlo.

The Poet rung the changes upon these eight several Words and by that Means made his Verses almost as numerous as the Virtues and the Stars which they celebrated.—ADDISON: *Spectator*, No. lx.

(2) to swindle one over a transaction by bamboozling him in changing money. For example: A man goes to a tavern and asks for a glass of beer (8d.); he lays a ten-shilling note on the bar and receives nine shillings and fourpence in change. "Oh!" says the man, "give me the note back, I have such a lot of change." He offers ten shillings in silver as he is handed the note, but just before the barmaid takes it he puts the lot together and says, "There, let's have a quid instead of the note and silver." This is done, and, of course, the barmaid loses ten shillings by the transaction.

Riot. In Common Law there are five elements necessary to make a tumult, or disturbance of the peace, a riot, viz.:—

(1) A number of persons, three at least; (2) common purpose; (3) execution or conception of the common purpose; (4) an intent to help one another by force if necessary against any person who may oppose them in the execution of their common purpose; (5) force or violence not merely used in demolishing, but displayed in such a manner as to alarm at least one person of reasonable firmness and courage.

If there are twelve persons or more present and they continue riotously and tumultuously together for one hour after the proclamation in the king's name ordering them to disperse has been read by a justice of the peace or other authorized person, the rioters are guilty of felony and can be punished by penal servitude for life (formerly it was a capital offence). This proclamation is popularly known as "reading the Riot Act," for it is the opening section of the Riot Act of 1714 that is read on such occasions.

To run riot. To act without restraint or control; to act in a very disorderly way. The phrase was originally used of hounds which had lost the scent.

Rip Van Winkle. *See* WINKLE.

Ripon. A cathedral city in Yorkshire. **True as Ripon steel.** Ripon used to be famous for its steel spurs, which were the best in the world. The spikes of a Ripon spur would strike through a shilling-piece without turning the point.

Ripping. Exccllent, tip-top.

Rise. On the rise. Going up in price; becoming more valuable, especially of stocks and shares.

To get a rise. Colloquial for to have an increase in salary.

To take a rise out of one. To raise a laugh at his expense, to make him a butt. Hotten says this is a metaphor from fly-fishing; the fish *rise* to the fly, and are caught.

Rising in the Air. *See* LEVITATION.

Rivals. Originally "persons dwelling on opposite sides of a river" (Lat. *rivalis*, a river-man). Cælius says there was no more fruitful source of contention than river-right, both with beasts and men, not only for the benefit of its waters, but also because rivers are natural boundaries.

Rivers. The following are miles in length:
About 3,500, the Nile, the longest river in Africa.
About 2,400, the Volga, the longest river in Europe.
About 3,200, the Yang-tze-Kiang, the longest river in Asia.
About 3,900, the Lower Mississippi and the Missouri. The Mississippi itself, the longest river in North America, is 2,553 miles from mouth to source.
About 4,700, the Amazon, the longest river in South America and in the world.
About 228, the Thames, the longest river in Great Britain.

Riviera, The. The name given to the Mediterranean coasts of France and Italy for a distance of about 300 miles, with its centre at Genoa. From west to east the principal resorts are: Hyères, Cannes, Nice, Monte Carlo, Mentone, San Remo, Bordighera, Rapallo, Savona, Spezzia.

Road. All roads lead to Rome. All efforts of thought converge in a common centre. As, from the centre of the ancient world, roads radiated to every part of the Empire, so any road, if followed to its source, must lead to the great capital city, Rome.

Gentlemen of the road or **knights of the road.** Highwaymen.

In the mountain districts of North America a highwayman used to be called a *road agent*, and the term is still applied to bandits who hold up trains, motor-cars, etc.

On the road. Progressing towards; as, *On the road to recovery*; said also of actors when "on tour," and of commercial travellers.

Road hog. *See* HOG.

The rule of the road—
The rule of the road is a paradox quite,
In riding or driving along;

If you go to the left you are sure to go right,
If you go to the right you go wrong.

This is the rule in Great Britain, Austria, Hungary, Portugal, Sweden, Czechoslovakia, and Yugoslavia; also in certain cities, *e.g.* Rome. In other European countries and in America traffic keeps to the right.

To take to the road. To turn highwayman or become a tramp.

Roadhouse. An inn, hotel, etc., by the roadside, usually at some distance outside a town, where parties can go out by car for meals, dancing, etc.

Roads or **Roadstead,** as "Yarmouth Roads," a place where ships can safely *ride* at anchor. *Road*, A.S. *rad*, comes from *ridan*, to ride.

Roan. A reddish-brown. This word used to be derived from Rouen, the town, because this was an Old French spelling of it (*un cheval rouen*); but there can be no connexion, as the Italian was *rovano* or *roano*, and its etymology is unknown. Rouen may have given its name to *roan*, the soft sheepskin leather.

Roan Barbary. The famous charger of Richard II, which ate from his royal hand.
Oh, how it yearned my heart when I beheld
In London streets, that coronation day,
When Bolingbroke rode on roan Barbary,
That horse that thou so often hast bestrid,
That horse that I so carefully have dressed.
Richard II, v, 5.

Roar. Roarer. A broken-winded horse is so called from the noise it makes in breathing.

He drives a roaring trade. He does a great business.

Roaring boys. The riotous blades of Ben Jonson's time, whose delight it was to annoy quiet folk. At one time their pranks in London were carried to an alarming extent.
And bid them think on Jones amidst this glee,
In hope to get such roaring boys as he.
Legend of Captain Jones (1659)
Dekker and Middleton wrote a play (1611) on Moll Cutpurse (*q.v.*) which they called *The Roaring Girl*.

Roast. To roast a person is to banter him unmercifully; also, to give him a dressing-down. Shakespeare, in *Hamlet*, speaks of roasting "in wrath and fire."

To rule the roast. To have the chief direction; to be paramount.

The phrase was common in the 15th century, and it is possible that *roast* was originally *roost*, the reference being to a cock, who decides which hen is to roost nearest to him; but it is unlikely; in Thomas Heywood's *History of Women* (about 1630) we read of "her that ruled the roast in the kitchen."

John, Duke of Burgoyne, ruled the rost, and governed both King Charles . . . and his whole realme.—
HALL: *Union* (1548).

Ah, I do domineer, and rule the roast.
    CHAPMAN: *Gentleman Usher*, V, i (1606).

Geate you nowe up into your pulpittes like bragginge cocks on the rowst, flappe your winges and crowe out aloude.—BP. JEWELL (*d.* 1571).

Rob. To rob Peter to pay Paul. To take away from one person in order to give to another; or merely to shift a debt—to pay it off by incurring another one. Fable has it that the phrase alludes to the fact that on December 17th, 1550, the abbey church of St. Peter, Westminster, was advanced to the dignity of a cathedral by letters patent; but ten years later it was joined to the diocese of London again, and many of its estates appropriated to the repairs of St. Paul's Cathedral. But it was a common saying long before this date, and had been used by Wyclif about 1380:—

How should God approve that you rob Peter, and give this robbery to Paul in the name of Christ?—*Select Works*, III, 174.

The hint of the President, Viglius, to the Duke of Alva when he was seeking to impose ruinous taxation in the Netherlands (1569) was that—

it was not desirable to rob St. Peter's altar in order to build one to St. Paul.

Rob Roy (*Robert the Red*). A nickname given to Robert M'Gregor (1671-1734), a noted Scottish outlaw and freebooter, on account of his red hair. He assumed the name of Campbell about 1716, and was protected by the Duke of Argyle. He may be termed the Robin Hood of Scotland.

Rather beneath the middle size than above it, his limbs were formed upon the very strongest model that is consistent with agility. . . . Two points in his person interfered with the rules of symmetry; his shoulders were so broad . . . as to give him the air of being too square in respect to his stature; and his arms, though round, sinewy, and strong, were so very long as to be rather a deformity.—SCOTT: *Rob Roy*, ch. xxiii.

Robert. The personal name is sometimes applied to the "man in blue," the policeman. The allusion is to Sir Robert Peel—*cp.* PEELER, and BOBBY.

Highwaymen and bandits are called *Robert's men* from *Robin Hood*.

Robin. A diminutive of Robert.

Robin Goodfellow. A "drudging fiend," and merry domestic fairy, famous for mischievous pranks and practical jokes; also known as "Puck," the son of Oberon, and the fairies' jester. The story is that at night-time he will sometimes do little services for the family over which he presides. The Scots call this domestic spirit a *brownie*; the Germans, *kobold* or *Knecht Ruprecht*. The Scandinavians called it *Nissë God-dreng*.

Either I mistake your shape and making quite,
Or else you are that shrewd and knavish sprite
Called Robin Goodfellow. . . .
Those that Hob-goblin call you, and sweet Puck,
You do their work, and they shall have good luck.
    Midsummer Night's Dream, ii, 1.

Robin Hood. This traditional outlaw and hero of English ballads is mentioned by Langland in the *Vision of Piers Plowman*, Bk. v, 402 (*q.v.*). It is doubtful whether he ever lived—the truth probably being that the stories associated with his name crystallized gradually round the personality of some popular local hero of the early 13th century—but the legends are that he was born in 1160 at Locksley, Notts, or, alternatively, that he was the outlawed Earl of Huntingdon, Robert Fitzooth, in disguise. Fitz- being omitted leaves Ooth, and converting *th* into *d* it became "Ood."

Another suggestion (Ten Brink) is that in the Robin Hood legends we have a late reminder of the old Scandinavian mythology of our ancestors. About the 12th century Woden was given the name "Robin," and the tales of outlawry may be a later form of the legend of the Wild Huntsman, connected with Woden.

According to Stow, he was an outlaw in the reign of Richard I (12th century). He entertained one hundred tall men, all good archers, with the spoil he took, but "he suffered no woman to be oppressed, violated, or otherwise molested; poore men's goods he spared, abundantlie relieving them with that which by theft he got from abbeys and houses of rich earles."

Robin Hood's companions in Sherwood Forest and Barnsdale, Yorks, were Little John, Friar Tuck, Will Scarlet, Allen-a-dale, George-a-Greene, and Maid Marian who do not appear in the earlier ballads; indeed, Friar Tuck does not figure until 1475, and Maid Marian not until 1500. According to one tradition, Robin Hood and Little John were two heroes defeated with Simon de Montfort at the battle of Evesham, in 1265. Fuller, in his *Worthies*, considers the outlaw an historical character, but Thierry says he simply represents the remnant of the old Saxon race, which lived in perpetual defiance of the Norman oppressors from the time of Hereward.

The traditions about Fulk FitzWarine, great-grandson of Warine of Metz, so greatly resemble those connected with "Robin Hood," that some suppose them to be both one. FitzWarine quarrelled with John, and when

John was king he banished Fulk, who became a bold forester.

The first published collection of ballads about the hero was the *Lytel Geste of Robin Hood*, printed by Wynkyn de Worde about 1490.

The stories about him formed the basis of early dramatic representations and were later amalgamated with the morris dances (*q.v.*) and May-day revels.

A Robin Hood wind. A cold thaw-wind. Tradition runs that Robin Hood used to say he could bear any cold except that which a thaw-wind brought with it.

Bow and arrow of Robin Hood. The traditional bow and arrow of Robin Hood are religiously preserved at Kirklees Hall, Yorkshire, the seat of Sir George Armytage; and the site of his grave is pointed out in the park.

Death of Robin Hood. He was bled to death treacherously by a nun, instigated to the foul deed by his kinsman, the prior of Kirklees, near Halifax.

Epitaph of Robin Hood.
Hear, underneath his latil stean,
Laiz Robert earl of Huntington;
Nea arcir ver az hie sae geud,
An pipl kauld him Robin Heud.
Sich utlaz az he an hiz men
Vll England nivr si agen.
                    Obit. 24, *Kalend Dikembris,* 1247.

Notwithstanding this epitaph Robin Hood lived into the reign of Edward II, and died in 1325. One of the ballads relates how Robin Hood took service under Edward II.

Many talk of Robin Hood who never shot with his bow. Many brag of deeds in which they took no part. Many talk of Robin Hood, and wish their hearers to suppose they took part in his adventures, but they never put a shaft to one of his bows; nor could they have bent it even if they had tried.

They cry out with an open mouth, as if they out-shot Robin Hood, that Plato banished them (*i.e.*, the Poets) out of his Commonwealth. — SIDNEY: *Apologie for Poetrie.*

Robin Hood and Guy of Gisborne. Robin Hood and Little John, having had a tiff, part company, when Little John falls into the hands of the sheriff of Nottingham, who binds him to a tree. Meanwhile, Robin Hood meets with Guy of Gisborne, sworn to slay the "bold forrester." The two bowmen struggle together, but Guy is slain, and Robin Hood rides till he comes to the tree where Little John, is bound. The Sheriff mistakes him for Guy of Gisborne, and gives him charge of the prisoner. Robin cuts the cord, hands Guy's bow to Little John, and the

two soon put to flight the sheriff and his men. (Percy: *Reliques.*)

Robin Hood's larder. *See* OAK.

To go round Robin Hood's barn. To arrive at the right conclusion by very roundabout methods.

To sell Robin Hood's pennyworth is to sell things at half their value. As Robin Hood stole his wares, he sold them, under their intrinsic value, for just what he could get.

Robin Redbreast. The tradition is that when our Lord was on His way to Calvary, a robin picked a thorn out of His crown, and the blood which issued from the wound falling on the bird dyed its breast with red.

Another fable is that the robin covers dead bodies with leaves; this is referred to in Webster's *White Devil*, v, 1 (1612): —
Call for the robin-red-breast and the wren,
Since o'er shady groves they hover,
And with leaves and flowers do cover
The friendless bodies of unburied men.

And in the ballad *The Babes in the Wood* —
No burial this pretty pair
From any man receives,
Till Robin Redbreast piously
Did cover them with leaves.

Cp. RUDDOCK.

Robin Redbreasts. Bow Street runners were so called from their red waistcoats.

A round robin. *See* ROUND.

Robin and Makyne. An ancient Scottish pastoral. Robin is a shepherd for whom Makyne sighs. She goes to him and tells her love, but Robin turns a deaf ear, and the damsel goes home to weep. After a time the tables are turned, and Robin goes to Makyne to plead for her heart and hand; but the damsel replies —
The man that will not when he may
Sall have nocht when he wald.
                    PERCY: *Reliques, etc.,* series ii.

Robinson Crusoe. Defoe's novel (1719) is founded on the adventures of Alexander Selkirk (1676-1723), a buccaneer who, at his own request, was marooned, in 1704, on the uninhabited island of Juan Fernandez, off the coast of Chile. He remained there for over four years, being finally rescued by Captain Woodes Rogers in 1709.

Though Robinson Crusoe's adventures are based on those of Selkirk, whom it is unlikely that Defoe ever met, the actual island he describes was not Juan Fernandez but more probably Tobago, from the mention of Trinidad in the distance, and the descriptions of tropical plants. Defoe himself had never been to the West Indies.

Robot (rō′ bot). An automaton with semi-human powers and intelligence. From this the term is often extended to mean a person who works automatically without employing initiative. The name comes from the mechanical creatures in Karel Capek's play *R.U.R.* (Rossum's Universal Robots) which was successfully produced in London in 1923.

Robot Bomb, or **Pilotless Plane,** is the official name of the "Flying Bombs," "Buzz Bombs," or "Doodlebugs" launched against England by the Germans in June 1944. They were officially known in Germany as VI, or Vergeltungswaffe Ein (Reprisal Weapon No. 1).

Roc (rok). A fabulous white bird of enormous size, and such strength that it can "truss elephants in its talons," and carry them to its mountain nest, where it devours them. (*Arabian Nights; The Third Calender, and Sinbad the Sailor.*)

Roche (rōsh). **Sir Boyle Roche's bird.** Sir Boyle Roche (1743-1807) was an Irish M.P., noted for his "bulls." On one occasion in the House, quoting from Jevon's play. *The Devil of a Wife,* he said, "Mr. Speaker, it is impossible I could have been in two places at once, unless I were a bird."

You may make a remark on the ubiquitous nature of certain cards, which, like Sir Boyle Roche's bird, are in two places at once.—*Drawing-room Magic.*

Rock. "The Rock," *par excellence*, is Gibraltar (*cp.* ROCK ENGLISH, *below*). As applied to pigeons—as in **Plymouth rock** and **blue rock**—the word is short for *rock-dove* or *rock-pigeon*. "The Rock of Ages" (*see below*) is used of Jesus Christ as the unshakable and eternal foundation.

In U.S.A. thieves' slang a *rock* is a diamond or other precious stone.

In the sense of swinging backwards and forwards **to rock** is a term in jazz music meaning to work up an exciting rhythm.

A house builded upon a rock. Typical of a person or a thing whose foundations are sure. The allusion is to *Matt*, vii, 24.

Captain Rock. A fictitious name assumed by the leader of the Irish insurgents in 1822.

On the rocks. "Stony broke," having no money; a phrase from seafaring; a ship that is on the rocks will very quickly go to pieces unless she can be got off.

Rock of Ages cleft for me. It is said that this well-known hymn was written by Augustus Montague Toplady (1740-78) while seated by a great cleft rock near Cheddar, Somerset. Another story, which may belong to the realm of fable, has it that the first verse was written on the ten of diamonds in the interval between two rubbers of whist at Bath. Hence a *Toplady ring* is a ring set with ten stones in the form of the pips on a ten of diamonds. The phrase itself, as applied to Christ, is considerably older, and is traced to the marginal note to *Is*. xxvi, 4, where the words "everlasting strength" are stated to be, in the Hebrew, "Rock of Ages." In one of his hymns Wesley had written (1788)—

Hell in vain against us rages;
Can it shock
Christ the Rock
Of eternal Ages?
Praise by all to Christ is given.

Southey also has—
These waters are the Well of Life, and lo!
The Rock of Ages there, from whence they flow.
Pilgrimage to Waterloo, Pt. ii, ca. iii.

Rockefeller Foundation (rok′ e fel′ er). This was established by John D. Rockefeller (1839-1937) in order "to promote the welfare of mankind throughout the world." From it grants have been made to educational and other societies, including the universities of Oxford, Cambridge, and London. The capital is over £32,000,000. The Rockefeller Institute for Medical Research was founded in New York City in 1901. John D. Rockefeller built and endowed the buildings at a cost of £800,000.

Rockefeller Center is a collection of 14 separate buildings covering almost 12 acres in New York City. Radio City occupies 5 buildings in one section, and the whole Center, grouped round a 70-storey skyscraper, has a daily population of some 151,000. It was completed in 1940.

Rocket, To give someone a. To reprimand severely. An expression much used by the British in World War II.

Rococo (rō kō′ kō). An 18th-century European decorative style, characterized by motifs taken from shells (*rocaille*). It is seen at its best in the furniture and architecture of France during the reign of Louis XV.

Rod. A rod in pickle. A scolding or punishment in store. Birch-rods used to be laid in brine to keep the twigs pliable.

Spare the rod and spoil the child. An old saying drawing attention to the folly of allowing childish faults to go unreproved; founded on *Prov*. xiii, 24, "He that spareth his rod hateth his child: but he that loveth him chasteneth him betimes."

Love is a boy, by poets styled,
Then spare the rod, and spoil the child.
BUTLER: *Hudibras*, II, i, 842.

Rodeo (rō′ de ō, or rō dā′ ō). A public exhibition of horsemanship, cattle rounding-up, etc., by cowboys.

Roderick or **Rodrigo.** A Spanish hero round whom many legends have collected. He was the thirty-fourth and last of the Visigothic kings, came to the throne in 710, and was routed, and probably slain, by the Moors under Tarik in 711. Southey took him as the hero of his *Roderick, the last of the Goths* (1814), where he appears as the son of Theodofred, and grandson of King Chindasuintho. Witiza, the usurper, put out the eyes of Theodofred, and murdered Favila, a younger brother of Roderick; but Roderick, having recovered his father's throne, put out the eyes of the usurper. The sons of Witiza, joining with Count Julian, invited the aid of Muza ibn Nozeir, the Arab chief, who sent Tarik into Spain with a large army. Roderick was routed at the battle of Guadalete, near Xeres de la Frontera (711); he himself disappeared from the battlefield, and the Spaniards transformed him into a hero who would come again to save his country. One legend relates that he was befriended by a shepherd who was rewarded with the royal chain and ring. Roderick passed the night in the cell of a hermit, who told him that by way of penance he must pass certain days in a tomb full of snakes, toads, and lizards. After three days the hermit went to see him, and he was unhurt, "because the Lord kept His anger against him." The hermit went home, passed the night in prayer, and went again to the tomb, when Rodrigo said, "They eat me now, they eat me now, I feel the adder's bite." So his sin was atoned for, and he died.

Roderigo (rod e rē′ gō). A Venetian gentleman in Shakespeare's *Othello.* He was in love with Desdemona, and when the lady eloped with Othello, hated the "noble Moor." Iago took advantage of this temper for his own ends, told his dupe the Moor would change; therefore "put money in thy purse." The burden of his advice was always the same—"Put money in thy purse."

Rogation Days. The Monday, Tuesday, and Wednesday before Ascension Day. Rogation is the Latin equivalent of the Greek word "Litany," and on the three Rogation days "the Litany of the Saints" is appointed to be sung by the clergy and people in public procession. ("Litany," Gr. *litaneia,* supplication. "Rogation," Lat. *rogatio,* same meaning.)

The Rogation Days used to be called *Gang Days,* from the custom of *ganging* round the country parishes to beat the bounds (*See*

BOUNDS) at this time. Similarly, the weed milkwort is still called *Rogation* or *Gangflower,* from the custom of decorating the pole (carried on such occasions by the charity children) with these flowers.

Roger. The cook in Chaucer's *Canterbury Tales.* "He cowde roste, sethe, broille, and frie, make mortreux, and wel bake a pye;" but Harry Baily, the host, said to him—

Now telle on Roger, and loke it be good;
For many a Jakk of Dover hastow sold,
That hath be twyës hoot and twyës cold.
Prologue to Cook's Tale.

In World War II **Roger** was a simple code word of American origin used in wireless conversations to denote "message understood." Like many war terms it passed for a time into civilian speech.

The Jolly Roger. The black flag with skull and cross-bones, the favourite ensign of pirates.

Roger's Rangers. A body of daring troops raised by an American colonial Major Robert Rogers, to fight with the British Army during the French and Indian war, 1756. Rogers fought at Quebec and occupied Detroit, but his Rangers were most successful in the vast Canadian forests. They may be regarded as a prototype of the modern Commando. Rogers could not repeat his success in the Revolutionary War and was rejected by both sides, eventually dying in London in drunken obscurity, 1795.

Rogero. Ruggiero, or **Rizieri** (ro jēr′ ō, ruj ēr′ o, ritz i ēr′ i) of Risa (in *Orlando Furioso*), was brother of Marphisa, and son of Rogero and Galacella. His mother was slain by Agolant and his sons, and he was nursed by a lioness. He deserted from the Moorish army to Charlemagne, and was baptized, and his marriage with Bradamant, Charlemagne's niece, and election to the crown of Bulgaria conclude the poem.

Rogue. One of the "canting" words used first in the 16th century to describe sturdy beggars and vagrants (perhaps from some outstanding member of the class named Roger). There is a good description of them in Harman's *Caveat for Common Cursitors vulgarly called Vagabones,* ch. iv. The expression *rogues and vagabonds* has since 1572 been applied in the Vagrancy Acts to all sorts of wandering, disorderly, or dissolute persons.

It is Ordered and Ordained by the Lords and Commons in this present Parliament assembled and by Authority of the same, That all Stage-players and Players of Interludes and Common Plays are hereby declared to be, and are and shall be taken to be Rogues and punishable within the Statutes of the Thirty ninth year of the

Reign of Queen Elizabeth and the seventh year of the Reign of King James . . . whether they be wanderers or no.—*Ordinance for Suppression of all Stage-Plays and Interludes*, Feb. 11th, 1647.

Roi Panade (*King of Slops*). Louis XVIII was so nicknamed (1755, 1814-24).

Roland or (in Ital.) **Orlando.** The most famous of Charlemagne's paladins, slain at the battle of Roncesvalles (778), called "The Christian Theseus" and "the Achilles of the West." He was Count of Mans and Knight of Blaives, and son of Duke Milo of Aiglant, his mother being Bertha, the sister of Charlemagne. Fable has it that he was eight feet high, and had an open countenance, which invited confidence, but inspired respect; and he is represented as brave, loyal, and simple-minded. On the return of Charlemagne from Spain Roland, who commanded the rearguard, fell into the ambuscade at Roncesvalles, in the Pyrenees, and perished with all the flower of the Frankish chivalry.

His achievements are recorded in the Chronicle attributed to Turpin (d. 794), Archbishop of Rheims, which was not written till the 11th or 12th century, and he is the hero of the *Song of Roland* (*See below*), Boiardo's *Orlando Innamorato*, and Ariosto's *Orlando Furioso*. In Pulci's *Morgante Maggiore* he is also a principal character, and converts the giant Morgante to Christianity.

In *Orlando Furioso* (*i.e.* "Orlando mad"), although married to Aldabella he fell in love with Angelica, daughter of the infidel king of Cathay; she married Medoro, a Moor, with whom she fled to India, whereupon Orlando went mad, or rather his wits were taken from him for three months by way of punishment, and deposited in the moon. Astolpho went to the moon in Elijah's chariot, and St. John gave him an urn containing the lost wits. On reaching earth again, Astolpho first bound the madman, then, holding the urn to his nose, Orlando was cured of both his madness and his love.

Childe Roland. Youngest brother of the "fair burd Helen" in the old Scottish ballad. Guided by Merlin, he undertook to bring his sister from Elf-land, whither the fairies had carried her, and succeeded in his perilous exploit.

> Childe Roland to the dark tower came;
> His word was still "Fie, foh, and fum,
> I smell the blood of a Britishman."
> *King Lear*, iii, 4.

Browning's poem, *Child Roland to the Dark Tower Came,* is not connected in any way (except by the first line) with the old ballad.

Like the blast of Roland's horn. Roland had a wonderful ivory horn, named "Olivant," that he won from the giant Jutmundus. When he was set upon by the Gascons at Roncesvalles he sounded it to give Charlemagne notice of his danger. At the third blast it cracked in two, but it was so loud that birds fell dead and the whole Saracen army was panic-struck. Charlemagne heard the sound at St. Jean Pied de Port, and rushed to the rescue, but arrived too late.

> Oh, for one blast of that dread horn
> On Fontarabian echoes borne,
>   That to King Charles did come.
> Scott: *Marmion*, vi. 33.

The Song (Chanson) of Roland. The 11th-century *chanson de geste* ascribed to the Norman trouvère Théroulde, or Turoldus, which tells the story of the death of Roland and all the paladins at Roncesvalles, and of Charlemagne's vengeance. When Charlemagne had been six years in Spain he sent Ganelon on an embassy to Marsillus, the pagan king of Saragossa. Ganelon, out of jealousy, betrayed to Marsillus the route which the Christian army designed to take on its way home, and the pagan king arrived at Roncesvalles just as Roland was conducting through the pass a rearguard of 20,000 men; he fought till 100,000 Saracens lay slain, and only 50 of his own men survived. At this juncture another army, consisting of 50,000 men, poured from the mountains. Roland now blew his enchanted horn, and blew so loudly that the veins of his neck started. Charlemagne heard the blast, but Ganelon persuaded him that it was only his nephew hunting the deer. Roland died of his wounds.

The *Song* runs to 4,000 lines, and it was probably parts of this that—as we are told by Wace in the *Roman de Rou*—the Norman minstrel sang to encourage William's soldiers at the battle of Hastings:—

> Taillefer, the minstrel-knight, bestrode
> A gallant steed, and swiftly rode
> Before the Duke, and sang the song
> Of Charlemagne, of Roland strong,
>   Of Oliver, and those beside
>   Brave knights at Roncevaux that died.
> *Arthur S. Way's rendering.*

To die like Roland. To die of starvation or thirst. One legend has it that Roland escaped the general slaughter in the defile of Roncesvalles, and died of hunger and thirst in seeking to cross the Pyrenees. He was buried at Blayes, in the church of St. Raymond; but his body was removed afterwards to Roncesvalles.

Rolling stock. All the wheeled equipment of a railway that is fitted to run on rails; the locomotives, passenger coaches, vans, goods trucks, etc.

Roller-Coaster. An open-air railway set in pleasure grounds, etc., running up and down steep inclines; an improvement on the old-fashioned switchback railway.

Rolls, The. The former building in Chancery Lane where the records in the custody of the Master of the Rolls were kept; now replaced by the Public Record Office. It included a court of justice and a chapel, and was originally built by Henry III as a *Domus Conversorum* (house for lay monks) for converted Jews. In the time of Edward III it was devoted to the purpose of storing records.

The Master of the Rolls. The head of the Public Record Office, an ex-officio Judge of the Court of Appeal and a member of the Judicial Committee, ranking next after the Lord Chief Justice. His jurisdiction was formerly exercised in Chancery as the deputy of the Lord Chancellor, and he also sat independently in the Rolls Chapel.

Roly-poly. A crust with jam rolled up into a pudding; a little fat child. Roly is a thing rolled with the diminutive added. In some parts of Scotland the game of ninepins is called *rouly pouly*.

Romaic. Modern or Romanized Greek.

Roman. Pertaining to Rome, especially ancient Rome, or to the Roman Catholic Church. As a surname or distinctive title the adjective has been applied to Giulio Pippi, *Giulio Romano* (1492-1546), the Italian artist.

Adrian van Roomen (1581-1615), the famous mathematician, *Adrianus Romanus*.

Stephen Picart (1631-1721), the French engraver, *le Romain*.

Jean Dumont (1700-81), the French painter, *le Romain*.

Marcus Terentius Varro (116-27 B.C.) was called the *Most Learned of the Romans*, and Rienzi (1313-54), the Italian patriot and "last of the Tribunes," was known as *Ultimus Romanorum*, the Last of the Romans—an honorific title later applied to Horace Walpole, Charles James Fox, and others.

King of the Romans. The title usually assumed by the sovereign of the Holy Roman Empire previous to his actual coronation in the Holy City. Napoleon's son, afterwards the Duke of Reichstadt, was styled the King of Rome at his birth in 1811.

Roman architecture. A style of architecture, distinguished by its massive character and abundance of ornament, which combines the Greek orders with the use of the arch. It is largely a corruption of the Doric and Ionic.

The most remarkable of the numerous **Roman remains in England** are probably—

The pharos, church, and trenches in Dover, Chilham Castle, Richborough, and Reculver forts; the amphitheatres at Silchester (Berkshire), Dorchester, Nisconium (Salop), and Caerleon; Hadrian's wall (*q.v.*); the wall, baths, and Newport Gate of Lincoln; the earthworks at Verulam, near St. Albans; York (Eboracum), where Severus and Constantius Chlorus died, and Constantine the Great was born; and the ancient parts of Bath.

Roman type. Ordinary type, as distinguished from italic, clarendon, gothic or "black letter," etc.; so called because founded on that used in ancient Roman inscriptions and manuscripts.

The Holy Roman Empire. *See* HOLY.

The Last of the Romans. *See above, also* LAST.

The Roman Empire. The Empire established on the ruins of the Republic by Augustus in 27 B.C., and lasting till A.D. 395, when it was divided into the Western or Latin Empire, and the Eastern or Greek.

The Roman Empire was a power, and not a nation. . . . The name *Roman*, in the use of Procopius, when it does not refer geographically to the elder Rome means any man, of whatever race, who is a subject of the Roman Empire or who serves in the Roman armies. His nationality may not be only Greek, Macedonian, or Thracian, but Gothic, Persian, or Hunnish.—FREEMAN: *Historical Essays*, III, 246.

The Roman Republic was established about 509 B.C. after the overthrow of the last of the seven kings, Tarquinius Superbus, and survived till it was superseded in 27 B.C. by the Empire.

For a few months in 1848-49, after the flight of Pius IX, the people of Rome declared themselves a republic under the triumvirate of Mazzini, Saffi, and Armellini. It is one of the ironies of history that this Roman Republic was destroyed by the army of Republican France.

Romance. Applied in linguistics to the languages, especially Old French, sprung from the Latin spoken in the European province of the Roman Empire; hence, as a noun, the word came to mean a mediæval tale in Old French or Provençal describing, usually in mixed prose and verse, the marvellous adventures of a hero of chivalry; the transition to the modern meanings—a work of fiction in which the scenes, incidents, etc., are more or less removed from common life and are surrounded by a halo of mystery—or the atmosphere of strangeness and imaginary adventure itself—is simple.

The mediæval romances fall into three main groups or *cycles*, viz., the Arthurian, the Charlemagne cycle, and the cycle of Alexander the Great. Nearly, but not quite, all the romances are connected with one or other of these.

Romance languages. Those languages which are the immediate offspring of Latin, as the Italian, Spanish, Portuguese, and French. Early French is emphatically so called; hence Bouillet says, *"Le romain était universellement parlé en Gaule au dixième siècle."*

> Frankis speech is called Romance,
> So say clerks and men of France.
> ROBERT LE BRUN.

Romanesque (rō mán esk'). A simple and severe style of European architecture which preceded the Gothic; in England it was approximately synonymous with the Norman. The name comes from the fact that the style was the Christian adaptation of, or evolution from Roman architecture. It has two main characteristics — the use of the rounded as opposed to the pointed arch; and great strength, used as a safety measure to overcome an ignorance of stresses which were finally mastered by Gothic architects.

Romantic Revival, The. The literary movement that began in Germany in the last quarter of the 18th century having for its object a return from the Augustan or classical formalism of the time to the freer fancies and methods of romance. It was led by Schiller, Goethe, Novalis, and Tieck; spread to England, where it affected the work of Collins and Gray and received an impetus from the publication of Percy's *Reliques* and Macpherson's *Ossian*; and, immensely stimulated by the French Revolution, effected a transformation of English literature through the writings of Keats, Byron, Wordsworth, Shelley, Coleridge, Scott, etc. In France its chief exponents were Chénier, Lamartine, de Musset, and Victor Hugo.

Romany. A gipsy; or the gipsy language, the speech of the Roma or Zincali. The word is from Gipsy *rom*, a man, or husband.

> A learned Sclavonian . . . said of Rommany, that he found it interesting to be able to study a Hindu dialect in the heart of Europe. — LELAND: *English Gipsies*, ch. viii.

Rome. The greatest city of the ancient world, according to legend founded (753 B.C.) by Romulus (*q.v.*) and named after him; but in all probability so called from Greek *rhoma* (strength), a suggestion confirmed by its other name Valentia, from *valens* (strong).

Oh, that all Rome had but one head, that I might strike it off at a blow! Caligula, the

Roman emperor, is said to have uttered this sentiment.

Rome penny, Rome scot. The same as Peter's penny (*q.v.*).

Rome was not built in a day. Achievements of great pith and moment are not accomplished without patient perseverance and a considerable interval of time. It is an old saying, and is to be found in Heywood's *Collection* (1562).

When you go to Rome, do as Rome does. Conform to the manners and customs of those amongst whom you live; "Don't wear a brown hat in Friesland." St. Monica and her son St. Augustine said to St. Ambrose: "At Rome they fast on Saturday, but not so at Milan; which practice ought to be observed?" To which St. Ambrose replied, "When I am at Milan, I do as they do at Milan; but when I go to Rome, I do as Rome does!" (*Epistle* xxxvi). *Cp. 2 Kings* v, 18.

The saying is to be found in that great storehouse of proverbs, Porter's *Two Angry Women of Abingdon* (1599).

Romeo and Juliet (rō mē ō, joo' li et). Shakespeare's tragedy (first published 1597) is founded on the story of the lovers of Verona as told in Arthur Brooke's poem, *The Tragicall Historye of Romeus and Juliet, containing a rare example of love constancie; with the subtill counsels and practices of an old Fryer* (1562), and a story in Painter's *Palace of Pleasure* (1576). Its earliest appearance in literature is in Masuccio's *Novelle* (Naples, 1476); next, as *La Giulietta*, by Luigi da Porta (1535); and then in Bandello's *Novella* (Lucca, 1554). It was the French translation of this latter by Pierre Belleforest that was followed by Brooke and Painter.

Girolamo della Corte's *History of Verona* to 1560 places the story in 1303, when a member of the Scala family (transformed by Shakespeare to *Escalus*) was ruling in Verona, and in Dante's *Divina Commedia* (about 1300-18) the Capulets and Montagues appear among the quarrelsome inhabitants of the town.

Romulus (rom' ūlûs). With his twin brother, Remus, the legendary and eponymous founder of Rome. They were sons of Mars and Rhea Silvia, who, because she was a vestal virgin, was condemned to death, while the sons were exposed. They were, however, suckled by a she-wolf, and eventually set about founding a city but quarrelled over the plans, and Remus was slain by his brother in anger. Romulus was later taken to the heavens by his father, Mars, in a fiery chariot, and was worshipped by the Romans under the name of Quirinus.

Roncesvalles (rons' val). A defile in the Pyrenees, famous for the disaster which here befell the rear of Charlemagne's army, on the return march from Saragossa (778). Ganelon betrayed Roland (*q.v.*) to Marsillus, king of the Saracens, and an ambuscade attacking the Franks killed every man of them, including Roland, Oliver, and all the paladins. *See* SONG OF ROLAND *under* ROLAND.

Roncesvalles is said to have left its name to *rouncival* peas, a large kind of garden pea. *See* ROUNCIVAL. In his *Glossographia* (1674) Blount has—

Rounceval Peas, a sort of great Peas, well known, and took name from Ronceval, a place at the foot of the Pyrenean Mountains from whence they first came to us.

But there is no confirmation of this.

Ronyon or **Runnion** (ron' yon, rŭn' yon). A term of contempt to a woman. It is probably the French *rogneux* (scabby, mangy).

You hag, you baggage, you polecat, you ronyon! out, out!—*Merry Wives of Windsor*, iv, 2.

"Aroint thee, witch!" the rump-fed ronyon cries.—*Macbeth*, i, 3.

Roodselken. An old country name for vervain, or "the herb of the cross."

Hallowed by thou, vervain, as thou growest in the ground,
For in the Mount of Calvary thou wast found.
Thou healedst Christ our Saviour, and staunchedst His bleeding wound;
In the name of Father, Son and Holy Ghost, I take thee from the ground.
FOLKARD: *Plant Lore*, p. 47.

Rook. A cheat. "To rook," to cheat; "to rook a pigeon," to fleece a greenhorn. Sometimes it simply means to win from another at a game of chance or skill.

Rook, the castle in chess, is through French and Spanish from Persian *rukh*, which is said to have meant a warrior.

Rookery. Any low, densely populated neighbourhood, especially one frequented by thieves and vagabonds. The allusion is to the way in which rooks build their nests clustered closely together. Colonies of seals, and places where seals or seabirds collect in the breeding season are also known as "rookeries."

Room. Your room is better than your company. Your absence is more to be wished than your presence. An old phrase; it occurs in Stany-hurst's *Description of Ireland* (1577), Greene's *Quip for an Upstart Courtier* (1592), etc.

Roost. A strong current or furious tide betwixt island groups, especially in the Orkneys and Shetlands.

To rule the roost. *See* ROAST.

Root. Root and branch. The whole of it without any exceptions or omissions; "lock, stock, and barrel." The Puritans of about 1640 who wanted to extirpate the episcopacy altogether were known as "Root-and-branch men," or "Rooters," and the term has since been applied to other political factions who are anxious to "go the whole hog."

To root (U.S.A.). To support a sporting team.

The root of the matter. Its true inwardness, its actual base and foundation. The phrase comes from *Job* xix, 28—

But ye should say, Why persecute we him, seeing the root of the matter is found in me?

To take or strike root. To become permanently or firmly established.

Rope. A taste of the rope's end. A flogging— especially among seamen.

Fought back to the ropes. Fought to the bitter end. A phrase from the prize-ring, the "ropes" forming the boundary of the "ring."

It is a battle that must be fought game, and right back to the ropes.—BOLDREWOOD: *Robbery Under Arms*, ch. xxxiii.

Ropes of sand. *See* SAND.

She is on her high ropes. In a distant and haughty temper; "high and mighty." The allusion is to a rope-dancer, who looks down on the spectators.

The Rope-walk. Former barristers slang for an Old Bailey practice. Thus, "Gone into the rope-walk" means, he has taken up practice in the Old Bailey. The allusion is to the murder trials taking place there, a convicted murderer "getting the rope."

To come to the end of one's rope or tether. *See* TETHER.

To fight with a rope round one's neck. To fight with a certainty of losing your life unless you conquer.

You must send in a large force; . . . for, as he fights with a rope round his neck, he will struggle to the last.— KINGSTON: *The Three Admirals*, viii.

To give one rope enough. To permit a person to continue in wrongdoing till he reaps the consequences. "Give him rope enough and he'll hang himself" is a common saying of one addicted to evil courses.

To know the ropes. To be up to all the tricks and dodges; to know exactly what is the proper thing to do.

To rope one in. To get him to take part in some scheme, enterprise, etc. An expression from the western states of America, where horses and cattle are roped in with a lasso.

Ropey. A phrase widely used by the British armed forces in World War II to denote anything inferior or worn-out—synonymous, in this connexion, with "old-fashioned."

Roque, St. *See* ROCH.

Rosalia, or **Rosalie, St.** (rō zā′ li a, roz′ e lē). The patron saint of Palermo, in art depicted in a cave with a cross and skull, or else in the act of receiving a rosary or chaplet of roses from the Virgin. She lived in the 12th century, and is said to have been carried by angels to an inaccessible mountain, where she dwelt for many years in the cleft of a rock, a part of which she wore away with her knees in her devotions. A chapel has been built there, with a marble statue, to commemorate the event.

Rosalind (roz′ à lind). The anagrammatic name under which Spenser introduces his early love, Rosa Daniel (sister of Samuel Daniel, the poet), into the *Shepherd's Calendar*, he himself figuring as "Colin Clout." She was the wife of John Florin, the lexicographer who is caricatured in *Love's Labour's Lost* as "Holofernes" (*i.e.* [Jo]h[an]rres Floreo).

In Shakespeare's As *You Like It* Rosalind is the daughter of the banished duke, brought up with Celia in the court of Frederick, the duke's brother, and usurper of his dominions. After sundry adventures, in the course of which she disguises herself as a youth and Celia as a peasant-girl, she obtains her father's consent to marry her lover, Orlando.

Rosamond, The Fair (roz′ a mŭnd). Higden, monk of Chester, writing about 1350, says: "She was the fayre daughter of Walter, Lord Clifford, concubine of Henry II, and poisoned by Queen Elianor, A.D. 1177. Henry made for her a house of wonderful working, so that no man or woman might come to her. This house was named Labryrinthus, and was wrought like unto a knot in a garden called a maze. But the queen came to her by a clue of thredde, and so dealt with her that she lived not long after. She was buried at Godstow, in an house of nunnes, with these verses upon her tombe:—

Hic jacet in tumba Rosa mundi, non Rosa munda;
Non redolet, sed olet, que redolerë solet."
Here Rose the graced, not Rose the chaste, reposes;
The smell that rises is no smell of roses.

This "evidence," dating nearly 200 years after the supposed event, is all the substantiation we have for the popular legend about the labyrinth; and there is none for the stories that Rosamund Clifford was the mother of William Longsword and Geoffrey, Archbishop of York. A subterranean labyrinth in Blenheim Park, near Woodstock, is still pointed out as "Rosamund's Bower."

Jane Clifford was her name, as books aver
Fair Rosamund was but her *nom de guerre*.
DRYDEN: *Epilogue to Henry II.*

Rosary (rō′ zàr i). The bead-roll employed by Roman Catholics for keeping count of their repetitions of certain prayers; also, these prayers themselves. The rope of beads consists of three parts, each of which symbolizes five mysteries connected with Christ or His virgin mother. The word is said by some to be derived from the chaplet of beads, perfumed with roses, given by the Virgin to St. Dominic. (This cannot be correct, as it was in use A.D. 1100.) Others say the first chaplet of the kind was made of rosewood; others, again, maintain that it takes its name from the "Mystical Rose," one of the titles of the Virgin. The set is sometimes called "fifteens," from its containing 15 "doxologies," 15 "Our Fathers," and 10 times 15, or 150, "Hail Marys."

The "Devotion of the Rosary" takes different forms:—(1) *the Greater Rosary*, or recitation of the whole fifteen mysteries; (2) *the Lesser Rosary*, or recitation of one of the mysteries; and (3) *the Living Rosary*, or the recitation of the fifteen mysteries by fifteen different persons in combination.

Rose. Mediæval legend asserts that the first roses appeared miraculously at Bethlehem as the result of the prayers of a "fayre Mayden" who had been falsely accused and was sentenced to death by burning. As Sir John Mandeville tells the tale (*Travels*, ch. vi), after her prayer

sche entered into the Fuyer; and anon was the Fuyr quenched and oute; and the Brondes that weren brennynge, becomen red Roseres; and the Brondes that weren not kyndled, becomen white Roseres, fulle of Roses. And these weren the first Roseres and Roses, both white and rede, that evere any Man saughe. And thus was this Mayden saved be the Grace of God.

The *Rose* has been an emblem of England since the time of the Wars of the Roses (*see below*), when the Lancastrians adopted a *red* rose as their badge, and the Yorkists a *white*. When the parties were united in the person of Henry VII the united Tudor rose was taken as his device.

The Red Rose of Lancaster was, says Camden, the accepted badge of Edmund Plantagenet, second son of Henry III, and of the first Duke of Lancaster, surnamed Crouch-back. It was also the cognizance of John of Gaunt, second Duke of Lancaster, in virtue of his wife, who was godchild of Edmund Crouch-back, and his sole heir; and, in later times, of the Richmonds. Hence the rose in the mouth of one of the foxes which figure in the sign of the Holland Arms, Kensington. The daughter of the Duke of Richmond (Lady Caroline Lennox) ran away with Mr. Henry Fox, afterwards Baron Holland of Foxley; the *Fox* ran off with the *Rose*.

The White Rose was not first adopted by the Yorkists during the contest for the crown, as Shakespeare says. It was an hereditary cognizance of the House of York, and had been borne by them ever since the title was first created. It was adopted by the Jacobites as an emblem of the Pretender, because his adherents were obliged to abet him *sub rosa* (in secret). Cecily Nevill, wife of Richard, Duke of York, and mother of Edward IV and Richard III, was known as *The White Rose of Raby*. She was a daughter of Ralph, Earl of Westmoreland, and granddaughter of John of Gaunt, and was the youngest of twenty-one children.

In heraldry the **Rose** is also used as the mark of cadency for a seventh son.

In Christian symbolism the *Rose*, as being emblematic of a paragon or one without peer, is peculiarly appropriated to the Virgin Mary, one of whose titles is "The Mystical Rose." It is also the attribute of St. Dorothea, who carries roses in a basket; of St. Casilda, St. Elizabeth of Portugal, and St. Rose of Viterbo, who carry roses in either their hands or caps; of St. Therese of Lisieux, who scatters red roses; and of St. Rosalie, St. Angelus, St. Rose of Lima, St. Ascylus, and St. Victoria, who wear crowns of roses.

In the language of flowers, different roses have a different signification. For example:—

The Burgundy Rose signifies simplicity and beauty.

The China Rose, grace or beauty ever fresh.

The Daily Rose, a smile.

The Dog Rose, pleasure mixed with pain.

A Faded Rose, beauty is fleeting.

The Japan Rose, beauty your sole attraction.

The Moss Rose, voluptuous love.

The Musk Rose, capricious beauty.

The Provence Rose, my heart is in flames.

The White Rose Bud, too young to love.

The White Rose full of buds, secrecy.

A wreath of Roses, beauty and virtue rewarded.

The Yellow Rose, infidelity.

Rose Coffee-house, The. The tavern at the corner of Russell Street and Bow Street, Covent Garden, where Dryden presided over the genius of the town. Formerly known as "The Red Cow," it was subsequently "Will's."

Rose of Jericho, The. The popular name of *Anastatica hierochuntina*, a small branching plant native to the sandy deserts of Arabia, Egypt, and Syria. When it is dry, if it is exposed to moisture, the branches uncurl. Also called the *rose of the Virgin, or Rosa Mariæ.*

Rose, The Romance of the. An early French poem of over 20,000 lines; an elaborate allegory on the Art of Love beneath which can be seen a faithful picture of contemporary life. It was begun by Guillaume de Lorris in the latter half of the 13th century, and continued by Jean de Meung in the early part of the 14th. The poet is accosted by Dame Idleness, who conducts him to the Palace of Pleasure, where he meets Love, accompanied by Sweet-looks, Riches, Jollity, Courtesy, Liberality, and Youth, who spend their time in dancing, singing, and other amusements. By this retinue the poet is conducted to a bed of roses, where he singles out one and attempts to pluck it, when an arrow from Cupid's bow stretches him fainting on the ground, and he is carried far away from the flower of his choice. As soon as he recovers, he finds himself alone, and resolves to return to his rose. Welcome goes with him; but Danger, Shameface, Fear, and Slander obstruct him at every turn. Reason advises him to abandon the pursuit, but this he will not do; whereupon Pity and Liberality aid him in reaching the rose of his choice, and Venus permits him to touch it with his lips. Meanwhile, Slander rouses up Jealousy, who seizes Welcome, whom he casts into a strong castle, and gives the key of the castle door to an old hag. Here the poet is left to mourn over his fate, and the original poem ends.

In the second part—which is much the longer—the same characters appear, but the spirit of the poem is altogether different, the author being interested in life as a whole instead of solely in love; and directing his satire especially against women.

A 15th-century English version is often published with Chaucer's works, and it is probable that the first 1,700 lines or so are by Chaucer.

Rose Sunday. The fourth Sunday in Lent, when the Pope blesses the "Golden Rose"(*q.v.*).

A bed of roses. *See* BED.

No rose without a thorn. There is always something to detract from pleasure—"every sweet has its sour," "there is a crook in every lot."

Under the rose (Lat. *sub rosa*). In strict confidence. The origin of the phrase is wrapped in obscurity, but the story is that Cupid gave Harpocrates (the god of silence) a rose, to bribe him not to betray the amours of Venus. Hence the flower became the emblem of silence, and was sculptured on the ceilings of banquet-rooms, to remind the guests that what was spoken *sub vino* was not to be uttered *sub divo*. In 1526 it was placed over confessionals.

The Wars of the Roses. A civil contest that lasted thirty years, in which eighty princes of the blood, a large portion of the English nobility, and some 100,000 common soldiers were slain. It was a struggle for the crown between the houses of York (*White rose*) and Lancaster (*Red*), York (Edward IV and V and Richard III) deriving from Edmund of Langley, Duke of York, and youngest son of Edward III, and Lancaster (Henry IV, V, and VI) from John of Gaunt, Duke of Lancaster, an elder brother of Edmund. The wars started in the reign of Henry VI with a Yorkist victory at St. Albans (1455) and ended with the defeat and death of the Yorkist Richard III at Bosworth (1485). His successor, Henry VII, was descended from John of Gaunt and married a descendant of Edmund of Langley, thus uniting the two houses.

Rosemary (rōz' mȧ ri) is *Ros-marinus* (sea-dew), and is said to be "useful in love-making." The reason is this: Both Venus, the love goddess, and Rosemary or sea-dew, were offspring of the sea; and as Love is Beauty's son, Rosemary is her nearest relative.

> The sea his mother Venus came on;
> And hence some reverend men approve
> Of rosemary in making love.
> <div align="right">BUTLER: <i>Hudibras</i>, Pt. ii, c. 1.</div>

Rosemary, an emblem of remembrance. Thus Ophelia says, "There's rosemary, that's for remembrance." According to ancient tradition, this herb strengthens the memory. As Hungary water, it was once very extensively taken to quiet the nerves. It was much used in weddings, and to wear rosemary in ancient times was as significant of a wedding as to wear a white favour. When the Nurse in *Romeo and Juliet* asks, "Doth not rosemary and Romeo begin both with a [*i.e.* one] letter?" she refers to these emblematical characteristics of the herb. In the language of flowers it means "Fidelity in love."

Rosemordris Circle. *See* MERRY MAIDENS.

Rosetta Stone, The (rō zet' ȧ). A stone found in 1799 by M. Boussard, a French officer of engineers, in an excavation made at Fort St. Julien, near Rosetta, in the Nile delta. It has an inscription in three different languages—the hieroglyphic, the demotic, and the Greek. It was erected 195 B.C. in honour of Ptolemy Epiphanes, because he remitted the dues of the sacerdotal body. The great value of this stone is that it furnished the key whereby the Egyptian hieroglyphics were deciphered.

Ross (Celtic). A headland; as Roslin, Culross, Rossberg, Montrose, Roxburgh, Ardrossan, etc.

Ross, from the Welsh *rhos* (a moor); found in Welsh and Cornish names, as Rossal, Rusholme, etc.

The Man of Ross. A name given to John Kyrle (1637-1724), a native of Whitehouse, in Gloucestershire. He resided the greater part of his life in the village of Ross, Herefordshire, and was famous for his benevolence and for supplying needy parishes with churches. The Kyrle Society (*q.v.*) was named in his honour.

> Who taught that heaven-directed spire to rise?
> "The Man of Ross," each lisping babe replies.
> <div align="right">POPE: <i>Moral Essays.</i></div>

Rosse. A famous sword which the dwarf Alberich gave to Otwit, King of Lombardy. It struck so fine a cut that it left no "gap," shone like glass, and was adorned with gold.

> This sword to thee I give: it is all bright of hue;
> Whatever it may cleave, no gap will there ensue,
> From Almari 1 brought it, and Rossë is its name;
> Wherever swords are drawn, 'twill put them all to shame.
> The Heldenbuch.

Rostrum (ros' trŭm). A pulpit, or stand for public speakers, in Latin; the beak of a ship. In Rome, the platform in the Forum from, which orators addressed the public was ornamented with the *rostra*, or ship-prows, taken from the Antiates in 338 B.C.

Rota (rō' tȧ). A short-lived political club, founded in London in 1659 by James Harrington, author of *Oceana* (1656). Its objects were to introduce rotation in Government offices and voting by ballot. It met at the Turk's Head, in New Palace Yard, Westminster, and did not survive the Restoration. Its republican principles are outlined in *Oceana*.

Rota Romana. A Roman Catholic ecclesiastical court composed of auditors under the presidency of a dean, who hear appeals and adjudicate when a conflict of rights occurs. The name is said to allude to the wheel-like (Lat. *rota*, wheel) plan of the room in which the court used to sit.

Rotary Club. A movement among business men which takes for its motto "Service not Self." The idea originated with Paul Harris, a Chicago lawyer, in 1905. In 1911 it took root in Britain and there are now clubs in all the large towns. Membership in each club is restricted to one member each of any trade, calling, or profession; lectures are delivered by experts at the weekly meetings of the clubs.

Rote. To learn by rote is to learn by means of repetition, *i.e.* by going over the same beaten track or *route* again and again. *Rote* is really the same word as *route*.

Take hackney'd jokes from Miller got by rote.
                         Byron: *English Bards, etc.*

Rothschild. A family of Jewish financiers, deriving their name from the red shield by which their parent house was known in Frankfort. The family was founded by Meyer Anselm Rothschild (1743-1812) who made a fortune during the French campaigns in Germany. On his death his five sons separated, extending the business throughout Europe. Nathan Meyer Rothschild (1777-1836) went to London in 1805 and is reputed to have made a fortune through advance knowledge of the defeat of Napoleon at Waterloo. His son Lionel (1808-79) was best known by his work for Jewish emancipation. Lionel's son Nathaniel Meyer (1840-1915) was made a baron in 1885. Through the network of their continental connexions the Rothschilds have exerted great influence in many directions.

Roué (roo' ā), The profligate Duke of Orleans, Regent of France, first used this word in its modern sense (about 1720). It was his ambition to collect round him companions as worthless as himself, and he used facetiously to boast that there was not one of them who did not deserve to be broken on the *wheel*—that being the most ordinary punishment for malefactors at the time; hence these profligates went by the name of Orleans' *roués* or wheels. The most notorious *roués* were the Dukes of Richelieu, Broglie, Biron, and Brancas, together with Canillac and Nocé; in England, the Dukes of Rochester and Buckingham.

Rouen (roo' on). **Aller à Rouen.** To go to ruin. The French are full of these puns, and our forefathers indulged in them also, as, *You are on the highway to Needham* (a market town in Suffolk), *i.e.* your courses will lead you to poverty.

The Bloody Feast of Rouen (1356). Charles the Dauphin gave a banquet to his private friends at Rouen, to which his brother-in-law Charles the Bad was invited. While the guests were at table King John the Good entered the room with a numerous escort, exclaiming, "Traitor, thou art not worthy to sit at table with my son!" Then, turning to his guards, he added, "Take him hence! By holy Paul, I will neither eat nor drink till his head be brought me!" Then, seizing an iron mace from one of the men at arms, he struck another of the guests between the shoulders, exclaiming, "Out, proud traitor!

by the soul of my father, thou shalt not live!" Four of the guests were beheaded on the spot.

Rouge (roozh) (Fr., red). **Rouge Croix.** One of the pursuivants of the Heralds' College (*q.v.*). So called from the red cross of St. George, the patron saint of England.

Rouge Dragon. The pursuivant founded by Henry VII. The Red Dragon was the ensign of Cadwalader, the last Welsh king of the Britons, an ancestor of Henry VII, who employed it as the dexter supporter of his coat of arms.

Rouge et Noir (Fr., red and black). A game of chance; so called because of the red and black diamond-shaped compartments on the board. The dealer deals out to *noir* first till the sum of the pips exceeds thirty, then to *rouge* in the same manner. That packet which comes nearest to thirty-one is the winner of the stakes.

Rough. Rough-hewn. Shaped in the rough, not finished, unpolished, ill-mannered, raw; as a "rough-hewn seaman" (Bacon); a "rough-hewn discourse" (Howe).

There's a divinity that shapes our ends,
Rough-hew them how we will.
                              Hamlet, v, 2.

Riding rough-shod over one. Treating one without the least consideration. The shoes of a horse that is *rough-shod* has the nails projecting to prevent it slipping.

Rough and Ready. So General Zachary Taylor (1784-1850) twelfth president of the United States, was called.

There was a Colonel Rough in the battle of Waterloo; fable tells that the Duke of Wellington used to say "Rough and ready, colonel," and that the family adopted the words as their motto.

Rouncival (rown' si val). Large; of gigantic size. Certain large bones of extinct animals were at one time said to be the bones of the heroes who fell with Roland in Roncesvalles (*q.v.*). "Rounceval peas" are those large peas called "marrowfats," and a very large woman is called a *rouncival*.

Hereof, I take it, it comes that seeing a great woman we say she is a *rouncival.*—Mandeville.

Round. There is an archaic verb *to round* (A.S. *runian*), meaning to whisper, or to communicate confidentially. Browning uses it more than once, *e.g.* —

First make a laughing-stock of me and mine,
Then round us in the ears from morn to night
(Because we show wry faces at your mirth)
That you are robbed, starved, beaten and what not!
                    The Ring and the Book, iv, 599.

Bunyan, in the *Pilgrim's Progress*, speaks of "that lesson which I will round you in the ear."

Cp. also—

France . . . rounded in the ear with [by] . . .
commodity [self-interest] hath resolved to [on] a most
base . . . peace.—*King John,* ii, 1.

And ner the feend he drough as nought ne were,
Full privëly, and rounëd in his eere,
"Herkë, my brother, herkë, by thi faith . . ."
　　　　　　　　CHAUCER: *Canterbury Tales,* 7132.

A good round sum. A large sum of money.

Three Thousand ducats; 'tis a good round sum
　　　　　　　　Merchant of Venice, i. i.

A round peg in a square hole. *See* PEG.

A round robin. A petition or protest signed
in a circular form, so that no name heads the
list. The device is French, and the term seems
to be a corruption of *rond* (round) *ruban*
(a ribbon). It was first adopted by the officers
of government as a means of making known
their grievances.

In round numbers. In whole numbers,
without regarding the fractions. Thus we say
the population of the British Isles in 1931 was
forty-nine millions, in round numbers, and that
of Greater London eight millions. The idea is
that what is round is whole or perfect, and, of
course, fractions, being broken numbers, cannot
belong thereto.

Round Table, The. The Table fabled to
have been made by Merlin at Carduel for
Uther Pendragon. Uther gave it to King Leodegraunce, of Cameliard, who gave it to King
Arthur when the latter married Guinever, his
daughter. It was circular to prevent any jealousy
on the score of precedency; it seated 150
knights, and a place was left in it for the San
Graal. The first reference to it is in Wace's
Roman de Brut (1155); these legendary details
are from Malory's *Morte d'Arthur,* III, i and ii.

The table shown at Winchester was recognized as ancient in the time of Henry III, but its
anterior history is unknown. It is of wedge-
shaped oak planks, and is 17 ft. in diameter and
$2\frac{3}{4}$ in. thick. At the back are 12 mortice holes in
which 12 legs probably used to fit. It was for the
accommodation of twelve favourite knights.
Henry VIII showed it to Francis I, telling him
that it was the one used by the British king. The
Round Table was not peculiar to the reign of
King Arthur, but was common in all the ages of
chivalry. Thus the King of Ireland, father of the
fair Christabelle, says in the ballad

Is there never a knighte of my round tablë
　　　　This matter will undergo? *Sir Cauline.*

In the eighth year of Edward I, Roger de
Mortimer established a Round Table at Kenil-
worth for "the encouragement of military
pastimes." At this foundation 100 knights and as

many ladies were entertained at the founder's
expense. About seventy years later, Edward III
erected a splendid table at Windsor. It was 200 ft.
in diameter, and the expense of entertaining
the knights thereof amounted to £100 a week.

Knights of the Round Table. According to
Malory (*Morte d'Arthur,* III, i, ii) there were
150 knights who had "sieges" at the table. King
Leodegraunce brought 100 when, at the wedding of his daughter Guinever, he gave the
table to King Arthur; Merlin filled up twenty-
eight of the vacant seats, and the king elected
Gawaine and Tor; the remaining twenty were
left for those who might prove worthy.

A list of the knights and a description of their
armour is given in the *Theatre of Honour* by
Andrew Fairne (1622). According to this list, the
number was 151; but in *Lancelot of the Lake* (vol.
ii, p. 81), they are said to have amounted to 250.

These knights went forth into all countries
in quest of adventures, but their chief exploits
occurred in quest of the San Graal (*q.v.*) or Holy
Cup, brought to Britain by Joseph of Arimathea.

Sir Lancelot is meant for a model of fidelity, bravery,
frailty in love, and repentance; Sir Galahad of chastity;
Sir Gawain of courtesy; Sir Kay of a rude, boastful
knight; and Sir Modred of treachery.

There is still a "Knights of the Round Table"
Club, which claims to be the oldest social club
in the world, having been founded in 1721.
Garrick, Dickens, Toole, Sir Henry Irving, Tenniel,
are among those who have been members.

A round table conference. A conference
between political parties in which each has
equal authority, and at which it is agreed that
the questions in dispute shall be settled amica-
bly and with the maximum amount of "give
and take" on each side.

The expression came into prominence in
connexion with a private conference in the house
of Sir William Harcourt, January 14th, 1887,
with the view of reuniting, if possible, the Liberal
party, broken up by Gladstone's Irish policy.

Roundabout. A large revolving machine at
fairs, circuses, etc., with wooden horses or the
like, which go round and round ridden by passengers, to the strains of a mechanical brass band.
From this arises the device at a crossroads, whereby
traffic circulates in one direction only, thus doing
away with the need for holding up vehicles on
one road while traffic from another crosses it.

Rouse. A good, hearty bumper; a drinking
bout. *See* CAROUSE.

Rout. A common term in the 18th century for
a large evening party or fashionable assemblage.
Cp. DRUM; HURRICANE; etc.

Routes. In N.W. Europe Allied routes were signposted in World War II with simple emblems instead of place names, to enable drivers to reach a destination without the use of maps. The British roads, reaching from Caen to the Baltic, were easily recognizable, among them being "Hat," "Bottle," and "Diamond." These were chosen by Brig. Sir Henry Floyd and Lt.-Col. J. C. Cockburn for an exercise in Yorkshire in which 8 Corps practised the battle they were to fight six months later south of Caen; hence when the real thing took place the same signs were used, and the routes beginning there continued across Europe. The most famous American road was the Red Ball Route—a supply line for fast-moving traffic only, kept rolling 24 hours a day to maintain the impetus of Gen. Patton's sensational advance across France. The name came from an old American railway tradition of marking priority freight with a red ball.

Routiers, or **Rutters** (roo′ ti erz, rŭt′ erz). Mediæval adventurers who made war a trade and let themselves out to anyone who would pay them. So called because they were always on the *route* or moving from place to place.

Rove. The original meaning was to shoot with arrows at marks that were selected at haphazard, the distance being unknown, with the object of practising judging distance. Hence—

To shoot at rovers. To shoot at random without any distinct aim.

Unbelievers are said by Clobery to "shoot at rovers."— *Divine Glimpses,* p. 4 (1659).

Running at rovers. Running wild; being without restraint.

Row (rou). A disturbance, noise, or tumult is late 18th-century slang; the origin of the word is unknown.

"I shall now and then kick up a row in the street."— *Loiterer,* No. 12.

Rowdy. A ruffian brawler, a "rough," a riotous or turbulent fellow, whose delight is to make a row or disturbance. Hence *rowdyism* and *rowdy-dowdy.* The term was originally American (early 19th century) and denoted a wild and lawless backwoodsman.

Rowley (rō′ li). **Old Rowley.** Charles II was so called from his favourite race-horse. A portion of the Newmarket racecourse is still called Rowley Mile, from the same horse.

The Rowley Poems. *See* FORGERIES.

Roxburghe Club, The (roks′ brŏ). An association of bibliophiles founded in 1812 for the purpose of printing rare works or MSS. It was named after John, Duke of Roxburghe, a celebrated collector of ancient literature (1740-1804), and remains the most distinguished gathering of bibliophiles in the world. It was the forerunner of a number of similar printing clubs, as the Camden, Cheetham, Percy, Shakespeare, Surtees, and Wharton, in England; the Abbotsford, Bannatyne, Maitland, and Spalding, in Scotland; and the Celtic Society of Ireland.

Roy, Le, or **la Reine, s'avisera** (the *king,* or *queen, will consider it*). This is the royal veto, last put in force March 11th, 1707, when Queen Anne refused her assent to a Scottish Militia Bill.

During the agitation for Catholic emancipation, George III threatened a veto, but the matter was not brought to the test.

Royal. A standard size of writing papers measuring 19×24 in. In printings it is 20×25 in. or $20 \times 25\frac{1}{2}$ in.; hence a royal octavo book measures $10 \times 6\frac{1}{4}$ in. (untrimmed).

Super Royal in printing papers measures (with slight variations) 20×27 in., and in writing papers 19×27 in.

Royal Academy. *See* ACADEMY.

Royal American Regiment. The original name of the King's Royal Rifle Corps, which was first raised under that title in Maryland and Pennsylvania, 1755.

Royal and Ancient. The name by which the game of golf has been known since early days. In 1834 the St. Andrews Golf Club (founded in 1754) took the name of Royal and Ancient Golf Club; except in U.S.A. this club is the recognized authority on golf throughout the world, governing the game, framing rules, and settling questions and disputes.

Royal Society. The premier scientific society in Britain. It originated in London in 1645 when a number of learned enquirers met to discuss and experiment in various branches of science. The society was organized in 1660, meeting at Gresham College until 1710, when a move was made to Crane Court, Fleet Street. In 1780 the Society moved again to Somerset House, finally settling in its present home at Burlington House in 1857. Its fellowship, the F.R.S., is the greatest honour in the scientific and philosophical world.

Royal Titles. *See* RULERS, TITLES OF.

Rozinante, Rocinante (roz i năn′ ti). The wretched jade of a riding-horse belonging to Don Quixote (*q.v.*). Although it was nothing but skin and bone—and worn out at that—he regarded it as a priceless charger surpassing "the Bucephalus of Alexander and the Babieca of the Cid." The name, which is applied to similar hacks, is from Span. *rocin*, a jade, the *ante* (before) implying that once upon a time, perhaps, it *had* been a horse.

Rub. An impediment. The expression is taken from bowls, where "rub" means that something hinders the free movement of your bowl.

Without rub or interruption.—*Swift.*

Like a bowle that runneth in a smooth allie without anie rub.—*Stanihurst*, p. 10.

Don't rub it in! Yes, I know I've made a fool of myself, but you needn't go on emphasizing the fact!

Rub of the green. A golf term for any unsuspected misfortune to which the best played stroke may sometimes be subject.

Rubber. In whist, bridge, and some other games, a set of three games, the best two out of three, or the third game of the set. The origin of the term is uncertain, but it may be a transference from bowls, in which the collision of two balls is a *rubber*, because they rub against each other.

Rubberneck-wagon. An excursion or sightseeing-bus in which the passengers stretch their necks to look at views or monuments.

Rubicon (roo' bi kon). **To pass the Rubicon.** To take some step from which it is not possible to recede. Thus, when the Austrians, in 1859, passed the Ticino, the act was a declaration of war against Sardinia; in 1866, when the Italians passed the Adige, it was a declaration of war against Austria; and in August 1914, when the Germans crossed the frontier into Belgium it was impossible to avoid the armed intervention of Great Britian.

The Rubicon was a small river separating ancient Italy from Cisalpine Gaul (the province allotted to Julius Cæsar). When, in 49 B.C., Cæsar crossed this stream he passed beyond the limits of his own province and became an invader of Italy, thus precipitating the Civil War.

Rubric (roo' brik) (Lat. *rubrica*, red ochre, or vermilion). An ordinance or law was by the Romans called a rubric, because it was written with vermilion, in contradistinction to prætorian edicts or rules of the court, which were posted on a *white* ground (*Juvenal*, xiv, 192).

Rubrica vetavit = the law has forbidden it.—(*Persius*, v, 99.)

The liturgical directions, titles, etc., in a Prayer Book are known as the *Rubric* because these were (and in many cases still are) printed in red. Milton has an allusion to the custom of printing the names of certain saints (*cp.* RED LETTER DAY) in red in the Prayer Book Calendar.

No date prefix'd
Directs me in the starry rubric set.
Paradise Regained, iv, 392.

Ruby. The ancients considered the ruby to be an antidote to poison, to preserve persons from plague, to banish grief, to repress the ill effects of luxuries, and to divert the mind from evil thoughts.

It has always been a very valuable stone, and even to-day a fine Burma ruby will cost more than a diamond of the same size.

Who can finde a virtuous woman? for her price is far above rubies.—*Prov.* xxxi, 10; *cp.* also *Job* xxviii, 18, and *Prov.* viii, 11.

Marco Polo said that the king of Ceylon had the finest ruby ever seen. "It is a span long, as thick as a man's arm, and without a flaw." Kublai Khan offered the value of a city for it, but the king would not part with it though all the treasures of the world were to be laid at his feet.

The perfect ruby. An alchemist's term for the elixir, or philosopher's stone.

He that once has the flower of the sun,
The perfect ruby, which we call elixir, . . .
Can confer honour, love, respect, long life,
Give safety, valour, yea, and victory,
To whom he will.
BEN JOHNSON: *The Alchemist*, ii, 1.

Rue (roo), called "herb of grace" (*q.v.*), because it was employed for sprinkling holy water. *See also* DIFFERENCE. Ophelia says—

There's rue for you, and here's some for me! we may call it "herb of grace" o' Sundays.—*Hamlet*, iv, 5.

Ruff. An early forerunner of whist, very popular in the late 16th and early 17th centuries, later called *slamm*. The act of trumping at whist, etc., especially when one cannot follow suit, is still called "the ruff."

Ruffian Hall. That part of West Smithfield, later the horse-market, where in the 16th century "tryals of skill were plaid by ordinary ruffianly people with sword and buckler" (*Blount*, p. 562).

The field commonly called West-Smith field, was for many yeares called *Ruffians Hall*, by reason it was the usuall place of Frayes and common fighting, during the Time that Sword-and-Bucklers were in use.—*Howes' continuation of Stow's "Annals"* (1631), p. 1024.

Rufus. (*The Red.*) William II of England (1056, 1087-1100).

Otho II of Germany (973-83), son of the emperor Otho the Great.

Gilbert de Clare, Earl of Gloucester, son-in-law of Edward I. (Slain 1313.)

Rule, or **Regulus, St.** A priest of Patræ in Achaia, who is said to have come to Scotland in the 4th century, bringing with him relics of St. Andrew, and to have founded the town and bishopric of St. Andrews. The name Killrule (*Cella Regul.*) perpetuates his memory.

Rule, Britannia. Words by James Thomson. (1700-48), author of *The Seasons*; music by Dr. Arne (1740). It first appeared in a masque entitled *Alfred*, in which the name of David Mallett is associated with that of Thomson. There are, however, no grounds whatever for supposing that Mallet wrote a single line of the Ode. In the rising of 1745 "Rule Britannia" was sung by the Jacobites with modifications appropriate to their cause.

Rulers, Titles of. Titles of sovereigns and other rulers may be divided into two classes, viz. (1) designations that correspond more or less to our *King* or *Emperor* (such as *Bey*, *Mikado*, *Sultan*), and (2) appellatives that were originally the proper name of some individual ruler (as *Cæsar*).

Akhoond. King and high priest of the Swat (N.W. Provinces, India).

Ameer, Amir. Ruler of Afghanistan, Sind, etc.

Archon. Chief of the nine magistrates of ancient Athens. The next in rank was called *Basileus*, and the third *Polemarch* (field marshal).

Beglerbeg. See BEY,

Begum. A queen, princess, or lady of high rank in India.

Bey—of Tunis. In Imperial Turkey, a bey was usually a superior military officer, though the title was often assumed by those who held no official position.

Brenn or *Brenhin* (war-chief) of the ancient Gauls. A dictator appointed by the Druids in times of danger.

Bretwalda (wielder of Britain). A title of some of the Anglo-Saxon kings who held supremacy over the rest; a king of the Heptarchy (*q.v.*).

Cacique. See CAZIQUE.

Caliph or *Calif* (successor). Successors of Mohammed in temporal and spiritual matters; after the first four successors of Mohammed the caliphate passed through various dynasties— Umayyad, Abbasid, Seljuk, Turkoman, etc. In 1538 the Sultan of Turkey, Selim I, declared himself Caliph and the title rested with the sultanate until 1922 when both sultanate and caliphate were suppressed.

Caudillo (Span., "leader"). The head of the Spanish State, Don Francisco Franco Bahamonde.

Cazique or *Cacique*. A native prince of the ancient Peruvians, Cubans, Mexicans, etc.

Chagan. The chief of the Avars.

Cham. See KHAN.

Cral. (from Carolus = Charlemagne). The ruler of ancient Serbia.

Czar. See TSAR.

Dey. Governor of Algiers, before it was annexed to France in 1830; also the 16th-century rulers of Tunis and Tripoli (Turk. *dāi*, uncle).

Diwan. The native chief of Palanpur, India.

Doge (= Duke). The ruler of the old Venetian Republic (697-1797); also of that of Genoa (1339-1797).

Duce (Ital., "leader"). Head of the Fascist State of Italy, 1922-45, Benito Mussolini.

Duke. The ruler of a duchy; formerly in many European countries of sovereign rank. (Lat. *Dux*, a leader.)

Elector. A Prince of the Holy Roman Empire (of sovereign rank) entitled to take part in the election of the Emperor.

Emir. The independent chieftain of certain Arabian provinces, as Bokhara, Nejd, etc.; also given to Arab chiefs who claim descent from Mohammed.

Emperor. The paramount ruler of an empire, especially, in mediæval times, the Holy Roman Empire; from Lat. *Imperator*, one who commands.

Exarch. The title of a viceroy of the Byzantine Emperors, especially the *Exarch* of Ravenna, who was *de facto* governor of Italy.

Führer (Ger., "leader"). Prime Minister and President of the Nazi German State, 1933-45, Adolf Hitler.

Gaekwar. Formerly the title of the monarch of the Mahrattas; now that of the native ruler of Baroda (his son being the *Gaekwad*). The word is Marathi for a cowherd.

Gauleiter (Ger., "region leader"). The ruler of a province under the Nazi regime, 1933-45.

Holkar. The title of the Maharajah of Indore.

Hospodar. The title borne by the princes of Moldavia and Wallachia before the union of those countries with Rumania (Slavic, lord, master).

Imperator. See EMPEROR.

Inca. The title of the sovereigns of Peru up to the conquest by Pizarro (1531).

Kabaka. The native ruler of the Buganda province of the Uganda Protectorate.

Kaiser. The German form of Lat. *Cæsar* (*See below, also* TSAR): the old title of the Emperor of the Holy Roman Empire, and of the Emperors of Germany and of Austria.

Khan. The chief rulers of Tartar, Mongol, and Turkish tribes, as successors of Genghis Khan (d. 1227). The word means lord or prince.

Khedive. The title conferred in 1867 by the Sultan of Turkey on the viceroy or governor of Egypt. *Cp.* VALI.

King. The Anglo-Saxon *cyning*, literally "a man of good birth" (*cyn*, tribe, kin, or race, with the patronymic *-ing*).

Lama. The priest-ruler of Tibet. *See* LAMA.

Maharajah. (Hind., "the great king"). The title of many of the native rulers of Indian States.

Maharao. The title of the native rulers of Cutch, Kotah, and Sirohi, India.

Maharao Rajah. The native ruler of Bundi, India.

Maharawal. The native rulers of Banswara, Dungarpur, Jaisalmer, and Partabgarh, India.

Mikado. The popular title of the hereditary ruler of Japan—officially styled "Emperor." The name (like the Turkish *Sublime Porte*) means "The August Door." *Cp.* SHOGUN.

Mir. The native ruler of Khairpur, India.

Mogul or *Great Mogul.* The Emperors of Delhi, and rulers of the greater part of India from 1526 to 1857, of the Mongol line founded by Baber.

Mpret. The old title of the Albanian rulers (from Lat. *imperator*), revived in 1913 in favour of Prince William of Wied, whose Mpretship lasted only a few months.

Nawab. The native rulers of Bhopal, Tonk, Jaora, and some other Indian States.

Negus (properly *Negus Negust*, meaning "king of kings"). The native name of the sovereign of Abyssinia—officially styled "Emperor."

Nizam. The title of the native ruler of Hyderabad, Deccan, since 1713.

Padishah (Pers., protecting lord). A title of the former Sultan of Turkey, the Shah of Persia, and of the former Great Moguls.

Pendragon. The title assumed by the ancient British overlord.

Polemarch. See ARCHON.

Prince. Formerly in common use as the title of a reigning sovereign, as it still is in a few cases, such as the Prince of Monaco and Prince of Liechtenstein.

Rajah. Hindustani for *king* (*cp.* MAHARAJAH): specifically the title of the native rulers of Cochin, Ratlam, Tippera, Chamba, Faridkot, Mandi, Pudukota, Rajgarh, Rajpipla, Sailana, and Tehri (Garhwal). *Cp.* REX.

Rex (*regem*), the Latin equivalent of our "king," connected with *regere*, to rule, and with Sanskrit *rajan* (whence RAJAH), a king.

Sachem, Sagamore. Chieftains of certain tribes of North American Indians.

Satrap. The governor of a province in ancient Persia.

Shah (Pers., king). The supreme ruler of Persia and of some other Eastern countries. *Cp.* PADISHAH.

Shaikh or *Sheikh.* An Arab chief, or head man of a tribe.

Shogun. The title of the virtual rulers of Japan (representing usurping families who kept the true Emperor in perpetual imprisonment) from about the close of the 12th century to the revolution of 1867-68. It means "leader of an army," and was originally the title of military governors. Also called the Tycoon.

Sindhia. The special title of the Maharajah of Gwalior.

Sirdar. The commander-in-chief of the Egyptian army and military governor of Egypt during the British occupation, 1882-1936.

Stadholder. Originally a viceroy in a province of the Netherlands, but later the chief executive officer of the United Provinces.

Sultan (formerly also *Soldan*). The title of the rulers of certain Mohammedan States.

Tetrarch. The governor of the fourth part of a province in the ancient Roman Empire.

Thakur Sahib. The title of the native ruler of Gondal, India.

Tsar (from Lat. *Cæsar; cp.* KAISER). The popular title of the former Emperors of Russia (assumed in 1547 by Ivan the Terrible), but officially his only as King of Poland and a few other parts of his Empire. His wife was the *Tsarina*, his son the *Tsarevich*, and his daughter the *Tsarevna*.

Tycoon. An alternative title of the Japanese Shogun (*q.v.*). The word is from Chinese and means "great sovereign."

Vali. The title of the governors of Egypt prior to 1867, when the style *Khedive* (*q.v.*) was granted by the Sultan.

Voivode, or *Vaivode.* Properly (Russ.) "the leader of an army," the word was for a time assumed as a title by the Princes of Moldavia and Wallachia, later called Hospodars (*q.v.*):

Wali. A title of the native ruler, or Khan, of Kalat, India.

(2) The following names have been adopted in varying degrees as royal titles among the peoples mentioned:—

Abgarus (The Grand). So the kings of Edessa were styled.

Abimelech (my father the king). The chief ruler of the ancient Philistines.

Attabeg (father prince). Persia, 1118.

Augustus. The title of the reigning Emperor of Rome, when the heir presumptive was styled "Cæsar."

Cæsar. Proper name adopted by the Roman emperors. *See* KAISER; TSAR.

Candace. Proper name adopted by the queens of Ethiopia.

Cyrus (mighty). Ancient Persia.

Darius. Latin form of *Darawesh* (king). Ancient Persia.

Melech (king). Ancient Semitic tribes.

Pharaoh (light of the world). Ancient Egypt.

Ptolemy. Proper name adopted by Egypt after the death of Alexander.

Sophy or *Sophi.* A former title of the kings of Persia, from Çafi-ud-din, the founder of the ancient dynasty of the Çafi or Çafavi.

Ruminate. To think, to meditate upon some subject; properly, "to chew the cud" (Lat. *rumino,* from *rumen,* the throat).

> To chew the cud of sweet and bitter fancy.—
> MILTON.

> On a flowery bank he chews the cud.—DRYDEN.

Rump, The. The end of the backbone, with the buttocks. The term was applied contemptuously to the remnant of the Long Parliament that was left after Pride's Purge (*q.v.*) in 1648, and lasted till it was eventually ejected by Cromwell in April, 1653; also to the later remnant of the same Parliament that was restored in May, 1659, and dissolved by Monk in the following February. The "Rump" was composed of those members who most strenuously opposed Charles I and the Restoration.

> The few,
> Because they're wasted to the stumps,
> Are represented best by rumps.
> BUTLER: *Hudibras,* Pt. iii, 2.

Rumpelstilzchen (rŭm pel stilts′ chen). A passionate little deformed dwarf of German folktale. A miller's daughter was enjoined by a king to spin straw into gold, and the dwarf did it for her, on condition that she would give him her first child. The maiden married the king, and grieved so bitterly when the child was born that the dwarf promised to relent if within three days she could find out his name. Two days were spent in vain guesses, but the third day one of the queen's servants heard a strange voice singing—

> Little dreams my dainty dame
> Rumpelstilzchen is my name.

The child was saved, and the dwarf killed himself with rage.

Run. A long run, a short run. We say of a drama, "It had a long run," meaning it attracted the people to the house, and was represented over and over again for many nights. The allusion is to a runner who continues his race for a long way. The drama ran on night after night without change.

In the long run. In the final result. This allusion is to race-running: one may get the start for a time, but in the long run, or entire race, the result may be different. The hare got the start, but in the long run the patient perseverance of the tortoise won the race.

On the run. Moving from place to place and hiding from the authorities; said specially of rebels.

To have the run of the house. To have free access to it and liberty to partake of whatever comes to table.

To run down. To cease to go or act from lack of motive force, or a clock when the spring is fully unwound.

To run into the ground. To pursue too far; to exhaust a topic.

To run the show. To take charge of it, generally with ostentation; to make oneself responsible for its success.

Runner-up. The competitor or team that finishes in the second place, after the winner.

Runners. *See* REDBREASTS.

His shoes are made of running leather. He is given to roving. There may be a pun between *roan* and *run.*

Quite out of the running. Quite out of court, not worthy of consideration; like a horse which has been scratched for some race and so is not "in the running."

Running footmen. Men servants in the early part of the 18th century, when no great house was complete without some half-dozen of them. Their duty was to run beside the fat Flemish mares of the period, and advise the innkeeper of the coming guests. The pole which they carried was to help the cumbrous coach out of the numerous sloughs. It is said that the notorious "Old Q" was the last to employ running footmen.

Running water. No enchantment can subsist in a living stream; if, therefore, a person can interpose a brook betwixt himself and the witches, sprites, or goblins chasing him, he is in perfect safety. Burns's tale of *Tam o' Shanter* turns upon this superstition.

Running the Hood. It is said that an old lady was passing over Haxey Hill, when the wind blew away her hood. Some boys began tossing it from one to the other, and the old lady so enjoyed the fun that she bequeathed thirteen acres of land, that thirteen candidates might be induced to renew the sport on the 6th of every January.

Runcible Spoon. The plate and cutlery trades have no knowledge of this utensil, which is mentioned in Edward Lear's *Owl and the Pussy Cat*:

> They dined on mince and slices of quince
> Which they ate with a runcible spoon.

Some who profess to know describe it as a kind of fork having three broad prongs, one of which has a sharp cutting edge.

Rune (roon). A letter or character of the earliest alphabet in use among the Gothic tribes of Northern Europe. Runes were employed for purposes of secrecy or for divination; and the word is also applied to ancient lore or poetry expressed in runes. *Rune* is related to A.S. *rān*, secret.

There were several sorts of runes employed by the Celts, as (1) the *Evil Rune*, when evil was to be invoked; (2) the *Securable Rune*, to secure from misadventure; (3) the *Victorious Rune*, to procure victory over enemies; (4) *Medicinal Rune*, for restoring to health the indisposed, or for averting danger, etc.

Runic Staff, or **Wand**. *See* CLOG ALMANAC.

Rupert. Prince Rupert's drops. Bubbles made by dropping molten glass into water. Their form is that of a tadpole, and if the smallest portion of the "tail" is nipped off, the whole flies into fine dust with explosive violence. These toys were named after Prince Rupert (1619-82), grandson of James I and the leader of Royalist cavalry in the Civil Wars, who introduced them into England.

The first production of an author . . . is usually esteemed as a sort of Prince Rupert's drop, which is destroyed entirely if a person make on it but a single scratch.—*Household Words*.

Russel. A common name given to a fox, from its russet colour.

> Daun Russel, the fox, stert up at oones,
> And by the garget hente Chaunteclere
> And on his bak toward the wood him bere.
>
> CHAUCER: The Nonnes Prestes Tale.

Russia Leather. A fine leather of a smooth texture, originally produced in Russia. It is the result of tanning and dyeing (usually of a red colour) by a particular process and the distinctive smell comes from the distillation of birch bark used in the manufacture.

Rustam, or **Rustem.** The Persian Hercules, the son of Zal, prince of Sedjistan, famous for his victory over the white dragon Asdeev. His combat for two days with Prince Isfendiar is a favourite subject with the Persian poets. Matthew Arnold's poem *Sohrab and Rustam* gives an account of Rustam fighting with and killing his son Sohrab.

> Let Zâl and Rustrum bluster as they will,
> Or Hātim call to Supper—heed not you.
>
> FITZGERALD: Rubaiyat of Omar Khayyam, x.

Rusty. He turns rusty. Like a rusty bolt, he sticks and will not move; he's obstinate.

Ryot. A tenant in India who pays a usufruct for his occupation. The Scripture parable of the husbandmen refers to such a tenure; the lord sent for his rent, which was not money but fruits, and the husbandmen stoned those who were sent, refusing to pay their "lord." Ryots have an hereditary and perpetual right of occupancy so long as they pay the usufruct, but if they refuse or neglect payment may be turned away.

S

S. The nineteenth letter of the English alphabet (eighteenth of the ancient Roman), representing the Phœnician and Hebrew *shin*.

S in the nautical log-book signifies *smooth* (of the sea) or *snowy* (weather).

Collar of S.S. or Esses. *See* COLLAR.

$. The typographical sign for the dollar. It is thought to be a variation of the 8 with which "pieces of eight" (*q.v.*) were stamped, and was in use in the United States before the adoption of the Federal currency in 1785. Another, perhaps fanciful, derivation is from the letters U.S.

S O S. The arbitrary code signal used by wireless operators on board ship to summon the assistance of any vessels within call; hence, an urgent appeal for help.

The letters have been held to stand for *save our souls* or *save our ship*, but they were adopted merely for convenience, being 3 dots, 3 dashes, and 3 dots, . . . — — — . . .

S.P.Q.R. Senatus Populusque Romanus (the Roman Senate and People). Letters inscribed on the standards, etc., of ancient Rome.

S.T.P. Sanctæ Theologiæ Professor. *Professor* is the Latin equivalent of the scholastic *Doctor*. "D.D."—*i.e.* Doctor of Divinity—is the English equivalent of "S.T.P."

Sabaism (săb′ ā izm). The worship of the stars, or the "host of heaven" (from Heb. *Caba*, host). The term is sometimes erroneously applied to the religion of the Sabians. *See* SABIANISM.

Sabaoth (să bā′ oth). The Bible phrase *Lord God of Sabaoth* means *Lord God of Hosts*, not *of the Sabbath*, *Sabaoth* being Hebrew for "armies" or "hosts." The epithet has been frequently misunderstood; see, for instance, the last stanza of Spenser's *Faerie Queene* (VII, viii, 2):—

All that moveth doth in change delight:
But thenceforth all shall rest eternally
With Him that is the God of Sabaoth hight:
O! that great Sabaoth God, grant me that Sabbath's
sight!

Sabbath (săb′ ăth) (Heb. *shabath*, to rest). Properly, the seventh day of the week, enjoined on the ancient Hebrews by the fourth Commandment (*Exod.* xx, 8-11) as a day of rest and worship; the Christian Sunday, "the Lord's Day,"

the first day of the week, is often, wrongly, alluded to as "the Sabbath."

A Sabbath Day's journey (*Exod.* xvi, 29; *Acts* i, 12), with the Jews was not to exceed the distance between the ark and the extreme end of the camp. This was 2,000 cubits, somewhat short of an English mile.

Up to the hill by Hebron, seat of giants old,
No journey of a Sabbath Day, and loaded so.
MILTON: *Samson Agonistes*.

Days set apart as Sabbaths. *Sunday* by Christians; *Monday* by the Greeks; *Tuesday* by the Persians; *Wednesday* by the Assyrians; *Thursday* by the Egyptians; *Friday* by the Mohammedans; *Saturday* by the Jews.

Witches Sabbath. *See* WITCH.

Sabbathians (să bā′ thi ănz). The disciples of Sabbathais Zwi, or Tsebhi of Smyrna (1626-76), perhaps the most remarkable "Messiah" of modern times. At the age of fifteen he had mastered the Talmud, and at eighteen the Cabbala. When in a Turkish prison he embraced Mohammedanism, and later formed a half-Mohammedan and half-Jewish sect of Cabalists.

Sabbatical Year (să băt′ i kăl). One year in seven, when all land with the ancient Jews was to lie fallow for twelve months. This law was founded on *Exod.* xxiii, 10, etc.; *Lev.* xxv, 2-7; *Deut.* xv. 1-11. In certain American and other universities the custom of allowing professors every seven years one full year during which he is free to study or travel without the obligation of teaching or lecturing.

Sabean. *See* SABÆANS.

Sabellianism (să bel′ i ăn izm). The tenets of the *Sabellians*, an obscure sect founded in the 3rd century by Sabellius, a Libyan priest. Little is known of their beliefs, but they were Unitarians and held that the Trinity merely expressed three relations or states of one and the same God. *See* PERSON (*Confounding the Persons*).

Sabines, The (săb′ īnz). An ancient people of central Italy, living in the Apennines N. and NE. of Rome, and subjugated by the Romans about 290 B.C.

The Rape of the Sabine Women. The legend connected with the founding of Rome is that as Romulus had difficulty in providing his followers with wives he invited the men of the neighbouring tribes to a celebration of games. In the absence of the menfolk the Roman youths raided the Sabine territory and carried off all the women they could find. The incident has frequently been treated in art; Rubens' canvas depicting the scene (now in the National Gallery, London) is one of the best known examples.

Sable. The heraldic term for *black*, shown in engraving by horizontal lines crossing perpendicular ones. The fur of the animal of this name is, of course, brown; but it is probable that in the 15th century, when the heraldic term was first used, the fur was dyed black, as seal fur is to-day.

Sable fur was always much sought after, and very expensive.

By the Statute of Apparel (24 Henry VIII c. 13) it is ordained that none under the degree of an earl shall use sables. Bishop tells us that a thousand ducats were sometimes given for a "face of sables" (*Blossoms*, 1577). Ben Jonson says, "Would you not laugh to meet a great councillor of state in a flat cap, with trunk-hose . . . and yond haberdasher in a velvet gown trimmed with sables?" (*Discoveries.*)

A suit of sables. A rich courtly dress.
So long? Nay, then, let the devil wear black, for I'll have a suit of sables.—*Hamlet*, iii, 2.

Sabotage (săb' ō tazh). Wilful and malicious destruction of tools, plant, machinery, materials, etc., by discontented workmen or strikers. The term came into use after the great French railway strike in 1912, when the strikers cut the shoes (*sabots*) holding the railway lines.

Sabreur (sa brer'). **Le beau sabreur,** the handsome swordsman. This was the name given to Joachim Murat (1767-1815), King of Naples and brother-in-law of Napoleon. He was in command of the cavalry in many of Napoleon's greatest battles.

Sacco Benedetto or **San Benito** (săk' ō ben é det' ō, săn bé nē' tō) (Span., the blessed sack or cloak). The yellow linen robe with two crosses on it, and painted over with flames and devils, in which persons condemned by the Spanish Inquisition were arrayed when they went to the stake. *See* AUTO DA FÉ. In the case of those who expressed repentance for their errors, the flames were directed downwards. Penitents who had been taken before the Inquisition had to wear this badge for a stated period. Those worn by Jews, sorcerers, and renegades bore a St. Andrew's cross in red on back and front.

Sack. A bag. According to tradition, it was the last word uttered before the tongues were confounded at Babel.

Sack was used of any loose upper garment hanging down the back from the shoulders; hence "sac-friars" or *fratres saccati.*

To get the sack, or **To be sacked.** To get discharged by one's employer. The phrase was current in France in the 17th century (*On luy a donné son sac*); and the probable explanation of the term is that mechanics carried their implements in a bag or sack, and when discharged received it back so that they might replace in it their tools, and seek a job elsewhere. The Sultan used to put into a sack, and throw into the Bosporus, any one of his harem he wished out of the way; but there is no connexion between this and our saying.

A sack race. A village sport in which each runner is tied up to the neck in a sack. In some cases the candidates have to make short leaps, in other cases they are at liberty to run as well as the limits of the sack will allow them.

Sack. Any dry wine, as sherry sack, Madeira sack, Canary sack, and Palm sack. (From Fr. *sec*, dry.)

Sackerson (săk' er són). The famous bear kept at Paris Garden (*q.v.*) in Shakespeare's time.

Sacrament. Originally "a military oath" (Lat. *sacramentum*) taken by the Roman soldiers not to desert their standard, turn their back on the enemy, or abandon their general. We also, in the sacrament of baptism, take a military oath "to fight manfully under the banner of Christ." The early Christians used the word to signify "a sacred mystery," and hence its application to baptism, the Eucharist, marriage, confirmation, etc.

The five sacraments are Confirmation, Penance, Orders, Matrimony, and Extreme Unction. These are not counted "Sacraments of the Gospel." *See Thirty-nine Articles*, Article xxv.

The seven sacraments are Baptism, Confirmation, the Eucharist, Penance, Orders, Matrimony, and Extreme Unction.

The two sacraments of the Protestant Churches are Baptism and the Lord's Supper.

Sacred. Applied to that which is consecrated (Lat. *sacrare*, to consecrate), or dedicated to, or set apart for, religious use.

The Sacred Band. A body of 300 Theban "Ironsides" who fought against Sparta in the 4th century B.C. They specially distinguished themselves at Leuctra (371), and the Band was annihilated at Chæronea (338).

The Sacred City. *See* HOLY CITY.

The Sacred College. The College of Cardinals (*q.v.*) at Rome.

The Sacred Heart. The "Feast of the Sacred Heart of Jesus" owes its origin to a French nun of the 17th century, St. Mary Margaret Alacoque, of Burgundy, who practised devotion to the Saviour's heart in consequence of a vision. The devotion was sanctioned by Pope Clement XII in 1732, and extended to the whole Church by Pius IX in 1856. It is observed on the Friday after the octave of Corpus Christi.

The Sacred Isle, or **Holy Island.** An epithet used of Ireland because of its many saints, and of Guernsey for its many monks. The island referred to by Moore in his *Irish Melodies* is Scattery, to which St. Senanus retired, and vowed that no woman should set. foot thereon.

Oh, haste and leave this sacred isle,
Unholy bark, ere morning smile.
St. Senanus and the Lady.

Enhallow (from the Norse *Eyinhalga*, holy isle) is the name of a small island in the Orkney group, where cells of the Irish anchorite fathers are said still to exist.

See also HOLY ISLE.

Sacred Majesty, a title applied to the sovereigns of Great Britain in the 17th and 18th centuries.

The Sacred War. In Greek history, one of the wars waged by the Amphictyonic League in defence of the temple and oracle of Delphi.

(1) Against the Cirrhæans (594-587 B.C.).

(2) For the restoration of Delphi to the Phocians, from whom it had been taken (448-447 B.C.).

(3) Against Philip of Macedon (346 B.C.).

The Sacred Way. *See* VIA SACRA.

The Sacred Weed, Vervain (*see Herba Sacra*), or—humorously—tobacco.

Sacy's Bible. *See* BIBLES SPECIALLY NAMED.

Sad. He's a sad dog. A playful way of saying a man is a debauchee.

Sadism (sā' dizm). The unscientific term for the obtaining of sexual satisfaction through the infliction of pain or humiliation on another person or even an animal. The word is also applied to the morbid pleasure certain psychological states experience in being cruel or in watching acts of cruelty. The term comes from the Marquis de Sade (1740-1814), a French writer, of notorious ill behaviour and perversion, whose novels *Justine* (1791) and *Les crimes de l'amour* (1800) exhibited this psychological state of mind.

Saddle. A saddle of mutton. The two loins with the connecting vertebræ.

Boot and saddle. *See* BOOT.

Lose the horse and win the saddle. *See* LOSE.

Saddle-bag furniture. Chairs and so on upholstered in a cheap kind of carpeting, the design of which is based on that of the saddle-bags carried by camels in the East.

Set the saddle on the right horse. Lay the blame on those who deserve it.

To be in the saddle. To be in a position of authority, in office; also to be ready for work and eager to get on with it.

To saddle with the responsibility. To put the responsibility on, to make responsible for.

Sadler's Wells (near Islington, London). There was a well at this place called *Holy Well*, once noted for "its extraordinary cures." The priests of Clerkenwell Priory used to boast of its virtues. At the Reformation it was stopped up, and was wholly forgotten till 1683, when a certain Sadler, in digging gravel for his garden, accidentally discovered it again. Hence the name. In 1765 a builder named Rosoman converted Sadler's garden into a theatre that became famous for burlettas, musical interludes and pantomimes. In 1772 the famous comedian Thomas King took over the management until he succeeded Sheridan at Drury Lane. Edmund Kean, Dibdin and many other great actors appeared at Sadler's Wells, and the great clown Grimaldi made his fame there. In 1844 Phelps took over the theatre and produced Shakespeare, but the boom in the West End theatres cast the Wells into the shade, though it enjoyed some popularity from 1875 until 1881 under the management of Mrs. Bateman. In 1931 Lilian Baylis (d. 1937), who for over thirty years had managed the Old Vic, opened Sadler's Wells for the production of ballet and opera and made it one of the leading houses in London.

Safety. Safety bicycle. *See* PENNYFARTHING.

Safety matches. In 1847 Schrotter, an Austrian chemist, discovered that red phosphorus gives off no fumes, and is virtually inert; but being mixed with chlorate of potash under slight pressure it explodes with violence. In 1855 Herr Böttger, of Sweden, put the one on the *box* and the other on the *match*; and later improvements have resulted in the match being tipped with a mixture of chlorate of potash, sulphide of antimony, bichromate of potassium and red lead, while on the box is a mixture of non-poisonous amorphous phosphorus and black oxide of manganese, so that the match must be rubbed on the box to bring the two together. *Cp.* PROMETHEANS; LUCIFERS.

Saffron. He hath slept in a bed of saffron (Lat. *dormivit in sacco croci*). He has a very light heart, in reference to the exhilarating effects of saffron.

> With genial joy to warm his soul,
> Helen mixed saffron in the bowl.

Saga (plural **Sagas**) (sa' gà). The Teutonic and Scandinavian mythological and historical traditions, chiefly compiled in the 12th and three following centuries. The most remarkable are those of *Lodbrog, Hervara, Vilkina, Voluspa, Volsunga, Blomsturvalla, Ynglinga, Olaf Tryggva-Sonar,* with those of *Jomsvikingia* and of *Knytlinga* (which contain the legendary history of Norway and Denmark), those of *Sturlinga* and *Eryrbiggia* (which contain the legendary history of Iceland), and the collections, the *Heims-Kringla* and *New Edda,* due to Snorro-Sturleson. *Cp.* EDDA.

Sagamore. *See* SACHEM.

Sages, The Seven. *See* WISE MEN.

Sagittarius (săj i târ' i ŭs) (Lat., the archer). One of the old constellations, the ninth sign of the Zodiac, which the sun enters about November 22nd. It represents the centaur Chiron, who at death was converted into the constellation.

Sagittary (săj' i tà ri). The name given in the mediæval romances to the centaur, a mythical monster half horse and half man, whose eyes sparkled like fire and struck dead like lightning, fabled to have been introduced into the Trojan armies.

> The dreadful Sagittary
> Appals our numbers.
> > *Troilus and Cressida,* v, 5.

The "Sagittary" referred to in *Othello* i, 1: —

> Lead to the Sagittary the raised search,
> And there will I be with him,

was probably an inn, but may have been the Arsenal.

Sail. Sailing under false colours. Pretending to be what you are not with the object of personal advantage. The allusion is to pirate vessels, which hoist any colours to elude detection.

To sail before the wind, close to the wind, etc. *See* WIND.

To set sail. To start a voyage.

To strike sail. *See* STRIKE.

You may hoist sail. Be off. Maria saucily says to Viola, dressed in man's apparel —

> Will you hoist sail, sir? Here lies your way. — *Twelfth Night,* i, 5.

Saint. Individual saints who have a place in this *Dictionary of Phrase and Fable* will be found entered under their names. For symbols of saints *see* SYMBOLS.

Alexander III (1159-81) was the first Pope to restrict the right of canonization (*i.e.* the making of a saint) to the Holy See; before his time it was performed by a synod of bishops and

merely ratified by the Pope. It was not till the 4th century that persons other than martyrs were canonized, and none was inscribed on the Roll of the Saints until 608, when Boniface IV dedicated the Pantheon to St. Mary of the Martyrs. The first saint to be made direct by a Pope was St. Swidborg, canonized in 752 by Stephen II at the request of Pepin. St. Alban, the English protomartyr, was canonized in 749 by Hadrian I, to please the Mercian King, Offa.

Popes who have been canonized. From the time of St. Peter to the end of the 4th century all the Popes (with a few minor and doubtful exceptions) are popularly entitled "Saint"; since then the following are the chief of those bearing the title: —

Innocent I (402-17).
Leo the Great (440-61).
John I (523-26).
Gregory the Great (590-604).
Deusdedit I (615-19).
Martin I (649-54).
Leo II (682-84).
Sergius I (687-701).
Zacharias (741-52).
Paul I (757-67).
Leo III (795-816).
Paschal I (817-24).
Nicholas the Great (858-67).
Leo IX (1049-54).
Gregory VII, *Hildebrand* (1073-85).
Celestine V (1294).
Pius V (1566-72).

Among the **kings and royalties** so called are—

Edward the Martyr (961, 975-78).
Edward the Confessor (1004, 1042-66).
Eric IX of Sweden (? 1155-61).
Ethelred I, king of Wessex (? 866-871).
Ferdinand III of Castile and Leon (1200, 1217-52).
Irene (d. 1124), the Empress; daughter of the king of Hungary and consort of John Comnenus, Byzantine Emperor.
Lawrence Justiniani, Patriarch of Venice (1390, 1451-55).
Louis IX of France (1215, 1226-70).
Margaret (d. 1093), queen of Scotland, wife of William III.
Olaus II of Norway, brother of Harald III, called "St. Olaf the Double Beard" (984. 1026-30).
Stephen I of Hungary (979, 997-1038).
Theodora (d. 867), Empress; consort of the Byzantine Emperor, Theophilus.
Wenceslaus (910, 928-936), king of Bohemia.

It is only rarely that persons are canonized now; Joan of Arc was canonized in 1909; in 1935 Pius XI canonized Sir Thomas More (1478-1535) and John Fisher (1459-1535), Bishop of Rochester, who had suffered for the Faith under Henry VIII.

The City of Saints. See CITY.

The Latter-day Saints. The Mormons (*q.v.*).

St. Befana. There is no saint of this name, which is a corruption of *Epiphany*. See BEFANA.

St. Cloud. A palace where many important events in French history took place, formerly stood some mile and a half west of Paris, on the Seine. It was built on the site of an older chateau in 1658 by Louis XIV, and given to his brother the Duke of Orleans. Louis XVI bought it from that family and gave it to Marie Antoinette; it was later a favourite residence of Napoleon and Napoleon III. It was badly damaged during the Franco-Prussian War of 1870, and on the fall of the Empire was demolished by the Communards in 1871.

St. Cyr, or **St.-Cyr-l'Ecole.** The famous French military academy, about 14 miles southwest of Paris. The building was formerly occupied by the girls' school founded by Mme de Maintenon, where Racine's *Esther* and *Athalie* were first acted. The girls' school was suppressed at the Revolution, and in 1808 Napoleon moved the military school thither from Fontainebleau. The building was destroyed by the R.A.F. in World War II.

St. Elmo, or **St. Elmo's Fire.** The corposant (Port. *corpo santo*, sacred body), or compozant, an electrical luminosity often seen on the masts and rigging of ships on dark, stormy nights. There is no saint of this name, and the suggestions are that "Elmo" is a corruption of St. *Anselm* (of Lucca), St. *Erasmus* (the patron saint of Neapolitan sailors), or of *Helena*, sister of Castor and Pollux (*q.v.*), by which twin-name the St. Elmo's Fire is also known.

St. Martin's le Grand. The familiar name for the central offices of the General Post Office, because from 1825 its headquarters have been on and about the site of the ancient church and monastery of this name (dating from pre-Conquest times) at the south-west corner of Aldersgate Street, London.

St. Petersburg. The former name of the capital of the old Russian Empire, so called in honour of Peter the Great, who founded it in 1703. Soon after the outbreak of World War I it was changed by Imperial rescript to *Petrograd*, this being the Russian, while the other is a German, equivalent of *Peter's Town*. In 1924 the name of the place was changed again, to Leningrad, in honour of Lenin (1870-1924) the virtual founder of the U.S.S.R. Leningrad withstood one of the greatest sieges of World War II, from 1941 until 1944.

St. Stephen's. The Houses of Parliament are so called, because, at one time, the Commons used to sit in St. Stephen's Chapel.

St. Stephen's Loaves. Stones; the allusion, of course, is to the stoning of St. Stephen (*Acts* vii, 54-60).

> Having said this, he took up one of St. Stephen's loaves, and was going to hit him with it.—RABELAIS: *Pantagruel*, v, 8.

Sake. A form of the obsolete word *sac* (A.S. *sacu*, a dispute or lawsuit), meaning some official right or privilege, such as that of holding a manorial court.

The common phrases *For God's sake, for conscience' sake, for goodness' sake*, etc., mean "out of consideration for" God, conscience, etc.

For old sake's sake. For the sake of old acquaintance, past times.

For one's name's sake. Out of regard for one's character or good name.

Sakes! or **Sakes alive!** Expressions of surprise, admiration, etc., commoner in the United States than in England.

Saker (sā' ker). A piece of light artillery, used, especially on board ship, in the 16th and 17th centuries. The word is borrowed from the saker hawk (falcon).

> The cannon, blunderbuss, and saker,
> He was the inventor of and maker.
> BUTLER: *Hudibras*, i, 2.

Sakuntala (sá kun' ta la). The heroine of Kalidasa's great Sanskrit drama, *Sakuntala*. She was the daughter of a sage, Viswamita, and Menakâ, a water-nymph, and was brought up by a hermit. One day King Dushyanta came to the hermitage during a hunt, and persuaded her to marry him; and later, giving her a ring, returned to his throne. A son was born, and Sakuntala set out with him to find his father. On the way, while bathing, she lost the ring, and the king did not recognize her owing to enchantment. Subsequently it was found by a fisherman in a fish he had caught (*cp.* KENTIGERN), the king recognized his wife, she was publicly proclaimed his queen, and Bhârata, his son and heir, became the founder of the glorious race of the Bhâratas.

Sakya-Muni (sak' ya mū' ni). One of the names of Gautama Siddartha, the Buddha (*q.v.*), founder of Buddhism.

Salaam (så lam'). An Oriental salutation of a ceremonious nature, often with a profound obeisance. In Arabic the word means "peace."

Salad. A pen'orth of salad oil. A strapping; a castigation. It is a joke on All Fool's Day to send one to the saddler's for a "pen'orth of salad oil." The pun is between "salad oil," as above, and the French *avoir de la salade*, "to be flogged." The French *salader* and *salade* are derived from the *salle* or saddle on which schoolboys were at one time birched. A block for the purpose is still kept as a curiosity in some of our public schools.

Salad days. Days of inexperience, when persons are very green.

> My salad days.
> When I was green in judgment.
> *Antony and Cleopatra*, i, 5.

Salamander (săl' å măn der) (Gr. *salamandra*, a kind of lizard). The name is now given to a family of amphibious urodela (newts, etc.), but anciently to a mythical lizard-like monster that was supposed to be able to live in fire, which, however, it quenched by the chill of its body. Pliny tells us he tried the experiment once, but the creature was soon burnt to a powder (*Nat. Hist*, x, 67; xxix, 4). It was adopted by Paracelsus as the name of the elemental being inhabiting fire (*gnomes* being those of the earth, *sylphs* of the air, and *undines* of the water), and was hence taken over by the Rosicrucian system, from which source Pope introduced salamanders into his *Rape of the Lock*.

> When the Fair in all their Pride expire,
> To their first Elements the Souls retire:
> The Sprites of fiery Termagants in Flame
> Mount up, and take a Salamander's name.
> *Rape of the Lock*, i, 57.

François I of France adopted as his badge a lizard in the midst of flames, with the legend *Nutrisco et extinguo* (I nourish and extinguish). The Italian motto from which this legend was borrowed was *Nutrisco il buono e spengo il reo* (I nourish the good and extinguish the bad). Fire purifies good metal, but consumes rubbish.

Falstaff calls Bardolph's nose "a burning lamp," "a salamander," and the drink that made such "a fiery meteor" he calls "fire."

> I have maintained that salamander of yours with fire any time this two-and-thirty years. — 1 *Henry IV*, iv, 3.

Salamander's wool. Asbestos, a fibrous mineral, affirmed by the Tartars to be made "of the root of a tree." It is sometimes called "mountain flax," and is not combustible.

Salary. Originally "salt rations" (Lat. *salarium*, *sal*, salt). The ancient Romans served out rations of salt and other necessaries to their soldiers and civil servants. The rations altogether were called by the general name of *salt*, and when money was substituted for the rations the stipend went by the same name.

Sales Resistance. The negative attitude of a possible buyer which hinders or prevents the sale of a commodity.

Saliens, The. In ancient Rome, a college of twelve priests of Mars traditionally instituted by Numa. The tale is that a shield (*see* ANCILE) fell from heaven, and the nymph Egeria predicted that wherever it was preserved the people would be the dominant people of the earth. To prevent its being surreptitiously taken away, Numa had eleven others made exactly like it, and appointed twelve priests as guardians. Every year these young patricians promenaded the city, singing and dancing, and they finished the day with a most sumptuous banquet, insomuch that *saliares cœna* became proverbial for a most sumptuous feast. The word "saliens" means dancing.

> Nunc est bibendum . . .
> . . . nunc Saliaribus
> Ornare pulvinar Deorum
> Tempus erat dapibus.
> HORACE: 1 *Odes*, xxxvii, 2-4.

Salisbury Crags. These rocky hills, near Arthur's Seat just outside Edinburgh, are so called from the Earl of Salisbury who accompanied Edward III on an expedition against the Scots.

Sallee-man, or **Sallee rover.** A pirate-ship; so called from Sallee, a seaport on the west coast of Morocco, the inhabitants of which were formerly notorious for their piracy.

Sally Lunn. A tea-cake; so called from a woman pastrycook of that name in Bath, who used to cry them about in a basket at the close of the 18th century. Dalmer, the baker, bought her recipe, and made a song about the buns.

Salmacis (săl' må sis). A fountain of Carĭa, which rendered effeminate all those who bathed therein. It was in this fountain that Hermaphroditus changed his sex. (Ovid: *Metamorphoses*, iv, 285, and xvi, 319.)

Salmagundi (săl' må gŭn' di). A mixture of minced veal, chicken, or turkey, anchovies or pickled herrings, and onions, all chopped together and served with lemon-juice and oil. The word appeared in the 17th century; its origin is unknown, but fable has it that it was the name of one of the ladies attached to the suite of Mary de Medicis, wife of Henri IV of France, who either invented or popularized the dish.

In 1807 Washington Irving published a humorous periodical with this as the title.

Salop. *See* SHROPSHIRE.

Salt. Flavour, smack. The salt of youth is that vigour and strong passion which then predominates.

Though we are justices, and doctors, and churchmen, Master Page, we have some salt of our youth in us.— *Merry Wives of Windsor*, ii, 3.

Shakespeare uses the term on several occasions for strong amorous passion. Thus Iago refers to it as "hot as monkeys, salt as wolves in pride" (*Othello*, iii, 3). The Duke calls Angelo's base passion his "salt imagination," because he supposed his victim to be Isabella, and not his betrothed wife whom the Duke forced him to marry (*Measure for Measure*, v, 1.)

A sailor of large experience is often called an *old salt*, the reason is obvious—he has been well *salted* by the sea.

Spilling salt was held to be an unlucky omen by the Romans, and the superstition remains to this day, though, with us, the evil may be averted if he who spills the salt throw a pinch of it over the *left* shoulder with the *right* hand. In Leonardo da Vinci's famous picture of the Lord's Supper, Judas Iscariot is known by the salt-cellar knocked over accidentally by his arm. Salt was used in sacrifice by the Jews, as well as by the Greeks and Romans; and it is still used in baptism by Roman Catholics. It was an emblem of purity and the sanctifying influence of a holy life on others. Hence our Lord tells his disciples they are "the salt of the earth" (*Matt.* v, 13). Spilling the salt after it was placed on the head of the victim was a bad omen, hence the superstition.

It is still not uncommon to put salt into a coffin; for it is said that Satan hates salt, because it is the symbol of incorruption and immortality; and in Scotland it was long customary to throw a handful of salt on the top of the mash when brewing, to keep the witches from it. Salt really has some effect in moderating the fermentation and fining the liquor.

Not worth your salt. Not worth your wages. The reference is to the *salary* (*q.v.*) composed of rations of salt and other necessaries served out by the Romans to their soldiers, etc.

The salt of the earth. Properly, the elect; the perfect, or those approaching perfection (*see Matt.* v, 13).

To eat a man's salt. To partake of his hospitality. Among the Arabs to eat a man's salt was a sacred bond between the host and guest. No one who has eaten of another's salt should speak ill of him or do him an ill turn.

Why dost thou shun the salt? that sacred pledge, Which, once partaken, blunts the sabre's edge,

Makes even contending tribes in peace unite, And hated hosts seem brethren to the sight!
BYRON: *The Corsair*; ii, iv.

True to his salt. Faithful to his employers. Here *salt* means salary (*q.v.*).

With a grain of salt (Lat. *Cum grano salis*). With great reservations or limitation; allowing it merely a *grain* of truth. As salt is sparingly used in condiments, so is truth in remarks to which this phrase is applied.

Salt Hill. The mound at Eton where the Eton scholars used to collect money for the Captain at the Montem (*q.v.*). All the money collected was called *salt* (*cp.* SALARY).

Salt lick. A place where salt is found naturally and in a position available to animals which resort thither to lick it from the rocks, etc.

Salute, Salutation. According to tradition, on the triumphant return of Maximilian to Germany, after his second campaign, the town of Augsburg ordered 100 rounds of cannon to be discharged. The officer on service, fearing to have fallen short of the number, caused an extra round to be added. The town of Nuremberg ordered a like salute, and the custom became established.

Salute in the British navy, between two ships of equal rank, is made by firing an equal number of guns. If the vessels are of unequal rank, the superior fires the fewer rounds.

Royal salute, in the British navy, consists (1) in firing twenty-one great guns, (2) in the officers lowering their sword-points, and (3) in dipping the colours.

In the Army a Royal Salute is 101 guns fired at intervals of 10 seconds.

Discharging guns as a salute. To show that no fear exists, and therefore no guns will be required. This is like "burying the hatchet" (*q.v.*).

Lowering swords. To express a willingness to put yourself unarmed in the power of the person saluted, from a full persuasion of his friendly feeling.

Shaking hands. A relic of the ancient custom of adversaries, in treating of a truce, taking hold of the weapon-hand to ensure against treachery.

Lady's curtsy. A relic of the ancient custom of women going on the knee to men of rank and power, originally to beg mercy, afterwards to acknowledge superiority.

Salvation Army. A religious organization founded by William Booth, a Methodist minister. Its origin was the East End Revival Society, which became the Christian Mission in 1865.

Booth selected the name Salvation Army in 1877 and organized it on semi-military lines, himself being called "General" having under him "Colonels," "Adjutants," "Corporals," etc. The motto adopted was "Through Blood and Fire," and the activities of the Army were turned to the relief, moral, spiritual and physical, of the poorest and least educated of the population. The work has spread to every part of the world and immense good has been done by the selfless devotion of its rank and file.

Salve. Latin "hail," "welcome." The word is often woven on door-mats.

Salve, Regina! An antiphonal hymn to the Virgin Mary sung in Roman Catholic churches from Trinity Sunday to Advent, after lauds and compline. So called from the opening words. *Salve, regina mater misericordiæ!* (Hail holy Queen, Mother of Mercy).

Uncle Sam. The personification of the Government, or the people, of the United States—a facetious adaptation of the initials U.S. (Uncle Sam) placed on government property. The expression arose about 1812 and quickly became popular.

Upon my Sam (or **Sammy**)! A humorous form of asseveration; also, *'pon my sacred Sam!*

Samaritan. A good Samaritan, A philanthropist, one who attends upon the poor to aid them and give them relief (*Luke* x, 30-37).

Sambo. A pet name given to one of Negro race; properly applied to the male offspring of a Negro and mulatto. (Span. *zambo*, bow-legged; Lat. *scambus*.)

Samian (sā′ mi ȧn). **The Samian letter.** The letter Y, the Letter of Pythagoras (*q.v.*), employed by him as the emblem of the straight and narrow path of virtue, which is one, but, if once deviated from, the farther the lines are extended the wider becomes the breach.

> When reason doubtful, like the Samian letter,
> Points him two ways, the narrower the better.
> <div align="right">POPE: <i>Dunciad</i>, iv.</div>

The Samian Poet. Simonides the satirist, born at Samos (about 556 B.C.).

The Samian Sage, or **The Samian.** Pythagoras born at Samos (6th cent. B.C.).

> 'Tis enough,
> In this late age, adventurous to have touched
> Light on the numbers of the Samian sage.
> THOMSON.

Samite (săm′ īt). A rich silk fabric with a warp of six threads, generally interwoven with gold, held in high esteem in the Middle Ages. So called after the Gr. *hexamiton, hex,* six, *mitos,* a thread. *Cp.* DIMITY.

Sampford Ghost, The. A kind of exaggerated "Cock Lane ghost" (*q.v.*) or Poltergeist, which haunted Sampford Peverell, Devon, for about three years in the first decade of the 19th century. Besides the usual knockings, the inmates were beaten; in one instance a powerful "unattached arm" flung a folio Greek Testament from a bed into the middle of a room. The Rev. Charles Caleb Colton (credited as the author of these freaks) offered £100 to anyone who could explain the matter except on supernatural grounds. No one, however, claimed the reward. Colton died 1832.

Samson. Any man of unusual strength; so called from the ancient Hebrew hero (*Judges* xiii-xvi). The name has been specially applied to Thomas Topham (d. 1753), the "British Samson," son of a London carpenter. He lifted three hogshead of water (1,836 lb.) in the presence of thousands of spectators at Cold-bath Fields, May 28th, 1741, and eventually committed suicide; and to Richard Joy, the "Kentish Samson," who died 1742, at the age of 67. His tombstone is in St. Peter's churchyard, Isle of Thanet.

Samurai (săm′ ū rī). The military class of old Japan. In early feudal times the term was applied to all who bore arms (it means "guard") but eventually it corresponded roughly to the mediæval squires as distinguished from the "daimio" or nobles. On the abolition of the feudal system in 1871 the samurai were forbidden to wear swords, and in 1878 the designation was changed to that of "shizoku," or gentry.

San Benito. *See* SACCO BENEDETTO.

Sance-bell. Same as "Sanctus bell." *See* SACRING-BELL.

Sancho Panza (săn′ chō păn zȧ). The squire of Don Quixote (*q.v.*), in Cervantes's romance, who became governor of Barataria; a short, potbellied rustic, full of common sense, but without a grain of "spirituality." He rode upon an ass, Dapple, and was famous for his proverbs. Panza, in Spanish, means *paunch.*

A Sancho Panza. A rough and ready, sharp and humorous justice of the peace. In allusion to Sancho, as judge in the isle of Barataria.

Sancho Panza's wife, is called Teresa, Pt. ii, i, 5; Maria, Pt. ii, iv, 7; Juana, Pt. i, 7; and Joan, Pt. i, 21.

Sanctions. The word employed in International Law to describe the action taken by one or more states to force another state to carry out its legal or treaty obligations.

Sanctum Sanctorum (săng′ tùm săng tôr′ ùm) (Lat., Holy of Holies). A private room into

which no one uninvited enters; properly the
Holy of Holies in the Jewish Temple, a small
chamber into which none but the high priest
might enter, and that only on the Great Day of
Atonement.

Sand. A rope of sand. Something nominally
effective and strong, but in reality worthless and
untrustworthy.

The sand-man is about. A playful remark
addressed to children who are tired and "sleepy-
eyed." *Cp.* DUSTMAN.

The sands are running out. Time is getting
short; there will be little opportunity for doing
what you have to do unless you take advantage
of *now*. Often used in reference to one who evidently has not much longer to live. The allusion
is to the hour-glass.

> Alas! dread lord, you see the case wherein I stand,
> and how little sand is left to run in my poor glass.—
> *Reynard the Fox,* iv.

To plough or **to number the sands.** To undertake an endless or impossible task.

> Alas! poor duke, the task he undertakes
> Is numbering sands and drinking oceans dry
> *Richard II,* ii, 2.

Sand-blind. Dim-sighted; not exactly blind,
but with eyes of very little use. *Sand-* is here a
corruption of the obsolete prefix *sam-,* meaning
"half." English used to have *sam- dead, sam-ripe,*
etc., and *sam-sodden* still survives in some dialects.
In the *Merchant of Venice* Launcelot Gobbo
connects it with *sand,* the gritty earth.

> This is my true-begotten father, who, being more
> than sand-blind, high-gravel blind, knows me not.—
> *Merchant of Venice,* ii, 2.

Sandabar or **Sindibad** (sănd' a bàr, sind' i
bad). Names given to a mediæval collection of
tales that are very much the same as those in
the Greek *Syntipas the Philosopher* and the
Arabic *Romance of the Seven Viziers* (known in
Western Europe as *The Seven Sages* (*Wise Masters*), and derived from the *Fables of Bidpai*
(*q.v.*). These names do not, in all probability,
stand for the author or compiler, but result
from Hebrew mistransliterations of the Arabic
equivalent of *Bidpai* or *Pilpay*.

Sandal. A man without sandals. A prodigal;
so called by the ancient Jews, because the seller
gave his sandals to the buyer as a ratification of
his bargain (*Ruth* iv, 7).

Sandemanians or **Glassites** (sănd è mān' i
ānz). A religious party expelled from the Church
of Scotland for maintaining that national
churches, being "kingdoms of this world," are
unlawful. Called *Glassites* from John Glas
(1695-1773), the founder (1728), and called
Sandemanians from Robert Sandeman (1718-71),

a disciple of his, who published a series of
letters on the subject in 1755. Members are
admitted by a "holy kiss," and abstain from all
animal food which has not been drained of
blood; they believe in the community of property, and hold weekly communions.

Sandwich. A piece of meat between two slices
of bread; so called from the fourth Earl of Sandwich (1718-92—the noted "Jemmy Twitcher"),
who passed whole days in gambling, bidding
the waiter bring him for refreshment a piece of
meat between two pieces of bread, which he ate
without stopping from play. This contrivance
was not first hit upon by the earl in the reign of
George III, for the Romans were very fond of
"sandwiches" called by them *offula*.

Sandwichman. A perambulating advertise-
ment-displayer, with an advertisement-board
before and behind.

Sang-de-bœuf (săng de berf) (Fr., bullock's
blood). The deep red with which ancient Chinese porcelain is often coloured.

Sang-froid (Fr., cold blood). Freedom from
excitement or agitation. One does a thing "with
perfect *sang-froid*" when one does it coolly and
collectedly, without unnecessary display.

> . . . cross-legg'd, with great sang-froid
> Among the scorching ruins he sat smoking
> Tobacco on a little carpet.
> BYRON: *Don Juan,* VIII, cxxi.

Sangrado, Dr. (săn gra' dō). A name often
applied to an ignorant or "fossilized" medical
practitioner, from the humbug in Le Sage's *Gil
Bias* (1715), a tall, meagre, pale man, of very
solemn appearance, who weighed every word he
uttered, and gave an emphasis to his sage dicta.
"His reasoning was geometrical, and his opinions angular." He prescribed warm water and
bleeding for every ailment, for his great theory
was that "It is a gross error to suppose that blood
is necessary for life."

Sanguine (săng' gwin) (Lat. *sanguis, san-
guinis,* blood). The term used in heraldry for
the deep red or purplish colour usually known
as *murrey* (from the mulberry). In engravings it
is indicated by lines of vert and purpure
crossed, that is, diagonals from left to right. This
is a word with a curious history. Its actual meaning is bloody, or of the colour of blood; hence it
came to be applied to one who was ruddy,
whose cheeks were red with good health and
well-being. From this it was easy to extend the
meaning to one who was full of vitality, vivacious, confident and hopeful.

Sanhedrin (săn' i drin) (Gr. *syn,* together;
hedra, a seat; *i.e.* a sitting together). The supreme

council of the ancient Jews, consisting of seventy priests and elders, and a president who, under the Romans, was the high priest. It took its rise soon after the exile from the municipal council of Jerusalem, and was in existence till about A.D. 425, when Theodosius the Younger forbade the Jews to build synagogues. All questions of the "Law" were dogmatically settled by the Sanhedrin, and those who refused obedience were excommunicated.

In Dryden's *Absalom and Achitophel* (*q.v.*), the *Sanhedrim* stands for the English Parliament.

> The Sanhedrim long time as chief he ruled,
> Their reason guided, and their passion cooled.

San Marino (săn mȧ rē′ nō). The smallest republic in the world. Surrounded by Italian territory it lies 12 m. SW. of Rimini, and consists of only 38 sq. miles. In 1631 the Pope formally acknowledged its independence which was recognized by Italy in 1862.

Sans. (Fr., without.)

Sans Culottes (Fr., without knee-breeches). A name given during the French Revolution to the extremists of the working-classes. Hence *Sansculottism*, the principles, etc., of "red republicans."

Sans peur et sans reproche (Fr., without fear and without reproach). Pierre du Terrail, Chevalier dé Bayard (1476-1524) was called *Le chevalier sans peur et sans reproche*.

Sans Souci (Fr.). Free and easy, void of care. It is the name given by him to the palace built by Frederick the Great near Potsdam (1747).

The Philosopher of Sans-Souci. Frederick the Great (1712, 1740-86).

Enfans Sans Souci. The mediæval French Tradesmen's company of actors, as opposed to the Lawyers', the "Basochians" (*q.v.*). It was organized in the reign of Charles VIII, for the performance of short comedies, in which public characters and the manners of the day were turned into ridicule; *Maitre Pathelin* (*see* MOUTONS), an immense favourite with the Parisians, was one of their pieces. The manager of the "Care-for-Nothings" (*sans souci*) was called "The Prince of Fools."

Santa Casa (Ital., the holy house). The reputed house in which the Virgin Mary lived at Nazareth, miraculously translated to Dalmatia, and finally to Italy. *See* LORETTO.

Santa Claus. A contraction of Santa Nikolaus (*i.e.* St. Nicolas), the patron saint in Germany of children. His feast-day is December 6th, and the vigil is still held in some places, but for the most part his name is now associated with Christmastide. The old custom used to be for someone, on December 5th, to assume the costume of a bishop and distribute small gifts to "good children." The present custom, introduced in England from Germany about 1840, is to put toys and other little presents into a stocking late on Christmas Eve, when the children are asleep, and when they wake on Christmas morn they find in the stocking at the bedside the gift sent by Santa Claus. *See* NICHOLAS.

Sappho (săf′ ō). The Greek poetess of Lesbos, known as "the Tenth Muse." She lived about 600 B.C., and is fabled to have thrown herself into the sea from the Leucadian promontory in consequence of her advances having been rejected by the beautiful youth Phaon.

Pope used the name in his *Moral Essays* (II) for Lady Mary Wortley Montagu (*cp.* ATOSSA). *See also* SAPHO, *above*.

Sapphics. A four-lined verse-form of classical lyric poetry, named after the Greek poetess Sappho, who employed it, the fourth line being an Adonic. There must be a cæsura at the fifth foot of each of the first three lines, which run thus:—

$$- \cup | - - | - \| \cup \cup | - \cup | - \cup$$

The Adonic is—

$$- \cup \cup | - \cup \; or \; - -$$

The first and third stanzas of the famous *Ode* of Horace, *Integer vitæ* (i, 22), may be translated thus, preserving the metre:—

> He of sound life, who ne'er with sinners wendeth,
> Needs no Moorish bow, such as malice bendeth,
> Nor with poisoned darts life from harm defendeth,
>   Fuscus believe me.
> Once I, unarmed, was in a forest roaming,
> Singing love lays; when i' the secret gloaming
> Rushed a huge wolf, which though in fury foaming,
>   Did not aggrieve me.
> E.C.B.

Probably the best example of Sapphics in English is Canning's *Needy Knife-grinder*.

Saracen (săr′ ȧ sen). Ducange derives the word from *Sarah* (Abraham's wife); Hottinger from the Arabic *saraca* (to steal); Forster from *sahra* (a desert); but probably it is the Arabic *sharakyoun* or *sharkeyn* (the eastern people), as opposed to Magharibe (the western people— *i.e.* of Morocco). In mediæval romance the term was applied to Moslems generally; but among the Romans it denoted any of the nomadic tribes that raided the Syrian borders of the Empire.

Saragossa (săr ȧ gos′ ȧ). **The Maid of Saragossa.** Augustina, a young Spanish girl (d. 1857) noted for her bravery in the defence of Saragossa against the French, 1808. She was only twenty-two when, her lover being shot, she mounted the battery in his place.

Saratoga Trunk (săr á tō' gà). A huge trunk, such as used to be taken by fashionable ladies to the watering place of that name in New York State.

Sarcenet. *See* SARSENET.

Sarcode. *See* PROTOPLASM.

Sarcophagus (sar kof' á gus) (Gr. *sarx*, flesh, *phagein*, to eat). A stone coffin; so called because it was made of stone which, according to Pliny, consumed the flesh in a few weeks. The stone was sometimes called *lapis Assius*, because it was found at Assos of Lycia.

Sardanapalus (sar dà năp' á lus). The Greek name of Asurbanipal (mentioned in *Ezra* iv, 10, as *Asenappar*), king of Assyria in the 7th century B.C. Byron, in his poetic drama of this name (1821), makes him a voluptuous tyrant whose effeminacy led Arbaces, the Mede, to conspire against him. Myrra, his favourite concubine, roused him to appear at the head of his armies. He won three successive battles, but was then defeated, and was induced by Myrra to place himself on a funeral pile. She set fire to it, and, jumping into the flames, perished with her master.

The name is applied to any luxurious, extravagant, self-willed tyrant.

Sardonic Smile, Laughter. A smile of contempt; bitter, mocking laughter; so used by Homer.

The Sardonic or Sàrdinian laugh. A laugh caused, it was supposed, by a plant growing in Sardinia, of which they who ate died laughing. — TRENCH: *Words*, lecture iv, p. 176.

The *Herba Sardonia* (so called from Sardis, in Asia Minor) is so arid that it produces a convulsive movement of the nerves of the face, resembling a painful grin.

'Tis envy's safest, surest rule
To hide her rage in ridicule;
The vulgar eye the best beguiles
When all her snakes are decked with smiles,
Sardonic smiles by rancour raised.
SWIFT: *Pheasant and Lark*.

Sardonyx (sar' don iks). A precious stone composed of white chalcedony alternating with layers of sard, which is an orange-brown variety of cornelian. Pliny says it is called *sard* from Sardis, in Asia Minor, where it is found, and *onyx*, the nail, because its colour resembles that of the skin under the nail (*Nat. Hist.* xxxvii, 6).

Sarsen Stones (sar' sen). The sandstone boulders of Wiltshire and Berkshire are so called. The early Christian Saxons used the word *Saresyn* (*i.e.* Saracen, *q.v.*) as a synonym of pagan or heathen, and as these stones were popularly associated with Druid worship, they were called *Saresyn* (or heathen) *stones*. Robert Ricart says of Duke Rollo, "He was a Saresyn come out of Denmark into France."

Sarsenet (sar' sen et). A very fine, soft, silk material, so called from its Saracenic or Oriental origin. The word is sometimes used adjectivally of soft and gentle speech.

SAS. Special Air Service. British volunteer troops raised in World War II to drop by parachute behind the enemy's lines in uniform (as distinct from spies or agents in civilian clothes) to damage specific targets or enemy communications in general. They were evolved from the Long Range Desert Patrol (*q.v.*).

Satan (sā' tàn), in Hebrew, means *adversary* or *enemy*.

To whom the Arch-enemy
(And hence in heaven called Satan).
MILTON: *Paradise Lost*, Bk. i, 81, 82.

In the Bible the term is usually applied to a human adversary or opposer, and only in three cases (*Zech.* iii, *Job* i, 2, and 1 *Chron.* xxi, 1) does it denote an evil spirit.

The name is often used of a person of whom one is expressing abhorrence. Thus, the Clown says to Malvolio —

Fie, thou dishonest Satan! I call thee by the most modest terms; for I am one of those gentle ones that will use the devil himself with courtesy. — *Twelfth Night*, iv, 2.

Satire (săt' īr). Scaliger's derivation of this word from satyr is untenable. It is from *satura* (full of variety), *satura lanx*, a hotchpotch or olla podrida. The term originally denoted a medley of hotchpotch in verse; now it is applied to compositions in verse or prose in which folly, vice, or individuals are held up to ridicule. *See* Dryden's Dedication prefixed to his *Satires*.

Saturday. The seventh day of the week; called by the Anglo-Saxons Sæter-dæg, after the Latin Saturni dies, the day of Saturn. *See* BLACK SATURDAY.

Saturn (săt' ùrn). A Roman deity, identified with the Greek Kronos (*time*) (*q.v.*). He devoured all his children except Jupiter (*air*), Neptune (*water*), and Pluto (*the grave*). These Time cannot consume. The reign of Saturn was celebrated by the poets as a "Golden Age." According to the old alchemists and astrologers, Saturn typified lead, and was a very evil planet to be born under. "The children of the sayd Saturne shall be great jangeleres and chyders . . . and they will never forgyve tyll they be revenged on theyr quarell." (*Compost of Ptholomeus*.)

Saturn's tree. An alchemist's name for the Tree of Diana, or Philosopher's Tree (*q.v.*).

Saturnalia. A time of unrestrained disorder and misrule. With the Romans it was the festival of Saturn, and was celebrated the 17th, 18th, and 19th of December. During its continuance no public business could be transacted, the law courts were closed, the schools kept holiday, no war could be commenced, and no malefactor punished. Under the empire the festival was extended to seven days.

Saturnian. Pertaining to Saturn; with reference to the "Golden Age," to the god's sluggishness, or to the baleful influence attributed to him by the astrologers.

Then rose the seed of Chaos and of Night
To blot out order and extinguish light.
Of dull and venal a new world to mould,
And bring Saturnian days of lead and gold.
POPE: *Dunciad*, iv, 13.

Lead to indicate dullness, and *gold* to indicate venality.

Saturnian verses. A rude metre in use among the Romans before the introduction of Greek metres. Also a peculiar metre, consisting of three iambics and a syllable over, joined to three trochees, as:—

The queen was in the par-lour . . .
The maids were in the garden . . .

The Fescennine and Saturnian were the same, for as they were called Saturnian from their ancientness, when Saturn reigned in Italy, they were called Fescennine from Fescennina [*sic*] where they were first practised.— DRYDEN: *Dedication of Juvenal*.

Satyr (săt' ir). One of a body of forest gods or demons who, in classical mythology, were the attendants of Bacchus. Like the fauns (*q.v.*) they are represented as having the legs and hind-quarters of a goat, budding horns, and goat-like ears, and they were very lascivious.

Hence, the term is applied to a brutish or lustful man; and the psychological condition among males characterized by excessive venereal desire is known as *satyriasis*.

Sauce means "salted food" (Lat. *salsus*), for giving a relish to meat, as pickled roots, herbs, and so on.

In familiar phrase it means "cheek," impertinence, the kind of remarks one may expect from a *saucebox*—an impudent youngster.

Saucy. Cheeky, impertinent (*see* SAUCE); *also* rakish, irresistible, that care-for-nobody, jaunty, daring behaviour which has won for many of our regiments and ships the term as a compliment.

How many saucy airs we meet,
From Temple Bar to Aldgate Street!
GAY: *The Barley-Mow and Dunghill*.

In Scotland the adjective is applied to one who is fastidious or dainty in eating.

Saucer. Originally a dish for holding sauce, the Roman *salsarium*.

Saucer eyes. Big, round, glaring eyes.

Yet when a child (bless me!) I thought
That thou a pair of horns had'st got,
With eyes like saucers staring.
PETER PINDAR: *Ode to the Devil*.

Flying Saucers. Alleged mysterious celestial phenomena resembling revolving, partially luminous discs that shoot across the sky at a high velocity and a great height. No feasible explanation has been put foward for these objects, nor has any really authenticated proof been given of their existence.

Saul, in Dryden's *Absalom and Achitophel*, is meant for Oliver Cromwell.

They who, when Saul was dead, without a blow
Made foolish Ishbosheth [Richard Cromwell] the crown forego.
Pt, i, 57, 58.

Sauria (saw' ri à). This is the name formerly applied to the order of reptiles which includes the lizards and snakes, but modern zoologists usually divide this order into lacertilia (lizards) and ophidia (snakes) leaving the term Sauria for certain extinct reptiles.

Sauve qui peut (sōv kē pèr) (Fr., save himself who can). One of the first uses of the phrase is by Boileau (1636-1711). The phrase thus became to mean a rout. Thackeray writes of "that general *sauve qui peut* among the Tory party."

Savanna. A Spanish word, deriving from the Carib, for the natural grass land in tropical countries. In Venezuela savannas are known as "llanos," as "campos" in Brazil, as "downs" in Australia, and as "park lands" in S. Africa.

Savannah was the first ship fitted with steam power to cross the Atlantic. She was built at Savannah, Georgia. Actually the greater part of the voyage to Liverpool, which took place in 1819, was done under sail; she crossed the Atlantic in 25 days.

Save. To save appearances. To do something to obviate or prevent exposure or embarrassment.

Savoir-faire (săv' wa fâr) (Fr.). Ready wit; skill in getting out of a scrape; hence *Vivre de son savoir-faire*, to live by one's wits.

Savoy, The. A precinct off the Strand, London, noted for the palace built there by Peter of Savoy, who came to England about 1245 to visit his niece Eleanor, wife of Henry III. At his death the palace became the property of the queen, who gave it to her second son, Edmund Lancaster, whence it was attached to the Duchy of Lancaster. When the Black Prince brought Jean le Bon, King of France, captive to London (1356), he lodged him in the

Savoy Palace, and there he died in 1364. The rebels under Wat Tyler burnt down the old palace in 1381; but it was rebuilt in 1505 by Henry VII, and converted into a hospital for the poor, under the name of St. John's Hospital, which was used by Charles II for wounded soldiers and sailors.

Here, in 1552, was established the first flint-glass manufactory in England.

The Chapel Royal of the Savoy (first made a Chapel Royal by George III in 1773) was built about 1510 on the ruins of John of Gaunt's earlier chapel. This, largely rebuilt, is the only one of the old buildings remaining, the rest of the site being occupied by the Savoy Hotel and Savoy Theatre.

In **Savoy Hill** were the first studios of the British Broadcasting Company, with the designation of 2LO. It was opened in 1922 and remained headquarters after the Company had become the British Broadcasting Corporation, until 1932.

Savoy Operas. The comic operas with words by W. S. Gilbert (1836-1911) and music by Arthur Sullivan (1842-1900), produced by R. D'Oyly Carte. Nearly all of them first appeared at the Savoy Theatre, which Carte built specially for these productions. The players performing in the operas were known as "Savoyards." The Gilbert and Sullivan operas are the following:—

Thespis, 1871, at the Royalty.
Trial by Jury, 1872, at the Royalty.
The Sorcerer, 1877, Opera Comique.
H.M.S. Pinafore, 1878, Opera Comique.
The Pirates of Penzance, 1880, Opera Comique.
Patience, 1881, Opera Comique, then transferred to the Savoy, where all the following appeared.
Iolanthe, 1882.
Princess Ida, 1884.
The Mikado, 1885.
Ruddigore, 1887.
The Yeomen of the Guard, 1888.
The Gondoliers, 1889.
Utopia Limited, 1893.
The Grand Duke, 1896.

Saw. In Christian art an attribute of St. Simon and St. James the Less, in allusion to the tradition of their being sawn to death in martyrdom.

Sawny or **Sandy.** A Scotchman; a contraction of "Alexander."

Saxifrage (săks' i frāj). A member of a genus of small plants (*Saxifraga*) probably so called because they grow in the clefts of rocks (Lat.

saxum, a rock, *frangere*, to break). Pliny, and later writers following him, held that the name was due to the supposed fact that the plant had a medicinal value in the breaking up and dispersal of stone in the bladder.

Saxons. A Teutonic people who ravaged the coasts of the North Sea and the English Channel at the end of the 3rd century and settled in districts of south-eastern England. Essex, Sussex, Middlesex, and Wessex are names that commemorate their colonization.

Saxon Characteristics (architectural).

(1) The quoining consists of a long stone set at the corner, and a short one lying on it and bonding into the wall.

(2) The use of large heavy blocks of stone in some parts, while the rest is built of Roman bricks.

(3) An arch with straight sides to the upper part instead of curves.

(4) The absence of buttresses.

(5) The use in windows of rude balusters.

(6) A rude round staircase west of the tower, for the purpose of access to the upper floors.

(7) Rude carvings in imitation of Roman work. (Rickman.)

Saxon Shore. The coast of Norfolk, Suffolk, Essex, Kent, Sussex, and Hampshire, where were castles and garrisons, under the charge of a count or military officer, called *Comes Littoris Saxonici per Britanniam*.

Branodunum (Barncaster) was on the Norfolk coast.
Gariannonum (Burgh) was on the Suffolk coast
Othona (Ithanchester) was on the Essex coast.
Regulbium (Reculver), Rutupiæ; (Richborough), Dubris (Dover), P. Lemanis (Lyme), were on the Kentish coast.
Anderida (Hastings or Pevensey), Portus Adurni (Worthing), were on the Sussex coast.

Say. To take the say. To taste meat or wine before it is presented, in order to prove that it is not poisoned. *Say* is short for *assay*, a test; the phrase was common in the reign of Queen Elizabeth I.

Sbirri (sbir' ē) (Ital. sing, *sbirro*). The Italian police, especially the force which existed in the Papal States. They were notorious as spies, informers, and agents provocateurs.

Scales. From time immemorial the scales have been one of the principal attributes of Justice, it being impossible to out-weigh even a little Right with any quantity of Wrong.

. . . first the right he put into one scale,
And then the Giant strove with puissance strong
To fill the other scale with so much wrong.
But all the wrongs that he therein could lay,
Might not it peise.
SPENSER: *Faerie Queene*, V, ii, 46.

Call these foul offenders to their answers;
And poise the cause in justice' equal scales,
Whose beam stands sure, whose rightful cause prevails.
2 Henry VI, ii, 1.

According to the Koran, at the Judgment Day everyone will be weighed in the scales of the archangel Gabriel. The good deeds will be put in the scale called "Light," and the evil ones in the scale called "Darkness"; after which they will have to cross the bridge Al Sīrát, not wider than the edge of a scimitar. The faithful will pass over in safety, but the rest will fall into the dreary realms of Jehennam.

Scallawag or **Scalawag.** A scamp or rascal. The term was originally applied in the American Civil War to a Southerner who aided the Federals.

Scallop Shell. The emblem of St. James of Compostella (and hence of pilgrims to his shrine), adopted, says Erasmus, because the shore of the adjacent sea abounds in them. Pilgrims used them for cup, spoon, and dish. On returning home, the pilgrim placed his scallop shell in his hat to command admiration, and adopted it in his coat-armour.

I will give thee a palmer's staff of ivory and a scallop-shell of beaten gold.—PEELE: *Old Wives' Tale* (1590).

Scalp Lock. A long lock of hair allowed to grow on the scalp by the men of certain North American Indian tribes as a challenge to their scalp-hunting enemies.

Scambling Days. *See* SKIMBLE-SKAMBLE.

Scammozzi's Rule (skà mot' ziz). The jointed two-foot rule used by builders, and said to have been invented by Vincenzio Scammozzi (1552-1616), the famous Italian architect.

Scamp. A deserter "from the field," *ex campo*; one who *decamps* without paying his debts.

Scandal (Gr. *skandalon*) means properly a pitfall or snare laid for an enemy; hence a stumbling-block, and morally an aspersion.

In *Matt.* xiii, 41-2, we are told that the angels shall gather "all things that offend . . . and shall cast them into a furnace"; here the Greek word is *skandalon*, and *scandals* is given as an alternative in the margin; the Revised version renders the word "all things that cause stumbling." *Cp. also* 1 *Cor.* i, 23.

Scapegoat. Part of the ancient ritual among the Hebrews for the Day of Atonement laid down by Mosaic law (*see Lev.* xvi) was as follows: Two goats were brought to the altar of the tabernacle and the high priest cast lots, one for the Lord, and the other for Azazel (*q.v.*). The Lord's goat was sacrificed, the other was the *scapegoat*; and the high priest having, by confession, transferred his own sins and the sins of the people to it, it was taken to the wilderness and suffered to escape.

Similar rites are not uncommon among primitive peoples. The aborigines of Borneo, for instance, annually launch a small boat laden with all the sins and misfortunes of the nation, which they imagine will fall on the crew that first meets with it.

Scaphism (skā' fizm) (Gr. *skaphe*, anything scooped out). A mode of torture formerly practised in Persia. The victim was enclosed in the hollowed trunk of a tree, the head, hands, and legs projecting. These were anointed with honey to invite the wasps. In this situation the sufferer must linger in the burning sun for several days.

Scapin (ska' pin). The knavish and intriguing valet, who makes his master his tool, in Molière's *Les Fourberies de Scapin*, 1671.

Scapular. A garment made of two strips of cloth put on over the head so that one falls in front and one behind. It is usually the width of the shoulders and reaches to the ankles; it originated in the working frock of the Benedictines— a sort of overall—but it is now regarded as the distinctively monastic part of many religious habits. Another form of scapular is worn by lay people of various R.C. confraternities. It consists of two pieces of cloth about 3 in. by 2 in., joined by strings and worn back and front next the skin.

Scarab (scă' ráb). An ancient gem in the form of a dung-beetle, especially *Scarabaeus sacer*. It originated in pre-dynastic Egypt as an amulet, being made of polished or glazed stone, metal, or glazed faience, and was perforated lengthwise for suspension. By the XIIth Dynasty scarabs became used as seals, worn as pendants or mounted as signet rings.

Scaramouch (skăr' à mouch). The English form of Ital. *Scaramuccia* (through Fr. *Scaramouche*) a stock character in Old Italian farce, introduced into England soon after 1670. He was a braggart and fool, very valiant in words, but a poltroon, and was usually dressed in a black Spanish costume caricaturing the dons. The Neapolitan actor, Tiberio Fiurelli (1608-94), was surnamed *Scaramouch Fiurelli*. He came to England in 1673, and astonished John Bull with feats of agility.

Stout Scaramoucha with rash lance rode in,
And ran a tilt with centaur Arlequin.
DRYDEN: *Epilogue to The Silent Woman*.

Scarborough Warning. Blow first, warning after. In Scarborough robbers used to be dealt with in a very summary manner by a sort of Halifax gibbet-law, lynch-law, or an *à la lanterne*. Another origin is given of this phrase: It is said that Thomas Stafford, in 1557, seized the castle of Scarborough, not only without warning, but even before the townsfolk knew he was afoot.

This term *Scarborrow warning*, grew, some say,
By hasty hanging for rank robbery there.
Who that was met but suspect in that way,
Straight he was trust up, whatever he were.
J. HEYWOOD.

Scarlet. The colour of certain official costumes, as those of judges and cardinals; hence, sometimes applied to these dignitaries. The scarlet coat worn by foxhunters is not technically *scarlet*, but *pink* (*see* PINK).

Scarlet Letter. In the rigid Puritan regime of New England in the early days a scarlet "A," for "adulteress" used to be branded or sewn on a guilty woman's dress. The theme of Hawthorne's novel of this name (1850) is based on this custom.

Scarlet Pimpernel. An elusive intriguer. The phrase comes from the nickname of the hero of several novels by Baroness Orczy. In 1905 *The Scarlet Pimpernel* told the adventures of a royalist partizan in the French Revolution, who took the pimpernel as his emblem when he saved victims from the guillotine, and played other tricks on the Sansculottes.

Scarlet, Will. One of the companions of Robin Hood (*q.v.*).

The Scarlet Woman, or **Scarlet Whore.** The woman seen by St. John in his vision "arrayed in purple and scarlet colour," sitting "upon a scarlet coloured beast, full of names of blasphemy, having seven heads and ten horns," "drunken with the blood of the saints, and with the blood of the martyrs," upon whose forehead was written "MYSTERY, BABYLON THE GREAT, THE MOTHER OF HARLOTS AND ABOMINATIONS OF THE EARTH" (*Rev.* xvii, 1-6).

St. John was probably referring to Rome, which, at the time he was writing, was "drunken with the blood of the saints"; some controversial Protestants have applied the words to the Church of Rome, and some Roman Catholics to the Protestant churches generally.

Scat Singing. In jazz a form of singing without words, using the voice as a musical instrument. Said to have been started by Louis Armstrong in the 1920s when he forgot the words or dropped the paper on which they were written while singing a number; Jelly Roll Morton, on the other hand, claims to have sung scat as early as 1906.

Scent. We are not yet on the right scent. We have not yet got the right clue. The allusion is to dogs following game by the scent.

Sceptic (skep' tik) literally means one who thinks for himself, and does not receive on another's testimony (from Gr. *skeptesthai*, to examine). Pyrrho founded the philosophic sect called "Sceptics," and Epictetus combated their dogmas. In theology we apply the word to those who do not accept revelation.

Sceptre (sep' ter) (Gr., a staff). The gold and jewelled wand carried by a sovereign as emblem of royalty; hence, royal authority and dignity.

This hand was made to handle nought but gold:
I cannot give due action to my words,
Except a sword, or sceptre balance it.
A sceptre shall it have, have I a soul,
On which I'll toss the flower-de-luce of France.
2 Henry VI, v, 1.

The sceptre of the kings and emperors of Rome was of ivory, bound with gold and surmounted by a golden eagle; the British sceptre is of richly jewelled gold, and bears immediately beneath the cross and ball the great Cullinan diamond (*q.v.*).

Homer says that Agamemnon's sceptre was made by Vulcan, who gave it to the son of Saturn. It passed successively to Jupiter, Mercury, Pelops, Atreus, and Thyestes till it came to Agamemnon. It was looked on with great reverence, and several miracles were attributed to it.

Scheherazade (she hēr' a zād). The mouthpiece of the tales related in the *Arabian Nights* (*q.v.*), daughter of the grand vizier of the Indies. The Sultan Schahriah, having discovered the infidelity of his sultana, resolved to have a fresh wife every night and have her strangled at daybreak. Scheherazade entreated to become his wife, and so amused him with tales for a thousand and one nights that he revoked his cruel decree, bestowed his affection on her, and called her "the liberator of the sex."

Schism, The Great. The term is usually applied to the ecclesiastical dispute which rent Europe into two parties in the 14th century. Three months after the election of Urban VI, in 1378, the fifteen electing cardinals declared that the election was invalid because it had been made under fear of violence from the Roman mob. Urban retorted by naming twenty-eight new cardinals; the others at once proceeded to elect a new pope, Clement VII, who went to reside at Avignon. Spain, Naples, France, Provence and Scotland adhered to Clement; England, Germany, Scandinavia, Flanders and Hungary stood by Urban. The Church was torn from top to bottom by the schism, both sides being in good faith and no one knowing to whom allegiance was due. This confusion lasted until 1417, when Martin V was elected at the Council of Constance.

Scholasticism. The philosophy and doctrines of the "Schoolmen" (*q.v.*) of the Middle Ages (9th to 16th cents.) which were based on the logical works of Aristotle and the teachings of the Christian Fathers. It was an attempt to give a rational basis to Christianity, but the methods of the Scholastics degenerated into mere verbal subtleties, academic disputations, and quibblings, till, at the time of the Renaissance, the remnants were only fit to be swept away before the current of new learning that broke upon the world. *Cp.* DIALECTICS.

Schoolmaster. The schoolmaster is abroad. Education is spreading—and it will bear fruit. Lord Brougham said, in a speech (1828) on the general diffusion of education, and of intelligence arising therefrom, "Let the soldier be abroad, if he will; he can do nothing in this age. There is another personage abroad . . . the schoolmaster is abroad; and I trust to him, armed with his primer, against the soldier in full military array."

Schoolmistress, The. A quietly humorous poem in the Spenserian stanza by Shenstone (1742). The character is designed for a "portrait of Sarah Lloyd," the dame who first taught the poet himself.

Schooner (skoo′ ner). In the U.S.A., a large glass or mug for beer. Sometimes also called a "prairie schooner."

Prairie schooner was the name given to the large covered wagon in which American pioneer settlers moved west across the prairies in the mid-19th century.

Science. Literally "knowledge," the Lat. *scientia* from the pres. part, of *scire*, to know. The old, wide meaning of the word is shown in this from Shakespeare:—

> Plutus himself,
> That knows the tinct and multiplying medicine,
> Hath not in nature's mystery more science
> Than I have in this ring.
> *All's Well*, v, 3.

The Dismal Science. Economics; a name given to it by Carlyle:—

The social science—not a "gay science," but a rueful—which finds the secret of this Universe in "supply and demand" . . . what we might call, by way of eminence, the dismal science.—CARLYLE: *On the Nigger Question* (1849).

The Noble Science. Boxing, or fencing; the "noble art of self-defence."

The Seven Sciences. A mediæval term for the whole group of studies, viz. Grammar,

Logic, and Rhetoric (the *Trivium*), with Arithmetic, Music, Geometry, and Astronomy (the *Quadrivium*).

Science Persecuted. Anaxagoras of Clazomenæ (d. about 430 B.C.) held opinions in natural science so far in advance of his age that he was accused of impiety, thrown into prison, and condemned to death. Pericles, with great difficulty, got his sentence commuted to fine and banishment.

Galileo (1564-1642) was imprisoned by the Inquisition for maintaining that the earth moved. To get his liberty he abjured the heresy, but as he went his way is said, on very flimsy authority, to have whispered, "*E pur si muove*" (but nevertheless it does move).

Roger Bacon (1214-94) was excommunicated and imprisoned for diabolical knowledge, chiefly on account of his chemical researches. Dr. Dee (*q.v.*) and Robert Grosseteste (d. 1253), Bishop of Lincoln, were treated in much the same way. Of the latter it is said that as he was accused of dealings in the black arts the Pope sent a letter to the King of England ordering that his bones should be disinterred and burnt to powder.

Averroes, the Arabian philosopher, who flourished in the 12th century, was denounced as a heretic and degraded solely on account of his great eminence in natural philosophy and medicine.

Andrew Crosse (1784-1855), the electrician, was accused of impiety and shunned as a "profane man" who wanted, to arrogate to himself the creative power of God, because he asserted that he had seen certain animals of the genus *Acarus*, which had been developed by him out of inorganic matter.

Scio's Blind Old Bard (sī′ ō). Homer. Scio is the modern name of Chios, in the Ægean Sea one of the "seven cities" that claimed the honour of being his birthplace.

Smyrna, Chios, Colophon, Salamis, Rhodos, Argos, Athenæ,
Your just right to call Homer your son you must settle between ye.

Scire facias (sī′ re fā′ si ás) (Lat., make him to know). A judicial writ enforcing the execution or the annulment of judgments, etc.; so called from its opening words. These writs were formerly the common procedure, but they are now rarely issued except for the revocation of royal charters.

Sciron (sī′ ron). A robber of Greek legend, slain by Theseus. He infested the parts about Megara, and forced travellers over the rocks into the sea, where they were devoured by a sea monster.

Scissors. The Latin *cisorium*, from *cædere*, to cut. In English the word was for centuries spelt without the *c*; the *sc-* spelling appeared in the 16th century, and seems to be due to confusion with Lat. *scissor*, the noun from *scindere*, to split or rend. *Scythe*, formerly *sithe*, has suffered in the same way.

In Johnson's Dictionary the word is entered in the singular; but the singular form has never been in common use, except in compounds such as *scissor-blade, scissor-tooth*, etc. (*cp. billiard-ball* from *billiards, trouser-button* from *trousers*, etc.).

Sconce (skons). A word with several meanings:—a wall bracket for holding one or more candles or lights; the small, detached fortified earthwork or fort; the head.

Scone (skōn). A parish about 2 miles north of Perth, the site of the castle where the ancient Scottish kings were crowned. It was from here that Edward I, in 1296, brought the great coronation stone on which the kings of Scotland used to be crowned, and which, ever since, has formed part of the Throne ("Edward the Confessor's Chair") in Westminster Abbey which British monarchs occupy at their coronation. It was stolen at Christmas, 1950, but was restored some months later and replaced in the Confessor's Chair in February, 1952.

More than one fable has attached itself to this stone. The monks gave out that it was the very "pillow" on which Jacob rested his head when he had the vision of angels ascending and descending between heaven and earth (*Gen.* xxviii, 11); and it was also said to be the original "Lia-faill" or "Tanist Stone" (*q.v.*), brought from Ireland by Fergus, son of Eric, who led the Dalriads to Argyleshire, and removed thence by King Kenneth (in the 9th cent.) to Scone.

Scorched Earth. A phrase coined to describe the Chinese policy (as old as war) of retreating before the Japanese and burning the countryside as they went, in the war which began in 1937. It was a phrase much used in World War II.

Score. Twenty; a reckoning; to make a reckoning; so called from the custom of marking off "runs" or "lengths," in games by the score feet.

To pay off old scores. To settle accounts; used sometimes of money debts, but usually in the sense of revenging an injury, "getting even" with one.

Scorpio, Scorpion (skôr' pi ō). Scorpio is the eighth sign of the zodiac, which the sun

enters about October 24th. Orion had boasted to Diana and Latona that he would kill every animal on the earth. These goddesses sent a scorpion which stung Orion to death. Jupiter later raised the scorpion to heaven.

Fable has it that scorpions—like the toad—carry with them an oil which is a remedy against their stings.

'Tis true, a scorpion's oil is said
To cure the wounds the venom made,
And weapons dressed with salve restore
And heal the hurts they gave before.
BUTLER: *Hudibras*, iii, 2.

This oil was extracted from the flesh and given to the sufferer as a medicine; it was also supposed to be "very useful to bring away the descending stone of the kidneys" (Boyle, 1663).

Another mediæval belief was that if a scorpion were surrounded by a circle of fire it would commit suicide by stinging itself with its own tail, Byron, in the *Giaour*, extracts a simile from the legend—

The mind that broods o'er guilty woes
Is like the Scorpion girt by fire; . . .
One sad and sole relief she knows,
The sting she nourish'd for her foes,
Whose venom never yet was vain
Gives but one pang, and cures all pain.

Scot. Payment, reckoning. The same word as shot (*q.v.*); we still speak of *paying one's shot*.

Scot and lot. A municipal levy on all according to their ability to pay. *Scot* is the tax, and *lot* the allotment or portion allotted. *To pay scot and lot*, therefore, is to pay the general assessment and also the personal tax allotted to you. The word comes from the Old Norse *skot*, a contribution, and it has no connexion with the Early Anglo-Saxon coin a *skeat*, for which *see* CHURCH SCOT.

To go scot-free. To be let off payment; to escape punishment or reprimand, etc.

Scotch, Scots, Scottish. These three adjectives all mean the same thing—belonging to, native of, or characteristic of, Scotland, but their application varies, and of late years their use has become something of a shibboleth.

Scotch. To make a scotch, *i.e.* a score or incision in, originally; but now the verb usually means to wound so that temporary disablement is caused, or to stamp out altogether. This application of the word arises from *Macbeth*, iii, 2, where Macbeth is made to say "We have scotch'd the snake, not killed it." *Macbeth* was not printed in Shakespeare's lifetime, and in the Folios the word appears as *scorch'd*; Theobald is responsible for the emendation (1726).

Out of all scotch and notch. Beyond all bounds; *scotch* was the line marked upon the ground in certain games, as **Hopscotch.**

The word *scotch* is also applied to a wedge placed before or behind a wheel, etc., to prevent its rolling.

Scotists (skō' tists). Followers of the 13th-century scholastic philosopher, Duns Scotus, who maintained the doctrine of the Immaculate Conception in opposition to Thomas Aquinas.

Scotland. St. Andrew is the patron saint of this country, and tradition says that his remains were brought by Regulus, a Greek monk, to the coast of Fife in 368.

The old royal arms of Scotland were:—Or, a lion rampant gules, armed and langued azure, within a double tressure flory-counter-flory of fleurs-de-lys of the second (this was quartered with the royal arms of the United Kingdom in 1603). *Supporters.* Two unicorns argent, imperially crowned, armed, crined, and unguled or, gorged with open crowns, with chains affixed thereto, and reflexed over the back, of the last. *Crest.* Upon the imperial crown proper, a lion sejant affrontée gules, crowned or, holding in the dexter paw, a sword and in the sinister a sceptre, both proper. *Mottoes,* "Nemo me impune lacessit" (*q.v.*), and, over the crest, "In Defence."

In Scotland now the royal arms of Great Britain are used with certain alterations; the lion supporter is replaced by another unicorn (crowned), the Scottish crest takes the place of the English, and the collar of the Thistle encircles that of the Garter.

Scotland a fief of England. Edward I founded his claim to the lordship of Scotland on four grounds, viz.—(1) the statement of certain ancient chroniclers that Scottish kings had occasionally paid homage to English sovereigns from time immemorial. (2) From charters of Scottish kings: as those of Edgar, son of Malcolm, William, and his son Alexander II. (3) From papal rescripts; as those of Honorius III, Gregory IX, and Clement IV. (4) From a passage in *The Life and Miracles of St. John of Beverley* (see Rymer's *Fœdera* I, Pt. ii, p. 771), which relates how a miracle was performed in the reign of Athelstan, King of the West Saxons and Mercians, 925-940. The king was repelling a band of marauding Scots and had reached the Tyne when he found that they had retreated. At midnight the spirit of St. John of Beverley appeared to him and bade him cross the river at daybreak, for he "should discomfit the foe:" Athelstan obeyed, and reduced the whole

kingdom to subjection. On reaching Dunbar on his return march, he prayed that some sign might be vouchsafed to him to satisfy all ages that "God, by the intercession of St. John, had given him the kingdom of Scotland." Then, striking the basaltic rocks with his sword, the blade sank into the solid flint "as if it had been butter," cleaving it asunder for "an ell or more," and the cleft remains to the present hour. This was taken as a sign from heaven that Athelstan was rightful lord of Scotland, and if Athelstan was, argued Edward, so was he, his successor.

Scotland Yard. The headquarters of the Metropolitan Police, whence all public orders to the force proceed. The original Scotland Yard, occupied by the Police from 1829-90, was a short street near Trafalgar Square, so called from a palace on the spot, given by King Edgar (about 970) to Kenneth II of Scotland when he came to London to pay homage, and subsequently used by the Scottish kings when visiting England. *New Scotland Yard,* as it is officially called, is on the Thames Embankment near Westminster Bridge.

Scotus, Duns. *See* DUNCE.

Scourers. *See* SCOWERERS.

Scourge. A whip or lash; commonly applied to diseases that carry off great numbers, as the scourge of influenza, the scourge of pneumonia, etc., and to persons who seem to be the instruments of divine punishment. Raleigh, for instance, was called the Scourge of Spain, and Spenser, in his *Sonnet upon Scanderbeg,* calls him "The scourge of Turkes and plague of infidels."

The Scourge of God (Lat. *flagellum Dei*). Attila (d. 453), king of the Huns, so called by mediæval writers because of the widespread havoc and destruction caused by his armies.

The Scourge of Homer. The carping critic, Zoilus. *See* ZOILISM.

The Scourge of Princes. Pietro Aretino (1492-1556), the Italian satirist.

Scout. This word comes from the old French *escoute,* a spy or eavesdropper, akin to the modern French *écouter,* to listen. It is now applied to a man, aeroplane, warship, etc., sent to observe the enemy's movements or obtain information of importance; some armies have organized bodies of Scouts. The word has other uses. In the early days of the game the fielders at cricket were called scouts; college servants at Oxford are still known by that name; it is often used for Boy Scouts (*q.v.*).

Scowerers. A set of rakes in the period about 1670 to 1720, who, with the Nickers and

Mohocks, committed great annoyances in London and other large towns.

> Who has not heard the Scowerers' midnight fame?
> Who has not trembled at the Mohocks' name?
> Was there a watchman took his hourly rounds,
> Safe from their blows and new-invented wounds?
> GUY: *Trivia*, iii.

Scrape. Bread and scrape. Bread and butter, with the butter spread very thin.

I've got into a bad scrape—an awkward predicament, an embarrassing difficulty. We use *rub*, *squeeze*, *pinch*, to express the same idea. Thus Shakespeare says, "Ay, there's the rub"; "I am come to a pinch" (difficulty).

To scrape along. To get along in the world with difficulty, finding it hard to "make both ends meet."

To scrape through. To pass an examination, etc., "by the skin of one's teeth," just to escape failure.

Scratch. There are two colloquial "sporting" uses of this word; a horse, or other entrant in a sporting event, is said to be *scratched* when its name is withdrawn (*scratched out*) from the list of competitors; the *scratch man* in a handicap is he who starts from *scratch*; *i.e.* the line marked out (originally *scratched*) to show the starting place.

A scratch crew, eleven, etc. A team got together anyhow; not the regular team.

A scratch race. A race of horses, men, boys, etc., without restrictions as to age, weight, previous winnings, etc., who all start from scratch.

Old Scratch. Old Nick; the devil. From *skratta*, an old Scandinavian word for a goblin or monster (modern Icelandic *skratti*, a devil).

Scratch cradle. Another form of "cat's cradle" (*q.v.*).

To come up to the scratch. To be ready when wanted; to fulfil expectations. In prizefighting a line was scratched on the ground, and the toe of the fighter must come up to the scratch.

Screw. Slang for wages, salary; probably because in some industry the weekly wage was handed out in a "screw of paper"; also a slang term for a prison warder.

An old screw. A miser who has amassed wealth by "putting on the screw" (*see below*), and who keeps his money tight, doling it out only in *screws*.

He has a screw loose. He is not quite *compos mentis*, he's a little mad. His mind is like a piece of machinery that needs adjusting—it won't work properly.

There's a screw loose somewhere. All is not right, there's something amiss. A figurative phrase from machinery, where one screw not tightened up may be the cause of a disaster.

His head is screwed on the right way. He is clear-headed and right-thinking; he knows what he's about.

To put on the screw. A phrase surviving from the days when the thumb screw was used as a form of torture to extract confessions or money. To press for payment, as a screw presses by gradually increasing pressure. Hence *to apply the screw*, *to give the screw another turn*, to take steps (or additional steps) to enforce one's demands.

To screw oneself up to it. To force oneself to face it, etc.; to get oneself into the right frame of mind for doing some unpleasant or difficult job.

Screw-ball. A colloquial American term for an erratic, eccentric, or unconventional person.

Scribe, in the New Testament, means a doctor of the law. Thus, in *Matt.* xxii, 35, we read, "Then one of them which was a *lawyer*, asked Him . . . Which is the great commandment of the law?" *Mark* (xii, 28) says, "One of the *scribes* came . . . and asked Him, 'Which is the first commandment of all?'" They were generally coupled with the Pharisees (*q.v.*) as being upholders of the ancient ceremonial tradition.

In the Old Testament the word is used more widely. Thus Seraiah is called the *scribe* (secretary) of David (2 *Sam.* viii, 17); "Shebna the scribe" (2 *Kings* xviii, 18) was secretary to Hezekiah; and Jonathan, Baruch, Gemariah, etc., who were princes, were called scribes. Ezra, however, called "a ready scribe in the law of Moses," accords with the New Testament usage of the word.

Scriblerus, Martinus (mar tī nùs skrib lēr' ùs). A merciless satire on the false taste in literature current in the time of Pope, for the most part written by Arbuthnot, and published in 1741. Cornelius Scriblerus, the father of Martin, was a pedant, who entertained all sorts of absurdities about the education of his son. Martin grew up a man of capacity; but though he had read everything, his judgment was vile and taste atrocious. Pope, Swift, and Arbuthnot founded a *Scriblerus Club* with the object of pillorying all literary incompetence.

Scrimmage. Originally, a *skirmish*, of which word this is a variant.

> Prince Ouffur at this skrymage, for all his pryde,
> Fled full and sought no guide.
> *MS. Lansdowne*, 200, f. 10.

Scrummage was another form of scrimmage; as *scrum* it still survives on the Rugby football field.

Scrimshaw (skrim' shaw). The term applied to the carved or scratched work on shells, ivory, etc., often in colours. This used to be done by sailors during the long sea voyages by sail. The word is sometimes used as a verb to describe the accomplishment of some intricate job neatly.

Scriptures, The, or **Holy Scripture** (Lat. *scriptura*, a writing). The Bible; hence applied allusively to the sacred writings of other creeds, as the Koran, *the Scripture* of the *Mohammedans*, the Vedas and Zendavesta, of the Hindus and Persians, etc.

Scripturists. Another name for the Caraites.

Scrounge. To purloin or annex something from nowhere particular or that has no obvious owner. A term much used in the army during World War I.

Scruple. The name of the weight (20 grains, or $\frac{1}{24}$ oz.), and the term for doubt or hesitation (as in a *scruple of conscience*), both come from Lat. *scrupulus*, meaning a sharp little pebble, such as will cause great uneasiness if it gets into one's shoe. The second is the figurative use; with the name of the little weight compare that of the big one—*stone*.

Scutage (skū' tij). In feudal times a payment in commutation of personal military service. To most knights and others liable to be summoned to follow the king to war it would be more convenient to pay the tax than set out on some distant expedition; at the same time the money they paid was of use to the king to enable him to employ more reliable troops. It was levied in varying rates between 1156 and 1385.

Scuttle. To scuttle a ship is to bore a hole in it in order to make it sink. The word is from the Old French *escoutilles*, hatches, and was first applied to a hole in a roof with a door or lid, then to a hatchway in the deck of a ship with a lid, then to a hole in the bottom of a ship.

Scuttle, for coals, is the A.S. *scutel*, a dish; from Lat. *scutella*, diminutive of *scutra*, a dish or platter. In auctioneers' jargon a coalscuttle is, quite unaccountably, called a perdonium.

To scuttle off, to make off hurriedly, was originally **To scuddle off,** scuddle being a frequentative of *scud*.

Scylla (sil' à). In Greek legend the name (1) of a daughter of King Nisus of Megara and (2) of a sea monster.

The daughter of Nisus promised to deliver Megara into the hands of her lover, Minos, and, to effect this, cut off a golden hair on her father's head, while he was asleep. Minos despised her for this treachery, and Scylla threw herself from a rock into the sea. At death she was changed into a lark, and Nisus into a hawk.

> Think of Scylla's fate.
> Changed to a bird, and sent to fly in air,
> She dearly pays for Nisus' injured hair.
>   POPE: *Rape of the Lock*, iii.

The sea monster dwelt on the rock Scylla, opposite Charybdis (*q.v.*), on the Italian side of the Straits of Messina. Homer says that she had twelve feet, and six heads, each on a long neck and each armed with three rows of pointed teeth, and that she barked like a dog. He makes her a daughter of Crataeis; but later accounts say that she was a nymph who, because she was beloved by Glaucus (*q.v.*), was changed by the jealous Circe into a hideous monster.

Scythian (sith' i àn). Pertaining to the peoples or region of Scythia, the ancient name of a great part of European and Asiatic Russia.

Scythian defiance. When Darius approached Scythia, an ambassador was sent to his tent with a bird, a frog, a mouse, and five arrows, then left without uttering a word. Darius, wondering what was meant, was told by Gobrias it meant this: Either fly away like a bird, hide your head in a hole like a mouse, or swim across the river, or in five days you will be laid prostrate by the Scythian arrows.

The Scythian or **Tartarian lamb.** The Russian barometz, the creeping root-stock and frondstalks of *Cibotium barometz*, a woolly fern, which, when inverted, was supposed to have some resemblance to a lamb. Mandeville in his *Travels* (ch. xxvi) gives a highly fanciful description of them.

Sea. Any large expanse of water, more or less enclosed; hence the expression "molten sea," meaning the great brazen vessel which stood in Solomon's temple (2 *Chron.* iv, 5, and 1 *Kings* vii, 26); even the Nile, the Euphrates, and the Tigris are sometimes called seas by the prophets. The world of water is the *Ocean*.

At sea, or **all at sea.** Wide of the mark; quite wrong; like a person in the open ocean without compass or chart.

The four seas. The seas surrounding Great Britain, on the north, south, east, and west.

The high seas. The open sea, the "main"; especially that part of the sea beyond "the three-mile limit," which forms a free highway to all nations.

The Old Man of the sea. A creature encountered by Sinbad the Sailor in his fifth voyage (*Arabian Nights*). This terrible Old Man got on Sinbad's back, and would neither dismount nor could be shaken off. At last Sinbad gave him some wine, which so intoxicated him that he relaxed his grip, and Sinbad made his escape. Hence the phrase is figuratively applied to bad habits, evil associates, etc., from which it is very difficult to free oneself.

The Seven Seas. *See* SEVEN.

Sea Deities. In classical myth, besides the fifty Nereids (*q.v.*), the Oceanides (daughters of Oceanus), the Sirens (*q.v.*), etc., there were a number of deities presiding over, or connected with, the sea. The chief of these are:—

Amphitrite, wife of Poseidon, queen goddess of the sea.

Glaucus, a fisherman of Bœotia, afterwards a marine deity.

Ino, who threw herself from a rock into the sea, and was made a sea-goddess.

Neptune, king of the ocean.

Nereus and his wife *Doris*. Their palace was at the bottom of the Mediterranean; his hair was sea-weed.

Oceanus and his wife *Tethys* (daughter of Uranus and Gē). Oceanus was god of the *Ocean*, which formed a boundary round the world.

Portumnus (Gr.; Lat. *Palemon*), the protector of harbours.

Poseidon, the Greek Neptune.

Proteus, who assumed every variety of shape.

Thetis, a daughter of Nereus and mother of Achilles.

Triton, son of Poseidon.

Sea-girt Isle, The. England. So called because, as Shakespeare has it, it is "hedged in with the main, that water-walled bulwark" (*King John*, ii, 1).

This precious stone set in the silver sea,
Which serves it in the office of a wall,
Or as a moat defensive to a house,
Against the envy of less happier lands.
Richard II, ii, 1.

Sea legs. He has got his sea legs. Is able to walk on deck when the ship is rolling; able to bear the motion of the ship without seasickness.

Sea serpent. A serpentine monster formerly supposed to inhabit the depths of the ocean. As stories of the "Great Sea Serpent" are usually received with incredulity, sailors are sometimes reluctant to report its appearance; but in spite of this there have been some circumstantial accounts and very vivid descriptions given by those who professed to have seen it. Pontoppidan in his *Natural History of Norway* (1755) speaks of sea serpents 600 ft. long.

See also LOCH NESS MONSTER.

Seabees. U.S. Naval Construction Battalions (C.B.s) in World War II. Their alleged motto was: "The difficult we do at once. The impossible takes a little longer."

Seal. The sire is called a *bull*, his females are *cows*, the offspring are called *pups*; the breeding-place is called a *rookery*, a group of young seals a *pod*, and a colony of seals a *herd*. The immature male is called a *bachelor*. A sealer is a seal-hunter, and seal-hunting is called sealing.

Sealed Orders. The term applied to orders delivered in a sealed package to naval or military commanders which they are not to read or consult before a certain time, or before reaching a certain locality, or except in certain specified conditions.

Seamy Side. The "wrong" or worst side; as the "seamy side of London," "the seamy side of life." In velvet, Brussels carpets, tapestry, etc., the "wrong" side shows the seams or threads of the pattern exhibited on the right side.

Seasons, The Four. Spring, Summer, Autumn, and Winter. *Spring* starts (officially) on March 21st, the Spring Equinox, when the sun enters Aries; *Summer* on June 22nd, the Summer Solstice, when the sun enters Cancer; *Autumn* on September 23rd, the Autumn Equinox, the sun entering Libra; and *Winter* on December 22nd, when the sun enters Capricornus.

The ancient Greeks characterized *Spring* by Mercury, *Summer* by Apollo, *Autumn* by Bacchus, and *Winter* by Hercules.

The London Season. The part of the year when the Court and fashionable society generally is in town—May, June, and July.

The silly season. *See* SILLY.

Season-ticket. A ticket giving the holder certain specified rights (in connexion with travelling, entrance to an exhibition, etc.) for a certain specified period.

Second. The next after the first (Lat. *secundus*). In duelling the *second* is the representative of the principal; he carries the challenge, selects the ground, sees that the weapons are in order, and is responsible for all the arrangements.

A second of time is so called because the division of the minute into sixtieths is the *second* of the sexagesimal operations, the first being the division of the hour into minutes.

One's second self. His *alter ego* (*q.v.*); one whose tastes, opinions, habits, etc., correspond so entirely with one's own that there is practically no distinction.

Second Adventists. Those who believe that the Second Coming of Christ (*cp.* 1 *Thess.* iv, 15) will precede the Millennium; hence sometimes also called *Premillenarians*.

Second-hand. Not new or original: what has already been the property of another, as, "second-hand" books, clothes, opinions, etc.

Second nature. Said of a habit, way of looking at things, and so on, that has become so ingrained in one that it is next to impossible to shake it off.

Second sight. The power of seeing things invisible to others; the power of foreseeing future events.

Second wind. *See* WIND.

Secondary colours. *See under* COLOURS (*Technical Terms*).

Secret. An open secret. A piece of information generally known, but not formally announced.

Un secret de polichinelle. No secret at all. A secret known to all the world; an open secret. Polichinelle is the Punch of the old French puppet-shows, and his secrets are "stage whispers" told to all the audience.

Entre nous, c'est qu'on appelle
Le secret de polichinelle.
                              La Mascotte, ii, 12.

Secret Service. A general unofficial term applied to the organization which exists in every country, in peace or war, for the collection of information about enemies, potential enemies and disaffected persons; also for counter-espionage. Such organizations have many ramifications, some quite public, others secret. In Great Britain the best known is MI5, a branch of Military Intelligence in the War Office. In France such matters come under the Deuxième Bureau.

Secular. From Lat. *sœcularis*, pertaining to the *sœculum*, *i.e.* the age of generation; hence, pertaining to this world in contradistinction to the next.

Secularism. The name given about 1851 by George Jacob Holyoake (1807-1906) to an ethical system founded on natural morality, and opposed to the tenets of revealed religion and ecclesiasticism.

Secular clergy. The Roman Catholic parish clergy who live in daily contact with the world, in contradistinction to monks, etc., who live in monasteries. Hierarchically they take precedence of regular clergy, and bishops are usually chosen from seculars.

Secular games. In ancient Rome the public games lasting three days and three nights that took place only once in an age (*sœculum*), or period of 100 years.

They were instituted in obedience to the Sibylline verses, with the promise that "the empire should remain in safety so long as this admonition was observed," and while the kings reigned were held in the Campus Martius, in honour of Pluto and Proserpine,

Date, quæ precamur
    Tempore sacro
Quo Sibyllini monuere versus.
                    HORACE: *Carmen Seculare*, A.U.C., 737.

Sedulous. To play the sedulous ape to. To study the style of another, and model one's own on his as faithfully and meticulously as possible: said, usually with more or less contempt, of literary men. The phrase is taken from R. L. Stevenson, who, in his essay, A *College Magazine* (*Memories and Portraits*), said that he had—

played the sedulous ape to Hazlitt, to Lamb, to Wordsworth, to Sir Thomas Browne, to Defoe, to Hawthorne, to Montaigne, to Baudelaire, and to Obermann. . . . That, like it or not, is the way to learn to write.

See. The seat or throne of a bishop (Lat. *sedes*, a seat). The term is applied to the place where the bishop's cathedral is located and from which he takes his title; and so is to be distinguished from *diocese*, the territory over which he has jurisdiction.

The Holy See. The Papacy, the papal jurisdiction and court.

Seel. To close the eyelids of a hawk by running a thread through them; to hoodwink. (Fr., *ciller, cil*, the eyelash).

She that so young could give out such a seeming,
To seel her father's eyes up, close as oak.
                                Othello, iii, 3.

Seian Horse, The (sī' ản). A possession which invariably brought ill luck with it. Hence the Latin proverb *Ille homo habet equum Seianum*. Cneius Seius had an Argive horse, of the breed of Diomed, of a bay colour and surpassing beauty, but it was fatal to its possessor. Seius was put to death by Mark Antony. Its next owner, Cornelius Dolabella, who bought it for 100,000 sesterces, was killed in Syria during the civil wars. Caius Cassius, who next took possession of it, perished after the battle of Philippi by the very sword which stabbed Cæsar. Antony had the horse next, and after the battle of Actium slew himself.

Like the gold of Tolosa and Hermione's necklace, the Seian or Sejan horse was a fatal possession.

Selah (sā' la). A Hebrew word occurring often in the *Psalms* (and three times in *Habakkuk* iii), indicating some musical or liturgical direction, such as a pause, a repetition, or the end of a section.

Select Man. In some of the New England States a member of a board of town officers who has been deputed to be responsible for the conduct of certain branches of local administration.

Selene (se lē' nē). The moon goddess of Greek mythology, daughter of Hyperion and Thea, and roughly corresponding to the Roman Diana (*q.v.*), the chaste huntress. Selene had fifty daughters by Endymion, and several by Zeus, one of whom was called "The Dew." Diana is represented with bow and arrow running after the stag; but Selene in a chariot drawn by two white horses, with wings on her shoulders, and a sceptre in her hand.

Self. Used in combination for a variety of purposes, such as (1) to express direct or indirect reflexive action, as in *self-command*; (2) action performed independently, or without external agency, as in *self-acting, self-fertilization*; (3) action or relation to the self, as in *self-conscious, self-suspicious*; (4) uniformity, naturalness, etc., as in *self-coloured, self-glazed*.

A self-made man. One who has risen from poverty and obscurity to opulence and a position of importance by his own efforts. The phrase was originally American.

Self-determination. The theory in political economy, that every nation, no matter how small or weak, has the right to decide upon its own form of government and to manage its own internal affairs. The phrase acquired its present significance during the attempts to resettle Europe after World War I; but difficulties arose (as in the case of Ireland) when it was discovered that an exact and comprehensive definition of the word *Nation* could not be agreed upon.

Seljuks (sel'jùks). A Perso-Turkish dynasty of eleven emperors over a large part of Asia, which lasted 138 years (1056-1194). It was founded by Togrul Beg, a descendant of Seljuk, chief of a small tribe which gained possession of Bokara.

Selkirk, Alexander, was probably the original of Robinson Crusoe. Born in 1676, the son of a Fifeshire shoemaker, he joined Dampier's expedition to the South Seas in 1703 and when off the island of Juan Fernandez asked to be set ashore in consequence of a quarrel with the captain. He remained on the island for 52 months and was eventually picked up by Captain Woodes Rogers, whose *Cruising Voyage Round the World*, in which he tells of Selkirk, is supposed to have given Defoe the idea of Robinson Crusoe. Selkirk died at sea, as mate of the *Weymouth*, in 1721.

Sell. Slang for a swindle, a hoax, a first-of-April trick; and the person hoaxed is said to be *sold*.

Semantics (se mǎn' tiks). The technical term for the study of the meanings of words rather than of their origins and derivations. As time passes the meanings and implications of words change, often imperceptibly; it is with these changes that semantics deals.

Semele (sem'ele). In Greek mythology, the daughter of Cadmus and Harmonia. By Zeus she was the mother of Dionysus, and was slain by lightning when he granted her request to appear before her as the God of Thunder.

Seminary. A college exclusively devoted to the training of candidates for the R.C. priesthood. The usual course is six years—two of philosophy and four of theology. Seminary priests is an historical and legal term to distinguish English priests ordained abroad from those ordained in England before the accession of Queen Elizabeth I. The latter are often called Marian priests, and they were treated more leniently by the penal laws. After 1585 it was high treason for a seminary priest even to be in England.

Semi-precious stones. Gems suitable for jewellery and for ornamenting other sorts of goldsmith's work; but not sufficiently beautiful, durable or rare to be ranked with such precious stones as diamonds, emeralds, rubies, and sapphires. Examples of semi-precious stones are amethysts, cairngorms, cornelian, lapis-lazuli, moonstones, and onyx.

Semiramis (se mir' á mis). In the Babylonian mythology, the mother of Ninus who was King of Assyria and founded Nineveh. She waged war against the Medes and the Chaldeans (c. 800 B.C.). After her death she became a legendary figure, identified with the Goddess Ishtar and her doves.

Semiramis of the North, The. Margaret of Denmark, Sweden, and Norway (1353-1412), and Catherine II of Russia (1729-96) have both been so called.

Semitic (se mit' ic). Pertaining to the descendants of Shem (*see Gen.* x), viz. the Hebrews, Arabs, Assyrians, Aramæans, etc., nowadays applied to the Jews.

The Semitic languages are the ancient Assyrian and Chaldee, Aramaic, Syriac, Arabic, Hebrew, Samaritan, Ethiopic, and old Phœnician. The great characteristic of this family of languages is that the roots of words consist of three consonants.

Senatus consultum (sen a' tus kon sǔl' tum). A decree of the Senate of Ancient Rome. The term was sometimes applied to a decree of any senate, especially that of the First Empire in France.

Send, To. That sends me. Amateurs of jazz use this phrase, meaning: The music sends me out of myself, or into ecstasies.

Seneschal (sen' e shàl). The majordomo or steward of a great house in the Middle Ages. He had full authority over the retainers and servants, supervised all ceremonial affairs, administered justice in the name of his master, and was in every way a personage of considerable importance.

Se'nnight. A week; seven nights. *Fort'night*, fourteen nights. These words are relics of the ancient Celtic custom of beginning the day at sunset, a custom observed by the ancient Greeks, Babylonians, Persians, Syrians, and Jews, and by the modern representatives of these people. In *Gen.* i we find the evening precedes the morning; as, "The evening and the morning were the first day," etc.

Sense. Common sense. *See* COMMON.

Scared out of my seven senses. According to ancient teaching the soul of man, or his "inward holy body," is compounded of the seven properties which are under the influence of the seven planets. Fire animates, earth gives the sense of feeling, water gives speech, air gives taste, mist gives sight, flowers give hearing, the south wind gives smelling. Hence the seven senses are animation, feeling, speech, taste, sight, hearing, and smelling (*see Ecclus.* xvii, 5).

Sentences, Master of the. The Schoolman, Peter Lombard (d. 1160), an Italian theologian and bishop of Paris, author of *The Four Books of Sentences* (*Sententiarum libri* iv), a compilation from the Fathers of the leading arguments pro and con, bearing on the hair-splitting theological questions of the Middle Ages.

The mediæval graduates in theology, of the second order, whose duty it was to lecture on the *Sentences*, were called **Sententiatory Bachelors.**

Separation, The. The name given in the 17th century to the body of Independents and Protestant dissenters generally—called individually **Separatists.** Thus the Amsterdam parson, Tribulation Wholesome, says:

These chastisements are common to the saints,
And such rebukes, we of the Separation,
    Must bear with willing shoulders, as the trials
Sent forth to tempt our frailties.
            BEN JONSON: *The Alchemist*, iii, 2.

Sephardim (sef ar' dim). The Jews of Spain and Portugal, so called from *Sepharad*, a district mentioned in *Obad.* 20, which was supposed by the rabbinical commentators to be intended

for Spain. As Jews were evidently in captivity at Sepharad at the time the passage was written this cannot possibly be the correct interpretation.

September. The seventh month from March, where the year used to commence.

The old Dutch name was *Herst-maand* (autumn-month); the old Saxon, *Gerst-monath* (barley-monath), or *Hœfest-monath*; and after the introduction of Christianity *Halig-monath* (holy-month, the nativity of the Virgin Mary being on the 8th, the exaltation of the Cross on the 14th, Holy-Rood Day on the 26th and St. Michael's Day on the 29th). In the French Republican calendar, it was called *Fructidor* (fruit-month, August 18th to September 21st).

September Bible. *See* BIBLE, SPECIALLY NAMED.

September massacres. An indiscriminate slaughter, during the French Revolution, of loyalists confined in the Abbaye and other prisons, lasting from September 2nd to 5th, 1792. Danton gave the order after the capture of Verdun by the allied Prussian army; as many as 8,000 persons fell, among whom was the Princess de Lamballe. Those who instigated or took part in the massacres were known as **Septembriseurs.**

Septentrional Signs (sep ten' tri ō nàl). The first six signs of the Zodiac, because they belong to the *northern* celestial hemisphere. The North was called the *septentrion* from the seven stars of the Great Bear (Lat. *septem*, seven, *triones*, plough oxen). *Cp.* URSA MAJOR.

Septuagint (sep' tū à jint). A Greek version of the Old Testament and Apocrypha, so called because it was traditionally said to have been made by seventy-two Palestinian Jews in the 3rd century B.C., at the command of Ptolemy Philadelphus. They worked on the island of Pharos and completed the translation in seventy-two days.

This tradition applies, however, only to the Pentateuch; Greek translations of the other books were added by later writers, some, perhaps, being as late as the Christian era. The name Septuagint is frequently printed LXX.

Sepulchre, The Holy. The cave outside the walls of Jerusalem in which the body of Christ is believed to have lain between His burial and resurrection. From at least the 4th century (*see* INVENTION OF THE CROSS, *under* CROSS) the spot has been covered by a Christian church.

Seraglio (sè ra' lyō). The palace of the Sultans of Turkey at Constantinople, situated on the Golden Horn, and enclosed by walls seven miles and a half in circuit. The chief entrance was the Sublime Gate (*cp.* SUBLIME PORTE); and the chief of the large edifices is the *Harem*, or "sacred spot," which contained numerous houses, one for each of the sultan's wives, and others for his concubines. The Seraglio might be visited by strangers; not so the Harem.

Seraphic (se răf' ik). **Seraphic Blessing.** The blessing written by St. Francis of Assisi at the request of Brother Leo on Mt. Alverna, in 1224. It is based on *Numbers* vi, 25: May the Lord bless thee and keep thee. May He shew His face to thee and have mercy on thee. May He turn His countenance to thee and give thee peace. May the Lord bless thee, Brother Leo.

The Seraphic Doctor. The scholastic philosopher, St. Bonaventura (1221-74).

The Seraphic Father, or **Saint**. St. Francis of Assisi (1182-1226); whence the Franciscans are sometimes called the *Seraphic Order*.

The Seraphic Hymn. The Sanctus "Holy, holy, holy" (*Is.* vi, 3), which was sung by the seraphim.

Seraphim. The highest of the nine choirs of angels, so named from the seraphim of *Is.* vi, 2. The word is probably the same as *saraph*, a serpent, from *saraph*, to burn (in allusion to its bite); and this connexion with burning suggested to early Christian interpreters that the seraphim were specially distinguished by the ardency of their zeal and love.

Seraphim is a plural form; the singular, *seraph*, was first used in English by Milton. Abdiel was

> The flaming Seraph, fearless, though alone,
> Encompassed round with foes.
>
> *Paradise Lost*, v, 875.

Serapis (se rā' pis). The Ptolemaic form of Apis, an Egyptian deity who, when dead, was honoured under the attributes of Osiris (*q.v.*), and thus became "osirified Apis" or [O]Sorapis. He was lord of the underworld, and was identified by the Greeks with Hades.

Serendipity (se ren dip' i ti). A happy coinage by Horace Walpole to denote the faculty of making lucky and unexpected "finds" by accident, In a letter to Mann (January 28th, 1754) he says that he formed it on the title of a fairy story, *The Three Princes of Serendip*, because the princes—

were always making discoveries, by accidents and sagacity, of things they were not in quest of.

Serendip is an ancient name of Ceylon.

Serene (Lat. *serenus*, clear, calm). A title formerly given to certain German princes. Those who used to hold under the empire were entitled *Serene* or *Most Serene Highnesses*.

It's all serene. All right (Span. *sereno*, all right—the sentinel's countersign).

The drop serene. See DROP.

Serif and **Sanserif** (ser' if, săn ser' if). The former is type with the wings or finishing stroke

(as T); the latter is type without the finishing strokes (as T).

Serjeants-at-Law. A superior order of barristers (*q.v.*) abolished in 1877. From the Low Latin *serviens ad legem*, one who serves (the king) in matters of law. Serjeants Inn, formerly in Chancery Lane and later in Fleet Street, was their inn at law.

Serpent. *See also* SNAKE. The serpent is symbolical of—

(1) Deity, because, says Plutarch, "it feeds upon its own body; even so all things spring from God, and will be resolved into deity again" (*De Iside et Osiride*, i, 2, p. 5; and *Philo Byblius*).

(2) Eternity, as a corollary of the former. It is represented as forming a circle, holding its tail in its mouth.

(3) Renovation and the healing art. It is said that when old it has the power of growing young again "like the eagle," by casting its slough, which is done by squeezing itself between two rocks. It was sacred to Æsculapius (*q.v.*), the Greek god of medicine, as it was supposed to have the power of discovering healing herbs. Hence, two serpents appear in the badge of the Royal Army Medical Corps. *See* CADUCEUS.

(4) Guardian spirit. It was thus employed by the ancient Greeks and Romans, and not unfrequently the figure of a serpent was depicted on their altars.

In the temple of Athena at Athens, a serpent, supposed to be animated by the soul of Ericthonius, was kept in a cage, and called "the Guardian Spirit of the Temple."

(5) Wisdom. "Be ye therefore wise as serpents, and harmless as doves" (*Matt.* x, 16).

(6) Subtlety. "Now the serpent was more subtle than any beast of the field" (*Gen.* iii, 1).

It is also symbolical of the devil, as the Tempter, and in early pictures is sometimes placed under the feet of the Virgin, in allusion to the promise made to Eve after the fall (*Gen.* iii, 15).

In Christian **art it is** an attribute of St. Cecilia, St. Euphemia, St. Patrick, and many other saints, either because they trampled on Satan, or because they miraculously cleared some country of snakes.

Fable has it that the cerastes hides in sand that it may bite the horse's foot and get the rider thrown. In allusion to this belief, Jacob says, "Dan shall be . . . an adder in the path, that biteth the horse heels, so that his rider shall fall backward" (*Gen.* xlix, 17). The Bible also tells us that the serpent stops up its ears that it may not be charmed by the charmers, "charming never so wisely" (*Ps.* lviii, 4).

Another old idea about snakes was that when attacked they would swallow their young and not eject them until reaching a place of safety.

It was in the form of a serpent, says the legend, that Jupiter Ammon appeared to Olympia and became by her the father of Alexander the Great.

Pharaoh's serpent. *See* PHARAOH.

Sea serpent. *See* SEA.

The serpent of old Nile. Cleopatra, so called by Antony.

He's speaking now,
Or murmuring "Where's my serpent of old Nile?"
For so he calls me.
                    Antony and Cleopatra, i, 5.

Their ears have been serpent-licked. They have the gift of foreseeing events, the power of seeing into futurity. This is a Greek superstition. It is said that Cassandra and Helenus were gifted with the power of prophecy, because serpents licked their ears while sleeping in the temple of Apollo.

To cherish a serpent in your bosom. To show kindness to one who proves ungrateful. The Greeks say that a husbandman found a frozen serpent, which he put into his bosom. The snake was revived by the warmth, and stung its benefactor. Shakespeare applies the tale to a serpent's egg:

Therefore think him as a serpent's egg
Which, hatched, would (as his kind) grow dangerous.
                    Julius Cæsar, ii, 1.

Serpentine Verses. Such as end with the same word as they begin with. The following are examples:—

Crescit amor nummi, quantum ipsa pecunia crescit.
(Greater grows the love of pelf, as pelf itself grows greater.)
Ambo florentes ætatibus, Arcades ambo.
(Both in the spring of life, Arcadians both.)

The allusion is to the old representations of snakes with their tails in their mouths—no beginning and no end.

Serve. I'll serve him out—give him a *quid pro quo*. This is the French *desserver*, to do an ill turn to one.

Serves you right! You've got just what you deserved.

To serve a sentence. To undergo the punishment awarded.

To serve one's time. To hold an office or appointment for the full period allowed; to go through one's apprenticeship; also, to serve one's sentence in prison.

Sesame (ses' á mi). **Open, Sesame.** The "password" at which the door of the robbers'

cave flew open in the tale of *The Forty Thieves* (*Arabian Nights*); hence, a key to a mystery, or anything that acts like magic in obtaining a favour, admission, recognition, etc.

Sesame is an East Indian annual herb, with an oily seed which is used as a food, a laxative, etc. In Egypt they eat sesame cakes, and the Jews frequently add the seed to their bread.

Sesquipedalian (ses kwi pé dā' li àn) is sometimes applied in heavy irony to cumbersome and pedantic words. It comes from Horace's *sesquipedalia verba*, words a foot and a half long.

Session, Court of. *See* COURT.

Sestina (ses tē' nà). A set form of poem, usually rhymed, with six stanzas of six lines each and a final triplet. The terminal words of stanzas 2 to 6 are the same as those of stanza 1 but arranged differently. Sestinas were invented by the Provençal troubadour Arnaut Daniel (13th cent.); Dante, Petrarch, and others employed them in Italy, Cervantes and Camoens in the Peninsula, and an early use in English was by Drummond of Hawthornden. Swinburne's sestinas are probably the best in English.

Set. The Egyptian original of the Greek Typhon (*q.v.*), the god of evil, brother (or son) of Osiris, and his deadly enemy. He is represented as having the body of a man and the head of some unidentified mythological beast with pointed muzzle and high square ears.

Set, To. A set scene. In theatrical parlance, a scene built up by the stage carpenters, or a furnished interior, as a drawing-room, as distinguished from an ordinary or shifting scene.

The setting of a jewel. The frame or mount of gold or silver surrounding a jewel in a ring, brooch, etc.

This precious stone set in the silver sea.
                    Richard II, ii, 1.

The setting of the sun, moon, or **stars.** Their sinking below the horizon. The saying, **The sun never sets on the British dominions,** was used long ago of other empires. Thus, in the *Pastor Fido* (1590) Guarini speaks of Philip II of Spain as—

that proud monarch to whom, when it grows dark [elsewhere] the sun never sets:

Captain John Smith in his *Advertisements for the Unexperienced* notes that—

the brave Spanish soldiers brag. The sunne never sets in the Spanish dominions, but ever shineth on one part or other we have conquered for our king:

and Thomas Gage in his *Epistle* Dedicatory to his *New Survey of the West Indies* (1648) writes—

It may be said of them [the Dutch], as of the Spaniards, that the Sun never sets upon their Dominions.

To set off to advantage. To display a thing in its best light, put the best construction on it. Perhaps a phrase from the jewellers' craft.

Setebos (set' e bos). A god or devil worshipped by the Patagonians, and introduced by Shakespeare into his *Tempest* as the god of Sycorax, Caliban's mother.

> His art is of such power,
> It would control my dam's god, Setebos.
> And make a vassal of him.   *Tempest*, i, 2.

The cult of Setebos was first known in Europe through Magellan's voyage round the world, 1519-21.

Seven. A mystic or sacred number; it is composed of four and three, which, among the Pythagoreans, were, and from time immemorial have been, accounted lucky numbers. Among the Babylonians, Egyptians, and other ancient peoples there were seven sacred planets; and the Hebrew verb *to swear* means literally "to come under the influence of seven things"; thus seven ewe lambs figure in the oath between Abraham and Abimelech at Beersheba (*Gen* xvi, 28), and Herodotus (III, viii) describes an Arabian oath in which seven stones are smeared with blood.

There are seven days in creation, seven days in the week, seven graces, seven divisions in the Lord's Prayer, seven ages in the life of man, climacteric years are seven and nine with their multiples by odd numbers, and the seventh son of a seventh son was always held notable.

Among the Hebrews every seventh year was sabbatical, and seven times seven years was the jubilee. The three great Jewish feasts lasted seven days, and between the first and second were seven weeks. Levitical purifications lasted seven days. The number is associated with a variety of occurrences in the Old Testament.

In the Apocalypse we have seven churches of Asia, seven candlesticks, seven stars, seven trumpets, seven spirits before the throne of God, seven horns, seven vials, seven plagues, a seven-headed monster, and the Lamb with seven eyes.

The old astrologers and alchemists recognized seven planets, each having its own "heaven" —

> The bodies seven, eek, lo hem heer anoon;
> Sol gold is, and Luna silver we threpe,
> Mars yren, Mercurie quyksilver we clepe;
> Saturnus leed, and Jubitur is tyn,
> And Venus coper, by my fader kyn.
> CHAUCER: *Prol. of the Canon's Yeoman's Tale.*

And from this very ancient belief sprang the theory that man was composed of seven substances, and has seven natures. *See under* SENSE.

Seven, The. Used of groups of seven people, especially (1) the "men of honest report"

chosen by the Apostles to be the first Deacons (*Acts* vi, 5), viz., Stephen, Philip, Prochorus, Nicanor, Timon, Parmenas, and Nicholas; (2) the Seven Bishops (*see below*); or (3) the Seven Sages of Greece (*see* WISE MEN). *See also* SEVEN NAMES, *below*.

Seven Against Thebes, The. The seven Argive heroes (Adrastus, Polynices, Tydeus, Amphiaraus, Capaneus, Hippomedon, and Parthenopæus), who, according to Greek legend, made war on Thebes with the object of restoring Polynices (son of Œdipus), who had been expelled by his brother Eteocles. All perished except Adrastus (*q.v.*), and the brothers slew each other in single combat. The legend is the subject of one of the tragedies of Æschylus. *See* NEMEAN GAMES.

Seven Champions, The. The mediæval designation of the national patron saints of England, Scotland, Wales, Ireland, France, Spain, and Italy. In 1596 Richard Johnson published a chap-book, *The Famous History of the Seven Champions of Christendom*. In this he relates that St. George of England was seven years imprisoned by the Almidor, the black king of Morocco; St. Denys of France lived seven years in the form of a hart; St. James of Spain was seven years dumb out of love to a fair Jewess; St. Anthony of Italy, with the other champions, was enchanted into a deep sleep in the Black Castle, and was released by St. George's three sons, who quenched the seven lamps by water from the enchanted fountain; St. Andrew of Scotland delivered six ladies who had lived seven years under the form of white swans; St. Patrick of Ireland was immured in a cell where he scratched his grave with his own nails; and St. David of Wales slept seven years in the enchanted garden of Ormandine, and was redeemed by St. George.

Seven Deadly or **Capital sins.** Pride, Wrath, Envy, Lust, Gluttony, Avarice, Sloth.

The Island of the Seven Cities. A land of Spanish fable, where seven bishops, who quitted Spain during the dominion of the Moors, founded seven cities. The legend says that many have visited the island, but no one has ever quitted it.

Seven Dials (London). A column with seven dials formerly stood facing the seven streets which radiated therefrom.

> Where famed St. Giles's ancient limits spread
> An in-railed column rears its lofty head,
> Here to seven streets seven dials count the day,
> And from each other catch the circling ray.
> GAY: *Trivia*, ii.

The district had at one time an unenviable reputation for squalor (*cp*. GILES, ST.); hence Sir W. S. Gilbert's —

Hearts just as pure and fair
May beat in Belgrave Square,
As in the lowly air
   Of Seven Dials.—*Iolanthe*.

Seven Gifts of the Spirit, The. Wisdom, Understanding, Counsel, Power or Fortitude, Knowledge, Righteousness, and Godly Fear.

Seven Gods of Luck, The. In Japanese folklore, Benten, goddess of love, Bishamon, god of war, Daikoku, of wealth, Ebisu, of self-effacement, Fukurokujin and Jurojin, gods of longevity, and Hstei, god of generosity. These are really popular conceptions of the seven Buddhist *devas* who preside over human happiness and welfare.

Seven Heavens, The. See HEAVEN.

Seven Hills. The walls of Ancient Rome, built about the 6th century B.C., included the seven hills, Palatine, Capitol, Aventine, Caelian, Esquiline, Viminal and Quirinal. The heart of the modern city clings to these hills, in some cases now scarcely perceptible rises in the street level.

Seven Names of God, The. The ancient Hebrews had many names for the Deity (*see under* NAME, *To take God's name in vain, and* ELOHISTIC), and the Seven over which the scribes had to exercise particular care were— El, Elohim, Adonai, YHWH (*i.e.* our *Jehovah*), Ehyeh-Asher-Ehyeh, Shaddai, and Zebaot. In mediæval times God was sometimes called simply, *The Seven*.

Now lord, for thy naymes sevyn, that made both moyn and starnys,
Well mo then I can neven thi will, lord, of me tharnys.
             Towneley Mysteries, xiii, 191 (about 1460).

Seven Planets, Sacraments, The. *See these headings*.

Seven Sages of Greece, The. See WISE MEN.

Seven Sciences, The. See SCIENCE.

Seven Seas, The. The Arctic and Antarctic, North and South Pacific, North and South Atlantic, and the Indian Oceans.

Seven Sisters, The. An old name of the Pleiades; also given to a set of seven cannon, cast by one Robert Borthwick and used at Flodden (1513).

Seven Sleepers, The. Seven Christian youths of Ephesus, according to the legend, who fled in the Decian persecution (250) to a cave in Mount Celion. After 230 years they awoke, but soon died, and their bodies were taken to Marseilles in a large stone coffin, still shown in Victor's church. Their names are Constantine, Dionysius, John, Maximian, Malchus, Martinian, and Serapion. This fable took its rise from a misapprehension of the words, "They fell asleep in the Lord"—*i.e.* died.

The mystic number is connected with other mediæval "Sleepers"; thus, Barbarossa turns himself once every seven years; once every seven years, also, Ogier the Dane thunders on the floor with his iron mace; and it was seven years that Tannhauser and Thomas of Ercildoune spent beneath the earth in magic enthralment.

Seven Sorrows. See MARY.

Seven Stars, The. Used formerly of the planets; also of the Pleiades and the Great Bear.

Fool: The reason why the seven stars are no more than seven is a pretty reason.
Lear: Because they are not eight?
Fool: Yes, indeed; thou wouldst make a good fool.
             King Lear, i, 5.

Seven Wonders of the World, The. See WONDERS.

Seven Works of Mercy, The. See MERCY.

Seven Years War, The (1756-1763) was waged by France, Austria, Russia, Sweden, Saxony, and Spain against Frederick the Great of Prussia, Great Britain, and Hanover. The prime cause of the war was fear of Frederick, coupled with Maria Theresa's eagerness to regain Silesia as an Austrian possession. The exhaustion of his enemies and his own superior generalship gave Frederick the victory. Britain gained most out of the war—the conquest of Bengal and the capture of Quebec and hence the whole of Canada.

In the seventh heaven. See HEAVEN.

Seventh-day Adventists. A small sect of millenarians holding very strict Sabbatarian views.

Seventh-day Baptists. Modern representatives of the Traskites (*q.v.*); more numerous in America than in England.

The seventh son of a seventh son. See SEVEN, *above*.

Several (late Lat. *sēparāte*, from *sēparāre*, to separate). The English word used simply to denote what is severed or separate; each, as "all and several."

Azariah was a leper, and dwelt in a several house.— 2 *Kings* xv, 5.

And it is still used in this way, as—

Three times slipping from the outer edge,
I bump'd the ice into three several stars.
             TENNYSON: *The Epic*, 12.

A several is the old legal term for a piece of enclosed ground adjoining a common field, or an enclosed pasture as opposed to an open field or common.

Severn. See SABRINA.

Severus, St. (se vēr' us). Patron saint of fullers, being himself of the same craft.

Sèvres Ware (sāvr). Porcelain of fine quality made at the French government works at Sèvres, near Paris. The factory was first established at Vincennes in 1745; in 1756 it was removed to Sèvres, and three years later was acquired by the state.

Sexagesima Sunday (seks à jes' i mà). The second Sunday before Lent; so called because in round numbers it is sixty days (Lat. *sexagesima dies*) before Easter.

Sextile (seks' tĭl). The aspect of two planets when distant from each other sixty degrees or two signs. This position is marked by astrologers thus *.

In sextile, square, and trine, and opposite
Of noxious efficacy.
MILTON: *Paradise Lost*, x, 659.

At Eton a sixth-form boy is called a *Sextile*.

Sexton. A corruption of *sacristan*, a church official who has charge of the *sacra*, or things attached to a specific church, such as vestments, cushions, books, boxes, tools, vessels, and so on.

Shaddock. A large kind of orange, now generally known as grape fruit (*citrus decumana*), so called from Captain Shaddock (early 18th century), who first transplanted one in the West Indies. It is a native of China and Japan.

Shade. Wine vaults with a lounge attached are often known as *shades*. The term originated at Brighton, where the Old Bank, in 1819, was turned into a smoking-room and bar. There was an entrance by the Pavilion *Shades*, or Arcade, and the name was soon transferred to the drinking-bar. It was not inappropriate, as the room was in reality shaded by the opposite house, occupied by Mrs. Fitzherbert.

Shadow. A word with a good many figurative and applied meanings, such as, a ghost; Macbeth says to the ghost of Banquo:—

Hence, horrible shadow! unreal mockery, hence!
Macbeth, iii, 4.

An imperfect or faint representation, as "I haven't the shadow of a doubt"; a constant attendant, as in Milton's "Sin and her shadow Death" (*Paradise Lost*, ix, 12); moral darkness or gloom—"He has outsoared the shadow of our night" (Shelley; *Adonais*, xl, 1); protecting influence—

Hither, like you ancient Tower,
Watching o'er the River's bed,
Fling the shadow of Thy power,
Else we sleep among the dead.
WORDSWORTH: *Hymn (Jesu! bless)*.

To be reduced to a shadow. Of people, to become thoroughly emaciated; of things, to become an empty form from which the substance has departed.

To shadow. To follow about like a shadow, especially as a detective, with the object of spying out all one's doings.

Shady. A shady character. A person of very doubtful reputation; one whose character would scarcely bear investigation in the light of day.

On the shady side of forty—the wrong side, meaning more than forty.

SHAEF. Mnemonic of Supreme Headquarters Allied Expeditionary Forces, the supreme directive military organization, under the command of General Eisenhower, in the later stages of World War II. SHAEF was disbanded in July, 1945.

Shah. The title of the king or emperor of Persia; that of his sons is *Shahzadah*. It is a corruption of *padishah* (*q.v.*).

Shake. A good shake up. Something sudden that startles one out of his lethargy and rouses him to action.

A shake of the head. An indication of refusal, disapproval, annoyance, etc.

I'll do it in a brace of shakes. Instantly, as soon as you can shake the dice-box twice.

No great shakes. Nothing extraordinary; no such mighty bargain. The reference is probably to gambling with dice.

In two shakes of a lamb's tail. Instantly. American expression originating in the early 19th century.

To shake hands. A very old method of salutation and farewell; when one was shaking hands one could not get at one's sword to strike a treacherous blow. When Jehu asked Jehonadab if his "heart was right" with him, he said, "If it be, give me thine hand," and Jehonadab gave him his hand (2 *Kings* x, 15). Nestor shook hands with Ulysses on his return to the Grecian camp with the stolen horses of Rhesus; Æneas, in the temple of Dido, sees his lost companions enter, and *avidi conjungere dextras ardebant* (*Æneid*, i, 514); and Horace, strolling along the Via Sacra, shook hands with an acquaintance. *Arreptâque manu, "Quid agis dulcissimĕ rerum?"*

Shakers. A sect of Second Adventists, founded in the 18th century in England by a secession from the Quakers, and transplanted in America by Ann Lee (1736-84), or "Mother Ann," as she is generally known. She was an uneducated factory hand, daughter of a Manchester blacksmith.

A sect of English Shakers, the "People of God," was founded in Battersea about 1864 by Mary Anne Girling (1827-86), a farmer's daughter; its chief seat was in the New Forest, and it disappeared soon after her death.

Shakespeare (1564-1616), the greatest poet and dramatist of all time and all countries. William Shakespeare born at Stratford-on-Avon, the third child of John Shakespeare, an alderman and bailiff of that town (variously described as a butcher, glover, and general trader), and Mary Arden, both of yeoman stock. He received a sound education at the Stratford grammar-school; in spite of Ben Jonson's remark that he had "small Latin and less Greek." Leaving Stratford in 1585 to avoid a prosecution for poaching by Sir Thomas Lucy ("Justice Shallow"), he came to London where he acted with the Earl of Leicester's company. His plays and poems were written between 1591 (*Love's Labour's Lost*) and 1611 (*The Tempest*). In the latter year he retired to Stratford, but visited London frequently, keeping up his relations with actors and poets until his death.

Ben Jonson calls him "Sweet Swan of Avon," also "The applause! delight! the wonder of our stage!" and says that "He was not for an age, but for all time" (*To the Memory of Shakespeare*). Milton calls him "Dear son of Memory, great heir of fame" (*An Epitaph*), and "Sweetest Shakespeare, fancy's child" (*L'Allegro*); to Collins he was "The perfect boast of Time" (*Epistle to Sir Thos. Hanmer*); to Coleridge, "Our myriad-minded Shakespeare" (*Biog. Lit.* xv); to Carlyle, "the greatest of intellects" (*Characteristics of Shakespeare*); to Christopher North, "the Poet Laureate of the Court of Faery"; to Landor, "not our poet, but the world's."

Dryden said of him—

Shakespeare's magic could not copied be;
Within that circle none durst walk but he.
Prologue to the Tempest.

And that he "was a man who of all modern and perhaps ancient poets, had the largest and most comprehensive soul." Young says—"He wrote the play the Almighty made"; (*Epistle to Lord Lansdowne*); Mallett—"Great above rule. . . . Nature was his own" (*Verbal Criticism*); Dr. Johnson—

Each change of many-colour'd life he drew;
Exhausted worlds, and then imagined new;
Existence saw him spurn her bounded reign,
And panting Time toiled after him in vain.
Prologue, 1747.

Pope—

Shakespear (whom you and every play-house bill
Style "the divine," "the matchless," what you will)
For gain, not glory, winged his roving flight,
And grew immortal in his own despite.
Imitations of Horace, Ep. 1.

And Matthew Arnold—

Others abide our question. Thou art free.
We ask and ask—Thou smilest and art still,
Out-topping knowledge—*Shakespeare.*

There are thirty-seven plays credited wholly or in part to Shakespeare, and an enthusiast has discovered that they contain 106,007 lines and 814,780 words, *Hamlet* being the longest, with 3,930 lines, and the *Comedy of Errors*, with 1,777 lines the shortest. The plays contain 1,277 speaking characters, of whom only 157 are females. The longest part is that of Hamlet, who has 11,610 words to deliver.

Shakespeare's descendants.

Shakespeare married (1582) Anne Hathaway, of Shottery, who was eight years his senior, and died in 1623. They had one son and two daughters—Susanna (b. 1583), and the twins Hamnet and Judith (1585). Hamnet died at the age of 11; Judith married Thomas Quiney, had three sons, all of whom died young and unmarried, and died in 1662. Susanna married John Hall and died in 1649, leaving only one child, Elizabeth, the last descendant of the dramatist. She married twice, but had no children; and died as Lady Bernard, wife of Sir John Bernard, of Abington Manor, Northampton, in 1670.

Shakespeare; the name. There is no way of spelling the dramatist's name that is *certainly* "correct" (*i.e.* as he would himself have spelt it), because the six unquestionably genuine signatures of his that we possess (viz., three on the Will, two on the Blackfriars conveyance and mortgage, and one on his deposition in the suit brought by Stephen Bellot against Christopher Mountjoy) vary, and are very difficult to decipher. The most usual modern spelling—Shakespeare—is that used throughout the First and Second Folios (1623 and 1632), and in all the Quartos with the exception of the 1598 *Love's Labour's Lost* ("Shakespere") and the first 1608, *King Lear* ("Shakspeare"), in the dedicatory epistles to *Venus and Adonis* (1593) and *Lucrece* (1594), and though on his own monument the name is given as "Shakspeare," on the tombs of his wife and daughter "Shakespeare" is the spelling. Theobald (1733) used this spelling; Rowe (1709), Pope (1725), and Hanmer (1744) all followed the Third and Fourth Folios, which spelt the name "Shakespear," Steevens and Malone (1778) preferred "Shakspeare."

The "Shakspere" spelling was used in Bell's edition of the works (1788), and in Knight's various editions (1839), etc., but its more recent adoption in literary circles is due to Sir Frederick Madden, who advocated it on the ground that this was the spelling of the most legible of the signatures—that in the copy of Florio's *Montaigne* (1603) now in the British

Museum—and to Furnivall having founded the "New *Shakspere* Society" to take the place of the defunct "*Shakespeare* Society." This signature is now, however, generally taken to be a forgery. The autograph in the Bellott-Mountjoy suit does not help matters, as it is abbreviated to "Willm Shak'p'"; and on the bond that Shakespeare took out for his marriage licence the name appears as "Shagspere." *See* J. R. Wise's *Autograph of William Shakespeare . . . together with 4,000 ways of spelling the name*, published at Philadephia in 1869.

Shakuntala. *See* SAKUNTALA.

Shaky. Not steady; not in good health; not strictly upright; not well prepared for examination; doubtfully solvent.

Shalott, The Lady of (shà lot'). A maiden of the Arthurian legends, who fell in love with Sir Lancelot of the Lake, and died because her love was not returned. Tennyson has a poem on the subject; and the story of Elaine (*q.v.*), "the lily maid of Astolat," is substantially the same.

Shamanism (sha' mà nizm). A primitive form of religion, in which those who practise it believe that the world and all events are governed by good and evil spirits who can be propitiated or bought off only through the intervention of a witch-doctor, or *Shaman*. The word is Slavonic; it comes from the Samoyeds and other Siberian peoples, but is now applied to Red Indian and other primitive worship.

Shamefast. Bashful; awkward through shyness; sheepish. This is the old form of *shamefaced* (which is properly an error), the *-fast* meaning "firmly fixed" or "restrained" (by shame).

Shamrock, the symbol of Ireland, because it was selected by St. Patrick to illustrate to the Irish the doctrine of the Trinity. According to the elder Pliny no serpent will touch this plant.

Shamus. An American term of disrespect. It derives from *shammus*, sexton of a Jewish synagogue.

Shandean (shăn' dē àn). Characteristic of Tristram Shandy or the Shandy family in Sterne's novel, *Tristram Shandy* (9 vols., 1759-67). Tristram's father, Walter Shandy, is a metaphysical Don Quixote in his way, full of superstitious and idle conceits. He believes in long noses and propitious names, but his son's nose is crushed, and his name becomes *Tristram* instead of *Trismegistus*. Tristram's Uncle Toby was wounded at the siege of Namur, and is benevolent and generous, simple as a child, brave as a lion, and gallant as a courtier. His modesty with Widow Wadman and his military

tastes are admirable. He is said to be drawn from Sterne's father. The mother was the *beau-ideal* of nonentity; and of Tristram himself, we hear almost more before he was born than after he had burst upon an astonished world.

Shanghai, To (shăng hī'). An old nautical phrase meaning to drug a man insensible in order to get him on board an outward bound vessel in need of crew. It would appear to have originated in the phrase "ship him to Shanghai," *i.e.* send him on a long voyage.

Shangri La (shăng gri la'). The hidden Buddhist lama paradise described in James Hilton's *Lost Horizon* (1933). In World War II the name was applied to the secret air base used by the U.S.A. Air Force for the great attack on Japan.

Shannon. Dipped in the Shannon. One who has been dipped in the Shannon is said to lose all bashfulness.

Shanties, Chanties. Songs sung by sailors at work, to ensure united action (Fr. *chanter*, to sing). They are in sets, each of which has a different cadence adapted to the work in hand. Thus, in sheeting topsails, weighing anchor, etc., one of the most popular of the shanty songs runs thus:—

I'm bound away, this very day,
 I'm bound for the Rio Grande.
 Ho, you, Rio!
Then fare you well, my bonny blue bell,
 I'm bound for the Rio Grande.

A shanty is also a small wooden house, or a roughly-built hut.

Shan Van Voght. This excellent song (composed 1798) has been called the Irish *Marseillaise*. The title of it is a corruption of *An t-sean bhean bhocht* (the poor old woman—*i.e.* Ireland). The last verse is—

Will Ireland then be free?
 Said, the Shan Van Voght. [repeat]
Yes, Ireland shall be free
From the centre to the sea,
Hurrah for liberty!
 Said the Shan Van Voght.

Shark. A swindler, a pilferer, an extortionate boarding-house keeper or landlord, etc.; one who snaps up things like a shark, which eats almost anything, and seems to care little whether its food is alive or dead, fish, flesh, or human bodies.

To shark up. To get a number of people, etc., together promiscuously, without consideration of their fitness.

Now, sir, young Fortinbras . . .
Hath in the skirts of Norway here and there
Shark'd up a list of lawless resolutes,
For food and diet, to some enterprise
That hath a stomach in't.

Hamlet, i, 1.

Sharp. A regular Becky Sharp. An unprincipled, scheming young woman, who by cunning, hypocrisy, and low smartness raises herself from obscurity and poverty to some position in Society, and falls therefrom in due course after having maintained a more or less precarious foothold. Of course she is good-looking, and superficial amiability is a *sine qua non*. Becky Sharp, the original of this, is the principal character in Thackeray's *Vanity Fair* (1848).

Shave. Just a grazing touch; *a near* or *close shave*, a narrow escape; *to shave through an examination*, only just to get through, narrowly to escape being "plucked." At Oxford a pass degree is sometimes called *a shave*.

Shaveling. Used in contempt—especially after the Reformation—of a priest. At a time when the laity wore moustaches and beards the clergy were not only usually clean shaven but invariably wore large shaven tonsures.

It maketh no matter how thou live here, so thou have the favour of the pope and his shavelings.—JOHN BRADFORD (1510-1555)-a Marian martyr.

Shavian (shā' vi àn). After the manner of George Bernard Shaw (1856-1950) or descriptive of his philosophy and style of humour.

She. She Bible, The. *See* BIBLE, SPECIALLY NAMED.

She Stoops to Conquer. Goldsmith's comedy (1773) owes its existence to an incident which actually occurred to its author. When he was sixteen years of age a wag residing at Ardagh directed him, when passing through that village, to Squire Fetherstone's house as the village inn. The mistake was not discovered for some time, and then no one enjoyed it more heartily than Oliver himself.

She-wolf of France. *See* WOLF.

Shear. God tempers the wind to the shorn lamb. *See* GOD.

Ordeal by sieve and shears. *See* SIEVE.

Shear or **Shere Thursday.** Maundy Thursday, the Thursday of Holy Week; so called, it is said, because in—

old fadres dayes the people wolde that day shere theyr hedes, and clyppe theyr berdes, and poll theyr hedes, and so make them honest agenst Ester day.

Sheathe. To sheathe the sword. To cease hostilities, make peace. In the early months of World War I the phrase "We will not sheathe the sword until the wrong done to Belgium has been righted" was a common slogan.

Sheba, The Queen of (shē' bà). The queen who visited Solomon (1 *Kings* x) is known to the Arabs as Bálkis, Queen of Saba (Koran, ch. xxvii). Sheba was thought by the Greeks and Romans to have been the capital of what is now Yemen, S.W. Arabia; and the people over whom the queen reigned were the Sabæans.

Shebang (she băng'). **Fed up with the whole shebang.** Tired of the whole concern and everything connected with it. *Shebang* is American slang for a hut or one's quarters; also for a cart; and also, in a humorously depreciatory way, for almost anything.

Shebeen (she bēn'). A place (originally only in Ireland) where liquor is sold without a licence; hence applied to any low-class public house.

You've been takin' a dhrop o' the crathur' an' Danny says "Troth, an' I been
Dhrinking yer health wid Shamus O'Shea at Katty's shebeen."
TENNYSON: *To-morrow.*

Shedem. *See* MAZIKEEN.

Sheep. *Ram* or *tup*, the sire; *ewe*, the dam; *lamb*, the young till weaned, when it is called a *tup-hogget* or *ewe-hogget*, as the case may be, or, if the tup is castrated, a *wether-hogget*.

After the removal of the *first* fleece, the tup-hogget becomes a *shearling*, the ewe-hogget a *gimmer*, and the wether-hogget a *dinmont*.

After the removal of the second fleece, the shearling becomes a *two-shear tup*, the gimmer an *ewe*, and the dinmont a *wether*.

After the removal of the *third* fleece, the ewe is called a *twinter-ewe*; and when it ceases to breed a *draft-ewe*.

Sheepish. Awkward and shy; bashful through not knowing how to deport oneself in the circumstances.

Sheep's head. A fool, a simpleton—
Gostanzo: What, sirrah, is that all?
No entertainment to the gentlewoman?
Valerio: Forsooth y'are welcome by my father's leave.
Gos.: What, no more compliment? Kiss her, you sheep's head!
Lady, you'll pardon our gross bringing up?
We dwell far off from court, you may perceive.
CHAPMAN: *All Fools*, ii, 1.

The Black Sheep (Kârâ-koin-loo). A tribe which established a principality in Armenia that lasted 108 years (1360-1468); so called from the device of their standard.

The White Sheep (Ak-koin-loo). A tribe which established a principality in Armenia, etc., on the ruin of the Black Sheep (1468-1508); so called from the device of their standard.

There's a black sheep in every flock. In every club or party of persons there's sure to be at least one shady character.

To cast sheep's eyes. To look askance, in a sheepish way, at a person to whom you feel lovingly inclined

But he, the beast, was casting sheep's eyes at her.—
COLMAN: *Broad Grins.*

Vegetable sheep. *See* SCYTHIAN LAMB.

Sheepskin (U.S.A.). A college diploma.

Sheer Thursday. *See* SHEAR.

Sheet. Three sheets in the wind. Very drunk;
just about as drunk as one can be. The *sheet* is
the rope attached to the lower end of a sail,
used for shortening and extending sail; if quite
free, the sheet is said to be "in the wind," and
the sail flaps and flutters without restraint. If all
the three sails were so loosened, the ship would
"reel and stagger like a drunken man."

Captain Cuttle looking, candle in hand, at Bunsby
more attentively, perceived that he was three sheets in
the wind, or, in plain words, drunk.—DICKENS: *Dombey
and Son.*

Sheikh (shēk, shek). A title of respect among
the Arabs (like the Ital. *signore.* Fr. *sieur,* Span.
señor, etc.), but properly the head of a Bedouin
clan, family, or tribe, or the headman of an Arab
village.

Sheikh-ul-Islam. The Grand Mufti, or
supreme head of the Mohammedan hierarchy
in Turkey.

Shekels (shek' elz). Colloquial for money.
The Hebrew shekel was a weight of about 250
grains troy, also a silver coin worth roughly 2s. 6d.

Shekinah (she kī' nà) (Heb. *shakan,* to reside).
The visible glory of the Divine Presence in the
shape of a cloud, which rested over the mercy-
seat between the Cherubim, and in the Temple
of Solomon (*See Exod.* xl, 34-38). The word
does not occur in the Bible, but is frequent in
the Targums, and was employed by the Jews as
a periphrasis for the Divine Name.

Sheldonian Theatre (shel dō' ni àn). The
Senate House of Oxford; so called from Gilbert
Sheldon (1598-1677), Archbishop of Canter-
bury, who built it.

Shelf. Laid on the shelf, or **shelved.** Put on
one side as of no further use; superannuated.
Said of officials and others no longer actively
employed; an actor no longer assigned a part; a
woman past the ordinary age of marriage; also
of a pawn at the broker's, a question started and
set aside, etc.

Shell (A.S. *scell*). The hard outside covering
of nuts, eggs, molluscs, tortoises, etc.; hence
applied to other hollow coverings, as a light or
inner coffin, and the hollow projectile filled
with explosives and missiles which will explode
on impact or at a set time.

Eggshells. Many persons, after eating a boiled
egg, break or crush the shell. This, according to
Sir Thomas Browne—

is but a superstitious relict . . . and the intent thereof was
to prevent witchcraft; for lest witches should draw or
prick their names therein, and veneficiously mischief
their persons, they broke the shell.—*Pseudodoxia
Epidemica,* V, xxii.

Scallop shells were the emblem of St. James
the Great (*q.v.*), and were hence carried by pilgrims, under whose special protection they were.

Shell shock. An acute neurasthenic condition due to a shock to the system caused by the
explosion of a shell or bomb at close quarters.
The term came into use in World War I.

To retire into one's shell. To become reti-
cent and uncommunicative, to withdraw oneself from society in a forbidding way. The allusion
is to the tortoise, which, once it has "got into its
shell," is quite unget-at-able.

See also NUTSHELL.

Shelter. In World War II this word, as an
abbreviation of Air Raid Shelter, was especially
applied to the various excavations, buildings, or
devices employed as a protection against aerial
bombing. Deep shelters, *e.g.* the London Tubes,
were sufficiently far below the ground level to
be immune from damage even by a direct hit.
Such shelters as the Anderson (half above and
half below ground, and made of corrugated
steel) or the Morrison (a sort of steel dining-table
with room for a bed beneath) afforded exiguous
protection from blast or falling masonry.

The Shepherd's Sundial. The scarlet pimpernel, which opens at a little past seven in the
morning and closes at a little past two. When rain
is at hand, or the weather is unfavourable, it
does not open at all.

The Shepherd's Warning
A red sky at night is the shepherd's delight,
But a red sky in the morning is the shepherd's warning.

The Italian saying is *Sera rosso e bianco mat-
tino allegra il pellegrino* (a red evening and a white
morning rejoice the pilgrim).

To shepherd. To guard and guide carefully
as a shepherd does his flock; in colloquial use, to
follow and spy on as a detective.

Sheppard, Jack (1702-24). A notorious highwayman, son of a carpenter in Smithfield, noted
for his two escapes from Newgate in 1724. He
was hanged at Tyburn the same year.

Sheriff (Sher' if). In mediæval and later
times the sheriff (shire reeve) was an official
who looked after the king's property in the various shires or counties. In England and Wales
each county has its sheriff, called the High
Sheriff, whose duty it is to keep the peace, administer justice under the direction of the
courts, execute writs by deputy, preside over

parliamentary elections, etc. There are sheriffs in certain cities such as Bristol, Norwich, etc., and the City of London has two.

In U.S.A. the sheriff is the officer in a county commissioned with the enforcement of law and order.

Sheriffmuir. There was mair lost at the Shirramuir. Don't grieve for your losses, for worse have befallen others before now. The battle of Sheriffmuir, in 1715, between the Jacobites and Hanoverians was very bloody; both sides sustained heavy losses, and both sides claimed the victory.

Sherlock Holmes. The most important figure in detective fiction, the creation of Arthur Conan Doyle (1859-1930). His solutions of crimes and mysteries were related in a series of sixty stories that appeared in the *Strand Magazine* off and on between 1891 and 1927. The character was based on Dr. Joseph Bell, of the Edinburgh Infirmary, whose methods of deduction suggested a system that Holmes developed into a science; his stooge Watson was a skit on Doyle himself. Holmes's method is in itself simple — the observation of the minutest details and apparently insignificant circumstances; the correct interpretation and application of the information thus acquired enables him to solve the apparently unsolvable with a minimum of energy or detective apparatus.

Shibboleth (shib′ ō leth). The password of a secret society; the secret by which those of a party know each other; also a worn-out or discredited doctrine. The Ephraimites could not pronounce *sh*, so when they were fleeing from Jephthah and the Gileadites (*Judges* xii, 1-16) they were caught at the ford on the Jordan because Jephthah caused all the fugitives to say the word *Shibboleth* (meaning "a stream in flood"), which all the Ephraimites pronounced as *Sibboleth*.

Shield. The most famous shields in story are the *Shield of Achilles* described by Homer, of *Hercules* described by Hesiod, of *Æneas* described by Virgil, and the *Ægis* (*q.v.*).

Others are that of: —

Agamemnon, a gorgon.
Amycos (son of Poseidon), a crayfish, symbol of prudence.
Cadmus and his descendants, a dragon, to indicate their descent from the dragon's teeth.
Eteocles, one of the Seven Against Thebes, a man scaling a wall.
Hector, a lion.
Idomeneus, a cock.
Menelaus, a serpent at his heart; alluding to the elopement of his wife with Paris.

Parthenopæus, one of the Seven Against Thebes, a sphinx holding a man in its claws.
Ulysses, a dolphin. Whence he is sometimes called Delphinosemos.

Servius says that in the siege of Troy the Greeks had, as a rule, Neptune on their bucklers, and the Trojans Minerva.

It was a common custom, after a great victory, for the victorious general to hang his shield on the wall of some temple.

The clang of shields. When a chief doomed a man to death, he struck his shield with the blunt end of his spear by way of notice to the royal bard to begin the death-song.

Cairbar rises in his arms,
The clang of shields is heard.
OSSIAN: *Temora*, 1.

Shi'ites (Arab, *shi'ah*, a sect). Those Mohammedans who regard Ali as the first rightful Imam or Caliph (rejecting the three Sunni Caliphs), and do not consider the Sunna, or oral law of any authority, but look upon it as apocryphal. They wear *red* turbans, and are sometimes called "Red Heads." *Cp*. SUNNITES.

Shillelagh (Ir.). A cudgel of oak or blackthorn; so called from a village of this name in County Wicklow.

Shilling (A.S. *scilling*, which is connected either with O.Teut. *skel-*, to resound or ring, or *skil-*, to divide). The coin was originally made with a deeply indented cross, and could easily be divided into halves or quarters.

Shilly Shally. To hesitate, act in an undecided, irresolute way; a corruption of "Will I, shall I," or "Shall I, shall I?"

There's no delay, they ne'er stand shall I, shall I,
Hermogenes with Dallila doth dally.
Taylor's Workes, iii, 3 (1630).

Shindig (shin′ dig). A slang term for a dance, a noisy celebration party, etc.

Shindy. A row, a disturbance. *To kick up a shindy*, to make a row. The word is probably connected with *shinty* or *shinny*, a primitive kind of hockey played in the north.

Shine. To take the shine out of one. To humiliate him, "take him down a peg or two"; to outshine him.

Shiner. A black eye.

Shin Plaster. An old American and also Australian phrase still occasionally used for paper tokens issued by rural stores as small change. It is said that some storekeepers baked them to make them brittle so that they would powder to nothing in the recipient's pocket.

Shintoism, the national religion of Japan. Worship takes the form of offerings and prayers for temporal blessings, litanies read by priests, reverence for ancestors and an unquestioning loyalty to the State. The chief of numerous deities is Ameratasu, the sun goddess from whom the emperors claim descent.

Ship. In the printing-house the body of compositors engaged for the time being on one definite piece of work is known as a *ship*; this is said to be short for *companionship*, but it is worth noting that many printing-house terms (*cp.* CHAPEL, FRIAR, MONK) have an ecclesiastical origin, and *ship* was an old name for the nave of a church.

Ship-money. A tax formerly levied in time of war on ports and seaboard counties for the maintenance of the Navy. It was through Charles I levying this tax in 1634-7 without the consent of Parliament, and extending it to the inland counties illegally, that the Puritan party, led by Hampden, refused to pay and thus began the struggle which culminated in the Civil War.

Shipshape. As methodically arranged as things in a ship; in good order. When a vessel is sent out temporarily rigged, it is termed "jury-rigged," and when the jury rigging has been duly changed for ship rigging, the vessel is "shipshape," *i.e.* in due or regular order.

To take shipping. To set out on a voyage, to embark on board ship.

When my ship comes home. When my fortune is made. The allusion is to the argosies returning from foreign parts laden with rich freights, and so enriching the merchants who sent them forth.

Shipton, Mother. This so-called prophetess is first heard of in a tract of 1641, in which she is said to have lived in the reign of Henry VIII, and to have foretold the death of Wolsey, Cromwell, Lord Percy, etc. In 1677 the pamphleteering publisher, Richard Head, brought out a *Life and Death of Mother Shipton*, and in 1862 Charles Hindley brought out a new edition in which she was credited with having predicted steam-engines, the telegraph, and other modern inventions, as well as the end of the world in 1881.

Shire. When the Saxon kings created an earl, they gave him a *shire* (A.S. *scir*) or division of land to govern. *Scir* meant originally employment or government, and is connected with *scirian*, to appoint, allot. At the Norman Conquest *count* superseded the title *earl*, and the shire or earldom was called a *county*. Even to the present hour we call the wife of an earl a countess.

Knight of the Shire. *See* KNIGHT.

Shirt. A boiled shirt. An Americanism for a stiff white shirt, as opposed to an unstarched coloured one.

Close sits my shirt, but closer my skin. My property is dear to me, but dearer my life; my belongings sit close to my heart, but *Ego proximus mihi.*

Not a shirt to one's name. Nothing at all; penniless and propertyless.

The shirt of Nessus. *See* NESSUS.

To get one's shirt out. To lose one's temper, to get in a rage. A variant is *to get one's rag out.*

Shirty. Bad-tempered; very cross and offended; in the state one is when somebody has "got your shirt out."

To give the shirt off one's back. All one has.

To put one's shirt on a horse. To back it with all the money one possesses.

Shivering Mountain. Mam Tor, a hill on the Peak of Derbyshire; so called from the waste of its mass by "shivering"—that is, breaking away in "shivers" or small pieces. This has been going on for ages, as the hill consists of alternate layers of shale and gritstone. The former, being soft, is easily reduced to powder, and, as it crumbles small "shivers" of the gritstone break away from want of support.

Shoddy. Worthless stuff masquerading as something that is really good; from the cheap cloth called *shoddy* which is made up out of cloth from old garments torn to pieces and shredded, mixed with new wool.

Shoddy characters. Persons of tarnished reputation, like cloth made of shoddy or refuse wool.

Shoe. It was at one time thought unlucky to put on the left shoe before the right, or to put either shoe on the wrong foot. It is said that Augustus Cæsar was nearly assassinated by a mutiny one day when he put on his left shoe first.

One of the sayings of Pythagoras was: "When stretching forth your feet to have your sandals put on, first extend your right foot, but when about to step into a bath, let your left foot enter first." Iamblichus says the hidden meaning is that worthy actions should be done heartily, but base ones should be avoided (*Protreptics*, symbol xii).

It has long been a custom to throw an old shoe, or several shoes, at the bride and bridegroom when they quit the bride's home, after the wedding breakfast, or when they go to church to get married.

Now, for goode luck caste an old shoe after me.—
HAYWOOD (1693-1756).

Ay, with all my heart, there's an old shoe after you.
—*The Parson's Wedding* (*Dodsley*, vol. ix, p. 499).

In Anglo-Saxon marriages the father delivered the bride's shoe to the bridegroom, who touched her with it on the head to show his authority; and it is said that in Turkey the bridegroom is chased by the guests, who either administer blows by way of adieux, or pelt him with slippers.

Some think this shoe-throwing represents an assault and refers to the notion that the bridegroom carried off the bride with force and violence. Others look upon it as a relic of the ancient law of exchange, implying that the parents of the bride give up henceforth all right of dominion to their daughter. Luther told the bridegroom at a wedding that he had placed the husband's shoe on the head of the bed so that he should take to himself the mastery and governing of his wife.

Loosing the shoe (*cp. Josh*, v, 15) is a mark of respect in the East to the present hour. The Mussulman leaves his slippers at the door of the mosque, and when making a visit of ceremony to a European visitor, at the tent entrance.

In *Deut.* xxv, 5-10 we read that the widow refused by the surviving brother, asserted her independence by "loosing his shoe"; and in the story of Ruth we are told "that it was the custom" in exchange to deliver a shoe in token of renunciation. When Boaz, therefore, became possessed of his lot, the kinsman's kinsman indicated his assent by giving Boaz his shoe. "A man without sandals" was a proverbial expression among the Jews for a prodigal, from the custom of giving one's sandals in confirmation of a bargain.

Another man's shoes. "To stand in another man's shoes" is to occupy the place of another. Among the ancient Northmen, when a man adopted a son, the person adopted put on the shoes of the adopter.

In *Reynard the Fox* (*q.v.*) Reynard, having turned the tables on Sir Bruin the Bear, asked the queen to let him have the shoes of the disgraced minister; so Bruin's shoes were torn off and put upon the new favourite.

To shake in one's shoes. To be in a state of nervous terror.

To shoe a goose. To engage in a silly and fruitless task.

To shoe the anchor. To cover the flukes of an anchor with a broad triangular piece of plank, in order that the anchor may have a stronger hold in soft ground.

To shoe the cobbler. To give a quick peculiar movement with the front foot in sliding.

To shoe the wild colt. To exact a fine called "footing" from a newcomer, who is called the "colt." Colt is a common synonym for a greenhorn, or a youth not broken in. Thus Shakespeare says—"Ay, that's a colt indeed, for he doth nothing but talk of his horse" (*Merchant of Venice*, i, 2.).

Shofar (shō' far). A Hebrew trumpet still used in the modern synagogue. It is made of the horn of a ram or any ceremonially clean animal, and produces only the natural series of harmonics from its fundamental note.

Shogun (shō' gŭn). The title of the actual ruler of Japan from the 12th century to the modernization of the country in 1868. The Shoguns were hereditary commanders-in-chief (the word means "army leader"), and took the place of the Mikados, whom they kept in a state of perpetual imprisonment. Also called the *Tycoon* (*q.v.*).

Shoot. *See also* SHOT.

Shooting-iron. Slang (originally American) for a firearm, especially a revolver.

Shooting stars. Incandescent meteors shooting across the sky, formerly, like comets, fabled to presage disaster—

A little ere the mightiest Julius fell,
The graves stood tenantless, and the sheeted dead
Did squeak and gibber in the Roman streets:
As stars with trains of fire and dews of blood,
Disasters in the sun.
Hamlet, i, 1.

They were called in ancient legends the "fiery tears of St. Lawrence," because one of the periodic swarms of these meteors is between August 9th and 14th, about the time of St. Lawrence's festival, which is on the 10th. Other periods are from November 12th to 14th, and from December 6th to 12th.

Shooting stars are said by the Arabs to be firebrands hurled by the angels against the inquisitive genii, who are for ever clambering up on the constellations to peep into heaven.

To go the whole shoot. To do all there is to do, go the whole hog, run through the gamut.

To shoot a line. To boast.

To shoot one's linen. To display an unnecessary amount of shirt-cuff; to show off.

To shoot the moon. To remove one's household goods by night to avoid distraint; to "do a moonlight flit."

To shoot the sun. A sailor's expression for taking the sun's meridional altitude, which is done by aiming at the reflected sun through the telescope of the sextant.

Shoot! Go ahead; say what you have to say. Let's have it! In motion pictures it is the word used in the studios for the cameras to begin turning when all is ready.

Shop. The Shop, in military slang, is the Royal Military Academy, Woolwich; on the Stock Exchange it is the South African gold market.

To talk shop. To talk about one's affairs or business; to draw allusions from one's business, as when Ollapod, the apothecary in Colman's *Poor Gentleman*, talks of a uniform with rhubarb-coloured facings.

Shopkeepers. A nation of shopkeepers. This phrase, applied to Englishmen by Napoleon in contempt, comes from Adam Smith's *Wealth of Nations* (iv, 7), a book well known to the Emperor. He says—

To found a great empire for the sole purpose of raising up a people of customers, may at first sight appear a project fit only for a nation of shopkeepers.

Ten years earlier, in 1766, J. Tucker had written in the third of his *Four Tracts:*—

A Shop-keeper will never get the more Custom by beating his Customers; and what is true of a Shopkeeper, is true of a Shop-keeping Nation.

Shoreditch, according to tradition, is so called from Jane Shore, the mistress of Edward IV, who, it is said, died there in a ditch. This tale comes from a ballad in Pepys' collection—

I could not get one bit of bread
Whereby my hunger might be fed. . . .
So, weary of my life, at length
I yielded up my vital strength
Within a ditch . . . which since that day
Is Shoreditch called, as writers say—

But the truth is, it appears in the Index to Kemble's *Codex Diplomaticus* as *Sordic*, in the 14th century as *Soerditch*, and Stow says that in the 12th century it was called *Soersditch*. It is probable that it is from a former Anglo-Saxon proprietor, *Soer*.

Jane Shore is supposed to have died about 1527, but the date and place are alike unknown.

The Duke of Shoreditch. The most successful of the London archers received this playful title.

Good king, make not good Lord of Lincoln Duke of Shoreditch!—*The Poore Man's Peticion to the Kinge* (1603).

Short. A drop of something short. A tot of whisky, gin, or other spirit, as opposed to a glass of beer.

Cut it short! Don't be so prolix, come to the point; "cut the cackle and come to the 'osses." Said to a speaker who goes round and round his subject.

To break off short. Abruptly, without warning, but completely.

To sell short. A Stock Exchange phrase meaning to sell stock that one does not at the moment possess on the chance that before the date of delivery the price will have fallen; the same as "selling for a fall," or "selling a bear."

To make short work of it. To dispose of it quickly, to deal summarily with it.

Shorter Catechism. The name given to a confession of faith which sets forth the Presbyterian doctrines of the Church of Scotland. Drawn up in 1647 it was called the "shorter" to distinguish it from the larger catechism which was too complicated and difficult for ordinary instruction.

Shorthand. The earliest shorthand was invented in Rome by M. Tullius Tiro (63 B.C.) who used it to take down Cicero's speeches. Various systems were in use during the Middle Ages, but in *The Arte of Stenographie*, 1602, John Willis devised a system based on sound rather than on spelling. This was improved on by Thomas Shelton (1630) in a system later employed by Samuel Pepys in setting down his diary. In 1786 Samuel Taylor published an essay attempting to set up a standard phonetic system which was, in 1840, improved and modified by Isaac Pitman. This is one of the two systems now in general use, the other being devised (1888) on a monoslope basis by John Robert Gregg. Gregg's shorthand is in general use in U.S.A. whereas Pitman's is the more popular in Great Britain.

Shot. A fool's bolt is soon shot. See BOLT.

Big shot. An important person. 20th-century development of the 19th-century "great gun" or "big bug."

He shot wide of the mark. He was altogether in error. The allusion is to shooting at the mark or bull's-eye of a target.

Like a shot. With great rapidity; or, without hesitation, most willingly.

Shoulder. Showing the cold shoulder. Receiving without cordiality someone who was once on better terms with you. See COLD.

Straight from the shoulder. With full force. A boxing term.

The government shall be upon his shoulder (*Is.* ix, 6). The allusion is to the key slung on the shoulder of Jewish stewards on public occasions, and as a key is emblematic of government and power, the metaphor is very striking.

Shouting, All over but the. Success is so certain that only the applause is lacking. The phrase perhaps originated in a hotly contested election.

Shrapnel. A type of shell containing a number of bullets which are released and travel forwards with a high velocity when the shell is shattered by the bursting charge. It was invented in 1784 by Col. Henry Shrapnel (1761-1842) and was adopted in 1803 by the British army. In World War II this type of projectile was not used, but the term was loosely applied to all high-explosive fragments.

Shrew-mouse. A small insectivorous mammal, resembling a mouse, formerly supposed to have the power of poisoning cattle and young children by running over them. To provide a remedy our forefathers used to plug the creature into a hole made in an ash-tree; then any branch from it would cure the mischief done.

Shrift. The **shriving** of a person; *i.e.* his confession to a priest, and the penance and absolution arising therefrom.

To give short shrift to. To make short work of. *Short shrift* was the few minutes in which a criminal about to be executed was allowed to make his confession.

Shrimp. A child, a puny little fellow, in the same ratio to a man as a shrimp to a lobster. *Fry*, and *small fry*, are also used for children.

It cannot be this weak and writhled shrimp
Would strike such terror to his enemies.
1 *Henry VI*, ii, 3.

Shrivatsa. *See* VISHNU.

Shroff. An Oriental term, in India applied to a money-changer or banker, in China to an expert who tests gold and silver coins for their genuineness.

Shropshire. The "shire of shrubs." The Anglo-Saxon name of Shrewsbury was *scrobbes byrg*, the burgh among the shrubs. The Normans could not pronounce *sc-*; so the A.S. name became *Salopesbury*, and for the name of the county the *-bury* (= town) was dropped, giving *Salop*, a name still used as an alternative for Shropshire; whence *Salopian*, a native of the county.

Shrovetide. The three days just before the opening of Lent, when people went to confession and afterwards indulged in all sorts of sports and merry-making.

Shrove Tuesday. The day before Ash Wednesday; "Pancake day." It used to be the great "Derby Day" of cock-fighting in England.

Or martyr beat, like Shrovetide cocks, with bats.
PETER PINDAR: *Subjects for Painters*.

Shun-pike (U.S.A.). A side-road is so called because it is used to avoid the pike, or turnpike, where toll had to be paid.

Shut Up. Hold your tongue. Shut up your mouth.

Shy. To have a shy at anything. To fling at it, to try and shoot it.

Shylock, A (shī′ lok). A grasping, stony-hearted moneylender; in allusion to the Jew in Shakespeare's *Merchant of Venice:*

A stony adversary, an inhuman wretch
Uncapable of pity, void and empty
From any dram of mercy.
iv, 1.

Shyster. A mean, tricky sort of person; originally American slang for a low-class lawyer hanging about the courts on the off-chance of exploiting petty criminals.

Si (sē), the seventh note in music, was not introduced till the 17th century. Guido d'Arezzo's original scale consisted of only six notes. *See* ARETINIAN SYLLABLES.

Si Quis (sī kwis) (Lat., if anyone). A notice to all whom it may concern, given in the parish church before ordination, that a resident means to offer himself as a candidate for holy orders; and *if anyone* knows any just cause or impediment thereto, he is to declare the same to the bishop.

Siamese Twins (sī′ a mēz). Yoke-fellows, inseparables; so called from the original pair, Eng and Chang, who were born of Chinese parents about 1814 and discovered at Mekong, Siam, in 1829, and were subsequently exhibited as freaks. Their bodies were united by a band of flesh, stretching from breast-bone to breastbone. They married two sisters, had offspring, and died within three hours of each other on January 17th, 1874.

Other so-called Siamese twins were Barnum's "Orissa twins," born at Orissa, Bengal, and joined by a band of cartilage at the waist only; "Millie-Christine," two joined South Carolina negresses who appeared all over the world as the "Two-headed Nightingale"; and Josepha and Roza Blazek, natives of Bohemia, who were joined by a cartilaginous ligament above the waist. They died practically simultaneously in Chicago (1922), Josepha leaving a son aged 12.

Sibyl (sib′ il). A prophetess of classical legend, who was supposed to prophesy under the inspiration of a deity; the name is now applied to any prophetess or woman fortune-teller. There were a number of sibyls, and they had their seats in widely separate parts of the world—Greece, Italy, Babylonia, Egypt, etc.

Plato mentions only one, viz., the *Erythræan*—identified with Amalthea, the *Cumæan Sibyl*, who was consulted by Æneas before his descent into Hades and who sold the Sibylline books (*q.v.*) to Tarquin; Martian Capella speaks of two, the *Erythræan and the Phrygian*; Ælian of four, the *Erythræan, Samian, Egyptian*, and *Sardian*; Varro tells us there were *ten*, viz. the *Cumæan*,

the *Delphic, Egyptian, Erythræan, Hellespon-
tine, Libyan, Persian, Phrygian, Samian* and
Tiburtine.

How know we but that she may be an eleventh
Sibyl or a second Cassandra?—RABELAIS: *Gargantua
and Pantagruel*, iii, 16.

The mediæval monks "adopted" the sibyls—
as they did so much of pagan myth; they made
them twelve, and gave to each a separate prophecy
and distinct emblem:—

(1) The *Libyan*: "The day shall come when
men shall see the King of all living things."
Emblem, a lighted taper.

(2) The *Samian*: "The Rich One shall be born
of a pure virgin." *Emblem*, a rose.

(3) The *Cuman*: "Jesus Christ shall come from
heaven, and live and reign in poverty on earth."
Emblem, a crown.

(4) The *Cumæan*: "God shall be born of a
pure virgin, and hold converse with sinners." *Emblem*, a cradle.

(5) The *Erythræan*: "Jesus Christ, Son of God,
the Saviour." *Emblem*, a horn.

(6) The Persian: "Satan shall be overcome
by a true prophet." *Emblem*, a dragon under the
sibyl's feet, and a lantern.

(7) The *Tiburtine*: "The Highest shall descend
from heaven, and a virgin be shown in the valleys of the deserts." *Emblem*, a dove.

(8) The *Delphic*: "The Prophet born of the
virgin shall be crowned with thorns." *Emblem*,
a crown of thorns.

(9) The *Phrygian*: "Our Lord shall rise again."
Emblem, a banner and a cross.

(10) The *European*: "A virgin and her Son
shall flee into Egypt." *Emblem*, a sword.

(11) *The Agrippine*: "Jesus Christ shall be
outraged and scourged." *Emblem*, a whip.

(12) The *Hellespontic*: "Jesus Christ shall
suffer shame upon the cross." *Emblem*, a T cross.

Sic (sik) (Lat., thus, so). A word used by re-
viewers, quoters, etc., after a doubtful word or
phrase, or a misspelling, to indicate that it is
here printed exactly as in the original and to call
attention to the fact that it is wrong in some way.

Sick Man, The. So Nicholas of Russia (in
1844) called the Ottoman Empire, which had
been declining ever since 1586.

I repeat to you that the sick man is dying; and we
must never allow such an event to take us by surprise.—
Annual Register, 1853.

Don John, Governor-General of the
Netherlands, writing in 1579 to Philip II of
Spain, calls the Prince of Orange *the sick man*,
because he was in the way, and he wanted him
"finished."

"Money" (he says in his letter) "is the gruel with which
we must cure this sick man [for spies and assassins are
expensive drugs]"—MOTLEY: *Dutch Republic*, Bk. v, 2.

Side. On the side of the angels. The famous
phrase with which Disraeli thought he had settled the questions raised by Darwin's theory of
the origin of species. It occurred in his speech
at the Oxford Diocesan Conference in 1864—

The question is this: Is man an ape or an angel? I, my
lord, am on the side of the angels.

It was the same statesman who said in the
House of Commons (May 14th, 1866), "Ignorance never settles a question."

Putting on side. Giving oneself airs; being
bumptious. *To put on side* in billiards is to give
your ball a twist or spin with the cue as you
strike it.

To side-track. Originally an American railroad term; hence, to get rid of, shelve, put on
one side indefinitely.

Sideburns (U.S.A.). Short side-whiskers worn
with a smooth chin. Originally called Burn-
sides from the Federal general A. E. Burnside
(1824-1881) who wore such whiskers and whose
face was familiar to many Americans.

Sidrac (sid' răk). An old French romance
which tells how Sidrac converted to Christianity
Boccus, an idolatrous king and magician of
India. Sidrac lived only 847 years after Noah,
and became possessed of Noah's wonderful
book on astronomy and the natural sciences.
This passed through various hands, including
those of a pious Chaldean, and Naaman the
Syrian, until, as legend relates, Roger of Palermo
translated it at Toledo into Spanish. The work is
more a romance of Arabian philosophy than of
chivalry. In Henry VI's reign an English metrical version was made by Hugh Campeden, and
this was printed in 1510 as *The Historye of King
Boccus and Sydracke.*

Siege Perilous. In the cycle of Arthurian
romances a seat at the Round Table which was
kept vacant for him who should accomplish
the quest of the Holy Grail. For any less a person
to sit in it was fatal. As the crown of his achievement Sir Galahad took his seat in the Siege
Perilous.

Siegfried (sēg' frēd). Hero of the first part of
the *Nibelungenlied*. He was the youngest son of
Siegmund and Sieglind, king and queen of the
Netherlands. He married Kriemhild, Princess of
Burgundy, and sister of Gunther. Gunther craved
his assistance in carrying off Brunhild from
Issland, and Siegfried succeeded by taking away
her talisman by main force. This excited the
jealousy of Gunther, who induced Hagen, the

Dane, to murder Siegfried. Hagen struck him with a spear in the only vulnerable part (between the shoulder-blades), while he stooped to quench his thirst at a fountain.

Siegfried's cloak of invisibility, called "tarnkappe" (*tarnen*, to conceal; *kappe*, a cloak). It not only made the wearer invisible, but also gave him the strength of twelve men.

Sierra (sē ĕr' à) (Span., a saw). A mountain whose top is indented like a saw; a range of mountains whose tops form a saw-like appearance; a line of craggy rocks; as *Sierra Morena* (where many of the incidents in *Don Quixote* are laid), *Sierra Nevada* (the snowy range) *Sierra Leone* (in West Africa, where lions abound), etc.

Siesta (sē es' tà). Spanish for "the sixth hour"— *i.e.* noon (Lat. *sexta hora*). It is applied to the short sleep taken in Spain during the midday heat.

Sieve and Shears. The oracle of sieve and shears. This method of divination is mentioned by Theocritus. The *modus operandi* was as follows:—The points of the shears were stuck in the rim of a sieve, and two persons supported them with their finger-tips. Then a verse of the Bible was read aloud, and St. Peter and St. Paul were asked if it was A, B, or C (naming the persons suspected). When the right person was named, the sieve would suddenly turn round.

Searching for things lost with a sieve and shears.— BEN JONSON: *Alchemist*, i, 1.

Sight, for "multitude," though now regarded as a colloquialism or as slang, is good old English, and was formerly in literary use, the earlier significance being "a show or display of something." Thus, Juliana Berners, lady prioress in the 15th century of Sopwell nunnery, speaks of a *bombynable syght of monkes* (a large number of friars); and in one of the *Paston Letters* (May 25th, 1449) we read—

ye sawe never suche a syght of schyppys take in to Englond thys c. [hundred] wynter.

A sight for sore eyes. Something that it is very pleasurable to see or witness, especially something unexpected.

Second light. See SECOND.

Sign. Royal Sign Manual. A stamp reproducing the royal signature, used when the sovereign is too ill to sign documents.

To sign off. In the 19th century this denoted leaving one religious denomination in a formal manner for another. In the 20th century it was for long used in radio as synonymous with the termination of a performance by a regular broadcaster known to the public, hence

Signature tune. A musical theme played regularly as a means of identification when introducing a well-known artist, dance band, etc.

Significavit (sig ni fi cā' vit). A writ of Chancery given by the ordinary to keep an excommunicate in prison till he submitted to the authority of the Church. The writ, which is now obsolete, used to begin with *Significavit nobis venerabilis pater*, etc. Chaucer says of his Sompnour—

And also ware him of a significavit.

Canterbury Tales (*Prologue*), 664.

Sigurd (sig' ĕrd). The Siegfried (*q.v.*) of the *Volsunga Saga*, the Scandinavian version of the *Niebelungenlied* (*q.v.*). He falls in love with Brynhild, but, under the influence of a love-potion, marries Gudrun, a union which brings about a volume of mischief.

Sikes, Bill. The type of a ruffianly house-breaker, from the fellow of that name in Dickens's *Oliver Twist*. The only rudiment of a redeeming feature he posessed was a kind of affection for his dog:

Sikh (sik) (Hindu *sikh*, disciple). The Sikhs were originally a monotheistic body founded in the Punjab by Nanak (1469-1539). They soon became a military community, and in 1764 formally assumed national independence. In 1809 their ruler, Rangit Singh made a treaty with Britain, but the anarchy following upon his death led to the Sikh Wars of 1845-46 and 1848-49. During the Mutiny they remained loyal to Britain.

Silence. Silence gives consent. A saying (common to many languages) founded on the old Latin law maxim—*Qui tacet consentire videtur* (who is silent is held to consent).

But that you shall not say I yield, being silent, I would not speak.

Cymbeline, ii, 3.

Silence is golden. *See under* SPEECH.

The rest is silence. The last words of the dying Hamlet (*Hamlet*, v, 2).

Towers of Silence. The small towers on which the Parsees and Zoroastrians place their dead to be consumed by birds of prey. The bones are picked clean in the course of a day, and are then thrown into a receptacle and covered with charcoal.

Parsees do not burn or bury their dead, because they consider a corpse impure, and they will not defile any of the elements. They carry it on a bier to the tower. At the entrance they look their last on the body, and the corpse-bearers carry it within the precincts and lay it down to be devoured by vultures which are constantly on the watch.

Two-minute Silence. A cessation of traffic and all other activities for two minutes at 11 a.m.

on November 11th, to commemorate those who died in World War I. It was first observed in 1919 and discontinued in 1947 when the day was named Remembrance Day in memory of the fallen in both World Wars, and observed on the Sunday preceding November 11th.

Silhouette (sil oo et'). A black profile, so called from Etienne de Silhouette (1709-67), Contrôleur des Finances, 1759, who made great savings in the public expenditure of France. Some say the black portraits were named after him in allusion to the sacrifices he demanded from the nobles—*silhouette* being the popular term for a figure reduced to its simplest form; others assert that he devised this way of taking likenesses to save expense.

Silk. To take silk. Said of a barrister who has been appointed a Queen's Counsel (Q.C.), because he then exchanges his stuff gown for a silk one.

You cannot make a silk purse of a sow's ear. You cannot make something good of what is by its nature bad or inferior in quality. "You cannot make a horn of a pig's tail."

Silly is the German *selig* (blessed) and used to mean in English "happy through being innocent"; whence the infant Jesus was termed "the harmless silly babe," and sheep were called "silly." As the "innocent" are easily taken in by worldly cunning, the word came to signify "gullible," "foolish."

The silly season. An obsolescent journalistic expression for the part of the year when Parliament and the Law Courts are not sitting (about August and September), when, through lack of news, the papers had to fill their columns with trivial items—such as news of giant gooseberries and sea serpents—and long correspondence on subjects of evanescent (if any) interest.

Silver. In England *standard silver* (*i.e.* that used for the coinage) formerly consisted of thirty-seven fortieths of fine silver and three fortieths of alloy (fineness, 925); but by an Act passed in 1920 the proportions, for reasons of economy, were changed to one half silver and one half alloy (fineness, 500). The Coinage Act of 1946 permitted copper-nickel coins, with no silver whatever, to replace the former silver coins.

Silver is not legal tender for sums over £2.

Silver articles are marked with five marks (*see* HALL MARK): the maker's private mark, the standard or assay mark, the hall mark, the duty mark, and the date mark. The standard mark states the proportion of silver, to which figure is added a *lion passant* for England, a *harp* crowned

for Ireland, a *thistle* for Edinburgh, and a *lion rampant* for Glasgow.

Among the ancient alchemists *silver* represented the Moon, or Diana; in heraldry it is known by its French name, *Argent* (which also gives its chemical symbol, "Ag."), and is indicated in engravings by the silver (argent) portion being left blank.

A silver lining. The prospect of better days, the promise of happier times. The saying, **Every cloud has a silver lining,** is an old one; thus in Milton's *Comus*, the Lady lost in the wood resolves to hope on, and sees a "sable cloud turn forth its silver lining to the night."

Born with a silver spoon in one's mouth. *See* BORN.

Silver of Guthrum. *See* GUTHRUM.

Silver Star. A U.S.A. military medal awarded to an officer or man who has been cited for gallantry in action of a less conspicuous nature than would warrant a citation for the Medal of Honor or the Distinguished Service Cross. It consists of a bronze star bearing a small silver star in its centre.

Silver-tongued. An epithet bestowed on many persons famed for eloquence; especially William Bates, the Puritan divine (1625-99); Anthony Hammond, the poet (1668-1738); Henry Smith, preacher (1550-1600); and Joshua Sylvester (1563-1618), translator of Du Bartas.

Silver Wedding. The twenty-fifth anniversary, when presents of silver plate (in Germany a silver wreath) are given to the happy pair.

Speech is silver. *See* SPEECH.

The Silver Age. The second of the Ages of the World (*q.v.*), according to Hesiod and the Greek and Roman poets; fabled as a period that was voluptuous and godless, and much inferior in simplicity and true happiness to the Golden Age.

The silver cooper. A kidnapper. "To play the silver cooper," to kidnap. A cooper is one who *coops up* another.

The Silver-Fork School. A name given in amused contempt (about 1830) to the novelists who were sticklers for the etiquette and graces of the Upper Ten and showed great respect for the affectations of gentility. Theodore Hook, Lady Blessington, and Bulwer Lytton might be taken as representatives of it.

The Silver Streak. The English Channel.

Thirty pieces of silver. The sum of money that Judas Iscariot received from the chief priest for the betrayal of his Master (*Matt.* xxvi, 15); hence used proverbially of a bribe or "blood-money."

With silver weapons you may conquer the world. The Delphic oracle to Philip of Macedon, when he went to consult it. Philip, acting on this advice, sat down before a fortress which his staff pronounced to be impregnable. "You shall see," said the king, "how an ass laden with silver will find an entrance."

Simeon, St. (sim' ē ón), is usually depicted as bearing in his arms the infant Jesus, or receiving Him in the Temple. His feast-day is February 18th.

St. Simeon Stylites. *See* STYLITES.

Similia similibus curantur (sim il' iá si mil' i bús kū răn' ter) (Lat.). Like cures like; or, as we say, "Take a hair of the dog that bit you."

Simkin. Anglo-Indian for champagne—of which word it is an Urdu mispronunciation.

Simnel Cakes. Rich cakes formerly eaten (especially in Lancashire) on Mid-Lent Sunday ("Mothering Sunday"), Easter, and Christmas Day. They were ornamented with scallops, and were eaten at Mid-Lent in commemoration of the banquet given by Joseph to his brethren, which forms the first lesson of Mid-Lent Sunday, and the feeding of five thousand, which forms the Gospel of the day.

The word *simnel* is through O.Fr. from late Lat. *siminellus*, fine bread, Lat. *simila*, the finest wheat flour.

Simon, St. (Zelotes), is represented with a saw in his hand, in allusion to the instrument of his martyrdom. He sometimes bears fish in the other hand, in allusion to his occupation as a fishmonger. His feast day is October 28th.

Simon Magus. Isidore tells us that Simon Magus died in the reign of Nero, and adds that he had proposed a dispute with Peter and Paul, and had promised to fly up to heaven. He succeeded in rising high into the air, but at the prayers of the two apostles he was cast down to earth by the evil spirits who had enabled him to rise.

Milman, in his *History of Christianity* (ii, p. 51) tells another story. He says that Simon offered to be buried alive, and declared that he would reappear on the third day. He was actually buried in a deep trench, "but to this day," says Hippolytus, "his disciples have failed to witness his resurrection."

His followers were known as Simonians, and the sin of which he was guilty, viz. the trafficking in sacred things, the buying and selling of ecclesiastical offices (*see Acts* viii, 18) is still called *simony*.

Simple Simon. A simpleton, a gullible booby; from the character in the well-known anonymous nursery tale, who "met a pie-man."

Simple, The. Charles III of France. (879, 893-929).

The simple life. A mode of living in which the object is to eliminate as far as possible all luxuries and extraneous aids to happiness, etc., returning to the simplicity of life as imagined by the pastoral poets.

Simplicity is *sine plica*, without a fold; as duplicity is *duplex plica*, a double fold. Conduct "without a fold" is *straightforward, simple*.

The flat simplicity of that reply was admirable.—
VANBRUGH: *The Provoked Husband*, i.

Disraeli spoke in the House of Commons (February 19th, 1850) of "The sweet simplicity of the Three per Cents," plagiarizing Lord Stowell, who had earlier spoken of their "elegant simplicity" (*see* Campbell's *Lives of the Chancellors*, vol. x).

Sin, according to Milton, is twin-keeper with Death of the gates of Hell. She sprang full-grown from the head of Satan.

 . . . Woman to the waist, and fair,
But ending foul in many a scaly fold
Voluminous and vast, a serpent armed
With mortal sting.
     Paradise Lost, ii, 650-653.

Original sin. That corruption which is born with us, and is the inheritance of all the offspring of Adam. Theology teaches that as Adam was founder of his race, when Adam fell the taint and penalty of his disobedience passed to all his posterity.

Sin-eaters. Persons hired at funerals in ancient times, to eat beside the corpse and so take upon themselves the sins of the deceased, that the soul might be delivered from purgatory.

Notice was given to an old sire before the door of the house, when some of the family came out and furnished him a cricket [low stool], on which he sat down facing the door; then they gave him a groat which he put in his pocket, a crust of bread which he ate, and a bowl of ale which he drank off at a draught. After this he got up from the cricket and pronounced the ease and rest of the soul departed, for which he would pawn his own soul.—
Bagford's letter on Leland's Collectanea, i, 76.

The Man of Sin. (2 *Thess.* ii, 3). Generally held to signify the Antichrist (*q.v.*), but applied by the old Puritans to the Pope of Rome, by the Fifth Monarchy men to Cromwell, and by many modern theologians to that "wicked one" (identical with the "last horn" of *Dan.* vii) who is immediately to precede the Second Advent.

The seven deadly sins. Pride, Wrath, Envy, Lust, Gluttony, Avarice, and Sloth.

To earn the wages of sin. To be hanged, or condemned to death.

The wages of sin is death.—*Rom.* vi, 23.

To sin one's mercies. To be ungrateful for the gifts of Providence.

Sinbad the Sailor (sin' băd). The hero of a story of this name in the *Arabian Nights Entertainments*. A wealthy citizen of Bagdad, he was called "The Sailor" because of his seven voyages in which, among other high adventures, he discovered the Roc's egg and the Valley of Diamonds, and killed the Old Man of the Sea who had got on his back and would not be dismounted.

Sine (Lat.). Without.

Sine die (Lat.). No time being fixed; indefinitely in regard to time. When a proposal is deferred *sine die*, it is deferred without fixing a day for its reconsideration, which is virtually "for ever."

Sine qua non (Lat.). An indispensable condition. Lat. *Sine qua non potest esse* or *fieri* (that without which [the thing] cannot be, *or* be done).

Sinecure (Lat. *sine cura*, without cure, or care). An enjoyment of the money attached to a benefice without having the trouble of the "cure"; applied to any office to which a salary is attached without any duties to perform.

Sinews of War. Essential funds for the prosecution of a war. Troops have to be paid and fed and the materials of war are costly.

The English phrase comes from Cicero's *Nervos belli pecuniam* (*Phil*. V. ii, 5), money makes the sinews of war. Rabelais (I, xlvi) uses the same idiom — *Les nerfs des batailles sont les pécunes*.

Victuals and ammunition,
And money too, the sinews of the war,
Are stored up in the magazine.
BEAUMONT AND FLETCHER: *Fair Maid of the Inn*, i, 1.

Sing. Singing bread (Fr. *pain à chanter*). An old term for the wafer used in celebration of the Mass, because singing was in progress during its consecration. The Reformers directed that the sacramental bread should be similar in fineness and fashion to the round bread and water *singing-cakes* used in private Masses.

To sing out. To cry or squeal from chastisement; formerly said also of a prisoner who turned informer against his comrades. *See above*.

To sing small. To cease boasting and assume a lower tone.

Sinis (sī' nis). A Corinthian robber of Greek legend, known *as the Pinebender*, because he used to fasten his victims to two pine-trees bent towards the earth, and then leave them to be rent asunder when the trees were released. He was captured by Theseus and put to death in this same way.

Sinister (sin' is ter) (Lat., on the left hand). Foreboding of ill; ill-omened. According to augury, birds, etc., appearing on the left-hand side forbode ill-luck; but on the right-hand side, good luck. Plutarch, following Plato and Aristotle, gives as the reason that the west (or left side of the augur) was towards the setting or departing sun.

Corva sinistra (a crow on the left-hand) is a sign of ill-luck which belongs to English superstitions as much as to the ancient Roman or Etruscan (Virgil: *Eclogues*, i, 18.)

That raven on you left-hand oak
(Curse on his ill-betiding croak)
Bodes me no good.
GAY: *Fable*, xxxvii.

Bar sinister. *See* BAR.

Sinn Fein (shin fān). Irish for "Ourselves alone" This was the Nationalist movement that finally brought about the establishment of the Irish Free State in 1921. The rebellion of 1916 was its first overt act of great importance; in the following year Eamonn de Valera was elected president of the movement and the new republican policy was inaugurated. In December, 1918, Sinn Fein candidates were elected for 73 out of 105 Irish seats in Parliament and these constituted themselves as Dail Eireann. The Irish republican army was organized and carried on a violent guerrilla warfare against the military and the police. In December, 1921, negotiations were opened between the Sinn Fein leaders and the British government, and the Treaty of independence of Eire was signed.

Sinon (sī' non). The Greek who induced the Trojans to receive the wooden horse (Virgil: *Æneid*, ii, 102, etc.). Anyone deceiving to betray is called "a Sinon."

Sioux (soo). A North American Indian tribe who call themselves Dakotas, Sioux being the termination of the French form of their Ojibwa name meaning "enemies." The name is used for the Siouan family generally, comprising many tribes in the Mississippi and Missouri basins.

Sir. Lat. *senex*, Span, *señor*, Ital. *signor*, Fr. *sieur, sire*.

As a title of honour prefixed to the Christian name of baronets and knights, *Sir* is of great antiquity; and the clergy had at one time *Sir* prefixed to their name. This is merely a translation of the university word *dominus* given to graduates, as, "*Dominus* Hugh Evans," etc. Spenser uses the title as a substantive, meaning a parson —

But this, good Sir, did follow the plaine word. —
Mother Hubberd's Tale, 390.

Sirat, Al. *See* AL-SIRAT.

Sirdar (ser' dar). A native noble in India. Also the former official title of the British commander-in-chief of the Egyptian army.

Siren (sī' ren). One of the mythical monsters, half woman and half bird, said by Greek poets (*see Odyssey*, xii) to entice seamen by the sweetness of their song to such a degree that the listeners forgot everything and died of hunger (Gr. *sirenes*, entanglers); hence applied to any dangerous, alluring woman.

In Homeric mythology there were but two sirens; later writers name three, viz. Parthenope, Ligea, and Leucosia; and the number was still further augmented by later writers.

Ulysses escaped their blandishments by filling his companions' ears with wax and lashing himself to the mast of his ship.

What Song the Syrens sang, or what name Achilles assumed when he hid himself among women, though puzzling questions are not beyond all conjecture. — SIR THOS. BROWNE: *Urn Burial.* v.

Plato says there were three kinds of sirens — the *celestial*, the *generative*, and the *cathartic*. The first were under the government of Jupiter, the second under that of Neptune, and the third of Pluto. When the soul is in heaven the sirens seek, by harmonic motion, to unite it to the divine life of the celestial host; and when in Hades, to conform them to the infernal regimen; but on earth they produce generation, of which the sea is emblematic. (Proclus: *On the Theology of Plato*, Bk. vi.)

In more recent times the word has been applied to the loud mechanical whistle sounded at a factory, etc., to indicate that work is to be started or finished for the day. Sirens with two or more recognizable notes were employed in World War II to give warning of the approach or departure of hostile aircraft.

Siren suit. A one-piece garment, on the lines of a boiler suit, sometimes worn in London during the bombing raids of World War II. It is so named from its being slipped on over the night clothes at the first moan of the siren.

Sirius (sir' i ús). The Dog-star; so called by the Greeks from the adjective *seirios*, hot and scorching. The Romans called it *canicula*, whence our Canicular days (*q.v.*), and the Egyptians *sept*, which gave the Greek alternative *sothis*. *See* SOTHIC YEAR.

Sirocco (si rok' ō). A wind from northern Africa that blows over Italy, Sicily, etc., producing extreme languor and mental debility.

Sise Lane. *See* TOOLEY STREET.

Sistine (sis' tīn, sis' tēn). **The Sistine Chapel.** The private chapel of the Pope in the Vatican, so called because built by Pope Sixtus IV (1471-84). It is decorated with the frescoes of Michelangelo and others.

Sistine Madonna, The, or the **Madonna di San Sisto.** The Madonna painted by Raphael (about 1518) for the church of St. Sixtus (San Sisto) at Piacenza; St. Sixtus is shown kneeling at the right of the Virgin. The picture was in the Royal Gallery, Dresden, but after World War II passed into Russian hands.

Sisyphus (sis' i fús). A legendary king of Corinth, crafty and avaricious, said to be the son of Æolus, or — according to later legend, which also makes him the father of Ulysses — of Autolycus. His task in the world of shades is to roll a huge stone up a hill till it reaches the top; as the stone constantly rolls back his work is incessant; hence "a labour of Sisyphus" or "Sisyphean toil" is an endless, heart-breaking job.

Sit. To make one sit up. To astonish or disconcert him considerably, to stir him up to action.

To sit on or **upon.** To snub, squash, smother, put in his place.

Sit on has other meanings also; thus *to sit on a corpse* is to hold a coroner's inquest on it; *to sit on the bench* is to occupy a seat as a judge or magistrate.

To sit on the fence. *See* FENCE.

To sit tight. To keep your own counsel; to remain in or as in hiding. The phrase is from poker, where, if a player does not want to continue betting and at the same time does not wish to throw in his cards, he "sits tight."

To sit under. A colloquialism for attending the ministrations of the clergyman named. The phrase was common three hundred years ago, and is still in use.

There would then also appear in pulpits other visages, other gestures, and stuff otherwise wrought than what we now sit under, oft-times to as great a trial of our patience as any other than they preach to us. — MILTON: *Of Education* (1644).

Sit-down strike. A strike in which the workers remain at their factory, etc., but refuse to work themselves or allow others to do so.

Sitting Bull. A famous warrior chief of the Sioux Indians, born on Grand River, South Dakota, in 1834. He commanded the Indians who defeated General Custer at Little Big Horn, 1876, but was killed on December 5th, 1890 while resisting arrest at Fort Yates, N. Dakota, during the Sioux rebellion of that year.

Siva or **Shiva** (sē' va, shē' va). The third person of the Hindu Trinity, or *Trimurti*, representing the destructive principle in life and also, as in Hindu philosophy restoration is involved in destruction, the reproductive or renovating power. He is a great worker of miracles through meditation and penance, and hence is a favourite deity with the ascetics. He is a god of the fine arts, and of dancing; and Siva, one only of his very many names, means "the Blessed One."

Six. At sixes and sevens. Higgledy-piggledy, in a state of confusion; or of persons, unable to come to an agreement. The phrase comes from dicing.

> The goddess would no longer wait;
> But rising from her chair of state,
> Left all below at six and seven,
> Harness'd her doves, and flew to heaven.
> SWIFT: *Cadenus and Vanessa (closing lines)*.

Six of one and half a dozen of the other. There is nothing to choose between them, they are both in the wrong—*Arcades ambo*.

The Six Articles. An Act of Parliament passed in 1539 (repealed 1547) enjoining belief in (1) the real presence of Christ in the Eucharist; (2) the sufficiency of communion in one kind; (3) the celibacy of the priests; (4) the obligation of vows of chastity; (5) the expediency of private masses; and (6) the necessity of auricular confession, and decreeing death on those who denied the doctrine of Transubstantiation. It was also known as *The Bloody Bill*, and the *Six Stringed Whip*.

The Six Nations. The confederacy of North American Indian tribes consisting of the Five Nations (*q.v.*) and the Tuscaroras (formerly of North Carolina but now of New York and Ontario) who joined about 1715.

Sizar (sī' zàr). An undergraduate of Cambridge, or of Trinity College, Dublin, who receives a grant from his college to assist in paying his expenses. Formerly sizars were expected to undertake certain menial duties now performed by college servants; and the name is taken to show that one so assisted received his *sizes* or *sizings* free.

Sizings. The allowance of food provided by the college for undergraduates at a meal; a pound loaf, two inches of butter, and a pot of milk used to be the "sizings" for breakfast; meat was provided for dinner, but any extras had to be *sized* for. The word is a contraction of *assize*, a statute to regulate the size or weight of articles sold.

> A size is a portion of bread or drinke; it is a farthing which schollers in Cambridge have at the buttery. It is noted with the letter S.—MINSHIEN: *Ductor* (1617).

Skains-mate. The meaning of the word is uncertain, but *skene* or *skean* is the long dagger formerly carried by the Irish and Scots (Gael. *scian, sgian*), so it may mean a dagger-comrade or fellow-cut-throat. Swift, describing an Irish feast (1720), says, "A cubit at least the length of their skains," and Greene, in his *Quip for an*

Upstart Courtier (1592), speaks of "an ill-favoured knave, who wore by his side a skane, like a brewer's bung-knife."

Skanda. *See* KARTTIKEYA.

Skedaddle. To run away hastily, make off in a hurry; to be scattered in rout. The Scots apply the word to the milk spilt over the pail in carrying it. During the American Civil War the word came into prominence with its present meaning.

Skeleton. The family skeleton, or **the skeleton in the cupboard.** Some domestic secret that the whole family conspires to keep to itself; every family is said to have at least one.

The story is that someone without a single care or trouble in the world had to be found. After long and unsuccessful search a lady was discovered whom all thought would "fill the bill"; but to the great surprise of the inquirers, after she had satisfied them on all points and the quest seemed to be achieved, she took them upstairs and there opened a closet which contained a human skeleton. "I try," said she, "to keep my trouble to myself, but every night my husband compels me to kiss that skeleton." She then explained that the skeleton was once her husband's rival, killed in a duel.

The skeleton at the feast. The thing or person that acts as a reminder that there are troubles as well as pleasures in life. Plutarch says in his *Moralia* that the Egyptians always had a skeleton placed in a prominent position at their banquets.

Skevington's Daughter. *See* SCAVENGER'S.

Skiddaw (skid' aw). **Whenever Skiddaw hath a cap, Scruffell wots full well of that** (Fuller: *Worthies*). When my neighbour's house is on fire mine is threatened; when you are in misfortune I also am a sufferer; when you mourn I have cause also to lament. Skiddaw and Scruffell, or Scawfell, are neighbouring hills in Cumberland. When Skiddaw is capped with clouds, it will be sure to rain ere long at Scawfell.

Skid Row (U.S.A.). A district populated by vicious characters or down-and-outs, *i.e.* those who have skidded from the path of virtue.

Skill. It skills not. It makes no difference; it doesn't matter one way or the other. The phrase was once very common, but is now looked upon as an archaism.

> Whether he [Callimachus] be now lyving I know not but whether he be or no, it skilleth not.—LYLY: *Euphues and his England* (1580).

Similarly, **What skills talking?** What is the use of talking?

Skimble-skamble. Rambling, worthless. "Skamble" is merely a variety of *scramble*, hence "scambling days," those days in Lent when no regular meals are provided, but each person "scrambles" or shifts for himself. "Skimble" is added to give force.

And such a deal of skimble-skamble stuff
As put me from my faith.
1 *Henry IV*, iii, 1.
With such scamble-scemble, spitter-spatter,
As puts me cleane beside the money-matter.
TAYLOR, *The Water Poet*, ii, 39 (1630).

Skimmington. It was an old custom in rural England and Scotland to make an example of nagging wives and unfaithful husbands by forming a ludicrous procession through the village for the purpose of ridiculing the offender. In cases of hen-pecking Grose tells us that the man rode behind the woman, with his face to the horse's tail. The man held a distaff, and the woman beat him about the jowls with a ladle. As the procession passed a house where the woman was paramount, each gave the threshold a sweep. This performance was called *riding Skimmington* (also *riding the stang*—*see* STANG), and the husband or wife was, for the time, known as *Skimmington*. The origin of the name is uncertain, but in an illustration of the procession of 1639 the woman is shown belabouring her husband with a *skimming*-ladle.

The custom was not peculiar to Britain; it prevailed in Scandinavia, Spain, and elsewhere. The procession is described at length in *Hudibras*, II, ii.

Skin. By the skin of one's teeth. Only just, by a mere hair's breadth. The phrase comes from the book of *Job* (xix, 20):—

My bone cleaveth to my skin and to my flesh, and I am escaped with the skin of my teeth.

Coverdale's rendering of the passage is—

My bone hangeth to my skynne, and the flesh is awaye only there is left me the skynne aboute my teth.

To save one's skin. To get off with one's life.

To skin a flint. To be very exacting in making a bargain. The French say, *Tondre sur un œuf*. The Latin *lana caprina* (goat's wool), means something as worthless as the skin of a flint or fleece of an eggshell. Hence a **skinflint**, a pinchfarthing, a niggard.

Skinners. A predatory band in the American Revolutionary War which roamed over Westchester County, New York, robbing and fleecing those who refused to take the oath of fidelity to the Republic.

Skull. Skull and crossbones. An emblem of mortality; specifically, the pirate's flag. The "crossbones" are two human thigh-bones laid across one another.

Sky. Rhyming slang for pocket, the missing word being *rocket*. *See* RHYMING SLANG.

If the sky falls we shall catch larks. A bantering reply to those who suggest some very improbable or wild scheme.

Lauded to the skies. Extravagantly praised; praised to the heights.

Sky-raker. A nautical term for any topsail; strictly speaking, a sail above the fore-royal, the main-royal, or the mizzen-royal.

Skyscraper. A very tall building, especially one in New York or some other American city. Some of them run to a hundred floors, and more. Also applied by sailors to a *sky-raker*.

Slam. A term in card-playing denoting winning all the tricks in a deal. In Bridge this is called *Grand slam*, and winning all but one, *Little slam*. *Cp.* RUFF.

Slander. Literally, a stumbling-block (*cp.* SCANDAL), or something which trips a person up (Gr. *skandalon*, through Fr. *esclandre*).

Slang. As denoting language or jargon of a low or colloquial type the word first appeared in the 18th century; its origin is not known, but it is probably connected with *sling* (*cp. mud-slinging*, for hurling abuse at one). Slang is of various sorts, fashionable, professional, schoolboy, sporting, etc. Some of it is introduced into the language from below, *i.e.* from the ranks of thieves, rogues, and vagabonds. It usually has an element of humour about it, through exaggeration or absurd juxtaposition. Slang is always invented by individuals and adopted later by the public. When the adoption becomes so general and so approved that the expression in question is accepted as standard English, it ceases to be slang.

See also BACK-SLANG; RHYMING SLANG.

To slang a person. To abuse him, give him a piece of your mind.

Slap-bang. At once, without hesitation—done with a slap and a bang. The term was formerly applied to cheap eating-houses, where one slapped one's money down as the food was banged on the table.

They lived in the same street, walked to town every morning at the same hour, dined at the same slap-bang every day.—DICKENS: *Sketches by Boz*, III, 36.

Slap-dash. In an off-hand manner done hurriedly as with a slap and a dash. Rooms used to be decorated by slapping and dashing the walls so as to imitate paper, and at one time slap-dash walls were very common.

Slap-up. First-rate, grand, stylish.

[The] more slap-up still have the shields painted on the panels with the coronet over.—THACKERAY.

Slapstick. Literally the two or more laths bound together at one end with which harlequins, clowns, etc., strike other performers with a resounding slap or crack; but more often applied to any broad comedy with knock-about action and horseplay.

Slate. Slate club. A sick benefit club for working-men. Originally the names of the members and the money paid in were entered on a folding slate.

To start with a clean slate. To be given another chance, one's past misdeeds having been forgiven and expunged, as writing is sponged from a slate.

Slave. This is an example of the strange changes which come over some words. The *Slavi* were a tribe which once dwelt on the banks of the Dnieper, and were so called from *slav* (noble, illustrious); but as, in the later stages of the Roman Empire, vast multitudes of them were spread over Europe as captives, the word acquired its present meaning.

Similarly, *Goths* means the good or godlike men; but since the invasion of the Goths the word has become synonymous with barbarous, bad, ungodlike.

In World War II a **slave** was a vehicle with electrical equipment designed to serve tanks—*i.e.* charge their batteries, and start them in the morning.

Sledge-hammer. A sledge-hammer argument. A clincher; an argument which annihilates opposition at a blow. The sledge-hammer (A.S. *slecge*) is the largest hammer used by smiths, and is wielded by both hands.

Sleep. To sleep away. To pass away in sleep, to consume in sleeping; as, "to sleep one's life away."

To sleep off. To get rid of by sleep.

To sleep on a matter. To let a decision on it stand over till to-morrow.

Sleeper, The. Epimenides, the Greek poet, is said to have fallen asleep in a cave when a boy, and not to have waked for fifty-seven years, when he found himself possessed of all wisdom.

In mediæval legend stories of those who have gone to sleep and have been—or are to be—awakened after many years are very numerous. Such legends hang round the names of King Arthur, Charlemagne, and Barbarossa. *Cp.* also the stories of the Seven Sleepers of Ephesus, Tannhäuser, Ogier the Dane, Kilmeny, and Rip van Winkle.

Sleeper Awakened, The. *See* SLY, CHRISTOPHER.

Sleeping Beauty, The. This charming nursery tale comes from the French *La Belle au Bois Dormant*, by Charles Perrault (1628-1703). (*Contes de ma mère l'Oye*, 1697). The Princess is shut up by enchantment in a castle, where she sleeps a hundred years, during which time an impenetrable wood springs up around. Ultimately she is disenchanted by the kiss of a young Prince, who marries her.

Sleeping partner. A partner in a business who takes no active share in running it beyond supplying capital.

Sleeping sickness. A West African disease caused by a parasite, *Trypanosoma Gambiense*, characterized by fever and great sleepiness, and usually terminating fatally. The disease known in England, which shows similar symptoms is usually called *Sleeping illness* or *Sleepy sickness* as a means of distinction; its scientific name is *Encephalitis lethargica.*

Sleepy. Pears are said to be "sleepy" when they are beginning to rot; and cream when, in the course of its making, the whole assumes a frothy appearance.

Sleepy hollow. Any village far removed from the active concerns of the outside world. The name given in Washington Irving's *Sketch Book* to a quiet old-world village on the Hudson.

Sleepy sickness. *See* SLEEPING SICKNESS, *above*.

Sleeve. To hang on one's sleeve. To listen devoutly to what one says: to surrender your freedom of thought and action to the judgment of another.

To have up one's sleeve. To hold in reserve; to have it ready to bring out in a case of emergency. The allusion is to conjurers, who frequently conceal in the sleeve the means by which they do the trick.

To laugh in one's sleeve. To ridicule a person not openly but in secret. At one time it was quite possible to conceal a laugh by hiding one's face in the large sleeves worn by men. The French say, *rire sous cape.*

To wear one's heart on one's sleeve, to expose all one's feelings to the eyes of the world. Iago wears his heart on his sleeve, displaying a feigned devotion to his master (*Othello*, i, 1).

Sleeveless. In the 16th century *sleeveless* was very commonly applied to *errand, answer, message*, etc., signifying that it was fruitless or futile, an errand, etc., that has no result. In *Eikonoclastes* Milton speaks of sleeveless reason, meaning reasoning that leads nowhere and proves nothing; and a *sleeveless message* was used of a kind of April fool trick—the messenger being dispatched merely so as to get rid of him for a time.

> If all these faile, a beggar-woman may
> A sweet love-letter to her hands convey,
> Or a neat laundresse or a hearb-wife can
> Carry a sleeveless message now and than.
> > *Taylor's Workes*, ii, 111 (1630).

Slick. Adroit, dextrous, smart; the word is a variant of *sleek*.

Sliding Scale. A scale of duties, prices, payment, etc., which slides up and down as the article to which it refers becomes dearer or cheaper, or by which such payments accommodate themselves to the fluctuations in other conditions previously named.

Slip. Many a slip 'twixt the cup and the lip. Everything is uncertain till you possess it. *Cp.* ANCÆUS.

> Multa cadunt inter calicem supremaque labra.—HORACE.

To give one the slip. To steal off unperceived; to elude pursuit. A sea phrase; a cable and buoy are fastened to the anchor-chain, which is let slip though the hawse-pipe, Done to save time in weighing anchor. The metaphor probably came originally from the action of "slipping" a hound, *i.e.* allowing it to run free by slipping the lead from its collar. In coursing the official who releases the greyhounds is still called the *slipper*.

Sloane MSS. 3,560 MSS. collected by Sir Hans Sloane (1660-1753), and left to the nation, together with his library (50,000 vols.) and other collections on condition that his heirs received £20,000, which was far less than their value. These collections were bought and housed in Montague House, and formed the nucleus of the British Museum.

Slogan (slō' găn). The war-cry of the old Highland clans (Gael. *sluagh*, host, *ghairm*, outcry). Hence, any warcry; and, in later use, a political party cry, an advertising catch-phrase, etc. *Cp.* SLUGHORN.

Slope. To decamp; to run away. The term came from the United States, and may be a contraction of *let's lope*, *lope* being a dialect variation of *loup* (leap), to run or jump away.

The slippery slope. The broad and easy way "that leadeth to destruction." *Facilis descensus Averno. See* AVERNUS.

Slops: Police; originally "ecilop." *See* BACK-SLANG.

> I dragged you in here and saved you,
> And sent out a gal for the slops;
> Ha! they're acomin', sir! Listen!
> The noise and the shoutin' stops.
> > SIMS: *Ballads of Babylon* (*The Matron's Story*).

Slough of Despond. A period of, or fit of, great depression. In Bunyan's *Pilgrim's Progress*, Pt. i, it is a deep bog which Christian has to cross in order to get to the Wicket Gate. Help comes to his aid, but Neighbour Pliable turns back.

Slow. Slow burn. A comedy routine invented by the Hollywood comedian Edgar Kennedy. It consists in struggling to preserve one's patience by passing the hands slowly over the face, but finally losing control and degenerating into hysteria. Kennedy's enormous success in exploiting this trick is undoubtedly due to the fact that it expresses to perfection the helpless exasperation of the little man in a bureaucratic and machine-ridden existence.

Slow-coach. A dawdle. As a slow coach in the old coaching-days got on slowly, so one that gets on slowly is a slow coach.

Slow-worm. *See* MISNOMERS.

Slubberdegullion (slŭb er de gŭl' yon). A nasty, paltry fellow. To *slubber* is to do things by halves, to perform a work carelessly; *degullion* is a fanciful addition (as in *rapscallion*).

> Quoth she, "Although thou hast deserved,
> Base slubber-degullion, to be served
> As thou didst vow to deal with me.
> > BUTLER: *Hudibras*, i, 3.

Slug (U.S.A.). A $50 gold piece.

Slugabed. A late riser. To *slug* used to be quite good English for to be thoroughly lazy. Sylvester has—

> The Soldier, slugging long at home in Peace,
> His wonted courage quickly doth decrease.
> > *Du Bartas*, I, vii, 340 (1591).

Slug-horn. A battle-trumpet; the word being the result of an erroneous reading by Chatterton of the Gaelic *slogan*. He thought the word sounded rather well; and, as he did not know what it meant, gave it a meaning that suited him:—

> Some caught a slughorne and an onsett wounde.—
> > *The Battle of Hastings*, ii, 99.

Browning adopted it in the last line but one of his *Childe Rolande to the Dark Tower Came*, and thus this "ghost-word" (*q.v.*) got a footing in the language.

Sly-boots. One who appears to be a dolt, but who is really wide awake; a cunning dolt.

> The frog called the lazy one several times, but in vain; there was no such thing as stirring him, though the sly-boots heard well enough all the while.—*Adventures of Abdalla*, p. 32 (1729).

You're a sly dog. A playful way of saying, You pretend to be disinterested, but I can read between the lines.

Small fry. A humorous way of referring to a number of young children, from the numerous fry or young of fish and other creatures.

Small holding. A small plot of land (but larger than an allotment) let by a local or county council to a tenant for agricultural purposes. The Act of 1892 lays down that a small holding shall be not less than one acre nor more than fifty, and should not exceed £50 in annual value.

The small hours. The hours from 1 A.M. to 4 or 5 A.M., when you are still in the small, or low, numbers.

The small of the back. The slenderer, narrower part, just above the buttocks.

To feel small. To feel humiliated, "taken down a peg or two."

To sing small. To adopt a humble tone; to withdraw some sturdy assertion and apologize for having made it.

Smalls. The undergraduates' name at Oxford for Responsions, *i.e.* the first of the three examinations for the B.A. degree; about corresponding to the Cambridge Little-go.

Smart Aleck. An American term for a bumptious, conceited know-all. The name goes back to the 1860s, but no record now remains of Aleck's identity.

Smart Money. Money paid by a person to obtain exemption from some disagreeable office or duty, or given to soldiers or sailors for injuries received in the service; in law it means a heavy fine. It either makes the person "smart," *i.e.* suffer, or else the person who receives it is paid for smarting.

Smear. A figurative sense of this word is to besmirch a reputation, to hint unpleasant things without specifying or doing more than suggest something derogatory.

Smectymnuus (smek tim' nùs). The name under which was published (1641) an anti-episcopalian tract in answer to Bishop Hall's *Divine Right of Episcopacy*. The name is a sort of acrostic, composed of the initials of the authors, viz.:—

Stephen Marshal, Edward Calamy, Thomas Young, Matthew Newcomen, and William Spurstow.

Milton published his *Apology for Smectymnuus*, another reply to Hall, in 1642.

Also contracted to **smec.**
The handkerchief about the neck,
Canonical cravat of Smec.
BUTLER: Hudibras, Pt. i, 5.

Smelfungus. *See* MUNDUNGUS.

Smell, To. Often used figuratively for to suspect, to discern intuitively, as in *I smell a rat* (*see* RAT), *to smell treason*, to discern indications of treason, etc.

Shakespeare has, "Do you smell a fault?" (*Lear*, i, 1); and Iago says to Othello, "One may smell in this a will most rank." St. Jerome says that St. Hilarion had the gift of knowing what sins or vices anyone was inclined to by simply smelling either the person or his garments, and by the same faculty could discern good feelings and virtuous propensities.

It smells of the lamp. *See* LAMP.

Smiler. Another name for shandy-gaff—a mixture of ale and lemonade or ginger-beer.

Smoke. To detect, or rather to get a scent of, some plot or scheme. The allusion may be to the detection of the enemy by smoke seen to issue from their place of concealment.

Cape smoke. A cheap and villainous kind of whisky sold in South Africa.

No smoke without fire. Every slander has some foundation. The reverse proverb, "No fire without smoke," means no good without some drawback.

Smoke-farthings, smoke-silver. An offering formerly given to the priest at Whitsuntide, according to the number of chimneys in his parish.

The Bishop of Elie hath out of everie parish in Cambridgeshire a certain tribute called . . . *smoke-farthings*, which the churchwardens do levie according to the number of . . . chimneys that be in a parish.—*MSS. Baker*, xxxix, 326.

To end in smoke. To come to no practical result. The allusion is to kindling, which smokes, but will not light a fire.

To smoke the pipe of peace. *See* CALUMET.

Snack (a variant of *snatch*).

To go snacks. To share and share alike.

To take a snack. To take a morsel.

Snag. To come up against a snag. To encounter some obstacle in your progress. The phrase is from the American lumber camps, a *snag* being a tree-trunk lodged in the bottom of the river and reaching the surface, or near it.

Snake. Rhyming-slang (*q.v.*) for a looking-glass, the missing portion being "in the grass."

It was an old idea that snakes in casting their sloughs annually gained new vigour and fresh strength; hence Shakespeare's allusion—

When the mind is quicken'd, out of doubt,
The organs, though defunct and dead before,
Break up their drowsy grave, and newly move
With casted slough and fresh legerity.
Henry V, ii, 1.

And another notion was that one could regain one's youth by feeding on snakes.

You have eat a snake
And are grown young, gamesome and rampant.
BEAUMONT AND FLETCHER: Elder Brother, iv, 4.

A snake in the grass. A hidden or hypocritical enemy, a disguised danger. The phrase is from Virgil (*Ecl.* iii, 93). *Latet anguis in herba*, a snake is lurking in the grass.

Snake-eyes. A double one, in throwing dice (U.S.A.).

Snake stones. The fossils called Ammonites (*q.v.*).

Snap. Not worth a snap of the fingers. Utterly worthless and negligible.

Snapdragon. The same as *"flapdragon"* (*q.v.*); also, a plant of the genus *Antirrhinum* with a flower opening like a dragon's mouth.

Snapshot. Formerly applied to a shot fired without taking aim, but now almost exclusively to an instantaneous photograph. Hence *to snapshot a person*, to take an instantaneous photograph of him.

Snap vote. A vote taken unexpectedly, especially in Parliament. The result of a "snap vote" has, before now, been the overthrow of the ministry.

Snark. The imaginary animal invented by Lewis Carroll as the subject of his mock heroic poem, *The Hunting of the Snark* (1876). It was most elusive and gave endless trouble, and when eventually the hunters thought they had tracked it down their quarry proved to be but a Boojum. The name (a "portmanteau word" of *snake* and *shark*) has hence sometimes been given to the quests of dreamers and visionaries.

It was one of Rossetti's delusions that in *The Hunting of the Snark* Lewis Carroll was caricaturing him.

Snarling Letter (Lat. *litera canina*). The letter *r*. *See* R.

Sneck Posset. To give one a sneck posset is to give him a cold reception, to slam the door in his face (Cumberland and Westmorland). The "sneck" is the latch of a door, and to "sneck the door in one's face" is to shut a person out.

Sneeze. St. Gregory has been credited with originating the custom of saying "God bless you" after sneezing, the story being that he enjoined its use during a pestilence in which sneezing was a mortal symptom. Aristotle, however, mentions a similar custom among the Greeks; and Thucydides tells us that sneezing was a crisis symptom of the great Athenian plague.

The Romans followed the same custom, their usual exclamation being *Absit omen!* The Parsees hold that sneezing indicates that evil spirits are abroad, and we find similar beliefs in India, Africa, ancient and modern Persia, among the North American Indian tribes, etc.

We are told that when the Spaniards arrived in Florida the Cazique sneezed, and all the court lifted up their hands and implored the sun to avert the evil omen.

It is not to be sneezed at—not to be despised.

Snickersnee. A large clasp-knife, or combat with clasp-knives. The word is a corruption of the old *snick and snee* or *snick or snee*, cut and thrust, from the Dutch.

Snide. A slang term for counterfeit, bogus. In the U.S.A. mean, contemptible.

Snidesman. An utterer of false coin.

Snob. A vulgar person who apes the ways of, and truckles to those in a higher social position than himself.

Thackeray calls George IV a snob, because he assumed to be "the first gentleman in Europe," but had not the genuine stamp of a gentleman's mind.

The word actually means a journeyman cobbler or a shoemaker's apprentice; at Cambridge it denotes a townsman as opposed to a gownsman.

Snood. The lassie lost her silken snood. The snood was a ribbon with which a Scots lass braided her hair, and was the emblem of her maiden character. When she married she changed the snood for the curch or coif; but if she lost the name of virgin before she obtained that of wife, she "lost her silken snood," and was not privileged to assume the curch.

In more recent times the word has been applied to the net in which women confine their hair.

Snooks. An exclamation of incredulity or derision. **To cock** or **pull a snook,** to make a gesture of contempt by putting the thumb to the nose and spreading the fingers.

Snotty. Sailors' slang for a midshipman.

Snow King, The. So the Austrians called Gustavus Adolphus of Sweden (1594, 1611-1632), because, said they, he "was kept together by the cold, but would melt and disappear as he approached a warmer soil."

Snuff. To be snuffed out—put down, eclipsed; killed. **To snuff it** is a euphemism for to die. The allusion is to a candle snuffed with snuffers.

'Tis strange the mind, that very fiery particle,
Should let itself be snuffed out by an article.
                    BYRON: *Don Juan*, xi, 60.

Took it in snuff—in anger, in huff.

You'll mar the light by taking it in snuff.
                    Love's Labour's Lost, v, 2.

Who . . . when it next came there, took it in snuff.—1 *Henry IV*, i, 3.

Up to snuff. Wide awake, knowing, sharp; not easily taken in or imposed upon.

Sob Stuff. A phrase describing newspaper, film, or other stories of a highly sentimental kind.

Sob Sister. A woman reporter.

Sobersides. A grave, steady-going, serious-minded person, called by some "a stick-in-the-mud"; generally **Old Sobersides.**

Social. Pertaining to society, the community as a whole, or to the intercourse and mutual relationships of mankind at large.

The social evil, or **plague.** Euphemisms for prostitution and venereal diseases.

Society. The upper ten thousand, or "the upper ten." When persons are in "society," they are on the visiting lists of the fashionable social leaders.

Society of Friends. *See* QUAKERS.

Society verse. *See* VERS DE SOCIÉTÉ.

Socinianism (so sin' yàn izm). A form of Unitarianism which, on the one hand, does not altogether deny the supernatural character of Christ, but, on the other, goes farther than Arianism, which, while upholding His divinity, denies that He is coequal with the Father. So called from the Italian theologian, Faustus Socinus (1539-1604), who, with his brother, Lælius (1525-62), propagated this doctrine.

Sock. The light shoe worn by the comic actors of Greece and Rome (Lat. *soccus*); hence applied to comedy itself.

> Then to the well-trod stage anon,
> If Jonson's learned sock be on.
> MILTON: L'Allegro.

The difference between the sock of comedy and the buskin (*q.v.*) of tragedy was that the sock reached only to the ankle, but the buskin extended to the knee.

Socrates (sok' rà tēz). The great Greek philosopher, born and died at Athens (about 470-399 B.C.). He used to call himself "the midwife of men's thoughts"; and out of his intellectual school sprang those of Plato and the Dialectic system, Euclid and the Megaric, Aristippus and the Cyrenaic, Antisthenes and the Cynic. Cicero said of him that "he brought down philosophy from the heavens to earth"; and he was certainly the first to teach that "the proper study of mankind is man." He was condemned to death for the corruption of youth by introducing new gods (thus being guilty of impiety) and drank hemlock in prison, surrounded by his disciples.

Socratic irony. Leading on your opponent in an argument by simulating ignorance, so that he "ties himself in knots" and eventually falls an easy prey—a form of procedure used with great effect by Socrates.

The Socratic method. The method of conducting an argument, imparting information, etc., by means of question and answer.

Soda-jerk. An attendant at an ice-cream soda fountain in the U.S.A.

Soho! (sō hō'). An exclamation used by huntsmen, especially in hare-coursing when a hare has been started. It is a very old call, dating from at least the 13th century, and corresponds to the "Tally-ho!" of fox-hunters when the fox breaks cover.

Soho, the district in London, is so called from a mansion which stood there in the time of Charles II, belonging to the Duke of Monmouth.

Soi-disant (swa dē' zon) (Fr.). Self-styled, would-be.

Soil. A son of the soil. One native to that particular place, whose family has been settled there for generations; especially if engaged in agriculture.

Sol. The Roman sun god; hence used for the sun itself.

> Sol through white curtains shot a timorous ray,
> And oped those eyes that must eclipse the day.
> POPE: Rape of the Lock, i, 13.

The name was given by the old alchemists to gold, and in heraldry it represents *or* (gold).

In music *sol* is the name of the fifth note of the diatonic scale (*see* DOH).

Solano (so la' nō). **Ask no favour daring the Solano.** A popular Spanish proverb, meaning— Ask no favour during a time of trouble or adversity. The *solano* (*solanus*, sun, *see* SOL) of Spain is a south-east wind, extremely hot, and loaded with fine dust; it produces giddiness and irritation.

Sold down the river (U.S.A.). Deceived or demoted. From the practice of selling slaves in the upper Southern States to the cotton and sugar plantation owners farther South, and so breaking up families and causing distress.

Soldier originally meant a hireling or mercenary; one paid a *solidus*, or wage, for military service; but hireling and soldier convey now very different ideas.

Soldier's battles. Engagements which are more of the nature of hand to hand encounters than regular pitched battles; those that have to be fought by the soldiers themselves, their leaders not having been able to take up strategical positions. The principal "Soldiers' Battles" of English history are Malplaquet, 1709, and Inkermann, 1854.

Soldiers of fortune. Men who live by their wits; *chevaliers de l'industrie*. Referring to those men in mediæval times who let themselves for hire into any army.

Solecism (sō' lē sizm). A deviation from correct idiom or grammar; from the Greek *soloikos*, speaking incorrectly, so named from Soloi, a town in Cilicia, the Attic colonists of which spoke a debased form of Greek.

The word is also applied to any impropriety or breach of good manners.

Solemn. The Solemn League and Covenant. A league entered into by the General Assembly of the Church of Scotland, the Westminster Assembly of English Divines, and the English Parliament in 1643, for the establishment of Presbyterianism and suppression of Roman Catholicism in both countries. Charles II swore to the Scots that he would abide by it and therefore they crowned him in 1651 at Dunbar; but at the Restoration he not only rejected the Covenant, but had it burnt by the common hangman.

Solid. In the 18th century this denoted a man of property and position, hence later it became synonymous with honest, genuine; in the 20th century it has kept the same meaning but only in U.S.A. slang—a fine jazz tune, for instance, being a *solid sender*.

Solipsism (sō lip' sizm) (Lat. *solus*, alone, *ipse*, self). Absolute egoism; the metaphysical theory that the only knowledge possible is that of oneself.

Solomon. King of Israel (d. about 930 B.C.). He was specially noted for his wisdom, hence his name has been used for wise men generally.

Solomon's Ring. Rabbinical fable has it that Solomon wore a ring with a gem that told him all he desired to know.

Solomon's Seal. *Polygonatum multiflorum*, a plant with drooping white flowers. As the stems decay the root-stalk becomes marked with scars that have some resemblance to seals; this, according to some, accounts for the name; but another explanation offered is that the root has medicinal value in *sealing* up and closing green wounds.

Solon (sō' lon). A wiseacre or sage; from the great lawgiver of ancient Athens (d. about 560 B.C.), one of the Seven Sages of Greece.

The Solon of Parnassus. So Voltaire called Boileau (1636-1711), in allusion to his *Art of Poetry*.

Solstice (sol' stis). The summer solstice is June 21st; the winter solstice is December 22nd; so called because on or about these dates the sun reaches its extreme northern and southern

points in the ecliptic and appears to stand still (Lat. *sol*, sun, *sistit*, stands) before it turns back on its apparent course.

Solyman (sol' i mán). King of the Turks (in *Jerusalem Delivered*), whose capital was Nice. Being driven from his kingdom, he fled to Egypt, and was there appointed leader of the Arabs (Bk. ix).

Soma (sō' ma). An intoxicating drink anciently made, with mystic rites and incantations, from the juice of some Indian plant by the priests, and drunk by the Brahmins as well as offered as libations to their gods. It was fabled to have been brought from heaven by a falcon, or by the daughters of the Sun; and it was itself personified as a god, and represented the moon. The plant was probably a species of *Asclepias*.

To drink the Soma. To become immortal, or as a god.

Some. Used—originally in America—with a certain emphasis as an adjective-adverb of all work, denoting some special excellence or high degree. "This is *some* book," for instance, means that it is a book that particularly fascinates, appeals to, or "intrigues" the speaker; "*some* golfer," a super-excellent golfer; "going *some*," going the pace.

Song. An old song. A mere trifle, something hardly worth reckoning, as "It went for an old song," it was sold for practically nothing.

Don't make such a song about it! Be more reasonable in your complaints; don't make such a fuss about it.

The Songs of Degrees. Another name for the Gradual Psalms (*q.v.*).

The Song of Roland. *See under* ROLAND.

The Song of Songs. The *Canticles*, or the *Song of Solomon*, in the Old Testament.

Sonnet. Prince of the sonnet. Joachim du Bellay, a French sonneteer (1526-60); but Petrarch (1304-74) better deserves the title.

Sooterkin. A kind of after-birth fabled to be produced by Dutch women through sitting over their stoves; hence an abortive proposal or scheme, and, as applied to literature, an imperfect or a supplementary work.

> For knaves and fools being near of kin
> As Dutch boors are f'a sooterkin,
> Both parties join'd to do their best
> To damn the public interest.
> BUTLER: *Hudibras*, III, ii, 145.

Soph. A student at Cambridge is a Freshman for the first term, a Junior Soph for the second year, and a Senior Soph for the third year. The word Soph is a contraction of "sophister," which is the Greek and Latin *sophistes* (a sophist). In former times these students had to maintain a given question in the schools by opposing the orthodox view of it. These opponencies are now limited to Law and Divinity degrees.

In American Universities *Soph* is an abbreviation of **Sophomore,** a term applied to students in their second year.

Sophia, Santa (sȯ fi′ å). The great metropolitan cathedral of the Orthodox Greek Church at Istanbul. It was built by Justinian (532-7), but since the capture of the city by the Turks (1453) has been used as a mosque. It was not dedicated to a saint named Sophia, but to the "Logos," or Second Person of the Trinity, called *Hagia Sophia* (Sacred Wisdom).

Sophist, Sophistry, Sophism, Sophisticator, etc. These words have quite run from their legitimate meaning. Before the time of Pythagoras (586-506 B.C.) the sages of Greece were called *sophists* (wise men). Pythagoras out of modesty called himself a *philosopher* (a wisdom-lover). A century later Protagoras of Abdera resumed the title, and a set of quibblers appeared in Athens who professed to answer any question on any subject, and took up the title discarded by the Wise Samian. From this movement *sophos* and all its family of words were applied to "wisdom falsely so called," and *philo-sophos* to the "modest search after truth."

Sophy, The. An old title of the rulers of Persia, first given to Sheik Juneyd u Dien, founder of the Safi dynasty (about 1500-1736).

Soppy. Mawkish (of people), ultra-sentimental (of stories, etc.). A *soppy boy* is one who is "tied to his mother's apron-strings."

Sorbonne. The institution of theology, science, and literature in Paris founded by Robert de Sorbon, Canon of Cambrai, in 1252. In 1808 the buildings, erected by Richelieu in the 17th century, were given to the University, and a great scheme of reconstruction was carried out in 1885. Since 1896 the Sorbonne has been the University of Paris.

Sordello (sȯr del′ ō). A Provençal troubadour (d. about 1255), mentioned a number of times by Dante in the *Purgatorio*, now remembered because of Browning's very obscure poem of this name (1840). It details, in a setting which shows the restless condition of northern Italy in the early 13th century, the conflict of a poet about the best way of making his influence felt, whether personally or by the power of song. Browning said of it:—

The historical decoration was purposely of no more importance than a background requires; and my stress lay on the incidents in the development of a soul; little else is worth study. I, at least, always thought so.

Tennyson's reference to *Sordello* is well known. He said he had done his best with it, but there were only two lines he understood— the first and the last—and they were both untrue. These are:—

Who will, may hear Sordello's story told.
Who would has heard Sordello's story told.

Sorites (sȯr′ ītz). A "heaped-up" (Gr. *soros* a heap) or cumulative syllogism, the predicate of one forming the subject of that which follows, the subject of the first being ultimately united with the predicate of the last. The following will serve as an example:—

All men who believe shall be saved.
All who are saved must be free from sin.
All who are free from sin are innocent in the sight of God.
All who are innocent in the sight of God are meet for heaven.
All who are meet for heaven will be admitted into heaven.
Therefore all who believe will be admitted into heaven.

The famous Sorites of Themistocles was: That his infant son commanded the whole world, proved thus:—

My infant son rules his mother.
His mother rules me.
I rule the Athenians.
The Athenians rule the Greeks.
The Greeks rule Europe.
And Europe rules the world.

Sorrow. The Seven Sorrows of the Virgin. *See* MARY.

Sort. Out of sorts. Not in good health and spirits. The French *être dérangé* explains the metaphor. If cards are *out of sorts* they are *deranged*, and if a person is *out of sorts* the health or spirits are out of order.

In printers' language *sorts* is applied to particular pieces of type considered as part of the fount, and a printer is *out of sorts* when he has run short of some particular letters, figures, stops, etc.

To run upon sorts. In printing, said of work which requires an unusual number of certain letters, etc.; as an index, which requires a disproportionate number of capitals.

S O S. *See under* S.

Sotadic Verse. *See* PALINDROME.

Soter (sȯ′ tĕr). Ptolemy I of Egypt (d. 283 B.C.) was given this surname, meaning *the Preserver* by the Rhodians because he compelled Demetrius to raise the siege of Rhodes (304 B.C.).

Sothic Period, Year. The Persian year consists of 365 days, so that a day is lost in four years, amounting in the course of 1,460 years to a year. This period of 1,460 years is called a *sothic period* (Gr. *sothis*, the dog-star, at whose rising it commences), and the reclaimed year made up of the bits is called a *sothic year. See* CANICULAR PERIOD.

Soul. Among the ancient Greeks the *soul* was the seat of the passions and desires, which animals have in common with man, and the *spirit* the highest and distinctive part of man. In 1 *Thess.* Paul says; "I pray God your whole spirit, soul, and body be preserved blameless unto the coming of our Lord Jesus Christ." *See also Heb.* iv, 12; 1 *Cor.* ii, 14 and 15; xv, 45, 46.

Heraclitus held the soul to be a spark of the stellar essence; *scintilla stellaris essentiœ* (Macrobius: *Somnium Scipionis,* i, 14).

> Vital spark of heavenly flame!
> Quit, oh quit this mortal frame.
> POPE: *The Dying Christian to his Soul.*

Both the Greeks and Romans seemed to think that the soul made its escape with life out of the death-wound.

The Moslems say that the souls of the faithful assume the forms of snow-white birds, and nestle under the throne of Allah until the resurrection, and hold that it is necessary, when a man is bow-strung, to relax the rope before death occurs to let the soul escape.

In Egyptian hieroglyphics the soul is represented by several emblems, as a basket of fire, a heron, a hawk with a human face, and a ram.

All Souls' Day. November 2nd, the day following All Saints' Day, set apart by the Roman Catholic Church for a solemn service for the repose of the departed. In England it was formerly observed by ringing the *soul bell* (or passing-bell), by making and distributing *soul cakes,* blessing beans, etc.

Sourdough (sour' dō). An oldtimer, a prospector, a cook (western U.S.A.). Sourdough is fermented flour with salt and water, a quantity of which is kept in a keg on the range or in mining camps for the making of bread; the keg is not cleaned out, but is merely topped up with further flour and water each time a lump of dough is removed.

South Paw (U.S.A.). In baseball, a left-handed pitcher or any left-handed player in games generally. A boxer who puts up his guard with his right forward.

Sovereign. A strangely misspelled word (from Lat. *superanus,* supreme), the last syllable being assimilated to *reign.* French *souverain* is nearer the Latin; Ital., *sovrano;* Span. *soberano.*

A gold coin of this name, value 22s. 6d., was issued by Henry VIII, and so called because he was represented on it in royal robes; but the modern sovereign of 20s. value was not issued till 1817. Just a hundred years later, during World War I, its issue was suspended in Britain and its place taken by paper Treasury Notes.

Sow (sou). **A pig of my own sow.** Said of that which is the result of one's own action.

A still sow. A cunning and selfish man; one wise in his own interest; one who avoids talking at meals that he may enjoy his food the better. So called from the old proverb, "The still sow eats the wash" or "draff."

> We do not act that often jest and laugh;
> 'Tis old, but true, "Still swine eat all the draugh."
> *Merry Wives of Windsor,* iv, 2.

As drunk as David's sow. Very drunk indeed.

To get the wrong sow by the ear. To capture the wrong individual, to take the wrong end of the stick, hit upon the wrong thing.

To send a sow to Minerva. To teach your grandmother how to suck eggs, to instruct one more learned in the subject than yourself. From the old Latin proverb, *Sus Minervam docet* (a pig teaching Minerva), which meant the same thing.

You cannot make a silk purse out of a sow's ear. *See* SILK.

See also PIG-IRON.

Spade. The spade of playing cards is so called from Span. *espada,* a sword, the suit in Spanish packs being marked with short swords; in French and British cards the mark—largely through the similarity in name—has been altered to something like the blade of a sharp-pointed spade.

To call a spade a spade. To be straightforward, outspoken, and blunt, even to the point of rudeness; to call things by their proper names without any beating about the bush.

> I have learned to call wickedness by its own terms: a fig a fig; and a spade a spade.—JOHN KNOX.

This is a translation of Erasmus's rendering of the old Latin proverb—*ficus ficus, ligonem ligonem vocat.*

Spagyric (spà jir' ik). Pertaining to alchemy; the term seems to have been invented by Paracelsus. Alchemy is "the spagyric art," and an alchemist a "spagyrist."

Spagyric food. Cagliostro's name for the elixir of immortal youth.

Spain. *See* HISPANIA.

Castles in Spain. *See* CASTLE.

Patron saint of Spain. St. James the Greater, who is said to have preached the Gospel in Spain, where his relics are preserved at Compostella.

Spanish fly. The cantharis, a coleopterous insect used in medicine. Cantharides are dried and used externally as a blister and internally as a stimulant to the genito-urinary organs; they were formerly considered to act as an aphrodisiac.

Spanish moss. A plant of the family Bromeliaceæ which hangs in long grey festoons from the branches of trees, especially the live oak, in tropical and sub-tropical American forests.

Spaniel. The Spanish dog from *español*, through the French

Spanker. Used of a fast horse, also—colloquially—of something or someone that is an exceptionally fine specimen, a "stunner."

In nautical language the *spanker* is the fore-and-aft sail set upon the mizen-mast of a three-masted vessel, and the jigger-mast of a four-masted vessel. There is no spanker in a one- or two-masted vessel of any rig.

Spare the rod, etc. *See* ROD.

Spartacists. An extreme Socialist group in Germany that flourished between 1916 and 1919. It was founded by Karl Liebknecht who, with Rosa Luxemburg led an attempted revolution in January of the latter year, in the suppression of which they were both killed. The movement was finally crushed by Ebert's government in the April. The original Spartacus was a Thracian who commanded a band of insurgents in the third Servile war of Rome, 71 B.C.

Spartan. The inhabitants of ancient Sparta, one of the leading city-states of Greece, were noted for their frugality, courage, and stern discipline; hence, one who can bear pain unflinchingly is termed "a Spartan," a very frugal diet is "Spartan fare," etc. It was a Spartan mother who, on handing her son the shield he was to carry into battle, said that he must come back either with it or on it.

Spartan dog. A blood-hound; a blood-thirsty man.

> O Spartan dog
> More fell than anguish, hunger or the sea,
> *Othello*, v, 2.

Spasmodic School. The. A name applied by Professor Aytoun to certain authors of the 19th century, whose writings were distinguished by forced conceits and unnatural style. The most noted are Bailey (author of *Festus*), Gerald Massey, Alexander Smith, and Sydney Dobell.

Spats. Short cloth or leather gaiters. The word comes from

Spatterdashes. Long gaiters, usually of cloth, worn to protect the stockings or trousers from mud. In military uniform they are generally waterproof and button or lace to some inches above the ankle.

Speak-easy. A place where alcoholic liquors are sold without a licence, or in some illegal way.

Speaker. The title of the presiding officer and official spokesman of the British House of Commons, the United States House of Representatives, and of some other legislative assemblies.

The Speaker of the House of Commons has autocratic and almost absolute power in the control of debates and internal arrangements of the House, etc.; he is elected by the members irrespective of party, and ceases to be a "party man," having no vote—except in cases of a tie, when he can give a casting vote. He holds office for the duration of that Parliament, but by custom (not law) is re-appointed unless he wishes to resign (in which case he goes to the House of Lords).

The Lord Chancellor is *ex officio* Speaker of the House of Lords.

To catch the Speaker's eye. The rule in the House of Commons is that the member whose rising to address the House is first observed by the Speaker is allowed precedence.

Speaking. A speaking likeness. A very good and lifelike portrait; one that makes you imagine that the subject is just going to speak to you.

They are not on speaking terms. Said of friends who have fallen out.

Spear. If a knight kept the point of his spear forward when he entered a strange land, it was a declaration of war; if he carried it on his shoulder with the point behind him, it was a taken of friendship. In Ossian (*Temora*, i) Cairbar asks if Fingal comes in peace, to which Morannal replies: "In peace he comes not, king of Erin, I have seen his forward spear."

The spear of Achilles. *See* ACHILLES' SPEAR; ACHILLEA.

The spear of Ithuriel. *See* ITHURIEL.

The spear-side. The male line of descent, called by the Anglo-Saxons *spere-healfe*. *Cp.* SPINDLE-SIDE.

To break a spear. To fight a tournament.

To pass under the spear. To be sold by auction, sold "under the hammer." Writing to Pepys (Aug. 12th, 1689) Evelyn speaks of "the noblest library that ever passed under the speare." The phrase is from the Latin *sub hasta vendere*.

Special Pleading. Quibbling; making your own argument good by forcing certain words or phrases from their obvious and ordinary meaning. A pleading in law means a written statement of a cause *pro* and *con*, and "special pleaders" are persons who have been called to the bar, but do not speak as advocates. They advise on evidence, draw up affidavits, state the merits and demerits of a cause, and so on. After a time most special pleaders go to the bar, and many get advanced to the bench.

Specie, Species, means literally "what is visible" (Lat. *species*, appearance). As things are distinguished by their visible forms, it has come to mean *kind* or *class*. As drugs and condiments at one time formed the most important articles of merchandise, they were called *species*—still retained in the French *épices*, and English *spices*. Again, as banknotes represent money, money itself is called *specie*, the thing represented.

Spectacles. In cricket, when a player scores a "duck's egg" (*i.e.* nothing at all) in each of his two innings of one match, he is said to make "a pair of spectacles."

Spectre of the Brocken. An optical illusion, first observed on the Brocken (the highest peak of the Hartz range in Saxony), in which shadows of the spectators, greatly magnified, are projected on the mists about the summit of the mountain opposite. In one of De Quincey's opium-dreams there is a powerful description of the Brocken spectre.

Spectrum, Spectra, Spectre (Lat. *specto*, I behold). In optics a *spectrum* is the image of a sunbeam beheld on a screen, after refraction by one or more prisms. *Spectra* are the images of objects left on the eye after the objects themselves are removed from sight. A *spectre* is the apparition of a person no longer living or not bodily present.

Speculate (spek' ū lāt) means to look out of a watch-tower, to spy about (Lat. *speculari*). Metaphorically, to look at a subject with the mind's eye, to spy into it; in *commerce*, to purchase articles or shares which you expect will prove profitable.

Specularis lapis, what we should now call window-glass, was some transparent stone or mineral, such as mica.

Speculum Humanæ Salvationis (*The Mirror of Human Salvation*). A kind of extended *Biblia Pauperum* (*q.v.*) telling pictorially the Bible story from the fall of Lucifer to the Redemption of Man, with explanations of each picture in Latin rhymes. MS copies of the 12th century are known; but its chief interest is that it was one of the earliest of printed books, having been printed about 1467.

Speech. Parts of speech. *See* PART. **Speech is silver (or silvern), silence is golden.** An old proverb, said to be of oriental origin, pointing to the advantage of keeping one's own counsel. The Hebrew equivalent is "If a word be worth one shekel, silence is worth two."

Spell. A turn of work done by a man or group of men in relief of another man or group; hence, the period of one's turn of work. The word was formerly applied to the gang itself, and is probably the A.S. *spala*, a substitute. *Spell*, in the sense of saying or writing the letters forming a word, is often used with the meaning to hint very broadly, especially of children.

Spell ho! An exclamation to signify that the allotted time has expired, and men are to be relieved by another set.

To spell is to relieve another at his work.

Spellbinders. Orators who hold their audience *spellbound*, that is, fascinated, charmed, as though bound by a spell or magic incantation. The word came into use in America in the presidential election of 1888, and has been used of British political orators of persuasive eloquence.

Spencean Philanthropists. Disciples of Thomas Spence (1750-1814) who, in 1775, devised a system of land nationalization. The inhabitants of each parish would form a corporation and appoint local officials to collect rents, deduct expenses, and divide what was left among the parishioners. No tax or toll would be required beyond the rent. A day of rest would be allowed every five days. "Whether the title of King, President, Consul or the like is assumed by the head of the country is quite indifferent to me." A number of hot-headed and woolly-minded persons thought that this plan heralded the Millennium and in 1816 "The Society of Spencean Philanthropists" was founded. That year they arranged the Spa Fields Meeting, Bermondsey, which ended in a riot. The Cato Street Conspirators and other dangerous demagogues were disciples of Spence.

Spencer. Now applied to a close-fitting bodice worn by women, but formerly the name of an outer coat without skirts worn by men; so named from the second Earl Spencer (1758-1834.)

. **Spenserian Metre.** The metre devised by Spenser (1592), founded on the Italian *ottava rima*, for his *Faerie Queene*. It is a stanza of nine iambic lines, all of ten syllables except the last, which is an Alexandrine. Only three different rhymes are admitted into a stanza, and these are disposed : a b a b b c b c c.

The stanza was used by Thomson (*Castle of Indolence*), Shenstone (*Schoolmistress*), Byron (*Childe Harold*), etc.

Spheres. In the Ptolemaic system of astronomy (*q.v.*) the earth, as the centre of the universe, was supposed to be surrounded by nine spheres of invisible space, the first seven carrying the "planets" as then known, viz., (1) Diana or the Moon, (2) Mercury, (3) Venus, (4) Apollo or the Sun, (5) Mars, (6) Jupiter, and (7) Saturn; the eighth, the Starry Sphere, carrying the fixed stars, and the ninth, the Crystalline Sphere, added by Hipparchus in the 2nd century B.C. to account for the precession of the equinoxes. Finally, in the Middle Ages, was added a tenth sphere, the *Primum mobile* (*q.v.*), a solid barrier which enclosed the universe and shut it off from Nothingness and the Empyrean. These last two spheres carried neither star nor planet.

> They pass the planets seven, and pass the fixed
> [starry sphere],
> And that crystalline sphere . . . and that First-Moved.
> MILTON: *Paradise Lost*, iii, 482.

The music, or **harmony, of the spheres.** Pythagoras, having ascertained that the pitch of notes depends on the rapidity of vibrations, and also that the planets move at different rates of motion, concluded that the planets must make sounds in their motion according to their different rates; and that, as all things in nature are harmoniously made, the different sounds must harmonize; whence the old theory of the "harmony of the spheres." Kepler has a treatise on the subject.

> There's not the smallest orb which thou behold'st
> But in his motion like an angel sings,
> Still quiring to the young-eyed cherubims.
> *Merchant of Venice*, v, 1.

Plato says that a siren sits on each planet, who carols a most sweet song, agreeing to the motion of her own particular planet, but harmonizing with all the others. Hence Milton speaks of the "celestial syrens' harmony that sit upon the nine enfolded spheres." (*Arcades*.)

Sphinx (sfingks). A monster of ancient mythology; in Greece represented as having the head of a woman, the body of a lion, and winged; in Egypt as a wingless lion with the head and breast of a man.

The Grecian Sphinx was generally said to be the daughter of Typhon and Chimæra; she infested Thebes, setting the inhabitants a riddle and devouring all those who could not solve it. The riddle was—

> What goes on four feet, on two feet, and three,
> But the more feet it goes on the weaker it be?

and it was at length solved by Œdipus (*q.v.*) with the answer that it was a man, who as an infant crawls upon all-fours, in manhood goes erect on his two feet, and in old age supports his tottering legs with a staff. On hearing this correct answer the Sphinx slew herself, and Thebes was delivered.

The Egyptian sphinx is a typification of Ra, the sun god. The colossal statue of the reclining monster was old in the days of Cheops, when the Great Pyramid, near which it lies, was built. It is hewn out of the solid rock; its length is 140 ft., and its head 30 ft. from crown to chin.

Spick and Span New. Quite and entirely new. A *spic* is a spike or nail, and a *span* is a chip. So that a spick and span new ship is one in which every nail and chip is new. According to Dr. Johnson, who, in recording the term says it is one which he "should not have expected to have found authorized by a polite writer," *span new* is from A.S. *spannan*, to stretch, and was originally used of cloth newly extended or dressed at the cloth-maker's, and *spick and span* is newly extended on the spikes or tenters. He gives quotations from Samuel Butler, Bishop Burnet, and Dean Swift, but cannot help adding "it is however a low word."

Spider. There are many old wives' fables about spiders, the most widespread being that they are venomous. Shakespeare alludes to this more than once—

> Let thy spiders, that suck up thy venom,
> And heavy-gaited toads lie in their way.
> *Richard II.* iii, 2.

> There may be in the cup
> A spider steep'd, and one may drink, depart,
> And yet partake no venom.
> *Winter's Tale*, ii, 1.

and in the examination into the murder of Sir Thomas Overbury, one of the witnesses deposed "that the countess wished him to get the strongest poison that he could . . ." Accordingly he brought seven great spiders.

Other tales were that spiders would never spin a web on a cedar roof, and that fever could be cured by wearing a spider in a nutshell round the neck.

Spiders were credited with other medicinal virtues. A common cure for jaundice in country parts of England was to swallow a large live house-spider rolled up in butter, while in the south of Ireland a similar remedy was given for ague.

Yet another story was that spiders spin only on dark days:—

> The subtle spider never spins
> But on dark days, his slimy gins.
> S. BUTLER: *On a Nonconformist*, iv.

Spigot. Spare at the spigot and spill at the bung. To be parsimonious in trifles and wasteful in great matters, like a man who stops his, beer-tub at the vent-hole and leaves it running at the bung-hole.

Spike. Slang for the workhouse; **to go on the spike** is to become a workhouse inmate.

To spike one's guns for him. To render his plans abortive, frustrate the scheme he has been laying, "draw his teeth." The allusion is to the old way of making a gun useless by driving a spike into the touch-hole.

To spike a drink. To add strong spirits to increase the alcoholic content.

Spill the Beans, To. To reveal a secret prematurely.

Spilt milk. *See* CRY.

Spindle-side. The female line of descent (*cp.* SPEAR-SIDE). The spindle was the pin on which the thread was wound from the spinning-wheel.

Spinner. Come in, Spinner. From the Australian national game of "Two Up"—spinning two coins, on which enormous sums are bet. When all bets are laid against the man who wishes to spin, he is told to come in (or spin) by the "boxer" (referee in charge of the game). The phrase is used derisively by one who has been taken in by a joke or trick.

Spinster. An unmarried woman. The fleece brought home by the Anglo-Saxons in summer, was spun and woven by the female part of each family during the winter. King Edward the Elder commanded his daughters to be instructed in the use of the distaff. Alfred the Great, in his will, calls the female part of his family the *spindle side*; and it was a regularly received axiom with our forefathers, that no young woman was fit to be a wife till she had spun for herself a set of body, table, and bed linen. Hence the maiden was termed a spinner or spinster.

It is said that the heraldic *lozenge*, in which the armorial bearings of a woman are depicted instead of, in the case of a man, on a *shield*, originally represented a spindle. Among the Romans the bride carried a distaff, and Homer tells us that Kryseis was to spin and share the king's bed.

Spirit. Properly, the breath of life, from Lat. *spiritus* (*spirare*, to breathe, blow):—

> And the Lord God formed man of the dust of the ground, and breathed into his nostrils the breath of life, and man became a living soul.—*Gen.* ii, 7.

Hence, life or the life principle, the soul; a disembodied soul (a ghost or apparition), or an immaterial being that never was supposed to have had a body (sprite), as a gnome, elf, or fairy; also, the temper or disposition of mind as animated by the breath of life, as *in good spirits*, *high-spirited*, *a man of spirit*.

The mediæval physiological notion (adopted from Galen) was that spirit existed in the body in three kinds, viz., (1) the *Natural spirit*, the principle of the "natural functions"—growth, nutrition, and generation, said to be a vapour rising from the blood and having its seat in the liver; (2) the *Vital spirit*, which arose in the heart by mixture of the air breathed in with the natural spirit and supplied the body with heat and life: and (3) the *Animal spirit*, which was responsible for the power of motion and sensation, and for the rational principle generally; this was a modification of the vital spirit, effected in the brain.

Spirit also came to mean any volatile or airy agent of essence; and hence, through the old alchemists, is still used of solutions in alcohol of a volatile principle and of any strong distilled alcoholic liquor. The alchemists named four substances only as "spirits," viz., mercury, arsenic, sal ammoniac, and sulphur:—

> The first spirit quyksilver called is:
> The secound orpiment; the thrid I wis
> Sal armoniac; and the ferth bremstoon.
> CHAUCER: *Canon's Yeoman's Prologue*.

The Elemental spirits of Paracelsus and the Rosicrucians, *i.e.* those which presided over the four elements, were—the *Salamanders* (or fire), *Gnomes* (earth), *Sylphs* (air), and *Undines* (water).

To spirit away. To kidnap, abduct; to make away with speedily and secretly. The phrase first came into use in the 17th century, in connexion with kidnapping youths and transporting them to the West Indian plantations.

Spiritualism. The belief that communication between the living and the spirits of the departed can and does take place, usually through the agency of a specially qualified person (a medium) and often by means of rapping, table-turning, or automatic writing; the system, doctrines, practice, etc., arising from this belief. Hence **Spiritualist**, one who maintains or practises this belief.

In Philosophy Spiritualism—the antithesis of materialism—is the doctrine that the spirit exists as distinct from matter, or as the only reality.

Spit. Spitting for luck. Spitting was a charm against enchantment among the ancient Greeks and Romans. Pliny says it averted witchcraft, and availed in giving an enemy a shrewder blow.

> Thrice on my breast I spit to guard me safe
> From fascinating charms. _Theocritus._

Countrymen spit for luck on a piece of money given to them; boxers spit on their hands, and costermongers on the first money they take in the day for the same reason.

Spitfire. An irascible person, whose angry words are like fire spit from the mouth of a fire-eater.

Splay is a contraction of _display_ (to unfold; Lat. _dis-plico_). A _splay window_ is one in a V-shape, the external opening being very wide, to admit as much light as possible, but the inner opening being very small. A _splay-foot_ is a foot displayed or turned outward. A _splay-mouth_ is a wide mouth, like that of a clown.

Spleen, the soft vascular organ placed to the left of the stomach and acting on the blood, was once believed to be the seat of melancholy and ill-humour. The fern _spleenwort_ was supposed to remove splenic disorders.

Splice. To marry. Very strangely, "splice" means to _split_ or _divide_ (Ger. _spleissen_, to split). The way it came to signify _unite_ is this: Ropes' ends are first untwisted or split before the strands are interwoven. Joining two ropes together by interweaving their strands is "splicing" them. Splicing wood is joining two boards together, the term being borrowed from the sailor.

To splice the main brace. See MAIN BRACE.

Split. To give away one's accomplices; betray secrets, "peach."

To split hairs. See HAIR.

To split with laughter. To laugh uproariously or unrestrainedly; to "split one's sides."

To split the infinitive. To interpose some word between _to_ and the verb, as "to thoroughly understand the subject." This construction is branded as a solecism by pedants, but it is as old as the English language, and there are few of our best writers who have not employed it.

> Without permitting himself to actually mention the name.—MATTHEW ARNOLD: _On Translating Homer_, iii.
>
> It becomes a truth again, after all, as he happens to newly consider it.—BROWNING: _A Soul's Tragedy_.
>
> Implore them to partially enlighten her.—GEO. MEREDITH: _The Egoist_.

Spoils System. The practice in the United States by which the victorious party in an election rewards its supporters by appointments to public office. Adopted and approved by Andrew Jackson at his election as President in 1829. "To the victors belong the spoils."

Spoke. To put a spoke in one's wheel. To interfere with his projects and frustrate them; to thwart him. When solid wheels were used, the driver was provided with a pin or spoke, which he thrust into one of the three holes made to receive it, to skid the cart when it went down-hill.

Sponge. To throw up the sponge. Give up; confess oneself beaten. The metaphor is from boxing matches, for when a second tossed a sponge into the air it was a sign that his man was beaten.

To sponge on a man. To live on him like a parasite, sucking up all he has as a dry sponge will suck up water.

A sponger is a mean parasite who is always accepting the hospitality of those who will give it and never make any adequate return.

Sponging House. A house where persons arrested for debt were kept for twenty-four hours, before being sent to prison. They were generally kept by a bailiff, and the person lodged was "sponged" of all his money before leaving.

Sponsored Programme. A wireless programme which is sponsored, _i.e._ chosen and paid for, by a commercial company, which utilizes a few moments at the beginning and the end of the programme for advertising its own product.

Spoon. A simpleton, a shallow prating duffer used to be called a _spoon_, and hence the name came to be applied to one who indulged in foolish, sentimental love-making, and such a one is said to be _spoony_, and to be _spoons on_ the girl.

In nautical phrase _to spoon_ is to scud before the wind; and in sculling to dip the sculls so lightly in the water as to do little more than skim the surface.

Apostle spoons. See APOSTLE.

He hath need of a long spoon that eateth with the devil. You will want all your wits about you if you ally yourself with evil. Shakespeare alludes to this proverb in the _Comedy of Errors_, iv, 3; and again in the _Tempest_, ii, 2, where Stephano says: "Mercy! mercy! this is a devil . . . I will leave him, I have no long spoon."

> Therefor behoveth hire a ful long spoon
> That schal ete with a feend.
> CHAUCER: _Squire's Tale_, 594.

To be born with a silver spoon in one's mouth. *See* BORN.

Spoonerism. A ludicrous form of metathesis (*q.v.*) that consists of transposing the initial sounds of words so as to form some laughable combination; so called from the Rev. W. A. Spooner (1844-1930), Warden of New College, Oxford. Some of the best attributed to him are— "We all know what it is to have a half warmed fish within us" (for "half-formed wish"); "Yes, indeed; the Lord *is* a shoving leopard"; and "Kingkering Kongs their titles take." Sometimes the term is applied to the accidental transposition of whole words, as when the tea-shop waitress was asked for "a glass bun and a bath of milk."

Sport. To sport one's oak. *See* OAK.

The figurative meaning of *to sport* is to exhibit in public in a somewhat ostentatious way; a young man for instance, may *sport* a highly coloured pair of socks, a new fashion in hats, or a monocle.

Spot. On the spot. At once; without having time to move away or do anything else; as— "He answered on the spot," immediately, without hesitation. A further colloquial meaning of *on the spot* is, in danger of death, in an embarrassing situation.

To knock spots off one. To excel him completely in something; originally an Americanism.

Spotting. The practice in the New Zealand settling days of buying up the land round all available creeks and streams, so that the adjoining territory would have no access to water and hence would find no buyer.

Spouse means one who has promised (Lat. *sponsus,* past part, of *spondere* to promise). In ancient Rome the friends of the parties about to be married met at the house of the woman's father to settle the marriage contract. This contract was called *sponsalia* (espousal); the man, *sponsus,* and the woman, *sponsa.*

Sprat. To throw a sprat to catch a mackerel. To give a small thing in the hope of getting something much more valuable.

Spread-eagle. The "eagle displayed" of heraldry, *i.e.* an eagle with legs and wings extended, the wings being elevated. It is the device of the United States.

In the navy a man was said to be **spread-eagled** when he was lashed to the rigging for flogging, with outstretched arms and legs.

Spread-eaglism in a United States citizen is very much the counterpart of the more aggressive and bombastic forms of Jingoism (*q.v.*) in the Briton.

Spread-eagle oratory. "A compound of exaggeration, effrontery, bombast, and extravagance, mixed with metaphors, platitudes, threats and irreverent appeals flung at the Almighty." (*North American Review,* November, 1858.)

Springers. The Wiltshire Regiment, raised in 1758, and so nicknamed from its speed of movement during the American War of Independence.

Spring Tide. The tide that springs or leaps or swells up. These full tides occur a day or two after the new and full moon, when the attraction of both sun and moon act in a direct line.

Spruce. Smart, dandified. The word is from the old Fr. *Pruce* (Ger. *Preussen*), Prussia, and was originally (16th cent.) applied to Prussian leather of which particularly neat and smart-looking jerkins were made.

And after them, came, syr Edward Haward, then admyral, and with him sir Thomas Parre, in doblettes of Crimosin velvet, voyded lowe on the backe, and before to the cannell bone, laced on the breastes with chaynes of silver, and over that shorte clokes of Crimosyn satyne, and on their heades hattes after dauncers fashion, with fesauntes fethers in theim; They were appareyled after the fashion of Prusia or Spruce.—*Hall's Chronicle: Henry VIII,* year 1 (1542).

Spruce beer is made from the leaves of the *spruce fir,* this being a translation of the German name of the tree, *Sprossen-fichte,* literally "sprouts-fir."

Spunging House. *See* SPONGING.

Spur. On the spur of the moment. Instantly; without stopping to take thought.

Spy Wednesday. A name given in Ireland to the Wednesday before Good Friday, when Judas bargained to become the spy of the Jewish Sanhedrin (*Matt.* xxvi, 3-5, 14-16).

Squab. Short and fat; plump; a person, cushion, etc., like this (a fat woman is *squabba* in Swedish). A young pigeon—especially an unfledged one—is called a *squab,* and a pie of mutton, apples, and onions is called a squab pie in some parts of the country.

Cornwall squab-pie, and Devon white-pot brings.
And Leicester beans and bacon, fit for kings.
KING: *Art of Cookery.*

Poet Squab. So Rochester called Dryden, who was very corpulent.

Squad, Squadron. *See* AWKWARD SQUAD.

Squalls. Look out for squalls. Expect to meet with difficulties. A nautical term, a squall being a succession of sudden and violent gusts of wind (Icel. *skvata*).

Square. On the square. Straight and above board, honest. Also said of a Freemason, with allusion to the Masonic emblem of a square and compasses.

To square a person. To bribe him, or to pay him for some extra trouble he has taken.

To square the circle. To attempt an impossibility. The allusion is to the impossibility of exactly determining the precise ratio between the diameter and the circumference of a circle, and thus constructing a circle of the same area as a given square. Popularly it is 3.14159 . . . the next decimals would be 26537, but the numbers would go on *ad infinitum.*

To square up to a person. To put oneself in a fighting attitude.

> Are you such fools
> To square for this?
> *Titus Andronicus,* ii, 1.

Squatter. Used first in the U.S.A. of a person settling on land without a legal title. Thence went to Australia in the early 19th century to describe ex-convicts who established themselves on unoccupied land and stole cattle from their more honest neighbours to enrich themselves.

> A squatter . . . is the horror of all his honest neighbours.—CHARLES DARWIN: *Voyage of the Beagle.*

Squib. A political joke, printed and circulated especially at election times against a candidate, with intent to bring him into ridicule, and to influence votes.

> Allowing that the play succeeds, there are a hundred squibs flying all abroad to show that it should not have succeeded.—GOLDSMITH: *Polite Learning.*

Squire. In mediæval times a youth of gentle birth attendant on a knight (*see* ESQUIRE); now a landed proprietor, the chief country gentleman of a place.

Squire of dames. Any cavalier who is devoted to ladies. Spenser, in his *Faerie Queene,* introduces the "squire," and records his adventures.

Stable. Locking the stable door after the horse is stolen. Taking precautions after the mischief is done.

The staff of life. Bread, which is the *support* of life.

> "Bread," says he, "dear brothers, is the staff of life."—SWIFT: *Tale of a Tub,* iv.

Shakespeare says, "The boy was the very staff of my age." The allusion is to a staff which supports the feeble in walking.

Stafford. He has had a treat in Stafford Court. He has been thoroughly cudgelled, a pun on the word *staff,* a stick. The French have a similar phrase: *Il a été au festin de Martin Baston* (he has been to Jack Drum's entertainment).

Similarly, **Stafford law** is club law—a good beating.

Stag. The reason why a stag symbolizes Christ is from the ancient idea that by its breath it draws serpents from their holes, and then tramples them to death. (Pliny: *Natural History,* viii, 50.)

Stag in Christian art. The attribute of St. Julian Hospitaller, St. Felix of Valois, and St. Aidan. When it has a crucifix between its horns it alludes to the legend of St. Hubert. When luminous it belongs to St. Eustachius.

Stag Line. At American dances, a number of extra men guests who stand at the edge of the dance-floor, without partners, but having the privilege of breaking in on any dancing couple and claiming the girl as a partner.

Stag party. A gathering of men only.

Stagirite or **Stagyrite** (stăj′ i rīt). Aristotle, who was born at Stagira, in Macedon (4th cent. B.C.).

> In one rich soul
> Plato, the Stagyrite, and Tully joined.
> THOMSON: *Summer,* 1541.
> And rules as strict his laboured work confine
> As if the Stagirite o'erlooked each line.
> POPE: *Essay on Criticism.*

Stakhanovism (stăk ăn ′ō vizm). Alexei Stakhanov, a Donetz coal miner, discovered in the 1930s that by concentrating on one aspect of his job and rationalizing the distribution of his work he could increase his daily output of coal by a substantial quantity. This aroused enthusiastic emulation among the younger and more skilled workers of his own and other trades, and was raised into a serious cult by the government.

Stalemate. To stalemate a person. To bring him to a standstill, render his projects worthless or abortive. The phrase is from chess, *stalemate* being the position in which the king is the only movable piece and he, though not in check, cannot move without becoming so. *Stale* in this word is probably from O.Fr. *estal* (our *stall*), a fixed position.

Stalingrad (sta′ lin grad), formerly Tsaritsyn, an important railway centre and manufacturing town on the Volga, in the S.E. Soviet Union. In 1917 Stalin defended Tsaritsyn against the White Army and its name was changed to commemorate the incident. In World War II Stalingrad was attacked by the Germans in their Caucasus drive in August 1942, but the Russians made a gallant defence that ended (Feb., 1943) in the capitulation of the Germans under Field-Marshal Paulus. From that time onward the Nazi offensive in Russia was turned into a retreat and eventually a rout.

Stamp. 'Tis of the right stamp.—has the stamp of genuine merit. A metaphor taken from current coin, which is stamped with a recognized stamp and superscription.

I weigh the man, not his title; 'tis not the king's stamp can make the metal heavier or better.—WYCHERLEY: *The Plain Dealer*, i, 1 (1677).

> The rank is but the guinea stamp;
> The man's the gowd for a' that!
>
> BURNS: *Is There, for Honest Poverty?*

Stand. To be at a stand. To be in doubt as to further progress, perplexed at what to do next.

To let a thing stand over. To defer consideration of it to a more favourable opportunity.

To stand by. To be ready to give assistance in case of need. A *stand-by* is a person or thing on which one can confidently rely.

To stand for a child. To be sponsor for it; to stand in its place and answer for it.

To stand in with. To go shares; also, to have an understanding or community of interests with.

To stand it out—persist in what one says. A translation of "persist" (Lat. *per-sisto* or *per-sto*).

To stand off and on. A nautical phrase for tacking in and out along the shore.

To stand Sam, stand to reason, stand treat, etc. *See these words.*

To stand to one's guns. To persist in a statement; not to give way. A military phrase.

To stand up for. Support, take his (or its) part.

To stand up for one's privilege or on punctilios. Quietly to insist on one's position, etc., being recognized; this is the Latin *insisto*.

Stand-in. In motion-picture parlance a substitute for a film star who takes his or her place during the preparations for lighting, etc.; performs any really dangerous stunts the part demands; and in general relieves the star of all but the glamorous, romantic, or publicity-value work of the part.

Standing orders. Rules or instructions constantly in force, especially those by-laws of the Houses of Parliament for the conduct of proceedings which stand in force till they are rescinded or suspended. Their suspension is generally caused by a desire to hurry through a Bill with unusual expedition.

The Standing Fishes Bible. *See* BIBLE, SPECIALLY NAMED.

Stand-offish. Unsociable, rather contemptuously reserved.

Standard. A banner as the distinctive emblem of a Royal House, an army, or a nation, etc. The word first came into use in England in connexion with the Battle of the Standard (*see below*), in telling of which Richard of Hexham (about 1139) says that the standard (a ship's mast with flags at the top) was so called because "it was there that valour took its *stand* to conquer or

die." The word is, however, from Lat. *extendĕre*, to stretch out, through O.Fr. *estandard*.

Standards were formerly borne by others than royalties and nations, and varied in size according to the rank of the bearer. Thus, that of an *emperor* was 11 yards in length; of a *king*, 9 yards; of a *prince*, 7 yards; of a *marquis*, $6\frac{1}{2}$ yards; of an *earl*, 6 yards; of a *viscount* or *baron*, 5 yards; of a *knight-banneret*, $4\frac{1}{2}$ yards; of a *baronet*, 4 yards. They generally contained the arms of the bearer, his cognizance and crest, his motto or war-cry, and were fringed with his livery.

The gold standard. A monetary standard based only on the value of gold.

The standard of living. A conventional term to express the supposed degree of comfort or luxury usually enjoyed by a man, a family, or a nation: this may be *high* or *low* according to circumstances.

Stang. To ride the stang. At one time a man who ill-treated his wife was made to sit on a *stang* (A.S. *stæng*, a pole) hoisted on men's shoulders. On this uneasy conveyance the "stanger" was carried in procession amidst the hootings and jeerings of his neighbours. *Cp.* SKIMMINGTON.

Stanhope (stăn' ŏp). The **Stanhope lens,** a cylindrical lens with spherical ends of different radii, and the **Stanhope press,** the first iron printing press to be used (1798), are so called from the inventor, Charles, 3rd Earl of Stanhope (1753-1816).

The light open-seated carriage, with two or four wheels, called a **Stanhope,** gets its name from Fitzroy Stanhope (1787-1864), for whom the first of these conveyances was made.

Star. Figuratively applied to a specially prominent film or other actor, of either sex, etc., hence **star part,** the part taken by a leading actor, **star turn,** etc.

In ecclesiastical art a number of saints may be recognized by the star depicted with them; thus, St. Bruno bears one on his breast; St. Dominic, St. Humbert, St. Peter of Alcantara, one over their head, or on their forehead, etc.

A star of some form constitutes part of the insignia of every order of knighthood; the Star and Garter, a common inn sign, being in reference to the Most Noble Order of the Garter.

The stars were said by the old astrologers to have almost omnioptent influence on the lives and destinies of man (*cp. Judges* v, 20—"The stars in their courses fought against Sisera"), and to this old belief is due a number of phrases still common, as—**Bless my stars! You may thank your lucky stars, star-crossed** (not favoured by the stars, unfortunate), **to be born under an evil star,** etc.

His star is in the ascendant. He is in luck's way; said of a person to whom some good fortune has fallen and who is very prosperous. According to astrology, those leading stars which are above the horizon at a person's birth influence his life and fortune; when those stars are in the ascendant, he is strong, healthy, and lucky; but when they are in the descendant below the horizon, his stars do not shine on him, he is in the shade and subject to ill-fortune. *Cp.* HOUSES, ASTROLOGICAL.

I'll make you see stars! "I'll put you through it"; literally, will give you such a blow in the eye with my fist that, when you are struck, you'll experience the optical illusion of seeing brilliant streaks, radiating and darting in all directions.

Star of Bethlehem. A bulbous plant of the lily family (*Ornithogallum umbellatum*), with star-shaped white flowers. The French peasants call it *La dame d'onze heures*, because it opens at eleven o'clock.

Star of David. A large yellow cloth star which Jews and persons of Jewish descent were forced to wear on their clothes under the Nazi and Fascist regimes. To express his disapproval of this racial indignity King Christian X of Denmark himself wore a Star of David during the German occupation of his country.

Star of India. A British order of knighthood, *The Most Exalted Order of the Star of India*, instituted in 1861 by Queen Victoria as a reward for services in and for India and a means of recognizing the loyalty of native rulers. Its motto is "Heaven's Light our Guide."

Stars and Bars. The flag of the eleven Confederate States of America who broke away from the Union in 1860. It consisted of two broad horizontal red bars with a narrow white bar between them; in the top left corner a blue union bearing eleven white stars arranged in a circle.

Stars and Stripes or the **Star-spangled Banner,** the flag of the United States of North America. The *stripes* are emblematic of the original thirteen States, and the *stars*—of which there are now forty-eight—of the States that now constitute the Union.

The first flag used in the Revolutionary War (1774) was a red flag bearing a Union Jack and the words "Liberty and Union." The next (1775) displayed a coiled snake and the words *Don't tread on me*; the third showed a pine tree and was also used in 1775. The first version of the Stars and Stripes was raised at the Siege of Boston on January 1, 1776, and consisted of thirteen stripes, alternately red and white, with a blue canton emblazoned with the crosses of St. George and St. Andrew.

By act of Congress dated June 14, 1777, the two crosses in the canton were replaced by thirteen stars in a circle, to a design by Francis Hopkinson. The prototype is said to have been embroidered by Betsy Ross, a Quaker widow who kept an upholsterer's shop in Arch Street Philadelphia, though this tradition is now regarded with grave doubts.

In 1794 (after the admission of Vermont and Kentucky) the stripes and stars were each increased to fifteen, but in 1818 it was decided that the original thirteen stripes should be restored, and stars added to signify the States in the Union. It was in 1818, also, that the stars were squared up for the first time.

Starboard and Laboard. Star- is the Anglo-Saxon *steor*, rudder, *bord*, side; meaning the right side of a ship (looking forwards). Larboard, for the left-hand side, is now obsolete, and "port" is used instead. The word was earlier *leereboard* (A.S. *lœre*, empty) that side being clear as the steersman stood on the star (*steer*) board.

Starvation Dundas. Henry Dundas, Horace Lord Melville (1740-1811) was so called by Walpole, because when the Opposition denounced the Bill for restraining trade and commerce with the New England colonies (1775) on the ground that it would cause a famine in which the innocent would suffer with the guilty, he said that he was "afraid" the Bill would not have this effect. The word "starvation" was first used by Dundas.

Starved With Cold. Half dead with cold (A.S. *steorfan*, to die).

States, The. A common term for the United States of America.

States General. The supreme legislative assembly of France before the Revolution of 1789. It was only summoned as a last resort, prior to 1789 not having been called since 1614. It consisted of the three Estates of the realm, nobles, clergy, and the Third Estate (*Tiers etat*) or commoners. The name is still applied to the parliament of the kingdom of the Netherlands.

Station. This word with the meaning of a place where people assemble for a specific duty or purpose has many applications; *e.g.* a railway station (U.S.A. depot); a police station, lifeboat station, etc. In Australia it was used as early as 1830 in the sense of a cattle farm or ranch. Thus, **station black,** an aboriginal; **station super,** a manager; **station mark,** a brand; **station jack,** a sort of meat pudding.

Stator (stā' tôr) (Lat., the stopper or arrester). When the Romans fled from the Sabines, they stopped at a certain place and made terms with the victors. On this spot they afterwards built a temple to Jupiter, and called it the temple of Jupiter Stator or Jupiter who caused them to stop in their flight.

Here, Stator Jove and Phœbus, god of verse
The votive tablet I suspend.
PRIOR.

Statute (Lat. *statutum*, from *statuere*, to cause
to stand; the same word, etymologically, as
statue). A law enacted by a legislative body, an
Act of Parliament; also laws enacted by the king
and council before there were any regular parliaments. Hence, a *statute mile*, a *statute ton*,
etc., is the measure as by law established and
not according to local custom.

Stolen sweets are always sweeter. Things
procured by stealth, and game illicitly taken,
have the charm of illegality to make them the
more palatable. Solomon says, "Stolen waters
are sweet, and bread eaten in secret is pleasant"
(*Prov.* ix, 17).

> From busie cooks we love to steal a bit
> Behind their backs and that in corners eat;
> Nor need we here the reason why entreat;
> All know the proverb, "Stolen bread is sweet."
> *History of Joseph*, n. d.

In one of the songs in Act iii, sc. iv, of
Randolph's *Amyntos* (1638) are the lines:—

> Furto cuncta magis bella,
> Furto dulçior Puella,
> Furto omnia decora,
> Furto poma dulciora,

which were translated by Leigh Hunt as:—

> Stolen sweets are always sweeter,
> Stolen kisses much completer,
> Stolen looks are nice in chapels,
> Stolen, stolen, be your apples.

Steelyard. A place (formerly a *yard* or enclosure) on the Thames just above London Bridge,
where the Hanse merchants had their depot. The
name is a mistranslation of Ger. *staalhof*, sample
yard, *staal* meaning both *sample* and *steel*.

Steeplechase. A horse-race across fields,
hedges, ditches, and other obstacles. The term
arose in the late 18th century from a party of fox-
hunters agreeing, on their return from an unsuccessful chase, to race in a direct line to the village
church, the steeple of which was in sight, regardless of anything that happened to lie in the way.

For the principal English steeplechases, *see*
RACES.

Steeple house. The old Puritan epithet for
a church.

Stentor (sten' tôr). **The voice of a Stentor.**
A very loud voice. Stentor was a Greek herald
in the Trojan war. According to Homer (*Iliad v.*
783), his voice was as loud as that of fifty men
combined; hence **stentorian**, loud voiced.

Step-. A prefix used before *father, mother,
brother, sister, son, daughter*, etc, to indicate
that the person spoken of is a relative only by
the marriage of a parent, and not by blood (A.S.
stéop, connected with *astieped*, bereaved). Thus,

a man who marries a widow with children becomes *stepfather* to those children, and if he has
children by her these and those of the widow's
earlier marriage are *stepbrothers* or *stepsisters*.
The latter are also called *half-brothers* and *half-
sisters*; but some make a distinction between
the terms, *half-brother* being kept for what we
have already defined as a *stepbrother*, this latter
term being applied only between the children
of former marriages when both parents have
been previously married.

Stephen, St. The first Christian martyr—the
"protomartyr." He was accused of blasphemy
and stoned to death (*Acts* vii, 58). He is commemorated on December 26th; the name means
"wreath" or "crown" (Gr. *stephanos*).

Fed with St. Stephen's bread. Stoned.

The Crown of St. Stephen. The crown of
Hungary, this St. Stephen being the first king of
Hungary (1000-38). He was a pagan, born at
Gran about 969, and was converted to Christianity about 995. During his reign the faith
became firmly established in his kingdom. He
was canonized by Benedict IX shortly after his
death, and is commemorated on September 2nd.

> If Hungarian independence should be secured
> through the help of Prince Napoleon, the Prince himself
> should receive the crown of St. Stephen.—KOSSUTH:
> *Memoirs of my Exile* (1880).

Sterling, when applied to coins and metal,
denotes that they are of standard value (92·5 parts
of silver to 7·5 of copper or other metal), genuine;
hence applied figuratively to anything of sound,
intrinsic worth, as A *man of sterling qualities*.
The word—first met with about the early 12th
century—has been held to be a corruption of
Easterlings, the Hanse merchants trading with
England; but this is unlikely, and the suggestions
are that it is either *steorling*, the coin with a star,
some of the early Norman coins having a small
star on them, or the bird *starling*, some of Edward
the Confessor's coins bearing four martlets.

Stet (Lat., let it stand). An author's or editor's
direction to the printer to cancel a correction
previously made in a MS., proof, etc.

Stetson. A large-brimmed hat habitually
worn by cattle men in the U.S.A., so called from
the best-known manufacturer, John B. Stetson.

Stew. In a stew. In a fix, a flurry; in a state of
mental agitation.

Irish stew. A dish made by stewing together
meat, onions, and potatoes. Called "Irish" from
the predominance of potatoes.

To stew in one's own juice. To suffer the
natural consequences of one's actions, to reap as
you have sown. Chaucer has:—

In his own gress I made him frie,
For anger and for verry jalousie.
                    Wife of Bath's Tale (Prologue).

The Russian ambassador, when Louis Philippe fortified Paris, remarked, if ever again Paris is in insurrection, it "can be made to stew in his own gravy (jus)."

Stick. An old stick-in-the-mud. A dull, unprogressive old fogy.

The wrong end of the stick. Not the true facts; a distorted version. *To have got hold of the wrong end of the stick* is to have misunderstood the story.

To stick at nothing. To be heedless of all obstacles in accomplishing one's desire; to be utterly unscrupulous.

To stick it up. Old slang for leaving one's "score" at the tavern to be paid later; a note of it was stuck, or chalked up, at the back of the door.

To stick up. Australian for to waylay and rob a coach, etc.; also in common use for raiding a bank and so on in daylight, the raiders closing the doors and covering all present with revolvers telling them to "stick 'em up," or hold up their hands above their heads.

Stuck up. Said of pretentious people who give themselves airs, nobodies who assume to be somebodies. The allusion is to the peacock, which sticks up its train to add to its "importance" and "awe down" antagonists.

Stickler. A stickler over trifles. One particular about things of no moment. *Sticklers* were the umpires in tournaments, or seconds in single combats, very punctilious about the minutest points of etiquette. The word is connected with A.S. *stihtan*, to arrange, regulate.

Stiff. Slang for a corpse; also for a horse that is sure to lose in a race; also (with reference to the stiff interest exacted by moneylenders) an I O U, a bill of acceptance.

His "stiff" was floating about in too many directions, at too many high figures.—OUIDA: *Under Two Flags*. ch. vii.

Stigmata (stig' mà tà). Marks developed on the body of certain persons, which correspond to some or all of the wounds received by our Saviour in His trial and crucifixion. It is a well-known psychological phenomenon and has been demonstrated in many modern instances. From Gr. *stigma*, the brand with which slaves and criminals in ancient Greece and Rome were marked; hence our verb stigmatize, to mark as with a brand of disgrace.

Among those who are said to have been marked with the stigmata are—

(1) MEN. St. Paul, who said "I bear in my body the marks of the Lord Jesus" (*Gal.* vi, 17); Angelo del Paz (all the marks); Benedict of Reggio (the crown of thorns), 1602; Carlo di Saeta (the lance-wound); Francis of Assisi (all the marks), September 15th, 1224; and Nicholas of Ravenna.

(2) WOMEN. Bianca de Gazeran; Catharine of Siena; Catharine di Raconisco (the crown of thorns), 1583; Cecilia di Nobili of Nocera 1655; Clara di Pugny (mark of the spear), 1514; "Estatica" of Caldaro (all the marks), 1842; Gabriella da Piezolo of Aquila (the spear-mark), 1472; Hieronyma Carvaglio (the spear-mark, which bled every Friday); Joanna Maria of the Cross; Maria Razzi of Chio (marks of the thorny crown); Maria Villani (ditto); Mary Magdalen di Pazzi; Mechtildis von Stanz; Ursula of Valencia; Veronica Giuliani (all the marks) 1694; Vincenza Ferreri of Valencia; Anna Emmerich, of Dülmen, Westphalia (d. 1824); Maria von Mörl (in 1839); Louise Lateau (1860), and Anne Girling, the foundress of the English "Shakers" (*q.v.*). Theresa Neumann, of Kennersreuth, Germany, (b. 1898) received her first stigmata on the tops of her hands and feet, on Good Friday, 1926. In subsequent years more marks appeared, on her side, shoulders, and brow. Stigmata, as studied in her case, never heal and never suppurate.

Stilo Novo (stī' lō nō' vō) (Lat., in the new style). Newfangled notions. When the calendar was reformed by Gregory XIII (1582), letters used to be dated *stilo novo*, which grew in time to be a cant phrase for any innovation.

And so I leave you to your *stilo novo.*
BEAUMONT AND FLETCHER: *Woman's Prize*, iv, 4.

Stirrup. Literally, a rope to climb by (A.S. *stirap*, from *stigan*, to climb, and *rāp*, a rope).

Stirrup cup. A "parting cup," given, especially in the Highlands, to guests on leaving when their feet are in the stirrups. *Cp.* DOCH-AN-DOROCH.

Lord Marmion's bugles blew to horse;
Then came the stirrup-cup in course;
Between the baron and his host
No point of courtesy was lost.
                    SCOTT: *Marmion*, i, 21.

Among the ancient Romans a "parting cup" was drunk in honour of Mercury to insure sound sleep. *See* Ovid, *Fasti*, ii, 635.

Stirrup oil. A beating; a variety of "strap oil" (*q.v.*).

Stiver (stī' vér). **Not a stiver.** Not a penny, not a cent. The stiver (*stuiver*) was a Dutch coin, equal to about a penny.

    Set him free,
And you shall have your money to a stiver
And present payment.
                    FLETCHER: *Beggars' Bush*, i, 3.

Stock. Originally, a tree-trunk, or stem (connected with *stick*); hence, in figurative uses, something fixed, also something regarded as the origin of families, groups, etc.; as **He comes of a good stock,** from a good stem, of good line of descent, **Languages of Indo-Germanic stock,** etc. **To worship stocks and stones** is to worship idols, *stock* here being taken as a type of a motionless, fixed thing, like a tree-stump. The village *stocks,* in which petty offenders were confined by the wrists and ankles, are so called from the stakes or posts at the side. In its financial meaning *stock* in the sense of a fund or capital derives from that part of the old wooden tally which the creditor took with him as evidence of the king's debt, the other portion, known as the counterstock remaining in the Exchequer. The word was applied to the money which this tally represented, *i.e.* money lent to the government.

Live stock. The cattle, sheep, pigs, horses, etc., belonging to a farmer; that part of his "stock in trade" which is alive. In slang use, lice or other parasitical vermin.

Lock, stock, and barrel. *See* LOCK.

Stock-broker, stock-jobber. The *broker* is engaged in the purchase of stocks and shares for clients on commission; the *jobber* speculates in stocks and shares so as to profit by market fluctuations, and acts as an intermediary between buying and selling brokers. The jobber must be a member of a Stock Exchange; but a broker need not necessarily be; if he is not he is known as an "outside broker" or a "kerbstone operator." *Cp.* BUCKET-SHOP.

Stock in trade. The fixed capital of a business; the goods, tools, and other requisites of a trade or profession.

Stock-rider. The Australian term for one in charge of cattle, *i.e.* stock. He uses a *stock-whip,* and herds his beasts in a *stock-yard.*

To take stock. To ascertain how one's business stands by taking an inventory of all goods and so on in hand, balancing one's books, etc.; hence, to survey one's position and prospects.

Stocking. Used of one's savings or "nest-egg," because formerly money used to be hoarded up in an old stocking, which was frequently hung up the chimney for safety.

Blue stocking. *See under* BLUE.

Stoic (stō′ik). A school of Greek philosophers (founded by Zeno, about 308 B.C.) who held that virtue was the highest good, and that the passions and appetites should be rigidly subdued.

It was so called because Zeno gave his lectures in the *Stoa Poikile,* the Painted Porch (*see* PORCH) of Athens.

Epictetus was the founder of the New Stoic school (1st cent. A.D.).

> The ancient Stoics in their porch
> With fierce dispute maintained their church,
> Beat out their brains in fight and study
> To prove that virtue is a body,
> That *bonum* is an animal,
> Made good with stout polemic bawl.
> BUTLER: *Hudibras,* ii, 2.

Stole (Lat. *stola*). An ecclesiastical vestment, also called the Orarium. Deacons wear the stole over the left shoulder, and loop the two parts together, that they may both hang on the right side. Priests wear it over both shoulders and hanging loose in front.

Stole, Groom of the. Formerly, the first lord of the bedchamber, a high officer of the Royal Household ranking next after the vice-chamberlain. The office was allowed to lapse on the accession of Queen Victoria; in the reign of Queen Anne it was held by a woman.

Stole, here, is not connected with Lat. *stola,* a robe, but refers to the king's *stool,* or privy. As late as the 16th century, when the king made a royal progress his close-stool formed part of the baggage and was in charge of a special officer or groom.

Stolen Things. *See under* STEAL.

Stomach. Used figuratively of inclination, appetite, etc.

> He who hath no stomach for this fight.—SHAKESPEARE: *Henry V,* iv, 3.
> Wolsey was a man of an unbounded stomach.—*Henry VIII,* iv, 2.
> Let me praise you while I have the stomach.—*Merchant of Venice,* iii, 5.

To stomach an insult. To swallow it and not resent it.

> If you must believe, stomach not all.—SHAKESPEARE: *Antony and Cleopatra,* iii, 4.

Stone. Used in a figurative sense in many ways when some characteristic of a stone is to be pointed out; as, *stone blind, stone cold, stone dead, stone still,* etc., as blind, cold, dead, or still as a stone.

> I will not struggle; I will stand stone still.
> *King John,* iv, 1.

In all ages stones, especially those of meteoric origin or those fabled to have "fallen from heaven," have been set up and worshipped by primitive peoples, and the great stone circles of Stonehenge, Avebury, the Orkneys, Carnac, etc., are relics of religious rites. Anaxagoras mentions a stone that fell from Jupiter in Thrace, a description of which is given by Pliny. The Ephesians asserted that their image of Diana came from Jupiter. The stone at Emessa, in Syria, worshipped as a symbol of the sun, was a similar meteorite. At Abydos and Potidæa similar stones were preserved. At Corinth was one venerated as Zeus. At Cyprus was one dedicated to Venus, a description of which is given by Tacitus and Maximus Tyrius. Herodian describes one in Syria, and the famous "black stone" (*see* HAJAR AL-ASWAD), set in the Kaaba of the Moslems, is a similar meteorite.

After the Moslem pilgrim has made his seven processions round the Kaaba, he repairs to Mount Arafat, and before sunrise enters the valley of Mena, where he throws seven stones at each of three pillars, in imitation of Abraham and Adam, who thus drove away the devil when he disturbed their devotions.

A rolling stone gathers no moss. One who is always "chopping and changing" and won't settle down will never become wealthy. So says the proverb (which is common to many languages), but it is not always borne out by facts— and its reverse does not hold true.

Tusser, in his *Five Hundred Points of Good Husbandrie* (1573) has—

The stone that is rolling can gather no moss,
For master and servant oft changing is loss.

Hag-stones. Flints naturally perforated, used in country places as charms against witches, the evil eye, etc. They are hung on the key of an outer door, round the neck for luck, on the bedpost to prevent nightmare, on a horse's collar to ward off disease, etc.

Stone soup or **St. Bernard's soup.** The story goes that a beggar asked alms at a lordly mansion, but was told by the servants they had nothing to give him. "Sorry for it," said the man, "but will you let me boil a little water to make some soup of this stone?" This was so novel a proceeding, that the curiosity of the servants was aroused, and the man was readily furnished with saucepan, water, and a spoon. In he popped the stone, and begged for a little salt and pepper for flavouring. Stirring the water and tasting it, he said it would be the better for any fragments of meat and vegetables they might happen to have. These were supplied, and ultimately he asked for a little ketchup or other sauce. When ready the servants tasted it, and declared that "stone soup" was excellent.

This story, which was a great favourite in the 16th and 17th centuries, was told with many variations, horseshoes, nails, ramshorns, etc., taking the place of the stone as narrated above.

The Stone Age. The period when stone implements were used by primitive man. It preceded the Bronze Age; and some peoples, such as certain tribes in Papua, have not yet emerged from it. *See* PALÆOLITHIC.

The stone jacket or **jug.** Slang for prison. *See* JUG.

To cast the first stone. To take the lead in criticizing, fault-finding, quarrelling, etc. The phrase is from *John* viii, 7:—

He that is without sin among you, let him first cast a stone at her.

To kill two birds with one stone. *See* BIRD.

To leave no stone unturned. To spare no trouble, time, expense, etc., in endeavouring to accomplish your aim. After the defeat of Mardonius at Platæa (477 B.C.), a report was current that the Persian general had left great treasures in his tent. Polycrates the Theban sought long but found them not. The Oracle of Delphi, being consulted, told him "to leave no stone unturned," and the treasures were discovered.

Stonehenge. The great prehistoric (Neolithic or early Bronze Age) monument on Salisbury Plain, originally consisting of two concentric circles of upright stones, enclosing two rows of smaller stones, and a central block of blue marble (18 ft. by 4 ft.), known as the Altar Stone. The Friar's Heel (*q.v.*) stands outside the circle to the NE. Many theories as to its original purpose and original builders have been propounded. It was probably used (if not built) by the Druids, and from its plotting, which had an astronomical basis, it is thought to have been the temple of a sun god and to have been built about 1680 B.C.

The *-henge* of the name seems to refer to something hanging (A.S. *hengen*) in, or supported in, the air, viz., the huge transverse stones; but Geoffrey of Monmouth connects it with Hengist, and says that Stonehenge was erected by Merlin to perpetuate the treachery of Hengist in falling upon Vortigern and putting him and his 400 attendants to the sword. Aurelius Ambrosius asked Merlin to devise a memento of this event, whereupon the magician transplanted from Ireland the "Giant's Dance" stones which had been brought thither from Africa by a race of giants and all of which possessed magic properties.

Stonewall, To. A cricketer's term for adopting purely defensive measures when at the wicket, blocking every ball and not attempting to score. It was originally Australian political slang and was used of obstructing business.

Stonewall Jackson. Thomas J. Jackson (1824-63), one of the Confederate generals in the American Civil War; so called because at the Battle of Bull Run (1861) General Bee, of South Carolina, observing his men to waver, exclaimed, "Look at Jackson's men; they stand like a stone wall!"

Stooge (stooj). The second partner in a comic music-hall act whose role is to be stupid, ask questions, and make the comedian say everything twice and very distinctly so that the jokes get over to the audience. Hence the term has passed into common parlance for a confederate or a decoy.

Stool Pigeon. A police spy or informer; also a person employed by gamblers, etc., as a decoy or secret confederate.

Store. Store cattle. Beasts kept on a farm for breeding purposes, or thin cattle bought for fattening.

To set store by. To value highly.

Stork. According to the Swedish legend, the stork received its name from flying round the cross of the crucified Redeemer, crying *Styrka! styrka!* (Strengthen! strengthen!).

Many fables and legends have grown up around this bird. Lyly refers to it more than once in his *Euphues* (1850), as—

Ladies use their lovers as the stork doth her young ones who pecketh them till they bleed with her bill, and then healeth them with her tongue.

And again—

Constancy is like unto the stork, who wheresoever she fly cometh into no nest but her own.

And—

It fareth with me . . . as with the stork, who, when she is least able carrieth the greatest burden.

Dutch and German mothers tell their children that babies are brought by storks; and another common belief was that the stork, like the secretary bird, will kill snakes "on sight";

'Twill profit when the stork, sworn foe of snakes, Returns, to show compassion to thy plants.

PHILIPS: *Cyder*, Bk. i.

Storm (Austr.). Young grass which has grown after a rainfall in dry areas. Travelling from storm to storm is to *storm along*.

A brain-storm. A sudden and violent upheaval in the brain, causing temporary loss of control, or even madness. *Nerve-storm* is used in much the same way of the nerves.

A storm in a teacup. A mighty to-do about a trifle; making a great fuss about nothing.

To take by storm. To seize by a sudden and irresistible attack; a military term used figuratively, as of one who becomes suddenly famous or popular; an actor, suddenly springing to fame, "takes the town by storm."

Stormy Petrel. *See* PETREL.

Stornello Verses (stôr nel' ō) are those in which certain words are harped on and turned about and about. They are common among the Tuscan peasants. The word is from *tornare* (to return).

I'll tell him the *white*, and the *green*, and the red,
Mean our country has flung the vile yoke from her head;
I'll tell him the *green*, and the *red*, and the *white*,
Would look well by his side as a sword-knot so bright;
I'll tell him the *red*, and the *white*, and the *green*,
Is the prize that we play for, a prize we will win.
Notes and Queries.

Storthing (stôr' ting). The Norwegian Parliament, elected every three years (*stor*, great; *thing*, assembly).

Stoush (stoush). Australian, a brawl. World War I was known by Australian troops as the *Big Stoush*. Probably from English *stashie* an uproar.

Stovepipe Hat. An old-fashioned tall silk hat, a chimney-pot hat (*q.v.*).

High collars, tight coats, and tight sleeves were worn at home and abroad, and, as though that were not enough, a stovepipe hat.—*Illustrated Sporting and Dramatic News*, Sept. 1891.

Strad. A colloquial name for a violin made by the famous maker Antonio Stradivarius (1644-1737) of Cremona. His best period was about 1700 to 1725; he sold his violins for about £4 each; they have since realized as much as £3,000, and one of his 'cellos £4,000.

Strafe (straf) (Ger. *strafen*, to punish). A word borrowed in good-humoured contempt from the Germans during World War I. One of their favourite slogans was *Gott strafe England!* The word was applied to any sharp and sudden bombardment.

Strain. The quality of mercy is not strained (*Merchant of Venice*, iv, 1)—constrained or forced, but cometh down freely as the rain, which is God's gift.

To strain a point. To go beyond one's usual, or the proper, limits; to give way a bit more than one has any right to.

To strain courtesy. To stand upon ceremony. Here, *strain* is to *stretch*, as parchment is strained on a drum-head.

Strand, The. One of the most famous of London thoroughfares, leading from the City of London to that of Westminster, along the Riverside, whence its name. It was little more than a country road until 1532 when it was paved. Nobles and no fewer than nine bishops had their inns or houses in the Strand, and no street in the metropolis has more historical or social associations, though within the last fifty years it has been widened and altered beyond recognition.

Stranger. Originally, a foreigner; from O.Fr. *estrangier* (Mod. Fr. *étranger*), which is the Latin *extraneus*, one without (*extra*, without).

It is said that Busiris, King of Egypt, sacrificed to his gods all strangers who set foot on his territories. Diomed (*q.v.*) gave strangers to his horses for food.

Floating tea-leaves in one's cup, charred pieces of wick that make the candle gutter, little bits of soot hanging from the bars of the grate, etc., are called "strangers," because they are supposed to foretell the coming of visitors.

I spy strangers! The recognized form of words by which a member of Parliament conveys to the Speaker the information that there is an unauthorized person in the House.

The little stranger. A new-born infant.

The stranger that is within thy gates. *See* PROSELYTES.

Strap. A taste of the strap, or a strapping is a flogging, properly with a leather strap.

A strapping young fellow. A big, sturdy chap; a robust, vigorous young woman is similarly termed a *strapper*.

Straphanger. One who cannot get a seat in a train, omnibus, etc., and so has to do his journey standing on the floor and clinging to a strap suspended from the roof for the purpose.

Strap oil. Slang for a thrashing. *See above.*

Strappado (strà pā' dō) (Ital. *strappare*, to pull). A mode of torture formerly practised for extracting confessions, retractations, etc. The hands were tied behind the back, and the victim was pulled up to a beam by a rope tied to them and then let down suddenly; by this means a limb was not infrequently dislocated.

Were I at the strappado or the rack, I'd give no man a reason on compulsion.—1 *Henry IV*, ii, 4.

Strassburg Goose. A goose fattened, crammed, and confined in order to enlarge its liver from which is made true paté de foie gras.

Straw. As used in phrases *straw* is generally typical of that which is worthless, as **Not worth a straw**, quite valueless, not worth a rap, a fig, etc.; **to care not a straw,** not to care at all.

A man of straw. A man without means, with no more substance than a straw doll; also, an imaginary or fictitious person put forward for some reason.

A straw shows which way the wind blows. Mere trifles often indicate the coming of momentous events. They are shadows cast before coming events.

The last straw. "'Tis the last straw that breaks the camel's back." There is an ultimate point of endurance beyond which calamity breaks a man down.

To catch at a straw. A forlorn hope. A drowning man will catch at a straw.

Strawberry. So called from *straw*, probably because the achenes with which the surface is dotted somewhat resemble finely chopped straw.

We may say of angling as Dr. Boteler said of strawberries, "Doubtless God could have made a better berry, but doubtless God never did."—IZAAK WALTON: *Compleat Angler*, ch. v.

Strawberry mark. A birthmark something like a strawberry. In Morton's *Box and Cox* the two heroes eventually recognize each other as long-lost brothers through one of them having a strawberry-mark on his left arm.

Strawberry preachers. So Latimer called the non-resident country clergy, because they "come but once a yeare and tarie not long" (*Sermon on the Plough*, 1549).

The strawberry leaves. A dukedom; the honour, rank, etc., of a duke. The ducal coronet is ornamented with eight strawberry leaves.

Street Arab. *See* BEDOUIN.

Strenia (strē' ni à). The goddess who presided over the New Year festivities in ancient Rome. Tatius, the legendary Sabine king, entered Rome on New Year's Day, and received from some augurs palms cut from the sacred grove, dedicated to her. After his seizure of the city, he ordained that January 1st should be celebrated by gifts to be called *strenœ*, consisting of figs, dates, and honey. The French *étrenne*, a New Year's gift, is from this goddess.

Strephon (stref' on). A stock name for a rustic lover; from the languishing lover of that name in Sidney's *Arcadia*.

Strike. A cessation of work by a body of employees with the object of inducing the employers to grant some demand, such as one for higher wages, shorter hours, better working conditions, etc., or sometimes for no direct reason, but out of sympathy for other workers or for the furtherance of some political object. **A lightning strike** is one of which no notice has been given; and the converse of a strike, *i.e.* the refusal of the masters to allow the men to work until certain conditions are agreed upon or rules complied with, is termed a *lock-out*.

The word first appears in this sense in 1768, and seems to have had a nautical origin; sailors who refused to go to sea because of some grievance *struck* (lowered) the yards of their ship.

Strike is the name of an old grain measure, still unofficially used in some parts of England,

and varying locally from half a bushel to four bushels. Probably so called because when filled the top of the measure was "struck off" and so levelled instead of being left heaped up.

It strikes me that . . . It occurs to me that . . . , it comes into my mind that . . .

Strike me dead! blind! etc. Vulgar expletives, or exclamations of surprise, dismay, wonder, and so on. Strike-me-dead is also sailor's slang for thin, wishy-washy beer.

Strike while the iron is hot. Act while the impulse is still fervent, *or* do what you do at the right time. The metaphor is taken from the blacksmith's forge; a horse-shoe must be struck while the iron is red-hot or it cannot be moulded into shape. Similar proverbs are: "Make hay while the sun shines," "Take time by the forelock."

To be struck all of a heap. *See* HEAP.

To be struck on a person. A colloquialism for to be much interested in him (or her), or to have fallen in love with the person named.

To strike an attitude. To pose; to assume an exaggerated or theatrical attitude.

To strike a balance. *See* BALANCE.

To strike a bargain (Lat. *fœdus ferire*). To determine or settle it. The allusion is to the ancient custom of making a sacrifice in concluding an agreement. After calling the gods to witness, they struck—*i.e.* slew—the victim which was offered in sacrifice. *Cp.* TO STRIKE HANDS *below*.

To strike lucky. To have an unexpected piece of good fortune; a phrase from the miner's camps. **To strike oil** (*see* OIL) means much the same thing, and has a similar origin.

To strike one's colours, or **flag.** *See* FLAG.

To strike out in another direction. To open up a new way for oneself, to start a new method, a fresh business.

To strike sail. To acknowledge oneself beaten; to eat humble pie. A nautical expression. When a ship in fight or on meeting another ship, let down her topsails at least half-mast high, she was said to *strike*, meaning that she submitted or paid respect to the other.

> Now Margaret
> Must strike her sail, and learn awhile to serve
> When kings command.
>
> 3 *Henry VI*, iii, 3.

To strike up. To begin, start operations; as *to strike up an acquaintance*, to set it going. Originally of an orchestra or company of singers, who "struck up" the music.

Willing to wound, and yet afraid to strike. Said of one who dare not do the injury or take the revenge that he wishes. The "tag" is from Pope's *Epistle to Dr. Arbuthnot* (1735).

String. Always harping on one string. Always talking on one subject; always repeating the same thing. The allusion is to the ancient harpers.

To have two strings to one's bow. *See* BOW.

Strip. To tear a strip off a person. To give him a severe reprimand.

Strip-tease. A theatrical or cabaret performance in which an actress slowly and provocatively undresses herself.

Stroke. The oarsman who sits on the bench next the coxswain, and sets the time of the stroke for the rest.

To stroke one the wrong way. To vex him, ruffle his temper.

Strong. A strong verb is one that forms inflexions by internal vowel-change (such as *bind*, *bound*; *speak*, *spoke*); **weak verbs** add a syllable, or letter (as *love*, *loved*; *refund*, *refunded*).

Going strong. Prospering, getting on famously; in excellent state of health.

To come it strong. *See* COME.

Strontium (stron' shùm). This element, a yellowish metal resembling calcium, receives its name from Strontian, in Argyllshire, where it was discovered in 1792 by Thomas Charles Hope (1766-1844).

Stuff Gown. A barrister (*q.v.*) who has not yet "taken silk," *i.e.* become a Q.C. *See* SILK.

Stuka (stū' kà). A German dive-bombing aeroplane in World War II, from *Stutzkampf-bomber*.

Stumer (stū' mer). A swindle, or a swindler, a forged banknote or "dud" cheque; a fictitious bet recorded by the bookmakers, and published in the papers, to deceive the public by running up the odds on a horse which is not expected to win.

Stump. A stump orator. A ranting, bombastic speaker, who harangues all who will listen to him from some point of vantage in the open air, such as the stump of a tree; a "tub-thumper," mob orator. Hence such phrases as *to stump the country*, *to take to the stump*, to go from town to town making inflammatory speeches.

To stump up. To pay one's reckoning, pay what is due. Ready money is called *stumpy* or *stumps*. An Americanism, meaning money paid down on the spot—*i.e.* on the stump of a tree. *Cp.* NAIL, ON THE.

Stunt. A feat, performance; especially one of a startling or sensational nature. Hence, *to stunt*, to do something surprising or hazardous, an aerobatic turn or trick; a newspaper stunt, a movement, party cry, sensation, etc., worked by a newspaper and boomed by publicity men.

The word was originally American college slang for some exceptional athletic feat.

Stupor Mundi. So the Emperor Frederick II (1194-1250) was called, as being the greatest sovereign, soldier, and patron of artists and scholars during the 13th century.

Sturm und Drang (stoorm und drang) (Ger., storm and stress). The name given to the intellectual awakening of Germany towards the close of the 18th century. It had a considerable effect on our own Romantic Movement, and was so called from a drama of that name by Friedrich Maximilian von Klinger (1752-1831). Goethe and Schiller contributed to the movement.

Sty, an inflamed pimple on the eyelid, is shortened from the earlier *styany* (taken as meaning *sty-on-eye*), which is from A.S. *stigend*, something that rises (*stigan*, to rise).

Stygian (sti' ji an). Infernal, gloomy; pertaining to the river Styx (*q.v.*).

At that so sudden blaze the Stygian throng
Bent their aspect.—MILTON: *Paradise Lost*, x, 453.

Style is from the Latin *stylus* (a metal pencil for writing on waxen tablets, etc.). The characteristic of a person's writing is called his style. Metaphorically it is applied to composition and speech. Good writing is *stylish*, and, by extension, smartness of dress and deportment is so called.

Style is the dress of thought, and a well-dressed thought like a well-dressed man, appears to great advantage.—CHESTERFIELD: *Letter* ccxl.

To do a thing in style. To do it splendidly, regardless of expense.

Styles. Tom Styles or **John a Styles,** connected with *John-a-Nokes* (*q.v.*) an imaginary plaintiff or defendant in a law suit or an ancient order of ejectment, like "John Doe" and "Richard Roe."

And, like blind Fortune, with a sleight
Convey men's interest and right
From Stiles's pocket into Nokes's.
BUTLER; *Hudibras*, iii, 3.

Stylites or **Pillar Saints** (stī lī' tēz). A class of early and mediæval ascetics, chiefly of Syria, who took up their abode on the tops of pillars, from which they never descended. The most celebrated are Simeon Stylites, of Syria, and Daniel the Stylite of Constantinople. Simeon (390-459) spent forty years on different pillars, each loftier and narrower than the preceding, the last being 66 feet high. Daniel (d. 494) lived thirty-three years on a pillar, and was not infrequently nearly blown from it by the storms from Thrace. This form of asceticism was in vogue as late as the 16th century.

Styx (stiks). The river of Hate (Gr. *stugein*, to hate)—called by Milton "abhorred Styx, the flood of burning hate" (*Paradise Lost*, ii, 577)—that, according to classical mythology, flowed nine times round the infernal regions.

The fables about the Styx are of Egyptian origin, and we are told that Isis collected the various parts of Osiris (murdered by Typhon) and buried them in secrecy on the banks of the Styx. Charon (*q.v.*), as Diodorus informs us, is an Egyptian word for a "ferryman." If the gods swore by the Styx, they dared not break their oath.

By the black infernal Styx I swear
(That dreadful oath which binds the Thunderer)
'Tis fixed!
POPE: *Thebais of Statius*, i.

Suaviter (swā' vi ter). *Suaviter in modo, fortiter in re* (Lat.), gentle in manner, resolute in action. Said of one who does what is to be done with unflinching firmness, but in the most inoffensive manner possible.

Subject and Object. In metaphysics the *Subject* is the ego, the mind, the conscious self, the substance or substratum to which attributes must be referred; the *Object* is an external as distinct from the ego, a thing or idea brought before the consciousness. Hence *subjective criticism, art,* etc., is that which proceeds from the individual mind and is consequently individualistic, fanciful, imaginative; while *objective criticism* is that which is based on knowledge of the externals.

Subject-object. The immediate object of thought as distinguished from the material thing of which one is thinking.

The thought is necessarily and universally subject-object. Matter is necessarily, and to us universally, object-subject.—LEWES: *History of Philosophy*, II 485.

Sublapsarian (or **Infralapsarian**) (sŭb lăp sâr' i an). A Calvinist who maintains that God devised His scheme of redemption *after* he had permitted the "lapse" or fall of Adam, when He elected some to salvation and left others to run their course. The *supra*-lapsarian maintains that all this was ordained by God from the foundation of the world, and therefore *before* the "lapse" or fall of Adam.

Sublime. From Lat. *sub,* up to, *limen,* the lintel; hence, lofty, elevated in thought or tone.

Submerged or **Submerged Tenth, The.** The proletariat, sunk or submerged in poverty.

All but the "submerged" were bent upon merry-making.— *Society,* Nov. 12th, 1892, p. 1273.

Subpœna (sŭb pē' na) (Lat., under penalty) is a writ commanding a man to appear in court usually unwillingly to bear witness or give evidence on a certain trial named. It is so called because the party summoned is bound to appear *sub pœna centum librorum* (under a penalty of £100). We have the verb to *subpœna.*

Subsidy (Lat. *sub-sedere*, to sit down). The *subsidii* of the Roman army were the troops held in reserve, the auxiliaries, supports; hence the word came to be applied to a support generally, and (in English) specially to financial support granted by Parliament to the king. It now usually means a contribution granted by the state in aid of some commercial venture of public importance.

Subsidiary, auxiliary, supplemental, is, of course, from the same word.

Subtle Doctor, The (*Doctor Subtilis*). The Scottish schoolman and Franciscan friar, Duns Scotus (about 1265-1308).

Succotash (U.S.A.). A dish of Indian corn and beans boiled together. Originally an Indian dish.

Succoth. The Jewish name for the Feast of Tabernacles (Heb. *sukkoth*, booths). *See* TABERNACLE.

Suck, or **Suck-in.** A swindle, hoax, deception; a fiasco.

Suède (swād). Undressed kid-skin; so called because the gloves made of this originally came from Sweden (Fr. *gants de Suède*).

Suffering. The Meeting for Sufferings. The standing representative Committee of the Yearly Meeting of the Society of Friends (Quakers), which deals with questions affecting the Society; so called because when originally appointed in the 17th century its chief function was to relieve the sufferings caused to Quakers by distraint for tithes, persecution, etc.

Suffrage. One's vote, approval, consent; or, one's right to vote, especially at parliamentary and municipal elections. The word is from Lat. *suffrago*, the hough or ankle-bone of a horse, which was used by the Romans for balloting with, whence the voting table came to be called *suffragium*.

Hence **Suffragette,** a woman (usually more or less "militant") who in the ten years or so preceding World War I "agitated" for the parliamentary vote. The Suffragettes' campaigns of disturbance, violence, assault, wanton destruction of public property, arson, and attempted terrorism (for which many women were imprisoned and went on "hunger-strike") reached alarming proportions; but it stopped dead on the outbreak of War, and in 1918 women of 30 were not only enfranchised but made eligible for seats in Parliament. In, 1928 enfranchisement was made on the same terms as for men.

The 19th Amendment of the Constitution of the United States of America enacted Woman Suffrage in August, 1920.

Sui generis (sū' ī jen' er is) (Lat., of its own kind). Having a distinct character of its own; unlike anything else.

Sui juris (Lat.). Of one's own right; the state of being able to exercise one's legal rights—*i.e.* freedom from legal disability.

Suicides were formerly buried ignominiously on the high-road, with a stake thrust through their body, and without Christian rites. (Lat. *sui*, of oneself, *-cidium*, from *cœdere*, to kill.)

> They buried Ben at four cross roads,
> With a stake in his inside.
> HOOD: Faithless Nelly Gray.

Suit. A suit of dittoes. *See* DITTO.

To follow suit. To follow the leader; to do as those do who are taken as your exemplars. The term is from games of cards.

Sultan (Arab., king, *cp.* SOLDAN). The chief ruler of Turkey, and of some other Mohammedan countries, as Oman, Zanzibar, and—since 1914 (*cp.* KHEDIVE)—Egypt.

The wife (or sometimes the mother, sister, or concubine) of the Sultan is the **Sultana,** a name also given to a small, seedless raisin grown near Smyrna and to the purple gallinule (*Porphyrio cœruleus*), a beautiful bird allied to the moorhen.

> Some purple-wing'd Sultana sitting
> Upon a column, motionless
> And glittering, like an idol-bird.
> MOORE: Paradise and the Peri.

Summer. The second or autumnal summer, said to last thirty days, begins shortly before the sun enters Scorpio (Oct. 23rd). It is variously called—

St. Martin's summer, a late spell of fine weather. St. Martin's Day is Nov. 11th.

> Expect St. Martin's summer, halcyon days.
> 1 Henry VI, i, 2.

All Saints' or All Hallows' summer (All Saints' is Nov. 1st).

> Farewell, All Hallowen summer.—1 Henry IV, i, 2.

St. Luke's little summer (St. Luke's day is Oct. 18th); and—especially in the United States—the Indian summer.

Sumptuary Laws. Laws to limit the expenses of food and dress, or any luxury. The Romans had their *leges sumptuarii*, and they have been enacted in many states at various times. Those of England were all repealed by 1 James I. c. 25; but during the two World Wars, with the rationing of food, coals, etc., and the compulsory lowering of the strength of beer and whisky we had a temporary return to sumptuary legislation.

Sun. The source of light and heat, and consequently of life, to the whole world; hence, regarded as a deity and worshipped as such by all primitive peoples and having a leading place in all mythologies. *Shamash* was the principal sun god of the Assyrians, *Merodach* of the Chaldees, *Ormuzd* of the Persians, *Ra* of the Egyptians, *Tezcatlipoca* of the Mexicans, and *Helios* (known to the Romans as *Sol*) of the Greeks. Helios drove his chariot daily across the heavens, rising from the sea at dawn and sinking into it in the west at sunset; the names of his snow-white, fire-breathing coursers are given as Brontē (*thunder*), Eoos (*day-break*), Ethiops (*flashing*), Ethon (*fiery*), Erythreos (*red-producer*), Philogea (*earth-loving*), and Pyrois (*fiery*).

The Scandinavian sun god, Sunna, who was in constant dread of being devoured by the wolf Fenris (a symbol of eclipses), was similarly borne through the sky by the horses Arvakur, Aslo, and Alsvidur.

Apollo was also a sun god of the Greeks, but he was the personification not of the sun itself but of its all-pervading light and life-giving qualities.

A place in the sun. A favourable position that allows room for development; a share in what one has a natural right to. The phrase was popularized by William II of Germany during the crisis of 1911. In his speech at Hamburg (Aug. 27th) he spoke of the German nation taking steps that would make them—

sure that no one can dispute with us the place in the sun that is our due.

It had been used by Pascal some two hundred years before.

The Southern Gate of the Sun. The sign Capricornus or winter solstice. So called because it is the most southern limit of the sun's course in the ecliptic.

The Sun of Righteousness. Jesus Christ. (*Mal.* iv, 2.)

To have been out in the sun, or **to have the sun in one's eyes.** To be slightly inebriated.

To make hay while the sun shines. *See* HAY.

Sundowner. Australian for a tramp who times his arrival at the houses of the hospitable at sundown, so as to get a night's lodging.

Sunday (A.S. *sunnendœg*). The first day of the week, so called because anciently dedicated to the sun, as Monday was to the moon (*see* WEEK, DAYS OF THE). *See also* SABBATH.

Not in a month of Sundays. Not in a very long time.

One's Sunday best, or **Sunday-go-to-meeting togs.** One's best clothes, kept for wearing on Sundays.

Sunday saint. One who observes the ordinances of religion, and goes to church on a Sunday, but is worldly, grasping, "indifferent honest," the following six days.

When three Sundays come together. Never.

Sundew, the *Drosera*, which is from the Greek *drosos*, dew. So called from the dew-like drops which rest on the hairy fringes of the leaves.

Sunflower. What we know as the sunflower is the *Helianthus*, so called, not because it follows the sun, but because it resembles a conventional drawing of the sun. A bed of these flowers will turn in every direction, regardless of the sun. The *Turnsole* (*Heliotropium*), belonging to quite another order of plants, is the flower that turns to the sun.

> The sunflower turns on the god, when he sets.
> The same look which she turned when he rose.
> T. MOORE: (*Believe me if all those endearing young charms*).

The Sunflower State (U.S.A.). Kansas.

Sunna (sŭn' à) (Arab., custom, divine law). Properly, the sayings and example of Mohammed and his immediate followers in so far as they conform to the Koran; hence applied to the collections of legal and moral traditions attributed to the Prophet, supplementary to the Koran as the Hebrew Mishna is to the Pentateuch.

Sunnites. The orthodox and conservative body of Moslems, who consider the Sunna as authentic as the Koran itself and acknowledge the first four caliphs to be the rightful successors of Mohammed. They form by far the largest section of Mohammedans, and are divided into four sects, viz., Hanbalites, Hanafites, Malikites, and Shafiites (*cp.* SHIITES).

Suo marte (sū' ō mar' te) (Lat.). By one's own strength or personal exertions.

Super (sū' per). In theatrical parlance, "supers" are supernumeraries, or persons employed to make up crowds, processions, dancing or singing choirs, messengers, etc., where little or no speaking is needed.

Supercilious. Having an elevated eyebrow (Lat. *super*, over, *cilium*, eyebrow); hence contemptuous, haughty.

Supererogation. Works of supererogation. The term used by theologians for good works which are performed but are not actually enjoined on Christians (Lat. *super*, over, above, *erogare*, to pay out). In common use as a phrase.

Superman. A hypothetical superior human being of high intellectual and moral attainments, fancied as evolved from the normally existing type. The term (*übermensch*) was invented by the German philosopher Nietzsche (d. 1900), and popularized in England by G. B. Shaw's play, *Man and Superman* (1903).

The wide popularity of the term gave rise to many compounds, such as *superwoman, super-critic, super-tramp, super-Dreadnought,* and *super-tax.*

Supernaculum. The very best wine. The word is Low Latin for "upon the nail" (*super unguem*), meaning that the wine is so good the drinker leaves only enough in his glass to make a bead on his nail. The French say of first-class wine, "It is fit to make a ruby on the nail" (*faire rubis sur l'ongle*). Nashe says that after a man had drunk his glass, it was usual, in the North, to turn the cup upside down, and let a drop fall upon the thumb-nail. If the drop rolled off, the drinker was obliged to fill and drink again (*Pierce Pennilesse*, 1592). Bishop Hall alludes to the same custom: "The Duke Tenterbelly . . . exclaims . . . 'Let never this goodly-formed goblet of wine go jovially through me;' and then he set it to his mouth, stole it off every drop, save a little remainder, which he was by custom to set upon his thumb-nail and lick off."

Hence, to *drink supernaculum* is to leave no heel-taps; to leave just enough not to roll off one's thumb-nail if poured upon it.

Supply. One who acts as a substitute, temporarily taking the place of another; used principally of clergymen, school teachers, and domestic servants.

In Parliamentary language **supplies** is used of money granted for the purposes of government which is not provided by the revenue. In Britain all money bills, *i.e.* those authorizing expenditure, must originate in the House of Commons.

The law of supply and demand. The economic statement that the competition of buyers and sellers tends to make such changes in price that the demand for any article in a given market will become equal to the supply. In other words, if the demand exceeds the supply the price rises, operating so as to reduce the demand and so enable the supply to meet it, and *vice versa*.

Surgeon. A contraction of the earlier *chirurgeon*, from Gr. *cheir*, hand, *egein*, to work—one who works with his hands, or works by manual operations instead of through the agency of physic (as does the *physician*). The word is, etymologically, identical with *manufacturer* (Lat. *manus*, hand, *facere*, to work).

Surloin. See SIRLOIN.

Surname. The name added to, or given over and above, the Christian or personal name (O.Fr. *sur-*, from Lat. *super-*, over, above). English surnames (of which, it is said, there are some 30,000) came into use in the latter part of the 10th century, but were not widely used till much later, In origin they are for the most part appellations denoting a trade or occupation, the place of residence, or some peculiar characteristic.

Surplice. Over the *pelisse* or fur robe. (Lat. *super-pellicium*, from *pellis*, skin.) The clerical robe worn over the bachelor's ordinary dress, which was anciently made of sheepskin.

Surrealism. A school of art beginning in 1924 which regarded the subconscious as the essential source of art drawing inspiration from "all that is contrary to the general appearance of reality." It falls into two groups: "hand painted dream photographs" (Dali), and an endeavour to achieve complete spontaneity of technique as well as subject matter by use of contrast. Chief exponents: Picasso, Max Ernst, Arp, Man Ray, Miró and Salvador Dali. The literary exponent was André Breton.

Sutras (sū' tràs). Ancient Hindu aphoristic manuals giving the rules of systems of philosophy, grammar, etc., and directions concerning religious ritual and ceremonial customs. They are so called from Sansk. *sutra*, a thread.

Suttee (sŭt' ē). The Hindu custom of burning the widow on the funeral pyre of her deceased husband; also, the widow so put to death (from Sansk. *sati*, a virtuous wife). In theory the practice, which lasted for some 2,000 years, was optional, but public opinion and the very severe form of ostracism the defaulting widow had to endure gave her practically no option. Women with child and mothers of children not yet of age could not perform suttee. The practice was declared illegal in British India in 1829.

Swag (connected with Norwegian *svagga*, to sway from side to side). One's goods carried in a pack or bundle; hence, the booty obtained by a burglary—which is often carried away in a sack. **To get away with the swag** is used figuratively of profiting by one's cleverness or sharp practice.

Swagger (frequentative of SWAG). To strut about with a superior or defiant air; to bluster, make oneself out a very important person; hence, ostentatiously smart or "swell"; as *a swagger dinner, a swagger car*, etc.

Swagger-stick. The small cane a soldier was formerly obliged to carry when walking out.

Swainmote. See SWANIMOTE.

Swallow. According to Scandinavian tradition, this bird hovered over the cross of our Lord, crying "*Svala! svala!*" (Console! console!) whence it was called *svalow* (the bird of consolation).

Ælian says that the swallow was sacred to the Penates or household gods, and therefore to injure one would be to bring wrath upon your own house. It is still considered a sign of good luck if a swallow or martin builds under the eaves of one's house.

Perhaps you failed in your foreseeing skill,
For swallows are unlucky birds to kill.
> DRYDEN: *Hind and Panther*, Pt. iii.

Longfellow refers to another old fable regarding this bird:—

Seeking with eager eyes that wondrous stone which the swallow
Brings from the shore of the sea to restore the sight of its fledglings. *Evangeline*, Pt. i.

One swallow does not make a summer. You are not to suppose summer has come to stay just because you have seen a swallow; nor that the troubles of life are over because you have surmounted one difficulty. The Greek proverb, "One swallow does not make a spring" is to be found in Aristotle's *Nico-machæan Ethics* (I, vii, 16).

Swan. The fable that the swan sings beautifully just before it dies is very ancient, though baseless. Swans do not "sing" at all, in the ordinary sense of the term, and the only one for which song of any kind can be claimed is the Whistling Swan (*Cygnus musicus*) of Iceland, of which it is reported—

during the long dark nights their wild song is often heard resembling the tones of a violin, though somewhat higher and remarkably pleasant.—NICOL: *Account of Iceland*.

The superstition was credited by Plato, Aristotle, Euripides, Cicero, Seneca, Martial, etc., and doubted by Pliny and Ælian.

Shakespeare refers to it more than once. Emilia, just before she dies says—

I will play the swan,
And die in music.
> *Othello*, v, 2.

In the *Merchant of Venice*, (iii, 2) Portia says—
He makes a swan-like end,
Fading in music.

And Lucrece (*Rape of Lucrece*, 1,1611)—
And now this pale swan in her watery nest
Begins the sad dirge of her certain ending.

Spenser speaks of the swan as though it sang quite regardless of death—

He, were he not with love so ill bedight,
Would mount as high and sing as soote [sweetly] as Swanne. *Shepheardes Calender*: October, 89.

And Coleridge, referring to poetasters of the time, gives the old superstition an epigrammatic turn—

Swans sing before they die; 'twere no bad thing
Did certain persons die before they sing.

One Greek legend has it that the soul of Apollo, the god of music, passed into a swan,

and in the *Phædo* Plato makes Socrates say that at their death swans sing—

not out of sorrow or distress, but because they are inspired of Apollo, and they sing as foreknowing the good things their god hath in store for them.

This idea made the Pythagorean fable that the souls of all good poets passed into swans hence, the *Swan of Mantua*, etc. (*see below*).

The male swan is called a *cob*, the female a *pen*; a young swan a *cygnet*.

See also FIONNUALA; LEDA; LOHENGRIN.

All your swans are geese. All your fine promises or expectations have proved fallacious. "Hope told a flattering tale." The converse, **All your geese are swans,** means all your children are paragons, and whatever you do is in your own eyes superlative work.

Swan-maidens. Fairies of northern folklore, who can become maidens or swans at will by means of the *swan shift*, a magic garment of swan's feathers. Many stories are told of how the swan shift was stolen, and the fairy was obliged to remain thrall to the thief until rescued by a knight.

Swan song. The song fabled to be sung by swans at the point of death (*see above*); hence, the last work of a poet, composer, etc.

The Knight of the Swan. Lohengrin (*q.v.*).

The Order of the Swan. An order of knighthood instituted by Frederick II of Brandenburg in 1440 (and shortly after in Cleves) in honour of the Lohengrin legend. It died out in the 16th century, but it is still commemorated in our *White Swan* public-house sign, which was first used in honour of Anne of Cleves, one of the wives of Henry VIII. The badge was a silver swan surmounted by an image of the Virgin.

Swanhild (swăn' hild). An old Norse legendary heroine, daughter of Sigurd and Gudrun. She was falsely accused of adultery with the son of the king who was wooing her, and the king had him hanged and her trampled to death by horses.

Swank. To behave in an ostentatious manner, to show off and "cut a dash" to impress the observers with one's cleverness, smartness, or rank, etc. It is an old dialect word adopted as, modern slang.

Swap. To exchange.

To swap horses in midstream. To change leaders at the height of a crisis. Abraham Lincoln, in an address, June 9th, 1864, referring to the fact that his fellow Republicans, though many were dissatisfied with his conduct of the Civil War, had renominated him for President, said that the Convention had concluded "that it is best not to swap horses while crossing the river."

Swashbuckler. A ruffian; a swaggerer. "From swashing," says Fuller (*Worthies*; 1662), "and making a noise on the buckler." The sword-players used to "swash" or tap their shield, as fencers tap their foot upon the ground when they attack. *Cp.* SWINGE-BUCKLER.

A brave, a swashbuckler, one that for money and good cheere will follow any man to defend him; but if any danger come, he runs away the first, and leaves him in the lurch. — FLORIO: *Worlde of Wordes* (1598).

Swastika. The gammadion, or fylfot (*q.v.*), an elaborated cross-shaped design used as a charm to ward off evil and bring good luck; the emblem of Nazi Germany, personally chosen as such by Adolf Hitler. The word is Sanskrit, from *svasti*, good fortune.

Swear, To. Originally used only of solemnly affirming, by the invocation of God or some sacred person or object as witness to the pledge, to take an oath. Swearing came later to mean using bad language by way of expletives, intensives, and in moments of sudden anger through the sacred expressions being used in a profane way in lightly and irreverently taking oaths.

The modern practice of swearing, in either its flippant or vituperative shape is derived from the break-up of the process once devised as a protection of truthfulness and fair dealing. . . . It must be remembered that the subject of vituperative swearing is interwoven with that of legal and religious ordinances. — SHARMAN: *A Cursory History of Swearing*, ch. ii (1884).

To swear black is white. To swear to any falsehood.

To swear like a trooper. To indulge in very strong blasphemy or profanity. — " 'Our armies swore terribly in Flanders,' cried my Uncle Toby" (Sterne: *Tristram Shandy*, II, xi).

Sweat. To sweat a person is to exact the largest possible amount of labour from him at the lowest possible pay, to keep him working at starvation wages. The term is also used of bleeding, or fleecing, a man; and of rubbing down coins so that one can obtain and use the gold or silver taken from them.

Sweat-box (U.S.A.). A form of punishment of long standing which consists of imprisoning a man in a box no bigger than himself often in the sun, so that he becomes exhausted by the terrific temperature. Hence, **to sweat it out of him** is to extort a confession or agreement by such use of threats and violence as may be necessary until the victim breaks under the ordeal.

Swedenborgians (swē' den bôr' ji ånz). Followers of Emanuel Swedenborg (1688-1772), called by themselves "the New Jerusalem Church" (*Rev.* xxi, 2). Their views of salvation, inspiration of Scripture, and a future state, differ widely from those of other Christians, and they believe the Trinity to be centred in the person of Jesus Christ (*Col.* ii, 9).

Sweep. To sweep the threshold. To announce to all the world that the woman of the house is paramount. When the procession called "Skimmington" (*q.v.*) passed a house where the woman "wore the breeches" everyone gave the threshold a sweep with a broom or bunch of twigs.

Sweepstakes. A race in which stakes are made by the owners of horses engaged, to be awarded to the winner or other horse in the race. Entrance money has to be paid to the race fund. If the horse runs, the full stake must be paid; but if it is withdrawn, a forfeit only is imposed.

Also a gambling arrangement in which a number of persons stake money on some event (usually a horse-race), each of whom draws a lot for every share bought, the total sum deposited being divided among the drawers of winners (or sometimes of starters). Some "sweeps" have very valuable prizes; as the "Calcutta Sweep" on the Derby (organized by the Calcutta Club), the first prize of which comes to over £100,000.

Sweet. The sweet singer of Israel. King David (about 1074-1001 B.C.).

To be sweet on. To be enamoured of, in love with.

To have a sweet tooth. To be very fond of dainties and sweet things generally.

Sweetness and light. A favourite phrase with Matthew Arnold. "Culture," he said, "is the passion for sweetness and light, and (what is more) the passion for making them prevail" (*Preface* to *Literature and Dogma*). The phrase was used by Swift (*Battle of the Books*, 1697) in an imaginary fable by Æsop as to the merits of the bee (the ancients) and the spider (the moderns). It concludes:—

The difference is that instead of dirt and poison, we have rather chosen to fill our hives with honey and wax, thus furnishing mankind with the two noblest of things, which are *sweetness* and *light*.

Swell. A person showily dressed; one who puffs himself out beyond his proper dimensions, like the frog in the fable; hence, a fashionable person, one of high standing or importance. In American usage as an adjective, fine, stylish, first rate, just right.

Swell mob. The better-dressed thieves and pickpockets.

Swelled head. An exaggerated sense of one's own dignity, usefulness, importance, etc.

Swim. In the swim. In a favourable position in society of any kind; a racing-man who is "in the swim" is one who mixes with the class from which he can get the best "tips"; and similarly with a diplomatist, a stockbroker, or a society lady. It is an angler's phrase. A lot of fish gathered together is called a *swim*, and when an angler can pitch his hook in such a place he is said to be "in a good swim."

Sink or swim. No matter what happens. Convicted witches were thrown into the water to "sink or swim"; if they sank they were drowned; if they swam it was clear proof they were in league with the Evil One; so it did not much matter, one way or the other.

To swim with the stream. To allow one's actions and principles to be guided solely by the force of public opinion.

Swindle. To cheat, defraud, gain a mean advantage by trickery. The verb is formed from the noun *swindler*, which was introduced into England by German Jews about 1760, from Ger. *schwindler*, a cheating company promoter (from *schwindeln*, to act heedlessly or extravagantly).

Swing. Captain Swing. The name assumed by certain persons who, about 1830, sent threatening letters to farmers who employed mechanical means, such as threshing machines, to save labour. "Captain Swing" was an entirely imaginary person but three so-called *Lives* of him appeared in 1830 and 1831.

> The neighbours thought all was not right,
> Scarcely one with him ventured to parley,
> And Captain Swing came in the night,
> And burnt all his beans and his barley.
> BARHAM: *Babes in the Wood* (*Ingoldsby Legends*).

A type of jazz with a catchy rhythm. The word originated in Negro parlance to describe really moving music well played, but later (1930s) came to denote a debased type of popular dance music which the uninformed imagined had some connection with jazz.

Swinge-buckler. A roisterer, a rake who went a bit further than a swashbuckler (*q.v.*), in that he *swinged* (beat) his man, as well as *swashed* his buckler. The continuation of Stow's *Annals* tells us that in Elizabeth's time the "blades" of London used to assemble in West Smithfield with sword and buckler for mock fights, called "bragging" fights. They swashed and swinged their bucklers with much show of fury, "but seldome was any man hurt."

> There was I, and little John Doit of Staffordshire, and black George Barnes, and Francis Pickbone, and Will Squele, a Cotswold man; you had not four such swinge-bucklers in all the Inns-of-court; and, I may say to you, we knew where the bona-robas were.—*2 Henry VI*, iii, 2.

Swiss. The nickname of a Swiss is "Colin Tampon."

Swithin, St. If it rains on St. Swithin's day (July 15th), **there will be rain for forty days.**

> St. Swithin's day, gif ye do rain, for forty days it will remain;
> St. Swithin's day, an ye be fair, for forty days 'twill rain nae mair.

The legend is that St. Swithin, Bishop of Winchester, who died 862, desired to be buried in the church-*yard* of the minster, that the "sweet rain of heaven might fall upon his grave." At canonization the monks thought to honour the saint by removing his body into the choir, and fixed July 15th for the ceremony; but it rained day after day for forty days, so that the monks saw the saint was averse to their project, and wisely abandoned it.

The St. Swithin of France is St. Gervais (*q.v.*; *and see* MÉDARD). The rainy saint in Flanders is St. Godelieve; in Germany, the Seven Sleepers.

Switzers. *See* SWISS.

Swollen Head. *See* SWELLED HEAD.

Sword. At sword's point. In deadly hostility, ready to fight each other with swords.

Fire and sword. Rapine and destruction perpetrated by an invading army.

Poke not fire with a sword. This was a precept of Pythagoras, meaning add not fuel to fire, or do not irritate an angry man by sharp words which will only increase his rage. (*See* Iamblichus: *Protreptics*, symbol ix.)

Sword and buckler. An old epithet for brag and bluster; as *a sword and buckler voice, sword and buckler men*, etc. Hotspur says of the future Henry V—

> And that same sword and buckler Prince of Wales,
> . . . . . .
> I'd have him poisoned with a pot of ale.
> *1 Henry IV*, i, 3.

Sword and Cloak Plays. *See* CLOAK AND SWORD.

Sword dance. A Scottish dance performed over two swords laid crosswise on the floor, or sometimes danced among swords placed point downwards in the ground: also a dance in which the men brandish swords and clash them together, the women passing under them when crossed.

Sword dollar. A Scottish silver coin of James VI, marked with a sword on the reverse. It was worth 30s. Scots (= 2s. 6d. in English contemporary money).

The sword of Damocles. *See* DAMOCLES.

The Sword of God. Khaled Ibn al Waled (d. 642), the Mohammedan conqueror of Syria, was so called for his prowess at the battle of Muta.

The Sword of Rome. Marcellus, who opposed Hannibal (216-14 B.C.).

The Sword of the Spirit. The Word of God (*Eph.* vi, 17).

To put to the sword. To slay.

Your tongue is a double-edged sword. Whatever you say wounds; your argument cuts both ways. The allusion is to the double-edged sword out of the mouth of the Son of Man—one edge to condemn, and the other to save (*Rev.* i, 16).

Yours is a Delphic sword—it cuts both ways. Erasmus says a Delphic sword is that which accommodates itself to the *pro* or *con* of a subject. The reference is to the double meanings of the Delphic oracles.

Some famous swords. In the days of chivalry a knight's horse and sword were his most treasured and carefully kept possessions, and his sword—equally with his horse—had its own name. The old romances, especially those of the Charlemagne and Arthurian cycles, are full of these names; we give below a list of the more noteworthy, and further particulars of these and others will be found throughout this Dictionary.

Angurvadal (stream of anguish), Frithiof's sword.

Arondight, the sword of Launcelot of the Lake.

Azoth, the sword of Paracelsus (Browning's *Paracelsus*, Bk. v).

Balisarda, Rogero's sword, made by a sorceress.

Balmung, one of the swords of Siegfried, made by Wieland.

Caliburn, another name of *Excalibur* (*q.v.*).

Chrysaor (sword, as good as gold), Artegal's sword (Spenser's *Faerie Queene*).

Colada, the Cid's sword.

Corrougue, Otuel's sword.

Courtain (the short sword), one of the swords of Ogier the Dane; *Sauvagine* was the other, and they both took Munifican three years to make.

Curtana, the blunted sword of Edward the Confessor.

Durandan, Durandal, or *Durandana* (the inflexible), Orlando's sword.

Excalibur, the sword of King Arthur. (*Ex cal*[*ce*]-*liber*[*are*], to liberate from the stone.)

Flamberge or *Floberge* (the flame-cutter), the name of one of Charlemagne's swords, and also that of Rinaldo's and Maugis or Maligigi's.

Frusberta, Rinaldo's sword.

Glorious, Oliver's sword, which hacked to pieces the nine swords made by Ansias, Galas, and Munifican.

Gram (grief), one of the swords of Siegfried.

Greysteel, the sword of Roll the Thrall.

Haute-claire (very bright), both Closamont's and Oliver's swords were so called.

Joyeuse (joyous), one of Charlemagne's swords: it took Gallas three years to make.

Merveilleuse (the marvellous), Doolin's sword.

Mimung, the sword that Wittich lent Siegfried.

Morglay (big glaive), Sir Bevis's sword.

Nagelring (nail-ring), Dietrich's sword.

Philippan. The sword of Antony, one of the triumvirs.

Quern-biter (a foot-breadth), both Haco I, and Thoralf Skolinson had a sword so called.

Sanglamore (the big bloody glaive), Braggadochio's sword (Spenser's *Faerie Queene*).

Sauvagine (the relentless): *see* COURTAIN *above*.

Sybarite (sī' bár īt). A self-indulgent person; a wanton. The inhabitants of Sybaris, in South Italy, were proverbial for their luxurious living and self-indulgence. A tale is told by Seneca of a Sybarite who complained that he could not rest comfortably at night, and being asked why, replied, "He found a rose-leaf doubled under him, and it hurt him."

Fable has it that the Sybarites taught their horses to dance to the pipe. When the Crotians marched against Sybaris they played on their pipes, whereupon all the Sybarite horses began to dance; disorder soon prevailed in the ranks, and the victory was quick and easy.

Sycamore and **Sycomore** (sik' à môr). The *Sycamore* is the common plane-tree of the maple family (*Acer pseudo-platănus*, or greater maple); the *sycomore* is the Egyptian fig-tree, and is the tree into which Zacchæus climbed (*Luke* xix, 4) to see Christ pass. Coverdale's, the Geneva, and other early English Bibles, call it the "wyld figge tre." Both words are from Gr. *sukon*, fig, and *moron*, mulberry.

Sycophant (sik' ō fănt). A sponger, parasite, or servile flatterer; the Greek *sukophantes* (*sukon*, fig, *phainein*, to show), which is said to have meant an informer against persons who exported figs or robbed the sacred fig-trees. There is no corroboration of this, but the widely accepted story is that the Athenians passed a law forbidding the exportation of figs, and there were always found mean fellows who, for their own private ends, impeached those who violated it; hence *sycophantes* came to signify first a government toady, and then a toady generally.

Sycorax (sī' kó răks). A witch, mother of Caliban, in Shakespeare's *Tempest*.

Syllogism (sil' ō jizm). A form of argument consisting of three propositions, a *major premise* or general statement, a *minor premise* or instance, and the *conclusion*, which is deduced from these.

The five hexameter verses which contain the symbolic names of all the different syllogistic figures are as follow:—

Barbara, Celarent, Darii, Ferioque, *prioris*.
Cesare, Camestres, Festino, Baroko, *secundœ*.
Tertia, Darapti, Disamis, Datisi, Felapton.
Bokardo, Ferison, *habet. Quarta insuper addit*
Bramantip, Camenes, Dimaris, Fesapo, Fresison.

The significance of these words lies in their vowels:

A universal affirmative.
E universal negative.
I particular affirmative.
O particular negative.

Taking the first line as the standard, the initials of all the words below it show to which standard the syllogism is to be reduced; thus, Baroko is to be reduced to "Barbara," Cesare to "Celarent," and so on.

Sylph (silf). An elemental spirit of air; so named in the Middle Ages by the Rosicrucians and Cabalists, from the Greek *silphe*, some kind of beetle, or a grub that turns into a butterfly. *Cp.* SALAMANDER.

Any mortal who has preserved inviolate chastity might enjoy intimate familiarity with these gentle spirits, and deceased coquettes were said to become sylphs, "and sport and flutter in the fields of air."

Whoever, fair and chaste,
Rejects mankind, is by some sylph embraced.
POPE: *Rape of the Lock*, i.

Symbolists. A group of French writers who, towards the end of the 19th century revolted against Naturalism and Parnassianism. Their aim was to suggest rather than to depict or transcribe, and their watchword was Verlaine's "Pas de couleur, rien que la nuance." Their precursors were Baudelaire, Banville, G. de Nerval and Villiers de l'Isle Adam. Chief Symbolists: in verse, Verlaine, Rimbaud, Mallarmé; in prose, Huysmans.

Symbols of Saints.

SAINTS.	SYMBOLS.
Agatha	With her severed breasts pierced by a sword or on a dish; also with a book in one hand, and a palm or pair of pincers in the other.
Agnes	With a lamb or a guardian angel at her side; sometimes standing on a flaming pyre with a sword in her hand.
Alban	As a Roman soldier, bearing a sword, and the palm or cross.
Ambrose	With a beehive.
Anastasius	With a hatchet; or carrying his cowled head on a plate.
Andrew	A saltire cross.
Andrew Corsini	Between a wolf and a lamb (in allusion to his unregenerate youth and saintly old age).
Anne	A book in her hand.
Antony	A tau cross, with a bell at the end, and a pig by his side, or with the bell tied to the neck of the pig.
Antony of Padua	Carrying the infant Jesus in his arms, or with a mule kneeling at his side.
Apollinaris	A bishop, bearing a sword or club, and having a raven at his side.
Appollonia	A tooth and palm branch, or a tooth grasped in a pair of forceps, She is applied to by those who suffer from toothache.
Arcadius	A torso (he was dismembered joint by joint, and limb by limb).
Augustine (of Hippo)	Holding a burning heart.
Barbara	With a three-windowed tower, and carrying a chalice with the Host above it.
Barbatus	A hatchet in his hand and a golden snake under his foot.
Barnabas	Carrying the Gospel in one hand, and a pilgrim's staff or a stone in the other.
Bartholomew	With a butcher's flaying knife (the instrument of his martyrdom), or a human skin with the face showing.
Benedict	Usually with his Rule in his hand and its first words (*Ausculta, O fili*) issuing on a scroll from his mouth; sometimes with his finger to his lip (enjoining silence), and with a scourge or rose-bush at his side and a broken goblet in his hand.
Bernard	With a hive of bees.
Bernard of Menthon	Bearing a blazing heart.
Bernardine of Siena	As a Minorite, with the "I.H.S." surrounded by rays on his breast, and at his side three mitres, in allusion to his frequent refusals of a bishopric.
Blaise	Iron combs, with which his body was torn to pieces.
Bridget (of Sweden)	A crozier and book.
Bruno (founder of the Carthusians)	Contemplating a crucifix with "O Bonitas" issuing on a scroll from his mouth, and sometimes carrying an olive-branch.
Catherine	An inverted sword, or large wheel.
Catherine of Siena	With a crown of thorns, receiving a ring from Christ, or exchanging hearts with Him.
Cecilia	Playing on a harp or organ.
Christopher	A gigantic figure carrying Christ over a river.
Clement	A papal crown, or an anchor. He was drowned with an anchor tied round his neck.
Cloud	With nails (he is the patron saint of nail-makers).
Crispin and Crispian	With shoemaker's tools, or with millstones round their necks.
Cuthbert	St. Osbald's head in his hand.
David	A leek, in commemoration of his victory over the Saxons.
Denys	Holding his mitred head in his hand.
Dominic	With a star on his brow.
Dorothy	Carrying a basket of fruit.
Edward the Confessor	Crowned with a nimbus, and holding a sceptre.

Elizabeth	St. John and the lamb at her feet.
Eloy (or Eligius) ..	Dressed as a farrier and holding a horse's leg (alluding to the legend that once when shoeing a restive horse he detached the leg, shod it, and then replaced it).
Eustace	With a stag bearing a crucifix between its horns.
Faith	A gridiron.
Felix	An anchor.
Francis of Assisi ..	Wearing the habit of his Order, bearded, and showing the stigmata in his hands.
Francis of Paula ..	Standing on his cloak, and with "Caritas" written across his breast; sometimes also with an ass beside a forge.
Frideswide	Beside a fountain, bearing a pastoral staff, and with an ox at her feet.
Gall	With a bear at his feet.
Geneviève	With the keys of Paris at her girdle, sometimes carrying a candle which an angel is relighting just after the devil has blown it out.
George	Mounted on horseback, and transfixing a dragon.
Gerasimus ..	With a tame lion.
Germanus ..	With an ass at his feet.
Gertrude ..	A pastoral staff with a mouse running up it.
Giles	A hind, with its head in the saint's lap.
Gregory the Great ..	In papal robes, with a dove, and a roll of music in his hand.
Guido, or Guy ..	As a pilgrim, with a horse and ox at his feet, two palms in his hand, and a harrow at his side.
Hedwige ..	Crowned and veiled, barefooted, with her shoes in her hand.
Hubert ..	In bishop's robes, with a stag bearing the crucifix between its horns.
Hugh	As a bishop, holding a ciborium above which is a Host with a child in the midst of the wafer; also, a swan at his own feet.
Humbert ..	With a cross marked on his head, and a docile bear at his side.
Ignatius	The monogram "I.H.S." on the breast or in the sky, circled with a glory.
Isidore	With a pen and a hive of bees.
James the Greater ..	A pilgrim's staff; or a scallop shell.
James the Less ..	A fuller's club; he was killed by Simon the fuller.
Jerome	Studying a large volume wearing the red hat of a cardinal (though he was never a cardinal), and with a lion crouching at his feet.
Joan of Arc ..	In armour; with a long pennant painted with a picture of Christ holding a globe in one hand and the other raised in benediction; the words "Jhesus—

	Maria" above; and the background powdered with the royal lilies in gold.
John the Baptist ..	A camel-hair garment, small rude cross, and a lamb at his feet.
John the Evangelist..	A chalice, out of which a dragon or serpent is issuing, and an open book; or a young man with an eagle in the background.
Jude	With a club, a cross, or a carpenter's square.
Kentigern (or Mungo)	With his episcopal cross in one hand, and in the other a salmon and a ring.
Lawrence ..	A book and gridiron.
Leger (or Leodegar)	With gimlets in his eyes, or holding them with pincers.
Louis	A king kneeling, with the arms of France at his feet; a bishop blessing him, and a dove descending on his head.
Loy (see ELOY).	
Lucy	With a short staff in her hand, and the devil behind her; or with eyes in a dish, and rays of light coming from a gash in her throat.
Luke	Sitting at a reading-desk, beneath which appears an ox's head; or painting the Virgin or a Bambino.
Marcellus	As a bishop, leading a dragon through the streets of Paris by his stole.
Margaret	Treading on a dragon, or piercing it with the cross.
Margaret of Cortona	Gazing at a skull, or a corpse, with a dog at her side.
Mark	A man seated writing, with a lion couchant at his feet.
Martin ..	On horseback, dividing his cloak with a beggar behind him on foot.
Mary Magdalen ..	A box of ointment.
Mary of Egypt ..	Carrying three loaves, and dressed as a hermit with very long hair.
Mary the Virgin ..	Carrying the child Jesus, a lily is somewhere displayed.
Matthew	With a halberd, with which Nadabar killed him, or with the Gospel, and a purse or money-box. As an evangelist, he holds a pen, with which he is writing on a scroll. His most ancient symbol is a man's face.
Maurus	With weights and measures (St. Benedict appointed him to decide on the allowance of bread, etc., for his monks).
Michael	In armour, with a cross, or else holding scales, in which he is weighing souls.
Neot	Ploughing with deer instead of oxen.
Nicholas	With three golden balls or purses; or with a tub with naked infants in it. He is patron saint of children.

Nicholas of Tolentino		With a star over his head, a lily in his hand, and Purgatory yawning at his feet.
Osyth	.. ..	Carrying her head in her hands.
Pancras	.. ..	A youth with a sword in one hand and a palm in the other.
Patrick	.. ..	A shamrock leaf (which he showed to the Irish heathen as a symbol of the Trinity).
Paul	.. ..	A sword and a book. Dressed as a Roman.
Peter	.. ..	Keys and a triple cross; or a fish; or a cock.
Peter Gonzales	..	In Dominican habit, and holding a blue candle.
Peter Martyr	..	With a hatchet sticking in a cleft in his head.
Philip	.. ..	A pastoral staff, surmounted with a cross; or carrying a basket containing loaves and fishes (John vi, 5-7).
Praxedis	.. ..	With a basin in one hand and palms in the other.
Roche	.. ..	A wallet, and a dog with a loaf in its mouth sitting by. He shows a boil in his thigh.
Sebastian	.. ..	Bound to a tree, his arms tied behind him, and his body transfixed with arrows.
Simeon	.. ..	An aged man, with a cross.
Simon Zelotes	..	A saw, because he was sawn asunder.
Stephen	.. ..	A book and a stone in his hand.
Theodora	.. ..	The devil holding her hand and tempting her.
Theodore	.. ..	Armed with a halberd in his hand, and with a sabre by his side.
Theresa	.. ..	With a flaming arrow piercing her heart.
Thomas	.. ..	With a builder's rule, or a stone in his hand, or holding the lance with which he was slain at Meliapour.
Ulric	.. ..	With an angel bestowing on him a cross.
Ursula	.. ..	A book and arrows. She was shot through with arrows by the Prince of the Huns.
Verena	.. ..	A comb.
Veronica	..	The sacred veil, which retained the impression of our Lord's face after she had wiped the sweat from his brow when on the way to Calvary.
Walburga	..	With a flask of oil.

(See APOSTLES, EVANGELISTS, etc.)

Symbols of other sacred characters.

Abraham	.. ..	An old man grasping a knife, ready to strike his son Isaac, who is bound on an altar. An angel arrests his hand, and a ram is caught in the thicket.
David	.. ..	Kneeling, above is an angel with a sword. Sometimes he is represented playing a harp.
Esau	.. ..	With bow and arrows, going to meet Jacob.
Gabriel	.. ..	A flower-pot full of lilies between him and the Virgin.
Job ..	.. ..	Sitting naked on the ground, with three friends talking to him.
Judas Iscariot	..	With a money bag. In the last supper he has knocked over the salt with his right elbow.
Judith	.. ..	With Holofernes' head in one hand, and a sabre in the other.
Noah	.. ..	Looking out of the ark window at a dove, which is flying to the ark, olive branch in its beak.
King Saul	..	Arrayed in a rich tunic and crowned. A harp is placed behind him.
Solomon	.. ..	In royal robes, standing under an arch.

Symplegades, The. See CYANEAN ROCKS.

Symposium (sim pō' zi ùm). Properly, a drinking together (Gr. *syn*, together, *posis*, drink); hence, a convivial meeting for social and intellectual entertainment; hence, a discussion upon a subject, and the collected opinions of different authorities printed and published in a review, etc.

The Symposium is the title given to a dialogue by Plato, and another by Xenophon, in which the conversation of Socrates and others is recorded.

Syndicalism. The doctrine in economics that all the workers in any industry should have a share in the control and in the profits arising from it, and that to compass this end the workers in the different trades should federate and enforce their demands by sympathetic strikes. The word was first used about 1907, and was coined from the French *chambre syndicate* (*syndic*, a delegate), a trade union.

Synecdoche (si nek' dō ke). The figure of speech which consists of putting a part for the whole, the whole for the part, a more comprehensive for a less comprehensive term, or *vice versa*. Thus, *a hundred bayonets* (for a hundred soldiers), *the town was starving* (for *the people in the town*).

Now will I remember you farther of that manner of speech which the Greekes call *Synecdoche*, and we the figure of *quick conceite* . . . as when one would tell me how the French king was overthrown at Saint Quintans, I am enforced to think that it was not the king himselfe in person, but the Constable of Fraunce with the French kings power.—PUTTENHAM: *Arte of English Poesie*, Bk. iii (1589).

T

T. The twentieth letter of the alphabet, representing Semitic *taw* and Greek *tau*, which meant "a mark." Our T is a modification of the earlier form, X. *See also* TAU.

It fits to a T. Exactly. The allusion is to work that mechanics square with a *T-square*, a ruler with a cross-piece at one end, especially useful in making right angles, and in obtaining perpendiculars and parallel lines.

Marked with a T. Notified as a felon. Persons convicted of felony, and admitted to the benefit of clergy, were branded on the thumb with the letter T (*thief*). The law authorizing this was abolished in 1827.

Taal (tal). The dialect of Dutch spoken in South Africa. It originated in the colloquial North Dutch of the 17th century but early underwent great changes. It is now frequently called Afrikaans.

Tabard (tăb' ard). A jacket with short pointed sleeves, whole before, open on both sides, with a square collar, winged at the shoulder like a cape, and worn by military nobles over their armour. It was generally emblazoned with heraldic devices. Heralds still wear tabards.

Tabernacles, Feast of. A Jewish festival lasting eight days and beginning on the 15th Tisri (towards the end of September). Kept in remembrance of the sojourn in the wilderness, it was also the Feast of Ingathering. It was formerly a time of great rejoicing.

Table. Apelles' table. A pictured board (Lat. *tabula*) or table, representing the excellency of sobriety on one side and the deformity of intemperance on the other.

Table d'hôte (Fr., the host's table). The "ordinary" at an hotel or restaurant; the meal for which one pays a fixed price whether one partakes of all the courses provided or not. In the Middle Ages, and even down to the reign of Louis XIV, the landlord's or host's table was the only public dining-place known in Germany and France.

Table-talk. Small talk, chit-chat, familiar conversation.

Table-turning. The turning of tables without the application of mechanical force, which in the early days of spiritualism was commonly practised at séances, and sank to the level of a parlour trick. It was said by some to be the work of departed spirits, and by others to be due to a force akin to mesmerism.

Table of Pythagoras. The common multiplication table, carried up to ten. The table is parcelled off into a hundred little squares or cells. The name first appears in a corrupt text of Boethius, who was really referring to the abacus (*q.v.*).

To lay on the table. The parliamentary phrase for postponing consideration of a motion, proposal, bill, etc., indefinitely. Hence, *to table a matter* is to defer it *sine die*.

To turn the tables. To reverse the conditions or relations; as, for instance, to rebut a charge by bringing forth a counter-charge. The phrase comes from the old custom of reversing the *table* or board, in games such as chess and draughts, so that the opponent's relative position is altogether changed.

Tableaux vivants (Fr., living pictures). Representations of statuary groups by living persons; said to have been invented by Madame de Genlis (1746-1830) while she had charge of the children of the Due d'Orléans.

Taboo, tabu. (Maori *tapu*). A custom among the South Sea Islanders of prohibiting the use of certain persons, places, animals, things, etc., or the utterances of certain names and words; it signifies that which is banned, interdicted, or "devoted" in a religious sense. Thus, a temple is *taboo*, and so is he who violates a temple, Not only so, but everyone and everything connected with what is taboo becomes taboo also; Captain Cook was *taboo* because some of his sailors took wood from a Hawaiian temple to supply themselves with fuel, and being "devoted," he was slain. The whole subject of taboo is a highly complicated and technical department of sociology.

With us, a person who is ostracized, or an action, custom, etc., that is altogether forbidden by Society, is said to be *taboo*, or *tabooed*.

Women, up till this
Cramped under worse than South-sea-isle taboo,
Dwarfs of the gynæceum, fail.
                    TENNYSON: *Princess*, iii, 278.

Tabula rasa (tăb' ū la rā zà) (Lat., a scraped tablet). A clean slate—literally and figuratively—on which anything can be written. Thus, we say that the mind of a person who has been badly taught must become a *tabula rasa* before he can learn anything properly.

Tace. Latin for candle. Silence is most discreet. *Tace* is Latin for "be silent," and candle is symbolical of *light*. The phrase means "keep it dark," do not throw light upon it. Fielding, in *Amelia* (ch. x), says, "*Tace*, madam, is Latin for candle." There is an historical allusion worth remembering. It was customary at one time to express disapprobation of a play or actor by throwing a candle on the stage, and when this was done the curtain was immediately drawn down. W. C. Oulton's *History of the Theatres of London* (1796) gives us an instance of this which occurred January 25th, 1772, at Covent Garden Theatre, when the piece before the public was *An Hour Before Marriage*. Someone threw a candle on the stage, and the curtain was dropped at once.

There are some auld stories that cannot be ripped up again with entire safety to all concerned. *Tace* is Latin for candle.—SCOTT: *Redgauntlet*, ch. xi.

Mum. William mum. *Tace* is Latin for candle.—W. B. YEATS: *Fairy Tales of the Irish Peasantry*, p. 205.

We have several of these phrases; *See* BRANDY IS LATIN FOR GOOSE.

Tack. The use of this word by sailors as meaning food is of unknown origin. **Hard Tack** is a large, coarse, hard biscuit baked with salt and at one time a staple of diet in the foc'sle mess. **Soft tack** is good, easily masticated food such as was served at the captain's table.

Tacky (U.S.A.). Small pony—a derogatory term.

Tactics, in the science of war is the art of manœuvring bodies of men, ships, etc., in contact with the enemy; strategy is the art of manœuvring before contact, so that when contact is made it will be to the enemy's disadvantage.

Taë-pings. Chinese rebels of about 1850 to 1864. The word means *Universal Peace*, and arose thus; Hung Hsiu-ch'uan, a man of humble birth, and an unsuccessful candidate for a government office, was converted to Christianity and gave out that he was the chosen instrument in God's hands to uproot idolatry and establish the dynasty of Universal Peace. He soon collected a numerous following, and in 1853 seized the city of Nanking. In 1864 Major Gordon ("Chinese Gordon") overthrew Hung's army, and the insurrection was put down, after the loss of over a million lives and incalculable property.

Taffeta or **Taffety** (tăf' e tà, tăf e ti). A material made of silk; at one time it was watered; hence Taylor says, "No taffaty more changeable than they." The word is from the Persian *taftan*, to twist or cure.

The fabric has often changed its character. At one time it was silk and linen, at another silk and wool. In the eighteenth century it was lustrous silk, sometimes striped with gold.

Taffeta phrases. Smooth sleek phrases, euphemisms. We also use the words *fustian, stuff, silken, shoddy, buckram, velvet*, etc., to qualify phrases and literary compositions spoken or written.

Taffata phrases, silken terms precise,
Three-piled hyperboless
                    Love'. Labour's Lost, v, 2.

Taffy. A Welshman. So called from *David*, a very common name in Wales. Familiarly *Davy*, it becomes in Welsh *Taffid, Taffy*.

Tag, is the usual American name for the British children's game of "He."

Tail. According to an old fable lions wipe out their footsteps with their tail, that they may not be tracked.

To tail is to follow a suspected person, keep him under observation, and prevent his escaping.

To turn tail. To turn one's back and run away.

With his tail between his legs. Very dejected, quite downcast. The allusion is to dogs.

Tail-end Charlie. An R.A.F. phrase in World War II for the last aircraft of a group on a mission—usually far behind the others and the recipient of spiteful attention from the enemy.

Taillefer (tī à fâr). A minstrel and warrior who accompanied William of Normandy to England in 1066. He went before the Norman army, singing of Charlemagne, Roland, and those who died at Roncesvalles. He obtained permission to strike the first blow in the Battle of Hastings, where he was killed.

Tailor. Nine tailors make a man. An old expression of contempt at the expense of tailors signifying that a tailor is so much more feeble than anyone else that it would take nine of them to make a man of average stature and strength. As a fact, the occupation of a tailor, and the cramped position in which he works, are not conducive to good physique; but it has been suggested that *tailor* is probably a facetious transformation of *teller*, a *teller* being a stroke on the bell at a funeral, three being given for a child, six for a woman, and *nine* for a *man*.

The number mentioned is sometimes only three:—

> Some foolish knave, I thinke, at first began
> The slander that three taylers are one man.
> <div align="right">TAYLOR: <i>Workes</i>, iii, 73 (1630).</div>

The three tailors of Tooley Street. Canning says that three tailors of Tooley Street, Southwark, addressed a petition of grievances to the House of Commons, beginning—"We, the people of England." Hence the phrase is used of any pettifogging coterie that fancies it represents the nation.

Taiping. *See* TAEPING.

Taj Mahal (taj ma hal'). A mausoleum near Agra, built in 1650 by the great Mogul emperor Shah Jehan in memory of his favourite wife, Mumtaz Mahal. The name comes from one of her titles—Taj Mahal, Crown of the Palace. Designed by Ustad Isa, a Turk or Persian, this white marble building is the supreme achievement of the Mogul style.

Take. To be taken aback. To be quite surprised for the moment, flabbergasted. From a nautical term, used when a ship's sails are so caught by the wind that they are forced back against the mast and thus impede any way the ship may have on her.

To have a taking way with one. To be of an ingratiating disposition, able to make one-self liked at once; *fetching way, winning way,* mean the same thing.

To take after. To have a strong resemblance to, physically, mentally, etc. "Doesn't little Johnny take after his father?" "Most of Lawrence's paintings seem to take after Romney."

To take back one's words. To withdraw them, to recant.

To take down a peg. *See* PEG.

To take in. To deceive, gull. Hence, a *regular take-in,* a hoax, swindle.

To take into one's head. To conceive the notion that . . . ; to resolve to do so and so.

To take it out of someone. To exact satisfaction, to get one's own back; or, of oneself, to become thoroughly exhausted, as "Working after midnight does take it out of me."

To take it upon oneself. To make oneself responsible (perhaps unwarrantably) to assume control.

To take off. To mimic or ridicule; also to start, especially of an aeroplane or of one in an athletic contest, as jumping or racing.

To take on. To be upset or considerably affected. In the U.S.A., to assume, or adopt.

To take over. To assume the management, control, or ownership.

Tale. A tally; a reckoning. In *Exod.* v, 8, we have *tale of bricks.* A measure by number, as of a shepherd counting his sheep:—

> And every shepherd tells his tale
> Under the hawthorn in the dale.
> <div align="right">MILTON: <i>L'Allegro</i>, 67.</div>

An old wife's tale. Any marvellous legendary story. The phrase was used by George Peele as the title of a play (1595), and by Arnold Bennett as that of a novel (1908).

A tale of a tub. *See* TUB.

To tell tales out of school. To utter abroad affairs not meant for the public ear.

Talent. Ability, aptitude, a "gift" for something or other. The word is borrowed from the parable in *Matt.* xxv, 14-30, and was originally the name of a weight and piece of money in Assyria, Greece, Rome, etc. (Gr. *talanton,* a balance). The value varied, the later Attic talent weighing about 57 lb. troy, and being worth about £250.

Tales (tā' lēz). Persons in the court from whom selection is made to supply the place of jurors who have been empanelled, but are not in attendance. It is the first word of the Latin sentence providing for this contingency—*Tales de circumstantibus, i.e.* "from such (persons) as are standing about."

> To serve for jurymen or tales.
> <div align="right">BUTLER: <i>Hudibras</i>, Pt. iii, 8.</div>

To pray a tales. To pray that the number of jurymen may be completed.

In the celebrated action Bardell *v.* Pickwick—

> It was discovered that only ten special jurymen were present. Upon this, Mr. Serjeant Buzfuz prayed a *tales;* the gentleman in black then proceeded to press into the special jury, two of the common jurymen; and a greengrocer and a chemist were caught directly.—DICKENS: *Pickwick Papers:* ch. xxxiv.

Those who supplement the jury are called *talesmen,* and their names are set down in the *talesbook.*

Talisman. A charm or magical figure or word, such as the Abraxas (*q.v.*), which is cut on metal or stone, under the influence of certain planets; it is supposed to be sympathetic, and to receive an influence from the planets which it communicates to the wearer.

In Arabia a talisman consisting of a piece of paper, on which are written the names of the Seven Sleepers and their dog, to protect a house from ghosts and demons, is still used; and in order to free any place of vermin a talisman consisting of the figure of the obnoxious animal is made in wax or consecrated metal, in a planetary hour.

> He swore that you had robbed his house,
> And stole his talismanic louse.
> <div align="right">BUTLER: <i>Hudibras</i>, pt. iii, 1.</div>

The word is the Arabic *tilasman* from late Greek *telesma*, mystery.

Tall anciently meant comely, fine, handsome; hence brave and valiant; and such phrases as *a tall and proper man, a tall ship* (*i.e.* one strong and well found in every respect) were used without any special reference to height.

> You were good soldiers, and tall fellows.—
> SHAKESPEARE: *Merry Wives of Windsor*, ii, 2.

> The undaunted resolution and stubborn ferocity of Gwenwyn . . . had long made him beloved among the "Tall Men" or champions of Wales.—SCOTT: *The Betrothed*, ch. i.

> Beyond the extreme sea-wall, and between the remote sea-gates,
> Waste water washes, and tall ships founder, and deep death waits.
>   SWINBURNE : *Hymn to Proserpine*.

A tall tale. An incredible story.

Tally. To correspond. The tally used in the Exchequer was a rod of wood, marked on one face with notches (Fr. *taille*, a notch or incision) corresponding to the sum for which it was an acknowledgment. Two other sides contained the date, the name of the payer, and so on. The rod was then cleft in such a manner that each half contained one written side and half of every notch. One part was kept in the Exchequer, and the other was circulated. When payment was required the two parts were compared, and if they "tallied," or made a tally, all was right; if not, there was some fraud, and payment was refused.

The last tally was issued in 1826. In 1834 orders were issued for their destruction. Two cartloads of them were lighted as a bonfire, and the conflagration set on fire the Houses of Parliament, which, with their offices and part of the Palace of Westminster, were burnt to the ground.

Tally-ho! The cry of fox-hunters on catching sight of the fox. It is the English form of the old French *taïant*, which was similarly used in deer-hunting, and also as a cry to the hounds when their share of the disembowelled stag was thrown to them.

Talmud, The (tăl' mŭd) (Heb., instruction). The body of Jewish civil and religious law not contained in, but largely derived from, the Pentateuch. The name was originally applied only to the Gemara (*q.v.*), but it now usually includes also the Mishna (*q.v.*).

When the *Talmud* is spoken of without any qualification the reference is to the *Babylonian Talmud*, one of the two recensions of the Gemara, the other being the *Palestinian Talmud*, which is of only about a fourth the volume of the *Babylonian*, and is considered by Jews of less

authority. The *Babylonian* codification dates from the 5th or 6th century, the *Palestinian* (or *Jerusalem*) from about a century earlier.

Talus (tā' lŭs). In Greek mythology, a man of brass, made by Hephæstus (Vulcan), the guardian of Crete. Whenever he caught a stranger on the island he made himself red-hot and embraced him to death.

He is introduced by Spenser into the *Faerie Queene* (Bk. v) as the "yron man" attendant upon Sir Artegal, and representing executive power—"swift as a swallow, and as lion strong."

Tamasha (tà ma' shà). A Hindustani word meaning a spectacle, an entertainment on a lavish scale, a show worth seeing.

Taming of the Shrew, The. Shakespeare's play (first printed in the 1623 Folio) was a rewriting of an anonymous comedy—*The Taming of A Shrew*—printed in 1594; its theme, a recipe for the management of wives, was very popular with contemporary audiences. *See* SLY.

Tammany Hall (tăm' à ni). The headquarters (in 14th Street, New York) of the controlling organization of the Democratic Party in New York City and State; hence, the Party itself, and, as this has been so frequently prosecuted and exposed for bribery and corruption, used figuratively for wholesale and systematic political or municipal malpractice.

Tammany was the name of a 17th-century Delaware chief, and the patriotic, anti-British leagues of pre-Revolutionary days adopted the name "St. Tammany" to ridicule the titles of loyalist organizations—Societies of St. George, St. Andrew, and so on. After the Revolution these leagues became anti-aristocratic clubs, but all soon died a natural death except "Tammany Society, No. 1," which was that of New York. This flourished, and was converted into a political machine by Aaron Burr in his conflict with Alexander Hamilton (about 1798), and in 1800 played a prominent part in the election of Jefferson to the Presidency.

Tam-o'-Shanter. The hero of Burns's poem of that name; the soft cloth headdress is so called from him.

Remember Tam-o'-Shanter's mare. You may pay too dear for your whistle, as Meg lost her tail, pulled off by Nannie of the "Cutty-sark," in Burns's poem.

> Think, ye may buy the joys owre dear—
> Remember Tam-o'-Shanter's mare.
>   BURNS: *Tam-o'-Shanter*.

Tandem. A pair of horses harnessed one behind the other; hence applied to a bicycle ridden by two persons in this position. The word is a punning use of the Latin *tandem*, at length, *i.e.* of time; the horses being "lengthways" instead of side by side.

Tangle. A water sprite of the Orkneys; from Dan. *tang*, sea-weed, with which it is covered. It is fabled to appear sometimes in human form, and sometimes as a little apple-green horse.

Tangram. A Chinese puzzle consisting of a square cut into seven pieces—a square, a rhomboid, and five triangles, which can be fitted together to form a number of shapes and figures.

Tanist (Gael. *tanaiste*). The elected heir presumptive to an ancient Irish chieftain, chosen generally from among the chief's relations. Hence, **tanistry**, the ancient Irish tenure of lands and chieftainship.

Tanist stone. The monolith erected by the ancient Gaelic kings at their coronation; especially that called *Liafail*, which, according to tradition, is identical with the famous stone of Scone (*q.v.*), now forming part of the Coronation Chair in Westminster Abbey. It is said to have been set up at Icolmkil for the coronation of Fergus I of Scotland, a contemporary of Alexander the Great (about 300 B.C.), and son of Ferchard, King of Ireland.

Tank. The heavily armoured military motor fort, running on "caterpillar" wheels, enclosed, and with room in the interior for quick-firing guns and several men, was so called by the War Office before it made its first appearance to prevent information as to its real nature leaking out to the enemy. Telegrams, etc., with inquiries about *tanks* would cause no suspicion if they fell into enemy hands. Tanks were invented during World War I, and were first used in the British attack on the German lines at Flers, September 15th, 1916.

Tanner. Slang for a sixpenny piece. The term has been in use for over a hundred years.

Tannhäuser (tăn′ hoi zcr). A lyrical poet, or *minnesinger*, of Germany, who flourished in the second half of the 13th century. He led a wandering life, and is said even to have visited the Far East; this fact, together with his *Buszlied* (song of repentance), and the general character of his poems, probably gave rise to the legend about him—which first appeared in a 16th-century German ballad. This relates how he spends a voluptuous year with Venus, in the Venusberg, a magic land reached through a subterranean cave; at last he obtains leave to visit the upper world, and goes to Pope Urban for absolution. "No," said His Holiness, "you can no more hope for mercy than this dry staff

can be expected to bud again." Tannhäuser departs in despair; but on the third day the papal staff bursts into blossom; the Pope sends in every direction for Tannhäuser, but the knight is nowhere to be found, for, mercy having been refused, he has returned to end his days in the arms of Venus.

Tansy. A yellow-flowered perennial herb, so called from Gr. *athanasia*, immortality, because it is a sort of everlasting flower.

Tantalus (tăn′ tá lus). In Greek mythology, the son of Zeus and Pluto (daughter of Himantes). He was a Lydian king, highly honoured and prosperous; but, because he divulged to mortals the secrets of the gods, he was plunged up to the chin in a river of Hades, a tree hung with clusters of fruit being just above his head. As every time he tried to drink, the waters receded from him, and as the fruit was just out of reach, he suffered agony from thirst, hunger, and unfulfilled anticipation.

Hence our verb, *to tantalize*, to excite a hope and disappoint it; and hence the name *tantalus* applied to a lock-up spirit chest in which the bottles are visible but un-get-at-able without the key.

Tantras, The (tăn′ tràs). Sanskrit religious writings, forming the Bible of the Shaktas, a Hindu religion the adherents of which worship the divine power in its female aspect.

The Tantras consist of magical formulas for the most part in the form of dialogues between Shiva and his wife, and treat of the creation and ultimate destruction of the world, divine worship, the attainment of superhuman power, and final union with the Supreme Spirit. They are of comparatively recent date (6th or 7th cent. A.D.).

Tantra is Sanskrit for thread, or warp, and hence is used of groundwork, order, or doctrine of religion.

Taoism (tā′ ō izm). One of the three great religious systems of China (Confucianism and Buddhism being the others), founded by the philosopher Lao-tsze (about 604-523 B.C.), and based on the *Tao-teh-king* (Book of Reason and Virtue), reputed to be by him.

Tap Dance. A quick-time dance in which the rhythm is beaten out on the floor with the dancer's toe or heel, or both alternately. On the stage shoes with a double sole are worn in order that the tap will be more readily audible.

Tapis (tăp′ ē). **On the tapis.** On the carpet; under consideration; now being ventilated. An English-French phrase, referring to the *tapis* or cloth with which the table of the council chamber is covered, and on which are laid the motions before the House.

My business comes now upon the tapis. — FARQUHAR: *The Beaux Stratagem,* iii, 3.

Tappit-hen. A Scots term, properly for a hen with a crest or tuft on its head, but generally used for a large beer or wine measure. Readers of *Waverley* will remember (in ch. xi) the Baron Bradwardine's tappit-hen of claret "containing at least three English quarts."

Weel she lo'ed a Hawick gill
And leugh to see a tappit-hen.

To have a tappit-hen under the belt is to have swallowed three quarts. *Cp.* HEN AND CHICKENS; JEROBOAM.

Tar. Jack Tar. A sailor; probably an abbreviation of *tarpaulin,* of which sailors' caps and overalls are made. Tarpaulins are tarred cloths, and are commonly used on board ship to keep articles from the sea-spray, etc.

To beat the tar out of. To belabour, or beat without mercy. The phrase possibly originated in the attempt to free a sheep's wool from the tar applied to heal any cuts received during shearing.

Tar-heel, the colloquial name for a native of North Carolina; that State is known as the Tar-heel State.

All tarred with the same brush. All alike to blame, all sheep of the same flock. The allusion is to the custom of distinguishing the sheep of any given flock by a common mark with a brush dipped in tar.

Tarred and feathered. Stripped to the skin, daubed with tar, and then rolled in feathers so that the feathers adhere; a common popular punishment in primitive communities, and still occasionally resorted to.

The first record of this punishment is in 1189 (1 *Rich.* I). A statute was made that any robber voyaging with the crusaders "shall be first shaved, then boiling pitch shall be poured upon his head, and a cushion of feathers shook over it." The wretch was then to be put on shore at the very first place the ship came to (Rymer: *Fœdera,* i, 65).

Tarantella (tăr én tel' à). A very quick Neapolitan dance (or its music) for one couple, said to have been based on the gyrations practised by those whom the tarantula had poisoned.

Tarantula (ta răn' tū là). A large and hairy venomous spider (so called from Taranto, Lat. *Tarentum,* a town in Apulia, Italy, where they abound), whose bite was formerly supposed to be the cause of the dancing mania hence

known as *tarantism.* This was an hysterical disease, common, epidemically, in southern Europe from the 15th to the 17th centuries.

At the close of the fifteenth century we find that Tarantism has spread beyond the boundaries of Apulia, and that the fear of being bitten by venomous spiders had increased. Nothing short of death itself was expected from the wound which these insects inflicted, and if those who were bitten escaped with their lives, they were said to be seen pining away in a desponding state of lassitude. — HECKER: *Epidemics of the Middle Ages* (1859).

Tariff. A table of duties or customs, payable on the importation or exportation of goods; hence, a table of charges generally, as of those at an hotel or restaurant. The word is the Arabic *tarif,* information, which was adopted in Old French as *tariffe,* for arithmetic.

Tariff reform. A political movement in Great Britain, inaugurated in 1903 by Joseph Chamberlain (1836-1914), for the extension of the tariff on imports, principally with the object of preventing "dumping" (*i.e.* the disposal in our own country of surplus or unsaleable goods manufactured abroad at such a price that the home markets are cut out), and for the protection of home industries.

Tarot Cards (tă' rot). Italian playing-cards, first used in the 14th century and still occasionally employed for fortune-telling. A pack contains 78 cards; 4 suits of numeral cards with four coat-cards, *i.e.* king, queen, chevalier, and valet, and in addition to the four suits 22 *atutti* cards, or trumps, known as *tarots.*

Tarpaulin. *See* TAR.

Tarquin (tar' kwin). The family name of a legendary line of early Roman kings, Tar-quinius Priscus, the fifth king of Rome, is dated 617-578 B.C. His son, Tarquinius Superbus, was the seventh (and last) king of Rome, and it was his son, Tarquinius Sextus, who committed the rape on Lucretia, in revenge for which the Tarquins were expelled from Rome and a Republic established.

Tarquin is also the name of a "recreant knight" figuring in the Arthurian cycle.

Tart. As applied to a harlot or girl of loose sexual morals this word dates back to Victorian times and in all probability is a contraction of "sweetheart."

Tartan Plaid. A plaid of a *tartan,* or chequered, pattern. A *plaid* is some twelve yards of narrow cloth wrapped round the waist, or over the chest and one shoulder, and reaching to the knees. It may be chequered or not; but the English use of the word in such a compound as *Scotch plaids,* meaning chequered cloth, is a blunder for *Scotch tartans.* The *tartan* is the chequered pattern, every clan having its own tartan. Though the thing is now typically Scottish, the word is from *Tartar* (Lat. *Tartenus*).

Tartarus. The infernal regions of classical mythology; used as equivalent to Hades (*q.v.*) by later writers, but by Homer placed as far beneath Hades as Hades is beneath the earth. It was here that Zeus confined the Titans. *Cp.* HELL.

Tartuffe (tar tuf'). The principal character of Molière's comedy so titled; a pedantic, obscene, and hypocritical poltroon, said to be drawn from the Abbé de Roquette, a parasite of the Prince de Condé. The name is from the Italian *tartuffoli* (truffles), and was suggested to Molière on seeing the sudden animation which lighted up the faces of certain monks when they heard that a seller of truffles awaited their orders.

Tattoo. The beat of drum at night to recall soldiers to barracks is so called from Dutch *tap-toe*, closed or put to. In the mid-17th century, when the word came into use, it was written *taptoo*, *tapp-too*, etc.

The other **tattoo**, to mark the skin by rubbing indelible pigments into small punctures, is one of our very few words from Polynesian. It is Tahitiah (*tatau*, mark), and was introduced by Captain Cook (1769).

The devil's tattoo. *See* DEVIL.

Torchlight tattoo. A military entertainment, carried out at night in the open air with illuminations, evolutions, and a lot of music.

Tau. The letter T in Greek and the Semitic languages. Anciently it was the last letter of the Greek alphabet (as it still is of the Hebrew); and in Middle English literature the phrase *Alpha to Omega* was not infrequently rendered *Alpha to Tau*.

Tau cross. A T-shaped cross, especially St. Anthony's cross.

Taurus (taw' rŭs) (Lat., the bull). The second zodiacal constellation, and the second sign of the Zodiac, which the sun enters about April 21st.

As bees
In spring-time, when the sun with Taurus rides,
Put forth their populous youth about the hive
In clusters.—MILTON: *Paradise Lost*, I, 768.

Taverner's Bible. *See* BIBLE, THE ENGLISH.

Tawdry. A corruption of *St. Audrey* (*Audrey* itself being a corruption of *Etheldrida*). At the annual fair of St. Audrey, in the isle of Ely, cheap jewellery, and showy lace called *St. Audrey's lace* was sold; hence *tawdry*, which is applied to anything gaudy, in bad taste, and of little value. *Cp.* TANTONY.

Come, you promised me a tawdry lace and a pair of sweet gloves.—*Winter's Tale*, iv, 4.

Taxi, short for **taximeter,** is the accepted term for a motor cab. In France the taximeter for registering distances and fares was employed on horse-drawn cabs or *fiacres* long before motor cabs were put on the road. In Britain the taximeter became common only with the appearance of motor cabs, and the term accordingly became associated with them. An aeroplane is said to taxi when it moves along the ground under its own power.

Taylor's Institute. The University Museum at Oxford. So called from Sir Robert Taylor (1714-88), who made large bequests towards its erection.

Te Deum, The (tē dē' um). This liturgical hymn, so called from the opening words of the Latin original, *Te Deum laudamus* ("Thee, God, we praise"). was formerly ascribed to St. Ambrose, but is probably of later date. The story was that St. Ambrose improvised it while baptizing St. Augustine (386). In allusion to this tradition, it is sometimes called "the Ambrosian Hymn," and in some of our early psalters it is entitled "Canticum Ambrosii et Augustini."

Tea. A nice old cup of tea. An ironical slang expression, which is applied to awkward occurrences, unpleasant situations, or muddles.

Not my cup of tea. Not at all in my line, not what I want or am suited for.

Teague. A contemptuous name for an Irishman (from the Irish personal name), rarely used nowadays but common in the 17th and 18th centuries.

Was't Carwell, brother James, or Teague,
That made thee break the Triple League?
ROCHESTER: *History of Insipids*.

Tear (târ). **To tear Christ's body.** To use imprecations. The common oaths of mediæval times were by different parts of the Lord's body; hence the preachers used to talk of "tearing God's body by imprecations."

Hir othes been so grete and so dampnable
That it is grisly for to heere hem swere;
Our blissed Lordes body thay to-tere.
CHAUCER: *Pardoner's Tale*, 144.

Tear (tēr). **Tear-shell.** A projectile which, on bursting, liberates gases which irritate the lachrymatory glands of all within range, causing the eyes to water and rendering them temporarily useless. Also called a "lachrymatory shell."

Tears of Eos. The dewdrops of the morning were so called by the Greeks. Eos was the mother of Memnon (*q.v.*), and wept for him every morning.

St. Lawrence's tears. *See* LAWRENCE.

The Vale of Tears. This world (*Cp.* BACA).

Tec, or **'Tec.** Slang for a detective.

Teeth. *See* TOOTH.

Teetotal. A word expressive of total abstinence from alcoholic liquors as beverages, coined about 1833 by Dick Turner, an artisan at Preston, Lancashire.

Turner's tombstone contains the inscription: "Beneath this stone are deposited the remains of Richard Turner, author of the word *Teetotal* as applied to abstinence from all intoxicating liquors, who departed this life on the 27th day of October, 1846, aged 56 years."

Telemachus (te lem' à kus). The only son of Ulysses and Penelope. After the fall of Troy he went, attended by Athene in the guise of Mentor, in quest of his father. He ultimately found him, and the two returned to Ithaca and slew Penelope's suitors.

Telemark (tel' e mark). The name of a swing or turn in ski-ing. Telemark is the district in Norway where ski-ing began as a sport, about 1860.

Telepathy (tè lep' à thi). The word invented in 1882 by F. W. H. Myers to describe "the communication of impressions of any kind from one mind to another independently of the recognized channels of sense." The term "thought-transference" is often used for this phenomenon and more nearly expresses its implications, for it indicates the communication of thought from one person to another without the medium of speech.

Telephus. *See* ACHILLEA.

Tell, William. The legendary national hero of Switzerland, whose deeds are based on a Teutonic myth of widespread occurrence in northern Europe.

Fable has it that Tell was the champion of the Swiss in the War of Independence against the Emperor Albert I (slain 1308). Tell refused to salute the cap of Gessler, the imperial governor, and for this act of independence was sentenced to shoot with his bow and arrow an apple from the head of his own son. He succeeded in this dangerous trial, but in his agitation dropped an arrow from his robe. The governor insolently demanded what the second arrow was for, and Tell fearlessly replied, "To shoot you with, had I failed in the task imposed upon me." Gessler now ordered him to be carried in chains across the lake, and cast into Küssnacht castle, a prey "to the reptiles that lodged there." He was, however, rescued by the peasantry, and, having shot Gessler, freed his country from the Austrian yoke.

The earliest form of the legend is found in the old Norse *Vilkina Saga* (based on Teutonic sources).

Saxo Grammaticus tells nearly the same story respecting Toki, who killed Harald, and similar tales are told of Adam Bell, Clym of the Clough, William of Cloudeslie and Henry IV, Olaf and Eindridi, etc.

Kissling's monument at Altorf (1892), has four reliefs on the pedestal: (1) Tell shooting the apple; (2) Tell's leap from the boat; (3) Gessler's death; and (4) Tell's death at Schachenbach.

Teller. Anciently, one who kept the tallies (Anglo-Fr. *talier*) and counted the money; now, a bank-clerk who receives and pays out money at the counter.

Up to 1834 there were four officers of the Exchequer known as *Tellers of the Exchequer*, whose duty was to receive and pay out moneys. *See* TALLY.

> When shall our prayers end?
> I tell thee (priest) . . .
> When proud surveyors take no parting pence,
> When Silver sticks not on the Teller's fingers,
> And when receivers pay as they receive.
> GASCOIGNE: *The Steel Glass* (1576).

Temora (tem' ôr à). One of the principal poems of Ossian (*q.v.*), in eight books, so called from the royal residence of the kings of Connaught.

Templars or **Knights Templar.** Nine French knights bound themselves, at the beginning of the 12th century, to protect pilgrims on their way to the Holy Land, and received the name of *Templars*, because their arms were kept in a building given to them for the purpose by the abbot of the convent on the site of the old Temple of Solomon, at Jerusalem. They used to call themselves the "Poor Soldiers of the Holy City."

Their habit was a long white mantle, to which subsequently was added a red cross on the left shoulder. Their war-cry was *Bauseant* (an old French name for a black and white horse), from their banner, which was striped black and white, and charged with a red cross. Their seal showed two knights riding on one horse, the story being that the first Master was so poor that he had to share a horse with one of his followers.

The Order afterwards became very wealthy and corrupt, and so powerful that its suppression (effected in 1312) was necessary for the peace of Europe.

In England the Order had its first house (built about 1121) near Holborn Bars, London, but a site between Fleet Street and the Thames was given to them by 1162, and here they were settled till Edward II suppressed the English branch and confiscated its possessions. The lands and buildings went to the Knights Hospitallers who, in the reign of Edward III, granted them to the "students of the Common laws of England" (Stow).

In Paris the stronghold of the Knights Templar was taken over in 1313 by the Knights of St. John. The old tower later became a prison where, in 1792, the royal family of France was incarcerated. Louis XVI, Marie Antoinette, and Princess Elizabeth went thence to the guillotine, and the Dauphin (Louis XVII) probably died within its walls. The tower was demolished by Napoleon in the early years of the Empire.

Temple, The. The site between Fleet Street and the Thames formerly occupied by the buildings of the Knights Templar (see TEMPLARS *above*), of which the Temple Church (dating from 1185) is the only portion now remaining though it was badly damaged in the air raids on London in 1940.

Since 1346 the Temple has been in the possession of doctors and students of the law, who, since 1609, have formed the two Inns of Court (*q.v.*) known as the *Inner* and *Middle Temples*. The badge of the former is the Winged Horse (*Pegasus*), that of the latter the Lamb (*Agnus Dei*).

The Inner Temple Hall is modern (1870), but that of the Middle Temple was one of the finest Elizabethan halls in existence. It was built in 1572, and Shakespeare's play of *Twelfth Night* was probably performed here in 1602. The Inner Temple was destroyed in the air raids of World War II and had to be rebuilt to new plans. The Middle Temple Hall was severely damaged but was restored almost entirely from the original woodwork.

Temple. The name of the place of worship is the Lat. *templum*, from Gr. *temenos*, a sacred enclosure, *i.e.* a space *cut off* from its surroundings (Gr. *temnein*, to cut). The Lat. *templum* originally denoted the space marked out by the augurs (*q.v.*) within which the sign was to occur.

Temple of Solomon, The. The central place of Jewish worship, erected by Solomon and his Tyrian workmen (probably on Phœnician models) on Mount Moriah, Jerusalem, about 1006 B.C. It was destroyed at the siege of Jerusalem by Nebuchadnezzar (588 B.C.), and some 70 years later the **Temple of Zerubbabel** was completed on its site. In 20 B.C. Herod the Great began the building of the last Temple—that of the New Testament—which was utterly destroyed during the siege of Jerusalem by Vespasian and Titus in A.D. 70. For many centuries the site has been covered by the Moslem mosque of Haram esh Sherif.

The chief emblems of the Jewish Temple were:—

The *golden candlestick*.

The *shewbread*. The twelve loaves representing the twelve tribes of Israel.

The *incense* of sweet spices. Prayer, which rises to heaven as incense.

The *Holy of Holies*. The nation of the Jews as God's peculiar people.

See Exod. xxv, 30-32; *Rev.* i, 12-20; *and see also* JACHIN AND BOAZ.

Tempora mutantur (Lat., the times are changed). The tag is founded on *Omnia mutantur, nos et mutamur in illis* (all things are changed, and we with them), a saying of Nicholas Borbonius, a Latin poet of the 16th century. Lothair, Emperor of the Holy Roman Empire, had, it is stated, already said, *Tempora mutantur, nos et mutamur in illis*.

Ten. Ten to one. Expressive of a very strong probability; as, "It's ten to one that it will rain to-night," *i.e.* it's extremely likely to; *a ten to one chance*, one in which it is very much more likely that you will win than lose.

The Ten Commandments. A humorous expression for the ten fingers, especially when used by an angry woman for scratching her opponent's face.

Could I come near your beauty with my nails,
I'd set my ten commandments in your face.
2 Henry VI, i, 3.

Ten-cent Jimmy. James Buchanan (1791-1868), 15th President of the U.S.A. (1857-61) was so nicknamed on account of his advocacy of low tariffs and low wages.

Tenner. A ten-pound note; as *fiver* is a five-pound note.

The Tenth Muse. A name given originally to Sappho (*q.v.*) there being *nine* true Muses (*see* MUSE), and afterwards applied to various literary women, as Mme de la Garde Deshoulières (1638-94), Mlle de Scudéry (1607-1701), Queen Christina of Sweden (1626-89), and the English novelist and essay-writer, Hannah More (1745-1833).

The tenth wave. *See* WAVE.

Tenant. One who holds property—land, house, etc.—anciently by any kind of title, in modern use from the owner or landlord for payment; the French *tenant*, holding (*tenir*, to hold; Lat. *tenere*). Theoretically, all land in the United Kingdom belongs to the Crown, and all landholders are therefore tenants.

Tenant at will. One who can at any moment be dispossessed of his tenancy at the will of the landlord or lessor.

Tenant-right. The right of an out-going tenant to claim from an incoming tenant compensation for the improvements he has made on the farm, etc., during his tenancy. In Elizabethan times the term denoted the right that certain tenants possessed of passing on the tenancy, at decease, to the eldest surviving issue; and it is now sometimes applied to the right of a well-behaved tenant to compensation if deprived of his tenancy.

Tender. *See* LEGAL TENDER.

Tenderfoot (pl. -foots or feet). A novice, an inexperienced person; a term originally applied in U.S.A. to newly-imported cattle not yet acclimatized to the hard ground of the prairies.

Tenderloin is the tender portion of meat lying under the short ribs of beef and pork, also a cut of beef between the sirloin and ribs. The word is also used as the name of the district in Chicago, where vice and police corruption are at their worst, the name thus arising from such a place being the "best cut" for political graft.

Tendon of Achilles. *See* ACHILLES.

Tennis. The real game of tennis (from which lawn tennis takes its name) is played with a ball and rackets by two or four persons on a walled court divided across the middle by a net. The court—96 ft. by 32 ft.—is surrounded by a wall from which a sloping roof, called the penthouse, extends on three sides to an inner wall, 7 ft. high. The server hits a ball with his racket so that it strikes the penthouse or the wall above it and rebounds into the court of his opponent's side of the net. The game is extremely complicated, strokes being won or lost according to how they strike or fail to strike the walls or penthouse. The old scoring of 15, 30, etc., with deuce and advantage have been adopted into lawn tennis.

Tennis is of great age. The king of France sent Henry V a box of tennis balls; all modern courts are modelled on that in which Henry VIII played at Hampton Court. Lawn tennis first became popular in the late 1870s.

Tenterhooks. I am on tenterhooks, or **on tenterhooks of great expectation.** My curiosity is on the full stretch, I am most curious or anxious to hear the issue. Cloth, after being woven, is stretched or "tentered" on hooks passed through the selvedges. (Lat. *tentus*, stretched, hence "tent," canvas stretched.)

Teraphim (ter' á fim). The idols or images of the ancient Hebrews and other Semitic peoples, worshipped by them as household gods or individual protecting deities, it was her father Laban's teraphim that Rachel stole and hid in the camel's saddle in *Gen.* xxxi, 17-35.

Term. In schools and the universities, the period during which instruction is given; in the law courts, the period during which the courts are in session.

At Oxford and Cambridge there are three terms in a year; at the latter, Lent, Easter, and Michaelmas, and at Oxford, viz., Hilary, Trinity, and Michaelmas.

LENT and HILARY—
Cambridge, begins January 13th, and ends on the Friday before Palm Sunday.
Oxford, begins January 14th, and ends on the Saturday before Palm Sunday.

EASTER and TRINITY—
Cambridge, begins on the Friday of Easter-week, and ends Friday nearest June 20th.
Oxford, begins on the Wednesday of Easter week, and ends Friday before Whit Sunday. The continuation, called "Trinity term," runs on till the second Saturday of July.

MICHAELMAS—
Cambridge, begins October 1st, and ends December 16th.
Oxford, begins October 10th, and ends December 17th.

The lawyers' terms, called, since 1873, law sessions, are:—
Michaelmas Sessions begin October 12th, and end December 21st.
Hilary Sessions begin January 11th, and end the Wednesday before Easter.
Easter Sessions begin the Tuesday after Easter week, and end the Friday before Whit Sunday.
Trinity Sessions begin the Tuesday after Trinity Sunday and end August 8th.

These are of Norman origin, and the Long Vacation was intended to coincide with the time of vintage.

To come to terms. To make an agreement with; decide the terms of a bargain.

Termagant. The name given by the Crusaders and in mediæval romances, to an idol or deity that the Saracens were popularly supposed to worship. He was introduced into the morality plays as a most violent and turbulent person in long, flowing Eastern robes, a dress that led to his acceptance as a woman, whence the name came to be applied to a shrewish violently abusive virago.

In the Romances his name was usually joined with that of Mohammed, and the *-magaunt* of *Termagaunt* may represent *Mahound*, but as an early version of the name was *Tervagant* it has been suggested that perhaps the word is the Latin *ter vagantem*, the thrice wandering, with reference to Selene, or the Moon.

Twas time to counterfeit, or that hot termagant Scot [Douglas] had paid me scot and lot too.—1 *Henry IV*, v, 4.

Terpsichore (tĕrp sik' ôr i). One of the nine Muses (*q.v.*) of ancient Greece, the Muse of dancing and the dramatic chorus, and later of lyric poetry. She is usually represented seated, and holding a lyre. Hence, *Terpsichorean*, pertaining to dancing.

Terra firma. Dry land, in opposition to water; the continents as distinguished from islands. The Venetians so called the mainland of Italy under their sway, and the continental parts of America belonging to Spain were called by the same term.

Terracotta. Unglazed earthenware of fine fired clay, either red or yellow. The ancient Greeks employed terracotta extensively in architecture and statuary. In the 14th century terracotta revived and was made much use of in the Renaissance age. In the later years of the 19th century the material was favoured for facing and decorating important buildings, *e.g.* the Natural History Museum, S. Kensington (1873-80).

Terrapin War (ter' a pin) (U.S.A.). The name for the war with Britain in 1812, so called because, through the blockade of foreign vessels and trade, the U.S.A. was shut up in its shell like a terrapin.

Terrible, The. Ivan IV (or II) of Russia. (1529, 1533-84).

Terrier. A dog that "takes the earth," or unearths his prey (Fr., from Lat. *terra*, earth); also formerly applied to the burrows of foxes, badgers, rabbits, and so on.

Also slang for a member of the Territorial Army.

A land-roll or description of estates is called a **terrier** from Fr. *papier terrier*, a register of land.

Territorial Army. The British home defence force which, in 1908, superseded the old Militia, Yeomanry, and Volunteers, on a territorial basis.

The infantry regiments of the line have been known as the *Territorial regiments* since 1881, when, following a new scheme of organization, each became associated in name, depot, etc., with some particular county or district.

Terror, The, or the **Reign of Terror.** The period in the French Revolution between the fall of the Girondists and the overthrow of Robespierre. It lasted 420 days, from May 31st, 1793, to July 27th, 1794. Also applied to similar cataclysms in the history of other nations, as the Russian Revolution (the *Red Terror*, March-Sept., 1917).

Tertium quid. A third party which shall be nameless; a third thing resulting from the combination of two things, but different from both. Fable has it that the expression originated with Pythagoras, who, defining bipeds, said:—

Sunt *bipes* homo, et avis, et tertium quid.

A man is a bipod, so is a bird, and a third thing (which shall be nameless).

Iamblichus says this third thing was Pythagoras himself.

In chemistry, when two substances chemically unite, the new substance is called a *tertium*

quid, as a neutral salt produced by the mixture of an acid and alkali.

Terza Rima. An Italian verse-form in triplets, the second line rhyming with the first and third of the succeeding triplet. In the first triplet lines 1 and 3 rhyme, and in the last there is an extra line, rhyming with its second.

Dante's *Divine Comedy* is in this metre; it was introduced into England by Sir Thomas Wyatt in the 16th century, and was largely employed by Shelley, as also by Byron in *The Prophecy of Dante*.

Test Act. An Act of Parliament directed against Roman Catholics and Nonconformists, especially that of 1673, which decreed that all holders of public offices must take the Oaths of Allegiance and Supremacy, receive the Church of England sacrament, renounce the doctrine of Transubstantiation, etc. It was repealed in 1828.

Hence, *to take the test*, to comply with the requirements of the Test Act.

Tête-à-tête (Fr., head to head). A confidential conversation, a heart to heart talk.

Tête du pont. The barbican or watch-tower placed on the head of a drawbridge.

Tether. He has come to the end of his tether. He has outrun his fortune; he has exhausted all his resources. The reference is to an animal tied to a rope (he can graze only so far as his tether can be carried out), or to a cable run out to the "bitter end" (*q.v.*).

Horace calls the end of life *ultima linea rerum*, the end of the goal, referring to the white chalk mark at the end of a racecourse.

Tethys. A sea goddess of the ancient Greeks, wife of Oceanus; hence, the sea itself.

Tetragrammaton. A word of four letters, especially the name of the Deity, JHVR (*see* JEHOVAH), which the ancient Jews never pronounced. The word means "I am," or "I exist" (*Exod.* iii, 14); but Rabbi Bechai says the letters include the three times—past, present, and future.

Pythagoras called Deity a Tetrad or Tetractys, meaning the "four sacred letters," and it is curious that in so many languages the name of the Supreme Being should be composed of four letters; thus there are the Greek *Zeus* and *θεος*, in Latin *Jove* and *Deus*; Fr. *Dieu*, Dutch *Godt*, Ger. *Gott*, Dan. *Godh*, Swed. *Goth*, Arab. *Alla*, Sansk. *Deva*, Span. *Dios*, Scand. *Odin*, and our *Lord*.

Such was the sacred Tetragrammaton.
Things worthy silence must not be revealed.
DRYDEN: *Britannia Rediviva.*

Tetrarch (tet' rark). Originally meaning the ruler of one of four parts of a region (Gr. *tettares*, four; *archein*, to rule) under the

Roman empire the term came to be applied to minor rulers, especially to the princes of Syria subject to the Roman Emperor. In World War II the name of a very light British Airborne tank which was landed by glider.

Teutons. The Germans, and Germanic peoples; from the Latin name, *Teutones*, for an ancient northern tribe, their own name for themselves being *Thiudans, i.e.* kings or lords. *Cp.* A.S. *theoden*, a king. Our *Dutch* and the German *Deutsch* are variations of the same word, originally written *Theodisk.*

Teutonic Cross. A cross potent, the badge of the order of Teutonic Knights. *See* POTENT.

Teutonic Knights. An order which arose at the time of the Crusades. Originally only Germans of noble birth were admitted to the order. Abolished by Napoleon in 1809, it was revived again in Austria in 1840.

Texarkana (teks ar kăn' á). A community formed of two cities, one in Texas and one in Arkansas, the States' boundary line running through the centre of the place. The cities have separate municipal governments, but they are socially and commercially one, much as its various boroughs are part of London.

Texas Rangers. A constabulary force enlisted in Texas in 1835 to control the lawlessness of cattle-thieves and other outlaws, and the hostile Indians. The Rangers' headquarters were at the fort now grown into the town of Ranger. Their resourcefulness and toughness have surrounded their name with a sort of legendary splendour in the annals of the Wild West.

Th (θ, *theta*). The sign given in the verdict of the Areopăgus of condemnation to death (*thanatos*).

Thalestris (thá les' tris). A queen of the Amazons, who went with 300 women to meet Alexander the Great, under the hope of raising a race of Alexanders.

Thalia (thá lī' á). One of the Muses (*q.v.*), generally regarded as the patroness of comedy. She was supposed by some, also, to preside over husbandry and planting, and is represented holding a comic mask and a shepherd's crook.

Thames (temz). The Latin *Thamesis* (the broad Isis, where *isis* is a mere variation of *esk, ouse, uisg,* etc., meaning water). It rises near Cirencester as the *Isis*, a name which has been applied to it as far as its junction with the *Thame*, near Dorchester.

> Around his throne the sea-born brothers stood;
> Who swell with tributary urns his flood:—
> First the famed authors of his ancient name.
> The winding Isis and the fruitful Thame!
> POPE: *Windsor Forest.*

Thammuz (thăm' ŭz). A Sumerian, Babylonian and Assyrian god who died every year and rose again in the spring. He is identified with the Babylonian Marduk and the Greek Adonis.

In *Ezek.* viii, 14, reference is made to the heathen "women weeping for Tammuz."

> Thammuz came next behind,
> Whose annual wound on Lebanon allured
> The Syrian damsels to lament his fate
> In amorous ditties all a summer's day,
> While smooth Adonis from his native rock
> Ran purple to the sea, supposed with blood
> Of Thammuz yearly wounded.
> MILTON: *Paradise Lost*, iii, 446.

Thamyris (thăm' i ris). A Thracian bard mentioned by Homer (*Iliad*, ii, 595). He challenged the Muses to a trial of skill, and, being overcome in the contest, was deprived by them of his sight and power of song. He is represented with a broken lyre in his hand.

> Blind Thamyris and blind Mæonides [Homer]
> And Tiresias and Phineus, prophets old,
> MILTON: *Paradise Lost*, iii, 35.

Thane. The name given in Anglo-Saxon England to a class of soldiers and landholders ranking between the earl and the churl. The rank of thane could be attained by a man of lower degree. After the Norman Conquest the word disappeared in England, giving place to *knight*. In Scotland a thane ranked with an earl's son, holding his land direct from the king; the title was given also to the chief of a clan who became one of the king's barons.

Thanksgiving Day. An annual holiday in U.S.A. usually held on the last Thursday in November and observed as an acknowledgement of the divine favours received during the year. It was first celebrated by the Plymouth Colony in 1621. After the Revolution it became general throughout the Republic, and since 1863 its observance has been annually recommended by the President.

That. Seven "thats" may follow each other, and make sense.

> For be it known that we may safely write
> Or say that "that *that*" that that man wrote was right;
> Nay, e'en that that *that*, that "that THAT" has followed,
> Through six repeats, the grammar's rule has hallowed;
> And that that *that* that *that* "that THAT" began
> Repeated seven times is right, deny't who can.
> My lords, with humble submission *that* that I say is this; That that that "that *that*" that that gentleman has advanced is not *that* that he should have proved to your lordships.—*Spectator*, No. 86.

Another *that* catch is to make sense of the following by supplying the missing punctuation:—

> that that is is that that is not is not is that it it is.

And that's that! A colloquial way of emphatically and triumphantly making one's point, closing the argument, and so on.

Thé dansant. An afternoon tea party, with dancing.

Theagenes and Chariclea (thē ăj′ ė nēz, chăr i klē′ á). The hero and heroine of an erotic romance in Greek by Heliodorus, Bishop of Trikka (4th century).

Thebes, called *The Hundred-Gated,* was not Thebes of Bœotia, but the chief town of the Thebaid, on the Nile in Upper Egypt, said to have extended over twenty-three miles of land. Homer says out of each gate the Thebans could send forth 200 war-chariots.

> The world's great empress on the Egyptian plain,
> That spreads her conquests o'er a thousand states,
> And pours her heroes through a hundred gates,
> Two hundred horsemen and two hundred cars
> From each wide portal issuing to the wars.
> POPE: *Iliad,* i.

It is here that the vocal statue of Memnon stood, and here too are the tombs of the kings, including the tomb of Tutankhamun (reigned 1360-1350 B.C.) which was discovered in 1932, with its wealth and equipment almost intact. The temple of Karnak, and large numbers of sculptures, sphinxes, etc., are to be seen in the village of Luxor, which now marks the site.

The Seven against Thebes. An expedition in Greek legend fabled to have taken place against Thebes of Bœotia before the Trojan War. The Seven were the Argive chiefs Adrastus, Polynices, Tydeus, Amphiaraus, Hippomedon, Capaneus, and Parthenopæus.

When Œdipus abdicated his two sons agreed to reign alternate years; but at the expiration of the first year, the elder, Eteocles, refused to give up the throne, whereupon Polynices, the younger brother, induced the six chiefs to espouse his cause. The allied army laid siege to Thebes, but without success, and all the heroes perished except Adrastus. Subsequently, seven sons of the chiefs, resolved to avenge their fathers' deaths, marched against the city, took it, and placed Terpander, one of their number, on the throne. These are known as the *Epigoni* (Gr., descendants). The Greek tragic poets Æschylus and Euripides dramatized the legend.

Thecla, St. (thek′ là). The first woman martyr, as St. Stephen is the protomartyr. All that is known of her is from the *Acts of Paul and Thecla,* pronounced apocryphal by Pope Gelasius. According to the legend she was born of a noble family in Iconium, and was converted by the preaching of St. Paul. Her feast day is 23rd September.

Theist, Deist, Atheist, Agnostic. A *theist* believes there is a God who made and governs all creation; but does not believe in the doctrine of the Trinity, nor in a divine revelation.

A *deist* believes there is a God who created all things, but does not believe in His superintendence and government. He thinks the Creator implanted in all things certain immutable laws, called the *Laws of Nature,* which act *per se,* as a watch acts without the supervision of its maker. Like the theist, he does not believe in the doctrine of the Trinity, or in a divine revelation.

The *atheist* disbelieves even the existence of a God. He thinks matter is eternal, and what we call "creation" is the result of natural laws.

The *agnostic* believes only what is knowable. He rejects revelation and the doctrine of the Trinity as "past human understanding." He is neither theist, deist, nor atheist, as all these subscribe to doctrines that are incapable of scientific proof.

Theodomas (thē od′ ō măs). A famous trumpeter at the siege of Thebes.

> At every court ther cam loud menstralcye
> That never tromped Joab for to heere,
> Ne he Theodomas yit half so cleere
> At Thebes, when the cite was in doute.
> CHAUCER: *Canterbury Tales,* 9,592.

Theodoric (thē od′ ō rik). A king of the East Goths (d. 526), who became celebrated in German legend as Dietrich of Bern (*q.v.*), and also has a place in the Norse romances and the *Nibelungen Saga.* He invaded Italy about 490, and three years later slew Odoacer and became sole ruler.

Theodosian Table. *See* ITINERARY.

Theon (thē′ on). A satirical poet of ancient Rome, noted for his mordant writings, Hence, *Theon's tooth,* the bite of an ill-natured or carping critic.

Dente Theonino circumrodi (Horace: *Ep.* i, 18, 82) to be nastily aspersed.

Theophany. *See* TIFFANY.

Theorbo (thē ôr′ bō). A large bass lute with a double neck, having two sets of tuning pegs. The lower set is applied to the strings over the fretted finger board, tuned in 4ths, with a 3rd in the middle; the upper pegs hold the bass strings, tuned in 2nds and played as open notes.

Theosophy (Gr., the wisdom of God). The name adopted by the Theosophical Society (founded in 1875 by Mme Blavatsky, Mrs. Besant, Col. Olcott, and others) to define their religious or philosophical system, which aims at the knowledge of God by means of intuition and contemplative illumination, or by direct communion. *Esoteric Buddhism* is another name for it; and its adherents claim that the doctrines of the great world religions are merely the exoteric expressions of their own esoteric traditions.

The Theosophist is a man who, whatever be his race, creed, or condition, aspires to reach this height of wisdom and beatitude by self-development.—OLCOTT: *Theosophy*, p. 144 (1885).

The name was formerly applied to the philosophical system of Boehme (d. 1624).

Therapeutæ (thĕr a pū' tē) (Gr., servants, ministers). A sect of Jewish mystics described in Philo's *De Vità Contemplativa*. They were a branch of the Essenes (*q.v.*) and were settled in Egypt in the 1st century A.D.

Therm. In physics the name given to the British thermal unit of heat (B.Th.U.) which is the amount of heat required to raise 1 lb. of water at its maximum density through 1° F. The calorie is the corresponding metric unit of heat; a therm equals nearly 252 calories. The gas therm, by which gas is charged to consumers, is equal to 100,000 B.Th.U. *Mr. Therm* is a small gnome-like figure resembling a flame who was introduced to advertise gas in Britain in the 1930s.

Thermidor (thĕr' mi dôr). The eleventh month of the French Republican calendar, containing thirty days from July 19th. So named from Gr. *therme* heat, *doron* a gift.

Thermopylœ (thĕr mop' i li). In ancient geography the pass from Thessaly to Locris, being the only passage for an army from northern to southern Greece. In 480 B.C. it was heroically defended against the invading Persians under Xerxes by some 300 men under Leonidas, King of Sparta. As the result of treachery the Persians got to the rear of the Greeks, who were all slain.

Theseus (thē' sūs). The chief hero of Attica in ancient Greek legend; son of Ægeus, and the centre of innumerable exploits. Among his deeds are the capture of the Marathonian bull, the slaying of the Minotaur (*q.v.*), his war against the Amazons, the Calydonian hunt, and his desertion of Ariadne in Naxos. He was foully murdered by Lycomedes in Scyros. *See* SINIS.

Theseus is also the name of the Duke of Athens in Chaucer's *Knight's Tale*. He married Hippolita, and as he returned home with his bride, and Emily her sister, was accosted by a crowd of female suppliants who complained of Creon, king of Thebes. The duke forthwith set out for Thebes, slew Creon, and took the city by assault. Many captives fell into his hands, amongst whom were the two knights, Palamon and Arcite (*q.v.*).

Shakespeare gives the same name to the Duke of Athens in *Midsummer Night's Dream*.

Thespians (thes' pi ǎnz). Actors; so called from Thespis, an Attic poet of the 6th century B.C., reputed to be the father of Greek tragedy.

> Thespis, the first professor of our art,
> At country wakes sang ballads from a cart.
>   DRYDEN : *Prologue to Sophonisba*.

Thestylis (thes' ti lis). A stock poetic name for a rustic maiden; from a young female slave of that name in the *Idylls* of Theocritus.

> And then in haste her bower she leaves,
> With Thestylis to bind the sheaves.
>   MILTON: *L'Allegro*.

Thetis (thē' tis). The chief of the Nereids (*q.v.*) of Greek legend. By Peleus she was the mother of Achilles.

Those two are very thick. They are very good friends, on excellent terms with one another. **As thick as thieves** is a similar saying.

Through thick and thin. Through evil and through good report; under any conditions; undauntedly.

> A griesly foster forth did rush . . .
> Through thick and thin, both over bank and bush
> In hope her to attain by hook or crook.
>   SPENSER: *Faerie Queene*, III, i, 17.

Thick-skinned. Not sensitive; not irritated by rebukes and slanders. **Thin-skinned,** on the contrary, means impatient of reproof or censure, having skin so thin that it is an annoyance to be touched.

Thimble. From A.S. *thymel*, a thumb-stall; so called because it was originally worn on the thumb, as sailors still wear their thimbles.

Just a thimbleful, A very little drop—usually of spirits. *Thimble* is sometimes used in place of *thimbleful*:—

> 'Tis true to her cottage still they came. . . .
> And never swallow'd a thimble the less
> Of something the Reader is left to guess.
>   HOOD: *A Tale of a Trumpet*.

Thimble-rigging. A form of cheating, carried on with three thimbles and a pea, principally on or about race courses. A pea is put on a table, and the manipulator places three thimbles over it in succession, and then, setting them on the table, asks you to say under which thimble the pea is. You are sure to guess wrong.

The term *thimble-rigging* is used allusively of any kind of mean cheating or jiggery-pokery.

Thing. The Old Norse word for the assembly of the people, the legislature, "parliament," court of law, etc. It is etymologically the same word as our *thing* (an object), the original meaning of which was a discussion (from *thingian*, to discuss), hence a cause, an object.

The great national diet of Norway is still called a *stor-thing* (great legislative assembly), and the two chambers which form it are the *lag-thing* (law assembly) and the *odels-thing* (free-holders' assembly).

A poor thing. A person (or, sometimes, an inanimate object) that is regarded with pity or disparagement. Touchstone's remark about Audrey—"An ill-favoured thing, sir, but mine own" (*As You Like It*, v, 4)—is frequently misquoted, "A *poor thing, but mine own*," when employed in half ironical disparagement of one's own work.

Old thing. A familiar mode of address between friends.

One's things. One's minor belongings, especially clothes, or personal luggage.

The thing. The proper thing to do; as, "It's not the thing to play leap-frog down Bond Street in a top-hat and spats."

The very thing. Just what I was wanting; just what will meet the case.

You can have too much of a good thing. "Enough is as good as a feast."

People may have too much of a good thing—
Full as an egg of wisdom thus I sing.
   PETER PINDAR: *The Gentleman and his Wife.*

Third. *See under* THREE.

Thirteen. It is said that the origin of sitting down thirteen at table being deemed unlucky is because, at a banquet in Valhalla, Loki once intruded, making thirteen guests, and Balder was slain.

In Christian countries the superstition was confirmed by the Last Supper of Christ and His twelve apostles, but the superstition itself is much anterior to Christianity.

The Italians never use the number in their lotteries; and in Paris no house bears it, and persons, called *Quartorzièmes*, are available to make a fourteenth at dinner parties. Sailors strongly object to leaving port on the 13th of the month—especially if it happens to be a Friday—and they always start on their thirteenth voyage with apprehension.

Thirteenpence-halfpenny. A hangman. So called because thirteenpence-halfpenny was at one time his wages for hanging a man.

Thirty. A man at thirty must be either a fool or a physician. A saying attributed by Tacitus (*Annals*, VI, xlvi) to the Emperor Tiberius, who died at the age of 77 in A.D. 37 (Plutarch gives the story, but changes the age to *sixty*). The idea seems to be that if a man has not learned to look after his health by the time he is thirty he must be a fool.

The Thirty Tyrants. *See* TYRANT.

Thirty Years War. A series of wars between the Catholics and Protestants of Germany in the 17th century, in which France, Sweden, and other peoples participated from time to time. It began in Bohemia in 1618, and ended in 1648 with the Peace of Westphalia.

Thirty-six Line Bible, The. *See* BIBLE, SPECIALLY NAMED.

Thirty-nine Articles, The. The articles of faith of the Church of England, the acceptance of which is obligatory on its clergy. They were originally issued in 1551 as forty-two, but in 1563 were modified and reduced to their present number. They received parliamentary authority in 1571.

Thisbe. *See* PYRAMUS.

Thistle. The heraldic emblem of Scotland; said to have been adopted at least as early as the 8th century in commemoration of an unsuccessful night attack by the Danes on Stirling Castle. Their presence was unsuspected, and was revealed through the barefooted scouts treading on thistles and suddenly crying out; the alarm was given, the Scots fell upon the party and defeated them with terrible slaughter.

With the thistle was adopted the motto *Nemo me impune lacessit*, "Nobody touches (or provokes) me with impunity."

Thomas. St. Thomas. The Apostle who doubted (*John* xxi, 25); hence the phrase, *a doubting Thomas* applied to a sceptic.

The story told of him in the Apocryphal *Acts of St. Thomas* is that he was deputed to go as a missionary to India, and, on refusing, Christ appeared and sold him as a slave to an Indian prince who was visiting Jerusalem. He was taken to India, where he baptized the prince and many others, and was finally martyred at Meliapore.

Another legend has it that Gondoforus, king of the Indies, gave him a large sum of money to build a palace. St. Thomas spent it on the poor, "thus erecting a superb palace in heaven." On account of this he is the patron saint of masons and architects, and his symbol is a builder's square.

Another legend relates that he once saw a huge beam of timber floating on the sea near the coast, and the king unsuccessfully endeavouring, with men and elephants, to haul it ashore. St. Thomas desired leave to use it in building a church, and, his request being granted, he dragged it easily ashore with a piece of packthread.

His feast day is December 21st.

Thomasing. Collecting small sums of money or obtaining drink from employers on St. Thomas's Day, a custom that still exists in some districts. In London on December 21st every one of the Common Council has to be either elected or re-elected.

Thomists. Followers of St. Thomas Aquinas (d. 1274)—styled "Doctor Angelicus" and, by Pius V, "the Fifth Doctor of the Church"—and opponents of the *Scotists*, or followers of Duns Scotus.

Scotists and Thomists now in peace remain.
   POPE: *Essay on Criticism*, 444.

Thone or **Thonis.** In Greek mythology the governor of a province of Egypt to which, it is said by post-Homeric poets, Paris took Helen, who was given by Polydamnia, wife to Thone, the drug *nepenthes*, to make her forget her sorrows.

Not that nepenthes which the wife of Thone
In Egypt gave to love-lorn Helena;
Is of such power to stir up joy as this.
MILTON: *Comus*, 695-697.

Thopas, Rime of Sir (thō′ pĕs). A burlesque on contemporary metrical romances, told as Chaucer's own tale in the *Canterbury Tales*.

Thor (thôr). Son of Woden, god of war, and the second god in the pantheon of the ancient Scandinavians—their Vulcan, and god of thunder. He had three principal possessions; a Hammer (*Mjolnir*), typifying thunder and lightning, and having the virtue of returning to him after it was thrown; a Belt (*Meginjardir*) which doubled his power; and Iron Gloves to aid him in throwing his hammer.

He was god of the household, and of peasants, and was married to Sip, a typical peasant woman. His name is still perpetuated in our *Thursday*, and in a number of place-names, as *Thorsby* (Cumberland), *Torthorwald* (Dumfries), and *Thurso* (Caithness).

Thorn. A thorn in the flesh. A source of constant irritation, annoyance, or affliction; said of objectionable and parasitical acquaintances, obnoxious conditions, of a "skeleton in the cupboard," etc. There was a sect of the Pharisees (*q.v.*) which used to insert thorns in the borders of their gaberdines to prick their legs in walking and make them bleed. The phrase is taken from St. Paul's reference to some physical complaint or misfortune, 2 *Cor.* xii, 7.

On thorns. In a state of painful anxiety and suspense; fearful that something is going wrong (*Cp.* TENTERHOOKS).

The Crown of Thorns. That with which our Saviour was crowned in mockery (*Matt.* xxvii, 29); hence sometimes used of a very special affliction with which one is unjustly burdened.

Calvin (*Admonitio de Reliquiis*) gives a long list of places claiming to possess one or more of the thorns which composed the Saviour's crown. To his list may be added Glastonbury Abbey, where was also the spear of Longius or Longinus.

The Glastonbury Thorn. *See* GLASTONBURY.

Thoroughbred. Of pure or unmixed breed, especially said of horses and cattle. A thoroughbred is a race horse of English breed remotely derived by crossing with Arab and other strains.

Thousand. He's one in a thousand. Said of a man who is specially distinguished by his excellent qualities; similarly, *a wife in a thousand*, a perfect wife, or one that exactly suits the speaker's ideas of what a wife should be.

Thousand is frequently used of large indefinite numbers; as in Byron's

A small drop of ink,
Falling like dew, upon a thought, produces
That which makes thousands, perhaps millions, think.
Don Juan, III, lxxxviii.

Thread. The thread of destiny. That on which destiny depends. According to Greek mythology, Clotho, one of the Fates (*q.v.*), spun from her distaff the destiny of man, and as she span her sister Lachesis worked out the events which were in store, and Atropos cut the thread at the point when death was to occur.

The Triple Thread. Brahminism. The ancient Brahmins wore a symbol of three threads, reaching from the right shoulder to the left. Faria says that their religion sprang from fishermen, who left the charge of the temples to their successors on the condition of their wearing some threads of their nets in remembrance of their vocation; but Osorius maintains that the triple thread symbolizes the Trinity.

Threadneedle Street. The street in the City of London leading from Bishopsgate to the Bank of England. The name first appears—as *Three needle Street*—in 1598, and previously it seems to have been called *Broad Street*, as forming part of the present *Old Broad Street*. The name may have arisen from the sign of an inn, *The Three Needles* (though none of that name is recorded in the neighbourhood), or from some connexion with the Needlemakers' Company, whose arms are "three needles in fesse argent."

Three. Pythagoras calls three the perfect number, expressive of "beginning, middle, and end," wherefore he makes it a symbol of Deity.

A Trinity is by no means confined to the Christian creed. The Brahmins represent their god with three heads; the world was supposed by the ancients to be under the rule of three gods, viz. Jupiter (heaven), Neptune (sea), and Pluto (Hades). Jove is represented with three-forked lightning, Neptune with a trident, and Pluto with a three-headed dog. The Fates are three, the Furies three, the Graces three, the Harpies three, the Sibylline books three times three (of which only three survived); the fountain from which Hylas drew water was presided over by three nymphs; the Muses were three times three; the pythoness sat on a three-legged stool, or tripod; and in Scandinavian mythology we hear of "the Mysterious Three," viz. "Har" (the Mighty), the "Like-Mighty," and the "Third Person," who sat on three thrones above the rainbow.

Man is threefold (body, soul, and spirit); the world is threefold (earth, sea, and air); the enemies of man are threefold (the world, the flesh, and the devil); the Christian graces are threefold (Faith, Hope, and Charity); the kingdoms of Nature are threefold (mineral, vegetable, and animal); the cardinal colours are three in number (red, yellow, and blue), etc. *Cp.* NINE, which is three times three.

Three·acres and a cow. A phrase which came into use after the formation by the Dukes of Argyll and Westminster of the National Land Company, in 1885. The object of this concern was to acquire large tracts of land and let it out for farming in small portions.

A three-cornered fight. A parliamentary (or other) contest in which there are three competitors.

Three Kings' Day. Epiphany or Twelfth Day, designed to commemorate the visit of the "three kings" or Wise Men of the East to the infant Jesus. *See* MAGI.

The three-legged mare. An obsolete slang term for the gallows, which at Tyburn was a triple erection in triangular plan.

Three Mile Limit. In International Law the limit of waters around its coast under the jurisdiction of a sovereign state.

Three Musketeers. Athos, Porthos, and Aramis, the three heroes of Dumas's novels *The Three Musketeers*, 1844; *Twenty Years Afterwards*, 1845; and *Vicomte de Bragelonne*, 1848-50. The Musketeers were a mounted guard of gentlemen in the service of the kings of France from 1661 until the Revolution, 1791. They formed two companies, called the Grey and the Black from the colour of their horses. The uniform was scarlet, hence their quarters were known as La Maison Rouge. In peacetime the Musketeers formed the king's bodyguard, but in war they fought on foot or on horseback with the army. Their ranks included many Scots, either Jacobite exiles or mere soldiers of fortune.

The Three R.'s. *See* R.

Three sheets in the wind. *See* SHEET.

Three-tailed bashaw. *See* BASHAW.

The three tailors of Tooley Street. *See* TAILOR.

Rule of Three. The rule of simple proportion; by which, given the relationship of two

entities, the proportional relationship of a third can be ascertained.

The Battle of the Three Emperors. The Battle of Austerlitz (December 2nd, 1805), when Napoleon inflicted a heavy defeat on the Russians and Austrians. The Emperors of the three Empires were all present in person.

To give one three times three. To give him a rousing ovation, cheer after cheer.

"When shall we three meet again?" — the title of a picture of *two* asses — is a similar "joke."

Threescore years and ten. A ripe old age — not necessarily (in allusive use) exactly 70 years. The reference is to *Ps.* xc, 10: —

The days of our years are threescore years and ten; and if by reason of strength they be fourscore years yet is their strength labour and sorrow; for it is soon cut off, and we fly away.

Third Degree. The highest degree, that of Master Mason, in British Freemasonry. In U.S.A. the term is applied to the use of exhaustive questioning and cross questioning by the police in the endeavour to extort a confession or compromising information from a criminal, accomplice, or witness.

Third Estate. The Commons, as the third estate of the realm coming after the Sovereign and the Peers. The term is a translation of the French *Tiers Etat*, being the third and lower body of representatives in the States General (*q.v.*).

To cut one's own throat. Figuratively, to adopt a policy, or take action that ruins one's own chances, plans, etc. Similarly, *to cut one another's throat* is to ruin one another by excessive competition.

To jump down a person's throat. To interrupt and affront him, suddenly, sharply, and decisively.

Throgmorton Street. The financial world at large, or the Stock Exchange, which is situated in this narrow London street. So named from Sir Nicholas Throckmorton (1515-71), head of the ancient Warwickshire family, and ambassador to France in the reign of Elizabeth I.

Throne, The. A comprehensive name for the office of King, *e.g.* He ascended the throne.

Thrones, principalities and powers, in the teachings of Fathers of the Church, are three choirs of the celestial hierarchy, or the assemblage of beneficent supernatural beings.

Through-stone. A flat gravestone, a stone coffin or sarcophagus; also a bond stone which extends over the entire thickness of a wall.

Throw. To throw away one's money. To spend it carelessly, recklessly, extravagantly.

To throw back. To revert to ancestral traits; hence, a *throw-back* is one (human or animal) who does this.

To throw oneself on someone. To commit oneself to his protection, favour, mercy, etc.

To throw in one's hand. To abandon one's projects. A metaphor from card-playing.

Thrums. The fringe of warp threads left when the web has been cut off; weavers' ends and fag-ends of carpet, used for common rugs.

Thug. A member of a religious body of northern India, worshippers of Kali (*q.v.*), who could be propitiated only by human victims who had been strangled. Hence, the Thugs became a professional fraternity of stranglers, and supported themselves by the plunder obtained from those they strangled. Their native name is *P'hansigars* (stranglers); that of *Thug* (*i.e.* cheat) was given them in 1810. Their methods were rigorously suppressed under British rule, and were practically extinct by 1840. In common parlance the word is used for a violent "tough."

Thuggee. The system of secret assassination preached by Thugs; the practice of Thugs.

Thumb. In the ancient Roman combats, when a gladiator was vanquished it rested with the spectators to decide whether he should be slain or not. If they wished him to live, they *shut up* their thumbs in their fists (*pollice compresso favor judicabatur*); if to be slain, they *turned out* their thumbs. *See* Pliny, xxviii, 2; Juvenal, iii, 36; Horace: I *Epist.* xviii, 66.

> Influenced by the rabble's bloody will,
> With thumbs bent back, they popularly kill.
> DRYDEN: *Third Satire.*

Our popular saying, **Thumbs up!** expressive of pleasure or approval, is probably a perversion of this custom.

Every honest miller has a thumb of gold. Even an honest miller grows rich with what he filches; for he simply can't help *some* of the flour that ought to go into the loaf sticking to his thumb! Chaucer says of his miller—

> Wel koude he stelen corn and tollen thries,
> And yet he hadded a thombe of gold, pardee.
> *Canterbury Tales: Prologue*, 562.

Rule of thumb. A rough, guesswork measure; practice or experience, as distinguished from theory. In some places the heat required in brewing is determined by dipping the thumb into the vat.

The pricking of one's thumb. In popular superstition, a portent of evil. The Second Witch in *Macbeth* (iv, 1) says:—

> By the pricking of my thumbs,
> Something wicked this way comes.

And Macbeth enters.

Another proverb says, **My little finger told me that.** When your *ears tingle* it is to indicate that someone is speaking about you; when a sudden fit of *shivering* occurs, it is because someone is treading on the place which is to form your grave; when the *eye itches*, it indicates the visit of a friend; when the *palm itches* it shows that a present will shortly be received; and when the *bones ache* a storm is prognosticated. Sudden pains and prickings are the warnings of evil on the road; sudden glows and pleasurable sensations are the couriers to tell us of joy close at hand.

In ancient Rome the augurs took special notice of the palpitation of the heart, the flickering of the eye, and the pricking of the thumb. In regard to the last, if the pricking was on the left hand it was considered a very bad sign, indicating mischief at hand.

Thumb index. Grooves cut in the pages of a book showing initial letters or other particulars to enable the reader to find a reference easily.

Thumb-nail. Used attributively of various things, especially sketches, portraits, and so on, that are on a very small scale.

To thumb a ride. To ask for a lift in a motor car by holding out the hand with the thumb pointing in the direction in which one wants to go.

Tom Thumb. *See* TOM.

Under one's thumb. Under the influence or power of the person named.

Thumbikins, Thumbscrew. An instrument of torture used largely by the Inquisition, whereby the thumbs are compressed between two bars of iron, by means of a screw. William Carstairs (1649-1715) was the last person put to the torture in Britain; as the Law of England would not permit torture, he was sent by the Privy Council for examination in Edinburgh, to elicit the names of the accomplices in the Rye House Plot (*q.v.*).

Thunder. Used figuratively of any loud noise, also of vehement denunciations or threats, as, the thunders of the Vatican, meaning the anathemas and denunciations of the Pope.

Jupiter was the god of thunder in the Roman mythology; hence Dryden's allusion to the inactivity of Louis XIV:—

> And threatening France, placed like a painted Jove,
> Kept idle thunder in his lifted hand.
> *Annus Mirabilis*, xxxix.

Sons of thunder. *See* BOANERGES.

To steal one's thunder. To forestall him; or to adopt his own special methods as one's own. The phrase comes from the anecdote of John Dennis (1657-1734), the critic and playwright who invented an effective device for producing stage thunder, for his play *Appius and Virginia*. The play was a failure and was withdrawn, but shortly afterwards Dennis heard his thunder used in a performance of *Macbeth*. "My God," he exclaimed, "The villains will play my thunder but not my plays!"

Thunderbolt. A missile or mass of heated matter that was formerly supposed on occasion to be discharged from thunder-clouds during a storm; used figuratively of an irresistible blow, a sudden and overwhelming shock (*Cp.* BOLT FROM THE BLUE).

> Be ready, gods, with all your thunderbolts;
> Dash him to pieces!
> *Julius Cæsar*, iv, 3.

Jupiter was depicted by the ancients as a man seated on a throne, holding a sceptre in his left hand and thunderbolts in his right.

Thursday. The day of the god Thor (*q.v.*), called by the French *jeudi*, that is, Jove's day. Both Jove and Thor were gods of thunder, and formerly Thursday was sometimes called *Thunderday*. *See also* BLACK, HOLY, MAUNDY THURSDAY.

Tiara (tē a′ rà). Anciently the name of the head-dress of the Persian kings; now applied to a coronet-like ornament, and especially to the triple crown of the Pope. This typifies the temporal claims of the papacy, and is composed of gold cloth encircled by three crowns and surmounted by a golden globe and cross.

Tradition has it that for the first five centuries the bishops of Rome wore a simple mitre like other bishops, and that Hormisdas (514-23) placed on his bonnet the crown sent him by Clovis. Boniface VIII (1294-1303) added a second crown during his struggles with Philip the Fair; and John XXII (1410-17) assumed the third.

There are other accounts of the original adoption of the crowns, and of their meanings; some say that the second was added in 1335 by Benedict XII, to indicate the prerogatives of spiritual and temporal power combined in the papacy; and that the third is indicative of the Trinity; and Pius IX, in 1871, spoke of it as:—

> The symbol of my threefold dignity, in heaven, upon earth, and in purgatory.

Still another suggestion is that as the Pope claims to be (1) Head of the Catholic or Universal Church; (2) Sole Arbiter of its Rights; and (3) Sovereign Father of all the kings of the earth, he wears one crown as High Priest, one as Emperor, and one as King.

The papal tiara is very richly ornamented, and contains 146 jewels of all colours, 11 brilliants, and 540 pearls.

Tib. The ace of trumps in the game of Gleek. Tom is the knave.

> That gamester needs must overcome,
> That can play both Tib and Tom.
> RANDOLPH : *Hermaphrodite*.

St. Tib's Eve. Never. A corruption of St. Ubes. There is no such saint in the calendar as St. Ubes, and therefore her eve falls on the "Greek Calends" (*q.v.*), neither before Christmas Day nor after it.

Tichborne Case. The most celebrated impersonation case in English law. In March, 1853, Roger Charles Tichborne, heir to an ancient Hampshire baronetcy, sailed for Valparaiso, and after travelling a while in S. America embarked on April 20th, 1854, in a sailing-ship named the *Bella*, bound for Jamaica. The ship went down, and nothing more was heard or seen of Roger Tichborne. In October, 1865, "R. C. Tichborne" turned up at Wagga Wagga, in Australia, in the person of a man locally known as Tom Castro. On Christmas Day, 1866, he landed in England as a claimant to the Tichborne baronetcy, asserting that he was the lost Roger. Lady Tichborne, the real Roger's mother, professed to recognize him, but the family could not be deceived. The case came into the Courts where the fellow's claims were proved to be false and he himself identified as Arthur Orton, the son of a Wapping butcher. A further trial for perjury ended in his being sentenced to 14 years penal servitude.

The Tichborne Case has been acknowledged as the greatest *cause célèbre* of English law; public feeling ran high, and a by-election was said to have been lost because the candidate expressed his doubts as to the claimant's genuineness.

Ticket (U.S.A.). The list of nominees for office: "I intend to vote the straight Republican ticket."

As a seafaring term **to get one's ticket** is to qualify for promotion.

That's the ticket or **That's the ticket for soup.** That's the right thing. The ticket to be shown in order to obtain something.

Ticket of leave. A warrant given to convicts to have their liberty on condition of good behaviour; hence, *Ticket-of-leave man*, a convict freed from prison but obliged to report himself to the police from time to time until his sentence was completed. The system is now discontinued.

Tide. Used figuratively of a tendency, a current or flow of events, etc., as in *a tide of feeling*, and in Shakespeare's—

> There is a tide in the affairs of men,
> Which, taken at the flood, leads on to fortune.
> *Julius Cæsar*, iv, 3.

Lose not a tide. Waste no time; set off at once on the business.

Tide-waiters. Custom-house officers who board ships entering ports and see that the customs regulations are carried out. The term has been figuratively applied to those who vote against their opinions.

To tide over a difficulty, hard times, etc. Just to surmount the difficulty, just to come through the hard times, by force of circumstances and a little luck, rather than by one's own endeavours.

Tidy means in *tide*, in season, in time. We retain the word in eventide, springtide, and so on. Tusser has the phrase, "If the weather be fair and tidy," meaning seasonable. Things done punctually and in their proper season are sure to be done orderly, and what is orderly done is neat and well arranged. Hence we get the notion of methodical, neat, well arranged, associated with tidy.

The word is also used in the sense of a thing being worth consideration **A tidy penny,** quite a good sum; **a tidy fortune,** an inheritance worth having.

Tiger. The nickname of the French statesman Georges Clemenceau (1841-1929).

A liveried servant who rides out with his master used to be called a *tiger*, also a boy in buttons, a page; but the expression is now obsolete. The same name is given in America to a final yell in a round of cheering.

Tiger is the lowest hand in poker that can be drawn—seven high, ace low, without pair, straight or flush. Great nerve is required to hold and bluff on such a hand, and the phrase is responsible for the title of the famous jazz, classic "Tiger Rag."

Tight. Intoxicated.

Blow me tight! An old expression of surprise, wonder, incredulity, etc.

> If there's a soul will give me food or find me in
> employ,
> By day or night, then blow me tight! (he was a vulgar
> boy).
> BARHAM: *Misadventures at Margate (Ingoldsby Legends)*.

Tike. A provincial word (from Old Norse) for a dog or cur; hence used of a low fellow, as in the contemptuous insult, *You dirty tike*.

A Yorkshire tike. A rustic of that county.

Tilde. The sign ~ placed over the letter *n* in Spanish words when this is to be pronounced like our *ni* in *bunion*, e.g. *cañon* (canyon). It is a relic of the small *n* placed over a word in Latin MSS. to indicate a contraction, and the name is a variant of Span, *titulo*, title.

The tilde is also occasionally placed over an *l* to indicate the sound in *million*, and in Portuguese (called *til*) over the first vowel of a diphthong to indicate that the diphthong is to have a nasal pronunciation. In Portuguese, too, our *ni* of *bunion* is represented by *nh*, not by *ñ*.

Tile. Old slang for a hat, this being to the head what the tiles are to a house.

He has a tile loose. He is not quite *compos mentis*, not all there.

In Freemasonry, **to tile a lodge** means to close and guard the doors to prevent anyone uninitiated from entering, the officer who does this being called the *Tiler*, sometimes spelled *tyler*.

Timber (U.S.A.). To take the tall timber; to depart or escape suddenly and unceremoniously.

Time. Summer time. The legal, as apart from Greenwich time during a certain portion of the year in Great Britain and some other countries. In the spring of 1916 the Summer Time Act was passed ordaining that—

During the prescribed period in each year during which this Act is in force the time for general purposes in Great Britain shall be one hour in advance of Greenwich Mean Time.

The scheme had been proposed in 1906 by William Willett, a Chelsea builder.

Until 1939 the prescribed period was "from two o'clock in the morning following the third Saturday in April . . . until two o'clock in the morning next following the first Saturday in October."

During World War II the dates were varied, and the actual period of Summer Time has since 1939 been annually prescribed by Order in Council.

Between the years 1941 and 1945 Double Summer Time was introduced, this enforcing the addition of an hour to the Summer Time, thus making legal time two hours ahead of Greenwich time.

Take time by the forelock. Seize the present moment; *Carpe diem*. Time called by Shakespeare "that bald sexton" (*King John* iii, 1), is represented with a lock of hair on his forehead but none on the rest of his head, to signify that time past cannot be used, but time present may be seized by the forelock. The saying is attributed to Pittacus of Mitylene, one of the Seven Sages of Greece.

Time and tide wait for no man. One of many sayings pointing the folly of procrastination. It appears in Ray's *Scottish Proverbs* as "Time bides na man."

For the next inn he spurs amain,
In haste alights, and scuds away—
But time and tide for no man stay.
    SOMERVILLE: *The Sweet-scented Miser.*

Time-expired. Applied to soldiers whose term of service is completed. Also used of convicts who have served their sentences.

Time lag, term given to the pause that elapses between a cause and its effect.

Time signal. A visual or wireless signal indicating exact noon or some other recognized hour.

Time zone. One of the 24 longitudinal divisions of the globe, corresponding mostly with meridians of 15° from the meridian of Greenwich. These divisions or zones are successively of one hour of time interval.

To know the time o' day. To be smart, wide awake.

Timeo Danaos. *See* GREEK GIFT.

Timoleon (tī mō' lē òn). The Greek general and statesman (d. about 336 B.C.) who so hated tyranny that he voted for the death of his own brother Timophanes when he attempted to make himself absolute in Corinth.

  The fair Corinthian boast
Timoleon, happy temper, mild and firm,
Who wept the brother while the tyrant bled.
    THOMSON: *Winter.*

Timon of Athens (tī'mon). An Athenian misanthrope of the late 5th century B.C., and the principal figure in Shakespeare's play so called. The play, was acted about 1607 and printed in 1623.

Macaulay uses the expression to "out-Timon Timon"—*i.e.* to be more misanthropical than even Timon.

Timur. *See* TAMBURLAINE.

Tin. Money. A depreciating synonym for silver, called by alchemists "Jupiter."

Tin-pan Alley. The district of New York City where popular music is published. The phrase is often used generically of the composers of this type of music.

Tintype. A positive photograph taken on a sensitized sheet of enamelled tin. Tintypes were cheap and very popular at fairs, amusement parks, etc.

Tincture. The heraldic term for a colour as opposed to a metal or fur.

Tip. A small present of money, such as that given to a waiter, porter, or schoolboy; from the cant verb (common in the 16th and 17th centuries) *to tip*, meaning to hand over, which also gives rise to the other signification of the verb, viz., private warning, such secret information as may guide the person *tipped* to make successful

bets or gain some other advantage. A *straight tip* comes straight or direct from the owner or trainer of a horse, or from one in a position to know.

Tip and Run Raid. A phrase used in World War II when hostile aircraft flew in across the sea, hurriedly—and often indiscriminately—dropped their bombs, and immediately sped homewards. So called from the light-hearted form of holiday cricket in which the batsman is forced to run every time he touches the ball.

Tip off. To warn or give a hint, especially timely warning of a police raid.

Tip-top. First rate, capital, splendid.

To have a thing on the tip of one's tongue. To have it so pat that it comes without thought; also, to have it on the verge of one's memory, but not quite perfectly remembered.

To tip one the wink. To make a signal to another by a wink.

Tiphany. The name given in the old romances to the mother of the Magi. It is a corruption of *Epiphany*. *See* TIFFANY.

Tiphys. The pilot of the Argonauts (*q.v.*); hence a generic name for pilots.

"Tipperary." This song, that will be forever associated with World War I, was composed by Jack Judge (d. 1938), of Oldbury, Birmingham. The words were by Harry J. Williams, of Temple Balsall, Warwickshire, and the first line of the song is engraved on his tombstone. "Tipperary" was composed in 1912 and was already popular on the music-hall stage by 1914. It was sung by troops embarking for France, by men "going over the top," by WAACS and WRENS. The refrain was:—

Goodbye Piccadilly; farewell Leicester Square
It's a long, long way to Tipperary.
My heart's right there.

Tippling House. A contemptuous name for a tavern or public-house. A *tippler* was formerly a tavern-keeper or tapster, and the tavern was called a *tippling house*. At Boston, Lincolnshire, in 1577, five persons were appointed "tipplers of Lincoln beer," and no "other tippler [might] draw or sell beer . . ." under penalties.

Tipstaff. A constable, bailiff, or sheriff's officer; so called because he carried a staff tipped with a bull's horn or with metal. In the documents of Edward III allusion is often made to his staff.

Tiresias (tī rē' si às). A Theban of Greek legend, who by accident saw Athene bathing, and was therefore struck with blindness by her splashing water in his face. She afterwards repented, and, as she could not restore his sight, conferred on him the power of soothsaying and of understanding the language of birds, and gave him a staff with which he could walk as safely as if he had his sight. He found death at last by drinking from the well of Tilphosa.

Tironian (tī rō′ ni àn). Pertaining to a system of shorthand said to have been invented by Tiro, the freedman and amanuensis of Cicero. Our "&" (*see* AMPERSAND) is still sometimes called the *Tironian sign*, for it represents the contraction of Lat. *et* introduced by Tiro.

With regard to this Maunde Thompson (*Handbook to Greek and Latin Palæography*, p. 84) says, "Suetonius has it that 'Vulgares notas *Ennius* primus mille et centum invenit'," and adds that more generally the name of Cicero's freedman, Tiro, is associated with the invention, the signs being commonly named "notæ Tironianæ." *See also* SHORTHAND.

Tirynthian (ti rin′ thi àn). Hercules is called by Spenser the *Tirynthian Swain* (*Faerie Queene*, VI, xii, 35), and the *Tirynthian Groom* (*Epithalamium*, 329), because he generally resided at Tiryns, an ancient city of Argolis in Greece, famous for its Cyclopean architecture, which is mentioned by Homer, and the ruins of which are still magnificent.

Tit for Tat. Retaliation; probably representing *tip for tap, i.e.* blow for blow. J. Bellenden Ker says this is the Dutch *dit vor dat* (this for that), Lat. *quid pro quo.* Heywood uses the phrase *tit for tat*, perhaps the French *tant pour tant*.

Titan (tī′ tan). Primordial being of Greek mythology, of enormous size and strength, and typical of lawlessness and the power of force. There were twelve, six male (Oceanus, Cœus, Crius, Hyperion, Japetus, and Cronus) and six female (Theia, Rhea, Themis, Mnemosyne, Phœbe, and Tethys), children of Uranus and Ge (Heaven and Earth). Legends vary, but one states that Cronus swallowed the rest of them, and that when liberated by Zeus (son of Cronus), they dethroned and emasculated their father, Uranus; whereupon they made war on Zeus, who, after defeating them, imprisoned them all—Oceanus alone excepted—in Tartarus.

By Virgil and Ovid the Sun was sometimes surnamed *Titan*; hence Shakespeare's:—

And flecked Darkness like a drunkard reels
From forth Day's path and Titan's fiery wheels.
                                Romeo and Juliet, ii, 3.

Titania (ti tan′ yà). Wife of Oberon (*q.v.*), and Queen of the Fairies in *A Midsummer Night's Dream*. Shakespeare was, apparently, the first to use this name.

Titanic. A White Star liner, at the time of her launching the biggest vessel in the world and reputed unsinkable. While on her maiden voyage from Southampton to New York she collided, it is believed, with a submerged iceberg and in less than three hours went to the bottom, at 2.20 a.m., April 15th, 1912. The *Carpathia* picked up about 700 survivors, but over 1,500 lives were lost.

Titular Bishops. The Roman Catholic dignitaries formerly known as bishops *in partibus*. *See* IN PARTIBUS.

Titus (tī′ tùs). An alternative name of the Penitent Thief. *See* DYSMAS.

The Arch of Titus. The arch built in Rome in commemoration of the capture of Jerusalem by Titus and Vespasian (A.D. 70) shortly after that event. It is richly sculptured, and the trophies taken at the destruction of the temple are shown in relief.

Tityrus (tit′ i rus). A poetical surname for a shepherd; from its use in Greek idylls and Virgil's first *Eclogue*. In the *Shepheardes Calendar* (*Feb., June*, and *Dec.*) Spenser calls Chaucer by this name.

Heroes and their feats
Fatigue me, never weary of the pipe
Of Tityrus, assembling as he sang
The rustic throng beneath his favourite beech.
                    COWPER: *The Winter Evening*, 750.

Tityre Tus. Dissolute young scapegraces of the late 17th century (*Cp.* MOHOCKS) whose delight was to annoy the watchmen, upset sedans, wrench knockers off doors, and insult pretty women. The name comes from the first line of Virgil's first Eclogue, *Tityre, tu patulæ recubans sub tegmine fagi*, because the Tityre Tus loved to lurk in the dark night looking for mischief.

Tityus (tit′ i ùs). A gigantic son of Zeus and Ge in Greek mythology whose body covered nine acres of land. He tried to defile Latona, but Apollo cast him into Tartarus, where a vulture fed on his liver, which grew again as fast as it was devoured. (*Cp.* PROMETHEUS.) He was the father of Europa.

Tiu. Son of Woden (Scandinavian mythology), and a younger brother of Thor. The wolf Fenrir bit off his hand.

Tizzy. A sixpenny-piece; a variant of *tester* (*q.v.*).

Tmesis (tme′ sis). The grammatical term for the separation of the parts of a compound word by inserting between them other words, or the re-arrangement in this manner of the words of a phrase; *e.g.* "A large meal and rich," instead of a large, rich meal. "The greatness of his power to usward" (*Eph.* i, 19) instead of The greatness of his power toward us.

To-do. Here's a pretty to-do. Disturbance.

To-remain Bible. *See* BIBLE, SPECIALLY NAMED.

Toads. The device of Clovis was three toads (or *botes*, as they were called in O.Fr.); legend relates that after his conversion and baptism the Arians assembled a large army under King Candat against him. While on his way to meet the heretics Clovis saw in the heavens his device miraculously changed into three lilies *or* on a banner *azure*. He instantly had such a banner made, and called it his *oriflamme*, and even before his army came in sight of King Candat, the host of the heretic lay dead, slain, like the army of Sennacherib, by a blast from the God of Battles (Raoul de Presles: *Grans Croniques de France*).

Toad-in-the-hole. A piece of beef, sausage, chop, etc., baked in batter.

Toast. The person, cause, object, etc., to which guests are invited to drink in compliment, as well as the drink itself. The word is taken from the piece of toast which used at one time to be put into the tankard, and which still floats in the loving-cups at the Universities.

The story goes that in the reign of Charles II a certain beau pledged a noted beauty in a glass of water taken from her bath; whereupon another roysterer cried out he would have nothing to do with the liquor, but would have the toast—*i.e.* the lady herself. (*Rambler*, No. 24.)

Let the toast pass, drink to the lass.—SHERIDAN: *School for Scandal.*

Say, why are beauties praised and honoured most,
The wise man's passion and the vain man's toast.

POPE: *Rape of the Lock*, canto i.

Toast-master. The official who announces the after-dinner speakers at a formal banquet. He must be a man of stentorian voice and enjoy a nice knowledge of precedence.

Toboso (tȯ bō' zō). The village home of Don Quixote's lady-love, whom he renamed Dulcinea (*q.v.*). It is a few miles east of Ciudad Real.

Toby. The dog in the puppet-show of Punch and Judy (*q.v.*). He wears a frill garnished with bells, to frighten away the devil from his master.

Toc H. The morse pronunciation of the letters T.H., the initials of Talbot House. The term was used in World War I, when the first Talbot House was founded, in December 1915, at Poperinghe, in memory of Gilbert Talbot, son of the Bishop of Winchester, who had been killed at Hooge in the preceding July. The Rev.

P. B. Clayton, M.C. made it a famous rest and recreation centre. In 1920 he founded a similar centre in London, also known as Toc H, which developed into an interdenominational association for Christian social service.

Tocsin (tok' sin). An alarm signal given by the ringing of church bells. As *tocksaine* it is an old English word coming through the French *toquesin*, from *toquer*, to touch, and *senh*, Provençal for a bell.

Toddy. Properly the juice obtained by tapping certain palms, fermented so as to become intoxicating (Hindu *tadi*, from *tar*, a palm). It is also applied to a beverage compounded of spirits, hot water, and sugar, a kind of punch.

Tofana (to fa' nà). An old woman of Naples (d. 1730) immortalized by her invention of a tasteless and colourless poison, called by her the *Manna of St. Nicola of Bari*, but better known as *Aqua Tofana*. Above 600 persons fell victims to this insidious drug.

Toga (tō' gà). The usual outer dress of a Roman citizen when appearing in public; the Romans were hence the *Gens togata* (*q.v.*), the "togaed people."

The toga consisted of a single piece of undyed woollen cloth, cut almost in a semicircle and worn in a flowing fashion round the shoulders and body.

Toga picta. The toga embroidered with golden stars that was worn by the emperor on special occasions, by a victorious general at his "triumph," etc.

Toga prætexta. The toga with a purple border that was worn by children, by those engaged in sacred rites, magistrates, etc.

Toga virilis. The toga worn by men (*virilis*, manly), assumed by boys when 15.

Toggle (U.S.A.). A verb meaning to fasten together with bits of rope. The word is a seaman's word of the 17th century, a toggle being a wooden pin passed through the eye or loop of a rope, or through a link of a chain. In World War II a toggle rope was a length of stout cord with a small bar of wood spliced into it at one end and a loop at the other; it was used for a variety of purposes and was carried by British Commandos.

Togs. Slang for clothes; hence *togged out in his best*, dressed in his best clothes; *toggery*, finery. The word may be connected with *toga* (*see above*).

Token Payment. A small payment made as a formal and binding acknowledgement of indebtedness. The word "token" is often used to describe some action or phrase used in lieu of—but acknowledging—a greater obligation.

Tokyo Rose. The name given by U.S. service men to a woman broadcaster of propaganda from Japan during World War II. Several U.S.A.-born Japanese (Nisei) girls were identified as taking part in these broadcasts, notably Iva Togori, of California, and Ruth Hayakawa.

Toledo (tŏ lē′ dō). A sword made at Toledo in Spain, which place, long before and after the Middle Ages, was specially famous for them.

> I give him three years and a day to match my Toledo
> And then we'll fight like dragons.
> MASSINGER: *The Maid of Honour*, ii, 2.

Tollbooth (tōl′ booth). Originally a booth or stall where taxes were collected.

> And whanne Jesus passide fro thennis, he saw a man, Matheu bi name, sittingge in a tolbothe.—WYCLIFFE, *Matt*, ix, 9.

In Scotland the term was applied to the town gaol, from the custom of confining offenders against the laws of a fair or market in the booth where market dues were collected.

Tolosa (to lō′ sa). He has got the gold of Tolosa. His ill-gotten wealth will do him no good. *See under* GOLD.

Tom, Tommy. Short for *Thomas*: used of the male of certain animals (especially the cat), and generically—like *Jack* (*q.v.*)—for a man. It is also a generic name for a little boy. When contrasted, *Jack* is usually the sharp, shrewd, active fellow, and *Tom* the honest dullard. No one would think of calling the thick-headed male cat a *Jack*, nor the pert, dexterous, thieving daw a *Tom*. The former is almost instinctively called a *Tom-cat*, and the latter a *Jack-daw*.

> The man that hails you Tom or Jack,
> And proves by thumps upon your back
>   How he esteems your merit,
> Is such a friend, that one had need
> Be very much his friend indeed
> To pardon or to bear it.
> COWPER: *Friendship*.

Tom and Jerry. Types of the roystering young man about town; from Pierce Egan's *Life in London; or, The Day and Night Scenes of Jerry Hawthorn, Esq., and his Elegant Friend Corinthian Tom* (1821). *Cp.* JERRYSHOP.

Tomboy. A romping girl. The word was formerly used of a loose or immodest woman, whence the slang, *Tom*, applied to a prostitute.

> A lady
> So fair . . . to be partner'd
> With tomboys.
> *Cymbeline*, i, 6.

Tom Collins. A long drink of gin, lemon or lime, and some sparkling aerated water—in England bitter beer. Many localities claim the original Tom Collins; whoever he was or wherever he lived he deserves well of posterity.

Tom, Dick, and Harry. A Victorian term for "the man in the street," more particularly persons of no note; persons unworthy notice. "Brown, Jones, and Robinson" are far other men; they are the vulgar rich, who give themselves airs, especially abroad, and look with scorn on all foreign manners and customs which differ from their own.

Tom o' Bedlam. A mendicant who levies charity on the plea of insanity. In the 16th and 17th centuries applications for admission to Bedlam (*q.v.*) became so numerous that many inmates were dismissed half cured. These "ticket-of-leave men" wandered about chanting mad songs, and dressed in fantastic dresses, to excite pity. Posing as these harmless "innocents," a set of sturdy rogues appeared, called *Abram men* (*q.v.*), who shammed lunacy, and committed great depredations.

> With a sigh like Tom o' Bedlam.
> SHAKESPEARE: *King Lear*, i, 2.

Tom Thumb. Any dwarfish or insignificant person is so called; from the pigmy hero of the old nursery tale, popular in the 16th century. *The History of Tom Thumb* was published by R. Johnson in 1621, and there is a similar tale by Perrault (*Le Petit Poucet*), in 1630.

The American dwarf Charles Sherwood Stratton (1838-83) was popularly called "General Tom Thumb" (*see* DWARFS); and Fielding wrote a burlesque (acted 1730) entitled *Tom Thumb the Great. See also* BOAST OF ENGLAND.

Tom Tiddler's ground. A place where it is easy to pick up a fortune or make a place in the world for oneself; from the old children's game in which a base-keeper, who is called Tom Tiddler, tries to keep the other children who sing:—

> Here we are on Tom Tiddler's ground
> Picking up gold and silver.

from crossing the boundary into his base.

Tom Tiller. A hen-pecked husband.

Tommy-cooker. A small individual stove using solid fuel, invented in the time of World War I and issued to Allied troops in World War II. It was also the name given by the Germans to the Sherman Tank, which caught fire very easily when hit.

Tommy gun. A Thompson short-barrelled, sub-machine gun.

Tommy rot. Utter nonsense, rubbish; a cock-and-bull story (*q.v.*).

Tommy shop. A shop where vouchers, given by an employer in lieu of money, can be exchanged for goods; commonly run by large employers of labour before the truck system was made illegal.

Tomahawk (tom′ à hawk). The war axe of the N. American Indians, pre-historically made of stone or deer-horn but after the coming of the white man of iron or steel with a wooden handle. Sometimes the blunt end of the head was hollowed into a pipe-bowl, the handle being bored to form a stem. It was the custom of the Indians to bury the tomahawk when making peace, and dig it up again on the outbreak of war—hence the phrase *To bury the hatchet*.

Tombland Fair. *See* Maundy Thursday.

To-morrow. To-morrow come never. Never at all—when two Sundays, or three Thursdays, meet.

To-morrow never comes. Because, when it *does* come it ceases to be *to-morrow* and becomes *to-day*; a reproof to those who defer till to-morrow what should be done to-day.

A similar—though more caustic—saying is:—
Treason doth never prosper; what's the reason?
For if it prosper, none dare call it treason.
            Sir John Harrington (d. 1612).

Tone Poem, or **Symphonic Poem, is** a form of orchestral work which is intended to describe some literary or other subject. As with other programme music it requires an accompanying explanatory description. The term Symphonic Poem was first used by Liszt, who wrote thirteen works of this description.

Tongue. A lick with the rough side of the tongue. A severe reprimand, a good slating.

The gift of tongues. Command of foreign languages; also the power claimed by the Early Church and by some later mystics (as the Irvingites) of conversing and understanding unknown tongues (from the miracle at Pentecost—*Acts* ii, 4).

The three tongues. *See* Three.

The tongue of the trump. The spokesman or leader of a party.

The tongue of the trump to them a'.
            Burns: *The Election Ballads,* III.

To give someone the length of one's tongue. To talk to him "like a Dutch uncle"; to tell him in unmeasured language what you really think of him.

To give tongue. Properly used of a dog barking when on the scent; hence sometimes applied to people. Thus Polonius says to his son:—

Give thy thoughts no tongue,
Nor any unproportioned thought his act.
            Hamlet, i, 3.

To hold one's tongue. To keep silent when one might speak; to keep a secret.

To lose one's tongue. To become tongue-tied or speechless through shyness, fear, etc.

To speak with one's tongue in one's cheek. Insincerely; saying one thing and meaning another.

Tongue-tied. Speechless, usually through bashfulness or modesty; also (literally) having an impediment of the speech through shortness of the frænum.

Tonic Sol-fa. A system of musical notation in which diatonic scales are written always in one way (the keynote being indicated), the tones being represented by syllables or initials, and time and accents by dashes and colons. *Tonic* is a musical term denoting pertaining to or founded on the keynote; *sol* and *fa* are two of the Aretinian Syllables (*q.v.*). *See also* Doh; Gamut.

Tonquin Bean. *See* Misnomers.

Tonsure. The sacerdotal custom among priests of "being tonsured," *i.e.* having the head, or part of it, shaved (Lat. *tonsura,* a shearing), dates from the 5th or 6th centuries, and symbolizes Christ's crown of thorns. That of the secular clergy is a round space about the size of a half-crown at the crown of the head. In Britain, U.S.A. and other countries where it would not be in accordance with the customs of the people the tonsure is not retained after ordination. Among regulars there is a great variety of tonsure; Carthusians and Camaldolese shave the whole head except for a horizontal strip (*corona*) about half an inch wide; Friars Minor, Cistercians, and Benedictines have a wider *corona*; Dominicans shave the whole crown above the top of the ears; these are all called the great tonsure. The tonsure of Eastern monks is a cruciform cutting of part of the hair. The Celtic tonsure was made by cutting off all the hair in front of a line drawn over the head from ear to ear.

Tontine (ton′ tēn). A form of annuity shared by several subscribers, in which the shares of those who die are added to the holdings of the survivors till the last survivor inherits all. So named from Lorenzo Tonti, a Neapolitan banker, who introduced the system into France in 1653. In 1765 the House of Commons raised £300,000 by way of tontine annuities at 3 per cent.; and so late as 1871 the *Daily News* announced a proposed tontine to raise £650,000 to purchase the Alexandra Palace and 100 acres of land.

Tool. To tool a coach. To drive one; generally applied to a gentleman driver who undertook stage-coach driving for his own amusement.

Tooley Street. A corruption of St. Olaf—*i.e.* 'T-olaf, Tolay, Tooley. Similarly, Sise Lane is St. Osyth's Lane.

The three tailors of Tooley Street. *See* TAILOR.

Toom Tabard (Scot., empty jacket). A nickname given to John Baliol (1249-1315), because of his poor spirit, and sleeveless appointment to the throne of Scotland. The honour was an "empty jacket," which he enjoyed only from 1292 to 1296. He died in Normandy.

Tooth, Teeth. Golden tooth. *See* GOLDEN.

Tooth and egg. An obsolete corruption of *tutenag* (from Arab, *tutiya*), an alloy rich in zinc, coming from China and the East Indies and largely used for lining tea-chests.

With tooth and nail. In right good earnest, with one's utmost power; as though biting and scratching.

By the skin of one's teeth. *See* SKIN.

From the teeth outwards. Merely talk; without real significance.

He has cut his eye-teeth. He is "wide awake," quite sophisticated; he has "his weather-eye open." The eye-teeth (*i.e.* the upper canines) are cut late:—

			Months.	
First set	5 to	8,	the	four central incisors.
	7 "	10	"	lateral incisors.
	12 "	16	"	anterior molars.
	14 "	20	"	eye-teeth.
			Years.	
Second set—	5 to	6,	the	anterior molars.
	7 "	8	"	incisors.
	9 "	10	"	bicuspids.
	11 "	12	"	eye-teeth.

See also EYE-TEETH.

His teeth are drawn. His power of doing mischief is taken from him. The phrase comes from the fable of the lion in love, who consented to have his teeth drawn and claws cut, in order that a fair damsel might marry him. When this was done the girl's father fell on the lion and slew him.

In the teeth of the wind. With the wind dead against one, blowing in or against the teeth.

> To strive with all the tempest in my teeth.
> POPE: *Epistles of Horace*, II, ii.

Top. *See also* MIZENTOP.

Over the top. One is said *to go over the top* when he takes the final plunge. A phrase from the trench warfare of World War I when, at zero hour, troops climbed over the parapet of the front-line trenches to advance across No-man's-land to attack the enemy front line.

The Big Top is the big circus tent in which the main performance takes place.

Top dog, the one who by skill, personality or violence obtains the mastery, as the dog who is on top of his adversary in a fight.

To blow one's top. To go mad; to lose all control of oneself.

The top o' the morning to ye! A cheery greeting on a fine day, especially in Ireland. It is about the same as "The best of everything to you!"

Top-heavy. Liable to tip over because the centre of gravity is too high; intoxicated.

Topsy. The little slave girl in Harriet Beecher Stowe's *Uncle Tom's Cabin* (1852); chiefly remembered because when asked by "Aunt Ophelia" about her parents she maintained that she had had neither father nor mother, her solution of her existence being "I 'spects I growed."

Topsy-turvy. Upside down; probably *top*, with *so* and obsolete *terve*, connected with A.S. *tearflian*, to turn or roll over. Shakespeare says, "Turn it topsy-turvy down" (1 *Henry IV*, iv, 1). *Cp.* HALF-SEAS OVER.

Torah (tôr' ȧ), The Hebrew term for the Pentateuch or Five Books of Moses. The word is also used collectively for the entire Scriptures and the corpus of Jewish religious literature.

Torch (U.S.A.). To carry the torch for someone means to admire or love that person—the torch being the torch of love.

Toreador (tor' e a dôr). A popular misnomer for *torero*, a Spanish bull-fighter.

Torso. A statue which has lost its head and limbs. The word is Ital. for a stump or stalk, from Lat. *thyrsus*, the attribute of Bacchus, consisting of a spear-shaft wreathed with ivy or vine branches and tipped with a fir-cone.

The *Torso Belvedere*, the famous torso of Hercules, in the Vatican, was discovered in the fifteenth century. It is said that Michael Angelo greatly admired it.

Tortoise. The name is given to the ancient Roman *testudo*, *i.e.* the screen formed by the overlapping shields held above their heads by soldiers when attacking a fort. The animal is frequently taken as the type of plodding perseverance—"slow but sure."

The tortoise which, according to Hindu myth, supports Maha-pudma, the elephant which, in its turn, supports the world, is Chukwa.

Achilles and the tortoise. *See* ACHILLES.

Like the hare and the tortoise. *See* HARE.

Tory (tôr' i). The name given in the 17th century to the Irish who were turned out of their holdings by English settlers, and so took to the hills and bogs and developed into brigands and outlaws (from *toraidhe*, a pursued person).

During the Revolution it was applied to the Catholics fighting for James II; hence to those in England who refused to concur in excluding James from the throne. Until the accession of George III the party had a Stuart bias, but it then decided vigorously to uphold the Crown, the Church as by law established, and all constituted authority. As the name of the political and parliamentary party it was gradually superseded after 1830 by "Conservative" (*q.v.*), but it has been retained to denote the principles and policy of the party. *Cp.* DIE-HARDS; LIBERAL; UNIONIST.

Totalitarian (tō tăl i târ′ i ȧn). An ugly neologism invented to describe an ugly thing—a form of government that neither tolerates nor recognizes any persons or parties holding views differing from its own.

Totem (tō′ tem). A North American Indian (Algonkin) word for some natural object, usually an animal, taken as the emblem of a person or clan on account of a supposed relationship. Totemism, which is common among primitive peoples, has a distinct value in preventing intermarriage among near relations, for if persons bearing the same totem (as, for instance, in the case of brothers and sisters) intermarry the punishment is death. Another custom is that one is not allowed to kill or eat the animal borne as one's totem.

This very extraordinary institution, whatever its origin, cannot have arisen except among men capable of conceiving kinship and all human relationships as existing between themselves and all animate and inanimate things. It is the rule and not the exception that all savage societies are founded upon this belief.—ANDREW LANG: *Myth, Ritual, and Religion.*

Totem pole. The post standing before a dwelling on which grotesque and, frequently, brilliantly coloured representations of the totem were carved or hung. It is often of great size, and sometimes so broad at the base that an archway is cut through it.

Touch and Go. A very narrow escape; a metaphor derived, perhaps, from driving when the wheel of one vehicle touches that of another passing vehicle without doing mischief. It was a *touch*, but neither vehicle was stopped, each could *go* on.

Touch down. In Rugby and American football, to score by touching the ball on the ground within a certain defined area behind the opponent's goal posts.

Touchy. Apt to take offence on slight provocation. *Ne touchez pas, Noli me tangere*, one not to be touched.

Touchstone. A dark flinty schist, jasper, or basanite (the *Lapis Lydius* of the ancients), so called because gold is tried by it. A series of needles are formed (1) of pure gold; (2) of 23 gold and 1 copper; (3) of 22 gold and 2 copper, and so on. The assayer selects one of these and rubs it on the touchstone, when it leaves a mark that is reddish in proportion to the quantity of alloy; the article to be tested is then similarly "touched" and the marks compared. Hence the word is often used of any criterion or standard.

Fable has it that Battus saw Mercury steal Apollo's oxen, and Mercury gave him a cow to secure his silence, but, being distrustful of the man, changed himself into a peasant, and offered him a cow and an ox if he would tell him where he got the cow. Battus, caught in the trap, told the secret, and Mercury changed him into a touchstone (Ovid: *Metamorphoses*, ii).

Men have a touchstone whereby to try gold; but gold is the touchstone whereby to try men.—FULLER: *Holy and Profane State (The Good Judge).*

Tour. The Grand Tour. In the 17th, 18th, and early 19th centuries it was the custom for families of rank and substance to finish their sons' education by sending them, under the guardianship of a tutor, on a tour through France, Switzerland, Italy, and home through western Germany. This was known as the Grand Tour and sometimes a couple of years were devoted to it. The young men were supposed to study the history, language, etc., of each country they visited.

Tour de force (Fr.). A feat of strength or skill.

Tournament (O.Fr. *torneiement*, from Lat. *tornare*, to turn). A tilt of knights; the chief art of the game being so to manœuvre or *turn* your horse as to avoid the adversary's blow.

Tours (toor). Geoffrey of Monmouth says; "In the party of Brutus was one Turones, his nephew, inferior to none in courage and strength, from whom Tours derived its name, being the place of his sepulture." This fable is wholly worthless historically. Tours is the city of the Turones, a people of Gallia Lugdunensis.

Tout ensemble (too ton sombl) (Fr.). The whole massed together; the general effect.

Tow. To take in tow. Take under guidance. A man who takes a lad in tow acts as his guide and director. To tow a ship or barge is to guide and draw it along by tow-lines.

Too proud for bards to take in tow my name.
PETER PINDAR: *Future Laureate*, Pt. ii.

Tower. Tower Liberty. The Tower of London, with the fortifications and Tower Hill.

This formed part of the ancient demesne of the Crown, with jurisdiction and privileges distinct from and independent of the City. *Cp. Liberty of the Fleet, under* LIBERTY.

Tower of London. The architect was Gundulphus, Bishop of Rochester, who also built or restored Rochester keep, in the time of William I. Tradition has it that the White Tower, the central and oldest portion, is on the site of a fort erected by Julius Cæsar to awe the ancient inhabitants; hence Gray's well-known allusion in *The Bard*:—

Ye Towers of Julius, London's lasting shame,
With many a foul and midnight murther fed.

In the precincts of the Tower lie buried Anne Boleyn and her brother; Catherine Howard and Lady Rochford her associate; the venerable Lady Salisbury, and Cromwell the minister of Henry VIII; the two Seymours, the admiral and the protector of Edward VI; the Duke of Norfolk and Earl of Sussex (Elizabeth I's reign); the Duke of Monmouth, son of Charles II; the Earls of Balmerino and Kilmarnock, and Lord Lovat; Bishop Fisher and his illustrious friend Sir Thomas More. The bones of the "little Princes," Edward V and his brother the Duke of York, murdered there by order of Richard III in 1483, were discovered in 1674 and removed to Westminster Abbey.

Towers of Silence. *See* SILENCE.

Town. A.S. *tun,* a plot of ground fenced round or enclosed by a hedge (connected with Ger. *zaun,* a hedge); a single dwelling; a number of dwelling-houses forming a village or burgh.

A man about town. *See* MAN.

A woman of the town. A prostitute.

Town and Gown. The two sections of a university town; composed of those who are not attached to the university and those who are; hence, a *town and gown row,* a collision, often leading to a fight, between the students and non-gownsmen. *Cp.* PHILISTINES.

Town crier. A municipal official who goes about the streets, usually in a robe, ringing a bell and crying, *Oyez! Oyez!* (*q.v.*) to attract attention to his proclamations of notices, coming events, lost property, etc.

Town house. One's residence in town as apart from that in the country.

Town is empty. The season (*q.v.*) is over; society has left town for the country. The few millions who live there and work do not count.

Town planning. The regulating of the ground plan or extension of a town with a view to securing the greatest advantages from the point of view of health, public amenities, convenience

in transport, etc. The Town Planning Act was passed in 1909—and various amending and other Acts came into force in subsequent years. In 1943 a Ministry of Town and Country Planning was constituted, with wide powers to originate and control development.

Going to town. Full of life and high spirits. An American expression, probably originating among backwoodsmen.

Toyshop of Europe, The. So Burke called Birmingham. Here the word "toy" does not refer to playthings for children, but to trinkets, knick-knacks, and similar articles.

Trade. Free Trade. *See* FREE.

The balance of trade. *See* BALANCE.

The Board of Trade. A Government department—officially a Committee of the Privy Council—dealing with commercial and industrial affairs, such as bankruptcy, company matters, railways, weights and measures, harbours, patents, trade and merchandise marks, etc. Originally established by Oliver Cromwell, it has grown in scope of its duties and power.

The trade. Usually the liquor trade, more particularly those engaged in the brewing and distilling industries; but applied also to the general body of persons engaged in the particular trade that is being spoken of.

To blow trade. *See* TRADE WINDS, *below.*

To trade something off. To barter or exchange it; to sell it as a "job lot."

To trade upon. To make use of so as to obtain some advantage. The phrase is usually employed to describe the unscrupulous use of private knowledge or even of a personal affliction to arouse sympathy.

Trade board. An official council set up to regulate the conditions of labour in certain trades that otherwise might be "sweated."

Trade dollar. A United States silver dollar formerly coined specially for Oriental trade. It weighed 420 gr., instead of the 412.5 gr. of the ordinary dollar, and has not been coined since 1887.

Trade mark. The name or distinctive device for an article made for sale, indicating that it was produced by the holder of this device. In most countries trade marks are protected by law, it being a misdemeanour to forge or counterfeit such a mark. In Britain and U.S.A. a trade mark must be registered with the Government in order to secure full protection.

Trade Union. An association of employees in a trade or industry, formed for the promotion and protection of their common interests in regard to conditions of labour, wages, etc., and often for providing its members with payments during temporary unemployment, sickness, or strikes, and pensions in old age.

The earliest forerunner of the modern trade union was probably the combination of London cordwainers against their overseers in 1387; but until the passing of the first Trade Union Act (1871), all trade unions were, in so far as their objects could be held to be "in restraint of trade," illegal associations.

As early as the time of Henry V it was decided that a contract imposing a general restraint upon trade was void, and agreements between workmen not to take work except upon certain terms are at common law bad, and consequently any association which exists to-promote such agreements or to enforce such terms is illegal. . . . By the Trade Union Act, 1871, it was declared that a Trade Union merely because its objects were in restraint of trade should not be held to be unlawful, and its agreements were made binding, so that they would be recognised in law.—*The Labour Year Book*, 1916 (p. 174).

The modern trade union, and the name, came into being about 1830.

Trade winds. Winds that *blow trade*, *i.e.* regularly in one track or direction (Low Ger. *trade*, track). In the northern hemisphere they blow from the *north-east*, and in the southern hemisphere from the *south-east*, about thirty degrees each side of the equator. In some places they blow six months in one direction, and six in the opposite. The term is sometimes applied to the Indian monsoons.

Tragedy. Literally, a goat-song (Gr. *tragos*, goat, *ode*, song), though why so called is not clear. Horace (*Ars Poetica*, 220) says, because the winner at choral competitions received a goat as a prize, but the explanation has no authority.

It was Aristotle (in his *Poetics*) who said that tragedy should move one "by pity and terror":—

The plot ought to be so constructed that, even without the aid of the eye, he who hears the tale told will thrill with horror and melt to pity at what takes place.—ARISTOTLE: *Poetics*, xix (*Butcher*).

The Father of Tragedy. A title given to Æschylus (d. 456 B.C.), author of the Orestean trilogy and many other tragedies, and to Thespis. *See* THESPIANS.

Trajan's Column. The great monument in Rome (dedicated A.D. 114) commemorating Trajan's victories. It is a Roman Doric column of marble, $127\frac{1}{2}$ ft. high, covered with reliefs representing over 2,000 persons, besides many animals. It formed the model for the column in the Place Vendôme, Paris, and is now surmounted by a statue of St. Peter.

Trajan's Wall. A line of fortifications stretching across the Dobrudja from Czernavoda to the Black Sea.

Tram. The old "popular" derivation of this word from the name of Benjamin *Outram*, who ran vehicles on stone rails at Little Eaton, Derbyshire, in 1800, is discredited. The word is connected with Low Ger. *traam*, a baulk or beam, and was applied as early as the 16th century to trucks used in coal mines, and run on long wooden beams as rails.

Trams are a kind of sledge on which coals are brought from the place where they are hewn to the shaft. A tram has four wheels, but a sledge is without wheels.—BRAND: *History of Newcastle-upon-Tyne*, vol. ii, p. 681 (1789).

Tramontane (tra' mon' tān). The north wind; so called by Italians because to them it comes from over the mountains (Lat. *trans*, across, *montem*, mountain). The Italians also apply the term to peoples, etc., north of the Alps. French lawyers, on the other hand, apply the word to Italian canonists, whom they consider too Romanistic.

Transept. An architectural term (from the Lat. *trans*, across; *septum*, enclosure) for the transverse portion of any building lying across the main body of that building. The transept became common in ecclesiastical architecture in the Middle Ages and almost universal in the Gothic period. The cross is often surmounted by a tower, spire or dome. In a basilica church the transept is the transverse portion in front of the choir.

Translator-General. So Fuller, in his *Worthies* (1662), calls Philemon Holland (1552-1637), who translated works by Pliny, Livy, Plutarch, and a large number of other Greek and Latin classics.

Trap. Slang for a policeman; also for the mouth. **Shut your trap**, be quiet.

Traps. Luggage, one's personal belongings, and so on (as in *Leave your traps at the station*), are called *traps* as short for *trappings*, bits of additional finery and decoration, properly ornamental harness or caparison for a horse. The word is also used for the row of pens from which the dogs are simultaneously released in greyhound racing.

Trappists. A religious order, so called from La Trappe, an abbey founded at Soligny la Trappe (Orne, France) in 1140, by Rotron, Count de Perche. It is a branch of the Cistercian order, and is noted for the extreme austerity of its rules which include perpetual silence except in cases of strict necessity.

Traskites. A sect of Puritan Sabbatarians founded by John Trask, a Somerset man, about

1620. They believed that the law as laid down for the ancient Hebrews was to be taken literally and applied to themselves and all men. Trask was brought before the Star Chamber and pilloried. He is said to have recanted later and to have become an Antinomian, and his followers became absorbed by the Seventh-day Baptists (*q.v.*).

Travellers' Tales. Tall yarns; exaggerated stories of wonderful adventures and sights. Telling such tales used to be called *tipping one the traveller*.

Travelogue (trăv é log'). A lecture or running commentary delivered to accompany a moving picture of travel.

Travertine (trăv ĕr tin). A limestone formed by the deposit of springs and rivers, of a browny-grey appearance and peculiarly suitable for building purposes. The stone has been extensively used in the building of Rome in all periods; it takes its name, indeed, from the Late Latin Tiburtino, or Tibur, now known as Tivoli, near Rome.

Tre, Pol, Pen. Very common prefixes for personal and place names in Cornwall —

> By their Tre, their Pol, and Pen,
> Ye shall know the Cornish men.

The extreme east of Cornwall is noted for *Tre* (old Cornish, or Welsh, for house), the extreme west for Pol (= pool), the centre for *Pen* (= height, peak).

On December 19th, 1891, the following; residents are mentioned by the *Launceston Weekly News* as attending the funeral of a gentleman who lived at Tre-hummer House, Tresmere: — Residents from Trevell, Tresmarrow, Treglith, Trebarrow, Treludick, etc., with Treleaven the Mayor of Launceston.

Treacle properly means an antidote against the bite of wild beasts (Gr. *theriake*, from *ther* a wild beast). The ancients gave the name to several sorts of antidotes, but ultimately it was applied chiefly to Venice treacle (*theriaca androchi*), a compound of some sixty-four drugs in honey.

Sir Thomas More speaks of "a most strong treacle [*i.e.* antidote] against these venomous heresies"; and in the *Treacle Bible, see* BIBLE, SPECIALLY NAMED, *balm* (Jer. viii, 22) is translated *treacle* — "Is there no tryacle in Gilead? Is there no phisitian there?"

Treadmill. A wheel turned by the weight of a person or persons treading on steps fixed to the periphery. It was formerly used in prisons as a means of discipline or as a part of hard labour, the power being sometimes employed for turning machinery or grinding corn.

Treason. Betrayal of a trust or of a person. **High Treason** is an act of treachery against the Sovereign or the State, a violation of one's allegiance; *petty treason* is the same against a subject, as the murder of a master by his servant.

Treasure. These are my treasures; meaning the sick and poor. So said St. Lawrence (*q.v.*) when the Roman prætor commanded him to deliver up his treasures.

One day a lady from Campania called upon Cornelia, the mother of the Gracchi, and after showing her jewels, requested in return to see those belonging to the famous mother-in-law of Africanus. Cornelia sent for her two sons, and said to the visitor, "These are my jewels, in which alone I delight."

Treasure Trove. The term applied to coins and other valuables of gold or silver found in the ground or some other hiding-place, whose owner is unknown. In the legal sense these objects must have been originally placed there with the purpose of concealment; gold ornaments, etc., found in tombs or tumuli where they were deliberately placed with no intention of concealment are not treasure trove. Treasure trove belongs to the Crown, but in practice the finder is usually given the market value of the objects found.

Treasury. Treasury Bills are a form of British government security issued in multiples of £1,000 and repayable in 3, 6, 9 or 12 months.

Treasury Bonds are for money borrowed for a number of years.

Treasury Notes were issued by the Treasury from 1914 to 1928 for £1 and 10s. Their place was then taken by notes issued by the Bank of England.

Tree. For particulars of some famous and patriarchal trees *see under* OAK *and* YEW.

In the Natural History Museum, South Kensington, is the section of a *Sequoia gigantea* with 1,335 rings, representing that number of years. There are, however, yet older trees still in full life in the forests of America.

The eight olive-trees on the Mount of Olives are said to have been flourishing when the Turks took Jerusalem in 1187; and there is a lime-tree in the Grisons which is supposed to be over 660 years old.

The spruce will reach the age of 1,200 years. Trees burst into leaf —

	earliest		latest	
Ash		May 13th,		June 14th.
Beech	"	April 19th,	"	May 7th.
Damson	"	March 28th,	"	May 13th.
Horse-chestnut	"	March 17th,	"	April 19th.
Larch	"	March 21st,	"	April 14th.
Lime		April 6th,	"	May 2nd.

Mulberry	"	May 12th,	"	June 23rd.
Oak	"	April 10th,	"	May 26th.
Poplar	"	March 6th,	"	April 19th.
Spanish chestnut	"	April 20th,	"	May 20th.
Sycamore	"	March 28th,	"	April 23rd.

The cross on which Our Lord was crucified is frequently spoken of in hymns and poetry *as the tree*. See *Acts* v, 30:—". . . Jesus, whom ye slew and hanged on a tree"; 1 *Pet*. ii, 24:—"Who his own self bare our sins in his own body on the tree."

The gallows is also called *the tree*, **Tyburn tree, the fatal tree,** etc.

The tree of Buddha, or of **Wisdom.** The botree (*q.v.*).

The Tree of the Universe. Yggdrasil (*q.v.*).

The treeness of the tree. The essential qualities that compose a tree; in the absence of which a tree would cease to be a tree. Hence, the absolute essentials of anything. The phrase is evidently modelled on Sterne's "Corregiosity of Corregio" (*Tristram Shandy* III, xii).

Up a tree. In a difficulty, in a mess, non-plussed. An American phrase, from 'coon hunting. As soon as the 'coon is driven up a tree he is helpless.

It is said that Spurgeon used to practise his students in extempore preaching, and that one of his young men, on reaching the desk and opening the note containing his text, read the single word "Zacchæus." He thought a minute or two, and then delivered himself thus:—

Zacchæus was a little man, so am I; Zacchæus was up a tree, so am I; Zacchæus made haste and came down, and so do I.

You cannot judge of a tree by its bark. Don't go by appearances; an old proverb.

Trench Fever. A remittent or relapsing fever affecting men living in trenches, dug-outs, etc., and transmitted by the excrement of lice. It first appeared in World War I, in the static warfare on the western front.

Trencher. A good trencher-man. A good eater. The trencher is the platter on which food is cut (Fr. *trancher*, to cut), by a figure of speech applied to food itself.

Trencher cap. The mortar-board (*q.v.*) worn at college; so called from the *trenchered* or split boards which form the top.

Treves (trēvz, trāv). **The Holy Coat of Treves.** A relic preserved in the cathedral of Treves. It is one of several said to be the seamless coat of our Saviour, which the soldiers would not rend, and therefore cast lots for (*John* xix, 23, 25), which, according to tradition, was found and preserved by the Empress Helena in the 4th century. Its written history goes back

only to the 12th century, whereas the Holy Coat of Argenteuil, with similar claims, is traced to Charlemagne. There is little to choose between the two traditions.

Tria Juncta in Uno (Lat., three combined in one). The motto of the Order of the Bath. It refers to the three classes of which the order consists, viz. Knights Grand Cross, Knights Commanders, and Companions.

Triads. Three subjects more or less connected treated as a group; as *the Creation, Redemption, and Resurrection; Brahma, Vishnu, and Siva: Alexander the Great, Julius Cæsar, and Napoleon; Law, Physic, and Divinity*.

The Welsh *Triads* are collections of historic facts, mythological traditions, moral maxims, or rules of poetry disposed in groups of three for mnemonic purposes.

Trials at Bar. *See* BAR.

Tribune (trib' ūn). A chief magistrate, and very powerful official among the ancient Romans. During the revolt of the plebs in 494 B.C. they appointed two tribunes as protectors against the patricians' oppression; later the number was increased to ten and their office put on a proper footing. They were personally inviolable, and could separately veto measures and proceedings.

As a military title *tribune* denoted the commander of a cohort.

A tribune of the people. A democratic leader.

The Last of the Tribunes. Cola di Rienzi (1313-54).

Trice. In a trice. In an instant; in a twinkling.

To tell you what conceyte
I had then in a tryce,
The matter were too nyse
      SKELTON: *Phyllyp Sparowe* (c. 1505).

Trice is probably the same word as *trice*, to haul, to tie up; the idea being "at a single tug." The older form was **At a trice.**

At door where this trull was,
I was at a tryce.
      JOHN T. HEYWOOD: *Play of Love*, 1534.

Trick. Besides its usual significance of a sly or mean deception, a clever device, a dodge, etc., this word denominates the cards played and won in a round; also a spell of duty as at a ship's wheel.

Tricolour. A flag of three broad strips of different colours, especially the national standard of France, blue, white, and red. The first flag of the Republicans was *green*. The tricolour was adopted July 11, 1789, when the people were disgusted with the king for dismissing Necker; the popular tale is that the insurgents had adopted for their flag the two colours, *red and blue* (the colours of the city of Paris) but that

Lafayette persuaded them to add the Bourbon *white*, to show that they bore no hostility to the king.

Other tricolours are the flags of:—

Belgium, black, yellow, red; divided vertically.
Bulgaria, white, green, red; horizontally.
Eire, green, white, yellow; vertically.
Holland, red, white, blue; horizontally.
Italy, green, white, red; vertically.
Persia, green, white, red; horizontally.
Romania, blue, yellow, red; vertically.
Serbia, red, blue, white; horizontally.
Bolivia, red, yellow, green; horizontally.
Mexico, green, white, red; vertically.
Venezuela, yellow, blue, red; horizontally.
Yugoslavia, blue, white, red; horizontally.

Trident. In Greek mythology the three-pronged spear which Poseidon (Roman Neptune) god of the sea, bore as the symbol of his sovereignty. It has come to be regarded as the emblem of sea power and as such is borne by Britannia. In gladiatorial combats in Rome the trident was used by the retiarii, whose skill lay in entangling their opponents in nets, and then despatching them with tridents.

Trigon (trī' gon). The junction of three signs. The zodiac is partitioned into four trigons, named respectively after the four elements; the *watery* trigon includes Cancer, Scorpio, and Pisces; the *fiery*, Aries, Leo, and Sagittarius; the *earthy*, Taurus, Virgo, and Capricornus; and the *airy*, Gemini, Libra, and Aquarius.

Trilogy (trīl' ō ji). A group of three tragedies. Everyone in Greece who took part in the poetic contest had to produce a trilogy and a satyric drama. There is only one complete specimen extant, viz. that embracing the *Agamemnon*, the *Choephorœ*, and the *Eumenides*, by Æschylus.

Trimmer. One who runs with the hare and hunts with the hounds. George Savile, Marquis of Halifax, adopted the term in the reign of Charles II to signify that he was neither an extreme Whig nor an extreme Tory.

Trine. In astrology, a planet distant from another one-third of the circle is said to be in trine; one-fourth, it is in square; one-sixth or two signs, it is in sextile; but when one-half distant, it is said to be "opposite."

> In sextile, square, and trine, and opposite
> Of noxious efficacy.
> MILTON: *Paradise Lost*, x, 659.

Planets distant from each other six signs or half a circle have opposite influences, and are therefore opposed to each other.

Trinity. The three Persons in one God—God the Father, God the Son, and God the Holy Ghost.

> And in this Trinity none is afore or after other; none is greater, or less than another; but the whole three Persons are co-eternal together and co-equal.—*The Athanasian Creed.*
> Cp. PERSONS (*Confounding the Persons*).

Tertullian (about 160-240) introduced the word into Christian theology, Almost every mythology has a threefold deity. *See* THREE.

Trinity House. The association, incorporated by Royal Charter and Acts of Parliament, and, for many purposes, forming a branch of the Board of Trade, constituting the chief pilotage authority of the United Kingdom and being responsible for lighthouses and seamarks in home waters; properly called The Corporation of Trinity House, from its headquarters on Tower Hill, London.

It was granted its first charter by Henry VIII in 1514, and now consists of a Master, ten Acting Elder Brethren, and a number of Honorary Elder Brethren, among whom are usually the King and other members of the Royal Family, Cabinet Ministers, etc. The Acting Elder Brethren (one a retired naval officer, and nine retired mercantile marine commanders) sit with the judges of the Admiralty Division as nautical assessors in marine causes.

Trinobantes (trin ō băn' tēz). Inhabitants of Middlesex and Essex, referred to in Cæsar's *Gallic Wars*. This word, converted into *Trinovantes*, gave rise to the myth that the people referred to came from Troy. *See* TROYNOVANT.

Tripe. Journalists' slang for very second-rate "copy" whose only use is as "fill-ups." Cp. BILGE-WATER.

Tripehound. In Australian slang a dog on a sheep station. The term has spread to England as a term of opprobrium.

Tripitaka (trip it' a ka) (Pali *tipitaka*, the three baskets). The three classes into which the sacred writings of the Buddhists are divided—viz. the *Sutrapitaka* (Basket of Aphorisms or Discourses) or *Sutras*, the *Vinayapitaka* (Basket of Disciplinary Directions), and *Abidhammapitaka* (Basket of Metaphysics).

Triple Alliance. A treaty entered into by England, Sweden, and Holland against Louis XIV in 1668. It ended in the treaty of Aix-la-Chapelle.

A treaty between England, France, and Holland against Spain in 1717. In the following year it was joined by Austria, and became a Quadruple Alliance.

The alliance between Germany, Austria and Italy, signed in 1882. It was renewed several times but finally broken in 1914 when Italy refused to join in the war against Britain and France.

Triptolemus (trip tol' ē ms). A Greek hero and demi-god, worshipped chiefly at Eleusis as the giver to man of grain and the first instructor in agriculture.

Triptych (trip' tik). In ecclesiastical painting a set of three upright panels joined together by hinges, each panel being painted with a separate subject. The wings were frequently painted on both sides so that when folded a fresh picture was presented. The Van Eycks and most of the great religious painters of the early Renaissance used the triptych, but it fell into disuse in the 16th century.

Trisagion (tris ăg' i on) (Gr., thrice holy). A hymn in the liturgies of the Greek and Eastern Churches in which (after *Is*. vi, 3) a threefold invocation to the Deity is the burden—"Holy God, Holy and Mighty, Holy and Immortal, have mercy upon us."

The name is sometimes applied to Bishop Heber's hymn for Trinity Sunday—

Holy, Holy, Holy! Lord God Almighty!
Early in the morning our song shall rise to Thee—

which is more properly called the *Ter-Sanctus*.

Triskelion (tri skel' i on) (Gr., three-legged). The emblem of the Isle of Man, and of Sicily; three human legs, bent at the knee, and joined at the thigh.

Trismegistus (tris me jis' tus) (Gr., thrice great). A name given to Hermes (*q.v.*), the Egyptian philosopher, or Thoth, councillor of Osiris, to whom is attibuted a host of inventions—amongst others the art of writing in hieroglyphics, the first code of Egyptian laws, harmony, astrology, the lute and lyre, magic, and all mysterious sciences.

Tristram, Sir (**Tristrem, Tristan,** or **Tristam**). A hero of mediæval romance whose exploits, though originally unconnected with it, became attached to the Arthurian cycle, he himself being named as one of the Knights of the Round Table. There are many versions of his story, which is, roughly, that he was cured of a wound by Iseult, or Ysolde, daughter of the king of Ireland, and on his return to Cornwall told his uncle, King Mark, of the beautiful princess. Mark sent him to solicit her hand in marriage, and was accepted. Tristram escorted her to England, but on the way they both unknowingly partook of a magic potion and became irretrievably enamoured of each other. Iseult married the king, and on Mark's discovering their liaison Tristram fled to Brittany and married Iseult, daughter of the Duke of Brittany.

Wounded by a poisoned weapon, he sent for Iseult of Ireland to come and heal him. The Vessel in which she was to come had orders to hoist a white sail if she was on board, otherwise a black sail. Tristram's wife, seeing the vessel approach, told her husband, from jealousy, that it bore a black sail. In despair, Tristram died; Iseult of Ireland, arriving too late, killed herself.

The name was originally *Drystan*, from the Pictish name *Drostan*, and the initial was changed to *T* apparently to connect it with Lat. *tristis*, sad.

Triton. Son of Poseidon and Amphitrite, represented as a fish with a human head. It is this sea god that makes the roaring of the ocean by blowing through his shell.

A Triton among the minnows. A great man amid a host of inferiors.

Triumph. A word formed from Gr. *thriambos*, the Dionysiac hymn, *Triumphe* being an exclamation used in the solemn processions of the Arval Brothers.

Some . . . have assigned the origin of . . . triumphal processions to the mythic pomps of Dionysus, after his conquests in the East, the very word *triumph* being . . . the Dionysiac hymn.—PATER: *Marius the Epicurean*, ch. xii.

The old Roman *triumphus* was the solemn and magnificent entrance of a general into Rome after having obtained a great or decisive victory. *Cp*. OVATION.

Triumvir (trī ŭm' vėr). In ancient Rome a member of a commission of three charged with some special duty, such as repairing tombs, coining money, or even founding colonies. The most famous triumvirate was that of Octavian, Antony, and Lepidus, 43 B.C., which was known as the Second Triumvirate to distinguish it from the private combination of Cæsar, Pompey, and Crassus in 60 B.C., popularly known as the First Triumvirate.

Trivet. Right as a trivet. See RIGHT.

Trivia. Gray's name for his invented goddess of streets and ways. His burlesque in three books so entitled (1716) is a mine of information on the outdoor life of Queen Anne's time.

Thou, Trivia, aid my song.
Through spacious streets conduct thy bard along . . .
To pave thy realm, and smooth the broken ways,
Earth from her womb a flinty tribute pays.
GAY: *Trivia*, Bk. 1.

Trivia is also the plural of *trivium*.

Trivium. The three roads (Lat. *tres*, three, *via*, a road) to learning in the Middle Ages, *i.e.* Grammar, Rhetoric, and Logic; forming the lower division of the seven liberal arts (*see* QUADRIVIUM).

Troglodytes. A people of Ethiopia, south-east of Egypt, so called from Gr. *trogle*, cave, *duein*, to go into, because they lived in cave dwellings, remains of which are still to be seen along the banks of the Nile. Hence applied to other cave-dwellers, and, figuratively to those who live in seclusion. There were troglodytes of Syria and Arabia also, according to Strabo, and Pliny (v, 8) asserts that they fed on serpents.

Troilus. The prince of chivalry, one of the sons of Priam, killed by Achilles in the siege of Troy (Homer's *Iliad*).

The loves of Troilus and Cressida, cele-brated by Shakespeare and Chaucer, form no part of the old classic tale. The story appears for the first time in the *Roman de Troie* by the 12th-century *trouvère*, Benoit de Ste. More. Guido delle Colonne included it in his *Historia Trojana* (about 1290), it thence passed to Boccaccio, whose *Il Filostrato* (1344)—where Pandarus first appears—was the basis of Chaucer's *Troilus and Criseyde*.

As true as Troilus. Troilus is meant by Shakespeare to be the type of constancy, and Cressida the type of female inconstancy.

> After all comparisons of truth . . .
> "As true as Troilus" : hall crown up the verse,
> And sanctify the numbers.
>
> *Troilus and Cressida*, iii, 2.

Trojan. He is a regular Trojan. A fine fellow, with courage and spirit, who works very hard, usually at an uncongenial task, indeed, doing more than could be expected of him. The Trojans in Homer's *Iliad* and Virgil's *Æneid* are described as truthful, brave, patriotic, and confiding.

> There they say right, and like true Trojans.
>
> BUTLER: *Hudibras*, i, 1.

Trojan War. The legendary war sung by Homer in the *Iliad* (*q.v.*) as having been waged for ten years by the confederated Greeks against the men of Troy and their allies, in conse-quence of Paris, son of Priam, the Trojan king, having carried off Helen, wife of Menelaus, king of Lacedemon (or of Sparta). The last year of the siege is the subject of the *Iliad*; the burn-ing of Troy and the flight of Æneas is told by Virgil in his *Æneid*.

There is no doubt whatever that the story of the siege of Troy has some historical basis, but when it took place is purely a matter of conjec-ture. Many dates, ranging from the 11th to the 14th centuries B.C. have been assigned to it.

Trolls. Dwarfs of Northern mythology, living in hills, underground in caverns or beneath; they are represented as stumpy, misshapen, and humpbacked, inclined to thieving, and fond of carrying off human children and substituting

their own. These hill people, as they are called, are especially averse to noise, from a recollec-tion of the time when Thor used to be for ever flinging his hammer after them.

Trooping. The trooping season. The season when the annual reliefs of the British forces in India were made, usually beginning in late February or March.

Trooping the colour. A military ceremonial parade in which the regimental flag, the *colour*, is carried between files of troops and received by the sovereign or a representative.

The ceremony dates from the 18th century (probably from Marlborough's time), and was originally a guard-mounting ceremony, the bat-talion finding the guards for the day "trooping" the colour to be carried on king's guard.

> Many years ago it became the custom to find the public guards on the King's birthday from the flank com-panies (picked companies) of the whole Brigade, instead of from one battalion, and it is from this custom that the ceremony of Trooping the Colour on his Majesty's birth-day by detachments of the flank companies of all the battalions in London originates. The Field-Officer-in-Brigade-Waiting always commands the troops on this parade, irrespective of the regiment to which he belongs.—*The Times*, 3 June, 1922.

Trophy. Originally the arms of a vanquished foe, collected and set up by the victors on the field of battle. The captured standards were hung from the branches of an oak tree, a portion of the booty being laid at the foot of the tree and dedicated to the tutelary deity. The Romans fre-quently bore their trophies to Rome; under the Empire the triumphs of the victorious generals were also celebrated with arches and columns.

Troubadours. Minstrels of the south of France in the 11th, 12th, and 13th centuries; so called from the Provencal verb *trobar*, to find or invent (*cp.* "poet," which means "a maker.") They wrote in the *langue d'oc*, or Provencal, principally on love and chivalry. *Cp.* TROUVÈRES.

Trouvères (troo' vâr). The troubadours of the north of France, in the 12th, 13th, and 14th centuries. So called from Fr. *trouver*, to find or invent (*cp.* TROUBADOURS). They wrote in the *langue d'oil* or *langue d'oui*, chiefly on amatory subjects.

Trows, or Drows. Dwarfs of Orkney and Shetland mythology, similar to the Scandinavian Trolls. There are land-trows and seatrows. "Trow tak' thee" is a phrase still used by the island women when angry with their children.

Troy. The Siege of Troy. *See* ILIAD; HELEN; TROJAN WAR; etc.

Troy Town. A Cornish expression for a labyrinth of streets, a regular maze. In several novels "Q" (Sir A. Quiller Couch) used the name as a disguise for Fowey. *Troy* was formerly used figuratively of any scene of disorder or confusion; a room with its disorder or confusion; a room with its furniture all higgledy-piggledy, for instance, would be called a *Troy fair*.

Troy weight. The system of weights used in weighing precious metals and gems, the pound of 12 ounces weighing 5760 grains as compared with the pound avoirdupois which weighs 7000 grains and is divided into 16 ounces (*cp.* AVOIRDUPOIS). Why so called is not certainly known, but probably it was the system used at the great fairs at Troyes, in France. 1 lb.troy = 0·822861 lb. av., rather over four-fifths.

Troynovant. The name given by the early chroniclers to London, anciently the city of the Trinobantes (*q.v.*); a corruption of *Trinovant*. As *Troynovant* was assumed to mean *The New Troy*, the name gave rise to the tradition that Brute, a Trojan refugee (from whom they derived the name *Britain*) came to England and founded London.

> For noble Britons sprong from Trojans bold,
> And Troy-novant was built of old Troyes ashes cold
> SPENSER: *Faerie Queen*, iii, 9.

Truce of God. In 1041 the Church attempted to limit private war, and decreed that there should be no hostilities between Lent and Advent or from the Thursday to the next Monday at the time of great festivals. This *Truce of God* was confirmed by the Lateran Council in 1179, and was agreed to by England, France, Italy, and other countries; but little attention was ever paid to it.

Truck System, The. The paying of employees otherwise than in current coin, or making it a condition that they shall buy food or other articles from some particular shop. In Britain this was made illegal by Acts passed in 1831, 1887, and 1896.

True. A true bill. See BILL.

True blue. See BLUE.

True-lovers' knot. A complicated double knot with two interlacing bows on each side and two ends, used as a symbol of love.

> Three times a true-love's knot I tie secure;
> Firm be the knot, firm may his love endure.
> *Gay's Pastorals: The Spell.*

True Thomas. Thomas the Rhymer. See RHYMER.

Truepenny. Hamlet says to the Ghost, "Art thou there, Truepenny?" Then to his comrades, "You hear this fellow in the cellarage" (i, 5). And again, "Well said, old mole; canst work?" The reference is to the sterling worth of his father—he was as honest and *true* as a genuine coin.

Trump. This word in such phrases as *a trumped up affair, trumpery*, etc., is the same word as *trumpet*; from Fr. *trompe*, a trumpet, whence *tromper* which, originally meaning "to play on a trumpet," came to mean to beguile, deceive, impose upon.

Trump in cards, is from Fr. *triomphe* (triumph), the name of an old variant of écarté.

The last trump. The final end of all things earthly; the Day of Judgment.

> We shall not all sleep, but we shall all be changed, in a moment, in the twinkling of an eye, at the last trump.—1 *Cor.* xv, 51, 52.

To play one's last trump. To be reduced to one's last expedient; a phrase from card-playing.

To turn up trumps. Unexpectedly to prove very friendly and helpful.

Trumpet. See TRUMP *above*.

The Feast of Trumpets. A Jewish festival, held on the first two days of Tisri (about mid Sept. to mid Oct.), the beginning of the ecclesiastical year, at which the blowing of trumpets formed a prominent part of the ritual. See *Num.* xxix, 1.

To blow one's own trumpet. To publish one's own praises, good deeds, etc. The allusion is to heralds, who used to announce with a flourish of trumpets the knights who entered a list. Similarly, *your trumpeter is dead* means that you are obliged to sound your own praises because no one will do it for you.

Trunk. In its sense of denominating the main body as opposed to the roots and branches, the word is used to describe the main lines of railway, postal, telephone systems, from which branch lines radiate. **A trunk call** is a telephone call on a trunk line from one town to another. **Trunk road** is a main highway between two principal towns. **Trunk hose** were a style of breeches worn in the 16th and 17th centuries, reaching from the waist to the middle of the thigh. **Trunk drawers**, or **trunks** are pants reaching only to the knee.

Trust. A combination of a number of companies or businesses doing similar trade, for the purpose of defeating competition or creating a monopoly, under one general control. So called because each member is on trust not to undersell the others, but to remain faithful to the terms agreed on.

Trusty. In American penology a well-behaved, long-term prisoner who is allowed to help the warders in some of their duties and is granted certain privileges not allowed to other convicts.

Truth. Pilate said, *"What is truth?"* (*John* xviii, 38). This was the great question of the Platonists. Plato said we could know truth if we could sublimate our minds to their original purity. Arcesilaus said that man's understanding is not capable of knowing what truth is. Carneades maintained that not only our understanding could not comprehend it, but even our senses are wholly inadequate to help us in the investigation. Gorgias the Sophist said, "What is right but what we prove to be right? and what is truth but what we believe to be truth?"

Pilate asked. *Quid est veritas?* And then some other matter took him in the head, and so up he rose and went his way before he had his answer. He deserved never to find what truth was.—BP. ANDREWS: *Sermon on the Resurrection* (1613)

Truth lies at the bottom of a well. This expression has been attributed to Heraclitus. Cleanthes, Democritus the Derider, and others,

Naturam accusa, quæ in profundo veritatem (ut ait Democritus) penitus abstruserit.—CICERO: *Academics*, i, 10.

Truth drug. Alkaloid scopolamin. An American doctor, R. E. House, used this drug to induce a state of lethargic intoxication in which the patient lost many of his defences and spoke the truth concerning matters about which he would normally have lied or prevaricated. The value of this and other truth drugs in penology has by no means been established.

Tuatha De Danann (twa' thà de dăn' àn). A legendary race of super-human heroes which invaded Ireland, overthrew the Firbolgs and Fomors, and were themselves overthrown by the Milesians, who later worshipped them as gods.

Tub. Tubs, in rowing slang, are gig pairs of college boat clubs, who practise for the term's races. They are pulled on one side when a pairoar boat in uniform makes its appearance.

Tubbing is taking out pairs under the supervision of a coach to train men for taking part in the races.

A tale of a tub. A cock-and-bull story; a rigmarole; a nonsensical romance.

There is a comedy of this name by Ben Jonson (produced 1633), and a prose satire by Swift (1704) which portrays allegorically the failings of the English, Roman, and Presbyterian Churches.

A tub of naked children. Emblematical in religious paintings of St. Nicholas (*q.v.*), in allusion to the two boys murdered and placed in a pickling tub by a landlord, but raised to life again by this saint.

Tub-thumper. A blustering, ranting public speaker; a "stump-orator." In allusion to the upturned tub frequently used as a rostrum at open-air meetings.

Tuck. This word, in the sense of eatables, is a mid-18th-century slang word, especially among schoolboys whose "tuck-box," brought from home at the beginning of term, contained sweets, jams, etc., to supplement school fare. From this came the phrase **To tuck in**, meaning to eat heartily and with relish. In Australia the word became **tucker**, meaning any kind of food, but particularly that carried on long journeys, etc.

To tuck one up. To finish him, do for him. The allusion is probably to tucking children up in bed for the night—they are finished with till next morning; but there may be some reference to the long narrow duellist's rapier formerly called a *tuck* (Fr. *étoc*, stock).

Tuck, Friar. *See* FRIAR TUCK.

Tucker. The ornamental frill of lace or muslin worn by women in the 17th and 18th centuries round the top of their dresses to cover the neck and shoulders. Hence, *with clean bib and tucker*, nicely dressed, looking fresh and spruce. *See also* TUCK.

Tuckahoe (tŭk' à hō) (U.S.A.). An inhabitant of that part of the State of Virginia that lies east of the Blue Ridge Mountains.

Tudor (tū' dòr). The general descriptive term given to the architecture, etc., characteristic of the late 15th and the whole of the 16th centuries, when the Tudor sovereigns Henry VII, Henry VIII, Edward VI, Mary I, and Elizabeth I reigned in England. Tudor architecture is of the late style of Gothic, with wide, broad-pointed windows and doorways.

Tuffet. A dialect variant of *tuft*. which was formerly used of a small grassy mound or hillock.

Little Miss Muffet
Sat on a tuffet
Eating her curds and whey
Nursery Rhyme.

Tug. A name by which Collegers are known at Eton; from the *tog* (*i.e. toga*) worn by them to distinguish them from the rest of the school.

Tug of war. A rural sport in which a number of men, divided into two bands, lay hold of a strong rope and pull against each other till one side has tugged the other over the dividing line.

When Greek meets Greek then is the tug of war. *See* GREEK.

Tuileries (twē' lé rē). A former palace in Paris, so named from the tile-yards (*tuileries*) once on the site. It stood between the Louvre and the Place de la Concorde. The palace was designed by Philibert de l'Orme for Catherine de' Medici, 1564, and long served as a residence for the sovereigns of France. In 1871 it was burned down by the Communards, but the gardens remain as a pleasant public open space.

Tulip Mania. A reckless mania for the purchase of tulip-bulbs that arose in Holland in the 17th century and was at its greatest height about 1634-1637. A root of the species called *Viceroy* sold for £250; *Semper Augustus*, more than double that sum. The mania spread all over Europe, and became a mere stock-jobbing speculation.

Tumbledown Dick. Anything that will not stand firmly. "Dick" is Richard Cromwell (1626-1712), the Protector's son, who was but a tottering wall at best.

Tumbler. A word with several meanings, all deriving from the verb "to tumble." Drinking tumblers are stemless glasses, now made with a flat bottom but originally with a rounded bottom that made the glass tumble over if set down on a table; hence requiring that it should be held until emptied. The performing tumbler was an acrobat whose turn consisted in somersaults, etc.; and thus a tumbler pigeon was one who performed such tricks in the air. The tumbler of a lock is a pivoted piece that has to be raised by the key for opening, and tumbles back into place when released, thus preventing the bolt from being drawn.

Tune. The tune the old cow died of. Advice instead of relief; remonstrance instead of help.

The reference is to the song—

> There was an old man, and he had an old cow,
>   But he had no fodder to give her,
> So he took up his fiddle and played her the tune;
>   "Consider, good cow, consider,
> This isn't the time for the grass to grow,
>   Consider, good cow, consider."

To change one's tune, or **sing another tune.** *See* SING.

To the tune of. To the amount of; as, "I had to pay up to the tune of £500."

Tuneful Nine, The. The nine Muses (*q.v.*).

> When thy young Muse invok'd the tuneful Nine,
> To say how LOUIS did not pass the RHINE,
> What Work had We with WAGENINGHEN, ARNHEIM,
> Places that could not be reduced to Rhime?
>   PRIOR: *Letter to Boileau Despréaux* (1704).

Turban. The head-dress of many Mohammedan races, consisting of a scarf of cotton or silk wound round the head, the manner of arranging the folds varying according to rank and country. The tarbush or fez is used as the foundation for a turban, and often as a headdress in itself, though in Turkey this was prohibited by law in 1925, when it was decreed that all Turks should wear European hats.

Turf, The. The racecourse; the profession of horse-racing, which is done on turf or grass. A *turfite* is one who lives by the turf, either by running horses or betting.

Turk. Applied to barbarous, savage, cruel men, because these qualities have been for centuries attributed to Turks; also to mischievous and unruly children, as *You little Turk!*

The Young Turks. The reforming party in the Ottoman Empire who, in the early part of the present century, introduced the methods of modern Europe into the government. Through many stormy scenes and much involved politics the party steered its country through World War I, and, dragged in divergent directions by the conflicting interests and policies of the European powers, survived in spite of all, to get rid (1922) of the decadent sultans of the House of Othman and declare Turkey a republic.

Turk Gregory. Falstaff's *ne plus ultra* of military valour—a humorous combination of the Sultan with Gregory VII (Hildebrand), probably the strongest of all the Popes.

> Turk Gregory never did such deeds in arms as I have done this day.— 1 *Henry IV*, v, 3.

Turkey. To talk turkey. (U.S.A.) To talk seriously.

Turkey rhubarb. *See* MISNOMERS.

Turn. Done to a turn. Cooked exactly right; another turn on the gridiron would be one too much.

One good turn deserves another. A benefit received ought to be repaid.

To turn down. To reject; a candidate at an examination, election, etc., who does not meet with success is said to be *turned down*.

In Eastern countries a glass is turned down at convivial gatherings as a memento of a recently departed companion:—

> And when thyself with shining feet shalt pass
> Among the guests star-scattered on the grass
>   And in thy joyous errand reach the spot
> Where I made one—turn down an empty glass!
>   FITZGERALD'S *Omar Khayyam*.

To turn-up. To arrive, often unexpectedly; to appear.

Waiting for something to turn up. Expectant that the luck will change, that good fortune will arrive without much effort on one's own part. Mr. Micawber's philosophy of life, in *David Copperfield*.

Turncoat. A renegade; one who deserts his principles or party.

Fable has it that a certain Duke of Saxony, whose dominions were bounded in part by France, hit upon the device of a coat *blue* one side, and *white* the other. When he wished to be thought in the French interest he wore the white outside; otherwise the blue. Whence a Saxon was nicknamed *Emmanuel Turncoat*.

Turnip. Common slang for a large, old-fashioned silver watch.

Turpin. A contemporary of Charlemagne, Archbishop of Rheims from 753 to 794, on whom has been fathered a French chronicle history, written in Latin in the first half of the 11th century. The probable author was a canon of Barcelona. It relates the expedition of Charlemagne to Spain in 777, and his return to France after subduing Navarre and Aragon.

Turret. A small tower, used for decorative purpose, on a building. In a battleship the turret is a circular armoured structure on the deck in which the heavy guns are mounted. By hydraulic or electrical power the turret can be moved round as required. Its under-structure goes to the bottom of the ship where are the magazines. In a tank it is a similar rotating structure, mounted on the hull, containing the main armament and periscope through which the commander may see when all the hatches are shut down.

Tut. A word used in Lincolnshire for a phantom, as the *Spittal Hill Tut. Tom Tut will get you* is a threat to frighten children. *Tut-gotten* is panic-struck.

Tutankhamun (too tăn kà moon'). A Pharaoh who lived in the middle of the 14th century B.C. In the winter of 1922/23 an expedition led by Howard Carter uncovered the burial place in the Valley of the Tombs of the Kings, in the face of the Nile cliffs. Unique treasure of mortuary furniture was found, most of which is now in the Cairo Museum. The mummy in its gorgeous coffin showed that the Pharaoh was little more than eighteen years old at the time of his death.

Tutivillus (tū ti vil' ŭs). The demon of mediæval legend who collects all the words skipped over or mutilated by priests in the celebration of the Mass. These scraps or shreds he deposits in that pit which is said to be paved with "good intentions" never brought to effect.

Tutor. A private teacher; in English universities a Fellow or other college official. He has the direction of the studies of a certain number of undergraduates who are placed under his care for the time they are up at the university. In Law a tutor is the guardian of a minor.

Tuxedo. The American term for a dinner-jacket; so called because it was first taken to U.S.A. from England by Griswold Lorillard, in 1886, and introduced by him at the Tuxedo Club, Tuxedo, N.Y.

Tweed. The origin of this name of a woollen cloth used for garments is to be found in a blunder. It should have been *tweal*, the Scots form of *twill*; but when the Scotch manufacturer sent a consignment to James Locke, of London, in 1826, the name was badly written and mis-read; and as the cloth was made on the banks of the Tweed, *tweed* was accordingly adopted. *Twill*, like *dimity* (*q.v.*), means "two-threaded."

Tweedledum and Tweedledee. Names invented by John Byrom (1692-1763) to satirize two quarrelling schools of musicians between whom the real difference was negligible. Hence used of people whose persons or opinions—are "as like as two peas."

> Some say compared to Bononcini
> That mynheer Handel's but a ninny;
> Others aver that he to Handel
> Is scarcely fit to hold a candle.
> Strange all this difference should be
> 'Twixt Tweedledum and Tweedledee.
>
> J. BYROM.

The Duke of Marlborough and most of the nobility took the side of G. B. Bononcini (d. about 1752), but the Prince of Wales, with Pope and Arbuthnot, was for Handel. *Cp.* GLUCKISTS.

Twelve, Twelfth. Each English archer carries twelve Scotsmen under his girdle. This was a common saying at one time, because the English were unerring archers, and each carried twelve arrows in his belt.

Twelve-note music. A modern system of musical composition in which the twelve notes of the chromatic scale have each exactly the same importance, not being centred round any one tone. By a selected order of tones these are unified for any given composition.

The twelve tables. The earliest code of Roman law, compiled by the Decemviri, and engraved on twelve bronze tablets (Livy, iii, 57; Diodorus, xii, 56).

Twelfth, The. The 12th of August, "St. Grouse's Day"; the first day of grouse-shooting.

Twelfth man. The reserve chosen for a cricket team of eleven, hence, anyone who just misses distinction.

Twelfth Night. January 5th, the eve of Twelfth Day, or the Feast of the Epiphany, twelve days after Christmas, Jan. 6th. Formerly this was a time of great merrymaking, and the games that took place were, with little doubt, a survival of the old Roman *Saturnalia*, which was held at the same season. By the Julian calendar Twelfth Day is Old Christmas Day.

Shakespeare's play of this name (produced in 1602) was so called because it was written for acting at the Twelfth Night festivities; the groundwork of the plot was ultimately drawn—through various sources—from the Italian of Bandello.

Twerp. A slang term of a mildly derogatory implication descriptive of a stupid and contemptible fellow.

Twickenham. The Bard of Twickenham. Alexander Pope (1688-1744), who lived there for thirty years.

Twins, The. A constellation and sign of the zodiac (May 21st to June 21st); representing Castor and Pollux (*q.v.*), the "great twin brethren" of classical mythology.

Twist. Like Oliver Twist, asking for more. Oliver Twist, the workhouse-boy hero of Dickens's novel of that name (1838), astonished the workhouse-master and caused general consternation by once actually asking for more gruel.

To twist it on one. Slang for to swindle one or to bamboozle him to one's own advantage. Also (with allusion to giving the screw another twist), to extract from a person all one can— and a bit over.

Twitcher, Jemmy. A cunning, treacherous highwayman in Gay's *Beggar's Opera*. The name was given about 1765, in a poem by Gray, to John, Lord Sandwich (1718-92), noted for his *liaison* with Miss Ray, who was shot by the Rev. "Captain" Hackman out of jealousy.

See Jemmy Twitcher shambles—stop, stop thief!

Two. The evil principle of Pythagoras. Accordingly the second day of the second month of the year was sacred to Pluto, and was esteemed unlucky.

The two eyes of Greece. Athens and Sparta.

To have two strings to one's bow. *See* BOW.

Two heads are better than one. Outside advice is often very useful. To the saying are sometimes added the words—*or why do folks marry?*

Two is company, three is none. An old saying, much used by lovers; it is given in Heywood's collection of proverbs (1546).

Two may keep counsel—if one of them's dead. A caustic saying expressive of the great difficulty of being *certain* that a secret is not told once it is imparted to someone else. Shakespeare has—

Two may keep counsel when the third's away.
Titus Andronicus, iv, 2.

And in *The Testament of Love*, formerly attributed to Chaucer, is—

For thre may kepe a counsel, if twain be awaie.

Two Gentlemen of Verona, The. Shakespeare's comedy (written certainly before 1598, but not printed till the Folio of 1623) is principally indebted for the story to the pastoral romance of *Diana*, by George of Monte-mayor, a Spaniard, a translation of which by Bartholomew Yonge was in existence in 1582, but not printed till 1598. Other Italian stories, and perhaps Sidney's *Arcadia*, were drawn upon, and the love adventure of Julia resembles that of Viola in *Twelfth Night*.

Twopenny. Often used slightingly of things of very little value.

Tybalt (tib' ălt). Formerly a name commonly given to cats (*cp.* TIBERT, in *Reynard the Fox*); hence the allusions to cats in connexion with Tybalt, one of the Capulet family in Shakespeare's *Romeo and Juliet*. Mercutio says, "Tybalt, you rat-catcher, will you walk?" (iii, 1); and again, when Tybalt asks, "What wouldst thou have with me?" Mercutio answers, "Good king of cats! nothing but one of your nine lives" (iii, 1).

Tyburn (tī' bĕrn). A former tributary of the Thames rising at Hampstead, which gave its name to the district where now stands the Marble Arch, and where public executions formerly took place. Hence **Tyburn tree,** the gallows, **to take a ride to Tyburn,** to go to one's hanging, **Lord of the Manor of Tyburn,** the common hangman, etc.

The site of the gallows is marked by three brass triangles let into the road pavement at the junction of Edgeware Road and Bayswater Road. The last criminal to be hanged there, in 1783, was one Ryland, a forger; after that date executions were carried out at Newgate, until that prison was demolished.

Tycoon (ti koon'). A title of the Shogun (*q.v.*); applied in the U.S.A. to an industrial magnate.

Tyke. *See* TIKE.

Tyler's Insurrection. An armed rebellion of peasants in southern England in 1381, led by Wat Tyler (an Essex man), in consequence of discontent aroused by the Statute of Labourers, and the heavy taxation, especially a poll-tax of three groats to defray the expenses of a war with France. Wat Tyler was slain by Sir William Walworth, the Lord Mayor, at Smithfield, the revolt was crushed, and many of the rebels executed.

Type. Before the introduction of the point system the principal sizes of printing type were:—

Great primer (pron. prim' er), a large, 18-pt. type, $4\frac{1}{4}$ lines to the inch.

Long primer, 10 pt., $7\frac{1}{2}$ lines to the inch.

These were so called from being used for the printing of primers, or prayer-books.

Pica. 12 pt., 6 lines to the inch.

Brevier, 8 pt., $9\frac{1}{2}$ lines to the inch. Many breviaries were printed in this.

Minion, 7 pt., 10 lines to the inch.

A fount of type. *See* LETTER.

In an ordinary fount the proportion of the various letters is usually as follows: —

a	..	8,500	h	..	6,400	o	..	8,000	v	 1,200
b	..	1,600	i	..	8,000	p	..	1,700	w	 2,000
c	..	3,000	j	..	400	q	..	500	x	 400
d	..	4,400	k	..	800	r	..	6,200	y	 2,000
e	..	12,000	l	..	4,000	s	..	8,000	z	 200
f	..	2,500	m	..	3,000	t	..	9,000	,	4,500 ; 800
g	..	1,700	n	..	8,000	u	..	3,400	.	2,000 : 600

Typographical Signs. ' An acute accent. In Greek it indicates a rise in the voice; in French vowel quality; in Spanish stress; in Bohemian and Hungarian a long vowel.

` A grave accent. In Greek indicating a fall of the voice; in French vowel quality, or sometimes a differentiation (as in *la*, *là*); and in English that the accented syllable is to be pronounced (as in *blessèd*).

^ A circumflex; in French usually indicating that an s has been dropped (as *être* for older estre), and that the marked vowel is long.

ˌ under the letter c in French, is called a *cedilla*, and indicated that the *c* (*ç*) is to be pronounced as s. It represents the Greek *zeta* (*z*), which formerly followed the *c* to indicate an s sound.

¨ over the second of two vowels, as in *reëstablish*, denotes that each vowel is to be sounded and is called the *diœresis*, in French, *trema*. In German it is the *umlaut* or *zweipunct* (*two dots*); and denotes a change in the vowel sound, a following vowel (usually *e*) having been dropped.

° over a vowel, is the Scandinavian form of the *umlaut* or *zweipunct* (*see above*).

~ The *tilde* (*q.v.*), used in Spanish, over the *n* (as *Oñoro*) to show that it is pronounced *ny*.

& And; the Tironian Sign, or Ampersand (*qq.v.*).

? The note of interrogation, or query mark; said to have been formed from the first and last letters of Lat. *Quœstio* (question), which were contracted to $\overset{Q}{\circ}$.

! The note of exclamation; representing the Latin *Io* (joy), written vertically $\overset{!}{\circ}$.

' The apostrophe; indicating that a letter (or figure has been omitted, as *don't*, *I'm*; *the rebellion of '98* (for 1798); also marking the possessive case (*John's book*).

*, †, ‡ The asterisk, dagger (or obelisk), and double dagger; used as reference marks, etc. Another reference mark is

⁎ or *⁎* The asterism.

§ The section mark; said to represent the old long initial s's (*ff*) of Lat. *signum sectionis* sign of a section.

☞ An index-hand, called by printers a "fist," to draw attention to a statement.

¶ A blind P (a modification of the initial letter of *paragraph*), marks a new paragraph.

() Called parentheses, and

[] Called brackets, separate some explanatory or collateral matter from the real sequence.

Typhœus (tī fe′ ŭs). A giant of Greek mythology, with a hundred heads, fearful eyes, and a terrible voice. He was the father of the Harpies. Zeus killed him with a thunderbolt, and he lies buried under Mount Etna.

Typhon (tī′ fon). Son of Typhœus. He was so tall that he touched the skies with his head. His offspring were Gorgon, Geryon, Cerberus, and the hydra of Lerne. Like his father, he lies buried under Etna. *See also* SET.

Tyrant. In ancient Greece the *tyrant* was merely the absolute ruler, the *despot*, of a state, and at first the word had no implication of cruelty or what we call *tyranny*. Many of the Greek tyrants were pattern rulers, as Pisistratus and Pericles, of Athens; Periander, of Corinth; Dionysius the Younger, Gelon, and his brother Hiero of Syracuse; Phidion, of Argos, Polycrates, of Samos; etc. The word (*turannos*) soon, however, obtained much the same meaning as it has with us.

A tyrant's vein. A ranting, bullying manner. In the old moralities the tyrants were made to rant, and the loudness of their rant was proportionate to the villainy of their dispositions.

The Thirty Tyrants. The thirty magistrates appointed by Sparta over Athens, at the termination of the Peloponnesian war. This "reign of terror," after one year's continuance, was overthrown by Thrasybulos (403 B.C.).

In the Roman empire those military usurpers who endeavoured, in the reigns of Valerian and Gallienus (253-268), to make themselves independent princes, are also called *the Thirty Tyrants*. The number must be taken with great latitude, as only nineteen are given, and their resemblance to those of Athens is extremely fanciful.

Tyrian Purple. This dye of ancient fame was, properly speaking, a crimson, produced from an animal juice found in the shell-fish *Murex*.

Tyrtæus (tĕr tē′ ŭs). A lame schoolmaster and elegiac poet of Athens who is said to have so inspired the Spartans by his songs that they defeated the Messenians (7th cent. B.C.). The name has hence been given to many martial poets who have urged on their countrymen to deeds of arms and victory.

U

U. The twenty-first letter of the English alphabet; in form a modification of V with which for many centuries it was interchangeable. Words beginning with U and V were (like those in I and J) not separated in English dictionaries till about 1800, and in 16th- and early-17th-century books spellings such as *vpon* and *haue* are the rule rather than the exception. The following from the title-page of *Polymanteia* (Anon., 1595) is a good example of the confusion:—

Polimanteia, or, The meanes . . . to ivdge of the fall of a Commonwealth, against the friuoulous and foolish coniectures of this age. Whereunto is added, a Letter . . . perswading them to a constant vnitie . . . for the defence of our . . . natiue country . . .—Printed by John Legate, Printer to the Vniversitie of Cambridge, 1595.

U and Non-U. A semi-humorous mark of distinction between social classes in England based on the usage of certain words. U is Upper Class, Non-U being Non-Upper Class. It is U to say "luncheon" for what Non-U folk call "lunch"; "napkin" and "serviette," "cycle" and "bike" are samples of this snobism.

U-boat. A German submarine; the term is adapted from the German *Unterseeboot* (underwater vessel).

Ugly Duckling. An unpromising child who develops into a beautiful and admired grownup; from this the term is extended to anything of an unprepossessing nature that may change with time into its very reverse. The phrase is taken from Hans Andersen's story of the ugly duckling that proved to be a cygnet and, to its foster-mother's surprise, grew up into a lovely swan.

Uitlander (oit' lan der). A S. African term for a foreigner—an out-lander. It is particularly applied to white inhabitants of other than Boer nationality, and was a term that aroused violent political feeling at the period of the Anglo-Boer War.

Ukelele (ū ke lā' le). A small 4-stringed instrument shaped like a guitar and used in the South Seas as the "small brother" of the Hawaiian guitar. It enjoyed a vogue in the U.S.A. and Britain in the 1920s.

Ulema (ū lē' má). The learned classes in Mohammedan countries, interpreters of the Koran and the law, from whose numbers are chosen the mollahs, imaums, muftis, cadis, etc. (ministers of religion, doctors of law, and administrators of justice). *Ulema* is the plural of *ulim*, a wise man.

Ulster. The northernmost province of Ireland, which was forfeited to the Crown in James I's reign in consequence of the rebellions of Tyrconnel and Tyrone, and colonized (1609-12) by English and Scottish settlers, who were forbidden to sell land to any Irishman. Since then the Ulstermen (*cp.* ORANGEMEN) have been intensely British and anti-Irish in sentiment and action, and have refused to form part of or have any share in the independent state of Eire.

The long loose overcoat known as an *ulster* is so called because originally made of Ulster frieze.

The Red, or Bloody, Hand of Ulster. The badge of Ulster, a sinister hand, erect, open, and couped at the wrist, gules; also carried as a charge on the coat of arms of baronets of England, Great Britain, and the United Kingdom, in commemoration of the fact that this order was created by James I (1611) with the ostensible object of raising funds for the settlement of Ulster. *See* BARONET.

Legend has it that in an ancient expedition to Ireland, it was given out that whoever first touched the shore should possess the territory which he touched; O'Neill, seeing another boat likely to outstrip his own, cut off his left hand and threw it on the coast. From this O'Neill the princes of Ulster were descended, and the motto of the O'Neills is to this day *Lamh dearg Eirin*, "red hand of Erin."

Ultima Thule. *See* THULE.

Ultimus Romanorum (ŭl' ti mùs rō má nôr' ùm) (Lat). The Last of the Romans. *See* LAST.

Ultor (ŭl' tôr) (Lat., the Avenger). A title given to Mars (*q.v.*) when, after defeating the murderers of Julius Cæsar, Augustus built a temple to him in the Forum at Rome.

Ulysses, or Odysseus (ū lis' ēz, o dis' ūs) ("the hater"). A mythical king of Ithaca, a small rocky island of Greece, one of the leading chieftains of the Greeks in Homer's *Iliad*, and the hero of his *Odyssey* (*q.v.*), represented by Homer as wise, eloquent, and full of artifices.

According to Virgil it was he who suggested the device of the wooden horse through which Troy was ultimately taken.

Ulysses' bow. Only Ulysses could draw his own bow, and he could shoot an arrow through twelve rings. By this sign Penelope recognized her husband after an absence of twenty years.

The bow was prophetic. It belonged at one time to Eurytus of Œchahlia.

Umble Pie. A pie made of umbles—*i.e.* the liver, kidneys, etc., of a deer. Such offal was the perquisite of the keeper, and umble pie was a dish for servants and inferiors.

> The keeper hath the skin, head, umbles, chine, and shoulders.—HOLINSHED: *Chronicle*, i, 204.

This is the origin of our phrase usually rendered "to eat *humble* pie."

Umbrage. (Lat. *umbra*, shade). **To take umbrage.** Originally to feel overshadowed, slighted and hence to take offence.

Umbrella. Used in China in the 11th century B.C., in ancient Babylon and Egypt, and known in England in Anglo-Saxon times, though not commonly in use till the early 18th century, and, apparently, not introduced into Scotland till 1780. Umbrellas are mentioned by Drayton in his *Muses Elizium* (1630)—

> And like umbrellas, with their feathers,
> Shield you in all sorts of weathers.

And Quarles in his *Emblems* (1635) uses the word to signify the Deity hidden in the manhood of Christ—"Nature is made th' umbrella of the Deity" (iv, 14). Another mention is in Swift's *City Shower* (1710), in Gay's *Trivia* (1711), and *The Tatler*, in No. 238 (Oct. 17th. 1710), says:

> The young gentlemen belonging to the Custom House . . . borrowed the umbrella from Wilk's coffeehouse.

Jonas Hanway (1712-86), the Persian traveller, seems to have popularized umbrellas, for his use of one in London to keep off the rain created a disturbance among the chairmen and public coachmen, showing that they were not commonly used in the streets at the time.

Umlaut (um' lout). The change or modification of sound characteristic of certain Germanic languages occasioned when a vowel is influenced by a following vowel. The second or modifying vowel can appear, or it can be replaced by a diaeresis, itself called an umlaut, as Goethe, Göthe; Duerer, Dürer.

U.N. The United Nations. This is the official designation, since the San Francisco meeting of June, 1945, of what had hitherto been known as U.N.O., the United Nations Organization. The preamble of its charter opens:—"We, the peoples of the United Nations, determined to save succeeding generations from the scourge of war . . . and to reaffirm faith in fundamental human rights, in dignity and worth of the human person, in the equal rights of men and women and of nations large and small . . . have resolved to combine our efforts to accomplish these aims."

U.N. formally came into existence October 24th, 1945, with its seat in U.S.A., temporarily at Lake Success, Long Island. Fifty-eight States were signatories to the Charter.

Una (ū' nà). The heroine of the first book of Spenser's *Faerie Queene*, typifying Truth (*Una*, the One).

Uncle Joe. A humorous nickname for Joseph Stalin, President of the U.S.S.R.

Uncle Remus (rē' mús). The old plantation Negro whose quaint and proverbial wisdom, and stories of Brer Rabbit and Brer Fox were related by Joel Chandler Harris (1848-1908) in *Uncle Remus, his Songs and Sayings* (1880), and *Nights with Uncle Remus* (1883).

Uncle Sam. *See* SAM.

Uncle Tom's Cabin. A story by Harriet Beecher Stowe (1811-96) that appeared in 1852. It tells of the sale of a pious and faithful old Negro slave to a bad owner. By its emphasis on the worst sides of negro slavery the book helped in no small degree to arouse the American nation to an understanding of the iniquities of the system. The original of Uncle Tom was a slave subsequently ordained as the Rev. J. Henson. He came to London in 1876 and was presented to Queen Victoria.

Unconscious, The. In psychology the mental processes which the individual cannot bring into consciousness—they are, indeed, often unknown to him.

Uncumber, St., formerly called St. Wilgefortis, a very mythical saint. "Women changed her name" (says Sir Thomas More) "because they reken that for a pecke of oats she will not faile to *uncumber* them of their husbondys." The tradition says that she was one of seven beautiful daughters born at a birth to a queen of Portugal; wishing to lead a single life she prayed that she might have a beard. The prayer was granted; and she was no more cumbered with lovers; but one of them, a prince of Sicily, was so enraged that he had her crucified.

> If a wife were weary of a husband, she offered oats at Poules . . . to St. Uncumber.—MICHAEL WOODE (1554).

Undecimilla. *See* URSULA.

Under-. Under-cover. Working out of sight. **An under-cover agent** is one who pursues his enquiries or work unknown to any but his employer.

Underground. A political or military movement carried on in secret against an oppressor government or an occupying enemy administration. During World War II there were many effectively organized underground movements in all countries occupied by German forces.

Underground Railroad. The route by which runaway slaves were secretly transported through the Northern States to Canada and freedom.

Undertaker. The application of this word to one who carries out funerals—in U.S.A. termed a mortician—dates from the 17th century, though its origin is unknown.

Underwriter. One who engages to buy at a certain prearranged price all the stock in a new company, of a new issue, etc., that is not taken up by the public. **An underwriter at Lloyd's** is one who insures a ship or its merchandise and undertakes other insurance to a stated amount. So called because he writes his name under the policy.

Undine (ŭn dēn′). One of the elemental spirits of Paracelsus (*cp.* SYLPH), the spirit of the waters. She was created without a soul; but had this privilege, that by marrying a mortal and bearing him a child she obtained a soul, and with it all the pains and penalties of the human race. She is the subject of a tale (*Undine*, 1811) by de la Motte Fouqué (1777-1843).

UNESCO. The United Nations Educational, Scientific, and Cultural Organization. Founded in 1945 as a specialized agency of the United Nations, "the purpose of the Organization is to contribute to peace and security by promoting collaboration among the nations through education, science and, culture."

Unfinished Symphony. Schubert's Symphony in B minor, of which only two movements were completed. Other work or disinclination caused the composer to leave unfinished the four movements he had originally designed.

Unfrock. In ecclesiastical parlance, to deprive a priest of his clerical robes and reduce him to lay estate. It is rarely done—so rarely in the R.C. Church that the last case of a solemn unfrocking was in Poland, in 1853, when a priest was publicly degraded before execution for a murder. After his death it was discovered that he had suffered innocently on behalf of another, of whose guilt he knew only under the seal of confession.

Unguem (ŭn′ gwem). **Ad unguem.** To the minutest point. To finish a statue *ad unguem* is to finish it so smoothly and perfectly that when the nail is run over the surface it can detect no imperfection. *See* FINGER (*to have it at one's fingers' ends*.)

Unhinged. I am quite unhinged. My nerves are shaken, my equilibrium of mind is disturbed; I am like a door which has lost one of its hinges.

Unhouseled. *See* UNANELED.

Unicorn (ū′ ni kôrn) (Lat. *unum cornu,* one horn). A mythical and heraldic animal, represented by mediæval writers as having the legs of a buck, the tail of a lion, the head and body of a horse, and a single horn, white at the base, black in the middle, and red at the tip, in the middle of its forehead. The body is white, the head red, and eyes blue. The oldest author that describes it is Ctesias (400 B.C.); the mediæval notions concerning it are well summarized in the following extract:

The unicorn has but one horn in the middle of its forehead. It is the only animal that ventures to attack the elephant; and so sharp is the nail of its foot, that with one blow it can rip the belly of that beast. Hunters can catch the unicorn only by placing a young virgin in his haunts. No sooner does he see the damsel, than he runs towards her, and lies down at her feet, and so suffers himself to be captured by the hunters. The unicorn represents Jesus Christ, who took on Him our nature in the virgin's womb, was betrayed by the Jews, and delivered into the hands of Pontius Pilate. Its one horn signifies the Gospel of Truth.—*Le Bestiaire Divin de Guillaume, Clerc de Normandie* (13th century).

Another popular belief was that the unicorn by dipping its horn into a liquid could detect whether or not it contained poison. In the designs for gold and silver plate made for the Emperor Rudolph II by Ottavio Strada is a cup on which a unicorn stands as if to assay the liquid.

The supporters of the old royal arms of Scotland are two Unicorns; when James VI of Scotland came to reign over England (1603) he brought one of the Unicorns with him, and with it supplanted the Red Dragon which, as representing Wales, was one of the supporters of the English shield, the other being the Lion.

The animosity which existed between the lion and the unicorn referred to by Spenser in his *Faerie Queene* (II, v)—

Like as a lyon, whose imperiall powre
A proud rebellious unicorn defyes—

is allegorical of that which once existed between England and Scotland.

Unilateral. One-sided. In a political sense this term implies action by one party to a treaty or agreement without the consent of the other party or parties involved.

Union. The Union. A short term for *the United States of America*, and (in England) a once familiar euphemism for the workhouse.

Union Jack. The national banner of Great Britain and Ireland. It consists of three united crosses—that of St. George for England, the saltire of St. Andrew for Scotland (added by James I), and the cross of St. Patrick for Ireland (added at the Union in 1801).

The white edging of St. George's cross shows the white field. In the saltire the cross is reversed on each side, showing that the other half of the cross is covered over. The broad white band is the St. Andrew's cross and should be uppermost at the top left-hand corner of the flag. The narrow white edge is the white field of St. Patrick's cross.

The Union Jack is technically described thus:—

The Union Flag shall be azure, the Crosses saltire of St. Andrew and St. Patrick quarterly per saltire, counterchanged, argent and gules, the latter fimbriated of the second, surmounted by the Cross of St. George of the third, fimbriated as the saltire.—*By order of the Council.*

For the word "Jack," *see* JACK.

Unionists. The Liberal and Radical party opposed to Home Rule in Ireland which was formed in 1886, and in 1895 joined the Conservative government; so named by Lord Randolph Churchill. After the formation of the Coalition Ministry in 1915 and, still more, after the granting of Home Rule to Ireland (1914 and 1920), the name tended to become obsolete though the party has never been formally dissolved.

Unitarians. Christians who deny the doctrine of the Trinity, maintaining that God exists in one Person only. Many of the early heretical sects were unitarian in belief though not in name; and at the time of the Reformation Servetus, Hetzer (*Switzerland*), Palæologus, Sega (*Italy*), Flekwyk (*Holland*), the "Holy Maid of Kent" (*England*), Aikenhead (*Scotland*), Catherine Vogel (*Poland*), Dolet (*France*), and hundreds of others were put to death for holding this opinion.

The modern Unitarians in England ascribe their foundation to John Biddle (1615-62), and among the famous men who have belonged to the body are Dr. Samuel Clarke, Joseph Priestley, Dr. Lardner, James Martineau, Sir Edward Bowring, and Joseph Chamberlain.

United Kingdom. The name adopted on January 1st, 1801, when Great Britain and Ireland were united.

United States. The forty-nine States, and one Federal District, composing the Federal Republic. Thirteen of these are original States, and seven were admitted without previous organization as Territories.

The nickname of a United States man is a *Yank*, or *Yankee* (*q.v.*); of the people in the aggregate *Brother Jonathan* (*q.v.*); and of the Government *Uncle Sam. See* SAM.

Most of the States have an official abbreviation and a familiar nickname, as the Cotton State for Alabama, the Apache State, Arizona, etc. The following is a list of the States with their abbreviations and nicknames:—

Alabama (Ala.), Cotton.
Alaska
Arizona (Ariz.), Apache.
Arkansas (Ark.) Wonder.
California (Calif.), Golden.
Colorado (Colo.), Centennial.
Connecticut (Conn.), Nutmeg.
Delaware (Del.), Diamond.
Florida (Fla.), Peninsular.
Georgia (Ga.), Goober, *i.e.* peanut.
Idaho (Id., Ida.), Gem.
Illinois (Ill.), Prairie.
Indiana (Ind.), Hoosier.
Iowa (Ia.), Hawkeye.
Kansas (Kan.), Sunflower.
Kentucky (Ky.), Blue Grass.
Louisiana (La.), Pelican.
Maine (Me.), Pine Tree.
Maryland (Md.), Old Line.
Massachusetts (Mass.), Bay.
Michigan (Mich.), Wolverine.
Minnesota (Minn.),Gopher.
Mississippi (Miss.), Magnolia.
Missouri (Mo.), Show-Me.
Montana (Mont.), Bonanza.
Nebraska (Neb.), Golden rod.
Nevada (Nev.), Sagebrush.
New Hampshire (N.H.), Granite.
New Jersey (N.J.), Garden.
New Mexico (N. Mex.), Sunshine.
New York (N.Y.), Empire.
North Carolina (N.C.), Tar Heel.
North Dakota (N. Dak.), Flickertail.
Ohio, Buckeye.
Oklahoma (Okla.), Sooner.
Oregon (Oreg.), Beaver.
Pennsylvania (Pa.), Keystone.
Rhode Island, (R.I.), Gun Flint.
South Carolina (S.C.), Palmetto.
South Dakota (S. Dak.), Coyote.
Tennessee (Tenn.), Volunteer.
Texas (Tex.), Lone Star.
Utah (Ut.), Mormon.
Vermont (Vt.), Green Mountain.
Virginia (Va.), The Old Dominion.
Washington (Wash.), Evergreen.
West Virginia (W. Va.), Panhandle.
Wisconsin (Wis.), Badger.
Wyoming (Wyo.), Equality.
Dist. of Columbia (D.C.)

Unities, The Dramatic. *See* DRAMATIC.

University. First applied to collegiate societies of learning in the 12th century, because the *universitas literarum* (entire range of literature) was taught in them—*i.e.* arts, theology, law, and physics, still called the "learned" sciences. Greek, Latin, grammar, rhetoric, and poetry are called *humanity studies,* or *humaniores literæ,* meaning "lay" studies in contradistinction to divinity, which is the study of *divine* things.

Unknown Warrior. The body of an unknown, and now unidentifiable, British soldier brought home from one of the battlefields of World War I and "buried among the kings" in Westminster Abbey. Several bodies of unknown soldiers were disinterred at random from battlefields of the Western Front; choice among these was again made at random, and one body was brought back to London to represent in splendid anonymity the 800,000 British warriors who fell in battle. On November 11th, 1920, the body was placed in the nave of the Abbey. Similar tombs are in the National Cemetery at Arlington, Virginia; beneath the Arc de Triomphe in Paris; and in the Unter den Linden, Berlin.

Unmentionables. One of the 19th-century prudish euphemisms for breeches, pantaloons, or trousers.

Corinthians and exquisites from Bond Street, sporting an eye-glass, . . . waiting-men in laced coats and plush unmentionables of yellow, green, blue, red, and all the primary colours.—REV. N. S. WHEATON: *Journal* (1830).

Unmerciful Parliament, The. Another name for the Wonderful Parliament (*q.v.*).

U.N.R.R.A. United Nations Relief and Rehabilitation Administration. An agency set up in U.S.A. in November, 1943, to help victims of World War II in liberated areas. Food, clothing, medicines, fuel, fertilizers, seeds, etc., were distributed by trained personnel and the administration also saw to the repatriation of millions of displaced persons. Its work having been largely completed by June, 1947, the Administration came to an end, passing over certain of its obligations to I.R.O., (International Refugee Organization) of United Nations.

Unrighteous Bible, The. *See* BIBLE, SPECIALLY NAMED.

Untouchables. The lowest caste in India, whose touch was believed to sully a high-caste Hindu. In 1948 such caste distinction was abolished, largely through influence of the teaching of Mahatma Gandhi.

Unwritten Law. Uncodified and unjudicial law which rests for its authority on the supposed right of the individual to take into his own hands the avenging of personal wrongs—especially sexual offences against his womenkind.

Up. The House is up. The business of the day is ended, and members of Parliament may go home.

"Up Guards, and at them!" In his *Fifteen Decisive Battles,* Creasy states that the Duke of Wellington gave this order in the final charge at the battle of Waterloo. It is impossible to say on what he based this odd statement; it was not the Guards, but the 52nd Light Infantry which broke the column of the French Imperial Guard in the final charge.

Up country. Remote from the coast, in the interior. The term, which is common in America and Australia, is sometimes used in the derogatory sense of unsophisticated, or rustic.

Up stage. As a technical theatrical direction this means at the back of the stage, which in many theatres slopes down slightly to the footlights. Colloquially the phrase *up-stage* means aloof, putting on airs of consequence or superiority.

Up State. In the U.S.A. the part of a State furthest north or distant from the coast; the term is used more particularly of the northern parts of New York State.

Upper Ten, The. *See* TEN.

Upanishads (ū păn' i shădz). The oldest speculative literature of the Hindus, a collection of treatises on the nature of man and the universe, forming part of the Vedic writings, the earliest dating from about the 6th century B.C. The name is Sanskrit, and means "a sitting down (at another's feet)," hence "a confidential talk," "esoteric doctrine."

Upset Price. The price at which goods sold by auction are first offered for competition. If no advance is made they fall to the person who made the upset price. *Reserved bid* is virtually the same thing.

Urania (ū rā' ni à). The Muse of Astronomy in Greek mythology, usually represented pointing at a celestial globe with a staff. Milton (*Paradise Lost,* vii, 1-20) makes her the spirit of the loftiest poetry, and calls her "heavenly born" (the name means "the heavenly one") and sister of Wisdom.

> Where was lorn Urania
> When Adonais died? With veiled eyes,
> 'Mid listening Echoes, in her Paradise
> She sate. SHELLEY:
>> *Adonais,* ii.

Uranus (ū' rà nus). In Greek mythology the personification of Heaven; son and husband of Ge (the earth), and father of the Titans, the Cyclops, the Furies, etc. He hated his children and confined them in Tartarus; but they broke out (*see* TITANS) and his son Kronos dethroned him.

The planet **Uranus** was discovered in 1781 by Herschell, and named by him *Georgium Sidus* in honour of George III. Its four satellites are named *Ariel*, *Umbriel*, *Titania*, and *Oberon*.

Urbanists. *See* FRANCISCANS.

Urbi et Orbi (er′ bī et ôr′ bī) (Lat., To the city [Rome] and the world). A phrase applied to the solemn blessing publicly given by the pope from the balcony of St. Peter's on special occasions, such as his election. The custom fell into abeyance after 1870 but at his election on February 22nd, 1922, Pope Pius XI gave the blessing Urbi et Orbi from the façade of St. Peter's.

Urdu (ĕr′ dū). One of the most important dialects of India, spoken by the Mohammedans; so named from Hindu *urdu-zaban*, the language of the camp.

Ur-Hamlet. *See* HAMLET.

Uriah (ū rī′ à). **Letter of Uriah.** A treacherous letter, importing friendship but in reality a death warrant. (*See II Sam*. xi, 15.)

Ursa Major. The Great Bear, or Charles's Wain (*q.v.*), the most conspicuous of the northern constellations.

The legend is that Calisto, daughter of Lycaon, was violated by Jupiter. Juno changed her into a bear, and Jupiter placed her among the stars that she might be more under his protection. Homer calls it *Arktos*, the Bear, and *Hamaxa*, the Wagon. The Romans called it *Ursa*, the Bear, and *Septemtriones*, the Seven Ploughing Oxen; whence *Septentrionalis* came to signify the north.

Boswell's father used to call Dr. Johnson *Ursa Major*.

Ursa Minor. The Little Bear; the northern constellation known also as *Cynosura*, or "Dog's tail," from its circular sweep. The Pole Star is *a* in the tail. *See* CYNOSURE.

Ursulines. An order of nuns founded by St. Angela Merici of Brescia about 1537, so called from their patron saint, St. Ursula. The chief work of the order is the education of girls.

Usher. From Fr. *huissier*, a door-keeper.

U.S.S.R. The initials of Union of Soviet Socialist Republics, in Russian S.S.S.R. (Soyuz Sovetskikh Sotsialisticheskickh Respublik), the government of Russia and Russian Asia that came into being after the revolution of 1917.

Utility. The name given during and after World War II to articles of wear, etc., the quality of which was sponsored by the Government. Utility goods were sold to the public at officially controlled prices.

Utilitarianism. The ethical doctrine that actions are right in proportion to their usefulness or as they tend to promote happiness; the doctrine that the end and criterion of public action is "the greatest happiness of the greatest number."

John Stuart Mill coined the word; but Jeremy Bentham, the official founder of the school, employed the word "Utility" to signify the doctrine which makes "the happiness of man" the one and only measure of right and wrong.

Utopia. Nowhere (Gr. *ou*, not, *topos*, a place). The name given by Sir Thomas More to the imaginary island in his political romance of the same name (1516), where everything is perfect— the laws, the morals, the politics, etc., and in which the evils of existing laws, etc., are shown by contrast. *See* COMMONWEALTHS, IDEAL.

This island has given us the adjective *Utopian*, applied to any highly desirable but impracticable scheme.

Rabelais (in Bk. II, ch. xxiv) sends Pantagruel and his companions to Utopia, where they find the citizens of its capital, Amaurot, most hospitable.

Utraquists (Lat. *utraque specie*, in both kinds). Another name for the Calixtines (*q.v.*), so called because they insisted that both the elements should be administered to all communicants in the Eucharist.

Utter and Inner Barristers. An *utter* or *outer barrister* means (in some cases at least) a full-fledged barrister, one licensed to practise. An *inner barrister* means a student.

Uzziel. One of the principal angels of rabbinical angelology, the name meaning "Strength of God." He was next in command to Gabriel, and in Milton's *Paradise Lost* (iv, 782) is commanded by Gabriel to "coast the south with strictest watch."

V

V. The twenty-second letter of the alphabet, formerly sharing its form with U (*q.v.*).

In the Roman notation it stands for 5, and represents ideographically the four fingers and thumb with the latter extended.

V-for Victory. On January 14th, 1941, M. Victor de Lavaleye, a member of the exiled Belgian government in London, proposed in a broadcast to Belgium that the letter V should be used as a simple substitute for the letters R.A.F. which were being chalked up on walls, etc., in Belgium. V had the advantage of standing for the word *Victory* in all Western European languages. The plan was immediately adopted and it soon became the most ambitious propaganda campaign of World War II. The Morse Code V (. . .—) was featured in every B.B.C. broadcast to Europe; this was followed by the use of the opening bar of Beethoven's 5th Symphony which has the same rhythm. "Colonel Britton" (Douglas E. Ritchie, director of the B.B.C. European news service) was responsible for this extensive and most powerful diffusion of the V-sign propaganda, which stiffened resistance and gave hope to the many thousands in bondage to the Germans. Winston Churchill popularized the sign of two up-raised fingers outspread in the form of a V.

V-1. Jet-propelled robot plane bomb sent against Britain by the Germans, June-August, 1944; subsequently sent by them against Antwerp. V = *Vergeltungswaffe* (Revenge weapon).

V-2. Jet-propelled rocket bomb, projected against England by the Germans in autumn, 1944.

V. D. M. I. Æ. Lat. *Verbum Dei manet in æternum, i.e.* the word of God endureth for ever. The inscription on the liveries of the servants of the Duke of Saxony and Landgrave of Hesse, the Lutheran princes, at the Diet of Spires in 1526.

V.E. Day. The end of hostilities in Europe after World War II, May 8th, 1945.

V.J. Day. The end of hostilities in the Far East, August 15th, 1945.

V-Mail (World War II). Reduced photostats of letters to and from soldiers overseas and their families, to save shipping space.

Vacuum (Lat. *vacare*, to be empty). A space from which air has been expelled. Descartes remarked, "If a vacuum could be effected in a vessel, the sides would be pressed into contact."

Nature abhors a vacuum. Galileo's way of accounting for the rise of water in pumps. *See* TORRICELLI.

Vagabond. An idle, disreputable person who wanders about from place to place without any settled home (late Lat. *vagabundas*, from *vagari*, to wander). Under the Vagrancy Act (1824) the term is applied to such as sleep out without visible means of subsistence. *Cp.* ROGUE.

Valentine. Valentine, St. A priest of Rome who was imprisoned for succouring persecuted Christians. He became a convert himself, and although he restored the sight of his gaoler's blind daughter he was martyred by being clubbed to death (February 14th, 269).

St. Valentine's Day. February 14th, the day when, according to ancient tradition, the birds choose their mates for the year. Chaucer refers to this (*Parliament of Foules*, 309), as also does Shakespeare:—

> Good morrow, friends! St. Valentine is past;
> Begin these wood-birds but to couple now?
> > *Midsummer Night's Dream*, iv, 1.

It was an old custom in England to draw lots for lovers on this day, the person drawn being the drawer's *valentine*, and given a present, sometimes of an expensive kind, but oftener of a pair of gloves. The valentine is now frequently represented by a greeting card of a sentimental, humorous, or merely vulgar character.

> If I stood affected that way [*i.e.* to marriage] I would choose my wife as men do Valentines—blindfold or draw cuts for them; for so I shall not be deceived in the choosing.—CHAPMAN: *Monsieur d'Olive*, I (1605).

The custom is said to have had its origin in a pagan practice connected with the worship of Juno on or about this day.

Valentine and Orson. An old French romance, connected with the Alexander cycle.

The heroes—from whom it is named—were the twin sons of Bellisant, sister of King Pepin and Alexander, and were born in a forest near Orleans. Orson (q.v.) was carried off by a bear, and became a wild man. While the mother was searching for him Valentine was carried off by his uncle, the king. Each had many adventures, but all ended happily, and Valentine married Clerimond, sister of the Green Knight, while Orson married a daughter of the Duke of Aquitaine.

Valhalla. In Scandinavian mythology, the hall in the celestial regions whither the souls of heroes slain in battle were borne by the Valkyries, to spend eternity in joy and feasting (valr, the slain, and hall).

Hence the name is applied to buildings, such as Westminster Abbey, used as the last resting-place of a nation's great men.

Valkyries, The (văl kir′ iz, văl kīr′ iz, văl′ ki riz) (Old Norse, The Choosers of the Slain). The twelve nymphs of Valhalla, who, mounted on swift horses, and holding drawn swords, rushed into the mêlée of battle and selected those destined to death. These heroes they conducted to Valhalla, where they waited upon them and served them with mead and ale in the skulls of the vanquished. The chief were Mista, Sangrida, and Hilda.

Vallary Crown. The same as a mural crown (see under CROWN).

Valley Forge. A village in south Pennsylvania where George Washington set up the winter quarters of his army, amid great privations, in the campaign of 1777-78.

Vamoose (và moos′). A slang word (deriving from the Spanish vamos, let us go) meaning to decamp, to make off hurriedly.

Vamp. To vamp up an old story, to refurbish it; to vamp an accompaniment to a song, to improvise as one goes along.

To vamp is properly to put new uppers to old boots; and vamps were short hose covering the feet and ankles (Fr. avant-pied, the forepart of the foot).

Another verb **To vamp** (derived from Vampire (q.v.) means to flirt outrageously or allure with the intent of gaining some personal end.

Vampire. A fabulous being, supposed to be the ghost of a heretic, excommunicated person, or criminal, that returns to the world at night in the guise of a monstrous bat and sucks the blood of sleeping persons who, usually, become vampires themselves.

> But first on earth, as vampire sent,
> Thy corse shall from the tomb be rent,
> Then ghastly haunt thy native place
> And suck the blood of all thy race.
>
> BYRON: The Giaour.

The word is applied to one who preys upon his fellows—a "blood-sucker."

One of the classics of English horror-romances, Dracula (1897) by Bram Stoker was centred on vampires.

Vandals. A Teutonic race from the Baltic (allied to the Wends, i.e. Wanderers), which in the 5th century A.D. ravaged Gaul and, under Genseric, captured Rome and despoiled it of its treasures of art, literature, and civilization generally.

The name is hence applied to those who wilfully or ignorantly destroy works of art, etc.

Vandyke (văn dīk′). To scallop an edge after the fashion of the collars painted by Van Dyck in the reign of Charles I. The scalloped edges are said to be vandyked.

Vandyke beard. A pointed beard such as those frequently shown in Van Dyck's portraits, especially of Charles I.

Vanity Fair. In Bunyan's Pilgrim's Progress, a fair established by Beelzebub, Apollyon, and Legion, in the town of Vanity, and lasting all the year round. Here were sold houses, lands, trades, places, honours, preferments, titles, countries, kingdoms, lusts, pleasures, and delights of all sorts.

Thackeray adopted the name for the title of his novel (1847) satirizing the weaknesses and follies of human nature.

Varuna. The Hindu Neptune. He is represented as an old man rising on a sea monster, with a club in one hand and a rope in the other. In the Vedic hymns he is the night sky, and Mitra the day sky. Varuna is said to set free the "waters of the clouds."

Vassal (văs′ ăl). A man in the feudal system who held his land with the obligation of rendering military service to his superior: hence the term was extended to include a servant or even a slave.

Vathek (văth′ ek). The hero of Beckford's oriental romance of the same name (1784). The ninth caliph of the Abbasside dynasty, he is a haughty, effeminate monarch, induced by a malignant genius to commit all sorts of crimes. He abjures his faith, and offers allegiance to Eblis, under the hope of obtaining the throne of the pre-Adamite sultans. This he gained, only to find that it was a place of torture and that he was doomed to remain in it for ever.

Vatican (văt′ i kån). The palace of the Pope; so called because it stands on the *Vaticanus Mons* (Vatican Hill) of ancient Rome, which got its name through being the headquarters of the *vaticinatores*, or soothsayers.

The City of the Vatican is the area of Rome recognized by the Treaty of the Lateran (1929) as constituting the territorial extent of the temporal power of the Holy See. Strictly speaking, the Vatican consists of the Papal palace, the court and garden of Belvidere, the library, and the museum, the Piazza of St. Peter, and contiguous buildings, in all an area of just under a square mile. Its population is about 500, of whom a number are clerics, and all male adults are in some way engaged in the immediate service of the Church. Under the pope it is governed by a layman.

The Council of the Vatican. The twenty-first Œcumenical Council (*q.v.*), opened at the Vatican in 1870 under Pius IX and not yet officially concluded.

Vaudeville (vōd′ vil). A corruption of *Val de Vire*, or in O.Fr. *Vau de Vire*, the native valley of Oliver Basselin, a Norman poet (d. 1418), author of convivial songs, which he called after the name of his birthplace. It is now applied to a variety entertainment.

Vaudois. See WALDENSIANS (*cp.* VOODOO).

Vauxhall (vawks′ awl). A part of Lambeth, London; so called from *Falkes* (or *Fulkes*) de Breauté, who was lord of the manor in the early 13th century.

Vauxhall Gardens. A very popular pleasure resort for Londoners, from 1661, when it was opened, till 1859. Pepys, who calls it Fox Hall, says the entertainments there are "mighty divertising"; and for the next two centuries its attractions and diversions furnished many writers and artists with incidents and scenes for their works.

Vedas or **Vedams.** The four sacred books of the Brahmans, comprising (1) the *Rig* or *Rish Veda*; (2) *Yajur Veda*; (3) the *Sama Veda*; and (4) the *Atharva Veda*. The first consists of prayers and hymns in verse, the second of prayers in prose, the third of prayers for chanting, and the fourth of formulas for consecration, imprecation, expiation, etc.

The word *Veda* means knowledge.

Vegetarianism. A movement which aims at making vegetable foods the sole diet of human beings. It began about 1850, although it had had many isolated adherents or sects through-out the preceding centuries. Strict vegetarians

(sometimes called Vegas) abstain from all food which comes from animals, such as milk, eggs, butter, cheese, etc. Akin to vegetarians are fruitarians who maintain life solely on fruit.

Velocipede (ve los′i pēd). An early form of bicycle, introduced about 1819. It consisted of two wheels connected by a bar on which was the rider's seat. Thus placed, with his feet touching the ground, he propelled himself along by the alternate thrust of each foot upon the ground. A later development was the introduction of treadles operating directly on cranks on the axle of the front wheel.

Vendée, War of La (la von′ dā). The rising of royalists against the French Republic in 1793-5 in La Vendée, a Department of western France, and Brittany. It was followed by the War of the Chouans (*see* CHOUAN), which was finally suppressed by Napoleon in 1800.

Vendetta (ven det′ à) (Lat. *vindicta*, revenge). The blood-feud, or duty of the nearest kin of a murdered man to kill the murderer. It prevailed in Corsica, Sicily, Sardinia, and Calabria, and in principle is not yet extinct.

Venerable (Lat. *venerabilis*, worthy of honour). The title applied to archdeacons in formally addressing them ("The Venerable the Archdeacon of Barset," or "The Venerable Archdeacon Brown"); and also, in the Roman Catholic Church, the title of one who has attained the first of the three degrees of canonization.

It specially belongs to Bede—the Venerable Bede—the monk of Jarrow, an English ecclesiastical historian (d. 735), and to William of Champeaux (d. 1121), the French scholastic philosopher and opponent of Abelard.

Veni, vidi, vici (Lat., "I came, I saw, I conquered"). According to Plutarch it vas thus that Julius Cæsar announced to his friend Amintius his victory at Zela (47 B.C.), in Asia Minor, over Pharnaces, son of Mithridates, who had rendered aid to Pompey.

Suetonius, however, says that the words were displayed before his title after his victories in Pontus, and does not ascribe them to Cæsar himself.

They are often used as an example of laconism, extreme concision.

Venial Sin. One that may be pardoned; one that does not forfeit grace. In the Catholic Church sins are of two sorts, *mortal* and *venial* (Lat. *venia*, grace, pardon). *See Matt*, xii, 31.

Venice Glass. The drinking-glasses of the Middle Ages, made at Venice, were said to break into shivers if poison were put into them.

> Doge: 'Tis said that our Venetian crystal has
> Such pure antipathy to poison, as
> To burst, if aught of venom touches it.
> BYRON: *The Two Foscari*, v, i.

Venice glass, from its excellency, became a synonym for *perfection*.

Venison. Anything taken in hunting or by the chase. Hence Isaac bids Esau to go and get *venison* such as he loved (*Gen.* xxvii, 3), meaning the wild kid. The word is the Latin *venatio*, hunting, but is now restricted to the flesh of deer.

Venom. The venom is in the tail. The real difficulty is the conclusion. The allusion is to the scorpion, which has a sting in its tail.

Ventose (von′ tōz) (Fr., windy). The sixth month of the French Revolutionary calendar. February 19th to March 20th.

Ventriloquism. The trick of producing vocal sounds so that they appear to come, not from the person producing them, but from some other quarter. So called from Lat. *venter*, belly, *loqui*, to speak (speaking from the belly), with the erroneous notion that the voice of the *ventriloquist* proceeded from his stomach.

Venus (vē′ nus). The Roman goddess of beauty and sensual love, identified with the Aphrodite (*q.v.*) of the Greeks. She is said in some accounts to have sprung from the foam of the sea, but in others to have been the daughter of Jupiter and Dione. Vulcan was her husband, but she had amours with Mars and many other gods and demi-gods; by Mercury she was the mother of Cupid, and by the hero Anchises the mother of Æneas, through whom she was regarded by the Romans as the foundress of their race. Her chief festival was April 1st (*see* VENUS VERTICORDIA, *below*).

Her name is given to the second planet from the sun, and in astrology "signifieth white men or browne . . . joyfull, laughter, liberall, pleasers, dauncers, entertayners of women, players, perfumers, musitions, messengers of love."

> Venus loveth ryot and dispense.
> CHAUCER: *Wife of Bath's Prol.*, 700.

By the alchemists *copper* was designated *Venus*, probably because mirrors were anciently made of copper. A mirror is still the astronomical symbol of the planet Venus.

The best cast at dice (three sixes) used to be called *Venus*, and the worst (three aces) *Canis* (dog); hence the phrase, "My Venus has turned out a whelp," equivalent to "all my swans are geese."

Venus Anadyomene. Venus rising from the sea, accompanied by dolphins. The name is given to the famous lost painting by Apelles, and to that by Botticelli in the Accademia delle Belle Arti at Florence.

Venus Callipyge (Gr., with the beautiful buttocks). The name given to a late Greek statue in the Museo Nazionale at Naples. There is no real ground for connecting the statue with Venus.

Venus de Medici. A famous statue, since 1860 in the Uffizzi Gallery, Florence, ranking as a canon of female beauty. It is supposed to date from the time of Augustus, and was dug up in the 17th century in the villa of Hadrian, near Tivoli, in eleven pieces. It was kept in the Medici Palace at Rome till its removal to Florence by Cosimo III.

Venus of Milo, or **Melos.** This statue, with three of Hermes, was discovered in 1820 by Admiral Dumont in Milo or Melos, one of the Greek islands. It dates from about 400 B.C., and is probably the finest single work of ancient art extant. It now stands in the Louvre.

Venus Victrix. Venus, as goddess of victory, represented on numerous Roman coins.

Venusberg. The Horselberg, or mountain of delight and love, situated between Eisenach and Gotha, in the caverns of which, according to mediæval German legend, the Lady Venus held her court. Human beings were occasionally permitted to visit her, as Heinrich von Limburg did, and the noble Tannhäuser (*q.v.*); but as such persons ran the risk of eternal perdition, Eckhardt the Faithful, who sat before the gate, failed not to warn them against entering.

Verdant Green. An excessively "green" or unsophisticated young man. The character was epitomized in the book of this name (1860) by "Cuthbert Bede" (Rev. Edward Bradley). Verdant's adventures at Oxford, whither he goes as a very green young undergraduate, the victim of endless practical jokes and impostures, make an entertaining and enlightening commentary on life at the University in the 1850s.

Verderer. In English forest law an official of the Crown having jurisdiction in the Royal Forests, with especial charge of the trees and undergrowth.

Veronica, St. (ve ron′ i kà). A late mediæval legend says that a maiden handed her handker chief to our Lord on His way to Calvary. H wiped the sweat from His brow, return the handkerchief to the owner, and went The handkerchief was found to bear a p likeness of the Saviour, and was called *Vera-Icon* (true likeness); the maiden became *St. Veronica*. It is one of the relics preserved in St. Peter's, Rome. In Spanish bull-fighting the most classic movement with the cape is called the Veronica, the cape being swung so slowly before the face of the charging bull that it resembles St. Veronica's wiping of the Holy Face.

Vers de société (Fr., Society verse). Light poetry of a witty or fanciful kind, generally with a slight vein of social satire running through it.

Versailles (vâr sī'). The great palace built by Louis XIV in the town of that name to the NNW. of Paris. The palace had been actually begun by Louis XIII, but the great enlargement was started in 1661 that made of Versailles the greatest palace in Europe. The splendours of the palace and grounds and the part it has played in French history make brief description impossible. Some of the royal and other apartments are kept in their original condition, but much of the palace is used as a national museum of French history. The first constitution of Germany was signed in the famous Galerie des Glaces in 1871, when the Prussians were in occupation. And in the same hall was also drawn up **The Treaty of Versailles,** the treaty made after World War I between the Allied states, 26 in number, on the one part, and Germany on the other. Its articles included the formation of the League of Nations, the cession of Alsace and Lorraine to France, of Posen and West Prussia to Poland, the prohibition of Germany possessing submarines, a military, naval, or air force beyond certain limits, and the occupation of the country for a certain period by Allied troops. As time went on most of these conditions were evaded, but the injustice of the Treaty of Versailles formed a never-failing subject for Adolf Hitler's fury and invective. The Treaty was signed on June 28th, 1919 and ratified on January 10th, 1920. China declined to sign, and the U.S.A. senate rejected it.

Vert (vĕrt). The heraldic (from French) term for *green*, said to signify love, joy, and abundance; in engravings it is indicated by lines running diagonally across the shield from right to left.

Vertumnus (vĕr tŭm' nus). The ancient Roman god of the seasons, and the deity presiding over gardens and orchards. He was the husband of Pomona. August 12th was his festival.

Vervain (vĕr' vān). Called "holy herb," from use in ancient sacred rites. Also called ons' grass," "Juno's tears," and "simpler's joy."

Supposed to cure scrofula, the bite of rabid animals, to arrest the diffusion of poison, to avert antipathies, to conciliate friendships, and to be a pledge of mutual good faith; hence it was anciently worn by heralds and ambassadors.

Verbena is its botanical name.

Vesica Piscis (ves' i ka pis' is) (Lat., fish-bladder). The ovoidal frame or glory which, in the 12th century, was much used, especially in painted windows, to surround pictures of the Virgin Mary and of our Lord. It is meant to represent a fish, from the anagram ICHTHUS (*q.v.*).

Vespers. The sixth of the seven canonical hours in the Greek and Roman Churches; sometimes also used of the Evening Service in the English Church. From Lat. *vesperus*, the evening, cognate with *Hesperus* (*q.v.*), Gr. *Hesperos*, the evening star.

Vesta. The virgin goddess of the hearth in Roman mythology, corresponding to the Greek *Hestia*, one of the twelve great Olympians. She was custodian of the sacred fire brought by Æneas from Troy, which was never permitted to go out lest a national calamity should follow. Wax matches are named from her.

Vestals. The six spotless virgins who tended the sacred fire brought by Æneas from Troy and preserved by the state in a sanctuary in the Forum at Rome. They were subjected to very severe discipline, and in the event of losing their virginity were buried alive.

Other duties of the Vestal Virgins were to prepare from the first fruits of the May harvest the sacrificial meal for the Lupercalia, the Vestalia, and the Ides of September.

The word *vestal* has been figuratively applied to any woman of spotless chastity. Thus, Shakespeare calls Elizabeth I—

A fair vestal, throned by the west.
Midsummer Night's Dream, ii, 1.

See also VENUS VERTICORDIA.

Veteran. Whereas in Britain this word is applied only to soldiers, etc., who have had long service under arms, in the U.S.A. one who has had any service or experience in some field of warfare, however brief or casual, is termed a veteran.

Veto (vē' tō) (Lat., I forbid). Louis XVI and Marie Antoinette were called *Monsieur* and *Madame Veto* by the Republicans, because the Constituent Assembly (1791) allowed the king to have the power of putting his veto upon any decree submitted to him and he abused it.

The power exercised by the head of a state to annul or negative a law or ordinance passed by a lower body; in brief, the right to say "No."

Via. A way (Lat. *via*). Our use of the word, as in *I'll go via Chester, i.e.* "by way of Chester," is *via*, the ablative of *via*.

Via Appia. The Appian Way (*q.v.*).

Via Dolorosa. The way our Lord went from the Mount of Olives to Golgotha, about a mile in length.

Via Lactea. The Milky Way (*q.v.*).

Via Sacra, the street in ancient Rome where Romulus and Tatius (the Sabine) swore mutual alliance. It does not mean the "holy street," but the "street of the oath."

Vial. Vials of wrath. Vengeance, the execution of wrath on the wicked. The allusion is to the seven angels who pour out upon the earth their vials full of wrath (*Rev.* xvi).

Viaticum (Lat.). The Eucharist administered to the dying. The word means "provision for a journey" and its application is obvious.

Vicar. A parish priest who receives a stipend, the tithes belonging to a chapter, religious house, layman, etc. (*cp.* CLERICAL TITLES). At the Reformation the rectorial offices and tithes of many parishes hitherto administered by the religious orders, were granted to laymen, colleges, etc., who were under obligation of appointing vicars to perform the sacred offices.

Lay vicar. A cathedral officer who sings those portions of the liturgy not reserved for the clergy. Formerly called a *clerk vicar.*

The Vicar of Bray. A semi-legendary vicar of Bray, Berkshire, who, between 1520 and 1560, was twice a Papist and twice a Protestant in successive reigns. His name has been given as Symonds, Alleyne, and Pendelton, and his date transferred to the time of Charles II. Historically nothing is known of him; the well-known song is said to have been written in Restoration times by an officer in Colonel Fuller's regiment.

Brome says of Simon Alleyn that he "lived in the reigns of Henry VIII, Edward VI, Mary, and Elizabeth. In the first two reigns he was Protestant, in Mary's reign he turned Papist, and in the next reign recanted—being resolved, whoever was king, to die Vicar of Bray."

The Vicar of Christ. A title given to the Pope, in allusion to his claim to be the representative of Christ on earth.

The Vicar of Hell. A name playfully given by Henry VIII to John Skelton, his "poet laureate," perhaps because Skelton was rector of Diss, in Norfolk, the pun being on Dis (*q.v.*). Milton refers to the story in his *Areopagitica:*—

I name not him for posterity's sake, whom Henry the Eighth named in merriment his vicar of hell.

Vice. The buffoon in the old English moralities. He wore a cap with ass's ears, and was generally named after some particular vice, as Gluttony, Pride, etc.

Vice versa (vī' si vĕr' sả) (Lat., *vicis*, change, *versa*, turned). The reverse; the terms of the case being reversed.

Vichy (vish' i). A little town in the Department of Allier, in central France, formerly fashionable on account of its thermal and medicinal springs. The name of Vichy will, however, be remembered in future as the seat of government set up by Marshal Pétain after the fall of France, in June, 1940. By the armistice of July 10th France was divided into two zones, one occupied by the Germans, the other unoccupied and a totalitarian state under the rule of Pétain. On the landing of the Allies in North Africa in the autumn of 1942 the Germans declared the whole country to be in danger of invasion and seized the excuse to occupy the *soi-disant* independent zone of France.

Vicious Circle. A chain of circumstances, in which the solving of a problem creates a new problem which makes the original problem more difficult of solution.

In logic, the fallacy of proving one statement by another which itself rests on the first for proof.

Victory Medal. A bronze medal with a double rainbow ribbon, awarded to Allied soldiers who served in a field of war in World War I.

Victrola (U.S.A.). Although the trade name of a certain make of phonograph (gramophone) the word is frequently used for any type of that instrument.

View Holloa. The shout of huntsmen when a fox breaks cover = "Gone away!" *Cp.* SOHO; TALLY-HO.

Vigilance Committee. A privately formed body of citizens taking upon themselves to assist in the maintenance of law and order in their town. The Southern States citizens sometimes form themselves into Vigilance Committees for the purpose of intimidating Negroes. During the Civil War (1861-65) they also strove to suppress the activities of loyalists to the Northern cause. Members of these committees are called *Vigilantes.*

Vignette (vi nyet). An engraving, especially on the title-page of a book, that is not enclosed within a border; properly, a likeness having a border of vine-leaves round it (Fr., little vine, tendril).

Viking (vik' ing, vī' king). A Norse pirate of about the 8th to 10th centuries A.D.; probably so called from Icel. *vig.* war, cognate with Lat. *vincere*, to conquer. The word is not connected with *king*. There were *sea-kings*, sometimes, but erroneously, called "vikings," connected with royal blood, and having small dominions on the coast, who were often *vikingr* or vikings, but the reverse is not true that every *viking* or pirate was a sea-king.

Villain means simply one attached to a villa or farm (late Lat. *villanus*, a farm-servant, from *villa*, a farm). In feudal times the lord was the great landowner, and under him were a host of tenants called *villains* (sometimes spelt *villein*, to differentiate this from the modern meaning). The highest class of villains were called *regardant*, and were annexed to the manor; then came the *Caliberti* or *Bures*, who were privileged vassals; then the *Bordarii* or cottagers (A.S. *bord*, a cottage), who rendered certain menial offices to their lord for rent; then the *Coscets*, *Cottarii*, and *Cotmanni*, who paid partly in produce and partly in menial service; and, lastly, the *villains in gross*, who were annexed to the person of the lord, and might be sold or transferred as chattels. The notion of wickedness and worthlessness associated with the word is simply the effect of aristocratic pride and exclusiveness.

I am no villain; I am the youngest son of Sir Rowland de Boys; he was my father, and he is thrice a villain that says such a father begot villains.—*As You Like It*, i, 1.

Vim. Slang for energy, force, "go." The accusative of Lat. *vis*, strength.

Vin. (Fr., wine).

Vin de Goutte. The last pressing of grapes, yielding an inferior wine.

Vin de Paille. A sweet wine from the Jura, made from grapes dried on straw before pressing.

Vin Gris. A cheap wine made in eastern France by mixing red and white grapes.

Vin ordinaire. A cheap wine served in restaurants when no style or mark is asked for.

Vin Rosé. Pink wine made in France by one of three methods; by mixing red and white grapes; by colouring white wine with cochineal; or from black grapes the skins of which are not left to ferment in the wine.

Vintage. Gathering of grapes. The year in which a certain wine was made. Since good vintages are more generally remembered, "a vintage year" has become a phrase descriptive of a year notable in any walk of life.

Vinaigret (vin ā gret'). A small bottle, usually delicately ornamented, containing aromatic vinegar, smelling salts, etc., in use among women when fainting was a more common expression of emotion.

Vincentian. A Lazarist (*q.v.*), a member of the order of Lazarites, founded by St. Vincent de Paul in the 17th century.

Vine. The Rabbis say that the fiend buried a lion, a lamb, and a hog at the foot of the first vine planted by Noah; and that hence men receive from wine ferocity, mildness, or wallowing in the mire.

Vinegar. Livy tells us that when Hannibal led his army over the Alps to enter Rome he used vinegar to dissolve the snow, and make the march less slippery. Nepos has left a short memoir of Hannibal, but says nothing about the vinegar. (Livy, 59 B.C. to A.D. 17; Nepos about the same time; Hannibal, 247-183 B.C.).

Vinland. The name given in the old Norse Sagas to a portion of the coast of North America discovered by wanderers from Denmark or Iceland about the opening of the 11th century. There have been many conjectures as to the locality, but scholars incline to the opinion that it was in or near Mount Hope Bay, Rhode Island, and got its old name because of grape-vines found growing there.

Vino (vī' nō). **In vino veritas** (Lat.). In wine is truth, meaning when persons are more or less intoxicated they utter many things they would at other times conceal or disguise.

Vintry Ward (London). So called from the site occupied by the Vintners or wine-merchants from Bordeaux, who anciently settled on this part of the Thames bank. They landed their wines here, and, till the 28th Edw. I, were obliged to sell what they landed within forty days.

Vinum Theologicum (vī' num thē ō loj' i kum). An old term for the best wine obtainable. Holinshed (i, 282) says it was so called because religious men would be sure "neither to drinke nor be served of the worst, or such as was anie waies vined by the vintner; naie, the merchant would have thought that his soule would have gone streightwaie to the devil if he would have served them with other than the best."

Violet. A flower, nowadays usually taken as the type of modesty, but fabled by the ancients to have sprung from the blood of the boaster Ajax.

The colour indicates the *love of truth* and the *truth of love*. For ecclesiastical and symbolical uses, *see* COLOURS.

In "flower language" the violet is emblematical of *innocence*, and Ophelia says in *Hamlet* that the King, the Queen, and even Hamlet himself, now he has killed Polonius, are unworthy of this symbol.

V.I.P. Very Important Person; a phrase originated in World War II to indicate one whose importance was considered such as to entitle him to preferential treatment in travelling, etc.

Viper (U.S.A.). A slang term for a smoker of marijuana.

Virago (vi ra' gō). Literally a man-like woman, but a term usually employed to designate a turbulent or scolding shrew.

Virgil (vĕr' jil). The greatest poet of ancient Rome, Publius Virgilius Maro (70-19 B.C.), born near Mantua (hence called *The Mantuan Swan*), a master of epic, didactic, and idyllic poetry. His chief works are the *Æneid*, the *Eclogues* or *Bucolics*, and the *Georgics*. From the *Æneid* grammarians illustrated their rules and rhetoricians selected the subjects of their declamations; and even Christians looked on the poet as half inspired; hence the use of his poems in divination. *See* SORTES.

In the Middle Ages Virgil came to be represented as a magician and enchanter, and it is this traditional character that furnishes Dante with his conception of making Virgil, as the personification of human wisdom, his guide through the infernal regions.

Virgil was wise, and as craft was considered a part of wisdom, especially over-reaching the spirits of evil, so he is represented by mediæval writers as outwitting the demon. On one occasion, the legend says, he saw an imp in a hole on a mountain, and the imp promised to teach the poet the black art if he released him. Virgil did so, and after learning all the imp could teach him, expressed amazement, that one of such imposing stature could be squeezed into so small a rift. The imp said, "Oh, that is not wonderful," and crept into the hole to show Virgil how it was done, whereupon Virgil closed up the hole and kept the imp there. This tale is almost identical with that of the *Fisherman and the Genie* in the *Arabian Nights*, indeed, most of the mediæval stories that have crystallized round the name of the great Roman poet (*see*, for instance, those in the *Gesta Romanorum*) have a strong Oriental colouring.

The Christian Virgil. Marco Girolamo Vida (d. 1566), an Italian Latin poet, author of *Christias* in six books (1535), an imitation of the *Æneid*.

The Virgil and Horace of the Christians. So Bentley calls Aurelius Clemens Prudentius

(fl. about A.D. 400). He was a native of Spain, and the author of several Latin hymns and religious poems.

Virgin. One of the ancient constellations (*Virgo*), and a sign of the Zodiac. (Aug. 23rd to Sept. 23rd). The constellation is the metamorphosis of Astræa (*q.v.*), goddess of justice, who was the last of the deities to quit our earth. *See* ICARIUS.

The word *virgin* is used as a prefix denoting that the article has never been used, tried, or brought into cultivation; as *paper of virgin whiteness*, paper that is unwritten, or unprinted upon, a *virgin fortress*, one that has never been captured; a *virgin forest*, one that man has never attempted to tame or make use of.

Virgin Birth. In theology the doctrine—in the R.C. Church the dogma—that the miraculous birth of Christ did not impair the virginity of His mother, our Lady, and that she remained a virgin to the day of her death.

The Virgin Queen. Elizabeth I; also called (by Shakespeare) "the fair Vestal."

Virginal. A musical instrument of the 16th and 17th centuries, also called *a pair of virginals*. It has been suggested that it was so called because it was used in convents to lead the *virginals* or hymns to the Virgin, but it is more probable that it was simply because it was adapted to the use of young girls. It was a quilled keyboard instrument of two or three octaves.

Virginia. The State of Virginia is the first of the original American colonies, having been founded by Sir Walter Raleigh in 1584 and named after Elizabeth I of England, the Virgin Queen. His colony was probably planted on Roanoke Island and was in what is now North Carolina, but for many years the whole seaboard from Florida to Newfoundland was known as Virginia.

Virtues, The Seven. Faith, Hope, Charity, Prudence, Justice, Fortitude, and Temperance. The first three are called the *supernatural*, *theological*, or *Christian* virtues; the remaining four are Plato's *Cardinal* virtues. *Cp.* SEVEN DEADLY SINS.

Virtuoso (vĕr tū ō' zō). An Italian word meaning skilled. It is now applied almost exclusively to a musical artist who has achieved an eminent mastery over the instrument upon which he performs.

Visa (vī' zà). The official endorsement made on a passport by the embassy or consulate of the country to which the traveller intends to Without such visa he would not be allowed e

Viscount (Vī' kount). A peer ranking next below an Earl and above a Baron. In 1440 the title became a degree of honour and was made hereditary, the first Viscount being John, Lord Beaumont. The coronet of a Viscount bears 16 silver balls, and he is styled by the Sovereign "Our right trusty and well-beloved Cousin."

Vishnu (vish' nū). The Preserver; the second member of the Hindu trinity, though worshipped by many Hindus as the supreme deity. He has had 9 incarnations, or *Avatars* (*q.v.*), and there is one—Kalki—still to come, during which Vishnu will at the end of four ages destroy sin, the sinful, and all the enemies of the world. He is usually represented as four-armed and carrying a club, a shell, a discus, and a lotus; a bow and sword are slung at his side, and on his breast is a peculiar mark called the *Shrivatsa*. He has millions of worshippers, especially under his Avatars as Rama and Krishna.

Vision of Piers Plowman, The. A long allegorical poem in Middle English alliterative verse, written between 1362 and 1400 by probably as many as four or five different authors. On internal evidence the first part has for long been ascribed to William Langland or Langley, who came from Shropshire and settled in London.

The title should really be "The Vision concerning Piers the Plowman," for in the earlier part Piers typifies the simple, pious, English labourer, and in the later Christ Himself. The poet supposes himself falling asleep on the Malvern Hills, and in his dream sees various visions of an allegorical character, bearing on the vices of the times. The whole poem consists of nearly 15,000 verses, and is divided into twenty parts, each part being called a *passus*.

As a whole the picture is confused and depressing, but in detail it is often very powerful, *e.g.* the description of the crowded scene in the first prologue; the figures of Holy Church, Lady Meed, the Seven Deadly Sins, Piers himself, the Rat Parliament, etc It lacks Chaucer's humorous and cultured touch, but atones by its earnestness and sympathy.—E. W. EDMUNDS: *Hist. Summary of Eng. Lit.*, II, D, iii,

Visitation. In common parlance this means an unwanted—and usually protracted—visit from an unwelcome person. As an ecclesiastical term it is applied to the official visit a bishop pays to every parish in his diocese. **A herald's visitation** was the tour a herald made among country towns and seats to ascertain and record ̄e genealogies and right to bear coat armour ̄ the nobility and gentry of England. This was ̄ ̄narily done for the purposes of taxation.

The Visitation is the term applied in theology to Our Lady's visit to St. Elizabeth before the birth of John. *Luke* i, 40 et seq. It is celebrated on 2 July.

Visual Aids. Instructive diagrams, pictures, pictorial maps, etc., hung on schoolroom walls to familiarize the scholars with the information contained on them.

Vitus, St. (vī' tùs). A Sicilian youth who was martyred with Modestus, his tutor, and Crescentia, his nurse, during the Diocletian persecution, 303. All three are commemorated on June 15th.

St. Vitus's dance. In Germany it was believed in the 16th century that good health for a year could be secured by anyone who danced before a statue of St. Vitus on his feast day; this dancing developed almost into a mania, and came to be confused with chorea, which was subsequently known as *St. Vitus's dance*, the saint being invoked against it.

Viva! (vī' và, vē' và). An exclamation of applause or joy; Italian, meaning (long) live.

Viva voce (Latin, with the living voice). Orally; by word of mouth. A *viva voce* examination is one in which the respondent answers by word of mouth.

Vivat regina (rex)! (Lat.). Long live the Queen (King)! At the coronation of British Sovereigns the boys of Westminster School have the privilege of acclaiming the King or Queen with shouts of "Vivat Rex (or Regina)."

Vivandière (vē von dē âr'). A woman officially attached to a French regiment for the purpose of selling liquor to the troops.

Vivien (viv' yėn). An enchantress of the Arthurian romances, called also *Nimue* and, because she lived in a palace in the middle of a magic lake, *The Lady of the Lake*. It was here that she brought up Launcelot, hence called *Launcelot of the Lake*.

Vixen (A.S. *fyxen*). A female fox. Metaphorically, a shrewish woman, one of villainous and ungovernable temper.

Vixere fortes ante Agamemnona. *See* AGAMEMNON.

Viz. A contraction of Lat. *videlicet*, meaning *namely, to wit*. The *z* represents 3, a common mark of contraction in the Middle Ages; as hab3—*habet*, omnib3—*omnibus*.

Vodka. A Russian spirituous liquor distilled from rye, barley, oats, potatoes, or maize. It contains up to 95 per cent, of alcohol, although for consumption this percentage is diluted down to about 50 per cent. It is thus one of the strongest spirituous beverages drunk.

Vogue (vōg). A French word. "In vogue" means in repute, in the fashion. The verb voguer means to sail or move forwards. Hence the idea of sailing with the tide.

Vogue la galère (Fr., lit., row the galley). Let the world go how it will; let us keep on, whatever happens; *arrive qui pourra*.

Volapük (vol' á puk). An artificial language invented in 1880 by Fr. F. Schleyer, an Austrian priest. It was supposed to be based on European languages, 40 per cent. being English; but the words were so distorted and twisted by terminations and modifications that no original was recognizable. For example, the name itself was said to be English:—*Vol*, "English" *world*; *pük*, "English" *speech*.

Vole (Fr. *voler*, to fly). **He has gone the vole.** He has been everything by turns. *Vole* is a deal at cards that draws the whole tricks. *To vole* is to win all the tricks.

Voltaire. The assumed name of François Marie Arouet (1694-1778), the great French philosopher, poet, dramatist, and author. He began to use the name on issuing from imprisonment in the Bastille, in 1718. *Voltaire* is an anagram of Arouet L. I. (*le jeune*).

Volume. The *word* shows the ancestry of the *thing*; for it comes from Lat. *volvere*, to roll, and anciently books were written on sheets fastened together lengthwise and *rolled* on a pin or roller.

Volund. *See* WAYLAND.

Voodoo, or **Voodooism.** A system of magic and witchcraft which includes snake-worship and, in its extreme forms, human sacrifices and cannibalism. It is said to be a relic of African barbarism and is still practised in Haiti and other parts of the West Indies and Southern American States.

The name is thought to have been first given to it by missionaries from Fr. *Vaudois*, a Waldensian, as these were accused of sorcery; but Sir Richard Burton derived it from *vodun*, a dialect form of Ashanti *obosum*, a fetish or tutelary spirit.

Voyageur (vwa ya zhĕr'). A French Canadian or half-breed hired as a guide to the remoter stations of a fur or trading company on account of his skill as a boatman, tracker, and woodsman.

Vox. Vox et præterea nihil (Lat., a voice, and nothing more). Empty words—"full of sound and fury, signifying nothing"; a threat not followed out. When the Lacedemonian plucked the nightingale, on seeing so little substance he exclaimed, *Vox tu es, et nihil præterea*. (Plutarch: *Apophthegmata Laconica*.)

Vox populi vox Dei (Lat., the voice of the people is the voice of God). This does not mean that the voice of the many is wise and good, but only that it is irresistible. After Edward II had been dethroned by the people in favour of his son (Edward III), Simon Mepham, Archbishop of Canterbury, preached from these words as his text.

Vulcan. A son of Jupiter and Juno, and god of fire, and the working of metals, and patron of handicraftsmen in mythology, identified with the Gr. Hephæstus, and called also Mulciber, *i.e.* the softener.

His workshop was on Mount Etna, where the Cyclops assisted him in forging thunderbolts for Jove. It is said that he took the part of Juno against Jupiter, and Jupiter hurled him out of heaven. He was nine days in falling, and at last was picked up, half dead and with one leg broken, by the fishermen of the island of Lemnos. It was he who, with the stroke of an axe, delivered Minerva from the head of Jupiter; and he was the author of Pandora, and the golden dogs of Alcinous, as he had the power of conferring life upon his creations. Venus was his wife, and in consequence of her amour with Mars he came to be regarded as the special patron of cuckolds.

Vulcanist. One who supports the Vulcanian or Plutonian theory, which ascribes the changes on the earth's surface to the agency of fire. These theorists say the earth was once in a state of igneous fusion, and that the crust has gradually cooled down to its present temperature. *Cp.* NEPTUNIAN.

Vulgate, The. The Latin translation of the Bible, made about 385-405 by St. Jerome (*q.v.*), still used, with some modifications, as the authorized version by Roman Catholics. In 1907 Pope Pius X entrusted to the Benedictines the revision of the Vulgate, and by 1949 the first eight books of the Old Testament had been issued by them.

VXL. A punning monogram on lockets, etc., standing for U XL (you excel). U and V were formerly interchangeable.

W

W. The twenty-third letter of the English alphabet. The form is simply a ligature of two V's (VV); hence the name; for V was formerly the symbol of U (*q.v.*) as well as of V.

Waac. The familiar name of a member of the *Women's Army Auxiliary Corps*, a body of women raised for non-combatant army service in World War I. In World War II they were termed A.T.S. (later R.A.T.S.) (Royal) Auxiliary Territorial Services.

W.A.C. (U.S.A.). In World War II the Women's Army Corps, equivalent to the British R.A.T.S.

Wad. A roll of paper money, and hence money itself.

Wadham College (Oxford) was founded in 1613 by a bequest from Nicholas Wadham (1532-1609).

Wafer. Ecclesiastically a thin disk of unleavened bread used in the Eucharist.

Before the device of gummed envelope flaps was introduced, thin round disks of dried paste or gelatine were inserted between the flap and the envelope—or, earlier still, between the outer sides of the folded letter—and having been moistened and pressed with a seal served the same purpose of keeping the paper closed.

Wag. Meaning a humorous person, this word comes from the Old English *wagge*, probably from the facetious use of *waghalter*, a merry rogue.

Wager. Anything staked or hazarded on the event of a contest, etc. Connected with *gage* and *wage* (low Lat. *wadiare*, to pledge.)

Wager of battle. The decision of a contested claim by single combat—a common and legal method in Anglo-Saxon and early Norman times. It had legal status in England until abolished by Act of Parliament in 1818.

Waggoner. An old sailors' name for a book of sea-charts, Dalrymple's Charts being known as the *English Waggoner*. A corruption of Lukas *Waganaar*, a Dutch geographer whose charts were in use for long after their first appearance in the 16th century.

Wagon. On the Wagon is an abbreviation of the older phrase "on the water-wagon" applied to one who has temporarily or permanently become a teetotaller.

Wagoner. *See* BOÖTES.

Wahabites (wa ha' bītz). A Mohammedan sect, whose object is to bring back the doctrines and observances of Islam to the literal precepts of the Koran; so called from the founder, Ibn-abd-ul-Wahab (d. 1787).

Wailing Wall of the Jews. An enclosure in Jerusalem containing a wall said to be built of stones from Solomon's Temple. Traditionally the Jews gather there every Friday for prayers and lamentations for the Dispersion and lost glories of Israel.

Wait. Wait and see. This frequently caricatured political phrase was first used by H. H. Asquith (Earl of Oxford & Asquith) as his answer to a question in the House of Commons, April 4th, 1910. No exception was taken to the answer at the moment, but when Asquith took to repeating it whenever posed with an awkward question, Members took it up and a time came when it was chanted by the whole Opposition when any question was put to him.

Lords in Waiting, Gentlemen in Waiting, Grooms in Waiting, etc., are functionaries in the Royal Household for personal attendance upon the sovereign.

Ladies in waiting (in the Queen's Household) are officially styled *Ladies of the Bedchamber*, *Bedchamber Women*, and *Maids of Honour*.

Waits. Street musicians, who serenade the principal inhabitants at Christmas-time, especially on Christmas Eve. From Rymer's *Fœdera* we learn it was the duty of musical watchmen "to pipe the watch" nightly in the king's court four times from Michaelmas to Shrove Thursday, and three times in the summer; and they had also to make "the bon gate" at every door, to secure them against "pyckeres and pillers." They form a distinct class from both the watch and the minstrels. Oboes were at one time called "waits."

Wake. The feast of the dedication of a church, which was formerly kept by watching all night; also the merrymaking held in connexion with this, hence merrymaking generally.

In Ireland the term denotes the watching of a dead body before the funeral by the friends and neighbours of the deceased, in which the lamentations were often followed by an orgy.

Waking a witch. If a witch were obdurate, the most effectual way of obtaining a confession was by what was termed *waking* her. An iron bridle or hoop was bound across her face with prongs thrust into her mouth; this was fastened to the wall by a chain in such a manner that the victim was unable to lie down; and men were constantly by to keep her awake, sometimes for several days.

Waldensians or **Waldenses** (wol den' zianz, wol den' zèz) (also called the *Vaudois*). Followers of Peter Waldo of Lyons, who began a reform movement in the Church about 1170. They threw off the authority of the Pope, bishops, and all clergy, appointed lay-preachers (women among them), rejected infant baptism and many other rites, and made themselves so obnoxious to the ecclesiastical powers that they met with considerable persecution celebrated in one of Milton's sonnets. This they survived, and their descendants in doctrine still exist, principally in the Alpine valleys of Dauphiné, and Piedmont.

Wales. The older form is *Wealthas* (plural of *Wealh*), an Anglo-Saxon word denoting foreigners, and applied by them to the ancient Britons; hence, also, *Corn-wall*, the horn occupied by the same "refugees." The Welsh proper are Cimbri, and call their country Cymru; those driven thither by the Teutonic invaders were refugees or strangers. *Cp.* WALNUT.

The Prince of Wales. The popular story is that the title arose thus: When Edward I subdued Wales, he promised the Welsh, if they would lay down their arms, that he would give them a native prince who could not speak a word of English. His queen (Eleanor) having given birth to a son in Wales, the newborn child was entitled Edward, Prince of Wales; and ever since then the eldest son of the British sovereign has retained the title.

The facts, however, are that Edward I obtained the submission of the Welsh in 1276; his eldest son, afterwards Edward II, was born at Carnarvon in 1284, and it was not till 1301 that he was created Prince of Wales.

The male heir apparent to the throne is born *Duke of Cornwall*, but is not *Prince of Wales* until this title is conferred upon him,

which it usually is. At death, or succession to the Throne, it lapses to the Crown and can only be renewed at the Sovereign's pleasure, Thus, when Edward VII became King his son did not immediately become Prince of Wales; the title was conferred on him eight months later.

Walk. This is a remarkable word. It comes from the A.S. *wealcan*, to roll; whence we get *wealcere*, a fuller of cloth. In Percy's *Reliques* we read: —

> She cursed the weaver and the walker,
> The cloth that they had wrought.

A walk-over. A very easy victory; as in a running match when one's rivals could be beaten by walking.

To walk into. To thrash; also, to partake heartily of, as "to walk into an apple tart."

To walk off with. To steal and decamp with.

To walk out with. To court, as a preliminary to marriage.

In America a strike is called a *walk out*.

To walk the chalk. An ordeal used at police stations, in barracks, on board ship, etc., as a test of sobriety. Two parallel lines are chalked on the floor and the delinquent must walk between them without stepping on either.

To walk through one's part. To repeat one's part at rehearsal verbally, but without dressing for it or acting it; to do anything appointed you in a listless, indifferent manner.

A walking-on part. A part in a play in which the actor has only to walk about on the stage, sometimes with a word or two to say.

Walk not in the public ways. The fifth symbol of the *Protreptics* of Iamblichus, meaning follow not the multitude in their evil ways; or, wide is the path of sin and narrow the path of virtue, few being those who find it.

> Broad is the way that leadeth to destruction.—*Matt,* vii, 13.

Walkie-Talkie. (World War II). American small portable short-range wireless (containing receiver and transmitter) for use by infantry. Its equivalent has been adopted elsewhere by police, etc.

Walking Stewart. The nickname of John Stewart (1749-1822). The son of a London linen-draper, he secured a post in the East India Company and went to Madras. After serious quarrels with his superiors he resigned and started out on his travels. During the following years he went on foot through Hindustan, Persia, Nubia, Abyssinia, across the Arabian Desert, through Europe from Constantinople to England, passing through most of the Continental countries. In 1791 he crossed to America and walked through what was then known of Canada and the United States. De Quincey says of him:—

A most interesting roan . . . contemplative and crazy . . . yet sublime and divinely benignant in his visionariness. This man as a pedestrian traveller had seen more of the earth's surface than any man before or since.

Wall. To give the wall. To allow another, as a matter of courtesy, to pass by on the pavement at the side farthest from the gutter; hence, to be courteous. At one time pedestrians *gave the wall* to persons of a higher rank than themselves.

Nathaniel Bailey's explanation of this phrase (1721) is worth perpetuating. He says it is—

a compliment paid to the female sex, or those to whom one would show respect, by letting them go nearest the wall or houses, upon a supposition of its being the cleanest. This custom is chiefly peculiar to England, for in most parts abroad they will give them the right hand, though at the same time they trust them into the kennel.

To go to the wall. To be put on one side; to be shelved. This is in allusion to another phrase, *Laid by the wall*—*i.e.* dead but not buried; put out of the way.

To hang by the wall. To hang up neglected; not to be made use of (*Cymbeline*, iii, 4).

To take the wall. To take the place of honour.

I will take the wall of any man or maid of Montague's.—*Romeo and Juliet*, i, 1.

Walls have ears. Things uttered in secret get rumoured abroad; there are listeners everywhere, and you'd better be careful. Certain rooms in the Louvre were said to be so constructed in the time of Catherine de' Medicis, that what was said in one room could be distinctly heard in another. It was by this contrivance that the suspicious queen became acquainted with state secrets and plots. The tubes of communication were called the *auriculaires*. *Cp.* DIONYSIUS'S EAR *under* EAR.

Wall Street. The thoroughfare in New York City which contains the Stock Exchange. The name is hence used as a synonym for the American stock market.

The Roman Wall, from the Tyne to Bowness, on the Solway Firth, a distance of 80 miles. Called—

The Roman Wall, because it was the work of the Romans.

Agricola's Wall, because Agricola made the south bank and ditch.

Hadrian's Wall, because Hadrian added another vallum and mound parallel to Agricola's.

The Wall of Severus, because Severus followed in the same line with a stone wall, having castles and turrets.

The Picts' Wall, because its object was to prevent the incursions of the Picts.

The Wall of Antoninus, now called *Graeme's Dyke*, from Dunglass Castle on the Clyde to Blackness Castle on the Forth, was made by Lollius Urbicus, legate of Antoninus Pius A.D. 140. It was a turf wall.

Wall-eyed. The M.E. *wald-eyed*, a corruption of Icel. *vald eygthr*, having a beam in the eye (*vagl*, beam). Persons are wall-eyed when the white is unusually large, and the sight defective, due to opacity of the cornea, or when they have a divergent squint. Shakespeare has *wall-eyed wrath or staring rage* (*King John*, iv, 3).

Wallaby. A small Australian kangaroo.

On the wallaby, or **on the wallaby track.** On the tramp—usually because out of work.

Wallflower. So called because it grows on old walls and ruined buildings. It is a native plant. Similarly, *wall cress, wall creeper*, etc., are plants which grow on dry, stony places, or on walls. *Wall fruit* is fruit trained against a wall. *Cp.* WALNUT.

Herrick has a pretty fancy on the origin of this flower. A fair damsel was long kept away from her lover; but at last.

Up she got upon a wall
'Tempting down to slide withal;
But the silken twist untied,
So she fell, and, bruised, she died.
Love, in pity of the deed,
And her loving luckless speed,
Turned her to this plant we call
Now the "Flower of the wall."

Girls who sit out against the wall, not having partners during a dance, are called "wallflowers."

Wallop (wol' ŏp). To thrash; properly, to boil with a noisy bubbling sound. The word is the same as *gallop*. It is also a slang term for ale.

Walnut. The foreign nut; called in M.E. *walnote*, from A.S. *wealh*, foreign. It came from Persia, and was so called to distinguish it from nuts native to Europe, as hazel, filbert, chestnut.

Some difficulty there is in cracking the name thereof. Why walnuts, having no affinity to a wall, should be so called. The truth is, *gual* or *wall* in the old Dutch signifieth "strange" or "exotic" (whence *Welsh* foreigners); these nuts being no natives of England or Europe.— FULLER: *Worthies of England*.

It is said that the walnut tree thrives best if the nuts are beaten off with sticks, and not gathered. Hence Fuller says, "Who, like a nut tree, must be manured by beating, or else would not bear fruit" (Bk. ii, ch. 11). The saying is well known that—

A woman, a dog, and a walnut tree,
The more you beat them the better they be.

Walpurgis Night (wol pĕr' gis). The eve of May Day, when the witch-world was supposed to hold high revelry under its chief on certain high places, particularly the Brocken, in Germany.

Walpurgis was an English nun concerned in the introduction of Christianity into Germany. She died Feb. 25th, 779.

Walstan, St. The patron saint in England of husbandmen. He was a rich Briton who gave up all his wealth, and supported himself by husbandry. He died mowing in 1016, and is usually depicted with a scythe in his hand, and cattle in the background.

Waltham Blacks. *See* BLACK ACT.

Waltzing Matilda. A song sung by the Australian forces in the Middle East in World War II, and sharing with *Lilli Marlene* (*q.v.*) pride of place as the best soldiers' song of the period. The phrase was originally "Walking Matilda," and as such is found in Australia in the late 19th century; it means carrying one's bag or roll, as a tramp does. The reason for a tramp's roll being called a "Matilda" is obscure; "to waltz" meaning to carry is American slang, and is found in Mark Twain's *Huckleberry Finn*, 1884.

> Once a jolly swagman camped by a billabong
> Under the shade of a coolibah tree,
> And he sang as he watched and waited till his billy boiled
> "You'll come a waltzing Matilda with me."

Wampum (wom' pum). Shell beads strung for ornament, currency, and tribal records by some North American Indian peoples. They are made of the perforated central columns of several kinds of marine shells. The name comes from the Algonquin *wompi*, white.

Wand. The long, slender rod used by magicians and conjurers; also by certain court functionaries as a staff of office, and by musical, conductors as a baton.

Wandering Jew, The. The central figure of a very widespread mediæval legend which tells how a Jew who refused to allow Christ to rest at his door while He was bearing his cross to Calvary, was condemned to wander over the face of the earth till the end of the world. The usual form of the legend says that he was Ahasuerus, a cobbler. The craftsman pushed Him away, saying, "Get off! Away with you, away!" Our Lord replied, "Truly I go away, and that quickly, but tarry thou till I come."

Another tradition has it that the Wandering Jew was Kartaphilos, the door-keeper of the judgment hall in the service of Pontius Pilate. He struck our Lord as he led Him forth, saying, "Go on faster, Jesus"; whereupon the Man of Sorrows replied, "I am going, but thou shalt tarry till I come again" (*Chronicle of St. Albans Abbey*; 1228).

The same *Chronicle*, continued by Matthew Paris, tells us that Kartaphilos was baptized by Ananias, and received the name of Joseph. At the end of every hundred years he falls into a trance, and wakes up a young man about thirty.

In German legend he is associated with John Buttadæus, seen at Antwerp in the 13th century, again in the 15th, and a third time in the 16th. His last appearance was in 1774 at Brussels. In the French version he is named Isaac Laquedem, or Lakedion; another story has it that he was Salathiel ben Sadi, who appeared and disappeared towards the close of the 16th century, at Venice, in so sudden a manner as to attract the notice of all Europe; and another connects him with the Wild Huntsman (*q.v.*).

Wangle. To achieve some object by sly, roundabout, or underhand methods; to cook accounts (for instance), to manipulate. The word came into wide use during World War I, but it was well-known slang among printers from very early times.

Wanion. With a wanion. An old imprecation; the word is pres. part. of *wanion*, to wane, and meant misfortune, ill-luck.

> Look how thou stirrest now! come away, or I'll fetch thee with a wannion.—*Pericles*, ii, 1.

Wantley, The Dragon of. An old story, preserved in Percy's *Reliques*, tells of this monster, which was slain by More, of More Hall. He procured a suit of armour studded with spikes, and kicked the Dragon in the mouth, where alone it was vulnerable. Percy says the Dragon was an overgrown, rascally attorney, who cheated some children of their estate, and was made to disgorge by one named More, who went against him, "armed with the spikes of the law," after which the attorney died of vexation. Wantley is Wharncliffe in Yorkshire.

Wapinshaw (wop' in shaw). The Scottish name for a meeting for rifle-shooting, curling, or similar sport. Formerly, the periodical review of clansmen under arms, a *weapon-show*.

War. A holy war. War undertaken from religious motives, such as the Crusades; or in defence of a religion.

On the war-path. Looking for one's adversary with every intention of catching him; thoroughly roused or incensed.

War game. A military training exercise consisting of a game played with maps, etc. for developing skill in manœuvring troops and designing both strategy and tactics.

War head. The explosive head of a torpedo or bomb.

War-horse. Used figuratively of a veteran who is overflowing with warlike memories; a "fire-eater."

War paint. The paint applied to their faces by Red Indians and other peoples to make their appearance terrifying before going out on the warpath. *Putting on one's war paint* is a phrase applied figuratively to getting ready to enter energetically into a dispute or to putting on lipstick, powder, etc., in order to overcome one's rivals.

Ward. A district under the charge of *a warden*. The word is applied to the subdivisions of Cumberland, Westmorland, and Durham, which, being contiguous to Scotland, were placed under the charge of lord wardens of the marches, whose duty it was to protect these counties from inroads. *See* HUNDRED.

The word has other applications:—The administrative division of a town or city; a large room or division of a hospital; each of the separate divisions of a prison (under a *warder*); a minor placed under the care of a guardian; a part of a lock or of a key.

Ward Room. In British warships a mess shared by the Commander—unless he is in command of the vessel, when he messes alone—and all other officers down to and including lieutenants. Junior officers mess in the gun room.

Warlock. An evil spirit; a wizard. A.S. *wærloga*, a traitor, one who breaks his word.

Warm. Used in slang with much the same force as *hot* (*q.v.*), as a *warm member*, said of a man who "goes the pace," of a sharper, or of one who is particularly notable in connexion with whatever happens to be the subject of discussion. *Warm thanks*, are hearty thanks; *he's in a warm corner* means he's in an awkward position.

A house-warming. An entertainment given by new occupiers of a house; a first welcoming of friends to a fresh residence.

Warming-pan. One who holds a place temporarily for another; used specially of a clergyman who officiates while the actual holder of the living is qualifying. In public schools it used to be the custom to make a fag warm his "superior's" bed by lying in it till the proper occupant was ready to turn him out.

Jacobites used to be nicknamed *Warming-pans*, because of the widely believed story that the "Old Pretender" was a child who was introduced into the lying-in-chamber of Mary of Modena, queen of James II, in a warming-pan, her own child having been stillborn.

Warp. The threads running the long way of a woven fabric, crossed by the *woof*, *i.e.* those running from selvedge to selvedge. *Warp* (A.S. *wearp*) is connected with Icel. *varpa*, to throw; *woof* with A.S. *wef*, web.

> Weave the warp and weave the woof,
> The winding-sheet of Edward's race;
> Give ample room and verge enough
> The characters of hell to trace.
> GRAY: *The Bard*.

To warp is a nautical term, meaning to shift the position of a vessel, which is done by means of a rope called a *warp*. *Kedging* is when the warp is bent to a kedge, which is let go, and the vessel is hove ahead by the capstan.

In Lancashire, *warping* means laying eggs; and boys, on finding a bird's nest, will ask— "And how many eggs has she warped?"

Warrant Officer. In the British navy this is a rank between a commissioned officer and petty officers and men. Warrant officers are promoted from the lower deck.

In the Army and Air Force warrant officer is a rank between that of commissioned officer and non-commissioned officer.

Warrior Queen, The. Boadicea, Queen of the Iceni, an ancient tribe of Eastern Britain subjugated by the Romans in A.D. 62.

> When the British warrior queen,
> Bleeding from the Roman rods,
> Sought, with an indignant mien,
> Counsel of her country's gods. . . .
> COWPER: *Boadicea*.

The Iceni were the faithful allies of Rome; but, on the death of Prasutagus, king of that tribe, the Roman procurator took possession of his kingdom, and when his widow Boadicea complained, the procurator had her beaten with rods like a slave.

Wash. It will all come out in the wash. Everything will turn out all right in the end. The phrase is Spanish, and occurs in *Don Quixote*.

Quite washed out. Thoroughly exhausted, done up, with no strength or spirit left.

That story won't wash! It won't do at all; you'll have to think of something better than *that*! Said of an excuse or explanation that is palpably false, far-fetched, or exaggerated.

To wash a brick. To engage in an utterly unprofitable enterprise; to do useless work. An old Latin proverbial expression (*laterem lavem*, Terence's *Phormio*, I, iv, 9).

To wash one's dirty linen in public. To expose the family skeletons to the public gaze; openly to discuss private affairs that are more or less discreditable.

Wash-out. A phrase made popular in World War I meaning a failure or fiasco. As an imperative verb it means, cancel, disregard—"Wash out that instruction," disregard that order, consider it as never having been given. It is really old Naval slang, dating from the times when signal messages were taken down on a slate which was washed clean when the message had been transmitted to the proper quarters.

To wash one's hands of. *See* HAND.

Wassail. A carouse, drinking bout, or other festive occasion.

> The king doth wake to-night and takes his rouse,
> Keeps wassail.
>
> *Hamlet*, i, 4.

Formerly a salutation used specially at the New Year over the spiced ale cup, hence called the "wassail bowl" (A.S. *Wæs hæl*, be whole, be well).

An old story has it that when Vortigern was invited to dine at the house of Hengist, Rowena, the daughter, of the host, brought a cup of wine which she presented to their royal guest, saying, "*Wæs hæl, hlaford cyning*' (Your health, lord king). Robert de Brunne (late 13th cent.) refers to this custom:—

> This is ther custom and hev gest
> When they are at the ale or fest:
> Ilk man that levis gware him drink
> Salle say "Wasseille" to him drink;
> He that biddis sall say "Wassaile,"
> The tother salle say again "Drinkaille."
> That says "Waisseille" drinks of the cup,
> Kiss and his felaw he gives it up.

Hence *wassailers*, those who join a wassail; revellers, drunkards.

> I should be loath
> To meet the rudeness and swilled insolence
> Of such late wassailers.
>
> MILTON: *Comus.*

Waster, wastrel. A good-for-nothing fellow; a prodigal, spendthrift.

Watch. In nautical usage, the time during which each division of a ship's crew is alternately on duty (four hours except during the *dogwatches* of two hours by which the change from night to day duty is arranged); also, either half (*starboard* or *port watch* from the position of the sailors' bunks in the forecastle) into which the officers and crew are divided, taking duty alternately.

12 to 4	p.m.	Afternoon watch.
4 to 6	"	First dog-watch.
6 to 8	"	Second dog-watch.
8 to 12	"	First night watch.
12 to 4	a.m.	Middle watch.
4 to 8	"	Morning watch.
8 to 12	"	Forenoon watch.

The Black Watch. *See* BLACK.

The Watch on the Rhine. A national song of the old German Empire, sharing the place of honour with *Deutschland über Alles* (Germany over all).

Watch and ward. Continuous vigilance; guard by night (*watch*) and by day (*ward*). In feudal times service "by watch and ward" was due by certain tenants in towns; later the term was applied to the constabulary.

Watch Night. December 31st, to see the Old Year out and the New Year in by a religious service. John Wesley grafted it on the religious system, and it has been adopted by many Christian communities.

Watchful Waiting. A phrase used by President Wilson in 1915 to describe the policy of the U.S.A. towards Mexico, whose attitude was extremely unfriendly and provocative.

Watchword. A word given to sentries as a signal that one has the right of admission, a password; hence, a motto, word, or phrase symbolizing or epitomizing the principles of a party, etc.

Water. Blood thicker than water. *See* BLOOD.

In deep water. In difficulties; in great perplexity; similarly, *in smooth water* means all is plain sailing, one's troubles and anxieties are things of the past.

It makes my mouth water. It is very alluring; it makes me long for it. Saliva is excited in the mouth by strong desire.

Of the first water. Of the highest type; very excellent. *See* DIAMOND.

Smooth, or **still, waters run deep.** Deep thinkers are persons of few words; he (or she) thinks a good deal more than is suspected; silent conspirators are the most dangerous; barking dogs do not bite. A calm exterior is far more to be feared than a tongue-doughty Bobadil.

> Smooth runs the water where the brook is deep;
> And in his simple show he harbours treason.
> The fox barks not when he would steal the lamb;
> No, no, my sovereign, Gloucester is a man
> Unsounded yet, and full of deep deceit.
>
> 2 *Henry VI*, iii, 1.

That won't hold water. That is not correct; it is not tenable. It is a vessel which leaks.

The Father of Waters. The Mississippi, the chief river of North America. The Missouri is its child. The Irrawaddy is so called also.

The water of jealousy. If a woman was known to have committed adultery she was to be stoned to death, according to the Mosaic law (*Deut.* xxii, 22). If, however, the husband had no proof, but only suspected his wife of infidelity, he might take her before the Sanhedrin to be examined, and if she denied it, she was given the "water of jealousy" to drink (*Numb.* v, 11-29). In this water some of the dust of the sanctuary was mixed, and the priest said to the woman, "If thou hast gone aside may Jehovah make this water bitter to thee, and bring on thee all the curses written in this law." He then wrote on a roll the curses, sprinkled the writing with the water, gave it to the woman, and then handed to her the "water of jealousy" to drink.

To back water. To row backwards in order to reverse the forward motion of a boat in rowing; hence, to go easy, to retrace one's steps, to retract.

To carry water to the river. To carry coals to Newcastle.

To fish in troubled waters. To seek to turn a state of disturbance to one's own advantage; to "profiteer" during a time of war, to seize power during a revolution, and so on.

To get into hot water. *See* HOT.

To keep one's head above water. *See* HEAD.

To throw cold water on a scheme. To discourage the proposal; to speak of it slightingly.

To turn on the waterworks. To cry, blubber.

To water stock. To add extra shares. Suppose a "trust" (*q.v.*) consists of 1,000 shares of £50 each, and the profit available for dividend is 40 per cent., the managers "water the stock," that is, add another 1,000 fully paid-up shares to the original 1,000. There are now 2,000 shares, and the dividend, instead of £40 per cent., is reduced to £20; but the shares are more easily sold, and the shareholders are increased in number.

Water-gall. The dark rim round the eyes after much weeping. A peculiar appearance in a rainbow which indicates more rain at hand.

> And round about her tear-distained eye
> Blue circles streamed, like rainbows in the sky;
> These watergalls . . . foretell new storms.
> > *Rape of Lucrece.*

Waterman. A boatman, especially one who rows a boat or skiff as a means of transport. The Thames watermen were a feature of old London, when much passenger traffic was carried by water from Westminster as far down as Greenwich.

Hackney-coach stands and cab ranks were each supplied with a licensed waterman whose duty it was to water the cab-horses and see that the drivers accepted fares in rotation.

Watermark. A design impressed into paper while in course of manufacture. Watermarks were employed as early as 1282, and served to identify the product of each paper mill, the designs chosen (many of them extremely complicated)

frequently also expressing emblematically the tenets of the manufacturers. The art of paper-making was almost entirely in the hands of the Huguenots and previous Protestants (Albigenses, Waldenses, Cathari, etc.), and the *Bull's head*, for instance, was an emblem of the Albigenses.

The watermark has in many cases been the origin of paper-trade terminology; thus the mark of the *cap and bells* gave us *Foolscap*, the *Post-horn*, *Post*, the *Pot*, *Pott*, and so on—all sizes of paper.

Waterloo. He met his Waterloo. He had a final and crushing defeat; in allusion, of course, to the decisive defeat inflicted on Napoleon by Wellington at Waterloo in 1815.

The Waterloo Cup. The "Derby" of the coursing fraternity; the great dog-race held annually at Altcar during three days in February.

It was founded in 1836 by a man named Lynn, the sporting owner of the Waterloo Hotel in Liverpool (whence its name). Lynn was also the founder of the Grand National, run at Aintree.

Watling Street. The great Roman road extending east and west across Britain. Beginning at Dover, it ran through Canterbury to London, thence through St. Albans, Dunstable, along the boundary of Leicester and Warwick to Wroxeter on the Severn, and so to Chester and Cardigan. *Watling* is said to be a corruption of *Vitellina strata*, the paved road of Vitellius, called by the Britons Guetalin.

Watson. *See* SHERLOCK HOLMES.

Wattle. Australian settlers built wattle-and-daub huts after the English manner from twigs of the abundant acacia trees, which hence became known as Wattles. *Wattle Day* is a national festival in Australia, held on August 1st, or September 1st according to the peak of the flowering of the wattle in each State.

Wave. The tenth wave. A notion prevails that the waves keep increasing in regular series till the maximum arrives, and then the series begins again. No doubt when two waves coalesce they form a large one, but this does not occur at fixed intervals.

The most common theory is that the *tenth* wave is the largest, but Tennyson says the *ninth*.

> And then the two
> Dropt to the cove, and watch'd the great sea fall,
> Wave after wave, each mightier than the last,
> Till last, a ninth one, gathering half the deep
> And full of voices, slowly rose and plunged
> Roaring, and all the wave was in a flame.
> > *The Holy Grail.*

Wax. Slang for temper, anger; *he's in an awful wax*, he's in a regular rage. Hence **waxy**, irritated, vexed, angry.

A man of wax. A model man; like one fashioned in wax. Horace speaks of the "waxen arms of Telephus," meaning model arms, or of perfect shape and colour; and the nurse says of Romeo, "Why, he's a man of wax (i, 3), which she explains by saying, "Nay, he's a flower, i' faith a very flower."

A nose of wax. Mutable and accommodating (faith). A waxen nose may be twisted any way.

Way. The way of all flesh. Death.

The way of the Cross. *See* STATIONS OF THE CROSS.

Ways and Means. A parliamentary term, meaning the method of raising the supply of money for the current requirements of the state.

Wayland. A wonderful and invisible smith of English legend, the English form of Scandinavian Volund, a supernatural smith and King of the Elves, a kind of Vulcan. He was bound apprentice to Mimi the smith. King Nidung cut the sinews of his feet, and cast him into prison, but he escaped in a feather boat. He and Amilias had a contest of skill in their handicraft. Wayland's sword, Balmung, cleft his rival down to the thighs, but it was so sharp that Amilias was not aware of the cut till he attempted to stir, when he divided into two pieces. Tradition has placed his forge near Lambourn, Berks (since called *Wayland Smith's Cave*), where it was said that if a traveller tied up his horse there, left sixpence for a fee, and retired from sight, he would find the horse shod on his return.

Wayzgoose. An annual dinner, picnic, or "beanfeast" given to, or held by, those employed in a printing-house. *Wayz* is an obsolete word for stubble, and a *wayzgoose* a "stubble goose," properly the crowning dish of the entertainment. *See* BEANFEAST.

We. Used of himself by a Sovereign, as representing his subjects, by the editor of a newspaper, as the public representative of a certain body of opinion, and by a writer of an unsigned article, as representing the journal for which he is writing.

Coke, in the *Institutes*, says the first king that wrote *we* in his grants was King John. All the kings before him wrote *ego* (I). This is not correct, as Richard *Lion-heart* adopted the royal "We." *See* Rymer's *Fœdera*.

"We are not amused!" A reproof attributed to Queen Victoria and frequently used as an ironical rebuke. There is no authority whatever for supposing that the Queen made this remark.

There is no record of her ever having used the royal "we" in other than official proclamations; nor is the spirit of the words in keeping with Queen Victoria's conversation or character.

Weal. A prosperous or sound state of affairs; the A.S. *wela*, cognate with *well.* Hence, the *common weal*, or the *public weal*, the welfare or prosperity of the community at large.

"Wearing of the Green, The." An immensely popular Irish revolutionary song, written about 1798, and known in Irish as "Shan Van Voght.

Weasel. Weasels suck eggs; hence Shakespeare:—

> The weazel Scot
> Comes sneaking, and so sucks the princely egg.
> *Henry V*, i, 2.

> I can suck melancholy out of a song, as a weazel sucks eggs.—*As You Like It*, ii, 5.

Pop Goes the Weasel. The title of this song is said to refer the habit of London hatters of "popping," or pawning, their "weasels," or accessories, on Saturday nights, to buy liquor.

(World War II.) A weasel is a jeep fitted with wide tracks instead of wheels, for carrying stores and personnel over deep mud. The load was reduced to $1\frac{1}{4}$ lb. per square inch, a remarkable achievement.

Weather. A weather breeder. A day of unusual fineness coming suddenly after a series of damp dull ones, especially at the time of the year when such a genial day is not looked for. Such a day is generally followed by foul weather.

Fair-weather friends. Those that stick to you so long as all is going well, but desert you as soon as storms gather round your head and you look as though you might "go under."

To keep the weather of. To get round, or get the better of. A phrase from the seaman's vocabulary.

> Mine honour keeps the weather of my fate:
> Life every man holds dear; but the dear man
> Holds honour far more precious dear than life.
> *Troilus and Cressida*, v, 3.

To make fair weather. To flatter, conciliate, make the best of things.

> But I must make fair weather yet awhile,
> Till Henry be more weak, and I more strong.
> 2 *Henry VI*, v, 1.

Weathercock. By a Papal enactment made in the middle of the 9th century, the figure of a cock was set up on every church steeple as the emblem of St. Peter. The emblem is in allusion to his denial of our Lord thrice before the cock crew twice. On the second crowing of the cock the warning of his Master flashed across his memory, and the repentent apostle "went out and wept bitterly."

A person who is always changing his mind is, figuratively, a *weathercock*.

Ther is no feith that may your herte embrace;
But, as a wedercock, that turneth his face
With every wind, ye fare.
CHAUCER (?): *Balade Against Women Unconstant*.

Web. *See* WARP.

The web of life. The destiny of an individual from the cradle to the grave. The allusion is to the three Fates who, according to Roman mythology, spin the thread of life, the pattern being the events which are to occur.

Wed, Wedding. Wed is Anglo-Saxon, and means a *pledge*. The ring is the pledge given by the man to avouch that he will perform his part of the contract.

Wedding Anniversaries. Fanciful names have been given to many wedding anniversaries, the popular idea being that they designate the nature of the gifts suitable for the occasion. The following list is fairly complete, and of these very few except the twenty-fifth and fiftieth are ever noticed.

First ..	.. Cotton Wedding.
Second ..	.. Paper Wedding.
Third ..	.. Leather Wedding,
Fifth ..	.. Wooden Wedding.
Seventh	.. Woollen Wedding.
Tenth ..	.. Tin Wedding.
Twelfth	.. Silk and Fine Linen Wedding.
Fifteenth	.. Crystal Wedding.
Twentieth	.. China Wedding.
Twenty-fifth	.. Silver Wedding.
Thirtieth	.. Pearl Wedding.
Fortieth	.. Ruby Wedding.
Fiftieth	.. Golden Wedding.
Seventy-fifth	.. Diamond Wedding.

The sixtieth anniversary is often reckoned the "Diamond Wedding" in place of the seventy-fifth; as the sixtieth year of Queen Victoria's reign was her "Diamond Jubilee."

Wedding Finger. The fourth finger of the left hand. Macrobius says the thumb is too busy to be set apart, the forefinger and little finger are only half protected, the middle finger is called *medicus*, and is too opprobious for the purpose of honour, so the only finger left is the *pronŭbus*.

Aulus Gellius tells us that Appianus asserts in his Egyptian books that a very delicate nerve runs from the fourth finger of the left hand to the heart, on which account this finger is used for the marriage ring.

The finger on which this ring [the wedding-ring] is to be worn is the fourth finger of the left hand, next unto the little finger; because by the received opinion of the learned . . . in ripping up and anatomising men's bodies, there is a vein of blood, called *vena amoris*, which passeth from that finger to the heart.—HENRY SWINBURNE: *Treaties of Spousals* (1680).

In the Roman Catholic Church, the thumb and first two fingers represent the Trinity; thus the bridegroom says, "In the name of the Father," and touches the thumb; "in the name of the Son," and touches the first finger; and "in the name of the Holy Ghost" he touches the long or second finger, with the word "Amen" he then puts it on the third finger and leaves it there. In some countries the wedding-ring is worn on the right hand; this was the custom generally in England until the end of the 16th century, and among Roman Catholics until much later.

In the Hereford, York, and Salisbury missals, the ring is directed to be put first on the thumb, then on the first finger, then on the long finger, and lastly on the ring-finger, *quia in illo digito est quædam vena procedens usque ad cor*.

Wedlock. This word comes from Old English *wed*, a pledge, and *lac*, a promise, the whole meaning the marriage vow. It does not, therefore, imply the unopenable lock of marriage, as has sometimes been supposed.

Wednesday. Woden-es or Odin-es Day, called by the French "Mercredi" (Mercury's Day). The Persians regard it as a "red-letter day," because the moon was created on the fourth day (*Gen*. i, 14-19).

Weeds. The mourning worn by a widow; from A.S. *wæde*, a garment. Spenser speaks of—

A goodly lady clad in hunter's weed.
Faerie Queene, II, iii, 21.

Shakespeare has—

And there the snake throws her enamell'd skin,
Weed wide enough to wrap a fairy in.
Midsummer Night's Dream, ii, 1.

And in *Timon of Athens* (i, 1) we get the modern meaning—

Hail, Rome, victorious in thy mourning weeds!

Week, Days of the. It is curious that while we owe the names of all the *months* to Rome, those of the *days* are Anglo-Saxon.

Sunday (A.S. *Sunnandæg*), day of the sun.
Monday (A.S. *Monandæg*), day of the moon.
Tuesday (A.S. *Tiwesdæg*), from Tiw, the god of war.
Wednesday (A.S. *Wodnesdæg*), from Odin the god of storms.
Thursday (A.S. *Thuresdæg*), day of Thor, the god of thunder.
Friday (A.S. *Frigedæg*), day of Freya, goddess of marriage.
Saturday (A.S. *Saterdæg*: Lat. *Dies Saturnus*), day of Saturn, the god of time.

A week of Sundays. A long time; an indefinite period.

Weeping. A notion long prevailed in this country that it augured ill for future married happiness if the bride did not weep profusely at the wedding.

As no witch could shed more than three tears, and those from her left eye only, a copious flow of tears gave assurance to the husband that the lady had not "plighted her troth" to Satan, and was no witch.

Weigh (A.S. *wegan*, to carry). **To weigh anchor.** To raise the anchor preparatory to sailing.

Under weigh. A solecism for *under way. See* WAY.

Weighed in the balance and found wanting. Tested, and proved to be at fault, or a failure. The phrase is from Daniel's interpretation of the vision of Belshazzar (*Dan.* v, 27).

A dead weight. *See* DEAD.

A weight-for-age race. A sort of handicap (*q.v.*), in which the weights carried are apportioned according to certain conditions. Horses of the same age carry similar weights, *cæteris paribus*.

Welch. An old spelling of *Welsh*; still retained in the name of the *Welch Regiment*.

Welcome Nugget. One of the largest nuggets of gold ever discovered. It was found at Baker's Hill, Ballarat, June 11, 1858. It weighed 2019⅔ oz. and was at the time worth £8,376.

Welfare Work. The organized work undertaken by carefully trained personnel to promote the well-being of factory workers, the employees of large businesses, etc. It is extended to many activities such as hospital almoners, police-court missionaries, and so forth, as well as to many tasks that have hitherto been left to the exertions of charity.

Wellington. The Duke of Wellington (1769-1852) left his name to two kinds of boot, a tree (of the sequoia family—the *Wellingtonia*), and as a term in cards. Men's riding-boots are called Wellingtons, with the front coming over the knee, and a shorter top-boot coming to just below the knee and often made of rubber. Half-Wellingtons are shorter boots of which the foot is made of patent leather, and the top part (of inferior and softer material) extends halfway up the calf inside the tight trousers of British army mess dress. In "Nap" a call of *Wellington* doubles *Napoleon*—*i.e.* the caller has to take all five tricks and wins (or loses) double stakes.

Welsh. Pertaining to Wales (*q.v.*), *i.e.* the country of foreigners (A.S. *wælse*, foreign). *Welsch* is German for *foreign*, and the Germans call Italy *Welschland. Taffy* is the generic name for a Welshman; from *David*, the patron saint.

Welsh harp. The musical instrument of the ancient Welsh bards; a large harp with three rows of strings, two tuned diatonically in unison, the third supplying the chromatic sharps and flats.

Welsh Main. In cock-fighting, another term for a battle royal (*q.v.*).

Welsh mortgage. A pledge of land in which no day is fixed for redemption.

Welsh rabbit. Cheese melted and spread over buttered toast. *Rabbit* is not a corruption of *rare-bit*; the term is on a par with "mock-*turtle*," "Bombay *duck*," etc.

Welter-weight. A boxer between light and middle weight, about 147 lb. In racing the term is applied to any extra heavy weight.

Weltpolitik (velt pol' i tik). The German phrase (world politics) for the policy a nation pursues in its relations with the world at large.

Wen. The Great Wen. So William Cobbett (1762-1835) in his *Rural Rides* called London, meaning that it was an abnormal growth, a blotch on the land.

Werewolf. *See* WERWOLF.

Wergild (wĕr' gild). The "blood-money" (*wer*, man, *gild*, payment) paid in Anglo-Saxon times by the kindred of the slayer to the kindred of the slain to avoid a blood-feud in cases of murder or manslaughter. There was a fixed scale:—1,200 shillings (about £24) for a free-man, 200 shillings for a villain, and 40 pence for a serf.

Werther (wĕr' ter). The sentimental hero of Goethe's romance, *The Sorrows of Werther* (1774), who was so overcome by his unrequited love for Lotte that he took his life. As Thackeray travestied the story—

Charlotte, having seen his body
Borne before her on a shutter,
Like a well-conducted person,
    Went on cutting bread and butter.

Werwolf (wĕr' wulf). A "man-wolf" (A.S. *wer*, man), *i.e.* a man who, according to mediæval belief, was turned—or could at will turn himself—into a wolf (the *loup-garou* of France). It had the appetite of a wolf, and roamed about at night devouring infants and sometimes exhuming corpses. Its skin was proof against shot or steel, unless the weapon had been blessed in a chapel dedicated to St. Hubert.

This belief was once common to almost all Europe, and still lingers in Brittany, Limousin, Auvergne, Servia, Wallachia, and White Russia; while in the 15th century a council of theologians, convoked by the Emperor Sigismund, decided that the werwulf was a reality.

The study of lycanthropy, *i.e.* of wolf-men, is, indeed, an important branch of the science of comparative religion. At one time or another the belief in animal-men has been prevalent in every part of the world, tigers, leopards, hyenas and other ferocious animals being thus associated with the magic.

Ovid tells the story of Lycaon, King of Acadia, turned into a wolf because he tested the divinity of Jupiter by serving up to him a "hash of human flesh"; Herodotus describes the Neuri as having the power of assuming once a year the shape of wolves; Pliny relates that one of the family of Antæus was chosen annually, by lot, to be transformed into a wolf, in which shape he continued for nine years; and St. Patrick, we are told, converted Vereticus, King of Wales, into a wolf.

Werewolves. (World War II). Term coined by the Germans for the fanatical saboteurs who, they said, were going to carry on harassing tactics against the Allies after the defeat of Germany in the field.

Wesleyan. A member of the Nonconformist church founded by John Wesley (1703-91) about 1739.

Wessex. The ancient kingdom of the West Saxons; it included Hants, Dorset, Wilts, Somerset, Surrey, Gloucestershire, and Bucks.

The Novelist of Wessex. Thomas Hardy (1840-1928), the scenes of whose novels are laid in this country.

West. The West End. The fashionable quarter of London, lying between Charing Cross and the western boundary of Hyde Park. Hence *West-end style*, ultra-fashionable.

To go west. Of persons, to die; of things, to be lost, rendered useless, never obtained, as *My chance of promotion has gone west*.

The phrase came into very wide use during World War I, but it is older than that, and originated in the United States, the reference being to the setting sun, which "goes west," and then expires. The idea is very old; it occurs in a Greek proverb, and *cp*. Tennyson's—

> My purpose holds
> To sail beyond the sunset, and the paths
> Of all the western stars, until I die. *Ulysses*.

West, Mae. *See* MAE WEST.

The Western Church. The Roman Catholic Church, which, after the Great Schism in the 9th century, acknowledged the headship of the Pope.

The Western Empire. The western division of the Roman Empire having Rome as capital, after the division into an Eastern and Western Empire by Theodosius in 395.

Wet. Slang for a drink; hence, **to have a wet**, to have a drink, and **to wet one's whistle**, meaning the same thing. This last is a very old phrase; Chaucer has "So was her joly whistle wel y-wet" (*Reeve's Tale*, 235), and in No. xiii of the *Towneley Plays* (about 1388) is

> Had she oones wett hyr Whystyll she could syng full clere
> Hyr pater noster.

A wet blanket. *See* BLANKET.

Wetback. An illegal immigrant to U.S.A. from Mexico. The term originates in the fact that such interlopers usually had to swim the Rio Grande.

Wet bob. At Eton a wet bob is a boy who goes in for boating; a dry bob one who chooses cricket.

Wet nurse. A woman employed to suckle children not her own.

White as whalebone. An old simile; whalebone is far from white. Our forefathers seemed to confuse the walrus with the whale; and "white as whalebone" is really a blunder for "white as walrus-ivory."

He knows what's what. He is a shrewd fellow not to be imposed on. One of the senseless questions of logic was *Quid est quid?*

> He knew what's what, and that's as high
> As metaphysic wit can fly.
> BUTLER: *Hudibras*, Pt. i, canto 1.

What-not. In Victorian drawing-room furniture a small stand with shelves for bibelots and knick-knacks of all sorts. Colloquially the phrase has come to be synonymous with "and so forth"—*e.g.* "Photos, sketches and what-not."

Whatever are you at? So Dr. W. G. Grace is reported to have called out when, in 1896, Ernest Jones, the Australian fast bowler, bowled through W. G.'s beard.

Wheatear. The stonechat, a bird with a white tail. The name has no connexion with either *wheat* or *ear*, but it is the A.S. *hwit*, white, *ears*—still in vulgar use as *arse*—the buttocks or rump. The French name of the bird, *culblanc*, signifies exactly the same thing.

Wheel. The invention of the wheel dates from late prehistoric times, its origin having been probably in Eastern Europe or Asia Minor. It was not known to the peoples of the Far East until much later, for the Asiatic emigrants to North America and the ancient civilizations of Central America knew nothing of this invention upon which the world's progress has so largely advanced. Emblematical of St. Catharine (*q.v.*).

St. Donatus bears a wheel set round with lights.

St. Euphemia and St. Willigis both carry wheels.

St. Quintin is sometimes represented with a broken wheel at his feet.

Broken on the wheel. *See* BREAK.

The wheel is come to full circle. Just retribution has followed. The line is from Shakespeare's *King Lear*, v, 3.

The wheel of Fortune. Fortuna, the goddess, is represented on ancient monuments with a wheel in her hand, emblematical of her inconstancy.

> Though Fortune's malice overthrow my state,
> My mind exceeds the compass of her wheel.
>   SHAKESPEARE: *3 Henry VI*, iv, 3.

To put a spoke in one's wheel. *See* SPOKE.

Wherewithal. In older writings this is a form of *wherewith* as in

> Wherewithal shall a young man cleanse his way.—
> *Ps.* cxix, 9.

Colloquially it is now used as a noun, with the connotation of *money*.

Whetstone. *See* ACCRUS NÆVIUS.

Lying for the whetstone. Said of a person who is grossly exaggerating or falsifying a statement. One of the Whitsun amusements of our forefathers was the lie-wage or lie-match; he who could tell the greatest lie was rewarded with a whetstone to sharpen his wit. The nature of these contests may be illustrated by the following: one of the combatants declared he could see a fly on the top of a church steeple; the other replied, "Oh, yes, I saw him wink his eye."

The Whetstone of Witte. A famous treatise on algebra (1556) by Robert Recorde. The old name for algebra was the "Cossic Art," and *Cos ingenii* rendered into English is "the Whetstone of Wit." In Scott's *Fortunes of Nigel* the maid told the belated traveller that her master had "no other books but her young mistress's Bible . . . and her master's *Whetstone of Witte*, by Robert Recorde."

Whig. The political party opposed to the Tories (q.v.); roughly speaking, the party in favour of gradual change towards more democratic government.

The name came into use in the later 17th century, and was supplanted by "Liberal" (*q.v.*) in the early 19th. It is from obsolete *whiggamore*, a nickname for certain Scots who came to buy corn at Leith, from *whiggam*, an old Scottish equivalent to our *Gee up!* addressed to horses, and was originally applied to the Covenanters.

The south-west counties of Scotland have seldom corn enough to serve them all the year round, and, the northern parts producing more than they used, those in the west went in summer to buy at Leith the stores that came from the north. From the word *whiggam*, used in driving their horses, all that drove were called the *whiggamors*, contracted into *whigs*. Now, in the year before the news came down of Duke Hamilton's defeat, the ministers animated their people to rise and march to Edinburgh; and they came up, marching at the head of their parishes with an unheard-of fury, praying and preaching all the way as they came. The Marquis of Argyle and his party came and headed them, they being about 6,000. This was called the "Whiggamors' Inroad"; and ever after that, all who opposed the court came in contempt to be called *whigs*. From Scotland the word was brought into England, where it is now one of our unhappy terms of disunion.—BISHOP BURNET: *Own Times* (1723).

The Whig Party in the U.S.A. was active from about 1824 to 1854 under the leadership of Henry Clay and Daniel Webster.

The Whig Bible. *See* BIBLE, SPECIALLY NAMED.

Whip. A member of Parliament appointed unofficially, and without salary (as such), whose duty is to see that the members of his party vote at important divisions, and to discipline them if they do not attend, or vote against the party. The Whips give notice to members that a motion is expected when their individual vote may be desirable. The circular, or *whip*, runs: "A motion is expected when your vote is 'earnestly' required." If the word "earnestly" has only one red-ink dash under it the receiver is *expected* to come, if it has two dashes it means that he *ought* to come, if it has three dashes, or is a "three-line whip," it means that he *must* come, if four dashes it means "stay away at your peril." These notices are technically called *Red whips* (*Annual Register*, 1877, p. 86).

A whip-round. An impromptu collection for some benevolent object.

The whip with six strings. *See under* SIX.

Whip-dog Day. October 18th, St. Luke's Day. Brand tells us (*Popular Antiquities*, ii, 273) that it is so called because a priest about to celebrate mass on St. Luke's Day happened to drop the pyx, which was snatched up by a dog.

Whipper-snapper. An inexperienced—and often cheeky—young man. The word probably derives from *whip snapper*, one who has nothing to do but crack a whip.

Whipping Boy. A boy kept to be whipped when a prince deserved chastisement. Mungo Murray stood for Charles I, Barnaby Fitzpatrick for Edward VI (Fuller: *Church History*, ii, 342). When Henry IV of France abjured Protestantism and was received into the Catholic Church in 1595, two ambassadors (D'Ossat and Du Perron, afterwards cardinals) were sent to Rome and knelt in the portico of St. Peter, singing the *Miserere*. At each verse a blow with a switch was given on their shoulders.

Whisky. *See* USQUEBAUGH. The light one-horse gig of this name from *whisk*, to flourish a thing about with a quick movement.

Whisky Insurrection. A riotous outbreak in Western Pennsylvania, in 1794, in protest against the excise laws on spirits. In the country districts many small stills were worked by private persons, and when the excise officers attempted to deal with these, they were repulsed with violence and organized resistance. President Washington sent the militia to repress this outbreak and enforce the law, and the insurrection was put down without bloodshed.

Whisper. Pig's whisper. *See* PIG.

To give the whisper. To give the tip, the warning; to pass some bit of secret information.

Whist. The card game originated in England (16th cent.) and was first called *Triumph* (whence *trump*), then *Ruff* or *Honours*, and then, early in the 17th century, *Whisk*, in allusion to the sweeping up of the cards. *Whist*, the later name, appears in Butler's *Hudibras* (1663), and was adopted through confusion with *Whist!* meaning Hush! Silence!

> Let nice Piquette the boast of France remain,
> And studious Ombre be the pride of Spain!
> Invention's praise shall England yield to none,
> While she can call delightful Whist her own.
> ALEXANDER THOMSON: *Whist* (2nd edn., 1792).

Whistle. To whistle down the wind. To defame a person. The cognate phrase "blown upon" is more familiar. The idea is to whistle down the wind that the reputation of the person may be blown upon.

To whistle for it. It was an old superstition among sailors that when a ship was becalmed a wind could be raised by whistling. By a perversion of sense the phrase "You can whistle for it" now means "You won't get it."

Worth the whistle. Worth calling; worth inviting; worth notice. The dog is worth the pains of whistling for. Thus Heywood, in one of his dialogues consisting entirely of proverbs, says, "It is a poor dog that is not worth the whistling." Goneril says to Albany—

> I have been worth the whistle.
> *King Lear*, iv, 2.

You paid too dearly for your whistle. You paid dearly for something you fancied, but found that it did not answer your expectation. The allusion is to a story told by Dr. Franklin of his nephew, who set his mind on a common whistle, which he bought of a boy for four times its value.

To wet one's whistle. To drink.

Whit Sunday. White Sunday. The seventh Sunday after Easter, to commemorate the descent of the Holy Ghost on the day of Pentecost, In the primitive Church the newly baptized wore *white* from Easter to Pentecost, and were called *albati* (white-robed). The last of the Sundays, which was also the chief festival, was called emphatically *Dominica in Albis* (Sunday in White).

As an old play on the name it was called *Wit* or *Wisdom* Sunday, the day when the Apostles were filled with wisdom by the Holy Ghost.

> This day Whit-sonday is cald,
> For wisdom and wit sevene fald.
> Was zonen to the Apostles as this day.
> *Cambr. Univer. MSS.*, Dd. i, 1, p. 234.

We ought to kepe this our Witsonday bicause the law of God was then of the Holy Wyght or Ghost deliured gostly vnto vs.—*Taverner* (1540).

This day is called Wytsonday because the Holy Ghost brought wytte and wysdom into Christis disciples . . . and filled them full of ghostly wytte.—*In die Pentecostis* (printed by Wynkyn de Worde).

Whitsun farthings. *See* QUADRAGESIMALS.

White denotes purity, simplicity, and candour; innocence, truth, and hope. *See* COLOURS, SYMBOLISM OF.

The ancient Druids, and indeed the priests generally of antiquity, used to wear white vestments. The magi also wore white robes.

The head of Osiris, in Egypt, was adorned with a white tiara; all his ornaments were white; and his priests were clad in white.

The priests of Jupiter, and the Flamen Dialis of Rome, were clothed in white, and wore white hats. The victims offered to Jupiter were white. The Roman festivals were marked with white chalk, and at the death of a Cæsar the national mourning was white; white horses were sacrificed to the sun, white oxen were selected for sacrifice by the Druids, and white elephants are held sacred in Siam.

The Persians affirm that the divinities are habited in white.

Whitebait Dinner. A dinner of Cabinet Ministers and prominent politicians that, until the early 1890s, was held at Blackwall or Greenwich toward the close of the parliamentary session. The time of meeting was Trinity Monday, or as near Trinity Monday as circumstances would allow.

Yesterday the Cabinet Ministers went down the River in the Ordnance barge to Lovegrove's "West India Dock Tavern," Blackwall, to partake of their annual fish dinner. Covers were laid for thirty-five gentlemen.—*The Times*, Sept. 10, 1835.

To hit the white. To be quite right, make a good shot. The phrase is from the old days of archery, the *white* being the inner circle of the target—the bull's eye.

The white bird. Conscience, or the soul of man. The Mohammedans have preserved the old Roman idea in the doctrine that the souls of the just lie under the throne of God, like white birds, till the resurrection morn. *Cp.* DOVE.

Whiteboys. A secret agrarian association organized in Ireland about the year 1760. So called because they wore white shirts in their nightly expeditions. In 1787 a new association appeared, the members of which called them-selves "Right-boys." The White-boys were origi-nally called Levellers (*q.v.*), from their throwing down fences and levelling enclosures.

White collar worker. The professional or clerical worker whose calling demands a certain nicety of attire.

White elephant. *See* ELEPHANT.

White-face. A nickname for a man from Hereford; from the white faces of Herefordshire cattle.

White flag. An all-white flag is universally used as the signal of surrender or of desiring to parley. A messenger bearing a white flag is by international decency immune from harm.

White Friars. The Carmelites (*q.v.*), so called because of the white mantle they wear over a brown habit. One of their houses, founded in London on the south side of Fleet Street in 1241, gives the name to that district, and was for many centuries a sanctuary.

The White Horse. The standard of the ancient Saxons; hence the emblem of Kent. A galloping white horse is the device of the House of Hanover, and it is from this that many public houses bear the sign of "The White Horse."

On Uffington Hill, Berks, there is formed in the chalk an enormous white horse, supposed to have been cut there after the battle in which Ethelred and Alfred defeated the Danes (871). This rude design is about 374 ft. long, and 1,000 ft. above the sea-level. It may be seen twelve or fifteen miles off, and gives its name to the *Vale of White Horse*, west of Abingdon.

An annual ceremony was once held, called "Scouring the White Horse."

Foam-crested waves are popularly called *White horses*.

> Now the great winds shoreward blow,
> Now the salt tides seaward flow;
> Now the wild white horses play,
> Champ and chafe and toss in the spray.
> MATTHEW ARNOLD: *The Forsaken Merman*.

White House. The presidential mansion in Washington, D.C. It is a building of freestone, painted white. The cornerstone was laid by Washington, and the house was remodelled in 1902. Figuratively, it means the Presidency of the U.S.A.

White Lady. A sort of ghostly spirit in many countries, the appearance of which generally forebodes death in the house. It is a relic of Teutonic mythology, representing Holda, or Berchta, the goddess who received the souls of maidens and young children.

German legend says that when the castle of Neuhaus, Bohemia, was being built a white lady appeared to the workmen and promised them a sweet soup and carp on the completion of the castle. In remembrance thereof, these dainties were for long given to the poor of Bohemia on Maundy Thursday. She is also said to have been heard to speak on two occasions, once in December, 1628, when she said, "I wait for judgment!" and once at Neuhaus, when she said to the princes, "'Tis ten o'clock."

The first recorded instance of this appari-tion was in the 16th century, and the name given to the lady is Bertha von Rosenberg. She last appeared, it is said, in 1879, just prior to the death of Prince Waldemar. She carries a bunch of keys at her side, and is always dressed in white.

In Normandy the White Ladies lurk in ravines, fords, bridges, and other narrow passes, and ask the passenger to dance. If they receive a courteous answer, well; but if a refusal, they seize the churl and fling him into a ditch, where thorns and briers may serve to teach him gentleness of manners.

The most famous of these ladies is *La Dame d'Aprigny*, who used to occupy the site of the present Rue St. Quentin, at Bayeux, and *La Dame Abonde*.

> One kind of these the Italians *Fata* name;
> The French call *Fée*; we *Sybils*; and the same
> Others *White Dames*, and those that them have seen,
> *Night Ladies* some, of which Habundia's queen.
> *Hierarchie*, viii, p. 507.

White League. A name of the Ku Klux Klan (*q.v.*).

A white lie. An excusable or pardonable un-truth.

White-livered. Mean or cowardly. It was an old notion that the livers of cowards were bloodless.

> How many cowards, whose hearts are all as false
> As stairs of sand, wear yet upon their chins
> The beards of Hercules and frowning Mars,
> Who, inward search'd, have livers white as milk!
> *Merchant of Venice*, iii, 2.

A white man. A thoroughly straightforward and honourable man.

White magic. Sorcery in which the devil was not invoked and played no part; opposed to black magic.

White Man's Burden. The duty supposed to be thrust on the white races, especially the British, to educate and govern the untutored coloured races for their own welfare. The phrase arose during the imperial fervour of the later 19th century:—

> Take up the White Man's Burden—
>   Send forth the best you breed
> Go bind your sons to exile
>   To serve the captives' need.
>   KIPLING.

A white night. A sleepless night; the French have the phrase *Passer une nuit blanche*.

White Paper. A publication issued by the British government giving information on matters of interest, reports of committees, etc., and on sale to the public. Since 1919 Government papers have been marked "Cmd.", command.

The White Rose. The House of York, whose emblem it was (*see under* ROSE).

White Rose League. A society adhering in theory to the claims of the House of Stuart to the throne of Great Britain. It is of a purely sentimental and historical nature, harbouring no disloyalty to the Crown.

White Satin. An old nickname for gin.

White Slave. A woman who is sold or forced into prostitution. The problem of White Slave Traffic, especially to South America, was taken up vigorously by the League of Nations, and in some measure the evil was mitigated through its exertions.

A white squall. One which produces no diminution of light, in contradistinction to a *black* squall, in which the clouds are black and heavy.

The White Tsar. An epithet of the former Tsars of Russia, as Tsars of Muscovy; the King of Muscovy was called the White King from the robes which he wore. The King of Poland was called the Black King.

Whitewash. Excuses made in palliation of bad conduct; a false colouring given to a person's character or memory to counteract disreputable allegations.

The term is also applied to the clearance by a bankrupt of his debts, not by paying them, but by judicial process.

White wine. Any wine of a light colour, not red; as champagne, hock, sauterne, moselle, etc.

White witch. One who practised white magic (*q.v.*) only.

Whittington, Dick. Sir Richard Whittington, "thrice Lord Mayor of London," about whom the well-known nursery story is told, was born about 1358, the son of Sir William de Whityngdon, lord of the manor of Pauntley, Gloucester. Being a younger son and unprovided for, he walked to London, was trained by a relative as a merchant, married his master's daughter and so prospered that he was able to lend Henry IV £1,000—equal to over £30,000 in present money.

He was Lord Mayor of London in 1397, 1406, and 1419, besides being once named by Richard II to succeed a mayor who had died in office. He died in 1423.

The legend that Whittington made his wealth largely through the agency of a cat seems to be founded on a confusion between Fr. *achat* and Eng. *a cat*. In the 14th and early 15th centuries trading, or buying and selling at a profit, was known among the educated classes as *achat* (French for "purchase"), which was written—and probably pronounced—*acat* (see Riley's *Introduction* to the *Liber Albus*).

Another suggestion is that it arose through confusion with the *cat*, a ship on the Norwegian model, having a narrow stern, projecting quarters, and deep waist, and used in the coal trade. According to tradition, Sir Richard made his money by trading in coals, which he conveyed in his "cat" from Newcastle to London. The black faces of his coalheavers gave rise to the tale about the Moors. But there are Eastern tales of the same kind, and it is probably one of these that became attached to the popular Lord Mayor.

Whoopee (woo pē') (Slang). Uproariousness, noisy merriment. As an exclamation it is one of excited pleasure.

Wide Boy. The predecessor of the Spiv (*q.v.*), active in the years 1920-40.

Widow, The. Old slang for the gallows. Also Victorian slang for champagne, from the well-known brand Veuve Cliquot.

Wife. A.S. *wif*, a woman. The ultimate root of the word is obscure; but it is "certainly not allied to *weave* (A.S. *weafn*), as the fable runs" (Skeat).

The old meaning, *a woman*, still appears in such combinations as *fish-wife*, *housewife*, etc., and in the phrase *an old wife's tale* (see 1 *Tim.* iv, 7) for an incoherent and unconvincing story.

The Wife-hater Bible. See BIBLE, SPECIALLY NAMED.

Wig. A shortened form of *periwig* (earlier, *perwig*), from Fr. *peruke*. In the middle of the

18th century we meet with thirty or forty different names for wigs: as the artichoke, bag, barrister's, bishop's, brush, bush (buzz), buckle, busby, chain, chancellor's, corded, wolf's paw, Count Saxe's mode, the crutch, the cut bob, the detached buckle, the Dalma-hoy (a bob wig worn by tradesmen), the drop, the Dutch, the full, the half natural, the Jan-senist bob, the judge's, the ladder, the long bob, the Louis, the pigeon's wing, the rhinoceros, the rose, the scratch, the she-dragon, the small back, the spinach seed, the staircase, the Welsh, the wild boar's back.

A bigwig. A magnate; in allusion to the large wigs that in the 17th and 18th centuries encumbered the head and shoulders of the aristocracy of England and France. They are still worn by the Lord Chancellor, judges, and barristers; bishops used to wear them in the House of Lords till 1880.

Wigwam (wig' worn). An American Indian term for a house or tent.

Wild fire. A very old English description of a composition of inflammable materials that catch fire quickly. It is now used figuratively in the phrase **To catch like wildfire,** to take on with the public instantaneously.

To lead one a wild-goose chase. To beguile one with false hopes, or put one on an impracticable pursuit, or after something that is not worth the chase. A wildgoose is very hard to catch, and very little use when caught.

To sow one's wild oats. *See* OAT.

Wild men. A term often applied, in politics, to intransigents, the extremists of either party who will not accommodate their views and actions to changing conditions or public opinion.

Women who took an active part in the movement for obtaining votes and political recognition were sometimes called *wild women.*

Wild West. The western frontier of the U.S.A. before a stable government was in being. The phrase really refers to the days of the mid-19th century before the whole continent was known and developed, and the ever-shifting frontiers of civilization in the west were the resort of desperadoes, cattle-thieves, etc. The term is often applied to stories of adventure dealing with that period and those localities.

Wilderness. To go into the wilderness. A figurative description of being deprived of political office through a change of government.

Wilhelmstrasse (vil' helm stra se). A street in Berlin where the principal government offices, including the Foreign Office, were situated. The term is usually applied to the German Foreign Office and its policy. In the Allied bombing of Berlin in World War II most of the street was levelled with the ground.

Will-o'-the-wisp. *See* FRIAR'S LANTHORN; IGNIS FATUUS.

William. One of the most popular of Christian names; Fr. *Guillaume,* Ger. *Wilhelm,* it means *a protector;* literally, *a resolute helmet*— Ger. *wille helm.*

The william pear. Properly the **William's pear,** or Bon Chrétien is so called from the name of its introducer into England. For a like reason it is known in the U.S.A. as the Bartlett Pear. Sweet william is an old English name for an old English flower, *Dianthus barbatus,* a member of the pink family.

Of the many saints of this name the following are perhaps the most noteworthy:—

St. William of Aquitaine. A soldier of Charlemagne's, who helped to chase the Saracens from Languedoc. In 808 he renounced the world, and died 812. He is usually represented as a mailed soldier.

St. William of Maleval. A French nobleman who went as pilgrim to Jerusalem, and on his return retired to the desert of Maleval, where he died in 1157. The *Guillemites* a branch of the Benedictine order, was founded by Albert, one of his disciples, and named in his honour. He is depicted in a Benedictine's habit, with armour lying beside him.

St. William of Montpelier is represented with a lily growing from his mouth, with the words *Ave Maria* in gold letters on the flower.

St. William of Monte Virgine (d. 1142) is shown with a wolf by his side.

St. William of Norwich was the child said to have been crucified by the Jews in 1137. He is represented crowned with thorns, or crucified, or holding a hammer and nails in his hands, or wounded in his side with a knife (*see* Drayton's *Polyolbion,* song xxiv).

In Percy's *Reliques* (Bk. i, 3) there is a tale of a lad named Hew, son of Lady Helen, of Merryland town (Milan), who was allured by a Jew's daughter with an apple. She stuck him with a penknife, rolled him in lead, and cast him into a well. Lady Helen went in search of her boy, and the child's ghost cried out from the bottom of the well—

The lead is wondrous heavy, mither,
  The well is wondrous deip;
A keen penknife sticks in my heirt, mither;
  A word I dauna speik.

St. William of York (d. 1154) was a nephew of King Stephen, and became Archbishop of

York in 1140. He was canonized by Honorius III about 1220 on account of the many miracles reported to have been performed at his tomb.

Willow. To handle the willow. To be a cricket-player. Cricket-bats are made of willow; hence the game is sometimes called *King Willow* (*see* the Harrow school song of this name).

To wear the willow. To go into mourning, especially for a sweetheart or bride.

The willow, especially the weeping willow, has from time immemorial been associated with sorrow and taken as an emblem of desolation or desertion. Fuller says, "The willow is a sad tree, whereof such as have lost their love make their mourning garlands," and the psalmist tells us that the Jews in captivity hung their harps upon the willows in sign of mourning (cxxxvii)

Desdemona says in *Othello* (iv, 3):—
My mother had a maid call'd Barbara;
She was in love, and he she lov'd prov'd mad
And did forsake her; she had a song of "willow";
An old thing 'twas, but it expressed her fortune,
And she died singing it.

And then comes the song—
The poor soul sat sighing by a sycamore tree,
Sing all a green willow;
Her hand on her bosom, her head on her knee,
Sing willow, willow, willow;
The fresh streams ran by her, and murmur'd her, moans;
Sing willow, willow, willow:
Her salt tears fell from her, and soften'd the stones;
Sing willow, willow, willow.

The Willow Pattern. A favourite design for blue china plates, imitating (but not copying) the Chinese style of porcelain decoration. It was introduced into England by Thomas Turner of Caughley about 1780, when the craze for things Chinese was at its height.

To the right is a mandarin's country seat, two stories high to show the rank and wealth of the possessor; in the foreground a pavilion, in the background an orange-tree, and to the right of the pavilion a peach-tree in full bearing. The estate is enclosed by a wooden fence, and a river crossed by a bridge, at one end of which is the famous willow-tree and at the outer the gardener's humble cottage. At the top of the pattern (left-hand side) is an island. The three figures on the bridge are the mandarin and the lovers, the latter also being shown in a boat on the river.

The willow pattern does not illustrate any Chinese story or legend, and is not Chinese in origin.

Willy-nilly. *Nolens volens*; willing or not. Will-he, nill-he, *nill* being *n'* (negative), *will*, just as Lat. *nolens* is *n'-volens*.

Wimbledon. A suburb of London, and home Off the All England Croquet Club. In the middle of the 1870s the Club, being in low water, added "Lawn Tennis" to its title, this being then a new game increasing in popularity. On the Club's courts the first lawn tennis Championship in the world was held in 1877. The annual tournament run by the All England Club at Wimbledon still ranks as the premier championship.

Wind. According to classical mythology, the north, south, east, and west winds (*Boreas, Notus, Eurus,* and *Zephyrus*) were under the rule of Æolus, who kept them confined in a cave on Mount Hæmus, Thrace. Other strong winds of a more destructive nature were the brood of Typhœus.

The story says that Æolus gave Ulysses a bag, tied with a silver string, in which were all the hurtful and unfavourable winds, so that he might arrive home without being delayed by tempests. His crew, however, opened the bag in the belief that it contained treasure, the winds escaped, and a terrible storm at once arose, driving the vessel out of its course and back to the island it had left.

Latin names for other winds are: north-east, *Argestes*; north-west, *Corus*; south-east, *Vol-turnus*; south-west, *Afer ventus, Africus, Africanus,* or *Libs*. The *Thrascias* is a north wind, but not due north. *Aquilo* is another name for the north wind, as *Auster* is of the south and *Favonius* of the west.

Boreas and Cæcias, and Argestes loud,
And Thrascias rend the woods, and seas upturn;
Notus and Afer, black with thunderous clouds,
From Serraliona. Thwart of these, as fierce,
Forth rush. . . . Eurus and Zephyr. . . .
Sirocco and Libecchio [Libycus].
MILTON: *Paradise Lost*, x, 699-706.

For some specially named winds *see* ETESIAN, HARMATTAN, KAMSIN, MISTRAL, MONSOON, PAMPERO, SIROCCO, SOLANO, TRADE WINDS, etc.

Second wind. Soon after the start in running, unless the runner is very fit he gets out of breath; but, as the body becomes heated, breathing becomes more easy, and endures till fatigue produces exhaustion; this is called the *second wind*.

There's something in the wind. There are signs that something is going to happen, some hitherto unanticipated development is about to take place.

Three sheets in the wind. *See* SHEET.

'Tis an ill wind that blows nobody any good. Someone profits by every loss; someone is benefited by every misfortune.
Except wind stands as never it stood,
It is an ill-wind turns none to good.
TUSSER: *Five Hundred Points of Good Husbandry*, xiii.

To know which way the wind blows. To be aware of the true state of affairs.

To sail close to the wind. In nautical use, to keep the vessel's head as near the quarter from which the wind is blowing as possible while keeping the sails filled; figuratively, to go to the very verge of what decency or propriety allow; to act so as just to escape the letter of the law.

To take the wind out of one's sails. To forestall him, "steal his thunder" (*see* THUNDER), frustrate him by utilizing his own material or methods. Literally, it is to sail to the windward of a ship and so rob its sails of the wind.

Windbag. A long-winded, bombastic speaker, who uses inflated phrases and promises far more than he can perform.

Windfall. An unexpected piece of good luck, especially an unexpected legacy; something worth having that comes to one without any personal exertion—like fruit which has fallen from the tree and so does not have to be picked.

Windjammer. A sailing ship, or one of its crew. The term is a modern one, born since steam superseded sail.

Windy City. Chicago.

Windmill. To fight with windmills. To face imaginary adversaries, combat chimeras. The allusion is to the adventure of Don Quixote who, when riding through the plains of Montiel, approached thirty or forty windmills, which he declared to Sancho Panza "were giants, two leagues in length or more." Striking his spurs into Rosinante, with his lance in rest, he drove at one of the "monsters dreadful as Typhœus" the lance lodged in the sail, and the latter lifted both man and beast into the air. When the valiant knight and his steed fell they were both much injured, and Don Quixote declared that the enchanter Freston, "who carried off his library with all the books therein," had changed the giants into windmills "out of malice" (Bk. i, ch. viii).

Window. Window dressing. Properly, the display of goods in a shop window for the purpose of attracting customers. Figuratively, the phrase is applied to the specious display of whatever is attractive in a project, plan, or the like.

Windsor. The House of Windsor. The official title of the reigning dynasty of Great Britain and the British Dominions beyond the Seas since July 17th, 1917, when King George V signed a proclamation adopting this style for the Royal Family and declared that—

all the descendants in the male line of Queen Victoria who are subjects of these realms, other than female descendants who may marry or may have married, shall bear the name of Windsor.

From the time of George I to the death of Queen Victoria the dynasty was known as the *House of Hanover*; from the accession of Edward VII to the date of this proclamation it was the *House of Saxe-Coburg*, so named from Edward VII's father, Albert, Duke of Saxony, Prince of Coburg and Gotha.

After his abdication, December 11th, 1936, King Edward VIII was created Duke of Windsor.

Wine. At the universities *a wine* is a convivial gathering at which wine, as a rule, is drunk.

Wine of ape (Chaucer). "I trow that ye have drunken win of ape"—*i.e.* wine to make you drunk; in French, *vin de singe*. There is a Talmud parable which says that Satan came one day to drink with Noah, and slew a lamb, a lion, a pig, and an ape, to teach Noah that man before wine is in him is a *lamb*, when he drinks moderately he is a *lion*, when like a sot he is a *swine*, but after that any further excess makes him an *ape* that senselessly chatters and jabbers.

See also VIN.

Wing. This word, naturally applied to the ailerons of an aeroplane, is used as a collective term in the R.A.F. for a group of three squadrons, under a Wing-Commander, ranking with a Commander in the Navy and a Lieut.-Colonel in the Army.

Don't try to fly without wings. Attempt nothing you are not fit for. A Latin saying, Plautus has (*Pœnulus* IV, ii, 47) *Sine pennis volare haud facile est*, It is by no means easy to fly without wings.

To clip one's wings. To take down one's conceit; to hamper one's freedom of action.

To take one under your wing. To patronize and protect. The allusion is to a hen gathering her chicks under her wing.

To take wing. To fly away; to depart without warning.

Oh, God! it is a fearful thing
To see the human soul take wing.
BYRON: *Prisoner of Chillon*.

Winifred, St. Patron saint of virgins, because she was beheaded by Prince Caradoc for refusing to marry him. She was Welsh by birth, and the legend says that where her head fell on the ground sprang up the famous healing well of St. Winifred in Flintshire. She is usually drawn like St. Denis, carrying her head in her hand. Holywell is St. Winifred's Well, celebrated for its "miraculous" virtues.

Wink. A nod is as good as a wink to a blind horse. *See* NOD.

Forty winks. A short nap, a doze.

Like winking. Old slang for very quickly; as in "to give an answer like winking."

To tip one the wink. To give him a hint privately; to "put him wise."

To wink at. To connive at, or to affect not to notice.

He knows not how to wink at human frailty
Or pardon weakness that he never felt.
ADDISON: *Cato*, v, 4.

Winkle, Rip van. The creation of Washington Irving, hero of one of the stories in the *Sketch Book* (1819) which tells how he, a Dutch colonist of New York in pre-Revolutionary days, met with a strange man in a ravine of the Catskill Mountains. Rip helps him to carry a keg, and when they reach the destination sees a number of odd creatures playing nine-pins, but no one utters a word. Master Winkle seizes the first opportunity to take a sip at the keg, falls into a stupor, and sleeps for twenty years. On waking, he finds that he is a tottering old man, his wife is dead and buried, his daughter is married, his native village has been remodelled, and America has become independent.

Winter's Tale, The. One of the last of Shakespeare's plays, acted in 1611 but not printed till 1623 (first Folio). It is founded on Greene's *Pandosto, The Triumph of Time* (1588), which was written round an actual incident that occurred in the Bohemian and Polish courts in the late 14th century.

In the play Polixenes, King of Bohemia, is invited to Sicily by King Leontes, and unwittingly excites the jealousy of his friend because he prolongs his stay at the entreaty of Queen Hermione. Leontes orders Camillo to poison the royal guest, but, instead of doing so, Camillo flees with him to Bohemia. In time Florizel, the son and heir of Polixenes, falls in love with Perdita, the lost daughter of Leontes. Polixenes forbids the match, and the young lovers, under the charge of Camillo, flee to Sicily. Polixenes follows the fugitives, the mystery of Perdita is cleared up, the lovers are married, and the two kings resume their friendship.

In Greene's romance Polixenes is *Pandosto*, Hermione *Bellaria*, Leontes *Egistus*, and Florizel and Perdita *Dorastus* and *Fawnia*.

Wipe. Old slang for a pocket-handkerchief.

Wiped out. Destroyed, annihilated; quite obliterated.

Wire. Used as a verb, meaning *to telegraph to.* "Wire me without delay," telegraph to me at once.

Wireless. Applied to telegraphic and telephonic communications sent through space instead of along a wire. A more colloquial term is "radio."

To pull the wires. To control events, politics, etc., clandestinely from behind the scenes, as the unseen operator manipulates the marionettes in a puppet-show.

Wisdom. Wisdom of Solomon. A book of the Old Testament Apocrypha, written by an Alexandrian Jew, probably between A.D. 1 and A.D. 40, to counteract the scepticism and Epicureanism presented in the Apocryphal book of Ecclesiasticus.

Wisdom tooth. The popular name for the third molar in each jaw. Wisdom teeth appear between the ages of 17 and 25.

The wisdom of many and the wit of one. Lord John Russell's definition of a proverb.

Wise. To put one wise. An Americanism, meaning to acquaint him with the facts, with the true position of affairs; to give him the necessary information.

Wisecrack. (Slang). A facetious or witty remark.

Wisest Fool in Christendom. James I of England (1566-1625).

The following have been surnamed **The Wise**:—

ALBERT II, Duke of Austria, called *The Lame and Wise.* (1289, 1330-58.)

ALFONSO X (or IX) of Leon, and IV of Castile, called *The Wise* and *The Astronomer.* (1203, 1252-85).

CHARLES V of France, called *Le Sage.* (1337, regent 1358-60, king 1364-80.)

FREDERICK II, Elector of Saxony. (1482, 1544-56.)

JOHN V of Brittany, called *The Good and Wise.* (1389, 1399-1442.)

Wise Men of Greece, The; also known as *The Seven Sages.*

Solon of Athens (about 638-559 B.C.), whose motto was, "Know thyself."

Chilo of Sparta (d. 597 B.C.)—"Consider the end." *See* DE MORTUIS.

Thales of Miletus (d. 548 B.C.)—"Who hateth suretyship is sure."

Bias of Priene (fl. 6th cent. B.C.)—"Most men are bad."

Cleobulus of Lindos (d. 564 B.C.)—"The golden mean," or "Avoid extremes."

Pittacus of Mitylene (d. 570 B.C.)—"Seize Time by the forelock."

Periander of Corinth (d. 585 B.C.)—"Nothing is impossible to industry."

The Wise Men of the East. *See* MAGI.

Wisest Man of Greece, The. So the Delphic oracle pronounced Socrates to be, and Socrates modestly made answer, "'Tis because I alone of all the Greeks know that I know nothing."

Wishing bone. *See* MERRYTHOUGHT.

Wishing cap. Fortunatus (*q.v.*) had an inexhaustible purse and a wishing cap, but these gifts proved the ruin of himself and his sons. The object of the tale is to show the vanity of human prosperity.

Wishful thinking. A popular psychoanalytical term that has gained general acceptance as describing the unconscious expression of one's desire in accordance with one's opinion; the thinking a thing to be true because one wants it to be so.

Wit. Understanding, intelligence (A.S. *witt*, knowledge); hence, the power of perceiving analogies and other relations between apparently incongruous ideas or of forming unexpected, striking, or ludicrous combinations of them; and so, a person distinguished for this power, a witty person.

At one's wits' end. Quite at a loss as to what to say or what to do next; "flummoxed."

To have one's wits about one. To be wide awake; observant of all that is going on and prepared to take advantage of any opportunity that offers.

To wit. Namely; that is to say.

Witch. (A.S. *wiccian*, to practise sorcery.) Innocent VIII issued the celebrated bull *Summis Desiderantes* in 1484, directing inquisitors and others to put to death all practisers of witchcraft and other diabolical arts, and it has been computed that as many as nine millions of persons have suffered death for witchcraft since that date.

By drawing the blood of a witch you deprive her of her power of sorcery. Glanvil says that when Jane Brooks, the demon of Tedworth, bewitched a boy, his father scratched her face and drew blood, whereupon the boy instantly exclaimed that he was well.

Blood will I draw on thee; thou art a witch.
1 Henry VI, i, 5.

John Fian, a schoolmaster at Saltpans, near Edinburgh, was tortured and then burnt at the stake on the Castle Hill of Edinburgh in 1591, because he refused to acknowledge that he had raised a storm at sea, to wreck James VI on his voyage to Denmark to visit his future queen.

Matthew Hopkins, the notorious "witch-finder," who, in the middle of the 17th century, travelled through the Eastern Counties to hunt out witches, is said to have hanged sixty in one year in Essex alone. At last he himself was tested by his own rule; when cast into a river he floated, and so was declared to be a wizard, and was put to death.

It is said that in England between three and four thousand persons suffered death for witchcraft between 1643 and 1661, and as late as 1705 two women were executed at Northampton

Witch hazel. A North American shrub (*Hamamelis virginiana*) having several large branches. It is so called because its twigs are used as divining rods.

Witchen. *See* ROWAN.

Withers. A horse's *withers* are the muscles uniting the neck and shoulders, or the ridge between the shoulder-blades; so called from A.S. *wither*, against, because this part is *against* the collar or load. Hamlet says (iii, 2):—

Let the galled jade wince, our withers are unwrung.

That is, let those wince who are galled; as for myself, my withers are not wrung. The skin of this part is often galled by the pommel of an ill-fitting saddle, and then the irritation of the saddle makes the horse wince. In 1 *Henry IV*, ii, 1, one of the carriers gives direction to the ostler to ease the saddle of his horse, Cut. "I prythee, Tom, beat Cut's saddle . . . the poor jade is wrung on the withers," that is, the muscles are wrung, and the skin galled by the saddle.

Wivern (wī' vern). A fabulous creature of heraldry consisting of a winged dragon ending in a barbed, serpent's tail.

Wizard of Oz. The central figure in a very popular children's book *The Wonderful Wizard of Oz*, (1900) by Lyman Frank Baum (1856-1919), a well-known American journalist. The musical comedy of the same name (1901) was a great success, which was carried on to the film of some years later.

We're off to see the Wizard
The Wonderful Wizard of Oz
We hear he's a whiz of a Wizard,
If ever a Wiz there was.

Woden (wō' den). The Anglo-Saxon form of *Odin* (*q.v.*), the name of the supreme god of the later Scandinavian pantheon, he having supplanted Thor. Woden was the god of agriculture, and on this account Wednesday (Woden's Day) was considered to be specially favourable for sowing.

Woe. Wo, or **Woe worth the day!** Cursed be the day! Evil betide it!

Thus saith the Lord God: Howl ye, woe worth the day!—*Ezek.* xxx, 2.

Worth here is A.S. *weothan*, to become.

Woebegone. Overwhelmed by woe, especially applied to the appearance—*A woebegone countenance*. At first sight it would seem that the words imply the reverse of this, but *begone* is the p.p. of the old English verb began, to surround. It thus means "surrounded with woe" rather than "woe go away, be gone."

The Knight of the Woeful Countenance. The title given by Sancho Panza to Don Quixote (Bk. iii, ch. v).

Wolf. The tradition that wolves were extirpated from Great Britain in the reign of Edgar (959-975) is based upon the words of William of Malmesbury, who says (Bk. ii, ch. viii) that the tribute paid by the King of Wales, consisting of 300 wolves, ceased after the third year, because he could find no more; but in 1076 we find that Robert de Umfraville, knight, held his lordship of Riddlesdale in Northumberland by service of defending that part of the kingdom from "wolves." In 1369 Thomas Engarne held lands in Pitchley, Northamptonshire, by service of finding dogs at his own cost for the destruction of "wolves" and foxes; and even as late as 1433 Sir Robert Plumpton held one bovate of land in the county of Notts by service of "frighting the wolves" in Sherwood Forest.

Wolf has been applied as an epithet to many persons of savage and inhuman disposition, especially to Isabella, the *She-wolf of France*, the queen of Edward II. According to tradition, she murdered her royal husband by thrusting a hot iron into his bowels.

She-wolf of France, with unrelenting fangs,
That tear'st the bowels of thy mangled mate.
                              GRAY: *The Bard*.

Dryden gave the name to the Presbytery in his *Hind and Panther*.

Unkennelled range in thy Polonian plains,
A fiercer foe the insatiate Wolf remains.

In music a discordant sound (occasioned by a faulty interval) in certain chords of the piano, was called a *wolf*. It has now been eliminated by modern tuning.

Nature hath implanted so inveterate a hatred atweene the wolfe and the sheepe, that, being dead, yet in the operation of Nature appeareth there a sufficient trial of their discording nature; so that the enmity betweene them seemeth not to dye with their bodies; for if there be put upon a harpe . . . strings made of the intralles of a sheepe, and amongst them . . . one made of the intralles of a wolfe . . . the musician . . . cannot reconcile them to a unity and concord of sounds, so

discording is that string of the wolfe.—FERNE: *Blazon of Gentrie* (1586).

The squeak made in *reed* instruments by unskilled players is termed a "goose."

Wolf call (U.S.A.). An admiring exclamation, usually whistled, at sight of a girl.

Wolf Cub. A Boy Scout of the most junior rank, aged from eight to eleven years.

A wolf in sheep's clothing. An enemy posing as a friend. The phrase is taken from the well-known fable of Æsop.

He put his head into the wolf's mouth. He exposed himself to needless danger. The allusion is to Æsop's fable of the crane that put its head into a wolf's (or fox's) mouth in order to extract a bone.

To cry "Wolf!" To give a false alarm. The allusion is to the well-known fable of the shepherd lad who so often cried "Wolf!" merely to make fun of the neighbours, that when at last the wolf came no one would believe him. This fable appears in almost every nation the world over.

To keep the wolf from the door. To ward off starvation. We say of a ravenous person "He has a wolf in his stomach," and one who eats voraciously is said *to wolf* his food. French *manger comme un loup* is to eat voraciously.

Wolf's-bane. A species of aconite, *Aconitum lycoctonum*. The name is said to have arisen through a curious double etymological confusion. *Bane* is a common term for poisonous plants, and by some early botanist it was translated into Gr. *kuamos*, which means *bean*. The plant has a pale yellow flower, and was so called the *white-bane* to distinguish it from the *blue* aconite. The Greek for white is *leukos*, hence *leukos-kuamos*; but *lukos* is the Greek for wolf, and by a blunder *leukos-kuamos* (white-bean) got muddled into *lukos-kuamos* (wolf-bean). Botanists, seeing the absurdity of calling aconite a *bean*, restored the original word *bane* but retained the corrupt word *lukos* (a wolf), and hence we get the name wolf's-bane for white aconite.

Another, more plausible, explanation would probably be that the plant is so called because meat saturated with its juice was supposed to be a wolf-poison.

Wolfe's Own. *See* REGIMENTAL NICKNAMES.

Woman's Suffrage. *See* SUFFRAGE.

Wonder. A nine days' wonder. Something that causes a sensational astonishment for a few days, and is then placed in the limbo of "things forgot." Three days' amazement, three days' discussion of details, and three days of subsidence.

> For whan men han wel cried, than let hem roune!
> For wonder last but nine night nevere in toune!
> CHAUCER: *Troilus and Criseyde*, iv, 587.

The Seven Wonders of the World.
The Pyramids of Egypt.
The Hanging Gardens of Babylon.
The Tomb of Mausolus.
The Temple of Diana at Ephesus.
The Colossus of Rhodes.
The Statue of Jupiter, by Phidias.
The Pharos of Alexandria.
A later list gives:—
The Coliseum of Rome.
The Catacombs of Alexandria.
The Great Wall of China.
Stonehenge.
The Leaning Tower of Pisa.
The Porcelain Tower of Nankin.
The Mosque of St. Sophia at Constantinople.

Wood, Wooden. Drawn from the wood. Taken direct from the cask to the tankard or glass. Said of beer, wines, and spirits.

Don't cry (or halloo) till you are out of the wood. Do not rejoice for having escaped danger till the danger has passed away. "Call no man happy till he is dead"; "there's many a slip 'twixt the cup and the lip."

One can't see the wood for the trees. There is such a mass of detail that it is almost impossible to arrive at a true estimate of the thing as a whole.

Woodbine. A name given in different localities to many plants that bind or wind themselves around trees; especially the honeysuckle and the convolvulus. In the first quotation below probably the former is intended; in the second the latter.

> Where the bee
> Strays diligent, and with extracted balm
> Of fragrant woodbine loads his little thigh.
> PHILLIPS.

Shakespeare says—
> So doth the woodbine, the sweet honeysuckle
> Gently entwist. *Midsummer Night's Dream*, iv, 1.

Woodchuck. A marmot (*Arctomys monax*) of North America, also called the *ground-hog*. Its name is a corruption of its North American Indian name, *wejack*, and has given rise to the punning conundrum—
How much wood would a woodchuck chuck, if a woodchuck could chuck wood?

Woodcock. Old slang for a simpleton; from the supposition that woodcocks are without brains. Polonius tells his daughter that protestations of love are "springes to catch woodcocks" (*Hamlet*, i, 3).

Wooden. Used of one who is awkward and ungainly, or of a spiritless, emotionless person.

The wooden horse of Troy. Virgil tells us that Ulysses had a monster wooden horse made after the death of Hector, and gave out that it was an offering to the gods to secure a prosperous voyage back to Greece. The Trojans dragged the horse within their city, but it was full of Grecian soldiers, who at night stole out of their place of concealment, slew the Trojan guards, opened the city gates, and set fire to Troy. Menelaus was one of the Greeks shut up in it. It was made by Epeios.

Wooden nutmegs. Connecticut was in the early 19th century referred to derisively as the land of wooden nutmegs because certain dishonest merchants from the State were said to have exported nutmegs made of wood and other worthless goods.

Woof. *See* WARP.

Wool. Great cry and little wool. *See* CRY.

Dyed in the wool. Cloth which is wool-dyed (not piece-dyed) is true throughout and will wash. Hence the phrase is used to describe anything or person absolutely genuine.

Your wits are gone wool-gathering. You are absent-minded; you're not thinking of the matter in hand. As children sent to gather wool from hedges wander hither and thither apparently aimlessly, so absent-minded persons can hold their minds to nothing, but wander in their thoughts from point to point.

Woollen. In 1666 an Act of Parliament was passed for "burying in woollen only," which was intended for "the encouragement of the woollen manufactures of the kingdom, and prevention of the exportation of money for the buying and importing of linen." The Act was repealed in 1814, but long before then it had fallen into abeyance.

> "Odious! in woollen! 'twould a saint provoke!"
> (Were the last words that poor Narcissa spoke).
> "No! let a charming chintz and Brussels lace
> Wrap my cold limbs, and shade my lifeless face.
> One would not, sure, be frightful when one's dead;
> And—Betty—give the cheeks a little red."
> POPE: *Moral Essays*, Ep. i.

Word. A man of his word. One whose word may be depended on; trustworthy; he is "as good as his word," and "his word is as good as his bond."

A word to the wise! Said when giving advice as a hint that it would be well for the recipient to follow it. The Latin *Verbum satis sapienti*, a word is enough to the wise.

By word of mouth. Orally. As "he took it down by word of mouth" (as it was spoken by the speaker).

I take you at your word. I will act in reliance upon what you tell me.

Pray, make no words about it. Don't mention it; make no fuss about it.

Put in a good word for me, please! Do your best to get me some privilege or favour; put my claims, my deeds, etc., in the best light possible.

The Word. The Scriptures; Christ as the Logos (*see John* i, 1).

To give, or pass one's word. To give a definite undertaking, make a binding promise.

To have words with one. To quarrel; to have an angry discussion. *To have a word with one.* is to have a brief conversation with him.

Upon my word. Assuredly; by my troth.

Upon my word and honour! A strong affirmation of the speaker as to the truth of what he has asserted.

World. A man or woman of the world. One who is acquainted with the ways of public and social life; not quite the same as a *worldly* man or woman, which expression would denote one that cares *only* for the things of this world.

In Shakespeare's time a *woman of the world* was merely a married woman: —

Touchstone: To-morrow will we be married.
Audrey: I do desire it with all my heart; and I hope It is no dishonest desire to be a woman of the world.—*As You Like It*, v, 3.
Everyone goes to the world but I, and I may sit in a corner and cry heigho! for a husband,—*Much Ado About Nothing*, ii, 1.

The world, the flesh, and the devil. "The world," *i.e.* the things of this world, in contradistinction to religious matters; "the flesh," *i.e.* love of pleasure and sensual enjoyments; "the devil," *i.e.* all temptations to evil of every kind, as theft, murder, lying, blasphemy, and so on.

From all the deceits of the world, the flesh, and the devil, Good Lord, deliver us.—*The Litany* (*Book of Common Prayer*).

World Court. The Permanent Court of International Justice, set up at The Hague under the Covenant of the League of Nations in September, 1921, and confirmed by the Charter of the United Nations in November, 1946. It has 15 judges elected by the Powers and it considers and passes judgment (from which appeal may be made to the Security Council) on all international disputes which may involve recourse to arms.

The World Turned Upside Down. An inn-sign alluding to Captain Cook's discovery of

Australia, where the inhabitants were thought of as hanging down into space.

World Wars. The name given generally—and throughout this book—to the two great wars of 1914-18 and 1939-45 in which most civilized nations of the world were participants.

World War II abbreviations. World War II was made a nightmare for those taking part by the habit of contracting all official names into initials which formed words easily remembered but seldom understood. Among the most frequently used were:—

AAF: American Air Force.
ABCA: Army Bureau of Current Affairs (British).
AIF: Australian Imperial Forces.
AMGOT: Allied Military Government of Occupied Territory.
ARP: Air Raid Precautions (British).
ATC: Air Transport Command, earlier Ferry Command. Main function was flying planes from U.S.A. to Britain.
ATS: Auxiliary Territorial Service, women in military service (British).
BAR: Browning automatic rifle (U.S.A.).
BAOR: British Army of the Rhine.
CARE: Cooperative for American Remittances to Europe. A non-profit making organization for sending food parcels to Europe, continued after the war.
COSSAC: Chief of Staff to the Supreme Allied Commander; the word Cossac became the code word for the Allied head-quarters in London.
DP: Displaced Person. Term applied to foreign forced labour and other refugees liberated by the Allied armies in Europe. Sarcastically referred to as "Displeased Persons" by the harassed troops who had to cope with the innumerable problems these thousands of broken lives presented.
DZ: Dropping Zone. The target area in which paratroops intended to land.
ETA: Estimated Time of Arrival.
ETO: European Theatre of Operations.
ETOUSA: European Theatre of Operations United States Army.
FFI: French Forces of the Interior.
GI: Government issue. From equipment its use extended to American enlisted men.
LDV: Local Defence Volunteers (British). Later Home Guard.
LCI: Landing Craft, Infantry.
LST: Landing Ship, Tank.
LZ: Landing Zone. The target area in which gliders intend to land.
MTOUSA: Mediterranean Theatre of Operations United States Army.
NATOUSA: North African Theatre of Operations United States Army.
OCS: Officer Candidate School (U.S.A.).
OCTU: Officer Cadet Training Unit (British).
OSS: Office of Strategic Services (U.S.A.). Organization for the gathering of strategic information and the execution of special missions in enemy territory.
OWI: Office of War Information (U.S.A.).

PIAT: Projectile Infantry Anti-Tank (British). A tank-destroying weapon operated on the same principle as the American bazooka and German Panzerfaust.

SAAFA: Soldiers', Army and Air Force Families Association (British). An organization to help deal with domestic problems of men absent in the forces.

SHAEF: Supreme Headquarters Allied Expeditionary Forces.

VIP: Very Important Person, requiring special accommodation or transport.

WAAC: Women's Army Auxiliary Corps (U.S.A.). Similar to British ATS.

WAAF: Women's Auxiliary Air Force.

WRNS: Women's Royal Naval Service, Wrens.

WVS: Women's Voluntary Services (British), started 1938.

Worm. The word was formerly used of dragons and great serpents, especially those of Teutonic and old Norse legend; it is now figuratively applied to miserable, grovelling creatures; also to the ligament under a dog's tongue.

To be food for worms. To be dead.

Your worm is your only emperor for diet; we fat all creatures else, to fat us; and we fat ourselves for maggots.—*Hamlet*, iv, 3.

To satisfy the worm. To appease one's hunger.

To worm out information. To elicit information indirectly and piecemeal.

To worm oneself into another's favour. To insinuate oneself into the good graces of another person.

Wormwood. The common name for the aromatic herbs of the genus *Artemisia*, especially *A. absinthium*, from which absinthe and vermouth are concocted. The name, which is of very great antiquity, almost certainly comes from the ancient legend that this plant sprang up in the track of the serpent as it writhed along the ground when driven out of Paradise.

Worship. Literally "worth-ship," honour, dignity, reverence; in its highest and now usual sense the respect and reverence man pays to God. In R.C. theology there are three kinds of worship—*latria*, the worship due to God alone; *hyperdulia*, the lesser worship paid to the B.V.M.; and *dulia*, the respect paid to the saints.

At one time the word carried a sense of personal respect. "Thou shalt have *worship* in the presence of them that sit at meat with thee" (*Luke* xiv, 10) means "Thou shalt have *worth-ship*—value or appreciation." In the marriage service the man says to the woman, "With my body I thee worship, and with all my worldly goods I thee endow"—that is, I confer on you my rank and dignities, and endow you with my wealth; the worthship attached to my person I share with you, and the wealth which is mine is thine also.

Magistrate and mayors are addressed as *Your Worship*, and in writing a mayor is *The Worshipful Mayor, Mr. A.*

Worst. If the worst comes to the worst. Even if the very worst occurs.

To get the worst of it. To come off second best; to be defeated, worsted.

Worsted (wĕr' sted). Yarn or thread made of wool; so called from Worsted, a village near Norwich, once the centre of an extensive woollen-weaving industry. The name occurs as early as the 13th century.

Worthies, the Nine. Nine heroes—three from the Bible, three from the classics, and three from romance—who were frequently bracketed together, as in the burlesque Pageant of the Nine Worthies in Shakespeare's *Love's Labour's Lost*. They are—Joshua, David, and Judas Maccabæus; Hector, Alexander, and Julius Cæsar; Arthur, Charlemagne, and Godfrey of Bouillon.

Nine worthies were they called, of different rites—
Three Jews, three pagans, and three Christian knights.
DRYDEN: *The Flower and the Leaf.*

Wound. Bind the wound, and grease the weapon. A Rosicrucian maxim. *See* WEAPON-SALVE.

Wove. Applied to papers made on an ordinary dandy roll or mould in which the wires are woven. Used in contradistinction to *laid* (*q.v.*).

Wowser (wou' zer). An Australian term dating from about 1900, meaning a narrow-minded bigot who criticizes and seeks to interfere with civil liberties and the amusements of the people—a splendid Australian word which has not taken root elsewhere.

Wraith (rāth). The phantom or spectral appearance of a still living person, usually taken as a warning that that person is very shortly going to die. It appears to persons at a distance, and forewarns them of the event.

Wrenning Day. St. Stephen's Day (Dec. 26th) used to be so called, because it was a custom among villagers to stone a wren to death on that day in commemoration of the saint's martyrdom.

Wrinkle. Familiar slang for a useful bit of information, a "tip" or a dodge. For instance, if a man were going abroad for the first time he might go to a friend who was a frequent visitor *to get a wrinkle or two, i.e.* learn about the things to see, the way of living there, how to get through the Customs, etc.

Write. A.S. *writan*, connected with Icel. *rita*, to tear, cut, scratch out, etc.

To write down, besides meaning to commit to writing, means to criticize unfavourably, to depreciate. Contrariwise, **to write up** is to puff, to bring into public notice or estimation by favourable criticisms or accounts.

To write off a debt. To cancel it.

To write oneself out. To exhaust one's powers of literary production.

Wroth Money or Wroth Silver. Money paid to the lord in lieu of castle guard for military service; a tribute paid for killing accidentally some person of note; a tribute paid in acknowledgement of the tenancy of unenclosed land. Dugdale, in his *History of Warwickshire*, says:—

There is a certain rent due unto the lord of this Hundred (*i.e.* of Knightlow, the property of the Duke of Buccleuch) called wroth money, or warth-money, or swarff-penny.

The rent must be paid on Martinmas Day (Nov. 11th), in the morning at Knightlow Cross, before sunrise. The party paying it must go thrice about the cross and say, "The wrath-money," and then lay it (varying from 1d. to 2s. 3d.) in a hole in the said cross before good witnesses, or forfeit a white bull with red nose and ears. The amount thus collected reached in 1892 to about 9s., and all who complied with the custom were entertained at a substantial breakfast at the Duke's expense, and were toasted in a glass of rum and milk.

Wuyck's Bible. *See* BIBLE.

Wych Hazel. *See* WITCH HAZEL.

Wyclif's Bible. *See* BIBLE, THE ENGLISH.

X

X. The twenty-fourth letter of the alphabet, representing the fourteenth letter of the Greek alphabet (*ksi*), and denoting in Roman numeration 10, or, on its side (⋈) 1,000, and with a dash over it (X̄) 10,000.

In algebra and mathematics generally *x* denotes an unknown quantity. The reason of this is that algebra came into use in Europe from Arabia, and that Arabic *shei*, a thing, a something (*cp. cosa* under COSS, RULE OF) was used in the Middle Ages to designate the mathematically "unknown," and that this was transcribed as *xei*.

X on beer casks formerly indicated beer which had paid the old 10s. duty, and hence it came to mean beer of a given quality. Two or three crosses are mere trade-marks, intended to convey the impression that the beer so marked was twice or thrice as strong as that which paid this duty.

Xanthippe or **Xantippe** (zăn tip′ i). Wife of the philosopher Socrates. Her bad temper shown towards her husband has rendered her name proverbial for a conjugal scold.

> Be she as foul as was Florentius' love,
> As old as Sibyl, and as curst and shrewd
> As Socrates' Xanthippe, or a worse,
> She moves me not.
> *Taming of the Shrew*, i, 2.

Xanthus (zăn′ thŭs) (Gr., reddish yellow). Achilles' wonderful horse, brother of Balios, Achilles' other horse, and offspring of Zephyrus and the harpy, Podarge. Being chid by his master for leaving Patroclus on the field of battle, Xanthus turned his head reproachfully, and told Achilles that he also would soon be numbered with the dead, not from any fault of his horse, but by the decree of inexorable destiny (*Iliad*, xix). (*Cp. Numb*, xxii, 28-30.)

Xanthus is also the ancient name of the Scamander and of a city on its banks. Elian and Pliny say that Homer called the Scamander "Xanthos" or the "Gold-red river," because it coloured with such a tinge the fleeces of sheep washed in its waters. Others maintain that it was so called because a Greek hero of this name defeated a body of Trojans on its banks, and pushed half of them into the stream.

Xerxes (zerks′ ēz). A Greek way of writing the Persian *Ksathra* or *Kshatra*. Xerxes I, the great Xerxes, is identical with the Ahasuerus of the Bible.

When Xerxes invaded Greece he constructed a pontoon bridge across the Dardanelles, which was swept away by the force of the waves; this so enraged the Persian despot that he "inflicted three hundred lashes on the rebellious sea, and cast chains of iron across it." This story is a Greek myth, founded on the peculiar construction of Xerxes' second bridge, which consisted of three hundred boats, lashed by iron chains to two ships serving as supporters.

Another story told of him is that when he reviewed his enormous army before starting for Greece, he wept at the thought of slaughter about to take place. "Of all this multitude, who shall say how many will return?" Similarly, it is said that Charlemagne viewed the fleet of the Norsemen in the Mediterranean with tears in his eyes, and remarked, "There was reason for these Xerxes' tears."

X.Y.Z. Correspondence. In 1797 the President of the U.S.A., John Adams, sent his agents Pinckney, Marshall, and Gerry to France to negotiate a treaty for the regulation of certain maritime matters. From Paris they reported that three French agents had intercepted them and demanded a large sum of money before the Directory would receive any American diplomats, alternatively a loan would have to be granted by U.S.A. to France. The Americans refused to negotiate on these terms, and the whole correspondence with the three French agents, whom they designated as X.Y. and Z., was published in Washington.

Y

Y. The twenty-fifth letter of the alphabet, is a differentiation of the Greek y (*see* SAMIAN LETTER) added by the Greeks to the Phœnician alphabet.

In Algebra it denotes the second unknown quantity (*cp.* X), and in the Middle Ages it was used in Roman numeration for 150. *See also* YE.

Yahoo (ya′ hoo). Swift's name, in *Gulliver's Travels*, for brutes with human forms and vicious propensities. They are subject to the *Houyhnhnms*, the horses with human reason. Hence applied to coarse, brutish, or degraded persons.

Yahweh. *See* JEHOVAH.

Yankee (yăng′ ki). Properly a New Englander or one of New England stock; but extended to mean, first, an inhabitant of the Northern as apart from the Southern United States, and later to comprise all United States citizens.

It is generally taken to be a North American Indian corruption of *English* (or of Fr. *Anglais*). The story is that in 1713 one Jonathan Hastings, a farmer of Cambridge, Massachusetts, used the word as a puffing epithet, meaning genuine, what cannot be surpassed, etc.; as, a "Yankee horse," "Yankee cider," and so on. The students at Harvard, catching up the term, called Hastings, "Yankee Jonathan." It soon spread, and became the jocose pet name of the New Englander.

Yankee Doodle. The quasi national air of the United States, the doggerel words of which are said to have been written by Dr. Shuckburgh, a surgeon in Lord Amherst's army during the French and Indian war of 1755.

The origin of the tune is disputed: some say that it comes from a mediæval church service, others that it was composed in England in Cromwell's time, others that it was played by the Hessian troops during the American Revolution and adopted by the revolutionaries in mockery. A Dutch origin has also been suggested.

Yarborough. A hand at bridge in which there is no card higher than a nine. So called because the second Lord Yarborough (early 19th cent.) used to lay 1,000 to 1 against such an occurrence in any named hand. The actual mathematical odds are 1,827 to 1 against.

Yashmak (yăsh′ măk). The veil worn by Moslem women. It consists of a white or a black veil, either covering the whole face or hanging from immediately below the eyes.

Year (connected with Gr. *horos*, a season, and Lat. *hora*, an hour). The period of time occupied by the revolution of the earth round the sun.

The Astronomical, Equinoctial, Natural, Solar, or Tropical year, is the time taken by the sun in returning to the same equinox, in mean length, 365 days 5 hours 48 min. and 46 sec.

The Astral or Sidereal year is the time in which the sun apparently returns to the same place in relation to the fixed stars: 365 days 6 hours 9 min. and 9 sec.

The Platonic, Great, or Perfect year (*Annus magnus*), was estimated by early Greek and Hindu astronomers at about 26,000 years, at the end of which all the heavenly bodies were imagined to return to the same places as they occupied at the Creation.

The Chaldean astronomers observed that the fixed stars shift their places at about the rate of a degree in seventy-two years, according to which calculation they will perform one revolution in 25,920 years, at the end of which time they will return to their "as you were." The Egyptians made it 30,000 years, and the Arabians 49,000.

For a year and a day. In law many acts are determined by this period of time—*e.g.* if a person wounded does not die within a year and a day, the offender is not guilty of murder; if an owner does not claim an estray within the same length of time, it belongs to the lord of the manor; a year and a day is given to prosecute appeals, etc.

Year of Grace. A year of the Christian era.

Year in year out. All the year round, without cessation.

Yellow (A.S. *geolo*, connected with Gr. *chloros*, green, and with *gall*, the yellowish fluid secreted by the bile). Indicating in symbolism jealousy, inconstancy, and adultery. In France the doors of traitors used to be daubed with yellow. In some countries the law ordained that Jews must be clothed in yellow, because they betrayed our Lord, hence Judas, in mediæval pictures, is arrayed in yellow. In Spain at an *auto-de-fé* the victims were robed in yellow, to denote heresy and treason.

In heraldry and in ecclesiastical symbolism yellow is frequently used in place of gold.

As a slang or colloquial term yellow is applied to a coward.

Yellow Jack. The yellow fever; also the flag displayed from lazarettos, naval hospitals, and vessels in quarantine.

Yellow Peril, The. A scare, originally raised in Germany in the late 'nineties of last century, that the yellow races of China and Japan would in a very few years have increased in population to such an extent that incursions upon the territories occupied by the white races—followed by massacres and every conceivable horror—were inevitable.

Yellow Press, The. Sensational and jingoist newspapers or journalism. The name arose in the United States about 1898 in consequence of scaring articles on the "Yellow Peril."

Yemen (ye' men). The south-west corner of the Arabian peninsula, called by the ancients Arabia Felix. *Felix* is a mistranslation by Ptolemy of *Yemen*, which means to the "right"—*i.e.* of Mecca.

Yeoman. Anciently, a forty-shilling freeholder, and as such qualified to vote and serve on juries, but not qualified to rank as one of the gentry. In more modern times it meant a farmer who cultivated his own freehold. Later still, an upper farmer, tenant, or otherwise, is often called a yeoman.

Yeoman's service. Hard work; effectual service; excellent service whether in a good or bad cause. The reference is to the yeomen of the Free Companies.

Hamlet says—

I once did hold it, as our statists do,
A baseness to write fair, and labour'd much
How to forget that learning; but, sir, now
It did me yeoman's service.

Hamlet, v, 2.

Yeomen of the Guard. The beefeaters (*q.v.*).

Yes-man. An expressive colloquialism for one who expresses agreement with his superior in everything, whatever his private opinion may be.

Yeth-hounds. Dogs without heads, of west country folklore; said to be the spirits of unbaptized children, which ramble among the woods at night, making wailing noises.

Yew. The yew is a British tree, and is commonly planted in churchyards because, as it is an evergreen, it is a symbol of immortality. It was planted by the Druids near their temples.

Some famous yews—

Of *Braburn*, in Kent, according to De Candolle, is 3,000 years old.

The *Scotch yew at Fortingal*, in Perthshire, is between 2,500 and 3,000 years.

Of *Darley churchyard*, Derbyshire, about 2,050 years.

Of *Crowhurst*, Surrey, about 1,400.

The three at *Fountains Abbey*, in Yorkshire, at least 1,200 years. Beneath these trees the founders of the abbey held their council in 1132.

The yew grove of *Norbury Park*, Surrey, was standing in the time of the Druids.

The yew trees at *Kingsley Bottom*, near Chichester, were standing when the sea-kings landed on the Sussex coast.

The yew tree of *Harlington churchyard*, Middlesex, is above 850 years old.

That at *Ankerwyke House*, near Staines, was noted when Magna Charta was signed in 1215, and it was the trysting tree for Henry VIII and Anne Boleyn.

Yggdrasil (ig' drà sil). The world tree of Scandinavian mythology that, with its roots and branches, binds together heaven, earth, and hell. It is an ash, and at the root is a fountain of wonderful virtues. In the tree, which drops honey, sit an eagle, a squirrel, and four stags.

The tree is a late addition to Scandinavian myth, and the name was probably originally that of one of the winds (*Yggr*, a name of Odin, and *dressill*, a horse).

Yiddish. A Middle German dialect developed in Poland under Hebrew and Slavic influence, written in Hebrew characters, and used as a language by Jews of Polish origin (Ger. *jüdisch*, Jewish).

Ymir (im' ir). The primeval being of Scandinavian mythology, the giant from whose body the world was created. He was nourished by the four milky streams which flowed from the cow Audhumla.

Yodel (yō' dèl). To sing with frequent alternations between the ordinary voice and falsetto. It is really peculiar to Switzerland and is a development of the Ranz des Vaches, or cowherd's call when driving the cattle to the mountain pastures with the coming of spring.

Like the cowhorn, the yodel has a restricted scale of natural harmonics.

Yoga (yō' gȧ). A practice of Hindu philosophy seeking to unite the human soul with the Universal Spirit by concentrating the mind on some eternal truth and withdrawing the physical senses from external objects. Adepts in yoga are able to hold their breath for protracted periods and do other things in apparent contravention of natural requirements.

Yom Kippur (yom ki pĕr'). The Jewish Day of Atonement, on the 10th day of the first month, Tishri. It is observed by a strict fast and ceremonies of supplication mostly dating from the 3rd century B.C.

Yorkist. A partisan of the White Rose in the Wars of the Roses. *See* ROSE.

Yours truly. This conventional ending to letters is sometimes used vulgarly to indicate the speaker—"There were X., Y., and Yours truly."

Ysolde (**Yseult, Isolde,** etc.). The name of two heroines of Arthurian romance, the more important *Ysolde the Fair*, King Mark's wife, being the lover of Tristram (*q.v.*), the other, *Ysolde of the White Hands*, or *Ysolde o Brittany*, being his wife, with whom he made a "Maiden Marriage" after he had been discovered by King Mark and had been obliged to flee.

It was through the treachery of Ysolde of the White Hands that Sir Tristram died, and that Ysolde the Fair died in consequence. The story has it that King Mark buried the two in one grave, and planted over it a rose-bush and vine, which so intermingled their branches as they grew up that no man could separate them.

Yuga. One of the four ages of the world into which, according to Hindu cosmogony, mundane time is divided.

Yule, Yuletide. Christmas time. A.S. *geola*, from Icel. *jol* (with which possibly our *jolly* is connected), the name of a heathen festival at the winter solstice.

Yule log. A great log of wood laid in ancient times across the hearth-fire on Christmas Eve. This was done with certain ceremonies and much merrymaking.

Yves or **Yvo, St.** (ēv, ē' vō). Patron saint of lawyers, being himself a lawyer. He was an ecclesiastical judge at Rennes, was ordained priest in 1285, died in 1303, and was canonized in 1347. As he used his knowledge of the law in defending the oppressed, he is still called in Brittany (where his festival is kept on May 19th) "the poor man's advocate."

Advocatus, sed non latro,
Res miranda populo.—*Hymn to St. Yves.*

Z

Z. The last letter of the alphabet, called *zed* in England, but in America *zee*. Its older English name was *izzard*.

In mathematics it denotes the third unknown quantity (*see* X); and in mediæval times it was used as a Roman numeral for 2,000.

Zadig. Possibly the best of Voltaire's short novels, published in 1748. Zadig was a Babylonian philosopher whose determination to lead a life of virtue and wisdom was rewarded by a series of ever-worsening calamities.

Zadikim. *See* CHASIDIM.

Zany (zā′ ni). The buffoon who mimicked the clown in the Commedia dell'Arte; hence a simpleton, one who "acts the goat." The name is the Italian *zanni*, a buffoon, fem. of *Giovanni* (*i.e.* John), our *Jane*.

> For indeed,
> He's like the zani to a tumbler
> That tries tricks after him to make men laugh.
> B. JONSON: *Every Man out of his Humour*, iv, 2.

Zeitgeist (zīt′ gīst) (Ger. *zeit*, time, *geist*, spirit). The spirit of the time; the moral or intellectual tendency characteristic of the period.

Zemindar (zem′ in dar). An Indian landowner holding direct from the Government and paying a fixed rent based on the revenue from his land.

Zemire. *See* AZOR'S MIRROR; BEAUTY AND THE BEAST.

Zemstvo (zemst′ vō). The elected local district and provincial administrative assembly in Russia under the old Empire. Theoretically it had large powers and was democratic; but it was always under the thumb of the great landowners, and all its decrees were subject to the approval of the Governor.

Zem Zem. The sacred well near the Kaaba at Mecca. According to Arab tradition, this is the very well that was shown to Hagar when Ishmael was perishing of thirst.

Zenana (ze na′ nà). The Hindu harem or apartment where the women of the family are kept secluded.

Zend-Avesta. The sacred writings of Zoroaster (or Zarathustra) that formed the basis of the religion that prevailed in Persia from the 6th century B.C. to the 7th century A.D. *Avesta* means the text, and *Zend* its interpretation into a more modern and intelligible language; hence the latter name has been given to the ancient Iranian language in which the *Zend-Avesta* is written.

Zenith, Nadir (zen′ ith, năd′ ir) (Arabic). *Zenith* is the point of the heavens immediately over the head of the spectator. *Nadir* is the opposite point, immediately beneath the spectator's feet. Hence, **to go from the zenith of prosperity to the nadir** is to fall from the height of fortune to the depths of poverty.

Zephyr (zef′ ir). The west wind in classical mythology; son of Æolus and Aurora, and lover of Flora; hence, any soft, gentle wind.

> Fair laughs the Morn and soft the Zephyr blows.
> While proudly riding o'er the azure realm
> In gallant trim the gilded vessel goes;
> Youth on the prow, and Pleasure at the helm.
> GRAY: *The Bard*.

Zero (zē′ rō) (Arabic, a cipher). The figure 0; nothing; especially the point on a scale (such as that of a thermometer) from which positive and negative quantities are measured; on the Centigrade and Réaumur thermometers fixed at the freezing-point of water, on the Fahrenheit 32° below this.

Absolute zero is the point at which it would be impossible for a body to get any colder; *i.e.* that at which it is totally devoid of heat (estimated at about—273° C.).

Zero hour. A military term (first used in World War I) for the exact time at which an attack etc., is to be begun. From this are timed the consequent operations, *e.g.* zero + 3 means 3 minutes after zero hour. Succeeded in World War II by H-hour.

Zero point. In *Time*, 12 o'clock, midday; the time at which 24-hour clocks begin the day.

Zeus (zūs). The Grecian Jupiter (*q.v.*). The word means the "living one" (Sanskrit *Djaus*, heaven).

Zincali or **Zingari** (zing′ ka li). Gipsies; so called in Spain from *Sinte* or *Sind* (India) and *calo* (black), on the supposition that they came from India which no doubt is true. The Persian *Zangi* means an Ethiopian or Egyptian.

875

Zion (Heb. *Tsīyon*, a hill). **Daughter of Zion.** Jerusalem or its people. The city of David stood on Mount Zion.

In *Pilgrim's Progress* Bunyan calls the Celestial City (*i.e.* Heaven) *Mount Zion.*

Zodiac (Gr. *zodiakos*, pertaining to animals; from *zōon*, an animal). The imaginary belt or zone in the heavens, extending about eight degrees each side of the ecliptic which the sun traverses every year.

Signs of the Zodiac. The zodiac was divided by the ancients into twelve equal parts, proceeding from west to east; each part of thirty degrees, and distinguished by a sign; these originally corresponded to the zodiacal constellations bearing the same names, but now, through the precession of the equinoxes, they coincide with the constellations bearing the names next in order.

Beginning with Aries, we have first six on the north side and six on the south side of the equator; beginning with Capricornus, we have six *ascending* and then six *descending* signs— *i.e.* six which ascend higher and higher towards the north, and six which descend lower and lower towards the south. The six northern signs are: *Aries* (the ram), *Taurus* (the bull), *Gemini* (the twins), spring signs; *Cancer* (the crab), *Leo* (the lion), *Virgo* (the virgin), summer signs. The six southern are: *Libra* (the balance), *Scorpio* (the scorpion), *Sagittarius* (the archer), autumn signs; *Capricornus* (the goat), *Aquarius* (the water-bearer), and *Pisces* (the fishes), winter signs.

Our vernal signs the RAM begins.
Then comes the BULL in May the TWINS;
The CRAB in June, next LEO shines,
And VIRGO ends the northern signs.
The BALANCE brings autumnal fruits,
The SCORPION stings, the ARCHER shoots;

December's GOAT brings wintry blast,
AQUARIUS rain, the FISH come last.—*E.C.B.*

Zoilus. A Greek rhetorician of the 4th century B.C., a literary Thersites. shrewd, witty, and spiteful, nicknamed *Homeromastix* (Homer's scourge), because he mercilessly assailed the epics of Homer, and called the companions of Ulysses in the island of Circe "weeping porkers" (*"choiridia klaionta"*). He also flew at Plato, Isocrates, and other high game.

Zombie (zom′ bi). The python god of certain West African tribes. Its worship was carried to the West Indies with the slave trade, and still somewhat covertly flourishes in Voodoo ceremonies in Haiti and some of the Southern States of the U.S.A. The word *zombie* is commonly applied to an alleged dead body brought by Voodoo magic to life in a more or less cataleptic or automaton state.

Zoot-suit (U.S.A.). An exaggerated style of clothing adopted in the late 1930s by *hepcats* (*q.v.*) and followers of fashionable swing music. It usually consisted of baggy trousers caught in at the bottom, a long coat resembling a frock coat, a broad-brimmed hat, and a flowing tie, all in vivid colours. An essential article of equipment was a vast key-chain.

Zounds! A minced oath; euphemistic for *God's wounds.*

Zuchetto (zu ket′ ō). The small skull-cap worn by Roman Catholic clergy; white for the pope, red for a cardinal, purple for a bishop, and black for others.

Zurich Bible, The. *See* BIBLE, SPECIALLY NAMED.

Zwichau Prophets, The. *See* ABECEDARIAN.